D1540302

Latin-American Spanish English Reference Dictionary

David L. Gold

Revised and Updated by

Kathleen O'Connor

Berlitz Publishing Company, Inc.

Princeton   Mexico City   Dublin   Eschborn   Singapore

Trademarks

Published by arrangement with Random House Reference & Information Publishing, a division of Random House, Inc.

ISBN 2-8315-7330-0

Printed in Canada

Contents

Preface

New Second Edition

This is a revised Second Edition of *Random House Latin-American Spanish Dictionary*, first published in 1997. New to this edition are pronunciations for all Spanish and English main entries, using IPA (International Phonetic Alphabet) symbols. The IPA symbols are explained in the pronunciation key for English on page vii and for Spanish on page xiii. Also included in this dictionary are detailed guides to the pronunciation of both languages.

Selection of Vocabulary

This dictionary emphasizes Spanish of the Western Hemisphere, featuring words and meanings unique to Central America, South America, and the Caribbean. It also tries to convey some of the regional variation that may be found from country to country within these areas. It covers the distinctive dialects of countries such as Argentina, Uruguay, Mexico, Chile, Venezuela, Bolivia, Costa Rica, Cuba, the Dominican Republic, Guatemala, and Peru.

Hundreds of new words and meanings have been added to this edition. The aim of this dictionary is to cover as much current vocabulary as possible, as well as certain terms found in standard works of modern Spanish and English literature.

Spanish Spelling and Alphabetization

On January 1, 1959, the Spanish language academies changed certain spelling rules and on April 27, 1994, they eliminated **ch** and **ll** as separate letters of the alphabet. Thus, whereas words like **chico** and **chocolate** were formerly alphabetized under their own letter (**ch,** which came between **c** and **d**) and words like **llamar** and **llegar** were formerly alphabetized under their own letter (**ll,** which came between **l** and **m**), words containing **ch** or **ll**, in whatever part of the word they may appear, are now alphabetized as they would be in English (**chico** therefore now appears under **c** and **llegar** under **l**).

Regional Labels for Spanish

Regional variation in Spanish ranges from nonexistent to extreme. On one hand, the words for "flower" and "mother-in-law," for example, are everywhere **flor** and **suegra** respectively. On the other hand, the language has many words for "bus" and "ballpoint pen."

Regional labels are given in this dictionary when a less than universal usage is found in a certain region or country. Certain usages are labeled *Lat. Am.* or *West. Hem.* (if they are in general use throughout Latin America or the Western Hemisphere) and others are given more restricted labels, like *Argentina* and *Mexico* (if they appear to be limited to just certain countries).

A regional label should be interpreted as meaning that the usage so labeled is found in that particular place, but it may also be found elsewhere. For instance, the regional label *Mexico* means that the usage so labeled is found in Mexico, but further research would be necessary to determine whether the usage is present or absent in other countries.

Field Labels

Only essential field labels are given in this dictionary. For example, the label *medicine* or *pathology* is unnecessary at **flebitis** "phlebitis" (in the Spanish–English section) because both the Spanish and English words refer only to the medical condition so called in those languages.

In contrast to that entry, we do need a label at **foca** "seal" (in the Spanish–English section) because English **seal** has several meanings and only the zoological one is intended here. English speakers looking up **foca** thus need the label *zoology* (Spanish speakers need no label because they know that **foca** is the name of an animal).

Subentries

If a main entry head is repeated in a subentry in exactly the same form, it is abbreviated to its first letter (for instance, at **fin** in the Spanish–English section we find **a f. de,** which stands for **a fin de**). If the main entry head appears in any other form, the full form is given in the subentry (thus, at **fin,** the subentry head **a fines de** is spelled without abbreviation).

Irregular Spanish Verbs and the Direction "See…"

If a Spanish verb is irregular, it has been treated in one of two ways: either its principal parts are shown (see for example the end of the entry for **caber**) or you are referred to an analogous irregular verb for guidance (see for example the end of the entry for **comparecer,** where you are directed to **conocer**). Thus, since the irregular form **conozco** is shown at **conocer,** you may infer that **comparecer** has the irregular form **comparezco.**

If "See…" is all you find at an entry, you are being directed to a synonym. Thus, "**descompasarse** See **descomedirse**" means that the translations of **descomedirse** are those of **descompasarse** too.

Spanish Equivalents of "you"

Today's Spanish, when taken as a whole, has at least six equivalents of "you": **tú, vos, usted** (abbreviated to **Vd.**), and **su merced** (all of which are used in addressing one person); and **ustedes** (abbreviated to **Vds.**), **vosotros, vosotras,** and **sus mercedes** (all used in addressing more than one person).

When **you** occurs in this dictionary, usually only one of those words has been chosen to translate it, though three are never used here: **su merced** and **sus mercedes,** because they are now limited to only a small area of the Spanish-speaking world (the Cundinamarca Savanna, in Colombia) and even there they are now obsolescent; and **vos,** because the verb forms corresponding to this pronoun often vary from country to country.

The editors of this *Second Edition* of the *Random House Latin-American Spanish Dictionary* are always grateful to receive suggestions for new words to add to subsequent editions. Any suggestions or queries should be sent to:

Random House Reference & Information Publishing
201 East 50th Street
New York, NY 10022

Guía de Pronunciación del inglés
Pronunciation Key for English

Símbolos del AFI
IPA Symbols

Ejemplos
Examples

Vocales y Diptongos

/æ/	*ingl.* hat; como la **a** de *esp.* paro, pero más cerrada
/ei/	*ingl.* stay; *esp.* reina
/ɛə/ [followed by /r/]	*ingl.* hair; *esp.* ver
/ɑ/	*ingl.* father; similar a las **as** de *esp.* casa, pero más larga
/ɛ/	*ingl.* bet; *esp.* entre
/i/	*ingl.* bee; como la **i** de *esp.* vida, pero más larga
/ɪə/ [followed by /r/]	*ingl.* hear; como la **i** de *esp.* venir, pero menos cerrada
/ɪ/	*ingl.* sit; como la **i** de *esp.* Chile, pero menos cerrada
/ai/	*ingl.* try; *esp.* hay
/ɒ/	*ingl.* hot; *esp.* poner
/ou/	*ingl.* boat; similar a la **o** de *esp.* saco, pero más cerrada
/ɔ/	*ingl.* saw; similar a la **o** de *esp.* corte, pero más cerrada
/ɔi/	*ingl.* toy; *esp.* hoy
/ʊ/	*ingl.* book; como la **u** de *esp.* insulto, pero menos cerrada
/u/	*ingl.* too; como la **u** de *esp.* luna, pero más larga
/au/	*ingl.* cow; *esp.* pausa
/ʌ/	*ingl.* up; entre la **o** de *esp.* borde y la **a** de *esp.* barro
/ɜ/ [followed by /r/]	*ingl.* burn; *fr.* fleur
/ə/	*ingl.* alone; *fr.* demain
/ə/	*ingl.* fire (fiᵊr); *fr.* bastille

Símbolos del AFI IPA Symbols	Ejemplos Examples
Consonantes	
/b/	*ingl.* **b**oy; como la **b** de *esp.* **b**oca, pero más aspirada
/tʃ/	*ingl.* **ch**ild; *esp.* mu**ch**o
/d/	*ingl.* **d**ad; *esp.* **d**ar
/f/	*ingl.* **f**or; *esp.* **f**echa
/g/	*ingl.* **g**ive; *esp.* **g**ato
/h/	*ingl.* **h**appy; como la **j** de *esp.* **j**abón, pero más aspirada y menos aspera
/dʒ/	*ingl.* **j**ust; *it.* **gi**orno
/k/	*ingl.* **k**ick; similar a la **k** de *esp.* **k**ilogramo, pero más aspirada
/l/	*ingl.* **l**ove; *esp.* **l**ibro
/m/	*ingl.* **m**other; *esp.* li**mb**o
/n/	*ingl.* **n**ow; *esp.* **n**oche
/ŋ/	*ingl.* si**ng**; *esp.* bla**n**co
/p/	*ingl.* **p**ot; como las **ps** de *esp.* **p**apa, pero más aspirada
/r/	*ingl.* **r**ead; como la **r** de *esp.* pa**r**a, pero con la lengua elevada hacia el paladar, sin tocarlo
/s/	*ingl.* **s**ee; *esp.* ha**s**ta
/ʃ/	*ingl.* **sh**op; *fr.* **ch**er**ch**er
/t/	*ingl.* **t**en; similar a la **t** de *esp.* **t**omar, pero más aspirada
/θ/	*ingl.* **th**ing; *esp.* (en España) **c**erdo, **z**apato
/ð/	*ingl.* fa**th**er; *esp.* co**d**o
/v/	*ingl.* **v**ictory; como la **b** de *esp.* ha**b**a, pero es labiodental en vez de bilabial
/w/	*ingl.* **w**itch; como la **u** de *esp.* p**u**esto, pero con labios más cerrados
/y/	*ingl.* **y**es; *esp.* **y**acer
/z/	*ingl.* **z**ipper; *fr.* **z**éro
/ʒ/	*ingl.* plea**s**ure; *fr.* **j**eune

Las consonantes /l̩/, /m̩/, y /n̩/ son similar a las **l**, **m**, y **n** del español, pero alargada y resonante.

Los sonidos del inglés americano

Vocales y diptongos

a Cuando representa el sonido /æ/, se pronuncia más cerrada que la *a* de *paro* (por ejemplo: **act, at, bat, hat, marry**); también se encuentra este sonido en palabras deletreadas con: -ah- (d*ah*lia), -ai- (pl*ai*d), -al- (h*al*f), -au- (l*au*gh), -ua- (g*ua*rantee).

a Cuando representa el sonido /ei/, se pronuncia más cerrada que la *e* de *hablé* y como si fuera seguido de *i* (por ejemplo: **age, gate, rate**); también se encuentra este sonido en palabras deletreadas con: -ai- (r*ai*n, *ai*r), -aigh- (str*aigh*t), -au- (g*au*ge), -ay- (s*ay*), -ea- (st*ea*k), -ei- (v*ei*l, w*ei*gh), -ey- (ob*ey*).

a /ɑ/ Equivale aproximadamente a la *a* de *sentado* y *bajo* (por ejemplo: **ah, father, part**); también se encuentra este sonido en palabras deletreadas con: -al- (c*al*m), -e(r)- (s*er*geant), -ea(r)- (h*ear*t), -ua- (g*ua*rd).

a /ə/ Equivale aproximadamente a la *e* de las palabras francesas *de* y *le* (por ejemplo: **alone, about**); también se encuentra este sonido en palabras deletreadas con: -e- (syst*e*m), -i- (eas*i*ly), -o- (gall*o*p), -u- (circ*u*s), -y- (mart*y*r).

e /ɛ/ Equivale aproximadamente a la *e* de *templo* y *perro* (por ejemplo: **edge, set, merry**); también se encuentra este sonido en palabras deletreadas con: a-, -a- (*a*ny, m*a*ny), -ai- (s*ai*d), -ay- (s*ay*s), -ea- (l*ea*ther), -ei- (h*ei*fer), -eo- (j*eo*pardy), -ie- (fr*ie*nd).

e /i/ Equivale aproximadamente a la *i* de *Chile* (por ejemplo: **be, equal, secret**); también se encuentra este sonido en palabras deletreadas con: ea- *(ea*ch, t*ea*), -ee- (f*ee*, k*ee*p), -ei- (rec*ei*ve), -eo- (p*eo*ple), -ey- (k*ey*), -ie- (f*ie*ld), -y (cit*y*).

i /ɪ/ Se pronuncia menos cerrada que la *i* de *Chile* (por ejemplo: **if, big, fit, mirror**); también se encuentra este sonido en palabras deletreadas con: e- (*E*ngland), -ee- (b*ee*n), -ei- (counterf*ei*t), -ia- (carr*ia*ge), -ie- (s*ie*ve), -o- (w*o*man), (b)u(s)- (b*u*siness), -y- (s*y*mpathetic).

i /ai/ Equivale aproximadamente a la *ai* de *aire, baile* (por ejemplo: **bite, ice, pirate**); también se encuentra este sonido en palabras deletreadas con: ais- (*ai*sle), -ei- (h*ei*ght, st*ei*n), -eye- *(eye)*, -ie (p*ie*), -igh- (h*igh*), is- (*i*sland), -uy- (b*uy*), -y (cycle, sky), -ye (l*ye*).

o /ou/ Se pronuncia más cerrada que la *o* de *supo* (por ejemplo: **hope, go, oh, over**); también se encuentra este sonido en palabras deletreadas con: -au- (m*au*ve), -aux (f*aux* pas), -eau- (b*eau*), -ew (s*ew*), -oa- (r*oa*d), -oe (t*oe*), -oo- (br*oo*ch), -ot (dep*ot*), -ou- (s*ou*l), -ow (fl*ow*), -owe- *(owe)*.

o /ɔ/ Se pronuncia más cerrada que la *o* de *corre* (por ejemplo: **alcohol, order, raw**); también se encuentra este sonido en palabras deletreadas con: -a- (t*a*ll), -al- (w*al*k), au- (*au*thor, v*au*lt), -augh- (c*augh*t), -oa- (br*oa*d), -oo- (fl*oo*r), -ough- (s*ough*t).

oi /oi/ Equivale aproximadamente a la *oy* de *doy* (por ejemplo: **oil, joint, voice**); también se encuentra este sonido en palabras deletreadas con: -awy- (l*awy*er), -oy- (b*oy*).

oo /ʊ/ Se pronuncia menos cerrada que la *u* de *insulto* (por ejemplo: **book, foot**); también se encuentra este sonido en palabras deletreadas con: -o- (w*o*lf), -ou- (t*ou*r), -u- (p*u*ll).

oo /u/ Se pronuncia más largo que la *u* de *susto* (por ejemplo: **too, ooze, fool**); también se encuentra este sonido en palabras deletreadas con: -eu- (man*eu*ver), -ew (gr*ew*), -o (wh*o*), -o...e (m*o*ve), -oe (can*oe*), -ou- (tr*ou*pe), -u...e (r*u*le), -ue (fl*ue*), -ui- (s*ui*t).

ou /au/ Equivale aproximadamente a la *au* de *aurora* (por ejemplo: **loud, out**); también se encuentra este sonido en palabras deletreadas con -ow (br*ow*, c*ow*, pl*ow*).

u /yiu/ Equivale aproximadamente a la *iu* de *ciudad* (por ejemplo: **cue, use, utility**); también se encuentra este sonido en palabras deletreadas con: -eau- (b*eau*ty), -eu- (f*eu*d), -ew (f*ew*), (h)u- (h*u*man), (h)u...e (h*u*ge), -iew (v*iew*), you *(you)*, yu...e *(yule)*.

u /ʌ/ Es sonido intermedio entre la *o* de *borro* y la *a* de *barro*, algo parecido a la pronunciación de la *eu* francesa de *peur;* (por ejemplo: **up, sun, mud**); también se encuentra este sonido en palabras deletreadas con: o- (other), -o- (s*o*n), -oe- (d*oe*s), o...e (l*o*ve), -oo- (bl*oo*d), -ou (tr*ou*ble).

Consonantes

b Se pronuncia igual que la *p* española salvo que en la pronunciación de la *b* suenan las cuerdas vocales. La *b* inglesa es más fuerte (más aspirada) que la española. Se encuentra en palabras escritas con *b* (**bed, amber, rub**) y también en palabras deletreadas con -bb- (ho*bb*y).

c Como la *c* española, lleva dos sonidos, /s/ y /k/. La /s/ se pronuncia igual que la *s* española y se encuentra en palabras deletreadas con ce- (**center**) y ci- (**city**). La /k/ es semejante a la *c* española cuando aparece delante de -a, -o, y -u *(católica, cómo, cuándo)* pero se pronuncia más fuerte (más aspirada). La /k/ se encuentra en palabras deletreadas con ca-, co-, y cu- (**cat, account, cut**).

ch Equivale aproximadamente a la *ch* española (por ejemplo: **chief, beach**); también se encuentra en palabras deletreadas con: -tch- (ca*tch*, bu*tch*er), -te- (righ*te*ous), -ti- (ques*ti*on), -tu- (na*tu*ral). A veces equivale a la /ʃ/ de la palabra francese *chèrie* (**chef**), o a la /k/ de *cómo* (**character**).

d Equivale aproximadamente a la *d* de *onda* (por ejemplo: **do, odor, red**); también se encuentra en palabras deletreadas con -dd- (la*dd*er) y -de- (fa*de*). La *d* inglesa es siempre más fuerte (más aspirada) que la española y no se pronuncia nunca /dʒ/ como la *d* de *padre* o las *d*'s de *Madrid*.

f Equivale aproximadamente a la *f* española (por ejemplo: **feed, safe**); también se encuentra en palabras deletreadas con -ff- (mu*ff*in) y -fe (li*fe*).

g Equivale aproximadamente a la *g* de *globo* (por ejemplo: **give, fog**); también se encuentra en palabras deletreadas con -gg- (e*gg*), gh- (*gh*ost), y -gue (pla*gue*). La *g* cuando cae delante de -i y -e se pronuncia /dʒ/ (**George, gem, legitimate**). El sonido /dʒ/ es semejante a, pero más fuerte que, la *y* y la *ll* españolas de *yo* y *llevar*. Véase *j*.

h Se pronuncia más aspirada pero menos áspera que la *j* española en *jabón* (por ejemplo: **hit, hope**); tambièn se encuentra en palabras deletreadas con wh- (*wh*o).

j   Equivale aproximadamente a la *y* de *yo* en su pronunciación enfática (p.ej. . . . *yo, y yo sólo soy el dueño aquí!*) o como la *y* de *cónyuge* en ciertas modalidades del español (por ejemplo: **just, joke**); también se encuentra en palabras deletreadas con: -dg- (ju*dg*e), -di- (sol*di*er), -ge (sa*ge*), -gg- (exa*gg*erate), gi- (*gi*n). La pronunciación de la *j* y de la *g* delante de -i y -e /dʒ/ es igual que la de la *ch* española, salvo que suenan las cuerdas vocales en la pronunciación del sonido /dʒ/.

k (Por ejemplo: **keep, make, token**) equivale a la *qui-* y *que* españolas pero se pronuncia más fuerte (más aspirada). La *k* inglesa no se pronuncia cuando cae delante de una *n* (**knife, knight, knee**).

l   Se pronuncia aproximadamente como la *l* de *lago* (por ejemplo: **leap, sail**); también se encuentra en palabras deletreadas con -le (mi*le*) y -ll (ca*ll*).

m Equivale aproximadamente a la *m* española (por ejemplo: **more, drum, him, summer**). Tengan cuidado de pronunciar la *m* al final de una palabra igual que se pronuncia en medio de la palabra y de no convertir el sonido en *n*.

n   Equivale aproximadamente a la *n* de *bueno* (por ejemplo: **now, sunny**); también se encuentra en palabras deletreadas con gn- (*gn*at) y kn- (*kn*ife).

ng (Por ejemplo: **sing, Washington**) equivale aproximadamente a la *n* de *blanco.*

p   (Por ejemplo: **pool, spool, supper, stop**) tras consonante equivale aproximadamente a la *p* española, pero lleva más aspiración. La *p* delante de una *s* (**psychologist, psyche**) no se pronuncia.

r   Se pronuncia con la punta de la lengua elevada hacia el paladar (sin tocarlo) y doblada para atrás (por ejemplo: **red, hurry, near**); también se encuentra en palabras deletreadas con: -re (pu*re*), rh- (*rh*ythm), y wr- (*wr*ong).

s   Equivale aproximadamente a la *s* de *salir,* pero algo más tensa y larga (por ejemplo: **see, kiss**).

sh Equivale aproximadamente a la *ch* de las palabras francesas *changer* and *chapeau* (por ejemplo: **ship, wash**); también se encuentra en palabras deletreadas con: -ce- (o*ce*an), -ch- (ma*ch*ine), -ci- (spe*ci*al), s(u)- (*su*gar), -sci- (con*sci*ence), -si- (man*si*on), -ss- (ti*ss*ue, mi*ssi*on), -ti- (cap*ti*on).

t   (Por ejemplo: **team, ten, steam, bit**) tras consonante equivale aproximadamente a la *t* española salvo con más aspiración; también se encuentra en palabras deletreadas con: -bt (dou*bt*), -cht (ya*cht*), -ed (talk*ed*), -ght (bou*ght*), -te (bi*te*), th- (*th*yme), -tt- (bo*tt*om), tw- (*tw*o).

th (Por ejemplo: **thin, ether, path**) equivale aproximadamente a la *z* española en el norte de España.

th (Por ejemplo: **that, the, either, smooth**) equivale aproximadamente a la *d* de *adoptar.*

v   (Por ejemplo: **voice, river, live**) equivale aproximadamente a la *b* de *haba* pero es labiodental en vez de bilabial. La pronunciación de la *v* inglesa es igual que la de la *f,* salvo que suenan las cuerdas vocales en la pronunción de la *v.*

w (Por ejemplo: **west, witch, away**) equivale aproximadamente a la *u* de *puesto.*

y (Por ejemplo: **yes, beyond**) equivale aproximadamente a la *i* de
bien; también se encuentra en palabras deletreadas con -i-
(on*i*on, un*i*on), -j- (hallelu*j*ah), y -ll- (torti*ll*a).

z Tiene dos sonidos: /z/ y /zh/. La /z/, la más común (por ejemplo:
zoo, lazy, zone), equivale aproximadamente a la *s* de *isla* y
mismo en ciertas modalidades del español, pero con más sonoridad. Este sonido se pronuncia igual que la *s* española, salvo que
en la pronunciación de la /z/ suenan las cuerdas vocales. Se encuentra el sonido /z/ en algunas palabras deletreadas con: -s-
(ha*s*), -se (ri*s*e), x- (*x*ylophone), y -zz- (bu*zz*ard, fu*zz*). El sonido
/zh/ que se encuentra en **azure** y **brazier** equivale aproximadamente a la *ll* del español de la gente mayor de la cuidad de
Buenos Aires (o sea, como la *j* de la palabra francesa *bonjour*).
El sonido /zh/ también se encuentra en ciertas palabras deletreadas con -ge (gara*g*e, mira*g*e), -si- (vi*si*on), y su- (plea*s*ure).

Pronunciation Key for Spanish
Guía de Pronunciación del español

IPA Symbols Símbolos del AFI	Key Words Ejemplos	Approximate Equivalents
a	alba, banco, cera	father, depart
e	esto, del, parte, mesa	bet; like rain when e ends syllable and is not followed by r, rr, or t
i	ir, fino, adiós, muy	like beet, but shorter
o	oler, flor, grano	like vote, but shorter
u	un, luna, cuento, vergüenza, guarda	fool, group
b	bajo, ambiguo, vaca	by, abet
β	hablar, escribir, lavar	like vehicle, but with lips almost touching
d	dar, desde, andamio, dueña	deal, adept
ð	pedir, edredón, verdad	that, gather
f	fecha, afectar, golf	fan, after
g	gato, grave, gusto, largo, guerra	garden, ugly
h	gemelo, giro, junta, bajo	horse
k	cacao, claro, cura, cuenta, que, quinto	kind, actor
l	lado, lente, habla, papel	lot, altar
ʎ	(in Spain) llama, calle, olla	like million, but with tongue behind teeth
m	mal, amor	more, commit
n	nada, nuevo, mano, bien	not, enter
ɲ	ñapa, año	canyon, companion
ŋ	angosto, aunque	ring, anchor
p	peso, guapo	pill, applaud
r	real, faro, deber	like rice, but with single flap of tongue on roof of mouth
rr	perro, sierra	like rice, but with trill, or vibration of tongue, against upper teeth

IPA Symbols	Key Words	Approximate Equivalents
s	sala, espejo, mas; (in Latin America) cena, hacer, vez	say, clasp
θ	(in Spain) cena, hacer, cierto, cine, zarzuela, lazo, vez	thin, myth
t	tocar, estado, cenit	table, attract
y	ya, ayer; (in Latin America) llama, calle	you, voyage
tʃ	chica, mucho	chill, batch

Diphthongs

ai	baile, hay	high, rye
au	audacia, laudable	out, round
ei	veinte, seis, rey	ray
ie	miel, tambien	fiesta
oi	estoico, hoy	coin, loyal
ua	cuanto	quantity
ue	buena, suerte	sway, quaint

The Basics of Standard Spanish Pronunciation

Whereas the fit between English spelling and pronunciation has for centuries been less than ideal (think, for example, of the various pronunciations of -ough, as in **although, bough, cough,** and **slough**), the fit between today's Spanish spelling and pronunciation is quite good, thanks to the regulatory efforts of the Spanish academies.

The following instructions thus take spelling as their starting point. Pronunciation is described in two ways: with phonetic symbols (enclosed in slashes) and by way of approximate comparisons with English. A wavy line separates variants (like **esnob ~ snob**). A stress mark (') means that the syllable following it is stressed (as in /re'lo/). An asterisk indicates a nonexistent form (like English *llion). A right-facing "arrow" (>), or "greater than" sign, means "became in Spanish" (as in English **rum** and French **rhum** > **ron ~ romo**).

As may be expected of a language that has been used for many centuries, over a vast area, and by many diverse people, Spanish is now pronounced in various ways. Of the many current pronunciations, two are offered as most suitable for speakers of Spanish as a second language. The two standards are identical to a large extent, differing chiefly with respect to the pronunciation of **c** before **e**; **c** before **i**; **z** in any position; and, optionally, **ll**, **g**, and **j**.

To the extent that the two standards differ, features belonging to just one of them are labeled either *Standard 1* or *Standard 2* below.

Features labeled *Standard 1* are accepted as standard in Spain but not in the Western Hemisphere. Features labeled *Standard 2* are accepted as standard in the Western Hemisphere but not in Spain. If you speak Spanish mostly with Spaniards or mostly with people from the Western Hemisphere, your choice of standard will thus be straightforward. If you speak with people from both areas, you can either try to master both standards or, if you want to follow just one of them no matter to whom you speak, pick Standard 2.

a is pronounced /a/, which is similar to the second vowel of the English interjection **aha!** and the vowel of the English interjection **ah,** although much shorter in duration. See also "Diphthongs and Triphthongs" below.

b has three pronunciations. At the beginning of an utterance, after /m/ (whether represented by **m** or by **n**), or after /n/ (whether represented by **n** or by **m**), the letter **b** is pronounced /b/, which is similar to the pronunciation of the first consonant of English **beach, broth, pebble,** etc. For example, in the sentence **Bulgaria envió a ambos embajadores en un barco japonés,** each of the four instances of **b** (and the one instance of **v**) is pronounced in this way.

At the end of a word, more than one pronunciation of **b** may be heard. For example, **club** may be /klub/, /kluβ/, or /klu/. Its plural, **clubs,** may be /klups/, /klus/, and possibly /kluβs/, unless the plural **clubes** is used, whose universal pronunciation is /kluβεs/ (see the next paragraph for interpreting /β/, and **e** for interpreting /ε/). All of the foregoing holds for compounds of **club,** like **aeroclub.** In **esnob ~ snob,** the final **b** is pronounced /b/.

In all other positions (for example, **hablas, hablar,** and **habré**), **b** is pronounced /β/, a sound absent in English, which is made by bringing the lips close together without letting them touch each other (as if you were blowing dust away or blowing out a match or candle), expelling air through the mouth, and vibrating the vocal cords. This sound is thus similar to /v/ (as in English **very** and **vowel**), except that the latter is made by making the lower lip touch the upper teeth. English-speakers should not mistake Spanish /β/ for English /v/.

It follows from the foregoing that if the position of **b** in the utterance changes, its pronunciation may change. For example, when the word **baba** is pronounced in isolation, the first **b** is rendered /b/ and the second one /β/, but in the phrase **la baba,** the first **b** is no longer at the beginning of an utterance (nor is it preceded by the sounds /m/ or /n/), hence the phrase is pronounced /laβaβa/.

These rules of pronunciation also hold true for the letter **v,** which is pronounced /b/ at the beginning of words, and /β/ in the middle. See also **v.**

c has several pronunciations. If it is followed by **e** or **i,** the letter **c** is pronounced /θ/ in Standard 1 and /s/ in Standard 2. The pronunciation of /θ/ in Spanish is similar to that of **th** in English **thatch, think,** etc., but made with somewhat more protrusion of the tongue. The sound /s/ is similar to the pronunciation of **s** in English **say, simple,** etc.

Although Standard 1 has /θ/ for **c** before **e** or **i,** people who use that pronunciation will not be put off if they hear you pronounce the **c** as /s/, because the latter is widespread (though not standard) in Spain. In the Western Hemisphere, **c** before **e** or **i** is always pronounced /s/ and never /θ/. Speakers of Western Hemispheric Spanish will react to /θ/ either as "the correct pronunciation" ("though we don't use it") or as a pretentious pronunciation (unless it comes from people to the manner born, i.e., many Spaniards). Thus, whereas it is desirable though not obligatory that you use Standard 1 in Spain, you would be well advised to use only Standard 2 in the Western Hemisphere, where /θ/ is bound to elicit a sharp reaction of one kind or another (as sharp as British **drawing pin, lorry,** or **trunk call** instead of **thumbtack, truck,** and **long-distance call** would probably elicit in the United States).

ch, wherever it is found, is always pronounced as /tʃ/, which is similar to the pronunciation of **ch** in English **church, child,** etc.

If **c** ends a syllable (for instance, **accionista, facsimíl,** and **técnico**), **c** is pronounced as /k/. Spanish /k/ is similar to the pronunciation of **c** in English **escape, scandal,** etc. To achieve a good rendition of Spanish /k/, hold your open palm in front of your mouth and pronounce first **cape** and **coop,** then **escape** and **scandal.** When pronouncing the first two words, you felt a noticeable puff of air on your palm, but in the last two words you felt almost no puff at all. A noticeable puff of air accompanying a speech sound is called *aspiration;* sounds pronounced with aspiration are *aspirated,* and those pronounced without it are *unaspirated.* Spanish /k/ (like Spanish /p/ and /t/) is always unaspirated, wherever it occurs. Thus, you should have no trouble with Spanish **escapar** and **escandalo** because here /k/ occurs after /s/, and as an English speaker you will automatically pronounce it as unaspirated, just as you would the **c** of the English cognates of those words: **escape** and **scandal.** It is in other positions that you have to be careful not to aspirate: **claro, crear,** etc. (contrast them with their English cognates, both of which have an aspirated /k/: **clear, create**).

See also **k, ll** (under **l**), **q, s,** and **z.**

d has several pronunciations. At the beginning of an utterance, after /n/, or after /l/, this letter is pronounced /d/, which is similar to the pronunciation of **d** in English **dear, dust,** etc., with this difference: in the production of Spanish /d/, the tongue touches the lower edge of the upper front incisors.

When between two vowels, when preceded by a vowel and followed by **r,** or when at the end of a word and not preceded by **r** (as in **pedir, Pedro,** and

libertad), the letter **d** is pronounced /ð/, which is similar to the pronunciation of **th** in English **that, there,** etc., but less interdental than English /ð/ (in the production of the Spanish sound, the tip of the tongue gently touches the lower edge of the upper incisors).

It follows from the foregoing that if the position of **d** in the utterance changes, its pronunciation may change. Contrast, for example, these three utterances: (1) **Dinamarca mandó embajadores a doce países,** (2) **En Dinamarca viven unos cuantos americanos,** and (3) **Iremos a Dinamarca.** In (1), the **d** of **Dinamarca** is pronounced /d/ because it comes at the beginning of an utterance; in (2) the same **d** is also pronounced /d/ because it comes after /n/; but in (3) the same **d** is pronounced /ð/ because none of the conditions for pronouncing it /d/ is met. Similarly, when the word **dedo** is pronounced in isolation, the first **d** is rendered /d/ (and the second one /ð/), but in the phrase **mi dedo,** the first **d** is no longer at the beginning of an utterance (nor is it preceded by /n/ or /l/); hence the phrase is pronounced /miðeðo/.

e has two pronunciations. The instruction given in some books that **e** is pronounced /e/ when stressed and /ɛ/ when unstressed does not hold true for today's Spanish and may never have been an accurate description of its pronunciation in any variety of the language.

Here are better guidelines for **e** (except when it is part of a diphthong or triphthong):

If **e** is found in a syllable ending in a consonant (see "Syllabification" below), it is pronounced /ɛ/, which is similar to the pronunciation of **è** in French or to the vowel of **bet, let, met,** etc., as pronounced in Standard English, that is, with considerable lowering of the jaw, for example, **embaldosar, fresco, hablen,** and **mestizo.**

If **e** ends a syllable and the next one begins with **r, rr,** or **t,** it is pronounced /ɛ/, for instance, **pero, caballete** (the first **e**), **cerrar,** and **jinete.**

Otherwise, **e** is pronounced /e/, which is similar to the pronunciation of **é** in French, that is, the jaw is lowered only minimally (the closest English comes to having a sound like /e/ is the vowel of **ache, rake, stake,** etc.), for example, **caballete** (the second **e**), **hablé,** and **mesa.** In this dictionary, the sounds /e/ and /ɛ/ are both represented by /e/.

See also "Diphthongs and Triphthongs" below.

g has several pronunciations. At the beginning of an utterance and when followed by **a, o, u,** or a consonant letter except **n** (as in **gato, goma, gusto,** or **glaciar**), **g** is pronounced /g/, which is similar to the pronunciation of **g** in English **get, go, gumption,** etc.

At the beginning of a word and when followed by **n,** the letter **g** is silent (as in **gnomo**). That pronunciation is in fact so widespread and reputable that a **g**-less spelling is now acceptable and is in fact preferred in this dictionary (see "Miscellaneous" below).

When **g** occurs at the end of a syllable and is preceded by **n,** it is silent, as in **búmerang.** In older borrowings from other languages, that **g** was systematically or sometimes omitted, as in **sterling > esterlina, pudding > pudín.**

Before **e** or **i** (as in **gemir** and **gigante**), except if it comes at the end of a word, the letter **g** is pronounced /x/, which is absent in most varieties of current English. This sound is similar to the pronunciation of **ch** in German **Bach,** that of **ch** in Israeli Hebrew **zecher,** and that of **ch** in Scots English **loch, Lochaber,** etc. Press the back of the tongue against the soft palate, expel air (as if coughing), and do not vibrate the vocal chords. **g** before **e** or **i** can also be pronounced /h/, as in English **"house,"** which is common in Latin America and in southern Spain. In this dictionary, both /x/ and /h/ are represented by /h/.

If **g** ends a syllable that is not the last syllable of the word (as in **dogma** and the first syllable of **zigzag**), this letter is pronounced /g/. In such cases, the next syllable always begins with a consonant.

Otherwise, **g** is pronounced /ɣ/, a sound absent in English, which is made by bringing the back of the tongue close to the soft palate (without letting them touch), expelling air through the mouth, and vibrating the vocal chords. Examples are **hago** and **hígado**. In this dictionary, both sounds, /g/ and /ɣ/, are represented by /g/.

h is silent.

i is pronounced /i/, which is similar to the vowel of English **beet, feet, sheen,** etc., but shorter (for instance, **dicho, isla,** and **cursi**).

See also **y**.

j is almost always pronounced /x/, although a pronunciation as /h/ is also acceptable in parts of Latin America and southern Spain (see **g** for interpreting these symbols). A notable exception is **reloj,** which many speakers pronounce /re'lo/. That pronunciation of **reloj** is so widespread that **reló** is an alternate spelling of the singular form, but only in informal writing. In the plural, everyone pronounces /x/ or /h/ and therefore writes the **j: relojes.**

l when not doubled is pronounced /l/, which is formed by putting the tip of the tongue against the sockets of the upper incisors, the remainder of the tongue lying flat. Spanish /l/ thus does not have the hollow sound of English /l/, in whose formation the back of the tongue rises toward the palate.

ll has two pronunciations, /ʎ/ and /y/, which vary by region and class rather than by placement within a word. /ʎ/, a sound similar to the Italian **gli,** has no real equivalent in English, although the **lli** of **million** comes close. While /ʎ/ is held to be the "correct" pronunciation by Spanish radio and television guidelines, it is almost never used in Latin America, except among some academics and the very wealthy. In Spain it is only heard in the northern regions of Castile. Much more common, and almost universally accepted today, is the pronunciation /y/, which is similar to our **y** in **yes** or **yam.**

In the Southern Cone of Latin America, a third pronunciation, /ʒ/ (like the French **Geneviève**), is also used.

Traditionally, Spanish does not have /m/ at the end of a word when it is pronounced in isolation. However, a few words (all learned borrowings from other languages) end in **m** (for example, **álbum, factótum, ídem, médium, memorándum, ultimátum,** and **vademécum**), and that letter always appears in the Spanish names of many places outside Spanish-speaking areas, like **Bírmingham, Búckingham, Siam,** and **Vietnam.** Both /m/ and /n/ are heard in such words, depending on people's ability to pronounce /m/ at the end of a word (as more and more Spanish-speakers study other languages, they find it easier to produce that sound in that position) and their interest in maintaining the supposedly "correct" (i.e., non-Spanish) pronunciation of that letter.

n has several pronunciations. If immediately followed by a labial consonant (represented by **b, f, m, p,** or **v**) whether in the same word or in the next one, it is pronounced /m/ (as in the words **anfitrión, inmediato, anverso,** or the sentences **insiste en bucear, insiste en pelear,** and **en muchos casos hay más**). Since /m/ + /m/ is reduced to a single /m/, **en muchos casos** actually has just one /m/.

However, /m/ + /n/ (as in **insomne**) is not reduced.

Before /k/ or /g/ (as in **aunque** and **angosto**), **n** is pronounced /ŋ/, which is similar to the final consonant of **sing, long,** and **song** as pronounced in English.

In all other positions (as in **Anatolia, andan,** and **nombrar**), **n** is pronounced /n/, which is similar to the pronunciation of **n** in English **hand, near,** etc.

ñ is pronounced /ɲ/, which is similar to the pronunciation of **ny** in English **canyon** or **ni** in English **onion.**

o is pronounced similarly to the **o** in the English words **tote** and **gloat.** English speakers, however, must be careful not to end the pronunciation of this vowel with an "off-glide" (an "off-glide," in this case, would close the **o** into a **u** sound at the end of the vowel). Thus, the Spanish **no** and the English **no** are not exactly alike, as the Spanish ends in a pure /o/ sound, while the English "off-glides" into a /u/, producing /nou/.

p, where it is pronounced, stands for /p/, which is similar to the pronunciation of **p** in English **space, spare, spook,** etc., but different from that of **p** in English **pike, peak, poke,** etc., in that it is not aspirated (see **c** for definitions of aspirated and unaspirated sounds).

Spanish **ps** at the beginning of a word is pronounced /s/.

q is always followed by **ue** or **ui.** The sequence **que** is pronounced /ke/ and **qui** is pronounced /ki/ (for example, **quince**).

To represent the sound sequences /kue/ and /kui/, Spanish has **cue** and **cui** respectively (as in **cueva** and **cuidar**).

Because **q** is always followed by **u,** if Spanish-speakers borrow words containing just **q** from other languages, that letter is changed to **k.** Thus, the Spanish names of Iraq and Qatar, for example, are **Irak** and **Katar.**

r has two pronunciations. At the beginning of a word or when it comes after **l, n,** or **s** (for example, **reir, alrededor, enrojecer,** and **Israel**), this letter has the same pronunciation as **rr** (see below).

In all other positions, **r** is pronounced with one flip of the upper part of the tongue against the sockets of the upper incisors (for instance, **leer, para, pera, pero, tercero,** and **treinta**).

rr is pronounced with a trill (several flips) of the upper front part of the tongue against the sockets of the upper incisors (for instance, **parra, perra, perro,** and **sierra**). Thus, **para** and **parra** are different words, with different meanings. The same applies to **caro** and **carro, pera** and **perra, pero** and **perro, torero** and **torrero,** and other pairs of words.

s has several pronunciations. When it represents the plural ending of nouns recently borrowed from other languages, it is silent in certain words, like **cabarets, carnets, complots, conforts, superávits, tíckets, trusts, vermuts.**

Before the letters **b, v, d, g** (but only when the letter is not followed by **e** or **i**), **l, m, n,** or **r** (whether any of those eight letters appear in the same word as **s** or they appear in the next word), you have an alternative in both standards if **s** is not the last letter of the word: it may be pronounced /z/ (a sound similar to the pronunciation of **z** in English **zebra, zoo,** etc.) or /s/ (see **c** for interpreting that symbol): **esbelto, esdrújulo, esgrimir, isla, esmalte, Israel, los baúles, los varones, los dedos, los guantes, los lagos, los maestros, los nervios, los ratones,** etc. If **s** is the last letter, only /s/ is found (for instance, in the family name **Pons**).

If **s** is followed by **r** (whether in the same word or in the next one), besides the two pronunciations suggested above, /s/ or /z/, a third possibility is not to pronounce the **s** at all and, as compensation, trill the **r** more. The word **Israel** (and its derivatives) thus has three pronunciations: /isrrael/, /izrrael/, and /irrrael/.

Otherwise, **s** is pronounced /s/ (as in **ese, especial, hablas, hasta, insistir, seco**).

If **s** is followed by **h,** the foregoing paragraph applies, except in the case of Spanish words recently borrowed from other languages or words modeled on such recently borrowed words, in which **sh** constitutes a unit, to be pronounced /ʃ/ (a sound similar to the pronunciation of **sh** in English **shall, sheet, should,** etc.). Thus, in **deshacer,** an old Spanish word not recently borrowed from another language, the instructions about **s** apply and the **h** is silent (hence the first two syllables of that word are /desa/), whereas in **riksha, sh** is pronounced /ʃ/.

See also **b, c, t, z,** and "Syllabification" below.

t is pronounced /t/, which is similar to the pronunciation of **t** in English **stoop, stake, steer,** etc., but different from that of **t** in English **take, teak, took,** etc., in that it is less aspirated (see **c**).

The Spanish /t/ is made by touching the tip of the tongue against the upper incisors (in contrast to English /t/, in whose production the tongue touches the gums). In two positions, **t** may not be pronounced as described above. First, before **l** or **m** in the same word (as in **atleta, aritmético,** and **ritmo**) you have an alternative: **t** may be pronounced as described or it may be pronounced /ð/ (see **d** for interpreting that symbol).

Second, the **t** at the end of a word may be silent. Probably many, most, or all Spanish-speakers pronounce it in **cenit, déficit, fagot, mamut, superavít,** and **el Tíbet ~ el Tibet,** whereas in other words the **t** is silent, for instance **cabaret, carnet, complot, tícket, trust,** and **vermut,** which are pronounced as if written *cabaré, *carné, *compló, *tique, *trus, and *vermú (the plurals are pronounced identically to their singulars). In still other words you have an alternative: **confort** is pronounced either /kom'for/ or /kom'fort/ (the plural **conforts** has both variants too).

u has two pronunciations. In the combinations **gue, gui, que,** and **qui,** the letter **u** is silent, for example, **guedeja** /geðeha/, **quedar** /keðar/, and **quien** /kien/ (see **q** and **e** on the pronunciation of those letters).

In all other cases, it is pronounced /u/, which is similar to the vowel sound of English **who** and **cool.** Thus, **puesto** and **seudonónimo,** for example, are pronounced /puesto/ and /seuðonónimo/.

v has two pronunciations. At the beginning of an utterance or after **n** (which in this position is pronounced /m/), the letter **v** is pronounced /b/, which is similar to the first consonant of English **beach, broth,** etc. In all other positions, this letter is pronounced /β/ (see **b** for interpreting that symbol). For example, in the sentence **¿Es verdad que en el anverso de la medalla se ve un pavo real?,** the second and sixth words have /b/ and the eleventh and thirteenth have /β/.

The instructions for pronouncing **b** and those for pronouncing **v** are identical (depending on the position of those letters in the utterance), as a consequence of which pairs of words like **baca** and **vaca** or **hube** and **uve** are homophones in today's Spanish and, as a further consequence of which, if you hear /b/ or /β/, you cannot tell whether it is to be represented by **b** or by **v** unless you know how to spell the word.

See also **b.**

w, which is found only in borrowings from Germanic languages and French, has several pronunciations. In several words, it is pronounced as if it were **b** or **v** and in such cases alternate spellings with **v** are found too: **wagneriano ~ vagneriano, Westfalia ~ Vestfalia.** The forms with **v** are preferable.

In at least a few words, **w** is pronounced /w/ (a sound similar to the first sound of English **win** and **won**), and for one of them an alternate spelling with **u** exists: **Malawi, Taiwán, Zimbabwe.**

In **whisky,** the letter combination **wh** is pronounced /w/ or /gw/.

x has several pronunciations. If **x** occurs before a consonant (as in **experiencia, extremidad,** and **mixto**), pronounce it /ks/. That pronunciation is probably the most frequent in words beginning with the prefix **ex-** followed by a consonant, for example **excelente,** widely pronounced /eksselente/ in Latin America, or /eksθelente/ in Castile.

If **x** occurs between vowels, you have an alternative in certain words (**examen** and **exiguo,** for example, may be pronounced with /ks/ or /gz/, but not in others (for instance, all Spanish-speakers, it seems, now pronounce **sexo** with /ks/).

At the end of a word, the pronunciation of **x** is in flux. In **ántrax, Benelux, dux, fénix, látex,** and **tórax,** /ks/ seems to be the most frequent if not universal pronunciation today, although /s/ is also heard.

At least some exceptions to those pronunciations are heard in words of Native American origin: for example, in **México** and **mexicano,** the **x** is now always pronounced /x/ (those are the spellings official and universal in Mexico; elsewhere, **Méjico** and **mejicano** are used); in **Xochimilco** (a Mexican place name), the **x** is always pronounced /s/.

Further exceptions are certain given and family names, which are found in two variants: one preserving a now archaic spelling with **x** (like **Xavier** and **Ximénez**) and the other spelled in modern fashion with **j** (**Javier** and **Jiménez**). Here, **x** is pronounced /h/, that is, just like **j.**

y has several pronunciations. In the word **y,** it is pronounced /i/ (see **i** for interpreting that symbol).

When it represents the first or last segment of a diphthong or triphthong (see "Diphthongs and Triphthongs" below), as in **ya, yegua, yunque, ley, rey, soy,** and **Paraguay,** the letter **y** is pronounced /y/ (see **ll** for interpreting that symbol).

In certain varieties of Spanish, **y** is pronounced with more occlusion, so that it has come to be close to /ʒ/ if not actually that sound (see **ll** for interpreting the latter symbol); and in still other varieties it is pronounced with so much occlusion that is has come to be close to /dʒ/ if not actually that (/dʒ/ is similar to the first consonant of English **Jacob, Jerusalem, Jew,** etc.)

Certain family names have two spelling variants, an archaic one with **y** and one spelled in modern fashion with **i** (like **Yglesias ~ Iglesias**). Here, **y** is pronounced /i/, that is, just like **i.**

z has several pronunciations. In Standard 1, you have an alternative: (1) In all positions, pronounce it /θ/ (see **c** for interpreting that symbol). Or, (2) Before the letters **b, v, d, g, l, m, n,** or **r** (whether in the same word or in the next one), pronounce it /ð/ (see **d** for interpreting that symbol), and in all other positions pronounce it /θ/.

In Standard 2, you have an alternative: (3) In all positions, pronounce it /s/ (see **c** for interpreting that symbol). Or, (4) Before the letters **b, v, d, g, l, m, n,** or **r** (whether in the same word or in the next one), pronounce it /z/, and in all other positions pronounce it /s/.

Diphthongs and Triphthongs

Spanish has fifteen diphthongs and eight triphthongs.

Eight of the diphthongs begin with a semivowel:

ia /ia/ is spelled **ya** at the beginning of a word, e.g., **desahuciar, yámbico.**
ua /ua/, e.g., **guardar.**
ie /ie/ is spelled **ye** at the beginning of a word, e.g., **agüero, bien, higiene, siete, yema.**
ue /ue/ is spelled **üe** after **g** that is not pronounced /h/, e.g., **huelga, hueste, huevo, vergüenza.**
io /io/ e.g., **biombo, piojo.** The spelling **io** at the beginning of a word is an imitation of Greek.
uo /uo/, e.g., **arduo.**
iu /iu/ is spelled **yu** at the beginning of a word, e.g., **yuca, yugo, triunfo.**
ui /ui/ (spelled **uy** in **muy**), e.g., **cuidar, muy.** For **uy** representing /uy/, see **uy** in the next section.

Take care to pronounce diphthongs beginning with a semivowel as diphthongs and not as two syllables. Thus, whereas English **barrio** has three syllables, Spanish **barrio** has two (**ba-rrio**), pronounced /barrio/.

Seven of the diphthongs end in a semivowel:
ai /ai/ is spelled **ay** at the end of most words; rarely, **ay** is found in the middle of a word, e.g., **aimará ~ aymará, hay, Raimundo, Seychelles.** If **ay** occurs before a vowel in the same word, it represents not a diphthong but /a/ + /y/, and each of those sounds belongs to a different syllable (thus, **aya** and **haya** for example are syllabified **a-ya** and **ha-ya**).
au /au/, e.g., **caudillo.**
ei is almost always pronounced /ey/ and is almost always spelled **ey** at the end of a word, e.g., **reina, rey.** A pronunciation exception is **reir,** which is pronounced as if it is spelled *reír.* If **ey** occurs before a vowel in the same word, it represents not a diphthong but /e/ + /y/, and each of those sounds belongs to a different syllable (thus, **reyes** and **leyenda** for instance are syllabified **re-yes** and **le-yen-da**).
eu /eu/, e.g., **seudonónimo.**
oi is almost always pronounced /oi/ and is spelled **oy** at the end of a word, e.g., **hoy,** and in certain family names in other positions too (like **Goytisolo**). A pronunciation exception is **oir,** which is pronounced as if spelled *oír.* If **oy** occurs before a vowel in the same word, it represents not a diphthong but /o/ + /y/ and each of those sounds belongs to a different syllable (thus, **Goya** is syllabified **Go-ya**).
uy, which always occurs at the end of a word, is almost always pronounced /ui/ (as in ¡**huy!, Jujuy**). The exception is **muy,** whose pronunciation is given in the previous section. If **uy** occurs before a vowel in the same word, it represents not a diphthong but /u/ + /y/ and each of those sounds belongs to a different syllable (thus, **cuyo** and **tuyas** are syllabified **cu-yo** and **tu-yas**).

The triphthongs are:
iai /iai/ e.g., **despreciáis.**
iau /iau/ e.g., **miau.**
iei /iei/ e.g., **despreciéis.**
uai /uai/ (spelled **uay** at the end of a word), e.g., **evaluáis, Uruguay.**
uau /uau/ e.g., **guau.**
uei /uei/ (spelled **uey** at the end of a word), e.g., **evaluéis, buey.**

List of Abbreviations Used in this Dictionary

a adjective
Abbr. abbreviation
acc accusative
adv adverb
Aer. aeronautics
Agr. agriculture
Anat. anatomy
Archit. architecture
Archeol. archeology
art. article
art art
Astron. astronomy
Astrol. astrology
Auto. automobiles
aux auxiliary
Biol. biology
Bot. botany
Cards. card games
Chem. chemistry
Com. commerce
Compar. comparative
condit conditional
conjunc conjunction
Cul. culinary
Dance. dancing
dat dative
dim diminutive
Eccl. ecclesiastical
Educ. education
Elec. electricity
Engin. engineering
Ent. entomology
esp. español, Spanish
Euph. euphemism
f feminine
Fig. figurative
Fig. Inf. used
  figuratively in
  informal speech
  or writing
fut future
gen generally; genitive

Geog. geography
Geol. geology
Geom. geometry
Gram. grammar
Gym. gymnastics
Herald. heraldry
Hist. history
Ichth. ichthyology
imperf imperfect
impers impersonal
indic indicative
indef art indefinite
  article
Inf. informal
infin infinitive
ing. inglés, English
insep inseparable
interj interjection,
  exclamation
interr interrogative
Ironic. ironical
irr irregular
Lat. Am. Latin America
Law. law
Ling. linguistics
Lit. literature
m masculine
Mas. masonry
Math. mathematics
Mech. mechanics
Med. medical
Metall. metallurgy
mf masculine or feminine
Mil. military
Mineral. mineralogy
Mus. music
Myth. mythology
n noun
Naut. nautical
Nav. naval
neut neuter

Obs obsolete
Opt. optics
Ornith. ornithology
part participle
Pers. personal; person
Pharm. pharmacy
Philos. philosophy
Phonet. phonetics
Photo. photography
Phys. physics
Physiol. physiology
pl plural
Poet. poetic
Polit. political
Polit. Econ. political
  economy
poss possessive
prep preposition
pres present
Print. printing
pron pronoun
Psychol. psychology
Radio. radio
Rail. railway
Sew. sewing
sing singular
Spirit. spiritualism
Sports. sports
subjunc subjunctive
Superl superlative
Surg. surgery
Surv. surveying
Tan. tanning
Theat. theater
Theol. theology
v aux auxiliary verb
vi intransitive verb
vr reflexive verb
vt transitive verb
West. Hem. Western
  Hemispheric Spanish
Zool. zoology

Spanish–English
Dictionary

A

a /a/ *f*, name of the letter A
a /a/ *prep* to; at; on; by; in, into; up to; according to; if, etc. 1. Denotes the direct complement of verb before objects representing specified persons or animals, personified nouns, pronouns referring to specific persons (**alguien, entrambos, cualquiera,** etc.), demonstrative or relative pronouns, collective nouns representing persons (**el público, la muchedumbre,** etc.), names of countries, cities, rivers, etc., except where these invariably take the def. art., e.g. *Dejé a Varsovia,* I left Warsaw, *but Dejé el Perú,* I left Peru. 2. Introduces indirect obj. when this is a noun governed by a verb implying motion, or an emphatic pers. pron., e.g. *Nos conviene a ti y a mí,* It suits both you and me. It is also used before indirect obj. to avoid ambiguity when there is both an indirect and direct obj. 3. Denotes the complement of verb when this is an infin., e.g. *Enseñó a pintar a María,* He taught Mary to paint. 4. Indicates direction or destination, e.g. *Vamos a Edimburgo,* We are going to Edinburgh. 5. Signifies location, or point of time when action takes place, e.g. *Vinieron a las doce.* They came at twelve o'clock. 6. Describes position of persons or things, e.g. *Se sentaron a la puerta,* They sat down at the door. *La casa queda a la derecha,* The house is on the right. 7. Denotes interval of time or place between one thing and another, e.g. *de tres a cinco de la tarde,* from three to five in the afternoon, *de calle a calle,* from street to street. 8. Expresses manner of action, e.g. *a la francesa,* in the French way, *bordado a mano,* embroidered by hand. 9. Indicates rate or price, e.g. *a cuatro pesetas la libra,* at four pesetas the lb. 10. Indicates difference or comparison, e.g. *Va mucho de querer a hacer,* There's a difference between wishing and doing. 11. Sometimes is synonymous with *hasta, según, hacia* and governs almost all parts of speech. Has many idiomatic uses. 12. Before infin. sometimes has conditional sense, e.g. *A haber sabido las noticias no lo hubiéramos hecho,* If we had heard the news we would not have done it. 13. Before infin. expresses "to be," e.g. *la nueva constitución a implementar en dos semanas...,* the new constitution to be implemented in two weeks.... 14. With certain nouns, adjectives, and infinitives forms adverbial phrases, e.g. *poco a poco,* little by little, *a veces,* sometimes, *a ciegas,* blindly, etc. *¡a ver!* let's see!; *Colombia* hello! (on telephone). **A + el** becomes **al,** e.g. *al rey,* to the king. *Al* + infin. means when or on, e.g. *al marcharme yo,* when I left (on my leaving); *Lat. Am.* **al año** a year later; *Lat. Am.* **a la semana** a week later; *Lat. Am.* **al mes** a month later
abacería /aβase'ria; aβaθe'ria/ *f,* grocery shop
abacero /aβa'sero; aβa'θero/ **(-ra)** *n* grocer
ábaco /'aβako/ *m, Archit.* abacus; counting frame
abad /a'βað/ *m,* abbot
abajo /a'βaho/ *adv* under; underneath; below; down. Used immediately after noun in adverbial phrases, e.g. *cuesta a., escalera a.,* downhill, downstairs. *interj* Down with! e.g., *¡A. el rey!* Down with the king! *venirse a.,* to fall down; *Fig.* collapse
abalanzamiento /aβa,lansa'miento; aβa,lanθa'miento/ *m,* balancing; rushing upon; dashing
abalanzar /aβalan'sar; aβalan'θar/ *vt* to balance; impel violently; *vr* throw oneself upon; attack, rush upon; *(with prep a)* rush into, risk. **Se abalanzó hacia ellos,** He rushed toward them
abalear /aβale'ar/ *vt, Lat. Am.* to shoot at
abalorio /aβa'lorio/ *m,* glass bead; bead work
abanderado /aβande'raðo/ *m,* standardbearer; *Argentina* valedictorian
abanderizar /aβanderi'sar; aβanderi'θar/ *vt* to organize in groups; *vr* band together
abandonado /aβando'naðo/ *a* deserted; forlorn; helpless; indolent, careless; slovenly

abandonamiento /a,βandona'miento/ *m,* desertion; forlornness; helplessness; carelessness; slovenliness
abandonar /aβando'nar/ *vt* to forsake, desert; neglect; leave; give up; renounce; *vr* neglect oneself; grow discouraged; *(with prep a)* give oneself over to
abandono /aβan'dono/ *m,* abandonment; defenselessness; forlornness; dilapidation; renunciation; neglect; slovenliness; debauchery
abanicar /aβani'kar/ *vt* to fan
abanico /aβa'niko/ *m,* fan; anything fan-shaped; *Inf.* sword; railway signal; *Naut.* derrick. **en a.,** fan-shaped
abaniqueo /aβani'keo/ *m,* fanning; swinging, oscillation; gesticulation
abaratar /aβara'tar/ *vt* to lower the price; make less expensive; *vr* fall in price
abarca /a'βarka/ *f,* leather sandal, worn chiefly in the Basque provinces
abarcador /aβarka'ðor/ **(-ra)** *n* one who clasps or embraces; monopolist
abarcadura /aβarka'ðura/ *f,* **abarcamiento** /aβarka'miento/ *m,* inclusion; scope
abarcar /aβar'kar/ *vt* to clasp, encircle; include, comprise; undertake, attempt; monopolize
abarquillar /aβarki'yar; aβarki'ʎar/ *vt* to shape into a roll; roll; curl
abarracar /aβarra'kar/ **(se)** *vi* and *vr Mil.* to go into barracks
abarrancadero /aβarranka'ðero/ *m,* rough road; ravine, precipice; *Fig.* difficult situation
abarrancar /aβarran'kar/ *vt* to ditch; make a ravine; *vr* fall into a pit; stick (in the mud, etc.); get into difficulties; *Naut.* run aground
abarrotería /aβarrote'ria/ *f, Mexico* grocery store, grocery, grocer's
abarrotero, -a /aβarro'tero/ *mf Lat. Am.* grocer
abarrotes /aβa'rrotes/ *m pl, Lat. Am.* groceries
abastar /aβas'tar/ see **abastecer**
abastecedor /aβastese'ðor; aβasteθe'ðor/ **(-ra)** *a* provisioning, supplying. *n* provider; purveyor, supplier; caterer
abastecer /aβaste'ser; aβaste'θer/ *vt irr* to supply, provide; purvey. See **conocer**
abastecimiento /aβastesi'miento; aβasteθi'miento/ *m,* providing; supply, provision; catering; supplies
abasto /a'βasto/ *m,* provisions, food; *Com.* supply. *adv* plentifully, abundantly
abate /a'βate/ *m,* abbé
abatido /aβa'tiðo/ *a* dejected, depressed; spiritless; discouraged; crushed, humbled; *Com.* depreciated
abatimiento /aβati'miento/ *m,* dejection, depression; humiliation; discouragement; falling; lowering; *(Aer. Naut.)* drift
abatir /aβa'tir/ *vt* to knock down; overthrow; demolish; lower, take down; droop; humiliate; discourage; *Naut.* dismantle; *vi (Aer. Naut.)* drift; or be despondent, despair; humble oneself; swoop down (of birds). **a. el vuelo,** to fly down
ABC /aβe'se; aβe'θe/ *m,* ABCs (e.g. *el ABC de la física,* the ABCs of physics)
abdicación /aβðika'sion; aβðika'θion/ *f,* abdication
abdicar /aβði'kar/ *vt* to abdicate; revoke, cancel; give up (rights, opinions)
abdomen /aβ'ðomen/ *m,* abdomen
abdominal /aβðomi'nal/ *a* abdominal
abecé /aβe'se; aβe'θe/ *m,* ABCs
abecedario /aβese'ðario; aβeθe'ðario/ *m,* ABCs, alphabet; reading book, primer
abedul /aβe'ðul/ *m,* birch tree; birch wood
abeja /a'βeha/ *f,* bee. **a. maestra,** queen bee. **a. obrera,** worker
abejar /aβe'har/ *m,* beehive
abejero /aβe'hero/ **(-ra)** *n* beekeeper
abejón /aβe'hon/ *m,* drone; hornet
abejorro /aβe'horro/ *m,* bumblebee

aberración /aβerra'sion; aβerra'θion/ *f*, deviation; error, lapse; (*Astron. Phys. Biol.*) aberration

abertura /aβer'tura/ *f*, opening; aperture, gap, hole; fissure, cleft; mountain pass; naturalness, frankness

abeto /a'βeto/ *m*, fir tree

abierto /a'βierto/ *a* open, not enclosed; open, full-blown (flowers); frank, sincere. *adv* openly. *m*, open (tournament); *Colombia* clearing

abigarrado /aβiga'rraðo/ *a* variegated; varied; speckled

abigotado /aβigo'taðo/ *a* having a thick mustache

abintestato /aβintes'tato/ *a Law*. intestate

abismal /aβis'mal/ *a* abysmal

abismar /aβis'mar/ *vt* to plunge into an abyss; depress, sadden; *vr* despair; be plunged in thought; be amazed

abismo /a'βismo/ *m*, chasm, abyss, gulf; hell

abjuración /aβhura'sion; aβhura'θion/ *f*, abjuration

abjurar /aβhu'rar/ *vt* to forswear, retract

ablactar /aβlak'tar/ *vt* to wean

ablandamiento /aβlanda'miento/ *m*, softening; placating

ablandante /aβlan'dante/ *a* softening; placatory

ablandar /aβlan'dar/ *vt* to soften; appease, placate; loosen; relax; *vi* and *vr* be softened; be appeased; grow less stormy; (elements) decrease in force

ablandecer /aβlande'ser; aβlande'θer/ *vt irr* to soften. See **conocer**

ablución /aβlu'sion; aβlu'θion/ *f*, ablution

abnegación /aβnega'sion; aβnega'θion/ *f*, abnegation, self-sacrifice

abnegado /aβne'gaðo/ *a* self-sacrificing

abnegarse /aβne'garse/ *vr irr* to deprive oneself, sacrifice oneself. See **cegar**

abobado /aβo'βaðo/ *a* bewildered; foolish-looking, silly

abobar /aβo'βar/ *vt* to daze, bewilder; make stupid

abocado /aβo'kaðo/ *a* full-flavored, pleasant (of wine)

abocar /aβo'kar/ *vt* to seize with the mouth; bring nearer; transfer (contents of one jug to another); *vr* meet, assemble; *vi Naut.* enter (a channel, port, etc.).

abocarse (con...), to contact (...), get in touch (with...)

abocetado /aβose'taðo; aβoθe'taðo/ *a Art.* unfinished; sketchy

abochornado /aβotʃor'naðo/ *a* flushed (of the face); ashamed; embarrassed

abochornar /aβotʃor'nar/ *vt* to overheat, make flushed; shame; embarrass; *vr* (plants) dry up

abofetear /aβofete'ar/ *vt* to slap, hit; buffet

abogacía /aβoga'sia; aβoga'θia/ *f*, legal profession; practice of law; advocacy

abogaderas, abogaderías /aβoga'ðeras/ *f pl Lat. Am.* hair-splitting, specious arguments, legalistics

abogado /aβo'gaðo/ **(-da)** *n* lawyer

abogar /aβo'gar/ *vi* to defend at law; intercede for; advocate, champion

abolengo /aβo'lengo/ *m*, lineage, descent, family; inheritance

abolición /aβoli'sion; aβoli'θion/ *f*, abolition

abolir /aβo'lir/ *vt* to abolish; cancel; annul

abolladura /aβoya'ðura; aβoʎa'ðura/ *f*, bruise; dent; embossment

abollar /aβo'yar; aβo'ʎar/ *vt* to bruise; dent

abombado /aβom'baðo/ *a* convex; domed; *Mexico* tight (tipsy)

abombar /aβom'bar/ *vt* to make convex; *Inf.* deafen, bewilder; *vr* begin to putrefy; get intoxicated; *Mexico* become tight, get tight (tipsy)

abominable /aβomi'naβle/ *a* abominable

abominación /aβomina'sion; aβomina'θion/ *f*, abomination; loathing, detestation

abominar /aβomi'nar/ *vt* to abominate, loathe, detest

abonable /aβo'naβle/ *a* subscribable; payable

abonado /aβo'naðo/ **(-da)** *a* trustworthy, reliable; ready, prepared, inclined. *n* subscriber; season ticket holder (for concerts, etc.)

abonanzar /aβonan'sar; aβonan'θar/ *vi impers* to clear up, be fine (weather)

abonar /aβo'nar/ *vt* to guarantee; go surety for; improve, better; manure; ratify, confirm; pay; *Com.* place to the credit of; *vr* subscribe, become a subscriber; take out (season tickets, etc.)

abonaré /aβona're/ *m, Com.* due bill; promissory note, I.O.U.

abono /a'βono/ *m*, subscription; voucher; guarantee; manure. **a. verde,** leaf mold. **en a. de,** in payment of; in support of

aboquillado /aβoki'yaðo; aβoki'ʎaðo/ *a* tipped (of cigarettes)

abordar /aβor'ðar/ *vt Naut.* to board a ship; *Naut.* collide, run into; accost, tackle; undertake; *vi Naut.* put into port

aborigen /aβor'ihen/ *a* aboriginal

aborígenes /aβo'rihenes/ *m pl*, aborigines

aborrachado /aβorra'tʃaðo/ *a* bright red; highly colored; flushed

aborrascarse /aβorras'karse/ *vr* to grow stormy

aborrecedor /aβorrese'ðor; aβorreθe'ðor/ **(-ra)** *a* hateful. *n* hater, loather

aborrecer /aβorre'ser; aβorre'θer/ *vt irr* to hate, loathe; desert offspring (animals, birds). See **conocer**

aborrecible /aβorre'siβle; aβorre'θiβle/ *a* hateful, detestable

aborrecimiento /aβorresi'miento; aβorreθi'miento/ *m*, hate, detestation; dislike

abortar /aβor'tar/ *vt* to abort; foil (a plot); *vi Med.* miscarry; fail, go awry

abortivo /aβor'tiβo/ *a* abortive

aborto /a'βorto/ *m*, abortion; miscarriage; failure

abotagarse /aβota'garse/ *vr* to swell up, become bloated

abotonador /aβotona'ðor/ *m*, button-hook

abotonar /aβoto'nar/ *vt* to button; *vi* bud, sprout

abra /'aβra/ *f*, cove, small bay; narrow gorge; fissure, cleft; *Argentina* clearing (in a forest)

abrasador /aβrasa'ðor/ *a* burning, flaming

abrasamiento /aβrasa'miento/ *m*, burning; ardor, heat

abrasar /aβra'sar/ *vt* to burn; dry up, parch (plants); squander, waste; shame; *vi* burn; *vr* be very hot, glow; burn with passion

abrasión /aβra'sion/ *f*, abrasion

abrasivo /aβra'siβo/ *a* and *m*, abrasive

abrazadera /aβrasa'ðera; aβraθa'ðera/ *f*, clasp; clamp

abrazamiento /aβrasa'miento; aβraθa'miento/ *m*, embracing

abrazar /aβra'sar; aβra'θar/ *vt* to embrace, clasp in one's arms; follow, adopt; engage in; seize, take advantage of; comprise, include; surround; take in hand; clamp; clasp. **abrazarse a,** to clutch, hang on to

abrazo /a'βraso; a'βraθo/ *m*, embrace

abrelatas /aβre'latas/ *m*, can opener

abrevar /aβre'βar/ *vt* to water cattle; irrigate, water

abreviación /aβreβia'sion; aβreβia'θion/ *f*, abbreviation, shortening; summary; hastening

abreviador /aβreβia'ðor/ *m*, abridger; condenser

abreviar /aβre'βiar/ *vt* to abbreviate, shorten; hasten, accelerate; condense, abridge. **a. tiempo,** to save time. **Y para a....,** And, to make a long story short...

abreviatura /aβreβia'tura/ *f*, abbreviation, contraction; shorthand

abridor /aβri'ðor/ *m*, opener. **a. de guantes,** glove-stretcher. **a. de láminas,** engraving needle. **a. de tas,** can opener

abridura /aβri'ðura/ *f*, (act of) opening (e.g. of a trunk)

abrigada /aβri'gaða/ *f*, **abrigadero** *m*, sheltered place

abrigar /aβri'gar/ *vt* to shelter, protect (against the cold, etc.); defend, help; hold (opinions); nurse (a hope, etc.); cover; *vr* take shelter; wrap oneself up

abrigo /a'βrigo/ *m*, shelter; defense; protection; help; sheltered place; wrap, coat; *Naut.* haven

abril /a'βril/ *m*, April; youth; *pl Poet.* years

abrillantar /aβriyan'tar; aβriʎan'tar/ *vt* polish, burnish; cause to shine

abrir /a'βrir/ *vt* to open; reveal; unlock; slide the bolt of; extend, spread out; cleave; engrave; clear (the way, etc.); begin; head, lead; separate; dig; inaugurate. *vi* unfold (flowers); expand; **en un abrir y cerrar de ojos,** in the twinkling of an eye, in the wink of an eye; *vr* open; expand; (*with con*) confide in. **a. el camino (a...),** to pave the way (for...).

abrirse camino, to make one's way; **abrirse paso a codazos,** to elbow one's way out, (or through)

abrochador /aβrotʃa'ðor/ *m,* button-hook

abrochar /aβro'tʃar/ *vt* to button; fasten, clasp; hook up (a dress, etc.); buckle; *Lat. Am.* **abrocharse (con...)** struggle (with...), wrestle (with...)

abrogar /aβro'gar/ *vt* to repeal, annul

abrojo /a'βroho/ *m,* thistle; *Bot.* caltrops; thorn, prickle; *pl* submerged rocks in sea

abroncar /aβron'kar/ *vt Inf.* to bore, annoy

abrumador /aβruma'ðor/ *a* burdensome, crushing, oppressive; troublesome, tiresome; exhausting

abrumar /aβru'mar/ *vt* to weigh down; overwhelm, oppress; weary, exhaust; *vr* grow misty

abrupto /a'βrupto/ *a* sudden, abrupt; rough, broken (ground); rugged

absceso /aβ'sseso; aβ'sθeso/ *m,* abscess

absentismo /aβsen'tismo/ *m,* absenteeism

ábside /'aβsiðe/ *mf, Archit.* apse. *m, Astron.* apsis

absolución /aβsolu'sion; aβsolu'θion/ *f,* (*Eccl.* and *Law.*) absolution; remission, pardon

absoluta /aβso'luta/ *f, Mil.* discharge

absolutista /aβsolu'tista/ *mf* absolutist

absoluto /aβso'luto/ *a* absolute; categorical; *Inf.* despotic. **en a.,** absolutely

absolver /aβsol'βer/ *vt irr* to absolve; acquit (of a charge). *Law.* **a. de la instancia,** to dismiss the case. See **mover**

absorbente /aβsor'βente/ *a* and *m,* absorbent

absorber /aβsor'βer/ *vt* to absorb; consume, use up; attract, hold (the attention, etc.); imbibe

absorción /aβsor'sion; aβsor'θion/ *f,* absorption

absortar /aβsor'tar/ *vt* to amaze, dumbfound

absorto /aβ'sorto/ *a* amazed, astounded; abstracted, lost in thought

abstemio /aβs'temio/ *a* abstemious; *mf,* teetotaler

abstención /aβsten'sion; aβsten'θion/ *f,* abstention

abstenerse /aβste'nerse/ *vr irr* to refrain; abstain. See **tener**

abstinencia /aβsti'nensia; aβsti'nenθia/ *f,* abstinence; fasting

abstinente /aβsti'nente/ *a* abstinent; temperate

abstracción /aβstrak'sion; aβstrak'θion/ *f,* abstraction; preoccupation; absent-mindedness

abstracto /aβ'strakto/ *a* abstract. **en a.,** in the abstract

abstraer /aβstra'er/ *vt irr* to abstract; consider separately; *vi* (*with de*) do without, exclude; *vr* be preoccupied; let one's thoughts wander. See **traer**

abstraído /aβstra'iðo/ *a* retired, recluse; preoccupied; absent-minded

abstruso /aβ'struso/ *a* abstruse

absurdidad /aβsurði'ðað/ *f,* absurdity; folly, nonsense

absurdo /aβ'surðo/ *a* ridiculous, absurd. *m,* piece of folly, nonsense

abuchear /aβutʃe'ar/ *vt vi* to boo, hoot, jeer

abuela /a'βuela/ *f,* grandmother

abuelo /a'βuelo/ *m,* grandfather; *gen pl* ancestor; *pl* grandparents

abulia /a'βulia/ *f,* lack of will-power, abulia

abúlico /a'βuliko/ *a* abulic, lacking will-power

abultado /aβul'taðo/ *a* bulky, large; voluminous; exaggerated

abultamiento /aβulta'miento/ *m,* bulkiness; enlargement, increase; mound; exaggeration

abultar /aβul'tar/ *vt* to enlarge, increase; exaggerate; model in rough (sculpture); *vi* be bulky; be large

abundancia /aβun'dansia; aβun'danθia/ *f,* abundance, plenty

abundante /aβun'dante/ *a* abundant, plentiful; abounding (in)

abundar /aβun'dar/ *vi* to be plentiful, abound

aburrido /aβu'rriðo/ *a* (*with ser*) boring, tedious, dull; tired, weary; (*with estar*) bored

aburrimiento /aβurri'miento/ *m,* boredom, dullness; wearisomeness, tediousness

aburrir /aβu'rrir/ *vt* to bore; *Inf.* spend (time, money); (birds) desert the nest; *vr* grow bored; be weary

¡abusado! /aβu'saðo/ *Mexico* careful!, look out!, watch out!

abusar /aβu'sar/ *vi* to abuse; exceed one's rights, go too far; (*with de*) take advantage of

abusivo /aβu'siβo/ *a* abusive

abuso /a'βuso/ *m,* abuse. **a. de confianza,** abuse of trust

abyección /aβyek'sion; aβyek'θion/ *f,* degradation, misery; abjectness, servility

abyecto /aβ'yekto/ *a* abject, wretched; servile

acá /a'ka/ *adv* here; at this time, now. **desde ayer a.,** from yesterday until now. **por a.,** around here

acabable /aka'βaβle/ *a* terminable, finishable; achievable

acabado /aka'βaðo/ *a* complete; perfect; expert, consummate; old, worn out; ill, infirm. *m,* finish

acabamiento /akaβa'miento/ *m,* finishing, completion; end; death, decease

acabar /aka'βar/ *vt* to end, terminate; finish; complete, perfect; kill; (*with con*) destroy, finish off; suppress; squander; *vi* end; die; be destroyed; (*with de* + *infin*) to have just (e.g. *Acaba de salir,* He has just gone out); *vr* end, be exhausted, run out of (e.g. *Se le acabó el dinero,* His money ran out); fade, grow weak; be destroyed. **Se les acabaron las dudas,** Their doubts were cleared up. **a. de desconcertar,** to nonplus completely; **a. de decidirse,** to come to a decision; **a. de saber,** to finally learn

acacia /a'kasia; a'kaθia/ *f, Bot.* acacia

academia /aka'ðemia/ *f,* academy

académico /aka'ðemiko/ **(-ca)** *a* academic. *n* academician. **a. de la lengua,** member of the Royal Spanish Academy

acaecer /akae'ser; akae'θer/ *vi irr* to happen, occur. See **conocer**

acaecimiento /akaesi'miento; akaeθi'miento/ *m,* happening, occurrence, event

acalambrarse /akalam'brarse/ (muscle) to contract with cramps. **Estar acalambrado,** to have cramps

acalenturarse /akalentu'rarse/ *vr* to grow feverish

acallar /aka'yar; aka'ʎar/ *vt* to quieten, hush; soothe, appease

acalorado /akalo'raðo/ *a* hot; fervent; *Fig.* heated

acaloramiento /akalora'miento/ *m,* excitement, agitation, vehemence; ardor

acalorar /akalo'rar/ *vt* to warm; aid, encourage; excite, stimulate; stir, move (to enthusiasm); inflame, rouse; tire (by exercise); *vr* grow hot; become agitated or excited; become heated (arguments)

acamar /aka'mar/ *vt* to lay flat (plants by the wind); *vr* be flattened (plants); lie down (animals); go rotten (fruit)

acampar /akam'par/ *vi* and *vt* to encamp

acanalar /akana'lar/ *vt* to groove, striate, flute; corrugate; furrow, channel

acantilado /akanti'laðo/ *a* steep, precipitous; shelving (ocean-bed). *m,* cliff

acanto /a'kanto/ *m,* (*Archit. Bot.*) acanthus

acantonamiento /akantona'miento/ *m,* billeting; cantonment

acantonar /akanto'nar/ *vt* to billet or quarter troops

acaparador /akapara'ðor/ **(-ra)** *n* monopolist

acaparar /akapa'rar/ *vt Com.* to monopolize, corner; seize, take possession of

acápite /a'kapite/ *m, West. Hem.* new paragraph

acaracolado /akarako'laðo/ *a* spiral, winding, twisting

acardenalar /akarðena'lar/ *vt* to bruise; *vr* be bruised; be covered with livid marks

acarear /akare'ar/ *vt* to face; face up to, meet with courage

acariciador /akarisia'ðor; akariθia'ðor/ **(-ra)** *a* caressing, loving. *n* fondler

acariciar /akari'siar; akari'θiar/ *vt* to caress; brush, touch lightly; cherish, treat affectionately; toy with (a suggestion)

acarraladura /akarrala'ðura/ f, Lat. Am. run (in a stocking)

acarreador /akarrea'ðor/ (-ra) n carrier, carter

acarreamiento, acarreo /akarrea'miento, aka'reo/ m, cartage, carting; transport, carriage; occasioning

acarrear /akarre'ar/ vt to cart, transport; occasion, bring (gen. evil). **La guerra acarreó la carestía,** The war brought scarcity

acartonado /akarto'naðo/ a shriveled; shrunken; of cardboard; Fig. forced (dialogue)

acaso /a'kaso/ m, chance. adv by chance; perhaps, perchance. **por si a.,** in case (e.g. Por si a. venga, In case he comes)

acatable /aka'taβle/ a venerable, worthy

acatamiento /akata'miento/ m, respect; reverence; observance

acatar /aka'tar/ vt to treat with respect, honor, revere; observe

acatarrar /akata'rrar/ vt, Lat. Am. to annoy, bother, pester

acatarrarse /akata'rrarse/ vr to catch a cold; Argentina booze up, tank up

acaudalado /akauða'laðo/ a wealthy, well-to-do

acaudalar /akauða'lar/ vt to make money; hoard up wealth; acquire (learning, etc.)

acaudillar /akauði'yar; akauði'ʎar/ vt Mil. to command, lead; head (a party, etc.)

acceder /akse'ðer; akθe'ðer/ vi (with prep a) to concede, grant; accede to, agree to

accesibilidad /ak,sesiβili'ðað; ak,θesiβili'ðað/ f, accessibility; approachableness

accesible /akse'siβle; akθe'siβle/ a accessible; approachable

accesión /akse'sion; akθe'sion/ f, agreement, acquiescence; accession; accessory; feverish attack

acceso /ak'seso; ak'θeso/ m, access; paroxysm, outburst; Med. attack

accesorio /akse'sorio; akθe'sorio/ a accessory

accesorios /akse'sorios; akθe'sorios/ m pl, accessories; Theat. properties

accidentado /aksiðen'taðo; akθiðen'taðo/ a rough, uneven; stormy, troubled (life, etc.)

accidentar /aksiðen'tar; akθiðen'tar/ vt to cause (someone) an accident; vr to be the victim of an accident; be seized by a fit

accidente /aksi'ðente; akθi'ðente/ m, chance; accident, mishap; illness, indisposition; Med. fit; Gram. accidence; Mus. accidental. **a. del trabajo,** accident at work. **por a.,** by chance, accidentally

acción /ak'sion; ak'θion/ f, action; battle; skirmish; Mech. drive; Com. share; gesture; lawsuit; Lit. action (of play, etc.); Com. posture, pose. **a. de gracias,** thanksgiving; Com. **a. liberada,** paid-up share. **a. privilegiada,** preference share

accionar /aksio'nar; akθio'nar/ vi to gesture, gesticulate; Lat. Am. act, be active

accionista /aksio'nista; akθio'nista/ mf Com. shareholder

acechar /ase'tʃar; aθe'tʃar/ vt to spy upon, watch; lie in ambush for

acecho /a'setʃo; a'θetʃo/ m, spying upon, watch; waylaying, ambush. **al a.,** in ambush; on the watch

acechona /ase'tʃona; aθe'tʃona/ f, waylaying; ambush

acecinar /asesi'nar; aθeθi'nar/ vt to salt and dry (meat); vr (persons) wither, dry up

acedar /ase'ðar; aθe'ðar/ vt to make bitter, sour; embitter, displease; vr turn sour; wither (plants)

acefalía /asefa'lia; aθefa'lia/ f, acephalia, headlessness

acéfalo /a'sefalo; a'θefalo/ a acephalous

aceitar /asei'tar; aθei'tar/ vt to oil, lubricate; rub with oil

aceite /a'seite; a'θeite/ m, olive oil; oil. **a. de hígado de bacalao,** cod-liver oil. **a. de linaza,** linseed oil. **a. de ricino,** castor-oil. **a. de trementina,** oil of turpentine

aceitera /asei'tera; aθei'tera/ f, woman who sells oil; oil can; oil bottle; pl cruet

aceitero /asei'tero; aθei'tero/ m, oil seller. a oil

aceitoso /asei'toso; aθei'toso/ a oily

aceituna /asei'tuna; aθei'tuna/ f, Bot. olive

aceitunado /aseitu'naðo; aθeitu'naðo/ a olive-colored

aceitunero /aseitu'nero; aθeitu'nero/ (-ra) n olive picker; olive seller. m, warehouse for storing olives

aceituno /asei'tuno; aθei'tuno/ m, olive tree; a, Lat. Am. olive-colored

aceleración /aselera'sion; aθelera'θion/ f, speed, acceleration

aceleradamente /asele,raða'mente; aθele,raða'mente/ adv hastily, swiftly

acelerador /aselera'ðor; aθelera'ðor/ a accelerating. m, hastener; Auto. accelerator

acelerar /asele'rar; aθele'rar/ vt to speed up; accelerate

acémila /a'semila; a'θemila/ f, beast of burden, mule

acendrado /asen'draðo; aθen'draðo/ a pure, unblemished, spotless

acendrar /asen'drar; aθen'drar/ vt to refine (metals); purify, make spotless

acento /a'sento; a'θento/ m, accent; tone, inflection; Poet. voice, words. **a. agudo,** acute accent. **a. circunflejo,** circumflex accent. **a. grave,** grave accent. **a. ortográfico,** graphic accent, written accent. **a. tónico,** tonic accent

acentuación /asentua'sion; aθentua'θion/ f, accentuation, stress; emphasis

acentuar /asen'tuar; aθen'tuar/ vt to accent; stress, emphasize; vr become evident, become marked, be noticeable

aceña /a'seɲa; a'θeɲa/ f, water-mill; irrigation water-wheel; chain-well

acepción /asep'sion; aθep'θion/ f, meaning, significance, acceptation. **a. de personas,** partiality, preference

acepilladura /ase,piya'ðura; aθe,piʎa'ðura/ f, brushing; planing; wood-shaving

acepillar /asepi'yar; aθepi'ʎar/ vt to brush; plane; Inf. brush up, polish up

aceptabilidad /a,septaβili'ðað; a,θeptaβili'ðað/ f, acceptability

aceptable /asep'taβle; aθep'taβle/ a acceptable

aceptación /asepta'sion; aθepta'θion/ f, acceptance; popularity; approval

aceptador /asepta'ðor; aθepta'ðor/ (-ra) a accepting. n acceptor

aceptar /asep'tar; aθep'tar/ vt to accept; approve; accept a challenge; Com. honor

acequia /ase'kia; aθe'kia/ f, ditch, trench; irrigation channel

acera /a'sera; a'θera/ f, sidewalk, pavement. **a. del sol,** sunny side of the street

acerado /ase'raðo; aθe'raðo/ a steel; steel-like; strong, tough; mordant, incisive

acerar /ase'rar; aθe'rar/ vt to steel; treat (liquids) with steel; harden, make obdurate

acerbidad /aserβi'ðað; aθerβi'ðað/ f, bitterness, acerbity, sourness; harshness, cruelty

acerbo /a'serβo; a'θerβo/ a sour, tart, bitter; cruel, harsh

acerca de /a'serka de; a'θerka de/ adv about, concerning

acercamiento /aserka'miento; aθerka'miento/ m, approach

acercar /aser'kar; aθer'kar/ vt to bring nearer; vr be near at hand, draw near; (with prep a) approach

acerico /ase'riko; aθe'riko/ m, small cushion; pincushion

acero /a'sero; a'θero/ m, steel; blade, sword; pl bravery, spirit; Inf. good appetite. **a. inoxidable,** stainless steel

acérrimo /a'serrimo; a'θerrimo/ a sup extremely strong, mighty; most harsh; most resolute, unflinching; very strong (taste, smell)

acerrojar /aserro'har; aθerro'har/ vt to lock, padlock; bolt

acertado /aser'taðo; aθer'taðo/ *a* well-aimed; fitting, suitable; wise; successful

acertar /aser'tar; aθer'tar/ *vt irr* to hit the mark; find, come across; succeed (in), achieve; guess, find out; **No acertaba a explicármelo,** I couldn't quite understand it. *a.* **por chambra,** to make a lucky guess. *vi* be successful; thrive (of plants); (*with prep a* + *infin*) happen, occur, come to pass. *Pres. Ind.* **acierto, aciertas, acierta, aciertan.** *Pres. Subjunc.* **acierte, aciertes, acierte, acierten**

acertijo /aser'tiho; aθer'tiho/ *m,* riddle

acervo /a'serβo; a'θerβo/ *m,* pile, heap; *Fig.* storehouse, wealth (e.g. of words)

acetaminofén /aθetamino'fen/ *m,* acetaminophen

acetato /ase'tato; aθe'tato/ *m,* acetate

acetileno /aseti'leno; aθeti'leno/ *m,* acetylene

achacar /atʃa'kar/ *vt* to attribute, impute, assign.

achacable a, imputable to

achacoso /atʃa'koso/ *a* ailing, ill, sickly

achantarse /atʃan'tarse/ *vr Inf.* to hide from danger; put up with, bear

achaparrado /atʃapa'rraðo/ *a* stocky

achaque /a'tʃake/ *m,* ailment, illness (permanent); *Inf.* period, menstruation; pregnancy; matter, affair; pretext; failing, bad habit. **En a. de...,** Re..., concerning...

achatamiento /atʃata'miento/ *m,* flattening

achatar /atʃa'tar/ *vt* to flatten, make flat

achicado /atʃi'kaðo/ *a* childish

achicar /atʃi'kar/ *vt* to make smaller, diminish; drain, bail out; depreciate, belittle

achicarse /atʃi'karse/ *Inf.* to get smaller

achicharrar /atʃitʃa'rrar/ *vt Cul.* to overcook; overheat; annoy, importune

achicoria /atʃi'koria/ *f,* chicory

achique /a'tʃike/ *m,* bailing, draining

achispado /atʃis'paðo/ *a Inf.* tipsy

achubascarse /atʃuβas'karse/ *vr* to become overcast, grow stormy

achuchar /atʃu'tʃar/ *vt Inf.* to squeeze, hug; jostle, push against

achuchón /atʃu'tʃon/ *m, Inf.* shove, push; hug, squeeze

achulado /atʃu'laðo/ *a Inf.* brazen, tough

aciago /a'siago; a'θiago/ *a* unhappy, ill-omened; fateful

acíbar /a'siβar; a'θiβar/ *m,* aloe tree; bitter aloes; sorrow, bitterness

acibarar /asiβa'rar; aθiβa'rar/ *vt* to add bitter aloes to; embitter, sadden

acicalado /asika'laðo; aθika'laðo/ *a* polished; neat; well-groomed. *m,* polishing, burnishing (of weapons)

acicalador /asikala'ðor; aθikala'ðor/ **(-ra)** *a* polishing. *n* polisher. *m,* burnisher (machine)

acicalar /asika'lar; aθika'lar/ *vt* to burnish (weapons); adorn, deck; *vr* dress oneself with care

acicate /asi'kate; aθi'kate/ *m,* Moorish spur; incitement, stimulus

acicatear /asikate'ar; aθikate'ar/ *vt* to induce, spur on. *a.* **la curiosidad,** arouse curiosity

acidez /asi'ðes; aθi'ðeθ/ *f,* acidity, bitterness

acidia /a'siðia; a'θiðia/ *f,* indolence; sluggishness

ácido /'asiðo; 'aθiðo/ *a* acid; sour; harsh. *m,* acid. **a. fénico,** carbolic acid. **a. graso,** fatty acid

acidular /asiðu'lar; aθiðu'lar/ *vt Chem.* to acidulate

acídulo /a'siðulo; a'θiðulo/ *a Chem.* acidulous

acierto /a'sierto; a'θierto/ *m,* good hit, bull's-eye; success; achievement; cleverness; dexterity, skill; wisdom, sense; tact

acimut /asi'mut; aθi'mut/ *m, Astron.* azimuth

aclamación /aklama'sion; aklama'θion/ *f,* acclamation; shout of acclamation. **por a.,** unanimously

aclamador /aklama'ðor/ **(-ra)** *a* acclaiming. *n* applauder, acclaimer

aclamar /akla'mar/ *vt* to acclaim; applaud

aclaración /aklara'sion; aklara'θion/ *f,* explanation; elucidation

aclarado /akla'raðo/ *m,* rinse; rinsing

aclarador, aclaratorio /aklara'ðor, aklara'torio/ *a* explanatory

aclarar /akla'rar/ *vt* to clarify, purify; clear; rinse (clothes); explain; thin; *vi* clear; (sky) clear up; dawn

aclimatación /aklimata'sion; aklimata'θion/ *f,* acclimatization; *Lat. Am.* air-conditioning

aclimatar /aklima'tar/ *vt* to acclimatize

acné /ak'ne/ *m,* acne

acobardar /akoβar'ðar/ *vt* to intimidate, frighten

acocear /akose'ar; akoθe'ar/ *vt* to kick; *Inf.* insult, humiliate

acocharse /ako'tʃarse/ *vr* to squat, crouch

acocil /ako'sil; ako'θil/ *m, Mexico* freshwater shrimp

acodalar /akoða'lar/ *vt* to prop

acodiciar /akoði'siar; akoði'θiar/ *vt* to yearn for, covet, desire

acogedizo /akohe'ðiso; akohe'ðiθo/ *a* gathered haphazardly

acogedor /akohe'ðor/ **(-ra)** *a* welcoming, friendly; inviting (e.g. a place or room); *n* protector

acoger /ako'her/ *vt* to receive, welcome, admit; protect, harbor; *vr* take refuge; (*with prep a*) make use of, resort to; **acogerse a sagrado,** seek sanctuary

acogida /ako'hiða/ *f,* reception, welcome; protection; shelter; meeting place; confluence (of waters). **tener buena a.,** to be well received

acogollar /akogo'yar; akogo'ʎar/ *vt* to protect, cover (plants); *vi* sprout, shoot

acogotar /akogo'tar/ *vt* to fell by a blow on the neck; *Inf.* knock out

acolada /ako'laða/ *f,* accolade

acolitar /akoli'tar/ *vi* to serve as an altar boy, serve as an altar girl

acólito /a'kolito/ *m,* acolyte

acomedido, -a /akome'ðiðo/ *Lat. Am.* helpful, obliging

acometedor /akome'teðor/ **(-ra)** *a* capable, enterprising; aggressive. *n* aggressor, attacker

acometer /akome'ter/ *vt* to attack furiously; undertake; take in hand; overcome (of sleep, etc.)

acometida /akome'tiða/ *f,* **acometimiento** *m,* assault, onrush; undertaking

acometividad /akometiβi'ðað/ *f,* aggressiveness; *Argentina* touchiness

acomodable /akomo'ðaβle/ *a* easily arranged

acomodación /akomoða'sion; akomoða'θion/ *f,* adjustment; adaptation; accommodation

acomodadizo /akomoða'ðiso; akomoða'ðiθo/ *a* accommodating, easy-going

acomodado /akomo'ðaðo/ *a* suitable; convenient; wealthy, well-off; comfort-loving; moderate, low (of price)

acomodador /akomoða'ðor/ **(-ra)** *n* theater attendant, usher

acomodamiento /akomoða'miento/ *m,* agreement, transaction; accommodation

acomodar /akomo'ðar/ *vt* to arrange, adjust, accommodate; adapt; appoint; place; reconcile; employ, take on; equip, provide; lodge; *vi* suit, be convenient; *vr* compromise, agree

acomodaticio /akomoða'tisio; akomoða'tiθio/ *a* accommodating

acomodo /ako'moðo/ *m,* post, employment; arrangement; settlement

acompañamiento /akompaɲa'miento/ *m,* accompaniment; following, retinue; *Mus.* accompaniment; *Theat.* crowd, chorus

acompañanta /akompa'ɲanta/ *f,* chaperon; maid; servant

acompañante /akompa'ɲante/ *m, Mus.* accompanist

acompañar /akompa'ɲar/ *vt* to accompany; follow, escort; enclose (a letter, etc.); *Mus.* accompany

acompasado /akompa'saðo/ *a* rhythmic; deliberate, slow

acondicionado /akondisio'naðo; akondiθio'naðo/ *a* conditioned; (*with* **bien** *or* **mal**) in good or bad condition; of good or bad quality; good- or ill-natured. **reflejo acondicionado** *Med.* conditioned reflex

acondicionar /akondisio'nar; akondiθio'nar/ *vt* to prepare; mend, repair; *vr* condition oneself

acongojar /akongo'har/ *vt* to sadden, grieve; oppress

aconsejable /akonse'haβle/ a advisable

aconsejar /akonse'har/ vt to advise; vr (with con) consult, ask advice of

acontecedero /akontese'ðero; akonteθe'ðero/ a possible

acontecer /akonte'ser; akonte'θer/ vi irr impers to happen. See **conocer**

acontecimiento /akontesi'miento; akonteθi'miento/ m, event, occurrence

acopiar /ako'piar/ vt to collect, amass, gather

acopio /a'kopio/ m, collection, store; accumulation, gathering

acopladura /akopla'ðura/ f, **acoplamiento** m, (Mech.) joint; coupling; yoking; mating (of animals)

acoplar /ako'plar/ vt to join, couple; yoke; mate (animals); reconcile (opinions); vr Inf. fall in love

acoquinar /akoki'nar/ vt Inf. to intimidate, terrify

acorazado /akora'saðo; akora'θaðo/ a (Nav. Mil.) armored, iron-clad. m, iron-clad, battleship

acorcharse /akor'tʃarse/ vr to dry up, shrivel; go numb (limbs)

acordadamente /akor,ðaða'mente/ adv by common consent, unanimously; deliberately, after due thought

acordar /akor'ðar/ vt irr to decide unanimously; resolve; remind; tune; harmonize (colors); vi agree; vr remember; come to an agreement. **Si mal no me acuerdo,** If memory serves me well. Pres. Ind. **acuerdo, acuerdas, acuerda, acuerdan.** Pres. Subjunc. **acuerde, acuerdes, acuerde, acuerden**

acorde /a'korðe/ a agreed; in harmony; in agreement. m, Mus. chord; harmony

acordeón /akorðe'on/ m, accordion; (slang) crib sheet

acordonar /akorðo'nar/ vt to lace; cordon off, surround; mill (coins)

acornear /akorne'ar/ vt to butt, toss (bulls)

acorralado /akorra'laðo/ a at bay, intimidated

acorralamiento /akorrala'miento/ m, corralling, penning

acorralar /akorra'lar/ vt to corral, pen; confine; corner, silence (in argument); frighten; harass

acorrer /ako'rrer/ vt to aid, assist; vi run, hasten; vr take refuge

acortamiento /akorta'miento/ m, shortening

acortar /akor'tar/ vt to shorten; vr be speechless, be shy. **a. las velas,** to take in sail

acosador /akosa'ðor/ (-ra) a persecuting. n persecutor

acosamiento /akosa'miento/ m, persecution

acosar /ako'sar/ vt to persecute relentlessly; annoy, harass

acostado /ako'staðo/ a in bed; stretched out; Herald. couchant

acostar /ako'star/ vt irr to lay down, stretch out; put to bed; vi lean, tilt; vr lie down; go to bed; Naut. come alongside. See **contar**

acostumbrado /akostum'braðo/ a accustomed, usual

acostumbrar /akostum'brar/ vt to habituate, accustom; vi be in the habit of (e.g. Acostumbramos ir a la playa en el verano, We generally go to the seashore in summer); vr (with prep a) become used to

acotación /akota'sion; akota'θion/ f, noting; marginal note; stage direction; ordnance survey number

acotar /ako'tar/ vt to annotate; mark out boundaries; fix, establish; accept; Inf. choose; testify; fix in elevation figures (on a map); vr seek refuge

acotejar /akote'har/ vt, Lat. Am. to arrange, put in order

acre /'akre/ a bitter, sour; harsh; biting, mordant. m, acre (land measure)

acrecencia /akre'sensia; akre'θenθia/ f, **acrecentamiento** m, increase; addition

acrecentar /akresen'tar; akreθen'tar/ vt irr to increase; augment; promote, prefer. See **acertar**

acrecer /akre'ser; akre'θer/ vt irr to increase; augment. See **conocer**

acreción /akre'sion; akre'θion/ f, accretion

acreditado /akreði'taðo/ a accredited, well-reputed; respected

acreditar /akreði'tar/ vt Inf. to prove; verify; accredit;

recommend; sanction, authorize; vouch for, guarantee; Com. credit

acreedor /akree'ðor/ (-ra) n creditor; claimant. a deserving. **a. hipotecario,** mortgagee

acreencia /akre'ensia; akre'enθia/ f, debt; Com. claim

acribillar /akriβi'yar; akriβi'ʎar/ vt to riddle with holes; wound repeatedly; pelt; torment; Inf. pester, harass

acriminación /akrimina'sion; akrimina'θion/ f, accusation

acriminador /akrimina'ðor/ (-ra) a incriminating. n accuser

acriminar /akrimi'nar/ vt to accuse, charge

acrimonia /akri'monia/ f, acrimony

acriollarse /akrio'jarse; akrio'ʎarse/ vr, Lat. Am. to adopt local customs, go native

acrisolar /akriso'lar/ vt to refine, purify (metals); perfect; clarify, elucidate

acrobacia /akro'βasia; akro'βaθia/ f, acrobatics

acróbata /a'kroβata/ mf acrobat

acrobático /akro'βatiko/ a acrobatic

acromatópsico /akroma'topsiko/ a color-blind

acróstico /a'krostiko/ a and m, acrostic

acta /'akta/ f, minutes, record; certificate of election (as deputy to Cortes, etc.); pl deeds (of a martyr). **a. matrimonial,** marriage register

actitud /akti'tuð/ f, attitude

activar /akti'βar/ vt to stimulate, make active; accelerate, hasten

actividad /aktiβi'ðað/ f, activity; movement, bustle. **en a.,** in action; at work

activo /ak'tiβo/ a active. m, Com. assets

acto /'akto/ m, act, deed, action; act, law; act (of a play); public ceremony; pl minutes (of a meeting), proceedings (of a conference). **a. continuo** or **a. seguido,** immediately afterwards. **a. vandálico,** act of vandalism. **los Actos de los Apóstoles,** Acts of the Apostles. **en a.,** in the act (of doing). **en el a.,** in the act; immediately

actor /ak'tor/ m, actor; Law. plaintiff

actriz /ak'tris; ak'triθ/ f, actress

actuación /aktua'sion; aktua'θion/ f, operation, functioning; action; pl legal functions, judicial acts

actual /ak'tual/ a present; contemporary

actualidad /aktuali'ðað/ f, present, present time; topic of interest. **actualidades,** current events. **en la a.,** at the present time

actuar /ak'tuar/ vt to operate, set in motion; vi act; exercise legal functions

actuario /ak'tuario/ (de seguros) m, actuary

acuarela /akua'rela/ f, water-color painting

acuarelista /akuare'lista/ mf water-colorist

acuario /a'kuario/ m, aquarium; Aquarius

acuartelamiento /a,kuartela'miento/ m, billeting (of troops); billet, quarters

acuartelar /akuarte'lar/ vt to billet

acuático, acuátil /a'kuatiko, a'kuatil/ a aquatic

acuatinta /akua'tinta/ f, aquatint

acuatizar /akuati'sar; akuati'θar/ vi, Lat. Am. to land on water, touch down on water

acuchillado /akutʃi'yaðo; akutʃi'ʎaðo/ a taught by experience, schooled

acuchillar /akutʃi'yar; akutʃi'ʎar/ vt to hack, cut about; stab, put to the sword; slash (sleeves, etc.); vr fight with swords, daggers

acucia /a'kusia; a'kuθia/ f, fervor, zeal; yearning, longing

acuciar /aku'siar; aku'θiar/ vt to incite; goad; stimulate; encourage

acuciosidad /akusiosi'ðað; akuθiosi'ðað/ f, eagerness, fervor, zeal

acucioso /aku'sioso; aku'θioso/ a eager, fervent, keen, zealous

acuclillarse /akukli'yarse; akukli'ʎarse/ vr to squat, crouch

acudir /aku'ðir/ vi to go, repair (to); come; go or come to the aid of; attend, be present; **No me acude ningún ejemplo a la memoria,** No example comes to mind; resort (to); seek protection; reply, respond

acueducto /akue'ðukto/ *m*, aqueduct

acuerdo /a'kuerðo/ *m*, motion, resolution; decision; harmony, agreement; opinion, belief; remembrance; report; meeting (of members of a tribunal); *Art.* harmony (of colors). **de a.,** in agreement, in conformity; unanimously; *Inf.* OK. **estar de a. (con),** to agree (with). **estar de acuerdo en** (+ infin.), to agree to (+ infin.) **ponerse de a.,** to come to an understanding

acuilmarse /akuil'marse/ *vr Central America* to get depressed, get the blues

acuitar /akui'tar/ *vt* to distress, trouble; grieve

acumulación /akumula'sion; akumula'θion/ *f*, accumulation, collection

acumulador /akumula'ðor/ **(-ra)** *a* accumulative. *m*, accumulator, car battery. *n* collector, accumulator

acumulamiento /akumula'miento/ *m*, accumulation (act)

acumular /akumu'lar/ *vt* to accumulate, amass, collect; accuse, charge with

acuñación /akuɲa'sion; akuɲa'θion/ *f*, minting, coining; wedging

acuñador /akuɲa'ðor/ **(-ra)** *n* coiner, stamper; wedge. *m*, coining machine

acuñar /aku'ɲar/ *vt* to mint, stamp, coin; wedge

acuoso /a'kuoso/ *a* aqueous, watery

acurrucarse /akurru'karse/ *vr* to huddle; curl up; crouch

acusación /akusa'sion; akusa'θion/ *f*, accusation; *Law.* charge; *Law.* prosecution

acusado /aku'saðo/ **(-da)** *a* accused; prominent; well-defined. *n* accused; *Law.* defendant

acusador /akusa'ðor/ **(-ra)** *a* accusing. *n* accuser; *Law.* prosecutor

acusar /aku'sar/ *vt* to accuse; blame; denounce; *Com.* acknowledge receipt; *Law.* prosecute; *Law.* charge. **acusarle a uno las cuarenta,** *inf* to give someone a piece of one's mind

acusatorio /akusa'torio/ *a* accusatory

acusón /aku'son/ **(-ona)** *n Inf.* telltale, sneak, informer

acústica /a'kustika/ *f*, acoustics

acústico /a'kustiko/ *a* acoustic

adagio /a'ðahio/ *m*, adage; *Mus.* adagio

adalid /aða'lið/ *m*, chieftain; head, leader

adamado /aða'maðo/ *a* refined; genteel; effeminate

adamantino /aðaman'tino/ *a* adamantine

adaptabilidad /aðaptaβili'ðað/ *f*, adaptability

adaptación /aðapta'sion; aðapta'θion/ *f*, adaptation

adaptar /aðap'tar/ *vt* to adapt, make suitable; *vr* adapt oneself

adarme /a'ðarme/ *m*, tittle, jot. **por adarmes,** in bits and pieces, in drabs and driblets

adecentar /aðesen'tar; aðeθen'tar/ *vt* to tidy up; *vr* tidy oneself

adecuación /aðekua'sion; aðekua'θion/ *f*, adequacy; suitability

adecuado /aðe'kuaðo/ *a* adequate; suitable

adecuar /aðe'kuar/ *vt* to proportion, fit; *Fig.* tailor

adefesio /aðe'fesio/ *m*, *Inf.* folly, absurdity (gen. *pl*); extravagant attire; guy, sight

adelantado /aðelan'taðo/ *a* precocious; forward, pert; fast (clocks); early (of fruit); excellent; capable, proficient. *m*, *Obs.* provincial governor *or* chief justice *or* captain-general (Spanish history). **por a.,** in advance

adelantamiento /aðelanta'miento/ *m*, promotion, furtherance; progress, advancement; betterment, improvement; *Obs.* office of **adelantado;** anticipation

adelantar /aðelan'tar/ *vt* to advance, move on; hasten; forestall; overtake; move forward (the hands of clocks); improve, better; beat, excel; place in front; *vi* progress, advance; be fast (clocks); grow, develop; *vr* come forward

adelante /aðe'lante/ *adv* on, forward; further on; straight ahead. **¡A.!** Onward!; Come in! **de hoy en a.,** henceforth, from today

adelanto /aðe'lanto/ *m*, anticipation; progress; *Com.* payment in advance. **el a. de la hora,** moving the clock forward

adelgazamiento /aðel,gasa'miento; aðel,gaθa'miento/ *m*, loss of weight; slenderness; thinness

adelgazar /aðelga'sar; aðelga'θar/ *vt* to make slender or thin; *Fig.* split hairs; whittle, taper; *vi* grow slender *or* thin

ademán /aðe'man/ *m*, posture, attitude; gesture; *pl* behavior, manners

además /aðe'mas/ *adv* besides, in addition; moreover. **a. de,** as well as

adentro /a'ðentro/ *adv* inside, within

adentros /a'ðentros/ *m pl*, private thoughts (e.g. *Pensé para mis adentros,* I thought to myself). *Interj* **¡Adentro!** Come in!; Go in!

adepto /a'ðepto/ *a* affiliated; adept, proficient

aderezamiento /aðe,resa'miento; aðe,reθa'miento/ *m*, dressing; seasoning; embellishment

aderezar /aðere'sar; aðere'θar/ *vt* to deck, embellish; cook; *Cul.* season; *Cul.* dress; prepare; repair, mend; guide, direct; dress (cloth)

aderezo /aðe'reso; aðe're θo/ *m*, dressing, adornment; beautifying; finery, ornament; preparation; seasoning; set of jewels; horse's trappings; gum starch (for dressing cloth); equipment

adeudar /aðeu'ðar/ *vt* to owe; be dutiable (goods); *Com.* debit; *vi* become related (by marriage); *vr* run into debt

adeudo /a'ðeuðo/ *m*, debt; customs duty; *Com.* debit

adherencia /aðe'rensia; aðe'renθia/ *f*, adherence; adhesion

adherente /aðe'rente/ *a* adhesive; connected, attached. *mf* adherent, follower; *m pl.* **adherentes,** accessories, requisites

adherirse /aðe'rirse/ *vr irr* to adhere, stick; follow; believe (in). See **herir**

adhesión /aðe'sion/ *f*, adhesion; adherence

adhesivo /aðe'siβo/ *a* adhesive

adición /aði'sion; aði'θion/ *f*, addition; *Argentina* check (in a restaurant)

adicional /aðisio'nal; aðiθio'nal/ *a* additional, extra

adicionar /aðisio'nar; aðiθio'nar/ *vt* to add up; add to

adicto /a'ðikto/ **(-ta)** *a* addicted. *n* addict; *Lat. Am.* (drug) addict

adiestrador /aðiestra'ðor/ **(-ra)** *n* trainer, coach; guide, teacher

adiestrar /aðies'trar/ *vt* to train, coach; guide, teach; lead; *vr* practice, perfect oneself

adietar /aðie'tar/ *vt Med.* to put on a diet

adifés /aði'fes/ *adv*, *Central America* deliberately, on purpose

adinerado /aðine'raðo/ *a* wealthy, well-off, rich

adiós /a'ðios/ *interj* Good-bye! *m*, farewell

aditamento /aðita'mento/ *m*, addition, appendix

adive /a'ðiβe/ *m*, jackal

adivinación /aðiβina'sion; aðiβina'θion/ *f*, divination; guess

adivinanza /aðiβi'nansa; aðiβi'nanθa/ *f*, divination; riddle; puzzle. **adivinanzas,** guessing games. **no estar para jugar a las a.,** to be in no mood for guessing games

adivinar /aðiβi'nar/ *vt* to prophesy, foretell; divine, guess; solve, guess (riddles, etc.)

adivino /aði'βino/ **(-na)** *n* soothsayer, prophet

adjetivo /aðhe'tiβo/ *a* adjectival. *m*, adjective

adjudicación /aðhuðika'sion; aðhuðika'θion/ *f*, adjudication, award

adjudicador /aðhuðika'ðor/ **(-ra)** *n* adjudicator

adjudicar /aðhuði'kar/ *vt* to adjudge; award; *vr* appropriate

adjudicatario /aðhuðika'tario/ **(-ia)** *n* recipient (of a prize, etc.); grantee

adjuntar /aðhun'tar/ *vt* to enclose (with a letter, etc.)

adjunto /að'hunto/ *a* attached; enclosed, accompanying; assistant, deputy; adjectival. *m*, addition, supplement; adjunct (professor)

administración /aðministra'sion; aðministra'θion/ *f*, administration; direction, control; administratorship

administrador /aðministra'ðor/ **(-ra)** *a* administrative. *n* administrator. **a. de correos,** postmaster

administrar /aðminis'trar/ *vt* to control, manage; provide, supply; administer. **administrarse el tiempo,** to budget one's time

administrativo /aðministra'tiβo/ *a* administrative, executive

admirable /aðmi'raβle/ *a* admirable

admirablemente /aðmi,raβle'mente/ *adv* admirably, excellently

admiración /aðmira'sion; aðmira'θion/ *f,* amazement; admiration; wonder; exclamation mark

admirador /aðmira'ðor/ **(-ra)** *a* admiring. *n* admirer

admirar /aðmi'rar/ *vt* to admire; surprise, amaze (e.g. *Me admira su acción,* His action surprises me); to see (e.g. *Desde la colina se pueden admirar varios edificios de la ciudad,* From the hill several buildings in the city can be seen); *vr (with de)* be surprised at or by

admisibilidad /aðmisiβili'ðað/ *f,* allowability, permissibility

admisible /aðmi'siβle/ *a* admissible; permissible

admisión /aðmi'sion/ *f,* admission; acceptance; allowance

admitir /aðmi'tir/ *vt* to admit; receive, accept; tolerate, brook; allow, permit

admonición /aðmoni'sion; aðmoni'θion/ *f,* admonition, warning; reprimand

adobar /aðo'βar/ *vt* to prepare; *Cul.* garnish; pickle (meat); cook; dress (hides)

adobe /a'ðoβe/ *m,* adobe, mudbrick

adobo /a'ðoβo/ *m,* repairing; dressing (for cloth, leather); *Cul.* savory sauce; pickling sauce; make-up, cosmetic

adocenado /aðose'naðo; aðoθe'naðo/ *a* ordinary; narrow-minded

adoctrinar /aðoktri'nar/ *vt* to instruct

adolecer /aðole'ser; aðole'θer/ *vi irr* to fall ill; *(with de)* suffer from (diseases, defects); *vr* be sorry for, regret. See **conocer**

adolescencia /aðoles'sensia; aðoles'θenθia/ *f,* adolescence

adolescente /aðoles'sente; aðoles'θente/ *a* and *mf* adolescent

adonde /a'ðonde/ *adv (interr* a **dónde)** where to, whither (e.g. *¿A dónde fuiste?* Where did you go to?)

adondequiera /a,ðonde'kiera/ *adv* wherever

adopción /aðop'sion; aðop'θion/ *f,* adoption

adoptador /aðopta'ðor/ **(-ra)** *a* adopting. *n* adopter

adoptar /aðop'tar/ *vt* to adopt (children); make one's own, embrace (opinions); take (decisions)

adoptivo /aðop'tiβo/ *a* adoptive

adoquín /aðo'kin/ *m,* cobble-stone; *Fig.* blockhead

adoquinado /aðoki'naðo/ *m,* cobbling, paving. *m,* cobbled pavement

adoquinar /aðoki'nar/ *vt* to pave with cobble-stones

adorable /aðo'raβle/ *a* adorable

adoración /aðora'sion; aðora'θion/ *f,* worship, adoration. **A. de los Reyes,** Adoration of the Magi; Epiphany

adorador /aðora'ðor/ **(-ra)** *a* adoring. *n* adorer

adorar /aðo'rar/ *vt* to adore; worship; *(with en)* dote on; *vi* pray

adormecedor /aðormese'ðor; aðormeθe'ðor/ *a* soporific, drowsy

adormecer /aðorme'ser; aðorme'θer/ *vt irr* to make drowsy; soothe, lull; hush to sleep; *vr* go to sleep (limbs); fall asleep; *(with en)* persist in. See **conocer**

adormecimiento /aðormesi'miento; aðormeθi'miento/ *m,* sleepiness; lulling asleep; numbness

adormitarse /aðormi'tarse/ *vr* to doze, take a nap, snooze

adornamiento /aðorna'miento/ *m,* adornment, decoration

adornar /aðor'nar/ *vt* to deck, beautify; decorate; trim, embellish; adorn (of virtues, etc.)

adorno /a'ðorno/ *m,* decoration, adornment; ornament; trimming. **de a.,** ornamental; flowering (shrubs)

adquiridor /aðkiri'ðor/ **(-ra)** *a* acquiring. *n* acquirer

adquirir /aðki'rir/ *vt irr* to acquire, get; achieve, obtain. *Pres. Ind.* **adquiero, adquieres, adquiere, ad-**

quieren. *Pres. Subjunc.* **adquiera, adquieras, adquiera, adquieran**

adquisición /aðkisi'sion; aðkisi'θion/ *f,* acquirement; acquisition. **poder de a.,** purchasing power

adquisidor /aðkisi'ðor/ **(-ra)** *a* acquiring. *n* acquirer, obtainer

adquisitivo /aðkisi'tiβo/ *a* acquisitive

adquisividad /aðkisiβi'ðað/ *f,* acquisitiveness

adrazo /a'ðraso; a'ðraθo/ *m,* salt-water still

adrede /a'ðreðe/ *adv* on purpose, intentionally

adrenalina /aðrena'lina/ *f,* adrenaline

adscribir /aðskri'βir/ *vt* to ascribe, attribute; appoint (to a post, etc.). See **escribir**

adscripción /aðskrip'sion; aðskrip'θion/ *f,* ascription, attribution; appointment

aduana /a'ðuana/ *f,* customs house, customs. **pasar por la a.,** to go through customs

aduanero /aðua'nero/ *a* customs. *m,* customs officer

aducir /aðu'sir; aðu'θir/ *vt irr* to adduce, allege, cite; add. See **conducir**

adueñarse /aðue'parse/ **(de)** *vr* to appropriate, take possession (of)

adulación /aðula'sion; aðula'θion/ *f,* adulation, flattery

adulador /aðula'ðor/ **(-ra)** *a* fawning. *n* flatterer

adular /aðu'lar/ *vt* to flatter, fawn over, adulate

adulonería /aðulone'ria/ *f, Lat. Am.* flattery, fawning

adulteración /aðultera'sion; aðultera'θion/ *f,* adulteration; falsification

adulterador /aðultera'ðor/ **(-ra)** *a* adulterant. *n* adulterator; falsifier; coiner

adulterar /aðulte'rar/ *vi* to commit adultery; *vt* adulterate; falsify

adulterino /aðulte'rino/ *a* adulterous; false

adulterio /aðul'terio/ *m,* adultery

adúltero /a'ðultero/ **(-ra)** *a* adulterous; corrupt. *n* adulterer

adulto /a'ðulto/ **(-ta)** *a* and *n* adult

adunar /aðu'nar/ *vt* to join, unite; unify, combine

adusto /a'ðusto/ *a* extremely hot (of climate); grave, austere; standoffish, reserved

advenedizo /aðβene'ðiso; aðβene'ðiθo/ *a* foreign, unknown; upstart; newly rich. *m,* newcomer, social climber; *Lat. Am.* novice, tyro

advenimiento /aðβeni'miento/ *m,* advent, arrival; ascension (to the throne)

advenir /aðβe'nir/ *vi irr* to come, arrive; happen, befall. See **venir**

adventicio /aðβen'tisio; aðβen'tiθio/ *a* casual, accidental; *Bot.* adventitious

adverbio /að'βerβio/ *m,* adverb

adversario /aðβer'sario/ **(-ia)** *n* adversary, rival; opponent

adversidad /aðβersi'ðað/ *f,* adversity, misfortune, sorrow

adverso /að'βerso/ *a* unfavorable, contrary, adverse; opposite

advertencia /aðβer'tensia; aðβer'tenθia/ *f,* warning; introduction, preface; remark

advertido /aðβer'tiðo/ *a* capable, clever; experienced; expert

advertir /aðβer'tir/ *vt irr* to warn; advise; point out, indicate; inform; discover. See **sentir**

adyacencia /aðja'sensia; aðja'θenθia/ *f, Argentina* nearness, proximity

adyacente /aðja'sente; aðja'θente/ *a* adjacent, near-by, neighboring

aeración /aera'sion; aera'θion/ *f,* aeration

aéreo /'aereo/ *a* aerial; airborne; airy; air; aeronautic; unsubstantial, fantastic. **correo a.,** airmail. **línea aérea** airline

aerobismo /aero'βismo/ *m,* aerobics

aerodinámica /aeroði'namika/ *f,* aerodynamics

aeromozo, -a /aero'moso; aero'moθo/ *mf, Lat. Am.* flight attendant

aeronauta /aero'nauta/ *mf* aeronaut, balloonist

aeronáutica /aero'nautika/ *f,* aeronautics

aeronáutico /aero'nautiko/ *a* aeronautic

aeropuerto /aero'puerto/ *m,* airport

aeróstato /ae'rostato/ *m,* dirigible

afabilidad /afaβili'ðað/ f, affability, geniality, friendliness

afable /a'faβle/ a affable, genial, pleasant

afamado /afa'maðo/ a famous, well-known

afamar /afa'mar/ vt to make famous

afán /a'fan/ m, effort; manual labor; desire, anxiety. **a. de mando,** thirst for power

afanar /afa'nar/ vt to press, urge on; filch; vr toil, labor; (with por) work hard to, try to

afanoso /afa'noso/ a hard, laborious; hard-working, painstaking; eager, anxious

afasia /a'fasia/ f, Med. aphasia

afear /afe'ar/ vt to make ugly; distort, deform; blame; criticize

afección /afek'sion; afek'θion/ f, fondness, affection; complaint, ailment, trouble

afectación /afekta'sion; afekta'θion/ f, affectation

afectado /afek'taðo/ a affected

afectar /afek'tar/ vt to feign, assume; affect; move, touch; Law. encumber; Lat. Am. damage, hurt, injure

afectivo /afek'tiβo/ a affective

afecto /a'fekto/ a fond, affectionate; Law. encumbered; (with prep a) addicted to. m, emotion, sentiment; affection

afectuosidad /afektuosi'ðað/ f, affectionateness

afectuoso /afek'tuoso/ a affectionate, fond

afeitada /afei'taða/ f, shave, shaving

afeitadora /afeita'ðora/ f, razor

afeitar /afei'tar/ vt to shave; make up (one's face); adorn, beautify

afeite /a'feite/ m, cosmetic; make-up (for the complexion)

afelpado /afel'paðo/ a velvet-like, plushy

afeminación /afemina'sion; afemina'θion/ f, effeminacy; weakness, languor

afeminado /afemi'naðo/ a effeminate

afeminar /afemi'nar/ vt to make effeminate; vr grow effeminate

aferradamente /aferraða'mente/ adv tenaciously, persistently, obstinately

aferramiento /aferra'miento/ m, seizing, clutching; Naut. furling; Naut. grappling; mooring, anchoring; obstinacy

aferrar /afe'rrar/ vt to seize, clutch; Naut. take in, furl; Naut. grapple; vi Naut. anchor; vr (with con, en, a) persist in, insist on

afestonado /afesto'naðo/ a festooned

Afganistán /afganis'tan/ Afghanistan

afgano /af'gano/ (-na) a and n Afghan

afianzamiento /afiansa'miento; afianθa'miento/ m, fastening, fixing; propping; grasping; guarantee, security

afianzar /afian'sar; afian'θar/ vt to fasten, fix; prop; consolidate (e.g. one's power); guarantee, be security for; grasp

afición /afi'sion; afi'θion/ f, propensity, inclination; fondness. **tomar a. (a),** to take a liking to

aficionado /afisio'naðo; afiθio'naðo/ (-da) a amateur. n amateur, fan, enthusiast. **ser a a.,** to be fond of, have a liking for

aficionar /afisio'nar; afiθio'nar/ vt to inspire liking or affection; vr (with prep a) take a liking to, grow fond of; become an enthusiast of

afijo /a'fiho/ m, Gram. affix

afiladera /afila'ðera/ f, whetstone, grindstone

afilado /afi'laðo/ a sharp, keen (of edges)

afilador /afila'ðor/ m, grinder (of scissors, etc.); razor strop

afilalápices /afila'lapises; afila'lapiθes/ m, pencil sharpener

afilar /afi'lar/ vt to sharpen; grind, whet; taper; Lat. Am. flatter; Lat. Am. court, woo; vr grow thin; taper

afiliación /afilia'sion; afilia'θion/ f, affiliation

afiliar /afi'liar/ vt (with prep a) to affiliate with; vr (with prep a) become affiliated with; join, become a member of

afiligranado /afiligra'naðo/ a filigree; delicate, fine; slender

afilón /afi'lon/ m, steel, knife sharpener; razor-strop

afín /a'fin/ a nearby, contiguous; similar, related. mf relative by marriage

afinador /afina'ðor/ m, tuning key; tuner (of pianos, etc.)

afinar /afi'nar/ vt to finish, perfect; Fig. polish, refine; tune (musical instruments); refine (metals); vi sing in tune; vr grow refined

afinidad /afini'ðað/ f, affinity, analogy; relationship (by marriage); Chem. affinity

afirmación /afirma'sion; afirma'θion/ f, affirmation, statement

afirmadamente /afir‚maða'mente/ adv firmly

afirmar /afir'mar/ vt to make firm; fix, fasten; affirm; vr steady oneself; hold on to

afirmativa /afirma'tiβa/ f, affirmative

afirmativo /afirma'tiβo/ a affirmative

aflicción /aflik'sion; aflik'θion/ f, affliction, grief

aflictivo /aflik'tiβo/ a sorrowful, grievous

afligir /afli'hir/ vt to sadden; afflict, trouble; vr lament, mourn

aflojamiento /afloha'miento/ m, slackening; loosening; diminution

aflojar /aflo'har/ vt to slacken; loosen; vi relax, weaken; abate, diminish. **a. el paso,** to slow down

afluencia /a'fluensia; a'fluenθia/ f, crowd, concourse; eloquence, fluency

afluente /a'fluente/ a fluent, eloquent. m, tributary (river)

afluir /aflu'ir/ vi irr to crowd, swarm; flow (into). See **huir**

afonía /afo'nia/ f, Med. aphonia, loss of voice; hoarseness

afónico /a'foniko/ a hoarse

aforismo /afo'rismo/ m, aphorism

aforrador /aforra'ðor/ **(-ra)** n one who lines jackets, etc.

aforrar /afo'rrar/ vt to line (clothes, etc.); vr wrap oneself up; Inf. gormandize

afortunadamente /afortu‚naða'mente/ adv luckily, fortunately

afortunado /afortu'naðo/ a lucky, fortunate; happy, stormy

afortunar /afortu'nar/ vt to bring luck to, make happy

afrancesado /afranse'saðo; afranθe'saðo/ **(-da)** a Francophile; Frenchified. n Francophile

afrancesamiento /afransesa'miento; afranθesa'miento/ m, adoption of the French way of life; servile imitation of everything French

afrancesar /afranse'sar; afranθe'sar/ vt to make French, gallicize; Frenchify; vr become a Francophile

afrenta /a'frenta/ f, insult, affront; disgrace

afrentar /afren'tar/ vt to insult; vr be ashamed

afrentoso /afren'toso/ a insulting, outrageous; disgraceful

África /'afrika/ Africa

africanismo /‚afrikan'ismo/ m, Africanism

africano /afri'kano/ **-na** a and n African

afroamericano /afroameri'kano/ **(-na)** a and n African-American

afrodisíaco /afroði'siako/ a and m, aphrodisiac

afrontar /afron'tar/ vt to place opposite; confront; face (danger, etc.)

afuera /a'fuera/ adv outside, out

afueras /a'fueras/ f pl, suburbs, outskirts

afusilar /afusi'lar/ vt, Lat. Am. to shoot

agachada /aga'tʃaða/ f, crouch, duck; jerk

agachar /aga'tʃar/ vt Inf. bend, bow; vr Inf. crouch down; lie low, hide

agalla /a'gaya; a'gaλa/ f, oak-apple; tonsil (gen. pl); Zool. gill; Inf. gall, cheek

agalludo, -a /aga'juðo; aga'λuðo/ a, Argentina mean, stingy, tight; bold, daring

ágape /'agape/ m, agape; banquet, feast

Agar /a'gar/ Hagar

agárico /a'gariko/ m, Bot. agaric

agarrada /aga'rraða/ f, Inf. brawl, scuffle

agarradero /agarra'ðero/ m, handle; heft; Inf. influence, pull

agarrado /aga'rraðo/ a Inf. tight-fisted, mean

agarrar /aga'rrar/ *vt* to grip, grasp; seize, take; *Inf.* nab (jobs); *vr* grip, hold on

agarro /a'garro/ *m,* hold; grip, grasp

agarrotar /agarro'tar/ *vt* to garrotte; tighten (ropes, etc.); press, squeeze; *vr* (limbs) go numb

agasajar /agasa'har/ *vt* to indulge, spoil, pet; receive kindly; entertain; caress

agasajo /aga'saho/ *m,* indulgence, kindness; affability, geniality; entertainment; gift, offering

agauchado /agau'tʃaðo/ *a* gaucho-like

agazapar /agasa'par; agaθa'par/ *vt Inf.* to nab, catch; *vr Inf.* squat, crouch

agencia /a'hensia; a'henθia/ *f,* influence, agency

agenciar /ahen'siar; ahen'θiar/ *vt* to negotiate, arrange; procure, manage

agenda /a'henda/ *f,* notebook; agenda

agente /a'hente/ *m,* agent. **a. de bolsa** *or* **a. de cambio,** bill broker. **a. de negocios,** business agent. **a. de policía,** police officer. **a. fiscal,** revenue officer

agestado /ahes'taðo/ *a* used generally with advs. **bien** *or* **mal,** well *or* ill-featured

agigantado /ahigan'taðo/ *a* enormous, gigantic; outstanding, extraordinary

ágil /'ahil/ *a* agile, nimble; easy to use (e.g. *un libro ágil,* a book easy to use)

agilidad /ahili'ðað/ *f,* agility, nimbleness

agilizar /ahili'sar; ahili'θar/ *vt* to make agile, limber; refresh one's knowledge of (e.g. *Quiero agilizar mi español,* I want to refresh my knowledge of Spanish); to enable; *vr* limber up

agitación /ahita'sion; ahita'θion/ *f,* shaking; agitation, excitement

agitador /ahita'ðor/ **(-ra)** *a* stirring; agitating. *n* agitator. *m,* stirrer, stirring rod

agitar /ahi'tar/ *vt* to stir; shake; agitate, excite. **a. una cuestión,** raise a question; discuss a question

aglomeración /aglomera'sion; aglomera'θion/ *f,* agglomeration

aglomerar /aglome'rar/ *vt* to agglomerate, amass

aglutinación /aglutina'sion; aglutina'θion/ *f,* agglutination

aglutinar(se) /agluti'nar,se,/ *vt* and *vr* to stick, agglutinate

agnóstico /ag'nostiko/ **(-ca)** *a* and *n* agnostic

agobiar /ago'βiar/ *vt* to bow, bend down; *Fig.* weigh down, oppress; overwhelm; *vr* bend (beneath a weight)

agobio /a'goβio/ *m,* bowing, bending down; oppression, burden, weight

agolparse /agol'parse/ *vr* to rush, crowd, swarm

agonía /ago'nia/ *f,* agony, anguish

agonizante /agoni'sante; agoni'θante/ *a* dying

agonizar /agoni'sar; agoni'θar/ *vt* to attend a dying person; *Inf.* pester, annoy; *vi* be dying (gen. **estar agonizando**)

agorar /ago'rar/ *vt* to prophesy, foretell

agorero /ago'rero/ **(-ra)** *a* prophetic; ill-boding. *n* seer, augur

agostarse /agos'tarse/ *vr* and *vr* to dry up, shrivel

agosto /a'gosto/ *m,* August; harvest. *Inf.* **hacer su a.,** to make hay while the sun shines

agotable /ago'taβle/ *a* exhaustible

agotado /ago'taðo/ *a* exhausted; out of print (of books)

agotador /agota'ðor/ *a* exhausting; exhaustive

agotamiento /a,gota'miento/ *m,* exhaustion

agotar /ago'tar/ *vt* to drain off (water); empty (a glass); exhaust; run through (money); study thoroughly, examine closely (a subject)

agraciado /agra'siaðo; agra'θiaðo/ *a* graceful; pretty

agraciar /agra'siar; agra'θiar/ *vt* to lend grace to; make pretty; favor

agradable /agra'ðaβle/ *a* agreeable, pleasant

agradar /agra'ðar/ *vi* to be pleasing, like, please (e.g. *Me agrada su sinceridad,* I like his sincerity)

agradecer /agraðe'ser; agraðe'θer/ *vt irr* to be grateful for; thank for; *Fig.* repay, requite. See **conocer**

agradecido /agraðe'siðo; agraðe'θiðo/ *a* grateful; thankful

agradecimiento /agraðesi'miento; agraðeθi'miento/ *m,* gratitude; thankfulness

agrado /a'graðo/ *m,* pleasure; desire, liking; amiability, affability

agrandar /agran'dar/ *vt* to enlarge

agrario /a'grario/ *a* agrarian

agrarismo /agra'rismo/ *m, Mexico* farmers' movement, peasant movement

agravación /agraβa'sion; agraβa'θion/ *f,* **agravamiento** *m,* aggravation, worsening

agravador /agraβa'ðor/ *a* aggravating; worsening; increasing

agravar /agra'βar/ *vt* to aggravate, increase; oppress (taxes, responsibilities); make worse; exaggerate; *vr* grow worse

agraviador /agraβia'ðor/ **-ra** *a* offensive. *n* offender

agraviar /agra'βiar/ *vt* to offend; wrong; *vr* take offense, be insulted

agravio /a'graβio/ *m,* offense, insult; wrong, injury

agraz /a'gras; a'graθ/ *m,* unripened grape; verjuice; *Fig.* bitterness

agredir /agre'ðir/ *vt* to attack; assault

agregación /agrega'sion; agrega'θion/ *f,* association, aggregation; total, collection, aggregate

agregado /agre'gaðo/ *m,* aggregate; assistant; attaché; *Lat. Am.* sharecropper

agregar /agre'gar/ *vt* to add; collect, amass; appoint (to a post). **agregarse a...,** to join... (e.g. an association)

agresión /agre'sion/ *f,* aggression

agresivo /agre'siβo/ *a* aggressive

agresor /agre'sor/ **(-ra)** *a* and *n* aggressor

agreste /a'greste/ *a* rural, rustic; wild; uncouth, rude

agriar /a'griar/ *vt* to make bitter or sour; exasperate, provoke

agrícola /a'grikola/ *a* agricultural; *mf* agriculturalist, farmer

agricultura /agrikul'tura/ *f,* agriculture

agridulce /agri'ðulse; agri'ðulθe/ *a* bitter-sweet

agrietarse /agrie'tarse/ *vr* to crack, split

agrimensor /agrimen'sor/ *m,* surveyor

agrimensura /agrimen'sura/ *f,* surveying

agrio /'agrio/ *a* bitter, sour; rough, uneven (ground); brittle; sharp (of color contrast); unsociable; disagreeable

agriparse /agri'parse/ *vr* to catch a cold, come down with a cold

agronomía /agrono'mia/ *f,* agronomy

agrónomo /a'gronomo/ *a* agronomic. *m,* agronomist

agrupación /agrupa'sion; agrupa'θion/ *f,* congregation, assembly; group; crowd; crowding, grouping

agrupar /agru'par/ *vt* to assemble, group; *vr* crowd, cluster

agrura /a'grura/ *f,* bitterness; sourness; asperity

agua /'agua/ *f,* water; rain; slope of a roof; *pl* shot or watered effect on silks, etc.; medicinal waters; waves; water (of precious stones). **a. abajo,** down-stream. **a. arriba,** upstream. **a. bendita,** holy water. **a. cruda,** hard water. **a. de colonia,** eau de Cologne. **a. dulce,** fresh water. **a. fresca,** cold water. **a. nieve,** sleet. **a. oxigenada,** hydrogen peroxide. *Fig. Inf.* **estar con el agua al cuello,** to be in low water. *Fig. Inf.* **estar entre dos aguas,** to be between two fires. *Naut.* **hacer a.,** to leak. **Todo eso es ya a. pasada,** That's all water under the bridge

aguacate /agua'kate/ *m,* avocado

aguacero /agua'sero; agua'θero/ *m,* heavy rainfall, shower

aguada /a'guaða/ *f,* water supply on board ship; flood (in mines); watering station; *Art.* water color

aguadero /agua'ðero/ *m,* (animals') watering place

aguado /a'guaðo/ *a* watery; abstemious; watered

aguador /agua'ðor/ **(-ra)** *n* water carrier; water seller; drawer (of water)

aguafiestas /,agua'fiestas/ *mf fig inf* wet blanket

aguafuerte /,agua'fuerte/ *f,* etching

aguaje /a'guahe/ *m,* tide, waves; sea current; water supply (on board ship); wake (of a ship)

aguamanil /aguama'nil/ *m,* washstand; pitcher, ewer

aguamanos /agua'manos/ *m*, water for washing hands; pitcher

aguamarina /aguama'rina/ *f*, aquamarine

aguamiel /agua'miel/ *f*, honey and water, hydromel

aguantable /aguan'taβle/ *a* tolerable, bearable

aguantar /aguan'tar/ *vt* to bear, tolerate, endure; restrain, resist, oppose; *vr* bear in silence, keep quiet

aguante /a'guante/ *m*, patience, endurance; resistance

aguar /a'guar/ *vt* to water down (wine, etc.); spoil (fun, etc.); *vr* be filled with water; be flooded; become watery or thin

aguardar /aguar'ðar/ *vt* to await; expect; allow time to (debtors)

aguardentería /aguar,ðente'ria/ *f*, liquor shop

aguardentoso /aguarðen'toso/ *a* spirituous, containing **aguardiente** hoarse, husky (of the voice)

aguardiente /aguar'ðiente/ *m*, liquor. **a. de caña,** rum

aguarrás /agua'rras/ *m*, oil of turpentine

aguatinta /agua'tinta/ *f*, aquatint

aguatocha /agua'totʃa/ *f*, pump (for water, etc.)

aguaturma /agua'turma/ *f*, Jerusalem artichoke

agudeza /agu'ðesa; agu'ðeθa/ *f*, sharpness; keenness; distinctness; alertness, cleverness; witty sally, repartee; wit; swiftness

agudo /a'guðo/ *a* sharp; alert, clever; (*Geom. Med.*) acute; fine, keen; rapid; high-pitched; strong (of scents, etc.)

agüero /a'guero/ *m*, omen, sign; prophecy, prediction

aguerrido /age'rriðo/ *a* veteran, war-hardened

aguerrir /age'rrir/ *vt defective* to harden to war; toughen

aguijada /agi'haða/ *f*, goad, spur

aguijar /agi'har/ *vt* to prick (with a goad); urge on, encourage (animals); incite, instigate; spur on; *vi* walk swiftly

aguijón /agi'hon/ *m*, goad; sting; thorn, prickle; spur; incitement, stimulus. **tener aguijones,** to be on pins and needles

aguijonazo /agiho'naso; agiho'naθo/ *m*, prick (with a goad)

águila /'agila/ *f*, eagle; master mind. **a. caudal** *or* **a. real,** royal eagle. **á. o sol,** *Mexico* heads or tails

aguileña /agi'leɲa/ *f*, *Bot.* columbine

aguileño /agi'leɲo/ *a* aquiline

aguilón /agi'lon/ *m*, *Archit.* gable; boom (of a crane)

aguinaldo /agi'naldo/ *m*, Christmas present; New Year's gift

aguja /a'guha/ *f*, needle; hand, pointer; hatpin; engraver's burin; switch; *Rail.* point; *Rail.* rail; obelisk; spire; bodkin; knitting needle; crochet hook; (compass) needle. *pl Bot.* plumelet. **a. capotera, a. de zurcir,** darning needle. **a. de marear** *Naut.*, binnacle; mariner's compass. **a. de media,** knitting needle. **a. espartera,** packing needle

agujerear /aguhere'ar/ *vt* to perforate, make holes in

agujero /agu'hero/ *m*, hole, aperture; needle maker or seller; needle case

agujeta /agu'heta/ *f*, lace (for shoes, etc.); *pl* muscular pains, aches; tip, gratuity

agusanarse /agusa'narse/ *vr* to become worm-infested

aguzadura /agusa'ðura; aguθa'ðura/ *f*, sharpening, grinding, whetting

aguzar /agu'sar; agu'θar/ *vt* to sharpen; grind, whet; stimulate, encourage; urge on, incite

ahechadura /aetʃa'ðura/ *f*, chaff (of grain)

ahembrado /aem'braðo/ *a* effeminate

aherrojar /aerro'har/ *vt* to put (a prisoner) in irons; oppress

aherrumbrar /aerrum'brar/ *vt* to give the color or taste of iron to; *vr* taste or look like iron; get rusty; rust

ahí /a'i/ *adv* there; over there. **de a.,** thus, so. **por a.,** somewhere about, near at hand.

ahidalgado /aiðal'gaðo/ *a* gentlemanly; noble, generous

ahijado /ai'haðo/ **(-da)** *n* godchild; protégé

ahijar /ai'har/ *vt* to adopt (children); mother (animals); attribute, impute; *vi* bring forth offspring; *Bot.* sprout. See **prohibir**

ahincado /ain'kaðo/ *a* earnest, eager

ahincar /ain'kar/ *vt* to urge, press; *vr* hurry, hasten. See **prohibir**

ahínco /a'inko/ *m*, earnestness, eagerness

ahitar /ai'tar/ *vt* to stuff with food; bore, disgust. See **prohibir**

ahíto /a'ito/ *a* full of food; *Fig.* fed up. *m*, indigestion

ahogado /ao'gaðo/ **(-da)** *a* drowned; suffocated; stuffy, unventilated; stifling. *n* drowned person; victim of suffocation

ahogamiento /aoga'miento/ *m*, drowning; suffocation

ahogar /ao'gar/ *vt* to drown; suffocate; put out (the fire); stifle (yawns, etc.); suppress, extinguish; tire; overwater (plants); *vr Naut.* sink, founder; drown; suffocate

ahogo /a'ogo/ *m*, anxiety, grief; difficulty in breathing, oppression; asthma; embarrassment; suffocation; straitened circumstances

ahondamiento /aonda'miento/ *m*, in-depth treatment (e.g. *el a. de un problema,* in-depth treatment of a problem)

ahondar /aon'dar/ *vt* to deepen; excavate, dig; go into thoroughly; go deep into, penetrate; *vr* (earth) subside

ahora /a'ora/ *adv* now; very soon; just now, a short time ago. *conjunc* whether; now. **a. bien,** well now, given that. **a. mismo,** immediately, at once. **por a.,** for the present

ahorcado /aor'kaðo/ **(-da)** *n* hanged man

ahorcar /aor'kar/ *vt* to execute by hanging, hang. *Inf.* **a. los hábitos,** to leave the priesthood, cease to be an ecclesiastic

ahorita /ao'rita/ *adv*, *Mexico* right away, right now; *elsewhere in Lat. Am.* in a little while

ahormar /aor'mar/ *vt* to adjust, shape; break in (new shoes); make (a person) see reason

ahorrar /ao'rrar/ *vt* to save, economize; avoid, eschew; *vr* avoid; remove clothing

ahorro /a'orro/ *m*, economy, thrift; *pl* savings

ahuchar /au'tʃar/ *vt* to hoard; expel, drive away

ahuciar /au'siar; au'θiar/ *vt* take possession of (a house)

ahuecar /aue'kar/ *vt* to hollow out; loosen; shake out; puff out, inflate; put on a solemn voice; hoe; dig; *Inf. vr* puff oneself out; put on airs

ahumada /au'maða/ *f*, smoke signal

ahumado /au'maðo/ *a* smoked; smoky

ahumar /au'mar/ *vt* to smoke (herrings, etc.); fill with smoke; *vi* smoke, burn; *vr* be full of smoke; taste smoked; *Inf.* get drunk. See **desahuciar**

ahusado /au'saðo/ *a* spindle-shaped

ahuyentar /auyen'tar/ *vt* to frighten off; drive away; dismiss, banish (anxiety, etc.); *vr* flee

airadamente /airaða'mente/ *adv* wrathfully, angrily

airado /ai'raðo/ *a* angry

airar /ai'rar/ *vt* to annoy, anger; *vr* grow annoyed

aire /'aire/ *m*, air; atmosphere (sometimes *pl*); breeze, wind; bearing, appearance; vanity; (horse's) gait; futility, frivolity; grace, charm; gracefulness; *Mus.* air; *Mus.* tempo. **a. popular,** popular tune. **al a. libre,** in the open air, outdoors. *Inf.* **beber los aires (por),** to yearn (for)

aireación /airea'sion; airea'θion/ *f*, airing; ventilation

airear /aire'ar/ *vt* to air; ventilate; aerate; *vr* take the air; catch a chill

airecito /aire'sito; aire'θito/ *m*, *Lat. Am.* breeze; gentle wind

airosidad /airosi'ðað/ *f*, gracefulness; jauntiness

airoso /ai'roso/ *a* airy, open; windy, breezy, fresh; graceful; handsome; jaunty; victorious, successful

aislacionismo /aislasio'nismo/ **aisla-θiona'mismo/** *m*, *Polit.* isolationism

aislacionista /aislasion'ista; aislaθion'ista/ *mf Polit.* isolationist

aislado /ais'laðo/ *a* isolated; remote; individual; single; *Elec.* insulated

aislador /aisla'ðor/ *m, Phys.* insulator
aislamiento /aisla'miento/ *m,* isolation; *Phys.* insulation
aislante /ais'lante/ *a* isolating; insulating
aislar /ais'lar/ *vt* to isolate; *Elec.* insulate; *vr* become a recluse; become isolated
¡ajá! /a'ha/ *interj Inf.* Aha! Good!
ajar /a'har/ *vt* to crease, crumple, spoil; humiliate; *vr* fade, wither (flowers)
ajedrecista /aheðre'sista; aheðre'θista/ *mf* chess player
ajedrez /ahe'ðres; ahe'ðreθ/ *m,* chess
ajenjo /a'henho/ *m, Bot.* wormwood; absinthe
ajeno /a'heno/ *a* alien; belonging to another; various, diverse; free, exempt; unsuitable; irrelevant
ajetrear /ahetre'ar/ *vt* to tire out, exhaust; *vr* be overtired
ajetreo /ahe'treo/ *m,* exhaustion, fatigue
ají /a'hi/ *m, Lat. Am.* chili, red pepper; chili sauce; **estar hecho un ají** to be hopping mad, be fuming
ajo /'aho/ *m,* garlic; *Inf.* make up, paint; disreputable affair, shady business; curse, oath. *Inf.* **revolver el a.,** to stir up trouble
ajorca /a'horka/ *f,* bracelet; slave bangle
ajornalar /ahorna'lar/ *vt* to hire by the day
ajuar /ahu'ar/ *m,* trousseau; household equipment
ajustado /ahus'taðo/ *a* exact; tight-fitting; trim
ajustador /ahusta'ðor/ **(-ra)** *a* adjusting. *n* adjuster. *m,* tight-fitting jacket
ajustamiento /ahusta'miento/ *m,* adjustment; agreement
ajustar /ahus'tar/ *vt* to adjust; fit; arrange; make an agreement about; reconcile; settle (accounts); engage, employ; retain (a barrister); regulate; tune up (a motor); *vi* fit; *vr* adapt oneself. *Inf.* **a. cuentas viejas,** to settle old accounts
ajuste /a'huste/ *m,* fitting; adjustment; agreement; arrangement; *Print.* make-up; reconciliation; settlement; regulation; engagement, appointment
ajusticiado /ahusti'siaðo; ahusti'θiaðo/ **(-da)** *n* executed person
ajusticiar /ahusti'siar; ahusti'θiar/ *vt* to put to death
al /al/ (contraction of *a + el*). 1. *prep a + m. def. art.,* to the, e.g. *Han ido al mar,* They have gone to the sea. 2. *prep a + el* used as *dem. pron* to that, to the one, e.g. *Mi sombrero se parece mucho al que tiene Vd.,* My hat is very similar to the one you have. *al + infin.* means when, as, at the same time as, e.g. *Al llamar a la puerta la vi en el jardín,* As I was knocking at the door, I saw her in the garden
ala /'ala/ *f, Zool.* wing; row, line; brim (of a hat); eaves; (*Archit. Aer. Mil. Bot.*) wing; blade (of propeller); fin (of fish); *pl* courage. **a. del corazón,** *Anat.* auricle. **arrastrar la a.,** to woo, flirt with. *Fig.* **cortar** (*or* **quebrar**) **las alas (a),** to clip a person's wings
alabador /alaβa'ðor/ **(-ra)** *n* praiser, extoller
alabanza /ala'βansa; ala'βanθa/ *f,* praise; eulogy
alabar /ala'βar/ *vt* to praise; *vr* brag, boast
alabastrino /alaβas'trino/ *a* alabastrine, alabaster
alabastro /ala'βastro/ *m,* alabaster
alacena /ala'sena; ala'θena/ *f,* cupboard; recess; closet; safe (for food)
alacrán /ala'kran/ *m,* scorpion
alacre /a'lakre/ *a, Mexico* agile, nimble
alacridad /alakri'ðað/ *f,* alacrity, eagerness; *Mexico* agility, nimbleness
alado /a'laðo/ *a* winged; feathered; *Fig.* soaring
alambicado /alambi'kaðo/ *a* sparing, frugal; subtle; euphuistic
alambicar /alambi'kar/ *vt* to distill; examine carefully, scrutinize; make over-subtle or euphuistic (of style)
alambique /alam'bike/ *m,* still
alambrada /alam'braða/ *f, Mil.* wire-entanglement
alambrado /alam'braðo/ *m,* wire-netting; *Mil.* wire-entanglement; wire cover
alambrar /alam'brar/ *vt* to wire (fence)
alambre /a'lambre/ *m,* wire; sheep bells. **a. espinoso,** barbed wire

alambrera /alam'brera/ *f,* wire fence; wire-netting; wire cover
alambrista /alam'brista/ *mf* tight-rope walker; (Mexico) wetback
alameda /ala'meða/ *f,* poplar wood or grove; avenue of poplars
álamo /'alamo/ *m,* poplar. **a. temblón,** aspen tree
alano /a'lano/ *m,* mastiff
alarde /a'larðe/ *m, Mil.* parade; display, ostentation. **hacer a. de,** to brag about
alargamiento /alarga'miento/ *m,* lengthening; stretching
alargar /alar'gar/ *vt* to lengthen; prolong; pass, hand (things); pay out (ropes, etc.); increase; *vr* go away, depart; be wordy, spread oneself; lengthen
alarido /ala'riðo/ *m,* yell, shout; shriek, scream; howl; yelp; cry (of a seagull)
alarma /a'larma/ *f,* alarm. **a. aérea,** air-raid warning
alarmante /alar'mante/ *a* alarming
alarmar /alar'mar/ *vt* to give the alarm; frighten; *vr* be alarmed
alarmista /alar'mista/ *mf* alarmist
alazán /ala'san; ala'θan/ *a* sorrel-colored. *m,* sorrel horse
alazo /a'laso; a'laθo/ *m,* flap or stroke of the wings
alba /'alβa/ *f,* dawn; *Eccl.* alb, vestment. **al a.,** at dawn
albacea /alβa'sea; alβa'θea/ *mf* executor, executrix; testator
albanés /alβa'nes/ **(-esa)** *a* and *n* Albanian. *m,* Albanian language
albañil /alβa'ɲil/ *m,* mason, bricklayer
albañilería /alβaɲile'ria/ *f,* masonry; bricklaying
albarda /al'βarða/ *f,* pack-saddle; *Lat. Am.* saddle
albardilla /alβar'ðiya; alβar'ðiʎa/ *f,* small saddle; pad; small pillow; *Archit.* coping
albaricoque /alβari'koke/ *m,* apricot
albaricoquero /alβariko'kero/ *m,* apricot tree
albarrada /alβa'rraða/ *f,* stone wall; mud fence
albatros /alβa'tros/ *m,* albatross
albear /alβe'ar/ *vi* to become white, whiten
albedrío /alβe'ðrio/ *m,* free will; fancy, caprice
albéitar /al'βeitar/ *m,* veterinary surgeon; farrier
alberca /al'βerka/ *f,* reservoir, tank; vat; artificial lake; *Lat. Am.* (swimming) pool
albergar /alβer'gar/ *vt* to shelter; nourish; harbor; *vi* and *vr* take refuge or shelter; lodge
albergue /al'βerge/ *m,* shelter, refuge; den, lair; hospitality; lodging; asylum
albo /'alβo/ *a* pure white
albóndiga /al'βondiga/ *f,* meat ball, rissole
albor /al'βor/ *m,* whiteness; dawnlight, dawn. **a. de la vida,** life's dawning, childhood
alborada /alβo'raða/ *f,* dawn; reveille; *Mil.* dawn attack; *Mus.* aubade
alborear /alβore'ar/ *vi* to grow light, dawn
albornoz /alβor'nos; alβor'noθ/ *m,* burnouse
alborotado /alβoro'taðo/ *a* impulsive; turbulent; noisy; excitable
alborotar /alβoro'tar/ *vt* to disturb; *vi* make a noise; be gay; *vr* riot; grow rough (sea)
alboroto /alβo'roto/ *m,* noise; confusion; tumult; riot; rejoicing, gaiety
alborotos /alβo'rotos/ *mpl, Argentina, Central America, Peru* popcorn
alborozar /alβoro'sar; alβoro'θar/ *vt* to overjoy, gladden; *vr* rejoice, be glad
alborozo /alβo'roso; alβo'roθo/ *m,* gladness, rejoicing, joy
albricias /al'βrisias; al'βriθias/ *f pl,* reward for bringer of good tidings. *interj* **¡A.!** Joy! Congratulations!
álbum /'alβum/ *m,* album
albúmina /al'βumina/ *f,* albumin
albur /al'βur/ *m, Ichth.* dace; chance, risk. **al a. de,** at the risk of
alcachofa /alka'tʃofa/ *f,* artichoke
alcahuete /alka'uete/ *m,* procurer, go-between, pimp; keeper; *Fig. Inf.* protector, screen; *Inf.* scandalmonger
alcahuetear /alkauete'ar/ *vt* to procure, act as a go-between for; *vi* be a pimp or a procuress

alcaide /al'kaiðe/ *m*, governor of a fortress *Obs.*; governor of a prison

alcalde /al'kalde/ **(-desa)** *n* mayor; magistrate. *Inf.* **tener el padre a.**, to have a friend at court

alcaldía /alkal'dia/ *f*, office or authority of an alcalde

álcali /'alkali/ *m*, *Chem.* alkali

alcalino /alka'lino/ *a* alkaline

alcance /al'kanse; al'kanθe/ *m*, reach, reaching, attainment; range (of firearms, etc.); scope; arm's length or reach; pursuit; stop press *or* extra edition (newspapers); *Com.* deficit; importance; *pl* talent; capacity. **al a. de la voz,** within call. **hombre de cortos alcances,** a limited, dull man. **poner al a. de,** to make available to; make intelligible to

alcancía /alkan'sia; alkan'θia/ *f*, money-box; coin bank, piggy bank

alcanfor /alkan'for/ *m*, camphor

alcantarilla /alkanta'riya; alkanta'riʎa/ *f*, little bridge; sewer; culvert; bed for electric cable

alcantarillado /alkantari'yaðo; alkantari'ʎaðo/ *m*, sewage system; main sewer

alcanzable /alkan'saβle; alkan'θaβle/ *a* obtainable; attainable

alcanzadizo /alkansa'ðiso; alkanθa'ðiθo/ *a* attainable, easily reached

alcanzar /alkan'sar; alkan'θar/ *vt* to overtake; reach; range (of guns, etc.); attain, achieve; understand; *Fig.* equal (in attainments); live at the same time as, be contemporaneous with; be capable of, be able; *vi* reach; share, participate in; be enough

alcaparra /alka'parra/ *f*, *Bot.* caper; caper bush

alcaucil /alkau'sil; alkau'θil/ *m*, (in most places) wild artichoke; (in some places) cultivated artichoke

alcazaba /alka'saβa; alka'θaβa/ *f*, fortress (within a walled town or city), casbah

alcázar /al'kasar; al'kaθar/ *m*, fortress; royal residence, castle; *Naut.* quarterdeck

alción /al'sion; al'θion/ *m*, *Ornith.* kingfisher

alcista /al'sista; al'θista/ *mf* speculator (on Stock Exchange)

alcoba /al'koβa/ *f*, bedroom; alcove, recess; Moorish flute

alcohol /al'kool/ *m*, alcohol; spirits of wine. **a. desnaturalizado,** industrial alcohol, methylated spirit. **a. metílico,** wood alcohol

alcohólico /alko'oliko/ *a* alcoholic

alcoholismo /alkool'ismo/ *m*, alcoholism

Alcorán /alko'ran/ *m*, Koran

alcornoque /alkor'noke/ *m*, cork tree; dolt

alcorzar /alkor'sar; alkor'θar/ *vt Cul.* to ice, cover with sugar; decorate, adorn

alcurnia /al'kurnia/ *f*, lineage, family, descent

alcuza /al'kusa; al'kuθa/ *f*, oil-bottle; oil-can; cruet

aldaba /al'daβa/ *f*, door knocker; bolt, latch; *pl* protectors, influential helpers. *Inf.* **tener buenas aldabas,** to have plenty of pull

aldabada /alda'βaða/ *f*, rap with the knocker; sudden shock

aldabeo /alda'βeo/ *m*, knocking

aldea /al'dea/ *f*, village

aldeano /alde'ano/ **(-na)** *a* village; country, ignorant. *n* villager; countryman, peasant

aldehído /alde'iðo/ *m*, *Chem.* aldehyde

aleación /alea'sion; alea'θion/ *f*, alloy

alear /ale'ar/ *vi* to flutter, beat the wings; flap one's arms; recuperate, grow well; *vt* alloy

aleatorio /alea'torio/ *a* accidental, fortuitous

aleccionamiento /aleksiona'miento; alekθiona'miento/ *m*, teaching, training, coaching

aleccionar /aleksio'nar; alekθio'nar/ *vt* to teach, train, coach

aledaño /ale'ðaɲo/ *a* adjoining; border. *m*, boundary, border

alegación /alega'sion; alega'θion/ *f*, allegation, statement

alegar /ale'gar/ *vt* to allege, state; cite; *vi Law.* bring forward, adduce

alegato /ale'gato/ *m*, *Law.* speech (for the prosecution or defense)

alegoría /alego'ria/ *f*, allegory

alegórico /ale'goriko/ *a* allegorical

alegorizar /alegori'sar; alegori'θar/ *vt* to interpret allegorically, treat as an allegory

alegrar /ale'grar/ *vt* to make happy, gladden, rejoice; adorn, beautify; stir (fires); *vr* be glad, rejoice; *Inf.* be merry (tipsy)

alegre /a'legre/ *a* joyful, glad; cheerful, gay; bright (colors, etc.); pretty, attractive; *Inf.* risqué; *Inf.* flirtatious, light

alegría /ale'gria/ *f*, joy, gladness; cheerfulness, gaiety; *pl* public rejoicings

alegrón /ale'gron/ *m*, sudden unexpected joy; *Inf.* flash of light. *a Inf.* flirtatious

alejamiento /aleha'miento/ *m*, placing at a distance, removal; withdrawal

Alejandría /alehan'dria/ Alexandria

alejar /ale'har/ *vt* to place at a distance, remove; withdraw; ward off (dangers, etc.); *vr* depart, go away; withdraw. **alejarse de,** to abandon (a belief, custom, superstition, etc.)

alelar /ale'lar/ *vt* to make silly or stupid

aleluya /ale'luya/ *mf*, alleluia. *m*, Eastertide. *f*, small Easter cake; *Inf.* daub, poor painting; *Inf.* doggerel; joy, rejoicing

alemán /ale'man/ **(-ana)** *a* and *n* German. *m*, German language.

Alemania /ale'mania/ Germany

alentada /alen'taða/ *f*, deep breath

alentado /alen'taðo/ *a* valiant, spirited; proud; *Argentina* strong, vigorous

alentador /alenta'ðor/ *a* encouraging, inspiring, stimulating

alentar /alen'tar/ *vi irr* to breathe; *vt* encourage, inspire; *vr* be encouraged. See **sentar**

alerce /a'lerse; a'lerθe/ *m*, larch tree and wood

alergia /a'ler'hia/ *f*, allergy

alergólogo /aler'gologo/ *m*, allergist

alero /a'lero/ *m*, projecting roof; splashboard (of carriages); eaves; gable end

alerón /ale'ron/ *m*, *Aer.* aileron

alerta /a'lerta/ *adv* watchfully. *interj* Take care! Look out! **estar ojo a.,** to be on the watch

alerto /a'lerto/ *a* watchful, alert

aleta /a'leta/ *f*, dim small wing; fin

aletargado /aletar'gaðo/ *a* lethargic; comatose

aletargamiento /aletarga'miento/ *m*, lethargy

aletargar /aletar'gar/ *vt* to cause lethargy; *vr* become lethargic

aletazo /ale'taso; ale'taθo/ *m*, flapping, beating (of wings); *Inf.* theft

aletear /alete'ar/ *vi* to flap the wings, flutter; move the arms up and down; become convalescent

aleteo /ale'teo/ *m*, fluttering, flapping of wings; beating, palpitation (of heart)

aleve /a'leβe/ *a* See **alevoso**

alevosía /aleβo'sia/ *f*, *Law.* malice; treachery

alevoso /ale'βoso/ *a Law.* malicious; treacherous

alfabético /alfa'βetiko/ *a* alphabetical

alfabetización /alfaβetisa'sion; alfaβetiθa'θion/ *f*, literacy work

alfabetizador /alfaβetisa'ðor; alfaβetiθa'ðor/ *m*, literacy worker

alfabeto /alfa'βeto/ *m*, alphabet. **a. manual,** sign language

alfalfa /al'falfa/ *f*, *Bot.* alfalfa, lucerne

alfandoque /alfan'doke/ *m*, *Lat. Am.* cheesecake; maraca

alfanje /al'fanhe/ *m* cutlass; *Mexico* machete

alfar /al'far/ *m*, potter's workshop; pottery, earthenware

alfarería /alfare'ria/ *f*, pottery shop; potter's workshop; potter's craft

alfarero /alfa'rero/ *m*, potter

alfeñique /alfe'ɲike/ *m*, *Cul.* icing, sugarpaste; *Inf.* affectation

alférez /al'feres; al'fereθ/ *m*, *Mil.* ensign; second lieutenant; lieutenant. *Nav.* **a. de fragata,** sub-lieutenant. **a. de navío,** lieutenant

alfil /al'fil/ *m*, bishop (in chess)

alfiler /alfi'ler/ *m*, pin; brooch with a pin; tiepin; *pl*

pin-money, dress-allowance; *Fig. Inf.* **no estar uno con sus alfileres,** to have a slate loose. *Inf.* vestido de veinticinco alfileres, dressed to the nines
alfiletero /alfile'tero/ *m*, needle-case
alfombra /al'fombra/ *f*, carpet; rug
alfombrado /alfom'braðo/ *m*, carpeting
alfombrar /alfom'brar/ *vt* to carpet
alfombrilla eléctrica /alfom'briya e'lektrika; alfom'briʎa e'lektrika/ *f*, electric pad or blanket
alfombrista /alfom'brista/ *m*, carpet merchant; layer of carpets
alforja /al'forha/ *f*, saddle-bag; *Mil.* knapsack
alforza /al'forsa; al'forθa/ *f*, *Sew.* tuck; *Inf.* scar
alforzar /alfor'sar; alfor'θar/ *vt Sew.* to tuck
alga /'alga/ *f*, alga, seaweed
algarabía /algara'βia/ *f*, Arabic; *Inf.* gibberish; din of voices, uproar
algarada /alga'raða/ *f*, troop of horse; uproar, hubbub; outcry
algarroba /alga'rroβa/ *f*, *Bot.* carob bean
algazara /alga'sara; alga'θara/ *f*, Moorish war cry; rejoicing, merriment; noise, clamor
álgebra /'alheβra/ *f*, algebra; art of bone setting
algebrista /alhe'βrista/ *mf* bonesetter; algebraist
álgido /'alhiðo/ *a* icy cold
algo /'algo/ *indef pron* some, something (e.g. *Se ve que hay a. que le molesta,* You can see that something is irritating him). *adv* somewhat, a bit. **en a.,** in some way
algodón /algo'ðon/ *m*, cotton plant; cotton flower; cotton fabric; candy floss (UK), cotton candy (USA). **a. en rama,** cotton-wool. **a. hidró-filo,** absorbent cotton wool. **a. pólvora,** nitrocellulose
algodonal /algoðo'nal/ *m*, cotton plantation
alguacil /algua'sil; algua'θil/ *m*, policeman, constable; *Obs.* city governor; short-legged spider
alguien /'algien/ *indef pron* someone, somebody, e.g. *Dime si viene a.,* Tell me if anyone comes
algún /al'gun/ *abb* of **alguno** bef. *m sing* noun, e.g. *a. libro*
alguno /al'guno/ *a* (*abb* **algún** bef. *m*, *sing*) some, any. *indef pron* someone, somebody; *pl* some, some people. **alguno que otro,** a few
alhaja /al'aha/ *f*, jewel; ornament; treasure, precious object; *Inf.* gem, excellent person (also ironic, e.g. *Es una a.,* He's a fine fellow)
alhajar /ala'har/ *vt* to adorn with jewels, bejewel; furnish, equip
alharaca /alar'aka/ *f*, vehemence, demonstration, fuss (gen. *pl*)
alheña /al'eɲa/ *f*, *Bot.* privet; henna
alhóndiga /al'ondiga/ *f*, corn exchange; public granary
aliado /a'liaðo/ (**-da**) *a* allied. *n* ally
alianza /a'liansa; a'lianθa/ *f*, alliance; pact, agreement; relationship (by marriage); sum total, whole (of factors, etc.); wedding-ring
aliarse /a'liarse/ *vr* to join together, become allies; be associated
alicaído /alika'iðo/ *a* drooping; *Inf.* weak, exhausted; discouraged, downhearted; come down in the world
alicates /ali'kates/ *m pl*, pincers, pliers
aliciente /ali'siente; ali'θiente/ *m*, attraction, inducement
alícuota /a'likuota/ *f*, *a* aliquot; proportional. **partes alícuotas,** aliquot parts
alienación /aliena'sion; aliena'θion/ *f*, alienation
alienado /alie'naðo/ *a* insane, mad
alienar /alie'nar/ *vt* See **enajenar**
alienista /alie'nista/ *mf Med.* alienist
aliento /a'liento/ *m*, breathing; breath; courage, spirit; encouragement. **el posterior a.,** one's last breath. **cobrar a.,** to regain one's breath; take heart. **de un a.,** in one breath; without stopping
alifafe /ali'fafe/ *m*, *Inf.* ailment; tumor on horse's hock
aligación /aliga'sion; aliga'θion/ *f*, binding together, alligation
aligeramiento /a,lihera'miento/ *m*, lightening, reduction in weight

aligerar /alihe'rar/ *vt* to lighten, make less heavy; quicken, hasten; ease, alleviate; moderate; shorten, abbreviate
alimaña /ali'maɲa/ *f*, destructive animal, predator
alimentación /alimenta'sion; alimenta'θion/ *f*, nourishment; feeding
alimentar /alimen'tar/ *vt* to feed; nourish; encourage, foment; assist, aid; keep, support
alimenticio /alimen'tisio; alimen'tiθio/ *a* nourishing; feeding
alimento /ali'mento/ *m*, food, nourishment; stimulus, encouragement; *pl* alimony; allowance
alindar /alin'dar/ *vt* to mark the boundary of; beautify, adorn; *vi* border, be contiguous
alineación /alinea'sion; alinea'θion/ *f*, alignment
alinear /aline'ar/ *vt* to align, range in line; dress (troops); *vr* fall into line
aliñar /ali'ɲar/ *vt* to decorate, adorn; *Cul.* season; prepare; set (bones)
aliño /a'liɲo/ *m*, decoration, ornament; preparation; condiment, seasoning; setting (bones)
aliquebrado /alike'βraðo/ *a* broken-winged; *Inf.* down in the mouth
alisador /alisa'ðor/ (**-ra**) *a* smoothing; polishing. *n* polisher
alisar /ali'sar/ *vt* to smooth; polish; sleek; plane; comb lightly
alisios /a'lisios/ *m pl*, trade winds
aliso /a'liso/ *m*, alder tree and wood
alistador /alista'ðor/ *m*, enroller
alistamiento /alista'miento/ *m*, enlistment; conscription; enrolment
alistar /alis'tar/ *vt* to enroll, list; enlist; conscript; prepare, get ready; enroll; *Mil.* enlist; get ready
alitranca /ali'tranka/ *f*, *Chile, Peru* brake
aliviar /ali'βiar/ *vt* to lighten; alleviate, mitigate; relieve; ease; quicken (one's step); hasten, speed up; steal
alivio /a'liβio/ *m*, lightening; relief; alleviation; ease
aljaba /al'haβa/ *f*, quiver (for arrows); *Lat. Am.* fuchsia
aljibe /al'hiβe/ *m*, tank, cistern; watership or tanker
aljófar /al'hofar/ *m*, small irregular shaped pearl; dew-drop, raindrop, tear drop
aljofifa /alho'fifa/ *f*, floorcloth
allá /a'ya; a'ʎa/ *adv* there; to that place. **más a.,** farther on, beyond. Used in conjunction with phrases of time, indicates remoteness, e.g. *a. en tiempos de los Reyes Católicos,* long ago in the time of the Catholic Monarchs. *a. por 1900,* way back in 1900
allanamiento /ayana'miento; aʎana'miento/ *m*, leveling, flattening; condescension, affability; (police) raid, (police) search acceptance of a judicial finding
allanar /aya'nar; aʎa'nar/ *vt* to level, flatten; overcome (difficulties); soothe; break into (a house, etc.); give entrance to the police; *vr* collapse (buildings, etc.); abide by, adapt oneself (to); condescend, be affable. **a. el camino (a...),** to pave the way (for...)
allegado /aye'gaðo; aʎe'gaðo/ (**-da**) *a* near, allied; related. *n* follower, ally
allegar /aye'gar; aʎe'gar/ *vt* to gather, collect; draw nearer; *Agr.* reap; add; *vi* arrive
allende /a'yende; a'ʎende/ *adv* beyond; besides. **de a. el mar,** from beyond the sea
allí /a'yi; a'ʎi/ *adv* there; in that place, thereto; thereupon, then. **por a.,** through there; that way
alma /'alma/ *f*, soul; living person; essence, core; vivacity, animation; energy, vitality; spirit, ghost; core (of a rope). **a. de cántaro,** fool, ninny. **a. de Dios,** simple soul, kind person. **a. en pena,** soul in purgatory. **¡A. mía!** My darling! **con todo el a.,** with all my heart. **Lo siento en el a.,** I feel it deeply
almacén /alma'sen; alma'θen/ *m*, warehouse; store, shop
almacenaje /almase'nahe; almaθe'nahe/ *m*, act of storing, cost of storage
almacenar /almase'nar; almaθe'nar/ *vt* to store; put in store; hoard
almacenero /almase'nero; almaθe'nero/ *m*, warehouseman, storekeeper

almacenista /almase'nista; almaθe'nista/ *mf* owner of a store; assistant, salesman (saleswoman)
almáciga /al'masiga; al'maθiga/ *f*, mastic; tree plantation or nursery
almagre /al'magre/ *m*, *Mineral.* red ocher; stain, mark
almanaque /alma'nake/ *m*, calendar, almanac
almeja /al'meha/ *f*, *Ichth.* clam
almenara /alme'nara/ *f*, beacon fire
almendra /al'mendra/ *f*, almond; kernel; crystal drop (of chandeliers, etc.); cocoon; bean (of cocoa tree, etc.). **a. garapiñada,** sugar almond
almendro /al'mendro/ *m*, almond tree
almendruco /almen'druko/ *m*, green almond
almete /al'mete/ *m*, casque, helmet; helmeted soldier
almiar /al'miar/ *m*, haystack, hayrick
almíbar /al'miβar/ *m*, sugar syrup; nectar
almibarado /almiβa'raðo/ *a* syrupy; *Inf.* sugary
almibarar /almiβa'rar/ *vt* to coat with sugar; preserve (fruit) in syrup; flatter with sweet words
almidón /almi'ðon/ *m*, starch
almidonado /almiðo'naðo/ *a* starched; *Fig. Inf.* stiff, unbending; prim, starchy
almidonar /almiðo'nar/ *vt* to starch
alminar /almi'nar/ *m*, minaret (of mosque)
almirantazgo /almiran'tasgo; almiran'taθgo/ *m*, Admiralty; admiralship; Admiralty Court
almirante /almi'rante/ *m*, admiral
almizcle /al'miskle; al'miθkle/ *m*, musk
almizcleño /almis'kleɲo; almiθ'kleɲo/ *a* musk (of scents)
almizclero /almis'klero; almiθ'klero/ *a* musky. *m*, *Zool.* musk-deer
almocafre /almo'kafre/ *m*, *Agr.* hoe; trowel, dibble
almohada /almo'aða/ *f*, pillow; pillowcase; cushion. *Inf.* **aconsejarse** *or* **consultar con la a.,** to think over (a matter) carefully, sleep on it
almohadilla /almoa'ðiya; almoa'ðiʎa/ *f*, *dim* small cushion; lace or sewing cushion; pin cushion
almohadillado /almoaði'yaðo; almoaði'ʎaðo/ *a* cushioned; padded
almoneda /almo'neða/ *f*, auction; furniture sale
almonedear /almoneðe'ar/ *vt* to auction; sell off (furniture)
almorranas /almo'rranas/ *f pl*, hemorrhoids
almorzar /almor'sar; almor'θar/ *vi irr* to lunch; breakfast. See **forzar**
almuecín, almuédano /almue'sin, al'mueðano; almue'θin, al'mueðano/ *m*, muezzin
almucería /almuerse'ria; almuerθe'ria/ *f*, *Mexico* lunch counter, luncheonette
almuerzo /al'muerso; al'muerθo/ *m*, luncheon; breakfast (not so usual)
alocado /alo'kaðo/ *a* feather-brained, reckless; crazy, wild
alocución /aloku'sion; aloku'θion/ *f*, allocution, address, harangue
áloe /'aloe/ *m*, *Bot.* aloe
alojado /alo'haðo/ **(-da)** *m*, billeted soldier. *n* lodger, guest
alojamiento /aloha'miento/ *m*, lodging; dwelling; *Mil.* billeting; *Naut.* steerage; camp, encampment
alojar /alo'har/ *vt* to lodge; billet, quarter (troops); insert, introduce; *vi* and *vr* lodge; live, dwell
alondra /a'londra/ *f*, *Ornith.* lark
alopatía /alopa'tia/ *f*, *Med.* allopathy
alpaca /al'paka/ *f*, alpaca (animal and fabric); nickel silver
alpargata /alpar'gata/ *f*, sandal with hemp sole
alpargatero /alparga'tero/ **(-ra)** *n* manufacturer or seller of alpargatas
Alpes, los /'alpes, los/ the Alps
alpestre /al'pestre/ *a* Alpine; rock (of plants); mountainous, lofty
alpinismo /alpi'nismo/ *m*, mountaineering
alpinista /alpi'nista/ *mf* mountaineer, climber
alpino /al'pino/ *a* Alpine
alpiste /al'piste/ *m*, bird seed
alquería /alke'ria/ *f*, farmstead

alquiladizo /alkila'ðiso; alkila'ðiθo/ *a* rentable, hirable
alquilador /alkila'ðor/ **(-ra)** *n* hirer
alquilamiento /alkila'miento/ *m*, See **alquiler**
alquilar /alki'lar/ *vt* to rent; hire out; hire; *vr* hire oneself out, serve on a wage basis
alquiler /alki'ler/ *m*, hiring out; renting; rental; hire; wages. **de a.,** for hire, on hire
alquimia /al'kimia/ *f*, alchemy
alquimista /alki'mista/ *mf* alchemist
alquitrán /alki'tran/ *m*, tar, pitch. **a. mineral,** coal tar
alquitranado /alkitra'naðo/ *a* tarred. *m*, *Naut.* tarpaulin
alrededor /alreðe'ðor/ *adv* around, about. **a. de,** around; approximately, about (e.g. *a. de cinco dólares,* about $5)
alrededores /alreðe'ðores/ *m pl*, environs, surrounding country
Alsacia /al'sasia; al'saθia/ Alsace
alsaciano /alsa'siano; alsa'θiano/ **(-na)** *a* and *n* Alsatian
alta /'alta/ *f*, certificate of discharge from hospital
altanería /altane'ria/ *f*, hawking; haughtiness, disdain; superciliousness
altanero /alta'nero/ *a* soaring, high-flying (of birds); supercilious; haughty, disdainful
altar /al'tar/ *m*, altar. **a. mayor,** high altar
altavoz /ˌalta'βos; ˌalta'βoθ/ *m*, loudspeaker; megaphone
altearse /alte'arse/ *vr* to rise, grow steep (of land)
alterabilidad /alteraβili'ðað/ *f*, alterability, changeability
alteración /altera'sion; altera'θion/ *f*, alteration, change; debasement (of coinage); agitation
alterar /alte'rar/ *vt* to change, alter; debase (coinage); disturb, agitate; *vr* grow angry; become excited
altercación /alterka'sion; alterka'θion/ *f*. **altercado** *m*, altercation, quarrel
altercar /alter'kar/ **(se)** *vi* and *vr* to quarrel, dispute, altercate
alternación /alterna'sion; alterna'θion/ *f*, alternation
alternado /alter'naðo/ *a* alternate
alternador /alterna'ðor/ *a* alternating. *m*, *Elec.* alternator
alternante /alter'nante/ *a* alternating
alternar /alter'nar/ *vt* to alternate; make one's debut as a **matador;** *vi* alternate; *(with con)* have dealings with, know
alternativa /alterna'tiβa/ *f*, alternative, option; service performed by turns; alternation
alternativo /alterna'tiβo/ *a* alternative
alterno /al'terno/ *a* alternative; *Bot.* alternate
alteza /al'tesa; al'teθa/ *f*, altitude, height; sublimity, perfection; **(A.)** Highness (title)
altibajo /alti'βaho/ *m*, embossed velvet; *pl Inf.* rough ground; *Inf.* vicissitudes of fortune
altillo /al'tiyo; al'tiʎo/ *m*, hillock; loft, garret, attic
altímetro /al'timetro/ *m*, *Aer.* altimeter
altiplanicie /altipla'nisie; altipla'niθie/ *f*, plateau; highland
altiplano /alti'plano/ *m* plateau; **el A.** the High Andes, the high Andean plateau
altisonante /altiso'nante/ *a* sonorous; sublime; high-flown, pompous
altitud /alti'tuð/ *f*, altitude, height
altivez /alti'βes; alti'βeθ/ *f*, arrogance, haughtiness
altivo /al'tiβo/ *a* arrogant, haughty
alto /'alto/ *a* high; tall; difficult, arduous; sublime; deep; most serious (of crimes, etc.); expensive (of price); small, early (hours). *m*, height; hill; story; floor; *Mil.* halt; rest light (traffic light). *adv* up, above, on high; loudly. *interj* **¡A.!** *Mil.* Halt! *Mil.* **A. Mando,** High Command. **las altas horas de la noche,** the wee (or early) hours. **en alta voz,** in a loud voice. **en alto,** on high; up above. **hacer alto,** to halt, stop
altozano /alto'sano; alto'θano/ *m*, mound, hillock; viewpoint, open space
altruismo /altru'ismo/ *m*, altruism
altruista /altru'ista/ *a* altruistic. *mf* altruist

altura /al'tura/ *f*, height; altitude; *Geom.* altitude or height; top, peak; sublimity; tallness
alucinación /alusina'sion; aluθina'θion/ *f*, **alucinamiento**, *m*, hallucination
alucinado /alusi'naðo; aluθi'naðo/ *m*, person suffering from hallucinations
alucinador /alusina'ðor; aluθina'ðor/ *a* hallucinatory, deceptive
alucinar /alusi'nar; aluθi'nar/ *vt* to dazzle, fascinate; deceive
alud /a'luð/ *m*, avalanche
aludir /alu'ðir/ *vi* to allude (to); refer (to), cite
alumbrado /alum'braðo/ *m*, lighting; *pl* illuminati
alumbramiento /alumbra'miento/ *m*, lighting, supply of light; childbirth
alumbrar /alum'brar/ *vt* to light, illuminate; give sight to the blind; instruct, teach; inflict (blows); hoe vine roots; *vi* give birth to a child; *vr Inf.* grow tipsy
alumbre /a'lumbre/ *m*, alum
aluminio /alu'minio/ *m*, aluminum
alumno /a'lumno/ **(-na)** *n* ward, adopted child; pupil. **a. externo,** day pupil. **a. interno,** boarder
alunizaje /aluni'sahe; aluni'θahe/ *m*, landing on the moon, moon-landing
alunizar /aluni'sar; aluni'θar/ *vi* to land on the moon
alusión /alu'sion/ *f*, allusion
alusivo /alu'siβo/ *a* allusive, suggestive; hinting
aluvial /alu'βial/ *a* alluvial
aluvión /alu'βion/ *m*, alluvium. **de a.,** alluvial
alverjana /alβer'hana/ *f*, *Lat. Am.* pea
alza /'alsa; 'alθa/ *f*, rise (of temperature, etc.); increase (in price); front sight (of guns)
alzacuello /alsa'kueyo; alθa'kueʎo/ *m*, high collar, clerical collar; neck stock
alzada /al'saða; al'θaða/ *f*, horse's stature; mountain pasture; *Law.* appeal
alzado /al'saðo; al'θaðo/ *a* fraudulent (of bankruptcy); fixed (of price); *Mexico* haughty, proud *m*, theft; *Lat. Am.* wild; insolent; rebellious; *Archit.* front elevation
alzamiento /alsa'miento; alθa'miento/ *m*, raising, lifting; higher bid (at auction); rising, rebellion; fraudulent bankruptcy
alzaprima /alsa'prima; alθa'prima/ *f*, lever; wedge; bridge (of string instruments)
alzar /al'sar; al'θar/ *vt* to raise; lift up; elevate (the Host); steal, remove; hide; gather in the harvest; build, construct; *Naut.* heave; *vr* rise (of temperature, mercury, price, etc.); make a fraudulent bankruptcy; *Law.* appeal; (*with con*) run off with, steal. *Naut.* **a. la vela,** to set sail
ama /'ama/ *f*, mistress of the house; owner; housekeeper; wet nurse. **a. de casa,** homemaker, housewife. **a. de leche,** foster-mother. **a. de llaves** *or* **a. de gobierno,** housekeeper. **a. seca,** children's nurse
amabilidad /amaβili'ðað/ *f*, lovableness; kindness; niceness, goodness, helpfulness
amable /a'maβle/ *a* lovable; kind; nice, good, helpful
amador /ama'ðor/ **(-ra)** *a* loving. *n* lover, admirer
amadrigar /amaðri'gar/ *vr* to welcome, receive well; *vr* go into a burrow or lair; go into seclusion
amaestrar /amaes'trar/ *vt* to train, instruct; tame; break in (horses)
amagar /ama'gar/ *vt* and *vi* to threaten; *vt* show signs of (diseases, etc.); *vr Inf.* hide
amago (**contra...**), /a'mago/ threat (to...), menace (to...)
amainar /amai'nar/ *vt Naut.* to take in the sails; *vi* drop (of the wind); *vi* and *vt* relax (efforts, etc.)
amaine /a'maine/ *m*, dropping, abatement (of the wind)
amalgama /amal'gama/ *f*, *Chem.* amalgam
amalgamación /amalgama'sion; amalgama'θion/ *f*, amalgamation
amalgamar /amalga'mar/ *vt* to amalgamate; *vr* be amalgamated
amamantamiento /amamanta'miento/ *m*, suckling, nursling
amamantar /amaman'tar/ *vt* to suckle

amancillar /amansi'yar; amanθi'ʎar/ *vt* to discredit, dishonor; tarnish; stain
amanecer /amane'ser; amane'θer/ *vi irr* to dawn; arrive *or* be somewhere *or* be doing, at dawn (e.g. *Amanecimos en el barco,* Dawn came while we were on the ship. *Amanecimos escribiendo la carta,* The day broke as we were writing the letter); appear at daybreak; begin to appear. *m*, dawn, daybreak. See **conocer**
amanerado /amane'raðo/ *a* mannered; affected
amaneramiento /amanera'miento/ *m*, manneredness; mannerism
amanerarse /amane'rarse/ *vr* to acquire mannerisms or tricks of style; become affected
amansador /amansa'ðor/ **(-ra)** *a* soothing, calming. *n* appeaser
amansar /aman'sar/ *vt* to tame; appease, moderate; soothe, pacify; break in (horses)
amante /a'mante/ *a* loving. *mf* lover
amanuense /ama'nuense/ *mf* amanuensis, secretary, clerk
amanzanar /amansa'nar/ to lay out the streets of
amañar /ama'ɲar/ *vt* to execute with skill; *vr* grow skillful
amaño /a'maɲo/ *m*, skill, dexterity; *pl* schemes, intrigues; tools, equipment
amapola /ama'pola/ *f*, poppy
amar /a'mar/ *vt* to love
amaranto /ama'ranto/ *m*, *Bot.* amaranth
amarar /ama'rar/ *vi* to alight on the water (of hydroplanes)
amarchantarse con /amartʃan'tarse kon/ *vr*, *Lat. Am.* deal regularly with, do business with
amargar /amar'gar/ *vi* to taste or be bitter; *vt* make bitter; embitter
amargo /a'margo/ *a* bitter; embittered; grievous, sad. *m*, bitterness; *pl* bitters
amargor /amar'gor/ *m*, **amargura,** *f*, bitter taste, bitterness; trouble, affliction, pain
amaricado /amari'kaðo/ *a Inf.* effeminate
amarillear /amariye'ar; amariʎe'ar/ *vi* to look yellow; turn yellow; tend to yellow
amarillento /amari'yento; amari'ʎento/ *a* yellowish, turning yellow
amarilleo /amari'yeo; amari'ʎeo/ *m*, yellowing
amarillez /amari'yes; amari'ʎeθ/ *f*, yellowness
amarillo /ama'riyo; ama'riʎo/ *a*, yellow
amarilloso /amari'joso; amari'ʎoso/ *a*, *Lat. Am.* yellowish, turning yellow
amarra /a'marra/ *f*, *Naut.* cable, thick rope
amarradero /amarra'ðero/ *m*, *Naut.* mooring berth; mooring-post; hitchingpost or ring
amarraje /ama'rrahe/ *m*, *Naut.* mooring charge
amarrar /ama'rrar/ *vt* to tie up, hitch; moor
amarre /a'marre/ *m*, mooring; hitching
amartelar /amarte'lar/ *vt* to make jealous; court, woo, make love to; *vr* be jealous; fall madly in love
amartillar /amarti'yar; amarti'ʎar/ *vt* to hammer; knock; cock (firearms)
amasadera /amasa'ðera/ *f*, kneading-trough
amasador /amasa'ðor/ **(-ra)** *a* kneading. *n* kneader
amasar /ama'sar/ *vt* to knead; massage; cement
amasia /a'masia/ *f*, concubine
amasiato /ama'siato/ *m*, concubinage
amasijo /ama'siho/ *m*, *Cul.* dough; kneading; portion of plaster or mortar; *Inf.* hotchpotch; mixture; scheme, plot
amatista /ama'tista/ *f*, amethyst
amazacotado /a,masako'taðo; a,maθako'taðo/ *a* heavy, dense; *Fig.* stodgy (of writings, etc.)
amazona /ama'sona; ama'θona/ *f*, Amazon; independent woman; woman rider; woman's riding habit
ambages /am'bahes/ *m pl*, maze, intricate paths; circumlocutions
ámbar /'ambar/ *m*, amber. **a. gris,** ambergris
ambarino /amba'rino/ *a* amber
Amberes /am'beres/ Antwerp
ambición /ambi'sion; ambi'θion/ *f*, ambition

ambicionar /ambisio'nar; ambiθio'nar/ *vt* to long for; desire eagerly; be ambitious to

ambicioso /ambi'sioso; ambi'θioso/ *a* ambitious; eager, desirous

ambidextro /ambi'ðekstro/ *a* ambidextrous

ambiente /am'biente/ *a* ambient, surrounding. *m*, air, atmosphere; environment

ambigú /ambi'gu/ *m*, cold buffet; buffet (in theaters, etc.)

ambigüedad /ambigue'ðað/ *f*, ambiguity

ambiguo /am'biguo/ *a* ambiguous

ámbito /'ambito/ *m*, precincts; boundary, limit; compass, scope

amblar /am'blar/ *vi* to pace (of a horse)

ambos, /'ambos,/ *a m pl*, **ambas** *a f pl*, both, e.g. *ambas casas*, both houses

ambulancia /ambu'lansia; ambu'lanθia/ *f*, ambulance. **a. de correos,** railway post office. **a. fija,** field-hospital

ambulante /ambu'lante/ *a* walking; traveling, wandering

amedrentar /ameðren'tar/ *vt* to frighten, scare; intimidate

ameliorar /amelio'rar/ *vt* to better, improve

amelonado /amelo'naðo/ *a* melon-shaped; *Inf.* madly in love

amén /a'men/ *m*, amen, so be it. **a. de,** besides, in addition to. *Inf.* **en un decir a.,** in a split second

amenaza /ame'nasa; ame'naθa/ *f*, threat

amenazador, amenazante /amenasa'ðor, amena'sante; amenaθa'ðor, amena'θante/ *a* menacing, threatening

amenazar /amena'sar; amena'θar/ *vt* to threaten; *vt* and *vi* presage, be pending

amenguamiento /amengua'miento/ *m*, lessening, diminution; discredit; loss of prestige

amenguar /amen'guar/ *vt* to lessen, decrease; dishonor, discredit

amenidad /ameni'ðað/ *f*, amenity; agreeableness

amenizar /ameni'sar; ameni'θar/ *vt* to make pleasant or attractive

ameno /a'meno/ *a* pleasant; entertaining; agreeable, delightful

América /a'merika/ America

América del Norte /a'merika del 'norte/ North America

América del Sur /a'merika del sur/ South America

americana /ameri'kana/ *f*, (man's) jacket

americanismo /amerika'nismo/ *m*, usage typical of Western-Hemisphere Spanish

americano /ameri'kano/ **(-na)** *a* Western Hemispheric; *mf* native of the Western Hemisphere; resident of the Western Hemisphere

ameritar /ameri'tar/ *vt WH* to deserve, merit

ametrallador /ametraya'ðor; ametraʎa'ðor/ *m*, machine-gunner

ametralladora /ametraya'ðora; ametraʎa'ðora/ *f*, machine-gun

amianto /a'mianto/ *m*, *Mineral.* amianthus, asbestos

amiba /a'miβa/ *f*, *Zool.* ameba

amicísimo /ami'sisimo; ami'θisimo/ *a sup.* **amigo,** most friendly

amiga /a'miga/ *f*, woman friend; mistress, lover; dame, schoolmistress; dame school

amigabilidad /amigaβili'ðað/ *f*, friendliness, amicability

amigable /ami'gaβle/ *a* friendly, amicable; harmonious; suitable

amígdala /a'migðala/ *f*, tonsil

amigdalitis /amigða'litis/ *f*, tonsillitis

amigo /a'migo/ **(-ga)** *a* friendly; fond, addicted. *n* friend. *m*, lover. *Inf.* **ser muy a. de,** to be very friendly with; be very keen on or fond of

amilanado /amila'naðo/ *a* cowed, spiritless

amilanar /amila'nar/ *vt* to terrify, intimidate; *vr* grow discouraged

aminorar /amino'rar/ *vt* to diminish, lessen

amistad /amis'tað/ *f*, friendship; liaison; favor; *pl* acquaintances, friends

amistar /amis'tar/ *vt* to introduce, make known to

each other; bring about a reconciliation between or with

amistoso /amis'toso/ *a* friendly

amnesia /am'nesia/ *f*, amnesia

amnistía /amnis'tia/ *f*, amnesty

amnistiar /amnisti'ar/ *vt* to concede an amnesty, pardon

amo /'amo/ *m*, head of the house; master; owner; overlord; overseer. **a. de huéspedes,** keeper of a boarding house. **Nuestro A.** Our Lord. *Inf.* **ser el a. del cotarro,** to rule the roost

amoblado /amo'βlaðo/ *m*, *Central America, Mexico* furniture

amodorramiento /amoðorra'miento/ *m*, stupor, deep sleep

amodorrarse /amoðo'rrarse/ *vr* to fall into a stupor; fall into a heavy sleep

amoladera /amola'ðera/ *f*, whetstone

amolador /amola'ðor/ *m*, scissors grinder; knife grinder; sharpener

amoladura /amola'ðura/ *f*, grinding, whetting, sharpening

amolar /amo'lar/ *vt irr* to grind, sharpen; *Inf.* pester, annoy. See **colar**

amoldar /amol'dar/ *vt* to mold; adjust; *vr* adapt oneself

amonedar /amone'ðar/ *vt* to coin, mint

amonestación /amonesta'sion; amonesta'θion/ *f*, warning; advice. **correr las amonestaciones,** to publish banns of marriage

amonestador /amonesta'ðor/ **(-ra)** *a* warning, admonitory. *n* admonisher

amonestar /amones'tar/ *vt* to warn; advise; rebuke; *Eccl.* publish bans of marriage

amoníaco /amo'niako/ *m*, ammonia

amontillado /amonti'yaðo; amonti'ʎaðo/ *m*, kind of pale, dry sherry

amontonamiento /amontona'miento/ *m*, accumulation; gathering, collection; piling up, heaping

amontonar /amonto'nar/ *vt* to pile up, heap; gather; collect; accumulate; *vr Inf.* fly into a rage

amor /a'mor/ *m*, love; beloved; willingness, pleasure; *pl* love affairs; caresses. **a. propio,** self-esteem; vanity. *Inf.* **con mil amores,** with great pleasure. **por a. de,** for love of; for the sake of

amoral /amo'ral/ *a* amoral

amoratado /amora'taðo/ *a* livid, bluish

amorcillo /amor'siyo; amor'θiʎo/ *m*, *Dim.* little love; unimportant love affair; Cupid

amordazar /amorða'sar; amorða'θar/ *vt* to muzzle; gag; prevent speaking

amorfo /a'morfo/ *a* amorphous

amorío /amo'rio/ *m*, *Inf.* wooing, love making; *pl* love affairs

amoroso /amo'roso/ *a* loving; gentle; mild, balmy

amorrar /amo'rrar/ *vi Inf.* to hang one's head; sulk, be sullen

amortajar /amorta'har/ *vt* to wrap in a shroud; enshroud

amortiguador /amortigua'ðor/ *m*, *Mech.* shock absorber. *Auto.* **a. de los muelles,** shock-absorber

amortiguamiento /amortigua'miento/ *m*, softening, deadening; mitigation, lessening

amortiguar /amorti'guar/ *vt* to soften, deaden; absorb (shocks); moderate, mitigate; soften (colors)

amortización /amortisa'sion; amortiθa'θion/ *f*, amortization

amortizar /amorti'sar; amorti'θar/ *vt* to amortize; recover, redeem; suppress, abolish (posts)

amoscarse /amos'karse/ *vr Inf.* to be piqued or annoyed; become agitated

amostazar /amosta'sar; amosta'θar/ *vt Inf.* to annoy; *vi* become peeved

amotinador /amotina'ðor/ **(-ra)** *a* mutinous, rebellious. *n* rebel, mutineer; rioter

amotinar /amoti'nar/ *vt* to incite to rebellion; unbalance, unhinge (mind); *vr* rebel; riot; *Fig.* be unhinged

amovible /amo'βiβle/ *a* movable, removable; removable (of officials, etc.)

amovilidad /amoβili'ðað/ *f*, movability, removability; liability to discharge or dismissal
amparador /ampara'ðor/ **(-ra)** *a* protective; sheltering. *n* protector, defender, helper; shelterer
amparar /ampa'rar/ *vt* to protect, favor, help; shelter; *vr* take refuge, take shelter; defend oneself
amparo /am'paro/ *m*, shelter, refuge; protection, favor, help; defense
amper /am'per/ *m*, *Elec.* ampere
amperímetro /ampe'rimetro/ *m*, *Elec.* ammeter
amperio /am'perio/ *m*, *Elec.* ampere
ampliable /am'pliaβle/ *a* amplifiable
ampliación /amplia'sion; amplia'θion/ *f*, enlargement, increase, extension; *Photo.* enlargement
ampliador /amplia'ðor/ **(-ra)** *a* enlarging. *n* enlarger
ampliadora /amplia'ðora/ *f*, *Photo.* enlarger
ampliar /amp'liar/ *vt* to extend, enlarge, increase; *Photo.* enlarge
amplificación /amplifika'sion; amplifika'θion/ *f*, extension, amplification; *Photo.* enlargement
amplificar /amplifi'kar/ *vt* to enlarge; extend; increase; amplify, expatiate upon
amplio /'amplio/ *a* wide; extensive; roomy, ample; prolix
amplitud /ampli'tuð/ *f*, extension; width; spaciousness, amplitude
ampolla /am'poya; am'poʎa/ *f*, blister; ampoule; bubble; *Elec.* bulb
ampulosidad /ampulosi'ðað/ *f*, pomposity, redundancy (of style)
ampuloso /ampu'loso/ *a* pompous, high-flown (style)
amputación /amputa'sion; amputa'θion/ *f*, amputation
amputar /ampu'tar/ *vt* to amputate
amuchachado /amutʃa'tʃaðo/ *a* boyish
amueblar /amue'βlar/ *vt* to furnish; provide with furniture
amuinar /amui'nar/ *vt*, *Mexico* to anger, make angry
amuleto /amu'leto/ *m*, amulet, charm
amurallar /amura'yar; amura'ʎar/ *vt* to surround with a wall, wall
amurrarse /amu'rrarse/ *vr*, *Lat. Am.* get depressed, get the blues
amusgar /amus'gar/ *vt* and *vi* to flatten the ears (animals); *vt* screw up the eyes (to see better)
anacardo /ana'karðo/ *m*, cashew (nut)
anacoreta /anako'reta/ *mf* anchorite, hermit
anacreóntico /anakre'ontiko/ *a* Anacreontic
anacrónico /ana'kroniko/ *a* anachronous
anacronismo /anakro'nismo/ *m*, anachronism
ánade /'anaðe/ *mf* duck
anadear /anaðe'ar/ *vi* to waddle (like a duck)
anadeo /ana'ðeo/ *m*, waddle
anadino /ana'ðino/ **(-na)** *n* duckling
anadón /ana'ðon/ *m*, drake
anáfora /a'nafora/ *f*, anaphora
anafrodisíaco /anafroði'siako/ *a* anaphrodisiac
anagrama /ana'grama/ *m*, anagram
analectas /ana'lektas/ *f*, *pl* analects
anales /a'nales/ *m*, *pl* annals
analfabetismo /analfaβe'tismo/ *m*, illiteracy
analfabeto /analfa'βeto/ **(-ta)** *a* and *n* illiterate
analgesia /anal'hesia/ *f*, analgesia
analgésico /anal'hesiko/ *a* and *m*, *Med.* analgesic
análisis /a'nalisis/ *m*, analysis; *Gram.* parsing
analista /ana'lista/ *mf* analyst
analizar /anali'sar; anali'θar/ *vt* to analyse
analogía /analo'hia/ *f*, analogy
analógico, análogo /ana'lohiko, a'nalogo/ *a* analogous
ananás /ana'nas/ *m*, pineapple
anaquel /ana'kel/ *m*, shelf, ledge
anaranjado /anaran'haðo/ *a* and *m*, orange (color)
anarquía /anar'kia/ *f*, anarchy
anárquico /a'narkiko/ *a* anarchical
anarquismo /anar'kismo/ *m*, anarchism
anarquista /anar'kista/ *mf* anarchist
anatema /ana'tema/ *mf.* anathema
anatomía /anato'mia/ *f*, anatomy

anatómico /ana'tomiko/ *a* anatomical
anca /'anka/ *f*, croup, hindquarters of a horse
ancho /'antʃo/ *a* wide, broad. *m*, width, breadth. *Inf.* *a mis* **(tus, sus,** etc.) **anchas** *or* **anchos,** at my (your, his, etc.) ease, with complete freedom
anchoa /an'tʃoa/ *f*, anchovy
anchura /an'tʃura/ *f*, width, breadth; ease, freedom; extent
anchuroso /antʃu'roso/ *a* very wide; extensive; spacious
ancianidad /ansiani'ðað; anθiani'ðað/ *f*, old age; seniority; oldness
anciano /an'siano; an'θiano/ **(-na)** *a* old; ancient. *n* old person
ancla /'ankla/ *f*, anchor. **a. de la esperanza,** sheet anchor. **echar anclas,** to anchor
ancladero, anclaje /ankla'ðero, an'klahe/ *m*, anchorage
anclar /an'klar/ *vi* to anchor
ancón /an'kon/ *m*, cove, *Mexico* corner
áncora /'ankora/ *f*, anchor; refuge, haven
andada /an'daða/ *f*, wandering, roving; hard bread roll; pasture; *pl* trail, tracks. *Fig. Inf.* **volver a las andadas,** to return to one's old tricks
andaderas /anda'ðeras/ *f pl*, go-cart (for learning to walk)
andador /anda'ðor/ *a* walking; swift walking; wandering. *m*, walker; garden path; *pl* leading-strings, reins
andadura /anda'ðura/ *f*, walk, gait; pace, step
Andalucía /andalu'sia; andalu'θia/ Andalusia
andaluz /anda'lus; anda'luθ/ **(-za)** *a* and *n* Andalusian
andaluzada /andalu'saða; andalu'θaða/ *f*, *Inf.* exaggeration, tall story
andamio /an'damio/ *m*, scaffolding; stand, platform
andanada /anda'naða/ *f*, *Naut.* broadside; cheapest priced seat in a bullring; *Inf.* dressing-down, scolding
andante /an'dante/ *a* walking, strolling; errant (of knights). *a* and *m*, *Mus.* andante
andanza /an'dansa; an'danθa/ *f*, happening, occurrence; *pl* doings, deeds. **buena a.,** good fortune
andar /an'dar/ *vi irr* to walk; move; work, operate, run (machines, etc.); progress, get along (negotiations, etc.); be, feel; elapse (of time); be occupied; behave; (*with prep a*) administer (blows, etc.); (*with en*) upset, turn over (papers, etc.); ride in or on (cars, bicycles, etc.); be engaged in; (*with con*) use, handle; *vt* traverse. *m*, gait, walk. **a. por los cuarenta,** to be in one's forties. **a. con paños tibios,** not to be firm. **a. con pies de plomo,** to be extremely cautious. **a. tras,** to follow, go after; persecute; desire ardently (things). **andarse a la flor del berro,** to sow one's wild oats. *Fig. Inf.* **andarse por las ramas,** to beat about the bush. **¡Anda!** Get along with you!; Hurry up!; You don't say so! **¡Andando!** Let's get going!; Let's get a move on it! *Preterite* **anduve,** etc. *Imperf subjunc* **anduviese,** etc.
andariego /anda'riego/ **(-ga)** *a* swift walking; wandering, vagrant. *n* walker.
andarín (-ina) /anda'rin/ *n* good walker; professional walker
andas /'andas/ *f pl*, kind of stretcher; bier
andén /an'den/ *m*, railway platform; *Lat. Am.* sidewalk
andero /an'dero/ *m*, bearer (of a bier)
andinismo /andi'nismo/ *m*, *Lat. Am.* mountain climbing **andinista** *mf Lat. Am.* mountain climber
andino /an'dino/ *a* Andean
andorrano (-na) /ando'rrano/ *a* and *n* Andorran
andrajo /an'draho/ *m*, rag, wisp of cloth, tatter
andrajoso /andra'hoso/ *a* ragged, tattered
andurriales /andu'rriales/ *m pl*, byways, unfrequented paths; remote places
anécdota /a'nekðota/ *f*, anecdote
anecdótico /anek'ðotiko/ *a* anecdotal
anegación /anega'sion; anega'θion/ *f*, drowning; flooding, inundation
anegar /ane'gar/ *vt* to drown; inundate; shipwreck; *vr* drown; be flooded

anejo /a'neho/ *a* attached, annexed. *m*, annexed borough

anemia /a'nemia/ *f*, anemia

anémico /a'nemiko/ *a* anemic

anémona, anémone /a'nemona, a'nemone/ *f*, anemone. **anémona de mar,** sea-anemone

anestesia /anes'tesia/ *f*, anesthesia

anestesiador (-ra) /anestesia'ðor/ *n* anesthetist

anestesiar /aneste'siar/ *vt* to anesthetize

anestésico /anes'tesiko/ *a* and *m*, anesthetic

aneurisma /aneu'risma/ *mf Med.* aneurism

anexar /anek'sar/ *vt* to annex

anexión /anek'sion/ *f*, annexation

anexo /a'nekso/ *a* attached, joined. *m*, annex

anfibio /an'fiβio/ *a* amphibious. *m*, amphibian

anfiteatro /anfite'atro/ *m*, amphitheater; operating theater; dissecting room; morgue; *Theat.* dress-circle

anfitrión /anfitri'on/ *m, Inf.* host, one who entertains guests

ánfora /'anfora/ *f*, amphora; *Lat. Am.* ballot box

angarillas /aŋga'riɟas; aŋga'riʎas/ *f pl*, hand barrow; table cruet; yoke and panniers

ángel /'anhel/ *m*, angel; *Lat. Am.* (hand) microphone **á. de la guarda,** guardian angel. **estar con los ángeles,** to be in Heaven (euphem. for "to be dead")

angelical, angélico /anheli'kal, an'heliko/ *a* angelic; divine, excellent

angina /an'hina/ *f, Med.* angina, tonsillitis. **a. de pecho,** angina pectoris

anglicanismo /aŋglika'nismo/ *m*, Anglicanism

anglicano (-na) /aŋgli'kano/ *a* and *n* Anglican

anglicismo /aŋgli'sismo; aŋgli'θismo/ *m*, anglicism

anglo (-la) /'aŋglo/ *a* and *n* Angle. *a* Anglo-

anglófilo (-la) /aŋglo'filo/ *n* Anglophile

anglosajón (-ona) /aŋglosa'hon/ *a* and *n* Anglo-Saxon. *m*, Anglo-Saxon language

angostar /aŋgos'tar/ *vi* and *vt* to narrow; tighten

angosto /aŋ'gosto/ *a* narrow; tight

angostura /aŋgos'tura/ *f*, narrowness; tightness; narrow pass; strait; *Fig.* tight corner, fix

anguila /aŋ'gila/ *f*, eel; *pl Naut.* slipway, slips

angula /aŋ'gula/ *f*, elver (young eel)

ángulo /'aŋgulo/ *m*, angle. **á. inferior izquierdo,** lower lefthand corner. **á. inferior derecho,** lower righthand corner. **á. superior izquierdo,** upper lefthand corner. **á. superior derecho,** upper righthand corner. **á. recto,** right angle

anguloso /aŋgu'loso/ *a* angulate; angular, gaunt; cornered

angustia /aŋ'gustia/ *f*, anguish, grief

angustiante /aŋgus'tiante/ *a* distressing

angustiar /aŋgus'tiar/ *vt* to grieve; afflict; *vr* be full of anguish

anhelación /anela'sion; anela'θion/ *f*, panting, hard breathing; yearning, longing

anhelar /ane'lar/ *vi* to pant, breathe with difficulty; *vi* and *vt* long for, yearn for, desire

anhélito /a'nelito/ *m*, pant, hard breathing

anhelo (de) /a'nelo/ *m*, longing (for), desire (for), yearning (for)

anheloso /ane'loso/ *a* difficult, labored (of breathing); anxious, longing

anidar /ani'ðar/ *vi* to nest (birds); swell; *vt* shelter, protect; *vr* nest; dwell; nestle

anilla /a'niɟa; a'niʎa/ *f*, curtain ring; *pl* gymnastic rings

anillo /a'niɟo; a'niʎo/ *m*, finger ring; small ring; coil (of serpents and ropes). **a. de compromiso** *Mexico* engagement ring. *Inf.* **venir como a. al dedo,** to fit like a glove; come just at the right moment

ánima /'anima/ *f*, soul, spirit; soul in purgatory; bore (of firearms); *pl* prayer bell for the souls of the departed

animación /anima'sion; anima'θion/ *f*, liveliness, gaiety; animation, vivacity; bustle, movement

animal /ani'mal/ *m*, animal; *Inf.* dolt, brute. *a* animal; *Inf.* brutish, doltish

animalada /anima'laða/ *f, Inf.* stupidity, foolishness

animalidad /animali'ðaθ/ *f*, animalism

animar /ani'mar/ *vt* to animate; encourage, incite; invigorate, enliven; cheer up; make attractive, adorn; *vr* take heart; make up one's mind; cheer up

animismo /ani'mismo/ *m*, animism

ánimo /'animo/ *m*, soul, spirit; courage; endurance, fortitude; will, intention; mind

animosidad /animosi'ðaθ/ *f*, hatred, animosity, dislike

animoso /ani'moso/ *a* spirited, lively; valiant

aniñado /ani'ɲaðo/ *a* childlike, childish

aniquilable /aniki'laβle/ *a* destructible

aniquilación /anikila'sion; anikila'θion/ *f*, destruction, annihilation; suppression; decay

aniquilador (-a) /anikila'ðor/ *a* destructive, annihilating. *n* destroyer

aniquilamiento /anikila'miento/ *m*, See **aniquilación**

aniquilar /aniki'lar/ *vt* to annihilate, destroy completely; *vr* waste away, decay

anís /a'nis/ *m*, aniseed, anise; anisette (liqueur)

anisar /ani'sar/ *vt* to flavor with aniseed

anisete /ani'sete/ *m*, anisette

aniversario /aniβer'sario/ *a* annual. *m*, anniversary

Anjeo /an'heo/ Anjou

ano /'ano/ *m*, anus

anoche /a'notʃe/ *adv* last night

anochecer /anotʃe'ser; anotʃe'θer/ *vi irr* to grow night; become dark; be in a place *or* be doing something at nightfall (e.g. *Anochecimos en Lérida,* We were in Lerida at nightfall). *vr Poet.* be obscured or darkened. *m*, nightfall, dusk. See **conocer**

anochecida /anotʃe'siða; anotʃe'θiða/ *f*, dusk, late twilight

anodino /ano'ðino/ *a Med.* anodyne; ineffective, useless; inoffensive. *m*, anodyne

anomalía /anoma'lia/ *f*, anomaly, inconstancy, irregularity; *Astron.* anomaly

anómalo /a'nomalo/ *a* anomalous, abnormal, unusual

anonadación /anonaða'sion; anonaða'θion/, *f*, **anonadamiento** *m*, destruction, annihilation; despair, melancholy; suppression

anonadar /anona'ðar/ *vt* to destroy, annihilate; suppress; *Fig.* overwhelm, depress; humble

anónimo /a'nonimo/ *a* anonymous. *m*, anonymity; anonymous letter; unsigned literary work

anorexia /ano'reksia/ *f*, anorexia

anormal /anor'mal/ *a* abnormal; irregular, unusual. *mf* abnormal person

anormalidad /anormali'ðaθ/ *f*, abnormality; irregularity, inconsistency

anotación /anota'sion; anota'θion/ *f*, annotation; *Lat. Am.* score (in sports)

anotador (-a) /anota'ðor/ **(-ra)** *n* annotator

anotar /ano'tar/ *vt* to annotate; note down

anquilostoma /ankilos'toma/ *m, Med.* hookworm

ánsar /an'sar/ *m*, goose; drake

ansarino /ansa'rino/ *a* goose. *m*, gosling

anseático /anse'atiko/ *a* Hanseatic

ansia (de) /'ansia/ *f*, anxiety, trouble; grief; longing (for), yearning (for); greed

ansiar /an'siar/ *vt* to long for, yearn for; covet, desire

ansiedad /ansie'ðaθ/ *f*, anxiety, anguish, worry

ansión /an'sion/ *f*, intense desire

ansioso /an'sioso/ *a* anxious; grievous, painful; eager, desirous; greedy

antagónico /anta'goniko/ *a* antagonistic

antagonismo /antago'nismo/ *m*, antagonism

antagonista /antago'nista/ *mf* antagonist, adversary

antaño /an'taɲo/ *adv* last year, yesteryear; long ago

antártico /an'tartiko/ *a* antarctic

ante /'ante/ *m, Zool.* elk; suede; buffalo

ante /'ante/ *prep* in the presence of, before; regarding, in the face of (e.g. *a. deber tan alto,* in the face of so noble a duty)

anteado /ante'aðo/ *a* beige, buff-colored, fawn

anteanoche /antea'notʃe/ *adv* the night before last

anteayer /antea'yer/ *adv* the day before yesterday

antebrazo /ante'βraso; ante'βraθo/ *m*, forearm

antecámara /ante'kamara/ *f*, antechamber

antecedente /antese'ðente; anteθe'ðente/ m, antecedent. **antecedentes** m pl background (of a case, situation, etc.)

antecedentemente /antese,ðente'mente; anteθe,ðente'mente/ adv previously

anteceder /antese'ðer; anteθe'ðer/ vt to precede

antecesor /antese'sor; anteθe'sor/ (-ra) a previous. n predecessor. m, forebear, ancestor

antecoger /anteko'her/ vt to carry in front, lead before; pick too soon

antecomedor /antekome'ðor/ m, breakfast nook, breakfast room

antedata /ante'ðata/ f, antedate

antedatar /anteða'tar/ vt to backdate

antedicho /ante'ðitʃo/ a aforementioned, aforesaid

antediluviano /anteðilu'βiano/ a antediluvian

antelación /antela'sion; antela'θion/ f, advance, anticipation

antellevar /anteje'βar; anteʎe'βar/ vt, Mexico to knock down, run over

antemano, de /ante'mano, de/ adv in advance, beforehand

antemeridiano /antemeri'ðiano/ a antemeridian, forenoon

antena /an'tena/ f, antenna; Radio. aerial

antenacido /antena'siðo; antena'θiðo/ a born prematurely

antenombre /ante'nombre/ m, title (placed before name)

anteojera /anteo'hera/ f, horse's blinker; eyeglass case

anteojo /ante'oho/ m, spy-glass, small telescope; pl horse's blinkers; eyeglasses, glasses; spectacles; goggles. **anteojos para el sol,** sunglasses

antepagar /antepa'gar/ vt to pay in advance

antepalco /ante'palko/ m, vestibule of a box in a theater

antepasado /antepa'saðo/ a previous, past. m, ancestor (gen. pl)

antepecho /ante'petʃo/ m, parapet; windowsill; railing, balustrade; front (of a theater box, etc.); Naut. bulwark

antepenúltimo /antepe'nultimo/ a antepenultimate, third to last

anteponer /antepo'ner/ vt irr to place before; prefer, favor. See **poner**

anteproyecto /antepro'yekto/ m, first sketch, preliminary work or plan

antepuerta /ante'puerta/ f, door-curtain, portiere; Mil. anteport

anterior /ante'rior/ a previous, former; anterior; aforementioned, preceding

anteriormente /anterior'mente/ adv beforehand, previously

antes /'antes/ adv before; rather, on the contrary; previously. **a. bien,** rather, sooner. **a. con a.** or **cuanto a.,** or **lo a. posible,** as soon as possible

antesala /ante'sala/ f, antechamber

antevíspera /ante'βispera/ f, two days previously

antiaéreo /anti'aereo/ a antiaircraft. m pl. **(cañones) antiaéreos,** A.A. guns

anticiclón /antisi'klon; antiθi'klon/ m, anticyclone

anticipación /antisipa'sion; antiθipa'θion/ f, anticipation; advance. **con a.,** ahead of time

anticipada /antisi'paða; antiθi'paða/ f, foul thrust (in fencing, etc.)

anticipadamente /antisi,paða'mente; antiθi,paða'mente/ adv in advance; prematurely

anticipado /antisi'paðo; antiθi'paðo/ a in advance; premature

anticipador /antisipa'ðor; antiθipa'ðor/ a anticipatory

anticipar /antisi'par; antiθi'par/ vt to anticipate; foresee; forestall; advance (money); lend; vr happen before time; (with prep a) act in advance of, anticipate; get ahead of oneself

anticipo /anti'sipo; anti'θipo/ m, anticipation, advance; advance payment; sum of money lent

anticlerical /antikleri'kal/ a anticlerical

anticlímax /anti'klimaks/ m, anticlimax

anticonstitucional /antikonstitusio'nal; antikonstituθio'nal/ a unconstitutional

anticuado /anti'kuaðo/ a antiquated, ancient

anticuario /anti'kuario/ m, antiquarian, antique dealer

antídoto /an'tiðoto/ m, antidote

antiesclavista /antieskla'βista/ a antislavery. mf antislavist

antiespasmódico /antiespas'moðiko/ a and m, Med. antispasmodic

antiestético /anties'tetiko/ a unesthetic

antietimológico /antietimo'lohiko/ a non-etymological, unetymological

antifaz /anti'fas; anti'faθ/ m, mask; face-covering

antiflogístico /antiflo'histiko/ a and m, Med. antiphlogistic

antigramatical /antigramati'kal/ a ungrammatical

antigualla /anti'guaya; anti'guaʎa/ f, antique; ancient custom; anything out-of-date

antiguamente /antigua'mente/ adv in time past, formerly

antiguamiento /antigua'miento/ m, seniority

antigüedad /antigue'ðað/ f, antiquity; ancients; length of service, seniority (in employment); pl antiquities

antiguo /an'tiguo/ a ancient, very old; antique; senior (in an employment); former. m, senior member (of a community, etc.). m pl, ancients. **A. Testamento,** Old Testament. **de a.,** from ancient times. **en lo antiguo,** in ancient times; in former times, in days of yore

antillano /anti'yano; anti'ʎano/ (-na) a and n of or from the Antilles

Antillas, las /an'tiyas, las; an'tiʎas, las/ the Antilles

antílope /an'tilope/ m, antelope

antimacasar /antimaka'sar/ m, antimacassar

antimilitarismo /antimilita'rismo/ m, antimilitarism

antimilitarista /antimilita'rista/ a antimilitaristic

antimonárquico /antimo'narkiko/ a antimonarchical

antimonio /anti'monio/ m, Metall. antimony

antipalúdico /antipa'luðiko/ a antimalarial

antipara /anti'para/ f, screen, shield

antiparras /anti'parras/ f pl, Inf. spectacles; eyeglasses, glasses

antipatía /antipa'tia/ f, antipathy

antipático /anti'patiko/ a disagreeable; unattractive

antipatriótico /antipa'triotiko/ a unpatriotic

antípoda /an'tipoða/ a and m, or f, antipode

antiquísimo /anti'kisimo/ a sup, **antiguo,** most ancient

antisemita /antise'mita/ a anti-Semitic. mf anti-Semite

antisemitismo /antisemi'tismo/ m, anti-Semitism

antiséptico /anti'septiko/ a and m, antiseptic

antisifilítico /antisifi'litiko/ a Med. anti-syphilitic

antisocial /antiso'sial; antiso'θial/ a antisocial

antítesis /an'titesis/ f, antithesis

antitético /anti'tetiko/ a antithetical, contrasted

antófago /an'tofago/ a anthophagous, flower-eating

antojadizo /antoha'ðiso; antoha'ðiθo/ a capricious, fanciful, whimsical

antojarse /anto'harse/ vr to have a fancy for, want (e.g. Se me antoja marcharme al campo, I have a yen to go to the country); suspect, imagine

antojito /anto'hito/ m, Mexico typical Mexican dish (of food)

antojo /an'toho/ m, caprice, fancy, whim; desire, will; pl birthmark

antología /antolo'hia/ f, anthology

antólogo /an'tologo/ m, anthologist

antonomasia /antono'masia/ f, antonomasia. **por a.,** by analogy, by transference

antorcha /an'tortʃa/ f, torch, flambeau

antracita /antra'sita; antra'θita/ f, anthracite

ántrax /'antraks/ m, Med. anthrax

antro /'antro/ m, cave, cavern; Anat. antrum

antropofagia /antropo'fahia/ f, cannibalism, anthropophagy

antropófago /antro'pofago/ **(-ga)** a cannibalistic. n cannibal

antropología /antropolo'hia/ f, anthropology
antropológico /antropo'lohiko/ a anthropological
antropólogo /antro'pologo/ m, anthropologist
antropometría /antropome'tria/ f, anthropometry
antropomorfo /antropo'morfo/ a anthropomorphous
antroposofía /antroposo'fia/ f, anthroposophy
antruejo /antru'eho/ m, three days of carnival before Lent
anual /a'nual/ a yearly, annual
anualidad /anuali'ðað/ f, annuity
anuario /a'nuario/ m, directory, yearbook, handbook
anubarrado /anuβa'rraðo/ a covered with clouds, cloudy
anublado /anu'βlaðo/ a lowering, overcast; clouded
anublar /anu'βlar/ vt to cloud; darken, obscure; blight (plants); vr cloud over; become blighted or mildewed
anudar /anu'ðar/ vt to knot; tie, fasten; join; continue; **a. amistad de,** to strike up a friendship with. **a. la corbata,** to put on one's tie, tie one's tie; vr grow stunted
anulable /anu'laβle/ a annulable, voidable
anulación /anula'sion; anula'θion/ f, annulment, abrogation
anular /anu'lar/ a annular, ring-shaped. vt to annul, cancel; Math. cancel out
anuloso /anu'loso/ a annulate, formed of rings
anunciación /anunsia'sion; anunθia'θion/ f, Eccl. Annunciation; announcement
anunciador /anunsia'ðor; anunθia'ðor/ (**-ra**), n **anunciante** mf announcer; advertiser
anunciar /anun'siar; anun'θiar/ vt to announce; publish, proclaim; advertise; foretell, presage. **Anuncian lluvia,** The forecast calls for rain
anuncio /a'nunsio; a'nunθio/ m, announcement; publication, proclamation; advertisement; T.V. commercial; presage, omen. **a. luminoso,** sky-sign
anverso /am'berso/ m, obverse, face
anzuelo /an'suelo; an'θuelo/ m, fish-hook; Cul. fritter; Inf. attraction, inducement
añadido /aɲa'ðiðo/ m, hair-switch; make-weight
añadidura /aɲaði'ðura/ f, addition; make-weight, extra
añadir /aɲa'ðir/ vt to add; increase
añagaza /aɲa'gasa; aɲa'gaθa/ f, decoy bird; enticement, lure
añejo /a'ɲeho/ a very old
añicos /a'ɲikos/ m pl, fragments, small pieces. **hacer a.,** to break into fragments
añil /a'ɲil/ m, indigo; indigo blue
año /'aɲo/ m, year; pl birthday. **a. bisiesto,** leap-year. **a. económico,** fiscal year. **A. Nuevo,** New Year. **tener (siete) años,** to be (seven) years old. **los Años Bobos,** the period from 1875 to 1898 in Spain
añoranza /aɲo'ransa; aɲo'ranθa/ f, homesickness, loneliness; nostalgia
añorar /aɲo'rar/ vi to be homesick or lonely
añoso /a'ɲoso/ a very old, full of years
añublo /a'ɲuβlo/ m, mildew
aojamiento /aoha'miento/ m, evil eye, wicked spell
aojar /ao'har/ vt to bewitch, place under a spell; spoil, frustrate
aojo /a'oho/ m, evil eye; magic spell
aorta /a'orta/ f, Anat. aorta
aovillarse /aoβi'yarse; aoβi'ʎarse/ vr to roll oneself into a ball; curl up
apabullante /apaβu'yante; apaβu'ʎante/ a crushing, flattening
apacentadero /apasenta'ðero; apaθenta'ðero/ m, grazing land, pasture
apacentamiento /apasenta'miento; apaθenta'miento/ m, pasturage; grazing
apacentar /apasen'tar; apaθen'tar/ vt irr to put out to grass; teach, instruct; satisfy (one's desires); vr graze (cattle). See **acertar**
apachurrar /apatʃu'rrar/ vt, Mexico to press (button, etc.)
apacibilidad /apasiβili'ðað; apaθiβili'ðað/ f, agreeableness; mildness; peaceableness

apacible /apa'siβle; apa'θiβle/ a agreeable; mild; peaceable; calm, peaceful
apaciguamiento /a,pasigua'miento; a,paθigua'miento/ m, appeasement, soothing, pacification
apaciguar /apasi'guar; apaθi'guar/ vt to appease, pacify; calm
apadrinar /apaðri'nar/ vt to act as godfather to; be best man to (at a wedding); act as a second for (in a duel); sponsor; favor
apagable /apa'gaβle/ a extinguishable
apagado /apa'gaðo/ a timid, nervous; pale (of colors); dull, lusterless
apagador /apaga'ðor/ (**-ra**) a quenching. n extinguisher. m, candle-snuffer; damper (of a piano)
apagaincendios /a,pagain'θendios; a,pagain'sendios/ m, ship's fire-extinguisher
apagamiento /apaga'miento/ m, quenching, extinguishment
apagar /apa'gar/ vt to extinguish, put out; Fig. quench, moderate; slake (lime); Art. tone down (colors); shut off (engines)
apagarrisas /apaga'rrisas/ mf crapehanger, killjoy, wet blanket
apagavelas /apaga'βelas/ m, candle-snuffer
apalabrar /apala'βrar/ vt to make an appointment with; discuss, consider
apaleamiento /apalea'miento/ m, beating, thrashing
apalear /apale'ar/ vt to beat, thrash; knock down with a stick
apandillarse /apandi'yarse; apandi'ʎarse/ vr to form a gang or group
apañar /apa'ɲar/ vt to take away, remove; seize; steal; dress, get ready; Inf. wrap up; patch, repair; vr Inf. grow skillful
apaño /a'paɲo/ m, dexterity, skill; craft, guile
aparador /apara'ðor/ m, sideboard; workshop; Eccl. credence (table); Mexico (shop) window
aparato /apa'rato/ m, apparatus; equipment, utensils; pomp, ostentation; symptoms; sign, circumstance, token. **a. digestivo,** digestive system; digestive tract. **a. fonador,** speech apparatus
aparatoso /apara'toso/ a showy, ostentatious. **incendio. a.,** conflagration, large fire
aparear /apare'ar/ vt to match, make equal; pair; mate (animals); vr form up in pairs
aparecer /apare'ser; apare'θer/ (**se**) vi and vr irr to appear; seem; be. See **conocer**
aparecido /apare'siðo; apare'θiðo/ m, apparition; specter
aparejador /apareha'ðor/ m, overseer, foreman; Naut. rigger
aparejar /apare'har/ vt to prepare, make ready; saddle (horses); prime, size; rig (a ship)
aparejo /apa'reho/ m, preparation, arrangement; harness, trappings; Naut. rigging; Naut. gear; priming, sizing; Mech. tackle; pl equipment
aparentar /aparen'tar/ vt to pretend, simulate
aparente /apa'rente/ a seeming, apparent; obvious, visible; suitable, proper
aparición /apari'sion; apari'θion/ f, appearance, arrival; apparition, phantom
apariencia /apa'riensia; apa'rienθia/ f, appearance, looks, probability, likelihood; outward semblance; pl Theat. scenery
apartadamente /apartaða'mente/ adv apart, in private; secretly
apartadero /aparta'ðero/ m, passing place for cars; railway siding; grass verge. **a. ferroviario,** railway marshaling yard
apartado /apar'taðo/ a distant, far off; secluded; different. m, post-office box; secluded room; smelting house; sorting of cattle; selection of bulls for a bull-fight
apartamento /aparta'mento/ m Lat. Am. (except Argentina) apartment
apartamiento /aparta'miento/ m, separation; withdrawal, retiral; seclusion; apartment, flat; Law. withdrawal of an action
apartar /apar'tar/ vt to separate; remove (e.g. an obstacle), take away; Rail. shunt; dissuade; sort; vr ob-

tain a divorce; *Law.* withdraw an action. **apartarse de la tradición,** to depart from tradition **aparte** /a'parte/ *adv* aside, on one side; separately; *Theat.* aside; besides; beyond. *m, Theat.* aside; paragraph; space between words. **¡Aparte!** Move to one side!

apartidario /aparti'ðario/ *a* non-partisan
apasionado /apasio'naðo/ **(-da)** *a* impassioned; fervent, devoted; passionate; enthusiastic. *n* admirer, lover; enthusiast
apasionamiento /apasiona'miento/ *m,* passion
apasionar /apasio'nar/ *vt* to arouse to passion; pain; *vr* (*with por*) grow passionately fond of; become enthusiastic for
apatía /apa'tia/ *f,* apathy
apático /a'patiko/ *a* apathetic
apeadero /apea'ðero/ *m,* mounting-block; halt, stopping place; wayside railway station; pied-à-terre, occasional dwelling
apear /ape'ar/ *vt* to dismount; hobble (horse); survey, map out; fell a tree; *Fig.* overcome (difficulties); *Inf.* dissuade; prop; remove, bring down; scotch (a wheel); *vr* dismount; alight, step off
apechugar /apetʃu'gar/ *vi* to push with the breast; *Inf.* put up with reluctantly
apedazar /apeða'sar; apeða'θar/ *vt* to tear; break; mend, repair
apedrear /apeðre'ar/ *vt* to stone; stone to death; *vi impers* hail; *vr* be damaged by hail (crops)
apegarse /ape'garse/ *vr* to grow fond (of), become attached (to)
apego /a'pego/ *m,* fondness, inclination; affection, attachment
apelación /apela'sion; apela'θion/ *f, Law.* appeal; *Inf.* doctor's consultation
apelante /ape'lante/ *a* and *mf Law.* appellant
apelar /ape'lar/ *vi Law.* to appeal; (*with prep a*) have recourse to; *vi* be of the same color (horses)
apellidar /apeyi'ðar; apeʎi'ðar/ *vt* to name, call; acclaim; call to arms; *vr* be named
apellido /ape'yiðo; ape'ʎiðo/ *m,* surname; nickname; call to arms; clamor; name
apenar /ape'nar/ *vt* to grieve, afflict; cause sorrow
apenarse /ape'narse/ *vr Lat. Am.* to be ashamed
apenas /a'penas/ *adv* scarcely; immediately, as soon as; with trouble or difficulty
apéndice /a'pendise; a'pendiθe/ *m,* appendix, supplement; *Anat.* appendix
apendicitis /apendi'sitis; apendi'θitis/ *f,* appendicitis
Apeninos, los /ape'ninos, los/ the Apennines
apeo /a'peo/ *m,* survey; scaffolding; prop, support
apercibimiento /apersiβi'miento; aperθiβi'miento/ *m,* preparation; provision; warning; *Law.* summons
apercibir /apersi'βir; aperθi'βir/ *vt* to prepare, furnish; warn; *Law.* summon
apergaminarse /apergami'narse/ *vr Inf.* to shrivel, dry up (with old age, etc.)
aperitivo /aperi'tiβo/ *a* aperitive. *m,* aperient; appetizer
apertura /aper'tura/ *f,* opening; inauguration; reading (of a will)
apesadumbrar /apesaðum'brar/ *vt* to sadden, afflict, grieve
apestar /apes'tar/ *vt* to infect with the plague; catch the plague; *Fig.* corrupt; *Inf.* pester, annoy; *vi* stink
apestoso /apes'toso/ *a* stinking, putrid
apetecer /apete'ser; apete'θer/ *vt irr* to want, desire; attract. See **conocer**
apetecible /apete'siβle; apete'θiβle/ *a* attractive, desirable
apetencia /ape'tensia; ape'tenθia/ *f,* appetite; desire
apetito /ape'tito/ *m,* appetite
apetitoso /apeti'toso/ *a* appetizing; tasty, savory; attractive
apiadarse /apia'ðarse/ *vr* (*with de*) to have compassion on, be sorry for
ápice /'apise; 'apiθe/ *m,* apex; tip, point; peak, summit, top; orthographic accent; iota, tittle; crux (of a problem)
apicultor /apikul'tor/ **(-ra)** *n* apiarist, beekeeper

apicultura /apikul'tura/ *f,* apiculture, beekeeping
apilar /api'lar/ *vt* to pile, heap
apimplado, -a /apim'plaðo/ *a, Lat. Am.* boozed up, drunk
apiñado /api'ɲaðo/ *a* crowded, serried
apiñamiento /apiɲa'miento/ *m,* crowding; congestion
apiñar /api'ɲar/ *vt* to group together, crowd; *vr* crowd
apio /'apio/ *m,* celery
apisonadora /apisona'ðora/ *f,* steam-roller; roller
apisonar /apiso'nar/ *vt* to roll, stamp, flatten, ram down; tamp, pack down (e.g. tobacco in a pipe)
apizarrado /apisa'rraðo; apiθa'rraðo/ *a* slate-colored
aplacable /apla'kaβle/ *a* appeasable, placable
aplacamiento /aplaka'miento/ *m,* appeasement
aplacar /apla'kar/ *vt* to appease, calm; moderate, mitigate
aplacible /apla'siβle; apla'θiβle/ *a* agreeable, pleasant
aplanacalles /aplana'kajes; aplana'kaʎes/ *mf, Lat. Am.* idler, lay about, lazybones
aplanar /apla'nar/ *vt* to flatten, level; roll (pastry); *Inf.* dumbfound, overwhelm; *vr* collapse (buildings); lose heart
aplastar /aplas'tar/ *vt* to flatten, squash, crush; *Inf.* squash flat, floor
aplaudir /aplau'ðir/ *vt* to applaud, clap; praise, commend, approve
aplauso /a'plauso/ *m,* applause; clapping, plaudit; approbation, commendation
aplazamiento /aplasa'miento; aplaθa'miento/ *m,* postponement; appointment; summons
aplazar /apla'sar; apla'θar/ *vt* to summon, arrange a meeting; postpone; adjourn
aplicabilidad /aplikaβili'ðað/ *f,* applicability
aplicable /apli'kaβle/ *a* applicable
aplicación /aplika'sion; aplika'θion/ *f,* application; diligence, assiduity; appliqué, ornamentation
aplicado /apli'kaðo/ *a* diligent, hardworking; appliqué
aplicar /apli'kar/ *vt* to apply; impute; intend, destine (for processions); *Law.* adjudge; *vr* engage in; apply oneself. **a. el oído,** to listen intently. **a. sanciones,** *Polit.* to impose sanctions
aplomado /aplo'maðo/ *a* self-possessed, dignified; leaden, lead-colored
aplomar /aplo'mar/ *vt* and *vi* to plumb, test with a plumb-line; *vr* collapse, fall down
aplomo /a'plomo/ *m,* self-possession, dignity; sangfroid
apocado /apo'kaðo/ *a* spiritless, timid; base, mean
Apocalipsis /apoka'lipsis/ *m,* Apocalypse
apocalíptico /apoka'liptiko/ *a* apocalyptic
apocamiento /apoka'miento/ *m,* timidity, pusillanimity; depression, discouragement; shyness, baseness, meanness
apocar /apo'kar/ *vt* to diminish, reduce; humiliate, scorn
apócrifo /a'pokrifo/ *a* fictitious, false; apocryphal. **Apócrifos,** Apocrypha
apodar /apo'ðar/ *vt* to nickname
apoderado /apoðe'raðo/ *a* authorized. *m,* attorney; deputy; proxy
apoderar /apoðe'rar/ *vt* to authorize; grant powers of attorney to; *vr* (*with de*) seize, take possession of
apodo /a'poðo/ *m,* nickname
apogeo /apo'heo/ *m, Astron.* apogee; *Fig.* zenith, peak (of fame, etc.)
apolillar /apoli'yar; apoli'ʎar/ *vt* to eat clothes (moths); *vr* be moth-eaten
apologista /apolo'hista/ *mf* apologist
apólogo /a'pologo/ *m,* apologue, moral fable
apoltronarse /apoltro'narse/ *vr* to grow idle
apoplejía /aople'hia/ *f,* apoplexy
aporrear /aporre'ar/ *vt* to beat, cudgel; *vr* work hard, slog away
aportación /aporta'sion; aporta'θion/ *f,* contribution; occasionment
aportar /apor'tar/ *vt* to cause, occasion; contribute; *vi Naut.* reach port; **El buque aportó a Nueva York,**

The ship reached New York, The ship sailed into New York harbor; arrive at an unexpected place

aposentador /aposenta'ðor/ *m*, usher; *Mil.* billeting officer

aposentar /aposen'tar/ *vt* to lodge, give hospitality to; *vr* lodge, settle down

aposento /apo'sento/ *m*, room; suite, apartments; lodging, accommodation; *Theat.* box

aposición /aposi'sion; aposi'θion/ *f*, *Gram.* apposition

apósito /a'posito/ *m*, poultice, external application; (medical) dressing

apostadero /aposta'ðero/ *m*, *Naut.* naval station; placing or stationing (of soldiers)

apostar /apos'tar/ *vt irr* to bet; station (soldiers); *vi* compete, rival. See **contar**

apostasía /aposta'sia/ *f*, apostasy

apóstata /a'postata/ *mf* apostate

apostilla /apos'tiya; apos'tiʎa/ *f*, marginal note, gloss

apóstol /a'postol/ *m*, apostle

apostólico /apos'toliko/ *a* apostolic

apóstrofe /a'postrofe/ *m*, or *f*, apostrophe, hortatory exclamation

apóstrofo /a'postrofo/ *m*, *Gram.* apostrophe

apostura /apos'tura/ *f*, neatness, spruceness

apotegma /apo'tegma/ *m*, apothegm, maxim

apoteosis /apote'osis/ *f*, apotheosis

apoyar /apo'yar/ *vt* (*with en*) to lean against; rest upon; *vt* uphold, favor; confirm, bear out; droop the head (horses); second (a motion); *vi* (*with en*) rest on; lean against; *vr* (*with en*) rest on; lean against; **apoyarse de codos,** to lean on one's elbows; be upheld by; *Fig.* be founded on; *Fig.* depend on, lean on

apoyo /a'poyo/ *m*, support, prop; windowsill, sill; assistance; backing, support

apreciable /apresia'βle; apreθia'βle/ *a* appreciable; estimable; important

apreciación /apresia'sion; apreθia'θion/ *f*, appreciation; valuation, estimate

apreciador /apresia'ðor; apreθia'ðor/ **(-ra)** *a* appreciatory. *n* appraiser

apreciar /apre'siar; apre'θiar/ *vt* to estimate (values); appreciate; like, esteem, have a regard for

apreciativo /apresia'tiβo; apreθia'tiβo/ *a* appreciative

aprecio /a'presio; a'preθio/ *m*, valuation; appreciation, regard

aprehender /apreen'der/ *vt* to apprehend, catch; seize (contraband); understand, grasp

aprehensión /apreen'sion/ *f*, seizure, apprehension

apremiador, apremiante /apremia'ðor, apre'miante/ *a* urgent, pressing

apremiar /apre'miar/ *vt* to hurry; urge, press; force, oblige; burden, oppress (with taxes)

apremio /a'premio/ *m*, insistence, pressure; compulsion; demand note

aprendedor /aprende'ðor/ **(-ra)** *n* learner

aprender /apren'der/ *vt* to learn. **a. de memoria,** to learn by heart

aprendiz /apren'dis; apren'diθ/ **(-za)** *n* apprentice

aprendizaje /aprendi'sahe; aprendi'θahe/ *m*, apprenticeship. **hacer el a.,** to serve an apprenticeship

aprensión /apren'sion/ *f*, capture; fear, apprehension; suspicion, fancy; prejudice, scruple

aprensivo /apren'siβo/ *a* apprehensive, nervous, fearful

apresar /apre'sar/ *vt* to nab, catch; capture (a ship); imprison; fetter

aprestar /apres'tar/ *vt* to prepare, arrange; dress (fabrics)

apresto /a'presto/ *m*, preparation, arrangement; dressing (for cloth)

apresurar /apresu'rar/ *vt* to quicken; *vr* hasten, be quick

apretado /apre'taðo/ *a* difficult, dangerous; tight; crabbed (of handwriting); clustered (e.g. *casas apretadas alrededor de la sinagoga,* houses clustered around the synagogue). *Inf.* mean, close-fisted. *m*, small close handwriting

apretadura /apreta'ðura/ *f*, tightening, compression

apretar /apre'tar/ *vt irr* to tighten; compress; urge

on, press; harass, vex; trouble, worry; speed up; squeeze; press (bells, gun triggers, etc.); *vi* increase, grow worse (storms, heat, etc.); pinch, hurt (shoes). **a. los pasos,** to quicken one's pace. *Inf.* **a. a correr,** to take to one's heels. **¡Aprieta!** *Inf.* Nonsense! It can't be! See **acertar**

apretón /apre'ton/ *m*, squeeze, grip, pressure; *Inf.* sprint, spurt; *Inf.* fix, pickle. **a. de manos,** handshake

apretujamiento /apretuha'miento/ *m*, squeezing together

apretujar /apretu'har/ *vt Inf.* to squeeze, hug

aprieto /a'prieto/ *m*, crowd, crush; urgency; *Inf.* jam, trouble, fix

aprisa /a'prisa/ *adv* quickly, in a hurry

aprisco /a'prisko/ *m*, cattle-shed; sheepfold

aprisionar /aprisio'nar/ *vt* to imprison; bind, fetter; tie

aprobación /aproβa'sion; aproβa'θion/ *f*, approbation, approval, commendation; ratification (of a bill); pass (in an examination)

aprobado /apro'βaðo/ *m*, pass certificate (in examinations)

aprobar /apro'βar/ *vt irr* to approve; pass (in an examination). See **contar**

aprontar /apron'tar/ *vt*, *Lat. Am.* to pay in advance, prepay

apropiación /apropia'sion; apropia'θion/ *f*, appropriation; application; adaptation

apropiado /apro'piaðo/ *a* appropriate, suitable, proper

apropiar /apro'piar/ *vt* to appropriate; adapt, fit; *vr* appropriate, take possession

aprovechable /aproβe'tʃaβle/ *a* usable, available

aprovechado /aproβe'tʃaðo/ *a* advantageous; assiduous, conscientious; capable; thrifty

aprovechador /aproβetʃa'ðor/ *a* self-seeking

aprovechamiento /aproβetʃa'miento/ *m*, utilization, employment; exploitation; profitable use

aprovechar /aproβe'tʃar/ *vi* to be advantageous or useful; be beneficial; make progress (in studies, etc.); *vt* use; profit by; *vr* take advantage of, make use of. **¡Que aproveche!** May it do you good! (said to anyone eating)

aprovisionar /aproβi'sionar/ *vt* to provision, supply

aproximación /aproksima'sion; aproksima'θion/ *f*, approximation; consolation prize (in a lottery)

aproximadamente /aproksimaða'mente/ *adv* approximately; nearly, almost

aproximar /aproksi'mar/ *vt* to bring or draw nearer; *vr* approach; be almost, be approximately; draw closer

aptitud /apti'tuð/ *f*, aptitude, ability; fitness; propensity

apto /'apto/ *a* suitable, fitting; competent. **no apta para menores,** not suitable for children (of films, etc.)

apuesta /a'puesta/ *f*, bet, wager; competition

apuestas benéficas de fútbol /a'puestas be'nefikas de 'futβol/ football pools

apuesto /a'puesto/ *a* elegant; handsome, well set-up

apuntación /apunta'sion; apunta'θion/ *f*, noting down; note; *Mus.* notation

apuntador /apunta'ðor/ **(-ra)** *n* note-taker; observer. *m*, *Theat.* prompter; *Theat.* stage-manager

apuntalar /apunta'lar/ *vt* to prop, prop up, underpin, bolster

apuntamiento /apunta'miento/ *m*, summary; *Law.* indictment, minute

apuntar /apun'tar/ *vt* to aim (a gun, etc.); point to, indicate; note down; mark; sketch; sharpen; bet (at cards); fasten temporarily; *Inf.* mend; *Theat.* prompt; suggest, hint (e.g. *La fecha está apuntada en varios manuscritos,* The date is hinted at in various manuscripts); *vi* begin to appear. *Inf.* **a. y no dar,** to promise and do nothing

apunte /a'punte/ *m*, abstract; note; annotation; sketch; *Theat.* prompt *or* prompter *or* prompt book *or* cue; stake in a card game

apuñalado /apuɲa'laðo/ *a* dagger-shaped

apuñalar /apuɲa'lar/ *vt* to stab, attack with a dagger

apurado /apu'raðo/ *a* poor, needy; dangerous; difficult; accurate, exact; hurried
apurar /apu'rar/ *vt* to purify; drain; exhaust; finish, conclude; examine closely, scrutinize (e.g. *apurar una materia*, to exhaust a subject, examine a subject thoroughly); irritate, make impatient; urge on, hasten; *vr* be anxious, fret; *Lat. Am.* hurry, hurry up
apuro /a'puro/ *m,* difficulty, fix; poverty, want; anxiety, worry. **pasar apuros,** to have a hard time
aquejar /ake'har/ *vt* to afflict; weary, beset, harass; *vr* complain
aquel, /a'kel,/ *a m* **aquella,** *a f* **aquellos,** *a m pl* **aquellas** *a f pl,* that, those; that or those over there (farther off than **ese**)
aquel /a'kel,/ *m,* charm, attraction, it
aquél, aquélla, aquéllos, aquéllas /a'kel,/ *dem pron m, f,* sing. and pl., that, the one, those, those ones; the former. e.g. *La casa que ve usted a lo lejos aquélla es la vivienda de mi tío,* The house that you see in the distance, that is my uncle's dwelling. *Éste no me gusta pero aquél sí,* I do not like the latter, but I like the former
aquelarre /ake'larre/ *m,* witches' sabbath
aquello /a'keyo; a'keʎo/ *dem pron neut* that; the fact; the matter, the affair, the former (remark, idea, etc.). e.g. *Todo a. por fin acabó,* All that came to an end at last. *a. de,* the fact that
aquí /a'ki/ *adv* here. **de a.,** hence the fact that. **¡He a.!** Behold!
aquietar /akie'tar/ *vt* to calm, soothe
aquilatar /akila'tar/ *vt* to assay; scrutinize; examine, weigh up (persons)
aquistar /akis'tar/ *vt* to attain, acquire
ara /'ara/ *f,* altar; **en aras de,** in honor of; for the sake of
árabe /'araβe/ *a* Arab, Arabic. *mf* Arab. *m,* Arabic (language)
arabesco /ara'βesko/ *a* Arabic. *m, Art.* arabesque
Arabia Saudita /a'raβia sau'ðita/ Saudi Arabia
arábigo /a'raβigo/ *a* Arabic. *m,* Arabic (language)
arácnido /a'raknið o/ *m, Zool.* arachnid
arado /a'raðo/ *m,* plow
arador /ara'ðor/ *a* plowing. *m,* plowman. **a. de la sarna,** *Ent.* scabies mite
aragonés /arago'nes/ **(-esa)** *a* and *n* Aragonese
araguato /ara'guato/ *m, Lat. Am.* howler monkey
arahuaco /ara'uako/ *a* and *n* Arawak, Arawakian
arancel /aran'sel; aran'θel/ *m,* tariff, duty, tax
arancelar /aranse'lar; aranθe'lar/ to charge tuition for (e.g. *a. la universidad,* charge tuition for college studies)
arancelario /aranse'lario; aranθe'lario/ *a* tariff, tax; customs
arándano /a'randano/ *m, Bot.* bilberry
arandela /aran'dela/ *f,* candle-dripper; *Mech.* washer; wall candelabrum
araña /a'raɲa/ *f,* spider; chandelier; *Lat. Am.* whore
arañacielos /a,raɲa'sielos; a,raɲa'θielos/ *m,* sky-scraper
arañar /ara'ɲar/ *vt* to scratch; *Inf.* scrape together; hoard
arañazo /ara'ɲaso; ara'ɲaθo/ *m,* scratch
arar /a'rar/ *vt* to plow. **a. en el mar,** to labor in vain
arbitrador /arβitra'ðor/ **(-ra)** *n* arbitrator
arbitraje /arβi'trahe/ *m,* arbitration; decision; arbitrage
arbitrar /arβi'trar/ *vt* to judge freely; *Law.* arbitrate, mediate; devise; invent; marshal (money, resources, etc.); draft (a law) *vr* make shift, contrive
arbitrariedad /arβitrarie'ðað/ *f,* arbitrariness
arbitrario /arβi'trario/ *a* arbitral, mediatory; arbitrary, capricious
arbitrio /ar'βitrio/ *m,* free will; arbitration; means; way; discretion; arbitrament; judgment; *pl* rates, municipal taxes
árbitro /'arβitro/ **(-ra)** *a* arbitrary. *n* arbiter. *m, Sports.* umpire; referee
árbol /'arβol/ *m,* tree; *Mech.* shaft; *Naut.* mast; axis of a winding stair. **a. de amor** *or* **a. de Judas,** Judas tree. **a. de la ciencia** (**del bien y del mal**), Tree of

Knowledge (of good and evil). **a. de levas,** *Mech.* camshaft. **a. del pan,** breadfruit tree. *Naut.* **a. mayor,** mainmast. **a. motor** *Mech.*, drivingshaft
arbolado /arβo'laðo/ *a* tree-covered, wooded. *m,* copse, woodland
arboladura /arβola'ðura/ *f, Naut.* masts and spars
arbolar /arβo'lar/ *vt* to hoist (flags); *Naut.* fit with masts; place upright; *vr* rear, prance (horses)
arboleda /arβo'leða/ *f,* copse, grove, spinney
arbotante /arβo'tante/ *m,* flying buttress
arbusto /ar'βusto/ *m,* shrub, woody plant
arca /'arka/ *f,* chest; money-box, coffer; ark; *pl* (treasury) vaults. **a. caudal,** strong box. **a. de agua,** water-tower. **a. de la alianza.** *or* **a. del testamento,** Ark of the Covenant (Bible). **a. de Noé,** Noah's Ark; lumber box
arcabucero /arkaβu'sero; arkaβu'θero/ *m,* arquebusier; maker of arquebuses
arcabuz /arka'βus; arka'βuθ/ *m,* arquebus
arcada /ar'kaða/ *f,* arcade; series of arches; *pl* sickness, nausea
árcade /'ar'kaðe/ *a* and *mf* Arcadian
arcaico /ar'kaiko/ *a* archaic
arcaísmo /arka'ismo/ *m,* archaism
arcángel /ar'kanhel/ *m,* archangel
arcano /ar'kano/ *a* secret. *m,* mystery, arcanum
arce /'arse; 'arθe/ *m, Bot.* maple tree
archifeliz /artʃife'lis; artʃife'liθ/ *a* extremely happy, in bliss
archimillonario /artʃimiyo'nario; artʃimiʎo'nario/ **(-ia)** *a* and *n* multimillionaire
archipiélago /artʃi'pielago/ *m,* archipelago
Archipiélago de Colón /artʃi'pielago de ko'lon/ *m,* Galapagos Islands
archivar /artʃi'βar/ *vt* to place in an archive; file (papers)
archivero /artʃi'βero/ *m,* archivist, keeper of the archives; librarian; registrar; (Mexico) file cabinet, filing cabinet
archivista /artʃi'βista/ *mf* archivist; file clerk, filing clerk
archivo /ar'tʃiβo/ *m,* archives, file
arcilla /ar'siya; ar'θiʎa/ *f,* clay
arcilloso /arsi'yoso; arθi'ʎoso/ *a* clayey, like or full of clay
arcipreste /arsi'preste; arθi'preste/ *m,* archpriest
arco /'arko/ *m, Geom.* arc; *Mil.* bow; bow (of a stringed instrument); hoop (of casks, etc.); *Archit.* arch; *Lat. Am.* goal (in sports). **a. del cielo** *or* **a. de San Martín** *or* **a. iris,** rainbow. **a. voltaico,** electric arc. *Mus.* **para a.,** for strings
arder /ar'ðer/ *vi* to burn; shine, gleam; *Fig.* burn (with passion, etc.); *vt* to set alight, burn
ardid /ar'ðið/ *a* crafty. *m,* trick, stratagem
ardiente /ar'ðiente/ *a* burning; ardent, passionate; vehement; enthusiastic; flame-colored; fiery-red
ardilla /ar'ðiya; ar'ðiʎa/ *f,* squirrel; *Lat. Am.* wheeler-dealer
ardite /ar'ðite/ *m,* ancient Spanish coin of little value; *Fig.* farthing, fig, straw. **no valer un a.,** to be not worth a straw
ardor /ar'ðor/ *m,* great heat; zeal, earnestness; passion, ardor; courage
ardoroso /arðo'roso/ *a* ardorous
arduo /'arðuo/ *a* arduous
área /'area/ *f,* area; small plot of ground; common threshing floor; arc (surface measure)
arena /a'rena/ *f,* sand; arena; grit, gravel. **a. movediza,** quicksand
arenal /are'nal/ *m,* quicksand; sand pit; sandy place
arenero /are'nero/ **(-ra)** *n* sand merchant. *m,* sandbox (carried by railway engines)
arenga /a'reŋga/ *f,* harangue, discourse *Argentina* argument, fight, quarrel
arenilla /are'niya; are'niʎa/ *f,* sand (for drying writing)
arenisca /are'niska/ *f,* sandstone
arenisco /are'nisko/ *a* sandy
arenque /a'renke/ *m,* herring
arete /a'rete/ *m,* earring

argamasa /arga'masa/ f, mortar
argayo /ar'gayo/ m, landslide; (Asturias) **a. de nieve,** avalanche
Árgel /'arhel/ Algiers
Argelia /ar'helia/ Algeria
argelino /arhe'lino/ **(-na)** a and n Algerian
argentado /arhen'taðo/ a silvered; silvery
argénteo /ar'henteo/ a silver; silvery
argentífero /arhen'tifero/ a silver-yielding
Argentina /arhen'tina/ Argentina
argentino /arhen'tino/ **(-na)** a silvery. a and n Argentinian. m, Argentinian gold coin
argento /ar'hento/ m, silver. **a. vivo,** mercury
argolla /ar'goya; ar'goʎa/ f, thick metal ring (for hitching, etc.); croquet (game); stocks, pillory; hoop, iron arch; *Lat. Am.* wedding ring
argonauta /argo'nauta/ m, *Myth.* Argonaut; *Zool.* paper nautilus, argonaut
argucia /ar'gusia; ar'guθia/ f, sophism, quibble; subtlety
argüir /ar'guir/ vt irr to deduce, imply; prove; reveal, manifest; accuse; vi argue, debate; dispute, oppose. See **huir**
argumentador /argumenta'ðor/ **(-ra)** a argumentative. n arguer
argumentar /argumen'tar/ vi to argue; dispute; oppose
argumento /argu'mento/ m, contention, case; theme (of a book, etc.); argument, discussion
aridez /ari'ðes; ari'ðeθ/ f, aridity, dryness; drought; sterility, barrenness; dullness, lack of interest
árido /'ariðo/ a dry, arid; sterile, barren; uninteresting, dull
ariete /a'riete/ m, *Mil.* battering ram
arisco /a'risko/ a unsociable, surly; wild, shy (animals)
arista /a'rista/ f, *Bot.* arista, awn, beard; pebble; edge, side
aristocracia /aristo'krasia; aristo'kraθia/ f, aristocracy
aristócrata /aris'tokrata/ mf aristocrat
aristocrático /aristo'kratiko/ a aristocratic
aristotélico /aristo'teliko/ a Aristotelian
aritmética /arit'metika/ f, arithmetic
aritmético /arit'metiko/ **(-ca)** a arithmetical. n arithmetician
arlequín /arle'kin/ m, harlequin; *Inf.* fool, buffoon; Neapolitan ice-cream
arma /'arma/ f, weapon; *Mil.* arm, branch; bull's horn; pl troops, army; means, way; arms, coat of arms. **a. arrojadiza,** missile. **a. blanca,** steel weapon. **a. de fuego,** fire-arm. **¡Armas al hombro!** Shoulder Arms! **armas portátiles,** small arms. *Inf.* **de armas tomar,** belligerent; resolute. **pasar por las armas,** *Mil.* to shoot. **presentar las armas,** *Mil.* to present arms. **ser a. de dos filos,** *Fig.* to cut both ways
armada /ar'maða/ f, navy, armada; fleet, squadron; *Argentina* lasso
armadía /arma'ðia/ f, raft, pontoon
armador /arma'ðor/ **(-ra)** n supplier, outfitter. m, shipowner; pirate, privateer; jacket; assembler, fitter
armadura /arma'ðura/ f, armature, armor; frame, framework; skeleton (of a building); skeleton (of vertebrates); *Phys.* armature; plate armor (of persons)
armamento /arma'mento/ m, *Mil.* armament; arms, military equipment
armar /ar'mar/ vt to arm; *Mech.* mount; man (guns); put together, assemble; roll (a cigarette); reinforce (concrete); *Inf.* arrange, prepare; *Inf.* occasion (quarrels); *Inf.* outfit; *Naut.* equip; commission (a ship); vr prepare oneself, arm oneself. **a. caballero,** to knight. **a. los remos,** to ship the oars. *Inf.* **armarla,** to cause a row or quarrel
armario /ar'mario/ m, cupboard; wardrobe. **a. de luna,** wardrobe with a mirror
armatoste /arma'toste/ m, unwieldy piece of furniture; *Fig. Inf.* dead weight, clumsy person; snare
armazón /arma'son; arma'θon/ f, frame, framework; ship's hulk. m, *Anat.* skeleton
armenio /ar'menio/ **(-ia)** a and n Armenian. m, Armenian language

armería /arme'ria/ f, armory; heraldry; gunsmith's craft or shop
armero /ar'mero/ m, gunsmith, armorer; stand for weapons
armiño /ar'miɲo/ m, ermine
armisticio /armis'tisio; armis'tiθio/ m, armistice
armón de artillería /ar'mon de artiye'ria; ar'mon de artiʎe'ria/ m, gun-carriage
armonía /armo'nia/ f, harmony; friendship, concord; *Mus.* harmony
armónica /ar'monika/ **(de boca)** f, mouth-organ
armónico /ar'moniko/ a harmonious. a and m, *Mus.* harmonic
armonio /ar'monio/ m, harmonium
armonioso /armo'nioso/ a harmonious
armonización /armonisa'sion; armoniθa'θion/ f, *Mus.* harmonization
armonizar /armoni'sar; armoni'θar/ vt to bring into harmony; *Mus.* harmonize
arnero /ar'nero/ m, *Lat. Am.* sieve
arnés /ar'nes/ m, armor; harness; pl horse trappings; *Inf.* equipment, tools
aro /'aro/ m, hoop; rim (of wheel, etc.); napkin-ring; croquet hoop; *Bot.* wild arum; child's hoop; *Lat. Am.* earring **a. de empaquetadura,** *Mech.* gasket
aroma /a'roma/ m, aroma, fragrance; balsam; sweet-smelling herb
aromático /aro'matiko/ a aromatic
arpa /'arpa/ f, harp. **a. eolia,** Eolian harp
arpar /ar'par/ vt to scratch, claw; tear, rend
arpegio /ar'pehio/ m, *Mus.* arpeggio
arpía /ar'pia/ f, harpy
arpicordio /arpi'korðio/ m, harpsichord
arpista /ar'pista/ mf harpist, harp player
arpón /ar'pon/ m, harpoon
arponear /arpone'ar/ vt to harpoon
arponero /arpo'nero/ m, harpooner; harpoon maker
arquear /arke'ar/ vt to arch; bend; beat (wool); gauge (ship's capacity); vi retch
arqueo /ar'keo/ m, arching; bending, curving; *Naut.* tonnage; gauging (of ship's capacity); *Com.* examination of deposits and contents of safe
arqueología /arkeolo'hia/ f, archeology
arqueológico /arkeo'lohiko/ a archeological
arqueólogo /arke'ologo/ m, archeologist
arquero /ar'kero/ m, *Com.* cashier, treasurer; *Mil.* archer
arquitecto /arki'tekto/ m, architect. **a. de jardines,** landscape gardener
arquitectura /arkitek'tura/ f, architecture
arquitrabe /arki'traβe/ m, architrave
arrabal /arra'βal/ m, suburb, district; pl outskirts
arracada /arra'kaða/ f, pendant-earring
arracimarse /arrasi'marse; arraθi'marse/ vr to cluster; group
arraigadamente /arrai̯ˌgaða'mente/ adv deeply, firmly
arraigado /arrai'gaðo/ a deep-rooted; firm; convinced
arraigar /arrai'gar/ vi to take root; vi and vr *Fig.* become established, take hold; vr settle; take up residence
arraigo /a'rraigo/ m, rooting; settlement; establishment; landed property
arrancaclavos /aˌrranka'klaβos/ m, nail-puller
arrancadero /aˌrranka'ðero/ m, *Sports.* starting-point
arrancar /arran'kar/ vt to uproot; pull out; wrench; tear off; extirpate; obtain by threats; clear one's throat; vt and vi *Naut.* put on speed; vi start (a car); *Inf.* leave, quit; derive, originate **¡Arrancan!** And they're off! (races)
arrancarse /arran'karse/ vr, *Lat. Am.* to kick the bucket, pop off
arranque /a'rranke/ m, uprooting; extirpation; wrenching, pulling, seizing; stimulus (of passion); sudden impulse; *Mech.* start; *Mech.* starter. **a. automático,** self-starter
arras /'arras/ f pl, dowry; coins given by bridegroom to his bride; earnest money, token

arrasamiento /arrasa'miento/ *m*, demolition, destruction; leveling

arrasar /arra'sar/ *vt* to demolish, destroy; level; fill to the brim; *vi* and *vr* clear up (sky). **ojos arrasados de lágrimas,** eyes brimming with tears

arrastrado /arras'traðo/ *a Inf.* poverty-stricken, wretched; *Inf.* knavish; unhappy, unfortunate

arrastrar /arras'trar/ *vt* to drag; trail; convince; haul; *vi* trail along or touch the ground; trump (at cards); *vr* crawl, creep; shuffle along; humble oneself

arrastre /a'rrastre/ *m*, dragging, trailing; haulage; trumping (at cards); *Central America, Mexico* clout, pull

¡arre! /'arre/ *interj* Gee up! Get along!

arrear /arre'ar/ *vt* to spur on, whip up (horses, etc.). *interj Inf.* **¡Arrea!** Hurry up! Get on!

arrebañar /arreβa'ɲar/ *vt* to pick clean, clear; eat or drink up

arrebatado /arreβa'taðo/ *a* precipitate, headlong; rash; flushed, red

arrebatador /arreβata'ðor/ *a* overwhelming; violent; bewitching, captivating; delightful

arrebatamiento /arreβata'miento/ *m*, abduction; seizure; fury; ecstasy

arrebatar /arreβa'tar/ *vt* to abduct, carry off; seize, grab; attract, charm; grip (the attention); *vr* be overcome with rage

arrebatiña /arreβa'tiɲa/ *f*, grab; scuffle, scrimmage

arrebato /arre'βato/ *m*, fit (gen. of anger); ecstasy, rapture

arrebozar /arreβo'sar/ arreβo'θar/ *vt* to muffle; envelop

arrebujarse /arreβu'harse/ *vr* to huddle; wrap oneself up

arrechucho /arre'tʃutʃo/ *m*, *Inf.* fit of rage; sudden slight ailment

arreciar /arre'siar/ arre'θiar/ *vi* to increase in intensity; *vr* grow strong

arrecife /arre'sife/ arre'θife/ *m*, reef (in the sea); stone-paved road

arredrar /arre'ðrar/ *vt* to separate, remove; force back, repel; terrify

arregazar /arrega'sar/ arrega'θar/ **(se)** *vt* and *vr* to tuck up one's skirts

arreglado /arre'glaðo/ *a* regular; regulated; ordered; methodical

arreglar /arre'glar/ *vt* to regulate; arrange; adjust, put right; tidy; make up (the face); *vr* (*with prep a*) conform to; (*with con*) reach an agreement with. **Me voy a a.,** I am going to make myself presentable. *Inf.* **arreglárselas,** to shift for oneself

arreglo /a'rreglo/ *m*, arrangement; rule; regulation; method, order; agreement; adjustment; compromise

arrellanarse /arreya'narse/ arreʎa'narse/ *vr* to settle comfortably in one's chair; be happy in one's work

arremangar /arremaŋ'gar/ *vt* to roll up (sleeves, trousers, etc.); *vr Inf.* make a decision

arremango /arre'maŋgo/ *m*, rolling or tucking up (of sleeve, etc.)

arremetedor /arremete'ðor/ **(-ra)** *n* attacker, assailant

arremeter /arreme'ter/ *vt* to attack, assail; *vi* launch oneself (at); *Fig.* spoil the view, shock the eye

arremetida /arreme'tiða/ *f*, attack, assault

arremolinarse /arremoli'narse/ *vr* to crowd, cluster, group

arrendador /arrenda'ðor/ **(-ra)** *n* landlord; renter; hirer; tenant

arrendamiento /arrenda'miento/ *m*, renting; hiring; rental; agreement, lease

arrendar /arren'dar/ *vt irr* to let, lease; hire; rent (as a tenant); train (horses); tie up (horses); restrain; mimic, imitate. See **recomendar**

arrendatario /arrenda'tario/ **(-ia)** *a* rent, lease. *n* tenant; lessee; hirer. **a. de contribuciones,** tax farmer

arreo /a'rreo/ *m*, ornament; apparel; *pl* horse trappings; appurtenances, equipment

¡Arrepa! /a'rrepa/ But look!, Hold on!, Hold your horses!, Not so fast!

arrepentimiento /arrepenti'miento/ *m*, repentance

arrepentirse /arrepen'tirse/ *vr irr* to repent, to change one's mind. See **sentir**

arrestado /arres'taðo/ *a* courageous, audacious, bold

arrestar /arres'tar/ *vt* to arrest, detain; *vr* be bold, dare

arresto /a'rresto/ *m*, arrest; detention; imprisonment; audacity, boldness

arriada /a'rriaða/ *f*, lowering (of a boat); taking in (of sail)

arriar /a'rriar/ *vt Naut.* to strike (colors); take in (sail); pay out (ropes, etc.); lower (boats); flood, inundate

arriate /a'rriate/ *m*, garden border; avenue, walk; trellis (for plants)

arriba /a'rriβa/ *adv* up, above; overhead; upstairs; earlier, before; upwards (with prices). *interj* **¡A.!** Up with!; Long live! **de a. abajo,** from head to foot, from one end to the other; completely, wholly

arribada /arri'βaða/ *f*, *Naut.* arrival. **de a.,** emergency (port)

arribar /arri'βar/ *vi Naut.* to arrive; put into an emergency port; reach, arrive at; *Inf.* convalesce; attain; *Naut.* drift

arribista /arri'βista/ *mf* social climber

arriero /a'rriero/ *m*, farrier; muleteer

arriesgado /arries'gaðo/ *a* dangerous, risky; rash, daring

arriesgar /arries'gar/ *vt* to risk; *vr* run into danger; dare, risk

arrimado /arri'maðo/ *m*, *Mexico* parasite

arrimar /arri'mar/ *vt* to bring or draw near; abandon (professions, etc.); lay aside, discard; *Inf.* administer (blows); *Naut.* stow (cargo); *vr* (*with prep a*) lean against, rest on; join, go with; seek the protection of. **Cada cual se arrima a su cada cual,** Birds of a feather flock together

arrimo /a'rrimo/ *m*, bringing or placing near; leaning or resting against; abandonment, giving up; protection; staff, support

arrinconado /arrinko'naðo/ *a* remote, secluded; forgotten, neglected

arrinconar /arrinko'nar/ *vt* to discard, lay aside; corner, besiege; set aside, dismiss; forsake; *vr* go into retirement, withdraw

arriscado /arris'kaðo/ *a* craggy, rugged; bold, resolute; sprightly, handsome

arriscarse /arris'karse/ *vr Lat. Am.* to dress up kill, dress to the nines

arro, arro, arro /'arro, 'arro, 'arro/ purrrr (echoic of a cat's purr)

arrobamiento /arroβa'miento/ *m*, ecstasy, rapture; trance

arrobar /arro'βar/ *vt* to charm, entrance; *vr* be enraptured; be in ecstasy

arrodillar /arroði'yar/ arroði'ʎar/ *vt* to cause to kneel down; *vi* and *vr* kneel down

arrogancia /arro'gansia/ arro'ganθia/ *f*, arrogance; courage; majesty, pride

arrogante /arro'gante/ *a* arrogant, haughty; courageous; proud, majestic

arrogar /arro'gar/ *vt* to adopt (as a son); *vr* usurp, appropriate

arrojadizo /arroha'ðiso/ arroha'ðiθo/ *a* easily cast or hurled; projectile

arrojado /arro'haðo/ *a* bold, determined; rash

arrojar /arro'har/ *vt* to throw, hurl, cast; shed (light, etc.; e.g. *La cuenta arroja un total de cien dólares,* The bill shows a total of a hundred dollars); *Com.* show (a balance, etc.); put out (sprouts); dismiss, send away; *vr* cast oneself; (*with prep a*) hurl oneself against or upon; undertake, venture upon. **a. de sí** (**a**), to get rid of, dismiss

arrojo /a'rroho/ *m*, daring, intrepidity; boldness

arrollar /arro'yar/ arro'ʎar/ *vt* to roll; make into a roll, roll up; defeat (the enemy); silence, confound; rock to sleep; bear along, carry off

arromar /arro'mar/ *vt* to blunt; flatten

arropar /arro'par/ *vt* to wrap up, cover

arrostrar /arros'trar/ *vt* to confront, defy, face up to; *vr* fight hand to hand. **a. las consecuencias,** *Fig.* to face the music

arroyada /arro'yaða/ *f*, gorge, gully; course, channel; flood

arroyo /a'rroyo/ *m*, stream, brook; street gutter; road, street; *Fig.* flood, plenty

arroz /a'rros; a'rroθ/ *m*, rice

arrozal /arro'sal; arro'θal/ *m*, rice field

arruga /a'rruga/ *f*, wrinkle; fold, pleat; crease

arrugamiento /arruga'miento/ *m*, wrinkling; fold, pleating; crumpling, creasing; corrugation

arrugar /arru'gar/ *vt* to wrinkle; pleat; corrugate; crumple, crease. **a. el ceño,** to knit one's brow, scowl

arruinamiento /arruina'miento/ *m*, ruin, decay, decline

arruinar /arrui'nar/ *vt* to ruin; destroy, damage severely

arrullar /arru'yar; arru'ʎar/ *vt* to bill and coo (doves); lull to sleep; *Inf.* whisper sweet words to, make love to

arrullo /a'rruyo; a'rruʎo/ *m*, cooing of doves; lullaby

arrumaco /arru'mako/ *m*, *Inf.* embrace, caress (gen. *pl*); ornament in bad taste

arrumaje /arru'mahe/ *m*, *Naut.* stowage; clouds on the horizon

arrurruz /arru'rrus; arru'rruθ/ *m*, arrowroot

arsenal /arse'nal/ *m*, dockyard; arsenal; *Fig.* store (of information, etc.)

arsénico /ar'seniko/ *m*, arsenic

arte /'arte/ *mf*, art; skill; ability, talent; guile, craftiness. **las bellas artes,** fine arts. *Inf.* **no tener a. ni parte en,** to have nothing to do with, have no part in

artefacto /arte'fakto/ *m*, machine, mechanism, apparatus; device, appliance. **a. atómico,** atomic bomb

arteria /ar'teria/ *f*, *Med.* artery; main line (of communication)

artería /ar'teria/ *f*, craftiness, guile

arterial /arte'rial/ *a* arterial

artesa /ar'tesa/ *f*, wooden trough; kneading bowl

artesano /arte'sano/ **(-na)** *n* artisan; mechanic

artesiano /arte'siano/ *a* artesian

artesón /arte'son/ *m*, bucket, pail; *Archit.* curved ceiling-panel; paneled ceiling

artesonado /arteso'naðo/ *a Archit.* paneled (ceiling). *m*, paneled ceiling

ártico /'artiko/ *a* Arctic

articulación /artikula'sion; artikula'θion/ *f*, joint, articulation; jointing; enunciation, pronunciation

articular /artiku'lar/ *vt* to joint, articulate; enunciate; pronounce clearly

articulista /artiku'lista/ *mf* article writer

artículo /ar'tikulo/ *m*, finger knuckle; heading; article; *Anat.* joint; *Gram.* article; *pl* goods, things. **a. de fondo,** leading article (in a newspaper). **a. de primera necesidad,** prime necessity, essential

artífice /ar'tifise; ar'tifiθe/ *mf* craftsman, artificer; author, creator; forger

artificial /artifi'sial; artifi'θial/ *a* artificial

artificio /arti'fisio; arti'fiθio/ *m*, skill, art; appliance; contraption, mechanism; trick, cunning device; guile, craftiness

artificioso /artifi'sioso; artifi'θioso/ *a* skilful; artificial; crafty, cunning

artillería /artiye'ria; artiʎe'ria/ *f*, artillery. **a. de costa,** coastal guns. **a. ligera, a. montada, a. rodada** *or* **a. volante,** field artillery

artillero /arti'yero; arti'ʎero/ *m*, gunner

artimaña /arti'maɲa/ *f*, trick, ruse, stratagem

artista /ar'tista/ *mf* artist; performer

artístico /ar'tistiko/ *a* artistic

artrítico /ar'tritiko/ *a Med.* arthritic

artritis /ar'tritis/ *f*, *Med.* arthritis

arveja /ar'βeha/ *f*, *Bot.* vetch; *Lat. Am.* pea

arzobispo /arso'βispo; arθo'βispo/ *m*, archbishop

as /as/ *m*, Roman copper coin; ace (*Aer.* cards, etc.)

asa /'asa/ *f*, handle; pretext, excuse

asadero /asa'ðero/ *m*, *Mexico* cottage cheese

asado /a'saðo/ *m*, *Cul.* roast

asador /asa'ðor/ *m*, *Cul.* roasting-spit; roaster

asadura /asa'ðura/ *f*, *Cul.* chitterlings; offal

asalariar /asala'riar/ *vt* to fix a salary for

asaltador /asalta'ðor/ **(-ra)** *a* attacking. *n* assailant, attacker

asaltar /asal'tar/ *vt* to storm, besiege; assault, attack; occur to (ideas); come on suddenly (illness)

asalto /a'salto/ *m*, storming, besieging; assault, attack; bout (in fencing, boxing, wrestling); round (in a fight)

asamblea /asam'βlea/ *f*, congregation, assembly; meeting; legislative assembly; *Mil.* assembly (bugle call)

asambleísta /asamble'ista/ *mf* member of an assembly

asar /a'sar/ *vt Cul.* to roast; grill; *vr* be burning-hot; *Fig.* burn (with enthusiasm)

asaz /a'sas; a'saθ/ *adv* sufficiently, enough; very; in abundance. *a* sufficient; many

asbesto /as'βesto/ *m*, asbestos

ascalonia /aska'lonia/ *f*, *Bot.* shallot

ascendencia /assen'densia; asθen'denθia/ *f*, lineage, ancestry, origin

ascendente /assen'dente; asθen'dente/ *a* ascending

ascender /assen'der; asθen'der/ *vi irr* to ascend; climb; be promoted; (*with prep a*) amount to (bills, etc.); *vt* promote. See **entender**

ascendiente /assen'diente; asθen'diente/ *mf* ancestor, forbear. *m*, influence, ascendancy

ascensión /assen'sion; asθen'sion/ *f*, ascension; promotion; *Astron.* exaltation

ascenso /as'senso; as'θenso/ *m*, ascent; promotion, preferment

ascensor /assen'sor; asθen'sor/ *m*, lift, elevator

ascensorista /assenso'rista; asθenso'rista/ *mf* elevator operator

asceta /as'seta; as'θeta/ *mf* ascetic

ascético /as'setiko; as'θetiko/ *a* ascetic

ascetismo /asse'tismo; asθe'tismo/ *m*, asceticism

asco /'asko/ *m*, nausea; repugnance, loathing; revolting thing. *Inf.* **Me da a.,** It sickens me

ascua /'askua/ *f*, live coal, ember. **estar como una a. de oro,** to be as bright as a new pin. **estar en ascuas,** *Fig.* to be on pins

aseado /ase'aðo/ *a* clean, tidy

asear /ase'ar/ *vt* to tidy, make neat; clean up; decorate, adorn

asechanza /ase'tʃansa; ase'tʃanθa/ *f*, ambush; trick, snare, stratagem

asechar /ase'tʃar/ *vt* to ambush, waylay; *Fig.* lay snares for

asediador /aseðia'ðor/ **(-ra)** *n* besieger

asediar /ase'ðiar/ *vt* to besiege; pester, importune

asedio /a'seðio/ *m*, siege; importunity

asegurado /asegu'raðo/ **(-da)** *a* insured. *n* insured person

asegurador /asegura'ðor/ **(-ra)** *a* insuring. *n* insurer

asegurar /asegu'rar/ *vt* to fasten, make secure; pinion, grip; reassure, soothe; assert, state; *Com.* insure; guarantee; ensure, secure; *vr Com.* insure oneself; (*with de*) make sure of

asemejar /aseme'har/ *vt* to imitate, copy; make similar to; *vr* (*with prep a*) be like, be similar to

asenderear /asendere'ar/ *vt* to make a pathway through; persecute, harass

asenso /a'senso/ *m*, assent. **dar a.,** to believe, give credence (to)

asentaderas /asenta'ðeras/ *f pl*, *Inf.* buttocks, seat

asentado /asen'taðo/ *a* prudent, circumspect; permanent, stable

asentamiento /asenta'miento/ *m*, seating; settlement, residence; prudence, judgment

asentar /asen'tar/ *vt irr* to seat; place; fasten, fix; found; plant (flags); pitch (a tent); establish, make firm; smooth; hone (razors); estimate, budget, arrange, set forth; note down; affirm, believe; *Com.* enter (in an account); *vi* fit (clothes); *vr* seat oneself; alight (birds); settle (liquids); *Archit.* settle, subside; to be located (e.g. *El edificio se asienta en una esquina,* The building is located on a corner). **a. la mano en,** to strike hard. See **acertar**

asentimiento /asenti'miento/ *m*, assent; consent, approval

asentir /asen'tir/ *vi irr* to assent, agree; (*with en*) consent to. See **sentir**

aseñorado /aseɲo'raðo/ *a* refined, gentlemanly; ladylike; presumptuous

aseo /a'seo/ *m,* cleanliness, neatness

asepsia /a'sepsia/ *f,* asepsis

asequible /ase'kiβle/ *a* attainable; obtainable

aserción /aser'sion; aser'θion/ *f,* assertion

aserradero /ase'rraðero/ *m,* sawmill; saw-pit

aserrador /aserra'ðor/ *(-ra)* *n* sawyer

aserrar /ase'rrar/ *vt irr* to saw. See **acertar**

aserrín /ase'rrin/ *m,* sawdust

aserruchar /aserru'tʃar/ *vt, Lat. Am.* to saw

asertivo /aser'tiβo/ *a* assertive

aserto /a'serto/ *m,* assertion

asesinar /asesi'nar/ *vt* to assassinate, murder

asesinato /asesi'nato/ *m,* assassination, murder

asesino /ase'sino/ *mf* assassin, murderer; murderess

asesor /ase'sor/ *(-ra)* *n* assessor

asesorar /aseso'rar/ *vt* to give advice; *vr* take legal advice; seek advice

asestar /ases'tar/ *vt* to aim (firearms); fire; deal (a blow)

aseveración /aseβera'sion; aseβera'θion/ *f,* assertion, statement

aseveradamente /aseβeraða'mente/ *adv* affirmatively

aseverar /aseβe'rar/ *vt* to affirm, assert

asfaltado /asfal'taðo/ *m,* asphalting; asphalt pavement

asfaltar /asfal'tar/ *vt* to asphalt

asfalto /as'falto/ *m,* asphalt

asfixia /as'fiksia/ *f, Med.* asphyxia

asfixiante /asfik'siante/ *a* asphyxiating

asfixiar /asfik'siar/ *vt* to asphyxiate

así /a'si/ *adv* thus, so, in this way; like this (e.g. *en días a.,* on days like this); even if; so that, therefore. **a. a.,** so-so. **a. como,** as well as; as soon as. **a. las cosas,** that being the case, **a. que,** as soon as, immediately; consequently, thus

asiático /a'siatiko/ *(-ca)* *a* and *n* Asiatic

asidero /asi'ðero/ *m,* hold, grasp; handle, haft; pretext, excuse

asido a /a'siðo a/ wedded to (e.g. a belief)

asiduo /a'siðuo/ *a* assiduous

asiento /a'siento/ *m,* seat; place, position; site; base (of a vase, etc.); lees, sediment; indigestion; *Archit.* subsidence, settling; treaty, pact; contract; note, reminder; *Com.* entry; permanence, stability; prudence; bit (of a bridle); *pl* buttocks, seat. **estar de a.,** to be established (in a place)

asignación /asigna'sion; asigna'θion/ *f,* assignation; appropriation (of money); salary; portion, share

asignar /asig'nar/ *vt* to assign; apportion; destine, intend; appoint

asignatario, -a /asigna'tario/ *mf Lat. Am.* heir, heiress, legatee

asignatura /asigna'tura/ *f,* subject (of study in schools, etc.)

asilar /asi'lar/ *vt* to give shelter to; receive; put into an institution

asilo /a'silo/ *m,* shelter, refuge; sanctuary, asylum; *Fig.* protection, defense; home, institution

asimetría /asime'tria/ *f,* asymmetry

asimétrico /asi'metriko/ *a* asymmetrical

asimiento /asi'miento/ *m,* hold, grasp; attachment, affection

asimilación /asimila'sion; asimila'θion/ *f,* assimilation

asimilar /asimi'lar/ *vt* to compare, liken; (*Bot. Zool. Gram.*) assimilate; *vi* resemble, be like; *Fig.* assimilate, digest (ideas)

asimismo /asi'mismo/ *adv* similarly, likewise

asir /a'sir/ *vt irr* to grasp, take hold of; seize; *vi* take root (plants); *vr* (*with de*) lay hold of; take advantage of; make an excuse to. *Pres. Ind.* **asgo, ases,** etc. *Pres. Subjunc.* **asga,** etc.

asirio /a'sirio/ *(-ia)* *a* and *n* Assyrian. *m,* Assyrian language

asistencia /asistensia; asis'tenθia/ *f,* presence, attendance; minimal attendance required (e.g. *Los alumnos*

tienen que completar una a.*, Pupils must attend a certain number of classes) assistance, help; service, attendance; medical treatment; remuneration; *pl* allowance. **a. pública,** Public Assistance. **a. social,** social work

asistenta /asis'tenta/ *f,* daily maid; waiting-maid

asistente /asis'tente/ *m,* assistant; *Mil.* orderly

asistir /asis'tir/ *vt* to accompany; assist, help; attend, treat; (*with de*) act as; *vi* (*with prep a*) be present at, attend; follow suit (in cards)

asma /'asma/ *f,* asthma

asmático /as'matiko/ *(-ca)* *a* asthmatic. *n* asthma sufferer

asnal /as'nal/ *a* asinine; brutish, stupid

asno /'asno/ *m,* ass

asociación /asosia'sion; asoθia'θion/ *f,* association; company, partnership; society, fellowship

asociado /aso'siaðo; aso'θiaðo/ *(-da)* *n* associate; member; partner

asociar /aso'siar; aso'θiar/ *vt* to associate; *vr* associate oneself; join together; form a partnership

asolar /aso'lar/ *vt irr* to destroy, devastate, lay flat; *vr* wither; settle (liquids). See **contar**

asoldar /asol'dar/ *vt irr* to employ, engage, hire. See **contar**

asolear /asole'ar/ *vt* to expose to the sun; *vr* sun oneself; become sunburnt

asomada /aso'maða/ *f,* brief appearance; vantage point

asomar /aso'mar/ *vt* to show, allow to appear, put forth; *vi* begin to show; *vr* show oneself, appear; *Inf.* be flushed (with wine); (*with prep a, por*) look out of. **asomarse a la ventana,** to show oneself at, or look out of, the window

asombrar /asom'βrar/ *vt* to shade, shadow; darken (a color); terrify; amaze

asombro /a'sombro/ *m,* fright, terror; amazement; wonder, marvel

asombroso /asom'βroso/ *a* amazing; marvelous, wonderful

asonancia /aso'nansia; aso'nanθia/ *f,* assonance; congruity, harmony

asordar /asor'ðar/ *vt* to deafen

asorocharse /asoro'tʃarse/ *vr, Peru* to come down with altitude sickness, get altitude sickness

aspa /'aspa/ *f,* cross; sail of a windmill

aspaviento /aspa'βiento/ *m,* exaggerated display of emotion; gesture (of horror, etc.); **hacer aspavientos,** to make a fuss

aspecto /as'pekto/ *m,* look, appearance; aspect, outlook

aspereza /aspe'resa; aspe'reθa/ *f,* roughness, harshness; ruggedness, rockiness; severity, asperity

áspero /'aspero/ *a* rough, harsh; uneven, rocky; jarring, grating; hard, severe

aspersión /asper'sion/ *f, Eccl.* aspersion; sprinkling

áspid /'aspið/ *m,* asp, viper

aspiración /aspira'sion; aspira'θion/ *f,* breath; breathing; aspiration, desire; *Mus.* pause

aspirador /aspira'ðor/ **(de polvo)** *m,* vacuum cleaner

aspirante /aspi'rante/ *m,* aspirant, novice; office-seeker; applicant

aspirar /aspi'rar/ *vt* to breathe in, inhale; *Gram.* aspirate; (*with prep a*) aspire to, desire

aspirina /aspi'rina/ *f,* aspirin

asquear /aske'ar/ *vi* and *vt* to hate, loathe

asquerosidad /askerosi'ðað/ *f,* filthiness, loathsomeness; vileness, hatefulness

asqueroso /aske'roso/ *a* nauseating; loathsome, revolting; vile, hateful

asta /'asta/ *f,* lance, spear, pike; horn (of bull); antler; flagstaff; shaft. **a media a.,** at half-mast

asterisco /aste'risko/ *m,* asterisk

astigmático /astig'matiko/ *a* astigmatic

astigmatismo /astigma'tismo/ *m,* astigmatism

astil /as'til/ *m,* handle, pole, shaft; bar of a balance; beam feather

astilla /as'tiya; as'tiʎa/ *f,* splinter

astillar /asti'yar; asti'ʎar/ *vt* to splinter, chip

astillero /asti'yero; asti'ʎero/ *m*, shipyard; rack for lances and pikes
astilloso /asti'yoso; asti'ʎoso/ *a* splintery, fragile
astracán /astra'kan/ *m*, astrakhan
astringente /astrin'hente/ *a* astringent
astringir /astrin'hir/ *vt* to tighten up; compress; constrain
astro /'astro/ *m*, heavenly body
astrolatría /astrola'tria/ *f*, astrolatry, star worship
astrología /astrolo'hia/ *f*, astrology
astrológico /astro'lohiko/ *a* astrological
astrólogo /as'trologo/ **(-ga)** *n* astrologist
astronauta /astro'nauta/ *m*, astronaut
astronomía /astrono'mia/ *f*, astronomy
astronómico /astro'nomiko/ *a* astronomical
astrónomo /as'tronomo/ *m*, astronomer
astucia /as'tusia; as'tuθia/ *f*, astuteness, guile, craftiness
asturiano /astu'riano/ **(-na)** *a* and *n* Asturian
astuto /as'tuto/ *a* guileful, crafty, astute
asueto /a'sueto/ *m*, day's holiday
asumir /asu'mir/ *vt* to assume; adopt, appropriate
asunción /asun'sion; asun'θion/ *f*, assumption. **La Asunción,** the Feast of the Assumption
asunto /a'sunto/ *m*, matter, theme, subject; business, affair
asustadizo /asusta'ðiso; asusta'ðiθo/ *a* timid, nervous, easily frightened
asustar /asus'tar/ *vt* to frighten; **que asusta,** terribly (e.g. *Es de una ñoñería que asusta,* It's a terribly timid thing to do) *vr* be frightened
atablar /ata'βlar/ *vt* to roll, flatten (earth)
atacado /ata'kaðo/ *a Inf.* hesitant; mean, stingy
atacador /ataka'ðor/ **(-ra)** *a* attacking. *n* aggressor, attacker
atacar /ata'kar/ *vt* to attack; fasten, button; fit (clothes); ram (guns); *Fig.* press hard, corner (persons). **a. a los nervios,** to jar on the nerves
ataché /ata'tʃe/ *m. Central America* (paper) clip
atadero /ata'ðero/ *m*, rope, tie, cord; hook, ring, etc. (for hitching); hindrance, impediment; hitching or fastening point
atado /a'taðo/ *m*, bundle, roll
atadura /ata'ðura/ *f*, tying, stringing, fastening, tie; knot; connection
atajar /ata'har/ *vi* to take a short cut; *vt* intercept, cut off; screen off, divide; impede, stop; interrupt (people); **atajarle la palabra a uno,** to cut somebody off, interrupt *vr* be overcome (by fear, shame, etc.)
atajo /a'taho/ *m*, short cut, quick way; cutting, abbreviation; division. *Inf.* **echar por el a.,** to go to the root of (a matter)
atalaya /ata'laya/ *f*, look out, watch tower; observation point. *m*, lookout
atalayar /atala'yar/ *vt* to scan, watch; spy upon
atalón /ata'lon/ *m*, atoll, coral island
atañadero /ataɲa'ðero/ *n*: **en lo atañadero a** with regard to, with respect to
atañer /ata'ɲer/ *vi impers* to concern, affect; belong, pertain
ataque /a'take/ *m*, (*Mil. Med.*) attack; quarrel, fight
atar /a'tar/ *vt* to tie; fasten; lace; stop, paralyse; *vr* get in a fix; confine oneself. **a. cabos,** to put two and two together
atardecer /atarðe'ser; atarðe'θer/ *vi irr impers* to grow dusk. See **conocer**
atardecer /atarðe'ser; atarðe'θer/ *m*, dusk, evening
atarear /atare'ar/ *vt* to set to work, assign work to; *vr* work hard
atarugar /ataru'gar/ *vt* to wedge; stop up; plug; block; *Inf.* silence, shut up; stuff, cram; *vr Fig. Inf.* lose one's head
atasajar /atasa'har/ *vt* to cut up, jerk (beef, etc.)
atascadero /ataska'ðero/ *m*, deep rut, boggy place; impediment, obstacle
atascar /atas'kar/ *vt* to plug; block up; stop (a leak); hinder, obstruct; *vr* stick in the mud; be held up or delayed; *Inf.* get stuck in a speech
atasco /a'tasko/ *m*, obstruction, block
ataúd /ata'uð/ *m*, coffin

ataviar /ata'βiar/ *vt* to deck, apparel, adorn
atavío /ata'βio/ *m*, get-up, dress, apparel; *pl* ornaments
atavismo /ata'βismo/ *m*, atavism
ate /'ate/ *m, Mexico* kind of Turkish delight
ateísmo /ate'ismo/ *m*, atheism
atejonarse /ateho'narse/ *vr Mexico* to hide
ateleje /ate'lahe/ *m*, team, yoke (of horses); trappings, harness; *Inf.* trousseau
atemperación /atempera'sion; atempera'θion/ *f*, moderation, mitigation; tempering
atemperar /atempe'rar/ *vt* to moderate, mitigate; adapt, adjust; temper, cool. **atemperarse a la realidad,** to adjust to reality
Atenas /a'tenas/ Athens
atenazar /atena'sar; atena'θar/ *vt* to grip, grasp; torture
atención /aten'sion; aten'θion/ *f*, attention; solicitude, kindness; courtesy, civility; *pl* business affairs. *interj* ¡**A.!** Take care! Look out!; *Mil.* Attention! **en a.** (**a**), taking into consideration. **estar en a.,** (patient) to be under treatment
atender /aten'der/ *vt irr* to await, expect; take care of, look after; *vi* (*with prep a*) attend to, listen to; *vi* remember. See **entender**
ateneo /ate'neo/ *m*, atheneum. *a* Athenian
atenerse /ate'nerse/ *vr irr* (*with prep a*) to abide by; resort to, rely on. See **tener**
ateniense /ate'niense/ *a* and *mf* Athenian
atentado /aten'taðo/ *a* prudent, sensible; secret, silent. *m*, infringement, violation; attempt (on a person's life); crime
atentar /aten'tar/ *vt irr* to do illegally; attempt a crime; *vr* proceed cautiously; restrain oneself. See **acertar**
atento /a'tento/ *a* attentive; courteous, civil. *adv* taking into consideration. **su atenta (atta),** *Com.* your favor
atenuación /atenua'sion; atenua'θion/ *f*, attenuation, diminution
atenuante /ate'nuante/ *a* attenuating; extenuating (of circumstances)
atenuar /ate'nuar/ *vt* to attenuate, diminish; extenuate
ateo /a'teo/ **(-ea)** *a* atheistic. *n* atheist
aterirse /ate'rirse/ *vr defective* to grow stiff with cold
aterrador /aterra'ðor/ *a* terrifying, dreadful
aterraje /ate'rrahe/ *m*, (*Aer., Naut.*) landing
aterramiento /aterra'miento/ *m*, horror, terror; terrorization; *Naut.* landing; ruin, demolition
aterrar /ate'rrar/ *vt irr* to demolish; discourage; cover with earth; *vi* land; *vr Naut.* draw near to land. See **acertar**
aterrizaje /aterri'sahe; aterri'θahe/ *m, Aer.* landing. **a. forzoso,** forced landing. **campo de a.,** landing field
aterrizar /aterri'sar; aterri'θar/ *vt* Aer. to land, touch down
aterrorizar /aterrori'sar; aterrori'θar/ *vt* to terrify; terrorize
atesar /ate'sar/ *vt Lat. Am.* to tighten (up)
atesorar /ateso'rar/ *vt* to hoard, treasure up
atestación /atesta'sion; atesta'θion/ *f*, attestation, affidavit
atestar /ates'tar/ *vt irr* to stuff, cram; insert, pack; *Inf.* stuff with food; crowd, fill with people; attest, testify. See **acertar**
atestiguación /atestigua'sion; atestigua'θion/ *f*, deposition, testimony
atestiguar /atesti'guar/ *vt* to testify, attest
atetar /ate'tar/ *vt* to suckle; *vi* suck
atezado /ate'saðo; ate'θaðo/ *a* bronzed, sunburnt; black
ático /'atiko/ *a* Attic. *m*, penthouse
atiesar /atie'sar/ *vt* to stiffen
atildar /atil'dar/ *vt* to place a tilde over; blame, criticize; decorate, ornament
atimia /a'timia/ *f*, loss of status
atinado /ati'naðo/ *a* pertinent, relevant
atinar /ati'nar/ *vi* to find by touch; discover by chance; guess; hit the mark

atinente a... /ati'nente a / concerning...
atingencia /atiŋ'gensia; atiŋ'genθia/ f, Lat. Am. connection, relationship
atingir /atiŋ'gir/ vt, Lat. Am. to concern, relate to
atisbadura /atisβa'ðura/ f, watching, spying, prying
atisbar /atis'βar/ vt to spy upon, watch
atisbo /a'tisβo/ m, prying, watching; suspicion, hint
atisbón /atis'βon/ a penetrating (mind, vision)
atizador /atisa'ðor; atiθa'ðor/ m, poker (for the fire)
atizar /ati'sar; ati'θar/ vt to poke (the fire); dowse, snuff; trim (lamps); excite, rouse; Inf. slap, wallop
atlántico /at'lantiko/ a Atlantic. m, Atlantic Ocean
atleta /at'leta/ m, athlete
atlético /at'letiko/ a athletic
atletismo /atle'tismo/ m, athletics
atmósfera /at'mosfera/ f, atmosphere
atmosférico /atmos'feriko/ a atmospheric
atolladero /atoya'ðero; atoʎa'ðero/ m, rut; mud; bog
atolón /ato'lon/ m, atoll, coral island
atolondrado /atolon'draðo/ a scatter-brained, flighty
atolondramiento /atolondra'miento/ m, rashness, recklessness; bewilderment
atolondrar /atolon'drar/ vt to bewilder, confuse
atómico /a'tomiko/ a atomic
átomo /'atomo/ m, atom; speck, particle
atónito /a'tonito/ a amazed, astounded
atontar /aton'tar/ vt to confuse, daze; make stupid; stun
atormentador /atormenta'ðor/ (-ra) a torturing. n tormentor; torturer
atormentar /atormen'tar/ vt to torment; torture; grieve, harass
atorrante /ato'rrante/ a and mf (Argentina) good-for-nothing
atracadero /atraka'ðero/ m, jetty, landingstage
atracar /atra'kar/ vt Inf. to stuff with food; Naut. tie up, moor; hold up, rob; vi Naut. moor, stop; vr Inf. guzzle, gorge
atracción /atrak'sion; atrak'θion/ f, attraction
atraco /a'trako/ (a) m, hold up (of), ambush (of)
atracón /atra'kon/ m, Inf. gorge, fill; surfeit. **darse atracones de,** to gorge oneself on
atractivo /atrak'tiβo/ a attractive. m, attraction, charm
atractriz /atrak'tris; atrak'triθ/ a attracting; f, force of attraction; (fig.) lure
atraer /atra'er/ vt irr to attract; charm, enchant. See **traer**
atragantarse /atragan'tarse/ vr to choke; Inf. be at a loss, dry up (in conversation)
atraíble /atra'iβle/ a attractable, able to be attracted
atrancar /atran'kar/ vt to bar the door; obstruct, block; hinder; vi Inf. stride; skip (in reading)
atrapar /atra'par/ vt Inf. grab, seize, catch; net, obtain; deceive
atrás /a'tras/ adv behind, back; past; previously. **¡A.!** Back! **años a.,** years ago
atrasado /atra'saðo/ a slow (of clocks); backward; old-fashioned; hard-up, poor. **a. mental,** retarded person
atrasar /atra'sar/ vt to delay, retard; fix a later date than the true one; put back (clocks). vi be slow (clocks); be late; be left behind
atraso /a'traso/ m, delay; backwardness, dullness; slowness (clocks); lateness; pl arrears. **El reloj lleva cinco minutos de a.,** The watch is five minutes slow
atravesado /atraβe'saðo/ a slightly squint-eyed; mongrel, crossbreed; half-caste; ill-intentioned
atravesar /atraβe'sar/ vt irr to lay across, put athwart; cross, traverse; pierce; obstruct; Naut. lie to; vr be among, mingle (with); interrupt; interfere, take part; quarrel; occur, arise. See **confesar**
atrayente /atra'yente/ a attractive
atreverse /atre'βerse/ vr to dare, risk, venture; be overbold or insolent
atrevido /atre'βiðo/ a bold, audacious; hazardous, dangerous; brazen, impudent
atribución /atriβu'sion; atriβu'θion/ f, attribution; perquisite, attribute

atribuible /atri'βuiβle/ a attributable
atribuir /atri'βuir/ vt irr to impute, attribute; assign, turn over to; vr take upon oneself, assume. See **huir**
atributo /atri'βuto/ m, attribute, quality
atril /a'tril/ m, lectern, reading desk; music stand
atrincherar /atrintʃe'rar/ vt to protect with entrenchments; vr entrench oneself
atrio /'atrio/ m, atrium; hall, vestibule; Archit. parvis
atrocidad /atrosi'ðað; atroθi'ðað/ f, atrocity, cruelty; Inf. terrific amount; enormity, crime
atrofia /a'trofia/ f, atrophy
atrofiarse /atro'fiarse/ vr to atrophy
atrojarse /atro'harse/ vr Mexico to be stumped, be stuck (for an answer)
atronado /atro'naðo/ a harebrained, foolish
atronar /atro'nar/ vt irr to deafen, stun with noise; confuse, daze. See **tronar**
atropelladamente /atropeyaða'mente; atropeʎaða'mente/ adv in disorder, helter-skelter
atropellado /atrope'yaðo; atrope'ʎaðo/ a rash, foolhardy
atropellar /atrope'yar; atrope'ʎar/ vt to trample upon; thrust out of the way; knock down; run over (with a vehicle); crash; disregard, violate (feelings); insult, abuse; transgress; do hastily; vr act rashly
atropello /atro'peyo; atro'peʎo/ m, trampling; road accident; knocking over; upsetting; violation; outrage
atroz /a'ntros; a'troθ/ a atrocious, savage; monstrous, outrageous; Inf. terrific, enormous
atufar /atu'far/ vt to irritate, vex; vr grow irritated; turn sour (wine, etc.)
atún /a'tun/ m, tuna fish, tuna
aturdido /atur'ðiðo/ a reckless, scatterbrained, silly; thoughtless; stunned
aturdimiento /aturði'miento/ m, daze; confusion, bewilderment
aturdir /atur'ðir/ vt to daze; confuse, bewilder; amaze; stun
atusar /atu'sar/ vt to trim (hair, beard); Agr. prune; smooth down (hair); vr dress over-carefully
audacia /au'ðasia; au'ðaθia/ f, audacity
audaz /au'ðas; au'ðaθ/ a audacious, daring
audibilidad /auðiβili'ðað/ f, audibility
audición /auði'sion; auði'θion/ f, audition
audiencia /au'ðiensia; au'ðienθia/ f, audience, hearing; Law. audience; audience chamber
audífono /au'ðifono/ m, hearing aid
audioteca /auðio'teka/ f, audio library
auditor /auði'tor/ m, magistrate, judge
auditorio /auði'torio/ a auditory. m, audience
auge /'auhe/ m, Fig. zenith, height; Astron. apogee
augusto /au'gusto/ a august, awesome
aula /'aula/ f, lecture or class room; Poet. palace
aullar /au'yar; au'ʎar/ vi to howl; bay
aullido /au'yiðo; au'ʎiðo/ m, howl; baying
aumentar /aumen'tar/ (se) vt vi vr to increase, augment
aumentativo /aumenta'tiβo/ a Gram. augmentative
aumento /au'mento/ m, increase; progress; enlargement; Mexico postscript **ir en a.,** to increase; advance, progress; prosper
aun /a'un/ adv even. **A. los que viven lejos han de oíros,** Even those who live far must hear you. **a. así** or **a. siendo así,** even so. **a. ayer,** only yesterday. **a. cuando,** even if. **más a.,** even more. **ni a. si,** not even if.
aún /a'un/ adv still, yet. **A. no te creen** or **No te creen a.,** They still don't believe you ¿**A. se lo darás?** or ¿**Se lo darás a.?** You still give it to her?
aunque /'aunke/ conjunc although, even if, even though. It takes the Indicative referring to statement of fact and Subjunctive referring to a hypothesis, e.g. A. vino, no lo hizo, Although he came, he did not do it. A. él cantase yo no iría allí, Even though he sang (were to sing), I should not go there
aura /'aura/ f, zephyr, gentle breeze; popularity, approbation; aura. **a. epiléptica,** Med. epileptic aura
áureo /'aureo/ a gold, gilt; golden
auricular /auriku'lar/ a auricular. m, little finger; receiver, ear-piece (of a telephone); earphone (radio)

aurífero /au'rifero/ a gold-yielding, auriferous
auriga /au'riga/ m, charioteer
aurora /au'rora/ f, dawn; genesis, beginnings. **a. boreal,** aurora borealis, Northern Lights
auscultación /auskulta'sion; auskulta'θion/ f, Med. auscultation
auscultar /auskul'tar/ vt Med. to auscultate
ausencia /au'sensia; au'senθia/ f, absence. **en ausencia de,** in the absence of
ausentar /ausen'tar/ vt to send away; vr absent oneself
ausente /au'sente/ a absent. mf absent person
auspicio /aus'pisio; aus'piθio/ m, augury, prediction; favor, patronage; pl auspices
austeridad /austeri'ðað/ f, austerity; mortification of the flesh
austero /aus'tero/ a austere, ascetic; severe, harsh; honest, upright
austral /aus'tral/ a southerly, austral
australiano /austra'liano/ (**-na**) a and n Australian
austríaco /aus'triako/ (**-ca**) a and n Austrian
austrófilo /aus'trofilo/ a and n Austrophile
autenticación /autentika'sion; autentika'θion/ f, authentication
autenticar /autenti'kar/ vt to authenticate, attest; prove genuine
autenticidad /autentisi'ðað; autentiθi'ðað/ f, authenticity
auténtico /au'tentiko/ a authentic
autero, -a /au'tero/ mf, Lat. Am. car thief
auto /'auto/ m, Law. sentence, decision; Theat. one-act allegory (gen. religious); pl proceedings. **a. de fe,** auto-da-fé. **a. de reconocimiento,** search-warrant. **a. sacramental,** one-act religious drama on theme of mystery of the Eucharist. **hacer a. de fe de,** to burn at the stake
autobiografía /autoβiogra'fia/ f, autobiography
autobús /auto'βus/ m, motor bus, bus
autocitarse /autosi'tarse; autoθi'tarse/ vr to quote from one's own works
autoclave /auto'klaβe/ m, pressure cooker
autocracia /auto'krasia; auto'kraθia/ f, autocracy
autócrata /au'tokrata/ mf autocrat
autocrático /auto'kratiko/ a autocratic
autocrueldad /autokruel'dað/ f, self-inflicted pain
autodescubrimiento /autoðeskuβri'miento/ m, self-discovery
autodidacto /autoði'ðakto/ a autodidactic; self-educated, self-taught
autódromo /au'toðromo/ m, speedway
autógeno /au'toheno/ a autogenous, self-generating
autogiro /auto'hiro/ m, Aer. autogyro
autografía /autogra'fia/ f, autography
autográfico /auto'grafiko/ a autographic, in lithographic reproduction
autógrafo /au'tografo/ a autographical. m, autograph
autoinducción /autoinduk'sion; autoinduk'θion/ f, self-induction
autómata /au'tomata/ m, automaton
automático /auto'matiko/ a automatic. m, Sew. press stud
automatismo /automa'tismo/ m, automatism
automejoramiento /autome,hora'miento/ m, self-improvement
automóvil /auto'moβil/ m, automobile, motor car. a automatic
automovilismo /automoβi'lismo/ m, motoring
automovilista /automoβi'lista/ mf motorist
autonombrarse /autonom'βrarse/ vr to call oneself, go by the name of
autonomía /autono'mia/ f, autonomy
autónomo /au'tonomo/ a autonomous
autopista /auto'pista/ f, motor road
autopsia /au'topsia/ f, Med. autopsy, post-mortem
autor /au'tor/ (**-ra**) n agent, originator; author; inventor; Law. perpetrator
autoridad /autori'ðað/ f, authority; pomp, show
autoritario /autori'tario/ a authoritarian; authoritative

autorización /autorisa'sion; autoriθa'θion/ f, authorization
autorizado /autori'saðo; autori'θaðo/ a approved, authorized, responsible
autorizar /autori'sar; autori'θar/ vt to authorize; Law. attest, testify; cite, prove by reference; approve; exalt
autorretratarse /autorretra'tarse/ vr to have one's portrait painted, sit for one's portrait
autorretrato /autorre'trato/ m, self-portrait
autostopista /autosto'pista/ mf hitchhiker
autosugestión /autosuhes'tion/ f, autosuggestion
auxiliador /auksilia'ðor/ (**-ra**) a assistant; helpful. n helper, assistant
auxiliar /auksi'liar/ vt to help, aid; attend (the dying). m, Educ. assisting
auxiliaría /auksilia'ria/ f, Educ. lectureship
auxilio /auk'silio/ m, help, aid, assistance
aval /a'βal/ m, Com. endorsement; voucher
avalar /aβa'lar/ vt to enhance. **avalado por la tradición,** hallowed by tradition
avalentado /aβalen'taðo/ a boastful, bragging
avalorar /aβalo'rar/ vt to value, estimate; put spirit into, encourage
avance /a'βanse; a'βanθe/ m, advance; advance payment; balance sheet; attack
avanzada /aβan'saða; aβan'θaða/ f, Mil. advance guard
avanzado /aβan'saðo; aβan'θaðo/ a advanced, progressive
avanzar /aβan'sar; aβan'θar/ vt to advance; promote; vi advance; attack; grow late (time)
avanzo /a'βanso; a'βanθo/ m, balance sheet; price estimate
avaricia /aβa'risia; aβa'riθia/ f, greed, avarice
avaricioso, avariento /aβari'sioso, aβari'riento; aβari'θioso, aβa'riento/ a avaricious, greedy
avaro /a'βaro/ (**-ra**) a miserly; greedy. n miser
avasallador /aβasaya'ðor; aβasaʎa'ðor/ a dominating; Fig. overwhelming; enslaving
avasallar /aβasa'yar; aβasa'ʎar/ vt to subdue, dominate; vr become a vassal; surrender, yield
ave /'aβe/ f, bird. **a. de paso,** migratory bird; Fig. bird of passage. **a. de rapiña,** bird of prey. **a. fria,** Ornith. plover. **ave cantora,** songbird
avecinarse /aβesi'narse; aβeθi'narse/ vr to be approaching (e.g. el año que avecina, the coming year)
avellana /aβe'yana; aβe'ʎana/ f, hazel nut
avellano /aβe'yano; aβe'ʎano/ m, Bot. hazel
avemaría /aβema'ria/ f, Hail Mary (prayer); Angelus; rosary bead. Inf. **en un a.,** in a split second
avena /a'βena/ f, oats; Poet. oaten pipe. **a. loca,** wild oats
avenal /aβe'nal/ m, oatfield
avenar /aβe'nar/ vt to drain (land); drain off (liquids)
avenencia /aβe'nensia; aβe'nenθia/ f, agreement, arrangement; transaction; conformity, harmony
avenida /aβe'niða/ f, flood, spate; avenue; abundance; way, approach (to a place)
avenido /aβe'niðo/ a (with bien or mal) well or ill-suited
avenidor /aβeni'ðor/ (**-ra**) n arbitrator, mediator
avenir /aβe'nir/ vt irr to reconcile; vi happen (used in infinitive and third singular and plural); vr be reconciled; agree; compromise, give way; harmonize (things); (with con) get on with, agree with. See **venir**
aventador /aβenta'ðor/ m, Agr. winnower; pitchfork
aventajado /aβenta'haðo/ a outstanding, talented; advantageous. m, Mil. private who enjoys extra pay
aventajar /aβenta'har/ vt to improve, better; promote, prefer; excel; vr (with prep a) surpass, excel. **Te aventajo en diez años,** I'm ten years older than you
aventamiento /aβenta'miento/ m, winnowing
aventar /aβen'tar/ vt irr to fan; air, ventilate; winnow; Inf. drive away, expel; (of beasts) be inflated; Inf. flee; smell (bad meat). See **sentar**
aventón /aβen'ton/ m, Mexico hitch, lift, ride
aventura /aβen'tura/ f, adventure; chance, luck; risk, danger

aventurar /aβentu'rar/ *vt* to risk, hazard

aventurero /aβentu'rero/ **(-ra)** *a* adventurous; unscrupulous, intriguing; undisciplined (of troops). *n* adventurer

avergonzar /aβergon'sar/ aβergon'θar/ *vt irr* to shame; make shy, abash; *vr* be ashamed; be shy or sheepish. *Pres. Ind.* **avergüenzo, avergüenzas, avergüenza, avergüenzan.** *Pres. Subjunc.* **avergüence, avergüences, avergüence, avergüencen**

avería /aβe'ria/ *f,* aviary; damage (to merchandise); loss, harm; *Elec.* fault; breakdown. **a. gruesa,** general average (marine insurance)

averiarse /aβe'riarse/ *vr* to be damaged; deteriorate; break down

averiguable /aβeri'guaβle/ *a* examinable, investigable; discoverable

averiguación /aβerigua'sion; aβerigua'θion/ *f,* inquiry, investigation; discovery

averiguar /aβeri'guar/ *vt* to investigate, inquire into; discover, ascertain. **¡averígüelo Vargas!** Beats me!, Search me!

averigüetas /aβeri'guetas/ *mf, Lat. Am.* snoopers, nosy parker

averío /aβe'rio/ *m,* flock of birds

aversión /aβer'sion/ *f,* aversion, repugnance

avestruz /aβes'trus; aβes'truθ/ *m,* ostrich

avetado /aβe'taðo/ *a* veined, mottled, streaked

avezar /aβe'sar; aβe'θar/ *vt* to accustom; *vr* grow accustomed (to)

aviación /aβia'sion; aβia'θion/ *f,* aviation

aviador /aβia'ðor/ *m,* aviator

aviar /a'βiar/ *vt* to outfit, equip; prepare, make ready; *Inf.* speed up; caulk (ship). *Fig. Inf.* **estar aviado,** to be in a mess

avidez /aβi'ðes; aβi'ðeθ/ *f,* avidity, greed; longing, desire

ávido /'aβiðo/ *a* avid, greedy

avieso /a'βieso/ *a* twisted, crooked; ill-natured; sinister; *m Colombia* abortion

avillanado /aβiya'naðo; aβiʎa'naðo/ *a* countrified; gross, vulgar; boorish

avío /a'βio/ *m,* preparation, provision; picnic lunch; money advanced (to miners or laborers); *pl Inf.* equipment, tools. **avíos de pesca,** fishing tackle

avión /a'βion/ *m,* airplane; *Ornith.* martin or swift. **a. de bombardeo,** bomber. **a. de caza,** fighter plane. **a. de combate nocturno,** night fighter. **a. de hostigamiento,** interceptor. **a. de reacción,** jet airplane. **a. de transporte,** *Aer.* transport. **a. en picado,** divebomber. **a. taxi,** air taxi. **por a.,** by airmail **«Avión»** "Airmail"

avioneta /aβio'neta/ *f,* light airplane, small airplane

avisado /aβi'saðo/ *a* shrewd, sensible. **mal a.,** illadvised, imprudent

avisar /aβi'sar/ *vt* to inform, acquaint; warn; advise

aviso /a'βiso/ *m,* notice, announcement; warning; advice; care, caution; attention; shrewdness, prudence. **estar sobre a.,** to be on call; be on the alert

avispa /a'βispa/ *f,* wasp

avispado /aβis'paðo/ *a Inf.* smart, clever, quick; wide-awake

avispar /aβis'par/ *vt* to goad, prick; *Inf.* rouse, incite; *vr* be uneasy, fret

avispero /aβis'pero/ *m,* wasp's nest; swarm of wasps; *Fig. Inf.* hornet's nest

avispón /aβis'pon/ *m,* hornet

avistamiento /aβista'miento/ *m,* sighting, spotting (e.g. of a ship)

avistar /aβis'tar/ *vt* to descry, sight, spot; *vr* **avistarse con,** to interview

avituallar /aβitua'yar; aβitua'ʎar/ *vt* to victual, supply with food

avivar /aβi'βar/ *vt* to enliven; stimulate, encourage; stir (fire); trim (wicks); brighten (colors); inflame; vivify, invigorate; *vr* revive, recover

avizor /aβi'sor; aβi'θor/ *m,* watcher, spy. *a* watchful, vigilant

avizorar /aβiso'rar; aβiθo'rar/ *vt* to watch, spy upon

avutarda /aβu'tarða/ *f,* bustard

axila /ak'sila/ *f, Bot.* axil; *Anat.* axilla, armpit

axioma /ak'sioma/ *m,* axiom

axiomático /aksio'matiko/ *a* axiomatic

¡ay! /ai/ *interj* Alas! Woe is me! *m,* complaint, sigh

ayer /a'yer/ *adv* yesterday; a short while ago; in the past. *m,* past

ayllu /'aiju; 'aiʎu/ *m, Peru* Native American commune

ayo /'ayo/ *mf,* tutor

ayote /a'yote/ *m, Mexico, Central America* pumpkin

ayuda /a'yuða/ *f,* help, assistance; enema; clyster; watch dog. *m,* **a. de cámara,** valet

ayudador /ayuða'ðor/ **(-ra)** *a* helping, assisting. *n* helper

ayudante /ayu'ðante/ *m,* assistant; teaching assistant; *Mil.* adjutant. **a. a cátedra,** *Educ.* assistant lecturer. **a. de plaza,** post adjutant

ayudar /ayu'ðar/ *vt* to assist; help, aid; *vr* make an effort; avail oneself of another's help

ayunador /ayuna'ðor/ **(-ra)** *a* fasting. *n* faster; abstainer

ayunar /ayu'nar/ *vi* to fast

ayuno /a'yuno/ *m,* fast. *a* fasting; ignorant, unaware. **en a.** *or* **en ayunas,** before breakfast, fasting; *Inf.* ignorant, unaware

ayuntamiento /ayunta'miento/ *m,* meeting, assembly; municipal government; town hall; sexual union

azabache /asaβatʃe; aθa'βatʃe/ *m, Mineral.* jet

azada /a'saða; a'θaða/ *f,* spade; hoe

azadón /asa'ðon; aθa'ðon/ *m, Agr.* hoe

azafata /asa'fata; aθa'fata/ *f,* queen's waiting-maid *Obs.*; flight attendant

azafate /asa'fate; aθa'fate/ *m,* flat basket; small tray

azafrán /asa'fran; aθa'fran/ *m, Bot.* saffron; crocus

azafranado /asafra'naðo; aθafra'naðo/ *a* saffroncolored

azahar /asa'ar; aθa'ar/ *m,* flower of orange, lemon or sweet lime tree

azar /a'sar; a'θar/ *m,* chance, hazard; unexpected misfortune; losing card or throw of dice

azararse /asa'rarse; aθa'rarse/ *vr* to go wrong, fail (negotiations, etc.); grow nervous; become confused; blush

azaroso /asa'roso; aθa'roso/ *a* unlucky, ill-omened; hazardous

ázimo /'asimo; 'aθimo/ *a* unleavened (bread)

ázoe /'asoe; 'aθoe/ *m,* nitrogen

azogar /aso'gar; aθo'gar/ *vt* to silver (mirrors, etc.); slake lime; *vr* suffer from mercury poisoning; *Inf.* grow uneasy, be agitated

azogue /a'soge; a'θoge/ *m, Mineral.* mercury, quicksilver; market-place

azolve /a'solβe; a'θolβe/ *m,* silt

azoramiento /asora'miento; aθora'miento/ *m,* alarm, terror; confusion, stupefaction; incitement

azorar /aso'rar; aθo'rar/ *vt* to alarm, terrify; confuse, stun, dumbfound; excite, stimulate; encourage

azotacalles /asota'kayes; aθota'kaʎes/ *mf Inf.* idler, street loafer

azotaina /aso'taina; aθo'taina/ *f, Inf.* whipping, spanking

azotamiento /asota'miento; aθota'miento/ *m,* flogging, beating, whipping

azotar /aso'tar; aθo'tar/ *vt* to whip, beat, flog; scourge, ravage; lash against or strike repeatedly

azotazo /aso'taso; aθo'taθo/ *m,* spank

¡azote /a'sote; a'θote/ *m,* whip; scourge; lash, blow with a whip; spank, slap; misfortune, disaster. *Inf.* **azotes y galeras,** monotonous diet

azotea /aso'tea; aθo'tea/ *f,* flat terrace roof

azotera /aso'tera; aθo'tera/ *f, Lat. Am.* beating, thrashing

azozobrar /asosoβ'rar; aθoθoβ'rar/ *vt* party whip, whip

azteca /as'teka; aθ'teka/ *a* and *mf* Aztec

azúcar /a'sukar; a'θukar/ *m,* sugar. **a. blanco** *or* **a. de flor,** white sugar. **a. de pilón,** loaf sugar. **a. moreno,** brown sugar. **a. quebrado,** brown sugar. **a. y canela,** sorrel gray (of horses)

azucarado /asuka'raðo; aθuka'raðo/ *a* sugared, sugar-coated; *Inf.* honeyed, flattering

azucarar /asuka'rar; aθuka'rar/ *vt* to coat with sugar;

sweeten; *Inf.* soften, mitigate; *vr* crystallize; go sugary (jam)

azucarera /asuka'rera; aθuka'rera/ *f*, sugar-basin

azucarero /asuka'rero; aθuka'rero/ *a* sugar-producing (e.g. province)

azucarillo /asuka'riyo; aθuka'riʎo/ *m*, *Cul.* bar made of white of egg and sugar for sweetening water

azucena /asu'sena; aθu'θena/ *f*, white lily. **a. de agua,** water-lily

azuela /a'suela; a'θuela/ *f*, adze

azufre /a'sufre; a'θufre/ *m*, sulphur

azul /a'sul; a'θul/ *a* and *m*, blue. **a. celeste,** sky blue, azure. **a. de mar** *or* **a. marino,** navy blue. **a. de ultramar,** ultramarine. **a. turquí,** indigo

azulado /asu'laðo; aθu'laðo/ *a* bluish, blue

azulear /asule'ar; aθule'ar/ *vi* to look bluish, have a blue tint

azulejo /asu'leho; aθu'leho/ *m*, ornamental glazed tile

azurumbado /asurum'βaðo; aθurum'βaðo/ *m*, *Central America* dumb, silly, stupid; boozed up, drunk

azuzar /asu'sar; aθu'θar/ *vt* to set on (dogs); irritate, provoke; incite, urge

B

baba /'baβa/ *f*, saliva; secretion (of snails, etc.); viscous fluid (of plants). *Inf.* **caérsele (a uno) la b.,** to ooze satisfaction; be dumbfounded

babador, babero /baβa'ðor, ba'βero/ *m*, bib, feeder

babear /baβe'ar/ *vi* to dribble, slaver; *Fig. Inf.* slobber over, be sloppy

babel /ba'βel/ *m*, babel

babélico /ba'βeliko/ *a* Babelian, Babel-like; confused; unintelligible

Babia, estar en /'baβia, es'tar en/ to be daydreaming

babieca /ba'βieka/ *mf Inf.* stupid person. **Babieca** *f*, the Cid's horse

Babilonia /baβi'lonia/ Babylon

babilónico /baβi'loniko/ *a* Babylonian

bable /'baβle/ *m*, Asturian (language)

babor /ba'βor/ *m*, *Naut.* larboard, port

babosa /ba'βosa/ *f*, slug; young onion

baboso /ba'βoso/ *a* slavering; *Fig. Inf.* "sloppy"; *Inf.* incompetent, useless; *Lat. Am.* dumb, stupid

babucha /ba'βutʃa/ *f*, heelless slipper, babouche

babuino /ba'βuino/ *m*, *Zool.* baboon

baca /'baka/ *f*, luggage carrier (on roof of bus, etc.)

bacalao /baka'lao/ *m*, codfish

bacanales /baka'nales/ *f pl*, Bacchanalia

bacante /ba'kante/ *f*, Bacchante

bacará /baka'ra/ *m*, baccarat (card game)

baceta /ba'seta; ba'θeta/ *f*, pool (in card games)

bache /'batʃe/ *m*, rut (in road); pothole

bacheo /ba'tʃeo/ *m*, repairing of streets

bachiller /batʃi'yer; batʃi'ʎer/ *mf* high-school graduate *m*, *Inf.* babbler. *f.* **bachillera,** *Inf.* blue-stocking; garrulous woman

bachillerarse /batʃiye'rarse; batʃiʎe'rarse/ *vr* to graduate as a bachelor

bachillerato /batʃiye'rato; batʃiʎe'rato/ *m*, baccalaureate, bachelor's degree

bacho /'batʃo/ *m*, *Peru* fib, tall tale

bacía /ba'sia; ba'θia/ *f*, bowl; barber's circular shaving-dish; barber's trade sign

bacilar /basi'lar; baθi'lar/ *a* bacillary

bacilo /ba'silo; ba'θilo/ *m*, bacillus

bacterial, bacteriano /bakte'rial, bakte'riano/ *a* bacterial

bactericida /bakteri'siða; bakteri'θiða/ *m*, bactericide

bacteriología /bakteriolo'hia/ *f*, bacteriology

bacteriológico /bakterio'lohiko/ *a* bacteriological

bacteriólogo /bakte'riologo/ *m*, bacteriologist

báculo /'bakulo/ *m*, staff; walking-stick; *Fig.* support. **b. episcopal,** bishop's crozier

badajo /ba'ðaho/ *m*, clapper (of a bell); chatterbox, gossip

badana /ba'ðana/ *f*, cured sheepskin, chamois leather, washleather; sweat band; *Inf.* **zurrar (a uno) la b.,** to take the hide off; insult

badén /ba'ðen/ *m*, channel made by rain, furrow; conduit

badulaque /baðu'lake/ *m*, *Inf.* good-for-nothing

bagaje /ba'gahe/ *m*, *Mil.* baggage; beast of burden, transport animal; luggage

bagatela /baga'tela/ *f*, trifle, oddment, bagatelle

bagazo /ba'gaso; ba'gaθo/ *m*, oilcake, bagasse

bagual /ba'gual/ *a WH* untamed, wild; doltish, dull. *m*, untamed horse, wild horse

bahía /ba'ia/ *f*, bay, harbor

bailable /bai'laβle/ *a* dance (of music). *m*, *Theat.* dance number

bailador /baila'ðor/ **(-ra)** *n* dancer

bailar /bai'lar/ *vi* to dance; spin around. **b. al son que le toca,** to adapt oneself to circumstances

bailarín /baila'rin/ *a* dancing. *m*, professional dancer. **b. de cuerda, bailarín de la cuerda floja,** tightrope dancer

bailarina /baila'rina/ *f*, ballerina

baile /'baile/ *m*, dance; ball; ballet. **b. de máscaras, b. de trajes,** fancy-dress ball. **b. de San Vito,** St. Vitus' dance. **b. ruso,** ballet

bailotear /bailote'ar/ *vi* to jig about; dance

baja /'baha/ *f*, drop, diminution; fall (in price, etc.); *Mil.* casualty; discharge. *Inf.* **darse de b.,** to leave an employment

bajada /ba'haða/ *f*, descent, fall; slope, incline; hollow, depression. **b. de aguas,** roof gutter

bajalato /baha'lato/ *m*, pashalik

bajamar /baha'mar/ *f*, low tide

bajamente /baha'mente/ *adv* basely, abjectly

bajar /ba'har/ *vi* to descend; go down; get off; drop; fall, decrease; *vt* lower, take down, bring down; let down; dismount, alight; bend, droop; drop; reduce (price); *Fig.* lower (voices); humiliate, humble; download. **b. a tierra,** to step ashore; **b. la cabeza ante,** to submit to (e.g. a judgment) *vr* alight, dismount; humble oneself

bajel /ba'hel/ *m*, *Naut.* galley, ship

bajeza /ba'hesa; ba'heθa/ *f*, base action; meanness; *Fig.* humble estate, lowliness. **b. de ánimo,** timorousness

bajío /ba'hio/ *m*, *Naut.* shallows, shoal; depression, hollow

bajista /ba'hista/ *mf* speculator, bear (Stock Exchange)

bajo /'baho/ *a* low; short, not tall; downcast; under; subordinate; pale (of colors); humble (origin); base; coarse, vulgar; cheap (price); low (sounds). *m*, depth; shoal, sand bank; *Mus.* bass; *pl* petticoats, skirts; horses' hoofs. *adv* beneath, below. *prep* under, beneath. **b. juramento,** upon oath. **bajo relieve,** bas relief. **en voz baja,** in a low voice. **planta baja,** ground floor. **por lo b.,** in a whisper; in secret, on the sly

bajolatino /bahola'tino/ *a* Low Latin

bajón /ba'hon/ *m*, *Mus.* bassoon; bassoon player; *Fig. Inf.* downfall

bajonista /baho'nista/ *mf* bassoon player

bala /'bala/ *f*, bullet, ball; bale. **b. fría,** spent bullet. **b. luminosa,** tracer bullet. **b. perdida,** stray bullet. *Inf.* **como una b.,** like a shot

balacear /balase'ar; balaθe'ar/ *vt*, *Central America, Mexico* to shoot (at)

balada /ba'laða/ *f*, ballad, song

baladí /bala'ði/ *a* worthless, insignificant

baladro /ba'laðro/ *m*, yell, outcry, shout

baladrón /bala'ðron/ *a* braggart

baladronada /balaðro'naða/ *f*, bravado, bragging

balagar /bala'gar/ *m*, straw rick

balance /ba'lanse; ba'lanθe/ *m*, balance; swinging, oscillation; rolling, rocking (of a ship, etc.); doubt, insecurity, *Com*. balance; *Com*. balance sheet **b. de situación** *Lat. Am*. balance sheet

balancear /balanse'ar; balanθe'ar/ *vi* to swing; oscillate; vacillate, hesitate; *vt* balance; *vr* balance oneself; rock or swing oneself

balanceo /balan'seo; balan'θeo/ *m*, balancing; rocking; swinging; rolling (of a ship, etc.)

balancín /balan'sin; balan'θin/ *m*, swing-bar; whipple-tree; balance beam; tight-rope dancer's pole; minting-mill; yoke (for carrying pails); *pl Naut*. lifts

balandra /ba'landra/ *f*, *Naut*. sloop, cutter

balanza /ba'lansa; ba'lanθa/ *f*, balance; scale; judgment; comparison. **b. de comercio**, balance of trade. **en balanzas**, in doubt or danger, in the balance

balar /ba'lar/ *vi* to bleat (sheep)

balasto /ba'lasto/ *m*, *Rail*. ballast

balaustrada /balaus'traða/ *f*, balustrade

balaustre /bala'ustre/ *m*, baluster

balazo /ba'laso; ba'laθo/ *m*, shot; bullet wound

balbuceo /balβu'seo; balβu'θeo/ *m*, stammering; babbling; lisping; **balbuceos** *Fig*. beginnings, early stages (e.g. *los b. de la literatura yídica*, the beginnings of Yiddish literature)

balbuciente /balβu'siente; balβu'θiente/ *a* stammering; babbling; lisping

balbucir /balβu'sir; balβu'θir/ *vi irr defective* to stammer; lisp; babble; read hesitantly. See **lucir**

Balcanes, los /bal'kanes, los/ the Balkans

balcón /bal'kon/ *m*, balcony

baldaquín /balda'kin/ *m*, canopy, baldachin

baldar /bal'dar/ *vt* to cripple; impede, obstruct

balde /'balde/ *m*, bucket

balde /'balde/ **(en)** *adv* in vain. **de b.**, gratis, free of charge

baldear /balde'ar/ *vt Naut*. to wash the decks

baldío /bal'dio/ *a* untilled; fallow; useless, worthless; vagrant

baldón /bal'don/ *m*, insult; dishonor

baldonar /baldo'nar/ *vt* to insult

baldosa /bal'dosa/ *f*, paving stone; tile

baldrufa /bal'drufa/ *f*, top, spinning top

balduque /bal'duke/ *m*, red tape

Baleares, las Islas /bale'ares, las 'islas/ the Balearic Islands

baleárico /bale'ariko/ *a* Balearic

balido /ba'liðo/ *m*, bleat, bleating

balística /ba'listika/ *f*, ballistics

baliza /ba'lisa; ba'liθa/ *f*, *Naut*. buoy, beacon

balizamiento /balisa'miento; baliθa'miento/ *m*, marking with beacons, marking with buoys; traffic signs and signals

ballena /ba'yena; ba'ʎena/ *f*, whale; whalebone

ballenero /baye'nero; baʎe'nero/ *a* whaling. *m*, whaler

ballesta /ba'yesta; ba'ʎesta/ *f*, crossbow; spring (of carriages)

ballestería /bayeste'ria; baʎeste'ria/ *f*, archery; crossbowmen

ballestero /bayes'tero; baʎes'tero/ *m*, archer; crossbowman; crossbow maker

balneario /balne'ario/ *a* pertaining to public baths; bathing; holiday; spa. *m*, watering place, spa

balompié /balom'pie/ *m*, football (game)

balón /ba'lon/ *m*, large ball; football; *Chem*. balloon; bundle; bale. **b. de ensayo**, *Fig*. feeler

baloncesto /balon'sesto; balon'θesto/ *m*, *Sports*. basketball

balota /ba'lota/ *f*, ballot

balotaje /balo'tahe/ *m*, balloting; run-off election

balotar /balo'tar/ *vi* to ballot

balsa /'balsa/ *f*, pond; raft

balsadera /balsa'ðera/ *f*, ferry

bálsamo /'balsamo/ *m*, balm

balsero /bal'sero/ *m*, ferryman; rafter (person fleeing a country by raft, rowboat, etc.)

báltico /'baltiko/ *a* Baltic. **el Mar Báltico** the Baltic Sea

baluarte /ba'luarte/ *m*, bulwark; bastion; protection, defense

bamboleante /bambole'ante/ *a* swaying, swinging; *Fig*. tottering (e.g. empire)

bambolearse /bambole'arse/ *vr* to sway; swing; totter; be shaky; stagger

bamboleo /bambo'leo/ *m*, rocking; swinging; tottering; staggering; reeling

bambolla /bam'βoya; bam'βoʎa/ *f*, *Inf*. ostentation, swank

bambú /bam'βu/ *m*, bamboo

banal /ba'nal/ *a* banal, commonplace

banana /ba'nana/ *f*, banana

banasta /ba'nasta/ *f*, big basket

banastero /banas'tero/ **(-ra)** *n* basket maker or dealer

banca /'banka/ *f*, bench; card game; stall; *Com*. banking

bancada /ban'kaða/ *f*, rowing seat

bancal /ban'kal/ *m*, oblong garden plot; terrace

bancario /ban'kario/ *a* banking, bank, banker

bancarrota /banka'rrota/ *f*, bankruptcy. **hacer b.**, to go bankrupt

banco /'banko/ *m*, form, bench; rowing seat; settle; seat; bench; *Com*. bank; *Naut*. bar, shoal; school (of fish). **b. azul**, government benches in Spanish Parliament. **b. de arena**, sand-bank. **b. de descuento**, discount bank. **b. de emisión, banco emisor**, bank of issue. **b. de hielo**, iceberg. **b. de nivel**, benchmark

banda /'banda/ *f*, wide ribbon; sash; ribbon, insignia; strip; border; party, group; gang; flock (of birds); zone, belt; side (of ship); *Mus*. band; cushion (billiards); *Herald*. bar, bend. **b. elástica**, rubber band. *Naut*. **dar a la b.**, to lie along

bandada /ban'daða/ *f*, flock (of birds)

bandeja /ban'deha/ *f*, tray, salver

bandera /ban'dera/ *f*, banner, flag; colors, standard. **b. de popa**, ensign. **jurar la b.**, (*Mil. Nav*.) to take the oath of allegiance

banderilla /bande'riya; bande'riʎa/ *f*, banderilla (bullfighting)

banderillear /banderiye'ar; banderiʎe'ar/ *vt* to put banderillas on bulls

banderillero /banderi'yero; banderi'ʎero/ *m*, man who puts banderillas on bulls

banderín /bande'rin/ *m*, *dim* small flag; recruiting post

banderizo /bande'riso; bande'riθo/ *a* factious; vehement, excitable

banderola /bande'rola/ *f*, banderole, pennon; bannerole

bandido /ban'diðo/ **(-da)** *a* and *n* outlaw, fugitive. *m*, bandit; highwayman; rogue, desperado

bando /'bando/ *m*, proclamation; order; faction, group, party

bandola /ban'dola/ *f*, *Mus*. pandora, pandore

bandolerismo /bandole'rismo/ *m*, brigandage

bandolero /bando'lero/ *m*, robber, footpad, brigand

bandolín /bando'lin/ *m*, mandolin

bandurria /ban'durria/ *f*, *Mus*. mandolin

banjo /'banho/ *m*, banjo

banquero /ban'kero/ *m*, banker

banqueta /ban'keta/ *f*, three-legged stool; seat; footstool; *Mexico* sidewalk

banquete /ban'kete/ *m*, banquet, feast

banquetear /bankete'ar/ *vt* and *vi* to banquet

banqueteo /banke'teo/ *m*, banqueting, feasting

bañadera /baɲa'ðera/ *f*, *Argentina* bathtub

bañado /ba'ɲaðo/ *m*, chamber pot; *WH* marshy land, marsh; **bañados** *pl* marsh

bañador /baɲa'ðor/ **(-ra)** *a* bathing. *n* bather. *m*, bathing dress; bath, vat

bañar /ba'ɲar/ *vt* to bathe; coat, cover; dip; lave, wash; *Fig*. bathe (of sunlight, etc.). *vr* take a bath; bathe

bañera /ba'ɲera/ *f*, bath attendant; bathtub

bañista /ba'ɲista/ *mf* bather; one who takes spa waters

baño /'baɲo/ *m*, bathing; bath; bathroom; bathtub; bagnio, Turkish prison; covering, coat; *pl* mineral baths, spa. **b. de China** *Argentina* shower bath, shower **b. de mar,** sea bath. **b. de María,** double saucepan. **b. de sol,** sunbath. **casa de baños,** public baths. **cuarto de b.,** bathroom

bao /'bao/ *m, Naut.* beam

baptisterio /baptis'terio/ *m,* baptistery; *Eccl.* font

baquelita /bake'lita/ *f,* bakelite

baqueta /ba'keta/ *f,* ramrod; *pl* drumsticks; *Mil.* gauntlet

bar /bar/ *m,* bar; café

barahúnda /bara'unda/ *f,* See **baraúnda**

baraja /ba'raha/ *f,* pack (of cards); game of cards

barajar /bara'har/ *vt* to shuffle (cards); jumble, mix; *vi* quarrel

baranda /ba'randa/ *f,* handrail, banister; cushion (of billiard table)

barandilla /baran'diya; baran'diʎa/ *f, dim* railing

barata /ba'rata/ *f, Mexico* bargain sale, sale

baratija /bara'tiha/ *f,* (gen. *pl*) trifle, oddment

baratillo /bara'tiyo; bara'tiʎo/ *m,* second-hand article, frippery; second-hand shop or stall; bargain counter

barato /ba'rato/ *a* cheap. *m,* bargain sale. *adv* cheaply

baratura /bara'tura/ *f,* cheapness

baraúnda /bara'unda/ *f,* uproar, confusion

barba /'barβa/ *f,* chin; beard; whiskers; fin; barb (of a feather); *m,* actor who plays old men. *f pl,* fibers of plants. **b. bien poblada,** a thick beard. **barbas de ballena,** whalebone. *Fig. Inf.* **echar a las barbas,** to throw in a person's face. **en la barba, en las barbas,** to ones face (e.g. *Me lo dijeron en las barbas.* They told me so to my face). **hacer la b.,** to shave; *Inf.* annoy

barbacoa /barβa'koa/ *f, West Hem.* barbecue; trellis (for climbing plants)

barbado /bar'βaðo/ *a* bearded. *m,* shoot; sucker; transplanted plant

barbárico /bar'βariko/ *a* barbarian; barbaric

barbaridad /barβari'ðað/ *f,* barbarity; blunder; atrocity; outrage; *Inf.* huge amount. **¡Qué b.!** How awful! You don't say so!

barbarie /bar'βarie/ *f,* barbarism; barbarity, cruelty

barbarismo /barβa'rismo/ *m,* barbarism; cruelty; barbarians

bárbaro /'barβaro/ **(-ra)** *a* and *n* barbarian. *a* fierce; headstrong; uncivilized. **como un b.,** like crazy (e.g. *estudiar como un b.,* to study like crazy)

barbechar /barβe'tʃar/ *vt* to plow; leave fallow

barbecho /bar'βetʃo/ *m, Agr.* fallow; first plowing

barbería /barβe'ria/ *f,* barber shop

barbero /bar'βero/ *m,* barber; *Guatemala, Mexico* flatterer

barbihecho /bar'βietʃo/ *a* fresh-shaved

barbilampiño /barβilam'piɲo/ *a* smooth-faced, beardless, clean-shaven

barbilindo /barβi'lindo/ *a* dandified, dappy; *m,* dandy

barbilla /bar'βiya; bar'βiʎa/ *f,* point of the chin; chin. **acariciar la b.** (**de**), to chuck under the chin

barbiquejo /barβi'keho/ *m, Naut.* bobstay; hat-guard

barbudo /bar'βuðo/ *a* heavily bearded

barbulla /bar'βuya; bar'βuʎa/ *f, Inf.* babble, chatter, murmur of voices

barca /'barka/ *f,* small boat; bark; barge. **b. de pasaje,** ferryboat. **b. plantaminas** minelayer

barcada /bar'kaða/ *f,* boat-load; ferry crossing

barcaza /bar'kasa/ *f, Naut.* lighter; barge. **b. de desembarco,** landingcraft

barcelonés /barselo'nes/ **(-esa)** *a* and *n* of or from Barcelona

barcino /bar'sino; bar'θino/ *a* ruddy (of animals); fawn and white; *Inf.* turncoat (of politicians)

barco /'barko/ *m,* boat; ship; hollow, rut. **b. barredero,** trawler. **b. siembraminas,** minelayer

barda /'barða/ *f,* horse armor; thatch; shingle; (Mexico) cement fence, cement wall

bardal /bar'ðal/ *m,* thatched wall; mud wall

bardar /bar'ðar/ *vt* to thatch

bardo /'barðo/ *m,* poet, bard

bario /'bario/ *m,* barium

barítono /ba'ritono/ *m,* baritone

barloventear /barloβente'ar/ *vi Naut.* to tack; ply to windward; *Inf.* wander about

barlovento /barlo'βento/ *m, Naut.* windward

barnacla /bar'nakla/ *m,* barnacle

barniz /bar'nis; bar'niθ/ *m,* varnish; glaze; smattering, veneer

barnizar /barni'sar; barni'θar/ *vt* to varnish; glaze

barométrico /baro'metriko/ *a* barometric

barómetro /ba'rometro/ *m,* barometer

barón /ba'ron/ *m,* baron

baronesa /baro'nesa/ *f,* baroness

barquero /bar'kero/ *m,* boatman; bargee; *Ent.* waterboatman

barquillero /barki'yero; barki'ʎero/ *m,* seller of wafers; waffle-iron

barquillo /bar'kiyo; bar'kiʎo/ *m,* wafer, cornet

barquín /bar'kin/ *m,* furnace bellows

barra /'barra/ *f,* bar; ingot; railing (in courtroom); sandbank; fault (in cloth); lever, crossbar; (in cricket) bail; *Mus.* bar. **b. de jabón de afeitar,** shaving-soap. **a barras derechas,** without deceit

barrabasada /barraβa'saða/ *f, Inf.* wilfulness, escapade

barraca /ba'rraka/ *f,* cabin, hut; stall; sideshow; *Lat. Am.* barracks. **b. de tiro,** shooting gallery

barracón /barra'kon/ *m,* side-show; stall

barragana /barra'gana/ *f,* concubine, mistress

barranca /ba'rranka/ *f,* **barranco** *m,* furrow, channel, rut; gorge; difficulty, fix

barrancoso /barran'koso/ *a* rutty, uneven

barredor /barre'ðor/ **(-ra)** *n* sweeper

barredura /barre'ðura/ *f,* sweeping; *pl* sweepings; rubbish

barrena /ba'rrena/ *f,* borer, gimlet, drill, auger. *Aer.* **b. de cola,** tail-spin

barrenar /barre'nar/ *vt* to drill, bore; blast (in quarries)

barrendero /barren'dero/ **(-ra)** *n* sweeper, scavenger

barrenero /barre'nero/ *m,* driller; blaster

barreno /ba'rreno/ *m,* blast hole; bore, drill; vanity; *Lat. Am.* mania, pet peeve

barreño /ba'rreno/ *m,* earthenware bowl (for dish washing, etc.)

barrer /ba'rrer/ *vt* to sweep; *Fig.* clear, make a clean sweep

barrera /ba'rrera/ *f,* barrier; barricade; *Fig.* obstacle. **b. de golpe,** automatic gate (at level crossings, etc.). **b. de minas,** minefield

barriada /ba'rriaða/ *f,* district; quarter (of a city); *Peru* slum, shanty town

barrica /ba'rrika/ *f,* cask; barrel

barricada /barri'kaða/ *f,* barricade

barriga /ba'rriga/ *f, Inf.* belly

barrigón, barrigudo /barri'gon, barri'guðo/ *a* pot-bellied

barril /ba'rril/ *m,* barrel; cask; water-butt

barrilero /barri'lero/ *m,* cooper

barrio /'barrio/ *m,* district, quarter; suburb. **barrios bajos,** slums, back streets. **el otro b.,** the other world, Eternity

barrizal /barri'sal; barri'θal/ *m,* muddy place; claypit

barro /'barro/ *m,* mud; clay; earthenware drinking vessel; *Inf.* money

barroco /ba'rroko/ *a* baroque

barroso /ba'rroso/ *a* muddy; pimpled; mud-colored

barrote /ba'rrote/ *m,* thick iron bar; stave, bond

barruntar /barrun'tar/ *vt* to conjecture; suspect

barrunto /ba'rrunto/ *m,* conjecture; indication, sign

bártulos /'bartulos/ *m pl,* household goods; *Fig.* means, wherewithal

barullo /ba'ruyo; ba'ruʎo/ *m, Inf.* confusion, disorder; mob

basa /'basa/ *f,* base; *Archit.* pedestal; foundation, basis

basalto /ba'salto/ *m,* basalt

basar /ba'sar/ *vt* to base, place on a base; *Fig.* found, base; *vr* (*with en*) rely upon, base oneself on

basca /'baska/ *f,* (gen. *pl*) nausea; retching; wave of anger

báscula /'baskula/ *f*, weighing-machine; platform-scale; weigh-bridge
base /'base/ *f*, base; (*Chem. Geom. Mil.*) base; basis; *Archit.* pedestal; *Mus.* root. **sin b.**, baseless
básico /'basiko/ *a* basic
Basilea /basi'lea/ Basel, Basle
basílica /ba'silika/ *f*, palace; church, basilica
basquear /baske'ar/ *vi* to retch; feel squeamish
bastante /bas'tante/ *a* sufficient, enough. *adv* sufficiently; enough; fairly; a good deal; somewhat. **Hace b. calor,** It is quite hot. **Tengo b.,** I have enough. **Tenemos b. tiempo,** We have sufficient time
bastar /bas'tar/ *vi* to suffice. **¡Basta!** Enough! No more! Stop! **¡Basta de...!** Enough of...! **Basta decir que...,** Suffice it to say that...
bastardía /bastar'ðia/ *f*, bastardy, illegitimacy; baseness, meanness
bastardilla /bastar'ðiya; bastar'ðiʎa/ *f*, *Print.* italics
bastardo /bas'tarðo/ **(-da)** *a* bastard; spurious. *n* bastard
bastear /baste'ar/ *vt Sew.* to baste
bastidor /basti'ðor/ *m*, embroidery frame; *Art.* stretcher (for canvas); *Theat.* wing; *Mech.* underframe; chassis, carriage; frame (of a window). *Fig.* **entre bastidores,** behind the scenes
bastilla /bas'tiya; bas'tiʎa/ *f*, *Sew.* hem; bastille
bastimentar /bastimen'tar/ *vt* to provision; supply
bastimento /basti'mento/ *m*, supplies; provisioning
bastión /bas'tion/ *m*, bastion
basto /'basto/ *m*, pack-saddle; ace of clubs; clubs (cards). *a* rude; tough; *Fig.* unpolished, rough
bastón /bas'ton/ *m*, cane, walking-stick; rod (of office); truncheon. **b. de junquillo,** Malacca cane. **empuñar el b.,** to take control, take over. **meter el b.,** to mediate
bastonear /bastone'ar/ *vt* to cane; stir with a stick
basura /ba'sura/ *f*, rubbish, refuse; dung; sweepings
basural /basu'ral/ *m*, *Lat. Am.* garbage dump
basurero /basu'rero/ *m*, garbage collector; dunghill, garbage dump; kitchen middens; trash bin
bata /'bata/ *f*, dressing-gown; smoking-jacket; old-fashioned dress; overall, smock
batacazo /bata'kaso; bata'kaθo/ *m*, bump, noise of a fall; *Polit.* dark horse
batahola /bata'ola/ *f*, *Inf.* hurly-burly, hubbub
batalla /ba'taya; ba'taʎa/ *f*, battle; *Fig.* struggle, conflict; tournament; *Art.* battle-piece. **b. campal,** pitched battle
batallador /bataya'ðor; bataʎa'ðor/ *a* fighting, warlike
batallar /bata'yar; bata'ʎar/ *vi* to battle, fight; dispute, argue; hesitate
batallón /bata'yon; bata'ʎon/ *m*, battalion
batata /ba'tata/ *f*, sweet potato, yam
batayola /bata'yola/ *f*, *Naut.* rail
batea /ba'tea/ *f*, wooden tray; punt
bateador, -a /batea'ðor/ *mf*, *Lat. Am.* batter (baseball)
batear /bate'ar/ *vt*, *Lat. Am.* to bat
batería /bate'ria/ *f*, (*Mil. Elec. Naut.*) battery. **b. de cocina,** kitchen utensils. **b. de pilas secas,** dry battery. **b. de teatro,** stage lights. **b. eléctrica,** electric battery
baticola /bati'kola/ *f*, crupper
batida /ba'tiða/ *f*, game drive; attack; *Metall.* beating
batido /ba'tiðo/ *a* beaten (of metals); shot (of silk); trodden, worn (roads, etc.). *m*, *Cul.* batter; hunting party
batidor /bati'ðor/ *m*, beater; scout; outrider; hair comb; *Cul.* whisk. **b. de oro** (*or* **de plata**)**,** gold (*or* silver) beater
batiente /ba'tiente/ *m*, jamb (of door, etc.); damper (piano); leaf (of door); place where sea beats against cliffs, etc.
batihoja /bati'oha/ *m*, gold beater; metal worker
batimiento /bati'miento/ *m*, beating
batín /ba'tin/ *m*, smoking-jacket; man's dressing-gown
batintín /batin'tin/ *m*, Chinese gong
batir /ba'tir/ *vt* to beat, slap; demolish; dismantle,

take down (stall, etc.); hammer, flatten; batter; *Fig.* beat (of sun, etc.); stir; pound; churn; comb (hair); vanquish, defeat; coin; reconnoiter, beat; throw down or drop; *vr* fight; swoop (birds of prey). **b. palmas,** to clap, applaud
batista /ba'tista/ *f*, cambric, batiste
baturrillo /batu'rriyo; batu'rriʎo/ *m*, hodgepodge (gen. food); *Inf.* farrago, medley
batuta /ba'tuta/ *f*, baton, conductor's wand. **llevar la b.,** *Inf.* boss the show, call the music, be in charge, to rule the roost
baúl /ba'ul/ *m*, trunk; *Inf.* belly; *Lat. Am. also* trunk (of a car) **b. escaparate** *or* **b. mundo,** wardrobe trunk
bauprés /bau'pres/ *m*, *Naut.* bowsprit
bausán /bau'san/ **(-ana)** *n* guy, strawman; puppet; fool, idiot; lazybones
bautismo /bau'tismo/ *m*, baptism
bautista /bau'tista/ *m*, baptizer, baptist. **San Juan B.,** St. John the Baptist
bautisterio /bautis'terio/ *m*, baptistery
bautizar /bauti'sar; bauti'θar/ *vt* to baptize, christen; *Inf.* nickname; *Inf.* water (wine); accidentally shower with water
bautizo /bau'tiso; bau'tiθo/ *m*, baptism; christening party
baya /'baia/ *f*, berry
bayeta /ba'yeta/ *f*, baize; flannel
bayo /'bayo/ **(-ya)** *a* bay (of horses)
Bayona /ba'yona/ Bayonne
bayoneta /bayo'neta/ *f*, bayonet. **b. calada,** fixed bayonet
bayonetazo /bayone'taso; bayone'taθo/ *m*, bayonet thrust
baza /'basa; 'baθa/ *f*, tricks taken (playing cards). *Fig. Inf.* **meter b.,** to stick one's oar in
bazar /ba'sar; ba'θar/ *m*, bazaar; shop, store; department store
bazo /'baso; 'baθo/ *m*, *Anat.* spleen. *a* yellow-brown
bazucar, bazuquear /basu'kar, basuke'ar; baθu'kar, baθuke'ar/ *vt* to shake or stir (liquids)
bazuqueo /basu'keo; baθu'keo/ *m*, shaking or stirring of liquids
be /be/ *f*, letter B. *m*, baa
beata /be'ata/ *f*, devout woman; *Inf.* pious hypocrite, prude; Sister of Mercy; over-religious woman
beatería /beate'ria/ *f*, sanctimoniousness; bigotry
beatificación /beatifika'sion; beatifika'θion/ *f*, beatification
beatificar /beatifi'kar/ *vt* to make happy; sanctify; beatify
beatífico /bea'tifiko/ *a* beatific
beatitud /beati'tuð/ *f*, blessedness, beatitude; happiness
beato /be'ato/ **(-ta)** *a* happy; blessed, beatified; devout; prudish. *n* devout person; over-pious person
beba /'beβa/ *f*, *Argentina* baby (girl)
bebé /be'βe/ *m*, baby
bebedero /beβe'ðero/ *a* drinkable. *m*, drinking trough or place
bebedizo /beβe'ðiso; beβe'ðiθo/ *a* drinkable. *m*, draught of medicine; love-potion; poisonous drink
bebedor /beβe'ðor/ **(-ra)** *a* drinkable. *n* drinker; toper
beber /be'βer/ *vt* to drink; absorb; *vi* toast, drink to the health (of); tipple. *m*, drinking; drink
bebida /be'βiða/ *f*, drink; beverage; alcoholic liquor
beca /'beka/ *f*, academic scarf or sash; scholarship, exhibition
becado /be'kaðo, be'kario/ *m*, exhibitioner, scholarship holder
becerra /be'serra; be'θerra/ *f*, calf; *Bot.* snapdragon
becerro /be'serro; be'θerro/ *m*, bullock; bull calf; calf-skin. **b. marino,** *Zool.* seal
Beda el Venerable /'beða el bene'raβle/ the Venerable Bede
bedel /be'ðel/ *m*, beadle; servitor; university porter
beduino /be'ðuino/ **(-na)** *a* and *n* Bedouin. *m*, savage, bloodthirsty man
befar /be'far/ *vt* to mock, ridicule

befo /'befo/ *a* thick-lipped; knock-kneed. *m*, animal's lip

begonia /be'gonia/ *f*, *Bot.* begonia

bejín /be'hin/ *m*, *Bot.* puff-ball; spoiled child

bejuco /be'huko/ *m*, rattan

beldad /bel'daδ/ *f*, beauty; belle

beldar /bel'dar/ *vt Agr.* to winnow

Belén /be'len/ Bethlehem

belén /be'len/ *m*, nativity, manager; *Inf.* bedlam; *Inf.* gossip

belfo /'belfo/ *a* thick-lipped

belga /'belga/ *a* and *mf* Belgian

Bélgica /'belhika/ Belgium

bélgico /'belhiko/ *a* Belgian

Belgrado /bel'graδo/ Belgrade

Belice /be'lise; be'liθe/ Belize

belicista /beli'sista; beli'θista/ *adj* war, militaristic; *mf* warmonger

bélico /'beliko/ *a* warlike, military

belicoso /beli'koso/ *a* bellicose, aggressive; warlike

beligerancia /belihe'ransia; belihe'ranθia/ *f*, belligerency

beligerante /belihe'rante/ *a* and *mf* belligerent

belitre /be'litre/ *a Inf.* knavish, cunning

bellaco /be'yako; be'ʎako/ *f* (**-ca**) *a* artful, cunning. *n* knave; *Lat. Am.* untamed horse

belladona /beya'δona; beʎa'δona/ *f*, belladonna

bellaquería /beyake'ria; beʎake'ria/ *f*, roguery, knavery, cunning

bellasombra /beya'sombra; beʎa'sombra/ *f*, umbra tree

belleza /be'yesa; be'ʎeθa/ *f*, beauty, loveliness

bello /'beyo; 'beʎo/ *a* beautiful

bellota /be'yota; be'ʎota/ *f*, acorn; carnation bud; ornamental button, knob

bemol /be'mol/ *a* and *m*, *Mus.* flat. *Inf.* **tener bemoles,** to be thorny, be difficult

bencina /ben'sina; ben'θina/ *f*, benzine; gasoline, gas

bendecir /bende'sir; bende'θir/ *vt irr* to praise, extol; bless; dedicate, consecrate. See **decir**

bendición /bendi'sion; bendi'θion/ *f*, benediction; blessing; consecration; *pl* marriage ceremony. **b. de la mesa,** grace before meals

bendito /ben'dito/ *a* holy, blessed; fortunate; simple. **ser un b.,** to be a simpleton; be a good soul. **¡Benditos los ojos que te ven!** It's so nice to see you!

benedictino /beneδik'tino/ (**-na**) *a* and *n* Benedictine. *m*, Benedictine liqueur

beneficencia /benefi'sensia; benefi'θenθia/ *f*, beneficence; charitable institutions

beneficiación /benefisia'sion; benefiθia'θion/ *f*, benefaction

beneficiado /benefi'siaδo; benefi'θiaδo/ *n* (**-da**) *n* beneficiary. *m*, incumbent of a benefice

beneficiador /benefisia'δor; benefiθia'δor/ (**-ra**) *n* benefactor

beneficiar /benefi'siar; benefi'θiar/ *vt* to benefit; improve; cultivate (land); exploit (mine); purchase (directorship, etc.); sell at a loss (bonds, etc.)

beneficiario /benefi'siario; benefi'θiario/ (**-ia**) *n* beneficiary

beneficiencia /benefi'siensia; benefi'θienθia/ *f*, beneficence, charity

beneficio /bene'fisio; bene'fiθio/ *m*, benefit; profit; cultivation (land, etc.); working (mine); *Eccl.* benefice; *Theat.* benefit

beneficioso /benefi'sioso; benefi'θioso/ *a* beneficial; useful

benéfico /be'nefiko/ *a* beneficent; kind, helpful; charitable

benemérito /bene'merito/ *a* benemeritus, worthy, meritorious

beneplácito /bene'plasito; bene'plaθito/ *m*, approbation; consent

benevolencia /beneβo'lensia; beneβo'lenθia/ *f*, benevolence, goodwill

benévolo /be'neβolo/ *a* benevolent, kind

Bengala /beŋ'gala/ Bengal

bengalí /beŋga'li/ *a* and *mf* Bengali

benignidad /benigni'δaδ/ *f*, kindness; mildness (of the weather, etc.)

benigno /be'nigno/ *a* kind; benign; mild; balmy

beodo /be'oδo/ (**-da**) *a* drunk, intoxicated. *n* drunkard

berbén /ber'βen/ *m*, *Mexico* scurvy

Berbería /berβe'ria/ Barbary

bereber /bere'βer/ *a* and *mf* Berber

berenjena /beren'hena/ *f*, eggplant

bergante /ber'gante/ *m*, rascal, rogue

berilo /be'rilo/ *m*, beryl

Berlín /ber'lin/ Berlin

berlinés /ber'lines/ (**-esa**) *a* and *n* of or from Berlin

bermejear /bermehe'ar/ *vi* to be or look reddish

bermejo /ber'meho/ *a* reddish; red; redgold; carroty (of hair)

bermellón /berme'yon; berme'ʎon/ *m*, vermilion

bernardina /bernar'δina/ *f*, lie; boast; gibberish

bernardo /ber'narδo/ (**-da**) *a* and *n* *Eccl.* Bernardine (Order of St. Bernard)

berquelio /ber'kelio/ *m*, berkelium

berrear /berre'ar/ *vi* to low, bellow; yell, squall; shriek; *vr* reveal, confess

berrido /be'rriδo/ *m*, lowing, bellowing; *Inf.* yell

berrinche /be'rrintʃe/ *m*, *Inf.* tantrum, fit, fit of sulks

berro /'berro/ *m*, watercress

berroqueña /berro'keɲa/ *f*, granite

berza /'bersa; 'berθa/ *f*, cabbage

besamanos /besa'manos/ *m*, ceremony of kissing royal hand, levee; kissing fingers (in salute)

besar /be'sar/ *vt* to kiss; *Inf.* brush against, touch (of things); *vr* kiss one another; *Inf.* bang into, knock against one another

beso /'beso/ *m*, kiss; knock, collision

bestia /'bestia/ *f*, quadruped (especially horses or mules); beast. *mf Inf.* nasty piece of work. **b. de carga,** beast of burden. **como una b.,** like a dog (e.g. *Trabajo como una b.* I work like a dog)

bestial /bes'tial/ *a* bestial; brutal; beastly

bestialidad /bestiali'δaδ/ *f*, brutality; bestiality; beastliness

bestialismo /bestia'lismo/ *m*, bestiality (sexual orientation)

besuquear /besuke'ar/ *vt Inf.* to cover with kisses; *vr Inf.* spoon, make love

besuqueo /besu'keo/ *m*, *Inf.* kissing and spooning

betabel /beta'βel/ *m*, *Mexico* beetroot

bético /'betiko/ *a* Andalusian

betún /be'tun/ *m*, bitumen; shoe blacking; kind of cement. **b. de Judea** or **b. judaico,** asphalt

bezo /'beso; 'beθo/ *m*, blubber lip; proud flesh (of a wound)

bezudo /be'suδo; be'θuδo/ *a* thick-lipped

biberón /biβe'ron/ *m*, feeding bottle

Biblia /'biβlia/ *f*, Bible

bíblico /'biβliko/ *a* biblical

bibliófilo /bi'βliofilo/ *m*, bibliophile

bibliografía /biβliogra'fia/ *f*, bibliography

bibliográfico /biβlio'grafiko/ *a* bibliographical

biblioteca /biβlio'teka/ *f*, library; book series. **b. por subscripción,** circulating library

bibliotecario /biβliote'kario/ (**-ia**) *n* librarian

biblioteconomía, **bibliotecología,** **biblioteconomía** /biβlio'teknia, biβlioteko'lohia, biβliotekono'mia/ *f*, library science

bicarbonato /bikarβo'nato/ *m*, bicarbonate

bíceps /'biseps; 'biθeps/ *m*, biceps

bicherío /bitʃe'rio/ *m*, *Lat. Am.* bugs, insects

bicho /'bitʃo/ *m*, any small animal or reptile; quadruped; fighting bull; scarecrow, sight. **b. viviente,** *Inf.* living soul. **mal b.,** rogue

bicicleta /bisi'kleta; biθi'kleta/ *f*, bicycle, bike. **ir** (or **andar** or **montar**) **en b.,** to bicycle, bike, go by bicycle, go by bike

bicoca /bi'koka/ *f*, *Inf.* trifle, bagatelle

bicolor /biko'lor/ *a* bicolored

bidé /bi'δe/ *m*, bidet

biela /'biela/ *f*, axle-tree; connecting-rod; big-end

bielda /'bielda/ *f*, pitchfork; *Agr.* winnowing

bien /bien/ *m*, ideal goodness, perfection; benefit, advantage; welfare; *pl* property, wealth. *adv* well; willingly; happily; perfectly; easily; enough, sufficient; all right! very well! **b. que**, although. **b. de equipo**, capital good. **bienes muebles**, movables, goods and chattels. **bienes raíces**, real estate. **el B. y el Mal**, Good and Evil. **¡Está b.!** All right! **no b.**, scarcely, as soon as. **si b.**, although, even if. **¿Y b.?** And so what? Well, then; What next?

bienal /bie'nal/ *a* biennial
bienamado /biena'maðo/ *a* dearly beloved
bienandante /bienan'dante/ *a* prosperous; happy
bienandanza /bienan'dansa; bienan'danθa/ *f*, happiness, welfare; prosperity
bienaventurado /bienaβentu'raðo/ *a* blessed, holy; happy; *Inf.* over-simple, innocent, foolish
bienaventuranza /bienaβentu'ransa; bienaβentu'ranθa/ *f*, blessedness
bienestar /bienes'tar/ *m*, wellbeing; ease; comfort
bienhablado /biena'βlaðo/ *a* well-spoken; civil, polite
bienhadado /biena'ðaðo/ *a* fortunate, happy
bienhechor /biene'tʃor/ **(-ra)** *a* kind, helpful. *n* benefactor
bienintencionado /bienintensio'naðo; bieninten-θio'naðo/ *a* well-meaning
bienio /'bienio/ *m*, biennium, space of two years, period of two years
bienquisto /bien'kisto/ *a* respected; generally esteemed
bienvenida /biembe'niða/ *f*, safe or happy arrival; welcome. **dar la b.**, to welcome
bienvivir /biembi'βir/ *vi* to live comfortably; live decently or uprightly
bies /bies/ *m*, bias, cross; slant
bife /'bife/ *m Argentina* beefsteak, steak
biftec /bif'tek/ *m*, beefsteak, steak
bifurcación /bifurka'sion; bifurka'θion/ *f*, bifurcation; fork, branch, junction
bifurcarse /bifur'karse/ *vr* to fork, branch
bigamia /bi'gamia/ *f*, bigamy
bígamo /'bigamo/ **(-ma)** *a* bigamous. *n* bigamist
bigornia /bi'gornia/ *f*, anvil
bigote /bi'gote/ *m*, mustache; *pl* whiskers
bigotudo /bigo'tuðo/ *a* moustached, whiskered
bikini /bi'kini/ *m*, bikini
bilateral /bilate'ral/ *a* bilateral
bilingüe /bi'liŋgue/ *a* bilingual
bilioso /bi'lioso/ *a* bilious
bilis /'bilis/ *f*, bile
billar /bi'yar; bi'ʎar/ *m*, billiards; billiard table
billete /bi'yete; bi'ʎete/ *m*, note, short letter; ticket; banknote. **b. circular**, excursion ticket. **b. de abono**, season ticket. **b. de andén**, platform ticket. **b. de banco**, banknote. **b. de favor**, free ticket. **b. de ida y vuelta**, round trip ticket. **b. entero**, full fare. **b. kilométrico**, tourist ticket. **b. sencillo**, one-way. **medio b.**, half-fare
billón /bi'yon; bi'ʎon/ *m*, billion
bimestral /bimes'tral/ *a* bimonthly
bimestre /bi'mestre/ *a* bimonthly. *m*, two months' duration; money paid or received at two-monthly intervals
bimotor /bimo'tor/ *a* two-motor. *m*, twin-engined aircraft
binario /bi'nario/ *a* binary
bincha /'bintʃa/ *f*, *Lat. Am.* hairband
binóculo /bi'nokulo/ *m*, opera glasses
biodedegradable /βioðeðgradaβle/ *a* biodegradable
biodegradable /bioðegra'ðaβle/ *a* biodegradable
biodiversidad /biodiβersiðað/ *f*, biodiversity
biofísica /bio'fisika/ *f*, biophysics
biografía /biogra'fia/ *f*, biography
biográfico /bio'grafiko/ *a* biographical
biógrafo /'biografo/ **(-fa)** *n* biographer; (Chile) movie theater (e.g. *¡Vamos al biógrafo!* Let's go to the movies!)
biología /biolo'hia/ *f*, biology
biológico /bio'lohiko/ *a* biological
biólogo /'biologo/ *m*, biologist

biombo /'biombo/ *m*, screen
bioquímica /bio'kimika/ *f*, biochemistry
bioquímico /bio'kimiko/ *m*, biochemist
bipartido /bipar'tiðo/ *a* bipartite
bípedo /'bipeðo/ *a* and *m*, biped
biplano /bi'plano/ *m*, biplane
biplaza /biplasa; bi'plaθa/ *a* two-seater
birla /'birla/ *f*, skittle
birlar /bir'lar/ *vt* to bowl from where the bowl stopped; *Inf.* knock down; snatch away; *Inf.* rob
birlocha /bir'lotʃa/ *f*, child's kite
Birmania /bir'mania/ Burma
birmano /bir'mano/ **(-na)** *a* and *n* Burmese
birreta /bi'rreta/ *f*, biretta
birrete /bi'rrete/ *m*, biretta; university cap; cap
bis /bis/ *adv* twice; repeat; encore. *a* duplicate; **B** (in addresses, e.g., *Calle de Alcalá 18bis*, 18b Alcalá St.)
bisabuela /bisa'βuela/ *f*, great-grandmother
bisabuelo /bisa'βuelo/ *m*, great-grandfather
bisagra /bi'sagra/ *f*, hinge; shoemaker's polisher
bisbís /bis'βis/ *m*, game of chance
bisbisar /bisβi'sar/ *vt Inf.* to mutter; whisper
bisbiseo /bisβi'seo/ *m*, *Inf.* muttering; murmuring; whispering
bisecar /bise'kar/ *vt* to bisect
bisección /bisek'sion; bisek'θion/ *f*, *Geom.* bisection
bisectriz /bisek'tris; bisek'triθ/ *f*, bisector
bisel /bi'sel/ *m*, bevel, chamfer
bisiesto /bi'siesto/ *a* leap and *m*, leap (year)
bisílabo /bi'silaβo/ *a* two-syllabled
bismuto /bis'muto/ *m*, bismuth
bisnieto /bis'nieto/ **(-ta)** *n* great-grandchild
bisonte /bi'sonte/ *m*, bison
bisoño /bi'soɲo/ **(-ña)** *a* inexperienced, raw. *n* recruit; *Inf.* greenhorn
bistec /bis'tek/ *m*, beef steak
bisturí /bistu'ri/ *m*, surgical knife
bisunto /bi'sunto/ *a* grubby, greasy
bituminoso /bitumi'noso/ *a* bituminous
bivalvo /bi'βalβo/ *a* bivalve
Bizancio /bi'sansio; bi'θanθio/ Byzantium
bizantinismo /bisanti'nismo; biθanti'nismo/ *m*, Byzantinism
bizarría /bisa'rria; biθa'rria/ *f*, handsomeness; dash; verve; gallantry, courage; magnificence; liberality; whim, caprice
bizarro /bi'sarro; bi'θarro/ *a* handsome; dashing; gallant, courageous; liberal; splendid, magnificent
bizcaitarrismo /biskaita'rrismo; biθkaita'rrismo/ *m*, doctrine of Basque autonomy; Basque autonomy movement
bizco /'bisko; 'biθko/ *a* squint-eyed, cross-eyed
bizcocho /bis'kotʃo; biθ'kotʃo/ *m*, biscuit; spongecake; bisque
bizma /'bisma; 'biθma/ *f*, poultice. **poner bizmas**, to poultice
biznieto /bis'nieto; biθ'nieto/ *n* See **bisnieto**
blanca /'blanka/ *f*, old Spanish coin; *Inf.* penny; *Mus.* minim. **sin b.**, penniless
blanco /'blanko/ *a* white; fair-skinned; blank, vacant; *Inf.* cowardly. *m*, target; blank left in writing; white person; interval. **b. de España**, whiting. **b. de la uña**, half-moon of the nail. **dar en el b.**, to hit the mark. **en b.**, blank, unused; *Inf.* in vain; uncomprehendingly; (of nights) sleepless
blancor /blan'kor,/ *m*. **blancura** *f*, whiteness; fairness (of skin)
blandear /blande'ar/ *vt* to moderate, soothe; brandish; *vi Fig.* give way, yield
blandir /blan'dir/ *vt* to brandish, wield, flourish
blando /'blando/ *a* soft; mild (weather); delicate; kind; peaceable, delicate, effeminate; *Inf.* cowardly
blandón /blan'don/ *m*, wax taper
blandura /blan'dura/ *f*, softness; poultice; blandishment, compliment; mildness (of weather); gentleness; affability; luxury
blanquear /blanke'ar/ *vt* to bleach; whitewash; whiten; *vi* appear white; show white

blanquecino /blanke'sino; blanke'θino/ *a* whitish

blanqueo /blan'keo/ *m,* whitening; whitewashing; bleaching

blanquillo /blan'kijo; blan'kiʎo/ *m, Central America, Mexico* egg; *Chile, Peru,* white peach

blanquizal /blanki'sal; blanki'θal/ *m,* pipe-clay

blasfemador /blasfema'ðor/ **(-ra)** *a* blaspheming. *n* blasphemer

blasfemar /blasfe'mar/ *vi* to blaspheme; curse, swear

blasfemia /blas'femia/ *f,* blasphemy; insult

blasfemo /blas'femo/ **(-ma)** *n* blasphemer. *a* blasphemous

blasón /bla'son/ *m,* heraldry; escutcheon; glory, honor. **una familia con antiguos blasones,** a family of ancient lineage

blasonar /blaso'nar/ *vt* to blazon; *vi* boast, brag, blazon abroad

bledo /'bleðo/ *m,* blade, leaf. **no importar un b.,** not to matter a straw

blenda /'blenda/ *f, Mineral.* blende

blindado /blin'daðo/ *a Nav.* armored, ironclad

blindaje /blin'dahe/ *m, Nav.* armor-plating; *Mil.* blindage

blindar /blin'dar/ *vt* to plate with armor, to case with steel

blofista /blo'fista/ *mf, Lat. Am.* bluffer

blonda /'blonda/ *f,* blonde (of lace)

blondo /'blondo/ *a* fair, blond, flaxen-haired

bloque /'bloke/ *m,* block, slab

bloquear /bloke'ar/ *vt* to blockade; besiege. **¡No me bloquees!** Don't cut me off!

bloqueo /blo'keo/ *m,* blockade; siege; blocking; freezing (of assets). **violar el b.,** to run the blockade

blusa /'blusa/ *f,* blouse

boa /'boa/ *f,* boa, large snake. *m,* boa (fur)

boato /bo'ato/ *m,* outward show, ostentation

bobería /boβe'ria/ *f,* foolishness, stupidity

bóbilis, bóbilis /'boβilis, 'boβilis/ **(de)** *adv Inf.* free of charge; without effort

bobina /bo'βina/ *f,* bobbin, spool, reel; *Elec.* coil; spool (of fishing rod)

bobo /'boβo/ **(-ba)** *a* stupid, idiotic; simple, innocent. *n* fool. *m,* clown, jester

boca /'boka/ *f,* mouth; pincers (of crustaceans); entrance or exit; mouth (of a river), gulf, inlet; orifice, opening; muzzle (of guns); cutting edge (of tools); taste (of wine, etc.). **b. abajo,** face down, prone. **b. arriba,** on one's back, face up, supine. **b. del estómago,** pit of the stomach. **b. rasgada,** large mouth. **a b.,** verbally. **a b. de jarro,** point-blank. **a pedir de b.,** just as one would wish. **de b.,** by word of mouth. *Inf.* **sin decir esta b. es mía,** without a word, in silence

bocacalle /boka'kaye; boka'kaʎe/ *f,* entrance (to a street); street junction

bocadillo /boka'ðiyo; boka'ðiʎo/ *m,* narrow ribbon; sandwich

bocado /bo'kaðo/ *m,* mouthful. **b. de reyes,** delicacy, exquisite dish (of food); snack; bite; (horse's) bit; bridle; *pl* preserved fruit cut up

bocamanga /boka'manga/ *f,* wrist (of sleeve)

bocana /bo'kana/ *f, Lat. Am.* estuary

bocanada /boka'naða/ *f,* mouthful (of liquid); cloud (of smoke). **b. de aire,** gust of wind

boceto /bo'seto; bo'θeto/ *m,* sketch; outline; rough-cast model

bocha /'botʃa/ *f, Sports.* bowl; *pl* bowls

bochorno /bo'tʃorno/ *m,* sultry weather; heat, stuffiness; blush, hot flush; shame

bochornoso /botʃor'noso/ *a* sultry; shameful

bocina /bo'sina; bo'θina/ *f,* trumpet; megaphone; foghorn; hooter; *Auto.* horn; horn (of gramophone); *Astron.* Ursa Minor

bocio /'bosio; 'boθio/ *m, Med.* goiter

bocoy /bo'koi/ *m,* hogshead; large cask

boda /'boða/ *f,* wedding, marriage. **bodas de oro,** fiftieth (golden) anniversary. **bodas de plata,** silver wedding anniversary

bodega /bo'ðega/ *f,* wine-cellar; storeroom; stockroom; granary; *Puerto Rico* grocery store; *Naut.* hold (of ship)

bodegón /boðe'gon/ *m,* eating-house; tavern; *Art.* still-life; genre picture

bofes /'bofes/ *m pl,* lungs, lights. *Inf.* **echar los b.,** to work oneself to death

bofetada /bofe'taða/ *f.* **bofetón** *m,* blow, slap; box on the ear

boga /'boga/ *f,* rowing; fashion, vogue; *Mech.* bogie. *mf* oarsman, rower. **estar en b.,** to be fashionable

bogador /boga'ðor/ **(-ra)** *n* rower, oarsman

bogar /bo'gar/ *vi* to row

bogavante /boga'βante/ *m,* lobster

bogotano /bogo'tano/ **(-na)** *a* and *n* of or from Bogotá

bohemio /bo'emio/ **(-ia)** *a* and *n* gipsy; bohemian; Bohemian. *m,* archer's short cloak

bohío /bo'io/ *m, Lat. Am.* hut

boicot, boicoteo /boi'kot, boiko'teo/ *m,* boycott

boicotear /boikote'ar/ *vt* to boycott

boina /'boina/ *f,* Basque cap; beret

bola /'bola/ *f,* globe; ball; *Sports.* bowl; *Archit.* balloon; *Inf.* trick, lie; (Cuba) rumor; *Mexico* shoeshine, shine. **b. de nieves,** snowball. *Inf.* **dejar rodar la b.,** to let things slide

bolardo /bo'larðo/ *m,* bollard

bolchevismo /boltʃe'βismo/ *m,* Bolshevism

bolea /bo'lea/ *f,* (tennis) volley; throw

bolera /bo'lera/ *f,* bowling alley

bolero /bo'lero/ *m,* bolero; dancer; *Inf.* top hat; *Mexico* bootblack

boleta /bo'leta/ *f,* admission ticket; billet ticket; warrant, voucher; summons, ticket, traffic ticket

boletería /bolete'ria/ *f. Lat. Am.* ticket office, box office

boletín /bole'tin/ *m,* bulletin; admission ticket; pay warrant; *Com.* price list; learned periodical. **b. de noticias,** news bulletin. **b. meteorológico,** weather report

boleto /bo'leto/ *m. Lat. Am.* ticket

boliche /bo'litʃe/ *m,* jack (in bowls); cup-and-ball toy; small oven (for charcoal); dragnet; *Mexico* bowling **juego de b.,** bowls

bólido /'boliðo/ *m, Astron.* bolide, meteor

bolígrafo /bo'ligrafo/ *m,* ballpoint pen

bolillo /bo'liyo; bo'liʎo/ *m,* bobbin (lace making); *Mexico* roll (food)

bolina /bo'lina/ *f, Naut.* bowline; *Naut.* sounder; *Inf.* uproar, tumult

bolita /bo'lita/ *f,* pellet

Bolivia /βo'liβia/ Bolivia

boliviano /boli'βiano/ **(-na)** *a* and *n* Bolivian. *m,* silver coin

bollo /'boyo; 'boʎo/ *m,* bread roll; bun; bulge, bruise (in metal); *Med.* lump

bollón /bo'yon; bo'ʎon/ *m,* round-headed or brass-headed nail; *Bot.* bud (especially vines)

bolo /'bolo/ *m,* skittle, ninepin; pillow (for lace making); Cuban coin; *Med.* large pill; *Fig. Inf.* blockhead; *pl* skittles (game of)

bolsa /'bolsa/ *f,* purse; bag; footmuff; fold, pucker; pouch; exchange, stock exchange, capital, money; prize money; *Med.* sac; *Mineral.* pocket. **b. de estudio,** scholarship grant. **b. de trabajo,** labor exchange. **b. de valores,** stock exchange. **bajar** (*or* **subir**) **la b.,** to fall (or rise) (of stock exchange quotations). **jugar a la b.,** to speculate on the stock exchange

bolsillo /bol'siyo; bol'siʎo/ *m,* pocket; purse; money

bolsista /bol'sista/ *mf* stock-broker; speculator (on the stock exchange)

bomba /'bomba/ *f, Mech.* pump; pumping engine; bomb; *Mil.* shell; lamp globe; *Inf.* improvised verses; *Inf.* drinking bout. **¡B.!** Listen! Here goes! **b. de incendios,** fire-engine. **b. marina,** waterspout. **b. de mecha atrasada,** time bomb. **b. volante,** flying-bomb. **a prueba de b.,** bombproof. **arrojar bombas,** to bomb. *Inf.* **caer como una b.,** to be a bombshell

bombachos /bom'βatʃos/ *a* baggy, loose-fitting; *m pl,* plus fours

bombardear /bombarðe'ar/ *vt* to bombard; bomb; shell
bombardeo /bombar'ðeo/ *m*, bombardment, bombing; shelling
bombardero /bombar'ðero/ *m*, gunner, bombardier; *Aer.* bomber. **b. pesado,** *Aer.* heavy bomber. **Servicio de b.,** Bomber Command
bombástico /bom'βastiko/ *a* bombastic, high sounding
bombazo /bom'βaso; bom'βaθo/ *m*, bombshell; bomb crater; noise of an exploding bomb
bombear /bombe'ar/ *vt* to pump; bombard, shell; praise
bombero /bom'βero/ *m*, worker of a pressure pump; fireman; mortar, howitzer
bombilla /bom'βiya; bom'βiʎa/ *f, Naut.* lantern; (*Elec. Phys.*) bulb; small pump; straw for drinking maté *West Hem.*
bombillo /bom'βiyo; bom'βiʎo/ *m*, w.c. siphon; handpump
bombo /'bombo/ *m*, big drum or player of it; *Naut.* barge, ferry; ballot box; exaggerated praise
bombón /bom'βon/ *m*, bonbon, sweet
bombonera /bombo'nera/ *f*, box for toffee, etc.
bonachón /bona'tʃon/ *a Inf.* genial, good-natured
bonaerense /bonae'rense/ *a* and *mf* of or from the Province of Buenos Aires
Bonaira /bo'naira/ Bonaire
bonancible /bonan'siβle; bonan'θiβle/ *a* calm (of weather, sea)
bonanza /bo'nansa; bo'nanθa/ *f*, fair weather; prosperity
bondad /bon'daθ/ *f*, goodness; kindness, helpfulness. **Tenga la b. de...,** Be good enough to..., Please...
bondadoso /bonda'ðoso/ *a* good, kind
bonete /bo'nete/ *m*, academic cap; *Zool.* reticulum (ruminants); *Eccl.* biretta. **gran b.,** important person. *Inf.* **a tente b.,** insistently
bonetero /bone'tero/ **(-ra)** *n* seller or maker of caps and birettas
boniato /bo'niato/ *m, Lat. Am.* sweet potato, yam
bonificación /bonifika'sion; bonifika'θion/ *f*, bonus; allowance, discount
bonito /bo'nito/ *a* pretty; graceful; (ironical) fine. *m, Ichth.* tuna, bonito
bono /'bono/ *m*, voucher; *Com.* bond, certificate. **b. postal,** postal money order. **bono del gobierno,** government bond
boñiga /bo'niga/ *f*, cow-dung, animal manure
boqueada /boke'aða/ *f*, gasp, opening of the mouth. **dar las boqueadas, estar en las últimas boqueadas,** to be at the last gasp
boquear /boke'ar/ *vi* to gasp; be dying; *Inf.* be at last gasp (of things); *vt* say, utter
boquera /bo'kera/ *f*, sluice (in irrigation canal)
boquerón /boke'ron/ *m*, large opening; *Ichth.* anchovy (fish); whitebait
boquete /bo'kete/ *m*, narrow entrance, aperture; gap, breach; hole
boquiabierto /bokia'βierto/ *a* open-mouthed; amazed
boquiancho /bo'kiantʃo/ *a* wide-mouthed
boquiasombrado /bokiasom'βraðo/ *a* gaping
boquilla /bo'kiya; bo'kiʎa/ *f*, dim small mouth; mouthpiece (of wind instruments, etc.); cigar- or cigarette-holder; gas-burner; nozzle; tip (of cigarettes)
boquirroto /boki'rroto/ *a Inf.* loquacious, indiscreet
borbollar /borβo'yar; borβo'ʎar/ *vi* to bubble, foam, froth
borbollón, borbotón /borβo'yon, borβo'ton; borβo'ʎon, borβo'ton/ *m*, gushing, bubbling, welling up. **a borbollones,** in a torrent; hastily, impetuously
borbotar /borβo'tar/ *vi* to gush out, well up
borda /'borða/ *f*, hut, cabin; *Naut.* gunwale
bordado /bor'ðaðo/ *m*, embroidery
bordador /borða'nðor/ **(-ra)** *n* embroiderer
bordar /bor'ðar/ *vt* to embroider; *Fig.* perform perfectly
borde /'borðe/ *m*, edge; fringe; verge; rim; mount (of a picture); brim (of a hat); side (of ship). *a* wild

(of plants); illegitimate. **estar lleno hasta los bordes,** to be full to the brim
bordear /borðe'ar/ *vt* to border, trim with a bordear; line (a street, e.g. *Diez mil personas bordearon las calles durante el desfile,* Ten thousand people lined the streets during the parade)
bordillo /bor'ðiyo; bor'ðiʎo/ *m*, curbstone, curb.
bordo /'borðo/ *m*, side (of ships); border, edge. **a b.,** on board
bordón /bor'ðon/ *m*, pilgrim's staff; monotonous repetition; refrain; *Mus.* bass string; *Fig.* guide, stay
borgoña /bor'goɲa/ *m*, Burgundy wine
borgoñón /borgo'ɲon/ **(-ona)** *a* and *n* Burgundian
bórico /'boriko/ *a* boric
boricua /bori'kua/ *a*, **borinqueño, -a** *a, mf* Puerto Rican
borla /'borla/ *f*, tassel; puff (for powder). *Fig.* **tomar la b.,** to take one's doctorate, graduate
bornear /borne'ar/ *vt* to bend, twist; *Archit.* hoist into position; *vr* warp (wood)
borra /'borra/ *f*, yearling ewe; thickest wool; wadstuffing; lees, sediment; fluff, dust; *Inf.* trash. **b. de algodón,** cotton-waste
borrachera /borra'tʃera/ *f*, drunkenness; orgy, carousal; *Inf.* blunder
borrachín /borra'tʃin/ **(-ina)** *n* tippler, toper
borrachito /borra'tʃito/ *a* high (on liquor), tipsy
borracho /bo'rratʃo/ **(de)** *a* drunk (on), intoxicated (with); *Inf.* blind (with rage, etc.). *n* tippler, drunkard
borrador /borra'ðor/ *m*, rough draft. **en borrador,** in the works (e.g. *Tiene dos ensayos en borrador,* She has two essays in the works). **estar en borrador,** to be in the works
borradura /borra'ðura/ *f*, erasure
borrajear /borrahe'ar/ *vt* to scribble
borrar /bo'rrar/ *vt* to erase; cross out; blot out; *Fig.* obliterate
borrasca /bo'rraska/ *f*, storm, tempest; peril, danger; *Inf.* orgy
borrascosidad /borraskosi'ðaθ/ *f*, storminess
borrascoso /borras'koso/ *a* stormy; disordered, turbulent
borrego /bo'rrego/ **(-ga)** *n* lamb; *Inf.* nincompoop, simpleton; *m pl*, fleecy clouds; white horses (waves)
borrico /bo'rriko/ **(-ca)** *a* donkey; fool. *m*, sawinghorse
borrón /bo'rron/ *m*, blot; rough draft; defect; *Fig.* stigma
borroso /bo'rroso/ *a* blurred, indistinct; full of dregs, muddy
boscaje /bos'kahe/ *m*, grove, group of trees, thicket
Bósforo, el /'bosforo, el/ the Bosporus
bosque /'boske/ *m*, wood, forest
bosquejar /boske'har/ *vt Art.* to sketch; sketch out, draft; model in rough (sculpture); outline
bosquejo /bos'keho/ *m*, outline, sketch; rough plan or idea; unfinished work. **en bosquejo,** grosso modo
bostar /bos'tar/ *m*, ox barn
bostezar /boste'sar; boste'θar/ *vi* to yawn
bostezo /bos'teso; bos'teθo/ *m*, yawning; yawn
bota /'bota/ *f*, small wineskin; barrel, butt; boot. **b. de montar,** riding boot. **botas de campaña,** topboots. **botas de vadear,** waders
botada, botadura /bo'taða, bota'ðura/ *f*, launching (of a ship)
botador /bota'ðor/ *m*, thrower; boating-pole; nailpuller
botafuego /bota'fuego/ *m, Mil.* linstock; *Inf.* quicktempered, irascible person
botalón /bota'lon/ *m, Naut.* boom. **b. de foque,** jibboom
botana /bo'tana/ *f, Lat. Am.* bite (to eat), snack
botánica /bo'tanika/ *f*, botany
botánico /bo'taniko/ **(-ca)** *a* botanical. *n* botanist
botar /bo'tar/ *vt* to fling; launch (boat); *Lat. Am.* to discard, throw away, throw out *Naut.* shift the helm; *vi* jump; bounce, rebound; rear, prance (horses)
botarate /bota'rate/ *m, Inf.* madcap, devil-may-care
botarel, botarete /bota'rel, bota'rete/ *m*, arch abutment, buttress, flying buttress

botarga /bo'targa/ f, motley; harlequin

bote /'bote/ m, thrust (with lance, etc.); rearing (of horse); rebound; *Aer.* bump; open boat; small bottle, jar. **b. salvavidas,** lifeboat. *Inf.* **de b. en b.,** chockful

botella /bo'teya; bo'teʎa/ f, bottle; bottleful; flask

botica /bo'tika/ f, chemist's shop; medicines, remedies; physic; store, shop; medicine chest

boticario /boti'kario/ m, apothecary, chemist

botija /bo'tiha/ f, earthen jug; *Slang.* chunky person

botijo /bo'tiho/ m, earthenware jar with spout and handle

botillería /botiye'ria; botiʎe'ria/ f, ice-cream bar

botín /bo'tin/ m, gaiter; buskin; booty

botiquín /boti'kin/ m, first-aid kit; medicine chest

botón /bo'ton/ m, bud; button; knob, handle; switch (electric); press button (bell); *Bot.* center; button (on a foil); *Mech.* stud

botonero /boto'nero/ **(-ra)** n button maker or seller

bóveda /b'oβeða/ f, *Archit.* vault, arch; crypt; cavern. **b. celeste,** sky

boxeador /boksea'ðor/ m, boxer

boxear /bokse'ar/ vi *Sports.* to box

boxeo /bok'seo/ m, *Sports.* boxing

boya /'boya/ f, *Naut.* buoy; float

boyante /bo'yante/ a floating; light, buoyant; prosperous

boyar /bo'yar/ vi *Naut.* to float

boyero /bo'yero/ m, cowherd

boza /'bosa; 'boθa/ f, painter (of a boat)

bozal /bo'sal; bo'θal/ m, muzzle; nosebag; harness bells. *mf Inf.* greenhorn; a wild, untamed (horses)

bozo /'boso; 'boθo/ m, down which precedes beard; muzzle; headstall; lips, snout

bracero /bra'sero; bra'θero/ m, one who offers his arm (to a lady); day laborer; strong man. **de b.,** arm-in-arm

bracete /bra'sete; bra'θete/ m, small arm. **de b.,** arm-in-arm

bracmán /brak'man/ m, Brahmin

braga /'braga/ f, (gen. *pl*) breeches; knickerbockers; hoist or pulley rope

bragazas /bra'gasas; bra'gaθas/ m, *Inf.* weak-willed, fellow, soft specimen

braguero /bra'gero/ m, *Med.* truss

bragueta /bra'geta/ f, fly (of trousers)

brahmanismo /brama'nismo/ m, Brahmanism

bramante /bra'mante/ a roaring. m, twine, packthread

bramar /bra'mar/ vi to roar; rage; *Fig.* howl (of the wind, etc.)

bramido /bra'miðo/ m, bellowing; roaring; yell of rage; *Fig.* howling (wind, sea, etc.)

brancada /bran'kaða/ f, drag net

branquia /'brankia/ f, (gen. *pl*) *Ichth.* gill

branquial /bran'kial/ a branchiate

braquicefalia /bra,kise'falia; bra,kiθe'falia/ f, brachycephaly

braquiotomía /brakioto'mia/ f, *Surg.* brachiotomy, amputation of the arms

brasa /'brasa/ f, live coal. **estar como en brasas,** to be like a cat on hot bricks

brasero /bra'sero/ m, brazier; *Mexico* fireplace

Brasil /bra'sil/ Brazil

brasileño /brasi'leɲo/ **(-ña)** a and n Brazilian

bravata /bra'βata/ f, bravado; threat

braveza /bra'βesa; bra'βeθa/ f, ferocity, savageness; valor; violence, fury (of elements)

bravío /bra'βio/ a savage, untamed; wild (plants); uncultured

bravo /'braβo/ a valiant; surly, rude; independent, strong-minded, good, excellent; savage (animals); stormy (sea); rough, rugged; violent, angry; *Inf.* sumptuous, magnificent.

bravura /bra'βura/ f, ferocity (animals); courage (persons); boastful threat

braza /'brasa; 'braθa/ f, *Naut.* fathom; stroke (in swimming)

brazado /bra'saðo; bra'θaðo/ m, armful

brazal /bra'sal; bra'θal/ m, armlet, brassard

brazalete /brasa'lete; braθa'lete/ m, bracelet; brassard

brazo /'braso; 'braθo/ m, arm; upper arm; front paw; *Mech.* arm; branch (of chandelier, etc.); bough; arm (of chair); power, courage; *pl* protectors; workmen, hands. **b. de mar,** firth, arm of the sea. **a b. partido,** in unarmed fight, man to man. **con los brazos abiertos,** welcomingly; willingly, gladly. **dar los brazos (a),** to embrace. *Inf.* **hecho un b. de mar,** dressed up to the nines

brea /'brea/ f, pitch, tar; sacking, canvas

brebaje /bre'βahe/ m, beverage; unpleasant drink; *Naut.* draft (of beer, grog, etc.)

brecha /'bretʃa/ f, *Mil.* breach; opening; *Fig.* impression (on mind). **morir en la b.,** to fight to the last ditch; die in harness

brécol /'brekol/ m, *Bot.* broccoli

brega /'breɣa/ f, fight; quarrel; disappointment, trick. **andar a la b.,** to work hard. **dar b.,** to play a trick

bregar /bre'gar/ vi to fight; work hard; *Fig.* struggle; **bregarse con,** to tackle (a problem)

breña /'breɲa/ f, rough ground, bramble patch

breñal /bre'ɲal/ m, scrub, brushwood

breñoso /bre'ɲoso/ a rugged, rocky

Bretaña /bre'taɲa/ Brittany

brete /'brete/ m, fetters, shackles; *Fig.* fix, squeeze, tight spot, tight squeeze (e.g. *Estoy en un brete.* I'm in a tight spot)

bretón /bre'ton/ **(-ona)** a and n Breton. m, Breton (language)

breva /'breβa/ f, early fig; early acorn; *Fig.* advantage, "plum"; *Inf.* peach (girl); *Inf.* windfall, piece of luck; Havana cigar

breve /'breβe/ a brief; concise. m, papal brief. f, *Mus.* breve. **en b.,** shortly, concisely; in a short while, soon

brevedad /breβe'ðað/ f, brevity **a la mayor b.,** *Lat. Am.* as soon as possible

breviario /bre'βiario/ m, breviary

brezal /bre'sal; bre'θal/ m, heath, moor

brezo /'breso; 'breθo/ m, *Bot.* heath

bribón /bri'βon/ **(-ona)** n rogue, ruffian. a knavish, dishonest; lazy

bribonada /briβo'naða/ f, knavery, mischievous trick

bribonear /briβone'ar/ vi to idle; play tricks, be a rogue

bribonería /briβone'ria/ f, rascality, vagrant life

brida /'briða/ f, bridle

brigada /bri'gaða/ f, *Mil.* brigade; *Naut.* division of fleet; beasts of burden. **b. millonaria,** (Castroist Cuba) team of thirty sugarcane cutters who cut a million or more arrobas in one harvest

brillante /bri'yante; bri'ʎante/ a sparkling, brilliant; *Fig.* outstanding. m, diamond

brillantez /briyan'tes; briʎan'teθ/ f, brightness, luster; fame; *Fig.* brilliance

brillantina /briyan'tina; briʎan'tina/ f, brilliantine

brillar /bri'yar; bri'ʎar/ vi to shine, sparkle, gleam, glisten; *Fig.* be brilliant or outstanding

brillo /'briyo; 'briʎo/ m, brilliancy, brightness, shine; fame, glory; distinction, brilliance, splendor

brincar /brin'kar/ vi to spring, leap, frisk; *Fig. Inf.* skip, omit; *Inf.* grow angry; vt jump a child up and down

brinco /'brinko/ m, leap, spring; skip, frolicking

brindar /brin'dar/ vi to invite, provoke (of things); (*with prep a or por*) drink the health of, toast; vt and vi give, present; offer; vr offer one's services

brindis /'brindis/ m, toast (drink)

brío /'brio/ m, vigor; spirit, courage; gusto, verve

brioso /'brioso/ a vigorous, enterprising; spirited, courageous; dashing, lively

briqueta /bri'keta/ f, briquette

brisa /'brisa/ f, breeze; grape pressings

británico /bri'taniko/ a British

brizna /'brisna; 'briθna/ f, shred, paring; blade (grass); filament, fiber; string (of bean-pod, etc.); splinter, chip

briznar /bris'nar; briθ'nar/ vi, *Lat. Am.* to drizzle

broca /'broka/ *f,* reel; tack (shoemaker's); *Mech.* drill, bit

brocado /bro'kaðo/ *m,* brocade. *a* brocade or embroidered like brocade

brocal /bro'kal/ *m,* puteal (of a well); mouthpiece (of wineskin); metal ring (of sword-sheath)

brocamantón /brokaman'ton/ *m,* large jeweled brooch

brocatel /broka'tel/ *m,* imitation brocade

brocha /'brotʃa/ *f,* brush. **b. de afeitar,** shaving brush. **de b. gorda,** crudely painted. **pintor de b. gorda,** decorator

brochada /bro'tʃaða/ *f,* stroke (of the brush)

brochado /bro'tʃaðo/ *a* brocaded, embossed

brochadura /brotʃa'ðura/ *f,* fastening, set of hooks and eyes

broche /'brotʃe/ *m,* clasp, fastening; brooch; hooks and eyes; *Lat. Am.* (paper) clip

brochón /bro'tʃon/ *m,* whitewash brush

broma /'broma/ *f,* merriment; joke, jest; ship-worm. **b. literaria,** literary hoax

bromear /brome'ar/ **(se)** *vi* and *vr* to joke, make fun

bromista /bro'mista/ *a* joking, jesting; mischievous. *mf* genial person; prankster, tease

bromo /'bromo/ *m,* bromine

bronca /'bronka/ *f, Inf.* shindy

bronce /'bronse; 'bronθe/ *m,* bronze; brass; *Poet.* gun, bell, trumpet; bronze statue; sunburn

bronceado /bronse'aðo; bronθe'aðo/ *a* bronzed; sunburned. *m,* sunburn

broncear /bronse'ar; bronθe'ar/ *vt* to bronze; sunburn

bronco /'bronko/ *a* rough, coarse; brittle; (of metals); harsh (voice, musical instruments); rigid, stiff; surly

bronconeumonía /,bronkoneumo'nia/ *f,* bronchopneumonia

bronquial /bron'kial/ *a* bronchial

bronquio /'bronkio/ *m,* (gen. *pl*) bronchi

bronquitis /bron'kitis/ *f,* bronchitis

broquel /bro'kel/ *m,* shield; *Fig.* protection

broquelero /broke'lero/ *m,* shield maker; quarrelsome man

broqueta /bro'keta/ *f,* skewer

brotadura /brota'ðura/ *f,* budding

brotar /bro'tar/ *vi* to germinate, sprout; gush forth (water); issue forth, burst out; *Fig.* appear (of rash); *Fig.* begin to appear; *vt* to bring forth; produce (of earth)

brote /'brote/ *m,* bud, sprout; *Fig.* germ, genesis; iota, jot, atom

broza /'brosa; 'broθa/ *f,* garden rubbish; debris; thicket

bruces /'bruses; 'bruθes/ **(a** *or* **de)** *adv* face downwards. **caer de b.,** to fall flat. Also with other verbs: *dar, echarse,* etc.

bruja /'bruha/ *f,* witch; owl; *Inf.* hag

brujear /bruhe'ar/ *vi* to practice witchcraft

brujería /bruhe'ria/ *f,* witchcraft

brujo /'bruho/ *m,* magician, wizard

brújula /'bruhula/ *f,* magnetic needle; compass; mariner's compass. **b. de bolsillo,** pocket compass. **b. giroscópica,** gyrocompass

bruma /'bruma/ *f,* haze; sea-mist

brumoso /bru'moso/ *a* misty, hazy

bruno /'bruno/ *a* dark brown

bruñido /bru'ɲiðo/ *m,* polishing; burnish

bruñidor /bruɲi'ðor/ **(-ra)** *a* polishing. *n* burnisher. *m,* polisher (instrument)

bruñir /bru'ɲir/ *vt* to polish, burnish; *Inf.* apply make up

brusco /'brusko/ *a* brusque, rude; blunt; sudden, unexpected; sharp (of bends)

Bruselas /bru'selas/ Brussels

bruselense /bruse'lense/ *a* and *mf* of or from Brussels

brusquedad /bruske'ðað/ *f,* brusquerie, rudeness; bluntness; suddenness, unexpectedness; sharpness (of a bend)

brutal /bru'tal/ *a* brutal

brutalidad /brutali'ðað/ *f,* brutality; *Fig.* brutishness; viciousness

bruto /'bruto/ *a* stupid, unreasonable; vicious; unpolished, rough. *m,* animal (gen. quadruped). **en b.,** in the rough; *Com.* in bulk. **diamante en b.,** an uncut diamond

bruza /'brusa; 'bruθa/ *f,* strong brush; scrubbing brush

Bs. As. /,buenos 'aires/ abbrev. of Buenos Aires

bu /bu/ *m, Inf.* bogey man

buba /'buβa/ *f,* pustule; *pl* buboes

bubónico /bu'βoniko/ *a* bubonic

bucal /bu'kal/ *a* buccal

bucanero /buka'nero/ *m,* buccaneer

búcaro /'bukaro/ *m,* arsenican clay; jar made of arsenican clay

buceador /busea'ðor; buθea'ðor/ *m,* diver

bucear /buse'ar; buθe'ar/ *vi* to dive, work as a diver; swim under water; *Fig.* investigate

bucéfalo /bu'sefalo; bu'θefalo/ *m,* bucephalus; *Inf.* fool, blockhead

buceo /bu'seo; bu'θeo/ *m,* diving; dive; *Fig.* investigation

buchaca /bu'tʃaka/ *f, Lat. Am.* saddlebag; billiard pocket

buche /'butʃe/ *m,* craw or crop; mouthful; wrinkle, pleat; *Inf.* stomach, belly. *Fig. Inf.* inmost heart

bucle /'bukle/ *m,* ringlet, curl

bucólico /bu'koliko/ *a* bucolic

budín /bu'ðin/ *m,* pudding

budismo /bu'ðismo/ *m,* Buddhism

budista /bu'ðista/ *a* and *mf* Buddhist

buen /buen/ *a abb* of **bueno,** good. Used before *m,* singular nouns and infinitives used as nouns, e.g. *un b. libro,* a good book. **el b. cantar,** good singing

buenamente /buena'mente/ *adv* easily; comfortably, conveniently; willingly

buenaventura /buenaβen'tura/ *f,* good luck; fortune told from hand

bueno /'bueno/ (see **buen**) *a* good; kind; useful; convenient; pleasant; healthy; large (drink, etc.); simple, innocent; suitable; sufficient; opportune. **¡B.!** Good!; Enough!; *Mexico* Hello! (on telephone); All right! **a buenas,** willingly. **de buenas a primeras,** at first sight, from the beginning. **hacer b.,** to prove, justify (a claim)

buey /buei/ *m,* ox. **b. suelto,** *Inf.* freelance; bachelor

búfalo /'bufalo/ **(-la)** *n* buffalo

bufanda /bu'fanda/ *f,* scarf

bufar /bu'far/ *vi* to bellow; snort; *Inf.* snort with rage

bufete /bu'fete/ *m,* desk, writing table; lawyer's office or practice; sideboard

bufido /bu'fiðo/ *m,* snort; bellow

bufo /'bufo/ *a* comic. *m,* clown, buffoon

bufón /bu'fon/ *m,* buffoon, clown; jester. *a* comical, clownish

bufonada /bufo'naða/ *f,* buffoonery, clowning; raillery, taunt

bufonear /bufone'ar/ **(se)** *vr* and *vi* to joke, jest, parody

bufonería. /bufone'ria/ See **bufonada**

buhardilla /buar'ðiya; buar'ðiʎa/ *f,* garret; skylight

búho /'buo/ *m,* owl; *Inf.* hermit, unsociable person

buhonería /buone'ria/ *f,* peddling, hawking; peddler's wares

buhonero /buo'nero/ *m,* pedler

buido /'buiðo/ *a* sharp-pointed; sharp

buitre /'buitre/ *m,* vulture

bujía /bu'hia/ *f,* candle; candlestick; *Elec.* candlepower; *Auto.* sparking plug

bula /'bula/ *f,* (Papal) bull

bulbo /'bulβo/ *m, Bot.* bulb. **b. dentario,** pulp (of teeth)

bulboso /bul'βoso/ *a* bulbous

bulevar /bule'βar/ *m,* boulevard, promenade

bulimia /bu'limia/ *f,* bulimia

bulla /'buya; 'buʎa/ *f,* noise; bustle; confusion; fuss. *Inf.* **meter a b.,** to throw into great confusion

bullebulle /buye'βuye; buʎe'βuʎe/ *mf* busybody; madcap

bullente /bu'yente; bu'ʎente/ *adj* boiling, bubbling; frothy (beer); swarming, teeming. **b. de sol,** drenched in sunlight, sun-drenched

bullicio /bu'yisio; bu'ʎiθio/ *m*, noise, bustle; rioting; uproar

bullicioso /buyi'sioso; buʎi'θioso/ *a* noisy, merry, boisterous; rebellious; lively, restless

bullir /bu'yir; bu'ʎir/ *vi* to boil; foam, bubble; *Fig.* seethe; *Fig.* swarm (insects); bustle; *vt* move, stir; *vr* stir, give signs of life

bulto /'bulto/ *m*, bulk, mass, size; form of person, etc., seen indistinctly; swelling; bust, statue; bundle, package, piece of luggage; pillowcase. *Fig. Inf.* **poner de b.,** to put clearly, emphasize. **ser de b.,** to be obvious

bumerang /bume'raŋ/ *m*, boomerang

buñolería /buɲole'ria/ *f*, bun or waffle shop

buñuelo /bu'ɲuelo/ *m*, bun; waffle, fritter; *Fig.* botch

buque /'buke/ *m*, ship, vessel; capacity of ship; ship's hull. **b. barreminas,** minesweeper. **b. de guerra,** battleship, man-of-war. **b. de vapor,** steamer. **b. de vela,** sailing ship. **b. escuela,** trainingship. **b. mercante,** merchant vessel. **b. submarino,** submarine. **b. transbordador,** train-ferry

burbuja /bur'βuha/ *f*, bubble

burbujear /burβuhe'ar/ *vi* to bubble

burdel /bur'ðel/ *m*, brothel; *Inf.* untidy, noisy place. *a* lascivious

burdo /'burðo/ *a* coarse, tough

burgalés /burga'les/ **(-esa)** *a* and *n* of or from Burgos

burgo /'burgo/ *m*, borough, burgh

burgomaestre /burgoma'estre/ *m*, burgomaster

burgués /bur'ges/ **(-esa)** *a* and *n* bourgeois

burguesía /burge'sia/ *f*, bourgeoisie

buriel /bu'riel/ *a* dark red

buril /bu'ril/ *m*, burin, engraver's tool

burla /'burla/ *f*, mockery; joke, jest; trick. **b. burlando,** without effort; negligently. **de burlas,** in fun. **entre burlas y veras,** half-jokingly

burlador /burla'ðor/ *a* mocking. *m*, libertine, rake; deceiver

burlar /bur'lar/ *vt* to play a trick on; deceive; disappoint; *vr* and *vi* (*with de*) make fun of, laugh at, ridicule

burlesco /bur'lesko/ *a* jocular, comic, burlesque

burlón /bur'lon/ **(-ona)** *a* joking; mocking, scoffing. *n* joker; scoffer

buró /bu'ro/ *m*, bureau, writing-desk; *Mexico* night table

burocracia /buro'krasia; buro'kraθia/ *f*, bureaucracy

burócrata /bu'rokrata/ *mf* bureaucrat

burocrático /buro'kratiko/ *a* bureaucratic

burocratismo /burokra'tismo/ *m*, bureaucracy, red tape

burra /'burra/ *f*, she-ass; foolish, unteachable woman; painstaking, patient woman

burrajo /bu'rraho/ *m*, dry stable dung used as fuel

burro /'burro/ *m*, ass, donkey; sawing-horse; card game

bursátil /bur'satil/ *a* *Com.* relating to the stock exchange; financial

busca /'buska/ *f*, search; hunting party; research; pursuit

buscado /bus'kaðo/ *adj* deliberate, intentional (negligence, etc.)

buscador /buska'ðor/ **(-ra)** *n* searcher; investigator. *m*, finder (of a camera, etc.)

buscapié /buska'pie/ *m*, hint or suggestion; *Fig.* feeler

buscapiés /buska'pies/ *m*, squib, cracker, firecracker

buscapleitos /buska'pleitos/ *mf* *Lat. Am.* troublemaker

buscar /bus'kar/ *vt* to search, look for; pursue. **ir a b.,** to go to look for, go and get; bring, fetch

buscarruidos /buska'rruiðos/ *mf* *Inf.* quarrel maker

buscavidas /buska'βiðas/ *mf* *Inf.* busybody; *Inf.* go-getter

buscón /bus'kon/ **(-ona)** *n* searcher; pickpocket, thief, swindler, rogue

buscona /bus'kona/ *f*, prostitute

busilis /bu'silis/ *m*, *Inf.* knotty problem, snag; **ahí está el b.,** there's the rub; core, main point

búsqueda /'buskeða/ **(de)** *f*, search (for)

busto /'busto/ *m*, *Art.* bust, head and shoulders

butaca /bu'taka/ *f*, armchair; *Theat.* orchestra stall; seat (in movies, etc.); *Lat. Am.* stool

butifarra /buti'farra/ *f*, sausage made principally in Catalonia and the Balearic Islands; *Inf.* badly fitting stocking

buzo /'buso; 'buθo/ *m*, diver

buzón /bu'son; bu'θon/ *m*, mailbox; letter-box; canal, channel; sluice

C

C. /k/ abbrev. of ciudadano

¡ca! /ka/ *interj* Fancy! Oh no!

cabal /ka'βal/ *a* just, exact; perfect; complete; faultless. *interj* Exactly! **por sus cabales,** according to plan; perfectly

cábala /'kaβala/ *f*, cabala; divination; *Inf.* intrigue. **hacer cábalas,** to venture a guess

cabalgada /kaβal'gaða/ *f*, cavalcade; foray, raid

cabalgador /kaβalga'ðor/ **(-ra)** *n* rider, horseman

cabalgadura /kaβalga'ðura/ *f*, riding horse; beast of burden

cabalgar /kaβal'gar/ *vi* to ride a horse; ride in procession

cabalístico /kaβa'listiko/ *a* cabalistic; mysterious

caballa /ka'βaya; ka'βaʎa/ *f*, mackerel

caballada /kaβa'yaða; kaβa'ʎaða/ *f*, pack of horses; stud (of horses)

caballeresco /kaβaye'resko; kaβaʎe'resko/ *a* gentlemanly; knightly; chivalrous

caballería /kaβaye'ria; kaβaʎe'ria/ *f*, riding animal; cavalry; knightly deed or quest; any of Spanish Military Orders; knight-errantry; knighthood; chivalry; share of the spoils of war; horsemanship. **c. andante,** knight-errantry. **c. ligera,** *Mil.* light horse. **c. mayor,** horses, mares, mules. **c. menor,** asses, donkeys

caballeriza /kaβaye'risa; kaβaʎe'riθa/ *f*, stable; stud of horses; staff of a stable

caballerizo /kaβaye'riso; kaβaʎe'riθo/ *m*, head sta-

ble-groom. **c. mayor del rey,** Master of the King's Horse

caballero /kaβa'yero; kaβa'ʎero/ *m*, gentleman; cavalier; knight. **c. andante,** knight-errant. *Inf.* **c. de industria,** adventurer, sharper. **el C. de la Mancha,** the Knight of La Mancha. **el C. Sin Miedo y Sin Tacha,** the Seigneur de Bayart. **c. del hábito,** knight of one of the Spanish Military Orders. **c. novel,** untried knight. **armar c.,** to dub a knight

caballerosidad /kaβayerosi'ðað; kaβaʎerosi'ðað/ *f*, gentlemanliness; nobility; generosity; chivalry

caballeroso /kaβaye'roso; kaβaʎe'roso/ *a* gentlemanly; noble; generous; chivalrous

caballete /kaβa'yete; kaβa'ʎete/ *m*, ridge (of a roof); *Mil.* wooden horse; brake (for flax and hemp); *Agr.* furrow; easel; sawing-frame; trestle; bridge (of the nose)

caballito /kaβa'yito; kaβa'ʎito/ *m*, *dim* little horse; *pl* merry-go-round; automatic horse gambling game; circus equestrian act. **c. del diablo,** dragonfly

caballo /ka'βayo; ka'βaʎo/ *m*, horse; (chess) knight; (Spanish cards) queen; sawing-frame; *pl* cavalry. **c. balancín,** rocking horse. **c. de batalla,** war-horse; *Fig.* hobby-horse; forte; crux. **c. de cartón,** hobbyhorse; rocking horse. **c. de carrera,** racehorse. **c. de tiro,** draft-horse. **c. de vapor,** horsepower. **c. marino,** sea-horse. **a c.,** on horseback. **A c. regalado no le mires el diente,** Never look a gift horse in the mouth. **caer bien a c.,** to have a good seat (on a horse). **ser**

un c. loco en una cacharrería, to be like a bull in a china shop
cabaña /ka'βaɲa/ *f,* hut, cabin, cottage; flock (of sheep); drove (of mules); *Argentina* cattle ranch; *Art.* pastoral scene; balk (billiards)
cabaret /kaβa'ret/ *m,* cabaret, nightclub
cabaretero /kaβare'tero/ *m,* nightclub owner
cabeceada /kaβese'aða; kaβeθe'aða/ *f, Lat. Am.* nod (of the head)
cabecear /kaβese'ar; kaβeθe'ar/ *vi* to nod; shake the head in disapproval; move the head from side to side; toss the head (horses); (*Aer. Naut.*) pitch; sway (of a carriage); lean; *vt* refoot (socks); head (wine)
cabeceo /kaβe'seo; kaβe'θeo/ *m,* nod, shake (of head); (*Naut. Aer.*) pitching; lurching (of a carriage, etc.); bight (of river)
cabecera /kaβe'sera; kaβe'θera/ *f,* top, upper portion, head; seat of honor; bed-head; river source; capital (country or county); illustrated chapter heading; pillow; inscription, heading
cabecilla /kaβe'siya; kaβe'θiʎa/ *dim f,* small head. *mf Inf.* hothead. *m,* rebel leader
cabellera /kaβe'yera; kaβe'ʎera/ *f,* head of long hair; hair-switch; tail (of comet)
cabello /ka'βeyo; ka'βeʎo/ *m,* hair; head of hair; silk (of maize). *Fig. Inf.* **asirse de un c.,** to clutch at a straw
cabelludo /kaβe'yuðo; kaβe'ʎuðo/ *a* hairy; *Bot.* fibrous
caber /ka'βer/ *vi irr* to be room for, contain; fit into, go into (e.g. *No cabemos todos en este coche,* There isn't room for all of us in this car); happen, befall, have (e.g. *No les cupo tal suerte,* They did not have such luck--Such luck did not befall them); be possible (e.g. *Todo cabe en Dios,* All things are possible with God). **No cabe más,** There's no room for anything else; *Fig.* That's the limit. *Fig.* **no c. en sí,** to be beyond oneself (with joy, pride, etc.). **No cabe duda de que,** There's no doubt that. *Pres. Ind.* **quepo, cabes, etc.** *Fut.* **cabré, etc.** *Condit.* **cabría, etc.** *Preterite* **cupe, cupiste, etc.** *Pres. Subjunc.* **quepa, quepas, etc.** *Imperf. Subjunc.* **cupiese, etc.**
cabestrar /kaβes'trar/ *vt* to halter
cabestrillo /kaβes'triyo; kaβes'triʎo/ *m,* sling; thin chain (for ornament). **en c.,** in a sling (e.g. *Tenía el brazo en c.,* His arm was in a sling)
cabestro /ka'βestro/ *m,* halter; sling; leading ox
cabeza /ka'βesa; ka'βeθa/ *f,* head; top, upper end; nail-head; brain; mind; judgment; self-control; edge (of book); peak, summit; source, origin; individual, person; head of cattle; capital city. *m,* leader, chief, head. *Mech.* **c. de biela,** big-end. *Inf.* **c. de chorlito,** scatterbrain (person). **c. de hierro,** blockhead. *Mil.* **c. de puente,** bridgehead. **c. de partido,** principal town of a region. **c. de turco,** scapegoat. **irse la c.** **(a alguien),** to feel giddy. *Fig. Inf.* **meter a uno en la c.,** to put into someone's head. *Inf.* **quebrarse la c.,** to rack one's brains. *Inf.* **quitar a uno de la c.** **(una cosa),** to dissuade; get an idea out of someone's head
cabezada /kaβe'saða; kaβe'θaða/ *f,* blow with or on the head; nod; headshake; headstall; *Naut.* pitching. **dar cabezadas,** to nod, go to sleep
cabezal /kaβe'sal; kaβe'θal/ *m,* small head pillow; *Surg.* pad; bolster; narrow mattress; *Mech.* head
cabezo /ka'βeso; ka'βeθo/ *m,* summit (of mountain); hill; *Naut.* reef
cabezón /kaβe'son; kaβe'θon/ *m,* tax-register; collar-band; head-opening (of a garment)
cabezudo /kaβe'suðo; kaβe'θuðo/ *a* large-headed; *Inf.* obstinate; *Inf.* heady (of wine). *m,* carnival grotesque
cabida /ka'βiða/ *f,* space, capacity; extent, area
cabildear /kaβilde'ar/ *vi* to canvass votes, lobby
cabildo /ka'βildo/ *m, Eccl.* chapter; municipal council; meeting, or meeting place of council. **c. abierto,** town meeting
cabina /ka'βina/ *f,* cabin. **c. telefónica** phone booth
cabinero, -a /kaβi'nero/ *mf, Lat. Am.* flight attendant
cabizbajo /kaβis'βaho; kaβiθ'βaho/ *a* crestfallen; pensive, melancholy
cable /'kaβle/ *m,* cable; string (of bridge); cable's

length; **c. aéreo,** overhead cable. **c. alimentario,** feed line. **c. eléctrico,** electric cable
cabo /'kaβo/ *m,* end, extremity; stump, stub; handle, shaft, haft; leader; *Geog.* cape; end, conclusion; *Naut.* rope; ply (of wool, etc.); *Mil.* corporal; *pl* accessories (clothes); horse's tail and mane. **c. de maestranza,** foreman. **c. de mar,** naval quartermaster. **c. furriel,** *Mil.* quartermaster. **al c.,** in the end. **llevar a c.,** to finish
Cabo de Hornos /'kaβo de 'ornos/ Cape Horn
cabotaje /kaβo'tahe/ *m, Naut.* coasting trade
cabra /'kaβra/ *f,* nanny-goat; goat. **c. montesa,** wild goat
cabrerizo /kaβreriso; kaβre'riθo/ **(-za)** *a* goatish. *m,* goatherd
cabrero /ka'βrero/ **(-ra)** *m,* goatherd; *a Argentina* bad-tempered, cantankerous
cabria /'kaβria/ *f,* winch, hoist
cabrilla /ka'βriya; ka'βriʎa/ *f,* saw-horse; *pl Astron.* Pleiades; burn marks on legs from sitting too near fire; white crests (of waves)
cabrillear /kaβriye'ar; kaβriʎe'ar/ *vi* to foam, froth (the sea)
cabrío /ka'βrio/ *a* goatish. *m,* herd of goats. **macho c.,** male goat, he-goat
cabriola /ka'βriola/ *f,* fouetté (in dancing); spin in the air (acrobats); curvet (horses); caper
cabriolar /kaβrio'lar/ *vi* to curvet; caper, skip
cabriolé /kaβrio'le/ *m,* cabriolet; short cape with or without sleeves
cabritilla /kaβri'tiya; kaβri'tiʎa/ *f,* dressed kid; lambskin, etc.
cabrito /ka'βrito/ *m, Zool.* kid; *pl* toasted maize, popcorn
cabrón /ka'βron/ *m,* billy goat, buck, he-goat; *Inf.* complaisant husband, cuckold; *Chile* owner or operator of a brothel; *vulgar, Mexico* bastard
cabrona /ka'βrona/ *f, Chile* bawd
cabruno /ka'βruno/ *a* goatish
cabujón /kaβu'hon/ *m, Mineral.* uncut gem; unpolished ruby; *pl* vignettes
cacahual /kaka'ual/ *m,* cacao plantation
cacahuete /kaka'uete/ *m, Bot.* peanut, monkey nut
cacao /ka'kao/ *m, Bot.* cacao tree; cacoanut
cacarear /kakare'ar/ *vi* to crow, cackle; *vt Inf.* boast
cacareo /kaka'reo/ *m,* crowing, cackling; *Inf.* boast
cacatúa /kaka'tua/ *f,* cockatoo
cacera /ka'sera; ka'θera/ *f,* irrigation channel
cacería /kase'ria; kaθe'ria/ *f,* hunting party; hunting bag, booty; *Art.* hunting scene
cacerola /kase'rola; kaθe'rola/ *f,* stew-pot, casserole
cachalote /katʃa'lote/ *m,* sperm whale
cachano /ka'tʃano/ *m,* Old Nick
cachar /ka'tʃar/ *vt* to break in fragments; split (wood)
cacharrería /katʃarre'ria/ *f,* crockery store
cacharro /ka'tʃarro/ *m,* coarse earthenware vessel; *Inf.* decrepit, worthless object
cachazudo /katʃa'suðo; katʃa'θuðo/ *a* phlegmatic, slow
cachear /katʃe'ar/ *vt* to search (a person) for weapons
Cachemira /katʃe'mira/ Kashmir
cachemira /katʃe'mira/ *f,* cashmere
cacheo /ka'tʃeo/ *m,* search (of persons) for weapons
cachetada /katʃe'taða/ *f, Lat. Am.* slap (in the face)
cachete /ka'tʃete/ *m,* blow on the head or face with one's fist; cheek (especially fat one)
cachetero /katʃe'tero/ *m,* dagger
cachetina /katʃe'tina/ *f,* hand-to-hand fight
cachimba /ka'tʃimβa/ *f, Lat. Am.* pipe (for smoking)
cachiporra /katʃi'porra/ *f,* club, bludgeon
cachivache /katʃi'βatʃe/ *m, Inf.* (gen. *pl*) trash; pots, pans, utensils
cacho /'katʃo/ *m,* small slice (gen. of bread or fruit)
cachón /ka'tʃon/ *m,* breaker, wave; small waterfall
cachorro /ka'tʃorro/ **(-rra)** *n* puppy; cub. *m,* small pistol
cacillo /ka'siyo; ka'θiʎo/ *m,* ladle; basting spoon
cacique /ka'sike; ka'θike/ *m,* Indian chief, cacique; *Inf.* political "boss"

caciquismo /kasi'kismo; kaθi'kismo/ *m*, political "bossism"

caco /'kako/ *m*, pickpocket, thief; *Inf*. poltroon

cacofonía /kakofo'nia/ *f*, cacophony

cacografía /kakogra'fia/ *f*, cacography

cacto /'kakto/ *m*, cactus

cacumen /ka'kumen/ *m*, *Inf*. brains, acumen

cada /'kaða/ *a* every, each. **c. cual**, each. **c. que**, whenever; every time that. **c. y cuando que**, whenever

cadalso /ka'ðalso/ *m*, scaffold; platform, stand

cadáver /ka'ðaβer/ *m*, corpse

cadavérico /kaða'βeriko/ *a* cadaverous, ghastly

cadena /ka'ðena/ *f*, chain; link, tie; *Fig*. bond; *Fig*. sequence (of events); *Law*. imprisonment; *Archit*. buttress; grand chain (dancing); **c. de montañas**, range of mountains. **c. perpetua**, life imprisonment

cadencia /ka'ðensia; ka'ðenθia/ *f*, cadence; rhythm; *Mus*. measure, time; *Mus*. cadenza

cadencioso /kaðen'sioso; kaðen'θioso/ *a* rhythmic

cadente /ka'ðente/ *a* falling, declining; decaying, dying; rhythmic

cadera /ka'ðera/ *f*, hip; flank

cadete /ka'ðete/ *m*, *Mil*. cadet

cadi /'kaði/ *mf* caddy

Cádiz /'kaðis; 'kaðiθ/ Cadiz

caducar /kaðu'kar/ *vi* to become senile; become invalid, be annulled; expire, lapse; *Fig*. be worn out

caduceo /kaðu'seo; kaðu'θeo/ *m*, Mercury's wand

caducidad /kaðusi'ðað; kaðuθi'ðað/ *f*, decrepitude; lapse, expiration

caduco /ka'ðuko/ *a* senile; decrepit; perishable; lapsed; obsolete

caduquez /kaðu'kes; kaðu'keθ/ *f*, senility

caedizo /kae'ðiso; kae'ðiθo/ *a* ready to fall; timid, cowardly, weak

caer /ka'er/ *vi* irr to fall, drop; drop out or off; suit, fit, become; fail; fade (colors); *Fig*. drop (voice); (*with sobre*) attack, fall upon; (*with en*) fall in or on to; decay, collapse; understand; (*with preps. a, hacia*) *Fig*. look on to, face; (*with por, en*) *Fig*. fall on, occur on; *vr Aer*. crash; fly off (buttons, etc.). **c. de cabeza**, to fall head foremost. **c. en conflicto (con)**, to come into conflict (with). **c. en las manos de uno**, to come into somebody's possession (come to be owned by somebody). **c. en gracia**, to make a good impression, arouse affection. **caerse de suyo**, to be self-evident. **c. por tierra**, (plan, etc.) to fall through. **Cayó enfermo**, He was taken ill. **cayendo y levantado**, dying. **Se me cayó**, It dropped (I dropped it). *Pres. Ind*. **caigo, caes, etc.** *Pres. Part*. **cayendo**. *Preterite* **cayó cayeron**. *Pres. Subjunc*. **caiga, etc.**

café /ka'fe/ *m*, coffee (tree, berry, drink); café, coffee-house. **c. con leche**, café au lait. **c. negro** *Lat. Am*. (*except Columbia*) black coffee. **c. solo** *Spain* black coffee. **c. tinto** *Colombia* black coffee

cafeína /kafe'ina/ *f*, caffeine

cafetal /kafe'tal/ *m*, coffee plantation

cafetera /kafe'tera/ *f*, coffeepot; *Peru* cab, taxi

cafeto /ka'feto/ *m*, coffee tree

cafiche /ka'fitʃe/ *m*, *Argentina, Chile* pimp

caficultor /kafikul'tor/ *m*, coffee-grower

caficultura /kafikul'tura/ *f*, coffee-growing

cafúa /ka'fua/ *f*, *Argentina* clink, slammer

cagadas /ka'gaðas/ *f pl*, droppings, dung

cagar /ka'gar/ **(se)** *vi vt vr* to evacuate (bowels); *vt Inf*. spoil, make a botch of

cagarruta /kaga'rruta/ *f*, dung of sheep, deer, rabbits, etc.

caída /ka'iða/ *f*, falling; fall; ruin; failure; close (of day); *Fig*. falling off; hanging (curtains, etc.); diminution; incline; *pl* coarse wool; *Inf*. repartee. **a la c. de la tarde**, at the end of the afternoon. **a la c. del sol**, at sunset

caído /ka'iðo/ **(-da)** *a* debilitated, languid; lapsed; (of a shoulder) sloping. **los caídos**, the fallen, the dead (in war, etc.)

caimán /kai'man/ *m*, alligator; *Inf*. shark, astute person

caite /'kaite/ *m*, *Central America* sandal

caja /'kaha/ *f*, box; safe, cash box; coffin; (of a vehicle) body; *Mus*. drum; case (of piano, watch, etc.); cavity; well (of a stair); *Com*. cash; cash-desk; cashier's office; *Bot*. sheath. **c. de ahorros**, savings bank. **c. de caudales**, strong-box. *Print*. **c. de imprenta**, type case. **c. de música**, musical box. **c. de reclutamiento**, recruiting office. **c. de velocidades**, gearbox. **c. registradora**, cash register. **c. torácica**, rib cage, thoracic cage

cajero /ka'hero/ **(-ra)** *m*, boxmaker; *n Com*. cashier; peddler. **c. automática**, automatic-teller machine, ATM, cash machine

cajetilla /kahe'tiya; kahe'tiʎa/ *f*, packet (cigarettes, etc.)

cajón /ka'hon/ *m*, chest, locker, case; drawer. **c. de municiones**, ammunition-box

cajonera /kaho'nera/ *f*, *Eccl*. chest of drawers in sacristy; *Agr*. frame

cal /kal/ *f*, lime. **c. muerta**, slaked lime. **c. viva**, quicklime. *Fig. Inf*. **de c. y canto**, tough, strong

cala /'kala/ *f*, sample slice (of fruit); *Naut*. hold; *Surg*. probe; cove, small bay; *Bot*. iris

calabacera /kalaβa'sera; kalaβa'θera/ *f*, *Bot*. pumpkin or gourd plant

calabacín /kalaβa'sin; kalaβa'θin/ *m*, kind of vegetable marrow; *Inf*. dolt

calabaza /kala'βasa; kala'βaθa/ *f*, *Bot*. pumpkin (plant and fruit); gourd; *Inf*. dolt. **dar calabazas**, to refuse (suitor); flunk (an examinee). *Inf*. **llevar calabazas**, to get the sack; be jilted

calabobos /kala'βoβos/ *m*, *Inf*. drizzle

calabocero /kalaβo'sero; kalaβo'θero/ *m*, jailer

calabozo /kala'βoso; kala'βoθo/ *m*, dungeon; prison cell; pruning knife

calada /ka'laða/ *f*, soaking, wetting through; flight of bird of prey; swoop. **dar una c.**, *Fig. Inf*. to dress down

calado /ka'laðo/ *a* soaked, wet through. *m*, *Sew*. open-work; fretwork; *Naut*. draft of a ship; water level; *pl* lace. **c. hasta los huesos**, soaked to the skin; madly in love

calador /kala'ðor/ *m*, one who does open or fretwork; caulking iron; borer; *Surg*. probe

calafate /kala'fate/ *m*, caulker

calafatear /kalafate'ar/ *vt Naut*. to caulk

calamaco /kala'mako/ *m*, *Mexico* kidney bean

calamar /kala'mar/ *m*, *Zool*. squid, calamary

calambre /ka'lambre/ *m*, cramp. **c. del escribiente**, writer's cramp

calamidad /kalami'ðað/ *f*, misfortune, calamity

calamina /kala'mina/ *f*, *Mineral*. calamine

calamitoso /kalami'toso/ *a* calamitous; unfortunate, unhappy

cálamo /'kalamo/ *m*, ancient flute; stalk (of grass); *Poet*. pen

calamocano /kalamo'kano/ *a* maudlin, tipsy

calandria /ka'landria/ *f*, *Ornith*. calender, lark; *Mech*. calender; treadmill. *mf Inf*. malingerer

calaña /ka'lapa/ *f*, sample; model; pattern; kind, quality; temperament; cheap fan

calar /ka'lar/ *vt* to permeate, soak through; pierce; do openwork (in cloth, paper, metal); cut a sample slice from fruit; pull (hat, etc.) well down on head; put down (an eyeshade or visor); fix (bayonets, etc.); *Inf*. understand (persons); *Inf*. guess, realize; *Naut*. let down; *vi Naut*. draw (water); *vr* be drenched, wet through; swoop (birds of prey); *Inf*. sneak in. *a* calcareous

calar /ka'lar/ *m*, limestone deposit or region

calatear /kalate'ar/ *vt*, *Peru* to undress

calato, -a /ka'lato/ *a*, *Peru* naked, nude; broke, penniless

calavera /kala'βera/ *f*, skull. *m*, dare-devil, madcap; roué; *Mexico* taillight

calaverada /kalaβe'raða/ *f*, *Inf*. dare-devilment, foolishness; escapade

calcañar /kalka'ɲar/ *m*, heel (of foot)

calcar /kal'kar/ *vt* to trace (drawing); press with foot; copy servilely, imitate

calcáreo /kal'kareo/ *a* calcareous

calce /'kalse; 'kalθe/ *m,* rim of a wheel; wedge; tire

calcés /kal'ses; kal'θes/ *m, Naut.* masthead

calceta /kal'seta; kal'θeta/ *f,* stocking; fetter. *Inf.* **hacer c.,** to knit

calcetería /kalsete'ria; kalθete'ria/ *f,* hosiery shop; hosiery trade

calcetero /kalse'tero; kalθe'tero/ **(-ra)** *n* hosier; hose maker or darner

calcetín /kalse'tin; kalθe'tin/ *m,* sock

calcificación /kalsifika'sion; kalθifika'θion/ *f, Med.* calcification

calcinación /kalsina'sion; kalθina'θion/ *f,* calcination

calcinar /kalsi'nar; kalθi'nar/ *vt* to calcine

calcio /'kalsio; 'kalθio/ *m,* calcium

calco /'kalko/ *m,* tracing (drawing)

calcografía /kalkogra'fia/ *f,* chalcography

calcografiar /kalkogra'fiar/ *vt* to transfer; make chalcographies of

calcomanía /kalkoma'nia/ *f,* transfer

calculación /kalkula'sion; kalkula'θion/ *f,* calculation

calculado /kalku'laðo/ *a* calculated

calculador /kalkula'ðor/ *a* calculating. *m,* calculating machine, calculator

calcular /kalku'lar/ *vt* to calculate

cálculo /'kalkulo/ *m,* calculation; *Math.* estimate; investigation; conjecture; *Math. Med.* calculus. **c. hepático,** *Med.* gallstone

calda /'kalda/ *f,* heating; *pl* hot mineral baths

caldear /kalde'ar/ *vt* to heat

caldeo /kal'deo/ *m,* heating

caldera /kal'dera/ *f,* cauldron; cauldron full; *West. Hem.* teapot; *Engin.* boiler. **c. de vapor,** steam-boiler

calderería /kaldere'ria/ *f,* coppersmith's trade and shop

calderero /kalde'rero/ *m,* boiler maker; coppersmith; tinker

calderilla /kalde'riya; kalde'riʎa/ *f,* holy water stoup; any copper coin

caldero /kal'dero/ *m,* small cauldron; casserole; kettle

calderón /kalde'ron/ *m,* large cauldron; *Mus.* rest; *Mus.* trill; pause

caldo /'kaldo/ *m,* broth; salad dressing; *pl Agr.* oil, wine, vegetable juices

calefacción /kalefak'sion; kalefak'θion/ *f,* heating. **c. central,** central heating

calendario /kalen'dario/ *m,* calendar. **c. deportivo,** fixture card. **c. gregoriano,** Gregorian calendar

calendas /ka'lendas/ *f pl,* calends. **en las c. griegas,** at the Greek calends

caléndula /ka'lendula/ *f,* marigold

calentador /kalenta'ðor/ *a* heating, warming. *m,* heater; warming-pan

calentamiento /kalenta'miento/ *m,* heating, warming

calentar /kalen'tar/ *vt irr* to heat, warm; rev-up (an engine); hasten; *Inf.* spank; *vr* warm oneself; be in heat (animals); grow excited. See **acertar**

calentura /kalen'tura/ *f,* fever

calenturiento /kalentu'riento/ *a* feverish

calera /ka'lera/ *f,* lime-pit; lime-kiln; fishing smack

calesa /ka'lesa/ *f,* calash, calèche, chaise (two-wheeled carriage)

calesita /kale'sita/ *f, Lat. Am.* merry-go-round

caleta /ka'leta/ *f,* cove, creek

caletre /ka'letre/ *m, Inf.* discernment, head, sense

calibrar /kali'βrar/ *vt* to calibrate; gauge

calibre /ka'liβre/ *m, Mech.* gauge; bore, caliber; diameter (tubes, pipes, etc.)

calidad /kali'ðað/ *f,* quality; role; character, temperament; condition, requisite; importance, gravity; personal particulars; nobility; *pl* qualities of the mind. **c. originaria,** rank and birth. **c. de oficio,** justification for action. **en c. de,** in the capacity of

cálido /'kaliðo/ *a* warm, hot; warming, heating; vehement, ardent; *Art.* warm

calidoscopio /kaliðos'kopio/ *m,* kaleidoscope

calientalibros /kalienta'liβros/ *mf,* bookworm (person)

calientapiés /kalienta'pies/ *m,* footwarmer

calientaplatos /kalienta'platos/ *m,* hot plate, platewarmer

caliente /ka'liente/ *a* warm, hot; excited; *Art.* warm

calientito /kalien'tito/ *a* piping hot

califa /ka'lifa/ *m,* caliph

calificable /kalifi'kaβle/ *a* classifiable; qualifiable

calificación /kalifika'sion; kalifika'θion/ *f,* classification; qualification; judgment; grade, place (examinations)

calificar /kalifi'kar/ *vt* to class; grade (exams); authorize; judge (qualities); *Fig.* ennoble; *vr* prove noble descent

calificativo /kalifika'tiβo/ *a Gram.* qualifying. *m,* epithet

californio /kali'fornio/ **(-ia)** *a* and *n* Californian

caliginoso /kalihi'noso/ *a* murky, dark

caligrafía /kaligra'fia/ *f,* calligraphy

calígrafo /ka'ligrafo/ *m,* calligraphist

calistenia /kalis'tenia/ *f,* callisthenics

cáliz /'kalis; 'kaliθ/ *m,* chalice; *Poet.* cup; *Bot.* calyx

caliza /ka'lisa; ka'liθa/ *f,* limestone

calizo /ka'liso; ka'liθo/ *a* calcareous

callado /ka'yaðo; ka'ʎaðo/ *a* silent; reserved; secret

callar /ka'yar; ka'ʎar/ **(se)** *vi* and *vr* to say nothing, keep silent; stop speaking; stop making any sound (persons, animals, things); *vt* conceal, keep secret; omit, leave out; *Inf. interj* **¡Calle!** You don't say so! **Quien calla otorga,** Silence gives consent

calle /'kaye; 'kaʎe/ *f,* street. **c. de un sentido, c. de una corrida** *Mexico* one-way street. **c. de una sola mano** *Argentina* one-way street *Inf.* **abrir c.,** to clear the way. *Inf.* **dejar en la c.,** to leave destitute. *Inf.* **echar a la c.,** put out of the house, to throw out of the house; make known, publish. **ponerse en la c.,** to go out

calleja, callejuela /ka'yeha, kaye'huela; ka'ʎeha, kaʎe'huela/ *f,* small street, alley, side street

callejear /kayehe'ar; kaʎehe'ar/ *vi* to walk the streets, wander about the streets, loaf around the streets

callejero /kaye'hero; kaʎe'hero/ *a* fond of gadding. *m,* street directory

callejón /kaye'hon; kaʎe'hon/ *m,* alley, lane. **c. sin salida,** cul-de-sac; *Fig.* impasse

callicida /kayi'siða; kaʎi'θiða/ *m,* corn cure

callista /ka'yista; ka'ʎista/ *mf* chiropodist

callo /'kayo; 'kaʎo/ *m,* corn, callosity; *Med.* callus; *pl* tripe

calloso /ka'yoso; ka'ʎoso/ *a* callous, horny

calma /'kalma/ *f,* calm, airlessness; serenity, composure; quiet, tranquillity, peace. **c. chicha,** dead calm. **en c.,** at peace; tranquil; calm (of the sea)

calmante /kal'mante/ *a* calming, soothing. *Med. a* and *m,* sedative, tranquilizer

calmar /kal'mar/ *vt* to soothe, calm; moderate, mitigate; pacify; quench (thirst); *vi* grow calm; moderate; be becalmed

calmoso /kal'moso/ *a* calm, tranquil; *Inf.* sluggish, lazy; imperturbable

calor /ka'lor/ *m,* heat; ardor, vehemence; cordiality; *Fig.* heat (of battle); excitement

caloría /kalo'ria/ *f, Phys.* calorie

calórico /ka'loriko/ *a Phys.* caloric, thermic

calorífero /kalo'rifero/ *a* heat-giving. *m,* heater, radiator

calumnia /ka'lumnia/ *f,* calumny; *Law.* slander

calumniador /kalumnia'ðor/ **(-ra)** *a* slandering. *n* calumniator, slanderer

calumniar /kalumni'ar/ *vt* to calumniate; *Law.* slander

calumnioso /kalum'nioso/ *a* calumnious, slanderous

caluroso /kalu'roso/ *a* hot, warm; cordial, friendly; enthusiastic; ardent, impassioned; excited

calva /'kalβa/ *f,* bald patch on head; worn place (cloth, etc.); bare spot, clearing (trees, etc.)

Calvario /kal'βario/ *m,* Calvary; *Inf.* series of disasters; *Inf.* debts

calvero /kal'βero/ *m,* clearing (in a wood); chalk or marl pit

calvicie /kal'βisie; kal'βiθie/ *f,* baldness

calvo /'kalβo/ *a* bald; bare, barren (land); worn (cloth, etc.)

calza /'kalsa; 'kalθa/ *f*, breeches (gen. *pl*); wedge; *Inf.* stocking. *Inf.* **tomar calzas,** to beat it

calzada /kal'saða; kal'θaða/ *f*, roadway. **c. romana,** Roman road

calzado /kal'saðo; kal'θaðo/ *m*, footwear, shoes

calzador /kalsa'ðor; kalθa'ðor/ *m*, shoehorn

calzadura /kalsa'ðura; kalθa'ðura/ *f*, wedging (of a wheel); act of putting on shoes; felloe of a wheel

calzar /kal'sar; kal'θar/ *vt* to put on shoes; wear (spurs, gloves, etc.); wedge, block (wheel); scotch (a wheel). *Fig. Inf.* **c. el coturno,** don the buskin; write in the sublime style; write a tragedy, write tragedies. **calzarse a una persona,** to have a person in one's pocket

calzón /kal'son; kal'θon/ *m*, long underwear, *Lat. Am.* panties. *Fig. Inf.* **ponerse los calzones,** (of a woman) to wear the pants

calzonazos /kalso'nasos; kalθo'naθos/ *m*, *Inf.* weak-willed, easily led fellow

calzoncillos /kalson'siyos; kalθon'θiʎos/ *m pl*, drawers, pants

calzoneras /kalso'neras; kalθo'neras/ *fpl*, *Mexico* pants buttoned down the sides

cama /'kama/ *f*, bed; bedstead; bedhanging; lair, form; floor (of a cart); check (of bridle) (gen. *pl*). **c. de campaña,** camp bed. **c. de matrimonio,** double bed. **c. de monja,** single bed. **c. de operaciones,** operating table. **c. turca,** settee-bed. **guardar c.,** to stay in bed

camada /ka'maða/ *f*, brood, litter; *Inf.* gang

camafeo /kama'feo/ *m*, cameo

camaleón /kamale'on/ *m*, chameleon; *Inf.* changeable person

cámara /'kamara/ *f*, chamber; hall; house (of deputies); granary; *Naut.* state room; chamber (firearms, mines); *Phys.* camera; human excrement; *Auto.* inner tube. **c. acorazada,** strong-room. **c. alta,** Upper House, **c. baja** or **c. de los comunes,** lower house, house of commons. **c. de comercio,** chamber of commerce. **c. oscura,** (optics) dark room

camarada /kama'raða/ *mf* pal, companion, comrade

camaradería /kamaraðe'ria/ *f*, comradeship, companionship

camarera /kama'rera/ *f*, waitress; chambermaid; stewardess

camarero /kama'rero/ *m*, waiter; papal chamberlain; chamberlain; steward; valet. **c. mayor,** lord chamberlain

camarilla /kama'riya; kama'riʎa/ *f*, palace or other clique, coterie; *Inf.* back-scratch

camarín /kama'rin/ *m*, *Theat.* dressing-room; closet; boudoir; cage (of a lift); niche

camarón /kama'ron/ *m*, prawn, shrimp; tip, reward

camarote /kama'rote/ *m*, cabin; berth

cambalache /kamβa'latʃe/ *m*, *Lat. Am.* secondhand shop; exchange

cambalachear /kambalatʃe'ar/ *vt Inf.* to barter

cámbaro /'kambaro/ *m*, sea-crab

cambiable /kam'βiaβle/ *a* exchangeable; changeable

cambiante /kam'βiante/ *a* exchanging; changing. *m*, sheen, luster (gen. *pl*); money changer

cambiar /kam'βiar/ *vt* to exchange; convert. *vt* and *vi* change, alter; *vi* and *vr* to veer (wind). **c. de aguas,** *Poet.* to move (change one's residence). **c. de aire,** get a change of scenery. **c. de frente,** to face about; *Fig.* change front

cambio /'kambio/ *m*, exchange; change; *Com.* rate of exchange; money change; *Com.* premium on bills of exchange. **a c. de, en c. de,** in exchange for; instead of. **en c.,** instead, on the other hand. **c. de velocidad,** *Auto.* gear-changing. **letra de c.,** bill of exchange. **libre c.,** free trade

cambista /kam'/'βista/ *mf* money changer. *m*, banker

cambullón /kamβu'jon; kamβu'ʎon/ *m*, *Lat. Am.* swindle

cambur /kam'βur/ *m*, *Venezuela* banana

camelar /kame'lar/ *vt Inf.* to woo; seduce

camelia /ka'melia/ *f*, camelia. **c. japonesa,** japonica

camellero /kame'yero; kame'ʎero/ *m*, camel keeper or driver

camello /ka'meyo; ka'meʎo/ *m*, camel. **c. pardal,** giraffe

camellón /kame'yon; kame'ʎon/ *m*, furrow; drinking trough; *Mexico* island, traffic island, median strip

camelo /ka'melo/ *m*, *Inf.* eyewash

camilla /ka'miya; ka'miʎa/ *f*, couch; small round skirted table with brazier underneath; stretcher, litter

camillero /kami'yero; kami'ʎero/ *m*, *Mil.* stretcher-bearer

caminador /kamina'ðor/ *a* in the habit of walking a great deal

caminante /kami'nante/ *mf* walker, traveler

caminar /kami'nar/ *vi* to travel; walk; *Fig.* move on, go (inanimate things). *Fig. Inf.* **c. derecho,** to walk uprightly

caminata /kami'nata/ *f*, long, tiring walk; excursion

caminejo /kami'neho/ *m*, worn path

camino /ka'mino/ *m*, road; route; journey; way, means; **c. de hierro,** railway. **c. de mesa,** table-runner. **c. de sirga,** towpath. **c. real,** highway, main road. **de c.,** on the way, in passing. **ponerse en c.,** to set out

camión /ka'mion/ *m*, truck. **c. de volteo, c. volquete** dump truck; *Mexico* bus; truck

camionera /kamio'nera/ *f*, *Mexico* bus station

camioneta /kamio'neta/ *f*, light truck, pick-up truck; *WH* station wagon

camisa /ka'misa/ *f*, shirt, stiff shirt; thin skin (of fruit); sloughed skin of snakes; coat (of whitewash, etc.); *Mech.* jacket; mantle (gas). **c. de fuerza,** strait-jacket. **dejar sin c.,** *Inf.* to leave penniless

camisería /kamise'ria/ *f*, shirt shop or factory

camisero /kami'sero/ **(-ra)** *n* shirt maker or seller

camiseta /kami'seta/ *f*, undershirt, T-shirt. **c. de fútbol,** soccer player's jersey

camisola /kami'sola/ *f*, stiff shirt; ruffled shirt

camisón /kami'son/ *m*, large wide shirt; night shirt

camomila /kamo'mila/ *f*, chamomile

camorra /ka'morra/ *f*, *Inf.* brawl, shindy. **armar c.,** to start a row

camote /ka'mote/ *m*, *Lat. Am.* sweet potato

campal /kam'pal/ *a* field, country

campamento /kampa'mento/ *m*, camping; *Mil.* encampment; camp; jamboree

campana /kam'pana/ *f*, bell; anything bell-shaped; church, parish. **c. de chimenea,** mantelpiece. **c. de hogar,** hood, shutter (of a fireplace)

campanada /kampa'naða/ *f*, peal of a bell; scandal

campanario /kampa'nario/ *m*, belfry, bell tower

campanear /kampane'ar/ *vi* to ring bells frequently

campaneo /kampa'neo/ *m*, bell-ringing; chime

campanero /kampa'nero/ *m*, bell-founder; bell ringer

campanil /kampa'nil/ *m*, small belfry, campanile

campanilla /kampa'niya; kampa'niʎa/ *f*, hand-bell; bubble; any bell-shaped flower

campante /kam'pante/ *a* outstanding; *Inf.* proud, satisfied

campanudo /kampa'nuðo/ *a* bell-shaped; sonorous (of words); pompous (of speech)

campaña /kam'paɲa/ *f*, level country; campaign. *Naut.* voyage, cruise. **correr la c.,** to reconnoiter. **la C. del Desierto,** the War against the Gauchos (in Argentina)

campar /kam'par/ *vi* to camp. *Inf.* **c. por sus respetos,** to stand on one's own feet

campeador /kampea'ðor/ *a* mighty in battle

campear /kampe'ar/ *vi* to go out to graze; grow green (crops); excel; *Mil.* be engaged in a campaign, reconnoiter

campechano /kampe'tʃano/ *a Inf.* hearty; frank; cheerful; generous

campeche /kam'petʃe/ *m*, *Bot.* logwood

campeón /kampe'on/ *m*, champion; advocate, defender

campeonato /kampeo'nato/ *m*, championship

campesinado /kampesi'naðo/ *m*, peasantry

campesino /kampe'sino/ **(-na)** *a* rural, rustic. *n* country dweller

campestre /kam'pestre/ *a* rural

campiña /kam'piɲa/ *f*, expanse of cultivated land; countryside, landscape

campo /'kampo/ *m*, country (as opposed to urban areas); field; *Fig.* sphere, province; (*Phys. Herald. Mil.*) field; *Art.* ground; *Mil.* camp, army; plain ground (of silks, etc.). **«C. Abierto»**, "Miscellaneous" (e.g. as the title of a section in a book catalog). **c. de aterrizaje**, *Aer.* landing-field. **c. de batalla**, battlefield. **c. de concentración**, concentration camp. **c. de experimentación**, testing ground. **c. de golf**, golf course. **c. de prisioneros** *Mil.* prison camp. **c. de tiro**, rifle-range. **c. santo**, graveyard. **c. visual**, field of vision. **a c. abierto**, in the open air. **a c. travieso**, cross-country

camuflaje /kamu'flahe/ *m*, camouflage

camuflar /kamu'flar/ *vt* to camouflage

can /kan/ *m*, dog; trigger; *Archit.* modillion; *Astron.* Dog Star

cana /'kana/ *f*, gray hair

Canadá /kana'ða/ Canada

canadiense /kana'ðiense/ *a* and *mf* Canadian

canal /ka'nal/ *m*, canal. *mf, Geol.* subterranean waterway; channel; *Anat.* canal, duct; defile, narrow valley; gutter; drinking trough; animal carcass. **abrir en c.**, to open up, split open

canalera /kana'lera/ *f*, roof gutter

canaleta /kana'leta/ *f*, (wooden) trough; gutter (on roof)

canalete /kana'lete/ *m*, paddle

canalización /kanalisa'sion; kanaliθa'θion/ *f*, canalization; *Elec.* main, mains; piping, tubing

canalizar /kanali'sar; kanali'θar/ *vt* to make canals or channels; regulate waters of rivers, etc.; canalize

canalla /ka'naya; ka'naʎa/ *f, Inf.* mob, rabble. *m, Inf.* scoundrel

canallesco /kana'yesko; kana'ʎesko/ *a* scoundrelly, knavish; despicable

canalón /kana'lon/ *m*, gutter, spout; shovel hat; pantile

canana /ka'nana/ *f*, cartridge belt

canapé /kana'pe/ *m*, sofa

canario /ka'nario/ **(-ia)** *m*, canary. *a* and *n* pertaining to or native of the Canary Islands.

canasta /ka'nasta/ *f*, hamper, basket; card game

canastilla /kanas'tiya; kanas'tiʎa/ *f*, small basket; layette

canastillo /kanas'tiyo; kanas'tiʎo/ *m*, basket-work tray

cáncamo /'kankamo/ *m*, ring-bolt

cancamusa /kanka'musa/ *f, Inf.* trick, deception

cancel /kan'sel; kan'θel/ *m*, draftscreen; *Eccl.* screen

cancela /kan'sela; kan'θela/ *f*, wrought-iron door

cancelación /kansela'sion; kanθela'θion/ *f*, cancellation; expunging

cancelar /kanse'lar; kanθe'lar/ *vt* to cancel; expunge, annul; abolish, blot out; pay off, clear (a mortgage)

cancelaría /kanse'laria; kanθe'laria/ *f*, papal chancery

cancelario /kanse'lario; kanθe'lario/ *m*, chancellor (universities)

cáncer /'kanser; 'kanθer/ *m*, cancer

cancerar /kanse'rar; kanθe'rar/ *vt* to consume; weaken; mortify; *vr* suffer from cancer; become cancerous

cancerbero /kanser'βero; kanθer'βero/ *m, Myth.* Cerberus; *Fig.* unbribable guard

canceroso /kanse'roso; kanθe'roso/ *a* cancerous

cancha /'kantʃa/ *f, Sports.* fronton; (tennis) court; cockpit; yard; hippodrome; widest part of a river; road; toasted maize. **estar en su cancha** *Argentina, Chile* to be in one's element. **tener cancha** *Argentina* to be experienced; *Venezuela* have charisma, charm, allure

canciller /kansi'yer; kanθi'ʎer/ *m*, chancellor; foreign minister; assistant vice-consul

cancillería /kansiye'ria; kanθiʎe'ria/ *f*, chancellorship; chancellery; foreign ministry

canción /kan'sion; kan'θion/ *f*, song; lyric poem; musical accompaniment; old name for any poetical composition. **volver a la misma c.**, *Fig.* to be always harping on the same theme

cancionero /kansio'nero; kanθio'nero/ *m*, collection of songs and verses; songbook

cancionista /kansio'nista; kanθio'nista/ *mf* singer; song writer

candado /kan'daðo/ *m*, padlock; earring

candeal /kande'al/ *a* white (of bread)

candela /kan'dela/ *f*, candle; horse-chestnut flower; candlestick; *Inf.* fire. **en c.**, *Naut.* vertical (of masts, etc.)

candelabro /kande'laβro/ *m*, candelabrum

candelero /kande'lero/ *m*, candlestick; lamp; candle maker or seller; *Naut.* stanchion

candente /kan'dente/ *a* candescent, red-hot

candidatear /kandiðate'ar/ *vi* to run (for office)

candidato /kandi'ðato/ **(-ta)** *n* candidate

candidatura /kandiða'tura/ *f*, candidature

candidez /kandi'ðes; kandi'ðeθ/ *f*, simplicity, ingenuousness; candidness

cándido /'kandiðo/ *a* white; simple, ingenuous; candid, frank

candil /kan'dil/ *m*, oil lamp; Greek lamp; tips of stag's horns; *Inf.* cock of a hat

candileja /kandi'leha/ *f*, oil reservoir of lamp; *pl* footlights, floats

candor /kan'dor/ *m*, extreme whiteness; sincerity, candor; simplicity, innocence

candoroso /kando'roso/ *a* candid, open; simple, honest

canela /ka'nela/ *f, Bot.* cinnamon; *Fig.* anything exquisitely perfect

canelo /ka'nelo/ *m*, cinnamon tree. *a* cinnamon-colored

cangilón /kanhi'lon/ *m*, pitcher, jar; bucket (for water); dredging bucket

cangreja /kaŋ'greha/ *f, Naut.* gaffsail. **c. de mesana,** *Naut.* jigger

cangrejo /kaŋ'greho/ *m*, crab. **c. de mar,** sea-crab. **c. ermitaño,** hermit crab

canguro /kaŋ'guro/ *m*, kangaroo

caníbal /ka'niβal/ *a* and *mf* cannibal

canibalismo /kaniβa'lismo/ *m*, cannibalism

canica /ka'nika/ *f*, marble (for playing with)

canícula /ka'nikula/ *f*, dog days; *Astron.* Dog star

caniculares /kaniku'lares/ *m pl* dog days

canijo /ka'niho/ *a Inf.* delicate, sickly; anemic, stunted

canilla /ka'niya; ka'niʎa/ *f*, long bone of leg or arm; any principal bones in bird's wing; tap, faucet; spool, reel; fault (in cloth)

canillera /kani'jera; kani'ʎera/ *f, Lat. Am.* cowardice; fear

canillito, -a /kani'jito; kani'ʎito/ *mf, Lat. Am.* newsboy, newsgirl

canino /ka'nino/ *a* canine

canje /'kanhe/ *m*, (*diplomacy, mil., com.*) exchange, substitution. **c. de prisioneros,** exchange of prisoners

canjear /kanhe'ar/ *vt* to exchange

cano /'kano/ *a* white-haired, hoary; ancient; *Poet.* white

canoa /ka'noa/ *f*, canoe; launch. **c. automóvil,** motor launch

canódromo /ka'noðromo/ *m*, dog-race track

canoero /kano'ero/ **(-ra)** *n* canoeist

canon /'kanon/ *m*, rule; (*Eccl. Print.*) canon; catalog; part of the Mass; *Mus.* canon, catch; tax. *pl* canon law

canónico /ka'noniko/ *a* canonic, canonical

canónigo /ka'nonigo/ *m*, canon; prebendary

canonización /kanonisa'sion; kanoniθa'θion/ *f*, canonization

canonizar /kanoni'sar; kanoni'θar/ *vt* to canonize; extol, exalt; approve, acclaim

canonjía /kanon'hia/ *f*, canonry, canonship; *Inf.* sinecure

canoso /ka'noso/ *a* white-haired, hoary

cansado /kan'saðo/ **(-da)** *a* tired; weary; exhausted; decadent; tiresome; *Inf.* fed up. *n* bore, tedious person

cansancio /kan'sansio; kan'sanθio/ *m*, fatigue, weariness

cansar /kan'sar/ *vt* to tire, weary; *Agr.* exhaust soil; bore; badger, annoy; *vr* be tired; grow weary

cansino /kan'sino/ *a* worn-out (of horses, etc.)

cantable /kan'taβle/ *a* singable; *Mus.* cantabile

cantábrico /kan'taβriko/ **(-ca)** *a* and *n* Cantabrian

cantante /kan'tante/ *a* singing. *mf* professional singer

cantar /kan'tar/ *vi* to sing; twitter, chirp; extol; *Inf.* squeak, creak; *Fig.* call (cards); *Inf.* squeal, confess. *m*, song. **C. de los Cantares,** Song of Songs. **cantarlas claras,** to call a spade a spade

cántara /'kantara/ *f*, pitcher, jug

cantárida /kan'tariða/ *f*, Spanish fly

cántaro /'kantaro/ *m*, pitcher, jug; jugful; varying wine measure; ballot box; tax on spirits and oil. **llover a cántaros,** to rain heavily; pour

cantata /kan'tata/ *f*, cantata

cantatriz /kanta'tris; kanta'triθ/ *f*, singer, prima donna

cante /'kante/ *m*, song; singing

cantera /kan'tera/ *f*, *Mineral.* quarry; capacity, talent

cantería /kante'ria/ *f*, stone-cutting; quarrying; building made of hewn stone

cantero /kan'tero/ *m*, stone-cutter; quarryman

cántico /'kantiko/ *m*, *Eccl.* canticle; *Poet.* poem

cantidad /kanti'ðað/ *f*, quantity; large part; portion; sum of money; quantity (prosody). **c. llovida,** rainfall

cantiga /kan'tiga/ *or* **cántiga** *f*, old poetic form designed to be sung

cantil /kan'til/ *m*, cliff; steep rock

cantimplora /kantim'plora/ *f*, water cooler; canteen (of water); siphon

cantina /kan'tina/ *f*, wine cellar; canteen; refreshment room

cantinero /kanti'nero/ *m*, sutler; owner of a canteen

canto /'kanto/ *m*, singing; song; canto; epic or other poem; end, rim, edge; non-cutting edge (knives, swords); pebble, stone; angle (of a building). *Mus.* **c. llano,** plain-song. **al c. del gallo,** at cockcrow. **de c.,** on edge

cantón /kan'ton/ *m*, province, region; corner (of a street); cantonment; *Herald.* canton, quartering

cantonera /kanto'nera/ *f*, corner-piece (books, furniture, etc., as ornament); angle-iron; bracket, small shelf

cantor /kan'tor/ **(-ra)** *a* singing. *n* singer; song-bird

cantuja /kan'tuha/ *f*, *Peru* underworld slang

canturía /kantu'ria/ *f*, singing exercise; vocal music; monotonous song; droning; *Mus.* execution, technique

canturreo, /kantu'rreo,/ *m*, **canturria** *f*, humming; droning

canturriar /kantu'rriar/ *vi* *Inf.* to hum, sing under one's breath

caña /'kaɲa/ *f*, stalk; reed; bone of arm or leg; leg (of a trouser, stocking, boot, etc.); marrow; *Bot.* cane; tumbler, glass; wine measure; gallery (of mine); *pl* mock joust on horseback using **cañas** as spears. **c. de azúcar,** sugar-cane. **c. de pescar,** fishing rod. **c. del timón,** tiller *Naut.*

cañada /ka'ɲaða/ *f*, glen, gulch, gully, hollow, ravine, vale, cattle path; *West Hem.* brook, cattle track

cañal /ka'ɲal/ *m*, cane-break; weir (for fish)

cañamazo /kaɲa'maso; kaɲa'maθo/ *m*, hempen canvas; embroidery canvas; embroidered canvas

cañamelar /kaɲame'lar/ *m*, sugar-cane plantation

cáñamo /'kaɲamo/ *m*, hemp; *Lat. Am.* marijuana

cañar /ka'ɲar/ *m*, canebrake; growth of reeds; fishgarth made of reeds

cañavalera /kaɲaβa'lera/ *f*, canefield

cañaveral /kaɲaβe'ral/ *m*, cane-brake; *West Hem.* bamboo field

cañazo /ka'ɲaso; ka'ɲaθo/ *m*, blow with a cane

cañería /kaɲe'ria/ *f*, conduit; pipe; piping

cañero /ka'ɲero/ *m*, pipe layer

caño /'kaɲo/ *m*, pipe, tube, sewer; organ pipe; jet (of water); mine gallery

cañón /ka'ɲon/ *m*, pipe, cylindrical tube; flue; quill (of birds); cannon; soft down; *Archit.* shaft (of column); stack (of a chimney). **c. antiaéreo,** A.A. gun. **c. antitanque,** anti-tank gun. **c. de escalera,** well of a staircase; *Slang.* terrific-looking, absolutely gorgeous (e.g. mujer cañón)

cañonazo /kaɲo'naso; kaɲo'naθo/ *m*, cannon shot; roar of a cannon

cañoneo /kaɲo'neo/ *m*, cannonade; bombardment

cañonería /kaɲone'ria/ *f*, *Mil.* group of cannon; *Mus.* set of organ pipes

cañonero /kaɲo'nero/ *m*, gunboat

cañuto /ka'ɲuto/ *m*, *Bot.* internode; small pipe or tube; *Inf.* tale-bearer

caoba /ka'oβa/ *f*, *Bot.* mahogany

caos /'kaos/ *m*, chaos; confusion

caótico /ka'otiko/ *a* chaotic

capa /'kapa/ *f*, cloak; cape; *Eccl.* cope; coating; layer; cover; coat (animals); *Fig.* cloak, disguise; *Geol.* stratum. **la c. del cielo,** the canopy of heaven. *Fig. Inf.* **echar la c. al toro,** to throw one's cap over the windmill. *Naut.* **estarse** (*or* **ponerse**) **a la c.,** to lie to

capacete /kapa'sete; kapa'θete/ *m*, helmet

capacha /ka'patʃa/ *f* basket; *Argentina, Chile* clink, jug (jail)

capacidad /kapasi'ðað; kapaθi'ðað/ *f*, capacity; extension, space; mental capacity, talent; opportunity; means; *Law.* capacity. **c. de compra,** buying power, purchasing power. **c. de producción,** output

capacitación /kapasita'sion; kapaθita'θion/ *f*, qualification, (act of) qualifying; (act of) training

capacitar /kapasi'tar; kapaθi'tar/ *vt* to capacitate, qualify, enable

capadura /kapa'ðura/ *f*, castration

capar /ka'par/ *vt* to castrate, geld; *Inf.* diminish, reduce

caparazón /kapara'son; kapara'θon/ *m*, caparison, horse blanket; waterproof cover; hood (of carriages); nosebag; shell (insects, crustaceans)

capataz /kapa'tas; kapa'taθ/ *m*, foreman; steward; overseer

capaz /ka'pas; ka'paθ/ *a* capacious; large, spacious; capable, competent; *Law.* able

capcioso /kap'sioso; kap'θioso/ *a* deceitful, artful; captious, carping

capear /kape'ar/ *vt* to steal a cape; play the bull with a cape (bullfighting); *Inf.* put off with excuses, deceive; *Naut.* lie to

capellán /kape'yan; kape'ʎan/ *m*, chaplain; any ecclesiastic

capelo /ka'pelo/ *m*, cardinal's hat; cardinalate

capeo /ka'peo/ *m*, playing the bull with a cape (bullfighting)

caperuza /kape'rusa; kape'ruθa/ *f*, hood, pointed cap; *Archit.* coping-stone

capigorrón /kapigo'rron/ *a* *Inf.* loafing. *m*, loafer, idler

capilar /kapi'lar/ *a* capillary

capilaridad /kapilari'ðað/ *f*, capillarity

capilla /ka'piya; ka'piʎa/ *f*, cowl, hood; chapel; *Eccl.* chapter; *Eccl.* choir. **c. ardiente,** chapelle ardente. **estar en c.,** to await execution (criminals); *Inf.* be in suspense, await anxiously

capillero /kapi'yero; kapi'ʎero/ *m*, sexton; churchwarden

capillo /ka'piyo; ka'piʎo/ *m*, baby's bonnet; cocoon of silkworm; flowerbud

capirotazo /kapiro'taso; kapiro'taθo/ *m*, box on the ear; fillip

capirote /kapi'rote/ *m*, academic hood and cap; hood (falconry); tall pointed cap. **ser tonto de c.,** *Inf.* to be a complete fool

capitación /kapita'sion; kapita'θion/ *f*, poll-tax, capitation

capital /kapi'tal/ *a* relating to the head; capital (sins, etc.); main, principal. *m*, capital, patrimony; *Com.* capital stock. *f*, capital (city). **c. pagado,** paid-in capital stock

capitalino, -a /kapita'lino/ *Lat. Am.* *a* of the capital; *n* native of the capital; resident of the capital

capitalismo /kapita'lismo/ *m*, capitalism

capitalista /kapita'lista/ *a* capitalistic. *mf* capitalist

capitalización /kapitalisa'sion; kapitaliθa'θion/ f, capitalization
capitalizar /kapitali'sar; kapitali'θar/ vt to capitalize
capitán /kapi'tan/ m, captain, skipper; chief, leader; ringleader. *Aer.* **c. de aviación,** group captain. **c. de fragata,** *Nav.* commander. **c. de puerto,** harbor master. **c. general de ejército,** field-marshal
capitana /kapi'tana/ f, admiral's ship; *Inf.* captain's wife
capitanear /kapitane'ar/ vt to captain, command; *Fig.* guide, lead
capitanía /kapita'nia/ f, captaincy; captainship
capitolio /kapi'tolio/ m, dignified building; *Archit.* acropolis; Capitol
capitulación /kapitula'sion; kapitula'θion/ f, agreement, pact; capitulation; pl marriage articles
capitular /kapitu'lar/ a capitulary, belonging to a Chapter. m, capitular, member of a Chapter. vi to make an agreement; capitulate; sing prayers; arrange order
capítulo /ka'pitulo/ m, *Eccl.* Chapter; meeting of town council, etc.; chapter (of book); item (in a budget); determination, decision
capó /ka'po/ m, *Auto.* hood
capón /ka'pon/ a castrated; gelded. m, capon; bundle of firewood or vines
caponera /kapo'nera/ f, coop for fattening capons; *Inf.* jail; *Inf.* place where one lives well free of charge
capota /ka'pota/ f, *Bot.* head of teasel; bonnet; hood (of vehicles)
capote /ka'pote/ m, short, brightly colored cape (used by bullfighters); cape coat; (cards) slam; *Inf.* scowl
capricho /ka'pritʃo/ m, caprice, fancy; strong desire
caprichoso /kapri'tʃoso/ a capricious; whimsical
caprichudo /kapri'tʃuðo/ a headstrong; capricious
cápsula /'kapsula/ f, cartridge-case; bottlecap; (*Bot. Med. Chem. Zool.*) capsule
captar /kap'tar/ vt assume, attract (goodwill, attention, etc.); *Mech.* collect; monitor (foreign broadcasts)
captor /kap'tor/ m, capturer
captura /kap'tura/ f, *Law.* capture; seizing, arrest
capturar /kaptu'rar/ vt to capture; arrest, apprehend
capucha /ka'putʃa/ f, hood; cowl; *Print.* circumflex accent
capuchina /kapu'tʃina/ f, Capuchin nun; *Bot.* nasturtium; table-lamp with an extinguisher
capucho /ka'putʃo/ m, cowl
capullo /ka'puyo; ka'puʎo/ m, cocoon; flower bud; acorn cup; *Anat.* prepuce
caqui /'kaki/ m, khaki; khaki color
cara /'kara/ f, face; likeness, aspect; façade, front; surface; side (of metal, etc.); mien. **c. a c.,** face to face; frankly; openly. *Inf.* **c. de juez,** severe face. *Inf.* **c. de pascua,** smiling face. *Inf.* **c. de vinagre,** sour face. **c. o cruz,** heads or tails. **c. o sello** *Argentina, Chile,* heads or tails **de c.,** opposite. **hacer a dos caras,** to be deceitful, be two-faced. **hacer c. (a),** to stand up to
caraba /ka'raβa/ f, *Slang.* 25-centimo coin
cárabe /'karaβe/ m, amber
carabina /kara'βina/ f, carbine; rifle
carabinazo /karaβi'naso; karaβi'naθo/ m, report of a carbine
carabinero /karaβi'nero/ m, carabineer; customs' guard, revenue guard; customs officer, customs official
caracol /kara'kol/ m, snail; snail's shell; cure; *Zool.* cochlea; winding stair. **c. marino,** periwinkle. **¡Caracoles!** Fancy!
caracola /kara'kola/ f, conch shell used as a horn
caracolear /karakole'ar/ vi to prance from side to side (horses)
carácter /ka'rakter/ m, sign, mark; character, writing (gen. pl); style of writing; brand (animals); nature, temperament; character, individuality, strong-mindedness, energy, firmness; condition, state, capacity. **comedia de c.,** psychological play. **en su c. de,** as in one's capacity as. **caracteres de imprenta,** printing types

característica /karakte'ristika/ f, quality, characteristic; *Math.* characteristic; actress who plays the part of an old woman
característico /karakte'ristiko/ a characteristic, distinctive. m, actor who plays roles of old men
caracterización /karakterisa'sion; karakteriθa'θion/ f, characterization; *Theat.* make-up
caracterizar /karakteri'sar; karakteri'θar/ vt to characterize; confer an office, honor, dignity, on; *Theat.* create a character; vr *Theat.* to make up, dress as, a character
caraíta /kara'ita/ a and mf Karaite
¡caramba! /ka'ramba/ interj gosh!; blast!
carámbano /ka'rambano/ m, icicle
carambola /karam'βola/ f, cannon (billiards); *Inf.* double effect; *Inf.* trick, deception
caramelo /kara'melo/ m, caramel; toffee
caramillo /kara'miyo; kara'miʎo/ m, flageolet; small flute, pipe; gossip, intrigue
carancho /ka'rantʃo/ m, *Argentina* vulture; *Peru* owl
carantamaula /karanta'maula/ f, *Inf.* hideous mask; ugly person
carapacho /kara'patʃo/ m, carapace, shell
carátula /ka'ratula/ f, mask; *Fig.* dramatic art, the theater
caravana /kara'βana/ f, caravan, group of traders, pilgrims, etc. (especially in East); *Inf.* crowd of excursionists, picnickers, etc.
¡caray! /ka'rai/ interj blast!; gosh!
carbólico /kar'βoliko/ a carbolic
carbón /kar'βon/ m, coal; charcoal; black chalk, crayon. **c. bituminoso,** soft coal. **c. de coque,** coke. **c. de leña,** charcoal. **c. mineral,** coal, anthracite. **mina de c.,** coal-mine
carbonada /karβo'naða/ f, *Lat. Am.* meat stew
carboncillo /karβon'siyo; karβon'θiʎo/ m, charcoal crayon
carbonear /karβone'ar/ vt to turn into charcoal; *Naut.* coal
carboneo /karβo'neo/ m, coaling
carbonera /karβo'nera/ f, coal-cellar, coal-house, etc.; coal-scuttle; woman who sells charcoal or coal; charcoal burner
carbonería /karβone'ria/ f, coal or charcoal merchant's office
carbonero /karβo'nero/ a relating to coal or charcoal. m, collier; charcoal maker; coal merchant; *Naut.* coal-ship
carbónico /kar'βoniko/ a *Chem.* carbonic
carbonífero /karβo'nifero/ a carboniferous
carbonizar /karβoni'sar; karβoni'θar/ vt to carbonize
carbono /kar'βono/ m, *Chem.* carbon
carbunco /kar'βunko/ m, *Med.* carbuncle
carbúnculo /kar'βunkulo/ m, carbuncle, ruby
carburador /karβura'ðor/ m, carburetor
carcaj /kar'kah/ m, quiver (for arrows); *Mexico* rifle case
carcajada /karka'haða/ f, burst of laughter, guffaw. **reírse a carcajadas,** to roar with laughter
carcajearse /karkahe'arse/ vi to guffaw
carcamal /karka'mal/ m, *Inf.* dotard
cárcel /'karsel; 'karθel/ f, prison, jail
carcelario /karse'lario; karθe'lario/ a prison, jail
carcelero /karse'lero; karθe'lero/ (-ra) a jail. n jailer
cárcola /'karkola/ f, treadle (of a loom)
carcoma /kar'koma/ f, wood-worm; dry rot; *Fig.* gnawing care; spendthrift
carcomer /karko'mer/ vt to gnaw wood (worms); *Fig.* undermine (health, etc.); vr be worm-eaten
carda /'karða/ f, card, carding; teasel head; card brush; *Inf.* reprimand
cardador /karða'ðor/ (-ra) n carder, comber
cardadura /karða'ðura/ f, carding; carding frame
cardar /kar'ðar/ vt to card, tease; brush up (felt, etc.)
cardenal /karðe'nal/ m, cardinal; cardinal bird; bruise
cardenalato /karðena'lato/ m, cardinalate, cardinalship
cardenillo /karðe'niyo; karðe'niʎo/ m, verdigris; *Art.* verditer

cárdeno /'karðeno/ *a* livid
cardíaco /kar'ðiako/ *a* Med. cardiac
cardinal /karði'nal/ *a* principal; cardinal (point); *Gram.* cardinal (number)
cardiógrafo /kar'ðiografo/ *m*, Med. cardiograph
cardiograma /karðio'grama/ *m*, Med. cardiogram
cardo /'karðo/ *m*, Bot. thistle
carear /kare'ar/ *vt* to confront; compare; *vi* turn towards, face; *vr* meet; come together
carecer /kare'ser; kare'θer/ *vi irr* to be short; lack, need (e.g. *Carece de las condiciones necesarias*, It lacks the necessary conditions). See **conocer**
carencia /ka'rensia; ka'renθia/ *f*, shortage, lack
carestía /kares'tia/ *f*, shortage, scarcity; famine; dearness, high price
careta /ka'reta/ *f*, mask; beekeeper's veil; fencing mask. *Fig.* **quitar la c. (a),** to unmask
carey /ka'rei/ *m*, Zool. shell turtle; tortoise-shell
carga /'karga/ *f*, loading; *Elec.* charging, charge; load; burden, weight; cargo; explosive charge; *Fig.* imposition; tax; duty, obligation. *Naut.* **c. de profundidad,** depth charge
cargadero /karga'ðero/ *m*, place where goods are loaded or unloaded
cargado /kar'gaðo/ *a* loaded; heavy, sultry; strong (tea, coffee). **c. de cadenas,** (prisoner, etc.) in chains. **c. de espaldas,** round-shouldered
cargador /karga'ðor/ *m*, loader; porter; dockhand; pitchfork; rammer; *Mech.* stoker; *Elec.* charger
cargamento /karga'mento/ *m*, Naut. cargo, freight, shipload
cargar /kar'gar/ *vt* to load; charge (guns, etc.); stoke; overburden; tax, impose; blame for, charge with; *Inf.* annoy, bore; *Argentina Inf.* to kid, tease; (*with con*) carry away; be loaded with (fruit); assume responsibility; (*with sobre*) importune, urge; lean against; *vr* turn (head, etc.); lower, grow darker (sky); (*with de*) be abundant (in or with); load oneself with
cargazón /karga'son; karga'θon/ *f*, cargo; loading; heaviness; darkness (of the sky)
cargo /'kargo/ *m*, loading; load, weight; post, office; duty, obligation; management, charge; care; *Com.* debit; accusation. *Com.* **el c. y la data,** debit and credit. **hacerse c. de,** to take charge of; understand; consider carefully. **ser en c. (a),** to be debtor (to)
cargosear /kargose'ar/ *vt*, Lat. Am. to annoy, pester
cargoso, -a /kar'goso/ *a*, Lat. Am. annoying, pestering
cariacontecido /kariakonte'siðo; kariakonte'θiðo/ *a* crestfallen, disappointed; glum
cariancho /kari'antʃo/ *a* Inf. broadfaced
cariarse /ka'riarse/ *vr* to become carious
caribe /ka'riβe/ *a* Caribbean. *mf* cannibal, savage
caricatura /karika'tura/ *f*, caricature
caricaturista /karikatu'rista/ *mf* caricaturist
caricaturizar /karikaturi'sar; karikaturi'θar/ *vt* to caricature
caricia /ka'risia; ka'riθia/ *f*, caress
caridad /kari'ðað/ *f*, charity; charitableness; alms
caries /'karies/ *f*, caries, tooth decay
carilargo /kari'largo/ *a* Inf. long-faced
carilla /ka'riya; ka'riʎa/ *f*, *dim* small face; mask; page (of a book)
carilleno /kari'yeno; kari'ʎeno/ *a* Inf. plump-faced, round-faced
carillón /kari'yon; kari'ʎon/ *m*, peal (of bells)
cariño /ka'riɲo/ *m*, affection; love; caress affectionately (gen. *pl*); fondness, inclination. **con c.,** affectionately
cariñoso /kari'ɲoso/ *a* affectionate; loving; kind
carioca /ka'rioka/ *a* of Rio de Janeiro; *n* native of Rio de Janeiro; resident of Rio de Janeiro
carirredondo /karirre'ðondo/ *a* Inf. roundfaced
carismático /karis'matiko/ *a* charismatic
caritativo /karita'tiβo/ *a* charitable
cariz /ka'ris; ka'riθ/ *m*, appearance of the sky; look, face; aspect; *Inf.* outlook (for a business deal, etc.)
carlista /kar'lista/ *a* and *mf* Carlist

carmelita /karme'lita/ *a* and *mf* Carmelite
carmen /'karmen/ *m*, country house and garden (Granada); song; poem
carmesí /karme'si/ *a* crimson. *m*, crimson color; cramoisy
carmín /kar'min/ *m*, red, carmine color; red wild rose-tree and flower
carnada /kar'naða/ *f*, bait
carnaje /kar'nahe/ *m*, salted meat
carnal /kar'nal/ *a* carnal; lascivious; materialistic, worldly; related by blood
carnalidad /karnali'ðað/ *f*, carnality
carnaval /karna'βal/ *m*, carnival. **martes de c.,** Shrove Tuesday
carnavalesco /karnaβa'lesko/ *a* carnival
carne /'karne/ *f*, flesh; meat; pulpy part of fruit; carnality, **c. concentrada,** meat extract. **c. congelada,** frozen meat. **c. de gallina** *Fig.* gooseflesh. **c. de membrillo,** quince cheese or conserve. **c. y hueso,** *Fig.* flesh and blood. *Inf.* **cobrar carnes,** to put on weight. **poner toda la c. en el asador,** *Inf.* to put all one's eggs in one basket
carné de conductor /'karne de konduk'tor/ *Argentina* driver's license
carnerada /karne'raða/ *f*, flock of sheep
carnerero /karne'rero/ **(-ra)** *n* shepherd
carnero /kar'nero/ *m*, sheep; mutton; mortuary; charnel-house; family burial vault. **c. marino,** Zool. seal
carnestolendas /karnesto'lendas/ *f pl* three days of carnival before Ash Wednesday
carnet /kar'net/ *m*, notebook, diary; identity card; membership card, pass. **c. de chófer,** driver's license
carnicería /karnise'ria; karniθe'ria/ *f*, butcher's shop; carnage, slaughter
carnicero /karni'sero; karni'θero/ *a* carnivorous; inhuman, cruel. *m*, butcher
carnívoro /kar'niβoro/ *a* carnivorous. *m*, carnivore
carnosidad /karnosi'ðað/ *f*, proud flesh; local fat; fatness
carnoso /kar'noso/ *a* meaty; fleshy; full of marrow; *Bot.* pulpy, juicy
caro /'karo/ *a* beloved; expensive; dear. *adv* expensively; dear
carolingio /karo'linhio/ **(-ia)** *a* and *n* Carolingian
carótida /ka'rotiða/ *f*, carotid artery
carpa /'karpa/ *f*, Ichth. carp. **c. dorada,** goldfish; *Lat. Am.* tent; awning
carpanta /kar'panta/ *f*, *Inf.* violent hunger; *Mexico* gang
Cárpatos, los Montes /'karpatos, los 'montes/ the Carpathian Mountains
carpeta /kar'peta/ *f*, table or chest cover, doily; writing case; portfolio; docket, letter file
carpetazo, dar /karpe'taso, dar; karpe'taθo, dar/ *vt* to shelve (a project, etc.)
carpintear /karpinte'ar/ *vi* to carpenter
carpintería /karpinte'ria/ *f*, carpenter's shop; carpentry
carpinteril /karpinte'ril/ *a* carpentering
carpintero /karpin'tero/ *m*, carpenter, joiner; *Theat.* scene-shifter. **c. de carretas,** wheelwright. **c. de ribera,** shipwright
carraca /ka'rraka/ *f*, rattle; ratchet-drill
Carrapempe /karra'pempe/ *m*, Old Nick
carrascal /karras'kal/ *m*, field of pinoaks
carraspear /karraspe'ar/ *vi* to clear one's throat, cough
carraspera /karras'pera/ *f*, *Inf.* hoarseness
carrera /ka'rrera/ *f*, run; race; racing; racecourse; *Astron.* course; high road; route; *Mas.* layer, course; line, row; *Fig.* run (in stockings, etc.); course; duration (of life); career, profession; *Mexico* major (academic); conduct; girders. **c. de fondo,** long-distance race. **c. de relevos, c. de equipos,** relay race. **a c. abierta, a c. tendida,** at full speed
carrerista /karre'rista/ *mf* racing enthusiast; professional racer
carreta /ka'rreta/ *f*, long, narrow two-wheeled cart; wagon; tumbril

carretada /karre'taða/ *f,* cart-load; *Inf.* great deal, mass

carretaje /karre'tahe/ *m,* cartage; carriage, transport

carrete /ka'rrete/ *m,* spool, reel, bobbin; fishing reel; *Elec.* coil; *Photo.* film spool

carretear /karrete'ar/ *vt* to cart; drive a cart

carretera /karre'tera/ *f,* high road; highway

carretería /karrete'ria/ *f,* number of carts; carting trade; cartwright's yard

carretero /karre'tero/ *m,* cartwright; carter, driver

carretilla /karre'tiya; karre'tiʎa/ *f,* wheelbarrow; hand cart; railway truck; squib. **de c.,** *Inf.* mechanically, without thought; (*with saber, repetir,* etc.) by rote

carretón /karre'ton/ *m,* truck, trolley; hand cart

carril /ka'rril/ *m,* wheel mark; furrow, rut; cart road, narrow road; rail (railways, etc.)

carrillera /karri'yera; karri'ʎera/ *f,* jaw (of some animals); chin strap; *pl* bonnet strings, etc.

carrillo /ka'rriyo; ka'rriʎo/ *m,* cheek; jowl

carriola /ka'rriola/ *f,* truckle bed; curricle

carro /'karro/ *m,* cart; cartload; car, chariot; carriage (of a typewriter, etc.); chassis; *Astron.* Plow, Great Bear; *Lat. Am.* automobile, auto, car; *Mil.* **c. blindado,** armored car. *Mil.* **c. de asalto,** tank. **c. de mudanzas,** moving van. **c. de regar,** watercart

carrocería /karrose'ria; karroθe'ria/ *f,* place where carriages are made, sold, repaired; *Auto.* coachwork, body shop

carrocha /ka'rrotʃa/ *f,* eggs (of insects)

carrochar /karro'tʃar/ *vi* to lay eggs (insects)

carromato /karro'mato/ *m,* road wagon; covered wagon

carroña /ka'rroɲa/ *f,* putrid flesh, carrion

carroza /ka'rrosa; ka'rroθa/ *f,* elegant coach; state coach; carriage; float (for tableaux, etc.); *Naut.* awning

carruaje /ka'rruahe/ *m,* carriage; any vehicle

carta /'karta/ *f,* letter; charter; royal order; playing card; chart, map. **c. certificada,** registered letter. **c. de amparo,** safe-conduct. **c. de crédito,** *Com.* letter of credit. **c. de marear,** sea chart. **c. de naturaleza,** naturalization papers. **c. de pésame,** letter of condolence. **c. de venta,** *Com.* bill of sale. **c. ejecutoria de hidalguía,** letters patent of nobility. **carta-poder,** letter of proxy, proxy. **cartas rusas,** (game of) consequences. **poner las cartas boca arriba,** *Fig.* to lay one's cards on the table

cartabón /karta'βon/ *m,* set-square; shoemaker's slide; quadrant

cartaginés /kartahi'nes/ **(-esa)** *a* and *n* Carthaginian

Cartago /'kartago/ Carthage

cartapacio /karta'pasio; karta'paθio/ *m,* note-book; schoolbag, satchel; file, batch of papers

cartear /karte'ar/ *vi* Cards. to play low; *vr* to correspond by letter

cartel /kar'tel/ *m,* placard, poster; cartel; pasquinade, lampoon. **fijar carteles,** to placard

cartela /kar'tela/ *f,* tablet (for writing); slip (of paper, etc.); *Archit.* console, bracket

cartelera /karte'lera/ *f,* billboard

cartelero /karte'lero/ *m,* billpaster, billsticker

carteo /kar'teo/ *m,* correspondence (by letter)

cartera /kar'tera/ *f,* pocketbook; wallet; dispatch-case; portfolio; notebook; pocket flap; office of a cabinet minister; *Com.* shares

cartería /karte'ria/ *f,* sorting room (in a post-office)

carterista /karte'rista/ *mf* pickpocket

cartero /kar'tero/ **(-ra)** *n* mail carrier

cartesiano /karte'siano/ **(-na)** *a* and *n* Cartesian

Cartesio /kar'tesio/ Descartes

carteta /kar'teta/ *f,* lansquenet (card game)

cartilaginoso /kartilahi'noso/ *a* cartilaginous

cartílago /kar'tilago/ *m,* cartilage

cartilla /kar'tiya; kar'tiʎa/ *f,* first reading book; primer; certificate of ordination; note-book; liturgical calendar. **c. de racionamiento,** ration book

cartografía /kartogra'fia/ *f,* cartography

cartógrafo /kar'tografo/ *m,* map maker

cartón /kar'ton/ *m,* pasteboard, cardboard; *Archit.* bracket; *Art.* cartoon, design

cartucho /kar'tutʃo/ *m,* cartridge; paper cone

cartuja /kar'tuha/ *f,* Carthusian Order or monastery

cartujano /kartu'hano/ *a* Carthusian

cartujo /kar'tuho/ *m,* Carthusian monk; *Inf.* taciturn, reserved man

cartulina /kartu'lina/ *f,* Bristol board, oaktag, pasteboard, card

carúncula /ka'runkula/ *f,* caruncle, comb of cock, etc.

casa /'kasa/ *f,* house; home; household; residence, dwelling; family house; *Com.* firm. **c. consistorial,** town hall. **c. cuna,** crèche. **c. de campo,** country-house. **c. de empeño,** pawnshop. **c. de huéspedes,** boarding house, lodging-house. **c. de los sustos,** haunted house (at amusement park). **c. de moneda,** mint. **c. de socorro,** First Aid Post. **c. de vecindad,** tenement. **c. mala,** house of ill repute. **c. solar** *or* **c. solariega,** family seat. **en c.,** at home (also sport usage). **poner c.,** to set up house

casaca /ka'saka/ *f,* dress coat. **volver la c.,** to become a turncoat, change one's allegiance

casación /kasa'sion; kasa'θion/ *f,* *Law.* cassation

casadero /kasa'ðero/ *a* marriageable

casadoro /kasa'ðoro/ *m,* *Costa Rica* bus

casamiento /kasa'miento/ *m,* marriage; wedding

casar /ka'sar/ *vt* to marry (of a priest); *Law.* repeal; *Inf.* marry off; join; match, harmonize; *vi* and *vr* (*with con*) to get married

casar /ka'sar/ *m,* group of houses

casca /'kaska/ *f,* grape skin; tan (bark); shell, peel, rind

cascabel /kaska'βel/ *m,* small bell (for harness, etc.). **serpiente de c.,** rattlesnake. *Inf.* **ser un c.,** to be feather-brained

cascabeleo /kaska'βeleo/ *m,* jingling of bells

cascabillo /kaska'βiyo; kaska'βiʎo/ *m,* husk (of cereals)

cascada /kas'kaða/ *f,* cascade; waterfall

cascadura /kaska'ðura/ *f,* cracking, crack

cascajo /kas'kaho/ *m,* gravel, shingle; *Inf.* broken, old things, junk; nuts

cascanueces /kaska'nueses; kaska'nueθes/ *m,* nutcrackers

cascar /kas'kar/ *vt* to crack, split, break; *Inf.* beat; *Fig. Inf.* break down (of health); *vi Inf.* talk, chatter

cáscara /'kaskara/ *f,* shell; peel, rind; bark. *Med.* **c. sagrada,** cascara

cascarón /kaska'ron/ *m,* eggshell; *Archit.* vault

cascarrabias /kaska'rraβias/ *mf Inf.* spitfire

cascarriento, -a /kaska'rriento/ *Argentina* filthy; greasy

casco /'kasko/ *m,* cranium; broken fragment of china, glass, etc.; crown of hat; helmet; tree of saddle; bottle; tank, pipe; barrel; *Naut.* hull; hoof; quarter (of fruit); *pl Inf.* head. **c. colonial,** sun-helmet. **c. respiratorio,** smoke-helmet

cascote /kas'kote/ *m,* rubble, ruins

caseoso /kase'oso/ *a* cheesy

caserío /kase'rio/ *m,* group of houses; country house

casero /ka'sero/ *a* home made; home bred; familiar; informal; *Inf.* domesticated, home-loving; domestic. *m,* landlord; caretaker; tenant

caserón /kase'ron/ *m,* large tumbledown house, mansion, hall

caseta /ka'seta/ *f,* hut; cottage; booth, stall. **c. de baños,** bathing van

casi /'kasi/ *adv* almost, nearly. **c. c.,** very nearly

casilla /ka'siya; ka'siʎa/ *f,* hut; cabin; lodge; ticket office; pigeon-hole; *Argentina, Chile* post-office box. *Aer.* **c. del piloto,** cockpit

casillero /kasi'yero; kasi'ʎero/ *m,* file cabinet; filing cabinet; locker (as in a locker room); set of pigeon-holes; *Sports.* scoreboard; *Rail.* crossing guard

casino /ka'sino/ *m,* casino; club

caso /'kaso/ *m,* happening, event; chance, hazard; occasion, opportunity; case, matter; (*Med. Gram.*) case. **en el c. de,** in a position to (e.g. *No estamos en el c. de pagar tanto dinero.* We are in no position to pay so much money). **en tal c.,** in such a case. **en**

todo c., in any case. **no hacer c. de,** to take no notice of. **venir al c.,** to be opportune

caspa /'kaspa/ *f,* dandruff; scab

¡cáspita! /'kaspita/ *interj* Amazing! Wonderful!

casquete /kas'kete/ *m,* helmet; skullcap; half wig

casquijo /kas'kiho/ *m,* gravel

casquillo /kas'kiyo; kas'kiʎo/ *m,* tip, cap, ferrule; socket; arrow-head; metal cartridge-case

casquivano /kaski'βano/ *a Inf.* giddy, feather-brained

casta /'kasta/ *f,* race; caste; breed (animals); kind, species, quality. **de buena c.,** pedigree (e.g. *perros de buena c.,* pedigree dogs)

castaña /kas'taɲa/ *f, Bot.* chestnut; knot, bun (of hair)

castañar /kasta'ɲar/ *m,* chestnut plantation or grove

castañetear /kastaɲete'ar/ *vi* to play the castanets; snap one's fingers; chatter (of teeth); knock together (of knees)

castaño /kas'taɲo/ *a* chestnut-colored. *m,* chestnut tree; chestnut wood. **c. de Indias,** horse-chestnut tree

castañuela /kasta'ɲuela/ *f,* castanet. **tocar las castañuelas,** to play the castanets

castellán /kaste'yan; kaste'ʎan/ *m,* castellan

castellano /kaste'yano; kaste'ʎano/ **(-na)** *n* Castilian; Spaniard. *m,* Spanish (language); castellan. *a* Castilian; Spanish

casticismo /kasti'sismo; kasti'θismo/ *m,* purity (of language); Spanish spirit; traditionalism

castidad /kasti'ðað/ *f,* chastity

castigador /kastiga'ðor/ *a* punishing. *m,* punisher; *Inf.* lady-killer

castigadora /kastiga'ðora/ *f, Inf.* man-hunter

castigar /kasti'gar/ *vt* to punish; chastise; chasten, advise; pain, grieve; correct, edit; decrease (expenses); *Com.* allow a discount

castigo /kas'tigo/ *m,* punishment; emendation, correction

Castilla /kas'tiya; kas'tiʎa/ Castile

castillo /kas'tiyo; kas'tiʎo/ *m,* castle; howdah. **c. de naipes,** house of cards. **c. de proa,** *Naut.* forecastle. **c. fuerte,** fortified castle. *Inf.* **hacer castillos en el aire,** to build castles in the air or in Spain

castizo /kas'tiso; kas'tiθo/ *a* pure-blooded; prolific; pure (of language); typically Spanish; traditional

casto /'kasto/ *a* chaste; pure, unsullied

castor /kas'tor/ *m, Zool.* beaver (animal and fur); soft, woollen cloth

castración /kastra'sion; kastra'θion/ *f,* castration, gelding

castrado /kas'traðo/ *a* castrated. *m, Inf.* eunuch

castrador /kastra'ðor/ *m,* castrator, gelder

castrapo /kas'trapo/ *m,* mixed Spanish and Galician spoken in Galicia, Spain

castrar /kas'trar/ *vt* to castrate, geld; prune; remove honeycomb from hives; weaken

castrense /kas'trense/ *a* military

castrista /kas'trista/ *v* and *mf* Castroite

casual /ka'sual/ *a* accidental, casual

casualidad /kasuali'ðað/ *f,* chance, coincidence. **por c.,** by chance. **ser mucha c. que...,** to be too much of a coincidence that...

casucha /ka'sutʃa/ *f, Inf.* tumbledown hut

casuista /ka'suista/ *a* casuistic. *mf* casuist

casuística /ka'suistika/ *f,* casuistry

casulla /ka'suya; ka'suʎa/ *f,* chasuble

cata /'kata/ *f,* tasting; taste, sample; *Lat. Am.* parrot

catabolismo /kataβo'lismo/ *m,* catabolism

cataclismo /kata'klismo/ *m,* cataclysm

catacumbas /kata'kumbas/ *f pl,* catacombs

catador /kata'ðor/ *m,* taster, sampler

catadura /kata'ðura/ *f,* tasting; look, countenance (gen. qualified)

catafalco /kata'falko/ *m,* catafalque

catalán /kata'lan/ **(-ana)** *a* and *n* Catalan, Catalonian. *m,* Catalan (language)

catalejo /kata'leho/ *m,* telescope

cataléptico /kata'leptiko/ *a* cataleptic

catálisis /ka'talisis/ *f, Chem.* catalysis

catalítico /kata'litiko/ *a* catalytic

catalogar /katalo'gar/ *vt* to catalog, list

catálogo /ka'talogo/ *m,* catalog, list

Cataluña /kata'luɲa/ Catalonia

cataplasma /kata'plasma/ *f,* cataplasm

catapulta /kata'pulta/ *f,* catapult

catar /ka'tar/ *vt* to taste, sample; see, examine; inspect; regard

catarata /kata'rata/ *f,* cataract, waterfall; *Med.* cataract (of the eyes)

catarral /kata'rral/ *a* catarrhal

catarro /ka'tarro/ *m,* catarrh; common cold

catástrofe /ka'tastrofe/ *f, Lit.* tragic climax; catastrophe

catastrófico /katas'trofiko/ *a* catastrophic

catavino /kata'βino/ *m,* taster (cup)

catavinos /kata'βinos/ *mf,* professional wine taster; *Inf.* tippler, tavern haunter

cate /'kate/ *m, slang* flunk (failure in a course at school)

catecismo /kate'sismo; kate'θismo/ *m,* catechism

catecúmeno /kate'kumeno/ **(-na)** *n* catechumen

cátedra /'kateðra/ *f,* university chair; chair in a Spanish **instituto;** professorship; university lecture room; subject taught by professor; reading desk, lectern; *Eccl.* throne; *Eccl.* see. **c. del espíritu santo,** pulpit. **c. de San Pedro,** Holy See

catedral /kate'ðral/ *f,* and *a* cathedral

catedrático /kate'ðratiko/ **(-ca)** *n* professor

categoría /katego'ria/ *f, Philos.* category; class, rank

categórico /kate'goriko/ *a* categorical, downright

cateo /ka'teo/ *m, West Hem.* sampling; prospecting; house search (by the police)

catequismo /kate'kismo/ *m,* catechism; question and answer method of teaching

catequista /kate'kista/ *mf* catechist

catequizar /kateki'sar; kateki'θar/ *vt* to catechize; persuade, induce

caterva /ka'terβa/ *f,* crowd, throng; jumble, collection

catéter /ka'teter/ *m, Surg.* probe; catheter

catoche /ka'totʃe/ *m, Lat. Am.* bad temper

catódico /ka'toðiko/ *a Elec.* cathodic

cátodo /'katoðo/ *m,* cathode

catolicidad /katolisi'ðað; katoliθi'ðað/ *f,* catholicity; catholic world

catolicismo /katoli'sismo; katoli'θismo/ *m,* Catholicism

católico /ka'toliko/ **(-ca)** *a* universal, catholic; infallible. *a* and *n* Catholic (by religion)

catorce /ka'torse; ka'torθe/ *a* fourteen; fourteenth. *m,* number fourteen; fourteenth (of days of month)

catorzavo /kator'saβo; kator'θaβo/ *a* fourteenth

catre /'katre/ *m,* camp-bed; truckle-bed; cot

Cáucaso, el /'kaukaso, el/ the Caucasus

cauce /'kause; 'kauθe/ *m,* river or stream bed; ditch, irrigation canal

cauchal /kau'tʃal/ *m,* rubber plantation

cauchera /kau'tʃera/ *f,* rubber tree

cauchero /kau'tʃero/ *m,* rubber planter; rubber-plantation worker

caucho /'kautʃo/ *m,* caoutchouc, rubber; *Lat. Am.* tire

caución /kau'sion; kau'θion/ *f,* caution, precaution; surety; security

caucional /kausio'nal; kauθio'nal/ *a* See **libertad**

caudal /kau'ðal/ *m,* wealth, capital; flow, volume (of water); plenty, abundance (e.g. *un c. de conocimientos,* a wealth of knowledge)

caudaloso /kauða'loso/ *a* carrying much water; wealthy; abundant

caudillo /kau'ðiyo; kau'ðiʎo/ *m,* head, leader; chieftain. **el C.,** (title of Francisco Franco)

causa /'kausa/ *f,* cause; reason, motive; lawsuit; *Law.* trial. **c. final,** *Philos.* final cause. **c. pública,** public welfare. **ser c. bastante para...,** to be reason enough to...

causador /kausa'ðor/ **(-ra)** *a* motivating. *n* occasioner, originator

causalidad /kausali'ðað/ *f,* causality

causante /kau'sante/ *a* causative, causing. *m, Law.* principal; *Mexico* taxpayer

causar /kau'sar/ *vt* to cause; occasion

causticidad /kaustisi'ðað; kaustiθi'ðað/ *f*, causticity; mordacity

cáustico /'kaustiko/ *a* burning, caustic; scathing; mordant; *Surg.* caustic

cautela /kau'tela/ *f*, caution; astuteness, cunning

cauteloso /kaute'loso/ *a* cautious; cunning

cauterio /kau'terio/ *m*, cautery

cauterización /kauterisa'sion; kauteriθa'θion/ *f*, cauterization

cauterizar /kauteri'sar; kauteri'θar/ *vt* to cauterize

cautivar /kauti'βar/ *vt* to capture; captivate, charm; attract; *vi* become a prisoner

cautiverio /kauti'βerio/ *m*, captivity

cautivo /kau'tiβo/ (**-va**) *a* and *n* captive

cauto /'kauto/ *a* cautious; prudent; sly

cava /'kaβa/ *f*, digging (especially vines); wine cellar in royal palaces

cavador /kaβa'ðor/ (**-ra**) *n* digger, hoer

cavadura /kaβa'ðura/ *f*, digging, hoeing; sinking (wells)

cavar /ka'βar/ *vt* to dig, hoe; sink (wells); *vi* hollow; *Fig.* go deeply into a thing

caverna /ka'βerna/ *f*, cavern, cave; *Med.* cavity (generally in the lung)

cavernícola /kaβer'nikola/ *a* cave. **hombre c.**, caveman

cavernoso /kaβer'noso/ *a* cavernous; caverned; *Fig.* hollow (cough, etc.); deaf

cavidad /kaβi'ðað/ *f*, cavity; sinus; cell

cavilación /kaβila'sion; kaβila'θion/ *f*, caviling

cavilar /kaβi'lar/ *vt* to cavil; criticize

caviloso /kaβi'loso/ *a* captious

caz /kas; kaθ/ *m*, channel, canal; head-race, flume

caza /'kasa; 'kaθa/ *f*, hunting; hunt, chase; game. *m*, *Aer.* fighter. *Aer.* **c. lanzacohetes**, rocket-launching aircraft. **c. nocturno**, night fighter. *Naut.* **dar c.**, to pursue

cazaautógrafos /ˌkasaau'tografos; ˌkaθaau'tografos/ *mf*, autograph hunter

cazabombardero /ˌkasaβombar'ðero; ˌkaθaβombar'ðero/ *m*, *Aer.* fighter bomber

cazadero /kasa'ðero; kaθa'ðero/ *m*, hunting ground

cazador /kasa'ðor; kaθa'ðor/ *a* hunting. *m*, *Mil.* chasseur; huntsman

cazadora /kasa'ðora; kaθa'ðora/ *f*, huntress; jacket; forage cap

cazadotes /kasa'ðotes; kaθa'ðotes/ *m*, dowry hunter

cazafortunas /kasafor'tunas; kaθafor'tunas/ *mf* fortune hunter

cazar /ka'sar; ka'θar/ *vt* to hunt, chase; *Fig. Inf.* run to earth; *Fig. Inf.* catch out; *Inf.* overcome by flattery

cazasubmarino /kasasuβma'rino; kaθasuβma'rino/ *m*, submarine chaser

cazatorpedero /kasatorpe'ðero; kaθatorpe'ðero/ *m*, *Naut.* torpedo-boat destroyer

cazo /'kaso; 'kaθo/ *m*, ladle; dipper

cazolada /kaso'laða; kaθo'laða/ *f*, panful

cazoleta /kaso'leta; kaθo'leta/ *f*, small pan; bowl (of pipe, etc.); sword guard; boss of a shield; pan (of a firelock)

cazuela /ka'suela; ka'θuela/ *f*, earthenware cooking dish; stew-pot; part of theater formerly reserved for women; *Theat.* gallery

cazumbrón /kasum'βron; kaθum'βron/ *m*, cooper

cazurro /ka'surro; ka'θurro/ *a Inf.* unsociable; surly, boorish

c.c.p. /sese'pe; θeθe'pe/ abbrev. of **con copia para**

ce /se; θe/ *f*, name of the letter C. *interj* Look! Chist! **ce por be**, in detail

cebada /se'βaða; θe'βaða/ *f*, barley (plant and grain). **c. perlada**, pearl barley

cebadal /seβa'ðal; θeβa'ðal/ *m*, barley field

cebadera /seβa'ðera; θeβa'ðera/ *f*, nose-bag; barley bin

cebadero /seβa'ðero; θeβa'ðero/ *m*, barley dealer

cebado /se'βaðo; θe'βaðo/ *a* on the prowl; having tasted human flesh (animal)

cebar /se'βar; θe'βar/ *vt* to feed or fatten (animals); fuel, feed (furnace, etc.); prime, charge (fire-arms, etc.); start up (machines); bait (fish hook); stimulate

(passion, etc.); *vi* stick in, penetrate (nails, screws, etc.); *vr* put one's mind to; grow angry. **cebarse en vanas esperanzas**, to nurture vain hopes

cebiche /θe'bitʃe/ *m*, dish of marinated raw fish

cebo /'seβo; 'θeβo/ *m*, fodder; detonator; encouragement, food; bait

cebolla /se'βoya; θe'βoʎa/ *f*, onion; onion bulb; any bulbous stem; oil bulb (of lamp). **c. escalonia**, shallot

cebollana /seβo'yana; θeβo'ʎana/ *f*, chive

cebollero /seβo'yero; θeβo'ʎero/ (**-ra**) *n* onion seller

cebolleta /seβo'yeta; θeβo'ʎeta/ *f*, leek; young onion

cebollino /seβo'yino; θeβo'ʎino/ *m*, onion seed; onion bed; chive

cebra /'seβra; 'θeβra/ *f*, zebra

ceca /'seka; 'θeka/ *f*, mint (for coining money); name of mosque in Cordova. **de C. en Meca**, from pillar to post, hither and thither

cecear /sese'ar; θeθe'ar/ *vi* to lisp

ceceo /se'seo; θe'θeo/ *m*, lisping, Spanish pronunciation of s as T

ceceoso /sese'oso; θeθe'oso/ *a* lisping

cecial /se'sial; θe'θial/ *m*, dried fish

cecina /se'sina; θe'θina/ *f*, dried salt meat

cedazo /se'ðaso; θe'ðaθo/ *m*, sieve, strainer

ceder /se'ðer; θe'ðer/ *vt* to cede, give up; transfer; *vi* give in, yield; diminish, decrease (fever, storm, etc.); fail, end; happen, turn out; sag, give, stretch. **No c. la fama a**, to be no less famous than. **ceda el paso**, yield right of way

cedro /'seðro; 'θeðro/ *m*, cedar tree; cedar wood. **c. dulce**, red cedar

cédula /'seðula; 'θeðula/ *f*, document, certificate, card. *Eccl.* **c. de comunión**, Communion card. **c. personal**, identity card. **c. real**, royal letters patent

céfiro /'sefiro; 'θefiro/ *m*, west wind; *Poet.* zephyr

cegajoso /sega'hoso; θega'hoso/ *a* blear-eyed

cegar /se'gar; θe'gar/ *vi irr* to become blind; *vt* to put out the eyes; *Fig.* blind; wall up, close up, stop up; infatuate. *Pres. Ind.* **ciego, ciegas, ciega, ciegan.** *Pres. Subjunc.* **ciegue, ciegues, ciegue, cieguen**

cegato /se'gato; θe'gato/ *a Inf.* short-sighted

ceguedad, ceguera /sege'ðað, se'gera; θege'ðað, θe'gera/ *f*, blindness; delusion; ignorance

Ceilán /sei'lan; θei'lan/ Ceylon

ceja /'seha; 'θeha/ *f*, eyebrow; cloud cap; mountain peak; *Mus.* bridge (of stringed instruments). *Fig.* **quemarse las cejas**, to burn the midnight oil

cejar /se'har; θe'har/ *vi* to go backwards; give way, hesitate

cejijunto /sehi'hunto; θehi'hunto/ *a* having eyebrows that almost meet, beetle-browed

cejo /'seho; 'θeho/ *m*, river mist

cejudo /se'huðo; θe'huðo/ *a* having long thick eyebrows

celada /se'laða; θe'laða/ *f*, helmet; ambush; fraud, trick

celador /sela'ðor; θela'ðor/ (**-ra**) *a* watchful, zealous. *n* supervisor; caretaker; guard (at a museum, etc.)

celaje /se'lahe; θe'lahe/ *m*, sky with scudding clouds (gen. *pl*); skylight; window; promising sign, presage

celar /se'lar; θe'lar/ *vt* to be zealous in discharge of duties; spy upon; watch; oversee, superintend; conceal; engrave

celda /'selda; 'θelda/ *f*, cell

celdilla /sel'diya; θel'diʎa/ *f*, cell (bees, wasps, etc.). (*Zool. Bot.*) cell; *Bot.* capsule

celebérrimo /sele'βerrimo; θele'βerrimo/ *a sup* **célebre** most celebrated

celebración /seleβra'sion; θeleβra'θion/ *f*, celebration; applause

celebrador /seleβra'ðor; θeleβra'ðor/ (**-ra**) *n* celebrator; applauder

celebrante /sele'βrante; θele'βrante/ *a* celebrating. *m*, *Eccl.*

celebrar /sele'βrar; θele'βrar/ *vt* to celebrate; applaud; praise; venerate; hold, conduct; **c. que** + *subj*, to be happy that, be glad that. *vt* and *vi Eccl.* officiate; *vr* take place

célebre /'seleβre; 'θeleβre/ *a* famous

celebridad /seleβri'ðað; θeleβri'ðað/ f, fame, celebrity; magnificence, show, pomp

celeridad /seleri'ðað; θeleri'ðað/ f, celerity

celeste /se'leste; θe'leste/ a celestial, heavenly

celestial /seles'tial; θeles'tial/ a celestial, heavenly; perfect, delightful; *Inf.* foolish (ironical)

celestina /seles'tina; θeles'tina/ f, procuress (allusion to *Tragicomedia de Calixto y Melibea*); *Inf.* matchmaker

celibato /seli'βato; θeli'βato/ m, celibacy; *Inf.* bachelor

célibe /'seliβe; 'θeliβe/ a celibate, unmarried. *mf* unmarried person

celo /'selo; 'θelo/ m, enthusiasm, ardor; religious zeal; devotion; jealousy; heat, rut; *pl* jealousy, suspicion. **dar celos (a,** to make jealous

celosía /selo'sia; θelo'sia/ f, lattice; Venetian blind

celoso /se'loso; θe'loso/ a zealous; jealous; suspicious

célula /'selula; 'θelula/ f, cell

celular /selu'lar; θelu'lar/ a cellular

celuloide /selu'loiðe; θelu'loiðe/ f, celluloid

celulosa /selu'losa; θelu'losa/ f, cellulose

celuloso /selu'loso; θelu'loso/ a cellular

cementación /sementa'sion; θementa'θion/ f, cementation

cementar /semen'tar; θemen'tar/ vt to cement

cementerio /semen'terio; θemen'terio/ m, cemetery

cemento /se'mento; θe'mento/ m, cement

cena /'sena; 'θena/ f, evening meal; supper. **La Última Cena,** Last Supper

cenacho /se'natʃo; θe'natʃo/ m, marketing bag

cenáculo /se'nakulo; θe'nakulo/ m, cenacle

cenador /sena'ðor; θena'ðor/ m, diner out; arbor, pergola

cenagal /sena'gal; θena'gal/ m, quagmire; *Fig.* impasse

cenagoso /sena'goso; θena'goso/ a miry, muddy

cenar /se'nar; θe'nar/ vi to dine, sup; vt eat for evening meal, sup off

cenceño /sen'seɲo; θen'θeɲo/ a slim, thin

cencerrada /sense'rraða; θenθe'rraða/ f, noisy mock serenade given to widows or widowers on the first night of their new marriage

cencerrear /senserre'ar; θenθerre'ar/ vi to jingle; *Inf.* play out of tune; bang in the wind, rattle; squeak

cencerreo /sense'rreo; θenθe'rreo/ m, jingling; jangle; rattling; squeaking

cencerro /sen'serro; θen'θerro/ m, cow-bell

cendal /sen'dal; θen'dal/ m, gauze; *Eccl.* stole; barbs of a feather

cenefa /se'nefa; θe'nefa/ f, border; valance, flounce; edging

cenicero /seni'sero; θeni'θero/ m, ash-pan; ash-pit; ash-tray

ceniciento /seni'siento; θeni'θiento/ a ash colored, ashen. **la Cenicienta,** Cinderella

cenit /'senit; 'θenit/ m, *Astron.* zenith; *Fig.* peak, summit

ceniza /se'nisa; θe'niθa/ f, ash, cinders

cenotafio /seno'tafio; θeno'tafio/ m, cenotaph

cenote /se'note; θe'note/ m, *Central America, Mexico* cenote (deep natural well or sinkhole)

censo /'senso; 'θenso/ m, census; agreement for settlement of an annuity; annual ground rent; leasehold

censor /sen'sor; θen'sor/ m, censor; censorious person; *Educ.* proctor

censual /sen'sual; θen'sual/ a pertaining to census, annuity, rents

censualista /sensua'lista; θensua'lista/ mf annuitant

censura /sen'sura; θen'sura/ f, censorship; criticism; blame, reproach; scandal, gossip; *Psychol.* censorship

censurable /sensu'raβle; θensu'raβle/ a reprehensible; censorable

censurar /sensu'rar; θensu'rar/ vt to judge; censure; criticize

centauro /sen'tauro; θen'tauro/ m, *Myth.* centaur

centavo /sen'taβo; θen'taβo/ m, hundredth part; cent; *Lat. Am.* centavo

centella /sen'teya; θen'teʎa/ f, lightning; spark; flash; *Fig.* spark (of anger, affection, etc.)

centellador /senteya'ðor; θenteʎa'ðor/ a flashing

centellear /senteye'ar; θenteʎe'ar/ vi to flash; twinkle; sparkle

centelleo /sente'yeo; θente'ʎeo/ m, scintillation; sparkle; flash

centén /sen'ten; θen'ten/ m, Spanish gold coin once worth 100 reals and later 25 pesetas

centena /sen'tena; θen'tena/ f, hundred

centenal, centenar /sente'nal, sente'nar; θente'nal, θente'nar/ m, hundred; centenary; rye field. **a centenares,** by the hundred, in crowds

centenario /sente'nario; θente'nario/ (**-ia)** a centenary. n centenarian. m, centenary

centeno /sen'teno; θen'teno/ m, *Bot.* rye

centésimo /sen'tesimo; θen'tesimo/ a and m, hundredth

centígrado /sen'tigraðo; θen'tigraðo/ a centigrade

centigramo /senti'gramo; θenti'gramo/ m, centigram

centilitro /senti'litro; θenti'litro/ m, centiliter

centímetro /senti'metro; θenti'metro/ m, centimeter. **c. cúbico,** cubic centimeter, milliliter

céntimo /'sentimo; 'θentimo/ a hundredth. m, centime (coin)

centinela /senti'nela; θenti'nela/ mf *Mil.* sentry, sentinel; person on watch. **estar de c.,** to be on sentry duty; be on guard

centolla /sen'toya; θen'toʎa/ f, marine crab

centón /sen'ton; θen'ton/ m, patchwork quilt

central /sen'tral; θen'tral/ a central; centric. f, head office; central depot; mother house. **c. de fuerza,** power-house. **c. telefónica,** telephone exchange

centralilla, centralita /sentra'liya, sentra'lita; θentra'liʎa, θentra'lita/ f, local exchange, private exchange

centralismo /sentra'lismo; θentra'lismo/ m, centralism

centralización /sentralisa'sion; θentraliθa'θion/ f, centralization

centralizador /sentralisa'ðor; θentraliθa'ðor/ a centralizing

centralizar /sentrali'sar; θentrali'θar/ vt to centralize

centrar /sen'trar; θen'trar/ vt to center

céntrico /'sentriko; 'θentriko/ a central, centric; centrally located; downtown

centrífugo /sen'trifugo; θen'trifugo/ a centrifugal

centrípeto /sen'tripeto; θen'tripeto/ a centripetal

centro /'sentro; 'θentro/ m, center; headquarters, meeting place, club; center, hub; middle; core (of a rope); *Fig.* focus. *Phys.* **c. de gravedad,** center of gravity. **c. de mesa,** table center-piece. *Anat.* **centro nervioso,** nerve center

Centroamérica /sentroa'merika; θentroa'merika/ f. Central America

centroamericano /sentroameri'kano; θentroameri'kano/ (**-na)** a and n. Central American

céntuplo /'sentuplo; 'θentuplo/ a centuple

centuria /sen'turia; θen'turia/ f, century

ceñidamente /seɲiða'mente; θeɲiða'mente/ tightly (e.g. un argumento c. organizado, a tightly organized plot)

ceñido /se'ɲiðo; θe'ɲiðo/ a thrifty; wasp-waisted, slender waisted; fitting (of garments)

ceñidor /seɲi'ðor; θeɲi'ðor/ m, girdle, belt

ceñir /se'ɲir; θe'ɲir/ vt irr to girdle; surround; shorten, abbreviate; vr be moderate (speech, expenditure, etc.); conform, confine oneself (to). **ceñirse a las reglas,** to abide by the rules. Pres. Ind. **ciño, ciñes, ciñen.** Pres. Part. **ciñendo.** Preterite **ciñó, ciñeron.** Pres. Subjunc. **ciña, etc.** Imperf. Subjunc. **ciñese, etc.**

ceño /'seɲo; 'θeɲo/ m, band, hoop; frown; *Fig.* dark outlook

ceñudo /se'ɲuðo; θe'ɲuðo/ a frowning

cepa /'sepa; 'θepa/ f, stump; vine-stock; root (tails, antlers, etc.); *Fig.* origin, trunk (of a family); *Biol.* strain. **de la más pura c.,** of the best quality

cepillar /sepi'yar; θepi'ʎar/ *vt* to brush; plane; smooth

cepillo /se'piyo; θe'piʎo/ *m*, brush; plane; poor-box, offertory-box. **c. para los dientes,** toothbrush. **c. para ropa,** clothes-brush. **c. para el suelo,** scrubbing-brush. **c. para las uñas,** nail-brush

cepo /'sepo; 'θepo/ *m*, bough; wooden stocks; snare; trap; poor-box; collecting-box

cera /'sera; 'θera/ *f*, beeswax; wax; wax candles, etc., used at a function. *Inf.* **ser como una c.,** to be like wax (in the hands of)

cerador /sera'ðor; θera'ðor/ *m*, floor waxer (person)

ceradora /sera'ðora; θera'ðora/ *f*, floor waxer (machine)

cerámica /se'ramika; θe'ramika/ *f*, ceramics; ceramic art, pottery

cerámico /se'ramiko; θe'ramiko/ *a* ceramic

cerbatana /serβa'tana; θerβa'tana/ *f*, blow-pipe, popgun; pea-shooter; ear-trumpet

cerca /'serka; 'θerka/ *f*, fence, wall

cerca /'serka; 'θerka/ *adv* near. **c. de,** near to; almost, nearly (e.g. *c. de las once,* nearly eleven o'clock)

cercado /ser'kaðo; θer'kaðo/ *m*, enclosure, fenced in place; fence

cercanía /serka'nia; θerka'nia/ *f*, nearness, proximity; (gen. *pl*) outskirts, surroundings

cercano /ser'kano; θer'kano/ *a* near, neighboring; impending, early

cercar /ser'kar; θer'kar/ *vt* to enclose; build a wall or fence round; to lay siege to; crowd round; *Mil.* surround

cercenamiento /sersena'miento; θerθena'miento/ **(a)** *m*, curtailment (of)

cercenar /serse'nar; θerθe'nar/ *vt* to lop off the ends, clip; curtail, diminish; abridge; whittle

cerciorar /sersio'rar; θerθio'rar/ *vt* to assure, confirm; *vr* make sure

cerco /'serko; 'θerko/ *m*, ring, hoop; fence; siege; small conversational circle; spin, circling; halo (sun, moon); frame; sash (of a window). **poner c. (a),** to lay siege to, blockade

cerda /'serða; 'θerða/ *f*, sow; bristle

Cerdeña /ser'ðeɲa; θer'ðeɲa/ Sardinia

cerdo /'serðo; 'θerðo/ *m*, pig, hog

cerdoso /ser'ðoso; θer'ðoso/ *a* bristly

cereal /sere'al; θere'al/ *a* and *m*, cereal

cerebelo /sere'βelo; θere'βelo/ *m*, *Anat.* cerebellum

cerebral /sere'βral; θere'βral/ *a* cerebral

cerebro /se'reβro; θe'reβro/ *m*, cerebrum; brain; intelligence

cerebro-espinal /se'reβro-espi'nal; θe'reβro-espi'nal/ *a* cerebrospinal

ceremonia /sere'monia; θere'monia/ *f*, ceremony; function, display; formality. **de c.,** ceremonial; formally. **por c.,** for politeness' sake

ceremonial /seremo'nial; θeremo'nial/ *a* ceremonial. *m*, ceremony; rite; protocol (rules of behavior)

ceremonioso /seremo'nioso; θeremo'nioso/ *a* ceremonious; formal, over-courteous

cerero /se'rero; θe'rero/ *m*, wax-chandler

cereza /se'resa; θe're θa/ *f*, cherry

cerezal /sere'sal; θere'θal/ *m*, cherry orchard

cerezo /se'reso; θe'reθo/ *m*, cherry tree; cherry wood

cerilla /se'riya; θe'riʎa/ *f*, wax taper; match; ear wax

cerillo /se'rijo; θe'riʎo/ *m*, *Mexico* matchstick

cerner /ser'ner; θer'ner/ *vt irr* to sieve; watch, observe; *Fig.* sift, clarify; *vi* bolt (of plants); drizzle; *vr* waddle; hover; threaten (of evil, etc.). *Pres. Ind.* **cierno, ciernes, cierne, ciernen.** *Pres. Subjunc.* **cierna, ciernas, cierna, ciernan**

cernícalo /ser'nikalo; θer'nikalo/ *m*, *Ornith.* kestrel; *Inf.* lout

cernidillo /serni'ðiyo; θerni'ðiʎo/ *m*, drizzle; teetering walk

cernido /ser'niðo; θer'niðo/ *m*, sifting, sieving; sifted flour

cerniduras /serni'ðuras; θerni'ðuras/ *f pl*, siftings

cero /'sero; 'θero/ *m*, *Math.* zero; naught; (tennis) love. *Fig. Inf.* **ser un c.,** to be a mere cipher

cerote /se'rote; θe'rote/ *m*, cobbler's wax. *Inf.* fear

cerquillo /ser'kiyo; θer'kiʎo/ *m*, tonsure; welt (of a shoe); *Lat. Am.* fringe

cerquita /ser'kita; θer'kita/ *adv* very near, hard by

cerradero, /serra'ðero,; θerra'ðero/ *m*, **cerradera** *f*, bolt staple; catch of a lock; clasp or strings of a purse

cerradizo /serra'ðiso; θerra'ðiθo/ *a* closable, lockable

cerrado /se'rraðo; θe'rraðo/ *a* closed; compact; incomprehensible, obscure; overcast, cloudy; *Inf.* taciturn; secretive. *m*, enclosure

cerradura /serra'ðura; θerra'ðura/ *f*, fastening, lock; closing, locking

cerraja /se'rraha; θe'rraha/ *f*, lock (of a door); bolt

cerrajería /serrahe'ria; θerrahe'ria/ *f*, locksmith's craft; locksmith's workshop or shop

cerrajero /serra'hero; θerra'hero/ *m*, locksmith

cerramiento /serra'miento; θerra'miento/ *m*, closing, locking up; fence; enclosure, shooting preserve; partition wall

cerrar /se'rrar; θe'rrar/ *vt irr* to close; lock, fasten, bolt; shut up; *Mech.* shut off, turn off; fold up; block or stop up; seal (letters, etc.); close down; terminate; obstruct; (*with con*) attack; *vi* close; close in (of night, etc.); *vr* heal up (wounds); close (flowers); *Radio.* close down; crowd together; *Fig.* stand firm. *Inf.* **cerrarse la espuela,** to take a nightcap, have a last drink. **c. la marcha,** to bring up the rear. **al c. la edición,** stop press. See **acertar**

cerrazón /serra'son; θerra'θon/ *f*, dark, overcast sky heralding a storm

cerril /se'rril; θe'rril/ *a* rough, rocky; wild, untamed (cattle, horses); *inf* boorish

cerro /'serro; 'θerro/ *m*, neck of an animal; spine, backbone; hill. *Fig.* **irse por los cerros de Úbeda,** to go off the track, indulge in irrelevancies

cerrojo /se'rroho; θe'rroho/ *m*, bolt (of a door, etc.); lock (of a door, gun, etc.)

certamen /ser'tamen; θer'tamen/ *m*, contest; competition; match

certero /ser'tero; θer'tero/ *a* well-aimed; sure, well-timed; knowledgeable, sure

certeza, certidumbre /ser'tesa, serti'ðumbre; θer'teθa, θerti'ðumbre/ *f*, certitude, assurance

certificación /sertifika'sion; θertifika'θion/ *f*, certification; certificate; affidavit

certificado /sertifi'kaðo; θertifi'kaðo/ *a* certified; registered. *m*, registered letter; certificate

certificar /sertifi'kar; θertifi'kar/ *vt* to certify; register (letter, etc.)

certificatorio /sertifika'torio; θertifika'torio/ *a* certifying or serving to certify

certísimo /ser'tisimo; θer'tisimo/ *a* learned form of the superlative of **cierto** (see **certísimo**)

certitud /serti'tuð; θerti'tuð/ *f*, certitude

cervantino /serβan'tino; θerβan'tino/ *a* Cervantine

cervecería /serβese'ria; θerβeθe'ria/ *f*, brewery; ale-house

cervecero /serβe'sero; θerβe'θero/ **(-ra)** *n* brewer; beer seller

cerveza /ser'βesa; θer'βeθa/ *f*, beer, ale. **c. negra,** stout

cerviz /ser'βis; θer'βiθ/ *f*, cervix, nape (of neck). **doblar** (*or* **bajar**) **la c.,** to humble oneself

cesación /sesa'sion; θesa'θion/ *f*, cessation, stopping

cesante /se'sante; θe'sante/ *a* dismissed; pensioned off. **declarar c. (a),** to dismiss (a person from a post)

estar c., to be out of a job

cesantía /sesan'tia; θesan'tia/ *f*, status of dismissed or retired official; retirement pension

cesar /se'sar; θe'sar/ *vi* to cease, stop, leave an employment; desist; retire

cesáreo /se'sareo; θe'sareo/ *a* Cesarean; imperial

cese /'sese; 'θese/ *m*, stopping of payment for an employment

cesión /se'sion; θe'sion/ *f*, cession; transfer; resignation; *Law.* release

cesionario /sesio'nario; θesio'nario/ **(-ia)** *n* cessionary, transferee

césped /'sespeð; 'θespeð/ *m*, grass, sward; sod, lawn

cesta /'sesta; 'θesta/ *f*, basket, hamper; *Sports.* racket; cradle (for a wine bottle)

cestada /ses'taða; θes'taða/ *f*, basketful
cestería /seste'ria; θeste'ria/ *f*, basketmaking, basketweaving; basket factory; basket shop; basketwork
cestero /ses'tero; θes'tero/ **(-ra)** *n* basket maker or seller
cesto /'sesto; 'θesto/ *m*, basket, hamper, skip
cesura /se'sura; θe'sura/ *f*, cesura
cetorrino /seto'rrino; θeto'rrino/ *m*, basking shark
cetrería /setre'ria; θetre'ria/ *f*, falconry
cetrino /se'trino; θe'trino/ *a* greenish-yellow; sallow; citrine; melancholy; reserved, aloof
cetro /'setro; 'θetro/ *m*, scepter; verge; reign
chabacanería /tʃaβakane'ria/ *f*, bad taste; vulgarity
chabacano /tʃaβa'kano/ *a* vulgar, common; rude, uncouth
chacal /tʃa'kal/ *m*, *Zool.* jackal
cháchara /'tʃatʃara/ *f*, *Inf.* empty chatter; verbiage
chacharear /tʃatʃare'ar/ *vi* to chatter; gabble, cackle
chacharero /tʃatʃa'rero/ *a* *Inf.* chattering; talkative
chacolotear /tʃakolote'ar/ *vi* to clatter, clink (loose horseshoe)
chacota /tʃa'kota/ *f*, merriment, mirth
chacotear /tʃakote'ar/ *vi* *Inf.* to be merry, have fun
chacotón /tʃako'ton/ *a* of a boisterous humor
chacra /'tʃakra/ *f*, *Lat. Am.* small farm, small holding
chafado /tʃa'faðo/ *a* taken aback; disappointed
chafallar /tʃafa'yar; tʃafa'ʎar/ *vt* *Inf.* to mend carelessly, botch
chafandín /tʃafan'din/ *m*, vain fool
chafar /tʃa'far/ *vt* to flatten; crumple, crease (clothes); *Inf.* heckle
chafarrinar /tʃafarri'nar/ *vt* to stain, mark, blot
chaflán /tʃa'flan/ *m*, bevel edge, chamfer
chagrén /tʃa'gren/ *m*, shagreen leather
chagüe /'tʃage/ *m*, *Central America* bog, marsh, swamp
chal /tʃal/ *m*, shawl
chalán /tʃa'lan/ *m*, horse-dealer
chalana /tʃa'lana/ *f*, *Naut.* wherry, lighter
chalanear /tʃalane'ar/ *vt* to bargain; indulge in sharp practice
chalar /tʃa'lar/ *vt* to drive mad; enamor
chaleco /tʃa'leko/ *m*, waistcoat; cardigan
chalequear /tʃaleke'ar/ *vt*, *Mexico* to pilfer, swipe
chalina /tʃa'lina/ *f*, flowing scarf, artist's bow
Chalo /'tʃalo/ pet form of the male given name *Carlos* "Charles", hence = English *Chuck; Bud, Mac* (in direct address to a male whose name one does not know)
chalote /tʃa'lote/ *m*, shallot
chalupa /tʃa'lupa/ *f*, shallop; launch; canoe; long boat, ship's boat
chamar /tʃa'mar/ *vt* *Inf.* to palm off, barter
chamarasca /tʃama'raska/ *f*, brushwood, tinder
chamarilero /tʃamari'lero/ **(-ra)** *n* secondhand dealer
chamarreta /tʃama'rreta/ *f*, sheepskin jacket; *Mexico* jacket
chambergo /tʃam'βergo/ *a* pertaining to the Chambergo regiment. *m*, broad-brimmed hat
chambón /tʃam'βon/ *a* *Inf.* awkward, clumsy; lucky
chambonada /tʃambo'naða/ *f*, *Inf.* blunder; fluke, chance
chambra /'tʃambra/ *f*, dressing-jacket, peignoir, negligee
chamicera /tʃami'sera; tʃami'θera/ *f*, piece of scorched earth (woodland, etc.)
chamorro /tʃa'morro/ *a* close-cropped, shorn (hair), crew-cut
champán /tʃam'pan/ *m*, champagne. **c. obrero**, *humorous* cider
champaña /tʃam'paɲa/ *m*, champagne
champar /tʃam'par/ *vt* *Inf.* to cast in a person's face, remind
champú /tʃam'pu/ *m*, shampoo
chamuscar /tʃamus'kar/ *vt* to scorch; singe
chamusquina /tʃamus'kina/ *f*, scorching; singeing; *Inf.* brawl
chanada /tʃa'naða/ *f*, *Inf.* trick, mischievous act
chancaca /tʃan'kaka/ *f*, *Lat. Am.* syrup cake

chancada /tʃan'kaða/ *f*, *Lat. Am.* dirty trick
chancearse /tʃanse'arse; tʃanθe'arse/ *vr* to joke
chancero /tʃan'sero; tʃan'θero/ *a* joking, facetious
chancho, -a /'tʃantʃo/ *mf*, *Lat. Am.* pig
chanchollada /tʃantʃo'yaða; tʃantʃo'ʎaða/ *f*, dirty trick, foul play, trick
chanchullo /tʃan'tʃuyo; tʃan'tʃuʎo/ *m*, *Inf.* fraud
chanciller /tʃansi'yer; tʃanθi'ʎer/ *m*, chancellor
chancillería /tʃansiye'ria; tʃanθiʎe'ria/ *f*, chancery
chancla /'tʃankla/ *f*, down at heel shoe; heelless slipper
chancleta /tʃan'kleta/ *f*, heelless slipper, babouche. *mf Inf.* ninny
chanclo /'tʃanklo/ *m*, overshoe; Wellington
chanfaina /tʃan'faina/ *f*, *Cul.* savory fricassee
chanflón /tʃan'flon/ *a* tough, coarse; ungainly
changador /tʃaŋga'ðor/ *m*. *Argentina* porter
chantaje /tʃan'tahe/ *m*, blackmail
chantajista /tʃanta'hista/ *mf* blackmailer
chantar /tʃan'tar/ *vt* to put on, clothe; *Inf.* tell plainly. *Inf.* **c. sus verdades**, to tell hometruths
chanza /'tʃansa; 'tʃanθa/ *f*, joke, jest
chanzoneta /tʃanso'neta; tʃanθo'neta/ *f*, canzonetta; *Inf.* joke
¡chao! /'tʃao/ *Argentina, Chile* bye!
chapa /'tʃapa/ *f*, plate, sheet; veneer; clasp; *Inf.* prudence, common sense; rouge. **c. de hierro**, sheet-iron. **c. de identidad**, number plate
chapado a la antigua /tʃa'paðo a la an'tigua/ *a* old-fashioned
chapalear /tʃapale'ar/ *vi* to dabble in water; splash; clatter (of a horseshoe)
chapaleo /tʃapa'leo/ *m*, dabbling, paddling; splash; clattering, clink (of a horseshoe)
chapaleteo /tʃapale'teo/ *m*, lapping of water; splashing (of rain)
chaparrear /tʃaparre'ar/ *vi* to pour with rain
chaparrón /tʃapa'rron/ *m*, heavy shower of rain, downpour
chapear /tʃape'ar/ *vt* to veneer; *vi* clatter (loose horseshoe)
chaperón /tʃape'ron/ *m*, hood
chapeta /tʃa'peta/ *f*, *dim* clasp; red flush or spot on cheek
chapetón /tʃape'ton/ **(-ona)** *n* *West Hem.* recently arrived European, especially Spaniard
chapín /tʃa'pin/ *m*, cork-soled leather overshoe (for women) *Obs.*
chapino /tʃa'pino/ *a* and *m*, *Mexico contemptuous* Guatemalan
chapodar /tʃapo'ðar/ *vt* to prune, lop off branches; cut down, reduce
chapotear /tʃapote'ar/ *vt* to sponge, moisten, damp; *vi* paddle, splash; dabble or trail the hands (in water)
chapoteo /tʃapo'teo/ *m*, moistening, sponging; paddling, splashing; dabbling
chapucear /tʃapuse'ar; tʃapuθe'ar/ *vt* to botch, do badly; bungle
chapuceramente /tʃapusera'mente; tʃapuθera'mente/ *adv* awkwardly. **hablar el japonés c.**, to speak broken Japanese
chapucería /tʃapuse'ria; tʃapuθe'ria/ *f*, roughness, poor workmanship; botch
chapucero /tʃapu'sero; tʃapu'θero/ *a* rough, badly finished; bungling, clumsy, awkward
chapurrado /tʃapu'rraðo/ *a* broken (e.g. *hablar un italiano c.*, to speak broken Italian)
chapurrar, chapurrear /tʃapu'rrar, tʃapurre'ar/ *vt* to speak badly (a language); jabber; *Inf.* mix (drinks)
chapuz /tʃa'pus; tʃa'puθ/ *m*, ducking, submerging; plunge; unimportant job; clumsiness
chapuzar /tʃapu'sar; tʃapu'θar/ *vt* to duck, submerge; plunge
chaqué /tʃa'ke/ *m*, morning coat; morning suit
chaqueta /tʃa'keta/ *f*, jacket; *Mech.* casing
chaquete /tʃa'kete/ *m*, backgammon
chaquetilla /tʃake'tiya; tʃake'tiʎa/ *f*, short jacket; coatee; blazer
chaquetón /tʃake'ton/ *m*, short coat. **c. de piloto**, *Aer.* pea-jacket

charabán /tʃara'βan/ *m*, charabanc
charada /tʃa'raða/ *f*, charade
charamusca /tʃara'muska/ *f*, *Lat. Am.* firewood, kindling
charanguero /tʃaraŋ'guero/ *a* rough, badly finished; clumsy. *m*, Andalusian boat
charca /'tʃarka/ *f*, pond, pool; reservoir
charco /'tʃarko/ *m*, puddle; *Inf.* sea
charla /'tʃarla/ *f*, *Inf.* chatter; conversation; talk, informal lecture
charlar /'tʃarlar/ *vi Inf.* to prattle, chatter; chat, converse; give a talk (on)
charlatán /tʃarla'tan/ **(-ana)** *a* loquacious, garrulous; indiscreet; fraudulent, false. *n* charlatan; chatterer
charlatanería /tʃarlatane'ria/ *f*, loquacity, garrulity; quackery
charlatanismo /tʃarlata'nismo/ *m*, charlatanism, quackery
charnela /tʃar'nela/ *f*, hinge; hinged joint
charol /tʃa'rol/ *m*, varnish; patent leather
charolar /tʃaro'lar/ *vt* to varnish
charolista /tʃaro'lista/ *mf*, varnisher
charpa /'tʃarpa/ *f*, pistol-belt; sling
charrán /tʃa'rran/ **(-ana)** *n* rogue, trickster
charranada /tʃarra'naða/ *f*, roguery, knavery
charrería /tʃarre'ria/ *f*, tawdriness; gaudiness
charretera /tʃarre'tera/ *f*, *Mil.* epaulet; garter
charro /'tʃarro/ *a* churlish, coarse; flashy, tawdry
chasca /'tʃaska/ *f*, brushwood, firewood
chascar /tʃas'kar/ *vi* to creak, crack; clack (the tongue); swallow
chascarrillo /tʃaska'rriyo; tʃaska'rriʎo/ *m*, *Inf.* amusing anecdote, good story
chasco /'tʃasko/ *m*, trick, practical joke; disappointment. **llevarse un c.**, to meet with a disappointment
chasis /'tʃasis/ *m*, *Auto.* chassis; *Photo.* plate-holder; *Mech.* underframe
chasquear /tʃaske'ar/ *vt* to play a trick on; wag (one's tongue); crack (a whip, one's knuckles); break a promise, disappoint; *vi* creak, crack; meet with a disappointment
chasquido /tʃas'kiðo/ *m*, crack (of whip); creaking (of wood); click (of the tongue)
chatarra /tʃa'tarra/ *f*, scrap iron; junk
chato /'tʃato/ *a* flat-nosed; flat
chauvinismo /tʃauβi'nismo/ *m*, chauvinism
chaval /tʃa'βal/ *a Inf.* young. *m*, lad
chaveta /tʃa'βeta/ *f*, *Mech.* bolt, pin, peg, cotter, key
checo /'tʃeko/ **(-ca)** *a* and *n* Czech. Czech (language)
Chejov /tʃe'hoβ/ Chekhov
chelín /tʃe'lin/ *m*, shilling
Chengis-Jan /tʃenhis-'han/ Genghis Khan
chepa /'tʃepa/ *f*, *Inf.* hunch (back); hump
cheque /'tʃeke/ *m*, check. **c. cruzado**, crossed check
chica /'tʃika/ *f*, girl; *Inf.* dear
chicana /tʃi'kana/ *f*, chicanery
chicano /tʃi'kano/ **(-na)** *a* and *n* Chicano, American of Mexican ancestry
chicha /'tʃitʃa/ *f*, *Lat. Am.* corn liquor
chícharo /'tʃitʃaro/ *m*, pea
chicharrón /tʃitʃa'rron/ *m*, *Cul.* crackling; burnt meat; *Inf.* sunburned person
chichón /tʃi'tʃon/ *m*, bruise, bump
chichonera /tʃitʃo'nera/ *f*, child's protective hat (something like a straw crash-helmet)
chicle /'tʃikle/ *m*, chewing gum
chiclero /tʃi'klero/ *m*, chicle-gatherer
chico /'tʃiko/ *a* little, small; young. *m*, little boy; youth; *Inf.* old boy, dear. **Es un buen c.**, He's a good fellow
chicoleo /tʃiko'leo/ *m*, *Inf.* compliment
chicote /tʃi'kote/ *mf* sturdy child. *m*, *Inf.* cigar; *Lat. Am.* whip
chifla /'tʃifla/ *f*, whistling, whistle; tanner's paring knife
chiflado /tʃi'flaðo/ *a Inf.* cracked, daft; crack-brained
chifladura /tʃifla'ðura/ *f*, whistling; *Inf.* whim, mania, hobby
chiflar /tʃi'flar/ *vi* to whistle; *vt* to make fun of, hiss;

pare or scrape leather; *Inf.* swill, tipple; *vr Inf.* have a slate loose; be slightly mad; *Inf.* lose one's head over, adore
chifle /'tʃifle/ *m*, whistle, whistling; decoy call (birds)
chiflón /tʃi'flon/ *m*, *Lat. Am.* draft (of air)
chile /'tʃile/ *m*, *Bot.* red pepper, chilli
chileno /tʃi'leno/ **(-na)** *a* and *n* Chilean
chilla /'tʃija; 'tʃiʎa/ *f*, *Argentina* fox
chillador /tʃiya'ðor; tʃiʎa'ðor/ *a* screaming, shrieking
chillar /tʃi'yar; tʃi'ʎar/ *vi* to scream, shriek; creak; squeak; jabber (monkeys, etc.); *Art.* be strident (of colors)
chillería /tʃiye'ria; tʃiʎe'ria/ *f*, shrieking, screaming
chillido /tʃi'yiðo; tʃi'ʎiðo/ *m*, scream, shriek; squeak (of mice, etc.); jabber (of monkeys, etc.)
chillón /tʃi'yon; tʃi'ʎon/ *a Inf.* screaming, yelling; strident, piercing; crude, loud (colors)
chimenea /tʃime'nea/ *f*, chimney; funnel; fireplace; kitchen range
chimpancé /tʃimpan'se; tʃimpan'θe/ *m*, chimpanzee
china /'tʃina/ *f*, pebble; porcelain, china; Chinese silk
chinche /'tʃintʃe/ *f*, bedbug; thumbtack, drawing-pin. *mf Inf.* bore
chinchona /tʃin'tʃona/ *f*, quinine
chinchorrería /tʃintʃorre'ria/ *f*, *Inf.* impertinence, tediousness; gossip
chinela /tʃi'nela/ *f*, mule, slipper; overshoe, patten *Obs.*
chinero /tʃi'nero/ *m*, china cupboard
chinesco /tʃi'nesko/ *a* Chinese. **a la chinesca**, in Chinese fashion
chingana /tʃiŋ'gana/ *f*, *Lat. Am.* bar
chino /'tʃino/ **(-na)** *a* and *n* Chinese. *m*, Chinese (language)
Chipre /'tʃipre/ Cyprus
chiquero /tʃi'kero/ *m*, pigsty; stable for bulls
chiquillada /tʃiki'yaða; tʃiki'ʎaða/ *f*, childishness, puerility
chiquillería /tʃikiye'ria; tʃikiʎe'ria/ *f*, *Inf.* crowd of children
chiquillo /tʃi'kiyo; tʃi'kiʎo/ **(-lla)** *n* small boy
chiquito /tʃi'kito/ **(-ta)** *a dim* **chico**, tiny, very small. *n* little one, small boy
chiripa /tʃi'ripa/ *f*, (billiards) fluke; *Inf.* happy coincidence, stroke of luck; lucky guess
chirivía /tʃiri'βia/ *f*, *Bot.* parsnip; *Ornith.* wagtail
chirlar /tʃir'lar/ *vi Inf.* to gabble, talk loudly
chirlo /'tʃirlo/ *m*, knife wound, saber cut; knife scar
chirona /tʃi'rona/ *f*, *Inf.* jail
chirriador /tʃirria'ðor/ *a* sizzling, crackling; creaking, squeaking
chirriar /tʃi'rriar/ *vi* to sizzle, crackle; creak, squeak; squawk; *Inf.* croak, sing out of tune
chirrido /tʃi'rriðo/ *m*, squawk; croaking; noise of grasshoppers; squeaking; creaking, creak
¡chis! /tʃis/ *interj* Shh! Silence!
chisme /'tʃisme/ *m*, gossip, tale; *Inf.* small household utensil, trifle
chismear /tʃisme'ar/ *vt* to tell tales, gossip
chismero /tʃis'mero/ **(-ra), chismoso (-sa)** *a* gossiping, talebearing. *n* gossip, tale bearer
chispa /'tʃispa/ *f*, spark; ember; *Elec.* spark; tiny diamond; small particle; wit; quickwittedness; *Inf.* drunkenness. **c. del encendido**, ignition spark
chispazo /tʃis'paso; tʃis'paθo/ *m*, flying out of a spark, sparking; damage done by spark; *Inf.* gossip, rumor
chispeante /tʃispe'ante/ *a* sparking; sparkling; *Fig.* scintillating (with wit etc.)
chispear /tʃispe'ar/ *vi* to throw out sparks, spark; sparkle, gleam; *Fig.* scintillate; drizzle gently
chisporrotear /tʃisporrote'ar/ *vi Inf.* to sputter; fizz
chisposo /tʃis'poso/ *a* sputtering, throwing out sparks
chistar /tʃis'tar/ *vi* to speak, break silence (gen. used negatively)
chiste /'tʃiste/ *m*, witticism, bon mot; amusing incident; joke
chistera /tʃis'tera/ *f*, creel (for fish); *Inf.* top-hat, tile
chistoso /tʃis'toso/ *a* joking; amusing, funny

chiticallando /tʃitika'yando; tʃitika'ʎando/ *adv* quietly, stealthily; *Inf.* on the quiet, in secret

¡chito! ¡chitón! /'tʃito tʃi'ton/ *interj* Hush! Sh!

chiva /'tʃiβa/ *f, Colombia, Panama* bus; *Venezuela* beard, goatee; **chivas** *f, Venezuela* hand-me-downs

chivo /'tʃiβo/ *n Zool.* kid.

c. expiatorio, scapegoat

chocante /tʃo'kante/ *a* colliding; provoking; shocking; surprising

chocar /tʃo'kar/ *vi* to collide; strike (against); run into; fight, clash; *vt* clink (glasses); provoke, annoy; surprise, shock. **¡Choca cinco!** Clasp five!, Gimme five!, Put it there!, Give some skin! (invitation to shake hands)

chocarrería /tʃokarre'ria/ *f,* coarse joke

chochear /tʃotʃe'ar/ *vi* to be senile; *Fig. Inf.* dote (on)

chocho /'tʃotʃo/ *a* senile; *Fig. Inf.* doting

choco /'tʃoko/ *m,* small hump, hunchback

chocolate /tʃoko'late/ *m,* chocolate; drinking chocolate. **c. a la española,** thick chocolate. **c. a la francesa,** French drinking chocolate

chocolatería /tʃokolate'ria/ *f,* chocolate factory or shop

chocolatero /tʃokola'tero/ **(-ra)** *a* fond of chocolate. *n* chocolate maker or seller

chófer /'tʃofer/ *m,* chauffeur; driver

chompa /'tʃompa/ *f, Lat. Am.* jumper, pullover

chonta /'tʃonta/ *f, Lat. Am.* palm tree

chopera /tʃo'pera/ *f,* grove or plantation of black poplar trees

chopo /'tʃopo/ *m, Bot.* black poplar; *Inf.* gun

choque /'tʃoke/ *m,* collision; shock; jar; *Med.* concussion; fight; clink (of glasses); clash; *Mil.* skirmish

choricera /tʃori'sera; tʃori'θera/ *f,* sausage-making machine

choricero /tʃori'sero; tʃori'θero/ **(-ra)** *n* sausage maker

chorizo /tʃo'riso; tʃo'riθo/ *m,* kind of pork sausage; counterweight

chorrear /tʃorre'ar/ *vi* to spout; jet; drip; *Fig. Inf.* trickle, arrive slowly

chorreo /tʃo'rreo/ *m,* drip, dripping; spouting, gushing

chorrera /tʃo'rrera/ *f,* spout; drip; jabot, lace front

chorro /'tʃorro/ *m,* jet; stream (of water, etc.); *Fig.* shower. **a chorros,** in a stream; in abundance, plentifully

chova /'tʃoβa/ *f,* rook; carrion crow; jackdaw

choza /'tʃosa; 'tʃoθa/ *f,* hut, cabin; cottage

chubasco /tʃu'βasko/ *m,* squall, downpour; storm; transitory misfortune

chuchería /tʃutʃe'ria/ *f,* gewgaw, trinket; savory titbit; snaring, trapping

chucruta /tʃu'kruta/ *f,* sauerkraut

chueca /'tʃueka/ *f,* round head of a bone; small ball; game like shinty; *Inf.* practical joke

chueco /'tʃueko/ *a Mexico* bent, crooked, twisted

chufa /'tʃufa/ *f, Bot.* chufa; *Inf.* joke, trick

chufería /tʃufe'ria/ *f,* place where drink made of **chufas** is sold

chufla /'tʃufla/ *f,* flippant remark

chufleta /tʃu'fleta/ *f, Inf.* joke; taunt

chulada /tʃu'laða/ *f,* mean trick, base action; drollery

chulería /tʃule'ria/ *f,* drollness; attractive personality

chuleta /tʃu'leta/ *f, Cul.* cutlet, chop; mutton-chop; *Inf.* slap

chulo /'tʃulo/ *a* droll, amusing; attractive. *m,* slaughterhouse worker; bullfighter's assistant; pimp; rogue

chumbera /tʃum'βera/ *f,* prickly pear; Indian fig

chupada /tʃu'paða/ *f,* sucking; suck; suction

chupado de cara, c. de mofletes /mof'letes; tʃu'paðo de 'kara/ *a* lantern-jawed

chupador /tʃupa'ðor/ *a* sucking. *m,* baby's comforter or dummy

chupar /tʃu'par/ *vt* to suck; absorb (of plants); *Fig. Inf.* drain, rob; *vr* grow thin. **chuparse los dedos,** *Inf.* to lick one's lips; be delighted

chupatintas /tʃupa'tintas/ *mf, Inf.* scrivener, clerk (scornful)

churdón /tʃur'ðon/ *m,* raspberry cane; raspberry; raspberry vinegar

churrería /tʃurre'ria/ *f,* place where **churros** are made or sold

churrero /tʃu'rrero/ **(-ra)** *n* maker or seller of **churros**

churrigueresco /tʃurrige'resko/ *a* Churrigueresque

churro /'tʃurro/ *a* coarse (of wool). *m, Cul.* a kind of fritter eaten with chocolate, coffee, etc.

churumbela /tʃurum'βela/ *f, Mus.* pipe; reed for drinking mate *West Hem.*

chusco /'tʃusko/ *a* droll, witty, amusing

chusma /'tʃusma/ *f,* galley hands, crew; rabble, mob

chutar /tʃu'tar/ *vt Sports.* to shoot (a goal)

chuzo /'tʃuso; 'tʃuθo/ *m, Mil.* pike

chuzón /tʃu'son; tʃu'θon/ *a* wily, suspicious, cunning

cianuro /sia'nuro; θia'nuro/ *m,* cyanide

ciar /siar; θiar/ *vi* to go backwards; *Naut.* row backwards; *Fig.* make no headway (negotiations)

ciática /'siatika; 'θiatika/ *f,* sciatica

ciático /'siatiko; 'θiatiko/ *a* sciatic

ciberespacio /siβeres'pasio; θiβeres'paθio/ *m,* cyberspace

cicatería /sikate'ria; θikate'ria/ *f,* niggardliness, avarice

cicatero /sika'tero; θika'tero/ *a* avaricious, niggardly, mean

cicatriz /sika'tris; θika'triθ/ *f,* cicatrice; *Fig.* scar, mark, impression

cicatrizar /sikatri'sar; θikatri'θar/ *vt* to cicatrize, heal; *vr* scar over

cíclico /'sikliko; 'θikliko/ *a* cyclic, cyclical

ciclismo /si'klismo; θi'klismo/ *m,* bicycling

ciclista /si'klista; θi'klista/ *mf* cyclist

ciclo /'siklo; 'θiklo/ *m,* cycle (of time). **c. artúrico, c. de Artús,** Arthurian Cycle. **c. de conferencias,** series of lectures

ciclón /si'klon; θi'klon/ *m,* cyclone

ciclópeo /si'klopeo; θi'klopeo/ *a* cyclopean

cicuta /si'kuta; θi'kuta/ *f,* hemlock

cid /sið; θið/ *m,* great warrior, chief. **el Cid,** national hero of Spanish wars against the Moors

cidra /'siðra; 'θiðra/ *f,* citron

cidro /'siðro; 'θiðro/ *m,* citron tree

ciego /'siego; 'θiego/ *a* blind; dazed, blinded; choked up. *m,* blind man; *Anat.* cæcum. **a ciegas,** blindly; heedlessly

cielo /'sielo; 'θielo/ *m,* sky, firmament; atmosphere; climate; paradise; Providence; bliss, glory; roof, canopy; *Inf.* darling. **a c. abierto,** in the open air. **parecer un c.,** to be heavenly

ciempiés /siem'pies; θiem'pies/ *m,* centipede

cien /sien; θien/ *a* abb. **ciento,** hundred. Used always before substantives (e.g. *c. hombres,* 100 men)

ciénaga /'sienaga; 'θienaga/ *f,* swamp; morass

ciencia /'siensia; 'θienθia/ *f,* science; knowledge; erudition, ability. **ciencias naturales,** natural science. **a c. cierta,** for certain, without doubt (gen. with *saber*)

cienmilésimo /siemi'lesimo; θiemi'lesimo/ *a* hundred-thousandth

cieno /'sieno; 'θieno/ *m,* slime, mud; silt

científico /sien'tifiko; θien'tifiko/ *a* scientific. *m,* scientist

ciento /'siento; 'θiento/ (cf. **cien**) *a* hundred; hundredth. *m,* hundred. **por c.,** per cent.

cierne, en /'sierne, en; 'θierne, en/ in flower; *Fig.* in the early stages, in embryo

cierre /'sierre; 'θierre/ *m,* closing, shutting; closing time of shops, etc.; fastening; fastener; clasp (of a necklace, handbag, etc.). **c. cremallera,** zip fastener. **c. metálico,** doorshutter

ciertamente /sierta'mente; θierta'mente/ *adv* certainly; undoubtedly; indeed

ciertísimo /sier'tisimo; θier'tisimo/ *a* everyday form of the superlative of **cierto** (see **certísimo**)

cierto /'sierto; 'θierto/ *a* certain, sure; true; particular (e.g. *c. hombre,* a certain man (note no *def. art.*)). **un c. sabor,** a special flavor. **una cosa cierta,** something certain. **no, por c.,** no, certainly not. **por c.,** truly, indeed

cierva /'sierβa; 'θierβa/ *f,* hind

ciervo /'sierβo; 'θierβo/ *m, stag.* **c. volante,** stagbeetle

cierzo /'sierso; 'θierθo/ *m,* northerly wind

cifra /'sifra; 'θifra/ *f*, number; figure; sum total; cipher, code; monogram; abbreviation

cifrar /si'frar; θi'frar/ *vt* to write in cipher; summarize, abridge; (*with en*) be dependent on; depend on

cigarra /si'garra; θi'garra/ *f*, *Ent.* cicada, harvest fly

cigarral /siga'rral; θiga'rral/ *m*, (Toledo) countryhouse and garden or orchard

cigarrera /siga'rrera; θiga'rrera/ *f*, woman who makes or sells cigars; cigar-cabinet; cigar-case

cigarrería /sigarre'ria; θigarre'ria/ *f*, *Lat. Am.* tobacco shop

cigarrillo /siga'rriyo; θiga'rriʎo/ *m*, cigarette

cigarro /si'garro; θi'garro/ *m*, cigar; *Lat. Am.* cigarette

cigüeña /si'gueɲa; θi'gueɲa/ *f*, *Ornith.* stork; *Mech.* crank

ciliar /si'liar; θi'liar/ *a* ciliary

cilicio /si'lisio; θi'liθio/ *m*, hairshirt

cilindrar /silin'drar; θilin'drar/ *vt* to roll; calendar; bore

cilindrero /silin'drero; θilin'drero/ *m*, organ grinder

cilíndrico /si'lindriko; θi'lindriko/ *a* cylindrical

cilindro /si'lindro; θi'lindro/ *m*, cylinder; roller

cima /'sima; 'θima/ *f*, summit; top of trees; apex; *Archit.* coping; head (thistle, etc.); *Fig.* aim, goal, end

cimbalero /simba'lero; θimba'lero/ **(-ra)** *n* cymbalist

címbalo /'simbalo; 'θimbalo/ *m*, cymbal

cimborrio /sim'βorrio; θim'βorrio/ *m*, *Archit.* cupola; cimborium

cimbrar, cimbrear /sim'βrar, simbre'ar; θim'βrar, θimbre'ar/ *vt* to bend; brandish; *vr* sway (in walking)

cimbreño /sim'βreɲo; θim'βreɲo/ *a* graceful, lithe, willowy

cimbreo /sim'βreo; θim'βreo/ *m*, swaying, bending

cimbrón /sim'βron; θim'βron/ *m*, *Lat. Am.* vibration

cimentar /simen'tar; θimen'tar/ *vt irr* to lay foundations; refine (gold, metals, etc.); found; *Fig.* ground (in virtue, etc.). See **acertar**

cimera /si'mera; θi'mera/ *f*, crest of helmet

cimiento /si'miento; θi'miento/ *m*, foundation (of a building); bottom; groundwork; origin, base. **abrir los cimientos,** to lay the foundations

cimitarra /simi'tarra; θimi'tarra/ *f*, scimitar

cinabrio /si'naβrio; θi'naβrio/ *m*, cinnabar; vermilion

cinc /sink; θink/ *m*, zinc

cincel /sin'sel; θin'θel/ *m*, chisel; burin, engraver

cincelador /sinsela'ðor; θinθela'ðor/ **(-ra)** *n* engraver; chiseler

cincelar /sinse'lar; θinθe'lar/ *vt* to chisel; carve; engrave

cincha /'sintʃa; 'θintʃa/ *f*, girth of a saddle

cinchar /sin'tʃar; θin'tʃar/ *vt* to tighten the saddle girths

cincho /'sintʃo; 'θintʃo/ *m*, belt, girdle; iron hoop

cinco /'sinko; 'θinko/ *a* and *m*, five; fifth. **a las c.,** at five o'clock

cincuenta /sin'kuenta; θin'kuenta/ *a* and *m*, fifty; fiftieth

cincuentavo /sinkuen'taβo; θinkuen'taβo/ *a* fiftieth

cincuentenario /sinkuente'nario; θinkuente'nario/ *m*, fiftieth anniversary

cincuentón /sinkuen'ton; θinkuen'ton/ **(-ona)** *a* and *n* fifty years old (person)

cine, cinema /'sine, si'nema; 'θine, θi'nema/ *m*, cinema, movies. **c. sonoro,** sound film

cinemática /sine'matika; θine'matika/ *f*, *Phys.* kinematics

cinematografía /sinematogra'fia; θinematogra'fia/ *f*, cinematography

cinematografiar /sinematogra'fiar; θinematogra'fiar/ *vt* to film

cinematográfico /sinemato'grafiko; θinemato'grafiko/ *a* cinematographic

cinematógrafo /sinema'tografo; θinema'tografo/ *m*, motion-picture camera; cinema

cínico /'siniko; 'θiniko/ *a* cynical; impudent; untidy. *m*, cynic

cinismo /si'nismo; θi'nismo/ *m*, cynicism

cinta /'sinta; 'θinta/ *f*, ribbon; tape; strip; film (cinematograph). **c. métrica,** tape-measure

cintillo /sin'tiyo; θin'tiʎo/ *m*, hatband; small ring set with gems

cinto /'sinto; 'θinto/ *m*, belt, girdle. **c. de pistolas,** pistol-belt

cintoteca /sinto'teka; θinto'teka/ *f*, tape library

cintura /sin'tura; θin'tura/ *f*, waist; belt, girdle

cinturón /sintu'ron; θintu'ron/ *m*, large waist; belt girdle; sword-belt; that which encircles or surrounds. **c. de seguridad,** seat belt

ciprés /si'pres; θi'pres/ *m*, *Bot.* cypress tree or wood

cipresal /sipre'sal; θipre'sal/ *m*, cypress grove

cipresino /sipre'sino; θipre'sino/ *a* cypress; cypress-like

circasiano /sirka'siano; θirka'siano/ **(-na)** *a* and *n* Circassian

circo /'sirko; 'θirko/ *m*, circus; amphitheater

circón /sir'kon; θir'kon/ *m*, zircon

circuir /sir'kuir; θir'kuir/ *vt. irr* to surround, encircle. See **huir**

circuito /sir'kuito; θir'kuito/ *m*, periphery; contour; (*Elec. Phys.*) circuit. **corto c.,** short circuit

circulación /sirkula'sion; θirkula'θion/ *f*, circulation; traffic. **c. de la sangre,** circulation of the blood. **calle de gran c.,** busy street

circular /sirku'lar; θirku'lar/ *a* circular. *f*, circular. *vt* to pass round; *vi* circle; circulate; move in a circle; move about; run, travel (traffic)

circulatorio /sirkula'torio; θirkula'torio/ *a* circulatory

círculo /'sirkulo; 'θirkulo/ *m*, circle; circumference; circuit; casino, social club

circuncidar /sirkunsi'ðar; θirkunθi'ðar/ *vt* to circumcise; modify, reduce

circuncisión /sirkunsi'sion; θirkunθi'sion/ *f*, circumcision

circunciso /sirkun'siso; θirkun'θiso/ *a* circumcised

circundar /sirkun'dar; θirkun'dar/ *vt* to surround

circunferencia /sirkunfe'rensia; θirkunfe'renθia/ *f*, circumference

circunflejo /sirkun'fleho; θirkun'fleho/ *a* circumflex. **acento c.,** circumflex accent

circunlocución /sirkunloku'sion; θirkunloku'θion/ *f*, circumlocution

circunnavegación /sirkunnaβega'sion; θirkunnaβega'θion/ *f*, circumnavigation

circunnavegar /sirkunnaβe'gar; θirkunnaβe'gar/ *vt* to circumnavigate

circunscribir /sirkunskri'βir; θirkunskri'βir/ *vt* to circumscribe. *Past Part.* **circunscrito**

circunscripción /sirkunskrip'sion; θirkunskrip'θion/ *f*, circumscription

circunspección /sirkunspek'sion; θirkunspek'θion/ *f*, circumspection; seriousness, dignity

circunspecto /sirkuns'pekto; θirkuns'pekto/ *a* circumspect; serious, dignified

circunstancia /sirkuns'tansia; θirkuns'tanθia/ *f*, circumstance; incident, detail; condition. **c. agravante,** aggravating circumstance. **c. atenuante,** extenuating circumstance. **bajo las circunstancias,** under the circumstances. **de circunstancias,** occasional (e.g. *poesías de circunstancias,* occasional verse). **estar a nivel de las circunstancias,** to rise to the occasion

circunstanciado /sirkunstan'siaðo; θirkunstan'θiaðo/ *a* circumstantiated, detailed

circunstancial /sirkunstan'sial; θirkunstan'θial/ *a* circumstantial; occasional (e.g. *poesías circunstanciales,* occasional verse)

circunstante /sirkuns'tante; θirkuns'tante/ *a* surrounding; present. *mf* person present, bystander

circunvecino /sirkumbe'sino; θirkumbe'θino/ *a* adjacent, neighboring

circunvolución /sirkumbolu'sion; θirkumbolu'θion/ *f*, circumvolution

cirial /si'rial; θi'rial/ *m*, processional candlestick

cirio /'sirio; 'θirio/ *m*, wax candle

cirro /'sirro; 'θirro/ *m*, *Med.* scirrhus; *Bot.* tendril; *Zool.* cirrus

cirrosis /si'rrosis; θi'rrosis/ *f*, cirrhosis

cirroso /si'rroso; θi'rroso/ *a* Med. scirrhous; (*Zool. Bot.*) cirrose

ciruela /si'ruela; θi'ruela/ *f*, plum; prune. **c. claudia, c. veidal,** greengage. **c. damascena,** damson

ciruelo /si'ruelo; θi'ruelo/ *m*, plum tree

cirugía /siru'hia; θiru'hia/ *f*, surgery

cirujano /siru'hano; θiru'hano/ *m*, surgeon

cisco /'sisko; 'θisko/ *m*, coal dust, slack coal; *Inf.* hubbub, quarrel

cisma /'sisma; 'θisma/ *m*, or *f*, schism; disagreement, discord. **el C. de Occidente,** the Western Schism

cismático /sis'matiko; θis'matiko/ *a* schismatic; discordant, inharmonious

cisne /'sisne; 'θisne/ *m*, swan

cisterciense /sister'siense; θister'θiense/ *a* Cistercian

cisterna /sis'terna; θis'terna/ *f*, water-tank, cistern

cístico /'sistiko; 'θistiko/ *a* cystic

cistitis /sis'titis; θis'titis/ *f*, cystitis

cita /'sita; 'θita/ *f*, appointment; quotation, citation

citable /si'taβle; θi'taβle/ *a* quotable

citación /sita'sion; θita'θion/ *f*, quotation; *Law.* summons

citar /si'tar; θi'tar/ *vt* to make an appointment; cite, quote; *Law.* summon. **c. en comparecencia,** to summon to appear in court

cítara /'sitara; 'θitara/ *f*, *Mus.* zither

citatorio /sita'torio; θita'torio/ *m*, summons

citerior /site'rior; θite'rior/ *a* hither, nearer

citrato /si'trato; θi'trato/ *m*, *Chem.* citrate

cítrico /'sitriko; 'θitriko/ *a* citric

ciudad /siu'ðað; θiu'ðað/ *f*, city; municipal body. **la c. señorial,** the Aristocratic City (Ponce, Puerto Rico)

ciudadanía /siuðaða'nia; θiuðaða'nia/ *f*, citizenship

ciudadano /siuða'ðano; θiuða'ðano/ **(-na)** *a* city; civic, born in or belonging to a city. *n* citizen; burgess; bourgeois. **c. de honor,** freeman (of a city)

ciudadela /siuða'ðela; θiuða'ðela/ *f*, citadel

cívico /'siβiko; 'θiβiko/ *a* civic; patriotic; *Lat. Am.* police officer

civicultura /siβikul'tura; θiβikul'tura/ *f*, raising of civets

civil /si'βil; θi'βil/ *a* civil; civilian; polite

civilidad /siβili'ðað; θiβili'ðað/ *f*, politeness, civility

civilización /siβilisa'sion; θiβiliθa'θion/ *f*, civilization

civilizador /siβilisa'ðor; θiβiliθa'ðor/ *a* civilizing

civilizar /siβili'sar; θiβili'θar/ *vt* to civilize; educate; *vr* grow civilized; be educated

civismo /si'βismo; θi'βismo/ *m*, civism; patriotism; civics

cizalla /si'saya; θi'θaʎa/ *f*, shears, shearing machine; metal filings

cizaña /si'saɲa; θi'θaɲa/ *f*, *Bot.* darnel, weed, tare; vice, evil; dissension, discord (gen. with *meter* and *sembrar*)

clac /klak/ *m*, opera-hat; tricorne

clamar /kla'mar/ *vi* to cry out; *Fig.* demand (of inanimate things); vociferate; speak solemnly

clamor /kla'mor/ *m*, outcry, shouting; shriek, complaint; knell, tolling of bells

clamorear /klamore'ar/ *vt* to implore, clamor (for); *vi* toll (of bells)

clamoroso /klamo'roso/ *a* noisy, clamorous

clandestino /klandes'tino/ *a* clandestine, secret

clangor /klaŋ'gor/ *m*, *Poet.* blare, bray (of trumpet)

claqué /kla'ke/ *m*, tap-dance

clara /'klara/ *f*, white of egg; bald patch (in fur); *Inf.* fair interval on a rainy day

claraboya /klara'βoya/ *f*, skylight; *Archit.* clerestory

claramente /klara'mente/ *adv* clearly, evidently

clarear /klare'ar/ *vt* to clear; give light to; *vi* to dawn; grow light; *vr* be transparent; *Inf.* reveal secrets unwittingly

clarete /kla'rete/ *m*, claret (wine); claret color. *a* claret; claret-colored

claridad /klari'ðað/ *f*, clearness; transparency; lightness, brightness; distinctness; clarity; good reputation, renown; plain truth, home truth (*gen. pl*)

clarificación /klarifika'sion; klarifika'θion/ *f*, clarification; purifying, refining

clarificar /klarifi'kar/ *vt* to illuminate; clarify, purify; refine (sugar, etc.)

clarín /kla'rin/ *m*, bugle; clarion; organ stop; bugler

clarinete /klari'nete/ *m*, clarinet; clarinet player

clarión /kla'rion/ *m*, white chalk, crayon

clarividencia /klariβi'ðensia; klariβi'ðenθia/ *f*, perspicuity, clear-sightedness, clairvoyance

clarividente /klariβi'ðente/ *a* perspicacious, clear-sighted, clairvoyant

claro /'klaro/ *a* clear; light, bright; distinct; pure, clean; transparent, translucent; light (of colors); easily understood; evident, obvious; frank; cloudless; shrewd, quick-thinking; famous. *m*, skylight; space between words; break in a speech; space in procession, etc.; *Art.* (gen. *pl*) high lights. *interj* ¡C.! or ¡C. está! Of course! **a las claras,** openly, frankly

claroscuro /klaros'kuro/ *m*, chiaroscuro; monochrome

clase /'klase/ *f*, class, group; kind, sort, quality; class (school, university); lecture room; lecture, lesson; order, family. **c. dirigente,** ruling class. **c. media,** middle class. **c. social,** social class

clasicismo /klasi'sismo; klasi'θismo/ *m*, classicism

clasicista /klasi'sista; klasi'θista/ *a* and *mf* classicist

clásico /'klasiko/ *a* classic; notable; classical. *m*, classic

clasificación /klasifika'sion; klasifika'θion/ *f*, classification

clasificador /klasifika'ðor/ **(-ra)** *n* classifier. **c. de billetes,** ticket-punch

clasificar /klasifi'kar/ *vt* to classify, arrange. **c. correspondencia,** to file letters

claudicación /klauðika'sion; klauðika'θion/ *f*, limping; negligence; hesitancy, weakness; backing down

claudicar /klauði'kar/ *vi* to limp; be negligent; hesitate, give way

claustral /klaus'tral/ *a* cloistral

claustro /'klaustro/ *m*, cloister; council, faculty, senate (of university); monastic rule

claustrofobia /klaustro'foβia/ *f*, claustrophobia

cláusula /'klausula/ *f*, clause. **c. de negación implícita,** contrary-to-fact clause. **c. principal,** main clause. **c. subordinada,** dependent clause, subordinate clause. **c. sustantiva,** noun clause

clausura /klau'sura/ *f*, sanctum of convent; claustration; solemn ending ceremony of tribunal, etc. **la vida de c.,** monastic or conventual life

clava /'klaβa/ *f*, club, truncheon; *Naut.* scupper

clavadizo /klaβa'ðiso; klaβa'ðiθo/ *a* nail-studded (doors, etc.)

clavar /kla'βar/ *vt* to nail; fasten with nails; pierce, prick; set gems (jeweler); spike (cannon, gum); *Fig.* fix (eyes, attention, etc.); *Inf.* cheat

clave /'klaβe/ *m*, clavichord. *f*, code, key; *Mus.* clef; *Archit.* keystone; plug (telephones); **c. (de),** key to. *Mus.* **c. de sol,** treble clef

clavel /kla'βel/ *m*, *Bot.* carnation plant and flower

clavelito /klaβe'lito/ *m*, *Bot.* pink plant and flower

clavero /kla'βero/ **(-ra)** *n* keeper of the keys. *m*, clove tree

clavetear /klaβete'ar/ *vt* to stud with nails; *Fig.* round off (business affairs)

clavicordio /klaβi'korðio/ *m*, clavichord

clavícula /kla'βikula/ *f*, clavicle

clavija /kla'βiha/ *f*, peg, pin; plug; peg of stringed instrument; axle-pin

clavo /'klaβo/ *m*, nail, spike, peg; corn (on foot); anguish. **c. de especia,** clove. **c. de herradura,** hob-nail

claymore /klai'more/ *f*, claymore

clemátide /kle'matiðe/ *f*, *Bot.* clematis

clemencia /kle'mensia; kle'menθia/ *f*, mildness; clemency; mercy

clemente /kle'mente/ *a* mild; clement; merciful

cleptomanía /kleptoma'nia/ *f*, kleptomania

cleptómano /klep'tomano/ **(-na)** *a* and *n* kleptomaniac

clerecía /klere'sia; klere'θia/ *f*, clergy

clerical /kleri'kal/ *a* belonging to the clergy; clerical

clericalismo /klerika'lismo/ *m*, clericalism

clerigalla /kleri'gaya; kleri'gaʎa/ f, (contemptuous) dog-collar men

clérigo /'klerigo/ m, cleric, clergyman; clerk (in Middle Ages)

clero /'klero/ m, clergy

cliente /'kliente/ mf client, customer; protégé, ward

clientela /klien'tela/ f, patronage, protection; clientele

clima /'klima/ m, climate, clime

climatérico /klima'teriko/ a climacteric

climático /kli'matiko/ a climatic

climatología /klimatolo'hia/ f, climatology

clímax /'klimaks/ m, climax

clínica /'klinika/ f, clinic, nursing home; department of medicine or surgery

clínico /'kliniko/ a clinical

clíper /'kliper/ m, (Aer. and Naut.) clipper

clisar /kli'sar/ vt Print. to cast from a mold, stereotype

clisé /kli'se/ m, Print. stereotype plate

cloaca /klo'aka/ f, sewer, drain; Zool. cloaca

cloquear /kloke'ar/ vi to go broody (hen); cluck

cloqueo /klo'keo/ m, cluck, clucking

cloquera /klo'kera/ f, broodiness (hens)

clorato /klo'rato/ m, chlorate

clorhídrico /klor'iðriko/ a hydrochloric

cloro /'kloro/ m, chlorine

clorofila /kloro'fila/ f, chlorophyll

cloroformizar /kloroformi'sar; kloroformi'θar/ vt to chloroform

cloroformo /kloro'formo/ m, chloroform

clorosis /klo'rosis/ f, chlorosis

cloruro /klo'ruro/ m, chloride

club /kluβ/ m, club

clueca /'klueka/ f, broody hen

clueco /'klueko/ a broody (hens); Inf. doddering

coacción /koak'sion; koak'θion/ f, coercion

coactivo /koak'tiβo/ a coercive

coadjutor /koaðhu'tor/ m, co-worker, assistant

coadunar /koaðu'nar/ vt to join or mingle together

coadyuvar /koaðyu'βar/ vt to assist

coagulación /koagula'sion; koagula'θion/ f, coagulation

coagular /koagu'lar/ vt to coagulate; clot; curdle

coágulo /ko'agulo/ m, clot; coagulation; congealed blood

coalición /koali'sion; koali'θion/ f, coalition

coartada /koar'taða/ f, alibi. **probar la c.,** to prove an alibi

coartar /koar'tar/ vt to limit, restrict

coautor /koau'tor/ (**-ra**) n co-author

cobalto /ko'βalto/ m, cobalt

cobarde /ko'βarðe/ a cowardly; irresolute. m, coward

cobardía /koβar'ðia/ f, cowardice

cobayo /ko'βayo/ m, guinea-pig

cobertera /koβer'tera/ f, lid, cover

cobertizo /koβer'tiso; koβer'tiθo/ m, overhanging roof; shack, shed, hut. **c. de aeroplanos,** Aer. hangar

cobertura /koβer'tura/ f, covering; coverlet; wrapping

cobija /ko'βiha/ f, imbrex tile; cover; Lat. Am. blanket

cobijar /koβi'har/ vt to cover; shelter

cobra /'koβra/ f, Zool. cobra; rope or thong for yoking oxen; retrieval (of game)

cobradero /koβra'ðero/ a that which can be collected, recoverable

cobrador /koβra'ðor/ m, collector, receiver. a collecting. **c. de tranvía,** tram conductor

cobranza /ko'βransa; ko'βranθa/ f, receiving, collecting; collection of fruit or money

cobrar /ko'βrar/ vt to collect (what is owed); charge; earn; regain, recover; feel, experience (emotions); wind, pull in (ropes, etc.); gain, acquire; retrieve (game); vr recuperate. **c. ánimo,** to take courage. **c. cariño (a),** to grow fond of. **c. fuerzas,** to gather strength. **c. importancia,** to gain importance. **¿Cuánto cobra Vd.?** How much do you charge?; How much do you earn?

cobre /'koβre/ m, Mineral. copper; copper kitchen utensils; pl Mus. brass; Lat. Am. (copper) cent, centavo

cobrizo /ko'βriso; ko'βriθo/ a containing copper; copper-colored

cocacolismo /kokako'lismo/ n Inf. economic dependence on the United States and adoption of its pop culture

cocacolonización /kokakolonisa'sion; kokakoloniθa'θion/ f, economic domination by the United States and introduction of its pop culture

cocacolonizar /kokakoloni'sar; kokakoloni'θar/ vt (United States) to gain economic control of… and introduce unto its pop culture

cocaína /koka'ina/ f, cocaine

cocción /kok'sion; kok'θion/ f, coction

coceador /kosea'ðor; koθea'ðor/ a inclined to kick; kicking (animals)

coceadura /kosea'ðura; koθea'ðura/ f, kicking

cocear /kose'ar; koθe'ar/ vi to kick; Inf. kick against, oppose

cocedero /kose'ðero; koθe'ðero/ a easily cooked

cocer /ko'ser; ko'θer/ vt. irr to boil; cook; bake (bricks, etc.); digest; Surg. suppurate; vi boil (of a liquid); ferment; vr suffer pain or inconvenience over a long period. Pres. Ind. **cuezo, cueces, cuece, cuecen.** Pres. Subjunc. **cueza, cuezas, cueza, cuezan**

cochayuyo /kotʃa'yujo/ m, Lat. Am. edible seaweed

coche /'kotʃe/ m, carriage, car. **c. camas,** sleeping car. **c. -camioneta,** station wagon. **c. cerrado,** Auto. sedan. **c. de muchos caballos,** high-powered car. **c. de plaza,** hackney-carriage. **c. fúnebre,** hearse. **c. -línea,** intercity bus. f, Ecuador puddle

cochera /ko'tʃera/ f, coach house; tramway depot

cochero /ko'tʃero/ m, coachman; driver. a easily cooked

¡cochi! /'kotʃi/ (call to pigs)

cochina /ko'tʃina/ f, sow

cochinería /kotʃine'ria/ f, Inf. filthiness; mean trick

cochinilla /kotʃi'niya; kotʃi'niʎa/ f, wood louse; cochineal insect; cochineal

cochinillo /kotʃi'niyo; kotʃi'niʎo/ m, sucking-pig. **c. de Indias,** guinea-pig

cochino /ko'tʃino/ m, pig; Inf. filthy person. a filthy

cocido /ko'siðo; ko'θiðo/ a boiled, cooked, baked. m, dish of stewed meat, pork, chicken, with peas, etc.

cociente /ko'siente; ko'θiente/ m, quotient

cocimiento /kosi'miento; koθi'miento/ m, cooking; decoction

cocina /ko'sina; ko'θina/ f, kitchen; pottage; broth; cookery. **c. de campaña,** field-kitchen. **c. económica,** cooking range

cocinar /kosi'nar; koθi'nar/ vt to cook; vi Inf. meddle, interfere

cocinería /kosine'ria/ f, Naut. galley

cocinero /kosi'nero; koθi'nero/ (**-ra**) n cook, chef

cocinilla /kosi'niya; koθi'niʎa/ f, spirit-stove

coco /'koko/ m, Bot. coconut tree and fruit; coconut shell; grub, maggot; bogeyman; hobgoblin; Inf. grimace. Inf. **ser un c.,** to be hideously ugly

cocodrilo /koko'ðrilo/ m, crocodile

cócora /'kokora/ mf Inf. bore, nosy Parker

cocotal /koko'tal/ m, grove of coconut palms

cocotero /koko'tero/ m, coconut palm

coctel /kok'tel/ m, cocktail

cocuyo /ko'kuyo/ m, firefly

codal /ko'ðal/ a cubital. m, shoot of a vine; prop, strut; frame of a hand-saw

codazo /ko'ðaso; ko'ðaθo/ m, blow or nudge of the elbow. **dar codazos,** to elbow, shoulder out of the way

codear /koðe'ar/ vi to jostle; elbow, nudge; vr be on terms of equality with

codeína /koðe'ina/ f, codeine

codelincuente /koðelin'kuente/ mf partner in crime, accomplice

codera /ko'ðera/ f, elbow rash; elbow-piece or patch

codeso /ko'ðeso/ m, laburnum

códice /'koðise; 'koðiθe/ m, codex

codicia /ko'ðisia; ko'ðiθia/ f, covetousness; greed

codiciar /koðisi'ar; koðiθi'ar/ vt to covet

codicilo /koði'silo; koði'θilo/ *m*, codicil

codicioso /koðisi'oso; koðiθi'oso/ **(-sa)** *a* covetous; *Inf.* hardworking. *n* covetous person

codificación /koðifika'sion; koðifika'θion/ *f*, codification

codificar /koðifi'kar/ *vt* to codify, compile

código /'koðigo/ *m*, code of laws. **c. de barras,** bar code. **c. civil,** civil laws. **c. de la circulación, c. de la vía pública,** highway code, traffic code. *Naut.* **c. de señales,** signal code. **c. penal,** criminal laws. **c. postal,** zip code

codillo /ko'ðiyo; ko'ðiʎo/ *m*, knee (of quadrupeds); shaft (of branch); bend (pipe, tube); stirrup

codo /'koðo/ *m*, elbow; angle, bend (pipe, tube); cubit. *Inf.* **hablar por los codos,** to chatter

codorniz /koðor'nis; koðor'niθ/ *f*, *Ornith.* quail

coeducación /koeðuka'sion; koeðuka'θion/ *f*, coeducation

coeficiente /koefi'siente; koefi'θiente/ *m*, coefficient

coercer /koer'ser; koer'θer/ *vt* to restrain, coerce

coerción /koer'sion; koer'θion/ *f*, *Law.* coercion

coercitivo /koersi'tiβo; koerθi'tiβo/ *a* coercive

coetáneo /koe'taneo/ **(-ea)** *a* contemporaneous. *n* contemporary

coevo /ko'eβo/ *a* coeval

coexistencia /koeksis'tensia; koeksis'tenθia/ *f*, coexistence

coexistir /koeksis'tir/ *vi* to co-exist

cofia /'kofia/ *f*, hairnet; coif

cofín /ko'fin/ *m*, basket

cofradía /kofra'ðia/ *f*, confraternity, brotherhood or sisterhood **c. de gastronomía,** eating club (US), dining society (UK)

cofre /'kofre/ *m*, trunk, chest (for clothes); coffer

cogedor /kohe'ðor/ *m*, collector, gatherer; dustpan; coal-shovel

coger /ko'her/ *vt* to seize, hold; catch; take, collect, gather; have room for; take up or occupy space; find; catch in the act; attack, surprise; reach; **c. un berrinche,** have a fit, have a tantrum. *vi* have room, fit

cogida /ko'hiða/ *f*, gathering, picking; *Inf.* fruit harvest; toss (bullfighting)

cogido /ko'hiðo/ *m*, pleat, fold; crease. **estar c. de tiempo** to be pressed for time.

cogitabundo /kohita'βundo/ *a* very pensive

cognación /kogna'sion; kogna'θion/ *f*, cognation; kinship

cognoscitivo /kognossi'tiβo; kognosθi'tiβo/ *a* cognitive. **las ciencias cognoscitivas,** cognitive science

cogollo /ko'goyo; ko'goʎo/ *m*, heart (of lettuce, etc.); shoot; topmost branches of pine tree

cogote /ko'gote/ *m*, nape (of neck)

cogulla /ko'guya; ko'guʎa/ *f*, monk's habit

cohabitación /koaβita'sion; koaβita'θion/ *f*, cohabitation

cohabitar /koaβi'tar/ *vt* to cohabit

cohechador /koetʃa'ðor/ **(-ra)** *a* bribing. *n* briber

cohechar /koe'tʃar/ *vt* to bribe, corrupt, suborn

cohecho /ko'etʃo/ *m*, bribing; bribe

coherencia /koe'rensia; koe'renθia/ *f*, coherence, connection

coherente /koe'rente/ *a* coherent

cohesión /koe'sion/ *f*, cohesion

cohesivo /koe'siβo/ *a* cohesive

cohete /ko'ete/ *m*, rocket

cohetero /koe'tero/ *m*, firework manufacturer

cohibir /koi'βir/ *vt* to restrain; repress. See **prohibir**.

cohombrillo /koom'briyo; koom'briʎo/ *m*, *dim* gherkin

cohombro /ko'ombro/ *m*, cucumber

cohonestar /koones'tar/ *vt* *Fig.* to gloss over, cover up; make appear decent (actions, etc.)

cohorte /ko'orte/ *f*, cohort

coima /'koima/ *f*, *Lat. Am.* bribe

coincidencia /koinsi'ðensia; koinθi'ðenθia/ *f*, coincidence

coincidir /koinsi'ðir; koinθi'ðir/ *vt* to coincide; (two or more people) be in the same place at the same time. **c. con que...** to agree that...

coito /'koito/ *m*, coitus

cojear /kohe'ar/ *vi* to limp; wobble, be unsteady (of furniture); *Fig. Inf.* go wrong or astray; *Inf.* suffer from (vice, bad habit)

cojera /ko'hera/ *f*, lameness, limp

cojijoso /kohi'hoso/ *a* peevish

cojín /ko'hin/ *m*, cushion; pad; pillow (for lace-making)

cojinete /kohi'nete/ *m*, small cushion; *Mech.* bearing. **c. de bolas,** ball-bearing

cojo /'koho/ *a* lame; unsteady, wobbly (of furniture, etc.)

col /kol/ *f*, cabbage. **c. de Bruselas,** Brussels sprouts

cola /'kola/ *f*, tail; train (of gown); shank (of a button); queue; tailpiece (of a violin, etc.); appendage; glue. **c. de milano,** dovetail. **c. de pescado,** isinglass. **formar c.,** to line up, queue up

colaboración /kolaβora'sion; kolaβora'θion/ *f*, collaboration. **en c.,** joint (e.g. *obra en colaboración,* joint work)

colaboracionista /kolaβorasio'nista; kolaβoraθio'nista/ *mf* collaborationist

colaborador /kolaβora'ðor/ **(-ra)** *n* collaborator

colaborar /kolaβo'rar/ *vt* to collaborate

colación /kola'sion; kola'θion/ *f*, conferment of a degree; collation (of texts); light repast; cold supper; area of a parish

colada /ko'laða/ *f*, wash; bleaching; mountain path; *Metall.* casting; *Inf.* trusty sword (allusion to name of one of the Cid's swords)

coladero /kola'ðero/ *m*, colander, sieve, strainer; narrow path

colador /kola'ðor/ *m*, colander

coladura /kola'ðura/ *f*, straining, filtration; *Inf.* untruth; *Inf.* howler, mistake

colapso /ko'lapso/ *m*, *Med.* prostration, collapse

colar /ko'lar/ *vt irr* to filter, strain; bleach; *Metall.* cast; *vi* go through a narrow place; *Inf.* drink wine; *vr* thread one's way; *Inf.* enter by stealth, steal in; *Inf.* tell untruths. *Pres. Ind.* **cuelo, cuelas, cuela, cuelan.** *Pres. Subjunc.* **cuele, cueles, cuele, cuelen**

colateral /kolate'ral/ *a* collateral

colcha /'koltʃa/ *f*, bedspread, counterpane, quilt

colchadura /koltʃa'ðura/ *f*, quilting

colchero /kol'tʃero/ *m*, quilt maker

colchón /kol'tʃon/ *m*, mattress. **c. de muelles,** spring-mattress. **c. de viento,** air-bed

colchoneta /koltʃo'neta/ *f*, pad, thin mattress

coleada /kole'aða/ *f*, wag of the tail

colear /kole'ar/ *vi* to wag the tail

colección /kolek'sion; kolek'θion/ *f*, collection

coleccionador /koleksiona'ðor; kolekθiona'ðor/ **(-ra)** *n* collector

coleccionar /koleksio'nar; kolekθio'nar/ *vt* to collect

coleccionista /koleksio'nista; kolekθio'nista/ *mf* collector

colecta /ko'lekta/ *f*, assessment; collection (of donations); *Eccl.* collect; voluntary offering

colectivero /kolekti'βero/ *m*, bus driver

colectividad /kolektiβi'ðað/ *f*, collectivity; body of people

colectivismo /kolekti'βismo/ *m*, collectivism

colectivista /kolekti'βista/ *a* collectivist

colectivo /kolek'tiβo/ *a* collective; *Argentina* (local) bus

colector /kolek'tor/ *m*, gatherer; collector; tax-collector; water-pipe; water-conduit; *Elec.* commutator, collector

colega /ko'lega/ *m*, colleague

colegiado /kole'hiaðo/ *a* collegiate

colegial /kole'hial/ **(-la)** *a* college, collegiate. *n* student; pupil; *Fig. Inf.* novice.

colegiarse /kole'hiarse/ *vr* to meet as an association (professional, etc.)

colegiata /kole'hiata/ *f*, college church

colegiatura /kolehia'tura/ *f*, scholarship, fellowship (money granted a student); tuition (fee paid by a student), tuition fee, tuition fees

colegio /ko'lehio/ *m*, college; school; academy; association (professional); council, convocation; college or school buildings. **c. de abogados,** bar association.

c. de cardenales, College of Cardinals. **c. electoral**, polling-booth. **c. militar**, military academy
colegir /kole'hir/ *vt irr* to collect, gather; deduce, infer. See **elegir**
cólera /'kolera/ *f*, bile, anger. *m*, cholera. **montar en c.**, to fly into a rage
colérico /ko'leriko/ *a* angry; choleric; suffering from cholera
colesterina /koleste'rina/ *f*, *Chem.* cholesterol
coleta /ko'leta/ *f*, pigtail; queue; *Inf.* postscript
coletazo /kole'taso; kole'taθo/ *m*, blow with one's tail, lash with one's tail; lash of a dying fish; *Fig.* last hurrah
coleto /ko'leto/ *m*, leather jerkin; *Inf.* body of a man
colgadero /kolga'ðero/ *a* able to be hung up. *m*, coat-hanger, hook
colgadizo /kolga'ðiso; kolga'ðiθo/ *a* hanging. *m*, overhanging roof
colgadura /kolga'ðura/ *f*, hangings, drapery, tapestries. **c. de cama**, bedhangings
colgajo /kol'gaho/ *m*, tatter; bunch (of grapes, etc.); *Surg.* skin lap
colgar /kol'gar/ *vt irr* to hang up; decorate with hangings; *Inf.* hang, kill; *vi* hang, be suspended; *Fig.* be dependent. See **contar**
colibrí /koli'βri/ *m*, hummingbird
cólico /'koliko/ *m*, colic
colicuar /koli'kuar/ *vt* to dissolve
coliflor /koli'flor/ *f*, cauliflower
coligarse /koli'garse/ *vr* to confederate, unite
colilla /ko'liya; ko'liʎa/ *f*, stub (of a cigar or cigarette)
colina /ko'lina/ *f*, hill; cabbage seed; *Chem.* choline
colindante /kolin'dante/ *a* adjacent, contiguous
coliseo /koli'seo/ *m*, coliseum; theater
colisión /koli'sion/ *f*, collision; abrasion, bruise; *Fig.* clash (of ideas)
colitis /ko'litis/ *f*, colitis
collado /ko'yaðo; ko'ʎaðo/ *m*, hill, hillock
collar /ko'yar; ko'ʎar/ *m*, necklace; chain of office or honor; collar (dogs, etc.)
collera /ko'yera; ko'ʎera/ *f*, horse collar; *Chile* cuff link
collerón /koje'ron; koʎe'ron/ *m*, horse collar
colmado /kol'maðo/ *a* abundant. *m*, provision shop
colmar /kol'mar/ *vt* to fill to overflowing; bestow generously, heap upon
colmena /kol'mena/ *f*, beehive
colmenero /kolme'nero/ **(-ra)** *n* beekeeper
colmillo /kol'miyo; kol'miʎo/ *m*, canine tooth; tusk; fang
colmilludo /kolmi'yuðo; kolmi'ʎuðo/ *a* having large canine teeth; tusked; fanged; sagacious
colmo /'kolmo/ *m*, overflow; highest point; completion, limit, end. **ser el c.**, *Inf.* to be the last straw. **el c. de los colmos**, the absolute limit
colocación /koloka'sion; koloka'θion/ *f*, placing, putting; situation, place; employment; *Sports.* placing; order, arrangement; *Ling.* collocation
colocar /kolo'kar/ *vt* to place, put, arrange; place in employment. **c. bajo banderas**, to draft (into the armed forces). *vr* place oneself
colocho /ko'lotʃo/ *m*, *Guatemala* (naturally) curly hair
colofón /kolo'fon/ *m*, *Print.* colophon
colofonia /kolo'fonia/ *f*, solid resin (for bows of stringed instruments, etc.)
colombiano /kolom'biano/ **(-na)** *a* and *n* Colombian
colombina /kolom'bina/ *f*, columbine
colombofilia /kolombo'filia/ *f*, pigeon fancying
colonia /ko'lonia/ *f*, colony; plantation
coloniaje /kolo'niahe/ *m*, *Lat. Am.* colonial period; colonial government
colonial /kolo'nial/ *a* colonial
colonización /kolonisa'sion; koloniθa'θion/ *f*, colonization
colonizador /kolonisa'ðor; koloniθa'ðor/ **(-ra)** *a* colonizing. *n* colonizer
colonizar /koloni'sar; koloni'θar/ *vt* to colonize; settle
colono /ko'lono/ *m*, settler, colonist; farmer

coloquio /ko'lokio/ *m*, colloquy, conversation, talk; colloquium
color /ko'lor/ *m*, color; dye; paint; rouge; coloring; pretext, excuse; character, individuality; *pl* natural colors. **c. estable, c. sólido**, fast color. **mudar de c.**, to change color. **de c.**, of color (people). **so c.**, under the pretext. **ver las cosas c. de rosa**, to see things through rose-colored glasses
colorado /kolo'raðo/ *a* colored. *West Hem.* red, reddish; *Inf.* blue, obscene; specious
colorante /kolo'rante/ *a* coloring. *m*, dyestuff; coloring (substance)
colorar /kolo'rar/ *vt* to color; dye
colorear /kolore'ar/ *vt* to color; pretext; *Fig.* whitewash, excuse; *vi* show color; be reddish; grow red, ripe (tomatoes, cherries, etc.)
colorero /kolo'rero/ *m*, dyer
colorete /kolo'rete/ *m*, rouge
colorido /kolo'riðo/ *m*, coloring, color
colorín /kolo'rin/ *m*, goldfinch; bright color
colosal /kolo'sal/ *a* colossal, enormous; extraordinary, excellent
coloso /ko'loso/ *m*, colossus; *Fig.* outstanding person or thing, giant; **el C. del Norte, el Gran C. del Norte**, (contemptuous epithet for the United States of America)
columbino /kolum'bino/ *a* pertaining to a dove; dovelike; candid, innocent; purply-red
columbrar /kolum'brar/ *vt* to discern in the distance, glimpse; conjecture, guess
columna /ko'lumna/ *f*, *Mil. Archit. Print.* column; *Fig.* protection, shelter; *Naut.* stanchion. **c. cerrada**, *Mil.* etc. mass formation. **c. de los suspiros**, agony column (in a newspaper)
columnata /kolum'nata/ *f*, colonnade
columpiar /kolum'piar/ *vt* to swing; dangle (one's feet); *vr Inf.* sway in walking; swing
columpio /ko'lumpio/ *m*, swing
colusión /kolu'sion/ *f*, collusion
colusorio /kolu'sorio/ *a* collusive
coma /'koma/ *f*, *Gram.* comma. *m*, *Med.* coma
comadre /ko'maðre/ *f*, best female friend, midwife; *Inf.* procuress, go-between; *Inf.* pal, gossip
comadrear /komaðre'ar/ *vi Inf.* to gossip
comadreja /koma'ðreha/ *f*, *Zool.* weasel
comadrón /koma'ðron/ *m*, accoucheur
comadrona /koma'ðrona/ *f*, midwife
comandancia /koman'dansia; koman'danθia/ *f*, *Mil.* command; commandant's H.Q.
comandante /koman'dante/ *m*, commandant; commander; major; squadron-leader. *a Mil.* commanding. **c. en jefe**, commanding officer
comandar /koman'dar/ *vt Mil.* to command
comandita /koman'dita/ *f*, *Com.* sleeping partnership; private company
comando /ko'mando/ *m*, *Mil.* commando
comarca /ko'marka/ *f*, district, region
comatoso /koma'toso/ *a* comatose
comba /'komba/ *f*, bend, warping; jump rope, skipping-rope; camber (of road)
combadura /komba'ðura/ *f*, curvature; warping; camber (of a road)
combar /kom'bar/ *vt* to bend; twist; warp; camber
combate /kom'bate/ *m*, fight, combat; mental strife; contradiction, opposition. **c. judicial**, trial by combat. **dejar fuera de c.**, (a) (boxing) to knock out
combatiente /komba'tiente/ *m*, combatant, soldier
combatir /komba'tir/ *vi* to fight; *vt* attack; struggle against (winds, water, etc.); contradict, oppose; *Fig.* disturb, trouble (emotions)
combi /'komβi/ *m*, *Mexico* minibus
combinación /kombina'sion; kombina'θion/ *f*, combination; list of words beginning with same letter; project; concurrence; underskirt, petticoat. **estar en c. (con)**, to be in cahoots (with), connive (with)
combinar /kombi'nar/ *vt* to combine; (*Mil. Nav.*) join forces; arrange, plan; *Chem.* combine; **combinar para + inf.** (two or more people) to make arrangements to + inf.
combustible /kombus'tiβle/ *a* combustible. *m*, fuel

combustión /kombus'tion/ *f*, combustion. **c. activa,** rapid combustion. **c. espontánea,** spontaneous combustion

comedero /kome'ðero/ *a* edible. *m*, feeding-trough; dining-room

comedia /ko'meðia/ *f*, comedy; play; theater; comic incident; *Fig.* play-acting, theatricalism. **c. alta,** art theater. **c. de costumbres,** comedy of manners. **c. de enredo,** play with very involved plot. *Inf.* **hacer la c.,** to play-act, pretend

comedianta /kome'ðianta/ *f*, actress

comediante /kome'ðiante/ *m*, actor; *Inf.* dissembler.

comedido /kome'ðiðo/ *a* courteous; prudent; moderate

comedimiento /komeði'miento/ *m*, courtesy; moderation; prudence

comedir /kome'ðir/ *vt irr* to prepare, premeditate; *vr* restrain oneself, be moderate; offer one's services. See **pedir**

comedor /kome'ðor/ *a* voracious. *m*, dining-room

comendador /komenda'ðor/ *m*, knight commander

comendatorio /komenda'torio/ *a* commendatory (of letters)

comensal /komen'sal/ *mf* table companion

comentador /komenta'ðor/ **(-ra)** *n* commentator

comentar /komen'tar/ *vt* explain (document); *Inf.* comment

comentario /komen'tario/ **(a)** *m*, commentary (on)

comentarista /komenta'rista/ *mf* commentator

comento /ko'mento/ *m*, comment; commentary

comenzante /komen'sante; komen'θante/ *mf* beginner, novice. *a* initial

comenzar /komen'sar; komen'θar/ *vt vi irr* to begin, commence. See **empezar**

comer /ko'mer/ *m*, eating; food. *vi* to eat; feed; dine. *vt* eat; *Inf.* enjoy an income; waste (patrimony); consume, exhaust; fade (of colors); *vr* be troubled, uneasy, remorseful. **ser de buen c.,** to have a good appetite; taste good. **tener que c.,** to be obliged to eat; have to eat; have enough to eat

comerciable /komer'siaβle; komer'θiaβle/ *a* marketable; sociable, pleasant (of persons)

comercial /komer'sial; komer'θial/ *a* commercial

comerciante /komer'siante; komer'θiante/ *a* trading. *mf* merchant, trader

comerciar /komer'siar; komer'θiar/ *vt* to trade; have dealings (with)

comercio /ko'mersio; ko'merθio/ *m*, trade, commerce; intercourse, traffic; illicit sexual intercourse; shop, store; tradesmen; commercial quarter of town

comestible /komes'tiβle/ *a* edible, eatable. *m*, (gen. *pl*) provisions

cometa /ko'meta/ *m*, *Astron.* comet. *f*, kite (toy). **c. celular,** box-kite

cometedor /komete'ðor/ **(-ra)** *n* perpetrator

cometer /kome'ter/ *vt* to entrust, hand over to; commit (crime, sins, etc.); *Com.* order

cometido /kome'tiðo/ *m*, charge, commission; moral obligation; function

comezón /kome'son; kome'θon/ *f*, itching, irritation; hankering, longing.

cómico /'komiko/ *a* comic; funny, comical. *m*, actor; comedian. **c. de la legua,** strolling player

comida /ko'miða/ *f*, food; meal; dinner; eating. **c. corrida** *Mexico* table d'hôte. **c. de gala,** state banquet. **c. de prueba,** *Med.* test meal

comienzo /ko'mienso; ko'mienθo/ *m*, beginning, origin

comillas /ko'miyas; ko'miʎas/ *f pl*, *Gram.* inverted commas, quotation marks. **entre c.,** in quotes

comilón /komi'lon/ **(-ona)** *a Inf.* gluttonous. *n* glutton

comino /ko'mino/ *m*, *Bot.* cumin. **no valer un c.,** to be not worth a jot

comisar /komi'sar/ *vt* to confiscate, sequestrate

comisaría /komisa'ria/ *f*, commissaryship; commissariat. **c. de policía,** police station

comisario /komi'sario/ *m*, deputy, agent; commissary, head of police; commissioner; *Argentina,*

purser. **alto c.,** high commissioner. **c. propietario,** stockholders' representative

comisión /komi'sion/ *f*, perpetration, committal; commission; committee; *Com.* commission

comisionado /komisio'naðo/ **(-da)** *a* commissioned. *m*, commissary

comisionar /komisio'nar/ *vt* to commission

comisionista /komisio'nista/ *mf Com.* commission agent

comiso /ko'miso/ *m*, *Law.* confiscation, sequestration; contraband

comité /komi'te/ *m*, committee

comitiva /komi'tiβa/ *f*, retinue, following

como /'komo/ *adv* like, as; in the same way; thus, accordingly; in the capacity of; so that; since. *conjunc* if *(followed by subjunc.)*; because. **c. no,** unless. **¿Cómo?** How? In what way? Why? Pardon? What did you say? *interj* **¡Cómo!** What! You don't say! **¡Cómo no!** Why not! Of course! Surely! **¿Cómo que...?** What do you mean that...?

cómo /'komo/ *m*, the wherefore. **no saber el porqué ni el c.,** not to know the why or wherefore

cómoda /'komoða/ *f*, chest of drawers

comodidad /komoði'ðað/ *f*, comfort; convenience; advantage; utility, interest

comodín /komo'ðin/ *m*, (in cards) joker

cómodo /'komoðo/ *a* comfortable; convenient; opportune

comodón /komo'ðon/ *a Inf.* comfort-loving; easygoing; egoistical

comodoro /komo'ðoro/ *m*, *Naut.* commodore

comoquiera que /komo'kiera ke/ *adv* by any means that, anyway; whereas, given that

compacto /kom'pakto/ *a* compact, dense; close (type)

compadecer /kompaðe'ser; kompaðe'θer/ *vt irr* to pity; *vr (with de)* sympathize with; pity; harmonize, agree with. See **conocer**

compadre /kom'paðre/ *m*, best friend, *Inf.* pal; *Argentina* bully

compaginación /kompahina'sion; kompahina'θion/ *f*, joining, fixing; *Print.* making-up

compaginar /kompahi'nar/ *vt* to fit together; join, put in order; harmonize, square (e.g. *compaginé una cuenta con la otra,* I squared one account with the other); *Print.* make up

compañero /kompa'ɲero/ **(-ra)** *n* companion, comrade; fellow-member; partner (games); *Fig.* pair, fellow, mate (things). **c. de armas,** brother-in-arms, companion-at-arms. **c. de cabina,** boothmate. **c. de exilio,** companion in exile, fellow exile. **c. de generación,** contemporary, person of the same generation. **c. de viaje,** traveling companion; *Polit.* fellow traveler (communist sympathizer)

compañía /kompa'ɲia/ *f*, company; society, association; theatrical company; *(Com. Mil.)* company. **C. de Jesús,** Society of Jesus. **c. de la zarza,** guild of guards and woodcutters for autos de fe. **c. de navegación,** shipping company. **c. por acciones,** joint stock company

comparable /kompa'raβle/ *a* comparable

comparación /kompara'sion; kompara'θion/ *f*, comparison

comparar /kompa'rar/ *vt* to compare; collate

comparativo /kompara'tiβo/ *a* comparative

comparecencia /kompare'sensia; kompare'θenθia/ *f*, (gen. *Law.*) appearance

comparecer /kompare'ser; kompare'θer/ *vi irr Law.* to appear (before tribunal, etc.); present oneself. See **conocer**

comparendo /kompa'rendo/ *m*, *Law.* summons

comparsa /kom'parsa/ *f*, retinue; *Theat.* chorus; troop of carnival revelers dressed alike. *mf Theat.* supernumerary actor

comparte /kom'parte/ *mf Law.* partner; accomplice

compartimiento /komparti'miento/ *m*, share, division; railway carriage. *Naut.* **c. estanco,** compartment

compartir /kompar'tir/ *vt* to share, share out, divide; participate

compás /kom'pas/ *m*, compasses; callipers; size; compass, time; range of voice; *(Naut. Mineral.)* compass; *Mus.* time, rhythm, bar, marking time. **c. de mar,** mariner's compass. **c. de puntas,** dividers, callipers. **fuera de c.,** *Mus.* out of time; out of joint (of the times). *Mus.* **llevar el c.,** to beat time

compasar /kompa'sar/ *vt* to measure with compasses; arrange or apportion accurately; *Mus.* put into bars

compasillo /kompa'siyo; kompa'siʎo/ *m, Mus.* $\frac{4}{4}$ measure

compasivo /kompa'siβo/ *a* compassionate; tenderhearted

compatibilidad /kompatiβili'ðað/ *f,* compatibility

compatible /kompa'tiβle/ *a* compatible

compatriota /kompa'triota/ *mf* compatriot

compeler /kompe'ler/ *vt* to compel, force

compendiar /kompen'diar/ *vt* to abridge, summarize

compendio /kom'pendio/ *m,* compendium. **en c.,** briefly

compendioso /kompen'dioso/ *a* summary, condensed; compendious

compenetración /kompenetra'sion; kompenetra'θion/ *f,* co-penetration; intermingling

compenetrado /kompene'traðo/ **(de)** *a* thoroughly convinced (of)

compenetrarse /kompene'trarse/ *vr* to co-penetrate; intermingle

compensación /kompensa'sion; kompensa'θion/ *f,* compensating; compensation

compensar /kompen'sar/ *vt* to equalize, counterbalance; compensate

compensatorio /kompensa'torio/ *a* compensatory; equalizing

competencia /kompe'tensia; kompe'tenθia/ *f,* competition, contest; rivalry; competence; aptitude; *Law.* jurisdiction

competente /kompe'tente/ *a* adequate, opportune; rightful, correct; apt, suitable; learned, competent

competer /kompe'ter/ *vi irr* to belong to; devolve on; concern. See **pedir**

competición /kompeti'sion; kompeti'θion/ *f,* competition

competidor /kompeti'ðor/ **(-ra)** *n* competitor

competir /kompe'tir/ *vi irr* to compete, contest; be equal (to), vie (with). See **pedir**

compilación /kompila'sion; kompila'θion/ *f,* compilation

compilador /kompila'ðor/ **(-ra)** *n* compiler. *a* compiling

compilar /kompi'lar/ *vt* to compile

compinche /kom'pintʃe/ *mf Inf.* pal, chum

complacencia /kompla'sensia; kompla'θenθia/ *f,* satisfaction, pleasure

complacer /kompla'ser; kompla'θer/ *vt irr* to oblige, humor; *vr* (*with en*) be pleased or satisfied with; delight in, like to. See **nacer**

complaciente /kompla'siente; kompla'θiente/ *a* pleasing; obliging, helpful

complejidad /komplehi'ðað/ *f,* complexity

complejo /kom'pleho/ *a* complex; intricate. *m,* complex. **c. de inferioridad,** inferiority complex

complementario /komplemen'tario/ *a* complementary

complemento /komple'mento/ *m,* complement (all meanings)

completar /komple'tar/ *vt* to complete; perfect

completo /kom'pleto/ *a* full; finished; perfect

complexión /komplek'sion/ *f,* physical constitution

complexo /kom'plekso/ *a* complex; intricate

complicación /komplika'sion; komplika'θion/ *f,* complication

complicar /kompli'kar/ *vt* to complicate; muddle, confuse; *vr* be complicated; be muddled or confused

cómplice /'komplise; 'kompliθe/ *mf* accomplice

complicidad /komplisi'ðað; kompliθi'ðað/ *f,* complicity

complot /kom'plot/ *m, Inf.* conspiracy, plot, intrigue

complutense /komplu'tense/ *a* native of, or belonging to, Alcalá de Henares

componedor /kompone'ðor/ **(-ra)** *n* repairer; arbitrator; bone-setter; *Mus.* writer, arranger; *Print.* compositor

componenda /kompo'nenda/ *f,* mending, repair; *Inf.* settlement; compromise, arbitration; *Inf.* shady business

componente /kompo'nente/ *a* and *m,* component

componer /kompo'ner/ *vt irr* to construct, form; *Mech.* resolve; compose, create; *Print.* compose; prepare, concoct, mend, repair; settle (differences); remedy; trim; correct, adjust; *Lit. Mus.* compose; add up to, amount to; *vi* write (verses); *Mus.* compose; *vr* dress oneself up. **c. el semblante,** to compose one's features; *Inf.* **componérselas,** to fix matters, use one's wits. See **poner**

componible /kompo'niβle/ *a* reparable, mendable; able to be arranged or adjusted

comportamiento /komporta'miento/ *m,* conduct; deportment

comportar /kompor'tar/ *vt* to tolerate; *vr* behave, comport oneself

composición /komposi'sion; komposi'θion/ *f,* composition; repair; arrangement; *Print.* composition; *Gram.* compound; *Chem.* constitution; *Mech.* resolution

compositor /komposi'tor/ **(-ra)** *n Mus.* composer; *Print.* compositor

Compostela /kompos'tela/ Compostella

compostura /kompos'tura/ *f,* composition, structure; repair; neatness (of person); adulteration; arrangement, agreement; discretion, modesty

compota /kom'pota/ *f,* fruit preserve, compote; thick sauce

compotera /kompo'tera/ *f,* jam or preserve dish

compra /'kompra/ *f,* buying; marketing, shopping; purchase. **estar de compras,** *Euph.* to be in the family way. **ir de compras,** to go shopping

comprable /kom'praβle/ *a* purchasable

comprador /kompra'ðor/ **(-ra)** *a* purchasing. *n* purchaser; buyer; shopper

comprar /kom'prar/ *vt* to buy

comprender /kompren'der/ *vt* to encircle, surround; include, comprise, contain; understand

comprensible /kompren'siβle/ *a* comprehensible

comprensión /kompren'sion/ *f,* comprehension, understanding

comprensivo /kompren'siβo/ *a* understanding; comprehensive

compresa /kom'presa/ *f, Med.* compress, swab; pack (for the face, etc.)

compresión /kompre'sion/ *f,* compression; squeeze

compresivo /kompre'siβo/ *a* compressive

compresor /kompre'sor/ *m,* compressor; *Auto. Aer.* supercharger

comprimido /kompri'miðo/ *m,* tablet, pill

comprimir /kompri'mir/ *vt* to compress; squeeze; restrain; *vr* restrain oneself

comprobación /komproβa'sion; komproβa'θion/ *f,* verification; checking; proof

comprobante /kompro'βante/ *a* verifying; confirmatory

comprobar /kompro'βar/ *vt irr* to verify, check; confirm, prove. See **probar**

comprobatorio /komproβa'torio/ *a* confirmatory; verifying; testing

comprometedor /kompromete'ðor/ *a Inf.* compromising; jeopardizing

comprometer /komprome'ter/ *vt* to submit to arbitration; compromise; imperil, jeopardize; *vr* pledge oneself; *Inf.* compromise oneself

comprometido /komprome'tiðo/ *a* awkward, embarrassing; (e.g. literature of a writer) committed, engagé

compromiso /kompro'miso/ *m,* commitment, compromise, agreement, arbitration, obligation; appointment, engagement; jeopardy; difficulty

compuerta /kom'puerta/ *f,* half-door, wicket, hatch; floodgate, sluice. **c. flotante,** floating dam

compuesto /kom'puesto/ *a* and *past part* made-up, built-up; composite; circumspect; *Bot. Gram.* compound. *m,* composite; preparation, compound

compulsar /kompul'sar/ *vt* to collate; *Law.* make a transcript of

compulsivo /kompul'siβo/ *a* compelling

compunción /kompun'sion; kompun'θion/ *f*, compunction

compungir /kompun'hir/ *vt* to cause remorse or pity; *vr* repent; sympathize with, pity

computable /kompu'taβle/ *a* computable

computación /komputa'sion; komputa'θion/ *f*, **cómputo** *m*, calculation, computation

computador /komputa'ðor/ (**-ra**) *n* computer

computar /kompu'tar/ *vt* to compute

cómputo /'komputo/ *m*, computation; estimate

comulgar /komul'gar/ *vt* to administer Holy Communion; *vi* receive Holy Communion

comulgatorio /komulga'torio/ *m*, communion rail, altar rail

común /ko'mun/ *a* general, customary, ordinary; public, communal; universal, common; vulgar, low. *m*, community, population; water-closet. **en c.,** in common; generally. **por lo c.,** generally. **sentido c.,** common sense

comuna /ko'muna/ *f*, *Lat. Am.* district

comunal /komu'nal/ *a* communal; common. *m*, commonalty

comunero /komu'nero/ *a* popular, affable, democratic. *m*, joint owner; commoner; *Hist.* commune

comunicable /komuni'kaβle/ *a* communicable; communicative, sociable

comunicación /komunika'sion; komunika'θion/ *f*, communication; (telephone) call, message; letter (to the press); *Mil.* communiqué; *pl* lines of communication, transport

comunicado /komuni'kaðo/ *m*, official communication, communiqué; letter (to the press)

comunicante /komuni'kante/ *a* communicating

comunicar /komuni'kar/ *vt* to communicate; transmit; impart, share; *vr* **comunicarse con,** (door) to open onto (e.g. *Esta puerta se comunica con el jardín.* This door opens onto the garden); communicate, converse, correspond with each other

comunicativo /komunika'tiβo/ *a* communicative; talkative, not reserved

comunidad /komuni'ðað/ *f*, the common people; community; generality, majority; *pl Hist.* Commune

comunión /komu'nion/ *f*, communion; intercourse, fellowship; *Eccl.* Communion

comunismo /komu'nismo/ *m*, communism

comunista /komu'nista/ *a* and *mf* communist

comúnmente /komu'mente/ *adv* commonly, generally; frequently

con /kon/ *prep* with; by means of; in the company of; towards, to; although (followed by *infin.,* but generally translated by an inflected verb, e.g. *C. ser almirante, no le gusta el mar,* Although he is an admiral, he doesn't like the sea); by (followed by *infin.* and generally translated by a gerund, e.g. *c. hacer todo esto,* by doing all this). **c. bien,** safe and sound, safely (e.g. *Llegamos con bien.* We arrived safely.) **c. cuentagotas,** sparingly; stingily. **c. que,** so, then. **c. tal que,** provided that, on condition that. **c. todo,** nevertheless. **¿Con...?** Is this...? (on the telephone, e.g. *¿Con el Sr. Piñangos?* Is this Mr. Piñangos?)

conato /ko'nato/ *m*, effort, endeavor; tendency; *Law.* attempted crime

concatenación /konkatena'sion; konkatena'θion/ *f*, concatenation

concavidad /konkaβi'ðað/ *f*, concavity; hollow

cóncavo /'konkaβo/ *a* concave. *m*, concavity; hollow

concebible /konse'βiβle; konθe'βiβle/ *a* conceivable

concebimiento /konseβi'miento; konθeβi'miento/ *m*, See **concepción**

concebir /konse'βir; konθe'βir/ *vi irr* to become pregnant; conceive, imagine; understand; *vt* conceive, acquire (affection, etc.). See **pedir**

concedente /konse'ðente; konθe'ðente/ *a* conceding

conceder /konse'ðer; konθe'ðer/ *vt* to confer, grant; concede; agree to

concejal /konse'hal; konθe'hal/ *m*, councillor; alderman

concejil /konse'hil; konθe'hil/ *a* pertaining to a municipal council; public

concejo /kon'seho; kon'θeho/ *m*, town council; town hall; council meeting

concentración /konsentra'sion; konθentra'θion/ *f*, concentration

concentrado /konsen'traðo; konθen'traðo/ *a* concentrated; (of persons) reserved

concentrar /konsen'trar; konθen'trar/ *vt* to concentrate

concéntrico /kon'sentriko; kon'θentriko/ *a* concentric

concepción /konsep'sion; konθep'θion/ *f*, conception; idea, concept; *Eccl.* Immaculate Conception

conceptismo /konsep'tismo; konθep'tismo/ *m*, *Lit.* Concetism

concepto /kon'septo; kon'θepto/ *m*, idea, concept; epigram; opinion. **en mi c.,** in my opinion; judgment. **por c. de,** in payment of

conceptuar /konsep'tuar; konθep'tuar/ *vt* to judge, take to be; believe; imagine

conceptuoso /konsep'tuoso; konθep'tuoso/ *a* witty, ingenious

concernencia /konser'nensia; konθer'nenθia/ *f*, respect, relation

concerniente /konser'niente; konθer'niente/ *a* concerning

concernir /konser'nir; konθer'nir/ *vi irr defective* to concern. See **discernir**

concertadamente /konsertaða'mente; konθertaða'mente/ *adv* methodically, orderly; by arrangement, or agreement

concertar /konser'tar; konθer'tar/ *vt irr* to arrange, settle, adjust; bargain; conclude (business deal); harmonize; compare, correlate; tune instruments; *vi* reach an agreement. See **acertar**

concertina /konser'tina; konθer'tina/ *f*, concertina

concertista /konser'tista; konθer'tista/ *mf Mus.* performer, soloist; *Mus.* manager. **c. de piano,** concert pianist

concesión /konse'sion; konθe'sion/ *f*, conceding, grant; concession; lease

concesionario /konsesio'nario; konθesio'nario/ *m*, *Law.* concessionaire, leaseholder

concha /'kontʃa/ *f*, shell; turtle-shell; prompter's box; cove, creek; anything shell-shaped. *Fig.* **meterse en su c.,** to retire into one's shell. *Inf.* **tener más conchas que un galápago,** to be very cunning

conchado /kon'tʃaðo/ *a* scaly, having a shell

concho /'kontʃo/ *m*, *Lat. Am.* dregs, sediment

conciencia /kon'siensia; kon'θienθia/ *f*, consciousness; conscience; conscientiousness. **c. doble,** dual personality. **ancho de c.,** broad-minded. **a c.,** conscientiously

concienzudo /konsien'suðo; konθien'θuðo/ *a* of a delicate conscience, scrupulous; conscientious

concierto /kon'sierto; kon'θierto/ *m*, methodical arrangement; agreement; *Mus.* concert; *Mus.* concerto. **de c.,** by common consent

conciliable /konsi'liaβle; konθi'liaβle/ *a* reconcilable, compatible

conciliábulo /konsi'liaβulo; konθi'liaβulo/ *m*, conclave, private meeting; secret meeting

conciliación /konsilia'sion; konθilia'θion/ *f*, conciliation; similarity, affinity; protection, favor

conciliador /konsilia'ðor; konθilia'ðor/ *a* conciliatory

conciliar /konsi'liar; konθi'liar/ *m*, councilor. *vt* to conciliate; *Fig.* reconcile (opposing theories, etc.). **c. el sueño,** to induce sleep, woo sleep. *vr* win liking (or sometimes dislike)

concilio /kon'silio; kon'θilio/ *m*, council; *Eccl.* assembly; conciliary decree; findings of council

concisión /konsi'sion; konθi'sion/ *f*, conciseness, brevity

conciso /kon'siso; kon'θiso/ *a* concise

concitar /konsi'tar; konθi'tar/ *vt* to stir up, foment

conciudadano /konsiuða'ðano; konθiuða'ðano/ (**-na**) *n* fellow citizen; fellow countryman

cónclave /'konklaβe/ *m*, conclave; meeting

concluir /kon'kluir/ *vt irr* to conclude, finish; come to a conclusion, decide; infer, deduce; convince by reasoning; *Law.* close legal proceedings; *vr* expire, terminate. **c. con,** to put an end to. See **huir**

conclusión /konklu'sion/ *f*, finish, end; decision;

close, denouement; theory, proposition (gen. *pl*); deduction, inference; *Law.* close. **en c.,** in conclusion
conclusivo /konklu'siβo/ *a* final; conclusive
concluyente /konklu'yente/ *a* concluding; convincing; conclusive
concomer /konko'mer/ *vi Inf.* to give a shrug, shrug one's shoulders; fidget with an itch. **c. de placer,** to itch with pleasure
concomitancia /konkomi'tansia; konkomi'tanθia/ *f,* concomitance
concomitante /konkomi'tante/ *a* and *m,* concomitant
concordable /konkor'ðaβle/ *a* conformable, agreeable
concordador /konkorða'ðor/ **(-ra)** *a* peacemaking. *n* peacemaker
concordancia /konkor'ðansia; konkor'ðanθia/ *f,* harmony, agreement; (*Mus. Gram.*) concord; *pl* concordance
concordar /konkor'ðar/ *vt irr* to bring to agreement; *vi* agree. See **acordar**
concordato /konkor'ðato/ *m,* concordat
concorde /kon'korðe/ *a* agreeing; harmonious
concordia /kon'korðia/ *f,* concord, agreement, harmony; written agreement
concreción /konkre'sion; konkre'θion/ *f,* concretion
concretar /konkre'tar/ *vt* to combine, bring together; make concise; resume; *vr Fig.* confine oneself (to a subject) to hammer out, work out (an agreement)
concreto /kon'kreto/ *a* concrete, real, not abstract. **en c.,** in definite terms; finally, to sum up
concubina /konku'βina/ *f,* concubine, mistress
concubinato /konkuβi'nato/ *m,* concubinage
conculcación /konkulka'sion; konkulka'θion/ *f,* trampling, treading; violation
conculcador /konkulka'ðor/ *m,* violator
conculcar /konkul'kar/ *vt* to trample under foot, tread on; break, violate
concupiscencia /konkupis'sensia; konkupis'θenθia/ *f,* concupiscence, lust; greed
concupiscente /konkupis'sente; konkupis'θente/ *a* concupiscent, lustful; greedy
concurrencia /konku'rrensia; konku'rrenθia/ *f,* assembly; coincidence; attendance; help, influence
concurrido /konku'rriðo/ *a* crowded; busy; frequented
concurrir /konku'rrir/ *vi* to coincide; contribute; meet together; agree, be of same opinion; compete (in an examination, etc.)
concurso /kon'kurso/ *m,* crowd, concourse; conjunction, coincidence; help; competition; (tennis) tournament; competitive examination; invitation to offer tenders. **c. de acreedores,** creditors' meeting. **c. interno,** competitive examination for a position open to staff members only
concusión /konku'sion/ *f,* concussion; shock; extortion
condado /kon'daðo/ *m,* earldom; county
condal /kon'dal/ *a* of an earl, earl's; of a count, count's; of Barcelona
conde /'konde/ *m,* earl; king of the gypsies
condecir /konde'sir; konde'θir/ **(con)** *vi* to agree (with)
condecoración /kondekora'sion; kondekora'θion/ *f,* conferment of an honor, decoration; medal
condecorar /kondeko'rar/ *vt* to confer a decoration or medal
condena /kon'dena/ *f, Law.* sentence; punishment; penalty
condenable /konde'naβle/ *a* culpable, guilty; worthy of damnation
condenado /konde'naðo/ **(-da)** *a* damned; wicked, harmful. *n Law.* convicted criminal
condenador /kondena'ðor/ *a* condemning; incriminating; blaming
condenar /konde'nar/ *vt Law.* to pronounce sentence (on), convict; condemn; disapprove; wall or block or close up. **c. a galeras,** to condemn to the gallies. *vr* blame oneself; be eternally damned
condenatorio /kondena'torio/ *a* condemnatory; incriminating

condensación /kondensa'sion; kondensa'θion/ *f,* condensation
condensador /kondensa'ðor/ *a* condensing. *m,* (*Elec. Mech. Chem.*) condenser
condensante /konden'sante/ *a* condensing
condensar /konden'sar/ *vt* to condense; thicken; abridge
condesa /kon'desa/ *f,* countess
condescendencia /kondessen'densia; kondesθen'denθia/ *f,* affability, graciousness
condescender /kondessen'der; kondesθen'der/ *vi irr* to be obliging, helpful, agreeable. See **entender**
condescendiente /kondessen'diente; kondesθen'diente/ *a* affable, gracious
condestable /kondes'taβle/ *m, Hist.* constable, commander-in-chief
condición /kondi'sion; kondi'θion/ *f,* condition; quality; temperament; character; (social) position; rank, family; nobility, circumstance; stipulation, condition, requirement. **estar en condiciones de,** to be in a position to. **no estar en condiciones de,** to be in no condition to
condicional /kondisio'nal; kondiθio'nal/ *a* conditional
condicionar /kondisio'nar; kondiθio'nar/ *vi* to come to an agreement, arrange; *vt* impose conditions
condigno /kon'digno/ *a* condign
condimentación /kondimenta'sion; kondimenta'θion/ *f, Cul.* seasoning
condimentar /kondimen'tar/ *vt* to flavor, season (food)
condimento /kondi'mento/ *m,* condiment, flavoring
condiscípulo /kondis'sipulo; kondis'θipulo/ *m,* schoolfellow
condolencia /kondo'lensia; kondo'lenθia/ *f,* compassion; condolence
condolerse /kondo'lerse/ *vr* (*with de*) to sympathize with, be sorry for. See **doler**
condominio /kondo'minio/ *m,* condominium
condón /kon'don/ *m,* condom
condonar /kondo'nar/ *vt* to condone
conducción /konduk'sion; konduk'θion/ *f.* **conducencia,** *f,* transport, conveyance, carriage; guiding; direction, management; *Phys.* conduction; *Mech.* control-gear. *Auto.* **c. a izquierda,** left-hand drive
conducente /kondu'sente; kondu'θente/ *a* conducting, conducive
conducir /kondu'sir; kondu'θir/ *vt irr* to transport, convey, carry; *Phys.* conduct; guide, lead; manage, direct; *Auto.* drive; conduce; *vi* be suitable; *vr* behave, conduct oneself. *Pres. Ind.* **conduzco,** etc. *Preterite* **conduje, condujiste,** etc. *Pres. Subjunc.* **conduzca, conduzcas,** etc. *Imperf. Subjunc.* **condujese,** etc.
conducta /kon'dukta/ *f,* transport, conveyance; management, conduct, direction; behavior
conductibilidad /konduktiβili'ðað/ *f, Phys.* conductivity
conductivo /konduk'tiβo/ *a* conductive
conducto /kon'dukto/ *m,* pipe, conduit, drain, duct; *Fig.* channel, means; *Anat.* tube
conductor /konduk'tor/ **(-ra)** *n* guide; leader; driver (vehicles); *m, Phys.* conductor. **c. de caballos,** teamster. **c. de entrada,** *Radio.* lead-in. **c. del calor,** heat-conductor. **c. eléctrico,** electric wire or cable
conección /konek'sion/ *f,* connection; *Elec.* switching on, connection; joint; joining; *pl* friends, connections; *Elec.* wiring
conectar /konek'tar/ *vt Elec.* to connect, switch on; couple; attach, join
conectivo /konek'tiβo/ *a* connective; (*Elec. Mech.*) connecting
conejera /kone'hera/ *f,* rabbit-warren; *Inf.* low dive or haunt
conejillo de Indias /kone'hiyo de 'indias; kone'hiʎo de 'indias/ *m,* guineapig
conejo /ko'neho/ *m,* rabbit
conejuna /kone'huna/ *f,* rabbit fur, cony
conejuno /kone'huno/ *a* rabbit, rabbit-like
conexo /ko'nekso/ *a* connected

confabulación /konfaβula'sion; konfaβula'θion/ f, confabulation, conspiracy

confabular /konfaβu'lar/ vi to confer; vr scheme, plot

confalón /konfa'lon/ m, standard, banner

confección /konfek'sion; konfek'θion/ f, making; confection; making-up; concoction, remedy; ready-made garment

confeccionador /konfeksiona'ðor; konfekθiona'ðor/ **(-ra)** n maker (of clothes, etc.)

confeccionar /konfeksio'nar; konfekθio'nar/ vt to make; prepare; make up (pharmaceuticals)

confederación /konfeðera'sion; konfeðera'θion/ f, alliance, pact; confederacy, federation

confederarse /konfeðe'rarse/ vr to confederate, be allied

conferencia /konfe'rensia; konfe'renθia/ f, conference, meeting; lecture; (telephone) long-distance call

conferenciante /konferen'siante; konferen'θiante/ mf lecturer

conferenciar /konferen'siar; konferen'θiar/ vi to confer

conferencista /konferen'sista; konferen'θista/ mf, Lat. Am. lecturer

conferir /konfe'rir/ vt irr to grant, concede; consider, discuss; compare, correlate. See **herir**

confesable /konfe'saβle/ a acknowledgeable, avowable

confesar /konfe'sar/ vt irr to avow, declare; acknowledge, admit; Eccl. hear confession; vr Eccl. confess. Pres. Ind. **confieso, confiesas, confiesa, confiesan.** Pres. Subjunc. **confiese, confieses, confiese, confiesen**

confesión /konfe'sion/ f, confession

confesional /konfesio'nal/ a confessional

confesionario, confesonario, confesorio /konfesio'nario, konfeso'nario, konfe'sorio/ m, Eccl. confessional

confeso /konfe'so/ a confessed; converted (of Jews). m, Eccl. lay brother

confesor /konfe'sor/ m, confessor

confeti /kon'feti/ m, confetti

confianza /kon'fiansa; kon'fianθa/ f, confidence, trust; assurance, courage; over-confidence, conceit; intimacy; familiarity. **de c.,** reliable (e.g. persona de c., reliable person); informal (e.g. reunión de c., informal meeting). **en c.,** in confidence, confidentially

confianzudo /konfian'suðo; konfian'θuðo/ a Inf. overconfident

confiar /kon'fiar/ vi (with en) to trust in, hope; vt (with prep a or en) entrust, commit to the care of; confide in

confidencia /konfi'ðensia; konfi'ðenθia/ f, trust; confidence; confidential information

confidencial /konfiðen'sial; konfiðen'θial/ a confidential

confidente /konfi'ðente/ **(-ta)** a trustworthy, true. m, seat for two. n confidant(e); spy

configuración /konfigura'sion; konfigura'θion/ f, configuration, form, lie

configurar /konfigu'rar/ vt to shape

confín /kon'fin/ m, boundary, frontier; limit. a boundary

confinado /konfi'naðo/ a banished. m, Law. prisoner

confinar /konfi'nar/ vi (with con) to be bounded by, contiguous to; vt banish; place in confinement

confirmación /konfirma'sion; konfirma'θion/ f, corroboration; Eccl. confirmation

confirmar /konfir'mar/ vt to corroborate; uphold; Eccl. confirm

confiscación /konfiska'sion; konfiska'θion/ f, confiscation

confiscar /konfis'kar/ vt to confiscate

confitar /konfi'tar/ vt to candy, crystallize or preserve (fruit, etc.); Fig. sweeten

confite /kon'fite/ m, bonbon, sugared almond, etc.

confitería /konfite'ria/ f, confectionery

confitero /konfi'tero/ **(-ra)** n confectioner

confitura /konfi'tura/ f, preserve, jam

conflagración /konflagra'sion; konflagra'θion/ f, conflagration, blaze; uprising, rebellion

conflicto /kon'flikto/ m, strife, struggle; spiritual conflict; Fig. difficult situation

confluencia /kon'fluensia; kon'fluenθia/ f, confluence; crowd

confluir /kon'fluir/ vi irr to meet, flow together (rivers); run together (roads); crowd. See **huir**

conformación /konforma'sion; konforma'θion/ f, conformation; make-up, structure (e.g. of an organization)

conformar /konfor'mar/ vt to fit, adjust; vr agree, be of the same opinion; submit, comply; to make up (e.g. los grupos sociales que conforman este país, the social groups who make up this country)

conforme /kon'forme/ a similar, alike; consistent; in agreement; long-suffering, resigned. adv according (to), in proportion (to)

conformidad /konformi'ðað/ f, conformity; similarity; resignation; agreement, harmony; proportion, symmetry. **de c.,** by common consent. **en c.,** according to

confort /kon'fort/ m, comfort

confortante /konfor'tante/ a comforting; consoling; strengthening (of beverages)

confortar /konfor'tar/ vt to comfort, reassure; encourage; console

confortativo /konforta'tiβo/ a comforting; comfortable; strengthening, warming (of beverages); encouraging, cheering

confrontación /konfronta'sion; konfronta'θion/ f, confrontment; comparison (of texts, etc.)

confrontar /konfron'tar/ vt to bring face to face; compare, correlate; vi face; (with con) be contiguous to, border on

confucianismo /konfusia'nismo; konfuθia'nismo/ m, Confucianism

confundible /konfun'diβle/ a mistakable, liable to be confused

confundimiento /konfundi'miento/ m, confounding; mistaking; confusion

confundir /konfun'dir/ vt to mix, confuse; jumble together; mistake; Fig. confound (in argument); humble; bewilder, perplex; vr be mixed together; mistake, confuse; be ashamed; be bewildered

confusión /konfu'sion/ f, confusion; perplexity; shame; jumble

confuso /kon'fuso/ a mixed, upset; jumbled; obscure; indistinct; blurred; bewildered

confutación /konfuta'sion; konfuta'θion/ f, confutation

confutar /konfu'tar/ vt to confute

conga /'koŋga/ f, conga (dance; drum)

congelación /konhela'sion; konhela'θion/ f, freezing; congealment. **punto de c.,** freezing point

congelar /konhe'lar/ vt to congeal; freeze

congeniar /konhe'niar/ vi to be congenial

congénito /kon'henito/ a congenital

congestión /konhes'tion/ f, Med. congestion

congestionar /konhestio'nar/ vt to congest; vr Med. be overcharged (with blood)

conglomeración /koŋglomera'sion; koŋglomera'θion/ f, conglomeration

conglomerar /koŋglome'rar/ vt to conglomerate

congoja /koŋ'goha/ f, anguish, anxiety, grief

congraciarse /koŋgra'siarse; koŋgra'θiarse/ (con), vr to ingratiate oneself (with), get into the good graces (of)

congratulación /koŋgratula'sion; koŋgratula'θion/ f, congratulation

congratular /koŋgratu'lar/ vt to congratulate; vr congratulate oneself

congratulatorio /koŋgratula'torio/ a congratulatory

congregación /koŋgrega'sion; koŋgrega'θion/ f, gathering, meeting, congregation; brotherhood, guild

congregar /koŋgre'gar/ **(se)** vt and vr to meet, assemble

congresista /koŋgre'sista/ mf member of a congress

congreso /koŋ'greso/ m, congress; conference, meeting; sexual intercourse

congrio /'koŋgrio/ m, conger eel

congruencia /koŋ'gruensia; koŋ'gruenθia/ *f*, suitability, convenience; *Math*. congruence

congruente /koŋ'gruente/ *a* convenient, opportune; *Math*. congruent

cónico /'koniko/ *a* conical, tapering *Math*. conic

conifera /ko'nifera/ *f*, conifer

conifero /ko'nifero/ *a* coniferous

conjetura /konhe'tura/ *f*, conjecture

conjetural /konhetu'ral/ *a* conjectural

conjeturar /konhetu'rar/ *vt* to conjecture, surmise

conjugación /konhuga'sion; konhuga'θion/ *f*, conjugation

conjugar /konhu'gar/ *vt* to conjugate

conjunción /konhun'sion; konhun'θion/ *f*, connection, union association; (*Astron. Gram.*) conjunction

conjuntivitis /konhunti'βitis/ *f*, conjunctivitis

conjunto /kon'hunto/ *a* united, associated adjoining; mingled, mixed (with) bound, affiliated. *m*, whole; combo, ensemble (of musicians). **c. habitacional,** housing complex, housing project

conjura, conjuración /kon'hura, konhura'sion; kon'hura, konhura'θion/ *f*, conspiracy, plot

conjurador /konhura'ðor/ **(-ra)** *n* conspirator, plotter; exorcist

conjurar /konhu'rar/ *vi* to conspire, plot *vt* swear, take an oath; exorcise; implore, beg; ward off (danger)

conjuro /kon'huro/ *m*, plot, conspiracy, spell, incantation; entreaty

conllevar /konye'βar/ konʎe'βar/ *vt* to share (troubles) bear, put up with; endure

conmemoración /komemora'sion; komemora'θion/ *f*, commemoration

conmemorar /komemo'rar/ *vt* to commemorate

conmemorativo /komemora'tiβo/ *a* commemorative

conmensurable /komensu'raβle/ *a* commensurable

conmigo /ko'migo/ *pers. pron* 1st pers. sing. *mf* with myself, with me

conminar /komi'nar/ *vt* to threaten

conminatorio /komina'torio/ *a* threatening

conmiseración /komisera'sion; komisera'θion/ *f*, commiseration, compassion, pity

conmoción /komo'sion; komo'θion/ *f*, disturbance (mind or body); upheaval, commotion. **c. eléctrica,** electric shock

conmovedor /komoβe'ðor/ *a* moving, pitiful; stirring, thrilling

conmover /komo'βer/ *vt irr* to perturb, stir; move to pity. **c. los cimientos de,** to shake the foundations of; *vr* be emotionally moved. See **mover**

conmutable /komu'taβle/ *a* commutable

conmutación /komuta'sion; komuta'θion/ *f*, commutation

conmutador /komuta'ðor/ *m*, *Elec.* commutator; change-over switch

conmutar /komu'tar/ *vt* to commute; *Elec.* switch, convert

conmutatriz /komuta'tris; komuta'triθ/ *f*, *Elec.* converter

connato /kon'nato/ *a* contemporary

connatural /konnatu'ral/ *a* innate, inborn

connaturalizar /konnaturali'sar; konnaturali'θar/ *vt* to connaturalize

connaturalizarse /konnaturali'sarse; konnaturali'θarse/ **(con)** *vr* to become accustomed (to), become acclimated (to)

connivencia /konni'βensia; konni'βenθia/ *f*, connivance

connotación /konnota'sion; konnota'θion/ *f*, connotation

connotado, -a /konno'taðo/ *a*, *Lat. Am.* well-known

connotar /konno'tar/ *vt* to connote

cono /'kono/ *m*, (*Geom. Bot.*) cone. **el C. Sur,** the Southern Cone

conocedor /konose'ðor; konoθe'ðor/ **(-ra)** *n* one who knows; connoisseur; expert

conocer /kono'ser; kono'θer/ *vt irr* to know; understand; observe, perceive; meet, be acquainted (with); conjecture; confess, acknowledge; know carnally; *vr* know oneself; know one another. **conocerle a uno la**

voz, to recognize somebody's voice (e.g. *Le conozco la voz.* I recognize her by her voice.) **conocerle a uno en su manera de andar,** to recognize somebody by his gait, recognize somebody by his walk. *Pres. Indic.* conozco, conoces, etc. *Pres. Subjunc.* conozca, etc.

conocido /kono'siðo; kono'θiðo/ **(-da)** *a* illustrious, distinguished. *n* acquaintance

conocimiento /konosi'miento; konoθi'miento/ *m*, knowledge; understanding; intelligence; acquaintance (*not* friend); consciousness; *Com.* bill of lading; *pl* knowledge, learning

conque /'konke/ *conjunc* so, so that (e.g. *¿C. Juan se va?* So John's going away?)

conquista /kon'kista/ *f*, conquest

conquistador /konkista'ðor/ **(-ra)** *a* conquering. *n* conqueror

conquistar /konkis'tar/ *vt* to conquer; *Fig.* captivate, win

consabido /konsa'βiðo/ *a* aforesaid, beforementioned

consagración /konsagra'sion; konsagra'θion/ *f*, consecration; dedication

consagrar /konsa'grar/ *vt* to consecrate; dedicate, devote; deify; *vr* (*with prep a*) dedicate oneself to, engage in

consanguíneo /konsaŋ'guineo/ *a* consanguineous

consciente /kons'siente; kons'θiente/ *a* conscious; aware; sane. *m*, *Psychol.* conscious

conscripción /konskrip'sion; konskrip'θion/ *f*, conscription

conscripto /kons'kripto/ *m*, conscript

consecución /konseku'sion; konseku'θion/ *f*, obtainment; attainment

consecuencia /konse'kuensia; konse'kuenθia/ *f*, consequence, outcome; logical consequence, conclusion; importance; consistence (of people)

consecuente /konse'kuente/ *a* consequent, resultant; consistent. **c. consigo mismo,** self-consistent *m*, consequence; *Math.* consequent

consecutivo /konseku'tiβo/ *a* consecutive, successive

conseguir /konse'gir/ *vt irr* to obtain, achieve. See **seguir**

conseja /kon'seha/ *f*, story, fairy-tale; old wives' tale

consejero /konse'hero/ **(-ra)** *n* adviser; member of council. *m*. **c. de estado,** counselor of state

consejo /kon'seho/ *m*, advice; council, commission; board; council chamber or building. **c. de administración,** board of directors. **c. de guerra,** council of war. **c. del reino,** council of the realm. **c. privado,** privy council

consenso /kon'senso/ *m*, consensus of opinion, unanimity

consentido /konsen'tiðo/ *a* complaisant (of husband); spoiled, over-indulged

consentimiento /konsenti'miento/ *m*, consent; assent

consentir /konsen'tir/ *vt irr* to permit, allow; believe; tolerate, put up with; over-indulge, spoil; *vr* crack, give way (furniture, etc.). **c. en,** to consent to; to agree to. See **sentir**

conserje /kon'serhe/ *m*, concierge, porter; warden or keeper (of castle, etc.)

conserjería /konserhe'ria/ *f*, conciergerie, porter's lodge; warden's dwelling (in castles, etc.)

conserva /kon'serβa/ *f*, jam; preserve; pickles; *Naut.* convoy. **en c.,** preserved, tinned

conservación /konserβa'sion; konserβa'θion/ *f*, upkeep; preservation, maintenance; *Cul.* preserving; conservation. **c. refrigerada,** cold storage

conservador /konserβa'ðor/ **(-ra)** *a* keeping, preserving. *a* and *n* preserver; *Polit.* conservative; traditionalist. *m*, curator

conservadurismo /konserβaðu'rismo/ *m*, conservatism

conservar /konser'βar/ *vt* to keep, maintain, preserve; keep up (custom, etc.); guard; *Cul.* preserve. **c. en buen estado,** to keep in repair

conservatorio /konserβa'torio/ *m*, conservatoire; academy; *Lat. Am.* greenhouse. **c. de música,** academy of music, conservatoire

considerable /konsiðe'raβle/ *a* considerable; worthy

of consideration, powerful; numerous; large; important

consideración /konsiðera'sion; konsiðera'θion/ *f,* consideration, attention; reflection, thought; civility; importance. **en c. de,** considering

considerado /konsiðe'raðo/ *a* considerate; prudent; distinguished; important

considerar /konsiðe'rar/ *vt* to consider, reflect upon; treat with consideration (persons); judge, estimate, feel (e.g. *Considero que...* I feel that...)

consigna /kon'signa/ *f, Mil.* watchword; left luggage office

consignador /konsigna'ðor/ **(-ra)** *n Com.* consigner, sender

consignar /konsig'nar/ *vt* to assign, lay aside; deposit; *Com.* consign; entrust, commit; put in writing; *Law.* deposit in trust; book (a suspect)

consignatario /konsigna'tario/ *m, Law.* trustee; mortgagee; *Com.* consignee. **c. de buques,** shipping agent

consigo /kon'sigo/ *pers. pron* 3rd sing. and pl. *mf* with himself, herself, oneself, yourself, yourselves, themselves

consiguiente /konsi'giente/ *a* consequent, resulting. *m,* consequence. **por c.,** in consequence

consistencia /konsis'tensia; konsis'tenθia/ *f,* solidity; consistence, density; consistency, congruity, relevance

consistente /konsis'tente/ *a* of a certain consistency; solid

consistir /konsis'tir/ *vi (with en)* to consist in; be comprised of; be the result of

consistorio /konsis'torio/ *m,* consistory; municipal council (in some Spanish towns); town hall

consola /kon'sola/ *f,* console table; piertable; *Mech.* bracket

cónsola /kon'sola/ *f,* radio cabinet

consolación /konsola'sion; konsola'θion/ *f,* consolation

consolador /konsola'ðor/ **(-ra)** *n* comforter, consoler

consolar /konso'lar/ *vt* to comfort, console. **consolarse de + inf.,** to console oneself for + *pp.* See **contar**

consolidación /konsoliða'sion; konsoliða'θion/ *f,* consolidation; stiffening

consolidar /konsoli'ðar/ *vt* to consolidate; strengthen; combine, unite; *vr Law.* unite

consomé /konso'me/ *m,* consommé

consonancia /konso'nansia; konso'nanθianb/ *f,* harmony; agreement

consonante /konso'nante/ *a* consonant, consistent. *m,* rhyme. *f, Gram.* consonant

consonantismo /konsonan'tismo/ *m,* consonantism, consonant system

consorcio /kon'sorsio; kon'sorθio/ *m,* partnership; trust; intimacy, common life; consortium

consorte /kon'sorte/ *mf* consort; companion, associate, partner; spouse

conspicuo /kons'pikuo/ *a* outstanding, distinguished; conspicuous

conspiración /konspira'sion; konspira'θion/ *f,* conspiracy

conspirador /konspira'ðor/ **(-ra)** *n* conspirator

conspirar /konspi'rar/ *vi* to conspire; plot, scheme; tend, combine

constancia /kons'tansia; kons'tanθia/ *f,* constancy, steadfastness; stability, steadiness; transcript (of grades); *Lat. Am. law* deposition. **c. de estudios,** transcript (of grades)

constante /kons'tante/ *a* constant; durable; *Mech.* steady, non-oscillating. *m,* constant

Constantinopla /konstanti'nopla/ Constantinople

Constanza /kons'tansa; kons'tanθa/ Constance (female given name and lake)

constar /kons'tar/ *vi* to be evident, be clear; *(with de)* be composed of, consist of, comprise

constelación /konstela'sion; konstela'θion/ *f,* *Astron.* constellation; climate

consternación /konsterna'sion; konsterna'θion/ *f,* dismay, alarm

consternarse /konster'narse/ *vr* to be dismayed or alarmed

constipado /konsti'paðo/ *m, Med.* cold; chill

constiparse /konsti'parse/ *vr* to catch a cold or chill

constitución /konstitu'sion; konstitu'θion/ *f,* constitution; composition, make-up (e.g. *la c. del suelo,* the make-up of the soil)

constitucional /konstitusio'nal; konstituθio'nal/ *a* constitutional

constituir /konsti'tuir/ *vt irr* to constitute, form; found, establish; *(with en)* appoint, nominate; *Fig.* place in (a difficult situation, etc.); *vr (with en or por)* be appointed or authorized; be under (an obligation). See **huir**

constituyente, constitutivo /konstitu'yente, konsti-tu'tiβo/ *a* and *m,* constituent

constreñir /konstre'ɲir/ *vt irr* to constrain, oblige; constrict; constipate. See **ceñir**

constricción /konstrik'sion; konstrik'θion/ *f,* constriction; contraction, shrinkage

construcción /konstruk'sion; konstruk'θion/ *f,* construction; art or process of construction; fabric, structure; *Gram.* construction; building, erection. **c. de caminos,** road making. **c. naval,** shipbuilding

constructor /konstruk'tor/ **(-ra)** *a* building, constructive. *n* builder; constructor

construir /kons'truir/ *vt irr* to construct; build, make; *Gram.* construct. See **huir**

consuelo /kon'suelo/ *m,* consolation; comfort, solace; joy, delight

cónsul /'konsul/ *m,* consul

consulado /konsu'laðo/ *m,* consulate. **c. general,** consulate general

consulta /kon'sulta/ *f,* deliberation, consideration; advice; reference; conference, consultation

consultar /konsul'tar/ *vt* to discuss, consider; seek advice, consult. **consultarlo con la almohada,** *Fig.* to sleep on it, think it over, mull it over

consultor /konsul'tor/ **(-ra)** *a* consultative, advisory; consulting. *n* consultant; adviser. **c. externo,** outside consultant

consultorio /konsul'torio/ *m, Med.* consulting rooms; surgery; technical information bureau

consumación /konsuma'sion; konsuma'θion/ *f,* consummation; completion, attainment; extinction, end

consumado /konsu'maðo/ *a* consummate; *Inf.* thorough, perfect

consumar /konsu'mar/ *vt* to consummate; complete, accomplish, perfect

consumido /konsu'miðo/ *a Inf.* emaciated, wasted away; timid, spiritless

consumidor /konsumi'ðor/ **(-ra)** *a* consuming. *n* consumer, user

consumir /konsu'mir/ *vt* to destroy; consume, use; waste away, wear away; *Eccl.* take communion; *Inf.* grieve; *vr* be destroyed; *Inf.* be consumed with grief

consumo /kon'sumo/ *m,* consumption; demand. **c. de combustible,** fuel consumption

contabilidad /kontaβili'ðað/ *f,* bookkeeping; accounts; accounting

contable /kon'taβle/ *m,* bookkeeper

contacto /kon'takto/ *m,* contact (also *Elec. Mil.*). **en c.,** in common (e.g. *Los dos libros tienen mucho en c.* The two books have much in common.)

contado /kon'taðo/ *a* few; infrequent; rare. **al c.,** *Com.* cash down. **por de c.,** presumably; of course, naturally

contador /konta'ðor/ *m,* a counting. *m,* accountant; *Law.* auditor; counter (in banks); *Elec.* meter, counter; *Naut.* purser. **c. oficial,** *Argentina* certified public accountant. **c. público titulado,** certified public accountant

contaduría /kontaðu'ria/ *f,* accountancy; counting house; accountant's office; auditorship; *Theat.* box-office; *Naut.* purser's office

contagiar /konta'hiar/ *vt* to infect; corrupt, pervert; *vr (with con, de or por)* be infected by or through

contagio /kon'tahio/ *m,* infection; contagious disease; *Fig.* contagion, perversion, corruption

contagioso /konta'hioso/ *a* infectious; *Fig.* catching, contagious

contaminación /kontamina'sion; kontamina'θion/ *f*, contamination, pollution

contaminar /kontami'nar/ *vt* to pollute, contaminate; infect; *Fig.* corrupt

contante /kon'tante/ *a* ready (of money)

contar /kon'tar/ *vt irr* to count; recount, tell; place to account; include, count among; *vi* calculate, compute. **contarle a uno las cuarenta,** *inf* to give someone a piece of one's mind. **c. con,** to rely upon; reckon upon. *Pres. Ind.* **cuento, cuentas, cuenta, cuentan.** *Pres. Subjunc.* **cuente, cuentes, cuente, cuenten**

contemplación /kontempla'sion; kontempla'θion/ *f*, meditation, contemplation; consideration

contemplar /kontem'plar/ *vt* to consider, reflect upon; look at, contemplate; indulge, please

contemplativo /kontempla'tiβo/ *a Eccl.* contemplative; reflective, thoughtful; kind, indulgent

contemporáneo /kontempo'raneo/ **(de)** *a* contemporaneous (to *or* with) *n* contemporary

contemporizar /kontempori'sar; kontempori'θar/ *vi* to temporize, gain time

contencioso /konten'sioso; konten'θioso/ *a* contentious, argumentative; *Law.* litigious

contender /konten'der/ *vi irr* to contain; restrain, hold back; comprise; *vr* control oneself. See **entender**

contendiente /konten'diente/ *mf* contestant

contener /konte'ner/ *vt irr* to contain; include; comprise; hold back; restrain; check, repress; hold down, subdue; suppress, put down; *vr* contain oneself; keep one's temper; keep quiet; refrain. See **tener**

contenido /konte'niðo/ *m*, contents. *a* contained; *Fig.* restrained; reserved (of persons)

contentamiento /kontenta'miento/ *m*, contentment

contentar /konten'tar/ *vt* to satisfy, please; *Com.* endorse; *vr* be pleased or satisfied

contento /kon'tento/ *a* happy; content; satisfied; pleased. *m*, pleasure; contentment. **no caber de c.,** to be overjoyed

contestación /kontesta'sion; kontesta'θion/ *f*, reply, answer; discussion, argument, dispute

contestar /kontes'tar/ *vt* to reply, answer; confirm, attest; *vi* accord, harmonize

contexto /kon'teksto/ *m*, context

contextura /konteks'tura/ *f*, structure; context; physique, frame

contienda /kon'tienda/ *f*, struggle, fight; quarrel, dispute; discussion

contigo /kon'tigo/ *pers. pron* 2nd sing. *mf* with thee, with you

contigüidad /kontigui'ðað/ *f*, proximity, nearness

contiguo /kon'tiguo/ *a* adjacent, near, contiguous

continencia /konti'nensia; konti'nenθia/ *f*, moderation, self-restraint; continence; chastity; containing

continental /konti'nental/ *a* continental. *m*, express messenger service; *Puerto Rico* person from the mainland United States

continente /konti'nente/ *a* continent. *m*, container; demeanor, bearing; *Geog.* continent; mainland

contingencia /kontin'hensia; kontin'henθia/ *f*, contingency; risk, danger

contingente /kontin'hente/ *a* incidental; fortuitous; dependent; *m, Mil.* taskforce, contingent

continuación /kontinua'sion; kontinua'θion/ *f*, continuation; prolongation; sequel (of a story, etc.)

continuador /kontinua'ðor/ **(-ra)** *n* continuer

continuar /konti'nuar/ *vt* to continue; *vi* continue; last, remain, go on; *vr* be prolonged

continuidad /kontinui'ðað/ *f*, continuity

continuo /kon'tinuo/ *a* continuous, steady, uninterrupted; persevering, tenacious; persistent, lasting, unremitting. *m*, a united whole. **de c.,** continuously

contonearse /kontone'arse/ *vr* to swing the hips (in walking); strut

contorno /kon'torno/ *m*, contour, outline; (gen. *pl*) environs, surrounding district

contorsión /kontor'sion/ *f*, contortion

contorsionista /kontorsio'nista/ *mf* contortionist

contra /'kontra/ *prep* against, counter, athwart; opposed to, hostile to; in front of, opposite; towards. *m*,

opposite view or opinion. *f, Inf.* difficulty, trouble. **c. la corriente,** upstream. **el pro y el c.,** the pros and cons. **en c.,** in opposition, against

contraalmirante /kontraalmi'rante/ *m*, rear admiral

contraataque /kontraa'take/ *m*, counterattack

contraaviso /kontraa'βiso/ *m*, countermand

contrabajo /kontra'βaho/ *m*, doublebass; player of this instrument; deep bass voice

contrabalancear /kontraβalanse'ar; kontraβalanθe'ar/ *vt* to counterbalance; *Fig.* compensate

contrabandista /kontraβan'dista/ *a* smuggling. *mf* smuggler

contrabando /kontra'βando/ *m*, contraband; smuggling

contracción /kontrak'sion; kontrak'θion/ *f*, contraction; shrinkage; abridgment; abbreviation

contracubierta /kontraku'βierta/ *f*, book jacket, jacket

contradanza /kontra'ðansa; kontra'ðanθa/ *f*, square dance

contradecir /kontraðe'sir; kontraðe'θir/ *vt irr* to contradict; *vr* contradict oneself. See **decir**

contradicción /kontraðik'sion; kontraðik'θion/ *f*, contradiction

contradictorio /kontraðik'torio/ *a* contradictory

contraer /kontra'er/ *vt irr* to shrink, reduce in size, shorten; abridge; contract (matrimony, obligations); *Fig.* acquire (diseases, habits); *vr* shorten, contract, shrink. See **traer**

contrafuerte /kontra'fuerte/ *m*, buttress, counterfort, abutment; *Geog.* spur

contrahacer /kontraa'ser; kontraa'θer/ *vt irr* to forge, counterfeit; mimic; imitate. See **hacer**

contrahecho /kontra'etʃo/ *a* deformed

contralor /kontra'lor/ *m*, comptroller

contraloría /kontralo'ria/ *f*, comptrollership, office of comptroller (position); comptroller's office (place)

contralto /kon'tralto/ *m*, contralto (voice)

contraluz /kontra'lus; kontra'luθ/ *f*, counterlight

contramaestre /kontrama'estre/ *m, Naut.* boatswain; overseer, superintendent, foreman

contramarcha /kontra'martʃa/ *f*, retrogression; *Mil.* countermarch

contramedida /kontrame'ðiða/ *f*, counter-measure

contraorden /kontra'orðen/ *f*, countermand

contrapedalear /kontrapeðale'ar/ *vi* to backpedal

contrapelo /kontra'pelo/ *a adv* the wrong way of the hair, against the grain; *Inf.* reluctantly, distastefully

contrapeso /kontra'peso/ *m*, counterpoise, counterweight; balancing-pole (acrobats); *Fig.* counterbalance; makeweight

contraponer /kontrapo'ner/ *vt irr* to compare; place opposite; oppose. See **poner**

contraproducente /kontraproðu'sente; kontraproðu'θente/ *a* counteractive, counterproductive, unproductive, self-deceiving; self-defeating

contrapuesto /kontra'puesto/ *a* opposing, divergent

contrapunto /kontra'punto/ *m*, counterpoint

contrariar /kontra'riar/ *vt* to counter, oppose; impede; vex, annoy

contrariedad /kontrarie'ðað/ *f*, contrariety, opposition; obstacle; vexation, trouble

contrario /kon'trario/ **(-ia)** *a* opposite; hostile, opposed; harmful; adverse, unfavorable. *n* adversary; opponent. *m*, obstacle. **c. contraria,** contrary, opposite. **al contrario,** on the contrary. **llevar la contraria (a),** to oppose; contradict

contrarreforma /kontrarre'forma/ *f*, counter-Reformation

contrasentido /kontrasen'tiðo/ *m*, wrong sense, opposite sense (of words); contradiction of initial premise; self-contradiction; nonsense

contraseña /kontra'seɲa/ *f*, countersign; *Mil.* password

contrastar /kontras'tar/ *vt* to contrast; oppose; resist; check (weights and measures); assay; *Mech.* calibrate, gauge; *vi* contrast

contraste /kon'traste/ *m*, contrast; opposition; difference; weights and measures inspector; dispute, clash. **en c. a,** in contrast to

contrata /kon'trata/ f, See **contrato**
contratación /kontrata'sion; kontrata'θion/ f, hiring; *Com.* transaction; commerce, trade
contratapa /kontra'tapa/ f, back cover (of a periodical, etc.)
contratar /kontra'tar/ vt to contract, enter into an agreement; make a bargain (with), deal (with); hire, contract
contratiempo /kontra'tiempo/ m, mishap, accident
contratista /kontra'tista/ mf contractor
contrato /kon'trato/ m, contract. **contrato de arrendamiento,** lease
contratorpedero /kontratorpe'ðero/ m, torpedoboat destroyer
contravención /kontraβen'sion; kontraβen'θion/ f, contravention; violation. **en c. a,** in violation of
contraveneno /kontraβe'neno/ m, *Med.* antidote; remedy, precaution
contravenir /kontraβe'nir/ vt irr to infringe, contravene. See **venir**
contraventana /kontraβen'tana/ f, shutter (for windows)
contravidriera /kontraβið'riera/ f, storm window
contrayente /kontra'yente/ a contracting. mf contracting party (used of matrimony)
contribución /kontriβu'sion; kontriβu'θion/ f, contribution; tax. **c. sobre la propiedad,** property tax
contribuir /kontri'βuir/ vt irr to pay (taxes); contribute. See **huir**
contribuyente /kontriβu'yente/ a contributing; contributory. mf contributor; taxpayer
contrición /kontri'sion; kontri'θion/ f, contrition
contrincante /kontrin'kante/ m, competitor, candidate (public examinations); rival, opponent
contrito /kon'trito/ a contrite
control /kon'trol/ m, control; checking. **c. de precios,** price control
controlar /kontro'lar/ vt to control
controversia /kontro'βersia/ f, controversy
controvertir /kontroβer'tir/ vi and vt irr to dispute, argue against, deny. See **sentir**
contumacia /kontu'masia; kontu'maθia/ f, obstinacy; *Law.* contumacy
contumaz /kontu'mas; kontu'maθ/ a stubborn; impenitent; *Law.* contumacious; *Med.* obstinate, resistant (to cure)
contumelia /kontu'melia/ f, contumely
conturbar /kontur'βar/ vt to perturb, make anxious, disturb; vr be perturbed
contuso /kon'tuso/ a contused, bruised
convalecencia /kombale'sensia; kombale'θenθia/ f, convalescence; convalescent home
convalecer /kombale'ser; kombale'θer/ vi irr to convalesce, get better; *Fig.* recover, regain (influence, etc.). See **conocer**
convaleciente /kombale'siente; kombale'θiente/ a and mf convalescent
convalidar /kombali'ðar/ vt to ratify, confirm
convecino /kombe'sino; kombe'θino/ a nearby; neighboring
convencedor /kombense'ðor; kombenθe'ðor/ a convincing
convencer /komben'ser; komben'θer/ vt to convince; prove beyond doubt, demonstrate to (persons); be convincing (e.g. *No convence,* It's not convincing; He's not convincing.) vr be convinced
convencimiento /kombensi'miento; kombenθi'miento/ m, conviction, belief, assurance
convención /komben'sion; komben'θion/ f, pact, formal agreement; harmony, conformity; convention
convencional /kombensio'nal; kombenθio'nal/ a conventional (all meanings)
convencionalismo /kombensiona'lismo; kombenθiona'lismo/ m, conventionality
convenido /kombe'niðo/ a agreed
conveniencia /kombe'niensia; kombe'nienθia/ f, conformity, harmony, adjustment; experience, suitability, convenience; advantage; agreement, pact; post as domestic; ease, comfort; pl income; social conventions

conveniente /kombe'niente/ a convenient, opportune; suitable, fitting; profitable; useful; decorous. **tener por c. + inf,** to think it fitting to + *Inf.*, find it appropriate to + *Inf.*
convenio /kom'benio/ m, pact, treaty; *Com.* agreement, contract
convenir /kombe'nir/ vi irr to agree; assemble, congregate; belong; be suitable; vr agree; suit oneself. **No me conviene salir esta tarde,** It does not suit me to go out this afternoon. **Me convendría pasar un mes allí,** It would be a good idea (or a wise thing) for me to spend a month there. See **venir**
conventillo /komben'tijo; komben'tiʎo/ m, *Lat. Am.* tenement
convento /kom'bento/ m, convent; monastery; religious community
conventual /komben'tual/ a conventual; monastic. m, *Eccl.* conventual
convergencia /komber'hensia; komber'henθia/ f, convergence
convergir /komber'hir/ vi to converge; *Fig.* coincide (views, etc.)
conversación /kombersa'sion; kombersa'θion/ f, conversation; intercourse, company; *Law.* criminal conversation
conversar /komber'sar/ vi to converse; chat; live with others; know socially
conversión /komber'sion/ f, conversion; change, transformation; *Com.* conversion; *Mil.* wheel; wheeling
converso /kom'berso/ **(-sa)** n convert (especially a Jew forced to convert during Spanish Inquisition)
convertible /komber'tiβle/ a convertible
convertir /komber'tir/ vt irr to change, transform; convert; reform; vr to become; be transformed; be converted; be reformed. See **sentir**
convexo /kom'bekso/ a convex
convicción /kombik'sion; kombik'θion/ f, conviction; certitude; *Law.* conviction
convicto /kom'bikto/ **(-ta)** a and n *Law.* convict
convidado /kombi'ðaðo/ **(-da)** n guest
convidar /kombi'ðar/ vt to invite (persons); encourage, provoke; entice, attract; vr invite oneself; offer one's services
convincente /kombin'sente; kombin'θente/ a convincing
convite /kom'bite/ m, invitation; banquet; party
convivencia /kombi'βensia; kombi'βenθia/ f, coexistence, common life, life together. **c. pacífica,** peaceful coexistence
convivial /kombi'βial/ a convivial
convivir /kombi'βir/ vi to live together, live under the same roof
convocación /komboka'sion; komboka'θion/ f, convocation
convocar /kombo'kar/ vt to convene, convoke
convoy /kom'boi/ m, convoy; escort; following; cruet-stand
convoyar /kombo'yar/ vt to convoy, escort
convulsión /kombul'sion/ f, convulsion
convulsivo /kombul'siβo/ a convulsive
conyugal /konyu'gal/ a conjugal
cónyuge /'konyuhe/ mf husband and (and) wife (used gen. in pl)
coñac /ko'nak/ m, brandy
coñete /ko'nete/ a, *Chile, Peru* mean, stingy
cooperación /koopera'sion; koopera'θion/ f, cooperation
cooperador /koopera'ðor/ **(-ra)** a cooperative. n cooperator, collaborator
cooperar /koope'rar/ vt to cooperate
cooperativa /koopera'tiβa/ f, cooperative society
cooperativo /koopera'tiβo/ a cooperative
coordenada /koorðe'naða/ f, coordinate
coordinación /koorðina'sion; koorðina'θion/ f, coordination
coordinar /koorði'nar/ vt to coordinate, classify
copa /'kopa/ f, wineglass, goblet; glassful; top branches (of trees); crown (of hat); *Cards.* heart; gill

(liquid measure); *Inf.* drink, glass; *pl Cards.* hearts (in Spanish pack, goblets)

copal /ko'pal/ *m, Central America, Mexico* resin

copartícipe /kopar'tisipe; kopar'tiθipe/ *mf* co-partner, partaker, participant

copec /'kopek/ *m,* kopeck

Copenhague /kope'nage/ Copenhagen

copernicano /koperni'kano/ *a* Copernican

copero /ko'pero/ *m,* cupbearer; sideboard; cocktail cabinet

copete /ko'pete/ *m,* lock, tress (hair); tuft, crest; forelock (horses); head, top (ice-cream, drinks); *Inf.* **de alto c.,** aristocratic; socially prominent

copetudo, -a /kope'tuðo/ *a, Lat. Am.* tufted, crested; haughty, stuck-up

copia /'kopia/ *f,* abundance, plenty; copy, reproduction; transcript; imitation

copiador /kopia'ðor/ **(-ra)** *a* copying. *n* copier; transcriber. *m,* copybook

copiar /ko'piar/ *vt* to copy

copioso /ko'pioso/ *a* abundant, plentiful

copla /'kopla/ *f,* couplet; popular four-line poem; couple, pair; *pl Inf.* verses

coplero /ko'plero/ **(-ra)** *n* balladmonger; poetaster

copo /'kopo/ *m,* cop (of a spindle); snowflake, ball (of cotton)

copón /ko'pon/ *m,* large goblet; *Eccl.* ciborium, chalice

coprófago /ko'profago/ *a* coprophagous

copropietario /kopropie'tario/ **(-ia)** *n* coproprietor, coowner

copto /'kopto/ **(-ta)** *n* Copt

cópula /'kopula/ *f,* connection; coupling; joining; copulation

copular /kopu'lar/ *vi* to copulate

coque /'koke/ *m,* coke

coqueluche /koke'lutʃe/ *f,* whooping cough

coqueta /ko'keta/ *f,* coquette, flirt

coquetear /kokete'ar/ *vi* to flirt

coqueteo /koke'teo/ *m,* coquetry; flirtation

coquetería /kokete'ria/ *f,* coquetry

coquetón /koke'ton/ *a* coquettish

coraje /ko'rahe/ *m,* courage, valor; anger; *Mexico Inf.* fury. **¡Qué c.!** What nerve!

coral /ko'ral/ *m,* coral. *f,* coral snake. *m, Bot.* coral tree; *pl* coral beads

coral /ko'ral/ *a* choral

coralina /kora'lina/ *f,* coral (polyp)

coraza /ko'rasa; ko'raθa/ *f,* cuirass; shell (of tortoise); armor-plate, armor (ships, etc.)

corazón /kora'son; kora'θon/ *m,* heart; courage, spirit; love, tenderness; goodwill, benevolence; core (of a fruit); *Fig.* pith. **de c.,** sincerely. **tener el c. en la mano,** to wear one's heart on one's sleeve

corazonada /koraso'naða; koraθo'naða/ *f,* feeling, instinct; presentiment, apprehension

corbata /kor'βata/ *f,* necktie; scarf; ribbon (insignia)

corbatería /korβate'ria/ *f,* necktie shop

corbatero /korβa'tero/ *m,* necktie maker; necktie dealer; tie rack

Córcega /'korsega; 'korθega/ Corsica

corchea /kor'tʃea/ *f, Mus.* quaver

corchete /kor'tʃete/ *m, Sew.* hook and eye; hook

corcho /'kortʃo/ *m, Bot.* cork, cork bark; stopper; cork; cork mat; bee hive

corcova /kor'koβa/ *f,* hump, abnormal protuberance

corcovado /korko'βaðo/ **(-da)** *a* hunchbacked, crooked. *n* hunchback

corcovear /korkoβe'ar/ *vi* to curvet, caper

cordaje /kor'ðahe/ *m, Naut.* cordage, tackling, rope

cordel /kor'ðel/ *m,* cord; *Naut.* line. **a c.,** in a straight line

cordelería /korðele'ria/ *f,* rope making; ropeyard; cordage

cordelero /korðe'lero/ **(-ra)** *n* rope maker

cordera /kor'ðera/ *f,* ewe lamb; sweet, gentle woman

corderillano, -a /korðeri'jano; korðeri'ʎano/ *a, Argentina, Chile* Andean

cordero /kor'ðero/ *m,* lamb; dressed lambskin; peaceable, mild man; Jesus (gen. **Divino C.**)

cordial /kor'ðial/ *a* warming, invigorating; affectionate, loving, friendly. *m, Med.* cordial

cordialidad /korðiali'ðað/ *f,* cordiality, friendliness

cordillera /korði'yera; korði'ʎera/ *f,* mountain range

Córdoba /'korðoβa/ Cordova

cordobán /korðo'βan/ *m,* cured goatskin; Cordovan leather, Spanish leather

cordobés /korðo'βes/ **(-esa)** *a* and *n* Cordovan

cordón /kor'ðon/ *m,* cord; cordon; *Eccl.* rope girdle; *Archit.* string-course

cordoncillo /korðon'siyo; korðon'θiʎo/ *m,* rib (in cloth); ridge, milling (of coins); *Sew.* piping

cordura /kor'ðura/ *f,* good sense, prudence

Corea /ko'rea/ Korea

coreografía /koreogra'fia/ *f,* choreography; art of dancing

coreográfico /koreo'grafiko/ *a* choreographic

coreógrafo /kore'ografo/ *m,* choreographer

corintio /ko'rintio/ **(-ia)** *a* and *n* Corinthian

Corinto /ko'rinto/ Corinth

corista /ko'rista/ *m, Eccl.* chorister. *mf Theat.* member of the chorus

cornada /kor'naða/ *f,* horn thrust or wound (bulls, etc.)

cornamenta /korna'menta/ *f,* horns (bulls, deer, etc.)

córnea /'kornea/ *f,* cornea

corneja /kor'neha/ *f,* carrion or black crow

córneo /'korneo/ *a* horny, corneous

corneta /kor'neta/ *f, Mus.* bugle; *Mus.* cornet; swineherd's horn; *Mil.* pennon. *m,* bugler; *Mil.* cornet. **c. de monte,** hunting horn

cornetín /korne'tin/ *m, dim* **corneta,** *Mus.* cornet; cornet player

cornezuelo /korne'suelo; korne'θuelo/ *m, dim* little horn; *Med.* ergot; *Bot.* variety of olive

cornisa /kor'nisa/ *f,* cornice

cornucopia /kornu'kopia/ *f,* cornucopia, horn of plenty; sconce; mirror

cornudo /kor'nuðo/ *a* horned. *m,* cuckold. **el C.,** the Devil

coro /'koro/ *m,* choir; chorus; *Archit.* choir. **hacer c. (a),** to listen to, support. **saber de c.,** to know by heart

corolario /koro'lario/ *m,* corollary

corona /ko'rona/ *f,* garland, wreath; halo; (*Astron. Archit.*) corona; crown (of tooth); crown (of head); tonsure; crown (coin); royal power; kingdom; triumph; reward; summit, height, peak; circlet (for candles)

coronación /korona'sion; korona'θion/ *f,* coronation; coping stone

coronamiento /korona'miento/ *m,* coronation; coping stone; *Fig.* crowning touch; *Naut.* taffrail

coronar /koro'nar/ *vt* to crown; crown (in checkers); complete, round off; *vr* be crowned; crown oneself; be tipped or capped

coronel /koro'nel/ *m,* colonel

coronela /koro'nela/ *f, Inf.* colonel's wife

coronelía /korone'lia/ *f,* colonelcy

coronilla /koro'niya; koro'niʎa/ *f, dim* small crown; crown of head; *Fig. Inf.* **estar hasta la c.,** to be fed up

coroza /ko'rosa; ko'roθa/ *f,* dunce's cap

corpiño /kor'piɲo/ *m,* bodice

corporación /korpora'sion; korpora'θion/ *f,* corporation, body, association

corporal /korpo'ral/ *a* and *m, Eccl.* corporal

corporativo /korpora'tiβo/ *a* corporate, corporative

corpóreo /kor'poreo/ *a* corporeal

corporizar /korpori'sar; korpori'θar/ *vt* to embody

corpulento /korpu'lento/ *a* corpulent, stout

Corpus /'korpus/ *m,* Corpus Christi

corpúsculo /kor'puskulo/ *m,* corpuscle

corral /ko'rral/ *m,* yard; pen, enclosure, corral; old-time theater. **c. de madera,** timber yard. *Inf.* **hacer corrales,** to play truant

corralón /ko'rrea/ *f,* leather strap or paring; flexibility; *Mech.* belt, band

corrección /korrek'sion; korrek'θion/ *f,* correction;

correctness; punishment; emendation. **c. de pruebas,** proofreading, proofing, reading proof

correcional /korre'sional; korre'θional/ *a* correctional. *m,* reformatory

correcto /ko'rrekto/ *a* correct; well-bred; unexceptionable, irreproachable; regular (of features)

corredera /korre'ðera/ *f,* link (engines); *Mech.* slide; *Naut.* log; racecourse; *Inf.* procuress

corredizo /korre'ðiso; korre'ðiθo/ *a* easy to untie; running (of knots); sliding

corredor /korre'ðor/ **(-ra)** *n* runner. *m, Com.* broker; corridor; *Inf.* meddler; *Inf.* procurer, pimp. *a* running. **c. de bolsa,** stockbroker

corregible /korre'hiβle/ *a* corrigible

corregidor /korrehi'ðor/ *m,* Spanish magistrate; *Obs.* mayor

corregidora /korrehi'ðora/ *f,* wife of corregidor; mayoress

corregir /korre'hir/ *vt irr* to correct; scold, punish; moderate, counteract; *Mech.* adjust; *vr* mend one's ways. **c. pruebas,** to read proof. *Pres. Ind.* **corrijo, corriges, corrige, corrigen.** *Pres. Part.* **corrigiendo.** *Pres. Subjunc.* **corrija, corrijas, etc.** *Imperf. Subjunc.* **corrigiese, etc.**

correligionario /korrelihio'nario/ **(-ia)** *n* coreligionist; fellow-supporter or believer

correlón, -ona /korre'lon/ *a Mexico, Venezuela* cowardly

correntada /korren'taða/ *f, Argentina* rapids

correo /ko'rreo/ *m,* courier; mail; post-office; letters. **c. aéreo,** air-mail. **c. certificado,** registered mail. **c. de voz,** voice mail. **c. electrónico,** e-mail, electronic mail. **a vuelta de c.,** by return of mail. **tren c.,** mail train

correr /ko'rrer/ *vi* to run; race; sail, steam; flow; blow; flood; extend, stretch; pass (of time); fall due (salary, etc.); be current or general; (*with con*) be in charge of or responsible for; *vt* run (a horse); fasten, slide (bolts, etc.); draw (curtains); undergo, suffer; sell, auction; *Inf.* steal; *Fig.* embarrass; spread (a rumor, etc.); catch, make (bus, train, etc.); *vr* slide, glide, slip; run (of colors); *Inf.* spread oneself, talk too much. **c. cañas,** to participate in a mock joust using reeds as spears

correría /korre'ria/ *f,* raid, foray; excursion, trip

correspondencia /korrespon'densia; korrespon'denθia/ *f,* relationship, connection; intercourse, communication; correspondence, letters; equivalence, exact translation

corresponder /korrespon'der/ *vi* to requite, repay; be grateful; belong to, concern; devolve upon, fall to; suit, harmonize (with); fit; *vr* correspond by letters; like or love each other

correspondiente /korrespon'diente/ *a* suitable; proportionate; corresponding; *mf* correspondent

corresponsal /korrespon'sal/ *mf* correspondent (especially professional); *Com.* agent

corretear /korrete'ar/ *vi* to wander about the streets; gad

correveidile /korreβei'ðile/ *mf Inf.* tale-bearer, gossip

corrida /ko'rriða/ *f,* race, run; *Aer.* taxying; bull fight (abb. for **c. de toros**)

corrido /ko'rriðo/ *a* extra, over (of weight); embarrassed; experienced

corriente /ko'rriente/ *a* current, present; well-known; usual, customary; fluent (style); ordinary, average; easy. *f,* flow, stream; *Fig.* course (of events, etc.); *Elec.* current. *adv* quite, exactly. *Elec.* **c. alterna,** alternating current. **c. continua,** direct current. **c. de aire,** draft. **cuenta c.,** savings account. **estar al c.,** to be informed (of something)

Corriente del Golfo /ko'rriente del 'golfo/ Gulf Stream

corrillo /ko'rriyo; ko'rriʎo/ *m,* knot, group, huddle (of people)

corro /'korro/ *m,* circle, group; ring (for children's games)

corroboración /korroβora'sion; korroβora'θion/ *f,* corroboration, confirmation

corroborar /korroβo'rar/ *vt* to fortify; corroborate, support

corroer /korro'er/ *vt irr* to corrode, waste away; *Fig.* gnaw. See **roer**

corromper /korrom'per/ *vt* to rot; mar; spoil, ruin; seduce; corrupt (texts); bribe; *Fig.* contaminate, corrupt; *vi* stink; *vr* putrefy, not; be spoiled; *Fig.* be corrupted

corrosión /korro'sion/ *f,* corrosion

corrosivo /korro'siβo/ *a* corrosive

corrugación /korruga'sion; korruga'θion/ *f,* corrugation, wrinkling

corrupción /korrup'sion; korrup'θion/ *f,* rot, putrefaction; corruption, depravity; decay; stink; bribery; falsification (of texts); corruption (of language, etc.)

corrupto /ko'rrupto/ *a* corrupt

corruptor /korrup'tor/ **(-ra)** *n* corrupter

corsario /kor'sario/ *m,* pirate; privateer

corsé /kor'se/ *m,* corset

corsetería /korsete'ria/ *f,* corset shop or manufactory

corso /'korso/ **(-sa)** *a* and *n* Corsican

corta /'korta/ *f,* felling, cutting

cortacircuitos /kortasir'kuitos; kortaθir'kuitos/ *m, Elec.* circuit breaker, cut-out; disconnecting switch

cortado /kor'taðo/ *a* fitting, proportioned; disjointed (style); confused, shamefaced

cortador /korta'ðor/ *m,* cutter; cutter-out (dresses, etc.); butcher

cortadura /korta'ðura/ *f,* cut, wound; cutting (from periodicals); defile; *pl* clippings, cuttings

cortafrío /korta'frio/ *m,* cold chisel; hammer-head chisel

cortalápices /korta'lapises; korta'lapiθes/ *m,* pencil sharpener

cortante /kor'tante/ *a* cutting; sharp; piercing (of wind, etc.); trenchant; *m, Argentina* scissors *pl.*

cortapapel /kortapa'pel/ *m,* paper-knife

cortapisa /korta'pisa/ *f,* condition, stipulation

cortaplumas /korta'plumas/ *m,* penknife

cortapuros /korta'puros/ *m,* cigar cutter

cortar /kor'tar/ *vt* to cut out (dresses, etc.); switch off, shut off (water, electricity, etc.); cleave, divide; cut (cards); pierce (wind, etc.); interrupt, impede; omit, cut; *Fig.* interrupt (conversation); decide, determine; *vr* be confused or shamefaced; curdle, turn sour (e.g. *Se cortó la leche,* The milk turned sour); split, fray; chap. **Se cortó el pelo,** She cut her hair

cortavidrios /korta'βiðrios/ *m,* diamond, glasscutter

cortaviento /korta'βiento/ *m,* windscreen

corte /'korte/ *f,* court (royal); retinue; yard; *pl* Spanish parliament. *m,* cutting, cut; blade, cutting edge; cutting out, dressmaking; length, material required for garment, shoes, etc.; cut, fit; style; book edge; *Archit.* section; means, expedient; counting of money (in a till). **c. de caja,** counting of money (in a till). **c. trasversal,** side view

cortedad /korte'ðað/ *f,* shortness, brevity; smallness; stupidity, dullness; timidity, shyness. **c. de fuerzas,** lack of strength

cortejar /korte'har/ *vt* to accompany, escort; woo, court

cortejo /kor'teho/ *m,* courtship, wooing; suite, accompaniment; gift, present; homage, attention; *Inf.* lover, beau

cortés /kor'tes/ *a* polite, attentive, courteous, civil

cortesana /korte'sana/ *f,* courtesan

cortesano /korte'sano/ *a* court; courtly; *m,* courtier

cortesía /korte'sia/ *f,* politeness, courtesy; attentiveness; civility; gift, present; favor. **c. internacional,** courtesy of nations. **c. de boca mucho vale y poco cuesta.** Courtesy is worth much and costs little

corteza /kor'tesa; kor'teθa/ *f, Bot.* bark; *Anat.* cortex; skin, peel, crust; aspect, appearance; roughness. **c. terrestre,** Earth's crust, crust of the Earth. **de c.,** superficial (e.g. explanation)

cortijo /kor'tiho/ *m,* farmhouse and land

cortina /kor'tina/ *f,* curtain; *Fig.* veil; *Inf.* heel taps; *Mil.* curtain, screen. **c. de fuego de artillería,** antiaircraft barrage. **c. de globos de intercepción,** balloon barrage. **c. de humo,** smoke screen. **c. metálica,** metal shutter

cortinaje /korti'nahe/ *m*, curtains, hangings
corto /'korto/ *a* short, brief; timid, bashful; concise; defective; stupid, dull; tongue-tied, inarticulate. **c. circuito,** *Elec.* short-circuit. **c. de alcances,** dull-witted. **c. de vista,** short-sighted
coruscar /korus'kar/ *vi* to glitter, shine
corvadura /korβa'ðura/ *f*, bend; curvature
corveta /kor'βeta/ *f*, curvet, prancing; *a, Central America* bow-legged
corvetear /korβete'ar/ *vi* to curvet
corzo /'korso; 'korθo/ *m*, roe-deer, fallow-deer
cosa /'kosa/ *f*, thing. **cualquier c.,** anything. **c. rara,** strange to relate; an extraordinary thing. **como si tal c.,** as though nothing had happened. *Inf.* **poquita c.,** a person of no account
cosaco /ko'sako/ **(-ca)** *a* and *n* Cossack
coscorrón /kosko'rron/ *m*, blow on the head, cuff
cosecha /ko'setʃa/ *f*, harvest; harvest time; reaping, gathering, lifting; yield, produce; crop, shower (of honors, etc.). **c. de vino,** vintage
cosechar /kose'tʃar/ *vi* and *vt* to harvest, reap
coseno /ko'seno/ *m*, cosine
coser /ko'ser/ *vt* to sew, stitch; join, unite; press together (lips, etc.). **c. a puñaladas,** to stab repeatedly
Cosme /'kosme/ Cosmo
cosmético /kos'metiko/ *a* and *m*, cosmetic
cósmico /'kosmiko/ *a* cosmic
cosmografía /kosmogra'fia/ *f*, cosmography
cosmógrafo /kos'mografo/ *m*, cosmographer
cosmonave /kosmo'naβe/ *f*, spaceship
cosmopolita /kosmopo'lita/ *a* and *mf* cosmopolitan
cosmopolitismo /kosmopoli'tismo/ *m*, cosmopolitanism
cosmos /'kosmos/ *m*, cosmos
cospel /kos'pel/ *m*, blank (from which to stamp coins); to ken; subway to ken
cosquillas /kos'kiyas; kos'kiʎas/ *f pl*, tickling. **hacer c.** (a), to tickle. **¿tienes c.?** Are you ticklish?
cosquillear /koskiye'ar; koskiʎe'ar/ *vt* to tickle
cosquilleo /koski'yeo; koski'ʎeo/ *m*, tickle, tickling
cosquilloso /koski'yoso; koski'ʎoso/ *a* ticklish; hypersensitive, touchy
costa /'kosta/ *f*, cost; expense; coast; *pl Law.* costs. **a c. de,** by dint of; at the cost of. **a toda c.,** at all costs
Costa del Oro, la /'kosta del 'oro, la/ the Gold Coast
Costa de Marfil /'kosta de mar'fil/ Ivory Coast
costado /kos'taðo/ *m, Anat.* side; *Mil.* flank; side; *pl* line of descent, genealogy. *Naut.* **dar el c.,** to be broadside on
costal /kos'tal/ *m*, sack, bag
costanero /kosta'nero/ *a* sloping; coast, coastal
costar /kos'tar/ *vi irr* to cost; cause. See **contar**
costarricense /kostarri'sense; kostarri'θense/ *a* and *n* Costa Rican
coste /'koste/ *m*, cost, price
costear /koste'ar/ *vt* to pay for, defray the expense of; *Naut.* coast; *Argentina* pasture; *vr* pay (for itself)
costilla /kos'tiya; kos'tiʎa/ *f*, (*Anat. Aer. Naut. Archit.*) rib; *Fig. Inf.* better half, wife; *pl Inf.* back, behind
costillaje, costillar /kosti'yahe, kosti'yar; kosti'ʎahe, kosti'ʎar/ *m, Anat.* ribs; *Naut.* ship's frame
costoso /kos'toso/ *a* expensive, costly; valuable; dear, costly, difficult
costra /'kostra/ *f*, crust; scab; rind (of cheese)
costumbre /kos'tumbre/ *f*, habit; custom
costumbrista /kostum'brista/ *mf* writer on everyday life and customs. *a* (of literary work) dealing with life and customs
costura /kos'tura/ *f*, sewing; seam; needlework; joint; riveting
costurar, costurear /kostu'rar/ *vi*, *Lat. Am.* to sew
costurera /kostu'rera/ *f*, seamstress
costurero /kostu'rero/ *m*, work-box, sewing bag
cota /'kota/ *f*, *Surv.* elevation, height; coat (of mail); quota. **c. de malla,** chain-mail
cotangente /kotan'hente/ *f*, cotangent
cotejar /kote'har/ *vt* to compare; collate
cotejo /ko'teho/ *m*, comparison; collation
cótel /'kotel/ *m*, cocktail, drink

cotelera /kote'lera/ *f*, cocktail shaker
cotidiano /koti'ðiano/ *a* daily
cotizable /koti'saβle; koti'θaβle/ *a* valued at; (of prices, shares) quoted
cotización /kotisa'sion; kotiθa'θion/ *f, Com.* quotation; *Com.* rate. **boletín de c.,** price list (of shares, etc.)
cotizar /koti'sar; koti'θar/ *vt Com.* to quote (prices, rates)
coto /'koto/ *m*, enclosed ground; boundary stone; preserve, covert; hand's breadth; end, stop, limit. **c. de caza,** game preserve
cotorra /ko'torra/ *f*, small green parrot; magpie; *Inf.* chatterbox
cotufa /ko'tufa/ *f*, earthnut; titbit; *Inf.* **pedir cotufas en el golfo,** to ask for the moon; **cotufas** *f pl Venezuela* popcorn
coyote /ko'yote/ *m*, coyote, prairie wolf; *Mexico* fixer (anyone who can pull strings to cut red tape or achieve something illegally); smuggler (of goods or people)
coyuntura /koyun'tura/ *f, Anat.* joint; juncture, occasion
coz /kos; koθ/ *f*, kick, recoil (of gun); butt (of a rifle); *Inf.* slap in the face, unprovoked rudeness. **dar coces,** to kick
craneal /krane'al/ *a* cranial
cranearse /krane'arse/ *vr, Chile* to burn the midnight oil
cráneo /'kraneo/ *m*, cranium, skull
crápula /'krapula/ *f*, drunkenness; depravity, immorality, debauchery
craquear /krake'ar/ *vt* to crack (petroleum)
crasitud /krasi'tuð/ *f*, greasiness; fatness; crassness
craso /'kraso/ *a* fat, greasy; thick; unpardonable, crass (often with *ignorancia*). *m*, fatness; ignorance
creación /krea'sion; krea'θion/ *f*, creation; universe, world; foundation; establishment; appointment (dignitaries)
creador /krea'ðor/ **(-ra)** *n* creator, originator; *m*, God. *a* creative
crear /kre'ar/ *vt* to create; found, institute, establish; make, appoint
crecer /kre'ser; kre'θer/ *vi irr* to grow; grow up; increase in size; grow longer; wax (moon); come in (of the tide); increase in value (money); *vr* become more sure of oneself; swell with pride; grow in authority. See **nacer**
creces /'kreses; 'kreθes/ *f pl*, increase, interest. **con c.,** fully, amply. **pagar con c.,** *Fig.* to pay with interest
crecida /kre'siða; kre'θiða/ *f*, swollen river or stream; food; rising (of the tide)
crecido /kre'siðo; kre'θiðo/ *a* grown up; considerable; abundant, plentiful; large; full; serious, important
crecidos /kre'siðos; kre'θiðos/ *m pl*, widening stitches (knitting)
creciente /kre'siente; kre'θiente/ *a* growing; rising (of the tide); crescent (moon). *m, Herald.* crescent. *f*, rising of the tide; crescent moon
crecimiento /kresi'miento; kreθi'miento/ *m*, growing; growth, development; increase (in value, money); waxing (of moon)
credenciales /kreðen'siales; kreðen'θiales/ *f pl*, credentials
credibilidad /kreðiβili'ðað/ *f*, credibility
crédito /'kreðito/ *m*, belief, credence; assent, acquiescence; reputation, name; favor, popularity, acceptance; *Com.* credit; *Com.* letter of credit. **créditos activos,** assets. **créditos pasivos,** liabilities. **a c.,** on credit
credo /'kreðo/ *m*, creed. *Inf.* **en un c.,** in a jiffy
credulidad /kreðuli'ðað/ *f*, credulity
crédulo /'kreðulo/ *a* credulous
creencia /kre'ensia; kre'enθia/ *f*, belief; religion, sect, faith
creer /kre'er/ *vt irr* to believe; think, consider, opine; think likely or probable. **¡Ya lo creo!** I should just think so! Rather! **creerse la divina garza,** *Mexico* to think one is God's gift to the world. **creerse descender del sobaco de Jesucristo,** to think one is

God's gift to the world. *Pres. Part.* **creyendo.** *Preterite* **creyó, creyeron.** *Imperf. Subjunc.* **creyese, etc.**

creíble /kre'iβle/ *a* credible

creído, -a /kre'iðo/ *a*, *Lat. Am.* credulous, trusting

crema /'krema/ *f*, cream (off milk); custard mold, cream, shape; face cream; cold cream; elect, flower (of society, etc.)

cremación /krema'sion; krema'θion/ *f*, cremation; burning, incineration

cremallera /krema'yera; krema'ʎera/ *f*, *Mech.* rack, ratch; zipper. **colgar la c.,** to give a house-warming

crematístico /krema'tistiko/ *a* economic, financial

crematorio /krema'torio/ *m*, crematorium. *a* burning; cremating

cremor /kre'mor/ *m*, *Chem.* cream of tartar

cremoso /kre'moso/ *a* creamy

crencha /'krentʃa/ *f*, parting (of the hair); each side of parting

crepitación /krepita'sion; krepita'θion/ *f*, crackling, sputtering; hissing; roar (of a fire); *Med.* crepitation

crepitar /krepi'tar/ *vi* to crackle; sputter; hiss; roar (of a fire); *Med.* crepitate

crepuscular /krepusku'lar/ *a* twilight

crepúsculo /kre'puskulo/ *m*, twilight, half light

cresa /'kresa/ *f*, maggot; cheese-mite; fly's egg

Creso /'kreso/ Croesus

crespo /'krespo/ *a* curly, frizzy (hair); rough (of animal's fur); curled (leaves); artificial, involved (style)

crespón /kres'pon/ *m*, crape

cresta /'kresta/ *f*, comb (of cock, etc.); tuft, topknot (birds); plume; summit, top (of mountains); crest (of a wave); *Herald.* crest

Creta /'kreta/ Crete

creta /'kreta/ *f*, chalk

cretense /kre'tense/ *a* Cretan

cretinismo /kreti'nismo/ *m*, cretinism

cretino /kre'tino/ **(-na)** *a* and *n* cretin

creyente /kre'yente/ *a* believing; religious. *mf* believer

cría /'kria/ *f*, rearing; bringing up; nursing; suckling; breeding; brood; litter

criadero /kria'ðero/ *m*, *Mineral.* vein, deposit; tree nursery, plantation; breeding farm or place. *a* prolific

criado /kri'aðo/ **(-da)** *n* servant. *a* bred, brought up (used with *bien* or *mal*, well or badly brought up)

criador /kria'ðor/ **(-ra)** *n* breeder, keeper, raiser. *a* creating; rearing; creative; fertile, rich

criandera /krian'dera/ *f*, *Lat. Am.* nursemaid, wet nurse

crianza /kri'ansa; kri'anθa/ *f*, feeding, suckling; lactation; manners. **buena** (or **mala**) **c.,** good (or bad) breeding or upbringing

criar /kri'ar/ *vt* to create; procreate; rear, educate, bring up; feed, nurse, suckle; raise (birds, animals); inspire, give rise to. **Me crié raquítico,** I grew up delicate

criatura /kria'tura/ *f*, being, creature; man, human being; infant; small child; fetus; *Fig.* puppet, tool

criba /'kriβa/ *f*, sieve, cribble

cribar /kri'βar/ *vt* to sieve; riddle (earth, etc.)

crimen /'krimen/ *m*, crime. **c. pasional,** crime of passion

criminal /krimi'nal/ *a* and *m*, criminal

criminalidad /kriminali'ðað/ *f*, guilt; crime ratio; delinquency

criminalista /krimina'lista/ *mf* criminal lawyer; criminologist

criminología /kriminolo'hia/ *f*, criminology

crin /krin/ *f*, horsehair; (gen. *pl*) mane

crinolina /krino'lina/ *f*, crinoline

crío /'krio/ *m*, *Inf.* kid, brat

criollo /'krioyo; 'krioʎo/ **(-lla)** *n* creole, descendant of Europeans born in colonial Spanish America. *a* creole

cripta /'kripta/ *f*, crypt

criptografía /kriptogra'fia/ *f*, cryptography

criquet /kri'ket/ *m*, *Sports.* cricket

crisantemo /krisan'temo/ *m*, chrysanthemum

crisis /'krisis/ *f*, crisis. **c. de desarrollo,** growing pains. **c. de vivienda,** housing shortage

crisma /'krisma/ *m*, or *f*, chrism

crisol /kri'sol/ *m*, crucible; melting pot

crispado /kris'paðo/ *a* stiffened

crispar /kris'par/ *vt* to cause to contract or twitch; *vr* twitch. *Inf.* **Se me crispan los nervios,** My nerves are all on edge

cristal /kri'stal/ *m*, crystal; glass; windowpane; mirror; water. **c. tallado,** cut glass

cristalería /kristale'ria/ *f*, glassware; glass manufacture; glass panes; glass and china shop

cristalino /krista'lino/ *a* crystalline. *m*, lens (of the eye)

cristalización /kristalisa'sion; kristaliθa'θion/ *f*, crystallization

cristalizar /kristali'sar; kristali'θar/ *vi* to crystallize; *Fig.* take shape; *vt* cause to crystallize

cristalografía /kristalogra'fia/ *f*, crystallography

cristiandad /kristian'dað/ *f*, Christendom

cristianismo /kristia'nismo/ *m*, Christianity; Christendom

cristianizar /kristiani'sar; kristiani'θar/ *vt* to convert to Christianity, christianize

cristiano /kris'tiano/ **(-na)** *a* and *n* Christian. *a Inf.* watered (of wine). *m*, *Inf.* Spanish (contrasted with other languages); *Inf.* person

cristino /kris'tino/ **(-na)** *a* and *n* supporting, or follower of, Queen Regent Maria Cristina during Carlist wars

Cristo /'kristo/ *m*, Christ; **cristo,** crucifix. *Inf.* **donde C. dio las tres voces,** in the middle of nowhere

cristus /'kristus/ *m*, Christ-cross; alphabet. **no saber el c.,** to be extremely ignorant

criterio /kri'terio/ *m*, criterion, standard; judgment; discernment; opinion. **a c. de,** in the opinion of. **según mi c.,** in my opinion

crítica /'kritika/ **(a)** *f*, criticism (of)

criticar /kriti'kar/ *vt* to criticize; censure, find fault with, blame

crítico /'kritiko/ *a* critical; censorious; dangerous, difficult; *Med.* critical. *m*, critic; fault-finder

criticón /kriti'kon/ **(-ona)** *a* censorious, hyper-critical. *n* fault-finder

Croacia /kro'asia; kro'aθia/ Croatia

croar /kro'ar/ *vi* (frog) to croak

croata /kro'ata/ *a* and *mf* Croatian

croché /kro'tʃe/ *m*, crochet work

crol /krol/ *m*, crawl (swimming)

cromado /kro'maðo/ *a* chromium-plated

cromático /kro'matiko/ *a* chromatic

crómico /'kromiko/ *a* chromic

cromo /'kromo/ *m*, chrome; chromium; chromolithograph

crónica /'kronika/ *f*, chronicle; diary of events

crónico /'kroniko/ *a* chronic; inveterate

cronista /kro'nista/ *mf* chronicler

cronología /kronolo'hia/ *f*, chronology

cronológico /krono'lohiko/ *a* chronological

cronómetro /kro'nometro/ *m*, stop-watch

croqueta /kro'keta/ *f*, croquette

croquis /'krokis/ *m*, sketch, outline, drawing. **c. de nivel,** (optical) foresight

crótalo /'krotalo/ *m*, rattlesnake; snapper (kind of castanet)

cruce /'kruse; 'kruθe/ *m*, crossing; point of intersection; crossroads

crucero /kru'sero; kru'θero/ *m*, *Eccl.* cross-bearer; crossroads; *Archit.* transept; *Astron.* Cross; *Naut.* cruiser

crucificar /krusifi'kar; kruθifi'kar/ *vt* to crucify; *Fig. Inf.* torment, torture

crucifijo /krusi'fiho; kruθi'fiho/ *m*, crucifix

crucifixión /krusifik'sion; kruθifik'sion/ *f*, crucifixion

crucigrama /krusi'grama; kruθi'grama/ *m*, crossword puzzle

cruda /'kruða/ *f*, *Mexico* hangover

crudelísimo /kruðe'lisimo/ *a sup* **cruel,** most cruel, exceedingly cruel

crudeza /kru'ðesa; kru'ðeθa/ *f*, rawness, uncookedness; unripeness; rawness (silk, etc.); crudeness; harshness; *Inf.* boasting

crudo /'kruðo/ *a* uncooked, raw; green, unripe; indi-

gestible; raw, natural, unbleached; harsh, cruel; cold, raw; *Inf.* boastful. **crudos de petróleo,** *m pl* crude oil
crueldad /kruel'daθ/ *f,* cruelty; harshness
cruento /'kruento/ *a* bloody
crujía /kru'hia/ *f,* passage, corridor; *Naut.* midship gangway
crujidero /kruhi'θero/ *a* crackling; creaking; crispy; clattering; rustling; chattering
crujido /kru'hiθo/ *m,* creak, crack, crackling, rustle
crujir /kru'hir/ *vi* to creak, crackle, rustle
crup /krup/ *m,* croup
crupié /kru'pie/ *m,* croupier
crustáceo /krus'taseo; krus'taθeo/ *a* and *m,* crustacean
cruz /krus; kruθ/ *f,* cross; tails (of coin); withers (of animals); insignia, decoration; affliction, trouble; *Astron.* Southern Cross; *Print.* dagger, obelisk, obelus. **c. doble,** diesis, double dagger. **c. de mayo,** May cross. **c. gamada,** swastika. *Inf.* **¡C. y raya!** An end to this! **en c.,** in the shape of a cross. *Inf.* **hacerse cruces,** to be left speechless, be dumbfounded
cruza /'krusa; 'kruθa/ *f, Lat. Am.* intersection
cruzada /kru'saða; kru'θaða/ *f,* crusade; crossroads; campaign
cruzado /kru'saðo; kru'θaðo/ *a* cross; double-breasted (of coats). *m,* crusader; member of military order
cruzamiento /krusa'miento; kruθa'miento/ *m,* crossing; intersection
cruzar /kru'sar; kru'θar/ *vt* to cross; intersect; interbreed; bestow a cross upon; *Naut.* cruise; *Chile, Peru* quarrel with; *vr* take part in a crusade; cross one another; coincide; *Geom.* intersect
cu /ku/ *f,* name of the letter Q
cuaco /'kuako/ *m, Lat. Am.* horse
cuacuac /kua'kuak/ *m,* quack (of a duck)
cuaderna /kua'ðerna/ *f, Naut.* ship's frame, timber; double fours (backgammon)
cuaderno /kua'ðerno/ *m,* notebook, jotter, account book; *Inf.* card pack. *Naut.* **c. de bitácora,** logbook
cuadra /'kuaðra/ *f,* stable; ward, dormitory; hall, large room; quarter of a mile; *Lat. Am.* block (of houses)
cuadrado /kua'ðraðo/ *a* square; perfect, exact. *m,* square; (*Mil. Math.*) square; window-frame; clock (of a stocking)
cuadragésima /kuaðra'hesima/ *f,* Quadragesima
cuadragésimo /kuaðra'hesimo/ *a* fortieth
cuadrángulo /kua'ðraŋgulo/ *m,* quadrangle
cuadrante /kua'ðrante/ *m,* quadrant; dial, face
cuadrar /kua'ðrar/ *vt* (*Math.*) to square; make square; *vi* correspond, tally; fit, be appropriate. *vr Mil.* stand at attention; *Fig. Inf.* dig one's heels in
cuadrática /kua'ðratika/ *f,* quadratic equation
cuadrático /kua'ðratiko/ *a* quadratic
cuadratura /kuaðra'tura/ *f,* squareness; (*Math. Astron.*) quadrature
cuadrienio /kua'ðrienio/ *m,* space of four years
cuadriga /kua'ðriga/ *f,* quadriga
cuadrilátero /kuaðri'latero/ *m,* quadrilateral; boxing ring. *a* quadrilateral
cuadrilla /kua'ðriya; kua'ðriʎa/ *f,* gang; company, band, group; police patrol; quadrille (dance); matadors and their assistants (at a bull fight). **c. carrillana,** track gang
cuadrilongo /kuaðri'loŋgo/ *a* and *m,* oblong
cuadrimotor /kuaðrimo'tor/ *a* Aer. four-engined
cuadrivio /kua'ðriβio/ *m,* quadrivium
cuadro /'kuaðro/ *m,* square; picture-frame; frame (of bicycle); flowerbed; *Theat.* tableau, scene; spectacle, sight; board (of instruments); description (in novel, etc.); *Mil.* command, officers; square (of troops). **c. de distribución,** *Elec.* main switchboard. **c. enrejado,** play pen. **cuadro de costumbres,** word-picture of everyday life and customs. **cuadro vivo,** tableau vivant. **a cuadros,** checked, in squares
cuadrúpedo /kua'ðrupeðo/ (**-da**) *a* and *n* quadruped
cuadruple /kua'ðruple/ *a* quadruple
cuadruplicar /kuaðrupli'kar/ *vt* to quadruple
cuajada /kua'haða/ *f,* curd (of milk)

cuajar /kua'har/ *m,* maw (of a ruminant)
cuajar /kua'har/ *vt* to coagulate; curdle; *vi Inf.* achieve, get away with; *vr* be coagulated or curdled; *Inf.* be packed or chock full; get stuck (e.g. a piece of food in one's throat)
cuajarón /kuaha'ron/ *m,* clot (of blood, etc.)
cuajo /'kuaho/ *m,* rennet; coagulation; curdling; *Anat.* abomasum
cual /kual/ *rel. pron* sing. *mf* and *neut pl* **cuales,** which; who; such as (e.g. **Le detuvieron sucesos cuales suelen ocurrir,** He was detained by events such as usually happen). **a c. mas,** vying (with) (e.g. *Los dos canónigos a c. más grueso,* The two canons each fatter (vying in fatness) than the other). **c.** is used with *def. art* **el (la, lo, los, las) cual(es),** who; which, when the antecedent is a noun (e.g. *Juan saltó en el barco, el c. zarpó en seguida,* John jumped into the boat which sailed at once). **por lo c.,** for which reason. *adv* like (gen. literary or poet.). **¿cuál? interr. pron** (no article) which? what? e.g. *Aquí tienes dos cuadros, ¿cuál de ellos te gusta?* Here are two pictures, which one do you like? Also expresses an implicit question, e.g. *No sé cuál te guste,* I don't know which you will like. **¡cuál!** *adv interj* how! **c.... c. indef pron** some... some
cualesquier /kuales'kier/ *a pl* de **cualquier**
cualesquiera /kuales'kiera/ *a pl* de **cualquiera**
cualidad /kuali'ðaθ/ *f,* quality; characteristic; talent
cualitativo /kualita'tiβo/ *a* qualitative
cualquier /kual'kier/ *abb* of **cualquiera,** any; *pl* **cualesquier.** Only used as abb. *before* noun
cualquiera /kual'kiera/ *a mf* any, e.g. *una canción c.,* any song. *pron* anybody, each, anyone whatsoever, whoever (e.g. *¡C. diría que no te gusta!* Anyone would say you don't like it!) *Inf.* **un c.,** a nobody
cuán /ku'an/ *adv* how (e.g. *¡C. bello es!* How beautiful it is!). Used only before *a* or *adv.* Abbr. of **cuánto**
cuando /'kuando/ *adv* when; if. *interr* **¿cuándo?** *conjunc* although; since; sometimes; *prep* during (e.g. *c. la guerra,* during the war) **c. más,** at most, at best. **c. menos,** at the least. **c. no,** if not (e.g. *Es agnóstica cuando no atea,* She's an agnostic, if not an atheist) **de c. en c.,** from time to time
cuandoquiera /kuando'kiera/ *adv* whenever
cuanta, teoría de la /'kuanta, teo'ria de la/ *f,* quantum theory
cuantía /kuan'tia/ *f,* quantity, amount; importance, rank, distinction
cuantiar /kuan'tiar/ *vt* to value, estimate; tax
cuantidad /kuanti'ðaθ/ *f,* quantity
cuantioso /kuan'tioso/ *a* large, considerable; numerous; plentiful, abundant
cuantitativo /kuantita'tiβo/ *a* quantitative
cuanto /'kuanto/ *a* as much as, all the; *pl* as many as, all the (e.g. *Te daré cuantas muñecas tengas allí,* I'll give you all the dolls you see there). *a. correlative* the... the, as... as (e.g. *C. más tanto, mejor,* The more the better). **cuánto,** *a* and *pron interr* and *interj* how much; *pl* how many (e.g. *¡Cuánto tiempo sin verla!* How long without seeing her!) *pron neut* **cuanto,** as much as, all that you wish). *adv* **cuanto,** as soon as. **c. antes,** as soon as possible. **c. a** or **en c. a,** concerning. *adv* and *conjunc* **c. más,** all the more (e.g. *Se lo diré c. más que tenía esa intención,* I shall tell him all the more because I meant to do so). *adv* **en c.,** as soon as, immediately (e.g. *Lo haré en c. venga,* I shall do it immediately he comes). **en c. a,** with regard to. **por c.,** inasmuch, for this reason. *adv interr* **¿Cuánto?** How much? How long? *adv interj* How! How much! (e.g. *¡Cuánto me gustaría ir!* How much I should like to go!)
cuaquerismo /kuake'rismo/ *m,* Quakerism
cuáquero /'kuakero/ (**-ra**) *n* Quaker
cuarenta /kua'renta/ *a* and *m,* forty; fortieth. **esas son otras cuarenta** *Argentina, Peru* That's a different story, that's a horse of another color
cuarentena /kuaren'tena/ *f,* fortieth; period of forty days, months or years; Lent; quarantine
cuarentón /kuaren'ton/ (**-ona**) *n* person forty years old

cuaresma /kua'resma/ *f*, Lent
cuaresmal /kuares'mal/ *a* Lenten
cuarta /'kuarta/ *f*, quarter, fourth; hand's breadth; *Mus.* fourth; *Astron.* quadrant
cuarteadura /kuartea'ðura/ *f*, crack
cuartear /kuarte'ar/ *vt* to quarter, divide into quarters; cut or divide into pieces
cuartel /kuar'tel/ *m*, barracks; *Naut.* hatch; quarter, fourth; *Herald.* quarter; district, ward; flowerbed; *Inf.* house, accommodation; *Mil.* quarter, mercy; *Mil.* billet, station. *Mil.* **c. general,** general headquarters
cuartelada /kuarte'laða/ *f*, *Naut.* quarter; military rebellion, military uprising, mutiny
cuartelazo /kuarte'laso; kuarte'laθo/ *m*, military rebellion, military uprising, mutiny
cuarteta /kuar'teta/ *f*, quatrain
cuarteto /kuar'teto/ *m*, *Mus.* quartet; *Poet.* quatrain
cuartilla /kuar'tiya; kuar'tiλa/ *f*, sheet of paper; liquid measure; quarter of an arroba; pastern (horses)
cuarto /'kuarto/ *m*, room; quarter, fourth; point (of compass); watch (on battleships); *Astron.* quarter, phase; portion, quarter; joint (of meat); *pl* quarters (of animals); *Inf.* penny, farthing. *a* quarter, fourth. **c. creciente,** first phase (of moon). **c. de hora,** quarter of an hour. **c. doble** *Mexico* double room. **c. sencillo** *Mexico* single room. **en c.,** *Print.* in quarto. *Inf.* **no tener un c.,** to be broke
cuarzo /'kuarso; 'kuarθo/ *m*, quartz
cuasidelito /kuasiðe'lito/ *m*, *Law.* technical offense
cuasimodo /kuasi'moðo/ *m*, *Eccl.* Low Sunday, Quasimodo
cuatrillón /kuatri'yon; kuatri'λon/ *m*, quadrillion
cuatrimestre /kuatri'mestre/ *a* of four months' duration. *m*, space of four months
cuatrimotor /kuatrimo'tor/ *m*, *Aer.* four-engine airplane
cuatrisílabo /kuatri'silaβo/ *a* quadrisyllabic
cuatro /'kuatro/ *a* four; fourth. *m*, figure four; fourth (of days of months); playing-card with four spots; *Mus.* quartet. **el c. de mayo,** the fourth of May. **Son las c.,** It is four o'clock
cuatrocientos /kuatro'sientos; kuatro'θientos/ *a* four hundred; four hundredth.
cuba /'kuβa/ *f*, barrel, cask; tub, vat; *Inf.* pot-bellied person; *Inf.* drunkard, toper
Cuba /'kuβa/ Cuba
cubano /ku'βano/ **(-na)** *a* and *n* Cuban
cubería /kuβe'ria/ *f*, cooperage
cubeta /ku'βeta/ *f*, *dim* keg, small cask; bucket, pail; *Photo.* developing dish
cubicar /kuβi'kar/ *vt* *Math.* to cube; *Geom.* measure the volume of
cúbico /'kuβiko/ *a* cubic
cubículo /ku'βikulo/ *m*, cubicle
cubierta /ku'βierta/ *f*, cover; envelope; casing; deck (of ship); tire cover; book-jacket; pretext, excuse. **c. de escotilla,** *Naut.* companion-hatch. **c. de paseo,** promenade deck
cubierto /ku'βierto/ *m*, cover, place at table; course (of a meal); table d'hôte, complete meal; roof. **un c. de doscientas pesetas,** a two hundred peseta meal
cubil /ku'βil/ *m*, lair, den (of animals)
cubilete /kuβi'lete/ *m*, *Cul.* mold; dice box; conjurer's cup
cubismo /ku'βismo/ *m*, cubism
cubista /ku'βista/ *mf* cubist. *a* cubistic
cubo /'kuβo/ *m*, bucket, pail; *Mech.* socket; *Math.* cube; hub (of a wheel); mill-pond
cubrecama /kuβre'kama/ *m*, bedspread
cubrimiento /kuβri'miento/ *m*, covering
cubrir /ku'βrir/ *vt* to cover; *Mil.* defend; spread over, extend over; conceal, hide; *Com.* cover; dissemble; *Archit.* roof; *vr* cover one's head; pay, meet (debts, etc.); cover or protect oneself (by insurance, etc.). *Past Part.* **cubierto**
cucaña /ku'kaɲa/ *f*, greasy pole; *Inf.* snip, cinch, bargain
cucaracha /kuka'ratʃa/ *f*, cockroach
cuchara /ku'tʃara/ *f*, spoon; ladle; *Naut.* boat scoop; scoop, dipper. *Fig.* **meter c.,** to stick one's oar in

cucharada /kutʃa'raða/ *f*, spoonful; ladleful
cucharita /kutʃa'rita/ *f*, *Lat. Am.* teaspoonful
cuchí /'kutʃi/ *m*, *Peru* hog
cúchi /'kutʃi/ *a inf* *Venezuela* cute, sweet
cuchicheador /kutʃitʃea'ðor/ **(-ra)** *n* whisperer
cuchichear /kutʃitʃe'ar/ *vi* to whisper
cuchicheo /kutʃi'tʃeo/ *m*, whisper; whispering; murmur
cuchillada /kutʃi'yaða; kutʃi'λaða/ *f*, knife thrust or wound; *pl* (in sleeves, etc.) slashes; fight, blows
cuchillero /kutʃi'yero; kutʃi'λero/ *m*, cutler
cuchillo /ku'tʃiyo; ku'tʃiλo/ *m*, knife; *Sew.* gore, gusset (gen. *pl*); authority, power; anything triangular in shape. **pasar a c.,** to put to the sword
cuclillas, en /ku'kliyas, en; ku'kliλas, en/ *adv* in a squatting position
cuclillo /ku'kliyo; ku'kliλo/ *m*, *Ornith.* cuckoo; *Inf.* cuckold
cuco /'kuko/ *a* *Inf.* pretty, cute; crafty, smart
Cucufo /'kukufo/ *m*, the Devil
cuculla /ku'kuya; ku'kuλa/ *f*, cowl, hood
cucurucho /kuku'rutʃo/ *m*, paper cornet
cueca /'kueka/ *f*, *Chile* cueca (Chilean dance)
cuello /'kueyo; 'kueλo/ *m*, *Anat.* neck; neck (of bottle, etc.); *Sew.* neck; collar; necklet (of fur, etc.)
cuenca /'kuenka/ *f*, socket (of eye); *Geog.* catchment-basin; gorge, deep valley. **c. de un río,** river-basin
cuenta /'kuenta/ *f*, count, counting; calculation; account; bead; charge, responsibility; reckoning; explanation, reason; *Com.* bill. **c. a cero, c. a la inversa, c. atrás,** countdown. **c. corriente,** savings, day-to-day account. **cuentas alegres, cuentas galanas,** *inf* idle dreams, illusions. **c. pendiente,** outstanding account. *Inf.* **caer en la c.,** to tumble to. **darse c. de,** to realize. **llevar la c.,** to reckon, keep account. **sin c.,** countless. **tener en c.,** to bear in mind
cuentacorrentista /kuentakorren'tista/ *mf* one who has a bank account
cuentagotas /kuenta'gotas/ *m*, dropper, dropping tube
cuentakilómetros /kuentaki'lometros/ *m*, speedometer
cuentapasos /kuenta'pasos/ *m*, pedometer
cuentista /kuen'tista/ *mf* storyteller; *Inf.* gossip
cuento /'kuento/ *m*, story, tale; narrative; calculation; *Inf.* gossip, fairytale; *Math.* million. **c. de viejas,** old wives' tale. *Fig.* *Inf.* **dejarse de cuentos,** to go straight to the point. *Inf.* **Va de c.,** It is told, they say
cuerda /'kuerða/ *f*, rope; cord; string; *Geom.* chord; *Mus.* string; catgut; chain (of clock); *Mus.* chord; vocal range. **dar c.** (**a),** to wind up (a watch); lead on, make talk. **de cuerdas cruzadas,** overstrung (of a piano)
cuerdo /'kuerðo/ *a* sane; prudent; levelheaded
cuerno /'kuerno/ *m*, *Anat.* horn; feeler, antenna; *Mus.* horn; horn (of the moon). **c. de abundancia,** horn of plenty. *Inf.* **poner en los cuernos de la luna,** to praise to the skies
cuero /'kuero/ *m*, hide, pelt; leather. **c. charolado,** patent leather. **en cueros,** stark naked
cuerpo /'kuerpo/ *m*, *Anat.* body or trunk; flesh (as opposed to spirit); bodice; volume, book; main portion; collection; size, volume; physical appearance; corpse; group, assembly; corporation, association; *Geom.* solid; *Chem.* element; thickness, density; *Mil.* corps. **c. de bomberos,** fire brigade. **c. de guardia,** guardhouse. **c. de la vida,** staff of life; *Inf.* **dar con el c. en tierra,** to fall flat. **de c. entero,** *Art.* full-length (portrait). **en c.,** without a coat, lightly clad. **un c. a c.,** a clinch (in wrestling)
cuervo /'kuerβo/ *m*, raven; crow
cuesco /'kuesko/ *m*, stone, seed, pip
cuesta /'kuesta/ *f*, slope, incline, gradient. **c. abajo (arriba),** down (up) hill. **a cuestas,** on one's back; having the responsibility of
cuestión /kues'tion/ *f*, problem, question; quarrel, disagreement; affair, matter; torture
cuestionable /kuestio'naβle/ *a* doubtful, questionable
cuestionar /kuestio'nar/ *vt* to discuss, debate
cuestionario /kuestio'nario/ *m*, questionnaire

cueva /'kueβa/ f, cave, cavern; basement, cellar. *Fig.* **c. de ladrones,** den of thieves

cuévano /'kueβano/ m, hamper, basket

cui /kui/ m, *Lat. Am.* guinea pig

cuico, -a /'kuiko/ mf, *Argentina, Chile* foreigner, outsider; *Mexico, informal* cop (police officer)

cuidado /kui'ðaðo/ m, carefulness, pains; attention; charge, care, responsibility; anxiety, fear. *interj* ¡**C.!** Careful! Look out! **Me tiene sin c. su opinión,** I am not interested in his (your) opinion. *Inf.* **estar al c. de,** to be under the direction of. **estar de c.,** to be dangerously ill

cuidadoso /kuiða'ðoso/ **(de)** a careful (about or with); anxious (about); concerned (with); watchful; conscientious

cuidar /kui'ðar/ vt to care for; tend; take care of, look after; mind, be careful of; vr look after oneself

cuita /'kuita/ f, misfortune, anxiety, trouble

cuitado /kui'taðo/ a unfortunate, worried; timid, bashful, humble

cuitla /'kuitla/ f, *Mexico* poultry manure

culata /ku'lata/ f, *Anat.* haunch; butt (of fire-arms); back, rear; *Auto.* sump. **salir por la c.,** to backfire

culebra /ku'leβra/ f, snake; *Inf.* trick, joke; *Inf.* sudden uproar. **hacer c.,** to stagger along

culebrear /kuleβre'ar/ vi to wriggle; grovel; meander, wind

culí /ku'li/ m, coolie

culinario /kuli'nario/ a culinary

culminación /kulmina'sion; kulmina'θion/ f, culmination, peak; *Astron.* zenith

culminante /kulmi'nante/ a culminating; *Fig.* outstanding

culminar /kulmi'nar/ vi to culminate (in)

culo /'kulo/ m, buttocks, seat; rump; anus; base, bottom. **c. de lámpara,** *Archit.* pendant; *Print.* tail-piece

culpa /'kulpa/ f, fault; blame. **echar la c.** (a), to blame. **por c. de,** through the fault of. **tener la c.,** to be to blame

culpabilidad /kulpaβili'ðað/ f, guilt

culpable /kul'paβle/ a culpable

culpado /kul'paðo/ **(-da)** n culprit

culpar /kul'par/ vt to blame, accuse; criticize, censure

cultígeno /kul'tiheno/ m, cultigen

cultismo /kul'tismo/ m, cultism (Gongorism); learned form, learnedism, learned word

cultivación /kultiβa'sion; kultiβa'θion/ f, cultivation; culture

cultivador /kultiβa'ðor/ **(-ra)** n cultivator; planter

cultivar /kulti'βar/ vt to cultivate; develop; exercise, practice (professions); culture (bacteriology)

cultivo /kul'tiβo/ m, cultivation; farming; culture (bacteriological)

culto /'kulto/ a cultivated; educated; cultured; elegant, artificial (style). m, worship; cult; religion; creed; homage; religious service (Protestant)

cultura /kul'tura/ f, cultivation; culture. **de c. universitaria,** college-educated

cultural /kultu'ral/ a cultural

cumbre /'kumbre/ f, peak, crest, summit; *Fig.* zenith, acme

cumpleaños /kumple'aɲos/ m, birthday

cumplidamente /kumpliða'mente/ adv fully, completely

cumplido /kum'pliðo/ a complete; thorough; long; plentiful; courteous, punctilious; fulfilled. m, courtesy, attention, formality. **gastar cumplidos,** to stand on ceremony; be formal

cumplimentar /kumplimen'tar/ vt to congratulate; perform, carry out

cumplimentero /kumplimen'tero/ a overcomplimentary; *Inf.* gushing

cumplimiento /kumpli'miento/ m, fulfillment, performance; courtesy, formality; completion; complement

cumplir /kum'plir/ vt to perform, carry into effect; reach (of age); keep (promises). **c. su palabra,** to keep one's word; vi perform a duty; expire, fall due; serve the required term of military service; be neces-

sary, behove; vr be fulfilled, come true. **por c.,** as a matter of form

cumulativo /kumula'tiβo/ a cumulative

cúmulo /'kumulo/ m, heap, pile; great many, host, mass, myriad; (cloud) cumulus, thunderhead

cuna /'kuna/ f, cradle; foundling hospital; birthplace; origin, genesis; *pl* cat's cradle (game)

cundir /kun'dir/ vi to extend, spread (gen. liquids); be diffused (news); expand, grow

cuneco, -a /ku'neko/ mf *Venezuela* baby of the family

cuneiforme /kunei'forme/ a wedge-shaped, cuneiform

cunero /ku'nero/ **(-ra)** n foundling, orphan

cuña /'kuɲa/ f, wedge; *Mech.* quoin. *Mil.* **practicar una c.,** to make a wedge

cuñada /ku'ɲaða/ f, sister-in-law

cuñado /ku'ɲaðo/ m, brother-in-law

cuño /'kuɲo/ m, die, stamp; *Fig.* impression; mark on silver, hallmark. **de viejo c.,** old-guard (e.g. socialites)

cuota /'kuota/ f, quota; share; subscription; fee

cupé /ku'pe/ m, coupé

Cupido /ku'piðo/ m, Cupid; philanderer

cuplé /ku'ple/ m, couplet; song

cupo /'kupo/ m, quota; share; tax rate; *Mil.* contingent

cupón /ku'pon/ m, coupon

cúpula /'kupula/ f, *Archit.* dome, cupola; *Bot.* cup

cuquería /kuke'ria/ f, craftiness, smartness; cuteness, prettiness

cura /'kura/ m, parish priest; *Inf.* Roman Catholic priest. f, cure (e.g. *La enfermedad tiene c.,* The illness can be cured); healing; remedy. **c. de almas,** cure of souls. **primera c.,** first aid. *inf* **c. de misa y olla,** ignorant priest

curación /kura'sion; kura'θion/ f, cure, remedy; healing

curador /kura'ðor/ **(-ra)** n curer, salter. m, (*Scots Law.*) curator. a curing; healing

curaduría /kuraðu'ria/ f, *Law.* guardianship

curanderismo /kurande'rismo/ m, quackery, charlatanism; quack medicine

curandero /kuran'dero/ **(-ra)** n quack doctor; charlatan

curar /ku'rar/ vi to heal, cure; (*with de*) take care of; care about, mind; vt cure, salt; treat medically (bandage, give medicines, etc.); cure (leather); bleach (cloth); season (timber); *Fig.* remedy (an evil)

curasao /kura'sao/ m, curaçao (drink)

curativo /kura'tiβo/ a curative

curato /ku'rato/ m, *Eccl.* parish, cure

Curazao /kura'sao; kura'θao/ Curaçao

cúrcuma /'kurkuma/ f, turmeric

cureña /ku'reɲa/ f, gun-carriage

curia /'kuria/ f, *Law.* bar; tribunal; *Eccl.* curia; care, attention

curiana /ku'riana/ f, cockroach

curiche /ku'ritʃe/ m, swamp

curiosear /kuriose'ar/ vi to pry; be curious (about); meddle, be a busybody

curiosidad /kuriosi'ðað/ f, curiosity; inquisitiveness, meddlesomeness; neatness; carefulness, conscientiousness; curio

curioso /ku'rioso/ a curious; inquisitive; interesting; odd; neat, clean; conscientious, careful

Curita /ku'rita/ f, *trademark* Band-Aid

cursado /kur'saðo/ a experienced; versed

cursante /kur'sante/ m, student

cursar /kur'sar/ vt to frequent, visit; do repeatedly; study, attend classes, take courses (e.g. *¿En qué escuela cursas?* At what school are you studying?); expedite (public admin.)

cursi /'kursi/ a *Inf.* vulgar, in bad taste; loud, crude

cursilería /kursile'ria/ f, *Inf.* vulgarity, bad taste

cursillo /kur'siyo; kur'siʎo/ m, minicourse, short course; short series of lectures

cursiva /kur'siβa/ f, italics. **en c.,** in italics, italicized

cursivo /kur'siβo/ a cursive

curso /'kurso/ m, course, direction; duration, passage

(time); progress; route; course of study; academic year; succession, series; *Com.* tender

curtido /kur'tiðo/ *m*, tanning; leather; tanned leather (gen. *pl*)

curtidor /kurti'ðor/ *m*, tanner

curtiduría /kurtiðu'ria/ *f*, tannery

curtimiento /kurti'miento/ *m*, tanning; effect of weather on the complexion; toughening-up; hardening

curtir /kur'tir/ *vt* to tan; *Fig.* bronze (complexions); make hardy, harden up; *vr* be weatherbeaten; be hardy. *Inf.* **estar curtido en,** to be experienced in; be expert at

curul /ku'rul/ *a* **curule** *m*, seat (in parliament)

curva /'kurβa/ *f*, curve; bend. *Surv.* **c. de nivel,** contour line

curvatura, curvidad /kurβa'tura, kurβi'ðað/ *f*, curvature

curvo /'kurβo/ *a* curved; bent. *m*, curve

cusma /'kusma/ *f*, *Lat. Am.* sleeveless shirt, tunic

cúspide /'kuspiðe/ *f*, peak, summit; (*Geom. Archit.*) cusp

custodia /kus'toðia/ *f*, custody; guardianship, care; *Eccl.* monstrance; custodian, keeper; guardian; guard

custodiar /kusto'ðiar/ *vt* to watch, guard; look after, care for; *Naut.* convoy

custodio /kus'toðio/ *a* guardian; guarding; custodial. *m*, custodian; guard. **angel c.,** guardian angel

cutama /ku'tama/ *f*, *Argentina* blanket; *Chile* bag, sack

cutáneo /ku'taneo/ *a* cutaneous, skin

cúter /'kuter/ *m*, *Naut.* cutter

cutícula /ku'tikula/ *f*, cuticle

cutis /'kutis/ *m*, complexion; skin (sometimes *f*)

cuyo /'kuyo/ (**cuya, cuyos, cuyas**) *rel pron poss* whose, of which (e.g. *el viejo cuya barba era más blanca que la nieve,* the old man whose beard was whiter than snow). *interr* **¿Cúyo?** Whose? (e.g. *¿Cúyos son estos lápices?* Whose pencils are these?) (gen. **de quién** or **de quiénes** is used rather than **cúyo**). *m*, beau, lover

D

dable /'daβle/ *a* practicable, possible

daca /'daka/ Give me!

dactilografía /daktilogra'fia/ *f*, typewriting

dactilógrafo /dakti'lografo/ (**-fa**) *n* typist

dactilología /daktilolo'hia/ *f*, dactylology

dadista /da'ðista/ *mf*, *Mexico* gambler

dádiva /'daðiβa/ *f*, gift, present

dadivoso /daði'βoso/ *a* generous, liberal

dado /'daðo/ *m*, die; *Archit.* dado. *conjunc* **d. que,** given that, supposing that. **cargar los dados,** to load the dice

dador /da'ðor/ (**-ra**) *n* giver, donor. *m*, *Com.* bearer; *Com.* drawer (of a bill of exchange)

daga /'daga/ *f*, dagger

daguerrotipo /dagerro'tipo/ *m*, daguerreotype

daifa /'daifa/ *f*, concubine

¡dale! /'dale/ *interj* Stop! No more about...!

dalia /'dalia/ *f*, *Bot.* dahlia

dallar /da'yar; da'ʎar/ *vt* to scythe (grass)

dalle /'daye; 'daʎe/ *m*, scythe

dálmata /'dalmata/ *a* and *mf* Dalmatian

daltoniano /dalto'niano/ *a* color-blind

daltonismo /dalto'nismo/ *m*, color-blindness

dama /'dama/ *f*, lady; noblewoman; lady-in-waiting; lady-love; mistress, concubine; queen (chess); king (checkers); *Theat.* **d. primera,** leading lady

damajuana /dama'huana/ *f*, demijohn

damas /'damas/ *f pl*, checkers (game)

damasceno /damas'seno; damas'θeno/ (**-na**) *a* and *n* Damascene

Damasco /da'masko/ Damascus

damasco /da'masko/ *m*, damask

damasquino /damas'kino/ *a* damascened (swords, etc.)

damería /dame'ria/ *f*, prudery, affectation

damisela /dami'sela/ *f*, damsel; *Inf.* woman of the town

damnificar /damnifi'kar/ *vt* to injure

dandi /'dandi/ *m*, dandy

dandismo /dan'dismo/ *m*, dandyism

danés /da'nes/ (**-esa**) *a* Danish. *n* Dane. *m*, Danish (language)

danta /'danta/ *f*, *Zool.* tapir

dantesco /dan'tesko/ *a* Dantesque

danubiano /da'nuβiano/ *a* Danubian

Danubio, el /da'nuβio, el/ the Danube

danza /'dansa; 'danθa/ *f*, dance; set (of dancers); *Fig. Inf.* dirty business. **d. de arcos,** dance of the arches. **d. de cintas,** maypole dance. **d. de monos,** amusing spectacle

danzador /dansa'ðor; danθa'ðor/ (**-ra**) *n* dancer; *a* dancing

danzante /dan'sante; dan'θante/ (**-ta**) *n* dancer; *Fig. Inf.* live wire; *Inf.* busybody

danzar /dan'sar; dan'θar/ *vt* and *vi* to dance; *vi* jump up and down, rattle; *Inf.* interfere, meddle

danzarín /dansa'rin; danθa'rin/ (**-ina**) *n* good dancer; *Inf.* meddler; *Inf.* playboy

danzón /dan'son; dan'θon/ *m*, Cuban dance

dañable /da'ɲaβle/ *a* harmful; worthy of condemnation

dañado /da'ɲaðo/ *a* evil, perverse; damned; spoiled, damaged

dañador /daɲa'ðor/ (**-ra**) *a* harmful. *n* injurer, offender

dañar /da'ɲar/ *vt* to hurt, harm; damage, spoil; *vr* spoil, deteriorate

dañino /da'ɲino/ *a* destructive (often of animals); hurtful, harmful. **animales dañinos,** vermin, pests

daño /'daɲo/ *m*, hurt; damage; loss. *Law.* **daños y perjuicios,** damages. **hacerse d.,** to hurt oneself

dañoso /da'ɲoso/ *a* hurtful, harmful

dar /dar/ *vt irr* to give; hand over; concede, grant; produce, yield; cause, create; sacrifice; propose, put forward; take (a walk); believe, consider; deliver (blows, etc.); administer (medicine); provide with; apply, coat with; occasion; perform (plays); propose (a toast); give forth, emit; set (norms), render (thanks, etc.); hold (banquets, etc.); proffer, hold out; *vi* to strike (clocks); (*with prep a*) overlook, look on to (e.g. *Su ventana da a la calle,* His window looks on to the street); (*with con*) find, meet (things, persons); (*with de*) fall on, fall down (e.g. *Dio de cabeza,* He fell head first. *Dio de espaldas,* He fell on his back); (*with en*) fall into, incur; insist on or persist in (doing something); acquire the habit of (e.g. *Dieron en no venir a vernos,* They took to not coming to see us); solve, guess (riddles, etc.); strike, wound, hurt (e.g. *La bala le dio en el brazo,* The bullet struck him in the arm); (*with por*) decide on (e.g. *Di por no hacerlo,* I decided not to do it). *vr* to yield, give in; (*with prep a*) engage in, devote oneself to; (*with por*) think or consider oneself (e.g. *Me di por muerto,* I gave myself up for dead). **d. alas a,** to propagate, spread (a belief). **darse a la vela,** to set sail. **darse cuenta de,** to realize. **darse la mano,** to shake hands. **darse por buenos,** to make up a quarrel, be friends. **darse prisa,** to hurry up, make haste. **darse uno a conocer,** to make oneself known. **darse uno por entendido,** to show that one understands; be grateful. **No se me da un bledo,** I couldn't care less. **d. abajo,** to fall down. **d. bien por mal,** to return good for evil. **d. a conocer,** to make known. **d. a entender,** to suggest, hint. **d. a luz,** to give birth; publish, issue. **d. cuenta de,** to give an account of. **d. de baja,** *Mil.* to muster out, discharge. **d. de comer,** to feed. **d. de sí,** to stretch, expand; produce, yield; give of itself (oneself, himself, themselves) (either in good or bad sense). **d. diente con diente**, to chatter (of teeth), shiver. **d. el pésame**, to tender condolences. **d. en cara**, *Fig. Inf.* to throw in one's face. **d. en el clavo**, *Fig.* to hit the mark. **d. en qué pensar**, to make suspicious, cause to think. **d. fe**, to certify, attest. **d. fiado**, to give on credit. **d. fianza**, to give security. **d. fin a**, to finish. **d. licencia**, to permit, allow. **d. los buenos días**, to wish good day or good morning. **d. mal**, to have bad luck at cards. **d. parte de**, to announce; issue a communiqué about (e.g. *Dieron parte de la pérdida del buque*, They announced the loss of the ship). **d. prestado**, to lend. **d. qué decir**, to cause a scandal. **d. qué hacer**, to cause trouble. **d. razón de**, to give an account of. **d. sobre uno**, to assault a person. **d. un abrazo**, to embrace. **d. voces**, to shriek; call out. *Inf.* **Donde las dan las toman**, It's only tit-for-tat. *Inf.* **No me da la real gana**, I darn well don't want to. *Pres. Ind.* **doy, das**, etc. *Preterite* **di, diste**, etc. *Pres. Subjunc.* **dé**, etc. *Imperf. Subjunc.* **diese, etc.**

Dardanelos, los /darða'nelos, los/ the Dardanelles

dardo /'darðo/ *m*, (*Mil. Sports.*) dart; *Ichth.* dace; lampoon

dares y tomares /dares i tomares/ *m, pl* give and take; *Inf.* back-chat. Generally used with *andar, haber* or *tener*

dársena /'darsena/ *f, Naut.* dock

darviniano /darβi'niano/ *a* Darwinian

darvinismo /darβi'nismo/ *m*, Darwinism

darvinista /darβi'nista/ *mf* Darwinian

data /'data/ *f*, date (calendar); *Com.* credit

datar /'datar/ *vt* to date; *vi* (*with de*) date from; *vr Com.* credit

dátil /'datil/ *m, Bot.* date

datilado /datil'aðo/ *a* date-like or date-colored

datilera /datil'era/ *f, Bot.* date-palm

dativo /da'tiβo/ *m, Gram.* dative

dato /'dato/ *m*, datum; basis, fact

davídico /da'βiðiko/ *a* Davidic

de /de/ *f*, name of letter D. *prep* of (possessive) (e.g. *Este cuadro es de Vd.*, This picture is yours); from (place and time) (e.g. *Vengo de Madrid*, I come from Madrid. *de vez en cuando*, from time to time); with, of, from, as the result of (e.g. *Lloraban de miedo*, They were crying with fright. *Murió de un ataque del corazón*, He died from a heart attack); for, to (e.g. *Es hora de marchar*, It is time to leave); with (of characteristics) (e.g. *el señor de los lentes*, the gentleman with the eyeglasses. *el cuarto de la alfombra azul*, the room with the blue carpet); when, as (e.g. *De niños nos gustaban los juguetes*, When we were children we liked toys); by (e.g. *Es un ensayo del mismo autor*, It is an essay by the same author. *Fue amado de todos*, He was loved by all. *Es hidalgo de nacimiento*, He is a gentleman by birth). Indicates the material of which a thing is made (e.g. *La mesa es de mármol*, The table is marble). Indicates contents of a thing (e.g. *un vaso de leche*, a glass of milk). Shows manner in which an action is performed (e.g. *Lo hizo de prisa*, He did it hurriedly). Shows the use to which an article is put (e.g. *una mesa de escribir*, a writing-table. *una máquina de coser*, a sewing-machine. *un caballo de batalla*, a war-horse). Sometimes used for emphasis (e.g. *El tonto de tu secretario*, That fool of a secretary of yours). Used by Spanish married women before husband's family name (e.g. *Señora Martínez de Cabra*, Mrs. Cabra (née Martínez)). Used after many adverbs (generally of time or place) to form prepositional phrases (e.g. *detrás de*, behind. *enfrente de*, opposite to; in front of. *de acá para allá*, here and there. *de allí a poco*, shortly afterward. *de allí a pocos días*, a few days later. *de bamba*, by chance. *de cabo a rabo*, from cover to cover. *además de*, besides, etc.). Used at beginning of various adverbial phrases (e.g. *de noche*, at night. *de día*, by day. *de antemano*, previously, *la persona de mi derecha* the person at my right, etc.). Used partitively before nouns, pronouns, adjectives (e.g. *Estas historias tienen algo de verdad*, These stories have some truth in them. *¿Qué hay de nuevo?* What's the news?) Forms many compound words (e.g. *deponer, denegar*, etc.). With **"uno"**

means "at" (e.g. *Lo cogió de un salto*, He caught it at one bound). **de a** is used before expressions of price, weight, etc. (e.g. *un libro de a cinco pesetas*, a five-peseta book)

dea /dea/ *f, Poet.* goddess

deán /de'an/ *m*, dean

debajo /de'βaho/ *adv* underneath; below

debate /de'βate/ *m*, discussion, debate; dispute

debatible /deβa'tiβle/ *a* debatable

debatir /deβa'tir/ *vt* to discuss, debate, argue

debe /'deβe/ *m, Com.* debtor

debelación /deβela'sion; deβela'θion/ *f*, conquest

debelador /deβela'ðor/ **(-ra)** *a* conquering. *n* conqueror

debelar /deβe'lar/ *vt* to conquer, overthrow

deber /de'βer/ *vt* to owe (e.g. *Le debo mil pesetas*, I owe him one thousand pesetas). Used as auxiliary verb followed by infinitive, ought to, be obliged to (e.g. *Debía haberlo hecho*, I ought to have done it. *Deberá hacerlo*, He will have to do it); be destined to (e.g. *La princesa que más tarde debió ser reina*, The princess who later was destined to be queen); be essential, must (e.g. *La cuestión debe ser resuelta*, The question must be settled); (*with de* + *infin.*) be probable (indicates supposition) (e.g. *Debe de tener cincuenta años*, He is probably about fifty. *Debía de sufrir del corazón*, He probably suffered from heart trouble); (preceded by a negative *with de* + *infin.*) be impossible (e.g. *No debe de ser verdad*, It can't be true)

deber /de'βer/ *m*, duty, obligation; debt. **hacer su d.**, to do one's duty

debidamente /deβiða'mente/ *adv* justly, rightly; duly

debido /de'βiðo/ *a* correct, due. **d. a**, owing to, because of

débil /'deβil/ *a* weak; *Fig.* spineless; frail

debilidad /deβili'ðað/ *f*, weakness; feebleness

debilitación /deβilitasion; deβilita'θion/ *f*, debilitation

debilitante /deβili'tante/ *a* weakening

debilitar /deβili'tar/ *vt* to weaken; *vr* become weak

débito /'deβito/ *m*, debit, debt; duty

debutar /deβu'tar/ *vi* to appear for the first time, make one's début

década /'dekaða/ *f*, decade

decadencia /dekaðensia; deka'ðenθia/ *f*, decadence, decline

decadente /deka'ðente/ *a* decadent, decaying

decaer /deka'er/ *vi irr* to fail (persons); decay, decline. See **caer**

decagramo /deka'gramo/ *m*, decagram

decaimiento /dekai'miento/ *m*, decadence; *Med.* prostration

decalaje /deka'lahe/ *m, Aer.* stagger

decalitro /deka'litro/ *m*, decaliter

decálogo /de'kalogo/ *m*, decalogue, the Ten Commandments

decámetro /de'kametro/ *m*, decameter

decampar /de'kampar/ *vi Mil.* to decamp

decanato /dekan'ato/ *m*, deanery; *Educ.* dean's rooms

decano /de'kano/ *m*, senior member; *Educ.* dean

decantación /dekantasion; dekanta'θion/ *f*, decantation

decantar /dekan'tar/ *vt* to decant (wines); praise

decapitación /dekapitasion; dekapita'θion/ *f*, decapitation

decapitar /dekapi'tar/ *vt* to decapitate, behead

decena /de'sena; de'θena/ *f*, ten; *Mus.* tenth

decenal /de'senal; de'θenal/ *a* decennial

decenario /dese'nario; deθe'nario/ *m*, decade

decencia /de'sensia; de'θenθia/ *f*, propriety, decency; decorum, modesty

decenio /de'senio; de'θenio/ *m*, decade

deceno /de'seno; de'θeno/ *a* tenth

decentar /desen'tar; deθen'tar/ *vt irr* to begin, cut (loaves, etc.); *Fig.* undermine (health, etc.); *vr* suffer from bedsores. See **acertar**

decente /de'sente; de'θente/ a decent, honest; respectable; suitable; tidy
decepción /desep'sion; deθep'θion/ f, disillusionment, disappointment
dechado /de'tʃaðo/ m, model, ideal; Sew. sampler; exemplar, ideal
decible /de'siβle; de'θiβle/ a expressible
decidero /de'siðero; de'θiðero/ a that which can be safely said
decidido /desi'ðiðo; deθi'ðiðo/ a decided; resolute, determined
decidir /desi'ðir; deθi'ðir/ vt to resolve, decide; vr make up one's mind
decidor /desi'ðor; deθi'ðor/ (-ra) a talkative, fluent, eloquent. n good talker
decigramo /desi'gramo; deθi'gramo/ m, decigram
décima /'desima; 'deθima/ f, tenth; ten-line stanza of eight-syllable verse
decimal /desi'mal; deθi'mal/ a decimal; pertaining to tithes. **sistema d.,** metric system
decímetro /de'simetro; de'θimetro/ m, decimeter
décimo /'desimo; 'deθimo/ a tenth. m, tenth part; tenth of a lottery ticket
decimoctavo /desimok'taβo; deθimok'taβo/ a eighteenth
decimocuarto /desimo'kuarto; deθimo'kuarto/ a fourteenth
decimonono /desimo'nono; deθimo'nono/ a nineteenth
decimoquinto /desimo'kinto; deθimo'kinto/ a fifteenth
decimoséptimo /desimo'septimo; deθimo'septimo/ a and m, seventeenth
decimosexto /desimo'seksto; deθimo'seksto/ a sixteenth
decimotercio /desimoter'sio; deθimoter'θio/ a thirteenth
decir /de'sir; de'θir/ vt irr to say; name; indicate, show; tell. **d. bien,** to go with, suit; speak the truth; be eloquent. **d. entre** (or **para**) **sí,** to say to oneself. Inf. **d. nones,** to refuse. **¿Cómo se dice... en español?** How do you say... in Spanish? **¡Diga!** Hello! (telephone). Inf. **el que dirán,** public opinion (what will people say!). **Es d.,** That is to say. **Se dice,** It is said, people say. Pres. Ind. **digo, dices, etc.** Pres. Part. **diciendo.** Past Part. **dicho.** Fut. **diré, etc.** Condit. **diría, etc.** Preterite **dije, etc.** Pres. Subjunc. **diga, etc.** Imperf. Subjunc. **dijese, etc.**
decir /de'sir; de'θir/ m, saying, saw; maxim, witticism (often pl.)
decisión /desi'sion; deθi'sion/ f, decision, resolution; Law. judgment; firmness, strength (of character)
decisivo /desi'siβo; deθi'siβo/ a decisive
declamación /deklama'sion; deklama'θion/ f, declamation, oration; Theat. delivery; recitation
declamador /deklama'ðor/ (-ra) a declamatory. n reciter; orator
declamar /dekla'mar/ vi to make a speech, declaim; recite
declamatorio /deklama'torio/ a declamatory, rhetorical
declaración /deklara'sion; deklara'θion/ f, declaration; exposition, explanation; confession; statement; Law. deposition. **d. jurada,** affidavit, sworn statement
declaradamente /deklaraða'mente/ adv avowedly
declarante /dekla'rante/ a declaring. mf Law. deponent
declarar /dekla'rar/ vt to declare; make clear, explain; Law. find; vi Law. give evidence; vr avow, confess (one's sentiments, etc.); show, reveal itself
declarativo, declaratorio /deklara'tiβo, deklara'torio/ a explanatory, declarative
declinación /deklina'sion; deklina'θion/ f, fall, descent; decadence, decay; Astron. declination; Gram. declension. Inf. **no saber las declinaciones,** not to know one's ABC, be very ignorant
declinante /dekli'nante/ a declining; sloping
declinar /dekli'nar/ vi to slope; diminish, fall; decline, deteriorate; Fig. near the end; vt Gram. decline
declive, **/de'kliβe,/ m. **declividad f, slope, incline; gradient

decocción /dekok'sion; dekok'θion/ f, decoction
decoloración /dekolora'sion; dekolora'θion/ f, decoloration; decolorization
decomisar /dekomi'sar/ vt to confiscate, seize
decoración /dekora'sion; dekora'θion/ f, decoration; ornament, embellishment; Theat. scenery
decorado /deko'raðo/ m, Theat. scenery, décor
decorador /dekora'ðor/ m, decorator
decorar /deko'rar/ vt to adorn, ornament; Poet. decorate, honor
decorativo /dekora'tiβo/ a decorative
decoro /de'koro/ m, respect, reverence; prudence, circumspection; decorum, propriety; integrity, decency; Archit. decoration
decoroso /deko'roso/ a decorous, honorable, decent
decrecer /dekre'ser; dekre'θer/ vi irr to decrease, grow less. See **conocer**
decreciente /dekre'siente; dekre'θiente/ a decreasing
decrepitación /dekrepita'sion; dekrepita'θion/ f, Chem. decrepitation, crackling
decrepitar /dekrepi'tar/ vi Chem. to decrepitate, crackle
decrépito /de'krepito/ a decrepit
decrepitud /dekrepi'tuð/ f, decrepitude
decretar /dekre'tar/ vt to decree, decide; Law. give a judgment (in a suit)
decreto /de'kreto/ m, decree, order; judicial decree
decuplar, decuplicar /dekup'lar, dekupli'kar/ vt to multiply by ten
décuplo /'dekuplo/ a tenfold
decurso /de'kurso/ m, course, lapse (of time)
dedada /de'ðaða/ f, thimbleful, finger; pinch
dedal /de'ðal/ m, thimble; finger-stall
dédalo /'deðalo/ m, labyrinth
dedeo /de'ðeo/ m, Mus. touch
dedicación /deðika'sion; deðika'θion/ f, dedication (all meanings)
dedicar /deði'kar/ vt to dedicate; devote; consecrate; vr (with prep a) dedicate oneself to, engage in
dedicatoria /deðika'toria/ f, dedication (of a book, etc.)
dedicatorio /deðika'torio/ a dedicatory
dedil /'deðil/ m, finger-stall
dedillo, saber al /de'ðiyo, saβer al; de'ðiʎo, saβer al/ Fig. to have at one's fingertips, know perfectly
dedo /'deðo/ m, finger; toe; finger's breadth. **d. anular,** third (ring) finger. **d. de en medio** or **del corazón,** middle finger. **d. índice,** forefinger. **d. meñique,** little finger. **d. pulgar,** thumb or big toe. Fig. Inf. **a dos dedos de,** within an inch of. Fig. Inf. **chuparse los dedos,** to smack one's lips over. Inf. **estar unidos como los dedos de la mano,** to be as thick as thieves
deducción /deðuk'sion; deðuk'θion/ f, inference, deduction; derivation; (Mus. Math.) progression
deducente /deðu'siente; deðu'θiente/ a deductive
deducir /deðu'sir; deðu'θir/ vt irr to deduce, infer; deduct, subtract; Law. plead, allege in pleading. See **conducir**
deductivo /deðuk'tiβo/ a deductive
defecación /defeka'sion; defeka'θion/ f, purification; defecation
defecar /defe'kar/ vt to clarify, purify; defecate
defección /defek'sion; defek'θion/ f, defection
defectible /defek'tiβle/ a deficient; imperfect
defecto /de'fekto/ m, defect, fault; imperfection
defectuoso /defek'tuoso/ a imperfect, defective
defender /defen'der/ vt irr to defend, protect; maintain, uphold; forbid; hinder; vr defend oneself. See **entender**
defendible /defen'diβle/ a defensible
defensa /de'fensa/ f, defense; protection; (hockey) pad; Law. defense; Sports. back; pl Mil. defenses; Naut. fenders. **d. química,** chemical warfare. Mil. **defensas costeras,** coastal defenses
defensiva /defen'siβa/ f, defensive
defensivo /defen'siβo/ a defensive. m, safeguard
defensor /defen'sor/ (-ra) n defender. m, Law. counsel for the defense
deferencia /defe'rensia; defe'renθia/ f, deference

deferente /defe'rente/ a deferential
deferir /defe'rir/ vi irr to defer, yield; vt delegate. Pres. Ind. **defiero, defieres, defiere, defieren.** Pres. Part. **defiriendo.** Preterite **defirió, defirieron.** Pres. Subjunc. **defiera, etc.** Imperf. Subjunc. **defiriese, etc.**
deficiencia /defi'siensia; defi'θienθia/ f, defect, deficiency
deficiente /defi'siente; defi'θiente/ a faulty, deficient
déficit /'defisit; 'defiθit/ m, deficit
definible /defi'niβle/ a definable
definición /defini'sion; defini'θion/ f, definition; decision
definido /defi'niðo/ a definite
definir /defi'nir/ vt to define; decide
definitivo /defini'tiβo/ a definitive. **en definitiva,** definitely; in short
deflagración /deflagra'sion; deflagra'θion/ f, sudden blaze, deflagration
deflagrador /deflagra'ðor/ m, Elec. deflagrator
deflagrar /defla'grar/ vi to go up in flames
deformación /deforma'sion; deforma'θion/ f, deformation; Radio. distortion
deformado /defor'maðo/ a deformed; misshapen
deformador /deforma'ðor/ **(-ra)** a disfiguring, deforming. n disfigurer
deformar /defor'mar/ vt to deform; vr become deformed or misshapen
deformidad /deformi'ða ð/ f, deformity; gross error; vice, lapse
defraudación /defrauða'sion; defrauða'θion/ f, defrauding; deceit
defraudador /defrauða'ðor/ **(-ra)** n defrauder
defraudar /defrau'ðar/ vt to defraud; usurp; frustrate, disappoint; impede
defuera /de'fuera/ adv outwardly, externally
defunción /defun'sion; defun'θion/ f, decease, death
degeneración /dehenera'sion; dehenera'θion/ f, degeneration. **d. grasienta,** fatty degeneration
degenerado /dehene'raðo/ **(-da)** a and n degenerate
degenerar /dehene'rar/ vi to degenerate
deglución /deglu'sion; deglu'θion/ f, swallowing, deglutition
deglutir /deglu'tir/ vi and vt to swallow
degollación /degoya'sion; degoʎa'θion/ f, decollation, throat slitting
degolladero /degoya'ðero; degoʎa'ðero/ m, slaughterhouse; execution block
degollador /degoya'ðor; degoʎa'ðor/ m, executioner
degolladura /degoya'ðura; degoʎa'ðura/ f, slitting of the throat
degollar /dego'yar; dego'ʎar/ vt irr to behead; slit the throat; Fig. destroy; (Fig. Theat.) murder; Inf. annoy, bore. Pres. Ind. **degüello, degüellas, degüella, degüellan.** Pres. Subjunc. **degüelle, degüelles, degüellen**
degollina /dego'yina; dego'ʎina/ f, Inf. massacre
degradación /degraða'sion; degraða'θion/ f, degradation; humiliation, debasement; Art. gradation, shading (colors, light)
degradante /degra'ðante/ a degrading, humiliating
degradar /degra'ðar/ vt to degrade; humiliate; Art. grade, blend; vr degrade oneself
degüello /de'gueyo; de'gueʎo/ m, decollation; havoc, destruction; haft (of swords, etc.)
degustación /degusta'sion; degusta'θion/ f, act of tasting or sampling
dehesa /de'esa/ f, pasture, meadow
deicida /dei'siða; dei'θiða/ mf deicide (person)
deicidio /dei'siðio; dei'θiðio/ m, deicide (act)
deidad /dei'ðað/ f, divinity; deity, idol
deificación /deifika'sion; deifika'θion/ f, deification
deificar /deifi'kar/ vt to deify; overpraise
deífico /de'ifiko/ a deific, divine
deísmo /de'ismo/ m, Deism
deísta /de'ista/ mf deist. a deistic
dejación /deha'sion; deha'θion/ f, relinquishment, abandonment
dejadez /deha'ðes; deha'ðeθ/ f, slovenliness; neglect; laziness; carelessness

dejado /de'haðo/ a lazy; neglectful; slovenly; discouraged, depressed
dejamiento /deha'miento/ m, relinquishment; negligence; lowness of spirits; indifference
dejar /de'har/ vt to leave; omit, forget, allow, permit (e.g. Déjame salir, Let me go out); yield, produce, entrust, leave in charge; believe, consider; intend, appoint; cease, stop; forsake, desert; renounce, relinquish; bequeath; give away; vr neglect oneself; engage (in); lay oneself open to, allow oneself; abandon oneself (to), fling oneself (into); Fig. be depressed or languid; (with de + infin.) cease to (e.g. Se dejó de hacerlo, He stopped doing it); vi (with de + adjective) be none the less, be rather (e.g. No deja de ser sorprendente, It isn't any the less surprising). **d. aparte,** to omit, leave out. **d. atrás,** to overtake; Fig. leave behind, beat. **d. caer,** to let fall. **dejarse caer,** to let oneself fall; Fig. Inf. to let fall, utter; appear suddenly. **dejarse vencer,** to give way, allow oneself to be persuaded
dejo /'deho/ m, relinquishment; end; accent (of foreign languages); savor, after-taste; negligence; Fig. touch, flavor
del /del/ contraction of **de** + **el,** (def. art. m.) of the (e.g. del perro, of the dog)
delación /dela'sion; dela'θion/ f, accusation, denunciation
delantal /delan'tal/ m, apron
delante /de'lante/ adv before, in front, in the presence (of)
delantera /delan'tera/ f, front, front portion; Theat. orchestra stall, front seat; front (of garment). **tomar la d.,** to take the lead; Inf. steal a march on
delantero /delan'tero/ a fore, front. m, postilion; Sports. forward. **d. centro,** Sports. centerforward
delatable /dela'taβle/ a impeachable; blameworthy
delatar /dela'tar/ vt to inform against, accuse; impeach
delator /dela'tor/ **(-ra)** a denunciatory, accusing. n denouncer, informer
delectación /delekta'sion; delekta'θion/ f, delectation, pleasure
delegación /delega'sion; delega'θion/ f, delegation; proxy
delegado /dele'gaðo/ **(-da)** n delegate; proxy
delegar /dele'gar/ vt to delegate
deleitable /delei'taβle/ a delightful
deleitar /delei'tar/ vt to delight, charm, please; vr delight (in)
deleite /de'leite/ m, delight; pleasure
deleitoso /delei'toso/ a delightful, pleasant
deletéreo /dele'tereo/ a deleterious; poisonous
deletrear /deletre'ar/ vi to spell; Fig. decipher
deletreo /dele'treo/ m, spelling; Fig. decipherment
deleznable /deles'naβle; deleθ'naβle/ a fragile, brittle; slippery; brief, fugitive, transitory
délfico /'delfiko/ a Delphic
delfín /del'fin/ m, (Ichth. Astron.) dolphin; dauphin
delfina /del'fina/ f, dauphiness
Delfos /'delfos/ Delphi
delgadez /delga'ðes; delga'ðeθ/ f, thinness; slenderness, leanness
delgado /del'gaðo/ a slim; thin; scanty; poor (of land); sharp, perspicacious
delgaducho /delga'ðutʃo/ a slenderish, somewhat thin
deliberación /deliβera'sion; deliβera'θion/ f, deliberation; consideration; discussion
deliberadamente /deliβeraða'mente/ adv deliberately
deliberante /deliβe'rante/ a deliberative, considering
deliberar /deliβe'rar/ vi to deliberate, consider; vt decide after reflection; discuss
delicadez /delika'ðes; delika'ðeθ/ f, weakness; delicacy; hypersensitiveness; amiability
delicadeza /delika'ðesa; delika'ðeθa/ f, delicacy; fastidiousness; refinement; subtlety; sensitiveness; consideration, tact; scrupulosity
delicado /deli'kaðo/ a courteous; tactful; fastidious; weak, delicate; fragile, perishable; delicious, tasty;

exquisite; difficult, embarrassing; refined, discriminating, sensitive; scrupulous; subtle; hypersensitive, suspicious. **d. de salud,** in poor health
delicia /deli'sia; deli'θia/ f, pleasure, delight; sensual pleasure
delicioso /deli'sioso; deli'θioso/ a delightful, agreeable, pleasant
delimitar /delimi'tar/ vt to delimit
delincuencia /delin'kuensia; delin'kuenθia/ f, delinquency, default
delincuente /delin'kuente/ a and mf delinquent, in default
delineación /delinea'sion; delinea'θion/ f, delineation; diagram, design, plan
delineador /delinea'ðor/ (**-ra**), n delineante m, draftsman, designer
delineamiento /delinea'miento/ m, delineation
delinear /deline'ar/ vt to delineate; sketch; describe
delinquimiento /delinki'miento/ m, delinquency; crime
delinquir /delin'kir/ vi irr to commit a crime. Pres. Ind. **delinco.** Pres. Subjunc. **delinca**
deliquio /deli'kio/ m, faint, swoon
delirante /deli'rante/ a delirious
delirar /deli'rar/ vi to be delirious; act or speak foolishly
delirio /de'lirio/ m, delirium; frenzy; foolishness, nonsense. **d. de grandezas,** illusions of grandeur
delito /de'lito/ m, delict, offense against the law, crime
delta /'delta/ f, fourth letter of Greek alphabet. m, delta (of a river)
delusorio /delu'sorio/ a deceptive
demacración /demakrasion; demakra'θion/ f, emaciation
demacrado /dema'kraðo/ a emaciated
demacrarse /dema'krarse/ vr to become emaciated
demagogia /dema'gohia/ f, demagogy
demagógico /dema'gohiko/ a demagogic
demagogo /dema'gogo/ (**-ga**) n demagogue
demanda /de'manda/ f, petition, request; collecting (for charity); collecting box; want ad; question; search; undertaking; Com. order or demand; Law. claim
demandadero /demanda'ðero/ (**-ra**) n convent or prison messenger; errandboy
demandado /deman'daðo/ (**-da**) n Law. defendant; Law. respondent
demandante /deman'dante/ mf Law. plaintiff
demandar /deman'dar/ vt to ask, request; desire, yearn for; question; Law. claim
demarcación /demarka'sion; demarka'θion/ f, demarcation, limit
demarcar /demar'kar/ vt to fix boundaries, demarcate
demás /de'mas/ a other. adv besides. **lo d., the** rest. **los (las) d.,** the others. **por d.,** useless; superfluous. **por lo d.,** otherwise; for the rest
demasía /dema'sia/ f, excess; daring; insolence; guilt, crime. **en d.,** excessively
demasiado /dema'siaðo/ a too; too many; too much. adv excessively
demencia /de'mensia; de'menθia/ f, madness, insanity
demencial /demen'sial; demen'θial/ a insane
dementar /demen'tar/ vt to render insane; vr become insane
demente /de'mente/ a insane, mad. mf lunatic
demérito /de'merito/ m, demerit, fault
demeritorio /demeri'torio/ a undeserving, without merit
demisión /demi'sion/ f, submission, acquiescence
democracia /demo'krasia; demo'kraθia/ f, democracy
demócrata /de'mokrata/ mf democrat
democrático /demo'kratiko/ a democratic
democratizar /demokrati'sar; demokrati'θar/ vt to make democratic
demoledor /demole'ðor/ (**-ra**) a demolition. n demolisher

demoler /demo'ler/ vt irr to demolish, destroy, dismantle. See **moler**
demolición /demoli'sion; demoli'θion/ f, demolition, destruction, dismantling
demoníaco /demo'niako/ a devilish; possessed by a demon
demonio /de'monio/ m, devil; evil spirit. interj **¡Demonios!** Deuce take it! Inf. **tener el d.,** to be always on the move, be very energetic
demontre /de'montre/ m, Inf. devil
demora /de'mora/ f, delay; Naut. bearing; Com. demurrage
demorar /demo'rar/ vt to delay; vi stay, remain, tarry; Naut. bear
demorón, -ona /demo'ron/ a, Lat. Am. slow
demostrable /demos'traβle/ a demonstrable
demostración /demostra'sion; demostra'θion/ f, demonstration; proof
demostrador /demostra'ðor/ (**-ra**) a demonstrating. n demonstrator
demostrar /demos'trar/ vt irr to demonstrate, explain; prove; teach. See **mostrar**
demostrativo /demostra'tiβo/ a demonstrative. Gram. **pronombre d.,** demonstrative pronoun
demudación /demuða'sion; demuða'θion/ f, change; alteration
demudar /demu'ðar/ vt to change, vary; alter, transform; vr change suddenly (color, facial expression, etc.); grow angry
denario /de'nario/ a denary. m, denarius
denegación /denega'sion; denega'θion/ f, denial; refusal
denegar /dene'gar/ vt irr to deny, refuse. See **acertar**
dengoso /deŋ'goso/ a fastidious, finicky
dengue /'deŋgue/ m, affectation, faddiness, fastidiousness
denigrable /deni'graβle/ a odious
denigración /denigra'sion; denigra'θion/ f, slander, defamation (of character)
denigrante /deni'grante/ a slanderous
denigrar /deni'grar/ vt to slander; insult
denodado /deno'ðaðo/ a valiant, daring
denominación /denomina'sion; denomina'θion/ f, denomination
denominador /denomina'ðor/ a denominating m, Math. denominator
denominar /denomi'nar/ vt to name, designate
denostada /denos'taða/ f, insult
denostar /denos'tar/ vt irr to revile, insult. See **acordar**
denotar /deno'tar/ vt to denote, indicate
densidad /densi'ðað/ f, density; closeness, denseness; Phys. specific gravity; obscurity
denso /'denso/ a compact, close; thick, dense; crowded; dark, confused
dentado /den'taðo/ a toothed; pronged; dentate
dentadura /denta'ðura/ f, set of teeth (real or false). **d. de rumiante,** teeth like an ox. **d. postiza,** false teeth
dental /den'tal/ a dental
dentar /den'tar/ vt irr to provide with teeth, prongs, etc.; vi cut teeth. See **sentar**
dentellada /dente'yaða; dente'ʎaða/ f, gnashing or chattering of teeth; bite; toothmark
dentellar /dente'yar; dente'ʎar/ vi to chatter, grind, gnash (teeth)
dentellear /denteye'ar; denteʎe'ar/ vt to bite, sink the teeth into
dentera /den'tera/ f, (**dar**) to set one's teeth on edge; Fig. Inf. make one's mouth water
dentición /denti'sion; denti'θion/ f, teething, dentition
dentífrico /den'tifriko/ m, toothpaste
dentista /den'tista/ mf dentist
dentro /'dentro/ adv within, inside. **d. de poco,** soon, shortly. **por d.,** from the inside; on the inside
dentudo /den'tuðo/ a having large teeth
denudación /denuða'sion; denuða'θion/ f, denudation; Geol. erosion
denudar /denu'ðar/ vt to denude

denuedo /de'nueðo/ *m*, courage, daring
denuesto /de'nuesto/ *m*, insult
denuncia /de'nunsia; de'nunθia/ *f*, denunciation, accusation
denunciante /denun'siante; denun'θiante/ *a* accusing. *mf Law.* denouncer
denunciar /denun'siar; denun'θiar/ *vt* to give notice, inform; herald, presage; declare, proclaim; denounce; *Law.* accuse
denunciatorio /denunsia'torio; denunθia'torio/ *a* denunciatory
deparar /depa'rar/ *vt* to furnish, offer, present
departamental /departamen'tal/ *a* departmental
departamento /departa'mento/ *m*, department; compartment (railway); branch, section; *Argentina* apartment. **d. de lactantes,** nursery (in a hospital)
departir /depar'tir/ *vi* to converse
depauperación /depaupera'sion; depaupera'θion/ *f*, impoverishment; *Med.* emaciation
depauperar /depaupe'rar/ *vt* to impoverish; *vr Med.* grow weak, become emaciated
dependencia /depen'densia; depen'denθia/ *f*, dependence; subordination; dependency; *Com.* branch; firm, agency; business affair; kinship or affinity; *pl Archit.* offices; *Com.* staff; accessories
depender /depen'der/ *vi* (*with de*) to be subordinate to; depend on; be dependent on, need
dependiente /depen'diente/ **(-ta)** *a* and *n* dependent, subordinate. *m*, employee; shop assistant
depilar /depi'lar/ *vt* to pluck, wax; *vr* to shave, wax (legs, etc.)
depilatorio /depila'torio/ *m*, depilatory
deplorar /deplo'rar/ *vt* to deplore, lament
deponente /depo'nente/ *a* deposing; affirming. *mf* deponent. *Gram.* **verbo d.,** deponent verb
deponer /depo'ner/ *vt irr* to lay aside; depose, oust; affirm, testify; remove, take from its place; *Law.* depose; *Central America, Mexico* throw up, vomit. See **poner**
deportación /deporta'sion; deporta'θion/ *f*, deportation
deportar /depor'tar/ *vt* to exile; deport
deporte /de'porte/ *m*, sport; *pl* games. **d. de vela,** sailing; boating
deportismo /depor'tismo/ *m*, sport
deportista /depor'tista/ *a* sporting. *mf* sportsman (sportswoman)
deportivo /depor'tiβo/ *a* sporting
deposición /deposi'sion; deposi'θion/ *f*, affirmation, statement; *Law.* deposition; degradation, removal (from office, etc.)
depositador /deposita'ðor/ **(-ra)** *a* depositing. *n* depositor
depositar /deposi'tar/ *vt* to deposit; place in safety; entrust; lay aside, put away; *vr Chem.* settle
depositaría /deposita'ria/ *f*, depository; trusteeship; accounts office
depositario /deposi'tario/ **(-ia)** *a* pertaining to a depository. *n* depositary, trustee
depósito /de'posito/ *m*, deposit; depository; *Com.* depot, warehouse; *Chem.* deposit, sediment; tank, reservoir; *Mil.* depot. **d. de bencina, d. de gasolina,** gas tank; service station. **d. de municiones,** munitions dump. *Com.* **en d.,** in bond. **Queda hecho el d. que marca la ley,** Copyright reserved
depravación /depraβa'sion; depraβa'θion/ *f*, depravity
depravar /depra'βar/ *vt* to deprave, corrupt; *vr* become depraved
deprecación /depreka'sion; depreka'θion/ *f*, supplication, petition; deprecation
deprecar /depre'kar/ *vt* to supplicate, petition; deprecate
depreciación /depresia'sion; depreθia'θion/ *f*, depreciation, fall in value
depreciar /depre'siar; depre'θiar/ *vt* to depreciate, reduce the value (of)
depredación /depreða'sion; depreða'θion/ *f*, depredation, robbery
depredar /depre'ðar/ *vt* to pillage

depresión /depre'sion/ *f*, depression. **d. nerviosa,** nervous breakdown
depresivo /depre'siβo/ *a* depressive; humiliating
deprimir /depri'mir/ *vt* to depress, compress, press down; depreciate, belittle; *vr* be compressed
depuración /depura'sion; depura'θion/ *f*, cleansing, purification; *Polit.* purge
depurar /depu'rar/ *vt* to cleanse, purify; *Polit.* purge
derecha /de'retʃa/ *f*, right hand; *Polit.* (gen. *pl*) Right. *Mil.* **¡D.!** Right Turn! **a la d.,** on the right
derechamente /deretʃa'mente/ *adv* straight, directly; prudently, justly; openly, frankly
derechera /dere'tʃera/ *f*, direct road
derechista /dere'tʃista/ *mf Polit.* rightist
derecho /de'retʃo/ *a* straight; upright; right (not left); just, reasonable; *Sports.* forehand. *adv* straightaway. *m*, right; law; just claim; privilege; justice, reason; exemption; right side (cloth, etc.); *pl* dues, taxes; fees. **d. a la vía,** right of way. **d. de apelación,** right to appeal. **d. de visita,** (international law) right of search. **derechos de aduana,** customhouse duties. **derechos de entrada,** import duties. **según d.,** according to law. **usar de su d.,** to exercise one's right
derechura /dere'tʃura/ *f*, directness, straightness; uprightness; *Lat. Am.* good luck
deriva /de'riβa/ *f*, (*Naut. Aer.*) drift, leeway. **d. continental,** continental drift
derivación /deriβa'sion; deriβa'θion/ *f*, origin, derivation; inference, consequence; *Gram.* derivation
derivar /deri'βar/ *vi* to originate; *Naut.* drift; *vt* conduct, lead; *Gram.* derive; *Elec.* tap
dermatología /dermatolo'hia/ *f*, dermatology
dermatólogo /derma'tologo/ *m*, dermatologist
derogación /deroga'sion; deroga'θion/ *f*, repeal, annulment; deterioration
derogar /dero'gar/ *vt* to annul, repeal; destroy, suppress
derogatorio /deroga'torio/ *a Law.* repealing
derrama /de'rrama/ *f*, apportionment of tax
derramado /derra'maðo/ *a* extravagant, wasteful
derramamiento /derrama'miento/ *m*, pouring out; spilling; scattering
derramar /derra'mar/ *vt* to pour out; spill; shed (blood); scatter; apportion (taxes); publish abroad, spread; *vr* be scattered; overflow
derrame /de'rrame/ *m*, spilling; leakage; overflow; scattering; slope
derredor /derre'ðor/ *m*, circumference. **al** (*or* **en**) **d.,** round about
derrelicto /derre'likto/ *a* abandoned; derelict. *m*, *Naut.* derelict
derrengado /derreŋ'gaðo/ *a* crooked; crippled
derretimiento /derreti'miento/ *m*, melting; thaw; liquefaction; *Inf.* burning passion
derretir /derre'tir/ *vt irr* to melt, liquefy; waste, dissipate; *vr* be very much in love; *Inf.* be susceptible (to love); *Inf.* long, be impatient. See **pedir**
derribar /derri'βar/ *vt* to demolish; knock down; fell; throw down; *Aer.* shoot down; throw (in wrestling); *Fig.* overthrow; demolish, explode (a myth); control (emotions); *vr* throw down; prostrate oneself; throw oneself down. **d. el chapeo,** *humorous* to doff one's hat
derribo /de'rriβo/ *m*, demolition; debris, rubble; throw (in wrestling)
derrocadero /derroka'ðero/ *m*, rocky precipice
derrocar /derro'kar/ *vt* to throw down from a rock; demolish (buildings); overthrow, oust
derrochador /derrotʃa'ðor/ **(-ra)** *a* wasteful, extravagant. *n* spendthrift
derrochar /derro'tʃar/ *vt* to waste, squander
derroche /de'rrotʃe/ *m*, squandering
derrota /de'rrota/ *f*, road; route, path; *Naut.* course; *Mil.* defeat
derrotar /derro'tar/ *vt* to defeat; overthrow (government); destroy, harm; *Mil.* defeat; *vr Naut.* drift, lose course; be a failure
derrotero /derro'tero/ *m*, *Naut.* course. *Naut.* ship's itinerary; number of sea charts; means to an end, course of action

derrotismo /derro'tismo/ *m*, defeatism

derrotista /derro'tista/ *mf* defeatist

derruir /de'rruir/ *vt irr* to demolish (a building). See **huir**

derrumbadero /derrumba'ðero/ *m*, precipice; risk, danger

derrumbamiento /derrumba'miento/ *m*, landslide; collapse, downfall

derrumbar /derrum'bar/ *vt* to precipitate; *vr* throw oneself down, collapse, tumble down (buildings, etc.)

derrumbe /de'rrumbe/ *m*, collapse; subsidence

derviche /der'βitʃe/ *m*, dervish

desabarrancar /desaβarran'kar/ *vt* to pull out of a ditch or rut; extricate (from a difficulty)

desabillé /desaβi'ye; desaβi'ʎe/ *m*, deshabille

desabor /desa'βor/ *m*, insipidity

desabotonar /desaβoto'nar/ *vt* to unbutton; *vi* open (flowers)

desabrido /desa'βriðo/ *a* insipid, poor-tasting; inclement (weather); disagreeable; unsociable; homely, plain (woman)

desabrigar /desaβri'gar/ *vt* to uncover; leave without shelter

desabrigo /desa'βrigo/ *m*, want of clothing or shelter; poverty, destitution

desabrimiento /desaβri'miento/ *m*, insipidity; harshness, disagreeableness; melancholy, depression

desabrir /desa'βrir/ *vt* to give a bad taste (to food); annoy, trouble

desabrochar /desaβro'tʃar/ *vt* to unbutton, untie; open; *vr Inf.* confide, open up

desacatar /desaka'tar/ *vt* to behave disrespectfully (towards); disobey; lack reverence

desacato /desa'kato/ *m*, irreverence; disrespect

desacertado /desaser'taðo; desaθer'taðo/ *a* wrong, erroneous; imprudent

desacertar /desaser'tar; desaθer'tar/ *vi irr* to be wrong; act imprudently. See **acertar**

desacierto /desa'sierto; desa'θierto/ *m*, mistake, miscalculation, blunder

desacomodado /desakomo'ðaðo/ *a* lacking means of subsistence; poor; unemployed (servants); troublesome

desacomodar /desakomo'ðar/ *vt* to incommode, make uncomfortable, inconvenience; dismiss, discharge

desaconsejado /desakonse'haðo/ *a* ill-advised

desaconsejar /desakonse'har/ *vt* to advise against, dissuade

desacoplar /desakop'lar/ *vt* to disconnect

desacordar /desakor'ðar/ *vt irr Mus.* to put out of tune; *vr* (*with de*) forget. See **acordar**

desacorde /desa'korðe/ *a* discordant, inharmonious; *Mus.* out of tune

desacostumbrado /desakostum'braðo/ *a* unaccustomed; unusual

desacostumbrar /desakostum'brar/ *vt* to break of a habit

desacotar /desako'tar/ *vt* to remove (fences); refuse, deny; *vi* withdraw (from agreement, etc.)

desacreditar /desakreði'tar/ *vt* to discredit

desacuerdo /desa'kuerðo/ *m*, disagreement, discord; mistake; forgetfulness; swoon, loss of consciousness

desadeudar /desaðeu'ðar/ *vt* to free from debt

desadornar /desaðor'nar/ *vt* to denude of ornaments

desadorno /desa'ðorno/ *m*, lack of ornaments; bareness

desafecto /desa'fekto/ *a* disaffected; hostile. *m*, disaffection

desaferrar /desafe'rrar/ *vt irr* to untie, unfasten; *Fig.* wean from; *Naut.* weigh anchor. See **acertar**

desafiador /desafia'ðor/ **(-ra)** *a* challenging. *n* challenger. *m*, duelist

desafiar /desa'fiar/ *vt* to challenge; compete with; oppose; *Mexico* fight

desafinar /desafi'nar/ *vi Mus.* to go out of tune; *Fig. Inf.* speak out of turn

desafío /desa'fio/ *m*, challenge; competition; duel

desaforado /desafo'raðo/ *a* lawless; outrageous; enormous

desaforar /desafo'rar/ *vt* to infringe (laws, etc.); *vr* be disorderly

desaforrar /desafo'rrar/ *vt* to remove the lining of or from

desafortunado /desafortu'naðo/ *a* unfortunate

desafuero /desa'fuero/ *m*, act of injustice; outrage, excess

desagarrar /desaga'rrar/ *vt Inf.* to release, loosen; unhook

desagraciado /desagra'siaðo; desagra'θiaðo/ *a* ugly, unsightly

desagraciar /desagra'siar; desagra'θiar/ *vt* to disfigure, make ugly

desagradable /desagra'ðaβle/ *a* disagreeable; unpleasant

desagradar /desagra'ðar/ *vi* to be disagreeable, displease (e.g. *Me desagrada su voz*, I find his voice unpleasant)

desagradecer /desagraðe'ser; desagraðe'θer/ *vt irr* to be ungrateful (for). See **conocer**

desagradecido /desagraðe'siðo; desagraðe'θiðo/ *a* ungrateful

desagradecimiento /desagraðesimiento; desagraðeθi'miento/ *m*, ingratitude

desagrado /desa'graðo/ *m*, displeasure, dislike, dissatisfaction

desagraviar /desagra'βiar/ *vt* to make amends, apologize; indemnify

desagravio /desa'graβio/ *m*, satisfaction, reparation; compensation

desagregar /desagre'gar/ **(se)** *vt* and *vr* to separate

desaguadero /desagua'ðero/ *m*, drain, waste pipe

desaguar /desa'guar/ *vt* to drain off; dissipate; *vi* flow (into sea, etc.)

desagüe /de'sague/ *m*, drainage; outlet, drain; catchment

desaguisado /desagi'saðo/ *a* outrageous, lawless. *m*, offense, insult

desahogado /desao'gaðo/ *a* brazen, insolent; clear, unencumbered; in comfortable circumstances

desahogar /desao'gar/ *vt* to ease, relieve; *vr* unburden oneself; recover (from illness, heat, etc.); get out of debt; speak one's mind

desahogo /desa'ogo/ *m*, relief, alleviation; ease; comfort, convenience; freedom, frankness; unburdening (of one's mind). *Inf.* **vivir con d.,** to be comfortably off

desahuciar /desau'siar; desau'θiar/ *vt* to banish all hope; give up, despair of the life of; put out (tenants); *Chile* dismiss

desahucio /desa'usio; desa'uθio/ *m*, ejection, dispossession (of tenants); *Chile* dismissal

desahumar /desau'mar/ *vt* to clear of smoke

desairado /desai'raðo/ *a* unattractive, graceless, ugly; unsuccessful, crestfallen; slighted

desairar /desai'rar/ *vt* to disdain, slight, disregard; underrate (things)

desaire /des'aire/ *m*, gracelessness, ugliness; insult, slight

desalabanza /desala'βansa; desala'βanθa/ *f*, disparagement; criticism

desalabar /desala'βar/ *vt* to censure, disparage

desalación /desala'sion; desala'θion/ *f*, desalinization

desalado /desa'laðo/ *a* anxious, precipitate, hasty

desalar /desa'lar/ *vt* to remove the salt from; take off wings; *vr* walk or run at great speed; long for, yearn

desalentar /desalen'tar/ *vt irr* to make breathing difficult (work, fatigue); discourage; *vr* be depressed or sad. See **sentar**

desaliento /desa'liento/ *m*, depression, discouragement, dismay

desalinear /desaline'ar/ *vt* to throw out of the straight

desaliñado /desali'ɲaðo/ *a* slovenly; slipshod

desaliñar /desali'ɲar/ *vt* to disarrange, make untidy, crumple

desaliño /desa'liɲo/ *m*, untidiness, slovenliness; negligence, carelessness

desalmado /desal'maðo/ *a* soulless, conscienceless; cruel

desalmamiento /desalma'miento/ *m*, inhumanity, consciencelessness; cruelty

desalmidonar /desalmiðo'nar/ *vt* to remove starch from

desalojamiento /desaloha'miento/ *m*, dislodgement, ejection

desalojar /desalo'har/ *vt* to dislodge, remove, eject; *vi* move out, remove

desalquilado /desalki'laðo/ *a* untenanted, vacant

desalquilar /desalki'lar/ *vt* to leave, or cause to leave, rented premises

desalterar /desalte'rar/ *vt* to soothe, calm

desamar /desa'mar/ *vt* to cease to love; hate

desamarrar /desama'rrar/ *vt* to untie; separate; *Naut.* unmoor

desamor /desa'mor/ *m*, indifference; lack of sentiment or affection; hatred

desamotinarse /desamoti'narse/ *vr* to cease from rebellion; submit

desamparar /desampa'rar/ *vt* to abandon, forsake; leave (a place)

desamparo /desam'paro/ *m*, desertion; need

desamueblado /desamue'βlaðo/ *a* unfurnished

desamueblar /desamue'βlar/ *vt* to empty of furniture

desandar lo andado /desan'dar lo an'daðo/ *vt irr* to retrace one's steps. See **andar**

desangrar /desaŋ'grar/ *vt Med.* to bleed; drain (lake, etc.); impoverish, bleed; *vr* lose much blood

desangre /de'saŋgre/ *m*, *Lat. Am.* bleeding, loss of blood

desanidar /desani'ðar/ *vi* to leave the nest; *vt* eject, expel

desanimado /desani'maðo/ *a* downhearted; (of places) dull, quiet

desanimar /desani'mar/ *vt* to discourage, depress

desanublar /desanu'βlar,/ *vt* **desanublarse** *vr* to clear up (weather)

desanudar /desanu'ðar/ *vt* to untie; disentangle

desaojar /desao'har/ *vt* to cure of the evil eye

desapacibilidad /desapasiβili'ðað; desapaθiβili'ðað/ *f*, disagreeableness, unpleasantness

desapacible /desapa'siβle; desapa'θiβle/ *a* disagreeable; unpleasant; unsociable

desaparecer /desapare'ser; desapare'θer/ *vt irr* to disappear; *vi* and *vr* disappear. **hacer d.**, to cause to disappear. See **conocer**

desaparecido /desapare'siðo; desapare'θiðo/ *a* late (deceased); *Mil.* missing

desaparejar /desapare'har/ *vt* to unharness

desaparición /desapari'sion; desapari'θion/ *f*, disappearance

desapegar /desape'gar/ *vt* to unstick, undo; *vr* be indifferent, cast off a love or affection

desapego /desa'pego/ *m*, lack of affection or interest, coolness

desapercibido /desapersi'βiðo; desaperθi'βiðo/ *a* unnoticed; unprovided, unprepared

desapestar /desapes'tar/ *vt* to disinfect

desapiadado /desapia'ðaðo/ *a* merciless

desaplicación /desaplika'sion; desaplika'θion/ *f*, laziness, lack of application; carelessness, negligence

desaplicado /desapli'kaðo/ *a* lazy; careless

desapoderado /desapoðe'raðo/ *a* precipitate, uncontrolled; furious, violent

desapoderar /desapoðe'rar/ *vt* to dispossess, rob; remove from office

desapolillar /desapoli'yar; desapoli'ʎar/ *vt* to free from moths; *vr Inf.* take an airing

desaposentar /desaposen'tar/ *vt* to evict; drive away

desapreciar /desapre'siar; desapre'θiar/ *vt* to scorn

desaprensivo /desapren'siβo/ *a* unscrupulous

desapretar /desapre'tar/ *vt* and *vr irr* to slacken. See **acertar**

desaprisionar /desaprisio'nar/ *vt* to release from prison

desaprobación /desaproβa'sion; desaproβa'θion/ *f*, disapproval

desaprobar /desapro'βar/ *vt irr* to disapprove; disagree with. See **probar**

desapropiamiento /desapropia'miento/ *m*, renunciation or transfer of property

desapropiarse /desapropi'arse/ *vr* to renounce or transfer (property)

desaprovechado /desaproβe'tʃaðo/ *a* unprofitable; backward; unintelligent

desaprovechar /desaproβe'tʃar/ *vt* to take no advantage of, waste; *vi Fig.* lose ground, lose what one has gained

desapuntar /desapun'tar/ *vt* to unstitch; lose one's aim

desarbolar /desarβo'lar/ *vt Naut.* to unmast

desarenar /desare'nar/ *vt* to clear of sand

desarmador /desarma'ðor/ *m*, *Mexico* screwdriver

desarmar /desar'mar/ *vt* to disarm; dismantle, dismount; appease

desarme /de'sarme/ *m*, disarming; disarmament

desarraigar /desarrai'gar/ *vt* to pull up by root (plants); extirpate, suppress; eradicate (opinion, etc.); exile

desarraigo /desa'rraigo/ *m*, uprooting; extirpation; eradication; exile

desarrebujar /desarreβu'har/ *vt* to disentangle, uncover; explain

desarreglado /desarre'glaðo/ *a* disarranged; untidy; intemperate, immoderate

desarreglar /desarre'glar/ *vt* to disarrange

desarreglo /desa'rreglo/ *m*, disorder; disarrangement; irregularity

desarrendar /desarren'dar/ *vt irr* to unbridle a horse; end a tenancy or lease. See **recomendar**

desarrollar /desarro'yar; desarro'ʎar/ *vt* to unroll; increase, develop, grow, unfold; explain (theory); develop, grow

desarrollo /des'arroyo; desa'rroʎo/ *m*, unrolling; development, growth; explanation

desarropar /desarro'par/ *vt* to uncover, remove the covers, etc. from

desarrugar /desarru'gar/ *vt* to take out wrinkles or creases

desarticulación /desartikula'sion; desartikula'θion/ *f*, disarticulation

desarticular /desartiku'lar/ *vt* to disarticulate; *Mech.* disconnect

desaseado /desase'aðo/ *a* dirty; unkempt, slovenly

desaseo /desa'seo/ *m*, dirtiness; slovenliness

desasimiento /desasi'miento/ *m*, loosening; liberality; disinterestedness; indifference, coldness

desasir /desa'sir/ *vt irr* to loosen, undo. *vr* disengage oneself. See **asir**

desasosegar /desasose'gar/ *vt irr* to disturb, make anxious. See **cegar**

desasosiego /desaso'siego/ *m*, uneasiness, disquiet

desastre /de'sastre/ *m*, disaster, calamity

desastroso /desas'troso/ *a* unfortunate, calamitous

desatacar /desata'kar/ *vt* to unfasten, undo, unbutton

desatadura /desata'ðura/ *f*, untying

desatar /desa'tar/ *vt* to untie; melt, dissolve; elucidate, explain; *vr* loosen the tongue; lose self control; lose all reserve; unbosom oneself

desatascar /desatas'kar/ *vt* to pull out of the mud; free from obstruction; extricate from difficulties

desataviar /desata'βiar/ *vt* to strip of ornaments

desatavío /desata'βio/ *m*, carelessness in dress, slovenliness

desatención /desaten'sion; desaten'θion/ *f*, inattention, abstraction; incivility

desatender /desaten'der/ *vt irr* to pay no attention to; disregard, ignore. See **entender**

desatentado /desaten'taðo/ *a* imprudent, ill-advised; excessive, immoderate

desatento /desa'tento/ *a* inattentive, abstracted; discourteous

desatinado /desati'naðo/ *a* foolish, imprudent, wild

desatinar /desati'nar/ *vt* to bewilder; *vi* behave foolishly; lose one's bearings

desatino /desa'tino/ *m*, folly, foolishness, imprudence, rashness; blunder, faux pas, mistake

desatracar /desatra'kar/ *vi Naut.* to push off

desatrancar /desatran'kar/ *vt* to unbar the door; remove obstacles

desaturdir /desatur'ðir/ *vt* to rouse (from torpor, etc.)

desautorizar /desautori'sar; desautori'θar/ *vt* to remove from authority; discredit

desavenencia /desaβe'nensia; desaβe'nenθia/ *f*, disharmony, disagreement

desavenido /desaβe'niðo/ *a* disagreeing, discordant

desavenir /desaβe'nir/ *vt irr* to upset. See **venir**

desaventajado /desaβenta'haðo/ *a* disadvantageous; unfavorable, inferior

desaviar /desa'βiar/ *vt* to lead astray; deprive of a necessity; *vr* lose one's way

desavisado /desaβi'saðo/ *a* unaware, unprepared

desavisar /desaβi'sar/ *vt* to take back one's previous advice

desayunador /desayuna'ðor/ *m*, breakfast nook

desayunarse /desayu'narse/ *vr* to have breakfast, eat breakfast

desayuno /desa'yuno/ *m*, breakfast

desazón /desa'son; desa'θon/ *f*, insipidity, lack of flavor; poorness (soil); anxiety, trouble; vexation

desazonar /desaso'nar; desaθo'nar/ *vt* to make insipid; make anxious, worry; vex; *vr* feel out of sorts

desbancar /desβan'kar/ *vt* to break the bank (gambling); supplant

desbandada /desβan'daða/ *f*, dispersal, rout. **a la d.,** in confusion or disorder

desbandarse /desβan'darse/ *vr* to disband, retreat in disorder; *Mil.* desert

desbaratado /desβara'taðo/ *a Inf.* corrupt, vicious

desbaratar /desβara'tar/ *vt* to spoil, destroy; dissipate, waste; foil, thwart (a plot); *Mil.* rout; *vi* talk foolishly; *vr* go too far, behave badly

desbarbado /desβar'βaðo/ *a* beardless

desbastar /desβas'tar/ *vt* to plane, dress; polish, refine, civilize

desbocado /desβo'kaðo/ *a* (of tools) blunt; runaway (of a horse); *Inf.* foul-tongued; *Lat. Am.* overflowing (its banks)

desbocar /desβo'kar/ *vt* to break the spout or neck (of jars, etc.); *vi* run (into) (of streets, etc.); *vr* bolt (horses); curse, swear

desboquillar /desβoki'yar; desβoki'ʎar/ *vt* to remove or break a stem or mouthpiece

desbordamiento /desβorða'miento/ *m*, overflowing, flood

desbordarse /desβor'ðarse/ *vr* to overflow; lose self-control. **d. en alabanzas para,** to heap praise on

desbravar /desβra'βar/ *vt* to break in (horses, etc.); *vi* grow less savage; lose force, decrease

desbrozar /desβro'sar; desβro'θar/ *vt* to free of rubbish, clear up

descabalgadura /deskaβalga'ðura/ *f*, alighting (from horses, etc.)

descabalgar /deskaβal'gar/ *vi* to alight (from horse); *vt* dismantle (gun)

descabellado /deskaβe'yaðo; deskaβe'ʎaðo/ *a* disheveled; ridiculous, foolish

descabellar /deskaβe'yar; deskaβe'ʎar/ *vt* to disarrange, ruffle (hair)

descabezado /deskaβe'saðo; deskaβe'θaðo/ *a* headless; rash, impetuous

descabezar /deskaβe'sar; deskaβe'θar/ *vt* to behead; cut the top off (trees, etc.); *Fig. Inf.* break the back of (work); *vi* abut, join; *vr* (*with con* or *en*) rack one's brains about

descacharrado, -a /deskatʃa'rraðo/ *a*, *Central America* dirty, filthy, slovenly

descafeinado /deskafei'naðo/ *a* decaffeinated

descalabazarse /deskalaβa'sarse; deskalaβa'θarse/ *vr Inf.* to rack one's brains

descalabradura /deskalaβra'ðura/ *f*, head wound or scar

descalabrar /deskala'βrar/ *vt* to wound in the head; wound; harm

descalabro /deska'laβro/ *m*, misfortune, mishap

descalzar /deskal'sar; deskal'θar/ *vt* to remove the shoes and stockings; undermine; *vr* remove one's shoes and stockings; lose a shoe (horses)

descalzo /des'kalso; des'kalθo/ *a* barefoot

descaminar /deskami'nar/ *vt* to lead astray; pervert, corrupt

descamisado /deskami'saðo/ **(-da)** *a Inf.* shirtless; ragged, poor. *n Inf.* down and out, outcast; vagabond

descansadero /deskansa'ðero/ *m*, resting place

descansado /deskan'saðo/ *a* rested, refreshed; tranquil

descansar /deskan'sar/ *vi* to rest, repose oneself; have relief (from anxiety, etc.); sleep; *Agr.* lie fallow; sleep in death; (*with en*) have confidence in; (*with sobre*) lean on or upon; *vt* (*with sobre*) rest (a thing) on another. **¡Que en paz descanse!** May he rest in peace!

descanso /des'kanso/ *m*, rest, repose; relief (from care); landing of stairs; *Mech.* bench, support; *Mil.* stand easy

descarado /deska'raðo/ *a* impudent, brazen

descararse /deska'rarse/ *vr* to behave impudently

descarbonizar /deskarβoni'sar; deskarβoni'θar/ *vt* to decarbonize

descarga /des'karga/ *f*, unloading; *Naut.* discharge of cargo; *Elec.* discharge; *Mil.* volley. **d. cerrada,** dense volley, fusillade

descargadero /deskarga'ðero/ *m*, wharf

descargador /deskarga'ðor/ *m*, unloader, docker; *Elec.* discharger

descargar /deskar'gar/ *vt* to unload; *Mil.* fire; unload (fire-arms); *Elec.* discharge; rain (blows) upon; *Fig.* free, exonerate; download. *vi* disembogue (of rivers); burst (clouds); *vr* relinquish (employment); shirk responsibility; *Law.* clear oneself

descargo /des'kargo/ *m*, unloading; *Com.* acquittance; *Law.* answer to an impeachment

descargue /des'karge/ *m*, unloading

descarnado /deskar'naðo/ *a* fleshless; scraggy; spare, lean

descarnador /deskarna'ðor/ *m*, dental scraper; tanner's scraper

descarnar /deskar'nar/ *vt* to scrape off flesh; corrode; inspire indifference to earthly things

descaro /des'karo/ *m*, impudence

descarriar /deska'rriar/ *vt* to lead astray; *vr* be lost, be separated (from others); *Fig.* go astray

descarrilamiento /deskarrila'miento/ *m*, derailment

descarrilar /deskarri'lar/ *vi* to run off the track, be derailed

descarrío /deska'rrio/ *m*, losing one's way

descartar /deskar'tar/ *vt* to put aside; *vr* discard (cards); shirk, make excuses

descarte /des'karte/ *m*, discard (cards); excuse, pretext

descascarar /deskaska'rar/ *vt* to peel; shell; *vr* peel off

descendencia /dessen'densia; desθen'denθia/ *f*, descendants, offspring; lineage, descent

descender /dessen'der; desθen'der/ *vi irr* to descend; flow (liquids); (*with de*) descend from, derive from; *vt* lower, let down. See **entender**

descendiente /dessen'diente; desθen'diente/ *mf* descendant, offspring. *a* descending

descendimiento /dessendi'miento; desθendi'miento/ *m*, descent

descenso /des'senso; des'θenso/ *m*, descent; lowering, letting down; degradation

descentralizar /dessentrali'sar; desθentrali'θar/ *vt* to decentralize

desceñir /desse'ɲir; desθe'ɲir/ **(se)** *vt* and *vr irr* to ungird, remove a girdle, etc. See **ceñir**

descepar /desse'par; desθe'par/ *vt* to tear up by the roots; *Fig.* extirpate

descercado /desser'kaðo; desθer'kaðo/ *a* unfenced, open

descercar /desser'kar; desθer'kar/ *vt* to pull down a wall or fence; *Mil.* raise a siege

descerrajar /desserra'har; desθerra'har/ *vt* to remove the locks (of doors, etc.)

descifrable /dessi'fraβle; desθi'fraβle/ *a* decipherable

descifrador /dessifra'ðor; desθifra'ðor/ *m*, decipherer, decoder

descifrar /dessi'frar; desθi'frar/ vt to decipher; decode

descinchar /dessin'tʃar; desθin'tʃar/ vt to loosen or remove girths (of horse)

desclavar /deskla'βar/ vt to remove nails; unnail, unfasten

descoagular /deskoagu'lar/ vt to liquefy, dissolve, melt

descobijar /deskoβi'har/ vt to uncover; undress

descocado /desko'kaðo/ a Inf. brazen, saucy

descoco /des'koko/ m, Inf. impudence

descogollar /deskogo'yar; deskogo'ʎar/ vt to prune a tree of shoots; remove hearts (of lettuces, etc.)

descolar /desko'lar/ vt irr to cut off or dock an animal's tail; Mexico slight, snub. See **colar**

descolgar /deskol'gar/ vt irr to unhang; lower; vr lower oneself (by rope, etc.); come down, descend; Inf. come out (with), utter. See **volcar**

descollar /desko'yar; desko'ʎar/ vi irr to excel, be outstanding. See **degollar**

descoloramiento /deskolora'miento/ m, discoloration

descolorar /deskolo'rar/ vt to discolor; vr be discolored

descolorido /deskolo'riðo/ a discolored; pale-colored; pallid

descomedido /deskome'ðiðo/ a excessive, disproportionate; rude

descomedimiento /deskomeði'miento/ m, disrespect, lack of moderation, rudeness

descomedirse /deskome'ðirse/ vr irr to be disrespectful or rude. See **pedir**

descompasarse /deskompa'sarse/ vr See **descomedirse**

descomponer /deskompo'ner/ vt irr to disorder, disarrange; Chem. decompose; unsettle; vr go out of order; rot, putrefy; be ailing; lose one's temper. See **poner**

descomposición /deskomposi'sion; deskomposi'θion/ f, disorder, confusion; discomposure; Chem. decomposition; putrefaction

descompostura /deskompos'tura/ f, decomposition; slovenliness, dirtiness, untidiness; impudence, rudeness

descompuesto /deskom'puesto/ a rude, impudent; Lat. Am. tipsy; Venezuela ill, sick

descomunal /deskomu'nal/ a enormous, extraordinary

desconcertar /deskonser'tar; deskonθer'tar/ vt irr to disorder, disarrange; dislocate (bones); disconcert, embarrass; vr disagree; be impudent. See **acertar**

desconcharse /deskon'tʃarse/ vr to flake off, peel

desconcierto /deskon'sierto; deskon'θierto/ m, disorder, disarrangement; dislocation; embarrassment; disagreement; impudence

desconectar /deskonek'tar/ vt to disconnect; switch off

desconfianza /deskon'fiansa; deskon'fianθa/ f, lack of confidence

desconfiar /deskon'fiar/ vi to lack confidence, mistrust

desconformidad /deskonformi'ðað/ f, See **disconformidad**

desconformismo /deskonfor'mismo/ m, nonconformism

desconocer /deskono'ser; deskono'θer/ vt irr to forget; be unaware of; deny, disown; pretend ignorance; not to understand (persons, etc.). See **conocer**

desconocido /deskonos'iðo; deskono'θiðo/ (-da) a unknown; ungrateful. n stranger; ingrate

desconocimiento /deskonosi'miento; deskonoθi'miento/ m, unawareness; ignorance; ingratitude

desconsiderado /deskonsiðe'raðo/ a inconsiderate; discourteous; rash

desconsolación /deskonsola'sion; deskonsola'θion/ f, affliction, trouble

desconsolar /deskonso'lar/ vt irr to afflict, make disconsolate; vr grieve, despair. See **colar**

desconsuelo /deskon'suelo/ m, anguish, affliction, despair

descontar /deskon'tar/ vt irr Com. to make a discount; ignore, discount; take for granted, leave aside. See **contar**

descontentadizo /deskontenta'ðiso; deskontenta'ðiθo/ a discontented, difficult to please; fastidious, finicky

descontentar /deskonten'tar/ vt to displease; vr be dissatisfied

descontento /deskon'tento/ m, discontent, dissatisfaction

descontextualizar /deskontekstuali'sar; deskontekstuali'θar/ vt to take out of context

descontrolarse /deskontro'larse/ vr to lose control, lose control of oneself

desconveniencia /deskombe'niensia; deskombe'nienθia/ f, inconvenience, unsuitability, disagreement

desconvenir /deskombe'nir/ vi irr to disagree; be unsuitable, unsightly or odd (things). See **venir**

descorazonamiento /deskorasona'miento; deskoraθona'miento/ m, depression, despair

descorazonar /deskoraso'nar; deskoraθo'nar/ vt to tear out the heart; depress, discourage

descorchar /deskor'tʃar/ vt to take the cork from cork tree; draw a cork (bottles); force, break into (safes)

descorrer /desko'rrer/ vt to re-run (race, etc.); draw back (curtains, etc.); vi run, flow (liquids)

descorrimiento /deskorri'miento/ m, overflow (liquids)

descortés /deskor'tes/ a impolite

descortesía /deskorte'sia/ f, impoliteness, discourtesy

descortezadura /deskortesa'ðura; deskorteθa'ðura/ f, peeling (of bark)

descortezar /deskorte'sar; deskorte'θar/ vt to decorticate; remove crust (bread, etc.); polish, civilize

descoser /desko'ser/ vt Sew. to unpick; vr be unpicked; be indiscreet or tactless

descosido /desko'siðo/ a tactless, talkative; Fig. disjointed; desultory; unsewn. m, Sew. rent, hole

descoyuntamiento /deskoyunta'miento/ m, dislocation (bones); irritation, bore; ache, pain

descoyuntar /deskoyun'tar/ vt to dislocate (bones); bore, annoy; vr be dislocated

descrédito /des'kreðito/ m, fall in value (things); discredit (persons)

descreer /deskre'er/ vt irr to disbelieve; depreciate; disparage (persons). See **creer**

descreído /deskre'iðo/ (-da) a unbelieving. n unbeliever; infidel

descremar /deskre'mar/ vt, Lat. Am. to skim (milk)

describir /deskri'βir/ vt to describe; outline, sketch. Past Part. **descrito**

descripción /deskrip'sion; deskrip'θion/ f, description; Law. inventory

descriptible /deskrip'tiβle/ a describable

descriptivo /deskrip'tiβo/ a descriptive

descuajar /deskua'har/ vt to liquefy; Inf. discourage; Agr. pull up by the root

descuartizar /deskuarti'sar; deskuarti'θar/ vt to quarter; joint (meat); Inf. carve, cut into pieces, break up

descubierto /desku'βierto/ a bareheaded; exposed. m, deficit. **al d.,** openly; in the open, without shelter. **girar en d.,** to overdraw (a bank account)

descubridero /deskuβri'ðero/ m, viewpoint, lookout

descubridor /deskuβri'ðor/ (-ra) n discoverer; inventor; explorer. m, Mil. scout

descubrimiento /deskuβri'miento/ m, find; discovery; revelation; newly discovered territory

descubrir /desku'βrir/ vt to reveal; show; discover; learn; unveil (memorials, etc.); vr remove one's hat; show oneself, reveal one's whereabouts. Past Part. **descubierto**

descuello /des'kueyo; des'kueʎo/ m, extra height; Fig. pre-eminence; arrogance

descuento /des'kuento/ m, reduction; Com. rebate, discount

descuidado /deskui'ðaðo/ a negligent; careless; untidy; unprepared

descuidar /deskui'ðar/ vt to relieve (of responsibility, etc.); distract, occupy (attention, etc.); *vi* and *vr* be careless; *vr* (*with de* or *en*) neglect

descuido /des'kuiðo/ *m*, carelessness, negligence; oversight, mistake; incivility; forgetfulness; shameful act

desde /'desðe/ *prep* since, from (time or space); after (e.g. *d. hoy*, from today). **d. la ventana**, from the window. **d. allá**, from the other world. **d. aquella época**, since that time

desdecir /desðe'sir; desðe'θir/ *vi irr* (*with de*) to degenerate, be less good than; be discordant, clash; be unworthy of; *vr* unsay one's words, retract. See **decir**

desdén /des'ðen/ *m*, indifference, coldness; disdain, scorn

desdentado /desðen'taðo/ *a* toothless; *Zool.* edentate

desdentar /desðen'tar/ *vt* to remove teeth

desdeñar /desðe'ɲar/ *vt* to scorn; *vr* (*with de*) dislike, be reluctant

desdeñoso /desðe'ɲoso/ *a* disdainful, scornful

desdibujado /desðiβu'haðo/ *a* badly drawn; blurred, confused

desdicha /des'ðitʃa/ *f*, misfortune; extreme poverty, misery. **por d.**, unfortunately

desdichado /desði'tʃaðo/ *a* unfortunate; *Inf.* timid, weak-kneed

desdicharse /desði'tʃarse/ *vr* to bewail one's fate

desdinerarse una fortuna /desðine'rarse 'una for'tuna/ *vr* to spend a fortune

desdoblar /desðo'βlar/ *vt* to unfold

desdorar /desðo'rar/ *vt* to remove the gilt; *Fig.* tarnish, sully

desdoro /des'ðoro/ *m*, discredit, dishonor

deseable /dese'aβle/ *a* desirable

desear /dese'ar/ *vt* to desire; yearn or long for

desecar /dese'kar/ *vt* to dry; *vr* be desiccated

desechar /dese'tʃar/ *vt* to reject, refuse; scorn; cast out, expel; put away (thoughts, etc.); cast off (old clothes); turn (key); give up

desecho /de'setʃo/ *m*, residue, rest, remains; cast-off; scorn; *Lat. Am.* shortcut

desegregación /desegrega'θion/ *f*, desegregation

desembalar /desemba'lar/ *vt* to unpack

desembanastar /desembana'star/ *vt* to take out of a basket; *Inf.* unsheath (sword); *vr* break loose (animals); *Inf.* get out, alight

desembarazar /desembara'sar; desembara'θar/ *vt* to clear of obstruction; disembarrass, free; vacate; *vr* *Fig.* rid oneself of obstacles

desembarazo /desemba'raso; desemba'raθo/ *m*, freedom, insouciance, naturalness

desembarcadero /desembarka'ðero/ *m*, landing-stage

desembarcar /desembar'kar/ *vt* to unload; *vi* disembark; alight from vehicle

desembarco /desem'barko/ *m*, disembarkation, landing; staircase landing

desembargar /desembar'gar/ *vt* to free of obstacles or impediments; *Law.* remove an embargo

desembargo /desem'bargo/ *m*, *Law.* removal of an embargo

desembarque /desem'barke/ *m*, disembarkation, landing

desembarrancar /desembarran'kar/ *vt* and *vi* *Naut.* to refloat

desembaular /desembau'lar/ *vt* to unpack from a trunk; disinter, empty; *Inf.* unbosom oneself

desembocadero /desemboka'ðero/ *m*, exit, way out; mouth (rivers, etc.)

desembocadura /desemboka'ðura/ *f*, mouth (rivers, etc.); street opening

desembocar /desembo'kar/ *vi* (*with en*) to lead to, end in; flow into (rivers)

desembolsar /desembol'sar/ *vt* to take out of a purse; pay, spend

desembolso /desem'bolso/ *m*, disbursement; expenditure

desemboscarse /desembos'karse/ *vr* to get out of the wood; extricate oneself from an ambush

desembozar /desembo'sar; desembo'θar/ *vt* to unmuffle

desembragar /desembra'gar/ *vt* *Mech.* to disengage (the clutch, etc.)

desembravecer /desembraβe'ser; desembraβe'θer/ *vt* *irr* to tame, domesticate. See **conocer**

desembriagar /desembria'gar/ *vt* and *vr* to sober up (after a drinking bout)

desembrollar /desembro'yar; desembro'ʎar/ *vt* *Inf.* to disentangle, unravel

desemejanza /deseme'hansa; deseme'hanθa/ *f*, unlikeness

desemejar /deseme'har/ *vi* to be unlike; *vt* disfigure, deform

desempacar /desempa'kar/ *vt* to unpack

desempapelar /desempape'lar/ *vt* to unwrap, remove the paper from; remove wallpaper

desempaquetar /desempake'tar/ *vt* to unpack

desemparejar /desempare'har/ *vt* to split (a pair); make unequal

desemparentado /desemparen'taðo/ *a* without relatives

desempedrar /desempe'ðrar/ *vt* *irr* to take up the flags (of a pavement). See **acertar**

desempeñar /desempe'ɲar/ *vt* to redeem (pledges); free from debt; fulfill (obligations, etc.); take out of pawn; hold, fill (an office); extricate (from difficulties, etc.); perform, carry out; *Theat.* act

desempeño /desempe'ɲo/ *m*, redemption of a pledge; fulfillment (of an obligation, etc.); performance, accomplishment; *Theat.* acting of a part

desempolvar /desempol'βar/ *vt* to free from dust, dust

desenamorar /desenamo'rar/ *vt* to kill the affection of; *vr* fall out of love

desencadenar /desenkaðe'nar/ *vt* to unchain, unfetter; *Fig.* unleash, let loose; *vr* *Fig.* break loose

desencajamiento /desenkaha'miento/ *m*, disjointedness, dislocation; ricketiness, broken-down appearance

desencajar /desenka'har/ *vt* to disconnect, disjoint; dislocate; *vr* be out of joint; be contorted (of the face); be tired looking

desencaje /desen'kahe/ *m*, See **desencajamiento**

desencantar /desenkan'tar/ *vt* to disenchant

desencanto /desen'kanto/ *m*, disenchantment; disillusionment

desencerrar /desense'rrar; desenθe'rrar/ *vt* *irr* to set at liberty; unlock; disclose, reveal. See **acertar**

desenchufar /desentʃu'far/ *vt* to disconnect, unplug (electric plugs, etc.)

desenclavijar /desenklaβi'har/ *vt* to remove the pegs or pins; disconnect, disjoint

desencoger /desenko'her/ *vt* to unfold, spread out; *vr* grow bold

desencolerizar /desenkoleri'sar; desenkoleri'θar/ *vt* to placate; *vr* lose one's anger, grow calm

desenconar /desenko'nar/ *vt* to reduce (inflammation); appease (anger, etc.); *vr* become calm

desencono /desen'kono/ *m*, reduction of inflammation; appeasement (of anger, etc.)

desencordelar /desenkorðe'lar/ *vt* to untie the ropes (of), unstring

desencorvar /desenkor'βar/ *vt* to straighten (curves, etc.)

desenfadado /desenfa'ðaðo/ *a* expeditious; natural, at ease; gay; forward, bold; wide, spacious

desenfadar /desenfa'ðar/ *vt* to appease, make anger disappear

desenfado /desen'faðo/ *m*, freedom; ease; unconcern, frankness

desenfrailar /desenfrai'lar/ *vi* to leave the cloister, become secularized; *Inf.* emancipate oneself

desenfrenar /desenfre'nar/ *vt* to unbridle (horses); *vr* give rein to one's passions, etc.; break loose (storms, etc.)

desenfreno /desen'freno/ *m*, license, lasciviousness; complete freedom from restraint

desengalanar /deseŋgala'nar/ *vt* to strip of ornaments

desenganchar /deseŋgan'tʃar/ *vt* to unhook; uncouple; unfasten; unharness

desengañador /deseŋgaɲa'ðor/ *a* undeceiving
desengañar /deseŋga'ɲar/ *vt* to undeceive, disillusion
desengaño /deseŋ'gaɲo/ *m*, undeceiving, disabuse; disillusionment
desengarzar /deseŋgar'sar; deseŋgar'θar/ *vt* to loosen from its setting; unlink, unhook, unclasp
desengastar /deseŋgas'tar/ *vt* to remove from its setting (jewelry, etc.)
desengrasar /deseŋgra'sar/ *vt* to remove the grease from, clean; *vi Inf.* grow thin
desenlace /desen'lase; desen'laθe/ *m*, loosening, untying; *Lit.* denouement, climax (of play, etc.)
desenlatar /desenla'tar/ *vt*, *Lat. Am.* to open (canned food)
desenlazar /desenla'sar; desenla'θar/ *vt* to untie, unloose; *Lit.* unravel (a plot)
desenlosar /desenlo'sar/ *vt* to remove flagstones
desenmarañar /desemara'ɲar/ *vt* to disentangle; *Fig.* straighten out
desenmascarar /desemaska'rar/ *vt* to remove the mask from; *Fig.* unmask
desenmudecer /desemuðe'ser; desemuðe'θer/ *vi irr* to be freed of a speech impediment; break silence, speak. See **conocer**
desenojar /deseno'har/ *vt* to soothe, appease; *vr* distract oneself, amuse oneself
desenojo /dese'noho/ *m*, relenting, abatement of anger
desenredar /desenre'ðar/ *vt* to disentangle; *Fig.* set right; straighten out; *vr* extricate oneself, get out of a difficulty
desenredo /desen'reðo/ *m*, disentanglement; *Lit.* climax
desenroscar /desenros'kar/ *vt Lat. Am.* to unscrew
desentablar /desenta'βlar/ *vt* to tear up planks or boards; disorder, disrupt
desentenderse /desenten'derse/ *vr irr* (*with de*) to pretend to be ignorant of; take no part in. See **entender**
desenterrador /desenterra'ðor/ *m*, disinterrer, unearther
desenterramiento /desenterra'miento/ *m*, disinterment; *Fig.* unearthing, recollection
desenterrar /desente'rrar/ *vt irr* to unbury, disinter; rummage out; *Fig.* unearth, bring up, recall. See **acertar**
desentoldar /desentol'dar/ *vt* to take away an awning; *Fig.* strip of ornament
desentonar /desento'nar/ *vt* to humiliate; *vi Mus.* be out of tune; speak rudely; *vr* be inharmonious; raise the voice (anger, etc.), behave badly
desentono /desen'tono/ *m*, bad behavior, rudeness; *Mus.* discord; grating quality or harshness (of voice)
desentorpecer /desentorpe'ser; desentorpe'θer/ *vt irr* to restore feeling to (numbed limbs); free from torpor; *vr* become bright and intelligent. See **conocer**
desentramparse /desentram'parse/ *vr Inf.* free oneself from debt
desentrañar /desentra'ɲar/ *vt* to disembowel; *Fig.* unravel, penetrate; *vr* give away one's all
desentumecer /desentume'ser; desentume'θer/ *vt irr* to free from numbness (limbs); *vr* be restored to feeling (numb limbs). See **conocer**
desenvainar /desembai'nar/ *vt* to unsheath; *Inf.* reveal, bring into the open
desenvoltura /desembol'tura/ *f*, naturalness, ease, freedom; eloquence, facility (of speech); effrontery, audacity, shamelessness (especially in women)
desenvolver /desembol'βer/ *vt irr* to unroll; unfold; *Fig.* unravel, explain; *Fig.* develop, work out (theories, etc.); *vr* unroll; unfold; lose one's timidity, blossom out; be over-bold; extricate oneself (from a difficulty). See **resolver**
desenvuelto /desem'buelto/ *a* natural, easy; impudent, bold
deseo /de'seo/ *m*, desire, will, wish
deseoso /dese'oso/ *a* desirous, wishful
desequilibrar /desekili'βrar/ (**se**) *vt* and *vr* to unbalance

desequilibrio /deseki'liβrio/ *m*, lack of balance; confusion, disorder; mental instability
deserción /deser'sion; deser'θion/ *f*, *Mil.* desertion.
d. estudiantil, school dropout
desertar /deser'tar/ *vt Mil.* to desert; *Inf.* quit
desertor /deser'tor/ *m*, *Mil.* deserter; *Inf.* quitter
deservicio /deserβisio; deser'βiθio/ *m*, disservice
desesperación /desespera'sion; desespera'θion/ *f*, desperation, despair; frenzy, violence
desesperado /desespe'raðo/ *a* desperate, hopeless; frenzied
desesperanza /desespe'ransa; desespe'ranθa/ *f*, despair; hopelessness
desesperanzar /desesperan'sar; desesperan'θar/ *vt* to render hopeless; *vr* despair, lose hope
desesperar /desespe'rar/ *vt* to make hopeless; *Inf.* annoy, make furious; *vr* lose hope, despair; be frenzied
desestañar /desesta'ɲar/ *vt* to unsolder
desestimación /desesti'sion; desestima'θion/ *f*, disrespect, lack of esteem; rejection
desestimar /desesti'mar/ *vt* to scorn; reject
desfachatado /desfatʃa'taðo/ *a Inf.* impudent, brazen
desfachatez /desfatʃa'tes; desfatʃa'teθ/ *f*, *Inf.* effrontery, cheek
desfalcador /desfalka'ðor/ *a* embezzling. *n* embezzler
desfalcar /desfal'kar/ *vt* to remove a part of; embezzle
desfalco /des'falko/ *m*, diminution, reduction; embezzlement
desfallecer /desfaye'ser; desfaʎe'θer/ *vt irr* to weaken; *vi* grow weak; faint, swoon. See **conocer**
desfallecimiento /desfayesi'miento; desfaʎeθi'miento/ *m*, weakness, languor; depression, discouragement; faint, swoon
desfavorable /desfaβo'raβle/ *a* unfavorable; hostile, contrary
desfavorecer /desfaβore'ser; desfaβore'θer/ *vt irr* to withdraw one's favor, scorn; disfavor; oppose. See **conocer**
desfiguración /desfigura'sion; desfigura'θion/ *f*, deformation; disfigurement
desfigurar /desfigu'rar/ *vt* to deform, misshape; disfigure; *Fig.* disguise, mask; obscure, darken; distort, misrepresent; *vr* be disfigured (by rage, etc.)
desfijar /desfi'har/ *vt* to unfix, pull off, remove
desfiladero /desfila'ðero/ *m*, defile, gully
desfilar /desfi'lar/ *vi* to walk in file; *Inf.* file out; *Mil.* file or march past
desfile /des'file/ *m*, *Mil.* march past; parade; walk past; procession
desflecarse /desfle'karse/ (**en**) *vr* to disintegrate (into)
desfloración /desflora'sion; desflora'θion/ *f*, defloration
desflorar /desflo'rar/ *vt* to tarnish, stain; deflower, violate; *Fig.* touch upon, deal lightly with
desfortalecer /desfortale'ser; desfortale'θer/ *vt irr Mil.* to dismantle a fortress. See **conocer**
desfruncir /desfrun'sir; desfrun'θir/ *vt* to unfold, shake out
desgaire /des'gaire/ *m*, untidiness, slovenliness; affectation of carelessness (in dress); scornful gesture. **al d.,** with an affectation of carelessness, negligently
desgajar /desga'har/ *vt* to tear off a tree branch; break; *vr* break off; dissociate oneself (from)
desgalgar /desgal'gar/ *vt* to throw headlong
desgana /des'gana/ *f*, lack of appetite; lack of interest, indifference; reluctance
desganar /desga'nar/ *vt* to dissuade; *vr* lose one's appetite; become bored or indifferent, lose interest
desgarbado /desgar'βaðo/ *a* slovenly, slatternly; gawky, graceless
desgarrado /desga'rraðo/ *a* dissolute, vicious; impudent, brazen
desgarrador /desgarra'ðor/ *a* tearing; heart-rending
desgarrar /desga'rrar/ *vt* to tear; *vr* leave, tear oneself away

desgarro /des'garro/ *m*, tearing; rent, breach; boastfulness, impudence, effrontery; *Lat. Am.* phlegm

desgastar /desgas'tar/ *vt* to corrode, wear away; spoil, corrupt; *vr* lose one's vigor, grow weak; wear away

desgaste /des'gaste/ *m*, attrition; wearing down or away; corrosion; wear and tear

desgobernado /desɡoβer'naðo/ *a* uncontrolled (of persons)

desgobernar /desɡoβer'nar/ *vt irr* to upset or rise against the government; dislocate (bones); *Naut.* neglect the tiller; *vr* affect exaggerated movements in dancing. See **recomendar**

desgobierno /desɡo'βierno/ *m*, misgovernment; mismanagement; maladministration; disorder, tumult

desgomar /desɡo'mar/ *vt* to ungum (fabrics)

desgorrarse /desɡo'rrarse/ *vr* to doff one's cap, doff one's hat

desgoznar /desɡos'nar/ desɡoθ'nar/ *vt* to unhinge; *vr Fig.* lose one's self-control

desgracia /des'grasia; des'graθia/ *f*, misfortune, adversity; mishap, piece of bad luck; disgrace, disfavor; disagreeableness, brusqueness; ungraciousness. **por d.**, unhappily, unfortunately

desgraciado /desgra'siaðo; desgra'θiaðo/ *a* unfortunate, unhappy; unlucky; dull, boring; disagreeable

desgraciar /desgra'siar; desgra'θiar/ *vt* to displease; spoil the development (of), destroy; maim; *vr* fall out of friendship; be out of favor; turn out badly, fail; be destroyed or spoiled; be maimed

desgranar /desgra'nar/ *vt Agr.* to thresh, flail; *vr* break (string of beads, etc.)

desgrasante /desgra'sante/ *m*, grease remover

desgreñar /desgre'ɲar/ *vt* to dishevel the hair; *vr Inf.* pull each other's hair, come to blows

desguarnecer /desguarne'ser; desguarne'θer/ *vt irr* to strip of trimming; *Mil.* demilitarize; *Mil.* disarm; dismantle; unharness. See **conocer**

desguazar /desgua'sar; desgua'θar/ *vt* to break up (ships)

deshabitado /desaβi'taðo/ *a* uninhabited, empty

deshabitar /desaβi'tar/ *vt* to desert, quit, leave (a place)

deshabituar /desaβi'tuar/ *vt* to disaccustom; *vr* lose the habit, become unaccustomed

deshacer /desa'ser; desa'θer/ *vt irr* to undo; destroy; *Mil.* rout, defeat; take to pieces; melt; pulp (paper); untie (knots, etc.); open (parcels); diminish, decrease; break in pieces, smash; *Fig.* obstruct, spoil; *vr* be wasted or spoiled; be full of anxiety; vanish; try or work very hard; injure oneself; be emaciated, grow extremely thin; (*with de*) part with. **d. agravios**, to right wrongs. See **hacer**

desharrapado /desarra'paðo/ *a* tattered, shabby

deshebillar /deseβi'yar; deseβi'ʎar/ *vt* to unbuckle

deshebrar /dese'βrar/ *vt* to unravel; shred

deshecha /des'etʃa/ *f*, pretense, evasion; courteous farewell; obligatory departure

deshechizar /desetʃi'sar; desetʃi'θar/ *vt* to disenchant

deshecho /des'etʃo/ *a* torn; undone; (of storms) violent

deshelar /dese'lar/ *vt irr* to thaw, melt. See **acertar**

desherbar /deser'βar/ *vt irr* to pull up weeds. See **acertar**

desheredar /desere'ðar/ *vt* disinherit; *vr Fig.* lower oneself

desherrar ,dese'rrar/ *vt irr* to unfetter, unchain; strike off horseshoes; *vr* lose a shoe (horses). See **acertar**

desherrumbrar /deserrum'brar/ *vt* to remove the rust from; clean off rust from

deshidratación /desiðrata'sion; desiðrata'θion/ *f*, dehydration

deshidratar /desiðra'tar/ *vt* to dehydrate

deshielo /des'ielo/ *m*, thaw, thawing out

deshilado /desi'laðo/ *a* in single file. *m*, *Sew.* drawn-thread work (gen. *pl*). **a la deshilada**, *Mil.* in file formation; secretly

deshiladura /desila'ðura/ *f*, unraveling

deshilar /desi'lar/ *vt* to unravel; *Sew.* draw threads; *Cul.* shred, grate

deshilvanado /desilβa'naðo/ *a Fig.* disjointed, disconnected

deshilvanar /desilβa'nar/ *vt Sew.* to remove the tacking threads

deshincar /desin'kar/ *vt* to pull out, remove, draw out

deshinchar /desin'tʃar/ *vt* to remove a swelling; deflate; lessen the anger of; *vr* decrease, subside (swellings); deflate; *Inf.* grow humble

deshojar /deso'har/ *vt* to strip the leaves from, strip the petals from; *Lat. Am.* husk (corn); peel (fruit)

deshollejar /desoye'har; desoʎe'har/ *vt* to skin, peel (fruit); shell (peas, etc.)

deshollinador /desoyina'ðor; desoʎina'ðor/ *m*, chimney-sweep; wall-brush; chemical chimney cleaner

deshollinar /desoyi'nar; desoʎi'nar/ *vt* to sweep chimneys; clean down walls; *Inf.* examine closely

deshonestidad /desonesti'ðað/ *f*, immodesty, shamelessness; indecency

deshonesto /deso'nesto/ *a* shameless, immodest; dissolute, vicious; indecent

deshonor /deso'nor/ *m*, dishonor; disgrace, insult

deshonra /de'sonra/ *f*, dishonor

deshonrabuenos /desonra'βuenos/ *mf Inf.* slanderer; degenerate

deshonrador /desonra'ðor/ **(-ra)** *a* dishonorable. *n* dishonorer

deshonrar /deson'rar/ *vt* to dishonor; insult; seduce (women)

deshonroso /deson'roso/ *a* dishonorable, insulting, indecent

deshora /de'sora/ *f*, inconvenient time. **a d.**, *or* **a deshoras**, at an inconvenient time, unseasonably; extempore

deshuesar /desue'sar/ *vt* to bone, remove the bone (from meat); stone (fruit)

deshumedecer /desumeðe'ser; desumeðe'θer/ *vt irr* to dry; *vr* become dry. See **conocer**

desidia /de'siðia/ *f*, negligence; laziness

desidioso /desi'ðioso/ *a* negligent; lazy

desierto /de'sierto/ *a* deserted, uninhabited, solitary. *m*, desert; wilderness

designación /designa'sion; designa'θion/ *f*, designation; appointment

designar /desig'nar/ *vt* to plan, intend; designate; appoint

designio /de'signio/ *m*, intention, idea

desigual /desi'gual/ *a* unequal; uneven (ground); rough; arduous, difficult; changeable

desigualar /desigua'lar/ *vt* to make unequal; *vr* prosper

desigualdad /desigual'dað/ *f*, inequality; unevenness, rockiness; *Fig.* changeability; variability

desilusión /desilu'sion/ *f*, disillusionment; disappointment

desilusionar /desilusio'nar/ *vt* to disillusion; *vr* become disillusioned; be undeceived

desinclinar /desinkli'nar/ *vt* to dissuade

desinfectante /desinfek'tante/ *a* and *m*, disinfectant

desinfectar /desinfek'tar/ *vt* to disinfect

desinflar /desin'flar/ *vt* to deflate

desinterés /desinte'res/ *m*, disinterestedness

desinteresado /desintere'saðo/ *a* disinterested; generous

desinteresarse /desintere'sarse/ *vr* to lose interest, grow indifferent

desistencia, /desis'tensia,; desis'tenθia,/ *f*, **desistimiento** *m*, desistance, ceasing

desistir /desis'tir/ *vi* to desist; cease; *Law.* renounce

desjuntamiento /deshunta'miento/ *m*, separation; division

desjuntar /deshun'tar/ **(se)** *vt* and *vr* to separate; divide

deslavado /desla'βaðo/ *a* brazen, impudent

deslavar /desla'βar/ *vt* to wash superficially; spoil by washing, take away the body of (cloth, etc.)

desleal /desle'al/ *a* disloyal, treacherous

deslealtad /desleal'tað/ *f*, disloyalty

desleír /desle'ir/ *vt irr* to dissolve; dilute. See **reír**

deslenguado /deslen'gwaðo/ *a* shameless, foul-mouthed

deslenguar /deslen'gwar/ *vt* to remove the tongue; *vr Inf.* be insolent

desliar /des'liar/ *vt* to untie, undo, unloose

desligadura /desliga'ðura/ *f*, untying, loosening

desligar /desli'gar/ *vt* to unfasten, unbind; *Fig.* solve, unravel; relieve of an obligation; *Mus.* play staccato; *vr* come unfastened, grow loose. **desligarse de,** to weasel out of, wiggle out of (a promise)

deslindador /deslinda'ðor/ *m*, one who fixes boundaries or limits

deslindar /deslin'dar/ *vt* to fix the boundaries (of); limit, circumscribe

deslinde /des'linde/ *m*, demarcation, boundary

desliz /des'lis; des'liθ/ *m*, slipping, slip, slide; skid; indiscretion, slip; peccadillo, trifling fault

deslizadero /deslisa'ðero; desliθa'ðero/ *m*, slippery place; chute

deslizadizo /deslisa'ðiso; desliθa'ðiθo/ *a* slippery

deslizar /desli'sar; desli'θar/ *vt* to slip, slide; skid; *vr* commit an indiscretion; speak or act unwisely; escape, slip away; slip; skid

deslucido /des'lusiðo; des'luθiðo/ *a* fruitless, vain; stupid, clumsy, awkward; discolored; tarnished, dull; unsuccessful

deslucimiento /deslusi'miento; desluθi'miento/ *m*, clumsiness, gracelessness; failure, lack of success

deslucir /deslu'sir; deslu'θir/ *vt irr* to fade; discolor, stain; tarnish; spoil; sully the reputation of; *vr* do a thing badly, fail at. See **lucir**

deslumbrador /deslumbra'ðor/ *a* dazzling

deslumbramiento /deslumbra'miento/ *m*, brilliant light, glare, dazzle; bewilderment, confusion

deslumbrar /deslumb'rar/ *vt* to dazzle; confuse, bewilder; *Fig.* daze (with magnificence)

deslustrar /deslus'trar/ *vt* to dull, dim, tarnish; frost (glass); discredit, sully (reputation)

deslustre /des'lustre/ *m*, dullness, tarnish; frosting (of glass); disgrace, stigma

deslustroso /deslus'troso/ *a* ugly, unsuitable, unbecoming

desmadejar /desmaðe'har/ *vt* to debilitate, enervate

desmalezar /desmale'sar; desmale'θar/ *vt*, *Lat. Am.* to clear the underbrush from; weed

desmán /des'man/ *m*, outrageous behavior; disaster, misfortune

desmandado /desman'daðo/ *a* disobedient

desmandar /desman'dar/ *vt* to cancel, revoke (orders); withdraw (an offer). *vr* behave badly; stray

desmantelado /desmante'laðo/ *a* dismantled, dilapidated

desmantelamiento /desmantela'miento/ *m*, dismantling; dilapidation

desmantelar /desmante'lar/ *vt* to dismantle; abandon, forsake

desmaña /des'maɲa/ *f*, lack of dexterity, clumsiness, awkwardness

desmañado /desma'ɲaðo/ *a* clumsy, awkward, unhandy

desmayado /desma'yaðo/ *a* pale, faint (of colors); weak (of a voice)

desmayar /desma'yar/ *vt* to cause to faint; *vi* grow discouraged, lose heart; *vr* swoon, faint

desmayo /des'mayo/ *m*, depression, discouragement; faint, swoon

desmedido /desme'ðiðo/ *a* disproportionate; excessive

desmedirse /desme'ðirse/ *vr* to misbehave, go too far

desmedrado /desme'ðraðo/ *a* thin, emaciated; deteriorated, spoiled

desmedrar /desme'ðrar/ *vt* to spoil, ruin; *vi* deteriorate; decline

desmedro /des''meðro/ *m*, impairment; decline, deterioration. **en d. de,** to the detriment of

desmejora /desme'hora/ *f*, deterioration

desmejorar /desmeho'rar/ *vt* to spoil, impair, cause to deteriorate; *vr* deteriorate; *vi* and *vr* decline in health; lose one's beauty

desmelenar /desmele'nar/ *vt* to ruffle or dishevel the hair

desmembración /desmembrasion; desmembra'θion/ *f*, dismemberment

desmembrar /desmem'brar/ *vt* to dismember; separate, divide

desmemoriarse /desmemo'riarse/ *vr* to forget, lose one's memory

desmenguar /desmen'guar/ *vt* to reduce, decrease; *Fig.* diminish

desmentida /desmen'tiða/ *f*, action of giving the lie to

desmentir /desmen'tir/ *vt irr* to give the lie to; contradict, deny; lower oneself; behave unworthily; *vi* deviate (from right direction, etc.). See **sentir**

desmenuzar /desmenu'sar; desmenu'θar/ *vt* to crumble, break into small pieces; *Fig.* examine in detail; *vr* be broken up

desmeollar /desmeo'yar; desmeo'ʎar/ *vt* to remove the marrow of

desmerecedor /desmerese'ðor; desmereθe'ðor/ *a* unworthy

desmerecer /desmere'ser; desmere'θer/ *vt irr* to become undeserving of; *vi* deteriorate; be inferior to. See **conocer**

desmesura /desme'sura/ *f*, insolence; disproportion; excess

desmesurado /desmesu'raðo/ *a* disproportionate; excessive, enormous; insolent, uncivil

desmesurar /desmesu'rar/ *vt* to disarrange, disorder; *vr* be insolent

desmigajar /desmiga'har/ **(se)** *vt* and *vr* to crumble

desmigar /desmi'gar/ *vt Cul.* to make breadcrumbs

desmilitarizar /desmilitari'sar; desmilitari'θar/ *vt* to demilitarize

desmochar /desmo'tʃar/ *vt* to lop off the top; pollard (trees)

desmonetización /desmonetisa'sion; desmoneti'θa'θion/ *f*, demonetization; conversion of coin into bullion

desmonetizar /desmoneti'sar; desmoneti'θar/ *vt* to convert money into bullion; demonetize; *vr* depreciate (shares, etc.)

desmontable /desmon'taβle/ *a* movable; sectional

desmontadura /desmonta'ðura/ *f*, clearing; deforestation; leveling; dismounting, dismounting

desmontar /desmon'tar/ *vt* to clear wholly or partly of trees or shrubs; clear up (rubbish); level (ground); dismantle; dismount; uncock (firearms); *vi* and *vr* dismount (from horse, etc.)

desmonte /des'monte/ *m*, clearing of trees and shrubs; clearing, cleared ground; timber remaining

desmoralización /desmoralisa'sion; desmorali'θa'θion/ *f*, demoralization, corruption

desmoralizador /desmoralisa'ðor; desmoraliθa'ðor/ *a* demoralizing

desmoralizar /desmorali'sar; desmorali'θar/ *vt* to demoralize, corrupt

desmoronamiento /desmorona'miento/ *m*, crumbling; decay, ruin

desmoronar /desmoro'nar/ *vt* to destroy, decay; crumble; *vr* crumble away, fall into ruin; decline, decay; wane, fade (power, etc.)

desmovilización /desmoβilisa'sion; desmoβili'θa'θion/ *f*, demobilization

desmovilizar /desmoβili'sar; desmoβili'θar/ *vt* to demobilize

desnacificación /desnasifika'sion; desnaθifika'θion/ *f*, denazification

desnatar /desna'tar/ *vt* to skim; *Fig.* take the cream or best

desnaturalización /desnaturalisa'sion; desnaturali'θa'θion/ *f*, denaturalization

desnaturalizar /desnaturali'sar; desnaturali'θar/ *vt* to denaturalize; exile; deform, disfigure, pervert; *vr* give up one's country

desnivel /desni'βel/ *m*, unevenness; slope, drop

desnivelar /desniβe'lar/ **(se)** *vi* and *vr* to become uneven

desnudar /desnu'ðar/ *vt* to undress; *Fig.* despoil, strip, denude; *vr* undress oneself; deprive oneself

desnudez /desnu'ðes; desnu'ðeθ/ *f*, nudity; nakedness; bareness; plainness

desnudo /des'nuðo/ *a* nude; ill-clad; bare, naked; clear, patent; *Fig.* destitute (of grace, etc.). *m*, *Art.* nude

desnutrición /desnutri'sion; desnutri'θion/ *f*, malnutrition

desobedecer /desoβeðe'ser; desoβeðe'θer/ *vt irr* to disobey. See **conocer**

desobediencia /desoβeðien'sia; desoβeðien'θia/ *f*, disobedience

desobediente /desoβe'ðiente/ *a* disobedient

desobligar /desoβli'gar/ *vt* to free from obligation; offend, hurt

desocupación /desokupa'sion; desokupa'θion/ *f*, lack of occupation; leisure

desocupado /desoku'paðo/ *a* idle; vacant, unoccupied

desocupar /desoku'par/ *vt* to empty; vacate; *vr* give up an employment or occupation

desodorante /desoðo'rante/ *a* and *m*, deodorant

desoir /deso'ir/ *vt irr* to pay no attention, pretend not to hear. See **oir**

desolación /desola'sion; desola'θion/ *f*, destruction, desolation; affliction

desolador /desola'ðor/ *a* desolate; grievous

desolar /deso'lar/ *vt irr* to lay waste, destroy; *vr* grieve, be disconsolate. See **contar**

desoldar /desol'dar/ *vt* to unsolder; *vr* become unsoldered

desolladero /desoya'ðero; desoʎa'ðero/ *m*, slaughterhouse

desollado /deso'yaðo; deso'ʎaðo/ *a Inf.* impertinent, barefaced. *m*, carcass

desolladura /desoya'ðura; desoʎa'ðura/ *f*, flaying, skinning; *Inf.* slander

desollar /deso'yar; deso'ʎar/ *vt irr* to flay, skin; harm, discredit. **d. vivo**, *Inf.* to extort an exorbitant price; slander. See **contar**

desopinado /desopi'naðo/ *a* discredited

desopinar /desopi'nar/ *vt* to discredit, defame

desorden /des'orðen/ *m*, disorder, disarray; confusion; excess

desordenado /desorðe'naðo/ *a* disordered; vicious; licentious

desordenar /desorðe'nar/ *vt* to disorder; confuse; *vr* go beyond the just limits; behave badly; be impertinent

desorganización /desorganisa'sion; desorganiθa'θion/ *f*, disorganization

desorganizador /desorganisa'ðor; desorganiθa'ðor/ *a* disorganizing

desorganizar /desorgani'sar; desorgani'θar/ *vt* to disorganize; disband

desorientación /desorienta'sion; desorienta'θion/ *f*, disorientation, loss of bearings; lack of method, confusion

desorientar /desorien'tar/ *vt* to disorient; perplex, confuse; *vr* lose one's way; be disoriented

desovar /deso'βar/ *vi* to spawn

desove /de'soβe/ *m*, spawning; spawning season

desovillar /desoβi'yar; desoβi'ʎar/ *vt* to unwind; uncoil; uncurl; explain, clarify

despabiladeras /despaβila'ðeras/ *f pl*, snuffers

despabilado /despaβi'laðo/ *a* alert, wide-awake; watchful, vigilant

despabiladura /despaβila'ðura/ *f*, snuff of a candle, lamp, etc.

despabilar /despaβi'lar/ *vt* to snuff (a candle); trim (lamps); hasten, expedite; finish quickly; steal, rob; *Fig.* quicken (intelligence, etc.); *Inf.* kill; *vr* rouse oneself, wake up

despachador /despatʃa'ðor/ **(-ra)** *n* dispatcher, sender

despachar /despa'tʃar/ *vt* to expedite; dispatch, conclude; forward, send; attend to correspondence; sell; dismiss; *Inf.* serve in a shop; *Inf.* kill; *vi* hasten; carry letters to be signed (in offices, etc.); *vr* get rid of

despachero, -a /despa'tʃero/ *mf Chile* shopkeeper, storekeeper

despacho /despa'tʃo/ *m*, transaction, execution; study; office, room; department; booking-office; dispatch, shipment; expedient; commission, warrant; dispatch (diplomatic); telegram; telephone message. **d. particular**, private office

despachurrar /despa'tʃurrar/ *vt Inf.* to crush, squash; recount in a muddled fashion; *Fig.* squash flat, confound

despacio /des'pasio; des'paθio/ *adv* slowly, little by little; deliberately, leisurely. *interj* Careful! Gently now!

despacito /despa'sito; despa'θito/ *adv Inf.* very slowly

despalmador /despalma'ðor/ *m*, dockyard

despampanar /despampa'nar/ *vt Agr.* to prune vines; *Inf.* amaze, stun, astound; *vi Inf.* relieve one's feelings; *vr Inf.* receive a serious injury (through falling)

desparpajar /desparpa'har/ *vt* to spoil; *vi Inf.* chatter

desparpajo /despar'paho/ *m*, *Inf.* loquaciousness, pertness; disorder, muddle

desparramar /desparra'mar/ *vt* to disperse, scatter; squander, waste (money, etc.); *vr* amuse oneself; be dissipated

despavorido /despaβo'riðo/ *a* terrified, panicstricken

despechar /despe'tʃar/ *vt* to anger; make despair; *Inf.* wean; *vr* be angry; be in despair

despecho /des'petʃo/ *m*, rancor, malice; despair. **a d. de**, in spite of

despechugar /despetʃu'gar/ *vt* to cut off the breast (fowls); *vr Inf.* show the bosom

despectivo /despek'tiβo/ *a* contemptuous, depreciatory

despedazar /despeða'sar; despeða'θar/ *vt* to cut or break into pieces; *Fig.* break (heart, etc.)

despedida /despe'ðiða/ *f*, dismissal, discharge; seeing off (a visitor, etc.); farewell, good-by

despedir /despe'ðir/ *vt irr* to throw out, emit, cast up; dismiss, discharge; see off (on a journey or after a visit); banish (from the mind); get rid of; *vr* say good-by; leave (employment). See **pedir**

despedregar /despeðre'gar/ *vt* to clear of stones

despegadamente /despegaða'mente/ *adv* uninterestedly, unconcernedly, indifferently

despegado /despe'gaðo/ *a Inf.* indifferent, unconcerned, cold

despegar /despe'gar/ *vt* to unstick; unglue; separate, detach; *vr* become estranged; come apart or unstuck; *vi Aer.* take off. **sin d. los labios**, without saying a word

despegue /des'pege/ *m*, *Aer.* take-off

despeinar /despei'nar/ *vt* to disarrange the hair; undo the coiffure

despejado /despe'haðo/ *a* lively, sprightly; logical, clear-cut; cloudless; spacious, unobstructed, clear, clear skies (in weather reports)

despejar /despe'har/ *vt* to clear, free of obstacles; **d. el camino de,** to clear the way for; *Fig.* elucidate, solve; *Math.* find the value of; *vr* smarten up, grow gay; amuse oneself; clear up (weather, sky, etc.); improve (a patient)

despejo /des'peho/ *m*, freeing of obstacles; smartness, gaiety; grace, elegance; perkiness; clearsightedness, intelligence

despellejar /despeʎe'har; despe'ʎehar/ *vt* to flay, skin; slander

despeluzar /despelu'sar; despelu'θar/ *vt* to disorder the hair; cause the hair to stand on end; horrify; *vr* stand on end (hair); be horrified or terrified

despeluznante /despelus'nante; despeluθ'nante/ *a* hair-raising, terrifying

despendedor /despende'ðor/ **(-ra)** *n* spendthrift, waster

despender /despen'der/ *vt* to spend; waste

despensa /des'pensa/ *f*, larder, pantry; store (of food); *Naut.* steward's room; stewardship

despensero /despen'sero/ **(-ra)** *n* steward; caterer; victualler; *Naut.* steward

despeñadero /despeɲa'ðero/ *m*, precipice, crag; dangerous undertaking, risk. *a* steep, precipitous

despeñar /despe'ɲar/ *vt* to precipitate, fling down from a height, hurl down; *vr* fling oneself headlong; throw oneself into (vices, etc.)

despeño /des'peɲo/ *m*, precipitation; headlong fall; *Fig.* collapse, ruin

despepitar /despepi'tar/ *vt* to remove seeds or pips; *vr* vociferate; act wildly; *Inf.* desire, long (for)

desperdiciador /desperði'siaðor; desperði'θiaðor/ **(-ra)** *a* squandering, wasting. *n* squanderer

desperdiciar /desperði'siar; desperði'θiar/ *vt* to squander; *Fig.* misspend, waste

desperdicio /desper'ðisio; desper'ðiθio/ *m*, waste; remains, leftovers (gen. *pl*)

desperdigar /desperði'gar/ *vt* to separate, sever; scatter

desperecerse /despere'serse; despere'θerse/ *vr irr* to crave, yearn (for). See **conocer**

desperezarse /despere'sarse; despere'θarse/ *vr* to stretch oneself

desperfecto /desper'fekto/ *m*, imperfection, flaw; slight deterioration

despernado /desper'naðo/ *a* weary, footsore

despertador /desperta'ðor/ **(-ra)** *a* awakening. *n* awakener. *m*, alarm clock; incentive, stimulus

despertar /desper'tar/ *vt irr* to awaken; bring to mind, recall; incite, stimulate; *vi* waken; *Fig.* wake up, become more intelligent. See **acertar**

despiadado /despia'ðaðo/ *a* cruel, merciless

despicar /despi'kar/ *vt* to satisfy, content; *vr* revenge oneself

despierto /des'pierto/ *a* wide-awake, clever

despilfarrado /despilfa'rraðo/ *a* ragged, shabby; wasteful; spendthrift

despilfarrar /despilfa'rrar/ *vt* to squander, waste

despilfarro /despil'farro/ *m*, slovenliness; waste, extravagance; mismanagement, poor administration

despintar /despin'tar/ *vt* to paint out; wash off the paint; efface, blot out; disfigure, deform; *vi* be unlike or unworthy (of); *vr* fade (colors); forget

despiojar /despio'har/ *vt* to remove lice, delouse; *Inf.* rescue from misery

despique /des'pike/ *m*, vengeance, revenge

despistar /despis'tar/ *vt* to throw off the scent; mislead

desplacer /despla'ser; despla'θer/ *vt irr* to displease. *m*, disgust, displeasure, sorrow. See **placer**

desplantar /desplan'tar/ **(se)** *vt* and *vr* to deviate from the vertical

desplazamiento /desplasa'miento; desplaθa'miento/ *m*, *Naut.* displacement

desplegadura /desplega'ðura/ *f*, unfolding

desplegar /desple'gar/ *vt irr* to unfold; spread open; *Fig.* reveal, disclose, explain; evince, display; *Mil.* deploy troops; *vr* unfold, open (flowers, etc.); *Mil.* deploy. See **cegar**

despliegue /des'pliege/ *m*, unfolding; spreading out; evincing, demonstration; *Mil.* deployment

desplomar /desplo'mar/ *vt* to put out of the straight, cause to lean (walls, buildings); *vr* lean, tilt (buildings); topple, fall down (walls, etc.); collapse (people); be ruined

desplome /des'plome/ *m*, collapse

desplomo /des'plomo/ *m*, tilt, cant, deviation from vertical

desplumar /desplu'mar/ *vt* to remove feathers, pluck; rob, despoil

despoblación /despoβla'sion; despoβla'θion/ *f*, depopulation. **d. forestal,** deforestation

despoblado /despo'βlaðo/ *m*, wilderness; deserted place

despoblar /despo'βlar/ *vt* to depopulate; despoil, rob; *vr* become depopulated

despojador /despoha'ðor/ **(-ra)** *a* robbing, despoiling. *n* despoiler

despojar /despo'har/ *vt* to plunder, despoil; dispossess; *vr* (*with de*) remove (garments, etc.); relinquish, give up

despojo /des'poho/ *m*, pillaging, spoliation; booty,

plunder; butcher's offal; *pl* remains, leavings; debris, rubble; corpse

despolvorear /despolβore'ar/ *vt* to remove dust; *Fig.* shake off

desposado /despo'saðo/ *a* recently married; fettered, handcuffed. **los desposados,** the newlyweds

desposar /despo'sar/ *vt* to perform the marriage ceremony; *vr* become betrothed; marry

desposeer /despose'er/ *vt* to dispossess; *vr* renounce one's possessions. See **creer**

desposeimiento /desposei'miento/ *m*, dispossession

desposorio /despo'sorio/ *m*, betrothal, promise of marriage; (gen. *pl*) wedding, marriage

déspota /'despota/ *m*, despot, tyrant

despótico /des'potiko/ *a* tyrannical

despotismo /despo'tismo/ *m*, despotism

despotricarse /despotri'karse/ *vr* to rave (against), rail (against)

despreciable /despre'siaβle; despre'θiaβle/ *a* worthless, contemptible

despreciar /despre'siar; despre'θiar/ *vt* to scorn, despise; *vr* despise oneself

despreciativo /despresia'tiβo; despreθia'tiβo/ *a* contemptuous, scornful

desprecio /des'presio; des'preθio/ *m*, contempt, scorn

desprender /despren'der/ *vt* to loosen, remove, unfix; give off (gases, etc.); *vr* work loose, give way; deduce, infer; give away, deprive oneself (of)

desprendido /despren'diðo/ *a* disinterested; generous

desprendimiento /desprendi'miento/ *m*, loosening; removal, separation; emission; indifference, lack of interest; generosity; impartiality

despreocupación /despreokupa'sion; despreokupa'θion/ *f*, fair mindedness, impartiality; lack of interest

despreocupado /despreoku'paðo/ *a* unprejudiced, broadminded; indifferent, uninterested

despreocuparse /despreoku'parse/ *vr* to shake off prejudice; (*with de*) pay no attention to; set aside

desprestigiar /despresti'hiar/ *vt* to discredit; *vr* lose prestige; lose caste

desprestigio /despres'tihio/ *m*, loss of prestige, discredit

desprevenido /despreβe'niðo/ *a* unprepared, improvident

desproporción /despropor'sion; despropor'θion/ *f*, disproportion

desproporcionado /desproporsio'naðo; despropor-θio'naðo/ *a* disproportionate; out of proportion

despropósito /despro'posito/ *m*, nonsense, absurdity

desproveer /desproβe'er/ *vt irr* to deprive of necessities. See **creer**

despueble /des'pueβle/ *m*, depopulation

después /des'pues/ *adv* afterwards, after, next (of time and place)

despuntar /despun'tar/ *vt* to blunt the point; *Naut.* double, sail round; *vi* show green, sprout; appear (the dawn); grow clever; *Fig.* stand out, excel

desquiciamiento /deskisia'miento; deskiθia'miento/ *m*, unhinging; disconnecting; *Fig.* upsetting, throwing out of gear; downfall, fall from favor

desquiciar /deski'siar; deski'θiar/ *vt* to unhinge; disconnect; *Fig.* throw out of gear, upset; banish from favor; *vr* become unhinged; *Fig.* be disordered; upset

desquitar /deski'tar/ **(se)** *vt* and *vr* to retrieve a loss; take revenge, retaliate

desquite /des'kite/ *m*, compensation; revenge

desrielar /desrie'lar/ *vt*, *Lat. Am.* to derail

destacamento /destaka'mento/ *m*, *Mil.* detachment

destacar /desta'kar/ *vt Mil.* to detach; *vr* excel; be prominent; be conspicuous; *Art.* stand out

destajador /destaha'ðor/ *m*, smith's hammer

destajar /desta'har/ *vt* to cut (cards); set forth conditions, stipulate, contract; *Lat. Am.* cut up

destajista /desta'hista/ *mf* pieceworker; jobber (worker)

destajo /des'taho/ *m*, piecework; job. **a d.,** quickly and diligently. *Inf.* **hablar a d.**, to chatter, talk too much

destapar /desta'par/ *vt* to remove the cover or lid; reveal, uncover; *vr* be uncovered; reveal oneself. **no destaparse**, to keep quiet, be mum

destartalado /destarta'laðo/ *a* tumble-down, rickety; poverty-stricken

destechado /deste'tʃaðo/ *a* roofless

destejar /deste'har/ *vt* to remove tiles or slates; leave unprotected

destejer /deste'her/ *vt* to unweave, unravel; *Fig.* undo, spoil

destello /deste'yo; des'teʎo/ *m*, gleam, sparkle, brilliance; flash, beam, ray; *Fig.* gleam (of talent)

destemplado /destem'plaðo/ *a* out of tune; inharmonious; intemperate; *Art.* inharmonious; *Inf.* out of sorts, indisposed

destemplanza /destem'plansa; destem'planθa/ *f*, inclemency, rigor (weather); intemperance, excess, abuse; *Inf.* indisposition; lack of moderation (actions, speech)

destemplar /destem'plar/ *vt* to disturb, upset, alter; *Mus.* put out of tune; put to confusion; *vr* be unwell; *Fig.* go too far, behave badly; lose temper (metals)

destemple /des'temple/ *m, Mus.* being out of tune; *Med.* indisposition; uncertainty (weather); lack of temper (metals); disturbance, disorder; intemperance, excess, confusion

desternillarse de risa /desterni'yarse de 'rrisa; desterni'ʎarse de 'rrisa/ to shake with laughter

desterrado /deste'rraðo/ **(-da)** *a* exiled. *n* exile

desterrar /deste'rrar/ *vt irr* to exile; shake off the soil; *Fig.* discard, lay aside; extirpate (an error). See **recomendar**

destetar /deste'tar/ *vt* to wean

destete /des'tete/ *m*, weaning

destiempo, a /des'tiempo, a/ *adv* untimely, inopportunely

destierro /des'tierro/ *m*, banishment, exile; place of exile; remote place

destilación /destila'sion; destila'θion/ *f*, distillation

destilador /destila'ðor/ **(-ra)** *n* distiller. *m*, still

destilar /desti'lar/ *vt* to distill; filter; *vi* to drip

destilatorio /destila'torio/ *a* distilling. *m*, distillery; still

destilería /destile'ria/ *f*, distillery

destinar /desti'nar/ *vt* to destine; appoint; assign

destino /des'tino/ *m*, fate, destiny; post, appointment; destination. **con d. a,** going to, bound for

destitución /destitu'sion; destitu'θion/ *f*, destitution; discharge, dismissal

destituir /destitu'ir/ *vt irr* (*with de*) to dismiss or discharge from (employment); deprive of. See **huir**

destorcer /destor'ser; destor'θer/ *vt irr* to untwist; straighten out; *vr Naut.* drift. See **torcer**

destornillado /destorni'yaðo; destorni'ʎaðo/ *a* reckless; *Fig. Inf.* with a screw loose

destornillador /destorni'yaðor; destorni'ʎaðor/ *m*, screwdriver

destornillamiento /destorniya'miento; destorniʎa'miento/ *m*, unscrewing

destornillar /destorni'yar; destorni'ʎar/ *vt* to unscrew; *vr* act rashly

destrenzar /destren'sar; destren'θar/ *vt* to unbraid. **destrenzarse las cintas,** to unlace one's shoes

destreza /des'tresa; des'treθa/ *f*, dexterity; agility

destrón /des'tron/ *m*, blind person's guide

destronamiento /destrona'miento/ *m*, dethronement

destronar /destro'nar/ *vt* to dethrone, depose; oust

destroncamiento /destronka'miento/ *m*, detruncation

destroncar /destron'kar/ *vt* to lop, detruncate (trees); dislocate, disjoint; mutilate; *Fig.* ruin, seriously harm; tire out; *Lat. Am.* uproot *or* be exhausted or tired

destrozar /destro'sar; destro'θar/ *vt* to destroy; break in pieces, shatter; *Mil.* wipe out, annihilate; squander, dissipate

destrozo /des'troso; des'troθo/ *m*, destruction, ruin; shattering; *Mil.* rout; dissipation, waste

destrozón /destro'son; destro'θon/ *a* hard on wearing apparel, shoes, etc.

destrucción /destruk'sion; destruk'θion/ *f*, destruction; ruin, irreparable loss

destructible /destruk'tiβle/ *a* destructible

destructivo /destruk'tiβo/ *a* destructive

destructor /destruk'tor/ **(-ra)** *a* destructive. *n* destroyer. *m, Nav.* destroyer

destruible /destruiβle/ *a* destructible

destruir /destru'ir/ *vt irr* to destroy, ruin, annihilate; frustrate, blast, disappoint; deprive of means of subsistence; squander, waste; *vr Math.* cancel. See **huir**

desuello /desue'yo; desue'ʎo/ *m*, flaying, skinning; forwardness, impertinence; extortion, fleecing. *Fig. Inf.* **¡Es un d.!** It's highway robbery!

desunión /desu'nion/ *f*, disunion, separation; *Fig.* discord, disharmony

desunir /desu'nir/ *vt* to disunite, separate; *Fig.* cause discord or disharmony

desusarse /desu'sarse/ *vr* to fall into disuse, become obsolete

desuso /de'suso/ *m*, disuse

desvaído /desβa'iðo/ *a* gaunt, lanky; pale, faded, dull (of colors)

desvainar /desβai'nar/ *vt* to shell (peas, beans)

desvalido /des'βaliðo/ *a* unprotected, helpless

desvalijar /desβali'har/ *vt* to rifle (a suitcase, etc.); swindle

desvalimiento /desβali'miento/ *m*, defenselessness, lack of protection; lack of favor; desertion, abandonment

desvalorización /desβalorisa'sion; desβaloriθa'θion/ *f*, devaluation

desván /des'βan/ *m*, garret

desvanecer /desβane'ser; desβane'θer/ *vt irr* to cause to disappear; disintegrate; make vain; remove; *vr* evaporate; faint, swoon; grow vain or conceited. See **conocer**

desvanecimiento /desβanesimiento; desβaneθi'miento/ *m*, faintness, loss of consciousness; vanity, conceit

desvarar /desβa'rar/ *vt* to slip, slide; *Naut.* refloat

desvariar /desβa'riar/ *vi* to be delirious; rave, talk wildly

desvarío /desβa'rio/ *m*, foolish action, absurdity; delirium; monstrosity; whim, caprice

desvedar /desβe'ðar/ *vt* to raise a ban or prohibition

desvelar /desβe'lar/ *vt* to keep awake; *vr* be sleepless; (*with por*) take great care over

desvelo /des'βelo/ *m*, sleeplessness, vigil; care, attention, vigilance; anxiety. **con d.,** watchfully

desvencijar /desβensi'har; desβenθi'har/ *vt* to loosen, disconnect, disjoint; *vr* work loose, become disjointed

desventaja /desβen'taha/ *f*, disadvantage. **estar en d.,** to be at a disadvantage

desventajoso /desβenta'hoso/ *a* disadvantageous

desventura /desβen'tura/ *f*, misfortune

desventurado /desβentu'raðo/ *a* unfortunate; timid, faint-hearted; miserly

desvergonzado /desβergonsaðo; desβergon'θaðo/ *a* shameless, brazen, impudent

desvergonzarse /desβergon'sarse; desβergon'θarse/ *vr irr* to be brazen, be impudent. See **avergonzar**

desvergüenza /desβer'guensa; desβer'guenθa/ *f*, insolence; shamelessness

desvestir /desβes'tir/ **(se)** *vt* and *vr irr* to undress. See **pedir**

desviación /desβia'sion; desβia'θion/ *f*, deviation, deflection

desviadero /desβia'ðero/ *m*, diversion; *Rail.* siding

desviar /des'βiar/ *vt* to divert, deflect; dissuade

desvío /des'βio/ *m*, deviation; indifference, coldness; repugnance

desvirgar /desβir'gar/ *vt* to deflower

desvirtuar /desβir'tuar/ *vt* to decrease in strength or merit

desvivirse /desβi'βirse/ *vr* (*with por*) to adore, love dearly; yearn for, be dying to; do one's best to please, (e.g. *Juan se desvive por servirme*, John does his best to help me)

detallar /deta'yar; deta'ʎar/ *vt* to tell in detail; relate

detalle /de'taye; de'taʎe/ *m*, retail account; detail, particular; *Com.* itemized bill

detallismo /deta'yismo; deta'ʎismo/ *m*, meticulous attention to details

detective /de'tektiβe/ *mf* detective

detector /detek'tor/ *m*, detector; *Radio.* catwhisker

detención /deten'sion; deten'θion/ *f*, stop, halt; delay; prolixity; arrest, detention. **con d.**, carefully, meticulously

detener /dete'ner/ *vt irr* to detain, stop; arrest; retain, keep; *vr* go slowly; tarry; halt, stop; (*with en*) pause over, stop at. See **tener**

detenido /dete'niðo/ *a* timid, irresolute; miserable, mean

deterioración /deteriora'sion; deteriora'θion/ *f*, deterioration

deteriorar /deterio'rar/ **(se)** *vt* and *vr* to deteriorate

determinación /determina'sion; determina'θion/ *f*, determination; daring; decision

determinado /determi'naðo/ *a* resolute, determined

determinar /determi'nar/ *vt* to determine, limit; discern, distinguish; specify, appoint; decide, resolve; *Law.* define, judge; *vr* make up one's mind

determinativo /determina'tiβo/ *a* determining

determinismo /determi'nismo/ *m*, determinism

determinista /determi'nista/ *mf* determinist. *a* deterministic

detersorio /deter'sorio/ *a* and *m*, detergent

detestable /detes'taβle/ *a* detestable

detestación /detesta'sion; detesta'θion/ *f*, detestation

detestar /detes'tar/ *vt* to abominate, detest

detonación /detona'sion; detona'θion/ *f*, detonation

detonador /detona'ðor/ *m*, detonator

detonar /deto'nar/ *vi* to detonate

detractor /detrak'tor/ **(-ra)** *a* slandering *n* detractor, slanderer

detraer /detra'er/ *vt irr* to detract, take away; separate; slander. See **traer**

detrás /de'tras/ *adv* behind, after (place). **por d.**, in the rear; *Fig.* behind one's back

detrimento /detri'mento/ *m*, detriment; moral harm. **en d. de,** to the detriment of

deuda /'deuða/ *f*, debt; fault, offense; sin. **d. exterior,** foreign debt. **estar en d. con,** to be indebted to. **Perdónanos nuestras deudas,** Forgive us our trespasses

deudo /'deuðo/ *m*, relative, kinsman; kinship, relationship

deudor /deu'ðor/ **(-ra)** *a* indebted. *n* debtor. **d. hipotecario,** mortgagor

devanadera /deβana'ðera/ *f*, bobbin, reel, spool; winder (machine)

devanador /deβana'ðor/ **(-ra)** *n* winder (person). *m*, spool, bobbin

devanar /deβa'nar/ *vt* to reel, wind. *Inf.* **devanarse los sesos,** to rack one's brains

devanear /deβane'ar/ *vi* to rave, talk nonsense

devaneo /deβa'neo/ *m*, delirium; foolishness, nonsense; dissipation; love affair

devastación /deβasta'sion; deβasta'θion/ *f*, devastation

devastar /deβas'tar/ *vt* to devastate, lay waste; *Fig.* destroy, ruin

develador /deβela'ðor/ *m*, betrayer

devengar /deβeŋ'gar/ *vt* to have a right to, earn (salary, interest, etc.)

devoción /deβo'sion; deβo'θion/ *f*, piety; affection, love; pious custom; prayer

devocionario /deβosio'nario; deβoθio'nario/ *m*, prayer book

devolución /deβolu'sion; deβolu'θion/ *f*, restitution, return; its devolution

devolutivo /deβolu'tiβo/ *a Law.* returnable

devolver /deβol'βer/ *vt irr* to restore to original state; return, give back; repay; **devolverse** *vr Lat. Am.* to come back, go back, return. See **resolver**

devorador /deβora'ðor/ **(-ra)** *a* devouring. *n* devourer

devorar /deβo'rar/ *vt* to devour; destroy, consume

devoto /de'βoto/ **(-ta)** *a* devout, pious; devoted, fond. *n* devotee. *m*, object of devotion

día /dia/ *m*, day; daylight; *pl* name or saint's day; birthday (e.g. *Hoy son los días de María*, This is Mary's saint's day (or birthday)). **d. de Año Nuevo,** New Year's Day. **d. de asueto,** day off. **d. de ayuno** or **de vigilia,** fast day. **d. del cura,** *humorous* wedding day. **d. del juicio,** Day of Judgment. **d. de los difuntos,** All Souls' Day. **d. de recibo,** at home day. **d. de Reyes,** Epiphany (when Spanish children receive their Christmas presents). **d. de trabajo** or **d. laborable,** working day. **d. por medio,** every other day. **días caniculares,** dog days. **d. por d.,** day by day. **al d.,** up to date; per day. **al otro d.,** next day. **¡Buenos días!** Good morning! Good day! **de d.,** by day. **de d. en d.,** from day to day. **de un d. a otro,** any time now, very soon. **el d. de mañana,** tomorrow, the near future. **un d. sí y otro no,** every other day. **vivir al d.,** to live up to one's income

diabético /dia'βetiko/ *a* diabetic

diablillo /dia'βliyo; dia'βliʎo/ *m*, *dim* devilkin, imp; *Inf.* madcap

diablo /'diaβlo/ *m*, devil; Satan; *Fig.* fiend. *Inf.* **d. cojuelo,** mischievous devil; *Fig. Inf.* imp. *Inf.* **Anda el d. suelto,** The Devil's abroad, there's trouble. *Inf.* **tener el d. en el cuerpo,** to be as clever as the Devil; be mischievous

diablura /dia'βlura/ *f*, mischief, prank; devilry

diabólico /dia'βoliko/ *a* diabolical, devilish; *Inf.* fiendish, iniquitous

diaconisa /diako'nisa/ *f*, deaconess

diácono /'diakono/ *m*, deacon

diadema /dia'ðema/ *f*, diadem; crown; tiara

diafanidad /diafani'ðað/ *f*, transparency

diáfano /'diafano/ *a* transparent, diaphanous

diafragma /dia'fragma/ *m*, *Anat. Mech.* diaphragm; sound-box (of a phonograph)

diagnosticar /diagnosti'kar/ *vt Med.* to diagnose

diagnóstico /diag'nostiko/ *a* diagnostic. *m*, diagnosis. **d. precoz,** early diagnosis

diagonal /diago'nal/ *a* diagonal; oblique

diagrama /dia'grama/ *m*, diagram

diagramación /diagrama'sion; diagrama'θion/ *f*, layout (of a publication)

dialectal /dialek'tal/ *a* dialect

dialéctica /dia'lektika/ *f*, dialectic. **La d. de Hegel,** Hegelian dialectic

dialéctico /dia'lektiko/ *a* dialectic. *m*, logician

dialecto /dia'lekto/ *m*, dialect

dialogar /dialo'gar/ *vi* to hold dialogue, converse; *vt* write dialogue

diálogo /'dialogo/ *m*, dialogue

diamante /dia'mante/ *m*, diamond; miner's lamp; glass-cutting diamond. **d. bruto,** rough diamond

diamantífero /diaman'tifero/ *a* diamond-bearing

diamantino /diaman'tino/ *a* diamantine; *Poet.* adamant

diamantista /diaman'tista/ *mf* diamond-cutter; diamond merchant

diámetro /'diametro/ *m*, diameter

diana /'diana/ *f*, *Mil.* reveille; bull's-eye (of a target); the moon

¡diantre! /'diantre/ *interj Inf.* the deuce!

diapasón /diapa'son/ *m*, *Mus.* tuning fork; diapason; neck (of violins, etc.). **d. normal,** tuning fork. **d. vocal,** pitch-pipe

diapositiva /diaposi'tiβa/ *f*, *Photo.* diapositive; (lantern) slide

diario /'diario/ *a* daily. *m*, diary; daily paper; daily expenses. **d. del navegación,** ship's diary. **d. de viaje,** travel diary, trip journal

diarismo /dia'rismo/ *m*, *Lat. Am.* journalism

diarista /dia'rista/ *mf* journalist, diarist

diarrea /dia'rrea/ *f*, diarrhea

diatónico /dia'toniko/ *a Mus.* diatonic

diatriba /dia'triβa/ *f*, diatribe

diávolo /'diaβolo/ *m*, diabolo (game)

dibujante /diβu'hante/ *m*, sketcher; draftsman; designer

dibujar /diβu'har/ *vt Art.* to draw; describe, depict; *vr* appear, be revealed; be outlined, stand out

dibujo /di'βuho/ *m*, drawing; sketch, design, pattern; depiction, description. **d. a la pluma**, pen-and-ink drawing. **d. a pulso**, freehand drawing. **d. del natural**, drawing from life

dicción /dik'sion; dik'θion/ *f*, word; diction, language, style

diccionario /diksio'nario; dikθio'nario/ *m*, dictionary

díceres /'diseres; 'diθeres/ *m pl West Hem.* news

dicha /'ditʃa/ *f*, happiness; good fortune. **por d.**, by chance; fortunately

dicharacho /ditʃa'ratʃo/ *m*, *Inf.* vulgar expression, slangy expression

dicho /'ditʃo/ *m*, saying, phrase, expression; witty remark; *Law.* declaration; *Inf.* insult. *a* said, aforementioned. *past part* **decir**, **"said." D. y hecho,** No sooner said than done. **Del d. al hecho hay muy gran trecho,** There's many a slip 'twixt the cup and the lip. **Lo d. d.,** The agreement stands

dichoso /di'tʃoso/ *a* happy; lucky; *Inf.* blessed, wretched, darn

diciembre /di'siembre; di'θiembre/ *m*, December

dictado /dik'taðo/ *m*, title of honor; dictation; *pl* promptings (of heart, etc.). **escribir al d.**, to write to dictation

dictador /dikta'ðor/ *m*, dictator

dictadura /dikta'ðura/ *f*, dictatorship

dictamen /dik'tamen/ *m*, judgment, opinion

dictaminar /diktami'nar/ *vi* to give judgment or opinion

dictar /dik'tar/ *vt* to dictate; suggest, inspire; *Lat. Am.* give (a lecture). **dictar fallo,** to hand down a decision, render judgment

dictatorial, dictatorio /diktato'rial, dikta'torio/ *a* dictatorial

dicterio /dik'terio/ *m*, taunt, insult

didáctica /di'ðaktika/ *f*, didactics

didáctico /di'ðaktiko/ *a* didactic

diecinuevavo /diesinue'βeaβo; dieθinue'βeaβo/ *a* and *m*, nineteenth

diecinueve /diesi'nueβe; dieθi'nueβe/ *a* and *m*, nineteen

dieciochavo /diesio'tʃaβo; dieθio'tʃaβo/ *a* and *m*, eighteenth

dieciocheno /diesio'tʃeno; dieθio'tʃeno/ *a* See **décimoctavo**

dieciocho /die'siotʃo; die'θiotʃo/ *a* and *m*, eighteen

dieciséis /diesi'seis; dieθi'seis/ *a* and *m*, sixteen

dieciseisavo /diesisei'saβo; dieθisei'saβo/ *a* and *m*, sixteenth

dieciseiseno /diesisei'seno; dieθisei'seno/ *a* See **décimosexto**

diecisiete /diesi'siete; dieθi'siete/ *a* and *m*, seventeen

diecisieteavo /diesisiete'aβo; dieθisiete'aβo/ *a* and *m*, seventeenth

diente /diente/ *m*, tooth; tooth (of saw, etc.); tusk; cog (of wheel); prong (of fork); tongue (of a buckle). **d. de leche**, milk-tooth. *Bot.* **d. de león,** dandelion. **d. de perro,** *Sew.* feather-stitch. *Inf.* **dar d. con d.,** to chatter (teeth). *Fig. Inf.* **enseñar** (*or* **mostrar**) **los dientes,** to show one's teeth; threaten. *Inf.* **estar a d.,** to be famished. **hablar entre dientes,** to mutter; fume, grumble. *Inf.* **tener buen d.,** to have a good appetite. **traer a uno entre dientes,** to loathe someone; speak scandal of

diestra /'diestra/ *f*, right hand; protection

diestro /'diestro/ *a* right (hand); skillful, dextrous; shrewd; astute, cunning; favorable, happy. *m*, expert fencer; bullfighter; halter; bridle

dieta /'dieta/ *f*, *Med.* diet; *Inf.* fast, abstinence; legislative assembly; travel allowance (gen. *pl*); day's journey of ten leagues; daily fee (gen. *pl*)

dietario /die'tario/ *m*, household accounts' book

dietética /die'tetika/ *f*, dietetics

dietético /die'tetiko/ *a* dietetic

dietista /die'tista/ *mf* dietician

diez /dies; dieθ/ *a* ten; tenth. *m*, ten; decade of rosary

diezmar /dies'mar; dieθ'mar/ *vt* to tithe; decimate; punish every tenth person

diezmero /dies'mero; dieθ'mero/ **(-ra)** *n* tax-gatherer

diezmesino /diesme'sino; dieθme'sino/ *a* ten months old

diezmillo /dies'mijo; dieθ'miʎo/ *m*, *Mexico* sirloin

diezmo /'diezmo; 'dieθmo/ *m*, ten per cent tax; tithe

difamación /difama'sion; difama'θion/ *f*, defamation, libel

difamador /difama'ðor/ **(-ra)** *a* libeling. *n* libeler

difamar /difa'mar/ *vt* to libel; denigrate

difamatorio /difama'torio/ *a* libelous, defamatory

diferencia /dife'rensia; dife'renθia/ *f*, unlikeness, dissimilarity; *Math.* difference; dissension, disagreement. **a d. de,** unlike; in contrast to

diferenciación /diferensia'sion; diferenθia'θion/ *f*, differentiation. **d. del trabajo,** division of labor

diferencial /diferen'sial; diferen'θial/ *a* differential

diferenciar /diferen'siar; diferen'θiar/ *vt* to differentiate; change the function (of); *vi* dissent, disagree; *vr* be different, differ; distinguish oneself

diferente /dife'rente/ *a* different, various

diferir /dife'rir/ *vt irr* to delay, retard; postpone; suspend, interrupt; *vi* be different. See **discernir**

difícil /di'fisil; di'fiθil/ *a* difficult

dificultad /difikul'taδ/ *f*, difficulty; impediment, obstacle; objection

dificultar /difikul'tar/ *vt* to raise difficulties; put obstacles in the way; *vi* think difficult (of achievements)

dificultoso /difikul'toso/ *a* difficult; *Inf.* ugly (face, figure, etc.)

difidencia /difi'ðensia; difi'ðenθia/ *f*, mistrust; lack of faith, doubt

difidente /difi'ðente/ *a* mistrustful

difracción /difrak'sion; difrak'θion/ *f*, diffraction

difractar /difrak'tar/ *vt* to diffract

difteria /dif'teria/ *f*, diphtheria

difundir /difun'dir/ *vt* to diffuse (fluids); spread, publish, divulge; *Radio.* broadcast

difunto /di'funto/ **(-ta)** *a* and *n* deceased. *m*, corpse

difusión /difu'sion/ *f*, diffusion; prolixity; *Radio.* broadcasting

difusivo /difu'siβo/ *a* diffusive

difuso /di'fuso/ *a* widespread, diffuse; prolix, wordy

digerible /dihe'riβle/ *a* digestible

digerir /dihe'rir/ *vt irr* to digest; bear patiently; consider carefully; *Chem.* digest. See **sentir**

digestible /dihes'tiβle/ *a* easily digested

digestivo /dihes'tiβo/ *a* digestive

digesto /di'hesto/ *m*, *Law.* digest

digitación /dihita'sion; dihita'θion/ *f*, *Mus.* fingering

digital /dihi'tal/ *a* digital. *f*, *Bot.* foxglove, digitalis

dígito /'dihito/ *a* digital. *m*, (*Astron. Math.*) digit

dignación /digna'sion; digna'θion/ *f*, condescension

dignarse /dig'narse/ *vr* to deign, condescend

dignatario /digna'tario/ *m*, dignitary

dignidad /digni'ðaδ/ *f*, dignity, stateliness; serenity, loftiness; high office or rank; high repute, honor; *Eccl.* dignitary

dignificar /dignifi'kar/ *vt* to dignify

digno /'digno/ *a* worthy, deserving; upright, honorable; fitting, suitable, appropriate

digresión /digre'sion/ *f*, digression

dije /'dihe/ *m*, charm; trinket, any small piece of jewelry; *Inf.* person of excellent qualities, jewel

dilacerar /dilase'rar; dilaθe'rar/ *vt* to lacerate, tear flesh; *Fig.* discredit

dilación /dila'sion; dila'θion/ *f*, delay

dilapidación /dilapiða'sion; dilapiða'θion/ *f*, waste, dissipation, squandering

dilapidar /dilapi'ðar/ *vt* to waste, squander

dilatación /dilata'sion; dilata'θion/ *f*, expansion; enlargement, widening; prolongation; *Surg.* dilatation; respite (in trouble)

dilatador /dilata'ðor/ *a* dilating. *m*, *Surg.* dilater

dilatar /dila'tar/ *vt* to dilate, enlarge; expand; delay, postpone; spread, publish abroad; prolong; *vr* expand; be prolix, spread oneself; *Lat. Am.* to be slow, take a long time

dilatorio /dila'torio/ *a* procrastinating, dilatory

dilección /dilek'sion; dilek'θion/ *f,* affection, love

dilema /di'lema/ *m,* dilemma

diletantismo /diletan'tismo/ *m,* dilettantism

diligencia /dili'hensia; dili'henθia/ *f,* care, conscientiousness; industry; haste, briskness; diligence (coach); *Inf.* business, occupation. **hacer diligencias,** to run errands. **hacer sus diligencias,** to try one's best

diligenciar /dilihen'siar; dilihen'θiar/ *vt* to set on foot, put into motion

diligente /dili'hente/ *a* diligent, conscientious, industrious; speedy, prompt

dilucidación /dilusiδa'sion; diluθiδa'θion/ *f,* elucidation, clarification

dilucidar /dilusi'δar; diluθi'δar/ *vt* to elucidate, clarify

dilución /dilu'sion; dilu'θion/ *f,* dilution

diluir /di'luir/ *vt irr* to dilute. See **huir**

diluviar /dilu'βiar/ *vi* to teem with rain

diluvio /di'luβio/ *m,* flood, inundation; *Inf.* very heavy rain, deluge; overabundance

dimanación /dimana'sion; dimana'θion/ *f,* emanation, source

dimanar /dima'nar/ *vi* (*with de*) to rise in (rivers); proceed from, originate in

dimensión /dimen'sion/ *f,* dimension; size, extent

dimes y diretes /'dimes i di'retes/ *m pl, Inf.* chat

diminutivo /diminu'tiβo/ *a* diminutive; diminishing; *Gram.* diminutive

diminuto /dimi'nuto/ *a* defective, incomplete; minute, very small

dimisión /dimi'sion/ *f,* resignation (of office, etc.)

dimisorias /dimi'sorias/ *f pl, Eccl.* letter dimissory. *Inf.* **dar d. a uno,** to give a person his marching orders, dismiss

dimitente /dimi'tente/ *a* resigning; retiring. *mf* resigner (of a post)

dimitir /dimi'tir/ *vt* to resign (office, post, etc.)

Dinamarca /dina'marka/ Denmark

dinamarqués /dinamar'kes/ **(-esa)** *a* Danish. *n* Dane

dinámica /di'namika/ *f,* dynamics

dinámico /di'namiko/ *a* dynamic

dinamita /dina'mita/ *f,* dynamite

dinamo /'dinamo/ *f,* dynamo

dinasta /di'nasta/ *mf* dynast

dinastía /dinas'tia/ *f,* dynasty

dinástico /di'nastiko/ *a* dynastic

dineral /dine'ral/ *m,* large amount of money, fortune

dinero /di'nero/ *m,* money; Peruvian coin; wealth, fortune; currency. **d. contante, d. junto,** ready cash, **Poderoso caballero es Don D.,** Money talks

dinosauro /dino'sauro/ *m,* dinosaur

dintel /'dintel/ *m,* lintel; *Lat. Am.* threshold

diocesano /diose'sano; dioθe'sano/ *a* diocesan

diócesis /'diosesis; 'dioθesis/ *f,* diocese

Dios /dios/ *m,* God; deity. **¡D. le guarde!** God keep you! **¡D. lo quiera!** God grant it! **D. mediante,** God willing (D.V.). **¡D. mío!** Good gracious! **De menos nos hizo D.,** Nothing is impossible, Never say die. **¡No lo quiera D.!** God forbid! **¡Plegue a D.!** Please God! **¡Por D.!** For goodness sake! Heavens! **¡Válgame D.!** Bless me! **¡Vaya Vd. con D.!** Goodbye! Off with you! Depart! **¡Vive D.!** By God!

diosa /'diosa/ *f,* goddess

diploma /di'ploma/ *m,* license, bull; diploma. **d. de suficiencia,** general diploma

diplomacia /diplo'masia; diplo'maθia/ *f,* diplomacy; tactfulness; *Inf.* astuteness

diplomarse /diplo'marse/ *vr, Lat. Am.* to get one's degree, receive one's degree

diplomático /diplo'matiko/ *a* diplomatic; tactful; *Inf.* astute. *m,* diplomat. **cuerpo d.,** diplomatic corps

dipsomanía /dipsoma'nia/ *f,* dipsomania

diptongo /dip'tongo/ *m,* diphthong

diputación /diputa'sion; diputa'θion/ *f,* deputation; mission

diputado /dipu'taδo/ **(-da)** *n* deputy, delegate. **d. a**

Cortes, member of the Spanish Parliament, congressman

diputar /dipu'tar/ *vt* to appoint, depute; delegate; empower

dique /'dike/ *m,* dike; dam; dry dock; *Fig.* bulwark, check; **d. flotante,** floating dock

dirección /direk'sion; direk'θion/ *f,* direction; management, control, guidance; directorate; instruction; information; order, wish, command; editorial board; directorship, managership; (postal) address; managerial office. **d. cablegráfica,** cable address **d. particular,** home address

directiva /direk'tiβa/ *f,* board, governing body

directivo /direk'tiβo/ *a* directive, control, ling; guiding, managing

directo /di'rekto/ *a* direct; straight

director /direk'tor/ **(-ra)** *a* directing, controlling. *n* director; manager; principal, head (schools, etc.); editor. **d. del ceremonial,** chief of protocol. **d. de escena,** stagemanager. **d. espiritual,** *Eccl.* father confessor. **d. gerente,** managing director

directorio /direk'torio/ *a* directory, advising. *m,* directory; directorate, board of directors

dirigible /diri'hiβle/ *m,* airship

dirigir /diri'hir/ *vt* to direct; regulate; govern; supervise; guide; *Mus.* conduct; address (an envelope, etc.); keep (a shop, etc.); edit; put (a question); point (a gun); cast (a glance); *vr* go; plan one's way. **d. la palabra (a),** to speak to, address. **d. la vista a,** to look towards, look in the direction of, turn towards, turn in the direction of. **dirigirse a,** to go towards; make one's way to; address (someone)

dirimir /diri'mir/ *vt* to annul, make void; break, dissolve; settle (disputes, etc.)

discernimiento /disserni'miento; disθerni'miento/ *m,* discernment; judgment; discrimination

discernir /disser'nir; disθer'nir/ *vt irr* to discern, distinguish. *Pres. Ind.* **discierno, disciernes, discierne, disciernen.** *Pres. Subjunc.* **discierna, disciernas, discierna, disciernan**

disciplina /dissi'plina; disθi'plina/ *f,* discipline; system, philosophy, education; submission, obedience; subject (arts or science); *pl* scourge

disciplinante /dissipli'nante; disθipli'nante/ *a* disciplinary. *m,* scourge

disciplinar /dissipli'nar; disθipli'nar/ *vt* to train; educate; scourge, beat; discipline; *vr* scourge oneself

disciplinario /dissipli'nario; disθipli'nario/ *a* disciplinary

discipulado /dissipu'laδo; disθipu'laδo/ *m,* pupilship, studentship; education, teaching; discipleship; body of pupils (of a school, etc.)

discípulo /dis'sipulo; dis'θipulo/ **(-la)** *n* pupil, student; disciple, follower

disco /'disko/ *m,* discus; disk; phonograph record; *Astron.* disk. **d. compacto,** compact disc. **d. de señales,** railway signal. **d. giratorio,** turntable (of a phonograph)

discóbolo /dis'koβolo/ *m,* discus thrower

díscolo /'diskolo/ *a* willful, unmanageable

disconformidad /diskonformi'δaδ/ *f,* disagreement; disconformity

discontinuo /diskon'tinuo/ *a* intermittent, discontinuous

discordancia /diskor'δansia; diskor'δanθia/ *f,* discord, disagreement

discordar /diskor'δar/ *vi* to be discordant; disagree; *Mus.* be out of tune

discorde /dis'korδe/ *a* discordant; *Mus.* dissonant

discordia /dis'korδia/ *f,* discord, disagreement

discreción /diskre'sion; diskre'θion/ *f,* discretion; circumspection; prudence, good sense; shrewdness; pithy or clever saying. **a d.,** at discretion; at will; voluntarily. *Mil.* **darse (or entregarse) a d.,** to surrender unconditionally

discrecional /diskresio'nal; diskreθio'nal/ *a* optional, voluntary

discrepancia /diskre'pansia; diskre'panθia/ *f,* discrepancy; disagreement

discrepar /diskre'par/ *vi* to be discrepant; differ; disagree

discreto /dis'kreto/ *a* discreet; ingenious, witty

disculpa /dis'kulpa/ *f*, excuse

disculpabilidad /diskulpaβili'ðað/ *f*, pardonableness

disculpable /diskul'paβle/ *a* excusable

disculpar /diskul'par/ *vt* to excuse; forgive, pardon; *vr* apologize; excuse oneself

discurrir /disku'rrir/ *vi* to wander, roam; flow, run (rivers, etc.); (*with en*) consider, think about; (*with sobre*) discourse on; *vt* invent; conjecture

discursivo /diskur'siβo/ *a* discursive; thoughtful, reflective

discurso /dis'kurso/ *m*, reasoning power; oration, discourse; consideration, reflection; speech, conversation; dissertation. **d. aceptatorio,** acceptance speech

discusión /disku'sion/ *f*, discussion

discutible /disku'tiβle/ *a* debatable; disputable

discutir /disku'tir/ *vt* to discuss, debate, consider

disecar /dise'kar/ *vt Anat.* to dissect; stuff animals; mount plants

disección /disek'sion; disek'θion/ *f*, dissection

disector /disek'tor/ *m*, dissector, anatomist

diseminación /disemina'sion; disemina'θion/ *f*, dissemination

diseminar /disemi'nar/ *vt* to disseminate; spread

disensión /disen'sion/ *f*, dissension

disentería /disente'ria/ *f*, dysentery

disentimiento /disenti'miento/ *m*, dissent

disentir /disen'tir/ *vi irr* to dissent; disagree. See **sentir**

diseñador /diseɲa'ðor/ *m*, delineator, drawer

diseñar /dise'ɲar/ *vt* to outline, sketch

diseño /di'seɲo/ *m*, outline, sketch; plan; description

disertación /diserta'sion; diserta'θion/ *f*, dissertation

disertar /diser'tar/ *vi* (*with sobre*) to discourse on, discuss, treat of

diserto /di'serto/ *a* eloquent

disfavor /disfa'βor/ *m*, disfavor, discourtesy, slight

disforme /dis'forme/ *a* deformed; ugly; enormous

disfraz /dis'fras; dis'fraθ/ *m*, disguise; mask; fancy dress; pretense

disfrazar /disfra'sar; disfra'θar/ *vt* to disguise; dissemble, misrepresent; *vr* disguise oneself; wear fancy dress

disfrutar /disfru'tar/ *vt* to enjoy (health, comfort, friendship, etc.); reap the benefit of; *vi* take pleasure in, enjoy

disfrute /dis'frute/ *m*, enjoyment, use, benefit

disgregación /disgrega'sion; disgrega'θion/ *f*, separation, disjunction

disgregar /disgre'gar/ *vt* to separate, disjoin

disgustado /disgus'taðo/ *a* annoyed; discontented, dissatisfied; melancholy, depressed

disgustar /disgus'tar/ *vt* to displease, dissatisfy; annoy; *Fig.* depress; *vr* quarrel, fall out. **Me disgusta la idea de marcharme,** I don't like the idea of going away

disgusto /dis'gusto/ *m*, displeasure, dissatisfaction; discontent; annoyance; affliction, sorrow, trouble; quarrel; boredom; repugnance

disidente /disi'ðente/ *a* dissenting. *mf* dissenter, nonconformist

disidir /disi'ðir/ *vi* to dissent

disímil /di'simil/ *a* dissimilar, different, unlike

disimulación /disimula'sion; disimula'θion/ *f*, dissimulation, pretense

disimulado /disimu'laðo/ *a* feigned, pretended

disimular /disimu'lar/ *vt* to dissemble; pretend, feign; put up with, tolerate; misrepresent, misinterpret

disimulo /di'simulo/ *m*, pretense, dissimulation; tolerance, patience

disipación /disipa'sion; disipa'θion/ *f*, dispersion; dissipation, frivolity; immorality

disipado /disi'paðo/ *a* spendthrift; dissipated, frivolous

disipar /disi'par/ *vt* to disperse; squander; *vr* evaporate; vanish, fade, disappear

dislate /dis'late/ *m*, absurdity, nonsense

dislexia /dis'leksia/ *f*, dyslexia.

dislocación /disloka'sion; disloka'θion/ *f*, dislocation

dislocar /dislo'kar/ *vt* to dislocate; *vr* dislocate; sprain

disminución /disminu'sion; disminu'θion/ *f*, diminution. **ir** (**una cosa**) **en d.,** to diminish, decrease; taper, grow to a point

disminuido físico /dismi'nuiðo 'fisiko/ *m*, physically impaired person, physically handicapped person

disminuir /dismi'nuir/ *vt* and *vi irr* to diminish, decrease. See **huir**

disociación /disosia'sion; disoθia'θion/ *f*, dissociation. **d. nuclear,** nuclear fission

disociar /diso'siar; diso'θiar/ *vt* to dissociate, separate; *Chem.* dissociate

disoluble /diso'luβle/ *a* dissoluble

disolución /disolu'sion; disolu'θion/ *f*, dissolution; immorality, laxity; disintegration; loosening, relaxation

disolutivo /disolu'tiβo/ *a* dissolvent, solvent

disoluto /diso'luto/ *a* dissolute, vicious

disolvente /disol'βente/ *m*, dissolvent, solvent

disolver /disol'βer/ *vt irr* to loosen, undo; *Chem.* dissolve; separate, disintegrate; annul. See **resolver**

disonancia /diso'nansia; diso'nanθia/ *f*, dissonance; disagreement; *Mus.* dissonant

disonante /diso'nante/ *a* dissonant; discordant, inharmonious

disonar /diso'nar/ *vi irr* to be inharmonious; disagree. See **sonar**

dísono /di'sono/ *a* dissonant

dispar /dis'par/ *a* unequal; unlike, different

disparadero /dispara'ðero/ *m*, trigger of a firearm

disparador /dispara'ðor/ *m*, shooter, firer; trigger (of firearms); ratchet (of watch); *a, Mexico* lavish

disparar /dispa'rar/ *vt* to shoot, fire; throw or discharge with violence; *vr* run precipitately; rush (towards); bolt (horses); race (of a machine); explode, go off; *Inf.* go too far, misbehave; *Mexico* spend lavishly

disparatado /dispara'taðo/ *a* foolish; absurd, unreasonable

disparatar /dispara'tar/ *vi* to act or speak foolishly

disparate /dispa'rate/ *m*, foolishness, nonsense

disparidad /dispari'ðað/ *f*, disparity, dissimilarity

disparo /dis'paro/ *m*, shooting; explosion; racing (of an engine); discharge; foolishness

dispendio /dis'pendio/ *m*, squandering, extravagance

dispendioso /dispen'dioso/ *a* costly, expensive

dispensa /dis'pensa/ *f*, dispensation; privilege

dispensable /dispen'saβle/ *a* dispensable; excusable

dispensación /dispensa'sion; dispensa'θion/ *f*, dispensation; exemption

dispensar /dispen'sar/ *vt* to grant, concede, distribute; exempt; excuse, forgive

dispensario /dispen'sario/ *m*, dispensary

dispepsia /dis'pepsia/ *f*, dyspepsia

dispéptico /dis'peptiko/ (**-ca**) *a* and *n* dyspeptic

dispersar /disper'sar/ *vt* to disperse, scatter, separate; *Mil.* rout

dispersión /disper'sion/ *f*, dispersion

disperso /dis'perso/ *a* dispersed, scattered; *Mil.* separated from regiment

displicencia /displi'sensia; displi'θenθia/ *f*, disagreeableness, coldness; hesitation, lack of enthusiasm

displicente /displi'sente; displi'θente/ *a* unpleasant, disagreeable; difficult, peevish

disponer /dispo'ner/ *vt irr* to arrange, dispose; direct, order; decide; prepare, get ready; *vi* (*with de*) dispose of, make free with; possess; have at one's disposal; *vr* prepare oneself to die; make one's will; get ready. See **poner**

disponible /dispo'niβle/ *a* disposable; available

disposición /disposi'sion; disposi'θion/ *f*, arrangement; order, instruction; decision; preparation; aptitude, talent; disposal; condition of health; temperament; grace of bearing; promptitude, competence; measure, step, preliminary; *Archit.* plan; proviso, stipulation; symmetry. **A la d. de Vd,** I (we, he, it, etc.) am at your disposal. **hallarse en d. de hacer una cosa,** to be ready to do something. **última d.,** last will and testament

dispositivo /disposi'tiβo/ a directory, advisory
dispuesto /dis'puesto/ a ready, prepared; handsome, gallant; clever, wide-awake. **bien d.**, well-disposed; well, healthy. **mal d.**, ill-disposed; disinclined; out of sorts, indisposed
disputa /dis'puta/ f, dispute. **sin d.**, undoubtedly
disputar /dispu'tar/ vt to argue, debate; dispute, question; *Fig.* fight for
disquisición /diskisi'sion; diskisi'θion/ f, disquisition
distancia /dis'tansia; dis'tanθia/ f, distance; interval of time; difference, dissimilarity; unfriendliness, coolness
distanciar /distan'siar; distan'θiar/ vt to separate, place farther apart
distante /dis'tante/ a separated; distant; far off
distar /dis'tar/ vi to be distant (time and place); be different, unlike
distender /disten'der/ (se) vt and vr *Med.* to distend, swell
distinción /distin'sion; distin'θion/ f, distinction, differentiation; difference, individuality; privilege, honor; clarity, order; distinction (of bearing or mind). **a d. de**, unlike, different from
distinguible /distiŋ'guiβle/ a distinguishable
distinguido /distiŋ'guiðo/ a distinguished, illustrious
distinguir /distiŋ'guir/ vt to distinguish, discern; differentiate; characterize; esteem, honor, respect; discriminate; see with difficulty; make out; vr be different; excel, distinguish oneself
distintivo /distin'tiβo/ a distinguishing; distinctive. m, distinguishing mark
distinto /dis'tinto/ a different; distinct; clear
distracción /distrak'sion; distrak'θion/ f, distraction; abstraction, heedlessness, absentmindedness; pleasure, amusement; licentiousness
distraer /distra'er/ vt irr to lead astray; distract (attention); influence for bad; amuse. vr be absentminded; amuse oneself. See **traer**
distraído /distra'iðo/ a abstracted, absentminded; inattentive; licentious *Lat. Am.* slovenly
distribución /distriβu'sion; distriβu'θion/ f, distribution; (gen. pl) share
distribuidor /distriβui'ðor/ (-ra) a distributing. n distributor
distribuir /distri'βuir/ vt irr to distribute; share out, divide. See **huir**
distributivo /distriβu'tiβo/ a distributive
distrito /dis'trito/ m, district
disturbio /dis'turβio/ m, disturbance
disuadir /disua'ðir/ vt to dissuade
disuasión /disua'sion/ f, dissuasion
disuasivo /disua'siβo/ a dissuasive
disyunción /disyun'sion; disyun'θion/ f, disjunction
dita /'dita/ f, *Lat. Am.* debt
ditirambo /diti'rambo/ m, dithyramb; excessive praise
diurético /diu'retiko/ a diuretic
diurno /'diurno/ a diurnal
diva /'diβa/ f, prima donna; woman singer
divagación /diβaga'sion; diβaga'θion/ f, wandering, roaming; digression
divagar /diβa'gar/ vi to wander, roam; digress
diván /di'βan/ m, divan (Turkish supreme council); divan, sofa; collection of Arabic, Persian or Turkish poems
divergencia /diβer'hensia; diβer'henθia/ f, divergence; disagreement
divergente /diβer'hente/ a divergent, conflicting, dissentient
divergir /diβer'hir/ vi to diverge; dissent
diversidad /diβersi'ðað/ f, diversity, unlikeness, difference; variety
diversificar /diβersifi'kar/ vt to differentiate; vary
diversión /diβer'sion/ f, pastime, amusement; *Mil.* diversion
diverso /di'βerso/ a diverse, unlike; pl various, many
divertido /diβer'tiðo/ a amusing, funny, entertaining
divertir /diβer'tir/ vt irr to lead astray, turn aside; entertain; *Mil.* create a diversion. vr amuse oneself. See **sentir**

dividendo /diβi'ðendo/ m, dividend. *Com.* **d. activo,** dividend
dividir /diβi'ðir/ vt to divide; distribute; stir up discord; vr (with de) part company with, leave
divieso /di'βieso/ m, *Med.* boil
divinamente /diβina'mente/ adv divinely; excellently, admirably, perfectly
divinidad /diβini'ðað/ f, divinity, Godhead; person or thing of great beauty
divino /di'βino/ a divine; excellent, admirable, superb
divisa /di'βisa/ f, badge, emblem; *Herald.* motto
divisar /diβi'sar/ vt to glimpse, descry
divisibilidad /diβisiβili'ðað/ f, divisibility
divisible /diβi'siβle/ a divisible
división /diβi'sion/ f, division, partition; discord; (*Math. Mil.*) division; hyphen; apportionment; district, ward
divisor /diβi'sor/ (-ra) a dividing, separating. m, *Math.* divisor. n divider, separator
divisoria /diβi'soria/ f, dividing line
divisorio /diβi'sorio/ a dividing
divorciar /diβor'siar; diβor'θiar/ vt to divorce; separate; vr be divorced, be separated
divorcio /di'βorsio; di'βorθio/ m, divorce
divulgación /diβulga'sion; diβulga'θion/ f, spreading, publication, propagation
divulgar /diβul'gar/ (se) vt and vr to spread abroad, publish
DNA DNA, m
do /do/ m, *Mus.* doh, C. *Poet.* where
dobladillo /doβla'ðiyo; doβla'ðiʎo/ m, *Sew.* hem; turn-up (of a trouser)
doblado /do'βlaðo/ a stocky, thickset, sturdy, rocky, rough, uneven; dissembling. m, garret
dobladura /doβla'ðura/ f, fold, crease; crease mark
doblamiento /doβla'miento/ m, doubling; folding
doblar /do'βlar/ vt to double, multiply by two; fold, double; bend; persuade, induce; *Naut.* double, sail round; turn, walk round; vi *Eccl.* ring the passing bell; *Theat.* double a role; vr fold, double; bend; bow; stoop; allow oneself to be persuaded
doble /'doβle/ a double, twofold; duplicate; insincere, false; thick (cloth); *Bot.* double (flowers); hardy, robust. m, fold, crease; *Eccl.* passing-bell; Spanish dance step. adv double, twice. *Eccl.* **rito d.,** full rites
doblegar /doβle'gar/ vt to fold; bend; brandish; dissuade in favor of another proposition; vr submit, give way, acquiesce
doblete /do'βlete/ a of medium thickness. m, imitation jewel
doblez /do'βleθ/ m, fold, crease; fold mark. mf, double dealing; treachery
doblilla /do'βliya; do'βliʎa/ f, twenty-real coin
doblón /do'βlon/ m, doubloon
doce /'dose; 'doθe/ a twelve. m, twelve; twelfth (of the month). **las d.,** twelve o'clock
docena /do'sena; do'θena/ f, dozen. **la d. del fraile,** baker's dozen
docente /do'sente; do'θente/ a teaching
dócil /'dosil; 'doθil/ a docile; obedient; flexible, easily worked (metals, etc.)
docilidad /dosili'ðað; doθili'ðað/ f, docility, obedience; flexibility
docto /'dokto/ a learned, erudite
doctor /dok'tor/ (-ra) n doctor; physician; teacher. f, *Inf.* blue-stocking
doctorado /dokto'raðo/ m, doctorate
doctorarse /dokto'rarse/ vr to get one's doctorate
doctrina /dok'trina/ f, doctrine; instruction, teaching; theory, conception; *Eccl.* sermon
doctrinar /doktri'nar/ vt to teach, instruct
documentación /dokumenta'sion; dokumenta'θion/ f, documentation; collection of documents, papers
documental /dokumen'tal/ a documental. m, documentary film
documentar /dokumen'tar/ vt to document
Dodecaneso, el /doðeka'neso, el/ the Dodecanese

dogal /do'gal/ *m*, halter; noose; slipknot. *Fig.* **estar con el d.** **a la garganta,** to be in a fix

dogma /'dogma/ *m*, dogma

dogmático /dog'matiko/ *a* dogmatic

dogmatizar /dogmati'sar; dogmati'θar/ *vt* to teach heretical doctrines; dogmatize

dólar /'dolar/ *m*, dollar

dolencia /do'lensia; do'lenθia/ *f*, ailment; pain; ache

doler /do'ler/ *vi irr* to be in pain; be reluctant; *vr* be sorry, regretful; grieve; sympathize, be compassionate; complain. *Pres. Ind.* **duelo, dueles, duele, duelen.** *Pres. Subjunc.* **duela, duelas, duela, duelan**

doliente /do'liente/ *a* suffering; ill; afflicted, sad. *mf* sufferer, ill person. *m*, chief mourner

dolo /'dolo/ *m*, fraud; deception; deceit; *Law.* premeditation

dolor /do'lor/ *m*, pain, ache; mental suffering. **d. sordo,** dull pain

dolorido /dolo'riðo/ *a* painful; afflicted, sad

doloroso /dolo'roso/ *a* sad, regrettable; mournful, sorrowful; pitiful; painful

doloso /do'loso/ *a* deceitful, fraudulent

domable /do'maβle/ *a* tamable; controllable

domador /doma'ðor/ **(-ra)** *n* subduer, controller; wild animal tamer; horsebreaker

domadura /doma'ðura/ *f*, taming, breaking in; controlling (emotions)

domar /do'mar/ *vt* to tame, break in; control, repress (emotions)

domesticable /domesti'kaβle/ *a* tamable; domesticable

domesticar /domesti'kar/ *vt* to tame; domesticate; *vr* grow tame; become domesticated

domesticidad /domestisi'ðað; domestiθi'ðað/ *f*, domesticity

doméstico /do'mestiko/ **(-ca)** *a* domestic, domesticated; tame. *n* domestic worker

domiciliar /domisi'liar; domiθi'liar/ *vt* to domicile; *vr* become domiciled, settle down; *Mexico* address (a piece of mail)

domiciliario /domisi'liario; domiθi'liario/ *a* domiciliary

domicilio /domi'silio; domi'θilio/ *m*, domicile; house

dominación /domina'sion; domina'θion/ *f*, domination; power, authority; command (of a military position, etc.); *Mil.* high ground; *pl* dominions, angels

dominador /domina'ðor/ *a* dominating; overbearing

dominante /domi'nante/ *a* dominating; overbearing, domineering; dominant. *f*, *Mus.* dominant

dominar /domi'nar/ *vt* to dominate; repress, subdue; *Fig.* master (branch of knowledge); *vi* stand out; *vr* control oneself

dómine /'domine/ *m*, *Inf.* teacher; pedant, know-all

domingo /do'mingo/ *m*, Sunday. **d. de Cuasimodo,** Low Sunday. **d. de Pentecostés,** Pentecost Sunday. **d. de Ramos,** Palm Sunday. **d. de Resurrección,** Easter Sunday

dominguero /domiŋ'guero/ *a* *Inf.* Sunday; special, excursion (trains)

dominicano /domini'kano/ **(-na)** *a* and *n* Dominican; native of Santo Domingo

dominio /'dominio/ *m*, authority, power; rule, sovereignty; dominion (country); domain

dominó /domi'no/ *m*, domino; game of dominoes

don /don/ *m*, gift; quality, characteristic; talent. **d. de gentes,** the human touch; charm

don /don/ *m*, title of respect equivalent to English Mr. or Esquire. Used only before given name and *not* before a family name, e.g. *don Juan Martínez,* or *don Juan*

donación /dona'sion; dona'θion/ *f*, donation, gift, grant

donador /dona'ðor/ **(-ra)** *a* donating. *n* donor

donaire /do'naire/ *m*, discretion, wit; witticism; gracefulness, elegance

donar /do'nar/ *vt* to bestow, give; transfer; grant

donatario /dona'tario/ *m*, recipient, grantee

doncel /don'sel; don'θel/ *m*, squire, youth not yet armed; knight; male virgin; king's page

doncella /don'seya; don'θeʎa/ *f*, virgin, maid; maidservant; lady's maid

donde /'donde/ *adv* where, wherein. Sometimes used as relative pronoun "in which" (e.g. *La casa d. estaba,* The house in which I was); *Lat. Am.* at the house of, at...'s; to the house of, to...'s (e.g. *Mi tía está donde mis abuelos* My aunt is at my grandparents' *Mi tío no fue donde mis primos* My uncle did not go to my cousins') *interrog* **¿dónde? ¿A dónde va Vd.?** Where are you going to? **¿De dónde viene Vd.?** Where do you come from? **¿Por dónde se va a Madrid?** Which is the way to Madrid?

dondequiera /donde'kiera/ *adv* wherever, anywhere, everywhere

donoso /do'noso/ *a* witty; graceful

donostiarra /donos'tiarra/ *a* and *mf* of or from San Sebastian (N. Spain)

donosura /dono'sura/ *f*, wit; grace; dash, verve

doña /'doɲa/ *f*, feminine equivalent of **don** (e.g. *D. Catalina Palacios*)

dorado /do'raðo/ *a* golden, gilded; fortunate, happy. *m*, gilding

dorador /dora'ðor/ *m*, gilder

doradura /dora'ðura/ *f*, gilding

dorar /do'rar/ *vt* to gild; make golden; *Fig.* gild the pill; *Cul.* toast lightly; *vr* become golden

dormidero /dormi'ðero/ *a* soporiferous, narcotic; *m*, *Lat. Am.* roost (of chickens)

dormilón /dormi'lon/ **(-ona)** *a* *Inf.* sleepy. *n* sleepyhead

dormir /dor'mir/ *vi irr* to sleep; spend the night; *Fig.* grow calm, sleep (tops); (*with sobre*) sleep on, consider; *vt* put to sleep; *vr* go to sleep; go slow over, neglect; be dormant; go numb (limbs). **d. como un lirón,** to sleep like a top. *Inf.* **d. la mona,** to sleep oneself sober. **entre duerme y vela,** half-awake. *Pres. Ind.* **duermo, duermes, duerme, duermen.** *Pres. Part.* **durmiendo.** *Preterite* **durmió, durmieron.** *Pres. Subjunc.* **duerma, duermas, duerma, duerman**

dormitar /dormi'tar/ *vi* to doze

dormitorio /dormi'torio/ *m*, dormitory; bedroom

dorso /'dorso/ *m*, back; dorsum

dos /dos/ *a* two; second (of the month). **las d.,** two o'clock. **d. a d.,** two against two. **de d. en d.,** two by two. *Inf.* **en un d. por tres,** in a twinkling

doscientos /dos'sientos; dos'θientos/ *a* and *m*, two hundred; two hundredth

dosel /do'sel/ *m*, canopy; dais

dosis /'dosis/ *f*, dose; quantity

dotación /dota'sion; dota'θion/ *f*, endowment; *Naut.* crew; staff, workers; equipment

dotar /do'tar/ *vt* to give as dowry; endow, found; *Fig.* endow (with talents, etc.); equip; apportion (salary)

dote /'dote/ *mf*, dowry. *f*, (gen. *pl*) gifts, talents. **dotes de mando,** capacity for leadership

dracma /'drakma/ *f*, drachma; dram

draga /'draga/ *f*, dredger

dragado /dra'gaðo/ *m*, dredging

dragaminas /draga'minas/ *m*, *Nav.* minesweeper

dragar /dra'gar/ *vt* to dredge

dragón /dra'gon/ *m*, dragon; *Bot.* snapdragon; *Mil.* dragoon; *Zool.* dragon, giant lizard; *Astron.* Draco

dragona /dra'gona/ *f*, female dragon; *Mil.* shoulderstrap

dragonear /dragone'ar/ *vi*, *Lat. Am.* to boast, brag

drama /'drama/ *m*, play; drama. **d. lírico,** opera

dramática /dra'matika/ *f*, dramatic art

dramático /dra'matiko/ *a* dramatic; vivid, unexpected, moving

dramaturgo /drama'turgo/ *m*, dramatist, playwright

drenaje /dre'nahe/ *m*, drainage (of land and wounds)

dril /dril/ *m*, drill, cotton cloth

droga /'droga/ *f*, drug; falsehood, deception; nuisance

droguería /droge'ria/ *f*, chemist's shop; drug trade

droguero /dro'gero/ **(-ra)** *n* chemist, druggist

dromedario /drome'ðario/ *m*, *Zool.* dromedary

druida /'druiða/ *m*, Druid

dualidad /duali'ðaθ/ f, duality
ducado /du'kaðo/ m, dukedom; duchy; ducat
ducentésimo /dusen'tesimo; duθen'tesimo/ a two hundredth
ducha /'dutʃa/ f, shower-bath; douche; stripe in cloth; furrow
ducho /'dutʃo/ a experienced, skillful
ductilidad /duktili'ðaθ/ f, ductility; adaptability
duda /'duða/ f, doubt, hesitation; problem. **sin d.**, doubtless
dudable /du'ðaβle/ a doubtful
dudar /du'ðar/ vi to be in doubt; vt doubt, disbelieve
dudoso /du'ðoso/ a doubtful; uncertain, not probable
duela /'duela/ f, hoop, stave
duelista /due'lista/ mf dueler; duelist
duelo /'duelo/ m, sorrow, grief; mourning; mourners; duel; (gen. pl) troubles, trials. **duelos y quebrantos,** Cul. fried offal. **sin d.,** in abundance
duende /'duende/ m, imp, elf, sprite, ghost
dueña /'dueɲa/ f, owner, proprietress, mistress; duenna; married lady Obs.
dueño /'dueɲo/ m, owner, proprietor; master (of servants). **d. de sí mismo,** self-controlled
Duero, el /'duero, el/ the Douro
duetista /due'tista/ mf duetist
dula /'dula/ f, common pasture ground or herds
dulce /dulse; 'dulθe/ a sweet; fresh, pure; fresh, not salty; fragrant; melodious; pleasant, agreeable; tender, gentle; soft (metals). m, sweetmeat, bonbon. **d. de almíbar,** preserved fruit.
dulcedumbre /dulse'ðumbre; dulθe'ðumbre/ f, sweetness; softness
dulcémele /dulse'mele; dulθe'mele/ m, dulcimer
dulcera /dul'sera; dul'θera/ f, preserve dish, fruit dish
dulcería /dulse'ria; dulθe'ria/ f, See **confitería**

dulcificar /dulsifi'kar; dulθifi'kar/ vt to make sweet; alleviate, sweeten
dulcinea /dul'sinca; dul'θinea/ f, Inf. sweetheart; ideal
dulzaina /dul'saina; dul'θaina/ f, Mus. flageolet
dulzura /dul'sura; dul'θura/ f, sweetness; gentleness; pleasure; meekness; agreeableness
duna /'duna/ f, (gen. pl) sand and dune
Dunquerque /dun'kerke/ Dunkirk
dúo /'duo/ m, Mus. duet
duodécimo /duoðesimo; duo'ðeθimo/ a twelfth
duodeno /duo'ðeno/ a twelfth. m, Anat. duodenum
duplicación /duplika'sion; duplika'θion/ f, duplication
duplicado /dupli'kaðo/ m, duplicate
duplicar /dupli'kar/ vt to duplicate; double
duplicidad /duplisi'ðaθ; dupliθi'ðaθ/ f, duplicity, falseness
duplo /'duplo/ a double
duque /'duke/ m, duke
duquesa /du'kesa/ f, duchess
duración /dura'sion; dura'θion/ f, duration; durability
duradero /dura'ðero/ a lasting; durable
durante /du'rante/ adv during
durar /du'rar/ vi to continue; endure, last
dureza /du'resa; du'reθa/ f, hardness; Med. callosity; severity, harshness
durmiente /dur'miente/ a sleeping. mf sleeper; m, Archit. dormant
duro /'duro/ a hard; firm, unyielding; vigorous, robust; severe, inclement; exacting, cruel; Mus. metallic, harsh; Art. crude, too sharply defined; miserly, avaricious; obstinate; self-opinionated; unbearable, intolerable; merciless, hard; harsh (style). m, Spanish coin worth five pesetas

E

e /e/ f, letter E. conjunc used instead of y (and) before words beginning with i or hi, provided this last is not followed by a diphthong (e.g. e invierno, e hijos, but y hierro)
¡ea! /'ea/ interj Well!; Come on!; Let's see! (often used with **pues**)
ebanista /eβa'nista/ mf cabinetmaker
ebanistería /eβaniste'ria/ f, cabinetmaker's shop; cabinetmaking or work
ébano /'eβano/ m, ebony
ebonita /eβo'nita/ f, ebonite, vulcanite
ebrio /'eβrio/ a intoxicated, inebriated
ebullición /eβuyi'sion; eβuʎi'θion/ f, boiling, ebullition
ebúrneo /e'βurneo/ a eburnine, ivory-like
echada /e'tʃaða/ f, throw, cast; pitch; fling; length of a man
echador /etʃa'ðor/ (-ra) n thrower. m, Inf. chuckerout
echadura /etʃa'ðura/ f, sitting on eggs to hatch them; (gen. pl) gleanings
echamiento /etʃa'miento/ m, throw, fling; throwing, casting; expulsion; rejection
echar /e'tʃar/ vt to throw, fling; eject, drive away; cast out, expel; put forth, sprout; emit, give forth; cut (teeth); dismiss, discharge; couple (animals); pour (liquids); place, apply; put into, fill; turn (keys, locks); impute; attribute; impose (penalty, taxes, etc.); play (game); try one's luck; distribute; publish, make known; perform (plays); (with por) go in direction of; (with prep a + infin.) begin to (e. **a andar,** to begin to walk); vr throw oneself down, lie down; sit on eggs (birds); abate, calm (wind); apply oneself, concentrate on; rush (towards), fling oneself (upon). **e. abajo,** to overthrow; demolish. **e. aceite al fuego,** to add fuel to the flames. **e. a perder,** to spoil, deteriorate. Naut. **e. a pique,** to sink. **e. a vuelo,** to ring (bells). **e. carnes,** to put on weight, grow fat. **e. cuentas,** to reckon up. **e. de menos,** to miss; mourn

absence of. **e. de ver,** to notice. Fig. **e. en cara,** to throw in one's face, reproach. **echarla de majo,** to play the gallant. **e. las cartas al correo,** to post the letters. **e. las cartas,** to tell fortunes. **e. el pie atrás,** Fig. to climb down; Fig. back out. **e. raíces,** to take root; **e. las bases de, e. los cimientos de,** to lay the foundation of, lay the foundation for. Fig. become established. **e. rayos por la boca,** to fly into a rage. **e. suertes,** to draw lots. **echarlo todo a rodar,** to spoil everything. **e. una mano,** to lend a hand. **echar un volado** Mexico to toss a coin
echazón /etʃa'son; etʃa'θon/ f, throw, cast; jetsam
eclecticismo /eklekti'sismo; eklekti'θismo/ m, eclecticism
ecléctico /e'klektiko/ (-ca) a and n eclectic
eclesiástico /ekle'siastiko/ a ecclesiastical. m, ecclesiastic, clergyman. **Eclesiástico,** Ecclesiasticus
eclipsar /e'klip'sar/ vt Astron. to eclipse; surpass, outvie; vr Astron. be in eclipse; disappear
eclipse /e'klipse/ m, Astron. eclipse; retirement, withdrawal
eco /'eko/ m, echo; verse-echo; muffled sound; slavish imitation or imitator
ecología /ekolo'hia/ f, ecology
economato /ekono'mato/ m, trusteeship; cooperative store
econometría /ekonome'tria/ f, econometrics
economía /ekono'mia/ f, economy, thrift; structure, organization; poverty, shortage; saving (of time, labor, etc.); pl savings. **e. dirigida,** planned economy. **e. doméstica,** domestic economy. **e. política,** political economy
económico /eko'nomiko/ a economic; thrifty; avaricious; cheap
economista /ekono'mista/ mf economist
economizar /ekonomi'sar; ekonomi'θar/ vt to economize; save
ecónomo /e'konomo/ m, trustee, guardian
ecosistema /ekosis'tema/ m, ecosystem

ecuación /ekua'sion; ekua'θion/ f, (*Math.* and *Astron.*) equation

ecuador /ekua'ðor/ m, equator

ecuánime /ekua'nime/ a calm, unruffled; impartial

ecuanimidad /ekuanimi'ðað/ f, calmness, serenity; impartiality

ecuatorial /ekuato'rial/ a equatorial

ecuatoriano /ekuato'riano/ **(-na)** a and n Ecuadorian

ecuestre /e'kuestre/ a equestrian

ecuménico /eku'meniko/ a ecumenical

eczema /'eksema; 'ekθema/ m, eczema

edad /e'ðað/ f, age; epoch; period. **e. de piedra,** Stone Age. **e. media,** Middle Ages. **de cierta e.,** middle-aged. **ser mayor de e.,** to have attained one's majority. **ser menor de e.,** to be a minor

edecán /eðe'kan/ m, aide-de-camp

edema /e'ðema/ m, edema

Edén /e'ðen/ m, Eden; *Fig.* paradise

edición /eði'sion; eði'θion/ f, edition. **e. diamante,** miniature edition. **e. príncipe,** first edition

edicto /e'ðikto/ m, edict, decree; public notice

edificación /eðifika'sion; eðifika'θion/ f, building, construction; edification

edificador /eðifika'ðor/ **(-ra)** a uplifting, edifying; building. n builder

edificante /eðifi'kante/ a building, constructing; edifying

edificar /eðifi'kar/ vt to build, construct; edify

edificio /eði'fisio; eði'fiθio/ m, building, structure

Edimburgo /eðim'burgo/ Edinburgh

editar /eði'tar/ vt (of a publisher) to publish; edit

editor /eði'tor/ **(-ra)** n publisher; editor

editorial /eðito'rial/ a publishing; editorial. m, editorial, leading article

edredón /eðre'ðon/ m, down of an eiderduck; eiderdown, quilt

eduardiano /eðuar'ðiano/ **(-na)** a and n Edwardian

educable /eðu'kaβle/ a educable

educación /eðuka'sion; eðuka'θion/ f, upbringing; education; good breeding, good manners

educado /eðu'kaðo/ a educated. **ser mal e.,** to be badly brought up; be ill-mannered or impolite

educador /eðuka'ðor/ **(-ra)** a educating. n educator

educando /eðu'kando/ **(-da)** n pupil

educar /eðu'kar/ vt to educate; bring up, train, teach, develop

educativo /eðuka'tiβo/ a educational, educative

educción /eðuk'sion; eðuk'θion/ f, eduction; inference, deduction

educir /eðu'sir; eðu'θir/ vt irr to educe; infer, deduce. See **conducir**

efe /'efe/ f, name of letter F

efectismo /efek'tismo/ m, sensationalism; striving after effect

efectista /efek'tista/ a (*Art. Lit.*) striking, sensational

efectivo /efek'tiβo/ a effective; real. m, cash. **hacer e.,** to put into effect

efecto /e'fekto/ m, effect, result; purpose, intent; impression; pl assets; goods, chattels. **efectos de escritorio,** stationery. **efectos públicos,** public securities. **en e.,** in fact, actually. **llevar a e.,** to put into effect; make effective

efectuación /efektua'sion; efektua'θion/ f, accomplishment, execution

efectuar /efek'tuar/ vt to accomplish, effect; make (a payment); vr be effected; happen, take place

eferente /efe'rente/ a efferent

efervescencia /eferβes'sensia; eferβes'θenθia/ f, effervescence; excitement, enthusiasm

efervescente /eferβes'sente; eferβes'θente/ a effervescent

Éfeso /e'feso/ Ephesus

eficacia /efi'kasia; efi'kaθia/ f, efficacy; effectiveness

eficaz /efi'kas; efi'kaθ/ a efficacious; effective

eficiencia /efi'siensia; efi'θienθia/ f, efficiency

eficiente /efi'siente; efi'θiente/ a efficient, effective

efigie /e'fihie/ f, effigy; image, representation, symbol

efímero /e'fimero/ a ephemeral; brief

eflorescencia /eflores'sensia; eflores'θenθia/ f, *Chem.* efflorescence

efluvio /e'fluβio/ m, effluvium; exhalation

efugio /e'fuhio/ m, subterfuge, evasion

efusión /efu'sion/ f, effusion; *Fig.* spate (of words, etc.)

efusivo /efu'siβo/ a effusive, expansive

Egeo, Mar /e'heo, mar/ Aegean Sea

égida /'ehiða/ f, shield; egis, protection

egipcíaco /ehip'siako; ehip'θiako/ **(-ca), egipcio (-ia)** a and n Egyptian

Egipto /e'hipto/ Egypt

egiptólogo /ehip'tologo/ **(-ga)** n Egyptologist

egoísmo /ego'ismo/ m, egoism, selfishness

egoísta /ego'ista/ a egoistic. mf egoist, selfish person

egolatría /egola'tria/ f, self-love

egotismo /ego'tismo/ m, egotism

egotista /ego'tista/ a egotistical. mf egotist

egregio /e'grehio/ a distinguished, celebrated

egresado /egre'saðo/ m, graduate (of a certain school)

egresar (de...) /egre'sar/ vi, Lat. Am. to go out (of...), leave (...); be graduated (from...)

egreso /e'greso/ m, Lat. Am. departure, leaving; graduation

eje /'ehe/ m, axis; axle-tree; shaft; pivot, fundamental idea. **e. trasero,** rear-axle. *Mexico* **ejes viales,** main highways

ejecución /eheku'sion; eheku'θion/ f, accomplishment, performance; execution, technique; death penalty

ejecutable /eheku'taβle/ a feasible, practicable

ejecutante /eheku'tante/ mf *Mus.* executant, performer

ejecutar /eheku'tar/ vt to discharge, perform; put to death; (*Art. Mus.*) execute; serve (a warrant, etc.); *Law.* seize (property)

ejecutivo /eheku''tiβo/ a executive; urgent

ejecutor /eheku'tor/ m, executor

ejecutoria /eheku'toria/ f, letters patent of nobility; *Law.* judgment, sentence

ejemplar /ehem'plar/ a exemplary. m, copy, specimen; precedent; example; warning

ejemplificar /ehemplifi'kar/ vi to exemplify

ejemplo /e'hemplo/ m, example, precedent; illustration, instance; specimen. **dar e.,** to set an example. **por e.,** for example

ejercer /eher'ser; eher'θer/ vt to practice (a profession); perform, fulfill; exercise, use

ejercicio /eher'sisio; eher'θiθio/ m, exercise; practice; performance; exertion, effort; *Mil.* exercises (gen. pl). **ejercicios espirituales,** spiritual exercises. **ejercicios físicos,** physical training

ejercitar /ehersi'tar; eherθi'tar/ vt to exercise; train, teach; vr exercise; practice

ejército /e'hersito; e'herθito/ m, army

ejote /e'hote/ m, Central America, Mexico string bean

el /el/ def art. m, sing the

él /el/ pers pron sing m, he; it (f. **ella.** neut **ello**) (e.g. Lo hizo él, He did it). Also used with prep. (e.g. Lo hicimos por él, We did it for him)

elaboración /elaβora'sion; elaβora'θion/ f, elaboration, working out

elaborado /elaβo'raðo/ a elaborate

elaborar /elaβo'rar/ vt to elaborate; produce, work out

elasticidad /elastisi'ðað; elastiθi'ðað/ f, elasticity; adaptability

elástico /e'lastiko/ a elastic; adaptable. m, elastic tape; elastic material

ele /'ele/ f, name of letter L

elección /elek'sion; elek'θion/ f, choice; election; selection; discrimination

electivo /elek'tiβo/ a elective

elector /elek'tor/ **(-ra)** n elector, voter. m, German prince *Obs.*

electorado /elekto'raðo/ m, electorate

electoral /elekto'ral/ a electoral

electricidad /elektrisi'ðað; elektriθi'ðað/ f, electricity

electricista /elektri'sista; elektri'θista/ mf electrician

eléctrico /e'lektriko/ *a* electric; electrical
electrificación /elektrifika'sion; elektrifika'θion/ *f*, electrification
electrificar /elektrifi'kar/ *vt* to electrify
electrizar /elektri'sar; elektri'θar/ *vt* to electrify; startle; *vr* be electrified
electrocución /elektroku'sion; elektroku'θion/ *f*, electrocution
electrocutar /elektroku'tar/ *vt* to electrocute
electrodo /elek'troðo/ *m*, electrode
electroimán /elektroi'man/ *m*, electromagnet
electrólisis /elek'trolisis/ *f*, electrolysis
electrolizar /elektroli'sar; elektroli'θar/ *vt* to electrolyze
electromagnético /elektromag'netiko/ *a* electromagnetic
electromotriz /elektro'motris; elektro'motriθ/ *a* electromotive. **fuerza e.**, electromotive force
electrón /elek'tron/ *m*, electron
electroquímica /elektro'kimika/ *f*, electrochemistry
electroscopio /elektro'skopio/ *m*, electroscope
electrotecnia /elektro'teknia/ *f*, electrical engineering
electroterapia /elektrote'rapia/ *f*, *Med.* electrotherapy
elefante /ele'fante/ **(-ta)** *n* elephant
elefantíasis /elefan'tiasis/ *f*, elephantiasis
elefantino /elefan'tino/ *a* elephantine
elegancia /ele'gansia; ele'ganθia/ *f*, elegance, grace; fashionableness; *Lit.* beauty of style
elegante /ele'gante/ *a* elegant; graceful, lovely; fashionable, stylish
elegantoso, -a /elegan'toso/ *a*, *Lat. Am.* = **elegante**
elegía /ele'hia/ *f*, elegy
elegíaco /ele'hiako/ *a* elegiac
elegibilidad /elehiβili'ðað/ *f*, eligibility
elegible /ele'hiβle/ *a* eligible
elegir /ele'hir/ *vt irr* to select, prefer; elect. *Pres. Ind.* **elijo, eliges, elige, eligen.** *Pres. Part.* **eligiendo.** *Preterite* **eligió, eligieron.** *Pres. Subjunc.* **elija, etc.**
elemental /elemen'tal/ *a* elemental; fundamental; elementary
elemento /ele'mento/ *m*, element; component, constituent; *Elec.* element; *pl* rudiments. *Mil.* **elementos de choque**, shock troops
elenco /e'lenko/ *m*, *Lat. Am.* cast (of characters)
elevación /eleβa'sion; eleβa'θion/ *f*, lifting, raising; height, high ground; elevation; altitude; *Fig.* eminence; elevation, advancement; ecstasy; raising (of the voice)
elevado /ele'βaðo/ *a* sublime, lofty
elevar /ele'βar/ *vt* to raise, lift; *Fig.* exalt; *vr* be in ecstasy, be transported. **elevarse de categoría**, to rise in status
elfc /'elfo/ *m*, elf
elidir /eli'ðir/ *vt* (phonetics) to elide
eliminación /elimina'sion; elimina'θion/ *f*, elimination
eliminador /elimina'ðor/ *a* eliminatory. *m*, eliminator
eliminar /elimi'nar/ *vt* to eliminate
elíptico /e'liptiko/ *a* elliptic
elíseo /e'liseo/ *m*, Elysium. *a* Elysian. **campos elíseos**, Elysian fields
ella /'eya; 'eʎa/ *pers. pron 3rd sing. f* she; it. See **él**
elle /'eye; 'eʎe/ *f*, name of letter LL
ello /'eyo; 'eʎo/ *pers. pron 3rd sing. neut* that, the fact, it. **Ello es que...**, The fact is that... **No tengo tiempo para ello**, I have no time for that
ellos, **ellas** /'eyos, 'eyas; 'eʎos, 'eʎas/ *pers. pron 3rd pl. m* and *f*, they. See **él**
elocución /eloku'sion; eloku'θion/ *f*, elocution; style of speech
elocuencia /elo'kuensia; elo'kuenθia/ *f*, eloquence
elocuente /elo'kuente/ *a* eloquent
elogiador /elohia'ðor/ **(-ra)** *a* eulogistic. *n* eulogist
elogiar /elo'hiar/ *vt* to eulogize, praise
elogio /e'lohio/ *m*, eulogy, praise. **«Elogio de la Locura»,** "In Praise of Folly"
elote /e'lote/ *m*, *Central America, Mexico* ear of corn
elucidación /elusiða'sion; eluθiða'θion/ *f*, elucidation, explanation
elucidar /elusi'ðar; eluθi'ðar/ *vt* to elucidate, clarify

eludible /elu'ðiβle/ *a* escapable, avoidable
eludir /elu'ðir/ *vt* to elude, avoid
elusivo, -a /elu'siβo/ *a*, *Lat. Am.* evasive, tricky
emaciación /emasia'sion; emaθia'θion/ *f*, emaciation
emanación /emana'sion; emana'θion/ *f*, emanation; effluvium
emanar /ema'nar/ *vi* to emanate (from), originate (in)
emancipación /emansipa'sion; emanθipa'θion/ *f*, emancipation; enfranchisement
emancipador /emansipa'ðor; emanθipa'ðor/ **(-ra)** *a* emancipatory. *n* emancipator
emancipar /emansi'par; emanθi'par/ *vt* to emancipate, free; enfranchise; *vr* emancipate oneself; become independent; free oneself
emascular /emasku'lar/ *vt* to emasculate
embadurnar /embaður'nar/ *vt* to smear, smudge, daub
embajada /emba'haða/ *f*, embassy; ambassadorship; embassy building; *Inf.* message
embajador /embaha'ðor/ *m*, ambassador; emissary
embajadora /embaha'ðora/ *f*, wife of ambassador; woman ambassador
embalador /embala'ðor/ *m*, packer
embalaje /emba'lahe/ *m*, packing; bale; wrapper; packing charge
embalar /emba'lar/ *vt* to pack
embaldosado /embaldo'saðo/ *m*, tiled pavement or floor
embaldosar /embaldo'sar/ *vt* to tile, pave with tiles
embalsamador /embalsama'ðor/ *a* embalming. *m*, embalmer
embalsamar /embalsa'mar/ *vt* to embalm; perfume
embalse /em'balse/ *m*, dam; damming, impounding (of water)
embanastar /embanas'tar/ *vt* to place in a basket; crowd, squeeze
embarazada /embara'saða; embara'θaða/ *a f*, pregnant
embarazar /embara'sar; embara'θar/ *vt* to impede, hinder, embarrass; *vr* be hindered or embarrassed; be pregnant
embarazo /emba'raso; emba'raθo/ *m*, difficulty, impediment; pregnancy; timidity, embarrassment
embarazoso /embara'soso; embara'θoso/ *a* embarrassing; inconvenient; difficult, troublesome
embarcación /embarka'sion; embarka'θion/ *f*, ship, vessel; embarkation
embarcadero /embarka'ðero/ *m*, wharf, dock; quay; pier; jetty
embarcador /embarka'ðor/ *m*, shipper
embarcar /embar'kar/ *vt* to embark, ship; board (boat, train, etc.); *vr* embark; board
embarco /em'barko/ *m*, embarking, embarkation
embargar /embar'gar/ *vt* to obstruct, impede; *Law.* seize; suspend, paralyse
embargo /em'bargo/ *m*, *Law.* seizure; embargo. **sin e.,** nevertheless, however
embarque /em'barke/ *m*, loading, embarkation (goods)
embarrancar /embarran'kar/ *vi Naut.* to run aground; *vr Naut.* be stuck on a reef or in the mud
embarrilar /embarri'lar/ *vt* to barrel
embarullar /embaru'yar; embaru'ʎar/ *vt Inf.* to mix up, muddle; do hastily and badly
embastar /embas'tar/ *vt Sew.* to baste; tack
embaste /em'baste/ *m*, *Sew.* basting; tacking stitch
embate /em'bate/ *m*, beating of the waves; sudden attack; unexpected misfortune
embaucamiento /embauka'miento/ *m*, trick, deception
embaucar /embau'kar/ *vt* to deceive, hoodwink
embaular /embau'lar/ *vt* to pack in a trunk; *Inf.* stuff with food
embazar /emba'sar; emba'θar/ *vt* to dye brown; hinder; amaze; *vr* be amazed; be tired or bored; be satiated
embebecer /embeβe'ser; embeβe'θer/ *vt irr* to entertain, amuse; engross, fascinate; *vr* be dumbfounded. See **conocer**

embebecimiento /embeβesi'miento; embeβeθi'miento/ *m*, astonishment; absorption, engrossment

embeber /embe'βer/ *vt* to absorb; contain; shrink, contract; saturate; insert, introduce; incorporate; *vi* shrink; *vr* be amazed; master or absorb (a subject).

embedido en sus pensamientos, absorbed in thought

embelecar /embele'kar/ *vt* to dupe, deceive, trick

embeleco /embe'leko/ *m*, deception, fraud

embelesar /embele'sar/ *vt* to astonish; fascinate, enchant; *vr* be astonished or fascinated

embeleso /embe'leso/ *m*, astonishment; fascination; charm

embellecer /embeʎe'ser; embeʎe'θer/ *vt irr* to embellish; *vr* beautify oneself. See **conocer**

embellecimiento /embeyesi'miento; embeʎeθi'miento/ *m*, beautifying, embellishment

emberizo /embe'riso; embe'riθo/ *m*, *Ornith.* yellowhammer

embermejecer /embermehe'ser; embermehe'θer/ *vt irr* to dye red; shame, make blush; *vi* turn red or reddish; *vr* blush. See **conocer**

embestida /embes'tiða/ *f*, assault, attack, onrush; *Inf.* importunity

embestir /embes'tir/ *vt irr* to rush upon, assault; *Inf.* importune, be a nuisance to; *vi Fig. Inf.* clash, be inharmonious. See **pedir**

emblema /em'blema/ *m*, emblem; symbol; badge

emblemático /emble'matiko/ *a* emblematic; symbolical

embobamiento /emboβa'miento/ *m*, stupefaction, amazement

embobar /embo'βar/ *vt* to entertain, fascinate; *vr* be dumbfounded

embobecer /emboβe'ser; emboβe'θer/ *vt irr* to make stupid. See **conocer**

embobecimiento /emboβesi'miento; emboβeθi'miento/ *m*, stupefaction

embocadero /emboka'ðero/ *m*, narrow entrance, bottleneck; mouth of a channel

embocadura /emboka'ðura/ *f*, entrance by a narrow passage; *Mus.* mouthpiece; flavor (of wine); estuary, mouth of a river; *Theat.* proscenium

embocar /embo'kar/ *vt* to put in the mouth; go through a narrow passage; deceive; *Inf.* devour, wolf; initiate a business deal

embolador, -a /emboʎa'ðor/ *mf*, *Lat. Am.* bootblack

embolia /em'bolia/ *f*, embolism

émbolo /'embolo/ *m*, *Mech.* piston, plunger

embolsar /embol'sar/ *vt* to place money in a purse; collect (a debt, etc.)

emborrachar /emborra'tʃar/ *vt* to intoxicate; daze, stupefy; *vr* become intoxicated; run (of dyes)

emborrascarse /emborras'karse/ *vr* to be furious; become stormy (weather); *Fig.* go downhill (business concern)

emborronar /emborro'nar/ *vt* to blot; scribble, write hastily

emboscada /embos'kaða/ *f*, ambuscade, ambush; intrigue, spying

emboscar /embos'kar/ *vt Mil.* to set an ambush; *vr* lie in ambush

embosquecer /emboske'ser; emboske'θer/ *vi irr* to become wooded. See **conocer**

embotar /embo'tar/ *vt* to blunt (cutting edge); *vi Fig.* weaken; *vr* become blunt

embotellado /embote'yaðo; embote'ʎaðo/ *m*, bottling; *Fig.* bottleneck

embotellador /embote'yaðor; embote'ʎaðor/ **(-ra)** *n* bottler. *f.* **embotelladora,** bottling outfit

embotellar /embote'yar; embote'ʎar/ *vt* to bottle; bottle up, prevent from escaping

embotijar /emboti'har/ *vt* to put into jars; *vr Inf.* be enraged

embozar /embo'sar; embo'θar/ *vt Fig.* to cloak, dissemble; muffle; *vr* muffle oneself up

embozo /em'boso; em'boθo/ *m*, anything used to cover or muffle the face; pretense, pretext; facings (gen. *pl*); yashmak

embragar /embra'gar/ *vt* to sling, lift; *Mech.* let in the clutch

embrague /em'brage/ *m*, hoisting, slinging; *Mech.* clutch

embravecer /embraβe'ser; embraβe'θer/ *vt irr* to infuriate; *vr* be enraged; be boisterous (sea). See **conocer**

embravecimiento /embraβesi'miento; embraβeθi'miento/ *m*, fury, rage

embrazadura /embrasa'ðura; embraθa'ðura/ *f*, grasping, clasping; handle, clasp

embreadura /embrea'ðura/ *f*, tarring

embrear /embre'ar/ *vt* to tar, paint with pitch

embriagador /embriaga'ðor/ *a* intoxicating

embriagar /embria'gar/ *vt* to intoxicate; enrapture; *vr* become inebriated

embriaguez /embria'ges; embria'geθ/ *f*, intoxication, inebriation; rapture

embriología /embriolo'hia/ *f*, embryology

embrión /em'brion/ *m*, embryo; germ, rough idea

embrionario /embrio'nario/ *a* embryonic

embrollar /embro'yar; embro'ʎar/ *vt* to entangle; embroil

embrollo /em'broyo; em'broʎo/ *m*, tangle; falsehood; difficult situation

embromar /embro'mar/ *vt* to tease, chaff; trick, deceive; waste the time of; annoy; harm

embrujar /embru'har/ *vt* to bewitch

embrutecer /embrute'ser; embrute'θer/ *vt irr* to make brutish or stupid; *vr* become brutish. See **conocer**

embudo /em'buðo/ *m*, *Chem.* funnel

embullo /em'βujo; em'βuʎo/ *m*, *Central America* noise; excitement; revelry

embuste /em'buste/ *m*, lie, fraud; *pl* trinkets

embustero /embus'tero/ **(-ra)** *a* deceitful, knavish. *n* liar, cheat, trickster

embutido /embu'tiðo/ *m*, inlaid work; *Cul.* sausage

embutir /embu'tir/ *vt* to inlay; stuff full, cram; *vt* and *vr Inf.* stuff with food

eme /'eme/ *f*, name of letter M

emergencia /emer'hensia; emer'henθia/ *f*, emergence; accident, emergency

emergente /emer'hente/ *a* emergent

emerger /emer'her/ *vi* to emerge; have its source (rivers, etc.)

emérito /e'merito/ *a* emeritus

emético /e'metiko/ *a* and *m*, emetic

emigración /emigra'sion; emigra'θion/ *f*, emigration; migration; number of emigrants

emigrado /emi'graðo/ *m*, emigrant, emigré

emigrante /emi'grante/ *a* and *mf* emigrant

emigrar /emi'grar/ *vi* to emigrate; migrate

emigratorio /emigra'torio/ *a* emigratory

eminencia /emi'nensia; emi'nenθia/ *f*, highland; importance, prominence; outstanding personality, genius; title given to cardinals

eminente /emi'nente/ *a* high, elevated; prominent, illustrious

emirato /emi'rato/ *m*, emirate

emisario /emi'sario/ **(-ia)** *n* emissary

emisión /emi'sion/ *f*, emission; *Radio.* broadcast; *Com.* issue (bonds, etc.); floating (of a loan)

emisor /emi'sor/ *m*, *Elec.* transmitter

emisora /emi'sora/ *f*, *Radio.* broadcasting station

emitir /emi'tir/ *vt* to emit; *Radio.* broadcast; *Com.* issue (bonds, paper money, etc.); utter, give voice to

emoción /emo'sion; emo'θion/ *f*, emotion

emocional /emo'sional; emo'θional/ *a* emotional; emotive

emocionante /emosio'nante; emoθio'nante/ *a* moving, causing emotion; thrilling

emocionar /emosio'nar; emoθio'nar/ *vt* to cause emotion, move; *vr* be stirred by emotion; be thrilled

emoliente /emo'liente/ *a* and *m*, emollient

emolumento /emolu'mento/ *m*, emolument (gen. *pl*)

empachado /empa'tʃaðo/ *a* awkward, clumsy

empachar /empa'tʃar/ *vt* to hinder, impede; disguise, dissemble; *vr* overeat, stuff; be bashful

empacho /em'patʃo/ *m*, bashfulness, timidity; embarrassment, impediment; indigestion, satiety
empadronamiento /empaðrona'miento/ *m*, census
empadronar /empaðro'nar/ *vt* to take the census
empalagar /empala'gar/ *vt* to cloy (of food); tire, annoy
empalagoso /empala'goso/ *a* sickly, oversweet; cloying; *Fig.* sugary, honeyed
empalar /empa'lar/ *vt* to impale
empalizada /empali'saða; empali'θaða/ *f*, stockade, fencing
empalmar /empal'mar/ *vt* to dovetail; splice (ropes); clamp; *Fig.* combine (plans, actions, etc.); *vi* join (railroad lines); couple (railroad trains); *vr* palm (as in conjuring)
empalme /em'palme/ *m*, connection; splicing; *Fig.* combination (of plans, etc.); railroad junction; continuation; palming, secreting
empanada /empa'naða/ *f*, savory turnover or pie; secret negotiations, intrigue
empanar /empa'nar/ *vt* to bread; *Cul.* cover with breadcrumbs; *Agr.* sow grain
empantanar /empanta'nar/ *vt* to turn into marsh; embog; delay, embarrass
empañar /empa'ɲar/ *vt* to swaddle; tarnish, dim; blur; *Fig.* sully (fame, etc.)
empapar /empa'par/ *vt* to saturate; absorb; impregnate; *vr* be saturated; absorb; *Fig.* be imbued
empapelado /empape'laðo/ *m*, paperhanging; wallpaper
empapelador /empapela'ðor/ *m*, paperhanger
empapelar /empape'lar/ *vt* to wrap in paper; paper (a room, etc.)
empaque /em'pake/ *m*, packing; paneling; *Inf.* mien, air; pomposity
empaquetador /empaketa'ðor/ **(-ra)** *n* packer
empaquetar /empake'tar/ *vt* to pack; make up parcels or packages; overcrowd
emparedado /empare'ðaðo/ **(-da)** *a* cloistered, reclusive. *n* recluse. *m*, *Cul.* sandwich
emparedar /empare'ðar/ *vt* to shut up, immure; *vr* become a recluse
emparejar /empare'har/ *vt* to pair, match; equalize, make level; *vi* come abreast (of); be equal
emparentar /emparen'tar/ *vi irr* to become related by marriage. See **acertar**
emparrado /empa'rraðo/ *m*, vine arbor; vine prop; pergola
empastadura /empasta'ðura/ *f*, filling (of teeth)
empastar /empas'tar/ *vt* to cover with glue or paste; bind in boards (books); fill (teeth). **empastado en tela,** clothbound
empaste /em'paste/ *m*, pasting, gluing; filling (teeth)
empatar /empa'tar/ *vt* to equal, tie with
empate /em'pate/ *m*, tie, draw; dead heat
empavonarse /empaβo'narse/ *vr*, *Central America* to dress to the nines
empecatado /empeka'taðo/ *a* willful; evil-minded, wicked; incorrigible, impenitent; extremely unlucky
empecer /empe'ser; empe'θer/ *vt irr* to harm, damage; *vi* hinder. See **conocer**
empecinado, -a /empesi'naðo; empeθi'naðo/ *a*, *Lat. Am.* pigheaded, stubborn
empedernido /empeðer'niðo/ *a* stony-hearted, cruel
empedrado /empe'ðraðo/ *a* dappled (horses); *Fig.* flecked (with clouds). *m*, paving; pavement
empedrar /empe'ðrar/ *vt irr* to pave with stones. See **acertar**
empegar /empe'gar/ *vt* to coat with pitch; mark with pitch (sheep)
empeine /em'peine/ *m*, groin; instep
empellar /empe'ʎar/ *vt* to push, jostle
empellón /empe'ʎon; empe'ʎon/ *m*, hard push. *Inf.* **a empellones,** by pushing and shoving
empeñado /empe'ɲaðo/ *a* violent, heated (of disputes)
empeñar /empe'ɲar/ *vt* to pledge, leave as surety; pawn; oblige, compel; appoint as mediator; *vr* bind oneself, be under an obligation; (*with en*) insist on;

persist in; *vr* intercede; mediate; *Mil.* begin (a battle).
empeñado en, determined to, intent on
empeño /em'peɲo/ *m*, pledge, surety; obligation, engagement; fervent desire; purpose, intention; determination, resolve; guarantor; *Inf.* influence, favor
empeoramiento /empeora'miento/ *m*, worsening; deterioration
empeorar /empeo'rar/ *vt* to make worse; *vi* and *vr* deteriorate, grow worse
empequeñecer /empekeɲe'ser; empekeɲe'θer/ *vt irr* to diminish, lessen; make smaller; belittle. See **conocer**
emperador /empera'ðor/ *m*, emperor
emperatriz /empera'tris; empera'triθ/ *f*, empress
emperezar /empere'sar; empere'θar/ *vt* to obstruct, hinder; *vr* be lazy
empernar /emper'nar/ *vt* to peg, bolt
empero /em'pero/ *conjunc* but; nevertheless
empezar /empe'sar; empe'θar/ *vt irr* to begin, commence; initiate; *vi* begin. *Pres. Ind.* **empiezo, empiezas, empieza, empiezan.** *Preterite* **empecé, empezaste, etc.** *Pres. Subjunc.* **empiece, empieces, empiece, empecemos, empecéis, empiecen**
empicotar /empiko'tar/ *vt* to pillory
empiezo /em'pieso; em'pieθo/ *m*, *Lat. Am.* beginning
empilonar /empilo'nar/ *vt*, *Lat. Am.* to pile up
empinado /empi'naðo/ *a* steep; lofty; arrogant; exalted
empinar /empi'nar/ *vt* to raise; tip, tilt (drinking vessels); *vr* stand on tiptoe; rear, prance; tower, rise; *Aer.* zoom, climb steeply. *Inf.* **e. el codo,** to lift the elbow, tipple
empingorotado /empiŋgoro'taðo/ *a* important, prominent; *Inf.* stuck-up
empírico /em'piriko/ **(-ca)** *a* empiric. *n* quack, charlatan
empizarrado /empisa'rraðo; empiθa'rraðo/ *m*, slate roof
empizarrar /empisa'rrar; empiθa'rrar/ *vt* to roof with slate
emplastar /emplas'tar/ *vt* *Med.* to apply plasters; make up; paint; *Inf.* hinder, obstruct; *vr* be smeared
emplasto /em'plasto/ *m*, *Med.* plaster; poultice; *Inf.* put-up job, fraud
emplazamiento /emplasa'miento; emplaθa'miento/ *m*, placing, location; site; *Law.* summons; *Naut.* berth
emplazar /empla'sar; empla'θar/ *vt* to convene, arrange a meeting; *Law.* summon
empleado /emple'aðo/ **(-da)** *n* employee; clerk. **e. público,** civil servant
emplear /em'plear/ *vt* to employ; lay out, invest (money); use; *vr* be employed or occupied
empleo /em'pleo/ *m*, employment; investment; laying out (of money); occupation; post, office
emplomar /emplo'mar/ *vt* to lead, solder or cover with lead; affix lead seals on to; weight (a stick, etc.); *Argentina* fill (a tooth)
emplumar /emplu'mar/ *vt* to feather; decorate with feathers; tar and feather
emplumecer /emplume'ser; emplume'θer/ *vi irr* to fledge, grow feathers. See **conocer**
empobrecer /empoβre'ser; empoβre'θer/ *vt irr* to impoverish; *vi* and *vr* become poor; decay. See **conocer**
empobrecimiento /empoβresi'miento; empoβreθi'miento/ *m*, impoverishment
empollar /empo'ʎar; empo'ʎar/ *vt* to hatch (eggs); *vi* produce a brood (of bees); *Inf.* brood on, consider; *Inf.* grind, cram, swot (of students)
empollón /empo'ʎon; empo'ʎon/ **(-ona)** *n* *Inf.* plodder, grind, swot
empolvar /empol'βar/ *vt* to cover with dust; powder
emponzoñar /emponso'ɲar; emponθo'ɲar/ *vt* to poison; pervert, corrupt
emporio /em'porio/ *m*, emporium
emprotar /empro'tar/ *vt* to embed, implant; fix down
emprendedor /emprende'ðor/ *a* capable, efficient, enterprising

emprender /empren'der/ *vt* to undertake; (*with prep a or con*) *Inf.* accost, tackle, buttonhole

empresa /em'presa/ *f,* undertaking, task; motto, device; intention, design; management, firm; enterprise, deal

empresarial /empresa'rial/ *a* entrepreneurial

empresario /empre'sario/ *m,* contractor; theatrical manager

empréstito /em'prestito/ *m,* loan

empujar /empu'har/ *vt* to push; *Fig.* exert pressure, influence

empuje /em'puhe/ *m,* push; *Archit.* pressure; energy; power, influence

empujón /empu'hon/ *m,* violent thrust or push. *Inf.* **a empujones,** by pushing and shoving; intermittently

empuñar /empu'ɲar/ *vt* to grasp; grip; clutch

empurrarse /empu'rrarse/ *vr, Central America* to get angry

emu /'emu/ *m,* emu

emulación /emula'sion; emula'θion/ *f,* emulation, competition, rivalry

emulador /emula'ðor/ *a* emulative

emular /emu'lar/ *vt* to emulate, rival, compete with

émulo /'emulo/ **(-la)** *a* emulative, rival. *n* competitor, rival

emulsión /emul'sion/ *f,* emulsion

en /en/ *prep* in; into; on, upon; at; by. **en Madrid,** in Madrid. **en junio,** in June. **Se echó en un sillón,** He threw himself into an armchair. **Se transformó en mariposa,** It turned into a butterfly. **Hay un libro en la mesa,** There is a book on the table. **María está en casa,** Mary is at home. **Un precio muy alto,** at a very high price. **El número de candidatos ha disminuido en un treinta por ciento,** The number of candidates has decreased by thirty percent. **En** appears in a number of adverbial phrases, e.g. *en particular,* in particular, *en secreto,* in secret, *en seguida,* immediately. When it is used with a gerund, it means after, as soon as, when, e.g. *En llegando a la puerta llamó,* When he arrived at the door, he knocked. *En todas partes se cuecen habas,* That happens everywhere; It happens in the best of families

enaceitar /enasei'tar; enaθei'tar/ *vt, Argentina* to oil

enagua /e'nagua/ *f,* slip, crinoline, petticoat

enajenación /enahena'sion; enahena'θion/ *f,* transference, alienation (property); abstraction, absentmindedness. **e. mental,** lunacy

enajenar /enahe'nar/ *vt* to transfer (property)

enaltecer /enalte'ser; enalte'θer/ *vt irr* to elevate, raise; exalt. See **conocer**

enamoradizo /enamora'ðiso; enamora'ðiθo/ *a* susceptible, easily enamored; fickle

enamorado /enamo'raðo/ *a* in love, lovesick; easily enamored

enamorar /enamo'rar/ *vt* to arouse love in; court, make love to; *vr* fall in love; (with *de*) become fond of (things)

enano /e'nano/ **(-na)** *a* dwarf, dwarfed. *n* dwarf

enarbolar /enarβo'lar/ *vt* to hoist (flags); *vr* prance (horses); become angry

enardecer /enarðe'ser; enarðe'θer/ *vt irr* to kindle, stimulate (passion, quarrel, etc.); *vr* be afire (with passion); *Med.* be inflamed. See **conocer**

encabestrar /enkaβe'strar/ *vt* to halter; lead, dominate

encabestrarse /enkaβes'trarse/ *vr, Lat. Am.* to dig one's heels in

encabezamiento /enkaβesa'miento; enkaβeθa'miento/ *m,* census taking; tax register; tax assessment; heading, inscription, running head

encabezar /enkaβe'sar; enkaβe'θar/ *vt* to take the census of; put on the tax register; open a subscription list; put a heading or title to; lead, head; *vr* compound, settle by agreement (taxes, etc.)

encadenamiento /enkaðena'miento/ *m,* fettering, chaining; connection, link, relation

encadenar /enkaðe'nar/ *vt* to chain, fetter; *Fig.* link up, connect; *Fig.* paralyze. **encadenar el interés de,** to capture the interest of

encajar /enka'har/ *vt* to insert, fit one thing inside another; force in; fit tightly; *Inf.* be opportune, fit in

(often with *bien*); *vr* squeeze or crowd in; *Inf.* butt in, interfere

encaje /en'kahe/ *m,* fitting, insertion; socket, groove; joining; lace; inlay, mosaic

encajero, -a /enka'hero/ *mf,* lace maker; lace seller

encaladura /enkala'ðura/ *f,* whitewashing

encalar /enka'lar/ *vt* to whitewash

encalladero /enkaya'ðero; enkaʎa'ðero/ *m, Naut.* sandbank, reef, shoal

encallar /enka'yar; enka'ʎar/ *vi Naut.* to run aground; *Fig.* be held up (negotiations, etc.)

encalmado /enkal'maðo/ *a* calm; *Com.* dull

encalmarse /enkal'marse/ *vr* to become calm (wind, weather)

encalvecer /enkalβe'ser; enkalβe'θer/ *vi irr* to grow bald. See **conocer**

encamado /enka'maðo/ *a* bedridden, confined to one's bed; *m,* person confined to his bed

encamarse /enka'marse/ *vr* to go to bed (gen. illness); be laid flat (grain, etc.); crouch

encaminadura /enkamina'ðura/ *f,* **encaminamiento** *m,* directing, forwarding, routing

encaminar /enkami'nar/ *vt* to guide; direct; regulate; manage; promote, advance; *vr* (with *prep a*) make for, go in the direction of

encandecer /enkande'ser; enkande'θer/ *vt irr* to make incandescent. See **conocer**

encandilar /enkandi'lar/ *vt* to dazzle; mislead; *Inf.* poke (the fire); *vr* be bloodshot (eyes)

encanecer /enkane'ser; enkane'θer/ *vi irr* to grow gray- or white-haired; grow mold; grow old. See **conocer**

encanijar /enkani'har/ *vt* to make weak, sickly (gen. of babies); *vr* be delicate or ailing

encantado /enkan'taðo/ *a Inf.* daydreaming, abstracted; haunted; rambling (of houses)

encantador /enkanta'ðor/ *a* captivating, bewitching, delightful. *m,* sorcerer, magician. **e. de serpientes,** snake charmer

encantamiento /enkanta'miento/ *m,* enchantment, spell, charm

encantar /enkan'tar/ *vt* to enchant, weave a spell; delight, captivate, charm

encañada /enka'ɲaða/ *f,* gorge, ravine

encañado /enka'ɲaðo/ *m,* trellis; pipeline

encañar /enka'ɲar/ *vt* to run water through a pipe; stake plants; wind thread on a spool

encañonar /enkaɲo'nar/ *vt* to run into pipes; pleat, fold

encapotarse /enkapo'tarse/ *vr* to muffle oneself in a cloak; scowl; be overcast; lower (sky)

encapricharse /enkapri'tʃarse/ *vr* to take a fancy (to); insist on having one's own way, be stubborn

encaramar /enkara'mar/ *vt* to raise, lift; climb; praise, extol. **e. al poder,** to put in power (e.g. a dictator). **encaramarse por,** to climb up

encarar /enka'rar/ *vt* to place face to face; aim (at); *vt and vr* face; come face to face

encarcelación /enkarsela'sion; enkarθela'θion/ *f,* incarceration

encarcelar /enkarse'lar; enkarθe'lar/ *vt* to imprison; jail; clamp

encarecer /enkare'ser; enkare'θer/ *vt irr* to raise the price; overpraise, exaggerate; recommend strongly; *vi and vr* increase in price. See **conocer**

encarecimiento /enkaresi'miento; enkareθi'miento/ *m,* increase (in price); enhancement; exaggeration. **con e.,** insistently, earnestly

encargado /enkar'gaðo/ *m,* person in charge; manager; agent, representative. **e. de negocios,** chargé d'affaires

encargar /enkar'gar/ *vt* to enjoin; commission; recommend; advise; *Com.* order

encargo /en'kargo/ *m,* charge, commission; order; office, employ; responsibility

encariñarse /enkari'ɲarse/ (*con*), *vi* to become fond (of)

encarnación /enkarna'sion; enkarna'θion/ *f,* incarnation

encarnadino /enkarna'ðino/ *a* incarnadine

encarnado /enkar'naðo/ a incarnate; flesh-colored; red

encarnar /enkar'nar/ vi to incarnate; pierce the flesh; *Fig.* leave a strong impression; vt symbolize, personify; vr mingle, blend

encarnizado /enkarni'saðo; enkarni'θaðo/ a bloodshot (eyes); flesh-colored; bloody, cruel (gen. of battles)

encarnizamiento /enkarnisa'miento; enkarniθa'miento/ m, cruelty, fury

encarnizar /enkarni'sar; enkarni'θar/ vt to infuriate; vr devour flesh (animals); persecute, ill-treat. vr e. se con, to attack viciously

encaro /en'karo/ m, stare, gaze; aim

encarrilar /enkarri'lar/ vt to set on the track or rails (vehicles); *Fig.* put right, set on the right track

encartamiento /enkarta'miento/ m, proscription; charter

encartar /enkar'tar/ vt to proscribe, outlaw; place on the tax register; *Law.* summon, cite

encartonar /enkarto'nar/ vt to cover with cardboard; bind in boards (books)

encasar /enka'sar/ vt *Surg.* to set (a bone)

encasillado /enkasi'yaðo; enkasi'ʎaðo/ m, set of pigeonholes

encasillar /enkasi'yar; enkasi'ʎar/ vt to pigeonhole; file, classify

encasquetar /enkaske'tar/ (se) vt and vr to pull a hat well down on the head; vr get a fixed idea

encasquillador, -a /enkaskija'ðor; enkaskiʎa'ðor/ mf, *Lat. Am.* blacksmith

encastillar /enkasti'yar; enkasti'ʎar/ vt to fortify with castles; vr retire to a castle; be headstrong, obstinate

encauzamiento /enkausa'miento; enkauθa'miento/ m, channeling; *Fig.* direction

encauzar /enkau'sar; enkau'θar/ vt to channel; *Fig.* direct, guide

encefalitis /ensefa'litis; enθefa'litis/ f, encephalitis. **e. letárgica**, encephalitis lethargica, sleeping sickness.

enceguedor a blinding, dazzling

encéfalo /en'sefalo; en'θefalo/ m, *Anat.* brain

encenagarse /ensena'garse; enθena'garse/ vr to wallow in mire; muddy oneself; take to vice

encendedor /ensende'ðor; enθende'ðor/ a lighting. m, lighter. **e. de bolsillo**, pocket lighter

encender /ensen'der; enθen'der/ vt irr to light; switch on; set fire to, kindle; arouse (emotions); inflame, incite; vr blush. See **entender**

encendido /ensen'diðo; enθen'diðo/ a high-colored; inflamed; ardent. m, *Auto.* ignition

encerado /ense'raðo; enθe'raðo/ a wax-colored. m, oilskin; sticking plaster; blackboard; tarpaulin

enceramiento /ensera'miento; enθera'miento/ m, waxing

encerar /ense'rar; enθe'rar/ vt to wax, varnish with wax; stain with wax; inspissate (lime)

encercar /enser'kar; enθer'kar/ vt, *Lat. Am.* to encircle

encerotar /ensero'tar; enθero'tar/ vt to wax (thread)

encerrar /ense'rrar; enθe'rrar/ vt irr to shut up, imprison; include, contain; vr go into seclusion. See **acertar**

encerrona /ense'rrona; enθe'rrona/ f, *Inf.* voluntary retreat; *Fig. Inf.* tight corner

encespedar /ensespe'ðar; enθespe'ðar/ vt to cover with sod

enchilada /entʃi'laða/ f, *Mexico* rolled-up tortilla filled with meat or cheese and covered with sauce or cream

enchufar /entʃu'far/ vt to connect tubes; *Fig.* combine (jobs, etc.); *Elec.* plug, connect

enchufe /en'tʃufe/ m, joint, fitting together (of tubes); *Elec.* wall socket, plug; part-time post; *Inf.* cushy job. **e. de reducción**, *Elec.* adapter

encía /en'sia; en'θia/ f, gum (of the mouth)

encíclica /en'siklika; en'θiklika/ f, encyclical

enciclopedia /ensiklo'peðia; enθiklo'peðia/ f, encyclopedia

enciclopédico /ensiklo'peðiko; enθiklo'peðiko/ a encyclopedic

encierro /en'sierro; en'θierro/ m, act of closing or shutting up; prison; retreat, confinement

encima /en'sima; en'θima/ adv over; above; at the top; besides; (with de) on, on top of. **por e. de esto**, over and above this, besides this

encinta /en'sinta; en'θinta/ a f, pregnant

encintar /ensin'tar; enθin'tar/ vt to decorate with ribbons

enclavar /enkla'βar/ vt to nail; pierce; embed; *Inf.* deceive

enclenque /en'klenke/ a ailing, weak; puny, anemic

enclocar /enklo'kar/ vi irr to begin to brood (hens). See **contar**

encobar /enko'βar/ vi to hatch eggs

encoger /enko'her/ vt to shrink, contract, recoil; discourage; vi shrink (wood, cloth, etc.); vr shrink from, recoil; be discouraged; be timid or bashful

encogimiento /enkohi'miento/ m, shrinkage; contraction; depression, discouragement; timidity; bashfulness

encoladura /enkola'ðura/ f. **encolamiento** m, gluing; sizing

encolerizar /enkoleri'sar; enkoleri'θar/ vt to anger; vr be angry

encomendar /enkomen'dar/ vt irr to charge with, entrust; recommend, commend; vr (with prep a) put one's trust in; send greetings to. See **acertar**

encomiar /enko'miar/ vt to eulogize, praise

encomienda /enko'mienda/ f, commission, charge; knight commandership; insignia of knight commander; land with Indian residents formerly granted in America to conquistadores; recommendation, commendation; protection, defense; pl greetings, compliments, messages

encomio /en'komio/ m, eulogy; strong recommendation

enconar /enko'nar/ vt to irritate, exasperate; vr *Med.* be inflamed; be exasperated; (with en) burden one's conscience with

encono /en'kono/ m, rancor, resentment, ill will

encontrado /enkon'traðo/ a facing, opposite, in front; hostile, inimical, opposed (to)

encontrar /enkon'trar/ vt irr to meet; find; vi meet; encounter unexpectedly; (with con) run into, collide with; vr be antagonistic; find; feel, be; differ, disagree (opinions); (with con) meet, come across. **e. eco**, to strike a responsive chord. **encontrarse con el cura de su pueblo**, to find someone who knows all about, meet someone who knows all about. **¿Cómo se encuentra Vd?** How are you? *Pres. Ind.* **encuentro**, etc. *Pres. Subjunc.* **encuentre**, etc.

encontrón /enkon'tron/ m, collision, violent impact

encopetado /enkope'taðo/ a conceited, proud; of noble descent; important

encorajinar /enkora'har/ vt to encourage, inspire, hearten; vr be angry

encordelar /enkorðe'lar/ vt to cord, rope

encorsetar /enkorse'tar/ vt to correct

encorvadura /enkorβa'ðura/ f, bending, curving

encorvar /enkor'βar/ vt to bend, curve; vr have a leaning toward, favor

encostrar /enkos'trar/ vt to cover with a crust; vr form a crust

encrespador /enkrespa'ðor/ m, curling irons

encrespar /enkres'par/ vt to curl (hair); enrage; vr be curly (hair); stand on end (hair, feathers, from fright); be angry; grow rough (sea); become complicated, entangled

encrestado /enkres'taðo/ a crested; haughty, arrogant

encrestarse /enkres'tarse/ vr to stiffen the comb or crest (birds)

encrucijada /enkrusi'haða; enkruθi'haða/ f, crossroad, intersection; ambush

encrudecer /enkruðe'ser; enkruðe'θer/ vt irr to make raw-looking; annoy; vr be annoyed. See **conocer**

encuadernación /enkuaðerna'sion; enkuaðerna-'θion/ f, bookbinding; binding (of a book); bookbinder's workshop. **e. en tela**, cloth binding

encuadernador /enkuaðerna'ðor/ (**-ra**) n bookbinder

encuadernar /enkuaðer'nar/ vt to bind (a book)

encuadrar /enkuaðˈrar/ *vt* to frame; fit one thing into another, insert; limit; *Mil.* enlist

encubar /enkuˈβar/ *vt* to put into casks (wine, etc.)

encubiertamente /enkuβiertaˈmente/ *adv* secretly; deceitfully

encubierto /enkuˈβierto/ *a* concealed; secret

encubridor /enkuβriˈðor/ **(-ra)** *a* concealing, hiding. *n* hider; harborer; accomplice; receiver (of stolen goods); *Law.* accessory after the fact

encubrimiento /enkuβriˈmiento/ *m,* hiding, concealment; *Law.* accessory before (after) the fact; receiving (of stolen goods)

encubrir /enkuˈβˈrir/ *vt* to conceal; receive (stolen goods); *Law.* prosecute as an accessory. *Past Part.* **encubierto**

encuentro /enˈkuentro/ *m,* collision; meeting, encounter; opposition, hostility; *Mil.* fight, skirmish; *Archit.* angle. **ir al e. de,** to go in search of. **salir al e. (de),** to go to meet; resist

encuerado, -a /enkueˈraðo/ *a, Lat. Am.* naked, nude, in the buff

encuesta /enˈkuesta/ *f,* survey, investigation, inquiry

encumbrado /enkumˈbraðo/ *a* elevated, high

encumbramiento /enkumbraˈmiento/ *m,* act of elevating; height; aggrandizement, advancement

encumbrar /enkumˈbrar/ *vt* to raise, elevate; exalt, promote; ascend, climb to the top; *vr* be proud; be lofty, tower

encurtido /enkurˈtiðo/ *m,* pickle

encurtir /enkurˈtir/ *vt* to pickle

ende /ˈende/ *adv Obs.* there. **por e.,** therefore

endeble /enˈdeβle/ *a* weak, frail

endeblez /endeˈβles; endeˈβleθ/ *f,* weakness

endémico /enˈdemiko/ *a Med.* endemic

endemoniado /endemoˈniaðo/ *a* devil-possessed; *Inf.* fiendish, malevolent

endemoniar /endemoˈniar/ *vt* to possess with a devil; *Inf.* enrage

endentar /endenˈtar/ *vt irr Mech.* to cut the cogs (of a wheel); engage, interlock (gears, wheels, etc.). See **regimentar**

endentecer /endenteˈser; endenteˈθer/ *vi irr* to cut teeth. See **conocer**

enderezamiento /endresaˈmiento; endereθaˈmiento/ *m,* straightening; directing, guiding; putting right, correction

enderezar /endereˈsar; endereˈθar/ *vt* to straighten; direct, guide; put right, correct; *vi* take the right road; *vr* straighten oneself; prepare to

endeudarse /endeuˈðarse/ *vr* to contract debts; be under an obligation

endiablado /endiaˈβlaðo/ *a* ugly, monstrous; *Inf.* fiendish

endiosar /endioˈsar/ *vt* to deify; *vr* be puffed up with pride; be abstracted or lost in ecstasy

enditarse /endiˈtarse/ *vr, Lat. Am.* to go into debt

endocrino /endoˈkrino/ *a* endocrine

endocrinología /endokrinoloˈhia/ *f,* endocrinology

endomingarse /endomiŋˈgarse/ *vr* to put on one's Sunday best

endosante /endoˈsante/ *m,* endorser

endosar /endoˈsar/ *vt Com.* to endorse; transfer, pass on

endoso /enˈdoso/ *m, Com.* endorsement

endrogarse /endroˈgarse/ *vr, Mexico* = **enditarse**

endulzar /endulˈsar; endulˈθar/ *vt* to sweeten; soften, mitigate

endurecer /endureˈser; endureˈθer/ *vt irr* to harden; toughen, inure; make severe or cruel; *vr* grow hard; become hardened or robust; be harsh or cruel. **endurecerse al trabajo,** to become hardened to work. See **conocer**

endurecimiento /enduresiˈmiento; endureθiˈmiento/ *m,* hardness; obstinacy, tenacity

ene /ˈene/ *f,* name of letter N

enemigo /eneˈmigo/ **(-ga)** *a* hostile. *n* enemy; antagonist. *m,* devil

enemistad /enemisˈtað/ *f,* enmity, hostility

enemistar /enemisˈtar/ *vt* to make enemies of; *vr* (with con) become an enemy of; cease to be friendly with

energético, -a /enerˈhetiko/ *a, Lat. Am.* = **enérgico**

energía /enerˈhia/ *f,* energy, vigor

enérgico /eˈnerhiko/ *a* energetic, vigorous

energúmeno /enerˈgumeno/ **(-na)** *n* energumen

enero /eˈnero/ *m,* January

enervación /enerβaˈsion; enerβaˈθion/ *f,* enervation

enervar /enerˈβar/ *vt* to enervate, weaken; *Fig.* take the force out of (reasons, etc.)

enfadar /enfaˈðar/ *vt* to make angry; *vr* become angry; *Lat. Am.* to get bored

enfado /enˈfaðo/ *m,* anger; annoyance; trouble, toil

enfadoso /enfaˈðoso/ *a* vexatious; troublesome, wearisome

enfaldada /enfalˈdaða/ *f,* skirtful

enfaldar /enfalˈdar/ *vt* to tuck up the skirts; lop off lower branches (of trees)

enfangarse /enfaŋˈgarse/ *vr* to cover oneself with mud; *Inf.* dirty one's hands, sully one's reputation; wallow in vice

énfasis /ˈenfasis/ *m,* or *f,* emphasis

enfático /enˈfatiko/ *a* emphatic

enfermar /enferˈmar/ *vi* to fall ill; *vt* cause illness; *Fig.* weaken. **Enfermó del corazón,** He fell ill with heart trouble.

enfermedad /enfermeˈðað/ *f,* illness; *Fig.* malady, distemper. **e. del sueño,** sleeping sickness

enfermería /enfermeˈria/ *f,* infirmary; hospital; first-aid station

enfermero, -a /enferˈmero/ *mf* nurse

enfermizo /enferˈmiso; enferˈmiθo/ *a* ailing, delicate; unhealthy, unwholesome

enfermo /enˈfermo/ **(-ma)** *a* ill; *Fig.* corrupt, diseased; delicate, sickly. *n* patient. **e. venéreo,** person with a venereal disease

enfilar /enfiˈlar/ *vt* to place in line; string; *Mil.* enfilade

enflaquecer /enflakeˈser; enflakeˈθer/ *vt irr* to make thin; weaken, enervate; *vi* grow thin; lose heart. See **conocer**

enflaquecimiento /enflakesiˈmiento; enflakeθiˈmiento/ *m,* loss of flesh; discouragement

enfocar /enfoˈkar/ *vt* to focus; envisage

enfoque /enˈfoke/ *m,* focus

enfoscado /enfosˈkaðo/ *a* ill-humored; immersed in business matters

enfrascar /enfrasˈkar/ *vt* to bottle; *vr* (with en) plunge into, entangle oneself in (undergrowth, etc.); become engrossed or absorbed in

enfrenar /enfreˈnar/ *vt* to bridle; curb (a horse); restrain, repress; check

enfrente /enˈfrente/ *adv* in front, opposite, facing; in opposition

enfriadero /enfriaˈðero/ *m,* cooling place, cold cellar, root cellar

enfriamiento /enfriaˈmiento/ *m,* cooling

enfriar /enfˈriar/ *vt* to cool; *Fig.* chill, make indifferent; *vr* grow cold; *Fig.* grow stormy (weather)

enfurecer /enfureˈser; enfureˈθer/ *vt irr* to enrage. See **conocer**

enfurecimiento /enfuresiˈmiento; enfureθiˈmiento/ *m,* fury

enfurruñarse /enfurruˈɲarse/ *vr Inf.* to fume, be angry; be disgruntled

engalanar /eŋgalaˈnar/ *vt* to decorate, embellish. **engalanado como nunca,** dressed to the nines, dressed to kill

enganchar /eŋganˈtʃar/ *vt* to hook; couple, connect; hitch, harness, yoke; *Inf.* seduce, hook; *Mil.* bribe into army; *vr* be hooked or caught on a hook; *Mil.* enlist

enganche /eŋˈgantʃe/ *m,* hooking; coupling (of railroad trains, etc.); connection; yoke, harness; hook; *Inf.* enticement; *Mil.* enlistment; *Mexico* down payment

engañadizo /eŋgaɲaˈðiso; eŋgaɲaˈðiθo/ *a* easily deceived, simple

engañador /eŋgaɲaˈðor/ **(-ra)** *a* deceiving; deceptive. *n* deceiver, impostor

engañar /eŋga'ɲar/ *vt* to deceive; defraud, cheat; beguile, while away; hoax, humbug; *vr* be mistaken; deceive oneself. **e. como a un chino,** *Inf.* to pull the wool over a person's eyes. **Las apariencias engañan,** Appearances are deceptive

engañifa /eŋga'nhook;ifa/ *f, Inf.* swindle, fraud

engaño /eŋ'gaɲo/ *m,* deceit; deception, illusion; fraud; falsehood

engañoso /eŋga'ɲoso/ *a* deceitful, false; fraudulent; deceptive, misleading

engarabatar /eŋgaraβa'tar/ *vt Inf.* to hook; *vr* become hooked, curved, crooked

engaratusar /eŋgaratu'sar/ *vt, inf, Lat. Am.* = **engatusar**

engarce /eŋgarse/ eŋ'garθe/ *m,* hooking; coupling; setting (of jewels)

engarzar /eŋgar'sar; eŋgar'θar/ *vt* to link, couple, enchain; hook; curl; set (jewels)

engastar /eŋgas'tar/ *vt* to set (jewels)

engaste /eŋ'gaste/ *m,* setting (of jewels)

engatusar /eŋgatu'sar/ *vt Inf.* to wheedle, coax, flatter

engendrador /enhendra'ðor/ (**-ra**) *a* engendering; original. *n* begetter

engendrar /enhen'drar/ *vt* to procreate; engender, produce, cause

engendro /en'hendro/ *m,* fetus; abnormal embryo; literary monstrosity

engestarse /eŋges'tarse/ *vr, Mexico* to make a wry face

englobar /eŋglo'βar/ *vt* to include, comprise, embrace

engolfarse /eŋgol'farse/ *vr* to sail out to sea; (*with en*) *Fig.* be absorbed in

engomar /eŋgo'mar/ *vt* to gum

engordar /eŋgor'ðar/ *vt* to fatten; *vi* grow fat; *Inf.* prosper, grow rich

engorde /eŋ'gorðe/ *m,* fattening (of stock)

engorrar /eŋgo'rrar/ *vt, Lat. Am.* to annoy, needle

engorro /eŋ'gorro/ *m,* impediment, obstacle, difficulty

engorroso /eŋgo'rroso/ *a* difficult, troublesome

engranaje /eŋgra'nahe/ *m, Mech.* gearing, gear; *Fig.* connection, link

engrandecer /eŋgrande'ser; eŋgrande'θer/ *vt irr* to enlarge; augment; eulogize; promote, exalt. See **conocer**

engrandecimiento /eŋgrandesi'miento; eŋgrandeθi'miento/ *m,* enlargement; increase; exaggeration, eulogization; advancement, promotion

engrasador /eŋgrasa'ðor/ *m,* greaser, lubricator; oiler

engrasar /eŋgra'sar/ *vt* to grease; lubricate, oil; manure; stain with grease

engreimiento /eŋgrei'miento/ *m,* conceit, vanity

engreír /eŋgre'ir/ *vt irr* to make conceited; *vr* become vain or conceited. See **reír**

engrescar /eŋgres'kar/ (**se**) *vt* and *vr* to start a quarrel

engrosar /eŋgro'sar/ *vt irr* to fatten, thicken; *Fig.* increase, swell; manure; *vi* put on weight, grow fat. See **contar**

engrudar /eŋgru'ðar/ *vt* to paste, glue

engrudo /eŋ'gruðo/ *m,* paste, glue

enguijarrado /eŋguiha'rraðo/ *a* pebbled. *m,* pebbled path

engullir /eŋgu'yir; eŋgu'ʎir/ *vt* to gobble, swallow

enhebrar /ene'βrar/ *vt* to thread (needles); string

enhestar /enes'tar/ *vt irr* to erect; set upright; *vr* rise; rear up; straighten oneself up. See **acertar**

enhiesto /en'iesto/ *a* upright, erect

enhorabuena /enora'βuena/ *f,* congratulation. *adv* well and good. **dar la e.,** to congratulate

enhoramala /enora'mala/ *adv* in an evil hour. *Inf.* **¡Vete en e.!** Go to the devil!

enhorquetado /enorke'taðo/ *a* in the saddle

enigma /e'nigma/ *m,* enigma

enigmático /enig'matiko/ *a* enigmatical

enjabonar /enhaβo'nar/ *vt* to soap; *Inf.* soap down, flatter

enjaezar /enhae'sar; enhae'θar/ *vt* to harness (a horse)

enjalbegar /enhalβe'gar/ *vt* to whitewash

enjambrar /enhamb'rar/ *vt* to hive bees; *vi* multiply, increase

enjambre /en'hambre/ *m,* swarm (of bees); crowd

enjaretado /enhare'taðo/ *m,* latticework

enjaular /enhau'lar/ *vt* to cage; *Inf.* jail

enjoyar /enho'yar/ *vt* to adorn with jewels; beautify; set with precious stones

enjuagadura /enhuaga'ðura/ *f,* rinsing (the mouth); rinse water; mouthwash

enjuagar /enhua'gar/ *vt* to rinse; *vr* rinse the mouth

enjuague /en'huage/ *m,* rinse; rinsing; mouthwash; tooth mug; scheme, plan

enjugar /enhu'gar/ *vt* to dry; cancel, write off; wipe, mop (perspiration, tears, etc.); *vr* grow lean

enjuiciar /enhui'siar; enhui'θiar/ *vt* to submit a matter to arbitration; *Law.* prosecute; *Law.* render judgment; *Law.* adjudicate (a case)

enjundia /en'hundia/ *f,* animal fat or grease; *Fig.* substance, meat; strength, vigor; constitution, temperament

enjuto /en'huto/ *a* dry; lean. *m pl,* brushwood; *Cul.* canapés, savories

enlace /en'lase; en'laθe/ *m,* connection; link; tie; *Chem.* bond; alliance; relationship; marriage, *Phonet.* linking

enladrillado /enlaðri'yaðo; enlaðri'ʎaðo/ *m,* brick floor or pavement

enlardar /enlar'ðar/ *vt Cul.* to baste

enlazar /enla'sar; enla'θar/ *vt* to tie, bind; join, link; lasso; *vr* marry; be allied, related. **e. con,** to connect with (of trains); link up with

enlentecerse /enlente'serse; enlente'θerse/ *vr* to decelerate, go slow, slow down

enlodar /enlo'ðar/ *vt* to muddy; *Fig.* smirch, sully

enloquecer /enloke'ser; enloke'θer/ *vt irr* to drive insane; *vi* go mad. See **conocer**

enlosado /enlo'saðo/ *m,* tile floor

enlosar /enlo'sar/ *vt* to pave with flags

enlozar /enlo'sar; enlo'θar/ *vt, Lat. Am.* to enamel, glaze

enlucir /enlu'sir; enlu'θir/ *vt irr* to plaster (walls); polish (metals). See **lucir**

enlutar /enlu'tar/ *vt* to put in mourning, drape with crepe; darken, obscure; sadden; *vr* go into mourning; become dark

enmaderar /emaðe'rar/ *vt* to panel in wood, board up

enmarañar /emara'ɲar/ *vt* to tangle, disorder (hair, etc.); complicate, confuse; *vr* be tangled; be sprinkled with clouds

enmaridar /emari'ðar/ *vi* to become a wife

enmarillecerse /emariye'serse; emariʎe'θerse/ *vr irr* to grow yellow. See **conocer**

enmascarar /emaska'rar/ *vt* to mask; disguise, dissemble; *vr* be masked

enmasillar /emasi'yar; emasi'ʎar/ *vt* to putty

enmendar /emen'dar/ *vt irr* to correct, improve; reform; compensate, indemnify; *Law.* repeal; *vr* be improved or corrected; mend one's ways. See **acertar**

enmienda /e'mienda/ *f,* correction; reform; indemnity; compensation; amendment; *pl Agr.* fertilizers

enmohecer /emoe'ser; emoe'θer/ *vt irr* to rust; *vr* become moldy. See **conocer**

enmudecer /emuðe'ser; emuðe'θer/ *vt irr* to silence; *vi* become dumb; be silent. See **conocer**

enmugrecer /emugre'ser; emugre'θer/ *vt irr* to cover with grime; *vr* be grimy, dirty. See **conocer**

enmugrentar /emugren'tar/ *vt, Chile* = **enmugrecer**

ennegrecer /ennegre'ser; ennegre'θer/ *vt irr* to dye black; make black; *vr* become black; become dark or cloudy. See **conocer**

ennoblecer /ennoβle'ser; ennoβle'θer/ *vt irr* to ennoble; enrich, embellish; adorn, befit. See **conocer**

ennoblecimiento /ennoβlesi'miento; ennoβleθi'miento/ *m,* ennoblement; enrichment

enojadizo /enoha'ðiso; enoha'ðiθo/ *a* irritable, peevish

enojar /eno'har/ *vt* to anger; annoy, irritate; *vr* be angry; rage, be rough (wind, sea)

enojo /e'noho/ *m*, anger; resentment; vexations, troubles, trials (gen. *pl*). **con gran e. de,** much to the annoyance of

enojoso /eno'hoso/ *a* annoying; troublesome, tiresome

enorgullecer /enorguye'ser; enorguʎe'θer/ *vt* irr to make proud; *vr* be proud. See **conocer**

enorme /e'norme/ *a* enormous, huge; monstrous, heinous

enormidad /enormi'ðað/ *f*, hugeness; enormity; wickedness

enramar /enra'mar/ *vt* to intertwine branches; embower; *vi* branch (trees)

enrarecer /enrare'ser; enrare'θer/ *vt* irr to rarefy; *vr* become rarefied; grow rare. See **conocer**

enrarecimiento /enraresi'miento; enrareθi'miento/ *m*, rarefaction

enredadera /enreða'ðera/ *f*, convolvulus. *a f*, climbing, twining (plant)

enredador /enreða'ðor/ **(-ra)** *a* mischievous, willful; intriguing, scheming; *Inf.* gossiping, meddlesome. *n* intriguer; *Inf.* meddler

enredar /enre'ðar/ *vt* to catch in a net; put down nets or snares; entangle; sow discord; compromise, involve (in difficulties); *vi* be mischievous; *vr* be entangled; be involved (in difficulties)

enredo /en'reðo/ *m*, tangle; mischief, prank; intrigue, malicious falsehood; difficult situation; plot

enredoso /enre'ðoso/ *a* tangled; fraught with difficulties

enrejado /enre'haðo/ *m*, railing, paling; trellis or latticework; *Sew.* openwork

enrejar /enre'har/ *vt* to fence with a railing; cover with grating

enriquecer /enrike'ser; enrike'θer/ *vt* irr to enrich; exalt, aggrandize; *vi* grow rich; prosper, flourish. See **conocer**

enriscado /enris'kaðo/ *a* craggy, rocky

enristrar /enris''trar/ *vt* to couch (a lance); string (onions, etc.); *Fig.* surmount (difficulties); go straight to (a place)

enrojecer /enrohe'ser; enrohe'θer/ *vt* irr to redden; make blush; *vr* grow red; blush. See **conocer**

enroscar /enros'kar/ *vt* to twist, twine; *vr* turn (screw); twist; coil

ensaimada /ensai'maða/ *f*, Spanish pastry cake

ensalada /ensa'laða/ *f*, salad; hodgepodge

ensaladera /ensala'ðera/ *f*, salad bowl

ensalmar /ensal'mar/ *vt* *Surg.* to set (bones); cure by spells

ensalmo /en'salmo/ *m*, spell, charm. **por e.,** as if by magic, rapidly

ensalzar /ensal'sar; ensal'θar/ *vt* to exalt, promote; praise

ensamblador /ensambla'ðor/ *m*, joiner, assembler

ensambladura /ensambla'ðura/ *f*, assemblage, joinery; joining; dovetailing

ensamblar /ensam'blar/ *vt* to assemble; join, dovetail, mortise

ensanchador, -a /ensantʃa'ðor/ *mf*, glove stretcher

ensanchar /ensan'tʃar/ *vt* to widen, enlarge, extend; *Sew.* let out, stretch; *vr* put on airs

ensanche /en'santʃe/ *m*, dilatation, widening; stretch; extension; *Sew.* turnings, letting out; (city) extension

ensangrentar /ensaŋgren'tar/ *vt* irr to stain with blood; *vr* be bloodstained; be overhasty. See **regimentar**

ensañar /ensa'ɲar/ *vt* to irritate, infuriate; *vr* be merciless (with vanquished)

ensartar /ensar'tar/ *vt* to string (beads); thread (needles); spit, pierce; tell a string (of falsehoods)

ensayar /ensa'yar/ *vt* to try out; *Chem.* test; *Theat.* rehearse; assay

ensayista /ensa'yista/ *mf* essayist

ensayo /ensa'yo/ *m*, test, trial; *Lit.* essay; assay; experiment; rehearsal. **e. general,** dress rehearsal

ensenada /ense'naða/ *f*, cove, inlet

enseñanza /ense'ɲansa; ense'ɲanθa/ *f*, teaching; education; example, experience. **e. primaria,** elementary education. **e. secundaria,** secondary education. **e. superior,** higher education

enseñar /ense'ɲar/ *vt* to teach, instruct; train; point out; exhibit, show; *vr* become accustomed. **e. la oreja,** *Fig.* to show the cloven hoof

enseñorearse /enseɲore'arse/ *vr* to take possession (of)

enseres /en'seres/ *m pl*, household goods; utensils; equipment

ensilladero /ensiya'ðero; ensiʎa'ðero/ *m*, paddock

ensillar /ensi'yar; ensi'ʎar/ *vt* to saddle

ensimismarse /ensimis'marse/ *vr* to be lost in thought; *Lat. Am.* to become conceited, become self-absorbed

ensoberbecer /ensoβerβe'ser; ensoβerβe'θer/ *vt* irr to make haughty; *vr* become arrogant; grow rough (sea). See **conocer**

ensordecedor /ensorðese'ðor; ensorðeθe'ðor/ *a* deafening

ensordecer /ensorðe'ser; ensorðe'θer/ *vt* irr to deafen; *vi* become deaf; keep silent, refuse to reply. See **conocer**

ensuciar /ensu'siar; ensu'θiar/ *vt* to soil, dirty; *Fig.* sully; *vr* be dirty; *Inf.* accept bribes

ensueño /en'sueɲo/ *m*, dream; illusion, fancy

entabicar /entaβi'kar/ *vt*, *Lat. Am.* to partition off

entablado /enta'βlaðo/ *m*, stage, dais; wooden floor; planking

entablar /enta'βlar/ *vt* to plank, floor with boards; board up; *Surg.* splint; undertake, initiate (negotiations, etc.); begin (conversations, etc.); *vr* settle (winds). **e. acción judicial,** to take legal action

entalegar /entale'gar/ *vt* to put into sacks or bags; hoard (money)

entalladura /entaya'ðura; entaʎa'ðura/ *f*, carving; sculpture; mortise, notch

entallar /enta'yar; enta'ʎar/ *vt* to carve; sculpture; engrave; notch, groove; tap (trees); fit (well or ill) at the waist

entallecer /entaye'ser; entaʎe'θer/ *vi* irr to sprout (plants). See **conocer**

entapizar /entapi'sar; entapi'θar/ *vt* to hang with tapestry; upholster; *Fig.* cover, carpet

entarimado /entari'maðo/ *m*, wooden floor; dais

ente /'ente/ *m*, entity, being; *Inf.* object, individual

entechar /ente'tʃar/ *vt*, *Lat. Am.* to roof, to put a roof on

enteco /en'teko/ *a* sickly, ailing, delicate

entendederas /entende'ðeras/ *f pl*, *Inf.* understanding

entendedor /entende'ðor/ **(-ra)** *a* understanding, comprehending. *n* one who understands. **A buen entendedor pocas palabras,** A word to the wise is sufficient

entender /enten'der/ *vt* irr to comprehend, understand; know; deduce, infer; intend; believe; (with *de*) be familiar with or knowledgeable about; (with *en*) have as a profession or trade; be engaged in; have authority in; *vr* understand oneself; have a reason (for behavior); understand each other; have an amatory understanding; be meant, signify; (with *con*) have an understanding with. **a mi e.,** in my opinion, as I see it. *Pres. Ind.* **entiendo, entiendes, entiende, entienden.** *Pres. Subjunc.* **entienda, entiendas, entienda, entiendan**

entendido /enten'diðo/ *a* learned, knowledgeable

entendimiento /entendi'miento/ *m*, understanding; mind, reason, intelligence

enteramente /entera'mente/ *adv* completely, entirely, wholly

enterar /ente'rar/ *vt* to inform, advise

entereza /ente'resa; ente'reθa/ *f*, entirety; completeness; impartiality, integrity; fortitude, constancy; strictness, rigor

enternecer /enterne'ser; enterne'θer/ *vt* irr to soften, make tender; move to pity; *vr* be touched by compassion. See **conocer**

enternecimiento /enternesi'miento; enterneθi'miento/ *m*, compassion, pity; tenderness

entero /en'tero/ *a* entire; whole; robust, healthy; upright, just; constant, loyal; pure; *Inf.* strong, tough (cloth); *Math.* integral; *Lat. Am.* payment

enterrador /enterra'ðor/ *m*, gravedigger

enterrar /ente'rrar/ *vt irr* to inter; outlive; bury, forget. See **acertar**

entibiar /enti'βiar/ *vt* to make lukewarm; *Fig.* cool, temper

entidad /enti'ðað/ *f*, entity; value, importance

entierro /en'tierro/ *m*, interment, burial; grave; funeral; buried treasure

entoldar /entol'dar/ *vt* to cover with an awning; hang with tapestry, etc., drape; cover (sky, clouds)

entomología /entomolo'hia/ *f*, entomology

entomológico /entomo'lohiko/ *a* entomological

entomólogo /ento'mologo/ *m*, entomologist

entonación /entona'sion; entona'θion/ *f*, intonation; modulation (voice); conceit

entonado /ento'naðo/ *m*, haughty, conceited

entonar /ento'nar/ *vt* to modulate (voice); intone; blow (organ bellows); lead (song); *Med.* tone up; *Art.* harmonize; *vr* become conceited; *Com.* improve, harden (stock, etc.)

entonces /entonses; en'tonθes/ *adv* then, at that time; in that case, that being so

entonelar /entone'lar/ *vt* to put in barrels or casks

entontecer /entonteser; entonte'θer/ *vt irr* to make stupid or foolish; *vr* become stupid. See **conocer**

entornar /entor'nar/ *vt* to leave ajar; half-close; upset, turn upside down

entorpecer /entorpe'ser; entorpe'θer/ *vt irr* to numb, make torpid; confuse, daze; obstruct, delay; *vr* go numb; be confused. See **conocer**

entorpecimiento /entorpesi'miento; entorpe-θi'miento/ *m*, numbness, torpidity; stupidity, dullness; delay, obstruction

entrada /en'traða/ *f*, entrance; door, gate; admission; *Cul.* entree; admission ticket; *Theat.* house; takings, gate; *Mil.* entry; beginnings (of month, etc.); intimacy; right of entry. **entradas y salidas,** comings and goings; collusion; *Com.* ingoing and outgoing

entrampar /entram'par/ *vt* to trap (animals); swindle; *Fig. Inf.* entangle (business affairs); *Inf.* load with debts; *vr* be bogged down; *Inf.* be in debt

entrante /en'trante/ *a* incoming, entrant; next, coming (month)

entraña /en'traɲa/ *f*, entrail; *pl* heart; *Fig.* center, core; humaneness; temperament. *Inf.* **no tener entrañas,** to be heartless, be without feeling

entrañable /entra'ɲaβle/ *a* intimate; dearly loved

entrar /en'trar/ *vi* (*with en*) to enter, go into, come in; flow into; *Fig.* have access to; join, become a member; *Fig.* be taken by (fever, panic, etc.); *Mil.* enter; be an ingredient of; (*with por, en*) penetrate, pierce; (*with de*) embrace (professions, etc.); (*with prep a + infin*) begin to; (*with en + noun*) begin to be (e.g. *e. en calor,* begin to be hot) or begin to take part in (e.g. *e. en lucha,* begin to fight); *vt* introduce, make enter; *Mil.* (*with en*) occupy; *vr* (*with en*) squeeze in. **e. en apetito,** to work up an appetite, get an appetite. *Inf.* **no e. ni salir en,** to take no part in. *Inf.* **No me entra,** I don't understand it

entre /'entre/ *prep* between; among; to. **e. joyas,** among jewels. **E. las dos se escribió la carta,** Between them, they wrote the letter. **Dije e. mí,** I said to myself. **los días de e. semana,** weekdays. **e. tanto,** in the meanwhile.

entreabrir /entrea'βrir/ *vt* to leave ajar; half-open. *Past Part.* **entreabierto**

entreacto /entre'akto/ *m*, interval, entr'acte; small cigar

entrecano /entre'kano/ *a* going gray, grayish (hair)

entrecejo /entre'seho; entre'θeho/ *m*, space between the eyebrows; frown

entrecerrar /entrese'rrar; entreθe'rrar/ *vt*, *Lat. Am* to close halfway, half-close; leave ajar

entrecoger /entreko'her/ *vt* to intercept, catch; constrain, compel

entrecortado /entrekor'taðo/ *a* intermittent (sounds); faltering, broken (voice)

entrecubiertas /entreku'βiertas/ *f pl*, *Naut.* between decks

entredicho /entre'ðitʃo/ *m*, prohibition; *Eccl.* interdiction

entredós /en'treðos/ *m*, *Sew.* insertion

entrefino /entre'fino/ *a* middling, fairly fine

entrega /en'trega/ *f*, handing over; delivery; *Lit.* part, serial; installment. **por entregas,** as a serial, serial (of stories)

entregar /entre'gar/ *vt* to hand over; deliver; surrender; *vr* give oneself up; surrender; submit; (*with prep a*) engage in, be absorbed in; (*with prep a* or *en*) give oneself over to (vice, etc.)

entreguista /entre'gista/ *mf* defeatist

entrelazar /entrela'sar; entrela'θar/ *vt* to interlace, intertwine; interweave

entrelistado /entrelis'taðo/ *a* striped

entrelucir /entrelu'sir; entrelu'θir/ *vi irr* to show through, be glimpsed. See **lucir**

entremedias /entre'meðias/ *adv* in between, halfway; in the meantime

entremés /entre'mes/ *m*, hors d'oeuvres (gen. *pl*); interlude, one-act farce

entremeter /entreme'ter/ *vt* to place between or among; *vr* intrude; meddle, pry

entremetido /entreme'tiðo/ **(-da)** *a* meddlesome. *n* busybody, meddler

entremetimiento /entremeti'miento/ *m*, meddlesomeness

entremezclar /entremes'klar; entremeθ'klar/ *vt* to intermingle

entrenador /entrena'ðor/ **(-ra)** *n* trainer; *Sports.* coach

entrenamiento /entrena'miento/ *m*, training, exercise

entrenar /entre'nar/ **(se)** *vt* and *vr* to train; exercise; *Sports.* coach

entreoír /entreo'ir/ *vt* to overhear; hear imperfectly

entrepaño /entre'paɲo/ *m*, *Archit.* panel; pier (between windows, etc.)

entrepiernas /entre'piernas/ *f pl*, crotch

entresacar /entresa'kar/ *vt* to choose or pick out; thin out (plants); thin (hair)

entresuelo /entre'suelo/ *m*, mezzanine, entresol; ground floor

entresueño /entre'sueɲo/ *m*, daydream

entretallar /entreta'yar; entreta'ʎar/ *vt* to carve in bas-relief; engrave; *Sew.* do openwork; intercept; *vr* connect, dovetail

entretejer /entrete'her/ *vt* to interweave; interlace; *Lit.* insert

entretela /entre'tela/ *f*, *Sew.* interlining

entretener /entrete'ner/ *vt irr* to keep waiting; make more bearable; amuse, entertain; delay, postpone; maintain, upkeep; *vr* amuse oneself. See **tener**

entretenido /entrete'niðo/ *a* amusing, entertaining

entretenimiento /entreteni'miento/ *m*, amusement; pastime, diversion; upkeep, maintenance

entretiempo /entre'tiempo/ *m*, between seasons, spring or autumn

entreventana /entreβen'tana/ *f*, space between windows

entreverado /entreβe'raðo/ *a* variegated; streaky (of bacon)

entreverar /entreβe'rar/ *vt* to intermingle

entrevista /entre'βista/ *f*, meeting, interview

entristecer /entriste'ser; entriste'θer/ *vt irr* to sadden; *vr* grieve. See **conocer**

entristecimiento /entristesi'miento; entriste-θi'miento/ *m*, sadness

entrometer /entrome'ter/ *vt* See **entremeter**

entromparse /entrom'parse/ *vi*, *Lat. Am.* to get angry

entronar /entro'nar/ *vt* See **entronizar**

entroncar /entron'kar/ *vt* to prove descent; *vi* be related, or become related (by marriage)

entronerar /entrone'rar/ *vt* to pocket (in billiards)

entronizar /entroni'sar; entroni'θar/ *vt* to enthrone; exalt

entronque /entron'ke/ *m*, blood relationship, cognation; junction

entrucharse /entru'tʃarse/ *vr, Mexico* to meddle into other people's business
entumecer /entume'ser; entume'θer/ *vt irr* to numb; *vr* go numb; swell, rise (sea, etc.). See **conocer**
enturbiar /entur'βiar/ *vt* to make turbid or cloudy; confuse, disorder; *vr* become turbid; be in disorder
entusiasmar /entusias'mar/ *vt* to inspire enthusiasm; *vr* be enthusiastic
entusiasmo /entu'siasmo/ *m*, enthusiasm
entusiasta /entu'siasta/ *a* enthusiastic. *mf* enthusiast
enumeración /enumera'sion; enumera'θion/ *f*, enumeration
enumerar /enume'rar/ *vt* to enumerate
enunciación /enunsia'sion; enunθia'θion/ *f*, statement, declaration, enunciation
enunciar /enun'siar; enun'θiar/ *vt* to state clearly, enunciate
envainar /embai'nar/ *vt* to sheathe
envalentonamiento /embalentona'miento/ *m*, boldness; braggadocio, bravado
envalentonar /embalento'nar/ *vt* to make bold (gen. in a bad sense); *vr* strut, brag; take courage
envanecer /embane'ser; embane'θer/ *vt irr* to make vain or conceited; *vr* be vain; be conceited
envanecimiento /embanesi'miento; embaneθi-miento/ *m*, conceit, vanity
envasador /embasa'ðor/ **(-ra)** *n* packer. *m*, funnel
envasar /emba'sar/ *vt* to bottle; barrel; sack (grain, etc.); pack in any container; pierce (with sword)
envase /em'base/ *m*, bottling; filling; container; packing
envejecer /embehe'ser; embehe'θer/ *vt irr* to make old, wear out; *vi* grow old. See **conocer**
envenenador /embenena'ðor/ **(-ra)** *n* poisoner
envenenamiento /embenena'miento/ *m*, poisoning
envenenar /embene'nar/ *vt* to poison; corrupt, pervert; put a malicious interpretation on; embitter; *vr* take poison
envergadura /emberga'ðura/ *f*, wingspan
envés /em'bes/ *m*, wrong side of anything; *Inf.* back. **al e.**, wrong side out
enviado /em'biaðo/ *m*, messenger; envoy. **e. extraordinario**, special envoy
enviar /em'biar/ *vt* to send, dispatch
enviciar /embi'siar; embi'θiar/ *vt* to corrupt, make vicious; *vr* (*with con, en*) take to (drink, etc.)
envidia /em'biðia/ *f*, envy; emulation; desire (to possess)
envidiable /embi'ðiaβle/ *a* enviable
envidiar /embi'ðiar/ *vt* to envy, grudge; emulate
envidioso /embi'ðioso/ *a* envious
envilecer /embile'ser; embile'θer/ *vt irr* to debase; *vr* degrade oneself. See **conocer**
envinarse /embi'narse/ *vr, Mexico* to get drunk (on wine)
envío /em'bio/ *m*, *Com.* remittance; consignment, shipment. **fecha de e.**, date sent
envite /em'bite/ *m*, stake (at cards); offer; push, shove
enviudar /embiu'ðar/ *vi* to become a widow or widower
envoltorio /embol'torio/ *m*, bundle
envoltura /embol'tura/ *f*, swaddling clothes; covering; wrapping
envolver /embol'βer/ *vt irr* to enfold; envelop; wrap up, parcel; *Fig.* contain, enshrine; swaddle, swathe; roll into a ball; confound (in argument); *Mil.* outflank; implicate (person). See **mover**
enyesado /enye'saðo/ *m*, plastering; stucco
enyesar /enye'sar/ *vt* to plaster; *Surg.* apply a plaster bandage
enzarzar /ensar'sar; enθar'θar/ *vt* to fill or cover with brambles; *vr* be caught on brambles; set one person against another; get in difficulties; quarrel
eñe /'eɲe/ *f*, name of the letter Ñ
eón /e'on/ *m*, eon
eperlano /eper'lano/ *m*, smelt
épica /'epika/ *f*, epic
épico /'epiko/ *a* epic

epicúreo /epi'kureo/ **(-ea)** *a* epicurean; sensual, voluptuous. *n* epicure
epidemia /epi'ðemia/ *f*, epidemic
epidémico /epi'ðemiko/ *a* epidemic
epifanía /epifa'nia/ *f*, Epiphany, Twelfth Night
epiglotis /epi'glotis/ *f*, epiglottis
epígrafe /epi'grafe/ *m*, epigraph, inscription; title, motto
epigrafía /epigra'fia/ *f*, epigraphy
epigrama /epi'grama/ *m*, inscription; epigram
epigramático /epigra'matiko/ **(-ca)** *a* epigrammatic. *n* epigrammatist
epilepsia /epi'lepsia/ *f*, epilepsy
epiléptico /epi'leptiko/ **(-ca)** *a* and *n* epileptic
epilogar /epilo'gar/ *vt* to summarize, recapitulate
epílogo /e'pilogo/ *m*, recapitulation; summary, digest; epilogue
episcopado /episko'paðo/ *m*, episcopate; bishopric
episodio /epi'soðio/ *m*, episode; digression
epistolar /episto'lar/ *a* epistolary
epitafio /epi'tafio/ *m*, epitaph
epíteto /e'piteto/ *m*, epithet
epítome /e'pitome/ *m*, epitome; summary, abstract
época /'epoka/ *f*, epoch, period; space of time. **é. de celo**, mating season. **é. de lluvias**, rainy season. **é. de secas**, dry season. **en aquella é.**, at that time
épodo /'epoðo/ *m*, *Poet.* epode
epopeya /epo'peya/ *f*, epic poem; *Fig.* epic
equidad /eki'ða ð/ *f*, fairness; reasonableness; equity
equidistancia /ekiðis'tansia; ekiðis'tanθia/ *f*, equidistance
equidistante /ekiðis'tante/ *a* equidistant
equilibrar /ekili'βrar/ *vt* to balance; *Fig.* maintain in equilibrium, counterbalance
equilibrio /eki'liβrio/ *m*, equilibrium; equanimity; *Fig.* balance
equilibrista /ekili'βrista/ *mf* equilibrist, tightrope walker
equino /e'kino/ *a* equine. *m*, *Archit.* echinus; sea urchin
equinoccio /ekinoksio; eki'nokθio/ *m*, equinox
equipaje /eki'pahe/ *m*, luggage, baggage; *Naut.* crew
equipar /eki'par/ *vt* to equip, furnish
equipo /e'kipo/ *m*, outfitting, furnishing; equipment; team; trousseau
equis /'ekis/ *f*, name of the letter X
equitación /ekita'sion; ekita'θion/ *f*, horsemanship, riding
equitativo /ekita'tiβo/ *a* equitable, just, fair
equivalencia /ekiβalensia; ekiβa'lenθia/ *f*, equivalence, equality
equivalente /ekiβa'lente/ *a* equivalent
equivaler /ekiβa'ler/ *vi irr* to be equivalent; *Geom.* be equal. See **valer**
equivocación /ekiβoka'sion; ekiβoka'θion/ *f*, error, mistake
equivocadamente /ekiβokaða'mente/ *adv* mistakenly, by mistake
equivocar /ekiβo''kar/ *vt* to mistake; *vr* be mistaken or make a mistake. **equivocarse de medio a medio**, to be off by a long shot
equívoco /e'kiβoko/ *a* equivocal, ambiguous. *m*, equivocation
era /'era/ *f*, era; threshing floor; vegetable or flower bed
erario /e'rario/ *m*, public treasury; exchequer
erección /erek'sion; erek'θion/ *f*, raising; erection, elevation; foundation, institution
eremita /ere'mita/ *mf* hermit
erguir /er'gir/ *vt irr* to raise; straighten; lift up; *vr* straighten up; tower; grow proud. *Pres. Ind.* **irgo** (or **yergo**), **irgues**, **irguen**. *Pres. Part.* **irguiendo**. *Preterite* **irguió**, **irguieron**. *Pres. Subjunc.* **irga or yerga**, **etc.**
erial /e'rial/ *m*, uncultivated land
erigir /eri'hir/ *vt* to found, establish; promote, exalt. **erigirse contra**, to rise up against
erisipela /erisi'pela/ *f*, erysipelas
erizado /eri'saðo; eri'θaðo/ *a* standing on end (of hair); prickly, covered with bristles or quills. **e. de**

espinas, bristling with thorns; covered with bristles or quills

erizar /eri'sar; eri'θar/ *vt* to set on end (hair); beset with difficulties; *vr* stand on end, bristle (hair, quills, etc.)

erizo /e'riso; e'riθo/ *m*, hedgehog; husk (of some fruits); *Inf.* touch-me-not, unsociable person; *Mech.* sprocket wheel. **e. de mar,** sea urchin

ermita /er'mita/ *f*, hermitage

ermitaño /ermi'taɲo/ *m*, hermit

erogación /eroga'sion; eroga'θion/ *f*, *Lat. Am.* expenditure

erosión /ero'sion/ *f*, erosion

erótico /e'rotiko/ *a* erotic

errabundo /erra'βundo/ *a* wandering, errant, vagrant

erradamente /erraða'mente/ *adv* erroneously

erradicable /erraði'kaβle/ *a* eradicable

erradicación /erraðika'sion; erraðika'θion/ *f*, eradication

erradicar /erraði'kar/ *vt* to eradicate

errante /e'rrante/ *a* wandering; erring; errant

errar /e'rrar/ *vi irr* to err, fail; rove, roam; wander (attention, etc.); *vr* be mistaken. *Auto.* **e. el encendido,** to misfire. *Pres. Ind.* **yerro, yerras, yerra, yerran.** *Pres. Subjunc.* **yerre, yerres, yerre, yerren**

errata /e'rrata/ *f*, misprint

errático /e'rratiko/ *a* wandering, vagrant; *Med.* erratic

erre /'erre/ *f*, name of the letter R

erróneo /e'rroneo/ *a* erroneous, mistaken

error /e'rror/ *m*, error. **error de más,** an overestimate. **error de menos,** an underestimate

eructar /eruk'tar/ *vi* to eructate, belch

eructo /e'rukto/ *m*, eructation, belching

erudición /eruði'sion; eruði'θion/ *f*, erudition

erudito /eru'ðito/ *a* learned, erudite. *m*, scholar. **e. a la violeta,** pseudo-learned

erupción /erup'sion; erup'θion/ *f*, *Med.* rash; eruption

eruptivo /erup'tiβo/ *a* eruptive

es /es/ *irr* 3rd *pers. sing Pres. Ind.* of ser, is

esa /'esa/ *f*, *dem a* that. **ésa,** *f*, *dem. pron* that one; the former; the town in which you are (e.g. *Iré a é. mañana,* I shall come to your town tomorrow). Used generally in letters. See **ése**

esbeltez /esβel'tes; esβel'teθ/ *f*, slenderness

esbelto /es'βelto/ *a* tall and slim and graceful, willowy

esbozar /esβo'sar; esβo'θar/ *vt* to sketch, outline

esbozo /es'βoso; es'βoθo/ *m*, sketch; outline, rough plan, first draft

escabechar /eskaβe'tʃar/ *vt* to pickle; dye (the hair, etc.); *Inf.* kill in anger; *Inf.* fail (an examination)

escabeche /eska'βetʃe/ *m*, *Cul.* pickle; hair dye

escabechina /eskaβe'tʃina/ *f*, *Inf.* heavy failure (in an examination)

escabel /eska'βel/ *m*, footstool; small backless chair; *Fig.* steppingstone

escabioso /eska'βioso/ *a* scabby, scabious

escabro /es'kaβro/ *m*, scab, mange

escabroso /eska'βroso/ *a* rough; rocky; uneven; rude, unpolished, uncivil; risqué, improper

escabullirse /eskaβu'yirse; eskaβu'ʎirse/ *vr irr* to escape; run away; slip out unnoticed. See **mullir**

escafandra /eska'fandra/ *f*, diving suit, diving outfit

escala /es'kala/ *f*, ladder; (*Mus. Math.*) scale; dial (of machines); proportion, ratio; stage, stopping place; measuring rule; *Naut.* port of call. **e. de toldilla,** companion ladder. *Mus.* **e. mayor,** major scale. **e. menor,** minor scale. *Naut.* **hacer e. en un puerto,** to call at a port

escalada /eska'laða/ *f*, escalade

escalafón /eskala'fon/ *m*, salary scale; roll, list

escalamiento /eskala'miento/ *m*, scaling, climbing; storming

escalar /eska'lar/ *vt* to scale; climb, ascend; storm, assail, enter or leave violently

escaldadura /eskalda'ðura/ *f*, scalding; scald

escaldar /eskal'dar/ *vt* to scald; make red-hot; *vr* scald or burn oneself. *Gato escaldado del agua fría huye,* Once bitten, twice shy

escalera /eska'lera/ *f*, staircase; stair. **e. abajo,** below stairs. **e. de caracol,** spiral staircase. **e. de mano,** ladder. **e. de tijera,** stepladder. **e. móvil,** escalator

escalfar /eskal'far/ *vt* to poach (eggs); burn (bread)

escalinata /eskali'nata/ *f*, outside staircase or flight of steps, perron

escalofrío /eskalo'frio/ *m*, (gen. *pl*) shiver, shudder

escalón /eska'lon/ *m*, step, stair; rung (of a ladder); *Fig.* steppingstone; grade, rank. **en escalones,** in steps

escalpar /eskal'par/ *vt* to scalp

escalpelo /eskal'pelo/ *m*, scalpel

escama /es'kama/ *f*, *Zool.* scale; anything scale-shaped; flake; suspicion, resentment

escamar /eska'mar/ *vt* to scale (fish); make suspicious. *vr Inf.* be suspicious or disillusioned

escamondar /eskamon'dar/ *vt Agr.* to prune

escamoso /eska'moso/ *a* scaly

escamotear /eskamote'ar/ *vt* to make disappear; palm (in conjuring); steal

escamoteo /eskamo'teo/ *m*, disappearance; stealing

escampada /eskam'paða/ *f*, *Inf.* clear interval on a rainy day

escampar /eskam'par/ *vi* to cease raining; clear up (of the weather, sky); stop (work, etc.)

escamujar /eskamu'har/ *vt Agr.* to cut out superfluous wood (of trees, etc.)

escanciar /eskan'siar; eskan'θiar/ *vt* to pour out wine; *vi* drink wine

escandalizar /eskandali'sar; eskandali'θar/ *vt* to shock, scandalize; disturb with noise; *vr* be vexed or irritated

escandallo /eskan'dayo; eskan'daʎo/ *m*, *Naut.* deep-sea lead; random test

escándalo /es'kandalo/ *m*, scandal; commotion, uproar; bad example; viciousness; astonishment

escandaloso /eskanda'loso/ *a* disgraceful, scandalous; turbulent

Escandinavia /eskandi'naβia/ Scandinavia

escandinavo /eskandi'naβo/ *a* **(-va)** *a* and *n* Scandinavian

escantillón /eskanti'yon; eskanti'ʎon/ *m*, template, pattern; rule

escaño /es'kaɲo/ *m*, bench with a back

escapada /eska'paða/ *f*, escape; escapade

escapar /eska'par/ *vt* to spur on (a horse); *vi* escape; flee; avoid, evade; *vr* leak (gas, etc.). **Se me escapó su nombre,** His name escaped me. **e. por un pelo,** to have a narrow escape

escaparate /eskapa'rate/ *m*, showcase, cabinet; shop window

escapatoria /eskapa'toria/ *f*, escape, flight; *Inf.* way out, loophole

escape /es'kape/ *m*, flight; evasion; escape (gas, etc.); *Auto.* exhaust. **a e.,** at full speed

escápula /es'kapula/ *f*, scapula

escaque /es'kake/ *m*, square (chessboard or checkerboard); *pl* chess

escaqueado /eskake'aðo/ *a* checked, worked in squares

escara /es'kara/ *f*, scar

escarabajo /eskara'βaho/ *m*, beetle, scarab; *Fig. Inf.* dwarf; *pl Inf.* scrawl

escaramuza /eskara'musa; eskara'muθa/ *f*, skirmish

escaramuzar /eskaramu'sar; eskaramu'θar/ *vi* to skirmish

escarapela /eskara'pela/ *f*, cockade, rosette; brawl

escarbadientes /eskarβa'ðientes/ *m*, toothpick

escarbar /eskar'βar/ *vt* to scratch, scrabble (fowls); root, dig; rake out (the fire); inquire into

escarcha /es'kartʃa/ *f*, frost

escarchar /eskar'tʃar/ *vt Cul.* to frost, ice; spread with frosting; *vi* freeze lightly

escarda /es'karða/ *f*, weeding; *Fig.* weeding out

escardador /eskarða'ðor/ *m* **(-ra)** *n* weeder

escardar /eskar'ðar/ *vt* to weed; *Fig.* separate good from bad

escarificación /eskarifika'sion; eskarifika'θion/ *f*, scarification

escarlata /eskar'lata/ *f*, scarlet; scarlet cloth

escualidez

escarlatina /eskarla'tina/ f, scarlet fever, scarlatina
escarmentar /eskarmen'tar/ vt irr to reprehend or punish severely; vi learn from experience, be warned. See **acertar**
escarmiento /eskar'miento/ m, disillusionment, experience; warning; punishment, fine
escarnecedor /eskarneseðor; eskarneθe'ðor/ (-ra) a mocking. n mocker
escarnecer /eskarne'ser; eskarne'θer/ vt irr to mock. See **conocer**
escarnio /es'karnio/ m, gibe, jeer, Poet. scornful poem
escarola /eska'rola/ f, endive; frilled ruff
escarpa /es'karpa/ f, steep slope, declivity; escarpment; Mexico pavement
escarpado /eskar'paðo/ a steep, precipitous
escarpín /eskar'pin/ m, pump, slipper
escasear /eskase'ar/ vt to dole out, give grudgingly; save, husband; vi be scarce or short; grow less
escasez /eska'ses; eska'seθ/ f, meanness, frugality; want; shortage, scarcity
escaso /es'kaso/ a scarce; short; bare; parsimonious
escatimar /eskati'mar/ vt to cut down, curtail
escatimoso /eskati'moso/ a malicious, guileful
escayola /eska'yola/ f, plaster of Paris
escena /es'sena; es'θena/ f, Theat. stage; scene; scenery; theater, drama; spectacle, sight; episode, incident. **director de e.,** producer. **poner en e.,** Theat. to produce
escenario /esse'nario; esθe'nario/ m, Theat. stage; scenario
escénico /es'seniko; es'θeniko/ a scenic
escenografía /essenogra'fia; esθenogra'fia/ f, scenography
escenógrafo /esse'nografo; esθe'nografo/ (-fa) n scenographer, scene painter
escepticismo /essepti'sismo; esθepti'θismo/ m, scepticism
escéptico /es'septiko; es'θeptiko/ (-ca) a sceptical. n sceptic
escindir /essin'dir; esθin'dir/ vt to split
escisión /essi'sion; esθi'sion/ f, cleavage, split; splitting; schism; disagreement
esclarecer /esklare'ser; esklare'θer/ vt irr to illuminate; ennoble, make illustrious; Fig. enlighten; elucidate; vi dawn. See **conocer**
esclarecido /esklare'siðo; esklare'θiðo/ a distinguished, illustrious
esclavina /eskla'βina/ f, short cape
esclavitud /eskla'βi'tuð/ f, slavery
esclavizar /esklaβi'sar; esklaβi'θar/ vt to enslave
esclavo /es'klaβo/ (-va) n slave. a enslaved. f, slave bracelet; ID bracelet
esclerosis /eskle'rosis/ f, sclerosis
esclerótica /eskle'rotika/ f, sclerotic
esclusa /es'klusa/ f, lock; sluice gate; weir
esclusero, -a /esklu'sero/ mf, lock keeper
escoba /es'koβa/ f, broom, brush; Bot. yellow broom
escobada /esko'βaða/ f, sweep, stroke (of a broom)
escobar /esko'βar/ vt to sweep with a broom
escobazo /esko'βaso; esko'βaθo/ m, brush with a broom
escobero, -a /esko'βero/ brush maker; brush seller
escobilla /esko'βiya; esko'βiʎa/ f, brush
escocer /esko'ser; esko'θer/ vi irr to smart; Fig. sear; vr hurt, smart; be chafed. See **mover**
escocés /esko'ses; esko'θes/ (-esa) a Scots, Scottish. n Scot
Escocia /es'kosia; es'koθia/ Scotland
escoda /es'koða/ f, claw hammer
escofina /esko'fina/ f, rasp, file
escoger /esko'her/ vt to choose, select
escogido /esko'hiðo/ a choice, select
escolar /esko'lar/ a school; pupil. m, pupil
escolasticismo /eskolasti'sismo; eskolasti'θismo/ m, scholasticism
escolástico /esko'lastiko/ a scholastic
escoleta /esko'leta/ f, Mexico amateur band
escollera /esko'yera; esko'ʎera/ f, breakwater, sea wall, jetty

escollo /es'koyo; es'koʎo/ m, reef; danger, risk; difficulty, obstacle
escolopendra /eskolo'pendra/ f, centipede; hart's-tongue fern
escolta /es'kolta/ f, escort, guard
escoltar /eskol'tar/ vt to escort; guard, conduct
escombrar /eskom'brar/ vt to remove obstacles, free of rubbish; Fig. clean up
escombro /es'kombro/ m, debris, rubble, rubbish; mackerel
esconder /eskon'der/ vt to hide, conceal; Fig. contain, embrace; vr hide
escondidas, a /eskon'diðas, a/ adv secretly
escondite, escondrijo /eskon'dite, eskon'driho/ m, hiding place. **jugar al escondite,** to play hide-and-seek
escopeta /esko'peta/ f, shotgun. **e. de aire comprimido,** air gun, popgun. **e. de pistón,** repercussion gun. **e. de viento,** air gun
escopetazo /eskope'taso; eskope'taθo/ m, gunshot; gunshot wound; Fig. bombshell
escopetear /eskopete'ar/ vt to shoot repeatedly
escopetero /eskope'tero/ m, musketeer; gunsmith; man with a gun
escoplear /eskople'ar/ vt to notch; chisel; gouge
escoplo /es'koplo/ m, chisel
escorbuto /eskor'βuto/ m, scurvy
escoria /es'koria/ f, dross, slag; scoria, volcanic ash; Fig. dreɓs
escorial /esko'rial/ m, slag heap
escorpión /eskor'pion/ m, scorpion; Scorpio
escorzo /es'korso; es'korθo/ m, Art. foreshortening
escotado /esko'taðo/ a low-cut (of dresses)
escotadura /eskota'ðura/ a low neck (of a dress); piece cut out of something; Theat. large trapdoor; recess
escotar /esko'tar/ vt to cut low in the neck (of dresses); pay one's share (of expenses)
escote /es'kote/ m, low neck (of a dress); shortness (of sleeves); share (of expenses); lace yoke
escotilla /esko'tiya; esko'tiʎa/ f, Naut. hatch
escozor /esko'sor; esko'θor/ m, smart, pricking pain; irritation, prickle; heartache
escriba /es'kriβa/ m, (Jewish hist.) scribe
escribanía /eskriβa'nia/ f, secretaryship; notaryship; bureau, office; writing case; inkstand
escribiente /eskri'βiente/ mf clerk
escribir /eskri'βir/ vt to write; vr enlist; enroll; correspond by writing. Past Part. **escrito**
escrito /es'krito/ m, writing, manuscript; literary or scientific work; Law. writ. **por e.,** in writing
escritor /eskri'tor/ (-ra) n writer, author
escritorio /eskri'torio/ m, desk; Lat. Am. office
escritura /eskri'tura/ f, writing; handwriting; Law. deed; literary work. **Sagrada E.,** Holy Scripture
escrófula /es'krofula/ f, scrofula
escrofuloso /eskrofu'loso/ a scrofulous
escroto /es'kroto/ m, scrotum
escrúpulo /es'krupulo/ m, scruple, qualm; conscientiousness; scruple (pharmacy)
escrupulosidad /eskrupulosi'ðað/ f, conscientiousness, scrupulousness
escrupuloso /eskrupu'loso/ a scrupulous; exact, accurate
escrutadora /eskruta'ðor/ (-ra) n scrutinizer. a examining, inspecting
escrutar /eskru'tar/ vt to scrutinize, examine; count (votes)
escrutinio /eskru'tinio/ m, scrutiny, examination; count (votes)
escuadra /es'kuaðra/ f, carpenter's square; architect's square; Nav. fleet; Aer. squadron; Mil. squad. **e. de agrimensor,** Surv. cross-staff
escuadrar /eskuað'rar/ vt (and Mas.) to square
escuadrilla /eskuað'riya; eskuað'riʎa/ f, squadron (airplanes, small ships)
escuadrón /eskuað'ron/ m, squadron
escualidez /eskuali'ðes; eskuali'ðeθ/ f, squalor, sordidness

escuálido /es'kualiðo/ *a* filthy, squalid; sordid; thin

escucha /es'kutʃa/ *f*, listening; peephole; *Mil.* sentinel

escuchar /esku'tʃar/ *vt* to listen; attend to, heed; *vr* like the sound of one's own voice

escudar /esku'ðar/ *vt* to shield, protect

escudero /esku'ðero/ *m*, squire, page; gentleman; shield maker

escudete /esku'ðete/ *m*, escutcheon; shield; gusset; white water lily

escudilla /esku'ðiya; esku'ðiʎa/ *f*, bowl

escudo /es'kuðo/ *m*, shield; escudo; escutcheon; protection, defense; ward (of a keyhole)

escudriñador /eskuðriɲa'ðor/ **(-ra)** *a* searching; curious, prying. *n* scrutinizer; pryer

escudriñar /eskuðri'ɲar/ *vt* to scrutinize; scan; investigate; pry into

escuela /es'kuela/ *f*, school; school building; style; (*Lit.* and *Art.*) school. **e. de artes y oficios,** industrial school. **e. industrial,** technical school. **e. normal,** normal school

escuelante /eskue'lante/ *m*, *Mexico* schoolmaster

escueto /es'kueto/ *a* dry, bare, unadorned; simple, exact; unencumbered

escuincle /es'kuinkle/ *mf*, *Mexico* child

esculpir /eskul'pir/ *vt* to sculpture; engrave

escultor /eskul'tor/ **(-ra)** *n* sculptor

escultórico /eskul'toriko/ *a* sculptural

escultura /eskul'tura/ *f*, sculpture; carving; modeling

escupidera /eskupi'ðera/ *f*, spittoon

escupir /esku'pir/ *vi* to expectorate; *vt Fig.* spit out; cast away, throw out

escurreplatos /eskurre'platos/ *m*, dishrack, draining rack

escurrido /esku'rriðo/ *a* narrow-hipped; skintight (of skirts)

escurridor /eskurri'ðor/ *m*, colander, sieve; dishrack; drainingboard

escurriduras /eskurri'ðuras/ *f pl*, lees, dregs

escurrir /esku'rrir/ *vt* to drain to the dregs; wring, press out, drain; *vi* trickle, drip; slip, slide; *vr* slip away, edge away; escape, slip out; skid

esdrújulo /esðru'hulo/ *a Gram.* of words where the stress falls on the antepenultimate syllable

ese /'ese/ *f*, name of letter S; S-shaped link (in a chain). *Inf.* **andar haciendo eses,** to reel about drunkenly

ese /'ese/ *m*, *dem a* (*f*, **esa.** *pl* **esos, esas**) that; those. **ése,** *m*, *dem pron* (*f*, **ésa.** *neut* **eso.** *pl* **ésos, ésas**) that one; the former (e.g. *Me gusta éste, pero ése no me gusta,* I like this one, but I do not like that one)

esencia /e'sensia; e'senθia/ *f*, essence, nature, character; extract; *Chem.* essence

esencial /esen'sial; esen'θial/ *a* essential

esfera /es'fera/ *f*, *Geom.* sphere, globe, ball; sky; rank; face, dial; province, scope

esférico /es'feriko/ *a* spherical

esfinge /es'finhe/ *f*, sphinx

esforzado /esfor'saðo; esfor'θaðo/ *a* valiant, courageous; spirited

esforzador /esforsa'ðor; esforθa'ðor/ *a* encouraging

esforzar /esfor'sar; esfor'θar/ *vt irr* to encourage; invigorate; *vr* make an effort. See **contar**

esfuerzo /es'fuerso; es'fuerθo/ *m*, effort; courage; spirit; vigor; exertion, strain; *Mech.* stress. **sin e.,** effortless

esfumar /esfu'mar/ *vt Art.* shade; *Art.* stump; dim; *vr* disappear

esfumino /esfu'mino/ *m*, *Art.* stump

esgrima /es'grima/ *f*, (art of) fencing

esgrimidor /esgrimi'ðor/ *m*, fencer, swordsman

esgrimir /esgri'mir/ *vt* to fence; fend off

esguince /es'ginse; es'ginθe/ *m*, dodging, twist; expression or gesture of repugnance; *Med.* sprain

eslabón /esla'βon/ *m*, link (in a chain); steel for producing fire. **e. perdido,** *Fig.* missing link

eslabonar /eslaβo'nar/ *vt* to link; connect, unite

eslavo /es'laβo/ **(-va)** *a* Slavic. *n* Slav

eslora /es'lora/ *f*, *Naut.* length (of a ship)

eslovaco /eslo'βako/ **(-ca)** *a* Slovakian. *n* Slovak

esmaltador /esmalta'ðor/ **(-ra)** *n* enameler

esmaltar /esmal'tar/ *vt* to enamel; decorate, adorn

esmalte /es'malte/ *m*, enamel; enamelwork; smalt; brilliance

esmerado /esme'raðo/ *a* careful, painstaking

esmeralda /esme'ralda/ *f*, emerald

esmerar /esme'rar/ *vt* to polish; *vr* (*with en*) take great pains with (or to)

esmeril /es'meril/ *m*, emery

esmerilar /esmeri'lar/ *vt* to polish with emery

esmero /es'mero/ *m*, great care, conscientiousness

esmoladera /esmola'ðera/ *f*, grindstone

esnob /es'noβ/ *a* snobbish. *mf* snob

eso /'eso/ *neut dem pron* that; the fact that; that idea, affair, etc.; about (of time) (e.g. *Vendrá a e. de las nueve,* He will come about nine o'clock). **Eso** refers to an abstraction, never to one definite object. **No me gusta e.,** I don't like that kind of thing. **e. es,** that's it. **por e.,** therefore, for that reason

esófago /e'sofago/ *m*, esophagus

esotérico /eso'teriko/ *a* esoteric

espaciar /espa'siar; espa'θiar/ *vt* to space; *Print.* lead; *vr* spread oneself, enlarge (upon)

espacio /es'pasio; es'paθio/ *m*, space; capacity; interval, duration; slowness; *Print.* lead

espaciosidad /espasiosi'ðað; espaθiosi'ðað/ *f*, spaciousness; capacity

espada /es'paða/ *f*, sword; matador; swordsman; (cards) spade. **entre la e. y la pared,** *Fig.* between a rock and a hard place; between undesirable alternatives.

espadachín /espaða'tʃin/ *m*, good swordsman; bully, quarrelsome fellow

espadaña /espa'ðaɲa/ *f*, open belfry; gladiolus

espadería /espaðe'ria/ *f*, sword cutler's workshop or shop

espadero /espa'ðero/ *m*, sword cutler

espadín /espa'ðin/ *m*, small dress sword

espalda /es'palda/ *f*, *Anat.* back (often *pl*); *pl* rear, back portion; *Mil.* rear guard. **de espaldas,** with one's (its, his, etc.) back turned; on one's (its, etc.) back

espaldar /espal'dar/ *m*, backpiece of a cuirass; back (of chair); garden trellis, espalier

espaldarazo /espalda'raso; espalda'raθo/ *m*, accolade

espaldera /espal'dera/ *f*, espalier, trellis

espantadizo /espanta'ðiso; espanta'ðiθo/ *a* easily frightened

espantapájaros /espanta'paharos/ *m*, scarecrow

espantar /espan'tar/ *vt* to frighten, terrify; chase off; *vr* be amazed; be scared

espanto /es'panto/ *m*, terror, panic; dismay; amazement; threat

espantoso /espan'toso/ *a* horrible, terrifying; awesome; amazing

España /es'paɲa/ Spain

español /espa'ɲol/ **(-la)** *a* Spanish. *n* Spaniard. *m*, Spanish (language). **a la española,** in Spanish fashion

españolía /espaɲo'lia/ *f*, Spanish colony, Spanish community (outside Spain)

españolismo /espaɲo'lismo/ *m*, love of things Spanish; Hispanicism

españolizar /espaɲoli'sar; espaɲoli'θar/ *vt* to hispanicize; *vr* adopt Spanish customs

esparadrapo /espara'ðrapo/ *m*, court plaster

esparavel /espara'βel/ *m*, casting net

esparcimiento /esparsi'miento; esparθi'miento/ *m*, scattering; naturalness, frankness; geniality

esparcir /espar'sir; espar'θir/ *vt* to scatter, sprinkle, disperse; spread, publish abroad; entertain; *vr* be scattered; amuse oneself

espárrago /es'parrago/ *m*, asparagus

esparraguera /esparra'gera/ *f*, asparagus plant; asparagus bed; asparagus dish

Esparta /es'parta/ Sparta

espartano /espar'tano/ **(-na)** *a* and *n* Spartan

espartería /esparte'ria/ *f*, esparto industry, esparto shop

esparto /es'parto/ *m*, esparto grass

espasmo /es'pasmo/ *m*, spasm

espasmódico /espas'moðiko/ *a* spasmodic

espátula /es'patula/ *f*, spatula; palette knife

especia /es'pesia; es'peθia/ *f*, spice. **nuez de e.**, nutmeg

especial /espe'sial; espe'θial/ *a* special; particular

especialidad /espesiali'ðað; espeθiali'ðað/ *f*, specialty; branch (of learning)

especialista /espesia'lista; espeθia'lista/ *mf* specialist

especialización /espesialisa'sion; espeθialiθa'θion/ *f*, specialization

especializarse /espesiali'sarse; espeθiali'θarse/ *vr* to specialize

especie /es'pesie; es'peθie/ *f*, class, kind; species; affair, matter, case; idea, image; news; pretext, appearance

especiería /espesie'ria; espeθie'ria/ *f*, spice trade; spice shop

especiero /espe'siero; espe'θiero/ **(-ra)** *n* spice merchant; spice rack

especificación /espesifika'sion; espeθifika'θion/ *f*, specification. **e. normalizada,** standard specification

especificar /espesifi'kar; espeθifi'kar/ *vt* to specify, particularize

específico /espe'sifiko; espe'θifiko/ *a* and *m*, specific patent medicine

espécimen /es'pesimen; es'peθimen/ *m*, specimen, sample

especioso /espe'sioso; espe'θioso/ *a* lovely, perfect; specious

espectacular /espektaku'lar/ *a* spectacular

espectáculo /espek'takulo/ *m*, spectacle, sight; show, display

espectador /espekta'ðor/ **(-ra)** *n* spectator

espectral /espek'tral/ *a* spectral; faint, dim

espectro /es'pektro/ *m*, phantom, specter; *Phys.* spectrum

especulación /espekula'sion; espekula'θion/ *f*, conjecture; *Com.* speculation

especulador /espekula'ðor/ **(-ra)** *n* speculator

especular /espeku'lar/ *vt* to examine, look at; (*with en*) reflect on, consider; *vi Com.* speculate

especulativo /espekula'tiβo/ *a* speculative; thoughtful, meditative

espejería /espehe'ria/ *f*, mirror shop or factory

espejero /espe'hero/ *m*, mirror manufacturer or seller

espejismo /espe'hismo/ *m*, mirage; illusion

espejo /es'peho/ *m*, mirror; *Fig.* model. **e. de cuerpo entero,** full-length mirror. **e. retrovisor,** rearview mirror

espejuelo /espe'huelo/ *m*, small mirror; *Mineral.* selenite; *Mineral.* sheet of talc; *pl* lenses, eyeglasses

espeluznante /espelus'nante; espeluθ'nante/ *a* hairraising

espeluznar /espelus'nar; espeluθ'nar/ *vt* to dishevel; untidy (hair, etc.); *vr* stand on end (hair)

espera /es'pera/ *f*, waiting; expectation; *Law.* adjournment; caution, restraint; *Law.* respite

esperantista /esperan'tista/ *mf* Esperantist

esperanto /espe'ranto/ *m*, Esperanto

esperanza /espe'ransa; espe'ranθa/ *f*, hope

esperanzar /esperan'sar; esperan'θar/ *vt* to inspire hope in

esperar /espe'rar/ *vt* to hope; expect; await; (*with en*) have faith in. **e. sentado,** *Fig. Inf.* to whistle for

esperma /es'perma/ *f*, sperm, semen. **e. de ballena,** spermaceti

esperpento /esper'pento/ *m*, *Inf.* scarecrow, grotesque; folly, madness; fantastic dramatic composition

espesar /espe'sar/ *vt* to thicken; make closer; tighten (fabrics); *vr* thicken; grow denser or thicker

espeso /es'peso/ *a* thick; dense; greasy, dirty

espesor /espe'sor/ *m*, thickness; density

espesura /espe'sura/ *f*, thickness; density; thicket; filth

espetar /espe'tar/ *vt Cul.* to spit, skewer; pierce; *Inf.* utter, give; *vr* be stiff or affected; *Inf.* push oneself in, intrude

espetera /espe'tera/ *f*, kitchen or pot rack

espetón /espe'ton/ *m*, *Cul.* spit; poker; large pin

espía /es'pia/ *mf* spy. *f*, *Naut.* warp

espiar /es'piar/ *vt* to spy upon, watch; *vi Naut.* warp

espiche /es'pitʃe/ *m*, sharp-pointed weapon or instrument; spit, spike

espiga /es'piga/ *f*, *Bot.* spike, ear; sprig; peg; tang, shank (of sword); tenon, dowel; *Naut.* masthead; *Herald.* garb

espigador /espiga'ðor/ **(-ra)** *n* gleaner

espigar /espi'gar/ *vt* to glean; tenon; *vi Bot.* begin to show the ear or spike; *vr Bot.* bolt; shoot up, grow (persons)

espigón /espi'gon/ *m*, sting; sharp point; breakwater; bearded spike (corn, etc.)

espigueo /espi'geo/ *m*, gleaning

espiguero /espi'gero/ *m*, *Mexico* granary

espín /es'pin/ *m*, porcupine

espina /es'pina/ *f*, thorn; prickle; splinter; fish bone; *Anat.* spine; suspicion, doubt

espinaca /espi'naka/ *f*, spinach

espinal /espi'nal/ *a* spinal

espinar /espi'nar/ *m*, thorn brake; *Fig.* awkward position. *vt* to prick, wound, hurt

espinazo /espi'naso; espi'naθo/ *m*, backbone

espinilla /espi'niya; espi'niʎa/ *f*, shinbone; blackhead

espinoso /espi'noso/ *a* thorny; difficult, intricate

espión /es'pion/ *m*, See **espía**

espionaje /espio'nahe/ *m*, espionage; spying

espira /es'pira/ *f*, (*Geom. Archit.*) helix; turn, twist (of winding stairs); whorl (of a shell)

espiración /espira'sion; espira'θion/ *f*, expiration; respiration

espiral /espi'ral/ *a* spiral. *f*, *Geom.* spiral; spiral watchspring

espirar /espi'rar/ *vt* to exhale, breathe out; inspire; encourage; *vi* breathe; breathe out; *Poet.* blow (wind)

espiritismo /espiri'tisimo/ *m*, spiritualism

espiritista /espiri'tista/ *a* spiritualist. *mf* spiritualist

espiritoso /espiri'toso/ *a* lively, active, spirited; spirituous

espíritu /es'piritu/ *m*, spirit; apparition, specter; soul; intelligence, mind; mood, temper, outlook; underlying principle, spirit; devil (gen. *pl*) vigor, ardor, vivacity; *Chem.* essence; *Chem.* spirits; turn of mind. **E. Santo,** Holy Spirit

espiritual /espiri'tual/ *a* spiritual

espiritualidad /espirituali'ðað/ *f*, spirituality

espiritualismo /espiritua'lismo/ *m*, *Philos.* spiritualism

espita /es'pita/ *f*, spigot, tap; *Inf.* tippler

esplender /esplen'der/ *vi Poet.* to shine

esplendidez /esplendiðes; esplendi'ðeθ/ *f*, liberality, abundance; splendor, pomp

espléndido /es'plendiðo/ *a* magnificent; liberal; resplendent (gen. *pl*)

esplendor /esplen'dor/ *m*, splendor, brilliance; distinction, nobility

esplendoroso /esplendo'roso/ *a* splendid, brilliant, radiant

espliego /es'pliego/ *m*, lavender

esplín /es'plin/ *m*, spleen, melancholy

espolada /espo'laða/ *f*, prick with the spur

espolear /espole'ar/ *vt* to prick with the spur; encourage, stimulate

espoleta /espo'leta/ *f*, fuse (of explosives); breastbone (of fowls); wishbone. **e. de tiempo, e. graduada,** time fuse. **e. de seguridad,** safety fuse

espolón /espo'lon/ *m*, spur (of a bird or mountain range); *Naut.* ram; breakwater; buttress; *Naut.* fender

espolvorear /espolβore'ar/ *vt* to sprinkle with powder

esponja /es'ponha/ *f*, sponge

esponjadura /esponha'ðura/ *f*, sponging

esponjar /espon'har/ *vt* to make spongy; sponge; *vr* swell with pride; *Inf.* bloom with health

esponjera /espon'hera/ *f*, sponge holder

esponjosidad /esponhosi'ðað/ *f*, sponginess

esponjoso /espon'hoso/ *a* spongy, porous

esponsales /espon'sales/ *m pl*, betrothal; marriage contract

espontaneidad /espontanei'ðað/ f, spontaneity
espontáneo /espon'taneo/ a spontaneous
espora /es'pora/ f, spore
esporádico /espo'raðiko/ a sporadic
esportillo /espor'tiyo; espor'tiʎo/ m, bass, frail
esposa /es'posa/ f, wife; pl handcuffs
esposo /es'poso/ m, husband; pl husband and wife
espuela /es'puela/ f, spur; stimulus; (Ornith. Bot.) spur. **e. de caballero,** larkspur
espuelar /espue'lar/ vt, Lat. Am. to spur, spur on
espulgar /espul'gar/ vt to delouse; examine carefully
espuma /es'puma/ f, froth, foam; Cul. scum; Fig. the best of anything, flower; Fig. Inf. **crecer como la e.,** to flourish like weeds
espumadera /espuma'ðera/ f, skimming ladle
espumajear /espumahe'ar/ vi to foam at the mouth
espumajoso /espuma'hoso/ a frothy, foaming
espumar /espu'mar/ vt to skim (soup, etc.); vi foam; increase rapidly
espumilla /espu'mija; espu'miʎa/ f, Lat. Am. meringue
espumoso /espu'moso/ a frothy, foaming
espurio /es'purio/ a bastard; spurious
esputo /es'puto/ m, sputum
esqueje /es'kehe/ m, Agr. cutting
esquela /es'kela/ f, note; (printed) card
esqueleto /eske'leto/ m, skeleton; Mexico, blank, form (to be filled out) Inf. skinny person; framework
esquema /es'kema/ f, diagram, layout sketch; scheme, plan. **e. de una máquina,** drawing of a machine
esquemático /eske'matiko/ a schematic; diagrammatic
esquematizar /eskemati'sar; eskemati'θar/ vt to plan, outline
esquí /es'ki/ m, ski, snowshoe
esquiador, -a /eskia'ðor/ mf, skier
esquiar /es'kiar/ vi to ski
esquila /es'kila/ f, cattle bell; small bell, hand bell; sheep shearing; (Ichth.) squill
esquilador /eskila'ðor/ a shearing. m, sheep shearer
esquiladora /eskila'ðora/ f, shearing machine
esquilar /eski'lar/ vt to shear, clip (sheep, etc.)
esquileo /eski'leo/ m, shearing; shearing time or place
esquilmar /eskil'mar/ vt to harvest; impoverish
esquilmo /es'kilmo/ m, harvest
esquimal /eski'mal/ a and mf Eskimo
esquina /es'kina/ f, corner; Lat. Am. corner shop; village shop
esquinado /eski'naðo/ a having corners; Fig. difficult to approach (people)
esquirol /eski'rol/ m, Inf. strikebreaker, blackleg
esquisto /es'kisto/ m, Mineral. slate; shale
esquivada /eski'βaða/ f, Lat. Am. evasion
esquivar /eski'βar/ vt to avoid; vr slip away, disappear; excuse oneself
esquivez /eski'βes; eski'βeθ/ f, unsociableness; unfriendliness, aloofness
esquivo /es'kiβo/ a unsociable, elusive, aloof
estabilidad /estaβili'ðað/ f, stability; fastness (of colors)
estabilizar /estaβili'sar; estaβili'θar/ vt to stabilize
estable /es'taβle/ a stable; fast (of colors)
establecer /estaβle'ser; estaβle'θer/ vt irr to establish, found, institute; decree; vt take up residence; open (a business firm). See **conocer**
establecimiento /estaβlesi'miento; estaβleθi'miento/ m, law, statute; foundation, institution; establishment
establo /es'taβlo/ m, stable
estaca /es'taka/ f, stake, pole; Agr. cutting; cudgel
estacada /esta'kaða/ f, fence; Mil. palisade; place fixed for a duel
estacar /esta'kar/ vt to stake; fence; tie to a stake; vr Fig. be as still as a post
estación /esta'sion; esta'θion/ f, position, situation; season; station (railroad, etc.); depot; time, period; stop, halt; building, headquarters; Bot. habitat; (Surv. Geom. Eccl.) station

estacional /estasio'nal; estaθio'nal/ a seasonal; Astron. stationary
estacionamiento /estasiona'miento; estaθiona'miento/ m, stationing; Auto. parking
estacionar /estasio'nar; estaθio'nar/ vt to station, place; Auto. park (a car); vr remain stationary; place oneself
estacionario /estasio'nario; estaθio'nario/ a motionless; Astron. stationary. m, stationer
estacionómetro /estasio'nometro; estaθio'nometro/ m, Mexico parking meter
estada /es'taða/ f, sojourn
estadía /esta'ðia/ f, stay, sojourn; Art. sitting (of a model)
estadio /es'taðio/ m, racetrack; stadium; furlong
estadista /esta'ðista/ mf, statistician; statesman, stateswoman
estadística /esta'ðistika/ f, statistics
estadístico /esta'ðistiko/ a statistical
estadizo /esta'ðiso; esta'ðiθo/ a stagnant
estado /es'taðo/ m, state; condition; rank, position; Polit. state; profession; status; Com. statement. **e. de guerra,** state of war; martial law. **e. mayor central,** (Nav. Mil.) general staff. **e. tapón,** Polit. buffer state. **tomar e.,** to marry; Eccl. profess; be ordained a priest
Estados Unidos de América /es'taðos u'niðos de a'merika/ United States of America
estadounidense /estaðouni'ðense/ a United States
estafa /es'tafa/ f, swindle
estafador /estafa'ðor/ (-ra) n swindler
estafar /esta'far/ vt to swindle
estafeta /esta'feta/ f, courier, messenger; branch post office; diplomatic pouch
estagnación /estagna'sion; estagna'θion/ f, stagnation
estalactita /estalak'tita/ f, stalactite
estalagmita /estalag'mita/ f, stalagmite
estallar /esta'yar; esta'ʎar/ vi to explode; burst; Fig. break out
estallido /esta'yiðo; esta'ʎiðo/ m, explosion; report; crash, crack; Fig. outbreak; Auto. **e. de un neumático,** blowout (of a tire)
estambre /es'tambre/ m, woolen yarn, worsted; stamen
estameña /esta'mena/ f, serge
estampa /es'tampa/ f, illustration, picture; print; aspect; printing press; track, step; Metall. boss, stud
estampación /estampa'sion; estampa'θion/ f, stamping; imprinting; imprinting. **e. en seco,** tooling (of a book)
estampado /estam'paðo/ a printed (of textiles). m, textile printing; printed fabric
estampar /estam'par/ vt to print, stamp; leave the print (of); bestow, imprint. **e. en relieve,** to emboss. **e. en seco,** to tool (a book)
estampería /estampe'ria/ f, print or picture shop; trade in prints
estampero /estam'pero/ m, print dealer, picture dealer
estampido /estam'piðo/ m, report, bang, detonation; crash
estampilla /estam'piya; estam'piʎa/ f, rubber stamp; seal; Lat. Am (except Mexico), (postage) stamp
estampillar /estampi'yar; estampi'ʎar/ vt to stamp, imprint
estancación /estanka'sion; estanka'θion/ f, stagnation
estancado /estan'kaðo/ a stagnant; blocked, held up
estancar /estan'kar/ vt to check, stem; set up a monopoly; Fig. hold up (negotiations, etc.); vr be stagnant
estancia /es'tansia; es'tanθia/ f, stay, residence; dwelling; lounge, livingroom; stanza; West Hem. farm; ranch
estanciero /estan'siero; estan'θiero/ m, West Hem. farmer; rancher
estanco /es'tanko/ a Naut. watertight. m, monopoly; shop selling government monopoly goods; archive
estandarte /estan'darte/ m, standard, flag. **e. real,** royal standard

estanque /es'tanke/ *m*, tank; pool; reservoir

estanquero /estan'kero/ **(-ra)** *n* seller of government monopoly goods (tobacco, matches, etc.)

estante /es'tante/ *a* present; extant; permanent. *m*, shelf; bookcase; bin (for wine)

estantería /estante'ria/ *f*, shelving; shelves, bookcase

estantigua /estan'tigua/ *f*, hobgoblin, specter; *Fig. Inf.* scarecrow

estañador /estaɲa'ðor/ *m*, tinsmith

estañar /esta'ɲar/ *vt* to tin; solder

estaño /es'taɲo/ *m*, tin

estaquilla /esta'kiʝa; esta'kiʎa/ *f*, peg, cleat

estar /es'tar/ *vi irr* to be. Indicates: 1. Position or place (e.g. *Está a la puerta*, He is at the door). 2. State (e.g. *Las flores están marchitas*, The flowers are faded). 3. Used to form the continuous or progressive tense (e.g. **Siempre está** ɘscribiendo, He is (was) always writing). 4. In contras: to verb *ser*, indicates impermanency (e.g. *Está enfermo*, He is ill). 5. **Estar** forms an apparent passive where no action is implied (e.g. *El cuadro está pintado al óleo*, The picture is painted in oils). 6. Used in some impersonal expressions (e.g. *¡Bien está!* All right! *¡Claro está!* Of course! etc.). **e. de**, to be in, or on, or acting as (e.g. *e. de prisa*, to be in a hurry. *e. de capitán*, to be acting as a captain). **e. para**, to be on the point of; to be nearly; to be in the mood for. **e. para llover**, to be on the point of raining. **e. por**, to remain to be done; have a mind to (e.g. *La historia está por escribir*, The story remains to be written). **e. a mano (con...)** *Lat. Am.* to be even (with...), be quits (with...) **e. bien**, to be well (healthy). *Mech.* **e. bajo presión**, to have the steam up. *Polit.* **e. en el poder**, to be in office. **e. en una cuenca**, *Dominican Republic* to be broke. **¿A cómo** (*or* **A cuántos) estamos? ¿En qué día estamos?** What is the date? *Pres. Ind.* **estoy, estás, está, estamos, estáis, están.** *Preterite* **estuve, etc.** *Pres. Subjunc.* **esté, estés, esté, estén.** *Imperf. Subjunc.* **estuviese, etc.**

estarcir /estar'sir; estar'θir/ *vt* to stencil

estatal /esta'tal/ *a* state

estática /es'tatika/ *f*, *Mech.* statics

estático /es'tatiko/ *a* static

estatizar /estati'sar; estati'θar/ *vt*, *Lat. Am.* to nationalize

estatua /es'tatua/ *f*, statue

estatuaria /esta'tuaria/ *f*, statuary

estatuir /esta'tuir/ *vt irr* to establish, order. See **huir**

estatura /esta'tura/ *f*, stature, height (of persons)

estatuto /esta'tuto/ *m*, statute, law

estay /es'tai/ *m*, *Naut.* stay. **e. mayor,** *Naut.* mainstay

este /'este/ *m*, east

este /'este/ *m*, *dem a* this (*f*, **esta**, *pl* **estos, estas,** these). **éste,** *m*, *dem pron* this one; the latter. (*f*, **ésta,** *neut* **esto,** *pl* **éstos, éstas,** these ones; the latter) (e.g. *Aquel cuadro no es tan hermoso como éste,* That picture is not as beautiful as this one)

este /'este/ *interj* uh, um

estela /es'tela/ *f*, wake, track (of a ship)

estenografía /estenogra'fia/ *f*, shorthand

estenordeste /estenor'ðeste/ *m*, east-northeast

estentóreo /esten'toreo/ *a* stentorian

estepa /es'tepa/ *f*, steppe, arid plain

estera /es'tera/ *f*, matting

esterar /este'rar/ *vt* to cover with matting; *vi Inf.* muffle oneself up

estercoladura /esterkola'ðura/ *f*, manuring

estercolar /esterko'lar/ *vt* to manure

estercolero /esterko'lero/ *m*, manure pile; driver of a dung cart

estereoscopio /estereo'skopio/ *m*, stereoscope

esterería /estere'ria/ *f*, matting factory, matting shop

esterero /este'rero/ **(-ra)** *n* matting maker, matting seller

estéril /es'teril/ *a* sterile, barren; unfruitful, unproductive

esterilidad /esterili'ðað/ *f*, sterility; barrenness, unfruitfulness

esterilización /esterilisa'sion; esteriliθa'θion/ *f*, sterilization

esterilizador /esterilisa'ðor; esteriliθa'ðor/ *a* sterilizing. *m*, sterilizer

esterilizar /esterili'sar; esterili'θar/ *vt* to make barren; *Med.* sterilize

esterilla /este'riʝa; este'riʎa/ *a*, mat, matting

esterlina /ester'lina/ *a f*, sterling. **libra e.,** pound sterling

esternón /ester'non/ *m*, sternum

estero /es'tero/ *m*, salt marsh

estertor /ester'tor/ *m*, stertorous breathing, rattle

estesudeste /estesu'ðeste/ *m*, east-southeast

estética /es'tetika/ *f*, aesthetics. *a* aesthete

estético /es'tetiko/ *a* aesthetic. *m*, aesthete

estetoscopio /esteto'skopio/ *m*, stethoscope

esteva /es'teβa/ *f*, plow handle

estevado /este'βaðo/ *a* bandy-legged

estiaje /es'tiahe/ *m*, low water level (of rivers)

estibador /estiβa'ðor/ *m*, stevedore, dock worker

estibar /esti'βar/ *vt Naut.* to stow

estiércol /es'tierkol/ *m*, dung; manure

estigio /es'tihio/ *a* Stygian; (*Fig. Poet.*) infernal

estigma /es'tigma/ *m*, stigma

estigmatizar /estigmati'sar; estigmati'θar/ *vt* to brand; stigmatize; insult

estilar /esti'lar/ *vi* to be accustomed; *vt* draw up (document)

estilete /esti'lete/ *m*, stiletto, dagger; needle, hand, pointer; *Med.* stylet

estilista /esti'lista/ *mf* stylist

estilística /esti'listika/ *f*, stylism, stylistics

estilizar /estili'sar; estili'θar/ *vt* to stylize

estilo /es'tilo/ *m*, (*Art. Archit. Lit.*) style, writing instrument; gnomon, pointer; manner, way; *Bot.* style. **por el e.,** in some such way, like that

estilográfico /estilo'grafiko/ *a* stylographic. **pluma estilográfica,** fountain pen

estima /es'tima/ *f*, appreciation, esteem, consideration

estimable /esti'maβle/ *a* estimable

estimación /estima'sion; estima'θion/ *f*, valuation, estimate; regard, esteem. **e. prudente,** conservative estimate

estimado /esti'maðo/ **(-da)** *a* esteemed, respected. (correspondence) **estimados señores,** Dear Sirs/ Madams

estimar /esti'mar/ *vt* to value, estimate; esteem, judge

estimulante /estimu'lante/ *m*, *Med.* stimulant. *a* stimulating

estimular /estimu 'lar/ *vt* to stimulate, excite; goad on, encourage, incite

estímulo /es'timulo/ *m*, stimulus; incitement, encouragement

estío /es'tio/ *m*, summer

estipendiar /estipen'diar/ *vt* to pay a stipend to

estipendiario /estipen'diario/ *m*, stipendiary

estipendio /esti'pendio/ *m*, stipend, pay, remuneration

estipulación /estipula'sion; estipula'θion/ *f*, stipulation; *Law.* clause, condition

estipular /estipu'lar/ *vt* to stipulate; arrange terms; *Law.* covenant

estirado /esti'raðo/ *a* stretched out; tight, stiff; wire-drawn (metals); stiff, pompous; parsimonious

estirador /estira'ðor/ *m*, wire drawer

estirar /esti'rar/ *vt* to stretch; iron roughly (clothes); *Metall.* wire-draw; dole out (money); *Fig.* stretch, go beyond the permissible; *vr* stretch oneself

estirpe /es'tirpe/ *f*, race, stock, lineage

estival /esti'βal/ *a* summer

esto /'esto/ *dem pron neut* this, this matter, this idea, etc. Always refers to abstractions, never to a definite object. **e. de**, the matter of. **e. es**, that's it; namely. **por e.,** for this reason. **a todo e.,** meanwhile

estocada /esto'kaða/ *f*, sword thrust

Estocolmo /esto'kolmo/ Stockholm

estofa /es'tofa/ *f*, *Sew.* quilting; kind, quality

estofado /esto'faðo/ *m*, stew. *a Sew.* quilted; stewed

estofar /esto'far/ vt Sew. to quilt; make a stew
estoicismo /estoi'sismo; estoi'θismo/ m, stoicism
estoico /es'toiko/ (**-ca**) n stoic. a stoical
estolidez /estoli'ðes; estoli'ðeθ/ f, idiocy
estólido /es'toliðo/ (**-da**) a idiotic. n idiot
estomacal /estoma'kal/ a stomach
estómago /es'tomago/ m, stomach
estomático /esto'matiko/ a pertaining to the mouth, oral
estomatitis /estoma'titis/ f, stomatitis
estonio /es'tonio/ (**-ia**) a and n Estonian. m, Estonian (language)
estopa /es'topa/ f, tow; oakum
estopilla /esto'piya; esto'piʎa/ f, batiste, lawn; calico, cotton cloth
estopín /esto'pin/ m, Mil. quick march
estoque /es'toke/ m, rapier; narrow sword
estoquear /estoke'ar/ vt to wound or kill with a rapier
estoqueo /esto''keo/ m, swordplay
estorbador /estorβa'ðor/ (**-ra**) a obstructive. n obstructer
estorbar /estor'βar/ vt to obstruct, impede; hinder
estorbo /es'torβo/ m, obstruction; hindrance, nuisance
estornino /estor'nino/ m, starling
estornudar /estornu'ðar/ vi to sneeze
estornudo /estor'nuðo/ m, sneezing; sneeze
estrabismo /estra'βismo/ m, Med. strabismus, squint, cast
estrada /es'traða/ f, road, highway
estrado /es'traðo/ m, dais
estrafalario /estrafa'lario/ a Inf. slovenly, untidy; Inf. eccentric, odd
estragar /estra'gar/ vt to corrupt, spoil, vitiate; ruin, destroy
estrago /es'trago/ m, devastation, destruction, ruin, havoc
estrambólico, -a /estram'βoliko/ Lat. Am. = **estrambótico**
estrambote /estram'bote/ m, refrain
estrambótico /estram'botiko/ a Inf. eccentric, odd, outlandish
estrangul /estraŋ'gul/ m, Mus. mouthpiece
estrangulación /estraŋgula'sion; estraŋgula'θion/ f, strangulation; Auto. throttling
estrangulador /estraŋgula'ðor/ (**-ra**) a strangling. n strangler. m, Auto. throttle
estrangular /estraŋgu'lar/ vt to strangle
estraperlista /estraper'lista/ mf black marketeer
estraperlo /estra'perlo/ m, black market
estratagema /estrata'hema/ f, stratagem, trick
estrategia /estra'tehia/ f, strategy
estratégico /estra'tehiko/ a strategic
estratego /estra'tego/ m, strategist
estratificación /estratifika'sion; estratifika'θion/ f, stratification
estrato /es'trato/ m, Geol. stratum
estratosfera /estratos'fera/ f, stratosphere
estraza /es'trasa; es'traθa/ f, rag. **papel de e.,** brown paper
estrechar /estre'tʃar/ vt to make narrower, tighten; hold tightly, clasp; compel, oblige; vr tighten oneself up; reduce one's expenses; Fig. tighten the bonds (of friendship, etc.). **e. la mano,** to shake hands
estrechez /estre'tʃes; estre'tʃeθ/ f, narrowness; tightness; scantiness; poverty, want. **e. de miras,** narrow-mindedness
estrecho /es'tretʃo/ a narrow; tight; intimate, close; austere, rigid; meanspirited. m, Geog. strait
estregadera /estrega'ðera/ f, shoe scraper; scourer
estregar /estre'gar/ vt irr to rub, scour, scrub, scrape, scratch. See **cegar**
estrella /es'treya; es'treʎa/ f, star; fortune, fate; anything star-shaped; Fig. star. **e. de la pantalla,** movie star. **e. de mar,** starfish. **e. de rabo,** comet. **e. fugaz,** shooting star. **tener e.,** to be born under a lucky star
estrellado /estre'yaðo; estre'ʎaðo/ a star-shaped; full of stars, starry; shattered, broken; fried (eggs)

estrellamar /estreya'mar; estreʎa'mar/ f, starfish
estrellar /estre'yar; estre'ʎar/ vt Inf. to shatter, break into fragments; fry (eggs); vr be starry or sprinkled with stars; be dashed against; fail in, come up against
estrellón /estre'yon; estre'ʎon/ m, large, artificial star (painted or otherwise); star-like firework; Lat. Am. crash
estremecer /estreme'ser; estreme'θer/ vt irr to cause to tremble; perturb; vr shudder, tremble. See **conocer**
estremecimiento /estremesi'miento; estreme-θi'miento/ m, shudder, trembling; agitation
estrenar /estre'nar/ vt to use or do for the first time; inaugurate; give the first performance of (plays, etc.); vr do for the first time; Com. make the first sale of the day
estreno /es'treno/ m, commencement, inauguration; first appearance; Theat. first performance, opening night, premiere
estrenque /es'trenke/ m, strong esparto rope
estrenuo /es'trenuo/ a strong, energetic, agile
estreñimiento /estreni'miento/ m, constipation
estreñir /estre'nir/ vt to constipate
estrépito /es'trepito/ m, clamor, din, great noise; fuss, show
estrepitoso /estrepi'toso/ a noisy, clamorous
estreptomicina /estreptomi'sina; estreptomi'θina/ f, streptomycin
estría /es'tria/ f, Archit. fluting, stria
estribadero /estriβa'ðero/ m, prop, support, strut
estribar /estri'βar/ vi (with en) to lean on, rest on, be supported by; Fig. be based on
estribillo /estri'βiyo; estri'βiʎo/ m, refrain
estribo /es'triβo/ m, stirrup; footboard, step, running board (of vehicles); Archit. buttress or pier; Fig. stay, support; Anat. stapes; Mech. stirrup piece. **perder los estribos,** to lose patience, forget oneself
estribor /estri'βor/ m, starboard
estricnina /estrik'nina/ f, strychnine
estricto /es'trikto/ a strict, exact; unbending, severe
estridente /estri'ðente/ a strident, shrill
estridor /estri'ðor/ m, strident or harsh sound; screech; creak
estro /'estro/ m, inspiration
estrofa /es'trofa/ f, strophe; verse, stanza
estropajo /estro'paho/ m, scourer, dishcloth; worthless person or thing
estropajoso /estropa'hoso/ a Inf. indistinct, stammering; dirty and ragged; tough (meat, etc.)
estropear /estrope'ar/ vt to spoil, damage; ruin, undo, spoil (plans, effects, etc.); ill-treat, maim; vr hurt oneself, be maimed; spoil, deteriorate
estropicio /estro'pisio; estro'piθio/ m, Inf. crash (of china, etc.)
estructura /estruk'tura/ f, structure; Fig. construction
estructural /estruktu'ral/ a structural
estruendo /es'truendo/ m, din, clatter; clamor, noise; ostentation
estruendoso /estruen'doso/ a noisy
estrujar /estru'har/ vt to squeeze, crush (fruit); hold tightly, press, squeeze, bruise; Fig. Inf. squeeze dry
estrujón /estru'hon/ m, squeeze, pressure; final pressing (grapes)
estuario /es'tuario/ f, estuary
estucado /estu'kaðo/ m, stucco
estucar /estu'kar/ vt to stucco
estuche /es'tutʃe/ m, case; casket, box; cover; sheath
estuco /es'tuko/ m, stucco; plaster
estudiantado /estuðian'taðo/ m, Lat. Am. student body, students
estudiante /estu'ðiante/ mf student
estudiantil /estuðian'til/ a Inf. student
estudiantina /estuðian'tina/ f, strolling band of students playing and singing, usually in aid of charity
estudiantino /estuðian'tino/ a of students
estudiantón /estuðian'ton/ m, Inf. grind
estudiar /estu'ðiar/ vt to study. **e. de,** study to be a (e.g. e. de rabino, study to be a rabbi); learn; Art. copy
estudio /es'tuðio/ m, study; sketch; disquisition, dis-

sertation; studio; diligence; *Art.* study; reading room, den

estudiosidad /estuðiosi'ðað/ *f,* studiousness

estudioso /estu'ðioso/ *a* studious

estufa /es'tufa/ *f,* heating stove; hothouse; hot room (in bathhouses); drying chamber; *Elec.* heater

estufador /estufa'ðor/ *m,* stewpot or casserole

estufista /estu'fista/ *mf* stove maker or repairer, stove seller

estulto /es'tulto/ *a* foolish

estupefacción /estupefak'sion; estupefak'θion/ *f,* stupefaction

estupefacto /estupe'fakto/ *a* stupefied, stunned, amazed

estupendo /estu'pendo/ *a* wonderful, marvelous

estupidez /estupi'ðes; estupi'ðeθ/ *f,* stupidity

estúpido /es'tupiðo/ *a* stupid

estupor /estu'por/ *m, Med.* stupor; astonishment

estupro /es'tupro/ *m, Law.* rape

estuque /es'tuke/ *m,* stucco

estuquería /estuke'ria/ *f,* stuccowork

esturión /estu'rion/ *m,* sturgeon

esvástica /es'βastika/ *f,* swastika

etapa /e'tapa/ *f, Mil.* field ration; *Mil.* halt, camp; stage, juncture. **a pequeñas etapas,** by easy stages (of a journey)

etcétera /et'setera; et'θetera/ et cetera, and so on

éter /'eter/ *m,* ether; *Poet.* sky

etéreo /e'tereo/ *a* etheric; ethereal

eterizar /eteri'sar; eteri'θar/ *vt* to etherize

eternidad /eterni'ðað/ *f,* eternity

eternizar /eterni'sar; eterni'θar/ *vt* to drag out, prolong; eternize, perpetuate

eterno /e'terno/ *a* eternal, everlasting; lasting, enduring

ética /'etika/ *f,* ethics

ético /'etiko/ *a* ethical. *m,* moralist

etimología /etimolo'hia/ *f,* etymology

etimológico /etimo'lohiko/ *a* etymological

etimologista /etimolo'hista/ *mf* etymologist

etimólogo /eti'mologo/ *m,* etymologist

etiología /etiolo'hia/ *f,* etiology

etíope /e'tiope/, **etiope** *a* and *mf* Ethiopian

Etiopía /etio'pia/ Ethiopia

etiqueta /eti'keta/ *f,* etiquette; label

etiquetero /etike'tero/ *a* ceremonious, stiff; prim

étnico /'etniko/ *a* ethnic; heathen

etnografía /etnogra'fia/ *f,* ethnography

etnográfico /etno'grafiko/ *a* ethnographic

etnología /etnolo'hia/ *f,* ethnology

etnólogo /et'nologo/ *m,* ethnologist

etrusco /e'trusko/ **(-ca)** *a* and *n* Etruscan

eubolia /eu'βolia/ *f,* discretion in speech

eucalipto /euka'lipto/ *m,* eucalyptus

Eucaristía /eukaris'tia/ *f,* Eucharist

euclídeo /eu'kliðeo/ *a* Euclidean

eufemismo /eufe'mismo/ *m,* euphemism

eufonía /eufo'nia/ *f,* euphony

eufónico /eu'foniko/ *a* euphonious

euforia /eu'foria/ *f,* resistance to disease; buoyancy, well-being

eufuismo /eu'fuismo/ *m,* euphuism

eugenesia /euhe'nesia/ *f,* eugenics

eugenésico /euhe'nesiko/ *a* eugenic

eunuco /eu'nuko/ *m,* eunuch

euritmia /eu'ritmia/ *f,* eurythmics

eurítmico /eu'ritmiko/ *a* eurythmic

euro /'euro/ *m, Poet.* east wind

Europa /eu'ropa/ Europe

europeizar /europei'sar; europei'θar/ *vt* to Europeanize

europeo /euro'peo/ **(-ea)** *a* and *n* European

éuscaro /'euskaro/ *a* Basque. *m,* Basque (language)

eutanasia /euta'nasia/ *f,* euthanasia

evacuación /eβakua'sion; eβakua'θion/ *f,* evacuation

evacuar /eβa'kuar/ *vt* to vacate; evacuate, empty; finish, conclude (a business deal, etc.)

evadir /eβa'ðir/ *vt* to avoid, elude; *vr* escape; elope

evaluación /eβalua'sion; eβalua'θion/ *f,* valuation; estimation

evaluar /eβa'luar/ *vt* to evaluate, estimate; gauge; value

evangélico /eβan'heliko/ **(-ca)** *a* and *n* evangelical

evangelio /eβan'helio/ *m,* Gospel; Christianity; *Inf.* indisputable truth

evangelista /eβanhe'lista/ *m,* evangelist

evangelizar /eβanheli'sar; eβanheli'θar/ *vt* to evangelize

evaporación /eβapora'sion; eβapora'θion/ *f,* evaporation

evaporar /eβapo'rar/ **(se)** *vt* and *vr* to evaporate; disappear, vanish

evasión, evasiva /eβa'sion, eβa'siβa/ *f,* subterfuge, evasion; flight, escape

evasivo /eβa'siβo/ *a* evasive

evento /e'βento/ *m,* happening, event; contingency

eventual /eβen'tual/ *a* possible, fortuitous; accidental (expenses); extra (emoluments)

eventualidad /eβentuali'ðað/ *f,* eventuality

evicción /eβik'sion; eβik'θion/ *f, Law.* eviction

evidencia /eβi'ðensia; eβi'ðenθia/ *f,* proof, evidence. **ponerse en e.,** to put oneself forward

evidenciar /eβiðen'siar; eβiðen'θiar/ *vt* to show, make obvious

evidente /eβi'ðente/ *a* obvious, evident

evitable /eβi'taβle/ *a* avoidable

evitación /eβita'sion; eβita'θion/ *f,* avoidance

evitar /eβi'tar/ *vt* to avoid; shun, eschew

evocación /eβoka'sion; eβoka'θion/ *f,* evocation

evocador /eβoka'ðor/ *a* evocative

evocar /eβo'kar/ *vt* to evoke

evolución /eβolu'sion; eβolu'θion/ *f,* evolution; development; (*Mil. Nav.*) maneuver; change; *Geom.* involution

evolucionar /eβolusio'nar; eβoluθio'nar/ *vi* to evolve; (*Nav. Mil.*) maneuver; change, alter

evolucionismo /eβolusio'nismo; eβoluθio'nismo/ *m,* evolutionism

evolutivo /eβolu'tiβo/ *a* evolutional

ex /eks/ *prefix* out of; from; formerly

exacción /eksak'sion; eksak'θion/ *f,* exaction; tax

exacerbación /eksaserβa'sion; eksaθerβa'θion/ *f,* exacerbation

exacerbar /eksaser'βar; eksaθer'βar/ *vt* to exasperate; exacerbate

exactitud /eksakti'tuð/ *f,* exactitude; correctness; punctuality

exacto /ek'sakto/ *a* exact; correct; punctual

exactor /ek'sak'tor/ *m,* tax collector; tyrant, oppressor

exageración /eksahera'sion; eksahera'θion/ *f,* exaggeration

exagerador /eksahera'ðor/ **(-ra)** *a* given to exaggerating. *n* exaggerater

exagerar /eksahe'rar/ *vt* to exaggerate

exaltación /eksalta'sion; eksalta'θion/ *f,* exaltation

exaltar /eksal'tar/ *vt* to exalt, elevate; extol; *vr* grow excited or agitated

exalumna /eksa'lumna/ *f, Lat. Am.* alumna, graduate

exalumno /eksa'lumno/ *m, Lat. Am.* alumnus, graduate

examen /ek'samen/ *m,* inquiry; investigation; research; examination; *Geol.* survey. **e. parcial,** quiz (at school)

examinador /eksamina'ðor/ **(-ra)** *n* examiner

examinando /eksami'nando/ **(-da)** *n* candidate, examinee

examinar /eksami'nar/ *vt* to inquire into; investigate; inspect; examine; *vr* take an examination

exangüe /ek'saŋgue/ *a* bloodless, pale; exhausted; weak; dead

exánime /ek'sanime/ *a* lifeless; spiritless, weak

exasperación /eksaspera'sion; eksaspera'θion/ *f,* exasperation

exasperador, exasperante /eksaspera'ðor, eksaspe'rante/ *a* exasperating

exasperar /eksaspe'rar/ *vt* to exasperate; irritate, annoy

excarcelar /ekskarse'lar; ekskarθe'lar/ *vt* to release from jail

excavación /ekskaβa'sion; ekskaβa'θion/ *f*, excavation

excavador /ekskaβa'ðor/ **(-ra)** *n* excavator. *f*, *Mech.* excavator

excavar /ekska'βar/ *vt* to hollow; excavate; *Agr.* hoe (roots of plants)

excedente /eksse'ðente; eksθe'ðente/ *a* exceeding; excessive; surplus

exceder /eksse'ðer; eksθe'ðer/ *vt* to exceed; *vr* forget oneself, go too far

excelencia /eksse'lensia; eksθe'lenθia/ *f*, excellence, superiority; Excellency (title)

excelente /eksse'lente; eksθe'lente/ *a* excellent; *Inf.* first-rate

excelso /eks'selso; eks'θelso/ *a* lofty, high; eminent, mighty; sublime

excentricidad /ekssentrisi'ðað; eksθentriθi'ðað/ *f*, eccentricity

excéntrico /eks'sentriko; ek'θentriko/ *a* unconventional; erratic; *Geom.* eccentric

excepción /ekssep''sion; eksθep'θion/ *f*, exception

excepcional /ekssepsio'nal; eksθepθio'nal/ *a* exceptional

exceptuar /ekssep'tuar; eksθep'tuar/ *vt* to except

excerpta, excerta /eks'serpta, eks'serta; eks'θerpta, eks'θerta/ *f*, excerpt, extract

excesivo /eksse'siβo; eksθe'siβo/ *a* excessive

exceso /eks'seso; eks'θeso/ *m*, excess; *Com.* surplus; *pl* crimes, excesses. **e. de peso** *or* **e. de equipaje,** excess baggage

excisión /ekssi'sion; eksθi'sion/ *f*, excision

excitabilidad /ekssitaβili'ðað; eksθitaβili'ðað/ *f*, excitability

excitable /ekssi'taβle; eksθi'taβle/ *a* excitable, highstrung

excitación /ekssita'sion; eksθita'θion/ *f*, excitation; excitement

excitador /ekssita'ðor; eksθita'ðor/ *a* exciting, stimulating. *m*, *Phys.* exciter

excitar /ekssi'tar; eksθi'tar/ *vt* to excite, stimulate, provoke; *Elec.* energize; *vr* become agitated or excited

exclamación /eksklama'sion; eksklama'θion/ *f*, exclamation, interjection

exclamar /ekskla'mar/ *vi* to exclaim

excluir /eksk'luir/ *vt irr* to exclude, keep out; reject, bar. See **huir**

exclusiva /eksklu'siβa/ *f*, exclusion; special privilege, sole right

exclusive /eksklu'siβe/ *adv* exclusively; excluded

exclusivismo /eksklusi'βismo/ *m*, exclusivism

exclusivista /eksklusi'βista/ *a* exclusive. *mf* exclusivist

exclusivo /eksklu'siβo/ *a* exclusive

excomulgado /ekskomul'gaðo/ **(-da)** *a* and *n* *Eccl.* excommunicate; *Inf.* wicked (person)

excomulgar /ekskomul'gar/ *vt* to excommunicate

excomunión /ekskomu'nion/ *f*, excommunication

excoriar /eksko'riar/ *vt* to flay, excoriate; *vr* graze oneself

excrecencia /ekskre'sensia; ekskre'θenθia/ *f*, excrescence

excreción /ekskre'sion; ekskre'θion/ *f*, excretion

excremento /ekskre'mento/ *m*, excrement

excretar /ekskre'tar/ *vi* to excrete

excretorio /ekskre'torio/ *a* excretory

exculpación /ekskulpa'sion; ekskulpa'θion/ *f*, exoneration

exculpar /ekskul'par/ **(se)** *vt* and *vr* to exonerate

excursión /ekskur'sion/ *f*, excursion, outing, trip; *Mil.* incursion

excursionarse /ekskursio'narse/ *vr*, *Lat. Am.* to go on a trip, go on an outing, go on an excursion

excursionismo /ekskursio'nismo/ *m*, sightseeing; hiking

excursionista /ekskursio'nista/ *mf* excursionist; hiker

excusa /eks'kusa/ *f*, excuse

excusado /eksku'saðo/ *a* excused; exempt; unnecessary, superfluous; reserved, private. *m*, lavatory, toilet

excusar /eksku'sar/ *vt* to excuse; avoid, ward off, prevent; exempt; *vr* excuse oneself

execración /eksekra'sion; eksekra'θion/ *f*, execration

execrar /ekse'krar/ *vt* to execrate; denounce; loathe

exención /eksen'sion; eksen'θion/ *f*, exemption

exentar /eksen'tar/ *vt* to exempt

exento /ek'sento/ *a* exempt; free, liberated; open (of buildings, etc.)

exequias /ekse'kias/ *f pl*, funeral, obsequies

exfoliar /eksfo'liar/ *vt* to strip off; *vr* flake off

exhalación /eksala'sion; eksala'θion/ *f*, exhalation; shooting star; lightning; emanation, effluvium

exhalar /eksa'lar/ *vt* to exhale, give off; *Fig.* give vent to

exhibición /eksiβi'sion; eksiβi'θion/ *f*, exhibition

exhibicionismo /eksiβisio'nismo; eksiβiθio'nismo/ *m*, exhibitionism

exhibicionista /eksiβisio'nista; eksiβiθio'nista/ *mf* exhibitionist

exhibir /eksi'βir/ *vt* to exhibit, show

exhortación /eksorta'sion; eksorta'θion/ *f*, exhortation

exhortar /eksor'tar/ *vt* to exhort

exhumación /eksuma'sion; eksuma'θion/ *f*, exhumation

exhumar /eksu'mar/ *vt* to exhume, disinter

exigencia /eksi'hensia; eksi'henθia/ *f*, exigency; demand

exigente /eksi'hente/ *a* exigent

exigir /eksi'hir/ *vt* to exact, collect; need, require; demand

exigüidad /eksigui'ðað/ *f*, exiguousness

exiguo /ek'siguo/ *a* exiguous, meager

eximio /ek'simio/ *a* most excellent; illustrious

eximir /eksi'mir/ *vt* to exempt

existencia /eksis'tensia; eksis'tenθia/ *f*, existence; *pl Com.* stock on hand

existir /eksis'tir/ *vi* to exist, be; live

éxito /'eksito/ *m*, success; result, conclusion

exitoso, -a /eksi'toso/ *a*, *Lat. Am.* successful

exliado, -a /eks'liaðo/ *Lat. Am.* a exiled, in exile; *mf* exile

éxodo /'eksoðo/ *m*, exodus, emigration. **Éxodo,** Exodus. **é. rural,** rural depopulation

exoneración /eksonera'sion; eksonera'θion/ *f*, exoneration

exonerar /eksone'rar/ *vt* to exonerate; discharge (from employment)

exorbitancia /eksorβi'tansia; eksorβi'tanθia/ *f*, exorbitance

exorbitante /eksorβi'tante/ *a* exorbitant, excessive

exorcismo /eksor'sismo; eksor'θismo/ *m*, exorcism

exorcista /eksor'sista; eksor'θista/ *m*, exorcist

exorcizar /eksorsi'sar; eksorθi'θar/ *vt* to exorcize

exordio /ek'sorðio/ *m*, exordium, introduction

exornar /eksor'nar/ *vt* to adorn; embellish (*Lit.* style)

exótico /ek'sotiko/ *a* exotic, rare

expandir /ekspan'dir/ *vt* to expand

expansión /ekspan'sion/ *f*, expansion; recreation, hobby

expansivo /ekspan'siβo/ *a* expansive; communicative, frank

expatriación /ekspatria'sion; ekspatria'θion/ *f*, expatriation

expatriarse /ekspa'triarse/ *vr*, to emigrate, leave one's country

expectante /ekspek'tante/ *a* expectant

expectativa /ekspekta'tiβa/ *f*, expectancy; expectation

expectoración /ekspektora'sion; ekspektora'θion/ *f*, expectoration

expectorar /ekspekto'rar/ *vt* to expectorate

expedición /ekspeði'sion; ekspeði'θion/ *f*, expedition; speed, promptness; *Eccl.* bull, dispensation; excursion; forwarding, dispatch

expediente /ekspe'ðiente/ *a* Law. proceedings; file of documents; expedient, device, means; expedition, promptness; motive, reason; provision

expedir /ekspe'ðir/ *vt irr* to expedite; forward, send, ship; issue, make out (checks, receipts, etc.); draw up (documents); dispatch, deal with. See **pedir**

expedito /ekspe'ðito/ a expeditious, speedy

expeler /ekspe'ler/ vt to expel, discharge, emit

expendedor /ekspende'ðor/ **(-ra)** a spending. n spender; agent; retailer; seller; Law. **e. de moneda falsa,** distributor of counterfeit money

expendeduría /ekspendeðu'ria/ f, shop where government monopoly goods are sold (tobacco, stamps, etc.)

expender /ekspen'der/ vt to spend (money); Com. retail; Com. sell on commission; Law. distribute counterfeit money

expendio /eks'pendio/ m, Lat. Am. tobacco shop

expensas /eks'pensas/ f pl, costs, charges

experiencia /ekspe'riensia; ekspe'rienθia/ f, experience; practice, experiment

experimentación /eksperimenta'sion; eksperimenta'θion/ f, experiencing

experimentar /eksperimen'tar/ vt to test, try; experience; feel

experimento /eksperi'mento/ m, experiment

experto /ek'sperto/ **(-ta)** a practiced, expert. n expert

expiación /ekspia'sion; ekspia'θion/ f, expiation

expiar /eks'piar/ vt to expiate, atone for; pay the penalty of; Fig. purify

expiatorio /ekspia'torio/ a expiatory

expiración /ekspira'sion; ekspira'θion/ f, expiration

expirar /ekspi'rar/ vi to die; Fig. expire; die down; exhale, expire

explanación /eksplana'sion; eksplana'θion/ f, leveling; explanation, elucidation

explanada /ekspla'naða/ f, esplanade; Mil. glacis

explanar /ekspla'nar/ vt to level; explain

explayar /ekspla'yar/ vt to extend, enlarge; vr spread oneself, enlarge (upon); enjoy an outing; confide (in)

explicación /eksplika'sion; eksplika'θion/ f, explanation; elucidation

explicar /ekspli'kar/ vt to explain; expound; interpret, elucidate; vr explain oneself

explicativo /eksplika'tiβo/ a explanatory

explícito /eks'plisito; eks'pliθito/ a explicit, clear

exploración /eksploracion; eksplora'θion/ f, exploration

explorador /eksplora'ðor/ a exploring. m, explorer; prospector; boy scout; Mil. scout

explorar /eksplo'rar/ vt to explore; investigate; Med. probe

exploratorio /eksplora'torio/ a exploratory

explosión /eksplo'sion/ f, explosion; outburst, outbreak. **hacer falsas explosiones,** Mech. to misfire

explosivo /eksplo'siβo/ a and m, explosive. **e. violento,** high explosive

explotación /eksplota'sion; eksplota'θion/ f, development, exploitation

explotar /eksplo'tar/ vt to work (mines); Fig. exploit

expoliación /ekspolia'sion; ekspolia'θion/ f, spoliation

expoliar /ekspo'liar/ vt to despoil

exponente /ekspo'nente/ a and mf exponent. m, Math. index

exponer /ekspo'ner/ vt irr to show, expose; expound; interpret; risk, jeopardize; abandon (child). See **poner**

exportación /eksporta'sion; eksporta'θion/ f, exportation; export

exportador /eksporta'ðor/ **(-ra)** a export. n exporter

exportar /ekspor'tar/ vt to export

exposición /eksposi'sion; eksposi'θion/ f, exposition, demonstration; petition; exhibition; Lit. exposition; Photo. exposure; orientation, position

expósito /eks'posito/ **(-ta)** a and n foundling

expositor /eksposi'tor/ **(-ra)** a and n exponent. n exhibitor

expremijo /ekspre'miho/ m, cheese vat

exprés /eks'pres/ a express. m, messenger or delivery service; express train; transport office

expresar /ekspre'sar/ vt to express (all meanings)

expresión /ekspre'sion/ f, statement, utterance;

phrase, wording; expression; presentation; manifestation; gift, present; squeezing; pressing (of fruits, etc.)

expresivo /ekspre'siβo/ a expressive; affectionate

expreso /eks'preso/ a express; clear, obvious. m, courier, messenger

exprimelimones /eksprimeli'mones/ m, **exprimidera,** f, lemon squeezer

exprimidor de la ropa /eksprimi'ðor de la 'rropa/ m, wringer, mangle

exprimir /ekspri'mir/ vt to squeeze, press (fruit); press, hold tightly; express, utter

expropiación /ekspropia'sion; ekspropia'θion/ f, expropriation

expropiar /ekspro'piar/ vt to expropriate; commandeer

expugnar /ekspug'nar/ vt Mil. to take by storm

expulsar /ekspul'sar/ vt to expel, eject, dismiss

expulsión /ekspul'sion/ f, expulsion

expurgar /ekspur'gar/ vt to cleanse, purify; expurgate

expurgatorio /ekspurga'torio/ a expurgatory. m, Eccl. index

exquisitez /ekskisi'tes; ekskisi'teθ/ f, exquisiteness

exquisito /eks'kisito/ a exquisite, choice; delicate, delicious

extasiarse /eksta'siarse/ vr to fall into ecstasy; marvel (at), delight (in)

éxtasis /'ekstasis/ m, ecstasy; rapture

extático /eks'tatiko/ a ecstatic

extemporáneo /ekstempo'raneo/ a untimely; inopportune, inconvenient

extender /eksten'der/ vt irr to spread; reach, extend; elongate; enlarge, amplify; unfold, open out, stretch; draw up (documents); make out (checks, etc.); vr stretch out; lie down; spread, be generalized; extend; last (of time); record; stretch, open out. **extenderse en,** to expatiate on. See **entender**

extensión /eksten'sion/ f, extension; expanse; length; extent; duration; extension (logic)

extensivo /eksten'siβo/ a extensive, spacious; extensible

extenso /eks'tenso/ a extensive, vast

extensor /eksten'sor/ a extensor. m, chest expander

extenuación /ekstenua'sion; ekstenua'θion/ f, emaciation, weakness; extenuation

extenuar /ekste'nuar/ vt to exhaust, weaken; vr become weak

exterior /ekste'rior/ a external; foreign (trade, etc.). m, outside, exterior; outward appearance

exterioridad /eksteriori'ðað/ f, outward appearance; outside, externality; pl ceremonies, forms; ostentation

exteriorizar /eksteriori'sar; eksteriori'θar/ vt to exteriorize, reveal

exterminador /ekstermina'ðor/ **(-ra)** a exterminating. n exterminator

exterminar /ekstermi'nar/ vt to exterminate; devastate

exterminio /ekster'minio/ m, extermination; devastation

externado /ekster'naðo/ m, day school

externarse /ekster'narse/ vr to stand out

externo /eks'terno/ **(-na)** a external. n day

extinción /ekstin'sion; ekstin'θion/ f, extinction; extinguishment; abolition, cancellation

extinguir /ekstin'guir/ vt to extinguish; destroy

extintor /ekstin'tor/ m, fire extinguisher

extirpación /ekstirpa'sion; ekstirpa'θion/ f, extirpation

extirpador /ekstirpa'ðor/ **(-ra)** a extirpating. n extirpator

extirpar /ekstir'par/ vt to extirpate; Fig. eradicate

extorsión /ekstor'sion/ f, extortion

extorsionar /ekstorsio'nar/ vt to extort

extra /'ekstra/ prefix outside, without, beyond. prep besides. a extremely, most. m, Inf. extra

extracción /ekstrak'sion; ekstrak'θion/ f, extraction; drawing (lottery); origin, lineage; exportation

extractar /ekstrak'tar/ vt to abstract, summarize

extracto /eks'trakto/ a, abstract, summary; Chem. extract

extractor /ekstrak'tor/ a extracting. m, extractor

extradición /ekstraði'sion; ekstraði'θion/ f, extradition

extraer /ekstra'er/ vt irr to extract; draw out; export; Chem. extract. See **traer**

extranjero /ekstran'hero/ (-ra) a alien, foreign. n foreigner. m, abroad, foreign country

extrañar /ekstra'ɲar/ vt to exile; alienate, estrange; wonder at; miss, feel the loss of; vr be exiled; be estranged; be amazed (by); refuse (to do a thing)

extrañeza /ekstra'ɲesa; ekstra'ɲeθa/ f, strangeness; estrangement; surprise

extraño /eks'traɲo/ a strange, unusual; foreign, extraneous

extraoficial /ekstraofi'sial; ekstraofi'θial/ a unofficial

extraordinario /ekstraorði'nario/ a extraordinary; special. m, Cul. extra course

extraterrenal /ekstraterre'nal/ **extraterreno** a, Lat. Am. extraterrestrial, unearthly

extraterritorialidad /ekstraterritoriali'ðað/ f, exterritoriality

extravagancia /ekstraβa'gansia; ekstraβa'ganθia/ f, eccentricity; queerness; folly

extravagante /ekstraβa'gante/ a eccentric; queer, strange; absurd

extravertido /ekstraβer'tiðo/ m, extrovert

extraviar /ekstra'βiar/ vt to mislead; mislay; vr lose one's way; be lost (of things); Fig. go astray

extravío /ekstra'βio/ m, deviation, divergence; error; aberration, lapse

extremado /ekstre'maðo/ a extreme

extremar /ekstre'mar/ vt to take to extremes; vr do one's best

extremaunción /ekstremaun'sion; ekstremaun'θion/ f, extreme unction

extremidad /ekstremi'ðað/ f, end; extremity; remotest part; edge; limit; pl extremities

extremista /ekstre'mista/ a and mf extremist

extremo /eks'tremo/ a last, ultimate; extreme; furthest; great, exceptional; utmost. m, end, extreme; highest degree; extreme care; pl excessive emotional display

extremoso /ekstre'moso/ a immoderate, exaggerated; very affectionate

extrínseco /ekstrin'seko/ a extrinsic

exuberancia /eksuβeransia; eksuβe'ranθia/ f, abundance; exuberance

exuberante /eksuβe'rante/ a abundant, copious; exuberant

exudar /eksu'ðar/ vi and vt to exude

exultación /eksulta'sion; eksulta'θion/ f, exultation; rejoicing

exultante /eksul'tante/ a exultant

exultar /eksul'tar/ vi to exult

eyaculación /eyakula'sion; eyakula'θion/ f, Med. ejaculation

eyacular /eyaku'lar/ vt Med. to ejaculate

F

fa /fa/ m, Mus. fa, F

fabada /fa'βaða/ f, dish of broad beans with pork, sausage or bacon

fábrica /'faβrika/ f, manufacture; making; factory, works; fabric, structure, building; creation; invention. **f. de papel,** paper mill. **marca de f.,** trademark

fabricación /faβrika'sion; faβrika'θion/ f, make; making; construction. **f. en serie,** mass production

fabricador /faβrika'ðor/ (-ra) a creative, inventive. n fabricator; maker

fabricante /faβri'kante/ a manufacturing. m, manufacturer; maker

fabricar /faβri'kar/ vt to manufacture; make; construct, build; devise; invent, create

fabril /fa'βril/ a manufacturing

fabriquero /faβri'kero/ m, manufacturer; churchwarden; charcoal burner

fábula /'faβula/ f, rumor, gossip; fiction; fable; story, plot; mythology; myth; laughingstock; falsehood.

fabulista /faβu'lista/ mf fabulist; mythologist

fabulosidad /faβulosi'ðað/ f, fabulousness

fabuloso /faβu'loso/ a fabulous; fictitious; incredible, amazing

faca /'faka/ f, jackknife

facción /fak'sion; fak'θion/ f, rebellion; faction, party, band; feature (of the face) (gen. pl); military exploit; any routine military duty

faccionario /faksio'nario; fakθio'nario/ a factional

faccioso /fak'sioso; fak'θioso/ (-sa) a factional; factious, seditious. n rebel

faceta /fa'seta; fa'θeta/ f, facet (gems); aspect, view

facha /'fatʃa/ f, Inf. countenance, look, face; guy, scarecrow. Naut. **ponerse en f.,** to lie to

fachada /fa'tʃaða/ f, facade, front (of a building, ship, etc.); Inf. build, presence (of a person); frontispiece (of a book)

fachenda /fa'tʃenda/ f, Inf. boastfulness, vanity

fachinal /fatʃi'nal/ m, Argentina swamp

fachoso, -a /fa'tʃoso/ a, Lat. Am. elegant, smart

facial /fa'sial; fa'θial/ a facial; intuitive

fácil /'fasil; 'faθil/ a easy; probable; easily led; docile; of easy virtue (women). adv easy

facilidad /fasili'ðað; faθili'ðað/ f, easiness; facility, aptitude; ready compliance; opportunity

facilitar /fasili'tar; faθili'tar/ vt to facilitate, expedite; provide, deliver

facineroso /fasine'roso; faθine'roso/ a criminal, delinquent. m, criminal; villain

facistol /fasis'tol; faθis'tol/ m, Eccl. lectern; chorister's stand

facsímile /fak'simile/ m, facsimile

factibilidad /faktiβili'ðað/ f, feasibility, practicability

factible /fak'tiβle/ a feasible, practicable

facticio /fak'tisio; fak'tiθio/ a factitious, artificial

factor /fak'tor/ m, Com. factor, agent; Math. factor; element; consideration

factoría /fakto'ria/ f, agency; factorage; factory; merchants' trading post, especially in a foreign country

factótum /fak'totum/ m, Inf. factotum, handyman; Inf. busybody; confidential agent or deputy

factura /fak'tura/ f, Com. invoice, bill, account; Art. execution; workmanship; making

facturar /faktu'rar/ vt Com. to invoice; register (luggage on a railroad)

facultad /fakulta'ð/ f, faculty; mental or physical aptitude, capability; authority, right; science, art; Educ. faculty; license

facultar /fakul'tar/ vt to authorize, permit

facultativo /fakulta'tiβo/ a belonging to a faculty; optional, permissive. m, physician

facundia /fa'kundia/ f, eloquence

facundo /fa'kundo/ a eloquent

faena /fa'ena/ f, manual labor; mental work; business affairs (gen. pl)

faetón /fae'ton/ m, phaeton

fagocito /fago'sito; fago'θito/ m, phagocyte

fagot /fa'got/ m, bassoon

fagotista /fago'tista/ mf bassoon player

faisán /fai'san/ (-ana) Ornith. cock (hen) pheasant

faisanera /faisa'nera/ f, pheasantry

faja /'faha/ f, belt; sash, scarf; corset, girdle; Geog. zone; newspaper wrapper; Archit. fascia; swathing band

fajar /fa'har/ vt to swathe; swaddle (a child)

fajero /fa'hero/ m, swaddling band

fajín /fa'hin/ m, ceremonial ribbon or sash worn by generals, etc.

fajina /fa'hina/ f, stack; brushwood; (fort.) fascine; Mexico lunch

fajo /'faho/ m, bundle, sheaf; pl swaddling clothes

falacia /fa'lasia; fa'laθia/ f, fraud, deceit; deceitfulness; fallacy

falange /fa'lanhe/ *f*, *Mil.* phalanx; *Anat.* phalange; (*Spanish Pol.*) Falange
falangista /falan'hista/ *a* and *mf* Falangist
falaz /fa'las; fa'laθ/ *a* deceitful; fallacious
falda /'falda/ *f*, skirt; lap, flap, panel (of a dress); slope (of a hill); the lap; loin (of beef, etc.); brim of a hat; *pl Inf.* petticoats, women. **f. escocesa,** kilt. **f.-pantalón,** divided skirt, culottes.
faldellín /falde'yin; falde'ʎin/ *m*, skirt; underskirt
faldero /fal'dero/ *a* lap (dog); fond of the company of women
faldillas /fal'diyas; fal'diʎas/ *f pl*, coattails
faldistorio /faldis'torio/ *m*, faldstool
faldón /fal'don/ *m*, long, flowing skirt; shirttail; coattail
falibilidad /faliβili'ðað/ *f*, fallibility
falible /fa'liβle/ *a* fallible
falla /'faya; 'faʎa/ *f*, deficiency, defect; failure; *Geol.* displacement; bonfire (Valencia); *Mineral.* slide
fallar /fa'yar; fa'ʎar/ *vt Law.* to pass sentence; *vi* be deficient
fallecer /faye'ser; faʎe'θer/ *vi irr* to die; fail. See **conocer**
fallecimiento /fayesi'miento; faʎeθi'miento/ *m*, death, decease
fallido /fa'yiðo; fa'ʎiðo/ *a* frustrated; bankrupt
fallo /'fayo; 'faʎo/ *m*, *Law.* verdict; judgment
falsario /fal'sario/ *a* falsifying, forging, counterfeiting; deceiving, lying. *m*, falsifier, forger, counterfeiter
falseamiento /falsea'miento/ *m*, falsifying; forging
falsear /false'ar/ *vt* to falsify; forge; counterfeit; penetrate; *vi* weaken; *Mus.* be out of tune (strings)
falsedad /false'ðað/ *f*, falseness; falsehood
falsete /fal'sete/ *m*, spigot; *Mus.* falsetto voice
falsificación /falsifika'sion; falsifika'θion/ *f*, falsification; forgery
falsificador /falsifika'ðor/ *a* falsifying; forging. *m*, falsifier; forger
falsificar /falsifi'kar/ *vt* to forge, counterfeit; falsify
falso /'falso/ *a* false; forged, counterfeit; treacherous, untrue, deceitful; incorrect; sham; vicious (horses). **de f.,** falsely; deceitfully
falta /'falta/ *f*, lack, shortage; defect; mistake; *Sports.* fault; shortcoming; nonappearance, absence; deficiency in legal weight of coin; *Law.* offense. **f. de éxito,** failure. **hacer f.,** to be necessary. **sin f.,** without fail
faltar /fal'tar/ *vi* to be lacking; fail, die; fall short; be absent from an appointment; not to fulfill one's obligations. **hacer f.,** to be necessary, need. **f. a,** to be unfaithful to, break (e.g. *Faltó a su palabra,* He broke his promise). **Me hace falta dinero,** I need money. *Inf.* **¡No faltaba más!** I should think not!; That's the limit!
falto /'falto/ *a* lacking, wanting; defective; wretched, mean, timid. **f. de personal,** short-handed
faltriquera /faltri'kera/ *f*, pocket; hip pocket
falúa /fa'lua/ *f*, *Naut.* tender; longboat
falucho /fa'lutʃo/ *m*, felucca
fama /'fama/ *f*, rumor, report; reputation; fame
famélico /fa'meliko/ *a* ravenous
familia /fa'milia/ *f*, family; household; kindred. **ser de f.,** to run in the family
familiar /fami'liar/ *a* family; familiar; well known; unceremonious; plain, simple; colloquial (language). *m*, *Eccl.* familiar; servant; intimate friend; familiar spirit
familiaridad /familiari'ðað/ *f*, familiarity
familiarizar /familiari'sar; familiari'θar/ *vt* to familiarize; *vr* become familiar; accustom oneself
familiarmente /familiar'mente/ *adv* familiarly
famoso /fa'moso/ *a* famous; notorious; *Inf.* excellent; perfect; *Inf.* conspicuous
fámula /'famula/ *f*, *Inf.* female servant
fámulo /'famulo/ *m*, servant of a college; *Inf.* servant
fanal /fa'nal/ *m*, lantern (of a lighthouse); *Naut.* poop lantern; lantern; lamp glass
fanático /fa'natiko/ **(-ca)** *a* fanatical. *n* fanatic; *Inf.* fan, enthusiast
fanatismo /fana'tismo/ *m*, fanaticism

fanatizar /fanati'sar; fanati'θar/ *vt* to make fanatical; turn into a fanatic
fandango /fan'daŋgo/ *m*, lively Andalusian dance; *Lat. Am.* rowdy party
fanega /fa'nega/ *f*, grain measure about the weight of 1.60 bushel; land measure (about $1\frac{1}{2}$ acres)
fanfarrón /fanfa'rron/ **(-ona)** *a Inf.* boastful; swaggering. *n* swashbuckler; boaster
fanfarronear /fanfarrone'ar/ *vi* to swagger; brag
fanfarronería /fanfarrone'ria/ *f*, bragging
fango /'faŋgo/ *m*, mud, mire; degradation
fangoso /faŋ'goso/ *a* muddy, miry
fantasear /fantase'ar/ *vi* to let one's fancy roam; boast
fantasía /fanta'sia/ *f*, fancy, imagination; fantasy; caprice; fiction; *Inf.* presumption; *Mus.* fantasia
fantasma /fan'tasma/ *m*, ghost, phantom; vision; image, impression; presumptuous person. *f*, *Inf.* scarecrow; apparition
fantasmagoría /fantasmago'ria/ *f*, phantasmagoria
fantasmagórico /fantasma'goriko/ *a* phantasmagoric
fantástico /fan'tastiko/ *a* fanciful, imaginary; fantastic, imaginative; presumptuous, conceited
fantoche /fan'totʃe/ *m*, puppet; *Inf.* yes-man, mediocrity
faquín /fa'kin/ *m*, porter, carrier
faquir /fɑ'kir/ *m*, fakir
farabute /fara'βute/ *mf*, *Argentina* rogue
faradio /fa'raðio/ *m*, farad
faralá /fara'la/ *m*, flounce, frill
faramallear /faramaje'ar; faramaʎe'ar/ *vi*, *Lat. Am.* to boast, brag
farándula /fa'randula/ *f*, profession of low comedian; troupe of strolling players; cunning trick
farandulero /farandu'lero/ *m*, actor, strolling player. *a Inf.* plausible
faraón /fara'on/ *m*, pharaoh; faro (card game)
fardel /far'ðel/ *m*, bag, knapsack; bundle
fardo /far'ðo/ *m*, bundle, bale, package
farfulla /far'fuya; far'fuʎa/ *f*, *Inf.* mumbling; gibbering. *mf Inf.* mumbler
farfullar /farfu'yar; farfu'ʎar/ *vt Inf.* to mumble; gibber; *Inf.* act in haste
faringe /fa'rinhe/ *f*, pharynx
faríngeo /fa'rinheo/ *a* pharyngeal
faringitis /farin'hitis/ *f*, pharyngitis
farmacéutico /farma'seutiko; farma'θeutiko/ *a* pharmaceutical. *m*, pharmacist
farmacia /far'masia; far'maθia/ *f*, pharmacy
farmacología /farmakolo'hia/ *f*, pharmacology
farmacólogo /farma'kologo/ *m*, pharmacologist
faro /'faro/ *m*, lighthouse; beacon, guide; *Auto.* headlight
farol /fa'rol/ *m*, lantern, lamp; streetlamp; cresset
farola /fa'rola/ *f*, lamppost (generally with several branches); lantern
farolero /faro'lero/ *m*, lantern maker; lamplighter; lamp tender. *a Inf.* swaggering, braggart
fárrago /'farrago/ *m*, hodgepodge
farruto, -a /fa'rruto/ *a*, *Lat. Am.* sickly, weak
farsa /'farsa/ *f*, old name for a play; farce; theatrical company; poor, badly constructed play; sham, trick, deception
farsante /far'sante/ *m*, comedian; *Obs.* actor; *Fig. Inf.* humbug
fascinación /fassina'sion; fasθina'θion/ *f*, evil eye; enchantment, fascination
fascinador /fassina'ðor; fasθina'ðor/ **(-ra)** *a* bewitching; fascinating. *n* charmer
fascinante /fassi'nante; fasθi'nante/ *a* fascinating
fascinar /fassi'nar; fasθi'nar/ *vt* to bewitch, place under a spell; deceive, impose upon; attract, fascinate
fascismo /fas'sismo; fas'θismo/ *m*, fascism
fascista /fas'sista; fas'θista/ *a* and *mf* fascist
fase /'fase/ *f*, phase; aspect
fastidiar /fasti'ðiar/ *vt* to disgust, bore; annoy; *vr* be bored
fastidio /fasti'ðio/ *m*, sickness, squeamishness; annoyance, boredom; dislike, repugnance

fastidioso /fasti'ðioso/ a disgusting, sickening; annoying; boring, tiresome

fastuoso /fas'tuoso/ a ostentatious; pompous

fatal /fa'tal/ a fatal, mortal; predetermined, inevitable; ill-fated, unhappy, disastrous; evil

fatalidad /fatali'ðað/ f, fatality; inevitability; disaster, ill-fatedness

fatalismo /fata'lismo/ m, fatalism

fatalista /fata'lista/ a fatalistic. mf fatalist

fatalmente /fatal'mente/ adv inevitably, unavoidably; unhappily, unfortunately; extremely badly

fatídico /fa'tiðiko/ a prophetic (gen. of evil)

fatiga /fa'tiɣa/ f, fatigue; toil; difficult breathing; hardship, troubles (gen. pl.)

fatigar /fati'ɣar/ vt to tire; annoy; vr be tired

fatigoso /fati'ɣoso/ a tired; tiring; tiresome, annoying

fatuidad /fatui'ðað/ f, fatuousness, inanity, foolishness; conceit; priggishness

fatuo /fa'tuo/ a fatuous, foolish; conceited; priggish. m, self-satisfied fool. **fuego f.**, will-o'-the-wisp

fauces /'fauses/ 'fauθes/ f pl, snout, jaws (animal)

faul /faul/ m, Lat. Am. foul

faulear /faule'ar/ vt, Lat. Am. to foul

fauna /'fauna/ f, fauna

fauno /'fauno/ m, faun

fausto /'fausto/ a, pomp, magnificence, ostentation. a fortunate, happy

fautor /fau'tor/ m, protector, helper; accomplice. **f. de guerra,** warmonger

favonio /fa'βonio/ m, Poet. zephyr, westerly wind

favor /fa'βor/ m, aid, protection, support; favor, honor, service; love favor, sign of favor. **a f. de,** in favor of; on behalf of

favorable /faβo'raβle/ a kind, helpful; favorable

favorecedor /faβorese'ðor; faβoreθe'ðor/ **(-ra)** a favoring, helping. n helper; protector

favorecer /faβore'ser; faβore'θer/ vt irr to aid, protect, support; favor; do a service, grant a favor. See **conocer**

favoritismo /faβori'tismo/ m, favoritism

favorito /faβo'rito/ **(-ta)** a and n favorite

fax /faks/ m, fax

fayenza /fa'yensa; fa'yenθa/ f, faience

faz /fas; faθ/ f, face; external surface of a thing; side; frontage

fe /fe/ f, faith; confidence, trust, good opinion; belief; solemn promise; assertion; certificate, attestation; faithfulness. **f. de erratas,** Print. errata. **dar f., Law.** to testify. **de buena f.,** in good faith. **en f.,** in proof

fealdad /feal'dað/ f, ugliness; base action

febo /'feβo/ m, Phoebus; Poet. sun

febrero /fe'βrero/ m, February

febril /fe'βril/ a feverish; ardent, violent; passionate

fecha /'fetʃa/ f, date. **a la f.,** at present, now. **hasta la f.,** up to the present (day)

fechar /fe'tʃar/ vt to date, write the date

feculento /feku'lento/ a starchy; dreggy

fecundación /fekunda'sion; fekunda'θion/ f, fecundation

fecundar /fekun'dar/ vt to fertilize; fecundate

fecundidad /fekundi'ðað/ f, fecundity; fertility, fruitfulness

fecundizar /fekundi'sar; fekundi'θar/ vt to fertilize; make fruitful

fecundo /fe'kundo/ a fertile, fecund, prolific; abundant

federación /feðera'sion; feðera'θion/ f, federation, league

federal /feðe'ral/ a federal. mf federalist

federalismo /feðera'lismo/ m, federalism

federalista /feðera'lista/ a federal, federalist. mf federalist

federativo /feðera'tiβo/ a federative

fehaciente /fea'siente; fea'θiente/ a Law. authentic, attested

felicidad /felisi'ðað; feliθi'ðað/ f, happiness; contentment, satisfaction; good fortune

felicitación /felisita'sion; feliθita'θion/ f, congratulation

felicitar /felisi'tar; feliθi'tar/ vt to congratulate; wish well; vr congratulate oneself

feligrés /feli'gres/ **(-esa)** n parishioner

feligresía /feligre'sia/ f, parish

felino /fe'lino/ a and m, feline

feliz /fe'lis; fe'liθ/ a happy; fortunate; skillful, felicitous (of phrases, etc.)

felón /fe'lon/ **(-ona)** n felon

felonía /felo'nia/ f, felony

felpa /'felpa/ f, plush; Inf. drubbing, beating

felpilla /fel'piya; fel'piʎa/ f, chenille

felpudo /fel'puðo/ a plush

femenino /feme'nino/ a feminine; female; Fig. weak

fementido /femen'tiðo/ a sly, false, treacherous, unfaithful

feminismo /femi'nismo/ m, feminism

feminista /femi'nista/ a feminist. mf feminist

fémur /'femur/ m, femur, thigh bone

fenecer /fene'ser; fene'θer/ vt irr to conclude, finish; vi die; be ended. See **conocer**

fenecimiento /fenesi'miento; feneθi'miento/ m, end; death

fenicio /fe'nisio; fe'niθio/ **(-ia)** a and n Phoenician

fénico /'feniko/ a phenic, carbolic

fénix /'feniks/ f, phoenix

fenomenal /fenome'nal/ a phenomenal; Inf. terrific

fenómeno /fe'nomeno/ m, phenomenon; Inf. something of great size

feo /'feo/ a ugly; alarming, horrid; evil. m, Inf. slight, insult

feraz /'feras; 'feraθ/ a fruitful, fertile

féretro /'feretro/ m, coffin; bier

feria /'feria/ f, fair, market; workday; holiday; rest

feriar /fe'riar/ vt to buy at a fair; bargain. vi cease work, take a vacation. **día feriado,** holiday

fermentación /fermenta'sion; fermenta'θion/ f, fermentation

fermentar /fermen'tar/ vi to ferment; be agitated; vt cause to ferment

fermento /fer'mento/ m, ferment; leaven; Chem. enzyme

ferocidad /ferosi'ðað; feroθi'ðað/ f, ferocity, cruelty

feroz /fe'ros; fe'roθ/ a ferocious, cruel; Lat. Am. ugly

férreo /'ferreo/ a ferrous; hard, tenacious. **línea férrea,** railroad

ferrería /ferre'ria/ f, ironworks

ferretería /ferrete'ria/ f, ironworks; ironmonger's shop; ironware, hardware

férrico /'ferriko/ a ferric

ferrífero /fe'rrifero/ a iron-bearing

ferrocarril /ferroka'rril/ m, railroad, railway; railroad train. **f. de cremallera,** rack railroad. **f. funicular,** funicular railway

ferroso /fe'rroso/ a ferrous

ferroviario /ferro'βiario/ a railroad, railway. m, railroad employee

fértil /'fertil/ a fertile; fruitful, productive

fertilidad /fertili'ðað/ f, fertility

fertilización /fertilisa'sion; fertiliθa'θion/ f, fertilization

fertilizar /fertili'sar; fertili'θar/ vt to fertilize, make fruitful

férula /'ferula/ f, ferule; Surg. splint; Fig. yoke, rule

fervor /fer'βor/ m, intense heat; fervor, devotion; zeal

fervoroso /ferβo'roso/ a fervent, zealous, devoted

festejar /feste'har/ vt to feast, entertain; woo; celebrate; vr amuse oneself; Mexico to thrash

festejo /feste'ho/ m, feast, entertainment; courtship, wooing; pl public celebrations

festín /fes'tin/ m, private dinner or party; sumptuous banquet

festival /festi'βal/ m, musical festival; festival

festividad /festiβi'ðað/ f, festivity; Eccl. celebration, solemnity; witticism

festivo /fes'tiβo/ a joking, witty; happy, gay; solemn, worthy of celebration. **día f.,** holiday

festón /fes'ton/ m, garland, wreath; festoon; border; scalloped edging

festonear /festone'ar/ *vt* to garland, festoon; border

fetal /fe'tal/ *a* fetal

fetiche /fe'titʃe/ *m*, fetish

fetichismo /feti'tʃismo/ *m*, fetishism

fetidez /feti'ðes; feti'ðeθ/ *f*, fetidness, fetor, stink

fétido /'fetiðo/ *a* stinking, fetid

feto /'feto/ *m*, fetus

feudal /feu'ðal/ *a* feudal; despotic

feudalismo /feuða'lismo/ *m*, feudalism

fez /fes; feθ/ *m*, fez

fiado, al /'fiaðo, al/ *adv* on credit. **en f.,** on bail

fiador /fia'ðor/ **(-ra)** *n* guarantor; bail. *m*, fastener, loop (of a coat, clock, etc.); safety catch, bolt. **salir f.,** to be surety (for); post bail

fiambre /'fiambre/ *m*, cold meat, cold dish; *Inf.* stale, out-of-date news, etc.; *Inf.* corpse

fiambrera /fiam'brera/ *f*, lunchbox, lunchpail

fiambrería /fiamβre'ria/ *f* delicatessen

fianza /'fiansa; 'fianθa/ *f*, guarantee, bail; surety; security. *Law.* **dar f.,** to guarantee; post bail

fiar /fi'ar/ *vt* to go surety for, post bail; sell on credit; trust; confide; *vr* (*with de*) confide in; trust

fibra /'fiβra/ *f*, fiber; filament; energy, strength; *Mineral.* vein; grain (of wood)

fibroso /fi'βroso/ *a* fibrous; fibroid

ficción /fik'sion; fik'θion/ *f*, falsehood; invention; fiction, imaginative creation; pretense

ficha /'fitʃa/ *f*, chip, counter; domino; index card, filing card. **f. antropométrica,** personal particulars card

fichar /fi'tʃar/ *vt* to record personal particulars on a filing card; file, index

fichero /fi'tʃero/ *m*, filing cabinet; card catalog

fichú /fi'tʃu/ *m*, fichu, scarf

ficticio /fik'tisio; fik'tiθio/ *a* fictitious

fidedigno /fiðe'ðigno/ *a* trustworthy, bona fide

fidelidad /fiðeli'ðað/ *f*, fidelity, honesty; loyalty; punctiliousness

fideos /fi'ðeos/ *m pl*, vermicelli. *m*, *Inf.* scraggy person

fiduciario /fiðu'siario; fiðu'θiario/ *a Law.* fiduciary. *m*, *Law.* trustee

fiebre /'fieβre/ *f*, fever; great agitation, excitement. **f. de oro,** gold fever. **f. palúdica,** malarial fever. **f. puerperal,** puerperal fever. **f. tifoidea,** typhoid fever

fiel /fiel/ *a* faithful, loyal; true, exact. *m*, axis; pointer (of a scale or balance)

fieltro /'fieltro/ *m*, felt

fiera /'fiera/ *f*, wild beast; cruel person

fiereza /fie'resa; fie'reθa/ *f*, savageness, wildness; cruelty, fierceness; deformity

fiero /'fiero/ *a* wild, savage; ugly; huge, enormous; horrible, alarming; haughty

fiesta /'fiesta/ *f*, merriment, gaiety; entertainment, feast; *Inf.* joke; festivity, celebration; public holiday; caress, cajolery (gen. *pl*); *pl* holidays. **f. fija** *Eccl.* immovable feast. *Inf.* **estar de f.,** to be making merry. **hacer f.,** to take a holiday. *Inf.* **Se acabó la f.,** It's all over and done with

fifiriche /fifi'ritʃe/ *a*, *Central America*, *Mexico* sickly, weak

figón /fi'gon/ *m*, eating house, diner

figulino /figu'lino/ *a* fictile, made of terra cotta

figura /fi'gura/ *f*, shape, form; face; *Art.* image, figure; *Law.* form; court card; *Mus.* note; *Theat.* character, role; (*Geom. Gram. Dance.*) figure. **f. de nieve,** snowman. **f. de proa,** figurehead. *Fig.* **f. decorativa,** figurehead. *Fig.* **hacer f.,** to cut a figure

figurado /figu'raðo/ *a* figurative; rhetorical

figurar /figu'rar/ *vt* to shape, mold; simulate, pretend; represent; *vi* be numbered among; cut a figure; *vr* imagine

figurilla /figu'riya; figu'riʎa/ *mf Inf.* ridiculous, dwarfish figure. *f*, *Art.* statuette

figurín /figu'rin/ *m*, fashion plate or model

figuroso, -a /figu'roso/ *a*, *Lat. Am.* flashy, loud, showy

fijación /fiha'sion; fiha'θion/ *f*, fixing; nailing; sticking; posting; attention, fixity; *Chem.* fixation; firmness, stability

fijador /fiha'ðor/ *m*, (*Med. Photo.*) fixative; setting lotion; *Art.* varnish. *a* fixing

fijamente /fiha'mente/ *adv* firmly; attentively

fijar /fi'har/ *vt* to fix; glue, stick; nail; make firm; settle, appoint (a date); fix, concentrate (attention, gaze); (*Photo. Med.*) fix; *vr* decide; notice (e.g. *No me había fijado,* I hadn't noticed). **f. anuncios,** to post bills

fijeza /fi'hesa; fi'heθa/ *f*, fixedness; firmness, stability; constancy, steadfastness

fijo /'fiho/ *a* firm; fixed; stable; steadfast; permanent; exact. **de f.,** certainly, without doubt

fila /'fila/ *f*, line, row; *Mil.* rank; antipathy, hatred. **en f.,** in a line

filacteria /filak'teria/ *f*, phylactery

filamento /fila'mento/ *m*, filament

filantropía /filantro'pia/ *f*, philanthropy

filantrópico /filan'tropiko/ *a* philanthropic

filántropo /fi'lantropo/ *m*, philanthropist

filarmónico /filar'moniko/ *a* philharmonic

filatelia /fila'telia/ *f*, philately, stamp collecting

filatélico /fila'teliko/ *a* philatelic

filatelista /filate'lista/ *mf* philatelist, stamp collector

filete /fi'lete/ *m*, *Archit.* filet; *Cul.* small spit; filet (of meat or fish); thread of a screw; *Sew.* hem

filiación /filia'sion; filia'θion/ *f*, filiation; affiliation; relationship; *Mil.* regimental register

filial /fi'lial/ *a* filial; affiliated

filibustero /filiβus'tero/ *m*, filibuster

filiforme /fili'forme/ *a* filamentous

filigrana /fili'grana/ *f*, filigree; watermark (of paper); *Fig.* delicate creation

filípica /fi'lipika/ *f*, philippic

Filipinas, las /fi'lipinas, las/ *the* Philippines

filipino /fili'pino/ **(-na)** *a* and *n* Philippine

filisteo /filis'teo/ **(-ea)** *a* and *n* philistine

filmar /fil'mar/ *vt* to film

filo /'filo/ *m*, cutting edge; dividing line

filología /filolo'hia/ *f*, philology

filológico /filo'lohiko/ *a* philological

filólogo /fi'lologo/ *m*, philologist

filomela /filo'mela/ *f*, *Poet.* nightingale

filón /fi'lon/ *m*, *Mineral.* vein, lode; *Fig.* gold mine

filoso, -a /fi'loso/ *a*, *Lat. Am.* sharp

filosofar /filoso'far/ *vi* to philosophize

filosofía /filoso'fia/ *f*, philosophy. **f. moral,** moral philosophy. **f. natural,** natural philosophy

filosófico /filo'sofiko/ *a* philosophic

filósofo /fi'losofo/ *m*, philosopher. *a* philosophic

filoxera /filo'ksera/ *f*, phylloxera

filtración /filtra'sion; filtra'θion/ *f*, filtration

filtrar /fil'trar/ *vt* to filter; *vi* filter through, percolate; *vr Fig.* disappear (of money, etc.)

filtro /'filtro/ *m*, filter, strainer; love potion, philter

filudo, -a /fi'luðo/ *a*, *Lat. Am.* = **filoso**

fin /fin/ *m*, finish, end, conclusion; purpose, goal, aim; limit, extent. **a f. de,** in order to, so that. **a fines de,** toward the end of (with months, years, etc.) (e.g. *a fines de octubre,* toward the end of October). **en f.,** at last; in fine; well then! **por f.,** finally

finado /fi'naðo/ **(-da)** *n* deceased, dead person

final /fi'nal/ *a* final. *m*, end, finish; *Sports.* final (gen. *pl*)

finalidad /finali'ðað/ *f*, finality; purpose

finalista /fina'lista/ *mf Sports.* finalist

finalizar /finali'sar; finali'θar/ *vt* to conclude, finish; *vi* be finished; close (stock exchange)

finalmente /final'mente/ *adv* finally

financiar /finan'siar; finan'θiar/ *vt* to finance

financiero /finan'siero; finan'θiero/ *a* financial. *m*, financier

finanzas /fi'nansas; fi'nanθas/ *f pl*, finance

finar /fi'nar/ *vi* to die; *vr* desire, long for a thing

finca /'finka/ *f*, land, real estate; house property, country house, ranch

fineza /fi'nesa; fi'neθa/ *f*, fineness; excellence; goodness; kindness; expression of affection; good turn, friendly act; gift; beauty, delicacy

fingido /fin'hiðo/ *a* pretended; assumed; feigned; sham

fingimiento /finhi'miento/ *m*, pretense; affectation, assumption

fingir /fin'hir/ *vt* to pretend, feign; imagine

finiquitar /finiki'tar/ *vt* to close and pay up an account; *Inf.* end

finiquito /fini'kito/ *m*, closing of an account; final receipt, quittance; quietus

finito /fi'nito/ *a* finite

finlandés /finlan'des/ **(-esa)** *a* Finnish. *n* Finn. *m*, Finnish (language)

fino /'fino/ *a* fine; excellent, good; slim, slender, thin; delicate, subtle; dainty (of people); cultured, polished; constant, loving; sagacious, shrewd; *Mineral.* refined

finta /'finta/ *f*, feint (in fencing); menace, threat

finura /fi'nura/ *f*, fineness; excellence; delicacy; courtesy

fiordo /'fiorðo/ *m*, fjord

firma /'firma/ *f*, signature; act of signing; *Com.* firm name, firm

firmamento /firma'mento/ *m*, firmament

firmante /fir'mante/ *a* signing. *mf* signatory

firmar /fir'mar/ *vt* to sign

firme /'firme/ *a* firm; hard; steady, solid; constant, resolute, loyal. *m*, foundation, base. *Mil.* **¡Firmes!** Attention! **batir de f.,** to strike hard

firmeza /fir'mesa; fir'meθa/ *f*, stability, firmness; constancy, resoluteness, loyalty

fiscal /fis'kal/ *a* fiscal. *m*, attorney general; public prosecutor; meddler. **f. de quiebras,** official receiver

fiscalizar /fiskali'sar; fiskali'θar/ *vt* to prosecute; pry into; meddle with; censure, criticize

fisco /'fisko/ *m*, national treasury, exchequer, revenue

fisgar /fis'gar/ *vt* to harpoon; pry; *vi* mock, make fun of

fisgón /fis'gon/ **(-ona)** *a* prying; mocking. *n* pryer; mocker; eavesdropper

fisgoneo /fisgo'neo/ *m*, prying; eavesdropping

física /'fisika/ *f*, physics

físico /'fisiko/ *a* physical. *m*, physicist; physician; physique

fisiología /fisiolo'hia/ *f*, physiology

fisiológico /fisio'lohiko/ *a* physiological

fisiólogo /fisi'ologo/ *m*, physiologist

fisioterapia /fisiote'rapia/ *f*, physiotherapy

fisonomía /fisono'mia/ *f*, physiognomy

fistol /fis'tol/ *m*, *Mexico* tie pin; crafty person, sly person

fístula /'fistula/ *f*, pipe, conduit; *Mus.* pipe; *Surg.* fistula

fisura /fi'sura/ *f*, fissure

flaccidez /flaksi'ðes; flakθi'ðeθ/ *f*, flabbiness

fláccido /'flaksiðo; 'flakθiðo/ *a* flaccid, soft, flabby

flaco /'flako/ *a* thin; weak, feeble; *Fig.* weak-minded; dispirited. *m*, failing, weakness. *Inf.* **hacer un f. servicio,** to do an ill turn. **estar f. de memoria,** to have a weak memory

flagelación /flahela'sion; flahela'θion/ *f*, flagellation

flagelante /flahe'lante/ *m*, flagellant

flagelar /flahe'lar/ *vt* to scourge; *Fig.* lash

flagelo /fla'helo/ *m*, whip, scourge

flagrante /fla'grante/ *a* *Poet.* refulgent; present; actual. **en f.,** in the very act, flagrante delicto

flagrar /fla'grar/ *vi* *Poet.* to blaze, be refulgent

flamante /fla'mante/ *a* resplendent; brand-new; fresh, spick-and-span

flamenco /fla'menko/ **(-ca)** *m*, *Ornith.* flamingo. *a* and *n* Flemish. *a* Andalusian; gypsy; buxom, fresh

flan /flan/ *m*, baked custard, creme caramel. **estar como un f.,** to shake like a leaf, be nervous

flanco /'flanko/ *m*, side; *Mil.* flank

flanquear /flanke'ar/ *vt* *Mil.* to flank

flanqueo /flan'keo/ *m*, *Mil.* outflanking

flaquear /flake'ar/ *vi* to grow weak; weaken; totter (buildings, etc.); be disheartened, flag

flaqueza /fla'kesa; fla'keθa/ *f*, weakness; thinness; faintness, feebleness; frailty, fault; loss of zeal

flato /'flato/ *m*, flatulence, gas

flatulento /flatu'lento/ *a* flatulent, gassy

flauta /'flauta/ *f*, flute

flautín /flau'tin/ *m*, piccolo

flautista /flau'tista/ *mf* flutist

flebitis /fle'βitis/ *f*, phlebitis

flecha /'fletʃa/ *f*, arrow, dart

flechar /fle'tʃar/ *vt* to shoot an arrow or dart; wound or kill with arrows; *Inf.* inspire love; *vi* bend a bow to shoot

flechazo /fle'tʃaso; fle'tʃaθo/ *m*, wound with an arrow; *Inf.* love at first sight

flechero /fle'tʃero/ *m*, archer; arrow maker

fleco /'fleko/ *m*, fringe; fringe (of hair)

fleje /'flehe/ *m*, iron hoop (for barrels, etc.)

flema /'flema/ *f*, phlegm; sluggishness

flemático /fle'matiko/ *a* phlegmatic; sluggish

flemón /fle'mon/ *m*, gumboil; abscess

flequetero, -a /fleke'tero/ *a*, *Lat. Am.* dishonest, tricky

flequillo /fle'kiyo; fle'kiʎo/ *m*, fringe (of hair)

fletamento /fleta'mento/ *m*, chartering (a ship)

fletar /fle'tar/ *vt* to charter a ship; embark merchandise or people

flete /'flete/ *m*, freightage; cargo, freight

flexibilidad /fleksiβili'ðað/ *f*, flexibility; suppleness, adaptability

flexible /fle'ksiβle/ *a* pliant, supple; flexible, adaptable. *m*, *Elec.* flex

flirtear /flirte'ar/ *vi* to flirt

flirteo /flir'teo/ *m*, flirtation

flojedad /flohe'ðað/ *f*, flabbiness; weakness, feebleness; laziness, negligence

flojo /'floho/ *a* flabby; slack, loose; weak, feeble; lazy, slothful; poor (of a literary work, etc.)

floqueado /floke'aðo/ *a* fringed

flor /flor/ *f*, flower; best (of anything); bloom (on fruit); virginity; grain (of leather); compliment (gen. *pl*); menstruation (gen. *pl*). **f. de especia,** mace. **f. de la edad,** prime, youth. **f. del cuclillo,** mayflower. **f. del estudiante,** French marigold. **flores de mano,** artificial flowers. **flores de oblón,** hops. **a f. de,** on the surface of, level with. **andarse en flores,** *Fig.* to beat around the bush. **echar flores,** to pay compliments. **en f.,** in bloom

flora /'flora/ *f*, flora

floral /flo'ral/ *a* floral. **juegos florales,** poetry contest

florear /flore'ar/ *vt* to adorn with flowers; *vi* execute a flourish on the guitar

florecer /flore'ser; flore'θer/ *vi irr* to flower, bloom; flourish, prosper; *vr* grow mold (of cheese, etc.). See **conocer**

floreciente /flore'siente; flore'θiente/ *a* flowering; prosperous

florecimiento /floresi'miento; floreθi'miento/ *m*, flowering; prosperity

floreo /flo'reo/ *m*, witty conversation; flourish (on the guitar or in fencing)

florero /flo'rero/ *m*, vase; flower pot; *Art.* flower piece

florescencia /flores'sensia; flores'θenθia/ *f*, flowering; flowering season, florescence

floresta /flo'resta/ *f*, grove, wooded park, woodland; *Fig.* collector of beautiful things; anthology

florete /flo'rete/ *m*, fencing foil

floricultor /florikul'tor/ **(-ra)** *n* floriculturist

floricultura /florikul'tura/ *f*, floriculture

floridamente /floriða'mente/ *adv* elegantly, with a flourish

florido /flo'riðo/ *a* flowery; best, most select; florid, ornate

florilegio /flori'lehio/ *m*, anthology, collection

florín /flo'rin/ *m*, florin

florista /flo'rista/ *mf* artificial-flower maker; florist; flower seller

florón /flo'ron/ *m*, large flower; *Archit.* fleuron; honorable deed

flota /'flota/ *f*, fleet of merchant ships. **f. aérea,** air force

flotación /flota'sion; flota'θion/ *f*, floating. *Naut.* **línea de f.,** water line

flotador /flota'ðor/ a floating. m, float
flotamiento /flota'miento/ m, floating
flotante /flo'tante/ a floating
flotar /flo'tar/ vi to float on water or in air
flote /'flote/ m, floating. **a f.,** afloat; independent, solvent
flotilla /flo'tiya; flo'tiʎa/ f, flotilla; fleet of small ships. **f. aérea,** air fleet
fluctuación /fluktua'sion; fluktua'θion/ f, fluctuation; hesitation, vacillation
fluctuante /fluk'tuante/ a fluctuating
fluctuar /fluktu'ar/ vi to fluctuate; be in danger (things); vacillate, hesitate; undulate; oscillate
fluidez /flui'ðes; flui'ðeθ/ f, fluidity
flúido /'fluiðo/ a fluid; fluent. m, fluid; Elec. current
fluir /flu'ir/ vi irr to flow. See **huir**
flujo /'fluho/ m, flow, flux; rising tide. **f. de sangre,** hemorrhage
fluminense /flumi'nense/ formal a of Rio de Janeiro; mf native of Rio de Janeiro; resident of Rio de Janeiro
fluorescencia /fluores'sensia; fluores'θenθia/ f, fluorescence
fluorescente /fluores'sente; fluores'θente/ a fluorescent
flus /flus/ m, Colombia, Venezuela suit (of clothes)
fluvial /flu'βial/ a fluvial
flux /fluks/ m, flush (in cards)
foca /'foka/ f, Zool. seal
focal /fo'kal/ a focal
foco /'foko/ m, focus; center; origin; source; Theat. spotlight; core (of an abscess)
fofo /'fofo/ a spongy, soft; flabby
fogata /fo'gata/ f, bonfire
fogón /fo'gon/ m, fire, cooking area, kitchen range, kitchen stove; furnace of a steamboiler; vent of a firearm
fogonazo /fogo'naso; fogo'naθo/ m, powder flash
fogonero /fogo'nero/ m, stoker
fogosidad /fogosi'ðað/ f, enthusiasm; vehemence; ardor
fogoso /fo'goso/ a ardent; vehement; enthusiastic
folclórico /fol'kloriko/ a pertaining to folklore
folclorista /folklo'rista/ mf folklorist
folículo /fo'likulo/ m, follicle
folio /'folio/ m, leaf of a book or manuscript, folio. **en f.,** in folio
follaje /fo'yahe; fo'ʎahe/ m, foliage; leafy ornamentation; crude, unnecessary decoration; verbosity
folletín /foye'tin; foʎe'tin/ m, feuilleton, literary article; serial story; Inf. dime novel, potboiler
folletinista /foyeti'nista; foʎeti'nista/ mf pamphleteer
folleto /fo'yeto; fo'ʎeto/ m, pamphlet, leaflet
follisca /fo'jiska; fo'ʎiska/ f, Lat. Am. brawl
follón /fo'yon; fo'ʎon/ a lazy; caddish; craven
fomentación /fomenta'sion; fomenta'θion/ f, Med. fomentation, poultice
fomentador /fomenta'ðor/ a fomenting. m, fomenter
fomentar /fomen'tar/ vt to warm, foment; incite, instigate; Med. apply poultices
fomento /fo'mento/ m, heat, shelter; fuel; protection, encouragement; Med. fomentation
fonda /'fonda/ f, inn; restaurant
fondeadero /fondea'ðero/ m, anchorage, anchoring ground
fondear /fonde'ar/ vt Naut. to sound; search a ship; examine carefully; vi Naut. anchor; vr, Lat. Am. get rich
fondillos /fon'diyos; fon'diʎos/ m pl, seat (of the trousers)
fondista /fon'dista/ mf owner of an inn or restaurant
fondo /'fondo/ m, bottom (of a well, etc.); bed (of the sea, etc.); depth; rear, portion at the back; ground (of fabrics); background; Com. capital; Com. stock; Fig. fund (of humor, etc.); character, nature; temperament; Fig. substance, core, essence; Naut. bottom; pl Com. resources, funds. **f. de amortización,** sinking fund. **f. doble** or **f. secreto,** false bottom. **f. muerto, f. perdido** or **f. vitalicio,** life annuity. Com. **fondos inactivos,** idle capital. **a fondo,** com-

pletely, thoroughly. **artículo de f.,** editorial, lead article. Sports. **carrera de f.,** long-distance race. Naut. **irse a f.,** to sink, founder
fonética /fo'netika/ f, phonetics
fonético /fo'netiko/ a phonetic
fonetista /fone'tista/ mf phonetician
fonógrafo /fo'nografo/ m, phonograph
fonología /fonolo'hia/ f, phonology
fonológico /fono'lohiko/ a phonological
fontanar /fonta'nar/ m, spring, stream
fontanería /fontane'ria/ f, pipe laying, plumbing
fontanero /fonta'nero/ m, pipe layer; plumber
forajido /fora'hiðo/ **(-da)** a fugitive, outlawed. n robber, fugitive
foramen /fora'men/ m, Lat. Am. hole
forastero /foras'tero/ **(-ra)** a strange, foreign; alien, exotic. n stranger
forcejear /forsehe'ar; forθehe'ar/ vi to struggle; try, strive; oppose, contradict
forcejo /for'seho; for'θeho/ m, struggle; endeavor; opposition, hostility
fórceps /'forseps; 'forθeps/ m pl, forceps
forense /fo'rense/ a forensic
forillo /fo'riyo; fo'riʎo/ m, Theat. backdrop
forja /'forha/ f, forge
forjador /forha'ðor/ m, smith, ironworker
forjar /for'har/ vt to forge; fabricate; create; counterfeit
forma /'forma/ f, shape, form; arrangement; method; style; manifestation, expression; formula, formulary; ceremonial; Print. form; manner; means, way; mold, matrix; style of handwriting. Law. **en debida f.,** in due form
formación /forma''sion; forma'θion/ f, formation; form, contour, shape; (Mil. Geol.) formation. **f. del censo,** census taking
formador /forma'ðor/ a forming, shaping
formal /for'mal/ a apparent, formal; serious, punctilious, steady; truthful, reliable; sedate; orderly, regular, methodical
formaldehído /formalde'iðo/ m, formaldehyde
formalidad /formali'ðað/ f, orderliness, propriety; formality; requirement, requisite; ceremony; seriousness, sedateness; punctiliousness
formalismo /forma'lismo/ m, formalism; bureaucracy, red tape
formalizar /formali'sar; formali'θar/ vt to put into final form; legalize; formulate, enunciate; vr take seriously (a joke)
formar /for'mar/ vt to shape; form; educate, mold; Mil. form. **formarle causa a uno,** to bring charges against someone. vr develop, grow; Mexico get in line
formativo /forma'tiβo/ a formative
formato /for'mato/ m, Print. format; Chem. formate
formidable /formi'ðaβle/ a formidable, awe-inspiring; huge, enormous
fórmula /'formula/ f, formula; prescription; mode of expression. (Math. Chem.) **f. clásica,** standard formula
formular /formu'lar/ vt to formulate; prescribe
formulario /formu'lario/ m, Law. formulary; handbook; Lat. Am. form
formulismo /formu'lismo/ m, formulism; bureaucracy, red tape
fornicación /fornika'sion; fornika'θion/ f, fornication
fornicador /fornika'ðor/ **(-ra)** a and n fornicator
fornicar /forni'kar/ vi to fornicate
fornido /for'niðo/ a stalwart, muscular, strong
foro /'foro/ m, forum; law courts; law, bar, legal profession; Theat. back scenery; leasehold
forraje /fo'rrahe/ m, forage, fodder; foraging
forrajeador /forrahea'ðor/ m, forager
forrajear /forrahe'ar/ vt to gather forage, go foraging
forrar /fo'rrar/ vt Sew. to line; cover, encase, make a cover for
forro /'forro/ m, lining, inner covering; cover (of a book); Argentina condom; Lat. Am. fraud, swindle
fortalecedor /fortale se'ðor; fortaleθe'ðor/ a fortifying
fortalecer /fortale'ser; fortale'θer/ vt irr to fortify. See **conocer**

fortaleza /forta'lesa; forta'leθa/ *f*, vigor; fortitude; fortress; natural defense; *Lat. Am.* stench, stink. *Aer.* **f. volante,** flying fortress

fortificable /fortifi'kaβle/ *a* fortifiable

fortificación /fortifika'sion; fortifika'θion/ *f*, fortification

fortificador /fortifika'ðor/ *a* fortifying

fortificar /fortifi'kar/ *vt* to fortify

fortísimo /for'tisimo/ *a sup* **fuerte** extremely strong

fortuito /for'tuito/ *a* fortuitous, chance

fortuna /for'tuna/ *f*, fate, destiny; fortune, capital, estate; tempest. **por f.,** fortunately. **probar f.,** to try one's luck

forzado /for'saðo; for'θaðo/ *a* forced, obliged. *m*, convict condemned to the galleys

forzador /forsa'ðor; forθa'ðor/ *m*, violator, seducer

forzar /for'sar; for'θar/ *vt irr* to force, break open; take by force; rape, ravish; oblige, compel. *Pres. Ind.* **fuerzo, fuerzas, fuerza, fuerzan.** *Preterite* **forcé, forzaste, etc.** *Pres. Subjunc.* **fuerce, fuerces, fuerce, forcemos, forcéis, fuercen**

forzoso /for'soso; for'θoso/ *a* obligatory, unavoidable, necessary

forzudo /for'suðo; for'θuðo/ *a* brawny, stalwart

fosa /'fosa/ *f*, grave; socket (of a joint). **f. común,** potter's field.

fosar /fo'sar/ *vt* to undermine; dig a trench around

fosfato /fos'fato/ *m*, phosphate

fosforecer /fosfore'ser; fosfore'θer/ *vi irr* to phosphoresce. See **conocer**

fosforera /fosfo'rera/ *f*, matchbox

fosforero /fosfo'rero/ **(-ra)** *n* match seller

fosforescente /fosfores'sente; fosfores'θente/ *a* phosphorescent

fósforo /'fosforo/ *m*, phosphorus; match; morning star

fósil /'fosil/ *a* and *m*, fossil; *Inf.* antique

foso /'foso/ *m*, hole, hollow, pit; trench; pit (in garages); *Theat.* room under the stage.

foto /'foto/ *f*, snapshot, photo

fotocopia /foto'kopia/ *f*, photocopy

fotogénico /foto'heniko/ *a* photogenic

fotograbado /fotogra'βaðo/ *m*, photogravure

fotografía /fotogra'fia/ *f*, photography; photograph

fotografiar /fotogra'fiar/ *vt* to photograph

fotográfico /foto'grafiko/ *a* photographic

fotógrafo /fo'tografo/ *m*, photographer

fotograma /foto'grama/ *m*, (cinema) shot

fotoquímica /foto'kimika/ *f*, photochemistry

fotostato /toto'stato/ *m*, photostat

frac /frak/ *m*, tail coat

fracasar /fraka'sar/ *vi* to break, crumble, be shattered; collapse (of plans, etc.); fail; be disappointed, frustrate

fracaso /fra'kaso/ *m*, shattering; collapse (of plans, etc.); disaster; failure, disappointment, downfall, frustration

fracción /frak'sion; frak'θion/ *f*, division into parts; fraction. **f. impropia,** *Math.* improper fraction

fractura /frak'tura/ *f*, fracture. **f. conminuta,** compound fracture

fracturar /fraktu'rar/ *vt* to fracture

fragancia /fra'gansia; fra'ganθia/ *f*, fragrance, perfume; renown, good name

fragante /fra'gante/ *a* fragrant; perfumed; flagrant

fragata /fra'gata/ *f*, frigate

frágil /'frahil/ *a* fragile, brittle; perishable, frail; weak, sinful

fragilidad /frahili'ðað/ *f*, fragility; frailty, sinfulness

fragmentario /fragmen'tario/ *a* fragmentary

fragmento /frag'mento/ *m*, fragment

fragor /fra'gor/ *m*, noise, crash

fragosidad /fragosi'ðað/ *f*, roughness, rockiness, unevenness

fragoso /fra'goso/ *a* craggy, rocky; rough; noisy, clamorous

fragua /'fragua/ *f*, forge

fraguar /fra'guar/ *vt* to forge, work; plot, scheme; *vi* set (concrete, etc.)

fraile /'fraile/ *m*, friar, monk. *Inf.* **f. de misa y olla,** ignorant friar

frailesco /frai'lesko/ *a Inf.* pertaining to friars, friarlike

frambuesa /fram'buesa/ *f*, raspberry

francachela /franka'tʃela/ *f, Inf.* binge

francés /fran'ses; fran'θes/ **(-esa)** *a* French. *n* Frenchman (-woman). *m*, French (language). **a la francesa,** in French fashion

francesilla /franse'siya; franθe'siʎa/ *f, Cul.* French roll

Francia /'fransia; 'franθia/ France

francmasón /frankma'son/ **(-ona)** *n* Freemason

francmasonería /frankmasone'ria/ *f*, freemasonry

franco /'franko/ *a* generous, liberal; exempt; sincere, genuine, frank; duty-free; Frank; Franco (in compound words). *m*, franc (coin). **f. de porte,** post-free; prepaid

francotirador /frankotira'ðor/ *m*, sharpshooter, franc tireur

franela /fra'nela/ *f*, flannel; *Lat. Am.* undershirt; T-shirt

frangir /fran'hir/ *vt* to divide, quarter

frangollar /fraŋgo'yar; fraŋgo'ʎar/ *vt* to scamp, skimp (work); botch, bungle

franja /'franha/ *f*, fringe; border, trimming; stripe. *Radio.* **f. undosa,** wave band

franjar /fran'har/ *vt Sew.* to fringe, trim

franqueadora /frankea'ðora/ *f*, postage meter

franquear /franke'ar/ *vt* to exempt; make free, make a gift of; clear the way; stamp, prepay; free (slaves); *vr* fall in easily with others' plans; make confidences

franqueo /fran'keo/ *m*, exemption; bestowal, making free; postage, stamping; enfranchisement (of slaves)

franqueza /fran'kesa; fran'keθa/ *f*, exemption, freedom; generosity, liberality; sincerity, frankness

franquicia /fran'kisia; fran'kiθia/ *f*, exemption from excise duties

franquista /fran'kista/ *mf* Franquist, supporter of Franco

frasco /'frasko/ *m*, bottle, flask; powder flask or horn. **f. cuentagotas,** drop bottle

frase /'frase/ *f*, sentence; phrase; epigram; idiom, style. **f. hecha,** cliché

frasear /frase'ar/ *vt* to phrase

fraseología /fraseolo'hia/ *f*, phraseology; wording

fratás /fra'tas/ *m*, plastering trowel

fraternal /frater'nal/ *a* brotherly

fraternidad /fraterni'ðað/ *f*, fraternity, brotherhood

fraternizar /fraterni'sar; fraterni'θar/ *vi* to fraternize

fraterno /fra'terno/ *a* fraternal

fratricida /fratri'siða; fratri'θiða/ *a* fratricidal. *mf* fratricide

fratricidio /fratri'siðio; fratri'θiðio/ *m*, fratricide (act)

fraude /'frauðe/ *m*, fraud, deception

fraudulento /frauðu'lento/ *a* fraudulent

fray /frai/ *m*, *abb* **fraile.** Always followed by a proper name (e.g. *F. Bartolomé*, Friar Bartholomew)

frazada /fra'saða; fra'θaða/ *f*, blanket

frecuencia /fre'kuensia; fre'kuenθia/ *f*, frequency. **f. radioeléctrica,** radiofrequency

frecuentación /frekuenta'sion; frekuenta'θion/ *f*, frequenting, visiting

frecuentador /frekuenta'ðor/ **(-ra)** *n* frequenter

frecuentar /frekuen'tar/ *vt* to frequent

frecuente /fre'kuente/ *a* frequent

fregada /fre'gaða/ *f, Lat. Am.* bother, hassle, nuisance

fregadero /frega'ðero/ *m*, kitchen sink

fregado /fre'gaðo/ *m*, scrubbing; rubbing; scouring; washing; *Inf.* murky business

fregador /frega'ðor/ *m*, kitchen sink; scrub brush; dishcloth. **f. mecánico de platos,** dishwasher

fregandera /fregan'dera/ *f, Mexico* charwoman, cleaning woman

fregar /fre'gar/ *vt* to rub; scour; wash (dishes). See **cegar**

fregona /fre'gona/ *f*, kitchen maid

fregotear /fregote'ar/ *vt Inf.* to clean or scour inefficiently

freiduría /freiðu'ria/ f, fried-fish shop

freír /fre'ir/ vt irr Cul. to fry. See **reír**

frenar /fre'nar/ vt to restrain, hold back; bridle, check; Mech. brake

frenesí /frene'si/ m, madness, frenzy; vehemence, exaltation

frenético /fre'netiko/ a mad, frenzied; vehement, exalted

freno /'freno/ m, bridle; Mech. brake; restraint, check. **f. de pedal,** foot brake. **f. neumático,** vacuum brake, pneumatic brake

frente /'frente/ f, brow, forehead; front portion; countenance; head; heading; beginning (of a letter, etc.). m, Mil. front. mf facade; front; obverse (of coins). adv in front, opposite. **f. a f.,** face to face. **con la f. levantada,** with head held high; proudly; insolently. **de f.,** abreast

freo /'freo/ m, strait, narrow channel

fresa /'fresa/ f, strawberry plant and fruit (especially small or wild varieties); Mech. milling cutter, miller

fresadora /fresa'ðora/ f, milling machine

fresal /fre'sal/ m, strawberry bed

fresca /'freska/ f, cool air; fresh air; Inf. home truth

fresco /'fresko/ a cool; fresh, new; recent; buxom, fresh-colored; calm, serene; Inf. impudent, cheeky, bold; thin (cloths). m, coolness; fresh air; Art. fresco. **al f.,** in the open air. **hacer f.,** to be cool or fresh

frescote /fres'kote/ a Inf. ruddy and corpulent

frescura /fres'kura/ f, coolness; freshness; pleasant verdure and fertility; Inf. cheek, nerve; piece of insolence; unconcern, indifference; calmness, serenity

fresero /fre'sero/ **(-ra)** n strawberry seller

fresno /'fresno/ m, Bot. ash

fresón /fre'son/ m, strawberry (large, cultivated varieties)

fresquera /fres'kera/ f, meat locker; cool place

fresquería /freske'ria/ f, Mexico refreshment stand

fresquista /fres'kista/ mf fresco painter

friable /'friaβle/ a brittle; friable, powdery

frialdad /frial'daθ/ f, coldness, chilliness; Med. frigidity; indifference, lack of interest; foolishness; negligence

fríamente /fria'mente/ adv coldly; coolly, with indifference; dully, flatly

fricción /frik'sion; frik'θion/ f, friction

friccionar /friksio'nar; frikθio'nar/ vt to rub; give a massage

friega /'friega/ f, friction, massage

frigidez /frihi'ðes; frihi'ðeθ/ f, See **frialdad**

frígido /'frihiðo/ a frigid

frigio /'frihio/ a and n Phrygian

frigorífico /frigo'rifiko/ a refrigerative. m, refrigerator, cold-storage locker

frijol /fri'hol/ m, bean; Bot. kidney bean. **frijoles refritos con queso,** Mexico refried beans with cheese

frío /'frio/ a cold; Med. frigid; indifferent, uninterested; dull, uninteresting; inefficient. m, coldness, chill; cold

friolera /frio'lera/ f, bagatelle, trifle, mere nothing

friolero /frio'lero/ a sensitive to cold

frisa /'frisa/ f, frieze cloth

frisar /fri'sar/ vt to frizz, curl (cloth); scrub, rub; vi approach, be nearly (e.g. Frisa en los setenta años, He's nearly seventy)

friso /'friso/ m, frieze; dado, border

fritada /fri'taða/ f, Cul. fry, fried food

frito /'frito/ a fried

fritura /fri'tura/ f, frying; fried food

frivolidad /friβoli'ðaθ/ f, frivolity

frivolité /friβoli'te/ m, Sew. tatting

frívolo /'friβolo/ a frivolous, superficial; futile, unconvincing

fronda /'fronda/ f, Bot. leaf; frond (of ferns); pl foliage

frondoso /fron'doso/ a leafy

frontera /fron'tera/ f, frontier; facade

fronterizo /fronte'riso; fronte'riθo/ a frontier; facing, opposite

frontero /fron'tero/ a facing, opposite. m, (Obs. Mil.) frontier commander

frontispicio /frontis'pisio; frontis'piθio/ m, frontispiece; facade; Fig. Inf. face, dial

frontón /fron'ton/ m, pelota court; jai alai court; Archit. pediment; Mexico jai alai

frotamiento, frote /frota'miento, 'frote/ m, rubbing, friction

frotar /fro'tar/ vt to rub

frotis /'frotis/ m, Med. smear

fructífero /fruk'tifero/ a fruitful, fructiferous

fructuoso /fruk'tuoso/ a fruitful, fertile; useful

frufrú /fru'fru/ m, rustle (of silk, etc.)

frugal /fru'gal/ a frugal; saving, economical

frugalidad /frugali'ðaθ/ f, frugality, abstemiousness, moderation

fruición /frui'sion; frui'θion/ f, enjoyment; fruition; satisfaction

fruir /fruir/ vi irr to enjoy what one has long desired. See **huir**

frunce /'frunse; 'frunθe/ m, Sew. shirring; gather; ruffling; tuck; pucker; wrinkle

fruncimiento /frunsi'miento; frunθi'miento/ m, wrinkling; puckering; Sew. shirring

fruncir /frun'sir; frun'θir/ vt to frown; purse (the lips); pucker; Sew. shirr, pleat, gather; reduce in size; conceal the truth; vr pretend to be prudish. **f. el ceño,** to knit one's brow, scowl

fruslería /frusle'ria/ f, trifle, nothing

frustración /frustra'sion; frustra'θion/ f, frustration

frustrar /frus'trar/ vt to disappoint; frustrate, thwart

fruta /'fruta/ f, fruit; Inf. consequence, result. **f. bomba,** Cuba papaya **f. de hueso,** stone fruit. Cul. **f. de sartén,** fritter

frutal /fru'tal/ a fruit-bearing. m, fruit tree

frutar /fru'tar/ vi to bear fruit

frutería /frute'ria/ f, fruit

frutero /fru'tero/ **(-ra)** a fruit. n fruit seller. m, fruit dish; Art. painting of fruit; basket of imitation fruit

frútice /'frutise; 'frutiθe/ m, bush, shrub

fruticultura /frutikul'tura/ f, fruit farming

fruto /'fruto/ m, fruit; product, result; profit, proceeds; Agr. grain

fu /fu/ spitting (of cats). interj expression of scorn. Inf. **ni f. ni fa,** neither one thing nor the other

fucsia /'fuksia/ f, fuchsia

fuego /'fuego/ m, fire; conflagration; firing (of firearms); beacon; hearth, home; rash; ardor; heat (of an argument, etc.); interj **¡F.!** Mil. Fire! **fuegos artificiales,** fireworks. **a sangre y f.,** by fire and sword. Mil. **hacer f.,** to fire (a weapon). **pegar f.,** to set on fire

fuelle /'fueye; 'fueʎe/ m, bellows; bag (of a bagpipe); Sew. pucker, wrinkle; hood (of a carriage, etc.); wind cloud; Inf. talebearer. **f. de pie,** foot pump

fuente /'fuente/ f, stream, spring; fountain; meat dish; genesis, origin; source, headwaters; tap

fuera /'fuera/ adv outside, out. interj get out! **f. de,** besides, in addition to. **f. de alcance,** out of reach. **f. de sí,** beside oneself (with rage, etc.). **de f.,** from the outside. **por f.,** on the outside, externally

fuereño, -a /fue'reɲo/ mf, Mexico foreigner

fuero /'fuero/ m, municipal charter; jurisdiction; compilation of laws; legal right or privilege; pl Inf. arrogance. **los fueros de León,** the laws of León

fuerte /'fuerte/ a strong, resistant; robust; spirited, vigorous; hard (of diamonds, etc.); rough, uneven; impregnable; terrible, tremendous; overweight (of coins); active; efficacious, effective; expert, knowledgeable; Gram. strong; intense; loud; tough. m, fort; talent, strong point; Mus. forte. adv strongly; excessively. **tener genio f.,** to be quick-tempered

fuerza /'fuersa; 'fuerθa/ f, strength; power, might; force, efficacy; fortress; Mech. stiffening; Mech. power; violence; toughness, durability, solidity; potency; authority; courage; vigor; pl Fig. Inf. livewires, influential people. **a f. de,** by means of, by dint of. **a la f.,** forcibly. **en f. de,** because of, on account of. **por f.,** necessarily, unavoidably; by main force. **ser f.,** to be necessary **mayor,** by main force.

fuga /'fuga/ f, flight, escape, running away; leak (gas, etc.); elopement; Mus. fugue; ardor, strength. **f. de cerebros,** brain drain

fugarse /fu'garse/ vr to run away; elope; escape
fugaz /fu'gas; fu'gaθ/ a fugitive; fleeting, brief
fugitivo /fuhi'tiβo/ **(-va)** a fugitive; runaway, escaping; transient. n fugitive
fulano /fu'lano/ **(-na)** n so-and-so, such a person **f., zutano, y mengano,** Inf. Tom, Dick, and Harry
fulcro /'fulkro/ m, fulcrum
fulgente, fúlgido /ful'hente, 'fulhiðo/ a brilliant, shining
fulgor /ful'gor/ m, brilliance, brightness
fulgurar /fulgu'rar/ vi to shine, be resplendent, scintillate; flare
fulguroso /fulgu'roso/ a shining, sparkling
fullería /fuʎe'ria; fuʎe'ria/ f, cheating at play; craftiness, low guile
fullero /fu'ʎero; fu'ʎero/ **(-ra)** a cheating; crafty, astute. n cheat, cardsharper
fulminante /fulmi'nante/ a Med. fulminant; fulminating; thundering. m, percussion cap
fulminar /fulmi'nar/ vt to fulminate (all meanings)
fulminato /fulmi'nato/ m, Chem. fulminate
fulmíneo, fulminoso /ful'mineo, fulmi'noso/ a fulminous, pertaining to lightning
fumadero /fuma'ðero/ m, smoking room
fumador /fuma'ðor/ **(-ra)** a smoking. n smoker. **«No fumadores»,** "Nonsmoking" (area)
fumar /fu'mar/ vi to smoke; vr Inf. dissipate, waste
fumarola /fuma'rola/ f, fumarole
fumigación /fumiga'sion; fumiga'θion/ f, fumigation
fumigador /fumiga'ðor/ **(-ra)** n fumigator
fumigar /fumi'gar/ vt to fumigate
fumigatorio /fumiga'torio/ a fumigatory. m, perfume burner
fumista /fu'mista/ mf stove maker; stove dealer; Argentina joker, tease
fumistería /fumiste'ria/ f, stove factory or store
funámbulo /fu'nambulo/ n tightrope walker, acrobat
función /fun'sion; fun'θion/ f, function; working, operation; Theat. performance; activity, duty; ceremony; celebration; Math. function; Mil. battle
funcional /funsio'nal; funθio'nal/ a functional
funcionamiento /funsiona'miento; funθiona'miento/ m, functioning
funcionar /funsio'nar; funθio'nar/ vi to function, work. **«No funciona»,** "Out of order"
funcionario /funsio'nario; funθio'nario/ m, functionary, official; civil servant
funda /'funda/ f, case, cover, sheath; hold-all. **f. de almohada,** pillowcase
fundación /funda'sion; funda'θion/ f, foundation
fundadamente /fundaða'mente/ adv with reason, on good evidence
fundador /funda'ðor/ **(-ra)** n founder, creator; originator
fundamental /funda'mental/ a fundamental
fundamento /funda'mento/ m, Mas. foundation; basis; basic principle, reason; origin, root
fundar /fun'dar/ vt to build, erect; base; found, institute; create, establish; vr (with en) found, base upon. **f. una compañía,** Com. to float a company
fundición /fundi'sion; fundi'θion/ f, foundry; smelting, founding, casting; cast iron; Print. font
fundido fotográfico /fun'diðo foto'grafiko/ m, composite photograph

fundidor /fundi'ðor/ m, founder, smelter.
fundir /fun'dir/ vt to melt; found, smelt; cast (metals); vr join together, unite; Elec. blow (fuses)
fúnebre /'funeβre/ a funeral; dismal, lugubrious, mournful
funerala, /fune'rala,/ **(a la)** adv Mil. with reversed arms
funerales /fune'rales/ m pl, funeral; Eccl. memorial masses
funeraria /fune'raria/ f, funeral home, undertaker
funéreo /fu'nereo/ a funereal, mournful
funestidad /funesti'ðað/ f, Mexico calamity, catastrophe
funesto /fu'nesto/ a unlucky, unfortunate; mournful, melancholy, sad
fungoso /fuŋ'goso/ a spongy, fungous
funicular /funiku'lar/ a funicular. n cable car
furgón /fur'gon/ m, wagon; van; guard's van, baggage car, luggage cart. **f. postal,** mail truck
furia /'furia/ f, Myth. fury; rage, wrath; fit of madness; raging, violence (of the elements); speed, haste
furibundo /furi'βundo/ a frantic, furious; raging
fúrico /'furiko/ a stark raving mad
furioso /fu'rioso/ a furious, enraged; mad, insane; violent, terrible; enormous, excessive
furor /fu'ror/ m, fury, rage; poetic frenzy; violence; furor
furtivo /fur'tiβo/ a furtive; covert, clandestine; pirate (editions)
fusa /'fusa/ f, demisemiquaver
fusco /'fusko/ a dark
fuselado /fuse'laðo/ a streamlined
fuselaje /fuse'lahe/ m, fuselage
fusible /fu'siβle/ a fusible. m, Elec. fuse; fuse wire
fusil /fu'sil/ m, rifle
fusilamiento /fusila'miento/ m, execution by shooting
fusilar /fusi'lar/ vt to execute by shooting; Inf. plagiarize
fusilazo /fusi'laso; fusi'laθo/ m, rifle shot
fusión /fu'sion/ f, melting, liquefying; fusion; blending; mixture, union; Com. merger, amalgamation
fusionar /fusio'nar/ vt to blend, fuse, merge; vr Com. combine, form a merger
fusta /'fusta/ f, brushwood; whip
fustán /fus'tan/ m Lat. Am. skirt
fuste /'fuste/ m, wood, timber; Poet. saddle; Fig. core, essence; importance, substance; shaft of a lance; Archit. shaft. **hombre de buen f.,** a man with a good (physical) constitution
fustigar /fusti'gar/ vt to whip, lash; rebuke harshly
fútbol /'futβol/ m, football; soccer
futbolista /futβo'lista/ mf football player; soccer player
fútil /'futil/ a futile, ineffectual, worthless
futilidad /futili'ðað/ f, futility, worthlessness
futura /fu'tura/ f, Law. reversion (of offices); Inf. fiancée
futurismo /futu'rismo/ m, futurism
futurista /futu'rista/ mf futurist
futurístico /futu'ristiko/ a futuristic
futuro /fu'turo/ **(-ra)** a future. m, future. n Inf. betrothed

G

gabacho /ga'βatʃo/ **(-cha)** a and n (inf scornful) Frenchman
gabán /ga'βan/ m, overcoat; cloak
gabardina /gaβar'ðina/ f, gabardine; weatherproof coat
gabarra /ga'βarra/ f, Naut. lighter, gabbard, barge
gabarro /ga'βarro/ m, flaw (in cloth); knot (in stone); snag, drawback; slip, error (in accounts)
gabela /ga'βela/ f, duty, tax; imposition, burden
gabinete /gaβi'nete/ m, study, library; sitting room;

den; Polit. cabinet; collection, museum, gallery; laboratory; boudoir; studio; display cabinet. **g. de lectura,** reading room
gablete /ga'βlete/ m, Archit. gable
gaceta /ga'seta; ga'θeta/ f, bulletin, review, record; newspaper; gazette (official Spanish government organ); Inf. newshound
gacetero /gase'tero; gaθe'tero/ **(-ra)** n newsdealer. m, news reporter
gacetilla /gase'tiya; gaθe'tiʎa/ f, news in brief, mis-

cellany column, society news; gossip column; *Inf.* newshound
gacetillero /gaseti'yero; gaθeti'ʎero/ *m*, paragrapher, penny-a-liner; reporter
gacha /'gatʃa/ *f*, unglazed crock; *pl* pap; porridge
gaché /ga'tʃe/ *m*, (among the Romany) Andalusian; *Inf.* fellow
gacho /'gatʃo/ *a* drooping, bent downward; slouch (hat); (of ears) lop; *Mexico* unpleasant
gachón /ga'tʃon/ *a Inf.* attractive, charming
gaélico /ga'eliko/ *a* and *m*, Gaelic
gafar /ga'far/ *vt* to claw; seize with a hook, hook; mend with a bracket (pottery)
gafas /'gafas/ *f pl*, eyeglasses; goggles; spectacle earhooks; grapplehooks
gafete /ga'fete/ *m*, hook and eye; clasp
gaita /'gaita/ *f*, bagpipe; hand organ; kind of clarinet; *Inf.* neck. **g. gallega,** bagpipe
gaitería /gaite'ria/ *f*, crude, gaudy garment or ornament
gaitero /gai'tero/ *a Inf.* overmerry; loud, crude. *m*, piper
gajes /'gahes/ *m pl*, salary; emoluments; perquisites
gajo /'gaho/ *m*, branch, bough (gen. cut); little cluster (of grapes); bunch (of fruit); quarter (of oranges, etc.); prong (of forks, etc.)
gala /'gala/ *f*, evening or full dress; grace, wit; flower, cream, best; gala; *pl* finery; trappings; wedding presents. **de g.,** full dress. **hacer g. de,** to glory in, boast of
galactita /galak'tita/ *f*, fuller's earth
galaico /ga'laiko/ *a* See **gallego**
galán /ga'lan/ *m*, handsome, well-made man; lover, wooer, gallant; *Theat.* leading man or one of leading male roles
galancete /galan'sete; galan'θete/ *m*, handsome little man; *Theat.* male juvenile lead
galano /ga'lano/ *a* smart, well-dressed; agreeable, pleasing; beautiful; ornamented; *Fig.* elegant (speech, style, etc.)
galante /ga'lante/ *a* gallant, courtly, attentive; flirtatious (of women); licentious
galanteador /galantea'ðor/ *a* flirtatious. *m*, philanderer; wooer
galantear /galante'ar/ *vt* to court; flirt with; make love to; *Fig.* procure assiduously
galanteo /galan'teo/ *m*, courtship; flirtation; love-making; wooing
galantería /galante'ria/ *f*, courtesy; attention, compliment; elegance, grace; gallantry; generosity, liberality
galanura /gala'nura/ *f*, showiness, gorgeousness; elegance, grace; prettiness
galápago /ga'lapago/ *m*, freshwater tortoise; cleat
galardón /galar'ðon/ *m*, reward, recompense, prize
galardonar /galarðo'nar/ *vt* to reward, recompense
galbana /gal'βana/ *f*, *Inf.* laziness, inertia
galbanoso /galβa'noso/ *a Inf.* slothful
galdrufa /gal'drufa/ *f*, top, spinning top
galera /ga'lera/ *f*, van, wagon, cart; *Naut.* galley; prison for women; *Print.* galley; *Central America, Mexico* shed. **echar a galeras,** to condemn to the galleys
galerada /gale'raða/ *f*, galley proof
galería /gale'ria/ *f*, gallery; corridor, passage; collection of paintings; *Mineral.* gallery, drift; *Theat.* gallery
galerna /ga'lerna/ *f*, tempestuous northwest wind (gen. on Spanish north coast)
Gales /'gales/ Wales
galés /ga'les/ **(-esa)** *a* Welsh. *n* Welshman. *m*, Welsh (language)
galga /'galga/ *f*, boulder, rolling stone; female greyhound
galgo /'galgo/ *m*, greyhound. **g. ruso,** borzoi
Galia /'galia/ Gaul
gálibo /'galiβo/ *m*, *Naut.* mold; elegance
galicado /gali'kaðo/ *a* gallicized
galicismo /gali'sismo; gali'θismo/ *m*, gallicism
gálico /'galiko/ *m*, syphilis. *a* gallic
Galilea /gali'lea/ Galilee
galileo /gali'leo/ **(-ea)** *a* and *n* Galilean

galimatías /galima'tias/ *m*, *Inf.* gibberish, nonsense
gallardear /gayarðe'ar; gaʎarðe'ar/ *vi* to behave with ease and grace
gallardete /gayar'ðete; gaʎar'ðete/ *m*, pennant; bunting
gallardía /gayar'ðia; gaʎar'ðia/ *f*, grace, dignity; spirit, dash; courage; liveliness
gallardo /ga'yarðo; ga'ʎarðo/ *a* handsome, upstanding; gallant; spirited; fine, noble; lively
gallear /gaye'ar; gaʎe'ar/ *vi Inf.* to put on airs; be a bully; shout, bawl (with anger, etc.); *Fig. Inf.* stand out
gallego /ga'yego; ga'ʎego/ **(-ga)** *a* and *n* Galician. *m*, Galician (language)
galleta /ga'yeta; ga'ʎeta/ *f*, biscuit; cookie; cracker; *Inf.* slap; anthracite, lump coal; small jar or vessel
gallina /ga'yina; ga'ʎina/ *f*, hen. *mf Inf.* coward. **g. ciega,** blindman's buff. *Inf.* **acostarse con las gallinas,** to go to bed early
gallinaza /gayi'nasa; gaʎi'naθa/ *f*, hen dung
gallinero /gayi'nero; gaʎi'nero/ **(-ra)** *n* poultry dealer. *m*, henhouse; brood of hens; *Theat.* gallery; babel, noisy place
gallito /ga'yito; ga'ʎito/ *m*, small cock; cock of the walk; bully
gallo /'gayo; ga'ʎo/ *m*, *Ornith.* cock; *Inf.* false note (in singing); *Inf.* boss, chief. **g. de viento,** weathercock. *Inf.* **alzar el g.,** to put on airs, boast. **Cada g. canta en su muladar,** Every man is boss in his own house. *Inf.* **Otro g. nos cantara,** Our lot (or fate) would have been very different
gallofero /gayo'fero; gaʎo'fero/ **(-ra)** *a* mendicant, vagabond. *n* beggar
galocha /ga'lotʃa/ *f*, patten, clog; cap with earflaps
galón /ga'lon/ *m*, galloon, braid; *Mil.* stripe; gallon (measure)
galoneadura /galonea'ðura/ *f*, braiding, trimming
galonear /galone'ar/ *vt* to trim with braid
galopante /galo'pante/ *a* galloping (of consumption, etc.)
galopar /galo'par/ *vi* to gallop; *Mech.* wobble
galope /ga'lope/ *m*, gallop. **a** or **de g.,** at the gallop; on the run, quickly. **andar a g. corto,** to canter
galopillo /galo'piyo; galo'piʎo/ *m*, scullion
galopín /galo'pin/ *m*, ragamuffin, urchin; rogue, knave; *Inf.* clever rogue; *Naut.* cabin boy
galvanización /galβanisa'sion; galβaniθa'θion/ *f*, galvanization
galvanizar /galβani'sar; galβani'θar/ *vt Elec.* to galvanize; electroplate; *Fig.* shock into life
gama /'gama/ *f*, *Mus.* scale; gamut, range; doe
gamba /'gamba/ *f*, prawn
gambado /gam'βaðo/ *a Lat. Am.* knock-kneed
gambito /gam'bito/ *m*, gambit (in chess)
gamella /ga'meya; ga'meʎa/ *f*, trough (for washing, feeding animals, etc.)
gamo /'gamo/ *m*, buck (of the fallow deer)
gamuza /ga'musa; ga'muθa/ *f*, chamois; chamois leather
gana /'gana/ *f*, appetite; wish, desire. **de buena g.,** willingly. **de mala g.,** reluctantly. **tener ganas (de),** to wish, desire, want. **no tener g.,** to have no appetite, not be hungry. **No me da la g.,** I don't want (to), I won't
ganable /ga'naβle/ *a* attainable; earnable
ganadería /ganaðe'ria/ *f*, livestock; strain (of cattle); cattle raising; stock farm; cattle dealing
ganadero /gana'ðero/ *m*, cattle raiser or dealer; herdsman
ganado /ga'naðo/ *m*, livestock, herd; flock; hive (of bees); *Inf.* mob. **g. mayor,** cattle, mules, horses. **g. menor,** sheep, goats, etc. **g. moreno,** hogs, swine. **g. vacuno,** cattle
ganador /gana'ðor/ **(-ra)** *a* winning. *n* winner
ganancia /ga'nansia; ga'nanθia/ *f*, winning; gain, profit
ganancial, ganancioso /ganan'sial, ganan'sioso; ganan'θial, ganan'θioso/ *a* gainful, profitable; lucrative
ganapán /gana'pan/ *m*, laborer; porter; *Inf.* boor

ganar /ga'nar/ *vt* to gain; win; conquer; arrive at; earn; surpass, beat; achieve; acquire; *vi* prosper
ganchero /gan'tʃero/ *m*, lumberjack
ganchillo /gan'tʃiyo; gan'tʃiʎo/ *m*, crochet hook; crochet. **hacer g.,** to crochet
gancho /'gantʃo/ *m*, hook; stump (of a branch); shepherd's crook; crochet hook; *Inf.* trickster, pimp; *Inf.* scribble
ganchoso /gan'tʃoso/ *a* hooked; bent; curved
gandujar /gandu'har/ *vt Sew.* to pleat, tuck, shirr
gandul /gan'dul/ **(-la)** *a Inf.* lazy. *n* lazybones, loafer
gandulería /gandule'ria/ *f*, loafing, idleness
ganga /'gaŋga/ *f*, *Mineral.* gangue, matrix; bargain, cinch
ganglio /'gaŋglio/ *m*, ganglion
gangoso /gaŋ'goso/ *a* nasal; with a twang (of speech)
gangrena /gaŋ'grena/ *f*, gangrene
gangrenarse /gaŋgre'narse/ *vr* to become gangrenous, mortify
gangrenoso /gaŋgre'noso/ *a* gangrenous
ganguear /gaŋgue'ar/ *vi* to speak nasally, or with a twang
ganoso /ga'noso/ *a* wishful, desirous, anxious
gansada /gan'saða/ *f*, *Inf.* impertinence, foolishness
ganso /'ganso/ **(-sa)** *n* goose, gander; slow-moving person; yokel, bumpkin
ganuar /ga'nuar/ *vi Lat. Am.* to drizzle
ganzúa /gan'sua; gan'θua/ *f*, skeleton key; *Inf.* picklock, burglar; *Inf.* pumper, inquisitive person
gañán /ga'ɲan/ *m*, farm worker; day laborer; brawny fellow
gañido /ga'ɲiðo/ *m*, yowl, yelp, howl
gañir /ga'ɲir/ *vi irr* to yowl, yelp, howl (of dogs, etc.); crow, croak; *Inf.* talk hoarsely. See **mullir**
garabatear /garaβate'ar/ *vi* to hook, catch with hooks; scribble; *Fig. Inf.* beat around the bush
garabateo /garaβa'teo/ *m*, hooking; scribbling
garabato /gara'βato/ *m*, hook; *Agr.* weed clearer; scrawl, scribble; *Inf.* charm, sex appeal; pothook; boat hook; *pl* gestures, movements (with the hands)
garaje /ga'rahe/ *m*, garage
garambaina /garam'baina/ *f*, tawdry finery; gaudiness; *pl Inf.* grimaces of affectation; *Inf.* scribble, scrawl
garante /ga'rante/ *mf* guarantor; reference (person). *a* responsible, guaranteeing
garantía /garan'tia/ *f*, guarantee; security, pledge; *Law.* warranty
garantir /garan'tir/ *vt* to guarantee; warrant, vouch for
garañón /gara'ɲon/ *m Lat. Am.* stallion
garapiñar /garapi'ɲar/ *vt* to ice, freeze (drinks, syrups, etc.); *Cul.* candy, coat with sugar
garbanzo /gar'βanso; gar'βanθo/ *m*, chickpea. **g. negro,** *Fig.* black sheep
garbillar /garβi'yar; garβi'ʎar/ *vt Agr.* to sift; *Mineral.* riddle
garbo /'garβo/ *m*, jaunty air; grace, elegance; frankness; generosity, liberality
garboso /gar'βoso/ *a* attractive; handsome, sprightly, gay; graceful; munificent
garduña /gar'ðuɲa/ *f*, weasel; marten
garduño /gar'ðuɲo/ **(-ña)** *n Inf.* sneak thief
garete /ga'rete/ **(ir** or **irse al)** *Naut.* to be adrift
garfa /'garfa/ *f*, claw (of a bird or animal)
garfear /garfe'ar/ *vi* to catch with a hook, hook
garfio /'garfio/ *m*, grappling iron, hook, drag hook, cramp; gaff
gargajear /gargahe'ar/ *vi* to expectorate
gargajo /gar'gaho/ *m*, phlegm
garganta /gar'ganta/ *f*, throat; gullet; instep; defile; neck, shaft, narrowest part
gargantear /gargante'ar/ *vi* to warble, trill
gárgara /'gargara/ *f*, gargling (gen. *pl*). **hacer gárgaras,** to gargle
gargarismo /garga'rismo/ *m*, gargling; gargle
gárgol /'gargol/ *a* rotten (eggs). *m*, groove, mortise
gárgola /'gargola/ *f*, *Archit.* gargoyle; linseed
garguero /gar'gero/ *m*, windpipe; esophagus

garita /ga'rita/ *f*, sentry box; porter's lodge; hut; cabin. **g. de señales,** (railroad) signal box
garitero /gari'tero/ *m*, gambling house keeper; gambler
garito /ga'rito/ *m*, gambling house; profits of a gambling house
garra /'garra/ *f*, paw with claws; talon; hand; *Mech.* clamp, claw. *Fig.* **caer en las garras de,** to fall into the clutches (of)
garrafa /ga'rrafa/ *f*, decanter, carafe; carboy
garrapata /garra'pata/ *f*, *Ent.* tick
garrapatear /garrapate'ar/ *vi* to scribble
garrapaticida /garrapati'siða; garrapati'θiða/ *m*, *Lat. Am.* insecticide
garrapato /garra'pato/ *m*, scribble, scrawl
garrido /ga'rriðo/ *a* handsome; gallant; elegant; graceful
garroba /ga'rroβa/ *f*, carob bean
garrocha /ga'rrotʃa/ *f*, goad. **salto a la g.,** pole jumping
garrotazo /garro'taso; garro'taθo/ *m*, blow with a truncheon or cudgel. **dar garrotazos de ciego,** to lay about one
garrote /ga'rrote/ *m*, truncheon, club; *Med.* tourniquet; garrote. **dar g. (a),** to strangle
garrotillo /garro'tiyo; garro'tiʎo/ *m*, croup
garrucha /ga'rrutʃa/ *f*, pulley; *Mech.* gin block
garrulidad /garruli'ðað/ *f*, garrulity, loquaciousness
gárrulo /'garrulo/ *a* twittering, chirping (birds); garrulous; murmuring, babbling (wind, water, etc.)
garza /'garsa/ *f*, heron
garzo /'garso; 'garθo/ *a* blue (gen. of eyes)
gas /gas/ *m*, gas; fumes. **g. asfixiante,** poison gas. **cámara de g.,** gasbag, gas chamber
gasa /'gasa/ *f*, gauze. **tira de g.,** black mourning band
gasconada /gasko'naða/ *f*, bravado, gasconade
gaseosa /gase'osa/ *f*, aerated water
gaseoso /gase'oso/ *a* gaseous
gasista /ga'sista/ *mf* gas fitter; gasman
gasolina /gaso'lina/ *f*, gasoline, petrol
gasómetro /ga'sometro/ *m*, gas meter; gasometer
gastado /gas'taðo/ *a* worn; worn-out; exhausted
gastador /gasta'ðor/ **(-ra)** *a* extravagant, wasteful. *n* spendthrift. *m*, *Mil.* sapper; convict condemned to hard labor
gastar /gas'tar/ *vt* to spend (money); wear out; exhaust; ruin, destroy; display or have habitually; possess, use, wear; *vr* wear out; run down (of a battery)
gasto /'gasto/ *m*, spending; expenditure; consumption (of gas, etc.); expense, cost, charge; wear (and tear). **g. suplementario,** extra charge
gástrico /'gastriko/ *a* gastric
gastritis /gas'tritis/ *f*, gastritis
gastronomía /gastrono'mia/ *f*, gastronomy
gastronómico /gastro'nomiko/ *a* gastronomic
gastrónomo /gas'tronomo/ **(-ma)** *n* gastronome
gata /'gata/ *f*, she-cat; wreath of mist; *Inf.* Madrilenian woman. **a gatas,** on all fours
gatada /ga'taða/ *f*, *Inf.* sly trick
gatear /gate'ar/ *vi* to climb like a cat; *Inf.* crawl on all fours; *vt Inf.* scratch (of a cat); steal, pinch
gatillo /ga'tiyo; ga'tiʎo/ *m*, *dim* small cat; dental forceps; trigger (of gun); *Inf.* juvenile petty thief
gato /'gato/ *m*, cat; tomcat; moneybag or its contents; *Mech.* jack; mousetrap; *Inf.* cat burglar, sneak thief; *Inf.* Madrilenian; clamp. **g. atigrado,** tiger cat. **g. de algalia,** civet cat. **g. de Angora,** Persian cat. **g. montés,** wildcat. **g. romano,** tabby cat. **dar g. por liebre,** to serve cat for hare, to deceive; misrepresent. *Inf.* **Hay g. encerrado,** There's more to this than meets the eye
gatuno /ga'tuno/ *a* feline
gaucho /'gautʃo/ **(-cha)** *n* gaucho; cowboy, rider
gaveta /ga'βeta/ *f*, drawer (of a desk)
gavia /'gaβia/ *f*, main topsail; *pl* topsails; crow's-nest
gavilán /gaβi'lan/ *m*, sparrow hawk; thistle flower; *Lat. Am.* ingrown toenail
gavilla /ga'βiya; ga'βiʎa/ *f*, sheaf (of corn, etc.); gang, rabble

gaviota /ga'βiota/ f, seagull

gavota /ga'βota/ f, gavotte

gayo /'gayo/ a gay, happy; showy, attractive. **gaya ciencia,** minstrelsy, art of poetry

gazapera /gasa'pera; gaθa'pera/ f, rabbit warren; *Inf.* thieves' den; *Inf.* brawl

gazapo /ga'sapo; ga'θapo/ m, young rabbit; *Inf.* cunning fellow; fib, lie; slip, blunder

gazmoñería /gasmoɲe'ria; gaθmoɲe'ria/ f, prudery, priggish affectation

gazmoño /gas'moɲo; gaθ'moɲo/ a hypocritical, prudish, priggish

gaznápiro /gas'napiro; gaθ'napiro/ (-ra) n ninny, simpleton

gaznate /gas'nate; gaθ'nate/ m, windpipe

gazpacho /gas'patʃo; gaθ'patʃo/ m, cold soup containing tomatoes, onions, vinegar, oil, etc.

ge /he/ f, name of the letter G

gehena /he'ena/ m, gehenna, hell

géiser /'heiser/ m, geyser

gelatina /hela'tina/ f, gelatin. **g. incendiaria,** napalm. **g. seca,** cooking gelatin

gelatinoso /helati'noso/ a gelatinous

gélido /'heliðo/ a *Poet.* icy; very cold

gema /'hema/ f, gem; *Bot.* bud

gemelo /he'melo/ (-la) a and n twin. m pl, field or opera glasses, binoculars; cuff links; *Astron.* Gemini

gemido /he'miðo/ m, groan, lament, moan

gemidor /hemi'ðor/ a groaning, moaning; wailing (of the wind, etc.)

gemir /he'mir/ vi irr to moan, groan, lament; *Fig.* wail, howl. See **pedir**

gene /'hene/ m, gene

genealogía /henealo'hia/ f, genealogy

genealógico /henea'lohiko/ a genealogical

genealogista /henealo'hista/ mf genealogist

generación /henera'sion; henera'θion/ f, generation, reproduction; species; generation

generador /henera'ðor/ a generative. m, *Mech.* generator

general /hene'ral/ a general; universal; widespread; common, usual. m, (*Mil. Eccl.*) general. **g. de división,** *Mil.* major general. **en** or **por lo g.,** generally

generalato /henera'lato/ m, generalship

generalidad /henerali'ðað/ f, majority, bulk; generality

generalísimo /henerali'lisimo/ m, generalissimo, commander in chief

generalización /heneralisa'sion; heneraliθa'θion/ f, generalization

generalizar /henerali'sar; henerali'θar/ vt to generalize; vr become widespread or general

generar /hene'rar/ vt to generate

genérico /he'neriko/ a generic

género /'henero/ m, kind; class; way, mode; *Com.* goods; species, genus; *Gram.* gender; cloth, material. **g. chico,** short theatrical pieces (gen. one act). **g. humano,** humankind

generosidad /henerosi'ðað/ f, hereditary nobility; generosity, magnanimity; liberality, munificence; courage

generoso /hene'roso/ a noble (by birth); magnanimous; generous (of wine); munificent; courageous; excellent

genésico /he'nesiko/ a genetic

génesis /'henesis/ m, **Génesis,** Genesis. f, beginning, origin

genial /he'nial/ a of genius; highly talented; brilliant; characteristic, individual; pleasant; cheerful

genialidad /heniali'ðað/ f, genius; talent; brilliance; eccentricity, oddity

genio /'henio/ m, nature, individuality, temperament; temper; character; talent; genius; genie, spirit. **corto de g.,** unintelligent. **mal g.,** bad temper

genital /heni'tal/ a genital. m, testicle (gen. pl)

genitivo /heni'tiβo/ a reproductive, generative. m, *Gram.* genitive

Génova /'henoβa/ Genoa

gente /'hente/ f, people, a crowd; nation; army; *Inf.* family; followers, adherents. **g. baja,** rabble. **g. de bien,** honest folk; respectable people. **g. de paz,** friends (reply to sentinel's challenge). **g. fina,** nice, cultured people. **g. menuda,** children, small fry

gentecilla /hente'siya; hente'θiʎa/ f, dim *Inf.* rabble; contemptible people

gentil /hen'til/ a pagan, idolatrous; spirited, dashing, handsome; notable, extraordinary; graceful, charming

gentileza /henti'lesa; henti'leθa/ f, grace; elegance; beauty; verve, sprightliness; courtesy; show, ostentation

gentilhombre /hentil'ombre/ m, gentleman; handsome man; kind sir! **gentileshombres de cámara,** gentlemen-in-waiting

gentilicio /henti'lisio; henti'liθio/ a national; family

gentílico /hen'tiliko/ a pagan, idolatrous

gentilidad /hentili'ðað/ f, idolatry, paganism; heathendom

gentío /hen'tio/ m, crowd, throng

gentualla, gentuza /hen'tuaya, hen'tusa; hen'tuθa, hen'tuθa/ f, canaille, rabble

genuflexión /henuflek'sion/ f, genuflection

genuino /he'nuino/ a pure; authentic, genuine; *Colombia* great, wonderful

geodesia /heo'ðesia/ f, geodesy

geodésico /heo'ðesiko/ a geodesic

geografía /heogra'fia/ f, geography

geográfico /heo'grafiko/ a geographical

geógrafo /he'ografo/ m, geographer

geología /heolo'hia/ f, geology

geológico /heo'lohiko/ a geological

geólogo /he'ologo/ m, geologist

geometría /heome'tria/ f, geometry. **g. del espacio,** solid geometry

geométrico /heo'metriko/ a geometrical

geranio /he'ranio/ m, geranium

gerencia /he'rensia; he'renθia/ f, *Com.* managership; manager's office; management

gerente /he'rente/ m, *Com.* manager

germanía /herma'nia/ f, thieves' slang; association of thieves; sixteenth-century political brotherhood

germánico /her'maniko/ a germanic

germanófilo /herma'nofilo/ (-la) a and n germanophile

germen /'hermen/ m, germ, sprout; *Bot.* embryo; genesis, origin

germinación /hermina'sion; hermina'θion/ f, germination

germinar /hermi'nar/ vi to germinate, sprout; develop, grow

germinativo /hermina'tiβo/ a germinative

gerundio /he'rundio/ m, *Gram.* gerund; *Inf.* pompous ass; *Inf.* tub-thumper

gesta /'hesta/ f, heroic deed. **cantar de g.,** epic or heroic poem

gestación /hesta'sion; hesta'θion/ f, gestation

gestear /heste'ar/ vi to gesture, grimace

gesticulación /hestikula'sion; hestikula'θion/ f, gesticulation; grimace

gesticular /hestiku'lar/ vi to grimace, gesticulate. a gesticulatory

gestión /hes'tion/ f, negotiation; management, conduct; effort, exertion; measure

gestionar /hestio'nar/ vt to negotiate; conduct; undertake; take steps to attain

gesto /'hesto/ m, gesture; facial expression; grimace; face, visage

gestor /hes'tor/ (-ra) n manager; partner; promoter. a managing

Getsemaní /hetsema'ni/ Gethsemane

giba /'hiβa/ f, hump, hunchback; *Inf.* nuisance, inconvenience

gibón /hi'βon/ m, gibbon

giboso /hi'βoso/ a hunchbacked

gibraltareño /hiβralta'reɲo/ a Gibraltarian

giganta /hi'ganta/ f, giantess

gigante /hi'gante/ a gigantic. m, giant.

gigantesco /higan'tesko/ a giant, gigantic; *Fig.* outstanding

gigantez /higan'tes; higan'teθ/ f, gigantic size

gigantón /higan'ton/ **(-ona)** n enormous giant; carnival grotesque

gimnasia /him'nasia/ f, gymnastics

gimnasio /him'nasio/ m, gymnasium; school, academy

gimnasta /him'nasta/ mf gymnast

gimnástico /him'nastiko/ a gymnastic

gimotear /himote'ar/ vi Inf. to whine (often used scornfully)

gimoteo /himo'teo/ m, Inf. whining, whimpering

ginebra /hi'neβra/ f, gin (drink); confusion; babble, din

ginebrés /hine'βres/ **(-esa), ginebrino (-na)** a and n Genevan

gineceo /hine'seo; hine'θeo/ m, (Bot. and in ancient Greece) gynaecium

ginecología /hinekolo'hia/ f, gynecology

ginecológico /hineko'lohiko/ a gynecological

ginecólogo /hine'kologo/ **(-ga)** n gynecologist

girado /hi'raðo/ m, Com. drawee

girador /hira'ðor/ m, Com. drawer

giralda /hi'ralda/ f, weathercock in the shape of a person or animal; tower at Seville

girar /hi'rar/ vi to revolve; deal (with), concern; turn, branch (streets, etc.); Com. trade; Mech. turn on, revolve; vt and vi Com. draw, cash. **g. en descubierto,** Com. to overdraw

girasol /hira'sol/ m, sunflower

giratorio /hira'torio/ a revolving, gyrating; swiveling

giro /'hiro/ m, revolution, turn; revolving; trend; course (of affairs); style, turn (of phrase); threat; knife gash; Com. draft, drawing; Com. line of business, specialty. **g. postal,** postal order

giroscopio /hiro'skopio/ m, gyroscope

gis /his/ m Lat. Am. chalk; Mexico also pulque

gitanería /hitane'ria/ f, cajolery, wheedling; gypsies; gypsy saying or action

gitanesco /hita'nesko/ a gypsy, gypsy-like

gitano /hi'tano/ **(-na)** a gypsy; gypsy-like; seductive, attractive; sly. n gypsy

glaciar /gla'siar; gla'θiar/ m, glacier

gladiador /glaðia'ðor/ m, gladiator

glanco /'glanko/ a Lat. Am. light green

glándula /'glandula/ f, gland

glicerina /glise'rina; gliθe'rina/ f, glycerin, glycerol

globo /'gloβo/ m, Geom. sphere; globe, world; globe (Elec. Gas.); balloon. **g. aerostático,** air balloon. **g. terrestre,** world; geographical globe

globular /gloβu'lar/ a globular

glóbulo /'gloβulo/ m, globule.

globuloso /gloβu'loso/ a globulous

gloria /'gloria/ f, heavenly bliss; fame, glory; delight, pleasure; magnificence, splendor; Art. apotheosis, glory. m, Eccl. doxology

gloriar /glo'riar/ vr to praise; vr (with de or en) boast about; be proud of, rejoice in

glorieta /glo'rieta/ f, bower, arbor; open space in a garden; street square, traffic circle

glorificación /glorifika'sion; glorifika'θion/ f, glorification

glorificador /glorifika'ðor/ a glorifying

glorificar /glorifi'kar/ vt to exalt, raise up; glorify, extol; vr (with de or en) be proud of; glory in; boast of

glorioso /glo'rioso/ a glorious; Eccl. blessed; boastful, bragging

glosa /'glosa/ f, gloss; explanation, note

glosador /glosa'ðor/ **(-ra)** n glossator; commentator. a explanatory

glosar /glo'sar/ vt Lit. to gloss

glosario /glo'sario/ m, glossary

glosopeda /gloso'peða/ f, foot-and-mouth disease

glotón /glo'ton/ **(-ona)** a greedy, gluttonous. n glutton

glotonería /glotone'ria/ f, gluttony, greed

glucosa /glu'kosa/ f, glucose

glúteo /'gluteo/ a gluteal

glutinoso /gluti'noso/ a glutinous

gn- /gn-/ For words so beginning, see spellings without **g.**

gobernación /goβerna'sion; goβerna'θion/ f, government; governor's office or building; ministry of the interior, home office (abb. for **ministerio de G.**)

gobernador /goβerna'ðor/ **(-ra)** a governing, n governor

gobernalle /goβer'naye; goβer'naʎe/ m, helm

gobernante /goβer'nante/ a governing. m, Inf. self-appointed director or manager

gobernar /goβer'nar/ vt irr to govern, rule; lead, conduct; manage; steer; control; vi govern; Naut. obey the tiller. See **recomendar**

gobierno /go'βierno/ m, government (all meanings); Naut. helm; control (of machines, business, etc.)

goce /'gose; 'goθe/ m, enjoyment; possession

godo /'goðo/ **(da)** a Gothic; aristocratic, noble. n Goth; aristocrat

gol /gol/ m, Sports. goal

gola /'gola/ f, throat; gullet; gorget; tucker, bib

goleta /go'leta/ f, schooner

golf /golf/ m, golf. **palo de g.,** golf club

golfear /golfe'ar/ vi to loaf

golfería /golfe'ria/ f, loafing; vagabondage; loafers

golfo /'golfo/ **(-fa)** m, Geog. gulf; sea, ocean. n ragamuffin, urchin. m, Inf. loafer; lounge lizard, wastrel

golilla /go'liya; go'liʎa/ f, ruff; Lat. Am. scarf; m, Inf. magistrate

gollería /goye'ria; goʎe'ria/ f, dainty, tidbit; Inf. affectation, persnicketiness

gollete /go'yete; go'ʎete/ m, gullet; neck (of a bottle, etc.); Mech. nozzle

golondrina /golon'drina/ f, Ornith. swallow; Chile moving van. **g. de mar,** tern

golosina /golo'sina/ f, tidbit, delicacy; desire, caprice; pleasant useless thing

goloso /go'loso/ a fond of sweet things; greedy, desirous; appetizing

golpe /'golpe/ m, blow, knock; pull (at the oars); ring (of a bell); Mech. stroke; crowd; fall (of rain, etc.); mass, torrent; misfortune; shock, collision; spring lock; beating (of the heart); flap (of a pocket); Sew. passementerie; surprise; point, wit; bet. **g. de estado,** coup d'état. **g. de fortuna,** stroke of fortune. **g. de mano,** rising, insurrection. **g. en vago,** blow in the air; disappointment. **g. franco,** Sports. free kick. **de g.,** suddenly; quickly

golpeadura /golpea'ðura/ f. **golpeo** knocking, striking; beating, throbbing

golpear /golpe'ar/ vt and vi to knock, strike; beat, throb

goma /'goma/ f, gum, rubber; India rubber; rubber band, eraser

gomería /gome'ria/ f, tire store

gomero /go'mero/ m, gum; rubber. m, West Hem. rubber planter

gomoso /go'moso/ a gummy; gum

gónada /'gonaða/ f, gonad

góndola /'gondola/ f, gondola

gondolero /gondo'lero/ m, gondolier

gongorino /goŋgo'rino/ a gongoristic, euphuistic

gonorrea /gono'rrea/ f, gonorrhea

gordo /'gorðo/ a fat, stout; greasy, oily; thick (thread, etc.). m, animal fat, suet. Inf. **ganar el g.,** to win first prize (in a lottery, etc.)

gordura /gor'ðura/ f, grease, fat; stoutness, corpulence

gorgojo /gor'goho/ m, weevil; Fig. dwarf

gorgoritear /gorgorite'ar/ vi Inf. to trill, quaver

gorgorito /gorgo'rito/ m, Inf. quaver, tremolo, trill (gen. pl)

gorgoteo /gorgo'teo/ m, gurgle

gorjear /gorhe'ar/ vi to trill, warble; twitter; vr crow (of a baby)

gorjeo /gor'heo/ m, trill, shake; warbling, twitter; crowing, lisping (of a child)

gorra /'gorra/ f, cap; bonnet; Mil. busby; hunting cap. **vivir de g.,** Inf. to sponge

gorrión /go'rrion/ m, sparrow

gorrista /go'rrista/ mf Inf. parasite; sponger

gorro /'gorro/ m, cap; bonnet

gorrón /go'rron/ m, smooth, round pebble; Mech. pivot, gudgeon; sponger, waster. a parasitical

gota /'gota/ *f*, drop (of liquid); gout

gotear /gote'ar/ *vi* to drop, trickle, drip; leak; drizzle; give or receive in driblets

goteo /go'teo/ *m*, trickling, dripping

gotera /go'tera/ *f*, dripping; trickle; leak; leakage; valance

gotero /go'tero/ *m Lat. Am.* (medicine) dropper

gótico /'gotiko/ *a* Gothic; noble, illustrious

gotoso /go'toso/ **(-sa)** *a* gouty. *n* sufferer from gout

gozar /go'sar; go'θar/ *vt* to enjoy, have; take pleasure (in), delight (in); know carnally; *vi (with de)* enjoy; have, possess

gozne /'gosne; 'goθne/ *m*, hinge

gozo /'goso; 'goθo/ *m*, enjoyment, possession; gladness, joy; *pl* couplets in honor of the Virgin Mary or a saint. *Inf.* **¡Mi g. en el pozo!** I'm sunk! All is lost!

gozoso /go'soso; go'θoso/ *a* glad, happy. *adv* gladly; with pleasure

grabado /gra'βaðo/ *m*, engraver's art; engraving; illustration, picture. **g. al agua fuerte,** etching. **g. al agua tinta,** aquatint

grabador /graβa'ðor/ **(-ra)** *n* engraver

grabadura /graβa'ðura/ *f*, act of engraving

grabar /gra'βar/ *vt* to engrave; *Fig.* leave a deep impression

gracejo /gra'seho; gra'θeho/ *m*, humor, wit; cheerfulness

gracia /'grasia; 'graθia/ *f*, grace; attraction, grace; favor; kindness; jest, witticism; pardon, mercy; pleasant manner; obligingness, willingness; *pl* thanks, thank you. **gracias a,** thanks to. **¡Gracias a Dios!** Thank God! Thank goodness! **las Gracias,** the Three Graces

grácil /'grasil; 'graθil/ *a* slender; small

graciosidad /grasiosi'ðað; graθiosi'ðað/ *f*, beauty, perfection, grace

gracioso /gra'sioso; gra'θioso/ **(-sa)** *a* attractive, graceful, elegant; witty, humorous; free, gratis. *n Theat.* comic role; *m*, *Theat.* fool

grada /'graða/ *f*, step, stair; gradin, seat; stand, gallery; *Agr.* harrow; *Naut.* runway; *pl* perron, flight of stairs

gradación /graða'sion; graða'θion/ *f*, gradation; climax

gradería /graðe'ria/ *f*, flight of steps

grado /'graðo/ *m*, step, stair; degree (of relationship); university degree; grade, class (in schools); (*Fig. Geom. Phys.*) degree; will, desire. **de buen g.,** willingly. **en sumo g.,** in the highest degree

graduación /graðua'sion; graðua'θion/ *f*, graduation; *Mil.* rank; rating (of a ship's company). **g. de oficial,** *Mil.* commission

graduado /gra'ðuaðo/ *a* graded; *Mil.* brevet. *m*, graduate

gradual /gra'ðual/ *a* gradual

graduar /gra'ðuar/ *vt* to classify; *Mil.* grade; confer a degree on; measure; test; *Com.* standardize; *Mech.* calibrate; *vr* graduate, receive a degree. **g. la vista,** to test the eyes. **graduarse de oficial,** *Mil.* to get one's commission

gráfica /'grafika/ *f*, graph

gráfico /'grafiko/ *a* graphic; vivid

grafito /gra'fito/ *m*, graphite

grafología /grafolo'hia/ *f*, graphology

grajear /grahe'ar/ *vi* to caw; gurgle, burble (of infants)

grajo /'graho/ *m*, *Ornith.* rook

grama /'grama/ *f Dominican Republic, Venezuela* grass, lawn

gramática /gra'matika/ *f*, grammar. *Inf.* **g. parda,** horse sense

gramático /gra'matiko/ *a* grammatical. *m*, grammarian

gramo /'gramo/ *m*, gram

gran /gran/ *a abb* See **grande.** Used before a singular noun. big; great; grand

grana /'grana/ *f*, grain, seed; seed time; cochineal; kermes; red

granada /gra'naða/ *f*, *Mil.* grenade, shell; pomegranate

granadero /grana'ðero/ *m*, grenadier; *Inf.* very tall person; *Lat. Am.* riot policeman

granadilla /grana'ðiya; grana'ðiλa/ *f*, passionflower

granadina /grana'ðina/ *f*, grenadine

granar /gra'nar/ *vi Agr.* to seed; run to seed

granate /gra'nate/ *m*, garnet; dark red

Gran Bretaña /gran bre'taɲa/ Great Britain

grande /'grande/ *a* big, large; great, illustrious; grand. *m*, great man; grandee. **en g.,** in a large size; as a whole; in style, lavishly

grandeza /gran'desa; gran'deθa/ *f*, largeness; greatness, magnificence; grandeeship; vastness, magnitude

grandilocuencia /grandilo'kuensia; grandilo'kuenθia/ *f*, grandiloquence

grandílocuo /gran'dilokuo/ *a* grandiloquent

grandiosidad /grandiosi'ðað/ *f*, grandeur, greatness

grandioso /gran'dioso/ *a* grandiose, magnificent

grandor /gran'dor/ *m*, size

granear /grane'ar/ *vt Agr.* to sow; grain (of leather)

granero /gra'nero/ *m*, granary; grain-producing country

granito /gra'nito/ *m*, *dim* small grain; granite; small pimple

granizar /grani'sar; grani'θar/ *vi* to hail, sleet; *vi* and *vt Fig.* shower down, deluge

granizo /gra'niso; gra'niθo/ *m*, hail, sleet; hailstorm; *Fig.* shower, deluge

granja /'granha/ *f*, farm; farmhouse; dairy farm, dairy

granjear /granhe'ar/ *vt* to trade, profit, earn; obtain, acquire; *vr* gain, win

granjería /granhe'ria/ *f*, farming; agricultural profits; earnings, profits

granjero /gran'hero/ **(-ra)** *n* farmer

grano /'grano/ *m*, *Agr.* grain; seed; bean (coffee, etc.); particle; markings, grain (of wood, etc.); pimple; grain (measure). *Fig. Inf.* **ir al g.,** to go to the root of the matter; come to the point

granuja /gra'nuha/ *f*, grape pit. *m*, *Inf.* urchin; scamp; knave, rogue

granujiento /granu'hiento/ *a* pimply

gránulo /'granulo/ *m*, granule

granuloso /granu'loso/ *a* granulous

grapa /'grapa/ *f*, cramp, dowel, clamp; block hook; *Elec.* cleat; staple

grasa /'grasa/ *f*, fat; grease; oil; dripping, suet

grasiento /gra'siento/ *a* greasy; grubby, dirty

gratificación /gratifika'sion; gratifika'θion/ *f*, monetary reward; fee, remuneration; gratuity

gratificar /gratifi'kar/ *vt* to recompense; please, gratify

gratis /'gratis/ *a* and *adv* gratis

gratitud /grati'tuð/ *f*, gratitude

grato /'grato/ *a* pleasing, agreeable; free, gratuitous; *Lat. Am.* appreciative, grateful

gratuito /gra'tuito/ *a* gratuitous, free; baseless, unfounded

grava /'graβa/ *f*, gravel; stone chip, pebble; metal (of a road)

gravamen /gra'βamen/ *m*, obligation; burden; tax

gravar /gra'βar/ *vt* to burden, weigh upon; tax

grave /'graβe/ *a* heavy; important, momentous; grave; dignified, serious; sedate; tiresome; low-pitched, low; *Gram.* grave accent

gravedad /graβe'ðað/ *f*, *Phys.* gravity

gravitación /graβita'sion; graβita'θion/ *f*, *Phys.* gravitation; seriousness; sedateness; importance; enormity, gravity

gravitar /graβi'tar/ *vi* to gravitate; lean or rest (upon)

gravoso /gra'βoso/ *a* grievous, oppressive; onerous; costly

graznar /gras'nar; graθ'nar/ *vi* to caw; cackle; quack; croak; sing stridently, screech

graznido /gras'niðo; graθ'niðo/ *m*, caw; cackle; croaking; quack; screech

Grecia /'gresia; 'greθia/ Greece

greco /'greko/ **(-ca)** *a* and *n* Greek

gregario /gre'gario/ *a* gregarious

gregoriano /grego'riano/ *a* Gregorian

gregüescos /gre'gueskos/ *m pl*, wide breeches (sixteenth and seventeenth centuries)

gremial /gre'mial/ *a* pertaining to a guild, union, or association. *m*, member of a guild, union, or association

gremio /'gremio/ *m*, guild, corporation, union; society, association; (univ.) general council

greña /'greɲa/ *f*, tangled lock (of hair) (gen. *pl*); tangle, confused mass

gresca /'greska/ *f*, uproar, tumult; fight, row

grey /grei/ *f*, flock, drove, herd; *Eccl.* flock, company; people, nation

griego /'griego/ (**-ga**) *a* and *n* Greek. *m*, Greek (language); *Inf.* gibberish

grieta /'grieta/ *f*, fissure; crevice; chink; split; flaw; vein (in stone, etc.); *Mech.* leak

grietado /grie'taðo/ *a* fissured; cracked

grifo /'grifo/ *m*, griffin; tap; cock

grillo /'griyo; 'griʎo/ *m*, cricket; *Bot.* shoot; *pl* fetters, irons, chains; *Fig.* shackles

grima /'grima/ *f*, revulsion, horror

gringo /'griŋgo/ (**-ga**) *n Inf.* foreigner (scornful)

gripe /'gripe/ *f*, influenza; grippe

gris /gris/ *a* and *m*, gray

grisú /gri'su/ *m*, firedamp

gritador /grita'ðor/ (**-ra**) *a* shouting. *n* shouter

gritar /gri'tar/ *vi* to shout, yell, scream; howl down; hoot

gritería /grite'ria/ *f*, shouting, yelling, clamor

grito /'grito/ *m*, shout, yell, shriek, scream. *Inf.* **poner el g. en el cielo,** to cry to high heaven, complain. **el Grito de Dolores** the Proclamation of Mexican Independence (1810)

groenlandés /groenlan'des/ (**-esa**) *a* Greenland. *n* Greenlander

Groenlandia /groen'landia/ Greenland

grosella /gro'seya; gro'seʎa/ *f*, currant. **g. blanca,** gooseberry

grosería /grose'ria/ *f*, crudeness, insult; rudeness; roughness (of workmanship); ignorance; rusticity

grosero /gro'sero/ *a* coarse; rough; thick; unpolished, rude

grotesco /gro'tesko/ *a* grotesque, absurd

grúa /'grua/ *f*, *Mech.* crane, hoist, derrick. **g. de pescante,** jib crane. **g. móvil,** traveling crane

gruesa /'gruesa/ *f*, twelve dozen, gross

grueso /'grueso/ *a* stout, corpulent; large. *m*, bulk, body; major portion, majority; thick stroke (of a letter); thickness, density. **en g.,** in bulk

grulla /'gruya; 'gruʎa/ *f*, *Ornith.* crane

grumete /gru'mete/ *m*, ship's boy, cabin boy

grumo /'grumo/ *m*, clot; heart (of vegetables); bunch, cluster; bud

gruñido /gru'ɲiðo/ *m*, grunt; growl

gruñidor /gruɲi'ðor/ *a* grunting; growling

gruñir /gru'ɲir/ *vi* to grunt; growl; grumble; squeak, creak (doors, etc.). *Pres. Part.* **gruñendo.** *Pres. Ind.* **gruño, gruñes, etc.**

grupa /'grupa/ *f*, croup (of a horse); pillion (of a motorcycle)

grupera /gru'pera/ *f*, pillion (of a horse, etc.)

grupo /'grupo/ *m*, knot, cluster; band, group; *Art.* group; *Mech.* set

gruta /'gruta/ *f*, cavern, grotto

guacamayo /guaka'mayo/ *m*, macaw

guadamecí /guaðame'si; guaðame'θi/ *m*, embossed decorated leather

guadaña /gua'ðaɲa/ *f*, scythe

guagua /'guagua/, *f Caribbean* bus

gualdo /'gualdo/ *a* yellow, golden

gualdrapa /gual'drapa/ *f*, saddlecloth, trappings; *Inf.* tatter, rag

guante /'guante/ *m*, glove. **g. con puño,** gauntlet glove. **g. de boxeo,** boxing glove. **g. de cabritilla,** kid glove. **arrojar el g.,** to throw down the gauntlet; challenge, defy

guantelete /guante'lete/ *m*, gauntlet

guantería /guante'ria/ *f*, glove trade, shop, or factory

guantero /guan'tero/ (**-ra**) *n* glove maker or seller, glover

guapear /guape'ar/ *vi Inf.* to make the best of a bad job; *Inf.* pride oneself on being well dressed

guapeza /gua'pesa; gua'peθa/ *f*, prettiness; *Inf.* resolution, courage; *Inf.* smartness or showiness of dress; boastful act or behavior

guapo /'guapo/ *a* pretty; handsome; *Inf.* daring, enterprising; *Inf.* smart, well-dressed, foppish; *Inf.* handsome; *Dominican Republic* angry, mad. *m*, braggart, brawler; beau, lover; *Inf.* fine fellow, son of a gun

guaracha /gua'ratʃa/ *f*, *Cuba, Puerto Rico* guaracha (vigorous dance in triple meter; music for this dance)

guarda /'guarða/ *mf* keeper, guard. *f*, guarding, keeping, custodianship, preservation; guardianship; observance, fulfillment; flyleaf, end page (books); warder (of locks or keys); *Mech.* guard; guard (of a fan)

guardabarrera /guarðaβa'rrera/ *mf* gatekeeper at a level crossing (railroad)

guardabarro /guarða'βarro/ *m*, mudguard

guardabosque /guarða'βoske/ *mf* gamekeeper

guardabrisa /guarða'βrisa/ *m*, *Auto.* windshield; glass candle shield

guardacostas /guarða'kostas/ *m*, coast guard; *Naut.* revenue cutter

guardafrenos /guarða'frenos/ *m*, brakeman (railroad)

guardalmacén /guarðalma'sen; guarðalma'θen/ *mf* storekeeper

guardameta /guarða'meta/ *mf* goalkeeper

guardamuebles /guarða'mueβles/ *m*, furniture warehouse

guardapelo /guarða'pelo/ *m*, locket

guardapolvo /guarða'polβo/ *m*, dustcover; light overcoat; inner case of a pocket watch

guardar /guar'ðar/ *vt* to keep; preserve, retain; maintain, observe; save, put aside, lay away; defend, protect; guard; *vr* (*with de*) avoid, guard against. **g. compás con,** to be in tune with. **guardarse mucho,** to think twice before. **g. silencio,** to keep silent. **¡Guarda!** Take care! **¡Guárdate del agua mansa!** Still waters run deep!

guardarropa /guarða'rropa/ *m*, cloakroom. *mf* cloakroom attendant; keeper of the wardrobe. *m*, wardrobe, clothes closet

guardarropía /guarðarro'pia/ *f*, theatrical wardrobe

guardavía /guarða'βia/ *f*, signalman (railroad)

guardería /guarðe'ria/ *f*, day nursery, day-care center

guardia /'guarðia/ *f*, guard, escort; protection; guard (fencing). *m*, guardsman; policeman. **g. de asalto,** armed police. **g. de corps,** royal bodyguard. **g. civil,** civil guard. **g. marina,** midshipman. **g. municipal,** city police. *Mil.* **montar la g.,** to mount guard

guardián /guar'ðian/ (**-ana**) *n* keeper; custodian; warden. *m*, watchman; jailer

guardilla /guar'ðiya; guar'ðiʎa/ *f*, attic, garret

guarecer /guare'ser; guare'θer/ *vt irr* to shelter, protect, aid; preserve, keep; cure; *vr* take shelter. See **conocer**

guarida /gua'riða/ *f*, lair, den; refuge, shelter; haunt, resort

guarismo /gua'rismo/ *m*, *Math.* figure; number, numeral

guarnecer /guarne'ser; guarne'θer/ *vt irr* to decorate, adorn; *Sew.* trim, face, border; *Mil.* garrison; *Mas.* plaster. See **conocer**

guarnecido /guarne'siðo; guarne'θiðo/ *m*, *Mas.* plastering

guarnición /guarni'sion; guarni'θion/ *f*, *Sew.* trimming, ornament, border, fringe; *Mech.* packing; *Mil.* garrison; setting (of jewels); guard (of a sword, etc.); *pl* harness; fittings

guarnir /guar'nir/ *vt Naut.* to reeve

guasa /'guasa/ *f*, *Inf.* dullness, boringness; joke. **de g.,** jokingly

guasón /gua'son/ *a Inf.* dull, tedious; humorous, jocose

guatemalteco /guatemal'teko/ (**-ca**) *a* and *n* Guatemalan

guau /guau/ *m*, bowwow, bark of a dog

guayaba /gua'yaβa/ *f*, guava; guava jelly; *Lat. Am. also* hoax

Guayana /gua'yana/ Guiana

gubernamental /guβernamen'tal/ *a* governmental

gubernativo /guβerna'tiβo/ *a* governmental; administrative

gubia /'guβia/ *f*, chisel; gouge

guedeja /ge'ðeha/ *f*, long tress or lock of hair; forelock; lion's mane

Guernesey /gerne'sei/ Guernsey

guerra /'gerra/ *f*, war; struggle, fight; *Fig.* hostility. *Inf.* **dar g.,** to give trouble, annoy. **en g. con,** at war with. **la g. de Cuba,** the Spanish-American War

guerrear /gerre'ar/ *vi* to make war, fight; oppose

guerrero /ge'rrero/ **(-ra)** *a* war, martial; warrior; *Inf.* troublesome, annoying. *n* fighter. *m*, warrior, soldier

guerrillear /gerriye'ar; gerriʎe'ar/ *vi* to wage guerrilla warfare; fight as a guerrilla

guerrillero /gerri'yero; gerri'ʎero/ *m*, guerrilla fighter

guía /'gia/ *mf* guide, conductor; adviser, director. *f*, guide, aid; guidebook; *Mech.* guide, slide; directory; signpost. **g. de ferrocarriles,** train schedule, railroad timetable. **g. de teléfonos,** telephone directory

guiar /giar/ *vt* to guide; lead, conduct; *Mech.* work, control; *Auto.* drive; pilot; teach, direct, govern

guija /'giha/ *f*, pebble

guijarro /gi'harro/ *m*, smooth, round pebble; boulder; cobblestone

guijarroso /giha'rroso/ *a* pebbly, cobbled

guijo /'giho/ *m*, gravel; granite chips; pebble

guillotina /giyo'tina; giʎo'tina/ *f*, guillotine; paper-cutting machine

guillotinar /giyoti'nar; giʎoti'nar/ *vt* to guillotine, decapitate

guinda /'ginda/ *f*, mazard cherry; *Naut.* height of masts

guinea /gi'nea/ *f*, guinea

guinga /'giŋga/ *f*, gingham

guiñada /gi'ɲaða/ *f*, wink; blink; *Naut.* yaw

guiñapo /gi'ɲapo/ *m*, rag, tatter; sloven, ragamuffin

guiñar /gi'ɲar/ *vt* to wink; blink; *Naut.* yaw; *vr* wink at each other

guiño /'giɲo/ *m*, wink

guión /gi'on/ *m*, royal standard; banner; summary; leader of a dance; *Gram.* hyphen; subtitle (in films). **g. mayor,** *Gram.* dash

guirigay /giri'gai/ *m*, *Inf.* gibberish; uproar, babble

guirnalda /gir'nalda/ *f*, garland, wreath

guisa /'gisa/ *f*, way, manner; will, desire. **a g. de,** in the manner or fashion of

guisado /gi'saðo/ *m*, *Cul.* stew; cooked dish

guisante /gi'sante/ *m*, *Agr.* pea; pea plant. **g. de olor,** sweetpea

guisar /gi'sar/ *vt* to cook; stew; *Cul.* prepare, dress; adjust, arrange

guiso /'giso/ *m*, cooked dish

güisquisoda /giski'soða/ *f Spain* highball

guitarra /gi'tarra/ *f*, guitar

guitarrista /gita'rrista/ *mf* guitar player

guito /'gito/ *a* vicious (horses, mules)

gula /'gula/ *f*, greed, gluttony

gusaniento /gusa'niento/ *a* worm-eaten; maggoty

gusano /gu'sano/ *m*, worm; caterpillar; maggot; meek, downtrodden person. **g. de seda,** silkworm

gusanoso /gusa'noso/ *a* wormy

gustar /gus'tar/ *vt* to taste, savor; try; *vi* be pleasing, give pleasure; like. **Me gusta el libro,** I like the book. **La película me gustó,** I didn't like the film. **g. de,** to like, is used only when a person is the subject

gusto /'gusto/ *m*, taste; flavor, savor; pleasure, delight; will, desire; discrimination, taste, style, fashion; manner; whim, caprice. **a g.,** to taste; according to taste. **con mucho g.,** with great pleasure. **dar g.,** to please. **de buen g.,** in good taste. **mucho g. en conocerlo (-la),** pleased to meet you

gustoso /gus'toso/ *a* savory, palatable; willingly, with pleasure; pleasant, agreeable

gutapercha /guta'pertʃa/ *f*, guttapercha

gutural /gutu'ral/ *a* guttural

H

haba /'aβa/ *f*, broad bean; bean (coffee, cocoa, etc.). **h. de las Indias,** sweetpea. **Esas son habas contadas,** That's a certainty

Habana, la /a'βana, la/ Havana

habanero /aβa'nero/ **(-ra), habano (-na)** *a* and *n* Havanese, from Havana. *m*, **habano,** Havana cigar

haber /a'βer/ *m*, estate, property (gen. *pl*); income; *Com.* credit balance. **h. monedado,** specie

haber /a'βer/ *vt irr* to be there (*3rd pers. sing*), have in compound tenses; catch, lay hands on (e.g. *El reo fue habido,* The criminal was caught). *v aux* (e.g. *Hemos escrito la carta,* We have written the letter). *v impers* to happen, take place; be. *3rd pers. sing Pres. Ind.* **ha** is replaced by **hay,** meaning there is or there are (e.g. *No hay naranjas en las tiendas,* There are no oranges in the shops). In certain weather expressions, **hay** means it is (e.g. *Hay luna,* It is moonlight). Used of expressions of time, **haber** means to elapse and **ha** (*3rd pers. sing Pres. Ind.*) has adverbial force of "ago" (e.g. *muchos días ha,* many days ago). **h. de,** to be necessary (less strong than **h. que**) (e.g. *Hemos de verle mañana,* We must see him tomorrow. *He de hacer el papel de Manolo,* I am to play the part of Manolo). **h. que,** to be unavoidable, be essential. With this construction the form **hay** is used (e.g. *Hay que darse prisa,* We (or one) must hurry. **No hay que enojarse,** There's no need to get annoyed). **no h., más que pedir,** to leave nothing to be desired. **no h. tal,** to be no such thing. *Inf.* **habérselas con,** to quarrel or fall out with. **Hubo una vez...,** Once upon a time... **¡No hay de qué!,** Don't mention it!; Not at all!; You're welcome! **No hay para que...,** There's no point in.... **poco tiempo ha,** a little while ago. **¿Qué hay?** What's the matter?; What's new? **¿Qué hay de nuevo?** What's new? *Pres. Ind.* **he, has, ha, hemos,**

habéis, han. *Fut.* **habré, etc.** *Condit.* **habría, etc.** *Preterite* **hube, hubiste, hubo, hubimos, hubisteis, hubieron.** *Pres. Subjunc.* **haya, etc.** *Imperf. Subjunc.* **hubiese, etc.**

habichuela /aβi'tʃuela/ *f*, kidney bean

hábil /'aβil/ *a* clever; skillful; able; lawful

habilidad /aβili'ðað/ *f*, ability; skill; accomplishment; craftsmanship; workmanship

habilidoso /aβili'ðoso/ *a* accomplished; able; skillful

habilitación /aβilita'sion; aβilita'θion/ *f*, habilitation; paymastership; equipment; furnishing

habilitado /aβili'taðo/ *m*, paymaster

habilitar /aβili'tar/ *vt* to qualify; equip; furnish; habilitate; enable; *Com.* capitalize

habitabilidad /aβitaβili'ðað/ *f*, habitability

habitable /aβi'taβle/ *a* habitable

habitación /aβita'sion; aβita'θion/ *f*, habitation, dwelling; room in a house; residence; (*Bot. Zool.*) habitat; caretaking

habitante /aβi'tante/ *m*, inhabitant

habitar /aβi'tar/ *vt* to inhabit, reside in

hábito /'aβito/ *m*, attire; *Eccl.* habit; use, custom; skill, facility; *pl* vestments; gown, robe. **tomar el h.,** to become a monk or nun

habitual /aβi'tual/ *a* habitual, usual

habituar /aβi'tuar/ *vt* to accustom; *vr* accustom oneself; grow used (to)

habitud /aβi'tuð/ *f*, habit, custom; connection, relationship

habla /'aβla/ *f*, speech; language; dialect; discourse. **al h.,** within speaking distance. **de h. hispana,** Spanish-speaking

hablado /a'βlaðo/ *a* spoken. **bien h.,** well-spoken; courteous. **mal h.,** ill-spoken; rude

hablador /aβla'ðor/ **(-ra)** a talkative; gossipy; *Mexico* also boastful. n chatterbox; gossip

habladuría /aβlaðu'ria/ f, gossip; impertinent chatter

hablanchín /aβlan'tʃin/ a *Inf.* chattering, gossiping

hablar /a'βlar/ vi to speak; converse; express oneself; arrange; (*with de*) speak about, discuss; gossip about, criticize; (*with por*) intercede on behalf of; vt speak (a language); say, speak; vr speak to one another. **no hablarse,** to not be on speaking terms. **h. a gritos,** to shout. **h. alto,** to speak loudly or in strong terms. **h. bien** (*or* **mal**), to be well- (or ill-) spoken; be polite (or rude). **h. claro,** to speak frankly. **h. consigo** *or* **h. entre sí,** to talk to oneself. *Inf.* **h. cristiano, h. en cristiano,** to speak clearly or intelligibly; speak frankly. **hablarlo todo,** to talk too much. **h. por h.,** to talk for talking's sake. *Inf.* **h. por los codos,** to chatter. **h. sin ton ni son,** to speak foolishly

hablilla /a'βliya; a'βliʎa/ f, rumor, tittletattle, gossip

hacecillo /ase'siyo; aθe'θiʎo/ m, small sheaf; small bundle; *Bot.* fascicle; beam (of light)

hacedero /ase'ðero; aθe'ðero/ a feasible, practicable

hacedor /ase'ðor; aθe'ðor/ m, maker; steward, manager; Creator

hacendado /asen'daðo; aθen'daðo/ **(-da)** a landed. n landowner; *West. Hem.* cattle rancher

hacendista /asen'dista; aθen'dista/ mf political economist

hacendoso /asen'doso; aθen'doso/ a diligent, hardworking

hacer /a'ser; a'θer/ vt irr to make; fashion, form, construct; do, perform; cause, effect; arrange, put right; contain; accustom, harden; pack (luggage); imagine, invent, create; improve, perfect; compel, oblige; deliver (speeches); compose; earn; *Math.* add up to; suppose, imagine (e.g. *Sus padres hacían a María en casa,* Her parents imagined that Mary was at home); put into practice, execute; play the part of or act like (e.g. *h. el gracioso,* to play the buffoon); shed, cast (e.g. *El roble hace sombra,* The oak casts a shadow); assemble, convoke (meetings, gatherings); give off, produce (e.g. *La chimenea hace humo,* The chimney is smoking); perform (plays); (*with el, la, lo, and some nouns*) pretend to be (e.g. *Se hizo el desconocido,* He pretended to be ignorant). (**h.** followed by infin. is sometimes translated by a past participle in English (e.g. *Lo hice h.,* I had it done).) vi to matter, be important, signify (e.g. *Su llegada no hace nada al caso,* His arrival makes no difference to the case. *Se me hace muy poco...,* It matters to me very little...); be fitting or suitable; concern, be pertinent; match, go with; agree, be in harmony; (*with de*) act as, discharge duties of temporarily (e.g. *h. de camarero,* to be a temporary waiter); (*with por*) try to, attempt to (e.g. *Haremos por decírselo,* We shall try to tell him). vi impers Used in expressions concerning: 1. the weather. 2. lapse of time. English uses the verb "to be'' in both cases, e.g.: 1. *hace buen* (*or mal*) **tiempo,** it is fine (or bad) weather. **hace mucho frío,** it is very cold. **hace sol,** it is sunny. **hace viento,** it is windy. **¿Qué tiempo hace?** What is the weather like? 2. **hace** + an expression of time is followed by **que** introducing a clause (e.g. *Hace dos horas que llegamos,* We arrived two hours ago) or **hace** + an expression of time may be followed by **desde** + a noun (e.g. *Hace dos años desde aquel día,* It is two years since that day) When an action or state that has begun in the past is still continuing in the present, the Spanish verb is in the Pres. Ind., whereas the English verb is in the Perfect (e.g. *Hace un mes que la veo todos los días,* I have been seeing her every day for a month). This rule holds good with other tenses. English Pluperfect, Future Perfect, Conditional Perfect become in Spanish Imperfect, Future, Conditional, respectively. *Naut.* **h. agua,** to leak. **h. aguas,** to pass water, urinate. **h. alarde de,** to boast of. **h. América,** to strike it rich. **h. el amor a,** to make love to, court, woo. **h. autoridad,** to be authoritative. **h. a todo,** to have many uses; be adaptable. **h. bancarrota,** to go bankrupt. **h. un berrinche, hacerse un berrinche,** to have a fit, have a tantrum. *Fig. Inf.* **h. buena,** to justify. **h. calceta,** to knit. **h. cara** *or* **frente a,** to face; resist. **h. caso,** to take notice, mind (e.g. *¡No hagas*

caso! Never mind!). **h. causas,** to bring charges, institute proceedings. **h. cuentas,** to reckon up. **h. daño,** to harm. *Inf.* **h. de las suyas,** to behave in his usual manner or play one of his usual tricks. **h. diligencias por,** to endeavor to. **h. fiesta,** to take a holiday. **h. fuerza,** to struggle. **h. fuerza a,** *Fig.* to do violence to (e.g. *Hizo fuerza a sus creencias,* He did violence to his beliefs). **h. h.,** to cause to be made (e.g. *He hecho hacer un vestido,* I have had a dress made). **h. juego,** to make a set, match (e.g. *El sombrero hace juego con el traje,* The hat goes with the dress). **h. la corte (a),** to court, woo. *Fig. Inf.* **h. la vista gorda,** to turn a blind eye. **h. la vida del claustro,** to lead a cloistered existence. **h. mal,** to do wrong; be harmful (food, etc.). **h. pedazos,** to break. **h. pinos** (*or* **pinitos**) to totter; toddle; stagger. *Aer.* **h. rizos,** to loop the loop. **h. saber,** to make known; notify. **h. seguir,** to forward (letters). **h. señas,** to make signs (wave, beckon, etc.). *Inf.* **h. una que sea sonada,** to cause a big scandal. **¡Hágame el favor!** Please! *Pres. Ind.* **hago, haces, etc.** *Fut.* **haré, etc.** *Condit.* **haría, etc.** *Imperat.* **haz, haga, hagamos, haced, hagan.** *Preterite* **hice, hiciste, hizo, hicimos, hicisteis, hicieron.** *Pres. Subjunc.* **haga, etc.** *Imperf. Subjunc.* **hiciese, etc.**

hacerse /a'serse; a'θerse/ vr irr to become (e.g. *Se ha hecho muy importante,* It (or he) has become very important); grow up (e.g. *Miguel se ha hecho hombre,* Michael has grown up (become a man)); develop, mature; pass oneself off as, pretend to be; (*with prep a*) become accustomed to or used to (e.g. *Me haré a este clima,* I shall grow used to this climate); withdraw or retire to (of places); (*with de or con*) provide oneself with. **h. a la vela,** to set sail. **h. a (uno),** to seem (e.g. *Eso que me cuentas se me hace increíble,* What you tell me seems incredible). *Inf.* **h. chiquito,** to be modest. **h. tarde,** to grow late; *Fig.* be too late. See **hacer**

hacha /'atʃa/ f, large candle; torch; ax. **h. pequeña,** hatchet

hachazo /a'tʃaso; a'tʃaθo/ m, stroke of an ax

hache /'atʃe/ f, name of the letter H

hachero /a'tʃero/ m, candlestick; woodcutter, axman

hacho /'atʃo/ m, torch; beacon

hacia /'asia; 'aθia/ prep toward, near, about. **h. adelante,** forward, onward

hacienda /a'sienda; a'θienda/ f, country estate, land; property; pl domestic tasks; cattle. **h. pública,** public funds. **ministerio de h.,** national treasury, exchequer

hacina /a'sina; a'θina/ f, *Agr.* stack; heap, pile

hacinamiento /asina'miento; aθina'miento/ m, stacking, piling; accumulation

hacinar /asi'nar; aθi'nar/ vt *Agr.* to stack sheaves; accumulate, amass; pile up, heap

hada /'aða/ f, fairy

hado /'aðo/ m, fate; destiny

hagiografía /ahiogra'fia/ f, hagiography

hagiógrafo /a'hiografo/ m, hagiographer

Haití /ai'ti/ Haiti

haitiano /ai'tiano/ **(-na)** a and n Haitian

halagar /ala'gar/ vt to caress; flatter; coax; please, delight

halago /a'lago/ m, flattery; coaxing; caress; source of pleasure, delight

halagüeño /ala'gueɲo/ a flattering; pleasing; caressing; hopeful, promising

halar /a'lar/ vt *Naut.* to haul, tow

halcón /al'kon/ m, falcon

halconero /alko'nero/ m, hawker, hunter

hálito /'alito/ m, breath; vapor; *Poet.* breeze

hallado /a'yaðo; a'ʎaðo/ a and *Past Part.* found, met. **bien h.,** welcome; happy, contented. **mal h.,** unwelcome; uneasy, discontented

hallador /aya'ðor; aʎa'ðor/ **(-ra)** n finder

hallar /a'yar; a'ʎar/ vt to find; meet; observe; discover; find out; vr be present; find oneself

hallazgo /a'yasgo; a'ʎaθgo/ m, finding; thing found; finder's reward

halo /'alo/ m, halo

halterofilia /altero'filia/ f, weightlifting

hamaca /a'maka/ f, hammock

hambre /'ambre/ f, hunger; famine; desire, yearning. **tener h.,** to be hungry
hambriento /am'briento/ a hungry; famished; Fig. starved (of affection, etc.)
hamburguesa /ambur'gesa/ f, hamburger
hamo /'amo/ m, fishhook
hampa /'ampa/ f, rogue's life; gang of rogues; underworld, slum
hangar /aŋ'gar/ m, hangar
haragán /ara'gan/ **(-ana)** a lazy, idle. n idler, lazybones
harapiento /ara'piento/ a ragged
harapo /a'rapo/ m, tatter, rag
haraposo /ara'poso/ a ragged
harén /a'ren/ m, harem
harina /a'rina/ f, flour; powder; farina. Inf. **ser h. de otro costal,** to be a horse of another color
harinero /ari'nero/ a relating to flour. m, flour merchant; flour bin
harinoso /ari'noso/ a floury, mealy; farinaceous
harmónica /ar'monika/ f, (Phys. Math.) harmonic
harmonizar /armoni'sar; armoni'θar/ vt to arrange (music)
harnear /arne'ar/ vt Lat. Am. to sieve, sift
harnero /ar'nero/ m, sieve
harón /a'ron/ a slothful, slow; lazy, idle
harpillera /arpi'yera; arpi'ʎera/ f, sackcloth, sacking
hartar /ar'tar/ vt to satiate; tire, annoy; satisfy the appetite; shower (with blows, etc.)
hartazgo /ar'tasgo; ar'taθgo/ m, satiety
harto /'arto/ a satiated; tired (of), adv enough
hartón /ar'ton/ a Central America, Mexico gluttonous
hartura /ar'tura/ f, satiety; abundance
hasta /'asta/ prep until; as far as; down or up to. conjunc also, even. **h. la vista,** See you! Ciao! Au revoir! **h. mañana,** until tomorrow
hastial /as'tial/ m, gable, end wall; boor, lout
hastío /as'tio/ a, loathing; distaste; nausea
hato /'ato/ m, bundle of personal clothing; herd of cattle; gang (of suspicious characters); crowd, mob; Inf. group, party. Inf. **liar el h.,** to pack up
Hawai /'awai/ Hawaii
hay /ai/ there is; there are. See **haber**
haya /'aya/ f, beech tree; beechwood
hayal /a'yal/ a, wood of beech trees, beech plantation
hayuco /a'yuko/ m, beech mast
haz /as; aθ/ m, bundle, sheaf; Mil. file; pl fasces. f, visage; surface, face. **h. de la tierra,** face of the earth. **h. de luz,** beam of light. Fig. **ser de dos haces,** to be two-faced
haz /as; aθ/ 2nd pers Imperat **hacer**
hazaña /a'saɲa; a'θaɲa/ f, exploit, prowess
hazañoso /asa'ɲoso; aθa'ɲoso/ a heroic, dauntless, courageous
hazmerreír /asmerre'ir; aθmerre'ir/ m, Inf. laughingstock
he /e/ interj and adv Behold! **¡Heme aquí!** Here I am. **he aquí,** here is...
hebilla /e'βiya; e'βiʎa/ f, buckle, clasp
hebra /'eβra/ f, thread; fiber; flesh; Mineral. vein, streak; filament (textiles); grain (of wood); pl Poet. hair. Inf. **pegar la h.,** to start a conversation
hebraísmo /eβra'ismo/ m, Hebraism
hebraísta /eβra'ista/ m, Hebraist
hebreo /e'βreo/ **(-ea)** a Hebraic, Jewish. n Jew. m, Hebrew (language)
hecatombe /eka'tombe/ f, hecatomb; slaughter, massacre
hechicería /etʃise'ria; etʃiθe'ria/ f, sorcery; spell, enchantment
hechicero /etʃi'sero; etʃi'θero/ a bewitching; magic; charming, attractive
hechizar /etʃi'sar; etʃi'θar/ vt to bewitch; charm, attract, delight
hechizo /e'tʃiso; e'tʃiθo/ m, magic spell; fascination; charm; delight, pleasure; a Lat. Am. homemade, produced locally, locally produced
hecho /'etʃo/ a developed, mature; accustomed, used; perfected, finished; ready-made. **h. una furia,** like a

fury, very angry. **bien h.,** well-made, well-proportioned; well or rightly done
hecho /'etʃo/ m, deed, action; fact; happening, event. **los Hechos de los Apóstoles,** the Acts of the Apostles
hechura /e'tʃura/ f, making, make; creation; form; figure, statue; Lit. composition; build (of body); Fig. puppet, creature; pl price paid for work done. **de h.**, **sastre,** a tailor-made
hectárea /ekta'rea/ f, hectare
hectógrafo /ek'tografo/ m, hectograph
hectogramo /ekto'gramo/ m, hectogram
hectolitro /ekto'litro/ m, hectoliter
hectovatio /ekto'βatio/ m, hectowatt
heder /e'ðer/ vi irr to stink; be intolerable. See **entender**
hediondez /eðion'des; eðion'deθ/ f, stink, stench
hediondo /e'ðiondo/ a stinking; intolerable, pestiential; obscene
hedonismo /eðo'nismo/ m, hedonism
hedonista /eðo'nista/ mf hedonist
hegeliano /ehe'liano/ a Hegelian
hegemonía /ehemo'nia/ f, hegemony
helada /e'laða/ f, frost. **h. blanca,** hoarfrost
heladera /ela'ðera/ f, refrigerator
helado /e'laðo/ a frozen; ice-cold; astounded, disdainful. m, iced drink; sherbet, ice cream
helamiento /ela'miento/ m, icing; freezing
helar /e'lar/ vt irr to freeze; ice, chill; astound; discourage; vr become iced; freeze; become ice-cold. v impers to freeze. See **acertar**
helecho /e'letʃo/ m, fern
helénico /e'leniko/ a Hellenic
helenismo /ele'nismo/ m, Hellenism
helenista /ele'nista/ mf Hellenist
helenizar /eleni'sar; eleni'θar/ vt to Hellenize
hélice /'elise; 'eliθe/ f, spiral, helical line; screw, propeller; Geom. helix; Astron. Ursa Major
helicóptero /eli'koptero/ m, Aer. helicopter
helio /'elio/ m, helium
heliógrafo /e'liografo/ m, heliograph
helioscopio /elio'skopio/ m, helioscope
helióstato /e'liostato/ m, heliostat
helioterapia /eliote'rapia/ f, heliotherapy
heliotropismo /eliotro'pismo/ m, heliotropism
heliotropo /elio'tropo/ m, heliotrope; agate
helvecio /el'βesio; el'βeθio/ **(-ia)** a and n Helvetian
hembra /'embra/ f, female; Inf. woman; nut of a screw; eye of a hook. Inf. **una real h.,** a fine figure of a woman
hemiciclo /emi'siklo; emi'θiklo/ m, hemicycle; floor (of a legislative building)
hemisférico /emis'feriko/ a hemispherical
hemisferio /emis'ferio/ m, hemisphere
hemofilia /emo'filia/ f, hemophilia
hemoglobina /emoglo'βina/ f, hemoglobin
hemorragia /emo'rrahia/ f, hemorrhage
hemorroides /emo'rroiðes/ f, hemorrhoids
henchido /en'tʃiðo/ a swollen
henchimiento /entʃi'miento/ m, swelling; inflation; filling
henchir /en'tʃir/ vt irr to fill; stuff; swell. Pres. Ind. **hincho, hinches, hinche, hinchen.** Pres. Part. **hinchiendo.** Pres. Subjunc. **hincha,** etc. Imperf. Subjunc. **hinchiese,** etc. Imperat. **hinche, hincha, hinchamos, henchid, hinchan**
hendedura /ende'ðura/ f, fissure; rift
hender /en'der/ vt irr to split, crack; Fig. cleave (air, water, etc.); make one's way through. See **entender**
hendidura /endi'ðura/ f, split, fissure, crack, chink
hendija /en'diha/ f, Lat. Am. crack, crevice
henil /e'nil/ m, hayloft
heno /'eno/ m, hay
hepático /e'patiko/ a hepatic
heráldica /e'raldika/ f, heraldry
heráldico /e'raldiko/ a heraldic
heraldo /e'raldo/ m, herald; harbinger
herbaje /er'βahe/ m, herbage; pasture; grass; thick woolen cloth

herbario /er'βario/ *m*, herbalist, botanist; herbarium.
a herbal
herbívoro /er'βiβoro/ *a* herbivorous
herbolaria /erβo'laria/ *f*, herbal
hercúleo /er'kuleo/ *a* herculean
heredad /ere'ðað/ *f*, landed property; country estate
heredar /ere'ðar/ *vt* to inherit; make a deed of gift to; inherit characteristics, etc.; take as heir
heredera /ere'ðera/ *f*, heiress
heredero /ere'ðero/ *m*, heir; inheritor. **h. aparente**, heir apparent. **presunto h.**, heir presumptive
hereditario /ereði'tario/ *a* hereditary
hereje /e'rehe/ *mf* heretic
herejía /ere'hia/ *f*, heresy
herencia /e'rensia; e'renθia/ *f*, inheritance; heredity; heritage
heresiarca /ere'siarka/ *mf* heresiarch
herético /e'retiko/ *a* heretical
herida /e'riða/ *f*, wound; insult; anguish. **h. contusa**, contusion. **h. penetrante**, deep wound
herir /e'rir/ *vt irr* to wound; strike, harm; *Fig.* pierce (of sun's rays); *Fig.* pluck (strings of a musical instrument); impress (the senses); affect (the emotions); offend (gen. of words). *Pres. Part.* **hiriendo.** *Pres. Ind.* **hiero, hieres, hiere, hieren.** *Preterite* **hirió, hirieron.** *Pres. Subjunc.* **hiera, hieras, hiera, hiramos, hiráis, hieran.** *Imperf. Subjunc.* **hiriese, etc.**
hermafrodita /ermafro'ðita/ *a* and *mf* hermaphrodite
hermafroditismo /ermafroði'tismo/ *m*, hermaphroditism
hermana /er'mana/ *f*, sister; twin, pair (of things). **h. de leche**, foster sister. **h. política**, sister-in-law
hermanar /erma'nar/ *vt* to join; mate; harmonize; *Chile* to pair (like socks); *vt* and *vr* be the spiritual brother of, be compatible
hermanastra /erma'nastra/ *f*, stepsister, half-sister
hermanastro /erma'nastro/ *m*, stepbrother, half-brother
hermandad /erman'dað/ *f*, brotherhood; friendship; intimacy; relationship (of one thing to another); confraternity. **Santa H.**, Spanish rural police force instituted in the fifteenth century
hermano /er'mano/ *m*, brother; pair, twin (of things); *Eccl.* brother. **h. de raza**, member of the same race. **h. político**, brother-in-law
hermético /er'metiko/ *a* hermetic
hermosear /ermose'ar/ *vt* to embellish, beautify, adorn
hermoso /er'moso/ *a* beautiful; shapely; handsome; fine, wonderful (weather, view, etc.)
hermosura /ermo'sura/ *f*, beauty; pleasantness, attractiveness, perfection of form; belle
hernia /'ernia/ *f*, hernia
héroe /'eroe/ *m*, hero
heroicidad /eroisi'ðað; eroiθi'ðað/ *f*, heroism
heroico /e'roiko/ *a* heroic
heroína /ero'ina/ *f*, heroine
heroismo /ero'ismo/ *m*, heroism
herpes /'erpes/ *m pl*, or *f pl*, herpes
herrada /e'rraða/ *f*, pail
herradero /erra'ðero/ *m*, branding of livestock
herrador /erra'ðor/ *m*, blacksmith
herradura /erra'ðura/ *f*, horseshoe
herraje /e'rrahe/ *m*, ironwork; *Lat. Am.* horseshoe
herramienta /erra'mienta/ *f*, tool; set of tools
herrar /e'rrar/ *vt irr* to shoe horses; brand (cattle); decorate with iron. See **acertar**
herrería /erre'ria/ *f*, forge; ironworks; blacksmith's shop; clamor, tumult, confusion
herrero /e'rrero/ *m*, smith
herrete /e'rrete/ *m*, ferrule, tag
herrumbre /e'rrumbre/ *f*, rust
herrumbroso /errum'broso/ *a* rusty
hervidero /erβi'ðero/ *m*, boiling, bubbling; *Fig.* ebullition; swarm, crowd
hervir /er'βir/ *vi irr* to boil; foam and froth (sea); seethe (emotions); surge (crowds); (*with en*) abound in, swarm with. See **sentir**
hervor /er'βor/ *m*, boiling; ebullition, vigor, zest; seething, agitation

hesitación /esita'sion; esita'θion/ *f*, hesitation, doubt, uncertainty
hesitar /esi'tar/ *vi* to hesitate, vacillate
heterodina /etero'ðina/ *a f*, *Radio.* heterodyne
heterodoxia /etero'ðoksia/ *f*, heterodoxy
heterodoxo /etero'ðokso/ *a* heterodox
heterogeneidad /eterohenei'ðað/ *f*, heterogeneity
heterogéneo /etero'heneo/ *a* heterogeneous
heterosexual /eterosek'sual/ *mf* and *a* heterosexual
hético /'etiko/ *a* hectic, consumptive
hexagonal /eksago'nal/ *a* hexagonal
hexágono /e'ksagono/ *m*, hexagon
hexámetro /e'ksametro/ *m*, hexameter
hez /es; eθ/ *f*, (gen. *pl* **heces**) lees, dregs
hiato /'iato/ *m*, hiatus
hibernal /'iβernal/ *a* wintry
hibernés /iβer'nes/ *a* Hibernian
hibisco /i'βisko/ *m*, hibiscus
hibridación /iβriða'sion; iβriða'θion/ *f*, hybridization
hibridismo /iβri'ðismo/ *m*, hybridism
híbrido /'iβriðo/ *a* and *m*, hybrid
hidalgo /i'ðalgo/ **(-ga)** *n* noble, aristocrat. *a* noble; illustrious; generous
hidalguía /iðal'gia/ *f*, nobility; generosity, nobility of spirit
hidra /'iðra/ *f*, *Zool.* hydra; poisonous snake; *Astron.* Hydra
hidratar /iðra'tar/ *vt Chem.* to hydrate
hidrato /i'ðrato/ *m*, hydrate. **h. de carbono**, carbohydrate
hidráulica /i'ðraulika/ *f*, hydraulics
hidráulico /i'ðrauliko/ *a* hydraulic
hidroavión /iðroa'βion/ *m*, flying boat
hidrocarburo /iðrokar'βuro/ *m*, hydrocarbon
hidrocéfalo /iðro'sefalo; iðro'θefalo/ *a* hydrocephalic
hidrodinámica /iðroði'namika/ *f*, hydrodynamics
hidroeléctrico /iðroe'lektriko/ *a* hydroelectric
hidrofobia /iðro'foβia/ *f*, hydrophobia; rabies
hidrógeno /i'ðroheno/ *m*, hydrogen
hidrografía /iðrogra'fia/ *f*, hydrography
hidrología /iðrolo'hia/ *f*, hydrology
hidropesía /iðrope'sia/ *f*, dropsy
hidrópico /i'ðropiko/ *a* dropsical
hidroplano /iðro'plano/ *m*, seaplane
hidroquinona /iðroki'nona/ *f*, hydroquinone
hidroscopio /iðro'skopio/ *m*, hydroscope
hidrostática /iðro'statika/ *f*, hydrostatics
hidroterapia /iðrote'rapia/ *f*, hydrotherapy
hiedra /i'eðra/ *f*, ivy
hiel /iel/ *f*, gall, bile, bitterness, affliction; *pl* troubles
hielo /'ielo/ *m*, ice, frost; freezing, icing; stupefaction; indifference, coldness. *Inf.* **estar hecho un h.**, to be as cold as ice
hiena /'iena/ *f*, hyena
hierático /ie'ratiko/ *a* hieratical
hierba /'ierβa/ *f*, grass; small plant; herb. **h. cana**, groundsel. **mala h.**, weed
hierbabuena /ierβa'βuena/ *f*, *Bot.* mint
hierra /'ierra/ *f*, branding time
hierro /'ierro/ *m*, iron; brand with hot iron; iron or steel head of a lance, etc.; instrument or shape made of iron; weapon of war. *pl* fetters. **h. colado**, cast iron. **h. dulce**, wrought iron. **h. en planchas**, sheet iron. **h. viejo**, scrap iron
hígado /'igaðo/ *m*, liver; courage; *Central America, Mexico* also nuisance
higiene /i'hiene/ *f*, hygiene; cleanliness, neatness. **h. privada**, personal hygiene. **h. pública**, public health
higiénico /i'hieniko/ *a* hygienic
higo /'igo/ *m*, fig. **h. chumbo**, prickly pear
higrómetro /i'grometro/ *m*, hygrometer
higuera /i'gera/ *f*, fig tree
hija /'iha/ *f*, daughter; native of a place; offspring
hijastro /i'hastro/ **(-a)** *n* stepchild
hijo /'iho/ *m*, son; child; native of a place; offspring; shoot, sprout; *pl* descendants. **h. de la cuna**, foundling. **h. de leche**, foster child. **h. natural**, natural child. **h. político**, son-in-law
hijuela /i'huela/ *f*, little daughter; small mattress;

small drain; side road; accessory, subordinate thing; piece of material for widening a garment; *Law.* part of an inheritance; *Lat. Am.* rural property

hila /'ila/ *f,* row, line; gut; *Surg.* lint (gen. *pl*)

hilacha /i'latʃa/ *f,* thread raveled from cloth; fiber, filament. **h. de vidrio,** spun glass

hilado /i'laðo/ *m,* spinning; thread, yarn

hilandería /ilande'ria/ *f,* spinning; spinning mill; mill. **h. de algodón,** cotton mill

hilandero /ilan'dero/ **(-ra)** *n* spinner

hilar /i'lar/ *vt* to spin; reason, infer, discourse

hilaridad /ilari'ðað/ *f,* hilarity; quiet happiness

hilaza /i'lasa; i'laθa/ *f,* yarn

hilera /i'lera/ *f,* line, file, row; fine yarn; *Mil.* file, rank; *Metall.* wire drawer; *Mas.* course (of bricks)

hilo /'ilo/ *m,* thread; linen; wire; mesh (spiders, silkworm's web, etc.); edge (of a blade); thin stream (of liquid); thread (of discourse)

hilván /il'βan/ *m, Sew.* basting; tack

hilvanar /ilβa'nar/ *vt Sew.* to baste

himen /'imen/ *m,* hymen

himeneo /ime'neo/ *m,* marriage, wedding

himnario /im'nario/ *m,* hymnal

himno /'imno/ *m,* hymn

hin /in/ *m,* whinny, neigh

hincapié /inka'pie/ *m,* foothold. **hacer h.,** to insist, make a stand

hincar /in'kar/ *vt* to thrust in; drive in, sink; *vr* kneel. **h. el diente,** to bite. **h. la uña,** to scratch. **hincarse de rodillas,** to kneel down

hinchado /in'tʃaðo/ *a* puffed up, vain; pompous, high-flown, redundant (style)

hinchar /in'tʃar/ *vt* to inflate; puff out (the chest); swell (of a river, etc.); exaggerate (events); *vr* swell; grow vain, be puffed up

hinchazón /intʃa'son; intʃa'θon/ *f,* swelling; vanity, presumption; pomposity, euphuism (style)

hiniesta /i'niesta/ *f,* Spanish broom

hinojo /i'noho/ *m, Bot.* fennel; knee. **de hinojos,** on bended knee

hipar /i'par/ *vi* to hiccup; pant (of dogs); be overanxious; be overtired; sob, cry

hipérbole /i'perβole/ *f,* hyperbole

hiperbólico /iper'βoliko/ *a* hyperbolical

hipercrítico /iper'kritiko/ *m,* hypercritic. *a* hypercritical

hipertensión /iperten'θion/ *f,* hypertension

hipertrofiarse /ipertro'fiarse/ *vr* to hypertrophy

hípico /'ipiko/ *a* equine

hipnosis /ip'nosis/ *f,* hypnosis

hipnótico /ip'notiko/ *a* hypnotic. *m,* hypnotic drug

hipnotismo /ipno'tismo/ *m,* hypnotism

hipnotización /ipnotisa'sion; ipnotiθa'θion/ *f,* hypnotization

hipnotizar /ipnoti'sar; ipnoti'θar/ *vt* to hypnotize

hipo /'ipo/ *m,* hiccup; sob; longing, desire; dislike, disgust

hipocondría /ipokon'dria/ *f,* hypochondria

hipocondríaco /ipokon'driakʊ/ **(-ca)** *a* hypochondriacal. *n* hypochondriac

hipocrático /ipo'kratiko/ *a* Hippocratic

hipocresía /ipokre'sia/ *f,* hypocrisy

hipócrita /i'pokrita/ *a* hypocritical. *mf* hypocrite

hipodérmico /ipo'ðermiko/ *a* hypodermic

hipódromo /i'poðromo/ *m,* hippodrome, racetrack

hipopótamo /ipo'potamo/ *m,* hippopotamus

hipostático /ipo'statiko/ *a* hypostatic

hipoteca /ipo'teka/ *f,* mortgage

hipotecable /ipote'kaβle/ *a* mortgageable

hipotecar /ipote'kar/ *vt* to mortgage

hipotecario /ipote'kario/ *a* belonging to a mortgage

hipotenusa /ipote'nusa/ *f,* hypotenuse

hipótesis /i'potesis/ *f,* hypothesis

hipotético /ipo'tetiko/ *a* hypothetical

hirsuto /ir'suto/ *a* hirsute, hairy

hirviente /ir'βiente/ *a* boiling

hisca /'iska/ *f,* birdlime

hisopear /isope'ar/ *vt Eccl.* to sprinkle, asperse

hisopo /i'sopo/ *m, Bot.* hyssop; *Eccl.* hyssop, sprinkler; *Lat. Am. also* (paint)brush

hispánico /is'paniko/ *a* Spanish

hispanismo /ispa'nismo/ *m,* Hispanism

hispanista /ispa'nista/ *mf* Hispanist

hispano /is'pano/ *a* Hispanic, Spanish American.

hispanoamericano /ispanoameri'kano/ **(-na)** *a* and *n* Spanish-American, Hispano-American

histeria /is'teria/ *f,* hysteria

histérico /is'teriko/ *a* hysterical; hysteric

histerismo /iste'rismo/ *m, Med.* hysteria

histología /istolo'hia/ *f,* histology

histólogo /is'tologo/ *m,* histologist

historia /is'toria/ *f,* history; narrative, story; tale; *Inf.* gossip (gen. *pl*); *Art.* historical piece. **h. natural,** natural history. **h. sagrada,** biblical history. *Fig. Inf.* **dejarse de historias,** to stop beating around the bush

historiador /istoria'ðor/ **(-ra)** *n* historian

historiar /isto'riar/ *vt* to narrate, relate; record, chronicle

histórico /is'toriko/ *a* historical; historic

historieta /isto'rieta/ *f,* short story; anecdote

historiografía /istoriogra'fia/ *f,* historiography

historiógrafo /isto'riografo/ *m,* historiographer

histriónico /ist'rioniko/ *a* histrionic

hitlerismo /itle'rismo/ *m,* Hitlerism

hito /'ito/ *m,* milestone; boundary mark; *Fig.* mark, target. **de h. en h.,** from head to foot

hocico /o'siko; o'θiko/ *m,* snout; *Inf.* face, mug; *Inf.* angry gesture; *Naut.* prow. **meter el h.,** to stick one's nose into other people's business

hogaño /o'gaɲo/ *adv Inf.* during this year; at the present time

hogar /o'gar/ *m,* hearth, fireplace; home, house; family life; firebox (of a locomotive)

hoguera /o'gera/ *f,* bonfire

hoja /'oha/ *f, Bot.* leaf; petal; sheet (metal, paper, etc.); page (of book); blade (sharp instruments); leaf (door, window); sword. **h. de cálculo,** spreadsheet. **h. de servicios,** service or professional record. **h. de tocino,** side of bacon. **h. extraordinaria,** extra, special edition (of a newspaper). **h. volante,** handbill, supplement. **volver la h.,** to turn over (pages); change one's opinion; turn the conversation

hojalata /oha'lata/ *f,* tin plate

hojalatería /ohalate'ria/ *f,* tinware; tin shop

hojalatero /ohala'tero/ *m,* tinsmith

hojalda, hojalde /o'halda, o'halde/ *m* = **hojaldre**

hojaldre /o'haldre/ *m,* or *f,* puff pastry

hojarasca /oha'raska/ *f,* withered leaves; excessive foliage; rubbish, trash

hojear /ohe'ar/ *vt* to turn the leaves of a book; skip, skim, read quickly; *vi* exfoliate

hojuela /o'huela/ *f, dim* little leaf; *Bot.* leaflet; pancake

¡hola! /'ola/ *interj* Hi! Hello!

Holanda /o'landa/ Holland

holandés /olan'des/ **(-esa)** *a* and *n* Dutchman (-woman) *m,* Dutch (language)

holgado /ol'gaðo/ *a* leisured, free; loose, wide; comfortable; well-off, rich

holganza /ol'gansa; ol'ganθa/ *f,* repose, leisure, ease; idleness; pleasure

holgar /ol'gar/ *vi irr* to rest; be idle; be glad; be unused or unnecessary (things). *vr* enjoy oneself, amuse oneself; be glad. See **colgar**

holgazán /olga'san; olga'θan/ **(-ana)** *a* idle. *n* idler

holgazanear /olgasane'ar; olgaθane'ar/ *vi* to idle

holgazanería /olgasane'ria; olgaθane'ria/ *f,* idleness, sloth

holgorio /ol'gorio/ *m,* rejoicing, festivity, merriment

holgura /ol'gura/ *f,* enjoyment, merrymaking; width; comfort, ease; *Mech.* free play

hollar /o'yar; o'ʎar/ *vt irr* to trample under foot; humiliate. See **degollar**

hollejo /o'yeho; o'ʎeho/ *m,* peel, thin skin (of fruit); *Agr.* chaff

hollín /o'yin; o'ʎin/ *m,* soot

holocausto /olo'kausto/ *m,* holocaust. **el H.** the Holocaust

hológrafo /o'lografo/ *m*, holograph
hombradía /ombra'ðia/ *f*, manliness; courage
hombre /'ombre/ *m*, man; adult; omber (cards). *interj* ¡**h.**! *Inf*. Old fellow! You don't say so! ¡**h. al agua!** Man overboard! **h. de bien,** honest, honorable man. **h. de estado,** statesman. **h. de muchos oficios,** jack-of-all-trades. **h. de negocios,** businessman; man of affairs. **h. de pro,** worthy man; famous man. **ser muy h.,** to be a real man, be very manly
hombrera /om'brera/ *f*, epaulette; shoulderpad
hombro /'ombro/ *m*, shoulder. **echar al h.,** to shoulder; undertake, take the responsibility of. **encogerse de hombros,** to shrug one's shoulders; be indifferent or uninterested
hombruno /om'bruno/ *a Inf*. mannish (of a woman)
homenaje /ome'nahe/ *m*, allegiance; homage; veneration, respect
homeópata /ome'opata/ *a* homeopathic. *mf* homeopath
homeopatía /omeopa'tia/ *f*, homeopathy
homérico /o'meriko/ *a* Homeric
homicida /omi'siða; omi'θiða/ *a* murderous, homicidal. *mf* murderer (-ess)
homicidio /omi'siðio; omi'θiðio/ *m*, homicide (act)
homilía /omi'lia/ *f*, homily
homogeneidad /omohenei'ðað/ *f*, homogeneity
homogéneo /omo'heneo/ *a* homogeneous
homónimo /o'monimo/ *a* homonymous. *m*, homonym
homosexual /omose'ksual/ *a* and *mf* homosexual
honda /'onda/ *f*, sling, catapult, slingshot
hondear /onde'ar/ *vt Naut*. to sound, plumb; *Naut*. unload; *Lat. Am*. to hit with a slingshot
hondo /'ondo/ *a* deep; low; *Fig*. profound; deep, intense (emotion). *m*, depth
hondón /on'don/ *m*, depth, recess
hondonada /ondo'naða/ *f*, hollow; glen; valley
hondura /on'dura/ *f*, depth
Honduras /on'duras/ Honduras
hondureño /ondu'reɲo/ **(-ña)** *a* and *n* Honduran
honestidad /onesti'ðað/ *f*, honorableness; virtue; respectability; modesty; courtesy
honesto /o'nesto/ *a* honorable, virtuous; modest; honest, just
hongo /'oŋgo/ *m*, fungus; toadstool; bowler hat
honor /o'nor/ *m*, honor; fame; reputation (women); modesty (women); praise; *pl* rank, position; honors
honorable /ono'raβle/ *a* honorable
honorario /ono'rario/ *a* honorary. *m*, honorarium, fee
honorífico /ono'rifiko/ *a* honorary; honorable
honra /'onra/ *f*, self-respect, honor, personal dignity; reputation; chastity and modesty (women); *pl* obsequies
honradez /onra'ðes; onra'ðeθ/ *f*, honesty; honorableness, integrity; respectability
honrado /on'raðo/ *a* honest; honorable
honrar /on'rar/ *vt* to respect; honor; *vr* to be honored
honroso /on'roso/ *a* honor-giving, honorable
¡hopa! /'opa/ *interj Argentina* cut it out!, stop it!
hora /'ora/ *f*, hour; opportune moment; *pl* peak of hours. **horas hábiles,** working hours. **horas muertas,** wee hours; wasted time. **a la h.,** on time. **a última h.,** at the last minute. **dar la h.,** to strike the hour. **decir la h.,** tell time. **por h.,** per hour. **¿Qué h. es?** What time is it?
horadar /ora'ðar/ *vt* to bore, pierce
horario /o'rario/ *a* hourly. *m*, timetable; hour hand of a clock; watch
horca /'orka/ *f*, gallows; *Agr*. pitchfork; fork; prop for trees
horcajadas /orka'haðas/ **(a)** *adv* astride
horcajadura /orkaha'ðura/ *f*, crotch
horchata /or'tʃata/ *f*, drink made of chufas or crushed almonds
horda /'orða/ *f*, horde
horizontal /orison'tal; oriθon'tal/ *a* horizontal
horizonte /ori'sonte; ori'θonte/ *m*, horizon. **nuevos horizontes,** new opportunities
horma /'orma/ *f*, mold; cobbler's last; stone wall.

Fig. Inf. **hallar la h. de su zapato,** to find what suits one; meet one's match
hormiga /or'miga/ *f*, ant
hormigón /ormi'gon/ *m*, concrete. **h. armado,** reinforced concrete
hormiguear /ormige'ar/ *vi* to itch; crowd, swarm
hormiguero /ormi'gero/ *m*, anthill; crowd, swarm
hormona /or'mona/ *f*, hormone
hornero /or'nero/ **(-ra)** *n* baker
horno /'orno/ *m*, oven; furnace; kiln; bakery. **h. alfarero,** firing oven (for pottery). **h. de cocina,** kitchen stove. **h. de cuba,** blast furnace. **h. de ladrillo,** brick kiln. **alto h.,** iron-smelting furnace
horóscopo /o'roskopo/ *m*, horoscope
horquilla /or'kiya; or'kiʎa/ *f*, forked stick; hairpin; hatpin; *Agr*. fork; hook. **viraje en h.,** hairpin turn
horrendo /o'rrendo/ *a* horrible, frightful
hórreo /'orreo/ *m*, granary, barn
horribilidad /orriβili'ðað/ *f*, horribleness
horribilísimo /orriβi'lisimo/ *a sup* most horrible, exceedingly horrible
horrible /o'rriβle/ *a* horrible
horrífico /o'rrifiko/ *a* horrific
horripilante /orripi'lante/ *a* hair-raising, horrifying
horrísono /o'rrisono/ *a Poet*. horrid-sounding, terrifying
horror /o'rror/ *m*, horror; horribleness; atrocity, enormity
horrorizar /orrori'sar; orrori'θar/ *vt* to horrify; *vr* be horrified, be terrified
horroroso /orro'roso/ *a* dreadful, horrible; horrid; *Inf*. hideous, most ugly
hortaliza /orta'lisa; orta'liθa/ *f*, green vegetable, garden produce
hortelano /orte'lano/ *m*, market gardener
hortensia /or'tensia/ *f*, hydrangea
horticultura /ortikul'tura/ *f*, horticulture
hortícola /or'tikultu'ral/ *a* horticultural
hosanna /o'sanna/ *m*, hosanna
hosco /'osko/ *a* dark brown; unsociable, sullen; crabbed
hospedaje /ospe'ðahe/ *m*, lodging; board, payment
hospedar /ospe'ðar/ *vt* to lodge, receive as a guest; *vr* and *vi* lodge, stay
hospedería /ospeðe'ria/ *f*, hostelry, inn; lodging
hospedero /ospe'ðero/ **(-ra)** *n* innkeeper
hospicio /os'pisio; os'piθio/ *m*, hospice; almshouse, workhouse; lodging; orphanage
hospital /ospi'tal/ *m*, hospital; hospice. **h. de sangre,** field hospital
hospitalidad /ospitalari'ðað/ *f*, hospitableness; hospital
hospitalidad /ospitali'ðað/ *f*, hospitality; hospitableness; hospital
hostelero /oste'lero/ **(-ra)** *n* innkeeper
hostería /oste'ria/ *f*, hostelry; inn
hostia /'ostia/ *f*, *Eccl*. wafer, Host
hostigamiento /ostiga'miento/ *m*, harassment. **h. sexual,** sexual harassment
hostigar /osti'gar/ *vt* to chastise; harass; tease, annoy
hostil /os'til/ *a* hostile
hostilidad /ostili'ðað/ *f*, hostility
hostilizar /ostili'sar; ostili'θar/ *vt* to commit hostile acts against; antagonize
hotel /'otel/ *m*, hotel; villa
hotelero /ote'lero/ **(-ra)** *n* hotelkeeper
hoy /oi/ *adv* today; at present. **h. día** *or* **h. en día,** today. **h. por h.,** day by day; at the present time. **de h. en adelante,** from today forward
hoya /'oya/ *f*, hole; grave; valley, glen; bed (of a river)
hoyo /'oyo/ *m*, hole; pockmark; grave; hollow
hoyuelo /o'yuelo/ *m*, *dim* little hole; dimple
hoz /os; oθ/ *f*, sickle; defile
hozar /o'sar; o'θar/ *vt* to root (pigs, etc.)
hucha /'utʃa/ *f*, large chest; strongbox; savings
hueco /'ueko/ *a* empty; hollow; vain; hollow (sound); pompous (style); spongy, soft; inflated. *m*, hollow; interval of time or place; *Inf*. vacancy; gap in a wall, etc.

huelga /'uelɣa/ *f*, strike; leisure; lying fallow; merrymaking. **h. de brazos caídos,** sit-down strike. **h. patronal,** lockout strike
huelguista /uel'gista/ *mf* striker
huella /'ueya; 'ueʎa/ *f*, footprint, track; footstep; tread (of stairs); *Print.* impression; vestige, trace. **h. digital,** fingerprint
huérfano /'uerfano/ **(-na)** *n* orphan. *a* unprotected, uncared for
huero /'uero/ *a* addled; empty, hollow
huerta /'uerta/ *f*, vegetable garden; orchard; irrigation land
huerto /'uerto/ *m*, orchard; vegetable garden
hueso /'ueso/ *m*, bone; stone (of fruit); kernel, core; drudgery; cheap, useless thing of poor quality. *Inf.* **no dejar un h. sano,** to tear (a person) to pieces. **tener los huesos molidos,** to be tired out; be bruised
huésped /'uespeð/ **(-da)** *n* guest; host; innkeeper
hueste /'ueste/ *f*, (gen. *pl*) army on the march; host; party, supporters
huesudo /ue'suðo/ *a* bony
hueva /'ueβa/ *f*, fish roe
huevera /ue'βera/ *f*, egg seller; eggcup
huevo /'ueβo/ *m*, egg. **h. duro,** hard-boiled egg. **h. estrellado,** fried egg. **h. pasado por agua,** soft-boiled egg. **huevos revueltos,** scrambled eggs
hugonote /ugo'note/ **(-ta)** *a* and *n* Huguenot
huida /'uiða/ *f*, flight, escape; bolting (of a horse); outlet
huir /uir/ *vi irr* to flee; fly (of time); elope; run away, bolt; (*with de*) avoid. *Pres. Part.* **huyendo.** *Pres. Ind.* **huyo, huyes, huyen.** *Preterite* **huyó, huyeron.** *Pres. Subjunc.* **huya, etc.** *Imperf. Subjunc.* **huyese, etc.**
hule /'ule/ *m*, oilcloth; rubber; *Central America, Mexico* rubber tree
hulla /'uya; 'uʎa/ *f*, coal mine, coal, soft coal
hullera /u'yera; u'ʎera/ *f*, colliery, coal mine
humanidad /umani'ðað/ *f*, humanity; human nature; human weakness; compassion; affability; *Inf.* stoutness; *pl* study of humanities
humanismo /uma'nismo/ *m*, humanism
humanista /uma'nista/ *mf* humanist. *a* humanistic
humanitario /umani'tario/ *a* humanitarian
humanizar /umani'sar; umani'θar/ *vt* to humanize
humano /u'mano/ *a* human; understanding, sympathetic. *m*, human being
humareda /uma'reða/ *f*, cloud of smoke
humeante /ume'ante/ *a* smoking; smoky
humear /ume'ar/ *vi* to give forth smoke; give oneself airs; *Lat. Am.* fumigate; beat, thrash
humedad /ume'ðað/ *f*, humidity; dampness; moisture
humedecer /umeðe'ser; umeðe'θer/ *vt irr* to moisten, wet, damp; *vr* grow moist. See **conocer**

húmedo /'umeðo/ *a* humid; damp; wet
humildad /umil'dað/ *f*, humility; lowliness; humbleness
humilde /u'milde/ *a* meek; lowly; humble
humillación /umiya'sion; umiʎa'θion/ *f*, humiliation
humillante /umi'yante; umi'ʎante/ *a* humiliating; debasing; mortifying
humillar /umi'yar; umi'ʎar/ *vt* to humble; humiliate; *vr* humble oneself
humo /'umo/ *m*, smoke; vapor, fume; vanity, airs
humor /u'mor/ *m*, *Med.* humor; temperament, disposition; mood. **de buen h.,** good-tempered. **de mal h.,** ill-tempered
humorada /umo'raða/ *f*, humorous saying, extravagance, witticism
humorismo /umo'rismo/ *m*, humor, comic sense; humorousness
humorista /umo'rista/ *mf* humorist
humorístico /umo'ristiko/ *a* humorous
humoso /u'moso/ *a* smoky, reeky
hundible /un'diβle/ *a* sinkable
hundido /un'diðo/ *a* sunken (of cheeks, etc.); hollow, deep-set (of eyes)
hundimiento /undi'miento/ *m*, sinking; collapse; subsidence (of earth)
hundir /un'dir/ *vt* to sink; oppress; confound; destroy, ruin; *vr* collapse (building); sink; *Fig. Inf.* disappear
húngaro /'uŋgaro/ **(-ra)** *a* and *n* Hungarian. *m*, Hungarian (language)
Hungría /uŋ'gria/ Hungary
huracán /ura'kan/ *m*, hurricane
huraña /ura'ɲa/ *f*, shyness, unsociableness; diffidence; wildness (of animals, etc.)
huraño /u'raɲo/ *a* shy, unsociable; diffident; wild (of animals, etc.)
hurgar /ur'ɣar/ *vt* to stir; poke, rake; touch; rouse, incite. *vr* pick one's nose
hurgón /ur'ɣon/ *m*, fire rake, poker; *Inf.* sword
hurgonada /urɣo'naða/ *f*, raking (of the fire, etc.)
hurguete /ur'ɣete/ *mf*, *Argentina* busybody, nosy parker
hurón /u'ron/ **(-ona)** *n* ferret. *a* shy, unsociable
¡hurra! /'urra/ *interj* Hurrah!
hurtadillas /urta'ðiyas; urta'ðiʎas/ **(a)** *adv* by stealth, secretly, sneakily
hurtar /ur'tar/ *vt* to steal; encroach (sea, river); plagiarize; *vr* hide oneself
hurto /'urto/ *m*, theft. **coger con el h. en las manos,** *Fig.* to catch red-handed
husmear /usme'ar/ *vt* to sniff out; *Inf.* pry; *vi* smell bad (of meat)
huso /'uso/ *m*, spindle; bobbin
¡huy! /'ui/ *interj* (denoting pain or surprise) Oh!

I

ibérico /i'βeriko/ *a* Iberian
ibero /i'βero/ **(-ra)** *a* and *n* Iberian
íbice /'iβise; 'iβiθe/ *m*, ibex
icnografía /iknoɣra'fia/ *f*, ichnography
icnográfico /ikno'ɣrafiko/ *a* ichnographical
icono /i'kono/ *m*, icon
iconoclasta /ikono'klasta/ *a* iconoclastic. *mf* iconoclast
iconografía /ikonoɣra'fia/ *f*, iconography
ictericia /ikte'risia; ikte'riθia/ *f*, jaundice
ida /'iða/ *f*, setting out, departure, going; impetuous action; precipitancy; track, trail (of animals). **de i. y vuelta,** round trip (of tickets)
idea /i'ðea/ *f*, idea. *Inf.* **¡Qué ideas tienes!** What (odd) ideas you have!
ideal /i'ðeal/ *a* ideal; perfect. *m*, model; ideal
idealidad /iðeali'ðað/ *f*, ideality
idealismo /iðea'lismo/ *m*, idealism
idealista /iðea'lista/ *a* idealistic. *mf* idealist

idealización /iðealisa'sion; iðealiθa'θion/ *f*, idealization
idealizar /iðeali'sar; iðeali'θar/ *vt* to idealize
idear /iðe'ar/ *vt* to imagine; devise; plan; design; draft, draw up
ideático, -a /iðe'atiko/ *a*, *Lat. Am.* eccentric
ídem /'iðem/ *adv* idem
idéntico /i'ðentiko/ *a* identical
identidad /iðenti'ðað/ *f*, identity
identificable /iðentifi'kaβle/ *a* identifiable
identificación /iðentifika'sion; iðentifika'θion/ *f*, identification
identificar /iðentifi'kar/ *vt* to identify; recognize; *vr* (*with con*) identify oneself with
ideografía /iðeoɣra'fia/ *f*, ideography
ideograma /iðeo'ɣrama/ *m*, ideogram
ideología /iðeolo'hia/ *f*, ideology. **i. racista,** racial ideology
ideológico /iðeo'lohiko/ *a* ideological

ideólogo /iðe'ologo/ **(-ga)** n ideologist; dreamer, planner
idílico /i'ðiliko/ a idyllic
idilio /i'ðilio/ m, idyll
idioma /i'ðioma/ m, language, tongue
idiomático /iðio'matiko/ a idiomatic
idiosincrasia /iðiosin'krasia/ f, idiosyncrasy
idiosincrásico /iðiosin'krasiko/ a idiosyncratic
idiota /i'ðiota/ a idiot; idiotic. mf idiot
idiotez /iðio'tes; iðio'teθ/ f, idiocy
idólatra /iðo'latra/ a idolatrous; adoring. mf idolater, heathen
idolatrar /iðola'trar/ vt to idolize; worship, love excessively
idolatría /iðola'tria/ f, idolatry; adoration, idolization
ídolo /'iðolo/ m, idol
idoneidad /iðonei'ðað/ f, fitness, suitability; competence; capacity
idóneo /i'ðoneo/ a suitable; competent, fit
idus /i'ðus/ m pl, ides
iglesia /i'glesia/ f, church. **i. colegial,** collegiate church. **cumplir con la i.,** to discharge one's religious duties. **llevar a una mujer a la i.,** to lead a woman to the altar
ígneo /'igneo/ a igneous
ignición /igni'sion; igni'θion/ f, ignition
ignominia /igno'minia/ f, ignominy, disgrace
ignominioso /ignomi'nioso/ a ignominious
ignorancia /igno'ransia; igno'ranθia/ f, ignorance. **pretender i.,** to plead ignorance
ignorante /igno'rante/ a ignorant; unaware, uninformed. mf ignoramus
ignorar /igno'rar/ vt to be unaware of, not to know
ignoto /ig'noto/ a unknown, undiscovered
igual /i'gual/ a equal; level; even, smooth; very similar; alike; uniform; proportionate; unchanging; constant; indifferent; same. mf equal. m, Math. equal sign. **al i.,** equally. **sin i.,** peerless, without equal. **Me es completamente i.,** It's all the same to me
iguala /i'guala/ f, equalizing; leveling; agreement, arrangement; cash adjustment
igualación /iguala'sion; iguala'θion/ f, equalization; leveling; arrangement, agreement; matching; Math. equation
igualador /iguala'ðor/ a equalizing; leveling
igualar /igua'lar/ vt to equalize, make equal; match; pair; level, flatten; smooth; adjust; arrange, agree upon; weigh, consider; Math. equate; vi be equal
igualdad /igual'dað/ f, equality; uniformity, harmony; evenness; smoothness; identity, sameness. **i. de ánimo,** equability, equanimity
igualitario /iguali'tario/ a equalizing; egalitarian
igualmente /igual'mente/ adv equally; the same, likewise
ijada /i'haða/ f, side, flank; pain in the side
ijadear /ihaðe'ar/ vt to pant
ijar /i'har/ m, See **ijada**
ilación /ila'sion; ila'θion/ f, connection, reference
ilegal /ile'gal/ a illegal
ilegalidad /ilegali'ðað/ f, illegality
ilegible /ile'hiβle/ a illegible, unreadable
ilegitimidad /ilehitimi'ðað/ f, illegitimacy
ilegítimo /ile'hitimo/ a illegitimate; false
ileso /i'leso/ a unharmed, unhurt
iletrado /ile'traðo/ a unlettered, uncultured
Ilíada /i'liaða/ f, Iliad
iliberal /iliβe'ral/ a illiberal; narrow-minded
iliberalidad /iliβerali'ðað/ f, illiberality; narrow-mindedness
ilícito /i'lisito; i'liθito/ a illicit
ilicitud /ilisi'tuð; iliθi'tuð/ f, illicitness
ilimitado /ilimi'taðo/ a unlimited, boundless
iliterato /ilite'rato/ a illiterate, uncultured
ilógico /i'lohiko/ a illogical
iluminación /ilumina'sion; ilumina'θion/ f, illumination; lighting. **i. intensiva,** floodlighting
iluminador /ilumina'ðor/ **(-ra)** a lighting; illuminating. n Art. illuminator

iluminar /ilumi'nar/ vt to illuminate; light; Art. illuminate; enlighten; vr. Lat. Am. get drunk
iluminativo /ilumina'tiβo/ a illuminating
ilusión /ilu'sion/ f, illusion; illusoriness; hope; dream
ilusionarse /ilusio'narse/ vr to harbor illusions
ilusivo /ilu'siβo/ a deceptive, illusive
iluso /i'luso/ a deceived, deluded; dreamy; visionary
ilusorio /ilu'sorio/ a illusory; deceptive; null
ilustración /ilustra'sion; ilustra'θion/ f, illustration, picture; enlightenment; explanation; illustrated newspaper or magazine; erudition, knowledge; example, illustration. **La Ilustración,** the Age of Enlightenment
ilustrado /ilu'straðo/ a erudite, learned; knowledgeable, well-informed
ilustrador /ilustra'ðor/ **(-ra)** a illustrative. n illustrator
ilustrar /ilus'trar/ vt to explain, illustrate; enlighten, instruct; illustrate (books); make illustrious; inspire with divine light
ilustrativo /ilustra'tiβo/ a illustrative
ilustre /i'lustre/ a illustrious, distinguished
ilustrísimo /ilus'trisimo/ a sup most illustrious (title of bishops, etc.)
imagen /i'mahen/ f, image; effigy, statue; idea; metaphor, simile. **i. nítida,** sharp image
imaginable /imahi'naβle/ a imaginable
imaginación /imahina'sion; imahina'θion/ f, imagination
imaginar /imahi'nar/ vi to imagine; vt suppose, conjecture; discover, invent; imagine. **¡Imagínese!** Just imagine!
imaginario /imahi'nario/ a imaginary
imaginativa /imahina'tiβa/ f, imagination; common sense
imaginativo /imahina'tiβo/ a imaginative
imaginería /imahine'ria/ f, imagery
imán /i'man/ m, magnet; attraction, charm; imam
imanación /imana'sion; imana'θion/ f, magnetization
imanar /ima'nar/ vt to magnetize
imbécil /im'besil; im'beθil/ a imbecile; stupid, idiotic. mf imbecile
imbecilidad /imbesili'ðað; imbeθili'ðað/ f, imbecility; folly, stupidity
imberbe /im'berβe/ a beardless. Inf. **joven i.,** stripling
imbibición /imbiβi'sion; imbiβi'θion/ f, imbibing, absorption
imborrable /imbo'rraβle/ a ineffaceable
imbuir /im'buir/ vt irr to imbue. See **huir**
imitable /imi'taβle/ a imitable
imitación /imita'sion; imita'θion/ f, imitation; reproduction, copy
imitado /imi'taðo/ a imitation; imitated
imitador /imita'ðor/ **(-ra)** a imitation; imitative. n imitator
imitar /imi'tar/ vt to imitate; counterfeit
imitativo /imita'tiβo/ a imitative
impacción /impak'sion; impak'θion/ f, impact
impaciencia /impa'siensia; impa'θienθia/ f, impatience
impacientar /impasien'tar; impaθien'tar/ vt to make impatient, annoy; vr grow impatient
impaciente /impa'siente; impa'θiente/ a impatient
impacto /im'pakto/ m, impact. **i. de lleno,** direct hit
impago, -a /im'pago/ a Lat. Am. remaining to be paid, still to be paid, unpaid; m non-payment
impalpabilidad /impalpaβili'ðað/ f, impalpability
impalpable /impal'paβle/ a impalpable
impar /im'par/ a odd; unpaired; single, uneven. **número impar,** odd number
imparcial /impar'sial; impar'θial/ a impartial
imparcialidad /imparsiali'ðað; imparθiali'ðað/ f, impartiality
imparisílabo /imparisi'laβiko/ a imparisyllabic
impartible /impar'tiβle/ a indivisible
impasibilidad /impasiβili'ðað/ f, impassivity, indifference
impasible /impa'siβle/ a impassive
impavidez /impaβi'ðes; impaβi'ðeθ/ f dauntlessness;

serenity in the face of danger; *Lat. Am.* cheek, cheekiness, effrontery

impávido /im'paβiðo/ *a* dauntless; calm, composed, imperturbable; *Lat. Am.* cheeky, fresh

impecabilidad /impekaβili'ðað/ *f*, impeccability, perfection

impecable /impe'kaβle/ *a* impeccable, perfect

impedido /impe'ðiðo/ *a* disabled

impedimento /impeði'mento/ *m*, obstacle; hindrance; *Law.* impediment

impedir /impe'ðir/ *vt irr* to impede; obstruct; prevent; thwart; disable; delay; *Poet.* amaze. See **pedir**

impeler /impe'ler/ *vt* to push; incite; drive; urge

impender /impen'der/ *vt* to spend money

impenetrabilidad /impenetraβili'ðað/ *f*, impenetrability; imperviousness; obscurity, difficulty

impenetrable /impene'traβle/ *a* impenetrable, dense; impervious; *Fig.* unfathomable; obscure

impenitencia /impeni'tensia; impeni'tenθia/ *f*, impenitence

impenitente /impeni'tente/ *a* impenitent

impensado /impen'saðo/ *a* unexpected, unforeseen

imperante /impe'rante/ *a* ruling, dominant

imperar /impe'rar/ *vi* to rule; command

imperativo /impera'tiβo/ *a* commanding. *a* and *m*, *Gram.* imperative

imperatorio /impera'torio/ *a* imperial, imperatorial

imperceptible /impersep'tiβle; imperθep'tiβle/ *a* imperceptible

imperdible /imper'ðiβle/ *m*, safety pin

imperdonable /imperðo'naβle/ *a* unpardonable, inexcusable

imperecedero /imperese'ðero; impereθe'ðero/ *a* undying, eternal, everlasting

imperfección /imperfek'sion; imperfek'θion/ *f*, imperfection, inadequacy; fault, blemish; weakness

imperfecto /imper'fekto/ *a* imperfect; inadequate; faulty. *a* and *m*, *Gram.* imperfect

imperial /impe'rial/ *a* imperial. *f*, upper deck of a bus or streetcar

imperialismo /imperia'lismo/ *m*, imperialism

imperialista /imperia'lista/ *a* imperialistic. *mf* imperialist

impericia /impe'risia; impe'riθia/ *f*, inexpertness; unskillfulness, unhandiness

imperio /im'perio/ *m*, empire; rule, reign; command, sway; imperial dignity; arrogance, haughtiness. *Fig. Inf.* **valer un i.**, to be priceless

imperioso /impe'rioso/ *a* imperious

imperito /impe'rito/ *a* inexpert; clumsy, unskilled

impermeabilidad /impermeaβili'ðað/ *f*, watertightness; imperviousness; impermeability

impermeabilizar /impermeaβili'sar; impermeaβili'θar/ *vt* to waterproof

impermeable /imperme'aβle/ *a* watertight, impermeable; impervious. *m*, raincoat, mackintosh

impertérrito /imper'territo/ *a* unafraid, dauntless

impertinencia /impertinen'sia; impertinen'θia/ *f*, impertinence, insolence; peevishness; fancy, whim; overexactness, meticulousness; interference, intrusion

impertinente /imperti'nente/ *a* impertinent; irrelevant; inopportune; officious, interfering

imperturbabilidad /imperturβaβili'ðað/ *f*, imperturbability

imperturbable /impertur'βaβle/ *a* calm, imperturbable

impetrar /impe'trar/ *vt* to obtain by entreaty; implore

ímpetu /'impetu/ *m*, impetus, momentum; speed, swiftness; violence

impetuosidad /impetuosi'ðað/ *f*, impetuosity

impetuoso /impe'tuoso/ *a* impetuous; precipitate

impiedad /impie'ðað/ *f*, cruelty, harshness; irreligion

impío /im'pio/ *a* impious, wicked; irreverent, irreligious

implacabilidad /implakaβili'ðað/ *f*, implacability, relentless

implacable /impla'kaβle/ *a* implacable

implantación /implanta'sion; implanta'θion/ *f*, inculcation, implantation

implantar /implan'tar/ *vt* to inculcate, implant (ideas, etc.)

implicación /implika'sion; implika'θion/ *f*, implication; contradiction (in terms); complicity

implicar /impli'kar/ *vt* to implicate; imply, infer; involve, entangle; *vi* imply contradiction (gen. with negatives)

implicatorio /implika'torio/ *a* contradictory; implicated (in crime)

implícito /im'plisito; im'pliθito/ *a* implicit; implied

implorante /implo'rante/ *a* imploring

implorar /implo'rar/ *vt* to implore, entreat

implume /im'plume/ *a* without feathers, unfeathered

impolítico /impo'litiko/ *a* impolitic; unwise, inexpedient; tactless

imponderabilidad /imponderaβili'ðað/ *f*, imponderability

imponderable /imponde'raβle/ *a* imponderable, immeasurable; most excellent

imponencia /impo'nensia; impo'nenθia/ *f. Lat. Am.* impressiveness

imponente /impo'nente/ *a* imposing, impressive; awe-inspiring

imponer /impo'ner/ *vt irr* to exact, impressive; impose; malign, accuse falsely; instruct, acquaint; *Fig.* impress (with respect, etc.); invest or deposit (money); *Print.* impose; give, bestow (a name). *vr* assert oneself. See **poner**

imponible /impo'niβle/ *a* taxable; ratable

impopular /impopu'lar/ *a* unpopular

impopularidad /impopulari'ðað/ *f*, unpopularity

importable /impor'taβle/ *a* importable

importación /importa'sion; importa'θion/ *f, Com.* importation; import

importador /importa'ðor/ **(-ra)** *a* import, importing. *n* importer

importancia /impor'tansia; impor'tanθia/ *f*, importance; magnitude

importante /impor'tante/ *a* important

importar /impor'tar/ *vi* to matter; be important; concern, interest; *vt* amount to; import; include, comprise. **¡No importa!** It doesn't matter! Never mind!

importe /im'porte/ *m*, amount; value, cost. **i. bruto,** gross or total amount. **i. líquido** *or* **neto,** net amount

importunación /importuna'sion; importuna'θion/ *f*, importuning; importunity

importunadamente /importunaða'mente/ *adv* importunately

importunar /importu'nar/ *vt* to importune, pester

importunidad /importuni'ðað/ *(also* **importunación)** *f*, importunity

importuno /impor'tuno/ *a* importunate, inopportune, ill-timed; persistent; tedious

imposibilidad /imposiβili'ðað/ *f*, impossibility

imposibilitado /imposiβili'taðo/ *a* disabled, crippled; incapable, unable

imposibilitar /imposiβili'tar/ *vt* to disable; render unable; make impossible

imposible /impo'siβle/ *a* impossible

imposición /imposi'sion; imposi'θion/ *f*, imposition; exaction; tax, duty, tribute; *Print.* makeup **i. de manos,** *Eccl.* laying on of hands

impostor /impos'tor/ **(-ra)** *n* impostor

impostura /impos'tura/ *f*, swindle, imposture; aspersion, slur, imputation

impotable /impo'taβle/ *a* undrinkable

impotencia /impo'tensia; impo'tenθia/ *f*, impotence

impotente /impo'tente/ *a* impotent; powerless

impracticabilidad /impraktikaβili'ðað/ *f*, impracticability; impassability (of roads, etc.)

impracticable /imprakti'kaβle/ *a* impracticable; impossible; impassable (roads, etc.)

imprecación /impreka'sion; impreka'θion/ *f*, imprecation; curse, malediction

imprecar /impre'kar/ *vt* to imprecate, curse

impregnación /impregna'sion; impregna'θion/ *f*, impregnation, permeation, saturation

impregnar /impreg'nar/ *vt* impregnate; to permeate; *vr* become impregnated

impremeditado /impremeði'taðo/ *a* unpremeditated

imprenta /im'prenta/ *f*, printing; printing house or office; print; letterpress

impreparación /imprepara'sion; imprepara'θion/ *f*, unpreparedness

imprescindible /impressin'diβle; impresθin'diβle/ *a* indispensable, essential

impresión /impre'sion/ *f*, printing; impression; effect; influence; imprint, stamp; *Print.* impression; print. **impresión digital,** fingerprint

impresionable /impresio'naβle/ *a* impressionable, susceptible

impresionante /impresio'nante/ *a* imposing; moving, affecting

impresionar /impresio'nar/ *vt* to impress; affect; fix in the mind; *Fig.* move deeply, stir; (*Radio.* cinema) record

impresionismo /impresio'nismo/ *m*, impressionism

impresionista /impresio'nista/ *mf* impressionist. *a* impressionistic

impreso /im'preso/ *m*, (gen. *pl*) printed matter

impresor /impre'sor/ *m*, printer

imprevisión /impreβi'sion/ *f*, lack of foresight; improvidence

imprevisto /impre'βisto/ *a* unforeseen, unexpected, sudden

imprevistos /impre'βistos/ *m pl*, incidental expenses

imprimación /imprima'sion; imprima'θion/ *f*, priming (of paint, etc.)

imprimar /impri'mar/ *vt* to prime (of paint)

imprimir /impri'mir/ *vt* to print; stamp; impress upon (the mind)

improbabilidad /improβaβili'ðað/ *f*, improbability

improbable /impro'βaβle/ *a* improbable

improbo /im'proβo/ *a* vicious, corrupt, dishonest; hard, arduous

improductivo /improðuk'tiβo/ *a* unproductive; unprofitable, fruitless

impronta /im'pronta/ *f*, *Art.* cast, mold

impronunciable /impronun'siaβle; impronun'θiaβle/ *a* unpronounceable; ineffable

improperio /impro'perio/ *m*, insult, affront

impropiedad /impropie'ðað/ *f*, inappropriateness; unsuitableness; impropriety

impropio /im'propio/ *a* unsuitable; inappropriate; inadequate; improper

improporcionado /improporsio'naðo; improporθio'naðo/ *a* disproportionate, out of proportion

impróvido /im'proβiðo/ *a* improvident, heedless

improvisación /improβisa'sion; improβisa'θion/ *f*, improvisation

improvisador /improβisa'ðor/ (*-ra*) *n* improviser

improvisamente /improβisa'mente/ *adv* unexpectedly, suddenly

improvisar /improβi'sar/ *vt* to improvise

improviso, improvisto /impro'βiso, impro'βisto/ *a* unexpected, unforeseen. **al** (*or* **de**) **improviso,** unexpectedly

imprudencia /impru'ðensia; impru'ðenθia/ *f*, imprudence, rashness, indiscretion

imprudente /impru'ðente/ *a* imprudent, unwise, rash

impúbero /im'puβero/ *a* below the age of puberty

impudencia /impu'ðensia; impu'ðenθia/ *f*, impudence, impertinence

impudente /impu'ðente/ *a* brazen, impudent

impudicia /impu'ðisia; impu'ðiθia/ *f*, immodesty, brazenness

impúdico /im'puðiko/ *a* immodest, brazen

impuesto /im'puesto/ *m*, tax; duty. **i. de utilidades,** income tax. **i. sucesorio,** inheritance tax

impugnable /impug'naβle/ *a* impugnable, refutable

impugnación /impugna'sion; impugna'θion/ *f*, refutation; contradiction

impugnar /impug'nar/ *vt* to refute, contradict; oppose; criticize

impulsar /impul'sar/ *vt* to impel; prompt, cause; drive, operate, propel

impulsión /impul'sion/ *f*, impulse; impetus; *Mech.* operation, driving; propulsion

impulsivo /impul'siβo/ *a* impulsive; irreflexive, precipitate

impulso /im'pulso/ *m*, stimulus, incitement; impulse, desire; *Mech.* drive, impulse

impulsor /impul'sor/ (*-ra*) *a* driving, impelling. *n* driver, operator ·

impune /im'pune/ *a* unpunished

impunemente /impune'mente/ *adv* with impunity

impunidad /impuni'ðað/ *f*, impunity

impureza /impu'resa; impu'reθa/ *f*, impurity; lack of chastity; obscenity, indecency

impurificar /impurifi'kar/ *vt* to defile; make impure; adulterate

impuro /im'puro/ *a* impure; adulterated; polluted; immoral, unchaste

imputable /impu'taβle/ *a* imputable

imputación /imputa'sion; imputa'θion/ *f*, imputation

imputador /imputa'ðor/ (*-ra*) *n* imputer, attributer

imputar /impu'tar/ *vt* to impute; attribute

inacabable /inaka'βaβle/ *a* endless, interminable, ceaseless; wearisome

inaccesibilidad /inaksesiβili'ðað; inakθesiβili'ðað/ *f*, inaccessibility

inaccesible /inakse'siβle; inakθe'siβle/ *a* inaccessible; incomprehensible

inacción /inak'sion; inak'θion/ *f*, inaction

inaceptable /inasep'taβle; inaθep'taβle/ *a* unacceptable

inactividad /inaktiβi'ðað/ *f*, inactivity; quiescence; idleness

inactivo /inak'tiβo/ *a* inactive; idle; unemployed; *Naut.* laid-up

inadaptable /inaðap'taβle/ *a* inadaptable

inadecuado /inaðe'kuaðo/ *a* inadequate, insufficient

inadmisible /inaðmi'siβle/ *a* inadmissible

inadvertencia /inaðβer'tensia; inaðβer'tenθia/ *f*, inadvertence; oversight, mistake, slip

inadvertido /inaðβer'tiðo/ *a* unnoticed; inattentive; inadvertent, unintentional; negligent

inafectado /inafek'taðo/ *a* unaffected, natural

inagotable /inago'taβle/ *a* inexhaustible, unfailing; abundant

inaguantable /inaguan'taβle/ *a* unbearable, intolerable

inajenable /inahe'naβle/ *a* inalienable

inalámbrica /ina'lambrika/ *f*, radio station

inalienable /inalie'naβle/ *a* inalienable

inalterable /inalte'raβle/ *a* unalterable

inamovibilidad /inamoβiβili'ðað/ *f*, immovability

inamovible /inamo'βiβle/ *a* immovable

inanición /inani'sion; inani'θion/ *f*, inanition

inanimado /inani'maðo/ *a* inanimate

inapagable /inapa'gaβle/ *a* inextinguishable

inapelable /inape'laβle/ *a* unappealable; irremediable, inevitable

inapetencia /inape'tensia; inape'tenθia/ *f*, lack of appetite

inaplazable /inapla'saβle; inapla'θaβle/ *a* undeferable, unable to be postponed

inaplicable /inapli'kaβle/ *a* inapplicable

inaplicación /inaplika'sion; inaplika'θion/ *f*, laziness, inattention, negligence

inaplicado /inapli'kaðo/ *a* lazy; inattentive; careless

inapreciable /inapre'siaβle; inapre'θiaβle/ *a* inappreciable; invaluable

inarmónico /inar'moniko/ *a* unharmonious; discordant

inarticulado /inartiku'laðo/ *a* inarticulate

inasequible /inase'kiβle/ *a* unattainable; out of reach

inaudible /inau'ðiβle/ *a* inaudible

inaudito /inau'ðito/ *a* unheard of, unprecedented; extraordinary, strange

inauguración /inaugura'sion; inaugura'θion/ *f*, inauguration; induction; inception, commencement

inaugural /inaugu'ral/ *a* inaugural

inaugurar /inaugu'rar/ *vt* to inaugurate; induct

inaveriguable /inaβeri'guaβle/ *a* unascertainable

inca /'inka/ *mf* Inca

incaico /in'kaiko/ *a* Incan
incalculable /inkalku'laβle/ *a* incalculable; innumerable
incalificable /inkalifi'kaβle/ *a* indescribable, unclassable; vile
incandescencia /inkandes'sensia; inkandes'θenθia/ *f*, incandescence, white heat
incandescente /inkandes'sente; inkandes'θente/ *a* incandescent
incansable /inkan'saβle/ *a* indefatigable; unflagging; unwearying
incapacidad /inkapasi'ðað; inkapaθi'ðað/ *f*, incapacity; incompetence
incapacitar /inkapasi'tar; inkapaθi'tar/ *vt* to incapacitate; disable
incapaz /inka'pas; inka'paθ/ *a* incapable, incompetent; inefficient
incasable /inka'saβle/ *a* unmarriageable; antimarriage
incásico, -a /in'kasiko/ *a, Lat. Am.* Inca
incautarse /inkau'tarse/ *vr* to seize, take possession (of)
incauto /in'kauto/ *a* incautious; unwary
incendiar /insen'diar; inθen'diar/ *vt* to set on fire, set alight
incendiario /insen'diario; inθen'diario/ **(-ia)** *a* and *n* incendiary
incendiarismo /insendia'rismo; inθendia'rismo/ *m*, incendiarism
incendio /in'sendio; in'θendio/ *m*, conflagration, fire; consuming passion
incensar /insen'sar; inθen'sar/ *vt irr Eccl.* to cense, incense; flatter. See **acertar**
incensario /insen'sario; inθen'sario/ *m*, incense burner, incensory
incentivo /insen'tiβo; inθen'tiβo/ *m*, incentive; encouragement
incertidumbre /inserti'ðumbre; inθerti'ðumbre/ *f*, uncertainty, incertitude
incesable,   incesante /inse'saβle,   inse'sante; inθe'saβle, inθe'sante/ *a* incessant, continuous
incesto /in'sesto; in'θesto/ *m*, incest
incestuoso /inses'tuoso; inθes'tuoso/ *a* incestuous
incidencia /insi'ðensia; inθi'ðenθia/ *f*, incidence
incidente /insi'ðente; inθi'ðente/ *a* incidental. *m*, incident, event, occurrence
incidir /insi'ðir; inθi'ðir/ *vi (with en)* to incur, fall into (e.g. *Incidió en el pecado,* He fell into sin)
incienso /in'sienso; in'θienso/ *m*, incense; flattery
incierto /in'sierto; in'θierto/ *a* untrue, false; uncertain; unknown
incineración /insinera'sion; inθinera'θion/ *f*, incineration
incinerador /insinera'ðor; inθinera'ðor/ *m*, incinerator
incinerar /insine'rar; inθine'rar/ *vt* incinerate, reduce to ashes
incipiente /insi'piente; inθi'piente/ *a* incipient
incircunciso /insirkun'siso; inθirkun'θiso/ *a* uncircumcised
incisión /insi'sion; inθi'sion/ *f*, incision
incisivo /insi'siβo; inθi'siβo/ *a* sharp, keen; incisive, sarcastic, caustic
inciso /in'siso; in'θiso/ *m*, clause; comma
incitación /insita'sion; inθita'θion/ *f*, incitement; *Fig.* spur, stimulus
incitar /insi'tar; inθi'tar/ *vt* to incite; stimulate, encourage
incivil /insi'βil; inθi'βil/ *a* rude, discourteous, uncivil
incivilidad /insiβili'ðað; inθiβili'ðað/ *f*, rudeness, incivility
inclasificable /inklasifi'kaβle/ *a* unclassifiable
inclemencia /inkle'mensia; inkle'menθia/ *f*, harshness, severity; inclemency (of the weather). **a la i.,** at the mercy of the elements
inclemente /inkle'mente/ *a* inclement
inclinación /inklina'sion; inklina'θion/ *f*, inclination; slope; slant; tendency, propensity; predilection, fondness; bow (in greeting); *Geom.* inclination
inclinar /inkli'nar/ *vt* to incline, tilt, slant; bow; bend; influence; persuade; *vi* resemble; *vr* lean;

stoop; tilt; tend, incline (to), view favorably (e.g. *Me inclino a creerlo,* I am inclined to believe it)
ínclito /in'klito/ *a* famous, celebrated
incluir /in'kluir/ *vt irr* to comprise, embrace, contain; include, take into account. See **huir**
inclusa /in'klusa/ *f*, children's home
inclusión /inklu'sion/ *f*, inclusion; relationship, intercourse, friendship
inclusive /inklu'siβe/ *adv* including
inclusivo /inklu'siβo/ *a* inclusive
incluso /in'kluso/ *adv* including, inclusive. *prep* even
incoar /inko'ar/ *vt* to begin (especially lawsuits)
incobrable /inko'βraβle/ *a* irrecoverable; irredeemable
incógnita /in'kognita/ *f, Math.* X; unknown quantity; secret motive; unknown lady
incógnito /in'kognito/ *a* unknown. *m*, incognito, assumed name, disguise
incoherencia /inkoe'rensia; inkoe'renθia/ *f*, incoherence
incoherente /inkoe'rente/ *a* incoherent, disconnected, illogical
íncola /'inkola/ *mf* resident, dweller, inhabitant
incoloro /inko'loro/ *a* colorless, uncolored
incólume /in'kolume/ *a* unharmed, unscathed; untouched, undamaged
incombustibilidad /inkombustiβili'ðað/ *f*, incombustibility
incommensurabilidad /inkommensuraβili'ðað/ *f*, incommensurability
inconmutable /inkommu'taβle/ *a* unalterable, immutable, unchangeable
incomodar /inkomo'ðar/ *vt* to disturb, incommode, inconvenience; annoy; *vr* disturb oneself, put oneself out; grow angry. **¡No se incomode!** Please don't move!; Please don't be angry!
incomodidad /inkomoði'ðað/ *f*, discomfort; inconvenience; trouble, upset; annoyance
incómodo /in'komoðo/ *a* uncomfortable; inconvenient; troublesome, tiresome; *Argentina, Chile* fed up *m*, discomfort; inconvenience
incomparable /inkompa'raβle/ *a* incomparable
incompartible /inkompar'tiβle/ *a* indivisible
incompasivo /inkompa'siβo/ *a* unsympathetic, hard
incompatibilidad /inkompatiβili'ðað/ *f*, incompatibility
incompetencia /inkompe'tensia; inkompe'tenθia/ *f*, incompetence
incompetente /inkompe'tente/ *a* incompetent
incomplejo, incomplexo /inkom'pleho, inkom'plekso/ *a* noncomplex, simple
incompleto /inkom'pleto/ *a* incomplete
incomponible /inkompo'niβle/ *a* unrepairable, unmendable
incomprensibilidad /inkomprensiβili'ðað/ *f*, incomprehensibility
incomprensible /inkompren'siβle/ *a* incomprehensible
incomprensión /inkompren'sion/ *f*, incomprehension
incomunicado /inkomuni'kaðo/ *a* in solitary confinement (of a prisoner)
incomunicar /inkomuni'kar/ *vt* to sentence to solitary confinement; isolate, deprive of means of communication; *vr* become a recluse
inconcebible /inkonseβiβle; inkonθe'βiβle/ *a* inconceivable
inconciliable /inkonsi'liaβle; inkonθi'liaβle/ *a* irreconcilable
incondicional /inkondisio'nal; inkondiθio'nal/ *a* unconditional; *Lat. Am.* fawning, servile
inconexión /inkone'ksion/ *f*, disconnectedness
inconexo /inkone'kso/ *a* unconnected; incoherent
inconfeso /inkon'feso/ *a* unconfessed
incongruencia /inkoŋgru'ensia; inkoŋgru'enθia/ *f*, incongruity
incongruente /inkoŋgru'ente/ *a* incongruous, inappropriate
inconmovible /inkomo'βiβle/ *a* immovable; unflinching, unshakable

inconquistable /inkonkis'taβle/ *a* unconquerable; *Fig.* resolute, inflexible

inconsciencia /inkonssiensia; inkon'sθienθia/ *f*, unconsciousness; subconscious

inconsciente /inkons'siente; inkon'sθiente/ *a* unconscious, involuntary; subconscious

inconsecuencia /inkonse'kuensia; inkonse'kuenθia/ *f*, inconsequence; inconsistency

inconsecuente /inkonse'kuente/ *a* inconsequential; inconsistent

inconsideración /inkonsiðera'sion; inkonsiðera'θion/ *f*, thoughtlessness

inconsiderado /inkonsiðe'raðo/ *a* thoughtless; heedless, selfish

inconsiguiente /inkonsi'giente/ *a* illogical, inconsistent

inconsistencia /inkonsis'tensia; inkonsis'tenθia/ *f*, inconsistency

inconsistente /inkonsis'tente/ *a* inconsistent

inconsolable /inkonso'laβle/ *a* inconsolable

inconstancia /inkons'tansia; inkons'tanθia/ *f*, inconstancy, infidelity

inconstante /inkons'tante/ *a* inconstant, fickle

inconstitucional /inkonstitusio'nal; inkonstituθio'nal/ *a* unconstitutional

incontaminado /inkontami'naðo/ *a* uncontaminated

incontestable /inkontes'taβle/ *a* undeniable, unquestionable

incontinencia /inkonti'nensia; inkonti'nenθia/ *f*, incontinence

incontinente /inkonti'nente/ *a* incontinent

incontrastable /inkontras'taβle/ *a* insuperable, invincible; undeniable, unanswerable; *Fig.* unshakable, inconvincible

incontrovertible /inkontroβer'tiβle/ *a* undeniable, incontrovertible

inconvencible /inkomben'siβle; inkomben'θiβle/ *a* inconvincible

inconveniencia /inkombe'niensia; inkombe'nienθia/ *f*, discomfort; inconvenience; unsuitability

inconveniente /inkombe'niente/ *a* awkward, inconvenient; uncomfortable; inappropriate. *m*, inconvenience; obstacle, impediment; disadvantage

inconvertible /inkomber'tiβle/ *a* inconvertible

incorporación /inkorpora'sion; inkorpora'θion/ *f*, incorporation

incorporar /inkorpo'rar/ *vt* to incorporate; cause to sit up, lift up; *vr* sit up, raise oneself; become a member, join (associations); be incorporated; blend, mix

incorporeidad /inkorporei'ðað/ *f*, incorporeity

incorpóreo /inkor'poreo/ *a* incorporeal; immaterial

incorrección /inkorrek'sion; inkorrek'θion/ *f*, incorrectness; indecorum, impropriety

incorrecto /inko'rrekto/ *a* incorrect; indecorous, unbecoming, improper

incorregible /inkorre'hiβle/ *a* incorrigible

incorrupción /inkorrup'sion; inkorrup'θion/ *f*, incorruption; purity; integrity; wholesomeness

incorrupto /inko'rrupto/ *a* incorrupt; pure; chaste

incredibilidad /inkreðiβili'ðað/ *f*, incredibility

incredulidad /inkreðuli'ðað/ *f*, incredulity, scepticism

incrédulo /in'kreðulo/ *a* **(-la)** *a* incredulous; atheistic. *n* atheist; unbeliever, sceptic

increíble /inkre'iβle/ *a* incredible; marvelous, extraordinary

incremento /inkre'mento/ *m*, increment, increase

increpación /inkrepa'sion; inkrepa'θion/ *f*, scolding, harsh rebuke

increpar /inkre'par/ *vt* to scold, rebuke harshly

incriminante /inkrimi'nante/ *a* incriminating

incriminar /inkrimi'nar/ *vt* to incriminate, accuse; exaggerate (a charge, etc.)

incruento /inkru'ento/ *a* bloodless, unstained with blood

incrustación /inkrusta'sion; inkrusta'θion/ *f*, incrustation; *Art.* inlay

incubación /inkuβa'sion; inkuβa'θion/ *f*, hatching; *Med.* incubation

incubadora /inkuβa'ðora/ *f*, incubator (for chickens)

incubar /inku'βar/ *vi* to sit on eggs (of hens); *vt* hatch; *Med.* incubate

inculcación /inkulka'sion; inkulka'θion/ *f*, inculcation, instillment

inculcar /inkul'kar/ *vt* to press one thing against another; instill, inculcate; *vr* grow more fixed in one's views

inculpable /inkul'paβle/ *a* blameless, innocent

inculpar /inkul'par/ *vt* to blame; accuse

incultivable /inkulti'βaβle/ *a* uncultivatable; untillable

inculto /in'kulto/ *a* uncultivated, untilled; uncultured; uncivilized

incultura /inkul'tura/ *f*, lack of cultivation; lack of culture

incumbencia /inkumbensia; inkum'benθia/ *f*, obligation, moral responsibility, duty

incumbir /inkum'bir/ *vi* to be incumbent on; concern

incumplimiento /inkumpli'miento/ *m*, nonfulfilment

incurable /inku'raβle/ *a* incurable; inveterate, hopeless

incuria /in'kuria/ *f*, negligence, carelessness

incurioso /inku'rioso/ *a* incurious

incurrir /inku'rrir/ *vi* (*with en*) to fall into (error, etc.); incur (dislike, etc.)

incursión /inkur'sion/ *f*, incursion; inroad

indagación /indaga'sion; indaga'θion/ *f*, investigation, inquiry

indagador /indaga'ðor/ **(-ra)** *a* investigating, inquiring. *n* investigator

indagar /inda'gar/ *vt* to investigate, examine; inquire. **i. precios,** to inquire about prices

indebido /inde'βiðo/ *a* undue, immoderate improper; illegal, illicit

indecencia /inde'sensia; inde'θenθia/ *f*, indecency; obscenity; impropriety

indecente /inde'sente; inde'θente/ *a* indecent; obscene; improper

indecible /inde'siβle; inde'θiβle/ *a* unutterable, ineffable, unspeakable

indeciso /inde'siso; inde'θiso/ *a* undecided; hesitant, irresolute; vague; noncommittal

indeclinable /indekli'naβle/ *a* obligatory; unavoidable; *Gram.* indeclinable, uninflected

indecoro /inde'koro/ *m*, impropriety, indecorum

indecoroso /indeko'roso/ *a* indecorous, unbecoming; base, mean

indefectible /indefek'tiβle/ *a* unfailing; perfect

indefectiblemente /indefektiβle'mente/ *adv* invariably

indefendible /indefen'diβle/ *a* indefensible

indefenso /inde'fenso/ *a* unprotected, defenseless

indefinible /indefi'niβle/ *a* indefinable, vague; indescribable

indefinido /indefi'niðo/ *a* indefinite, vague; undefined; *Gram.* indefinite

indeleble /inde'leβle/ *a* indelible

indeliberado /indeliβe'raðo/ *a* unpremeditated; unconsidered

indemme /in'demme/ *a* unharmed, undamaged

indemnidad /indemni'ðað/ *f*, indemnity

indemnización /indemniza'sion; indemniθa'θion/ *f*, compensation, indemnification; indemnity

indemnizar /indemni'sar; indemni'θar/ *vt* to indemnify, compensate

indemostrable /indemo'straβle/ *a* indemonstrable, incapable of demonstration

independencia /indepen'densia; indepen'denθia/ *f*, independence

independiente /indepen'diente/ *a* independent; self-contained

indescifrable /indessi'fraβle; indesθi'fraβle/ *a* undecipherable; illegible

indestructible /indestruk'tiβle/ *a* indestructible

indeterminado /indetermi'naðo/ *a* indeterminate; vague, doubtful, uncertain; hesitant, irresolute; *Math.* indeterminate

indiano /in'diano/ **(-na)** *a* and *n* Indian; East Indian; West Indian. *m*, nouveau riche, one who returns rich from the Western Hemisphere

indicación /indika'sion; indika'θion/ *f*, indication; sign, evidence; intimation, hint
indicador /indika'ðor/ *a* indicative. *m*, indicator. **i. del nivel de gasolina,** gas gauge
indicar /indi'kar/ *vt* to indicate; show; point out; simply, suggest; intimate
indicativo /indika'tiβo/ *a* indicative. *a* and *m*, *Gram.* indicative
índice /'indise; 'indiθe/ *m*, index; indication, sign; library catalog; catalog room; hand (of a clock); pointer, needle (of instruments); gnomon (of a sundial); *Math.* index; forefinger. **I. expurgatorio,** the Index
indicio /in'disio; in'diθio/ *m*, indication; sign; evidence. **indicios vehementes,** circumstantial evidence
indiferencia /indife'rensia; indife'renθia/ *f*, indifference
indiferente /indife'rente/ *a* indifferent
indígena /in'dihena/ *a* native, indigenous. *mf* native
indigencia /indi'hensia; indi'henθia/ *f*, destitution, indigence; impecuniosity
indigenismo /indihe'nismo/ *m*, *Lat. Am.* Native American movement, indigenous peoples
indigente /indi'hente/ *a* destitute, indigent; impecunious
indigestión /indihes'tion/ *f*, indigestion
indigesto /indi'hesto/ *a* indigestible; *Lit.* muddled, confused; unsociable, brusque
indignación /indigna'sion; indigna'θion/ *f*, indignation, anger
indignado /indig'naðo/ *a* indignant
indignar /indig'nar/ *vt* to anger, make indignant; *vr* grow angry
indignidad /indigni'ðað/ *f*, unworthiness; indignity; personal affront
indigno /in'digno/ *a* unworthy; base, despicable
índigo /'indigo/ *m*, indigo
indio /'indio/ **(-ia)** *a* Indian; blue. *n* Indian. *m*, indium
indirecta /indi'rekta/ *f*, hint, covert suggestion, innuendo. *Inf.* **i. del padre Cobos,** strong hint
indirecto /indi'rekto/ *a* indirect
indisciplina /indissi'plina; indisθi'plina/ *f*, indiscipline
indisciplinado /indissipli'naðo; indisθipli'naðo/ *a* undisciplined
indiscreción /indiskre'sion; indiskre'θion/ *f*, indiscretion
indiscreto /indis'kreto/ *a* indiscreet
indiscutible /indisku'tiβle/ *a* unquestionable, undeniable
indisoluble /indiso'luβle/ *a* indissoluble
indispensable /indispen'saβle/ *a* indispensable
indisponer /indispo'ner/ *vt irr* to make unfit or incapable; indispose, make ill; (*with con or contra*) set against, make trouble with; *vr* be indisposed; (*with con or contra*) quarrel with. See **poner**
indisposición /indisposi'sion; indisposi'θion/ *f*, reluctance, disinclination; indisposition, brief illness
indistinguible /indistiŋ'guiβle/ *a* undistinguishable
indistinto /indis'tinto/ *a* indistinct; indeterminate; vague
individual /indiβi'ðual/ *a* individual; peculiar, characteristic. *m*, (tennis) single
individualidad /indiβiðuali'ðað/ *f*, individuality
individualismo /indiβiðua'lismo/ *m*, individualism
individualista /indiβiðua'lista/ *a* individualistic. *mf* individualist
individuo /indi'βiðuo/ **(-ua)** *a* individual; indivisible. *m*, individual; member, associate; *Inf.* self. *n Inf.* person
indivisibilidad /indiβisiβili'ðað/ *f*, indivisibility
indivisible /indiβi'siβle/ *a* indivisible
indiviso /indi'βiso/ *a* undivided
indochino /indo'tʃino/ **(-na)** *a* and *n* Indochinese
indócil /in'dosil; in'doθil/ *a* unmanageable; disobedient; brittle, unpliable (of metals)
indocilidad /indosili'ðað; indoθili'ðað/ *f*, indocility; disobedience; brittleness (of metals)
indoeuropeo /indoeuro'peo/ *a* Indo-European

indoísmo /indo'ismo/ *m*, Hinduism
índole /'indole/ *f*, temperament, nature; kind, sort
indolencia /indo'lensia; indo'lenθia/ *f*, idleness, indolence
indolente /indo'lente/ *a* nonpainful; indifferent, insensible; idle, indolent
indoloro /indo'loro/ *a* painless
indomable /indo'maβle/ *a* untamable; invincible; indomitable; ungovernable, unmanageable
indomado /indo'maðo/ *a* untamed
indómito /in'domito/ *a* untamed; untamable; unmanageable, unruly; indomitable
indonesio /indo'nesio/ **(-ia)** *a* and *n* Indonesian
indostanés /indosta'nes/ *a* Hindustani
indostani /indos'tani/ *m*, Hindustani (language)
indubitable /induβi'taβle/ *a* unquestionable
inducción /induk'sion; induk'θion/ *f*, persuasion; *Phys.* induction
inducir /indu'sir; indu'θir/ *vt irr* to persuade, prevail upon; induce; infer, conclude. See **conducir**
inductivo, inductor /induk'tiβo, induk'tor/ *a* inductive
indudable /indu'ðaβle/ *a* indubitable
indulgencia /indul'hensia; indul'henθia/ *f*, over-kindness, tenderness; *Eccl.* indulgence
indulgente /indul'hente/ *a* indulgent, tender; tolerant
indultar /indul'tar/ *vt* to pardon; exempt
indulto /in'dulto/ *m*, amnesty; exemption; forgiveness; *Eccl.* indult
indumentaria /indumen'taria/ *f*, clothing; outfit (of clothes)
industria /in'dustria/ *f*, assiduity, industriousness; pains, effort, ingenuity; industry. **i. pesada,** heavy industry. **i. cárnica,** meat industry. **i. extractivos,** mining industry
industrial /indus'trial/ *a* industrial. *m*, industrialist
industrialismo /industria'lismo/ *m*, industrialism
industrialización /industrialisa'sion; industriali θa'θion/ *f*, industrialization
industriar /indus'triar/ *vt* to teach, train; *vr* find a way, manage, succeed in
industrioso /indus'trioso/ *a* industrious; diligent, assiduous
inédito /i'neðito/ *a* unpublished; unedited
inefable /ine'faβle/ *a* ineffable
ineficacia /inefi'kasia; inefi'kaθia/ *f*, inefficiency; ineffectiveness
ineficaz /inefi'kas; inefi'kaθ/ *a* ineffective; inefficient
ineludible /inelu'ðiβle/ *a* unavoidable
ineptitud /inepti'tuð/ *f*, ineptitude
inepto /i'nepto/ *a* inept, incompetent; unfit, unsuitable
inequívoco /ine'kiβoko/ *a* unequivocal
inercia /i'nersia; i'nerθia/ *f*, inertia
inerme /i'nerme/ *a* defenseless, unprotected; (*Bot. Zool.*) unarmed
inerte /i'nerte/ *a* inert
inescrutable /ineskru'taβle/ *a* inscrutable, unfathomable
inesperado /inespe'raðo/ *a* unexpected, sudden
inestabilidad /inestaβili'ðað/ *f*, instability, unsteadiness, shakiness, unreliability, inconstancy
inestable /ines'taβle/ *a* unstable
inestimable /inesti'maβle/ *a* inestimable
inevitable /ineβi'taβle/ *a* inevitable
inexactitud /ineksakti'tuð/ *f*, inexactitude, inaccuracy; error, mistake
inexacto /ine'ksakto/ *a* inexact, inaccurate; erroneous
inexcusable /ineksku'saβle/ *a* inexcusable, unforgivable; indispensable
inexhausto /ineks'austo/ *a* inexhaustible
inexistente /ineksis'tente/ *a* nonexistent
inexorable /inekso'raβle/ *a* inexorable
inexperiencia /inekspe'riensia; inekspe'rienθia/ *f*, inexperience
inexperto /ineks'perto/ *a* inexperienced; inexpert
inexplicable /inekspli'kaβle/ *a* inexplicable
inexplorado /ineksplo'raðo/ *a* unexplored

inexplosible /ineksplo'siβle/ *a* inexplosive
inexpresivo /inekspre'siβo/ *a* inexpressive; reticent
inexpugnable /inekspuǥ'naβle/ *a* impregnable; *Fig.* unshakable, firm; obstinate
inextinguible /inekstiŋ'ǥ uiβle/ *a* inextinguishable; everlasting, perpetual
infalibilidad /infaliβili'ðað/ *f*, infallibility
infalible /infa'liβle/ *a* infallible
infamación /infama'sion; infama'θion/ *f*, defamation
infamador /infama'ðor/ (**-ra**) *a* slandering. *n* slanderer
infamar /infa'mar/ *vt* to defame, slander
infame /in'fame/ *a* infamous, vile
infamia /in'famia/ *f*, infamy; baseness, vileness
infancia /in'fansia; in'fanθia/ *f*, infancy, babyhood; childhood
infanta /in'fanta/ *f*, female child under seven years; infanta, any Spanish royal princess; wife of a Spanish royal prince
infantado /infan'taðo/ *m*, land belonging to an *infante* or *infanta*
infante /in'fante/ *m*, male child under seven years; infante, any Spanish royal prince except an heir-apparent; infantryman. **i. de coro,** choir boy
infantería /infante'ria/ *f*, infantry. **i. de marina,** Marine Corps
infanticida /infanti'siða; infanti'θiða/ *a* infanticidal. *mf* infanticide (person)
infanticidio /infanti'siðio; infanti'θiðio/ *m*, infanticide (act)
infantil /infan'til/ *a* infantile, babyish; innocent, candid
infatigable /infati'ǥaβle/ *a* unwearying, indefatigable
infatuación /infatua'sion; infatua'θion/ *f*, infatuation
infatuar /infa'tuar/ *vt* to infatuate; *vr* become infatuated
infausto /in'fausto/ *a* unlucky, unfortunate
infección /infek'sion; infek'θion/ *f*, infection
infeccioso /infek'sioso; infek'θioso/ *a* infectious
infectar /infek'tar/ *vt* to infect; corrupt, pervert; *vr* become infected; be corrupted
infecto /in'fekto/ *a* infected; corrupt, perverted; tainted
infecundidad /infekundi'ðað/ *f*, sterility
infecundo /infe'kundo/ *a* sterile, barren
infelice /infe'lise; infe'liθe/ *a Poet.* unhappy, unfortunate
infelicidad /infelisi'ðað; infeliθi'ðað/ *f*, unhappiness
infeliz /infe'lis; infe'liθ/ *a* unhappy; unfortunate; *Inf.* simple, good-hearted
inferencia /infe'rensia; infe'renθia/ *f*, inference, connection
inferior /infe'rior/ *a* inferior; lower; second-rate; subordinate. *mf* inferior, subordinate
inferioridad /inferiori'ðað/ *f*, inferiority
inferir /infe'rir/ *vt irr* to infer, deduce; involve, imply; occasion; inflict. See **sentir**
infernáculo /infer'nakulo/ *m*, hopscotch
infernal /infer'nal/ *a* infernal; devilish, fiendish; wicked, inhuman; *Inf.* confounded
infierno /in'ferno/ *a Poet.* infernal
infértil /in'fertil/ *a* infertile
infestación /infesta'sion; infesta'θion/ *f*, infestation
infestar /infes'tar/ *vt* to infest, swarm in; infect; injure, damage
infesto /in'festo/ *a Poet.* harmful, dangerous
inficionar /infisio'nar; infiθio'nar/ *vt* to infect; pervert, corrupt
infidelidad /infiðeli'ðað/ *f*, faithlessness, infidelity; disbelief in Christian religion; unbelievers, infidels
infidelísimo /infiðe'lisimo/, *a sup* **infiel** most disloyal; most incorrect; most incredulous, faithless
infidencia /infi'ðensia; infi'ðenθia/ *f*, disloyalty, faithlessness
infiel /in'fiel/ *a* unfaithful, disloyal; inaccurate, incorrect; infidel, unbelieving. *mf* infidel, nonbeliever
infierno /in'fierno/ *m*, hell; hades (gen. *pl*); *Fig. Inf.* inferno. **en el quinto i.,** very far off, at the end of the

world. **en los quintos infiernos,** at the end of nowhere
infiltración /infiltra'sion; infiltra'θion/ *f*, infiltration; inculcation, implantation
infiltrar /infil'trar/ *vt* to infiltrate; imbue, inculcate
ínfimo /'infimo/ *a* lowest; meanest, vilest, most base; cheapest, poorest (in quality)
infinidad /infini'ðað/ *f*, infinity; infinitude; great number
infinitivo /infini'tiβo/ *a* and *m, Gram.* infinitive
infinito /infi'nito/ *a* infinite; endless; boundless; countless. *m, Math.* infinite. *adv* excessively, immensely
infinitud /infini'tuð/ *f*, See **infinidad**
inflación /infla'sion; infla'θion/ *f*, inflation; distension; pride, vanity
inflacionismo /inflasio'nismo; inflaθio'nismo/ *m*, inflationism
inflacionista /inflasio'nista; inflaθio'nista/ *mf* inflationist
inflador /infla'ðor/ *m. Lat. Am.* bicycle pump
inflamabilidad /inflamaβili'ðað/ *f*, inflammability
inflamable /infla'maβle/ *a* inflammable
inflamación /inflama'sion; inflama'θion/ *f*, inflammation; *Engin.* ignition
inflamador /inflama'ðor/ *a* inflammatory
inflamar /infla'mar/ *vt* to set on fire; *Fig.* inflame, excite; *vr* take fire; *Med.* become inflamed; grow hot or excited
inflamatorio /inflama'torio/ *a Med.* inflammatory
inflar /in'flar/ *vt* to inflate; blow up, distend; throw out (one's chest); exaggerate; make haughty or vain; *vr* be swollen or inflated; be puffed up with pride
inflexibilidad /infleksiβili'ðað/ *f*, inflexibility; rigidity; immovability, constancy
inflexible /infle'ksiβle/ *a* inflexible
inflexión /infle'ksion/ *f*, bending, flexion; diffraction (optics); inflection
infligir /infli'hir/ *vt* to impose, inflict (penalties)
influencia /influ'ensia; influ'enθia/ *f*, influence; power, authority; *Elec.* charge
influir /in'fluir/ *vt irr* to influence; affect; (*with en*) cooperate in, assist with. See **huir**
influjo /in'fluho/ *m*, influence; flux, inflow of the tide
influyente /influ'yente/ *a* influential
información /informa'sion; informa'θion/ *f*, information; legal inquiry; report; research, investigation
informador /informa'ðor/ (**-ra**) *a* informing, acquainting. *n* informant
informal /infor'mal/ *a* informal, irregular; unreliable (of persons); unconventional
informalidad /informali'ðað/ *f*, irregularity; unconventionality; unreliability
informante /infor'mante/ *mf* informant
informar /infor'mar/ *vt* to inform, acquaint with; *vi Law.* plead; *vr* (*with de, en, or sobre*) find out about, investigate
informática /infor'matika/ *f*, computer science; information sciences
informativo /informa'tiβo/ *a* informative
informe /in'forme/ *a* formless, shapeless. *m*, report, statement; information; *Law.* plea; *pl* data, particulars; references
infortificable /infortifi'kaβle/ *a* unfortifiable
infortuna /infor'tuna/ *f, Astrol.* evil influence
infortunado /infortu'naðo/ *a* unfortunate
infortunio /infor'tunio/ *m*, misfortune, unhappiness; adversity; mischance, ill luck
infracción /infrak'sion; infrak'θion/ *f*, transgression, infringement
infracto /in'frakto/ *a* imperturbable
infractor /infrak'tor/ (**-ra**) *a* infringing. *n* transgressor, infringer
infrangible /infran'hiβle/ *a* unbreakable
infranqueable /infranke'aβle/ *a* insuperable, unsurmountable
infrarrojo /infra'rroho/ *a* infrared
infrascrito /infras'krito/ *a* undersigned; undermentioned

infrecuente /infre'kuente/ *a* infrequent

infringir /infrin'hir/ *vt* to infringe, transgress, break

infructífero /infruk'tifero/ *a* unfruitful; worthless, useless

infructuosidad /infruktuosi'ðað/ *f,* unfruitfulness; worthlessness, uselessness

infructuoso /infruk'tuoso/ *a* fruitless; useless, worthless

infumable /infu'maβle/ *a* unsmokable (of tobacco)

infundado /infun'daðo/ *a* unfounded, groundless

infundio /in'fundio/ *m, Inf.* nonsense, untruth

infundir /infun'dir/ *vt* to infuse, imbue with

infusión /infu'sion/ *f,* infusion

ingeniar /inhe'niar/ *vt* to devise, concoct, plan; *vr* contrive, find a way, manage

ingeniería /inhenie'ria/ *f,* engineering

ingeniero /inhe'niero/ *m,* engineer. **i. agrónomo,** agricultural engineer. **i. de caminos, canales y puertos,** civil engineer. **i. radiotelegrafista,** radio engineer. **cuerpo de ingenieros,** royal engineers

ingenio /in'henio/ *m,* mind; inventive capacity; imaginative talent; man of genius; talent, cleverness; ingeniousness; machine; guillotine (bookbinding)

ingeniosidad /inheniosi'ðað/ *f,* ingeniousness; witticism, clever remark

ingenioso /inhe'nioso/ *a* talented, clever; ingenious

ingénito /in'henito/ *a* unengendered, unconceived; innate, inborn

ingente /in'hente/ *a* huge, enormous

ingenuidad /inhenui'ðað/ *f,* ingenuousness, naiveté

ingenuo /in'henuo/ *a* ingenuous, naive, artless, unaffected

Inglaterra /ingla'terra/ England

ingle /'ingle/ *f,* groin

inglés /in'gles/ **(-esa)** *a* English; British. *n* Englishman; Briton. *m,* English (language); *Inf.* creditor. **a la inglesa,** in English fashion. **marcharse a la inglesa,** *Inf.* to take French leave

inglesismo /ingle'sismo/ *m,* Anglicism

ingobernable /ingoβer'naβle/ *a* ungovernable, unruly

ingratitud /ingrati'tuð/ *f,* ingratitude

ingrato /in'grato/ *a* ungrateful; irksome, thankless; disagreeable

ingrávido /in'graβiðo/ *a* light weight

ingrediente /ingre'ðiente/ *m,* ingredient; *Argentina* appetizer

ingresar /ingre'sar/ *vi* to return, come in (money); (*with en*) join, become a member of, enter

ingreso /in'greso/ *m,* joining, entering, admission; *Com.* money received; opening, commencement; *pl* earnings, takings, revenue

ingurgitación /ingurhita'sion; ingurhita'θion/ *f,* *Med.* ingurgitation

inhábil /in'aβil/ *a* unskillful; unpracticed; incompetent, unfit; unsuitable, ill-chosen

inhabilidad /inaβili'ðað/ *f,* unskillfulness; incompetence; unsuitability; inability

inhabilitación /inaβilita'sion; inaβilita'θion/ *f,* incapacitation; disqualification; disablement

inhabilitar /inaβili'tar/ *vt* to make ineligible; disqualify; incapacitate, make unfit; *vr* become ineligible; be incapacitated

inhabitable /inaβi'taβle/ *a* uninhabitable

inhabitado /inaβi'taðo/ *a* uninhabited, deserted

inhalación /inala'sion; inala'θion/ *f,* inhalation

inhalador /inala'ðor/ *m, Med.* inhaler

inhalar /ina'lar/ *vt* to inhale

inhallable /ina'yaβle; ina'ʎaβle/ *a* nowhere to be found, unfindable

inheredital /inereði'taβle/ *a* uninheritable

inherencia /ine'rensia; ine'renθia/ *f,* inherency

inherente /ine'rente/ *a* inherent, innate

inhestar /ines'tar/ *vt irr* to raise, lift up; erect. See **acertar**

inhibición /iniβi'sion; iniβi'θion/ *f,* inhibition

inhibir /ini'βir/ *vt Law.* to inhibit; *vr* inhibit or restrain oneself. See **prohibir**

inhibitorio /iniβi'torio/ *a Law.* inhibitory

inhonesto /ino'nesto/ *a* indecent, obscene; immodest

inhospedable, inhospitalario /inospe'ðaβle, inospita'lario/ *a* inhospitable; bleak, uninviting; exposed

inhospitalidad /inospitali'ðað/ *f,* inhospitality

inhumación /inuma'sion; inuma'θion/ *f,* inhumation, burial

inhumadora /inuma'ðora/ *f,* crematory

inhumanidad /inumani'ðað/ *f,* inhumanity; brutality

inhumano /inu'mano/ *a* inhuman; brutal, barbarous

inhumar /inu'mar/ *vt* to bury, inter

iniciación /inisia'sion; inisia'θion/ *f,* initiation

iniciador /inisia'ðor; iniθia'ðor/ **(-ra)** *a* initiating; *n* initiator

inicial /ini'sial; ini'θial/ *a* and *f,* initial

iniciar /ini'siar; ini'θiar/ *vt* to initiate; admit, introduce; originate; *vr* be initiated; *Eccl.* take minor or first orders

iniciativa /inisia'tiβa; iniθia'tiβa/ *f,* initiative

inicuo /ini'kuo/ *a* iniquitous, most unjust, wicked

inimaginable /inimahi'naβle/ *a* inconceivable

inimicísimo /inimi'sisimo; inimi'θisimo/ *a sup* **enemigo** most hostile

inimitable /inimi'taβle/ *a* inimitable

ininteligible /ininteli'hiβle/ *a* unintelligible

iniquidad /iniki'ðað/ *f,* iniquity, wickedness

injerir /inhe'rir/ *vt irr* to insert, place within, introduce; interpolate; *vr* meddle. See **sentir**

injertar /inher'tar/ *vt Agr.* to graft

injerto /in'herto/ *m, Agr.* graft; grafting; grafted plant, briar, or tree

injuria /in'huria/ *f,* insult; slander; outrage; wrong, injustice; harm, damage

injuriador /inhuria'ðor/ **(-ra)** *a* insulting. *n* offender, persecutor

injuriar /inhu'riar/ *vt* to insult; slander; outrage; wrong, persecute; harm, damage

injurioso /inhu'rioso/ *a* insulting; slanderous; offensive, abusive; harmful

injusticia /inhus'tisia; inhus'tiθia/ *f,* injustice; lack of justice; unjust action

injustificable /inhustifi'kaβle/ *a* unjustifiable

injustificado /inhustifi'kaðo/ *a* unjustified

injusto /in'husto/ *a* unjust; unrighteous

inllevable /inʎe'βaβle; inʎe'βaβle/ *a* unbearable, intolerable

inmaculado /inmaku'laðo/ *a* immaculate, pure

inmaturo /inma'turo/ *a* immature; unripe

inmanejable /inmane'haβle/ *a* unmanageable; uncontrollable

inmanencia /inma'nensia; inma'nenθia/ *f,* immanence

inmanente /inma'nente/ *a* immanent

inmarcesible, inmarchitable /inmarsesiβle, inmartʃitaβle; inmarθe'siβle, inmartʃi'taβle/ *a* unfading, imperishable

inmaterial /inmate'rial/ *a* incorporeal; immaterial

inmaterialidad /inmateriali'ðað/ *f,* incorporeity; immateriality

inmediación /imeðia'sion; imeðia'θion/ *f,* nearness, proximity; contact; *pl* outskirts, neighborhood, environs

inmediatamente /imeðiata'mente/ *adv* near; immediately, at once

inmediato /ime'ðiato/ *a* adjoining, close, nearby; immediate, prompt

inmejorable /imeho'raβle/ *a* unsurpassable, unbeatable

inmemorable, inmemorial /imemo'raβle, imemo'rial/ *a* immemorial

inmensidad /imensi'ðað/ *f,* vastness, huge extent; infinity; infinite space; immensity; huge number

inmenso /i'menso/ *a* vast; infinite; immense; innumerable

inmensurable /imensu'raβle/ *a* immeasurable, incalculable

inmerecido /imere'siðo; imere'θiðo/ *a* undeserved, unmerited

inmérito /i'merito/ *a* wrongful, unjust

inmeritorio /imeri'torio/ *a* unmeritorious, unpraiseworthy

inmersión /imer'sion/ *f,* immersion; dip

inmigración /imigra'sion; imigra'θion/ *f*, immigration
inmigrante /imi'grante/ *a* and *mf* immigrant
inmigrar /imi'grar/ *vi* to immigrate
inminencia /imi'nensia; imi'nenθia/ *f*, imminence
inminente /imi'nente/ *a* imminent
inmiscuir /imis'kuir/ *vt* to mix; *vr* meddle. May be conjugated regularly or like **huir**
inmisión /imi'sion/ *f*, inspiration
inmobiliario /imoβi'liario/ *a* concerning real estate
inmoble /i'moβle/ *a* immovable; motionless, immobile, stationary; *Fig.* unshakable, unflinching
inmoderación /imoðera'sion; imoðera'θion/ *f*, immoderateness, excess
inmoderado /imoðe'raðo/ *a* immoderate; unrestrained, excessive
inmodestia /imo'ðestia/ *f*, immodesty
inmodesto /imo'ðesto/ *a* immodest
inmolación /imola'sion; imola'θion/ *f*, immolation
inmolador /imola'ðor/ **(-ra)** *a* sacrificing. *n* immolator
inmolar /imo'lar/ *vt* to immolate; *Fig.* sacrifice, give up; *vr Fig.* sacrifice oneself
inmoral /imo'ral/ *a* immoral
inmoralidad /imorali'ðað/ *f*, immorality
inmortal /imor'tal/ *a* immortal
inmortalidad /imortali'ðað/ *f*, immortality
inmortalizar /imortali'sar; imortali'θar/ *vt* to immortalize
inmotivado /imoti'βaðo/ *a* unfounded, without reason
inmoto /i'moto/ *a* motionless, stationary
inmóvil /i'moβil/ *a* immovable, fixed; motionless; steadfast, constant
inmovilidad /imoβili'ðað/ *f*, immovability; immobility; constancy, steadfastness
inmovilizar /imoβili'sar; imoβili'θar/ *vt* to immobilize
inmueble /i'mueβle/ *m*, *Law.* immovable estate
inmundicia /imun'disia; imun'diθia/ *f*, filth, nastiness; dirt; rubbish, refuse; obscenity, indecency
inmundo /i'mundo/ *a* dirty, filthy; obscene, indecent; unclean
inmune /i'mune/ *a* exempt; *Med.* immune
inmunidad /imuni'ðað/ *f*, exemption; immunity
inmunizar /imuni'sar; imuni'θar/ *vt* to immunize
inmutabilidad /imutaβili'ðað/ *f*, immutability, changelessness; imperturbability
inmutable /imu'taβle/ *a* immutable, unchangeable; imperturbable
inmutación /imuta'sion; imuta'θion/ *f*, change, alteration, disturbance
inmutar /imu'tar/ *vt* to change, alter, vary; *vr* change one's expression (through fear, etc.)
innato /in'nato/ *a* innate; inherent; instinctive, inborn
innatural /innatu'ral/ *a* unnatural
innavegable /innaβe'gaβle/ *a* unnavigable; unseaworthy (of ships)
innecesario /innese'sario; inneθe'sario/ *a* unnecessary
innegable /inne'gaβle/ *a* undeniable; indisputable, irrefutable
innoble /in'noβle/ *a* plebeian; ignoble
innocuo /inno'kuo/ *a* harmless, innocuous
innovación /innoβa'sion; innoβa'θion/ *f*, innovation
innovador /innoβa'ðor/ **(-ra)** *a* innovative. *n* innovator
innovar /inno'βar/ *vt* to innovate, introduce innovations
innumerabilidad /innumeraβili'ðað/ *f*, countless number, multitude
innumerable /innume'raβle/ *a* innumerable, countless
innúmero /in'numero/ *a* countless, innumerable
inobediencia /inoβe'ðiensia; inoβe'ðienθia/ *f*, disobedience
inobediente /inoβe'ðiente/ *a* disobedient
inobjetable /inoβhe'taβle/ *a*, *Lat. Am.* unobjectionable
inobservable /inoβser'βaβle/ *a* unobservable
inobservancia /inoβser'βansia; inoβser'βanθia/ *f*, inobservance

inobservante /inoβser'βante/ *a* unobservant
inocencia /ino'sensia; ino'θenθia/ *f*, innocence; simplicity, candor; harmlessness
inocentada /inosen'taða; inoθen'taða/ *f*, *Inf.* naive remark or action; fool's trap; practical joke
inocente /ino'sente; ino'θente/ *a* innocent; candid, simple; harmless; easily deceived
inocentón /inosen'ton; inoθen'ton/ *a* *Inf.* extremely credulous and easily taken in
inocuidad /inokui'ðað/ *f*, innocuousness
inoculación /inokula'sion; inokula'θion/ *f*, inoculation
inoculador /inokula'ðor/ *m*, inoculator
inocular /inoku'lar/ *vt* to inoculate; pervert, corrupt; contaminate
inodoro /ino'ðoro/ *a* odorless. *m*, toilet, lavatory
inofensivo /inofen'siβo/ *a* inoffensive, harmless
inolvidable /inolβi'ðaβle/ *a* unforgettable
inoperable /inope'raβle/ *a* inoperable
inopia /i'nopia/ *f*, poverty; scarcity. *Inf.* **estar en la i.**, to be without a clue (about)
inopinable /inopi'naβle/ *a* indisputable, unquestionable
inopinado /inopi'naðo/ *a* unexpected, sudden
inoportunidad /inoportuni'ðað/ *f*, inopportuneness, unseasonableness; unsuitability
inoportuno /inopor'tuno/ *a* inopportune, untimely
inordenado /inorðe'naðo/ *a* inordinate, immoderate, excessive
inorgánico /inor'ganiko/ *a* inorganic
inoxidable /inoksi'ðaβle/ *a* rustless
inquebrantable /inkeβran'taβle/ *a* unbreakable; final, irrevocable
inquietador /inkieta'ðor/ **(-ra)** *a* disturbing. *n* disturber
inquietar /inkie'tar/ *vt* to disturb; trouble, make anxious, worry; *vr* be disquieted, worry
inquieto /in'kieto/ *a* restless; unquiet; fidgety; disturbed, anxious, worried, uneasy
inquietud /inkie'tuð/ *f*, restlessness; uneasiness; worry; trouble, care, anxiety
inquilinato /inkili'nato/ *m*, tenancy; rent; *Law.* lease; (rental) rates
inquilino /inki'lino/ **(-na)** *n* tenant; lessee; *Chile* tenant farmer
inquina /in'kina/ *f*, dislike, grudge
inquinar /inki'nar/ *vt* to contaminate, corrupt, infect
inquiridor /inkiri'ðor/ **(-ra)** *a* inquiring, examining. *n* investigator
inquirir /inki'rir/ *vt irr* to inquire; examine, look into. See **adquirir**
inquisición /inkisi'sion; inkisi'θion/ *f*, inquiry, investigation; *Eccl.* Inquisition
inquisidor /inkisi'ðor/ **(-ra)** *a* inquiring, investigating. *n* investigator. *m*, *Eccl.* inquisitor; judge
inquisitorial /inkisito'rial/ *a* inquisitorial
insaciabilidad /insasiaβili'ðað; insaθiaβili'ðað/ *f*, insatiability
insaciable /insa'siaβle; insa'θiaβle/ *a* insatiable
insalubre /insa'luβre/ *a* unhealthy
insanable /insa'naβle/ *a* incurable
insania /in'sania/ *f*, insanity
insano /in'sano/ *a* insane, mad
inscribir /inskri'βir/ *vt* to inscribe; record; enter (a name on a list, etc.), register, enroll; engrave; *Geom.* inscribe. *Past Part.* **inscrito**
inscripción /inskrip'sion; inskrip'θion/ *f*, inscription; record, enrollment; registration; government bond
insecable /inse'kaβle/ *a* undryable, undrying
insecticida /insekti'siða; insekti'θiða/ *a* insecticide
insecto /in'sekto/ *m*, insect
inseguridad /inseguri'ðað/ *f*, insecurity
inseguro /inse'guro/ *a* insecure; unsafe; uncertain
insensatez /insensa'teθ/ *f*, folly, foolishness
insensato /insen'sato/ *a* foolish, stupid, mad
insensibilidad /insensiβili'ðað/ *f*, insensibility; imperception; callousness, hard-heartedness
insensibilizar /insensiβili'sar; insensiβili'θar/ *vt* to make insensible (to sensations)

insensible /insen'siβle/ a insensible; imperceptive, insensitive; unconscious, senseless; imperceptible, inappreciable; callous

inseparabilidad /inseparaβili'ðað/ f, inseparability

inseparable /insepa'raβle/ a inseparable

insepulto /inse'pulto/ a unburied (of the dead)

inserción /inser'sion; inser'θion/ f, insertion; interpolation; grafting

insertar /inser'tar/ vt to insert; introduce; interpolate; vr (Bot. Zool.) become attached

inservible /inser'βiβle/ a useless; unfit; unsuitable

insidia /in'siðia/ f, insidiousness; snare, ambush

insidiador /insiðia'ðor/ (-ra) a ensnaring. n schemer, ambusher

insidiar /insi'ðiar/ vt to waylay, ambush; set a trap for; scheme against

insidioso /insi'ðioso/ a insidious; treacherous; scheming, guileful

insigne /in'signe/ a illustrious, famous; distinguished

insignia /in'signia/ f, symbol; badge; token; banner, standard; Naut. pennant; pl insignia

insignificancia /insignifi'kansia; insignifi'kanθia/ f, meaninglessness; unimportance, triviality; insignificance, insufficiency

insignificante /insignifi'kante/ a meaningless; unimportant; insignificant, small

insinuación /insinua'sion; insinua'θion/ f, insinuation; hint; implication; suggestion

insinuador /insinua'ðor/ a insinuating; suggestive, implicative

insinuar /insi'nuar/ vt to insinuate; suggest, hint; vr ingratiate oneself; creep in

insinuativo /insinua'tiβo/ a insinuative

insipidez /insipi'ðes; insipi'ðeθ/ f, tastelessness, insipidity; Fig. dullness

insípido /in'sipiðo/ a tasteless, insipid; dull, uninteresting, boring

insistencia /insis'tensia; insis'tenθia/ f, insistence

insistente /insis'tente/ a insistent

insistir /insis'tir/ vi (with en or sobre) to lay stress upon, insist on; persist in

ínsito /'insito/ a inherent, innate

insociabilidad /insosiaβili'ðað; insoθiaβili'ðað/ f, unsociability

insociable /inso'siaβle; inso'θiaβle/ a unsociable

insolación /insola'sion; insola'θion/ f, insolation, exposure to the sun; sunstroke

insolar /inso'lar/ vt to expose to the sun's rays; vr contract sunstroke

insoldable /insol'daβle/ a unsolderable, unable to be soldered

insolencia /inso'lensia; inso'lenθia/ f, insolence; impudence, impertinence

insolentarse /insolen'tarse/ vr to grow insolent; be impudent

insolente /inso'lente/ a insolent; impudent, impertinent

insólito /in'solito/ a unaccustomed; infrequent; unusual; unexpected

insolubilidad /insoluβili'ðað/ f, insolubility

insoluble /inso'luβle/ a insoluble

insoluto /inso'luto/ a unpaid, outstanding

insolvencia /insol'βensia; insol'βenθia/ f, insolvency

insolvente /insol'βente/ a insolvent

insomne /in'somne/ a sleepless

insomnio /in'somnio/ m, insomnia

insondable /inson'daβle/ a unfathomable, bottomless; inscrutable, secret

insoportable /insopor'taβle/ a intolerable, unbearable

insostenible /insoste'niβle/ a indefensible; arbitrary, baseless

inspección /inspek'sion; inspek'θion/ f, inspection; supervision; examination; inspectorship; inspector's office

inspeccionar /inspeksio'nar; inspekθio'nar/ vt to inspect; survey, examine. **i. una casa,** to view a house

inspector /inspek'tor/ (-ra) a inspecting, examining. n supervisor. m, inspector; surveyor

inspiración /inspira'sion; inspira'θion/ f, inspiration; inhalation

inspirador /inspira'ðor/ (-ra) a inspiring. n inspirer

inspirar /inspi'rar/ vt to breathe in, inhale; blow (of the wind); inspire; vr be inspired; (with en) find inspiration in, imitate

instalación /instala'sion; instala'θion/ f, plant, apparatus; erection, fitting; induction; installment, settling in

instalador /instala'ðor/ (-ra) n fitter; one who installs (electricity, etc.)

instalar /insta'lar/ vt to appoint, induct; erect (a plant, etc.); install, put in; lay on; Elec. wire; vr install oneself, settle down

instancia /ins'tansia; ins'tanθia/ f, instance; argument; suggestion; supplication; request; formal petition. **de primera i.,** in the first instance, firstly

instantánea /instan'tanea/ f, Photo. snapshot

instantáneo /instan'taneo/ a instantaneous

instante /ins'tante/ a urgent. m, second; instant, moment. **a cada i.,** every minute; frequently. **al i.,** at once, immediately. **por instantes,** continually; immediately

instar /ins'tar/ vt to press; persuade; insist upon; vi be urgent, press

instauración /instaura'sion; instaura'θion/ f, restoration; renewal; renovation; Lat. Am. establishment

instaurador /instaura'ðor/ (-ra) a renovating, renewing. n restorer, renovator

instaurar /instau'rar/ vt to restore; repair; renovate, renew; Lat. Am. establish, set up

instaurativo /instaura'tiβo/ a restorative

instigación /instiga'sion; instiga'θion/ f, instigation, incitement

instigador /instiga'ðor/ (-ra) n instigator

instigar /insti'gar/ vt to instigate, incite; induce

instilación /instila'sion; instila'θion/ f, instillment, pouring drop by drop; inculcation, implantation

instilar /insti'lar/ vt Chem. instill; implant, inculcate

instintivo /instin'tiβo/ a instinctive

instinto /ins'tinto/ m, instinct. **por i.,** by instinct, naturally

institución /institu'sion; institu'θion/ f, setting up, establishment; institution; teaching, instruction; pl institutes, digest

institucional /institusio'nal; instituθio'nal/ a institutional

instituir /insti'tuir/ vt irr to found, establish; institute; instruct, teach. See **huir**

instituto /insti'tuto/ m, institute; secondary school. **i. de belleza,** beauty parlor, beauty salon

institutor /institu'tor/ m, founder, instituter; tutor

institutriz /institu'tris; institu'triθ/ f, governess

instrucción /instruk'sion; instruk'θion/ f, teaching, instruction; knowledge, learning; education; pl orders; rules; instruction. **i. primaria,** primary education. **i. pública,** public education

instructivo /instruk'tiβo/ a instructive

instructor /instruk'tor/ (-ra) a instructive. n instructor

instruido /ins'truiðo/ a cultured, well-educated; knowledgeable

instruir /ins'truir/ vt irr to teach, instruct; train; inform, acquaint with; Law. formulate. See **huir**

instrumentación /instrumenta'sion; instrumenta'θion/ f, Mus. instrumentation

instrumentista /instrumen'tista/ mf Mus. instrumentalist; instrument maker

instrumento /instru'mento/ m, tool, implement; machine, apparatus; Mus. instrument; means, medium; legal document. **i. de cuerda,** string instrument. **i. de percusión,** percussion instrument. **i. de viento,** wind instrument

insuave /in''suaβe/ a unpleasant (to the senses); rough

insubordinación /insuβorðina'sion; insuβorðina'θion/ f, insubordination, rebellion

insubordinado /insuβorði'naðo/ a insubordinate, unruly

insubordinar /insuβorði'nar/ vt to rouse to rebellion; vr become insubordinate, rebel

insubsistencia /insuβsis'tensia; insuβsis'tenθia/ *f*, instability

insubsistente /insuβsis'tente/ *a* unstable; groundless, unfounded

insubstancial /insuβstan'sial; insuβstan'θial/ *a* insubstantial, unreal, illusory; pointless, worthless, superficial

insubstancialidad /insuβstansiali'ðað; insuβstanθiali'ðað/ *f*, superficiality, worthlessness

insuficiencia /insufi'siensia; insufi'θienθia/ *f*, insufficiency, shortage; incompetence, inefficiency

insuficiente /insufi'siente; insufi'θiente/ *a* insufficient, scarce, inadequate

insufrible /insu'friβle/ *a* insufferable, unbearable, intolerable

insular /insu'lar/ *a* insular

insulina /insu'lina/ *f*, insulin

insulsez /insul'ses; insul'seθ/ *f*, insipidity, tastelessness; dullness; tediousness

insulso /in'sulso/ *a* insipid, tasteless; tedious; dull

insultador /insulta'ðor/ (-ra) *a* insulting. *n* insulter

insultante /insul'tante/ *a* insulting

insultar /insul'tar/ *vt* to insult; call names; *vr* take offense

insulto /in'sulto/ *m*, insult; sudden attack; sudden illness, fit; *Argentina* fit of fainting; *Mexico* indigestion

insumable /insu'maβle/ *a* incalculable; excessive, exorbitant

insumergible /insumer'hiβle/ *a* unsinkable

insumiso /insu'miso/ *a* rebellious

insuperable /insupe'raβle/ *a* insuperable

insurgente /insur'hente/ *a* insurgent, rebellious. *m*, rebel

insurrección /insurrek'sion; insurrek'θion/ *f*, insurrection

insurreccionar /insurreksio'nar; insurrekθio'nar/ *vt* to incite to rebellion; *vr* rise in rebellion

insurrecto /insu'rrekto/ (-ta) *n* rebel

insustancial /insustan'sial; insustan'θial/ *a* See **insubstancial**

insustituible /insusti'tuiβle/ *a* indispensable

intachable /inta'tʃaβle/ *a* irreproachable; impeccable, perfect

intacto /in'takto/ *a* untouched; intact, uninjured; whole, entire; complete; pure

intangibilidad /intanhiβili'ðað/ *f*, intangibility

intangible /intan'hiβle/ *a* intangible

integración /integra'sion; integra'θion/ *f*, integration

integrar /inte'grar/ *vt* to integrate; *Com.* repay

integridad /integri'ðað/ *f*, wholeness; completeness; integrity, probity, honesty; virginity

íntegro /'integro/ *a* integral, whole; upright, honest

integumento /integu'mento/ *m*, integument; pretense, simulation

intelectiva /intelek'tiβa/ *f*, understanding

intelecto /inte'lekto/ *m*, intellect

intelectual /intelek'tual/ *a* intellectual

intelectualidad /intelektuali'ðað/ *f*, understanding, intellectuality; intelligentsia

inteligencia /inteli'hensia; inteli'henθia/ *f*, intelligence; intellect; mental alertness; mind; meaning, sense; experience, skill; understanding, secret agreement; information, knowledge; Intelligence, Secret Service

inteligente /inteli'hente/ *a* intelligent; clever; skillful; capable, competent

inteligible /inteli'hiβle/ *a* intelligible; understandable; able to be heard

intemperancia /intempe'ransia; intempe'ranθia/ *f*, intemperance, lack of moderation

intemperante /intempe'rante/ *a* intemperate

intemperie /intem'perie/ *f*, stormy weather. **a la i.**, at the mercy of the elements; in the open air

intempestivo /intempes'tiβo/ *a* inopportune, ill-timed

intención /inten'sion; inten'θion/ *f*, intention; determination, purpose; viciousness (of animals); caution. *Inf.* **con segunda i.**, with a double meaning, slyly

intencionado /intensio'naðo; intenθio'naðo/ *a* intentioned, disposed

intencional /intensio'nal; intenθio'nal/ *a* intentional, designed, premeditated

intendencia /inten'densia; inten'denθia/ *f*, management; supervision; administration; *Polit.* intendancy; *Argentina* mayoralty. *Mil.* **cuerpo de i.**, quartermaster corps, army supply corps

intendente /inten'dente/ *m*, director; manager; *Polit.* intendant; *Argentina* mayor. **i. de ejército,** quartermaster general

intensar /inten'sar/ *vt* to intensify

intensidad /intensi'ðað/ *f*, intensity; ardor; vehemence

intensificar /intensifi'kar/ *vt* to intensify

intensivo /inten'siβo/ *a* intensive

intenso /in'tenso/ *a* intense; ardent; fervent, vehement

intentar /inten'tar/ *vt* to intend, mean; propose; try, endeavor; initiate. **i. fortuna,** to try one's luck

intento /in'tento/ *m*, intention, determination; purpose. **de i.,** on purpose; knowingly

intentona /inten'tona/ *f*, *Inf.* foolhardy attempt

interacción /interak'sion; interak'θion/ *f*, interaction; reciprocal effect; *Chem.* reaction

intercalación /interkala'sion; interkala'θion/ *f*, interpolation; insertion

intercalar /interka'lar/ *vt* to intercalate; interpolate, include, insert

intercambiable /interkam'biaβle/ *a* interchangeable

intercambio /inter'kambio/ *m*, interchange

interceder /interse'ðer; interθe'ðer/ *vi* to intercede, plead for

interceptación /intersepta'sion; interθepta'θion/ *f*, interception

interceptar /intersep'tar; interθep'tar/ *vt* to intercept; interrupt; hinder

intercesión /interse'sion; interθe'sion/ *f*, intercession

intercesor /interse'sor; interθe'sor/ (-ra) *a* interceding. *n* intercessor

intercutáneo /interku'taneo/ *a* intercutaneous

interdecir /inter'ðesir; inter'ðeθir/ *vt irr* to forbid, prohibit. See **decir**

interdicción /interðik'sion; interðik'θion/ *f*, interdiction, prohibition

interdicto /inter'ðikto/ *m*, interdict

interés /inte'res/ *m*, interest; yield, profit; advantage; *Com.* interest; inclination, fondness; attraction, fascination; *pl* money matters. **i. compuesto,** compound interest. **intereses creados,** bonds of interest; vested interests

interesado /intere'saðo/ (-da) *a* involved, concerned; biased; selfish. *n Law.* interested party

interesante /intere'sante/ *a* interesting

interesar /intere'sar/ (se) *vi* and *vr* to be interested; *vt Com.* invest; interest

interfecto /inter'fekto/ (-ta) *n Law.* victim (of murder)

interferencia /interfe'rensia; interfe'renθia/ *f*, *Phys.* interference

interfoliar /interfo'liar/ *vt* to interleave (of books)

ínterin /'interin/ *m*, interim. *adv* meanwhile, in the meantime

interinamente /interina'mente/ *adv* in the interim; provisionally

interinar /interi'nar/ *vt* to discharge (duties) provisionally, act temporarily as

interino /inte'rino/ *a* acting, provisional, temporary

interior /inte'rior/ *a* interior; inner; inside; indoor; inland; internal, domestic (policies, etc.); inward, spiritual. *m*, interior, inside; mind, soul; *pl* entrails

interiorizar /interiori'sar; interiori'θar/ *vt*, *Lat. Am.* to investigate closely, look into, scrutinize

interjección /interhek'sion; interhek'θion/ *f*, *Gram.* interjection, exclamation

interlinear /interline'ar/ *vt* to write between the lines; *Print.* lead

interlocución /interloku'sion; interloku'θion/ *f*, dialogue, conversation

interlocutorio /interloku'torio/ *a Law.* interlocutory

intérlope /in'terlope/ *a* interloping. *mf* interloper

interludio /inter'luðio/ *m*, interlude

intermediario /interme'ðiario/ **(-ia)** *a* and *n* intermediary. *m, Com.* middleman

intermedio /inter'meðio/ *a* intermediate. *m*, interim; *Theat.* interval. **por i. de,** through, by the mediation of

intermisión /intermi'sion/ *f*, intermission, interval

intermitencia /intermi'tensia; intermi'tenθia/ *f*, intermittence

intermitente /intermi'tente/ *a* intermittent

intermitir /intermi'tir/ *vt* to interrupt, suspend, discontinue

internación /interna'sion; interna'θion/ *f*, going inside; penetration; taking into

internacional /internasio'nal; internaθio'nal/ *a* international

internacionalismo /internasiona'lismo; internaθiona'lismo/ *m*, internationalism

internacionalista /internasiona'lista; internaθiona'lista/ *mf* internationalist

internacionalización /internasionalisa'sion; internaθionaliθa'θion/ *f*, internationalization

internado /inter'naðo/ *m*, boarding school

internamiento /interna'miento/ *m*, internment

internar /inter'nar/ *vt* to take or send inland; *vi* penetrate; *vr* (*with en*) go into the interior of (a country); get into the confidence of; study deeply (a subject)

Internet /inter'net/ *m*, the Internet

interno /in'terno/ **(-na)** *a* interior; internal; inner; inside; boarding (student). *n* boarding school student; *Med.* intern

internuncio /inter'nunsio; inter'nunθio/ *m*, *Eccl.* internuncio; interlocutor; representative

interoceánico /interose'aniko; interoθe'aniko/ *a* interoceanic

interpaginar /interpahi'nar/ *vt* to interleave (of books)

interpelación /interpela'sion; interpela'θion/ *f*, *Law.* interpellation; appeal

interpelar /interpe'lar/ *vt Law.* to interpellate; appeal to, ask protection from

interpolación /interpola'sion; interpola'θion/ *f*, interpolation, insertion; interruption

interpolador /interpola'ðor/ **(-ra)** *n* interpolator; interrupter

interpolar /interpo'lar/ *vt* to interpolate; interject

interponer /interpo'ner/ *vt irr* to interpose, insert, intervene; designate as an arbitrator; *vr* intervene. See **poner**

interposición /interposi'sion; interposi'θion/ *f*, interposition; intervention; mediation, arbitration

interpresa /inter'presa/ *f*, *Mil.* surprise attack

interpretación /interpreta'sion; interpreta'θion/ *f*, interpretation; translation

interpretador /interpreta'ðor/ **(-ra)** *a* interpretative. *n* interpreter

interpretar /interpre'tar/ *vt* to interpret; translate; attribute; expound, explain. **i. mal,** to misconstrue; translate wrongly

intérprete /in'terprete/ *mf* interpreter

interregno /inte'rregno/ *m*, interregnum; *Lat. Am.* interim. **i. parlamentario,** parliamentary recess

interrogación /interroga'sion; interroga'θion/ *f*, interrogation, question; *Gram.* question mark

interrogador /interroga'ðor/ **(-ra)** *n* questioner

interrogante /interro'gante/ *a* interrogating. *m*, *Print.* question mark

interrogar /interro'gar/ *vt* to interrogate, question

interrogativo /interroga'tiβo/ *a* interrogative

interrogatorio /interroga'torio/ *m*, interrogatory

interrumpir /interrum'pir/ *vt* to interrupt; hinder, obstruct; *Elec.* break contact

interrupción /interrup'sion; interrup'θion/ *f*, interruption; stoppage (of work); *Elec.* break

interruptor /interrup'tor/ **(-ra)** *a* interrupting. *n* interrupter. *m*, *Elec.* switch, interruptor. **i. de dos direcciones,** *Elec.* two-way switch

intersticio /inter'stisio; inter'stiθio/ *m*, interstice, crack, crevice; interval, intervening space

intervalo /inter'βalo/ *m*, interval

intervención /interβen'sion; interβen'θion/ *f*, inter-

vention; mediation, intercession; auditing (of accounts)

intervenir /interβe'nir/ *vi irr* to take part (in); intervene, interfere; arbitrate, mediate; happen, occur; *vt Com.* audit. See **venir**

interventor /interβen'tor/ **(-ra)** *a* intervening. *n* one who intervenes. *m*, auditor; inspector

intervocálico /interβo'kaliko/ *a* intervocalic

intestado /intes'taðo/ **(-da)** *a* and *n Law.* intestate

intestino /intes'tino/ *a* intestinal. *m*, intestine

íntima, intimación /'intima, intima'sion; 'intima, intima'θion/ *f*, intimation, notification

intimar /inti'mar/ *vt* to intimate; inform, notify; *vr* penetrate; *vr* and *vi* become intimate or friendly

intimidación /intimiða'sion; intimiða'θion/ *f*, intimidation, terrorization

intimidad /intimi'ðað/ *f*, intimacy

intimidar /intimi'ðar/ *vt* to intimidate, terrorize, cow

íntimo /'intimo/ *a* intimate; deep-seated, inward; private, personal

intitular /intitu'lar/ *vt* to give a title to, entitle, call; *vr* call oneself

intolerable /intole'raβle/ *a* intolerable; unbearable

intolerancia /intole'ransia; intole'ranθia/ *f*, narrow-mindedness, intolerance, bigotry

intolerante /intole'rante/ *a* narrow-minded, illiberal; *Med.* intolerant

intonso /in'tonso/ *a* long-haired, unshorn; boorish, ignorant

intoxicación /intoksika'sion; intoksika'θion/ *f*, poisoning

intoxicar /intoksi'kar/ *vt* to poison

intraducible /intraðu'siβle; intraðu'θiβle/ *a* untranslatable

intramuros /intra'muros/ *adv* within the town walls, within the city

intranquilidad /intrankili'ðað/ *f*, disquiet, restlessness; anxiety

intranquilizador /intrankilisa'ðor; intrankiliθa'ðor/ *a* disquieting, perturbing

intranquilizar /intrankili'sar; intrankili'θar/ *vt* to disquiet, make uneasy, worry

intranquilo /intran'kilo/ *a* uneasy, anxious

intransferible /intransfe'riβle/ *a* untransferable, not transferable

intransigencia /intransi'hensia; intransi'henθia/ *f*, intolerance, intransigence

intransigente /intransi'hente/ *a* intolerant, intransigent

intransitable /intransi'taβle/ *a* impassable; unsurmountable

intransitivo /intransi'tiβo/ *a* intransitive

intrascendente /intrassen'dente; intrasθen'dente/ *a*, *Lat. Am.* unimportant

intratable /intra'taβle/ *a* intractable; impassable; rough; unsociable, difficult

intrauterino /intraute'rino/ *a* intrauterine. **dispositivo i.,** intrauterine device

intravenoso /intraβe'noso/ *a* intravenous

intrepidez /intrepi'ðes; intrepi'ðeθ/ *f*, intrepidity, dauntlessness, gallantry

intrépido /in'trepiðo/ *a* intrepid, dauntless, gallant

intriga /in'triga/ *f*, scheme, intrigue; entanglement; *Lit.* plot

intrigante /intri'gante/ *mf* intriguer, schemer

intrigar /intri'gar/ *vi* to intrigue, scheme, plot; **intrigarse** *Lat. Am.* to be intrigued, be puzzled

intrincación /intrinka'sion; intrinka'θion/ *f*, intricacy

intrincado /intrin'kaðo/ *a* intricate

intrincar /intrin'kar/ *vt* to complicate; obscure, confuse

intríngulis /in'tringulis/ *m*, *Inf.* ulterior motive

intrínseco /in'trinseko/ *a* intrinsic, inherent; essential

introducción /introðuk'sion; introðuk'θion/ *f*, introduction

introducir /introðu'sir; introðu'θir/ *vt irr* to introduce; insert; fit in; drive in; present, introduce; bring into use; cause, occasion; show in, bring in; *vr* interfere, meddle; enter. See **conducir**

introductor /introðuk'tor/ **(-ra)** *n* introducer

introito /introito/ *m*, preamble, introduction; *Eccl.* introit; *(Theat. Obs.)* prologue

intromisión /intromi'sion/ *f*, intromission; interference; *Geol.* intrusion

introspección /introspek'sion; introspek'θion/ *f*, introspection

introverso /intro'βerso/ *a* introvert

intruso /in'truso/ **(-sa)** *a* intruding, intrusive. *n* intruder

intuición /intui'sion; intui'θion/ *f*, intuition

intuir /in'tuir/ *vt irr* to know by intuition. See **huir**

intuitivo /intui'tiβo/ *a* intuitive

intuito /in'tuito/ *m*, glance, look, view

inulto /i'nulto/ *a Poet.* unavenged, unpunished

inundación /inunda'sion; inunda'θion/ *f*, flood; flooding; excess, superabundance

inundar /inun'dar/ *vt* to flood; swamp; *Fig.* inundate, overwhelm

inurbanidad /inurβani'ðað/ *f*, discourtesy, impoliteness

inurbano /inur'βano/ *a* discourteous, uncivil, impolite

inusitado /inusi'taðo/ *a* unusual, unaccustomed; rare

inútil /i'nutil/ *a* useless

inutilidad /inutili'ðað/ *f*, uselessness

inutilizar /inutili'sar; inutili'θar/ *vt* to render useless; disable, incapacitate; spoil, damage

invadeable /imbaðe'aβle/ *a* impassable, unfordable

invadir /imba'ðir/ *vt* to invade

invaginación /imbahina'sion; imbahina'θion/ *f*, invagination

invalidación /imbaliða'sion; imbaliða'θion/ *f*, invalidation

invalidar /imbali'ðar/ *vt* to invalidate

invalidez /imbali'ðes; imbali'ðeθ/ *f*, invalidity; disablement; infirmity

inválido /im'baliðo/ **(-da)** *a* weak, infirm; invalid; null; disabled. *n* invalid; disabled soldier

invariable /imba'riaβle/ *a* invariable

invariación /imbaria'sion; imbaria'θion/ *f*, invariableness

invariante /imba'riante/ *m*, invariant

invasión /imba'sion/ *f*, invasion, encroachment, incursion

invasor /imba'sor/ **(-ra)** *a* invading; *Med.* attacking. *n* invader

invectiva /imbek'tiβa/ *f*, invective

invencibilidad /imbensiβili'ðað; imbenθiβili'ðað/ *f*, invincibili.y

invencible /imben'siβle; imben'θiβle/ *a* invincible

invención /imben'sion; imben'θion/ *f*, invention, discovery; deception, fabrication, lie; creative imagination; finding (e.g. *i. de la Santa Cruz,* Invention of the Holy Cross)

invencionero /imbensio'nero; imbenθio'nero/ **(-ra)** *n* inventor; schemer, deceiver

invendible /imben'diβle/ *a* unsalable

inventar /imben'tar/ *vt* to invent; create; imagine; concoct, fabricate (lies, etc.)

inventariar /imbenta'riar/ *vt* to make an inventory of; *Com.* take stock of

inventario /imben'tario/ *m*, inventory; *Com.* stock taking

inventiva /imben'tiβa/ *f*, inventiveness, ingenuity; creativeness

inventivo /imben'tiβo/ *a* inventive

invento /im'bento/ *m*, See **invención**

inventor /imben'tor/ **(-ra)** *n* inventor, discoverer; liar, storyteller

inverecundia /imbere'kundia/ *f*, impertinence, impudence

inverecundo /imbere'kundo/ *a* shameless, brazen

inverisímil /imberi'simil/ *a* See **inverosímil**

invernáculo /imber'nakulo/ *m*, greenhouse; conservatory

invernada /imber'naða/ *f*, winter season; hibernation; *Lat. Am.* winter pasture

invernadero /imberna'ðero/ *m*, winter quarters; greenhouse

invernal /imber'nal/ *a* wintry; winter

invernar /imber'nar/ *vi irr* to winter; hibernate; be wintertime. See **acertar**

invernizo /imber'niso; imber'niθo/ *a* wintry, winter

inverosímil /imbero'simil/ *a* unlikely, improbable

inverosimilitud /imberosimili'tuð/ *f*, improbability

inversamente /imbersa'mente/ *adv* inversely

inverso /im'berso/ *a* inverse; inverted

inversor, -a /imber'sor/ *mf*, *Lat. Am.* investor

invertebrado /imberte'βraðo/ *a* and *m*, invertebrate

invertir /imber'tir/ *vt irr* to invert, transpose; reverse; *Com.* invest; spend (time). See **sentir**

investidura /imbesti'ðura/ *f*, investiture

investigación /imbestiga'sion; imbestiga'θion/ *f*, investigation, examination; research; inquiry

investigador /imbestiga'ðor/ **(-ra)** *a* investigating. *n* investigator; researcher

investigar /imbesti'gar/ *vt* to investigate, examine; research on

investir /imbes'tir/ *vt irr* to confer upon, decorate with; invest, appoint. See **pedir**

inveterado /imbete'raðo/ *a* inveterate

inviable /im'biaβle/ *a* unfeasible

invicto /im'bikto/ *a* invincible; unconquered

invierno /im'bierno/ *m*, winter; rainy season

inviolabilidad /imbiolaβili'ðað/ *f*, inviolability. **i. parlamentaria**, parliamentary immunity

inviolable /imbio'laβle/ *a* inviolable; infallible

inviolado /imbio'laðo/ *a* inviolate

invisibilidad /imbisiβili'ðað/ *f*, invisibility

invisible /imbi'siβle/ *a* invisible; *m*, *Argentina* hairpin; *Mexico* hairnet

invitación /imbita'sion; imbita'θion/ *f*, invitation

invitado /imbi'taðo/ **(-da)** *n* guest

invitar /imbi'tar/ *vt* to invite; urge, request; allure, attract

invocación /imboka'sion; imboka'θion/ *f*, invocation

invocador /imboka'ðor/ **(-ra)** *n* invoker

invocar /imbo'kar/ *vt* to invoke

involuntariedad /imboluntarie'ðað/ *f*, involuntariness

involuntario /imbolun'tario/ *a* involuntary

invulnerabilidad /imbulneraβili'ðað/ *f*, invulnerability

invulnerable /imbulne'raβle/ *a* invulnerable

inyección /inyek'sion; inyek'θion/ *f*, injection

inyectado /inyek'taðo/ *a* bloodshot (of eyes)

inyectar /inyek'tar/ *vt* to inject

ipecacuana /ipeka'kuana/ *f*, ipecac

iperita /i'perita/ *f*, mustard gas

ir /ir/ *vi irr* to go; suit, be becoming, fit (e.g. *El vestido no te va bien,* The dress doesn't suit you); extend; lead, go in the direction of (e.g. *Este camino va a Lérida,* This road leads to Lerida); get along, do, proceed, be (e.g. *¿Cómo te va estos días?* How are you getting along these days?); come (e.g. *Ahora voy,* I'm coming now); bet (e.g. *Van cinco pesetas que no lo hace,* I bet five pesetas he doesn't do it); be different, be changed (e.g. *¡Qué diferencia va entre esto y aquello!* What a difference there is between this and that!); *Math.* carry (e.g. *siete y van cuatro,* seven, and four to carry); *Math.* leave (e.g. *De quince a seis van nueve,* Six from fifteen leaves nine). With a gerund, **ir** indicates the continuance of the action, going (e.g. *Iremos andando hacia el mar,* We will go on walking toward the sea, or *Entre tanto iba amaneciendo,* In the meanwhile it was growing light); past participle, **ir** means "to be" (e.g. *Voy encantado de lo que he visto,* I am delighted with what I have seen). With *prep a + infin,* **ir** expresses the periphrastic future, and means to be (to do) or to intend (to do) or to be on the point of doing (e.g. *Van a cantar la canción que te gusta,* They are going (or preparing) to sing the song you like). With *prep a + noun,* **ir** indicates destination (e.g. *Voy al cine,* I'm going to the cinema. *¿A dónde vamos?* Where are we going to?). **ir** + *con* means to go in the company of, or to be in a certain manner (e.g. *Hemos de ir con cuidado,* We must go carefully). **ir** + *en* means to concern, interest (e.g.

¿Qué le va a él en este asunto? What has this affair to do with him?). **ir** + *por* means to follow the career of, become (e.g. *Juan va por abogado,* John is going to be a lawyer). It also means to go and bring, or to go for (e.g. *Iré por agua,* I shall go and bring (or for) water). *vr* to go away, leave, depart; die; leak (of liquids); evaporate; overbalance, slip (e.g. *Se le fueron los pies,* He slipped (and lost his balance)); be worn out, grow old, deteriorate; be incontinent; *Fig. Inf.* **irse a uno una cosa,** not to notice or not to understand a thing. *Naut.* **irse a pique,** to founder, sink. **Se le fueron los ojos tras María,** He couldn't keep his eyes off Mary. **i. a caballo,** to ride, go on horseback. **i. adelante,** to go on ahead, lead; *Fig. Inf.* forge ahead, go ahead. **i. al cuartel,** to go into the army. **i. a una,** to cooperate in. **i. bien** *Fig. Inf.* to go on well; be well. **i. de brazo,** to walk arm in arm. **i. de compras,** to go shopping. **i. de juerga** *Inf.* to go on a binge. **i. de bicicleta** *or* **en coche,** to go by bicycle or to ride (in a car or carriage). **i. por,** to do things in order, take one thing at a time. *Fig. Inf.* **i. tirando,** to carry on, manage. **¿Cómo le va?** How are things with you? How are you getting along? *Inf.* **no irle ni venirle a uno nada en un asunto,** to be not in the least concerned in (an affair). **¡Qué va!** Rubbish! Nothing of the sort! **¿Quién va?** *Mil.* Who goes there? **Vamos,** Let's go (also used as an exclamation: Good gracious! You don't say so! Well!) **Vamos a ver...,** Let's see.... **¡Vaya!** What a...!; Come now! Never mind! **¡Vaya a paseo!** *or* **¡Vaya con su música a otra parte!** Take yourself off! Get out! **¡Vaya con Dios!** God keep you! Good-bye! *Pres. Ind.* **voy, vas, va, vamos, váis, van.** *Pres. Part.* **yendo.** *Preterite* **fui, fuiste, fue, fuimos, fuisteis, fueron.** *Imperf.* **iba, etc.** *Pres. Subjunc.* **vaya, etc.** *Imperf. Subjunc.* **fuese, etc.** *Imperat.* **vé**

ira /'ira/ *f,* wrath, anger; vengeance; raging, fury (of elements); *pl* cruelties, acts of vengeance

iracundia /ira'kundia/ *f,* irascibility, irritability; anger

iracundo /ira'kundo/ *a* irascible, irritable, choleric; angry; raging, tempestuous

iranio /i'ranio/ **(-ia)** *a* and *n* Iranian

irascibilidad /irassiβili'ðað; irasθiβili'ðað/ *f,* irascibility; petulance

iridiscencia /iriðis'sensia; iriðis'θenθia/ *f,* iridescence

iridiscente /iriðis'sente; iriðis'θente/ *a* iridescent

iris /'iris/ *m,* rainbow; *Anat.* iris (of the eye)

irisación /irisa'sion; irisa'θion/ *f,* irisation

irisar /iri'sar/ *vi* to be iridescent

Irlanda /ir'landa/ Ireland

irlandés /irlan'des/ **(-esa)** *a* and *n* Irishman (woman)

ironía /iro'nia/ *f,* irony

irónico /i'roniko/ *a* ironical

iroqués /iro'kes/ **(-esa)** *a* and *n* Iroquois

irracional /irrasio'nal; irraθio'nal/ *a* irrational; illogical, unreasonable; *Math.* irrational, absurd

irracionalidad /irrasionali'ðað; irraθionali'ðað/ *f,* irrationality, unreasonableness

irradiación /irraðia'sion; irraðia'θion/ *f,* radiation, irradiation

irradiar /irra'ðiar/ *vt* to radiate, irradiate

irrazonable /irraso'naβle; irraθo'naβle/ *a* unreasonable

irreal /irre'al/ *a* unreal

irrealidad /irreali'ðað/ *f,* unreality

irrealizable /irreali'saβle; irreali'θaβle/ *a* unachievable, unattainable

irrebatible /irreβa'tiβle/ *a* irrefutable, evident

irreconciliable /irrekonsi'liaβle; irrekonθi'liaβle/ *a* irreconcilable, intransigent

irrecuperable /irrekupe'raβle/ *a* irretrievable

irredimible /irreði'miβle/ *a* irredeemable

irreemplazable /irreempla'saβle; irreempla'θaβle/ *a* irreplaceable

irreflexión /irreflek'sion/ *f,* thoughtlessness; impetuosity

irreflexivo /irreflek'siβo/ *a* thoughtless; rash, impetuous

irreformable /irrefor'maβle/ *a* unreformable

irrefragable /irrefra'gaβle/ *a* indisputable, unquestionable

irrefrenable /irrefre'naβle/ *a* unmanageable, uncontrollable

irrefutable /irrefu'taβle/ *a* irrefutable

irregular /irregu'lar/ *a* irregular; infrequent, rare

irregularidad /irregulari'ðað/ *f,* irregularity; abnormality; *Inf.* moral lapse

irreligión /irreli'hion/ *f,* irreligion

irreligiosidad /irrelihiosi'ðað/ *f,* impiety, godlessness

irreligioso /irreli'hioso/ *a* irreligious, impious

irremediable /irreme'ðiaβle/ *a* irremediable

irremediablemente /irremeðiaβle'mente/ *adv* unavoidably; hopelessly

irremisible /irremi'siβle/ *a* unpardonable, inexcusable

irremunerado /irremune'raðo/ *a* unremunerated, gratuitous

irreparable /irrepa'raβle/ *a* irreparable

irreprensible /irrepren'siβle/ *a* blameless, unexceptionable

irreprochable /irrepro't∫aβle/ *a* irreproachable

irresistible /irresis'tiβle/ *a* irresistible; ravishing

irresolución /irresolu'sion; irresolu'θion/ *f,* vacillation, indecision

irresoluto /irreso'luto/ *a* hesitant, irresolute

irrespetuoso /irrespe'tuoso/ *a* disrespectful

irresponsabilidad /irresponsaβili'ðað/ *f,* irresponsibility

irresponsable /irrespon'saβle/ *a* irresponsible

irreverencia /irreβe'rensia; irreβe'renθia/ *f,* irreverence

irreverente /irreβe'rente/ *a* irreverent

irrevocabilidad /irreβokaβili'ðað/ *f,* irrevocability, finality

irrevocable /irreβo'kaβle/ *a* irrevocable

irrigación /irriga'sion; irriga'θion/ *f,* irrigation

irrigador /irriga'ðor/ *m,* spray, sprinkler; *Med.* syringe, spray

irrigar /irri'gar/ *vt* (*Med. Agr.*) to irrigate

irrisible /irri'siβle/ *a* ridiculous, laughable, absurd

irrisión /irri'sion/ *f,* derision; laughingstock

irrisorio /irri'sorio/ *a* ridiculous; derisive

irritabilidad /irritaβili'ðað/ *f,* irritability, petulance, irascibility

irritable /irri'taβle/ *a* irritable

irritación /irrita'sion; irrita'θion/ *f, Med.* irritation; petulance, exasperation

irritador /irrita'ðor/ *a* irritating; exasperating. *m,* irritant

irritante /irri'tante/ *a* irritating; exasperating

irritar /irri'tar/ *vt* to exasperate, annoy; provoke, inflame; (*Med. Law.*) irritate

írrito /'irrito/ *a* Law. null, void

irrogar /irro'gar/ *vt* to occasion (damage, harm)

irrompible /irrom'piβle/ *a* unbreakable

irrumpir /irrum'pir/ *vi* to enter violently, break in

irrupción /irrup'sion; irrup'θion/ *f,* irruption, incursion, invasion

irruptor /irrup'tor/ *a* invading, attacking

isabelino /isaβe'lino/ *a* Isabelline (pertaining to Spanish Queen Isabella II (reigned 1830–68)); bay (of horses)

isla /'isla/ *f,* island; block (of houses)

islámico /is'lamiko/ *a* Islamic

islamismo /isla'mismo/ *m,* Islam

islamita /isla'mita/ *a* and *mf* Muslim

islandés /islan'des/ **(-esa),** **islándico (-ca)** *a* Icelandic. *n* Icelander. *m,* Icelandic (language)

Islandia /is'landia/ *f,* Iceland

isleño /is'leɲo/ **(-ña)** *a* island. *n* islander; native of the Canary Islands

isleta /is'leta/ *f,* islet

islote /is'lote/ *m,* small island, islet

isoca /i'soka/ *f, Argentina* caterpillar

isométrico /iso'metriko/ *a* isometric

isomorfo /iso'morfo/ *a* isomorphic

isotermo /iso'termo/ *a* isothermal

isótope, isótopo /i'sotope, i'sotopo/ *m,* isotope

israelita /israe'lita/ *mf* Israelite. *a* Israeli

istmeño /ist'meɲo/ **(-ña)** *n* native of an isthmus

ístmico /'istmiko/ *a* isthmian

istmo /'istmo/ *m*, isthmus
Istmo de Suez, el /'istmo de 'sues, el; 'istmo de 'sueθ, el/ the Suez Canal
Italia /i'talia/ Italy
italianismo /italia'nismo/ *m*, Italianism
italianizar /italiani'sar; italiani'θar/ *vt* to italianize
italiano /ita'liano/ **(-na)** *a* and *n* Italian. *m*, Italian (language)
itálico /i'taliko/ *a* italic
iteración /itera'sion; itera'θion/ *f*, iteration, repetition

iterar /ite'rar/ *vt* to repeat, reiterate
iterativo /itera'tiβo/ *a* iterative, repetitive
itinerario /itine'rario/ *a* and *m*, itinerary
izar /i'sar; i'θar/ *vt* Naut. to hoist
izote /i'sote; i'θote/ *m*, yucca
izquierda /is'kierða; iθ'kierða/ *f*, left, left-hand side; Polit. left. **¡I.!** Mil. Left face! **a la i.**, on the left
izquierdo /is'kierðo; iθ'kierðo/ *a* left, left-hand; left-handed; bent, twisted, crooked

JK

¡ja, ja, ja! /'ha, ha, ha/ *interj* Ha! ha! ha!
jaba /'haβa/ *f*, Lat. Am. basket; Mexico crate
jabalí /haβa'li/ *m*, wild boar
jabalina /haβa'lina/ *f*, sow of wild boar; javelin
jabato /ha'βato/ *m*, young wild boar
jabón /ha'βon/ *m*, soap. **j. blando**, soft soap. **j. de olor** or **j. de tocador, toilet** soap. **j. de sastre**, French chalk, steatite
jabonadura /haβona'ðura/ *f*, soaping; *pl* soapsuds, lather
jabonar /haβo'nar/ *vt* to soap; wash, put on soap; Inf. dress down, scold
jaboncillo /haβon'siyo; haβon'θiʎo/ *m*, toilet soap; steatite
jabonera /haβo'nera/ *f*, soapdish or box; soapwort
jabonería /haβone'ria/ *f*, soap factory or shop
jabonoso /haβo'noso/ *a* soapy
jaca /'haka/ *f*, pony; filly
jacal /ha'kal/ *m*, Mexico hut, shack
jácara /'hakara/ *f*, gay, roguish ballad; song and dance
jácena /'hasena; 'haθena/ *f*, Archit. beam, girder
jacinto /ha'sinto; ha'θinto/ *m*, hyacinth; jacinth. **j. de ceilán**, zircon. **j. occidental**, topaz. **j. oriental**, ruby
jaco /'hako/ *m*, short coat of mail; hack, jade
jactancia /hak'tansia; hak'tanθia/ *f*, bragging, boasting
jactancioso /haktan'sioso; haktan'θioso/ **(-sa)** *a* boastful. *n* braggart
jactarse /hak'tarse/ *vr* to brag, boast
jaculatoria /hakula'toria/ *f*, ejaculatory prayer
jade /'haðe/ *m*, Mineral. jade
jadeante /haðe'ante/ *a* panting
jadear /haðe'ar/ *vi* to pant
jadeo /ha'ðeo/ *m*, pant; panting; hard breathing
jaez /ha'es; ha'eθ/ *m*, harness (gen. *pl*); kind, sort; *pl* trappings
jaguar /ha'guar/ *m*, jaguar
jaiba /'haiβa/ *f*, Lat. Am. crab
jáibol /'haiβol/ *m*, Lat. Am. highball
jáilaif /'hailaif/ *m*, Lat. Am. high life
jalbegar /halβe'gar/ *vt* to whitewash; make up the face
jalbegue /hal'βege/ *m*, whitewash
jalde /'halde/ *a* bright yellow
jalea /ha'lea/ *f*, jelly. **j. de membrillo**, quince jelly
jalear /hale'ar/ *vt* to encourage, urge on (by shouts, etc.)
jaleo /ha'leo/ *m*, act of encouraging dancers by clapping, shouting, etc.; Andalusian song and dance, Inf. uproar
jalón /ha'lon/ *m*, surveying rod
jamaicano /hamai'kano/ **(-na)** *a* and *n* Jamaican
jamás /ha'mas/ *adv* never. **nunca j.**, never. **por siempre j.**, for always, forever
jamba /'hamba/ *f*, jamb (of a door or window)
jambarse /ham'βarse/ *vr*, Lat. Am. to overeat
jamelgo /ha'melgo/ *m*, sorry nag, miserable hack
jamón /ha'mon/ *m*, ham
jamona /ha'mona/ *f*, Inf. plumpish middle-aged woman
jansenista /hanse'nista/ *mf* and *a* Jansenist
Japón /ha'pon/ Japan

japonés /hapo'nes/ **(-esa)** *a* and *n* Japanese. *m*, Japanese (language)
jaque /'hake/ *m*, check (in chess); braggart. **j. mate**, checkmate. **en j.**, at bay
jaquear /hake'ar/ *vt* to check (in chess); Mil. harass the enemy
jaqueca /ha'keka/ *f*, migraine, sick headache. Inf. **dar una j.**, to annoy
jarabe /ha'raβe/ *m*, syrup, cough medicine. **j. tapatío**, Mexican hat dance
jarana /ha'rana/ *f*, roundhouse; Inf. revelry; fight, roughhouse; trick, deception
jarcia /'harsia; 'harθia/ *f*, equipment; Naut. tackle, rigging (gen. *pl*); fishing tackle; Inf. heap, mixture, medley
jardín /har'ðin/ *m*, garden
jardinar /harði'nar/ *vt* to landscape
jardinera /harði'nera/ *f*, plant stand, jardiniere; open streetcar
jardinería /harðine'ria/ *f*, gardening
jardinero /harði'nero/ **(-ra)** *n* gardener
jareta /ha'reta/ *f*, Sew. running hem; Naut. netting
jarra /'harra/ *f*, jar, jug. **en jarras**, arms akimbo
jarrero /ha'rrero/ *m*, jug seller or manufacturer
jarrete /ha'rrete/ *m*, calf (of the leg)
jarretera /harre'tera/ *f*, garter
jarro /'harro/ *m*, pitcher; jug; jar; vase
jarrón /ha'rron/ *m*, garden urn; vase
jaspe /'haspe/ *m*, jasper
jaspeado /haspe'aðo/ *a* marbled, mottled; dappled; frosted (of glass)
jauja /'hauha/ *f*, Fig. paradise, land of milk and honey
jaula /'haula/ *f*, cage; crate; miner's cage
jauría /hau'ria/ *f*, pack of hounds
jazmín /has'min; haθ'min/ *m*, jasmine. **j. amarillo**, yellow jasmine. **j. de la India**, gardenia
jefa /'hefa/ *f*, forewoman; manager; leader, head
jefatura /hefa'tura/ *f*, chieftainship; managership; leadership. **j. de policía**, police station or headquarters
jefe /'hefe/ *m*, chief; head, leader; manager; Mil. commanding officer. **j. de estado mayor**, chief of staff. **j. del tren**, railroad guard
jengibre /hen'hiβre/ *m*, ginger
jeque /'heke/ *m*, sheik
jerarca /he'rarka/ *m*, hierarch
jerarquía /herar'kia/ *f*, hierarchy
jerárquico /he'rarkiko/ *a* hierarchical
jerez /he'res; he'reθ/ *m*, sherry
jerga /'herga/ *f*, thick frieze cloth; jargon
jergón /her'gon/ *m*, straw or hay mattress; pallet; misfit (garments); Inf. fat, lazy person
Jericó /heri'ko/ Jericho
jerigonza /heri'gonsa; heri'gonθa/ *f*, jargon; gibberish
jeringa /he'ringa/ *f*, syringe
jeringar /herin'gar/ *vt* to inject; syringe; Inf. annoy
jeringuilla /herin'guiya; herin'guiʎa/ *f*, small syringe; mock orange
jeroglífico /hero'glifiko/ *a* hieroglyphic. *m*, hieroglyph
jersey /her'sei/ *m*, jersey, sweater
Jerusalén /herusa'len/ Jerusalem

jesuita /he'suita/ *m*, Jesuit

Jesús /he'sus/ *m*, Jesus. *interj* Goodness!; Bless you! (said to someone after sneezing). **¡ay J.!** Alas! *Inf.* **en un decir J.,** in a trice

jeta /'heta/ *f*, hog's snout; blubber lip; *Inf.* face, mug

jibia /'hiβia/ *f*, cuttlefish

jícama /'hikama/ *f*, *Central America* sweet turnip

jícara /'hikara/ *f*, small cup

jicote /hi'kote/ *m*, *Lat. Am.* wasp

jifa /'hifa/ *f*, meat offal

jifia /'hifia/ *f*, swordfish

jinete /hi'nete/ *m*, horseman, rider; horse soldier, cavalryman

jip /hip/ *m*, jeep

jipijapa /hipi'hapa/ *f*, very fine straw. **sombrero de j.,** panama hat

jira /'hira/ *f*, strip of cloth; picnic; tour

jirafa /hi'rafa/ *f*, giraffe

jirón /hi'ron/ *m*, rag; piece of a dress, etc.; portion of a whole

jitomate, /hito'mate/ *m*, *Mexico* tomato. See **tomate**

jiujitsu /hiu'hitsu/ *m*, jujitsu

jocosidad /hokosi'ðað/ *f*, pleasantry, jocularity; joke

jocoso /ho'koso/ *a* waggish; jocose, joyous

jocundidad /hokundi'ðað/ *f*, jocundity

jocundo /ho'kundo/ *a* jocund

jofaina /ho'faina/ *f*, washbowl

jónico /'honiko/ **(-ca)** *a* Ionic. *n* Ionian. *m*, (metrics) Ionic foot

jonrón /hon'ron/ *m*, home run

Jordán /hor'ðan/ Jordan (river)

jornada /hor'naða/ *f*, day's journey; journey, trip; *Mil.* expedition; duration of a working day; opportunity; span of life; act of a drama. **a grandes jornadas,** by forced marches, rapidly

jornal /hor'nal/ *m*, day's wages or labor

jornalear /hornale'ar/ *vi* to work by the day

jornalero /horna'lero/ **(-ra)** *n* day laborer; wage earner

joroba /ho'roβa/ *f*, hump; *Inf.* impertinence, nuisance

jorobado /horo'βaðo/ **(-da)** *a* humpbacked. *n* hunchback

jota /'hota/ *f*, name of letter J; popular Spanish dance; jot, tittle (always used negatively). **no saber j.,** to be completely ignorant

joven /'hoβen/ *a* young. *mf* young man or woman

jovenzuelo /hoβen'suelo; hoβen'θuelo/ **(-la)** *n* youngster, boy

jovialidad /hoβiali'ðað/ *f*, joviality, cheerfulness

joya /'hoia/ *f*, jewel; present; *Archit.* astragal; *Fig.* a jewel of a person

joyería /hoie'ria/ *f*, jeweler's shop or workshop

joyero /ho'iero/ *m*, jeweler; jewel box

juanete /hua'nete/ *m*, bunion; prominent cheekbone; *Naut.* topgallant sail

juanetudo /huane'tuðo/ *a* having bunions; with prominent cheekbones

jubilación /huβila'sion; huβːla'θion/ *f*, retirement; pensioning off; pension

jubilado /huβi'laðo/ *a* retired

jubilar /huβi'lar/ *vt* to pension off; excuse from certain duties; *Inf.* put aside as useless (things); *vr* rejoice; retire or be pensioned off

jubileo /huβi'leo/ *m*, jubilee

júbilo /'huβilo/ *m*, rejoicing, merriment. **j. de vivir,** joie de vivre

jubiloso /huβi'loso/ *a* jubilant, happy

jubón /hu'βon/ *m*, doublet; bodice

judaico /hu'ðaiko/ *a* Judaic

judaísmo /huða'ismo/ *m*, Judaism

judas /'huðas/ *m*, Judas; traitor

judería /huðe'ria/ *f*, Jewry

judesmo /hu'ðesmo/ *m*, Judezmo (Sephardic Spanish, Romance language of Jews)

judía /hu'ðia/ *f*, Jewish woman; Jewish quarter, Jewish neighborhood; haricot bean. **judías verdes,** string beans

judicatura /huðika'tura/ *f*, judicature; judgeship; judiciary

judío /hu'ðio/ **(-ía)** *a* Jewish. *n* Jew. **j. errante,** wandering Jew

juego /'huego/ *m*, play, sport; gambling; hand (of cards); set; suite; *Mech.* play, working. **j. de café,** coffee set. **j. de los cientos,** piquet. **j. de manos,** sleight of hand, conjuring. **j. de naipes,** game of cards. **j. limpio,** fair play. **j. sencillo,** single (at tennis). **j. sucio,** foul play. **juegos florales,** floral games, poetry contest. **juegos malabares,** juggling. **Juegos Olímpicos,** the Olympics. **en j.,** in operation; at stake. **entrar en j.,** to come into play. **hacer j.,** to match. **hacer juegos malabares,** to juggle

juerga /'huerga/ *f*, *Inf.* spree, binge. **ir de j.,** *Inf.* to go on a binge

jueves /'hueβes/ *m*, Thursday. **¡No es cosa del otro j.!** *Inf.* It's no great shakes! It's nothing to write home about!

juez /hues; hueθ/ *m*, judge. **j. arbitrador,** arbitrator; referee. **j. municipal,** magistrate

jugada /hu'gaða/ *f*, play; playing; move, throw; *Fig.* bad turn

jugador /huga'ðor/ **(-ra)** *a* gambling; playing. *n* gambler; player. **j. de manos,** conjurer

jugar /hu'gar/ *vi irr* to play; frolic; take part in a game; gamble; make a move (in a game); *Mech.* work; handle (a weapon); *Com.* intervene; *vt* play (a match); bet; handle (a weapon); risk. **j. el lance,** *Fig.* to play one's cards well. **j. limpio,** to play fair; *Fig. Inf.* be straightforward. **j. sucio,** to play foul. **jugarse el todo por el todo,** to stake everything. *Pres. Ind.* **juego, juegas, juega, juegan.** *Pres. Subjunc.* **juegue, juegues, juegue, jueguen**

jugarreta /huga'rreta/ *f*, *Inf.* bad play; dirty trick

juglar /hug'lar/ *m*, entertainer; buffoon, juggler; minstrel

juglaresco /hugla'resko/ *a* pertaining to minstrels

jugo /'hugo/ *m*, sap; juice; *Fig.* essence. **j. de muñeca,** elbow grease

jugosidad /hugosi'ðað/ *f*, juiciness, succulence; *Fig.* pithiness

jugoso /hu'goso/ *a* juicy, succulent; *Fig.* pithy

juguete /hu'gete/ *m*, toy; plaything; *Fig.* puppet

juguetear /hugete'ar/ *vi* to frolic, gambol

jugueteo /huge'teo/ *m*, gamboling; play, dalliance

juguetería /hugete'ria/ *f*, toy trade; toy shop

juguetón /huge'ton/ *a* playful

juicio /'huisio; 'huiθio/ *m*, judgment; wisdom, prudence; sanity, right mind; opinion; horoscope. **j. final,** Last Judgment. **j. sano,** right mind. **asentar el j.,** to settle down, become sensible. **estar fuera de j.,** to be insane. **pedir en j.,** to sue at law

juicioso /hui'sioso; hui'θioso/ *a* judicious; prudent

julepear /hulepe'ar/ *vt*, *Lat. Am.* to get scared, be terrified

julio /'hulio/ *m*, July; *Elec.* joule

jumento /hu'mento/ *m*, ass; beast of burden

juncal /hun'kal/ *a* reedy; rushy; *Inf.* slim, lissome

juncar /hun'kar/ *m*, reedy ground

junco /'hunko/ *m*, *Bot.* rush, reed; *Naut.* junk

junio /'hunio/ *m*, June

junquillo /hun'kiyo; hun'kiʎo/ *m*, jonquil; *Archit.* reed molding

junta /'hunta/ *f*, joint; assembly, council; committee; union, association; session, sitting; entirety, whole; board, management; junta. **j. de comercio,** board of trade. **j. directiva,** managerial board

juntamente /hunta'mente/ *adv* jointly; simultaneously

juntar /hun'tar/ *vt* to join, unite (*with prep a or con*); couple; assemble; amass; leave ajar (door); *vr* (*with con*) frequent company of; meet; join; copulate

junto /'hunto/ *a* united, together. *adv* (*with prep a*) near; together, simultaneously. **en j.,** altogether, in all

juntura /hun'tura/ *f*, joining; joint; seam; juncture

jura /'hura/ *f*, solemn oath; swearing

jurado /hu'raðo/ *m*, jury; jury

juramentar /huramen'tar/ *vt* to swear in; *vr* take an oath

juramento /hura'mento/ *m*, oath; curse, imprecation. **j. falso,** perjury, **prestar j.,** to take an oath
jurar /hu'rar/ *vt* to swear an oath; swear allegiance; *vi* curse, be profane
jurídico /hu'riðiko/ *a* juridical, legal
jurisconsulto /huriskon'sulto/ *m*, jurisconsult
jurisdicción /hurisðik'sion; hurisðik'θion/ *f*, *Law.* jurisdiction; boundary; authority
jurisprudencia /hurispru'ðensia; hurispru'ðenθia/ *f*, jurisprudence
jurista /hu'rista/ *mf* jurist
justa /'husta/ *f*, joust; tournament; contest
justar /hus'tar/ *vi* to joust
justicia /hus'tisia; hus'tiθia/ *f*, justice; equity, right; penalty, punishment; righteousness; court of justice; *Inf.* death penalty, execution. **administrar j.,** to dispense justice
justiciero /husti'siero; husti'θiero/ *a* just
justificable /hustifi'kaβle/ *a* justifiable
justificación /hustifika'sion; hustifika'θion/ *f*, justification, impartiality, fairness; convincing proof
justificar /hustifi'kar/ *vt* to justify, vindicate; adjust, regulate; prove innocent; *vr* justify oneself; prove one's innocence
justipreciar /hustipre'siar; hustipre'θiar/ *vt* to appraise, value
justiprecio /husti'presio; husti'preθio/ *m*, appraisement, valuation

justo /'husto/ *a* just; righteous; virtuous; exact, accurate; tight-fitting, close. *adv* justly; exactly; tightly
juvenil /huβe'nil/ *a* young
juventud /huβen'tuð/ *f*, youthfulness, youth; younger generation
juzgado /hus'gaðo; huθ'gaðo/ *m*, court of law; jurisdiction; judgeship
juzgar /hus'gar; huθ'gar/ *vt* to judge, pass sentence on; decide, consider
ka /ka/ *f*, name of the letter K
káiser /'kaiser/ *m*, kaiser
kan /kan/ *m*, khan
kantiano /kan'tiano/ *a* Kantian
Kenia /'kenia/ Kenya
kermese /ker'mese/ *f*, kermis, festival
kerosén /kero'sen/ *m*, kerosene
kilo /'kilo/ *prefix* meaning a thousand. *m*, *abb* kilogram
kilociclo /kilo'siklo; kilo'θiklo/ *m*, *Elec.* kilocycle
kilogramo /kilo'gramo/ *m*, kilogram (2.17 lb.)
kilolitro /kilo'litro/ *m*, kiloliter
kilometraje /kilome'trahe/ *m*, number of kilometers; mileage
kilométrico /kilo'metriko/ *a* kilometric. **billete k.,** tourist ticket
kilómetro /ki'lometro/ *m*, kilometer (about $\frac{5}{8}$ mile)
kilovatio /kilo'βatio/ *m*, *Elec.* kilowatt
kiosco /'kiosko/ *m*, kiosk
klaxon /klak'son/ *m*, *Mexico* horn

L

la /la/ *def art. f, sing* the (e.g. *la mesa,* the table). **la** is replaced by el *m, sing* before feminine nouns beginning with stressed *a* or *ha* (e.g. *el hambre,* hunger). **la** is sometimes used before names of famous women (e.g. *la Juana de Arco, la Melba* (Joan of Arc, Melba)) and is generally not translated. *pers pron acc f sing* her; it (e.g. *La veo venir,* I see her coming). *dem. pron* followed by *de,* or by *que* introducing relative clause, that of, that which, the one that, she who (e.g. *La casa está lejos de la que escribo,* The house is far from the one in which I write). **la de** is used familiarly for Mrs. (e.g. *la de Jiménez,* Mrs. Jimenez). **la** means some, any, one, as substitution for noun already given (e.g. *Su hija lo haría si la tuviera,* Her daughter would do it if she had one)
lábaro /'laβaro/ *m*, labarum, standard
laberíntico /laβe'rintiko/ *a* labyrinthine
laberinto /laβe'rinto/ *m*, labyrinth; *Fig.* tangle, complication; *Anat.* labyrinth of the ear
labia /'laβia/ *f*, *Inf.* blarney, gab
labial /la'βial/ *a* labial
labihendido /laβien'diðo/ *a* harelipped
labio /'laβio/ *m*, lip; rim, edge. **l. leporino,** harelip. **cerrar los labios,** to close one's lips; keep silent
labor /la'βor/ *f*, work, toil; sewing; needlework; husbandry, farming; silkworm egg; *Mineral.* working; trimming; plowing, harrowing; *Central America* small farm
laborable /laβo'raβle/ *a* workable; cultivable, tillable. **día l.,** workday
laborar /laβo'rar/ *vt* to work; till; plow; construct; *vi* scheme, plot, plan; *Central America* work
laboratorio /laβora'torio/ *m*, laboratory
laborear /laβore'ar/ *vt* to work; till, cultivate; *Naut.* reeve
laboreo /laβo'reo/ *m*, tilling, cultivation; working, development (of mines, etc.)
laboriosidad /laβoriosi'ðað/ *f*, laboriousness, diligence
laborioso /laβo'rioso/ *a* industrious, diligent; laborious, tedious, hard
laborista /laβo'rista/ *a* and *mf* belonging to the Labor Party
labra /'laβra/ *f*, stonecutting; carving or working (metal, stone, or wood)
labrada /la'βraða/ *f*, fallow land ready for sowing

labradero /laβra'ðero/ *a* workable; cultivable, tillable
labrado /la'βraðo/ *a* and *past part* worked; fashioned; carved; embroidered; figured, patterned. *m*, (gen. *pl*) cultivated ground
labrador /laβra'ðor/ *m*, laborer, worker; farmer; peasant
labradora /laβra'ðora/ *f*, peasant girl; farm girl
labradoresco, labradoril /laβraðo'resko, laβraðo'ril/ *a* rustic, peasant, farming
labrandera /laβran'dera/ *f*, seamstress
labrantío /labran'βtio/ *a* tillable, cultivable. *m*, farming
labranza /la'βransa; la'βranθa/ *f*, tillage, cultivation; farm; farmland; farming; employment, work
labrar /la'βrar/ *vt* to work, do; carve; fashion, construct, make; *Agr.* cultivate, till; plow; embroider; sew; bring about, cause; *vi Fig.* impress deeply, leave a strong impression
labriego /la'βriego/ **(-ga)** *n* agricultural laborer; peasant
laca /'laka/ *f*, lac; lacquer, varnish; *Art.* lake (pigment)
lacayo /la'kaio/ *m*, groom; lackey, footman
lacear /lase'ar; laθe'ar/ *vt Sew.* to trim with bows; tie, lace; snare, trap; *Lat. Am.* lasso
laceración /lasera'sion; laθera'θion/ *f*, laceration
lacerado /lase'raðo; laθe'raðo/ *a* unhappy, unfortunate; leprous
lacerar /lase'rar; laθe'rar/ *vt* to lacerate, mangle, tear; distress, wound the feelings of
lacería /lase'ria; laθe'ria/ *f*, poverty, misery; toil, drudgery; trouble, affliction
lacero /la'sero; la'θero/ *m*, cowboy, one who uses a lasso; poacher
lacio /'lasio; 'laθio/ *a* drooping; limp; withered, faded; straight (hair)
lacónico /la'koniko/ *a* laconic; concise; Laconian
lacra /'lakra/ *f*, aftereffect, trace (of illness); vice; fault; *Lat. Am.* sore, ulcer
lacrar /la'krar/ *vt* to impair the health; infect with an illness; injure, prejudice (the interests, etc.); seal with sealing wax
lacre /'lakre/ *m*, sealing wax. *a* red
lacrimoso /lakri'moso/ *a* tearful, lachrymose
lactancia /lak'tansia; lak'tanθia/ *f*, lactation

lactar /lak'tar/ *vt* to suckle; feed with milk; *vi* take or drink milk

lácteo /'lakteo/ *a* lacteal; milky

ladear /laðe'ar/ *vt* to incline; tilt; turn aside, twist; skirt, pass close to; reach by a roundabout way, go indirectly to; *vr* tilt; be in favor of, incline to; be equal to

ladeo /la'ðeo/ *m*, tilt; sloping; turning aside

ladera /la'ðera/ *f*, slope, incline; hillside

ladería /laðe'ria/ *f*, terrace on a hillside

ladero /la'ðero/ *a* lateral; *Argentina* helper

ladilla /la'ðiya; la'ðiʎa/ *f*, crab louse

ladino /la'ðino/ *a* eloquent; versatile linguistically; wily, crafty; *m*, Ladino (variety of Judezmo)

lado /'laðo/ *m*, side; edge, margin; slope, declivity; faction, party; side, flank; face (of a coin); *Fig.* aspect, view; line of descent; means, way; favor, protection; *pl* helpers, protectors; advisers. **al l.**, near at hand. *Inf.* **dar de l. (a),** to cool off, fall out with. **dejar a un l. (una cosa),** to omit, pass over (a thing). **mirar de l.** *or* **de medio l.,** to look upon with disapproval; steal a look at

ladrar /la'ðrar/ *vi* to bark; *Inf.* threaten without hurting

ladrido /la'ðriðo/ *m*, bark, barking; slander, gossip

ladrillado /laðri'yaðo; laðri'ʎaðo/ *m*, brick floor or pavement

ladrillar /laðri'yar; laðri'ʎar/ *vt* to floor or pave with bricks. *m*, brickyard; brickkiln

ladrillo /la'ðriyo; la'ðriʎo/ *m*, brick

ladrón /la'ðron/ **(-ona)** *a* robbing, thieving. *n* thief, robber; burglar. *m*. **l. de corazones,** ladykiller

ladronera /laðro'nera/ *f*, thieves' den; thieving, pilfering; strongbox

lagar /la'gar/ *m*, wine or olive press

lagarta /la'garta/ *f*, female lizard; *Inf.* she-serpent, cunning female

lagartera /lagar'tera/ *f*, lizard hole

lagartija /lagar'tiha/ *f*, wall lizard, small lizard

lagarto /la'garto/ *m*, lizard; *Inf.* sly, artful person, fox; *Inf.* insignia of Spanish Military Order of Santiago

lago /'lago/ *m*, lake

lagotear /lagote'ar/ *vi Inf.* to wheedle, play up to

lagotería /lagote'ria/ *f*, wheedling, coaxing, flattery

lágrima /'lagrima/ *f*, tear; drop (of liquid); exudation, oozing (from trees)

lagrimal /lagri'mal/ *a* lachrymal

lagrimear /lagrime'ar/ *vi* to shed tears

lagrimeo /lagri'meo/ *m*, weeping, crying; watering of the eyes

lagrimoso /lagri'moso/ *a* tearful; watery (of eyes); sad, tragic

laguna /la'guna/ *f*, small lake, lagoon; lacuna; gap, hiatus

lagunoso /lagu'noso/ *a* boggy, marshy

laicismo /lai'sismo; lai'θismo/ *m*, secularism, laity

laico /'laiko/ *a* lay, secular

laja /'laha/ *f*, *Lat. Am.* flagstone, slab

lama /'lama/ *f*, ooze, slime. *m*, lama, Buddhist priest

lambioche /lam'βiotʃe/ *a*, *Mexico* cringing, fawning

lameculos /lame'kulos/ *mf Inf.* toady

lamedura /lame'ðura/ *f*, licking; lapping

lamentable /lamen'taβle/ *a* lamentable

lamentación /lamenta'sion; lamenta'θion/ *f*, lamentation; lament

lamentador /lamenta'ðor/ **(-ra)** *a* lamenting, wailing. *n* wailer, mourner

lamentar /lamen'tar/ *vt* to mourn, lament, bewail; *vr* bemoan, bewail

lamento /la'mento/ *m*, lament

lamentoso /lamen'toso/ *a* lamenting, afflicted; lamentable

lamer /la'mer/ *vt* to lick; pass the tongue over; touch lightly; lap

lámina /'lamina/ *f*, sheet (of metal); lamina; engraving; illustration, picture; engraving plate

laminación /lamina'sion; lamina'θion/ *f*, lamination, rolling (of metals)

laminado /lami'naðo/ *a* laminate; rolled (metals). *m*, rolling (of metals)

laminador /lamina'ðor/ *m*, rolling mill (for metals)

laminar /lami'nar/ *a* laminate; laminated. *vt* to roll (metals); laminate; lick

lampa /'lampa/ *f*, *Chile, Peru* hoe

lámpara /'lampara/ *f*, lamp; radiance, light, luminous body; grease spot. **l. de los mineros** *or* **l. de seguridad,** safety lamp. **l. de soldar,** blowpipe. **l. termiónica,** *Radio.* thermionic valve. **atizar la l.,** to trim the lamp; *Inf.* refill drinking glasses

lamparería /lampare'ria/ *f*, lamp factory; lamp shop

lamparero /lampa'rero/ **(-ra),** *n* **lamparista** *mf* lamplighter; lamp maker or seller

lamparilla /lampa'riya; lampa'riʎa/ *f*, night-light; *Bot.* aspen; small lamp

lamparón /lampa'ron/ *m*, scrofula, king's evil; tumor (disease of horses)

lampazo /lam'paso; lam'paθo/ *m*, *Lat. Am.* (floor) mop

lampiño /lam'pino/ *a* beardless, clean-shaven; smooth-faced; *Bot.* nonhirsute

lampista /lam'pista/ *mf* See **lamparero**

lamprea /lam'prea/ *f*, lamprey

lana /'lana/ *f*, wool; fleece; woolen garments or cloth; woolen trade (gen. *pl*)

lanar /la'nar/ *a* wool; wool-bearing. **ganado l.,** sheep

lance /'lanse; 'lanθe/ *m*, throw, cast; casting a fishing line; catch of fish; crisis, difficult moment; *Lit.* episode; quarrel; move (in a game). *Fig.* **l. apretado,** difficult position, tight corner. **l. de fortuna,** chance, fate. **l. de honor,** affair of honor; duel

lancear /lanse'ar; lanθe'ar/ *vt* to wound with a lance; lance

lancero /lan'sero; lan'θero/ *m*, *Mil.* lancer; *pl* lancers (dance and music)

lanceta /lan'seta; lan'θeta/ *f*, lancet; *Lat. Am.* goad

lancha /'lantʃa/ *f*, *Naut.* launch; lighter; ship's boat; small boat; flagstone. **l. bombardera** *or* **l. cañonera,** gunboat. **l. de salvamento,** ship's lifeboat. **l. escampavía,** patrol boat

lancinar /lansi'nar; lanθi'nar/ *vt Med.* to lance

landa /'landa/ *f*, lande

landó /lan'do/ *m*, landau

lanero /la'nero/ *a* woolen. *m*, wool merchant; wool warehouse

langosta /lan'gosta/ *f*, locust; lobster. **l. migratoria,** locust

langostín /langos'tin/ *m*, crayfish

languidecer /languiðe'ser; languiðe'θer/ *vi irr* to languish, pine. See **conocer**

languidez /langui'ðes; langui'ðeθ/ *f*, lassitude, inertia; languor

lánguido /'languiðo/ *a* listless, weak, languid; half-hearted; languishing, languorous

lanolina /lano'lina/ *f*, lanolin

lanosidad /lanosi'ðað/ *f*, woolliness; down (on leaves, etc.)

lanoso, lanudo /la'noso, la'nuðo/ *a* woolly

lanza /'lansa; 'lanθa/ *f*, lance, spear; lancer; nozzle (of a hosepipe). **correr lanzas,** to joust (in a tournament). **estar con la l. en ristre,** to have the lance in rest; be prepared or ready. *Inf.* **ser una l.,** to be very clever

lanzabombas /lansa'βombas; lanθa'βombas/ *m*, (*Aer. Nav.*) bomb release

lanzada /lan'saða; lan'θaða/ *f*, lance or spear thrust

lanzadera /lansa'ðera; lanθa'ðera/ *f*, weaver's shuttle; sewing machine shuttle. *Inf.* **parecer una l.,** to be constantly on the go

lanzador /lansa'ðor; lanθa'ðor/ **(-ra)** *m*, batsman. *n* thrower, caster, tosser

lanzallamas /lansa'yamas; lanθa'ʎamas/ *m*, flamethrower

lanzamiento /lansa'miento; lanθa'miento/ *m*, throwing; cast, throw; *Law.* dispossession; *Naut.* launching

lanzaminas /lansa'minas; lanθa'minas/ *m*, minelayer

lanzar /lan'sar; lan'θar/ *vt* to throw, cast, hurl; *Naut.* launch; vomit; *Law.* dispossess; *Agr.* take root; *vr* hurl oneself, rush; take (to), embark (upon)

lanzatorpedos /lansator'peðos; lanθator'peðos/ (**tubo**) *m*, torpedo tube
lañar /la'ɲar/ *vt* to clamp; clean fish (for salting)
lapa /'lapa/ *f*, barnacle, limpet; *Mexico* scrounger
lapicera /lapi'sera; lapi'θera/ *f*, *Argentina* ballpoint (pen)
lapicero /lapi'sero; lapi'θero/ *m*, pencil holder, pencil case; mechanical pencil
lápida /'lapiða/ *f*, memorial tablet; gravestone
lapidar /lapi'ðar/ *vt* to stone, lapidate; throw stones at
lapidario /lapi'ðario/ *a* lapidary
lapislázuli /lapis'lasuli; lapis'laθuli/ *m*, lapis lazuli
lápiz /'lapis; 'lapiθ/ *m*, graphite; pencil; crayon. **l. para los labios,** lipstick
lapizar /lapi'sar; lapi'θar/ *m*, graphite mine. *vt* to pencil
lapón /la'pon/ (**-ona**) *a* Lappish. *n* Laplander. *m*, Sami (language)
lapso /'lapso/ *m*, lapse, period, passage; slip, error, failure
laquear /lake'ar/ *vt* to lacquer, paint
lardear /larðe'ar/ *vt* *Cul.* to baste
lardo /'larðo/ *m*, lard; animal fat
lardoso /lar'ðoso/ *a* greasy; fat; oily
larga /'larga/ *f*, longest billiard cue; delay (gen. *pl*). **a la l.,** in the long run
largamente /larga'mente/ *adv* fully, at length; generously; widely, extensively; comfortably
largar /lar'gar/ *vt* to slacken, loosen; *Naut.* unfurl; set at liberty; *Fig. Inf.* let fly (oaths, etc.); administer (blows, etc.); *vr Inf.* quit, leave (in a hurry or secretly); *Naut.* set sail
largo /'largo/ *a* long; generous, liberal; abundant, plentiful; protracted; prolonged; expeditious; *pl* many long (e.g. *por largos años*, for many long years). *m*, *Mus.* largo; length. *Inf.* **¡L. de aquí!** Get out! **a la larga,** in length; eventually, finally; slowly; with many digressions. **a lo l.,** lengthwise; along the length (of); in the distance, far off; along, the length (of). *Fig.* **ponerse de l.,** to make one's debut in society; come of age
largor /lar'gor/ *m*, largura *f*, length
largucho, -a /lar'gutʃo/ *a*, *Lat. Am.* lanky
largueza /lar'gesa; lar'geθa/ *f*, length; generosity, munificence
largura /lar'gura/ *f*, length
laringe /la'rinhe/ *f*, larynx
laríngeo /la'rinheo/ *a* laryngeal
laringitis /larin'hitis/ *f*, laryngitis
larva /'larβa/ *f*, larva; worm, grub; specter, phantom
las /las/ *def art. f pl*, of **la** the. *pers pron acc f pl*, of **la**, them
lascivia /las'siβia; las'θiβia/ *f*, lasciviousness
lascivo /las'siβo; las'θiβo/ *a* lascivious, lewd; wanton
lasitud /lasi'tuð/ *f*, lassitude, weariness, exhaustion
laso /'laso/ *a* weary, exhausted; weak; untwisted (of silk, etc.)
lástima /'lastima/ *f*, compassion, pity; pitiful sight; complaint, lamentation. **dar l.,** to cause pity. **Es l.,** It's a pity. **tener l.** (**a** *or* **de**) to be sorry for (persons)
lastimador /lastima'ðor/ *a* harmful, injurious; painful
lastimadura /lastima'ðura/ *f*, *Lat. Am.* injury, wound
lastimar /lasti'mar/ *vt* to hurt, harm, injure; pity; *Fig.* wound, distress; *vr* (*with de*) be sorry for or about; complain, lament
lastimero /lasti'mero/ *a* pitiful; mournful; injurious, harmful
lastimoso /lasti'moso/ *a* pitiful, heartbreaking; mournful
lastrar /las'trar/ *vt* to ballast
lastre /'lastre/ *m*, ballast; good sense, prudence
lata /'lata/ *f*, can; tin plate; can of food. **en l.,** canned, tinned (of food). *Inf.* **Es una l.,** It's a bore, It's an awful nuisance
latamente /lata'mente/ *adv* extensively, at length; broadly
latente /la'tente/ *a* latent
lateral /late'ral/ *a* lateral
látex /'lateks/ *m*, latex

latido /la'tiðo/ *m*, yelp, bark; beat; throb; palpitation
latifundios /lati'fundios/ *m pl*, latifundia (large agricultural estates)
latigazo /lati'gaso; lati'gaθo/ *m*, lash; crack of a whip; sudden blow of fate; *Inf.* draft (of wine, etc.); harsh scolding; *Naut.* jerk or flapping (of sails)
látigo /'latigo/ *m*, whip, lash; cinch, girth of a saddle
latín /la'tin/ *m*, Latin. **bajo l.,** low Latin. *Inf.* **saber l.,** to know the score; be smart
latinajo /lati'naho/ *m*, *Inf.* bad Latin
latinismo /lati'nismo/ *m*, Latinism
latinista /lati'nista/ *mf* Latinist
latinizar /latini'sar; latini'θar/ *vt* to latinize; *vi Inf.* use Latin phrases
latino /la'tino/ (**-na**) *a* and *n* Latin; Latin-American
latinoamericano /latinoameri'kano/ (**-na**) *a* and *n* Latin-American
latir /la'tir/ *vi* to yelp, howl; bark; throb, palpitate, beat **me late que...** *Mexico*, I have a hunch that...
latitud /lati'tuð/ *f*, latitude; area, extent; breadth
latitudinario /lati,tuði'nario/ *a* latitudinarian
lato /'lato/ *a* extensive; large; broad (of word meanings)
latón /la'ton/ *m*, brass
latonería /latone'ria/ *f*, brassworks; brass shop
latoso /la'toso/ *a* boring, troublesome, annoying
latrocinio /latro'sinio; latro'θinio/ *m*, larceny
latvio /'latβio/ (**-ia**) *a* and *n* Latvian
laúd /la'uð/ *m*, lute
laudable /lau'ðaβle/ *a* praiseworthy, laudable
laudatorio /lauða'torio/ *a* laudatory
laurear /laure'ar/ *vt* to crown with laurel; honor, reward
laurel /lau'rel/ *m*, bay tree. **l. cerezo,** laurel. **l. rosa,** rosebay, oleander
láureo /'laureo/ *a* laurel
lauréola /lau'reola/ *f*, laurel wreath
lauro /'lauro/ *m*, bay tree; glory, triumph
lava /'laβa/ *f*, lava
lavable /la'βaβle/ *a* washable
lavabo /la'βaβo/ *m*, sink, washbasin; cloakroom, lavatory
lavada /la'βaða/ *f*, load of wash, load
lavadedos /laβa'ðeðos/ *m*, fingerbowl
lavadero /laβa'ðero/ *m*, washing place; laundry
lavado /la'βaðo/ *m*, washing; cleaning; wash. **l. al seco,** dry cleaning
lavadura /laβa'ðura/ *f*, washing
lavamanos /laβa'manos/ *m*, sink; lavatory
lavamiento /laβa'miento/ *m*, washing, cleansing, ablution
lavanda /la'βanda/ *f*, lavender
lavandera /laβan'dera/ *f*, laundrywoman; washerwoman
lavandería /laβande'ria/ *f*, laundry
lavandero /laβan'dero/ *m*, laundry; laundryman
lavaplatos /laβa'platos/ *m*, dishwasher; *Chile, Mexico* (kitchen) sink
lavar /la'βar/ *vt* to wash; *Fig.* wipe out, purify; paint in watercolors. **l. al seco,** to dry-clean
lavativa /laβa'tiβa/ *f*, enema; syringe, clyster; *Inf.* nuisance, bore
lavatorio /laβa'torio/ *m*, washing, lavation; *Eccl.* lavabo; lavatory, washing place; *Eccl.* maundy
lavazas /la'βasas; la'βaθas/ *f pl*, dirty soapy water
laxante /lak'sante/ *a* and *m*, laxative
laxar /lak'sar/ *vt* to loosen, relax; soften
laxitud /laksi'tuð/ *f*, laxity, looseness
laxo /'lakso/ *a* lax; slack
laya /'laia/ *f*, *Agr.* spade; kind, sort, class
layar /la'jar/ *vt Agr.* to fork
lazar /la'sar; la'θar/ *vt* to lasso
lazareto /lasa'reto; laθa'reto/ *m*, leper hospital; quarantine hospital
lazarillo /lasa'riyo; laθa'riʎo/ *m*, boy who guides a blind person
lázaro /'lasaro; 'laθaro/ *m*, beggar. **Lázaro,** Lazarus
lazo /'laso; 'laθo/ *m*, bow; knot of ribbons; tie; ornamental tree; figure (in dancing); lasso; rope, bond;

lace (of a shoe); *Fig.* trap, snare; bond, obligation; slipknot. **l. corredizo,** running knot. *Fig. Inf.* **armar l.,** to set a trap. *Inf.* **caer en el l.,** to fall into the trap, be deceived

le /le/ *pers pron dat m,* or *f, 3rd pers sing* to him, to her, to it, to you (e.g. *María le dio el perro,* Mary gave him (her, you) the dog). Clarity may require the addition of **a él, a ella, a usted** (e.g. *Le dio el perro a ella,* etc.). *pers pron acc m, 3rd pers sing* him (e.g. *Le mandé a casa,* I sent him home)

leal /le'al/ *a* loyal; faithful (animals)

lealtad /leal'taθ/ *f,* loyalty; faithfulness; sincerity, truth

lebrel /le'βrel/ *m,* greyhound

lección /lek'sion; lek'θion/ *f,* reading; lesson; oral test; warning, example. **l. práctica,** object lesson. **dar l.,** to give a lesson. **tomar la l.,** to hear a lesson

leccionista /leksio'nista; lekθio'nista/ *mf* private teacher, coach, tutor

lechas /'letʃas/ *f pl,* soft roe; milt

leche /'letʃe/ *f,* milk; milky fluid of some plants and seeds; *Lat. Am.* good luck. *Inf.* **estar con la l. en los labios,** to be young and inexperienced

lechera /le'tʃera/ *f,* milkmaid; milk can or jug; *Lat. Am.* cow

lechería /letʃe'ria/ *f,* dairy; dairy shop; *Lat. Am.* meanness

lechero /le'tʃero/ **(-ra)** *a* dairy, milk; milky; milch, milk-giving. *n* milk seller. **industria lechera,** dairy farming

lecho /'letʃo/ *m,* bed; couch; animal's bed, litter; riverbed; bottom of the sea; layer; *Geol.* stratum

lechón /le'tʃon/ *m,* suckling pig; hog; *Inf.* slovenly man

lechosa /le'tʃosa/ *f, Dominican Republic, Venezuela,* papaya

lechoso /le'tʃoso/ *a* milky

lechudo, -a /le'tʃuðo/ *a, Lat. Am.* lucky

lechuga /le'tʃuga/ *f,* lettuce; frill, flounce. *Inf.* **como una l.,** as fresh as a daisy

lechuguero /letʃu'gero/ **(-ra)** *n* lettuce seller

lechuguilla /letʃu'giya; letʃu'giʎa/ *f,* ruff; ruche

lechuguina /letʃu'gina/ *f, Inf.* affected, overdressed young woman

lechuguino /letʃu'gino/ *m,* lettuce plant; *Inf.* young blood, gallant; *Inf.* foppish young man

lechuza /le'tʃusa; le'tʃuθa/ *f,* barn owl

lector /lek'tor/ **(-ra)** *n* reader; lecturer

lectura /lek'tura/ *f,* reading; lecture; culture, knowledge

ledo /'leðo/ *a* happy, content

leer /le'er/ *vt irr* to read; explain, interpret; teach; take part in an oral test. See **creer**

lega /'lega/ *f, Eccl.* lay sister

legación /lega'sion; lega'θion/ *f, Eccl.* legateship; legation

legado /le'gaðo/ *m,* legacy; legate

legajo /le'gaho/ *m,* bundle, docket; file

legal /le'gal/ *a* legal; legitimate; upright, trustworthy

legalidad /legali'ðaθ/ *f,* legality

legalización /legalisa'sion; legaliθa'θion/ *f,* legalization

legalizar /legali'sar; legali'θar/ *vt* to legalize

legamente /lega'mente/ *adv* ignorantly, stupidly

légamo /'legamo/ *m,* mud, slime

legamoso /lega'moso/ *a* slimy

legañoso /lega'ɲoso/ *a* bleary-eyed

legar /le'gar/ *vt* to bequeath; send as a legate

legatario /lega'tario/ **(-ia)** *n* legatee, one to whom a legacy is bequeathed

legendario /lehen'dario/ *a* legendary

legibilidad /lehiβili'ðaθ/ *f,* legibility

legible /le'hiβle/ *a* legible

legión /le'hion/ *f,* legion

legionario /lehio'nario/ *a* and *m,* legionary

legislación /lehisla'sion; lehisla'θion/ *f,* legislation

legislador /lehisla'ðor/ **(-ra)** *a* legislative. *n* legislator

legislar /lehis'lar/ *vi* to legislate

legislativo /lehisla'tiβo/ *a* legislative

legislatura /lehisla'tura/ *f,* legislature

legista /le'hista/ *mf* jurist; student of law

legítima /le'hitima/ *f,* portion of a married man's estate that cannot be willed away from his wife and children

legitimación /lehitima'sion; lehitima'θion/ *f,* legitimation

legitimar /lehiti'mar/ *vt* to legitimize

legitimidad /lehitimi'ðaθ/ *f,* legitimacy

legítimo /le'hitimo/ *a* legitimate; real, true

lego /'lego/ *a* lay, secular. *m,* layman

legua /'legua/ *f,* league (approximately 5.573 meters). **a la l., de cien leguas, desde media l.,** from afar

legumbre /le'gumbre/ *f,* pulse; vegetable

leída /le'iða/ *f, Lat. Am.* reading. **de una leída** in one reading, at one go

leído /le'iðo/ *a* well-read

leila /'leila/ *f,* nocturnal Moorish merrymaking or dance

lejanía /leha'nia/ *f,* distance

lejano /le'hano/ *a* distant, remote, far off

lejía /le'hia/ *f,* lye; bleaching solution; *Inf.* dressing-down, scolding

lejos /'lehos/ *adv* far off, far, distant. *m,* perspective, view from afar; *Art.* background. **a lo l.,** far off, in the distance. **de** or **desde l.,** from afar, from a distance

lelo /'lelo/ *a* stupid; fatuous, inane

lema /'lema/ *m,* chapter heading; argument, summary; motto; theme, subject

lémur /'lemur/ *m,* lemur

lencería /lense'ria; lenθe'ria/ *f,* linen goods; linen merchant's shop; linen closet

lencero /len'sero; len'θero/ *m,* linen merchant

lene /'lene/ *a* smooth, soft; kind, sweet, gentle; lightweight

lengua /'lengua/ *f, Anat.* tongue; mother tongue, language; clapper of a bell; information. *mf* spokes. **l. de escorpión** or **mala l.,** scandalmonger, backbiter. **l. de fuego,** *Eccl.* tongue of fire, flame. **l. del agua,** waterline, tidemark. **l. de oc,** langue d'oc. **l. de oil,** langue d'oil. **l. de tierra,** neck of land, promontory. **l. viva,** modern language. *Inf.* **andar en lenguas,** to be rumored, be famous. *Inf.* **hacerse lenguas de,** to praise to the skies. *Inf.* **irse (a uno) la l.,** to be indiscreet, talk too much. **poner l.** or **lenguas en,** to gossip about. *Inf.* **tener mucha l.,** to be very talkative. **tomar l.** or **lenguas,** to find out about, inform oneself on

lenguado /len'guaðo/ *m, Ichth.* sole

lenguaje /len'guahe/ *m,* language; style; speech, idiom. **l. vulgar,** common speech

lengüeta /len'gueta/ *f, dim* little tongue; *Mus.* tongue (of wind instruments); barb (of an arrow); needle (of a balance)

lengüeterías /lengüete'rias/ *Lat. Am.* gossip

lenidad /leni'ðaθ/ *f,* lenience, indulgence, mercy

lenitivo /leni'tiβo/ *a* lenitive; soothing. *m, Med.* lenitive; *Fig.* balm (of sorrow, etc.)

lente /'lente/ *m,* lens; *pl* eyeglasses. **l. de aumento,** magnifying glass. **l. de contacto,** contact lens

lenteja /len'teha/ *f,* lentil; lentil plant

lentejuela /lente'huela/ *f,* sequin

lentitud /lenti'tuθ/ *f,* lentitude; slowness, deliberation

lento /'lento/ *a* slow, deliberate; sluggish, heavy; *Med.* glutinous, adhesive

leña /'leɲa/ *f,* firewood; *Inf.* beating, birching. *Fig.* **echar l. al fuego,** to add fuel to the flame. *Fig.* **llevar l. al monte,** to carry coals to Newcastle

leñador /leɲa'ðor/ **(-ra)** *n* woodcutter; firewood dealer

leñera /le'ɲera/ *f,* woodpile; woodshed

leño /'leɲo/ *m,* wooden log; wood, timber; *Poet.* ship; *Inf.* blockhead

leñoso /le'ɲoso/ *a* woody, ligneous

león /le'on/ *m,* lion. *Astron.* Leo; valiant man; *Lat. Am.* puma. **l. marino,** sea lion

leona /le'ona/ *f,* lioness; *Chile* confusion, mixup

leonera /leo'nera/ *f,* lion cage; lion's den; *Inf.* gambling den; *Inf.* lumber room; *Mexico* whore house

leonero /leo'nero/ (-ra) n lionkeeper; *Inf.* keeper of a gambling house
leopardo /leo'parðo/ m, leopard
leperada /lepe'raða/ f, *Central America, Mexico* coarse remark
lepra /'lepra/ f, leprosy
leproso /le'proso/ a leprous
lerdo /'lerðo/ a slow, lumbering (gen. horses); stupid, slow-witted, dull
les /les/ pers pron dat 3rd pers pl mf, to them (e.g. *Les dimos las flores,* We gave them flowers. *Les hablé del asunto,* I spoke to them about the matter)
lesbio /'lesβio/ (-ia) a and n lesbian
lesión /le'sion/ f, lesion, wound; *Fig.* injury
lesionar /lesio'nar/ vt to wound; *Fig.* injure
lesna /'lesna/ f, awl
leso /'leso/ a wounded, hurt; offensive, injurious; *Fig.* unbalanced, perturbed (of the mind); *Lat. Am.* dumb, stupid. **crimen de lesa majestad,** crime of lèse-majesté
letal /le'tal/ a lethal; deadly
letanía /leta'nia/ f, *Eccl.* litany
letargia /le'tarhia/ f, *Med.* lethargy
letárgico /le'tarhiko/ a lethargic
letargo /le'targo/ m, lethargy; indifference, apathy
letra /'letra/ f, letter (of alphabet); *Print.* type; penmanship, hand; *Fig.* letter, literal meaning; words (of a song); inscription; *Com.* bill, draft; cunning, shrewdness; pl learning, knowledge. **l. abierta,** *Com.* open credit. **l. de cambio,** *Com.* bill of exchange. **l. gótica,** Gothic characters. **l. itálica,** italics. **l. mayúscula,** capital letter. **l. paladial,** palatal. **facultad de letras,** faculty of arts. **La l. con sangre entra,** Learning is acquired with pain. **primeras letras,** early education, first letters
letrado /le'traðo/ a learned, educated; *Inf.* presumptuous; pedantic. m, lawyer
letrero /le'trero/ m, label; inscription; poster, bill; sign, indicator. **l. luminoso,** illuminated sign
letrilla /le'triya; le'triʎa/ f, short poem, often set to music
letrina /le'trina/ f, latrine
leva /'leβa/ f, *Naut.* weighing anchor; *Mil.* levy, forced enrollment; tappet; *Mech.* lever; *Mech.* cam; *Inf.* **irse a l. y a monte,** to flee, beat it, quit
levadizo /leβa'ðiso; leβa'ðiθo/ a able to be raised or lowered (bridges). **puente l.,** drawbridge
levadura /leβa'ðura/ f, leaven, yeast; rising (of bread)
levantada /leβan'taða/ f, act of rising from bed
levantamiento /leβanta'miento/ m, raising, lifting; rebellion, revolt; ennoblement, elevation; settlement of accounts
levantar /leβan'tar/ vt to raise, lift; pick up; build, construct; cancel, remove; encourage, rouse; recruit, enlist; cut (cards); leave, abandon; survey; disturb (game); produce, raise (a swelling); found, institute; increase (prices); raise (the voice); *Fig.* ennoble, elevate; cause, occasion; libel, accuse falsely; vr rise; get up; stand up; stand out, be prominent; rebel; leave one's bed after an illness. **l. bandera,** to rebel. **l. el campo,** to break camp. **levantarse del izquierdo,** *Inf.* to get out of bed on the wrong side
levante /le'βante/ m, east; Levant; east wind
levar /le'βar/ vt *Naut.* to weigh anchor; vr set sail
leve /'leβe/ a light (in weight); unimportant, trifling
levedad /leβe'ðað/ f, lightness (in weight); unimportance, levity, flippancy
leviatán /leβia'tan/ m, leviathan
levita /le'βita/ m, Levite; deacon. f, frock coat
levitación /leβita'sion; leβita'θion/ f, levitation
levítico /le'βitiko/ a Levitical. m, **Levítico,** Leviticus
levitón /leβi'ton/ m, frock coat
léxico /'leksiko/ m, lexicon
lexicografía /leksikogra'fia/ f, lexicography
lexicógrafo /leksi'kografo/ m, lexicographer
lexicólogo /leksi'kologo/ m, lexicologist
ley /lei/ f, law; precept; regulation, rule; doctrine; loyalty, faithfulness; affection, love; legal standard (weights, measures, quality); ratio of gold or silver in

coins, jewelry; statute, ordinance; pl the Law. **l. de préstamo y arriendo,** Lend-Lease Act. **ley suntuaria,** sumptuary law. *Inf.* **a la l.,** with care and decorum. **a l. de caballero,** on the word of a gentleman. **de buena l.,** a excellent; adv genuinely; in good faith. **de mala l.,** a disreputable, base; adv in bad faith
leyente /le'iente/ a reading. mf reader
lezna /'lesna; 'leθna/ f, awl
lía /'lia/ f, plaited esparto rope; pl lees, dregs
liar /li'ar/ vt to fasten or tie up; wrap up, parcel; roll (a cigarette); *Inf.* entangle, embroil; vr take a lover, enter on a liaison. *Inf.* **liarlas,** to quit, sneak off; *Inf.* kick the bucket, die
libación /liβa'sion; liβa'θion/ f, libation
líbano, el /'liβano, el/ Lebanon
libar /li'βar/ vt to suck; perform a libation; sip, taste; sacrifice
libelista /liβe'lista/ mf libeler
libelo /li'βelo/ m, libel; *Law.* petition
libélula /li'βelula/ f, dragonfly
liberación /liβera'sion; liβera'θion/ f, liberation, freeing; receipt, quittance; *Law.* reconveyance (of mortgages)
liberador /liβera'ðor/ (-ra) a liberating, freeing. n liberator
liberal /liβe'ral/ a generous, openhanded; liberal, tolerant; learned (of professions). a and mf *Polit.* liberal
liberalidad /liβerali'ðað/ f, generosity, magnanimity
liberalismo /liβera'lismo/ m, liberalism
liberalizar /liβerali'sar; liβerali'θar/ vt to liberalize, make liberal
liberar /liβe'rar/ vt to liberate
libérrimo /li'βerrimo/ a sup extremely free, most free
libertad /liβer'tað/ f, liberty, freedom; independence; privilege, right (gen. pl); exemption; licentiousness; forwardness, familiarity; naturalness, ease of manner; facility, capacity; immunity. **l. caucional,** freedom on bail, release on bail. **l. de cultos,** freedom of worship; religious toleration. **l. vigilada,** *Law.* probation. **poner en l.,** to set at liberty; (with de) *Fig.* free from
libertador /liβerta'ðor/ (-ra) a liberating, freeing. n liberator, deliverer
libertar /liβer'tar/ vt to liberate, free; save, deliver; exempt
libertario /liβer'tario/ (-ia) a anarchistic. n anarchist
libertinaje /liβerti'nahe/ m, libertinage, licentiousness
libertino /liβer'tino/ (-na) a debauched, licentious. m, libertine. n child of a freed slave
liberto /li'βerto/ (-ta) n freed slave, freedman
Libia /'liβia/ Libya
libídine /li'βiðine/ f, lust
libidinoso /liβiði'noso/ a libidinous, lustful
libio /'liβio/ (-ia) a and n Libyan
libra /'liβra/ f, pound (measure, coinage); *Astron.* Libra. **l. esterlina,** pound sterling. **l. medicinal,** pound troy
libración /liβra'sion; liβra'θion/ f, oscillation; *Astron.* libration
librador /liβra'ðor/ (-ra) a freeing, liberating. n deliverer, liberator. m, *Com.* drawer (of bill of exchange, etc.)
libramiento /liβra'miento/ m, liberation, deliverance; *Com.* delivery; order of payment
libranza /li'βransa; li'βranθa/ f, *Com.* draft. **l. de correos, l. postal** *Lat. Am.* (postal) money order
librar /li'βrar/ vt to liberate, free; protect (from misfortune); *Com.* draw (a draft); *Com.* deliver; place confidence in; issue, enact; vi bring forth children; vr (with de) escape from; get rid of
libre /'liβre/ a free; at liberty, disengaged; unhampered, untrammeled; independent; bold, brazen; dissolute, vicious; exempt; vacant, unoccupied; unmarried; clear, free; mutinous, rebellious; isolated, remote; innocent; unharmed; *Mexico, Venezuela* taxi. **l. cambio,** free trade
librea /li'βrea/ f, livery
librecambio /liβre'kambio/ m, free trade

librecambista /liβrekam'βista/ *a* free trade. *mf* free trader

librepensador /liβrepensa'ðor/ **(-ra)** *a* freethinking. *n* freethinker

librepensamiento /liβrepensa'miento/ *m*, free thought

librera /li'βrera/ *f, Lat. Am.* bookcase

librería /liβre'ria/ *f*, bookshop; book trade, bookselling; bookcase

librero /li'βrero/ *m*, bookseller; *Lat. Am.* bookcase. **l. anticuario,** antiquarian bookseller; rare-book dealer

libreta /li'βreta/ *f, Cul.* 1-lb. loaf; notebook; passbook, bankbook

libretista /liβre'tista/ *mf* librettist

libreto /li'βreto/ *m*, libretto

librillo /li'βriyo; li'βriʎo/ *m, dim* small book; book of cigarette papers; tub, pail; *Zool.* omasum

libro /'liβro/ *m*, book; *Mus.* libretto; *Zool.* omasum. **l. copiador,** *Com.* letter book. **l. de actas,** minute book. **l. de caja,** *Com.* cash book. **l. de cheques,** checkbook. **l. de facturas,** *Com.* invoice book. **l. de reclamaciones,** complaint book. **l. de texto,** textbook. **l. diario,** *Com.* daybook. **l. mayor,** ledger. **l. talonario,** receipt book. *Fig. Inf.* **hacer l. nuevo,** to turn over a new leaf; introduce innovations

licencia /li'sensia; li'θenθia/ *f*, permission, license; licentiousness; boldness, insolence; *Educ.* bachelor's degree, licentiate. **l. absoluta,** *Mil.* discharge. **l. de manejar** *Lat. Am.* driver's license

licenciado /lisen'siaðo; liθen'θiaðo/ **(-da)** *a* pedantic; free, exempt; licensed. *n Educ.* bachelor; licentiate. *m*, discharged soldier

licenciar /lisen'siar; liθen'θiar/ *vt* to allow, permit; license; dismiss, discharge; confer degree of bachelor or licentiate; *Mil.* discharge; *vr* become licentious; receive bachelor's degree or licentiate

licenciatura /lisensia'tura; liθenθia'tura/ *f*, degree of licentiate or bachelor; graduation as such; licentiate course of study

licencioso /lisen'sioso; liθen'θioso/ *a* licentious, dissolute

liceo /li'seo; li'θeo/ *m*, lyceum; *Lat. Am.* secondary school, high school

licitación /lisita'sion; liθita'θion/ *f*, bidding (at auction)

licitador /lisita'ðor; liθita'ðor/ *m*, bidder (at auction); *Lat. Am.* auctioneer

licitar /lisi'tar; liθi'tar/ *vt* to bid for (at auction)

lícito /'lisito; 'liθito/ *a* permissible, lawful

licor /li'kor/ *m*, liquor, alcoholic drink; liquid

licorera /liko'rera/ *f*, liqueur set; decanter

licuadora /likua'ðora/ *f*, blender

licuar /li'kuar/ *vt* to liquefy

lid /liδ/ *f*, combat, fight; dispute, controversy. **en buena l.,** in fair fight; by fair means

líder /'liðer/ *m*, leader; chief

lidia /'liðia/ *f*, fighting; bullfight

lidiador /liðia'ðor/ **(-ra)** *n* combatant, fighter

lidiar /li'ðiar/ *vi* to fight; *Fig.* struggle; (*with contra or con*) oppose, fight against; *vt* fight (a bull). **¡Cuánto tienen que l. con...!** *Fig.* What a struggle they have with...!

liebre /'lieβre/ *f*, hare

liendre /'liendre/ *f*, nit

lienza /liensa; 'lienθa/ *f*, narrow strip (of cloth)

lienzo /'lienso; 'lienθo/ *m*, linen; cotton; cambric; hemp cloth; *Art.* canvas

liga /'liga/ *f*, garter; bandage; birdlime; mixture, blend; *Metall.* alloy; alliance, coalition; league (football, etc.)

ligación /liga'sion; liga'θion/ *f*, tying; binding; union

ligado /li'gaðo/ *m, Mus.* legato; *Mus.* tie

ligadura /liga'ðura/ *f*, bond, tie; binding, fastening; *Fig.* shackle, link; (*Surg. Mus.*) ligature; *Naut.* lashing

ligamento /liga'mento/ *m*, tie, bond; mixture; *Anat.* ligament

ligar /li'gar/ *vt* to tie, bind; *Metall.* alloy; join, connect; render impotent by sorcery; *Mus.* slur (notes); *vr* ally, join together; *Fig.* bind oneself. **l. cabos,** to put two and two together

ligazón /liga'son; liga'θon/ *f*, fastening; union; bond

ligereza /lihe'resa; lihe'reθa/ *f*, lightness (of weight); swiftness, nimbleness; fickleness; tactless remark, indiscretion

ligero /li'hero/ *a* light (in weight); swift, nimble; light (sleep); unimportant, insignificant; easily digested (food); thin (fabrics, etc.); fickle, changeable. **l. de cascos,** frivolous, gay. **a la ligera,** lightly; quickly; without fuss. **de l.,** impetuously, thoughtlessly; easily, with ease

lignito /lig'nito/ *m*, lignite

lija /'liha/ *f*, dogfish; sandpaper

lijar /li'har/ *vt* to sandpaper

lila /'lila/ *f*, lilac bush and flower; lilac color. *a Inf.* foolish, vain

lima /'lima/ *f*, sweet lime, citron fruit; lime tree; file (tool); filing, polishing. **Lima,** Lima

limadura /lima'ðura/ *f*, filing; polishing; *pl* filings

limar /li'mar/ *vt* to file, smooth with a file; *Fig.* touch up, polish

limazo /li'maso; li'maθo/ *m*, slime, viscosity (especially of snails, etc.)

limbo /'limbo/ *m*, limbo; edge, hem; (*Astron. Bot.*) limb; limb (of a quadrant, etc.). *Inf.* **estar en el l.,** to be bewildered or abstracted

limen /'limen/ *m, Poet.* threshold; *Psychol.* limen

limeño /li'meɲo/ **(-ña)** *a* and *n* native of or belonging to Lima (Peru)

limero /li'mero/ **(-ra)** *n* seller of sweet limes. *m*, sweet lime tree (citron)

limitación /limita'sion; limita'θion/ *f*, limitation; limit, extent, bound; district, area

limitado /limi'taðo/ *a* dull-witted, limited

limitar /limi'tar/ *vt* to limit; curb, restrict; bound

límite /'limite/ *m*, limit, extent; boundary, border; end, confine

limítrofe /li'mitrofe/ *a* bordering, contiguous

limo /'limo/ *m*, mud, mire, slime; *Lat. Am.* lime tree

limón /li'mon/ *m*, lemon; lemon tree

limonada /limo'naða/ *f*, lemonade. **l. seca,** lemonade powder

limonar /limo'nar/ *m*, lemon grove

limonero /limo'nero/ **(-ra)** *n* lemon seller. *m*, lemon tree

limosna /li'mosna/ *f*, alms

limosnear /limosne'ar/ *vi* to beg, ask alms

limosnero, -a /limos'nero/ *a* charitable, generous. *a* charitable, generous. *mf* almoner; *Lat. Am.* beggar

limoso /li'moso/ *a* slimy, muddy

limpiabarros /limpia'βarros/ *m*, shoe scraper

limpiabotas /limpia'βotas/ *m*, bootblack (person)

limpiachimeneas /limpiatʃime'neas/ *m*, chimneysweep

limpiador /limpia'ðor/ **(-ra)** *a* cleaning. *n* cleaner

limpiadura /limpia'ðura/ *f*, cleaning; *pl* rubbish

limpiamanos /limpia'manos/ *m, Central America, Mexico* towel

limpiamente /limpia'mente/ *adv* cleanly; dexterously, neatly; sincerely, candidly; generously, charitably

limpiametales /limpiame'tales/ *m*, metal polish

limpiaparabrisas /limpiapara'βrisas/ *m*, windshield wiper

limpiapipas /limpia'pipas/ *m*, pipe cleaner

limpiar /lim'piar/ *vt* to clean; *Fig.* cleanse, clear; empty, free (from); *Agr.* thin out; *Inf.* steal, pinch; *Inf.* win (gambling); *vr* clean oneself

limpidez /limpi'ðes; limpi'ðeθ/ *f, Poet.* limpidity

límpido /'limpiðo/ *a Poet.* limpid

limpieza /lim'piesa; lim'pieθa/ *f*, cleanliness; cleaning; chastity; purity; altruism; uprightness, integrity; neatness, tidiness; dexterity, skill, precision; fair play

limpio /'limpio/ *a* clean; pure, unalloyed, unmixed; neat, tidy; pure-blooded; unharmed, free. **en l.,** in substance; as a fair copy; clearly; *Com.* net

linaje /li'nahe/ *m*, lineage, family; offspring; kind; sort, quality

linajudo /lina'huðo/ **(-da)** *a* highborn. *n* noble, aristocrat; one who alleges his noble descent

linaza /li'nasa; li'naθa/ *f*, linseed

lince /'linse; 'linθe/ *m*, lynx; *Mexico* wild cat; *fig.* fox, crafty person
linchamiento /lintʃa'miento/ *m*, lynching
linchar /lin'tʃar/ *vt* to lynch
lindar /lin'dar/ *vi* to run together, be contiguous
linde /'linde/ *mf* limit, extent; boundary
lindero /lin'dero/ *a* bordering, contiguous. *m*, boundary. *Inf.* con **linderos y arrabales,** with many digressions
lindeza /lin'desa; lin'deθa/ *f*, beauty, loveliness; witticism; *pl* (*inf ironical*) insults
lindo /'lindo/ *a* lovely, beautiful; perfect, exquisite
línea /'linea/ *f*, line; kind, class; ancestry, lineage; limit, extent; *Mil.* file; equator. **l. aérea,** airline. **l. de abajo,** the bottom line. *Naut.* **l. de flotación,** waterline. **l. de toque,** touchline (in soccer). **l. recta,** direct line (of descent)
lineal /line'al/ *a* lineal; *computers* on-line
lineamento /linea'mento/ *m*, lineament
linear /line'ar/ *a* linear. *vt* to line, mark with lines; *Art.* sketch
linfa /'linfa/ *f*, *Med.* lymph; vaccine; *Poet.* water
linfático /lin'fatiko/ *a* lymphatic
lingote /liŋ'gote/ *m*, ingot; bar (of iron). **l. de fundición,** pig iron
lingüista /liŋ'guista/ *mf* linguist
lingüística /liŋ'guistika/ *f*, linguistics
lingüístico /liŋ'guistiko/ *a* linguistic
linimento /lini'mento/ *m*, liniment
lino /'lino/ *m*, *Bot.* flax; linen; *Poet.* ship's sail, canvas
linóleo /li'noleo/ *m*, linoleum
linotipia /lino'tipia/ *f*, linotype
linterna /lin'terna/ *f*, lantern; lighthouse; lamp. **l. sorda,** dark lantern
lío /'lio/ *m*, bundle; *Inf.* muddle, imbroglio; *Inf.* liaison, amour. *Inf.* **armar un l.,** to make a muddle, cause trouble. *Inf.* **hacerse un l.,** to get in a fix; get in a muddle
liposucción /liposuk'θion/ *f*, liposuction
liquen /'liken/ *m*, lichen
liquidable /liki'ðaβle/ *a* liquefiable
liquidación /likiða'sion; likiða'θion/ *f*, liquefaction; *Com.* clearance, sale; *Com.* settlement
liquidar /liki'ðar/ *vt* to liquefy; *Com.* settle; *Com.* liquidate; finish; *vr* liquefy; *Inf.* kill
liquidez /liki'ðes; liki'ðeθ/ *f*, liquidness
líquido /'likiðo/ *a* liquid; *Com.* net. *m*, liquid; *Com.* net profit
lira /'lira/ *f*, *Mus.* lyre; *Astron.* Lyra; lira (coin)
lírica /'lirika/ *f*, lyrical verse, lyric
lírico /'liriko/ *a* lyrical
lirio /'lirio/ *m*, lily. **l. cárdeno,** yellow flag (iris). **l. de los valles,** lily of the valley
lirismo /li'rismo/ *m*, lyricism
lirón /li'ron/ *m*, *Zool.* dormouse; *Inf.* sleepyhead
Lisboa /lis'βoa/ Lisbon
lisiado /li'siaðo/ *a* lame, crippled
lisiar /li'siar/ *vt* to cripple, lame; *vr* be disabled; be lame
liso /'liso/ *a* smooth; sleek; unadorned, plain; unicolored
lisonja /li'sonha/ *f*, flattery, adulation
lisonjear /lisonhe'ar/ *vt* to flatter; fawn upon; *Fig.* delight (the ear). **lisonjearse de...,** to flatter oneself on...
lisonjero /lison'hero/ (**-ra**) *a* flattering; sweet, pleasant (sounds). *n* flatterer
lista /'lista/ *f*, strip of cloth; streak; rib; stripe; catalog, list. **l. de correos,** general delivery; poste restante. **l. de platos,** bill of fare; *Mexico* **l. de raya** payroll. **pasar l.,** to call the roll; check the list
listado /lis'taðo/ *a* streaked; striped; ribbed. *m*, list, listing; printout
listo /'listo/ *a* clever; expeditious, diligent; ready, prepared
listón /lis'ton/ *m*, ribbon; strip (of wood)
lisura /li'sura/ *f*, smoothness; sleekness; flatness; sincerity
lisurero, -a, /lisu'rero/ *a*, *Peru* cheeky, impudent

litera /li'tera/ *f*, litter; *Naut.* berth
literal /lite'ral/ *a* literal
literario /lite'rario/ *a* literary
literatear /literate'ar/ *vi* to write on literary subjects
literato /lite'rato/ (**-ta**) *a* literary. *n* writer, litterateur. **los literatos,** the literati
literatura /litera'tura/ *f*, literature
litigación /litiga'sion; litiga'θion/ *f*, litigation
litigante /liti'gante/ *mf* litigant
litigar /liti'gar/ *vt* to litigate; *vi* dispute, argue
litigio /li'tihio/ *m*, lawsuit; dispute, argument
litigioso /liti'hioso/ *a* litigious; quarrelsome, disputatious
litisexpensas /litiseks'pensas/ *f pl*, *Law.* costs of a suit; legal expenses
litografía /litogra'fia/ *f*, lithography
litografiar /litogra'fiar/ *vt* to lithograph
litoral /lito'ral/ *a* and *m*, littoral
litro /'litro/ *m*, liter; *Chile* coarse woolen cloth
Lituania /li'tuania/ Lithuania
liturgia /li'turhia/ *f*, liturgy
litúrgico /li'turhiko/ *a* liturgical
liviandad /liβian'dað/ *f*, lightness (of weight); fickleness; unimportance; frivolity; lewdness; act of folly, indiscretion
liviano /li'βiano/ *a* light weight; fickle; unimportant; trifling, frivolous; lascivious
lividez /liβi'ðes; liβi'ðeθ/ *f*, lividness
lívido /'liβiðo/ *a* livid; *Lat. Am.* pale, pallid
liza /'lisa; 'liθa/ *f*, list (at a tournament); arena
llaga /'ʎaga; 'ʎaga/ *f*, ulcer; sore; grief, affliction; *Fig.* thorn in the flesh
llagar /ʎa'gar; ʎa'gar/ *vt* to ulcerate; make or produce sores; *Fig.* wound; *vr* be covered with sores
llama /'ʎama; 'ʎama/ *f*, flame; ardor, vehemence; marsh; *Zool.* llama
llamada /ʎa'maða; ʎa'maða/ *f*, call; *Mil.* call-to-arms, call. **l. molestosa,** annoyance call, nuisance call
llamado /ʎa'maðo; ʎa'maðo/ *a* called; so-called
llamador /ʎama'ðor; ʎama'ðor/ (**-ra**) *n* caller. *m*, door knocker; doorbell
llamamiento /ʎama'miento; ʎama'miento/ *m*, calling; call; divine summons, inspiration; invocation; appeal; summons, convocation
llamar /ʎa'mar; ʎa'mar/ *vt* to call; invoke, call upon; summon, convoke; name; attract; *vi* knock (at a door); ring (a bell); *vr* be named, be called; *Naut.* veer (wind). **Se llama Pedro,** His name is Peter
llamarada /ʎama'raða; ʎama'raða/ *f*, flame, flash; blaze, flare (of anger, etc.)
llamativo /ʎama'tiβo; ʎama'tiβo/ *a* striking, showy; provocative
llamear /ʎame'ar; ʎame'ar/ *vi* to throw out flames, blaze
llana /'ʎana; 'ʎana/ *f*, mason's trowel; plain; surface of a page
llanada /ʎa'naða; ʎa'naða/ *f*, plain
llanamente /ʎana'mente; ʎana'mente/ *adv* frankly, plainly; naturally, simply; candidly, sincerely
llanero /ʎa'nero; ʎa'nero/ (**-ra**) *n* plain dweller
llaneza /ʎa'nesa; ʎa'neθa/ *f*, naturalness; candor; familiarity; simplicity (of style)
llano /'ʎano; 'ʎano/ *a* flat, level; smooth, even; shallow (of receptacles); unaffected, homely, natural; plain (of dresses); manifest, evident; easy; straightforward, candid; informal; simple (of style). *m*, plain; level stretch of ground
llanta /'ʎanta; 'ʎanta/ *f*, *Auto.* tire; rim, felloe. **l. de refacción,** *Mexico* spare tire. **l. de rueda,** wheel, rim
llanto /'ʎanto; 'ʎanto/ *m*, weeping, flood of tears
llanura /ʎa'nura; ʎa'nura/ *f*, smoothness, evenness, levelness; plain
llave /'ʎaβe; 'ʎaβe/ (**de**) *f*, key (to); spigot (of), faucet (of), tap (of); spanner, wrench; *Elec.* switch; clock winder; *Mus.* key, clef; *Archit.* keystone; *Print.* brace; *Mech.* wrench; lock (of a gun); tuning key; piston (of musical instruments); lock (in wrestling); *Fig.* key (of a problem or a study). **l. de transmisión,** sender (telegraphy). **l. inglesa,** monkey-wrench; span-

ner. **l. maestra**, master key, skeleton key. **echar la l.**, to lock. **torcer la l.**, to turn the key

llavero /ya'βero; ʎa'βero/ **(-ra)** n keeper of the keys. m, key ring. **l. de cárcel**, turnkey

llavín /ya'βin; ʎa'βin/ m, yale key, latchkey

llegada /ye'gaða; ʎe'gaða/ f, arrival, advent

llegar /ye'gar; ʎe'gar/ vi to arrive; last, endure; reach; achieve a purpose; be sufficient, suffice; amount (to), make; vt bring near, draw near; gather; vr come near, approach; adhere. **l. a ser**, to become. **l. a un punto muerto**, to reach a deadlock. **l. hasta...**, to stretch as far as...

llena /'yena; 'ʎena/ f, spate, overflow

llenar /ye'nar; ʎe'nar/ vt to fill; occupy (a post); satisfy, please; fulfill; satiate; pervade; fill up (a form); vi be full (of the moon); vr Inf. stuff, overeat; Fig. Inf. be fed-up

lleno /'yeno; 'ʎeno/ a full; replete; abundant; complete. m, full moon; Theat. full house; Inf. glut, abundance; perfection. **de l., de l. en l.**, entirely, completely

llenura /ye'nura; ʎe'nura/ f, abundance, plenty

lleva, llevada /'yeβa, ye'βaða; 'ʎeβa, ʎe'βaða/ f, carrying, bearing

llevadero /yeβa'ðero; ʎeβa'ðero/ a tolerable, bearable

llevar /ye'βar; ʎe'βar/ vt to carry, transport; charge (a price); yield, produce; carry off, take away; endure; bear; persuade; guide, take; direct; wear (clothes); carry (a handbag, etc.); introduce, present; gain, achieve; manage (a horse); pass, spend (of time); (with past part) have (e.g. Llevo escrita la carta, I have written the letter); Math. carry; (with prep. a) surpass, excel. **l. a cabo**, to accomplish. **l. a cuestas**, to carry on one's back; support. **l. la correspondencia**, to look after the correspondence. **l. la delantera**, to take the lead. **l. luto**, to be in mourning. **1. por delante** Argentina, Chile to run over (e.g., a pedestrian) **llevarse bien**, to get on well, agree

llorar /yo'rar; ʎo'rar/ vi to weep, cry; drip; water (eyes); vt lament, mourn; bewail one's troubles

lloriquear /yorike'ar; ʎorike'ar/ vi to whine, snivel

lloriqueo /yori'keo; ʎori'keo/ m, whining, sniveling

lloro /'yoro; 'ʎoro/ m, weeping, crying; flood of tears

llorón /yo'ron; ʎo'ron/ a weeping; sniveling, whining. m, long plume. **niño llorón**, crybaby

lloroso /yo'roso; ʎo'roso/ a tearful; grievous, sad; sorrowful

llovedizo /yoβe'ðiso; ʎoβe'ðiθo/ a leaky; rainy

llover /yo'βer; ʎo'βer/ vi impers irr to rain; come in abundance (of troubles, etc.); vr leak (roofs, etc.). **l. a cántaros**, to rain in torrents, rain cats and dogs. **l. sobre mojado**, to add insult to injury. **como llovido**, unexpectedly. See **mover**

llovida /jo'βiða; ʎo'βiða/ f, Lat. Am. rain, shower

llovido /yo'βiðo; ʎo'βiðo/ m, stowaway

llovizna /yo'βisna; ʎo'βiθna/ f, drizzle, fine rain

llovixnar /yoβis'nar; ʎoβiθ'nar/ vi to drizzle

lluvia /'yuβia; 'ʎuβia/ f, rain; rainwater; Fig. shower; rose (of watering can) Chile, Nicaragua shower bath, shower

lluvioso /yu'βioso; ʎu'βioso/ a rainy, showery

lo /lo/ def art. neut the thing, part, fact, what, that which. Used before adjectives, past participles, sometimes before nouns and adverbs (e.g. Lo barato es caro, Cheap things are dear (in the long run).) **Lo mío es mío, pero lo tuyo es de ambos**, What's mine is mine, but what is yours belongs to both of us. **Juan siente mucho lo ocurrido**, John is very sorry for what has happened. **a lo lejos**, in the distance). **lo... que**, how (e.g. No sabes lo bueno que es, You don't know how good he is). pers pron acc m, or neut him, it; that, it (e.g. Lo harán mañana, They will do it to-morrow). Means some, any, one, as substitute for noun already mentioned (e.g. Carecemos de azúcar; no lo hay, We are short of sugar; there isn't any). **Lo cortés no quita lo valiente**, One can be courteous and still insistent

loa /'loa/ f, praise, eulogy; Theat. prologue; short dramatic piece; Obs.; dramatic eulogy

loable /lo'aβle/ a praiseworthy

loar /lo'ar/ vt to praise; commend

lobero /lo'βero/ a wolf; wolfish

lobo /'loβo/ **(-ba)** n wolf. m, (Bot. Anat.) lobe; Inf. drinking fit. **l. marino**, Zool. seal. Inf. **pillar un l.**, to get drunk

lóbrego /'loβrego/ a murky, dark; dismal; mournful, lugubrious

lobreguez /loβre'ges; loβre'geθ/ f, obscurity, gloom, darkness

lóbulo /'loβulo/ m, lobe

locación /loka'sion; loka'θion/ f, Law. lease; agreement, contract

local /lo'kal/ a local. m, premises; place, spot, scene

localidad /lokali'ðað/ f, location; locality; place, spot; seat (in theaters, etc.)

localización /lokalisa'sion; lokaliθa'θion/ f, localization, placing; place

localizar /lokali'sar; lokali'θar/ vt to localize

locamente /loka'mente/ adv insanely, madly; extraordinary, extremely

loción /lo'sion; lo'θion/ f, lotion

loco /'loko/ **(-ca)** a insane, mad; rash, foolish, crazy; excessive, enormous; amazing; extraordinary; infatuated. n lunatic; rash person. Fig. Inf. **Es un l. de atar**, He's completely crazy! **Ellos están locos conmigo**, They're crazy about me

locomoción /lokomo'sion; lokomo'θion/ f, locomotion

locomotor /lokomo'tor/ a locomotive

locomotora /lokomo'tora/ f, locomotive

locomóvil /loko'moβil/ a and f, locomotive

locro /'lokro/ m, Lat. Am. meat-and-vegetable stew

locuacidad /lokuasi'ðað; lokuaθi'ðað/ f, loquacity

locuaz /lo'kuas; lo'kuaθ/ a loquacious

locución /loku'sion; loku'θion/ f, style of speech; phrase, idiom; Gram. locution

locuelo /lo'kuelo/ **(-la)** n madcap

locura /lo'kura/ f, insanity, lunacy; madness, fury; folly, foolishness

locutor /loku'tor/ **(-ra)** n (radio) announcer; commentator

locutorio /loku'torio/ m, locutory; phone booth

lodazal, lodazar /loða'sal,. loða'sar; loða'θal, loða'θar/ m, muddy place; quagmire

lodo /'loðo/ m, mud

lodoso /lo'ðoso/ a muddy

logarítmico /loga'ritmiko/ a logarithmic

logaritmo /loga'ritmo/ m, logarithm

logia /'loxia/ f, (Freemason's) lodge

lógica /'loxika/ f, logic. Inf. **l. parda**, common sense

lógico /'loxiko/ **(-ca)** a logical. n logician

logística /lo'xistika/ f, logistics

lograr /lo'grar/ vt to achieve, attain, obtain; enjoy; (with infin) succeed in; vr succeed in, achieve; reach perfection

logrear /logre'ar/ vi to borrow or lend at interest

logrero /lo'grero/ **(-ra)** n moneylender; monopolist, profiteer

logro /'logro/ m, achievement, attainment; profit, gain; usury, money-lending

loma /'loma/ f, knoll, hill

lombarda /lom'βarða/ f, red cabbage

lombardo /lom'βarðo/ m, mortgage bank

lombriciento, -a /lomβri'siento; lomβri'θiento/ a, Lat. Am. having worms, suffering from worms

lombriz /lom'βris; lom'βriθ/ f, earthworm, common worm. **l. intestinal**, intestinal worm. **l. solitaria**, tapeworm

lomo /'lomo/ m, loin, back of a beast; ridge between furrows; pl ribs; loins

lona /'lona/ f, canvas, sailcloth

lonchería /lontʃe'ria/ f, Lat. Am. luncheonette, lunch counter, snack bar

Londres /'londres/ London

longaniza /loŋga'nisa; loŋga'niθa/ f, Cul. pork sausage

longevidad /lonxeβi'ðað/ f, longevity

longevo /lon'xeβo/ a long-lived

longísimo /lon'hisimo/ a sup **luengo** exceedingly long

longitud /lonhi'tuð/ *f*, length; longitude. **l. de onda,** *Radio.* wavelength

lonja /'lonha/ *f*, slice, rasher; *Com.* exchange; market; grocery store; woolen warehouse

lonjista /lon'hista/ *mf* provision merchant, grocer

lontananza /lonta'nansa; lonta'nanθa/ *f*, distance (also *Art.*). **en l.,** in the distance, far off

loor /lo'or/ *m*, praise

loquear /loke'ar/ *vi* to play the fool; romp

loro /'loro/ *m*, *Ornith.* parrot

los /los/ *def art. m pl*, the (e.g. *l. sombreros,* the hats). *pers. pron acc 3rd pers m pl,* them. **Tus cigarrillos no están sobre la mesa; los tengo en mi bolsillo,** Your cigarettes are not on the table; I have them in my pocket. Means some, any, ones, as substitution for noun already stated (e.g. *Los cigarros están en la caja si los hay,* The cigars are in the box, if there are any). Used demonstratively followed by *de* or *que* introducing relative clause, those of; those which, those who; the ones that (who) (e.g. *Estaba leyendo algunos libros de los que tienes en tu cuarto,* I was reading some books from among those which you have in your room)

losa /'losa/ *f*, flagstone; slab; tombstone

lote /'lote/ *m*, lot, portion, share

lotería /lote'ria/ *f*, lottery; lotto (game); lottery office

lotero /lo'tero/ **(-ra)** *n* seller of lottery tickets

loto /'loto/ *m*, lotus; lotus flower or fruit

loza /'losa; 'loθa/ *f*, porcelain, china

lozanía /losa'nia; loθa'nia/ *f*, luxuriance (of vegetation); vigor, lustiness; arrogance

lozano /lo'sano; lo'θano/ *a* luxuriant, exuberant; vigorous, lusty; arrogant

lubricación /luβrika'sion; luβrika'θion/ *f*, lubrication

lubricante /luβri'kante/ *a* lubricant

lubricar /luβri'kar/ *vt* to lubricate

lúbrico /'luβriko/ *a* slippery, smooth; lascivious, lustful

lucera /lu'sera; lu'θera/ *f*, skylight

lucerna /lu'serna; lu'θerna/ *f*, large chandelier; skylight

lucero /lu'sero; lu'θero/ *m*, evening star; any bright star; white star (on a horse's head); brilliance, radiance; *pl Poet.* eyes, orbs. **l. del alba,** morning star

lucha /'lutʃa/ *f*, fight; struggle; wrestling match; argument, disagreement. **l. grecorromana,** wrestling. **l. igualada,** close fight. **l. libre,** catch-as-catch-can

luchador /lutʃa'ðor/ **(-ra)** *n* fighter; struggler

luchar /lu'tʃar/ *vi* to fight hand to hand; wrestle; fight; struggle; argue

lucidez /lusi'ðes; luθi'ðeθ/ *f*, brilliance, shine; lucidity, clarity

lucido /lu'siðo; lu'θiðo/ *a* splendid, brilliant; sumptuous; fine, elegant

lúcido /'lusiðo; lu'θiðo/ *a Poet.* brilliant; lucid; clear

luciente /lu'siente; lu'θiente/ *a* bright, shining

luciérnaga /lu'siernaga; lu'θiernaga/ *f*, firefly, glowworm

lucimiento /lusi'miento; luθi'miento/ *m*, brilliance, luster; success, triumph; elegance; display, ostentation

lucir /lu'sir; lu'θir/ *vi irr* to shine, scintillate; excel, outshine; be successful; *vt* illuminate; display, show off; show; *vr* dress elegantly; be successful; excel, be brilliant. *Pres. Ind.* **luzco, luces,** etc. *Pres. Subjunc.* **luzca,** etc.

lucrativo /lukra'tiβo/ *a* lucrative

lucro /'lukro/ *m*, gain, profit

lucroso /lu'kroso/ *a* profitable

luctuoso /luk'tuoso/ *a* lugubrious, mournful

lucubración /lukuβra'sion; lukuβra'θion/ *f*, lucubration

ludibrio /lu'ðiβrio/ *m*, mockery, ridicule

luego /'luego/ *adv* immediately; afterward; later; then; soon, presently. *conjunc* therefore. **l. que,** as soon as. **desde l.,** at once; of course, naturally; in the first place. **hasta l.,** see you later, good-by for the present

lueguito /lue'gito/ *adv Lat. Am.* at once, right away, right now; *Central America, Chile, Mexico* near, nearby

luengo /'luengo/ *a* long

lugar /lu'gar/ *m*, place; spot; village, town, city; region, locality; office, post; passage, text; opportunity, occasion; cause, motive; place on a list; room, space; seat. **l. común,** commonplace. **en l. de,** instead of. **en primer l.,** firstly, in the first place. **hacer l.,** to make room, make way. *Law.* **No ha l.,** The petition is refused. **tener l.,** to take place; have the time or opportunity (to)

lugarejo /luga'reho/ *m*, hamlet

lugareño /luga'reɲo/ **(-ña)** *a* peasant, regional. *n* villager, peasant

lugarteniente /lugarte'niente/ *m*, lieutenant; substitute, deputy

lúgubre /'luguβre/ *a* lugubrious, dismal, mournful

luis /'luis/ *m*, louis (French coin)

lujo /'luho/ *m*, luxury; abundance, profusion. **artículos de l.,** luxury goods

lujoso /lu'hoso/ *a* luxurious; abundant, profuse

lujuria /lu'huria/ *f*, lasciviousness; excess, intemperance

lujuriante /luhu'riante/ *a* luxuriant, abundant, profuse

lujurioso /luhu'rioso/ *a* lascivious, voluptuous

lumbago /lum'βago/ *m*, lumbago

lumbre /'lumbre/ *f*, fire; light; splendor, luster; transom window, opening, skylight; *pl* tinderbox

lumbrera /lum'βrera/ *f*, luminary; skylight; dormer window; eminent authority; *Mexico* box (in a theater or bullring)

luminar /lumi'nar/ *m*, luminary (also *Fig.*)

luminaria /lumi'naria/ *f*, illumination; fairy lamp, small light; lamp burning before the Sacrament in Catholic churches

luminosidad /luminosi'ðað/ *f*, luminosity

luminoso /lumi'noso/ *a* luminous; bright

luna /'luna/ *f*, moon; mirror; satellite; sheet of plate glass. **l. creciente,** new or rising moon. **l. de miel,** honeymoon. **l. llena,** full moon. **l. menguante,** waning moon. **media l.,** crescent moon

lunado /lu'naðo/ *a* half-moon, crescent

lunar /lu'nar/ *m*, beauty spot; *Fig.* stain, blot (on reputation, etc.); blemish, slight imperfection. *a* lunar

lunático /lu'natiko/ **(-ca)** *a* and *n* lunatic

lunes /'lunes/ *m*, Monday

luneta /lu'neta/ *f*, lens (of eyeglasses), *Theat.* orchestra stall; (*Archit. Mil.*) lunette

lupa /'lupa/ *f*, magnifying glass

lupanar /lupa'nar/ *m*, brothel

lúpulo /'lupulo/ *m*, *Bot.* hop

luso /'luso/ **(-sa)** *n* Portuguese

lustrador /lustra'ðor/ *m*, polisher; *Lat. Am.* bootblack. **l. de piso,** floor polisher

lustrar /lus'trar/ *vt* to lustrate, purify; polish, burnish; roam, journey

lustre /'lustre/ *m*, polish, sheen, gloss; glory, luster

lustro /'lustro/ *m*, lustrum, period of five years; chandelier

lustroso /lus'troso/ *a* shining, glossy; brilliant; glorious, noble

luterano /lute'rano/ **(-na)** *a* and *n* Lutheran

luto /'luto/ *m*, mourning; grief, affliction; *pl* mourning draperies. **estar de l.,** to be in mourning

luxación /luksa'sion; luksa'θion/ *f*, *Surg.* luxation, dislocation

luz /lus/ *f*, light; glow; brightness, brilliance; information, news; *Fig.* luminary; day, daylight; *pl* culture, learning; windows. **luces de estacionamiento,** parking lights. **a buena l.,** in a good light; in a favorable light; after due consideration. **a primera l.,** at dawn. **dar a l.,** to publish (a book); bring forth (children); reveal. **entre dos luces,** in the dawn light; in the twilight; *Inf.* tipsy. **media l.,** half-light, twilight

M

maca /'maka/ *f*, bruise or blemish on fruit; defect, flaw; *Inf.* fraud, swindle
macabro /ma'kaβro/ *a* macabre
macagua /ma'kagua/ *f*, *Ornith.* macaw
macanudo /maka'nuðo/ *a* (*Inf. West Hem.*) extraordinary; enormous; robust; fine, excellent
macarrones /maka'rrones/ *m pl*, macaroni; *Naut.* stanchions
macarrónico /maka'rroniko/ *a* macaronic, recondite, stylized
macarse /ma'karse/ *vr* to go bad, rot (fruit)
maceración /masera'sion; maθera'θion/ *f*, maceration; steeping, soaking; mortification of the flesh
macerar /mase'rar; maθe'rar/ *vt* to macerate; steep, soak; mortify
macero /ma'sero; ma'θero/ *m*, mace bearer
maceta /ma'seta; ma'θeta/ *f*, *dim* small vase; handle, haft (of tools); stonecutter's hammer; flowerpot; *Lat. Am.* bouquet, bunch (of flowers)
macetero /mase'tero; maθe'tero/ *m*, flowerpot stand; *Lat. Am.* flowerpot
machaca /ma'tʃaka/ *f*, pestle; pulverizer. *mf Inf.* bore, tedious person
machacador /matʃaka'ðor/ (**-ra**) *a* crushing, pounding. *n* beater, crusher, pounder
machacar /matʃa'kar/ *vt* to crush, pound; *vi* importune; harp on a subject
machacón /matʃa'kon/ *a* tiresome, prolix
machado /ma'tʃaðo/ *m*, hatchet, ax
machete /ma'tʃete/ *m* machete
machetero /matʃe'tero/ *m*, one who cuts sugarcane with a machete
machihembrar /matʃiem'βrar/ *vt* to dovetail
machina /ma'tʃina/ *f*, derrick, crane; pile driver
macho /'matʃo/ *m*, male; male animal (he-goat, stallion, etc.); male plant; hook (of hook and eye); screw; *Metall.* core; tap (tool); *Inf.* dunderhead, fool; *Archit.* buttress. *a* male; stupid, ignorant; vigorous, strong. **m. cabrío**, he-goat
machucadura /matʃuka'ðura/ *f*, **machucamiento** *m*, pounding, crushing; bruising
machucar /matʃu'kar/ *vt* to crush, pound; bruise
machucho /ma'tʃutʃo/ *a* prudent, sensible; adult, mature
macicez /masi'ses; maθi'θeθ/ *f*, solidity; massiveness; thickness
macilento /masi'lento; maθi'lento/ *a* thin, lean, emaciated
macillo /ma'siyo; ma'θiʎo/ *m*, *dim* small mace; hammer (of a piano)
macis /'masis; 'maθis/ *f*, *Cul.* mace
macizar /masi'sar; maθi'θar/ *vt* to block up, fill up
macizo /ma'siso; ma'θiθo/ *a* massive; compact, solid; *Fig.* well-founded, unassailable; thick; strong. *m*, solidity, compactness; bulk, volume; flowerbed; solid tire
macrocosmo /makro'kosmo/ *m*, macrocosm
macuco, -a /ma'kuko/ *a*, *Lat. Am.* crafty, cunning, sly
mácula /'makula/ *f*, stain, spot; *Fig.* blot, blemish; *Inf.* trick, deception; *Astron.* macula
macuquero /maku'kero/ *m*, unauthorized worker of abandoned mines
madeja /ma'ðeha/ *f*, lock of hair; *Inf.* dummy, useless person
madera /ma'ðera/ *f*, wood; timber; *Inf.* kind, sort; *Mus.* wind instruments. **m. contrachapada**, plywood. **m. de construcción**, timber. **maderas de sierra**, lumber wood. *Inf.* **ser de mala m.**, to be a ne'er-do-well
maderada /maðe'raða/ *f*, lumber wood
maderaje /maðe'rahe/ *m*, woodwork, timber work
maderero /maðe'rero/ *m*, timber merchant; lumberjack; carpenter
madería /maðe'ria/ *f*, timber yard
madero /ma'ðero/ *m*, wooden beam; log, piece of

lumber; ship, vessel; *Inf.* blockhead or insensible person
madrastra /ma'ðrastra/ *f*, stepmother
madraza /ma'ðrasa; ma'ðraθa/ *f*, *Inf.* overindulgent mother
madre /'maðre/ *f*, mother; matron; cause, genesis; *Inf.* dame, mother; riverbed; dam; womb; main sewer; chief irrigation channel. **m. de familia**, mother; housewife. **m. de leche**, wet nurse. **m. política**, mother-in-law; stepmother. *Inf.* **sacar de m. (a)**, to provoke, irritate (a person)
madreperla /maðre'perla/ *f*, mother-of-pearl
madreselva /maðre'selβa/ *f*, honeysuckle
madrigado /maðri'gaðo/ *a* twice-married (women); *Inf.* experienced, wide-awake
madrigal /maðri'gal/ *m*, madrigal
madriguera /maðri'gera/ *f*, rabbit warren; burrow, den, hole, lair; haunt of thieves, etc.
madrina /ma'ðrina/ *f*, godmother; matron of honor or bridesmaid; sponsor; patroness; prop; stanchion
madroncillo /maðron'siyo; maðron'θiʎo/ *m*, strawberry
madroño /ma'ðroɲo/ *m*, strawberry tree; tuft, spot; tassel
madrugada /maðru'gaða/ *f*, dawn, daybreak; early rising. **de m.**, at dawn
madrugador /maðruga'ðor/ (**-ra**) *a* early rising. *n* early riser
madrugar /maðru'gar/ *vi* to get up early; gain time; anticipate, be beforehand
maduración /maðura'sion; maðura'θion/ *f*, ripening; mellowing; preparation; ripeness; maturity
madurador /maðura'ðor/ *a* ripening; maturing
maduramente /maðura'mente/ *adv* maturely; sensibly
madurar /maðu'rar/ *vt* to ripen; mature; think out; *vi* ripen; grow mature, learn wisdom
madurez /maðu'res; maðu're θ/ *f*, ripeness; maturity; mellowness; wisdom
maduro /ma'ðuro/ *a* ripe; mature; mellow; adult; wise
maestra /ma'estra/ *f*, schoolmistress; teacher, instructor; queen bee; guide, model
maestral /maes'tral/ *a* referring to the grand master of one of the Spanish military orders; teaching, pedagogic. *m*, mistral (wind); cell of a queen bee
maestranza /maes'transa; maes'tranθa/ *f*, *Lat. Am.* machine shop
maestrear /maestre'ar/ *vt* to direct, control, manage; prune vines; *vi Inf.* bully, domineer
maestría /maes'tria/ *f*, mastery, skill; *Educ.* master's degree
maestril /maes'tril/ *m*, queen cell (of bees)
maestro /ma'estro/ *a* masterly; excellent; chief, main; midship. *m*, master, expert; teacher; instructor; master craftsman; *Educ.* teacher; *Mus.* composer; *Naut.* mainmast. **m. de armas**, fencing master. **m. de capilla**, *Eccl.* choirmaster. **m. de obras**, building contractor; master builder. **El ejercicio hace m.**, Practice makes perfect
Magallanes, Estrecho de /maga'yanes; es'tretʃo de; maga'ʎanes, es'tretʃo de/ Straits of Magellan
magdalena /magða'lena/ *f*, madeleine (cake); magdalen, penitent. *Inf.* **estar hecha una M.,** to be inconsolable
magia /'mahia/ *f*, magic
mágica /'mahika/ *f*, magic; enchantress, sorceress
mágico /'mahiko/ *a* magic; marvelous, wonderful. *m*, magician; enchanter, wizard
magín /ma'hin/ *m*, *Inf.* imagination; head, mind
magisterio /mahis'terio/ *m*, teaching profession; teaching diploma; teaching post; pedantry, pompousness. **ejercer su m. en,** to be employed as a teacher in
magistrado /mahis'traðo/ *m*, magistrate; magistracy

magistral /mahis'tral/ *a* magistral; authoritative, magisterial; pedantic, pompous

magistratura /mahistra'tura/ *f*, magistracy

magnanimidad /magnanimi'ðað/ *f*, magnanimity; generosity, liberality

magnánimo /mag'nanimo/ *a* magnanimous, generous, noble

magnate /mag'nate/ *m*, magnate

magnavoz /magna'βos; magna'βoθ/ *m*, *Mexico* loudspeaker

magnesia /mag'nesia/ *f*, magnesia

magnesio /mag'nesio/ *m*, magnesium

magnético /mag'netiko/ *a* magnetic

magnetizar /magneti'sar; magneti'θar/ *vt* to magnetize; mesmerize

magneto /mag'neto/ *m*, magneto

magnificar /magnifi'kar/ *vt* to magnify, enlarge; praise, extol

magnificencia /magnifi'sensia; magnifi'θenθia/ *f*, magnificence, pomp, splendor

magnífico /mag'nifiko/ *a* magnificent; splendid, wonderful, fine; excellent

magnitud /magni'tuð/ *f*, magnitude; quantity; importance

magno /'magno/ *a* great; famous. **Alejandro M.**, Alexander the Great

magnolia /mag'nolia/ *f*, magnolia

mago /'mago/ *m*, magician; *pl* magi

magra /'magra/ *f*, rasher (of bacon, ham)

magrez, magrura /ma'gres, ma'grura; ma'greθ, ma'grura/ *f*, leanness; scragginess

magro /'magro/ *a* lean; scraggy. *m*, *Inf.* lean pork

magulladura /maguya'ðura; maguʎa'ðura/ *f*, **magullamiento** *m*, bruising; bruise, contusion

magullar /magu'yar; magu'ʎar/ *vt* to bruise

magullón /magu'jon; magu'ʎon/ *m*, *Lat. Am.* bruise

mahometano /maome'tano/ **(-na)** *a* and *n* Muslim

mahonesa /mao'nesa/ *f*, mayonnaise

maíz /ma'is; ma'iθ/ *m*, corn

maizal /mai'sal; mai'θal/ *m*, cornfield

maja /'maha/ *f*, belle

majada /ma'haða/ *f*, sheepfold; dung

majaderear /mahaðere'ar/ *vt*, *Lat. Am.* to nag, pester

majadería /mahaðe'ria/ *f*, impertinence, insolence

majadero /maha'ðero/ *a* persistent, tedious. *m*, bobbin (for lace making); pestle. *n* fool, bore

majador /maha'ðor/ *m*, pestle

majar /ma'har/ *vt* to pound, crush; *Inf.* importune, annoy

majestad /mahes'tað/ *f*, majesty (title); dignity; stateliness

majestuosidad /mahestuosi'ðað/ *f*, majesty; dignity

majestuoso /mahes'tuoso/ *a* majestic; stately; dignified

majo /'maho/ *a* arrogant, aggressive; gaudily attired, smart; dashing, handsome; attractive, pretty; elegant, well-dressed. *m*, beau, gallant, man about town

majuelo /ma'huelo/ *m*, new vine; species of white hawthorn

mal /mal/ *a abb* **malo**. Used only before *m sing* nouns (e.g. *un m. cuarto de hora*, a bad quarter of an hour). *m*, evil; damage; harm; misfortune; illness, disease; trouble (e.g. *El m. es*, The trouble is). **el bien y el m.**, good and evil. **m. de altura**, air sickness. **m. de ojo**, evil eye. **m. de piedra**, lithiasis, stone. **m. francés**, syphilis. **el m. menor**, the lesser of two evils. *interj* **¡M. haya!** A curse upon! **echar a m.**, to scorn (things); waste, squander. **llevar a m. (una cosa)**, to take (a thing) badly, complain. **No hay m. que por bien no venga**, It's an ill wind that blows no one any good, Every cloud has a silver lining. **parar en m.**, to come to a bad end

mal /mal/ *adv* badly; unfavorably; wrongly; wickedly; with difficulty; scarcely, barely. **m. que bien**, willingly or unwillingly; rightly or wrongly. **de m. en peor**, from bad to worse

mala /'mala/ *f*, mail, post. **m. real**, royal mail

malabarista /malaβa'rista/ *mf* juggler

malaconsejado /malakonse'haðo/ *a* ill-advised; imprudent

malacostumbrado /malakostum'βraðo/ *a* badly trained, spoiled; having bad habits

Málaga /'malaga/ Malaga

malandante /malan'dante/ *a* evildoing; unfortunate, miserable; poor

malandanza /malan'dansa; malan'danθa/ *f*, evildoing; misfortune, misery; poverty

malandrín /malan'drin/ *a* wicked, ill-disposed. *m*, scoundrel, miscreant

malanga /ma'laŋga/ *f*, *Central America* kind of tuber resembling a sweet potato

malaquita /mala'kita/ *f*, malachite

malaria /ma'laria/ *f*, malaria

malaventura /malaβen'tura/ *f*, misfortune, adversity, bad luck

malaventurado /malaβentu'raðo/ *a* unfortunate, unlucky

malayo /ma'laio/ **(-ya)** *a* Malay. *n* Malayan

malbaratador /malβarata'ðor/ **(-ra)** *a* wasteful, spendthrift. *n* squanderer, spendthrift

malbaratar /malβara'tar/ *vt* to squander, waste; sell at a loss

malcasado /malka'saðo/ *a* adulterous, unfaithful, unhappily married

malcasar /malka'sar/ **(se)** *vt* and *vr* to marry badly

malcomido /malko'miðo/ *a* underfed

malcontento /malkon'tento/ **(-ta)** *a* dissatisfied, discontented; rebellious. *n* malcontent, rebel

malcriado /mal'kriaðo/ *a* badly brought up; ill-bred; spoiled, peevish

maldad /mal'dað/ *f*, badness; depravity, wickedness

maldecidor /maldesi'ðor; maldeθi'ðor/ **(-ra)** *a* slanderous. *n* scandalmonger, slanderer

maldecir /malde'sir; malde'θir/ *vt irr* to curse; *vt* and *vi* slander, backbite. See **decir**

maldiciente /maldi'siente; maldi'θiente/ *a* defamatory, slanderous; cursing, reviling. *m*, slanderer; curser

maldición /maldi'sion; maldi'θion/ *f*, malediction; curse, imprecation

maldispuesto /maldis'puesto/ *a* indisposed, ill; reluctant

maldita /mal'dita/ *f*, *Inf.* tongue. *Inf.* **soltar la m.**, to say too much, go too far

maldito /mal'dito/ *a* accursed; wicked; damned; poor (of quality); *Inf.* not a...

maleabilidad /maleaβili'ðað/ *f*, malleability, flexibility

maleable /male'aβle/ *a* malleable, flexible

maleante /male'ante/ *a* rascally, villainous. *mf* evildoer

malecón /male'kon/ *m*, breakwater, wharf, seafront

maledicencia /maleði'sensia; maleði'θenθia/ *f*, slander, abuse, backbiting; cursing

maleficencia /malefi'sensia; malefi'θenθia/ *f*, wrongdoing

maleficio /male'fisio; male'fiθio/ *m*, (magic) curse; spell; charm

maléfico /ma'lefiko/ *a* malefic, harmful. *m*, sorcerer

malestar /males'tar/ *m*, indisposition, slight illness; discomfort

maleta /ma'leta/ *f*, suitcase, valise, grip; *m*, *Inf.* clumsy matador; duffer (at games, etc.). **hacer la m.**, to pack a suitcase; *Inf.* prepare for a journey, get ready to leave

maletero /male'tero/ *m*, seller or maker of traveling bags; porter

maletín /male'tin/ *m*, small suitcase or valise

malevolencia /maleβo'lensia; maleβo'lenθia/ *f*, malevolence, hatred, malice

malévolo /ma'leβolo/ *a* malevolent, malicious

maleza /ma'lesa; ma'leθa/ *f*, weeds; undergrowth; thicket

malgastador /malgasta'ðor/ **(-ra)** *a* thriftless, wasteful. *n* squanderer

malgastar /malgas'tar/ *vt* to waste (time); squander, throw away (money)

malhablado /mala'βlaðo/ *a* foul-tongued, indecent

malhadado /mala'ðaðo/ *a* ill-fated, unhappy

malhecho /mal'etʃo/ a deformed, twisted (persons). m, evil deed, wrongdoing

malhechor /male'tʃor/ **(-ra)** n malefactor; evildoer

malhumorado /malumo'raðo/ a ill-humored, bad-tempered

malicia /ma'lisia; ma'liθia/ f, wickedness, evil; malice, maliciousness; acuteness, subtlety, shrewdness; craftiness, guile; Inf. suspicion

maliciar /mali'siar; mali'θiar/ vt to suspect; spoil, damage; hurt, harm

malicioso /mali'sioso; mali'θioso/ a malicious; vindictive; wicked; shrewd, clever; Inf. suspicious; artful

malignidad /maligni'ðað/ f, malignancy, spite, ill will

maligno /ma'ligno/ a malignant, spiteful; wicked; Med. malignant

malintencionado /malintensio'naðo; malinten-θio'naðo/ a ill-intentioned, badly disposed

malla /'maya; 'maʎa/ f, mesh (of a net); coat of mail; pl Theat. tights. **m. de alambre,** wire netting. **cota de m.,** coat of mail

Mallorca /ma'yorka; ma'ʎorka/ Majorca

malmandado /malman'daðo/ a disobedient; reluctant, unwilling

malmaridada /malmari'ðaða/ f, adultress, faithless wife

malo /'malo/ a bad; wicked; evil; injurious; harmful; illicit; licentious; ill; difficult; troublesome, annoying; Inf. mischievous; knavish; rotten, decaying. interj **¡M.!** That's bad!; You shouldn't have done that!; That's a bad sign! **de malas,** unluckily, unhappily. **el M.,** the Evil One, the Devil. **estar m.,** to be ill. **Lo m. es,** The trouble is, The worst of it is. **por malas o por buenas,** willy-nilly, willingly or unwillingly. **ser m.,** to be wicked; be evil; behave badly (children)

malograr /malo'grar/ vt to lose (time); waste, throw away (opportunities); vr fall through, fail; wither, fade; die early, come to an untimely end

malogro /ma'logro/ m, loss, waste (time, opportunity); frustration; decline, fading; untimely death

malparar /malpa'rar/ vt to ill-treat; damage. **quedar malparado,** to get the worst of

malparir /malpa'rir/ vt Med. to miscarry

malparto /mal'parto/ m, miscarriage; abortion

malquerencia /malke'rensia; malke'renθia/ f, ill will, aversion, dislike

malquistar /malkis'tar/ vt to stir up trouble; make unpopular; estrange; vr make oneself disliked

malquisto /mal'kisto/ a unpopular, disliked

malsano /mal'sano/ a unhealthy

malta /'malta/ m, malt. **Malta,** Malta

malteada /malte'aða/ f, malted beverage

maltés /mal'tes/ **(-esa)** a and n Maltese

maltraer /maltra'er/ vt irr to ill-treat; insult. See **traer**

maltraído, -a /maltra'iðo/ a, Lat. Am. shabby

maltratamiento /maltrata'miento/ m, abuse, ill usage; damage, deterioration

maltratar /maltra'tar/ vt to ill-treat; abuse, insult; misuse, spoil, damage

maltrato /mal'trato/ m, maltreatment; misuse

maltrecho /mal'tretʃo/ a ill-treated, bruised; abused, insulted; damaged

maltusiano /maltu'siano/ a Malthusian

Malucas, las /ma'lukas, las/ the Moluccas

malucho /ma'lutʃo/ a Inf. off-color, below par, not well

malva /'malβa/ f, mallow. **m. real, m. rosa,** or **m. loca,** hollyhock. **ser como una m.,** Fig. Inf. to be a clinging vine

malvado /mal'βaðo/ a evil, malevolent, fiendish. n villain, fiend

malvasía /malβa'sia/ f, Bot. malvasia; malmsey (wine)

malvavisco /malβa'βisko/ m, Bot. marshmallow

malvender /malβen'der/ vt to sell at a loss

malversación /malβersa'sion; malβersa'θion/ f, malversation; maladministration; misappropriation (of funds)

malversador /malβersa'ðor/ **(-ra)** n bad or corrupt administrator

malversar /malβer'sar/ vt to misappropriate (funds)

Malvinas, las /mal'βinas/ fpl the Falkland Islands

mama /'mama/ f, Inf. breast; udder

mamá /'mama/ f, mama, mother

mamado, -a /ma'maðo/ a, Lat. Am. drunk, tipsy

mamar /ma'mar/ vt to suck (the breast); Inf. wolf, swallow; learn from an early age; enjoy, obtain unfairly; vr get drunk

mamario /ma'mario/ a mammary

mamarracho /mama'rratʃo/ m, Inf. scarecrow, dummy; anything grotesque looking

mameluco /mame'luko/ m, mameluke; Inf. ninny, fool

mamífero /ma'mifero/ a mammalian. m, mammal

mamotreto /mamo'treto/ m, notebook, memorandum; Inf. large book or bulky file of papers

mampara /mam'para/ f, folding screen; screen; partition

mamparo /mam'paro/ m, bulkhead

mampostería /mamposte'ria/ f, masonry, stonemasonry

mampostero /mampos'tero/ m, stonemason

maná /ma'na/ m, manna

manada /ma'naða/ f, handful; herd, flock; group, drove, crowd

manadero /mana'ðero/ m, herdsman, drover; spring, stream

manantial /manan'tial/ m, fountain, source, spring; head (of a river)

manar /ma'nar/ vi to flow, stream; be plentiful

manatí /mana'ti/ m, sea cow, manatee

mancar /man'kar/ vt to injure, maim; vi grow calm (elements)

manceba /man'seβa; man'θeβa/ f, concubine

mancebía /manse'βia; manθe'βia/ f, brothel; youth, young days

mancebo /man'seβo; man'θeβo/ m, youth, stripling; bachelor; shop assistant

mancha /'mantʃa/ f, spot, smear, stain; blotch; plot of ground; patch of vegetation; stigma, disgrace

manchar /man'tʃar/ vt to stain; smear; spot; speckle; disgrace; tarnish

manchuriano /mantʃu'riano/ **(-na)** a and n Manchurian

mancilla /man'siya; man'θiʎa/ f, stain; slur

mancillar /mansi'yar; manθi'ʎar/ vt to stain; Fig. smirch

manco /'manko/ **(-ca)** a maimed, disabled; one-handed; one-armed; armless; handless; incomplete, faulty. n disabled person. **El Manco de Lepanto,** Cervantes

mancomunidad /mankomuni'ðað/ f, association, society; community, union; commonwealth; regional legislative assembly

mancorna, mancuerna /man'korna/ f, Colombia cuff link **mancuerna, mancuernilla** f, Central America cuff link

manda /'manda/ f, offer, suggestion, proposition; legacy

mandadero /manda'ðero/ **(-ra)** n convent or prison messenger; errand boy (girl)

mandado /man'daðo/ m, order, command; errand

mandamiento /manda'miento/ m, order, command; Eccl. commandment; Law. writ; pl Inf. one's five fingers. **los diez mandamientos,** The Ten Commandments

mandar /man'dar/ vt to order, command; bequeath, will; send; control, drive; promise, offer; order (e.g. Mandó hacerse un traje, He ordered a suit to be made); vr walk unaided (convalescents, etc.); lead into one another (rooms, etc.); **¿Quién manda aquí?** Who is in charge here? **¡Mande!** Mexico Yes! (response to a call)

mandarín /manda'rin/ m, mandarin; Inf. bureaucrat; Lat. Am. bossy person, domineering person

mandarina /manda'rina/ f, mandarin (classical Chinese); mandarin orange

mandato /man'dato/ m, mandate; command; Eccl.

maundy. *Polit.* mandate. **cuarto m.**, fourth term (of President, Governor, etc.)

mandíbula /man'diβula/ *f*, jaw; jawbone, mandible

mandil /man'dil/ *m*, long leather apron; apron; Freemason's apron; close-meshed fishing net; *Lat. Am.* (horse) blanket

mandilón /mandi'lon/ *m*, *Inf.* coward, nincompoop

mandioca /man'dioka/ *f*, manioc, cassava; tapioca

mando /'mando/ *m*, authority, power; (*Mil. Nav.*) command; *Engin.* regulation; controls (of a machine, etc.). **m. a distancia,** remote control. *Aer.* **m. de dos pilotos,** dual-controlled. **mandos gemelos,** dual control. **al m. de,** under the command of; under the direction of

mandolín /mando'lin/ *m*. **mandolina** *f*, mandolin

mandón /man'don/ *a* domineering, bossy

mandril /man'dril/ *m*, *Mech.* mandrel, chuck; *Zool.* mandrill

manear /mane'ar/ *vt* to hobble (a horse); manage, control

manecilla /mane'siya; mane'θiʎa/ *f*, *dim* little hand; hand of a clock; *Print.* fist

manejable /mane'haβle/ *a* manageable, controllable

manejar /mane'har/ *vt* to handle; use, wield; control; manage, direct; ride (horses); *vr* manage to move around (after an accident, illness)

manejo /ma'neho/ *m*, handling; use, wielding; control; management, direction; horsemanship; intrigue

maneota /mane'ota/ *f*, hobble, shackle

manera /ma'nera/ *f*, manner, way, means; behavior, style (gen. *pl*); class (of people); *Art.* style, manner. **a la m. de,** like, in the style of. **de esa m.,** in that way; according to that, in that case. **de m. que,** so that. **en gran m.,** to a great extent. **sobre m.,** exceedingly

manga /'maŋga/ *f*, sleeve; bag; grip; handle; pipe (of a hose); strainer; waterspout; body of troops; beam, breadth of a ship; *pl* profits. **m. de viento,** whirlwind. **echar de m. a,** to make use of a person. *Inf.* **estar de m.,** to be in league. **tener m. ancha,** to be broad-minded. *Fig. Inf.* **traer (una cosa) en la m.,** to have (something) up one's sleeve. **de m. corta,** short-sleeved. **de m. larga,** long-sleeved

mangana /maŋ'gana/ *f*, lasso

manganilla /maŋga'niya; maŋga'niʎa/ *f*, sleight of hand; hoax, trick

mangle /'maŋgle/ *m*, mangrove tree

mango /'maŋgo/ *m*, handle, haft, stock; mango. **m. de cuchillo,** knife handle

mangonear /maŋgone'ar/ *vi Inf.* to loaf, roam about; interfere, meddle

mangonero /maŋgo'nero/ *a Inf.* meddlesome

mangosta /maŋ'gosta/ *f*, mongoose

mangote /maŋ'gote/ *m*, *Inf.* long, wide sleeve; black oversleeve

manguera /maŋ'guera/ *f*, hose; sleeve; tube; airshaft; waterspout

manguero /maŋ'guero/ *m*, fireman; hoseman

manguito /maŋ'guito/ *m*, muff; black oversleeve; wristlet, cuff; *Mech.* bush, sleeve

manía /ma'nia/ *f*, mania, obsession; whim, fancy

maniabierto, -a /mania'βierto/ *a*, *Lat. Am.* generous, giving, open-handed

maníaco /ma'niako/ **(-ca)** *a* maniacal; capricious, extravagant. *n* maniac

maniatar /mania'tar/ *vt* to handcuff; hobble (a cow, etc.)

maniático /ma'niatiko/ **(-ca)** *a* maniacal; capricious; faddy, fussy. *n* crank

manicomio /mani'komio/ *m*, insane asylum; mental hospital

manicura /mani'kura/ *f*, manicure

manicuro /mani'kuro/ **(-ra)** *n* manicurist

manida /ma'niða/ *f*, lair, den; dwelling, habitation

manifestación /manifesta'sion; manifesta'θion/ *f*, declaration; statement; exhibition; demonstration; *Eccl.* exposition of the Blessed Sacrament)

manifestante /manifes'tante/ *mf* demonstrator

manifestar /manifes'tar/ *vt irr* to declare, make

known, state; exhibit, show; *Eccl.* to expose (the Blessed Sacrament). See **acertar**

manifiesto /mani'fiesto/ *a* obvious, evident. *m*, manifesto; *Naut.* manifest; *Eccl.* exposition of the Blessed Sacrament. **poner de m.,** to show; make public; reveal

manigua /ma'nigua/ *f*, thicket, *Cuba* jungle

manija /ma'niha/ *f*, handle, stock, haft; hand lever; clamp; tether (for horses, etc.)

manileño /mani'leno/ **(ña)** *a* and *n* Manilan

manilla /ma'niya; ma'niʎa/ *f*, bracelet; handcuff, manacle

maniobra /ma'nioβra/ *f*, operation, process; *Mil.* maneuver; intrigue; tackle, gear; handling, management; *Naut.* working of a ship; *pl* shunting (trains)

maniobrar /manio'βrar/ *vi Mil.* to maneuver; *Naut.* handle, work (ships)

manipulación /manipula'sion; manipula'θion/ *f*, handling; manipulation; control, management

manipulador /manipula'ðor/ *a* manipulative. *m*, sending key (telegraphy)

manipular /manipu'lar/ *vt* to handle; manipulate; manage, direct

maniquete /mani'kete/ *m*, black lace mitten

maniquí /mani'ki/ *m*, mannequin; dummy; *Inf.* puppet, weak person

manirroto /mani'rroto/ **(-ta)** *a* wasteful, extravagant. *n* spendthrift

manivela /mani'βela/ *f*, *Mech.* crank, lever; *Lat. Am.* handle

manjar /man'har/ *m*, dish, food; pastime, recreation, pleasure. **m. blanco,** blancmange; *Lat. Am.* fudge

mano /'mano/ *f*, hand; coat, coating; quire (of paper); front paw (animals); elephant's trunk; side, hand; hand (of a clock); game (of cards, etc.); lead (at cards); way, means; ability; power; protection, favor; compassion; aid, help; scolding; *Mus.* scale; pestle; workers. *Inf.* editing, correction of a literary work (gen. by a person more skilled than the author). **m. de mortero,** pestle. **m. de obra,** (manual) labor. **manos muertas,** *Law.* mortmain. **m. sobre m.,** with folded hands; lazily, indolently. **a la m.,** at hand, nearby; within one's grasp. **a manos llenas,** in abundance, abundantly. **bajo m.,** in an underhand manner, secretly. **buenas manos,** cleverness, ability; dexterity. **de primera m.,** first-hand, new. **estar dejado de la m. de Dios,** to be very unlucky; be very foolish. **poner la m. en,** to ill-treat; slap, buffet. **Si a m. viene...,** If by chance... **tender la m.,** to put out one's hand, shake hands. **traer entre manos,** to have on hand, be engaged in

manojo /ma'noho/ *m*, bunch, handful. **a manojos,** in handfuls; plentifully, in abundance

manolo /ma'nolo/ **(-la)** *n* inhabitant of low quarters of Madrid noted for pride, gaiety, quarrelsomeness, and wit

manoseado /manose'aðo/ *a* hackneyed

manosear /manose'ar/ *vt* to handle; paw, touch repeatedly; finger

manoseo /mano'seo/ *m*, handling; fingering; *Inf.* pawing, feeling

manotada /mano'taða/ *f*, slap, cuff

manotear /manote'ar/ *vt* to slap, cuff; *vi* gesticulate, gesture with the hands

manoteo /mano'teo/ *m*, gesticulation with the hands

manquedad /manke'ðað/ *f*, disablement of hand or arm; lack of one of these; defect; incompleteness

mansalva /man'salβa/ *f*, *adv* without danger

mansedumbre /manse'ðumbre/ *f*, meekness; kindness; gentleness

mansión /man'sion/ *f*, stay, visit; dwelling, abode; mansion

manso /'manso/ *a* soft, gentle, meek, mild; tame; peaceable, amiable; calm

manta /'manta/ *f*, blanket; horse blanket; traveling rug; *Inf.* hiding, thrashing. **m. de viaje,** traveling rug. *Inf.* **a m. de Dios,** in abundance, by the score. **dar una m.,** to toss in a blanket. *Fig. Inf.* **tirar de la m.,** to let the cat out of the bag

manteamiento /mantea'miento/ *m*, tossing in a blanket

mantear /mante'ar/ *vt* to toss in a blanket
manteca /man'teka/ *f*, lard; cooking fat; grease; *Argentina* butter. **como m.,** as mild as milk, as soft as butter
mantecada /mante'kaða/ *f*, buttered toast
mantecado /mante'kaðo/ *m*, French ice cream
mantecoso /mante'koso/ *a* greasy
mantel /man'tel/ *m*, tablecloth; altar cloth
mantelería /mantele'ria/ *f*, table linen
mantelete /mante'lete/ *m*, (*Eccl. Mil.*) mantlet
mantener /mante'ner/ *vt irr* to maintain; keep, feed; support; continue, persevere with; uphold, affirm; keep up; *vr* support oneself; remain in a place; (*with en*) continue to uphold (views, etc.), persevere in. **mantenerse firme,** *Fig.* to stand one's ground. See **tener**
mantenimiento /manteni'miento/ *m*, maintenance; support; sustenance, nourishment; affirmation; upkeep; livelihood
manteo /man'teo/ *m*, tossing in a blanket; long cloak
mantequera /mante'kera/ *f*, churn; dairymaid; butter dish
mantequero /mante'kero/ *m*, dairyman; butter dish
mantequilla /mante'kiya; mante'kiʎa/ *f*, butter
mantero /man'tero/ *m*, blanket seller or maker
mantilla /man'tiya; man'tiʎa/ *f*, mantilla; saddlecloth. *pl* baby's long clothes. **estar en mantillas,** to be in swaddling clothes; *Fig.* be in early infancy
manto /'manto/ *m*, cloak; cover, disguise; *Zool.* mantle; *Mineral.* layer
mantón /man'ton/ *m*, shawl. **m. de Manila,** Manila shawl
mantuano /man'tuano/ **(-na)** *a* and *n* Mantuan
manuable /ma'nuaβle/ *a* easy to handle or use, handy
manual /ma'nual/ *a* manual; handy, easy to use; docile, peaceable. *m*, manual, textbook; *Eccl.* book of ritual; notebook
manubrio /ma'nuβrio/ *m*, handle, crank; *Lat. Am.* handlebars
manuela /ma'nuela/ *f*, open carriage (Madrid)
manufactura /manufak'tura/ *f*, manufacture; manufactured article; factory
manufacturar /manufaktu'rar/ *vt* to manufacture
manufacturero /manufaktu'rero/ *a* manufacturing
manuscrito /manus'krito/ *a* and *m*, manuscript
manutención /manuten'sion; manuten'θion/ *f*, maintenance; upkeep; protection
manzana /man'sana; man'θana/ *f*, apple; block (of houses); city square; Adam's apple; *Argentina* 2.5 acres; *Central America* 1.75 acres
manzanal /mansa'nal; manθa'nal/ *m*, apple orchard; apple tree
manzanar /mansa'nar; manθa'nar/ *m*, apple orchard
manzanilla /mansa'niya; manθa'niʎa/ *f*, white sherry wine; *Bot.* chamomile; chamomile tea; knob, ball (on furniture); pad (on an animal's foot)
manzano /man'sano; man'θano/ *m*, apple tree
maña /'maɲa/ *f*, skill, dexterity; craftiness, guile; vice, bad habit (gen. *pl*). **darse m. para,** to contrive to
mañana /ma'ɲana/ *f*, morning; tomorrow. *m*, future, tomorrow. *adv* tomorrow; in time to come; soon. **¡M.!** Tomorrow! Another day! Not now! (generally to beggars). **de m.,** early in the morning. **muy de m.,** very early in the morning. **pasado m.,** the day after tomorrow
mañanica /maɲa'nika/ *f*, early morning
mañear /maɲe'ar/ *vt* to arrange cleverly; *vi* behave shrewdly
mañero /ma'ɲero/ *a* shrewd, clever; easily worked; handy
mañoso /ma'ɲoso/ *a* clever, skillful; crafty; vicious, with bad habits
mañuela /ma'ɲuela/ *f*, low guile
mapa /'mapa/ *m*, map; card. **m. en relieve,** relief map. **m. del estado mayor,** ordnance map. *Inf.* **no estar en el m.,** to be off the map; be most unusual (of things)
mapache /ma'patʃe/ *m*, raccoon

maqueta /ma'keta/ *f*, (*Art. Archit.*) model
maquiavélico /makia'βeliko/ *a* Machiavellian
maquiladora /makila'ðora/ *f*, maquiladora (factory run by a U.S. company in Mexico to take advantage of cheap labor and lax regulation)
maquillaje /maki'yahe; maki'ʎahe/ *m*, makeup, cosmetics; making up (of the face)
maquillar /maki'yar; maki'ʎar/ **(se)** *vt* and *vr* to make up (the face, etc.)
máquina /'makina/ *f*, machine, mechanism; engine; apparatus; plan, scheme; machine, puppet; *Inf.* mansion, palace; plenty; locomotive; fantasy, product of the imagination. **m. fax,** fax machine. **m. de vapor,** steam engine. **m. de arrastre,** traction engine; tractor. **m. de coser,** sewing machine. **m. de escribir,** typewriter. **m. fotográfica,** camera. **m. de impresionar,** movie camera. **m. de imprimir,** printing machine. **m. herramienta,** machine tool. **m. neumática,** air pump
maquinación /makina'sion; makina'θion/ *f*, intrigue, machination
maquinador /makina'ðor/ **(-ra)** *n* intriguer, schemer
maquinal /maki'nal/ *a* mechanical
maquinar /maki'nar/ *vt* to intrigue, scheme, plot
maquinaria /maki'naria/ *f*, machinery; applied mechanics; mechanism
maquinista /maki'nista/ *mf* driver, enginer; mechanic; machinist; locomotive driver
mar /mar/ *mf* sea; great many, abundance. **m. bonanza** *or* **m. en calma,** calm sea. **m. de fondo** *or* **m. de leva,** swell. **alta m.,** high seas. **a mares,** plentifully. **arar en el m.,** to labor in vain. *Naut.* **hacerse a la m.,** to put out to sea. **la m. de historias,** a great number of stories
maraña /ma'raɲa/ *f*, undergrowth; tangle; *Fig.* difficult position; intrigue; silk waste
marasmo /ma'rasmo/ *m*, *Med.* marasmus, atrophy; inactivity, paralysis
maravilla /mara'βiya; mara'βiʎa/ *f*, marvel, wonder; admiration; amazement; marigold. **a m.,** wonderfully. **a las mil maravillas,** to perfection, excellently. **por m.,** by chance; occasionally
maravillar /maraβi'yar; maraβi'ʎar/ *vt* to amaze, cause admiration; *vr* (*with de*) marvel at, admire; be amazed by
maravilloso /maraβi'yoso; maraβi'ʎoso/ *a* marvelous, wonderful
marbete /mar'βete/ *m*, label, tag; edge, border
marca /'marka/ *f*, mark, sign; brand; frontier zone, border country; standard, norm (of size); make, brand; measuring rule; *Sports.* record. **m. de fábrica,** brand, trademark. **m. de ley,** hallmark. **m. registrada,** registered name. **de m.,** excellent, of excellent quality
marcado /mar'kaðo/ *a* marked; pronounced; strong (of accents)
marcador /marka'ðor/ *a* marking. *m*, marker; scoreboard; bookmark
marcar /mar'kar/ *vt* to mark; brand; embroider initials on linen; tell the time (watches); show the amount (cash register, etc.); dial (telephone); *Sports.* score (a goal); notice, observe; set aside, earmark; *vr* *Naut.* check the course. **m. el compás,** to beat time
marcha /'martʃa/ *f*, departure; running, working; *Mil.* march; speed (of trains, ships, etc.); *Mus.* march; progress, course (of events). **m. atrás,** backing, reversing. **m. de ensayo,** trial run. **m. forzada,** *Mil.* forced march. **a largas marchas,** with all speed. **a toda m.,** at top speed; full speed ahead; by forced marches; *Mil.* **batir la m.,** to strike up a march. **en m.,** underway; working; in operation
marchamero /martʃa'mero/ *m*, customs official who checks and marks goods
marchamo /mar'tʃamo/ *m*, customs mark on checked goods
marchante, -a /mar'tʃante/ *mf Lat. Am.* client, customer; dealer, merchant; peddler
marchar /mar'tʃar/ *vi* to run; work; function; go; leave, depart; progress, proceed; *Mil.* march; go (clocks); *vr* leave, go away
marchitable /martʃi'taβle/ *a* perishable, fragile

marchitar /martʃi'tar/ *vt* to wither, fade; blight, spoil; weaken; *vr* wither; be blighted

marchito /mar'tʃito/ *a* withered; faded; blighted, frustrated

marcial /mar'sial; mar'θial/ *a* martial; courageous, militant

marcialidad /marsiali'ðað; marθiali'ðað/ *f*, war-like spirit, militancy

marciano /mar'siano; mar'θiano/ *a* Martian

marco /'marko/ *m*, mark (German coin); boundary mark; frame (of a picture, etc.). **m. de ventana,** window frame

Mar de las Indias /'mar de las 'indias/ Indian Ocean

Mar del Norte /'mar del 'norte/ North Sea

marea /ma'rea/ *f*, tide; strand, water's edge; light breeze; drizzle; dew; street dirt. **m. creciente,** flood tide. **m. menguante,** ebb tide. **m. muerta,** neap tide

mareaje /ma'reahe/ *m*, seamanship; ship's course

marear /mare'ar/ *vt* to navigate; sell; sell publicly; *Inf.* annoy; *vr* be seasick; feel faint; feel giddy; be damaged at sea (goods)

marejada /mare'haða/ *f*, surge, swell; high sea; tidal wave; commotion, uproar

mareo /ma'reo/ *m*, seasickness; nausea, dizziness; *Inf.* irritation, tediousness

mareta /ma'reta/ *f*, movement of the waves; sound, noise (of a crowd)

marfil /mar'fil/ *m*, ivory

marfileño /marfi'leɲo/ *a* ivory; ivory-like

marfuz /mar'fus; mar'fuθ/ *a* spurned, rejected; deceitful

marga /'marga/ *f*, loam, marl

margarina /marga'rina/ *f*, margarine

margarita /marga'rita/ *f*, pearl; marguerite, oxeye daisy; daisy; periwinkle

margen /'marhen/ *mf* edge, fringe, border, verge; margin (of a book); opportunity; marginal note. **dar m. para,** to provide an opportunity for; give rise to

marginal /marhi'nal/ *a* marginal

margoso /mar'goso/ *a* loamy, marly

marica /ma'rika/ *f*, magpie. *m*, (*offensive*) homosexual; milksop

maricón /mari'kon/ *m*, (*offensive*) homosexual

maridable /mari'ðaβle/ *a* marital, matrimonial

maridaje /mari'ðahe/ *m*, conjugal union and harmony; intimate relationship (between things)

maridar /mari'ðar/ *vi* to get married; mate, live as husband and wife; *vt* unite, link, join together

marido /ma'riðo/ *m*, husband

marihuana /mari'uana/ *f*, marijuana

marimacho /mari'matʃo/ *m*, *Inf.* mannish woman

marina /ma'rina/ *f*, coast, seashore; *Art.* seascape; seamanship; navy, fleet. **m. de guerra,** navy. **m. mercante,** merchant navy

marinera /mari'nera/ *f*, sailor's blouse

marinería /marine'ria/ *f*, profession of a sailor; seamanship; crew of a ship; sailors (as a class)

marinero /mari'nero/ *m*, sailor, seaman. **m. de agua dulce,** freshwater sailor (a novice). **m. práctico,** able seaman. **a la marinera,** in a seaman-like fashion

marinesco /mari'nesko/ *a* seamanly

marino /ma'rino/ *a* marine, sea; seafaring; shipping. *m*, sailor, mariner

marioneta /mario'neta/ *f*, marionette, puppet

mariposa /mari'posa/ *f*, butterfly; night-light

mariposear /maripose'ar/ *vi* to flutter, flit, fly about; flirt, be fickle; follow about, dance attendance on

mariquita /mari'kita/ *f*, *Ent.* ladybird; parakeet.

marisabidilla /marisaβi'ðiya; marisaβi'ðiʎa/ *f*, *Inf.* blue-stocking, know-it-all

mariscal /maris'kal/ *m*, *Mil.* marshal; field marshal; blacksmith

marisco /ma'risko/ *m*, shellfish

marisma /ma'risma/ *f*, bog, morass, swamp

marital /mari'tal/ *a* marital

marítimo /ma'ritimo/ *a* maritime, sea

marjal /mar'hal/ *m*, marshland, fen

marmita /mar'mita/ *f*, stewpot; copper, boiler; *Mexico* kettle

marmitón /marmi'ton/ *m*, kitchen boy, scullion

mármol /'marmol/ *m*, marble; work executed in marble

marmolería /marmole'ria/ *f*, marble works; work executed in marble

marmolista /marmo'lista/ *mf* marble cutter; dealer in marble

marmóreo /mar'moreo/ *a* marble; *Poet.* marmoreal

marmota /mar'mota/ *f*, *Zool.* marmot; sleepyhead, dormouse

Mar Muerto /mar 'muerto/ Dead Sea

maroma /ma'roma/ *f*, rope, hawser; *Lat. Am.* tightrope

maromero, -a /maro'mero/ *mf*, *Lat. Am.* acrobat, tightrope walker; opportunist

marquesina /marke'sina/ *f*, marquee

marquetería /markete'ria/ *f*, marquetry

marrana /ma'rrana/ *f*, sow; *Inf.* slattern, slut

marrano /ma'rrano/ *m*, pig, hog; Marrano

marras /'marras/ (**de**) *adv* long ago, in the dim past

marrasquino /marras'kino/ *m*, maraschino liqueur

marro /'marro/ *m*, tick, tag (game)

marrón /ma'rron/ *a* maroon; brown. *m*, brown color; maroon color; quoit

marroquí /marro'ki/ *a* and *mf* Moroccan. *m*, Morocco leather

marroquín /marro'kin/ (**-ina**), **marrueco** (**-ca**) *a* and *n* Moroccan

Marruecos /ma'rruekos/ Morocco

marrullería /marruye'ria; marruʎe'ria/ *f*, flattery, cajolery

marrullero /marru'yero; marru'ʎero/ (**-ra**) *a* wheedling, flattering. *n* wheedler, cajoler

marsopa /mar'sopa/ *f*, porpoise

marta /'marta/ *f*, sable; marten

martajar /marta'har/ *vt*, *Lat. Am.* to grind, pound

Marte /'marte/ *m*, Mars

martes /'martes/ *m*, Tuesday. **m. de carnaval,** mardi gras

martillar /marti'yar; marti'ʎar/ *vt* to hammer; oppress

martillazo /marti'yaso; marti'ʎaθo/ *m*, hammer blow

martilleo /marti'yeo; marti'ʎeo/ *m*, hammering; noise of the hammer; clink, clatter

martillero, -a /marti'jero; marti'ʎero/ *mf*, *Lat. Am.* auctioneer

martillo /mar'tiyo; mar'tiʎo/ *m*, hammer; oppressor, tyrant; auction rooms. **a m.,** by hammering. **de m.,** wrought (of metals)

martinete /marti'nete/ *m*, hammer (of a pianoforte); pile driver; drop hammer. **m. de báscula,** tilt hammer

Martinica /marti'nika/ Martinique

martín pescador /mar'tin peska'ðor/ *m*, kingfisher

mártir /'martir/ *mf* martyr

martirio /mar'tirio/ *m*, martyrdom

martirizar /martiri'sar; martiri'θar/ *vt* to martyr; torture, torment, martyrize; tease, annoy

marxismo /mark'sismo/ *m*, Marxism

marzo /'marso; 'marθo/ *m*, March

mas /mas/ *conjunc* but; yet

más /mas/ *adv comp* more; in addition, besides; rather, preferably. *Math.* plus. **el** (**la**, etc.) **más,** *adv sup* the most, etc. **m. bien,** more; rather; preferably. **m. que,** only; but; more than; although, even if. **a lo m.,** at the most; at the worst. **a m.,** besides, in addition. **de m.,** superfluous, unnecessary, unwanted. **no... m. que,** only. **por m. que,** however; even if. **sin m. ni m.,** without further ado. **M. vale un mal arreglo que un buen pleito,** A bad peace is better than a good war

masa /'masa/ *f*, mass; dough; whole, aggregate; majority (of people); mortar. **en la m. de la sangre,** *Fig.* in the blood, in a person's nature

masada /ma'saða/ *f*, farmhouse and stock

masadero /masa'ðero/ *m*, farmer; farm laborer

masaje /ma'sahe/ *m*, massage

masajista /masa'hista/ *mf* masseur; masseuse

masato /ma'sato/ *m*, *Lat. Am.* drink made from bananas, fermented corn, yucca, etc.

mascadura /maska'ðura/ *f*, chewing

mascar /mas'kar/ *vt* to chew; masticate; *Inf.* mumble, mutter

máscara /'maskara/ *f*, mask; fancy dress; pretext, excuse. *mf* masquerader, reveler; *pl* masquerade. **m. para gases,** gas mask

mascarada /maska'raða/ *f*, masquerade; company of revelers

mascarero /maska'rero/ **(-ra)** *n* theatrical costumer, fancy-dress dealer

mascarilla /maska'riya; maska'riʎa/ *f*, death mask

mascarón /maska'ron/ *m*, large mask; *Archit.* gargoyle. **m. de proa,** *Naut.* figurehead

mascota /mas'kota/ *f*, mascot

masculinidad /maskulini'ðað/ *f*, masculinity

masculino /masku'lino/ *a* masculine; male; manly, vigorous

mascullar /masku'yar; masku'ʎar/ *vt Inf.* to chew; mutter, mumble

masera /ma'sera/ *f*, kneading bowl; cloth for covering dough

masilla /ma'siya; ma'siʎa/ *f*, mastic, putty

masón /ma'son/ **(-ona)** *n* Freemason

masonería /masone'ria/ *f*, freemasonry

masónico /ma'soniko/ *a* masonic

masoquismo /maso'kismo/ *m*, masochism

mastelero /maste'lero/ *m*, *Naut.* topmast

masticación /mastika'sion; mastika'θion/ *f*, mastication

masticar /masti'kar/ *vt* to masticate, eat; *Inf.* chew upon, consider

masticatorio /mastika'torio/ *a* masticatory

mástil /'mastil/ *m*, *Naut.* mast; upright, stanchion; pole (of a tent); stem, trunk; neck (of a guitar, etc.)

mastín /mas'tin/ *m*, mastiff

mastodonte /masto'ðonte/ *m*, mastodon

mastoides /mastoi'ðes/ *a* mastoid

mastuerzo /mas'tuerso; mas'tuerθo/ *m*, watercress; fool, blockhead

masturbación /masturβa'sion; masturβa'θion/ *f*, masturbation

masturbarse /mastur'βarse/ *vr* to masturbate

mata /'mata/ *f*, plant, shrub; stalk, sprig; grove, copse. **m. de pelo,** mat of hair

matacandelas /matakan'delas/ *m*, candle snuffer

matachín /mata'tʃin/ *m*, mummer; butcher; *Inf.* swashbuckler

matadero /mata'ðero/ *m*, slaughterhouse, abattoir; *Lat. Am.* brothel

matadura /mata'ðura/ *f*, sore (on animals)

matafuego /mata'fuego/ *m*, fire extinguisher; fireman

matalotaje /matalo'tahe/ *m*, ship's supplies, stores; *Inf.* hodgepodge

matamoros /mata'moros/ *a* swashbuckling, swaggering

matamoscas /mata'moskas/ *m*, fly swatter

matanza /ma'tansa; ma'tanθa/ *f*, killing, massacre, slaughter; butchery (animals); *Inf.* persistence, determination

matar /ma'tar/ *vt* to kill; quench (thirst); put out (fire, light); slake (lime); tarnish (metal); bevel (corners, etc.); pester, importune; suppress; compel; *Art.* tone down; *vr* kill oneself; be disappointed, grieve; overwork. **estar a m.,** to be at daggers drawn. **matarse por,** to try hard to; work hard for

matasanos /mata'sanos/ *m*, *Inf.* quack (doctor); bad doctor

matasellos /mata'seyos; mata'seʎos/ *m*, cancellation, postmark

mate /'mate/ *a* matte, unpolished, dull. *m*, checkmate (chess), maté, Paraguayan tea; gourd; vessel made from gourd, coconut, etc., traditional tea of Argentina and the Andes drunk from a gourd

matemáticas /mate'matikas/ *f pl*, mathematics. **m. prácticas,** applied mathematics. **m. teóricas,** pure mathematics

matemático /mate'matiko/ *a* mathematical; exact. *m*, mathematician

materia /ma'teria/ *f*, matter; theme, subject matter; subject (of study); matter, stuff, substance; pus, mat-

ter; question; subject; reason, occasion. **m. colorante,** dye. **materias plásticas,** plastics. **materias primas,** raw materials. **en m. de,** concerning; in the matter of

material /mate'rial/ *a* material; dull, stupid, limited. *m*, material; ingredient; plant, factory; equipment. **m. móvil ferroviario,** rolling stock (railroads)

materialidad /materiali'ðað/ *f*, materiality; external appearance (of things)

materialismo /materia'lismo/ *m*, materialism

materialista /materia'lista/ *a* materialistic. *mf* materialist; *Mexico* truckdriver

materializar /materiali'sar; materiali'θar/ *vt* to materialize; *vr* materialize; grow materialistic, grow less spiritual

maternidad /materni'ðað/ *f*, maternity, motherhood

materno /ma'terno/ *a* maternal

matiz /ma'tis; ma'tiθ/ *m*, combination of colors; tone, hue; shade (of meaning, etc.)

matizar /mati'sar; mati'θar/ *vt* to combine, harmonize (colors); tint, shade; tinge (words, etc.)

matojo /ma'toho/ *m*, shrub, bush

matorral /mato'rral/ *m*, thicket, bush, undergrowth

matraca /ma'traka/ *f*, rattle; *Inf.* scolding, dressing-down; insistence, importunity

matraquear /matrake'ar/ *vi* to make a noise with a rattle; *Inf.* scold

matriarcado /matriar'kaðo/ *m*, matriarchy

matrícula /ma'trikula/ *f*, list, register; matriculation; registration number (of a car, etc.). **m. de buques,** maritime register. **m. de mar,** mariner's register; maritime register

matriculación /matrikula'sion; matrikula'θion/ *f*, matriculation; registration

matricular /matriku'lar/ *vt* to matriculate; enroll; *Naut.* register; *vr* matriculate; enroll, register

matrimonial /matrimo'nial/ *a* matrimonial

matrimonio /matri'monio/ *m*, marriage, matrimony; married couple. **m. a yuras,** secret marriage. **m. de la mano izquierda** *or* **m. morganático,** morganatic marriage. **contraer m.,** to get married

matritense /matri'tense/ *a* and *mf* Madrilenian

matriz /ma'tris; ma'triθ/ *f*, uterus, womb; matrix, mold; *Mineral.* matrix; nut, female screw

matrona /ma'trona/ *f*, married woman; matron; midwife; female customs officer

matusalén /matusa'len/ *m*, Methuselah, very old man

matute /ma'tute/ *m*, smuggling; contraband; gambling den

matutero /matu'tero/ **(-ra)** *n* smuggler, contrabandist

matutino /matu'tino/ *a* matutinal, morning

maula /'maula/ *f*, trash; remnant; deception, fraud, trick. *mf Inf.* good-for-nothing; lazybones. *Inf.* **ser buena m.,** to be a trickster or a fraud

maulería /maule'ria/ *f*, remnant stall; trickery

maullar /mau'yar; mau'ʎar/ *vi* to meow, mew (cats)

maullido /mau'yiðo; mau'ʎiðo/ *m*, meow, cry of the cat

Mauricio, Isla de /mau'risio, 'isla de; mau'riθio, 'isla de/ Mauritius

mauritano /mauri'tano/ **(-na)** *a* and *n* Mauritian

mausoleo /mauso'leo/ *m*, mausoleum

maxilar /maksi'lar/ *a* maxillary. *m*, jaw

máxima /'maksima/ *f*, maxim, rule, precept, principle

máxime /'maksime/ *adv* principally, chiefly

máximo /'maksimo/ *a sup* **grande** greatest, maximum, top. *m*, maximum

maya /'maya/ *f*, common daisy; May queen

mayal /ma'yal/ *m*, flail

mayo /'mayo/ *m*, May; maypole; bouquet, wreath of flowers; *pl* festivities on eve of May Day

mayólica /ma'yolika/ *f*, majolica

mayonesa /mayo'nesa/ *f*, mayonnaise

mayor /ma'yor/ *a comp* **grande** bigger; greater; elder; main, principal; older; high (mass, etc.); *Mus.* major. *mf* major (of full age). *a sup* **grande. el, la, lo mayor, los (las) mayores,** the biggest, greatest; eldest; chief, principal. **por m.,** in short, briefly; *Com.*

wholesale. *m*, head, director; chief clerk; *Mil.* major; *pl* ancestors

mayoral /mayo'ral/ *m*, head shepherd; coachman, driver; foreman, overseer, supervisor, steward

mayorazgo /mayo'rasgo; mayo'raθgo/ *m*, *Law.* entail; entailed estate; heir (to an entail); eldest son; right of primogeniture

mayordoma /mayor'ðoma/ *f*, steward's wife; housekeeper; stewardess

mayordomo /mayor'ðomo/ *m*, steward, superintendent; butler; major-domo, royal chief steward

mayoreo /mayo'reo/ *m*, *Lat. Am.* wholesale

mayoría /mayo'ria/ *f*, majority

mayorista /mayo'rista/ *mf*, wholesaler

mayormente /mayor'mente/ *adv* chiefly; especially

mayúscula /ma'yuskula/ *f*, capital letter, upper-case letter

mayúsculo /ma'yuskulo/ *a* large; capital (letters). **letra mayúscula,** capital letter, upper-case letter

maza /'masa; 'maθa/ *f*, mallet; club, bludgeon; mace; bass drum stick; pile driver; bone, stick, etc., tied to dog's tail in carnival; *Inf.* pedant, bore; important person, authority; *Lat. Am.* hub (of a wheel). **m. de polo,** polo mallet

mazacote /masa'kote; maθa'kote/ *m*, concrete; roughhewn work of art; *Inf.* stodgy overcooked dish; bore, tedious person

mazamorra /masa'morra; maθa'morra/ *f*, dish made of cornmeal; biscuit crumbs; broken fragments, remains

mazapán /masa'pan; maθa'pan/ *m*, marzipan

mazmorra /mas'morra; maθ'morra/ *f*, dungeon

mazo /'maso; 'maθo/ *m*, mallet; bundle, bunch; importunate person; clapper (of a bell); *Argentina*, deck (of cards)

mazonería /masone'ria; maθone'ria/ *f*, stonemasonry

mazonero /maso'nero; maθo'nero/ *m*, stonemason

mazorca /ma'sorka; ma'θorka/ *f*, spindleful; spike, ear (of corn); cocoa berry; camarilla, group

mazurca /ma'surka; ma'θurka/ *f*, mazurka

me /me/ *pers pron acc* or *dat 1st sing mf* me; to me

meandro /me'andro/ *m*, meandering, twisting, winding; wandering

meato /me'ato/ *m*, meatus

mecánica /me'kanika/ *f*, mechanics; mechanism, machinery; *Inf.* worthless thing; mean action

mecánico /me'kaniko/ *a* mechanical; power-operated; base, ill-bred. *m*, engineer; mechanic

mecanismo /meka'nismo/ *m*, mechanism; works, machinery

mecanizar /mekani'sar; mekani'θar/ *vt* to mechanize

mecanografía /mekanogra'fia/ *f*, typewriting

mecanografiar /mekanografi'ar/ *vt* to typewrite, type

mecanográfico /mekano'grafiko/ *a* typewriting, typing; typewritten, typed

mecanografista /mekanogra'fista/ *mf* **mecanógrafo (-fa)** *n* typist

mecate /me'kate/ *m*, *Lat. Am.* twine; coarse person

mecedor /mese'ðor; meθe'ðor/ *a* rocking, swaying. *m*, swing; *Lat. Am.* rocking chair

mecedora /mese'ðora; meθe'ðora/ *f*, rocking chair

mecenas /me'senas; me'θenas/ *m*, Maecenas, patron

mecer /me'ser; me'θer/ *vt* to stir, mix; shake; rock; swing

mecha /'metʃa/ *f*, wick; bit, drill; fuse (of explosives); match (for cannon, etc.); fat bacon (for basting); lock of hair; skein, twist; *Lat. Am.* fright, scare

mechar /me'tʃar/ *vt* *Cul.* to baste, lard

mechero /me'tʃero/ *m*, gas burner; pocket lighter; socket of a candlestick

mechón /me'tʃon/ *m*, tuft, skein, bundle; lock of hair; wisp

medalla /me'ðaya; me'ðaʎa/ *f*, medal; medallion; plaque, round panel; *Inf.* piece of eight (coin)

medallón /meða'ʎon; meða'ʎon/ *m*, large medal; medallion; locket

media /'meðia/ *f*, stocking

mediación /meðia'sion; meðia'θion/ *f*, mediation, arbitration; intercession

mediado /me'ðiaðo/ *a* half-full. **a mediados (del mes,** etc.), toward the middle (of the month, etc.)

mediador /meðia'ðor/ **(-ra)** *n* mediator, arbitrator; intercessor

medianamente /meðiana'mente/ *adv* moderately; passably, fairly well

medianero /meðia'nero/ **(-ra)** *a* middle; intervening, intermediate; mediatory. *n* mediator. *m*, owner of a semidetached house or of one in a row

medianía /meðia'nia/ *f*, average; medium, mediocrity; moderate wealth or means

mediano /me'ðiano/ *a* medium, average; moderate; *Inf.* middling, passable, fair

medianoche /meðia'notʃe/ *f*, midnight

mediante /me'ðiante/ *a* mediatory. *adv* by means of, by, through

mediar /me'ðiar/ *vi* to reach the middle; get halfway; elapse half a given time; intercede, mediate; arbitrate; be in between or in the middle; intervene, take part

medicación /meðika'sion; meðika'θion/ *f*, medication

medicamento /meðika'mento/ *m*, medicine, remedy

medicar /meði'kar/ *vt* to medicate

medicastro /meði'kastro/ *m*, unskilled physician; quack, charlatan

medicina /meði'sina; meði'θina/ *f*, medicine

medicinar /meðisi'nar; meðiθi'nar/ *vt* to attend; treat (patients)

medición /meði'sion; meði'θion/ *f*, measuring; measurements; survey (land); scansion

médico /'meðiko/ **(-ca)** *a* medical. *n* doctor of medicine. **m. de cabecera,** family doctor. **m. general,** general practitioner

medida /me'ðiða/ *f*, measurement; measuring stick; measure, precaution (gen. with *tomar, adoptar,* etc.); gauge; judgment, wisdom; meter; standard. **a m. que,** while, at the same time as. **tomar las medidas (a),** *Fig.* to take a person's measure, sum him up. **tomar sus medidas,** to take his (their) measurements; take the necessary measures. **un traje hecho a m.,** a suit made to measure

medidor /meði'ðor/ *m* *Lat. Am.* gauge, meter. **m. de agua** water meter. **m. de gas** gas meter

medio /'meðio/ *a* half; middle; intermediate; halfway. *m*, half; middle; *Art.* medium; spiritualist medium; proceeding, measure, precaution; environment, medium; middle way, mean; *Sports.* halfback. **m. galope,** canter. **m. tiempo,** part-time (job), *Sports.* halftime. **a medias,** by halves; half, partly. **de por m.,** by halves; in between; in the way. **estar de por m.,** to be in the way; take part in. *Inf.* **quitar de en m.,** to get rid of. *Inf.* **quitarse de en m.,** to go away, remove oneself

mediocre /me'ðiokre/ *a* mediocre

mediodía /meðio'ðia/ *m*, noon, meridian; south

medioeval /meðioe'βal/ *a* medieval

mediquillo /meði'kiyo; meði'kiʎo/ *m*, *Inf.* quack; medicine man (in the Philippines)

medir /me'ðir/ *vt irr* to measure; (metrics) scan; survey (land); compare; *vr* measure one's words; act with restraint. See *pedir*

meditabundo /meðita'βundo/ *a* pensive, meditative, thoughtful

meditación /meðita'sion; meðita'θion/ *f*, meditation, consideration, reflection

meditador /meðita'ðor/ *a* meditative, thoughtful

meditar /meði'tar/ *vt* to meditate, consider, muse

meditativo /meðita'tiβo/ *a* meditative

mediterráneo /meðite'rraneo/ *a* mediterranean; inland, landlocked

médium /'meðium/ *m*, *Spirit.* medium

medra /'meðra/ *f*, progress; improvement; betterment; growth; prosperity

medrar /me'ðrar/ *vi* to flourish, grow; become prosperous or improve one's position

medro /'meðro/ *m*, improvement, progress. See **medra**

medroso /me'ðroso/ *a* timid, frightened; frightful, horrible

médula /'meðula/ *f*, marrow; *Bot.* pith; *Fig.* essence, core

medusa /me'ðusa/ *f*, jellyfish
mefistofélico /mefisto'feliko/ *a* Mephistophelian
mefítico /me'fitiko/ *a* noxious, mephitic, poisonous
megáfono /me'gafono/ *m*, megaphone
megalómano /mega'lomano/ **(-na)** *n* megalomaniac
mejicano /mehi'kano/ **(-na)** *a* and *n* Mexican
Méjico /'mehiko/ Mexico
mejilla /me'hiya; me'hiʎa/ *f*, *Anat.* cheek
mejillón /mehi'yon; mehi'ʎon/ *m*, sea mussel
mejor /me'hor/ *a comp* **bueno** better. *adv* better;
rather; sooner; preferably. *a sup* **bueno. el, la, lo me-**
jor; los, las mejores, the best; most preferable. **m.**
que m., better and better. *Inf.* **a lo m.,** probably, in
all probability. **tanto m.,** so much the better
mejora /me'hora/ *f*, improvement; bettering; progress; higher bid (at auctions)
mejorable /meho'raβle/ *a* improvable
mejoramiento /mehora'miento/ *m*, betterment, improvement
mejorar /meho'rar/ *vt* to improve; better; outbid; *vi*
grow better (in health); improve (weather); make
progress; rally (of markets). **Mejorando lo presente,**
Present company excepted
mejoría /meho'ria/ *f*, improvement, progress; betterment; superiority; advantage, profit
mejunje /me'hunhe/ *m*, *Inf.* brew, potion, cure-all,
stuff; *Lat. Am.* mess
melado /me'laðo/ *a* honey-colored. *m*, cane syrup
melancolía /melanko'lia/ *f*, melancholia; sadness, depression, melancholy
melancólico /melan'koliko/ *a* melancholy, sad; depressing
melaza /me'lasa; me'laθa/ *f*, molasses
melena /me'lena/ *f*, long side whiskers; loose, flowing hair (in women); overlong hair (in men); lion's
mane. *Inf.* **andar a la m.,** to start a fight or quarrel.
Inf. **traer a la m.,** to drag by the hair, force
melifluo /me'lifluo/ *a* mellifluous, sweet-voiced; honeyed
melindre /me'lindre/ *m*, honey fritter; affectation,
scruple, fastidiousness; narrow ribbon
melindroso /melin'droso/ *a* overfastidious, affected,
prudish
mella /'meya; 'meʎa/ *f*, nick, notch; dent; gap;
harm, damage (to reputation, etc.). **hacer m.,** *Fig.* to
make an impression (on the mind); *Mil.* breach, drive
a wedge
mellar /me'yar; me'ʎar/ *vt* to nick, notch; dent; damage
mellizo /me'yiso; me'ʎiθo/ **(-za)** *a* and *n* twin (fraternal)
melocotón /meloko'ton/ *m*, peach; peach tree
melocotonero /melokoto'nero/ *m*, peach tree
melodía /melo'ðia/ *f*, melody, tune; melodiousness
melódico /me'loðiko/ *a* melodic, melodious
melodioso /melo'ðioso/ *a* melodious, tuneful, sweet-
sounding
melodrama /melo'ðrama/ *m*, melodrama
melodramático /meloðra'matiko/ *a* melodramatic
melón /me'lon/ *m*, melon
melosidad /melosi'ðað/ *f*, sweetness
meloso /me'loso/ *a* honeyed; sweet; gentle; mellifluous
membrana /mem'brana/ *f*, membrane
membrete /mem'brete/ *m*, note, memorandum; note
or card of invitation; superscription, heading; address
(of person)
membrillo /mem'briyo; mem'briʎo/ *m*, quince tree;
quince; quince jelly
membrudo /mem'bruðo/ *a* brawny, strong, muscular
memo /'memo/ *a* silly, stupid
memorable /memo'raβle/ *a* memorable
memorándum /memo'randum/ *m*, notebook, jotter;
memorandum
memorar /memo'rar/ **(se)** *vt* and *vr* to remember, recall
memoria /me'moria/ *f*, memory; remembrance, recollection; monument; memorial; report; essay, article; codicil; memorandum; record, chronicle; *pl*
regards, compliments, greetings; memoirs; memo-

randa. *Inf.* **m. de grillo,** poor memory. **de m.,** by
heart. **flaco de m.,** forgetful. **hacer m.,** to remember
memorial /memo'rial/ *m*, notebook; memorial, petition
memorioso /memo'rioso/ *a* mindful, unforgetful
mena /'mena/ *f*, *Mineral.* ore
menaje /me'nahe/ *m*, household or school equipment
or furniture
mención /men'sion; men'θion/ *f*, mention. **m. hon-**
orífica, honorable mention. **hacer m. de,** to mention
mencionar /mensio'nar; menθio'nar/ *vt* to mention
mendacidad /mendasi'ðað; mendaθi'ðað/ *f*, mendacity, untruthfulness
mendaz /men'das; men'daθ/ *a* mendacious, untruthful
mendicante /mendi'kante/ *a* begging; *Eccl.* mendicant. *mf* beggar
mendicidad /mendisi'ðað; mendiθi'ðað/ *f*, mendicancy, begging
mendigar /mendi'gar/ *vt* to beg for alms; entreat,
supplicate
mendigo /men'digo/ **(-ga)** *n* beggar
mendoso /men'doso/ *a* mendacious, untruthful; mistaken
mendrugo /men'drugo/ *m*, crust of bread
menear /mene'ar/ *vt* to sway, move; wag; shake;
manage, control, direct; *vr Inf.* get a move on; sway,
move; wriggle
meneo /me'neo/ *m*, swaying movement; wagging;
shaking; wriggling; management, direction; *Aer.*
bump; *Inf.* spanking
menester /menes'ter/ *m*, lack, shortage; necessity;
occupation, employment; *pl* physical necessities; *Inf.*
tools, implements, equipment. **haber m.,** to need, require. **ser m.,** to be necessary or requisite
menesteroso /meneste'roso/ *a* indigent, poverty-
stricken, needy
menestra /me'nestra/ *f*, vegetable soup; dried vegetable (gen. *pl*)
mengano /men'gano/ **(-na)** *n* so-and-so (used instead of the name of the person)
mengua /'mengua/ *f*, decrease; lack, shortage; waning (of the moon, etc.); dishonor, disgrace; poverty
menguado /men'guaðo/ **(-da)** *a* timid, cowardly;
silly, stupid; mean, avaricious. *n* coward; fool; skinflint. *m*, narrowing stitch when knitting socks
menguante /men'guante/ *a* ebb; waning; decreasing. *f*, ebb tide; decadence, decline. **m. de la luna,**
waning of the moon
menguar /men'guar/ *vi* to decrease; decline, decay;
wane; ebb; narrow (socks); *vt* diminish; disgrace,
discredit
menina /me'nina/ *f*, child attendant (on Spanish royalty)
menino /me'nino/ *m*, Spanish royal page; little
dandy
menjurje /men'hurhe/ *m*, See **mejunje**
menopausia /meno'pausia/ *f*, menopause
menor /me'nor/ *a comp* less, smaller; younger, minor; *Mus.* minor. *m*, minor. *f*, (logic) minor. *a sup* **el,**
la, lo m.; los, las menores, the least; smallest;
youngest. **m. de edad,** minor (in age). **por m.,** at retail; in detail
menoría /meno'ria/ *f*, subordination, dependence; inferiority; minority (underage); childhood, youth
menorista /meno'rista/ *Lat. Am.*, *a* retail; *mf* retailer
menos /'menos/ *adv* less; minus; least; except. **m.**
de or **m. que,** less than. **al m.** or **por lo m.,** at least. **a**
m. que, unless. **De m. nos hizo Dios,** Never say die,
Nothing is impossible. **poco más o m.,** more or less,
about
menoscabar /menoska'βar/ *vt* to lessen, diminish;
decrease; deteriorate, damage; disgrace, discredit
menoscabo /menos'kaβo/ *m*, decrease, diminishment; harm, damage, loss
menospreciable /menospre'siaβle; menospre'θiaβle/
a despicable, contemptible
menospreciador /menospresia'ðor; menospreθia'ðor/ **(-ra)** *a* scornful. *n* scorner, despiser

menospreciar /menospre'siar; menospre'θiar/ *vt* to despise, scorn; underestimate, have a poor opinion of

menospreciativo /menospresia'tiβo; menospreθia'tiβo/ *a* scornful, slighting, derisive

menosprecio /menos'presio; menos'preθio/ *m*, scorn, derision; underestimation

mensaje /men'sahe/ *m*, message; official communication

mensajería /mensahe'ria/ *f*, carrier service; steamship line

mensajero /mensa'hero/ **(-ra)** *n* messenger; errand boy

menso, -a /'menso/ *a*, *Mexico* dumb, silly, stupid

menstruación /menstrua'sion; menstrua'θion/ *f*, menstruation

menstruar /menstru'ar/ *vi* to menstruate

mensual /men'sual/ *a* monthly

mensualidad /mensuali'ðað/ *f*, monthly salary, monthly payment

mensurable /mensu'raβle/ *a* measurable

mensurar /mensu'rar/ *vt* to measure

menta /'menta/ *f*, menthe, mint; peppermint

mentado /men'taðo/ *a* celebrated, distinguished, famous

mental /men'tal/ *a* mental

mentalidad /mentali'ðað/ *f*, mentality

mentalmente /mental'mente/ *adv* mentally

mentar /men'tar/ *vt irr* to mention. See **sentar**

mentas /'mentas/ *fpl*, *Argentina* reputation, gossip

mente /'mente/ *f*, mind; intelligence, understanding; will, intention

mentecatería /mentekate'ria/ *f*, folly, stupidity

mentecato /mente'kato/ **(-ta)** *a* foolish, silly; feebleminded, simple. *n* fool, idiot

mentir /men'tir/ *vi irr* to lie, be untruthful; deceive, mislead; falsify; *Poet.* belie; disagree, be incompatible; *vt* break a promise, disappoint. **m. como un bellaco,** to lie like a trooper. See **sentir**

mentira /men'tira/ *f*, lie, falsehood; error (in writing); *Inf.* white spot (on a fingernail); cracking (of fingerjoints). **m. oficiosa,** white lie. **Parece m.,** It seems incredible

mentiroso /menti'roso/ *a* lying, false; full of errors (literary works); deceptive

mentís /men'tis/ *m*, giving the lie (literally, you lie); proof, demonstration (of error)

mentol /'mentol/ *m*, menthol

mentón /men'ton/ *m*, chin

menú /me'nu/ *m*, menu

menudamente /menuða'mente/ *adv* minutely; in detail, circumstantially

menudear /menuðe'ar/ *vt* to do frequently; do repeatedly; *vi* happen frequently; describe in detail; *Com.* sell by retail

menudencia /menu'ðensia; menu'ðenθia/ *f*, minuteness, smallness; exactness, care, accuracy; trifle, worthless object; small matter; *pl* offal; pork sausages

menudeo /menu'ðeo/ *m*, repetition; description in detail; *Com.* retail. **al m.,** at retail

menudillos /menu'ðiyos; menu'ðiʎos/ *m pl*, giblets; offal

menudo /menu'ðo/ *a* minute, tiny; despicable; thin; small; vulgar; meticulous, exact; small (money). *m*, small coal; *m pl*, offal, entrails; small change (money). **a m.,** often, frequently. **por m.,** in detail, carefully; *Com.* in small lots

meñique /me'ɲike/ *a Inf.* very small. *m*, little finger (in full, **dedo m.**)

meollo /me'oyo; me'oʎo/ *m*, brain; *Anat.* marrow; *Fig.* essence, core, substance; understanding; *Inf.* **no tener m. (una cosa),** to be worthless, unsubstantial (things)

me palpita que... /me pal'pita ke / *Argentina*, I have a hunch that...

mequetrefe /meke'trefe/ *m*, *Inf.* coxcomb, whippersnapper

meramente /mera'mente/ *adv* solely, simply, merely

mercachifle /merkat'ʃifle/ *m*, peddler; small merchant

mercadear /merkaðe'ar/ *vi* to trade, traffic

mercadeo /merka'ðeo/ *m*, marketing (study of markets)

mercader /merka'ðer/ *m*, dealer, merchant, trader. **m. de grueso,** wholesaler

mercadería /merkaðe'ria/ *f*, See **mercancía**

mercado /mer'kaðo/ *m*, market; marketplace

mercancía /merkan'sia; merkan'θia/ *f*, goods, merchandise; commerce, trade, traffic

mercante /mer'kante/ *a* trading; commercial. *m*, merchant, dealer, trader

mercantil /merkan'til/ *a* mercantile, commercial

merced /mer'seð; mer'θeð/ *f*, salary, remuneration; favor, benefit, kindness; will, desire, pleasure; mercy, grace; courtesy title given to untitled person (e.g. *vuestra m.,* your honor. Has now become *usted* and is universally used). **m. a,** thanks to. **estar uno a m. de,** to live at someone else's expense, be dependent on

mercenario /merse'nario; merθe'nario/ **(-ia)** *n Eccl.* member of the Order of la Merced. *m*, *Mil.* mercenary; day laborer. *a* mercenary

mercería /merse'ria; merθe'ria/ *f*, haberdashery, mercery

mercerizar /merseri'sar; merθeri'θar/ *vt* to mercerize

mercero /mer'sero; mer'θero/ *m*, haberdasher, mercer

mercurio /mer'kurio/ *m*, mercury, quicksilver; *Astron.* Mercury

merecedor /merese'ðor; mereθe'ðor/ *a* deserving, worthy

merecer /mere'ser; mere'θer/ *vt irr* to deserve, be worthy of; attain, achieve; be worth; *vi* deserve, be deserving. **m. bien de,** to deserve well of; have a claim on the gratitude of. See **conocer**

merecido /mere'siðo; mere'θiðo/ *m*, due reward

merecimiento /meresi'miento; mereθi'miento/ *m*, desert; merit

merendar /meren'dar/ *vi irr* to have lunch; pry into another's affairs; *vt* have (a certain food) for lunch. *Inf.* **merendarse (una cosa),** to obtain (a thing), have it in one's pocket. See **recomendar**

merendero /meren'dero/ *m*, lunchroom; tearoom

merengue /me'reŋgue/ *m*, *Cul.* meringue. **el Merengue,** Latin dance and music originating in the Dominican Republic

meridiana /meri'ðiana/ *f*, daybed, chaise longue; siesta

meridiano /meri'ðiano/ *a* meridian. *m*, meridian. **a la meridiana,** at noon

meridional /meriðio'nal/ *a* meridional, southern

merienda /me'rienda/ *f*, tea, snack; lunch; *Inf.* hunchback. *Inf.* **juntar meriendas,** to join forces, combine interests

merino /me'rino/ *a* merino. *m*, merino wool; shepherd of merino sheep

mérito /'merito/ *m*, merit; desert; worth, excellence. **de m.,** excellent, notable. **hacer m. de,** to mention

meritorio /meri'torio/ *a* meritorious. *m*, unpaid worker, learner

merluza /mer'lusa; mer'luθa/ *f*, hake; *Inf.* drinking bout. *Inf.* **pescar una m.,** to get drunk

merma /'merma/ *f*, decrease, drop; loss, waste, reduction; leakage

mermar /mer'mar/ *vi* to diminish, waste away, decrease; evaporate; leak; *vt* filch, pilfer; reduce, decrease

mermelada /merme'laða/ *f*, preserve; jam; marmalade

mero /'mero/ *a* mere; simple; plain

merodeador /meroðea'ðor/ *a* marauding. *m*, marauder, raider

merodear /meroðe'ar/ *vi* to maraud, raid; *Mexico* make money illegally

merodeo /mero'ðeo/ *m*, raiding, marauding

mes /'mes/ *m*, month; menses, menstruation

mesa /'mesa/ *f*, table; board, directorate; meseta, tableland; staircase landing; flat (of a sword, etc.); game of billiards. **m. de batalla,** post office sorting table. **m. de caballete,** trestle table. **m. de noche,**

bedside table. **m. de tenis,** *Mexico* tennis court. **m. de tijeras,** folding table. **m. giratoria,** turntable. **alzar** (*or* **levantar**) **la m.,** to clear the table. **cubrir** (*or* **poner**) **la m.,** to set the table

mesada /me'saða/ *f,* monthly wages, monthly payment

mesadura /mesa'ðura/ *f,* tearing of the hair or beard

mesarse /me'sarse/ *vr* to tear one's hair or beard

mesenterio /mesen'terio/ *m,* mesentery

mesera /me'sera/ *f Mexico* waitress

mesero /me'sero/ *m Mexico* waiter

meseta /me'seta/ *f,* staircase landing; plateau, tableland

mesiánico /me'sianiko/ *a* Messianic

Mesías /me'sias/ *m,* Messiah

mesilla /me'siya; me'siʎa/ *f,* small table; laughing admonition; landing (of a stair)

mesnada /mes'naða/ *f,* association, company, society

mesocracia /meso'krasia; meso'kraθia/ *f,* mesocracy; middle class, bourgeoisie

mesón /me'son/ *m,* inn, tavern

mesonero /meso'nero/ **(-ra)** *n* innkeeper; *Venezuela* waiter, waitress

mesta /'mesta/ *f,* ancient order of sheep farmers; *pl* confluence, meeting (of rivers)

mester /'mester/ *m,* craft, occupation. **m. de clerecía,** learned poetic meter of the Spanish Middle Ages. **m. de juglaría,** popular poetry and troubadour songs

mestizo /mes'tiso; mes'tiθo/ *a* half-breed; crossbreed, *Lat. Am.* of mixed Castilian and Native American ancestry

mesura /me'sura/ *f,* sedateness; dignity; courtesy; moderation

mesurado /mesu'raðo/ *a* sedate; dignified; moderate, restrained, temperate

meta /'meta/ *f,* goalpost *Fig.* aim, end; goal; goalkeeper

metabolismo /metaβo'lismo/ *m,* metabolism

metáfora /me'tafora/ *f,* metaphor

metafórico /meta'foriko/ *a* metaphorical

metal /me'tal/ *m,* metal; brass; timbre of the voice; state, condition; quality, substance; *Herald.* gold or silver; *Mus.* brass (instruments)

metalario /meta'lario/ *m,* metalworker

metálico /me'taliko/ *a* metallic. *m,* metalworker; coin, specie; bullion

metalistería /metaliste'ria/ *f,* metalwork

metalizar /metali'sar; metali'θar/ *vt* to metallize, make metallic; *vr* become metallized; grow greedy for money

metalurgia /metalur'hia/ *f,* metallurgy

metalúrgico /meta'lurhiko/ *a* metallurgical. *m,* metallurgist

metamorfosis /metamor'fosis/ *f,* metamorphosis

metano /me'tano/ *m,* methane

metate /me'tate/ *m, Central America, Mexico* flat stone for grinding and pounding

metátesis /me'tatesis/ *f,* metathesis

metedor /mete'ðor/ **(-ra)** *n* placer, inserter; smuggler, contrabandist

metellón, -ona /mete'jon; mete'ʎon/ *a, Mexico* meddling, meddlesome

metempsicosis /metempsi'kosis/ *f,* metempsychosis

metemuertos /mete'muertos/ *Inf.* meddler, Nosy Parker

meteórico /mete'oriko/ *a* meteoric

meteorito /meteo'rito/ *m,* meteorite

meteoro /mete'oro/ *m,* meteor

meteorología /meteorolo'hia/ *f,* meteorology

meteorológico /meteoro'lohiko/ *a* meteorological

meteorologista /meteorolo'hista/ *mf* meteorologist; weather forecaster

meter /me'ter/ *vt* to place; put; introduce, insert; stake (gambling); smuggle; cause, occasion; place close together; persuade to take part in; *Sew.* take in fullness; deceive, humbug; cram in, pack tightly; *Naut.* take in sail; *vr* interfere, butt in; meddle (with); take up, follow (occupations); be overfamiliar; disembogue, empty itself (rivers, etc.); attack with the sword; (*with prep a*) follow (occupations); become,

turn (e.g. *meterse a predicar,* to turn preacher); (*with con*) pick a quarrel with. **meterse en precisiones,** to go into details. *Inf.* **meterse en todo,** to be very meddlesome

metesillas y sacamuertos /mete'siyas i saka'muertos; mete'siʎas i saka'muertos/ *m,* scene shifter, stagehand

metiche /me'titʃe/ *a, Mexico* = **metellón**

meticulosidad /metikulosi'ðað/ *f,* meticulosity; timorousness

meticuloso /metiku'loso/ *a* meticulous, fussy; timid, nervous

metido /me'tiðo/ *a* tight; crowded; crabbed (of handwriting). *m, Sew.* material for letting out (seams). **m. en años,** quite old (person)

metílico /me'tiliko/ *a* methylic

metimiento /meti'miento/ *m,* insertion, introduction; influence, sway

metódico /me'toðiko/ *a* methodical

método /'metoðo/ *m,* method

metodología /metoðolo'hia/ *f,* methodology

metralla /me'traya; me'traʎa/ *f, Mil.* grapeshot, shrapnel

métrica /'metrika/ *f,* metrics

métrico /'metriko/ *a* metric; metrical

metro /'metro/ *m,* (verse) meter; meter (measurement); subway, underground railway

metrónomo /me'tronomo/ *m,* metronome

metrópoli /me'tropoli/ *f,* metropolis, capital; see of a metropolitan bishop; mother country

metropolitano /metropoli'tano/ *a* metropolitan. *m,* metropolitan bishop

mexicano /meksi'kano/ *Lat. Am.* = **mejicano**

México /'mehiko/ *Lat. Am.* = **Méjico**

mezcla /'meskla; 'meθkla/ *f,* mixture; blend, combination; mixed cloth, tweed; mortar

mezclar /mes'klar; meθ'klar/ *vt* to mix, blend, combine; *vr* mix, mingle; take part; interfere, meddle; intermarry

mezcolanza /mesko'lansa; meθko'lanθa/ *f, Inf.* hodgepodge

mezquindad /meskin'dað; meθkin'dað/ *f,* poverty; indigence; miserliness; paltriness; meanness, poorness

mezquino /mes'kino; meθ'kino/ *a* needy, impoverished; miserly, stingy; small, diminutive; unhappy; mean, paltry

mezquita /mes'kita; meθ'kita/ *f,* mosque

mi /'mi/ *poss pron* my. *m, Mus.* mi, E

mí /'mi/ *pers pron acc gen dat 1st pers sing* me. Used only after prepositions (e.g. *Lo hicieron por mí,* They did it for me)

miaja /'miaha/ *f,* See **migaja**

miasma /'miasma/ *m,* miasma

miasmático /mias'matiko/ *a* miasmatic, malarious

miau /'miau/ *m,* meow

mica /'mika/ *f, Mineral.* mica; coquette, flirt

micho /'mitʃo/ **(-cha)** *n Inf.* puss, pussycat

micología /mikolo'hia/ *f,* mycology

micra /'mikra/ *f,* micron, thousandth part of a millimeter

micro /'mikro/ *m, Chile, Peru* (large, express) bus; *elsewhere in Lat. Am.* minibus

microbiano /mikro'βiano/ *a* microbial, microbic

microbio /mi'kroβio/ *m,* microbe

microbiología /mikroβiolo'hia/ *f,* microbiology

microbrigada /mikroβri'gaða/ *f,* team of volunteer workers (in Castroist Cuba)

microchip /mikro'tʃip/ *m,* microchip

microcosmo /mikro'kosmo/ *m,* microcosm

micrófono /mi'krofono/ *m,* microphone

microonda /mikro'onda/ *f,* microwave

microscópico /mikros'kopiko/ *a* microscopic

microscopio /mikros'kopio/ *m,* microscope

miedo /'mieðo/ *m,* fear, apprehension, terror. **m. al público,** stagefright. **tener m.,** to be afraid

miedoso /mie'ðoso/ *a Inf.* fearful, nervous

miel /miel/ *f,* honey. **m. de caña,** sugarcane syrup. *Inf.* **quedarse a media m.,** to see one's pleasure

snatched away. *Inf.* **ser de mieles,** to be most pleasant or agreeable
mielitis /mie'litis/ *f,* myelitis
miembro /mi'embro/ *m, Anat.* limb; penis; member, associate; part, portion, section; *Math.* member
miente /'miente/ *f,* thought, imagination, mind. **parar** *or* **poner mientes en,** to consider, think about. **venírsele a las mientes,** to occur to one's mind
mientras /'mientras/ *adv* while. **m. más...,** the more.... **m. que,** while (e.g. *m. que esperaba en el jardín,* while he was waiting in the garden). **m. tanto,** in the meanwhile
miércoles /'mierkoles/ *m,* Wednesday. **m. de ceniza,** Ash Wednesday
mies /'mies/ *f,* cereal plant, grain; harvest time; *pl* grain fields
miga /'miga/ *f,* breadcrumb; crumb; *Inf.* essence, core; substance; bit, scrap; *pl* fried breadcrumbs. *Inf.* **hacer buenas** (*or* **malas**) **migas,** to get on well (*or* badly) together
migaja /mi'gaha/ *f,* breadcrumb; bit, scrap; trifle, mere nothing; *pl* crumbs (from the table); remains, remnants
migajón /miga'hon/ *m,* crumb (of a loaf): *Fig. Inf.* essence, substance, core
migración /migra'sion; migra'θion/ *f,* migration; emigration
migraña /mi'graɲa/ *f,* migraine
migratorio /migra'torio/ *a* migratory
mijo /'miho/ *m,* millet; maize
mil /mil/ *a* thousand; thousandth; many, large number. *m,* thousand; thousandth. *Inf.* **Son las m. y quinientas,** It's extremely late (of the hour)
miladi /mi'laði/ *f,* my lady
milagrero /mila'grero/ *a Inf.* miraculous
milagro /mi'lagro/ *m,* miracle; marvel, wonder. **¡M.!** Amazing! Just fancy!
milagroso /mila'groso/ *a* miraculous; marvelous, wonderful
mildeu /'mildeu/ *m,* mildew
milenario /mile'nario/ *a* millenary; millennial. *m,* millenary; millennium
milésimo /mi'lesimo/ *a* thousandth
milicia /mi'lisia; mi'liθia/ *f,* militia; military; art of war; military profession
miliciano /mili'siano; mili'θiano/ *a* military. *m,* militiaman
milico /mi'liko/ *m, Lat. Am.,* derogatory soldier
miligramo /mili'gramo/ *m,* milligram
mililitro /mili'litro/ *m,* milliliter
milímetro /mi'limetro/ *m,* millimeter
militante /mili'tante/ *a* militant
militar /mili'tar/ *a* military. *m,* soldier. *vi* to fight in the army; struggle (for a cause); *Fig.* militate (e.g. *Las circunstancias militan en favor de* (*or contra*) *sus ideas,* Circumstances militate against his ideas)
militarismo /milita'rismo/ *m,* militarism
militarista /milita'rista/ *a* militaristic. *mf* militarist
militarizar /militari'sar; militari'θar/ *vt* to militarize; make war-like
milla /'miya; 'miʎa/ *f,* mile
millar /mi'yar; mi'ʎar/ *m,* thousand; vast number (gen. *pl*)
millón /mi'yon; mi'ʎon/ *m,* million
millonario /miyo'nario; miʎo'nario/ (**-ia**) *a* and *n* millionaire
millonésimo /miyo'nesimo; miʎo'nesimo/ *a* millionth
milmillonésimo /milmiyo'nesimo; milmiʎo'nesimo/ *a* billionth
milpa /'milpa/ *f, Central America, Mexico* corn field
milpero, -a /mil'pero/ *mf, Lat. Am.* corn grower
mimar /mi'mar/ *vt* to spoil, overindulge; caress, fondle
mimbre /'mimbre/ *mf* osier; willow tree. *m,* wicker
mimbrear /mimbre'ar/ *vi* to sway, bend
mimbrera /mim'brera/ *f,* osier; osier bed; willow
mímica /'mimika/ *f,* mimicry; mime
mímico /'mimiko/ *a* mimic

mimo /'mimo/ *m,* mimic, buffoon; mime; caress, expression of affection, tenderness; overindulgence
mimoso /mi'moso/ *a* affectionate, demonstrative
mina /'mina/ *f,* mine; excavation, mining; underground passage; lead (in a pencil); (*Mil. Nav.*) mine; *Fig.* gold mine. *Mil.* **m. terrestre,** landmine
minador /mina'ðor/ *m,* excavator; *Nav.* minelayer; *Mil.* sapper
minar /mi'nar/ *vt* to excavate, mine; *Fig.* undermine; (*Mil. Nav.*) mine; work hard for
minarete /mina'rete/ *m,* minaret
mineraje /mine'rahe/ *m,* exploitation of a mine, mining; mineral products
mineral /mine'ral/ *a* and *m,* mineral
mineralogía /mineralo'hia/ *f,* mineralogy
mineralógico /minera'lohiko/ *a* mineralogical
mineralogista /mineralo'hista/ *mf* mineralogist
minería /mine'ria/ *f,* mining, mineworking; mineworkers
minero /mi'nero/ *a* mining. *m,* miner, mineworker; source, origin
minga /'miŋga/ *f, Lat. Am.* voluntary communal labor
miniar /mini'ar/ *vt Art.* to illuminate
miniatura /minia'tura/ *f,* miniature
miniaturista /miniatu'rista/ *mf* miniaturist
mínima /'minima/ *f, Mus.* minim; very small thing or portion
mínimo /'minimo/ *a sup* **pequeño** smallest; minimum; meticulous, precise. *m,* minimum; (meteorological) trough
ministerial /ministe'rial/ *a* ministerial
ministerio /minis'terio/ *m,* office, post; *Polit.* cabinet; ministry; government office; government department.
ministrar /minis'trar/ *vt* and *vi* to fill; administer (an office); *vt* minister to; give, provide
ministro /mi'nistro/ *m,* instrument, agency; minister of state, cabinet minister; clergyman, minister; minister plenipotentiary; policeman. **m. de estado,** secretary of state. **m. de gobernación,** secretary of the interior. **m. de hacienda,** treasurer. **m. de relaciones extranjeras,** foreign secretary. **primer m.** prime minister
minoración /minora'sion; minora'θion/ *f,* reduction, decrease
minorar /mino'rar/ *vt* to diminish, decrease
minoría /mino'ria/ *f,* minority, smaller number; minority (of age)
minoridad /minori'ðað/ *f,* minority (of age)
minorista /mino'rista/ *mf, Lat. Am.* retailer
minucia /mi'nusia; minu'θia/ *f,* smallness; morsel, mite; *pl* details, trifles, minutiae
minucioso /minu'sioso; minu'θioso/ *a* meticulous, precise, minute
minúsculo /mi'nuskulo/ *a* minute, very small
minuta /mi'nuta/ *f,* memorandum, minute; note; list, catalogue
minutero /minu'tero/ *m,* minute hand (of a clock)
minuto /mi'nuto/ *a* minute, very small. *m,* minute
mío /'mio/ *m.* **mía,** *f,* (*m pl.* **míos,** *f pl.* **mías**) *poss pron* mine (e.g. *Las flores son mías,* The flowers are mine). **Mi** is used before nouns, *not* **mío.** Also used with article (e.g. *Este sombrero no es el mío,* This hat is not mine (my one)). **de mío,** by myself, without help. *Inf.* **¡Esta es la mía!** This is my chance!
miope /mi'ope/ *a* myopic. *mf* myopic person
miopía /mio'pia/ *f,* shortsightedness
miosota /mio'sota/ *f,* myosotis, forget-me-not
mira /'mira/ *f,* sight (optical instruments, guns); intention, design; *Mil.* watchtower; care, precaution. **andar, estar** *or* **quedar a la m.,** to be vigilant, be on the lookout
mirada /mi'raða/ *f,* look; gaze. **lanzar miradas de carnero degollado** (**a**), to cast sheep's eyes at
miradero /mira'ðero/ *m,* object of attention, cynosure; observation post, lookout
mirador /mira'ðor/ (**-ra**) *n* spectator. *m, Archit.* oriel; enclosed balcony; observatory
miramiento /mira'miento/ *m,* observation, gazing;

scruple, consideration; precaution, care; thoughtfulness

mirar /mi'rar/ *vt* to look at, gaze at; observe, behold; watch; consider, look after; value, appreciate; concern; believe, think; (*with prep a*) overlook, look on to; face; (*with por*) care for, protect; look after, consider. **m. contra el gobierno,** *Inf.* to be squint-eyed. **m. de hito en hito,** to look over, stare at. **mirarse en (una cosa),** to consider (a matter) carefully

miríada /mi'riaða/ *f,* myriad, huge number

mirilla /mi'riya; mi'riʎa/ *f,* peephole

miriñaque /miri'ɲake/ *m,* trinket, ornament; crinoline

mirlarse /mir'larse/ *vr Inf.* to give oneself airs

mirlo /'mirlo/ *m,* blackbird; *Inf.* pompous air

mirón /mi'ron/ *a* inquisitive, curious

mirra /'mirra/ *f,* myrrh

mirto /'mirto/ *m,* myrtle

misa /'misa/ *f,* (*Eccl. Mus.*) mass. **m. de difuntos,** requiem mass. **m. del gallo,** midnight mass. **m. mayor,** high mass. **m. rezada,** low mass. **como en m.,** in profound silence. **oír m.,** to attend mass

misal /mi'sal/ *m,* missal

misantropía /misantro'pia/ *f,* misanthropy

misantrópico /misan'tropiko/ *a* misanthropic

misántropo /mi'santropo/ *m,* misanthrope

miscelánea /misse'lanea; misθe'lanea/ *f,* medley, assortment, miscellany

misceláneo /misse'laneo; misθe'laneo/ *a* assorted, miscellaneous, mixed

miscible /mis'siβle; mis'θiβle/ *a* mixable

miserable /mise'raβle/ *a* miserable, unhappy; timid, pusillanimous; miserly, mean; despicable

miseria /mi'seria/ *f,* misery; poverty, destitution; avarice, miserliness; *Inf.* poor thing, trifle

misericordia /miseri'korðia/ *f,* mercy, compassion

misericordioso /miserikor'ðioso/ *a* merciful, compassionate

mísero /'misero/ *a Inf.* fond of churchgoing

misérrimo /mi'serrimo/ *a superl.* most miserable

misión /mi'sion/ *f,* mission; vocation; commission, duty, errand

misionar /misio'nar/ *vi* to missionize, act as a missionary; *Eccl.* conduct a mission

misionero /misio'nero/ *m,* missioner; missionary

Misisipi, el /misi'sipi, el/ the Mississippi

misiva /mi'siβa/ *f,* missive

mismo /'mismo/ *a* same; similar; self (e.g. *ellos mismos,* they themselves); very, same (e.g. *Ahora m. voy,* I'm going this very minute). **Me da lo m.,** It makes no difference to me. **por lo m.,** for that self-same reason

misógamo /mi'sogamo/ **(-ma)** *n* misogamist

misógino /mi'sohino/ *m,* misogynist

misterio /mis'terio/ *m,* mystery

misterioso /miste'rioso/ *a* mysterious

mística /'mistika/ *f,* **misticismo** *m,* mysticism

místico /'mistiko/ *a* mystic

mistificación /mistifika'sion/ *f,* mistifika'θion/ *f,* mystification; mystery; deception

mistificar /mistifi'kar/ *vt* to mystify; deceive

Misuri, el /mi'suri, el/ the Missouri

mitad /mi'taɗ/ *f,* half; middle, center. *Fig. Inf.* **cara m.,** better half. *Inf.* **mentir por la m. de la barba,** to lie barefacedly

mítico /'mitiko/ *a* mythical

mitigación /mitiga'sion; mitiga'θion/ *f,* mitigation

mitigador /mitiga'ðor/ **(-ra)** *a* mitigatory. *n* mitigator

mitigar /miti'gar/ *vt* to mitigate, moderate, alleviate; appease

mitin /'mitin/ *m,* mass meeting

mito /'mito/ *m,* myth

mitología /mitolo'hia/ *f,* mythology

mitológico /mito'lohiko/ *a* mythological

mitologista, mitólogo /mitolo'hista, mi'tologo/ *m,* mythologist

mitón /mi'ton/ *m,* mitten

mitra /'mitra/ *f,* miter; bishopric; archbishopric

mitrado /mi'traðo/ *a* mitred

mixto /'miksto/ *a* mixed, blended; hybrid; composite; mongrel. *m,* mixed train (carrying freight and passengers); sulphur match

mixtura /miks'tura/ *f,* mixture, blend; compound; mixture (medicine)

¡miz, miz! /'mis, mis; miθ, miθ/ puss, puss!

mobiliario /moβi'liario/ *a* movable (goods). *m,* furniture

moblaje /mo'βlahe/ *m,* household goods and furniture

mocasín /moka'sin/ *m,* moccasin

mocedad /mose'ðaɗ; moθe'ðaɗ/ *f,* youth, adolescence; mischief, prank. *Fig. Inf.* **correr sus mocedades,** to sow one's wild oats

mochila /mo'tʃila/ *f,* knapsack; nosebag; military rations for a march

mocho /'motʃo/ *a* blunted, topless, lopped; *Inf.* shorn, cropped. *m,* butt, butt end

mochuelo /mo'tʃuelo/ *m,* owl; *Inf.* difficult job

moción /mo'sion; mo'θion/ *f,* motion, movement; impulse, tendency; divine inspiration; motion (of a debate)

moco /'moko/ *m,* mucus; candle drips; snuff of a candle. *Inf.* **caérsele el m.,** to be very simple, be easily deceived

mocoso /mo'koso/ **(-sa)** *a* running of the nose, sniffling; unimportant, insignificant. *n* coxcomb, stripling; *Lat. Am.* child

moda /'moða/ *f,* fashion. **estar** *or* **ser de m.,** to be fashionable, be in fashion. **la última m.,** the latest fashion

modales /mo'ðales/ *m pl,* manners, behavior

modalidad /moðali'ðaɗ/ *f,* form, nature; *Mus.* modality

modelado /moðe'laðo/ *m,* *Art.* modeling

modelar /moðe'lar/ *vt Art.* to model; *vr* model oneself (on), copy

modelo /mo'ðelo/ *m,* example, pattern; model. *mf Art.* life model

módem /'moðem/ *m,* modem

moderación /moðera'sion; moðera'θion/ *f,* moderation; restraint, temperance, equability

moderado /moðe'raðo/ *a* moderate; restrained, temperate

moderador /moðera'ðor/ **(-ra)** *a* moderating. *n* moderator

moderantismo /moðeran'tismo/ *m,* moderate opinion; moderate political party

moderar /moðe'rar/ *vt* to moderate; temper, restrain; *vr* regain one's self-control; behave with moderation

modernidad /moðerni'ðaɗ/ *f,* modernity

modernismo /moðer'nismo/ *m,* modernism

modernista /moðer'nista/ *a* modernistic; modern. *mf* modernist

modernización /moðernisa'sion; moðerniθa'θion/ *f,* modernization

modernizar /moðerni'sar; moðerni'θar/ *vt* to modernize

moderno /mo'ðerno/ *a* modern. *m,* modern. **a la moderna,** in modern fashion

modestia /mo'ðestia/ *f,* modesty

modesto /mo'ðesto/ *a* modest

módico /'moðiko/ *a* moderate (of prices, etc.)

modificable /moðifi'kaβle/ *a* modifiable

modificación /moðifika'sion; moðifi'kaθion/ *f,* modification

modificador, modificante /moðifi'kaðor, moðifi'kante/ *a* modifying, moderating

modificar /moðifi'kar/ *vt* to modify; moderate

modismo /mo'ðismo/ *m,* idiom, idiomatic expression

modista /mo'ðista/ *mf* dressmaker; couturier; milliner

modo /'moðo/ *m,* mode, method, style; manner, way; moderation, restraint; civility, politeness (often *pl*); *Mus.* mode; *Gram.* mood. **m. de ser,** nature, temperament. **de m. que,** so that. **de ningún m.,** not at all, by no means. **de todos modos,** in any case

modorra /mo'ðorra/ *f,* deep sleep, stupor

modorro /mo'ðorro/ *a* drowsy, heavy

modoso /mo'ðoso/ *a* demure; well-behaved

modulación /moðula'sion; moðula'θion/ *f*, modulation

modulador /moðula'ðor/ **(-ra)** *a* modulative. *n* modulator, *m*, *Mus.* modulator

modular /moðu'lar/ *vt* and *vi* to modulate

mofa /'mofa/ *f*, mockery, ridicule, jeering

mofador /mofa'ðor/ **(-ra)** *a* jeering. *n* scoffer, mocker

mofarse /mo'farse/ *vr* (*with de*) to make fun of, jeer at

mofeta /mo'feta/ *f*, noxious gas; damp (gas); *Zool.* skunk

moflete /mo'flete/ *m*, *Inf.* plump cheek

mofletudo /mofle'tuðo/ *a* plump-cheeked

mogol /'mogol/ **(-la)** *a* and *n* Mongolian.

mogote /mo'gote/ *m*, hill; pyre, stack

mohín /mo'in/ *m*, grimace

mohína /mo'ina/ *f*, grudge, rancor; sullenness; sulkiness

mohíno /mo'ino/ *a* depressed, gloomy; sulky; black or black-nosed (of animals)

moho /'moo/ *m*, mold, fungoid growth; moldiness; moss. *Inf.* **no criar m.,** to be always on the move

mohoso /mo'oso/ *a* mossy; moldy

mojada /mo'haða/ *f*, wetting; *Inf.* stab; sop of bread

mojador /moha'ðor/ **(-ra)** *n* wetter. *m*, stamp moistener

mojar /mo'har/ *vt* to wet; moisten; *Inf.* stab, wound with a dagger; *vi* take part in; meddle, interfere; *vr* get wet

mojicón /mohi'kon/ *m*, kind of spongecake; *Inf.* slap in the face

mojiganga /mohi'gaŋga/ *f*, masquerade, mummer's show; farce; funny sight, figure of fun

mojigatería /mohigate'ria/ *f*, hypocrisy; sanctimoniousness; prudery

mojigato /mohi'gato/ **(-ta)** *a* hypocritical; sanctimonious; prudish. *n* hypocrite; bigot; prude

mojón /mo'hon/ *m*, boundary marker; milestone; heap. **m. kilométrico,** milestone

molar /mo'lar/ *a* molar

molde /'molde/ *m*, mold, matrix; *Fig.* model, pattern. **de m.,** printed; suitably, conveniently; perfectly. **letra de m.,** printed letters, print

moldeador /moldea'ðor/ **(-ra)** *n* molder

moldear /molde'ar/ *vt* to mold, cast

moldura /mol'dura/ *f*, molding

moldurar /moldu'rar/ *vt* to mold

mole /'mole/ *f* mass, bulk

molécula /mo'lekula/ *f*, molecule

molecular /moleku'lar/ *a* molecular

mole de guajolote /'mole de guaho'lote/ *m*, Mexico turkey served with a heavy dark sauce made of different kinds of chiles, spices, etc.

moler /mo'ler/ *vt* *irr* to grind, crush; tire, exhaust; illtreat; pester, annoy. **m. a palos,** to beat black and blue. *Pres. Ind.* **muelo, mueles, muele, muelen.** *Pres. Subjunc.* **muela, muelas, muela, muelan**

molestar /moles'tar/ *vt* to bother, annoy

molestia /mo'lestia/ *f*, inconvenience, trouble; annoyance; discomfort, pain; bore, nuisance. **Es una m.,** It's a nuisance

molesto /mo'lesto/ *a* inconvenient, troublesome; annoying; painful; uncomfortable; boring, tedious

molestoso, -a /moles'toso/ *a*, *Lat. Am.* annoying, bothersome

moletón /mole'ton/ *m*, flannelet

molicie /mo'lisie; mo'liθie/ *f*, softness, smoothness; effeminacy, weakness

molienda /mo'lienda/ *f*, milling; grinding; mill; portion ground at one time; *Inf.* exhaustion, fatigue; *Inf.* nuisance

molificar /molifi'kar/ *vt* to mollify, appease

molimiento /moli'miento/ *m*, milling; grinding; exhaustion, fatigue

molinera /moli'nera/ *f*, (woman) miller; miller's wife

molinero /moli'nero/ *a* mill. *m*, miller

molinillo /moli'niyo; moli'niʎo/ *m*, hand mill, small grinder; mincing machine; beater. **m. de café,** coffee mill

molino /mo'lino/ *m*, mill; harum-scarum, rowdy;

bore, tedious person; *Inf.* mouth. **m. de rueda de escalones,** treadmill. **m. de viento,** windmill

molleja /mo'yeha; mo'ʎeha/ *f*, gizzard

mollera /mo'yera; mo'ʎera/ *f*, crown of the head; brains, sense. *Inf.* **ser duro de m.,** to be obstinate; be stupid

molusco /mo'lusko/ *m*, mollusk

momentáneo /momen'taneo/ *a* momentary, brief; instantaneous, immediate

momento /mo'mento/ *m*, moment, minute; importance; *Mech.* moment. **al m.,** immediately. **a cada m.,** all the time; frequently. **por momentos,** continually; intermittently

momería /mome'ria/ *f*, mummery

momero /mo'mero/ **(-ra)** *n* mummer

momia /'momia/ *f*, mummy

momificación /momifika'sion; momifika'θion/ *f*, mummification

momificar /momifi'kar/ *vt* to mummify; *vr* become mummified

mona /'mona/ *f*, female monkey; *Inf.* imitator; drinking bout; drunk. *Inf.* **Aunque la m. se vista de seda, m. se queda,** Breeding will tell. *Inf.* **ser la última m.,** to be of no account, be unimportant

monacillo /mona'siyo; mona'θiʎo/ *m*, *Eccl.* acolyte

monada /mo'naða/ *f*, mischievous prank; affected gesture or grimace; small, pretty thing; childish cleverness; flattery; rash act; *pl* monkey shines

monaguillo /mona'giyo; mona'giʎo/ *m*, *Eccl.* acolyte

monarca /mo'narka/ *mf* monarch

monarquía /monar'kia/ *f*, monarchy

monárquico /mo'narkiko/ **(-ca)** *a* monarchic. *n* monarchist

monarquismo /monar'kismo/ *m*, monarchism

monasterio /mona'sterio/ *m*, monastery; convent

monástico /mo'nastiko/ *a* monastic

monda /'monda/ *f*, skinning, peeling; *Agr.* pruning; cleansing; *Lat. Am.* beating, thrashing

mondadientes /monda'ðientes/ *m*, toothpick

mondar /mon'dar/ *vt* to skin, peel; *Agr.* prune; cut the hair; cleanse; free of rubbish; *Inf.* deprive of possessions; *Lat. Am.* beat, beat up, thrash *vr* pick one's teeth

mondo /'mondo/ *a* simple, plain; bare; unadulterated, pure

mondongo /mon'doŋgo/ *m*, *Lat. Am.* tripe

moneda /mo'neða/ *f*, coin, piece of money; coinage; *Inf.* wealth; cash. **m. corriente,** currency. **m. metálica,** specie. **m. nacional,** national currency. **pagar en buena m.,** to give entire satisfaction. **pagar en la misma m.,** to pay back in the same coin, return like for like. *Inf.* **ser m. corriente,** to be usual or very frequent

monedero /mone'ðero/ *m*, coiner, mint; handbag; purse

monería /mone'ria/ *f*, mischievous trick; unimportant trifle; pretty thing; childish cleverness, pretty ways

monetario /mone'tario/ *a* monetary. *m*, collection of coins and medals

monetización /monetisa'sion; monetiθa'θion/ *f*, monetization

monigote /moni'gote/ *m*, *Inf.* boor; grotesque, puppet

monitor /moni'tor/ *m*, monitor

monitorio /moni'torio/ *a* monitory

monja /'monha/ *f*, nun; *pl* sparks

monje /'monhe/ *m*, monk

monjil /mon'hil/ *a* nun-like. *m*, nun's habit

mono /'mono/ *a* *Inf.* pretty, attractive; amusing, funny. *m*, monkey; person given to grimacing; rash youth; coverall. *Inf.* **estar de monos,** to be on bad terms

monocromo /mono'kromo/ *a* monochrome; monochromatic

monóculo /mo'nokulo/ *m*, monocle

monogamia /mono'gamia/ *f*, monogamy

monógamo /mo'nogamo/ *a* monogamous. *n* monogamist

monografía /monogra'fia/ *f*, monograph

monograma /mono'grama/ *m*, monogram

monolítico /mono'litiko/ a monolithic
monolito /mono'lito/ m, monolith
monólogo /mo'nologo/ m, monologue
monomanía /monoma'nia/ f, monomania, obsession
monomaníaco /monoma'niako/ **(-ca)** n monomaniac
monopatín /monopa'tin/ m, scooter
monoplano /mono'plano/ m, monoplane
monopolio /mono'polio/ m, monopoly
monopolista /monopo'lista/ mf monopolist
monopolizar /monopoli'sar; monopoli'θar/ vt to monopolize
monoteísmo /monote'ismo/ m, monotheism
monoteísta /monote'ista/ mf monotheist
monotipia /mono'tipia/ f, monotype
monotonía /monoto'nia/ f, monotony; monotone
monótono /mo'notono/ a monotonous
monroísmo /monro'ismo/ m, Monroe doctrine
monseñor /monse'ɲor/ m, monsignor
monserga /mon'serga/ f, Inf. rigmarole; jargon
monstruo /'monstruo/ m, monster; freak, monstrosity; cruel person; hideous person or thing
monstruosidad /monstruosi'ðað/ f, monstrousness, monstrosity
monstruoso /mon'struoso/ a monstrous, abnormal; enormous; extraordinary; atrocious, outrageous
monta /'monta/ f, mounting a horse; total; Mil. mounting signal; breeding station (horses)
montacargas /monta'kargas/ m, hoist, lift; freight elevator
montador /monta'ðor/ m, mounter; mounting block
montadura /monta'ðura/ f, mounting; mount, setting (of jewels)
montaje /mon'tahe/ m, assembling, setting up (machines); presentation (of a book); (cinema) montage
montano /mon'tano/ a hilly, mountainous
montante /mon'tante/ m, upright, stanchion; tent pole
montaña /mon'taɲa/ f, mountain; mountainous country. **montañas rusas,** roller coaster (at an amusement park)
montañés /mon'taɲes/ **(-esa)** a mountain. n mountain dweller; native of Santander
montañoso /monta'ɲoso/ a mountainous; hilly
montar /mon'tar/ vi to ascend, climb up, get on top; mount (a horse); ride (a horse); be important; vt get on top of; ride (a horse); total, amount to; set up (apparatus, machinery); Naut. sail around, double; set, mount (gems); cock (firearms); fine for trespassing; wind (a clock); command (a ship); Naut. carry, be fitted with (guns, etc.). **m. a horcajadas en,** to mount astride; straddle. **montarse en cólera,** to fly into a rage
montaraz /monta'ras; monta'raθ/ a mountain-dwelling; wild, savage; rude, uncivilized, uncouth. m, gamekeeper, forester
monte /'monte/ m, mount, hill; woodland; obstacle, impediment. **m. de piedad,** pawnshop. **m. pío,** savings fund
montepío /monte'pio/ m, Lat. Am. pawnshop
montera /mon'tera/ f, cap; glass roof
montería /monte'ria/ f, hunt, chase; art of hunting
montero /mon'tero/ **(-ra)** n hunter, huntsman
montés /mon'tes/ a wild, savage, untamed
montevideano /monteβiðe'ano/ **(-na)** a and n Montevidean
montículo /mon'tikulo/ m, mound, hill
montón /mon'ton/ m, heap, pile; Inf. abundance, lot, bunch. Inf. **a, de** or **en m.,** all jumbled up together. **a montones,** in abundance
montonero, -a /monto'nero/ mf domineering, overbearing
montuoso /mon'tuoso/ a mountainous
montura /mon'tura/ f, riding animal, mount; horse trappings; setting up, mounting (artillery, etc.)
monumento /monu'mento/ m, monument; document, record; tomb
monzón /mon'son; mon'θon/ mf, monsoon
moña /'moɲa/ f, doll; dressmaker's model; bow for the hair; bullfighter's black bow; baby's bonnet; Inf. drinking bout

moño /'moɲo/ m, bun, chignon; topknot (birds); bunch of ribbons; pl tawdry trimmings
moquete /mo'kete/ m, slap in the face
moquillo /mo'kiyo; mo'kiʎo/ m, distemper (of animals)
mora /'mora/ f, blackberry; mulberry; bramble; Moorish girl, Moorish woman
morada /mo'raða/ f, dwelling, abode; sojourn, stay
morado /mo'raðo/ a purple
morador /mora'ðor/ **(-ra)** n dweller; sojourner
moral /mo'ral/ a moral, ethical. f, morality, ethics; morale. m, blackberry bush
moraleja /mora'leha/ f, moral, lesson
moralidad /morali'ðað/ f, morality
moralista /mora'lista/ mf moralist
moralización /moralisa'sion; moraliθa'θion/ f, moralization
moralizador /moralisa'ðor; moraliθa'ðor/ **(-ra)** a moralizing. n moralizer
moralizar /morali'sar; morali'θar/ vt to reform, correct; vi moralize
moratoria /mora'toria/ f, moratorium
morbidez /mor'βiðes; mor'βiðeθ/ f, Art. morbidezza; softness
mórbido /'morβiðo/ a morbid, diseased; Art. delicate (of flesh tones); soft
morbo /'morβo/ m, illness. **m. gálico,** syphilis
morboso /mor'βoso/ a ill; morbid, unhealthy
morcilla /mor'siya; mor'θiʎa/ f, Cul. black pudding; (Inf. Theat.) gag
morcillero /morsi'yero; morθi'ʎero/ **(-ra)** n seller of black puddings; (Inf. Theat.) actor who gags
mordacidad /morðasi'ðað; morðaθi'ðað/ f, corrosiveness; mordacity, sarcasm; Cul. piquancy
mordaz /mor'ðas; mor'ðaθ/ a corrosive; sarcastic, caustic, mordant; Cul. piquant
mordaza /mor'ðasa; mor'ðaθa/ f, gag
mordedor /morðe'ðor/ a biting; scandalmongering
mordedura /morðe'ðura/ f, bite, biting
mordelón, -ona /morðe'lon/ mf, Central America, Mexico given to taking bribes
morder /mor'ðer/ vt irr to bite; nibble, nip; seize, grasp; corrode, eat away; slander; etch. Pres. Ind. **muerdo, muerdes, muerde, muerden.** Pres. Subjunc. **muerda, muerdas, muerda, muerdan.**
mordida /mor'ðiða/ f, Lat. Am. bite; Central America, Mexico also bribe
mordiente /mor'ðiente/ m, fixative (for dyeing); mordant. a mordant (of acid)
mordiscar /morðis'kar/ vt to nibble, bite gently; bite
mordisco /mor'ðisko/ m, nibble; nibbling; bite; biting; piece bitten off
morena /mo'rena/ f, moraine
moreno /mo'reno/ **(-na)** a dark brown; swarthy complexioned; dark (of people). n Inf. (ethnic) black, mulatto
morera /mo'rera/ f, mulberry bush
morería /more'ria/ f, Moorish quarter
morfina /mor'fina/ f, morphine
morfinómano /morfi'nomano/ **(-na)** n morphine addict
morfológico /morfo'lohiko/ a morphological
morganático /morga'natiko/ a morganatic
moribundo /mori'βundo/ **(-da)** a moribund, dying. n dying person
morillo /mo'riyo/ m, andiron, fire-dog
morir /mo'rir/ vi irr to die; fade, wither; decline, decay; disappear (years); long (to); go out (lights, fire); vr die; go numb (limbs); (with por) adore, be mad about. Inf. **m. vestido,** to die a violent death. **¡Muera!** Down with! Past Part. **muerto.** For other tenses see **dormir**
morisco /mo'risko/ **(-ca)** a Moorish. n Morisco, Moor converted to Christianity
mormón /mor'mon/ **(-ona)** n Mormon
mormonismo /mormo'nismo/ m, Mormonism
moro /'moro/ **(-ra)** a Moorish. n Moor; Mohammedan. Inf. **haber moros y cristianos,** to be the deuce of a row

moronga /mo'roŋga/ f, Central America, Mexico blood sausage

morosidad /morosi'ðað/ f, slowness, delay; sluggishness, sloth

moroso /mo'roso/ a slow, dilatory; sluggish, lazy

morra /'morra/ f, crown of the head

morral /mo'rral/ m, nose-bag; knapsack; game-bag; Inf. lout

morriña /mo'rriɲa/ f, cattle plague, murrain; Inf. depression, blues; homesickness

morro /'morro/ m, anything round; hummock, hillock; round pebble; headland, cliff

morrón /mo'rron/ m, Lat. Am. hot red pepper

morsa /'morsa/ f, walrus

mortaja /mor'taha/ f, shroud, winding sheet

mortal /mor'tal/ a mortal; fatal, deadly; on the point of death; great, tremendous; certain, sure. mf mortal

mortalidad /mortali'ðað/ f, humanity, human race; mortality, death-rate

mortandad /mortan'dað/ f, mortality, number of deaths

mortecino /morte'sino; morte'θino/ a dead from natural causes (animals); weak; fading; dull, dead (of eyes); flickering; on the point of death or extinction

mortero /mor'tero/ m, mortar (for building); Mil. mortar; pounding mortar

mortífero /mor'tifero/ a deadly, mortal

mortificación /mortifika'sion; mortifika'θion/ f, Med. gangrene; humiliation, wounding; mortification (of the flesh)

mortificar /mortifi'kar/ vt Med. to mortify; humiliate, wound, hurt; mortify (the flesh); vr become gangrenous

mortuorio /mor'tuorio/ a mortuary. m, funeral, obsequies

mosaico /mo'saiko/ a and m, mosaic

mosca /'moska/ f, fly; Inf. nuisance; bore, pest; cash; pl sparks. Inf. m. muerta, underhanded person. Inf. papar moscas, to gape, be dumbfounded. Inf. soltar la m., to give or spend money unwillingly

moscardón /moskar'ðon/ m, gadfly

moscatel /moska'tel/ a muscatel. m, muscatel (grapes and wine); Inf. pest, tedious person

Moscú /mos'ku/ Moscow

mosquear /moske'ar/ vt to drive off flies; reply crossly; whip; vr be exasperated; brush aside obstacles

mosquero /mos'kero/ m, flypaper

mosquete /mos'kete/ m, musket

mosquetería /moskete'ria/ f, musketry; (Obs. Theat.) male members of the audience who stood at the back of the pit

mosquetero /moske'tero/ m, musketeer; (Spanish theater of the sixteenth and seventeenth centuries) male member of the audience who stood at the back of the pit

mosquitero /moski'tero/ m, mosquito net

mosquito /mos'kito/ m, mosquito; midge, gnat; Inf. tippler, drunkard

mostacera /mosta'sera; mosta'θera/ f, mustard pot

mostacho /mos'tatʃo/ m, mustache, whiskers; Inf. smudge on the face

mostaza /mos'tasa; mos'taθa/ f, mustard plant or seed; Cul. mustard

mostela /mos'tela/ f, sheaf (of corn, etc.)

mosto /'mosto/ m, must, unfermented wine

mostrador /mostra'ðor/ (-ra) n one who shows, exhibitor. m, shop counter; face of a watch

mostrar /mos'trar/ vt irr to show; indicate, point out; demonstrate, prove; manifest, reveal; vr show oneself, be (e.g. Se mostró bondadoso, He showed himself to be kind). Pres. Ind. muestro, muestras, muestra, muestran. Pres. Subjunc. muestre, muestres, muestre, muestren

mostrenco /mos'trenko/ a Inf. stray, vagrant, homeless; Inf. dull, ignorant; Inf. fat, heavy

mota /'mota/ f, fault in cloth; mote, defect, fault; mound, hill; thread of cotton, speck of dust, etc.; fleck (of the sun, etc.); spot

mote /'mote/ m, maxim, saying; motto, device; catchword, slogan; nickname; Lat. Am. boiled corn

motear /mote'ar/ vt to speckle, dot, variegate, spot

motejar /mote'har/ vt to nickname, call names, dub

motete /mo'tete/ m, motet

motín /mo'tin/ m, mutiny; riot

motivar /moti'βar/ vt to motivate, cause; explain one's reasons

motivo /mo'tiβo/ a motive. m, cause, motive; Mus. motif. con m. de, on account of, because of. de m. propio, of one's own free will

motocicleta /motosi'kleta; motoθi'kleta/ f, motorcycle

motociclista /motosi'klista; motoθi'klista/ mf motorcyclist

motor /mo'tor/ (-ra) a motive, driving. m, motor, engine. n (person) mover, motive force. m. de combustión interna, internal combustion engine. m. de retroacción, jet engine

motorista /moto'rista/ mf motorist, driver

movedizo /moβe'ðiso; moβe'ðiθo/ a movable; insecure, unsteady; shaky; changeable, vacillating

mover /mo'βer/ vt irr to move; operate, drive; sway; wag; persuade, induce; excite; move (to pity, etc.); (with prep a) cause; vi sprout (plants); vr move. Pres. Ind. muevo, mueves, mueve, mueven. Pres. Subjunc. mueva, muevas, mueva, muevan

movible /mo'βiβle/ a movable; insecure, shaky. m, motive, cause, incentive

movilidad /moβili'ðað/ f, mobility; changeableness, inconstancy

movilización /moβilisa'sion; moβiliθa'θion/ f, mobilization

movilizar /moβili'sar; moβili'θar/ vt to mobilize

movimiento /moβi'miento/ m, movement; perturbation, excitement; Mus. movement; Lit. fire, spirit; Mech. motion, movement. Mil. m. envolvente, encircling movement

moza /'mosa; 'moθa/ f, maid; girl; waitress. m. de partido, party girl, prostitute. buena m., fine, upstanding young woman

mozalbete /mosal'βete; moθal'βete/ m, lad, stripling, boy

mozo /'moso; 'moθo/ a young, unmarried. m, boy, youth; bachelor; waiter; porter. m. de cordel or m. de esquina, street porter, message boy. m. de estación, railroad porter. buen m., fine, upstanding young man, Lat. Am. handsome

muaré /mua're/ m, moiré silk

mucama /mu'kama/ f, Argentina chambermaid

muceta /mu'seta; mu'θeta/ f, Educ. hood, short cape (of a graduate's gown)

muchacha /mu'tʃatʃa/ f, girl, lass; female servant

muchachada /mutʃa'tʃaða/ f, childish prank

muchachez /mutʃa'tʃes; mutʃa'tʃeθ/ f, boyhood; girlhood

muchachil /mutʃa'tʃil/ a boyish; girlish

muchacho /mu'tʃatʃo/ m, boy, youth; male servant

muchedumbre /mutʃe'ðumbre/ f, abundance, plenty; crowd, multitude; mass, mob

muchísimo /mu'tʃisimo/ a sup very much. adv very great deal, very much

mucho /'mutʃo/ a much; plenty of; very; long (time); pl many, numerous. adv a great deal; much; very much; yes, certainly; frequently, often; very (e.g. Me alegro m., I am very glad); to a great extent; long (time). con m., by far, easily. ni con m., nor anything like it, very far from it. ni m. menos, and much less. por m. que, however much

mucílago /mu'silago; mu'θilago/ m, mucilage, gum

mucosa /mu'kosa/ f, mucous membrane

mucoso /mu'koso/ a mucous

muda /'muða/ f, change, transformation; change of clothes; molting season; molt, sloughing of skin (snakes, etc.); change of voice (in boys)

mudable /mu'ðaβle/ a changeable, inconstant

mudanza /mu'ðansa; mu'ðanθa/ f, move (household); furniture removal; step, figure (in dancing); changeability, inconstancy

mudar /mu'ðar/ vt to change; alter, transform;

exchange; remove; dismiss (from employment); molt; slough the skin (snakes, etc.); change the voice (boys); *vr* alter one's behavior; change one's clothes; change one's residence, move; change one's expression; *Inf.* go away, depart

mudéjar /mu'ðehar/ *m, Archit.* style containing Moorish and Christian elements. *mf* Moor who remained in Spain under Christian rule

mudez /mu'ðes; mu'ðeθ/ *f,* dumbness; silence, muteness

mudo /'muðo/ *a* dumb; silent, mute, quiet

mueblaje /mue'βlahe/ *m,* household goods and furniture

mueble /'mueβle/ *m,* piece of furniture; furnishing

mueblería /mueβle'ria/ *f,* furniture store or factory

mueblista /mue'βlista/ *mf* furniture maker; furniture dealer

mueca /'mueka/ *f,* grimace

muela /'muela/ *f,* grindstone; molar (tooth); millstone; flat-topped hill. **m. del juicio,** wisdom tooth. **dolor de muelas,** toothache

muellaje /mue'yahe; mue'ʎahe/ *m,* wharfage, dock dues

muelle /'mueye; 'mueʎe/ *a* soft, smooth; voluptuous, sensuous; luxurious. *m,* spring (of a watch, etc.); wharf, quay; freight platform (railroad). **m. real,** mainspring (of a watch). **m. del volante,** hairspring.

muérdago /'muerðago/ *m,* mistletoe

muermo /'muermo/ *m,* boredom, apathy

muerte /'muerte/ *f,* death; destruction, annihilation; end, decline. *Inf.* **una m. chiquita,** a nervous shudder. **a m.,** to the death, with no quarter. **de m.,** implacably, inexorably (of hatred); very seriously (of being ill). **dar m.** (**a**), to kill. **estar a la m.,** to be on the point of death. **a cada m. de un obispo,** once in a blue moon

muerto /'muerto/ **(-ta)** *a* dead; slaked (lime); *Mech.* neutral; faded, dull (colors); languid, indifferent. **m.** is used in familiar speech as *past part* matar (e.g. *Le ha muerto,* He has killed him). *n* corpse. *Inf.* **desenterrar los muertos,** to speak ill of the dead. *Inf.* **echarle a uno el m.,** to pass the buck. *Inf.* **estar m. por,** to be dying, yearning for. **ser el m.,** to be dummy (at cards)

muesca /'mueska/ *f,* notch, mortise, groove

muestra /'muestra/ *f,* shop sign; sample, specimen; pattern, model; demeanor; watch or clock face; sign, indication; poster, placard; *Mil.* muster roll. **hacer m.,** to show

muestrario /mues'trario/ *m,* sample book, collection of samples

mufla /'mufla/ *f,* muffler (of a furnace)

mugido /mu'hiðo/ *m,* mooing or lowing (of cattle)

mugir /mu'hir/ *vi* to low or moo (cattle); bellow, shout; rage (elements)

mugre /'mugre/ *f,* grease, grime, dirt

mugriento /mu'griento/ *a* grimy, greasy

muguete /mu'gete/ *m,* lily of the valley

mujer /mu'her/ *f,* woman; wife. **m. de la vida airada** *or* **m. del partido** *or* **m. pública,** prostitute. **m. de la luna,** man in the moon. **m. de su casa,** good housewife. **tomar m.,** to take a wife

mujerero, -a /muhe'rero/ *a, Lat. Am.* fond of women

mujeriego /muhe'riego/ *a* (of men) womanizing, dissolute, given to philandering. **cabalgar a mujeriegas,** to ride sidesaddle

mujeril /muhe'ril/ *a* womanly, feminine

mula /'mula/ *f,* female mule; mule (heelless slipper); *Colombia* dope smuggler; *Mexico* junk, trash. *Inf.* **Se me fue la m.,** My tongue ran away with me

muladar /mula'ðar/ *m,* refuse heap, junkpile, dunghill

mular /mu'lar/ *a* mule; mulish

mulatero /mula'tero/ *m,* mule hirer; muleteer

mulato /mu'lato/ **(-ta)** *a* and *n* mulatto

muleta /mu'leta/ *f,* crutch; bullfighter's red flag; support, prop

mullir /mu'yir; mu'ʎir/ *vt irr* to make soft, shake out (wool, down, etc.); *Fig.* prepare the way; *Agr.* hoe the roots (of vines, etc.). *Pres. Part.* **mullendo.** *Preterite* **mulló, mulleron.** *Imperf. Subjunc.* **mullese, etc.**

mulo /'mulo/ *m,* mule

multa /'multa/ *f,* fine

multar /mul'tar/ *vt* to impose a fine on

multicolor /multiko'lor/ *a* multicolored

multiforme /multi'forme/ *a* multiform

multilátero /multi'latero/ *a* multilateral

multimillonario /multimiyo'nario; multimiʎo'nario/ **(-ia)** *a* and *n* multimillionaire

multiplicación /multiplika'sion; multiplika'θion/ *f,* multiplication

multiplicador /multiplika'ðor/ **(-ra)** *n* multiplier. *m, Math.* multiplier

multiplicando /multipli'kando/ *m,* multiplicand

multiplicar /multipli'kar/ **(se)** *vt* and *vr* to multiply; reproduce

multiplicidad /multiplisi'ðað; multipliθi'ðað/ *f,* multiplicity

múltiplo /'multiplo/ *m, Math.* multiple

multisecular /multiseku'lar/ *a* age-old, many centuries old

multitud /multi'tuð/ *f,* multitude, great number; crowd; rabble, masses, mob

mundanal, mundano /munda'nal, mun'dano/ *a* worldly, mundane

mundial /mun'dial/ *a* world, worldwide

mundo /'mundo/ *m,* world, universe; human race; earth; human society; world (of letters, science, etc.); secular life; *Eccl.* vanities of the flesh; geographical globe. **echar al m.,** to give birth to; produce, bring forth. **el Nuevo M.,** the New World, America. *Inf.* **el m. por montera,** to treat the world as one's oyster. **ser hombre/mujer del m.,** to be a man/woman of the world. *Inf.* **tener m.** *or* **mucho m.,** to be very experienced, know the world. **todo el m.,** everyone. **venir al m.,** to be born. **ver el m.,** to travel, see the world

mundología /mundolo'hia/ *f,* worldliness, experience of the world

munición /muni'sion; muni'θion/ *f, Mil.* munition; small shot. *Mil.* **m. de boca,** fodder and food supplies

municionero /munisio'nero; muniθio'nero/ **(-ra)** *n* purveyor, supplier

municipal /munisi'pal; muniθi'pal/ *a* municipal. *m,* policeman

municipalidad /munisipali'ðað; muniθipali'ðað/ *f,* municipality

municipio /muni'sipio; muni'θipio/ *m,* municipality, town council

munificencia /munifi'sensia; munifi'θenθia/ *f,* munificence, generosity

munífico /mu'nifiko/ *a* munificent, generous

muñeca /mu'ɲeka/ *f, Anat.* wrist; doll; puppet; dressmaker's dummy; polishing pad; mannequin; boundary marker; *Inf.* flighty young woman

muñeco /mu'ɲeko/ *m,* boy doll; puppet; *Inf.* playboy

muñir /mu'ɲir/ *vt irr* to summon, convoke; arrange, dispose. See **mullir**

muñón /mu'ɲon/ *m, Surg.* stump of an amputated limb; *Mech.* gudgeon

mural /mu'ral/ *a* mural

muralla /mu'raya; mu'raʎa/ *f,* town wall; rampart, fortification

murar /mu'rar/ *vt* to surround with a wall, wall in

murciélago /mur'sielago; mur'θielago/ *m, Zool.* bat

murga /'murga/ *f,* band of street musicians

murmullo /mur'muyo; mur'muʎo/ *m,* whisper; whispering; rustling; purling, lapping, splashing; mumbling, muttering

murmuración /murmura'sion; murmura'θion/ *f,* slander, backbiting, gossip

murmurador /murmura'ðor/ **(-ra)** *a* gossiping, slanderous. *n* gossip, backbiter

murmurar /murmu'rar/ *vi* to rustle (leaves, etc.); purl, lap, splash (water); whisper; mumble, mutter; *vi* and *vt Inf.* slander, backbite

murmurio /mur'murio/ *m,* rustling; lapping (of water); whispering; murmur; *Inf.* slander

muro /'muro/ *m,* wall; defensive wall, rampart

musaraña /musa'raɲa/ *f, Zool.* shrew; any small

animal; *Inf.* ridiculous effigy, guy. *Inf.* **mirar a las musarañas,** to be absent-minded
muscular /musku'lar/ *a* muscular
musculatura /muskula'tura/ *f,* musculature
músculo /'muskulo/ *m,* muscle; strength, brawn
musculoso /musku'loso/ *a* muscular; strong, brawny
muselina /muse'lina/ *f,* muslin
museo /mu'seo/ *m,* museum. **m. de pintura,** art gallery, picture gallery
musgo /'musɡo/ *m,* moss
musgoso /mus'ɡoso/ *a* mossy, moss-grown
música /'musika/ *f,* music; melody, harmony; musical performance; musical composition; group of musicians; sheet music. *Inf.* **m. celestial,** vain words, moonshine. *Inf.* **m. ratonera,** badly played music. *Inf.* **¡Vaya con su m. a otra parte!** Get out! Go to hell!
musical /musi'kal/ *a* musical
músico /'musiko/ **(-ca)** *a* music. *n* musician. **m. ambulante,** strolling musician. **m. mayor,** bandleader
musitar /musi'tar/ *vi* to mutter, mumble
muslo /'muslo/ *m,* thigh
mustango /mus'taŋɡo/ *m, Lat. Am.* mustang
mustio /'mustio/ *a* sad, disheartened, depressed; faded, withered; *Mexico* hypocritical
musulmán /musul'man/ **(-ana)** *a* and *n* Muslim

mutabilidad /mutaβili'ðað/ *f,* mutability, changeability
mutación /muta'sion; muta'θion/ *f,* change, mutation; sudden change in the weather; *Theat.* change of scene
mutilación /mutila'sion; mutila'θion/ *f,* mutilation; damage; defacement
mutilar /muti'lar/ *vt* to mutilate; spoil, deface, damage; cut short; reduce
mutis /'mutis/ *m, Theat.* exit. **hacer m.** *Theat.* to exit; keep quiet, say nothing
mutismo /mu'tismo/ *m,* mutism, dumbness; silence, speechlessness
mutualidad /mutuali'ðað/ *f,* reciprocity, mutuality, interdependence; principle of mutual aid; mutual aid society
mutualismo /mutua'lismo/ *m,* mutualism, organized mutual aid
mutualista /mutua'lista/ *mf* member of a mutual aid society
mutuante /mu'tuante/ *mf Com.* lender
mutuo /'mutuo/ *a* reciprocal, mutual, interdependent
muy /'mui/ *adv* very; very much; much. Used to form absolute superlative (e.g. *m. rápidamente,* very quickly). Can modify adjectives, nouns used adjectivally, adverbs, participles (e.g. *María es m. mujer,* Mary is very much a woman (very womanly)). **m. temprano,** very early. **M. señor mío,** Dear Sir (in letters)

N Ñ

naba /'naβa/ *f,* Swedish turnip
nabar /na'βar/ *m,* turnip field
nabo /'naβo/ *m,* turnip; turnip root; any root stem; *Naut.* mast; stock (of a horse's tail)
nácar /'nakar/ *m,* mother-of-pearl
nacarado, nacáreo /naka'raðo, na'kareo/ *a* nacreous, mother-of-pearl
nacer /na'ser; na'θer/ *vi irr* to be born; rise (rivers, etc.); sprout; grow (plumage, fur, leaves, etc.); descend (lineage); appear (stars, etc.); originate; *Fig.* issue forth; appear suddenly; (*with prep a* or *para*) be destined for, have a natural leaning toward. **n. con pajitas de oro en la cuna,** to be born with a silver spoon in one's mouth. *vr* grow; sprout; *Sew.* split at the seams. *Pres. Ind.* **nazco, naces, etc.** *Pres. Subjunc.* **nazca, etc.**
nacido /na'siðo; na'θiðo/ *a* and *past part* born; suitable, fit. *m,* (gen. *pl*) the living and the dead. **bien n.,** noble, well-born; well-bred. **mal n.,** base-born; illbred
naciente /na'siente; na'θiente/ *a* growing; nascent. *m,* east
nacimiento /nasi'miento; naθi'miento/ *m,* birth; source (of rivers, etc.); birthplace; origin; lineage; *Astron.* rising; nativity crib, manger. **de n.,** from birth; by birth; born
nación /na'sion; na'θion/ *f,* nation; country; *Inf.* birth
nacional /nasio'nal; naθio'nal/ *a* national; native. *mf* citizen, national
nacionalidad /nasionali'ðað; naθionali'ðað/ *f,* nationality
nacionalismo /nasiona'lismo; naθiona'lismo/ *m,* nationalism
nacionalista /nasiona'lista; naθiona'lista/ *a* and *mf* nationalist
nacionalización /nasionalisa'sion; naθionaliθa'θion/ *f,* naturalization; nationalization; acclimatization
nacionalizar /nasionali'sar; naθionali'θar/ *vt* to naturalize; nationalize
nacionalsindicalismo /nasio͵nalsindika'lismo; naθio͵nalsindika'lismo/ *m,* national syndicalism
nacionalsocialismo /nasio͵nalsosia'lismo; naθio͵nalsoθia'lismo/ *m,* national socialism, nazism
nada /'naða/ *f,* void, nothingness. *pron indef* nothing. *adv* by no means. **casi n.,** very little, practically noth-

ing. **¡De n.!** Not at all! Don't mention it! You're welcome! **No vale para n.,** He (it, she) is of no use
nadaderas /naða'ðeras/ *f pl,* water wings (for swimming)
nadador /naða'ðor/ **(-ra)** *n* swimmer. *a* swimming
nadar /na'ðar/ *vi* to swim; float; have an abundance (of); *Inf.* be too large (of garments, etc.). **n. y guardar la ropa,** *Fig.* to sit on the fence
nadería /naðe'ria/ *f,* trifle
nadie /'naðie/ *pron indef* no one. *m, Fig.* a nobody
nadir /na'ðir/ *m,* nadir
nado /'naðo/ *a* by swimming; afloat
nafta /'nafta/ *f,* naphtha; *Argentina* gas, gasoline
naftalina /nafta'lina/ *f,* naphthalene
naipe /'naipe/ *m,* playing card; pack of cards
naire /'naire/ *m,* elephant keeper or trainer
nalga /'nalɡa/ *f,* (gen. *pl*) buttock(s)
nana /'nana/ *f, Inf.* grandma; lullaby; *Mexico* wet nurse; nurserymaid
nao /'nao/ *f,* ship
napoleónico /napole'oniko/ *a* Napoleonic
Nápoles /'napoles/ Naples
napolitano /napoli'tano/ **(-na)** *a* and *n* Neapolitan
naranja /na'ranha/ *f,* orange. **n. dulce,** blood orange. **n. mandarina,** tangerine. *Inf.* **media n.,** better half
naranjada /naran'haða/ *f,* orangeade
naranjal /naran'hal/ *m,* orange plantation
naranjero /naran'hero/ **(-ra)** *n* orange seller
naranjo /na'ranho/ *m,* orange tree; *Inf.* lout, blockhead
narciso /nar'siso; nar'θiso/ *m,* narcissus; dandy, fop. **n. trompón,** daffodil
narcótico /nar'kotiko/ *a* and *m,* narcotic
narcotizar /narkoti'sar; narkoti'θar/ *vt* to narcotize
narcotraficante /narkotrafi'kante/ *mf* drug dealer
nardo /'narðo/ *m,* tuberose, spikenard, nard
narigudo /nari'ɡuðo/ *a* large-nosed; nose-shaped
nariz /na'ris; na'riθ/ *f,* nose; nostril; snout; nozzle; sense of smell; bouquet (of wine). **n. perfilada,** wellshaped nose. **n. respingona,** snub nose. *Inf.* **meter las narices,** to meddle, interfere
narración /narra'sion; narra'θion/ *f,* narration, account
narrador /narra'ðor/ **(-ra)** *a* narrative. *n* narrator
narrar /na'rrar/ *vt* to narrate, tell, relate

narrativa /narra'tiβa/ *f*, narrative; account; narrative skill

narrativo, narratorio /narra'tiβo, narra'torio/ *a* narrative

nata /'nata/ *f*, cream; *Fig.* the flower, elite; *pl* whipped cream with sugar

natación /nata'sion; nata'θion/ *f*, swimming. **n. a la marinera,** trudgen stroke

natal /na'tal/ *a* natal; native. *m*, birth; birthday

natalicio /nata'lisio; nata'liθio/ *a* natal. *a* and *m*, birthday

natalidad /natali'ðað/ *f*, birth rate

natatorio /nata'torio/ *a* swimming. *m*, swimming pool

natillas /na'tiyas; na'tiʎas/ *f pl*, custard

natividad /natiβi'ðað/ *f*, nativity; birth; Christmas

nativo /na'tiβo/ *a* indigenous; native; innate

nato /'nato/ *a* born; inherent; ex officio

natura /na'tura/ *f*, nature; *Mus.* major scale

natural /natu'ral/ *a* natural; native; indigenous; spontaneous; sincere, candid; physical; usual, ordinary; *Mus.* natural; unadulterated, pure; *Herald.* proper. *mf* native, citizen. *m*, temperament; disposition; instinct (of animals); natural inclination. **al n.,** naturally, without art. **del n.,** *Art.* from life

naturaleza /natura'lesa; natura'leθa/ *f*, nature; character; disposition; instinct; temperament; nationality, origin; naturalization; kind, class; constitution, physique. **n. humana,** humankind. **n. muerta,** *Art.* still life

naturalidad /naturali'ðað/ *f*, naturalness; nationality

naturalista /natura'lista/ *mf* naturalist

naturalización /naturalisa'sion; naturaliθa'θion/ *f*, naturalization; acclimatization

naturalizar /naturali'sar; naturali'θar/ *vt* to naturalize; acclimatize; *vr* become naturalized; become acclimatized

naturalmente /natural'mente/ *adv* naturally; of course

naturismo /natu'rismo/ *m*, nature cure

naufragar /naufra'gar/ *vi* to be shipwrecked; fail, be unsuccessful

naufragio /nau'frahio/ *m*, shipwreck; disaster, loss

náufrago /'naufrago/ **(-ga)** *n* shipwrecked person. *m*, shark

náusea /'nausea/ *f*, nausea (*pl* more usual); repugnance

nauseabundo, nauseoso /nausea'βundo, nause'oso/ *a* nauseous; nauseating, repugnant

nauta /'nauta/ *mf* mariner

náutica /'nautika/ *f*, navigation; yachting; seamanship

náutico /'nautiko/ *a* nautical

navaja /na'βaha/ *f*, razor; clasp knife; boar tusk; sting; *Inf.* slanderous tongue. **n. de afeitar,** (shaving) razor

navajada /naβa'haða/ *f*, slash with a razor

navajero /naβa'hero/ *m*, razor case

naval /na'βal/ *a* naval

Navarra /na'βarra/ Navarre

navarro /na'βarro/ **(-ra)** *a* and *n* Navarrese

nave /'naβe/ *f*, ship; *Archit.* nave. **n. aérea,** airship. *Archit.* **n. lateral,** aisle. **n. principal,** *Archit.* nave

navegable /naβe'gaβle/ *a* navigable

navegación /naβega'sion; naβega'θion/ *f*, navigation; sea voyage

navegante /naβe'gante/ *a* voyaging; navigating. *m*, navigator

navegar /naβe'gar/ *vi* to navigate; sail; fly

navidad /naβi'ðað/ *f*, nativity; Christmas; *pl* Christmastime

naviero /na'βiero/ *a* shipping. *m*, ship owner

navío /na'βio/ *m*, warship; ship. **n. de transporte,** transport. **n. de tres puentes,** three-decker

náyade /'naiaðe/ *f*, naiad, water nymph

nazareno /nasa'reno; naθa'reno/ **(-na)** *a* and *n* Nazarene; Christian

Nazaret /nasa'ret; naθa'ret/ Nazareth

nazismo /na'sismo; na'θismo/ *m*, nazism

neblina /ne'βlina/ *f*, fog; mist

nebulosidad /neβulosi'ðað/ *f*, nebulousness; cloudiness

nebuloso /neβu'loso/ *a* foggy; misty; cloudy; somber, melancholy; confused, nebulous

necedad /nese'ðað; neθe'ðað/ *f*, silliness, foolishness

necesario /nese'sario; neθe'sario/ *a* necessary; unavoidable

neceser /nese'ser; neθe'ser/ *m*, dressing case. *Sew.* **n. de costura,** workbox

necesidad /nesesi'ðað; neθesi'ðað/ *f*, necessity; poverty, want; shortage, need; emergency. **de n.,** necessarily

necesitado /nesesi'taðo; neθesi'taðo/ **(-da)** *a* needy, poor. *n* poor person

necesitar /nesesi'tar; neθesi'tar/ *vt* to necessitate; compel, oblige; *vi* be necessary, need

necio /'nesio; 'neθio/ *a* stupid; senseless; unreasonable, foolish

necrología /nekrolo'hia/ *f*, necrology, obituary

necromancia /nekroman'sia; nekroman'θia/ *f*, necromancy

neerlandés /neerlan'des/ *a* Dutch

nefando /ne'fando/ *a* iniquitous

nefario /ne'fario/ *a* nefarious

nefasto /ne'fasto/ *a* disastrous, ill-omened

nefrítico /ne'fritiko/ *a* nephritic

nefritis /ne'fritis/ *f*, nephritis

negable /ne'gaβle/ *a* deniable

negación /nega'sion; nega'θion/ *f*, negation; privation; negative; nay; *Gram.* negative particle; *Law.* traverse

negado /ne'gaðo/ *a* inept, unfitted; stupid

negar /ne'gar/ *vt irr* to deny; refuse; prohibit; disclaim; dissemble; disown; *Law.* traverse; *vr* refuse, avoid; decline (to receive visitors). See **acertar**

negativa /nega'tiβa/ *f*, denial; refusal; *Photo.* negative

negativo /nega'tiβo/ *a* negative

negligencia /negli'hensia; negli'henθia/ *f*, negligence; omission; carelessness; forgetfulness

negligente /negli'hente/ *a* negligent; careless; neglectful

negociable /nego'siaβle; nego'θiaβle/ *a* negotiable

negociación /negosia'sion; negoθia'θion/ *f*, negotiation; business affair, deal

negociado /nego'siaðo; nego'θiaðo/ *m*, department, section (of a ministry, etc.); business; *Chile* shop, store; *elsewhere in Lat. Am.* shady deal

negociante /nego'siante; nego'θiante/ *m*, businessman. *a* negotiating; trading

negociar /nego'siar; nego'θiar/ *vi* to trade, traffic; negotiate

negocio /ne'gosio; ne'goθio/ *m*, occupation; trade; business; employment; transaction; *Argentina* shop, store; *pl* business affairs. **hombre de negocios,** businessman

negra /'negra/ *f*, black girl, black woman; *Inf.* honey, *West Hem.* sweetheart

negrecer /negre'ser; negre'θer/ *vi irr* to become black. See **conocer**

negro /'negro/ *a* black; dark; *Herald.* sable. *m*, black; black (color). **n. de humo,** lampblack

negrura /ne'grura/ *f*, blackness

negruzco /ne'grusko; ne'gruθko/ *a* blackish

neme /'neme/ *m*, *Colombia* asphalt

nemotécnica /nemo'teknika/ *f*, mnemonics

nene /'nene/ **(-na)** *n Inf.* baby; darling

nenúfar /ne'nufar/ *m*, white water lily

neo /'neo/ *m*, neon

neófito /ne'ofito/ **(-ta)** *n* neophyte

neologismo /neolo'hismo/ *m*, neologism

neoyorquino /neoior'kino/ **(-na)** *a* New York. *n* New Yorker

nepotismo /nepo'tismo/ *m*, nepotism

Neptuno /nep'tuno/ *m*, *Astron.* Neptune; *Poet.* sea

nervio /'nerβio/ *m*, nerve; sinew; *Bot.* vein; vigor; *Mus.* string. **n. ciático,** sciatic nerve

nervioso /ner'βioso/ *a* nervous; overwrought; agitated; vigorous; neural; sinewy; jerky (of style, etc.)

nervosidad /nerβosi'ðað/ *f*, nervousness; nervosity;

flexibility (metals); jerkiness (of style, etc.); force, efficacy
nervudo /ner'βuðo/ a strong-nerved, vigorous
nesga /'nesga/ f, Sew. gore
neto /'neto/ a neat; clean; pure; Com. net. m, Archit. dado
neumático /neu'matiko/ a pneumatic. m, rubber tire
neumococo /neumo'koko/ m, pneumococcus
neurálgico /neu'ralhiko/ a neuralgic
neurastenia /neuras'tenia/ f, neurasthenia
neurasténico /neuras'teniko/ (-ca) a and n neurasthenic
neurología /neurolo'hia/ f, neurology
neurólogo /neu'rologo/ m, neurologist
neurosis /neu'rosis/ f, neurosis. n. de guerra, war neurosis; shell shock
neurótico /neu'rotiko/ (-ca) a and n neurotic
neutral /neu'tral/ a neutral; indifferent
neutralidad /neutrali'ðað/ f, neutrality; impartiality, indifference
neutralizar /neutrali'sar; neutrali'θar/ vt to neutralize; counteract, mitigate
neutro /'neutro/ a neuter; Chem. neutral; Mech. neuter; sexless
nevada /ne'βaða/ f, snowfall
nevado /ne'βaðo/ m, Lat. Am. snow-capped mountain
nevar /ne'βar/ vi irr impers to snow. Pres. Ind. **nieva.** Pres. Subjunc. **nieve**
nevazón /neβa'son; neβa'θon/ f, Lat. Am. blizzard, snowstorm
nevera /ne'βera/ f, refrigerator; icehouse
nevero /ne'βero/ m, ice-cream man; iceman
nevisca /ne'βiska/ f, light snowfall
nevoso /ne'βoso/ a snowy
nexo /'nekso/ m, nexus; connection; union
ni /ni/ conjunc neither, nor. **ni bien ni mal,** neither good nor bad. **ni siquiera,** not even. **¡Ni crea!, ¡Ni creas!** Nonsense!
niara /'niara/ f, haystack, rick
nicaragüeño /nikara'gueɲo/ (-ña) a and n Nicaraguan
nicho /'nitʃo/ m, niche; recess (in a wall)
nicotina /niko'tina/ f, nicotine
nidada /ni'ðaða/ f, nest full of eggs; brood, clutch
nidal /ni'ðal/ m, nest; nest egg; haunt; cause, foundation
nido /'niðo/ m, nest; den; hole; dwelling; haunt. **n. de ametralladoras,** Mil. pillbox
niebla /'n;əβla/ f, fog; mist; cloud; mildew; haze
nieto /'nieto/ (-ta) n ɡrandchild; descendant
nieve /'nieβe/ f, snow; whiteness. **deportes de n.,** winter sports
nigromancia /nigro'mansia; nigro'manθia/ f, necromancy
nigromante /nigro'mante/ m, necromancer
nihilismo /nii'lismo/ m, nihilism
nihilista /nii'lista/ mf nihilist
Nilo, el /'nilo, el/ the Nile
nimbo /'nimbo/ m, halo, nimbus
nimiedad /nimie'ðað/ f, prolixity; Inf. fussiness; fastidiousness, delicacy
nimio /'nimio/ a prolix; Inf. fussy; fastidious; Inf. parsimonious
ninfa /'ninfa/ f, nymph; Ent. chrysalis
ningún /niŋ'gun/ a abb of **ninguno.** Used before m, sing nouns only. **De n. modo,** In no way! Certainly not!
niña /'niɲa/ f, girl. **n. del ojo,** pupil (of the eye). **n. de los ojos,** apple of one's eye, darling
niñada /ni'ɲaða/ f, childishness, foolish act
niñera /ni'ɲera/ f, nursemaid
niñería /niɲe'ria/ f, childish act; trifle; childishness, folly
niñez /ni'ɲes; ni'ɲeθ/ f, childhood; beginning, early days; Fig. cradle
niño /'niɲo/ (-ña) a childish; young; inexperienced; imprudent. n child; young or inexperienced person. **n. de la doctrina,** charity child. **n. terrible,** enfant terrible. **desde n.,** from childhood

nipón /ni'pon/ (-ona) a and n Japanese
níquel /'nikel/ m, Chem. nickel
niquelar /nike'lar/ vt to chrome-plate
niquelera /nike'lera/ f, Colombia purse, change purse
nirvana /nir'βana/ m, nirvana
níspero /'nispero/ m, medlar tree; medlar
níspola /'nispola/ f, medlar
nitidez /niti'ðes; niti'ðeθ/ f, brightness, neatness, cleanliness
nítido /'nitiðo/ a bright, neat, clean (often poet.)
nitrato /ni'trato/ m, nitrate
nítrico /'nitriko/ a nitric
nitrógeno /ni'troheno/ m, nitrogen
nivel /ni'βel/ m, level; levelness. **n. de albañil,** plummet. **n. de burbuja,** spirit level. **a n.,** on the level. **estar al n. de las circunstancias,** to rise to the occasion; save the day
nivelación /niβela'sion; niβela'θion/ f, leveling
nivelador /niβela'ðor/ (-ra) a leveling. n leveler
nivelar /niβe'lar/ vt to level; Fig. make equal
níveo /'niβeo/ a snowy; snow-white
no /no/ adv no; not. **no bien,** no sooner. **no sea que,** unless. **no tal,** no such thing
noble /'noβle/ a noble, illustrious; generous; outstanding, excellent; aristocratic. mf nobleman (-woman)
nobleza /no'βlesa; no'βleθa/ f, nobility
noche /'notʃe/ f, night; darkness; confusion, obscurity. Inf. **n. toledana,** restless night. **¡Buenas noches!** Good night! **de n.,** by night. **esta n.,** tonight
nochebuena /notʃe'βuena/ f, Christmas Eve
nochebueno /notʃe'βueno/ m, yule log; Christmas cake
nocherniego /notʃer'niego/ a night, nocturnal
nochote /no'tʃote/ m, Mexico cactus beer
noción /no'sion; no'θion/ f, notion, idea; pl elementary knowledge
nocividad /nosiβi'ðað; noθiβi'ðað/ f, noxiousness
nocivo /no'siβo; no'θiβo/ a noxious
nocturno /nok'turno/ a nocturnal; melancholy. m, Mus. nocturne
nodriza /no'ðrisa; no'ðriθa/ f, wet nurse
nogal /no'gal/ m, walnut tree; walnut wood
nómada /'nomaða/ a nomadic
nomadismo /noma'ðismo/ m, nomadism
nombradía /nom'βraðia/ f, renown
nombramiento /nombra'miento/ m, naming; appointment; nomination
nombrar /nom'βrar/ vt to name; nominate; appoint; mention (in dispatches, etc.)
nombre /'nombre/ m, name; title; reputation; proxy; Gram. noun; Mil. password. **n. de pila,** Christian name. **por n.,** called; by name. **Su n. anda puesto en el cuerno de la Luna,** He (she) is praised to the skies
nomenclatura /nomenkla'tura/ f, nomenclature
nómina /'nomina/ f, list, register; payroll; amulet
nominación /nomina'sion; nomina'θion/ f, nomination, appointment
nominador /nomina'ðor/ (-ra) a nominating. n nominator
nominal /nomi'nal/ a nominal
nominalismo /nomina'lismo/ m, nominalism
nominalista /nomina'lista/ a nominalistic. mf nominalist
nomo /'nomo/ m, gnome
non /non/ a odd (of numbers)
nonada /no'naða/ f, nothing, practically nothing
nonagenario /nonahe'nario/ (-ia) a and n nonagenarian
nonagésimo /nona'hesimo/ a ninetieth
nones /'nones/ m, pl certainly not, definitely not, nope
nopal /no'pal/ m, nopal, prickly pear tree
noque /'noke/ m, tanner's vat
noquear /noke'ar/ vt (Box.) to knock out, K.O.
norabuena /nora'βuena/ f, congratulation
nordeste /nor'ðeste/ m, northeast
nórdico /'norðiko/ (-ca) a and n Nordic

noria /'noria/ *f*, water well; chain pump; *Inf*. hard, monotonous work

norma /'norma/ *f*, square (used by builders, etc.); *Fig*. norm, standard, model

normal /nor'mal/ *a* normal, usual; standard, average. *f*, normal school, teacher's college (also **escuela n.**)

normalidad /normali'ðað/ *f*, normality

normalista /norma'lista/ *mf* student at a teacher's college

normalización /normalisa'sion; normaliθa'θion/ *f*, normalization; standardization

normalizar /normali'sar; normali'θar/ *vt* to make normal; standardize

Normandía /norman'dia/ Normandy

normando /nor'mando/ **(-da)** *a* Norman. *n* Northman; Norman

nornordeste /nornor'ðeste/ *m*, northnortheast

nornorueste /norno'rueste/ *m*, northnorthwest

noroeste /noro'este/ *m*, northwest

norte /'norte/ *m*, north pole; north; north wind; polestar; *Fig*. guide

norteamericano /norteameri'kano/ **(-na)** *a* and *n* North American; (*U.S.A.*) American

norteño /nor'teɲo/ *a* northerly, northern

Noruega /no'ruega/ Norway

noruego /no'ruego/ **(-ga)** *a* and *n* Norwegian. *m*, Norwegian (language)

nos /nos/ *pers pron pl mf acc* and *dat* (direct and indirect object) of **nosotros,** us; to us (e.g. *Nos lo dio,* He gave it to us)

nosotros, nosotras /no'sotros, no'sotras/ *pers pron pl mf* we; us. Also used with preposition (e.g. *Lo hicieron por nosotros,* They did it for us)

nostalgia /nos'talhia/ *f*, nostalgia

nostálgico /nos'talhiko/ *a* nostalgic; melancholy; homesick

nóstico /'nostiko/ **(-ca)** *a* and *n* gnostic

nota /'nota/ *f*, mark, sign; annotation, comment; *Mus*. note; memorandum; *Com*. bill, account; criticism, imputation; mark (in exams); repute, renown; note (diplomatic)

notabilidad /notaβili'ðað/ *f*, notability

notable /no'taβle/ *a* notable, remarkable; outstanding, prominent; with distinction (examination mark). *m pl*, notabilities

notación /nota'sion; nota'θion/ *f*, (*Mus. Math.*) notation; annotation

notar /no'tar/ *vt* to mark, indicate; observe, notice; note down; annotate; dictate, read out; criticize, reproach; discredit

notaría /nota'ria/ *f*, profession of a notary; notary's office

notarial /nota'rial/ *a* notarial

notario /no'tario/ *m*, notary public

noticia /no'tisia; no'tiθia/ *f*, rudiment, elementary knowledge; information; news (gen. *pl*); *pl* knowledge. **atrasado de noticias,** *Fig*. behind the times

noticiar /noti'siar; noti'θiar/ *vt* to inform, give notice

noticiario /noti'siario; noti'θiario/ *m*, news bulletin, newsreel.

noticiero /noti'siero; noti'θiero/ *m*, newspaper

noticioso /noti'sioso; noti'θioso/ *a* informed; learned; newsy

notificación /notifika'sion; notifika'θion/ *f*, *Law*. notification. **n. de reclutamiento,** draft notice

notificar /notifi'kar/ *vt* to notify officially; inform; warn

noto /'noto/ *a* known. *m*, south wind

notoriedad /notorie'ðað/ *f*, notoriety, publicity; flagrancy; fame, renown

notorio /no'torio/ *a* well-known; notorious, obvious; flagrant

novatada /noβa'taða/ *f*, *Inf*. practical joke, hazing (of a freshman); blunder

novato /no'βato/ **(-ta)** *a* new, inexperienced. *n* novice, beginner

novecientos /noβe'sientos; noβe'θientos/ *a* and *m*, nine hundred

novedad /noβe'ðað/ *f*, newness, novelty; change, alteration; latest news; surprise; *pl* novelties. **sin n.,** no

change; all well (or as usual); safely, without incident

novel /no'βel/ *a* new; inexperienced

novela /no'βela/ *f*, novel; tale; falsehood. **n. caballista,** western, cowboy story. **n. por entregas,** serial (story)

novelero /noβe'lero/ **(-ra)** *a* fond of novelty and change; fond of novels; fickle. *n* newshound, gossip

novelesco /noβe'lesko/ *a* novelistic; imaginary

novelista /noβe'lista/ *mf* novelist

novelística /noβe'listika/ *f*, art of novel writing

novena /no'βena/ *f*, *Eccl*. novena, religious services spread over nine days

noveno /no'βeno/ *a* and *m*, ninth

noventa /no'βenta/ *a* and *m*, ninety; ninetieth

novia /'noβia/ *f*, bride; fiancée

noviar con /no'βiar kon/ *vi*, *Argentina* to court, woo

noviazgo /no'βiasgo; no'βiaθgo/ *m*, engagement, betrothal

noviciado /noβi'siaðo; noβi'θiaðo/ *m*, novitiate; training, apprenticeship

novicio /no'βisio; no'βiθio/ **(-ia)** *n* *Eccl*. novice; beginner, apprentice; unassuming person

noviembre /no'βiembre/ *m*, November

novillada /noβi'yaða; noβi'ʎaða/ *f*, herd of young bulls; bullock baiting

novillo /no'βiyo; no'βiʎo/ *m*, bullock. **hacer novillos,** to play truant

novilunio /noβi'lunio/ *m*, new moon

novio /'noβio/ *m*, bridegroom; fiancé; novice, beginner

novísimo /no'βisimo/ *a sup* **nuevo** newest; latest, most recent

nubada /nu'βaða/ *f*, cloudburst, rainstorm; abundance, plenty

nubarrón /nuβa'rron/ *m*, dense, lowering cloud, storm cloud

nube /'nuβe/ *f*, cloud; *Fig*. screen, impediment. **n. de verano,** summer cloud; passing annoyance

nublado /nu'βlaðo/ *a* cloudy; overcast. *m*, storm cloud; menace, threat; multitude, crowd

nublarse /nu'βlarse/ *vr* to cloud over

nubloso /nu'βloso/ *a* cloudy; unfortunate, unhappy

nuca /'nuka/ *f*, nape

núcleo /'nukleo/ *m*, kernel; stone, pip (of fruit); nucleus; *Fig*. core, essence

nudillo /nu'ðiyo; nu'ðiʎo/ *m*, knuckle; *Mas*. plug

nudo /'nuðo/ *m*, knot; (*Bot. Med.*) node; joint; *Naut*. knot; *Fig*. bond, tie; *Fig*. crux, knotty point. **n. al revés,** granny knot. **n. de comunicaciones,** communication center. **n. de marino,** reef knot. **n. de tejedor,** sheet bend (knot). **n. en la garganta,** *Fig*. lump in the throat (from emotion)

nudoso /nu'ðoso/ *a* knotted, knotty; gnarled

nuera /'nuera/ *f*, daughter-in-law

nuestro, nuestra /'nuestro, 'nuestra/ *poss pron 1st pers pl mf* our; ours. **los nuestros,** our friends, supporters, party, profession, etc.

nueva /'nueβa/ *f*, news

nuevamente /nueβa'mente/ *adv* again

Nueva Orleans /'nueβa orle'ans/ New Orleans

Nueva York /'nueβa york/ New York

Nueva Zelanda, Nueva Zelandia /'nueβa se'landa, se'landia; 'nueβa θe'landa, θe'landia/ New Zealand

nueve /'nueβe/ *a* nine; ninth. *m*, number nine; ninth (of the month) (e.g. *el nueve de marzo,* March 9th). **a las nueve,** at nine o'clock

nuevo /'nueβo/ *a* new; fresh; newly arrived; inexperienced; unused, scarcely worn. **de n.,** again. **¿Qué hay de n.?** What's the news? What's new?

Nuevo México /'nueβo 'meksiko/ *m* New Mexico

nuez /nues; nueθ/ *f*, walnut; *Anat*. Adam's apple. **n. moscada,** nutmeg

nulidad /nuli'ðað/ *f*, nullity; incompetence, ineptitude; worthlessness

nulo /'nulo/ *a* null, void; incapable; worthless

numen /'numen/ *m*, divinity; inspiration

numeración /numera'sion; numera'θion/ *f*, calculation; numbering

numerador /numera'ðor/ *m*, numerator

numerar /nume'rar/ *vt* to number; enumerate; calculate

numerario /nume'rario/ *a* numerary. *m*, cash

numérico /nu'meriko/ *a* numerical

número /'numero/ *m*, number; figure; numeral; size (of gloves, etc.); quantity; issue, copy; rhythm; *Gram.* number; item (of a program); *pl Eccl.* Numbers. **n. del distrito postal**, ZIP code. **n. quebrado**, *Math.* fraction. **sin n.**, numberless

numeroso /nume'roso/ *a* numerous; harmonious

numismática /numis'matika/ *f*, numismatics

nunca /'nunka/ *adv* never. **n. jamás**, nevermore. **N. digas «De esta agua no beberé!»** Never say "Never!"

nuncio /'nunsio/ 'nun θio/ *m*, messenger; papal nuncio; *Fig.* harbinger

nupcial /nup'sial; nup'θial/ *a* nuptial

nupcialidad /nupsiali'ðað; nupθiali'ðað/ *f*, marriage rate

nupcias /'nupsias; 'nupθias/ *f pl*, nuptials, marriage

nutria /'nutria/ *f*, otter, nutria

nutrición /nutri'sion; nutri'θion/ *f*, nourishment; nutrition

nutrido /nu'triðo/ *a* abundant; numerous

nutrimento /nutri'mento/ *m*, nutriment; nourishment; nutrition; *Fig.* food, encouragement

nutrir /nu'trir/ *vt* to nourish; encourage; *Fig.* fill

nutritivo /nutri'tiβo/ *a* nourishing, nutritive

ñácara /'ɲakara/ *f*, *Central America* sore, ulcer

ñaña /'ɲaɲa/ *f*, *Lat. Am.* wet nurse; nursemaid; elder sister

ñaques /'ɲakes/ *m pl*, odds and ends, rubbish

ñiquiñaque /ɲiki'ɲake/ *m*, *Inf.* good-for-nothing, wastrel; *Inf.* trash

ñoco, -a /'ɲoko/ *a*, *Lat. Am.* one-handed; missing a finger

ñoñería /ɲoɲe'ria/ *f*, *Inf.* drivel; folly, stupidity. **Déjate de ñoñerías**, *Inf.* Stop being a crybaby

ñoño /'ɲoɲo/ **(-ña)** *a Inf.* sentimental; foolish, idiotic. *n* fool.

O

o /o/ *f*, letter O. *conjunc* or, either. **o** becomes **u** before words beginning with **o** or **ho** (e.g. *gloria u honor*)

oasis /o'asis/ *m*, oasis; *Fig.* refuge, haven

obcecación /oβseka'sion; oβθeka'θion/ *f*, blindness; obstinacy; obsession

obcecar /oβse'kar; oβθe'kar/ *vt* to blind; obsess; *Fig.* dazzle; darken

obduración /oβðura'sion; oβðura'θion/ *f*, obstinacy, stubbornness, obduracy

obedecer /oβeðe'ser; oβeðe'θer/ *vt irr* to obey; *Fig.* respond; bend, yield (metals, etc.); *vi* result (from); arise (from). See **conocer**

obedecimiento /oβeðesi'miento; oβeðeθi'miento/ *m*, **obediencia** *f*, obedience

obediente /oβe'ðiente/ *a* obedient; docile

obelisco /oβe'lisko/ *m*, obelisk

obertura /oβer'tura/ *f*, *Mus.* overture

obesidad /oβesi'ðað/ *f*, obesity

obeso /o'βeso/ *a* obese

óbice /'oβise; 'oβiθe/ *m*, obstacle, impediment

obispado /oβis'paðo/ *m*, bishopric

obispo /o'βispo/ *m*, bishop. **o. sufragáneo**, suffragan bishop

óbito /'oβito/ *m*, death, demise

obituario /oβi'tuario/ *m*, obituary; obituary column

objeción /oβhe'sion; oβhe'θion/ *f*, objection

objetar /oβhe'tar/ *vt* to object to, oppose

objetivar /oβheti'βar/ *vt* to view objectively

objetividad /oβhetiβi'ðað/ *f*, objectivity

objetivo /oβhe'tiβo/ *a* objective. *m*, *Opt.* eyepiece; object finder; aim, goal

objeto /oβ'heto/ *m*, object; subject, theme; purpose; aim, goal. **sin o.**, without object; aimlessly

oblicuidad /oβlikui'ðað/ *f*, obliqueness

oblicuo /o'βlikuo/ *a* slanting, oblique

obligación /oβliga'sion; oβliga'θion/ *f*, obligation; *Com.* bond; *Com.* debenture; *pl* responsibilities; *Com.* liabilities

obligacionista /oβligasio'nista; oβligaθio'nista/ *mf Com.* bond holder, debenture holder

obligado /oβli'gaðo/ *m*, contractor (to a borough, etc.); *Mus.* obbligato

obligar /oβli'gar/ *vt* to compel, oblige, constrain; lay under an obligation; *Law.* mortgage; *vr* bind oneself, promise

obligatorio /oβliga'torio/ *a* obligatory

oblongo /o'βlongo/ *a* oblong

oboe /o'βoe/ *m*, oboe; oboe player, oboist

óbolo /'oβolo/ *m*, obol, ancient Greek coin

obra /'oβra/ *f*, work; anything made; literary, artistic, scientific production; structure, construction; repair, alteration (to buildings, etc.); means, influence, power; labor, time spent; action, behavior. **o. de**

caridad, charitable act. **o. maestra**, masterpiece. **obras públicas**, public works. **poner por o.**, to put into effect; to set to work on. **o. de**, about, approximately

obrar /o'βrar/ *vt* to work; make, do; execute, perform; affect; construct, build; *vi* be, exist (things); act, behave. **o. mal**, to behave badly, do wrong

obrero /o'βrero/ **(-ra)** *a* working. *n* worker; *pl* workers

obscenidad /oβsseni'ðað; oβsθeni'ðað/ *f*, obscenity

obsceno /oβs'seno; oβs'θeno/ *a* obscene

obsequiar /oβse'kiar/ *vt* to entertain; be attentive (to); give presents (to); court, make love to. **Me obsequia con un reloj**, He is presenting me with a watch

obsequio /oβ'sekio/ *m*, attention; gift; deference. **en o. de**, as a tribute to

obsequioso /oβse'kioso/ *a* obliging, courteous, attentive

observable /oβser'βaβle/ *a* observable

observación /oβserβa'sion; oβserβa'θion/ *f*, observation; remark

observador /oβserβa'ðor/ **(-ra)** *a* observing. *n* observer

observancia /oβser'βansia; oβser'βanθia/ *f*, observance; respect, reverence

observar /oβser'βar/ *vt* to notice; inspect, examine; fulfill; remark; watch, spy upon; *Astron.* observe

observatorio /oβserβa'torio/ *m*, observatory

obsesión /oβse'sion/ *f*, obsession

obsesionar /oβsesio'nar/ *vt* to obsess

obseso /oβ'seso/ *a* obsessed

obsidiana /oβsi'ðiana/ *f*, obsidian

obsolecer /oβsole'ser; oβsole'θer/ *vi* to obsolesce, become obsolete

obsoleto /oβso'leto/ *a* obsolete

obstáculo /oβs'takulo/ *m*, impediment; obstacle

obstante, no /oβs'tante, no/ *adv* in spite of; nevertheless

obstar /oβs'tar/ *vi* to impede, hinder

obstetra /oβs'tetra/ *mf* obstetrician

obstetricia /oβste'trisia; oβste'triθia/ *f*, obstetrics

obstinación /oβstina'sion; oβstina'θion/ *f*, obstinacy

obstinado /oβsti'naðo/ *a* obstinate, stubborn

obstinarse /oβsti'narse/ *vr* (*with en*) to persist in, insist on; be stubborn about

obstinaz /oβsti'nas; oβsti'naθ/ *a* obstinate

obstrucción /oβstruk'sion; oβstruk'θion/ *f*, obstruction

obstruccionismo /oβstruksio'nismo; oβstrukθio'nismo/ *m*, obstructionism, stonewalling

obstruir /oβstru'ir/ *vt*, *Lat. Am.* to obstruct, stonewall

obstruccionista /oβstruksio'nista; oβstrukθio'nista/ *mf* obstructionist

obstruir /oβs'truir/ *vt irr* to obstruct; block; hinder; *vr* become choked or stopped up (pipes, etc.). See **huir**

obtención /oβten'sion; oβten'θion/ *f*, obtainment; attainment, realization

obtener /oβte'ner/ *vt irr* to obtain; attain; maintain; preserve. See **tener**

obturador /oβtura'ðor/ *m*, stopper; shutter (of a camera)

obturar /oβtu'rar/ *vt* to stopper, plug; block, obstruct

obtuso /oβ'tuso/ *a* blunt, dull; (*Geom.* and *Fig.*) obtuse

obús /o'βus/ *m*, howitzer; *Mil.* shell

obviar /oβ'βiar/ *vt* to obviate

obvio /'oββio/ *a* obvious, evident, apparent

oca /'oka/ *f*, goose

ocasión /oka'sion/ *f*, occasion; opportunity; motive, cause; danger, risk; *Inf.* **asir la o. por la melena,** to take time by the forelock. **de o.,** second-hand

ocasional /okasio'nal/ *a* chance, fortuitous; occasional

ocasionar /okasio'nar/ *vt* to cause, occasion; excite, provoke; risk, endanger

ocaso /o'kaso/ *m*, sunset; west; dusk; decadence, decline

occidental /oksiðen'tal; okθiðen'tal/ *a* Western

occidente /oksi'ðente; okθi'ðente/ *m*, West, Occident

occiso /ok'siso; ok'θiso/ *a* murdered; killed

oceánico /ose'aniko; oθe'aniko/ *a* oceanic

océano /o'seano; o'θeano/ *m*, ocean; immensity, abundance

oceanografía /oseanogra'fia; oθeanogra'fia/ *f*, oceanography

ocelote /ose'lote; oθe'lote/ *m*, ocelot

ochava /o'tʃaβa/ *f*, eighth; *Eccl.* octave

ochavo /o'tʃaβo/ *m*, *Obs.* small Spanish copper coin

ochenta /o'tʃenta/ *a* and *m*, eighty; eightieth

ochentón /otʃen'ton/ **(-ona)** *n* octogenarian

ocho /'otʃo/ *a* eight; eighth. *m*, figure eight; playing card with eight pips; eight; eighth day (of the month). **las o.,** eight o'clock

ochocientos /otʃo'sientos; otʃo'θientos/ *a* and *m*, eight hundred; eight-hundredth

ocio /'osio; 'oθio/ *m*, leisure, idleness; *pl* pastimes; leisure time

ociosidad /osiosi'ðað; oθiosi'ðað/ *f*, idleness, laziness; leisure

ocioso /o'sioso; o'θioso/ **(-sa)** *a* idle; useless, worthless; unprofitable, fruitless. *n* idle fellow

ocozoal /okoso'al; okoθo'al/ *m*, *Mexico* rattlesnake

ocre /'okre/ *m*, ocher

octágono /ok'tagono/ *m*, octagon

octava /ok'taβa/ *f*, octave

octaviano /okta'βiano/ *a* Octavian

octavo /ok'taβo/ *a* eighth. *m*, eighth. **en o.,** in octavo

octeto /ok'teto/ *m*, octet; byte

octogenario /oktohe'nario/ **(-ia)** *a* and *n* octogenarian

octogésimo /okto'hesimo/ *a* eightieth

octubre /ok'tuβre/ *m*, October

óctuple /'oktuple/ *a* octuple, eightfold

ocular /oku'lar/ *a* ocular. *m*, eyepiece

oculista /oku'lista/ *mf* oculist

ocultación /okulta'sion; okulta'θion/ *f*, hiding, concealment

ocultamente /okulta'mente/ *adv* secretly

ocultar /okul'tar/ *vt* to hide, conceal; disguise; keep secret

ocultismo /okul'tismo/ *m*, occultism

oculto /o'kulto/ *a* hidden; secret; occult. **en o.,** secretly, quietly

ocupación /okupa'sion; okupa'θion/ *f*, occupancy; occupation, pursuit; employment, office, trade

ocupado /oku'paðo/ *a* occupied; busy

ocupante /oku'pante/ *n* occupant

ocupar /oku'par/ *vt* to take possession of; obtain or hold (job); occupy, fill; inhabit; employ; hinder, embarrass; hold the attention (of); *vr* (*with en*) be engaged in, be occupied with; (*with con*) concentrate on (a business affair, etc.)

ocurrencia /oku'rrensia; oku'rrenθia/ *f*, occurrence, incident; bright idea; witty remark

ocurrir /oku'rrir/ *vi* to anticipate; happen, take place; occur, strike (ideas)

oda /'oða/ *f*, ode

odalisca /oða'liska/ *f*, odalisque

odiar /o'ðiar/ *vt* to hate; *Chile* annoy, irk

odio /'oðio/ *m*, hatred; malevolence

odioso /o'ðioso/ *a* hateful, odious; *Argentina, Chile, Peru* annoying, irksome

odisea /oði'sea/ *f*, odyssey

odontología /oðontolo'hia/ *f*, odontology

odontólogo /oðon'tologo/ *m*, odontologist

odorífero /oðo'rifero/ *a* odoriferous, fragrant

odre /'oðre/ *m*, goatskin, wineskin; *Inf.* wine bibber

oesnorueste /oesno'rueste/ *m*, westnorthwest

oessudueste /oessu'ðueste/ *m*, westsouthwest

oeste /o'este/ *m*, west

ofender /ofen'der/ *vt* to ill-treat, hurt; offend, insult; anger, annoy; *vr* be offended

ofendido /ofen'diðo/ *a* offended; resentful

ofensa /o'fensa/ *f*, injury, harm; offense, crime

ofensiva /ofen'siβa/ *f*, *Mil.* offensive. **tomar la o.,** to take the offensive

ofensivo /ofen'siβo/ *a* offensive

ofensor /ofen'sor/ **(-ra)** *n* offender

oferta /o'ferta/ *f*, offer; gift; proposal; *Com.* tender. **o. y demanda,** supply and demand

oficial /ofi'sial; ofi'θial/ *a* official. *m*, official; officer; clerk; executioner; worker

oficiala /ofi'siala; ofi'θiala/ *f*, trained female worker

oficialidad /ofisiali'ðað; ofiθiali'ðað/ *f*, officialdom; officers

oficiar /ofi'siar; ofi'θiar/ *vt Eccl.* to celebrate or serve (mass); communicate officially, inform; *Inf.* (*with de*) act as

oficina /ofi'sina; ofi'θina/ *f*, workshop; office; pharmaceutical laboratory; *pl* cellars, basement (of a house)

oficinesco /ofisi'nesko; ofiθi'nesko/ *a* bureaucratic, red-tape

oficinista /ofisi'nista; ofiθi'nista/ *mf* clerk, office employee, office worker

oficio /o'fisio; o'fiθio/ *m*, occupation, employment; office, function, capacity; craft; operation; trade, business; official communication; office, bureau; *Eccl.* office. **Santo O.,** Holy Office. *Fig.* **buenos oficios,** good offices

oficiosidad /ofisiosi'ðað; ofiθiosi'ðað/ *f*, diligence, conscientiousness; helpfulness, friendliness; officiousness

oficioso /ofi'sioso; ofi'θioso/ *a* conscientious; helpful, useful; officious; meddlesome; unofficial, informal

ofrecer /ofre'ser; ofre'θer/ *vt irr* to offer; present; exhibit; consecrate, dedicate; *vr* occur, suggest itself; volunteer. **¿Qué se le ofrece?** What do you require? What would you like? See **conocer**

ofrecimiento /ofresi'miento; ofreθi'miento/ *m*, offer, offering

ofrenda /o'frenda/ *f*, *Eccl.* offering; gift, present

oftalmología /oftalmolo'hia/ *f*, ophthalmology

oftalmólogo /oftal'mologo/ *m*, oculist, ophthalmologist

ofuscación /ofuska'sion; ofuska'θion/ *f*. **ofuscamiento** *m*, obfuscation, dazzle, dimness of sight; mental confusion, bewilderment

ofuscar /ofus'kar/ *vt* to dazzle, daze; dim, obfuscate; confuse, bewilder

ogro /'ogro/ *m*, ogre

ohmio /'omio/ *m*, ohm

oídas, de /o'iðas, de/ *adv* by hearsay

oído /o'iðo/ *m*, sense of hearing; ear. **de o.,** by ear. **decir al o.,** to whisper in a person's ear. *Mus.* **duro de o.,** hard of hearing; having a bad ear (for music). **estar sordo de un o.,** to be deaf in one ear

oidor /oi'ðor/ *m*, hearer; judge, *Obs.* magistrate

oir /o'ir/ *vt irr* to hear; give ear to, listen; understand. *Pres. Part.* **oyendo.** *Pres. Ind.* **oigo, oyes, oye, oyen.** *Preterite* **oyó, oyeron.** *Pres. Subjunc.* **oiga,** etc. *Imperf. Subjunc.* **oyese,** etc.

oíslo /o'islo/ *mf Inf.* better half

ojal /o'hal/ *m,* buttonhole; slit, hole

¡ojalá! /oha'la/ *interj* If only that were so! God grant! O. **que venga,** I hope he comes (with *subjunc.*)

ojeada /ohe'aða/ *f,* glance

ojear /ohe'ar/ *vt* to look at, stare at; bewitch; scare, startle

ojera /o'hera/ *f,* dark shadow (under the eye); eye bath

ojeriza /ohe'risa; ohe'riθa/ *f,* ill-will, spite

ojeroso /ohe'roso/ *a* having dark shadows under the eyes, wan, haggard

ojete /o'hete/ *m,* eyelet

ojinegro /ohi'negro/ *a* black-eyed

ojiva /o'hiβa/ *f,* ogive

ojo /'oho/ *m,* eye; hole; slit; socket; keyhole; eye (of a needle); span (of a bridge); core (of a corn); attention, care; mesh; spring, stream; well (of a staircase); *pl* darling. **¡Ojo!** Take care! **o.** **avizor,** sharp watch; lynx eye. **Ojos que no ven, corazón que no siente,** Out of sight, out of mind. **o. saltón,** prominent, bulging eye. **o. vivo,** bright eye. **a o. de buen cubero,** at a guess. **a ojos vistas,** visibly; patently

ojota /o'hota/ *f, Chile,* sandal

ola /'ola/ *f,* billow; wave (atmospheric)

ole /'ole/ *m,* Andalusian dance

¡olé! /'ole/ *interj* Bravo!

oleada /ole'aða/ *f,* big wave, breaker; swell (of the sea); *Fig.* surge (of a crowd)

oleaginoso /oleahi'noso/ *a* oleaginous

oleaje /ole'ahe/ *m,* swell, surge, billowing

olear /ole'ar/ *vt* to administer extreme unction

óleo /'oleo/ *m,* oil; *Eccl.* holy oil (gen. *pl*). **al ó.,** in oils

oleoducto /oleo'ðukto/ *m,* oil pipeline

oler /o'ler/ *vt irr* to smell; guess, discover; pry, smell out; *vi* smell; (*with prep a*) smell of; smack of, be reminiscent of. *Pres. Ind.* **huelo, hueles, huele, huelen.** *Pres. Subjunc.* **huela, huelas, huela, huelan**

olfatear /olfate'ar/ *vt* to sniff, snuff, smell; *Inf.* pry into

olfativo, olfatorio /olfa'tiβo, olfa'torio/ *a* olfactory

olfato /ol'fato/ *m,* sense of smell; shrewdness

olfatorio /olfa'torio/ *a* olfactory

oliente /o'liente/ (**mal**) *a* evil-smelling

oligárquico /oli'garkiko/ *a* oligarchic

olímpico /o'limpiko/ *a* Olympic; Olympian

olisco, -a /o'lisko/ *a, Lat. Am.* spoiled, tainted (meat)

oliva /o'liβa/ *f,* olive tree; olive; barn owl; peace

olivar /oli'βar/ *m,* olive grove

olivo /o'liβo/ *m,* olive tree

olla /'oya; 'oʎa/ *f,* stew pot; Spanish stew; whirlpool. **o. podrida,** rich Spanish stew containing bacon, fowl, meat, vegetables, ham, etc. **las ollas de Egipto,** the fleshpots of Egypt

olmeda /ol'meða/ *f,* **olmedo** *m,* elm grove

olmo /'olmo/ *m,* elm tree

olor /o'lor/ *m,* odor, scent, smell; hope, promise; suspicion, hint; reputation. **o. de santidad,** odor of sanctity

oloroso /olo'roso/ *a* fragrant, perfumed

olvidadizo /olβiða'ðiso; olβiða'ðiθo/ *a* forgetful

olvidar /olβi'ðar/ (**se**) *vt* and *vr* to forget; neglect, desert. **Se me olvidó el libro,** I forgot the book. **Me olvidé de lo pasado,** I forgot the past

olvido /ol'βiðo/ *m,* forgetfulness; indifference, neglect; oblivion

ombligo /om'βligo/ *m,* navel; *Fig.* core, center

ominoso /omi'noso/ *a* ominous

omisión /omi'sion/ *f,* omission; carelessness, negligence; neglect

omiso /o'miso/ *a* omitted; remiss, careless. **hacer caso o. de,** to set aside, ignore

omitir /omi'tir/ *vt* to omit

ómnibus /'omniβus/ *m,* bus

omnímodo /om'nimoðo/ *a* all-embracing

omnipotencia /omnipo'tensia; omnipo'tenθia/ *f,* omnipotence

omnipotente /omnipo'tente/ *a* omnipotent, all-powerful

omnisciencia /omnis'siensia; omnis'θienθia/ *f,* omniscience

omniscio /om'nissio; om'nisθio/ *a* omniscient

omnívoro /om'niβoro/ *a* omnivorous

omoplato /omo'plato/ *m,* scapula, shoulder blade

once /'onse; 'onθe/ *a* eleven; eleventh. *m,* eleven; eleventh (of the month). **las o.,** eleven o'clock

onceno /on'seno; on'θeno/ *a* eleventh

onda /'onda/ *f,* wave; (of flames); *Sew.* scallop; *Phys.* wave; ripple; *pl* waves (in hair). *Radio.* **o. corta,** short wave. **o. etérea,** ether wave. **o. sonora,** sound wave

ondeado /onde'aðo/ *a* undulating; wavy; scalloped

ondeante /onde'ante/ *a* waving; flowing

ondear /onde'ar/ *vi* to wave; ripple; undulate; roll (of the sea); float, flutter, stream; *Sew.* scallop; *vr* swing, sway

ondeo /on'deo/ *m,* waving; undulation

ondulación /ondula'sion; ondula'θion/ *f,* undulation; wave; wriggling; twisting. **o. permanente,** permanent wave, perm

ondulado /ondu'laðo/ *a* wavy; undulating; scalloped

ondular /ondu'lar/ *vi* to writhe, squirm, wriggle; twist; coil; *vt* wave (in hair)

oneroso /one'roso/ *a* onerous, heavy; troublesome

ónice /'onise; 'oniθe/ *m,* onyx

onomástico /ono'mastiko/ *a* onomastic. **día o.,** saint's day

onomatopeya /onomato'peia/ *f,* onomatopoeia

onza /'onsa; 'onθa/ *f,* ounce. **por onzas,** by ounces; sparingly

onzavo /on'saβo; on'θaβo/ *a* and *m,* eleventh

opacidad /opasi'ðað; opaθi'ðað/ *f,* opacity; obscurity; gloom

opaco /o'pako/ *a* opaque; dark; gloomy, sad

opalino /opa'lino/ *a* opaline

ópalo /'opalo/ *m,* opal

opción /op'sion; op'θion/ *f,* option; choice, selection; *Law.* option

ópera /'opera/ *f,* opera

operación /opera'sion; opera'θion/ *f, Surg.* operation; execution, performance; *Com.* transaction

operar /ope'rar/ *vt Surg.* to operate; *vi* act, have an effect; operate, control; *Com.* transact

operario /ope'rario/ (**-ia**) *n* worker, hand; operator; mechanic

opereta /ope'reta/ *f,* operetta, light opera

opinar /opi'nar/ *vi* to have or form an opinion, think; judge, consider

opinión /opi'nion/ *f,* opinion, view; reputation

opio /'opio/ *m,* opium. **fumadero de o.,** opium den

opíparo /o'piparo/ *a* magnificent, sumptuous (banquets, etc.)

oponer /opo'ner/ *vt irr* to oppose; resist, withstand; protest against; *vr* oppose; be contrary or hostile (to); face, be opposite; object (to), set oneself against; compete (in public exams.). See **poner**

oporto /o'porto/ *m,* port (wine)

oportunidad /oportuni'ðað/ *f,* opportunity, occasion

oportunismo /oportu'nismo/ *m,* opportunism

oportunista /oportu'nista/ *a* and *mf* opportunist

oportuno /opor'tuno/ *a* opportune, timely

oposición /oposi'sion; oposi'θion/ *f,* opposition; resistance; antagonism; public competitive exam for a post; (*Astron. Polit.*) opposition

opositor /oposi'tor/ (**-ra**) *n* opponent; competitor

opresión /opre'sion/ *f,* oppression; hardship; pressure. **o. de pecho,** difficulty in breathing

opresor /opre'sor/ (**-ra**) *a* oppressive. *n* oppressor

oprimir /opri'mir/ *vt* to oppress; treat harshly; press, crush; choke

oprobio /o'proβio/ *m,* opprobrium

optar /op'tar/ *vt* to take possession of; (*with por*) choose

óptica /'optika/ *f, Phys.* optics; peepshow

óptico /'optiko/ *a* optic, optical. *m,* optician

optimismo /opti'mismo/ *m*, optimism
optimista /opti'mista/ *mf* optimist. *a* optimistic
óptimo /'optimo/ *a sup* **bueno** best, optimal, optimum
opugnar /opuɡ'nar/ *vt* to resist violently; *Mil.* assault, attack; impugn, challenge
opulencia /opu'lensia; opu'lenθia/ *f*, opulence, riches; excess, superabundance
opulento /opu'lento/ *a* opulent, rich
opúsculo /o'puskulo/ *m*, monograph, opuscule
oquedad /oke'ðað/ *f*, hollow, cavity; superficiality, banality
ora /'ora/ *adv* now
oración /ora'sion; ora'θion/ *f*, oration, speech; prayer; *Gram.* sentence
oráculo /o'rakulo/ *m*, oracle
orador /ora'ðor/ **(-ra)** *n* orator; speech maker. *m*, preacher
oral /o'ral/ *a* oral; verbal; buccal
orangután /oraŋgu'tan/ *m*, orangutan
orar /o'rar/ *vi* to harangue, make an oration; pray; *vt* request, beg
orate /o'rate/ *mf* lunatic
oratoria /ora'toria/ *f*, oratory, eloquence
oratorio /ora'torio/ *a* oratorical. *m*, oratory, chapel; *Mus.* oratorio
orbe /'orβe/ *m*, sphere; orb; world
órbita /'orβita/ *f*, *Astron.* orbit; *Fig.* sphere; *Anat.* orbit, eye socket
ordalía /orða'lia/ *f*, (medieval hist.) ordeal
orden /'orðen/ *mf* order, mode of arrangement; succession, sequence; group; system; orderliness, neatness; coherence, plan; *Eccl.* order, brotherhood; (*Zool. Bot.*) group, class; *Archit.* order; *Math.* degree. *f*, precept, command; *Com.* order; *pl Eccl.* ordination. (*Mil. Naut.*) **o. de batalla,** battle array. **o. de caballería,** order of knighthood. **o. del día,** order of the day. *Eccl.* **dar órdenes,** to ordain. **en o.,** in order; with regard to. **por su o.,** in its turn; successively
ordenación /orðena'sion; orðena'θion/ *f*, order, orderly arrangement, disposition; ordinance, precept; *Eccl.* ordination
ordenador /orðena'ðor/ *m Spain* computer
ordenamiento /orðena'miento/ *m*, ordaining; ordinance; edict
ordenancista /orðenan'sista; orðenan'θista/ *mf Mil.* martinet; disciplinarian
ordenanza /orðe'nansa; orðe'nanθa/ *f*, order, method; command, instruction; ordinance, regulation (gen. *pl*). *m*, *Mil.* orderly
ordenar /orðe'nar/ *vt* to put in order, arrange; command, give instructions to; decree; direct, regulate; *Eccl.* ordain; *vr* (*with de*) *Eccl.* be ordained as
ordeñadero /orðeɲa'ðero/ *m*, milk pail
ordeñar /orðe'ɲar/ *vt* to milk
ordinal /orði'nal/ *a* ordinal. *m*, ordinal number
ordinariez /orðina'ries; orðina'rieθ/ *f*, rudeness, uncouthness; vulgarity
ordinario /orði'nario/ *a* ordinary, usual; vulgar, coarse, uncultured; rude; commonplace, average, mediocre. *m*, *Eccl.* ordinary; carrier; courier. **de o.,** usually, ordinarily
orear /ore'ar/ *vt* to ventilate; *vr* dry; air; take the air
orégano /o'regano/ *m*, wild marjoram
oreja /o'reha/ *f*, external ear; lug; tab, flap; tongue (of a shoe). *Inf.* **con las orejas caídas,** down in the mouth, depressed
orejera /ore'hera/ *f*, earflap; mold board (of a plow)
orejudo /ore'huðo/ *a* large- or long-eared
oreo /o'reo/ *m*, zephyr; ventilation; airing
orfanato /orfa'nato/ *m*, orphanage, orphan asylum
orfandad /orfan'dað/ *f*, orphanhood; defenselessness, lack of protection
orfebre /or'feβre/ *mf* gold- or silversmith
orfebrería /orfeβre'ria/ *f*, gold- or silverwork
orfeón /orfe'on/ *m*, choral society
organdí /organ'di/ *m*, organdy
orgánico /or'ganiko/ *a* organic; harmonious; *Fig.* organized

organillero /organi'yero; organi'ʎero/ **(-ra)** *n* organ grinder
organillo /orga'niyo; orga'niʎo/ *m*, barrel organ
organismo /orga'nismo/ *m*, organism; organization, association
organista /orga'nista/ *mf* organist
organización /organisa'sion; organiθa'θion/ *f*, organization; order, arrangement
organizador /organisa'ðor; organiθa'ðor/ **(-ra)** *a* organizing. *n* organizer
organizar /organi'sar; organi'θar/ *vt* to organize; regulate; constitute
órgano /'organo/ *m*, *Mus.* organ; (*Anat. Bot.*) organ; means, agency. **o. de manubrio,** barrel organ
orgasmo /or'gasmo/ *m*, orgasm
orgía /or'hia/ *f*, orgy
orgullo /or'guyo; or'guʎo/ *m*, pride; arrogance
orgulloso /orgu'yoso; orgu'ʎoso/ *a* proud; haughty
orientación /orienta'sion; orienta'θion/ *f*, orientation; exposure, prospect; bearings
oriental /orien'tal/ *a* Oriental, Eastern. *mf* Oriental; *Argentina* Uruguayan
orientalismo /orienta'lismo/ *m*, Orientalism
orientalista /orienta'lista/ *mf* Orientalist
orientar /orien'tar/ *vt* to orientate; *vr* find one's bearings; familiarize oneself (with)
oriente /o'riente/ *m*, Orient, the East; luster (of pearls); youth, childhood; origin, source
orificio /ori'fisio; ori'fiθio/ *m*, orifice; hole
oriflama /ori'flama/ *f*, oriflamme; standard, flag
origen /o'rihen/ *m*, origin, source, root; stock, extraction; reason, genesis. **dar o. a,** to give rise to. **país de o.,** native land
original /orihi'nal/ *a* original; earliest, primitive; new, first-hand; novel, fresh; inventive, creative; eccentric; quaint. *m*, original manuscript; original; sitter (for portraits); eccentric
originalidad /orihinali'ðað/ *f*, originality
originar /orihi'nar/ *vt* to cause, originate; invent; *vr* spring from, originate (in)
originario /orihi'nario/ *a* original, primary; primitive; native (of)
orilla /o'riya; o'riʎa/ *f*, limit, edge; hem, border; selvage; shore, margin; bank (of a river, etc.); sidewalk; brink, edge. **a la o.,** on the brink; nearly
orillar /ori'yar; ori'ʎar/ *vt* to settle, arrange, concludɔ; *vi* reach the shore or bank; *Sew.* leave a hem; *Sew.* border; leave a selvage on cloth
orillo /o'riyo; o'riʎo/ *m*, selvage (of cloth)
orín /o'rin/ *m*, rust; *pl* urine
orinal /ori'nal/ *m*, chamber pot, urinal
orinar /ori'nar/ *vi* to urinate
oriundo /o'riundo/ *a* native (of); derived (from)
orla /'orla/ *f*, border, fringe; selvage (of cloth, garments); ornamental border (on diplomas, etc.)
orlar /or'lar/ *vt* to border; edge, trim
ornamentación /ornamenta'sion; ornamenta'θion/ *f*, ornamentation
ornamental /ornamen'tal/ *a* ornamental
ornamentar /ornamen'tar/ *vt* to ornament; embellish
ornamento /orna'mento/ *m*, ornament; decoration; gift, virtue, talent; *pl Eccl.* vestments
ornar /or'nar/ *vt* to ornament, adorn, embellish
ornato /or'nato/ *m*, decoration, ornament
ornitología /ornitolo'hia/ *f*, ornithology
ornitológico /ornito'lohiko/ *a* ornithological
ornitólogo /orni'tologo/ *m*, ornithologist
oro /'oro/ *m*, gold; gold coins or jewelry; *Fig.* riches; *pl* diamonds (cards). **o. batido,** gold leaf. **o. en polvo,** gold dust. *Fig.* **como un o.,** shining with cleanliness. **el as de oros,** the ace of diamonds
orondo /o'rondo/ *a* hollow; *Inf.* pompous; *Inf.* swollen, spongy
oropel /oro'pel/ *m*, brass foil; showy, cheap thing; trinket; tinsel
orquesta /or'kesta/ *f*, orchestra
orquestación /orkesta'sion; orkesta'θion/ *f*, orchestration
orquestal /orkes'tal/ *a* orchestral
orquestar /orkes'tar/ *vt* to orchestrate

orquídea /or'kiðea/ *f*, orchid
ortega /or'tega/ *f*, *Ornith.* grouse
ortiga /or'tiga/ *f*, *Bot.* nettle
orto /'orto/ *m*, rising (of sun, stars)
ortodoxia /orto'ðoksia/ *f*, orthodoxy
ortodoxo /orto'ðokso/ *a* orthodox
ortografía /ortogra'fia/ *f*, orthography
ortográfico /orto'grafiko/ *a* orthographical
ortopedia /orto'peðia/ *f*, orthopedics
ortopédico /orto'peðiko/ **(-ca)** *a* orthopedic. *n* orthopedist
ortopedista /ortope'ðista/ *mf* orthopedist
oruga /o'ruga/ *f*, caterpillar
orzuelo /or'suelo; or'θuelo/ *m*, *Med.* sty; trap (for wild animals)
os /os/ *pers pron 2nd pl mf dat* and *acc* of **vos** and **vosotros** you, to you
osa /'osa/ *f*, she-bear; *Astron.* **O. mayor,** Big Bear; **O. menor,** Little Bear
osadía /osa'ðia/ *f*, boldness, audacity
osado /o'saðo/ *a* daring, bold
osamenta /osa'menta/ *f*, skeleton; bones (of a skeleton)
osar /o'sar/ *vi* to dare; risk, venture
osario /o'sario/ *m*, charnel house, ossuary
oscilación /ossila'sion; osθila'θion/ *f*, oscillation
oscilante /ossi'lante; osθi'lante/ *a* oscillating
oscilar /ossi'lar; osθi'lar/ *vi* to oscillate, sway; hesitate, vacillate
ósculo /'oskulo/ *m*, kiss, osculation
oscurantismo /oskuran'tismo/ *m*, obscurantism
oscurantista /oskuran'tista/ *a* and *mf* obscurantist
oscurear /oskure'ar/ *Mexico* = **oscurecer**
oscurecer /oskure'ser; oskure'θer/ *vt irr* to darken; *Fig.* tarnish, dim, sully; confuse, bewilder; express obscurely; *Art.* shade; *v* grow dark; *vr* cloud over (sky); *Inf.* disappear (things, gen. by theft). See **conocer**
oscuridad /oskuri'ðað/ *f*, darkness; gloom, blackness; humbleness; obscurity, abstruseness
oscuro /os'kuro/ *a* dark; humble, unknown; abstruse, involved; obscure; uncertain, dangerous. **a oscuras,** in the dark; ignorant
óseo /'oseo/ *a* osseous
osera /o'sera/ *f*, bear's den
osezno /o'sesno; o'seθno/ *m*, bear cub
osificación /osifika'sion; osifika'θion/ *f*, ossification
osificarse /osifi'karse/ *vr* to ossify
ósmosis /'osmosis/ *f*, osmosis
oso /'oso/ *m*, bear. **o. blanco,** polar bear
ostensible /osten'sißle/ *a* ostensible; obvious

ostensión /osten'sion/ *f*, show, display, manifestation
ostensivo /osten'sißo/ *a* ostensive
ostentación /ostenta'sion; ostenta'θion/ *f*, manifestation; ostentation
ostentar /osten'tar/ *vt* to exhibit, show; boast, show off
ostentoso /osten'toso/ *a* magnificent, showy, ostentatious
osteópata /oste'opata/ *mf* osteopath
osteopatía /osteopa'tia/ *f*, osteopathy
ostión /os'tion/, *m*, *Mexico* oyster
ostra /'ostra/ *f*, oyster. **vivero de ostras,** oyster bed
ostracismo /ostra'sismo; ostra'θismo/ *m*, ostracism
otear /ote'ar/ *vt* to observe; look on at
otero /o'tero/ *m*, hill, height, eminence
otología /otolo'hia/ *f*, otology
otólogo /o'tologo/ *m*, otologist
otomana /oto'mana/ *f*, ottoman, couch
otomano /oto'mano/ *a* Ottoman
otoñal /oto'ɲal/ *a* autumnal, autumn, fall
otoño /o'toɲo/ *m*, autumn, fall
otorgamiento /otorga'miento/ *m*, granting; consent, approval; license, award
otorgar /otor'gar/ *vt* to grant; concede, approve; *Law.* grant, stipulate, execute
otro /'otro/ **(-ra)** *a* other, another. *n* another one
otrosí /otro'si/ *adv* besides, moreover
ovación /oßa'sion; oßa'θion/ *f*, ovation, triumph; applause
ovacionar /oßasio'nar; oßaθio'nar/ *vt* to applaud
oval /o'ßal/ *a* oval
óvalo /'oßalo/ *m*, oval
ovario /o'ßario/ *m*, ovary
oveja /o'ßeha/ *f*, ewe
overol /oße'rol/ *m Lat. Am.* overalls
ovillar /oßi'yar; oßi'ʎar/ *vi* to wind thread into a ball; *vr* curl up; huddle
ovillo /o'ßiyo; o'ßiʎo/ *m*, ball, bobbin (of thread); tangled heap (of things)
ovíparo /o'ßiparo/ *a* oviparous
OVNI /'oßni/ *m*, UFO
ovulación /oßula'sion; oßula'θion/ *f*, ovulation
óvulo /'oßulo/ *m*, ovule
oxidación /oksiða'sion; oksiða'θion/ *f*, oxidation
oxidar /oksi'ðar/ *vt* oxidize; *vr* become oxidized
óxido /'oksiðo/ *m*, oxide. **ó. de carbono,** carbon monoxide. **ó. de cinc,** zinc oxide
oxígeno /ok'siheno/ *m*, oxygen
oyente /o'iente/ *mf* hearer; *pl* audience
ozono /o'sono; o'θono/ *m*, ozone

P

pabellón /paße'yon; paße'ʎon/ *m*, pavilion; colors, flag; bell tent. **p. británico,** Union Jack. **p. de reposo,** rest home. **en p.,** stacked (of arms)
pábulo /'paßulo/ *m*, food; *Fig.* pabulum
pacedero /pase'ðero; paθe'ðero/ *a* Agr. grazing, meadow
pacer /pa'ser; pa'θer/ *vi irr* Agr. to graze; *vt* nibble away; eat away. See **nacer**
paciencia /pa'siensia; pa'θienθia/ *f*, patience
paciente /pa'siente; pa'θiente/ *a* patient; long-suffering; complacent. *mf Med.* patient
pacienzudo /pasien'suðo; paθien'θuðo/ *a* extremely patient or long-suffering
pacificación /pasifika'sion; paθifika'θion/ *f*, pacification; serenity, peace of mind
pacificador /pasifika'ðor; paθifika'ðor/ **(-ra)** *a* peace making; pacifying. *n* peace maker
pacificar /pasifi'kar; paθifi'kar/ *vt* to pacify; *vi* make peace; *vr* grow quiet, become calm (sea, etc.)
pacífico /pa'sifiko; pa'θifiko/ *a* pacific, meek, mild; peace-loving, peaceful. **el Océano P.,** the Pacific Ocean

pacifismo /pasi'fismo; paθi'fismo/ *m*, pacifism
pacifista /pasi'fista; paθi'fista/ *a* and *mf* pacifist
pacotilla /pako'tiya; pako'tiʎa/ *f*, goods. *Inf.* **hacer su p.,** to make one's packet or fortune. **ser de p.,** to be poor stuff; be jerry-built (of houses)
pactar /pak'tar/ *vt* to stipulate, arrange; contract
pacto /'pakto/ *m*, agreement, contract; pact
padecer /paðe'ser; paðe'θer/ *vt irr* to suffer; feel keenly; experience, undergo; tolerate. **p. desnudez,** to go unclothed. **p. hambre,** to go hungry. See **conocer**
padecimiento /paðesi'miento; paðeθi'miento/ *m*, suffering
padrastro /pa'ðrastro/ *m*, stepfather; cruel father; *Fig.* impediment, obstacle; hangnail
padrazo /pa'ðraso; pa'ðraθo/ *m*, *Inf.* indulgent father
padre /'paðre/ *m*, father; stallion; head (of the family, etc.); *Eccl.* father; genesis, source; author, creator; *pl* parents; ancestors. **p. adoptivo,** foster father. **p. de familia,** paterfamilias. **P. Eterno,** Eternal Father. **p. nuestro,** Lord's Prayer. **P. Santo,** Holy Father, the Pope

padrear /paðre'ar/ *vi* to take after one's father; *Zool.* reproduce, breed

padrejón /paðre'hon/ *m, Argentina* stallion

padrino /pa'ðrino/ *m*, godfather; sponsor; second (in duels, etc.); patron; best man

padrón /pa'ðron/ *m*, census; pattern; model; memorial stone

paella /pa'eya; pa'eʎa/ *f, Cul.* savory rice dish of shellfish, chicken, and meat

paga /'paga/ *f*, payment; amends, restitution; pay; payment of fine; reciprocity (in love, etc.)

pagadero /paga'ðero/ *a* payable. *m*, date and place when payment is due

pagador /paga'ðor/ **(-ra)** *n* payer. *m*, teller; wages clerk; paymaster

pagaduría /pagaðu'ria/ *f*, pay office

paganismo /paga'nismo/ *m*, paganism; heathenism

pagano /pa'gano/ **(-na)** *a* and *n* pagan; heathen

pagar /pa'gar/ *vt* to pay; make restitution, expiate; return, requite (love, etc.); *vr* (*with de*) become fond of; be proud of. **p. adelantado,** to prepay. *Com.* **p. al contado,** to pay cash. **p. la casa,** to pay the rent (for one's residence)

pagaré /paga're/ *m, Com.* promissory note, I.O.U.

página /'pahina/ *f*, page (of a book); episode

paginación /pahina'sion; pahina'θion/ *f*, pagination

paginar /pahi'nar/ *vt* to paginate

pago /'pago/ *m*, payment; recompense, reward; region of vineyards, olive groves, etc.; *Argentina* area, region

paguro /pa'guro/ *m*, hermit crab

pailebote /paile'βote/ *m*, schooner

país /pa'is/ *m*, country, nation; region; *Art.* landscape. **del p.,** typical of the country of origin (gen. of food)

paisaje /pai'sahe/ *m*, countryside; landscape, scenery

paisajista, paisista /paisa'hista, pai'sista/ *mf* landscape painter

paisano /pai'sano/ **(-na)** *n* compatriot; peasant; civilian

Países Bajos, los /pa'ises 'bahos, los/ the Low Countries, the Netherlands

paja /'paha/ *f*, straw; chaff; trash; *Fig.* padding. **ver la p. en el ojo del vecino y no la viga en el nuestro,** to see the mote in our neighbor's eye and not the beam in our own

pajar /pa'har/ *m*, barn

pájara /'pahara/ *f*, hen (bird); kite (toy); *Inf.* jay; prostitute. **p. pinta,** game of forfeits

pajarear /pahare'ar/ *vt* to snare birds; loaf, idle about

pajarera /paha'rera/ *f*, aviary

pajarero /paha'rero/ *m*, bird catcher or seller. *a Inf.* frivolous, giddy; *Inf.* gaudy (colors); *Lat. Am.* skittish (horse)

pajarita /paha'rita/ *f*, bow tie

pájaro /'paharo/ *m*, bird. **p. bobo,** penguin. **p. carpintero,** woodpecker. *Fig. Inf.* **p. gordo,** big gun. **p. mosca,** hummingbird

pajarota /paha'rota/ *f, Inf.* canard, false report

paje /'pahe/ *m*, page; *Naut.* cabin boy

pajera /pa'hera/ *f*, hayloft

pajizo /pa'hiso; pa'hiθo/ *a* made of straw; covered or thatched with straw; strawcolored

pala /'pala/ *f*, paddle; blade (of an oar); shovel; spade; baker's peel (long-handled shovel); cutting edge of a spade, hoe, etc.; *Sports.* racket; vamp, upper (of a shoe); pelota or jai alai racket; tanner's knife; *Inf.* guile, cunning; cleverness, dexterity. **p. de hélice,** propeller blade. **p. para pescado,** fish server. *Inf.* **corta p.,** ignoramus; blockhead

palabra /pa'laβra/ *f*, word; power of speech; eloquence; offer, promise; *pl* magic formula, spell. **p. de clave,** code word. **p. de matrimonio,** promise of marriage. **p. de rey,** inviolable promise. **palabras cruzadas,** crossword puzzle. **bajo p. de,** under promise of. **cuatro palabras,** a few words; short conversation. **de p.,** verbally, by word of mouth. **dirigir la p. a,** to address, speak to. **faltar a su p.,** to break one's promise. **llevar la p.,** to be spokesperson. **medias palabras,** half-words; hint, insinuation. **su p. empeñada,**

one's solemn word. **tener la p.,** to have the right to speak (in meetings, etc.) (e.g. *El señor Martínez tiene la p.,* Mr. Martinez has the floor)

palabrería /palaβre'ria/ *f*, verbosity, wordiness

palabrota /pala'βrota/ *f, Inf.* coarse language; long word

palaciego /pala'siego; pala'θiego/ **(-ga)** *a* pertaining to palaces; *Fig.* courtesan. *n* courtier

palacio /pa'lasio; pa'laθio/ *m*, palace; mansion

palada /pa'laða/ *f*, shovelful; spadeful; oar stroke

paladar /pala'ðar/ *m, Anat.* palate; taste; discernment, sensibility

paladear /palaðe'ar/ *vt* to taste with pleasure, savor; enjoy, relish

paladín /pala'ðin/ *m*, paladin

paladino /pala'ðino/ *a* public, clear, open

palafrén /pala'fren/ *m*, palfrey

palafrenero /palafre'nero/ *m*, groom; stablehand

palanca /pa'lanka/ *f, Mech.* lever; handle; bar; (high) diving board. **p. de arranque,** starting gear. **p. de cambio de velocidad,** gear-changing lever. **p. de mando,** control stick

palangana /palaŋ'gana/ *f*, washbasin

palanganear /palaŋgane'ar/ *vi, Lat. Am.* to show off

palanganero /palaŋga'nero/ *m*, washstand

palanqueta /palan'keta/ *f, dim* small lever; jimmy

palastro /pa'lastro/ *m*, sheet iron or steel

palatinado /palati'naðo/ *m*, Palatinate

palatino /pala'tino/ *a* palatine

palatizar /palati'sar; palati'θar/ *vt* to palatilize

palazón /pala'son; pala'θon/ *f*, woodwork

palco /'palko/ *m, Theat.* box; stand, raised platform, enclosure. **p. de platea,** orchestra

palenque /pa'lenke/ *m*, enclosure; stand; platform; palisade

paleografía /paleogra'fia/ *f*, paleography

paleógrafo /paleo'grafo/ *m*, paleographer

paleolítico /paleo'litiko/ *a* paleolithic

paleología /paleolo'hia/ *f*, paleology

paleontología /paleontolo'hia/ *f*, paleontology

palestra /pa'lestra/ *f*, tilt yard

paleta /pa'leta/ *f, dim* little shovel; trowel; *Art.* palette; fireplace shovel; mason's trowel; *Anat.* shoulder blade; blade (of a propeller, ventilator, etc.); *Chem.* spatula

paliacate /palia'kate/ *m, Mexico* kerchief

paliación /palia'sion; palia'θion/ *f*, palliation; excuse

paliar /pa'liar/ *vt* to dissemble, excuse; palliate, mitigate

paliativo /palia'tiβo/ *a* palliative; extenuating

palidecer /paliðe'ser; paliðe'θer/ *vi irr* to turn pale. See **conocer**

palidez /pali'ðes; pali'ðeθ/ *f*, pallor, paleness

pálido /'paliðo/ *a* pale, pallid

paliducho /pali'ðutʃo/ *a* somewhat pale, palish; sallow

palillo /pa'liyo; pa'liʎo/ *m, dim* small stick; toothpick; bobbin (for lacemaking); drumstick; chopstick; *Fig.* chatter; *pl* castanets

palimpsesto /palimp'sesto/ *m*, palimpsest

palinodia /pali'noðia/ *f, lit* palinode. **cantar la p.,** to eat one's words, recant

palio /'palio/ *m*, Greek mantle; cape; *Eccl.* pallium; canopy, awning

palique /pa'like/ *m, Inf.* chat. **estar de p.,** to be having a chat

paliquear /palike'ar/ *vi* to chat

paliza /pa'lisa; pa'liθa/ *f*, caning, beating

palizada /pali'saða; pali'θaða/ *f*, paling, fence; palisade, stockade. **p. de tablas,** hoarding

palma /'palma/ *f*, palm tree; palm leaf; date palm; palm (of the hand); hand; triumph. **llevarse la p.,** to bear away the palm; take the cake

palmada /pal'maða/ *f*, slap; *pl* hand-clapping

palmado /pal'maðo/ *a* web (of feet); palmy

palmar /pal'mar/ *a* palmaceous; palmar; clear, obvious. *m*, palm grove

palmatoria /palma'toria/ *f*, ferule, ruler; candlestick

palmear /palme'ar/ *vi* to clap hands

palmera /pal'mera/ *f*, palm tree

palmeta /pal'meta/ *f*, ferrule, ruler
palmetazo /palme'taso; palme'taθo/ *m*, slap on the hand with a ruler; *Fig.* slap in the face
palmo /'palmo/ *m*, span; hand's breadth. **p. a p.,** inch by inch, piecemeal
palmotear /palmote'ar/ *vt* to applaud; clap
palo /'palo/ *m*, stick; rod; pole; timber, wood; wooden log; *Naut.* mast; blow with a stick; execution by hanging; suit (of playing cards); fruit stalk; *Herald.* pale. **p. de Campeche,** logwood. **p. de hule,** rubber tree. **p. de rosa,** tulipwood. *Naut.* **p. mayor,** mainmast. *Naut.* **a p. seco,** under bare poles. **de tal p.,** tal astilla, a chip off the old block; like father like son. **estar del mismo p.,** to be of the same mind, agree
paloma /pa'loma/ *f*, dove; pigeon; gentle person; *pl Naut.* white horses. **p. buchona,** pouter pigeon. **p. mensajera,** carrier pigeon. **p. torcaz,** wood pigeon
palomar /palo'mar/ *m*, dovecote; pigeon loft
palomero /palo'mero/ **(-ra)** *n* pigeon fancier; pigeon dealer
palomino /palo'mino/ *m*, young pigeon
palomo /pa'lomo/ *m*, male pigeon; wood pigeon
palotes /pa'lotes/ *m pl*, drumsticks; pothooks (in writing)
palpabilidad /palpaβili'ðað/ *f*, palpability
palpable /pal'paβle/ *a* palpable, tangible
palpación /palpa'sion; palpa'θion/ *f*, palpation
palpar /pal'par/ *vt* to palpate, examine by touch; grope, walk by touch; *Fig.* see clearly
palpitación /palpita'sion; palpita'θion/ *f*, beating (of a heart); *Med.* palpitation; convulsive movement
palpitante /palpi'tante/ *a* palpitating; quivering; beating; (of a question) burning
palpitar /palpi'tar/ *vi* to beat (heart); throb, palpitate; shudder, move convulsively; *Fig.* manifest itself (passions, etc.)
palpo /'palpo/ *m*, palp, feeler
palta /'palta/ *f*, *Lat. Am.* avocado (pear)
palúdico /pa'luðiko/ *a* marshy, swampy; malarial
paludismo /palu'ðismo/ *m*, malaria; paludism
palurdo /pa'lurðo/ **(-da)** *a Inf.* gross, rude, boorish. *n* boor
palustre /pa'lustre/ *m*, mason's trowel. *a* marshy, swampy
pamela /pa'mela/ *f*, wide-brimmed straw sailor (woman's hat)
pamema /pa'mema/ *f*, *Inf.* unimportant trifle; *Inf.* caress
pampa /'pampa/ *f*, pampa, treeless plain
pamplina /pam'plina/ *f*, *Inf.* nonsense, rubbish
pan /pan/ *m*, bread; loaf; *Cul.* piecrust; *Fig.* food; wheat; gold leaf; *pl* cereals. **p. ázimo,** unleavened bread. **p. de oro,** gold leaf. **llamar al p. p. y al vino vino,** to call a spade a spade. **venderse como p. bendito,** to sell like hot cakes
pana /'pana/ *f*, velveteen, velour; *mf*, *Lat. Am. Inf.* pal
panacea /pana'sea; pana'θea/ *f*, panacea; cure-all
panadería /panaðe'ria/ *f*, bakery trade or shop; bakery
panadero /pana'ðero/ **(-ra)** *n* baker. *m pl*, Spanish dance
panadizo /pana'ðiso; pana'ðiθo/ *m*, *Med.* whitlow; *Inf.* ailing person, crock
panal /pa'nal/ *m*, honeycomb; wasp's nest
Panamá /pana'ma/ Panama
panamá /pana'ma/ *m*, *Lat. Am.* Panama hat
panameño /pana'meɲo/ **(-ña)** *a* and *n* Panamanian
panamericanismo /panamerika'nismo/ *m*, pan-Americanism
panarra /pa'narra/ *m*, *Inf.* simpleton
páncreas /'pankreas/ *m*, pancreas
pancreático /pankre'atiko/ *a* pancreatic
panda /'panda/ *f*, gallery of a cloister. *mf Zool.* panda
pandémico /pan'demiko/ *a* pandemic
pandemonio /pande'monio/ *m*, pandemonium
pandereta /pande'reta/ *f*, tambourine
pandero /pan'dero/ *m*, tambourine; *Inf.* windbag

pandilla /pan'diya; pan'diʎa/ *f*, league, group; gang (of burglars, etc.); party, crowd, band
pane /'pane/ *f*, breakdown
panecillo /pane'siyo; pane'θiʎo/ *m*, dim roll (of bread)
panegírico /pane'hiriko/ *a* and *m*, panegyric
panel /pa'nel/ *m*, panel
panetela /pane'tela/ *f*, panada
pánfilo /'panfilo/ **(-la)** *a* sluggish, phlegmatic, slow-moving. *n* sluggard
panfleto /pan'fleto/ *m*, pamphlet
paniaguado /pania'guaðo/ *m*, servant; favorite, protégé
pánico /'paniko/ *a* and *m*, panic
panoja /pa'noha/ *f*, *Bot.* panicle; *Bot.* ear, beard, awn
panoli /pa'noli/ *a Inf.* doltish, stupid
panorama /pano'rama/ *m*, panorama; view
panorámico /pano'ramiko/ *a* panoramic
pantalla /pan'taya; pan'taʎa/ *f*, lampshade; face screen; movie screen; shade, reflector
pantalón /panta'lon/ *m*, pant, trouser (gen. *pl*); knickers. **p. de corte,** striped trousers. **pantalones bombachos,** plus fours
pantano /pan'tano/ *m*, marsh, swamp; impediment; artificial pool
pantanoso /panta'noso/ *a* marshy, swampy; *Fig.* awkward, full of pitfalls
panteísmo /pante'ismo/ *m*, pantheism
panteón /pante'on/ *m*, pantheon; *Mexico* cemetery
pantera /pan'tera/ *f*, panther; *Venezuela* jaguar, ocelot
pantomima /panto'mima/ *f*, pantomime; mime
pantorrilla /panto'rriya; panto'rriʎa/ *f*, calf (of the leg)
pantuflo /pan'tuflo/ *m*, house slipper
panza /'pansa; 'panθa/ *f*, paunch, stomach; belly (of jugs, etc.). *Inf.* **un cielo de p. de burra,** a dark gray sky. **p. mojada** *Mexico* wetback
panzudo /pan'suðo; pan'θuðo/ *a* paunchy
pañal /pa'ɲal/ *m*, diaper; shirttail; *pl* long clothes, swaddling clothes; infancy
pañería /paɲe'ria/ *f*, drapery stores; drapery
pañero /pa'ɲero/ **(-ra)** *n* draper
paño /'paɲo/ *m*, woolen material; cloth, fabric; drapery, hanging; tapestry; linen, bandage; tarnish or other mark; *Naut.* canvas; *Sew.* breadth, width (of cloth); panel (in a dress); floor cloth, duster; livid mark on the face; *pl* garments. **p. de lágrimas,** consoler, sympathizer. **p. mortuorio,** pall (on a coffin). **paños menores,** underwear. **p. verde,** gambling table. **al p.,** *Theat.* from the wings, from without. *Inf.* **poner el p. al púlpito,** to hold forth, spread oneself
pañoleta /paɲo'leta/ *f*, kerchief, triangular scarf; fichu
pañuelo /pa'ɲuelo/ *m*, kerchief; handkerchief
papa /'papa/ *m*, pope; *f Inf.* potato; stupid rumor; nonsense; *pl* pap; *Cul.* sop; food
papá /'papa/ *m*, *Inf.* papa, daddy
papada /pa'paða/ *f*, double chin; dewlap
papado /pa'paðo/ *m*, papacy
papagayo /papa'gaio/ *m*, parrot
papal /pa'pal/ *m*, *Lat. Am.* potato field
papamoscas /papa'moskas/ *m*, *Ornith.* flycatcher; *Inf.* simpleton
papanatas /papa'natas/ *m*, *Inf.* simpleton
papar /pa'par/ *vt* to sip soft food; *Inf.* eat; neglect, be careless about
paparrucha /papa'rrutʃa/ *f*, *Inf.* stupid rumor; nonsense
papel /pa'pel/ *m*, paper; document; manuscript; *Theat.* role; part; pamphlet; sheet of paper; paper, monograph, essay; *pl* guise, role; *Theat.* character. **p. carbón,** carbon paper. **p. celofán,** cellophane. **p. cuadriculado,** graph paper, cartridge paper. **p. de calcar,** carbon paper; tracing paper. **p. de escribir,** writing paper. **p. de estaño,** tinfoil. **p. de estraza,** brown paper. **p. de fumar,** cigarette paper. **p. de lija,** emery- or sandpaper. **p. de paja de arroz,** rice paper. **p. de seda,** tissue paper. **p. de tornasol,** litmus paper. **p. del estado,** government bonds. **p.**

higiénico, toilet paper. **p. moneda,** paper money. **p. pintado,** wallpaper. **p. secante,** blotting paper. **p. sellado,** official stamped paper. **hacer buen (mal) p.,** to do well (badly). **hacer el p. (de),** *Theat.* to act the part (of). feign, pretend; **desempeñar el p.,** to play a part or role

papelear /papele'ar/ *vi* to turn over papers, search among them; *Inf.* cut a dash

papeleo /pape'leo/ *m,* bureaucracy, red tape

papelera /pape'lera/ *f,* mass of papers; desk (for keeping papers)

papelería /papele'ria/ *f,* heap of papers; stationer's shop; stationery

papelero /pape'lero/ **(-ra)** *a* paper, stationery. *n* paper maker; stationer

papeleta /pape'leta/ *f,* slip or scrap of paper

papelista /pape'lista/ *mf* paper maker; stationer; paperhanger

papelucho /pape'lutʃo/ *m,* old or dirty piece of paper; trash, worthless writing; *Inf.* rag (newspaper)

papera /pa'pera/ *f,* mumps

papilla /pa'piya; pa'piʎa/ *f,* pap; guile, wiliness

papillote /papi'yote; papi'ʎote/ *m,* curl-paper

papiro /pa'piro/ *m,* papyrus

papo /'papo/ *m,* dewlap; gizzard (of a bird); goiter. **p. de cardo,** thistledown

paquebote /pake'βote/ *m, Naut.* packet; mail boat; liner

paquete /pa'kete/ *m,* packet; parcel; package

paquidermo /paki'ðermo/ *m,* pachyderm

par /par/ *a* equal; alike; corresponding. *m,* pair, couple; team (of oxen, mules); peer (title); rafter (of a roof); *Mech.* torque, couple; *Elec.* cell. *f,* par. **a la p.,** jointly; simultaneously; *Com.* at par. **a pares,** two by two. **de p. en p.,** wide-open (doors, etc.). **sin p.,** peerless, excellent

para /'para/ *prep* in order to; for; to; for the sake of (e.g. *Lo hice p. ella,* I did it for her sake); enough to (gen. with *bastante,* etc.); in the direction of, toward; about to, on the point of (e.g. *Está p. salir,* He is about to go out). Expresses: 1. *Purpose* (e.g. *La educan p. bailarina,* They are bringing her up to be a dancer. *Lo dije p. ver lo que harías,* I said it to (in order to) see what you would do) 2. *Destination* (e.g. *Salió p. Londres,* He left for London) 3. *Use* (e.g. *seda p. medias,* silk for stockings. *un vaso p. flores,* a vase for flowers)

parábola /pa'raβola/ *f,* parable; *Geom.* parabola

parabrisas /para'βrisas/ *m,* windshield

paracaídas /paraka'iðas/ *m,* parachute

paracaidista /parakai'ðista/ *mf* parachutist

parachoques /para'tʃokes/ *m, Auto.* bumper; buffer (railroad)

parada /pa'raða/ *f,* stopping, halting; stop; stoppage, suspension; halt; *Mil.* review; interval, pause; cattle stall; dam; gambling stakes; parry (in fencing); relay (of horses). **p. de coches,** taxi rank. **p. de tranvía,** streetcar stop. **p. discrecional,** request stop (buses, etc.)

paradear /paraðe'ar/ **(con...)** *vi, Argentina* to brag (about...)

paradero /para'ðero/ *m,* railroad station; stopping place; end, conclusion; whereabouts

paradisíaco /paraði'siako/ *a* paradisaical

parado /pa'raðo/ *a* still; indolent, lazy; unoccupied, leisured; silent, reserved; timid; unemployed

paradoja /para'ðoha/ *f,* paradox

paradójico /para'ðohiko/ *a* paradoxical

parador /para'ðor/ *m,* inn, tavern, hostelry

parafina /para'fina/ *f,* paraffin

parafrasear /parafrase'ar/ *vt* to paraphrase

paráfrasis /pa'rafrasis/ *f,* paraphrase

paraguas /pa'raguas/ *m,* umbrella

paraguayo /para'guayo/ **(-ya)** *a* and *n* Paraguayan

paragüería /parague'ria/ *f,* umbrella shop

paragüero /para'guero/ **(-ra)** *n* umbrella maker, umbrella seller. *m,* umbrella stand

paraíso /para'iso/ *m,* paradise; garden of Eden; heaven; (*Inf. Theat.*) gallery, gods

paraje /pa'rahe/ *m,* place, locality; spot; state, condition

paralela /para'lela/ *f, Mil.* parallel; *pl* parallel bars (for gymnastic exercises)

paralelismo /parale'lismo/ *m,* parallelism

paralelo /para'lelo/ *a* parallel; analogous; similar. *m,* parallel, similarity; *Geog.* parallel

parálisis /pa'ralisis/ *f,* paralysis

paralítico /para'litiko/ **(-ca)** *a* and *n* paralytic

paralización /paralisa'sion; paraliθa'θion/ *f,* paralysis; cessation; *Com.* dullness, quietness

paralizar /parali'sar; parali'θar/ *vt* to paralyze; stop

paramento /para'mento/ *m,* ornament; trappings (of a horse); face (of a wall); facing (of a building). **paramentos sacerdotales,** liturgical vestments or ornaments

páramo /'paramo/ *m,* paramo, treeless plain; desert, wilderness

parangón /paraŋ'gon/ *m,* comparison; similarity

parangonar /paraŋgo'nar/ *vt* to compare

paraninfo /para'ninfo/ *m, Archit.* paranymph, university hall; best man (weddings); messenger of good

paranoico /para'noiko/ *m,* paranoiac

parapetarse /parape'tarse/ *vr* to shelter behind a parapet; take refuge behind

parapeto /para'peto/ *m,* parapet

parapoco /para'poko/ *mf Inf.* ninny, numskull

parar /pa'rar/ *vi* to stop, halt; end, finish; lodge; come into the hands of; *vt* stop; detain; prepare; bet, stake; point (hunting dogs); parry (fencing); *vr* halt; be interrupted; *Lat. Am.* to get up, stand up. **p. mientes en,** to notice; consider. **sin p.,** immediately, at once; without stopping

pararrayos /para'rraios/ *m,* lightning conductor

parasitario, parasítico /parasi'tario, para'sitiko/ *a* parasitic

parásito /pa'rasito/ *m,* parasite; *Fig.* sponger; *pl Radio.* interference. *a* parasitic

parasitología /parasitolo'hia/ *f,* parasitology

parasol /para'sol/ *m,* sunshade; *Bot.* umbel

paratifoidea /paratifoi'ðea/ *f,* paratyphoid

parca /'parka/ *f,* Fate; *Poet.* death. **las Parcas,** the Three Fates

parcela /par'sela; par'θela/ *f,* plot, parcel (of land); atom, particle

parchar /par'tʃar/ *vt, Lat. Am.* to mend, patch, patch up

parche /'partʃe/ *m, Med.* plaster; *Auto.* patch; drum; drumhead, parchment of drum; patch, mend

parcial /par'sial; par'θial/ *a* partial, incomplete; biased, prejudiced; factional, party; participatory

parcialidad /parsiali'ðað; parθiali'ðað/ *f,* partiality, bias, prejudice; party, faction, group; intimacy, friendship

parco /'parko/ *a* scarce, scanty; temperate, moderate; frugal

parcómetro /par'kometro/ *m Lat. Am.* (*except Argentina and Mexico*) parking meter

pardo /'parðo/ *a* brown; gray, drab, dun-colored; cloudy, dark; husky (voices). *m,* leopard

pardusco /par'ðusko/ *a* grayish; fawn-colored

parear /pare'ar/ *vt* to pair, match; put in pairs; compare

parecer /pare'ser; pare'θer/ *vi irr* to appear; look, seem; turn up (be found). *impers* believe, think (e.g. *me parece,* it seems to me, I think, my opinion is); *vr* look alike, resemble one another. See **conocer**

parecer /pare'ser; pare'θer/ *m,* opinion, belief; appearance, looks

parecido /pare'siðo; pare'θiðo/ *a* (*with bien or mal*) good- or bad-looking. *m,* resemblance

pared /pa'reð/ *f,* wall; partition wall; side, face. **p. maestra,** main wall. **p. medianera,** party wall. **Las paredes oyen,** The walls have ears. *Inf.* **pegado a la p.,** confused, taken aback

pareja /pa'reha/ *f,* pair; dance partner; couple. **p. desparejada,** mismatched pair. **parejas mixtas,** mixed doubles (in tennis). **correr parejas** *or* **correr a las parejas,** to be equal; go together; happen simultaneously; be on a par

parejo /pa'reho/ *a* equal; similar; smooth, flat; even, regular

parentela /paren'tela/ *f*, relatives, kindred; parentage

parentesco /paren'tesko/ *m*, kinship; relationship; affinity; *Inf.* connection, link

paréntesis /pa'rentesis/ *m*, parenthesis; digression. **entre p.**, incidentally

paresa /pa'resa/ *f*, peeress

paria /'paria/ *mf* pariah; outcast

parida /pa'riða/ *a f*, newly delivered of a child

paridad /pari'ðað/ *f*, parity; analogy, similarity

pariente /pa'riente/ **(-ta)** *n* relative, relation; *Inf.* husband (wife)

parihuela /pari'uela/ *f*, wheelbarrow; stretcher

parir /pa'rir/ *vt* to give birth to; *Fig.* bring forth; reveal, publish; *vi* lay eggs

París /pa'ris/ Paris

parisiense /pari'siense/ *a* and *mf* Parisian

parla /'parla/ *f*, speech; loquaciousness, eloquence; verbiage

parlamentar /parlamen'tar/ *vi* to converse; discuss (contracts, etc.); *Mil.* parley

parlamentario /parlamen'tario/ *a* parliamentarian. *m*, member of parliament

parlamentarismo /parlamenta'rismo/ *m*, parliamentarianism

parlamento /parla'mento/ *m*, legislative assembly; parliament; discourse, speech; *Theat.* long speech; *Mil.* parley

parlanchín /parlan'tʃin/ *a Inf.* talkative, chattering, loquacious

parlar /par'lar/ *vt* and *vi* to speak freely or easily; chatter; reveal, speak indiscreetly; babble (of streams, etc.)

parlero /par'lero/ *a* talkative; gossiping, indiscreet; talking (birds); *Fig.* expressive (eyes, etc.); prattling, babbling (brook, etc.)

parlotear /parlote'ar/ *vi Inf.* to chatter, gossip

parloteo /parlo'teo/ *m*, chattering, gossip

parnaso /par'naso/ *m*, Parnassus; anthology of verse

paro /'paro/ *m*, *Inf.* work stoppage; lockout; *Ornith.* tit. **p. forzoso**, unemployment

parodia /pa'roðia/ *f*, parody

parodiar /paro'ðiar/ *vt* to parody

parodista /paro'ðista/ *mf* parodist

parótida /pa'rotiða/ *f*, parotid gland; parotitis, mumps

parotiditis /paroti'ðitis/ *f*, parotitis, mumps

paroxismo /parok'sismo/ *m*, *Med.* paroxysm; frenzy, ecstasy, fit

parpadear /parpaðe'ar/ *vi* to blink

parpadeo /parpa'ðeo/ *m*, blinking

párpado /'parpaðo/ *m*, eyelid

parque /'parke/ *m*, park; depot, park; paddock, pen. **p. de atracciones**, pleasure ground. **p. de** (*or* **para**) **automóviles**, car park, parking lot

parquear /parke'ar/ *vt*, *vi*, *Lat. Am.* to park

parquedad /parke'ðað/ *f*, scarcity; moderation, temperance; parsimony, frugality

parquímetro /par'kimetro/ *m Spain*, *Venezuela* parking meter

parra /'parra/ *f*, vine. **hoja de p.**, *Fig.* fig leaf

párrafo /'parrafo/ *m*, paragraph; *Gram.* paragraph sign. **p. aparte**, new paragraph. **echar un p.**, to chat, gossip

parranda /pa'rranda/ *f*, *Inf.* binge; strolling band of musicians. **ir de p.**, to go on a binge

parricida /parri'siða; parri'θiða/ *mf* parricide (person)

parricidio /parri'siðio; parri'θiðio/ *m*, parricide (act)

parrilla /pa'rriya; pa'rriʎa/ *f*, *Cul.* griller, broiler; grill, gridiron; *Engin.* grate. *Cul.* **a la p.**, grilled

párroco /'parroko/ *m*, parish priest; parson

parroquia /pa'rrokia/ *f*, parish church; parish; clergy of a parish; clientele, customers

parroquial /parro'kial/ *a* parochial

parroquiano /parro'kiano/ **(-na)** *a* parochial. *n* parishioner; client, customer

parsimonia /parsi'monia/ *f*, frugality, thrift; prudence, moderation

parsimonioso /parsimo'nioso/ *a* parsimonious

parte /'parte/ *f*, part; share; place; portion; side, faction; *Law.* party; *Theat.* part, role. *m*, communication, message; telegraph or telephone message; (*Mil. Nav.*) communiqué. *f pl*, parts, talents. **p. actora**, *Law.* prosecution. **p. de la oración**, part of speech. **partes litigantes**, *Law.* contending parties. **dar p.**, to notify; (*Mil. Naut.*) report; give a share (in a transaction). **de algún tiempo a esta p.**, for some time past. **de p. de**, in the name of, from. **en p.**, partly. **por todas partes**, on all sides, everywhere. **ser p.** *a or* **ser p. para que**, to contribute to. **tener de su p.** (**a**), to count on the favor of. **la quinta p.**, one-fifth, etc.

partear /parte'ar/ *vt* to assist in childbirth

partera /par'tera/ *f*, midwife

partero /par'tero/ *m*, accoucheur

partición /parti'sion; parti'θion/ *f*, partition, distribution; (*Aer. Naut.*) accommodation

participación /partisipa'sion; partiθipa'θion/ *f*, participation; notice, warning; announcement (of an engagement, etc.); *Com.* share

participante /partisi'pante; partiθi'pante/ *a* and *mf* participant

participar /partisi'par; partiθi'par/ *vi* to participate, take part (in), share; *vt* inform; announce (an engagement, etc.)

partícipe /par'tisipe; par'tiθipe/ *a* sharing. *mf* participant

participio /parti'sipio; parti'θipio/ *m*, participle

partícula /par'tikula/ *f*, particle, grain; *Gram.* particle

particular /partiku'lar/ *a* private; peculiar; special, particular; unusual; individual. *mf* private individual. *m*, matter, subject. **en p.**, especially; privately

particularidad /partikulari'ðað/ *f*, individuality; specialty; rareness, unusualness; detail, circumstance; intimacy, friendship

particularizar /partikulari'sar; partikulari'θar/ *vt* to detail, particularize; single out, choose; *vr* (*with en*) be characterized by

partida /par'tiða/ *f*, departure; entry, record (of birth, etc.); certificate (of marriage, etc.); *Com.* item; *Com.* lot, allowance; *Mil.* guerrilla; armed band; expedition, excursion; game (of cards, etc.); rubber (at bridge, etc.); *Inf.* conduct, behavior; place, locality; death. *Com.* **p. doble**, double entry. **punto de p.**, point of departure. **Las siete Partidas**, code of Spanish laws compiled by Alfonso X (1252–84)

partidario /parti'ðario/ **(-ia)** *a* partisan. *n* adherent, disciple. *m*, partisan, guerrilla

partidarismo /partiða'rismo/ *m*, partisanship

partido /par'tiðo/ *m*, party, group, faction; profit; *Sports.* match; team; agreement, pact. **p. conservador**, *Polit.* conservative party. **p. obrero** *or* **p. laborista**, *Polit.* labor party. **buen p.**, *Fig.* good match, catch. **sacar p. de**, to take advantage of, make the most of. **tomar p.**, to enlist; join, become a supporter (of)

partidor /parti'ðor/ *m*, divider, apportioner; cleaver, chopper; hewer

partir /par'tir/ *vt* to divide; split; crack, break; separate; *Math.* divide; *vi* go, depart; start (from). **p. como el rayo**, be off like a flash. *vr* disagree, become divided; leave, depart

partitura /parti'tura/ *f*, *Mus.* score

parto /'parto/ *m*, parturition, birth; newborn child; *Fig.* creation, offspring; important event

parturienta /partu'rienta/ *a f*, parturient

parva /'parβa/ *f*, light breakfast; threshed or unthreshed grain; heap, mass

parvedad /parβe'ðað/ *f*, smallness; scarcity; light breakfast (taken on fast days)

parvo /'parβo/ *a* little, small

párvulo /'parβulo/ **(-la)** *n* child. *a* small; innocent, simple; lowly, humble

pasa /'pasa/ *f*, raisin; *Naut.* channel; passage, flight (of birds). **p. de Corinto**, currant

pasacalle /pasa'kaye; pasa'kaʎe/ *m*, *Mus.* lively march

pasada /pa'saða/ *f*, passing, passage; money sufficient to live on; passage, corridor. **dar p.**, to let pass, put up with. *Inf.* **mala p.**, bad turn, dirty trick

pasadera /pasa'ðera/ *f*, steppingstone

pasadero /pasa'ðero/ a passable, traversable; fair (health); tolerable, passable.

pasadizo /pasa'ðiso; pasa'ðiθo/ m, narrow corridor or passage; alley, narrow street; *Naut.* alleyway

pasado /pa'saðo/ m, past; pl ancestors. **Lo p., p.,** What's past is past. **p. de moda,** out of fashion, unfashionable

pasador /pasa'ðor/ m, bolt, fastener; *Mech.* pin, coupler; pin (of brooches, etc.); colander; *Naut.* marlin spike; shirt stud

pasajaretas /pasaha'retas/ m, bodkin

pasaje /pa'sahe/ m, passing; passage; fare; passage money; *Naut.* complement of passengers; channel, strait; (*Mus. Lit.*) passage; *Mus.* modulation, transition (of voice); voyage; passage; covered way; road; *Lat. Am.* dead-end street

pasajero /pasa'hero/ **(-ra)** a crowded public (thoroughfare); transitory, fugitive; passing; temporary. n passenger

pasamanería /pasamane'ria/ f, passementerie work, industry or shop

pasamano /pasa'mano/ m, passementerie; banister, handrail; *Naut.* gangway

pasante /pa'sante/ a *Herald.* passant. m, student teacher; articled clerk; apprentice; student. **p. de pluma,** law clerk

pasaporte /pasa'porte/ m, passport; license, permission. **dar el p. (a),** *Inf.* to give the sack (to)

pasar /pa'sar/ vt to pass; carry, transport; cross over; send; go beyond, overstep; run through, pierce; upset; overtake; transfer; suffer, undergo; sieve; study; dry (grapes, etc.); smuggle; surpass; omit; swallow (food); approve; dissemble; transform; spend (time); vi pass; be transferred; be infectious; have enough to live on; cease; last; die; pass away; pass (at cards); be transformed; be current (money); be salable (goods); (*with prep a + infin*) begin to; (*with por*) pass as; have a reputation as; visit; (*with sin*) do without. *impers.* happen, occur. vr end; go over to another party; forget; go stale or bad; *Fig.* go too far, overstep the mark; permeate. **p. contrato,** to draw up a contract; sign a contract. **p. la voz,** to pass the word along. **p. por alto (de),** to omit, overlook. **p. de largo,** to go by without stopping. **pasarse de listo,** to be too clever. **¡No pases cuidado!** Don't worry!

pasarela /pasa'rela/ f, gangplank

pasatiempo /pasa'tiempo/ m, pastime, hobby, amusement

pasavante /pasa'βante/ m, *Naut.* safe conduct; navicert

pascua /'paskua/ f, Passover; Easter; Christmas; Twelfth Night; Pentecost; pl twelve days of Christmas. **P. florida,** Easter Sunday. **dar las pascuas,** to wish a merry Christmas. **¡Felices pascuas!** Merry Christmas!

pascual /pas'kual/ a paschal

pase /'pase/ m, pass (with the hands and in football, etc.); safe conduct; free pass; thrust (in fencing)

paseante /pase'ante/ mf stroller, promenader, passerby

pasear /pase'ar/ vt to take a walk; parade up and down, display; vi take a walk; go for a drive; go for a ride (on horseback, etc.); stroll up and down; vr touch upon lightly, pass over; loaf, be idle; drift; float

paseo /pa'seo/ m, walk, stroll; drive; outing, expedition; promenade; boulevard. **p. a caballo,** ride on horseback

pasiega /pa'siega/ f, wet nurse

pasillo /pa'siyo; pa'siʎo/ m, gallery; corridor; lobby; railway corridor; *Sew.* basting stitch

pasión /pa'sion/ f, suffering; passivity; passion; desire; *Eccl.* passion. **con p.,** passionately

pasionaria /pasio'naria/ f, passionflower

pasividad /pasiβi'ðað/ f, passivity

pasivo /pa'siβo/ a passive; inactive; *Com.* sleeping (partner); *Gram.* passive. m, *Com.* liabilities

pasmar /pas'mar/ vt to freeze to death (plants); dumbfound, amaze, stun; chill; vr be stunned or amazed

pasmo /'pasmo/ m, amazement, astonishment; wonder, marvel; *Med.* tetanus, lockjaw

pasmoso /pas'moso/ a astounding, amazing; wonderful

paso /'paso/ a dried (of fruit)

paso /'paso/ m, step; pace; passage, passing; way; footstep; progress, advancement; passage (in a book); *Sew.* tacking stitch; occurrence, event; *Theat.* short play; gait, walk; strait, channel; migratory flight (birds); *Mech.* pitch; event or scene from the Passion; armed combat; death; *Lat. Am.* ford. pl measures, steps. adv softly, in a low voice; gently. **p. a nivel,** level crossing. **p. a p.,** step by step. **p. doble,** quick march; Spanish dance. **p. volante,** (gymnastics) giant stride. **a cada p.,** at every step; often. **al p.,** without stopping; on the way, in passing. **ceder el p.,** to allow to pass. **de p.,** in passing; incidentally. **llevar el p.,** to keep in step. **marcar el p.,** to mark time. **salir al p.,** to waylay, confront; oppose. **seguir los pasos (a),** to follow; spy upon

paspa /'paspa/ f, *Peru* chapped skin

paspadura /paspa'ðura/ f, *Argentina* = **paspa**

pasparse /pas'parse/ vr, *Lat. Am.* to chap, crack

pasquín /pas'kin/ m, **pasquinada** f, pasquinade, lampoon

pasta /'pasta/ f, *Cul.* dough; paste; pastry; piecrust; batter; *Cul.* noodle paste; paper pulp; board (bookbinding). **ser de buena p.,** to be good-natured

pastar /pas'tar/ vt to take to pasture; vi graze, pasture

pastel /pas'tel/ m, cake; *Art.* pastel; pie; *Inf.* plot, secret understanding; cheating (at cards); *Print.* pie; *Inf.* fat, stocky person

pastelear /pastele'ar/ vi *Inf.* to indulge in shady business (especially in politics)

pastelería /pastele'ria/ f, cake bakery; cake shop; confectioner's art; confectionery

pastelero /paste'lero/ **(-ra)** n confectioner, pastry cook; *Fig. Inf.* spineless person, jellyfish

pastelillo /paste'liyo; paste'liʎo/ m, *Cul.* turnover

pastelón /paste'lon/ m, meat or game pie

pasteurización /pasteurisa'sion; pasteuriθa'θion/ f, pasteurization

pasteurizar /pasteuri'sar; pasteuri'θar/ vt to pasteurize

pastilla /pas'tiya; pas'tiʎa/ f, tablet, cake; lozenge; pastille, drop; tread (of a tire)

pasto /'pasto/ m, grazing land, pasture; fodder; *Fig.* fuel, food; spiritual food. **a p.,** in plenty, abundantly. **de p.,** of daily use

pastor /pas'tor/ **(-ra)** n shepherd. m, *Eccl.* pastor

pastoral /pasto'ral/ a rustic, country; *Eccl.* pastoral, f, pastoral poem; *Eccl.* pastoral letter

pastorear /pastore'ar/ vt to graze, put to grass; *Eccl.* have charge of souls

pastorela /pasto'rela/ f, pastoral

pastoreo /pasto'reo/ m, pasturage, grazing

pastoril /pasto'ril/ a shepherd, pastoral

pastoso /pas'toso/ a doughy; mealy; pasty; mellow

pata /'pata/ f, paw and leg (animals); foot (of table, etc.); duck; *Inf.* leg. **p. de gallo,** blunder; crow's-foot, wrinkle. **meter la p.,** to interfere, put one's foot in one's mouth. *Inf.* **tener mala p.,** to be unlucky

patada /pa'taða/ f, kick, stamp; *Inf.* step, pace

patagón /pata'gon/ **(-ona)** a and n Patagonian

patalear /patale'ar/ vi to stamp (with the feet)

pataleo /pata'leo/ m, kicking; stamping

pataleta /pata'leta/ f, *Inf.* convulsion; feigned hysterics

patán /pa'tan/ m, *Inf.* yokel; boor, churl

patanería /patane'ria/ f, *Inf.* boorishness, churlishness

patarata /pata'rata/ f, trash, useless thing; extravagant courtesy

patata /pa'tata/ f, potato

patatal, patatar /pata'tal, pata'tar/ m, potato patch

patatús /pata'tus/ m, *Inf.* petty worry; mishap; *Med.* stroke, fit

patear /pate'ar/ vt *Inf.* to stamp; *Fig.* walk on, treat badly; *vi Inf.* stamp the feet; be furiously angry; (*golf*) putt

patena /pa'tena/ *f*, engraved medal worn by country women; *Eccl.* paten

patentar /paten'tar/ *vt* to issue a patent; take out a patent, patent

patente /pa'tente/ *a* obvious, patent; *f*, patent; warrant, commission; letters patent. **p. de invención,** patent. **p. de sanidad,** clean bill of health

patentizar /patenti'sar; patenti'θar/ *vt* to make evident

paternidad /paterni'ðað/ *f*, paternity

paterno /pa'terno/ *a* paternal

patético /pa'tetiko/ *a* pitiable; pathetic, moving

patiabierto /patia'βierto/ *a Inf.* knock-kneed

patibulario /patiβu'lario/ *a* heartrending, harrowing

patíbulo /pa'tiβulo/ *m*, scaffold

paticojo /pati'koho/ *a Inf.* lame; wobbly; unsteady

patilla /pa'tiya; pa'tiʎa/ *f*, side whisker (gen. *pl*); *pl* old Nick, the Devil

patín /pa'tin/ *m*, skate; runner (of a sled); (*Aer.* and of vehicles) skid; *Mech.* shoe. **p. del diablo,** scooter. **p. de ruedas,** roller skate

patinador /patina'ðor/ **(-ra)** *n* skater

patinaje /pati'nahe/ *m*, skating; skidding (of planes and vehicles)

patinar /pati'nar/ *vi* to skate; slip, lose one's footing; skid (vehicles and planes)

patinazo /pati'naso; pati'naθo/ *m*, skid (of a vehicle)

patinete /pati'nete/ *m*, child's scooter

patio /'patio/ *m*, courtyard; *Theat.* pit; *Mexico* shunting yard

patitieso /pati'tieso/ *a Inf.* paralyzed in the hands or feet; open-mouthed, amazed; stiff, unbending, proud

patituerto /pati'tuerto/ *a* crooked-legged; pigeon-toed; *Inf.* lopsided

patizambo /pati'sambo; pati'θambo/ *a* knock-kneed

pato /'pato/ *m*, duck; *Inf.* **pagar el p.,** to be a scapegoat

patógeno /pa'toheno/ *a* pathogenic

patojo /pa'toho/ *a* wadJling

patología /patolo'hia/ *f*, pathology

patológico /pato'lohiko/ *a* pathological

patólogo /pa'tologo/ *m*, pathologist

patoso /pa'toso/ *a Fig.* heavy, pedestrian, tedious

patraña /pa'traɲa/ *f*, nonsense, rubbish, fairy tale

patria /'patria/ *f*, motherland, native country; native place. **p. chica,** native region

patriarca /pa'triarka/ *m*, patriarch

patriarcado /patriar'kaðo/ *m*, patriarchy

patriarcal /patriar'kal/ *a* patriarchal

patricio /pa'trisio; pa'triθio/ **(-ia)** *a* and *n* patrician

patrimonio /patri'monio/ *m*, patrimony

patriota /pa'triota/ *mf* patriot

patriótico /pa'triotiko/ *a* patriotic

patriotismo /patrio'tismo/ *m*, patriotism

patrocinar /patrosi'nar; patroθi'nar/ *vt* to protect, defend; favor, sponsor; patronize

patrocinio /patro'sinio; patro'θinio/ *m*, protection, defense; sponsorship; patronage

patrón /pa'tron/ **(-ona)** *n* patron, sponsor; patron saint; landlord; employer. *m*, coxswain; *Naut.* master, skipper; pattern, model; standard. **p. de oro,** gold standard

patronato /patro'nato/ *m*, patronage, protection; employers' association; charitable foundation. **p. de turismo,** tourist bureau

patronímico /patro'nimiko/ *a* and *m*, patronymic

patrono /pa'trono/ **(-na)** *n* protector; sponsor; patron; patron saint; employer

patrulla /pa'truya; pa'truʎa/ *f*, *Mil.* patrol; group, band

patrullar /patru'yar; patru'ʎar/ *vi Mil.* patrol; march about

patudo /pa'tuðo/ *a Inf.* large-footed

paulatinamente /paulatina'mente/ *adv* slowly, by degrees

pauperismo /paupe'rismo/ *m*, destitution, pauperism

pausa /'pausa/ *f*, pause, interruption; delay; *Mus.* rest; *Mus.* pause. **a pausas,** intermittently

pausado /pau'saðo/ *a* deliberate, slow. *adv* slowly, deliberately

pausar /pau'sar/ *vi* to pause

pauta /'pauta/ *f*, standard, norm, design; *Fig.* guide, model

pava /'paβa/ *f*, *Argentina* kettle; *Venezuela* broad-brimmed straw hat, *inf* bad luck

pavada /pa'βaða/ *f*, flock of turkeys

pavana /pa'βana/ *f*, pavane, stately dance

pavero /pa'βero/ **(-ra)** *a* vain; strutting. *n* turkey keeper or vendor. *m*, broad-brimmed Andalusian hat; *mf*, *Chile*, *Peru* practical joker

pavimentación /paβimenta'sion; paβimenta'θion/ *f*, paving, flagging

pavimento /paβi'mento/ *m*, pavement

pavo /'paβo/ **(-va)** *n Ornith.* turkey. **p. real,** peacock. *Inf.* leap to, to serenade, court

pavón /pa'βon/ *m*, *Ornith.* peacock; peacock butterfly; preservative paint (for steel, etc.); gunmetal

pavonear /paβone'ar/ *vi* to strut, peacock (also *vr*); *Inf.* hoodwink, dazzle

pavor /pa'βor/ *m*, terror, panic

pavoroso /paβo'roso/ *a* fearful, awesome, dreadful

payador /paya'ðor/ *m*, *Argentina*, *Chile* gaucho minstrel

payasada /paia'saða/ *f*, clowning, practical joke; clown's patter

payasear /payase'ar/ *vi*, *Lat. Am.* to clown around

payaso /pa'iaso/ *m*, clown

paz /pas; paθ/ *f*, peace; harmony, concord; peaceableness. **¡P. sea en esta casa!** Peace be upon this house! (salutation). **estar en p.,** to be at peace; be quits, be even. **poner** (*or* **meter**) **p.,** to make peace (between dissentients). **venir en p.,** to come with peaceful intentions

pazguato /pas'guato; paθ'guato/ **(-ta)** *n* simpleton, *Inf.* dope

pe /pe/ *f*, name of the letter P. *Inf.* **de pe a pa,** from A to Z, from beginning to end

peaje /pe'ahe/ *m*, toll (on bridges, roads, etc.)

peatón /pea'ton/ *m*, pedestrian; walker; country postman

pebete /pe'βete/ *m*, joss stick; fuse; *Inf.* stench

peca /'peka/ *f*, mole, freckle

pecado /pe'kaðo/ *m*, sin; fault; excess; defect; *Inf.* the Devil. **p. capital,** mortal sin

pecador /peka'ðor/ *a* sinful. *m*, sinner. **¡P. de mí!** Poor me!

pecadora /peka'ðora/ *f*, sinner; *Inf.* prostitute

pecaminoso /pekami'noso/ *a* sinful

pecar /pe'kar/ *vi* to sin; trespass, transgress; (*with de*) be too... (e.g. *El libro peca de largo,* The book is too long)

peceño /pe'seɲo; pe'θeɲo/ *a* pitch-black (horses, etc.); tasting of pitch

pecera /pe'sera; pe'θera/ *f*, goldfish bowl; aquarium

pechera /pe'tʃera/ *f*, shirt front; chest protector; bib, tucker; shirt frill; *Inf.* bosom

pecho /'petʃo/ *m*, *Anat.* chest; breast; bosom; mind, conscience; courage; endurance; *Mus.* quality (of voice); incline, slope. **p. arriba,** uphill. **abrir su p. a** (*or* **con**), to unbosom oneself to. **dar el p. (a),** to suckle. **de pechos,** leaning on. **echar el p. al agua,** *Fig.* to embark courageously upon. **tomar a pechos** (**una cosa**), to take (a thing) very seriously; take to heart

pechuga /pe'tʃuga/ *f*, breast (of a bird); *Inf.* breast, bosom; slope, incline

pécora /'pekora/ *f*, sheep, head of sheep; *Inf.* wily woman, serpent

pecoso /pe'koso/ *a* freckled; spotted (with warts)

pecuario /pe'kuario/ *a Agr.* stock; cattle

peculiar /peku'liar/ *a* peculiar, individual

peculiaridad /pekuliari'ðað/ *f*, peculiarity

peculio /pe'kulio/ *m*, private money or property

pecunia /pe'kunia/ *f*, *Inf.* cash

pedagogía /peðago'hia/ *f*, education, pedagogy

pedagogo /peða'gogo/ *m*, schoolmaster; educationalist; *Fig.* mentor

pedal /pe'ðal/ *m*, *Mech.* treadle, lever, *Mus.* pedal;

Mus. sustained harmony. *Auto.* **p. de embrague,** clutch pedal

pedalear /peða'leːar/ *vi* to pedal

pedante /pe'ðante/ *a* pedantic. *mf* pedant

pedantería /peðante'ria/ *f*, pedantry

pedazo /pe'ðaso; pe'ðaθo/ *m*, bit, piece; lump; fragment, portion. *Inf.* **p. del alma, p. del corazón, p. de las entrañas,** loved one, dear one. **a pedazos** *or* **en pedazos,** in pieces, in bits. **hacer pedazos,** to break into fragments

pedernal /peðer'nal/ *m*, flint; anything very hard

pedestal /peðes'tal/ *m*, pedestal; base; stand; *Fig.* foundation

pedestre /pe'ðestre/ *a* pedestrian; dull, uninspired

pediatra /pe'ðiatra/ *mf* pediatrician

pedicuro /peði'kuro/ *m*, chiropodist

pedido /pe'ðiðo/ *m*, *Com.* order; request, petition

pedigüeño /peði'gueɲo/ *a* importunate, insistent

pedimento /peði'mento/ *m*, petition, demand; *Law.* claim; *Law.* motion

pedir /pe'ðir/ *vt irr* to ask, request; *Com.* order; demand; necessitate; desire; ask in marriage. **p. aventón** *Mexico* to hitch a ride **p. en juicio,** *Law.* to bring an action against. *Inf.* **pedírselo** (**a uno) el cuerpo,** to desire (something) ardently. **a p. de boca,** according to one's wish. *Pres. Part.* **pidiendo.** *Pres. Ind.* **pido, pides, pide, piden.** *Preterite* **pidió, pidieron.** *Pres. Subjunc.* **pida, etc.** *Imperf. Subjunc.* **pidiese, etc.**

pedo /'peðo/ *m*, fart

pedómetro /pe'ðometro/ *m*, pedometer

pedrada /pe'ðraða/ *f*, casting a stone; blow with a stone; innuendo

pedrea /pe'ðrea/ *f*, stone throwing; fight with stones; shower of hailstones

pedregal /peðre'gal/ *m*, stony ground, rocky ground

pedregoso /peðre'goso/ *a* stony

pedrera /pe'ðrera/ *f*, stone quarry

pedrería /peðre'ria/ *f*, precious stones

pedrisco /pe'ðrisko/ *m*, hailstone; shower of stones; pile of stones

pedrusco /pe'ðrusko/ *m*, *Inf.* rough, unpolished stone

pega /'pega/ *f*, sticking; cementing; joining; pitch; varnish; *Inf.* joke; beating; *Ornith.* magpie

pegadizo /pega'ðiso; pega'ðiθo/ *a* sticky, gummy, adhesive; detachable, removable; *Fig.* clinging, importunate (of people)

pegado /pe'gaðo/ *m*, sticking plaster; patch

pegajoso /pega'hoso/ *a* sticky, gluey; viscid; contagious, catching; *Inf.* oily, unctuous; *Fig. Inf.* cadging, sponging

pegar /pe'gar/ *vt* to stick; cement; join, fasten; press (against); infect with (diseases); hit, strike; give (a shout, jump, etc.); patch; *vi* spread, catch (fire, etc.); *Fig.* make an impression, have influence; be opportune; *vr Cul.* stick, burn; meddle; become enthusiastic about; take root in the mind. **p. un tiro (a),** to shoot

pegote /pe'gote/ *m*, sticking plaster; *Fig. Inf.* sponger; *Inf.* patch

peinado /pei'naðo/ *m*, hairdressing or style; headdress. *a Inf.* effeminate, overelegant (men); overcareful (style). **un p. al agua,** a finger wave

peinador /peina'ðor/ **(-ra)** *m*, peignoir, dressing gown; *Lat. Am.* dressing table. *n* hairdresser

peinadura /peina'ðura/ *f*, brushing or combing of hair; *pl* hair combings

peinar /pei'nar/ *vt* to comb, dress the hair; card (wool); cut away (rock)

peine /'peine/ *m*, comb; *Mech.* hackle, reed; instep; *Inf.* crafty person

peinería /peine'ria/ *f*, comb factory or shop

peinero /pei'nero/ *m*, comb manufacturer or seller

peineta /pei'neta/ *f*, high comb (for mantillas, etc.)

peladilla /pela'ðiya; pela'ðiʎa/ *f*, sugared almond; smooth, small pebble

pelado /pela'ðo/ *a* plucked; bare, unadorned; needy, poor; hairless; skinned; peeled; without shell; treeless

peladura /pela'ðura/ *f*, peeling; shelling; skinning; plucking (feathers)

pelafustán /pelafus'tan/ *m*, *Inf.* good-for-nothing, scamp

pelagatos /pela'gatos/ *m*, *Inf.* miserable wretch

pelágico /pe'lahiko/ *a* pelagian, oceanic

pelagra /pe'lagra/ *f*, pellagra

pelaje /pe'lahe/ *m*, fur, wool

pelamesa /pela'mesa/ *f*, brawl, fight; lock, tuft (of hair)

pelapatatas /pelapa'tatas/ *m*, potato peeler

pelar /pe'lar/ *vt* to tear out or cut the hair; pluck; skin; peel; shell; rob, fleece; *vr* lose one's hair

peldaño /pel'daɲo/ *m*, step, stair, tread, rung

pelea /pe'lea/ *f*, battle; quarrel, dispute; fight (among animals); effort, exertion; *Fig.* struggle

peleador /pelea'ðor/ *a* fighting; quarrelsome, aggressive

pelear /pele'ar/ *vi* to fight; quarrel; struggle, strive. **p. como perro y gato,** to fight like cat and mouse. *vr* come to blows; fall out, become enemies

pelechar /pele'tʃar/ *vi* to get a new coat (of animals); grow new feathers (of birds); *Inf.* prosper, flourish; grow well

pelele /pe'lele/ *m*, effigy; *Inf.* nincompoop

peletería /pelete'ria/ *f*, furrier; fur shop

peletero /pele'tero/ *m*, furrier; skinner

peliagudo /pelia'guðo/ *a* long-haired (animals); *Inf.* complicated, difficult; wily, downy

pelícano /pe'likano/ *m*, pelican

pelicorto /peli'korto/ *a* short-haired

película /pe'likula/ *f*, film. **p. fotográfica,** roll of film. **p. sonora,** sound film

peligrar /peli'grar/ *vi* to be in danger

peligro /pe'ligro/ *m*, danger, peril. **correr p.** *or* **estar en p.,** to be in danger

peligroso /peli'groso/ *a* dangerous, perilous, risky

pelilargo /peli'largo/ *a* long-haired

pelirrojo /peli'rroho/ *a* red-haired

pelleja /pe'yeha; pe'ʎeha/ *f*, hide, skin (of animals); sheepskin

pellejo /pe'yeho; pe'ʎeho/ *m*, hide; pelt; skin; wineskin; *Inf.* drunkard; peel, skin (of fruit)

pelliza /pe'yisa; pe'ʎiθa/ *f*, fur or fur-trimmed coat

pellizcar /peyis'kar; peʎiθ'kar/ *vt* to pinch, tweak, nip; pilfer

pellizco /pe'yisko; pe'ʎiθko/ *m*, pinch, nip, tweak; pilfering, pinching; bit, pinch

pelmazo /pel'maso; pel'maθo/ *m*, squashed mass; *Inf.* idler, sluggard; *Inf.* bore

pelo /'pelo/ *m*, hair; down (on birds and fruit); fiber, filament; hair trigger (firearms); hairspring (watches); kiss (in billiards); nap (of cloth), grain (of wood); flaw (in gems); raw silk. **p. chino,** *Mexico* (naturally) curly hair **p. de camello,** camel's hair. **a p.,** in the nude; without a hat; opportunely. **en p.,** bareback (of horses). **hacerse el p.,** to do one's hair; have one's hair cut. *Inf.* **no tener p. de tonto,** to be smart, clever. *Inf.* **no tener pelos en la lengua,** to be outspoken. *Inf.* **tomar el p. (a),** to pull a person's leg. **venir a p.,** to be apposite; come opportunely

pelón /pe'lon/ *a* hairless; *Fig. Inf.* broke, fleeced

pelonería /pelone'ria/ *f*, *Inf.* poverty, misery

pelota /pe'lota/ *f*, ball; ball game. **p. base,** baseball. **p. vasca,** pelota. **en p.,** stark naked

pelotari /pelo'tari/ *m*, professional pelota player

pelotazo /pelo'taso; pelo'taθo/ *m*, knock or blow with a ball

pelotear /pelote'ar/ *vt* to audit accounts; *vi* play ball; throw, cast; quarrel; argue

pelotera /pelo'tera/ *f*, *Inf.* brawl

pelotón /pelo'ton/ *m*, big ball; lump of hair; crowd, multitude; *Mil.* platoon. **p. de ejecución,** firing squad

peltre /'peltre/ *m*, pewter

peluca /pe'luka/ *f*, wig; periwig; *Inf.* scolding

peludo /pe'luðo/ *a* hairy. *m*, long-haired rug

peluquería /peluke'ria/ *f*, hairdressing establishment; hairdressing trade

peluquero /pelu'kero/ **(-ra)** *n* hairdresser; barber

peluquín /pelu'kin/ *m*, small wig

pelusa /pe'lusa/ *f*, down, soft hair; fluff, nap

pena /'pena/ *f*, punishment, penalty; grief; pain,

suffering; difficulty, trouble; mourning veil; hardship; anxiety; embarrassment; tail feather. **p. capital** *or* **p. de la vida,** capital punishment. **a duras penas,** with great difficulty. **so p. de,** under penalty of. **valer** (*or* **merecer**) **la p.,** to be worth while

penable /pe'naβle/ *a* punishable

penacho /pe'natʃo/ *m,* topknot, crest (of birds); plume, panache; *Inf.* pride, arrogance

penado /pe'naðo/ **(-da)** *a* difficult, laborious; painful, troubled, afflicted. *n* convict

penal /pe'nal/ *a* penal; punitive

penalidad /penali'ðað/ *f,* trouble, labor, difficulty; *Law.* penalty

penar /pe'nar/ *vt* to penalize; punish; *vi* suffer; undergo purgatorial pains; *vr* suffer anguish. **p. por,** to long for

penca /'penka/ *f, Bot.* fleshy leaf; lash, strap, cat-o'-nine-tails

penco /'penko/ *m, Inf.* wretched nag

pendejo /pen'deho/ *m,* pubic hair; *Inf.* coward; jerk

pendencia /pen'densia; pen'denθia/ *f,* fight; quarrel

pendenciar /penden'siar; penden'θiar/ *vi* to fight; quarrel

pendenciero /penden'siero; penden'θiero/ *a* quarrelsome, aggressive

pender /pen'der/ *vi* to hang; depend; be pending

pendiente /pen'diente/ *a* pending; hanging; *Com.* outstanding. *m,* earring; pendant. *f,* slope, incline; gradient

péndola /'pendola/ *f,* feather, plume; quill pen; pendulum (of a clock)

pendolista /pendo'lista/ *mf* calligrapher

pendón /pen'don/ *m,* pennon, banner; *Bot.* shoot; *Inf.* lanky, slatternly woman; *pl* reins

péndulo /'pendulo/ *a* pendulous, hanging. *m,* pendulum

pene /'pene/ *m,* penis

peneque /pe'neke/ *m, Mexico* roll of maize dough filled with cheese

penetrabilidad /penetraβili'ðað/ *f,* penetrability

penetración /penetra'sion; penetra'θion/ *f,* penetration; understanding, perspicuity; sagacity, shrewdness

penetrador /penetra'ðor/ *a* penetrating, perspicacious; sagacious, acute

penetrante /pene'trante/ *a* penetrating; deep; piercing (of sounds); acute, shrewd

penetrar /pene'trar/ *vt* to penetrate; permeate; master, comprehend; (*with en*) enter

penetrativo /penetra'tiβo/ *a* piercing

penicilina /penisi'lina; peniθi'lina/ *f,* penicillin

península /pe'ninsula/ *f,* peninsula. **la P.** the Iberian Peninsula

Península Ibérica, la /pe'ninsula i'βerika, la/ the Iberian Peninsula

penique /pe'nike/ *m,* penny

penitencia /peni'tensia; peni'tenθia/ *f,* penitence, repentance; penance

penitencial /peniten'sial; peniten'θial/ *a* penitential

penitenciaría /penitensia'ria; penitenθia'ria/ *f,* penitentiary

penitente /peni'tente/ *a* penitent, repentant. *mf* penitent

penoso /pe'noso/ *a* laborious, difficult; grievous; painful; troublesome; *Inf.* foppish; *Lat. Am.* shy, timid

pensado /pen'saðo/ *a* premeditated, deliberate. **de p.,** intentionally. **mal p.,** malicious, evil-minded

pensador /pensa'ðor/ *a* thinking; pensive. *m,* thinker

pensamiento /pensa'miento/ *m,* mind; thought; idea; suspicion, doubt; heartsease pansy; maxim; intention, project

pensar /pen'sar/ *vt irr* to think; purpose, intend; (*with en, sobre*) reflect upon; think about; *vt* feed (animals). **p. entre sí. p. para consigo** *or* **p. para sí,** to think to oneself. See **acertar**

pensativo /pensa'tiβo/ *a* reflective, pensive

pensil /pen'sil/ *a* hanging. *m,* hanging garden; delightful garden

pensión /pen'sion/ *f,* pension, allowance; boarding

house, private hotel; scholarship grant; cost of board; trouble, drudgery

pensionado /pensio'naðo/ **(-da)** *a* pensioned; retired. *n* scholarship holder. *m,* boarding school

pensionar /pensio'nar/ *vt* to pension, grant a pension to; charge a pension on

pensionista /pensio'nista/ *mf* pensioner; boarder

pentágono /pen'tagono/ *m,* pentagon. *a* pentagonal

pentámetro /pen'tametro/ *m,* pentameter

Pentateuco /penta'teuko/ *m,* Pentateuch

Pentecostés /pentekos'tes/ *m,* Pentecost, Whitsuntide

penúltimo /pe'nultimo/ *a* next to the last, penultimate

penuria /pe'nuria/ *f,* scarcity; want, penury

peña /'pena/ *f,* crag, rock; boulder; group of friends; club. **ser una p.,** to be stony-hearted

peñasco /pe'ɲasko/ *m,* craggy peak

peñascoso /peɲas'koso/ *a* craggy, rocky

peñón /pe'ɲon/ *m,* rock; cliff; peak

peón /pe'on/ *m,* pedestrian; laborer; *South America* farmhand; top (toy); piece (chess, checkers); *Mech.* axle; infantryman. **p. caminero,** road mender. **p. de ajedrez,** pawn (in chess)

peonada /peo'naða/ *f,* day's manual labor; gang of laborers

peonar /peo'nar/ *vi, Argentina* to do manual labor

peonía /peo'nia/ *f,* peony

peonza /pe'onsa; pe'onθa/ *f,* top; teetotum

peor /pe'or/ *a comp* **malo** worse. *adv comp* **mal,** worse. *a sup* **el (la, lo)** peor; los **(las)** peores, the worst. **p. que p.,** worse and worse. **tanto p.,** so much the worse

pepino /pe'pino/ *m,* cucumber plant; cucumber; *Fig.* pin, straw

pepita /pe'pita/ *f, Mineral.* nugget; pip, seed (of fruit)

péptico /'peptiko/ *a* peptic

pequeñez /peke'ɲes; peke'ɲeθ/ *f,* littleness, smallness; pettiness; childhood; infancy; trifle, insignificant thing; meanness, baseness

pequeño /pe'keɲo/ *a* little, small; petty; very young; short, brief; humble, lowly

pequero, -a /pe'kero/ *mf, Argentina* cardsharp

pera /'pera/ *f,* pear; goatee; *Fig.* plum, sinecure

peral /pe'ral/ *m,* pear tree; pearwood

perca /'perka/ *f, Ichth.* perch

percal /per'kal/ *m,* percale, calico

percalina /perka'lina/ *f,* percaline, binding cloth

percance /per'kanse; per'kanθe/ *m,* perquisite, attribute (gen. *pl*); disaster, mischance

percebe /per'seβe; per'θeβe/ *m,* (gen. *pl*) goose barnacle

percentaje /persen'tahe; perθen'tahe/ *m,* percentage

percepción /persep'sion; perθep'θion/ *f,* perception; idea, conception

perceptible /persep'tiβle; perθep'tiβle/ *a* perceptible

perceptivo /persep'tiβo; perθep'tiβo/ *a* perceptive

perceptor /persep'tor; perθep'tor/ **(-ra)** *a* perceptive. *n* observer

percha /'pertʃa/ *f,* stake, pole; coat hanger; perch (for birds); rack (for hay); hall stand, coat and hat stand, coatrack

perchero /per'tʃero/ *m,* hall stand; clothes rack; row of perches (for fowl, etc.)

percibir /persi'βir; perθi'βir/ *vt* to collect, draw, receive; perceive; understand, grasp

percibo /per'siβo; per'θiβo/ *m,* perceiving; collecting, drawing, receiving

percolador /perkola'ðor/ *m,* percolator (coffee)

percusión /perku'sion/ *f,* percussion; shock, vibration

percusor /perku'sor/ *m,* hammer (of a firearm)

percutir /perku'tir/ *vt* to percuss, strike

perdedor /perðe'ðor/ **(-ra)** *a* losing. *n* loser

perder /per'ðer/ *vt* to lose; throw away, squander; spoil, destroy; *vi* fade (of colors); *vr* lose one's way, be lost; be confused or perplexed; be shipwrecked; take to vice, become dissolute; be spoiled or destroyed; disappear; love madly. **p. la chaveta (por),** to go out of one's head (for), be wild (about). **p. la**

ocasión, to let the chance slip. **p. los estribos,** to lose patience. **p. terreno,** to lose ground. **perderse de vista,** to be lost to sight. **echarse a p.,** to spoil, be damaged. See **entender**

perdición /perði'sion; perði'θion/ f, loss; perdition, ruin; damnation; depravity, viciousness

pérdida /'perðiða/ f, loss; waste. **p. cuantiosa,** heavy losses

perdidamente /perðiða'mente/ adv ardently, desperately; uselessly

perdigón /perði'gon/ m, young partridge; decoy partridge; hailstone, pellet, shot

perdigonada /perðigo'naða/ f, volley of hailstone; hailstone wound

perdiguero /perði'gero/ (-ra) n game dealer; setter, retriever

perdiz /per'ðis; per'ðiθ/ f, partridge

perdón /per'ðon/ m, pardon, forgiveness; remission. **con p.,** with your permission; excuse me

perdonable /perðo'naβle/ a pardonable, excusable

perdonar /perðo'nar/ vt to pardon, forgive; remit, excuse; exempt; waste, lose; give up (a privilege)

perdonavidas /perðona'βiðas/ m, Inf. bully, braggart

perdulario /perðu'lario/ a careless, negligent; slovenly; vicious, depraved

perdurable /perðu'raβle/ a perpetual, everlasting; enduring, lasting

perdurar /perðu'rar/ vi to last, endure

perecedero /perese'ðero; pereθe'ðero/ a brief, fugitive, transient; perishable. m, Inf. poverty, want

perecer /pere'ser; pere'θer/ vi irr to end, finish; perish, die; suffer (damage, grief, etc.); be destitute; vr (with por) long for, crave; desire ardently. See **conocer**

peregrinación /peregrina'sion; peregrina'θion/ f, journey, peregrination; pilgrimage

peregrinamente /peregrina'mente/ adv rarely, not often; beautifully, perfectly

peregrinar /peregri'nar/ vi to journey, travel; make a pilgrimage

peregrino /pere'grino/ (-na) a and n pilgrim. a migratory (birds); rare, unusual; extraordinary, strange; beautiful, perfect

perejil /pere'hil/ m, parsley; Inf. ornament or apparel (gen. pl); pl honors, titles

perengano /peren'gano/ (-na) n so-and-so, such a one

perenne /pe'renne/ a incessant, constant; Bot. perennial

perennidad /perenni'ðað/ f, perpetuity

perentoriedad /perentorie'ðað/ f, peremptoriness; urgency

perentorio /peren'torio/ a peremptory; conclusive, decisive; urgent, pressing

pereza /pe'resa; pe'reθa/ f, laziness; languor, inertia; slowness, deliberateness

perezoso /pere'soso; pere'θoso/ a lazy; languid; slothful; slow, deliberate. m, Zool. sloth

perfección /perfek'sion; perfek'θion/ f, perfection; perfecting, perfect thing, virtue, grace

perfeccionamiento /perfeksiona'miento; perfekθiona'miento/ m, perfecting; progress, improvement

perfeccionar /perfeksio'nar; perfekθio'nar/ vt to perfect; complete

perfectamente /perfekta'mente/ adv perfectly; quite, entirely

perfecto /per'fekto/ a perfect; excellent, very good; complete; whole; Gram. perfect

perfidia /per'fiðia/ f, perfidy, treachery

pérfido /'perfiðo/ a perfidious, treacherous

perfil /per'fil/ m, ornament, decoration; outline, contour; profile; section (of metal); fine stroke (of letters); pl finishing touches; politeness, attention, courtesy. **de p.,** in profile; sideways

perfilado /perfi'laðo/ a long, elongated (of faces, etc.)

perfilar /perfi'lar/ vt to draw in profile; outline; vr place oneself sideways, show one's profile; Inf. dress up, titivate

perforación /perfora'sion; perfora'θion/ f, perforation, boring; hole

perforador /perfora'ðor/ a perforating, boring. m, Mech. drill

perforar /perfo'rar/ vt to perforate, pierce; bore, drill, make a hole in

perfumador /perfuma'ðor/ (-ra) a perfuming. n perfumer. m, perfume burner

perfumar /perfu'mar/ vt to perfume; vi give off perfume

perfume /per'fume/ m, perfume; scent, fragrance

perfumería /perfume'ria/ f, scent factory; perfumery; perfume shop

perfumista /perfu'mista/ mf perfumer

perfunctorio /perfunk'torio/ a perfunctory

pergamino /perga'mino/ m, parchment, vellum; document; diploma; pl aristocratic descent

pericardio /peri'karðio/ m, pericardium

pericia /pe'risia; pe'riθia/ f, expertness; skilled workmanship

pericial /peri'sial; peri'θial/ a expert, skillful

perico /pe'riko/ m, parakeet; giant asparagus

periferia /peri'feria/ f, periphery

periférico /peri'feriko/ a peripheral

perifollos /peri'foyos; peri'foʎos/ m pl, Inf. frills, flounces, finery

perifrástico /peri'frastiko/ a periphrastic

perilla /pe'riya; pe'riʎa/ f, pear-shaped ornament; goatee; imperial. **p. de la oreja,** lobe of the ear. **venir de p.,** to be most opportune

perillán /peri'yan; peri'ʎan/ m, Inf. rascal, rogue

perímetro /pe'rimetro/ m, perimeter; precincts

perínclito /pe'rinklito/ a distinguished, illustrious; heroic

perineo /peri'neo/ m, perineum

perínola /peri'nola/ f, top, teetotum

periodicidad /perioðisi'ðað; perioðiθi'ðað/ f, periodicity

periódico /pe'rioðiko/ a periodic. m, newspaper; periodical publication

periodicucho /perioði'kutʃo/ m, rag (bad newspaper)

periodismo /perio'ðismo/ m, journalism

periodista /perio'ðista/ mf journalist

periodístico /perio'ðistiko/ a journalistic

período /pe'rioðo/ m, period; Phys. cycle; menstruation period; Gram. clause; age, era

periostio /pe'riostio/ m, periosteum

peripatético /peripa'tetiko/ a peripatetic

peripecia /peri'pesia; peri'peθia/ f, sudden change of fortune, vicissitude

peripuesto /peri'puesto/ a Inf. overelegant, spruce; too well-dressed; smart

periquete /peri'kete/ m, Inf. jiffy, trice

periquito /peri'kito/ m, parakeet; budgerigar

periscopio /peris'kopio/ m, periscope

perito /pe'rito/ (-ta) a expert; skillful, experienced. n expert

peritoneo /perito'neo/ m, peritoneum

perjudicador /perhuðika'ðor/ (-ra) a injurious, prejudicial. n injurer

perjudicar /perhuði'kar/ vt to harm, damage, injure; prejudice

perjudicial /perhuði'sial; perhuði'θial/ a injurious, noxious, harmful; prejudicial

perjuicio /per'huisio; per'huiθio/ m, injury, damage; harm; Law. prejudice

perjurador /perhura'ðor/ (-ra) n perjurer

perjurar /perhu'rar/ vi to perjure oneself, commit perjury; swear, curse

perjurio /per'hurio/ m, perjury

perjuro /per'huro/ (-ra) a perjured, forsworn. n perjurer

perla /'perla/ f, pearl; Archit. bead; Fig. treasure, jewel, dear. **de perlas,** excellent; exactly right

perlero /per'lero/ a pearl

perlesía /perle'sia/ f, paralysis; palsy

perlino /per'lino/ a pearly, pearl-colored

permanecer /permane'ser; permane'θer/ vi irr to stay, remain. **p. en posición de firme,** to stand at attention. See **conocer**

permanencia /perma'nensia; perma'nenθia/ *f*, stay, sojourn; permanence

permanente /perma'nente/ *a* permanent; lasting, enduring

permeabilidad /permeaβili'ðað/ *f*, permeability

permisible /permi'siβle/ *a* permissible, allowable

permisivo /permi'siβo/ *a* permissive

permiso /per'miso/ *m*, permission, leave; permit; (*Mil.* etc.) pass. ¡**Con p.!** Excuse me!; Allow me!

permitir /permi'tir/ *vt* to permit, allow

permuta /per'muta/ *f*, exchange

permutación /permuta'sion; permuta'θion/ *f*, permutation, interchange

permutar /permu'tar/ *vt* to exchange

pernear /perne'ar/ *vi* to kick; *Inf.* bustle; fret, be impatient

pernetas, en /per'netas, en/ *adv* barelegged

perniciosidad /pernisiosi'ðað; perniθiosi'ðað/ *f*, perniciousness

pernicioso /perni'sioso; perni'θioso/ *a* pernicious

pernil /per'nil/ *m*, *Anat.* hock; ham; leg of pork; leg (of trousers)

pernio /'pernio/ *m*, hinge (of doors, windows)

perniquebrar /pernike'βrar/ *vt irr* to break the legs of. See **quebrar**

perno /'perno/ *m*, bolt, pin, spike

pernoctar /pernok'tar/ *vi* to spend the night (away from home)

pero /'pero/ *conjunc* but. *m*, *Inf.* defect; difficulty, snag

perogrullada /perogru'yaða; perogru'ʎaða/ *f*, *Inf.* truism

perol /pe'rol/ *m*, *Cul.* pan

peroné /pero'ne/ *m*, fibula

peronista /pero'nista/ *a*, *mf* Peronist

peroración /perora'sion; perora'θion/ *f*, peroration

perorar /pero'rar/ *vi* to make a speech; *Inf.* speak pompously; ask insistently

peróxido /pe'roksiðo/ *m*, peroxide

perpendicular /perpendiku'lar/ *a* perpendicular. *f*, perpendicular

perpetración /perpetra'sion; perpetra'θion/ *f*, perpetration

perpetrar /perpe'trar/ *vt* to perpetrate

perpetua /per'petua/ *f*, *Bot.* immortelle, everlasting

perpetuación /perpetua'sion; perpetua'θion/ *f*, perpetuation

perpetuar /perpe'tuar/ *vt* to perpetuate; *vr* last, endure

perpetuidad /perpetui'ðað/ *f*, perpetuity

perpetuo /per'petuo/ *a* everlasting; lifelong

perplejidad /perplehi'ðað/ *f*, perplexity, bewilderment, doubt

perplejo /per'pleho/ *a* perplexed, bewildered, doubtful

perquirir /perki'rir/ *vt irr* to search carefully. See **adquirir**

perra /'perra/ *f*, bitch; *Inf.* sot, drunkard; tantrums. **p. chica,** five-cent coin. **p. gorda,** ten-cent coin

perrada /pe'rraða/ *f*, pack of dogs; *Inf.* dirty trick

perramus /per'rramus/ *m*, *Argentina* raincoat

perrengue /pe'rrengue/ *m*, *Inf.* short-tempered person

perrera /pe'rrera/ *f*, dog kennel; useless toil; *Inf.* tantrums

perrería /perre'ria/ *f*, pack of dogs; *Inf.* dirty trick; fit of anger

perrero /pe'rrero/ *m*, dog fancier; kennel worker

perro /'perro/ *m*, dog. **p. caliente** hot dog. **p. danés,** Great Dane. **p. de aguas,** poodle; spaniel. **p. de casta,** thoroughbred dog. **p. de lanas** poodle. **p. de muestra,** pointer. **p. de presa,** bulldog. **p. de San Bernardo,** St. Bernard (dog). **p. de Terranova,** Newfoundland (dog). **p. del hortelano,** dog in the manger. **p. dogo** bulldog. **p. esquimal** husky. **p. faldero,** lap dog. **p. lobo,** wolfhound. **p. pachón,** dachshund. **p. pastor alemán** *or* **p. policía,** German shepherd. **p. pequinés,** Pekingese. **p. perdiguero,** retriever. **p. pomerano,** spitz, Pomeranian (dog). **p. sabueso español,** spaniel. **p. zorrero,** foxhound. *Inf.* **A p. viejo**

no hay tus tus, You can't fool an old dog. **vivir como perros y gatos,** Inf. to live like cat and dog

persa /'persa/ *a* and *mf* Persian. *m*, Persian (language)

persecución /perseku'sion; perseku'θion/ *f*, pursuit; persecution; annoyance, importuning

perseguidor /persegi'ðor/ **(-ra)** *a* pursuing; tormenting. *n* pursuer; tormentor, persecutor

perseguimiento /persegi'miento/ *m*, pursuit

perseguir /perse'gir/ *vi irr* to pursue; persecute, torment; importune. See **seguir**

perseverancia /perseβe'ransia; perseβe'ranθia/ *f*, perseverance

perseverante /perseβe'rante/ *a* persevering; constant

perseverar /perseβe'rar/ *vi* to persevere; last, endure

persiana /per'siana/ *f*, Venetian blind; flowered silk material

pérsico /'persiko/ *a* Persian. *m*, peach tree; peach

persignar /persig'nar/ *vr* to sign; make the sign of the cross over; *vr* cross oneself

persistencia /persis'tensia; persis'tenθia/ *f*, persistence

persistente /persis'tente/ *a* persistent

persistir /persis'tir/ *vi* to persist

persona /per'sona/ *f*, person; personage; character (in a play, etc.); (*Gram. Eccl.*) person. **de p. a p.,** in private, face to face

personaje /perso'nahe/ *m*, important person, personage; character (in a play, etc.)

personal /perso'nal/ *a* personal. *m*, staff, personnel

personalidad /personali'ðað/ *f*, personality

personalismo /persona'lismo/ *m*, personality; personal question

personalizar /personali'sar; personali'θar/ *vt* to become personal, be offensive

personalmente /personal'mente/ *adv* personally

personarse /perso'narse/ *vr* to present oneself, call, appear

personificación /personifika'sion; personifika'θion/ *f*, personification

personificar /personifi'kar/ *vt* to personify

perspectiva /perspek'tiβa/ *f*, perspective; view; outlook; aspect, appearance. **p. aérea,** bird's-eye view

perspicacia /perspi'kasia; perspi'kaθia/ *f*, perspicacity, shrewdness

perspicaz /perspi'kas; perspi'kaθ/ *a* perspicacious, clear-sighted

perspicuidad /perspikui'ðað/ *f*, perspicuity

perspicuo /pers'pikuo/ *a* lucid, clear

persuadir /persua'ðir/ *vt* to persuade

persuasible /persua'siβle/ *a* persuadable

persuasión /persua'sion/ *f*, persuasion; belief, conviction, opinion

persuasiva /persua'siβa/ *f*, persuasiveness

persuasivo /persua'siβo/ *a* persuasive

pertenecer /pertene'ser; pertene'θer/ *vi irr* to belong; relate, concern. See **conocer**

perteneciente /pertene'siente; pertene'θiente/ *a* belonging (to), pertaining (to)

pertenencia /perte'nensia; perte'nenθia/ *f*, ownership, proprietorship; property, accessory

pértiga /'pertiga/ *f*, long rod; pole. **salto de p.,** pole vaulting

pertinacia /perti'nasia; perti'naθia/ *f*, pertinacity, doggedness

pertinaz /perti'nas; perti'naθ/ *a* pertinacious, stubborn, dogged

pertinencia /perti'nensia; perti'nenθia/ *f*, relevance, appropriateness

pertinente /perti'nente/ *a* relevant, apposite; appropriate

pertrechar /pertre'tʃar/ *vt* to supply, equip; prepare, make ready

pertrechos /per'tretʃos/ *m pl*, *Mil.* armaments, stores; equipment, appliances

perturbación /perturβa'sion; perturβa'θion/ *f*, disturbance; agitation

perturbador /perturβa'ðor/ **(-ra)** *a* disturbing. *n* disturber; heckler

perturbar /pertur'βar/ *vt* to disturb; agitate

Perú /pe'ru/ *m* Peru. **la República del P.**, Peru
peruano /pe'ruano/ **(-na)** *a* and *n* Peruvian
perversidad /perβersi'ðað/ *f*, wickedness, depravity
perversión /perβer'sion/ *f*, perversion; wickedness, evil
perversivo /perβer'siβo/ *a* perversive
perverso /per'βerso/ *a* wicked, iniquitous, depraved
pervertir /perβer'tir/ *vt irr* to pervert, corrupt; distort. See **sentir**
pesa /'pesa/ *f*, weight; clock weight; gymnast's weight. **pesas y medidas,** weights and measures
pesacartas /pesa'kartas/ *m*, letter scale, letter balance
pesada /pe'saða/ *f*, weighing
pesadez /pesa'ðes; pesa'ðeθ/ *f*, heaviness; obesity; tediousness, tiresomeness; slowness; fatigue
pesadilla /pesa'ðiya; pesa'ðiʎa/ *f*, nightmare
pesado /pe'saðo/ *a* heavy; obese; deep (of sleep); oppressive (of weather); slow; unwieldy; tedious; impertinent; dull, boring; offensive
pesadumbre /pesa'ðumbre/ *f*, heaviness; grief, sorrow; trouble, anxiety
pésame /'pesame/ *m*, expression of condolence. **dar el p.,** to present one's condolences
pesantez /pesan'tes; pesan'teθ/ *f*, weight, heaviness; seriousness, gravity
pesar /pe'sar/ *m*, grief, sorrow; remorse. **a p. de,** in spite of
pesar /pe'sar/ *vi* to weigh; be heavy; be important; grieve, cause regret (e.g. *Me pesa mucho,* I am very sorry); influence, affect; *vt* weigh; consider. **Mal que me (te,** etc.**) pese...,** Much as I regret...
pesaroso /pesa'roso/ *a* regretful, remorseful; sorrowful
pesca /'peska/ *f*, fishery; angling, fishing; catch of fish. **p. a la rastra,** trawling. **p. deportiva** sport fishing. **p. mayor,** deep-sea fishing
pescadería /peskaðe'ria/ *f*, fishery; fish store; fish market
pescadilla /peska'ðiya; peska'ðiʎa/ *f*, *Ichth.* whiting
pescado /pes'kaðo/ *m*, fish (out of the water), cooked fish; salt cod
pescador /peska'ðor/ **(-ra)** *n* fisherman; angler
pescante /pes'kante/ *m*, driving seat; coach box; jib (of a crane)
pescar /pes'kar/ *vt* to fish; *Inf.* catch in the act; acquire. **p. a la rastra,** to trawl
pescozón /pesko'son; pesko'θon/ *m*, slap on the neck or head
pescuezo /pes'kueso; pes'kueθo/ *m*, neck; throat; haughtiness, arrogance. **torcer el p.,** to wring the neck (of chickens, etc.)
pesebre /pe'seβre/ *m*, manger, stable; feeding trough
pesero /pe'sero/ *m*, *Mexico* jitney, jitney taxi
pésimamente /'pesimamente/ *adv* extremely badly
pesimismo /pesi'mismo/ *m*, pessimism
pesimista /pesi'mista/ *a* pessimistic. *mf* pessimist
pésimo /'pesimo/ *a sup* **malo** extremely bad
peso /'peso/ *m*, weighing; weight; heaviness; gravity; importance; influence; load; peso (money); scale, balance. **p. bruto,** gross weight. **p. de joyería,** troy weight. **p. específico,** *Phys.* specific gravity. **p. pluma,** (*Box.*) featherweight
pespunte /pes'punte/ *m*, backstitch
pesquera /pes'kera/ *f*, fishing ground, fishery
pesquería /peske'ria/ *f*, fishing, angling; fisherman's trade; fishing ground, fishery
pesquero /pes'kero/ *a* fishing (of boats, etc.)
pesquisa /pes'kisa/ *f*, investigation, examination, search
pesquisar /peski'sar/ *vt* to investigate, look into; search
pestaña /pes'tana/ *f*, eyelash; *Sew.* edging, fringe; ear, lug; *Naut.* fluke
pestañear /pestane'ar/ *vi* to wink; blink; flutter one's eyelashes
pestañeo /pesta'neo/ *m*, winking; blinking
peste /'peste/ *f*, plague, pestilence; nauseous smell; epidemic; pest; vice; *Chile* smallpox; *pl* oaths, curses. **p. bubónica,** bubonic plague. **p. roja** syphilis. **p. de las abejas,** foul brood. **echar pestes,** to swear; fume

pestífero /pes'tifero/ *a* noxious
pestilencia /pesti'lensia; pesti'lenθia/ *f*, plague, pestilence
pestilente /pesti'lente/ *a* pestilential
pestillo /pes'tiyo; pes'tiʎo/ *m*, latch; lock bolt. **p. de golpe,** safety latch
petaca /pe'taka/ *f*, cigarette or cigar case; tobacco pouch; *Mexico* suitcase.
pétalo /'petalo/ *m*, petal
petardista /petar'ðista/ *mf* swindler, impostor
petardo /pe'tarðo/ *m*, detonator; torpedo; firecracker; fraud
petición /peti'sion; peti'θion/ *f*, petition, request
peticionar /petisio'nar; petiθio'nar/ *vt*, *Lat. Am.* to petition
peticionario /petisio'nario; petiθio'nario/ **(-ia)** *n* petitioner. *a* petitionary
petimetra /peti'metra/ *f*, stylish and affected young woman
petimetre /peti'metre/ *m*, fop
petirrojo /peti'rroho/ *m*, robin
petitorio /peti'torio/ *a* petitionary. *m*, *Inf.* importunity
peto /'peto/ *m*, breastplate; front (of a shirt); bib
pétreo /'petreo/ *a* petrous
petrificación /petrifika'sion; petrifika'θion/ *f*, petrifaction
petrificar /petrifi'kar/ *vt* to petrify; *vr* become petrified
petrografía /petrogra'fia/ *f*, petrology
petróleo /pe'troleo/ *m*, petroleum; oil, mineral oil. **p. bruto,** crude oil. **p. de lámpara,** kerosene
petrolero /petro'lero/ **(-ra)** *a* oil, petroleum. *n* petroleum seller; incendiarist. *m*, oil tanker
petrolífero /petro'lifero/ *a* oil-bearing
petulancia /petu'lansia; petu'lanθia/ *f*, insolence; vanity
petulante /petu'lante/ *a* insolent; vain
pez /pes; peθ/ *m*, fish; *pl* Pisces. *f*, *Chem.* pitch. **p. sierra,** swordfish
pezón /pe'son; pe'θon/ *m*, *Bot.* stalk; nipple; axle pivot; point (of land, etc.)
pezuña /pe'suna; pe'θuna/ *f*, cloven hoof (of cows, pigs, etc.)
piada /'piaða/ *f*, chirping, twittering
piadoso /pia'ðoso/ *a* compassionate; kind, pitiful; pious, religious
piafar /pia'far/ *vi* to stamp, paw the ground (horses)
pianista /pia'nista/ *mf* piano maker; piano dealer; pianist
piano /'piano/ *m*, pianoforte. **p. de cola,** grand piano. **p. de media cola,** baby grand. **p. vertical,** upright piano
piante /'piante/ *a* chirping, twittering
piar /piar/ *vi* to chirp, twitter
piara /'piara/ *f*, herd of swine; pack (of horses, etc.)
pibe, -a /'piβe/ *mf*, *Argentina* kid, child
pica /'pika/ *f*, *Mil.* pike; bullfighter's goad; pike soldier; stonecutter's hammer. **a p. seca,** in vain. **pasar por las picas,** to suffer hardship. **poner una p. en Flandes,** to triumph over great difficulties
picacho /pi'katʃo/ *m*, peak, summit
picada /pi'kaða/ *f*, prick; bite; peck; *Aer.* dive
picadero /pika'ðero/ *m*, riding school; paddock (of a racetrack)
picado /pi'kaðo/ *a Sew.* pinked. *m*, *Cul.* hash
picador /pika'ðor/ *m*, horse trainer; meat chopper; horseman armed with a goad (bullfights)
picadura /pika'ðura/ *f*, puncture; prick; sting; *Sew.* pinking; peck (of birds); cut tobacco; black tobacco; beginning of caries in teeth
picajoso /pika'hoso/ *a* hypersensitive, touchy, peevish
picamaderos /pikama'ðeros/ *m*, woodpecker
picanear /pikane'ar/ *vt*, *Lat. Am.* to goad on, spur on
picante /pi'kante/ *a* piquant; mordant; hot, highly seasoned. *m*, mordancy; pungency
picantería /pikante'ria/ *f*, *Lat. Am.* restaurant specializing in spicy foods

picapleitos /pika'pleitos/ *m*, *Inf*. shady lawyer, *Inf*. ambulance chaser

picaporte /pika'porte/ *m*, latch, door catch; door knocker

picar /pi'kar/ *vt* to prick; sting; peck; bite; chop fine; mince; nibble (of fishing); irritate (the skin); *Sew*. pink; burn (the tongue); eat (grapes); goad; spur; stipple (walls); stimulate, encourage; split, cleave; *Mil*. harass; vex; *Mus*. play staccato; *vi* burn (of the sun); smart (of cuts, etc.); eat sparingly; *Auto*. knock; (*with en*) knock at (doors, etc.); *vr* be motheaten; go rotten (fruit, etc.); grow choppy (of the sea); be piqued; boast

picardear /pikarðe'ar/ *vi* to play the rogue; behave mischievously

picardía /pikar'ðia/ *f*, knavery, roguery; mischievousness; practical joke; wantonness

picaresco /pika'resko/ *a* roguish, picaresque, knavish

pícaro /'pikaro/ (**-ra**) *a* knavish; base, vile; astute; mischievous. *n* rogue

picatoste /pika'toste/ *m*, kind of fritter

picaza /pi'kasa; pi'kaθa/ *f*, magpie

picazo /pi'kaso; pi'kaθo/ *m*, blow with a pike or anything pointed; peck, tap with a beak (of birds); sting

picazón /pika'son; pika'θon/ *f*, itch, irritation; annoyance

pícea /'pisea; 'piθea/ *f*, *Bot*. spruce

píceo /'piseo; 'piθeo/ *a* piscine, fish-like

pichincha /pi'tʃintʃa/ *f*, *Argentina* bargain

pichón /pi'tʃon/ (**-ona**) *m*, male pigeon. *n Inf*. darling

pico /'piko/ *m*, beak (of birds); peak; woodpecker; odd amount (e.g. *treinta y p.*, thirty-odd); sharp point; spout (of a jug, etc.); *Inf*. mouth; blarney, gab. **p. de cigüeña,** crane's-bill. **p. de oro,** silver-tongued orator

picor /pi'kor/ *m*, burning sensation in the mouth; smarting; itching, irritation

picoso /pi'koso/ *a* pitted, marked by smallpox; *Mexico* hot, spicy (food)

picota /pi'kota/ *f*, pillory; peak; spire

picotazo /piko'taso; piko'taθo/ *m*, peck; dab; sting, bite

picotear /pikote'ar/ *vt* to peck (of a bird); *vi* toss the head (of horses); *Inf*. chatter senselessly; *vr Inf*. slang each other

picotero /piko'tero/ *a Inf*. chattering, talkative; indiscreet

pictórico /pik'toriko/ *a* pictorial

picudo /pi'kuðo/ *a* pointed, peaked; having a spout; *Inf*. chattering; *Mexico* clever, crafty, sly

pie /pie/ *m*, foot; stand, support; stem (of a glass, etc.); standard (of a lamp); *Bot*. trunk, stem; sapling; lees, sediment; *Theat*. cue; foot (measure); custom; (metrics) foot; motive, cause; pretext; (metrics) meter. **p. de cabra,** crowbar. **p. de imprenta,** printer's mark, printer's imprint. **p. de piña,** clubfoot. **p. de rey,** calliper. **p. palmado,** webfoot. **al p. de la letra,** punctiliously. *Inf*. **andar con pies de plomo,** to walk warily. **a p.,** on foot. **a p. firme,** without budging, steadfastly. *Inf*. **buscar tres pies al gato,** to look for something that isn't there; twist a person's words. **de a p.,** on foot. **en p. de guerra,** on a wartime footing. *Inf*. **poner pies en polvorosa,** to quit

piedad /pie'ðað/ *f*, piety; pity, compassion; *Art*. pietà

piedra /'pieðra/ *f*, stone; tablet; *Med*. gravel. **p. de amolar,** whetstone, grindstone. **p. angular,** cornerstone (also *Fig*.). **p. caliza,** limestone. **p. clave,** keystone. **p. de construcción,** building stone; child's block. **p. de toque,** touchstone, test. **p. filosofal,** philosopher's stone. **p. fundamental,** foundation stone. **p. miliaria,** milestone. **p. mortuoria,** tombstone. *Fig*. *Inf*. **no dejar p. sin remover,** to leave no stone unturned. **no dejar p. sobre p.,** to demolish, destroy completely

piel /piel/ *f*, skin; fur; hide; leather; peel (of some fruits); rind (of bacon). **p. de gallina,** *Fig*. goose flesh. **p. de rata,** horse blanket. **p. de Rusia,** Russian leather.

piélago /'pielago/ *m*, high seas; sea, ocean; glut, superabundance

pienso /'pienso/ *m*, *Agr*. fodder

pierna /'pierna/ *f*, *Anat*. leg; *Mech*. shank; leg of a compass. *Inf*. **a p. suelta,** at one's ease. **en piernas,** barelegged

pietista /pie'tista/ *a* pietistic. *mf* pietist

pieza /'piesa; 'pieθa/ *f*, portion; piece; component part; room; *Theat*. play; roll (of cloth); piece (in chess, etc.); coin; piece (of music). **p. de recambio** *or* **p. de repuesto,** spare part. **p. de recibo,** reception room. *Inf*. **quedarse en una p.,** to be struck dumb

pífano /'pifano/ *m*, fife; fife player, fifer

pigmentación /pigmenta'sion; pigmenta'θion/ *f*, pigmentation

pigmento /pig'mento/ *m*, pigment

pignoración /pignora'sion; pignora'θion/ *f*, hypothecation; pawning; mortgage

pignorar /pigno'rar/ *vt* to hypothecate; pawn; mortgage

pigre /'pigre/ *a* lazy; negligent, careless

pigricia /pi'grisia; pi'griθia/ *f*, laziness; negligence *Chile*, *Peru* trifle

pijama /pi'hama/ *m*, pajamas

pila /'pila/ *f*, trough, basin; heap, pile; *Elec*. battery; *Eccl*. parish; pier, pile; *Phys*. cell. **p. atómica,** atomic pile. **p. bautismal,** *Eccl*. font

pilar /pi'lar/ *m*, fountain basin; milestone; pillar

pilastra /pi'lastra/ *f*, pier, pile; pilaster

pilche /'piltʃe/ *m*, *Lat. Am*. calabash, gourd

píldora /'pildora/ *f*, *Med*. pill; *Inf*. disagreeable news

pileta /pi'leta/ (**de natación**) *f*, *Argentina*, (swimming) pool

pillador /piʎa'ðor; piʎa'ðor/ (**-ra**) *a* pillaging, plundering. *n* plunderer

pillaje /pi'yahe; pi'ʎahe/ *m*, pillaging, looting; robbery, theft

pillar /pi'yar; pi'ʎar/ *vt* to pillage; steal, rob; seize, snatch; *Inf*. surprise, find out (in a lie, etc.). **pillarse el dedo,** to get one's finger caught (in a door, etc.)

pillastre /pi'yastre; pi'ʎastre/ *m*, *Inf*. rogue, ragamuffin

pillería /piye'ria; piʎe'ria/ *f*, *Inf*. gang of rogues; *Inf*. rogue's trick

pillo /'piyo; 'piʎo/ *m*, rogue, knave

pilón /pi'lon/ *m*, fountain basin; pestle; loaf sugar; pylon; *Mexico*, *Venezuela* gratuity, tip

pilongo /pi'loŋgo/ *a* thin, lean

píloro /'piloro/ *m*, pylorus

pilotaje /pilo'tahe/ *m*, pilotage; piling, pilework. **examen de p.,** flying test

pilotar /pilo'tar/ *vt* to pilot

pilote /pi'lote/ *m*, *Engin*. pile

pilotear /pilote'ar/ *vt* to pilot

piloto /pi'loto/ *m*, pilot; mate (in merchant ships). **p. de pruebas,** test pilo

pilsen /'pilsen/ *m*, *Chile* beer

pimentero /pimen'tero/ *m*, pepper plant; pepper shaker

pimentón /pimen'ton/ *m*, red pepper, cayenne

pimienta /pi'mienta/ *f*, pepper. **p. húngara,** paprika. *Inf*. **ser como una p.,** to be sharp as a needle

pimiento /pi'miento/ *m*, pimiento; capsicum; red pepper; pepper plant. **p. de cornetilla,** chili pepper

pimpollo /pim'poyo; pim'poʎo/ *m*, sapling, sprout, shoot; rosebud

pina /'pina/ *f*, conical stone; felloe (of a wheel)

pinacoteca /pinako'teka/ *f*, art gallery, picture gallery

pináculo /pi'nakulo/ *m*, pinnacle, summit; climax, culmination; *Archit*. finial

pinar /pi'nar/ *m*, pinewood

pincel /pin'sel; pin'θel/ *m*, paintbrush; artist, painter; painting technique. **p. para las cejas,** eyebrow pencil

pincelada /pinse'laða; pinθe'laða/ *f*, brushstroke. **dar la última p.,** to add the finishing touch

pincelero /pinse'lero; pinθe'lero/ (**-ra**) *n* seller or maker of paintbrushes; brush box

pinchadura /pintʃa'ðura/ *f*, prick, puncture, piercing; sting; nipping, biting

pinchar /pin'tʃar/ *vt* to prick; puncture; pierce; sting; nip, bite. *Inf*. **no p. ni cortar,** to be ineffective (of persons)

pinchazo /pin'tʃaso; pin'tʃaθo/ *m*, prick; puncture; sting; incitement

pinche /'pintʃe/ *m*, scullion, kitchen boy; *Argentina* minor office clerk; *a*, *Mexico* damn

pineda /pi'neða/ *f*, pinewood

pingajo /pin'gaho/ *m*, *Inf.* tatter, rag

pingajoso /pinga'hoso/ *a Inf.* tattered, ragged

pingo /'pingo/ *m*, *Inf.* tatter, rag; *pl Inf.* cheap clothes

pingüe /'pingue/ *a* fat, greasy; fertile, rich

pingüino /piŋ'guino/ *m*, penguin

pino /'pino/ *a* steep. *m*, *Bot.* pine, deal; *Poet.* ship. **p. de tea,** pitch pine. **p. silvestre,** red fir

pinta /'pinta/ *f*, spot; marking; mark; fleck; look, appearance; pint (measure); drop, drip; spot ball (in billiards)

pintamonas /pinta'monas/ *mf Inf.* dauber

pintar /pin'tar/ *vt* to paint; describe, picture; exaggerate; *vi* show, manifest itself; *vr* make up (one's face). *Inf.* **pintarse solo para,** to be very good at, excel at

pintiparado /pintipa'raðo/ *a* most similar, very alike; fitting, apposite

pintiparar /pintipa'rar/ *vt Inf.* to compare

pintor /pin'tor/ **(-ra)** *n* painter, artist. **p. callejero,** sidewalk artist, pavement artist. **p. de brocha gorda,** house painter

pintoresco /pinto'resko/ *a* picturesque, quaint, pretty

pintorrear /pintorre'ar/ *vt Inf.* to daub, paint badly

pintura /pin'tura/ *f*, painting; paint, pigment; picture, painting; description. **p. a la aguada,** watercolor painting. **p. al fresco,** fresco. **p. al látex,** latex paint. **p. al óleo,** oil painting. **p. al pastel,** pastel drawing

pinturería /pinture'ria/ *f*, paint store

pinturero /pintu'rero/ *a Inf.* affected, conceited; dandified, overdressed

pinza /'pinsa; 'pinθa/ *f*, clamp. **p. de la ropa,** clothes peg

pinzas /'pinsas; 'pinθas/ *f pl*, pincers; pliers; tweezers; forceps. **p. hemostáticas,** arterial forceps

piña /'piɲa/ *f*, pineapple; cluster, knot (of people, etc.); pinecone

piñón /pi'ɲon/ *m*, pine nut; *Mech.* pinion, chain wheel

pío /'pio/ *a* pious; compassionate; good; piebald. *m*, chirping, cheep; *Inf.* longing

piocha /'piotʃa/ *f*, *Lat. Am.* pickax

piojo /'pioho/ *m*, louse

piojoso /pio'hoso/ *a* lousy; avaricious, stingy

piola /'piola/ *f*, *Lat. Am.* cord, string; rope; tether

pionero /pio'nero/ *m*, pioneer

piorrea /pio'rrea/ *f*, pyorrhea

pipa /'pipa/ *f*, barrel, cask; tobacco pipe; pip (of fruits)

pipar /pi'par/ *vi* to smoke a pipe

pipeta /pi'peta/ *f*, pipette

pipiar /pi'piar/ *vi* to chirp, twitter

pique /'pike/ *m*, pique, resentment. **a p. de,** on the verge of, about to. **echar a p.,** *Naut.* to sink; destroy. **irse a p.,** to sink, founder

piqueta /pi'keta/ *f*, pick, mattock; mason's hammer

piquete /pi'kete/ *m*, puncture, small wound; *Mil.* picket; pole, stake; small hole (in garments); picket (in strikes)

pira /'pira/ *f*, funeral pyre; bonfire

piragua /pi'ragua/ *f*, piragua, canoe

pirámide /pi'ramiðe/ *f*, pyramid

piraña /pi'raɲa/ *f* piranha

pirarse /pi'rarse/ *vr Inf.* to slip away

pirata /pi'rata/ *a* piratical *mf* pirate; savage, cruel person

piratear /pirate'ar/ *vi* to play the pirate

piratería /pirate'ria/ *f*, piracy; plunder, robbery

pirático /pi'ratiko/ *a* piratical

pirca /'pirka/ *f*, *Lat. Am.* dry-stone wall

pirenaico, pirineo /pire'naiko, piri'neo/ *a* Pyrenean

pirético /pi'retiko/ *a* pyretic

piriforme /piri'forme/ *a* pear-shaped

Pirineos, los /piri'neos, los/ the Pyrenees

piropear /pirope'ar/ *vt Inf.* to pay compliments to

piropo /pi'ropo/ *m*, carbuncle; *Inf.* catcall, street comments, compliment. **echar piropos,** to pay compliments

pirotécnico /piro'tekniko/ *a* pyrotechnical. *m*, pyrotechnist

pirrarse /pi'rrarse/ *vr Inf.* to desire ardently

pírrico /'pirriko/ *a* Pyrrhic

pirueta /pi'rueta/ *f*, pirouette, twirl

pisada /pi'saða/ *f*, treading, stepping; footprint, footstep; stepping on a person's foot. **seguir las pisadas de alguien,** *Fig.* to follow in someone's footsteps, imitate someone

pisano /pi'sano/ **(-na)** *a* and *n* Pisan

pisapapeles /pisapa'peles/ *m*, paperweight

pisar /pi'sar/ *vt* to tread upon; trample upon; crush; *Mus.* press (strings); trespass upon; *vr*, *Argentina* to be mistaken

pisaverde /pisa'βerðe/ *m*, *Inf.* fop, dandy

piscicultura /pissikul'tura; pisθikul'tura/ *f*, pisciculture, fish farming

piscina /pis'sina; pis'θina/ *f*, fishpond; swimming pool; *Eccl.* piscina

piscolabis /pisko'laβis/ *m*, *Inf.* snack, light meal

piso /'piso/ *m*, treading, trampling; story, floor; flooring; apartment. **p. bajo,** ground floor

pisón /pi'son/ *m*, rammer, ram

pisotear /pisote'ar/ *vt* to trample; crush under foot; tread on; step on; humiliate, treat inconsiderately

pisoteo /piso'teo/ *m*, trampling under foot; treading

pista /'pista/ *f*, track, trail (of animals); circus ring; racetrack, racecourse. **p. de patinar,** skating rink. **p. de vuelo,** *Aer.* landing field. *Inf.* **seguir la p. a,** to spy upon

pistacho /pis'tatʃo/ *m*, pistachio

pistar /pis'tar/ *v* to pestle, pound

pistero /pis'tero/ *m*, feeding cup

pistilo /pis'tilo/ *m*, pistil

pisto, /'pisto/ *m*, *Central America, Slang.* dough (money)

pistola /pis'tola/ *f*, pistol. **p. ametralladora,** machine gun.

pistolera /pisto'lera/ *f*, holster; pistol case

pistolero /pisto'lero/ *m*, gangster

pistoletazo /pistole'taso; pistole'taθo/ *m*, pistol shot; pistol wound

pistón /pis'ton/ *m*, *Mus.* piston; *Mil.* percussion cap; *Mech.* piston

pitada /pi'taða/ *f*, blast on a whistle, whistling; impertinence

pitagórico /pita'goriko/ **(-ca)** *a* and *n* Pythagorean

pitanza /pi'tansa; pi'tanθa/ *f*, alms, charity; *Inf.* daily food; pittance, scanty remuneration

pitar /pi'tar/ *vi* to play the whistle; *vt* pay (debts); smoke; give alms to

pitido /pi'tiðo/ *m*, blast on a whistle; whistling (of birds)

pitillera /piti'yera; piti'ʎera/ *f*, cigarette case; female cigarette maker

pito /'pito/ *m*, whistle; *Mus.* fife. *Inf.* **Cuando pitos flautas, cuando flautas pitos,** It's always the unexpected that happens. *Inf.* **no valer un p.,** to be not worth a straw

pitoflero /pito'flero/ **(-ra)** *n* mediocre performer (gen. on a wind instrument); *Inf.* talebearer, gossip

pitón /pi'ton/ *m*, *Zool.* python; nascent horn (of goats, etc.); spout; protuberance; *Bot.* sprout

pitonisa /pito'nisa/ *f*, *Myth.* pythoness; witch, enchantress

pitorrearse /pitorre'arse/ *vr* to ridicule, mock

pituitario /pitui'tario/ *a* pituitary

pituso /pi'tuso/ *a* small and amusing (of children)

pivote /pi'βote/ *m*, pivot, swivel, gudgeon

piyama /pi'yama/ *m*, pajamas

pizarra /pi'sarra; pi'θarra/ *f*, slate; blackboard

pizarral /pisa'rral; piθa'rral/ *m*. **pizarrería** *f*, slate quarry

pizarrín /pisa'rrin; piθa'rrin/ *m*, slate pencil

pizca /'piska; 'piθka/ *f*, *Inf.* atom, speck, crumb; jot, whit. **¡Ni p.!** Not a scrap!

pizpireta /pispi'reta; piθpi'reta/ *a f*, *Inf.* coquettish; smart; dressed up

placa /'plaka/ *f*, plate, disk; *Art.* plaque; *Photo.* plate; star (insignia). **p. recordatorio,** commemorative plaque

placabilidad /plakaβili'ðað/ *f*, placability, appeasability

pláceme /'plaseme; 'plaθeme/ *m*, congratulation

placentero /plasen'tero; plaθen'tero/ *a* agreeable, pleasant

placer /pla'ser; pla'θer/ *vt irr* to please, give pleasure to, gratify. *m*, *Naut.* reef, sandbank; pleasure; wish, desire; permission, consent; entertainment, diversion. **a p.,** at one's convenience; at leisure. *Pres. Ind.* **plazco, places, etc.** *Preterite* **plugo, pluguieron.** *Pres. Subjunc.* **plazca, etc.** *Imperf. Subjunc.* **pluguiese, etc.**

placibilidad /plasiβili'ðað; plaθiβili'ðað/ *f*, agreeableness, pleasantness

placible /pla'siβle; pla'θiβle/ *a* agreeable, pleasant

placidez /plasi'ðes; plaθi'ðeθ/ *f*, placidity, calmness, serenity

plácido /'plasiðo; 'plaθiðo/ *a* placid, calm, serene

placiente /pla'siente; pla'θiente/ *a* pleasing, attractive

plácito /'plasito; 'plaθito/ *m*, decision, judgment, opinion

plafón /pla'fon/ *m*, ceiling light; *Archit.* panel

plaga /'plaga/ *f*, plague; disaster, calamity; epidemic; glut; pest; grief

plagar /pla'gar/ *vt* (*with de*) to infect with; *vr* (*with de*) be covered with; be overrun by; be infested with

plagiar /pla'hiar/ *vt* to plagiarize, copy; kidnap, hold for ransom

plagiario /pla'hiario/ **(-ia)** *n* plagiarist; *Lat. Am.* kidnapper

plagio /'plahio/ *m*, plagiary; kidnapping

plan /plan/ *m*, plan; scheme; plane. **p. quinquenal,** five-year plan

plana /'plana/ *f*, sheet, page; mason's trowel; plain. **p. mayor,** (*Mil. Nav.*) staff

planadora /plana'ðora/ *f*, steamroller

plancha /'plantʃa/ *f*, sheet, slab, plate; iron; horizontal suspension (in gymnastics); *Naut.* gangway, gangplank; *Inf.* howler

planchado /plan'tʃaðo/ *m*, ironing; ironing to be done or already finished

planchador /plantʃa'ðor/ **(-ra)** *n* ironer

planchar /plan'tʃar/ *vt* to iron, press with an iron

planchear /plantʃe'ar/ *vt* to plate (with metal)

planeador /planea'ðor/ *m*, *Aer.* glider

planear /plane'ar/ *vt* to plan out; make plans for; *vi Aer.* glide

planeo /pla'neo/ *m*, *Aer.* glide

planeta /pla'neta/ *m*, planet

planetario /plane'tario/ *a* planetary. *m*, planetarium

planicie /pla'nisie; pla'niθie/ *f*, levelness, evenness; plain

planilla /pla'nija; pla'niʎa/ *f*, *Lat. Am.* application, application form, blank; payroll; list; ballot

plano /'plano/ *a* flat, level; plane. *m*, *Geom.* plane; plan, map; *Aer.* aileron, wing

planta /'planta/ *f*, *Bot.* plant; sole (of the foot); plantation; layout, plan; position of the feet (in dancing, fencing); scheme, project. **p. baja,** ground floor. **p. vivaz,** perennial plant. *Inf.* **buena p.,** good appearance

plantación /planta'sion; planta'θion/ *f*, planting; plantation, nursery

plantador /planta'ðor/ **(-ra)** *n* planter. *m*, *Agr.* dibble. *f*, **plantadora,** mechanical planter

plantar /plan'tar/ *vt* to plant; erect; place; found, set up; pose (a problem); raise (a question, etc.); *Inf.* leave in the lurch; *vr* take up one's position; jib (of horses); oppose

planteamiento /plantea'ıniento/ *m*, execution; putting into practice; planning; statement (of problems)

plantel /plan'tel/ *m*, nursery garden; training school, nursery

plantilla /plan'tiya; plan'tiʎa/ *f*, young plant; insole (of shoes); *Mech.* template, jig

plantío /plan'tio/ *m*, plantation, afforestation; planting. *a* planted or ready for planting (ground)

plantón /plan'ton/ *m*, plant or sapling ready for transplanting; *Bot.* cutting; doorkeeper, porter. **dar un p.** (a), to keep (a person) waiting a long time

plañidero /plaɲi'ðero/ *a* mournful, piteous, anguished

plañido /pla'ɲiðo/ *m*, lament, weeping, wailing

plañir /pla'ɲir/ *vi* and *vt irr* to lament, wail, weep. See **tañer**

plasma /'plasma/ *m*, plasma

plasmar /plas'mar/ *vt* to mold, throw (pottery)

plástica /'plastika/ *f*, art of clay modeling; plastic

plástico /'plastiko/ *a* plastic; flexible, malleable, soft

plata /'plata/ *f*, silver; silver (coins); *Lat. Am.,* money; white. **p. labrada,** silverware

plataforma /plata'forma/ *f*, platform; running board (of a train); *Rail.* turntable

platal /pla'tal/ *m*, *Lat. Am.* wealth

plátano /'platano/ *m*, banana tree, banana; plantain; plane tree

platea /pla'tea/ *f*, *Theat.* pit. **butaca de p.,** pit stall

plateado /plate'aðo/ *a* silvered; silver-plated; silvery

plateador /platea'ðor/ *m*, plater

platear /plate'ar/ *vt* to electroplate, silver

platería /plate'ria/ *f*, silversmith's art or trade; silversmith's shop or workshop

platero /pla'tero/ *m*, silversmith; jeweler

plática /'platika/ *f*, conversation; exhortation, sermon; address, discourse

platicar /plati'kar/ *vt* and *vi* to converse (about)

platija /pla'tiha/ *f*, plaice

platillo /pla'tiyo; pla'tiʎo/ *m*, saucer; kitty (in card games); pan (of a scale); *pl* cymbals

platinado /plati'naðo/ *m*, plating

platino /pla'tino/ *m*, platinum

platívolo /pla'tiβolo/ *m*, flying saucer

plato /'plato/ *m*, plate; dish; *Cul.* course, dish; pan (of a scale). **p. sopero,** soup plate. **p. trinchero,** meat dish. *Inf.* **comer en un mismo p.,** to be on intimate terms. **nada entre dos platos,** much ado about nothing

platónico /pla'toniko/ *a* Platonic

platonismo /plato'nismo/ *m*, Platonism

platudo, -a /pla'tuðo/ *mf*, rich, wealthy, well-heeled

plausible /plau'siβle/ *a* plausible, reasonable; commendable

playa /'plaia/ *f*, beach, seashore, strand

plaza /'plasa; 'plaθa/ *f*, square (in a town, etc.); marketplace; fortified town; space; duration; employment, post.; *Com.* market. **p. de armas,** garrison town; military camp. **p. de toros,** bullring. **p. fuerte,** strong place, fortress. **sentar p.,** to enlist in the army

plazo /'plaso; 'plaθo/ *m*, term, duration; expiration of term, date of payment; installment. **a plazos,** *Com.* by installments, on the installment system

plazoleta /plaso'leta; plaθo'leta/ *f*, small square (in gardens, etc.)

pleamar /plea'mar/ *f*, *Naut.* high water

plebe /'pleβe/ *f*, common people; rabble, mob

plebeyo /ple'βeio/ **(-ya)** *a* plebeian. *n* commoner, plebeian

plebiscito /pleβis'sito; pleβis'θito/ *m*, plebiscite

plectro /'plektro/ *m*, plectrum, pick (musical instruments)

plegable /ple'gaβle/ *a* foldable

plegadera /plega'ðera/ *f*, folder; folding knife; paper folder

plegadizo /plega'ðiso; plega'ðiθo/ *a* folding; collapsible; jointed

plegado /ple'gaðo/ *m*, pleating; folding

plegador /plega'ðor/ *a* folding. *m*, folding machine

plegadura /plega'ðura/ *f*, folding, doubling; fold, pleat

plegar /ple'gar/ *vt irr* to fold; pleat; *Sew.* gather; *vr* submit, give in. See **acertar**

plegaria /ple'garia/ *f*, fervent prayer

pleitear /pleite'ar/ *vt* to go to court about; indulge in litigation

pleitista /plei'tista/ *a* quarrelsome, litigious

policromo

pleito /'pleito/ *m*, action, lawsuit; dispute, quarrel; litigation. **p. de familia,** family squabble. **ver el p.,** *Law.* to try a case

plenamente /plena'mente/ *adv* fully, entirely

plenario /ple'nario/ *a* full, complete; *Law.* plenary

plenilunio /pleni'lunio/ *m*, full moon

plenipotencia /plenipo'tensia; plenipo'tenθia/ *f*, full powers (diplomatic, etc.)

plenipotenciario /plenipoten'siario; plenipoten'θiario/ *a* and *m*, plenipotentiary

plenitud /pleni'tuð/ *f*, fullness, completeness; plenitude, abundance

pleno /'pleno/ *a* full. *m*, general meeting

pleonasmo /pleo'nasmo/ *m*, *Gram.* pleonasm

pleonástico /pleo'nastiko/ *a* pleonastic

pleuresía /pleure'sia/ *f*, pleurisy

plexo /'plekso/ *m*, plexus

pliego /'pliego/ *m*, sheet (of paper); letter, packet of papers

pliegue /'pliege/ *m*, fold, pleat; *Sew.* gather

plinto /'plinto/ *m*, *Archit.* plinth (of a column); baseboard

plisar /pli'sar/ *vt* to pleat; fold

plomada /plo'maða/ *f*, plummet; sounding lead; plumb, lead

plomería /plome'ria/ *f*, plumbing; plumbing business; lead roofing

plomero /plo'mero/ *m*, plumber

plomizo /plo'miso; plo'miθo/ *a* lead-like; lead-colored, gray

plomo /'plomo/ *m*, lead (metal); plummet; bullet; *Inf.* bore, tedious person

pluma /'pluma/ *f*, feather; pen; plumage; quill; penmanship; writer; writing profession. **p. estilográfica,** fountain pen. **a vuela p.,** as the pen writes, written in a hurry

plumado /plu'maðo/ *a* feathered

pluma fuente /'pluma 'fuente/ *f*, *Lat. Am.* fountain pen

plumaje /plu'mahe/ *m*, plumage, feathers; plume

plúmbeo /'plumbeo/ *a* plumbeous, leaden

plúmeo /'plumeo/ *a* feathered, plumed

plumero /plu'mero/ *m*, feather duster; plume, feather; plumage

plumón /plu'mon/ *m*, down; feather bed; *Lat. Am.* felt-tipped pen

plumoso /plu'moso/ *a* feathered

plural /plu'ral/ *a* and *m*, plural

pluralidad /plurali'ðað/ *f*, plurality; multitude, number

pluralizar /plurali'sar; plurali'θar/ *vt* to pluralize

plurilingüe /pluri'liŋgue/ *a* multilingual

pluscuamperfecto /pluskuamper'fekto/ *m*, pluperfect

plusmarquista /plusmar'kista/ *mf* *Sports.* recordholder

plutocracia /pluto'krasia; pluto'kraθia/ *f*, plutocracy

plutócrata /plu'tokrata/ *mf* plutocrat

plutocrático /pluto'kratiko/ *a* plutocratic

pluviómetro /plu'βiometro/ *m*, rain gauge

poblacho /po'βlatʃo/ *m*, miserable town or village

población /poβla'sion; poβla'θion/ *f*, peopling; population; town

poblado /po'βlaðo/ *m*, inhabited place; town; village

poblador /poβla'ðor/ **(-ra)** *a* populating. *n* colonist, settler

poblar /po'βlar/ *vt irr* to colonize; people, populate; breed fast; stock, supply; *vr* put forth leaves (of trees). See **contar**

pobre /'poβre/ *a* poor; indigent, needy; mediocre; unfortunate; humble, meek. *mf* beggar, pauper, needy person. *Inf.* **ser p. de solemnidad,** to be down and out

pobrero /po'βrero/ *m*, *Eccl.* distributor of alms

pobretería /poβrete'ria/ *f*, poverty; needy people

pobretón /poβre'ton/ *a* extremely needy

pobreza /po'βresa; po'βreθa/ *f*, poverty, need; shortage; timidity; *Mineral.* baseness; poorness (of soil, etc.)

pocero /po'sero; po'θero/ *m*, well digger

pocilga /po'silga; po'θilga/ *f*, pigsty; *Inf.* filthy place

poción /po'sion; po'θion/ *f*, potion, drink; mixture, dose

poco /'poko/ *a* little, scanty; *pl* few. *m*, small amount, a little. *adv* little; shortly, in a little while. **p. a p.,** by degrees, little by little; slowly. **p. más o menos,** more or less, approximately. **por p.,** almost, nearly (always used with the present tense, e.g. *Por p. me caigo,* I almost fell). **tener en p.** (a), to have a poor opinion of; undervalue

poda /'poða/ *f*, *Agr.* pruning; pruning season

podadera /poða'ðera/ *f*, pruning knife

podar /po'ðar/ *vt Agr.* to prune, trim

poder /po'ðer/ *vt*, power; authority, jurisdiction; *Law.* power of attorney; strength; ability; proxy; efficacy; possession; *pl* authority; power of attorney. **los poderes constituidos,** the established authorities; the powers that be. **p. de adquisición,** purchasing power. **casarse por poderes,** to be married by proxy

poder /po'ðer/ *vt irr* to be able to (e.g. *Podemos comprar estas naranjas,* We can (are able to) buy these oranges). **Dice que la calamidad podía haberse evitado,** He says that the disaster could have been averted). **p.** also expresses possibility (e.g. *Pueden haber ido a la ciudad,* They may have gone to the city. *¡Qué distinta pudo haber sido su vida!* How different his life might have been!). *impers* be possible. **a más no p.,** of necessity, without being able to help it; to the utmost. **no p. con,** to be unable to control or manage. **no p. hacer más,** to have no alternative, have to; be unable to do more. **no p. menos de,** to be obliged to, have no alternative but. **no p. contener su emoción,** to be overcome with emotion. **no p. ver a,** to hate (persons). *impers* **Puede que venga esta tarde,** He may come (perhaps he will come) this afternoon. *Pres. Part.* **pudiendo.** *Pres. Ind.* **puedo, puedes, puede, pueden.** *Fut.* **podré,** etc. *Condit.* **podría,** etc. *Preterite* **pude, pudiste,** etc. *Pres. Subjunc.* **pueda, puedas, pueda, puedan.** *Imperf. Subjunc.* **pudiese,** etc.

poderío /poðe'rio/ *m*, power, authority; sway, rule; dominion; wealth

poderoso /poðe'roso/ *a* powerful; opulent; effective, efficacious; mighty, magnificent

podredumbre /poðre'ðumbre/ *f*, decay; pus; *Fig.* canker, anguish

podredura, podrición /poðre'ðura, poðri'sion; poðre'ðura, poðri'θion/ *f*, putrefaction; decay

podrido /po'ðriðo/ *a* rotten; putrid; corrupt; decayed

podrir /po'ðrir/ *vt* See **pudrir**

poema /po'ema/ *m*, poem. **p. sinfónico,** tone poem

poesía /poe'sia/ *f*, poetry, verse; lyric, poem

poeta /po'eta/ *m*, poet

poetastro /poe'tastro/ *m*, poetaster

poética /po'etika/ *f*, poetics

poético /po'etiko/ *a* poetical

poetisa /poe'tisa/ *f*, poetess

poetizar /poeti'sar; poeti'θar/ *vi* to write verses; *vt* poeticize

polaco /po'lako/ **(-ca)** *a* Polish. *n* Pole. *m*, Polish (language)

polainas /po'lainas/ *f pl*, leggings, puttees, gaiters

polar /po'lar/ *a* polar

polaridad /polari'ðað/ *f*, polarity; polarization

polarización /polarisa'sion; polariθa'θion/ *f*, polarization

polarizar /polari'sar; polari'θar/ *vt* to polarize

polca /'polka/ *f*, polka

polea /po'lea/ *f*, pulley; *Naut.* block

polémica /po'lemika/ *f*, polemic, controversy, dispute

polémico /po'lemiko/ *a* polemical

polemista /pole'mista/ *mf* disputant, controversialist

polen /'polen/ *m*, pollen

polichinela /politʃi'nela/ *m*, Punchinello

policía /poli'sia; poli'θia/ *f*, police; government, polity, administration; civility, courtesy; cleanliness, tidiness. *m*, policeman. **p. urbana,** city police

policíaco /poli'siako; poli'θiako/ *a* police; detective

policial /poli'sial; poli'θial/ *a* police; *m*, *Lat. Am.* police officer

policromo /poli'kromo/ *a* polychrome

poliedro /po'lieðro/ *m*, polyhedron
polifacético /polifa'setiko; polifa'θetiko/ *a* many-sided
polifonía /polifo'nia/ *f*, polyphony
polifónico /poli'foniko/ *a* polyphonic
poligamia /poli'gamia/ *f*, polygamy
polígamo /po'ligamo/ **(-ma)** *a* polygamous. *n* polygamist
polígloto /poli'gloto/ **(-ta)** *n* polyglot. *f*, polyglot Bible
polígono /po'ligono/ *a* polygonal. *m*, polygon
polilla /po'liya; po'liʎa/ *f*, moth; moth grub; destroyer, ravager
polimorfismo /polimor'fismo/ *m*, *Chem.* polymorphism
polimorfo /poli'morfo/ *a* polymorphous
Polinesia /poli'nesia/ Polynesia
polinesio /poli'nesio/ **(-ia)** *a* and *n* Polynesian
polinización /polinisa'sion; poliniθa'θion/ *f*, pollination
poliomielitis /poliomie'litis/ *f*, poliomyelitis, polio
pólipo /'polipo/ *m*, *Zool.* polyp; octopus; *Med.* polyp
polisílabo /poli'silaβo/ *a* polysyllabic. *m*, polysyllable
polista /po'lista/ *mf* polo player
politécnico /poli'tekniko/ *a* polytechnic
politeísmo /polite'ismo/ *m*, polytheism
politeísta /polite'ista/ *a* polytheistic. *mf* polytheist
política /po'litika/ *f*, politics; civility, courtesy; diplomacy; tact; policy
politicastro /politi'kastro/ *m*, corrupt politician
político /po'litiko/ *a* political; civil, courteous; in-law, by marriage (relationships). *m*, politician
politiquear /politike'ar/ *vi Inf.* to dabble in politics, talk politics
politizarse /politi'sarse; politi'θarse/ *vr* to enter the political arena
póliza /'polisa; 'poliθa/ *f*, *Com.* policy; *Com.* draft; share certificate; revenue stamp; admission ticket; lampoon. **p. a prima fija,** fixed-premium policy. **p. de seguros,** insurance policy. **p. dotal,** endowment policy
polizón /poli'son; poli'θon/ *m*, loafer, tramp; stowaway; bustle (of a dress)
polla /'poya; 'poʎa/ *f*, pullet; *Inf.* flapper, young woman
pollada /po'yaða; po'ʎaða/ *f*, brood, hatch (especially of chickens)
pollastro /po'yastro; po'ʎastro/ **(-ra)** *n* pullet.
pollera /po'yera; po'ʎera/ *f*, female poultry breeder or seller; chicken coop; go-cart; *Argentina, Chile* skirt
pollería /poye'ria; poʎe'ria/ *f*, poultry market or shop
pollero /po'yero; po'ʎero/ *n* poultry breeder; poulterer. *m*, hen coop; *Lat. Am.* gambler
pollino /po'yino; po'ʎino/ **(-na)** *n* young ass; donkey
pollo /'poyo; 'poʎo/ *m*, chicken; *Inf.* youth, stripling; *Fig. Inf.* downy bird. *Inf.* **p. pera,** young blood, lad.
sacar pollos, to hatch chickens
polo /'polo/ *m*, pole (all meanings); *Fig.* support; popular Andalusian song; *Sports.* polo. **de p. a p.,** from pole to pole
polonés /polo'nes/ **(-esa)** *a* Polish. *n* Pole
Polonia /po'lonia/ Poland
poltrón /pol'tron/ *a* lazy, idle
poltronear /poltrone'ar/ *vi* to loaf about
poltronería /poltrone'ria/ *f*, idleness, laziness
polución /polu'sion; polu'θion/ *f*, *Med.* ejaculation
polvareda /polβa'reða/ *f*, dust cloud; storm, agitation
polvera /pol'βera/ *f*, powder bowl; powder puff; powder compact
polvillo /pol'βiyo; pol'βiʎo/ *m*, *Lat. Am.* blight
polvo /'polβo/ *m*, dust; powder; pinch (of snuff, etc.); *pl* face or dusting powder. **Se hizo como por polvos de la madre celestina,** It was done as if by magic. *Inf.* **limpio de p. y paja,** gratis, for nothing; net (of profit)
pólvora /'polβora/ *f*, gunpowder; bad temper. **p. de algodón,** guncotton.
polvorear /polβore'ar/ *vt* to powder, dust with powder

polvoriento /polβo'riento/ *a* dusty; powdery, covered with powder
polvorín /polβo'rin/ *m*, very fine powder; powder magazine; powder flask
polvoroso /polβo'roso/ *a* dusty; covered with powder
pomada /po'maða/ *f*, pomade; salve, ointment
pomar /po'mar/ *m*, orchard (especially an apple orchard)
pómez /'pomes; 'pomeθ/ *f*, pumice stone **(piedra p.)**
pomo /'pomo/ *m*, *Bot.* pome; pomander; nosegay; pommel, hilt (of a sword); handle; rose (of watering can)
pomología /pomolo'hia/ *f*, pomology, art of fruit growing
pompa /'pompa/ *f*, pomp, splendor; ceremonial procession; air bubble; peacock's outspread tail; *Naut.* pump; billowing of clothes in the wind
Pompeya /pom'peia/ Pompeii
pomposidad /pomposi'ðað/ *f*, pomposity
pomposo /pom'poso/ *a* stately, ostentatious, magnificent; inflated, pompous; florid, bombastic
pómulo /'pomulo/ *m*, cheekbone
ponchada /pon'tʃaða/ *f Lat. Am.* great deal, large amount
ponche /'pontʃe/ *m*, punch, toddy
ponchera /pon'tʃera/ *f*, punch bowl
poncho /'pontʃo/ *a* lazy, negligent. *m*, military cloak; poncho, cape
ponderación /pondera'sion; pondera'θion/ *f*, weighing; reflection, consideration; exaggeration
ponderador /pondera'ðor/ *a* reflective, deliberate; exaggerated
ponderar /ponde'rar/ *vt* to weigh; consider, ponder; exaggerate; overpraise
ponderosidad /ponderosi'ðað/ *f*, heaviness, ponderousness, dullness
ponderoso /ponde'roso/ *a* heavy; ponderous; circumspect
ponedero /pone'ðero/ *a* egg-laying (of hens). *m*, nest
ponencia /po'nensia; po'nenθia/ *f*, clause, section; office of referee or arbitrator; report, referendum, conference
poner /po'ner/ *vt irr* to place, put; arrange; set (the table); bet, stake; appoint (to an office); call, name; lay (eggs); set down (in writing); calculate, count; suppose; leave to a person's judgment; risk; contribute; prepare; need, take; cause, inspire (emotions); make, cause; adapt; add; cause to become (angry, etc.); insult; praise; (*with prep a + infin*) begin to. **p. a contribución,** to lay under contribution, turn to account, utilize. **ponerle el cascabel al gato** *or* **el collar al gato,** to bell the cat. **p. los cuernos (a),** to cuckold. **p. al corriente,** to bring up to date, inform. **p. a prueba,** to test. **p. casa,** to set up house. *Inf.* **p. colorado a,** to make blush. **p. coto a,** to put a stop to, check. **p. en comparación,** to compare. **p. conato en,** to put a great deal of effort into. **p. en cotejo,** to collate. **p. en limpio,** to make a fair copy (of). **p. en marcha,** to start, set in motion. **p. en práctica,** to put into effect. **p. por caso,** to take as an example (e.g. *Pongamos por caso...* For example,...). **p. por encima (de),** to prefer. *vr* to place oneself; become; put on (garments, etc.); dirty or stain oneself; set (of the sun, stars); oppose; deck oneself, dress oneself up; arrive; (*with prep a + infin*) begin to. **ponerse al corriente,** to bring oneself up to date. **ponerse al día,** to update. **ponerse bien,** to improve; get better (in health). **ponerse colorado,** to blush, flush. **p. una base racional a la fe,** to give faith a rational foundation. **p. los cimientos de,** to lay the foundation of, lay the foundations for. **p. una conferencia,** to make a long-distance call. *Pres. Ind.* **pongo, pones, etc.** *Fut.* **pondré,** etc. *Condit.* **pondría,** etc. *Imperat.* **pon.** *Past Part.* **puesto.** *Preterite* **puse, pusiste,** etc. *Pres. Subjunc.* **ponga,** etc. *Imperf. Subjunc.* **pusiese,** etc.
pongo /'poŋgo/ *m Bolivia, Peru* Native American serf
pongueaje /poŋgue'ahe/ *m* **Bolivia, Peru** Native American serfdom
ponientada /ponien'taða/ *f*, steady west wind
poniente /po'niente/ *m*, west; west wind

pontazgo /pon'tasgo; pon'taθgo/ *m*, bridge toll
pontear /ponte'ar/ *vt* to bridge; make bridges
pontificado /pontifi'kaðo/ *m*, pontificate, papacy
pontífice /pon'tifise; pon'tifiθe/ *m*, pontifex; pope, pontiff; archbishop; bishop
pontón /pon'ton/ *m*, *Mil.* pontoon; hulk used as a prison, hospital, store, etc.; wooden bridge
pontonero /ponto'nero/ *m*, pontonier, military engineer
ponzoña /pon'soɲa; pon'θoɲa/ *f*, poison, venom
ponzoñoso /ponso'ɲoso; ponθo'ɲoso/ *a* poisonous, venomous; noxious; harmful
popa /'popa/ *f*, *Naut.* stern, poop. **en p.,** abaft, astern, aft
popelina /pope'lina/ *f*, poplin
popote /po'pote/ *m*, *Mexico* (drinking) straw
populachería /populatʃe'ria/ *f*, cheap popularity with the rabble
populachero /popula'tʃero/ *a* mob, vulgar
populacho /popu'latʃo/ *m*, mob, rabble
popular /popu'lar/ *a* popular
popularidad /populari'ðað/ *f*, popularity
popularizar /populari'sar; populari'θar/ *vt* to popularize; *vr* grow popular
populoso /popu'loso/ *a* populous, crowded
popurrí /popu'rri/ *m*, *Cul.* stew; potpourri; miscellany
poquedad /poke'ðað/ *f*, paucity, scarcity; timidity, cowardice; trifle, mere nothing
poquísimo /po'kisimo/ *a sup* **poco** very little
poquito /po'kito/ *m*, very little
por /por/ *prep* for; by; through, along; during; because, as (e.g. *Lo desecharon p. viejo*, They threw it away because it was old); however (e.g. *p. bonito que sea*, however pretty it is); during; in order to (e.g. *Lo hice p. no ofenderla*, I did it in order not to offend her); toward, in favor of, for; for the sake of; on account of, by reason of (e.g. *No pudo venir p. estar enfermo*, He could not come on account of his illness); via, by (e.g. *p. correo aéreo*, by airmail); as for (e.g. *P. mí, lo rechazo*, As for me, I refuse it. *p. mi cuenta*, to my way of thinking; on my own); in exchange for (e.g. *Me vendió dos libros p. seis dólares*, He sold me two books for six dollars); in the name of, as a substitute for, instead of (e.g. *Hace mi trabajo p. mí*, He is doing my work for me); per. **Por** has several uses: 1. Introduces the agent after a passive (e.g. *La novela fue escrita p. él*, The novel was written by him). 2. Expresses movement through, along or about (e.g. *Andaban p. la calle*, They were walking along (or down) the street). 3. Denotes time at or during which an action occurs (e.g. *Ocurrió p. entonces un acontecimiento de importancia*, About that time an important event occurred). 4. Expresses rate or proportion (e.g. *seis por ciento*, six percent). 5. With certain verbs, means "to be" and expresses vague futurity (e.g. *El libro queda p. escribir*, The book remains to be written). **p. cortesía,** by courtesy, out of politeness. **p. cortesía de,** by courtesy of. **p. escrito,** in writing. **p. fas or p. nefas,** by fair means or foul; at any cost. **p. mucho que,** however great, however much; in spite of, notwithstanding. **¿P. qué?** Why? **p. si acaso,** in case, if by chance. **estar p.,** to be about to; be inclined to. **P. un clavo se pierde la herradura,** For want of a nail, the shoe was lost.
porcelana /porse'lana; porθe'lana/ *f*, porcelain, china; chinaware
porcentaje /porsen'tahe; porθen'tahe/ *m*, percentage
porche /'portʃe/ *m*, porch, portico
porcino /por'sino; por'θino/ *a* porcine. *m*, young pig; bruise
porción /por'sion; por'θion/ *f*, portion; *Com.* share; *Inf.* crowd; allowance, pittance
porcionista /porsio'nista; porθio'nista/ *mf* shareholder; sharer; boarding school student
pordiosear /porðiose'ar/ *vi* to ask alms, beg
pordioseo /porðio'seo/ *m*, asking alms, begging
pordiosero /porðio'sero/ **(-ra)** *a* begging. *n* beggar
porfía /por'fia/ *f*, obstinacy; importunity; tenacity. **a p.,** in competition

porfiadamente /porfiaða'mente/ *adv* obstinately
porfiado /por'fiaðo/ *a* obstinate, obdurate, persistent
porfiar /por'fiar/ *vi* to be obstinate, insist; persist
pórfido /'porfiðo/ *m*, porphyry
pormenor /porme'nor/ *m*, particular, detail (gen. *pl*); secondary matter
pormenorizar /pormenori'sar; pormenori'θar/ *vt* to describe in detail
pornografía /pornogra'fia/ *f*, pornography
pornográfico /porno'grafiko/ *a* pornographic, obscene
poro /'poro/ *m*, pore; *Lat. Am. also* leek
porongo /po'roŋgo/ *m*, *Lat. Am.* calabash, gourd
porosidad /porosi'ðað/ *f*, porosity, permeability
poroso /po'roso/ *a* porous, leaky
poroto /po'roto/ *m*, *Lat. Am.* bean; *Chile* child, kid
porque /'porke/ *conjunc* because, for; in order that
porqué /'porke/ *m*, reason, wherefore, why; *Inf.* money. **el cómo y el qué,** the why and the wherefore
porquería /porke'ria/ *f*, *Inf.* filth, nastiness; dirty trick; rudeness, gross act; trifle, thing of no account
porquerizo, porquero /porke'riso, por'kero; porke'riθo, por'kero/ *m*, swineherd
porra /'porra/ *f*, club, bludgeon; last player (in children's games); *Inf.* vanity, boastfulness; bore, tedious person
porrada /po'rraða/ *f*, blow with a club; buffet, knock, fall; *Inf.* folly; glut, abundance
porrazo /po'rraso; po'rraθo/ *m*, blow with a club; buffet, knock, fall
porrear /porre'ar/ *vi Inf.* to insist, harp on
porrería /porre'ria/ *f*, *Inf.* folly; obduracy, persistence
porreta /po'rreta/ *f*, green leaves of leeks, onions, and cereals. *Inf.* **en p.,** stark-naked
porrino /po'rrino/ *m*, seed of a leek; young leek plant
porrón /po'rron/ *m*, winebottle with a spout; earthenware jug
porsiacaso /porsia'kaso/ *m*, *Argentina, Venezuela* knapsack
portaaviones /portaa'βiones/ *m*, aircraft carrier
portachuelo /porta'tʃuelo/ *m*, defile, narrow mountain pass
portada /por'taða/ *f*, front, facade; frontispiece, title page; portal, doorway
portado /por'taðo/ (**bien** or **mal**) *a* well- or ill-dressed or behaved
portador /porta'ðor/ **(-ra)** *n* carrier. *m*, *Com.* bearer; *Mech.* carrier
portaestandarte /ˌportaestan'darte/ *m*, standard-bearer
portafolio /porta'folio/ *m*, portfolio; *Lat. Am. also* briefcase
portafusil /porta'fusil/ *m*, rifle sling
portal /por'tal/ *m*, entrance, porch; portico; city gate
portalámpara /porta'lampara/ *f*, lamp holder; *Elec.* socket
portalibros /porta'liβros/ *m*, bookstrap
portalón /porta'lon/ *m*, gangway
portamanteo /portaman'teo/ *m*, traveling bag
portamonedas /portamo'neðas/ *m*, pocketbook; handbag, purse
portanuevas /porta'nueβas/ *mf* bringer of news, newsmonger
portaobjetos /portaoβ'hetos/ *m*, stage (of a microscope)
portaplumas /porta'plumas/ *m*, pen holder
portar /por'tar/ *vt* to retrieve (of dogs); carry (arms); *vr* behave (well or badly); bear oneself, act; be well, or ill (in health)
portátil /por'tatil/ *a* portable
portavoz /porta'βos; porta'βoθ/ *m*, megaphone; spokesman, mouthpiece
portazgo /por'tasgo; por'taθgo/ *m*, toll; tollbooth
portazguero /portas'gero; portaθ'gero/ *m*, toll collector
portazo /por'taso; por'taθo/ *m*, bang of the door; slamming the door in a person's face
porte /'porte/ *m*, transport; *Com.* carriage; postage; freight; transport cost; porterage; behavior, conduct;

bearing, looks; capacity, volume; size, dimension; nobility (of descent); *Naut.* tonnage. **p. pagado,** charges prepaid

porteador /portea'ðor/ *m,* carrier; porter; carter

portear /porte'ar/ *vt* to carry, transport; *vr* migrate (of birds)

portento /por'tento/ *m,* marvel, prodigy, portent

portentoso /porten'toso/ *a* marvelous, portentous

porteño, -a /por'teɲo/ *a* of Buenos Aires; native of Buenos Aires; resident of Buenos Aires

porteo /por'teo/ *m,* porterage, cartage

portería /porte'ria/ *f,* porter's lodge; porter's employment; *Sports.* goal

portero /por'tero/ **(-ra)** *n* doorman, doorkeeper; porter; concierge; janitor; *Sports.* goalkeeper. **p. eléctrico,** door buzzer

portezuela /porte'suela; porte'θuela/ *f, dim* small door; carriage door; pocket flap

pórtico /'portiko/ *m,* portico, piazza; porch; vestibule, hall

portillo /por'tiyo; por'tiʎo/ *m,* breach, opening; defile, narrow pass; *Fig.* loophole

portón /por'ton/ *m,* hall door, inner door; *Chile* back door

portorriqueño /portorri'keɲo/ **(-ña)** *a* and *n* Puerto Rican

portuario /por'tuario/ *a* dock, port

Portugal /portu'gal/ Portugal

portugués /portu'ges/ **(-esa)** *a* and *n* Portuguese. *m,* Portuguese (language)

portuguesada /portuge'saða/ *f,* exaggeration

porvenir /porβe'nir/ *m,* future time

¡porvida! /por'βiða/ *interj* By the saints! By the Almighty!

pos /pos/ *prefix* after; behind. Also *adv* **en p.,** with the same meanings

posa /'posa/ *f,* tolling bell; *pl* buttocks

posada /po'saða/ *f,* dwelling; inn, tavern; lodging; hospitality

posaderas /posa'ðeras/ *f pl,* buttocks

posadero /posa'ðero/ **(-ra)** *n* innkeeper; boardinghouse keeper

posar /po'sar/ *vi* to lodge, live; rest; alight, perch; *vt* set down (a burden); *vr* settle (liquids); (*with en or sobre*) perch upon

posdata /pos'ðata/ *f,* P.S., postscript

pose /'pose/ *f, Photo.* time exposure; *Inf.* pose

poseedor /posee'ðor/ **(-ra)** *n* possessor, holder

poseer /pose'er/ *vt irr* to own, possess; know (a language, etc.); *vr* restrain oneself. **estar poseído por,** to be possessed by (passion, etc.); be thoroughly convinced of. See **creer**

posesión /pose'sion/ *f,* ownership, occupancy; possession; property, territory (often *pl*)

posesionarse /posesio'narse/ *vr* to take possession; lay hold (of)

poseso /po'seso/ *a* possessed of an evil spirit

posesor /pose'sor/ **(-ra)** *n* owner, possessor

posfecha /pos'fetʃa/ *f,* postdate

posguerra /pos'gerra/ *f,* postwar period

posibilidad /posiβili'ðað/ *f,* possibility; probability; opportunity, means, chance; *pl* property, wealth

posibilitar /posiβili'tar/ *vt* to make possible, facilitate

posible /po'siβle/ *a* possible. *m pl,* property, personal wealth. **hacer lo p.** *or* **hacer todo lo p.,** to do everything possible; do one's best

posición /posi'sion; posi'θion/ *f,* placing; position; situation; status

positivamente /positiβa'mente/ *adv* positively, definitely

positivismo /positi'βismo/ *m,* positivism

positivista /positi'βista/ *a* positivistic. *mf* positivist

positivo /posi'tiβo/ *a* positive; certain, definite; (*Math. Elec.*) plus; true, real

pósito /'posito/ *m,* public granary; cooperative association

posma /'posma/ *f, Inf.* sluggishness, sloth

poso /'poso/ *m,* sediment; lees, dregs; repose, quietness

posponer /pospo'ner/ *vt irr* (*with prep a*) to place after; make subordinate to; value less than. See **poner**

posta /'posta/ *f,* post horse; stage, post; stake (cards)

postal /pos'tal/ *a* postal. *f,* postcard, postal card

poste /'poste/ *m,* post, stake

postema /pos'tema/ *f,* tumor, abscess; bore, tedious person

postergación /posterga'sion; posterga'θion/ *f,* delay; delaying; relegation; disregard of seniority (in promotion)

postergar /poster'gar/ *vt* to delay; disregard a senior claim to promotion

posteridad /posteri'ðað/ *f,* descendants; posterity

posterior /poste'rior/ *a* back, rear; hind; subsequent

posteriormente /posterior'mente/ *adv* later, subsequently

postigo /pos'tigo/ *m,* secret door; grating, hatch; postern; shutter (of a window)

postillón /posti'yon; posti'ʎon/ *m,* postilion

postizo /pos'tiso; pos'tiθo/ *a* false, artificial, not natural. *m,* switch of false hair

postor /pos'tor/ *m,* bidder (at an auction)

postración /postra'sion; postra'θion/ *f,* prostration; exhaustion; depression, distress

postrar /pos'trar/ *vt* to cast down, demolish; prostrate, exhaust; *vr* kneel down; be prostrated or exhausted

postre /'postre/ *a* last (in order). *m, Cul.* dessert. **a la p.,** at last, finally

postrero /pos'trero/ *a* last (in order); rearmost, hindmost

postrimeramente /postrimera'mente/ *adv* lastly, finally

postrimería /postrime'ria/ *f, Eccl.* last period of life

postulación /postula'sion; postula'θion/ *f,* entreaty, request

postulado /postu'laðo/ *m,* assumption; supposition; working hypothesis; *Geom.* postulate

postulante /postu'lante/ **(-ta)** *n Eccl.* postulant, applicant, candidate

postular /postu'lar/ *vt* to postulate; *Lat. Am.* nominate

póstumo /'postumo/ *a* posthumous

postura /pos'tura/ *f,* posture, bearing; laying (of an egg); bid (at an auction); position; agreement, pact; bet, stake; planting; transplanted tree. **p. de vida,** way of life

potable /po'taβle/ *a* drinkable. **agua p.,** drinking water

potación /pota'sion; pota'θion/ *f,* potation, drink

potaje /po'tahe/ *m,* stew, potage; dried vegetables; mixed drink; hotchpotch

potasa /po'tasa/ *f,* potash

potasio /po'tasio/ *m,* potassium

pote /'pote/ *m,* pot; jar; flowerpot; *Cul.* cauldron; *Cul.* stew

potencia /po'tensia; po'tenθia/ *f,* power; potency; *Mech.* performance, capacity; strength, force; *Math.* power; rule, dominion

potencial /poten'sial; poten'θial/ *a* potential

potentado /poten'taðo/ *m,* potentate

potente /po'tente/ *a* potent; powerful; *Inf.* enormous

potestad /potes'tað/ *f,* authority, power; podesta, Italian magistrate; potentate; *Math.* power; *pl* angelic powers

potestativo /potesta'tiβo/ *a Law.* facultative

potingue /po'tiŋgue/ *m, Inf.* brew; mixture; lotion; medicine; filthy place, pigsty

poto /'poto/ *m, Lat. Am.* calabash; gourd; backside

potra /'potra/ *f,* filly

potrear /potre'ar/ *vt Inf.* to annoy

potro /'potro/ *m,* colt, foal; rack (for torture); vaulting horse. **p. mesteño,** mustang

poyo /'poyo/ *m,* stone seat

pozal /po'sal; po'θal/ *m,* pail, bucket

pozo /'poso; 'poθo/ *m,* well; shaft (in a mine). *Auto.* **p. colector,** crankcase

pozole, /po'sole; po'θole/ *m, Mexico* stew of pork, corn, chile, etc.

práctica /'praktika/ f, practice; custom, habit; method; exercise
practicabilidad /praktikaβili'ðað/ f, feasibility
practicable /prakti'kaβle/ a feasible, practicable
prácticamente /'praktikamente/ adv practically, in practice
practicante /prakti'kante/ m, medical practitioner; medical student; Med. intern; first-aid practitioner
practicar /prakti'kar/ vt to execute, perform; practice; make
práctico /'praktiko/ a practical; experienced, expert; workable. m, Naut. pilot
pradeño /pra'ðeɲo/ a meadow, prairie
pradera /pra'ðera/ f, meadow, field; lawn
pradería /praðe'ria/ f, meadowland, prairie
prado /'praðo/ m, meadow; grassland; field; lawn; walk (in cities)
Praga /'praga/ Prague
pragmatista /pragma'tista/ a pragmatic. mf pragmatist
pravedad /praβe'ðað/ f, wickedness, immorality, depravity
pravo /'praβo/ a wicked, immoral, depraved
pre /pre/ m, Mil. daily pay. prep insep pre-
preámbulo /pre'ambulo/ m, preamble, preface; importunate digression
prebenda /pre'βenda/ f, Eccl. prebend, benefice; Inf. sinecure
preboste /pre'βoste/ m, provost
precario /pre'kario/ a precarious, uncertain, insecure
precaución /prekau'sion; prekau'θion/ f, precaution, safeguard
precaucionarse /prekausio'narse; prekauθio'narse/ vr to take precautions, safeguard oneself
precautelar /prekaute'lar/ vt to forewarn; take precautions
precaver /preka'βer/ vt to prevent, avoid; vr (with de or contra) guard against
precavido /preka'βiðo/ a cautious, forewarned
precedencia /prese'ðensia; preθe'ðenθia/ f, priority, precedence; superiority; preference, precedence
precedente /prese'ðente; preθe'ðente/ a preceding. m, antecedent; precedent
preceder /prese'ðer; preθe'ðer/ vt to precede; have precedence over, be superior to
preceptivo /presep'tiβo; preθep'tiβo/ a preceptive; didactic
precepto /pre'septo; pre'θepto/ m, precept; order, injunction; rule, commandment. **de p.,** obligatory
preceptor /presep'tor; preθep'tor/ **(-ra)** n teacher, instructor, tutor, preceptor
preces /'preses; 'preθes/ f pl, Eccl. prayers; entreaties
preciado /pre'siaðo; pre'θiaðo/ a excellent, esteemed, precious; boastful
preciar /pre'siar; pre'θiar/ vt to esteem, value; valuate, price; vr boast
precintar /presin'tar; preθin'tar/ vt to seal; rope, string, tie up
precinto /pre'sinto; pre'θinto/ m, sealing; roping, tying up; strap
precio /'presio; 'preθio/ m, price, cost; recompense, reward; premium; rate; reputation, importance; esteem. **p. de tasa,** controlled price
preciosidad /presiosi'ðað; preθiosi'ðað/ f, preciousness; exquisiteness, fineness; richness; wittiness; Inf. loveliness, beauty; thing of beauty
precioso /pre'sioso; pre'θioso/ a precious; exquisite, fine, rare; rich; witty; Inf. lovely, delicious, attractive
preciosuna /presio'suna; preθio'suna/ f, Lat. Am. thing of beauty
precipicio /presi'pisio; preθi'piθio/ m, precipice; heavy fall; ruin, disaster
precipitación /presipita'sion; preθipita'θion/ f, precipitancy, haste; rashness; Chem. precipitation
precipitadamente /presipitaða'mente; preθipitaða'mente/ adv precipitately, in haste; rashly, foolishly
precipitado /presipi'taðo; preθipi'taðo/ a precipitate; rash, thoughtless. m, Chem. precipitate
precipitar /presipi'tar; preθipi'tar/ vt to precipitate,

hurl headlong; hasten; Chem. precipitate; vr hurl oneself headlong; hasten, rush
precipitoso /presipi'toso; preθipi'toso/ a precipitous; rash, heedless
precisamente /presisa'mente; preθisa'mente/ adv exactly, precisely, just; necessarily. **Y p. en aquel instante llegó,** And just at that moment he arrived
precisar /presi'sar; preθi'sar/ vt to fix, arrange; set forth, draw up, state; compel, force, oblige
precisión /presi'sion; preθi'sion/ f, accuracy, precision; necessity, conciseness, clarity; compulsion, obligation
preciso /pre'siso; pre'θiso/ a necessary, unavoidable; concise, clear; precise, exact
precitado /presi'taðo; preθi'taðo/ a aforementioned
preclaro /pre'klaro/ a illustrious, distinguished, celebrated
precocidad /prekosi'ðað; prekoθi'ðað/ f, precocity
precognición /prekogni'sion; prekogni'θion/ f, foreknowledge
precolombino, -a /prekolom'βino/ a pre-Columbian
preconcebido /prekonse'βiðo; prekonθe'βiðo/ a preconceived
preconcepto /prekon'septo; prekon'θepto/ m, preconceived idea, preconceived notion
preconizar /prekoni'sar; prekoni'θar/ vt to eulogize, praise publicly
preconocer /prekono'ser; prekono'θer/ vt irr to know beforehand; foresee. See **conocer**
precoz /pre'kos; pre'koθ/ a precocious
precursor /prekur'sor/ **(-ra)** a precursory; preceding, previous. n precursor
predecesor /preðese'sor; preðeθe'sor/ **(-ra)** n predecessor
predecir /preðe'sir; preðe'θir/ vt irr to foretell, prophesy. See **decir**
predestinación /preðestina'sion; preðestina'θion/ f, predestination
predestinado /preðesti'naðo/ **(-da)** a predestined; foreordained. n one of the predestined
predestinar /preðesti'nar/ vt to predestine, foreordain
predeterminar /preðetermi'nar/ vt to predetermine
prédica /'preðika/ f, inf (contemptuous) sermon
predicación /preðika'sion; preðika'θion/ f, preaching; homily, sermon
predicadera /preðika'ðera/ f, pulpit; pl Inf. talent for preaching
predicador /preðika'ðor/ **(-ra)** a preaching. n preacher
predicamento /preðika'mento/ m, predicament; reputation
predicar /preði'kar/ vt to publish; manifest; preach; vi overpraise; Inf. lecture, scold. **p. en el desierto, to** preach to the wind
predicción /preðik'sion; preðik'θion/ f, prediction, prophecy
predilección /preðilek'sion; preðilek'θion/ f, predilection, preference, partiality
predilecto /preði'lekto/ a favorite, preferred
predisponer /preðispo'ner/ vt irr to predispose. See **poner**
predisposición /preðisposi'sion; preðisposi'θion/ f, predisposition; tendency, prejudice
predominación /preðomina'sion; preðomina'θion/ f, predomination
predominante /preðomi'nante/ a predominant; prevailing
predominar /preðomi'nar/ vi and vt to predominate; prevail; tower above; overlook
predominio /preðo'minio/ m, predominance, ascendancy, preponderance
preeminencia /preemi'nensia; preemi'nenθia/ f, preeminence
preeminente /preemi'nente/ a preeminent
preexistencia /preeksis'tensia; preeksis'tenθia/ f, preexistence
preexistente /preeksis'tente/ a preexistent
preexistir /preeksis'tir/ vi to preexist, exist before
prefacio /pre'fasio; pre'faθio/ m, introduction, preface, prologue; Eccl. preface

prefecto /pre'fekto/ *m*, prefect
prefectura /prefek'tura/ *f*, prefecture
preferencia /prefe'rensia; prefe'renθia/ *f*, preference; superiority. **de p.**, preferred, favorite; preferably
preferente /prefe'rente/ *a* preferable; preferential; preferred (of stock)
preferible /prefe'riβle/ *a* preferable
preferir /prefe'rir/ *vt irr* to prefer; excel, exceed. *Pres. Part.* **prefiriendo.** *Pres. Ind.* **prefiero, prefieres, prefiere, prefieren.** *Preterite* **prefirió, prefirieron.** *Pres. Subjunc.* **prefiera, prefieras, prefiera, prefieran.** *Imperf. Subjunc.* **prefiriese, etc.**
prefijar /prefi'har/ *vt* to prefix
prefijo /pre'fiho/ *m*, prefix
prefinir /prefi'nir/ *vt* to fix a time limit for
prefulgente /preful'hente/ *a* brilliant, shining, resplendent
pregón /pre'gon/ *m*, public proclamation; marriage banns
pregonar /prego'nar/ *vt* to proclaim publicly; cry one's wares; publish abroad; eulogize, praise; proscribe, outlaw. **p. a los cuatro vientos,** *Inf.* to shout from the rooftops
pregonería /pregone'ria/ *f*, office of the town crier
pregonero /prego'nero/ *m*, town crier; court crier
preguerra /pre'gerra/ *f*, prewar period
pregunta /pre'gunta/ *f*, question; *Com.* inquiry; questionnaire, interrogation. *Inf.* **andar** (*or* **estar**) **a la cuarta p.**, to be very hard up, be on the rocks. **hacer una p.**, to ask a question
preguntador /pregunta'ðor/ **(-ra)** *a* questioning; inquisitive. *n* questioner; inquisitive person
preguntar /pregun'tar/ *vt* to question, ask; (*with por*) inquire for; *vr* ask oneself, wonder
prehistoria /preis'toria/ *f*, prehistory
prehistórico /preis'toriko/ *a* prehistoric
prejuicio /pre'huisio; pre'huiθio/ *m*, prejudice
prejuzgar /prehus'gar; prehuθ'gar/ *vt* to prejudge; judge hastily
prelacía /prela'sia; prela'θia/ *f*, prelacy
prelación /prela'sion; prela'θion/ *f*, preference
prelado /pre'laðo/ *m*, prelate
preliminar /prelimi'nar/ *a* preliminary, prefatory. *m*, preliminary
preludiar /prelu'ðiar/ *vi* and *vt Mus.* to play a prelude (to); *vt* prepare, initiate
preludio /pre'luðio/ *m*, introduction, prologue; *Mus.* prelude; *Mus.* overture
prematuro /prema'turo/ *a* premature, untimely; unseasonable; immature, unripe
premeditación /premeðita'sion; premeðita'θion/ *f*, premeditation
premeditar /premeði'tar/ *vt* to premeditate, plan in advance
premiador /premia'ðor/ **(-ra)** *a* rewarding. *n* rewarder
premiar /pre'miar/ *vt* to reward, requite
premio /'premio/ *m*, prize; reward; premium; *Com.* interest. **p. en metálico,** cash prize. *Inf.* **p. gordo,** first prize (in a lottery)
premioso /pre'mioso/ *a* tight; troublesome, annoying; stern, strict; slow-moving; burdensome, hard; labored (of speech or style)
premisa /pre'misa/ *f*, premise; sign, indication
premonitorio /premoni'torio/ *a* premonitory
premura /pre'mura/ *f*, urgency, haste
prenda /'prenda/ *f*, pledge; token, sign; jewel; article of clothing; talent, gift; loved one; *pl* game of forfeits
prendador /prenda'ðor/ **(-ra)** *n* pledger
prendamiento /prenda'miento/ *m*, pawning
prendar /pren'dar/ *vt* to pawn; charm, delight; *vr* (*with de*) take a liking to
prender /pren'der/ *vt* to seize; arrest; capture, catch; turn on (lights, radio). *vi* take root (plants); catch fire; be infectious
prendería /prende'ria/ *f*, second-hand shop
prendero /pren'dero/ **(-ra)** *n* second-hand dealer
prendimiento /prendi'miento/ *m*, seizure; capture; arrest
prenombre /pre'nombre/ *m*, given name, praenomen

prensa /'prensa/ *f*, press; printing press; newspapers; the press. **dar a la p.**, to publish
prensado /pren'saðo/ *m*, **prensadura** *f*, pressing; flattening; squeezing
prensar /pren'sar/ *vt* to press; squeeze
prensil /pren'sil/ *a* prehensile
preñado /pre'ɲaðo/ *a* pregnant; bulging, sagging (walls, etc.); swollen. *m*, pregnancy
preñez /pre'ɲes; pre'ɲeθ/ *f*, pregnancy; suspense
preocupación /preokupa'sion; preokupa'θion/ *f*, anxiety, preoccupation; prejudice
preocupadamente /preokupaða'mente/ *adv* preoccupiedly, absentmindedly; with prejudice
preocupar /preoku'par/ *vt* to preoccupy; make anxious; bias, prejudice; *vr* be anxious; be prejudiced
preordinar /preorði'nar/ *vt Eccl.* to predestine
preparación /prepara'sion; prepara'θion/ *f*, preparation; treatment; compound, specific
preparado /prepa'raðo/ *a* ready, prepared. *m*, preparation, patent food, etc.
preparar /prepa'rar/ *vt* to prepare; *vr* prepare oneself; qualify
preparativo /prepara'tiβo/ *a* preparatory. *m*, preparation
preparatorio /prepara'torio/ *a* preparatory
preponderancia /preponde'ransia; preponde'ranθia/ *f*, preponderance
preponderante /preponde'rante/ *a* preponderant; dominant
preponderar /preponde'rar/ *vi* to preponderate; dominate; outweigh
preponer /prepo'ner/ *vt irr* to put before. See **poner**
preposición /preposi'sion; preposi'θion/ *f*, preposition
prepósito /pre'posito/ *m*, chairman, head, president; *Eccl.* provost
prepucio /pre'pusio; pre'puθio/ *m*, prepuce, foreskin
prerrogativa /prerroga'tiβa/ *f*, prerogative
presa /'presa/ *f*, hold, grasp; seizure, capture; booty; dam; lock (on rivers, canals); weir; ditch, trench; embankment; slice, bit. **hacer p.**, to seize; take advantage of (circumstances)
presagiar /presa'hiar/ *vt* to prophesy, presage, bode
presagio /pre'sahio/ *m*, presage, sign; presentiment, foreboding
présbita /'presβita/ *a* long-sighted, farsighted
presbiterado /presβite'raðo/ *m*, priesthood; holy orders
presbiteriano /presβite'riano/ **(-na)** *a* and *n* Presbyterian
presbítero /pres'βitero/ *m*, priest
presciencia /pres'siensia; pres'θienθia/ *f*, prescience, foresight
presciente /pres'siente; pres'θiente/ *a* prescient, farsighted
prescindible /pressin'diβle; presθin'diβle/ *a* nonessential, able to be dispensed with
prescindir /pressin'dir; presθin'dir/ *vi* (*with de*) to pass over, omit; do without. **Prescindiendo de esto...,** Leaving this aside....
prescribir /preskri'βir/ *vt* to prescribe, order
prescripción /preskrip'sion; preskrip'θion/ *f*, prescription
presea /pre'sea/ *f*, jewel, object of value
presencia /pre'sensia; pre'senθia/ *f*, presence, attendance; appearance, looks; ostentation. **p. de ánimo,** presence of mind
presenciar /presen'siar; presen'θiar/ *vt* to be present at; witness, behold
presentación /presenta'sion; presenta'θion/ *f*, presentation; introduction; *Lat. Am. also* petition
presentar /presen'tar/ *vt* to show; present, make a gift of; introduce (persons); *vr* occur; present oneself; offer one's services
presente /pre'sente/ *a* present. *m*, gift; present time. *Law.* **Por estas presentes...,** By these presents.... **tener p.,** to remember
presentimiento /presenti'miento/ *m*, presentiment, apprehension

presentir /presen'tir/ *vt irr* to have a presentiment of. See **sentir**

preservación /preserβa'sion; preserβa'θion/ *f*, preservation, protection, saving

preservar /preser'βar/ *vt* to preserve, protect, save

preservativo /preserβa'tiβo/ *a* preservative. *m*, preservative, safeguard, protection

presidencia /presi'ðensia; presi'ðenθia/ *f*, presidency; chairmanship; presidential seat or residence

presidencial /presiðen'sial; presiðen'θial/ *a* presidential

presidenta /presi'ðenta/ *f*, female president; president's wife; chairwoman

presidente /presi'ðente/ *m*, president; chairman; head, director; presiding judge

presidiar /presi'ðiar/ *vt* to garrison

presidiario /presi'ðiario/ *m*, convict

presidio /pre'siðio/ *m*, garrison; garrison town; fortress; penitentiary; imprisonment; *Law.* hard labor; assistance, protection

presidir /presi'ðir/ *vt* to preside over; act as chairperson for; influence, determine

presilla /pre'siya; pre'siʎa/ *f*, loop, shank, noose; press stud; *Mexico* epaulet

presión /pre'sion/ *f*, pressure

preso /'preso/ **(-sa)** *n* prisoner, captive; convict

prestación /presta'sion; presta'θion/ *f*, lending, loan. **p. vecinal,** corvée

prestador /presta'ðor/ **(-ra)** *a* lending, loan. *n* lender

prestamente /presta'mente/ *adv* expeditiously, promptly

prestamista /presta'mista/ *mf* moneylender; pawnbroker

préstamo /'prestamo/ *m*, loan; lending. **casa de préstamos,** pawnshop

prestar /pres'tar/ *vt* to lend; assist; pay (attention); give; *Lat. Am.* to borrow; *vi* be useful; give, expand; *vr* be suitable; lend itself; offer oneself. **pedir/tomar prestado,** to borrow

prestatario /presta'tario/ **(-ia)** *n* money borrower, debtor

preste /'preste/ *m*, celebrant of high mass. **el p. Juan,** title of Prester John

presteza /pres'tesa; pres'teθa/ *f*, speed; promptness, dispatch

prestidigitación /prestiðihita'sion; prestiðihita'θion/ *f*, prestidigitation

prestidigitador /prestiðihita'ðor/ **(-ra)** *n* juggler, conjurer

prestigio /pres'tihio/ *m*, magic spell, sorcery; trick, illusion (of conjurers, etc.); influence, prestige

prestigioso /presti'hioso/ *a* illusory; influential

presto /'presto/ *a* quick, speedy; prompt, ready. *m*, pressure cooker. *adv* immediately; soon; quickly. **de p.,** speedily

presumido /presu'miðo/ *a* conceited, vain; presumptuous

presumir /presu'mir/ *vt* to suppose, presume; *vi* be conceited

presunción /presun'sion; presun'θion/ *f*, supposition, presumption; vanity, presumptuousness

presuntivo /presun'tiβo/ *a* presumptive

presuntuosidad /presuntuosi'ðað/ *f*, presumptuousness

presuntuoso /presun'tuoso/ *a* presumptuous, vain

presuponer /presupo'ner/ *vt irr* to presuppose, assume; budget, estimate. See **poner**

presuposición /presuposi'sion; presuposi'θion/ *f*, presupposition

presupuesto /presu'puesto/ *m*, motive, reason; supposition, assumption; estimate; *Com.* tender; national budget

presuroso /presu'roso/ *a* swift, speedy

pretencioso /preten'sioso; preten'θioso/ *a* pretentious, vain

pretender /preten'der/ *vt* to seek, solicit; claim; apply for; attempt, try; woo, court

pretendiente /preten'diente/ **(-ta)** *n* pretender; candidate; petitioner; suitor

pretensión /preten'sion/ *f*, pretension; claim; *pl* ambitions

pretérito /pre'terito/ *a* past. *m*, preterite

pretextar /preteks'tar/ *vt* to allege as a pretext or excuse

pretexto /pre'teksto/ *m*, pretext, excuse

prevalecer /preβale'ser; preβale'θer/ *vi irr* to prevail; be dominant; take root (plants). See **conocer**

prevaleciente /preβale'siente; preβale'θiente/ *a* prevailing; prevalent

prevaricador /preβarika'ðor/ **(-ra)** *n* prevaricator

prevaricar /preβari'kar/ *vi* to prevaricate

prevención /preβen'sion; preβen'θion/ *f*, prevention; precaution; prejudice; police station; *Mil.* guard room; foresight, prevision; preparation. **de p.,** as a precaution

prevenido /preβe'niðo/ *a* prepared; cautious, forewarned

prevenir /preβe'nir/ *vt irr* to prepare; prevent, avoid; warn; prejudice; occur, happen; *Fig.* overcome (obstacles); *vr* be ready; be forewarned. See **venir**

preventivo /preβen'tiβo/ *a* preventive

prever /pre'βer/ *vt irr* to foresee, forecast, anticipate. See **ver**

previamente /preβia'mente/ *adv* previously, in advance

previo /'preβio/ *a* previous, advance

previsión /preβi'sion/ *f*, forecast; foresight, prevision, prescience. **p. social,** social insurance

previsor /preβi'sor/ *a* farsighted, provident

prieto /'prieto/ *a* almost black, blackish; tight; mean, avaricious; *Lat. Am.* dark-skinned, swarthy

prima /'prima/ *f*, *Eccl.* prime; *Com.* premium; female cousin

primacía /prima'sia; prima'θia/ *f*, supremacy, preeminence; primacy; primateship

primada /pri'maða/ *f*, *Inf.* act of sponging on, taking advantage of

primado /pri'maðo/ *m*, primate; primateship

primario /pri'mario/ *a* primary. *m*, professor who gives the first lecture of the day

primavera /prima'βera/ *f*, springtime; primrose; figured silk material; beautifully colored thing; youth; prime

primaveral /primaβe'ral/ *a* spring, spring-like

primeramente /primera'mente/ *adv* first; in the first place

primerizo /prime'riso; prime'riθo/ **(-za)** *n* novice; beginner; apprentice; firstborn

primero /pri'mero/ *a* first; former; excellent, first-rate. *adv* first; in the first place. **primera enseñanza,** primary education. **primera materia,** raw material. **primer plano,** *Art.* foreground. **primera cura,** first aid. **de buenas a primeras,** all at once, suddenly

primicia /pri'misia; pri'miθia/ *f*, first fruits; offering of first fruits; *pl* first effects

primitivo /primi'tiβo/ *a* original, early; primitive

primo /'primo/ **(-ma)** *a* first; excellent, fine. *n* cousin; *Inf.* simpleton; *Inf.* pigeon, dupe. **p. carnal,** first cousin. *Inf.* **hacer el p.,** to be a dupe. *Inf.* **ser prima hermana de,** to be the twin of (of things)

primogénito /primo'henito/ **(-ta)** *a* and *n* firstborn

primogenitura /primoheni'tura/ *f*, primogeniture

primor /pri'mor/ *m*, exquisite care; beauty, loveliness; thing of beauty

primoroso /primo'roso/ *a* beautiful; exquisitely done; dexterous, skillful

princesa /prin'sesa; prin'θesa/ *f*, princess

principado /prinsi'paðo; prinθi'paðo/ *m*, principality; princedom; superiority, preeminence

principal /prinsi'pal; prinθi'pal/ *a* chief, principal; illustrious; fundamental, first. *m*, head, principal (of a firm); *Com.* capital, principal; first floor

principalmente /prinsipal'mente; prinθipal'mente/ *adv* principally, chiefly

príncipe /'prinsipe; 'prinθipe/ *m*, leader; prince. **p. de Asturias,** prince of Asturias. **p. de la sangre,** prince of the blood royal

principesco /prinsi'pesko; prinθi'pesko/ *a* princely

principiante /prinsi'piante; prinθi'piante/ **(-ta)** n beginner, novice; apprentice
principiar /prinsi'piar; prinθi'piar/ vt to begin, commence
principio /prin'sipio; prin'θipio/ m, beginning; principle; genesis, origin; rudiment; axiom; constituent. **al p.,** at first. **a principios,** at the beginning (of the month, year, etc.). **en p.,** in principle
pringar /prin'gar/ vt Cul. to soak in fat; stain with grease; Inf. wound; take part in a business deal; slander; vr Inf. appropriate, misuse (funds, etc.)
pringo /'pringo/ m, Lat. Am. drop (of a liquid)
pringoso /prin'goso/ a greasy
pringue /'pringue/ mf, animal fat, lard; grease spot
priora /'priora/ f, prioress
prioridad /priori'ðað/ f, priority
prisa /'prisa/ f, haste, speed; skirmish, foray. **a toda p.,** with all speed. **correr p.,** to be urgent. **dar p.,** to hasten, speed up. **darse** (or **estar de**) **p.,** to hurry
prisión /pri'sion/ f, prison, jail; seizure; captivity, imprisonment; Fig. bond; obstacle, shackle; pl fetters
prisma /'prisma/ m, prism
prismáticos /pris'matikos/ m pl, field glasses
prisonero /priso'nero/ **(-ra)** n prisoner; Fig. victim (of passion, etc.)
pristino /pris'tino/ a pristine
privación /priβa'sion; priβa'θion/ f, privation; lack, shortage; deprivation; degradation
privada /pri'βaða/ f, toilet, privy, water closet
privadamente /priβaða'mente/ adv privately; individually, separately
privado /pri'βaðo/ a private; individual, personal. m, favorite; confidant
privar /pri'βar/ vt to deprive; dismiss (from office); interdict, forbid; vi prevail, be in favor; vr swoon; deprive oneself
privilegiar /priβile'hiar/ vt to privilege; bestow a favor on
privilegio /priβi'lehio/ m, privilege; prerogative; concession; copyright; patent
pro /pro/ mf advantage, benefit. **el p. y el contra,** the pros and cons. **en p.,** in favor
proa /'proa/ f, prow, bow
probabilidad /proβaβili'ðað/ f, probability
probable /pro'βaβle/ a probable; likely; provable
probación /proβa'sion; proβa'θion/ f, proof, test; novitiate, probation
probado /pro'βaðo/ a tried, tested, proved
probar /pro'βar/ vt irr to prove; test; taste; try on (clothes); vi suit; (with prep a + infin) try to. **p. fortuna,** to try one's luck. Pres. Ind. **pruebo, pruebas, prueba, prueban.** Pres. Subjunc. **pruebe, pruebes, prueben**
probatorio /proβa'torio/ a probationary
probidad /proβi'ðað/ f, probity, trustworthiness, honesty
problema /pro'βlema/ m, problem
problemático /proβle'matiko/ a problematical, uncertain
probo /'proβo/ a honest, trustworthy
procacidad /prokasi'ðað; prokaθi'ðað/ f, insolence, pertness
procaz /pro'kas; pro'kaθ/ a insolent, pert, brazen
procedencia /prose'ðensia; proθe'ðenθia/ f, origin, source; parentage, descent; port of sailing or call
procedente /prose'ðente; proθe'ðente/ a arriving or coming from
proceder /prose'ðer; proθe'ðer/ vi to proceed; behave; originate, arise; continue, go on; act. Law. **p. contra,** to proceed against (a person)
procedimiento /proseði'miento; proθeði'miento/ m, proceeding, advancement; procedure; legal practice; process
proceloso /prose'loso; proθe'loso/ a tempestuous
prócer /'proser; 'proθer/ a exalted, eminent; lofty. m, exalted personage
procesado /prose'saðo; proθe'saðo/ **(-da)** n defendant
procesamiento /prosesa'miento; proθesa'miento/ m, suing, suit; indictment

procesar /prose'sar; proθe'sar/ vt Law. to proceed against, sue
procesión /prose'sion; proθe'sion/ f, proceeding, emanating; procession; Inf. train, string. **andar** (or **ir**) **por dentro la p.,** to feel keenly without betraying one's emotion
proceso /pro'seso; pro'θeso/ m, process; progress; advancement; lapse of time; lawsuit
proclama /pro'klama/ f, proclamation; announcement; publication of marriage banns
proclamación /proklama'sion; proklama'θion/ f, proclamation; acclaim, applause
proclamar /prokla'mar/ vt to proclaim; acclaim; publish abroad; reveal, show
proclividad /prokliβi'ðað/ f, proclivity, tendency
procomún /proko'mun/ m, social or public welfare
procreación /prokrea'sion; prokrea'θion/ f, procreation
procreador /prokrea'ðor/ **(-ra)** a procreative. n procreator
procrear /prokre'ar/ vt to procreate, beget, engender
procuración /prokura'sion; prokura'θion/ f, procurement; assiduity, care; Law. power of attorney; Law. attorneyship
procurador /prokura'ðor/ **(-ra)** m, proxy; Law. attorney; proctor. n procurer. **P. de la República,** Attorney General
procurar /proku'rar/ vt to try, attempt; procure, get; exercise the profession of a lawyer
prodigalidad /proðigali'ðað/ f, prodigality, lavishness; waste, extravagance
prodigar /proði'gar/ vt to waste, squander; lavish, bestow freely; vr make oneself cheap
prodigio /pro'ðihio/ m, marvel, wonder; prodigy; monster; miracle
prodigiosidad /proðihiosi'ðað/ f, prodigiousness
prodigioso /proði'hioso/ a wonderful; prodigious; monstrous; miraculous
pródigo /'proðigo/ **(-ga)** a wasteful, extravagant; lavish, generous. n spendthrift, wastrel, prodigal. **el hijo p.,** the prodigal son
producción /proðuk'sion; proðuk'θion/ f, production; output, yield; generation (of heat, etc.); crop
producir /proðu'sir; proðu'θir/ vt irr to produce; generate; yield, give; cause, occasion; publish; vr explain oneself; arise, appear, be produced. **p. efecto,** to have effect; take effect. See **conducir**
productividad /proðuktiβi'ðað/ f, productivity
productivo /proðuk'tiβo/ a productive; fertile; profitable
producto /pro'ðukto/ m, produce; product; profit; yield, gain; Math. product. Chem. **p. derivado,** by-product
productor /proðuk'tor/ **(-ra)** a productive. n producer
proemio /pro'emio/ m, prologue; preface; introduction
proeza /pro'esa; pro'eθa/ f, prowess, gallantry; skill; Lat. Am. boast
profanación /profana'sion; profana'θion/ f, profanation
profanador /profana'ðor/ **(-ra)** n profaner, transgressor
profanar /profa'nar/ vt to profane
profanidad /profani'ðað/ f, profanity
profano /pro'fano/ a profane; dissolute; pleasure-loving, worldly; immodest; lay, ignorant
profecía /profe'sia; profe'θia/ f, prophecy; Eccl. Book of the Prophets; opinion, view
proferir /profe'rir/ vt irr to utter, pronounce. See **herir**
profesar /profe'sar/ vt to exercise, practice (professions); Eccl. profess; believe in; teach
profesión /profe'sion/ f, profession; trade, occupation; avowal, admission
profesional /profesio'nal/ a professional
profesionalismo /profesiona'lismo/ m, professionalism
profeso /pro'feso/ **(-sa)** a Eccl. professed. n professed monk
profesor /profe'sor/ **(-ra)** n teacher; professor

profesorado /profeso'raðo/ m, teaching staff; teaching profession; professorship; professorate
profeta /pro'feta/ m, prophet; seer
profético /pro'fetiko/ a prophetic
profetisa /profe'tisa/ f, prophetess
profetizar /profeti'sar; profeti'θar/ vt to prophesy; imagine, suppose
proficiente /profi'siente; profi'θiente/ a proficient
profiláctico /profi'laktiko/ a and m, prophylactic
prófugo /'profugo/ (-ga) a and n fugitive from justice. m, Mil. one who evades military service
profundamente /profunda'mente/ adv profoundly; acutely, deeply
profundidad /profundi'ðað/ f, depth; profundity, obscurity; Geom. depth; concavity; intensity (of feeling); vastness (of knowledge, etc.)
profundizar /profundi'sar; profundi'θar/ vt to deepen; hollow out; Fig. go into deeply, fathom
profundo /pro'fundo/ a deep; low; Fig. intense, acute; abstruse, profound; Fig. vast, extensive; high. m, depth, profundity; Poet. ocean, the deep; Poet. hell
profuso /pro'fuso/ a profuse, abundant; extravagant, wasteful
progenie /pro'henie/ f, descendants
prognosis /prog'nosis/ f, prognosis; forecast
programa /pro'grama/ m, program; edict, public notice; plan, scheme; Educ. calendar; syllabus; timetable
programador /programa'ðor/ (-ra) n (computer) programmer
progresar /progre'sar/ vt and vi to make progress; progress, advance
progresión /progre'sion/ f, progression; advancement, progress
progresista /progre'sista/ a Polit. progressive. mf progressive
progresivo /progre'siβo/ a progressive; advancing
progreso /pro'greso/ m, progress, advancement; growth; improvement, development
prohibente /proi'βente/ a prohibitory, prohibitive
prohibición /proiβi'sion; proiβi'θion/ f, forbidding, prohibition
prohibicionista /proiβisio'nista; proiβiθio'nista/ mf prohibitionist. a prohibitionist
prohibir /proi'βir/ vt to forbid, prohibit. «**Prohibido el paso,**» "No thoroughfare". Pres. Indic. **prohíbo, prohíbes, prohíbe, prohíben.** Pres. Subjunc. **prohíba, prohíbas, prohíba, prohíban.**
prohibitivo, prohibitorio /proiβi'tiβo, proiβi'torio/ a prohibitive
prohijador /proiha'ðor/ (-ra) n adopter (of a child)
prohijamiento /proiha'miento/ m, child adoption; fathering (of a bill, etc.)
prohijar /proi'har/ vt to adopt (children, ideas); Fig. father. See **prohibir**
prohombre /pro'ombre/ m, master of a guild; respected, welliliked man
prójimo /'prohimo/ m, fellow man, brother, neighbor.
prole /'prole/ f, progeny, young offspring
proletariado /proleta'riaðo/ m, proletariat
proletario /prole'tario/ a poor; common, vulgar. m, plebeian; pauper; proletarian
prolífico /pro'lifiko/ a prolific; abundant, fertile
prolijidad /prolihi'ðað/ f, verbosity, prolixity; nicety, scruple; importunity, tediousness
prolijo /pro'liho/ a verbose, prolix; fussy, fastidious; tedious, importunate; Argentina indefatigable, untiring
prologar /prolo'gar/ vt to prologue; provide with a preface
prólogo /'prologo/ m, preface; prologue; introduction
prolongación /proloŋga'sion; proloŋga'θion/ f, lengthening; prolongation; protraction; extension
prolongado /proloŋ'gaðo/ a prolonged; oblong, long
prolongar /proloŋ'gar/ vt to lengthen; Geom. produce; prolong, spin out
promediar /prome'ðiar/ vt to distribute or divide into two equal portions; average; vi arbitrate; place oneself between two people; reach half-time
promedio /pro'meðio/ m, average; middle, center
promesa /pro'mesa/ f, promise; augury, favorable sign
prometedor /promete'ðor/ (-ra) a promising. n promiser
prometer /prome'ter/ vt to promise; attest, certify; vi promise well, look hopeful; vr devote oneself to service of God; anticipate confidently, expect; become engaged (marriage). Inf. **prometérselas muy felices,** to have high hopes
prometido /prome'tiðo/ (-da) n betrothed. m, promise
prometimiento /promet'imiento/ m, promise; promising
prominencia /promi'nensia; promi'nenθia/ f, prominence, protuberance; eminence, hill
prominente /promi'nente/ a prominent, protuberant; eminent, elevated
promiscuar /promis'kuar/ vi to eat meat and fish on fast days
promiscuidad /promiskui'ðað/ f, promiscuity; ambiguity
promiscuo /pro'miskuo/ a indiscriminate, haphazard, promiscuous; ambiguous
promisión /promi'sion/ f, promise
promisorio /promi'sorio/ a promissory
promoción /promo'sion; promo'θion/ f, promotion; batch, class, year (of recruits, students, etc.)
promontorio /promon'torio/ m, headland; promontory; cumbersome object
promotor /promo'tor/ (-ra) a promotive. n promoter; supporter
promover /promo'βer/ vt irr to promote, further, advance; promote (a person). **p. un proceso (a),** to bring a suit (against). See **mover**
promulgación /promulga'sion; promulga'θion/ f, promulgation
promulgar /promul'gar/ vt to publish officially, proclaim; promulgate. Law. **p. sentencia,** to pass judgment
pronombre /pro'nombre/ m, pronoun
pronosticación /pronostika'sion; pronostika'θion/ f, prognostication; presage
pronosticar /pronosti'kar/ vt to prognosticate, forecast; presage
pronóstico /pro'nostiko/ m, omen, prediction; almanac; prognosis; sign, indication. **p. del tiempo,** weather forecast
prontitud /pronti'tuð/ f, quickness, promptness; quick-wittedness; Fig. sharpness, liveliness; celerity; dispatch
pronto /'pronto/ a quick, speedy; prompt; ready, prepared. m, Inf. sudden decision. adv immediately; with all speed; soon. **de p.,** suddenly; without thinking. **por lo p.,** temporarily, provisionally
prontuario /pron'tuario/ m, compendium, handbook; summary
pronunciación /pronunsia'sion; pronunθia'θion/ f, pronunciation
pronunciamiento /pronunsia'miento/ m, pronunθia'miento/ m, military uprising; political manifesto; Law. pronouncement of sentence
pronunciar /pronun'siar; pronun'θiar/ vt to pronounce, articulate; decide, determine; Law. pronounce judgment; give or make (a speech)
propagación /propaga'sion; propaga'θion/ f, propagation; dissemination; transmission
propagador /propaga'ðor/ a propagative. m, propagator
propaganda /propa'ganda/ f, propaganda organization; propaganda
propagandista /propagan'dista/ mf propagandist
propagar /propa'gar/ vt to reproduce; propagate, disseminate; vr reproduce, multiply; propagate, spread
propalar /propa'lar/ vt to disseminate, spread abroad
propasarse /propa'sarse/ vr to go too far, forget oneself; overstep one's authority

propender /propen'der/ *vi* to be inclined, have a leaning toward
propensión /propen'sion/ *f*, propensity, inclination; tendency
propenso /pro'penso/ *a* inclined, disposed; liable
propiamente /propia'mente/ *adv* properly, suitably
propiciación /propisia'sion; propiθia'θion/ *f*, propitiation
propiciador /propisia'ðor; propiθia'ðor/ **(-ra)** *a* propitiatory. *n* propitiator
propiciar /propi'siar; propi'θiar/ *vt* to propitiate, appease
propiciatorio /propisia'torio; propiθia'torio/ *a* propitiatory
propicio /pro'pisio; pro'piθio/ *a* propitious, auspicious; kind, favorable
propiedad /propie'ðað/ *f*, estate, property; ownership; landed property; attribute, quality, property; *Art.* resemblance, naturalness
propietario /propie'tario/ **(-ia)** *a* proprietary. *n* proprietor, owner
propina /pro'pina/ *f*, gratuity, tip. *Inf.* **de p.**, in addition, extra
propinar /propi'nar/ *vt* to treat to a drink; administer (medicine); *Inf.* give (slaps, etc.)
propincuidad /propinkui'ðað/ *f*, propinquity, proximity
propincuo /pro'pinkuo/ *a* near, contiguous, adjacent
propio /'propio/ *a* own, one's own; typical, characteristic; individual, peculiar; suitable, apt; natural, real; same. *m*, messenger; *pl* public lands
proponente /propo'nente/ *a* proposing. *m*, proposer; *Com.* tenderer
proponer /propo'ner/ *vt irr* to propose, suggest; make a proposition; propose (for a post, office, etc.); *Math.* state; *vr* intend, purpose. **proponerse para un empleo,** to apply for a post. See **poner**
proporción /propor'sion; propor'θion/ *f*, proportion; chance, opportunity; size; *Math.* proportion
proporcionado /proporsio'naðo; proporθio'naðo/ *a* fit, suitable; proportionate; symmetrical
proporcional /proporsio'nal; proporθio'nal/ *a* proportional
proporcionar /proporsio'nar; proporθio'nar/ *vt* to allot, proportion; supply, provide, give; adapt
proposición /proposi'sion; proposi'θion/ *f*, proposition; motion (in a debate)
propósito /pro'posito/ *m*, proposal; intention, aim; subject, question, matter. **a p.**, suitable, apropos; by the way, incidentally. **de p.**, with the intention, proposing. **fuera de p.**, irrelevant
propuesta /pro'puesta/ *f*, proposal, tender
propugnar /propug'nar/ *vt* to defend, protect
propulsar /propul'sar/ *vt* to repulse, throw back; propel, drive
propulsión /propul'sion/ *f*, repulse; propulsion
propulsor /propul'sor/ *a* driving, propelling. *m*, propeller
prorrata /pro'rrata/ *f*, quota, share, apportionment. **a p.**, in proportion
prorratear /prorrate'ar/ *vt* to apportion, distribute proportionately, prorate
prorrogación /prorroga'sion; prorroga'θion/ *f*, prorogation, adjournment; extension (of time); renewal (of a lease, etc.)
prorrogar /prorro'gar/ *vt* to extend, prolong; defer, suspend, prorogue; renew (leases, etc.)
prorrumpir /prorrum'pir/ *vt* (*with en*) to burst out; utter, give vent to, burst into
prosa /'prosa/ *f*, prose; prosaism, prosaic style; *Inf.* dull verbosity; monotony, tediousness; *Lat. Am.* pomposity
prosaico /pro'saiko/ *a* prosaic; prosy; monotonous, tedious; matter-of-fact
prosapia /pro'sapia/ *f*, family, lineage, descent
proscenio /pros'senio; pros'θenio/ *m*, proscenium
proscribir /proskri'βir/ *vt* to proscribe, outlaw; forbid, prohibit. *Past Part.* **proscrito**
proscripción /proskrip'sion; proskrip'θion/ *f*, proscription

proscrito /pros'krito/ **(-ta)** *n* outlaw, exile
prosecución /proseku'sion; proseku'θion/ *f*, prosecution, performance; pursuit
proseguir /prose'gir/ *vt irr* to continue, proceed with. See **pedir**
proselitismo /proseli'tismo/ *m*, proselytism
prosélito /pro'selito/ *m*, convert, proselyte
prosificar /prosifi'kar/ *vt* to turn verse into prose
prosista /pro'sista/ *mf* prose writer
prosodia /pro'soðia/ *f*, prosody
prospecto /pros'pekto/ *m*, prospectus
prosperar /prospe'rar/ *vt* to prosper; protect; *vi* flourish, prosper
prosperidad /prosperi'ðað/ *f*, prosperity; wealth; success
próspero /'prospero/ *a* favorable, propitious, fortunate; prosperous. **¡P. año nuevo!** Happy New Year!
próstata /'prostata/ *f*, prostate
prostitución /prostitu'sion; prostitu'θion/ *f*, prostitution
prostituir /prosti'tuir/ *vt irr* to prostitute; *vr* become a prostitute; sell oneself, debase oneself. See **huir**
prostituta /prosti'tuta/ *f*, prostitute
protagonista /protago'nista/ *mf* hero or heroine, principal character; leading figure, protagonist
protección /protek'sion; protek'θion/ *f*, protection, defense; favor, aid
proteccionismo /proteksio'nismo; protekθio'nismo/ *m*, protectionism
proteccionista /proteksio'nista; protekθio'nista/ *mf* protectionist
protector /protek'tor/ *a* protective. *m*, protector; guard
protectorado /protekto'raðo/ *m*, protectorate
protectriz /protek'tris; protek'triθ/ *f*, protectress
proteger /prote'her/ *vt* to protect, defend; favor, assist
protegido /prote'hiðo/ **(-da)** *n* protégé
proteico /pro'teiko/ *a* protean
proteína /prote'ina/ *f*, protein
protervia /pro'terβia/ *f*, depravity, perversity
protervo /pro'terβo/ *a* depraved, perverse
protesta, protestación /pro'testa, protesta'sion; pro'testa, protesta'θion/ *f*, protest; protestation, declaration
protestante /protes'tante/ *a* and *mf* Protestant
protestantismo /protestan'tismo/ *m*, Protestantism
protestar /protes'tar/ *vt* to declare, attest; (*with contra*) protest against; (*with de*) affirm vigorously
protesto /pro'testo/ *m*, *Com.* protest; objection
protocolizar /protokoli'sar; protokoli'θar/ *vt* to protocol, draw up
protocolo /proto'kolo/ *m*, protocol
prototipo /proto'tipo/ *m*, model, prototype
protuberancia /protuβe'ransia; protuβe'ranθia/ *f*, protuberance, protrusion, swelling
provecho /pro'βetʃo/ *m*, gain, benefit; profit; advantage; progress, proficiency. **¡Buen p.!** Enjoy your food! Enjoy your meal! **ser de p.**, to be advantageous or useful
provechoso /proβe'tʃoso/ *a* beneficial; profitable; advantageous; useful
provecto /pro'βekto/ *a* ancient, venerable; mature, experienced
proveedor /proβee'ðor/ **(-ra)** *n* provider; purveyor, supplier
proveer /proβe'er/ *vt irr* to provide; furnish; supply; confer (an honor or office); transact, arrange. **p. de,** to furnish or supply with; fit with. See **creer**
provenir /proβe'nir/ *vi irr* (*with de*) to originate in, proceed from. See **venir**
provenzal /proβen'sal; proβen'θal/ *a* and *mf* Provençal. *m*, Provençal (language)
proverbio /pro'βerβio/ *m*, proverb; omen; *pl* Book of Proverbs
providencia /proβi'ðensia; proβi'ðenθia/ *f*, precaution, foresight; provision, furnishing; measure, preparation. **la Divina P.,** Providence
providencial /proβiðen'sial; proβiðen'θial/ *a* providential

próvido /'proβiðo/ a provident, thrifty, careful; kind, favorable

provincia /pro'βinsia; pro'βinθia/ f, province; *Fig.* sphere

provincial /proβin'sial; proβin'θial/ a provincial. m, *Eccl.* provincial

provincialismo /proβinsia'lismo; proβinθia'lismo/ m, provincialism

provinciano /proβin'siano; proβin'θiano/ (-na) a provincial. n provincial, rustic, countryman; native of Biscay

provisión /proβi'sion/ f, stock, store; provision; supply; food supply (gen. pl); catering; means, way

provisional /proβisio'nal/ a temporary, provisional

provisor /proβi'sor/ m, purveyor, supplier; *Eccl.* vicar general

provisorio, -a /proβi'sorio/ a, *Lat. Am.* = **provisional**

provocación /proβoka'sion; proβoka'θion/ f, provocation

provocador /proβoka'ðor/ (-ra) a provocative. n provoker; instigator

provocar /proβo'kar/ vt to provoke; incite; irritate; help, assist; *Inf.* vomit; *Lat. Am.* ¿te provoca ir al cine? Would you like to go to the movies?

provocativo /proβoka'tiβo/ a provocative

próximamente /'proksimamente/ adv proximately; soon; approximately

proximidad /proksimi'ðað/ f, nearness, proximity (in time or space)

próximo /'proksimo/ a near, neighboring; next; not distant (of time)

proyección /proiek'sion; proiek'θion/ f, projection (all meanings)

proyectante /proiek'tante/ a projecting, jutting

proyectar /proiek'tar/ vt to throw, cast; plan, contrive; design; project; vr jut out; be cast (a shadow, etc.)

proyectil /proyek'til/ m, projectile

proyectista /proiek'tista/ mf planner

proyecto /pro'iekto/ a placed in perspective. m, project, plan, scheme; planning; intention, idea

proyector /proiek'tor/ (-ra) n designer, planner. m, searchlight; spotlight; projector

prudencia /pru'ðensia; pru'ðenθia/ f, prudence, sagacity, caution; moderation

prudencial /pruðen'sial; pruðen'θial/ a prudent, discreet; safe

prudente /pru'ðente/ a prudent, cautious; provident

prueba /'prueβa/ f, proof; test; quiz (in school); testing; trial; fitting (of garments); sample; taste; *Law.* evidence; (*Photo. Print.*) proof. *Law.* **p. de indicios** or **p. indiciaria,** circumstantial evidence. *Photo.* **p. negativa,** negative. *Com.* **a p.,** on approval; on trial; up to standard, perfect. **a p. de,** proof against (water, etc.). **poner a p.,** to put to the test, try out

prurito /pru'rito/ m, pruritus; desire, longing

ps- /ps-/ For words so beginning (e.g. *psicología, psiquiatría*), see spellings without **p**

púa /'pua/ f, prong; tooth (of a comb); quill (of a porcupine); *Agr.* graft; plectrum (for playing the mandolin, etc.); anxiety, grief; pine needle; *Inf.* crafty person

púber /'puβer/ a pubescent

pubertad /puβer'tað/ f, puberty

púbico /'puβiko/ a pubic

publicación /puβlika'sion; puβlika'θion/ f, publication; announcement, proclamation; revelation; publishing of marriage banns

publicador /puβlika'ðor/ (-ra) a publishing. n publisher; announcer

publicar /puβli'kar/ vt to publish; reveal; announce, proclaim; publish (marriage banns)

publicidad /puβlisi'ðað; puβliθi'ðað/ f, publicity; advertising, propaganda

publicista /puβli'sista; puβli'θista/ mf publicist; publicity agent

público /'puβliko/ a well-known, universal; common, general; public. m, public; audience; gathering, attendance. **dar al p.** or **sacar al p.,** to publish

pucherazo /putʃe'raso; putʃe'raθo/ m, *Inf.* electoral fraud, vote-fixing

puchero /pu'tʃero/ m, *Cul.* kind of stew; stew pot; *Inf.* daily food; puckering of the face preceding tears

pudicia /pu'ðisia; pu'ðiθia/ f, modesty; bashfulness; chastity

púdico /'puðiko/ a modest; bashful; chaste

pudiente /pu'ðiente/ a rich, wealthy; powerful

pudín /pu'ðin/ m, pudding

pudor /pu'ðor/ m, modesty; bashfulness, shyness

pudoroso /puðo'roso/ a modest; shy

pudrir /pu'ðrir/ vt to rot, putrefy; irritate, worry, provoke; vi rot in the grave; vr rot; be consumed with anxiety

puebla /'pueβla/ f, town; population; gardener's seed setting

pueblada /pue'βlaða/ f, *Lat. Am.* riot; rebellion, revolt, uprising

pueblo /'pueβlo/ m, town; village, hamlet; people, population, inhabitants; common people; working classes; nation

puente /'puente/ mf bridge; *Mus.* bridge (of stringed instruments); *Naut.* bridge; crossbeam, transom. **p. colgante,** suspension bridge. **p. levadizo,** drawbridge. **hacer p. de plata (a),** to remove obstacles for, make plain sailing

puerco /'puerko/ m, pig; wild boar. a filthy; rough, rude; low, mean. **p. espín** or **p. espino,** porcupine. **p. marino,** dolphin. **p. montés** or **p. salvaje,** wild boar

puericultura /puerikul'tura/ f, child care

pueril /pue'ril/ a childish, puerile; foolish, silly; trivial

puerilidad /puerili'ðað/ f, puerility; foolishness; triviality

puerro /'puerro/ m, leek

puerta /'puerta/ f, door; gate; goal (football, soccer, hockey); means, way. **p. batiente,** swinging door. **p. caediza,** trapdoor. **p. corrediza,** sliding door. **p. de servicio,** tradesman's entrance. **p. falsa** or **p. secreta,** secret door; side door. **p. trasera,** back door. **a p. cerrada,** in camera; in secret. *Inf.* **dar con la p. en las narices (de),** to slam the door in a person's face; offend, insult. **llamar a la p.,** to knock at the door; be on the verge of happening. **tomar la p.,** to depart, go away

puerto /'puerto/ m, harbor; port; defile, narrow pass; refuge, haven. **p. fluvial,** river port. **p. franco,** free port. **tomar p.,** to put into port; take refuge

Puerto Rico /'puerto 'rriko/ Puerto Rico

puertorriqueño, -a /puertorri'keɲo/ a and mf Puerto Rican

pues /pues/ conjunc then; since, as; for, because; well. adv yes, certainly. conjunc **p. que,** since, as

puesta /'puesta/ f, *Astron.* setting, sinking; stake (in gambling). **p. al día,** aggiornamento, updating; modernization. **p. de largo,** coming of age; coming-out party. **p. del sol,** sunset

puesto /'puesto/ m, post, job; booth, stall; beat, pitch; place, position; state, condition; *Mil.* encampment, barracks; office, position. **p. de los testigos,** witness box. **p. de mando,** command, position of authority.

puesto /'puesto/ a (with bien or mal) well-or badly dressed. conjunc **p. que,** since, as; although

púgil /'puhil/ mf pugilist, boxer

pugilato /puhi'lato/ m, boxing; boxing match

pugilista /puhi'lista/ mf boxer

pugna /'pugna/ f, fight, struggle; rivalry, conflict

pugnante /pug'nante/ a hostile, conflicting, rival

pugnar /pug'nar/ vi to fight; quarrel; (*with con, contra*) struggle against, oppose; (*with por, para*) strive to

pugnaz /pug'nas; pug'naθ/ a pugnacious

puja /'puha/ f, outbidding (at an auction); higher bid; push, thrust

pujador /puha'ðor/ (-ra) n bidder or outbidder (at an auction)

pujante /pu'hante/ a strong, powerful, vigorous, pushy

pujanza /pu'hansa; pu'hanθa/ f, strength, vigor

pujar /pu'har/ *vt* to push on; bid or outbid (at an auction); *vi* stutter; hesitate, falter; *Inf.* show signs of weeping

pujo /'puho/ *m*, irresistible impulse; desire; will; purpose, intention

pulcritud /pulkri'tuð/ *f*, beauty, loveliness, delicacy; fastidiousness, subtlety

pulcro /'pulkro/ *a* beautiful, lovely; delicate, fine; fastidious, subtle

pulga /'pulga/ *f*, flea; small top (toy). **el juego de la p.**, tiddlywinks. *Inf.* **tener malas pulgas**, to be irritable. **mercado de p.**, flea market

pulgada /pul'gaða/ *f*, inch

pulgar /pul'gar/ *m*, thumb

pulgón /pul'gon/ *m*, aphid, greenfly

pulgoso /pul'goso/ *a* full of fleas

pulguiento /pul'giento/ *a*, *Lat. Am.* = **pulgoso**

pulidez /puli'ðes; puli'ðeθ/ *f*, elegance, fineness; polish, smoothness; neatness

pulido /pu'liðo/ *a* elegant, fine; polished, smooth; neat

pulidor /puli'ðor/ *m*, polisher (machine)

pulimentar /pulimen'tar/ *vt* to polish, burnish

pulir /pu'lir/ *vt* to polish, burnish; give the finishing touch to; beautify, decorate; *Fig.* polish up, civilize; *vr* beautify oneself; become polished and polite

pulla /'puya; 'puʎa/ *f*, lewd remark; strong hint; witty comment

pulmón /pul'mon/ *m*, lung

pulmonar /pulmo'nar/ *a* pulmonary

pulmonía /pulmo'nia/ *f*, pneumonia

pulpa /'pulpa/ *f*, fleshy part of fruit; *Anat.* pulp; wood pulp

pulpejo /pul'peho/ *m*, *Anat.* fleshy part, fat portion (of thumbs, etc.)

pulpería /pulpe'ria/ *f*, *West Hem.* grocery, grocery store, general store; bar, tavern

púlpito /'pulpito/ *m*, pulpit

pulpo /'pulpo/ *m*, octopus. *Inf.* **poner como un p.**, to beat to a pulp

pulposo /pul'poso/ *a* pulpy, pulpous

pulque /'pulke/ *m*, pulque (fermented maguey juice)

pulquérrimo /pul'kerrimo/ *a sup* **pulcro** most lovely, most exquisite

pulsación /pulsa'sion; pulsa'θion/ *f*, pulsation; throb, beat

pulsar /pul'sar/ *vt* to touch, feel; take the pulse of; *Fig.* explore (a possibility); *vi* beat (the heart, etc.)

pulsera /pul'sera/ *f*, bracelet; wrist bandage. **p. de pedida**, betrothal bracelet

pulso /'pulso/ *m*, pulse; steadiness of hand; tact, diplomacy, circumspection. **a p.**, freehand (drawing). **tomar a p. (una cosa)**, to try a thing's weight. **tomar el p. (a)**, to take a person's pulse

pulular /pulu'lar/ *vi* to pullulate, sprout; abound, be plentiful; swarm, teem; multiply (of insects)

pulverización /pulβerisa'sion; pulβeriθa'θion/ *f*, pulverization; atomization

pulverizador /pulβerisa'ðor; pulβeriθa'ðor/ *m*, atomizer, sprayer; scent spray

pulverizar /pulβeri'sar; pulβeri'θar/ *vt* to pulverize, grind, make into powder; atomize; spray

¡pum! /pum/ *interj* Bang! Thump!

pundonor /pundo'nor/ *m*, **(punto de honor)** point of honor, sense of honor

pundonoroso /pundono'roso/ *a* careful of one's honor; honorable, punctilious

pungir /pun'hir/ *vt* to prick, pierce; revive an old sorrow; *Fig.* wound, sting (passions)

punible /pu'niβle/ *a* punishable

punitivo /puni'tiβo/ *a* punitive, punitory

punta /'punta/ *f*, sharp end, point; butt (of a cigarette); end, point, tip; cape, headland; trace, touch, suspicion; nib (of a pen); pointing (pointer dogs); *Herald.* point; *pl* point lace. **p. de París**, wire nail. **p. seca**, drypoint, engraving needle. **cortar las puntas**, to trim one's hair. **sacar p.**, to sharpen; *Inf.* twist (a remark)

puntación /punta'sion; punta'θion/ *f*, dotting, placing dots over (letters)

puntada /pun'taða/ *f*, *Sew.* stitch; innuendo, hint

puntal /pun'tal/ *m*, *Naut.* draft, depth; stanchion, prop, brace, pile; *Fig.* basis, foundation; *Lat. Am.* bite (to eat), snack

puntapié /punta'pie/ *m*, kick

punteado /punte'aðo/ *m*, plucking the strings of a guitar, etc.; sewing

puntear /punte'ar/ *vt* to make dots; *Mus.* pluck the strings of; play the guitar; sew; *Art.* stipple; *vi Naut.* tack

puntera /pun'tera/ *f*, mend in the toe of a stocking; toe cap; new piece on the toe of shoe; *Inf.* kick

puntería /punte'ria/ *f*, aiming (of a firearm); aim, sight (of a firearm); marksmanship

puntero /pun'tero/ *a* of a good aim, having a straight eye. *m*, pointer, wand; stonecutter's chisel

puntiagudo /puntia'guðo/ *a* pointed, sharp-pointed

puntilla /pun'tiya; pun'tiʎa/ *f*, narrow lace edging; headless nail, wire nail; brad, tack. **de puntillas**, on tiptoe

puntilloso /punti'yoso; punti'ʎoso/ *a* punctilious; overfastidious, fussy

punto /'punto/ *m.*; dot; point; pen nib; gun sight; *Sew.* stitch; dropped stitch, hole; weaving stitch, mesh; *Gram.* full stop, period; hole (in belts for adjustment); place, spot; point, mark; subject matter; *Mech.* cog; degree, extent; taxi stand; instant; infinitesimal amount; opportunity, chance; vacation, recess; aim, goal; point of honor. **p. de congelación**, freezing point. **p. de ebullición**, boiling point. **p. de fuga**, vanishing point. **p. de fusión**, melting point. **p. de partida**, starting point. **p. de vista**, point of view. **p. final**, *Gram.* period, full stop. **p. interrogante**, question mark. **p. menos**, a little less. **p. y coma**, semicolon. **p. cardinal**, cardinal point. **p. suspensivo**, *Gram.* ellipsis point, suspension point, leader, dot. **a p.**, in readiness; immediately. **en p.**, sharp, prompt (e.g. *a las seis en p.*, at six o'clock sharp)

puntoso /pun'toso/ *a* many-pointed

puntuación /puntua'sion; puntua'θion/ *f*, punctuation; *Sports.* score

puntual /pun'tual/ *a* punctual; punctilious; certain, indubitable; suitable, convenient

puntualidad /puntuali'ðað/ *f*, punctuality; punctiliousness; certainty; exactitude, accuracy

puntualizar /puntuali'sar; puntuali'θar/ *vt* to describe in detail; give the finishing touch to, perfect; impress on the mind

puntualmente /puntual'mente/ *adv* punctually, carefully, diligently; exactly

puntuar /pun'tuar/ *vt* to punctuate

puntudo /pun'tuðo/ *a*, *Lat. Am.* = **puntiagudo**

punzada /pun'saða; pun'θaða/ *f*, prick, sting; puncture, piercing; sudden pain, twinge, stitch; *Fig.* anguish, pain

punzar /pun'sar; pun'θar/ *vt* to pierce, puncture; prick; punch, perforate; *vi* revive, make itself felt (pain or sorrow)

punzón /pun'son; pun'θon/ *m*, awl; punch; die; engraver's burin

puñado /pu'naðo/ *m*, handful; a few, some, a small quantity. **a puñados**, in handfuls; liberally, lavishly

puñal /pu'nal/ *m*, dagger

puñalada /puna'laða/ *f*, dagger thrust; stab, wound; *Fig.* unexpected blow (of fate). **p. por la espalda**, stab in the back

puñetazo /pune'taso; pune'taθo/ *m*, blow with the fist

puño /'puno/ *m*, fist; handful; cuff (of a sleeve); wristband; handle, head, haft; hilt (of a sword); *pl Inf.* guts, courage. **p. de amura**, *Naut.* tack. **p. de manillar**, handlebar grip. *Inf.* **meter en un p.**, to overawe. *Inf.* **ser como un p.**, to be tightfisted; be small (in stature)

pupila /pu'pila/ *f*, female child ward; *Anat.* pupil; *Inf.* cleverness, talent

pupilaje /pupi'lahe/ *m*, pupilage, minority; boarding house, guesthouse; boarding school; price of board residence; dependence; boarding

pupilo /pu'pilo/ *m*, ward, minor; boarder; boarding school student; *Lat. Am.* prostitute, whore

pupitre /pu'pitre/ *m*, desk, school desk

puquío /pu'kio/ *m Lat. Am.* spring (of water)

puramente /pura'mente/ *adv* purely; simply, solely; *Law.* unconditionally, without reservation

puré /pu're/ *m*, purée, thick soup

pureza /pu'resa; pu'reθa/ *f*, purity; perfection, excellence; chastity; disinterestedness, genuineness; clearness

purga /'purga/ *f*, laxative, purge; waste product

purgación /purga'sion; purga'θion/ *f*, purging; menstruation; gonorrhea

purgante /pur'gante/ *a* purgative. *m*, purge, cathartic

purgar /pur'gar/ *vt* to cleanse, purify; expiate, atone for; (*Med. Law.*) purge; suffer purgatorial pains; clarify, refine; *vr* rid oneself, purge oneself

purgativo /purga'tiβo/ *a* purgative

purgatorio /purga'torio/ *m*, purgatory. *a* purgatorial

puridad /puri'δaδ/ *f*, purity; secrecy, privacy. **en p.**, openly, without dissembling; secretly, in private

purificación /purifika'sion; purifika'θion/ *f*, purification; cleansing

purificador /purifika'δor/ **(-ra)** *a* purifying; cleansing. *n* purifier; cleanser

purificar /purifi'kar/ *vt* to purify; cleanse; *vr* be purified

purificatorio /purifika'torio/ *a* purificatory

Purísima /pu'risima/ **(la)** *f*, the Most Blessed Virgin

purista /pu'rista/ *mf* purist

puritano /puri'tano/ **(-na)** *a* puritanical. *n* Puritan

puro /'puro/ *a* pure; undiluted; unalloyed; unmixed; disinterested, honest; virgin; absolute, sheer; mere, simple. *m*, cigar. **de p.**, by sheer..., by dint of

púrpura /'purpura/ *f*, purple; *Poet.* blood; purpura; *Herald.* purpure; purple (cloth); dignity of an emperor, cardinal, consul

purpurear /purpure'ar/ *vi* to look like purple; be tinged with purple

purpurina /purpu'rina/ *f Lat. Am.* metallic paint

purulencia /puru'lensia; puru'lenθia/ *f*, purulence

purulento /puru'lento/ *a* purulent

pus /pus/ *m*, pus, matter

pusilánime /pusi'lanime/ *a* pusillanimous, timid, cowardly

pústula /'pustula/ *f*, pustule

putativo /puta'tiβo/ *a* putative

puto, -a /'puto/ *mf* prostitute

putrefacción /putrefak'sion; putrefak'θion/ *f*, putrefaction; rottenness, putrescence

putrefacto /putre'fakto/ *a* rotten, decayed

pútrido /'putriδo/ *a* putrid, rotten

puya /'puya/ *f*, goad

puyar /pu'yar/ *vt Lat. Am.* to jab, prick, stick; *Fig.* needle

puyazo /pu'yaso; pu'yaθo/ *m*, prick with a goad

Q

que /ke/ *pron rel* all genders sing. and pl. who; which; that; whom; when (e.g. *Un poema en que habla de su juventud,* A poem in which he speaks of his youth. *El libro que tengo aquí,* The book (that) I have here. **No es oro todo lo que reluce,** All that glitters is not gold. **Un día que nos vimos,** One day when we met —*interr* **¿qué?** what? *interj* what a ------! what! how! (e.g. *¿Qué hay?* What's the matter? *¡Qué día más hermoso!* What a lovely day! *¿qué de...?* what's up with...? *¿qué tal?* How are you? *Inf.* ¿Qué tal estás hoy? How are you today? *¿qué tanto?* how much?) **¿a qué?** why? for what reason? (e.g. *¿A qué negarlo?* Why deny it?) —*conjunc* that (e.g. *Me dijo que vendría,* He said (that) he would come). Means "so that," "that," "for," in commands (e.g. *Mandó que le trajesen el libro,* He ordered that they bring him the book (He ordered them to bring him the book)). Note that the translation of **que** is often omitted in English. In compound tenses where the participle is placed first, **que** means "when" (e.g. *llegado que hube,* when I had arrived). In comparisons, **que** means "than" (e.g. *más joven que yo,* younger than I). With subjunctives and expressing commands or wishes, **que** means "let" (e.g. *¡Que venga!* Let him come!) Preceding a subjunctive, **que** is generally translated by "to" (e.g. *Quiero, que venga or que llueva,* I want him to come *or* I want it to rain). Also means "may" (e.g. *¡Que lo pase bien!* May you enjoy yourself! (I hope you...)). **que le vaya bien,** May it go well with you (when saying goodbye). **es (era) que,** the fact is (was) that... **que... que,** whether... or...

quebrada /ke'βraδa/ *f*, mountain gorge, ravine; *Com.* bankruptcy; *Lat. Am.* brook, stream

quebradizo /keβra'δiso; keβra'δiθo/ *a* brittle, fragile; ailing, infirm; delicate, frail

quebrado /ke'βraδo/ **(-da)** *m*, *Math.* fraction; *n Com.* bankrupt. *a* rough, uneven (ground); *Med.* ruptured; bankrupt; ailing, brokcn-down

quebradura /keβra'δura/ *f*, snap, breaking; gap, crevice; hernia

quebraja /ke'βraha/ *f*, split, crack; flaw (in wood, metal, etc.)

quebrantahuesos /keβranta'uesos/ *m*, sea eagle, osprey; *Inf.* bore, tedious person

quebrantamiento /keβranta'miento/ *m*, crushing; splitting, cleaving; fracture, rupture; profanation; desecration; burglary; violation, breaking, infringement; fatigue; *Law.* annulment; exhaustion

quebrantanueces /keβranta'nueses; keβranta'nueθes/ *m*, nutcrackers

quebrantaolas /keβranta'olas/ *m*, breakwater

quebrantar /keβran'tar/ *vt* to break, shatter; crush, pound; transgress, infringe; break out, force; tone down, soften; moderate, lessen; bore, exhaust; move to pity; *Inf.* break in (horses); profane; overcome (difficulties); assuage, placate; *Law.* revoke (wills); *vr* be shaken or bruised, suffer from aftereffects

quebranto /ke'βranto/ *m*, breaking, shattering; crushing, pounding; infringement; breaking out (from prison); weakness, exhaustion; compassion, pity; loss, damage; pain, suffering

quebrar /ke'βrar/ *vt irr* to break, shatter; crush; impede, hinder; make pale (color, gen. of complexion); mitigate, moderate; bend, twist; overcome (difficulties); *vi* break off (a friendship); weaken, give way; go bankrupt; *vr Med.* suffer from hernia; be interrupted (of mountain ranges). **quebrarse los ojos,** to strain one's eyes. *Pres. Ind.* **quiebro, quiebras, quiebra, quiebran.** *Pres. Subjunc.* **quiebre, quiebres, quiebre, quiebren**

queda /'keδa/ *f*, curfew; curfew bell

quedada /ke'δaδa/ *f*, stay, sojourn

quedar /ke'δar/ *vi* to stay, sojourn; remain; be left over; (*with por + infin.*) remain to be (e.g. *Queda por escribir,* It remains to be written); (*with por*) be won by or be knocked down to; be, remain in a place; end, cease; (*with en*) reach an agreement (e.g. *Quedamos en no ir,* We have decided not to go). **q. en esta alternativa...,** to face this alternative:.... *vr* remain; abate (wind); grow calm (sea); (*with con*) keep, retain possession of. **q. bien o mal,** to behave well or badly, come off well or badly (in business affairs, etc.). **quedarse muerto,** to be astounded

quedo /'keδo/ *a* still, motionless; quiet, tranquil. *adv* in a low voice; quietly, noiselessly. **de q.,** slowly, gradually. *interj* **¡Q.!** Quiet!

quehacer /kea'ser; kea'θer/ *m*, odd job; task; business (gen. *pl*)

queja /'keha/ *f*, lamentation, grief; complaint, grudge; quarrel

quejarse /ke'harse/ *vr* to lament; complain, grumble; *Law.* lodge an accusation (against)

quejido /ke'hiδo/ *m*, complaint, moan

quejoso /ke'hoso/ *a* querulous, complaining

quejumbre /ke'humbre/ *f*, complaint, whine; querulousness

quejumbroso /kehum'βroso/ *a* complaining, grumbling

quelite /ke'lite/ *m*, *Central America*, *Mexico* vegetables

quema /'kema/ *f*, burn; burning; fire, conflagration

quemadero /kema'ðero/ *a* burnable. *m*, stake (for burning people)

quemado /ke'maðo/ *m*, burned patch of forest; *Inf.* anything burned or burning

quemador /kema'ðor/ **(-ra)** *m*, jet, burner. *n* incendiary

quemadura /kema'ðura/ *f*, burn; scald; burning

quemajoso /kema'hoso/ *a* smarting, burning, pricking

quemar /ke'mar/ *vt* to burn; dry up, parch; scorch; tan, bronze; scald; throw away, sell at a loss; *vi* burn, be excessively hot; *vr* be very hot; be dried up with the heat; burn with (passions); *Inf.* be near the attainment of a desired end. **quemarse las cejas,** to burn the midnight oil, study too hard

quemazón /kema'son; kema'θon/ *f*, burning; conflagration; intense heat; *Inf.* smarting; *Inf.* hurtful remark; *Inf.* vexation, soreness

quena /'kena/ *f* kind of Native American flute

querella /ke'reya; ke'reʎa/ *f*, complaint; quarrel, fight

querellarse /kere'yarse; kere'ʎarse/ *vr* to complain; lament, bemoan; *Law.* lodge an accusation; *Law.* contest a will

querelloso /kere'yoso; kere'ʎoso/ *a* complaining, grumbling, querulous

querencia /ke'rensia; ke'renθia/ *f*, love, affection; homing instinct; lair; natural inclination or desire

querer /ke'rer/ *vt irr* to desire, wish; want, will; attempt, endeavor; *(with a)* love. *impers* be on the point of. **q. decir,** to mean. **¿Qué quiere decir esto? What does this mean? sin q.,** unintentionally. See **entender**

querer /ke'rer/ *m*, affection, love

querido /ke'riðo/ **(-da)** *n* lover; beloved; darling. *a* dear

querub, querube /ke'ruβ, ke'ruβe/ *Poet.* **querubín** *m*, cherub

querúbico /ke'ruβiko/ *a* cherubic

quesadillas, /kesa'ðijas; kesa'ðiʎas/ *fpl*, *Mexico* maize dough with beans or cheese fried like a turnover

quesera /ke'sera/ *f*, dairymaid; dairy; cheese vat; cheese board; cheese dish

quesería /kese'ria/ *f*, dairy; cheese shop; season for making cheese

queso /'keso/ *m*, cheese. **q. rallado,** grated cheese

quetzal /ket'sal; ket'θal/ *m*, quetzal (monetary unit of Guatemala)

quevedos /ke'βeðos/ *m pl*, glasses, eyeglasses; pincenez

¡quia! /kia/ *interj Inf.* You don't say so!

quianti /'kianti/ *m*, chianti

quicial /ki'sial; ki'θial/ *m*, doorjamb

quicio /'kisio; 'kiθio/ *m*, threshold; hinge; *Mech.* bushing. **fuera de q.,** out of order; unhinged. **sacar de q.,** to displace (things); annoy, irritate; drive crazy

quiebra /'kieβra/ *f*, breach, crack; rut, fissure; loss; bankruptcy

quiebro /'kieβro/ *m*, twisting of the body, dodging; *Mus.* trill

quien /kien/ *rel pron mf pl* **quienes.** *interr* **quién, quiénes** who; whom; he (she, etc.) who, anyone who, whoever; which; whichever (e.g. *mis padres a quienes respeto,* my parents whom I respect. *Quien te quiere te hará llorar,* Whoever (he, those, who) love(s) you will make you weep. **¿Quién está a la puerta?** Who is at the door? **¿De quién es?** Whose is it? To whom does it belong?). *indef pron* one (*pl* some)

quienquiera /kien'kiera/ *indef pron mf pl* **quienesquiera,** whosoever, whichever, whomsoever

quietador /kieta'ðor/ **(-ra)** *a* tranquilizing, soothing. *n* soother

quieto /'kieto/ *a* quiet, still; peaceful, tranquil; virtuous, respectable

quietud /kie'tuð/ *f*, stillness, repose; peacefulness; rest, quietness

quif /kif/ *m*, hashish, marijuana

quijada /ki'haða/ *f*, jawbone, jaw; *Mech.* jaw

quijo /'kiho/ *m*, ore (gold or silver)

quijotada /kiho'taða/ *f*, quixotic action, quixotism

quijote /ki'hote/ *m*, cuisse; thigh guard; quixotic person

quijotesco /kiho'tesko/ *a* quixotic

quilate /ki'late/ *m*, carat; degree of excellence (gen. *pl*). *Inf.* **por quilates,** in small bits, parsimoniously

quilla /'kiya; 'kiʎa/ *f*, *Naut.* keel; breastbone (of birds)

quillotrar /kiyo'trar; kiʎo'trar/ *vt Inf.* to encourage, incite; woo, make love to; consider; *vr Inf.* fall in love; dress up; whine, complain

quillotro /ki'yotro; ki'ʎotro/ *m*, *Inf.* incentive; indication, sign; love affair; puzzle, knotty point; compliment; dressing up

quimera /ki'mera/ *f*, chimera; fancy, vision; quarrel, dispute

quimérico /ki'meriko/ *a* chimerical, fanciful

quimerista /kime'rista/ *mf* dreamer, visionary; quarreler, disputant

química /'kimika/ *f*, chemistry

químico /'kimiko/ *a* chemical. *m*, chemist. **productos químicos,** chemicals

quimioterapia /kimiote'rapia/ *f*, chemotherapy

quimono /ki'mono/ *m*, kimono

quina /'kina/ *f*, cinchona; quinine; *pl* Arms of Portugal. *Inf.* **tragar q.,** to suffer in patience, put up with

quinario /ki'nario/ *m*, *Argentina* mud hut

quincalla /kin'kaya; kin'kaʎa/ *f*, cheap jewelery; fancy goods

quincallería /kinkaye'ria; kinkaʎe'ria/ *f*, cheap jewelry shop; hardware factory or industry; cheap jewelry; fancy goods

quince /'kinse; 'kinθe/ *a* and *m*, fifteen; fifteenth

quinceañero /kinsea'ɲero; kinθea'ɲero/ *f*, sweet sixteen party, sweet sixteen (in Spanish-speaking areas, held at age fifteen)

quincena /kin'sena; kin'θena/ *f*, fortnight, two weeks; bimonthly pay; *Mus.* fifteenth

quincenal /kinse'nal; kinθe'nal/ *a* fortnightly; lasting a fortnight, lasting two weeks

quinceno /kin'seno; kin'θeno/ *a* fifteenth

quincuagenario /kinkuahe'nario/ *a* quinquagenarian

quincuagésimo /kinkua'hesimo/ *a* fiftieth

quindécimo /kin'desimo; kin'deθimo/ *a* fifteenth

quinientos /ki'nientos/ *a* five hundred; five-hundredth. *m*, five hundred

quinina /ki'nina/ *f*, quinine

quinqué /kin'ke/ *m*, oil lamp, student's lamp, table lamp; perspicuity, talent

quinquenio /kin'kenio/ *m*, period of five years, lustrum

quinta /'kinta/ *f*, country house; *Mus.* fifth; conscripting men into army by drawing lots; *Mil.* draft

quintaesencia /kintae'sensia; kintae'senθia/ *f*, quintessence

quintal /kin'tal/ *m*, hundredweight

quintar /kin'tar/ *vt* to draw one out of every five; draw lots for conscription into the army; *vi* reach the fifth (day, etc., gen. of the moon)

quintería /kinte'ria/ *f*, farm

quintero /kin'tero/ *m*, farmer; farmworker

quinteto /kin'teto/ *m*, quintet

Quintín, San. armarse /kin'tin, san ar'marse/ (*or* **haber**) **la de San Q.** to quarrel, make trouble; be a row

quinto /'kinto/ *a* fifth. *m*, one-fifth; *Mil.* conscript; duty of twenty percent; *Law.* fifth part of an estate. **quinta columna,** fifth column. **quinta esencia,** quintessence

quintuplicar /kintupli'kar/ *vt* to quintuplicate

quíntuplo /'kintuplo/ *a* fivefold, quintuple

quiñón /ki'ɲon/ *m*, share of land owned jointly, share of the profits

quiosco /'kiosko/ *m*, kiosk, stand; pavilion, pagoda. **q. de música,** bandstand

quipo /'kipo/ *m* quipu (Native American rope writing in Peru)
quiquiriquí /kikiri'ki/ *m*, cock-a-doodle-doo; *Fig. Inf.* cock of the walk
quiromancia /kiro'mansia; kiro'manθia/ *f*, chiromancy, palmistry
quiromántico /kiro'mantiko/ **(-ca)** *n* chiromancer, palmist
quirúrgico /ki'rurhiko/ *a* surgical
quirurgo /ki'rurgo/ *m*, surgeon
quisicosa /kisi'kosa/ *f*, *Inf.* riddle, puzzle, enigma
quisquilla /kis'kiya; kis'kiʎa/ *f*, trifle, quibble, scruple; prawn, shrimp
quisquilloso /kiski'yoso; kiski'ʎoso/ *a* quibbling, overscrupulous, fastidious; hypersensitive; irascible, touchy
quistarse /kis'tarse/ *vr* to make oneself well-liked or loved
quiste /'kiste/ *m*, *Med.* cyst
quita /'kita/ *f*, *Law.* discharge (of part of a debt)
quitaesmalte /kitaes'malte/ *m*, nail polish remover (for fingernails)

quitamanchas /kita'mantʃas/ *mf*, dry cleaner, clothes cleaner
quitamotas /kita'motas/ *mf Inf.* flatterer, adulator
quitanieve /kita'nieβe/ *m*, snowplow
quitanza /ki'tansa; ki'tanθa/ *f*, quittance; quietus
quitapesares /kitape'sares/ *m*, *Inf.* consolation, solace, comfort
quitar /ki'tar/ *vt* to remove; take off or away; clear (the table); rob, steal; prevent, impede; parry (in fencing); separate; redeem (pledges); forbid; annul, repeal (laws, etc.); free from (obligations); *vr* shed, take off, remove; get rid of; leave, quit. **quitarse de encima (a)**, to get rid of someone or something. **q. el polvo**, to dust. **de quita y pon**, detachable, removable; adjustable
quitasol /kita'sol/ *m*, parasol, sunshade
quitasueño /kita'sueɲo/ *m*, *Inf.* sleep banisher, anxiety
quite /'kite/ *m*, hindering, impeding; obstruction; parry (in fencing). **estar al q.**, to be ready to protect someone
quizá, quizás /ki'sa, ki'sas; ki'θa, ki'θas/ *adv* perhaps. **q. y sin q.**, without doubt, certainly

R

rabadán /rraβa'ðan/ *m*, head shepherd or herdsman
rabadilla /rraβa'ðiya; rraβa'ðiʎa/ *f*, rump, croup
rábano /'rraβano/ *m*, radish. **r. picante**, horseradish
rabel /rra'βel/ *m*, *Mus.* rebec; *Inf.* backside, seat
rabera /rra'βera/ *f*, tail-end; chaff, siftings
rabí /rra'βi/ *m*, rabbi
rabia /'rraβia/ *f*, rabies, hydrophobia; anger, fury. *Inf.* **tener r. (a)**, to hate
rabiar /rra'βiar/ *vi* to suffer from hydrophobia; groan with pain; be furious; (*with por*) yearn for, desire. **a r.**, excessively
rabieta /rra'βieta/ *f*, *Inf.* tantrum
rabínico /rra'βiniko/ *a* rabbinical
rabinismo /rraβi'nismo/ *m*, rabbinism
rabino /rra'βino/ *m*, rabbi. **gran r.**, chief rabbi
rabioso /rra'βioso/ *a* rabid; furious, angry; vehement. **perro r.**, mad dog
rabo /'rraβo/ *m*, tail; *Bot.* stalk; *Inf.* train (of a dress); shank (of a button). **r. del ojo**, corner of the eye. *Fig. Inf.* **ir r. entre piernas**, to have one's tail between one's legs
rabón /rra'βon/ *a* tailless, docked; bobtailed
rabonear /rraβone'ar/ *vi*, *Lat. Am.* to play hookey
rabudo /rra'βuðo/ *a* big-tailed
racimo /rra'simo; rra'θimo/ *m*, bunch (of grapes or other fruits); cluster; raceme
raciocinar /rrasiosi'nar; rraθioθi'nar/ *vi* to reason
raciocinio /rrasio'sinio; rraθio'θinio/ *m*, reasoning; ratiocination; discourse, speech
ración /rra'sion; rra'θion/ *f*, ration; portion (in a restaurant); meal allowance; *Eccl.* prebendary. *Inf.* **r. de hambre**, starvation diet; pittance, starvation wages
racional /rrasio'nal; rraθio'nal/ *a* reasonable, logical; rational
racionalidad /rrasionali'ðað; rraθionali'ðað/ *f*, reasonableness; rationality
racionalismo /rrasiona'lismo; rraθiona'lismo/ *m*, rationalism
racionalista /rrasiona'lista; rraθiona'lista/ *a* and *mf* rationalist. *a* rationalistic
racionalización /rrasionalisa'sion; rraθionaliθa'θion/ *f*, rationalization
racionamiento /rrasiona'miento; rraθiona'miento/ *m*, rationing. *f*. **cartilla de r.**, ration book
racionar /rrasio'nar; rraθio'nar/ *vt* to ration
racismo /rra'sismo; rra'θismo/ *m*, racism
rada /'rraða/ *f*, bay, cove; *Naut.* road, roadstead
radar /rra'ðar/ *m*, radar
radiación /rraðia'sion; rraðia'θion/ *f*, radiation; *Radio.* broadcasting
radiactividad /rraðiaktiβi'ðað/ *f*, radioactivity

radiactivo /rraðiak'tiβo/ *a* radioactive
radiador /rraðia'ðor/ *m*, radiator (for heating); *Auto.* radiator
radial /rra'ðial/ *a* radial
radiante /rra'ðiante/ *a Phys.* radiating; brilliant, shining; *Fig.* beaming (with satisfaction)
radiar /rra'ðiar/ *vi Phys.* to radiate; *vt* broadcast (by radio); *Lat. Am.* to cross off, delete, erase
radical /rra'ði'kal/ *a* radical; fundamental; *Polit.* radical. *m*, *Gram.* root; (*Math. Chem.*) radical. *mf Polit.* radical
radicalismo /rraðika'lismo/ *m*, radicalism
radicar /rraði'kar/ **(se)** *vi* and *vr* to take root. **r. una solicitud**, file an application, submit an application. *vi* be (in a place)
radio /'rraðio/ *m*, (*Geom. Anat.*) radius; radium. *f*, radio
radioaficionado /rraðioafisio'naðo; rraðioafiθio'naðo/ **(-da)** *n* radio amateur; *Inf.* ham, wireless fan or enthusiast
radioaudición /rraðioauði'sion; rraðioauði'θion/ *f*, radio broadcast
radiocomunicación /rraðiokomunika'sion; rraðiokomunika'θion/ *f*, radio transmission
radiodifundir /rraðioðifun'dir/ *vt Radio.* to broadcast
radiodifusión, radioemisión /rraðioðifu'sion, rraðioemi'sion/ *f*, *Radio.* broadcast; broadcasting
radiodifusora /rraðioðifu'sora/ *f*, *Lat. Am.* = **radioemisora**
radioemisora /rraðioemi'sora/ *f*, radio station; (radio) transmitter
radioescucha /rraðioes'kutʃa/ *mf* radio listener
radiofotografía /rraðiofotogra'fia/ *f*, radiophotography; x-ray photograph. **tomar una r. de**, to x-ray
radiofrecuencia /rraðiofre'kuensia; rraðiofre'kuenθia/ *f*, radiofrequency
radiografía /rraðiogra'fia/ *f*, radiography, x-ray
radiografiar /rraðiogra'fiar/ *vt* to x-ray, radiograph
radiografista /rraðiogra'fista/ *mf* radiographer
radiograma /rraðio'grama/ *m*, radiogram, cable
radiolocación /rraðioloka'sion; rraðioloka'θion/ *f*, radiolocation
radiología /rraðiolo'hia/ *f*, radiology
radiólogo /rra'ðiologo/ *mf* radiologist
radiometría /rraðiome'tria/ *f*, radiometry
radiómetro /rra'ðiometro/ *m*, radiometer
radiorreceptor /rraðiorresep'tor; rraðiorreθep'tor/ *m*, receiver, wireless set
radioscopia /rraðios'kopia/ *f*, radioscopy
radiotelefonía /rraðiotelefo'nia/ *f*, radiotelephony
radiotelegrafía /rraðiotelegra'fia/ *f*, radiotelegraphy

radiotelegráfico /rraðiotele'grafiko/ *a* radiotelegraphic, wireless

radiotelegrafista /rraðiotelegra'fista/ *mf* wireless operator

radiotelegrama /rraðiotele'grama/ *m*, radiogram, radiotelegram

radioterapia /rraðiote'rapia/ *f*, radiotherapy, radiotherapeutics

radiotransmisor /rraðiotransmi'sor/ *m*, (radio) transmitter

radioyente /rraðio'yente/ *mf* radio listener

raedera /rrae'ðera/ *f*, scraper

raedor /rrae'ðor/ *a* scraping; abrasive

raedura /rrae'ðura/ *f*, scraping; rubbing; fraying

raer /rra'er/ *vt irr* to scrape; abrade; fray; *Fig.* extirpate. See **caer**

ráfaga /'rrafaga/ *f*, gust or blast of wind; light cloud; flash (of light)

rafe /'rrafe/ *m*, eaves

rafia /'rrafia/ *f*, raffia

raicear /rraise'ar/ rraiθe'ar/ *vi*, *Lat. Am.* to take root

raído /'rraiðo/ *a* frayed, threadbare; brazen, barefaced

raíz /rra'is/ rra'iθ/ *f*, root. **r. amarga,** horseradish. **r. cuadrada (cúbica),** square (cubed) root. **r. pivotante,** tap root. **r. fuerte,** *Mexico* horseradish **a r.,** close to the root, closely. **a r. de,** as a result of; after. **de r.,** from the root, entirely. **echar raíces,** to take root

raja /'rraha/ *f*, split, crack; chip, splinter (of wood); slice (of fruit, etc.)

rajadura /rraha'ðura/ *f*, splitting; crack, split, crevice; *Geol.* break

rajar /rra'har/ *vt* to crack, split; slice; *vi Inf.* boast; chatter; *vr* crack, split; *Inf.* take back one's words

ralea /rra'lea/ *f*, kind, quality; (*inf* scornful) race, lineage

ralear /rrale'ar/ *vi* to grow thin (cloth, etc.); behave true to type (gen. in a bad sense)

rallador /rraʎa'ðor/ rraʎa'ðor/ *m*, *Cul.* grater

rallar /rra'yar/ rra'ʎar/ *vt Cul.* to grate; *Inf.* bother, annoy

rallo /'rrayo/ 'rraʎo/ *m*, *Cul.* grater; rasp

ralo /'rralo/ *a* sparse, thin

rama /'rrama/ *f*, bough, branch; *Fig.* branch (of family). *Fig. Inf.* **andarse por las ramas,** to beat around the bush. **en r.,** *Com.* raw; unbound (of books)

ramaje /rra'mahe/ *m*, thickness of branches, denseness of foliage

ramal /rra'mal/ *m*, strand (of rope); halter; branch line (of a railroad); fork (of a road, etc.); ramification, division

ramalazo /rrama'laso; rrama'laθo/ *m*, blow with a rope; mark left by this; bruise

rambla /'rrambla/ *f*, bed, channel, course; avenue, boulevard (in Catalonia)

ramera /rra'mera/ *f*, whore

ramificación /rramifika'sion; rramifika'θion/ *f*, ramification; *Anat.* bifurcation

ramificarse /rramifi'karse/ *vr* to branch, fork; *Fig.* spread

ramillete /rrami'yete; rrami'ʎete/ *m*, bouquet; table centerpiece; *Bot.* cluster

ramo /'rramo/ *m*, *Bot.* branch; twig, spray; bouquet; bunch; wreath; *Fig.* branch (of learning, etc.); *Com.* line (of business); *Fig.* touch, slight attack. **Domingo de Ramos,** Palm Sunday

ramoso /rra'moso/ *a* branchy, thick with branches

rampa /'rrampa/ *f*, gradient, incline; *Mil.* ramp; launching site

ramplón /rram'plon/ *a* stout, heavy (of shoes); coarse; vulgar; bombastic

rana /'rrana/ *f*, frog. **r. de San Antonio,** tree frog

ranchero /rran'tʃero/ *m*, *Mil.* cook; small farmer; *West Hem.* rancher

rancho /'rrantʃo/ *m*, mess, rations; settlement, camp; hut, cabin; *Inf.* group, huddle; *West Hem.* ranch; *Naut.* gang. **hacer r.,** *Inf.* to make room

rancidez /rransi'ðes; rranθi'ðeθ/ *f*, rancidness; staleness; rankness; antiquity

ranciedad /rransie'ðað; rranθie'ðað/ *f*, rancidness; antiquity, oldness; mustiness

rancio /'rransio; 'rranθio/ *a* rancid, rank; mellow (of wine); ancient; traditional; musty

rancotán /rranko'tan/ *adv*, *Lat. Am.* in cash

rango /'rrango/ *m*, grade, class; range; (*Mil. Nav.* and social) rank; file, line

ranura /rra'nura/ *f*, groove; rabbet; slot, notch

rapacidad /rrapasi'ðað; rrapaθi'ðað/ *f*, rapacity, avidity, greed

rapador /rrapa'ðor/ *a* scraping. *m*, *Inf.* barber

rapapolvo /rrapa'polβo/ *m*, *Inf.* severe scolding, dressing-down

rapar /rra'par/ **(se)** *vt* and *vr* to shave; *vt* crop, cut close (hair); *Inf.* steal, pinch

rapaz /rra'pas; rra'paθ/ *a* rapacious. *m*, young boy. **ave r.,** bird of prey

rapaza /rra'pasa; rra'paθa/ *f*, young girl

rape /'rrape/ *m*, *Inf.* hasty shave or haircut. **al r.,** close-cropped

rapidez /rrapi'ðes; rrapi'ðeθ/ *f*, speed, swiftness, rapidity

rápido /'rrapiðo/ *a* quick, swift; express (trains). *m*, torrent, rapid; express train

rapiña /rra'piɲa/ *f*, robbery, plundering, sacking

rapiñar /rrapi'ɲar/ *vt Inf.* to steal, pinch

raposa /rra'posa/ *f*, vixen, fox; *Inf.* wily person

raposear /rrapose'ar/ *vi* to behave like a fox

raposo /rra'poso/ *m*, (male) fox

rapsodia /rrap'soðia/ *f*, rhapsody

raptar /rrap'tar/ *vt* to abduct; rob

rapto /'rrapto/ *m*, abduction, rape; snatching, seizing; ecstasy, trance; *Med.* loss of consciousness

raptor /rrap'tor/ *m*, kidnapper, abductor

raquero /rra'kero/ *a* pirate. *m*, wrecker; pickpocket, dock rat

raqueta /rra'keta/ *f*, racket (tennis, badminton, squash rackets); croupier's rake. **r. de nieve,** snowshoe

raquianestesia /rrakianes'tesia/ *f*, spinal anesthesia

raquítico /rra'kitiko/ *a Med.* rachitic; small, minute; weak, feeble; rickety

raquitismo /rraki'tismo/ *m*, rickets

rarefacer /rrarefa'ser; rrarefa'θer/ **(se)** *vt* and *vr irr* to rarefy. See **satisfacer**

rareza /rra'resa; rra'reθa/ *f*, rareness, unusualness; eccentricity, whim; oddity, curio

raridad /rrari'ðað/ *f*, rarity; thinness; scarcity

raro /'rraro/ *a* rare, unusual, uncommon; notable, outstanding; odd, eccentric, queer; rarefied (gases, etc.). **rara vez,** seldom. **lo r. de,** the strange thing about (e.g. *Lo r. del caso es...,* the strange thing about the case is...)

ras /rras/ *m*, level. **a r.,** flush (with); nearly touching

rasa /'rrasa/ *f*, worn place in cloth; clearing, glade

rasar /rra'sar/ *vt* to level with a strickle; graze, brush, touch lightly; *vr* grow clear (of the sky, etc.)

rascacielos /rraska'sielos; rraska'θielos/ *m*, skyscraper

rascador /rraska'ðor/ *m*, scraper; ornamental hairpin

rascadura /rraska'ðura/ *f*, scraping; scratching

rascar /rras'kar/ *vt* to scratch; claw; scrape; twang (a guitar, etc.). *Inf.* **¡Que se rasque!** Let him put up with it! Let him lump it!

rascatripas /rraska'tripas/ *m*, *Inf.* caterwauler, squeaker (of violinists, etc.)

rascón /rras'kon/ *a* sour, tart

rasgado, -a /rras'gaðo/ *a*, *Lat. Am.* outspoken

rasgadura /rrasga'ðura/ *f*, tearing; tear, rip, rent

rasgar /rras'gar/ **(se)** *vt* and *vr* to tear, rip; *vt* strum the guitar

rasgo /'rrasgo/ *m*, flourish (of the pen); felicitous expression; characteristic, quality; *Lat. Am.* irrigation channel; *pl* features (of the face)

rasgón /rras'gon/ *m*, rip, tear

rasguear /rrasge'ar/ *vt* to strum, twang (the guitar); *vi* write with a flourish

rasgueo /rras'geo/ *m*, flourish (on a guitar); scratch (of a pen)

rasguñar /rrasgu'ɲar/ vt to scratch, scrape; claw; Art. sketch

rasguño /rras'guɲo/ m, scratch; Art. sketch, outline

raso /'rraso/ a flat; free of obstacles; glossy; clear (sky, etc.); plain; undistinguished; backless (chairs). m, satin. **al r.**, in the open air

raspa /'rraspa/ f, Bot. beard (of cereals); fishbone; bunch of grapes; Bot. husk; scraper

raspador /rraspa'ðor/ m, eraser; scraper, rasp

raspadura /rraspa'ðura/ f, scraping; erasing; shavings, filings; Lat. Am. brown sugar

raspar /rras'par/ vt to scrape; erase; rob, steal; burn, bite (wine, etc.); Lat. Am. scold; inf to fail (student), fire (employee)

rastra /'rrastra/ f, trace, sign; sled; string of onions, etc.; anything dragging; Agr. harrow; Agr. rake. **a la r.**, dragging; reluctantly. **pescar a la r.**, to trawl

rastreador /rrastrea'ðor/ m, Naut. minesweeper. a dragging

rastrear /rrastre'ar/ vt to trace, trail; drag, trawl; surmise, conjecture, investigate; vi Agr. rake; fly low

rastreo /rras'treo/ m, dragging (of lakes, etc.)

rastrero /rras'trero/ a dragging, trailing; low-flying; servile, abject; Bot. creeping. m, slaughterhouse employee

rastrillador /rrastriya'ðor; rrastriʎa'ðor/ (-ra) n raker; hackler

rastrilladora /rrastriya'ðora; rrastriʎa'ðora/ f, mechanical harrow

rastrillaje /rrastri'yahe; rrastri'ʎahe/ m, raking

rastrillar /rrastri'yar; rrastri'ʎar/ vt to rake; dress, comb (flax)

rastrillo /rras'triyo; rras'triʎo/ m, Agr. rake; hackle; portcullis; Agr. rack

rastro /'rrastro/ m, Agr. rake; track, trail; wholesale meat market; slaughterhouse; trace, vestige; second-hand market (in Madrid)

rastrojo /rras'troho/ m, stubble; stubble field

rasura /rra'sura/ f, shaving

rasurar /rrasu'rar/ (se) vt and vr to shave

rata /'rrata/ f, rat. m, Inf. pickpocket. **r. almizclera,** muskrat. Inf. **más pobre que las ratas,** poorer than a church mouse

rataplán /rrata'plan/ m, beating of a drum

ratear /rrate'ar/ vt to rebate pro rata; apportion; thieve on a small scale, filch; vi crawl, creep

ratería /rrate'ria/ f, filching, petty theft, shoplifting; picking pockets; meanness, parsimony

ratero /rra'tero/ (-ra) n pilferer, petty thief, pickpocket, shoplifter

ratificación /rratifika'sion; rratifika'θion/ f, ratification

ratificador /rratifika'ðor/ (-ra) n ratifier

ratificar /rratifi'kar/ vt to ratify

ratificatorio /rratifika'torio/ a ratifying, confirmatory

rato /'rrato/ m, short interval of time, while. **buen (mal) r.,** pleasant (unpleasant) time. **r. perdido,** leisure moment. **a ratos,** sometimes, occasionally. **de r. en r.,** from time to time. **pasar el r.,** Inf. to while away the time

ratón /rra'ton/ (-ona) n mouse

ratonera /rrato'nera/ f, mousetrap; mousehole; mouse nest; Lat. Am. hovel. Fig. **caer en la r.,** to fall into a trap

ratonero, ratonesco, ratonil /rrato'nero, rrato'nesko, rrato'nil/ a mousy

rauco /'rrauko/ a Poet. hoarse

raudal /rrau'ðal/ m, torrent, cascade; Fig. flood, abundance

raudo /'rrauðo/ a swift, rapid

ravioles /rra'βioles/ m pl, ravioli

raya /'rraya/ f, stripe, streak; limit, end; part (of the hair); boundary; Gram. dash; score (some games). m, Ichth. ray. **pasar de r.,** to go too far; misbehave

rayadillo /rraya'ðiyo; rraya'ðiʎo/ m, striped cotton

rayano /rra'yano/ a neighboring; border; almost identical, very similar

rayar /rra'yar/ vt to draw lines; streak; stripe; cross out; underline; rifle (a gun); vi verge (on), border

(on); appear (of dawn, daylight); excel; be similar. **Raya en los catorce años,** He is about fourteen

rayo /'rrayo/ m, Phys. beam, ray; thunderbolt; flash of lightning; spoke; quick-witted person; capable, energetic person; sudden pain; disaster, catastrophe. **r. de sol,** sunbeam. **r. catódico,** cathode ray. **r. x,** x-ray. Fig. **echar rayos,** to breathe forth fury

rayón /rra'yon/ m, rayon

raza /'rrasa; 'rraθa/ f, race; breed; lineage, family; kind, class; crack, crevice. **de r.,** purebred

razón /rra'son; rra'θon/ f, reason; reasoning; word, expression; speech, argument; motive, cause; order, method; justice, right, authority; explanation; Math. ratio, proportion. **r. de estado,** raison d'état, reasons of state. Com. **r. social,** firm, trade name. **a r. de,** at a rate of. **dar la r. (a),** to agree with. **estar puesto en r.,** to stand to reason. **tener r.,** to be right

razonable /rraso'naβle; rraθo'naβle/ a reasonable; moderate

razonador /rrasona'ðor; rraθona'ðor/ (-ra) n reasoner

razonamiento /rrasona'miento; rraθona'miento/ m, reasoning

razonar /rraso'nar; rraθo'nar/ vi to reason; speak; attest, confirm

razzia /'rrassia; 'rraθθia/ f, foray; pillaging, sacking; police raid

re /rre/ m, Mus. re, D

reabsorción /rreaβsor'sion; rreaβsor'θion/ f, reabsorption

reacción /rreak'sion; rreak'θion/ f, reaction. **r. de Bayardo,** quick reaction of someone always ready to help those in distress

reaccionar /rreaksio'nar; rreakθio'nar/ vi to react

reaccionario /rreaksio'nario; rreakθio'nario/ (-ia) a and n reactionary

reaccionarismo /rreaksiona'rismo; rreakθiona'rismo/ m, reactionism

reacio /rre'asio; rre'aθio/ a recalcitrant

reactivo /rreak'tiβo/ m, reagent. a reactive; reacting

readmisión /rreaðmi'sion/ f, readmission

readmitir /rreaðmi'tir/ vt to readmit

reajustar /rreahus'tar/ vt to readjust

real /rre'al/ a actual, real; kingly; royal; royalist; Fig. regal; Inf. fine, handsome. m, silver coin, real; m pl, encampment, camp. **alzar el r.,** Mil. to strike camp. **asentar el r.,** Mil. to encamp. **r. decreto,** royal decree. **sitio r.,** royal residence. **un r., sobre otro,** Inf. cash in full

realce /rre'alse; rre'alθe/ m, raised or embossed work; renown, glory; Art. high light

realeza /rrea'lesa; rrea'leθa/ f, royalty, royal majesty

realidad /rreali'ðað/ f, reality; sincerity; truth. **en r.,** in fact, actually

realismo /rrea'lismo/ m, realism; regalism; royalism

realista /rrea'lista/ a realistic; royalist. mf realist; royalist; regalist

realizable /rreali'saβle; rreali'θaβle/ a realizable; practicable

realización /rrealisa'sion; rrealiθa'θion/ f, realization; performance, execution

realizar /rreali'sar; rreali'θar/ vt to perform, execute, carry out; Com. realize. **r. beneficio,** to make a profit

realmente /rreal'mente/ adv really, truly; actually

realzar /rreal'sar; rreal'θar/ vt to heighten, raise; emboss; exalt; enhance; Art. intensify (colors, etc.)

reanimar /rreani'mar/ vt to reanimate; revive, restore, resuscitate; encourage

reanudación /rreanuða'sion; rreanuða'θion/ f, resumption, renewal

reanudar /rreanu'ðar/ vt to resume, continue

reaparecer /rreapare'ser; rreapare'θer/ vi irr to reappear. See **conocer**

reaparición /rreapari'sion; rreapari'θion/ f, reappearance

rearmamento /rrearma'mento/ m, rearmament

rearmar /rrear'mar/ vi to rearm

reasegurador /rreasegura'ðor/ m, underwriter

reasegurar /rreasegu'rar/ vt to reinsure; underwrite

reaseguro /rrease'guro/ m, reinsurance; underwriting

reasunción /rreasun'sion; rreasun'θion/ *f*, reassumption; resumption

reata /rre'ata/ *f*, string of horses or mules. **de r.**, in single file; *Inf*. blindly, unquestioningly; *Inf*. at once

rebaja /rre'βaha/ *f*, diminution; *Com*. discount, rebate; remission

rebajar /rreβa'har/ *vt* to lower; curtail, lessen; remit; *Com*. reduce in price; *Mech*. file; *Elec*. step down; humble, humiliate; *vr* cringe, humble oneself

rebajo /rre'βaho/ *m*, reduction (in price, etc.); rabbet

rebanada /rreβa'naða/ *f*, slice, piece (of bread, etc.)

rebanar /rreβa'nar/ *vt* to cut into slices; split

rebaño /rre'βaɲo/ *m*, flock, drove, herd; *Eccl*. flock

rebasar /rreβa'sar/ *vt* to exceed, go beyond; *Mil*. bypass

rebate /rre'βate/ *m*, altercation, dispute, quarrel

rebatiña /rreβa'tiɲa/ *f*, grab; scrimmage. **andar a la r.**, to scuffle

rebatir /rreβa'tir/ *vt* to repulse, repel; fight again; fight hard; oppose, resist; *Com*. deduct; refuse, reject

rebato /rre'βato/ *m*, alarm, tocsin; *Mil*. surprise attack; panic, dismay

rebeca /rre'βeka/ *f*, cardigan, jersey

rebeco /rre'βeko/ *m*, *Zool*. chamois

rebelarse /rreβe'larse/ *vr* to mutiny, rebel; oppose, resist

rebelde /rre'βelde/ *a* mutinous, rebellious; wilful, disobedient; stubborn. *mf* rebel

rebeldía /rreβel'dia/ *f*, rebelliousness; willfulness; stubbornness; *Law*. nonappearance

rebelión /rreβe'lion/ *f*, insurrection, revolt

rebenque /rre'βenke/ *m*, *Lat. Am*. whip

rebién /rre'βien/ *adv* very well, extremely well

rebisabuelo /rreβisa'βuelo/ **(-la)** *n*. See **tatarabuelo**

reblandecer /rreβlande'ser; rreβlande'θer/ *vt irr* to soften; *vr* become soft. See **conocer**

reblandecimiento /rreβlandesi'miento; rreβlandeθi'miento/ *m*, softening; *Med*. flabbiness

reborde /rre'βorðe/ *m*, rim, edge; *Mech*. flange. **r. de acera,** curb

rebordear /rreβorðe'ar/ *vt* to flange

rebosar /rreβo'sar/ *vi* to overflow, run over; *Fig*. abound; express one's feelings

rebotar /rreβo'tar/ *vi* to rebound; clinch (nails, etc.); refuse; *vr* change color; *Inf*. be vexed

rebote /rre'βote/ *m*, rebounding; rebound

rebotica /rreβo'tika/ *f*, back room of a pharmacy; back of a shop

rebozar /rreβo'sar; rreβo'θar/ *vt* to muffle up; coat with batte̞

rebozo /rre'βoso; rre'βoθo/ *m*, muffling up, hiding the face; head shawl; pretense, excuse. *Fig*. **sin r.,** openly

rebueno /rre'βueno/ *a Inf*. extremely good, fine

rebullicio /rreβu'yisio; rreβu'λiθio/ *m*, uproar, clamor

rebullir /rreβu'yir; rreβu'λir/ *vi* to stir, show signs of movement; *Fig*. swarm, seethe

rebusca /rre'βuska/ *f*, close search; gleaning; remains

rebuscado /rreβus'kaðo/ *a* affected, unnatural (of style)

rebuscar /rreβus'kar/ *vt* to search for; glean

rebuznar /rreβus'nar; rreβuθ'nar/ *vi* to bray

recadero /rreka'ðero/ **(-ra)** *n* messenger, errand boy

recado /rre'kaðo/ *m*, message; greeting, note; gift, present; daily marketing; outfit, implements; precaution, safeguard

recaer /rreka'er/ *vi irr* to fall again; *Med*. relapse; lapse, backslide; devolve, fall upon. See **caer**

recaída /rreka'iða/ *f*, falling again; *Med*. relapse; lapse

recalar /rreka'lar/ *vt* to impregnate; *Naut*. call at (a port), come within sight of land

recalcada /rrekal'kaða/ *f*, pressing down, squeezing; emphasis; *Naut*. list

recalcar /rrekal'kar/ *vt* to press down; squeeze; pack tight; stress, emphasize; *vi Naut*. list; *vr Inf*. say over and over, savor one's words

recalcitrante /rrekalsi'trante; rrekalθi'trante/ *a* obdurate, recalcitrant

recalentador /rrekalenta'ðor/ *m*, *Mech*. superheater

recalentar /rrekalen'tar/ *vt irr* to overheat; superheat; reheat. See **sentar**

recamado /rreka'maðo/ *m*, raised embroidery

recámara /rre'kamara/ *f*, dressing room; explosives chamber; breech of a gun; *Inf*. caution; *Mexico* room, bedroom

recamarera /rrekama'rera/ *f*, *Mexico* chambermaid

recambio /rre'kambio/ *m*, spare, spare part; *Com*. reexchange

recantación /rrekanta'sion; rrekanta'θion/ *f*, retraction, recantation

recapacitar /rrekapasi'tar; rrekapaθi'tar/ *vi* to search one's memory; think over

recapitulación /rrekapitula'sion; rrekapitula'θion/ *f*, summary, résumé

recapitular /rrekapitu'lar/ *vt* to recapitulate, summarize

recargar /rrekar'gar/ *vt* to recharge; load again; reaccuse; overcharge; overdress or overdecorate; *vr Med*. become more feverish. **r. acumuladores,** to recharge batteries

recargo /rre'kargo/ *m*, charge; new load; *Law*. new accusation; overcharge, extra cost; *Med*. temperature increase

recatado /rreka'taðo/ *a* prudent, discreet, circumspect; modest, shy

recatar /rreka'tar/ *vt* to hide, conceal; *vr* be prudent or cautious

recato /rre'kato/ *m*, caution, prudence; modesty, shyness, reserve

recelar /rrese'lar; rreθe'lar/ *vt* to suspect, fear, mistrust; *vr* (*with de*) be afraid or suspicious of

recelo /rre'selo; rre'θelo/ *m*, suspicion, mistrust, doubt, fear

receloso /rrese'loso; rreθe'loso/ *a* suspicious, distrustful, doubtful

recepción /rresep'sion; rreθep'θion/ *f*, receiving, reception; admission, acceptance; reception, party; *Law*. cross-examination

receptáculo /rresep'takulo; rreθep'takulo/ *m*, receptacle, container; *Fig*. refuge; *Bot*. receptacle

receptador /rresepta'ðor; rreθepta'ðor/ **(-ra)** *n* receiver (of stolen goods); accomplice

receptivo /rresep'tiβo; rreθep'tiβo/ *a* receptive

receptor /rresep'tor; rreθep'tor/ **(-ra)** *a* receiving. *n* recipient. *m*, *Elec*. receiver; wireless set. **r. de galena,** crystal set. **r. telefónico,** telephone receiver

receta /rre'seta; rre'θeta/ *f*, *Med*. prescription; *Cul*. recipe

recetar /rrese'tar; rreθe'tar/ *vt Med*. to prescribe; *Inf*. demand

rechapear /rretʃape'ar/ *vt* to replate

rechazar /rretʃa'sar; rretʃa'θar/ *vt* to repulse; resist; refuse; oppose, deny (the truth of); contradict

rechazo /rre'tʃaso; rre'tʃaθo/ *m*, recoil; rebound; refusal

rechinamiento, rechino /rretʃina'miento, rre'tʃino/ *m*, squeaking, creaking; gnashing (of teeth)

rechinar /rretʃi'nar/ *vi* to squeak, creak; gnash (teeth); chatter (teeth); do with a bad grace

rechoncho /rre'tʃontʃo/ *a* squat, stocky, thickset

reciamente /rresia'mente; rreθia'mente/ *adv* hard; strongly, firmly, vigorously

recibí /rresi'βi; rreθi'βi/ *m*, *Com*. receipt

recibidor /rresiβi'ðor; rreθiβi'ðor/ **(-ra)** *a* receiving. *n* recipient. *m*, reception room

recibimiento /rresiβi'miento; rreθiβi'miento/ *m*, reception; welcome, greeting; reception room, waiting room; hall, vestibule

recibir /rresi'βir; rreθi'βir/ *vt* to obtain, receive; support, bear; suffer, experience (attack, injury); approve; accept, receive; entertain; stand up to (attack); *vr* (*with de*) graduate as, take office as

recibo /rre'siβo; rre'θiβo/ *m*, reception; *Com.* receipt; reception room, waiting room; hall, vestibule. *Com.* **acusar r.,** to acknowledge receipt

reciclar /rresi'klar; rreθi'klar/ *vt* recycle

recidiva /rresi'ðiβa; rreθi'ðiβa/ *f*, *Med.* relapse

recién /rre'sien; rre'θien/ *adv* recently, newly. Shortened form of **reciente** before a past participle (e.g. *r. llegado*, newly arrived)

reciente /rre'siente; rre'θiente/ *a* recent; new; fresh

recinto /rre'sinto; rre'θinto/ *m*, precinct; neighborhood; premises, place

recio /'rresio; 'rreθio/ *a* strong; robust; bulky, thick; rough, uncouth; grievous, hard; severe (weather); impetuous, precipitate

recipiente /rresi'piente; rreθi'piente/ *a* receiving. *m*, receptacle, container, vessel

reciprocar /rresipro'kar; rreθipro'kar/ *vt* to reciprocate

reciprocidad /rresiprosi'ðað; rreθiproθi'ðað/ *f*, reciprocity; reciprocation

recíproco /rre'siproko; rre'θiproko/ *a* reciprocal

recitación /rresita'sion; rreθita'θion/ *f*, recitation

recitado /rresi'taðo; rreθi'taðo/ *m*, recitative

recitador /rresita'ðor; rreθita'ðor/ **(-ra)** *n* elocutionist, reciter

recitar /rresi'tar; rreθi'tar/ *vt* to recite, declaim

reclamación /rreklama'sion; rreklama'θion/ *f*, reclamation; objection, opposition; *Com.* claim

reclamar /rrekla'mar/ *vi* to oppose, object to; *Poet.* resound; *vt* call repeatedly; *Com.* claim; decoy (birds)

reclamo /rre'klamo/ *m*, decoy bird; enticement, allurement; *Law.* reclamation; advertisement. **objeto de r.,** advertising sample. **venta de r.,** bargain sale

reclinación /rreklina'sion; rreklina'θion/ *f*, reclining; leaning

reclinatorio /rreklina'torio/ *m*, couch; prie-dieu

recluir /rre'kluir/ *vt irr* to immure, shut up; detain, arrest. See **huir**

reclusión /rreklu'sion/ *f*, confinement, seclusion; prison

recluso /rre'kluso/ **(-sa)** *n* recluse

recluta /rre'kluta/ *f*, recruiting. *mf Mil.* recruit

reclutador /rrekluta'ðor/ *m*, recruiting office

reclutamiento /rrekluta'miento/ *m*, recruiting

reclutar /rreklu'tar/ *vt* to enlist recruits, recruit; *Argentina* round up

recobrar /rreko'βrar/ *vt* to recover, regain; *vr* recuperate; regain consciousness

recobro /rre'koβro/ *m*, recovery; *Mech.* pick-up

recocer /rreko'ser; rreko'θer/ *vt irr* to reboil; recook; overboil; overcook; anneal (metals); *vr Fig.* be tormented (by emotion), be all burned up. See **cocer**

recodo /rre'koðo/ *m*, bend, turn, loop

recogedor /rrekohe'ðor/ *a* sheltering. *m*, *Agr.* gleaner

recoger /rreko'her/ *vt* to gather, pick; pick up; retake; collect (letters from a mailbox, etc.); amass; shrink, narrow; keep; hoard; shelter; reap, pick; *vr* withdraw, retire; go home; go to bed; retrench, economize; give oneself to meditation

recogida /rreko'hiða/ *f*, collection (of letters from a mailbox); withdrawal; retirement; harvest

recogido /rreko'hiðo/ *a* recluse; cloistered, confined

recogimiento /rrekohi'miento/ *m*, gathering, picking; collection, accumulation; seclusion; shelter; women's reformatory

recolección /rrekolek'sion; rrekolek'θion/ *f*, summary, résumé; harvest; collection (of taxes, etc.); *Eccl.* convent of a reformed order; mystic ecstasy

recoleto /rreko'leto/ *a Eccl.* reformed (of religious orders); recluse

recomendable /rrekomen'daβle/ *a* commendable, recommendable

recomendación /rrekomenda'sion; rrekomenda'θion/ *f*, recommendation (all meanings)

recomendar /rrekomen'dar/ *vt irr* to recommend (all meanings); entrust, commend. *Pres. Ind.* **recomiendo, recomiendas, recomienda, recomiendan.** *Pres. Sub-*

junc. **recomiende, recomiendes, recomiende, recomienden**

recompensa /rrekom'pensa/ *f*, compensation; recompense, reward

recompensar /rrekompen'sar/ *vt* to compensate; requite; reward, recompense

recomposición /rrekomposi'sion; rrekomposi'θion/ *f*, recomposition

recomprar /rrekom'prar/ *vt* to repurchase

reconcentrar /rrekonsen'trar; rrekonθen'trar/ *vt* to concentrate; dissemble; *vr* withdraw into oneself, meditate

reconciliable /rrekonsi'liaβle; rrekonθi'liaβle/ *a* reconcilable

reconciliación /rrekonsilia'sion; rrekonθilia'θion/ *f*, reconciliation

reconciliador /rrekonsilia'ðor; rrekonθilia'ðor/ **(-ra)** *a* reconciliatory. *n* reconciler

reconciliar /rrekonsi'liar; rrekonθi'liar/ *vt* to reconcile; *Eccl.* reconsecrate; *Eccl.* hear a short confession; *vr* become reconciled; *Eccl.* make an additional confession

recondicionar /rrekondisio'nar; rrekondiθio'nar/ *vt* to rebuild, overhaul, recondition

recóndito /rre'kondito/ *a* recondite

reconocer /rrekono'ser; rrekono'θer/ *vt irr* to examine, inspect; recognize; admit, acknowledge; own, confess; search; *Polit.* recognize; *Mil.* reconnoiter; (*with por*) adopt as (a son, etc.); recognize as; *vr* be seen, show; acknowledge, confess; know oneself. **Bien se reconoce que no está aquí,** It's easy to see he's not here. See **conocer**

reconocido /rrekono'siðo; rrekono'θiðo/ *a* grateful

reconocimiento /rrekonosi'miento; rrekonoθi'miento/ *m*, examination, inspection; recognition; acknowledgement, admission; search; *Mil.* reconnoitering; adoption; gratitude

reconquista /rrekon'kista/ *f*, reconquest

reconquistar /rrekonkis'tar/ *vt* to reconquer; *Fig.* recover, win back

reconstitución /rrekonstitu'sion; rrekonstitu'θion/ *f*, reconstitution

reconstituir /rrekonsti'tuir/ *vt irr* to reconstitute. See **huir**

reconstituyente /rrekonstitu'yente/ *m*, *Med.* tonic

reconstrucción /rrekonstruk'sion; rrekonstruk'θion/ *f*, reconstruction

reconstruir /rrekons'truir/ *vt irr* to reconstruct, rebuild; recreate. See **huir**

reconvención /rrekomben'sion; rrekomben'θion/ *f*, rebuke, reproof; recrimination; *Law.* countercharge

reconversión /rrekomber'sion/ *f*, reconversion

recopilación /rrekopila'sion; rrekopila'θion/ *f*, summary, compendium; collection (of writings); digest (of laws)

recopilador /rrekopila'ðor/ *m*, compiler

recopilar /rrekopi'lar/ *vt* to compile, collect

recordar /rrekor'ðar/ *vt irr* to cause to remember, remind; remember; *vi* remember; awake. See **acordar**

recordatorio /rrekorða'torio/ *m*, reminder. *a* commemorative (e.g. a plaque)

recorrer /rreko'rrer/ *vt* to travel over; pass through; wander around; examine, inspect; read hastily; overhaul, renovate

recorrido /rreko'rriðo/ *m*, journey, run; *Mech.* stroke; overhaul. **r. de despegue,** *Aer.* take-off run

recortado /rrekor'taðo/ *a Bot.* jagged, incised. *m*, paper cutout

recortar /rrekor'tar/ *vt* to clip, trim, pare; cut out; *Art.* outline; *vr* stand out (against), be outlined (against)

recorte /rre'korte/ *m*, clipping, paring; cutting; cut-out; *Art.* outline; *pl* snippets, clippings. **r. de periódico,** newspaper cutting, newspaper clipping

recostar /rrekos'tar/ *vt irr* (*with en or contra*) to lean, rest against; *vr* (*with en or contra*) lean against, rest on; lean back; recline. See **contar**

recreación /rrekrea'sion; rrekrea'θion/ *f*, recreation, hobby

recrear /rrekre'ar/ *vt* to entertain, amuse; *vr* amuse oneself; delight (in), enjoy

recreo /rre'kreo/ *m*, recreation, hobby; playtime, recess (in schools); place of amusement. **salón de r.**, recreation room

recriminación /rrekrimina'sion; rrekrimina'θion/ *f*, recrimination

recriminador /rrekrimina'ðor/ *a* recriminatory

recriminar /rrekrimi'nar/ *vt* to recriminate

recrudecer /rrekruðe'ser; rrekruðe'θer/ **(se)** *vi* and *vr irr* to recur, return. See **conocer**

recrudescencia /rrekruðes'sensia; rrekruðes'θenθia/ *f*, recrudescence, recurrence

rectángulo /rrek'tangulo/ *m*, rectangle. *a* rectangular

rectificable /rrektifi'kaβle/ *a* rectifiable

rectificación /rrektifika'sion; rrektifika'θion/ *f*, rectification; *Mech.* grinding

rectificador /rrektifika'ðor/ *m*, rectifier

rectificar /rrektifi'kar/ *vt* to rectify; *Mech.* grind; *vr* mend one's ways; *Mil.* **r. el frente,** to straighten the line

rectilíneo /rrekti'lineo/ *a* rectilinear

rectitud /rrekti'tuð/ *f*, straightness; rectitude, integrity; exactness; righteousness

recto /'rrekto/ *a* straight; upright; erect; literal (meaning); just, fair; single-breasted (of coats); *m*, right angle; rectum

rector /rrek'tor/ **(-ra)** *n* director; principal, headmaster. *m*, *Eccl.* rector

rectorado /rrekto'raðo/ *m*, principalship, headmaster-(mistress-) ship, directorship; *Eccl.* rectorship

rectoría /rrekto'ria/ *f*, rectorate, rectorship

recua /'rrekua/ *f*, drove of beasts of burden; *Inf.* string or line (of things)

recubrir /rreku'βrir/ *vt* to re-cover; coat; plate. *Past Part.* **recubierto**

recuento /rre'kuento/ *m*, calculation; recount; inventory

recuerdo /rre'kuerðo/ *m*, memory, remembrance; souvenir, memento; *pl* greetings, regards

reculada /rreku'laða/ *f*, drawing back; recoil

recular /rreku'lar/ *vi* to recoil, draw back; *Inf.* go back on, give up

recuperable /rrekupe'raβle/ *a* recoverable, recuperable

recuperación /rrekupera'sion; rrekupera'θion/ *f*, recovery, recuperation; *Chem.* recovery

recurrente /rreku'rrente/ *a* recurrent

recurrir /rreku'rrir/ *vi* to recur; (*with prep a*) have recourse to; appeal to

recurso /rre'kurso/ *m*, recourse, resort; choice, option; reversion; petition; *Law.* appeal; *pl* means of livelihood; *Fig.* way out, last hope

recusar /rreku'sar/ *vt* to refuse; challenge the authority (of), *Law.* recuse

red /rreð/ *f*, net; network; hairnet; railing, grating; *Fig.* snare; system (of communications, etc.); *Fig.* combination (of events, etc.); *Elec.* mains. **r. de arrastre,** trawl net. **Red Mundial,** World Wide Web. *Fig. Inf.* **caer en la r.,** to fall into the trap

redacción /rreðak'sion; rreðak'θion/ *f*, phrasing; editorial office; editing; editorial board

redactar /rreðak'tar/ *vt* to write, phrase; draw up; edit

redactor /rreðak'tor/ **(-ra)** *a* editorial. *n* editor

redada /rre'ðaða/ *f*, cast (of a fishing net); haul, catch

redecilla /rreðe'siya; rreðe'θiʎa/ *f*, *dim* small net; netting; hairnet

redención /rreðen'sion; rreðen'θion/ *f*, redemption; ransom; deliverance, salvation; redeeming, paying off (a mortgage, etc.)

redentor /rreðen'tor/ **(-ra)** *a* redeeming, redemptive. *n* redeemer

redificar /rreðifi'kar/ *vt* to rebuild

redifusión /rreðifu'sion/ *f*, *Radio.* relay

redil /rre'ðil/ *m*, sheepfold

redimible /rreði'miβle/ *a* redeemable

redimir /rreði'mir/ *vt* to ransom; redeem, buy back; pay off (a mortgage, etc.); deliver, free; *Eccl.* redeem

reditar /rreði'tar/ *vt* to reprint, reissue

rédito /'rreðito/ *m*, *Com.* income, revenue, interest, profit

redoblamiento /rreðoβla'miento/ *m*, redoubling; bending back (of nails, etc.); rolling (of a drum)

redoblar /rreðo'βlar/ *vt* to redouble; repeat; bend back (nails, etc.); *vi* roll (a drum)

redoble /rre'ðoβle/ *m*, doubling; redoubling; repetition; roll (of a drum)

redoma /rre'ðoma/ *f*, flask, vial

redomado /rreðo'maðo/ *a* astute, crafty, sly; complete, perfect

redonda /rre'ðonda/ *f*, district; pasture ground; *Naut.* square sail; *Mus.* semibreve. **a la r.,** around

redondear /rreðonde'ar/ *vt* to make round; round; free (from debt, etc.); *vr* acquire a fortune; clear oneself (of debts, etc.)

redondel /rreðon'del/ *m*, traffic circle, rotary, roundabout

redondez /rreðon'des; rreðon'deθ/ *f*, roundness

redondo /rre'ðondo/ *a* round; circular; unequivocal, plain. *m*, round, circle; *Inf.* cash. **suma redonda,** lump sum (cash)

reducción /rreðuk'sion; rreðuk'θion/ *f*, reduction; *Mil.* defeat, conquest; decrease; *Com.* rebate; (*Math. Chem.*) reduction

reducir /rreðu'sir; rreðu'θir/ *vt irr* to reduce; decrease, cut down; break up; *Art.* scale down; *Elec.* step down; subdue; (*Chem. Math. Surg.*) reduce; exchange; divide into small fragments; persuade; *vr* be obliged to, have to; live moderately. See **conducir**

redundancia /rreðun'dansia; rreðun'danθia/ *f*, redundance

redundante /rreðun'dante/ *a* redundant

redundar /rreðun'dar/ *vi* to overflow; be excessive or superfluous; (*with en*) redound to

reduplicación /rreðuplika'sion; rreðuplika'θion/ *f*, reduplication

reduplicar /rreðupli'kar/ *vt* to reduplicate, redouble

ree For words so beginning (e.g. *reeditar, reexaminación*), see spellings with one **e**

refacción /rrefak'sion; rrefak'θion/ *f*, refection, light meal; compensation, reparation. **«cerrado por r.,»** "closed for repairs"

refaccionar /rrefaksio'nar; rrefakθio'nar/ *vt*, *Lat. Am.* to fix, repair

refajo /rre'faho/ *m*, skirt, underskirt; *Colombia* mild drink consisting of champagne, soda and beer

refectorio /rrefek'torio/ *m*, refectory

referencia /rrefe'rensia; rrefe'renθia/ *f*, report, account; allusion; regard, relation; *Com.* reference (gen. *pl*); consideration

referente /rrefe'rente/ *a* concerning, related (to)

referir /rrefe'rir/ *vt irr* to narrate; describe; direct, guide; relate, refer, concern; *vr* allude (to); refer (to); concern. See **sentir**

refinación /rrefina'sion; rrefina'θion/ *f*, refining

refinado /rrefi'naðo/ *a* refined; polished, cultured; crafty

refinador /rrefina'ðor/ *m*, refiner

refinamiento /rrefina'miento/ *m*, refinement, subtlety, care

refinar /rrefi'nar/ *vt* to refine, purify; polish, perfect

refinería /rrefine'ria/ *f*, refinery

reflector /rreflek'tor/ *a* reflecting. *m*, reflector; searchlight; shade (for lamps, etc.)

reflejar /rrefle'har/ *vi* *Phys.* to reflect; *vt* consider; show, mirror; *vr* *Fig.* be reflected, be seen

reflejo /rre'fleho/ *m*, reflection; image; glare. *a* reflex; considered, judicious

reflexión /rreflek'sion/ *f*, *Phys.* reflection; consideration, thought

reflexionar /rrefleksio'nar/ *vt* (*with en* or *sobre*) to consider, reflect upon

reflexivo /rreflek'siβo/ *a* *Phys.* reflective; thoughtful

reflorecer /rreflore'ser; rreflore'θer/ *vi irr* to flower again; return to favor (ideas, etc.). See **conocer**

reflujo /rre'fluho/ *m*, reflux, reflowrece; ebb tide

refocilar /rrefosi'lar; rrefoθi'lar/ *vt* to warm up, brace up; give pleasure to; *vr* enjoy oneself

reforma /rre'forma/ f, reform; improvement; reformation; Hist. Reformation

reformación /rreforma'sion; rreforma'θion/ f, reform, improvement

reformador /rreforma'ðor/ (-ra) a reformatory, reforming. n reformer

reformar /rrefor'mar/ vt to remake; reshape; repair, mend, restore; improve, correct; Eccl. reform; reorganize; vr mend one's ways, improve; control oneself

reformatorio /rreforma'torio/ m, reformatory. a reforming, reformatory

reformista /rrefor'mista/ mf reformist, reformer. a reformatory

reforzador /rreforsa'ðor; rreforθa'ðor/ m, Photo. reinforcing bath; Elec. booster

reforzamiento /rreforsa'miento; rreforθa'miento/ m, stiffening, reinforcing

reforzar /rrefor'sar; rrefor'θar/ vt irr to reinforce, strengthen, stiffen; encourage, inspirit. See **forzar**

refractar /rrefrak'tar/ vt to refract

refractario /rrefrak'tario/ a stubborn; (Phys. Chem.) refractory; unmanageable, unruly; fireproof

refrán /rre'fran/ m, proverb

refranero /rrefra'nero/ m, collection of proverbs

refregamiento /rrefrega'miento/ m, rubbing; scrubbing, scouring

refregar /rrefre'gar/ vt irr to rub; scrub, scour; Fig. Inf. rub in, insist on. See **cegar**

refrenamiento /rrefrena'miento/ m, curbing; control, restraint

refrenar /rrefre'nar/ vt to curb, rein in (horses); control, restrain

refrendar /rrefren'dar/ vt to countersign, endorse, legalize

refrescante /rrefres'kante/ a refreshing, cooling

refrescar /rrefres'kar/ vt to cool, chill; repeat; Fig. brush up, revise; vi be rested or refreshed; grow cooler; take the air; freshen (wind); take a cool drink; vr grow cooler; take the air; take a cool drink

refresco /rre'fresko/ m, refreshment; cool drink; Lat. Am. soft drink, soda, pop

refresquería /rrefreske'ria/ f, Lat. Am. refreshment stand

refriega /rre'friega/ f, affray, scuffle, rough-and-tumble

refrigeración /rrefrihera'sion; rrefrihera'θion/ f, refrigeration

refrigerador /rrefrihera'ðor/ m, refrigerator

refrigerante /rrefrihe'rante/ a refrigerative; chilling; cooling. m, cooling chamber, cooler

refrigerar /rrefrihe'rar/ vt to chill; cool; freeze, refrigerate; refresh

refrigerio /rrefri'herio/ m, coolness; consolation; refreshment, food

refringente /rrefrin'hente/ a Phys. refringent

refuerzo /rre'fuerso; rre'fuerθo/ m, reinforcement, strengthening; aid, help

refugiado /rrefu'hiaðo/ (-da) a and n refugee

refugiar /rrefu'hiar/ vt to protect, shelter; vr take refuge

refugio /rre'fuhio/ m, refuge, shelter, protection; traffic island. **r. antiaéreo,** air raid shelter. **r. para peatones,** traffic island

refulgencia /rreful'hensia; rreful'henθia/ f, resplendence, splendor, brilliance

refulgente /rreful'hente/ a resplendent, refulgent, dazzling

refulgir /rreful'hir/ vi to shine, be dazzling

refundición /rrefundi'sion; rrefundi'θion/ f, recasting (of metals); adaptation; rehash, refurbishing

refundir /rrefun'dir/ vr to recast (metals); include, comprise; adapt; rehash, refurbish; vi Fig. promote, contribute to

refunfuñador /rrefunfuɲa'ðor/ a grumbling, fuming

refunfuñar /rrefunfu'ɲar/ vi to grumble, growl, fume

refunfuño /rrefun'fuɲo/ m, grumble, fuming; snort

refutable /rrefu'taβle/ a refutable

refutación /rrefuta'sion; rrefuta'θion/ f, refutation

refutar /rrefu'tar/ vt to refute

regadera /rrega'ðera/ f, watering can; irrigation canal; sprinkler; Lat. Am. shower bath, shower

regadío /rrega'ðio/ m, irrigated land; irrigation, watering. a irrigated

regajal, regajo /rrega'hal, rre'gaho/ m, pool, puddle; stream, brook

regalado /rrega'laðo/ a delicate, highly bred; luxurious, delightful

regalar /rrega'lar/ vt to make a gift of, give; caress, fondle; indulge, cherish; entertain, regale; vr live in luxury

regalía /rrega'lia/ f, royal privilege; right, exemption; perquisite, emolument

regaliz /rrega'lis; rrega'liθ/ m, **regaliza** f, licorice

regalo /rre'galo/ m, gift, present; satisfaction, pleasure; entertainment, regalement; luxury, comfort

regalón /rrega'lon/ a Inf. pampered

regalonear /rregalone'ar/ vt, Lat. Am. to pamper, spoil

regañadientes, a /rregaɲa'ðientes, a/ adv unwillingly, grumblingly

regañar /rrega'ɲar/ vi to snarl (dogs); crack (skin of fruits); grumble, mutter; Inf. quarrel; vt Inf. scold

regaño /rre'gaɲo/ m, angry look or gesture; Inf. scolding

regañón /rrega'ɲon/ (-ona) a Inf. grumbling, complaining; scolding. n Inf. grumbler

regar /rre'gar/ vt irr to water, sprinkle with water; flow through, irrigate; spray; Fig. shower (with), strew. See **cegar**

regata /rre'gata/ f, regatta; small irrigation channel (for gardens, etc.)

regate /rre'gate/ m, twist of the body, sidestep; dribbling; (in soccer) Inf. dodging, evasion

regatear /rregate'ar/ vt to haggle over, beat down (prices); resell, retail; dribble (a ball); Fig. Inf. dodge, avoid; vi bargain, haggle; Naut. take part in a regatta, race

regateo /rrega'teo/ m, haggling, bargaining

regatero /rrega'tero/ (-ra) a retail. n retailer

regatón /rrega'ton/ (-ona) m, ferrule, tip. a haggling, bargaining. n haggler; retailer

regatonear /rregatone'ar/ vt to resell at retail

regazo /rre'gaso; rre'gaθo/ m, lap, knees; Fig. heart, bosom

regeneración /rrehenera'sion; rrehenera'θion/ f, regeneration

regenerador /rrehenera'ðor/ (-ra) n regenerator. a regenerative, reforming

regenerar /rrehene'rar/ vt to regenerate, reform

regenta /rre'henta/ f, wife of the president of a court of session

regentar /rrehen'tar/ vt to fill temporarily (offices); rule, govern; manage, run (businesses)

regente /rre'hente/ a ruling. mf regent. m, president of a court of session; manager

regicidio /rrehi'siðio; rrehi'θiðio/ m, regicide (act)

regidor /rrehi'ðor/ a ruling, governing. m, magistrate, alderman

régimen /'rrehimen/ m, administration, management; regime; (Med. Gram.) regimen; Mech. rating

regimentación /rrehimenta'sion; rrehimenta'θion/ f, regimentation

regimentar /rrehimen'tar/ vt irr to form into regiments; regiment. Pres. Ind. **regimento, regimientas, regimienta, regimientan.** Pres. Subjunc. **regimente, regimientes, regimiente, regimienten**

regimiento /rrehi'miento/ m, Mil. regiment; administration, rule; Lat. Am. crowd (of people)

regio /'rrehio/ a royal; magnificent, regal. **¡regio!** great!, wonderful!

región /rre'hion/ f, region, country; area, tract, space. **r. industrial,** industrial area

regionalismo /rrehiona'lismo/ m, regionalism

regionalista /rrehiona'lista/ mf regionalist. a regional

regir /rre'hir/ vt irr to govern, rule; administer, conduct; Gram. govern; vi be in force (laws, etc.); work, function; Naut. obey the helm. See **pedir**

registrador /rrehistra'ðor/ a recording. m, registrar,

keeper of records; recorder. **caja (registradora)**, (cash) register

registrar /rrehis'trar/ *vt* to examine, inspect; search; copy, record; mark the place (in a book); observe, note; (of thermometers, etc.) record, show; look on to (houses, etc.); *vr* register (hotels, etc.)

registro /rre'histro/ *m*, search; registration, entry; record; recording; reading (of a thermometer, etc.); *Mech.* damper; registry; register (book); *Mus.* range, compass (voice); *Mus.* register (organ); (*Mech. Print.*) register; bookmark. **r. civil**, register of births, marriages, and deaths

regla /'rregla/ *f*, ruler, measuring stick; rule, principle, guide, precept; system, policy; *Med.* period; moderation; method, order. **r. de cálculo,** slide rule. **r. T,** T-square. **en r.,** in due form. **por r.,** general, generally, as a rule

reglamentación /rreglamenta'sion; rreglamenta'θion/ *f*, regulation; rules and regulations

reglamentar /rreglamen'tar/ *vt* to regulate

reglamento /rregla'mento/ *m*, bylaw; regulation, ordinance

reglar /rre'glar/ *vt* to rule (lines); regulate; govern; control; *vr* restrain oneself, mend one's ways

regocijar /rregosi'har; rregoθi'har/ *vt* to cheer, delight; *vr* enjoy oneself, rejoice

regocijo /rrego'siho; rrego'θiho/ *m*, happiness, joy; cheer, merriment

regordete /rregor'ðete/ *a Inf.* chubby

regresar /rregre'sar/ *vi* to return

regresión /rregre'sion/ *f*, return; retrogression; regression

regreso /rre'greso/ *m*, return

reguera /rre'gera/ *f*, irrigation channel, ditch

regulación /rregula'sion; rregula'θion/ *f*, regulation; *Mech.* control, timing

regulador /rregula'ðor/ *m*, *Mech.* governor, regulator. *a* regulating, controlling

regular /rregu'lar/ *vt* to adjust, regulate; *Mech.* govern. *a* methodical, ordered; moderate; average, medium; (*Eccl. Mil. Geom. Gram.*) regular; so-so, not bad; probable. **por lo r.,** generally

regularidad /rregulari'ðað/ *f*, regularity

regularización /rregularisa'sion; rregulariθa'θion/ *f*, regularization; regulation

regularizar /rregulari'sar; rregulari'θar/ *vt* to regularize; regulate

regurgitar /rregurhi'tar/ *vi* to regurgitate

rehabilitación /rreaβilita'sion; rreaβilita'θion/ *f*, rehabilitation

rehabilitar /rreaβili'tar/ *vt* to rehabilitate; *vr* rehabilitate oneself

rehacer /rrea'ser; rrea'θer/ *vt irr* to remake; repair, mend; *vr* recover one's strength; control one's emotions; *Mil.* rally. See **hacer**

rehén /rre'en/ *m*, hostage (gen. *pl*); *Mil.* pledge, security

rehenchir /rreen'tʃir/ *vt irr* to restuff; refill, recharge. See **henchir**

reherir /rree'rir/ *vt irr* to repulse. See **herir**

rehilar /rrei'lar/ *vt* to spin too much or twist the yarn; *vi* totter, stagger; whizz (arrows, etc.). See **prohibir**

rehuir /rre'uir/ *vt irr* to withdraw; avoid; reject. See **huir**

rehusar /rreu'sar/ *vt* to refuse, reject. See **desahuciar**

reimponer /rreimpo'ner/ *vt irr* to reimpose. See **poner**

reimportación /rreimporta'sion; rreimporta'θion/ *f*, reimportation

reimpresión /rreimpre'sion/ *f*, reprint

reimprimir /rreimpri'mir/ *vt* to reprint

reina /'rreina/ *f*, queen; queen (in chess); queen bee; peerless beauty, belle

reinado /rrei'naðo/ *m*, reign; heyday, fashion

reinante /rrei'nante/ *a* reigning; prevalent

reinar /rrei'nar/ *vi* to reign; influence; endure, prevail

reincidencia /rreinsi'ðensia; rreinθi'ðenθia/ *f*, relapse (into crime, etc.), recidivism

reincidente /rreinsi'ðente; rreinθi'ðente/ *mf* backslider

reincidir /rreinsi'ðir; rreinθi'ðir/ *vi* to relapse (into crime, etc.)

reincorporar /rreinkorpo'rar/ *vt* to reincorporate; *vr* join again, become a member again

reingresar /rreiŋgre'sar/ *vi* to reenter

reingreso /rreiŋ'greso/ *m*, reentry

reino /'rreino/ *m*, kingdom

reinstalación /rreinstala'sion; rreinstala'θion/ *f*, reinstatement

reinstalar /rreinsta'lar/ *vt* to reinstate; *vr* be reinstalled

reintegración /rreintegra'sion; rreintegra'θion/ *f*, reintegration

reintegrar /rreinte'grar/ *vt* to reintegrate; *vr* be reinstated, recuperate, recover

reir /rre'ir/ *vi* to laugh; sneer, jeer; *Fig.* smile (nature); *vt* laugh at; *vr Inf.* (*with de*) scorn. **reírse a carcajadas,** to shout with laughter. *Pres. Part.* **riendo.** *Pres. Ind.* **río, ríes, ríe, rien.** *Preterite* **rió, rieron.** *Pres. Subjunc.* **ría,** etc. *Imperf. Subjunc.* **riese, etc.**

reiteración /rreitera'sion; rreitera'θion/ *f*, reiteration, repetition

reiteradamente /rreiteraða'mente/ *adv* repeatedly, reiteratively

reiterar /rreite'rar/ *vt* to reiterate, repeat

reivindicación /rreiβindika'sion; rreiβindika'θion/ *f*, *Law.* recovery

reivindicar /rreiβindi'kar/ *vt Law.* to recover

reja /'rreha/ *f*, colter, plowshare; plowing, tilling; grating, grille; *Lat. Am.* jail, prison

rejado /rre'haðo/ *m*, railing, grating

rejilla /rre'hiya; rre'hiʎa/ *f*, grating; grille, lattice; luggage rack (in a train); cane (for chairs, seats, etc.); wire mesh; small brazier; *Elec.* grid; *Mech.* grate

rejo /'rreho/ *m*, *Lat. Am.* whip

rejuntar /rrehun'tar/ *vt* to point (a wall)

rejuvenecer /rrehuβene'ser; rrehuβene'θer/ *vt irr* to rejuvenate; *Fig.* revive; bring up to date; *vi* and *vr* be rejuvenated, grow young again, rejuvenesce. See **conocer**

rejuvenecimiento /rrehuβenesi'miento; rrehuβeneθi'miento/ *m*, rejuvenation

relación /rrela'sion; rrela'θion/ *f*, relation; connection (of ideas); report, statement; narrative, account; *Math.* ratio; *Law.* brief; intercourse, association, dealings (gen. *pl*); list; analogy, relation. **tener relaciones con,** to have dealings with; be engaged or betrothed to; woo, court

relacionar /rrelasio'nar; rrelaθio'nar/ *vt* to recount, narrate, report; connect, relate; *vr* be connected

relajación /rrelaha'sion; rrelaha'θion/ *f*, relaxation; recreation; laxity, dissoluteness

relajar /rrela'har/ *vt* to relax; recreate, amuse; make less rigorous; *Law.* remit; *vr* become relaxed; be dissolute, lax, or vicious, *Dominican Republic* joking

relamer /rrela'mer/ *vt* to lick again; *vr* lick one's lips; *Fig.* overpaint, make up too much; ooze satisfaction, brag

relamido /rrela'miðo/ *a* overdressed; affected

relámpago /rre'lampago/ *m*, lightning; flash, gleam; streak of lightning (of quick persons or things); flash of wit, witticism

relampaguear /rrelampage'ar/ *vi* to lighten (of lightning); flash, gleam

relapso /rre'lapso/ *a* relapsed, lapsed (into error, vice)

relatar /rrela'tar/ *vt* to relate, narrate, report, relay

relatividad /rrelatiβi'ðað/ *f*, relativeness; *Phys.* relativity

relativo /rrela'tiβo/ *a* relevant, pertinent, relative, comparative; *Gram.* relative

relato /rre'lato/ *m*, narration, account, report

relator /rrela'tor/ **(-ra)** *a* narrating. *n* narrator. *m*, *Law.* reporter

relavar /rrela'βar/ *vt* to rewash, wash again

relección /rrelek'sion; rrelek'θion/ *f*, reelection

releer /rrele'er/ *vt irr* to reread; revise. See **creer**

relegación /rrelega'sion; rrelega'θion/ *f*, relegation

relegar /rrele'gar/ *vt* to banish; relegate, set aside

relegir /rrele'hir/ *vt irr* to reelect. See **elegir**
relente /rre'lente/ *m*, night dew, dampness; *Inf.* cheek, impudence
relevación /rreleβa'sion; rreleβa'θion/ *f*, *Art.* relief; release; remission, exemption
relevar /rrele'βar/ *vt Art.* to work in relief; emboss; relieve, free; dismiss; excuse, pardon; aid, succor; *Fig.* aggrandize; *Mil.* relieve; *vi* carve in relief
relevo /rre'leβo/ *m*, relay; *Mil.* relief
relieve /rre'lieβe/ *m*, *Art.* relief; *pl* leftovers, remains (of food). **alto r.**, high relief. **bajo r.**, low relief
religar /rreli'gar/ *vt* to retie, fasten again; fasten more securely; solder
religión /rreli'hion/ *f*, religion; creed, faith, philosophy; devotion, religious practice. **r. reformada,** Protestantism. **entrar en r.,** *Eccl.* to profess
religiosidad /rrelihiosi'ðað/ *f*, religiosity; religiousness; conscientiousness, punctiliousness
religioso /rreli'hioso/ **(-sa)** *a* religious; punctilious, conscientious; moderate. *n* religious
relinchar /rrelin'tʃar/ *vi* to whinny, neigh
reliquia /rre'likia/ *f*, residue (gen. *pl*); *Eccl.* relic; vestige, remnant, memento; permanent disability or ailment
rellanar /rre'yanar; rre'ʎanar/ *vt* to make level again; *vr* stretch oneself at full length
rellano /rre'yano; rre'ʎano/ *m*, landing (of a staircase); level stretch (of ground)
rellenar /rreye'nar; rreʎe'nar/ *vt* to refill, replenish; fill up; *Mas.* plug, point; *Cul.* stuff; *Inf.* cram with food (gen. *vr*)
relleno /rre'yeno; rre'ʎeno/ *m*, *Cul.* stuffing; replenishing; filling; *Fig.* padding (of speeches, etc.)
reloj /rre'loh/ *m*, clock; watch. **r. de arena,** hourglass. **r. de bolsillo,** watch. **r. de la muerte,** deathwatch beetle. **r. de péndulo,** grandfather clock. **r. de pulsera,** wristwatch. **r. de repetición,** repeater. **r. de sol** *or* **r. solar,** sundial
relojera /rrelo'hera/ *f*, clock stand; watch case
relojería /rrelohe'ria/ *f*, watch or clock making; jeweler, watch maker's shop
relojero /rrelo'hero/ **(-ra)** *n* watch maker, watch repairer
reluciente /rrelu'siente; rrelu'θiente/ *a* shining, sparkling; shiny
relucir /rrelu'sir; rrelu'θir/ *vi irr* to glitter, sparkle, gleam; *Fig.* shine, excel. See **lucir**
reluctante /rreluk'tante/ *a* unruly, refractory, disobedient
relumbrante /rrelum'βrante/ *a* resplendent, dazzling
relumbrar /rrelum'βrar/ *vi* to be resplendent, shine, glitter
remachar /rrema'tʃar/ *vt* to rivet; *Fig.* clinch
remache /rre'matʃe/ *m*, riveting; rivet
remaduro, -a /rrema'ðuro/ *a*, *Lat. Am.* overripe
remanente /rrema'nente/ *m*, remains, residue
remanso /rre'manso/ *m*, backwater; stagnant water; sloth, dilatoriness
remar /rre'mar/ *vi* to row, paddle, scull; toil, strive
rematadamente /rremataða'mente/ *adv* completely, entirely, absolutely
rematado, -a /rrema'taðo/ *a* beyond hope, extremely ill; utterly lost; *Law.* convicted
rematar /rrema'tar/ *vt* to end, finish; finish off, kill; knock down at auction; *Sew.* finish; *vi* end; *vr* be ruined or spoiled
remate /rre'mate/ *m*, end, conclusion; extremity; *Archit.* coping; *Archit.* terminal; highest bid; auction. **de r.,** utterly hopeless
rematista /rrema'tista/ *mf*, *Lat. Am.* auctioneer
rembarcar /rrembar'kar/ *vt* to reembark, reship
rembolsable /rrembol'saβle/ *a* repayable
rembolsar /rrembol'sar/ *vt* to recover (money); refund, return (money)
rembolso /rrem'βolso/ *m*, repayment. **contra r.,** cash on delivery, C.O.D.
remedar /rreme'ðar/ *vt* to copy, imitate; mimic
remediador /rremeðia'ðor/ **(-ra)** *a* remedying. *n* benefactor, helper

remediar /rreme'ðiar/ *vt* to remedy; aid, help; save from danger; prevent (trouble)
remedio /rre'meðio/ *m*, remedy; emendation, correction; help; refuge, protection; *Med.* remedy. **No hay más r.,** There's nothing else to do, It's the only way open. **no tener más r.,** to be unable to help (doing something), be obliged to
remedo /rre'meðo/ *m*, imitation; poor copy
remembranza /rremem'βransa; rremem'βranθa/ *f*, remembrance, memory
rememorar /rrememo'rar/ *vt* to remember, recall to mind
remendar /rremen'dar/ *vt irr* to mend, patch; darn; repair; correct. See **recomendar**
remendón /rremen'don/ **(-ona)** *n* cobbler; mender of old clothes
remero /rre'mero/ **(-ra)** *n* oarsman, rower; sculler
remesa /rre'mesa/ *f*, remittance; consignment, shipment
remesar /rreme'sar/ **(se)** *vt* and *vr* to pluck out (hair); *vt Com.* remit; consign
remezón /rreme'son; rreme'θon/ *m*, *Lat. Am.* (earth) tremor
remiendo /rre'miendo/ *m*, *Sew.* patch; mend, darn; emendation; *Inf.* insignia of one of the Spanish military orders. **a remiendos,** *Inf.* piecemeal
remilgarse /rremil'garse/ *vr* to preen oneself, be overdressed
remilgo /rre'milgo/ *m*, affectation; mannerism; prudery, squeamishness
reminiscencia /rreminis'sensia; rreminis'θenθia/ *f*, reminiscence; memory, recollection
remirado /rremi'raðo/ *a* wary, cautious, prudent, circumspect
remirar /rremi'rar/ *vt* to revise, go over again; *vr* take great care over; behold with pleasure
remise /rre'mise/ *m*, *Argentina* limousine, hired taxi
remisión /rremi'sion/ *f*, sending; remission; pardon, forgiveness; foregoing, relinquishment; abatement, diminution; *Lit.* reference, allusion
remiso /rre'miso/ *a* timid, spiritless; languid, slow
remitente /rremi'tente/ *mf* sender. *a* sending
remitir /rremi'tir/ *vt* to remit, send; pardon, forgive; defer, postpone; abate, diminish; relinquish, forgo; *Lit.* refer; *vr* remit, submit, consult; refer (to), cite
remo /'rremo/ *m*, oar, scull, paddle; arm or leg (of men or animals, gen. *pl*); wing (gen. *pl*); hard, continuous toil; galleys. **al r.,** by dint of rowing; *Inf.* struggling with hardships
remojar /rremo'har/ *vt* to soak, steep; celebrate by drinking
remojo /rre'moho/ *m*, soaking, steeping
remolacha /rremo'latʃa/ *f*, beet
remolcador /rremolka'ðor/ *m*, *Naut.* tow, tugboat. *a Naut.* towing
remolcar /rremol'kar/ *vt* (*Naut. Auto.*) to tow; *Fig.* press into service, use
remoler /rremo'ler/ *vi*, *Lat. Am.* to live it up, live the life of Riley
remolinar /rremoli'nar/ *vi* to spin, whirl, eddy; *vr* throng, swarm
remolino /rremo'lino/ *m*, whirlwind; eddy, swirl; whirlpool; crowd, throng, swarm; disturbance, riot
remolonear /rremolone'ar/ *vi Inf.* to loiter, lag; avoid work; be lax or dilatory
remolque /rre'molke/ *m*, towage, towing; towline; barge; *Auto.* trailer. **a r.,** on tow
remonta /rre'monta/ *f*, resoling (of shoes); leather gusset (of riding breeches); *Mil.* remount
remontar /rremon'tar/ *vt* to scare off (game); *Mil.* supply with fresh horses; resole (shoes); *Fig.* rise to great heights (of oratory, etc.); *vr* soar (of birds); (*with prep a*) date from, go back to; originate in
remoquete /rremo'kete/ *m*, blow with the fist; witticism; *Inf.* flirtation, courtship
rémora /'rremora/ *f*, *Ichth.* remora; delay, hindrance
remorder /rremor'ðer/ *vt irr* to bite again or repeatedly; *Fig.* gnaw, nag, cause uneasiness or remorse; *vr* show one's feelings. See **morder**
remordimiento /rremorði'miento/ *m*, remorse

remoto /rre'moto/ *a* distant, remote; unlikely, improbable

remover /rremo'βer/ *vt irr* to remove, move; stir; turn over; dismiss, discharge. See **mover**

remozar /rremo'sar; rremo'θar/ *vt* to cause to appear young; freshen up, bring up to date; *vr* look young

remplazar /rrempla'sar; rrempla'θar/ *vt* to replace; exchange, substitute; succeed, take the place of

remplazo /rrem'plaso; rrem'plaθo/ *m*, replacement; exchange, substitute; successor; *Mil.* replacement

remuda /rre'muða/ *f*, replacement, exchange

remudar /rremu'ðar/ *vt* to replace

remuneración /rremunera'sion; rremunera'θion/ *f*, remuneration; reward

remunerador /rremunera'ðor/ **(-ra)** *a* remunerative, recompensing. *n*

remunerar /rremune'rar/ *vt* to recompense, reward

remusgar /rremus'gar/ *vi* to suspect, imagine

renacentista /rrenasen'tista; rrenaθen'tista/ *a* renaissance

renacer /rrena'ser; rrena'θer/ *vi irr* to be reborn. See **nacer**

renacimiento /rrenasi'miento; rrenaθi'miento/ *m*, rebirth; Renaissance

renacuajo /rrena'kuaho/ *m*, tadpole; *Mech.* frog; *Inf.* twerp

rencarcelar /rrenkarse'lar; rrenkarθe'lar/ *vt* to reimprison

rencarnación /rrenkarna'sion; rrenkarna'θion/ *f*, reincarnation

rencarnar /rrenkar'nar/ **(se)** *vi* and *vr* to be reincarnated

rencilla /rren'siya; rren'θiʎa/ *f*, grudge, grievance, resentment

rencilloso /rrensi'yoso; rrenθi'ʎoso/ *a* peevish, easily offended, touchy

rencor /rren'kor/ *m*, rancor, spite, old grudge. **guardar r.**, to hold a grudge

rencoroso /rrenko'roso/ *a* rancorous, malicious, spiteful

rencuadernar /rrenkuaðer'nar/ *vt* to rebind (books)

rencuentro /rren'kuentro/ *m*, collision; *Mil.* encounter, clash

rendición /rrendi'sion; rrendi'θion/ *f*, surrender; yield, profit

rendido /rren'diðo/ *a* submissive, obsequious

rendija /rren'diha/ *f*, crevice, cleft, crack, fissure

rendimiento /rrendi'miento/ *m*, weariness, fatigue; submissiveness, obsequiousness; yield, profit; *Mech.* efficiency

rendir /rren'dir/ *vt irr Mil.* to cause to surrender; defeat; overcome, conquer; give back, return; yield, provide; tire, exhaust; vomit; pay, render; *vr* be exhausted, be worn out; surrender. *Mil.* **r. el puesto,** to retire from or give up a post. See **pedir**

renegado /rrene'gaðo/ **(-da)** *n* renegade, apostate; turncoat; *Inf.* malignant person. *a* renegade

renegador /rrenega'ðor/ **(-ra)** *n* blasphemer; foulmouthed person

renegar /rrene'gar/ *vt irr* to deny, disown; loathe, hate; *vi* (*with de*) apostatize; blaspheme; *Inf.* curse. See **cegar**

renganchar /rrengan'tʃar/ **(se)** *vt* and *vr Mil.* to reenlist

renganche /rren'gantʃe/ *m*, *Mil.* reenlistment

renglón /rren'glon/ *m*, *Print.* line; *pl* writing, composition, line (of a poem)

renguear /rrengue'ar/ *vi*, *Lat. Am.* to limp

renguera /rren'guera/ *f*, *Lat. Am.* limp

reniego /rre'niego/ *m*, blasphemy; *Inf.* foul language, cursing

renitencia /rreni'tensia; rreni'tenθia/ *f*, repugnance

renombrado /rrenom'βraðo/ *a* illustrious, famous

renombre /rre'nombre/ *m*, surname; renown, reputation, fame

renovable /rreno'βaβle/ *a* renewable, replaceable

renovación /rrenoβa'sion; rrenoβa'θion/ *f*, replacement; renewal; renovation; transformation, reform

renovador /rrenoβa'ðor/ **(-ra)** *n* reformer; renovator. *a* renovating; reforming

renovar /rreno'βar/ *vt irr* to renew; renovate; replace; exchange; reiterate, repeat. See **contar**

renta /'rrenta/ *f*, yield, profit; income; revenue; government securities; rent; tax

rentar /rren'tar/ *vt* to yield, produce an income

rentero /rren'tero/ **(-ra)** *n* tenant farmer. *m*, one who farms out land

rentista /rren'tista/ *mf* financier; bondholder; person who lives on a private income, rentier

rentístico /rren'tistiko/ *a* revenue, financial

renuente /rre'nuente/ *a* refractory, willful

renuevo /rre'nueβo/ *m*, *Bot.* shoot; renewal

renuncia /rre'nunsia; rre'nunθia/ *f*, renunciation; resignation; abandonment, relinquishment

renunciar /rrenun'siar; rrenun'θiar/ *vt* to renounce; refuse; scorn; abandon, relinquish; resign; revoke (at cards). **r. a,** to give up

renuncio /rre'nunsio; rre'nunθio/ *m*, revoke (cards); *Inf.* falsehood

reñidamente /rreɲi'ðamente/ *adv* strongly, stubbornly, fiercely

reñir /rre'ɲir/ *vi irr* to quarrel, dispute; fight; be on bad terms, fall out; *vt* scold; fight (battles, etc.). See **ceñir**

reo /'rreo/ *mf* criminal; offender, guilty party; *Law.* defendant

reojo /rre'oho/ *m*, **(mirar de)** to look out of the corner of the eye; *Fig.* look askance

reorganización /rreorganisa'θor; rreorganiθa'ðor/ **(-ra)** *a* reorganizing. *n* reorganizer

reóstato /rre'ostato/ *m*, rheostat

repantigarse /rrepanti'garse/ *vr* to stretch out one's legs, make oneself comfortable

reparable /rrepa'raβle/ *a* remediable, reparable; worthy of note

reparación /rrepara'sion; rrepara'θion/ *f*, repair, mending, reparation, satisfaction; indemnity, compensation

reparada /rrepa'raða/ *f*, shying (of horses)

reparador /rrepara'ðor/ *a* repairing, mending; faultfinding; restoring; satisfying, compensating

reparar /rrepa'rar/ *vt* to repair; restore; consider; correct, remedy; atone for, expiate; indemnify; hold up, detain; protect, guard; (*with en*) notice; *Lat. Am.* to ape, imitate, mimic; *vi* halt, be detained; *vr* control oneself

reparo /rre'paro/ *m*, repair; restoration; remedy; note, reflection; warning; doubt, scruple; guard, protection; parry (at fencing)

repartición /rreparti'sion; rreparti'θion/ *f*, distribution

repartidero /rreparti'ðero/ *a* distributable

repartidor /rreparti'ðor/ **(-ra)** *a* distributing. *n* distributor; tax assessor

repartimiento /rreparti'miento/ *m*, distribution, allotment; assessment

repartir /rrepar'tir/ *vt* to distribute; share out; allot; deal (cards); assess; *Com.* deliver

reparto /rre'parto/ *m*, distribution; assessment; delivery (of letters, etc.); *Theat.* cast; deal (at cards); *Lat. Am.* building site, construction site

repasador /rrepasa'ðor/ *m*, *Lat. Am.* dish cloth, dishrag

repasar /rrepa'sar/ *vt* to pass by again; peruse, reexamine; brush up, revise; skim, glance over; mend, repair (garments); edit, revise; hone

repaso /rre'paso/ *m*, second passage through; reexamination, perusal; revision, editing; brushing up, revision; repair, mending; *Inf.* dressing-down, scolding

repatriación /rrepatria'sion; rrepatria'θion/ *f*, repatriation

repatriado /rrepa'triaðo/ **(-da)** *n* repatriate

repatriar /rrepa'triar/ *vt* to repatriate; *vi* and *vr* return to one's own country

repecho /rre'petʃo/ *m*, steep slope. **a r.,** uphill

repelar /rrepe'lar/ *vt* to pull by the hair; put through its paces (of a horse); clip, cut; remove, diminish

repeler /rrepe'ler/ *vt* to repel, throw back; reject, refute

repelo /rre'pelo/ *m*, anything against the grain; *Inf.* skirmish; reluctance, repugnance

repente /rre'pente/ *m*, *Inf.* sudden or unexpected movement. **de r.**, suddenly

repentino /rrepen'tino/ *a* sudden, unexpected

repentizar /rrepenti'sar; rrepenti'θar/ *vi Mus.* to sight-read

repercusión /rreperku'sion/ *f*, repercussion; vibration

repercutir /rreperku'tir/ *vi* to recoil, rebound; *vr* reverberate; reecho; *Fig.* have repercussions; *vt Med.* repel

repertorio /rreper'torio/ *m*, repertory

repesar /rrepe'sar/ *vt* to reweigh, weigh again

repetición /rrepeti'sion; rrepeti'θion/ *f*, repetition; *Art.* replica, copy; repeater (in clocks); recital

repetidamente /rrepetiða'mente/ *adv* repeatedly

repetir /rrepe'tir/ *vt irr* to repeat, do over again; reiterate; *Art.* copy, make a replica of; recite. See **pedir**

repicar /rrepi'kar/ *vt* to chop, mince; peal (of bells); prick again; *vr* pride oneself (on), boast

repique /rre'pike/ *m*, chopping, mincing; peal, pealing (of bells); disagreement, grievance

repisa /rre'pisa/ *f*, *Archit.* bracket; ledge; shelf. **r. de chimenea**, mantelpiece

replantar /rreplan'tar/ *vt* to replant; transplant

repleción /rreple'sion; rreple'θion/ *f*, repletion, satiety

replegar /rreple'gar/ *vt irr* to refold, fold many times; *vr Mil.* retreat in good order. See **cegar**

repleto /rre'pleto/ *a* replete

réplica /'rreplika/ *f*, reply, answer; replica

replicar /rrepli'kar/ *vi* to contradict, dispute; answer, reply. **¡No me repliques!** *Inf.* Don't answer back!

repliegue /rre'pliege/ *m*, double fold, crease; doubling, folding; *Mil.* withdrawal

repoblación /rrepoβla'sion; rrepoβla'θion/ *f*, repeopling, repopulation

repoblar /rrepo'βlar/ *vt* to repeople, repopulate

repollo /rre'poɣo; rre'poʎo/ *m*, white cabbage; heart (of lettuce, etc.)

reponer /rrepo'ner/ *vt irr* to replace; reinstate; restore; reply; *vr* recover, regain (possessions); grow well again; grow calm. See **poner**

reportación /rreporta'sion; rreporta'θion/ *f*, serenity, moderation

reportaje /rrepor'tahe/ *m*, journalistic report

reportar /rrepor'tar/ *vt* to restrain, moderate; achieve, obtain; carry; bring; *vr* control oneself

reporte /rre'porte/ *m*, report, news; rumor

reporterismo /rreporte'rismo/ *m*, newspaper reporting

reportero /rrepor'tero/ **(-ra)** *a* news, report. *n* reporter

reposado /rrepo'saðo/ *a* quiet, peaceful, tranquil

reposar /rrepo'sar/ *vi* to rest, repose oneself; sleep, doze; lie in the grave; settle (liquids); rest (on)

reposición /rreposi'sion; rreposi'θion/ *f*, replacement; restoration; renewal; recovery (of health); *Theat.* revival

repositorio /rreposi'torio/ *m*, repository

reposo /rre'poso/ *m*, rest, repose; peace, tranquility; sleep

repostada /rrepos'taða/ *f*, *Lat. Am.* cheeky reply, saucy retort

repostería /rreposte'ria/ *f*, confectioner's shop; pantry; butler's pantry

repostero /rrepos'tero/ *m*, confectioner, pastry cook

repreguntar /rrepregun'tar/ *vt* to cross-examine

reprender /rrepren'der/ *vt* to scold, reprimand, rebuke

reprensible /rrepren'siβle/ *a* reprehensible, censurable

reprensión /rrepren'sion/ *f*, scolding, reprimand, rebuke

represa /rre'presa/ *f*, damming, holding back (water); dam, lock; restraining, controlling

represalia /rrepre'salia/ *f*, reprisal (gen. *pl*); retaliation

represar /rrepre'sar/ *vt* to dam, harness (water); *Naut.* retake, recapture; *Fig.* restrain, control

representación /rrepresenta'sion; rrepresenta'θion/ *f*, representation; *Theat.* performance; authority; dignity; *Com.* agency; portrait, image; depiction, expression; petition

representador /rrepresenta'ðor/ *a* representative

representante /rrepresen'tante/ *a* representative. *mf* representative; actor; performer

representar /rrepresen'tar/ *vt* to represent; *Theat.* perform; depict, express; describe, portray; *vr* imagine, picture to oneself

representativo /rrepresenta'tiβo/ *a* representative

represión /rrepre'sion/ *f*, repression; recapture

represivo /rrepre'siβo/ *a* repressive

reprimenda /rrepri'menda/ *f*, rebuke, reprimand

reprimir /rrepri'mir/ *vt* to repress, restrain, control; *vr* restrain oneself

reprobación /rreproβa'sion; rreproβa'θion/ *f*, censure; reprobation

reprobar /rrepro'βar/ *vt irr* to reprove; censure; fail (in an exam). See **probar**

réprobo /'rreproβo/ **(-ba)** *n* reprobate

reprochar /rrepro'tʃar/ *vt* to reproach

reproche /rre'protʃe/ *m*, reproaching; rebuke, reproach

reproducción /rreproðuk'sion; rreproðuk'θion/ *f*, reproduction. **r. a gran escala**, large-scale model

reproducir /rreproðu'sir; rreproðu'θir/ *vt irr* to reproduce. See **conducir**

reproductor /rreproðuk'tor/ **(-ra)** *a* reproductive. *n* breeding animal

reps /rreps/ *m*, rep (fabric)

reptil /rrep'til/ *a* reptilian; crawling. *m*, reptile

república /rre'puβlika/ *f*, republic; state, commonwealth. **la r. de las letras**, the republic of letters

República Dominicana /rre'puβlika domini'kana/ Dominican Republic

República Malgache /rre'puβlika mal'gatʃe/ Republic of Madagascar

republicanismo /rrepuβlika'nismo/ *m*, republicanism

republicano /rrepuβli'kano/ **(-na)** *a* and *n* republican

repudiación /rrepuðia'sion; rrepuðia'θion/ *f*, repudiation

repudiar /rrepu'ðiar/ *vt* to cast off (a wife); repudiate, renounce

repuesto /rre'puesto/ *a* retired, hidden. *m*, stock, provision; serving table; pantry; stake (at cards, etc.). **de r.**, spare, extra

repugnancia /rrepug'nansia; rrepug'nanθia/ *f*, inconsistency, contradiction; aversion, dislike; reluctance; repugnance

repugnante /rrepug'nante/ *a* repugnant, loathsome

repugnar /rrepug'nar/ *vt* to contradict, be inconsistent with; hate, be averse to (e.g. *La idea me repugna,* I hate the idea)

repujado /rrepu'haðo/ *m*, repoussé work

repujar /rrepu'har/ *vt* to work in repoussé

repulir /rrepu'lir/ *vt* to repolish, reburnish; *vt* and *vr* make up too much, overdress

repulsa /rre'pulsa/ *f*, snub, rebuff; rejection; repulse

repulsar /rrepul'sar/ *vt* to decline, reject; repulse; deny, refuse; rebuff

repulsión /rrepul'sion/ *f*, repulsion; rebuff; aversion, dislike

repulsivo /rrepul'siβo/ *a* repellent

repunta /rre'punta/ *f*, headland, cape; *Fig.* first sign; *Inf.* disgust; caprice; fight

reputación /rreputa'sion; rreputa'θion/ *f*, reputation

reputar /rrepu'tar/ *vt* to believe, consider (e.g. *Le reputo por honrado,* I believe him to be an honorable man); appreciate, esteem

requebrar /rreke'βrar/ *vt irr* to break into smaller pieces; make love to, woo; compliment, flatter. See **quebrar**

requemado /rreke'maðo/ *a* sunburned; brown

requemar /rreke'mar/ *vt* to burn again; overcook; dry up, parch (of plants, etc.); burn (the mouth) (of spicy foods, etc.); *vr Fig.* suffer inwardly

requerimiento /rrekeri'miento/ *m*, requirement, demand; *Law.* summons

requerir /rreke'rir/ *vt irr* to inform, notify; examine;

need, necessitate; require; summon; woo; persuade. See **sentir**

requesón /rreke'son/ m, cream cheese; curd

requetebién /rrekete'βien/ adv Inf. exceedingly well

requiebro /rre'kieβro/ m, compliment, expression of love; wooing, flirtation

requintar /rrekin'tar/ vt, Lat. Am. to tighten

requisa /rre'kisa/ f, inspection, visitation; Mil. requisitioning; Lat. Am. confiscation

requisar /rreki'sar/ vt Mil. to requisition

requisito /rreki'sito/ m, requisite

res /rres/ f, animal, beast; head of cattle. Lat. Am. **carne de r.**, steak

resabiar /rresa'βiar/ vt to make vicious, cause bad habits; vr contract bad habits or vices; be discontented; relish

resabio /rre'saβio/ m, disagreeable aftertaste; bad habit, vice

resaca /rre'saka/ f, surf, undertow, surge; Com. redraft

resacar /rresa'kar/ vt to distil

resalado /rresa'laðo/ a Inf. very witty; most attractive

resaltar /rresal'tar/ vi to rebound; project, jut out; grow loose, fall out; Fig. stand out, be prominent

resalto /rre'salto/ m, rebound; projection

resarcir /rresar'sir; rresar'θir/ vt to compensate, indemnify

resbaladizo /rresβala'ðiso; rresβala'ðiθo/ a slippery; difficult, delicate (of a situation)

resbalar /rresβa'lar/ vi to slip; slide; skid; err, fall into sin

resbalón /rresβa'lon/ m, slip; slide; skid; temptation, error

rescatador /rreskata'ðor/ (**-ra**) n ransomer; rescuer

rescatar /rreska'tar/ vt to ransom; redeem, buy back; barter; free, rescue; Fig. redeem (time, etc.)

rescate /rres'kate/ m, ransom; redemption; barter; amount of ransom

rescindir /rressin'dir; rresθin'dir/ vt to annul, repeal, rescind

rescoldo /rres'koldo/ m, ember, cinder; scruple, qualm, doubt

resentimiento /rresenti'miento/ m, deterioration, impairment; animosity, resentment

resentirse /rresen'tirse/ vr irr to deteriorate, be impaired; be hurt or offended. See **sentir**

reseña /rre'seɲa/ f, Mil. review; short description; review (of a book)

reseñar /rrese'ɲar/ vt Mil. to review; describe briefly, outline

reserva /rre'serβa/ f, store, stock; exception, qualification; reticence; restraint, moderation; (Eccl. Law.) reservation; (Mil. Naut.) reserve. **sin r.**, frankly, without reserve

reservación /rreserβa'sion; rreserβa'θion/ f, reservation; scruple

reservado /rreser'βaðo/ a reserved, reticent; prudent, moderate; kept, reserved. m, reserved compartment; private apartment, private garden, etc.

reservar /rreser'βar/ vt to keep, hold; postpone; reserve (rooms, etc.); exempt; keep secret; withhold (information); Eccl. reserve; vr await a better opportunity; be cautious

reservista /rreser'βista/ a (Mil. Nav.) reserved. mf reservist

resfriado /rres'friaðo/ m, Med. cold, chill

resfriar /rres'friar/ vt to chill; Fig. cool, moderate; vi grow cold; vr catch a cold; Fig. cool off (of love, etc.)

resguardar /rresguar'ðar/ vt to protect; shelter; vr take refuge; (with de) guard against; (with con) shelter by

resguardo /rres'guarðo/ m, protection, guard; Com. guarantee, security; Com. voucher; preservation; vigilance (to prevent smuggling, etc.); contraband guards

residencia /rresi'ðensia; rresi'ðenθia/ f, stay, residence; home, domicile; Eccl. residence

residencial /rresiðen'sial; rresiðen'θial/ a residential; resident, residentiary

residente /rresi'ðente/ a resident. mf inhabitant. m, resident, minister resident (diplomatic)

residir /rresi'ðir/ vi to live, inhabit; reside officially; be found, be, exist

residuo /rre'siðuo/ m, residue, remainder; Math. remainder; Chem. residue

resignación /rresigna'sion; rresigna'θion/ f, resignation; fortitude, submission

resignar /rresig'nar/ vt to resign, relinquish; vr submit, resign oneself

resina /rre'sina/ f, resin

resistencia /rresis'tensia; rresis'tenθia/ f, resistance, opposition; endurance; (Phys. Mech. Psychol.) resistance

resistente /rresis'tente/ a resistant; tough; hardy (of plants)

resistir /rresis'tir/ vt to resist, oppose; reject; vt endure, bear; resist; vr fight, resist

resollar /rreso'yar; rreso'ʎar/ vi irr to breathe; pant. See **degollar**

resolución /rresolu'sion; rresolu'θion/ f, decision; boldness, daring; determination, resolution; decree

resoluto /rreso'luto/ a resolute, bold; brief, concise; able, expert

resolver /rresol'βer/ vt irr to determine, decide; summarize; solve; dissolve; analyze; (Phys. Med.) resolve; vr decide, determine; be reduced to, become; Med. resolve. Pres. Ind. **resuelvo, resuelves, resuelve, resuelven**. Past Part. **resuelto**. Pres. Subjunc. **resuelva, resuelvas, resuelva, resuelvan**

resonancia /rreso'nansia; rreso'nanθia/ f, resonance, sonority, ring; fame, reputation

resonante /rreso'nante/ a resonant; resounding

resonar /rreso'nar/ vi irr to resound, echo. See **tronar**

resoplido, resoplo /rreso'pliðo, rre'soplo/ m, heavy breathing, pant, snort

resorber /rresor'βer/ vt to reabsorb

resorción /rresor'sion; rresor'θion/ f, reabsorption

resorte /rre'sorte/ m, Mech. spring; elasticity; Fig. means, instrument; Lat. Am. rubber band

respaldo /rres'paldo/ m, back (of chairs, etc.); reverse side (of a piece of paper), Com. endorsement

respectivo /rrespek'tiβo/ a respective

respecto /rres'pekto/ m, relation, regard, reference. **con r. a**, or **r. a**, with regard to, with respect to, concerning

respetabilidad /rrespetaβili'ðað/ f, respectability; worthiness

respetable /rrespe'taβle/ a worthy of respect; respectable; Fig. considerable, large

respetar /rrespe'tar/ vt to respect, revere

respeto /rres'peto/ m, respect, honor; consideration, reason. **de r.**, spare, extra; special, ceremonial

respetuoso /rrespe'tuoso/ a venerable, worthy of honor; respectful, courteous

respingar /rrespiŋ'gar/ vi to flinch, wince, kick; Inf. be uneven, rise (hem of garments); Inf. do (a thing) grumblingly

respingo /rres'piŋgo/ m, wincing; jerk, shake; Inf. gesture of reluctance or dislike

respiración /rrespira'sion; rrespira'θion/ f, breathing, respiration; ventilation

respiradero /rrespira'ðero/ m, ventilator; air hole, vent; rest, breathing space

respirador /rrespira'ðor/ a breathing; respiratory. m, respirator

respirar /rrespi'rar/ vi to breathe; exhale, give off; take courage; have a breathing space, rest; Inf. speak. **sin r.**, continuously, without stopping for breath

respiratorio /rrespira'torio/ a respiratory

respiro /rres'piro/ m, breathing; breathing space, respite

resplandecer /rresplande'ser; rresplande'θer/ vi irr to glitter, gleam; shine, excel. See **conocer**

resplandeciente /rresplande'siente; rresplande'θiente/ a glittering, resplendent, shining

resplandor /rresplan'dor/ m, radiance, brilliance; glitter, gleam; majesty, splendor

responder /rrespon'der/ vt to reply; satisfy, answer; vi reecho; requite, return; produce, provide; Fig. answer, have the desired effect; Com. (with de) answer for, guarantee; Com. correspond

respondón /rrespon'don/ *a Inf.* pert, impudent, cheeky, given to answering back

responsabilidad /rresponsaβili'ðað/ *f,* responsibility

responsable /rrespon'saβle/ *a* responsible

responso /rres'ponso/ *m, Ecl.* response, responsory

respuesta /rres'puesta/ *f,* answer, reply; response; refutation; repartee

resquebradura /rreskeβra'ðura/ *f,* fissure, crevice, crack

resquebrajarse /rreskeβra'harse/ *vr* to crack, split

resquemar /rreske'mar/ *vt* to bite, sting (of hot dishes)

resquicio /rres'kisio; rres'kiθio/ *m,* crack, chink, slit; opportunity; *Lat. Am.* sign, trace, vestige

resta /'rresta/ *f, Math.* subtraction; *Math.* remainder

restablecer /rrestaβle'ser; rrestaβle'θer/ *vt irr* to reestablish; restore; *vr* recover one's health; reestablish oneself. See **conocer**

restablecimiento /rrestaβlesi'miento; rrestaβleθi'miento/ *m,* reestablishment; restoration

restañar /rresta'ɲar/ *vt* to re-tin; staunch

restar /rres'tar/ *vt Math.* to subtract; deduct; return (a ball); *vi* remain. **No me resta más que decir adiós,** It only remains for me to say good-by

restauración /rrestaura'sion; rrestaura'θion/ *f,* restoration; renovation

restaurante /rrestau'rante/ *m,* restaurant

restaurantero /rrestauran'tero/ *m,* restaurant operator; restaurant owner; restaurateur

restaurar /rrestau'rar/ *vt* to recover, recuperate; renovate, repair; restore

restaurativo /rrestaura'tiβo/ *a* and *m,* restorative

restinga /rres'tiŋga/ *f,* sandbank, bar

restitución /rrestitu'sion; rrestitu'θion/ *f,* restitution

restituible /rresti'tuiβle/ *a* returnable, replaceable

restituir /rresti'tuir/ *vt irr* to return, give back; restore; reestablish; *vr* return to one's place of departure. See **huir**

resto /'rresto/ *m,* rest, balance; *Math.* remainder; *pl* remains

restorán /rresto'ran/ *m,* restaurant

restricción /rrestrik'sion; rrestrik'θion/ *f,* limitation, restriction

restrictivo /rrestrik'tiβo/ *a* restrictive; restraining

restringir /rrestriŋ'gir/ *vt* to limit, restrict; contract

resucitar /rresusi'tar; rresuθi'tar/ *vt* to raise from the dead; *Fig. Inf.* revive; *vi* resuscitate

resuello /rre'sueyo; rre'sueʎo/ *m,* breathing; panting, hard breathing

resuelto /rre'suelto/ *a* audacious, daring; resolute, capable

resulta /rre'sulta/ *f,* consequence, result; decision, resolution; vacant post. **de resultas de,** as the result of; in consequence of

resultado /rresul'taðo/ *m,* result, consequence, outcome

resultar /rresul'tar/ *vi* to result, follow; turn out, happen; result (in); *Inf.* turn out well. **El vestido no me resulta,** The dress isn't a success on me

resumen /rre'sumen/ *m,* summary. **en r.,** in short

resumir /rresu'mir/ *vt* to summarize, abridge; sum up, recapitulate; *vr* be contained, be included

resurgimiento /rresurhi'miento/ *m,* resurgence, revival

resurgir /rresur'hir/ *vi* to reappear, rise again, revive; resuscitate

resurrección /rresurrek'sion; rresurrek'θion/ *f,* resurrection

retablo /rre'taβlo/ *m, Archit.* altarpiece, retable; frieze; series of pictures

retador, -a /rreta'ðor/ *mf, Lat. Am.* challenger

retaguardia /rreta'guarðia/ *f,* rear guard. **a r.,** in the rear. **picar la r.,** to harass the rear guard

retajar /rreta'har/ *vt* to cut in the round; circumcise

retal /rre'tal/ *m,* clipping, filing, shaving; remnant

retama /rre'tama/ *f, Bot.* broom. **r. común** *or* **r. de olor,** Spanish broom. **r. de escobas,** common broom

retar /rre'tar/ *vt* to challenge; *Inf.* reproach, accuse

retardar /rretar'ðar/ *vt* to retard, delay

retardo /rre'tarðo/ *m,* delay, retardment

retazo /rre'taso; rre'taθo/ *m,* remnant, cutting; excerpt, fragment

retemblar /rretem'βlar/ *vi* to quiver, tremble constantly

retemplar /rretem'plar/ *vt, Lat. Am.* to cheer up

retén /rre'ten/ *m,* stock, reserve, provision; *Mil.* reserve

retención /rreten'sion; rreten'θion/ *f,* retention

retener /rrete'ner/ *vt irr* to keep, retain; recollect, remember; keep back; *Law.* detain; deduct. See **tener**

retenidamente /rreteniða'mente/ *adv* retentively

retentiva /rreten'tiβa/ *f,* retentiveness, memory

retentivo /rreten'tiβo/ *a* retentive

reticencia /rreti'sensia; rreti'θenθia/ *f,* reticence

reticente /rreti'sente; rreti'θente/ *a* reticent

retículo /rre'tikulo/ *m,* reticulum, network; *Phys.* reticle

retina /rre'tina/ *f,* retina

retintín /rretin'tin/ *m,* ringing; tinkling; *Inf.* sarcastic tone

retiñir /rreti'ɲir/ *vi* to tinkle, clink; jingle

retirada /rreti'raða/ *f,* withdrawal; retirement; seclusion, refuge; *Mil.* retreat

retirado /rreti'raðo/ *a* remote, secluded; *Mil.* retired

retirar /rreti'rar/ *vt* to withdraw; remove; repel, throw back; hide, put aside; *vr* withdraw; retire; *Mil.* retreat

retiro /rre'tiro/ *m,* withdrawal; removal; seclusion, privacy; *Mil.* retreat; retirement; *Eccl.* retreat. **dar el r. (a),** to place on the retired list

reto /'rreto/ *m,* challenge; threat

retocar /rreto'kar/ *vt* to touch again or repeatedly; *Photo.* retouch; restore (pictures); *Fig.* put the finishing touch to

retoñar /rreto'ɲar/ *vi* to sprout, shoot; *Fig.* revive, resuscitate

retoño /rre'toɲo/ *m,* sprout, shoot

retoque /rre'toke/ *m,* frequent touching; finishing touch; touch, slight attack

retorcer /rretor'ser; rretor'θer/ *vt irr* to twist; contort; confound with one's own argument; misconstrue, distort; *vr* contort; writhe. See **torcer**

retórica /rre'torika/ *f,* rhetoric; *pl Inf.* quibbling

retórico /rre'toriko/ **(-ca)** *a* rhetorical. *n* rhetorician

retornar /rretor'nar/ *vt* to return, give back; turn, twist; turn back; *vi* and *vr* return, go back

retorno /rre'torno/ *m,* return, going back; recompense, repayment; exchange; return journey

retorsión /rretor'sion/ *f,* twisting, writhing; *Fig.* misconstruction

retortijón /rretorti'hon/ *m,* twisting, curling. **r. de tripas,** stomachache

retozar /rreto'sar; rreto'θar/ *vi* to skip, frisk, frolic, gambol; romp; *Fig.* be aroused (passions)

retozón /rreto'son; rreto'θon/ *a* frolicsome

retracción /rretrak'sion; rretrak'θion/ *f,* drawing back, retraction

retractación /rretrakta'sion; rretrakta'θion/ *f,* retractation, recantation

retractar /rretrak'tar/ *vt* to retract, recant, withdraw

retráctil /rre'traktil/ *a* retractile

retraer /rretra'er/ *vt irr* to bring back again; dissuade; buy back, redeem; *vr* take refuge; retire; withdraw; go into seclusion. See **traer**

retraído /rretra'iðo/ *a* fugitive, refugee, retired, solitary; timid, nervous, unsociable

retraimiento /rretrai'miento/ *m,* withdrawal; seclusion, privacy; refuge, asylum, sanctuary; timidity, unsociability

retranca /rre'tranka/ *f, Lat. Am.* brake

retrancar /rretran'kar/ *vt, Lat. Am.* to brake

retrasar /rretra'sar/ *vt* to postpone, delay; turn back (the clock); *vi* be slow (of clocks); *vr* be behind time, be late; be backward (persons)

retraso /rre'traso/ *m,* lateness; delay, dilatoriness; loss of time (clocks); setting back (of the clock) (e.g. *El reloj lleva cinco minutos de r.,* The clock is five minutes slow)

retratar /rretra'tar/ *vt* to paint or draw the portrait of; portray, describe; photograph; copy, imitate

retratería /rretrate'ria/ *f, Lat. Am.* photographer's studio

retratista /rretra'tista/ *mf* portrait painter; photographer; portrayer

retrato /rre'trato/ *m,* portrait; portrayal; *Fig.* image, likeness

retrechería /rretretʃe'ria/ *f, Inf.* craftiness, evasiveness

retrete /rre'trete/ *m,* toilet

retribución /rretriβu'sion; rretriβu'θion/ *f,* recompense, reward

retribuir /rretri'βuir/ *vt irr* to recompense, reward. See **huir**

retroactivo /rretroak'tiβo/ *a* retroactive

retroceder /rretrose'ðer; rretroθe'ðer/ *vi* to withdraw, move back, draw back; recede

retroceso /rretro'seso; rretro'θeso/ *m,* retrocedence, withdrawal; *Med.* retrogression

retrogradación /rretrograða'sion; rretrograða'θion/ *f,* retrogression

retrógrado /rretro'graðo/ *a* retrogressive, retrograde; *Polit.* reactionary

retronar /rretro'nar/ *vi irr* to bang, thunder, resound with noise. See **tronar**

retrospectivo /rretrospek'tiβo/ *a* retrospective

retrotraer /rretrotra'er/ *vt irr* to antedate. See **traer**

retruécano /rre'truekano/ *m,* antithesis; play on words, pun

retumbante /rretum'βante/ *a* resounding; pompous, high-flown

retumbar /rretum'βar/ *vi* to resound, echo, reverberate; roll (of thunder); roar (of a cannon)

retumbo /rre'tumbo/ *m,* reverberation, echo; rumble; roll (of thunder); roar (of a cannon, etc.)

reuma /'rreuma/ *m,* rheumatism

reumático /rreu'matiko/ *a* rheumatic

reumatismo /rreuma'tismo/ *m,* rheumatism

reunión /rreu'nion/ *f,* reunion, union; meeting; assembly, gathering

reunir /rreu'nir/ *vt* to reunite; unite; join; gather, assemble; *vr* meet, assemble; unite

revacunación /rreβakuna'sion; rreβakuna'θion/ *f,* revaccination

revacunar /rreβaku'nar/ *vt* to revaccinate

revalidación /rreβaliðasion; rreβaliða'θion/ *f,* ratification, confirmation

revalidar /rreβali'ðar/ *vt* to ratify, confirm; *vr* pass a final examination

revejido /rreβe'hiðo/ *a* prematurely old

revelación /rreβela'sion; rreβela'θion/ *f,* revelation; *Photo.* developing

revelador /rreβela'ðor/ *a* revealing. *m, Photo.* developer

revelar /rreβe'lar/ *vt* to reveal; *Photo.* develop

revendedor /rreβende'ðor/ **(-ra)** *a* reselling, retail. *n* retailer

revender /rreβen'der/ *vt* to resell; retail (goods)

reventa /rre'βenta/ *f,* resale; retail

reventar /rreβen'tar/ *vi irr* to burst, explode; break in foam (waves); burst forth; *Fig.* burst (with impatience, etc.); *Inf.* explode (with anger, etc.); *vt* break, crush; *Fig.* wear out, exhaust; *Inf.* irritate, vex; *vr* burst; *Fig.* be exhausted. See **sentar**

reventón /rreβen'ton/ *a* bursting. *m,* explosion, bursting; steep hill; hole, fix, difficulty; uphill work, heavy toil

rever /rre'βer/ *vt irr* to look at again, revise; *Law.* retry. See **ver**

reverberación /rreβerβera'sion; rreβerβera'θion/ *f,* reflection (of light); reverberation, resounding

reverberar /rreβerβe'rar/ *vi* to reflect; resound, reverberate

reverbero /rreβer'βero/ *m,* reverberation; reflector; *Lat. Am.* small stove

reverdecer /rreβerðe'ser; rreβerðe'θer/ *vi irr* to grow green again; revive, acquire new vigor. See **conocer**

reverencia /rreβe'ren'sia; rreβeren'θia/ *f,* respect, veneration; bow; curtsy; *Eccl.* reverence (title)

reverencial /rreβeren'sial; rreβeren'θial/ *a* reverential, respectful

reverenciar /rreβeren'siar; rreβeren'θiar/ *vt* to revere; honor; respect

reverendo /rreβe'rendo/ *a* reverend; venerable; *Inf.* overprudent

reversión /rreβer'sion/ *f,* reversion

reverso /rre'βerso/ *m,* wrong side, back; reverse side (of coins)

reverter /rreβer'ter/ *vi irr* to overflow. See **entender**

revertir /rreβer'tir/ *vi Law.* to revert

revés /rre'βes/ *m,* wrong side, back, reverse; cuff, slap; backhand (in ballgames); check, setback, reverse; disaster, misfortune. **al r.,** on the contrary; wrong side out. **de r.,** from left to right, counterclockwise

revesado /rreβe'saðo/ *a* complicated, difficult; willful

revestimiento /rreβesti'miento/ *m, Mas.* lining, coating

revestir /rreβes'tir/ *vt* to dress; *Mas.* coat, line; *Fig.* cover, clothe; *vr* be dressed or dress oneself; *Fig.* be captivated (by an idea); become haughty or full of oneself; rise to the occasion, develop qualities necessary. See **pedir**

reviejo /rre'βieho/ *a* very old. *m,* dead branch (of trees)

revisar /rreβi'sar/ *vt* to revise; examine

revisión /rreβi'sion/ *f,* revision; reexamination; *Law.* retrial

revisor /rreβi'sor/ *a* revising, examining. *m,* reviser; ticket inspector

revista /rre'βista/ *f,* reexamination, revision; review, periodical; *Theat.* revue; reinspection; review (of a book, etc.); *Law.* new trial; *Mil.* review. **pasar r.,** to inspect; review

revivificación /rreβiβifika'sion; rreβiβifika'θion/ *f,* revivification

revivificar /rreβiβifi'kar/ *vt* to revivify, revive

revivir /rreβi'βir/ *vi* to resuscitate; revive

revocación /rreβoka'sion; rreβoka'θion/ *f,* revocation, cancellation, annulment

revocar /rreβo'kar/ *vt* to revoke, annul; dissuade; repel, throw back; wash (walls); *Law.* discharge

revolcadero /rreβolka'ðero/ *m,* bathing place (of animals)

revolcar /rreβol'kar/ *vt irr* to knock down, trample underfoot; lay flat (in an argument); *vr* wallow; dig one's heels in, be obstinate. See **volcar**

revolotear /rreβolote'ar/ *vi* to flutter, fly around; twirl; *vt* hurl, toss

revoltillo /rreβol'tiyo; rreβol'tiʎo/ *m,* jumble, hodgepodge; confusion, tangle; *Venezuela* scrambled eggs

revoltoso /rreβol'toso/ *a* rebellious; mischievous, willful; intricate

revoltura /rreβol'tura/ *f, Mexico* dish of eggs and vegetables

revolución /rreβolu'sion; rreβolu'θion/ *f,* turn, revolution; rebellion, uprising; revolution

revolucionar /rreβolusio'nar; rreβoluθio'nar/ *vt* to revolutionize

revolucionario /rreβolusio'nario; rreβoluθio'nario/ **(-ia)** *a* and *n* revolutionary

revolver /rreβol'βer/ *vt irr* to turn over; turn upside down; wrap up; revolve; stir; reflect upon; consider; upset, cause disharmony; search through; disorder (papers, etc.); *vr* move from side to side; change (in the weather). See **resolver**

revólver /rre'βolβer/ *m,* revolver

revoque /rre'βoke/ *m, Mas.* washing, whitewash; plastering

revuelco /rre'βuelko/ *m,* wallowing

revuelo /rre'βuelo/ *m,* second flight of birds; irregular course of flight; disturbance, upset

revuelta /rre'βuelta/ *f,* second turn or revolution; revolt, rebellion; quarrel, fight; turning point; change of direction, turn; change (of opinions, posts, etc.)

revueltamente /rreβuelta'mente/ *adv* in confusion, higgledy-piggledy

revulsión /rreβul'sion/ *f,* revulsion

rexaminación /rreksamina'sion; rreksamina'θion/ *f,* reexamination

rexpedir /rrekspe'ðir/ *vt* to forward, send on

rey /rrei/ *m*, king (in cards, chess); queen bee; *Inf.* swineherd; *Fig.* king, chief. *Herald.* **r. de armas,** king-of-arms. **reyes magos,** magi. **día de Reyes,** Twelfth Night. **servir al r.**, to fight for the king

reyerta /rre'yerta/ *f*, quarrel, row, rumpus

reyezuelo /rreye'suelo; rreye'θuelo/ *m*, kinglet, petty king; golden-crested wren

rezagar /rresa'gar; rreθa'gar/ *vt* to leave behind; postpone, delay; *vr* lag behind, straggle

rezar /rre'sar; rre'θar/ *vt* to pray, say prayers; say mass; *Inf.* state, say; *vi* pray; *Inf.* fume, grumble. **El edicto reza así,** The edict runs like this, The edict reads like this

rezo /'rreso; 'rreθo/ *m*, prayer; devotions

rezongar /rreson'gar; rreθoŋ'gar/ *vi* to grouse, grumble

rezumar /rresu'mar; rreθu'mar/ **(se)** *vr* and *vi* to percolate, ooze through; *Inf.* leak out, be known

ría /'rria/ *f*, estuary, river mouth, firth

riachuelo /rria'tʃuelo/ *m*, rivulet, stream

riada /'rriaða/ *f*, flood. *Aer.* **r. de acero,** rain of flak

ribaldería /rriβalde'ria/ *f*, ribaldry

ribaldo /rri'βaldo/ *a* ribald. *m*, knave

ribazo /rri'βaso; rri'βaθo/ *m*, slope, incline

ribera /rri'βera/ *f*, bank, margin, shore, strand; *Lat. Am.* slum

ribereño /rriβe'reɲo/ *a* (**-ña**) *a* and *n* riparian

ribero /rri'βero/ *m*, embankment, wall

ribete /rri'βete/ *m*, binding, border, trimming; stripe; increase, addition; dramatic touch, exaggeration; *pl* indications, signs

ribetear /rriβete'ar/ *vt Sew.* to bind, trim, edge

ricacho /rri'katʃo/ **(-cha)** *n Inf.* newly rich person, nouveau riche

ricahembra /rrika'embra/ *f*, lady; daughter or wife of a Spanish noble *Obs.*

ricamente /rrika'mente/ *adv* richly, opulently; beautifully, splendidly; luxuriously

ricino /rri'sino; rri'θino/ *m*, castor oil plant

rico /'rriko/ *a* wealthy, rich; abundant; magnificent, splendid; delicious. **r. como Creso,** rich as Croesus

ricohombre /rriko'ombre/ *m*, nobleman *Obs.*

ricura /rri'kura/ *f*, *Inf.* richness, wealth

ridiculez /rriðiku'les; rriðiku'leθ/ *f*, absurd action or remark; ridiculousness; affectation; folly

ridiculizar /rriðikuli'sar; rriðikuli'θar/ *vt* to ridicule, poke fun at

ridículo /rri'ðikulo/ *a* ridiculous, absurd; grotesque; preposterous, outrageous. *m*, reticule

riego /'rriego/ *m*, watering, spraying; irrigation

riel /'rriel/ *m*, ingot; rail (of a train or streetcar)

rielar /rrie'lar/ *vi* to glimmer, glisten; glitter; shimmer

rienda /'rrienda/ *f*, rein (gen.); restraint; *pl* administration, government. **a r. suelta,** swiftly; without restraint; *Fig.* with loose reins

riesgo /'rriesgo/ *m*, risk, danger

riesgoso, -a /rries'goso/ *a*, *Lat. Am.* dangerous, risky

rifa /'rrifa/ *f*, raffle; quarrel, disagreement

rifar /rri'far/ *vt* to raffle; *vi* quarrel, fall out

rifle /'rrifle/ *m*, rifle

rigidez /rrihi'ðes; rrihi'ðeθ/ *f*, stiffness; rigidity; harshness

rígido /'rrihiðo/ *a* stiff; rigid; inflexible; severe, harsh

rigor /rri'gor/ *m*, severity, sternness; rigor; hardness; inflexibility; *Med.* rigor. **en r.,** strictly speaking. **ser de r.,** to be essential, be indispensable

rigorista /rrigo'rista/ *mf* martinet

riguroso /rrigu'roso/ *a* rigorous; harsh, cruel; austere, rigid; strict, exact, scrupulous

rijoso /rri'hoso/ *a* quarrelsome; lascivious

rima /'rrima/ *f*, rhyme, rime; heap; *pl* lyrics

rimador /rrima'ðor/ **(-ra)** *a* rhyming, rimer. *n* rhymer, rimer

rimar /rri'mar/ *vi* to compose verses; *vi* and *vt* rhyme, rime

rimbombo /rrim'βombo/ *m*, reverberation (of a sound)

rimero /rri'mero/ *m*, heap, pile

Rin, el /rrin, el/ the Rhine

rincón /rrin'kon/ *m*, corner, angle; retreat, hiding place; *Inf.* home, nest, nook

rinconada /rrinko'naða/ *f*, corner, angle

rinconera /rrinko'nera/ *f*, corner cupboard; corner table

ringlera /rriŋ'glera/ *f*, file, line, row

ringlero /rriŋ'glero/ *m*, guiding line for writing

ringorrangos /rriŋgo'rraŋgos/ *m pl*, *Inf.* exaggerated flourishes in writing; *Inf.* unnecessary frills or ornaments

ringueletear /rriŋguelete'ar/ *vi*, *Lat. Am.* to wander through the streets

rinoceronte /rrinose'ronte; rrinoθe'ronte/ *m*, rhinoceros

riñón /rri'ɲon/ *m*, kidney; *Fig.* center, heart; *pl Anat.* back

río /'rrio/ *m*, river; *Fig.* stream, flood

rioja /'rrioha/ *m*, red wine from Rioja

rioplatense /rriopla'tense/ *a* of the River Plate area; *mf* native of the River Plate area; resident of the River Plate area

ripio /'rripio/ *m*, remains, rest; debris, rubbish; *Lit.* padding; verbiage, prolixity. **no perder r.,** to lose no occasion or opportunity

riqueza /rri'kesa; rri'keθa/ *f*, riches, wealth; abundance; richness, magnificence

risa /'rrisa/ *f*, laugh; laughter; cause of amusement, joke

risco /'rrisko/ *m*, crag

riscoso /rris'koso/ *a* craggy

risible /rri'siβle/ *a* laughable

risoles /rri'soles/ *m pl*, rissoles

risotada /rriso'taða/ *f*, loud laugh

ristra /'rristra/ *f*, string (of onions, etc.); file, line, row

risueño /rri'sueɲo/ *a* smiling; cheerful; pleasant, agreeable; favorable, hopeful

rítmico /'rritmiko/ *a* rhythmic

ritmo /'rritmo/ *m*, rhythm

rito /'rrito/ *m*, rite

ritualismo /rritua'lismo/ *m*, ritualism

ritualista /rritua'lista/ *mf* ritualist

rivalidad /rriβali'ðað/ *f*, rivalry, competition; hostility

rivalizar /rriβali'sar; rriβali'θar/ *vi* to compete, rival

rizado /rri'saðo; rri'θaðo/ *m*, curling; pleating, crimping; rippling, ruffling

rizar /rri'sar; rri'θar/ *vt* to curl (hair); ripple, ruffle (of water); pleat, crimp; *vr* be naturally wavy (of hair)

rizo /'rriso; 'rriθo/ *m*, curl, ringlet; cut velvet. *Aer.* **hacer el r.,** to loop the loop; *Naut.* to take in reefs

rizoso /rri'soso; rri'θoso/ *a* naturally curly or wavy (hair)

robador /rroβa'ðor/ **(-ra)** *a* robbing. *n* robber, thief. *m*, abductor

robar /rro'βar/ *vt* to rob; abduct; wash away, eat away (rivers, sea); remove honey from the hive; draw (in cards, dominoes); *Fig.* capture (love, etc.)

roblar /rro'βlar/ *vt* to reinforce, strengthen; clinch

roble /'rroβle/ *m*, oak tree; oak; *Fig.* bulwark, tower of strength

robledo /rro'βleðo/ *m*, oak grove

roblón /rro'βlon/ *m*, rivet

robo /'rroβo/ *m*, theft, robbery; booty

robustecer /rroβuste'ser; rroβuste'θer/ *vt irr* to strengthen. See **conocer**

robustez /rroβus'tes; rroβus'teθ/ *f*, strength, robustness

robusto /rro'βusto/ *a* vigorous, robust, hearty, strong

roca /'rroka/ *f*, rock; *Fig.* tower of strength

roce /'rrose; 'rroθe/ *m*, rubbing, brushing, touching, friction; social intercourse

rociada /rro'siaða; rro'θiaða/ *f*, dewing; sprinkling; dew-wet grass given as medicine to horses and mules; *Fig.* shower; general slander; harsh rebuke

rociar /rro'siar; rro'θiar/ *vi* to fall as dew; drizzle; *vt* sprinkle, spray; *Fig.* shower (with)

rocín /rro'sin; rro'θin/ *m*, sorry nag; hack; *Inf.* ignoramus, boor

rocinante /rrosi'nante; rroθi'nante/ *m*, poor nag (alluding to Don Quixote's horse)

rocío /'rrosio; 'rroθio/ *m*, dew; dewdrop; drizzle, light shower; *Fig.* sprinkling, spray

rocoso /rro'koso/ *a* rocky

rodaballo /rroða'βayo; rroða'βaʎo/ *m*, turbot; *Inf.* crafty man

rodada /rro'ðaða/ *f*, wheel mark or track

rodado /rro'ðaðo/ *a* dappled (of horses)

rodaje /rro'ðahe/ *m*, wheeling; shooting (of a film)

rodante /rro'ðante/ *a* rolling

rodar /rro'ðar/ *vi* to roll; revolve, turn; run on wheels; wander, roam; be moved about; be plentiful, abound; happen successively; (*with por*) fall down, roll down

rodear /rroðe'ar/ *vi* to walk around; go by a roundabout way; *Fig.* beat around the bush; *vt* encircle, surround; besiege; *West Hem.* round up (cattle)

rodela /rro'ðela/ *f*, round shield; buckler

rodeno /rro'ðeno/ *a* red (of rocks, earth, etc.)

rodeo /rro'ðeo/ *m*, encirclement; indirect and longer way; trick to evade pursuit; *West Hem.* rodeo, roundup; stockyard, cattle enclosure; *Fig.* beating around the bush; evasive reply

rodera /rro'ðera/ *f*, rail, track, line; cart rut or track

rodilla /rro'ðiya; rro'ðiʎa/ *f*, knee; floor cloth. **de rodillas,** on one's knees. **ponerse de rodillas,** *or* **hincar las rodillas,** to kneel down

rodillazo /rroði'yaso; rroði'ʎaθo/ *m*, push with the knee

rodillera /rroði'yera; rroði'ʎera/ *f*, kneecap, kneepad; mend at the knee of garments; bagginess of trouser knees

rodillo /rro'ðiyo; rro'ðiʎo/ *m*, roller; traction engine; *Print.* inking roller; garden roller. **r. de pastas,** *Cul.* rolling pin

rododendro /rroðo'ðendro/ *m*, rhododendron

rodrigón /rroðri'gon/ *m*, stake, prop (for plants); *Inf.* old retainer who serves as a ladies' escort

roedor /rroe'ðor/ *a* gnawing; *Fig.* nagging; biting. *a* and *m*, rodent

roedura /rroe'ðura/ *f*, biting, gnawing; corrosion

roer /rro'er/ *vt irr* to gnaw, nibble, eat; corrode, wear away; trouble, afflict. *Pres. Ind.* **roigo, roes, etc.** *Preterite* **royó, royeron.** *Imperf. Subjunc.* **royese, etc.**

rogación /rroga'sion; rroga'θion/ *f*, request, supplication, entreaty; *Eccl.* rogation

rogador /rroga'ðor/ **(-ra)** *a* requesting; beseeching. *n* suppliant

rogar /rro'gar/ *vt irr* to request; beseech, beg. See **contar**

rogativo /rroga'tiβo/ *a* supplicatory, petitioning

roído /rro'iðo/ *a* gnawed, eaten; *Inf.* miserable, stingy

rojal /rro'hal/ *a* red (of soil, etc.). *m*, red earth

rojear /rrohe'ar/ *vi* to appear red; be reddish

rojete /rro'hete/ *m*, rouge

rojez /rro'hes; rro'heθ/ *f*, redness

rojizo /rro'hiso; rro'hiθo/ *a* reddish

rojo /'rroho/ *a* red; fair; red-gold (of hair); *Polit.* radical, red

rol /rrol/ *m*, roll, list

roldana /rrol'dana/ *f*, pulley wheel

rollizo /rro'yiso; rro'ʎiθo/ *a* round; plump, sturdy. *m*, log

rollo /'rroyo; 'rroʎo/ *m*, roll; *Cul.* rolling pin; log; town cross or pillar; anything rolled (paper, etc.); twist (of tobacco)

Roma /'rroma/ Rome

romance /rro'manse; rro'manθe/ *a* and *m*, romance (language). *m*, Spanish; ballad; romance of chivalry; *pl Fig.* fairy tales, excuses. **en buen r.,** *Fig.* in plain words

romancear /rromanse'ar; rromanθe'ar/ *vt* to translate from Latin into the spoken language; translate into Spanish; paraphrase the Spanish to assist translation; *Lat. Am.* to flirt

romancero /rroman'sero; rroman'θero/ **(-ra)** *n* balladeer. *m*, collection of ballads

romancista /rroman'sista; rroman'θista/ *mf* romancist

románico /rro'maniko/ *a* *Archit.* Romanesque

romanista /rroma'nista/ *mf* expert in Roman law or Romance languages and literature

romanizar /rromani'sar; rromani'θar/ *vt* to romanize; *vr* become romanized

romano /rro'mano/ **(-na)** *a* and *n* Roman. **a la romana,** in the Roman way. **cabello a la romana,** *Inf.* bobbed hair

romanticismo /rromanti'sismo; rromanti'θismo/ *m*, romanticism

romántico /rro'mantiko/ **(-ca)** *a* romantic; emotional; fanciful. *n* romantic; romanticist

rombo /'rrombo/ *m*, rhombus

romería /rrome'ria/ *f*, pilgrimage; excursion, picnic (made on a saint's day)

romero /rro'mero/ **(-ra)** *m*, rosemary. *n* pilgrim

romo /'rromo/ *a* blunt, dull, unsharpened; flat (of noses); *m. Lat. Am.* rum

rompecabezas /rrompeka'βesas; rrompeka'βeθas/ *m*, bludgeon; knuckleduster; *Inf.* teaser, puzzle, riddle; jigsaw puzzle

rompeimágenes /rrompei'mahenes/ *mf* iconoclast

rompeolas /rrompe'olas/ *m*, jetty, breakwater

romper /rrom'per/ *vt* to break; shatter, break into fragments; spoil, ruin; break up, plow; *Fig.* cut, divide (of water, etc.); *Fig.* end, break; interrupt; infringe, break; *vi* break; break (of waves); sprout, flower; (*with prep a*) begin to. **Rompió a hablar,** He broke into speech. *Past Part.* **roto**

rompiente /rrom'piente/ *a* breaking. *m*, reef, shoal

rompimiento /rrompi'miento/ *m*, break, rupture; crack, split; breakage; infringement; plowing up; *Fig.* dividing (water, etc.); spoiling, ruining; opening (of buds, etc.)

ron /rron/ *m*, rum

roncar /rron'kar/ *vi* to snore; *Fig.* roar, howl (of the sea, wind, etc.); *Inf.* brag

roncear /rronse'ar; rronθe'ar/ *vi* to be dilatory or unwilling; *Inf.* flatter, cajole; *Naut.* lag behind, sail slowly

roncero /rron'sero; rron'θero/ *a* dilatory, slow; grumbling, complaining; cajoling, flattering; *Lat. Am.* sly

roncha /'rrontʃa/ *f*, wheal; bruise, bump; *Inf.* money lost through trickery; thin, round slice

ronco /'rronko/ *a* hoarse, husky

ronda /'rronda/ *f*, round, beat, patrol; serenading party; *Inf.* round (of drinks)

rondador /rronda'ðor/ *m*, watchman; roundsman; serenader; night wanderer

rondalla /rron'daya; rron'daʎa/ *f*, tale, fairy tale

rondar /rron'dar/ *vi* to patrol, police; walk the streets by night; serenade; *vt* haunt; hover about; *Inf.* overcome (of sleep, etc.)

ronquear /rronke'ar/ *vi* to be hoarse

ronquera /rron'kera/ *f*, hoarseness

ronquido /rron'kiðo/ *m*, snore; hoarse sound

ronronear /rronrone'ar/ *vi* to purr (of cats)

ronzal /rron'sal; rron'θal/ *m*, halter

ronzar /rron'sar; rron'θar/ *vt* to munch, crack with the teeth

roña /'rroɲa/ *f*, mange (in sheep); grime, filth; mold; moral corruption; *Inf.* stinginess; *Inf.* trick, deception

roñería /rroɲe'ria/ *f*, *Inf.* meanness, stinginess

roñoso /rro'ɲoso/ *a* scabby; filthy; rusty; *Inf.* mean, stingy

ropa /'rropa/ *f*, fabric, material, stuff; clothes, wearing apparel; garment; outfit; robe (of office). **r. blanca,** underclothes; (domestic) linen. **r. hecha,** ready-made clothing. **r. talar,** long gown; cassock

ropaje /rro'pahe/ *m*, clothes, garments; vestments; drapery; *Fig.* form, outline

ropavejería /rropaβehe'ria/ *f*, old-clothes shop

ropavejero /rropaβe'hero/ **(-ra)** *n* old-clothes dealer

ropería /rrope'ria/ *f*, clothier's shop or trade; wardrobe; cloakroom

ropero /rro'pero/ **(-ra)** *n* clothier; keeper of the wardrobe. *m*, wardrobe; charitable organization

ropilla /rro'piya; rro'piʎa/ *f*, doublet

ropón /rro'pon/ *m*, a loose-fitting gown generally worn over clothes

roque /'rroke/ *m*, rook (in chess)
roqueño /rro'keɲo/ *a* rocky; hard as rock
roquete /rro'kete/ *m*, *Eccl.* rochet; barb of a lance
rorro /'rrorro/ *m*, *Inf.* infant, baby
rosa /'rrosa/ *f*, rose; anything rose-shaped; artificial rose; red spot on the body; *Archit.* rose window; *pl* rosettes. *m*, rose color. **r. de los vientos,** mariner's compass. **r. laurel,** oleander
rosado /rro'saðo/ *a* rose-colored; rose; rosé (wines)
rosal /rro'sal/ *m*, rose tree. **r. de tallo,** standard rose tree
rosaleda, rosalera /rrosa'leða, rrosa'lera/ *f*, rose garden
rosario /rro'sario/ *m*, rosary; *Fig.* string; chain pump; *Inf.* backbone
rosbif /rros'ßif/ *m*, roast beef
rosca /'rroska/ *f*, screw and nut; *Cul.* twist (of bread or cake); spiral
roscado /rros'kaðo/ *a* twisted, spiral
rosear /rrose'ar/ *vi* to turn to rose, become rose-colored
róseo /'rroseo/ *a* rose-colored
roseta /rro'seta/ *f*, *dim* small rose; rosette; rose of a watering can; rosette copper; *pl* toasted maize. **r. de fiebre,** rush of fever
rosetón /rrose'ton/ *m*, large rosette; *Archit.* rose window
rosicler /rrosi'kler/ *m*, rose-pink (first flush of dawn)
rosillo /rro'siyo; rro'siʎo/ *a* light red; roan (of horses)
rosmaro /rros'maro/ *m*, manatee, sea cow
roso /'rroso/ *a* bald, worn; red
rosquete /rros'kete/ *m*, *Lat. Am.* bun
rosquilla /rros'kiya; rros'kiʎa/ *f*, ring-shaped cake
rosquillero /rroski'yero; rroski'ʎero/ **(-ra)** *n* seller of rosquillas
rostrituerto /rrostri'tuerto/ *a* *Inf.* wry-faced (from sadness or anger)
rostro /'rrostro/ *m*, face, visage. **conocer de r.,** to know by sight. **dar en r.,** *Fig.* to throw in one's face
rota /'rrota/ *f*, *Mil.* defeat; *Eccl.* Rota; *Bot.* rattan
rotación /rrota'sion; rrota'θion/ *f*, rotation. **r. de cultivos,** rotation of crops
rotativa /rrota'tißa/ *f*, rotary printing press
rotativo /rrota'tißo/ *a* rotary
rotatorio /rrota'torio/ *a* rotatory
rotisería /rrotise'ria/ *f*, *Lat. Am.* steakhouse; grillroom
roto /'rroto/ *a* broken, torn; shabby, ragged; vicious, debauched
rotograbado /rrotogra'ßaðo/ *m*, rotogravure
rotonda /rro'tonda/ *f*, rotunda
rótula /'rrotula/ *f*, rotula, patella
rotular /rrotu'lar/ *vt* to label; give a title or heading to
rótulo /'rrotulo/ *m*, title; poster, placard; label
rotundamente /rrotunda'mente/ *adv* tersely, roundly, plainly
rotundidad /rrotundi'ðað/ *f*, rotundity; roundness; finality (of words, etc.)
rotundo /rro'tundo/ *a* round; rotund; sonorous; final, plain (of words, etc.)
rotura /rro'tura/ *f*, breaking, shattering; plowing up; breakage; rupture
roturar /rrotu'rar/ *vt* *Agr.* to break up, plow up
roya /'rroya/ *f*, rust, mildew; tobacco
roza /'rrosa; 'rroθa/ *f*, *Agr.* clearing (of weeds, etc.); ground ready for sowing. **de r. abierta,** open cast (of mining)
rozador /rrosa'ðor; rroθa'ðor/ *m*, *Lat. Am.* machete
rozadura /rrosa'ðura; rroθa'ðura/ *f*, rubbing, friction; abrasion, chafing
rozagante /rrosa'gante; rroθa'gante/ *a* long and elaborate (dresses); upstanding; handsome; strapping, fine
rozamiento /rrosa'miento; rroθa'miento/ *m*, grazing, brushing, rubbing; discord, disharmony, disagreement; *Mech.* friction
rozar /rro'sar; rro'θar/ *vt* *Agr.* to clear of weeds; crop, nibble; scrape; brush against, touch; *vi* brush,

rub, touch; *vr* have dealings with, know; stammer; be like, resemble
rúa /'rrua/ *f*, village street; highway
ruar /rru'ar/ *vi* to walk or ride through the streets; parade through the streets flirting with the ladies
rubeola /rruße'ola/ *f*, rubella
rubí /rru'ßi/ *m*, ruby; jewel (of a watch)
rubia /'rrußia/ *f*, *Bot.* madder; blonde (girl, woman)
rubicundez /rrußikun'des; rrußikun'deθ/ *f*, rubicundity, ruddiness, redness
rubicundo /rrußi'kundo/ *a* red-gold; ruddy-complexioned; reddish
rubio /'rrußio/ *a* red-gold, gold; fair, blond
rubor /rru'ßor/ *m*, blush, flush; bashfulness
ruborizarse /rrußori'sarse; rrußori'θarse/ *vr* to blush; be shamefaced
ruboroso /rrußo'roso/ *a* shamefaced; blushing
rúbrica /'rrußrika/ *f*, rubric; personal mark, flourish added to one's signature
rubricar /rrußri'kar/ *vt* to sign and seal; sign with an X or other symbol; sign with a flourish
rubro /'rrußro/ *a* red
rucio /'rrusio; 'rruθio/ *a* fawn, light-gray (of animals); *Inf.* going gray, gray-haired
rudamente /rruða'mente/ *adv* rudely, abruptly, churlishly; roughly
rudeza /rru'ðesa; rru'ðeθa/ *f*, roughness; rudeness, uncouthness; stupidity
rudimentario /rruðimen'tario/ *a* rudimentary
rudimento /rruði'mento/ *m*, embryo; *pl* rudiments
rudo /'rruðo/ *a* rough; unfinished; uncouth, boorish, rude; stupid
rueca /'rrueka/ *f*, distaff (in spinning); spinning wheel; curve, twist
rueda /'rrueða/ *f*, wheel; group, circle; spread of a peacock's tail; roller, castor; round piece or slice; turn, chance; succession (of events); wheel (used for torture). **r. libre,** freewheeling. *Inf.* **hacer la r. (a),** to flatter, make a fuss of
ruedero /rrue'ðero/ *m*, wheelwright
ruedo /'rrueðo/ *m*, turning, rotation; circumference; lined hem of a cassock; circuit
ruego /'rruego/ *m*, request, entreaty
rufián /rru'fian/ *m*, ruffian; pimp
rufo /'rrufo/ *a* fair; red-haired; curly-haired
rugido /rru'hiðo/ *m*, roaring, roar; creaking; gnashing; rumbling
rugir /rru'hir/ *vi* to roar; squeak, creak; gnash (the teeth)
ruibarbo /rrui'ßarßo/ *m*, rhubarb
ruido /'rruiðo/ *m*, noise, din; disturbance; rumor. **hacer** (*or* **meter**) **r.,** to cause a sensation. *Inf.* **ser más el r. que las nueces,** to be much ado about nothing
ruidoso /rrui'ðoso/ *a* noisy; notable
ruin /rru'in/ *a* base, vile; despicable; mean; puny
ruina /'rruina/ *f*, ruin, downfall; financial ruin; fall, decline; *pl* ruins
ruinar /rrui'nar/ *vt* to ruin
ruindad /rruin'dað/ *f*, baseness; meanness; pettiness, unworthiness; mean trick, despicable action
ruinoso /rrui'noso/ *a* half-ruined; ruinous; useless, worthless
ruiseñor /rruise'ɲor/ *m*, nightingale
ruleta /rru'leta/ *f*, roulette
rumano /rru'mano/ **(-na)** *a* and *n* Romanian. *m*, Romanian (language)
rumba /'rrumßa/ *f* rumba; *Lat. Am.* party (celebration)
rumbo /'rrumbo/ *m*, *Naut.* course, way, route; direction; *Inf.* swank; *Lat. Am.* party (celebration) **con r. a,** headed for, in the direction of. **hacer r. a,** to sail for; make for
rumboso /rrum'ßoso/ *a* *Inf.* pompous, dignified; open-handed, generous
rumia /'rrumia/ *f*, rumination; cud
rumiante /rru'miante/ *a* and *mf* *Zool.* ruminant. *a* *Inf.* reflective, meditative
rumiar /rru'miar/ *vt* *Zool.* to ruminate; *Inf.* reflect upon, chew on; *Inf.* fume, rage

rumor /rru'mor/ *m*, noise; rumor; murmur, babble; dull sound
rúnico /'rruniko/ *a* runic
runrunearse /rrunrune'arse/ *v impers* to be rumored
rupia /'rrupia/ *f*, rupee
ruptura /rrup'tura/ *f*, *Fig*. rupture; *Surg*. hernia
rural /rru'ral/ *a* rustic, rural
ruralmente /rrural'mente/ *adv* rurally
Rusia /'rrusia/ Russia
rusificar /rrusifi'kar/ *vt* to russianize
ruso /'rruso/ **(-sa)** *a* and *n* Russian. *m*, Russian (language)
rusticación /rrustika'sion; rrustika'θion/ *f*, rustication

rusticar /rrusti'kar/ *vi* to rusticate
rusticidad /rrustisi'ðað; rrustiθi'ðað/ *f*, rusticity; boorishness, coarseness
rústico /'rrustiko/ *a* rustic, country; boorish, uncouth. *m*, countryman; yokel; peasant. **en rústica**, in paper covers (of books)
ruta /'rruta/ *f*, route; *Fig*. way. **r. de evitación**, bypass, detour
ruteno /rru'teno/ **(-na)** *a* and *n* Ruthenian. *m*, Ruthenian (language)
rutilante /rruti'lante/ *a Poet*. sparkling, glowing
rutilar /rruti'lar/ *vi Poet*. to gleam, sparkle
rutina /rru'tina/ *f*, routine
rutinario /rruti'nario/ *a* routine
rutinero /rruti'nero/ **(-ra)** *a* routinistic. *n* routinist

S

sábado /'saβaðo/ *m*, Saturday; Jewish sabbath. **s. de gloria**, Easter Saturday
sábalo /'saβalo/ *m*, *Ichth*. shad
sabana /sa'βana/ *f*, savannah
sábana /sa'βana/ *f*, bed sheet; altar cloth. *Inf*. **pegársele (a uno) las sábanas**, to be tied to the bed, get up late
sabandija /saβan'diha/ *f*, any unpleasant insect or reptile; *Fig*. vermin
sabanero /saβa'nero/ **(-ra)** *n* savannah dweller. *a* savannah
sabanilla /saβa'niya; saβa'niʎa/ *f*, small piece of linen (kerchief, towel, etc.); altar cloth
sabañón /saβa'ɲon/ *m*, chilblain
sabatario /saβa'tario/ *a* sabbatarian
sabático /sa'βatiko/ *a* sabbatical
sabatino /saβa'tino/ *a* Saturday, Sabbath
sabedor /saβe'ðor/ *a* aware; knowledgeable, knowing
sabelotodo /saβelo'toðo/ *mf Inf*. know-it-all
saber /sa'βer/ *m*, learning; wisdom
saber /sa'βer/ *vt irr* to know; to be able to, know how; *vi* know; be shrewd, be well aware of; (*with prep a*) taste of; be like or similar to. **s. al dedillo**, *Fig*. to have at one's fingertips. **a s.**, viz., namely. **no s. dónde meterse**, to be overcome by shame; have the jitters. **No sé cuántos**, I don't know how many. **No sé quién**, I don't know who (which person). **No sé qué**, I don't know what. **un no sé qué**, a certain something; a touch (of). **¡Quién sabe!** Who knows!; Time will tell. *Pres. Ind*. **sé, sabes, etc.** *Fut*. **sabré**, etc. *Condit*. **sabría**, etc. *Preterite* **supe**, etc. *Pres. Subjunc*. **sepa**, etc. *Imperf. Subjunc*. **supiese**, etc.
sabiamente /saβia'mente/ *adv* wisely, prudently
sabidillo /saβi'ðiyo; saβi'ðiʎo/ **(-lla)** *a* and *n Inf*. know-it-all
sabiduría /saβiðu'ria/ *f*, prudence, wisdom; erudition, learning; knowledge, awareness. **Libro de la S. de Salomón**, Book of Wisdom
sabiendas, a /sa'βiendas/, *a/ adv* knowingly, consciously
sabihondo /sa'βiondo/ **(-da)** *n Inf*. know-it-all
sabio /'saβio/ **(-ia)** *a* wise; learned, erudite; prudent, sagacious; knowing (of animals); performing (of animals). *n* wise person; scholar, erudite person
sablazo /sa'βlaso; sa'βlaθo/ *m*, saber thrust or wound; *Inf*. sponging, taking advantage of. **dar un s. (a)**, *Inf*. to sponge on; touch for money
sable /'saβle/ *m*, saber; *Herald*. sable; *Inf*. talent for sponging on people. *a Herald*. sable
sablear /saβle'ar/ *vi Inf*. to touch for invitations, loans, etc.; cadge
sablista /sa'βlista/ *mf Inf*. sponger, cadger
saboneta /saβo'neta/ *f*, hunting case watch, hunter
sabor /sa'βor/ *m*, taste, flavor; impression, effect. **a s.**, to taste; at pleasure
saboreamiento /saβorea'miento/ *m*, savoring; relishing, enjoyment
saborear /saβore'ar/ *vt* to flavor, season; relish, savor; appreciate, enjoy; *vr* relish, savor; enjoy
saboreo /saβo'reo/ *m*, tasting; savoring; relishing

sabotaje /saβo'tahe/ *m*, sabotage
saboteador /saβotea'ðor/ *m*, saboteur
Saboya /sa'βoya/ Savoy
saboyano /saβo'yano/ **(-na)** *a* and *n* Savoyard
sabroso /sa'βroso/ *a* tasty, savory, well-seasoned; delightful, delicious; *Inf*. piquant, racy; *Lat. Am*. garrulous, talkative
sabueso /sa'βueso/ *m*, cocker spaniel. **s. de artois**, hound
sabuloso /saβu'loso/ *a* sandy
saburra /sa'βurra/ *f*, fur (on the tongue)
saca /'saka/ *f*, drawing out, removing; export, transport, shipping; removal, extraction; legal copy (of a document). **estar de s.**, to be on sale; *Inf*. be marriageable (of women)
sacabocados /sakaβo'kaðos/ *m*, punch (tool); *Inf*. cinch, easy matter
sacabotas /saka'βotas/ *m*, bootjack
sacabrocas /saka'βrokas/ *m*, tack puller
sacabuche /saka'βutʃe/ *m*, *Mus*. sackbut; sackbut player; *Inf*. insignificant little man; *Naut*. hand pump
sacacorchos /saka'kortʃos/ *m*, corkscrew
sacacuartos /saka'kuartos/ *m*, *Inf*. catchpenny
sacada /sa'kaða/ *f*, territory cut off from a province
sacadineros /sakaði'neros/ *m*, *Inf*. catchpenny
sacamantas /saka'mantʃas/ *mf*. See **quitamanchas**
sacamantas /saka'mantas/ *m*, *Inf*. tax collector
sacamiento /saka'miento/ *m*, removing, taking out
sacamuelas /saka'muelas/ *mf* dentist; charlatan, quack; *Inf*. windbag
sacapotras /saka'potras/ *m*, *Inf*. unskilled surgeon
sacar /sa'kar/ *vt* to draw out; extract; pull out; take out; remove; dispossess, turn out; free from, relieve; examine, investigate; extort (the truth); extract (sugar, etc.); win (prizes, games); copy; discover, find out; elect by ballot; obtain, achieve; exclude; show, exhibit; quote, mention; produce, invent; manufacture; note down; put forth; unsheath (swords); bowl (in cricket); serve (in tennis). **s. a bailar**, to invite to dance. **s. a luz**, to publish, print; reveal, bring out. **s. a paseo**, to take for a walk. **s. de pila**, to be a godfather or godmother to. **s. en claro** or **s. en limpio**, to copy; conclude, infer, gather. **sacarse en conclusión que...**, the conclusion is that...
sacarificar /sakarifi'kar/ *vt* to saccharify
sacarina /saka'rina/ *f*, saccharin
sacasillas /saka'siyas; saka'siʎas/ *mf*, *Inf. Theat*. stagehand
sacerdocio /saser'ðosio; saθer'ðoθio/ *m*, priesthood
sacerdotal /saserðo'tal; saθerðo'tal/ *a* priestly
sacerdote /saser'ðote; saθer'ðote/ *m*, priest
sacerdotisa /saserðo'tisa; saθerðo'tisa/ *f*, priestess. **sumo s.**, high priestess
sachar /sa'tʃar/ *vt* to weed
sacho /'satʃo/ *m*, weeder
saciable /sa'siaβle; sa'θiaβle/ *a* satiable
saciar /sa'siar; sa'θiar/ *vt* to satisfy; satiate; *vr* be satiated
saciedad /sasie'ðað; saθie'ðað/ *f*, satiety, surfeit

saco /'sako/ *m*, sack, handbag; bag; sackful; sack coat; *Biol*. sac; *Mil*. sack, plundering. **s. de noche,** dressing case, weekend case. *Inf*. **no echar en s. roto,** not to forget, to remember

sacramentalmente /sakramental'mente/ *adv* sacramentally; in confession

sacramentar /sakramen'tar/ *vt* to consecrate; administer the Blessed Sacrament; hide, conceal

sacramentario /sakramen'tario/ **(-ia)** *n* sacramentalist; sacramentarian

sacramento /sakra'mento/ *m*, sacrament; *Eccl*. Host; *Eccl*. mystery. **s. del altar,** Eucharist. **con todos los sacramentos,** with all the sacraments; done in order, complete with all formalities. **recibir los sacramentos,** to receive the last sacraments

sacratísimo /sakra'tisimo/ *a* most sacred

sacrificadero /sakrifika'ðero/ *m*, place of sacrifice

sacrificador /sakrifika'ðor/ **(-ra)** *a* sacrificing. *n* sacrificer

sacrificar /sakrifi'kar/ *vt* to sacrifice; slaughter; *vr* consecrate oneself to God; sacrifice oneself; devote or dedicate oneself (to)

sacrificio /sakri'fisio; sakri'fiθio/ *m*, sacrifice; offering, dedication; surrendering, forgoing; compliance; submission. **s. del altar,** sacrifice of the mass

sacrilegio /sakri'lehio/ *m*, sacrilege

sacrílego /sa'krilego/ *a* sacrilegious

sacristán /sakris'tan/ *m*, sacristan; sexton; hoop (for dresses). *Inf*. **s. de amén,** yes-man. *Inf*. **ser gran s.,** to be very crafty

sacristana /sakris'tana/ *f*, wife of a sacristan or sexton; nun in charge of a convent sacristy

sacristanía /sakrista'nia/ *f*, office of a sacristan or sexton

sacristía /sakris'tia/ *f*, sacristy; vestry; office of a sacristan or sexton

sacro /'sakro/ *a* sacred; *Anat*. sacral

sacrosanto /sakro'santo/ *a* sacrosanct

sacudida /saku'ðiða/ *f*, shake, shaking; jerk, jar, jolt; twitch, pull; *Aer*. bump

sacudido /saku'ðiðo/ *a* unsociable; difficult, wayward; determined, bold

sacudidor /sakuði'ðor/ **(-ra)** *a* shaking; jerking. *n* shaker. *m*, carpet beater; duster

sacudidura /sakuði'ðura/ *f*, shaking (especially to remove dust); jerking

sacudimiento /sakuði'miento/ *m*, shake, shaking; jerk; twitch, pull; jolt

sacudir /saku'ðir/ *vt* to shake; flap, wave; jerk, twitch; beat, bang; shake off; *vr* shake off, avoid

sadismo /sa'ðismo/ *m*, sadism

sadista /sa'ðista/ *mf* sadist

sadístico /sa'ðistiko/ *a* sadistic

saduceo /saðu'seo; saðu'θeo/ **(-ea)** *a* Sadducean. *n* Sadducee

saeta /sa'eta/ *f*, arrow, dart; clock hand, watch hand; magnetic needle; short sung expression of religious ecstasy; *Astron*. Sagitta

saetada /sae'taða/ *f*, **saetazo** *m*, arrow wound

saetera /sae'tera/ *f*, loophole; small window

saetero /sae'tero/ *a* arrow, arrow-like. *m*, archer, bowman

safado, -a /sa'faðo/ *a*, *Lat. Am*. cheeky, impudent, saucy

saga /'saga/ *f*, saga

sagacidad /sagasi'ðað; sagaθi'ðað/ *f*, sagacity

sagaz /sa'gas; sa'gaθ/ *a* sagacious, shrewd; farseeing; quick on the scent (dogs)

sagital /sahi'tal/ *a* arrow-shaped

sagitario /sahi'tario/ *m*, archer; *Astron*. Sagittarius

sagrado /sa'graðo/ *a* sacred; holy; sacrosanct, venerable; accursed, detestable. *m*, sanctuary, refuge; haven

sagrario /sa'grario/ *m*, sanctuary; sacrarium

sagú /sa'gu/ *m*, sago

Sáhara, el /'saara, el/ the Sahara

sahornarse /saor'narse/ *vr* to chafe, grow sore

sahorno /sa'orno/ *m*, chafing, abrasion

sahumado /sau'maðo/ *a* improved, rendered more excellent; perfumed; fumigated

sahumador /sauma'ðor/ *m*, perfumer; fumigating vessel

sahumar /sau'mar/ *vt* to perfume; fumigate. See desahuciar

sahumerio /sau'merio/ *m*, perfuming; fumigation; fume, smoke

saín /sa'in/ *m*, fat, grease; sardine oil (for lamps); grease spot (on clothes)

sainar /sai'nar/ *vt* to fatten up (animals)

sainete /sai'nete/ *m*, *Cul*. sauce; *Theat*. one-act parody or burlesque; farce; delicacy, tidbit; delicate taste (of food)

sainetero /saine'tero/ *m*, writer of sainetes

sainetesco /saine'tesko/ *a* pertaining to sainetes; burlesque, satirical

sajar /sa'har/ *vt* *Surg*. to scarify

sajón /sa'hon/ **(-ona)** *a* and *n* Saxon

Sajonia /sa'honia/ Saxony

sal /sal/ *f*, salt; wit; grace, gracefulness. **s. de cocina,** common kitchen salt. **s. de la Higuera,** Epsom salts. **s. gema,** rock salt. **s. marina,** sea salt. **sales inglesas,** smelling salts. *Inf*. **estar hecho de s.,** to be full of wit. *Inf*. **hacerse s. y agua,** to melt away, disappear (of riches, etc.)

sala /'sala/ *f*, drawing room; large room, hall; *Law*. courtroom; *Law*. bench; **s. de apelación,** court of appeal. **s. de hospital,** hospital ward. **s. de justicia,** court of justice. **s. de lectura,** reading room. *Law*. **guardar s.,** to respect the court

salacidad /salasi'ðað; salaθi'ðað/ *f*, lewdness, salaciousness

saladero /sala'ðero/ *m*, salting or curing place; *West Hem*. meat packing factory

saladillo /sala'ðiyo; sala'ðiʎo/ *m*, salt pork

salado /sa'laðo/ *a* salty, briny; brackish; witty; attractive, amusing

salador /sala'ðor/ **(-ra)** *a* salting, curing. *n* salter, curer. *m*, curing place

saladura /sala'ðura/ *f*, salting, curing

salamandra /sala'mandra/ *f*, salamander; fire sprite

salar /sa'lar/ *vt* to salt; season with salt; oversalt; cure, pickle (meat, etc.); *m*, *Lat. Am*. salt marsh

salario /sa'lario/ *m*, salary

salaz /sa'las; sa'laθ/ *a* lewd, lecherous

salazón /sala'son; sala'θon/ *f*, salting, curing; salt meat or fish trade

salazonero /salaso'nero; salaθo'nero/ *a* salting, curing

salchicha /sal'tʃitʃa/ *f*, sausage

salchichería /saltʃitʃe'ria/ *f*, sausage shop

salchichero /saltʃi'tʃero/ **(-ra)** *n* sausage maker, sausage seller

salchichón /saltʃi'tʃon/ *m*, *Cul*. salami, kind of sausage

saldar /sal'dar/ *vt* *Com*. to settle, pay in full; sell out cheap; balance

saldista /sal'dista/ *mf* remnant buyer

saldo /'saldo/ *m*, *Com*. balance; closing of an account; bargain sale. **s. acreedor,** credit balance. **s. deudor,** debit balance. **s. líquido,** net balance

salero /sa'lero/ *m*, saltshaker, saltcellar; salt storage warehouse; *Inf*. wit

saleta /sa'leta/ *f*, *dim* small hall; royal antechamber; court of appeal

salida /sa'liða/ *f*, going out; leaving; departure; sailing; exit, way out; projection, protrusion; *Fig*. escape, way out; outcome, result; witty remark; *Mil*. sally; *Com*. outlay, expense; *Com*. opening, sale, salability; environs, outskirts; *Argentina* bathrobe **s. de dólares,** dollar drain. **s. de tono,** *Inf*. an impertinent remark. **dar s.,** *Com*. to enter on the credit side

salidero /sali'ðero/ *a* fond of going out; *m*, exit, way out

salidizo /sali'ðiso; sali'ðiθo/ *m*, *Archit*. projection. *a* projecting

saliente /sa'liente/ *a* outgoing; salient, projecting. *m*, east; projection; salient. **s. continental,** continental shelf

salina /sa'lina/ *f*, salt mine; saltworks

salinero /sali'nero/ *m*, salt merchant; salter; salt worker

salino /sa'lino/ *a* saline. *m, Med.* saline

salir /salir/ *vi irr* to go out; depart, leave; succeed in getting out; escape; appear (of the sun, etc.); sprout, show green; fade, come out (of stains); project, stand out; grow, develop; turn out, result; happen, take place; cost; sail; end (of seasons, time); lead off, start (some games); be published (books); do (well or badly), succeed or fail; appear, show oneself; be drawn, win (lottery tickets); balance, come out right (accounts); be elected; become; give up (posts); lead to (of streets, etc.); *Naut.* overtake; (*with prep a*) guarantee, be surety for; resemble, be like; (*with con*) utter, come out with; commit, do inopportunely; succeed in, achieve (e.g. *Salió con la suya,* He got his own way). **¿Cómo salieron las cosas?,** How did it (things) turn out? (*with de*) originate in; break away from (traditions, conventions); get rid of; (*with por*) stand up for, protect; go surety for, guarantee. *vr* leak; boil over; overflow; (*with con*) achieve, get; (*with de*) *Fig.* break away from. *Theat.* **s. a la escena,** to enter, come on to the stage. **Salió a su papá,** He's just like his father. **s. de,** to recover from (an illness). **no acabar de s. de,** to not be completely recovered from. **s. del apuro,** to get out of trouble. **s. de estampía,** to stampede (of animals). **s. pitando,** *Inf.* to get out in a hurry. **Esta idea no salió de Juan,** This wasn't John's idea. **salga lo que saliere,** *Inf.* come what may.... *Pres. Ind.* **salgo, sales,** etc. *Fut.* **saldré,** etc. *Condit.* **saldría,** etc. *Pres. Subjunc.* **salga,** etc.

salitral /sali'tral/ *a* nitrous. *m*, saltpeter bed

salitre /sa'litre/ *m*, saltpeter

salitrería /salitre'ria/ *f*, saltpeter works

salitrero /sali'trero/ *n* saltpeter worker or dealer

saliva /sa'liβa/ *f*, saliva. *Inf.* **tragar s.,** to put up with; be unable to speak through emotion

salivación /saliβa'sion; saliβa'θion/ *f*, salivation

salival /sali'βal/ *a* salivary

salivar /sali'βar/ *vi* to salivate; spit

sallar /sa'yar; sa'ʎar/ *vt* to weed

salmantino /salman'tino/ (**-na**) *a* and *n* Salamanca

salmear /salme'ar/ *vi* to intone psalms

salmista /sal'mista/ *mf* psalmist; psalmodist, psalm chanter

salmo /'salmo/ *m*, psalm

salmodia /sal'moðia/ *f*, psalmody; *Inf.* drone; psalter

salmodiar /salmo'ðiar/ *vi* to chant psalms; *vt* drone

salmón /sal'mon/ *m*, salmon

salmonado /salmo'naðo/ *a* salmon-like

salmonera /salmo'nera/ *f*, salmon net

salmonete /salmo'nete/ *m*, red mullet

salmuera /sal'muera/ *f*, brine

salobre /sa'loβre/ *a* salt, salty; brackish

salobridad /saloβri'ðað/ *f*, saltiness

salomar /salo'mar/ *vi Naut.* to sing chanteys

salón /sa'lon/ *m*, drawing room; large room or hall; reception room; salon, reception, social gathering. **s. de muestras,** showroom

saloncillo /salon'siyo; salon'θiʎo/ *m*, *dim* small room; *Theat.* greenroom; rest room

salpicadura /salpika'ðura/ *f*, sprinkling, spattering, splashing

salpicar /salpi'kar/ *vt* to sprinkle, scatter; bespatter, splash

salpicón /salpi'kon/ *m*, *Cul.* kind of salmagundi; *Inf.* hodgepodge; spattering

salpimentar /salpimen'tar/ *vt irr* to season (with pepper and salt; sprinkle; *Fig.* leaven, enliven (a speech, etc.). See **regimentar**

salpresar /salpre'sar/ *vt* to preserve in salt, salt

salpullido /salpu'yiðo; salpu'ʎiðo/ *m*, rash, skin eruption

salsa /'salsa/ *f*, sauce; gravy. **s. mahonesa** *or* **s. mayonesa,** mayonnaise sauce. **s. mayordoma,** sauce maître d'hôtel

salsera /sal'sera/ *f*, sauce boat, gravy boat

saltabanco /salta'βanko/ *m*, mountebank; street entertainer, juggler

saltabarrancos /saltaβa'rrankos/ *mf Inf.* madcap, harum-scarum

saltable /sal'taβle/ *a* jumpable

saltadero /salta'ðero/ *m*, jumping ground; fountain, jet

saltador /salta'ðor/ (**-ra**) *a* jumping. *n* jumper; acrobat. *m*, jump rope, skip rope

saltamontes /salta'montes/ *m*, grasshopper

saltaojos /salta'ohos/ *m*, peony

saltaparedes /saltapa'reðes/ *mf Inf.* madcap, romp

saltar /sal'tar/ *vi* to jump, leap, spring; prance; frisk; gambol; rebound; blow up; burst, break asunder; pop (of corks); fly off, come off (buttons, etc.); gush out, shoot up (liquids); break apart, be shattered; be obvious, stand out; come to mind, suggest itself; show anger; *Fig.* let slip, come out with (remarks); *vt* leap or jump over; poke out (eyes); cover (the female); omit, pass over; blow up, explode. **s. a la cuerda,** to jump rope, play with a skip rope. **s. a la vista,** to be obvious, leap to the eye. **s. diciendo,** *Inf.* to come out with, say

saltarín /salta'rin/ (**-ina**) *a* jumping, frolicking, dancing. *n* dancer

saltatriz /salta'tris; salta'triθ/ *f*, ballet dancer, female acrobat

saltatumbas /salta'tumbas/ *m*, (*inf* contemptuous) cleric who makes his living off funerals

salteador /saltea'ðor/ *m*, highwayman

salteamiento /saltea'miento/ *m*, highway robbery, holdup; assault, attack

saltear /salte'ar/ *vt* to hold up and rob; assault, attack; jump from one thing to another, do intermittently; forestall; surprise, amaze

salterio /sal'terio/ *m*, psaltery

saltimbanco, saltimbanqui /saltim'βanko, saltim-'βanki/ *m*, *Inf.* See **saltabanco**

salto /'salto/ *m*, jump, leap, bound; leapfrog (game); precipice, ravine; waterfall; assault; important promotion; omission (of words). **s. de agua,** waterfall. **s. de cama,** peignoir, bathrobe. **s. de campana,** overturning. *Inf.* **s. de mal año,** sudden improvement in circumstances. **s. de mata,** flight, escape. **s. mortal,** leap of death; somersault. **s. de pie,** spillway. **dar un s.,** to leap. **en un s.,** at one jump; swiftly

saltón /sal'ton/ *a* jumping, leaping; prominent (teeth, eyes). *m*, grasshopper

salubérrimo /salu'βerrimo/ *a sup* **salubre** most healthy

salubre /sa'luβre/ *a* salubrious, healthful

salubridad /saluβri'ðað/ *f*, healthfulness

salud /sa'luð/ *f*, health; salvation; welfare, well-being; *Eccl.* state of grace; *pl* civilities, greetings. **¡S. y pesetas!** Here's to your good health and prosperity! (on drinking). **gastar s.,** to enjoy good health. *Inf.* **vender** (*or* **verter**) **s.,** to look full of health

saludable /salu'ðaβle/ *a* healthy, wholesome

saludador /saluða'ðor/ (**-ra**) *a* greeting, saluting. *n* greeter. *m*, charlatan, quack

saludar /salu'ðar/ *vt* to greet, salute; hail (as king, etc.); send greetings to; bow; *Mil.* fire a salute

saludo /sa'luðo/ *m*, greeting, salutation; bow; (*Mil. Nav.*) salute

salutación /saluta'sion; saluta'θion/ *f*, greeting, salutation; Ave Maria

salutífero /salu'tifero/ *a* salubrious

salva /'salβa/ *f*, salutation, greeting; (*Mil. Nav.*) salvo, volley; salute (of guns); salver; ordeal (to establish innocence); solemn assurance, oath; sampling, tasting (of food, drink). **s. de veintiún cañonazos,** twenty-one-gun salute

salvación /salβa'sion; salβa'θion/ *f*, liberation, deliverance; salvation

salvado /sal'βaðo/ *m*, bran

salvador /salβa'ðor/ (**-ra**) *a* saving, redeeming. *n* deliverer. *m*, redeemer

salvadoreño /salβaðore'ɲo/ (**-ña**) *a* and *n* Salvadorean

salvaguardia /salβa'guarðia/ *m*, guard, watch. *f*, safeguard; protection, defense; safe conduct, passport

salvajada /salβa'haða/ *f*, savagery, brutal action

salvaje /sal'βahe/ *a* wild (plants, animals); rough, uncultivated; uncultured, uncivilized. *mf* savage

salvajismo /salβa'hismo/ *m*, savagery

salvamano, a /salβa'mano, a/ *adv* safely

salvamente /salβa'mente/ *adv* safely, securely

salvamento /salβa'mento/ *m*, salvation; deliverance, security, safety; place of safety; salvage

salvante /sal'βante/ *adv Inf.* except, save

salvar /sal'βar/ *vt* to save; *Eccl.* redeem; avoid (difficulty, danger); exclude, except; leap, jump; pass over, clear; *Law.* prove innocent; *Naut.* salve. **s. la diferencia,** to bridge the gap. *vi* taste, sample (food, drink); *vr* be saved from danger; *Eccl.* be redeemed

salvavidas /salβa'βiðas/ *m*, life belt; safety belt; life preserver; traffic island

¡salve! /'salβe/ *interj Poet.* hail! **¡S. María!,** Hail Mary. **¡S. Regina!,** Salve Regina

salvedad /salβe'ðað/ *f*, qualification, reservation

salvia /'salβia/ *f, Bot.* sage

salvilla /sal'βiya; sal'βiʎa/ *f*, salver

salvo /'salβo/ *a* safe, unharmed; excepting, omitting. *adv* except. **a s.,** safely, without harm. **a su s.,** to his (her, their) satisfaction; at his (her, etc.) pleasure. **dejar a s.,** to exclude, leave aside. **en s.,** in safety

salvoconducto /salβokon'dukto/ *m*, safe conduct, pass

samarita /sama'rita/ *a* and *mf* **samaritano (-na)** *a* and *n* Samaritan

samba /'samβa/ *f* samba

sambenito /sambe'nito/ *m*, penitent's gown (Inquisition); disgrace, dishonor

sambubia /sam'βuβia/ *f, Mexico* pineapple drink

Samotracia /samo'trasia; samo'traθia/ Samothrace

samotracio /samo'trasio; samo'traθio/ **(-ia)** *a* and *n* Samothracian

samoyedo /samo'yeðo/ **(-da)** *n* Samoyed

san /san/ *a abb* of **santo.** Used before masculine singular names of saints except **Santos Tomás** (or **Tomé**), **Domingo, Toribio**

sanable /sa'naβle/ *a* curable

sanador /sana'ðor/ **(-ra)** *a* healing, curing. *n* healer

sanalotodo /sanalo'toðo/ *m, Inf.* cure-all, universal remedy

sanar /sa'nar/ *vt* to cure, heal; *vi* recover, get well; heal

sanatorio /sana'torio/ *m*, sanatorium; convalescent home

sanción /san'sion; san'θion/ *f*, authorization, consent; sanction; penalty

sancionable /sansio'naβle; sanθio'naβle/ *a* sanctionable

sancionar /sansio'nar; sanθio'nar/ *vt* to authorize, approve; sanction

sancochar /sanko'tʃar/ *vt Cul.* to parboil, half-cook

sancocho /san'kotʃo/ *m*, parboiled meat

sandalia /san'dalia/ *f*, sandal

sándalo /'sandalo/ *m*, sandalwood

sandez /san'des; san'deθ/ *f*, foolishness, stupidity; folly

sandía /san'dia/ *f*, watermelon

sandio /'sandio/ *a* foolish, inane

sandunga /san'duŋga/ *f, Inf.* attractiveness, winsomeness, grace; *Lat. Am.* carousing

sandunguero /sanduŋ'guero/ *a Inf.* attractive, appealing, winsome

saneado /sane'aðo/ *a* unencumbered, nontaxable, free

saneamiento /sanea'miento/ *m*, guarantee, security; indemnity; stabilization (of currency); drainage

sanear /sane'ar/ *vt Com.* to guarantee, secure; indemnify; stabilize (currency); drain (land, etc.)

Sanedrín /sane'ðrin/ *m*, Sanhedrin

sangradera /saŋgra'ðera/ *f*, lancet; channel, sluice, drain

sangrador /saŋgra'ðor/ *m*, phlebotomist; outlet, drainage

sangradura /saŋgra'ðura/ *f*, inner bend of the arm; *Surg.* bleeding; draining off

sangrar /saŋ'grar/ *vt Surg.* to bleed; drain off; *Inf.* extort money, bleed; *Print.* indent; draw off resin (from pines, etc.); *vi* bleed; *vr* bleed; have oneself bled; run (of colors)

sangre /'saŋgre/ *f*, blood; lineage, family. **s. fría,** sang-froid. **a s. fría,** in cold blood, premeditated. **a s. y fuego,** by fire and sword, without quarter. *Inf.* **bullir la s.,** to have youthful blood in one's veins. **llevar en la s.,** *Fig.* to be in the blood. **subírsele la s. a la cabeza,** to grow excited. *Fig. Inf.* **tener s. de horchata,** to have milk and water in one's veins

sangría /saŋ'gria/ *f*, sangria (wine); *Surg.* bloodletting; resin cut (on pines, etc.)

sangriento /saŋ'griento/ *a* bloody, bloodstained; bloodthirsty, cruel; mortal (insults, etc.); *Poet.* blood-colored

sangüesa /saŋ'guesa/ *f*, raspberry

sanguijuela /saŋgi'huela/ *f*, leech; *Fig. Inf.* sponger

sanguinaria /saŋgi'naria/ *f*, bloodstone

sanguinario /saŋgi'nario/ *a* vengeful, bloody, cruel

sanguíneo /saŋ'gineo/ *a* blood; sanguineous; sanguine, fresh-complexioned; blood-colored

sanguinolento /saŋgino'lento/ *a.* See **sangriento**

sanidad /sani'ðað/ *f*, safety, security; healthiness; health department. **s. interior,** Public Health. **S. militar,** army medical corps

sanitario /sani'tario/ *a* sanitary, hygienic. *m, Mil.* medical officer

sano /'sano/ *a* healthy; safe, secure; healthful, wholesome; unhurt, unharmed; upright, honest; sincere; *Inf.* entire, undamaged; sane. **s. y salvo,** safe and sound. *Inf.* **cortar por lo s.,** to cut one's losses

San Pablo /san 'paβlo/ São Paulo

sánscrito /'sanskrito/ *a* and *m*, Sanscrit

santa /'santa/ *f*, female saint

santamente /santa'mente/ *adv* in a saintly manner; simply

santero /san'tero/ **(-ra)** *a* given to image worship. *n* accomplice (of a burglar); caretaker (of a hermitage); beggar; *Guatemala* artisan who crafts figurines of saints

¡Santiago! /san'tiago/ *interj* St. James! (Spanish war cry). *m*, attack, assault

santiamén /santia'men/ *m, Inf.* split second

santidad /santi'ðað/ *f*, sanctity; saintliness; godliness. **Su S.,** His Holiness

santificación /santifika'sion; santifika'θion/ *f*, sanctification

santificador /santifika'ðor/ **(-ra)** *a* sanctifying. *n* sanctifier

santificar /santifi'kar/ *vt* to sanctify, make holy; consecrate; dedicate; keep (feast days)

santiguada /santi'guaða/ *f*, crossing oneself; rough treatment, harsh reproof

santiguar /santi'guar/ *vt* to make the sign of the cross over; *Inf.* beat, rain blows on; *vr* cross oneself; *Inf.* be dumbfounded

santísimo /san'tisimo/ *a sup* most saintly, most holy

santo /'santo/ *a* holy; saintly; saint (see **san**); consecrated; inviolate, sacred; *Inf.* simple, sincere, ingenuous. *m*, saint; image of a saint; saint's day, name day (of a person); *Mil.* password. **Santa Hermandad,** Holy Brotherhood (former name of the Spanish rural police force). **S. Oficio,** Holy Office, Inquisition. **S. y bueno,** Well and good, All right! *Inf.* **alzarse con el s. y la limosna,** to take the lot, make off with everything. **llegar y besar el s.,** to do in a trice. *Inf.* **No es s. de mi devoción,** I'm not very keen on him. *Inf.* **todo el s. día,** the whole blessed day

santón /san'ton/ *m*, dervish, santon. *Inf.* hypocrite, sham saint

santoral /santo'ral/ *m*, book of saints; calendar of saints; choir book

santuario /san'tuario/ *m*, sanctuary

santurrón /santu'rron/ **(-ona)** *a* sanctimonious; hypocritical; prudish. *n* hypocrite

santurronería /santurrone'ria/ *f*, sanctimoniousness

saña /'saɲa/ *f*, fury, blind rage; lust for revenge, cruelty

sañoso, sañudo /sa'ɲoso, sa'ɲuðo/ *a* furious, blind with rage; cruel

sapidez /sapi'ðes; sapi'ðeθ/ *f*, flavor, sapidity

sápido /'sapiðo/ *a* tasty, savory

sapiencia /sa'piensia; sa'pienθia/ f, wisdom; knowledge; erudition
sapino /sa'pino/ m, fir (tree)
sapo /'sapo/ m, toad
saque /'sake/ m, Sports. serve, service; service or bowling line; Sports. server; Sports. bowler; bowling (in cricket)
saqueador /sakea'ðor/ (-ra) a looting, pillaging. n pillager, plunderer
saquear /sake'ar/ vt to pillage, plunder, sack
saqueo /sa'keo/ m, plundering, pillage, sacking
sarampión /saram'pion/ m, measles
sarao /sa'rao/ m, soirée, evening party
sarape /sa'rape/ m, Mexico woolen shawl or blanket worn by males
sarcasmo /sar'kasmo/ m, sarcasm
sarcástico /sar'kastiko/ a sarcastic
sarcia /'sarsia; 'sarθia/ f, load, cargo
sarcófago /sar'kofago/ m, sarcophagus
sarda /'sarða/ f, mackerel
sardana /sar'ðana/ f, traditional Catalonian dance
sardina /sar'ðina/ f, sardine. **s. arenque,** herring. **como sardinas en banasta,** Fig. packed like sardines
sardinal /sarði'nal/ m, sardine net
sardinero /sarði'nero/ (-ra) a sardine. n sardine seller or dealer. m, famous district of Santander
sardineta /sarði'neta/ f, sprat; small sardine; Mil. chevron
sardónico /sar'ðoniko/ a sardonic
sarga /'sarga/ f, (silk) serge; willow
sargentear /sarhente'ar/ vt to be in charge as a sergeant; command, captain; Inf. boss
sargento /sar'hento/ m, sergeant
sarita /sa'rita/ f. Peru straw hat
sarmentoso /sarmen'toso/ a vine-like; twining
sarmiento /sar'miento/ m, vine shoot
sarna /'sarna/ f, scabies. **s. perruna,** mange. **más viejo que la s.,** Inf. older than the plague
sarnoso /sar'noso/ a itchy; mangy
sarraceno /sarra'seno; sarra'θeno/ (-na) a Saracen. n Saracen; Moor
sarracina /sarra'sina; sarra'θina/ f, scuffle
sarrillo /sa'rriyo; sa'rriʌo/ m, death rattle, rale; arum lily
sarro /'sarro/ m, furry encrustation, scale; film; tartar (on teeth)
sarta /'sarta/ f, string, link (of pearls, etc.); file, line
sartén /sar'ten/ f, frying pan. **tener la s. por el mango,** Inf. to be top dog
sastra /'sastra/ f, female tailor; tailor's wife
sastre /'sastre/ m, tailor. **ser buen s.,** Inf. to be an expert (in)
sastrería /sastre'ria/ f, tailoring; tailor's shop
Satanás /sata'nas/ m, Satan; devil
satánico /sa'taniko/ a satanic
satélite /sa'telite/ m, satellite; follower, admirer, sycophant
satén /sa'ten/ m, sateen
satinar /sati'nar/ vt to calender; glaze; satin (paper)
sátira /'satira/ f, satire
satírico /sa'tiriko/ a satiric
satirizar /satiri'sar; satiri'θar/ vi to write satires; vt satirize
sátiro /'satiro/ m, satyr; Theat. indecent play
satisfacción /satisfak'sion; satisfak'θion/ f, settlement, payment; atonement, expiation; satisfaction; gratification; amends; complacency, conceit; contentment; apology. **tomar s.,** to avenge oneself
satisfacer /satisfa'ser; satisfa'θer/ vt irr to pay, settle; atone for, expiate; gratify; quench; fulfill, observe; compensate, indemnify; discharge, meet; convince, persuade; allay, relieve; reward; explain; answer, satisfy; vr avenge oneself; satisfy oneself. Pres. Ind. **satisfago, satisfaces, etc.** Fut. **satisfaré, etc.** Condit. **satisfaría, etc.** Preterite **satisfice, etc.** Past Part. **satisfecho.** Pres. Subjunc. **satisfaga, etc.** Imperf. Subjunc. **satisficiese, etc.**
satisfactorio /satisfak'torio/ a satisfactory
satisfecho /satis'fetʃo/ a self-satisfied, complacent; happy, contented

sátrapa /'satrapa/ m, satrap; Inf. cunning fellow
saturación /satura'sion; satura'θion/ f, saturation
saturar /satu'rar/ vt to satiate, fill; saturate
saturnino /satur'nino/ a saturnine, melancholy, morose
saturnismo /satur'nismo/ m, saturnism, lead poisoning
Saturno /sa'turno/ m, Saturn
sauce /'sause; 'sauθe/ m, willow. **s. llorón,** weeping willow
saúco /sa'uko/ m, elder tree
saurio /'saurio/ a and m, saurian
savia /'saβia/ f, sap; energy, zest
sáxeo /'sakseo/ a stone, stony
saxófono /sak'sofono/ or **saxofón** m, saxophone
saya /'saya/ f, skirt; long tunic
sayal /sa'yal/ m, thick woolen material
sayo /'sayo/ m, loose smock; Inf. any garment. **cortar un s.** (a), Inf. to gossip behind a person's back
sayón /sa'yon/ m, executioner; Inf. hideous-looking man
sazón /sa'son; sa'θon/ f, ripeness, maturity; season; perfection, excellence; opportunity; taste, flavor; seasoning. **a la s.,** at that time, then. **en s.,** in season; opportunely
sazonador /sasona'ðor; saθona'ðor/ (-ra) a seasoning. n seasoner
sazonar /saso'nar; saθo'nar/ vt Cul. to season; mature; vr mature, ripen
se /se/ object pron reflexive 3rd sing and pl mf 1. Used as accusative (direct object) himself, herself, yourself, themselves, yourselves (e.g. Juan se ha cortado, John has cut himself). 2. Used as dative or indirect object to himself, at himself, herself, themselves, etc. (e.g. María se mira al espejo, Mary looks at herself in the mirror). Reciprocity is also expressed by reflexive (e.g. No se hablan, They do not speak to one another). When a direct object pron. (accusative) and an indirect object pron., both in the 3rd pers. (sing. or pl.), are used together, the indirect object pron. becomes **se** (instead of **le** or **les**) (e.g. Se lo doy, I give it to him). Many Spanish reflexive verbs have English equivalents that are not reflexive (e.g. desayunarse, to breakfast, arrepentirse, to repent, quejarse, to complain). Some intransitive (neuter) verbs have a modified meaning when used reflexively (e.g. marcharse, to go away, dormirse, to fall asleep). The passive may be formed by using **se** + 3rd pers. sing. of verb (e.g. se dice, it is said, people say). A number of impersonal phrases are also formed in this way (e.g. «Se alquila,» "To Let," «Se vende,» "For Sale"). The imperative is used in the same way (e.g. Véase la página dos, See page two)
sebáceo /se'βaseo; se'βaθeo/ a sebaceous
sebo /'seβo/ m, tallow; candle grease; fat, grease
seboso /se'βoso/ a tallowy; fat, greasy
seca /'seka/ f, drought; Naut. unsubmerged sandbank
secadero /seka'ðero/ m, drying place, drying room
secadora /seka'ðora/ f, dryer, drying machine, clothesdryer. **s. de cabello,** hairdryer
secafirmas /seka'firmas/ m, blotting pad
secamente /seka'mente/ adv tersely, brusquely, curtly; dryly
secamiento /seka'miento/ m, drying
secano /se'kano/ m, nonirrigated land; Naut. unsubmerged sandbank; anything very dry
secante /se'kante/ a drying. a and f, Geom. secant. **papel s.,** blotting paper
secar /se'kar/ vt to dry; desiccate; annoy, bore; vr dry; dry up (of streams, etc.); wilt, fade (of plants); become parched; grow thin, become emaciated; be very thirsty; become hard-hearted
sección /sek'sion; sek'θion/ f, act of cutting; section, part, portion; Geom. Mil. section. **s. cónica,** conic section. **s. de amenidades,** entertainment section (of a newspaper). **s. de reserva,** Mil. reserve list
seccionar /seksio'nar; sekθio'nar/ vt to divide into sections, section
seccionario /seksio'nario; sekθio'nario/ a sectional
secesión /sese'sion; seθe'sion/ f, secession

secesionista /sesesio'nista; seθesio'nista/ a and mf secessionist

seco /'seko/ a dry; dried up, parched; faded, wilted; dead (plants); dried (fruits); thin, emaciated; unadorned; barren, arid; brusque, curt; severe, strict; indifferent, unenthusiastic; sharp (sounds); dry (wines). **a secas,** only; solely; simply, just. **en s.,** on dry land; curtly. *Inf.* **dejar s.** (a), to dumbfound, petrify

secreción /sekre'sion; sekre'θion/ f, segregation, separation; *Med.* secretion

secreta /se'kreta/ f, *Law.* secret trial or investigation; *Eccl.* secret(s); toilet, water closet

secretar /sekre'tar/ vt *Med.* to secrete

secretaría /sekreta'ria/ f, secretaryship; secretary's office, secretariat

secretario /sekre'tario/ **(-ia)** n secretary; amanuensis, clerk. m, actuary; registrar. **s. de asuntos exteriores** or **s. de asuntos extranjeros, foreign** secretary. **s. particular,** private secretary

secretear /sekrete'ar/ vi *Inf.* to whisper, have secrets

secreteo /sekre'teo/ m, *Inf.* whispering, exchanging of secrets

secreto /se'kreto/ m, secret; secrecy, silence; confidential information; mystery; secret drawer. a secret; private, confidential. **en s.,** in secret, confidentially. **s. a voces,** open secret

secta /'sekta/ f, sect

sectario /sek'tario/ **(-ia)** a and n sectarian. n fanatical believer

sectarismo /sekta'rismo/ m, sectarianism

sector /sek'tor/ m, sector

secuaz /se'kuas; se'kuaθ/ mf follower, disciple

secuela /se'kuela/ f, sequel, result

secuencia /se'kuensia; se'kuenθia/ f, *Eccl.* sequence; (cinema) sequence

secuestrador /sekuestra'ðor/ **(-ra)** a sequestrating. n sequestrator

secuestrar /sekues'trar/ vt to sequester; kidnap

secuestro /se'kuestro/ m, sequestration; kidnapping; *Surg.* sequestrum

secular /seku'lar/ a secular, lay; centennial; age-old, ancient; *Eccl.* secular

secularización /sekularisa'sion; sekulariθa'θion/ f, secularization

secularizar /sekulari'sar; sekulari'θar/ vt to secularize; vr become secularized

secundar /sekun'dar/ vt to second, aid

secundario /sekun'dario/ a secondary; accessory, subordinate; *Geol.* mesozoic

sed /seð/ f, thirst; desire, yearning, appetite. **apagar** (or **matar**) **la s.,** to quench one's thirst. **tener s.,** to be thirsty

seda /'seða/ f, silk; bristle (boar, etc.). **s. cordelada,** twist silk. **s. ocal,** floss silk. **s. vegetal** or **s. artificial,** artificial silk. *Inf.* **como una s.,** as smooth as silk; sweet-tempered; achieved without any trouble

sedación /seða'sion; seða'θion/ f, calming, soothing

sedal /se'ðal/ m, fish line

sedar /se'ðar/ vt to soothe, calm

sedativo /seða'tiβo/ a and m, *Med.* sedative

sede /'seðe/ f, *Eccl.* see; bishop's throne; *Fig.* seat (of government, etc.); Holy See (also **Santa S.**)

sedentario /seðen'tario/ a sedentary

sedeño /se'ðeɲo/ a silky; silken, made of silk

sedería /seðe'ria/ f, silk goods; silks; silk shop

sedero /se'ðero/ **(-ra)** a silk. n silk weaver or worker; silk merchant

sedición /seði'sion; seði'θion/ f, sedition

sedicioso /seði'sioso; seði'θioso/ a seditious

sediento /se'ðiento/ a thirsty; parched, dry (land); eager (for), desirous (of)

sedimentación /seðimenta'sion; seðimenta'θion/ f, sedimentation

sedimentar /seðimen'tar/ vt to leave a sediment; vr settle, form a sediment

sedimento /seði'mento/ m, sediment; dregs, lees; scale (on boilers)

sedoso /se'ðoso/ a silky, silk-like

seducción /seðuk'sion; seðuk'θion/ f, seduction; temptation, blandishment, wile; charm, allurement

seducir /seðu'sir; seðu'θir/ vt irr to seduce; tempt, lead astray; charm, attract; corrupt, bribe. See **conducir**

seductivo /seðuk'tiβo/ a tempting; seductive, charming

seductor /seðuk'tor/ **(-ra)** a tempting; charming. n seducer; charming person

sefardí /sefar'ði/ mf Iberian Jew; pl Sephardim. a Sephardic

segadera /sega'ðera/ f, sickle

segador /sega'ðor/ m, reaper, harvester

segadora /sega'ðora/ f, mowing machine, harvester; woman harvester

segar /se'gar/ vt irr to scythe, cut down; reap, harvest; mow. See **cegar**

seglar /seg'lar/ a secular, lay. mf layman

segmento /seg'mento/ m, segment; *Geom.* segment. **s. de émbolo,** piston ring

segoviano /sego'βiano/ **(-na)** a and n Segovian

segregación /segrega'sion; segrega'θion/ f, segregation

segregar /segre'gar/ vt to segregate, separate; *Med.* secrete

seguida /se'giða/ f, continuation, prolongation. **de s.,** continuously; immediately. **en s.,** at once, immediately

seguidamente /segiða'mente/ adv continuously; immediately

seguidilla /segi'ðiya; segi'ðiʎa/ f, popular Spanish tune and dance and verse sung to them; *Inf.* diarrhea

seguido /se'giðo/ a continuous, successive; direct, straight

seguidor /segi'ðor/ **(-ra)** a following. n follower, disciple

seguimiento /segi'miento/ m, following, pursuit; continuation, resumption

seguir /se'gir/ vt irr to follow; go after, pursue; prosecute, execute; continue, go on; accompany, go with; exercise (a profession); subscribe to, believe in; agree with; persecute, pester, annoy; imitate; *Law.* institute (a suit); handle, manage; vr result, follow as a consequence; follow in order, happen by turn; originate. *Pres. Part.* **siguiendo.** *Pres. Ind.* **sigo, sigues, sigue, siguen.** *Pres. Subjunc.* **siga,** etc. *Imperf. Subjunc.* **siguiese**

según /se'gun/ adv according to; as. **s. parece,** as it seems. **s. y como,** as, according to

segunda /se'gunda/ f, *Mus.* second

segundar /segun'dar/ vt to repeat, do again; vi to second, follow the first

segundero /segun'dero/ a *Agr.* of the second flowering or fruiting. m, second hand (of a watch)

segundo /se'gundo/ a second. m, second in command, deputy head; *Astron. Geom.* second. **segunda intención,** double meaning. **segunda velocidad,** *Auto.* second gear. **de segunda mano,** second-hand. **sin s.,** without peer or equal

segundogénito /segundo'henito/ **(-ta)** a and n secondborn

segundón /segun'don/ m, second son; any son but the eldest

segurador /segura'ðor/ m, surety, security (person)

seguramente /segura'mente/ adv securely, safely; surely, of course, naturally

seguridad /seguri'ðað/ f, security; safety; certainty; trustworthiness; *Com.* surety; *Mexico* clasp, lock (of a suitcase, trunk, etc) **con toda s.,** with complete safety, surely, absolutely. **de s.,** a safety

seguro /se'guro/ a secure; safe; certain, sure; firm, fixed; reliable, trustworthy; unfailing. m, clasp, fastener; certainty; haven, place of safety; *Mexico* safety pin; *Com.* insurance; permit; *Mech.* ratchet. **s. contra incendio, accidentes, robo,** fire, accident, burglary insurance. **s. sobre la vida,** life insurance. **de s.,** surely, certainly. **en s.,** in safety. **s. social** *Lat. Am.* social security

seis /seis/ a six; sixth. m, six; sixth (of the month); playing card or domino with six spots. **Son las s.,** It is six o'clock

seiscientos /seis'sientos; seis'θientos/ a six hundred; six-hundredth. m, six hundred

selección /selek'sion; selek'θion/ f, selection, choice. **s. natural,** natural selection

seleccionar /seleksio'nar; selekθio'nar/ vt to select, choose

selectivo /selek'tiβo/ a selective

selecto /se'lekto/ a choice, select, excellent

sellado /se'jaðo; se'ʎaðo/ m, Argentina postage

sellador /seya'ðor; seʎa'ðor/ (**-ra**) a sealing, stamping. n sealer, stamper

selladura /seya'ðura; seʎa'ðura/ f, sealing, stamping

sellar /se'yar; se'ʎar/ vt to seal; stamp; end, conclude; close

sello /'seyo; 'seʎo/ m, seal; stamp. **s. fiscal,** stamp duty. **s. postal,** postage stamp. **s. y cruz** Colombia, heads or tails

selva /'selβa/ f, forest, wood; jungle. **s. tropical,** rainforest

Selva Negra, la /'selβa 'negra, la/ the Black Forest

selvático /sel'βatiko/ a sylvan, wood, forest; wild

selvoso /sel'βoso/ a wooded, sylvan

semafórico /sema'foriko/ a semaphoric

semáforo /se'maforo/ m, traffic light.

semana /se'mana/ f, week; week's salary. **S. Mayor** or **S. Santa,** Holy Week. **entre s.,** during the week, on weekdays; weekdays

semanal /sema'nal/ a weekly; of a week's duration

semanario /sema'nario/ a weekly. m, weekly periodical

semanero, -a /sema'nero/ a employed by the week; paid by the week; person employed by the week; person paid by the week

semántica /se'mantika/ f, semantics

semántico /se'mantiko/ a semantic

semblante /sem'βlante/ m, facial expression, countenance; face; appearance, look, aspect. **componer el s.,** to pull oneself together, straighten one's face. **mudar de s.,** to change color, change one's expression; alter (of circumstances)

semblanza /sem'βlansa; sem'βlanθa/ f, biographical sketch. **s. literaria,** short literary biography

sembradera /sembra'ðera/ f, sowing machine

sembradío /sembra'ðio/ a Agr. ready for sowing

sembrado /sem'βraðo/ m, sown land

sembrador /sembra'ðor/ (**-ra**) a sowing. n sower

sembradura /sembra'ðura/ f, Agr. sowing

sembrar /sem'βrar/ vt irr Agr. to sow; scatter, sprinkle; spread, disseminate. See **sentar**

semeja /se'meha/ f, resemblance, similarity; indication, sign (gen. pl)

semejante /seme'hante/ a like, similar; such a; Math. similar. m, similarity, imitation. mf fellow man

semejanza /seme'hansa; seme'hanθa/ f, similarity, likeness. **a s. de,** in the likeness of; like

semejar /seme'har/ (**se**) vi and vr to resemble

semen /'semen/ m, semen; Bot. seed

semental /semen'tal/ a Agr. seed; breeding (of male animals). m, stallion

sementar /semen'tar/ vt Agr. to sow

sementera /semen'tera/ f, Agr. sowing; sown land; seedbed; seedtime; Fig. hotbed, nursery, genesis

sementero /semen'tero/ m, seed bag; seed bed

semestral /semes'tral/ a biannual, half-yearly; lasting six months

semestre /se'mestre/ a biannual. m, half-year, period of six months; six months' salary; semester

semicírculo /semi'sirkulo; semi'θirkulo/ m, semicircle

semidifunto /semiði'funto/ a half-dead

semidormido /semiðor'miðo/ a half-asleep

semilla /se'miya; se'miʎa/ f, Bot. seed; Fig. germ, genesis

semillero /semi'yero; semi'ʎero/ m, seedbed; nursery; Fig. hotbed, origin

seminario /semi'nario/ m, seedbed; nursery; genesis, origin; seminary; tutorial. **s. conciliar,** theological seminary

seminarista /semina'rista/ mf seminarist

semiótica /semi'otika/ f, Med. symptomatology; semiotics

semita /se'mita/ mf Semite. a Semitic

semítico /se'mitiko/ a Semitic

semitismo /semi'tismo/ m, Semitism

semitono /semi'tono/ m, Mus. semitone

semitransparente /semitranspa'rente/ a semitransparent

semivivo /semi'βiβo/ a half-alive

sémola /'semola/ f, semolina

sempiterna /sempi'terna/ f, everlasting flower; thick woolen material

sempiterno /sempi'terno/ a eternal

sen /sen/ m, senna

Sena, el /'sena, el/ the Seine

sena /'sena, el/ f, Bot. senna; six-spotted die

senado /se'naðo/ m, senate; senate house; any grave assembly

senador /sena'ðor/ m, senator

senaduría /sena'ðuria/ f, senatorship

senario /se'nario/ a senary

senatorio /sena'torio/ a senatorial

sencillez /sensi'yes; senθi'ʎeθ/ f, simplicity; naturalness; easiness; ingenuousness, candor

sencillo /sen'siyo; sen'θiʎo/ a simple; unmixed; natural; thin, light (fabric); easy; ingenuous, candid; unadorned, plain; single; sincere

senda /'senda/ f, path, footpath; way; means

senderear /sendere'ar/ vt to conduct along a path; make a pathway; vi attain by tortuous means

sendero /sen'dero/ m, footpath, path

sendos, sendas /'sendos, 'sendas/ a m, and f pl, one each (e.g. Les dio sendos lápices, He gave them each a pencil)

senectud /senek'tuð/ f, old age

senescal /senes'kal/ m, seneschal

senil /se'nil/ a senile

senilidad /senili'ðað/ f, senility

seno /'seno/ m, hollow; hole; concavity; bosom, breast; chest; uterus, womb; any internal cavity of the body; bay, cove; lap (of a woman); interior (of anything), heart; gulf; Math. sine; Anat. sinus

sensación /sensa'sion; sensa'θion/ f, sensation

sensacional /sensasio'nal; sensaθio'nal/ a sensational

sensacionalista /sensasiona'lista; sensaθiona'lista/ a sensationalist

sensatez /sensa'tes; sensa'teθ/ f, prudence, good sense

sensato /sen'sato/ a prudent, wise

sensibilidad /sensiβili'ðað/ f, sensibility

sensibilizar /sensiβili'sar; sensiβili'θar/ vt Photo. to sensitize

sensible /sen'siβle/ a sensible, sensitive; tender, feeling; perceptible; noticeable, definite; sensitive; sad, regrettable

sensiblemente /sensiβle'mente/ adv appreciably; perceptibly; painfully, sadly

sensiblería /sensiβle'ria/ f, sentimentality, sentimentalism

sensiblero /sensi'βlero/ a oversentimental

sensitiva /sensi'tiβa/ f, sensitive plant, mimosa

sensitivo /sensi'tiβo/ a sensuous; sensitive, sensible

sensorio /sen'sorio/ a sensory. m, sensorium

sensual /sen'sual/ a sensual; sensitive, sensible; carnal, voluptuous

sensualidad /sensuali'ðað/ f, sensuality; sensualism

sensualismo /sensua'lismo/ m, sensualism; Philos. sensationalism

sensualista /sensua'lista/ mf Philos. sensationalist; sensualist

sentadera /senta'ðera/ f, Lat. Am. seat (of a chair)

sentadero /senta'ðero/ m, resting place, improvised seat

sentado /sen'taðo/ a prudent, circumspect

sentar /sen'tar/ vt irr to seat; vi Inf. suit, agree with (e.g. No me sienta este vino (este plato), This climate (dish) doesn't suit me); fit, become; Inf. please, satisfy, be agreeable to; vr sit down; Inf. leave a mark on the skin. *Pres. Ind.* **siento, sientas, sienta, sientan.** *Pres. Subjunc.* **siente, sientes, siente, sienten**

sentencia /sen'tensia; sen'tenθia/ *f*, opinion, belief; maxim; *Law.* verdict, sentence; decision, judgment. *Law.* **fulminar** (*or* **pronunciar**) **la s.,** to pass sentence

sentenciador /sentensia'ðor; sentenθia'ðor/ *a Law.* sentencing

sentenciar /senten'siar; senten'θiar/ *vt Law.* to sentence; *Inf.* destine, intend

sentencioso /senten'sioso; senten'θioso/ *a* sententious

sentidamente /sentiða'mente/ *adv* feelingly; sadly, regretfully

sentido /sen'tiðo/ *m*, sense (hearing, seeing, touch, smell, taste); understanding, sense; meaning, interpretation, signification; perception, discrimination; judgment; direction, way. *a* and *past part* felt; expressive; hypersensitive, touchy. **s. común,** common sense. **costar un s.,** *Fig. Inf.* to cost a fortune. **perder el s.,** to lose consciousness

sentimental /sentimen'tal/ *a* emotional; sentimental; romantic

sentimentalismo /sentimenta'lismo/ *m*, emotional quality; sentimentalism

sentimiento /senti'miento/ *m*, feeling, sentiment; sensation, impression; grief, sorrow. **Le acompaño a usted en su s.,** I sympathize with you in your sorrow (bereavement)

sentina /sen'tina/ *f*, well (of a ship); *Naut.* bilge; cesspool; sink of iniquity

sentir /sen'tir/ *vt irr* to feel, experience; hear; appreciate; grieve, regret; believe, consider; envisage, foresee; *vr* complain; suffer; think or consider oneself; crack; feel, be; go rotten, decay (gen. with *estar* + *past part.*). *m*, view, opinion; feeling. **Lo siento,** I'm sorry. **Lo siento mucho,** I'm very sorry. **sin s.,** without feeling; without noticing. *Pres. Part.* **sintiendo.** *Pres. Ind.* **siento, sientes, siente, sienten.** *Preterite* **sintió, sintieron.** *Pres. Subjunc.* **sienta, sientas, sienta, sintamos, sintáis, sientan.** *Imperf. Subjunc.* **sintiese, etc.**

seña /'sena/ *f*, sign, mark; gesture; *Mil.* password; signal; *pl* address, domicile. **s. mortal,** definite or unmistakable sign. **dar señas,** to show signs, manifest. **hablar por señas,** to converse by signs

señal /se'nal/ *f*, mark, sign; boundary stone; landmark; scar; signal; trace, vestige; indication, symptom, token; symbol, sign; image, representation; prodigy, marvel; deposit, advance payment. **s. de aterrizaje,** *Aer.* landing signal. **s. de niebla,** fog signal. **señales horarias,** *Radio.* time signal. **en s.,** as a sign, in proof of. **s. luminosa de la circulación,** traffic light, traffic robot

señaladamente /senala'ðamente/ *adv* especially, particularly, notably

señalado /sena'laðo/ *a* famous, distinguished; important, notable

señalador /senala'ðor/ *m, Argentina* bookmark

señalamiento /senala'miento/ *m*, marking; pointing out; appointment, designation

señalar /sena'lar/ *vt* to mark; indicate, point out; fix, arrange; wound; signal; stamp; appoint (to office); *vr* excel

señero /se'nero/ *a* solitary, isolated

señor /se'nor/ *a Inf.* gentlemanly. *m*, owner, master; mister, esquire; **(S.)** the Lord; lord, sire. **s. de horca y cuchillo,** feudal lord, lord of life and death

señora /se'nora/ *f*, lady; owner, mistress; madam; wife. **s. de compañía,** chaperon; lady companion. **Nuestra S.,** Our Lady

señorear /senore'ar/ *vt* to control, run, manage; master; domineer; appropriate, seize; dominate, overlook; restrain (emotions); *vr* behave with dignity

señoría /seno'ria/ *f*, lordship (title and person); lordship, jurisdiction; area, territory; control, restraint

señoría /seno'ria/ *f*, dignity, sedateness; self-control

señorial /seno'rial/ *a* manorial; noble, dignified, lordly

señoril /seno'ril/ *a* lordly, noble, aristocratic

señorío /seno'rio/ *m*, lordship; jurisdiction; dominion

señorita /seno'rita/ *f*, young lady; miss; *Inf.* mistress of the house

señorito /seno'rito/ *m*, young gentleman; *Inf.* master of the house; master (address); *Inf.* young man about town

señuelo /se'nuelo/ *m*, decoy; bait; allurement, attraction. **caer en el s.,** *Fig. Inf.* to fall into the trap

sepancuantos /sepan'kuantos/ *m, Inf.* scolding, rebuke; spanking

separación /separa'sion; separa'θion/ *f*, separation

separado /sepa'raðo/ *a* separate

separador /separa'ðor/ **(-ra)** *a* separating. *n* separator. *m*, filter. **s. de aceite,** oil filter

separar /sepa'rar/ *vt* to separate; divide; dismiss (from a post); lay aside; *vr* retire, resign; separate

separatismo /separa'tismo/ *m*, separatism

separatista /separa'tista/ *a* and *mf* separatist

septeno /sep'teno/ *a.* see **séptimo**

septentrión /septen'trion/ *m, Astron.* Great Bear; north

septentrional /septentrio'nal/ *a* north; northern

septeto /sep'teto/ *m*, septet

septicemia /septi'semia; septi'θemia/ *f*, septicemia

séptico /'septiko/ *a* septic

septiembre /sep'tiembre/ *m*, September

septillo /sep'tiyo; sep'tiʎo/ *m, Mus.* septuplet

séptima /'septima/ *f, Mus.* seventh

séptimo /'septimo/ *a* and *m*, seventh

septuagenario /septuahe'nario/ **(-ia)** *a* and *n* septuagenarian

septuagésimo /septua'hesimo/ *a* seventieth; septuagesimal. *m*, seventieth

séptuplo /'septuplo/ *a* sevenfold

sepulcral /sepul'kral/ *a* sepulchral

sepulcro /se'pulkro/ *m*, sepulcher

sepultador /sepulta'ðor/ **(-ra)** *a* burying. *n* gravedigger; burier

sepultar /sepul'tar/ *vt* to inter, bury; hide, cover up

sepultura /sepul'tura/ *f*, interment; grave; tomb

sepulturero /sepultu'rero/ *m*, gravedigger

sequedad /seke'ðað/ *f*, dryness, barrenness; acerbity, sharpness

sequía /se'kia/ *f*, drought

séquito /'sekito/ *m*, following, suite, retinue; general approval, popularity

ser /ser/ *m*, essence, nature; being; existence, life. **El S. Supremo,** The Supreme Being, God

ser /ser/ *vi irr* to be (e.g. *El sombrero es azul,* The hat is blue). **Ser** may agree with either subject or complement, though when latter is *pl* the verb tends to be so too (e.g. *Son las once,* (*horas*), It is eleven o'clock. *Cien dólares son poco dinero,* A hundred dollars is a small amount). With verbal complement is pers. pron., **ser** agrees with it both in number and person (e.g. *Son ellos,* It is they. *Soy yo,* It is I). In impers. phrases the pron. is not expressed (e.g. *Es difícil,* It is difficult. *Es sorprendente,* It is surprising). **ser** means to exist (e.g. *Pienso luego soy,* I think, therefore I am). **ser** (also **ser de** with nouns or obj. prons.) means to belong to, be the property of (e.g. *Este gato es mío,* This cat is mine. *El libro es de Juan,* The book belongs to John). Signifies to happen, occur (e.g. *¿Cómo fue eso?* How did that happen?). Means to be suitable or fitting (e.g. *Este vestido no es para una señora mayor,* This dress is not suitable for an elderly lady). Expresses price, to be worth (e.g. *¿A cuánto es el dólar?* How much is the dollar worth?) Means to be a member of, belong to (e.g. *Es de la Academia Española,* He is a member of the Spanish Academy). Means to be of use, be useful for (e.g. *Esta casa no es para una familia numerosa,* This house is not for a large family). **Ser** expresses nationality (e.g. *Son francesas,* They are French. *Somos de Londres,* We are from London). *Auxiliary verb* used to form passive tense (e.g. *Esta historia ha sido leída por muchos,* This story has been read by many. *Fueron mandados al Japón,* They were sent to Japan. *s. de ver,* to be worth seeing. *s. para poco,* to be of little use, amount to little. *s. testigo de,* to witness. *¡Cómo es eso!* How can that be! Surely not! *¡Cómo ha de s.!* How should it be!; One must resign oneself. *Érase una vez or que érase,*

Once upon a time. *es a saber*, viz., that is to say. *un sí es no es*, a touch of, a suspicion of). *Pres. Part.* **siendo.** *Pres. Ind.* **soy, eres, es, somos, sois, son.** *Fut.* **seré, etc.** *Condit.* **sería, etc.** *Preterite* **fui, fuiste, fue, fuimos, fuisteis, fueron.** *Imperf.* **era, etc.** *Past Part.* **sido.** *Pres. Subjunc.* **sea, etc.** *Imperf. Subjunc.* **fuese, etc.** *Imperat.* **sé**

sera /'sera/ *f*, large frail

seráfico /se'rafiko/ *a* seraphic

serafín /sera'fin/ *m*, seraphim

serbal /ser'βal/ *m*, service tree

serena /se'rena/ *f*, serenade; *Inf.* dew

serenar /sere'nar/ *vt* to calm; soothe; clear; *vr* grow calm; clear up (weather); clear (liquids); be soothed or pacified

serenata /sere'nata/ *f*, serenade

serenidad /sereni'ðað/ *f*, serenity, composure, tranquility; Serene Highness (title)

sereno /se'reno/ *a* cloudless, fair; composed, serene. *m*, dew; night watchman. **al s.**, in the night air

sericultor /serikul'tor/ *m*, silk cultivator, sericulturist

sericultura /serikul'tura/ *f*, silk culture

serie /'serie/ *f*, series, sequence, succession; *Math.* progression; (*Biol. Elec.*) series; break (in billiards)

seriedad /serie'ðað/ *f*, seriousness, earnestness; gravity; austerity; sternness; importance; sincerity; solemnity

serigrafía /serigra'fia/ *f*, silkscreen printing

serio /'serio/ *a* serious, earnest; grave; austere; stern; important; sincere, genuine; solemn. **en s.**, seriously

sermón /ser'mon/ *m*, sermon; scolding. **dar un s.**, to give a sermon

sermonar /sermo'nar/ *vi* to preach

sermonear /sermone'ar/ *vi* to preach sermons; *vt* scold

sermoneo /sermo'neo/ *m*, *Inf.* scolding

seroja /se'roha/ *f*, withered leaves; brushwood

serpear /serpe'ar/ *vi* to wind, twist; wriggle, squirm; coil

serpenteado /serpente'aðo/ *a* winding

serpentear /serpente'ar/ *vi* to wind, twist, meander; stagger along; wriggle; coil; *Aer.* yaw

serpenteo /serpen'teo/ *m*, winding, twisting; wriggling; coiling; *Aer.* yaw

serpentín /serpen'tin/ *m*, *Chem.* worm; coil (in industry); *Mineral.* serpentine

serpentina /serpen'tina/ *f*, *Mineral.* serpentine; paper streamer

serpentino /serpen'tino/ *a* serpentine; *Poet.* winding, sinuous

serpiente /ser'piente/ *f*, snake, serpent; Satan, the Devil; *Astron.* Serpent. **s. de anteojos**, cobra. **s. de cascabel**, rattlesnake

serpollo /ser'poyo; ser'poʎo/ *m*, *Bot.* shoot, new branch; sprout; sucker

serrado /se'rraðo/ *a* serrate

serrallo /se'rrayo; se'rraʎo/ *m*, harem; seraglio; brothel

serranía /serra'nia/ *f*, mountainous territory

serrano /se'rrano/ **(-na)** *a* mountain, highland. *n* highlander, mountain dweller

serruchar /serru'tʃar/ *vt*, *Lat. Am.* to saw, saw off

serrucho /se'rrutʃo/ *m*, handsaw. **s. de calar**, fretsaw

Servia /'serβia/ Serbia

servible /ser'βiβle/ *a* serviceable; useful

servicial /serβi'sial; serβi'θial/ *a* useful, serviceable; obliging, obsequious

servicio /ser'βisio; ser'βiθio/ *m*, service; domestic service; cult, devotion; care, attendance; military service; set, service; department, section; present of money; cover (cutlery, etc., at table); domestic staff, servants. **s. informativo**, news service. **s. nocturno permanente**, all-night service. **hacer un flaco s. (a)**, *Inf.* to do someone an ill turn. **prestar servicios**, to render service, serve

servidor /serβi'ðor/ **(-ra)** *n* servant, domestic; name by which one refers to oneself (e.g. *Un s. lo hará con mucho gusto*, I (your servant) will do it with much pleasure). *m*, wooer, lover; bowler (in cricket). **los servidores de una ametralladora**, the crew (of a

gun). **Quedo de Vd. atento y seguro s.**, I remain your obedient servant (in letters), Yours faithfully

servidumbre /serβi'ðumbre/ *f*, serfdom; servitude; servants, domestic staff; obligation, duty; enslavement (by passions); right of way; use, service

servil /ser'βil/ *a* servile; humble

servilismo /serβi'lismo/ *m*, servility; abjectness; absolutism (Spanish history)

servilleta /serβi'yeta; serβi'ʎeta/ *f*, table napkin. **s. higiénica**, sanitary napkin

servilletero /serβiye'tero; serβiʎe'tero/ *m*, napkin ring

servio /'serβio/ **(-ia)** *a* and *n* Serbian

servir /ser'βir/ *vi irr* to be employed (by), be in the service (of); serve (as), perform the duties (of); be of use; wait (on), be subject to. *Mil.* serve in the armed forces; wait at table; be suitable or favorable; *Sports.* serve; perform a service; follow the lead (cards); (*with de*) act as, be a deputy for; be a substitute for; *vt* serve; worship; do a favor to; woo, court; serve (food, drink); *vr* be pleased or willing, deign; help oneself to (food); (*with de*) make use of. **no s. para nada**, to be good for nothing, be useless. **No sirves para tales cosas**, You are no good at this sort of thing. **Para servirle**, At your service. **¡Sírvase de...!** (followed by infin.), Please! **s. de**, to serve (e.g. *s. de base a*, to serve as a basis for). See **pedir**

sésamo /'sesamo/ *m*, sesame

sesenta /se'senta/ *a* and *m*, sixty; sixtieth

sesentavo /sesen'taβo/ *a* and *m*, sixtieth

sesentón /sesen'ton/ **(-ona)** *n Inf.* person of sixty

sesga /'sesga/ *f*, *Sew.* gore

sesgadamente /sesgaða'mente/ *adv* on the slant; askew; obliquely

sesgado /ses'gaðo/ *a* oblique, slanting

sesgar /ses'gar/ *vt Sew.* to cut on the bias; slant, slope; place askew, twist to one side

sesgo /'sesgo/ *a* slanting, oblique; serious-faced. *m*, slope, slant, obliquity; compromise, middle way. **al s.**, on the slant

sesión /se'sion/ *f*, session, meeting; conference, consultation; *Law.* sitting; term. **abrir la s.**, to open the meeting. **levantar la s.**, to adjourn the meeting

seso /'seso/ *m*, brain; prudence; *pl* brains. **perder el s.**, to go mad; *Fig.* lose one's head

sestear /seste'ar/ *vi* to take an afternoon nap; rest; settle

sesteo /ses'teo/ *m*, *Lat. Am.* nap, siesta

sesudez /sesu'ðes; sesu'ðeθ/ *f*, prudence, shrewdness

sesudo /se'suðo/ *a* sensible, prudent

seta /'seta/ *f*, mushroom. **s. venenosa**, poisonous toadstool

setal /se'tal/ *m*, mushroom bed, patch, or field

setecientos /sete'sientos; sete'θientos/ *a* and *m*, seven hundred; seven-hundredth

setenta /se'tenta/ *a* and *m*, seventy; seventieth

setentavo /seten'taβo/ *a* and *m*, seventieth

setentón /seten'ton/ **(-ona)** *n* septuagenarian

seter /'seter/ *m*, setter (dog)

setiembre /se'tiembre/ *m*. See **septiembre**

seto /'seto/ *m*, fence; hedge

seudo /'seuðo/ *a* pseudo

seudónimo /seu'ðonimo/ *m*, pseudonym

severamente /seβera'mente/ *adv* severely, harshly

severidad /seβeri'ðað/ *f*, severity; harshness; strictness, rigor; austerity, seriousness

severo /se'βero/ *a* severe; harsh; strict, rigid, scrupulous, exact; austere, serious

sevillanas /seβi'yanas; seβi'ʎanas/ *f pl*, Sevillian dance and its music

sevillano /seβi'yano; seβi'ʎano/ **(-na)** *a* and *n* of or from Seville, Sevillian

sexagenario /seksahe'nario/ **(-ia)** *n* sexagenarian

sexagésimo /seksa'hesimo/ *a* sixtieth

sexismo /sek'sismo/ *m*, sexism

sexo /'sekso/ *m*, sex; (sexual) organ

sexología /seksolo'hia/ *f*, sexology

sexólogo /sek'sologo/ **(-ga)** *n* sexologist

sexta /'seksta/ *f*, *Eccl.* sext; *Mus.* sixth

sexteto /seks'teto/ *m*, sextet

sexto /'seksto/ *a* sixth
sextuplicación /sekstuplika'sion; sekstuplika'θion/ *f,* multiplication by six
sextuplicar /sekstupli'kar/ *vt* to multiply by six, sextuple
séxtuplo /'sekstuplo/ *a* sixfold
sexualidad /seksuali'ðað/ *f,* sexuality
si /si/ *m, Mus.* B, seventh note of the scale. *conjunc* if; whether; even if, although. In conditional clause, **si,** meaning if, is followed by indicative tense unless statement be contrary to fact (e.g. *Si pierdes el tren, volverás a casa,* If you miss your train you will return home, *but Si hubieran venido habríamos ido al campo,* If they had come (but they didn't) we would have gone to the country). **Si** is used at the beginning of a clause to make expressions of doubt, desire, or affirmation more emphatic (e.g. *¡Si lo sabrá él, con toda su experiencia!* Of course he knows it, with all his experience. *¿Si será falsa la noticia?* Can the news be false?) **Si** also means whether (e.g. *Me preguntaron si era médico o militar,* They asked me whether I was a doctor or a soldier). Sometimes means even if, although (e.g. *Si viniesen no lo harían,* Even if they came they would not do it. *como si,* as if. *por si acaso,* in case, in the event of. *si bien,* although.
sí /si/ *pers pron reflexive 3rd pers m,* and *f, sing* and *pl* himself, herself, itself, themselves. Always used with prep. (e.g. *para sí,* for himself, herself, etc. *de por sí,* separately, on its own. *decir para sí,* to say to oneself)
sí /si/ *adv* yes. **sí** *or* **sí que** is frequently used to emphasize a verb generally in contrast to a previous negative (e.g. *Ellos no lo harán, pero yo sí,* They won't do it but I will). Often translated by "did" (e.g. *No lo vi todo, pero lo que sí vi,* I didn't see it all, but what I did see...). *m,* assent; yes; consent. **dar el sí,** to say yes; agree; accept an offer of marriage
siamés /sia'mes/ **(-esa)** *a* and *n* Siamese. *m,* Thai (language)
sibarita /siβa'rita/ *a* sybaritic. *mf* sybarite
sibarítico /siβa'ritiko/ *a* sybaritic; sensual
sibaritismo /siβari'tismo/ *m,* sybaritism
siberiano /siβe'riano/ **(-na)** *a* and *n* Siberian
sibila /si'βila/ *f,* sibyl
sibilante /siβi'lante/ *a* sibilant
sibilino /siβi'lino/ *a* sibylline
sicario /si'kario/ *m,* paid assassin
Sicilia /si'silia; si'θilia/ Sicily
siciliano /sisi'liano; siθi'liano/ **(-na)** *a* and *n* Sicilian
sicoanálisis /sikoa'nalisis/ *m,* psychoanalysis
sicoanalista /sikoana'lista/ *mf* psychoanalyst
sicoanalizar /sikoanali'sar; sikoanali'θar/ *vt* to psychoanalyze
sicofanta, sicofante /siko'fanta, siko'fante/ *m,* sycophant
sicología /sikolo'hia/ *f,* psychology
sicológico /siko'lohiko/ *a* psychological
sicólogo /si'kologo/ **(-ga)** *n* psychologist
sicomoro /siko'moro/ *m,* sycamore
sicopático /siko'patiko/ *a* psychopathic
sicosis /si'kosis/ *f, Med.* psychosis
sicoterapia /sikote'rapia/ *f,* psychotherapy
SIDA /'siða/ *m,* AIDS
sideral, sidéreo /siðe'ral, si'ðereo/ *a* sidereal
sidra /'siðra/ *f,* cider
siega /'siega/ *f,* reaping, harvesting; harvest time; harvest, crop
siembra /'siembra/ *f, Agr.* sowing; seedtime; sown field
siempre /'siempre/ *adv* always. **s. que,** provided that; whenever. **para s.,** forever. **por s. jamás,** for always, for ever and ever
siempreviva /siempre'βiβa/ *f, Bot.* everlasting flower. **s. mayor,** houseleek
sien /sien/ *f, Anat.* temple
sierpe /'sierpe/ *f,* serpent, snake; anything that wriggles; kite (toy); *Bot.* sucker; hideous person
sierra /'sierra/ *f,* saw; ridge of mountains; sawfish; slope; hillside. **s. de cerrojero,** hacksaw. **s. de cinta,** handsaw
siervo /'sierβo/ **(-va)** *n* slave; servant; serf

siesta /'siesta/ *f,* noonday heat; afternoon nap
siete /'siete/ *a* seven; seventh. *m,* seven; seventh (days of the month); playing card with seven spots; number seven. **las s.,** seven o'clock. *Inf.* **más que s.,** more than somewhat, extremely
sietemesino /siete'mesino/ **(-na)** *n* seven-month-old child; *Fig. Inf.* young cock
sífilis /'sifilis/ *f,* syphilis
sifilítico /sifi'litiko/ **(-ca)** *a* and *n* syphilitic
sifón /si'fon/ *m,* siphon; siphon bottle; soda water; *Mech.* trap
sigilar /sihi'lar/ *vt* to seal; hide, conceal
sigilo /si'hilo/ *m,* seal; secrecy, concealment; silence, reserve
sigiloso /sihi'loso/ *a* secret, silent
sigla /'sigla/ *f,* acronym
siglo /'siglo/ *m,* century; long time, age; social intercourse, society, world. **s. de oro,** golden age. **en** *or* **por los siglos de los siglos,** for ever and ever
signar /sig'nar/ *vt* to sign; make the sign of the cross over; *vr* cross oneself
signatario /signa'tario/ **(-ia)** *a* and *n* signatory
signatura /signa'tura/ *f, Print.* signature; mark, sign; *Mus.* signature
significación /signifika'sion; signifika'θion/ *f,* **significado** *m,* meaning; importance, significance
significante /signifi'kante/ *a* significant
significar /signifi'kar/ *vt* to signify, indicate; mean; publish, make known; *vi* represent, mean; be worth
significativo /signifika'tiβo/ *a* significant
signo /'signo/ *m,* sign, indication, token; sign, character; *Math.* symbol; sign of the zodiac; *Mus.* sign; *Med.* symptom; *Eccl.* gesture of benediction; destiny, fate
siguemepollo /sigeme'poyo; sigeme'poʎo/ *m, Inf.* streamer
siguiente /si'giente/ *a* following; next, subsequent. **el día s.,** the next day
sílaba /'silaβa/ *f,* syllable
silabario /sila'βario/ *m,* speller, spelling book
silabear /silaβe'ar/ *vi* and *vt* to pronounce by syllables, syllabize
silabeo /silaβe'o/ *m,* pronouncing syllable by syllable, syllabication
silábico /si'laβiko/ *a* syllabic
sílabo /'silaβo/ *m,* syllabus, list
silba /'silβa/ *f,* hissing (as a sign of disapproval)
silbador /silβa'ðor/ **(-ra)** *a* whistling; hissing. *n* whistler; one who hisses
silbar /sil'βar/ *vi* to whistle; whizz, rush through the air; *vi* and *vt Theat.* hiss
silbato /sil'βato/ *m,* whistle; air hole
silbido, silbo /sil'βiðo, 'silβo/ *m,* whistle, whistling; hiss, hissing
silenciador /silensia'ðor; silenθia'ðor/ *m,* (*Auto.* firearms) silencer
silenciar /silen'siar; silen'θiar/ *vt* to silence; keep secret
silenciario /silen'siario; silen'θiario/ *a* vowed to perpetual silence
silencio /si'lensio; si'lenθio/ *m,* silence; noiselessness, quietness; omission, disregard; *Mus.* rest. **en s.,** in silence; quietly; uncomplainingly. **pasar en s. (una cosa)** to pass over (something) in silence, omit. **s. de muerte,** deathly silence
silencioso /silen'sioso; silen'θioso/ *a* silent; noiseless; tranquil, quiet. *m,* (*Auto.* firearms) silencer
silfide /'silfiðe/ *f,* **silfo** *m,* sylph
silicato /sili'kato/ *m, Chem.* silicate
sílice /'silise; 'siliθe/ *f, Chem.* silica
silla /'siya; 'siʎa/ *f,* chair; riding saddle; *Mech.* rest, saddle; *Eccl.* see. **s. de manos,** sedan chair. **s. de montar,** riding saddle. **s. de posta,** post chaise. **s. de ruedas,** wheelchair. **s. de tijera,** deck chair; campstool. **s. giratoria,** swivel chair. **s. poltrona,** easy chair. *Inf.* **pegársele la s.,** to overstay one's welcome
sillar /si'yar; si'ʎar/ *m,* ashlar, stone, quarry stone; horseback
sillería /siye'ria; siʎe'ria/ *f,* set of chairs; pew, choir

stalls; chair factory; shop where chairs are sold; chair making; *Mas.* ashlar masonry

sillero /si'yero; si'ʎero/ **(-ra)** *n* chair maker or seller; saddler

silleta /si'yeta; si'ʎeta/ *f*, bedpan; fireman's lift

silletero /siye'tero; siʎe'tero/ *m*, runner, sedan chair carrier

sillín /si'yin; si'ʎin/ *m*, light riding saddle; seat, saddle (of bicycles, etc.)

sillón /si'yon; si'ʎon/ *m*, armchair; sidesaddle; *Lat. Am.* rocking chair. **s.-cama,** reclining chair. **s. de mimbres,** bamboo chair

silo /'silo/ *m*, *Agr.* silo; dark cavern, dark cave

silogismo /silo'hismo/ *m*, syllogism

silogístico /silo'histiko/ *a* syllogistic

silueta /si'lueta/ *f*, silhouette; figure

silúrico /si'luriko/ *a* silurian

siluro /si'luro/ *m*, catfish; *Nav.* self-propelling torpedo

silva /'silβa/ *f*, literary miscellany; metrical form

silvestre /sil'βestre/ *a Bot.* wild; sylvan; uncultivated; savage

silvicultor /silβikul'tor/ *m*, forester

silvicultura /silβikul'tura/ *f*, forestry

sima /'sima/ *f*, abyss, chasm

simbiosis /sim'biosis/ *f*, symbiosis

simbólico /sim'boliko/ *a* symbolical

simbolismo /simbo'lismo/ *m*, symbolism

simbolista /simbo'lista/ *mf* symbolist

simbolización /simbolisa'sion; simboliθa'θion/ *f*, symbolization

simbolizar /simboli'sar; simboli'θar/ *vt* to symbolize, represent

símbolo /'simbolo/ *m*, symbol. **s. de la fe,** *Eccl.* Creed

simetría /sime'tria/ *f*, symmetry

simétrico /si'metriko/ *a* symmetric; symmetrical

simetrizar /simetri'sar; simetri'θar/ *vt* to make symmetrical

símico /'simiko/ *a* simian

simiente /si'miente/ *f*, seed; semen; germ, genesis, origin

simiesco /si'miesko/ *a* apish, ape-like

símil /'simil/ *a* similar. *m*, comparison; simile

similar /simi'lar/ *a* similar

similitud /simili'tuð/ *f*, similarity

simio /'simio/ **(-ia)** *n* ape

simón /si'mon/ *m*, horse cab; cabdriver

simonía /simo'nia/ *f*, simony

simpatía /simpa'tia/ *f*, liking, understanding, affection; fellow feeling; sympathy

simpático /sim'patiko/ *a* friendly, nice, decent, congenial; sympathetic. **gran s.,** *Anat.* sympathetic

simpatizar /simpati'sar; simpati'θar/ *vi* to get on well, be congenial

simple /'simple/ *a* simple; single, not double; insipid; easy; plain, unadorned; stupid, silly; pure, unmixed; easily deceived, simple; naïve, ingenuous; mere; mild, meek. *mf* simpleton; fool

simpleza /sim'plesa; sim'pleθa/ *f*, foolishness, stupidity; simplicity

simplicidad /simplisi'ðað; simpliθi'ðað/ *f*, simplicity; candor, ingenuousness

simplícimo /simpli'sisimo; simpli'θisimo/ *a sup* most simple, exceedingly simple

simplificable /simplifi'kaβle/ *a* simplifiable

simplificación /simplifika'sion; simplifika'θion/ *f*, simplification, simplifying

simplificador /simplifika'ðor/ *a* simplifying

simplificar /simplifi'kar/ *vt* to simplify

simplista /sim'plista/ *mf* herbalist

simulación /simula'sion; simula'θion/ *f*, pretense, simulation

simulacro /simu'lakro/ *m*, image, simulacrum; vision, fancy; *Mil.* mock battle

simuladamente /simulaða'mente/ *adv* pretendedly

simulador /simula'ðor/ **(-ra)** *a* feigned. *n* dissembler

simular /simu'lar/ *vt* to feign, pretend

simultanear /simultane'ar/ *vt* to perform simultaneously

simultaneidad /simultanei'ðað/ *f*, simultaneousness

simultáneo /simul'taneo/ *a* simultaneous

simún /si'mun/ *m*, sandstorm

sin /sin/ *prep* without (e.g. *Lo hizo s. hablar,* He did it without speaking). **s. embargo,** nevertheless. **s. fin,** endless. **s. hilos,** radio, wireless

sinagoga /sina'goga/ *f*, synagogue

sinapismo /sina'pismo/ *m*, *Med.* mustard plaster; *Inf.* pest, bore

sincerarse /sinse'rarse; sinθe'rarse/ *vr* to justify oneself; vindicate one's actions

sinceridad /sinseri'ðað; sinθeri'ðað/ *f*, sincerity

sincero /sin'sero; sin'θero/ *a* sincere

síncopa /'sinkopa/ *f*, *Mus.* syncopation; *Gram.* syncope

sincopar /sinko'par/ *vt* to syncopate; abbreviate

síncope /'sinkope/ *m*, syncope

sincrónico /sin'kroniko/ *a* synchronous

sincronismo /sinkro'nismo/ *m*, synchronism

sincronizar /sinkroni'sar; sinkroni'θar/ *vt* to synchronize; *Radio.* tune in

sindéresis /sin'deresis/ *f*, discretion, good sense

sindicación /sindika'sion; sindika'θion/ *f*, syndication

sindicado /sindi'kaðo/ *m*, syndicate

sindical /sindi'kal/ *a* syndical

sindicalismo /sindika'lismo/ *m*, syndicalism, trade unionism

sindicalista /sindika'lista/ *mf* syndicalist, trade unionist. *a* syndicalistic, trade unionist

sindicar /sindi'kar/ *vt* to accuse, charge; censure; syndicate

sindicato /sindi'kato/ *m*, syndicate; trade union. **s. gremial,** trade union. **S. Internacional de Trabajadoras de la Aguja,** International Ladies' Garment Workers' Union

sindicatura /sindika'tura/ *f*, (official) receivership

síndico /'sindiko/ *m*, *Com.* receiver, trustee

síndrome /'sindrome/ *m*, syndrome. **síndrome de inmunidad deficiente adquirida** acquired immunity deficiency syndrome

sinecura /sine'kura/ *f*, sinecure

sinergia /si'nerhia/ *f*, synergy

sinfín /sin'fin/ *m*, countless number

sinfonía /sinfo'nia/ *f*, symphony

sinfónico /sin'foniko/ *a* symphonic

sinfonista /sinfo'nista/ *mf* composer of symphonies, player in a symphony orchestra

sinfonola /sinfo'nola/ *f*, jukebox

singladura /siŋgla'ðura/ *f*, *Naut.* day's sailing; nautical twenty-four hours (beginning at midday)

singlar /siŋ'glar/ *vi Naut.* to sail a given course

singular /siŋgu'lar/ *a* singular, single; individual; extraordinary, remarkable. *a* and *m*, *Gram.* singular

singularidad /siŋgulari'ðað/ *f*, individuality, peculiarity; strangeness, remarkableness; oddness, eccentricity

singularizar /siŋgulari'sar; siŋgulari'θar/ *vt* to particularize, single out; *Gram.* make singular, singularize; *vr* distinguish oneself, stand out; be distinguished (by)

sinhueso /sin'ueso/ *f*, *Inf.* tongue (organ of speech)

siniestra /si'niestra/ *f*, left, lefthand

siniestro /si'niestro/ *a* left (side); vicious, perverse; sinister; unlucky. *m*, viciousness, depravity (gen. *pl*); shipwreck, sinking; disaster, catastrophe; *Com.* damage, loss

sinnúmero /sin'numero/ *m*, countless number

sino /'sino/ *m*, fate, destiny. *conjunc* but; except (e.g. *No lo hicieron ellos s. yo,* They didn't do it, I did. *no... s.,* not..., but); only (e.g. *No sólo lo dijo él s. ella,* Not only he said it, but she did too)

sínodo /'sinoðo/ *m*, (*Eccl. Astron.*) synod; council

sinología /sinolo'hia/ *f*, sinology

sinólogo /si'nologo/ *m*, sinologist

sinonimia /sino'nimia/ *f*, synonymy

sinónimo /si'nonimo/ *a* synonymous. *m*, synonym

sinopsis /si'nopsis/ *f*, synopsis

sinóptico /si'noptiko/ *a* synoptic

sinrazón /sinra'son; sinra'θon/ *f*, injustice, wrong

sinsabor /sinsa'βor/ *m*, unpleasantness, trouble; grief, anxiety

sintáctico /sin'taktiko/ *a* syntactic

sintaxis /sin'taksis/ *f*, syntax

síntesis /'sintesis/ *f*, synthesis

sintético /sin'tetiko/ *a* synthetic

sintetizar /sinteti'sar; sinteti'θar/ *vt* to synthesize

síntoma /'sintoma/ *m*, symptom

sintomático /sinto'matiko/ *a* symptomatic

sintomatología /sintomatolo'hia/ *f*, symptomatology

sintonización /sintonisa'sion; sintoniθa'θion/ *f*, *Radio.* tuning in

sintonizador /sintonisa'ðor; sintoniθa'ðor/ *m*, *Radio.* tuner

sintonizar /sintoni'sar; sintoni'θar/ *vt Radio.* to tune in

sinuosidad /sinuosi'ðað/ *f*, sinuosity

sinuoso /sin'uoso/ *a* sinuous, winding

sinvergüenza /simber'guensa; simber'guenθa/ *mf* rascal, knave, rogue

sinvergüenzada /simberguen'saða; simberguen'θaða/ *f*, *Lat. Am.* dirty thing (to do)

Sión /'sion/ Zion

sionismo /sio'nismo/ *m*, Zionism

sionista /sio'nista/ *a* and *mf* Zionist

siquiatra /si'kiatra/ *m*, psychiatrist

siquiatría /sikia'tria/ *f*, psychiatry

síquico /'sikiko/ *a* psychic

siquiera /si'kiera/ *conjunc* although, even if. **s.... s.**, whether... or. *adv* at least; even (e.g. *Hay que pedir mucho para tener s. la mitad*, One must ask a great deal to get even half). **ni s.**, not even (e.g. *No había nadie, ni s. un perro*, There was no one, not even a dog)

Siracusa /sira'kusa/ Syracuse

siracusano /siraku'sano/ **(-na)** *a* and *n* Syracusan

sirena /si'rena/ *f*, mermaid, siren; siren; foghorn

sirga /'sirga/ *f*, towline

sirgar /sir'gar/ *vt Naut.* to track, tow

Siria /'siria/ Syria

sirio /'sirio/ **(-ia)** *a* and *n* Syrian. *m*, Sirius

siroco /si'roko/ *m*, sirocco

sirte /'sirte/ *f*, sandbank, submerged rock

sirvienta /sir'βienta/ *f*, female servant

sirviente /sir'βiente/ *a* serving. *m*, servant

sisa /'sisa/ *f*, pilfering; *Sew.* dart. **s. dorada,** gold lacquer

sisador /sisa'ðor/ **(-ra)** *n* filcher, pilferer

sisar /si'sar/ *vt* to pilfer, filch, steal; *Sew.* take in, make darts in

sisear /sise'ar/ *vi* and *vt* to hiss (disapproval); sizzle

sísmico /'sismiko/ *a* seismic

sismógrafo /sis'mografo/ *m*, seismograph

sismología /sismolo'hia/ *f*, seismology

sismológico /sismo'lohiko/ *a* seismological

sismómetro /sis'mometro/ *m*, seismometer

sistema /sis'tema/ *m*, system. **s. ferroviario,** railroad system. **s. métrico,** metric system

sistemático /siste'matiko/ *a* systematic

sistematización /sistematisa'sion; sistematiθa'θion/ *f*, systematization

sistematizar /sistemati'sar; sistemati'θar/ *vt* to systematize

sístole /'sistole/ *f*, systole

sitiador /sitia'ðor/ *a* besieging. *m*, besieger

sitiar /si'tiar/ *vt Mil.* to lay siege to; surround, besiege

sitio /'sitio/ *m*, place, spot; room, space; site; locality; *Mil.* siege, blockade; *Lat. Am.* taxi stand **No hay s.,** There's no room

sito /'sito/ *past part* situated, located

situación /situa'sion; situa'θion/ *f*, situation; position; circumstances; condition, state; location

situado /si'tuaðo/ *past part* situated, placed. *m*, income, interest

situar /si'tuar/ *vt* to situate, locate, place; assign funds; *vr* place oneself

snobismo /sno'βismo/ *m*, snobbery

so /so/ *prep* under (used only with **color, pena,** pretexto, capa) (e.g. *so color de*, under the pretext of). *interj* **¡So!** Whoa! (to horses); *Lat. Am.* Hush!

soba /'soβa/ *f*, rubbing; kneading; massage; beating; handling, touching

sobacal /soβa'kal/ *a* underarm, axillary

sobaco /so'βako/ *m*, armpit; *Bot.* axil

sobajar /soβa'har/ *vt* to squeeze, press

sobaquera /soβa'kera/ *f*, *Sew.* armhole; dress shield

sobar /so'βar/ *vt* to rub; knead; massage; beat, thrash; handle, touch, paw (persons); soften

soberanear /soβerane'ar/ *vi* to tyrannize, domineer

soberanía /soβera'nia/ *f*, sovereignty; dominance, sway, rule; dignity, majesty

soberano /soβe'rano/ **(-na)** *a* sovereign; superb; regal, majestic. *n* ruler, lord. *m*, sovereign (coin)

soberbia /so'βerβia/ *f*, arrogance, haughtiness; conceit, presumption; ostentation, pomp; rage, anger

soberbio /so'βerβio/ *a* haughty, arrogant; conceited; superb, magnificent; lofty, soaring; spirited (of horses)

sobón /so'βon/ *a Inf.* overdemonstrative, mushy; *Inf.* lazy

sobordo /so'βorðo/ *m*, *Naut.* manifest, freight list

sobornación /soβorna'sion; soβorna'θion/ *f*, bribing; bribery

sobornador /soβorna'ðor/ **(-ra)** *a* bribing. *n* briber

sobornar /soβor'nar/ *vt* to bribe

soborno /so'βorno/ *m*, bribing; bribe; inducement

sobra /'soβra/ *f*, excess, surplus; insult, outrage; *pl* leftovers (from a meal); remains, residue; rubbish, trash. **de s.,** in abundance; in excess, superfluous; unnecessary, superfluous; too well

sobradamente /soβraða'mente/ *adv* abundantly; in excess

sobrado /so'βraðo/ *a* excessive; brazen, bold; wealthy, rich. *m*, garret

sobrante /so'βrante/ *a* surplus, leftover, remaining. *m*, remainder, surplus, excess

sobrar /so'βrar/ *vt* to exceed; have too much of (e.g. *Me sobran mantas*, I have too many blankets); *vi* be superfluous; remain, be left. *Inf.* **Aquí sobro yo,** I am in the way here, My presence is superfluous

sobrasada /soβra'saða/ *f*, spicy sausage

sobre /'soβre/ *prep* upon, on; above, over; concerning, about; apart from, besides; about (e.g. *s. las nueve*, at about nine o'clock) (indicates approximation); toward; after. *m*, envelope; address, superscription. **s. cero,** above freezing (Fahrenheit); above zero (Centigrade). **s. el nivel del mar,** above sea level. **s. manera,** excessively, extremely. **s. todo,** especially

sobreabundancia /soβreaβun'dansia; soβreaβun'danθia/ *f*, superabundance, excess

sobreabundante /soβreaβun'dante/ *a* superabundant

sobreabundar /soβreaβun'dar/ *vi* to be superabundant

sobreagudo /soβrea'guðo/ *a* and *m*, *Mus.* treble (pitch)

sobrealiento /soβrea'liento/ *m*, heavy, painful breathing

sobrealimentación /soβrealimenta'sion; soβrealimenta'θion/ *f*, overfeeding; *Auto.* supercharge

sobrealimentar /soβrealimen'tar/ *vt Auto.* to supercharge

sobreasar /soβrea'sar/ *vt* to roast or cook again

sobrecama /soβre'kama/ *f*, bedspread, quilt

sobrecarga /soβre'karga/ *f*, overload; rope, etc., for securing bales and packs; additional trouble or anxiety

sobrecargar /soβrekar'gar/ *vt* to overload; weigh down; *Sew.* oversew, fell

sobrecargo /soβre'kargo/ *m*, *Naut.* purser; flight attendant

sobrecarta /soβre'karta/ *f*, envelope (for a letter)

sobreceja /soβre'seha; soβre'θeha/ *f*, brow, lower forehead; frown

sobrecejo /soβre'seho; soβre'θeho/ *m*, frown

sobrecielo /soβre'sielo; soβre'θielo/ *m*, canopy

sobrecoger /soβreko'her/ *vt* to take by surprise; *vr* be frightened or apprehensive

sobrecogimiento /soβrekohi'miento/ *m*, fright, apprehension

sobrecomida /soβreko'miða/ *f*, dessert

sobrecoser /soβreko'ser/ *vt Sew.* to oversew, whip

sobrecrecer /soβrekre'ser; soβrekre'θer/ *vi irr* to grow too much. See **conocer**

sobrecubierta /soβreku'βierta/ *f*, second lid or cover; dust jacket (of a book); *Naut.* upper deck

sobrecuello /soβre'kueyo; soβre'kueʎo/ *m*, overcollar; loose collar

sobredicho /soβre'ðitʃo/ *a* aforementioned, aforesaid

sobredorar /soβreðo'rar/ *vt* to gild (metals); make excuses for

sobreedificar /soβreeðifi'kar/ *vt* to build upon or above

sobreexcitar /soβreekssi'tar; soβreeksθi'tar/ *vt* to overexcite

sobrefaz /soβre'fas; soβre'faθ/ *f*, surface, exterior

sobreganar /soβrega'nar/ *vt* to make an excess profit

sobreguarda /soβre'guarða/ *m*, head guard; extra or second guard

sobreherido /soβree'riðo/ *a* lightly wounded

sobrehilar /soβrei'lar/ *vt* to oversew or overcast. See **prohibir**

sobrehumano /soβreu'mano/ *a* superhuman

sobrellenar /soβreye'nar; soβreʎe'nar/ *vt* to fill full

sobrellevar /soβreye'βar; soβreʎe'βar/ *vt* to help in the carrying of a burden; endure, bear; make excuses for, overlook; help

sobremesa /soβre'mesa/ *f*, tablecloth; after-dinner conversation. **de s.**, *Fig.* at the dinner table

sobrenadar /soβrena'ðar/ *vi* to float

sobrenatural /soβrenatu'ral/ *a* supernatural; extraordinary, singular

sobrenombre /soβre'nombre/ *m*, additional surname; nickname

sobrentender /soβrenten'der/ *vt irr* to take for granted, understand as a matter of course; *vr* go without saying. See **entender**

sobrepaga /soβre'paga/ *f*, overpayment; extra pay

sobreparto /soβre'parto/ *m*, time after parturition; afterbirth

sobrepasar /soβrepa'sar/ *vt* to exceed; outdo, excel

sobrepelliz /soβrepe'yis; soβrepe'ʎiθ/ *f*, surplice

sobreponer /soβrepo'ner/ *vt irr* to place over; overlap; *vr* rise above (circumstances); dominate (persons). See **poner**

sobreprecio /soβre'presio; soβre'preθio/ *m*, extra charge, rise in price

sobreproducción /soβreproðuk'sion; soβreproðuk'θion/ *f*, overproduction

sobrepuerta /soβre'puerta/ *f*, curtain pelmet; door curtain

sobrepujar /soβrepu'har/ *vt* to excel, surpass, outdo

sobrequilla /soβre'kiya; soβre'kiʎa/ *f*, *Naut.* keelson

sobrerrealismo /soβrerrea'lismo/ *m*, surrealism

sobrerrealista /soβrerrea'lista/ *a* and *mf* surrealist

sobresaliente /soβresa'liente/ *a* overhanging; projecting; distinctive, outstanding; excellent, remarkable. *m*, "excellent" (mark in examinations). *mf Theat.* understudy

sobresalir /soβresa'lir/ *vi irr* to overhang, project; stand out; be conspicuous or noticeable; excel; distinguish oneself. See **salir**

sobresaltar /soβresal'tar/ *vt* to assail, rush upon; startle, frighten suddenly; *vi Art.* stand out, be striking; *vr* be startled or frightened

sobresalto /soβre'salto/ *m*, sudden attack; unexpected shock; agitation; sudden fear. **de s.**, unexpectedly

sobresanar /soβresa'nar/ *vi* to heal superficially but not deeply; conceal, dissemble

sobrescribir /soβreskri'βir/ *vt* to label; address, superscribe. *Past Part.* **sobrescrito**

sobrescrito /soβres'krito/ *m*, address, superscription

sobresello /soβre'seyo; soβre'seʎo/ *m*, second seal

sobrestante /soβres'tante/ *m*, overseer; supervisor; foreman; inspector

sobresueldo /soβre'sueldo/ *m*, additional salary, bonus

sobresuelo /soβre'suelo/ *m*, second flooring

sobretarde /soβre'tarðe/ *f*, early evening, late afternoon

sobretodo /soβre'toðo/ *m*, overcoat

sobrevenida /soβreβe'niða/ *f*, sudden arrival

sobrevenir /soβreβe'nir/ *vi irr* occur, take place; supervene. See **venir**

sobrevidriera /soβreβi'ðriera/ *f*, storm window; wiremesh window guard

sobrevienta /soβre'βienta/ *f*, gust of wind; fury, violence; shock, surprise. **a s.**, suddenly

sobreviviente /soβreβi'βiente/ *a* surviving. *mf* survivor

sobrevivir /soβreβi'βir/ *vi* to survive

sobriedad /soβrie'ðað/ *f*, sobriety, moderation

sobrina /so'βrina/ *f*, niece

sobrino /so'βrino/ *m*, nephew

sobrio /'soβrio/ *a* sober, moderate, temperate

socaliña /soka'liɲa/ *f*, cunning, craft

socaliñero /sokali'ɲero/ **(-ra)** *a* cunning. *n* trickster

socalzar /sokal'sar; sokal'θar/ *vt Mas.* to underpin

socapa /so'kapa/ *f*, blind, pretext. **a s.**, secretly; cautiously

socarra /so'karra/ *f*, scorching, singeing; craftiness

socarrón /soka'rron/ *a* cunning, deceitful; malicious, sly (of humor, etc.)

socarronería /sokarrone'ria/ *f*, cunning, craftiness; slyness (of humor, etc.); knavish action

socava /so'kaβa/ *f*, undermining; *Agr.* hoeing round tree roots

socavar /soka'βar/ *vt* to undermine

sociabilidad /sosiaβili'ðað; soθiaβili'ðað/ *f*, sociability

sociable /so'siaβle; so'θiaβle/ *a* sociable; social

social /so'sial; so'θial/ *a* social

socialdemócrata /sosialde'mokrata; soθialde'mokrata/ *a* and *mf* social democrat

socialismo /sosia'lismo; soθia'lismo/ *m*, socialism

socialista /sosia'lista; soθia'lista/ *mf* socialist. *a* socialistic

socialización /sosialisa'sion; soθialiθa'θion/ *f*, socialization

socializar /sosiali'sar; soθiali'θar/ *vt* to socialize

sociedad /sosie'ðað; soθie'ðað/ *f*, society; association; *Com.* partnership; *Com.* company. *Com.* **S. anónima**, incorporated company, limited company. **S. de las Naciones**, League of Nations. **s. de socorros mutuos**, mutual aid society. **s. en comandita**, private company

socio /'sosio; 'soθio/ **(-ia)** *a* associate, partner; member. **s. comanditario**, *Com.* silent partner

sociología /sosiolo'hia; soθiolo'hia/ *f*, sociology

sociológico /sosio'lohiko; soθio'lohiko/ *a* sociological

sociólogo /so'siologo; so'θiologo/ **(-ga)** *n* sociologist

socollada /soko'yaða; soko'ʎaða/ *f*, *Naut.* flapping (of sails); pitching (of a ship)

socolor /soko'lor/ *m*, pretext. *adv* (also **so c.**) under pretext

socorredor /sokorre'ðor/ **(-ra)** *a* aiding, succoring. *n* helper

socorrer /soko'rrer/ *vt* to aid, succor, assist; pay on account

socorrido /soko'rriðo/ *a* helpful, generous, prompt to assist; well-equipped, well-furnished; well-supplied

socorro /so'korro/ *m*, aid, help, assistance; payment on account; *Mil.* relief (provisions or arms)

socrático /so'kratiko/ *a* socratic

sodio /'soðio/ *m*, sodium

sodomía /soðo'mia/ *f*, sodomy

sodomita /soðo'mita/ *mf* sodomite. *a* sodomitic

soez /so'es; so'eθ/ *a* base, vile; vulgar

sofá /so'fa/ *m*, sofa, couch

sofaldar /sofal'dar/ *vt* to tuck up the skirts; disclose, reveal

sofisma /so'fisma/ *m*, sophism, fallacy

sofista /so'fista/ *a* sophistic. *mf* sophist, quibbler

sofistería /sofiste'ria/ *f*, sophistry

sofístico /so'fistiko/ *a* sophistic, fallacious

soflama /so'flama/ *f*, thin flame; glow; flush, blush; specious promise, deception

soflamar /sofla'mar/ *vt* to shame, make blush; promise with intent to deceive, swindle; *vr Cul.* burn

sofocación /sofoka'sion; sofoka'θion/ *f*, suffocation, smothering; shame; anger

sofocador, sofocante /sofoka'ðor, sofo'kante/ *a* suffocating; stifling

sofocar /sofo'kar/ *vt* to suffocate, smother; extinguish; dominate, oppress; pester, importune; shame, make blush, make angry; agitate; *vr* be ashamed; be angry

sofocleo /sofo'kleo/ *a* Sophoclean

sofoco /so'foko/ *m*, mortification, chagrin; shame; anger; suffocation, smothering; hot flush

sofreír /sofre'ir/ *vt irr* to fry lightly. See **reír**

sofrenada /sofre'naða/ *f*, sudden check, pulling up short (of horses); harsh scolding; moral restraint

sofrenar /sofre'nar/ *vt* to pull up, check suddenly (horses); scold harshly; restrain, repress (emotions)

sofrito /so'frito/ *m*, sauce of sautéed tomatoes, peppers, onions, and garlic

software /'sofθwer/ *m*, software

soga /'soga/ *f*, rope; land measure (varies in length). *m*, *Inf.* rogue, knave

soguería /soge'ria/ *f*, rope making; rope walk; rope shop; ropes

soguero /so'gero/ *m*, rope maker or seller

soja /'soha/ *f*, soybean

sojuzgador /sohusga'ðor; sohuθga'ðor/ **(-ra)** *a* conquering, oppressive. *n* conqueror, oppressor

sojuzgar /sohus'gar; sohuθ'gar/ *vt* to conquer, oppress, subdue

sol /sol/ *m*, sun; sunlight; day; Peruvian coin; *Mus.* G, fifth note of the scale, sol. **de s. a s.,** from sunrise to sunset. **hacer s.,** to be sunny. **morir uno sin s. sin luz y sin moscas,** *Inf.* to die abandoned by all. **no dejar a s. ni a sombra,** *Inf.* to follow everywhere; pester constantly. **tomar el s.,** to bask in the sun

solado /so'laðo/ *m*, paving; tile floor

solador /sola'ðor/ *m*, tiler

solamente /sola'mente/ *adv* only; exclusively; merely, solely. **s. que,** only that; nothing but

solana /so'lana/ *f*, sunny corner; Solarium

solanera /sola'nera/ *f*, sunburn; sunny spot

solapa /so'lapa/ *f*, lapel; excuse, pretext. **de s.,** *Inf.* secretly

solapado /sola'paðo/ *a* cunning, sly

solapar /sola'par/ *vt Sew.* to provide with lapels; *Sew.* cause to overlap; dissemble; *vi Sew.* overlap

solapo /so'lapo/ *m*, lapel; *Inf.* slap, buffet. **a s.,** *Inf.* secretly, slyly

solar /so'lar/ *vt irr* to pave; sole (shoes). *m*, family seat, manor house; building site; lineage, family. *a* solar. See **colar**

solariego /sola'riego/ *a* memorial; of an old and noble family

solas, a /'solas, a/ *adv* alone, in private

solaz /so'las; so'laθ/ *m*, consolation; pleasure; relief, relaxation. **a s.,** enjoyably, pleasantly

solazar /sola'sar; sola'θar/ *vt* to solace, comfort; amuse, entertain; rest; *vr* be comforted; find pleasure (in)

soldada /sol'daða/ *f*, salary, wages, emoluments; (*Nav. Mil.*) pay

soldadesca /solda'ðeska/ *f*, soldiering, military profession; troops. **a la s.,** in a soldier-like way

soldadesco /solda'ðesko/ *a* military, soldier

soldado /sol'daðo/ *m*, soldier; defender, partisan. **s. raso,** *Mil.* private

soldador /solda'ðor/ *m*, solderer, welder; soldering iron

soldadura /solda'ðura/ *f*, welding, soldering; correction, emendation

soldar /sol'dar/ *vt irr* to weld; mend by welding; correct, put right; *Mil.* wipe out, liquidate. See **contar**

solecismo /sole'sismo; sole'θismo/ *m*, solecism

soledad /sole'ðað/ *f*, solitude; loneliness; homesickness; *pl* melancholy Andalusian song and dance (also *f pl.* **soleares**)

solemne /so'lemne/ *a* solemn; magnificent; formal; serious, grave, important; pompous; *Inf.* downright, complete

solemnidad /solemni'ðað/ *f*, solemnity; magnificence; formality; gravity, seriousness; solemn ceremony; religious ceremony; legal formality

solemnización /solemnisa'sion; solemniθa'θion/ *f*, solemnization

solemnizar /solemni'sar; solemni'θar/ *vt* to solemnize, celebrate; extol

soler /so'ler/ *vi irr defective* to be in the habit, be used; happen frequently (e.g. *Solía hacerlo los lunes,* I generally did it on Mondays. *Suele llover mucho aquí,* It rains a great deal here). See **moler**

solercia /so'lersia; so'lerθia/ *f*, shrewdness, ability, astuteness

solevantado /soleβan'taðo/ *a* agitated; restless

solevantar /soleβan'tar/ *vt* to raise, push up; incite to rebellion. **s. con gatos,** *Mech.* to jack up

solfa /'solfa/ *f*, *Mus.* sol-fa

solfear /solfe'ar/ *vt Mus.* to sing in sol-fa; *Inf.* spank, buffet; *Inf.* scold

solfeo /sol'feo/ *m*, *Mus.* sol-fa, solfeggio; *Inf.* spanking, drubbing

solicitación /solisita'sion; soliθita'θion/ *f*, request; application; solicitation; wooing; search (for a post); attraction, inducement

solicitador /solisita'ðor; soliθita'ðor/ **(-ra)** *a* soliciting. *n* solicitor. *m*, agent; applicant

solicitante /solisi'tante; soliθi'tante/ *mf* applicant, candidate

solicitar /solisi'tar; soliθi'tar/ *vt* to solicit; request; apply for; make love to, court; seek (posts, etc.); try to, attempt to; manage (business affairs); *Phys.* attract; appeal to

solícito /so'lisito; so'liθito/ *a* solicitous; conscientious; careful

solicitud /solisi'tuð; soliθi'tuð/ *f*, diligence, conscientiousness; solicitude; request; application (forms); appeal, entreaty; petition; *Com.* demand. **a s.,** on request

solidaridad /soliðari'ðað/ *f*, solidarity

solidario /soli'ðario/ *a Law.* jointly responsible or liable

solideo /soli'ðeo/ *m*, *Eccl.* small skullcap

solidez /soli'ðes; soli'ðeθ/ *f*, solidity; *Fig.* force, weight (of arguments, etc.)

solidificación /soliðifika'sion; soliðifika'θion/ *f*, solidification

solidificar /soliðifi'kar/ **(se)** *vt* and *vr* to solidify

sólido /'soliðo/ *a* compact, solid; thick; fast or lasting (of colors); indisputable, convincing. *m*, (*Geom. Phys.*) solid; solidus (ancient coin)

soliloquiar /solilo'kiar/ *vi Inf.* to soliloquize, talk to oneself

soliloquio /soli'lokio/ *m*, soliloquy

solio /'solio/ *m*, throne

solista /so'lista/ *mf* soloist

solitario /soli'tario/ **(-ia)** *a* abandoned, deserted; solitary; secluded; solitude-loving. *n* recluse. *m*, solitaire diamond; hermit; solitaire (card game). **hacer solitarios,** to play solitaire (card game)

sólito /'solito/ *a* accustomed, wonted; customary, habitual

soliviantar /soliβian'tar/ *vt* to rouse, incite, excite

soliviar /soli'βiar/ *vt* to help to lift up; *vr* half get up, raise oneself

sollastre /so'yastre/ *m*, scullion; brazen rogue

sollozante /soyo'sante; soʎo'θante/ *a* sobbing

sollozar /soyo'sar; soʎo'θar/ *vi* to sob

sollozo /so'yoso; so'ʎoθo/ *m*, sob

solo /'solo/ *a* sole, only; alone; lonely; deserted, forsaken. *m*, solo performance; (cards) solo; solitaire (card game). **a solas,** alone; without help, unaided

sólo /'solo/ *or* **solo** *adv* only; merely, solely; exclusively

solomillo /solo'miyo; solo'miʎo/ *m*, sirloin; filet (of meat)

solsticio /sols'tisio; sols'tiθio/ *m*, solstice. **s. hiemal,** winter solstice. **s. vernal,** summer solstice

soltar /sol'tar/ *vt irr* to loosen; let go; disengage; untie; release; let drop; let out (a laugh, etc.); solve; *Inf.* utter; turn on (taps); set free; *vr* work loose; grow skillful; (*with prep.* a + *infin.*) begin to do (something). See **contar**

soltera /sol'tera/ *f*, spinster

soltería /solte'ria/ *f*, bachelorhood; spinsterhood

soltero /sol'tero/ *a* unmarried, single. *m*, bachelor

solterón /solte'ron/ *m*, confirmed bachelor

solterona /solte'rona/ *f*, confirmed old maid

soltura /sol'tura/ *f*, loosening; untying; freedom from restraint; ease, independence; impudence; immorality, viciousness; facility of speech; *Law.* release

solubilidad /soluβili'ðað/ *f*, solubility

soluble /so'luβle/ *a* soluble, dissolvable; solvable

solución /solu'sion; solu'θion/ *f*, dissolution, loosening; (*Math. Chem.*) solution; answer, solution; payment, satisfaction; *Lit.* climax; conclusion, end (of negotiations)

solucionar /solusio'nar; soluθio'nar/ *vt* to solve, find a solution for

solvencia /sol'βensia; sol'βenθia/ *f*, *Com.* solvency

solventar /solβen'tar/ *vt* to pay or settle accounts; solve (problems, difficulties)

solvente /sol'βente/ *a Com.* solvent

somático /so'matiko/ *a* somatic, corporeal

sombra /'sombra/ *f*, shadow; shade; darkness, dimness; specter, phantom; defense, refuge, protection; resemblance, likeness; defect; *Inf.* luck; gaiety, charm; trace, vestige; *Art.* shading, shadow. **sombras chinescas,** shadow show. **a la s.,** in the shade; *Inf.* in jail. **hacer s.,** to shade; *Fig.* stand in the light, be an obstacle; protect. **ni por s.,** by no means; without warning. **no tener s. de,** to have not a trace of.... **tener buena s.,** *Inf.* to be witty or amusing and agreeable. **tener mala s.,** *Inf.* to bring bad luck, exert an evil influence upon; be dull and disagreeable

sombrear /sombre'ar/ *vt* to shadow, shade; *Art.* shade; *vi* begin to show (of mustaches, beards)

sombrerera /sombre'rera/ *f*, milliner; hatbox

sombrerería /sombrere'ria/ *f*, hat shop or trade; hat factory

sombrerero /sombre'rero/ *m*, hatter; hat manufacturer

sombrerete /sombre'rete/ *m*, *Mech.* bonnet; cap; cowl

sombrero /som'βrero/ *m*, hat; *Mech.* cap, cowl; sounding board; head (of mushrooms, toadstools). **s. calañés,** Andalusian hat. **s. chambergo,** broadbrimmed plumed hat. **s. de canal** *or* **teja,** shovel hat (worn by clergymen). **s. de copa,** top hat. **s. de jipijapa,** Panama hat. **s. de pelo** *Lat. Am.* top hat. **s. de tres picos,** three-cornered hat, cocked hat. **s. flexible,** soft felt hat. **s. hongo,** bowler (hat)

sombría /som'βria/ *f*, shady spot

sombrilla /som'βriya; som'βriʎa/ *f*, sunshade

sombrío /som'βrio/ *a* dark; shadowy; overcast; *Art.* shaded; gloomy, melancholy

someramente /somera'mente/ *adv* superficially; briefly, summarily

somero /so'mero/ *a* superficial, shallow; summary, rudimentary, brief

someter /some'ter/ *vt* to put down, defeat; submit; place before; subject. **s. a votación,** to put to a vote. *vr* yield, surrender; (*with prep* a) undergo

sometimiento /someti'miento/ *m*, defeat; submission (to arbitration, etc.); subjection

somnambulismo /somnambu'lismo/ *m*, somnambulism, sleepwalking

somnámbulo /som'nambulo/ (**-la**) *a* somnambulistic. *n* somnambulist

somnífero /som'nifero/ *a* soporiferous

somnílocuo /som'nilokuo/ *a* somniloquous, sleeptalking

somnolencia /somno'lensia; somno'lenθia/ *f*, somnolence

son /son/ *m*, sound; rumor; reason, motive; means,

way; guise, manner. **al s. de,** to the sound of; to the music of. **en s. de,** in the manner of, as, like, under pretext of

sonadera /sona'ðera/ *f*, nose blowing

sonado /so'naðo/ *a* famous; much admired or talked of. **hacer una que sea sonada,** *Inf.* to cause a great scandal; do something noteworthy

sonaja /so'naha/ *f*, metal jingles on a tambourine; baby's rattle

sonajero /sona'hero/ *m*, baby's rattle

sonar /so'nar/ *vi irr* to sound; be quoted, be mentioned; ring; *Inf.* be familiar, remember (e.g. *No me suena el nombre,* I don't remember the name); (*with prep* a) be reminiscent of; *vt* sound; ring; play on; clink; *vr* be rumored, be reported; blow one's nose. *Pres. Ind.* **sueno, suenas, suena, suenan.** *Pres. Subjunc.* **suene, suenes, suene, suenen**

sonata /so'nata/ *f*, sonata

sonda /'sonda/ *f*, *Naut.* taking of soundings, heaving the lead; sound, plummet, lead; dragrope; probe, sound

sondar /son'dar/ *vt Naut.* to take soundings; probe; *Inf.* sound, try to find out; bore, drill

sondeable /sonde'aβle/ *a* fathomable

sondeo /son'deo/ *m*, *Naut.* sounding; *Mineral.* drilling; probing

sonetear, sonetizar /sonete'ar, soneti'sar; sonete'ar, soneti'θar/ *vi* to write sonnets

sonetista /sone'tista/ *mf* sonneteer

soneto /so'neto/ *m*, sonnet

sonido /so'niðo/ *m*, sound; literal meaning; rumor, report

sonochar /sono'tʃar/ *vi* to keep watch in the early hours of the night

sonoridad /sonori'ðað/ *f*, sonorousness

sonoro /so'noro/ *a* sounding; resonant, loud; sonorous

sonreír, sonreírse /son'reir, sone'reirse/ *vi* and *vr irr* to smile; *vi* look pleasant (landscape, etc.); look favorable (of circumstances). **sonreír tras la barba,** to laugh to oneself. See **reír**

sonriente /son'riente/ *a* smiling

sonrisa /son'risa/ *f*, smile

sonrojar /sonro'har/ *vt* to cause to blush; *vr* blush

sonrosado /sonro'saðo/ *a* rosy, rose-colored; pink

sonrosar /sonro'sar/ *vt* to make rose-colored; *vr* blush, flush

sonroseo /sonro'seo/ *m*, blush, flush

sonsaca /son'saka/ *f*, removal by stealth; pilfering; enticement; *Fig.* pumping (of a person for information)

sonsacar /sonsa'kar/ *vt* to remove by stealth; steal, pilfer; entice away; *Fig.* pump (a person for information), draw out

sonsonete /sonso'nete/ *m*, rhythmic tapping or drumming; monotonous sound (gen. unpleasant); sarcastic tone of voice

soñador /soɲa'ðor/ (**-ra**) *a* dreamy, sleepy. *n* dreamer

soñar /so'ɲar/ *vt irr* to dream; imagine, conjure up; (*with con*) dream of; (*with prep* a) fear (of persons)

soñoliento /soɲo'liento/ *a* sleepy, drowsy; soothing; slow, leisurely

¡Soo! /soo/ *interj* Whoa! (command to horses, etc.)

sopa /'sopa/ *f*, sop, piece of bread; soup. **s. boba,** beggar's portion; life of ease at others' expense. **andar a la s.,** to beg one's way. **hecho una s.,** *Inf.* wet through

sopapo /so'papo/ *m*, chuck under the chin; *Inf.* slap; valve

sopera /so'pera/ *f*, soup tureen

sopero /so'pero/ *m*, soup plate, soup bowl. *a* fond of soup

sopesar /sope'sar/ *vt* to try the weight of

sopetón /sope'ton/ *m*, blow, cuff. **de s.,** suddenly

soplada /so'plaða/ *f*, puff of wind

soplado /so'plaðo/ (**-ra**) *a* Inf. overelegant; haughty, stiff. *m*, fissure, chasm

soplador /sopla'ðor/ (**-ra**) *a* instigatory. *m*, blower, fan. *n* instigator; blower

soplar /so'plar/ *vi* to blow; *vt* blow; blow away; inflate, blow up; filch, steal; instigate, inspire; accuse; fan; prompt, help out; *vr Inf.* eat and drink too much; *Inf.* be puffed up, grow haughty. *interj* **¡Sopla!** *Inf.* You don't say so!

soplete /so'plete/ *m,* blowpipe

soplo /'soplo/ *m,* blow; blowing; instant, trice; *Inf.* hint, tip; *Inf.* accusation; *Inf.* tale-bearer; puff, breath (of wind)

soplón /so'plon/ **(-ona)** *a Inf.* tale-bearing, backbiting. *n* tale-bearer. *m, Auto.* scavenger

soponcio /so'ponsio; so'ponθio/ *m, Inf.* fainting fit

sopor /so'por/ *m,* stupor; deep sleep

soporífero /sopo'rifero/ *a* soporiferous

soportable /sopor'taβle/ *a* bearable

soportador /soporta'ðor/ **(-ra)** *a* supporting. *n* supporter

soportal /sopor'tal/ *m,* portico

soportar /sopor'tar/ *vt* to bear; carry, support; put up with, tolerate

soporte /so'porte/ *m,* rest, support; *Mech.* bearing; *Mech.* bracket, support; backup (of a computer file)

sorbedor /sorβe'ðor/ **(-ra)** *a* supping, sipping. *n* sipper

sorber /sor'βer/ *vt* to suck; imbibe; swallow; *Fig.* absorb eagerly (ideas); sip

sorbete /sor'βete/ *m,* sherbet, iced drink; French ice cream

sorbo /'sorβo/ *m,* sucking; imbibition; swallow; sip; mouthful, gulp

sordamente /sorða'mente/ *adv* secretly, quietly

sordera /sor'ðera/ *f,* deafness

sórdido /'sorðiðo/ *a* dirty, squalid; mean, niggardly; sordid

sordina /sor'ðina/ *f, Mus.* sordine, mute; *Mus.* damper. **a la s.,** on the quiet, in secret

sordo /'sorðo/ *a* deaf; silent, quiet; dull, muted (of sounds); insensible, inanimate; obdurate, uncompliant. **a la sorda** *or* **a lo s.** *or* **a sordas,** in silence, quietly

sordomudez /sorðomu'ðes; sorðomu'ðeθ/ *f,* deaf-muteness, deaf-mutism

sordomudo /sorðo'muðo/ **(-da)** *a* and *n* deaf-mute

sorna /'sorna/ *f,* slowness, sluggishness; craftiness, guile, knavery; malice

soroche /so'rotʃe/ *m, Peru* altitude sickness, mountain sickness

sorprendente /sorpren'dente/ *a* surprising, amazing

sorprender /sorpren'der/ *vt* to surprise, amaze

sorpresa /sor'presa/ *f,* surprise; amazement; shock

sorpresivo, -a /sorpre'siβo/ *a, Lat. Am.* sudden, unexpected; surprising

sortear /sorte'ar/ *vt* to raffle; draw lots for; avoid artfully (difficulties, etc.); fight (bulls)

sorteo /sor'teo/ *m,* raffle; casting lots

sortero /sor'tero/ **(-ra)** *n* sorcerer; holder of a draw ticket

sortija /sor'tiha/ *f,* ring (for a finger); ring (for a curtain, etc.); curl

sortilegio /sorti'lehio/ *m,* sorcery, magic

sortílego /sor'tilego/ **(-ga)** *a* magic. *n* sorcerer, fortuneteller

sosa /'sosa/ *f,* sodium carbonate, soda ash. **s. cáustica,** sodiumhydroxide, caustic soda, soda

sosegado /sose'gaðo/ *a* tranquil, peaceful, calm

sosegador /sosega'ðor/ **(-ra)** *a* soothing, calming. *n* appeaser, soother

sosegar /sose'gar/ *vt irr* to soothe, quiet; reassure; appease, moderate; *vi* grow still; rest, sleep; *vr* grow quiet; calm down, be appeased; grow still. See **cegar**

sosería /sose'ria/ *f,* insipidness; lack of wit, dullness; stupidity

sosia /'sosia/ *m,* double, exact likeness (of persons)

sosiego /so'siego/ *m,* calm; peace, tranquility

soslayar /sosla'yar/ *vt* to slant, place in an oblique position; *Fig.* go around (a difficulty)

soslayo /sos'layo/ *a* slanting. **al s.,** obliquely, on the slant; askance

soso /'soso/ *a* saltless, insipid; dull, uninteresting; heavy (of people)

sospecha /sos'petʃa/ *f,* suspicion

sospechar /sospe'tʃar/ *vt* and *vi* to suspect

sospechoso /sospe'tʃoso/ *a* suspicious. *m,* suspect

sostén /sos'ten/ *m,* support; *Mech.* stand, support; brassiere, bra, bustier; steadiness (of a ship)

sostenedor /sostene'ðor/ **(-ra)** *a* supporting. *n* supporter

sostener /soste'ner/ *vt irr* to support; defend, uphold; bear, tolerate; help, aid; maintain, support. **s. una conversación,** to carry on a conversation. See **tener**

sostenido /soste'niðo/ *a Mus.* sostenuto, sustained. *a* and *m, Mus.* sharp

sostenimiento /sosteni'miento/ *m,* support; defense; toleration, endurance; maintenance, sustenance

sota /'sota/ *f,* jack, knave (in cards); *Inf.* baggage, hussy. *m,* foreman, supervisor. *prep* deputy, substitute (e.g. *sotamontero,* deputy huntsman)

sotabanco /sota'βanko/ *m,* attic, garret

sotana /so'tana/ *f,* gown, cassock, robe

sótano /'sotano/ *m,* basement, cellar

sotavento /sota'βento/ *m,* leeward. **a s.,** on the lee

sotechado /sote'tʃaðo/ *m,* hut, shed

soterrar /sote'rrar/ *vt irr* to bury in the ground; hide, conceal. See **acertar**

sotileza /soti'lesa; soti'leθa/ *f,* fine cord for fishing (in Santander province)

soto /'soto/ *m,* thicket, grove, copse

soviético /so'βietiko/ *a* soviet

sovietismo /soβie'tismo/ *m,* sovietism

sovietizar /soβieti'sar; soβieti'θar/ *vt* to sovietize

sovoz, a /so'βos, a; so'βoθ, a/ *adv* in a low voice

su, sus /su, sus/ *poss pron 3rd pers mf sing* and *pl* his, her, its, one's, your, their

suasorio /sua'sorio/ *a* suasive, persuasive

suave /'suaβe/ *a* soft, smooth; sweet; pleasant, harmonious, quiet; slow, gentle; meek; delicate, subtle

suavidad /suaβi'ðað/ *f,* softness, smoothness; sweetness; pleasantness; quietness; gentleness; meekness; delicacy

suavizador /suaβisa'ðor; suaβiθa'ðor/ *a* softening, smoothing; soothing, quietening. *m,* razor strop

suavizar /suaβi'sar; suaβi'θar/ *vt* to soften; smooth; strop (a razor); moderate, temper; *Mech.* steady; quieten; ease

subalpino /suβal'pino/ *a* a subalpine

subalternar /suβalter'nar/ *vt* to put down, subdue

subalterno /suβal'terno/ *a* subordinate. *m,* subordinate; *Mil.* subaltern

subarrendar /suβarren'dar/ *vt irr* to sublet. See **recomendar**

subarrendatario /suβarrenda'tario/ **(-ia)** *n* sublessee

subarriendo /suβa'rriendo/ *m,* sublease, sublet

subasta /su'βasta/ *f,* auction sale. **sacar a pública s.,** to sell by auction

subastar /suβas'tar/ *vt* to auction

subcentral /suβsen'tral; suβθen'tral/ *f,* substation

subclase /suβ'klase/ *f,* subclass

subcolector /suβkolek'tor/ *m,* assistant collector

subcomisión /suβkomi'sion/ *f,* subcommittee

subconsciencia /suβkons'siensia; suβkons'θienθia/ *f,* subconscious

subcutáneo /suβku'taneo/ *a* subcutaneous

subdelegar /suβðele'gar/ *vt* to subdelegate

subdirector /suβðirek'tor/ **(-ra)** *a* deputy, assistant director

súbdito /'suβðito/ **(-ta)** *a* dependent, subject. *n* subject (of a state)

subdividir /suβðiβi'ðir/ *vt* to subdivide

subdominante /suβðomi'nante/ *f, Mus.* subdominant

subgénero /suβ'henero/ *m,* subgenus

subgobernador /suβgoβerna'ðor/ *m,* deputy governor, lieutenant governor

subibaja /suβi'βaha/ *f,* seesaw, teetertotter

subida /su'βiða/ *f,* ascension, ascent; upgrade; rise; carrying up; raising (of a theater curtain)

subidero /suβi'ðero/ *m,* uphill road; mounting block; way up (to a higher level)

subido /su'βiðo/ *a* strong (of scents); deep (of colors); expensive, high-priced; best, finest

subidor /suβi'ðor/ *m,* porter, carrier; elevator

subintendente /suβinten'dente/ *m*, deputy or assistant intendant

subir /su'βir/ *vi* to ascend, climb, go up; mount; rise; *Com.* amount (to), reach; prosper, advance, be promoted; grow more acute (of illnesses); intensify; *Mus.* raise the pitch (of an instrument or voice); *vt* ascend, climb; pick up, take up; raise up; place higher; build up, make taller; straighten up, place in a vertical position; increase, raise (in price or value); *vr* ascend, climb. **s. a caballo,** to mount a horse. **subirse a la cabeza,** *Inf.* to go to one's head (of alcohol, etc.)

subitáneo /suβi'taneo/ *a* sudden

súbito /'suβito/ *a* unexpected, unforeseen; sudden; precipitate, impulsive. *adv* suddenly (also **de s.**)

subjefe /suβ'hefe/ *m*, deputy chief, second in command

subjetividad /suβhetiβi'ðað/ *f*, subjectivity

subjetivismo /suβheti'βismo/ *m*, subjectivism

subjetivo /suβhe'tiβo/ *a* subjective

subjuntivo /suβhun'tiβo/ *a* and *m*, subjunctive

sublevación /suβleβa'sion; suβleβa'θion/ *f*, **sublevamiento** *m*, rebellion, mutiny, uprising

sublevar /suβle'βar/ *vt* to rouse to rebellion; excite (indignation, etc.); *vr* rebel

sublimación /suβlima'sion; suβlima'θion/ *f*, sublimation

sublimado /suβli'maðo/ *m*, *Chem.* sublimate

sublimar /suβli'mar/ *vt* to exalt, raise up; *Chem.* sublimate

sublime /su'βlime/ *a* sublime

sublimidad /suβlimi'ðað/ *f*, sublimity, majesty, nobility

submarino /suβma'rino/ *a* submarine. *m*, submarine. **s. de bolsillo** *or* **s. enano,** midget submarine

suboficial /suβofi'sial; suβofi'θial/ *m*, *Mil.* subaltern; *Nav.* petty officer

subordinación /suβorðina'sion; suβorðina'θion/ *f*, dependence, subordination

subordinado /suβorði'naðo/ **(-da)** *a* and *n* subordinate

subordinar /suβorði'nar/ *vt* to subordinate

subprefecto /suβpre'fekto/ *m*, subprefect

subproducto /suβpro'ðukto/ *m*, by-product

subrayar /suβra'yar/ *vt* to underline; emphasize

subrepción /suβrep'sion; suβrep'θion/ *f*, underhand dealing; *Law.* subreption

subrepticio /suβrep'tisio; suβrep'tiθio/ *a* surreptitious; clandestine

subrogación /suβroga'sion; suβroga'θion/ *f*, surrogation

subrogar /suβro'gar/ *vt Law.* to surrogate, elect as a substitute

subs /suβs/ -- For words so beginning not found here, see **sus-**

subsanar /suβsa'nar/ *vt* to make excuses for; remedy, put right; indemnify

subscriptor /suβskrip'tor/ **(-ra)** *n* subscriber

subsección /suβsek'sion; suβsek'θion/ *f*, subsection

subsecretaría /suβsekreta'ria/ *f*, assistant secretaryship; assistant secretary's office

subsecretario /suβsekre'tario/ **(-ia)** *n* assistant secretary

subsecuente /suβse'kuente/ *a* subsequent

subsidiario /suβsi'ðiario/ *a* subsidized; subsidiary

subsidio /suβ'siðio/ *m*, subsidy

subsiguiente /suβsi'giente/ *a* subsequent; next

subsistencia /suβsis'tensia; suβsis'tenθia/ *f*, permanence; stability; subsistence, maintenance; livelihood

subsistir /suβsis'tir/ *vi* to last, endure; subsist, live; make a livelihood

subsuelo /suβ'suelo/ *m*, subsoil, substratum

subte /'suβte/ *m*, Argentina, *informal* subway

subteniente /suβte'niente/ *m*, *Mil.* second lieutenant

subterfugio /suβter'fuhio/ *m*, subterfuge, trick

subterráneo /suβte'rraneo/ *a* underground, subterranean. *m*, subterranean place

subtítulo /suβ'titulo/ *m*, subtitle; caption

subtropical /suβtropi'kal/ *a* subtropical

suburbano /suβur'βano/ **(-na)** *a* suburban. *n* suburbanite

suburbio /su'βurβio/ *m*, suburb

subvención /suββen'sion; suββen'θion/ *f*, subsidy, subvention, grant

subvencionar /suββensio'nar; suββenθio'nar/ *vt* to subsidize

subvenir /suββe'nir/ *vt irr* to help, succor; subsidize. See **venir**

subversivo /suββer'siβo/ *a* subversive

subvertir /suββer'tir/ *vt irr* to subvert, overturn, ruin. See **sentir**

subyugación /suβyuga'sion; suβyuga'θion/ *f*, subjugation

subyugador /suβyuga'ðor/ **(-ra)** *a* subjugating. *n* conqueror

subyugar /suβyu'gar/ *vt* to subjugate, overcome

succión /suk'sion; suk'θion/ *f*, suction

suceder /suse'ðer; suθe'ðer/ *vi* to follow, come after; inherit, succeed. *impers* happen, occur

sucedido /suse'ðiðo; suθe'ðiðo/ *m*, *Inf.* event, occurrence

sucesión /suse'sion; suθe'sion/ *f*, succession; series; offspring, descendants; *Law.* estate

sucesivo /suse'siβo; suθe'siβo/ *a* successive. **en lo s.,** in future

suceso /su'seso; su'θeso/ *m*, happening, occurrence; course (of time); outcome, result

sucesor /suse'sor; suθe'sor/ **(-ra)** *a* succeeding. *n* successor

suciedad /susie'ðað; suθie'ðað/ *f*, dirt; filth, nastiness; obscenity

sucinto /su'sinto; su'θinto/ *a* succinct, brief, concise

sucio /'susio; 'suθio/ *a* dirty, unclean; stained; easily soiled; *Fig.* sullied, spotted; obscene; dirty (of colors); *Fig.* tainted, infected. **jugar s.,** *Sports.* to play in an unsporting manner

suco /'suko/ *m*, juice

sucoso /su'koso/ *a* juicy

sucre /'sukre/ *m* sucre (monetary unit of Ecuador)

suculencia /suku'lensia; suku'lenθia/ *f*, succulence; juiciness

suculento /suku'lento/ *a* succulent; juicy

sucumbir /sukum'βir/ *vi* to yield, give in; die, succumb; lose a lawsuit

sucursal /sukur'sal/ *a* branch. *f*, *Com.* branch (of a firm)

sud /suð/ *m*, south (gen. **sur**). Used in combinations like **sudamericano**

sudadero /suða'ðero/ *m*, horse blanket; sudatorium, sweating bath

sudafricano /suðafri'kano/ **(-na)** *a* and *n* South African

Sudamérica /suða'merika/ *f* South America

sudamericano /suðameri'kano/ **(-na)** *a* and *n* South American

sudante /su'ðante/ *a* sweating, perspiring

sudar /su'ðar/ *vi* and *vt* to perspire, sweat; ooze; *vi Inf.* toil; *vt* bathe in sweat; *Inf.* give reluctantly. **s. frío,** to break out in a cold sweat. **s. la gota gorda,** *Fig. Inf.* to be in a stew

sudario /su'ðario/ *m*, shroud

sudeste /su'ðeste/ *m*, southeast; southeast wind

sudexpreso /suðeks'preso/ *m*, southern express

sudoeste /suðo'este/ *m*, southwest; southwest wind

sudor /su'ðor/ *m*, sweat, perspiration; toil; juice, moisture, sap, gum

sudoroso /suðo'roso/ *a* sweaty

sudsudeste /suðsu'ðeste/ *m*, southsoutheast

sudsudoeste /suðsuðo'este/ *m*, southsouthwest

Suecia /'suesia; 'sueθia/ Sweden

sueco /'sueko/ **(-ca)** *a* Swedish. *n* Swede. *m*, Swedish (language)

suegra /'suegra/ *f*, mother-in-law

suegro /'suegro/ *m*, father-in-law

suela /'suela/ *f*, sole (of a shoe); *Ichth.* sole; tanned leather; base. **no llegarle a uno a la s. del zapato,** *inf* to be not fit to hold a candle to.

sueldo /'sueldo/ *m*, salary, wages; *Obs.* Spanish coin. **a s.,** for a salary, salaried

suelo /'suelo/ *m*, ground, earth; soil; bottom, base; sediment, dregs; site, plot; floor; flooring; story; land, territory; hoof (of horses); earth, world; *pl* chaff of grain. **s. natal,** native land; **besar el s.,** *Inf.* to fall flat. **dar consigo en el s.,** to fall down. **dar en el s. con,** to throw down; damage, spoil. *Inf.* **estar (una cosa) por los suelos,** to be dirt cheap

suelta /'suelta/ *f*, loosening, unfastening; hobble (for horses); relay of oxen. **dar s. a,** to let loose, allow to go out for a time

sueltista /suel'tista/ *mf*, *Lat. Am.* freelance journalist, stringer

suelto /'suelto/ *a* swift; competent, efficient; odd, separate; licentious; flowing, easy (style); loose, unbound. *m*, single copy (of a newspaper); loose change; newspaper paragraph

sueño /'sueɲo/ *m*, dream; sleep; drowsiness, desire for sleep; vision, fancy. **s. pesado,** deep sleep. **conciliar el s.,** to court sleep. **echar un s.,** *Inf.* to take a nap. **en sueños,** in a dream; while asleep. **entre sueños,** between sleeping and waking. **¡Ni por sueño!** *Inf.* Certainly not! I wouldn't dream of it!

suero /'suero/ *m*, serum. **s. de la leche,** whey

suerte /'suerte/ *f*, chance, luck; good luck; destiny, fate; condition, state; kind, species, sort; way, manner; bullfighter's maneuver; parcel of land. **de s. que,** so that; as a result. **echar suertes,** to draw lots. **tener buena s.,** to be lucky

sueste /'sueste/ *m*, southeast; sou'wester (cap); *Lat. Am.* southeast wind

suéter /'sueter/ *m*, sweater

suficiencia /sufi'siensia; sufi'θienθia/ *f*, sufficiency; talent, aptitude; pedantry. **a s.,** enough

suficiente /sufi'siente; sufi'θiente/ *a* sufficient, enough; suitable

sufijo /su'fiho/ *m*, suffix

sufragar /sufra'ɡar/ *vt* to assist, aid; favor; pay, defray

sufragio /su'frahio/ *m*, aid, assistance; *Eccl.* suffragium, pious offering; vote; suffrage

sufragista /sufra'hista/ *f*, suffragette

sufrible /su'friβle/ *a* bearable, endurable

sufrido /su'friðo/ *a* long-suffering, resigned; complaisant (of husbands); dirt-resistant (colors)

sufrimiento /sufri'miento/ *m*, suffering, pain; affliction; tolerance

sufrir /su'frir/ *vt* to suffer, undergo, experience; bear, endure; tolerate, put up with; allow, permit; resist, oppose; expiate; *vi* suffer

sugerir /suhe'rir/ *vt irr* to suggest. See **sentir**

sugestión /suhes'tion/ *f*, suggestion

sugestionable /suhestio'naβle/ *a* easily influenced, open to suggestion

sugestionador /suhestiona'ðor/ *a* suggestive

sugestionar /suhestio'nar/ *vt* to suggest hypnotically; dominate, influence

sugestivo /suhes'tiβo/ *a* suggestive, stimulating

suicida /sui'siða; sui'θiða/ *a* suicidal, fatal. *mf* suicide (person)

suicidarse /suisi'ðarse; suiθi'ðarse/ *vr* to commit suicide

suicidio /sui'siðio; sui'θiðio/ *m*, suicide (act)

Suiza /'suisa; 'suiθa/ Switzerland

suiza /'suisa; 'suiθa/ *f*, row, rumpus, scrap

suizo /'suiso; 'suiθo/ **(-za)** *a* and *n* Swiss

sujeción /suhe'sion; suhe'θion/ *f*, subjection, domination; fastening, fixture; obedience, conformity

sujetador /suheta'ðor/ *m*, clamp; clip

sujetar /suhe'tar/ *vt* to fasten, fix; hold down; grasp, clutch; subdue; *vr* (*with prep a*) conform to, obey. **s. con alfileres,** to pin up. **s. con tornillos,** to screw down

sujeto /su'heto/ *a* liable, subject. *m*, topic, subject; person, individual; *Gram. Philos.* subject

sulfatar /sulfa'tar/ *vt* to sulphate

sulfato /sul'fato/ *m*, sulphate

sulfurar /sulfu'rar/ *vt* to sulphurate; *vr* grow irritated, become angry

sulfúrico /sul'furiko/ *a* sulphuric

sulfuro /sul'furo/ *m*, sulphide

sulfuroso /sulfu'roso/ *a* sulphurous

sultán /sul'tan/ *m*, sultan

sultana /sul'tana/ *f*, sultana

suma /'suma/ *f*, total; amount, sum; *Math.* addition; summary, digest; computation. **en s.,** in brief, in short, finally. *Com.* **s. redonda,** lump sum

sumador /suma'ðor/ **(-ra)** *n* summarizer; computator, adder

sumamente /suma'mente/ *adv* extremely, most

sumar /su'mar/ *vt* to sum up, summarize; *Math.* add up

sumaria /su'maria/ *f*, written indictment

sumariamente /sumaria'mente/ *adv* concisely, in brief; *Law.* summarily

sumario /su'mario/ *a* brief, concise, abridged; *Law.* summary. *m*, summary, résumé, digest

sumergible /sumer'hiβle/ *a* sinkable; submergible. *m*, submarine

sumergir /sumer'hir/ *vt* to dip, immerse; sink, submerge; *Fig.* overwhelm (with grief, etc.); *vr* sink; dive; be submerged

sumersión /sumer'sion/ *f*, immersion, dive, submersion

sumidero /sumi'ðero/ *m*, cesspool; drain; sink; pit, gully

suministración /suministra'sion; suministra'θion/ *f*. See **suministro**

suministrador /suministra'ðor/ **(-ra)** *n* purveyor

suministrar /suminis'trar/ *vt* to purvey, supply, provide

suministro /sumi'nistro/ *m*, purveyance; provision; supply

sumir /su'mir/ *vt* to sink; submerge; *Eccl.* consummate; *Fig.* overwhelm (with grief, etc.); *vr* fall in, become sunken (of cheeks, etc.); sink; be submerged; *Lat. Am.* cower, cringe

sumisión /sumi'sion/ *f*, submission, obedience; *Com.* estimate, tender

sumiso /su'miso/ *a* submissive, docile

sumista /su'mista/ *mf* quick reckoner, computator. *m*, condenser, summarizer, abridger

sumo /'sumo/ *a* supreme; high; tremendous, extraordinary. **a lo s.,** at the most; even if, although. **en s. grado,** in the highest degree

suntuosidad /suntuosi'ðað/ *f*, magnificence, luxury

suntuoso /sun'tuoso/ *a* magnificent, luxurious, sumptuous

supeditación /supeðita'sion; supeðita'θion/ *f*, subjection

supeditar /supeði'tar/ *vt* to oppress; overcome, conquer; subordinate

superabundancia /superaβun'dansia; superaβun'danθia/ *f*, superabundance, excess; glut

superabundante /superaβun'dante/ *a* superabundant, excessive

superádito /supe'raðito/ *a* superadded

superar /supe'rar/ *vt* to overcome, conquer; surpass; do better than

superávit /supe'raβit/ *m*, *Com.* balance, surplus

superchería /supertʃe'ria/ *f*, trickery, guile

superchero /super'tʃero/ *a* guileful, wily

superconsciencia /superkons'siensia; superkons'θienθia/ *f*, higher consciousness

supereminencia /superemi'nensia; superemi'nenθia/ *f*, supereminence, greatest eminence

supereminente /superemi'nente/ *a* supereminent

superentender /superenten'der/ *vt irr* to supervise, superintend. See **entender**

supererogación /supereroga'sion; supereroga'θion/ *f*, supererogation

superestructura /superestruk'tura/ *f*, superstructure

superficial /superfi'sial; superfi'θial/ *a* surface, shallow; superficial, rudimentary; futile

superficialidad /superfisiali'ðað; superfiθiali'ðað/ *f*, superficiality; futility; shallowness

superficie /super'fisie; super'fiθie/ *f*, area; surface; outside, exterior. **s. de rodadura,** tire tread

superfino /super'fino/ *a* superfine

superfluidad /superflui'ðað/ *f*, superfluity

superfluo /su'perfluo/ *a* superfluous, redundant

superfortaleza volante /superforta'lesa bo'lante; superforta'leθa bo'lante/ f, Aer. superfortress

superhombre /super'ombre/ m, superman

superintendencia /superinten'densia; superinten'denθia/ f, supervision; superintendentship; higher administration

superintendente /superinten'dente/ mf superintendent; supervisor

superior /supe'rior/ a higher, upper; excellent, fine; superior; higher (education, etc.). m, head, director; superior

superiora /supe'riora/ f, mother superior

superioridad /superiori'ðað/ f, superiority

superlativo /superla'tiβo/ a and m, superlative

superno /su'perno/ a supreme

supernumerario /supernume'rario/ (-ia) a and n supernumerary

superposición /superposi'sion; superposi'θion/ f, superposition

superproducción /superproðuk'sion; superproðuk'θion/ f, overproduction; superproduction

superrealismo /superrea'lismo/ m, surrealism

superrealista /superrea'lista/ a surrealist

superstición /supersti'sion; supersti'θion/ f, superstition

supersticioso /supersti'sioso; supersti'θioso/ a superstitious

supervención /superβen'sion; superβen'θion/ f, Law. supervention

supervigilancia /superβihi'lansia; superβihi'lanθia/ f, Lat. Am. supervision

supervivencia /superβi'βensia; superβi'βenθia/ f, survival

superviviente /superβi'βiente/ a surviving. mf survivor

supino /su'pino/ a supine; foolish, stupid. m, Gram. supine

suplantación /suplanta'sion; suplanta'θion/ f, supplanting

suplantador /suplanta'ðor/ (-ra) a supplanting. n supplanter

suplantar /suplan'tar/ vt to forge, alter (documents); supplant

suplefaltas /suple'faltas/ mf Inf. scapegoat

suplementario /suplemen'tario/ a supplementary, additional

suplemento /suple'mento/ m, supplement; supply, supplying; newspaper supplement; Geom. supplement

suplente /su'plente/ m, substitute, proxy; Fig. makeweight

súplica /'suplika/ f, supplication, prayer; request

suplicación /suplika'sion; suplika'θion/ f, entreaty, supplication; Law. petition

suplicante /supli'kante/ a supplicatory; Law. petitioning. mf supplicator; Law. petitioner

suplicar /supli'kar/ vt to beg, supplicate; request; Law. appeal

suplicio /su'plisio; su'pliθio/ m, torment, torture; execution; place of torture or execution; affliction, anguish. **último s.,** capital punishment

suplir /su'plir/ vt to supply, furnish; substitute, take the place of; overlook, forgive

suponer /supo'ner/ vt irr to suppose, take for granted; simulate; comprise, include; vi carry weight, wield authority. See **poner**

suposición /suposi'sion; suposi'θion/ f, supposition; conjecture, assumption; distinction, talent, importance; falsity, falsehood

supositorio /suposi'torio/ m, suppository

suprasensible /suprasen'siβle/ a supersensible

supremacía /suprema'sia; suprema'θia/ f, supremacy

supremo /su'premo/ a supreme; matchless, incomparable; last

supresión /supre'sion/ f, suppression; destruction; eradication; omission

suprimir /supri'mir/ vt to suppress; destroy, eradicate; omit, leave out. **s. una calle al tráfico,** to close a street to traffic, ban traffic from a street

supuesto /su'puesto/ a supposed; so-called; reputed.

m, supposition, hypothesis. **por s.,** of course, presumably; doubtless

supurar /supu'rar/ vi to suppurate

suputar /supu'tar/ vt to calculate, compute

sur /sur/ m, south; south wind

surcador /surka'ðor/ m, plowman

surcar /sur'kar/ vt to plow furrows; furrow, line; cut, cleave (water, etc.)

surco /'surko/ m, furrow; wrinkle, line; groove, channel; rut

surgidero /surhi'ðero/ m, Naut. road, roadstead

surgir /sur'hir/ vi to spout, gush, spurt; Naut. anchor; appear, show itself; come forth, turn up

surrealismo /surrea'lismo/ m, surrealism

surrealista /surrea'lista/ a and mf surrealist

surtida /sur'tiða/ f, hidden exit; false door; Naut. slipway

surtidero /surti'ðero/ m, outlet, drain; jet, fountain

surtido /sur'tiðo/ a mixed, assorted. m, variety, assortment; stock, range. **de s.,** in everyday use

surtidor /surti'ðor/ (-ra) n purveyor, supplier. m, fountain, jet. **s. de gasolina,** gasoline pump, gas pump

surtimiento /surti'miento/ m, assortment; stock

surtir /sur'tir/ vt to provide, supply, furnish; vi spurt, gush

surto /'surto/ a calm, reposeful; Naut. anchored

susceptibilidad /susseptiβili'ðað; susθeptiβili'ðað/ f, susceptibility

susceptible /sussep'tiβle; susθep'tiβle/ a susceptible, open to; touchy, oversensitive

suscitar /sussi'tar; susθi'tar/ vt to cause, originate; provoke, incite; vr arise, take place

suscribir /suskri'βir/ vt to sign; agree to; vr subscribe, contribute; take out a subscription (to a periodical, etc.). Past Part. **suscrito**

suscripción /suskrip'sion; suskrip'θion/ f, subscription; agreement, accession

susodicho /suso'ðitʃo/ a aforesaid

suspender /suspen'der/ vt to suspend, hang up; postpone, defer, stop; amaze, dumbfound; suspend (from employment); fail (an exam); adjourn (meetings); vr rear (of horses)

suspensión /suspen'sion/ f, suspension; postponement, stoppage, deferment; amazement; failure (in an exam); adjournment (of a meeting); springs (of a car). Com. **s. de pagos,** suspension of payments. **con mala s.,** badly sprung (of a car)

suspensivo /suspen'siβo/ a suspensive

suspensivos /suspen'siβos/ m, pl suspension points, ellipsis points

suspenso /sus'penso/ a amazed, bewildered. m, failure slip (in an exam). **en s.,** in suspense

suspensor /suspen'sor/ m, Lat. Am. suspender (for pants)

suspicacia /suspi'kasia; suspi'kaθia/ f, suspiciousness; mistrust, uneasiness

suspicaz /suspi'kas; suspi'kaθ/ a suspicious, mistrustful

suspirado /suspi'raðo/ a eagerly desired, longed for

suspirar /suspi'rar/ vt and vi to sigh. **s. por,** to long for

suspiro /sus'piro/ m, sigh; breath; glass whistle; Mus. brief pause, pause sign. **último s.,** Inf. last leg, end

suspirón /suspi'ron/ a given to sighing

sustancia /sus'tansia; sus'tanθia/ f, substance, juice, extract, essence; Fig. core, pith; Fig. meat; wealth, estate; worth, importance; nutritive part; Inf. common sense. Anat. **s. gris,** gray matter. **en s.,** in short

sustanciación /sustansia'sion; sustanθia'θion/ f, substantiation

sustancial /sustan'sial; sustan'θial/ a substantial, real; important, essential; nutritive; solid

sustanciar /sustan'siar; sustan'θiar/ vt to substantiate; summarize, extract, abridge

sustancioso /sustan'sioso; sustan'θioso/ a substantial; nutritive

sustantivo /sustan'tiβo/ a and m, Gram. substantive, noun

sustentable /susten'taβle/ a arguable, defensible
sustentación /sustenta'sion; sustenta'θion/ f, maintenance; defense
sustentar /susten'tar/ vt to sustain, keep; support, bear; nourish, feed; uphold. advocate. **s. un ciclo de conferencias,** to give a series of lectures
sustento /sus'tento/ m, maintenance, preservation; nourishment, sustenance; support
sustitución /sustitu'sion; sustitu'θion/ f, substitution
sustituible /susti'tuiβle/ a substitutive, replaceable
sustituir /susti'tuir/ vt irr to substitute. See **huir**
sustitutivo /sustitu'tiβo/ a substitutive
sustituto /susti'tuto/ **(-ta)** n substitute
susto /'susto/ m, fright, shock; apprehension. **dar un s.** (a), to scare
sustracción /sustrak'sion; sustrak'θion/ f, subtraction
sustraer /sustra'er/ vt irr to remove, separate; rob, steal; Math. subtract; vr depart, remove oneself; avoid. See **traer**
sustrato /sus'trato/ m, substratum
susurrador /susurra'ðor/ **(-ra)** a whispering; murmuring; rustling. n whisperer
susurrante /susu'rrante/ a whispering; murmuring; rustling
susurrar /susu'rrar/ vi to whisper; murmur; rustle;

babble, purl, prattle (of water); vi and vr be whispered abroad
susurro /su'surro/ m, whispering, whisper; murmur; rustle; lapping
sutil /'sutil/ a fine, thin; penetrating, subtle, keen
sutileza, sutilidad /suti'lesa, sutili'ðað; suti'leθa, sutili'ðað/ f, fineness, thinness; subtlety, penetration.
sutileza de manos, dexterity; light-fingeredness; sleight of hand
sutilizaciones /sutilisa'siones; sutiliθa'θiones/ f, pl casuistry, hairsplitting, quibbling
sutilizar /sutili'sar; sutili'θar/ vt to make thin, refine; Fig. finish, perfect; Fig. split hairs, make subtle distinctions
sutura /su'tura/ f, suture
suyo, suya /'suyo, 'suya/ m, and f, pl **suyos, suyas,** poss pron and a 3rd pers his; hers; its; yours; theirs; of his, of hers, etc. (e.g. Este libro es suyo, This book is his (hers, yours, theirs). **Este libro es uno de los suyos,** This book is one of his (hers, etc.). **(suyo** is often used with def. art. **el, la,** etc.) **los suyos,** his (hers, yours, etc.) family, following, adherents, etc. **de suyo,** of its very nature, of itself; spontaneously. **salirse con la suya,** to get one's own way. Inf. **ver la suyo,** to see one's opportunity

T

tabacal /taβa'kal/ m, tobacco plantation
tabacalero /taβaka'lero/ **(-ra)** a tobacco. n tobacco merchant; tobacco planter
tabaco /ta'βako/ m, tobacco plant, tobacco leaf; tobacco; cigar. **t. de pipa,** pipe tobacco. **t. flojo,** mild tobacco. **t. rubio,** Virginia tobacco
tabalear /taβale'ar/ **(se)** vt and vr to rock, sway, swing; vi drum with the fingers
tabaleo /taβa'leo/ m, swaying, rocking; drumming with the fingers
tabanco /ta'βanko/ m, market stall
tábano /'taβano/ m, Ent. horsefly, gadfly
tabanque /ta'βanke/ m, potter's wheel
tabaque /ta'βake/ m, small osier basket (for fruit, sewing, etc.); large tack
tabaquera /taβa'kera/ f, tobacco jar, tobacco tin; bowl of pipe tobacco; tobacco pouch; snuffbox
tabaquería /taβake'ria/ f, tobacconist's shop
tabaquero /taβa'kero/ **(-ra)** n tobacco grower; tobacco merchant; tobacco factory worker; tobacconist
tabaquismo /taβa'kismo/ m, nicotinism, nicotine poisoning
tabaquista /taβa'kista/ mf tobacco expert; heavy smoker
tabardillo /taβarðiyo; taβar'ðiʎo/ m, fever. **t. de tripas,** typhoid. **t. pintado,** typhus
tabardo /ta'βarðo/ m, tabard
taberna /ta'βerna/ f, public house, tavern
tabernáculo /taβer'nakulo/ m, tabernacle
tabernario /taβer'nario/ a public house, tavern; low, vulgar
tabernera /taβer'nera/ f, publican's wife; barmaid
tabernero /taβer'nero/ m, publican; barman, drawer
tabicar /taβi'kar/ vt to wall or board up; hide, cover up
tabique /ta'βike/ m, partition wall, inside wall; thin wall
tabla /'taβla/ f, plank of wood, board; Metall. plate; slab; flat side, face (of wood); Sew. box pleat; table (of contents, etc.); Art. panel; vegetable garden; butcher's slab; butcher's stall; pl tablets (for writing); (Math. etc.) tables; stalemate (chess, checkers); draw (in an election); Theat. boards, stage. **t. de armonía,** sounding board (of musical instruments). **t. de lavar,** washboard. **t. de materias,** table of contents. **t. de multiplicación,** multiplication table. **t. rasa,** clean sheet (of paper, etc.); complete ignorance. **T. Redonda,** Round Table (of King Arthur). **escapar** or **salvarse en una t.,** to have a narrow escape, escape in the nick of time

tablacho /ta'βlatʃo/ m, sluice gate. **echar el t.,** Inf. to interrupt the flow of someone's remarks
tablado /ta'βlaðo/ m, flooring; platform; Theat. stage; scaffold, gibbet. **sacar al t.,** to produce, put on the stage; to make known, publish
tablazón /taβla'son; taβla'θon/ f, planks, boards; flooring; Naut. deck planks or sheathing
tablear /taβle'ar/ vt to saw into planks; Sew. make box pleats in; hammer iron into sheets
tablero /ta'βlero/ m, board (of wood); paneling, boarding; slab; shop counter; board (checkers, chess). **t. de instrumentos,** dashboard; instrument panel
tableta /ta'βleta/ f, tablet; pastille, lozenge
tablilla /ta'βliya; ta'βliʎa/ f, small board; tablet; bulletin board, notice board
tablón /ta'βlon/ m, thick plank; wooden beam; Inf. drinking bout
tabú /ta'βu/ m, taboo
tabuco /ta'βuko/ m, miserable little room; hovel
taburete /taβu'rete/ m, stool; tabouret
tacañería /takaɲe'ria/ f, miserliness, niggardliness; craftiness
tacaño /ta'kaɲo/ a miserly, niggardly, Inf. cheap; crafty
tacha /'tatʃa/ f, imperfection, defect; spot, stain; fault; large tack. **poner t.,** to criticize, object to
tachable /ta'tʃaβle/ a censurable, blameworthy
tachar /ta'tʃar/ vt to criticize; blame; cross out, erase; charge, accuse
tacho de basura /'tatʃo de ba'sura/ m, Argentina garbage can
tachón /ta'tʃon/ m, round-headed ornamental nail; Sew. gold or silver studs, trimming; crossing out, erasure
tachonar /tatʃo'nar/ vt to stud with round-headed nails; Sew. trim with gold or silver studs or trimming
tachoso /ta'tʃoso/ a imperfect, defective, faulty; spotted, stained
tachuela /ta'tʃuela/ f, tack
tácito /'tasito; 'taθito/ a silent, unexpressed; tacit, implied
taciturnidad /tasiturni·oað; taθiturni'ðað/ f, taciturnity; reserve; melancholy
taciturno /tasi'turno; taθi'turno/ a taciturn; reserved; dismal, gloomy, melancholy
taco /'tako/ m, stopper, plug; billiard cue; rammer; wad, wadding (in a gun); pop gun; taco (filled tortilla); tear-off calendar; Argentina, heel (of a shoe) Inf. snack; obscenity, oath. **t. de papel,** writing tablet

tacón /ta'kon/ *m*, heel (of a shoe)
taconear /takone'ar/ *vi* to stamp with one's heels; walk heavily on one's heels; walk arrogantly
taconeo /tako'neo/ *m*, drumming or stamping of one's heels (gen. in dancing)
táctica /'taktika/ *f*, method, technique; *Mil.* tactics; policy, way, means
táctico /'taktiko/ *a* tactical. *m*, *Mil.* tactician
táctil /'taktil/ *a* tactile
tacto /'takto/ *m*, sense of touch; touch, feel; touching; skill; tact
tafetán /tafe'tan/ *m*, taffeta; *pl* flags, standards. **t. de heridas** *or* **t. inglés,** court plaster
tafilete /tafi'lete/ *m*, morocco leather
tahalí /taa'li/ *m*, sword shoulder belt
tahona /ta'ona/ *f*, horse mill; bakery; baker's shop
tahonero /tao'nero/ **(-ra)** *n* miller; baker
tahúr /ta'ur/ *m*, gambler; cardsharper
tahurería /taure'ria/ *f*, gambling den; gambling; cheating at cards
Tailandia /tai'landia/ Thailand
taimado /tai'maðo/ *a* knavish, crafty; obstinate, headstrong
taimería /taime'ria/ *f*, cunning, craftiness
taita /'taita/ *m*, daddy
taja /'taha/ *f*, cut, cutting; slice; washboard
tajada /ta'haða/ *f*, slice; strip, portion; steak, filet; *Inf.* cough; drinking bout; hoarseness
tajadera /taha'ðera/ *f*, cheese knife; chisel; *pl* sluice gate
tajado /ta'haðo/ *a* steep, sheer (of cliffs, etc.)
tajadura /taha'ðura/ *f*, cutting, dividing, dissection
tajar /ta'har/ *vt* to cut, chop; sharpen, trim (quill pens)
tajea /ta'hea/ *f*, culvert; aqueduct; drain; watercourse
tajear /tahe'ar/ *vt*, *Lat. Am.* to cut up
Tajo, el /'taho, el/ the Tagus
tajo /'taho, el/ *m*, cut, incision; task; cutting (in a mountain, etc.); cut, thrust (of sword); executioner's block; chopping board; washboard; steep cliff, precipice
tajón /ta'hon/ *m*, butcher block; chopping board
tal /tal/ *a pl* **tales,** such; said (e.g. *el t. Don Juan,* the so called Don Juan). **tal** is always used before nouns and (except when meaning "the said") without def. art. **un t.,** a certain (e.g. *un t. hombre,* a certain man). *pron* some, some people; someone; such a thing. *adv* so, thus. **t. para cual,** two of a kind, a well-matched pair; tit for tat. **con t. que,** *conjunc* on condition that, provided that. **No hay t.,** There is no such thing. *Inf.* **¿Qué t.?** How are you? What's the news? What's new? *Inf.* **fulano de t.,** whatsisname
tala /'tala/ *f*, felling or cutting down (of trees); cropping of grass (ruminants)
talabarte /tala'βarte/ *m*, sword belt
talabartería /talaβarte'ria/ *f*, saddlery
talador /tala'ðor/ **(-ra)** *a* felling, cutting; destructive. *n* feller, cutter; destroyer
taladrar /tala'ðrar/ *vt* to drill, bore, gouge holes; pierce, perforate; punch (a ticket); assail or hurt the ear (sounds); *Fig.* go into deeply (a subject)
taladro /ta'laðro/ *m*, drill, gimlet, gouge; drill hole, bore; puncher (for tickets, etc.)
tálamo /'talamo/ *m*, marriage bed; (*Bot. Anat.*) thalamus
talán /ta'lan/ *m*, peal, tolling (of a bell)
talanquera /talan'kera/ *f*, barricade; parapet; fence, wall; refuge, asylum; safety, security
talante /ta'lante/ *m*, mode of execution, technique; personal appearance, mien; disposition, temperament; wish, desire; aspect, appearance. **de buen (mal) t.,** willingly (unwillingly)
talar /ta'lar/ *a* full-length, long (of gowns, robes, etc.)
talar /ta'lar/ *vt* to fell, chop down (trees); ravage, lay waste; prune (gen. olive trees)
talco /'talko/ *m*, *Mineral.* talc; sequin, tinsel
talcualillo /talkua'liyo; talkua'liʎo/ *a Inf.* not too bad, fairly good; slightly better (of health)
taled /ta'leð/ *m*, prayer shawl, tales, tallit

talega /ta'lega/ *f*, sack, bag; sackful; money bag; *pl Inf.* cash wealth
talego /ta'lego/ *m*, narrow sack; *Inf.* dumpy person
talento /ta'lento/ *m*, talent (Greek coin); talent, gift, quality; intelligence, understanding; cleverness
talentoso /talen'toso/ *a* talented
talero /ta'lero/ *m*, *Argentina* whip
talión /ta'lion/ *m*, (**ley de**) law of retaliation
talismán /talis'man/ *m*, talisman
talla /'taya; 'taʎa/ *f*, carving (especially wood); cutting (of gems); reward for apprehension of a criminal; ransom; stature, height, size; height measuring rod
tallado /ta'yaðo; ta'ʎaðo/ *a* **bien** (*or* **mal**), well (or badly) carved; well (or badly) proportioned, of a good (or bad) figure
tallado /ta'yaðo; ta'ʎaðo/ *m*, carving
tallador /taya'ðor; taʎa'ðor/ *m*, metal engraver; die sinker
tallar /ta'yar; ta'ʎar/ *vt Art.* to carve; engrave; cut (gems); value, estimate; measure height (of persons)
tallarín /taya'rin; taʎa'rin/ *m*, (gen. *pl*) *Cul.* noodle
talle /'taye; 'taʎe/ *m*, figure, physique; waist; fit (of clothes); appearance, aspect. *Inf.* **largo de t.,** long-waisted; long drawn out, overlong. **tener buen t.,** to have a good figure
tallecer /taye'ser; taʎe'θer/ *vi irr Bot.* to sprout, shoot. See **conocer**
taller /ta'yer; ta'ʎer/ *m*, workshop; factory; mill; workroom, atelier; industrial school; school of arts and crafts; studio
tallista /ta'yista; ta'ʎista/ *mf* engraver; wood carver; sculptor
tallo /'tayo; 'taʎo/ *m*, *Bot.* stalk; shoot; slice of preserved fruit; cabbage. **t. rastrero,** *Bot.* runner
talludo /ta'yuðo; ta'ʎuðo/ *a* long-stalked; lanky, overgrown; no longer young, aging (of women); habit-ridden
talmúdico /tal'muðiko/ *a* Talmudic
talón /ta'lon/ *m*, heel; heel (of a shoe); *Com.* counterfoil; luggage receipt; *Com.* sight draft; coupon; heel (of a violin bow). *Inf.* **apretar los talones,** to take to one's heels. *Inf.* **pisarle (a uno) los talones,** to follow on a person's heels; rival successfully
talonada /talo'naða/ *f*, dig in with the spurs
talonario /talo'nario/ *m*, stub book
tamaño /ta'maɲo/ *a comp* so big; so small (e.g. *La conocí tamaña,* I knew her when she was so high) (indicating her size with a gesture)); so great, so large (e.g. *tamaña empresa,* so great an undertaking). *m*, size
tamarindo /tama'rindo/ *m*, tamarind
tambaleante /tambale'ante/ *a* tottering, rickety; staggering
tambalear /tambale'ar/ (**se**) *vi* and *vr* to totter, sway, shake; reel, stagger
tambaleo /tamba'leo/ *m*, swaying; tottering; rocking; shaking; staggering, reeling
tambarillo /tamba'riyo; tamba'riʎo/ *m*, chest with an arched lid
también /tam'bien/ *adv* also, too; in addition, as well
tambor /tam'bor/ *m*, *Mus.* drum; drummer; embroidery frame; *Mech.* drum, cylinder; roaster (for coffee, chestnuts, etc.). **t. mayor,** drum major. **a t.** (*or* **con t.**) **>batiente,** with drums beating; triumphantly, with colors flying
tamborear /tambore'ar/ *vi* to totter, sway, stagger, reel
tamboreo /tambo'reo/ *m*, tottering, swaying; staggering, reeling
tamboril /tambo'ril/ *m*, tabor
tamborilada /tambori'laða/ *f*, *Inf.* slap on the back or face; *Inf.* fall on the bottom
tamborilear /tamborile'ar/ *vi* to play the tabor; *vt* eulogize, extol
tamborilero /tambori'lero/ *m*, tabor player
tamborín /tambo'rin/ *m*, tabor
Támesis, el /'tamesis, el/ the Thames
tamiz /ta'mis; ta'miθ/ *m*, sieve
tamizar /tami'sar; tami'θar/ *vt* to sieve

tarjar

tamo /'tamo/ *m*, fluff; chaff

tampoco /tam'poko/ *adv* neither, not... either, nor... either; no more (e.g. *No lo ha hecho María t.,* Mary hasn't done it either)

tampón /tam'pon/ *m*, stamp moistener; *Surg.* tampon

tan /tan/ *adv abb* **tanto** so, as. Used before adjectives and adverbs, excepting **más, mejor, menos, peor,** which need **tanto. t.... como,** as... as. **t. siquiera,** even (see **siquiera**). **t. sólo,** only, solely (e.g. *No vengo t. sólo para saludarte,* I do not come merely to greet you). **qué... t.,** what a... (e.g. *¡Qué día t. hermoso!* What a lovely day!)

tanda /'tanda/ *f*, turn; opportunity; task; shift, relay; game (of billiards); bad habit; collection, batch, group; round (of a game); (*Dance.*) set

tándem /'tandem/ *m*, tandem bicycle

tandeo /tan'deo/ *m*, allowance of irrigation water, turn for using water

Tangañica /taŋga'ɲika/ Tanganyika

tangente /tan'hente/ *a* and *f*, *Geom.* tangent

Tánger /'tanher/ Tangier

tangerino /tanhe'rino/ **(-na)** *a* and *n* of or from Tangier, Tangerine

tanque /'tanke/ *m*, *Mil.* tank; cistern, tank, reservoir; ladle, dipper

tanteador /tantea'ðor/ *m*, *Sports.* scorer, marker; scoreboard

tantear /tante'ar/ *vt* to measure, compare; consider fully; test, try out; *Fig.* probe, pump (persons); estimate roughly; *Art.* sketch, block in; *vt* and *vi Sports.* keep the score of

tanteo /tan'teo/ *m*, measurement, comparison; test; rough estimate; *Sports.* score

tanto /'tanto/ *a* so much; as much; very great; as great; *pl* **tantos,** so many; as many (e.g. *Tienen tantas flores como nosotros,* They have as many flowers as we). In comparisons **tanto** is used before **más, mejor, menos, peor,** but generally **tan** is used before adjectives and adverbs (e.g. *¡Tanto peor!* So much the worse!). *pron dem* that (e.g. *por lo t.,* therefore, on that account). *m,* so much, a certain amount; copy of a document; man, piece (in games); point (score in games); *Com.* rate (e.g. *el t. por ciento,* the percentage, the rate); *pl* approximation, odd (e.g. *Llegaron cien hombres y tantos,* A hundred-odd men arrived). *adv* so much; as much; so, in such a way. **t.... como,** the same as, as much as. **t.... cuanto,** as much as. **t. más,** the more. **t. menos,** the less (e.g. *Cuanto más* (*menos*) **dinero tiene t. más** (**menos**) **quiere,** The more (less) money he has, the more (less) he wants). **t. más** (**menos**)... **cuanto que,** all the more (less)... because. **algún t.,** a certain amount, somewhat. **al t. de** (**una cosa**), aware of, acquainted with (a thing). **en t.** *or* **entre t.,** meanwhile. **las tantas,** *Inf.* late hour, wee hours. **No es para t.,** *Inf.* It's not as bad as that, there's no need to make such a fuss; he (she, it) isn't equal to it. **otro t.,** the same, as much; as much more. **un t.,** a bit, somewhat

tañedor /taɲe'ðor/ **(-ra)** *n Mus.* player

tañer /ta'ɲer/ *vt irr Mus.* to play; *vi* sway, swing. **t. la occisa,** to sound the death (in hunting). *Pres. Part.* **tañendo.** *Preterite* **tañó, tañeron.** *Imperf. Subjunc.* **tañese, etc.**

tañido /ta'ɲiðo/ *m*, tune, sound, note; toll, peal; ring

taoísmo /tao'ismo/ *m*, Taoism

taoísta /tao'ista/ *mf* Taoist

tapa /'tapa/ *f*, lid; cover; cover (of books)

tapaboca /tapa'βoka/ *m*, blow on the mouth; *f*, scarf, muffler; *Inf.* remark that silences someone

tapada /ta'paða/ *f*, veiled woman, one whose face is hidden

tapadera /tapa'ðera/ *f*, loose lid, top, cover

tapadero /tapa'ðero/ *m*, stopper

tapado /ta'paðo/ *m*, *Argentina* coat, overcoat

tapador /tapa'ðor/ **(-ra)** *a* covering. *n* coverer. *m*, stopper; lid; cover

tapagujeros /tapagu'heros/ *m*, *Inf.* unskilled mason or bricklayer; *Fig. Inf.* stopgap (person)

tapar /ta'par/ *vt* to cover; cover with a lid; muffle up, veil; hide, keep secret; close up, stop up

taparrabo /tapa'rraβo/ *m*, loincloth; swimming trunks

tapete /ta'pete/ *m*, rug; tablecover. *Inf.* **t. verde,** gaming table. *Fig.* **estar sobre el t.,** to be on the carpet, be under consideration

tapia /'tapia/ *f*, adobe; mud wall; fence. *Inf.* **más sordo que una t.,** as deaf as a post

tapiar /ta'piar/ *vt* to wall up; put a fence around, fence in

tapicería /tapise'ria/ tapiθe'ria/ *f*, set of tapestries; tapestry work; art of tapestry making; upholstery; tapestry storehouse or shop

tapicero /tapi'sero; tapi'θero/ *m*, tapestry weaver or maker; upholsterer; carpet layer; furnisher

tapioca /ta'pioka/ *f*, tapioca

tapisca /ta'piska/ *f Central America, Mexico* corn harvest

tapiz /ta'pis; ta'piθ/ *m*, tapestry; carpet

tapizar /tapi'sar; tapi'θar/ *vt* to cover with tapestry; cover, clothe; upholster; carpet; hang with tapestry; furnish with hangings or drapes

tapón /ta'pon/ *m*, stopper; cork (of a bottle); plug; *Surg.* tampon

taponar /tapo'nar/ *vt* to stopper, cork; plug; *Surg.* tampon; *Mil.* seal off

tapujarse /tapu'harse/ *vr* to wrap oneself up, muffle oneself

tapujo /ta'puho/ *m*, scarf, muffler, face covering; disguise; *Inf.* pretense, subterfuge

taquera /ta'kera/ *f*, rack (for billiard cues)

taquería /take'ria/ *f*, taco stand

taquigrafía /takigra'fia/ *f*, shorthand

taquigrafiar /takigra'fiar/ *vt* to write in shorthand

taquigráfico /taki'grafiko/ *a* shorthand

taquígrafo /ta'kigrafo/ **(-fa)** *n* shorthand writer, stenographer

taquilla /ta'kiya; ta'kiʎa/ *f*, booking office; box office; grille, window (in banks, etc.); rolltop desk, cupboard for papers; *Theat.* takings, cash

taquillero /taki'yero; taki'ʎero/ **(-ra)** *n* booking office clerk

tara /'tara/ *f*, tally stick; *Com.* tare

taracea /tara'sea; tara'θea/ *f*, inlaid work, marquetry

taracear /tarase'ar; taraθe'ar/ *vt* to inlay

tarambana /taram'bana/ *mf Inf.* madcap

tarántula /ta'rantula/ *f*, tarantula

tararear /tarare'ar/ *vt* to hum a tune

tarareo /tara'reo/ *m*, humming, singing under one's breath

tarasca /ta'raska/ *f*, figure of a dragon (carried in Corpus Christi processions); *Inf.* hag, trollop

tarascada /taras'kaða/ *f*, bite, nip; *Inf.* insolent reply

tarascar /taras'kar/ *vt* to bite; wound with the teeth

tardanza /tar'ðansa; tar'ðanθa/ *f*, delay, tardiness; slowness

tardar /tar'ðar/ *vi* to delay; be tardy, arrive late; take a long time. **a más t.,** at the latest

tarde /'tarðe/ *f*, afternoon. *adv* late. **¡Buenas tardes!** Good afternoon! **de t. en t.,** from time to time, sometimes. **hacerse t.,** to grow late. **Más vale t. que nunca,** Better late than never. **de la t. a la mañana,** overnight

tardecer /tarðe'ser; tarðe'θer/ *vi impers irr* to grow dusk. See **conocer**

tardecica, tardecita /tarðe'sika, tarðe'sita; tarðe'θika, tarðe'θita/ *f*, dusk, late afternoon

tardíamente /tar'ðiamente/ *adv* late; too late

tardío /tar'ðio/ *a* late; backward; behind; slow, deliberate

tardo /'tarðo/ *a* slow, slothful, tardy; late; dilatory; stupid, slow-witted; badly spoken, inarticulate

tarea /ta'rea/ *f*, task, work

tarifa /ta'rifa/ *f*, price list; tariff

tarifar /tari'far/ *vt* to put a tariff on

tarima /ta'rima/ *f*, stand, raised platform

tarín barín /ta'rin ba'rin/ *adv Inf.* more or less, about. *Inf.* **beber sobre t.,** to drink on credit

tarjar /tar'har/ *vt* to reckon by tally; *Lat. Am.* cross out, erase

tarjeta /tar'heta/ f, buckler, small shield; *Archit.* tablet bearing an inscription; title (of maps and charts); visiting card; invitation (card). **t. de visita,** visiting card. **t. postal,** postcard, postal card
tarquín /tar'kin/ m, mud, mire
tárraga /'tarraga/ f, old Spanish dance
tarro /'tarro/ m, jar, pot; *Lat. Am.* top hat
tarso /'tarso/ m, *Anat.* tarsus, ankle; *Zool.* hock; *Ornith.* shank
tarta /'tarta/ f, cake pan; cake; tart
tártago /'tartago/ m, spurge; *Inf.* misfortune, disappointment
tartajear /tartahe'ar/ vi to stammer; stutter
tartajeo /tarta'heo/ m, stammering; stutter
tartajoso /tarta'hoso/ **(-sa)** a stammering; stuttering. n stutterer
tartalear /tartale'ar/ vi *Inf.* to stagger, totter; be speechless, be dumbfounded
tartamudear /tartamuðe'ar/ vi to stammer, stutter
tartamudeo /tartamu'ðeo/ m. **tartamudez** f, stammering; stuttering
tartamudo /tarta'muðo/ **(-da)** n stammerer
tartán /tar'tan/ m, tartan
tartana /tar'tana/ f, *Naut.* tartan; covered two-wheeled carriage
tartáreo /tar'tareo/ a *Poet.* infernal, hellish
tártaro /'tartaro/ **(-ra)** m, cream of tartar; tartar (on teeth); *Poet.* hell, hades. a and n Tartar
tartufo /tar'tufo/ m, hypocrite
tarugo /ta'rugo/ m, thick wooden peg; stopper; wooden block; a *Lat. Am.* dumb, stupid
tasa /'tasa/ f, assessment, valuation; valuation certificate; fixed price; standard rate; measure, rule. *Com.* **t. de cambio,** exchange rate
tasación /tasa'sion; tasa'θion/ f, valuation; assessment
tasador /tasa'ðor/ m, public assessor; valuer
tasajo /ta'saho/ m, salt meat; piece of meat
tasar /ta'sar/ vt to value; price; fix remuneration; tax; regulate; rate; dole out sparingly
tasca /'taska/ f, gambling den; tavern
tascar /tas'kar/ vt to dress (hemp, etc.); graze, crop the grass
tasquera /tas'kera/ f, *Inf.* quarrel, row, rumpus
tasquil /tas'kil/ m, wood splinter, chip
tata /'tata/ m, *Inf. West Hem.* daddy
tatarabuela /tatara'βuela/ f, great-great-grandmother
tatarabuelo /tatara'βuelo/ m, great-great-grandfather
tataradeudo /tatara'ðeuðo/ **(-da)** n very old relative; ancestor
tataranieta /tatara'nieta/ f, great-great-granddaughter
tataranieto /tatara'nieto/ m, great-great-grandson
tatas, andar a /'tatas, an'dar a/ vt to walk on all fours
¡tate! /'tate/ interj Stop!; Be careful!; Go slowly!; Now I understand!, Of course!
tatuaje /ta'tuahe/ m, tattooing
tatuar /tatu'ar/ vt to tattoo
taumaturgia /tauma'turhia/ f, thaumaturgy, wonder-working
taumaturgo /tauma'turgo/ m, thaumaturge, magician
taurino /tau'rino/ a taurine; pertaining to bullfights
Tauro /'tauro/ m, Taurus
tauromaquia /tauro'makia/ f, bullfighting, tauromachy
tautología /tautolo'hia/ f, tautology
taxi /'taksi/ m, taxi
taxidermia /taksi'ðermia/ f, taxidermy
taxidermista /taksiðer'mista/ mf taxidermist
taxista /tak'sista/ m, taxi driver
taxonomía /taksono'mia/ f, taxonomy
taza /'tasa; 'taθa/ f, cup; cupful; basin (of a fountain)
tazar /ta'sar; ta'θar/ **(se)** vt and vr to fray (of cloth)
taz a taz /tas a tas; taθ a taθ/ adv in exchange, without payment; even
tazón /ta'son; ta'θon/ m, large cup; bowl
te /te/ f, name of the letter T. mf dat. and acc. of pers pron 2nd pers sing thee; you; to thee, to you. Never used with a preposition

té /te/ m, tea
tea /tea/ f, torch; firebrand
teatral /tea'tral/ a theatrical
teatralidad /teatrali'ðað/ f, theatricality
teatro /te'atro/ m, theater; stage; dramatic works; dramatic art; drama, plays. **t. de variedades,** music hall. **t. por horas,** theater where short, one-act plays are staged hourly
teca /'teka/ f, teak
techado /te'tʃaðo/ m, ceiling; roof
techador /tetʃa'ðor/ m, roofer
techar /te'tʃar/ vt to roof
techo /'tetʃo/ m, roof; ceiling; dwelling, habitation
techumbre /te'tʃumbre/ f, ceiling; roof
tecla /'tekla/ f, key (of keyed instruments); typewriter, linotype, or calculating machine key; *Fig.* difficult or delicate point. *Inf.* **dar en la t.,** to hit on the right way of doing a thing
teclado /te'klaðo/ m, keyboard
tecleado /tekle'aðo/ m, *Mus.* fingering
teclear /tekle'ar/ vi to finger the keyboard; run one's fingers over the keyboard; *Inf.* drum or tap with the fingers; vt tap (the keys, etc.); *Inf.* try out various schemes
tecleo /te'kleo/ m, fingering the keys; *Inf.* drumming with the fingers; scheme, means
técnica /'teknika/ f, technique
tecnicismo /tekni'sismo; tekni'θismo/ m, technical jargon; technicality, technical term
técnico /'tekniko/ a technical. m, technician
tecnicolor /tekniko'lor/ m, technicolor
tecnología /teknolo'hia/ f, technology
tecnológico /tekno'lohiko/ a technological
tecnólogo /tek'nologo/ m, technologist
tecolote /teko'lote/ m, *Central America, Mexico* owl; *Mexico* cop (police officer)
tedero /te'ðero/ m, torch seller; torch holder
tedio /'teðio/ m, tedium, boredom, ennui
tedioso /te'ðioso/ a tedious, boring
teísmo /te'ismo/ m, theism
teísta /te'ista/ a theistic. mf theist
teja /'teha/ f, tile, slate. *Inf.* **de tejas abajo,** in the normal way; in the world of men. **de tejas arriba,** in a supernatural way; in heaven
tejadillo /teha'ðiyo; teha'ðiʎo/ m, roof (of a vehicle)
tejado /te'haðo/ m, roof
tejano, -a /te'hano/ a and m. Texan. **tejanos** jeans
tejar /te'har/ m, tile works. vt to roof with tiles
Tejas /'tehas/ m Texas
tejavana /teha'βana/ f, penthouse, open shed
tejedor /tehe'ðor/ **(-ra)** a weaving; *Inf.* scheming. n weaver; *Inf.* schemer
tejedura /tehe'ðura/ f, weaving; fabric; texture
tejeduría /teheðu'ria/ f, art of weaving; weaving shed or mill
tejemaneje /tehema'nehe/ m, *Inf.* cleverness, knack
tejer /te'her/ vt to weave; plait; spin a cocoon; arrange, regulate; concoct, hatch (schemes); wind in and out (in dancing)
tejero /te'hero/ m, tile manufacturer
tejido /te'hiðo/ m, texture, weaving; textile; *Anat.* tissue; fabric, material
tejón /te'hon/ m, quoit, discus; metal disk; yew tree
tejón /te'hon/ m, *Zool.* badger
tela /'tela/ f, fabric, material, cloth; membrane; film (on liquids); spiderweb, cobweb; inner skin (of fruit, vegetables); film over the eye; matter, subject; scheme, plot. **t. metálica,** wire gauze. **en t. de juicio,** under consideration, in doubt. **llegarle a uno a las telas del corazón,** to hurt deeply, cut to the quick
telar /te'lar/ m, loom, weaving machine; *Theat.* gridiron
telaraña /tela'rana; tela'raɲa/ f, spider web, cobweb; mere trifle, bagatelle. *Inf.* **mirar las telarañas,** to be absent-minded. **Telaraña Global,** World Wide Web.
telarañoso /telara'ɲoso/ a cobwebby
telecomunicación /telekomunika'sion; teleko-munika'θion/ f, telecommunication
telefonear /telefone'ar/ vt to telephone, call

telefonía /telefo'nia/ *f*, telephony. **t. sin hilos,** wireless telephony, broadcasting

telefónico /tele'foniko/ *a* telephonic

telefonista /telefo'nista/ *mf* telephone operator

teléfono /te'lefono/ *m*, telephone. **t. celular,** cellular phone. **llamar por t. (a),** to telephone, call

telefundir /telefun'dir/ *vt* to telecast

telegrafía /telegra'fia/ *f*, telegraphy. **t. sin hilos,** wireless telegraphy

telegrafiar /telegra'fiar/ *vt* to telegraph

telegráfico /tele'grafiko/ *a* telegraphic

telegrafista /telegra'fista/ *mf* telegraph operator

telégrafo /te'legrafo/ *m*, telegraph. **t. sin hilos,** wireless telegraph. *Inf.* **hacer telégrafos,** to talk by signs

telegrama /tele'grama/ *m*, telegram

telemetría /teleme'tria/ *f*, telemetry

telémetro /te'lemetro/ *m*, telemeter, rangefinder

teleología /teleolo'hia/ *f*, teleology

telepatía /telepa'tia/ *f*, telepathy

telepático /tele'patiko/ *a* telepathic

telescópico /teles'kopiko/ *a* telescopic

telescopio /teles'kopio/ *m*, telescope

telespectador /telespekta'ðor/ *m*, TV viewer, member of the television audience

teletipo /tele'tipo/ *m*, teleprinter

televisión /teleβi'sion/ *f*, television

telilla /te'liya; te'liʎa/ *f*, film (on liquids); thin fabric

telón /te'lon/ *m*, *Theat.* curtain; drop scene. **t. contra incendios, t. de seguridad,** *Theat.* safety curtain. **t. de boca,** drop curtain. **t. de foro,** drop scene

tema /'tema/ *m*, theme, subject; *Mus.* motif, theme; thesis, argument. *f*, obstinacy; obsession, mania; hostility, grudge, rancor

temático /te'matiko/ *a* thematic; pigheaded, obstinate

temblador /tembla'ðor/ *a* trembling, shaking. *n* Quaker

temblante /tem'blante/ *a* shaking; quivering. *m*, bracelet

temblar /tem'blar/ *vi irr* to tremble, shake; wave, quiver; shiver with fear. See **acertar**

temblequear, tembletear /tembleke'ar, temblete'ar/ *vi Inf.* tremble; shake with fear

temblón /tem'blon/ *a Inf.* trembling, shaking. *m*, *Inf.* aspen

temblor /tem'blor/ *m*, shake, trembling, shiver. **temblor (de tierra)** earthquake

tembloroso, tembloso /temblo'roso, tem'bloso/ *a* trembling, shaking, shivering, quivering

temedero /teme'ðero/ *a* fearsome, dread

temedor /teme'ðor/ **(-ra)** *a* fearful. *n* fearer, dreader

temer /te'mer/ *vt* to fear, dread; suspect, imagine; *vi* be afraid

temerario /teme'rario/ *a* reckless, impetuous; thoughtless, hasty

temeridad /temeri'ðað/ *f*, recklessness, impetuosity, temerity; thoughtlessness; act of folly; rash judgment

temerón /teme'ron/ *a Inf.* swaggering, bombastic

temeroso /teme'roso/ *a* frightening, dread; fearful, timid; afraid, suspicious

temible /te'miβle/ *a* dread, awesome

temor /te'mor/ *m*, fear

temoso /te'moso/ *a* obstinate, headstrong

témpano /'tempano/ *m*, tabor; drumhead; block, flat piece; side of bacon. **t. de hielo,** iceberg, ice floe

temperación /tempera'sion; tempera'θion/ *f*, tempering

temperamento /tempera'mento/ *m*, temperament, nature; compromise, agreement

temperar /tempe'rar/ *vt* to temper; *Lat. Am.* spend the summer

temperatura /tempera'tura/ *f*, temperature

temperie /tem'perie/ *f*, weather conditions

tempestad /tempes'tað/ *f*, storm

tempestividad /tempestiβi'ðað/ *f*, opportuneness, seasonableness

tempestivo /tempes'tiβo/ *a* opportune, seasonable

tempestuoso /tempes'tuoso/ *a* stormy

templa /'templa/ *f*, tempera; *pl Anat.* temples

templado /tem'plaðo/ *a* moderate; temperate (of

regions); lukewarm; *Mus.* in tune; restrained (of style); *Inf.* brave, long-suffering. **estar bien (or mal) templado,** *Inf.* to be well (or badly) tuned (of musical instruments); be in a good (or bad) temper; be good- (or ill-) natured

templador /templa'ðor/ **(-ra)** *n* tuner. *m*, tuning key

templadura /templa'ðura/ *f*, tuning; tempering

templanza /tem'plansa; tem'planθa/ *f*, moderation; sobriety; mildness of climate

templar /tem'plar/ *vt* to tune; *Metall.* temper; moderate; warm; allay, appease; anneal; *Art.* harmonize, blend; *Naut.* trim the sails; *vr* control oneself, be moderate; *vi* grow warm

temple /'temple/ *m*, weather conditions; temperature; temper (of metals, etc.); nature, disposition; bravery; mean, average; *Mus.* tuning. **al t.,** in tempera

templete /tem'plete/ *m*, *dim* shrine; niche (for statues); kiosk, pavilion

templo /'templo/ *m*, temple

temporada /tempo'raða/ *f*, space of time, season, while. **de t.,** seasonal; temporary. **estar de t.,** to be out of town, on holiday

temporal /tempo'ral/ *a* temporal; temporary; secular, lay; transient, fugitive. *m*, storm, tempest; rainy period; seasonal laborer

temporalidad /temporali'ðað/ *f*, secular character; temporality secular possession (gen. *pl*)

temporáneo, temporario /tempora'neo, tempo'rario/ *a* temporary, impermanent, fleeting

témporas /'temporas/ *f pl*, Ember days

temporejar /tempore'har/ *vt Naut.* to lie to in a storm

temporero /tempo'rero/ *a* temporary (of work)

temporizar /tempori'sar; tempori'θar/ *vi* to while away the time; temporize

tempranal /tempra'nal/ *a* early fruiting

tempranear /temprane'ar/ *vi*, *Lat. Am.* to get up early

tempranero /tempra'nero/ *a* early

temprano /tem'prano/ *a* early. *adv* in the early hours; prematurely, too soon

temulento /temu'lento/ *a* intoxicated, drunken

tenacear /tenase'ar; tenaθe'ar/ *vi* to insist, be obstinate

tenacidad /tenasi'ðað; tenaθi'ðað/ *f*, adhesiveness; resistance, toughness; obstinacy, tenacity

tenacillas /tena'siyas; tena'θiʎas/ *f pl*, *dim* small tongs; candle snuffers; sugar tongs; curling irons; tweezers

tenaz /te'nas; te'naθ/ *a* adhesive; hard, resistant, unyielding; tenacious, obstinate

tenaza /te'nasa; te'naθa/ *f*, claw (of a lobster, etc.); *pl* tongs; pincers; pliers; dental forceps

tenazada /tena'saða; tena'θaða/ *f*, seizing with tongs; strong bite, snap; rattle of tongs

tenazón /tena'son; tena'θon/ **(a** or **de)** *adv* without taking aim, wildly; unexpectedly

tención /ten'sion; ten'θion/ *f*, retention, holding; grip

ten con ten /ten kon ten/ *m*, *Inf.* tact, diplomacy

tendal /ten'dal/ *m*, awning; sheet for catching olives; *Lat. Am.* heap, lot, pile, large amount, large number

tendedero /tende'ðero/ *m*, drying ground

tendedura /tende'ðura/ *f*, laying out; stretching

tendencia /ten'densia; ten'denθia/ *f*, tendency

tendencioso /tenden'sioso; tenden'θioso/ *a* tendentious, biased

tender /ten'der/ *vt irr* to hang out; unfold, spread out; extend, hold out; *Mas.* plaster; *vi* tend, incline; *vr* lie down at full length; place one's cards on the table; gallop hard (of horses). See **entender**

tendero /ten'dero/ **(-ra)** *n* shopkeeper; retailer. *m*, tent maker

tendido /ten'diðo/ *m*, row of seats in a bullfight arena; clothes hung out to dry; clear sky; *Mas.* plaster

tendón /ten'don/ *m*, tendon

tenducha /ten'dutʃa/ *f*, *Inf.* wretched little shop

tenebroso /tene'βroso/ *a* dark, gloomy

tenedero /tene'ðero/ *m*, *Naut.* anchoring ground, anchorage

tenedor /tene'ðor/ *m*, table fork; possessor, retainer; *Com.* holder; payee. **t. de libros,** bookkeeper

teneduría /teneðu'ria/ *f*, employment of a bookkeeper. **t. de libros,** bookkeeping

tenencia /te'nensia; te'nenθia/ *f*, possession; tenancy, occupation; lieutenancy

tener /te'ner/ *vt irr* to have; hold; grasp; possess, own; uphold, maintain; contain; include; hold fast, grip; stop; keep (promises); lodge, accommodate; (*with en*) value, estimate (e.g. *Le tengo en poco,* I have a poor opinion of him); (*with para*) be of the opinion that (e.g. *tengo para mí,* my opinion is); (*with por*) believe, consider; *vi* be wealthy; *vr* steady oneself; hold on to; lean (on); rest (on); defend oneself; uphold; rely on; (*with por*) consider oneself as. **tener** is used to express: 1. Age (e.g. *¿Cuántos años tiene Vd?* How old are you?). 2. *Possession* (e.g. *Tenemos muchos sombreros,* We have a great many hats). 3. *Measurements* (e.g. *El cuarto tiene dieciocho metros de largo,* The room is eighteen meters long). Translated by "be' when describing some physical and mental states (e.g. *Tenemos miedo,* We are afraid. *Tengo sueño,* I am sleepy. *Tienen frío (calor),* They are cold (hot)). Used as *auxiliary verb* replacing **haber** in compound tenses of transitive verbs (e.g. *Tengo escritas las cartas,* I have written the letters). **t. a bien,** to think fit, please, judge convenient. **t. algo en cuenta a uno,** to hold something against someone. **a menos de hacer (una cosa),** to scorn to do (a thing). **t. cruda,** to have a hangover. **t. curiosidad por,** to be curious about. **t. curiosidad por que +** *subj* to be interested that. **t. en aprecio,** to appreciate, esteem, value. **t. en cuenta,** to bear in mind. **t. en menos (a),** to despise (a person). **t. gana,** to want, wish; feel disposed; have an appetite. **t. lugar,** to take place, occur. **t. muchas partes cruzadas,** to be well-traveled. **t. mucho colegio** to be well-educated. **t. muy en cuenta,** to certainly bear in mind. **t. poco colegio,** to have had little education. **t. presente,** to remember. **t. que,** to have to (e.g. *tengo que hacerlo,* I must do it). **t. que ver (con),** to have something to do (with), be related to. **no tenerlas todas consigo,** *Inf.* to have the jitters. *Pres. Indic.* **tengo, tienes, tiene, tenemos, tenéis, tienen.** *Preterite* **tuve,** etc. *Fut.* **tendré,** etc. *Condit.* **tendría,** etc. *Pres. Subjunc.* **tenga,** etc. *Imperf. Subjunc.* **tuviese, etc.**

tenguerengue, en /teŋgue'reŋgue, en/ *adv* *Inf.* rickety, insecure

tenia /'tenia/ *f*, tapeworm; *Archit.* fillet, narrow molding

teniente /te'niente/ *a* owning, holding; unripe (of fruit); *Inf.* slightly deaf; stingy, mean. *m*, deputy, substitute; *Mil.* first lieutenant, lieutenant. **t. coronel,** lieutenant colonel. **t. de navío,** naval lieutenant. **t. general,** *Mil.* lieutenant general. **t. general de aviación,** air marshal

tenis /'tenis/ *m*, tennis

tenor /te'nor/ *m*, import, contents (of a letter, etc.); constitution, composition; *Mus.* tenor

tenorio /te'norio/ *m*, rake, Don Juan, philanderer

tensar /ten'sar/ *vt* to tighten; tense

tensión /ten'sion/ *f*, tautness; tension; strain, stress; *Elec.* tension

tenso /'tenso/ *a* taut; tight; tense

tentación /tenta'sion; tenta'θion/ *f*, temptation; attraction, inducement

tentáculo /ten'takulo/ *m*, tentacle; feeler

tentadero /tenta'ðero/ *m*, yard for trying out young bulls for bullfighting

tentador /tenta'ðor/ **(-ra)** *a* tempting; attractive. *n* tempter. *m*, the Devil

tentalear /tentale'ar/ *vt* to examine by touch

tentar /ten'tar/ *vt irr* to touch, feel; examine by touch; incite, encourage; try, endeavor; test; tempt; *Surg.* probe. See **sentar**

tentativa /tenta'tiβa/ *f*, endeavor, attempt; preliminary exam (at some univs.)

tentativo /tenta'tiβo/ *a* tentative, experimental

tentemozo /tente'moso; tente'moθo/ *m*, support, prop; tumbler (toy)

tentempié /tentem'pie/ *m*, *Inf.* snack, bite

tenue /'tenue/ *a* thin; slender, delicate; trivial, worthless, insignificant; pale; faint

tenuidad /tenui'ðað/ *f*, slenderness; delicacy; triviality, insignificance; paleness; faintness

teñidura /teɲi'ðura/ *f*, dyeing, staining

teñir /te'ɲir/ *vt irr* to dye; *Art.* darken; color, tinge; *vr* be dyed; be tinged or colored. See **ceñir**

teocracia /teo'krasia; teo'kraθia/ *f*, theocracy

teocrático /teo'kratiko/ *a* theocratic

teodolito /teoðo'lito/ *m*, theodolite

teologal /teolo'gal/ *a* theological

teología /teolo'hia/ *f*, theology, divinity

teológico /teo'lohiko/ *a* theological

teologizar /teolohi'sar; teolohi'θar/ *vi* to theologize

teólogo /te'ologo/ *a* theological. *m*, theologian, divine; student of theology

teorema /teo'rema/ *m*, theorem

teoría /teo'ria/ *f*, theory

teórica /te'orika/ *f*, theory

teórico /te'oriko/ *a* theoretical, speculative. *m*, theorist

teorizar /teori'sar; teori'θar/ *vt* to consider theoretically, theorize about

teoso /te'oso/ *a* resinous, gummy

teosofía /teoso'fia/ *f*, theosophy

teosófico /teo'sofiko/ *a* theosophical

teósofo /te'osofo/ *m*, theosophist

tepe /'tepe/ *m*, sod, cut turf

tequila /te'kila/ *f* *Mexico* tequila, maguey brandy

terapeuta /tera'peuta/ *mf* therapeutist

terapéutica /tera'peutika/ *f*, therapeutics

terapéutico /tera'peutiko/ *a* therapeutic

terapia /te'rapia/ *f*, therapy. **t. física,** physical therapy

teratología /teratolo'hia/ *f*, teratology

tercena /ter'sena; ter'θena/ *f*, warehouse for storing government monopoly goods (tobacco, etc.)

tercenista /terse'nista; terθe'nista/ *mf* person in charge of a tercena

tercer /ter'ser; ter'θer/ *a* *abb* of **tercero** third. Used before *m*, *sing* nouns

tercera /ter'sera; ter'θera/ *f*, procuress; *Mus.* third

tercería /terse'ria; terθe'ria/ *f*, arbitration, mediation; temporary occupation of a fortress, etc.

tercero /ter'sero; ter'θero/ **(-ra)** *a* third; mediatory. *n* third; mediator. *m*, pimp; *Eccl.* tertiary; tithes collector; third person. **¡A la tercera va la vencida!** Third time lucky!

terceto /ter'seto; ter'θeto/ *m*, tercet, triplet

tercia /'tersia; 'terθia/ *f*, one-third; *Eccl.* tierce, third hour; storehouse for tithes. **tercias reales,** royal share of ecclesiastical tithes

terciana /ter'siana; ter'θiana/ *f*, tertian fever

terciar /ter'siar; ter'θiar/ *vt* to slant; sling sideways; divide into three; equalize weight (on beasts of burden); plow or dig for the third time; *Agr.* prune; *vr* be opportune, come at the right time. *vi* mediate, arbitrate; make up a number (for cards, etc.); reach the third day (of the moon); take part, participate

tercio /'tersio; 'terθio/ *a* third. *m*, one-third; *Mil.* infantry regiment; *Obs.,* body of foreign volunteers; fishermen's association; *pl* brawny limbs of a man. **hacer t.,** to take part in; make up the number of. **hacer buen** (*or* **mal**) **t. a alguien,** to do someone a good (or bad) turn

terciopelo /tersio'pelo; terθio'pelo/ *m*, velvet; velveteen

terco /'terko/ *a* pigheaded, obstinate; hard, tough

tergiversación /terhiβersa'sion; terhiβersa'θion/ *f*, tergiversation, confusion

tergiversar /terhiβer'sar/ *vt* to tergiversate, shuffle, vacillate

termal /ter'mal/ *a* thermal

termas /'termas/ *f* *pl*, thermal springs, hot mineral baths; thermal

térmico /'termiko/ *a* thermic

terminable /termi'naβle/ *a* terminable

terminación /termina'sion; termina'θion/ *f*, conclusion, termination; end, finish; ending of a word; *Gram.* termination

terminador /termina'ðor/ **(-ra)** *a* concluding. *n* finisher

terminal /termi'nal/ *a* terminal; final. *m, Elec.* terminal. **t. de carga,** cargo terminal

terminante /termi'nante/ *a* conclusive, definite; categorical

terminar /termi'nar/ *vt* to end, conclude; complete; *vr* and *vi* end

término /'termino/ *m,* limit, end; term, expression; boundary marker; district, suburb; space, period; state, condition; boundary; object, aim; appearance, demeanor, behavior (gen. *pl*); completion; *Mus.* tone; (*Math. Law. Logic.*) term. **t. medio,** *Math.* average; medium; compromise, middle way. **correr el t.,** to lapse (of time). **en primer t.,** *Art.* in the foreground. **medios términos,** evasions, excuses. **primer t.,** (cinema) closeup

terminología /terminolo'hia/ *f,* terminology

termita /ter'mita/ *f,* thermite. *m,* termite

termodinámica /termoði'namika/ *f,* thermodynamics

termoeléctrico /termoe'lektriko/ *a* thermoelectric

termómetro /ter'mometro/ *m,* thermometer

termos /'termos/ *m,* thermos, vacuum bottle

termoscopio /termos'kopio/ *m,* thermoscope

termostático /termos'tatiko/ *a* thermostatic

termóstato /ter'mostato/ *m,* thermostat

terna /'terna/ *f,* triad, trio; set of dice

ternario /ter'nario/ *a* ternal, ternary

terne /'terne/ *a* *Inf.* bullying, braggartly; persistent, obstinate; robust. *mf* bully

ternera /ter'nera/ *f,* female calf; veal

ternero /ter'nero/ *m,* male calf

terneza /ter'nesa; ter'neθa/ *f,* tenderness, kindness; softness; softheartedness; endearment, caress, compliment (gen. *pl*)

ternilla /ter'niya; ter'niʎa/ *f,* cartilage, gristle

ternísimo /ter'nisimo/ *a sup* **tierno** most tender

terno /'terno/ *m,* triad; suit of clothes, three-piece suit; oath, curse

ternura /ter'nura/ *f,* softness; softheartedness; tenderness, kindness, sweetness

terquedad, terquería, terqueza /ter'kesa; terke'ðaθ, terke'ria, ter'keθa/ *f,* obstinacy, obduracy

terracota /terra'kota/ *f,* terra cotta

terrado /te'rraðo/ *m,* flat roof

Terranova /terra'noβa/ *m,* Newfoundland

terraplén /terra'plen/ *m,* embankment; *Mil.* terreplein

terraplenar /terraple'nar/ *vt* to fill up with earth; fill in (a hollow); make into an embankment; terrace

terrateniente /terrate'niente/ *mf* landowner

terraza /te'rrasa; te'rraθa/ *f,* terrace; flat roof; flower border (of a garden)

terrazgo /te'rrasgo; te'rraθgo/ *m,* tillable land; rent for farming land

terregoso /terre'goso/ *a* lumpy, full of clods (of soil)

terremoto /terre'moto/ *m,* earthquake

terrenal /terre'nal/ *a* terrestrial

terreno /te'rreno/ *a* terrestrial. *m,* ground, land; *Fig.* sphere; region; soil; plot of land. **ganar t.,** *Fig.* to win ground, make progress. **medir el t.,** *Fig.* to feel one's way

térreo /'terreo/ *a* earthy

terrero /te'rrero/ *a* earthly; low-flying, almost touching the ground; humble. *m,* flat roof; pile or mound of earth; deposit of earth, alluvium; target; mineral refuse

terrestre /te'rrestre/ *a* terrestrial, earthly

terrezuela /terre'suela; terre'θuela/ *f,* poor soil

terribilidad /terriβili'ðaθ/ *f,* terribleness, horribleness; rudeness

terribilísimo /terriβi'lisimo/ *a sup* most terrible

terrible /te'rriβle/ *a* terrible, horrible; rude, unsociable, ill-humored; enormous, huge

terrífico /te'rrifiko/ *a* terrible, frightful

territorial /territo'rial/ *a* territorial

territorialidad /territoriali'ðaθ/ *f,* territoriality

territorio /terri'torio/ *m,* territory; jurisdiction. **t. bajo mandato,** mandated territory

terrizo /te'rriso; te'rriθo/ *a* earthen

terrón /te'rron/ *m,* clod (of earth); lump; *pl* lands, landed property. **t. de azúcar,** lump of sugar

terrorismo /terro'rismo/ *m,* terrorism

terrorista /terro'rista/ *mf* terrorist

terrosidad /terrosi'ðaθ/ *f,* earthiness

terroso /te'rroso/ *a* earthy; earthen

terruño /te'rruɲo/ *m,* plot of ground; native earth; country; soil

terso /'terso/ *a* smooth, shiny, glossy; *Lit.* elegant, polished (style)

tersura /ter'sura/ *f,* smoothness, glossiness; elegance (of style)

tertulia /ter'tulia/ *f,* regular social meeting (gen. in cafés); conversational group; party; part of Spanish cafés set apart for players of chess, etc. **hacer t.,** to meet for conversation

tertuliano /tertu'liano/ **(-na)** *n* **tertuliante,** *mf* **tertulio (-ia),** *n* member of a tertulia

terzuelo /ter'suelo; ter'θuelo/ *m,* third, third part

Tesalia /te'salia/ Thessaly

tesar /te'sar/ *vt Naut.* to make taut; *vi* step backward, back (oxen)

tesela /te'sela/ *f,* tessera, square used in mosaic work

teselado /tese'laðo/ *a* tessellated

tesina /te'sina/ *f,* master's essay, thesis

tesis /'tesis/ *f,* thesis

teso /'teso/ *a* tight, taut, tense. *m,* hilltop; bulge, lump

tesón /te'son/ *m,* persistence, obstinacy, tenacity

tesonería /tesone'ria/ *f,* stubbornness, obstinacy

tesorería /tesore'ria/ *f,* treasury; treasuryship

tesorero /teso'rero/ **(-ra)** *n* treasurer

tesoro /te'soro/ *m,* treasure; public treasury; hoard; *Fig.* gem, excellent person; thesaurus. **t. de duende,** fairy gold

tespíades /tes'piaðes/ *f pl,* the muses

testa /'testa/ *f,* head; face, front; *Inf.* sense, acumen. **t. coronada,** crowned head

testación /testa'sion; testa'θion/ *f,* erasure, crossing out

testado /tes'taðo/ *a* testate

testador /testa'ðor/ **(-ra)** *n* testator

testaferro /testa'ferro/ *m, Fig.* figurehead, proxy

testamentar /testamen'tar/ *vt* to bequeath

testamentaria /testamen'taria/ *f,* execution of a will; *Law.* estate; executors' meeting

testamentario /testamen'tario/ *a* testamental, testamentary

testamento /testa'mento/ *m, Law.* will; testament. **Antiguo T.,** Old Testament. **ordenar** (*or* otorgar) **su t.,** to make one's will

testar /tes'tar/ *vi* to make a will; *vt* erase, cross out

testarada /testa'raða/ *f,* a blow with the head; pigheadedness, stubbornness

testarrón /testa'rron/ *a Inf.* pigheaded

testarudez /testaru'ðes; testaru'ðeθ/ *f,* obstinacy, obduracy

testarudo /testa'ruðo/ *a* stubborn, obstinate

testera /tes'tera/ *f,* front, face; front seat (in a vehicle); upper half of an animal's face; tester, canopy

testículo /tes'tikulo/ *m,* testicle

testificación /testifika'sion; testifika'θion/ *f,* testification

testificar /testifi'kar/ *vt* to testify; affirm, assert; attest, prove

testigo /tes'tigo/ *mf* witness. *m,* proof, evidence. *Law.* **t. de cargo,** witness for the prosecution. *Law.* **t. de descargo,** witness for the defense. **t. de vista,** eyewitness. *Law.* **hacer testigos,** to bring forward witnesses

testimonial /testimo'nial/ *a* confirmatory, proven

testimoniar /testimo'niar/ *vt* to attest, confirm, bear witness to

testimoniero /testimo'niero/ **(-ra)** *a* slanderous; hypocritical. *n* slanderer, hypocrite

testimonio /testi'monio/ *m,* testimony, proof; slander; affidavit

testuz /tes'tus; tes'tuθ/ *m*, front of the head (of some animals); nape (of animals)

teta /'teta/ *f*, mammary gland, breast; teat, dug, udder. **dar la t.** (a), to suckle

tétano, tétanos /'tetano, 'tetanos/ *m*, tetanus

tetera /te'tera/ *f*, teapot; teakettle; *Lat. Am.* (feeding) bottle

tetilla /te'tiya; te'tiʎa/ *f*, *dim* rudimentary teat or nipple; nipple (of a nursing bottle)

tétrico /'tetriko/ *a* gloomy; somber

teutón /teu'ton/ **(-ona)** *n* Teuton. *a* Teutonic

teutónico /teu'toniko/ *a* Teutonic

textil /teks'til/ *a* and *m*, textile

texto /'teksto/ *m*, text; quotation, citation; textbook

textorio /teks'torio/ *a* textile

textual /teks'tual/ *a* textual

textualista /tekstua'lista/ *mf* textualist

textura /teks'tura/ *f*, texture; weaving; structure (of a novel, etc.); animal structure

tez /tes; teθ/ *f*, complexion, skin

ti /ti/ *pers pron 2nd sing mf dat acc abl* thee, you. Always used with prep. (e.g. *por ti*, by thee (you))

tía /'tia/ *f*, aunt; *Inf.* wife, mother, dame; *Inf.* coarse creature. **t. abuela,** grandaunt, great-aunt. *Inf.* **quedarse para t.,** to be left an old maid

tianguis /'tiaŋguis/ *m*, *Central America, Mexico* open-air market

tiara /'tiara/ *f*, ancient Persian headdress; papal tiara; coronet; dignity and power of the papacy

tiberino /tiβe'rino/ *a* Tiberine

tibetano /tiβe'tano/ **(-na)** *a* and *n* Tibetan. *m*, Tibetan (language)

tibia /'tiβia/ *f*, flute; tibia

tibieza /ti'βiesa; ti'βieθa/ *f*, tepidity; indifference, lack of enthusiasm

tibio /'tiβio/ *a* tepid, lukewarm; indifferent, unenthusiastic

tiburón /tiβu'ron/ *m*, shark

ticket /'tikket/ *m*, ticket; pass, membership card

tico, -a /'tiko/ *mf inf* Costa Rican

tictac /tik'tak/ *m*, ticktock (of a clock)

tiempo /'tiempo/ *m*, time; season; epoch, period; chance, opportunity; leisure, free time; weather; *Mus.* tempo; *Gram.* tense; *Naut.* storm. **t. ha,** many years ago, long ago. **t. medio** *or* **medio t.,** *Sports.* halftime. **abrir el t.,** to clear up (of the weather). **ajustar los tiempos,** to fix the date (chronology). **a largo t.,** after a long time. **andando el t.,** in the course of time. **a su t.,** in due course, at the proper time. **a t.,** in time, at the right time. **a un t.,** simultaneously, at the same time. **cargarse el t.,** to cloud over (of the sky). **con t.,** in advance, with time; in time. **correr el t.,** to pass, move on (of time). **de t. en t.,** from time to time. **engañar** (*or* **entretener**) **el t.,** to kill time, while away the hours. *Inf.* **en t., de Maricastaña** *or* **del rey Perico,** long, long ago. **fuera de t.,** unseasonably, inopportunely; out of season. **ganar t.,** to gain time; *Inf.* hurry. **hacer t.,** to wait, cool one's heels; *Fig.* mark time. **perder el t.,** to waste time; misspend or lose time. **sentarse el t.,** to clear up (of the weather). **tomarse t.** (**para**), to postpone, take time for (or to)

tienda /'tienda/ *f*, tent; *Naut.* awning, canopy; shop, store. **t. de abarrotes** *Lat. Am.* grocery store, grocery, grocer's. **t. de antigüedades,** antique shop. **t. de campaña,** bell tent, pavilion. **t. oxigena,** oxygen tent

tienta /'tienta/ *f*, astuteness; cleverness; *Surg.* probe; trying out young bulls for the bullring. **a tientas,** by touch, gropingly

tientaparedes /tientapa'reðes/ *mf* one who gropes one's way

tiento /'tiento/ *m*, touching, feeling; touch, feel; blind person's cane; tightrope walker's pole; manual control, steady hand; caution, care, tact; *Mus.* preliminary flourish; *Inf.* slap buffet; tentacle. **a t.,** by touch; unsurely, gropingly

tierno /'tierno/ *a* soft; tender; kind; sweet; delicate; softhearted; fresh, recent; affectionate

tierra /'tierra/ *f*, world, planet; earth; soil; ground; cultivated ground, land; homeland, native land; region; district, territory. **t. adentro,** inland. **t. de batán,** fuller's earth. **t. de Promisión,** Promised Land. **t. de Siena,** sienna. **besar la t.,** *Inf.* to fall down. **dar en t. con,** to throw down; demolish. **echar en t.,** *Naut.* to put ashore, land. **echar por t.,** *Fig.* to overthrow, destroy. **echar t. a,** *Fig.* to bury, forget. *Inf.* **la t. de María Santísima,** Andalusia. **por t.,** overland. **saltar en t.,** to land, disembark. **venir** (*or* **venirse**) **a t.,** to fall down, topple over

Tierra Santa /'tierra 'santa/ Holy Land

tieso /'tieso/ *a* hard, rigid, stiff; healthy, robust; taut; spirited, courageous; obstinate, stiff-necked; distant, formal. *adv* firmly, strongly

tiesto /'tiesto/ *m*, flowerpot; broken piece of earthenware

tiesura /tie'sura/ *f*, hardness, rigidity, stiffness; physical fitness; courageousness; obstinacy; formality, stiffness

tifoidea /tifoi'ðea/ *f*, typhoid

tifón /ti'fon/ *m*, typhoon

tifus /'tifus/ *m*, typhus. **t. exantemático,** trench fever

tigre /'tigre/ *m*, tiger; ferocious person; *Lat. Am.* jaguar

tijera /ti'hera/ *f*, scissors (gen. *pl*); any scissor-shaped instrument; shears; drainage channel; carpenter's horse; scandalmonger, gossip

tijeretada /tihere'taða/ *f*, cut or snip with scissors

tijeretear /tihere'te'ar/ *vt* to cut with scissors; *Inf.* interfere arbitrarily

tijereteo /tihere'teo/ *m*, scissor cut; click of the scissors

tila /'tila/ *f*, lime tree or flower; linden tree or flower; infusion made of lime flowers

tildar /til'dar/ *vt* to cross out, erase; stigmatize; place a tilde over a letter

tilde /'tilde/ *mf*, bad reputation; tilde; *f*, jot, iota

tilín /ti'lin/ *m*, tinkle, peal (of a bell)

tillar /ti'yar; ti'ʎar/ *vt* to lay wood floors

tilo /'tilo/ *m*, lime tree

timador /tima'ðor/ **(-ra)** *n* *Inf.* swindler, sharper, cheat

timar /ti'mar/ *vt* to swindle, cheat, deceive; *vr Inf.* exchange looks or winks

timba /'timba/ *f*, *Inf.* casino, gambling den; game of chance

timbal /tim'bal/ *m*, kettledrum

timbalero /timba'lero/ *m*, kettledrum player

timbrador /timbra'ðor/ *m*, stamper; stamping machine; rubber stamp

timbrar /tim'brar/ *vt* to stamp; place the crest over a coat of arms

timbre /'timbre/ *m*, postage stamp; heraldic crest; excise stamp; bell, push-button; *Mus.* timbre; noble deed; personal merit; *Mexico* (postage) stamp; *Lat. Am.* description (of a person or goods)

timidez /timi'ðes; timi'ðeθ/ *f*, timidity; nervousness

tímido /'timiðo/ *a* timid, nervous

timo /'timo/ *m*, *Inf.* swindling, trick; thymus

timón /ti'mon/ *m*, *Naut.* helm; rudder; management, direction; stick of a rocket. **t. de dirección,** *Aer.* tailfin

timonear /timone'ar/ *vi Naut.* to steer

timonel, timonero /timo'nel, timo'nero/ *m*, helmsman, coxswain

timorato /timo'rato/ *a* godfearing; timid, vacillating

tímpano /'timpano/ *m*, *Anat.* eardrum, tympanum; *Mus.* kettledrum; *Archit.* tympanum; *Print.* tympan

tina /'tina/ *f*, vat; flour bin; large earthenware jar; wooden tub; bath

tinaco /ti'nako/ *m*, *Mexico* (water) tank

tinada /ti'naða/ *f*, woodpile; cow shed

tinaja /ti'naha/ *f*, large earthenware jar; jarful

tinajero /tina'hero/ *m*, seller of earthenware jars

tinelo /ti'nelo/ *m*, servants' hall

tinerfeño /tiner'feɲo/ **(-ña)** *a* and *n* of or from Tenerife

tinglado /tiŋ'glaðo/ *m*, overhanging roof; open shed; penthouse; intrigue

tiniebla /ti'nieβla/ *f*, gloom, darkness (gen. *pl*); *pl* profound ignorance; confusion of mind; *Eccl.* tenebrae

tino /'tino/ *m*, skilled sense of touch; good eye, accurate aim; judgment, shrewdness; vat. **sacar de t.** (a)**,** to bewilder, confuse; irritate, exasperate. **sin t.,** without limit, excessively

tinta /'tinta/ *f*, color, tint; ink; staining, dyeing; dye, stain; *pl* shades, colors; *Art.* mixed colors ready for painting. **t. china,** India ink. **t. simpática,** invisible ink. **recargar las tintas,** *Fig.* to overpaint, lay the colors on too thick. *Inf.* **saber de buena t.** (**una cosa**)**,** to learn (a thing) from a reliable source

tintar /tin'tar/ *vt* to dye; color, tinge, stain

tinte /'tinte/ *m*, dyeing, staining; color; dye; stain; dye house; pretext, disguise

tintero /tin'tero/ *m*, inkwell. *Inf.* **dejar** (*or* **quedársele a uno**) **en el t.,** to forget, omit (to say, write)

tintín /tin'tin/ *m*, ring, peal; clink; chink

tintinar /tinti'nar/ *vi* to ring, tinkle; clink; jingle

tintineo /tinti'neo/ *m*, ringing, tinkling; clinking; jingle

tinto /'tinto/ *a* red (of wine). *m*, red wine; dark red

tintorera /tinto'rera/ *f*, *Lat. Am.* shark

tintorería /tintore'ria/ *f*, dyeing industry; dyeing and dry-cleaning shop

tintorero /tinto'rero/ (**-ra**) *n* dyer; dry cleaner

tintura /tin'tura/ *f*, dyeing, staining; color, tint; dye; stain; tincture; smattering, slight knowledge

tinturar /tintu'rar/ *vt* to dye; color, tinge, stain; give a superficial notion of

tiña /'tiɲa/ *f*, ringworm; *Inf.* meanness, stinginess

tiñoso /ti'ɲoso/ *a* mangy; afflicted with ringworm; *Inf.* mean, stingy

tiñuela /ti'ɲuela/ *f*, shipworm

tío /'tio/ *m*, uncle; gaffer; fellow, chap; fool; stepfather; father-in-law. **t. abuelo,** granduncle, great-uncle

tiovivo /tio'βiβo/ *m*, merry-go-round

típico /'tipiko/ *a* typical

tiple /'tiple/ *m*, soprano or treble voice. *mf* soprano

tipo /'tipo/ *m*, model, pattern; type; print, type; species, group (of animals, etc.); *Inf.* guy, chap. *Com.* **t. de cambio,** exchange rate

tipografía /tipogra'fia/ *f*, typography

tipográfico /tipo'grafiko/ *a* typographical

tipógrafo /ti'pografo/ *m*, typographer

tipula /'tipula/ *f*, daddy-longlegs

tiquismiquis /tikis'mikis/ *m pl*, ridiculous scruples; affected courtesies. *a Inf.* faddy, fussy

tira /'tira/ *f*, strip, band, ribbon; stripe, rib. **t. cómica,** comic strip

tirabotas /tira'βotas/ *m*, buttonhook

tirabuzón /tiraβu'son/ tiraβu'θon/ *m*, corkscrew; ringlet, curl; hair curler

tirada /tira'raða/ *f*, throwing; drawing, pulling; cast, throw; distance, space; *Print.* edition, issue; circulation (of a newspaper, etc.); stroke (in golf); lapse, interval (of time). **t. aparte,** reprint (of an article, etc.)

tiradero /tira'ðero/ *m*, shooting butt

tirado /ti'raðo/ *a Inf.* dirt-cheap. *m*, wire drawing

tirador /tira'ðor/ (**-ra**) *n* thrower, caster; drawer, puller; marksman. *m*, handle, knob; *Mech.* trigger; bell rope, bell pull; *Print.* pressman. **t. de bota,** boot tag. **t. de gomas,** catapult. **t. de oro,** gold wire drawer

tiralíneas /tira'lineas/ *m*, ruling pen

tiramiento /tira'miento/ *m*, pulling; stretching

tiramira /tira'mira/ *f*, long, narrow mountain range; long line of persons or things; distance

tiranía /tira'nia/ *f*, tyranny, despotism

tiranicida /tirani'siða/ tirani'θiða/ *mf* tyrannicide (person)

tiranicidio /tirani'siðio/ tirani'θiðio/ *m*, tyrannicide (act)

tiránico /ti'raniko/ *a* tyrannical

tiranización /tiranisa'sion/ tiraniθa'θion/ *f*, tyranny, tyrannization

tiranizar /tirani'sar/ tirani'θar/ *vt* to tyrannize over

tirano /ti'rano/ (**-na**) *a* tyrannous, tyrannical; *Fig.* overwhelming, dominating. *n* tyrant

tirante /ti'rante/ *a* taut; tense, strained. *m*, trace (of a harness); shoulderstrap; suspender (gen. *pl*); *Archit.* tie

tirantez /tiran'tes/ tiran'teθ/ *f*, tautness; tension, strain; straight distance between two points. **estado de t.,** *Polit.* strained relations

tiranuelo /tira'nuelo/ *m*, petty tyrant

tirar /ti'rar/ *vt* to throw, cast; fling, aim, toss; throw down, overthrow; pull; draw; discharge, shoot; stretch, pull out; rule, draw (lines); squander, waste; *Print.* print; *vi* attract; pull; (*with prep a*) turn to, turn in the direction of; incline, tend to; incline toward, have a tinge of (colors); try, aspire to; (*with de*) wield, unsheath, draw out (firearms, arms); *vr* cast oneself, precipitate oneself; throw oneself on. *Inf.* **ir tirando,** to carry on, get along somehow

tirilla /ti'riya; ti'riʎa/ *f*, *Sew.* shirt neckband

tiritaña /tiri'taɲa/ *f*, thin silk material; *Inf.* mere nothing, trifle

tiritar /tiri'tar/ *vi* to shiver with cold

tiritón /tiri'ton/ *m*, shiver, shudder

Tiro /'tiro/ Tyre

tiro /'tiro/ *m*, throwing; throw, cast; toss, fling; try (in football); shooting; piece of artillery; report, shot (of a gun); discharge (firearms); shooting range or gallery; team (of horses); range (of firearms, etc.); hoisting cable; flight (of stairs); *Mineral.* shaft; *Inf.* trick; robbery, theft; innuendo, insinuation; grave harm or injury; *pl* sword belt. **t. de pichón,** pigeon shooting. **t. par,** four-in-hand. **a t.,** within firing range; within reach. **de tiros largos,** *Inf.* in full regalia

tirocinio /tiro'sinio; tiro'θinio/ *m*, apprenticeship

tiroideo /tiroi'ðeo/ *a* thyroid

tiroides /ti'roiðes/ *f*, thyroid gland

tirón /ti'ron/ *m*, novice, beginner; pull, tug, heave. **de un t.,** with one tug; at one stroke, at one blow

tiroriro /tiro'riro/ *m*, *Inf.* sound of a wind instrument; *pl Inf.* wind instruments

tirotearse /tirote'arse/ *vr Mil.* to exchange fire; indulge in repartee

tiroteo /tiro'teo/ *m*, shooting, exchange of shots; crackle (of rifle fire)

Tirreno, el Mar /ti'rreno, el mar/ the Tyrrhenian Sea

tirria /'tirria/ *f*, *Inf.* hostility, grudge, dislike

tirulato /tiru'lato/ *a* dumbfounded, stupefied

tisana /ti'sana/ *f*, tisane

tísico /'tisiko/ (**-ca**) *a* tuberculous. *n* sufferer from tuberculosis, consumptive

tisis /'tisis/ *f*, tuberculosis

tisú /ti'su/ *m*, silver or gold tissue

titánico /ti'taniko/ *a* titanesque; colossal, huge

títere /'titere/ *m*, puppet; *Fig. Inf.* dummy, grotesque; *Inf.* fool; obsession, fixed idea; *pl Inf.* circus; Punch and Judy show. *Inf.* **echar los títeres a rodar,** to upset the whole show; quarrel, fall out with. *Inf.* **no dejar t. con cabeza,** to destroy entirely, smash up completely; leave no one

titerero /tite'rero/ (**-ra**)**, titiritero** (**-ra**)**,** *n* **titerista** *mf* puppet showman; acrobat; juggler

tití /ti'ti/ *m*, marmoset

titilación /titila'sion/ titila'θion/ *f*, quiver, tremor; twinkling, winking, gleam

titilador, titilante /titila'ðor, titi'lante/ *a* quivering, trembling; twinkling

titilar /titi'lar/ *vi* to quiver, tremble; twinkle

titiritaina /titiri'taina/ *f*, *Inf.* muffled strains of musical instruments; merrymaking, uproar

titiritar /titiri'tar/ *vi* to tremble, shiver, shudder

titiritero /titiri'tero/ (**-ra**) *n* puppet master; acrobat

titubear /tituβe'ar/ *vi* to totter, sway, rock; stutter, stammer; toddle; hesitate, vacillate

titubeo /titu'βeo/ *m*, tottering, swaying, stuttering; hesitation

titulado /titu'laðo/ *m*, titled person; one who holds an academic title

titular /titu'lar/ *a* titular. *vt* to entitle, call; *vi* obtain a title (of nobility); *vr* style oneself, call oneself

título /'titulo/ *m*, title; heading; inscription; pretext, excuse; diploma, certificate; claim, right; noble title and its owner; section, clause; (univ.) degree; *Com.*

stock certificate, bond; *Com.* title; caption; qualification, right, merit; basis of a claim or privilege; *pl Com.* securities, stocks. **t. de la columna,** *Print.* running title. **títulos de propiedad,** title deeds. **t. del reino,** title of nobility. **a t.,** under pretext

tiza /'tisa; 'tiθa/ *f,* chalk; whiting; calcined stag's antler

tiznar /tis'nar; tiθ'nar/ *vt* to make sooty; dirty, stain, begrime; *Fig.* sully, tarnish

tizne /'tisne; 'tiθne/ *m,* (sometimes *f*) soot; charcoal; stain (on one's honor, etc.); *Agr.* blight

tizón /ti'son; ti'θon/ *m,* firebrand; *Agr.* blight; *Fig.* stain (on one's honor, etc.)

tizona /ti'sona; ti'θona/ *f, Inf.* sword (by allusion to name of that of the Cid)

tizonear /tisone'ar; tiθone'ar/ *vi* to poke or rake the fire

toalla /to'aya; to'aʎa/ *f,* towel. **t. continua,** roller towel. **t. rusa,** Turkish towel

toallero /toa'yero; toa'ʎero/ *m,* towel rail

tobillera /toβi'yera; toβi'ʎera/ *f, Inf.* girl, flapper

tobillo /to'βiyo; to'βiʎo/ *m,* ankle

tobogán /toβo'gan/ *m,* toboggan; chute (in apartment buildings or amusement parks)

toca /'toka/ *f,* headdress; toque; wimple; coif

tocable /to'kaβle/ *a* touchable

tocado /to'kaðo/ *a Fig.* touched, half-crazy. *m,* headdress; coiffure, hairdressing

tocador /toka'ðor/ **(-ra)** *n Mus.* player. *m,* dressing table; kerchief; boudoir; cloakroom; dressing room; dressing case

tocamiento /toka'miento/ *m,* touching, feeling; touch; *Fig.* inspiration

tocante /to'kante/ *a* touching. **t. a,** concerning, with regard to

tocar /to'kar/ *vt* to touch, feel; *Mus.* play; knock, rap; summon; ring, peal; brush against; discover by experience; persuade, inspire; mention, touch upon; *Naut.* touch bottom; *Art.* retouch, touch up. *vi* belong; stop (at), touch at; be one's turn; concern, interest; be one's lot; adjoin; be near to; be opportune; be allied or closely related to; find the scent (of dogs). **t. en un puerto,** *Naut.* to touch at a port. **Ahora me toca a mí,** Now it's my turn. **Es un problema que me toca de cerca,** It is a problem that touches me very nearly. **a toca teja,** *Inf.* in ready cash

tocayo /to'kayo/ **(-ya)** *n* namesake

tochedad /totʃe'ðað/ *f,* boorishness, loutishness

tocho /'totʃo/ *a* boorish, loutish, countrified. *m,* iron bar

tocinería /tosine'ria; toθine'ria/ *f,* pork butcher's shop

tocinero /tosi'nero; toθi'nero/ *m,* pork butcher

tocino /to'sino; to'θino/ *m,* bacon; salt pork

tocología /tokolo'hia/ *f,* tokology, obstetrics

tocón /to'kon/ *m,* stump (of a tree or an amputated limb)

todavía /toða'βia/ *adv* still; even; nevertheless; yet. **No han venido t.,** They have not come yet. **Queda mucho que hacer t.,** There is still much to be done.

todo /'toðo/ *a* all; whole, entire; every, each. *m,* whole, entirety; whole word (in charades); all; *pl* all; everyone. *adv* wholly, entirely. **t. lo posible,** everything possible; all one can, one's best. **t. lo que,** all that which. **ante t.,** in the first place; especially, particularly. **así y t.,** nevertheless. **a t. esto,** in the meanwhile. **con t.** or **con t. esto** or **con t. y esto,** nevertheless, in spite of this. **del t.,** wholly, completely. **jugar el t. por el t.,** to risk everything on the outcome. **sobre t.,** especially. **y t.,** in addition, as well. **Todos somos hijos de Adán y Eva, sino que nos diferencia la lana y la seda,** We are all equal, but some of us are more equal than others

todopoderoso /toðopoðe'roso/ *a* all-powerful, almighty. *m,* the Almighty, God

toga /'toga/ *f,* toga; robe, gown

Tokio /'tokio/ Tokyo

tolda /'tolda/ *f* canvas; tent; shelter

toldadura /tolda'ðura/ *f,* awning; canopy; hanging; curtain

toldillo /tol'diyo; tol'diʎo/ *m,* covered litter or sedan chair; *West Hem.* mosquito net

toldo /'toldo/ *m,* awning; canopy; pomp, show

tole /'tole/ *m,* outcry, uproar, tumult

toledano /tole'ðano/ **(-na)** *a* and *n* Toledan

tolerable /tole'raβle/ *a* bearable, tolerable

tolerancia /tole'ransia; tole'ranθia/ *f,* tolerance, forbearance; permission

tolerante /tole'rante/ *a* tolerant, broad-minded

tolerantismo /toleran'tismo/ *m,* religious toleration

tolerar /tole'rar/ *vt* to put up with, bear, tolerate; overlook, allow, forgive

tolla /'toya/ *f, 'toʎa/ f,* marsh, bog

tollina /to'yina; to'ʎina/ *f, Inf.* spanking, whipping

tolmo /'tolmo/ *m,* tor

tolondro /to'londro/ *a* stupid, heedless, reckless. *m,* bump, bruise

tolva /'tolβa/ *f,* chute (for grain, etc.)

toma /'toma/ *f,* taking; receiving; conquest, capture; dose (of medicine)

tomada /to'maða/ *f,* taking; take; capture

tomadero /toma'ðero/ *m,* handle, haft

tomadura /toma'ðura/ *f,* taking; receiving; dose (of medicine). *Inf.* **t. de pelo,** leg-pull, joke

tomar /to'mar/ *vt* to take; pick up; conquer; eat; drink; adopt, employ; contract (habits); engage (employees); rent; understand; steal; remove; buy; suffer; *Fig.* overcome (by laughter, sleep, etc.); choose; possess physically; *vi* (*with por*) go in the direction of; *vr* grow rusty; go moldy; (*with con*) quarrel with. **t. a chacota,** to take as a joke. **t. a pechos,** to take to heart. **t. el fresco,** to take the air. **tomarla con,** to contradict, oppose; bear a grudge. **t. la delantera,** to take the lead; excel, beat. **t. las de Villadiego,** *Inf.* to quit, show one's heels. **t. por su cuenta,** to undertake, take charge of; take upon oneself. **t. su desquite con,** to get even with. **Más vale un toma que dos te daré,** A little help is worth a lot of promises. **¡Toma!** *Inf.* Fancy! You don't say!; Of course! There's nothing new about that!

tomatal /toma'tal/ *m,* tomato bed, tomato patch; *Lat. Am.* tomato plant

tomate /to'mate/ *m,* tomato; tomato plant; *Mexico* small green tomato; *Inf.* hole, potato (in stockings, etc.)

tomatera /toma'tera/ *f,* tomato plant

tomatero /toma'tero/ **(-ra)** *n* tomato seller

tómbola /'tombola/ *f,* raffle (gen. for charity); jumble sale

tomillo /to'miyo; to'miʎo/ *m,* thyme

tomo /'tomo/ *m,* volume, book; importance, worth

ton /ton/ *m, abb* **tono. sin t. ni son,** *Inf.* without rhyme or reason

tonada /to'naða/ *f,* words of a song and its tune

tonadilla /tona'ðiya; tona'ðiʎa/ *f, dim* short song; comic song; *Theat.* musical interlude *Obs.*

tonadillero /tonaði'yero; tonaði'ʎero/ **(-ra)** *n* composer or singer of tonadillas

tonal /to'nal/ *a* tonal

tonalidad /tonali'ðað/ *f,* tonality

tonar /to'nar/ *vi Poet.* to thunder or lightning

tonel /to'nel/ *m,* barrel; cask; butt

tonelada /tone'laða/ *f,* ton

tonelería /tonele'ria/ *f,* cooperage; collection or stock of casks and barrels

tonelero /tone'lero/ *m,* cooper

tonga, tongada /'toŋga, toŋ'gaða/ *f,* layer, stratum; *Inf.* task

tónica /'tonika/ *f, Mus.* keynote

tónico /'toniko/ *a* tonic. *m, Med.* tonic; pick-me-up

tonificador, tonificante /tonifika'ðor, tonifi'kante/ *a* strengthening, invigorating tonic

tonillo /to'niyo; to'niʎo/ *m, dim* monotonous singsong voice; regional accent

tonina /to'nina/ *f,* tuna; dolphin

tono /'tono/ *m,* inflection, modulation; (*Mus. Med. Art.*) tone; pitch, resonance; energy, strength; style; manner, behavior; *Mus.* key; mode of speech. **bajar el t.,** *Fig. Inf.* to change one's tune. *Inf.* **darse t.,** to put on side, give oneself airs. **de buen (mal) t.**, in good (bad) taste

tonsila /ton'sila/ f, tonsil

tonsilitis /tonsi'litis/ f, tonsillitis

tonsura /ton'sura/ f, shearing; hair cutting; Eccl. tonsure

tonsurar /tonsu'rar/ vt to shear, clip; cut the hair off; Eccl. tonsure

tontaina /ton'taina/ mf Inf. ninny, fool

tontear /tonte'ar/ vi to behave foolishly; play the fool

tontería /tonte'ria/ f, foolishness, stupidity; piece of folly; trifle, bagatelle

tontillo /ton'tiyo; ton'tiʎo/ m, dress bustle; hoop (for dresses)

tontiloco /tonti'loko/ a Inf. crazy, daft

tontivano /tonti'βano/ a vain, conceited

tonto /'tonto/ (**-ta**) a silly, stupid, simple; foolish, absurd. n fool, idiot. m, short coat, stroller. **t. de capirote,** Inf. an utter fool. **a tontas y a locas,** without rhyme or reason, topsy-turvy. **volver t. (a),** Fig. Inf. to drive crazy

topacio /to'pasio; to'paθio/ m, topaz

topar /to'par/ vt (with con) to run into, collide with, hit; meet unexpectedly; come across, find; vi butt (of horned animals); take a bet (in cards); consist in (of obstacles); meet with (difficulties); Inf. be successful

tope /'tope/ m, projection, part that juts out; obstacle, impediment; collision, bump; crux, difficult point; quarrel, fight; Mech. stop; Naut. masthead; Rail. buffer; Mexico speed bump. **hasta el t.,** completely full, full to the brim

topera /to'pera/ f, molehill

topetada /tope'taða/ f, butt (of horned animals); Inf. knock, bang

topetar /tope'tar/ vt and vi to butt (of horned animals); vt meet, run into

topetón /tope'ton/ m, butt; collision, impact, bump; blow on the head

tópico /'topiko/ a topical. m, topic, theme

topo /'topo/ m, Zool. mole; Inf. clumsy or short-sighted person; dolt, ninny

topografía /topogra'fia/ f, topography

topográfico /topo'grafiko/ a topographical

topógrafo /to'pografo/ m, topographer

toque /'toke/ m, touch, touching; pealing, ringing (of bells); crux, essence; test, proof; touchstone; Metall. assay; warning; Inf. tap (on the shoulder, etc.); Art. touch. **t. de luz,** Art. light (in a picture). **t. de obscuro,** Art. shade (in a picture). **t. de queda,** curfew. **t. de tambor,** beating of a drum. **dar un t. a,** Inf. to put to the test; pump (for information)

toquero /to'kero/ (**-ra**) n manufacturer of headdresses

toquetear /tokete'ar/ vt to keep touching, handle repeatedly

toquilla /to'kiya; to'kiʎa/ f, hatband, hat trimming; kerchief; small shawl

torácico /to'rasiko; to'raθiko/ a thoracic

toral /to'ral/ a principal, chief, main

tórax /'toraks/ m, thorax

torbellino /torβe'yino; torβe'ʎino/ m, whirlwind; spate of things; Inf. madcap. **t. de ideas,** brainstorm

torcedero /torse'ðero; torθe'ðero/ a twisted, crooked

torcedor /torse'ðor; torθe'ðor/ a twisting. m, twister; cause of continual anxiety

torcedura /torse'ðura; torθe'ðura/ f, twisting; sprain, wrench

torcer /tor'ser; tor'θer/ vt irr to twist; bend; turn, bear (of roads, etc.); slant, slope, incline; misconstrue, pervert; dissuade; wrench, sprain (muscles); corrupt (justice). **t. el gesto,** to make a wry face. vr turn sour (of wine, milk); Fig. go astray; turn out badly (of negotiations). Pres. Ind. **tuerzo, tuerces, etc.** Pres. Subjunc. **tuerza, tuerzas, tuerza, tuerzan**

torcida /tor'siða; tor'θiða/ f, wick (of lamps, etc.)

torcido /tor'siðo; tor'θiðo/ a bent, crooked, sloping, inclined; curved; dishonest, tortuous. m, silk twist

torcijón /torsi'hon; torθi'hon/ m, stomachache

torcimiento /torsi'miento; torθi'miento/ m, twisting; twist, turn; circumlocution; digression

tordo /'torðo/ a piebald, black-and-white. m, Ornith. thrush. **t. de campanario** or **t. de Castilla,** starling

toreador /torea'ðor/ m, bullfighter

torear /tore'ar/ vi and vt to fight bulls; vt ridicule; exasperate, provoke; Inf. string along, deceive

toreo /to'reo/ m, bullfighting

torera /to'rera/ f, bullfighter's jacket

torero /to'rero/ a Inf. bullfighting. m, bullfighter

torete /to'rete/ m, dim small bull; Inf. problem, difficult question; engrossing topic of conversation

toril /to'ril/ m, pen for fighting bulls

torio /'torio/ m, thorium

tormenta /tor'menta/ f, storm; misfortune, calamity; indignation, agitation

tormento /tor'mento/ m, torment; torture; pain; anxiety, anguish. **dar t. (a),** to torture; inflict pain (on)

tormentoso /tormen'toso/ a stormy, tempestuous; Naut. pitching, rolling

torna /'torna/ f, return; restitution; backwater

tornaboda /torna'βoða/ f, day after a wedding; rejoicings of this day

tornada /tor'naða/ f, return home; return visit, revisit; Poet. envoy

tornadizo /torna'ðiso; torna'ðiθo/ (**-za**) a Inf. changeable. n turncoat

tornamiento /torna'miento/ m, return; change, transformation

tornar /tor'nar/ vt to return, give back; change, transform; vi return, go back; continue

tornasol /torna'sol/ m, sunflower; sheen, changing light; Chem. litmus

tornasolado /tornaso'laðo/ a shot (of silk, etc.)

tornasolar /tornaso'lar/ vt to look iridescent; change the color of, cause to appear variegated

tornátil /tor'natil/ a turned (in a lathe); inconstant, changeable; Poet. spinning, revolving

tornatrás /torna'tras/ mf half-caste

tornaviaje /torna'βiahe/ m, return journey

tornavoz /torna'βos; torna'βoθ/ m, soundboard, sounding board

torneador /tornea'ðor/ m, turner; jouster, fighter in a tournament

tornear /torne'ar/ vt Sports. to put a spin on (balls); turn in a lathe; vi turn around, spin; fight in a tournament; turn over in the mind

torneo /tor'neo/ m, tournament

tornería /torne'ria/ f, turnery

tornero /tor'nero/ m, turner; lathe maker; convent messenger

tornillero /torni'yero; torni'ʎero/ m, (Inf. Mil.) deserter

tornillo /tor'niyo; tor'niʎo/ m, screw; (Inf. Mil.) desertion

torniquete /torni'kete/ m, turnstile; tourniquet. **dar t. (a),** to pervert, misinterpret (meanings)

torniscón /tornis'kon/ m, Inf. slap, buffet, blow; pinch

torno /'torno/ m, lathe; turntable (of a convent, etc.); turn, rotation; windlass; dumbwaiter; axletree; spinning wheel; bend, loop (in a river). **en t.,** round about, around; in exchange

toro /'toro/ m, bull; Taurus; pl bullfight. Inf. **t. corrido,** tough nut to crack, wise guy. Inf. **Ciertos son los toros,** So it's true (gen. of bad news)

toronja /to'ronha/ f, grapefruit

toroso /to'roso/ a strong, vigorous, robust

torpe /'torpe/ a heavy, slow, encumbered; torpid; clumsy, unskilled; stupid, dull-witted; obscene, indecent; base, infamous; ugly

torpedeamiento /torpeðea'miento/ m, torpedoing, sinking

torpedear /torpeðe'ar/ vt to torpedo

torpedeo /torpe'ðeo/ m, torpedoing

torpedero /torpe'ðero/ m, torpedo boat

torpedo /tor'peðo/ m, Ichth. torpedo fish, electric ray; torpedo; sports car. **t. automóvil,** self-propelling torpedo

torpeza /tor'pesa; tor'peθa/ f, slowness, heaviness;

torpidity; stupidity; lack of skill, clumsiness; indecency; ugliness; baseness, infamy

tórpido /'torpiðo/ a torpid

torrar /to'rrar/ vt to toast, brown

torre /'torre/ f, tower; belfry, steeple; turret; rook (in chess); *Naut.* gun turret; stack, pile (of chairs, etc.); country house with a garden. **t. del tráfico,** traffic light. **t. de viento,** castle in the air, castle in Spain

torrefacción /torrefak'sion; torrefak'θion/ f, toasting (of coffee, etc.)

torrencial /torren'sial; torren'θial/ a torrential, rushing

torrente /to'rrente/ m, torrent; *Fig.* spate, rush; crowd

torrentoso, -a /torren'toso/ a, *Lat. Am.* = **torrencial**

torreón /to'rreon/ m, large fortified tower

torrero /to'rrero/ m, lighthouse keeper; gardener

torreznero /torres'nero; torreθ'nero/ **(-ra)** n *Inf.* lazybones, idler

torrezno /to'rresno; to'rreθno/ m, rasher of bacon

tórrido /'torriðo/ a torrid

torsión /tor'sion/ f, twisting, torsion

torta /'torta/ f, cake; pastry, tart; *Inf.* slap. **t. de reyes,** traditional Twelfth Night cake

tortada /tor'taða/ f, meat pie, game pie

tortedad /torte'ðað/ f, twistedness, crookedness

tortera /tor'tera/ f, cake pan; baking dish; whorl (of a spindle)

tortícolis /tor'tikolis/ m, crick (in the neck)

tortilla /tor'tiya; tor'tiʎa/ f, omelet; *Central America, Mexico* tortilla (corn pancake) **t. a la española,** potato omelet. **hacer t.,** to smash to atoms. **Se volvió la t.,** *Inf.* The tables are turned

tortillero, -a /torti'jero; torti'ʎero/ mf *Central America, Mexico* tortilla vendor

tórtola /'tortola/ f, turtledove

tórtolo /'tortolo/ m, male turtledove; *Inf.* devoted lover

tortuga /tor'tuga/ f, turtle; tortoise. **a paso de t.,** at a snail's pace

tortuosidad /tortuosi'ðað/ f, tortuousness; winding; indirectness; deceitfulness

tortuoso /tor'tuoso/ a tortuous; winding; disingenuous, deceitful

tortura /tor'tura/ f, twistedness; torture, torment; anguish, grief. **una t. china,** excruciating torture

torturador /tortura'ðor/ a torturing, tormenting

torturar /tortu'rar/ vt to torture

torva /'torβa/ f, squall of rain or snow

torzal /tor'sal; tor'θal/ m, sewing silk; twist, plait

tos /tos/ f, cough. **t. ferina,** whooping cough

tosco /'tosko/ a rough, unpolished; coarse; boorish, uncouth

toser /to'ser/ vi to cough

tósigo /'tosigo/ m, poison, venom; anguish; affliction

tosigoso /tosi'goso/ a poisoned, venomous

tosquedad /toske'ðað/ f, roughness, lack of polish; coarseness; boorishness, uncouthness

tostada /tos'taða/ f, *Cul.* toast

tostadera /tosta'ðera/ f, toasting fork

tostado /tos'taðo/ a golden brown, tanned. m, roasting (of coffee, etc.)

tostador /tosta'ðor/ **(-ra)** n toaster (of peanuts, etc.). m, toaster (utensil); coffee or peanut roaster

tostadura /tosta'ðura/ f, toasting; roasting (of coffee, etc.)

tostón /tos'ton/ m, buttered toast; anything overtoasted; roast pig; *Inf.* nuisance, bore

total /to'tal/ a total, entire, whole; general. m, total. adv in short; so, therefore

totalidad /totali'ðað/ f, whole; aggregate, entirety

totalitario /totali'tario/ a totalitarian

tótem /'totem/ m, totem

toxicidad /toksisi'ðað; toksiθi'ðað/ f, toxicity

tóxico /'toksiko/ a toxic. m, toxic substance

toxicología /toksikolo'hia/ f, toxicology

toxicológico /toksiko'lohiko/ a toxicological

tozo /'tozo; 'toθo/ a dwarfish, small

tozudez /tosu'ðes; toθu'ðeθ/ f, obstinacy

tozudo /to'suðo; to'θuðo/ a obstinate, obdurate

tozuelo /to'suelo; to'θuelo/ m, scruff, fat nape (of animals)

traba /'traβa/ f, setting (of a saw's teeth); tether (for horses); difficulty, obstacle; fastening; bond, tie; shackle; *Law.* distraint

trabacuenta /traβa'kuenta/ f, mistake in accounts; argument, difference of opinion

trabajado /traβa'haðo/ a and past part wrought; fashioned; labored, exhausted, weary

trabajador /traβaha'ðor/ **(-ra)** a working; conscientious. n worker

trabajar /traβa'har/ vi to work; function; stand the strain, resist (of machines, etc.); exert oneself, strive; toil, labor; operate, work; produce, yield (the earth fruits, etc.); vt work; till, cultivate; exercise (a horse); worry, annoy, weary; operate, drive; vr make every effort, work hard

trabajo /tra'βaho/ m, work; toil, labor; operation, working; difficulty, obstacle; literary work; hardship, trouble; process; pl poverty; hardship. **t. a destajo,** piecework. **t. al ralenti,** go-slow tactics. **trabajos forzados** (or **forzosos**), *Law.* hard labor. **pasar trabajos,** to undergo hardships

trabajosamente /traβahosa'mente/ adv painstakingly

trabajoso /traβa'hoso/ a difficult, hard; ailing, delicate; needy; afflicted

trabalenguas /traβa'lenguas/ m, *Inf.* tongue twister, jawbreaker

trabamiento /traβa'miento/ m, joining, fastening; uniting; initiation, commencement; shackling; hobbling (of horses)

trabar /tra'βar/ vt to join, unite, fasten; grasp, seize; set the teeth (of a saw); thicken; begin, initiate; hobble (of horses); reconcile, bring together, harmonize; shackle; *Law.* distrain; vr speak with an impediment; stutter, hesitate. **t. amistad,** to make friends. **t. conversación,** to get into conversation. **Se me trabó la lengua,** I began to stutter

trabazón /traβa'son; traβa'θon/ f, join, union, fastening; connection; thickness, consistency

trabilla /tra'βiya; tra'βiʎa/ f, vest strap; dropped stitch (in knitting)

trabuca /tra'βuka/ f, squib, Chinese firecracker, riprap

trabucar /traβu'kar/ vt to turn upside down, upset; confuse, bewilder; mix up, confuse (news, etc.); pronounce or write incorrectly

trabucazo /traβu'kaso; traβu'kaθo/ m, shot or report of a blunderbuss; *Inf.* calamity, unexpected misfortune

trabuco /tra'βuko/ m, *Mil.* catapult; blunderbuss

trabuquete /traβu'kete/ m, catapult

tracalada /traka'laða/ f, *Lat. Am.* crowd (of people); lot (large amount)

tracamundana /trakamun'dana/ f, *Inf.* barter, exchange of trash; hubbub, uproar

tracción /trak'sion; trak'θion/ f, pulling; traction

tracoma /tra'koma/ f, trachoma

tracto /'trakto/ m, tract, area, expanse; lapse of time

tractor /trak'tor/ m, tractor. **t. de orugas,** caterpillar tractor

tractorista /trakto'rista/ mf driver of a tractor, tractor driver

tradición /traði'sion; traði'θion/ f, tradition

tradicional /traðisio'nal; traðiθio'nal/ a traditional

tradicionalismo /traðisiona'lismo; traðiθiona'lismo/ m, traditionalism

tradicionalista /traðisiona'lista; traðiθiona'lista/ a traditionalistic. mf traditionalist

traducción /traðuk'sion; traðuk'θion/ f, translation; interpretation, explanation

traducible /traðu'siβle; traðu'θiβle/ a translatable

traducir /traðu'sir; traðu'θir/ vt irr to translate; interpret, explain; express. See **conducir**

traductor /traðuk'tor/ **(-ra)** n translator; interpreter

traedizo /trae'ðiso; trae'ðiθo/ a portable, movable

traer /tra'er/ vt irr to bring; attract; cause, occasion; wear, have on; quote, cite (as proof); compel, force; persuade; conduct, lead (persons); be engaged in; vr dress (well or badly). **t. consigo,** to bring with; have or carry or bring with one. **t. entre manos,** to have on hand. *Pres. Ind.* **traigo, traes, etc.** *Pres. Part.*

trayendo. *Preterite* **traje, trajiste, etc.** *Pres. Subjunc.*
traiga, etc. *Imperf. Subjunc.* **trajese, etc.**

trafagador /trafaga'ðor/ *m,* dealer, trafficker, merchant

tráfago /'trafago/ *m,* traffic, trade; toil, drudgery

trafalmejas /trafal'mehas/ *a Inf.* rowdy, crazy, *mf Inf.* rowdy

traficante /trafi'kante/ *mf* dealer, merchant, trader

traficar /trafi'kar/ *vi* to trade; travel

tráfico /'trafiko/ *m,* traffic; trade, commerce

tragaderas /traga'ðeras/ *f pl,* throat, gullet. *Inf.* **tener buenas t.,** to be very credulous; be tolerant (of evil)

tragadero /traga'ðero/ *m,* throat, gullet; sink, drain; hole, plug

tragador /traga'ðor/ **(-ra)** *n* glutton, guzzler

tragahombres /traga'ombres/ *mf Inf.* braggart, bully

trágala /'tragala/ *m,* **(trágala tú, servilón),** title of Spanish Liberal song aimed at Absolutists; *Inf.* take that!

tragaleguas /traga'leguas/ *mf Inf.* fast walker

tragaluz /traga'lus; traga'luθ/ *m,* skylight; fan light

tragantón /tragan'ton/ **(-ona)** *a Inf.* guzzling, greedy. *n* glutton

tragantona /tragan'tona/ *f, Inf.* spread, large meal; swallowing with difficulty; *Fig. Inf.* hard pill to swallow

tragaperras /traga'perras/ *m, Inf.* vending machine, catchpenny

tragar /tra'gar/ *vt* to swallow; eat ravenously, devour; engulf, swallow up; believe, take in; tolerate, put up with; dissemble; consume, absorb

tragedia /tra'heðia/ *f,* tragedy

trágico /'trahiko/ **(-ca)** *a* tragic. *n* tragedian; writer of tragedies

tragicomedia /trahiko'meðia/ *f,* tragicomedy

tragicómico /trahi'komiko/ *a* tragicomic

trago /'trago/ *m,* swallow, gulp, draft; *Fig. Inf.* bitter pill. **a tragos,** *Inf.* little by little, slowly

tragón /tra'gon/ **(-ona)** *a Inf.* greedy, gluttonous. *n* glutton

tragonear /tragone'ar/ *vt Inf.* to devour, eat avidly

traición /trai'sion; trai'θion/ *f,* treason, treachery. **a t.,** treacherously

traicionar /traisio'nar/ traiθio'nar/ *vt* to betray

traicionero /traisio'nero; traiθio'nero/ **(-ra)** *a* treacherous. *n* traitor

traída /tra'iða/ *f,* conduction. **t. de aguas,** water supply

traidor /trai'ðor/ **(-ra)** *a* treacherous. *n* traitor

trailla /tra'iya; tra'iʎa/ *f,* lead, leash (for animals)

traje /'trahe/ *m,* dress, apparel; outfit, costume; suit. **t. de americana,** lounge suit. **t. de baño,** swimsuit. **t. de ceremonia** *or* **t. de etiqueta,** full-dress uniform; evening dress (men). **t. de luces,** bullfighter's gala outfit. **t. de montar,** riding habit. **t. de noche,** evening dress (women). **t. paisano,** civilian dress; lounge suit

trajín /tra'hin/ *m,* carriage, transport; busyness, moving around; bustle; clatter

trajinar /trahi'nar/ *vt* to carry, transport; *Argentina* cheat, swindle; *vi* be busy, go about one's business

tralla /'traya; 'traʎa/ *f,* rope, cord; lash (of a whip); whip

trama /'trama/ *f,* woof, texture (of cloth); twisted silk; intrigue, scheme; *Lit.* plot; olive flower

tramar /tra'mar/ *vt* to weave; prepare, hatch (plots); *Fig.* prepare the way for; *vi* flower (of trees, especially olive)

tramitación /tramita'sion; tramita'θion/ *f,* transaction, conduct; procedure, method

tramitar /trami'tar/ *vt* to transact, conduct, settle

trámite /'tramite/ *m,* transit; negotiation, phase of a business deal; requirement, condition, *Inf. pl* red tape

tramo /'tramo/ *m,* plot of ground; flight of stairs, staircase; stretch, expanse, reach, tract

tramontana /tramon'tana/ *f,* north wind; arrogance, haughtiness

tramontano /tramon'tano/ *a* ultramontane, from beyond the mountains

tramontar /tramon'tar/ *vi* to cross the mountains;

sink behind the mountains (of the sun); *vr* run away, escape

tramoya /tra'moya/ *f, Theat.* stage machinery; trick, deception, hoax

tramoyista /tramo'yista/ *mf* stage carpenter; stagehand; scene-shifter; trickster, impostor, swindler

trampa /'trampa/ *f,* trap, snare; trapdoor; flap of a shop counter; trouser fly; trick, swindle; overdue debt. *Fig. Inf.* **caer en la t.,** to fall into the trap. *Inf.* **coger en la t.,** to catch in a trap; catch in the act

trampal /tram'pal/ *m,* bog, marsh

trampantojo /trampan'toho/ *m, Inf.* optical illusion, swindle

trampeador /trampea'ðor/ *a Inf.* swindling. *n* trickster, swindler

trampear /trampe'ar/ *vi Inf.* to obtain money on false pretenses; struggle on (against illness, etc.); keep oneself alive, make shift; *vt* defraud, swindle

trampolín /trampo'lin/ *m,* springboard; diving board; *Fig.* jumping-off place

tramposo /tram'poso/ **(-sa)** *n* debtor; cardsharper; swindler

tranca /'tranka/ *f,* thick stick, cudgel; bar (of a window, etc.)

trancada /tran'kaða/ *f,* stride

trancar /tran'kar/ *vt* to bar the door; *vi Inf.* oppose, resist; *vr, Lat. Am.* be constipated

trancazo /tran'kaso; tran'kaθo/ *m,* blow with a stick; influenza, flu

trance /'transe; 'tranθe/ *m,* crisis, difficult juncture; danger, peril. **t. de armas,** armed combat. **a todo t.,** at all costs, without hesitation

tranco /'tranko/ *m,* stride; threshold. *Inf.* **en dos trancos,** in a trice

tranquera /tran'kera/ *f,* stockade, palisade

tranquilar /tranki'lar/ *vt Com.* to check off

tranquilidad /trankili'ðað/ *f,* tranquility, peace, quietness; composure, serenity

tranquilizador /trankilisa'ðor; trankiliθa'ðor/ *a* tranquilizing, soothing

tranquilizar /trankili'sar; trankili'θar/ *vt* to calm, quiet; soothe

tranquilo /tran'kilo/ *a* tranquil, quiet, peaceful; serene, composed

tranquiza /tran'kisa; tran'kiθa/ *f, Mexico* beating, thrashing

transacción /transak'sion; transak'θion/ *f,* compromise, arrangement; transaction, negotiation, deal

transalpino /transal'pino/ *a* transalpine

transandino /transan'dino/ *a* transandean

transatlántico /transat'lantiko/ *a* transatlantic. *m,* (transatlantic) liner

transbordar /transβor'ðar/ *vt* to transship; transfer, remove goods from one vehicle to another

transbordo /trans'βorðo/ *m,* transshipment, transshipping; transfer, removal

transcendencia /transsen'densia; transθen'denθia/ *f* See **trascendencia**

transcendental /transsenden'tal; transθenden'tal/ *a.* See **trascendental**

transcribir /transkri'βir/ *vt* to transcribe; copy. *Past Part.* **transcrito**

transcripción /transkrip'sion; transkrip'θion/ *f,* transcription; copy, transcript

transcurrir /transku'rrir/ *vi* to elapse, pass (time)

transcurso /trans'kurso/ *m,* passage, lapse, course (of time)

transepto /tran'septo/ *m,* transept

transeúnte /tran'seunte/ *a* transient, temporary. *mf* passerby; visitor, sojourner

transferencia /transfe'rensia; transfe'renθia/ *f,* transfer (from one place to another); *Law.* conveyance, transference. **t. bancaria,** bank draft

transferidor /transferi'ðor/ **(-ra)** *a* transferring. *n* transferrer; *Law.* transferor

transferir /transfe'rir/ *vt irr* to transfer, move from one place to another; *Law.* convey (property, etc.); postpone. See **sentir**

transfiguración /transfigura'sion; transfigura'θion/ *f,* transfiguration

transfigurar /transfigu'rar/ vt to transfigure

transfijo /trans'fiho/ a transfixed

transfixión /transfik'sion/ f, transfixion

transformable /transfor'maβle/ a transformable

transformación /transforma'sion; transforma'θion/ f, transformation

transformador /transforma'ðor/ a transformative. m, Elec. transformer

transformar /transfor'mar/ vt to transform; reform (persons); vr be transformed; reform, mend one's ways

transfregar /transfre'gar/ vt irr to rub, scrub. See **cegar**

transfretar /transfre'tar/ vt Naut. to cross the sea; vi spread

tránsfuga /'transfuga/ mf **tránsfugo** m, fugitive; political turncoat

transfundir /transfun'dir/ vt to transfuse, pour from one vessel to another; imbue, transmit

transfusor /transfu'sor/ a transfusive

transgredir /transgre'ðir/ vt to transgress, infringe

transgresión /transgre'sion/ f, infringement, violation, transgression

transgresor /transgre'sor/ **(-ra)** a infringing. n transgressor, violator

transición /transi'sion; transi'θion/ f, transition, change

transido /tran'siðo/ a exhausted, worn-out, spent; niggardly, mean

transigencia /transi'hensia; transi'henθia/ f, tolerance, forbearance, indulgence

transigente /transi'hente/ a tolerant, forbearing

transigir /transi'hir/ vi to be tolerant; be broadminded. vt put up with, tolerate

transitable /transi'taβle/ a passable, traversable

transitar /transi'tar/ vi to cross, pass through; travel

transitivo /transi'tiβo/ a transitive

tránsito /'transito/ m, passage, crossing; transit; stopping place; transition, change; gallery of a cloister; Eccl. holy death. **de t.,** temporarily; in transit (of goods). **hacer tránsitos,** to break one's journey, stop

transitorio /transi'torio/ a transitory, fugitive, fleeting

translimitación /translimita'sion; translimita'θion/ f, trespass; bad behavior; armed intervention in a neighboring state

translimitar /translimi'tar/ vt to overstep the boundaries (of a state, etc.); overstep the limits (of decency, etc.)

translucidez /translusi'ðes; transluθi'ðeθ/ f, translucence, semitransparency

translúcido /trans'lusiðo; trans'luθiðo/ a translucent, semitransparent

transmarino /transma'rino/ a transmarine

transmigración /transmigra'sion; transmigra'θion/ f, transmigration

transmigrar /transmi'grar/ vi to migrate; transmigrate (of the soul)

transmisión /transmi'sion/ f, transmission. **t. del pensamiento,** thought transference

transmisor /transmi'sor/ a transmitting. m, Elec. transmitter, sender

transmitir /transmi'tir/ vt to transmit; Mech. drive

transmutable /transmu'taβle/ a transmutable

transmutación /transmuta'sion; transmuta'θion/ f, transmutation, transformation, change

transmutar /transmu'tar/ vt to transmute, transform, change

transoceánico /transose'aniko; transoθe'aniko/ a transoceanic

transpacífico /transpa'sifiko; transpa'θifiko/ a transpacific

transparencia /transpa'rensia; transpa'renθia/ f, transparency; obviousness

transparentarse /transparen'tarse/ vr to be transparent; show through; Fig. reveal, give away (secrets)

transparente /transpa'rente/ a transparent; translucent; evident, obvious. m, windowshade, blind

transpiración /transpira'sion; transpira'θion/ f, perspiration

transpirar /transpi'rar/ vi to perspire

transponer /transpo'ner/ vt irr to move, transfer; transplant; transpose; vr hide behind; sink behind the horizon (of the sun, stars); be half-asleep. See **poner**

transportable /transpor'taβle/ a transportable

transportación /transporta'sion; transporta'θion/ f. See **transporte**

transportador /transporta'ðor/ **(-ra)** a transport. n transporter. m, Geom. protractor

transportamiento /transporta'miento/ m. See **transporte**

transportar /transpor'tar/ vt to transport; Mus. transpose; carry; vr Fig. be carried away by (anger, rapture)

transporte /trans'porte/ m, transport, carriage; cartage; Naut. transport; strong emotion, transport, ecstasy

transposición /transposi'sion; transposi'θion/ f, transposition

transpositivo /transposi'tiβo/ a transpositive

transubstanciación /transuβstansia'sion; transuβstanθia'θion/ f, transubstantiation

transubstanciar /transuβstan'siar; transuβstan'θiar/ vt to transubstantiate, transmute

transversal, transverso /transβer'sal, trans'βerso/ a transverse

tranvía /tram'bia/ m, street railway; streetcar. **t. de sangre,** horse-drawn streetcar.

tranviario /tram'biario/ a streetcar. m, streetcar employee

trapacear /trapase'ar; trapaθe'ar/ vi to cheat, swindle

trapacete /trapa'sete; trapa'θete/ m, Com. daybook

trapacista /trapa'sista; trapa'θista/ mf trickster, swindler, knave

trapajoso /trapa'hoso/ a ragged, shabby, tattered

trápala /'trapala/ f, noise, confusion, hubbub; noise of horse's hoofs, gallop; Inf. trick, swindle; prattling, babbling. mf Inf. babbler, prattler; trickster

trapalear /trapale'ar/ vi to walk noisily, tramp; Inf. chatter, babble

trapatiesta /trapa'tiesta/ f, Inf. brawl, row, quarrel

trapaza /tra'pasa; tra'paθa/ f, hoax, swindle

trapeador /trapea'ðor/ m, Lat. Am. (floor) mop

trapear /trape'ar/ vt, Lat. Am. to mop (the floor)

trapecio /tra'pesio; tra'peθio/ m, trapeze; Geom. trapezium, trapezoid

trapería /trape'ria/ f, old-clothes shop; old clothes, rags, trash, frippery

trapero /tra'pero/ **(-ra)** n old-clothes seller; rag merchant; ragpicker

trapezoide /trape'soiðe; trape'θoiðe/ m, trapezium, trapezoid

trapichear /trapitʃe'ar/ vi Inf. to make shift, endeavor

trapiento /tra'piento/ a ragged, shabby

trapillo /tra'piyo; tra'piʎo/ m, Inf. poverty-stricken lover; nest egg, savings. Inf. **de t.,** in a state of undress, in négligé

trapío /tra'pio/ m, Inf. spirit of a fighting bull; verve, dash, independent air (of women)

trapisonda /trapi'sonda/ f, Inf. uproar, brawl; hubbub, bustle; snare, fix

trapisondear /trapisonde'ar/ vi Inf. to be given to brawling; scheme, intrigue

trapisondista /trapison'dista/ mf brawler; schemer, trickster

trapo /'trapo/ m, rag; Naut. canvas; bullfighter's cape; pl garments, bits and pieces. Inf. **poner como un t.** (a), to dress down, scold. **soltar el t.,** to burst out crying or laughing

trapujo /tra'puho/ m, Inf. trick; subterfuge

traque /'trake/ m, report, bang (of a rocket, etc.); fuse (of a firework)

tráquea /'trakea/ f, trachea

traqueotomía /trakeoto'mia/ f, tracheotomy

traquetear /trakete'ar/ vi to crack, bang, go off with a report; rattle; jolt (of trains, etc.). vt shake, stir; Inf. paw, handle too much

traqueteo /trake'teo/ m, banging (of fireworks); creaking; rattling; jolting (of trains, etc.)

traquido /tra'kiðo/ *m*, report (of a gun); crack (of a whip); creak

tras /tras/ *prep* after; behind; following, in pursuit of; trans- (in compounds). *m*, *Inf.* buttock; sound of a blow, bang, bump. **t. t.**, knocking (at a door); banging

trasalcoba /trasal'koβa/ *f*, dressing room

trasbarrás /trasβa'rras/ *m*, bang, bump, noise

trasbocar /trasβo'kar/ *vt*, *Lat. Am.* to vomit

trascendencia /trassen'densia; trasθen'denθia/ *f*, transcendence, excellence; consequence, result

trascendental /trassenden'tal; trasθenden'tal/ *a* transcendental; important, farreaching

trascender /trassen'der; trasθen'der/ *vi irr* to spread to, influence; become known, leak out; exhale a scent; *vt* investigate, discover. See **entender**

trascocina /trasko'sina; trasko'θina/ *f*, back kitchen

trascolar /trasko'lar/ *vt irr* to filter, strain; cross over, traverse. See **colar**

trascordarse /traskor'ðarse/ *vr irr* to mix up, make a muddle of, forget. See **acordar**

trasechar /trase'tʃar/ *vt* to ambush, waylay

trasegar /trase'gar/ *vt irr* to upset, turn upside down; transfer, move from one place to another; empty, pour out, upset (liquids). See **cegar**

traseñalar /traseɲa'lar/ *vr* to re-mark, mark again

trasera /tra'sera/ *f*, rear, back, rear portion

trasero /tra'sero/ *a* rear, back. *m*, hindquarters, rump; buttocks, seat; *pl Inf.* ancestors

trasgo /'trasgo/ *m*, imp, sprite, puck

trashumante /trasu'mante/ *a* nomadic (of flocks)

trashumar /trasu'mar/ *vi* to go from winter to summer pasture (or vice versa) (of flocks). See **desahuciar.**

trasiego /tra'siego/ *m*, emptying, pouring out, upsetting (of liquids); decanting (of wines)

traslación /trasla'sion; trasla'θion/ *f*, removal, transfer; alteration (of the date for a meeting); metaphor

trasladable /trasla'ðaβle/ *a* removable, movable, transferable

trasladar /trasla'ðar/ *vt* to remove, transfer; move from one place to another; alter (the date of a meeting); translate; copy, transcribe; *vr* remove (from a place)

traslado /tras'laðo/ *m*, removal; transfer; transcription

traslapar /trasla'par/ *vt* to cover, overlap

traslapo /tras'lapo/ *m*, overlap, overlapping

traslucirse /traslu'sirse; traslu'θirse/ *vr irr* to be transparent or translucent; shine through; come out (of secrets); infer, gather. See **lucir**

traslumbramiento /traslumbra'miento/ *m*, dazzle, glare, brilliance

traslumbrar /traslum'βrar/ *vt* to dazzle; *vr* flicker, glimmer; fade quickly, disappear

trasluz /tras'lus; tras'luθ/ *m*, reflected light. **al t.,** against the light

trasminar /trasmi'nar/ *vt* to undermine, excavate; *vi* percolate, ooze; penetrate, spread

trasnochada /trasno'tʃaða/ *f*, previous night, last night; night's vigil; sleepless night; *Mil.* night attack

trasnochado /trasno'tʃaðo/ *a* stale, old; weary; hackneyed; drawn, pinched

trasnochador /trasnotʃa'ðor/ **(-ra)** *n* one who watches by night or stays up all night; *Inf.* night owl, reveler

trasnochar /trasno'tʃar/ *vi* to stay up all night; watch through the night; spend the night; *vt* sleep on, leave for the following day

trasnoche, trasnocho /tras'notʃe, tras'notʃo/ *m*, *Inf.* night out; night vigil

trasoir /traso'ir/ *vt irr* to hear incorrectly, misunderstand. See **oir**

trasojado /traso'haðo/ *a* haggard, tired-eyed

trasoñar /traso'ɲar/ *vt irr* to imagine, mistake a dream for reality. See **contar**

traspalar /traspa'lar/ *vt* to fork (grain); shovel; transfer, move

trasparencia /traspa'rensia; traspa'renθia/ *f*. See **transparencia**

traspasar /traspa'sar/ *vt* to transfer, move; cross; *Law.* convey, make over to; pierce; transgress, flout; exceed one's authority; *Fig.* go too far; reexamine, go over again; give intolerable pain (of illness, grief). **se traspasa,** to be disposed of (houses, etc.)

traspaso /tras'paso/ *m*, transport, transfer; *Law.* conveyance; property transferred; price agreed upon

traspatio /tras'patio/ *m*, *Lat. Am.* backyard

traspié /tras'pie/ *m*, slip, catching of the foot, stumble; heel of the foot. **dar traspiés,** *Inf.* to blunder

trasplantación /trasplanta'sion; trasplanta'θion/ *f*, **trasplante** *m*, transplantation; emigration

trasplantar /trasplan'tar/ *vt Agr.* to transplant; *vr* emigrate

trasplante /tras'plante/ *m*, planting out

traspuesta /tras'puesta/ *f*, transposition; back quarters; rear (of a house); back yard

traspunte /tras'punte/ *m*, *Theat.* prompter

traspuntín /traspun'tin/ *m*, *Auto.* folding seat

trasquilar /traski'lar/ *vt* to cut the hair unevenly; shear (sheep); *Inf.* cut down, diminish

trasquilón /traski'lon/ *m*, cropping (of hair); shearing; *Inf.* money stolen by pilfering

trastada /tras'taða/ *f*, *Inf.* dirty trick, mean act

traste /'traste/ *m*, fret (of stringed instruments); tasting cup. **dar al t. con,** to spoil, upset, damage. *Inf.* **sin trastes,** topsy-turvy, without method

trastear /traste'ar/ *vt* to play well (on the mandolin, etc.); *Inf.* manage tactfully; *vi* move around, change (furniture, etc.); discuss excitedly

trastejar /traste'har/ *vt* to repair the roof; renew slates; overhaul

trastienda /tras'tienda/ *f*, back of a shop; room behind a shop; *Inf.* wariness, caution

trasto /'trasto/ *m*, piece of furniture; (household) utensil; lumber, useless furniture; *Theat.* wing or set piece; *Inf.* useless person, ne'er-do-well; oddment, thing; *pl* implements, equipment

trastornable /trastor'naβle/ *a* easily overturned or upset; easily agitated

trastornar /trastor'nar/ *vt* to turn upside down; perturb, disturb; *Fig.* overpower (of scents, etc.); disorder, upset; dissuade; make mad; derange the mind

trastorno /tras'torno/ *m*, upset; perturbation, anxiety; disorder; mental derangement; confusion (of the senses)

trastrabillar /trastraβi'yar; trastraβi'ʎar/ *vi* to stumble, slip; totter, sway; hesitate; stutter, be tongue-tied

trastrás /tras'tras/ *m*, *Inf.* last but one (in games)

trastrocamiento /trastroka'miento/ *m*, alteration, change; disarrangement

trastrocar /trastro'kar/ *vt irr* to alter, change, disarrange; change the order of. See **contar**

trasudar /trasu'ðar/ *vt* to perspire

trasudor /trasu'ðor/ *m*, light perspiration

trasuntar /trasun'tar/ *vt* to copy, transcribe; summarize

trasunto /tra'sunto/ *m*, copy, transcript; imitation

trasver /tras'βer/ *vt irr* to see through or between, glimpse; see incorrectly. See **ver**

trasverter /trasβer'ter/ *vi irr* to overflow. See **entender**

trata /'trata/ *f*, slave trade. **t. de blancas,** white slave traffic

tratable /tra'taβle/ *a* easily accessible, sociable, unpretentious

tratadista /trata'ðista/ *mf* writer of a treatise; expert, writer on special subjects

tratado /tra'taðo/ *m*, pact, agreement; treaty; treatise

tratador /trata'ðor/ **(-ra)** *n* arbitrator

tratamiento /trata'miento/ *m*, treatment; courtesy title; address, style; *Med.* treatment; process

tratante /tra'tante/ *m*, merchant, dealer

tratar /tra'tar/ *vt* to handle; use; conduct; manage; have dealings with, meet, know (e.g. *Yo no le trato,* I don't know him); behave well or badly toward; care for, treat; discuss, deal with (e.g. *¿De qué trata el libro?* What is the book about?); propose, suggest; *Chem.* treat; (*with de*) address as, call; *vi* have amorous relations; (*with de*) try to, endeavor to; (*with* *en*) trade in; *vr* look after oneself, treat oneself; conduct oneself

trato /'trato/ *m*, use, handling; management; conduct, behavior; manner, demeanor; appellation, title; commerce, traffic; dealings, intercourse; treatment; agreement, arrangement. **t. colectivo,** collective bargaining

traumático /trau'matiko/ *a* traumatic

traumatismo /trauma'tismo/ *m*, traumatism

través /tra'βes/ *m*, slant, slope; mishap; (*Mil. Archit.*) traverse. **a t.** *or* **al t.,** across; through. **de t.,** athwart; through

travesaño /traβe'saɲo/ *m*, crossbar; bolster; rung (of a ladder); traverse

travesear /traβese'ar/ *vi* to run about, romp, be mischievous; lead a vicious life; speak wittily; move ceaselessly (of water, etc.)

travesía /traβe'sia/ *f*, crossing; traverse; crossroad; side road or street; distance, space; sea crossing; crosswise position; stretch of road within a town

travestido /traβes'tiðo/ *a* disguised, dressed up

travesura /traβe'sura/ *f*, romping, frolic; mischief; prank; quick-wittedness

traviesa /tra'βiesa/ *f*, sleeping car, sleeper (railroad); *Archit.* rafter; distance between two points

travieso /tra'βieso/ *a* transverse, crosswise; mischievous, willful; debauched; clever, subtle; ever-moving (of streams, etc.)

trayecto /tra'yekto/ *m*, run, distance, journey; stretch, expanse, tract; fare stage

trayectoria /trayek'toria/ *f*, trajectory; journey

traza /'trasa/ 'traθa/ *f*, plan, design, draft; scheme, project; idea, proposal; aspect, appearance; means, manner. **Hombre pobre todo es trazas,** A poor man is full of schemes (for bettering himself)

trazado /tra'saðo; tra'θaðo/ *m*, designing, drawing; design, draft, model, plan; course, direction (of a canal, etc.)

trazador /trasa'ðor; traθa'ðor/ **(-ra)** *n* draftsman, designer; planner, schemer

trazar /tra'sar; tra'θar/ *vt* to plan, draft, design; make a drawing of; trace; describe; map out, arrange

trazo /'traso; 'traθo/ *m*, line, stroke; outline, contour, form, line; *Art.* fold in drapery; stroke of the pen

trebejar /treβe'har/ *vi* to frolic, skip, play

trebejo /tre'βeho/ *m*, chessman, chess piece; utensil, article (gen. *pl*); plaything

trébol /'treβol/ *m*, clover

trece /'trese; 'treθe/ *a* and *m*, thirteen, thirteenth. *m*, thirteenth (day of the month)

trecemesino /treseme'sino; treθeme'sino/ *a* thirteen months old

trecho /'tretʃo/ *m*, distance, space; interval (of time). **a trechos,** at intervals. **de t. en t.,** from time to time

trefe /'trefe/ *a* pliable, flexible; light; spurious (of coins)

tregua /'tregua/ *f*, truce; *Mil.* ceasefire; respite, rest. **dar treguas,** to afford relief, give a respite; give time

treinta /'treinta/ *a* and *m*, thirty; thirtieth. *m*, thirtieth (day of the month)

treintavo /trein'taβo/ *a* thirtieth

treintena /trein'tena/ *f*, thirtieth (part)

tremebundo /treme'βundo/ *a* fearsome, dread

tremedal /treme'ðal/ *m*, bog; quagmire

tremendo /tre'mendo/ *a* fearful, formidable; awesome; *Inf.* tremendous, enormous

trementina /tremen'tina/ *f*, turpentine

tremolar /tremo'lar/ *vt* and *vi* to wave, fly (of banners); *Fig.* make a show of

tremolina /tremo'lina/ *f*, noise of the wind; *Inf.* hubbub, confusion

trémulo /'tremulo/ *a* trembling, tremulous

tren /tren/ *m*, supply, provision; outfit; equipment; pomp, show; railroad train; following, train; *Mexico* *also* streetcar, trolley car, trolley. **t. ascendente,** up train (from coast to interior). *Inf.* **t. botijo,** excursion train. **t. con coches corridos,** corridor train. **t. correo,** mail train. **t. descendente,** down train (from interior to coast). **t. mixto,** train carrying passengers

and freight. **t. ómnibus,** accommodation train, slow, stopping train. **t. rápido,** express

trencilla /tren'siya; tren'θiʎa/ *f*, braid, trimming

trencillar /trensi'yar; trenθi'ʎar/ *vt* to trim with braid, braid

trenza /'trensa; 'trenθa/ *f*, plait, braid; plait of hair; bread twist; *Lat. Am.* string (of onions). **en t.,** in plaits, plaited (of hair)

trenzadera /trensa'ðera; trenθa'ðera/ *f*, linen tape

trenzar /tren'sar; tren'θar/ *vt* to plait, braid; *vi* curvet, prance *Lat. Am.* **trenzarse (en...)** get involved (in...), e.g. *trenzarse en una disputa* get involved in a dispute

trepa /'trepa/ *f*, perforation, boring, piercing; climbing; creeping; *Inf.* half-somersault; grain, surface (of wood); craftiness, slyness; deception, fraud; beating, drubbing

trepador /trepa'ðor/ *a* climbing; crawling; *Bot.* creeping, climbing. *m*, climbing place

trepanación /trepana'sion; trepana'θion/ *f*, trepanning

trepanar /trepa'nar/ *vt* to trepan

trepante /tre'pante/ *a* creeping; *Bot.* twining, climbing

trepar /tre'par/ *vi* to climb, ascend; *Bot.* climb or creep; bore, perforate

trepatrepa /trepa'trepa/ *m*, jungle gym, monkey bars

trepidación /trepiða'sion; trepiða'θion/ *f*, trepidation, dread; vibration; jarring; shaking

trepidar /trepi'ðar/ *vi* to shiver, shudder; vibrate; shake; jar; *Lat. Am.* hesitate

trépido /'trepiðo/ *a* shuddering, shivering; vibrating

tres /tres/ *a* three; third. *m*, figure three; third (day of the month); three (of playing cards); trio. *Inf.* **como t. y dos son cinco,** as sure as two and two make four

trescientos /tres'sientos; tres'θientos/ *a* and *m*, three hundred; three-hundredth

tresillo /tre'siyo; tre'siʎo/ *m*, omber (card game); *Mus.* triplet

tresnal /tres'nal/ *m*, *Agr.* stook, cock, sheaf

treta /'treta/ *f*, scheme; trick, hoax; feint (in fencing)

trezavo /tre'saβo; tre'θaβo/ *a* thirteenth

tría /'tria/ *f*, selection, choice; worn place (in cloth)

triangulación /triangula'sion; triangula'θion/ *f*, triangulation

triángulo /tri'angulo/ *a* triangular. *m*, (*Geom. Mus.*) triangle. **t. acutángulo,** acute triangle. **t. obtusángulo,** obtuse triangle. **t. rectángulo,** right-angled triangle

triar /triar/ *vt* to select, pick out; *vi* fly in and out of the hive (of bees); *vr* grow threadbare, become worn

tribu /'triβu/ *f*, tribe; species, family

tribulación /triβula'sion; triβula'θion/ *f*, tribulation, suffering

tribuna /tri'βuna/ *f*, tribune; platform, rostrum, pulpit; spectators' gallery; stand. **t. de la prensa,** press gallery. **t. del jurado,** jury box. **t. del órgano,** organ loft

tribunado /triβu'naðo/ *m*, tribunate

tribunal /triβu'nal/ *m*, law court; *Law.* bench; judgment seat; tribunal; board of examiners. **t. de menores,** children's court, juvenile court. *Naut.* **t. de presas,** prize court. **t. de primera instancia,** *Law.* petty sessions. **t. militar,** court-martial

tribuno /tri'βuno/ *m*, tribune; political speaker

tributar /triβu'tar/ *vt* to pay taxes; offer, render (thanks, homage, etc.)

tributario /triβu'tario/ **(-ia)** *a* tributary; tax-paying, contributive. *n* taxpayer. *m*, tributary (of a river)

tributo /tri'βuto/ *m*, contribution; tax; tribute, homage; census

tricenal /trise'nal/ *a* of thirty years' duration; occurring every thirty years

tricentésimo /trisen'tesimo; triθen'tesimo/ *a* three-hundredth

triciclo /tri'siklo; tri'θiklo/ *m*, tricycle

tricolor /triko'lor/ *a* three-colored

tricorne /tri'korne/ *a* *Poet.* three-cornered, three-horned

tricornio /tri'kornio/ *a* three-cornered. *m*, three-cornered hat

tricotomía /trikoto'mia/ *f*, trichotomy, division into three

tricromía /trikro'mia/ *f*, three-color process

tridente /tri'ðente/ *a* tridentate, three-pronged. *m*, trident

trienal /trie'nal/ *a* triennial

trienio /'trienio/ *m*, space of three years

trifásico /tri'fasiko/ *a* three-phase

trifolio /tri'folio/ *m*, trefoil

trigal /tri'gal/ *m*, wheat field

trigésimo /tri'hesimo/ *a* thirtieth

trigo /'trigo/ *m*, wheat plant; ear of wheat; wheat field (gen. *pl*); wealth, money. **t. sarraceno,** buckwheat. **t. tremés** *or* **t. trechel** *or* **t. tremesino** *or* **t. de marzo,** summer wheat

trigonometría /trigonome'tria/ *f*, trigonometry

trigueño /tri'geɲo/ *a* brunette, dark

triguero /tri'gero/ *a* wheat; wheat-growing. *m*, grain sieve; grain merchant

trilátero /tri'latero/ *a* three-sided, trilateral

trilingüe /tri'liŋgue/ *a* trilingual

trilla /'triya; 'triʎa/ *f*, red mullet; *Agr.* harrow; threshing; threshing season

trillado /tri'yaðo; tri'ʎaðo/ *a* frequented, trodden, worn (of paths); hackneyed

trilladora /triya'ðora; triʎa'ðora/ *f*, threshing machine

trillar /tri'yar; tri'ʎar/ *vt* to thresh; *Inf.* frequent; ill-treat

trillo /'triyo; 'triʎo/ *m*, threshing machine; harrow

trillón /tri'yon; tri'ʎon/ *m*, trillion

trilogía /trilo'hia/ *f*, trilogy

trimestral /trimes'tral/ *a* quarterly; terminal (in schools, etc.)

trimestre /tri'mestre/ *a* quarterly; terminal. *m*, quarter, three months; term (in schools, etc.); quarterly payment; quarterly rent

trinado /tri'naðo/ *m*, *Mus.* trill; twittering, shrilling (of birds)

trinar /tri'nar/ *vi Mus.* to trill; twitter, shrill; *Inf.* get in a temper, be furious

trincapiñones /trinkapi'ɲones/ *m*, *Inf.* scatterbrained youth

trincar /trin'kar/ *vt* to fasten securely; tie tightly; pinion; *Naut.* lash, make fast; cut up, chop; *Inf.* tipple; *vi Naut.* sail close to the wind

trincha /'trintʃa/ *f*, vest strap

trinchante /trin'tʃante/ *m*, table carver; carving fork; stonecutter's hammer

trinchar /trin'tʃar/ *vt* to carve (at table); *Inf.* decide, dispose

trinche /'trintʃe/ *m Mexico* pitchfork; *elsewhere in Lat. Am.* fork

trinchera /trin'tʃera/ *f*, *Mil.* trench; cutting (for roads, etc.); trench coat

trinchero /trin'tʃero/ *m*, platter, trencher; serving table, side table

trineo /tri'neo/ *m*, sled, sledge, sleigh

trinidad /trini'ðað/ *f*, trinity

trinitaria /trini'taria/ *f*, *Bot.* pansy, heartsease

trinitario /trini'tario/ **(-ia)** *a* and *n Eccl.* Trinitarian

trino /'trino/ *a* triune; ternary. *m*, *Mus.* trill

trinomio /tri'nomio/ *m*, trinomial

trinquete /trin'kete/ *m*, *Naut.* mainmast; mainsail; *Sports.* rackets; *Mech.* ratchet

trinquis /'trinkis/ *m*, *Inf.* draft, drink

trío /'trio/ *m*, trio

tripa /'tripa/ *f*, entrail, gut; *Inf.* belly; inside (of some fruits). **hacer de tripas corazón,** *Inf.* to take heart, buck up. **revolver las tripas (a),** *Fig. Inf.* to make one sick

tripartición /triparti'sion; triparti'θion/ *f*, tripartition

tripartito /tripar'tito/ *a* tripartite

tripicallos /tripi'kayos; tripi'kaʎos/ *m pl*, *Cul.* tripe

triple /'triple/ *a* triple; three-ply (of yarn)

triplicación /triplika'sion; triplika'θion/ *f*, trebling

triplicar /tripli'kar/ *vt* to treble

trípode /'tripoðe/ *m*, (sometimes *f*) three-legged stool or table; tripod; trivet

tríptico /'triptiko/ *m*, triptych

triptongo /'triptoŋgo/ *m*, triphthong

tripulación /tripula'sion; tripula'θion/ *f*, crew (ships and aircraft)

tripulante /tripu'lante/ *m*, crew member

tripular /tripu'lar/ *vt* to provide with a crew, man; equip, furnish; serve in, work as the crew of

trique /'trike/ *m*, crack, creak. *Inf.* **a cada t.,** at every moment

triquiñuela /triki'ɲuela/ *f*, *Inf.* evasion, subterfuge

triquitraque /triki'trake/ *m*, tap, rap; crack; firework

tris /tris/ *m*, crack, noise of glass, etc., cracking; *Inf.* instant, trice. **estar en un t. (de),** to be on the verge (of), within an inch (of)

trisar /tri'sar/ *vt* to crack, break, splinter (of glass); *vi* chirp, twitter (especially of swallows)

trisca /'triska/ *f*, cracking, crushing, crackling (of nuts, etc.); noise, tumult

triscar /tris'kar/ *vi* to make a noise with the feet; gambol, frolic; creak, crack; *vt* blend, mingle; set the teeth of a saw

trisecar /trise'kar/ *vt* to trisect

trisemanal /trisema'nal/ *a* three times weekly; every three weeks

trisílabo /tri'silaβo/ *a* trisyllabic

trismo /'trismo/ *m*, lockjaw, trismus

triste /'triste/ *a* unhappy, sorrowful; melancholy, gloomy; sad; piteous, unfortunate; useless, worthless; *m*, *Lat. Am.* sad love song

tristeza, tristura /tris'teθa, tris'tura; tris'tesa/ *f*, unhappiness; melancholy, gloom; sadness; piteousness

tritón /tri'ton/ *m*, merman

triturar /tritu'rar/ *vt* to crumble, crush; chew; masticate; ill-treat, bruise; refute, contradict

triunfada /triun'faða/ *f*, trumping (at cards)

triunfador /triunfa'ðor/ **(-ra)** *a* triumphant. *n* victor

triunfal /triun'fal/ *a* triumphal

triunfante /triun'fante/ *a* triumphant

triunfar /triun'far/ *vi* to triumph; be victorious, win; trump (at cards); spend ostentatiously

triunfo /'triunfo/ *m*, triumph; victory; trump card; success; booty, spoils of war; conquest

trivial /tri'βial/ *a* well-known, hackneyed; frequented, trodden; commonplace, mediocre, trivial, unimportant

trivialidad /triβiali'ðað/ *f*, banality, triteness, mediocrity; triviality

trivio /'triβio/ *m*, road junction

triza /'trisa; 'triθa/ *f*, fragment, bit; *Naut.* rope. **hacer trizas,** to smash to bits

trizar /tri'sar; tri'θar/ *vt* to smash up, destroy

trocable /tro'kaβle/ *a* exchangeable

trocada, a la /tro'kaða, a la/ *adv* contrariwise; in exchange

trocador /troka'ðor/ **(-ra)** *n* exchanger

trocar /tro'kar/ *vt irr* to exchange; vomit; distort, misconstrue, mistake; *vr* change, alter one's behavior; change places with another; be transferred. See **contar**

trocear /trose'ar; troθe'ar/ *vt* to divide into pieces

trocha /'trotʃa/ *f*, short cut; trail, path, track

trochemoche, a /trotʃe'motʃe, a/ *adv Inf.* without rhyme or reason, pell-mell

trofeo /tro'feo/ *m*, trophy; victory; military booty

troglodita /troglo'ðita/ *a* and *mf* troglodyte. *m*, *Fig.* savage, barbarian. *mf* glutton

troj /troh/ *f*, granary

trojero /tro'hero/ *m*, granary keeper

trola /'trola/ *f*, *Inf.* lie, nonsense, hoax

trole /'trole/ *m*, trolley

trolebús /trole'βus/ *m*, trolley car

trolero /tro'lero/ *a Inf.* deceiving, lying

tromba /'tromba/ *f*, waterspout

trombón /trom'bon/ *m*, trombone; trombone player. **¡Trombones y platillos!** Great Scot!

trombosis /trom'bosis/ *f*, thrombosis

trompa /'trompa/ *f*, elephant's trunk; *Mus.* horn;

proboscis (of insects); waterspout; humming top. **t. de Falopio,** fallopian tube

trompada /trom'paða/ f, *Inf.* bang, bump; blow, buffet, slap; collision

trompazo /trom'paso; trom'paθo/ m, heavy blow, knock, bang

trompear /trompe'ar/ *vi* to play with a top; *vt* knock about

trompero /trom'pero/ m, top maker. a deceiving, swindling

trompeta /trom'peta/ f, trumpet; bugle. m, trumpeter; bugler; *Inf.* ninny. **t. de amor,** sunflower

trompetada /trompe'taða/ f, *Inf.* stupid remark, piece of nonsense

trompetazo /trompe'taso; trompe'taθo/ m, bray of a trumpet; bugle blast; *Inf.* stupid remark

trompetear /trompete'ar/ *vi Inf.* to play the trumpet or bugle

trompeteo /trompe'teo/ m, trumpeting, trumpet call; sound of the bugle

trompetería /trompete'ria/ f, collection of trumpets; metal organ pipes

trompetero /trompe'tero/ m, trumpet or bugle maker or player

trompetilla /trompe'tiya; trompe'tiʎa/ f, *dim* little trumpet; ear trumpet

trompicar /trompi'kar/ *vt* to make stumble, trip. *vi* stumble, trip up

trompicón /trompi'kon/ m, stumble

trompo /'trompo/ m, humming or spinning top; *Inf.* dolt, idiot

tronada /tro'naða/ f, thunderstorm

tronado /tro'naðo/ a worn-out; threadbare, old; poor, poverty-stricken; down at the heels

tronar /tro'nar/ *v impers irr* to thunder; *vi* growl, roar (of guns); *Inf.* go bankrupt, be ruined; *Inf.* protest against, attack; *Central America, Mexico* execute, shoot; (*with con*) quarrel with. *Pres. Ind.* **trueno, truenas, truena, truenan.** *Pres. Subjunc.* **truene, truenes, truene, truenen**

troncal /tron'kal/ a trunk; main, principal

troncha /'trontʃa/ f, *Lat. Am.* piece; slice

tronchar /tron'tʃar/ *vt* to break off, lop off (branches)

troncho /'trontʃo/ m, *Bot.* stem, stalk, branch

tronco /'tronko/ m, *Anat. Bot.* trunk; main body or line (of communications); trunk line; common origin, stock; *Inf.* blockhead, dolt; callous person. *Fig.* **estar hecho un t.,** to lie like a log; sleep like a log

tronera /tro'nera/ f, *Naut.* porthole; embrasure; slit window; pocket of a billiards table. *mf Inf.* madcap, harumscarum

tronido /tro'niðo/ m, roll of thunder

trono /'trono/ m, throne; *Eccl.* tabernacle; shrine; kingly might; *pl* thrones, hierarchy of angels

tronzador /tronsa'ðor; tronθa'ðor/ m, two-handled saw

tronzar /tron'sar; tron'θar/ *vt* to smash, break into bits; *Sew.* pleat; exhaust, overtire

tropa /'tropa/ f, crowd (of people); troops, military; *Mil.* call to arms; *pl* army. **t. de línea,** regiment of the line. **tropas de asalto,** storm troopers. **tropas de refresco,** fresh troops. **en t.,** in a crowd; in groups

tropel /tro'pel/ m, rush, surge (of crowds, etc.); bustle, confusion; crowd, multitude; heap, jumble (of things). **en t.,** in a rush; in a crowd

tropelía /trope'lia/ f, rush, dash; violence; outrage

tropezar /trope'sar; trope'θar/ *vi irr* to stumble, slip; (*with con*) meet unexpectedly or accidentally come up against, be faced with (difficulties); quarrel with or oppose; fall into (bad habits). See **empezar**

tropezón /trope'son; trope'θon/ m, stumbling, slipping; stumbling block, obstacle. **a tropezones,** *Inf.* stumblingly; by fits and starts

tropical /tropi'kal/ a tropical

trópicos /'tropikos/ m *pl,* tropics

tropiezo /tro'pieso; tro'pieθo/ m, stumble; stumbling block, obstacle; hitch; impediment; slip, peccadillo, fault; difficulty, embarrassment; fight, skirmish; quarrel

tropo /'tropo/ m, trope, figure of speech

troquel /tro'kel/ m, die, mold

trotaconventos /trotakom'bentos/ f, *Inf.* go-between, procuress

trotamundos /trota'mundos/ mf, *Inf.* globetrotter

trotar /tro'tar/ *vi* to trot; *Inf.* hurry, get a move on

trote /'trote/ m, trot; toil, drudgery. **t. corto,** jog-trot. **al t.,** with all speed

trotón /tro'ton/ (-ona) a trotting. m, horse. f, chaperone

trova /'troβa/ f, verse; song, lay, ballad; love song

trovador /troβa'ðor/ (-ra) m, troubadour, minstrel. n poet

trovadoresco /troβaðo'resko/ a pertaining to minstrels, troubadour

trovar /tro'βar/ *vi* to compose verses; write ballads; misconstrue, misinterpret

Troya /'troia/ *Troy*

troyano /tro'iano/ (-na) a and n Trojan

trozo /'troso; 'troθo/ m, part, fragment; piece, portion; *Lit.* selection. **t. de abordaje,** *Nav.* landing party

trucha /'trutʃa/ f, trout. **t. asalmonada,** salmon trout

truchuela /tru'tʃuela/ f, small trout; salt cod

truco /'truko/ m, trick, deception

truculencia /truku'lensia; truku'lenθia/ f, harshness, cruelty, truculence

truculento /truku'lento/ a fierce, harsh, truculent

trueco /'trueko/ m, exchange. **a t. de,** in exchange for; on condition that

trueno /'trueno/ m, thunder; report, noise (of firearms); *Inf.* rake, scapegrace

trueque /'trueke/ m, exchange. **a.** (*or* **en**) **t.,** in exchange

trufa /'trufa/ f, *Bot.* truffle; nonsense, idle talk

trufar /tru'far/ *vt Cul.* to stuff with truffles; *vi Inf.* lie, tell fibs

truhán /tru'an/ (-ana) a knavish, roguish, comic. n knave, rogue; clown, buffoon

truhanear /truane'ar/ *vi* to be a trickster, behave like a knave; play the clown

truhanería /truane'ria/ f, knavery, act of a rogue; clowning, buffoonery; collection of rogues

truhanesco /trua'nesko/ a knavish, scoundrelly; clownish

trujal /tru'hal/ m, oil or grape press; oil mill; vat for soap making

trujar /tru'har/ *vt* to partition off

trulla /'truya; 'truʎa/ f, uproar, tumult; crowd, throng

truncar /trun'kar/ *vt* to shorten, truncate; decapitate, mutilate; omit, cut out (words, etc.); curtail, abridge; mutilate, deform (texts, etc.)

truque /'truke/ m, card game; kind of hopscotch

trusa /'trusa/ f, *Cuba,* bathing suit

trust /trust/ m, *Com.* trust

tú /tu/ *pers pron 2nd sing mf* thou, you. **tratar de t.** (**a**), to address familiarly; be on intimate terms with

tu /tu/ *poss pron mf* thy, your. Used only before nouns

tuberculina /tuβerku'lina/ f, tuberculin

tubérculo /tu'βerkulo/ m, (*Zool. Med.*) tubercle; *Bot.* tubercle, tuber

tuberculoso /tuβerku'loso/ a tubercular, tuberculous

tubería /tuβe'ria/ f, piping, tubing; pipe system; pipe factory

tuberosa /tuβe'rosa/ f, tuberose

tuberoso /tuβe'roso/ a tuberous

tubo /'tuβo/ m, pipe, tube; lamp chimney; flue; *Anat.* duct, canal. **t. acústico,** speaking tube. **t. de ensayo,** test tube. **t. de escape,** exhaust pipe. **t. lanzatorpedos,** torpedo tube. **t. termiónico,** *Radio.* thermionic valve

tubular /tuβu'lar/ a tubular

tucán, tucano /tu'kan/ m toucan

tudesco /tu'ðesko/ a German

tueco /'tueko/ m, stump (of a tree); wormhole (in wood)

tuerca /'tuerka/ f, nut (of a screw)

tuerto /'tuerto/ a one-eyed. m, *Law.* tort; *pl* afterpains. **a t.,** unjustly

tueste /'tueste/ m, toasting

tuétano /'tuetano/ *m*, marrow. *Inf.* **hasta los tuétanos,** to the depths of one's being

tufillas /tu'fiyas; tu'fiʎas/ *mf Inf.* easily irritated person

tufo /'tufo/ *m*, strong smell, poisonous vapor; *Inf.* stink; side, airs, conceit (often *pl*); lock of hair over the ears

tugurio /tu'gurio/ *m*, shepherd's hut; miserable little room; *Inf.* haunt, low dive

tul /tul/ *m*, tulle

tulipa /tu'lipa/ *f*, small tulip; lampshade

tulipán /tuli'pan/ *m*, tulip

tullido /tu'yiðo; tu'ʎiðo/ *a* partially paralyzed; maimed, crippled

tullir /tu'yir; tu'ʎir/ *vt irr* to maim, cripple; paralyze; *vr* become paralyzed; be crippled. See **mullir**

tumba /'tumba/ *f*, tomb; tumble, overbalancing; somersault; Catherine wheel

tumbar /tum'bar/ *vt* to knock down; kill, drop; *Inf.* overpower, overcome (of odors, wine). *vi* fall down; *Naut.* run aground; *vr Inf.* lie down, stretch oneself out

tumbo /'tumbo/ *m*, tumble, overbalancing; undulation (of ground); rise and fall of sea waves; imminent danger; book containing deeds and privileges of monasteries and churches

tumbón /tum'bon/ *a Inf.* crafty, sly; idle, lazy. *m*, trunk with an arched lid

tumefacción /tumefak'sion; tumefak'θion/ *f*, swelling

tumefacto, túmido /tume'fakto, 'tumiðo/ *a* swollen

tumor /tu'mor/ *m*, tumor

túmulo /'tumulo/ *m*, tumulus; catafalque; mound of earth

tumulto /tu'multo/ *m*, riot, uprising; tumult, commotion, disturbance

tumultuario, tumultuoso /tumul'tuario, tumul'tuoso/ *a* noisy, tumultuous, confused

tuna /'tuna/ *f*, prickly pear tree or fruit; vagrant life; strolling student musicians (playing to raise money for charity)

tunante /tu'nante/ *a* rascally, roguish. *mf* rascal, scoundrel

tunantuelo /tunan'tuelo/ **(-la)** *n Inf.* imp, little rascal

tunda /'tunda/ *f*, shearing of cloth; *Inf.* sound beating, hiding

tundear /tunde'ar/ *vt* to beat, drub, buffet

tundidora /tundi'ðora/ *f*, woman who shears cloth; cloth-shearing machine; lawn mower

tundir /tun'dir/ *vt* to shear (cloth); mow (grass); *Inf.* beat, wallop

tunecino /tune'sino; tune'θino/ **(-na)** *a* and *n* Tunisian

túnel /'tunel/ *m*, tunnel

túnica /'tunika/ *f*, tunic, chiton; tunicle; robe

tuno /'tuno/ **(-na)** *a* knavish, rascally. *n* rascal, scoundrel

tupé /tu'pe/ *m*, forelock (of a horse); toupee; *Inf.* cheek, nerve

tupición /tupi'sion; tupi'θion/ *f*, *Lat. Am.* blockage, obstruction; cold (in the head)

tupido /tu'piðo/ *a* thick, dense; obtuse, dull, stupid; *Lat. Am.* blocked up, obstructed

tupir /tu'pir/ *vt* to thicken, make dense; press tightly; *vr* stuff oneself with food or drink

turba /'turβa/ *f*, crowd, multitude; peat

turbación /turβa'sion; turβa'θion/ *f*, disturbance; upset; perturbation; bewilderment, confusion; embarrassment

turbador /turβa'ðor/ **(-ra)** *a* disturbing, upsetting. *n* disturber, upsetter

turbamulta /turβa'multa/ *f*, *Inf.* mob, rabble

turbante /tur'βante/ *a* upsetting, perturbing. *m*, turban

turbar /tur'βar/ *vt* to disturb, upset; make turbid, muddy; bewilder, confuse; embarrass

turbera /tur'βera/ *f*, peat bog

turbiedad /turβie'ðað/ *f*, muddiness (of liquids); obscurity

turbina /tur'βina/ *f*, turbine

turbio /'turβio/ *a* turbid, muddy; troublous; turbulent, disturbed; obscure, confused (style); indistinct, blurred, *m pl*, lees, sediment (of oil)

turbión /tur'βion/ *m*, brief storm, squall; *Fig.* shower, rush

turbulencia /turβu'lensia; turβu'lenθia/ *f*, turbidity, muddiness; turbulence, commotion; disturbance, confusion

turbulento /turβu'lento/ *a* muddy, turbid; turbulent, disturbed; confused

turca /'turka/ *f*, *Inf.* drinking bout

turco /'turko/ **(-ca)** *a* Turkish. *n* Turk. *m*, Turkish (language)

turgencia /tur'hensia; tur'henθia/ *f*, swelling, turgidity

turgente /tur'hente/ *a Med.* turgescent; *Poet.* turgid, prominent, swollen

turismo /tu'rismo/ *m*, touring, tourist industry. **coche de t.,** touring car

turista /tu'rista/ *mf* tourist

turno /'turno/ *m*, turn. **por t.,** in turn

turquesa /tur'kesa/ *f*, turquoise

Turquía /tur'kia/ Turkey

turrón /tu'rron/ *m*, kind of nougat; almond paste; *Inf.* soft job, sinecure; civil service job

turulato /turu'lato/ *a Inf.* dumbfounded, speechless, inarticulate

tusa /'tusa/ *f*, *Central America* corncob; whore; *Argentina* mane (of a horse)

tutear /tute'ar/ *vt* to address as tú (instead of the formal usted); treat familiarly

tutela /tu'tela/ *f*, guardianship; tutelage; protection, defense

tuteo /tu'teo/ *m*, the use in speaking to a person of the familiar tú instead of the formal usted

tutor /tu'tor/ **(-ra)** *n* guardian. *m*, stake (for plants); protector, defender

tutoría /tuto'ria/ *f*. See **tutela**

¡tus! /tus/ *interj* word for calling dogs. **sin decir t. ni mus,** *Inf.* without saying anything

tuyo, tuya, tuyos, tuyas /'tuyo, 'tuya, 'tuyos, 'tuyas/ *poss pron 2nd sing* and *pl mf* thine, yours. Used sometimes with def. art. (e.g. *Este sombrero es el tuyo,* This hat is yours)

U

u /u/ *f*, letter U. *conjunc* Used instead of **o** or before words beginning with **o** or **ho** (e.g. *fragante u oloroso*)

ubérrimo /u'βerrimo/ *a sup* most fruitful; very abundant

ubicación /uβika'sion; uβika'θion/ *f*, situation, position, location

ubicar /uβi'kar/ *vt* to place, situate; *vi* and *vr* be situated

ubicuidad /uβikui'ðað/ *f*, ubiquity

ubicuo /u'βikuo/ *a* omnipresent; ubiquitous

ubre /'uβre/ *f*, udder

Ucrania /u'krania/ Ukraine

ucranio /u'kranio/ **(-ia)** *a* and *n* Ukrainian

¡uf! /uf/ *interj* ugh!

ufanarse /ufa'narse/ *vr* to pride oneself, put on airs

ufanía /ufa'nia/ *f*, pride, conceit

ufano /u'fano/ *a* conceited, vain; satisfied, pleased; expeditious, masterly

ujier /u'hier/ *m*, usher

úlcera /'ulsera; 'ulθera/ *f*, ulcer

ulcerar /ulse'rar; ulθe'rar/ **(se)** *vt* and *vr* to ulcerate

ulceroso /ulse'roso; ulθe'roso/ *a* ulcerous

ulpo /'ulpo/ *m*, *Chile, Peru* corn gruel

ulterior /ulte'rior/ *a* farther, ulterior; subsequent
ulteriormente /ulterior'mente/ *adv* subsequently, later
ultimación /ultima'sion; ultima'θion/ *f*, ending, finishing
ultimar /ulti'mar/ *vt* to end, conclude
ultimátum /ulti'matum/ *m*, ultimatum
último /'ultimo/ *a* last; farthermost; ultimate; top; final, definitive; most valuable, best; latter; recent. **«Última Hora.»** "Stop Press." **a última hora,** *Fig.* at the eleventh hour. **en estos últimos años,** in recent years. **a últimos de mes,** towards the end of the month. **el ú. piso,** the top floor. **por ú.,** finally. *Inf.* **estar en las últimas,** to be at the end, be finishing
ultra /'ultra/, *adv* besides; (with words like *mar*) beyond; (as prefix) excessively
ultrajar /ultra'har/ *vt* to insult; scorn, despise
ultraje /ul'trahe/ *m*, insult, outrage
ultrajoso /ultra'hoso/ *a* offensive, insulting, abusive
ultramar /ultra'mar/ *m*, overseas, abroad
ultramarino /ultrama'rino/ *a* oversea; ultramarine. *m,* foreign produce (gen. *pl*)
ultramontano /ultramon'tano/ *a* ultramontane
ultrarrojo /ultra'rroho/ *a* infrared
ultratumba /ultra'tumba/ *adv* beyond the grave
ultravioleta /ultraβio'leta/ *a* ultraviolet
úlula /'ulula/ *f*, screech owl
ululación /ulula'sion; ulula'θion/ *f*, screech, howl; hoot of an owl
ulular /ulu'lar/ *vi* to howl, shriek, screech; hoot (of an owl)
ululato /ulu'lato/ *m*, ululation
umbilical /umbili'kal/ *a* umbilical
umbral /um'bral/ *m*, threshold; *Fig.* starting point; *Archit.* lintel. **atravesar** (*or* **pisar**) **los umbrales,** to cross the threshold
umbría /um'bria/ *f*, shady place
umbrío /um'brio/ *a* shady, dark
umbroso /um'broso/ *a* shady
un /un/ *abb* of **uno, a,** one. Used before *m, sing f,* **una,** *indef art.* a, an; a; one
unánime /u'nanime/ *a* unanimous
unanimidad /unanimi'ðað/ *f*, unanimity. **por u.,** unanimously
unción /un'sion; un'θion/ *f*, anointing; *Eccl.* Extreme Unction; unction, fervor
uncir /un'sir; un'θir/ *vt* to yoke
undécimo /un'desimo; un'deθimo/ *a* eleventh
undísono /un'disono/ *a* *Poet.* sounding, sonorous (waves, etc.)
undoso /un'doso/ *a* wavy, rippling
undulación /undula'sion; undula'θion/ *f*, undulation; *Phys.* wave
undular /undu'lar/ *vi* to undulate; wriggle; float, wave (flags, etc.)
undulatorio /undula'torio/ *a* undulatory
ungimiento /unhi'miento/ *m*, anointment
ungir /un'hir/ *vt* to anoint
ungüento /uŋ'guento/ *m*, ointment; lotion; *Fig.* balm, unguent
unicelular /uniselu'lar; uniθelu'lar/ *a* unicellular
único /'uniko/ *a* unique; sole, solitary, only. **Lo ú. que se puede hacer es...,** The only thing one can do is...
unicolor /uniko'lor/ *a* of one color
unicornio /uni'kornio/ *m*, unicorn
unidad /uni'ðað/ *f*, unity; unit; (*Math. Mil.*) unit. **u. de bagaje,** piece of baggage. (of drama) **u. de lugar,** unity of place. **u. de tiempo,** unity of time
unidamente /uniða'mente/ *adv* jointly; harmoniously
unificación /unifika'sion; unifika'θion/ *f*, unification
unificar /unifi'kar/ **(se)** *vt* and *vr* to unify, unite
uniformación /uniforma'sion; uniforma'θion/ *f*, standardization
uniformar /unifor'mar/ *vt* to make uniform, standardize; put into uniform; *vr* become uniform
uniforme /uni'forme/ *a* uniform; same, similar. *m,* uniform
uniformidad /uniformi'ðað/ *f*, uniformity

unigénito /uni'henito/ *a* only-begotten. *m,* Christ
unilateral /unilate'ral/ *a* one-sided, unilateral
unión /u'nion/ *f*, union; correspondence, conformity; agreement; marriage; alliance, federation; composition, mixture; combination; proximity, nearness; (mystic) union
unionista /unio'nista/ *mf Polit.* unionist
Unión Soviética /u'nion so'βietika/ Soviet Union
unir /u'nir/ *vt* to unite, join; mix, combine; bind, fasten; connect, couple; bring together; marry; *Fig.* harmonize, conciliate; *vr* join together, unite; be combined; marry; (*with prep* a *or con*) be near to; associate with
unísono /u'nisono/ *a* unisonant. **al u.,** in unison; unanimously
unitario /uni'tario/ **(-ia)** *a* and *n* Unitarian
universal /uniβer'sal/ *a* universal; well-informed; widespread
universalidad /uniβersali'ðað/ *f*, universality
universalizar /uniβersali'sar; uniβersali'θar/ *vt* to make universal, generalize
universidad /uniβersi'ðað/ *f*, university; universality; universe
universitario /uniβersi'tario/ *a* university
universo /uni'βerso/ *a* universal. *m,* universe
uno /'uno/ (*f*, **una**) *a* a, one; single, only; same; *pl* some; about, nearly. *m,* one (number). **Tiene unos doce años,** He is about twelve. **unas pocas manzanas,** a few apples. *pron* someone; one thing, same thing; *pl* some people. **No sabe uno qué creer,** One doesn't know what to believe. **Unos dicen que no, otros que sí,** Some (people) say no, others yes. **Juan no tiene libros y le voy a dar uno,** John has no books and I am going to give him one. **Todo uno,** It's all the same. **u. a u.,** one by one. **u. que otro,** a few. **u. y otro,** both. **unos cuantos,** a few, some. **Es la una,** It is one o'clock
untar /un'tar/ *vt* to anoint; grease, oil; *Inf.* bribe; *vr* smear oneself with grease or similar thing; *Fig. Inf.* line one's pockets. **u. el carro,** *Fig.* to grease the wheels
unto /'unto/ *m*, grease; animal fat; *Fig.* balm; *Chile* shoe polish
untuoso /un'tuoso/ *a* fat, greasy
uña /'uɲa/ *f*, nail (of fingers or toes); hoof, trotter, claw; stinging tail of scorpion; thorn; stump of tree branch; *Naut.* fluke; *Fig. Inf.* light fingers (gen. *pl*). **afilarse las uñas,** to sharpen one's claws, prepare for trouble. **comerse las uñas,** to bite one's nails. **caer en las uñas de,** to fall into the clutches of. **hincar la u. (en),** to stick the claws into; to defraud, overcharge. **ser u. y carne,** to be devoted friends. **sacarle las uñas,** to use any means available
uñarada /uɲa'raða/ *f*, scratch with nails
uñero /u'ɲero/ *m*, ingrowing nail, ingrown nail
¡upa! /'upa/ *interj* Up you get! Up you go! Upsy daisy! (gen. to children)
uranio /u'ranio/ *m*, uranium
urbanidad /urβani'ðað/ *f*, civility, good manners, urbanity
urbanismo /urβa'nismo/ *m*, town planning; housing scheme
urbanización /urβanisa'sion; urβaniθa'θion/ *f*, urbanization
urbanizar /urβani'sar; urβani'θar/ *vt* to civilize, polish; urbanize
urbano /ur'βano/ *a* urban, city; urbane
urbe /'urβe/ *f*, city, metropolis
urbícola /ur'βikola/ *mf* city dweller
urdemalas /urðe'malas/ *mf*, schemer, intriguer
urdidera /urði'ðera/ *f*, warping-frame
urdimbre /ur'ðimbre/ *f*, warp; scheming, plotting
urdir /ur'ðir/ *vt* to warp; weave; scheme, intrigue
uréter /u'reter/ *m*, ureter
uretra /u'retra/ *f*, urethra
urgencia /ur'hensia; ur'henθia/ *f*, urgency; necessity; compulsion
urgente /ur'hente/ *a* urgent
urgir /ur'hir/ *vi* to be urgent; be valid, be in force (laws)

urinario /uri'nario/ *a* urinary. *m*, urinal
urna /'urna/ *f*, urn; ballot box; glass case
urraca /u'rraka/ *f*, magpie
Uruguay /uru'guai/ *m* Uruguay
uruguayo /uru'guayo/ **(-ya)** *a* and *n* Uruguayan
usado /u'saðo/ *a* worn out; accustomed, efficient. *Com.* **al u.**, in the usual form. **ropa usada,** secondhand clothing, worn clothing
usanza /usansa/ u'sanθa/ *f*, custom, usage
usar /u'sar/ *vt* to use; wear, make use of; follow (trade, occupation); *vi* be accustomed
usina /u'sina/ *f*, *Argentina* power plant
uso /'uso/ *m*, use; custom; fashion; habit; wear and tear. **al u.**, according to custom. **al u. de,** in the manner of
usted /us'teð/ *mf* you. *pl* **ustedes.** Often abbreviated to **Vd, V, Vds, VV** or **Ud, Uds**
usual /u'sual/ *a* usual; general, customary; sociable
usufructo /usu'frukto/ *m*, *Law.* usufruct; life-interest; profit
usura /u'sura/ *f*, usury; profiteering. **pagar con u.**, to pay back a thousandfold
usurario /usu'rario/ *a* usurious
usurear /usure'ar/ *vi* to lend or borrow with usury; profiteer, make excess profits
usurero /usu'rero/ **(-ra)** *n* usurer; profiteer

usurpación /usurpa'sion; usurpa'θion/ *f*, usurpation
usurpador /usurpa'ðor/ **(-ra)** *a* usurping. *n* usurper
usurpar /usur'par/ *vt* to usurp
utensilio /uten'silio/ *m*, utensil; tool, implement (gen. *pl*)
uterino /ute'rino/ *a* uterine
útero /'utero/ *m*, uterus
útil /'util/ *a* useful; profitable; *Law.* lawful (of days, etc.). *m*, usefulness, profit; *pl* **útiles,** utensils, tools
utilidad /utili'ðað/ *f*, utility; usefulness; profit
utilitario /utili'tario/ *a* utilitarian
utilitarismo /utilita'rismo/ *m*, utilitarianism
utilizable /utilisaβle; utili'θaβle/ *a* utilizable
utilización /utilisa'sion; utiliθa'θion/ *f*, utilization
utilizar /utili'sar; utili'θar/ *vt* to utilize
utillaje /uti'yahe; uti'ʎahe/ *m*, machinery
utópico /u'topiko/ *a* Utopian
uva /'uβa/ *f*, grape. **u. espina,** kind of gooseberry. **u. moscatel,** muscatel grape. *Inf.* **hecho una u.,** dead-drunk
uvero /u'βero/ **(-ra)** *a* pertaining or relating to grapes, grape. *n* grape seller
uxoricidio /uksori'siðio; uksori'θiðio/ *m*, uxoricide (act)
uxorio /uk'sorio/ *a* uxorious

V

---

v /be/ *f*, letter V. **v doble** *or* **doble v,** letter W. **V** *or* **Vd, VV,** *abbs* **vuestra (s) merced (es),** *mf sing* and *pl* you
vaca /'baka/ *f*, cow. **v. de San Antón,** *Ent.* ladybug
vacación /baka'sion; baka'θion/ *f*, vacation, holiday (gen. *pl*); vacancy; act of vacating (employment). **vacaciones retribuidas,** paid vacation
vacada /ba'kaða/ *f*, herd of cows
vacancia /ba'kansia; ba'kanθia/ *f*, vacancy
vacante /ba'kante/ *a* vacant. *f*, vacancy
vacar /ba'kar/ *vi* to be vacant; take a holiday; retire temporarily; (*with prep a*) dedicate oneself to, engage in
vaciadero /basia'ðero; baθia'ðero/ *m*, rubbish dump; sewer, drain
vaciado /ba'siaðo; ba'θiaðo/ *m*, plaster cast; *Archit.* excavation
vaciamiento /basia'miento; baθia'miento/ *m*, emptying; molding, casting; depletion
vaciar /ba'siar; ba'θiar/ *vt* to empty; drain, drink; mold, cast; *Archit.* excavate; hone; copy; *vi* flow (into) (rivers); *vr Inf.* blurt out
vaciedad /basie'ðað; baθie'ðað/ *f*, emptiness; foolishness, inanity
vacilación /basila'sion; baθila'θion/ *f*, swaying; tottering; staggering; hesitation, perplexity
vacilada /basi'laða; baθi'laða/ *Mexico,* *f* joke, trick (played on someone)
vacilante /basi'lante; baθi'lante/ *a* swaying; tottering; staggering; hesitating, vacillating
vacilar /basi'lar; baθi'lar/ *vi* to sway; totter; stagger; flicker; hesitate
vacío /ba'sio; ba'θio/ *a* empty, void; fruitless, vain; unoccupied, vacant, deserted; imperfect; hollow, empty; conceited, immature. *m*, hollow; *Anat.* flank; vacancy; shortage; *Phys.* vacuum. **v. de aire,** airpocket. **de v.,** unloaded (carts, etc.). **en v.,** in vacuo. *Inf.* **hacer el v. (a),** to send to Coventry
vacuidad /bakui'ðað/ *f*, emptiness; vacuity
vacuna /ba'kuna/ *f*, cowpox; vaccine. **v. antivariolosa,** smallpox vaccine
vacunación /bakuna'sion; bakuna'θion/ *f*, vaccination
vacunar /baku'nar/ *vt* to vaccinate; inoculate
vacuno /ba'kuno/ *a* bovine
vacuo /'bakuo/ *a* empty; vacant. *m*, void; vacuum
vadeable /baðe'aβle/ *a* fordable (rivers, etc.); *Fig.* surmountable
vadear /baðe'ar/ *vt* to ford, wade; *Fig.* overcome (ob-

stacles); *Fig.* sound, find out the opinion (of); *vr* behave
vademécum /baðe'mekum/ *m*, vade mecum; school satchel
vado /'baðo/ *m*, ford; expedient, help
vagabundear /bagaβunde'ar/ *vi* to wander, roam, loiter
vagabundeo /bagaβun'deo/ *m*, vagabondage
vagabundo /baga'βundo/ **(-da)** *a* roving, wandering; vagrant. *n* tramp, vagabond
vagamundear /bagamunde'ar/ *vi.* See **vagabundear**
vagancia /ba'gansia; ba'ganθia/ *f*, vagrancy
vagar /ba'gar/ *m*, leisure; interval, pause. *vi* be idle or at leisure; wander, roam
vagido /ba'hiðo/ *m*, cry, wail (infants)
vago /'bago/ **(-ga)** *a* vagrant, idle; vague; *Art.* indefinite, blurred. *n* idler. *m*, tramp; loafer. **en v.,** unsuccessfully, vainly
vagón /ba'gon/ *m*, wagon; (railway) coach. **v. comedor,** dining car
vagoneta /bago'neta/ *f*, open truck (railways, mines, etc.)
vaguear /bage'ar/ *vi* to roam, wander; loaf
vaguedad /bage'ðað/ *f*, vagueness; vague remark
vaharada /baa'raða/ *f*, whiff, exhalation
vahído /ba'iðo/ *m*, vertigo, dizzy spell
vaho /'bao/ *m*, vapor, fume
vaina /'baina/ *f*, scabbard; *Bot.* sheath, pod; case (scissors, etc.); *Dominican Republic* thing; *Colombia* hassle. **¡Qué vaina!** What a hassle!
vainilla /bai'niya; bai'niʎa/ *f*, *Bot.* vanilla; *Sew.* drawn-thread work
vaivén /bai'βen/ *m*, swing, sway, seesaw; instability, fluctuation
vajilla /ba'hiya; ba'hiʎa/ *f*, china; dinner service
val /bal/ *m*, *abb* **valle**
Valdepeñas /balde'peɲas/ *m*, red wine from Valdepeñas
vale /'bale/ *m*, *Com.* bond, I.O.U.; promissory note; voucher; valediction; *Lat. Am.* buddy, pal
valedero /bale'ðero/ *a* valid, binding
valedor /bale'ðor/ **(-ra)** *n* protector, sponsor
valencia /ba'lensia; ba'lenθia/ *f*, valency
valenciano /balen'siano; balen'θiano/ **(-na)** *a* and *n* Valencian
valentía /balen'tia/ *f*, bravery; heroic deed; boast; (*Art. Lit.*) dash, imagination, fire; superhuman effort
valentón /balen'ton/ *a* boastful, blustering

valer /ba'ler/ *vt irr* to protect; defend; produce (income, etc.); cost; *vi* be worth; deserve; have power or authority; be of importance or worth; be a protection; be current (money); be valid; *vr* (*with de*) make use of. *m,* value, worth. **Vale,** *Spain* OK. **v. la pena,** to be worthwhile. **v. tanto como cualquiera,** to be as good as the next guy, be as good as the next fellow. **¡Válgame Dios!** Heavens! Bless me! **Más vale así,** It's better thus. **Vale más ser cola de león que cabeza de ratón.** Better a big frog in a small puddle than a small frog in a big puddle. *Pres. Ind.* **valgo, vales,** etc. *Fut.* **valdré,** etc. *Condit.* **valdría,** etc. *Pres. Subjunc.* **valga,** etc.

valeriana /bale'riana/ *f,* valerian

valeroso /bale'roso/ *a* active, energetic; courageous; powerful

valetudinario /baletuði'nario/ *a* valetudinarian

valía /ba'lia/ *f,* value, price; influence, worth; faction, party. **a las valías,** at the highest price

validación /baliða'sion; baliða'θion/ *f,* validation; force, soundness

validar /bali'ðar/ *vt* to make strong; validate

validez /bali'ðes; bali'ðeθ/ *f,* validity

valido /ba'liðo/ *a* favorite, esteemed. *m,* court favorite; prime minister

válido /ba'liðo/ *a* firm, sound, valid; strong, robust

valiente /ba'liente/ *a* strong, robust; courageous; active; excellent; excessive, enormous (gen. *Ironic.*); boastful

valija /ba'liha/ *f,* valise, suitcase, grip; mail bag; mail

valimiento /bali'miento/ *m,* value; favor; protection, influence

valioso /ba'lioso/ *a* valuable; powerful; wealthy

valisoletano /balisole'tano/ **(-na)** *a* and *n* of or from Valladolid

valla /'baya; 'baʎa/ *f,* barricade, paling; stockade; *Fig.* obstacle. **v. publicitaria,** billboard

vallado /ba'yaðo; ba'ʎaðo/ *m,* stockade; enclosure; *Mexico* deep ditch

valle /'baye; 'baʎe/ *m,* valley; vale; river-basin

valor /ba'lor/ *m,* worth, value; price; courage; validity; power; yield, income; insolence; *pl Com.* securities

valoración /balora'sion; balora'θion/ *f,* valuation; appraisement

valorar /balo'rar/ *vt* to value; appraise

valorización /balorisa'sion; baloriθa'θion/ *f,* valuation

valquiria /bal'kiria/ *f,* Valkyrie

vals /bals/ *m,* waltz

valsar /bal'sar/ *vi* to waltz

valuación /balua'sion; balua'θion/ *f.* See **valoración**

valuar /balu'ar/ *vt* to value; appraise; assess

valva /'balβa/ *f, Zool.* valve

válvula /'balβula/ *f, Mech.* valve. *Auto.* **v. de cámara (del neumático),** tire-valve. **v. de seguridad,** safety-valve

vampiro /bam'piro/ *m,* vampire; *Fig.* bloodsucker

vanagloria /bana'gloria/ *f,* vaingloriousness, conceit

vanagloriarse /banaglo'riarse/ *vr* to be conceited

vanaglorioso /banaglo'rioso/ **(-sa)** *a* conceited. *n* boaster

vanamente /bana'mente/ *adv* vainly; without foundation; superstitiously; arrogantly

vandálico /ban'daliko/ *a* Vandal

vandalismo /banda'lismo/ *m,* vandalism; destructiveness

vándalo /'bandalo/ **(-la)** *a* and *n* Vandal

vanguardia /baŋ'guarðia/ *f,* vanguard; *pl* outerworks. **a v.,** in the forefront

vanidad /bani'ðað/ *f,* vanity; ostentation; empty words; illusion. *Inf.* **ajar la v. de,** to take (a person) down a peg

vanidoso /bani'ðoso/ **(-sa)** *a* vain; ostentatious. *n* conceited person

vano /'bano/ *a* vain; hollow, empty; useless, ineffectual; unsubstantial, illusory. *m,* span (bridge). **v. único,** single span. **en v.,** uselessly, in vain

vapor /ba'por/ *m,* steam, vapor; fainting fit; steamboat; *pl* hysterics. **v. de ruedas, v. de paleta,** paddle steamer. **v. volandero,** tramp steamer. **al v.,** full steam ahead; *Inf.* with all speed

vaporable /bapo'raβle/ *a* vaporizable

vaporación /bapora'sion; bapora'θion/ *f,* evaporation

vaporización /baporisa'sion; baporiθa'θion/ *f,* vaporization

vaporizador /baporisa'ðor; baporiθa'ðor/ *m,* vaporizer; spray, sprayer

vaporizar /bapori'sar; bapori'θar/ *vt* to vaporize; spray

vaporoso /bapo'roso/ *a* vaporous; ethereal; gauzy

vapulación /bapula'sion; bapula'θion/ *f,* **vapulamiento** *m,* whipping

vapular /bapu'lar/ *vt* to whip

vapuleo /bapu'leo/ *m,* whipping, spanking

vaquería /bake'ria/ *f,* herd of cattle; dairy; dairy farm

vaquero /ba'kero/ **(-ra)** *n* cowboy; **vaqueros,** *m, pl* jeans

vaquilla /ba'kiya; ba'kiʎa/ *f,* heifer

vara /'bara/ *f,* staff; rod; wand (of authority); vara (2.8 feet); shaft (of cart). **v. de aforar,** water gauge

varada /ba'raða/ *f, Naut.* running aground

varadero /bara'ðero/ *m,* shipyard

varar /ba'rar/ *vi Naut.* to run aground; *Fig.* be held up (negotiations, etc.); *vt Naut.* put in dry dock

varear /bare'ar/ *vt* to knock down (fruit from tree); beat (with a rod); measure with a vara; sell by the rod; *vr* grow thin

variabilidad /bariaβili'ðað/ *f,* variableness

variable /ba'riaβle/ *a* variable; changeable, inconsistent

variación /baria'sion; baria'θion/ *f,* variation

variado /ba'riaðo/ *a* varied; variegated

variante /ba'riante/ *a* varying. *f,* variant; discrepancy

variar /ba'riar/ *vt* to vary; change; *vi* change; be different

varice /ba'rise; ba'riθe/ *f,* varix

varicela /bari'sela; bari'θela/ *f,* chicken pox

varicoso /bari'koso/ *a* varicose

variedad /barie'ðað/ *f,* variety; change; inconstancy, instability; alteration; variation; *Biol.* variety

varilla /ba'riya; ba'riʎa/ *f, dim* rod; rib (fan, umbrella). **v. de virtudes,** conjurer's wand. *Mech.* **v. percusora,** tappet rod

vario /'bario/ *a* different, diverse; inconstant, changeable; variegated; *pl* several, a few

variopinto /bario'pinto/ *a* motley

varón /ba'ron/ *m,* male; man

varonil /baro'nil/ *a* male; manly

Varsovia /bar'soβia/ *f,* Warsaw

varsoviano /barso'βiano/ **(-na)** *a* and *n* of or from Warsaw

vasallaje /basa'yahe; basa'ʎahe/ *m,* vassalage; dependence; tribute money

vasallo /ba'sayo; ba'saʎo/ **(-lla)** *n* vassal. *a* vassal; dependent

vasco /'basko/ **(-ca), vascongado (-da)** *a* and *n* Basque

vascuence /bas'kuense; bas'kuenθe/ *m,* Basque (language); *Inf.* gibberish

vaselina /base'lina/ *f,* vaseline

vasija /ba'siha/ *f,* vessel, receptacle, jar

vaso /'baso/ *m,* receptacle; glass, tankard, mug; glassful; (*Naut. Anat. Bot.*) vessel; garden-urn; vase

vástago /'bastago/ *m,* stem, shoot; offspring, descendant; piston rod

vastedad /baste'ðað/ *f,* extensiveness, largeness, vastness

vasto /'basto/ *a* vast, extensive

vate /'bate/ *m,* bard; seer

vaticano /bati'kano/ *a* and *m,* Vatican

vaticinar /batisi'nar; batiθi'nar/ *vt* to prophesy, foretell

vaticinio /bati'sinio; bati'θinio/ *m,* prediction

vatímetro /ba'timetro/ *m,* water meter

vatio /'batio/ *m,* watt. **v. hora,** watt hour

ve /be/ *f,* name of the letter V. **v. doble** *or* **doble v.,** name of the letter W

vecinal /besi'nal; beθi'nal/ *a* neighboring, adjacent

vecindad /besin'daθ; beθin'daθ/ f, neighborhood; *Lat. Am.* slum. **buena v.,** good neighborliness. **hacer mala v.,** to be a nuisance to one's neighbors

vecindario /besin'dario; beθin'dario/ m, neighborhood; population of a district

vecino /be'sino; be'θino/ **(-na)** a neighboring; near; similar. n neighbor; citizen; inhabitant

vector /bek'tor/ m, carrier (of disease)

veda /'beða/ f, close season; prohibition

vedamiento /beða'miento/ m, prohibition

vedar /be'ðar/ vt to forbid; prevent

vedija /be'ðiha/ f, tangled lock of hair; piece of matted wool; curl (of smoke)

veedor /bee'ðor/ **(-ra)** a prying. n busy-body. m, inspector; overseer

vega /'bega/ f, fertile lowland plain; meadow

vegada /be'gaða/ f. See **vez**

vegetable /behe'taβle/ a and m, vegetable

vegetación /beheta'sion; beheta'θion/ f, vegetation

vegetal /behe'tal/ a vegetal; plant. m, vegetable, plant

vegetar /behe'tar/ vi to flourish, grow (plants); *Fig.* vegetate

vegetarianismo /behetaria'nismo/ m, vegetarianism

vegetariano /beheta'riano/ **(-na)** a and n vegetarian

vegetativo /beheta'tiβo/ a vegetative

vehemencia /bee'mensia; bee'menθia/ f, vehemence

vehemente /bee'mente/ a vehement; vivid

vehículo /be'ikulo/ m, vehicle; means, instrument

veinte /'beinte/ a and m, twenty; twentieth

veintena /bein'tena/ f, a score

veinticinco /beinti'sinko; beinti'θinko/ a and m, twenty-five; twenty-fifth

veinticuatro /beinti'kuatro/ a and m, twenty-four; twenty-fourth

veintidós /beinti'ðos/ a and m, twenty-two; twenty-second

veintinueve /beinti'nueβe/ a and m, twenty-nine; twenty-ninth

veintiocho /bein'tiotʃo/ a and m, twenty-eight; twenty-eighth

veintiséis /beinti'seis/ a and m, twenty-six; twenty-sixth

veintisiete /beinti'siete/ a and m, twenty-seven; twenty-seventh

veintitrés /beinti'tres/ a and m, twenty-three; twenty-third

veintiuno /bein'tiuno/ a and m, twenty-one; twenty-first. Abbreviates to **veintiún** before a noun (even if one or more adjectives intervene)

vejación /beha'sion; beha'θion/ f, ill-treatment, persecution

vejamen /be'hamen/ m, irritation, provocation; taunt; lampoon

vejar /be'har/ vt to ill-treat, persecute; plague

vejatorio /beha'torio/ a vexing, annoying

vejete /be'hete/ m, *Inf.* silly old man

vejez /be'hes; be'heθ/ f, oldness; old age; platitude. **vejeces,** pl ailments of old age. *Inf.* **a la v.,** **viruelas,** the older the madder

vejiga /be'higa/ f, bladder; blister. **v. natatoria,** float (of a fish)

vela /'bela/ f, vigil; watch; pilgrimage; sentinel; watchman; candle; *Naut.* sail; awning; night work, overtime. **v. de cangreja,** boom sail. **v. de mesana,** mizzen sail. **v. de trinquete,** foresail. **v. latina,** lateen sail. **a toda v.,** with all speed. **alzar velas,** to hoist sail. **en v.,** wakeful, without sleep. *Inf.* **estar entre dos velas,** to be tipsy

velación /bela'sion; bela'θion/ f, vigil; watch; marriage ceremony of veiling (gen. *pl*)

velada /be'laða/ f, vigil; watch; evening party

velado /be'laðo/ a veiled; dim; (of voice) thick, indistinct

velador /bela'ðor/ **(-ra)** a watchful; vigilant. m, candlestick; small round table; *Mexico* lampshade. n watcher, guard

velar /be'lar/ vi to watch, be wakeful; work overtime or at night; *Eccl.* watch; *Fig.* (with *por*) watch over,

defend; vt veil; conceal; *Photo.* blur; (with *prep* a) wake (corpse); sit with (patient at night)

veleidad /belei'ðað/ f, velleity; fickleness

veleidoso /belei'ðoso/ a inconstant, changeable

velero /be'lero/ **(-ra)** m, sailing ship; sailmaker. n candlemaker

veleta /be'leta/ f, weathercock; float, quill (fishing). *mf* changeable person

velís /be'lis/ m, *Mexico* suitcase.

vello /'beyo; 'beʎo/ m, down, soft hair

vellocino /beyo'sino; beʎo'θino/ m, wool; fleece

vellón /be'yon; be'ʎon/ m, fleece; copper and silver alloy formerly used in sense of "sterling'; *Obs.* copper coin

vellosidad /beyosi'ðað; beʎosi'ðað/ f, downiness, hairiness

velloso /be'yoso; be'ʎoso/ a downy, hairy

velludo /be'yuðo; be'ʎuðo/ a hairy, downy. m, plush, velvet

velo /'belo/ m, veil; curtain; *Eccl.* humeral veil; excuse, pretext; *Zool.* velum. **v. del paladar,** soft palate. **correr el v.,** to disclose a secret. **tomar el v.,** to take the veil, become a nun

velocidad /belosi'ðað; beloθi'ðað/ f, speed; *Mech.* velocity. *Aer.* **v. ascensional,** rate of climb. *Mech.* **v. del choque,** speed of impact. **en gran v.,** by passenger train. **en pequeña v.,** by goods train

velocímetro /belo'simetro; belo'θimetro/ m, *Mexico* speedometer

velódromo /be'loðromo/ m, velodrome

velón /be'lon/ m, oil lamp

velorio /be'lorio/ m, *Lat. Am.* (funeral) wake; dull party

veloz /be'los; be'loθ/ a swift; quick-thinking or acting

vena /'bena/ f, (*Bot. Anat.*) vein; streak, veining (in wood or stone); *Mineral.* seam; underground spring; inspiration. **estar de v.,** to be in the mood; be inspired

venablo /be'naβlo/ m, javelin

venado /be'naðo/ m, venison; deer

venal /be'nal/ a venous; saleable; venal

venalidad /benali'ðað/ f, saleableness; venality

vencedor /bense'ðor; benθe'ðor/ **(-ra)** a conquering. n conqueror

vencer /ben'ser; ben'θer/ vt to conquer; defeat; overcome, rise above; outdo, excel; restrain, control (emotions); convince, persuade; vi succeed, triumph; *Com.* fall due, mature; *Com.* expire; vr control oneself; twist, incline; *Argentina* wear out. **La habitación vence a las doce,** Check-out time is twelve o'clock

vencible /ben'siβle; ben'θiβle/ a conquerable; superable

vencimiento /bensi'miento; benθi'miento/ m, defeat; conquest, victory; bend, twist (of things); *Com.* expiration; *Com.* maturity (of a bill)

venda /'benda/ f, bandage; fillet. **tener v. en los ojos,** to be blind (to the truth)

vendaje /ben'dahe/ m, bandage

vendar /ben'dar/ vt to bandage; *Fig.* blind (generally passions)

vendaval /benda'βal/ m, strong wind

vendedor /bende'ðor/ **(-ra)** a selling. n seller

vender /ben'der/ vt to sell; betray; vr sell oneself; be sold; risk all (for someone); *Fig.* give away (secret); (with *por*) sell under false pretences. **al contado,** to sell for cash. **v. al por mayor,** to sell wholesale. **v. al por menor,** to sell retail. **venderse caro,** to be unsociable

vendí /ben'di/ m, *Com.* certificate of sale

vendible /ben'diβle/ a purchasable; saleable

vendimia /ben'dimia/ f, vintage; profit, fruits

vendimiar /bendi'miar/ vt to harvest the grapes; take advantage of; *Inf.* kill

veneno /be'neno/ m, poison; venom; danger (to health or soul); evil passion

venenoso /bene'noso/ a poisonous, venomous

venera /be'nera/ f, scallop-shell (pilgrim's badge); badge, decoration

veneración /benera'sion; benera'θion/ *f*, respect, veneration

venerador /benera'ðor/ **(-ra)** *a* venerating. *n* venerator, respector

venerar /bene'rar/ *vt* to venerate; worship

venéreo /be'nereo/ *a* venereal

venero /be'nero/ *m*, spring of water; horary line on sundial; origin, genesis; *Mineral.* bed

venezolano /beneso'lano; beneθo'lano/ **(-na)** *a* and *n* Venezuelan

vengador /beŋga'ðor/ **(-ra)** *a* avenging. *n* avenger

venganza /beŋ'gansa; beŋ'ganθa/ *f*, revenge

vengar /beŋ'gar/ *vt* to avenge; *vr* avenge oneself

vengativo /beŋga'tiβo/ *a* vindictive

venia /'benia/ *f*, pardon, forgiveness; permission; inclination of head (in greeting); *Law.* license issued to minors to manage their own estate

venial /be'nial/ *a* venial

venialidad /beniali'ðað/ *f*, veniality

venida /be'niða/ *f*, arrival, coming; return; attack (fencing); precipitancy

venidero /beni'ðero/ *a* future. *Poet.* **la vida venidera**, the hereafter

venideros /beni'ðeros/ *m pl*, successors; posterity

venir /be'nir/ *vi irr* to come; arrive; turn up (at cards); fit, suit; consent, agree; *Agr.* grow; follow, come after, succeed; result, originate; occur (to the mind); feel, experience; (*with prep a* + *infin.*) happen finally, come to pass; (*with en*) decide, resolve; *vr* ferment. **v. a menos**, to deteriorate, decline; come upon evil days. **v. a pelo**, to come opportunely, be just right. **v. a ser**, to become. **venirse abajo**, to fall, collapse. **¿A qué viene este viaje?** What is the purpose of this journey? **el mes que viene**, next month. **El vestido te viene muy ancho**, The dress is too wide for you. **Me vino la idea de marcharme**, It occurred to me to leave. **en lo por venir**, in the future. *Pres. Ind.* **vengo, vienes, viene, venimos, venís, vienen.** *Pres. Part.* **viniendo.** *Fut.* **vendré, etc.** *Condit.* **vendría, etc.** *Preterite* **vine, viniste, vino, vinimos, vinisteis, vinieron.** *Pres. Subjunc.* **venga, etc.** *Imperf. Subjunc.* **viniese, etc.**

venta /'benta/ *f*, selling; sale; inn; *Inf.* wilderness; *pl Com.* turnover. **v. pública,** auction. **a la v.,** on sale. **la V. de la Mesilla,** the Gadsden Purchase

ventada /ben'taða/ *f*, gust of wind

ventaja /ben'taha/ *f*, advantage; profit

ventajoso /benta'hoso/ *a* advantageous; *Lat. Am.* unscrupulous

ventana /ben'tana/ *f*, window. **v. de guillotina,** sash window. **v. salediza,** bay window. **echar algo por la v.,** to waste a thing

ventanal /benta'nal/ *m*, large window

ventanilla /benta'niya; benta'niλa/ *f*, small window (as in railway compartments); grill (ticket office, bank, etc.); nostril

ventarrón /benta'rron/ *m*, high wind

ventear /bente'ar/ *v impers* to blow (of the wind); *vt* sniff air (animals); air, dry; investigate; *Lat. Am.* brand (an animal); *vr* be spoiled by air (tobacco, etc.)

ventero /ben'tero/ **(-ra)** *n* innkeeper

ventilación /bentila'sion; bentila'θion/ *f*, ventilation; ventilator; current of air

ventilador /bentila'ðor/ *m*, ventilating fan; ventilator

ventilar /benti'lar/ *vt* to ventilate; shake, winnow; air; discuss

ventisca /ben'tiska/ *f*, snowstorm

ventiscar, ventisquear /bentis'kar, bentiske'ar/ *v impers* to snow with a high wind

ventisquero /bentis'kero/ *m*, glacier; snowfield, snowdrift; snowstorm

ventolera /bento'lera/ *f*, gust of wind; *Inf.* boastfulness; whim, caprice

ventolina /bento'lina/ *f*, *Lat. Am.* sudden gust (of wind)

ventor /ben'tor/ **(-ra)** *n* pointer (dog)

ventosa /ben'tosa/ *f*, vent (pipes, etc.); *Zool.* sucker; *Surg.* cupping glass

ventoso /ben'toso/ *a* windy; flatulent

ventrículo /ben'trikulo/ *m*, ventricle

ventrílocuo /ben'trilokuo/ **(-ua)** *a* ventriloquial. *n* ventriloquist

ventriloquia /bentri'lokia/ *f*, ventriloquism

ventrudo /ben'truðo/ *a* big-bellied

ventura /ben'tura/ *f*, happiness; chance, hazard; risk, danger. **a la v.,** at a venture. **buena v.,** good luck. **por v.,** perhaps; by chance; fortunately

venturoso /bentu'roso/ *a* fortunate

Venus /'benus/ *m*, Venus. *f*, beautiful woman, beauty

ver /ber/ *vt irr* to see; witness, behold; visit; inspect, examine; consider; observe; know, understand; *Lat. Am.* look at, watch (television, etc.) (*with de* + *infin.*) try to; *vr* be seen; show oneself, appear; experience, find oneself; exchange visits; meet. **v. mundo,** to travel. **V. y creer,** Seeing is believing. **A mi v.,** In my opinion. **¡A v.!** Let's see!; Wait and see! **no tener nada que v. con,** to have no connection with, nothing to do with. **Veremos,** Time will tell. **Verse en la casa,** to be a stay-at-home. **Ya se ve,** Of course, Naturally. *Pres. Ind.* **veo, ves, etc.** *Imperf.* **veía, etc.** *Past Part.* **visto.** *Pres. Subjunc.* **vea, etc.** *Imperf. Subjunc.* **viese, etc.**

vera /'bera/ *f*, edge; border; shore. **a la v.,** on the edge, on the verge

veracidad /berasi'ðað; beraθi'ðað/ *f*, truthfulness, veracity

veranada /berana'ðero/ *m*, summer pasture

veraneante /berane'ante/ *mf* summer resident, summer vacationist, holiday-maker

veranear /berane'ar/ *vi* to spend the summer

veraneo /bera'neo/ *m*, summer vacation, summer holidays, summering

veraniego /bera'niego/ *a* summer; light, unimportant

verano /be'rano/ *m*, summer; dry season *West Hem.*

veras /'beras/ *f pl*, reality, truth; fervor, earnestness. **de v.,** really; in earnest

veraz /be'ras/ *a* truthful, veracious

verbal /ber'βal/ *a* verbal; oral

verbena /ber'βena/ *f*, *Bot.* verbena, vervain; fair held on eve of a saint's day

verbigracia /berβi'grasia; berβi'graθia/ *adv* for instance. *m*, example

verbo /'berβo/ *m*, word; vow; *Gram.* verb. **v. activo** *or* **v. transitivo,** active or transitive verb. **v. auxiliar,** auxiliary verb. **v. intransitivo** *or* **v. neutro,** intransitive or neuter verb. **v. reflexivo** *or* **v. recíproco,** reflexive verb

verbosidad /berβosi'ðað/ *f*, verbosity

verboso /ber'βoso/ *a* verbose, prolix

verdad /ber'ðað/ *f*, truth, veracity; reality. **a la v.,** indeed; without doubt. **en v.,** in truth; indeed. **cantar cuatro verdades a alguien,** to tell someone a few home truths. **la pura v.,** the plain truth

verdadero /berða'ðero/ *a* true; real; sincere; truthful

verdal /ber'ðal/ *a* green. **ciruela v.,** greengage

verde /'berðe/ *a* green; unripe; fresh (vegetables); youthful; immature, undeveloped; obscene, dissolute. *m*, green (color); verdure, foliage

verdear /berðe'ar/ *vi* to look green; be greenish; grow green

verdecer /berðe'ser; berðe'θer/ *vi irr* to grow green, be verdant. See **conocer**

verdegay /berðe'gai/ *a* and *m*, bright green

verdemar /berðe'mar/ *a* and *m*, sea-green

verdín /ber'ðin/ *m*, verdure; mold; verdigris

verdinegro /berði'negro/ *a* dark green

verdor /ber'ðor/ *m*, verdure; greenness; strength; youth (also *pl*)

verdoso /ber'ðoso/ *a* greenish

verdugo /ber'ðugo/ *m*, hangman, executioner; wale, mark; shoot of tree; switch; whip; *Fig.* scourge; tyrant

verdulera /berðu'lera/ *f*, greengrocer; market woman; *Inf.* harridan

verdulería /berðule'ria/ *f*, greengrocer's shop

verdulero /berðu'lero/ *m*, greengrocer

verdura /ber'ðura/ *f*, verdure; green garden produce, vegetables (gen. *pl*); *Art.* foliage; obscenity

verecundo /bere'kundo/ *a* bashful

vereda /be'reða/ *f*, footpath; sheep track; *Argentina, Chile, Peru* sidewalk

veredicto /bere'ðikto/ *m*, *Law.* verdict; judgment, considered opinion

verga /'berga/ *f*, steel bow of crossbow; *Naut.* yard; *Inf.* penis

vergajo /ber'gaho/ *m*, rod (for punishment)

vergel /ber'hel/ *m*, orchard

vergonzoso /bergon'soso; bergon'θoso/ **(-sa)** *a* shameful; bashful, shamefaced. *n* shy person

vergüenza /ber'guensa; ber'guenθa/ *f*, shame; self-respect; bashfulness, timidity; shameful act; public punishment

vericueto /beri'kueto/ *m*, narrow, stony path

verídico /be'riðiko/ *a* veracious; true, exact

verificación /berifika'sion; berifika'θion/ *f*, verification, checking; *Law.* **v. de un testamento,** probate

verificador /berifika'ðor/ **(-ra)** *a* verifying, checking. *n* inspector, checker

verificar /berifi'kar/ *vt* to prove; verify; *vr* take place, happen; check; come true. *Elec.* **v. las conexiones,** to check the connections

verisímil /beri'simil/ *a* credible, probable

verisimilitud /berisimili'tuð/ *f*, credibility

verismo /be'rismo/ *m*, realism; truthfulness

verja /'berha/ *f*, grating, grill; railing

vermífugo /ber'mifugo/ *a* and *m*, vermifuge

vermut /ber'mut/ *m*, vermouth

vernáculo /ber'nakulo/ *a* native, vernacular

vernal /ber'nal/ *a* vernal

verónica /be'ronika/ *f*, *Bot.* speedwell; veronica (bull-fighting)

verosímil /bero'simil/ *a* credible, probable

verosimilitud /berosimili'tuð/ *f*, verisimilitude, probability

verraco /be'rrako/ *m*, boar

verruga /be'rruga/ *f*, *Med.* wart; *Inf.* bore; defect

versar /ber'sar/ *vi* to revolve; (*with sobre*) concern, deal with (book, etc.); *vr* become versed (in). **La campaña versó en torno sobre tres temas,** The campaign revolved around three issues

versátil /ber'satil/ *a* *Zool.* versatile; changeable; fickle

versatilidad /bersatili'ðað/ *f*, *Zool.* versatility; changeableness; fickleness

versículo /ber'sikulo/ *m*, versicle; verse (of the Bible)

versificación /bersifika'sion; bersifika'θion/ *f*, versification

versificador /bersifika'ðor/ **(-ra)** *n* versifier

versificar /bersifi'kar/ *vi* to write verses; *vt* put into verse, versify

versión /ber'sion/ *f*, translation; version; account

verso /'berso/ *m*, poetry, verse; stanza; line (of a poem). **v. suelto,** blank verse

vertebrado /berte'βraðo/ *a* and *m*, *Zool.* vertebrate

vertedor /berte'ðor/ *m*, drain, sewer; chute

verter /ber'ter/ *vt irr* to pour; spill; empty; translate; *vi* flow. See **entender**

vertical /berti'kal/ *a* and *f*, vertical

verticalidad /bertikali'ðað/ *f*, verticality

vértice /'bertise; 'bertiθe/ *m*, vertex

vertiente /ber'tiente/ *a* emptying. *mf*, slope; incline; watershed; *Lat. Am. also* spring (of water)

vertiginoso /bertihi'noso/ *a* giddy; vertiginous

vértigo /'bertigo/ *m*, giddiness, faintness

vesícula /be'sikula/ *f*, blister; (*Anat. Bot.*) vesicle

vespertino /besper'tino/ *a* evening

vestíbulo /bes'tiβulo/ *m*, hall, vestibule foyer

vestido /bes'tiðo/ *m*, dress; clothes; *Panama, Peru* suit

vestidura /besti'ðura/ *f*, garment; *pl* vestments

vestigio /bes'tihio/ *m*, footprint; trace; mark; remains; *Fig.* vestige

vestir /bes'tir/ *vt irr* to clothe; dress; adorn; embellish (ideas); *Fig.* disguise (truth); simulate, pretend; *vi* be dressed; *vr* dress oneself; *Fig.* be covered. See **pedir**

vestuario /bes'tuario/ *m*, clothing, dress; *Theat.* wardrobe or dressing room; *Eccl.* vestry; *Mil.* uniform

Vesubio /be'suβio/ Vesuvius

veta /'beta/ *f*, vein; stripe, rib (fabric)

veterano /bete'rano/ **(-na)** *a* and *n* veteran

veterinaria /beteri'naria/ *f*, veterinary science

veterinario /beteri'nario/ *a* veterinary. *m*, veterinary surgeon

veto /'beto/ *m*, veto; prohibition

vetustez /betus'tes; betus'teθ/ *f*, antiquity, oldness

vetusto /be'tusto/ *a* ancient, very old

vez /bes; beθ/ *f*, time, occasion; turn; *pl* proxy, deputy, substitute. **a la v.,** simultaneously. **alguna v.,** sometime. **a su v.,** in its (her, his, their) turn. **a veces,** sometimes. **de una v.,** at the same time, all at once. **de v. en cuando,** from time to time. **en v. de,** instead of. **hacer las veces de,** to be a substitute for. **otra v.,** again. **Su cuarto es dos veces más grande que éste,** His room is twice as large as this one

vía /'bia/ *f*, way; road; railway track or gauge; *Anat.* tract; (mystic) way; route; conduct; *pl* procedure. **v. ancha,** broad gauge (railway). **v. angosta,** narrow gauge. **v. de agua,** *Naut.* leak. *Law.* **v. ejecutiva,** seizure, attachment. **v. férrea,** railway. **v. láctea,** Milky Way. **v. muerta,** railway siding. **v. principal,** main line. **v. pública,** public thoroughfare. **v. romana,** Roman road. **v. secundaria,** *Rail.* side line. **por v. aérea,** by air, by airplane

viabilidad /biaβili'ðað/ *f*, viability

viable /'biaβle/ *a* viable; practicable; workable; passable

viaducto /bia'ðukto/ *m*, viaduct

viajante /bia'hante/ *mf* traveling salesman, commercial traveler

viajar /bia'har/ *vi* to travel, journey, voyage

viaje /'biahe/ *m*, journey; voyage; water-supply; travel journal; *Naut.* **v. de ensayo,** trial trip. **v. redondo,** circular tour. **¡Buen v.!** Have a good trip! Bon voyage!

viajero /bia'hero/ **(-ra)** *a* traveling. *n* traveler; passenger

vianda /'bianda/ *f*, viand, victual (gen. *pl*); meal

viático /'biatiko/ *m*, *Eccl.* viaticum; provisions for a journey

víbora /'biβora/ *f*, viper; *Lat. Am.* poisonous snake

viborezno /biβo'resno; biβo'reθno/ *m*, young viper

vibración /biβra'sion; biβra'θion/ *f*, vibration; jar, jolt; thrill

vibrante /bi'βrante/ *a* shaking; vibrant; thrilling

vibrar /bi'βrar/ *vt* to shake, oscillate; *vi* vibrate; jar, jolt; quiver, thrill

vibratorio /biβra'torio/ *a* vibratory, vibrative

vicaría /bika'ria/ *f*, vicarage; vestry

vicario /bi'kario/ *a* vicarious. *m*, vicar; curate; deputy

vicecónsul /bise'konsul; biθe'konsul/ *m*, vice-consul

viceconsulado /bisekonsu'laðo; biθekonsu'laðo/ *m*, vice-consulate

vicepresidente /bisepresi'ðente; biθepresi'ðente/ **(-ta)** *n* vice president

vicesecretario /bisesekre'tario; biθesekre'tario/ **(-ia)** *n* assistant secretary

viciar /bi'siar; bi'θiar/ *vt* to corrupt; adulterate; forge; annul; interpret maliciously, misconstrue; *vr* become vicious

vicio /'bisio; 'biθio/ *m*, vice; defect; error, fraud; bad habit; excess, exaggerated desire; viciousness (animals); overgrowth (plants); mischief (children). **tener el v. de,** to have the bad habit of. **el v. del juego,** fondness for gambling

vicioso /bi'sioso; bi'θioso/ *a* vicious; vigorous, overgrown; abundant; *Inf.* spoiled (children)

vicisitud /bisisi'tuð; biθisi'tuð/ *f*, vicissitude

víctima /'biktima/ *f*, victim

victimar /bikti'mar/ *vt*, *Lat. Am.* to murder

victimario, -a /bikti'mario/ *mf*, *Lat. Am.* killer, murderer

¡víctor! /'biktor/ *interj* Victor!; Long live!; Hurrah!

victoria /bik'toria/ *f*, victory, triumph; victoria

victoriano /bikto'riano/ **(-na)** *a* and *n* Victorian

victorioso /bikto'rioso/ *a* victorious

vicuña /bi'kuɲa/ *f* vicuna

vid /bið/ *f*, vine

vida /'biða/ *f*, life; livelihood; human being;

biography; vivacity. **v. airada,** dissolute life. **la v. allende la muerte,** life after death. **de por v.,** for life. **darse buena v.,** to live comfortably; enjoy one's life. **dar mala v.,** to ill-treat. **en la v.,** in life; never. **ganarse la v.,** to make one's living

vidente /bi'ðente/ *m,* clairvoyant; seer

videocámara /biðeo'kamara/ *f,* video camera; camcorder.

videograbación /biðeograβa'sion; biðeograβa'θion/ *f,* videotape

vidriar /bi'ðriar/ *vt* to glaze (earthenware)

vidriera /bi'ðriera/ *f,* glass window (gen. stained or colored)

vidriero /bi'ðriero/ *m,* glazier. *a* made of glass

vidrio /'biðrio/ *m,* glass; anything made of glass; fragile thing; touchy person. **v. inastillable,** safetyglass. **v. jaspeado,** frosted glass. **v. pintado** *or* **v. de color,** stained glass. **v. plano,** plate glass. **v. soplado,** blown glass

vidrioso /bi'ðrioso/ *a* brittle; slippery; fragile; hypersensitive; *Fig.* glazed (eyes)

vieja /'bieha/ *f,* old woman

viejo /'bieho/ *a* old; ancient; former; old-fashioned; worn out. *m,* old man

Viena /'biena/ Vienna

vienés /bie'nes/ **(-esa)** *a* and *n* Viennese

viento /'biento/ *m,* wind; scent (of game, etc.); guy (rope); upheaval; vanity. **v. en popa,** *Naut.* following wind; without a hitch, prosperously. **vientos alisios,** trade-winds. **v. terral,** land wind. **a los cuatro vientos,** in all directions. **contra v. y marea,** *Fig.* against all obstacles. **correr malos vientos,** to be unfavorable (of circumstances). **refrescar el v.,** to stiffen (of the breeze)

vientre /'bientre/ *m,* stomach; belly; vitals; *Law.* venter

viernes /'biernes/ *m,* Friday. **V. Santo,** Good Friday

viga /'biga/ *f,* beam, rafter; girder; joist; mill beam. **v. maestra,** main beam or girder. **la v. de tu ojo,** the beam in your eye

vigente /bi'hente/ *a* valid; in force (laws, customs)

vigésimo /bi'hesimo/ *a* twentieth

vigía /bi'hia/ *f,* watch tower; (gen. *m*) look-out, watch

vigilancia /bihi'lansia; bihi'lanθia/ *f,* watchfulness, vigilance; watch patrol

vigilante /bihi'lante/ *a* watchful. *m,* watcher; watchman. **v. escolar,** truant officer

vigilar /bihi'lar/ *vi* to watch over; supervise

vigilia /bi'hilia/ *f,* vigil; wakefulness; night study; *Eccl.* vigil, eve; wake; *Mil.* watch. **día de v.,** fast-day

vigor /bi'gor/ *m,* strength; activity; vigor, efficiency; validity

vigorizar /bigori'sar; bigori'θar/ *vt* to invigorate; exhilarate; encourage

vigoroso /bigo'roso/ *a* strong, vigorous

vihuela /bi'uela/ *f,* lute

vil /bil/ *a* vile, infamous; base; despicable; untrustworthy

vileza /bi'lesa; bi'leθa/ *f,* baseness; vileness, infamy

vilipendiar /bilipen'diar/ *vt* to revile

vilipendio /bili'pendio/ *m,* vilification; contempt

villa /'biya; 'biʎa/ *f,* villa; country house; town. **v. miseria** *Argentina* slum

villancico /biyan'siko; biʎan'θiko/ *m,* carol

villanesco /biya'nesko; biʎa'nesko/ *a* peasant; rustic, country

villanía /biya'nia; biʎa'nia/ *f,* humbleness of birth; vileness; villainy

villano /bi'yano; bi'ʎano/ **(-na)** *n* peasant. *a* rustic, country; boorish; base

vilo, en /'bilo, en/ *adv* hanging in the air; *Fig.* in suspense

vilorta /bi'lorta/ *f,* hoop; *Mech.* washer

vilote /bi'lote/ *mf, Lat. Am.* chicken, coward

vinagre /bi'nagre/ *m,* vinegar

vinagrera /bina'grera/ *f,* vinegar bottle; table cruet; *Lat. Am.* heartburn

vinagreta /bina'greta/ *f,* vinegar sauce

vinagroso /bina'groso/ *a* vinegary; *Inf.* bad-tempered, acid

vinatero /bina'tero/ **(-ra)** *n* wine merchant. *a* wine

vincapervinca /binkaper'βinka/ *f, Bot.* periwinkle

vinculación /binkula'sion; binkula'θion/ *f, Law.* entail

vincular /binku'lar/ *vt Law.* to entail; *Fig.* base; *vr* perpetuate. *a Law.* entail

vínculo /'binkulo/ *m,* tie, bond; *Law.* entail

vindicación /bindika'sion; bindika'θion/ *f,* vindication; justification; excuse

vindicador /bindika'ðor/ **(-ra)** *n* vindicator. *a* vindicative

vindicar /bindi'kar/ *vt* to avenge; vindicate; justify; excuse

vindicativo /bindika'tiβo/ *a* avenging; vindicatory

vinería /bine'ria/ *f, Lat. Am.* wineshop

vinícola /bi'nikola/ *a* wine-growing; wine

vinicultor /binikul'tor/ **(-ra)** *n* wine grower, viniculturalist

vinicultura /binikul'tura/ *f,* wine-growing, viniculture

vinificación /binifika'sion; binifika'θion/ *f,* vinification

vinillo /bi'niyo; bi'niʎo/ *m,* thin, weak wine

vino /'bino/ *m,* wine; fermented fruit juice. **v. de Oporto,** port wine. **v. generoso,** well-matured wine. **v. tinto,** red wine

vinoso /bi'noso/ *a* vinous; fond of wine

viña /'biɲa/ *f,* vineyard

viñador /biɲa'ðor/ *m,* vineyard-keeper; vine-cultivator

viñedo /bi'ɲeðo/ *m,* vineyard

viñeta /bi'ɲeta/ *f,* vignette

viola /'biola/ *f, Mus.* viola; *Bot.* viola, pansy. *mf* viola player

violación /biola'sion; biola'θion/ *f,* violation; infringement; rape

violado /bio'laðo/ *a* violet

violador /biola'ðor/ **(-ra)** *n* violator seducer, rapist

violar /bio'lar/ *vt* to violate; infringe; rape; spoil, harm

violencia /bio'lensia; bio'lenθia/ *f,* violence; outrage; rape

violentar /biolen'tar/ *vt* to force; falsify, misinterpret; force an entrance; *vr* force oneself

violento /bio'lento/ *a* violent; repugnant; impetuous; hasty-tempered; unnatural, false; unreasonable

violeta /bio'leta/ *f, Bot.* violet. *m,* violet color. **v. de febrero,** snowdrop

violín /bio'lin/ *m,* violin

violinista /bioli'nista/ *mf* violinist

violón /bio'lon/ *m,* double-bass, bass viol; double-bass player

violoncelista /biolonse'lista; biolonθe'lista/ *mf* cellist

violoncelo /biolon'selo; biolon'θelo/ *m,* cello

viperino /bipe'rino/ *a* viperine; venomous, evil

vira /'bira/ *f,* welt (of a shoe); dart

viraje /bi'rahe/ *m, Auto.* change of direction; bend, turn

virar /bi'rar/ *vt Naut.* to put about; *Photo.* tone; *vi Naut.* tack; *Auto.* change direction. **v. de bordo,** *Naut.* to lay off

virgen /'birhen/ *mf* virgin; *f, Astron.* Virgo

virginal /birhi'nal/ *a* virginal; pure, unspotted

virginidad /birhini'ðað/ *f,* virginity

virgulilla /birgu'liya; birgu'liʎa/ *f,* comma; cedilla; accent; apostrophe; fine line

viril /bi'ril/ *a* manly, virile. *m,* clear glass screen

virilidad /birili'ðað/ *f,* virility

virote /bi'rote/ *m,* arrow; shaft; *Inf.* young blood; *Mexico* roll (bread)

virreina /bi'rreina/ *f,* vicereine

virreinato /birrei'nato/ *m,* viceroyship

virrey /bi'rrei/ *m,* viceroy

virtual /bir'tual/ *a* virtual; implicit

virtualidad /birtuali'ðað/ *f,* virtuality

virtualmente /birtual'mente/ *adv* virtually; tacitly

virtud /bir'tuð/ *f,* virtue; power; strength, courage; efficacy. **en v. de,** in virtue of

virtuosidad /birtuosi'ðað/ *f*, virtuosity
virtuoso /bir'tuoso/ *a* virtuous; powerful, efficacious. *m*, virtuoso, artist
viruela /bi'ruela/ *f*, smallpox (gen. *pl*)
virulencia /biru'lensia; biru'lenθia/ *f*, virulence
virulento /biru'lento/ *a* virulent
virus /'birus/ *m*, virus
viruta /bi'ruta/ *f*, wood-shaving
visa /'bisa/ *f*, *Lat. Am.* visa
visado /bi'saðo/ *m*, *Spain* visa
visaje /bi'sahe/ *m*, grimace
visar /bi'sar/ *vt* to visa; endorse
vis cómica /bis 'komika/ *f*, the comic spirit
viscosidad /biskosi'ðað/ *f*, viscosity
viscoso /bis'koso/ *a* viscous, sticky
visera /bi'sera/ *f*, visor; eye-shade; peak (of a cap)
visibilidad /bisiβili'ðað/ *f*, visibility
visillo /bi'siyo; bi'siʎo/ *m*, window-blind
visión /bi'sion/ *f*, seeing, sight; queer sight; vision; hallucination; *Inf.* scarecrow, sight
visionario /bisio'nario/ **(-ia)** *a* and *n* visionary
visir /bi'sir/ *m*, vizier. **gran v.**, grand vizier
visita /bi'sita/ *f*, visit; visitor; inspection. **v. de cumplido**, formal call. **v. de sanidad**, health inspection. **hacer una v.**, to pay a call
visitación /bisita'sion; bisita'θion/ *f*, visitation; visit
visitador /bisita'ðor/ **(-ra)** *n* regular visitor. *m*, inspector. *a* visiting; inspecting
visitar /bisi'tar/ *vt* to visit; inspect; *Med.* attend; *Eccl.* examine. **v. los monumentos**, to see the sights, go sightseeing
visiteo /bisi'teo/ *m*, receiving or paying of visits
vislumbrar /bislum'βrar/ *vt* to glimpse; surmise, conjecture
vislumbre /bis'lumbre/ *f*, glimmer, glimpse; surmise, glimmering (gen. *pl*); semblance, appearance
viso /'biso/ *m*, view point, elevation; glare; shimmer, gleam; colored slip under transparent dress; semblance. **de v.**, prominent (persons)
visón /bi'son/ *m*, mink
víspera /'bispera/ *f*, eve; *Eccl.* day before festival; prelude, preliminary. *pl Eccl.* vespers. **en vísperas de**, on the eve of
vista /'bista/ *f*, vision, sight; view; eyes; eyesight; meeting, interview; *Law.* hearing (of a case); apparition; picture of a view; clear idea; connection (of things); proposition, intention; glance; *pl* window, door, skylight, opening for light. **v. corta**, short sight. **v. de lince**, sharp eyes. **a primera v.**, at first sight. **a v. de,** in sight of; in the presence of. **conocer de v.,** to know by sight. **dar una v.,** to take a look. **doble v.,** second sight; clairvoyance. **en v. de,** in view of, considering. **estar a la v.,** to be evident. *Inf.* **hacer la v. gorda,** to turn a blind eye. **¡Hasta la v.!** Good-bye! **perder de v. (a),** to lose sight of
vistazo /bis'taso; bis'taθo/ *m*, glance. **echar un v.,** to cast a glance. **Dale un v.,** Look it over
visto /'bisto/ *past part irr* **ver**. *Law.* whereas. **bien v.,** approved. **mal v.,** disapproved. **V. Bueno (Vº Bº)** Approved, Passed. **v. que,** since, inasmuch as
vistoso /bis'toso/ *a* showy, gaudy; beautiful
visual /bi'sual/ *a* visual
vital /bi'tal/ *a* vital; essential
vitalicio /bita'lisio; bita'liθio/ *a* lifelong. *m*, life-insurance
vitalidad /bitali'ðað/ *f*, vitality
vitamina /bita'mina/ *f*, vitamin
vitando /bi'tando/ *a* odious; bad; vital
vitela /bi'tela/ *f*, vellum
vitícola /bi'tikola/ *a* viticultural. *mf* viticulturist
viticultura /bitikul'tura/ *f*, viticulture
¡vítor! /'bitor/ *interj* Victor!; Hurrah!; Long live!
vitorear /bitore'ar/ *vt* to cheer; applaud, acclaim
vítreo /'bitreo/ *a* glassy, vitreous
vitrificar /bitrifi'kar/ **(se)** *vt* and *vr* to vitrify
vitrina /bi'trina/ *f*, show-case; display cabinet; *Argentina, Chile, Venezuela* (shop) window
vitriólico /bi'trioliko/ *a* vitriolic
vitriolo /bi'triolo/ *m*, vitriol

vitualla /bi'tuaya; bi'tuaʎa/ *f*, (gen. *pl*) victuals, provisions
vituperable /bitupe'raβle/ *a* blameworthy, vituperable
vituperador /bitupera'ðor/ **(-ra)** *a* vituperative. *n* vituperator
vituperar /bitupe'rar/ *vt* to censure, blame, vituperate
vituperio /bitu'perio/ *m*, vituperation
viuda /'biuða/ *f*, widow
viudedad /biuðe'ðað/ *f*, widow's pension
viudez /biu'ðes; biu'ðeθ/ *f*, widowhood
viudita /biu'ðita/ *f*, young widow
viudo /'biuðo/ *m*, widower
¡viva! /'biβa/ *interj* Long live!; Hurrah!
vivacidad /biβasi'ðað; biβaθi'ðað/ *f*, vivacity, gaiety; ardor, warmth; brightness
vivamente /biβa'mente/ *adv* quickly, lively
vivandera /biβan'dera/ *f*, vivandiere
vivandero /biβan'dero/ *m*, sutler
vivaque /bi'βake/ *m*, bivouac
vivaquear /biβake'ar/ *vi* to bivouac
vivar /bi'βar/ *m*, warren; aquarium; breeding ground; well (of a fishing boat); *vt*, *Lat. Am.* to cheer, shout hurrah (for...)
vivaracho /biβa'ratʃo/ *a Inf.* sprightly, cheery, lively
vivaz /bi'βas; bi'βaθ/ *a* vigorous; quick-witted; sprightly; *Bot.* perennial; vivid, bright
víveres /'biβeres/ *m pl*, provisions; *Mil.* stores
vivero /bi'βero/ *m*, *Bot.* nursery; vivarium; small marsh
viveza /bi'βesa; bi'βeθa/ *f*, quickness, briskness; vehemence; perspicuity; witticism; resemblance; brightness (eyes, colors); thoughtless word or act
vividero /biβi'ðero/ *a* habitable
vívido /'biβiðo/ *a Poet.* vivid
vividor /biβi'ðor/ **(-ra)** *a* frugal, thrifty; dissolute. *n* liver; long-liver; libertine, rake
vivienda /bi'βienda/ *f*, dwelling
viviente /bi'βiente/ *a* living
vivificación /biβifika'sion; biβifika'θion/ *f*, vivification
vivificante /biβifi'kante/ *a* vivifying
vivificar /biβifi'kar/ *vt* to vivify; comfort
vivir /bi'βir/ *vi* to be alive, live; last, endure; (*with en*) inhabit. *m*, life. **¿Quién vive?** *Mil.* Who goes there? **v. a costillas ajenas,** to live at someone else's expense, live off someone else
vivisección /biβisek'sion; biβisek'θion/ *f*, vivisection
vivo /'biβo/ *a* alive; intense, strong; bright; *Mil.* active; subtle, ingenious; precipitate; *Fig.* lasting, enduring; diligent; hasty; persuasive, expressive. *m*, edge. **al v., a lo v.,** to the life; vividly
vizcaíno /bis'kaino; biθ'kaino/ **(-na)** *a* and *n* Biscayan
Vizcaya, el Golfo de /bis'kaya, el 'golfo de; biθ'kaya, el 'golfo de/ the Bay of Biscay
vizconde /bis'konde; biθ'konde/ *m*, viscount
vizcondesa /biskon'desa; biθkon'desa/ *f*, viscountess
vocablo /bo'kaβlo/ *m*, word
vocabulario /bokaβu'lario/ *m*, vocabulary
vocación /boka'sion; boka'θion/ *f*, vocation; trade, profession
vocal /bo'kal/ *a* vocal; oral. *f*, *Gram.* vowel. *mf* voting member
vocalización /bokalisa'sion; bokaliθa'θion/ *f*, vocalization
vocalizar /bokali'sar; bokali'θar/ *vi* to vocalize
voceador, -a /bosea'ðor; boθea'ðor/ *mf*, *Lat. Am.* newsvendor
vocear /bose'ar; boθe'ar/ *vi* to cry out, shout; *vt* proclaim; call for; acclaim
vocerío /bose'rio; boθe'rio/ *m*, shouting, clamor, outcry
vociferación /bosifera'sion; boθifera'θion/ *f*, vociferation, outcry
vociferar /bosife'rar; boθife'rar/ *vt* to boast (of); *vi* shout, vociferate
vocinglería /bosiŋgle'ria; boθiŋgle'ria/ *f*, clamor; babble, chatter

vocinglero /bosiŋ'glero/ boθiŋ'glero/ a vociferous; prattling, babbling
vodca /'booka/ m, vodka
volada /bo'laða/ f, short flight; *Mexico* flat tire, flat. *Mech.* **v. de grúa,** jib
voladura /bola'ðura/ f, explosion; blasting
volandas (en), volandillas (en) /bolan'diyas; bo'landas, bolan'diʎas/ *adv* in the air, as though flying; *Inf.* in a trice
volante /bo'lante/ a flying; wandering, restless. *m,* frill, flounce; screen; fan (of a windmill); *Mech.* flywheel; *Mech.* balance wheel (watches); coiner's stamp mill; shuttle-cock. *Auto.* **v. de dirección,** steering-wheel
volantón /bolan'ton/ (-ona) *n* fledgling
volar /bo'lar/ *vi irr* to fly (birds, insects, aviation); float in the air; hurry; disappear suddenly; burst, explode; jut out (buttresses, etc.); cleave (air) (arrows, etc.); *Fig.* spread (rumors); *vt* explode; blast; anger. See **contar**
volatería /bolate'ria/ f, fowling; fowls; poultry; flock of birds; *Fig.* crowd (of ideas)
volátil /bo'latil/ a volatile; inconstant
volatilizar /bolatili'sar; bolatili'θar/ *vt* to volatilize
volatinero /bolati'nero/ (-ra) *n* tight-rope walker, acrobat
volcán /bol'kan/ m, volcano; violent passion. **v. extinto,** extinct volcano
volcánico /bol'kaniko/ a volcanic
volcar /bol'kar/ *vt irr* to overturn, capsize; make dizzy; cause a change (of opinion); annoy; *vi* overturn. *Pres. Ind.* **vuelco, vuelcas, vuelca, vuelcan.** *Preterite* **volqué, volcaste, etc.** *Pres. Subjunc.* **vuelque, vuelqués, vuelque, vuelquen**
volear /bole'ar/ *vt* to strike in the air, volley; *Agr.* sow broadcast
voleo /bo'leo/ m, volley (tennis, etc.); high kick; straight punch
volframio /bol'framio/ m, wolfram, tungsten
volición /boli'sion; boli'θion/ f, volition
volquete /bol'kete/ m, tip-cart
voltaico /bol'taiko/ a voltaic
voltaje /bol'tahe/ m, voltage
voltario /bol'tario/ a versatile; capricious; headstrong
volteador /boltea'ðor/ (-ra) *n* acrobat
voltear /bolte'ar/ *vt* to whirl, turn; overturn; change place (of); *Archit.* construct an arch or vault; *vi* revolve; tumble, twirl (acrobats)
volteo /bol'teo/ m, turning, revolution; whirl; overturning; twirling; *Elec.* voltage
voltereta /bolte'reta/ f, somersault
volteriano /bolte'riano/ a Voltairian
voltímetro /bol'timetro/ m, voltmeter
voltio /'boltio/ m, volt
volubilidad /boluβili'ðað/ f, inconstancy, fickleness
voluble /bo'luβle/ a easily turned; inconstant, changeable; *Bot.* twining
volumen /bo'lumen/ m, bulk, size; volume, book
voluminoso /bolumi'noso/ a voluminous, bulky
voluntad /bolun'tað/ f, will, volition; wish; decree; free will; intention; affection; free choice; consent. **a v.,** at will; by choice. **de buena v.,** of good will; willingly, with pleasure. **de su propia v.,** of one's own free will. **mala v.,** hostility, ill-will
voluntario /bolun'tario/ (-ia) a voluntary; strong-willed. *n* volunteer
voluntarioso /bolunta'rioso/ a self-willed
voluptuosidad /boluptuosi'ðað/ f, voluptuousness
voluptuoso /bolup'tuoso/ a voluptuous
volver /bol'βer/ *vt irr* to turn; turn over; return; pay back; direct, aim; translate; restore; change, alter; close (doors, etc.); vomit; reflect, reverberate; *vi* come back; continue (speech, etc.); bend, turn (roads); (*with prep a* + *infin.*) do something again (e.g. *v. a leer,* to read over again); (*with por* + *noun*)

protect; *vr* become; go sour; turn. **v. a las filas,** *Mil.* to reduce to the ranks. **v. en sí,** to regain consciousness. **v. la cabeza,** to turn one's head. **volverse** **atrás,** *Fig.* to back out. **volverse loco,** to go mad. See **resolver**
vomitar /bomi'tar/ *vt* to vomit; *Fig.* vomit forth; *Fig.* spit out (curses, etc.); *Inf.* burst into confidences
vomitivo /bomi'tiβo/ a and m, emetic
vómito /'bomito/ m, vomit
voracidad /borasi'ðað; boraθi'ðað/ f, voracity
vorágine /bo'rahine/ f, vortex, whirlpool
voraz /bo'ras; bo'raθ/ a voracious; *Mexico* bold
vórtice /'bortise; 'bortiθe/ m, whirlpool; *Fig.* vortex
vortiginoso /bortihi'noso/ a vortical
vos /bos/ *pers pron 2nd pers sing* and *pl* you; *Central America* you (familiar)
vosear /bose'ar/ *vt* to use the pronoun *vos*; address (someone) as *vos*
vosotros, vosotras /bo'sotros, bo'sotras/ *pers pron 2nd pers pl mf* you
votación /bota'sion; bota'θion/ f, voting
votador /bota'ðor/ (-ra) *n* voter; swearer
votar /bo'tar/ *vi* and *vt* to vote; make a vow; curse, swear. **v. una proposición de confianza,** to pass a vote of confidence
votivo /bo'tiβo/ a votive
voto /'boto/ m, vote; vow; voter; prayer; curse; desire; opinion. **v. de calidad,** casting vote. **v. de confianza,** vote of confidence
voz /bos; boθ/ f, voice; sound, noise; cry, shout (gen. *pl*); word; expression; *Mus.* singer or voice; *Gram.* mood; vote; rumor; instruction, order. **v. común,** general opinion. **a voces,** in a shout, loudly. **llevar la v. cantante,** *Inf.* to have the chief say
vuelco /'buelko/ m, overturning
vuelo /'buelo/ m, flight; wing; *Sew.* skirt-fullness; ruffle, frill; *Archit.* buttress. **v. a ciegas,** *Aer.* blind flying. **v. de distancia,** long-distance flight. **v. de patrulla,** patrol or reconnaissance flight. **v. de reconocimento,** reconnaissance flight. **v. nocturno,** *Aer.* night flying. **v. sin parar,** non-stop flight. **al v.,** on the wing; in passing; quickly. **alzar** (*or* **levantar**) **el v.,** to take flight
vuelta /'buelta/ f, revolution; turn; bend; curve; return; restitution; recompense; repetition; wrong side; beating; *Sew.* facing, cuff; change (money); conning (lessons, etc.); stroll, walk; change; vault, ceiling; *Sports.* round; *Mech.* **vueltas por minuto,** revolutions per minute. **a v. de correo,** by return mail, by return of post. **a la v.,** on returning; overleaf. **dar la v.,** to turn round, make a détour. **dar una v.,** to take a stroll. **dar vueltas,** to revolve; search (for); consider. **media v.,** half turn
vuelto /'buelto/ m, *Lat. Am.* change (money returned)
vuestro, vuestra, vuestros, vuestras /'buestro, 'buestra, 'buestros, 'buestras/ *poss pron 2nd pl mf* your, yours
vulcanizar /bulkani'sar; bulkani'θar/ *vt* to vulcanize
vulgar /bul'gar/ a popular; general, common; vernacular; mediocre
vulgaridad /bulgari'ðað/ f, vulgarity
vulgarismo /bulga'rismo/ m, vulgarism
vulgarización /bulgariθa'sion; bulgariθa'θion/ f, vulgarization; popularization
vulgarizar /bulgari'sar; bulgari'θar/ *vt* to vulgarize; popularize; translate into the vernacular; *vr* grow vulgar
vulgata /bul'gata/ f, Vulgate
vulgo /'bulgo/ *adv* commonly known as. *mpl,* the masses
vulnerabilidad /bulneraβili'ðað/ f, vulnerability
vulnerable /bulne'raβle/ a vulnerable
vulpeja /bul'peha/ f, vixen
vulpino /bul'pino/ a vulpine; crafty

WXYZ

wagneriano /wagne'riano/ a Wagnerian

wáter /'water/ m, toilet, water-closet

whisky /'wiski/ m, whiskey

xenofobia /seno'foβia/ f, xenophobia, hatred of foreigners

xilófago /si'lofago/ a xylophagous, wood-boring. m, wood-borer

xilófono /si'lofono/ m, xylophone

xilografía /silogra'fia/ f, xylography

y /i/ conjunc and. See **e**

ya /ya/ adv already; formerly; soon; now; finally; immediately; well, yes, quite. Used of past, present and future time, and in various idiomatic ways. **Ha venido ya,** He has already come. **¡Ya caerá!** His time will come!, He will get his comeuppance! **Ya vendrá,** He will come soon. **¡Ya voy!** Coming! **¡Ya verás!** You'll see! **¡Ya lo creo!** Of course!; I should think so! **¡Ya!** Quite!; I understand. **ya no,** no longer. **ya que,** since

yacaré /yaka're/ m, Lat. Am. alligator

yacente /ya'sente; ya'θente/ a recumbent, reclining (statues, etc.)

yacer /ya'ser; ya'θer/ vi irr to be lying at full length; lie (in the grave); be situated, be; lie (with), sleep (with); graze by night. Pres. Ind. **yazgo** or **yazco, yaces,** etc. Pres. Subjunc. **yazga** or **yazca,** etc.

yacija /ya'siha; ya'θiha/ f, bed; couch; tomb

yacimiento /yasi'miento; yaθi'miento/ m, Geol. bed, deposit

yacio /'yasio; 'yaθio/ m, india-rubber tree

yaguré /yagu're/ m, Lat. Am. skunk

yak /yak/ m, yak

yanqui /'yanki/ a and mf contemptuous and offensive North American (gen. U.S.A.)

yarda /'yarða/ f, yard (English measure)

yate /'yate/ m, Naut. yacht

ye /ye/ f, name of the letter Y

yegua /'yegua/ f, mare

yelmo /'yelmo/ m, helmet

yema /'yema/ f, bud; yolk (of egg); sweetmeat; Fig. best of anything. **y. del dedo,** finger-tip

yerba mate /'yerβa 'mate/ m mate (drink)

yermo /'yermo/ a uninhabited, deserted; uncultivated. m, wilderness, desert

yerno /'yerno/ m, son-in-law

yerro /'yerro/ m, error; mistake; fault

yerto /'yerto/ a stiff, rigid

yesca /'yeska/ f, tinder; fuel; stimulus

yeso /'yeso/ m, gypsum, calcium sulphate; plaster; plaster cast

yesquero /yes'kero/ m, Lat. Am. (cigarette) lighter

yidish /'yiðis/ n and a Yiddish

yip /yip/ m jeep

yo /yo/ pers pron 1st sing mf I. **el yo,** the ego

yodo /'yoðo/ m, iodine

yuca /'yuka/ f, yucca

yucateco /yuka'teko/ (-ca) a and n Yucatecan

yugo /'yugo/ m, yoke; nuptial tie; oppression; Naut. transom; Fig. **sacudir el y.,** to throw off the yoke

yugular /yugu'lar/ a Anat. jugular. m, jugular vein

Yukón, el /yu'kon, el/ the Yukon

yunque /'yunke/ m, anvil; patient, undaunted person; hard worker; Anat. incus

yunta /'yunta/ f, yoke (of oxen, etc.)

yute /'yute/ m, jute fiber or fabric

yuxtaponer /yukstapo'ner/ vt irr to juxtapose. See **poner**

yuxtaposición /yukstaposi'sion; yukstaposi'θion/ f, juxtaposition

zabarcera /saβar'sera; θaβar'θera/ f, vegetable seller

zaborda /sa'βorða; θa'βorða/ f, **zabordamiento** m, grounding, stranding

zabordar /saβor'ðar; θaβor'ðar/ vi Naut. to run aground, strand

zacatín /saka'tin; θaka'tin/ m, street or square where clothes are sold

zafadura /safa'ðura; θafa'ðura/ f, Lat. Am. dislocation, sprain

zafar /sa'far; θa'far/ vt to embellish, garnish, adorn; Naut. lighten (a ship); vr escape, hide oneself; (with de) excuse oneself, avoid; get rid of

zafarrancho /safa'rrantʃo; θafa'rrantʃo/ m, Naut. clearing the decks; Inf. damage; Inf. scuffle

zafiedad /safie'ðað; θafie'ðað/ f, rudeness, ignorance, boorishness

zafio /'safio; 'θafio/ a rude, unlettered, boorish

zafiro /sa'firo; θa'firo/ m, sapphire

zafra /'safra; 'θafra/ f, olive oil container; sugar crop or factory; Mineral. waste

zaga /'saga; 'θaga/ f, rear. m, last player. **en z.,** behind. Inf. **no quedarse en z.,** not to be left behind; be not inferior

zagal /sa'gal; θa'gal/ m, youth; strong, handsome lad; young shepherd; full skirt

zagala /sa'gala; θa'gala/ f, maiden, girl; young shepherdess

zagual /sa'gual; θa'gual/ m, paddle

zaguán /sa'guan; θa'guan/ m, entrance hall; vestibule

zaguero /sa'gero; θa'gero/ a loitering, straggling. m, Sports. back

zahareño /saa'reɲo; θaa'reɲo/ a untamable, wild (birds); unsociable, disdainful

zaherimiento /saeri'miento; θaeri'miento/ m, upbraiding; nagging

zaherir /sae'rir; θae'rir/ vt irr to upbraid, reprehend; nag. See **herir**

zahína /sa'ina; θa'ina/ f, Bot. sorghum

zahón /sa'on; θa'on/ m, leather apron (worn by cowboys)

zahorí /sao'ri; θao'ri/ m, soothsayer; waterfinder; sagacious person

zahúrda /sa'urða; θa'urða/ f, pigsty

zaino /'saino; 'θaino/ a treacherous; vicious (horses); chestnut (horses); black (cows)

zalagarda /sala'garða; θala'garða/ f, ambush; skirmish; snare, trap; Inf. trick, ruse; Inf. mock battle

zalamería /salame'ria; θalame'ria/ f, adulation, flattery

zalamero /sala'mero; θala'mero/ (-ra) a wheedling, flattering. n flatterer

zalea /sa'lea; θa'lea/ f, sheepskin

zalear /sale'ar; θale'ar/ vt to shake; frighten away (dogs)

zalema /sa'lema; θa'lema/ f, salaam

zamacuco /sama'kuko; θama'kuko/ m, Inf. oaf, dolt; Inf. drinking bout

zamarra /sa'marra; θa'marra/ f, sheepskin jacket

zamarrear /samarre'ar; θamarre'ar/ vt to worry, shake (prey); Fig. Inf. beat up; Inf. floor, confound

zambo /'sambo; 'θambo/ (-ba) a knock-kneed. n, Lat. Am. person of mixed African and indigenous origin

zambomba /sam'βomba; θam'βomba/ f, rustic drum

zambuco /sam'βuko; θam'βuko/ m, Inf. concealment (especially of cards)

zambullida /sambu'yiða; θambu'ʎiða/ f, plunge, submersion; thrust (in fencing)

zambullir /sambu'yir; θambu'ʎir/ vt to plunge in water, submerge; vr hide oneself, cover oneself

zampar /sam'par; θam'par/ vt to conceal (one thing in another); eat greedily; (with en) arrive suddenly

zampatortas /sampa'tortas; θampa'tortas/ mf Inf. glutton

zampoña /sam'poɲa; θam'poɲa/ f, rustic flute; Inf. unimportant word

zanahoria /sana'oria; θana'oria/ f, carrot

zanca /'sanka; 'θanka/ f, long leg (birds); Inf. long thin leg; Archit. stringboard (of stairs)

zancada /san'kaða; θan'kaða/ f, swift stride
zancadilla /sanka'ðiya; θanka'ðiʎa/ f, trip (wrestling); Inf. trick, deceit. **echar la z.** (a), to trip up
zancajear /sankahe'ar; θankahe'ar/ vi to stride about
zancajo /san'kaho; θan'kaho/ m, heel-bone; torn heel (stocking, shoe); Inf. ill-shaped person. Inf. **no llegarle al z.**, to be immensely inferior to someone
zancajoso /sanka'hoso; θanka'hoso/ a flatfooted; slovenly
zanco /'sanko; 'θanko/ m, stilt. Fig. Inf. **andar** (or **estar**) **en zancos**, to have gone up in the world
zancudo /san'kuðo; θan'kuðo/ a long-legged
zangandungo /saŋgan'duŋgo; θaŋgan'duŋgo/ (**-ga**) n Inf. loafer
zanganear /saŋgane'ar; θaŋgane'ar/ vi Inf. to loaf
zángano /'saŋgano; 'θaŋgano/ m, Ent. drone; Inf. idler, parasite
zangolotear /saŋgolote'ar; θaŋgolote'ar/ vt Inf. to shake violently; vi fuss about, bustle; vr rattle (windows, etc.)
zangoloteo /saŋgolo'teo; θaŋgolo'teo/ m, shaking; rattling
zanguango /saŋ'guaŋgo; θaŋ'guaŋgo/ m, Inf. lazybones
zanja /'sanha; 'θanha/ f, trench, ditch; drain; furrow
zanjar /san'har; θan'har/ vt to excavate; Fig. remove (obstacles)
Zanzíbar /san'siβar; θan'θiβar/ Zanzibar
zapa /'sapa; 'θapa/ f, shovel, spade; Mil. sap; sandpaper
zapador /sapa'ðor; θapa'ðor/ m, Mil. sapper
zapapico /sapa'piko; θapa'piko/ m, pick-ax; mattock
zapaquilda /sapa'kilda; θapa'kilda/ f, Inf. she-cat
zapar /sa'par; θa'par/ vi Mil. to sap
zaparrastrar /saparras'trar; θaparras'trar/ vi Inf. to trail along the floor (dresses)
zapata /sa'pata; θa'pata/ f, half-boot; piece of leather used to stop creaking of a hinge; Archit. lintel; (Naut. Mech.) shoe
zapatazo /sapa'taso; θapa'taθo/ m, blow with a shoe; fall, thud; stamping (horses); flap (of sail)
zapateado /sapate'aðo; θapate'aðo/ m, dance in which rhythmic drumming of heels plays important part
zapatear /sapate'ar; θapate'ar/ vt to hit with a shoe; stamp feet; drum heels (in dancing); Inf. ill-treat; thump ground (rabbits); vi stamp (horses); Naut. flap (sails); vr Fig. stand one's ground
zapateo /sapa'teo; θapa'teo/ m, stamping; rhythmic drumming of heels
zapatera /sapa'tera; θapa'tera/ f, cobbler's wife; woman who makes or sells shoes
zapatería /sapate'ria; θapate'ria/ f, shoemaking; shoe shop
zapatero /sapa'tero; θapa'tero/ m, shoemaker; shoe seller. **z. remendón**, cobbler
zapateta /sapa'teta; θapa'teta/ f, caper, leap
zapatilla /sapa'tiya; θapa'tiʎa/ f, slipper; trotter, hoof
zapato /sa'pato; θa'pato/ m, shoe. **z. de hule** Mexico, galosh, rubber
zapatón /sapa'ton; θapa'ton/ m, Lat. Am. galosh, overshoe
¡zape! /'sape; 'θape/ interj Inf. shoo! Used for frightening away cats; exclamation of surprise or warning
zapear /sape'ar; θape'ar/ vt to scare away cats; Inf. frighten off
zaque /'sake; 'θake/ m, leather bottle, wineskin; Inf. drunkard, sot
zaquizamí /sakisa'mi; θakiθa'mi/ m, garret; dirty little house or room
zar /sar; θar/ m, tsar
zarabanda /sara'βanda; θara'βanda/ f, saraband; Inf. racket, row
zaragata /sara'gata; θara'gata/ f, Inf. fight, brawl
Zaragoza /sara'gosa; θara'goθa/ Saragossa
zaragozano /sarago'sano; θarago'θano/ (**-na**) a and n Saragossan
zaragüelles /sara'gueyes; θara'gueʎes/ m, pl wide pleated breeches

zaranda /sa'randa; θa'randa/ f, sieve, strainer, colander
zarandajas /saran'dahas; θaran'dahas/ f, pl Inf. odds and ends
zarandar /saran'dar; θaran'dar/ vt to sieve (grapes, grain); strain; Inf. pick out the best; vr Inf. move quickly
zarandillo /saran'diyo; θaran'diʎo/ m, small sieve, strainer; Inf. a live wire, energetic person; Spanish dance
zaraza /sa'rasa; θa'raθa/ f, chintz
zarcillo /sar'siyo; θar'θiʎo/ m, earring; Bot. tendril; Agr. trowel
zarco /'sarko; 'θarko/ a light blue (generally eyes or water)
zarpa /'sarpa; 'θarpa/ f, Naut. weighing anchor; paw
zarpada /sar'paða; θar'paða/ f, blow with a paw
zarpar /sar'par; θar'par/ vt and vi Naut. to weigh anchor, sail
zarza /'sarsa; 'θarθa/ f, Bot. bramble, blackberry bush
zarzal /sar'sal; θar'θal/ m, bramble patch
zarzamora /sarsa'mora; θarθa'mora/ f, blackberry
zarzaparrilla /sarsapa'rriya; θarθapa'rriʎa/ f, sarsaparilla
zarzo /'sarso; 'θarθo/ m, hurdle; wattle
zarzoso /sar'soso; θar'θoso/ a brambly
zarzuela /sar'suela; θar'θuela/ f, comic opera; musical comedy
zarzuelista /sarsue'lista; θarθue'lista/ mf writer or composer of comic operas
¡zas! /sas; θas/ m, sound of a bang or blow
zascandil /saskan'dil; θaskan'dil/ m, Inf. busybody
zatara /sa'tara; θa'tara/ f, raft
zeda /'seða; 'θeða/ f, name of the letter Z
zedilla /se'ðiya; θe'ðiʎa/ f, cedilla
zenit /'senit; 'θenit/ m. See **cenit**
zepelín /sepe'lin; θepe'lin/ m, Zeppelin
zeta /'seta; 'θeta/ f. See **zeda**
zigzag /sig'sag; θig'θag/ m, zigzag
zigzaguear /sigsage'ar; θigθage'ar/ vi to zigzag
zinc /sink; θink/ m, zinc
zipizape /sipi'sape; θipi'θape/ m, Inf. row, quarrel
zoca /'soka; 'θoka/ f, square
zócalo /'sokalo; 'θokalo/ m, Archit. socle; Mexico main square
Zócalo, el /'sokalo; 'θokalo/ m, the Main Square of Mexico City)
zoclo /'soklo; 'θoklo/ m, clog, sabot
zoco /'soko; 'θoko/ m, square; market; clog, sabot
zodiaco /so'ðiako; θo'ðiako/ m, zodiac
zona /'sona; 'θona/ f, girdle, band; strip (of land); zone; Med. shingles. **z. de depresión,** air pocket. **z. templada,** temperate zone. **z. tórrida,** torrid zone
zonal /so'nal; θo'nal/ a zonal
zoncear /sonse'ar; θonθe'ar/ vi, Lat. Am. to behave stupidly
zonzo, -a /'sonso; 'θonθo/ a, Lat. Am. silly, stupid
zoología /soolo'hia; θoolo'hia/ f, zoology
zoológico /soo'lohiko; θoo'lohiko/ a zoological
zoólogo /so'ologo; θo'ologo/ m, zoologist
zopenco /so'penko; θo'penko/ a Inf. oafish
zopo /'sopo; 'θopo/ a maimed, deformed (hands, feet)
zoquete /so'kete; θo'kete/ m, block; dowel; hunk of bread; Inf. short, ugly man; Inf. dunderhead
zorcico /sor'siko; θor'θiko/ m, Basque song and dance
zorra /'sorra; 'θorra/ f, vixen; fox; Inf. cunning person; Inf. prostitute; Inf. drinking bout; truck, dray
zorrera /so'rrera; θo'rrera/ f, foxhole
zorrería /sorre'ria; θorre'ria/ f, foxiness; Inf. cunning
zorro /'sorro; 'θorro/ m, fox; fox-skin; Inf. knave
zóster /'soster; 'θoster/ f, Med. shingles
zote /'sote; 'θote/ a dull, ignorant
zozobra /so'soβra; θo'θoβra/ f, Naut. foundering, capsizing; anxiety
zozobrar /soso'βrar; θoθo'βrar/ vi Naut. to founder, sink; Naut. plunge, shiver; be anxious, vacillate
zueco /'sueko; 'θueko/ m, sabot, clog

zulú /su'lu; θu'lú/ *a* and *mf* Zulu

zumaque /su'make; θu'make/ *m, Bot.* sumach tree; *Inf.* wine

zumba /'sumba; 'θumba/ *f,* cow bell; jest

zumbar /sum'βar; θum'βar/ *vi* to buzz, hum; ring (of the ears); whizz; twang (of a guitar, etc.); *Fig. Inf.* be on the brink

zumbido /sum'βiðo; θum'βiðo/ *m,* buzzing, humming; ringing (in the ears); whizz; twanging (of a guitar, etc.); *Inf.* slap, blow

zumbón /sum'βon; θum'βon/ *a* humming (motor), buzzing (insect); joke playing, teasing

zumo /'sumo; 'θumo/ *m,* sap; juice; profit, advantage

zumoso /su'moso; θu'moso/ *a* succulent, juicy

zupia /'supia; 'θupia/ *f,* wine lees; cloudy wine; *Fig.* dregs

zurcido /sur'siðo; θur'θiðo/ *m, Sew.* darn; mend

zurcidor /sursi'ðor; θurθi'ðor/ **(-ra)** *n* darner, mender. **z. de voluntades,** *humorous* pimp

zurcidura /sursi'ðura; θurθi'ðura/ *f,* darning; mending; darn

zurcir /sur'sir; θur'θir/ *vt* to darn; mend, repair; join; *Fig.* concoct, weave

zurdo /'surðo; 'θurðo/ *a* left-handed

zurra /'surra; 'θurra/ *f, Tan.* currying; *Inf.* spanking; *Inf.* quarrel

zurrador /surra'ðor; θurra'ðor/ *m, Tan.* currier, dresser

zurrapa /su'rrapa; θu'rrapa/ *f,* (gen. *pl*) sediment, lees, dregs

zurrar /su'rrar; θu'rrar/ *vt* to curry (leather); *Inf.* spank; *Inf.* dress down, scold

zurriagazo /surria'gaso; θurria'gaθo/ *m,* lash with a whip; *Fig.* blow of fate

zurriago /su'rriago; θu'rriago/ *m,* whip

zurribanda /surri'βanda; θurri'βanda/ *f, Inf.* whipping; fight, quarrel

zurriburri /surri'βurri; θurri'βurri/ *m, Inf.* ragamuffin; mob; uproar

zurrido /su'rriðo; θu'rriðo/ *m, Inf.* blow; dull noise

zurrir /su'rrir; θu'rrir/ *vi* to have a confused sound, hum, rattle

zurrón /su'rron; θu'rron/ *m,* shepherd's pouch; leather bag; *Bot.* husk

zutano /su'tano; θu'tano/ **(-na)** *n Inf.* so-and-so, such a one

English–Spanish
Dictionary

A

a /ei/ *n* (letter) a, *f*; *Mus.* la, *m*. **symphony in A major,** sinfonía en la mayor, *f*. **A1,** de primera clase; de primera calidad, excelente

a, an /ə; ən; *when stressed* ei; æn/ *indef art.* (one) un, *m*; una, *f*; (with weights, quantities) el, *m*; la, *f*; (with weeks, months, years, etc.) por, al, *m*; a la, *f*. The indef. art. is omitted in Spanish before nouns expressing nationality, profession, rank, and generally before a noun in apposition. It is omitted also before certain words such as **mil, ciento, otro, semejante, medio,** etc. Not translated in book titles, e.g., *A History of Spain,* Historia de España. *prep* a. In phrases such as *to go hunting,* ir a cazar. As prefix, see *abed, ashore,* etc. *Madrid, a Spanish city,* Madrid, ciudad de España. *three times a month,* tres veces al mes. *ten dollars an hour,* diez dólares por hora. *thirty miles an hour,* treinta millas por hora. *a certain Mrs. Brown,* una tal Sra. Brown. *a thousand soldiers,* mil soldados. *half an hour later,* media hora después

aback /ə'bæk/ *adv Naut.* en facha; *Fig.* sorprendido, desconcertado. **to take a.,** desconcertar, coger desprevenido (a)

abacus /'æbəkəs/ *n* ábaco, *m*

abandon /ə'bændən/ *vt* abandonar; dejar; desertar, desamparar; renunciar; entregar. *n* entusiasmo, fervor, *m*; naturalidad, *f*. **to a. oneself to,** (despair, vice, etc.) entregarse a

abandoned /ə'bændənd/ *a* entregado a los vicios, vicioso

abandonment /ə'bændənmənt/ *n* abandono, *m*; renunciación, *f*; deserción, *f*

abase /ə'beis/ *vt* humillar; degradar; abatir

abasement /ə'beismənt/ *n* humillación, degradación, *f*; abatimiento, *m*

abash /ə'bæʃ/ *vt* avergonzar; confundir, desconcertar

abashed /ə'bæʃt/ *a* avergonzado, confuso, consternado

abate /ə'beit/ *vt* disminuir, reducir; (a price) rebajar; (suppress) suprimir, abolir; (remit) condonar, remitir; (annul) anular; (moderate) moderar; (of pain) aliviar. *vi* disminuir; moderarse; (of the wind and *Fig.*) amainar; cesar; apaciguarse, calmarse

abatement /ə'beitmənt/ *n* disminución, *f*; reducción, *f*; mitigación, *f*; (of price) rebaja, *f*; supresión, *f*; remisión, *f*; (annulment) anulación, *f*; (of the wind and of enthusiasm, etc.) amaine, *m*; (of pain, etc.) alivio, *m*

abattoir /'æbə,twɑr/ *n* matadero, *m*

abbey /'æbi/ *n* abadía, *f*

abbreviate /ə'brivi,eit/ *vt* abreviar; condensar, resumir

abbreviation /ə,brivi'eiʃən/ *n* abreviación, *f*; resumen, *m*, condensación, *f*; (of a word) abreviatura, *f*

abdicate /'æbdɪ,keit/ *vt* renunciar; (a throne) abdicar

abdication /,æbdɪ'keiʃən/ *n* renuncia, *f*; abdicación, *f*

abdomen /'æbdəmən/ *n* abdomen, *m*

abdominal /æb'dɒmənl/ *a* abdominal

abduct /æb'dʌkt/ *vt* raptar, secuestrar

abduction /æb'dʌkʃən/ *n* rapto, *m*; (*Anat. Philos.*) abducción, *f*

abductor /æb'dʌktər/ *n Anat.* abductor, *m*; raptor, *m*

aberration /,æbə'reiʃən/ *n* aberración (also *Astron. Phys. Biol.*), *f*

abet /ə'bɛt/ *vt* ayudar, apoyar, favorecer; incitar, alentar; (in bad sense) ser cómplice de

abetment /ə'bɛtmənt/ *n* ayuda, *f*, apoyo, *m*; instigación, *f*

abettor /ə'bɛtər/ *n* instigador (-ra); cómplice, *mf*

abeyance /ə'beiəns/ *n* suspensión, *f*; expectativa, esperanza, *f*. **in a.,** en suspenso; vacante; latente

abhor /æb'hɔr/ *vt* detestar, odiar, aborrecer; repugnar

abhorrence /æb'hɔrəns/ *n* detestación, *f*, odio, aborrecimiento, *m*; repugnancia, *f*

abhorrent /æb'hɔrənt/ *a* detestable, odioso, aborrecible; repugnante

abide /ə'baid/ *vi* morar, quedar. *vt* aguardar; *Inf.*

aguantar, sufrir. **to a. by,** atenerse a, cumplir; sostener

abiding /ə'baidɪŋ/ *a* permanente, constante, perenne

ability /ə'bɪlɪti/ *n* habilidad, facultad, *f*, poder, *m*; talento, *m*, capacidad, *f*. **to the best of my a.,** lo mejor que yo pueda

abject /'æbdʒɛkt/ *a* abyecto; vil; servil

abjure /æb'dʒʊr/ *vt* abjurar; renunciar; retractar

ablaze /ə'bleiz/ *adv* en llamas, ardiendo. *a* brillante; (with, of anger, etc.) dominado por

able /'eibəl/ *a* capaz (de); (clever) hábil; competente; en estado (de); *Law.* apto legalmente, capaz; bueno, excelente. **to be a. to,** poder; ser capaz de; (know how) saber. **a.-bodied,** fuerte, fornido. **a.-bodied seaman,** marinero práctico, *m*

abloom /ə'blum/ *adv* en flor

ablution /ə'bluʃən/ *n* ablución, *f*

ably /'eibli/ *adv* hábilmente; competentemente

abnegation /,æbnɪ'geiʃən/ *n* abnegación, *f*

abnormal /æb'nɔrməl/ *a* anormal; irregular

abnormality /,æbnɔr'mælɪti/ *n* anormalidad, *f*; irregularidad, *f*

abnormally /æb'nɔrməli/ *adv* anormalmente; demasiado

aboard /ə'bɔrd/ *adv* a bordo. *prep* a bordo de. **to go a.,** embarcarse, ir a bordo. **All a.!** ¡Viajeros a bordo!; (a train) ¡Viajeros al tren!

abode /ə'boud/ *n* morada, habitación, *f*; residencia, *f*; (stay) estancia, *f*

abolish /ə'bɒlɪʃ/ *vt* abolir, suprimir, anular

abolition /,æbə'lɪʃən/ *n* abolición, supresión, *f*; anulación, *f*

abolitionist /,æbə'lɪʃənɪst/ *n* abolicionista, *mf*

abominable /ə'bɒmənəbəl/ *a* abominable, aborrecible; repugnante, execrable; *Inf.* horrible

abominably /ə'bɒmənəbli/ *adv* abominablemente

abominate /ə'bɒmə,neit/ *vt* abominar, aborrecer, detestar

abomination /ə,bɒmə'neiʃən/ *n* abominación, *f*; aborrecimiento, *m*; horror, *m*

aboriginal /,æbə'rɪdʒənl/ *a* aborigen; primitivo

aborigines /,æbə'rɪdʒə,niz/ *n pl* aborígenes, *m pl*

abort /ə'bɔrt/ *vi* abortar, malparir; *Fig.* malograrse

abortion /ə'bɔrʃən/ *n* aborto, *Colombia* avieso *m*; *Fig.* fracaso, malogro, *m*

abortive /ə'bɔrtɪv/ *a* abortivo

abound /ə'baund/ *vi* abundar (en)

about /ə'baut/ *adv* (around) alrededor; (round about) a la redonda, en torno; (all over) por todas partes; (up and down) acá y acullá; por aquí, por ahí; en alguna parte; por aquí; (in circumference) en circunferencia; (almost) casi, aproximadamente; (by turns) por turnos, en rotación. *prep* alrededor de; en torno; por; (near to) cerca de; (on one's person) sobre; (on the subject of) sobre; (concerning) acerca de; (over) por, a causa de; en; (of) de; (with time by the clock) a eso de, sobre; (towards) hacia; (engaged in) ocupado en; (on the point of) a punto de. **a. here,** por aquí. **a. nothing,** por nada. **a. supper time,** hacia la hora de cenar. **a. three o'clock,** a eso de las tres. **A. turn!** ¡Media vuelta! (a la izquierda o a la derecha). **He wandered a. the streets,** Vagaba por las calles. **somewhere a.,** en alguna parte. **to be a. to,** (tratar de + infin.), estar para, estar a punto de. **to bring a.,** ocasionar. **to come a.,** suceder. **to know a.,** saber de. **to set a.,** empezar, iniciar; (a person) acometer. **What are you thinking a.?** ¿En qué piensas?

above /ə'bʌv/ *adv* arriba; en lo alto; encima; (superior) superior; (earlier) antes; (higher up on a page, etc.) más arriba; (in heaven) en el cielo. *prep* encima de; por encima de; sobre; (beyond) fuera de; fuera del alcance de; (superior to) superior a; (more than) más de; (too proud to) demasiado orgulloso para; (too good to) demasiado bueno para; (in addition to) además de, en adición a; (with degrees of temperature) sobre. *a* anterior; (with past participles) antes. **from a., desde arriba. a. all,** sobre todo. **over and a.,** además de. **a. board,** *adv* abiertamente, con las cartas boca arriba. *a* franco y abierto. **a. mentioned,** supradicho, susodicho, antes citado

abrasion /ə'breiʒən/ *n* abrasión, *f*; rozadura, *f*; *Geol.* denudación, *f*

abrasive /ə'breisɪv/ *a* abrasivo. *n* substancia abrasiva, *f*, abrasivo, *m*

abreast /ə'brɛst/ *adv* de frente, al lado uno de otro; *Naut.* por el través. **to keep a. of the times,** mantenerse al día. **to ride six a.,** cabalgar a seis de frente. **a. with,** al nivel de, a la altura de

abridge /ə'brɪdʒ/ *vt* abreviar; resumir, condensar, compendiar; disminuir; reducir

abridgment /ə'brɪdʒmənt/ *n* abreviación, *f*; resumen, *m*, sinopsis, *f*; disminución, *f*; reducción, *f*

abroad /ə'brɔd/ *adv* (out) fuera, afuera; (gone out) salido; ausente; (everywhere) en todas partes; (in foreign lands) en el extranjero. **to go a.,** ir al extranjero; (of rumors, etc.) propagarse, rumorearse

abrogation /ˌæbrə'geiʃən/ *n* abrogación, anulación, *f*

abrupt /ə'brʌpt/ *a* (precipitous) escarpado, precipitado, abrupto; (unexpected) repentino, inesperado; (of persons) brusco, descortés; (of style) seco

abruptly /ə'brʌptli/ *adv* bruscamente; repentinamente

abruptness /ə'brʌptnɪs/ *n* precipitación, *f*; brusquedad, *f*

abscess /'æbsɛs/ *n* absceso, *m*

abscond /æb'skɒnd/ *vi* evadirse; huir, escaparse; (with money) desfalcar

absence /'æbsəns/ *n* ausencia, *f*; alejamiento, *m*; (of mind) abstracción, *f*, ensimismamiento, *m*; (lack) falta, *f*. **leave of a.,** permiso para ausentarse, *m*; *Mil.* licencia, *f*, permiso, *m*

absent /ə 'æbsənt/ *v* æb'sɛnt/ *a* ausente; alejado (de); (in mind) abstraído, ensimismado, distraído. *vt* ausentarse; alejarse. **the a.,** los ausentes. **a.-mindedness,** ensimismamiento, *m*, abstracción, *f*

absentee /ˌæbsən'ti/ *n* ausente, *mf*

absenteeism /ˌæbsən'tiizəm/ *n* absentismo, *m*

absently /'æbsəntli/ *adv* distraídamente

absinthe /'æbsɪnθ/ *n* ajenjo, *m*

absolute /'æbsə,lut/ *a* absoluto; perfecto; puro; (unconditional) incondicional; (true) verdadero; (unlimited) ilimitado. **the a.,** lo absoluto

absolutely /ˌæbsə'lutli/ *adv* absolutamente; enteramente, completamente; realmente, categóricamente

absolution /ˌæbsə'luʃən/ *n* (*Eccl. Law.*) absolución, *f*

absolutism /'æbsəlu,tɪzəm/ *n* absolutismo, despotismo, *m*

absolutist /'æbsə,lutɪst/ *n* absolutista, *mf*

absolve /æb'zɒlv, -'sɒlv/ *vt* absolver; (free) exentar, eximir; librar; exculpar

absorb /æb'sɔrb, -'zɔrb/ *vt* absorber; (drink) beber; (use) gastar; (of shocks) amortiguar; (*Fig.* digest) asimilar; (engross) ocupar (el pensamiento, etc.). **to be absorbed in,** *Fig.* enfrascarse en, engolfarse en, estar entregado a

absorbent /æb'sɔrbənt, -'zɔr-/ *a* and *n* absorbente, *m*. **a. cotton,** algodón hidrófilo, *m*

absorbing /æb'sɔrbɪŋ, -'zɔr-/ *a* absorbente; *Fig.* sumamente interesante

absorption /æb'sɔrpʃən, -'zɔrp-/ *n* absorción, *f*; (*Fig.* digestion) asimilación, *f*; (engrossment) enfrascamiento, *m*, preocupación, abstracción, *f*

abstain /æb'stein/ *vi* abstenerse (de); evitar

abstemious /æb'stimiəs/ *a* abstemio, abstinente; sobrio; moderado

abstention /æb'stɛnʃən/ *n* abstención, *f*; abstinencia, *f*; privación, *f*

abstinence /'æbstənəns/ *n* abstinencia, *f*. **day of a.,** día de ayuno, *m*

abstinent /'æbstənənt/ *a* abstinente; sobrio

abstract /*a*, *v* æb'strækt, 'æbstrækt; *n* 'æbstrækt/ *a* abstracto. *n* extracto, resumen, *m*; abstracción, *f*. *vt* abstraer; separar; extraer; (précis) resumir; (steal) substraer. **in the a.,** en abstracto

abstraction /æb'strækʃən/ *n* abstracción, *f*; (of mind) preocupación, desatención, *f*; (stealing) substracción, *f*

abstruse /æb'strus/ *a* abstruso, ininteligible; obscuro; recóndito

absurd /æb'sɜrd/ *a* absurdo, grotesco; ridículo, disparatado; cómico

absurdity /æb'sɜrdɪti/ *n* absurdidad, ridiculez, *f*; disparate, *m*, tontería, *f*

abundance /ə'bʌndəns/ *n* abundancia, copia, *f*; muchedumbre (de), multitud (de), *f*; riqueza, *f*; prosperidad, *f*

abundant /ə'bʌndənt/ *a* abundante, copioso; rico

abundantly /ə'bʌndəntli/ *adv* en abundancia, abundantemente

abuse /*n* ə'byus; *v* ə'byuz/ *n* abuso, *m*; (bad language) insulto, *m*, injuria, *f*. *vt* (ill-use) maltratar; (misuse) abusar (de); (revile) insultar, injuriar; (deceive) engañar

abuser /ə'byuzər/ *n* abusador (-ra); injuriador (-ra); (defamer) denigrante, *mf*

abusive /ə'byusɪv/ *a* abusivo; (scurrilous) insultante, injurioso, ofensivo

abusively /ə'byusɪvli/ *adv* insolentemente, ofensivamente

abysmal /ə'bɪzməl/ *a* abismal

abyss /ə'bɪs/ *n* abismo, *m*, sima, *f*; (hell) infierno, *m*

acacia /ə'keiʃə/ *n* acacia, *f*

academic /ˌækə'dɛmɪk/ *a* académico

academician /ˌækədə'mɪʃən/ *n* académico, miembro de la Academia, *m*

academy /ə'kædəmi/ *n* academia, *f*; conservatorio, *m*; (school) colegio, *m*; (of riding, etc.) escuela, *f*. **A. of Music,** Conservatorio de Música, *m*

accede /æk'sid/ *vi* (to a throne) ascender (al trono); tomar posesión (de); (join) hacerse miembro (de); aceptar; (agree) acceder (a), consentir (en), convenir (en)

accelerate /æk'sɛlə,reit/ *vt* acelerar; apresurar; (shorten) abreviar

acceleration /æk,sɛlə'reiʃən/ *n* aceleración, *f*

accelerator /æk'sɛlə,reitər/ *n* (of a vehicle) acelerador, *m*

accent /'æksɛnt/ *n* acento (all meanings), *m*. *vt* acentuar

accentuate /æk'sɛntʃu,eit/ *vt* acentuar; dar énfasis a

accept /æk'sɛpt/ *vt* aceptar; (believe) creer; recibir; admitir; (welcome) acoger

acceptability /æk,sɛptə'bɪlɪti/ *n* aceptabilidad, *f*; mérito, *m*

acceptable /æk'sɛptəbəl/ *a* aceptable; admisible; agradable; (welcome) bien acogido

acceptably /æk'sɛptəbli/ *adv* aceptablemente; agradablemente

acceptance /æk'sɛptəns/ *n* aceptación, *f*. **a. speech** discurso aceptatorio; (approval) aprobación, *f*; (welcome) buena acogida, *f*; *Com.* aceptación, *f*

access /'æksɛs/ *n* acceso, *m*; entrada, *f*; (way) camino, *m*; *Med.* ataque, *m*; (fit) transporte, *m*; (advance) avance, *m*. **easy of a.,** accesible; fácil de encontrar. *vt* tener acceso a

accessibility /æk,sɛsə'bɪlɪti/ *n* accesibilidad, *f*

accessible /æk'sɛsəbəl/ *a* accesible; asequible

accession /æk'sɛʃən/ *n* (to the throne, etc.) advenimiento, *m*; aumento, *m*; (acquisition) adición, *f*; adquisición, *f*; *Law.* accesión, *f*

accessory /æk'sɛsəri/ *a* accesorio; secundario; suplementario, adicional. *n* accesorio, *m*; *Law.* cómplice, *mf*. **a. before the fact,** instigador (-ra). **a. after the fact,** encubridor (-ra)

accident /'æksɪdənt/ *n* accidente, *m*; (chance) casualidad, *f*; (mishap) contratiempo, *m*. **by a.,** por casualidad, accidentalmente. **a. insurance,** seguro contra accidentes, *m*

accidental /ˌæksɪ'dɛntl̩/ *a* accidental, casual, fortuito. *n Mus.* accidente, *m*

accidentally /ˌæksɪ'dɛntl̩i/ *adv* accidentalmente; por casualidad; sin querer

acclaim /ə'kleim/ *vt* aclamar; proclamar; vitorear, aplaudir

acclamation /ˌæklə'meiʃən/ *n* aclamación, *f*; aplauso, vítor, *m*

acclimatization /ə'klaimətə,zeishən/ *n* aclimatación, *f*

acclimatize /ə'klaimə,taiz/ vt aclimatar

accolade /'ækə,leid/ n acolada, f, espaldarazo, m

accommodate /ə'kɒmə,deit/ vt acomodar; ajustar; adaptar; (reconcile) reconciliar; (provide) proveer, proporcionar; (oblige) complacer; (fit) poner, instalar; (lodge) hospedar; (lend) prestar; (hold) tener espacio para, contener; (give a seat to) dar un sitio a. **to a. oneself to,** adaptarse a

accommodating /ə'kɒmə,deitıŋ/ a acomodadizo; (obliging) servicial

accommodation /ə,kɒmə'deiʃən/ n acomodación, f; ajuste, m; adaptación, f; (arrangement) arreglo, m; (reconciliation) reconciliación, f; (lodging) alojamiento, m; (Aer. Naut.) partición, f; (space, room or seat) sitio, m; (loan) préstamo, m

accompaniment /ə'kʌmpənimənt/ n acompañamiento, m

accompanist /ə'kʌmpənist/ n acompañante (-ta)

accompany /ə'kʌmpəni/ vt acompañar

accompanying /ə'kʌmpəniiŋ/ a anexo n acompañamiento, m

accomplice /ə'kɒmplis/ n cómplice, comparte, mf

accomplish /ə'kɒmpliʃ/ vt llevar a cabo, efectuar; terminar; (fulfill) cumplir; perfeccionar; (achieve) conseguir, lograr

accomplished /ə'kɒmpliʃt/ a consumado; perfecto; culto; (talented) talentoso

accomplishment /ə'kɒmpliʃmənt/ n efectuación, f; realización, f, logro, m; (fulfilment) cumplimiento, m; (gift) prenda, f, talento, m; pl **accomplishments,** partes, dotes, f pl; conocimientos, m pl

accord /ə'kɔrd/ n acuerdo, m; unión, f; consentimiento, m; concierto, m, concordia, f; voluntad, f. vt otorgar, conceder. vi estar de acuerdo (con); armonizar (con). **of one's own a.,** espontáneamente. **with one a.,** unánimemente

accordance /ə'kɔrdns/ n acuerdo, m, conformidad, f; arreglo, m. **in a. with,** de acuerdo con, según, con arreglo a

according /ə'kɔrdiŋ/ adv según, conforme. **a. as,** conforme a, a medida que. **a. to,** según

accordingly /ə'kɔrdiŋli/ adv en consecuencia, por consiguiente; pues

accordion /ə'kɔrdiən/ n acordeón, m

accost /ə'kɔst/ vt abordar, molestar

account /ə'kaunt/ vt (judge) considerar, creer, juzgar, tener por. vi (for) explicar; (understand) comprender; (be responsible) responder de, dar razón de; justificar

account /ə'kaunt/ n (bill) cuenta, f; factura, f; (narrative) narración, relación, f; (description) descripción, f; historia, f; versión, f; (list) enumeración, f; (reason) motivo, m, causa, f; (importance) importancia, f; (weight) peso, m; (news) noticias, f pl; (advantage) provecho, m, ventaja, f. **by all accounts,** según lo que se oye, según voz pública. **outstanding a.,** cuenta pendiente, f. **on a.,** a cuenta. **on a. of,** a causa de, por motivo de. **on no a.,** de ninguna manera. **on that a.,** por lo tanto. **savings a.,** cuenta corriente, f. **to be of no a.,** ser insignificante; ser de poca importancia; Inf. ser la última mona. **to give an a.,** contar, hacer una relación (de). **to give an a. of oneself,** explicarse. **to keep a.,** llevar la cuenta. **to settle accounts,** ajustar cuentas. **to take into a.,** considerar. **to turn to a.,** sacar provecho de. **a. book,** libro de cuentas, m

accountability /ə,kauntə'biliti/ n responsabilidad, f

accountable /ə'kauntəbəl/ a responsable

accountancy /ə'kauntnsi/ n contabilidad, f

accountant /ə'kauntnt/ n contador, m. **chartered a.,** contador autorizado, m. **accountant's office,** contaduría, f

accouterment /ə'kutərmənt/ n atavío, m; equipo, m

accredit /ə'kredit/ vt acreditar

accretion /ə'kriʃən/ n acrecentamiento, aumento, m; Law. accesión, f

accrue /ə'kru/ vi resultar (de), proceder (de), originarse (en); aumentar

accumulate /ə'kyumyə,leit/ vt acumular; amontonar, atesorar. vi acumularse; aumentarse, crecer

accumulation /ə,kyumyə'leiʃən/ n acumulación, f; amontonamiento, m

accumulative /ə'kyumyə,leitiv/ a acumulador; adquisitivo, ahorrador

accumulator /ə'kyumyə,leitər/ n Elec. acumulador, m

accuracy /'ækyərəsi/ n exactitud, corrección

accurate /'ækyərit/ a exacto, correcto, fiel; (of persons) exacto, minucioso; (of apparatus) de precisión

accurately /'ækyəritli/ adv con exactitud, correctamente; con precisión

accursed /ə'kɜrsid, ə'kɜrst/ a maldito.

accusation /,ækyu'zeiʃən/ n acusación, f. **to lodge an a.,** querellarse ante el juez

accusatory /ə'kyuzə,tɔri/ a acusatorio

accuse /ə'kyuz/ vt acusar

accused /ə'kyuzd/ n Law. acusado (-da)

accuser /ə'kyuzər/ n acusador (-ra)

accustom /ə'kʌstəm/ vt acostumbrar (a), habituar (a)

accustomed /ə'kʌstəmd/ a acostumbrado, usual; general; característico

ace /eis/ n as, m; Fig. pelo, m

acerbity /ə'sɜrbiti/ n acerbidad, f; Fig. aspereza, f; severidad, f; sequedad, f

acetaminophen /ə,sitə'minəfən/ n acetaminofén, m

acetate /'æsi,teit/ n acetato, m

acetic /ə'sitik/ a acético

acetylene /ə'sɛtl,in/ n acetileno, m. **a. lamp,** lámpara de acetileno, f

ache /eik/ n dolor, m; pena, f. vi doler. **My head aches,** Me duele la cabeza, Tengo dolor de cabeza

achievable /ə'tʃivəbəl/ a alcanzable, asequible; factible

achieve /ə'tʃiv/ vt conseguir, lograr; (reach) alcanzar; (obtain) obtener, ganar

achievement /ə'tʃivmənt/ n logro, m, realización, f; obtención, f; (deed) hazaña, f; (work) obra, f; (success) éxito, m; (discovery) descubrimiento, m; (victory) victoria, f

aching /'eikiŋ/ n dolor, m; pena, angustia, f. a doliente; afligido

achromatic /,eikrə'mætik/ a acromático

achromic /ei'kroumik/ a acrómico

acid /'æsid/ a and n ácido, m. **fatty a.,** ácido graso, m

acidify /ə'sidə,fai/ vt acidificar

acidity /ə'siditi/ n acidez, f

acidosis /,æsi'dousis/ n Med. acidismo, m

acid rain n lluvia ácida, f

acknowledge /æk'nɒlidʒ/ vt reconocer; confesar; (reply to) contestar a; (appreciate) agradecer. **to a. receipt,** Com. acusar recibo

acknowledgment /æk'nɒlidʒmənt/ n reconocimiento, m; confesión, f; (appreciation) agradecimiento, m; (reward) recompensa, f; (of a letter) acuse de recibo, m

acme /'ækmi/ n cumbre, f; Fig. auge, apogeo, m

acne /'ækni/ n acné, m

acolyte /'ækə,lait/ n acólito, monacillo (male) m, acólita, monacilla, f, (female)

acorn /'eikɔrn/ n bellota, f. **a. cup,** capullo de bellota, m. **a.-shaped,** en forma de bellota, abellotado

acoustic /ə'kustik/ a acústico

acoustics /ə'kustiks/ n pl acústica, f

acquaint /ə'kweint/ vt dar a conocer, comunicar, informar (de), dar parte (de); familiarizar (con). **to be acquainted with,** conocer; saber. **to make oneself acquainted with,** familiarizarse con; entablar amistad con

acquaintance /ə'kweintns/ n conocimiento, m; (person) conocido (-da); pl **acquaintances,** amistades, f pl. **to make their a.,** conocer (a), llegar a conocer (a)

acquiesce /,ækwi'ɛs/ vi asentir (en), consentir (a)

acquiescence /,ækwi'ɛsəns/ n acquiescencia, f, consentimiento, m

acquiescent /,ækwi'ɛsənt/ a conforme; resignado

acquire /ə'kwaiⁱr/ vt adquirir, obtener; (diseases, habits) contraer; ganar; (learn) aprender

Acquired Immune Deficiency Syndrome /ə'kwaiⁱrd/ n el Síndrome de Inmunodeficiencia Adquirida, m

acquirement /ə'kwaiⁱrmənt/ n adquisición, f; (learning) conocimiento, m; (talent) talento, m

acquirer /ə'kwaiⁱrər/ n adquisidor (-ra)

acquisition /,ækwə'ziʃən/ n adquisición, f

acquisitive /ə'kwızıtıv/ a adquisitivo
acquit /ə'kwıt/ vt (a debt) pagar; exonerar; Law. absolver; (a duty) cumplir. **to a.** oneself well (badly), portarse bien (mal); salir bien (mal)
acquittal /ə'kwıtl/ n (of a debt) pago, m; Law. absolución, f; (of a duty) cumplimiento, m
acquittance /ə'kwıtn̩s/ n descargo, m; quitanza, f
acre /'eikər/ n (measure) acre, m; pl **acres,** terrenos, campos, m pl. **1.75 acres** Central America manzana f.
2.5 acres Argentina manzana f
acreage /'eikərıdʒ/ n acres, m pl
acrid /'ækrıd/ a acre
acrimonious /,ækrə'mouniəs/ a acrimonioso, áspero; mordaz, sarcástico
acrimony /'ækrə,mouni/ n acrimonia, acritud, f; sarcasmo, m
acrobat /'ækrə,bæt/ n acróbata. Lat. Am. also maromero (-ra) mf
acrobatic /,ækrə'bætık/ a acrobático
acrobatics /,ækrə'bætıks/ n pl acrobacia, f
acronym /'ækrənım/ n sigla, f
acropolis /ə'krɒpəlıs/ n acrópolis, f
across /ə'krɔs/ adv a través, de través, transversalmente; (on the other side) al otro lado; de una parte a otra; (of the arms, etc.) cruzados, m pl. prep. **He** went a. the road, Cruzó la calle. **to run a.,** correr por; tropezar con; dar con. **a.** country, a campo travieso. **a. the way,** en frente
acrostic /ə'krɔstık/ n (poema) acróstico, m, a acróstico
act /ækt/ n acción, obra, f, hecho, m; acto, m; Law. ley, f; Theat. acto, m. **in the act,** en el acto. **in the act (of doing),** en acto de (hacer algo). **in the very act,** en flagrante. **the Acts of the Apostles,** los Actos de los Apóstoles. **act of God,** fuerza mayor, f. **act of indemnity,** bill de indemnidad, m
act /ækt/ vt (a play) representar, hacer; (a part) desempeñar, hacer (un papel); (pretend) simular, fingir. vi obrar, actuar, Lat. Am. accionar; (behave) portarse, conducirse; (function) funcionar; producir su efecto; (feign) fingir; (as a profession) ser actor. **to act as,** hacer de; cumplir las funciones de. **to act as a second,** (in a duel) apadrinar. **to act for,** representar; ser el representante de. **to act upon,** obrar sobre; afectar; influir en
acting /'æktıŋ/ n (of a play) representación (de una comedia), f; (of an actor) interpretación (de un papel), f; (as a hobby) el hacer comedia; (dramatic art) arte dramática, f. a interino, suplente; comanditario. **He is a. captain,** Está de capitán. **a. partner,** socio (-ia) comanditario (-ia)
action /'ækʃən/ n acción, f; función, f; operación, f; (movement) movimiento, m; (effect) efecto, m; influencia, f; Law. proceso, m; Mil. batalla, acción, f; Lit. acción, f. **in a.,** en actividad; en operación; Mil. en el campo de batalla. **man of a.,** hombre de acción, m. **to be killed in a.,** morir en el campo de batalla. **to bring an a. against,** pedir en juicio, entablar un pleito contra. **to put into a.,** hacer funcionar; introducir. **to take a.,** tomar medidas (para). **to take a. against,** prevenirse contra; Law. proceder contra
actionable /'ækʃənəbəl/ a procesable, punible
active /'æktıv/ a activo; ágil; diligente; Mil. vivo; enérgico; Gram. activo. **be a.** Lat. Am. accionar. **to make a.,** activar, estimular
activity /æk'tıvıti/ n actividad, f
actor /'æktər/ n actor, m; (in comedy) comediante, m
actress /'æktrıs/ n actriz, f; (in comedy) comedianta, f
actual /'æktʃuəl/ a actual, existente; real, verdadero
actuality /,æktʃu'ælıti/ n realidad, f
actually /'æktʃuəli/ adv en efecto, realmente, en realidad
actuary /'æktʃu,ɛri/ n actuario de seguros, m
actuate /'æktʃu,eit/ vt mover, animar, excitar
acumen /ə'kyumən/ n cacumen, m, agudeza, sagacidad, f
acute /ə'kyut/ a agudo; (shrewd) perspicaz; (of a situation) crítico. **a. accent,** acento agudo, m. **a.-angled,** acutángulo

acutely /ə'kyutli/ adv agudamente; (deeply) profundamente
acuteness /ə'kyutnıs/ n agudeza, f; (shrewdness) perspicacia, penetración, f
ad /æd/ n anuncio, m. See **advertisement**
adage /'ædıdʒ/ n refrán, proverbio, decir, m
Adam /'ædəm/ n Adán, m. **Adam's apple,** nuez de la garganta, f
adamant /'ædəmənt/ a firme, duro, inexorable
adamantine /,ædə'mæntin/ a adamantino
adapt /ə'dæpt/ vt adaptar; ajustar, acomodar; aplicar; (a play, etc.) refundir, arreglar; Mus. arreglar
adaptability /ə,dæptə'bılıti/ n adaptabilidad, f
adaptable /ə'dæptəbəl/ a adaptable
adaptation /,ædəp'teiʃən/ n adaptación, f; (of a play, etc.) refundición, f; (Mus. etc.) arreglo, m
adapter /ə'dæptər/ n (of a play, etc.) refundidor (-ra); Elec. enchufe de reducción, m
add /æd/ vt añadir; juntar; (up) sumar. **add insult to injury,** al mojado echarle agua, añadir a una ofensa otra mayor. **to add up,** añadir a; (increase) aumentar, acrecentar. **to add up,** sumar. **to add up to,** subir a; (mean) querer decir
adder /'ædər/ n víbora, serpiente, f
addict /'ædıkt/ n adicto (-ta). **to a. oneself to,** dedicarse a, entregarse a
addicted /ə'dıktıd/ a aficionado (a), amigo (de), dado (a); adicto (a)
addiction /ə'dıkʃən/ n afición, propensión, f; adicción, f
addition /ə'dıʃən/ n añadidura, f; Math. adición, suma, f. **in a. (to),** además (de), también
additional /ə'dıʃənl/ a adicional
addled /'ædl̩d/ a huero, podrido; Fig. confuso
address /n ə'drɛs, 'ædrɛs; v ə'drɛs/ n (on a letter) sobrescrito, m; (of a person) dirección, f, señas, f pl; (speech) discurso, m; (petition) memorial, m, petición, f; (dedication) dedicatoria, f; (invocation) invocación, f; (deportment) presencia, f; (tact) diplomacia, habilidad, f; pl **addresses,** corte, f. vt (a ball) golpear; (a letter) dirigir, poner el sobrescrito a, Mexico domiciliar; (words, prayers) dirigir (a); hablar, hacer un discurso. **to a. oneself to a task,** dedicarse a (or entregarse a or emprender) una tarea. **to deliver an a.,** pronunciar un discurso. **to pay one's addresses to,** cortejar, hacer la corte (a), galantear
addressee /,ædrɛ'si/ n destinatario (-ia)
adduce /ə'dus/ vt aducir, alegar; aportar
Aden /'ɑdn̩/ Adén m
adenoids /'ædn̩,ɔidz/ n pl amígdalas, f pl
adept /a ə'dɛpt; n 'ædɛpt/ a adepto, versado, consumado. n adepto, m
adequacy /'ædıkwəsi/ n adecuación, f; suficiencia, f; competencia, f
adequate /'ædıkwıt/ a adecuado; proporcionado; suficiente; competente; a la altura (de)
adequately /'ædıkwıtli/ adv adecuadamente
adhere /æd'hıər/ vi adherirse; pegarse; ser fiel (a); persistir (en)
adherence /æd'hıərəns/ n Fig. adhesión, f
adherent /æd'hıərənt/ n partidario (-ia)
adhesion /æd'hiʒən/ n adherencia, f; (to a party, etc.) adhesión, f
adhesive /æd'hisıv/ a adhesivo; (sticky) pegajoso. **a. tape,** esparadrapo, m; Elec. cinta aisladora adherente, f
adipose /'ædə,pous/ a adiposo
adjacent /ə'dʒeisənt/ a próximo, contiguo, adyacente, vecino
adjective /'ædʒıktıv/ n adjetivo, m
adjoin /ə'dʒɔin/ vt estar contiguo a, lindar con; juntar. vi colindar
adjoining /ə'dʒɔinıŋ/ a vecino, de al lado, adyacente, cercano
adjourn /ə'dʒɜrn/ vt aplazar, diferir (a meeting, etc.) suspender, levantar. vi retirarse. **The debate was adjourned,** Se suspendió el debate. **to a. a meeting,** levantar la sesión
adjournment /ə'dʒɜrnmənt/ n aplazamiento, m (a meeting) suspensión (de la sesión), f
adjudicate /ə'dʒudı,keit/ vt adjudicar; Law. declarar;

juzgar. *vi* ejercer las funciones del juez; fallar, dictar sentencia

adjudication /ə,dʒudɪ'keiʃən/ *n* adjudicación, *f*; *Law*. fallo, *m*, sentencia, *f*; (of bankruptcy) declaración (de quiebra), *f*; concesión, *f*, otorgamiento, *m*

adjudicator /ə'dʒudɪ,keitər/ *n* adjudicador (-ra)

adjunct /'ædʒʌŋkt/ *n* atributo, *m*; accesorio, *m*; adjunto, *m*; *Gram.* adjunto, *m*

adjure /ə'dʒʊr/ *vt* conjurar; rogar encarecidamente

adjust /ə'dʒʌst/ *vt* ajustar; regular; arreglar; (correct) corregir; adaptar

adjustable /ə'dʒʌstəbəl/ *a* ajustable; regulable; desmontable; de quita y pon

adjustment /ə'dʒʌstmənt/ *n* ajuste, *m*; regulación, *f*; arreglo, *m*; (correction) corrección, *f*; adaptación, *f*; *Com.* prorrateo, *m*

adjutant /'ædʒətənt/ *n* *Mil.* ayudante, *m*

administer /æd'mɪnəstər/ *vt* administrar; (laws) aplicar; (blows, etc.) dar; (an office) ejercer; (govern) regir, gobernar; (provide) suministrar; (an oath) tomar; (justice) hacer; (the sacraments) administrar; (with to) contribuir a. **to a. an oath,** tomar juramento (a)

administration /æd,mɪnə'streiʃən/ *n* administración, *f*; (government) gobierno, *m*; dirección, *f*; (of laws) aplicación, *f*; distribución, *f*

administrative /æd'mɪnə,streitɪv/ *a* administrativo; gubernativo

administrator /æd'mɪnə,streitər/ *n* administrador (-ra)

admirable /'ædmərəbəl/ *a* admirable

admirably /'ædmərəbli/ *adv* admirablemente

admiral /'ædmərəl/ *n* almirante, *m*. **A. of the Fleet,** almirante supremo, *m*. **admiral's ship,** capitana, *f*

admiration /,ædmə'reiʃən/ *n* admiración, *f*

admire /æd'maiᵊr/ *vt* sentir admiración por; (love) amar; (like) gustar; (respect) respetar

admirer /æd'maiᵊrər/ *n* admirador (-ra); (amateur) aficionado (-da), apasionado (-da); (partisan) satélite, *m*; (lover) enamorado, amante, *m*

admiring /æd'maiərɪŋ/ *a* admirativo, de admiración

admissible /æd'mɪsəbəl/ *a* admisible; aceptable; lícito, permitido

admission /æd'mɪʃən/ *n* admisión, *f*; recepción, *f*; entrada, *f*; confesión, *f*, reconocimiento, *m*. **Free a.,** Entrada libre. **No a.!** Entrada prohibida. **right of a.,** derecho de entrada, *m*. **a. ticket,** entrada, *f*

admit /æd'mɪt/ *vt* admitir; recibir; dejar entrar; hacer entrar, introducir; (hold) contener; (concede) conceder; (acknowledge) reconocer, confesar. **to a. of,** permitir; sufrir

admittance /æd'mɪtns/ *n* admisión, *f*; entrada, *f*. **No a.!** Prohibida la entrada. **to gain a.,** lograr entrar

admittedly /æd'mɪtɪdli/ *adv* según opinión general; sin duda

admonish /æd'mɒnɪʃ/ *vt* (advise) aconsejar; amonestar, advertir; (reprimand) reprender

admonition /,ædmə'nɪʃən/ *n* amonestación, *f*; advertencia, *f*; admonición, *f*

admonitory /æd'mɒnɪ,tɔri/ *a* amonestador

ad nauseam /'æd nɔziəm/ *adv* hasta la saciedad

ado /ə'du/ *n* (noise) ruido, *m*; (trouble) trabajo, *m*, dificultad, *f*; (fuss) barahúnda, *f*. **much ado about nothing,** mucho ruido y pocas nueces, nada entre dos platos. **without further ado,** sin más ni más

adolescence /,ædl'ɛsəns/ *n* adolescencia, *f*

adolescent /,ædl'ɛsənt/ *a* and *n* adolescente, *mf*

adopt /ə'dɒpt/ *vt* adoptar. **a. local customs** *Lat. Am.* acriollarse

adopted /ə'dɒptɪd/ *a* adoptivo

adoption /ə'dɒpʃən/ *n* adopción, *f*; (choice) elección, *f*

adoptive /ə'dɒptɪv/ *a* adoptivo

adorable /ə'dɔrəbəl/ *a* adorable

adoration /,ædə'reiʃən/ *n* adoración, *f*. **A. of the Magi,** Adoración de los Reyes, *f*

adore /ə'dɔr/ *vt* adorar

adorer /ə'dɔrər/ *n* adorador (-ra); amante, *m*

adoringly /ə'dɔrɪŋli/ *adv* con adoración

adorn /ə'dɔrn/ *vt* adornar, embellecer; (*Fig.* of persons) adornar con su presencia

adornment /ə'dɔrnmənt/ *n* adorno, *m*; ornamento, *m*; embellecimiento, *m*

adrenalin /ə'drɛnlɪn/ *n* adrenalina, *f*

Adriatic, the /,eidri'ætɪk/ el (Mar) Adriático, *m*

adrift /ə'drɪft/ *a* and *adv* a merced de las olas; a la ventura. **to turn a.,** *Inf.* poner de patitas en la calle

adroit /ə'drɔit/ *a* hábil

adulate /'ædʒə,leit/ *vt* adular

adulation /,ædʒə'leiʃən/ *n* adulación, *f*

adulatory /'ædʒələ,tɔri/ *a* adulador

adult /ə'dʌlt/ *a* and *n* adulto (-ta)

adult education *n* educación de los adultos, *f*

adulterate /*v* ə'dʌltə,reit; *a* ə'dʌltə,reit; -tərit/ *vt* adulterar; falsificar; contaminar. *a* adulterado; falsificado; impuro

adulteration /ə,dʌltə'reiʃən/ *n* adulteración, *f*; falsificación, *f*; impureza, *f*; contaminación, *f*

adulterer /ə'dʌltərər/ *n* adúltero, *m*

adulteress /ə'dʌltərɪs/ *n* adúltera, *f*

adulterous /ə'dʌltərəs/ *a* adúltero

adultery /ə'dʌltəri/ *n* adulterio, *m*. **to commit a.,** cometer adulterio, adulterar

advance /æd'væns/ *n* avance, *m*; (progress) progreso, adelantamiento, *m*; (improvement) mejora, *f*; (of shares) alza, *f*; (of price) subida, *f*; (loan) préstamo, *m*; (in rank) ascenso, *m*; *pl* **advances,** (overtures) avances, *m pl*; (proposals) propuestas, *f pl*; (of love) requerimientos amorosos, *m pl.* **in a.,** de antemano, con anticipación, con tiempo, previamente; (of money) por adelantado. **a. guard,** *Mil.* avanzada, *f*. **a. payment,** anticipo, *m*, paga por adelantado, *f*

advance /æd'væns/ *vt* avanzar; (suggest) sugerir, proponer; (encourage) fomentar; (a person) ascender; (improve) mejorar; (of events, dates) adelantar; (of prices, stocks) hacer subir; (money) anticipar; (of steps) tomar. *vi* avanzar; (progress) progresar; (in rank, studies, etc.) adelantar; (of prices) subir

advanced /æd'vænst/ *a* avanzado; (developed) desarrollado; (mentally, of children) precoz; (course) superior. **a. research,** investigaciones superiores. **a. standing,** equivalencias, *f pl.* **a. views,** ideas avanzadas, *f pl*

advancement /æd'vænsmənt/ *n* adelantamiento, *m*; progreso, *m*; (encouragement) fomento, *m*; (in employment) promoción, *f*; prosperidad, *f*

advancing /æd'vænsɪŋ/ *a* que avanza; (of years) que pasan

advantage /æd'væntɪdʒ/ *n* ventaja, *f*; superioridad, *f*; (benefit) provecho, beneficio, *m*; interés, *m*; ocasión favorable, oportunidad, *f*; (tennis) ventaja, *f*. **to have the a. of,** tener la ventaja de. **to show to a.,** embellecer, realzar; aumentar la belleza (etc.) de. **to take a. of,** sacar ventaja de, aprovecharse de; (deceive) engañar. **to take a. of the slightest pretext,** asirse de un cabello

advantageous /,ædvən'teidʒəs/ *a* ventajoso, provechoso. **to be a.,** ser de provecho

advent /'ædvɛnt/ *n* advenimiento, *m*, llegada, *f*; *Eccl.* Adviento, *m*

adventitious /,ædvən'tɪʃəs/ *a* adventicio (all uses)

adventure /æd'vɛntʃər/ *n* aventura, *f*; riesgo, *m*; (chance) casualidad, *f*; *Com.* especulación, *f*, *vt* aventurar, arriesgar. *vi* arriesgarse, osar

adventurer /æd'vɛntʃərər/ *n* aventurero (-ra) (one living by his or her wits) caballero de industria, *m*; (in commerce) especulador (-ra)

adventuresome /æd'vɛntʃərsəm/ *a* de aventura

adventurous /æd'vɛntʃərəs/ *a* aventurero; osado, audaz; (dangerous) peligroso, arriesgado

adverb /'ædvɜrb/ *n* adverbio, *m*

adversary /'ædvər,sɛri/ *n* adversario (-ia)

adverse /æd'vɜrs/ *a* adverso; hostil (a); malo; desfavorable; (opposite) opuesto

adversity /æd'vɜrsɪti/ *n* adversidad, *f*

advertise /'ædvər,taiz/ *vt* anunciar. *vi* poner un anuncio; (oneself) llamar la atención

advertisement /,ædvər'taizmənt, æd'vɜrtɪsmənt/ *n* anuncio, *m*; (poster) cartel, *m*; (to attract attention) reclamo, *m*. **to put an a. in the paper,** poner un anuncio en el periódico

advertiser /'ædvər,taizər/ *n* anunciante, *mf*

advertising /'ædvər,taizɪŋ/ n anuncios, m pl; publicidad, propaganda, f; medios publicitarios, m pl
advice /æd'vais/ n consejo, m; (warning) advertencia, amonestación, f; (news) noticia, f, aviso, m; Com. comunicación, f; (belief) parecer, m, opinión, f. **piece of a.**, consejo, m. **to follow the a.** of, seguir los consejos de. **to give a.**, dar consejos
advisability /æd,vaizə'bılıti/ n conveniencia, f; prudencia, f
advisable /æd'vaizəbəl/ a conveniente, aconsejable; prudente
advise /æd'vaiz/ vt aconsejar; (inform) avisar, informar
advised /æd'vaizd/ a avisado; premeditado. **ill-a.**, mal aconsejado; imprudente. **well-a.**, bien aconsejado; prudente
adviser /æd'vaizər/ n consejero (-ra), asesor
advisory /æd'vaizəri/ a asesor, consultivo, consultativo
advocacy /'ædvəkəsi/ n defensa, f; apología, f; abogacía, intercesión, f
advocate /n 'ædvəkɪt; v -,keit/ n Law. abogado (-da); defensor (-ra); (champion) campeón, m. vt abogar; defender; sostener, apoyar; recomendar
adze /ædz/ n azuela, f
Aegean, the /ə'dʒiən/ el (Mar) Egeo, m
aegis /'idʒis/ n égida, f; protección, f
aerated /'ɛə,reitid/ a aerado; (of lemonade, etc.) gaseoso. **a. waters,** aguas gaseosas, f pl
aeration /,ɛə'reiʃən/ n aeración, f
aerial /'ɛəriəl/ a aéreo, de aire; etéreo; fantástico. n (radio) antena, f. **indoor a.,** antena interior, f
aerobics /ɛə'roubiks/ n aerobismo m
aerodynamics /,ɛəroudai'næmiks/ n aerodinámica, f
aeronaut /'ɛərə,nɔt/ n aeronauta, mf
aeronautical /,ɛərə'nɔtikəl/ a aeronáutico
aeronautics /,ɛərə'nɔtiks/ n aeronáutica, f
afar /ə'fɑr/ adv a lo lejos, en la distancia. **from a.**, desde lejos
affability /,æfə'bılıti/ n afabilidad, condescendencia, urbanidad, f
affable /'æfəbəl/ a afable, condescendiente
affably /'æfəbli/ adv afablemente
affair /ə'fɛər/ n asunto, m, cosa, f; cuestión, f; (business) negocio, m; (Fam. applied to a machine, carriage, etc.) artefacto, m; (of the heart) amorío, m. **a. of honor,** lance de honor, m
affect /ə'fɛkt/ vt afectar; influir; Med. atacar; (move) impresionar, conmover; enternecer; (harm) perjudicar; (frequent) frecuentar; (like) gustar de; (love) amar; (wear) vestir; (use) gastar, usar; (feign) aparentar; (boast) hacer alarde de
affectation /,æfɛk'teiʃən/ n afectación, f
affected /ə'fɛktɪd/ a afectado; influido; Med. atacado; (moved) conmovido, impresionado; enternecido; (inclined) dispuesto, inclinado; (artificial) artificioso; amanerado, afectado; (of style) rebuscado, artificial
affecting /ə'fɛktɪŋ/ a conmovedor, emocionante
affection /ə'fɛkʃən/ n afecto, cariño, m; amor, m; apego, m; simpatía, f; (emotion) emoción, f, sentimiento, m; Med. afección, enfermedad, f
affectionate /ə'fɛkʃənɪt/ a afectuoso, cariñoso; mimoso; (tender) tierno; expresivo
affectionately /ə'fɛkʃənɪtli/ adv afectuosamente. **Yours a.**, tu cariñoso..., tu..., que te quiere
affective /'æfɛktɪv/ a afectivo
affidavit /,æfi'deivit/ n declaración jurada, declaración jurídica, f, atestiguación, f
affiliate /ə'fıli,eit/ vt afiliar; adoptar; Law. imputar; Law. legitimar. n afiliado, socio, m
affiliation /ə,fıli'eiʃən/ n afiliación, f; adopción, f; legitimación de un hijo, f
affinity /ə'fınıti/ n afinidad, f
affirm /ə'fɜrm/ vt afirmar, aseverar, declarar; confirmar. vi Law. declarar ante un juez
affirmation /,æfər'meiʃən/ n afirmación, aserción, f; confirmación, f; Law. declaración, deposición, f
affirmative /ə'fɜrmətɪv/ a afirmativo. n afirmativa, f
affix /v ə'fıks; n 'æfıks/ vt fijar; pegar; añadir; (seal, one's signature) poner. n Gram. afijo, m

afflict /ə'flıkt/ vt afligir, atormentar, aquejar
affliction /ə'flıkʃən/ n aflicción, f; tribulación, pesadumbre, f; calamidad, f; miseria, f; (ailment) achaque, m
affluence /'æfluəns/ n afluencia, f; abundancia, f; riqueza, f; opulencia, f
affluent /'æfluənt/ a abundante; rico; opulento
afflux /'æflʌks/ n afluencia, f; Med. aflujo, m
afford /ə'fɔrd/ vt dar, proporcionar; producir; ofrecer; (bear) soportar; poder con; (financially) tener medios para; permitirse el lujo de; (be able) poder. **I could not a. to pay so much,** No puedo (podía) pagar tanto
afforest /ə'fɔrɪst/ vt convertir en bosque
afforestation /ə,fɔrə'steiʃən/ n conversión en bosque, f; plantación de un bosque, f
affray /ə'frei/ n riña, refriega, f
affront /ə'frʌnt/ n afrenta, f, insulto, agravio, m. vt insultar, ultrajar, afrentar; (offend) ofender
Afghan /'æfgæn/ a and n afgano (-na)
Afghanistan /æf'gænə,stæn/ Afganistán, m
afield /ə'fild/ adv en el campo; lejos. **to go far a.**, ir muy lejos
afire /ə'faiər/ adv en fuego, en llamas; Fig. ardiendo
aflame /ə'fleim/ adv en llamas; Fig. encendido
afloat /ə'flout/ adv a flote; Naut. a bordo; (solvent) solvente; en circulación; (floating) flotante; (swamped) inundado; (in full swing) en marcha, en movimiento
afoot /ə'fʊt/ adv a pie; en marcha, en movimiento; en preparación. **to set a.,** iniciar, poner en marcha
aforementioned /ə'fɔr,mɛnʃənd/ a antedicho, ya mencionado
aforesaid /ə'fɔr,sɛd/ a consabido, dicho, susodicho
afraid /ə'freid/ a espantado; temeroso, miedoso. **I'm a. that...,** Me temo que.... **to be a.,** tener miedo. **to make a.,** dar miedo (a)
afresh /ə'frɛʃ/ adv de nuevo, otra vez
African /'æfrɪkən/ a and n africano (-na)
African-American /'æfrɪkən ə'mɛrɪkən/ n afroamericano (-na)
aft /æft/ adv en popa; a popa. **fore and aft,** de proa a popa
after /'æftər/ prep (of place) detrás de; (of time) después de; (behind) en pos de; (following) tras; (in spite of) a pesar de; (in consequence of) después de, a consecuencia de; (in accordance with) según; (in the style of) al estilo de, en imitación de. adv (later) después, más tarde; (subsequently) después (que); (when) cuando. a futuro, venidero. **day a.** day, día tras día. **on the day a.,** al día siguiente. **soon a.,** poco después. **to look a.,** cuidar de. **to go a.,** ir a buscar; seguir. **the day a. tomorrow,** pasado mañana. **What are you a.?** ¿Qué buscas? **a. all,** después de todo. **the manner of,** a la moda de, según la moda de; al estilo de. **a.-dinner conversation,** conversación de sobremesa, f. **a. glow,** resplandor crepuscular, reflejo del sol poniente en el cielo, m. **a. life,** vida futura, f. **a. pains,** dolores de sobreparto, m pl. **a. taste,** gusto, paladar, m
afterbirth /'æftər,bɜrθ/ n placenta, f
aftermath /'æftər,mæθ/ n consecuencias, f pl, resultado, m
afternoon /,æftər'nun/ n tarde, f. **Good a.!** ¡Buenas tardes! **a. nap,** siesta, f
afterthought /'æftər,θɔt/ n reflexión tardía, f; segunda intención, f. **to have an a.,** pensar en segundo lugar
afterwards /'æftərwərdz/ adv después; más tarde
again /ə'gɛn/ adv (once more) otra vez, de nuevo; por segunda vez, dos veces; (on the other hand) por otra parte; (moreover) además; (likewise) también; (returned) de vuelta. Sometimes translated by prefix **re** in verbs. **as much a.,** otro tanto. **never a.,** nunca más. **not a.,** no más. **now and a.,** de vez en cuando. **to do a.,** volver a hacer, hacer de nuevo. **a. and a.,** repetidas veces
against /ə'gɛnst/ prep (facing) enfrente de; contra; (in preparation for) para; (contrary to) contrario a; (opposed to) opuesto a; (near) cerca de. **to be a.,** oponer; estar enfrente de. **a. the grain,** a contrapelo
agate /'ægɪt/ n ágata, f; heliotropo, m

age /eidʒ/ n edad, f; (generation) generación, f; (epoch) siglo, período, m; época, f; (old age) vejez, f; (majority) mayoría de edad, f, vi envejecer. **at any age,** a cualquier edad. **the golden age,** la edad de oro; (in literature, etc.) el siglo de oro. **from age to age,** por los siglos de los siglos. **to be of age,** ser mayor de edad. **to be under age,** ser menor de edad. **to come of age,** llegar a la mayoría de edad. **She is six years of age,** Ella tiene seis años. **age-old,** secular

aged /eidʒd/ 'eidʒɪd/ a de la edad de; (old) anciano, viejo. **a girl a. four,** una niña de cuatro años

ageless /'eidʒlɪs/ a siempre joven; eterno

agency /'eidʒənsi/ n órgano, m, fuerza, f; acción, f; influencia, f; intervención, f; mediación, f; Com. agencia, f. **through the a. of,** por la mediación (or influencia) de

agenda /ə'dʒɛndə/ n agenda, f

agent /'eidʒənt/ n agente, m; Com. representante, mf; Law. apoderado (-da). **business a.,** agente de negocios, m

agglomerate /ə'glɒmə,reit/ vt and vi aglomerar(se)

agglomeration /ə,glɒmə'reiʃən/ n aglomeración, f

agglutinate /ə'glutn̩,eit/ vt and vi aglutinar(se)

aggrandize /ə'grændaiz/ vt engrandecer

aggrandizement /ə'grændɪzmənt/ n engrandecimiento, m

aggravate /'ægrə,veit/ vt agravar, hacer peor; intensificar; (annoy) irritar, exasperar

aggravating /'ægrə,veitɪŋ/ a agravante, agravador; (tiresome) molesto; (annoying) irritante. **a. circumstance,** circunstancia agravante, f

aggravation /,ægrə'veiʃən/ n agravación, f, intensificación, f; (annoyance) irritación, f

aggregate /'ægrɪgɪt, -,geit/ a total. n agregado, conjunto, m. **in the a.,** en conjunto

aggression /ə'grɛʃən/ n agresión, f

aggressive /ə'grɛsɪv/ a agresivo, a

aggressiveness /ə'grɛsɪvnɪs/ n carácter agresivo, m, belicosidad, f

aggressor /ə'grɛsər/ a and n agresor (-ra)

aggrieved /ə'grivd/ a afligido; ofendido; lastimero

aghast /ə'gæst/ a horrorizado, espantado; (amazed) estupefacto

agile /'ædʒəl/ a ágil; ligero, Mexico alacre; vivo

agility /æ'dʒɪlɪti/ n agilidad, f; ligereza, f, Mexico alacridad

agitate /'ædʒɪ,teit/ vt agitar; excitar; inquietar, perturbar; discutir. **to a. for,** luchar por; excitar la opinión pública en favor de

agitating /'ædʒɪ,teitɪŋ/ a agitador

agitation /,ædʒɪ'teiʃən/ n agitación, f; perturbación, f; discusión, f

agitator /'ædʒɪ,teitər/ n agitador (-ra); (apparatus) agitador, m

aglow /ə'glou/ a and adv brillante, fulgente; encendido

agnostic /æg'nɒstɪk/ a and n agnóstico (-ca)

agnosticism /æg'nɒstə,sɪzəm/ n agnosticismo, m

ago /ə'gou/ adv hace. **a short while ago,** hace poco. **How long ago?** ¿Cuánto tiempo hace? **long ago,** hace mucho. **many years ago,** hace muchos años. **I last saw him ten years ago,** La última vez que le vi fue hace diez años

agog /ə'gɒg/ a agitado; ansioso; excitado; impaciente; curioso. adv con agitación; con ansia; con curiosidad

agonize /'ægə,naiz/ vt atormentar. vi sufrir intensamente; retorcerse de dolor

agonizing /'ægə,naizɪŋ/ a (of pain) intenso, atormentador

agonizingly /'ægə,naizɪŋli/ adv dolorosamente

agony /'ægəni/ n agonía, f; angustia, f; paroxismo, m. **a. column,** columna de los suspiros, f

agrarian /ə'grɛəriən/ a agrario

agree /ə'gri/ vi estar de acuerdo. **Do you a.?** ¿Estás de acuerdo?; convenir (en); acordar; ponerse de acuerdo, entenderse; (suit) sentar bien, probar; (consent) consentir (en); Gram. concordar, (get on well) llevarse bien; (correspond) estar conforme (con). **to**

a. to, convenir en, consentir en. **to a. with,** estar de acuerdo con, apoyar; dar la razón a; (suit) sentar bien; Gram. concordar

agreeable /ə'griəbəl/ a agradable; afable, amable; (pleasant) ameno, grato; conforme; dispuesto a (hacer algo); conveniente

agreeableness /ə'griəbəlnɪs/ n (of persons) afabilidad, amabilidad, f; amenidad, f; deleite, m; conformidad, f

agreeably /ə'griəbli/ adv agradablemente; de acuerdo (con), conforme (a)

agreed /ə'grid/ a convenido, acordado; (approved) aprobado. interj ¡convenido! ¡de acuerdo!

agreement /ə'grimənt/ n acuerdo, m; pacto, m; acomodamiento, concierto, m; contrato, m; Com. convenio, m; conformidad, f; consentimiento, m; Gram. concordancia, f. **in a.,** conforme. **in a. with,** de acuerdo con; según. **to reach an a.,** ponerse de acuerdo

agricultural /,ægrɪ'kʌltʃərəl/ a agrícola. **a. engineer,** ingeniero agrónomo, m. **a. laborer,** labriego, m. **a. show,** exposición agrícola, f

agriculturalist /,ægrɪ'kʌltʃərəlɪst/ n agrícola, mf

agriculture /'ægrɪ,kʌltʃər/ n agricultura, f

agronomist /ə'grɒnəmɪst/ n agrónomo, m

agronomy /ə'grɒnəmi/ n agronomía, f

aground /ə'graund/ adv Naut. varado, encallado. **running a.,** varada, f. **to run a.,** varar

ague /'eigyu/ n fiebre intermitente, f; Fig. escalofrío, m

ah! /ɑ/ interj ¡ah! ¡ay!

aha! /ɑ'hɑ/ interj ¡ajá!

ahead /ə'hɛd/ adv delante; enfrente; al frente (de); a la cabeza (de); adelante; hacia delante; Naut. por la proa. **Go a.!** ¡Adelante! **It is straight a.,** Está derecho. **to go straight a.,** ir hacia delante; seguir (haciendo algo)

ahoy! /ə'hɔi/ interj ¡ah del barco!

aid /eid/ n ayuda, f; socorro, auxilio, m; subsidio, m. vt ayudar; socorrer, auxiliar. **in aid of,** pro, en beneficio de. **first aid,** primera cura, f. **first aid post,** puesto de socorro, m. **to come or go to the aid of,** acudir en defensa de

aide-de-camp /'eid də 'kæmp/ n edecán, m

AIDS /eidz/ n el SIDA, m

ail /eil/ vt afligir, doler; pasar. vi estar indispuesto (or enfermo). **What ails you?** Inf. ¿Qué te pasa?

ailing /'eilɪŋ/ a enfermizo, enclenque, achacoso

ailment /'eilmənt/ n enfermedad, f, achaque, m

aim /eim/ n (of firearms) puntería, f; (mark) blanco, m; Fig. objeto, fin, m; Fig. intención, f, propósito, m, vt (a gun) apuntar; dirigir; (throw) lanzar; (a blow) asestar. vi apuntar (a); (a remark at) decir por; aspirar (a); intentar, proponerse. **Is your remark aimed at me?** ¿Lo dices por mí? **to aim high,** apuntar alto; Inf. picar alto. **to miss one's aim,** errar el tiro. **to take aim,** apuntar. **with the aim of,** con objeto de, a fin de

aimless /'eimlɪs/ a **aimlessly,** adv sin objeto, a la ventura

air /ɛər/ n aire, m, (all meanings). **by air,** en avión, (of mail) por avión; (of goods) por vía aérea. **in the air,** al aire; al aire libre; (as though flying) en volandas. **in the open air,** al aire libre, al fresco, a la intemperie. **to be on the air,** Radio. hablar por radio. **to give oneself airs,** darse tono, tener humos. **to take the air,** tomar el fresco; despejar. **air balloon,** globo aerostático, m; (toy) globo, m. **air-base,** base aérea, f. **air-bed,** colchón de viento, m. **air-borne (to become),** levantar el vuelo, despegar. **air-brake,** Mech. freno neumático, m. **air-chamber,** cámara de aire, f. **air chief marshal,** general del ejército del aire, m. **air-cock,** válvula de escape de aire, f. **air commodore,** general de brigada de aviación, m. **air conditioning,** purificación de aire, f, Lat. Am. aclimatación, f. **air-cooled,** enfriado por aire. **air crash,** accidente de aviación, m. **air current,** corriente de aire, f. **air-cushion,** almohadilla neumática, f. **air-field,** campo de aviación, m. **air fleet,** flotilla aérea, f. **air force,** fuerza aérea, flota aérea, f. **air-gun,** escopeta de viento, f. **air-hole,** respiradero, m. **air-hostess,** azafata, f. **air-lift,** puente aéreo, m. **air-liner,** avión de air 306

pasajeros, *m.* **airline** linea aérea, aerolínea, *f.* **airmail,** correo aéreo, *m.* **by airmail,** por avión. **air marshal,** teniente general de aviación, *m.* **air-pocket,** bolsa (or vacío, *m*) de aire, *f.* **air pollution** contaminación atmosférica, *f.* **air pump,** bomba neumática, *f.* **air raid,** bombardeo aéreo, *m.* **air-raid shelter,** refugio antiaéreo, *m.* **air-raid warning,** alarma aérea, *f.* **airroute,** vía aérea, *f.* **air-screw,** hélice de avión, *f.* **airshaft,** respiradero de mina, *m.* **air shuttle,** puente aéreo, *m.* **air squadron,** escuadrilla aérea, *f.* **air stream,** chorro de aire, *m.* **air taxi,** avión taxi, *m.* **air-tight,** herméticamente cerrado. **air valve,** válvula de aire, *f.* **air vice-marshal,** general de división de aviación, *m*

air /ɛər/ *vt* airear, orear; secar al aire; ventilar; *Fig.* sacar a lucir, emitir; *Fig.* ostentar

aircraft /'ɛər,kræft/ *n* aeronave, avión, *m.* **a. barrage,** cortina de fuego de artillería, *f.* **a.-carrier,** portaaviones, *m.* **a. factory,** fábrica de aeroplanos, *f*

airily /'ɛərəli/ *adv* ligeramente, sin preocuparse; alegremente

airiness /'ɛərɪnɪs/ *n* airosidad, *f;* ventilación, *f;* situación airosa, *f;* (lightness) ligereza, *f;* alegría, *f;* frivolidad, *f*

airing /'ɛərɪŋ/ *n* aireación, *f;* ventilación, *f;* secamiento, *m;* (walk) vuelta, *f*, paseo, *m.* **to take an a.,** dar una vuelta

airless /'ɛərlɪs/ *a* sin aire; falto de ventilación; sofocante

airman /'ɛərmən/ *n* aviador, *m*

airplane /'ɛər,plein/ *n* aeroplano, avión, *m.* **jet-propelled a.,** aeroplano de reacción, *m.* **model a.,** aeroplano en miniatura, *m*

airport /'ɛər,pɔrt/ *n* aeropuerto, *m*

airsick /'ɛər,sɪk/ *a* mareado en el aire, mareado

airway /'ɛər,wei/ *n* vía aérea, *f*

airwoman /'ɛər,wʊmən/ *n* aviadora, *f*

airy /'ɛəri/ *a* aéreo; (breezy) airoso; ligero; vaporoso; alegre; (vain) vano; (flippant) frívolo

aisle /ail/ *n* nave lateral, ala, *f*

ajar /ə'dʒɑr/ *a* entreabierto, entornado. **to leave a.,** dejar entreabierto, entornar

akimbo /ə'kɪmbou/ *adv* en jarras. **with arms a.,** con los brazos en jarras

akin /ə'kɪn/ *a* consanguíneo, emparentado; análogo; relacionado; semejante

alabaster /'ælə,bæstər/ *n* alabastro, *m*, a alabastrino

alacrity /ə'lækrɪti/ *n* alacridad, *f*

alarm /ə'lɑrm/ *n* alarma, *f*, toque de alarma, *m;* (tocsin) rebato, *m;* sobresalto, *m*, alarma, *f. vt* alarmar; *Mil.* dar la alarma (a); asustar. **to give the a.,** dar la alarma. **a. bell,** timbre de alarma, *m.* **a. clock,** despertador, *m.* **a. signal,** señal de alarma, *f*

alarming /ə'lɑrmɪŋ/ *a* alarmante

alarmingly /ə'lɑrmɪŋli/ *adv* de un modo alarmante; espantosamente

alarmist /ə'lɑrmɪst/ *n* alarmista, *mf*

alas! /ə'læs/ *interj* ¡ay!

alb /ælb/ *n* alba, *f*

Albanian /æl'beiniən/ *a* and *n* albanés (-esa) and *n* (language) albanés, *m*

albatross /'ælbə,trɔs/ *n* albatros, *m*

albeit /ɔl'bit/ *conjunc* aunque, si bien; sin embargo

albinism /'ælbə,nɪzəm/ *n* albinismo, *m*

albino /æl'bainou/ *a* albino

album /'ælbəm/ *n* álbum, *m*

albumin /æl'byumən/ *n* albúmina, *f*

alchemist /'ælkəmɪst/ *n* alquimista, *m*

alchemy /'ælkəmi/ *n* alquimia, *f*

alcohol /'ælkə,hɔl/ *n* alcohol, *m.* **industrial a.,** alcohol desnaturalizado, *m.* **wood a.,** alcohol metílico, alcohol de madera, *m*

alcoholic /,ælkə'hɔlɪk/ *a* alcohólico

alcoholism /'ælkəhɔ,lɪzəm/ *n* alcoholismo, *m*

alcove /'ælkouv/ *n* alcoba, *f;* nicho, *m*

alder /'ɔldər/ *n* (tree and wood) aliso, *m*

alderman /'ɔldərmən/ *n* concejal, *m*

ale /eil/ *n* cerveza, *f.* **ale-house,** cervecería, *f*

alert /ə'lɜrt/ *a* alerto; vigilante; despierto; vivo. *n* si-

rena, *f.* **to be on the a.,** estar sobre aviso; estar vigilante

alertly /ə'lɜrtli/ *adv* alertamente

alertness /ə'lɜrtnɪs/ *n* vigilancia, *f;* viveza, *f;* prontitud, *f*

Alexandria /,ælɪg'zændriə/ Alejandría, *f*

algae /'ældʒi/ *n* algas, *f pl*

algebra /'ældʒəbrə/ *n* álgebra, *f*

algebraic /,ældʒə'breiɪk/ *a* algebraico

Algeria /æl'dʒɪəriə/ Argelia, *f*

Algerian /æl'dʒɪəriən/ *a* and *n* argelino (-na)

Algiers /æl'dʒɪərz/ Argel, *m*

alias /'eiliəs/ *adv* alias, por otro nombre. *n* nombre falso, seudónimo, *m*

alibi /'ælə,bai/ *n Law.* coartada, *f.* **to prove an a.,** probar la coartada

alien /'eiliən/ *a* ajeno; (foreign) extranjero; extraño; contrario. *n* extranjero (-ra). **a. to,** ajeno a; repugnante a

alienable /'eiliənəbəl/ *a* enajenable

alienate /'eiliə,neit/ *vt* alejar, hacer indiferente; (property) enajenar, traspasar

alienation /,eiliə'neiʃən/ *n* desvío, *m;* enajenación, *f;* traspaso, *m;* enajenación mental, *f*

alight /ə'lait/ *vi* apearse (de), bajar (de); desmontar (de); (of birds, etc.) posarse (sobre)

align /ə'lain/ *vt* alinear

alignment /ə'lainmənt/ *n* alineación, *f*

alike /ə'laik/ *a* semejante; igual. *adv* del mismo modo; igualmente

alimentary /,ælə'mɛntəri/ *a* nutritivo; alimenticio. **a. canal,** tubo digestivo, *m*

alimentation /,æləmɛn'teiʃən/ *n* alimentación, *f*

alimony /'ælə,mouni/ *n Law.* alimentos, *m pl*, pensión alimenticia, *f*

alive /ə'laiv/ *a* viviente; vivo; del mundo; (busy) animado, concurrido; (aware) sensible; (alert) lleno de vida, enérgico, despierto. **He is still a.,** Aún vive. **He is the best man a.,** Es el mejor hombre que existe, Es el mejor hombre del mundo. **half-a.,** semivivo. **while a.,** en vida. **a. to,** consciente de, sensible de. **a. with,** plagado de, lleno de

alkali /'ælkə,lai/ *n* álcali, *m*

alkaline /'ælkə,lain/ *a* alcalino

alkaloid /'ælkə,lɔid/ *n* alcaloide, *f*

all /ɔl/ *a* todo, *m;* toda, *f;* todos, *m pl;* todas, *f pl;* (in games) iguales. *adv* enteramente, completamente; del todo; absolutamente. **after all,** después de todo; sin embargo. **at all,** nada; de ninguna manera; en absoluto. **fifteen all,** (tennis) quince iguales. **for good and all,** para siempre. **if that's all,** si no es más que eso. **in all,** en conjunto. **It is all one to me,** Me da igual. **not at all,** de ningún modo, nada de eso; nada; (never) jamás; (as a polite formula) No hay de qué. **once for all,** una vez por todas; por última vez. **That is all,** Eso es todo. **all along,** (of time) siempre, todo el tiempo; (of place) a lo largo de, de un extremo a otro de. **all but,** (almost) casi, por poco; (except) todo menos. **all joking aside,** fuera de burla. **all of** /,ɔl ev/ (with ns. and pr.): todas ellas, *f pl.* **All right!** ¡Bien! ¡Está bien! ¡Entendido! **all that,** todo eso; (as much as) cuanto. **all that which,** todo lo que. **all those who,** todos los que, *m pl;* todas las que, *f pl.* **all the more,** cuanto más. **all the same,** sin embargo, a pesar de todo. **all the worse,** tanto peor

all /ɔl/ *n* todo, *m;* todos, *m pl;* todas, *f pl;* (everyone, all men) todo el mundo. **to lose one's all,** perder el todo. **All is lost,** Todo se ha perdido. **all told,** en conjunto

all /ɔl/ (in compounds) **all-absorbing,** que todo lo absorbe; sumamente interesante. **all-bountiful,** de suma bondad. **all-conquering,** invicto. **all-consuming,** que todo lo consume; interesadísimo; ardiente. **all-enduring,** resignado a todo. **All Fools' Day,** Día de los Inocentes, *m,* (December 28). **all-fours,** a cuatro patas; a gatas. **to go on all fours,** andar a gatas. **All hail!** ¡Salud! ¡Bienvenido! **all-important,** sumamente importante. **all-in insurance,** seguro contra todo riesgo, *m.* **all-in wrestling,** lucha libre, *f.* **all-loving,** de un amor infinito. **all-merciful,** de una compasión infinita, sumamente misericordioso. **all-powerful,** omnipo-

tente, todo poderoso. **all-round,** completo, cabal; universal. **an all-round athlete,** un atleta completo. **All Souls' Day,** Día de las Ánimas, Día de los difuntos, *m.* **all-wise,** omniscio
allay /ə'lei/ *vt* calmar; (relieve) aliviar; apaciguar
allaying /ə'leiɪŋ/ *n* alivio, *m;* apaciguamiento, *m*
allegation /ˌælɪ'geiʃən/ *n* alegación, *f*
allege /ə'lɛdʒ/ *vt* afirmar, declarar; alegar
allegiance /ə'lidʒəns/ *n* lealtad, *f;* fidelidad, *f;* obediencia, *f*
allegorical /ˌælɪ'gɔrɪkəl/ *a* alegórico
allegory /'ælə,gɔri/ *n* alegoría, *f*
alleluia /ˌælə'luyə/ *n* aleluya, *mf*
allergic /ə'lɜrdʒɪk/ *a* alérgico
allergist /'ælərdʒɪst/ *n* alergólogo, *m*
allergy /'ælərdʒi/ *n* alergia, *f*
alleviate /ə'livi,eit/ *vt* aliviar
alleviation /ə,livi'eiʃən/ *n* alivio, *m;* mitigación, *f*
alley /'æli/ *n* callejuela, *f,* callejón, *m;* avenida, *f;* (skittle a.) pista de bolos, *f.* **a.-way,** *Naut.* pasadizo, *m*
alliance /ə'laiəns/ *n* alianza, *f;* parentesco, *m*
allied /'ælaid/ *a* aliado; allegado
alligator /'ælɪ,geitər/ *n* caimán, *m*
alliteration /ə,lɪtə'reiʃən/ *n* aliteración, *f*
allocate /'ælə,keit/ *vt* asignar, destinar; distribuir, repartir
allocation /ˌælə'keiʃən/ *n* asignación, *f;* distribución, *f,* repartimiento, *m*
allotment /ə'lɒtmənt/ *n* repartimiento, *m,* distribución, *f;* porción, *f;* lote, *m;* parcela de tierra, huerta, *f*
allow /ə'lau/ *vt* permitir; autorizar; dejar; tolerar, sufrir; (provide) dar; conceder, otorgar; (acknowledge) admitir; confesar; (a pension) hacer; deducir. **to a. for,** tener en cuenta; ser indulgente con; deducir; dejar (espacio, etc.) para
allowable /ə'lauəbəl/ *a* admisible, permisible; lícito, legítimo
allowance /ə'lauəns/ *n* ración, *f;* (discount) descuento, *m;* pensión, *f;* concesión, *f;* excusa, *f;* (subsidy) subsidio, *m;* (bonus) abono, *m;* (monthly) mesada, *f.* **to make a. for,** tener presente; hacer excusas para, ser indulgente con
alloy /*n* 'ælɔi, *v* ə'lɔi/ *n* aleación, *f;* liga, *f;* mezcla, *f. vt* alear, ligar; mezclar
allspice /'ɔl,spais/ *n* guindilla de Indias, *f*
all-star game /'ɔl,star/ *n* juego de estrellas, *m*
allude /ə'lud/ *vi* aludir (a), referirse (a)
allure /ə'lur/ *vt* convidar, provocar; atraer; seducir, fascinar
allurement /ə'lurmənt/ *n* (snare) añagaza, *f;* atracción, *f;* tentación, seducción, *f*
alluring /ə'lurɪŋ/ *a* atractivo, seductor, tentador; (promising) halagüeño
allusion /ə'luʒən/ *n* alusión, referencia, *f;* insinuación, *f*
allusive /ə'lusiv/ *a* alusivo
ally /*n* 'ælai, *v* ə'lai/ *n* aliado (-da), allegado (-da); asociado (-da); (state) aliado, *m. vt* unir. **to become allies,** aliarse
almanac /'ɔlmə,næk/ *n* almanaque, *m*
almighty /ɔl'maiti/ *a* omnipotente
almond /'amənd/ *n* almendra, *f;* (tree) almendro, *m.* **bitter a.,** almendra amarga, *f.* **green a.,** almendruco, *m.* **milk of almonds,** horchata de almendras, *f;* (for the hands) loción de almendras, *f.* **sugar a.,** almendra garapiñada, *f.* **a.-eyed,** con, or de, ojos rasgados. **a. paste,** pasta de almendras, *f.* **a.-shaped,** en forma de almendra, almendrado
almoner /'ælmənər, 'amə-/ *n* limosnero (-ra) *mf*
almost /'ɔlmoust/ *adv* casi; por poco
alms /amz/ *n* limosna, *f.* **to ask a.,** pedir limosna, mendigar. **to give a.,** dar limosna. **a.-box,** cepillo de limosna, *m*
almsgiving /'amz,gɪvɪŋ/ *n* caridad, *f*
aloe /'ælou/ *n* áloe, *m;* *pl* **aloes,** *Med.* acíbar, *m*
aloft /ə'lɔft/ *adv* arriba, en alto
alone /ə'loun/ *a* solo; solitario. *adv* a solas, sin compañía; solamente; únicamente. **to leave a.,** dejar solo; dejar en paz
along /ə'lɔŋ/ *adv* a lo largo; todo el tiempo. *prep* a lo

largo de; por; al lado (de); en compañía (de). **Come a.!** ¡Ven! **all a.,** todo el tiempo, desde el principio; a lo largo de. **a. with,** junto con; en compañía de
alongside /ə'lɔŋ'said/ *adv* al lado; *Naut.* al costado. *prep* junto a, al lado de; *Naut.* al costado de. **to bring a.,** *Naut.* abarloar. **to come a.,** *Naut.* acostarse
aloof /ə'luf/ *adv* a distancia; lejos. *a* altanero, esquivo; reservado. **to keep a.,** mantenerse alejado
aloofness /ə'lufnɪs/ *n* alejamiento, *m;* esquivez, *f;* reserva, *f*
aloud /ə'laud/ *adv* en alta voz, alto
alpaca /æl'pækə/ *n* alpaca, *f*
alphabet /'ælfə,bɛt/ *n* alfabeto, *m;* abecedario, *m*
alphabetical /ˌælfə'bɛtɪkəl/ *a* alfabético
Alpine /'ælpain/ *a* alpestre, alpino
Alps, the /ælps/ los Alpes, *m*
already /ɔl'rɛdi/ *adv* ya; previamente
Alsatian /æl'seiʃən/ *a* and *n* alsaciano (-na†. **A. dog,** perro policía, perro pastor alemán, perro lobo, *m*
also /'ɔlsou/ *adv* también, igualmente, además
altar /'ɔltər/ *n* altar, *m.* **high a.,** altar mayor, *m.* **to lead a woman to the a.,** llevar a una mujer a la iglesia. **a.-cloth,** mantel del altar, *m.* **a.-piece,** retablo, *m.* **a.-rail,** mesa del altar, *f*
altar boy *n* acólito, monaguillo, *m*
altar girl *n* acólita, monaguilla *f*
altar server *n* acólito, monaguillo, *m* (male), acólita, monaguilla, *f* (female)
alter /'ɔltər/ *vt* cambiar; alterar; modificar; corregir; transformar; (clothes) arreglar. *vi* cambiar
alterable /'ɔltərəbəl/ *a* alterable
alteration /ˌɔltə'reiʃən/ *n* cambio, *m,* alteración, *f;* modificación, *f;* corrección, *f;* innovación, *f;* (to buildings, etc.) reforma, *f,* renovación, *f;* arreglo, *m*
altercation /ˌɔltər'keiʃən/ *n* altercación, *f*
alternate /*a* 'ɔltərnɪt; *v* -,neit/ *a* alternativo; (*Bot.* and of rhymes) alterno. *vt* and *vi* alternar
alternately /'ɔltərnɪtli/ *adv* alternativamente; por turno
alternating /'ɔltər,neitɪŋ/ *a* alternador. **a. current,** *Elec.* corriente alterna, *f*
alternation /ˌɔltər'neiʃən/ *n* alternación, *f;* (of time) transcurso, *m;* turno, *m*
alternative /ɔl'tɜrnətɪv/ *n* alternativa, *f, a* alternativo, alterno. **to have no a. but,** no poder menos de
alternatively /ɔl'tɜrnətɪvli/ *adv* alternativamente
alternative medicine *n* medicina alternativa; salud natural, *f*
alternator /'ɔltər,neitər/ *n Elec.* alternador, *m*
although /ɔl'ðou/ *conjunc* aunque, bien que; si bien; no obstante, a pesar de
altimeter /æl'tɪmɪtər/ *n Aer.* altímetro, *m*
altitude /'æltɪ,tud/ *n* altitud, elevación, *f;* altura, *f*
alto /'æltou/ *n* (voice) contralto, *m;* (singer) contralto, *mf;* viola, *f*
altogether /ˌɔltə'gɛðər/ *adv* completamente; del todo; en conjunto
altruism /'æltru,ɪzəm/ *n* altruismo, *m*
altruist /'æltruist/ *n* altruista, *mf*
aluminum /ə'lumənəm/ *n* aluminio, *m*
aluminum foil *n* hoja de aluminio, *f*
alumna /ə'lʌmnə/ *n Lat. Am.* exalumna, *f*
alumnus /ə'lʌmnəs/ *n Lat. Am.* exalumno, *m*
always /'ɔlweiz/ *adv* siempre
amalgam /ə'mælgəm/ *n* amalgama, *f;* mezcla, *f*
amalgamate /ə'mælgə,meit/ *vt* amalgamar; combinar, unir. *vi* amalgamarse; combinarse, unirse
amalgamation /ə,mælgə'meiʃən/ *n* amalgamación, *f;* combinación, *f;* mezcla, *f*
amanuensis /ə,mænyu'ɛnsɪs/ *n* amanuense, *mf;* secretario (-ia)
amass /ə'mæs/ *vt* acumular, amontonar
amateur /'æmə,tʃur/ *a* and *n* aficionado (-da), (sports) no profesional. **a. theatricals,** función de aficionados, *f.* **a. band,** *Mexico* escoleta, *f*
amateurish /'æmə,tʃurɪʃ/ *a* no profesional; de aficionado; superficial; (clumsy) torpe
amatory /'æmə,tɔri/ *a* amatorio
amaze /ə'meiz/ *vt* asombrar, sorprender; pasmar; confundir

amazed /ə'meizd/ a asombrado; sorprendido; admirado; asustado
amazement /ə'meizmənt/ n asombro, pasmo, m; sorpresa, f; (wonderment) admiración, f; estupor, m
amazing /ə'meiziŋ/ a asombroso, pasmoso; sorprendente
amazingly /ə'meiziŋli/ adv asombrosamente
Amazon /'æmə,zɒn/ n amazona, f
Amazon River, the el (Río de las) Amazonas, m
ambassador /æm'bæsədər/ n embajador (-ra)
amber /'æmbər/ n ámbar, m, a ambarino
ambidextrous /,æmbɪ'dekstrəs/ a ambidextro
ambiguity /,æmbɪ'gyuɪti/ n ambigüedad, f
ambiguous /æm'bɪgyuəs/ a ambiguo, equívoco
ambition /æm'bɪʃən/ n ambición, f
ambitious /æm'bɪʃəs/ a ambicioso. **to be a. to,** ambicionar
amble /'æmbəl/ n (of a horse) paso de andadura, m; paso lento, m. vi (of a horse) andar a paso de andadura; andar lentamente
ambulance /'æmbyələns/ n ambulancia, f. **a. corps,** cuerpo de sanidad, m. **a. man,** sanitario, m
ambulatory /'æmbyələ,tɔri/ n paseo, m; claustro, m, a ambulante
ambush /'æmbʊʃ/ n acecho, m, asechanza, f; Mil. emboscada, f. vt acechar, asechar; Mil. emboscar; sorprender. **to be in a.,** emboscarse, estar en acecho
amelioration /ə,milyə'reiʃən/ n mejora, f
amen /'ei'mɛn, 'ɑ'mɛn/ n amén, m
amenable /ə'minəbəl/ a sujeto (a); responsable; dócil; fácil de convencer, dispuesto a ser razonable; dispuesto a escuchar. **to make a. to reason,** hacer razonable
amend /ə'mɛnd/ vt enmendar; modificar. vi reformarse
amendment /ə'mɛndmənt/ n enmienda, f; modificación, f
amends /ə'mɛndz/ n pl reparación, f; satisfacción, f; compensación, f. **to make a.,** dar satisfacción
amenity /ə'mɛniti/ n amenidad, f
America /ə'mɛrikə/ América, f
American /ə'mɛrikən/ n americano (-na); (U.S.A.) norteamericano (-na), Lat. Am. estadounidense. a americano, de América; norteamericano, de los Estados Unidos. **Central A.,** a and n centroamericano (-na). **A. bar,** bar americano, m
Americanism /ə'mɛrikə,nizəm/ n americanismo, m
Americanize /ə'mɛrikə,naiz/ vt americanizar
amethyst /'æməθɪst/ n amatista, f
amiability /,eimiə'bɪliti/ n amabilidad, afabilidad, cordialidad, f
amiable /'eimiəbəl/ a amable, afable, cordial
amiably /'eimiəbli/ adv amablemente, con afabilidad
amianthus /,æmi'ænθəs/ n amianto, m
amicable /'æmɪkəbəl/ a amigable, amistoso
amice /'æmɪs/ n amito, f
amid, amidst /ə'mɪd; ə'mɪdst/ prep en medio de; entre; rodeado por
amidships /ə'mɪd,ʃɪps/ adv en el centro del buque, en medio del navío
amiss /ə'mɪs/ adv mal; de más; (ill) indispuesto, enfermo; (inopportunely) inoportunamente. a malo
ammeter /'æm,mitər/ n Elec. amperímetro, m
ammonia /ə'mounyə/ n amoníaco, m
ammoniacal /,æmə'naiəkəl/ a amoniacal
ammunition /,æmyə'nɪʃən/ n munición, f. **a. box,** cajón de municiones, m
amnesia /æm'niʒə/ n amnesia, f
amnesty /'æmnəsti/ n amnistía, f. **to concede an a. to,** amnistiar
amok /ə'mʌk/ **(to run a.)** atacar a ciegas
among /ə'mʌŋ/ prep en medio de; entre; con
amoral /ei'mɔrəl/ a amoral
amorality /,eimə'ræliti/ n amoralidad, f
amorous /'æmərəs/ a amoroso; (tender) tierno
amorousness /'æmərəsnɪs/ n erotismo, m; galantería, f
amorphous /ə'mɔrfəs/ a amorfo
amortization /,æmərtə'zeiʃən/ n amorcización, f
amortize /'æmər,taiz/ vt amortizar

amount /ə'maunt/ n importe, m, suma, f; cantidad, f. vi (to) subir a, ascender a, llegar a; valer; reducirse a. **gross a.,** importe bruto, m. **net a.,** importe líquido, importe neto, m. **It amounts to the same thing, then,** Es igual entonces, Viene a ser lo mismo pues. **What he says amounts to this,** Lo que dice se reduce a esto
amperage /'æmpərɪdʒ/ n amperaje, m
ampere /'æmpɪər/ n amper, amperio, m
amphibian /æm'fɪbiən/ n anfibio, m
amphibious /æm'fɪbiəs/ a anfibio
amphitheater /'æmfə,θiətər/ n anfiteatro, m
amphora /'æmfərə/ n ánfora, f
ample /'æmpəl/ a amplio; abundante; extenso, vasto; (sufficient) bastante, suficiente
amplification /,æmpləfɪ'keiʃən/ n amplificación, f
amplifier /'æmplə,faiər/ n amplificador, m
amplify /'æmplə,fai/ vt amplificar; aumentar, ampliar
amplitude /'æmplɪ,tud/ n amplitud, f; abundancia, f; extensión, f
amply /'æmpli/ adv ampliamente; abundantemente; suficientemente
amputate /'æmpyʊ,teit/ vt amputar
amputation /,æmpyʊ'teiʃən/ n amputación, f
amulet /'æmyəlɪt/ n amuleto, m
amuse /ə'myuz/ vt divertir, entretener, distraer. **to a. oneself,** divertirse; pasarlo bien
amusement /ə'myuzmənt/ n diversión, f, entretenimiento, m; (hobby) pasatiempo, m. **a. park,** parque de atracciones, m
amusing /ə'myuzɪŋ/ a divertido, entretenido; (of people) salado
amusingly /ə'myuzɪŋli/ adv de un modo divertido, entretenidamente
an. /ən/ See **a**
Anabaptism /,ænə'bæptɪzəm/ n anabaptismo, m
Anabaptist /,ænə'bæptɪst/ n anabaptista, mf
anachronism /ə'nækrə,nɪzəm/ n anacronismo, m
anachronistic /ə,nækrə'nɪstɪk/ a anacrónico
anagram /'ænə,græm/ n anagrama, m
analects /'ænḷ,ɛkts/ n pl analectas, f pl
analgesia /,ænḷ'dʒiziə/ n analgesia, f
analgesic /,ænḷ'dʒizɪk/ a and n analgésico, m
analogous /ə'næləgəs/ a análogo
analogy /ə'nælədʒi/ n analogía, f
analysis /ə'næləsɪs/ n análisis, m
analyst /'ænḷɪst/ n analista, mf
analytical /,ænḷ'ɪtɪkəl/ a analítico
analyze /'ænḷ,aiz/ vt analizar
anaphora /ə'næfərə/ n anáfora, f
anaphrodisiac /æn,æfrə'dizi,æk/ a anafrodisíaco
anarchic /æn'ɑrkɪk/ a anárquico
anarchism /'ænər,kɪzəm/ n anarquismo, m
anarchist /'ænərkɪst/ n anarquista, mf
anarchy /'ænərki/ n anarquía, f
anastigmatic /,ænəstɪg'mætɪk/ a anastigmático
anathema /ə'næθəmə/ n anatema, mf
anathematize /ə'næθəmə,taiz/ vt anatematizar
anatomic /,ænə'tɒmɪk/ a anatómico
anatomically /,ænə'tɒmɪkli/ adv anatómicamente; físicamente
anatomist /ə'nætəmɪst/ n anatomista, mf
anatomy /ə'nætəmi/ n anatomía, f
ancestor /'ænsɛstər/ n antepasado, abuelo, m
ancestral /æn'sɛstrəl/ a de sus antepasados; de familia; hereditario. **a. home,** casa solariega, f
ancestry /'ænsɛstri/ n antepasados, m pl; linaje, abolengo, m; estirpe, f; nacimiento, m; origen, m
anchor /'æŋkər/ n ancla, f. Fig. áncora, f. vt sujetar con el ancla. vi anclar, echar anclas, fondear. **at a.,** al ancla. **drag a.,** ancla flotante, ancla de arrastre, f. **sheet a.,** ancla de la esperanza, f; Fig. ancla de salvación, f. **to drop a.,** anclar. **to ride at a.,** estar al ancla. **to weigh a.,** levar el ancla
anchorage /'æŋkərɪdʒ/ n ancladero, fondeadero, m; derechos de anclaje, m pl
anchovy /'ænʧouvi/ n anchoa, f, boquerón, m
ancient /'einʃənt/ a anciano; antiguo. n pl **ancients,**

los antiguos. **from a. times,** de antiguo. **most a.,** antiquísimo

and /ænd, ənd/ *conjunc* y; (before stressed i or hi) e; (after some verbs and before infin.) de, a; que; (with) con; (often not translated before infins.). **Better and better,** Mejor que mejor. **I shall try and do it,** Trataré de hacerlo. **to come and see,** venir a ver. **We shall try and speak to him,** Procuraremos hablar con él

Andalusia /ˌændl̩ˈuʒə/ Andalucía, *f*

Andalusian /ˌændl̩ˈuʒən/ *a* andaluz. *n* andaluz (-za). **A. hat,** sombrero calañés, *m*

Andean /ˈændiən/ *a* andino (-na), *Argentina, Chile also* corderillano (-na)

Andes, the /ˈændiz/ los Andes, *f*

andiron /ˈænd‚aiˀrn/ *n* morillo, *m*

Andorran /ænˈdɔrən/ *n* andorrano (-na)

androgynous /ænˈdrɒdʒənəs/ *a* andrógino

anecdotal /ˈænɪkˌdoutl̩/ *a* anecdótico

anecdote /ˈænɪkˌdout/ *n* anécdota, *f*

anemia /əˈnimiə/ *n* anemia, *f*

anemic /əˈnimɪk/ *a* anémico

anemometer /ˌænəˈmɒmɪtər/ *n* anemómetro, *m*

anemone /əˈnɛməˌni/ *n* anémona, anémone, *f*

aneroid /ˈænəˌrɔid/ *a* aneroide. *n* barómetro aneroide, *m*

anesthesia /ˌænəsˈθiʒə/ *n* anestesia, *f*

anesthetic /ˌænəsˈθɛtɪk/ *a* and *n* anestésico, *m*.

anesthetist /əˈnɛsθɪtɪst/ *n* anestesiador (-ra)

anesthetize /əˈnɛsθɪˌtaiz/ *vt* anestesiar

aneurism /ˈænyəˌrɪzəm/ *n* aneurisma, *mf*

angel /ˈeindʒəl/ *n* ángel, *m*

angelic /ænˈdʒɛlɪk/ *a* angélico

angelica /ænˈdʒɛlɪkə/ *n* angélica, *f*

anger /ˈæŋɡər/ *n* cólera, ira, *f*, enojo, *m*, *vt* enojar, encolerizar; hacer rabiar, *Mexico* amuinar

angina /ænˈdʒainə/ *n* angina, *f*. **a. pectoris,** angina de pecho, *f*

angle /ˈæŋɡəl/ *n* ángulo, *m*; rincón, *m*; esquina, *f*; (of a roof) caballette, *m*; *Fig.* punto de vista, *m*, *vi* pescar con caña. **at an a.,** a un lado. **a.-iron,** hierro angular, *m*. **to a. for,** pescar; *Fig.* procurar obtener

Angle /ˈæŋɡəl/ *a* and *n* anglo (-la)

angler /ˈæŋɡlər/ *n* pescador (-ra) de caña

Anglican /ˈæŋɡlɪkən/ *a* and *n* anglicano (-na)

Anglicanism /ˈæŋlɪkəˌnɪzəm/ *n* anglicanismo, *m*

Anglicism /ˈæŋɡlɪˌsɪzəm/ *n* anglicismo, inglesismo, *m*

Anglicize /ˈæŋɡləˌsaiz/ *vt* inglesar

angling /ˈæŋɡlɪŋ/ *n* pesca con caña, *f*

Anglo- (in compounds) anglo-. **A.-American,** *a* and *n* angloamericano (-na). **A.-Saxon,** *a* and *n* anglosajón (-ona); (language) anglosajón, *m*

anglomania /ˌæŋɡləˈmeiniə/ *n* anglomanía, *f*

anglophile /ˈæŋɡləˌfail/ *n* anglófilo (-la)

anglophobia /ˌæŋɡləˈfoubiə/ *n* anglofobia, *f*

angora /æŋˈɡɔrə/ *n* angora, *f*. **a. cat,** gato de angora, *m*. **a. rabbit,** conejo de angora, *m*

angrily /ˈæŋɡrəli/ *adv* airadamente

angry /ˈæŋɡri/ *a* (of persons) enfadado, enojado, airado; (of waves, etc.) furioso, *Med.* inflamado; (red) rojo; (scowling) cenudo; (dark) obscuro. **to be a.,** estar enojado. **to get angry, to grow a.,** enojarse, enfadarse, *Lat. Am.* entromparse; (of waves) encresparse; (of the sky) obscurecerse. **to make a.,** enojar

anguish /ˈæŋɡwɪʃ/ *n* agonía, *f*, dolor, *m*; angustia, *f*. *vt* angustiar

angular /ˈæŋɡyələr/ *a* angular; (of features, etc.) anguloso

angularity /ˌæŋɡyəˈlærɪti/ *n* angulosidad, *f*

anhydrous /ænˈhaidrəs/ *a* anhidro

aniline /ˈænlɪn/ *n* anilina, *f*

animal /ˈænəməl/ *a* and *n* animal *m*. **a. fat,** grasa animal, *f*. **a. kingdom,** reino animal, *m*. **a. spirits,** *Philos.* espíritus animales, *m pl*

animalism /ˈænəməˌlɪzəm/ *n* animalidad, *f*; sensualidad, *f*

animate /*v* ˈænəˌmeit; *a* -mɪt/ *vt* animar; inspirar. *a* vivo; viviente

animated /ˈænəˌmeitɪd/ *a* animado; vivo, lleno de vida

animation /ˌænəˈmeiʃən/ *n* animación, *f*; vivacidad, *f*; calor, fuego, *m*

animism /ˈænəˌmɪzəm/ *n* animismo, *m*

animosity /ˌænəˈmɒsɪti/ *n* animosidad, hostilidad, *f*

aniseed /ˈænəˌsid/ *n* anís, *m*

anisette /ˌænəˈsɛt/ *n* (liqueur) anisete, *m*

ankle /ˈæŋkəl/ *n* tobillo, *m*. **a. bone,** hueso del tobillo, *m*. **a. sock,** calcetín corto, *m*

anklet /ˈæŋklɪt/ *n* brazalete para el tobillo, *m*; (support) tobillera, *f*

annals /ˈæn‚lz/ *n pl* anales, *m pl*

anneal /əˈnil/ *vt* (metals) recocer; (glass) templar; (with oil) atemperar

annex /*v* əˈnɛks; ˈænɛks; *n* ˈænɛks/ *vt* unir, juntar; anexar. *n* anexo, *m*

annexation /ˌænɪkˈseiʃən/ *n* anexión, *f*

annihilate /əˈnaiəˌleit/ *vt* aniquilar

annihilation /əˌnaiəˈleiʃən/ *n* aniquilación, *f*

anniversary /ˌænəˈvɜrsəri/ *a* and *n* aniversario, *m*.

annotate /ˈænəˌteit/ *vt* anotar, acotar, comentar; hacer anotaciones a

annotation /ˌænəˈteiʃən/ *n* anotación, *f*; nota, *f*

annotator /ˈænəˌteitər/ *n* anotador (-ra), comentador (-ra)

announce /əˈnauns/ *vt* proclamar; declarar; publicar; anunciar

announcement /əˈnaunsmənt/ *n* proclama, *f*; declaración, *f*; publicación, *f*; anuncio, *m*; (of a betrothal) participación, *f*

announcer /əˈnaunsər/ *n* anunciador (-ra); (radio or TV) locutor (-ra)

annoy /əˈnɔi/ *vt* exasperar, irritar, disgustar; molestar, incomodar, *Lat. Am.* acatarrar, cargosear, engorrar

annoyance /əˈnɔiəns/ *n* disgusto, *m*, exasperación, *f*; molestia, *f*, fastidio, *m*

annoying /əˈnɔiɪŋ/ *a* enojoso, molesto, fastidioso, *Lat. Am.* cargoso

annual /ˈænyuəl/ *a* anual. *n* anuario, *m*; calendario, *m*; planta anual, *f*

annually /ˈænyuəli/ *adv* anualmente, cada año

annuitant /əˈnuitn̩t/ *n* censualista, *mf*

annuity /əˈnuiti/ *n* anualidad, pensión vitalicia, *f*

annul /əˈnʌl/ *vt* anular

annulment /əˈnʌlmənt/ *n* anulación, *f*

annunciation /əˌnʌnsiˈeiʃən/ *n* anunciación, *f*. **the A.,** la Anunciación

anodyne /ˈænəˌdain/ *a* and *n* anodino, *m*

anoint /əˈnɔint/ *vt* untar; (before death) olear; (a king, etc.) ungir

anointing /əˈnɔintɪŋ/ *n* unción, *f*

anomalous /əˈnɒmələs/ *a* anómalo

anomaly /əˈnɒməli/ *n* anomalía, *f*

anonymity /ˌænəˈnɪmɪti/ *n* anónimo, *m*

anonymous /əˈnɒnəməs/ *a* anónimo. **a. letter,** anónimo, *m*

anorexia /ˌænəˈrɛksiə/ *n* anorexia, *f*

another /əˈnʌðər/ *a* otro; (different) distinto. *n* otro, *m*; otra, *f*. **For one thing... and for a.,** En primer lugar... y además (y por otra cosa). **one after a.,** uno después de otro. **They love one a.,** Ellos se aman. **They sent it from one to a.,** Lo mandaron de uno a otro

answer /ˈænsər/ /ˈɑn-/ *n* contestación, respuesta, *f*; (refutation) refutación, *f*; (pert reply) réplica, *f*; (solution) solución, *f*; *Math.* resultado, *m*; *Law.* contestación a la demanda, *f*

answer /ˈænsər, ˈɑn-/ *vt* responder, contestar; (a letter, etc.) contestar a; (refute) refutar; (reply pertly) replicar; (write) escribir; (return) devolver; (suit) servir; (a bell, etc.) acudir a; (the door) abrir. *vi* contestar; (succeed) tener éxito; dar resultado. **to a. by return,** contestar a vuelta de correo, **to a. back,** replicar. **to a. for,** ser responsable por; ser responsable de; (speak for) hablar por; (guarantee) garantizar, responder de

answerable /ˈænsərəbəl/ *a* responsable; refutable; (adequate) adecuado. **to make a. for,** hacer responsable de

answering machine /'ænsərɪŋ/ n contestador telefónico, contestador, m
ant /ænt/ n hormiga, f. **ant-eater,** oso hormiguero, m. **ant-hill,** hormiguero, m
antagonism /æn'tægə,nɪzəm/ n antagonismo, m, hostilidad, oposición, f
antagonist /æn'tægənɪst/ n antagonista, mf
antagonistic /æn,tægə'nɪstɪk/ a antagónico, hostil
antagonize /æn'tægə,naɪz/ vt contender; hacer hostil (a)
antarctic /ænt'ɑrktɪk/ a antártico. n polo antártico, m
antecedent /,æntə'sidn̩t/ a and n antecedente, m.
antechamber /'ænti,tʃeimbər/ n antecámara, antesala, f
antedate /'ænti,deit/ vt antedatar; anticipar
antediluvian /,æntidɪ'luviən/ a antediluviano
antelope /'ænt̩,oup/ n antílope, m
antenna /æn'tenə/ n antena, f
anterior /æn'tɪəriər/ a anterior
anthem /'ænθəm/ n antífona, f
anthologist /æn'θɒlədʒɪst/ n antólogo, m
anthology /æn'θɒlədʒi/ n antología, floresta, f
anthracite /'ænθrə,sait/ n antracita, f, carbón mineral, m
anthrax /'ænθræks/ n ántrax, m
anthropological /,ænθrəpə'lɒdʒɪkəl/ a antropológico
anthropologist /,ænθrə'pɒlədʒɪst/ n antropólogo, m
anthropology /,ænθrə'pɒlədʒi/ n antropología, f
anti-aircraft /,ænti'eər,kræft, ,æntai-/ a antiaéreo. **A.A. gun,** cañon antiaéreo, m
antibody /'ænti,bɒdi/ n anticuerpo, m
antic /'æntɪk/ n travesura, f
Antichrist /'ænti,kraist/ n Anticristo, m
anticipate /æn'tɪsə,peit/ vt (foresee) prever; anticipar; adelantarse a; (hope) esperar; (frustrate) frustrar; (enjoy) disfrutar con anticipación de
anticipation /æn,tɪsə'peiʃən/ n anticipación, f; adelantamiento, m; esperanza, expectación, f. **in a. of,** en espera de
anticipatory /æn'tɪsəpə,tɔri/ a anticipador
anticlerical /,ænti'klerɪkəl, ,æntai-/ a anticlerical
anticlericalism /,ænti'klerɪkə,lɪzəm, ,æntai-/ n anticlericalismo, m
anticlimax /,ænti'klaimæks, ,æntai-/ n anticlímax, m
antidote /'ænti,dout/ n antídoto, contraveneno, m
antifreeze /'ænti,friz/ n anticongelante, m
Antilles, the /æn'tɪliz/ las Antillas, f
antimony /'æntə,mouni/ n antimonio, m
antipathetic /,æntɪpə'θetɪk/ a antipático
antipathy /æn'tɪpəθi/ n antipatía, f
antipode /'ænti,poud/ n pl antípodas, mf pl
antiquarian /,ænti'kweəriən/ a anticuario
antiquary /'ænti,kweri/ n anticuario, m
antiquated /'ænti,kweitɪd/ a anticuado
antique /æn'tik/ a antiguo. n antigüedad, antigualla, f. **a. dealer,** anticuario, m. **a. shop,** tienda de antigüedades, f
antiquity /æn'tɪkwɪti/ n antigüedad, f; ancianidad, f
antireligious /,æntirɪ'lɪdʒəs, ,æntai-/ a antirreligioso
anti-Semitic /,æntisə'mɪtɪk, ,æntai-/ a antisemita
anti-Semitism /,ænti'semɪ,tɪzəm, ,æntai-/ n antisemitismo, m
antiseptic /,æntə'septɪk/ a and n antiséptico, m
antisocial /,ænti'souʃəl, ,æntai-/ a antisocial
antithesis /æn'tɪθəsɪs/ n antítesis, f
antithetic /,ænti'θetɪk/ a antitético
antitoxin /,ænti'tɒksɪn/ n antitoxina, f
antler /'æntlər/ n asta, f
antonym /'æntənɪm/ n contrario, m
antrum /'æntrəm/ n antro, m
Antwerp /'æntwɔrp/ n Amberes, m
anus /'einəs/ n ano, m
anvil /'ænvɪl/ n yunque, m, bigornia, f
anxiety /æŋ'zaiɪti/ n inquietud, intranquilidad, f; preocupación, f; ansiedad, f; curiosidad, f; impaciencia, f; (wish) deseo, afán, m
anxious /'æŋkʃəs, 'æŋʃəs/ a inquieto, intranquilo; preocupado; ansioso; impaciente; deseoso. **to be a.,** estar inquieto; apurarse. **to be a. to,** ansiar, tener de-

seos de. **to make a.,** preocupar, inquietar, intranquilizar
anxiously /'æŋkʃəsli, 'æŋʃəs-/ adv con inquietud; ansiosamente; impacientemente
any /'eni/ a cualquiera; (before the noun only) cualquier; (some) algún, m; alguna, f; (every) todo; (expressing condition or with interrogatives or negatives, following the noun) alguno, m; alguna, f, (is often not translated in a partitive sense, e.g. *Have you any butter?* ¿Tienes mantequilla?) pron algo; (with the relevant noun) algún, etc.; lo, m, and neut; la, f; los, m pl; las, f pl. **He hasn't any pity,** No tiene piedad alguna. **at any rate,** de todos modos; por lo menos. **If there is any,** Si lo (la, etc.) hay. **in any case,** venga lo que venga. **not any,** ninguno, m; ninguna, f. **Whether any of them...,** Si alguno de ellos... **any further,** más lejos. **any longer,** (ya no + infin.), **He doesn't drink any longer,** ya no toma; más largo; (of time) más tiempo. **any more,** nada más; nunca más
anybody /'eni,bɒdi/ n and pron (someone) alguien; cualquiera, mf; (everyone) todo el mundo; (with a negative) nadie; (of importance) persona de importancia, f. **hardly a.,** casi nadie
anyhow /'eni,hau/ adv de cualquier modo; (with a negative) de ningún modo; de cualquier manera; (at least) por lo menos, en todo caso; (carelessly) sin cuidado
anyone /'eni,wʌn/ n. See **anybody**
anything /'eni,θɪŋ/ n algo, m, alguna cosa, f; (negative) nada; cualquier cosa, f; todo (lo que). **a. but,** todo menos
anyway /'eni,wei/ adv de todos modos, con todo; venga lo que venga; (anyhow) de cualquier modo
anywhere /'eni,weər/ adv en todas partes, dondequiera; en cualquier parte; (after a negative) en (or a) ninguna parte
aorta /ei'ɔrtə/ n aorta, f
apart /ə'pɑrt/ adv aparte; a un lado; separadamente; separado (de); apartado (de). **a. from,** aparte de, dejando a un lado. **to keep a.,** mantener aislado; distinguir (entre). **to take a.,** desarmar. **wide a.,** muy distante
apartment /ə'pɑrtmənt/ n cuarto, m, habitación, f; piso, *Argentina* apartamento, *elsewhere in Lat. Am.* apartamento m
apathetic /,æpə'θetɪk/ a apático; indiferente
apathy /'æpəθi/ n apatía, f; indiferencia, f
ape /eip/ n simio, m
Apennines, the /'æpə,nainz/ los Apeninos, m
aperitive /ə'perɪtɪv/ a and n aperitivo, m
aperture /'æpərtʃər/ n abertura, f; agujero, m; orificio, m
apex /'eipeks/ n ápice, m
aphasia /ə'feiʒə/ n afasia, f
aphorism /'æfə,rɪzəm/ n aforismo, m
aphrodisiac /,æfrə'dizi,æk/ a and n afrodisíaco, m
apiary /'eipi,eri/ n colmenar, f
apiece /ə'pis/ adv cada uno; por persona
apish /'eipɪʃ/ a simiesco, de simio; (affected) afectado; (foolish) tonto
aplomb /ə'plɒm/ n confianza en sí, f, aplomo, m
apocalypse /ə'pɒkəlɪps/ n Apocalipsis, m
apocalyptic /ə,pɒkə'lɪptɪk/ a apocalíptico
apocopate /ə'pɒkə,peit/ vt apocopar
Apocrypha /ə'pɒkrəfə/ n libros apócrifos, m pl
apocryphal /ə'pɒkrəfəl/ a apócrifo
apogee /'æpə,dʒi/ n apogeo, m
apologetic /ə,pɒlə'dʒetɪk/ a apologético. n **apologetics,** apologética, f
apologist /ə'pɒlədʒɪst/ n apologista, mf
apologize /ə'pɒlə,dʒaiz/ vi presentar sus excusas; disculparse, excusarse; (regret) sentir
apology /ə'pɒlədʒi/ n excusa, disculpa, f; defensa, apología, f; (makeshift) substituto, m
apoplectic /,æpə'plektɪk/ a and n apoplético (-ca)
apoplexy /'æpə,pleksi/ n apoplegía, f
apostasy /ə'pɒstəsi/ n apostasía, f
apostate /ə'pɒsteit/ n apóstata, mf. renegado (-da)
apostatize /ə'pɒstə,taiz/ vi apostatar, renegar

apostle /ə'pɒsəl/ n apóstol, m. **Apostles' Creed,** el Credo de los Apóstoles

apostolic /ˌæpə'stɒlɪk/ a apostólico

apostrophe /ə'pɒstrəfi/ n apóstrofe, mf; (punctuation mark) apóstrofo, m

apothecaries' weight /ə'pɒθəˌkɛriz/ peso de boticario, m

apothegm /'æpəˌθɛm/ n apotegma, m

apotheosis /əˌpɒθi'ousɪs/ n apoteosis, f

appall /ə'pɔl/ vt horrorizar, espantar, aterrar

appalling /ə'pɔlɪŋ/ a espantoso, horrible

apparatus /ˌæpə'rætəs/ n aparato, m; máquina, f; instrumentos, m pl

apparel /ə'pærəl/ n ropa, f; vestiduras, f pl; ornamento, m. vt vestir

apparent /ə'pærənt/ a aparente; visible; evidente, manifiesto; (of heirs) presunto. **to become a.,** manifestarse

apparently /ə'pærəntli/ adv al parecer, aparentemente

apparition /ˌæpə'rɪʃən/ n aparición, f, fantasma, espectro, m

appeal /ə'pil/ n súplica, f; llamamiento, m; (charm) atracción, f, encanto, m; Law. apelación, alzada, f. vi (to) suplicar (a); hacer llamamiento (a); poner por testigo (a); recurrir a; llamar la atención de; interesar (a); (attract) atraer, encantar; Law. apelar. **It doesn't a. to him,** No le atrae, No le gusta. **to allow an a.,** revocar una sentencia apelada. **without a.,** inapelable

appealing /ə'pilɪŋ/ a suplicante; atrayente

appealingly /ə'pilɪŋli/ adv de un modo suplicante

appear /ə'pɪər/ vi (of persons and things) aparecer; (seem) parecer; (before a judge) comparecer, presentarse (ante el juez); (of books) publicarse; (of lawyers) representar; (of the dawn) rayar; (of the sun, etc.) salir; (show itself) manifestarse. **to cause to a.,** hacer presentarse; (show) hacer ver; (prove) demonstrar, probar

appearance /ə'pɪərəns/ n aparición, f; (show, semblance or look, aspect) apariencia, f; presencia, f; aspecto, m; (in court of law) comparecencia, f; (of a book) publicación, f; (arrival) llegada, f; (view) perspectiva, f; (ghost) aparición, f, fantasma, m. **first a.,** (of an actor, etc.) debut, m; (of a play) estreno, m. **to all appearances,** según las apariencias. **to make one's first a.,** aparecer por primera vez; Theat. debutar. **Appearances are deceptive,** Las apariencias engañan

appease /ə'piz/ vt apaciguar, aplacar, pacificar; satisfacer

appeasement /ə'pizmənt/ n apaciguamiento, aplacamiento, m, pacificación, f; satisfacción, f

appellant /ə'pɛlənt/ a and n Law. apelante, mf

appellation /ˌæpə'leɪʃən/ n nombre, m; título, m

append /ə'pɛnd/ vt añadir; (a seal) poner; (enclose) incluir, anexar

appendage /ə'pɛndɪdʒ/ n accesorio, m; (Bot. Zool.) apéndice, m

appendicitis /əˌpɛndə'saitɪs/ n apendicitis, f

appendix /ə'pɛndɪks/ n apéndice, m

appertain /ˌæpər'teɪn/ vi pertenecer (a)

appetite /'æpɪˌtaɪt/ n apetito, m; Fig. hambre, f; deseo, m. **to have a bad a.,** no tener apetito, estar desganado. **to have a good a.,** tener buen apetito. **to whet the a.,** abrir el apetito

appetizer /'æpɪˌtaɪzər/ n aperitivo, m, Argentina ingrediente, m

appetizing /'æpɪˌtaɪzɪŋ/ a apetitoso

applaud /ə'plɔd/ vt and vi aplaudir; aclamar, ovacionar; celebrar

applause /ə'plɔz/ n aplauso, m; ovación, f; aprobación, alabanza, f

apple /'æpəl/ n manzana, f. **the a. of one's eye,** la niña de los ojos. **a. orchard,** manzanar, m. **a. sauce,** compota de manzanas, f. **a. tart,** pastel de manzanas, m. **a. tree,** manzano, m

appliance /ə'plaɪəns/ n aparato, m; instrumento, m; utensilio, m; máquina, f

applicability /ˌæplɪkə'bɪlɪti/ n aplicabilidad, f

applicable /'æplɪkəbəl/ a aplicable

applicant /'æplɪkənt/ n candidato, m; aspirante, m; solicitante, mf

application /ˌæplɪ'keɪʃən/ n aplicación, f; solicitud, f; petición, f; empleo, m. **on a.,** a solicitar

appliqué /ˌæplɪ'keɪ/ a aplicado. n aplicación, f

apply /ə'plaɪ/ vt aplicar; (use) emplear; (place) poner; (give) dar; (the brakes) frenar; vi ser aplicable; ser a propósito; dirigirse (a); acudir (a); (for a post) proponerse para. **a. for,** solicitar, pedir; (a post) proponerse para. **a. for admission (to...),** solicitar el ingreso (en...). **a. oneself to,** ponerse a; dedicarse a, consagrarse a

appoint /ə'pɔɪnt/ vt (prescribe) prescribir, ordenar; señalar; asignar; (furnish) amueblar; equipar; (create) crear, establecer; (to a post) nombrar, designar; (manage) gobernar; organizar. **at the appointed hour,** a la hora señalada. **well-appointed,** bien amueblado; bien equipado

appointive /ə'pɔɪntɪv/ a por nombramiento

appointment /ə'pɔɪntmənt/ n (assignation) cita, f; (to a post) nombramiento, m; (post, office) cargo, m; creación, f. **By Royal A.,** Proveedor de la Real Casa. **to make an a. with,** citar

apportion /ə'pɔrʃən/ vt dividir; distribuir; prorratear; (taxes) derramar

apportionment /ə'pɔrʃənmənt/ n repartimiento, m, distribución, f; división, f; prorrateo, m

apposite /'æpəzɪt/ a a propósito, pertinente, oportuno; justo

appositeness /'æpəzɪtnɪs/ n pertinencia, oportunidad, f

appraisal /ə'preɪzəl/ n valoración, valuación, f; estimación, f

appraise /ə'preɪz/ vt valorar, tasar; estimar

appraiser /ə'preɪzər/ n apreciador (-ra), evaluador (-ra)

appreciable /ə'priʃəbəl/ a apreciable, perceptible

appreciably /ə'priʃəbli/ adv sensiblemente

appreciate /ə'priʃiˌeɪt/ vt (understand) darse cuenta de, comprender; estimar; apreciar; (distinguish) distinguir. vi encarecer, aumentar en valor; (of shares) subir, estar en alza

appreciation /əˌpriʃi'eɪʃən/ n (understanding) comprensión, f; apreciación, f; (recognition, etc.) aprecio, reconocimiento, m; (in value) aumento (en valor), m; subida de precio, f

appreciative /ə'priʃətɪv/ a apreciativo

appreciatively /ə'priʃətɪvli/ adv con aprecio

appreciator /ə'priʃieɪtər/ n apreciador (-ra)

apprehend /ˌæprɪ'hɛnd/ vt aprehender, prender; comprender, aprehender; (fear) temer

apprehension /ˌæprɪ'hɛnʃən/ n aprehensión, comprensión, f; (fear) aprensión, f; (seizure) aprehensión, presa, f

apprehensive /ˌæprɪ'hɛnsɪv/ a aprehensivo; (fearful) aprensivo

apprehensiveness /ˌæprɪ'hɛnsɪvnɪs/ n aprehensión, f; (fear) aprensión, f, temor, m

apprentice /ə'prɛntɪs/ n aprendiz (-za). **to bind a.,** poner de aprendiz

apprenticeship /ə'prɛntɪsˌʃɪp/ n aprendizaje, m. **to serve an a.,** hacer el aprendizaje

apprise /ə'praɪz/ vt dar parte (de), informar (de)

approach /ə'proutʃ/ vt acercarse a; aproximarse a; (pull, etc. nearer) acercar, aproximar; (resemble) parecerse a, ser semejante a; (seek to) hablar con; (of night, etc.) avanzar, m; (entrance) entrada, f; (to a subject) punto de vista (sobre), concepto (de), m; (introduction) introducción, f; pl **approaches,** (environs) alrededores, m pl, inmediaciones, f pl; (seas) mares, m pl; (overtures) avances, m pl

approachable /ə'proutʃəbəl/ a accesible

approaching /ə'proutʃɪŋ/ a venidero, próximo, cercano

approbation /ˌæprə'beɪʃən/ n asentimiento, m; aprobación, f

appropriate /a ə'proupriɪt; v -ˌeɪt/ a apropiado; conveniente; *vt* adueñarse de, tomar posesión de, apropiar

appropriately /ə'proupriitli/ *adv* propiamente; convenientemente; justamente

appropriateness /ə'proupriitnis/ *n* conveniencia, *f*; justicia, *f*

appropriation /ə,proupri'eifən/ *n* apropiación, *f*; aplicación, *f*; empleo, *m*

approval /ə'pruvəl/ *n* aprobación, *f*; consentimiento, *m*. **on a.,** a prueba

approve /ə'pruv/ *vt* aprobar; confirmar; (sanction) autorizar, sancionar; ratificar; estar contento (de); (oneself) demostrarse. *vi* aprobar

approved /ə'pruvd/ *a* aprobado; bien visto; (on documents) Visto Bueno (V° B°)

approximate /a ə'prɒksəmit/ *v* -,meit/ *a* aproximado. *vt* acercar. *vi* aproximarse (a)

approximately /ə'prɒksəmitli/ *adv* aproximadamente, poco más o menos

approximation /ə,prɒksə'meifən/ *n* aproximación, *f*

appurtenance /ə'pɜrtnəns/ *n* accesorio, *m*, pertenencia, *f*

apricot /'æpri,kɒt/ *n* albaricoque, *m*. **a. tree,** albaricoquero, *m*

April /'eiprəl/ *n* abril, *m*, *a* abrileño. **A. Fool's Day,** el 1° de abril; (in Spain) el Día de los Inocentes (December 28)

apron /'eiprən/ *n* delantal, *m*; (of artisans and freemasons) mandil, *m*. **to be tied to a mother's a.-strings,** estar cosido a las faldas de su madre. **a.-stage,** proscenio, *m*. **a.-string,** cinta del delantal, *f*

apse /æps/ *n* ábside, *mf*

apt /æpt/ *a* apto, listo; propenso (a), inclinado (a); expuesto (a); (suitable) apropiado, oportuno

aptitude /'æpti,tud/ *n* aptitud, disposición, facilidad, *f*

aptly /'æptli/ *adv* apropiadamente; justamente, bien

aquamarine /,ækwəmə'rin/ *n* aguamarina, *f*

aquarelle /,ækwə'rɛl/ *n* acuarela, *f*

aquarellist /,ækwə'rɛlist/ *n* acuarelista, *mf*

aquarium /ə'kwɛəriəm/ *n* acuario, *m*

Aquarius /ə'kwɛəriəs/ *n* Acuario, *m*

aquatic /ə'kwætik/ *a* acuático

aquatint /'ækwə,tint/ *n* acuatinta, *f*

aqueduct /'ækwi,dʌkt/ *n* acueducto, *m*

aqueous /'ækwiəs/ *a* ácueo, acuoso

aquiline /'ækwə,lain/ *a* aguileño

Arab /'ærəb/ *a* árabe, *mf*

arabesque /,ærə'bɛsk/ *n* arabesco, *m*

Arabian /ə'reibiən/ *a* árabe, arábigo. **The A. Nights,** Las Mil y Una Noches

Arabic /'ærəbik/ *a* arábigo. *n* (language) arábigo, árabe, *m*

Arabist /'ærəbist/ *n* arabista, *mf*

arable /'ærəbəl/ *a* cultivable, labrantío

Aragonese /,ærəgə'niz/ *a* and *n* aragonés (-esa)

arbiter /'ɑrbitər/ *n* árbitro (-ra), arbitrador (-ra)

arbitrariness /'ɑrbi,trerinis/ *n* arbitrariedad, *f*

arbitrary /'ɑrbi,treri/ *a* arbitrario

arbitrate /'ɑrbi,treit/ *vi* arbitrar, juzgar como árbitro; someter al arbitraje

arbitration /,ɑrbi'treifən/ *n* arbitraje, *m*

arbitrator /'ɑrbi,treitər/ *n* See **arbiter**

arbor /'ɑrbər/ *n* glorieta, *f*, emparrado, *m*

arc /ɑrk/ *n* arco, *m*. **arc-light,** lámpara de arco, *f*

arcade /ɑr'keid/ *n* arcada, *f*; galería, *f*; pasaje, *m*

arch /ɑrtʃ/ *n* arco, *m*; (vault) bóveda, *f*. *vt* abovedar; arquear; encorvar

arch /ɑrtʃ/ *a* (roguish) socarrón; (coy) coquetón

arch- *prefix* archi-

archaic /ɑr'keiik/ *a* arcaico

archaism /'ɑrki,izəm/ *n* arcaísmo, *m*

archangel /'ɑrk,eindʒəl/ *n* arcángel, *m*

archbishop /'ɑrtʃ'bifəp/ *n* arzobispo, *m*

archenemy /'ɑrtʃ'enəmi/ *n* mayor enemigo (-ga); Demonio, *m*

archeological /,ɑrkiə'lɒdʒikəl/ *a* arqueológico

archeologist /,ɑrki'ɒlədʒist/ *n* arqueólogo, *m*

archeology /,ɑrki'ɒlədʒi/ *n* arqueología, *f*

archer /'ɑrtʃər/ *n* flechero, saltero, *m*; *Mil.* arquero, *m*

archery /'ɑrtʃəri/ *n* ballestería, *f*

archery range *n* campo de tiro con arco, *m*

archfiend /'ɑrtʃ'find/ *n* demonio, *m*

arching /'ɑrtʃiŋ/ *n* arqueo, *m*

archipelago /,ɑrkə'pɛlə,gou/ *n* archipiélago, *m*

architect /'ɑrki,tɛkt/ *n* arquitecto, *m*

architectural /,ɑrki'tɛktʃərəl/ *n* arquitectónico

architecturally /,ɑrki'tɛktʃərəli/ *adv* arquitectónicamente; desde el punto de vista arquitectónico

architecture /'ɑrki,tɛktʃər/ *n* arquitectura, *f*

archive /'ɑrkaiv/ *n* archivo, *m*

archivist /'ɑrkəvist/ *n* archivero, *m*

archness /'ɑrtʃnis/ *n* coquetería, *f*; malicia, *f*

archway /'ɑrtʃ,wei/ *n* arcada, *f*, pasaje abovedado, *m*; arco, *m*

arctic /'ɑrktik, 'ɑrtik/ *a* ártico; muy frío. **A. Circle,** Círculo ártico, *m*

ardent /'ɑrdn̩t/ *a* ardiente; apasionado, vehemente; fogoso

ardently /'ɑrdn̩tli/ *adv* ardientemente; con vehemencia, apasionadamente

ardor /'ɑrdər/ *n* ardor, *m*

arduous /'ɑrdʒuəs/ *a* arduo, difícil

arduousness /'ɑrdʒuəsnis/ *n* dificultad, arduidad, *f*

are /ɑr/ *pl* of present indicative of **be**. See **be. There are,** Hay

area /'ɛəriə/ *n* área, *f*; superficie, *f*; (extent) extensión, *f*; espacio, *m*; región, *f*; (of a house) patio, *m*; (of a concert hall, etc.) sala, *f*

area code *n* característica, *f*, (Chile) código territorial (Spain), prefijo (Spain), código interurbano, código (Argentina), *m*

arena /ə'rinə/ *n* arena, *f*

argent /'ɑrdʒənt/ *n* Poet. blancura, *f*; Herald. argén, *m*

Argentina /,ɑrdʒən'tinə/ Argentina

Argentinian /,ɑrdʒən'tiniən/ *a* and *n* argentino (-na)

argonaut /'ɑrgə,nɔt/ *n* (Zool. and Myth.) argonauta, *m*

argot /'ɑrgou, -gət/ *n* jerga, *f*; (thieves') germanía, *f*

arguable /'ɑrgyuəbəl/ *a* discutible

argue /'ɑrgyu/ *vt* discutir; persuadir; (prove) demostrar. *vi* argüir, discutir; sostener. **to a. against,** hablar en contra de, oponer

arguing /'ɑrgyuiŋ/ *n* razonamiento, *m*; argumentación, *f*; discusión, *f*

argument /'ɑrgyəmənt/ *n* argumento, *m*, Argentina arenga *f*

argumentative /,ɑrgyə'mɛntətiv/ *a* argumentador; contencioso

arid /'ærid/ *a* árido, seco

aridity /ə'riditi/ *n* aridez, *f*

Aries /'ɛəriz/ *n* Aries, *m*

arise /ə'raiz/ *vi* levantarse; (appear) surgir, aparecer; ofrecerse, presentarse; (of sound) hacerse oír; provenir (de); proceder (de); (result) hacerse sentir; (rebel) sublevarse

aristocracy /,ærə'stɒkrəsi/ *n* aristocracia, *f*

aristocrat /ə'ristə,kræt/ *n* aristócrata, *mf*

aristocratic /ə,ristə'krætik/ *a* aristocrático

Aristotelian /,ærəstə'tilyən/ *a* aristotélico

arithmetic /ə'riθmətik/ *n* aritmética, *f*

arithmetical /,æriθ'mɛtikəl/ *a* aritmético

ark /ɑrk/ *n* arca, *f*. **Noah's ark,** arca de Noé, *f*. **Ark of the Covenant,** arca de la alianza, *f*

arm /ɑrm/ *n* (Anat. Geog. Mech. of a chair, a cross, and Fig.) brazo, *m*; (lever) palanca, *f*; (of a tree) rama, *f*, brazo, *m*; (sleeve) manga, *f*; Naut. cabo de una verga, *m*; (weapon) arma, *f*, (Fig army, navy, etc.) ramo, *m pl.* **arms,** Herald. armas, *f pl*, escudo, *m*. **in arms,** en brazos; armado; en oposición. **To arms!** ¡A las armas! **to keep at arm's length,** guardar las distancias; tratar fríamente. **to lay down arms,** rendir las armas. **to present arms,** presentar las armas. **to receive with open arms,** recibir con los brazos abiertos. **to take up arms,** alzarse en armas, empuñar las armas. **under arms,** sobre las armas. **with folded arms,** con los brazos cruzados. **arm in arm,** del bracete, de bracero. **arm of the sea,** brazo de mar, *m*. **arm-rest,** brazo de sillón, *m*

arm /ɑrm/ *vt* armar; proveer (de); (Fig. fortify) fortificar. *vi* armarse

armada /ɑr'mɑdə/ n armada, f
armament /'ɑrməmənt/ n armamento, m
armchair /'ɑrm,tʃɛr/ n sillón, m, silla poltrona, f
armed /ɑrmd/ a armado
Armenian /ɑr'miniən/ a and n armenio (-ia); (language) armenio, m
armful /'ɑrm,fʊl/ n brazado, m
armhole /'ɑrm,houl/ n sobaquera, f
arming /'ɑrmɪŋ/ n armamento, m
armistice /'ɑrməstɪs/ n armisticio, m
armless /'ɑrmlɪs/ a sin brazos
armor /'ɑrmər/ n armadura, f; (for ships, etc.) blindaje, m. vt blindar, acorazar. **(to) a.-plate,** vt blindar. n coraza, plancha blindada, f
armored /'ɑrmərd/ a blindado, acorazado. **a. car,** carro blindado, m. **a. cruiser,** crucero acorazado, m
armory /'ɑrməri/ n armería, f
army /'ɑrmi/ n ejército, m; multitud, muchedumbre, f. **to be in the a.,** ser del ejército. **to go into the a.,** alistarse. **a. corps,** cuerpo del ejército, m. **a. estimates,** presupuesto del ejército, m. **a. list,** escalofón del ejército, m. **A. Medical Corps,** Sanidad Militar, f. **A. Supply Corps,** Cuerpo de Intendencia, m
aroma /ə'roumə/ n aroma, m
aromatic /,ærə'mætɪk/ a aromático
around /ə'raund/ prep alrededor de; por todas partes de; cerca de; (with words like corner) a la vuelta de. adv alrededor; a la redonda, en torno; por todas partes; de un lado para otro
arouse /ə'rauz/ vt despertar; excitar. **a. (someone's) suspicions,** despertar las sospechas (de fulano)
arpeggio /ɑr'pɛdʒi,ou/ n arpegio, m
arraign /ə'rein/ vt acusar; Law. procesar
arraignment /ə'reinmənt/ n acusación, f; Law. procesamiento, m
arrange /ə'reindʒ/ vt arreglar; acomodar; poner en orden, clasificar, Lat. Am. acotejar; (place) colocar; (order) ordenar, disponer; (contrive) agenciar; organizar; preparar; Mus. adaptar; (of differences) concertar, ajustar. vi convenir, concertarse; arreglar; hacer preparativos
arrangement /ə'reindʒmənt/ n arreglo, m; clasificación, f; disposición, f; (agreement) acuerdo, m; Mus. adaptación, f; pl **arrangements,** preparativos, m pl
array /ə'rei/ n (of troops) orden de batalla, mf; formación, f; colección, f; (dress) atavío, m, vt poner en orden de batalla; formar (las tropas, etc.); ataviar, adornar
arrears /ə'rɪərz/ n pl atrasos, m pl. **in a.,** atrasado
arrest /ə'rɛst/ vt detener, impedir; (the attention) atraer; (capture) arrestar, prender; (judgment) suspender. n (stop) interrupción, parada, f; (hindrance) estorbo, m; (detention) arresto, m, detención, f; (of a judgment) suspensión, f. **under a.,** bajo arresto
arresting /ə'rɛstɪŋ/ a que llama la atención, notable, muy interesante; asombroso, chocador
arrival /ə'raivəl/ n llegada, venida, f, advenimiento, m; Naut. arribada, f; entrada, f; el, m, (la, f), que llega. **on a.,** al llegar, a la llegada. **the new arrivals,** los recién llegados
arrive /ə'raiv/ vi llegar; aparecer; (happen) suceder; Naut. arribar; entrar. **to a. at,** (a place or conclusion) llegar a
arrogance /'ærəgəns/ n arrogancia, altivez, soberbia, f
arrogant /'ærəgənt/ a altivo, arrogante, soberbio
arrogate /'ærə,geit/ vt arrogar
arrow /'ærou/ n saeta, flecha, f. **a.-shaped,** en forma de flecha, sagital. **a. wound,** flechazo, saetazo, m
arsenal /'ɑrsənl/ n arsenal, m
arsenic /'ɑrsənɪk/ n arsénico, m
arson /'ɑrsən/ n incendio premeditado, m
art /ɑrt/ n arte, mf; (cleverness) habilidad, f; (cunning) artificio, m. **Faculty of Arts,** Facultad de Letras, f. **fine arts,** bellas artes, f pl. **art exhibition,** exposición de pinturas, f. **art gallery,** museo de pinturas, m. **art school,** colegio de arte, m
arterial /ɑr'tɪəriəl/ a arterial; (of roads) de primera clase. **a. forceps,** pinzas hemostáticas, f pl
artery /'ɑrtəri/ n arteria, f

artesian /ɑr'tiʒən/ a artesiano
artful /'ɑrtfəl/ a hábil, ingenioso; (crafty) astuto
artfully /'ɑrtfəli/ adv ingeniosamente; con astucia
artfulness /'ɑrtfəlnɪs/ n habilidad, ingeniosidad, f; astucia, maña, f
arthritic /ɑr'θrɪtɪk/ a artrítico
arthritis /ɑr'θraitɪs/ n artritis, f
artichoke /'ɑrtɪ,tʃouk/ n alcachofa, f. **Jerusalem a.,** aguaturma, f
article /'ɑrtɪkəl/ n artículo, m; (object) objeto, m, cosa, f; pl **articles,** escritura, f; contrato, m; estatutos, m pl. vt escriturar; contratar. **leading a.,** artículo de fondo, m. **articles of apprenticeship,** contrato de aprendizaje, m. **articles of association,** estatutos de asociación, m pl. **articles of war,** código militar, m
articulate /v ɑr'tɪkyə,leit; a -lɪt/ vt articular; pronunciar, articular. vi estar unido por articulación; articular. a articulado; claro; expresivo
articulation /ɑr,tɪkyə'leiʃən/ n articulación, f, (all meanings)
artifice /'ɑrtəfɪs/ n artificio, m; arte, m, or f, habilidad, f
artificial /,ɑrtə'fɪʃəl/ a artificial; falso, fingido; afectado. **a. flowers,** flores de mano, f pl. **a. silk,** seda artificial, seda vegetal, f
artificial intelligence n inteligencia artificial, f
artificiality /,ɑrtə,fɪʃi'ælɪti/ n artificialidad, f; falsedad, f; afectación, f
artificially /,ɑrtə'fɪʃəli/ adv artificialmente; con afectación
artillery /ɑr'tɪləri/ n artillería, f. **field a.,** artillería volante (or ligera o montada), f. **a. practice,** ejercicio de cañón, m
artilleryman /ɑr'tɪlərimən/ n artillero, m
artisan /'ɑrtəzən/ n artesano (-na)
artist /'ɑrtɪst/ n artista, mf; (painter) pintor (-ra)
artistic /ɑr'tɪstɪk/ a artístico
artistically /ɑr'tɪstɪkli/ adv artísticamente
artistry /'ɑrtɪstri/ n habilidad artística, f, arte, mf
artless /'ɑrtlɪs/ a natural; sencillo, cándido, inocente
artlessly /'ɑrtlɪsli/ adv con naturalidad; con inocencia
artlessness /'ɑrtlɪsnɪs/ n naturalidad, f; sencillez, candidez, inocencia, f
art museum n museo de arte, m
Aryan /'ɛəriən/ a ario
as /æz/ adv conjunc rel pron como; así como; (followed by infin.) de; (in comparisons) tan... como; (while) mientras; a medida que; (when) cuando, al (followed by infin.); (since) puesto que, visto que; (because) porque; (although) aunque; por; (according to) según; en; (in order that) para (que). **as a rule,** por regla general. **Once as he was walking,** Una vez mientras andaba. **as... as,** tan... como. **as far as,** hasta; en cuanto a. **as from,** desde. **as good as,** tan bueno como. **as if,** como si. **as it were,** por decirlo así, en cierto modo. **as many,** otros tantos (e.g. **six embassies as many countries,** seis embajadas en otros tantos países). **as many as,** tanto... como; todos los que. **as soon as,** en cuanto, luego que, así que. **as soon as possible,** cuanto antes, Lat. Am. a la mayor brevedad posible. **as sure as can be,** sin duda alguna. **as to,** en cuanto a. **as usual,** como de costumbre. **as well,** también. **as well as,** (besides) además de; (in comparisons) tan bien como. **as yet,** todavía
asbestos /æs'bɛstəs/ n asbesto, amianto, m
ascend /ə'sɛnd/ vt and vi subir; (on, in) subir a; ascender; (rise) elevarse; (a river) remontar. **to a. the stairs,** subir las escaleras. **to a. the pulpit,** subir al púlpito. **to a. the throne,** subir al trono
ascendancy /ə'sɛndənsi/ n ascendiente, influjo, m
ascendant /ə'sɛndənt/ n elevación, f. a ascendente; predominante. **to be in the a.,** Fig. ir en aumento; predominar
ascending /ə'sɛndɪŋ/ a ascendente
ascension /ə'sɛnʃən/ n subida, ascensión, f; (of the throne) advenimiento (al trono), m. **The A.,** La Ascensión
ascent /ə'sɛnt/ n subida, f, ascenso, m; elevación, f; (slope) cuesta, pendiente, f
ascertain /,æsər'tein/ vt averiguar, descubrir

ascertainable /ˌæsər'teinəbəl/ a averiguable, descubrible

ascertainment /ˌæsər'teinmənt/ n averiguación, f

ascetic /ə'sɛtɪk/ a ascético. n asceta, mf

asceticism /ə'sɛtəˌsɪzəm/ n ascetismo, m

ascribable /ə'skraibəbəl/ a imputable, atribuible

ascribe /ə'skraib/ vt atribuir, adscribir, imputar

ascription /ə'skrɪpʃən/ n atribución, adscripción, f

asepsis /ə'sɛpsɪs/ n asepsia, f

aseptic /ə'sɛptɪk/ a aséptico

asexual /ei'sɛkʃuəl/ a asexual

ash /æʃ/ n ceniza, f; cenizas, f pl; (tree and wood) fresno, m; pl **ashes,** cenizas, f pl; restos mortales, m pl. **mountain ash,** serbal, m. **ash-colored,** ceniciento. **ash grove,** fresneda, f. **ashtray,** cenicero, m. **Ash Wednesday,** miércoles de ceniza, m

ashamed /ə'ʃeimd/ a avergonzado. **to be a.** (of), avergonzarse (de), Mexico apenarse (de). **to be a. of oneself,** avergonzarse, tener vergüenza de sí mismo

ashen /'æʃən/ a ceniciento; (of ash wood) de fresno; pálido como un muerto

ashlar /'æʃlər/ n sillar, m

ashore /ə'ʃɔr/ adv a tierra; en tierra. **to go** or **put a.,** desembarcar

Asiatic /ˌeiʒi'ætɪk/ a and n asiático (-ca)

aside /ə'said/ adv a un lado; aparte. n Theat. aparte, m. **to set a.,** poner a un lado; (omit) dejar aparte; descontar; abandonar; (a judgment) anular. **to take a.,** llevar aparte

asinine /'æsəˌnain/ a asnal

ask /æsk/ vt (a question; enquire) preguntar; (request; demand) pedir; (beg) rogar; (invite) invitar. **to ask a question,** hacer una pregunta. **to ask about,** preguntar acerca de. **to ask after,** preguntar por. **to ask for,** pedir; preguntar por. **ask for the moon,** pedir cotofas en el golfo. **to ask in,** invitar (a alguien) a entrar. **to ask over,** invitar a bajar; invitar a visitar (a alguien)

askance /ə'skæns/ adv al (or de) soslayo, de reojo; con recelo

askew /ə'skyu/ adv oblicuamente; al lado; a un lado; sesgadamente

asleep /ə'slip/ a and adv dormido. **to be a.,** estar dormido. **to fall a.,** dormirse

asparagus /ə'spærəgəs/ n espárrago, m. **a. bed,** esparraguera, f

aspect /'æspɛkt/ n aspecto, m; vista, f; apariencia, f, semblante, m

asperity /ə'spɛriti/ n aspereza, f

aspersion /ə'spɜrʒən/ n Eccl. aspersión, f; calumnia, f; insinuación, f

asphalt /'æsfɔlt/ n asfalto, m, vt asfaltar

asphyxia /æs'fɪksiə/ n asfixia, f

asphyxiate /æs'fɪksiˌeit/ vt asfixiar

asphyxiating /æs'fɪksiˌeitɪŋ/ a asfixiante

aspirant /'æspərənt/ n aspirante, candidato, m

aspirate /v 'æspəˌreit/ n -pərɪt/ vt aspirar. n letra aspirada, f

aspiration /ˌæspə'reiʃən/ n aspiración, ambición, f; deseo, anhelo, m; Gram. aspiración, f

aspire /ə'spaiᵊr/ vi aspirar (a), pretender, ambicionar; alzarse

aspirin /'æspərɪn/ n aspirina, f

ass /æs/ n asno, m

assail /ə'seil/ vt atacar, acometer, arremeter

assailable /ə'seiləbəl/ a atacable

assailant /ə'seilənt/ n asaltador (-ra)

assassin /ə'sæsɪn/ n asesino, mf

assassinate /ə'sæsəˌneit/ vt asesinar

assassination /əˌsæsə'neiʃən/ n asesinato, m

assault /ə'sɔlt/ n asalto, m; acometida, embestida, f; Fig. ataque, m. vt asaltar; acometer, embestir; atacar. **to take by a.,** tomar por asalto

assay /n 'æsei; v æ'sei/ n ensayo, m. vt ensayar, aquilatar

assayer /æ'seiər/ n ensayador, m

assaying /æ'seiɪŋ/ n ensaye, m

assemblage /ə'sɛmblɪdʒ/ n reunión, f; (of a machine) montaje, m; (of people) muchedumbre, f, concurso, m; (of things) colección, f, grupo, m

assemble /ə'sɛmbəl/ vt (persons) reunir, convocar; (things and persons) juntar; (a machine, etc.) armar; ensamblar. vi reunirse, congregarse; acudir

assembly /ə'sɛmbli/ n asamblea, f; reunión, f; Eccl. concilio, m. **a. line,** cadena de montaje, línea de montaje, f. **a. room,** sala de reuniones, f; sala de baile, f

assent /ə'sɛnt/ n asentimiento, consentimiento, m; aprobación, f; (parliamentary, Law.) sanción, f. vi asentir (a), consentir (en); aprobar

assert /ə'sɜrt/ vt mantener, defender; declarar, afirmar; hacer valer, reclamar. **to a. oneself,** imponerse, hacerse sentir; hacer valer sus derechos

assertion /ə'sɜrʃən/ n aserción, afirmación, f; defensa, f; reclamación, f

assertive /ə'sɜrtɪv/ a afirmativo; dogmático

assess /ə'sɛs/ vt tasar, valorar; fijar, señalar; repartir (contribuciones, etc.)

assessment /ə'sɛsmənt/ n tasación, f; fijación, f; repartimiento, m

assessor /ə'sɛsər/ n Law. asesor (-ra); (of taxes) repartidor (-ra); (valuer) tasador, m. **public a.,** tasador, m

asset /'æsɛt/ n ventaja, f; adquisición, f; cualidad, f; pl **assets,** fondos, m pl; Com. activo, m, créditos activos, m pl, bienes m pl

assiduity /ˌæsɪ'dyuiti/ n asiduidad, f

assiduous /ə'sɪdʒuəs/ a asiduo

assiduously /ə'sɪdʒuəsli/ adv asiduamente, con asiduidad

assign /ə'sain/ vt Law. ceder; señalar, asignar; (appoint) destinar; fijar; atribuir, imputar. n cesionario (-ia)

assignation /ˌæsɪg'neiʃən/ n asignación, f; cita, f; Law. cesión, f

assignment /ə'sainmənt/ n (homework) tarea, f; Law. cesión, f; escritura de cesión, f; atribución, f; parte, porción, f

assimilable /ə'sɪmələbəl/ a asimilable

assimilate /ə'sɪməˌleit/ vt asimilar; incorporarse. vi mezclarse

assimilation /əˌsɪmə'leiʃən/ n asimilación, f; incorporación, f

assimilative /ə'sɪmələtɪv/ a asimilativo

assist /ə'sɪst/ vt ayudar; auxiliar, socorrer; (uphold) apoyar; (further) promover, fomentar. vi (be present) asistir (a)

assistance /ə'sɪstəns/ n ayuda, f; auxilio, socorro, m; apoyo, m; (furtherance) fomento, m. **public a.,** asistencia pública, f

assistant /ə'sɪstənt/ n ayudante, m; Eccl. asistente, m; (in any body) dependiente (-ta); colaborador (-ra); (university) auxiliar, m; sub-. **a. secretary,** subsecretario (-ia). **a. secretaryship,** subsecretaría, f

associate /n, a ə'souʃiit; v -si,eit/ n asociado (-da); miembro, m; socio (-ia); compañero (-ra), amigo (-ga); colega, m; colaborador (-ra); (confederate) cómplice, mf. a asociado; auxiliar. vt asociar; unir, juntar. **to a. oneself with,** asociarse con; asociarse a. **to a. with,** frecuentar la compañía de, ir con

association /əˌsousi'eiʃən/ n asociación, f; unión, f; sociedad, f; (company) corporación, f; (connection) relación, f

assonance /'æsənəns/ n asonancia, f

assort /ə'sɔrt/ vt clasificar; mezclar

assorted /ə'sɔrtɪd/ a surtido, mezclado. **They are a well-a. pair,** Son una pareja bien avenida

assortment /ə'sɔrtmənt/ n clasificación, f, arreglo, m; surtido, m, mezcla, f

assuage /ə'sweidʒ/ vt mitigar; suavizar; calmar; aliviar

assume /ə'sum/ vt asumir; tomar; apropiarse; (wear) revestir; (suppose) suponer; poner por caso

assumed /ə'sumd/ a fingido, falso; supuesto

assumption /ə'sʌmpʃən/ n asunción, f; apropiación, arrogación, f; suposición, f. **Feast of the A.,** Fiesta de la Asunción, f

assurance /ə'ʃurəns/ n garantía, f; promesa, f; confianza, seguridad, f; (in a good sense) aplomo, m; naturalidad, f; (impudence) presunción frescura, f; descaro, m; Com. seguro, m

assure /ə'ʃur/ vt asegurar

assured /ə'ʃurd/ a aseguardo; seguro

assuredly /əˈʃʊrɪdli/ adv seguramente

asterisk /ˈæstərɪsk/ n asterisco, m

astern /əˈstɜrn/ adv a popa; de popa; en popa; atrás

asthma /ˈæzmə/ n asma, f

asthmatic /æzˈmætɪk/ a asmático

astigmatic /ˌæstɪgˈmætɪk/ a astigmático

astigmatism /əˈstɪgməˌtɪzəm/ n astigmatismo, m

astir /əˈstɜr/ adv en movimiento; (out of bed) levantado; excitado

astonish /əˈstɒnɪʃ/ vt sorprender, asombrar

astonished /əˈstɒnɪʃt/ a atónito, estupefacto

astonishing /əˈstɒnɪʃɪŋ/ a sorprendente, asombroso

astonishment /əˈstɒnɪʃmənt/ n asombro, m, sorpresa, estupefacción, f

astound /əˈstaʊnd/ vt aturdir, pasmar. **to be astounded,** Inf. quedarse muerto

astounding /əˈstaʊndɪŋ/ a asombroso

astray /əˈstreɪ/ adv desviado, extraviado; por el mal camino. **to go a.,** errar el camino, perderse; Fig. descarriarse

astride /əˈstraɪd/ adv a horcajadas. prep a horcajadas sobre; a ambos lados de

astringent /əˈstrɪndʒənt/ a astringente

astrologer /əˈstrɒlədʒər/ n astrólogo (-ga)

astrological /ˌæstrəˈlɒdʒɪkəl/ a astrológico

astrology /əˈstrɒlədʒi/ n astrología, f

astronaut /ˈæstrəˌnɔt/ n astronauta, mf

astronomer /əˈstrɒnəmər/ n astrónomo, m

astronomical /ˌæstrəˈnɒmɪkəl/ a astronómico

astronomy /əˈstrɒnəmi/ n astronomía, f

astrophysics /ˌæstrouˈfɪzɪks/ n astrofísica, f

astute /əˈstut/ a astuto, sagaz; (with knave, etc.) redomado, pícaro

astuteness /əˈstutnɪs/ n astucia, sagacidad, f

asunder /əˈsʌndər/ adv en dos; separadamente; lejos uno de otro

asylum /əˈsaɪləm/ n asilo, m; (for the insane) manicomio, m

asymmetrical /ˌeɪsɪˈmɛtrɪkəl/ a asimétrico

asymmetry /eiˈsɪmɪtri/ n asimetría, f

at /æt/ prep a; en casa de; en; de; con; por; (before) delante de. Sometimes forms part of verb, e.g. to aim at, apuntar. to look at, mirar. May be translated by using pres. part., e.g. They were at play, Estaban jugando. at a bound, de un salto. at peace, en paz. at the doctor's, en casa del médico. at the crack of dawn, al rayar el alba, al romper el alba. at the head, a la cabeza. John is at Brighton, Juan está en Brighton. at the house of..., at...'s en casa de, Lat. Am. also donde (e.g., My cousin is at my grandmother's Mi primo está en casa de mi abuela, Mi primo está donde mi abuela) at first, al principio. at last, por fin. at no time, jamás. at once, en seguida. at most, a lo más. at one go Lat. Am. de una leída. at all events, en todo caso. What is he getting at? ¿Qué quiere saber? at home, en casa. at-home day, día de recibo, m

atavism /ˈætəˌvɪzəm/ n atavismo, m

atavistic /ˌætəˈvɪstɪk/ a atávico

atheism /ˈeɪθiˌɪzəm/ n ateísmo, m

atheist /ˈeɪθiɪst/ n ateo (-ea)

atheistic /ˌeɪθiˈɪstɪk/ a ateo

Athens /ˈæθɪnz/ Atenas, f

athlete /ˈæθlit/ n atleta, m

athletic /æθˈlɛtɪk/ a atlético

athletics /æθˈlɛtɪks/ n atletismo, m

athwart /əˈθwɔrt/ adv de través. prep al través de; contra

Atlantic /ætˈlæntɪk/ a and n atlántico m. **A. Charter,** Carta del Atlántico, f. **A. liner,** transatlántico, m

Atlantis /ætˈlæntɪs/ Atlántida, f

atlas /ˈætləs/ n atlas, m

ATM n cajera automática, f

atmosphere /ˈætməsˌfɪər/ n aire, m; atmósfera, f; Fig. ambiente, m

atmospheric /ˌætməsˈfɛrɪk/ a atmosférico

atmospherics /ˌætməsˈfɛrɪks/ n pl perturbaciones eléctricas atmosféricas, f pl

atoll /ˈætɒl/ n atolón, m

atom /ˈætəm/ n átomo, m. **splitting of the a.,** escisión del átomo, f

atomic /əˈtɒmɪk/ a atómico. **a. bomb,** bomba atómica, f. **a. pile,** pila atómica, f. **a. theory,** teoría atómica, f

atomize /ˈætəˌmaɪz/ vt pulverizar

atomizer /ˈætəˌmaɪzər/ n pulverizador, m

atone /əˈtoʊn/ vi (for) expiar

atonement /əˈtoʊnmənt/ n expiación, f

atonic /əˈtɒnɪk, eiˈtɒn-/ a átono, atónico

atrocious /əˈtroʊʃəs/ a atroz; horrible

atrocity /əˈtrɒsɪti/ n atrocidad, f

atrophy /ˈætrəfi/ n atrofia, f, vi atrofiarse

attach /əˈtætʃ/ vt (Law. of goods) embargar; (Law. of persons) arrestar; (fix) fijar; (tie) atar; (join) juntar; (stick) pegar; (connect) conectar; (hook) enganchar; (with a brooch, etc.) prender; (blame, etc.) imputar; (importance, etc.) dar, conceder; (assign) asignar; (attract) atraer; (enclose) adjuntar, incluir. vi pertenecer (a), ser indivisible (de). **to a. oneself to,** pegarse a; adherirse a, asociarse con; acompañar; hacerse inseparable de

attaché /ætæˈʃei/ n agregado, m. **a. case,** maletín, m

attachment /əˈtætʃmənt/ n (Law. of goods) embargo, m, vía ejecutiva, f; (Law. of persons) arresto, m; unión, f; conexión, f; (hooking) enganche, m; (with a brooch, etc.) prendimiento, m; (tying) atadura, f; (fixing) fijación, f; (affection) apego, cariño, m; (friendship) amistad, f

attack /əˈtæk/ n ataque, m; Mil. ofensiva, f; (access) acceso, m. vt atacar

attacker /əˈtækər/ n atacador (-ra), asaltador (-ra)

attain /əˈtein/ vt alcanzar, conseguir, lograr. vi llegar a; alcanzar

attainable /əˈteinəbəl/ a asequible, realizable; accesible

attainment /əˈteinmənt/ n consecución, obtención, f; logro, m; pl **attainments,** prendas, dotes, f pl

attempt /əˈtɛmpt/ vt (try) procurar, tratar de, intentar; ensayar; querer; Law. hacer una tentativa (de), atentar. n tentativa, prueba, f; esfuerzo, ensayo, m; (criminal) atentado, m, tentativa, f

attend /əˈtɛnd/ vi prestar atención (a); escuchar; (look after) cuidar (de); (serve) servir; (accompany) acompañar; (await) esperar. vt (be present) asistir (a); (of a doctor) visitar; (accompany) acompañar; (bring) acarrear, traer; (follow) seguir. **to be attended with,** traer consigo, acarrear

attendance /əˈtɛndəns/ n asistencia, presencia, f; (those present) público, m, concurrencia, f; servicio, m; (train) acompañamiento, m; Med. asistencia, f, tratamiento médico, m. **to be in a.,** acompañar (a)

attendant /əˈtɛndənt/ a que acompaña; que sigue; concomitante. n criado (-da); (keeper) guardián (-ana); (nurse) enfermero (-ra); (in a cloakroom) guardarropa, f; (in a theater) acomodador (-ra); (on a train) mozo, m; (waiter) camarero, m; (at baths) bañero (-ra)

attention /əˈtɛnʃən, əˌtɛnˈʃʌn/ n atención, f; cuidado, m. **A.!** ¡Atención!; Mil. ¡Firmes! **to pay a.,** prestar atención. **to stand at a.,** cuadrarse, permanecer en posición de firmes

attentive /əˈtɛntɪv/ a atento; solícito; cortés, obsequioso

attentively /əˈtɛntɪvli/ adv con atención, atentamente; solícitamente

attentiveness /əˈtɛntɪvnɪs/ n cuidado, m; cortesía, f

attenuate /əˈtɛnyuˌeit/ vt atenuar

attenuating /əˈtɛnyuˌeitɪŋ/ a atenuante. **a. circumstance,** circunstancia atenuante, f

attenuation /əˌtɛnyuˈeiʃən/ n atenuación, f

attest /əˈtɛst/ vt atestar. vi atestiguar, deponer, dar fe

attestation /ˌætɛˈsteiʃən/ n atestación, deposición, f; (certificate) certificado, m, fe, f

attic /ˈætɪk/ n buhardilla, guardilla, f, desván, sotabanco, m

Attic /ˈætɪk/ a ático

attire /əˈtaiᵊr/ n atavío, m; (dress) traje, m; (finery) galas, f pl, vt ataviar, vestir; engalanar

attitude /ˈætɪˌtud/ n actitud, f; postura, f; posición, f

attorney /əˈtɜrni/ n (solicitor) abogado (-da); (agent) apoderado (-da); (public) procurador, m. **power of a.,** poderes, m pl procuración, f. **A.-general,** fiscal, m

attract /ə'trækt/ vt atraer; (charm) seducir, cautivar, apetecer; (invite) convidar; (goodwill, etc.) captar

attraction /ə'trækʃən/ n atracción, f; atractivo, aliciente, encanto, m

attractive /ə'træktɪv/ a atrayente; atractivo, seductivo; apetecible; encantador

attractively /ə'træktɪvli/ adv atractivamente

attributable /ə'trɪbyʊtəbəl/ a imputable, atribuible

attribute /v ə'trɪbyut; n 'ætrə,byut/ vt atribuir (a), achacar (a), imputar (a). n atributo, m

attribution /,ætrə'byuʃən/ n atribución, imputación, f; atributo, m

attrition /ə'trɪʃən/ n atrición, f

auburn /'ɔbərn/ a castaño, rojizo

auction /'ɔkʃən/ n subasta, almoneda, f; venta pública, pública subasta, f, vt subastar. **to put up to a.,** sacar a pública subasta

auctioneer /,ɔkʃə'nɪər/ n subastador (-ra), Lat. Am. also licitador (-ra)

audacious /ɔ'deiʃəs/ a atrevido, audaz, osado, temerario; (shameless) descarado, impudente

audaciously /ə'deiʃəsli/ adv osadamente; descaradamente

audacity /ɔ'dæsɪti/ n audacia, osadía, temeridad, f, atrevimiento, m; (shamelessness) descaro, m, desvergüenza, f

audibility /,ɔdə'bɪlɪti/ n audibilidad, perceptibilidad, f

audible /'ɔdəbəl/ a audible, oíble

audibly /'ɔdəbli/ adv en forma audible, perceptiblemente, en alta voz

audience /'ɔdiəns/ n (interview and Law.) audiencia, f; oyentes, m pl, auditorio, público, m. **to give a.,** dar audiencia. **a. chamber,** sala de recepción, f

audiofrequency /'ɔdiou,frikwɛnsi/ n audiofrecuencia, f

audit /'ɔdɪt/ vt intervenir, examinar (cuentas). n intervención, f, ajuste (de cuentas), m

audition /ɔ'dɪʃən/ n audición, f

auditor /'ɔdɪtər/ n (hearer) oyente, mf; interventor, contador, m

auditorium /,ɔdɪ'tɔriəm/ n sala de espectáculos, f

auditory /'ɔdɪ,tɔri/ a auditivo, auditorio

Augean /ɔ'dʒiən/ a de Augeas; muy sucio

auger /'ɔgər/ n taladro, m

aught /ɔt/ n algo. **For a. I know,** Por lo que yo sepa

augment /ɔg'mɛnt/ vt aumentar, acrecentar. vi aumentarse, acrecentarse

augmentation /,ɔgmɛn'teiʃən/ n aumento, acrecentamiento, m; añadidura, f

augmentative /ɔg'mɛntətɪv/ a aumentativo

augur /'ɔgər/ n agorero (-ra). vt and vi presagiar, anunciar; pronosticar, augurar

augury /'ɔgyəri/ n predicción, f; agüero, presagio, pronóstico, m

August /'ɔgəst/ n agosto, m

august /ɔ'gəst/ a augusto

Augustan /ɔ'gʌstən/ a (of Roman emperor) augustal. **A. Age,** siglo de Augusto, m

Augustinian /,ɔgə'stɪniən/ a and n Eccl. agustino (-na)

aunt /ænt, ɑnt/ n tía, f. **great-a.,** tía abuela, f

aura /'ɔrə/ n exhalación, f; influencia psíquica, f; Med. aura, f

aural /'ɔrəl/ a auricular. **a. surgeon,** otólogo, m

auricle /'ɔrɪkəl/ n (of the heart) aurícula, ala del corazón, f; oreja, f, pabellón de la oreja, m

aurora /ə'rɔrə/ n aurora, f. **a. borealis,** aurora boreal, f

auspice /'ɔspɪs/ n auspicio, m

auspicious /ɔ'spɪʃəs/ a propicio, favorable, feliz

auspiciously /ɔ'spɪʃəsli/ adv prósperamente, felizmente

auspiciousness /ɔ'spɪʃəsnɪs/ n buenos auspicios, m pl; felicidad, f

austere /ɔ'stɪər/ a severo, austero, adusto; ascético; (of style) desnudo

austerity /ɔ'stɛrɪti/ n austeridad, severidad, f; ascetismo, m; (of style) desnudez, f

Australian /ɔ'streilyən/ a and n australiano (-na)

Austrian /'ɔstriən/ a and n austríaco (-ca)

authentic /ɔ'θɛntɪk/ a auténtico

authenticate /ɔ'θɛntɪ,keit/ vt autenticar

authentication /ɔ,θɛntɪ'keiʃən/ n autenticación, f

authenticity /,ɔθɛn'tɪsɪti/ n autenticidad, f

author /'ɔθər/ n autor (-ra)

author index n índice de autores, m

authoritarian /ə,θɔrɪ'tɛəriən/ a autoritario

authoritative /ə'θɔrɪ,teitɪv/ a autoritario

authority /ə'θɔrɪti/ n autoridad, f; poder, m. **to have on the best a.,** tener de muy buena fuente

authorization /,ɔθərə'zeiʃən/ n autorización, f

authorize /'ɔθə,raiz/ vt autorizar

authorship /'ɔθər,ʃɪp/ n profesión de autor, f; paternidad (literaria), f; origen, m

auto /'ɔtou/ n = **automobile**

autobiographical /,ɔtə,baiə'græfɪkəl/ a autobiográfico

autobiography /,ɔtəbai'bgrəfi/ n autobiografía, f

autocracy /ɔ'tɒkrəsi/ n autocracia, f

autocrat /'ɔtə,kræt/ n autócrata, mf

autocratic /,ɔtə'krætɪk/ a autocrático

autograph /'ɔtə,græf/ n autógrafo, m

autography /ɔ'tɒgrəfi/ n autografía, f

automatic /,ɔtə'mætɪk/ a automático. **a. gate,** (at level crossings, etc.) barrera de golpe, f. **a. pencil,** lapicero, m

automatically /,ɔtə'mætɪkəli/ adv automáticamente

automatism /ɔ'tɒmə,tɪzəm/ n automatismo, m

automaton /ɔ'tɒmə,tɒn/ n autómata, m

automobile /,ɔtəmə'bil/ n automóvil, coche, Lat. Am. carro m

autonomous /ɔ'tɒnəməs/ a autónomo

autonomy /ɔ'tɒnəmi/ n autonomía, f

autopsy /'ɔtɒpsi/ n autopsia, f

autosuggestion /,ɔtousəg'dʒɛstʃən/ n autosugestión, f

autumn /'ɔtəm/ n otoño, m

autumnal /ɔ'tʌmnl/ a otoñal, de otoño

auxiliary /ɔg'zɪlyəri/ n auxiliar. n auxiliador, m. **a. verb,** verbo auxiliar

avail /ə'veil/ vt servir; valer; importar. vt aprovechar. **to a. oneself of,** valerse de, aprovecharse de. **to no a.,** en balde

availability /ə,veilə'bɪlɪti/ n utilidad, f; disponibilidad, f; provecho, m; (validity) validez, f

available /ə'veiləbəl/ a útil; disponible; aprovechable; válido

avalanche /'ævə,læntʃ/ n alud, lurte, m

avarice /'ævərɪs/ n avaricia, f

avaricious /,ævə'rɪʃəs/ a avaro, avaricioso

ave /'ɑvei/ interj ¡ave! n avemaría, f; despedida, f

avenge /ə'vɛndʒ/ vt vengar; vindicar. **to a. oneself for,** vengarse de

avenger /ə'vɛndʒər/ n vengador (-ra)

avenging /ə'vɛndʒɪŋ/ a vengador

avenue /'ævə,nyu/ n avenida, f

aver /ə'vɜr/ vt afirmar, asegurar

average /'ævərɪdʒ/ n promedio, término medio, m; (marine insurance) avería, f, a de promedio; típico; corriente; normal. vt hallar el término medio (de); prorratear, proporcionar; ser por término medio. **general a.,** (marine insurance) avería gruesa, f. **on the a.,** por término medio

averse /ə'vɜrs/ a opuesto (a); desinclinado (a); enemigo (de); repugnante. **to be a. to,** no gustar de; oponerse a; estar desinclinado a; ser enemigo de; repugnar

aversion /ə'vɜrʒən/ n aversión, f; repugnancia, f

avert /ə'vɜrt/ vt apartar; (avoid) evitar

aviary /'eivi,ɛri/ n avería, pajarera, f

aviation /,eivi'eiʃən/ n aviación, f

aviator /'eivi,eitər/ n aviador (-ra)

avid /'ævɪd/ a ávido

avidity /ə'vɪdɪti/ n avidez, f

avidly /'ævɪdli/ adv ávidamente, con avidez

avocado /,ævə'kɑdou, ,ɑvə-/ n aguacate, m

avocation /,ævə'keiʃən/ n pasatiempo, m, distracción, f; ocupación, f; profesión, f

avoid /ə'vɔid/ vt evitar; (pursuit) evadir, eludir; guardarse de; rehuir; Law. anular

avoidable /ə'vɔidəbəl/ a evitable, eludible

avoidance /ə'vɔidns/ n evitación, f

avow /ə'vau/ *vt* confesar; declarar
avowal /ə'vauəl/ *n* confesión, admisión, *f*
avowedly /ə'vauɪdli/ *adv* por confesión propia
avuncular /ə'vʌŋkyələr/ *a* avuncular
await /ə'weit/ *vt* aguardar, esperar
awake /ə'weik/ *vt* despertar. *vi* despertarse. *a* despierto; vigilante; consciente (de); atento (a)
awakening /ə'weikənɪŋ/ *n* despertamiento, *m*
award /ə'wɔrd/ *n* sentencia, decisión, *f*; adjudicación, *f*; (prize) premio, *m*. *vt* adjudicar; otorgar, conceder. **She was awarded a professorship in Greek,** Ganó unas oposiciones para una cátedra de griego
aware /ə'wɛər/ *a* consciente, sabedor. **to be well a. of,** saber muy bien. **to make a. of,** hacer saber
awash /ə'wɒʃ/ *adv* a flor de agua
away /ə'wei/ *adv* a distancia, a lo lejos, lejos; (absent) ausente; (out) fuera; (unceasingly) sin parar, continuamente; (wholly) completamente; (visibly) a ojos vistas. In verbs of motion **a.** is rendered by the reflexive, e.g. *to go a.,* marcharse, irse. *to take a.,* quitar. *interj* ¡fuera de aquí! ¡márchese Vd.!; ¡vámonos! ¡adelante! **nine miles a.,** a nueve millas de distancia. **a. in the distance,** allá a lo lejos. **She sang a.,** Ella seguía cantando
awe /ɔ/ *n* temor reverente, *m*; horror, *m*; respeto, *m*; reverencia, *f*, *vt* intimidar, aterrar; infundir respeto (a). **to stand in awe of,** tener respeto (a), reverenciar
awesome /'ɔsəm/ *a* pavoroso, temible, aterrador; terrible; (august) augusto; (imposing) imponente
awestruck /'ɔ,strʌk/ *a* espantado, aterrado
awful /'ɔfəl/ *a* terrible, pavoroso; horrible; temible; atroz; *Inf.* enorme. **How a.!** *Inf.* ¡Qué barbaridad!

awfully /'ɔfəli, 'ɔfli/ *adv* terriblemente; horriblemente; *Inf.* muy
awfulness /'ɔfəlnɪs/ *n* lo terrible; lo horrible; atrocidad, *f*; (of a crime, etc.) enormidad, *f*
awkward /'ɔkwərd/ *a* difícil; peligroso; delicado; embarazoso; (of time, etc.) inconveniente, inoportuno; (of things) incómodo; (clumsy) torpe, desmañado; desagradable; (ungraceful) sin gracia. **the a. age,** la edad difícil
awkwardly /'ɔkwərdli/ *adv* torpemente; incómodamente; mal; con dificultad; sin gracia. **He is a. placed,** Se encuentra en una situación difícil
awkwardness /'ɔkwərdnɪs/ *n* dificultad, *f*; peligro, *m*; delicadeza, *f*; inconveniencia, inoportunidad, *f*; (clumsiness) torpeza, desmaña, *f*; (ungracefulness) falta de gracia, *f*
awl /ɔl/ *n* lezna, *f*, punzón, *m*
awning /'ɔnɪŋ/ *n* toldo, palio, *m*, *Lat. Am.* carpa *f*; *Naut.* toldilla, *f*
awry /ə'rai/ *adv* a un lado; oblicuamente; *Fig.* mal. *a* torcido; *Fig.* descarriado
ax /æks/ *n* hacha, *f*
axiom /'æksiəm/ *n* axioma, *m*
axiomatic /,æksiə'mætɪk/ *a* axiomático
axis /'æksɪs/ *n* eje, *m*; *Zool.* axis, *m*. **A. power,** nación del Eje
axle /'æksəl/ *n* eje, *m*; peón, árbol (de una rueda), *m*. **back a.,** eje trasero, *m*. **differential a.,** eje diferencial, *m*. **front a.,** eje delantero, *m*
ay /ai/ *interj* sí. *n* voto afirmativo, *m*
azalea /ə'zeilyə/ *n* azalea, *f*
Aztec /'æztɛk/ *a* and *n* azteca, *mf*
azure /'æʒər/ *n* azul celeste, *m*

B

b /bi/ *n* (letter) be, *f*; *Mus.* si, *m*
baa /bæ, ba/ *n* balido, be, *m*, *vi* balar, dar balidos
babble /'bæbəl/ *n* (chatter) charla, *f*; (of a child) gorjeo, *m*; (confused sound) vocinglería, barbulla, *f*, rumor, *m*; (of water) murmullo, susurro, *m*. *vi* charlar; (of children) gorjearse; (incoherently) balbucir; (water) murmurar, susurrar; (a secret) descubrir
babbler /'bæblər/ *n* charlatán (-ana)
babbling /'bæblɪŋ/ *n* garrulería, locuacidad, *f*; (incoherent speech) balbuceo, *m*. (of water) murmullo, *m*. *a* gárrulo, locuaz; balbuciente; murmurante
babel /'bæbəl/ *n* babel, *m*
baboon /bæ'bun/ *n* babuino, *m*
baby /'beibi/ *n* bebé, crío, *m*; niño (-ña) de pecho; *Fig.* gran bebé, *m*; niño mimado, *m*. *a* infantil. **b. blue,** azul claro, *m*. **b. doll,** muñeca bebé, *f*. **b. girl,** *Argentina* beba, *f*. **b. grand piano,** piano de media cola, *m*. **b. of the family,** *Venezuela* cuneco (-ca), *mf*
baby carriage *n* coche de niños, *m*
baby-faced /'beibi ,feist/ *a* con mejillas mofletudas
babyhood /'beibi,hʊd/ *n* infancia, niñez, *f*
babyish /'beibiɪʃ/ *a* infantil, aniñado, pueril
babysitter /'beibi,sɪtər/ *n* cuidaniños, *mf*
baccalaureate /,bækə'lɔriɪt, -'lɒr-/ *n* bachillerato, *m*
baccarat /,bɑkə'rɑ, ,bækə-/ *n* bacará, *m*
bachelor /'bætʃələr/ *n* soltero, célibe, *m*; (of a university) licenciado, bachiller, *m*; (as a title) caballero, *m*. **confirmed b.,** solterón, *m*. **degree of b.,** licenciatura, *f*. **to receive the degree of b.,** licenciarse, bachillerarse
bachelorhood /'bætʃələr,hʊd/ *n* soltería, *f*, celibato, *m*
bacillus /bə'sɪləs/ *n* bacilo, *m*
back /bæk/ *n* *Anat.* espalda, *f*; (of an animal) lomo, espinazo, *m*; (reins, loins) riñones, *m pl*; (of chairs, sofas) respaldo, *m*; (of a book) lomo, *m*; (back, bottom) fondo, *m*; parte posterior, parte de atrás, *f*; (of a hand, brush and many other things) dorso, *m*; (of a coin) reverso, *m*; el otro lado de alguna cosa; (in football, hockey) defensa, *m*; *Theat.* foro, *m*; (of firearms) culata, *f*; (of a knife) canto, *m*; (upper portion) parte superior, *f*. *a* posterior, trasero; de atrás; (remote) alejado, apartado; inferior; (overdue) past; out

of date) atrasado; (earlier) anterior; *Anat.* dorsal. **at the b.,** detrás; en el fondo; en la última fila. **at the b. of one's mind,** por sus adentros, en el fondo del pensamiento. **behind one's b.,** a espaldas de uno, en ausencia de uno. **half-b.,** medio, *m*. **on one's b.,** boca arriba; a cuestas. **to see the b. of,** *Inf.* ver por última vez, desembarazarse de. **to turn one's b. on,** volver la espalda (a). **with one's b. to the engine,** de espaldas a la máquina. **b. to b.,** espalda con espalda
back /bæk/ *vt* empujar hacia atrás; (a vehicle) dar marcha atrás; hacer retroceder; (line) reforzar; (support) apoyar; (sign) endosar; (bind) forrar; (bet on) apostar a; (a sail) fachear. *vi* retroceder; dar marchar atrás; (of the wind) girar; (with on to) dar sobre, dominar; (with down) abandonar (una pretensión, etc.). **to b. out,** salir, marcharse; volverse atrás; (retract) desdecirse
back /bæk/ *adv* detrás; atrás; otra vez, de nuevo; (returned) de vuelta; a alguna distancia; (at home) en casa. *interj* ¡atrás! **A few weeks b.,** Hace unas semanas, Unas semanas atrás. **It stands b. from the road,** Está a alguna distancia del camino. **to go b. to,** (of families, etc.) remontar a. **to come b.,** regresar. **to come b. again,** regresar de nuevo, regresar por segunda vez
back axle *n* eje trasero, *m*
backbite /'bæk,bait/ *vt* cortar (a uno) un sayo, desollarle (a uno) vivo, murmurar de
backbiter /'bæk,baitər/ *n* mala lengua, *f*, murmurador (-ra)
backbiting /'bæk,baitɪŋ/ *n* murmuración, detracción, maledicencia, *f*, a murmurador, detractor
backbone /'bæk,boun/ *n* espinazo, *m*, columna vertebral, *f*. **to the b.,** hasta la médula
backchat /'bæk,tʃæt/ *n* dimes y diretes, *m pl*; insolencia, *f*. **to indulge in b.-c.,** andar en dimes y diretes
back door *n* puerta trasera, puerta de servicio, *f*
backed /bækt/ *a* (lined) forrado; (in compounds; of persons) de espalda; (of chairs) de respaldo
backer /'bækər/ *n* (better) apostador, *m*; protector (-ra, -triz)

backfire /'bæk,faiᵊr/ n contrafuego m, falsa explosión, f
backgammon /'bæk,gæmən/ n chaquete, m
back garden n jardín de atrás, m
background /'bæk,graund/ n fondo, m; Art. último término, m. **in the b.,** en el fondo; Art. en último término; Fig. en las sombras; alejado, a distancia
backhand /'bæk,hænd/ n Sports. revés, m
backhanded /'bæk,hændɪd/ a de revés, dado con el revés de la mano; Fig. ambiguo, equívoco
backing /'bækɪŋ/ n forro, m; (lining) refuerzo, m; (of a vehicle) marcha atrás, f; retroceso, m; (betting) el apostar (a); (wagers) apuestas, f pl; (Fig. support) apoyo, m, ayuda, f; garantía, f
backlog /'bæk,lɔg/ n Com. rezago de pedidos, m
back number n (of a periodical) número atrasado, m
back pedal vi contrapedalear
back premises /'premɪsɪz/ n parte trasera (de una casa, etc.), f
backroom /'bæk'rum/ n cuarto interior, m, habitación trasera, f. **b. boy,** investigador ocupado en trabajos secretos para el gobierno, m
back seat n asiento trasero, m; fondo, m. **to take a b.-s.,** permanecer en el fondo, ceder el paso
back shop n trastienda, f
backside /'bæk,said/ n trasero, m, posaderas, nalgas, f pl
backslide /'bæk,slaid/ vi recaer, reincidir
backslider /'bæk,slaidər/ n (in religion or politics) apóstata, mf; reincidente, mf
backsliding /'bæk,slaidɪŋ/ n apostasía, f; reincidencia, f
backstage /'bæk'steidʒ/ n foro, fondo del escenario, m, adv hacia el foro; detrás de bastidores
back staircase n escalera de servicio, f; escalera secreta, f
backstairs /'bæk'stɛərz/ n escalera de servicio, f; Fig. vías secretas, f pl, a de cocina; Fig. secreto
backstitch /'bæk,stɪtʃ/ n Sew. pespunte, m, vt and vi pespuntar
back street n calle secundaria, callejuela, f; pl **back streets,** barrios bajos, m pl
backstroke /'bæk,strouk/ n reculada, f; Sports. revés, m
back tooth n muela, f
back view n vista de detrás, f
backward /'bækwərd/ a hacia atrás; vuelto hacia atrás; (in development) atrasado, poco avanzado; lento; negligente; (shy) modesto; (late) tardío; atrasado; retrógrado; (dull) torpe; retrospectivo. adv hacia atrás; atrás; al revés; (of falling) de espaldas; (of time) al pasado. **to go b. and forward,** ir y venir. **b. and forward,** de acá para allá
backwardness /'bækwərdnɪs/ n atraso, m; lentitud, f; negligencia, f; modestia, f; (lateness) tardanza, f; atraso, m; (dullness) torpeza, f; falta de progreso, f
backwards /'bækwərdz/ adv. See **backward**
backwash /'bæk,wɒʃ/ n agua de rechazo, f
backwater /'bæk,wɔtər/ n remanso, m
back wheel n rueda trasera, f, vi contrapedalear
backwoods /'bæk'wudz/ n monte, m, selva, f
back yard n corral, m
bacon /'beikən/ n tocino, m
bacteria /bæk'tɪriə/ n bacteria, f
bacterial /bæk'tɪriəl/ a bacterial, bacteriano
bactericide /bæk'tɪriə,said/ n bactericida, m
bacteriological /bæk,tɪriə'lɒdʒɪkəl/ a bacteriológico
bacteriologist /,bæktɪri'ɒlədʒɪst/ n bacteriólogo, m
bacteriology /,bæktɪri'ɒlədʒi/ n bacteriología, f
bad /bæd/ a malo; (wicked) perverso; (ill) enfermo, malo (with estar); (naughty; undutiful) malo (with ser); (of coins) falso; (of debts) incobrable; (rotten) podrido; (harmful) nocivo; (dangerous) peligroso; (of pains, a cold) fuerte; intenso; (of a shot) errado; (mistaken) equivocado; (unfortunate) desgraciado. n el mal, lo malo; (persons) los malos. **extremely bad,** pésimo. **from bad to worse,** de mal en peor. **It's too bad!** ¡Esto es demasiado! **to go bad,** (fruit) macarse; (food) estropearse. **bad habit,** mala costumbre, f, vicio, m. **to have the bad habit of,** tener el vicio de. **bad temper,** malhumor, mal genio, Lat. Am. catoche,

m. **bad-tempered,** malhumorado, Argentina cabrero.
bad turn, flaco servicio, m, mala pasada, f
badge /bædʒ/ n insignia, f; (decoration) condecoración, f; símbolo, emblema, m; (mark) marca, f
badger /'bædʒər/ n tejón, m, vt cansar, molestar
Bad Lands (of Nebraska and South Dakota) Tierras malas f pl; (of Argentina) la Travesía, f
badly /'bædli/ adv mal. **extremely b.,** pésimamente. **to want something b.,** necesitar algo con urgencia. **b. done,** mal hecho. **b. disposed,** malintencionado
badminton /'bædmɪntŋ/ n el juego del volante, m
badness /'bædnɪs/ n maldad, f; mala calidad, f; lo malo
bad-smelling /'bæd ,smɛlɪŋ/ a maloliente
baffle /'bæfəl/ vt desconcertar; (bewilder) tener perplejo (a); contrariar, frustrar; (obstruct) impedir; (avoid) evitar. **to b. description,** no haber palabras para describir
baffling /'bæflɪŋ/ a desconcertante; difícil; confuso; perturbador; (of people) enigmático
bag /bæg/ n saco, m; talega, f; (hand) bolsa, f, saco (de mano), m; (for tools) capacho, m; (for sewing) costurero, m; (of bagpipes) fuelle, m; (saddle) alforja, f; (briefcase) cartera, f; (suitcase) maleta, f; (under the eye) ojera, f; (game shot) caza, f. vt entalegar; coger, cazar; matar; tomar. vi (of garments) arrugarse. **to clear out bag and baggage,** liar el petate.
a bag of bones, (person) un manojo de huesos
bagatelle /,bægə'tɛl/ n bagatela, friolera, f; (game) billar romano, m
bagful /'bægful/ n saco, m; bolsa, f
baggage /'bægɪdʒ/ n equipaje, m; Mil. bagaje, m; (madcap) pícara, f; (jade) mujerzuela, f. **b. master,** (railway) factor, m. **b. car,** furgón de equipajes, m
baggage rack n (of automobile) portaequipajes, m
baggy /'bægi/ a suelto; (creased, of trousers) con rodilleras, arrugado; (wide) bombacho
bagpipe /'bæg,paip/ n gaita, f
bagpiper /'bæg,paipər/ n gaitero, m
Bahamas, the /bə'hɑməz/ las Islas Bahamas, las Islas Lucayas, f
bail /beil/ n Law. fianza, caución, f; (person) fiador (-ra); (cricket) travesaño, m; barra, f. vt Law. poner en libertad bajo fianza; salir fiador (por); (a boat) achicar. **on b.,** en fiado. **to go b.,** dar fianza, fiar
bailiff /'beilɪf/ n Law. agente ejecutivo, m; alguacil, m; mayordomo, m; capataz, m
bait /beit/ n cebo, m; anzuelo, m; (fodder) pienso, m, vt cebar; (feed) dar pienso (a); azuzar; atormentar; (attract) atraer
baiting /'beitɪŋ/ n cebadura, f; combate, m; tormenta, f
bake /beik/ vt cocer, hacer (pan, etc.). **I like to bake cakes,** Me gusta hacer pasteles; Fig. endurecer. vi cocerse
bakelite /'beiklait/ n bakelita, f
baker /'beikər/ n panadero, hornero, m. **a baker's dozen,** la docena del fraile
bakery /'beikəri, 'beikri/ n panadería, f
baking /'beikɪŋ/ n cocimiento, cocción, f; (batch) hornada, f; el hacer (pan, etc.); a Inf. abrasador. **b.-dish,** tortera, f. **b.-powder,** levadura química, f
balance /'bæləns/ n balanza, f; equilibrio, m; Com. balance, saldo, m; (in a bank) saldo (a favor del cuentacorrentista), m; Math. resto, m; Astron. Libra, f; (pendulum) péndola, f; (counterweight) contrapeso, m. **credit b.,** saldo acreedor, m. **debit b.,** saldo deudor, m. **net b.,** saldo líquido, m. **to lose one's b.,** perder el equilibrio. **to strike a b.,** hacer balance. **b. of power,** equilibrio político, m. **b. of trade,** balanza de comercio, f. **b.-sheet,** balance, avanzo, Lat. Am. balance de situación, m. **b. wheel,** (of watches) volante, m
balance /'bæləns/ vt balancear, abalanzar; contrapesar; (accounts) saldar; comparar; considerar, examinar. vi balancearse; ser de igual peso; equilibrarse; (accounts) saldarse
balance of trade n balanza comercial, f
balancing /'bælənsɪŋ/ n balanceo, m; Com. balance, m. **b.-pole,** balancín, m

baptize

balconied /'bælkənɪd/ *a* con balcones, que tiene balcones
balcony /'bælkənɪ/ *n* balcón, *m*; galería, *f*; *Theat.* anfiteatro, *m*
bald /bɔld/ *a* calvo; (of style) seco, pobre; *Fig.* desnudo, árido, pelado; sin adorno; (simple) sencillo. **to grow b.,** ponerse calvo, encalvecer
balderdash /'bɔldər,dæʃ/ *n* galimatías, *m*, jerigonza, *f*; disparate, *m*
baldly /'bɔldlɪ/ *adv* secamente; sencillamente
baldness /'bɔldnɪs/ *n* calvicie, *f*; (of style) sequedad, pobreza, *f*; (bareness) desnudez, aridez, *f*
bale /beɪl/ *n* (bundle) fardo, *m*; (of cotton, paper, etc.) bala, *f*
Balearic Islands, the /,bæli'ærɪk/ las Islas Baleares, *f*
baleful /'beɪlfəl/ *a* malicioso, siniestro, maligno
balk /bɔk/ *n* obstáculo, *m*; (beam) viga, *f*; (billiards) cabaña, *f*. *vt* frustrar; impedir. *vi* resistirse, rehusar
Balkans, the /'bɔlkənz/ los Balcanes, *m*
ball /bɔl/ *n* globo, *m*, esfera, *f*; (plaything) pelota, *f*; (as in billiards, cricket, croquet) bola, *f*; (in football, basket-ball) balón, *m*; (shot) bala, *f*; (of wool, etc.) ovillo, *m*; (of the eye) globo (del ojo), *m*; (of the thumb) yema (del pulgar), *f*; (of the foot) planta (del pie), *f*; (dance) baile, *m*. *vi* apelotonarse. **red b.,** (in billiards) mingo, *m*. **to play b.,** jugar a la pelota. **to roll oneself into a b.,** aovillarse, hacerse un ovillo. **b. -and-socket joint,** articulación esférica, *f*. **b.-bearing,** cojinete de bolas, *m*
ballad /'bæləd/ *n* romance, *m*; (song) balada, *f*
ballast /'bæləst/ *n* (*Naut.* and *Fig.*) lastre, *m*; *Rail.* balasto, *m*. *vt* lastrar; llenar de balasto
ballerina /,bælə'rinə/ *n* bailarina, *f*
ballet /bæ'leɪ/ *n* baile ruso, ballet, *m*; baile, *m*. **b. master,** director de ballet, *m*
ballistics /bə'lɪstɪks/ *n* balística, *f*
balloon /bə'lun/ *n* globo aerostático, *m*; *Chem.* balón, *m*; (toy) globo, *m*; *Archit.* bola, *f*. **captive b.,** globo cautivo, *m*. **b. barrage,** cortina de globos de intercepción, *f*. **b.-tire,** neumático balón, *m*
balloonist /bə'lunɪst/ *n* aeronauta, *mf*
ballot /'bælət/ *n* votación, *f*; papeleta para votar, cédula de votación, *f*. *vi* votar, balotar. **b. box,** urna electoral, *f*
ballpoint, ballpoint pen /'bɔl,pɔɪnt/ *n Argentina* biro *m*, *Argentina, Uruguay* birome *m*, *Spain* bolígrafo *m*, *Mexico* bolilápiz *m*, *Colombia* esfero *m*, *Colombia* esferográfica *f*, *Cuba* estenógrafo *m*, *Argentina* lapicera *f*, *Central America, Colombia* lapicero *m*, *Paraguay, Peru* lápiz de bolilla *m*, *Chile* lápiz de pasta *m*, *Spain* pluma esférica *f*, *Spain* pluma esferográfica *f*, *Venezuela* plumilla *f*, *Spain* polígrafo *m*, *Bolivia* punto bola, punto-bola, puntobola *f*, pluma de bola *f*, pluma atómica *f*
ballroom /'bɔl,rum/ *n* salón de baile, *m*; salón de fiestas, *m*
ballroom dancing *n* baile de salón, *m*
balm /bɑm/ *n* bálsamo, *m*; *Fig.* ungüento, *m*
balminess /'bɑmɪnɪs/ *n* fragancia, *f*; aroma, *m*; (gentleness) suavidad, *f*
balmy /'bɑmɪ/ *a* balsámico; fragante; aromático; (soft) suave; (soothing) calmante
balsam /'bɔlsəm/ *n* bálsamo, *m*
Baltic, the /'bɔltɪk/ el (Mar) Báltico, *m*
balustrade /'bælə,streɪd/ *n* balaustrada, barandilla, *f*, antepecho, *m*
bamboo /bæm'bu/ *n* bambú, *m*
bamboozle /bæm'buzəl/ *vt* engatusar, embaucar
bamboozler /bæm'buzlər/ *n* embaucador (-ra)
ban /bæn/ *n* interdicción, *f*; prohibición, *f*; bando, *m*. *vt* prohibir; proscribir
banal /bə'næl/ *a* banal, vulgar, trivial
banality /bə'nælɪtɪ/ *n* banalidad, vulgaridad, trivialidad, *f*
banana /bə'nænə/ *n* (tree and fruit) plátano, *m*; (fruit) banana, *f*, *Venezuela* cambur, *m*. **b. plantation,** platanar, *m*
band /bænd/ *n* lista, tira, *f*; zona, *f*; (black mourning) tira de gasa, *f*; (sash) faja, *f*; (ribbon) banda; cinta, *f*; (bandage) venda, *f*; *Mech.* correa, *f*; *Archit.* listón, *m*; *Mus.* banda, *f*; (group) pandilla, *f*, grupo,

m. *vt* congregar, reunir. *vi* reunirse, asociarse. **b.-saw,** sierra de cinta, *f*
bandage /'bændɪdʒ/ *n* venda, *f*, vendaje, *m*, *vt* vendar, poner un vendaje en (limbs, etc. or persons)
bandaging /'bændɪdʒɪŋ/ *n* vendaje, *m*
banderol /'bændə,rɔl/ *n* banderola, *f*
bandit /'bændɪt/ *n* bandido, bandolero, *m*
bandmaster /'bænd,mæstər/ *n* músico mayor, *m*; director de orquesta, *m*
bandsman /'bændzmən/ *n* músico, *m*
bandstand /'bænd,stænd/ *n* quiosco de música, *m*
bandy /'bændɪ/ *vt* cambiar, trocar; pasar de uno a otro
bandy-legged /'bændɪ ,lɛgɪd/ *a* estevado zanquituerto
bane /beɪn/ *n* (poison) veneno, *m*; perdición, ruina, *f*; (nuisance) plaga, *f*
baneful /'beɪnfəl/ *a* pernicioso, funesto; dañino; maligno
banefully /'beɪnfəlɪ/ *adv* funestamente; malignamente
bang /bæŋ/ *n* golpe, golpazo, *m*; (of an explosive, fire-arm) estallido, *m*, detonación, *f*; (of a firework) traque, *m*; (of a door) portazo, *m*; (with the fist) puñetazo, *m*; (noise) ruido, *m*; (fringe) flequillo, *m*. *vt* golpear; (beat) sacudir; (throw) lanzar, arrojar con violencia; (a door, etc.) cerrar de golpe, cerrar con violencia. *vi* golpear; estallar; (thunder) retronar; (in the wind) cencerrear. *interj* ¡pum! ¡zas!
banging /'bæŋɪŋ/ *n* golpeadura, *f*; sacudidura, *f*; detonación, *f*; ruido, *m*
bangle /'bæŋgəl/ *n* pulsera, *f*; brazalete, *m*; (for ankles) ajorca, *f*
banish /'bænɪʃ/ *vt* desterrar, apartar; (from the mind) despedir, ahuyentar; (suppress) suprimir
banishment /'bænɪʃmənt/ *n* destierro, *m*; expulsión, *f*; relegación, *f*; (suppression) supresión, *f*
banister /'bænɪstər/ *n* baranda, *f*, pasamano, *m*
banjo /'bændʒou/ *n* banjo, *m*
banjoist /'bændʒouɪst/ *n* tocador (-ra) de banjo
bank /bæŋk/ *n* (of rivers, etc.) ribera, orilla, *f*, margen, *m*; (of clouds) banda, capa, *f*; (of sand, fog, snow) banco, *m*; (embankment) terraplén, *m*; *Com.* banco, *m*; (gaming) banca, *f*; (for foreign exchange) casa de cambio, *f*. **b. account,** cuenta corriente, *f*. **b. book,** libreta de banco, *f*. **b. clerk,** empleado del banco, *m*. **b. holiday,** fiesta oficial, *f*. **b.-note,** billete de banco, *m*. **b. stock,** acciones de un banco, *f pl*
bank /bæŋk/ *vt* estancar, represar; amontonar; poner (dinero) en un banco, depositar en un banco. *vi* tener cuenta corriente en un banco; (gaming) tener la banca; ser banquero; *Aer.* inclinarse al virar
banker /'bæŋkər/ *n* bancario (-ia), banquero, *m*, (also at cards); (money-changer) cambista, *mf*
banking /'bæŋkɪŋ/ *n Com.* banca, *f*; *Aer.* vuelo inclinado, *m*, *a Com.* bancario. **b. house,** casa de banca, *f*
bankrupt /'bæŋkrʌpt/ *a* insolvente, quebrado. *n* quebrado (-da). **to go b.,** declararse en quiebra, hacer bancarrota
bankruptcy /'bæŋkrʌptsɪ/ *n* bancarrota, quiebra, *f*; *Fig.* pobreza, decadencia, *f*. **fraudulent b.,** quiebra fraudulenta, *f*. **b. court,** tribunal de quiebras, *m*
banner /'bænər/ *n* bandera, *f*
banns /bænz/ *n pl* amonestaciones, *f pl*. **to forbid the b.,** impedir las amonestaciones. **to publish the b.,** decir las amonestaciones
banquet /'bæŋkwɪt/ *n* banquete, *m*, *vt and vi* banquetear
banqueting /'bæŋkwɪtɪŋ/ *a* de banquetes. **b. hall,** sala de banquetes, *f*
bantam /'bæntəm/ *n* gallina enana, *f*. **b. weight,** (*Sports.*) *a* de peso gallo. *n* peso gallo, *m*
banter /'bæntər/ *vt and vi* tomar el pelo (a). *n* chistes, *m pl*, burlas, *f pl*
baptism /'bæptɪzəm/ *n* bautismo, *m*; *Fig.* bautizo, *m*
baptist /'bæptɪst/ *n* bautista, *m*. **St. John the B.,** San Juan Bautista
baptistry /'bæptəstrɪ/ *n* baptisterio, bautisterio, *m*
baptize /bæp'taɪz/ *vt* bautizar

baptizing /'bæp'taizɪŋ/ n bautizo, m
bar /bɑr/ n barra, f; (of chocolate, soap) pastilla, f;
Herald. banda, f; (on a window) reja, f; (of a door)
tranca, f, barrote, m; (bar lever) palanca, f; (of a balance) astil, m; *Mus.* barra, f; (in the sea, etc.) banco,
alfaque, m; (barrier) barrera, f; (legal profession)
foro, m, curia, f; *Fig.* tribunal, m; (in a court) barra,
f; *Fig.* impedimento, m; (of light) rayo, m; (stripe)
raya, f; (for refreshments) bar, m, *Lat. Am.* chingana,
f, mostrador del bar, m. *vt* atrancar, abarrotar; impedir, obstruir; prohibir; exceptuar, excluir; (streak)
rayar. **the b.,** el cuerpo de abogados. **to be called to
the b.,** ser recibido como abogado en los tribunales.
b.-tender, camarero del bar, m
bar association n colegio de abogados, m
barb /bɑrb/ n púa, f; (of an arrow, fish-hook, etc.)
lengüeta, f; (of a lance) roquete, m; (of fish) barbilla,
f; (of a feather) barba, f; (horse) caballo berberisco,
m. *vt* proveer de púas; armar de lengüetas
Barbados /bɑr'beidouz/ Isla de Barbados, f
barbarian /bɑr'bɛəriən/ a bárbaro, barbárico. n bárbaro (-ra)
barbaric /bɑr'bærɪk/ a barbárico, salvaje
barbarism /'bɑrbə,rɪzəm/ n barbarismo, salvajismo,
m; crueldad, f; (of style) barbarismo, m
barbarity /bɑr'bærɪti/ n barbaridad, ferocidad, f
barbarous /'bɑrbərəs/ a feroz, cruel, salvaje; inculto
barbarously /'bɑrbərəsli/ adv bárbaramente, cruelmente
barbarousness /'bɑrbərəsnɪs/ n barbaridad, f; crueldad, ferocidad, f
barbecue /'bɑrbɪ,kyu/ n barbacoa, f
barbed wire /'bɑrbd/ n alambre de púas, alambre espinoso, m
barber /'bɑrbər/ n barbero, m. **barber shop,** barbería, f
Barcelona /,bɑrsə'lounə/ (of or from) a and n barcelonés (-esa)
bar code n código de barras, m
bard /bɑrd/ n bardo, vate, m
bare /bɛər/ a desnudo; descubierto; vacío; (mere)
mero, solo; (worn) raído; pelado, raso; (unadorned)
sencillo; (unsheathed) desnudo; (arid) árido; (curt)
seco; (unprotected) desabrigado; pobre. *vt* desnudar;
descubrir; revelar. **He bared his head,** Se descubrió.
to lay b., dejar al desnudo; revelar
bareback /'bɛər,bæk/ a que monta en pelo. adv en
pelo
barefaced /'bɛər,feist/ a descarado, desvergonzado,
cínico
barefoot /'bɛər,fʊt/ a descalzo
bareheaded /'bɛər,hɛdɪd/ a sin sombrero, descubierto
barelegged /'bɛər,legɪd/ a en pernetas, en piernas
barely /'bɛərli/ adv apenas; escasamente; meramente,
solamente
bareness /'bɛərnɪs/ n desnudez, f; desadorno, m;
(aridity) aridez, f; pobreza, f
bargain /'bɑrgən/ n contrato, m; pacto, acuerdo, m;
(purchase) ganga, f. *vi* negociar; (haggle) regatear.
into the b., de añadidura, también. **It is a b.,** Es una
ganga; Trato hecho. **to get the best of the b.,** salir
ganando. **to strike a b.,** cerrar un trato. **b. counter,**
sección de saldos, f. **b. sale,** venta de saldos, *Mexico*
barata f
bargainer /'bɑrgənər/ n negociador (-ra); regatón
(-ona)
bargaining /'bɑrgənɪŋ/ n negociación, gestión, f;
(haggling) regateo, m
barge /bɑrdʒ/ n (for freight) barcaza, gabarra, f;
falúa, f; lancha, f. *vi* (into) tropezar con; dar empujones
baritone /'bærɪ,toun/ n barítono, m
barium /'bɛəriəm/ n *Chem.* bario, m
bark /bɑrk/ n (of a tree) corteza, f; (of a fountain) quina,
f; (boat, *Poet.*) barca, f; *Naut.* buque de tres palos, m;
(of a dog) ladrido, m; (of a wolf) aullido, m; (of a
gun) ruido, m. *vi* (of a dog) ladrar; (of a wolf) aullar;
(of a gun) tronar
barking /'bɑrkɪŋ/ n ladrido, m; (of stags) rebramo,
m; (of foxes) aullidos, m pl; (of guns) trueno, m

barley /'bɑrli/ n cebada, f, a de cebada. **pearl b.,** cebada perlada, f. **b.-bin,** cebadera, f. **b. dealer,** cebadero, m. **b. field,** cebadal, m. **b.-water,** hordiate, m
barm /bɑrm/ n (froth on beer) giste, m; (leaven)
levadura, f
barmaid /'bɑr,meid/ n moza de bar, camarera, f
barn /bɑrn/ n pajar, granero, hórreo, m. **b.-owl,**
lechuza, f
barnacle /'bɑrnəkəl/ n lapa, f, barnacla, m
barometer /bə'rɒmɪtər/ n barómetro, m
barometric /,bærə'metrɪk/ a barométrico
baron /'bærən/ n barón, m
baroness /'bærənɪs/ n baronesa, f
Baron Munchausen /'bærən 'mʊntʃ,hauzən/ el
Barón de la Castaña
baroque /bə'rouk/ a barroco. **the b.,** lo barroco
barracks /'bærəks/ n *Mil.* cuartel, m, caserna, *Lat.
Am.* barraca f. **to quarter in b.,** acuartelar
barrage /bə'rɑʒ/ n presa de contención, f; *Mil.* cortina de fuego, f; (barrier) barrera, f; (of questions)
lluvia, f. **b. balloon,** globo de intercepción, m
barrel /'bærəl/ n barril, m; tonel, m; cuba, f; (of a
gun) cañón, m; *Mech.* cilindro, m; (of an animal)
cuerpo, m. *vt* embarrilar, entonelar. **b.-organ,** organillo, órgano de manubrio, m
barrelled /'bærəld/ a embarrilado; (of guns, generally
in compounds) de... cañones. **double-b. gun,** escopeta de dos cañones, f
barren /'bærən/ a estéril; (of ground) árido; (fruitless) infructuoso, yermo
barrenness /'bærən,nɪs/ n esterilidad, f; aridez, sequedad, f; (fruitlessness) inutilidad, f
barricade /'bærɪ,keid/ n barricada, f; barrera, f, *vt*
cerrar con barricadas; obstruir
barricading /'bærɪ,keidɪŋ/ n el cerrar con barricadas;
la defensa con barricadas (de)
barrier /'bæriər/ n barrera, f; impedimento, m; (for
customs duties) portazgo, m
barring /'bɑrɪŋ/ prep salvo, excepto, con la excepción
de, menos
barrister /'bærəstər/ n abogado (-da)
barrow /'bærou/ n carretón, m; carretilla, f; (tumulus) túmulo, m
barter /'bɑrtər/ n cambio, trueque, m; tráfico, m, *vt*
and *vi* cambiar, trocar; traficar
barterer /'bɑrtərər/ n traficante, mf
basalt /bə'sɔlt/ n basalto, m
base /beis/ a bajo, vil, ruin; soez; indigno; impuro;
(of metals) de mala ley. n base, f; fundamento, m;
pie, m; *Archit.* pedestal, m; (*Mil. Chem. Geom.*) base,
f; (of a vase) asiento, m, *vt* basar; fundar. **b. action,**
bajeza, f. **b. line,** *Sports.* línea de base, f. **b. metal,**
metal común, m
baseball /'beis,bɔl/ n beisbol, m, pelota base, f
baseless /'beislɪs/ a sin base; sin fundamento, insostenible
basely /'beisli/ adv bajamente, vilmente
basement /'beismənt/ n sótano, m
baseness /'beisnɪs/ n bajeza, vileza, ruindad, f
bashful /'bæʃfəl/ a vergonzoso, ruboroso; tímido,
corto; (unsociable) huraño, esquivo
bashfully /'bæʃfəli/ adv vergonzosamente; tímidamente
bashfulness /'bæʃfəlnɪs/ n vergüenza, f, rubor, m;
encogimiento, m, timidez, cortedad, f; (unsociableness) huraña, esquivez, f
basic /'beisɪk/ a básico; fundamental
basic commodity n artículo básico, producto primario, m
basilica /bə'sɪlɪkə/ n basílica, f
basilisk /'bæsəlɪsk/ n basilisco, m
basil (sweet) /'bæzəl, 'bei-/ n *Bot.* albahaca, f
basin /'beisən/ n vasija, f; (for washing) jofaina, f;
(barber's) bacía, f; (of a fountain) taza, f; *Anat.* baci-
nete, m; (of a harbor) concha, f; (of a river) cuenca,
f; (in the earth) hoya, f; (dock) dársena, f
basis /'beisɪs/ n base, f; fundamento, m; elemento
principal, m
bask /bæsk/ *vi* calentarse (in the sun) tomar el sol
basket /'bæskɪt/ n cesta, f; canasta, capacha, *Lat.*

Am. jaba *f;* (frail) espuerta, *f.* **flat b.,** azafate, *m.*
large b., banasta, *f.* **b. with a lid,** excusabaraja, *f.* **b.**
ball, baloncesto, *m.* **b. maker** or **dealer,** banastero,
cestero, *m.* **b. work** or **shop** or **factory,** cestería, *f.* **b.**
work chair, sillón de mimbres, *m*
basketful /'bæskɪt,fʊl/ *n* cesta, cestada, *f*
Basque /bæsk/ *a* and *n* vasco (-ca), vascongado (-da).
n (language) vascuence, *m;* **B. Country,** el País Vasco
Basque Provinces, the las Provincias Vascongadas
bas-relief /,bɑrɪ'lif, ,bæs-/ *n* bajo relieve, *m*
bass /beis/ *n Mus.* bajo, *m;* (for tying) esparto, *m, a*
Mus. bajo. **double b.,** contrabajo, *m.* **figured b.,** bajo
cifrado, *m.* **b. clef,** clave de fa, *f.* **b. string,** bordón,
m. **b. voice,** voz baja, *f*
bassinet /,bæsə'nɛt/ *n* cochecito de niño, *m*
bassoon /bæ'sun/ *n Mus.* bajón, fagot, *m*
bassoonist /bæ'sunɪst/ *n* bajonista, fagotista, *mf*
bastard /'bæstərd/ *n* bastardo (-da), hijo (-ja) natural.
a bastardo, ilegítimo; espurio
baste /beist/ *vt Sew.* bastear, hilvanar, embastar; *Cul.*
enlardar, lardear
basting /'beistɪŋ/ *n Sew.* embaste, *m;* *Cul.* lardea-
miento, *m.* **b. spoon,** cacillo, *m.* **b. stitch,** pasillo, *m*
bastion /'bæstʃən/ *n* bastión, baluarte, *m.* **to fortify**
with bastions, abastionar
bastioned /'bæstʃənd/ *a* abastionado, con bastiones
bat /bæt/ *n Zool.* murciélago, *m;* (in baseball) bate,
m; (in cricket) paleta, *f;* (in table tennis) pala, *f. vi*
batear; (cricket) golpear con la paleta. See **without**
batch /bætʃ/ *n* (of loaves, etc.) hornada, *f;* lote, *m;*
(of recruits) promoción, *f*
bath /bæθ/ *n* baño, *m;* (room) cuarto de baño, *m;*
(vat) bañador, *m;* (for swimming) piscina cubierta, *f;*
(in the open air) piscina al aire libre, *f; Photo.* baño,
m, solución, *f. vt* bañar, lavar. **hot mineral baths,**
termas, *f pl.* **Order of the B.,** Orden del Baño, *f.* **pub-**
lic baths, casa de baños, *f.* **reinforcing b.,** *Photo.* reforzador, *m.* **to take a b.,** bañarse, tomar un baño. **b.**
-chair, cochecillo de inválido, *m.* **b.-robe,** bata de
baño, *f,* albornoz, *m.* **b. room,** cuarto de baño, *m.* **b.**
towel, toalla del baño, *f.* **b. tub,** bañera, *f,* baño, *m,*
bañadera *f*
bathe /beið/ *vt* bañar, lavar; (of light, etc.) bañar, envolver. *vi* bañarse. *n* baño, *m*
bather /'beiðər/ *n* bañista, *mf;* bañador (-ra)
bathing /'beiðɪŋ/ *a* de baño; balneario. *n* baño, *m.* **b.**
cap, gorro de baño, *m.* **b. gown,** albornoz, *m,* bata
de baño, *f.* **b. machine,** caseta de baño, *f.* **b.-pool,**
piscina, *f.* **b.-resort,** estación balnearia, *f.* **b.-shoes,**
calzado de baño, *m.* **b. suit,** traje de baño, *m*
bathos /'beiθɒs/ *n* paso de lo sublime a lo ridículo,
m; anticlímax, *m*
batiste /bə'tist/ *n;* batista, *f*
baton /bə'tɒn/ *n* bastón de mando, *m; Mus.* batuta,
f; (policeman's) porra, *f*
battalion /bə'tælyən/ *n* batallón, *m*
batter /'bætər/ *n Cul.* batido, *m;* pasta, *f; Sports.* lanzador, bateador, *m. vt* apalear, golpear; (demolish)
derribar, demoler; (with artillery) cañonear; batir. **to**
coat with b., rebozar. **to b. down,** derribar
battering ram /'bætərɪŋ/ *n* ariete, *m*
battery /'bætəri/ *n* (*Mil. Nav.*) batería, *f; Elec.* pila,
batería, *f; Law.* agresión, *f.* **dry b.,** batería de pilas, *f.*
storage b., acumulador, *m.* **b. cell,** pila de batería
eléctrica, *f*
battle /'bætl/ *n* batalla, *f;* pelea, *f,* combate, *m;*
(struggle) lucha, *f. vi* batallar, pelear; luchar. **b.-**
array, orden de batalla, *f.* **b.-axe,** hacha de combate,
f. **b.-cruiser,** acorazado, *m.* **b.-field,** campo de batalla, *m.* **b.-front,** frente de combate, *m.* **b.-piece,**
Art. batalla, *f.* **b.-ship,** buque de guerra, *m*
battlement /'bætlmənt/ *n* almenaje, *m;* muralla al-
menada, *f*
bauble /'bɔbəl/ *n* (trifle) chuchería, fruslería, *f;*
(fool's) cetro de bufón, *m*
bauxite /'bɔksait, 'bouzait/ *n* bauxita, *f*
Bavaria /bə'vɛəriə/ *n* Baviera, *f*
Bavarian /bə'vɛəriən/ *a* and *n* bávaro (-ra)
bawdy /'bɔdi/ *a* obsceno, indecente, escabroso
bawl /bɔl/ *vi* chillar, vocear
bawling /'bɔlɪŋ/ *n* vocerío, *m,* chillidos, *m pl*

bay /bei/ *n Geog.* bahía, *f;* (small) abra, *f; Bot.* laurel,
m; (horse) bayo, *m;* (howl) aullido, *m; Archit.* abertura, *f; Rail.* andén, *m. a* (of horses) bayo, isabelino.
vi aullar. **at bay,** en jaque, acorralado. **sick-bay,** enfermería, *f.* **to keep at bay,** tener a distancia; tener
alejado; entretener. **bay rum,** ron de malagueta, *m.*
bay window, ventana salediza, *f*
baying /'beiɪŋ/ *n* aullido, *m*
bayonet /'beiənɛt/ *n* bayoneta, *f, vt* herir o matar con
bayoneta. **fixed b.,** bayoneta calada, *f.* **b. charge,**
carga de bayoneta, *f.* **b. thrust,** bayonetazo, *m*
Bayonne /ba'yɒn/ Bayona, *f*
bazaar /bə'zɑr/ *n* bazar, *m*
be /bi/ *vi* ser; (of position, place, state, temporariness) estar; (exist) existir; (in impersonal expressions) haber; (of expressions concerning the weather
and time) hacer; (remain) quedar; (leave alone) dejar; (do) hacer; (of one's health) estar; (of feeling
cold, hot, afraid, etc. and of years of one's age) tener;
(live) vivir; (belong) ser (de), pertenecer (a); (matter,
concern) importar (a); (happen) ocurrir, suceder;
(find oneself) hallarse, encontrarse, estar; (arrive) llegar (a); (cost) costar; (be worth) valer; (celebrate,
hold) celebrarse, tener lugar; (forming continuous
tense with present participle active or passive) estar;
(with past participle forming passive) ser (this construction is often replaced by reflexive form when no
ambiguity is entailed); (with infinitive expressing
duty, intention) haber de; (must) tener que. **He is a**
soldier (doctor, etc.), Es soldado (médico, etc.). **He**
is on guard, Está de guardia. **They were at the door**
(in the house, etc.), Estaban a la puerta (en la casa,
etc.). **I am writing a letter,** Estoy escribiendo una
carta (but this form is often replaced by a simple
tense, e.g. escribo...). **It remains to be written,**
Queda por escribir. **What is to be done?** ¿Qué hay
que hacer? **Woe is me!** ¡Ay de mí! **to be hot (cold),**
(of things) estar caliente (frío); (of weather) hacer calor (frío); (of persons) tener calor (frío). **How is**
John? He is well, ¿Cómo está Juan? Está bien de salud. **It is daylight,** Es de día. **It is cloudy,** Está
nublado. **She is 10,** Tiene diez años. **They are afraid,**
Tienen miedo. **I am to go there tomorrow,** He de ir
allí mañana. **What is to be will be,** Lo que tiene que
ser será. **If John were to come we could go into**
the country, Si viniera Juan podríamos ir al campo.
Be that as it may, Sea como sea. **It is seven years**
since we saw him, Hace siete años que no le vemos.
We have been here for three years, Hace tres años
que estamos aquí, Llevamos tres años aquí. **There is**
or **there are,** Hay. **There will be many people,**
Habrá mucha gente. **There were many people,** Había mucha gente. **There are many people,** Hay
mucha gente. **It is three miles to the next village,**
Estamos a tres millas del pueblo próximo. **So be it!**
Así sea. **Your pen is not to be seen,** Tu pluma no se
ve. **It is to be hoped that...,** Se espera que...; ¡Ojalá
que...! **The door is open,** La puerta está abierta. **The**
door was opened by Mary, La puerta fue abierta por
María. **He was accused of being a fascist,** Lo acu-
saron de fascista. **to be about to,** estar por; (of a
more imminent action) estar para, estar a punto de.
to be in, estar dentro; estar en casa. **to be off,** marcharse, irse. **Be off!** ¡Márchate! ¡Vete!; ¡Fuera! **to be**
out, estar fuera; haber salido; no estar en casa; (of a
light, etc.) estar apagado. **to be up,** estar levantado.
to be up to, proyectar, traer entre manos; urdir,
maquinar
beach /bitʃ/ *n* playa, *f;* costa, *f. vt* (a boat) encallar
en la costa. **b. shoes,** playeras, *f pl.* **b. suit,** vestido
de playa, *m*
beach club *n* club de playa, *m*
beacon /'bikən/ *n* (lighthouse) faro, *m;* (buoy) baliza, *f,* fanal, *m;* (watch-tower) atalaya, *f; Fig.* guía, *f.*
vt iluminar. **b. fire,** almenara, *f*
bead /bid/ *n* cuenta, *f;* (of glass) abalorio, *m;* (drop)
gota, *f; Archit.* perla, *f;* (bubble) burbuja, *f;* (foam)
espuma, *f; pl* **beads,** rosario, *m, vt* adornar con aba-
lorios. **to tell one's beads,** rezar el rosario. **b. work,**
abalorio, *m*
beading /'bidɪŋ/ *n* abalorio, *m; Archit.* friso, listón, *m*
beadle /'bidl/ *n* bedel, *m*

beadleship /'bidəl,ʃɪp/ n bedelía, f

beagle /'bigəl/ n perro sabueso, m

beak /bik/ n pico, m; punta, f; Naut. espolón, m. **to tap with the b.,** picotear

beaked /'bikt/ a que tiene pico; (in compounds) de... pico

beaker /'bikər/ n copa, f; Chem. vaso de precipitado, m

beam /bim/ n Archit. madero, m, viga, f; (width of a ship) manga, f; (of a balance) palanca, f; (of a plough) cama, f; (of light) rayo, destello, m; Phys. rayo, m; (smile) sonrisa brillante, f; pl **beams,** (of a building) envigado, m; (of a ship) baos, m pl. **main b.,** Archit. viga maestra, f. **b. of light,** rayo de luz, haz de luz, m

beam /bim/ vt lanzar, emitir; difundir. vi brillar, fulgurar, destellar; estar radiante, estar rebosando de alegría

beaming /'bimɪŋ/ a brillante; radiante

bean /bin/ n haba, f; judía, alubia, f; (of coffee) grano, m. **broad b.,** haba, f. **French, haricot, kidney b.,** judía, f. **string b.,** judía verde, f. **b. field,** habar, m. **beans,** Mexico frijoles, m; Dominican Republic habichuelas, f

bear /bɛər/ n Zool. oso, m; (she-bear) osa, f; (Stock Exchange) bajista, mf. **Great B.,** Astron. Osa Mayor, f, Septentrión, m. **Little B.,** Astron. Osa Menor, f. **polar b.,** oso blanco, m. **b.-cub,** osezno, m. **bear's den,** osera, f. **b.-hunting,** caza de osos, f. **b.-like,** osuno. **b.-pit,** recinto de los osos, m

bear /bɛər/ vt and vi (carry) llevar; (show) ostentar; (company, etc.) hacer; (profess) profesar; (of spite, etc. and of relation) guardar; (have) tener; (fruit) dar; (give birth to) parir; (support) sostener; (endure) aguantar; (suffer) padecer, sufrir; (tolerate) tolerar, aguantar, sufrir; (a strain, an operation, etc.) resistir; (lean on) apoyarse en; (experience) experimentar; (produce) producir, dar; (enjoy) disfrutar de; (use) usar; (impel) empujar; (occupy, hold) ocupar; (go) dirigirse. **It was suddenly borne in on them that...,** De pronto vieron claro que... **I cannot b. any more,** No puedo más. **We cannot b. him,** No le aguantamos, No le sufrimos. **His language won't b. repeating,** Su lenguaje no puede repetirse. **to bring to b.,** ejercer (presión, etc.). **to b. a grudge,** guardar rencor (a), tener ojeriza (a). **to b. arms,** llevar armas; servir en el ejército o la milicia. **to b. company,** hacer compañía (a), acompañar (a). **to b. in mind,** tener en cuenta, tener presente; acordarse de. **to b. oneself,** conducirse, portarse. **to b. to the right,** ir hacia la derecha. **to b. witness,** atestiguar. **to b. false witness,** levantar falso testimonio. **to b. away,** llevarse; ganar. **to b. down,** hundir; derribar; bajar. **to b. down on,** avanzar rápidamente hacia; correr hacia; Naut. arribar sobre; (attack) caer sobre. **to b. in,** llevar adentro. **to b. off,** llevarse; ganar; Naut. apartarse de la costa. **to b. on, upon,** apoyarse en; (refer to) referirse a. **to b. out,** llevar fuera; confirmar; apoyar; justificar. **to b. up,** llevar arriba; llevar a la cumbre (de); sostener; (recover) cobrar ánimo; (against) resistir; hacer frente a. **to b. with,** soportar; sufrir; aguantar; llevar con paciencia; ser indulgente con

bearable /'bɛərəbəl/ a soportable; aguantable; tolerable

beard /bɪərd/ n barba, f; (of cereals) raspa, arista, f, vt desafiar. **thick b.,** barba bien poblada, f

bearded /'bɪərdɪd/ a con barba, barbudo

beardless /'bɪərdlɪs/ a barbilampiño, desbarbado, imberbe, lampiño

bearer /'bɛərər/ n llevador (-ra), portador (-ra); (of a bier) andero, m; Com. dador, portador, m. **good b.,** Agr. árbol fructífero, m. **to b.,** Com. al portador

bearing /'bɛərɪŋ/ n porte, m; postura, f; presencia, f; conducta, f; aspecto, m; relación, f; (meaning) significación, f; Naut. demora, orientación, f; Mech. cojinete, soporte, m; (endurance) tolerancia, f; pl **bearings,** (way) camino, m; Herald. escudo de armas, m. **ball b.,** cojinete de bolas, m; **to get one's bearings,** orientarse; encontrar el camino. **to lose one's bearings,** desorientarse; perderse. **to have a b. on,** tener relación con; tener que ver con; influir en

bearish /'bɛərɪʃ/ a osuno; rudo, áspero

bearskin /'bɛər,skɪn/ n piel de oso, f; birretina, f

beast /bist/ n animal, bruto, m; cuadrúpedo, m; (cattle) res, f; bestia, f. **wild b.,** fiera, f. **b. of burden,** acémila, bestia de carga, f. **b. of prey,** animal de rapiña, m

beastliness /'bistlinɪs/ n bestialidad, brutalidad, f; obscenidad, f

beastly /'bistli/ a bestial, brutal; obsceno; Inf. horrible

beat /bit/ n latido, m, pulsación, f; golpe, m; (of a drum) toque (de tambor), m; (of a clock) tictac, m; sonido repetido, m; vibración, f

beat /bit/ vt and vi batir; golpear; (thrash) pegar, dar una paliza (a), Lat. Am. humear; (to remove dust, etc.) sacudir; (shake) agitar; (the wings) aletear; (hunting) batir; (excel) exceder, superar; ganar; (defeat) vencer; (of the rain, etc.) azotar; (a drum) tocar; (of the sun) batir, dar (en); (throb) latir, palpitar, pulsar. **to b. about the bush,** andarse por las ramas. **to stop beating about the bush,** dejarse de historias. **to b. a retreat,** Mil. emprender la retirada; huir. **to b. black and blue,** moler a palos. **to b. hollow,** vencer completamente; ganar fácilmente; aventajar con mucho. **to b. it,** Inf. escaparse corriendo. **to b. time,** Mus. llevar el compás; triunfar sobre la vejez. **to b. to it,** Inf. tomar la delantera. **to b. against,** golpear contra; chocar contra. **to b. back,** rechazar; (sobs, etc.) ahogar; reprimir. **to b. down,** (prices) regatear; (of the sun) caer de plomo, caer de plano; reducir; suprimir; destruir. **to b. out,** hacer salir; (metals) batir; (a tune) llevar el compás (de). **to b. up,** Cul. batir; (a mattress) mullir; asaltar; maltratar

beaten /'bitn̩/ a (of paths) trillado; (conquered) vencido; (of metals) batido; (dejected) deprimido; (trite) trivial, vulgar

beater /'bitər/ n batidor, m; (for carpets) sacudidor (de alfombras), m; Cul. batidor, m

beatific /,biə'tɪfɪk/ a beatífico

beatification /bi,ætəfɪ'keiʃən/ n beatificación, f

beatify /bi'ætə,fai/ vt beatificar

beating /'bitɪŋ/ n batimiento, m; vencimiento, m; (thrashing) paliza, f., Lat. Am. also azotera, f.; (of the heart, etc.) palpitación, f, latido, m; (of metals) batida, f; (of a drum) rataplán, toque de tambor, m; (of waves) embate, m; (of wings) aleteo, aletazo, m

beatitude /bi'ætɪ,tud/ n beatitud, f

beau /bou/ n galán, m; (fop) petimetre, m

beautiful /'byutəfəl/ a bello, lindo, hermoso; magnífico; excelente; exquisito; elegante; encantador, delicioso

beautifully /'byutəfəli/ adv bellamente; (richly) ricamente; admirablemente; magníficamente; elegantemente

beautify /'byutə,fai/ vt embellecer; hermosear; adornar. **to b. oneself,** arreglarse, ponerse elegante

beautifying /'byutəfaɪŋ/ n embellecimiento, m; adorno, m

beauty /'byuti/ n belleza, hermosura, lindeza, f; magnificencia, f; excelencia, f; elegancia, f; encanto, m; (belle) beldad, Venus, f. **to lose one's b.,** desmejorarse, perder su hermosura. **b. contest,** concurso de belleza, m. **b. parlor,** salón de belleza, instituto de belleza, m. **b. sleep,** el primer sueño de la noche. **b. spot,** lunar, m; lunar postizo, m; (place) sitio hermoso, m. **b. treatment,** masaje facial, m

beaver /'bivər/ n castor, m; (hat) sombrero de copa, m; (of helmet) babera, f

because /bɪ'kɔz/ conjunc porque. **b. of,** debido a, a causa de

beckon /'bɛkən/ vt and vi hacer señas (a); llamar por señas, llamar con la mano

become /bɪ'kʌm/ vi volverse; llegar a ser, venir a ser; convertirse en; ponerse; hacerse; (befit) convenir; (suit) ir bien (a), favorecer. **He became red,** Se enrojeció. **The hat becomes you,** El sombrero te va bien. **He became king,** Llegó a ser rey. **What has b. of her?** ¿Qué es de ella?; (Where is she?) ¿Qué se ha hecho de ella? **b. binding,** adquirir carácter de compromiso

becoming /bɪ'kʌmɪŋ/ a propio; correcto; decoroso; (suitable) conveniente; (of dress) que favorece, que va bien. **This dress is b. to you,** Este vestido te favorece

becomingly /bɪˈkʌmɪŋli/ *adv* decorosamente

bed /bɛd/ *n* cama, *f*, lecho, *m*; (of sea) fondo, *m*; (of river) cauce, *m*; *Geol.* yacimiento, *m*; (in a garden) cuadro, macizo (de jardín), *m*; (of a machine) asiento, *m*; (of a building) cimiento, *m*; *Fig.* fundamento, *m*, base, *f*, *vt* (plants) plantar; (fix) fijar, poner. **double bed,** cama de matrimonio, *f.* **single bed,** cama de sencilla, *f.* **in bed,** en cama. **to be gone to bed,** haber ido a la cama. **to be in bed,** estar acostado. **to get into bed,** meterse en cama. **to get out of bed,** levantarse de la cama. **to go to bed,** acostarse, ir a la cama. **to make the beds,** hacer las camas. **to put to bed,** acostar. **to stay in bed,** quedarse en cama, guardar cama. **bed-bug,** chinche, *f.* **bed-clothes,** ropa de cama, *f.* **bed-cover,** cubrecama, colcha, *f.* **bed-head,** cabecera, *f.* **bed-pan,** silleta, *f.* **bed-sore,** úlcera de decúbito, *f*

bedaub, bedazzle. /bɪˈdɔb; bɪˈdæzəl/. See **daub, dazzle**

bedchamber /ˈbɛd,tʃeimbər/ *n* dormitorio, *m*, alcoba, *f*

bedded /ˈbɛdɪd/ *a* con... cama(s). **a double-b. room,** un cuarto con dos camas; un cuarto con cama de matrimonio

bedding /ˈbɛdɪŋ/ *n* ropa de cama, *f*; cama para el ganado, *f*

bedeck /bɪˈdɛk/ *vt* embellecer, adornar, engalanar

bedfellow /ˈbɛd,fɛlou/ *n* compañero de almohada, compañero de cama

bedlam /ˈbɛdləm/ *n* belén, manicomio, *m*; *Fig.* babel, *m*

bedraggled /bɪˈdrægəld/ *a* mojado y sucio

bedridden /ˈbɛd,rɪdn̩/ *a* postrado en cama, inválido

bedrock /ˈbɛd,rɒk/ *n* lecho de roca, *m*; *Fig.* principios fundamentales, fundamentos, *m pl*

bedroom /ˈbɛd,rum/ *n* cuarto de dormir, dormitorio, *m*, habitación, *f*

bedside /ˈbɛd,said/ *n* lado de cama, *m*; cabecera, *f.* **b. manner,** mano izquierda, diplomacia, *f.* **b.-table,** mesa de noche, *f*

bedspread /ˈbɛd,sprɛd/ *n* colcha, cubrecama, sobrecama, *f*

bedstead /ˈbɛd,stɛd/ *n* cama, *f*

bedtime /ˈbɛd,taim/ *n* hora de acostarse, *f*

bee /bi/ *n* abeja, *f*; (meeting) reunión, *f*, *a* abejuno. **queen bee,** rey, *m*, abeja maestra, *f.* **to have a bee in one's bonnet,** tener una manía (or idea fija). **to make a bee-line for,** ir directamente a. **bee-eater,** *Ornith.* abejaruco, *m.* **bee-hive,** colmena, *f*; abejar, *m.* **bee-keeper,** apicultor (-ra), colmenero (-ra), abejero (-ra). **bee's wax,** cera de abeja, *f*

beech /bitʃ/ *n* haya, *f.* **plantation of b. trees,** hayal, *m.* **b.-nut,** hayuco, *m*

beef /bif/ *n* carne de res, *f*; (flesh) carne, *f*; (strength) fuerza, *f.* **roast b.,** rosbif, *m.* **b.-tea,** caldo, *m*

beefsteak /ˈbif,steik/ *n* bistec, *f*, *Argentina* bife, *m*

beer /bɪər/ *n* cerveza, *f.* **b. barrel,** barril de cerveza, *m.* **b.-house,** cervecería, *f.* **b. mug,** jarro para la cerveza, *m*

beery /ˈbɪəri/ *a* de cerveza; (tipsy) achispado

beet /bit/ *n* remolacha, *f.* *Mexico* betabel, *m.* **b. sugar,** azúcar de remolacha, *Mexico* azúcar de betabel, *m*

beetle /ˈbitl/ *n* escarabajo, *m.* **b.-browed,** cejijunto

beetroot /ˈbit,rut/ *n* remolacha, *f*, *Mexico* betabel, *m*

befall /bɪˈfɔl/ *vi* acontecer, suceder, ocurrir. *vt* ocurrir (a), acontecer (a)

befit /bɪˈfɪt/ *vt* convenir (a), ser digno de

befitting /bɪˈfɪtɪŋ/ *a* conveniente, apropiado; digno; oportuno

before /bɪˈfɔr/ *adv* delante; al frente; (of time), antes, anteriormente; (of order) antes; (already) ya. *prep* delante de; en frente de; (of time, order) ante; (in the presence of) ante, en presencia de; (rather than) antes de. **b. going,** antes de marcharse. **B. I did it,** Antes de que lo hiciera; Antes de hacerlo. **as never b.,** como nunca. **b. long,** en breve, dentro de poco. **b.-mentioned,** antes citado. **b. the mast,** al pie del mástil, e.g. *two years b. the mast,* dos años al pie del mástil

beforehand /bɪˈfɔr,hænd/ *adv* previamente, de antemano

befoul /bɪˈfaul/ *vt* ensuciar; *Fig.* manchar, difamar

befriend /bɪˈfrɛnd/ *vt* proteger, ayudar, favorecer, amparar

beg /bɛg/ *vt* pedir, implorar, suplicar, rogar. *vi* mendigar, pordiosear; vivir de limosna. **I beg to propose,** Me permito proponer; Tengo el gusto de proponer; (the health of) Brindo a la salud de. **I beg your pardon!** ¡Vd. dispense!; (when passing in front of anyone, etc.) Con permiso; (in conversation for repetition of a word) ¿Cómo? **to beg the question,** dar por sentado lo mismo que se trata de probar. **His conduct begs description,** No hay palabras para su comportamiento

beget /bɪˈgɛt/ *vt* procrear, engendrar; causar; suscitar

begetter /bɪˈgɛtər/ *n* procreador (-ra); creador (-ra)

begetting /bɪˈgɛtɪŋ/ *n* procreación, *f*; origen, *m*, causa, *f*

beggar /ˈbɛgər/ *n* mendigo (-ga), pordiosero (-ra), *Lat. Am. also* llimosnero (-ra). **beggars can't be choosers,** a falta de pan, se conforma con tortillas (Mexico); *vt* empobrecer; arruinar. **to b. description,** no haber palabras para describir

beggarliness /ˈbɛgərlinɪs/ *n* mendicidad, *f*; pobreza, *f*

beggarly /ˈbɛgərli/ *a* miserable, pobre

beggary /ˈbɛgəri/ *n* miseria, pobreza, *f*

begging /ˈbɛgɪŋ/ *a* mendicante, pordiosero. *n* mendicidad, *f*, pordioseo, *m.* **to go b.,** andar mendigando. **b. letter,** carta pidiendo dinero, *f*

begin /bɪˈgɪn/ *vt* and *vi* empezar; comenzar; iniciar; (a conversation) entablar; (open) abrir; inaugurar; tener su principio; nacer. **to b. to,** empezar a; (start on) ponerse a; (with laughing, etc.) romper a. **to b. with,** empezar por; para empezar, en primer lugar

beginner /bɪˈgɪnər/ *n* principiante (-ta); (novice) novato (-ta); iniciador (-ra); autor (-ra)

beginning /bɪˈgɪnɪŋ/ *n* principio, comienzo, *Lat. Am.* empiezo. *m*; origen, *m.* **at the b.,** al principio; (of the month) a principios (de). **from the b. to the end,** desde el principio hasta el fin, *Inf.* de pe a pa. **in the b.,** al principio. **to make a b.,** comenzar, empezar

begone /bɪˈgɔn/ *interj* ¡fuera! ¡márchate! ¡vete!

begonia /bɪˈgounyə/ *n* begonia, *f*

begrudge /bɪˈgrʌdʒ/ *vt* envidiar

beguile /bɪˈgail/ *vt* engañar; defraudar; (time) entretener; (charm) encantar, embelesar

beguilement /bɪˈgailmənt/ *n* engaño, *m*; (of time) entretenimiento, *m*; (charm) encanto, *m*

beguilingly /bɪˈgailɪŋli/ *adv* encantadoramente

behalf /bɪˈhæf/ *n* (preceded by on or upon) por; (from) de parte (de); a favor (de); en defensa (de)

behave /bɪˈheiv/ *vi* (oneself) conducirse, portarse; (act) obrar, proceder. **to b. badly,** portarse mal; obrar mal. **B.!** ¡Pórtate bien!

behavior /bɪˈheivyər/ *n* conducta, *f*; comportamiento, *m*; proceder, *m*; (manner) modales, *m pl*; *Biol.* reacción, *f.* **b. science,** ciencias de la conducta, *f pl*

behaviorism /bɪˈheivyə,rɪzəm/ *n* *Psychol.* behaviorismo, *m*, conductismo, *m*

behead /bɪˈhɛd/ *vt* decapitar, descabezar

beheading /bɪˈhɛdɪŋ/ *n* decapitación, *f*

behest /bɪˈhɛst/ *n* precepto, mandato, *m*

behind /bɪˈhaind/ *adv* detrás; por detrás; atrás; hacia atrás; en pos; (of time and order) después; (late and in arrears) con retraso; (old-fashioned) atrasado. *prep* detrás de; por detrás de; inferior a; menos avanzado que. *n* *Inf.* trasero, *m.* **from b.,** por detrás. **to b. time,** retrasarse; llegar tarde. **b. the back of,** a espaldas de. **b. the scenes,** entre bastidores. **b. the times,** *Fig.* atrasado de noticias; pasado de moda. **the ideology b. the French Revolution,** la ideología que informó la Revolución Francesa.

behold /bɪˈhould/ *vt* ver, mirar, contemplar; presenciar. *interj* ¡he aquí! ¡mira!

beholden /bɪˈhouldən/ *a* obligado, agradecido

beholder /bɪˈhouldər/ *n* espectador (-ra). **the beholders,** los que lo presenciaban

beholding /bɪˈhouldɪŋ/ *n* contemplación, vista, *f*

behoove /bɪˈhuv/ *vt* incumbir, tocar, corresponder

beige /beiʒ/ *n* beige, color arena, *m*

being /'biːŋ/ *n* existencia, *f*; operación, *f*; ser, *m*; (spirit) alma, *f*, espíritu, *m*; esencia, *f*. **human b.**, ser humano, *m*, alma viviente, *f*. **for the time b.**, por ahora, por el momento

bejewel /bɪ'dʒuəl/ *vt* enjoyar, adornar con joyas

belabor /bɪ'leibər/ *vt* apalear, golpear

belated /bɪ'leitɪd/ *a* tardío

belay /bɪ'lei/ *vt* amarrar

belch /bɛltʃ/ *n* eructo, *m*; detonación, *f*; (of a volcano) erupción, *f*. *vi* eructar. *vt* vomitar; (curses, etc.) escupir; despedir, arrojar

belching /'bɛltʃɪŋ/ *n* eructación, *f*; (of smoke, etc.) vómito, *m*, emisión, *f*

beleaguer /bɪ'liɡər/ *vt* sitiar

belfry /'bɛlfri/ *n* campanario, *m*

Belgian /'bɛldʒən/ *a* and *n* belga, *mf*

Belgium /'bɛldʒəm/ Bélgica, *f*

Belgrade /'bɛlɡreid/ Belgrado, *m*

belie /bɪ'lai/ *vt* desmentir, contradecir; defraudar

belief /bɪ'lif/ *n* creencia, *f*; fe, *f*; opinión, *f*, parecer, *m*; (trust) confianza, *f*. **in the b. that**, creyendo que, en la creencia de que

believable /bɪ'livəbəl/ *a* creíble

believe /bɪ'liv/ *vt* and *vi* creer; opinar, ser de la opinión, parecer (a uno); confiar, tener confianza. **I b. not**, Creo que no, Me parece que no. **I b. so**, Creo que sí, Me parece que sí. **to make (a person) b.**, hacer (a uno) creer. **to b. in**, creer en; confiar en, tener confianza en

believer /bɪ'livər/ *n* persona que cree, *f*; creyente, *mf*

belittle /bɪ'lɪtl/ *vt* achicar; conceder poca importancia a

bell /bɛl/ *n* campana, *f*; (hand-bell) campanilla, *f*; (small, round) cascabel, *m*; (on cows, etc.) cencerro, *m*, esquila, *f*; (electric, push, or bicycle) timbre, *m*; (jester's) cascabeles, *m pl*; (cry of stag) bramido, *m*. *vt* poner un cascabel (a). *vi* (stags) bramar, roncar. **to ring the b.**, tocar el timbre; agitar la campanilla. **to ring the bells**, tocar las campanas. **to b. the cat**, ponerle el cascabel al gato, ponerle el collar al gato. **b.-boy**, botones, mozo de hotel, *m*. **b.-clapper**, badajo, *m*. **b.-flower**, campanilla, *f*. **b.-founder**, campanero, *m*. **b.-mouthed**, abocinado. **b.-pull**, tirador de campanilla, *m*. **b.-ringer**, campanero, *m*. **b.-shaped**, campanudo. **b.-tent**, pabellón, *m*. **b. tower**, campanario, *m*

belladonna /ˌbɛlə'dɒnə/ *n* belladona, *f*

belle /bɛl/ *n* beldad, *f*

belles-lettres /bɛl 'lɛtrə/ *n pl* bellas letras, *f pl*

bellicose /'bɛlɪˌkous/ *a* belicoso, agresivo

bellicosity /ˌbɛlɪ'kɒsɪti/ *n* belicosidad, *f*

belligerence /bə'lɪdʒərəns/ *n* beligerancia, *f*

belligerent /bə'lɪdʒərənt/ *a* beligerante; belicoso, guerrero. *n* beligerante, *mf*

bellow /'bɛlou/ *n* (shout) grito, *m*; rugido, bramido, *m*; (of guns) trueno, *m*. *vi* gritar, vociferar; rugir, bramar; tronar

bellowing /'bɛlouɪŋ/ *n*. See **bellow**

bellows /'bɛlouz/ *n* fuelle, *m*

belly /'bɛli/ *n* vientre, *m*, barriga, *f*; (of a jug, etc.) panza, *f*; estómago, *m*; (womb) seno, *m*. *vt* hinchar. *vi* hincharse

belong /bɪ'lɔŋ/ *vi* pertenecer (a); tocar (a), incumbir (a); (to a place) ser de; residir en

belongings /bɪ'lɔŋɪŋz/ *n pl* efectos, *m pl*; posesiones, *f pl*; (luggage) equipaje, *m*

beloved /bɪ'lʌvɪd/ *a* muy amado, muy querido. *n* querido (-da)

below /bɪ'lou/ *adv* abajo; (under) debajo; (further on) más abajo; (in hell) en el infierno; (in this world) en este mundo, aquí abajo. *prep* bajo; (underneath) debajo de; (after) después de; (unworthy of) indigno de; inferior a. **The valley lay b. us,** El valle se extendía a nuestros pies. **b. zero,** bajo cero

belt /bɛlt/ *n* cinturón, *m*; (of a horse) cincha, *f*; (corset) faja, *f*; *Geog.* zona, *f*; (of a machine) correa (de transmisión), *f*

beltway /'bɛltˌwei/ *n* anillo periférico, *m*

belvedere /'bɛlvɪˌdɪər/ *n* mirador, *m*

bemoan /bɪ'moun/ *vt* deplorar, lamentar

bemoaning /bɪ'mounɪŋ/ *n* lamentación, *f*

bemuse /bɪ'myuz/ *vt* confundir, desconcertar

bench /bɛntʃ/ *n* banco, *m*; (with a back) escaño, *m*; mesa de trabajo, *f*; (carpenter's, shoemaker's, in a boat, in parliament) banco, *m*; (judges) tribunal, *m*

bend /bɛnd/ *n* corvadura, curva, vuelta, *f*; (in a river, street) recodo, *m*; (on a road) codo viraje, *m*; (of the knee) corva, *f*; (in a pipe) codo, *m*; *Naut.* nudo, *m*; *Herald.* banda, *f*. **sheet b.,** (knot) nudo de tejedor, *m*

bend /bɛnd/ *vt* encorvar; doblegar; torcer; (the head) bajar; (the body) inclinar; (steps) dirigir, encaminar; (the mind) aplicarse, dedicarse. *vi* encorvarse; doblegarse; torcerse; (arch) arquear; inclinarse. **to b. the knee,** arrodillarse. **on bended knee,** de rodillas. **to b. back,** *vt* redoblar. *vi* redoblarse; inclinarse hacia atrás. **to b. down,** agacharse; inclinarse. **to b. forward,** inclinarse hacia delante. **to b. over,** inclinarse encima de

bendable /'bɛndəbəl/ *a* que puede doblarse; plegadizo; flexible

bending /'bɛndɪŋ/ *n* doblamiento, *m*; flexión, *f*; inclinación, *f*. *a* doblado; inclinado

beneath /bɪ'niθ/ *adv* abajo; debajo; (at one's feet) a los pies de uno. *prep* bajo; debajo de; al pie de; (unworthy, inferior) indigno

Benedictine /ˌbɛnɪ'dɪktɪn, -tin/ *a* benedictino. *n* benedictino, *m*; (liquor) benedictino, *m*

benediction /ˌbɛnɪ'dɪkʃən/ *n* bendición, *f*; gracia divina, merced, *f*

benefaction /'bɛnə,fækʃən/ *n* beneficiación, *f*; buena obra, *f*; beneficio, favor, *m*

benefactor /'bɛnəˌfæktər/ *n* bienhechor, *m*; protector, *m*; patrono, *m*; fundador, *m*

benefactress /'bɛnəˌfæktrɪs/ *n* bienhechora, *f*; protectora, *f*; patrona, *f*; fundadora, *f*

benefice /'bɛnəfɪs/ *n* beneficio eclesiástico, *m*, prebenda, *f*

beneficence /bə'nɛfəsəns/ *n* beneficiencia, caridad, *f*, buenas obras, *f pl*

beneficent /bə'nɛfəsənt/ *a* benéfico, caritativo

beneficial /ˌbɛnə'fɪʃəl/ *a* beneficioso; provechoso, útil

beneficiary /ˌbɛnə'fɪʃɪˌɛri/ *n* beneficiado (-da), beneficiario (-ia)

benefit /'bɛnəfɪt/ *n* beneficio, bien, *m*; provecho, *m*, utilidad, *f*; (favor) favor, *m*; *Theat.* beneficio, *m*; (help) ayuda, *f*, servicio, *m*. *vt* beneficiar; aprovechar; (improve) mejorar. *vi* (with by) sacar provecho de; ganar. **for the b. of,** para; en pro de, a favor de. **b. society,** sociedad benéfica, *f*

benevolence /bə'nɛvələns/ *n* benevolencia, bondad, *f*; liberalidad, *f*; caridad, *f*; favor, *m*

benevolent /bə'nɛvələnt/ *a* benévolo; bondadoso; caritativo. **b. society,** sociedad de beneficencia, *f*

benevolently /bə'nɛvələntli/ *adv* benignamente, con benevolencia

Bengal /bɛn'ɡɔl/ Bengala, *f*

benighted /bɪ'naitɪd/ *a* sorprendido por la noche; *Fig.* ignorante

benign, benignant /bɪ'nain; bɪ'nɪɡnənt/ *a* benigno

bent /bɛnt/ *n* talento, *m*; inclinación, afición, *f*, a torcido, *Mexico* chueco; encorvado; resuelto

benumb. /bɪ'nʌm/ See **numb**

bequeath /bɪ'kwɪð/ *vt* legar, dejar (en el testamento); transmitir

bequest /bɪ'kwɛst/ *n* legado, *m*

Berber /'bɜrbər/ *a* and *n* bereber, *mf*

bereave /bɪ'riv/ *vt* privar (de), quitar; arrebatar; afligir. **the bereaved parents,** los padres afligidos

bereavement /bɪ'rivmənt/ *n* privación, *f*; (by death) pérdida, *f*; aflicción, *f*

bereft /bɪ'rɛft/ *a* privado (de); desamparado; indefenso. **utterly b.,** completamente solo

beret /bə'rei/ *n* boina, *f*

Berlin /bər'lɪn/ *a* and *n* (of or from) berlinés (-esa). *f* (carriage) berlina, *f*

Bermudas, the /bər'myudəz/ *m* las Islas Bermudas

Bernard /'bɜrnərd/ *n* Bernardo, *f*. **St. B. dog,** perro de San Bernardo, *m*

Berne /bɜrn/ Berna, *f*

berry /'bɛri/ *n* baya, *f*; (of coffee, etc.) fruto, *m*, *vi* dar bayas; coger bayas
berth /bɜrθ/ *n* (bed) litera, *f*; (cabin) camarote, *m*; (anchorage) anclaje, fondeadero, *m*; (job) empleo, *m*, *vt* (a ship) fondear. **to give a wide b. to,** *Naut.* ponerse a resguardo de; apartarse mucho de; evitar
beseech /bɪ'sitʃ/ *vt* suplicar, rogar, implorar; (ask for) pedir con ahinco
beseeching /bɪ'sitʃɪŋ/ *a* suplicante, implorante. *n* súplica, *f*; ruego, *m*
beseechingly /bɪ'sitʃɪŋli/ *adv* suplicantemente
beset /bɪ'sɛt/ *vt* atacar, acosar; aquejar, acosar, perseguir. **beset by personal misfortune,** acosado por las desgracias personales; (block) obstruir; (surround) rodear, cercar
besetting /bɪ'sɛtɪŋ/ *a* usual, frecuente; obsesionante
beside, besides /bɪ'said; bɪ'saidz/ *prep* al lado de; cerca de; (compared with) en comparación de, comparado con; (in addition) además de; aparte de; excepto. *adv* además, también. **to be beside oneself,** estar fuera de sí
besiege /bɪ'sidʒ/ *vt* sitiar; (assail) asaltar, asediar; (surround) rodear; importunar
besieged /bɪ'sidʒd/ *n* sitiado (-da)
besieger /bɪ'sidʒər/ *n* sitiador, *m*
besieging /bɪ'sidʒɪŋ/ *a* sitiador. *n* sitio, asalto, *m*; asedio, *m*, importunación, *f*
besmear /bɪ'smɪər/ *vt* embadurnar, ensuciar
besotted /bɪ'sɒtɪd/ *a* estúpido; embrutecido; atontado
bespangled /bɪ'spæŋgəld/ *a* adornado con lentejuelas; brillante (con); (studded) salpicado (de)
bespatter /bɪ'spætər/ *vt* manchar; derramar; salpicar
bespeak /bɪ'spik/ *vt* reservar; (goods) encargar; (signify) demostrar, indicar, significar; *Poet.* hablar
besprinkle /bɪ'sprɪŋkəl/ *vt* rociar
best /bɛst/ *a sup* of **good** and **well,** mejor; el (la) mejor, *m, f.,* los (las) mejores, *m pl, f pl. adv* mejor; el mejor; (most) más. **as b. I can,** como mejor pueda. **at the b.,** cuando más, en el mejor caso. **He did it for the b.,** Lo hizo con la mejor intención. **the b.,** lo mejor. **to be at one's b.,** brillar; lucirse. **to do one's b.,** hacer todo lo posible. **to get the b. of,** llevar la mejor parte de; triunfar de (or sobre). **to make the b. of,** sacar el mayor provecho de. **The next b. thing to do is...,** Lo mejor que queda ahora por hacer es... **b. man,** padrino de boda, *m.* **to be b. man to,** apadrinar, ser padrino de. **b. seller,** libro que se vende más, libro favorito, *m*
bestial /'bɛstʃəl/ *a* bestial
bestiality /,bɛstʃi'æliti/ *n* bestialidad, *f*
bestir (oneself) /bɪ'stɜr/ *vr* menearse, moverse; preocuparse; (hurry) darse prisa
bestow /bɪ'stou/ *vt* (place) poner; (with upon) conferir, conceder, otorgar; (a present) regalar
bestowal /bɪ'stouəl/ *n* puesta, *f*; otorgamiento, *m*, concesión, *f*; (of a present) regalo, *m*, dádiva, *f*
bestride /bɪ'straid/ *vt* montar a horcajadas en; poner una pierna en cada lado de; cruzar de un tranco
bestseller /'bɛst'sɛlər/ *n* campeón de venta, éxito editorial, triunfo de librería, *m*
bet /bɛt/ *n* apuesta, postura, *f, vi* apostar; (gamble) jugar. **What do you bet?** ¿Qué apuesta Vd.?
bethink (oneself) /bɪ'θɪŋk/ *vr* pensar, reflexionar; (remember) recordar, hacer memoria; ocurrirse
Bethlehem /'bɛθli,hɛm/ Belén, *m*
betray /bɪ'trei/ *vt* traicionar; revelar, descubrir; (a woman) seducir; (show) dejar ver
betrayal /bɪ'treiəl/ *n* traición, *f*; (of confidence) abuso (de confianza), *m*; (of a woman) seducción, *f*
betrayer /bɪ'treiər/ *n* traidor (-ra)
betroth /bɪ'trouð/ *vt* desposar(se) con, prometer(se). **to be betrothed to,** estar desposado con
betrothal /bɪ'trouðəl/ *n* desposorio, *m*, esponsales, *m pl*; (duration) noviazgo, *m*
betrothed /bɪ'trouðd/ *n* desposado (-da), futuro (-ra)
better /'bɛtər/ *a comp* of **good,** mejor; superior. *adv* mejor; más. *vt* mejorar; exceder. *n* apostador (-ra). **He has bettered himself,** Ha mejorado su situación. **It is b. to...,** Es mejor..., Vale más... (followed by infin.). **little b.,** poco mejor; algo mejor; poco más.

much b., mucho mejor. **so much the b.,** tanto mejor. **the b. to,** para mejor. **to be b.,** ser mejor; (of health) estar mejor. **to get b.,** mejorar. **to get the b. of,** triunfar sobre, vencer. **b. half,** *Inf.* media naranja, *f.* **b. off,** mejor situado, más acomodado
betterment /'bɛtərmənt/ *n* mejora, *f*, mejoramiento, *m*; adelantamiento, avance, *m*
betting /'bɛtɪŋ/ *n* apuesta, *f*
bettor /'bɛtər/ *n* apostador (-ra)
between /bɪ'twin/ *prep* entre; en medio de; de. **the break b. Mr. X and Mrs. Y,** el rompimiento del Sr. X y la Sra. Y. *adv* en medio; entre los dos. **far b.,** a grandes intervalos. **b. now and then,** desde ahora hasta entonces. **b. one thing and another,** entre una cosa y otra. **b. ourselves,** entre nosotros
bevel /'bɛvəl/ *n* bisel, *m, vt* abiselar
beverage /'bɛvərɪdʒ/ *n* brebaje, *m*, bebida, *f*
bevy /'bɛvi/ *n* grupo, *m*; (of birds) bandada, *f*; (of roes) manada, *f*
bewail /bɪ'weil/ *vt* lamentar, llorar
bewailing /bɪ'weilɪŋ/ *n* lamentación, *f*
beware /bɪ'wɛər/ *vi* guardarse (de); cuidar (de); desconfiar (de). *interj* ¡cuidado! ¡atención! **B. of imitations!** ¡Desconfiad de las imitaciones!
bewilder /bɪ'wɪldər/ *vt* aturdir, abobar; dejar perplejo (a); confundir
bewildered /bɪ'wɪldərd/ *a* aturdido, abobado; perplejo; confuso
bewildering /bɪ'wɪldərɪŋ/ *a* incomprensible; complicado
bewilderment /bɪ'wɪldərmənt/ *n* aturdimiento, *m*; perplejidad, *f*; confusión, *f*
bewitch /bɪ'wɪtʃ/ *vt* hechizar; fascinar, encantar
bewitching /bɪ'wɪtʃɪŋ/ *a* encantador, hechicero, fascinante. *n* embrujamiento, encantamiento, *m*
bewitchingly /bɪ'wɪtʃɪŋli/ *adv* de un modo encantador
bewitchment /bɪ'wɪtʃmənt/ *n.* See **bewitching**
beyond /bɪ'ɒnd/ *prep* más allá de; más lejos que; (behind) tras, detrás de; (of time) después de; *Fig.* fuera del alcance de; (without) fuera de; (above) encima de; (not including) aparte. *adv* más allá; más lejos; detrás. **b. doubt,** fuera de duda. **b. question,** indiscutible. **b. the sea,** allende el mar. **That is b. me,** Eso es demasiado para mí; Eso no está en mi mano; Eso está fuera de mi alcance. **the B.,** la otra vida
Bhután /bu'tɑn/ Bután, *m*
bias /'baiəs/ *n* sesgo, bies, través, *f*; *Fig.* prejuicio, *m*; parcialidad, *f*, *vt* influir; predisponer. **to cut on the b.,** cortar al sesgo
biased /'baiəst/ *a* parcial; tendencioso
bib /bɪb/ *n* babero, *m*; pechera, *f*, *vi* beber mucho, empinar el codo
Bible /'baibəl/ *n* Biblia, *f*
biblical /'bɪblɪkəl/ *a* bíblico. **b. history,** historia sagrada, *f*
bibliographer /,bɪbli'ɒgrəfər/ *n* bibliógrafo (-fa)
bibliographical /,bɪbliə'græfɪkəl/ *a* bibliográfico
bibliography /,bɪbli'ɒgrəfi/ *n* bibliografía, *f*
bibliophile /'bɪbliə,fail/ *n* bibliófilo, *m*
bibulous /'bɪbyələs/ *a* bebedor, borrachín
bicarbonate /bai'karbənɪt/ *n* bicarbonato, *m*
bicentenary /,baisen'tɛnəri/ *n* segundo centenario, *m*
biceps /'baiseps/ *n* bíceps, *m*
bicker /'bɪkər/ *vi* disputar, altercar; (of stream, etc.) murmurar, susurrar; (of flame) bailar, centellear
bickering /'bɪkərɪŋ/ *n* altercado, argumento, *m*
bicycle /'baisikəl/ *n* bicicleta, *f*, *vi* andar en bicicleta, ir de bicicleta
bicycle pump *Lat. Am.* inflador, *m*
bicycling /'baisiklɪŋ/ *n* ciclismo, *m*
bicyclist /'baisiklist/ *n* bicyclista, *mf*
bid /bɪd/ *n* (at auction) postura, *f*; (bridge) puja, *f*; oferta, *f, vt* mandar, ordenar, invitar a; (at an auction) pujar, licitar. **to make a bid for,** (attempt) hacer un esfuerzo para; procurar. **to bid fair,** prometer; dar indicios de; dar esperanzas de. **to bid goodbye to,** decir adios (a), despedirse de. **to bid welcome,** dar la bienvenida (a)
biddable /'bɪdəbəl/ *a* obediente, dócil; manso

bidder /'bɪdər/ n postor, m, pujador (-ra). **the highest b.**, el mejor postor

bidding /'bɪdɪŋ/ n (order) orden, f; instrucción, f; invitación, f; (at an auction) postura, licitación, f. **to do a person's b.**, hacer lo que se le manda

bide /baid/ vt aguardar, esperar. **to b. by,** (fulfill) cumplir con

bidet /bi'dei/ n bidé, m

biennial /bai'ɛniəl/ a bianual, bienal

bier /bɪər/ n andas, f pl; féretro, ataúd, m

bifocal /bai'foukəl/ a bifocal

bifurcate /'baifər,keit/ vt and vi bifurcar(se)

bifurcation /,baifər'keiʃən/ n bifurcación, f

big /bɪg/ a grande; before n sing gran; grueso; (grown up) mayor; (tall) alto; voluminoso; (vast) extenso, vasto; (full) lleno (de); (with young) preñada; importante; tamaño. **to talk big,** echarla de importante. **big-boned,** huesudo. **big-end,** Auto. biela, f. **big game,** caza mayor, f. **big gun,** Inf. pájaro gordo, m

bigamist /'bɪgəmɪst/ n bígamo (-ma)

bigamous /'bɪgəməs/ a bígamo

bigamy /'bɪgəmi/ n bigamia, f

bight /bait/ n (in a rope) vuelta (de un cabo), f; (bay) ensenada, f

bigness /'bɪgnɪs/ n grandor, m; gran tamaño, m; altura, f; (tallness of a person) gran talle, m; (vastness) extensión, f; importancia, f

bigot /'bɪgət/ n fanático (-ca)

bigoted /'bɪgətɪd/ a fanático, intolerante

bigotry /'bɪgətri/ n fanatismo, m, intolerancia, f

bikini /bɪ'kini/ n bikini, m

bilberry /'bɪl,bɛri/ n arándano, m

bile /bail/ n bilis, hiel, f; mal humor, m, cólera, f

bilge /bɪldʒ/ n Naut. pantoque, m, sentina, f. **b. water,** agua de pantoque, f

bilingual /bai'lɪŋwəl/ a bilingüe

bilious /'bɪlyəs/ a bilioso

bill /bɪl/ n (parliamentary) proyecto de ley, m; Law. escrito, m; Com. cuenta, f; (poster) cartel, m; (program) programa, m; (cast) repertorio, m; (bank note) billete de banco, m; (of a bird) pico, m; (for pruning) podadera, f. **due b.,** Com. abonaré, m. **Post no bills!** Se prohíbe fijar carteles. **b. of exchange,** letra de cambio, f. **b. of fare,** lista de platos, f; Fig. programa, m. **b. of health,** patente de sanidad, f. **b. of lading,** conocimiento de embarque, m. **b. of rights,** declaración de derechos, f. **b. of sale,** contrato de venta, m, carta de venta, f. **b.-broker,** agente de bolsa, agente de cambio, m. **b.-poster,** fijador de carteles, cartelero, m

bill /bɪl/ vt anunciar; publicar; poner en el programa; fijar carteles en. **to b. and coo,** (doves) arrullar; Inf. besuquearse

billboard /'bɪl,bɔrd/ n tablero publicitario, m

billed /bɪld/ a (in compounds) de pico

billet /'bɪlɪt/ n alojamiento, m; (of wood) pedazo (de leña), m; (job) empleo, destino, m, vt alojar (en or con)

billeting /'bɪlɪtɪŋ/ n alojamiento, m. **b. officer,** Mil. aposentador, m; oficial encargado de encontrar alojamiento, m

billiards /'bɪlyərdz/ n pl billar, m. **billiard ball,** bola de billar, f. **billiard cue,** taco, m. **billiard cushion,** baranda de la mesa de billar, f. **billiard marker,** marcador, m. **billiard match,** partida de billar, f. **billiard player,** jugador (-ra) de billar. **billiard pocket,** Lat. Am. buchaca, f. **billiard room,** sala de billar, f. **billiard table,** mesa de billar, f

billing /'bɪlɪŋ/ n facturación, f

billion /'bɪlyən/ n billón, m; (U.S.A. and France) mil millones, m pl

billionth /'bɪlyənθ/ a billonésimo; (U.S.A. and France) milmillonésimo

bill of particulars /pər'tɪkyələrz/ n relación detallada, f

billow /'bɪlou/ n oleada, f; Poet. ola, f; Fig. onda, f. vi hincharse, encresparse; ondular

billowy /'bɪloui/ a ondulante, ondeado

bimonthly /bai'mʌnθli/ a bimestral

bin /bɪn/ n hucha, f, arcón, m; recipiente, m; depósito, m; cajón, m; (for wine) estante, m

binary /'bainəri/ a binario

bind /baind/ vt atar; unir, ligar; amarrar; (in sheaves) agavillar; (bandage) vendar; sujetar; fijar; aprisionar; (a book) encuadernar; Sew. ribetear; (oblige) obligar; comprometer; (constipate) estreñir; contratar (como aprendiz). **I feel bound to,** Me siento obligado a. **to b. over,** obligar a comparecer ante el juez

binder /'baindər/ n encuadernador (-ra); Agr. agavilladora, f

binding /'baindɪŋ/ a válido, valedero; obligatorio; **become b.,** adquirir carácter de compromiso; Med. constrictivo. n atadura, ligación, f; (of books) encuadernación, f; Sew. ribete, m

binge /bɪndʒ/ n parranda, juerga, f. **to go on the b.,** ir de parranda, ir de picos pardos, ir de juerga

binnacle /'bɪnəkəl/ n Naut. bitácora, f

binocular /bə'nɒkyələr/ a binocular. n pl **binoculars,** binóculos, gemelos, m pl

binomial /bai'noumiəl/ a and n binomio m.

biochemist /,baiou'kɛmɪst/ n bioquímico, m

biochemistry /,baiou'kɛməstri/ n bioquímica, f

biodegradable /,baioudɪ'greidəbəl/ a biodegradable

biodiversity /,baioudɪ'vɜrsɪti/ n biodiversidad, f

biographer /bai'ɒgrəfər/ n biógrafo (-fa)

biographical /,baiə'græfɪkəl/ a biográfico

biography /bai'ɒgrəfi/ n biografía, vida, f

biological /,baiə'lɒdʒɪkəl/ a biológico

biologist /bai'ɒlədʒɪst/ n biólogo, m

biology /bai'ɒlədʒi/ n biología, f

bipartite /bai'pɑrtait/ a bipartido

biped /'baiped/ n bípedo, m, a bípedo, bípede

birch /bɜrtʃ/ n Bot. abedul, m; (rod) vara, f. a de abedul. vt pegar con una vara, dar una paliza (a)

bird /bɜrd/ n pájaro, m; ave, f. **Birds of a feather flock together,** Cada cual se arrima a su cada cual. **hen b.,** pájara, f. **b.-call,** voz del pájaro, f, canto del ave, m. **b. catcher or vendor,** pajarero, m. **bird's-eye view,** vista de pájaro, perspectiva aérea, f. **b.-like,** como un pájaro; de pájaro. **b.-lime,** liga, f. **to go b.-nesting,** ir a coger nidos de pájaros. **b. of paradise,** ave del paraíso, f. **b. of passage,** ave de paso, f. **b. of prey,** ave rapaz, f. **b.-seed,** alpiste, m. **b.-watcher,** aficionado (-da) a las aves; criador (-ra) de pájaros

birth /bɜrθ/ n nacimiento, m; (act of) parto, m; origen, m; (childhood) infancia, f; (family) linaje, m, familia, f; Fig. creación, f. **from b.,** de nacimiento. **to give b. to,** dar a luz, echar al mundo, parir. **b. certificate,** partida de nacimiento, certificación de nacimiento, f. **b. control,** anticoncepcionismo, m, regulación de la fecundidad, f. **b.-mark,** antojo, m pl. **b.-place,** lugar de nacimiento, m. **b.-rate,** natalidad, f

birthday /'bɜrθ,dei/ n cumpleaños, m

birthright /'bɜrθ,rait/ n derecho de nacimiento, m; herencia, f

Biscay, the Bay of /'bɪskei/ el Golfo de Vizcaya, m

Biscayan /bɪs'keiən/ a and n vizcaíno (-na)

biscuit /'bɪskɪt/ n galleta, f; bizcocho, m. **b. box or maker,** galletero, m. **b.-like,** abizcochado

bisect /bai'sɛkt/ vt dividir en dos partes iguales; Geom. bisecar

bisexual /bai'sɛkʃuəl/ a bisexual

bishop /'bɪʃəp/ n obispo, m; (in chess) alfil, m. **bishop's crozier,** báculo episcopal, cayado, m

bismuth /'bɪzməθ/ n bismuto, m

bison /'baisən/ n bisonte, m

bisque /bɪsk/ n porcelana blanca, f, bizcocho, m

bistoury /'bɪstəri/ n bisturí, m

bit /bɪt/ n pedazo, m; (of grass, etc.) brizna, f; (moment) instante, m; (quantity) cantidad, f; (of a drill) mecha, f; (part) parte, f; (passage) trozo, m; (horse's) bocado, m; Inf. miga, f. **a bit,** un ʹanto, algo, un poco. **a little bit,** Mexico un poquito. **bit by bit,** poco a poco, gradualmente. **to give someone a bit of one's mind,** contarle cuatro verdades. **to take the bit between one's teeth,** desbocarse; Fig. rebelarse. **Wait a bit!** ¡Espera un momento!

bitch /bɪtʃ/ n (female dog) perra, f; (fox) zorra, f; (wolf) loba, f

bite /bait/ *n* mordedura, *f*; mordisco, *m*; (mouthful, snack) bocado, *m*, *Lat. Am.* botana, *f*; (of fish and insects) picada, *f*; (hold) asimiento, *m*; (sting, pain) picadura, *f*; (pungency) resquemor, *m*; (offer) oferta, *f*; (*Fig.* mordancy) mordacidad, acritud, *f. vt and vi* morder; (gnaw) roer; (of fish, insects) picar; (of hot dishes) resquemar; (of acids) corroer; (deceive) engañar, defraudar; (of wheels, etc.) agarrar; (hurt, wound) herir. **to b. one's tongue,** morderse la lengua. **to b. the dust,** caer al suelo

biting /'baitiŋ/ *a* (stinging) picante; (mordant) mordaz, acre; (of winds, etc.) penetrante; satírico. *n* mordedura, *f*; roedura, *f*

bitter /'bitər/ *a* amargo; (sour) agrio, ácido; (of winds) penetrante; (of cold) intenso; cruel. **to the b. end,** hasta la muerte; hasta el último extremo. **b.-sweet,** agridulce

bitterly /'bitərli/ *adv* amargamente; intensamente; cruelmente

bitterness /'bitərnis/ *n* amargura, *f*; (sourness) acidez, *f*; (of cold) intensidad, *f*; crueldad, *f*

bitters /'bitərz/ *n pl* (drink) bíter, *m*, angostura, *f*

bitumen /bai'tumən/ *n* betún, *m*

bivouac /'bivu,æk/ *n Mil.* vivaque, *m*, *vi* vivaquear

bizarre /bi'zɑr/ *a* raro, extravagante; grotesco

black /blæk/ *a* negro; obscuro; (sad) triste, melancólico; funesto; perverso; (sullen) malhumorado. *n* (color) negro, *m*; (mourning) luto, *m*; (person) negro (-a), *Lat. Am.* moreno (-a). *vt* ennegrecer; tiznar. **in b. and white,** por escrito. **to look on the b. side,** verlo todo negro. **b. art,** nigromancia, *f*. **b.-currant,** grosella negra, *f*. **b.-eyed,** ojinegro, con ojos negros. **b.-haired,** pelinegro, de pelo negro. **b.-lead,** plombagina, *f*. **b.-list,** lista negra, *f*. **b.-market,** estraperlo, mercado negro, *m*. **b.-marketeer,** estraperlista, contrabandista, *mf*. **b.-out,** oscurecimiento, apagamiento, *m*. **b. panther,** pantera negra, *f*. **b.-pudding,** morcilla, *f*. **b. sheep,** oveja negra, *f*; *Fig.* oveja descarriada, *f*; (of a family) garbanzo negro, *m*. **b.-water fever,** melanuria, *f*

blackberry /'blæk,beri/ *n* mora, zarzamora, *f*; (bush) zarza, *f*, moral, *m*

blackbird /'blæk,bɜrd/ *n* mirlo, *m*

blackboard /'blæk,bɔrd/ *n* encerado, *m*, pizarra, *f*

black coffee *n Spain* café solo, *Colombia* café tinto, *elsewhere in Lat. Am.* café negro *m*

blacken /'blækən/ *vt* ennegrecer; tiznar; *Fig.* manchar, desacreditar. *vi* ennegrecerse

black eye *n* ojo como un tomate, ojo morado, *m*

blackguard /'blægɑrd/ *n* tipo de cuidado, perdido, *m*

blackhead /'blæk,hed/ *n* espinilla, *f*

blacking /'blækiŋ/ *n* betún, *m*

blackish /'blækiʃ/ *a* negruzco

blackmail /'blæk,meil/ *n* chantaje, *m*, *vt* hacer víctima de un chantaje; arrancar dinero por chantaje (a)

blackmailer /'blæk,meilər/ *n* chantajista, *mf*

blackness /'blæknis/ *n* negrura, *f*; obscuridad, *f*

blacksmith /'blæk,smiθ/ *n* herrero (-ra) *mf*, *Lat. Am. also* encasquillador (-ra) *mf*. **blacksmith's forge,** herrería, *f*

bladder /'blædər/ *n Anat.* vejiga, *f*; ampolla, *f*; (of sea-plants) vesícula, *f*; (of fish) vejiga natatoria, *f*

blade /bleid/ *n* (leaf) hoja, *f*; (of grass, etc.) brizna, *f*; (of sharp instruments) hoja, *f*; (of oar) pala, *f*; (of propeller) paleta, ala, *f*

bladed /'bleidid/ *a* de... hojas. **a two-b. knife,** un cuchillo de dos hojas

blame /bleim/ *n* culpa, *f*; responsabilidad, *f*; censura, *f*. *vt* culpar, echar la culpa (a); tachar, censurar, criticar; acusar. **You are to b. for this,** Vd. tiene la culpa de esto

blameless /'bleimlis/ *a* inculpable; inocente; intachable; elegante

blamelessness /'bleimlisnis/ *n* inculpabilidad, inocencia, *f*; elegancia, *f*

blameworthy /'bleim,wɜrði/ *a* culpable, digno de censura, vituperable

blanch /blæntʃ/ *vt Cul.* mondar; hacer palidecer. *vi* palidecer, perder el color

blanching /'blæntʃiŋ/ *n* palidecimiento, *m*; *Cul.* mondadura, *f*

blancmange /blə'mɑndʒ/ *n* manjar blanco, *m*

bland /blænd/ *a* afable, cortés; dulce, agradable

blandish /'blændiʃ/ *vt* adular, halagar, acariciar

blandishment /'blændiʃmənt/ *n* adulación, *f*, halago, *m*, caricia, *f*

blandness /'blændnis/ *n* afabilidad, urbanidad, *f*; dulzura, *f*

blank /blæŋk/ *a* en blanco; (empty) vacío; desocupado; pálido; (confused) confuso, desconcertado; (expressionless) sin expresión; (of verse) suelto; sin adorno. *n* blanco, hueco, *m*; papel en blanco, *m*; laguna, *f*; (form to be filled out) hoja *f*, *Mexico* esqueleto, *m*. **b. cartridge,** cartucho para salvas, cartucho de fogueo, *m*. **b. verse,** verso suelto, *m*

blanket /'blæŋkit/ *n* manta, frazada, *Lat. Am.* cobija *f*; (of a horse) sudadero, *Lat. Am.* mandil *m*; *Fig.* capa, *f. vt* cubrir una manta. **to toss in a b.,** mantear. **wet b.,** aguafiestas, *mf*. **b. maker or seller,** mantero, *m*. **b. vote,** voto colectivo, *m*

blanketing /'blæŋkitiŋ/ *n* manteamiento, *m*

blankly /'blæŋkli/ *adv* con indiferencia; sin comprender; (flatly) categóricamente

blankness /'blæŋknis/ *n* confusión, *f*, desconcierto, *m*; (emptiness) vaciedad, *f*; indiferencia, *f*; incomprensión, *f*

blare /blɛər/ *n* sonido de la trompeta o del clarín, *Poet.* clangor, *m*; (of a car horn) ruido, *m. vi* sonar

blarney /'blɑrni/ *n* labia, *f. vt* lisonjear

blaspheme /blæs'fim/ *vi* blasfemar. *vt* renegar de, maldecir

blasphemer /blæs'fimər/ *n* blasfemador (-ra), blasfemo (-ma)

blasphemous /'blæsfəməs/ *a* blasfemo, blasfematorio

blasphemy /'blæsfəmi/ *n* blasfemia, *f*

blast /blæst/ *n* (of wind) ráfaga (de viento), *f*; (of a trumpet, etc.) trompetazo, son, *m*; (of a whistle) pitido, *m*; (draft) soplo, *m*; explosión, *f*; *Fig.* influencia maligna, *f. vt* (rock) barrenar, hacer saltar; (wither) marchitar, secar; *Fig.* destruir; (curse) maldecir. **in full b.,** en plena marcha. **b.-furnace,** alto horno, horno de cuba, *m*. **b. hole,** barreno, *m*

blaster /'blæstər/ *n* barrenero, *m*

blasting /'blæstiŋ/ *n* (of rock) voladura, *f*; (withering) marchitamiento, *m*; *Fig.* destrucción, ruina, *f*; (cursing) maldiciones, *f pl.* *a.* (destructor) *Fig.* funesto. **b. charge,** carga explosiva, *f*

blatant /'bleitnt/ *a* ruidoso; agresivo; llamativo; (boastful) fanfarrón

blaze /bleiz/ *n* llama, *f*; fuego, *m*; conflagración, *f*; luz brillante, *f*; (of anger, etc.) acceso, *m. vi* llamear, encenderse en llamas; brillar, resplandecer. **a b. of color,** una masa de color. **Go to blazes!** ¡Vete al infierno!

blazon /'bleizən/ *n Herald.* blasón, *m*; *Fig.* proclamación, *f*, *vt* blasonar; adornar; proclamar

bleach /blitʃ/ *n* lejía, *f. vt* blanquear; descolorar. *vi* ponerse blanco; descolorarse

bleaching /'blitʃiŋ/ *n* blanqueo, *m*. **b. powder,** hipoclorito de cal, *m*

bleak /blik/ *a* yermo, desierto; frío; expuesto; (sad) triste; severo

bleakness /'bliknis/ *n* situación expuesta, *f*; desnudez, *f*; frío, *m*; (sadness) tristeza, *f*; severidad, *f*

bleary-eyed /'bliəri ,aid/ *a* legañoso, cegajoso

bleat /blit/ *n* balido, *m*, *vt and vi* balar, dar balidos

bleating /'blitiŋ/ *a* balador, que bala. *n* balido, *m*

bleed /blid/ *vi* sangrar, echar sangre; sufrir. *vt* sangrar; arrancar dinero a

bleeding /'blidiŋ/ *n* hemorragia, *f*; sangría, *f*, *Lat. Am.* desangre *m*

blemish /'blemiʃ/ *n* imperfección, *f*, defecto, *m*; (on fruit) maca, *f*; (stain) mancha, *f*, deshonra, *f*

blend /blend/ *n* mezcla, mixtura, *f*; combinación, *f*; fusión, *f. vt* mezclar; combinar. *vi* mezclarse; combinarse

blende /blɛnd/ *n Mineral.* blenda, *f*

blending /'blɛndiŋ/ *n* mezcla, *f*; fusión, *f*

bless /blɛs/ *vt* bendecir; consagrar; (praise) alabar, glorificar; hacer feliz (a). **B. me!** ¡Válgame Dios!

blessed /'blɛsid/ *a* bendito; *Eccl.* beato, bienaventurado; (dear) querido; feliz; *Inf.* maldito

blessedness /'blɛsɪdnɪs/ n felicidad, f; bienaventuranza, f

blessing /'blɛsɪŋ/ n bendición, f; (grace) bendición de la mesa, f; (mercy) merced, gracia, f; favor, m; (good) bien, m. **He gave them his b.,** Les echó su bendición

Bless you! (to someone who has sneezed) ¡Salud!

blight /blait/ n Agr. tizne, tizón, m; (of cereals) añublo, m; (mould) roña, f; (greenfly) pulgón, m; Fig. influencia maligna, f; (frustration) desengaño, m; (spoil-sport) aguafiestas, mf. vt atizonar; anublar; (wither) marchitar, secar; Fig. frustrar, destruir; malograr

blighter /'blaitər/ n bribón, m

blind /blaind/ a ciego; (secret) secreto; (of a door, etc.) falso; (closed) cerrado, sin salida; (unaware) ignorante; sin apreciación (de). **to be b.,** ser ciego; Fig. tener una venda en los ojos. **to be b. in one eye,** ser tuerto. **to turn a b. eye,** hacer la vista gorda. **b. alley,** callejón sin salida, m. **b. as a bat,** más ciego que un topo. **b. flying,** Aer. vuelo a ciegas, m. **b. man,** ciego, hombre ciego, m. **b. obedience,** obediencia ciega, f. **b. side,** (of persons) lado débil, m. **b. woman,** ciega, mujer ciega, f

blind /blaind/ vt cegar; poner una venda en los ojos (de); (dazzle) deslumbrar; hacer cerrar los ojos a; hacer ignorar

blind /blaind/ n persiana, f; (Venetian) celosía, f; (deception) pretexto, m; velo, m

blindfold /'blaind,fould/ vt vendar los ojos (a); Fig. poner una venda en los ojos (de). a and adv con los ojos vendados; a ciegas; con los ojos cerrados

blindly /'blaindli/ adv ciegamente; a ciegas; ignorantemente

blindman's buff /'blaind,mænz 'bʌf/ n gallina ciega, f

blindness /'blaindnɪs/ n ceguedad, f; ofuscación, f; ignorancia, f

blink /blɪŋk/ n parpadeo, m, guiñada, f; (of light) destello, m; reflejo, m; vi parpadear, pestañear; (of lights) destellar

blinkers /'blɪŋkərz/ n pl anteojeras, f pl

bliss /blɪs/ n felicidad, f; deleite, placer, m; Eccl. gloria, f

blissful /'blɪsfəl/ a feliz

blissfulness /'blɪsfəlnɪs/ n. See **bliss**

blister /'blɪstər/ n Med. vesícula, f; ampolla, f; (bubble) burbuja, f. vt ampollar; Fig. herir

blithe /blaið/ a alegre

blithely /'blaiðli/ adv alegremente

blitheness /'blaiðnɪs/ n alegría, f

blitzkrieg /'blɪts,krig/ n blitzkrieg, m, guerra relámpago, f

blizzard /'blɪzərd/ n ventisca, nevasca, f

bloated /'bloutid/ a abotagado, hinchado; orgulloso

bloater /'bloutər/ n arenque ahumado, m

blob /blɒb/ n masa, f; mancha, f; gota, f

block /blɒk/ n bloque, m; (log) leño, m; Naut. polea, f; (for beheading and of a butcher) tajo, m; (for mounting) apeadero, m; (of shares, etc.) lote, m; (of houses) manzana, Lat. Am. cuadra f; (obstruction) obstrucción, f; (for hats) forma, f. **A chip off the old b.,** De tal palo tal astilla. **b. and tackle,** Naut. polea con aparejo. **b.-hook,** grapa, f. **b.-house,** Mil. blocao, m

block /blɒk/ vt bloquear; cerrar (el paso); (stop up) atarugar, atascar; (a wheel) calzar; (a bill, etc.) obstruir; (hats) poner en forma. **to b. the way,** cerrar el paso.

blockade /blɒ'keid/ n bloqueo, m, vt bloquear. **to run the b.,** violar el bloqueo

blockhead /'blɒk,hɛd/ n leño, zoquete, imbécil, m

blond(e) /blɒnd/ a (of hair) rubio; (of complexion) de tez blanca. n hombre rubio, m; (woman) rubia, mujer rubia, f. **peroxide b.,** rubia oxigenada, f. **b. lace,** blondina, f

blood /blʌd/ n sangre, f; (relationship) parentesco, m; (family) linaje, m, prosapia, f; (life) vida, f; (sap) savia, f; jugo, m; (horse) caballo de pura raza, m; (dandy) galán, m. vt sangrar. **bad b.,** mala sangre, f; odio, m; mala leche, f. **blue b.,** sangre azul, f. **in cold b.,** a sangre fría, f. **My b. is up,** Se me enciende

la sangre. **My b. runs cold,** Se me hiela la sangre. **to be in the b.,** llevar en la sangre. **b.-bank,** banco de sangre, m. **b.-bath,** matanza, f. **b.-colored,** de color de sangre, sanguíneo. **b.-feud,** venganza de sangre, f. **b.-guilt,** culpabilidad de homicidio, m. **b.-heat,** calor de sangre, m. **b.-letting,** sangría, f. **b. orange,** naranja dulce, f. **b.-plasma,** plasma sanguíneo, m. **b.-poisoning,** septicemia, f; infección, f. **b.-pressure,** presión sanguínea, f. **b. purity,** limpieza de sangre, f. **b.-red,** rojo como la sangre. **b.-relation,** pariente (-ta) consanguíneo(a). **b.-relationship,** consanguinidad, f. **b.-stain,** mancha de sangre, f. **b.-stained,** ensangrentado, manchado de sangre. **b.-stone,** sanguinaria, f. **b.-sucker,** sanguijuela, f; Fig. vampiro, m; (usurer) avaro (-ra). **b.-vessel,** vaso sanguíneo, m

blooded /'blʌdid/ a de sangre...; de casta...

bloodhound /'blʌd,haund/ n sabueso, m

bloodily /'blʌdɪli/ adv sangrientamente; cruentamente; con ferocidad, cruelmente

bloodiness /'blʌdɪnɪs/ n estado sangriento, m; crueldad, ferocidad, f

bloodless /'blʌdlɪs/ a exangüe; pálido; incruento; anémico; indiferente

bloodshed /'blʌd,ʃɛd/ n efusión de sangre, f; matanza, carnicería, f

bloodshot /'blʌd,ʃɒt/ a (of the eye) inyectado

bloodthirstiness /'blʌd,θɜrstinɪs/ n sed de sangre, f

bloodthirsty /'blʌd,θɜrsti/ a sanguinario, carnicero

bloody /'blʌdi/ a sangriento; (of battles) encarnizado; (cruel) sanguinario, cruel

bloom /blum/ n flor, f; florecimiento, m; (on fruit) flor, f; (prime) lozanía, f; (on the cheeks) color sano, m. vi florecer. **in b.,** en flor

blooming /'blumɪŋ/ a florido; en flor; fresco; lozano; brillante

blossom /'blɒsəm/ n flor, f. vi florecer. **to b. out into,** hacerse, llegar a ser; (wear) lucir; (buy) comprarse

blossomed /'blɒsəmd/ a con flores, de flores

blossoming /'blɒsəmɪŋ/ n floración, f

blot /blɒt/ n borrón, m; mancha, f. vt manchar; (erase) tachar; (dry) secar. **to b. out,** borrar; destruir; secar con papel secante

blotch /blɒtʃ/ n (on the skin, or stain) mancha, f

blotter /'blɒtər/ n Com. libro borrador, m; teleta, f

blotting paper /'blɒtɪŋ/ n papel secante, m

blouse /blaus/ n blusa, f

blow /blou/ n golpe, m; bofetada, f; (with the fist) puñetazo, m; (with the elbow) codazo, m; (with a club) porrazo, m; (with a whip) latigazo, m; (blossoming) floración, f; (disaster) desastre, m, tragedia, f. **to come to blows,** venirse a las manos. **at a b.,** con un solo golpe; de una vez. **b. below the belt,** golpe bajo, m. **b. in the air,** golpe en vago, m. **b. of fate,** latigazo de la fortuna, m

blow /blou/ vi (of wind) soplar (el viento), hacer viento, correr aire; (pant) jadear, echar resoplidos; (of fuses) fundirse. vt (wind instruments) tocar; soplar; (inflate) inflar; (swell) hinchar. **to b. a kiss,** tirar un beso. **to b. one's nose,** sonarse las narices. **to b. away,** disipar; ahuyentar; llevar (el viento). **to b. down,** echar por tierra, derribar; llevar (el viento). **to b. in,** llevar adentro, hacer entrar (el viento); (windows, etc.) quebrar (el viento). **to b. off,** quitar (el viento). **to b. open,** abrir (el viento). **to b. out,** hacer salir (el viento); llevar afuera (el viento); (a light) matar de un soplo, apagar soplando. **to b. over,** pasar por (el viento); soplar por; disiparse; olvidarse. **to b. up,** (inflate) inflar; (to fire avivar (el fuego); (explode) volar; (swell) hinchar

blowing /'blouɪŋ/ n soplo, m; violencia, f; (blossoming) florecimiento, m. **b. up,** voleo, m; explosión, f

blow-up /'blou ,ʌp/ n (photograph) fotografía ampliada, f

blubber /'blʌbər/ vi gimotear; berrear. n (of the whale) grasa de ballena, f. **b.-lip,** bezo, m. **b.-lipped,** bezudo

bludgeon /'blʌdʒən/ n cachiporra, porra, f; garrote, m; estaca, f. vt golpear con una porra, dar garrotazos (a)

blue /blu/ a azul; (with bruises) amoratado; (sad)

deprimido, melancólico; (obscene) verde; (dark) sombrío; (traditionalist) conservador. n azul, m; (sky) cielo, m; (for clothes) añil de lavandera, m; pl **blues,** melancolía, depresión, f; (homesickness) morriña, f. vt (laundry) añilar. **to look b.,** parecer deprimido; (of prospects, etc.) ser poco halagüeño. **b. black,** azul negro, m; (of hair) azabache, m. **b.-bottle,** Ent. moscón, m. **b.-eyed,** con ojos azules. **b. gum,** eucalipto, m. **B. Peter,** bandera de salida, f. **b. print,** fotocopia, f; plan, m

bluebell /'blu,bɛl/ n campanilla, f

bluestocking /'blu,stɒkɪŋ/ n marisabidilla, doctora, f

bluff /blʌf/ a (of cliffs, etc.) escarpado; (of persons) franco, campechano, brusco

bluffer /'blʌfər/ n Lat. Am. blofista mf

bluffness /'blʌfnɪs/ n franqueza, brusquedad, f

bluish /'bluɪʃ/ a azulado

bluishness /'bluɪʃnɪs/ n color azulado, m

blunder /'blʌndər/ n desacierto, desatino, m; equivocación, f; (in a translation, etc.) falta, f. vi tropezar (con); desacertar; equivocarse; Inf. meter la pata. vt manejar mal; estropear

blunderer /'blʌndərər/ n desatinado (-da)

blundering /'blʌndərɪŋ/ a desacertado; equivocado; imprudente n. See **blunder**

blunt /blʌnt/ a romo, embotado; obtuso; (abrupt) brusco; franco; descortés; (plain) claro. vt enromar, embotar; (the point) despuntar; Fig. hacer indiferente; (pain) mitigar

bluntly /'blʌntli/ adv sin filo; sin punta; bruscamente, francamente; claramente

bluntness /'blʌntnɪs/ n embotamiento, m; Fig. brusquedad, franqueza, f; claridad, f

blur /blɜr/ n borrón, m; mancha, f; imagen indistinta, f. vt borrar; manchar; Photo. velar

blurred /blɜrd/ a borroso; indistinto; turbio, nebuloso

blurt (out) /blɜrt/ vt proferir bruscamente; revelar sin querer

blush /blʌʃ/ n rubor, m; rojo, m. vi enrojecerse, ruborizarse, ponerse colorado; avergonzarse (por)

blushing /'blʌʃɪŋ/ a ruboroso; púdico

bluster /'blʌstər/ vi (of the wind) soplar con furia; (of waves) encresparse, embravecerse; (of persons) bravear, fanfarronear. n furia, violencia, f; tumulto, m; fanfarronería, f

blustering /'blʌstərɪŋ/ a (of wind) violento, fuerte; (of waves) tumultuoso; (of people) fanfarrón, valentón

boar /bɔr/ n verraco, m; (wild) jabalí, m

board /bɔrd/ n tabla, f; (for notices) tablón, m; (b. residence) pensión, f; (table) mesa, f; (food) comida, f; (for chess, checkers) tablero, m; (sign) letrero, m; (of instruments) cuadro, m; (bookbinding) cartón, m; Naut. bordo, m; (committee) junta, dirección, f; tribunal, m; pl **boards** Theat. tablas, f pl. **above b.,** abiertamente, sin disimulo. **free on b.,** (f.o.b.) franco a bordo. **in boards,** (of books) encartonado. **managerial b.,** junta directiva, f. **on b.,** a bordo. **on the boards,** Theat. en las tablas. **room and b.,** pensión completa, casa y comida, f. **to go on b.,** ir a bordo. **b. of directors,** consejo de administración, m. **b. of examiners,** tribunal de exámenes, m. **b. of trade,** junta de comercio, f; ministerio de comercio, m

board /bɔrd/ vt entablar, enmaderar; embarcar en; (Nav. a ship) abordar; (lodge) alojar, tomar a pensión

boarder /'bɔrdər/ n huésped (-da); (at school) pensionista, mf alumno (-na) interno (-na)

boarding /'bɔrdɪŋ/ n entablado, m; (planking) tablazón, f; (of a ship) abordaje, m; (of a train) subida (al tren), f. **b.-house,** casa de huéspedes, pensión, f. **b.-school,** pensionado, m

boarding gate n puerta de embarque, f

boast /boust/ n jactancia, f; ostentación, f; (honor) gloria, f. vi jactarse, vanagloriarse, Lat. Am. dragonear, Argentina faramallear; alabarse; ostentar. **to b. about,** jactarse de; hacer gala de; gloriarse en

boaster /'boustər/ n vanaglorioso (-sa), jactancioso (-sa)

boastful /'boustfəl/ a vanaglorioso, jactancioso; ostentador

boastfulness /'boustfəlnɪs/ n vanagloria, jactancia, f; fanfarronería, f; ostentación, f

boasting /'boustɪŋ/ n alardeo, m; fanfarronería, f

boat /bout/ n barco, m; bote, m; (in a fun fair) columpio, m, lancha, f; (for sauce or gravy) salsera, f. vi ir en barco; (row) remar; navegar. **to b. down,** bajar en barco. **to b. up,** subir en barco. **b. building,** construcción de barcos, f. **b. club,** club náutico, m. **b. crew,** tripulación de un barco, f. **b.-hook,** bichero, garabato, m. **b.-house,** cobertizo de las lanchas, m. **b.-load,** barcada, f. **b.-race,** regata, f. **b.-scoop,** achicador, m. **b.-shaped,** en forma de barco. **b.-train,** tren que enlaza con un vapor, m

boating /'boutɪŋ/ n pasear en bote, m; manejo de un bote, m; (rowing) remo, m. **b.-pole,** botador, m

boatman /'boutmən/ n barquero, m

boatswain /'bousən/ n contramaestre, m. **boatswain's mate,** segundo contramaestre, m

bob /bɒb/ n (curtsey) reverencia, f; (woman's hair) pelo a la romana, m; (of bells) toque (de campana), m. vi saltar; moverse. vt cortar corto. **long bob,** (hair) melena, f. **to bob up,** ponerse de pie; surgir. **to bob up and down,** subir y bajar; bailar. **bob-tail,** rabo corto, m. **bob-tailed,** rabón

bobbin /'bɒbɪn/ n carrete, huso, m; (of wool, etc.) ovillo, m; (of looms, sewing machines) bobina, f; (in lace-making) bolillo, palillo, m

bobsled /'bɒb,slɛd/ n trineo doble, m

bode /boud/ vt presagiar, prometer. **to b. ill,** prometer mal. **to b. well,** prometer bien

bodice /'bɒdɪs/ n corpiño, m

bodied /'bɒdid/ a (in compounds) de cuerpo

bodiless /'bɒdilɪs/ a incorpóreo

bodily /'bɒdˌli/ a del cuerpo; físico; corpóreo; real; material; (of fear) de su persona. adv corporalmente; en persona, personalmente; en conjunto, enteramente; en una pieza

boding /'boudɪŋ/ a ominoso, amenazador. n presagio, m; agüero, m

body /'bɒdi/ n Anat. cuerpo, m; (trunk) tronco, m; (corpse) cadáver, m; (of a vehicle) caja, f; (of a motor-car) carrocería, f; (of a ship) casco, m; (of a church) nave, f; (centre) centro, m; (of a book, persons, consistency and Astron.) cuerpo, m; (person) persona, f; corporación, f; grupo, m; (of an army) grueso (de ejercito), m; organismo, m. **in a b.,** en masa, juntos (juntas); en corporación. **to have enough to keep b. and soul together,** tener de que vivir. **b.-snatcher,** junta cadáveres mf ladrón de cadáveres, m. **b.-snatching,** robo de cadáveres, m

bodyguard /'bɒdi,gɑrd/ n guardia de corps, f; guardia, f; (escort) escolta, f

body language n el lenguaje del cuerpo, m

bog /bɒg/ n pantano, marjal, m, marisma, f, Central America chagüe m

bogey /'bougi; 'bʊgi/ n duende, m; (to frighten children) coco, m; (nightmare) pesadilla, f

boggy /'bɒgi/ a pantanoso, fangoso

bogus /'bougəs/ a postizo, falso

Bohemian /bou'himiən/ a and n bohemio (-ia)

boil /bɔil/ n bullir, hervir; (cook) cocer. vt hervir; cocer. n ebullición, f; Med. divieso, m. **to b. away,** consumirse hirviendo; Chem. evaporar a seco. **to b. over,** rebosar

boiler /'bɔilər/ n Cul. marmita, olla, f; (of a furnace) caldera, f. **double-b.,** baño de María, m. **steam-b.,** caldera de vapor, f. **b.-maker,** calderero, m. **b. room,** cámara de la caldera, f. **b.-suit,** mono, m

boiling /'bɔilɪŋ/ n ebullición, f, hervor, m; (cooking) cocción, f, a hirviente. **b. point,** punto de ebullición, m

boisterous /'bɔistərəs/ a (of persons) exuberante, impetuoso; (stormy) tempestuoso, borrascoso; violento

boisterously /'bɔistərəsli/ adv tempestuosamente, ruidosamente; tempestuosamente; con violencia

boisterousness /'bɔistərəsnɪs/ n exuberancia, impetuosidad, f; violencia, f; tempestuosidad, borrascosidad, f

bold /bould/ a intrépido, audaz, Argentina agulludo; (determined) resuelto; (forward) atrevido; (showy) llamativo; (clear) claro. **b.-faced,** descarado, desvergonzado. **b.-faced type,** letra negra, f

boldly /'bouldli/ *adv* intrépidamente; descaradamente; resueltamente; claramente

boldness /'bouldnıs/ *n* intrepidez, valentía, *f*; resolución, *f*; (forwardness) osadia, *f*, descaro, atrevimiento, *m*; claridad, *f*

Bolivia /bou'lıvıə/ Bolivia

Bolivian /bou'lıvıən/ *a* and *n* boliviano (-na)

Bolshevik /'boulʃəvık/ *a* and *n* bolchevique, *mf*

Bolshevist /'boulʃəvıst/ *n* bolchevista, *mf*

bolster /'boulstər/ *n* travesaño, *m*. *vt* apuntalar; *Fig.* apoyar

bolt /boult/ *n* pasador, cerrojo, *m*; (pin) perno, *m*; (knocker) aldaba, *f*; (roll) rollo, *m*; (flight) huida, *f*; (of a crossbow) flecha, *f*; (from the blue) rayo, *m*. *adv* (upright) recto como una flecha; enhiesto; rígido. **nut and b.**, perno y tuerca, *m*

bolt /boult/ *vt* echar el cerrojo (a); empernar; (*Fam.* eat) zampar. *vi* huir; (horses) desbocarse, dispararse; (plants) cerner. **to b. down,** cerrar con cerrojo. **to b. in,** entrar corriendo, entrar de repente. **to b. off,** marcharse corriendo. **to b. out,** *vi* salir de golpe. *vt* cerrar fuera

bolus /'boulas/ *n* bolo, *m*

bomb /bɒm/ *n* bomba, *f*, *vt* bombardear. **to be a b.-shell,** *Fig.* caer como una bomba. **b.-carrier,** portabombas, *m*. **b. crater,** bombazo, *m*. **b.-release,** (*Aer. Nav.*) lanzabombas, *m*. **b.-sight,** mira de avión de bombardeo, *f*

bombard /bɒm'bɑrd/ *vt* bombardear, bombear; *Fig.* llover (preguntas, etc.) sobre

bombardier /ˌbɒmbər'dıər/ *n* bombardero, *m*

bombardment /bɒm'bɑrdmənt/ *n* bombardeo, *m*

bombast /'bɒmbæst/ *n* ampulosidad, pomposidad, *f*

bombastic /bɒm'bæstık/ *a* bombástico, altisonante, pomposo

bomber /'bɒmər/ *n* avión de bombardeo, bombardero, *m*. **dive b.,** bombardero en picado, *m*. **heavy b.,** bombardero pesado, *m*. **light b.,** bombardero ligero, *m*. **b. command,** servicio de bombardeo, *m*

bombproof /'bɒm,pruf/ *a* a prueba de bomba

bonafide /'bounə,faid/ *a* fidedigno

bonbon /'bɒn,bɒn/ *n* bombón, confite, dulce, *m*. **b. box,** bombonera, *f*

bond /bɒnd/ *n* lazo, vínculo, *m*; *Chem.* enlace, *m*; (financial) obligación, *f*; (security) fianza, *f*; (Customs) depósito, *m*; *pl* **bonds,** cadenas, *f pl*, *a* esclavo. **in b.,** en depósito. **bonds of interest,** intereses creados, *m pl*. **b.-holder,** obligacionista, *mf*

bondage /'bɒndıdʒ/ *n* esclavitud, *f*; servidumbre, *f*; cautiverio, *m*; prisión, *f*

bone /boun/ *n* hueso, *m*; (of fish) espina (de pez), *f*; (whale b.) ballena, *f*; *pl* **bones,** cuerpo, *m*, *vt* deshuesar; poner ballenas (a or en). **to be all skin and bones,** estar en los huesos. **to have a b. to pick with,** tener que arreglar las cuentas con. **b.-ash,** cendra, *f*

boned /bound/ *a* (in compounds) de huesos; deshuesado, sin hueso

boner /'bounər/ *n* (blunder) gazapo, *m*, patochada, plancha, *f*

bonfire /'bɒn,faiər/ *n* fogata, hoguera, *f*

Bonn /bɒn/ Bonn, *f*

bonnet /'bɒnıt/ *n* capota, *f*; (of babies) gorra, *f*; (of men) boina, *f*; (of chimney and of machines) sombrerete, *m*

bonus /'bounəs/ *n* paga extraordinaria, bonificación, *f*; sobresueldo, *m*; (of food, etc.) ración extraordinaria, *f*

bon vivant /bɔ̃ vi'vɑ̃/ *m* alegre, vividor, *m*

bon voyage /bɔ̃ vwa'yaʒ/ *interj* ¡buen viaje! ¡feliz viaje!

bony /'bouni/ *a* huesudo; (of fish-bones) lleno de espinas; óseo

booby /'bubi/ *n* pazguato, bobo, *m*. **b.-prize,** último premio, *m*. **b.-trap,** trampa, *f*; *Mil.* mina, *f*

book /bʊk/ *n* libro, *m*; volumen, tomo, *m*; (of an opera) libreto, *m*; *vt* anotar en un libro; apuntar; (seats) tomar (localidades); (tickets) sacar (billetes); (of the issuing clerk) dar; (reserve) reservar; inscribir; consignar (a suspect); (engage) contratar; (invite) comprometer. **to turn the pages of a b.,** hojear un

libro. b.-ends, sostén para libros, sujetalibros, *m*. **b.-keeper,** tenedor de libros, *m*. **b.-keeping,** teneduría de libros, *f*. **b.-maker,** apostador de profesión, *m*. **b. of reference,** libro de consulta, *m*. **b.-plate,** exlibris, *m*. **b.-post,** tarifa de impresos, *f*. **b.-shop,** librería, *f*. **b.-trade,** venta de libros, *f*; comercio de libros, *m*

bookbinder /'bʊk,baindər/ *n* encuadernador (-ra) de libros

bookbinding /'bʊk,baindıŋ/ *n* encuadernación de libros, *f*

bookcase /'bʊk,keis/ *n* armario de libros, *Lat. Am.* librero *m*

booking /'bʊkıŋ/ *n* (of rooms, etc.) reservación, *f*; (of tickets) toma, *f*; *Com.* asiento, *m*; (engagement) contratación, *f*. **b.-clerk,** vendedor (-ra) de billetes. **b.-office,** despacho de billetes, *m*; taquilla, *f*

bookish /'bʊkıʃ/ *a* aficionado a los libros; docto, erudito

bookishness /'bʊkıʃnıs/ *n* afición a los libros, *f*; erudición, *f*

bookmark /'bʊk,mɑrk/ *n* marcador, *m*

bookseller /'bʊk,selər/ *n* librero, *m*

bookselling /'bʊk,selıŋ/ *n* venta de libros, *f*; comercio de libros, *m*

bookshelf /'bʊk,ʃelf/ *n* estante para libros, *m*, *Mexico* repisa, *f*

bookstall /'bʊk,stɔl/ *n* puesto de libros, *m*

bookstrap /'bʊk,stræp/ *n* portalibros, *m*

bookworm /'bʊk,wɜrm/ *n* polilla que roe los libros, *f*; *Fig.* ratón de biblioteca, *m*

boom /bum/ *n* *Naut.* botavara, *f*; (of a crane) aguilón, *m*; (noise) ruido, *m*; (of the sea) bramido, *m*; (thunder) trueno, *m*; (in a port) cadena de puerto, *f*; *Com.* actividad, *f*; (*Fig.* peak) auge, *m*, *vi* sonar; bramar; tronar; *Com.* subir; ser famoso. **b. sail,** vela de cangreja, *f*

boomerang /'bumə,ræŋ/ *n* bumerang, *m*

boon /bun/ *n* favor, *m*, merced, *f*; bien, *m*, ventaja, *f*; don, *m*; privilegio, *m*, *a* (of friends) íntimo

boor /bʊr/ *n* monigote, patán, palurdo, *m*

boorish /'bʊrıʃ/ *a* rudo, zafio, rústico, cerril

boorishness /'bʊrıʃnıs/ *n* zafiedad, patanería, tosquedad, *f*

boost /bust/ *vt* *Elec.* aumentar la fuerza (de); *Inf.* empujar; subir; (advertise) dar bombo (a)

boot /but/ *n* bota, *f*; (of a car) compartimiento para equipaje, *m*. **button-boots,** botas de botones, *f pl*. **riding-boots,** botas de montar, *f pl*. **to b. off,** además, de añadidura. **b.-maker,** zapatero, *m*. **b.-tag,** tirador de bota, *m*. **b.-tree,** horma de bota, *f*

bootblack /'but,blæk/ *n* limpiabotas, *Mexico* bolero (-ra), *elsewhere in Lat. Am.* embolador (-ra), lustrador (-ra)

booted /'butıd/ *a* con botas, calzado con botas; (in compounds) de botas...

bootee /bu'ti/ *n* botita, *f*

booth /buθ/ *n* puesto, *m*, barraca, *f*

bootlace /'but,leis/ *n* cordón para zapatos, *m*

bootlegger /'but,legər/ *n* contrabandista de alcohol, *m*

boots /buts/ *m* mozo de hotel, botones, *m*

booze /buz/ *vi* emborracharse. **b. up,** *Argentina* acatarrarse. *n* alcohol, *m*; borrachera, *f*

boozed up /buzd/ *Lat. Am.* apimplado (-da), *Argentina* acatarrado (-da), *Central America* azurumbado (-da)

boozer /'buzər/ *n* borracho (-cha)

boracic /bə'ræsık/ *a* bórico. *n* ácido bórico, *m*

borax /'bɒræks/ *n* bórax, *m*

Bordeaux /bɔr'dou/ *a* and *n* (of or from) bordelés (-esa). *n* (wine) vino de Burdeos, *m*

bordello /bɔr'delou/ *n* burdel, *m*

border /'bɔrdər/ *n* borde, *m*; (of a lake, etc.) orilla, *f*; (edge) margen, *m*; (of a diploma, etc.) orla, *f*; *Sew.* ribete, *m*, orla, *f*; (fringe) franja, *f*; (garden) arriate, *m*; (territory) frontera, *f*; límite, confín, *m*. *vt* orlar, ribetear; ornar (de); (of land) lindar con. **to b. on,** (of land) tocar, lindar con; (approach) rayar en. **b. country,** región fronteriza, *f*

borderer /'bɔrdərər/ *n* habitante de una zona fronteriza, *m*; escocés (-esa) de la frontera con Inglaterra

borderland /'bɔrdər,lænd/ n zona fronteriza, f; lindes, m pl

borderline /'bɔrdər,lain/ n frontera, f; límite, m; margen, m, a fronterizo; lindero; (uncertain) dudoso, incierto

bore /bɔr/ n taladro, barreno, m; perforación, f; (hole) agujero, m; (of guns) calibre, m; (wave) oleada, f; (nuisance) fastidio, m; (dullness) aburrimiento, tedio, m; (person) pelmazo, m, machaca, mf vt taladrar, barrenar, horadar; perforar; hacer un agujero (en); (exhaust) aburrir; fastidiar. **It's a b.,** Es una lata. **to be bored,** aburrirse, fastidiarse

boredom /'bɔrdəm/ n aburrimiento, m; tedio, hastío, m

boring /'bɔrɪŋ/ a aburrido, pesado, tedioso; molesto, fastidioso. n taladro, m; horadación, f; sondeo, m; perforación, f

born /bɔrn/ a nacido; (by birth) de nacimiento; (b. to be) destinado a; natural (de). **He was b. in 1870.** Nació en 1870. **to be b.,** nacer, venir al mundo. **to be b. again,** ecc. nacido de nuevo, renacer, volver a nacer. **well-b.,** bien nacido. **b. with a silver spoon in one's mouth,** Nacido de pie, Nacido un domingo

-borne /-bɔrn/ trasmitido por... (e.g. anthropod-b., trasmitido por los antrópodos)

borough /'bɜrou/ n burgo, m; villa, f; ciudad, f. **b. surveyor,** arquitecto municipal, m

borrow /'bɒrou/ vt pedir prestado; apropiarse, adoptar; copiar; (arithmetic) restar; (a book from a library) tomar prestado. **May I b. your pencil?** ¿Quieres prestarme tu lápiz?

borrower /'bɒrouər/ n el (la) que pide o toma prestado

borrowing /'bɒrouɪŋ/ n el pedir prestado, acto de pedir prestado, m

Bosnian /'bɒzniən/ a bosnio

bosom /'buzəm/ n pecho, m; (heart) corazón, m; (of the earth, etc.) seno, m. **b. friend,** amigo (-ga) del alma, amigo (-ga) íntimo (-ma)

Bosphorus, the /'bɒsfərəs/ el Bósforo, m

boss /bɒs/ n (of a shield) corcova saliente, f; tachón, m; Archit. pinjante, m. Inf. amo, m; jefe, m. vt mandar; dominar. **political b.,** cacique, m

bossism /'bɒsɪzəm/ n caudillaje, m

bossy /'bɒsi/ a mandón, autoritario. **b. person,** Lat. Am. mandarín, m

botanical /bə'tænɪkəl/ a botánico. **b. garden,** jardín botánico, m

botanist /'bɒtnɪst/ n botánico (-ca)

botany /'bɒtni/ n botánica, f

botch /bɒtʃ/ n (clumsy work) chapucería, f; remiendo, m. vt chapucear, chafallar; (patch) remendar

both /bouθ/ a and pron ambos, m pl; ambas, f pl; los dos, m pl; las dos, f pl, adv tan(to)... como; (and) y; a la vez, al mismo tiempo. **It appealed both to the young and the old,** Gustó tanto a los jóvenes como a los viejos. **b. of you,** ustedes dos, vosotros dos, vosotras dos. **b. pretty and useful,** bonito y útil a la vez

bother /'bɒðər/ n molestia, f, fastidio, m; (worry) preocupación, f; dificultad, f; (fuss) alboroto, m, Lat. Am. fregada f. vt molestar, fastidiar, Lat. Am. acatarrar; preocupar. vi preocuparse

bottle /'bɒtl/ n botella, f; (smaller) frasco, m; (babies) biberón, m; (for water) cantimplora, f, vt embotellar, envasar, enfrascar. **to b. up,** (liquids, capital, armies, navies) embotellar; (feelings) refrenar. **to bring up on the b.,** criar con biberón. **b.-green,** verde botella, m. **b.-neck,** (in an industry) embotellamiento, m; (in traffic) atascadero, m. **b.-washer,** fregaplatos, mf; (machine) máquina para limpiar botellas, f

bottle cap n corchalata, f

bottled /'bɒtld/ a en botella; (of fruit, vegetables) conservado

bottleful /'bɒtl,fʊl/ n botella, f

bottler /'bɒtlər/ n embotellador (-ra)

bottling /'bɒtlɪŋ/ n embotellado, m; envase, m. **b. outfit,** embotelladora, f; (for fruit, etc.) aparato para conservar frutas o legumbres, m

bottom /'bɒtəm/ n base, f; (deepest part) fondo, m; (last place) último lugar, m; (of a

chair) asiento, m; (of a page, table, mountain, etc.) pie, m; (posterior) culo, m; (of a river) lecho, m; (of the sea) fondo, m; (of a ship) casco, m; (of a skirt) orilla, f; (truth) realidad, verdad, f; (basis) origen, m, causa, f. **at b.,** en realidad. **at the b.,** en el fondo. **false b.,** fondo doble, fondo secreto, m. **to be at the b. of,** ocupar el último lugar en; ser el causante de. **to get to the b. of,** descubrir la verdad de; profundizar en, analizar. **to sink to the b.,** (of ships) irse a pique

bottomed /'bɒtəmd/ a (in compounds) de fondo...

bottomless /'bɒtəmlɪs/ a sin fondo; (of chairs, etc.) sin asiento; (unfathomable) insondable

boudoir /'budwɑr/ n tocador, gabinete de señora, m

bough /bau/ n rama, f, brazo (de un árbol) m

boulder /'bouldər/ n roca, peña, f; canto rodado, m; bloque de roca, m

boulevard /'bulə,vɑrd/ n bulevar, m

bounce /bauns/ n bote, rebote, m; salto, m; (boasting) fanfarronería, f, vi rebotar; saltar, brincar. vt hacer botar o saltar

bouncing /'baunsɪŋ/ a (healthy) sano, robusto; vigoroso, fuerte

bound /baund/ n límite, m; (jump) salto, brinco, m, vt limitar, confinar. vi saltar, brincar; (bounce) botar. **within bounds,** dentro del límite. **b. for,** con destino a; (of ships) con rumbo a

boundary /'baundəri/ n límite, lindero, término, m; frontera, f; raya, f. **b. stone,** mojón, m

bounden /'baundən/ a obligatorio, forzoso; indispensable

boundless /'baundlɪs/ a sin límites, infinito; inmenso

bounteous, bountiful /'bauntiəs; 'bauntɪfəl/ a dadivoso, generoso; bondadoso

bountifulness /'bauntɪfəlnɪs/ n munificencia, dadivosidad, generosidad, f

bounty /'baunti/ n generosidad, munificencia, f; don, m; (subsidy) subvención, f

bouquet /bou'kei, bu-/ n ramo, ramillete (de flores), m, Lat. Am. also maceta f; perfume, m; (of wine) nariz, f

Bourbon /'bɜrbən; 'bʊrbən/ a borbónico. n Borbón (-ona)

bourgeois /bʊr'ʒwɑ/ a and n burgués (-esa)

bourgeoisie /,bʊrʒwɑ'zi/ n burguesía, mesocracia, f

bout /baut/ n turno, m; (in fencing, boxing, wrestling) asalto, m; (of illness, coughing) ataque, m; (fight) lucha, f, combate, m; (of drinking) borrachera, f

bovine /'bouvain/ a bovino, vacuno

bow /bou/ n (weapon) arco, m; (of a saddle) arzón (de silla), m; Mus. arco, m; (knot) lazo, m; (greeting) saludo, m; reverencia, inclinación, f; (of a boat) proa, f. **to tie a bow,** hacer un lazo. **bow and arrows,** arco y flechas, m. **bow-legged,** patizambo, Central America corveta, f. **bow window,** ventana saliente, f

bow /bau/ vi inclinarse; hacer una reverencia, saludar; (remove the hat) descubrirse; Fig. inclinarse (ante); (submit) someterse (a), reconocer; agobiarse; Mus. manejar el arco. vt (usher in) introducir en, conducir a; doblar; inclinar. **to bow down (to),** humillarse ante; obedecer; (worship) reverenciar, adorar. **to bow out,** despedir con una inclinación del cuerpo

bowel /'bauəl/ n intestino, m; pl **bowels,** Fig. seno, m, entrañas, f pl

bower /'bauər/ n (arbor) enramada, f; glorieta, f; (boudoir) tocador de señora, f

bowing /'bouɪŋ/ n Mus. arqueada, f; saludo, m, a (of acquaintance) superficial

bowl /boul/ n receptáculo, m; (of a fountain) taza, f; (of a pipe) cazoleta, f; (barber's) bacía, f; (for washing) jofaina, f; (for punch) ponchera, f; (goblet) copa, f; (for soup) escudilla, f; (for fruit) frutero, m; (for a spoon) paleta, f; (ball) boliche, m. vt tirar; (in cricket) sacar; (a hoop) jugar con; (in ninepins) tumbar con una bola. **to b. along,** recorrer; ir en coche o carruaje (por). **to b. over,** Fig. dejar consternado (a), desconcertar

bowler /'boulər/ n (in cricket) servidor, m; (hat) sombrero hongo, m; (skittle player) jugador de bolos, m

bowling /'boulɪŋ/ n (in cricket) saque, m; (skittles) (juego de) bolos, m; (juego de) boliche, m. **b. alley,**

bolera, pista de bolos, *f*, salón de boliche, *m*. **b.-green,** bolera en cesped, *f*
bowls /boulz/ *n* juego de boliche, *m*
bowsprit /'bausprit/ *n* bauprés, *m*
bowstring /'bou,striŋ/ *n* cuerda de arco, *f*
bow tie /bou/ *n* pajarita, *f*
bow-wow /'bau ,wau/ *n* guau, *m*
box /bɒks/ *n* caja, *f*; (case) estuche, *m*; (luggage) baúl, *m*, maleta, *f*; (for a hat) sombrerera, *f*; *Bot.* boj, *m*; *Theat.* palco, *m*, *Mexico* lumbrera, *f*; (for a sentry, signalman, etc.) garita, casilla, *f*; (on a carriage) pescante, *m*; (blow) cachete, *m*, bofetada, *f*; (for a horse) vagón, *m*. **post office box,** apartado de correos, *m*. **box-kite,** cometa celular, *f*. **box-maker,** cajero, *m*. **box office,** taquilla, *f*, *Lat. Am.* boletería *f*. **box-pleat,** *Sew.* tabla, *f*
box /bɒks/ *vt* encajonar, meter en una caja. *vi* boxear. **to box the ears of,** calentar las orejas de. **to box up,** encerrar
boxer /'bɒksər/ *n Sports.* boxeador, pugilista, *m*
boxing /'bɒksiŋ/ *n* encajonamiento, *m*; envase, *m*; *Sports.* boxeo, pugilato, *m*. **B. Day,** Día de San Esteban, *m*, (A Spanish child receives Christmas presents on the Día de Reyes (Twelfth Night).) **b.-gloves,** guantes de boxeo, *m pl*. **b.-ring,** cuadrilátero de boxeo, *m*
box-office success /'bɒks ,ɔfis/ *n* éxito de taquilla, *m*
boy /bɔi/ *n* muchacho, niño, rapaz, *m*; (older) chico, joven, *m*. **new boy,** nuevo alumno, *m*. **old boy,** (of a school) antiguo alumno, *m*; (*Fam.* address) chico. **small boy,** chiquillo, pequeño, crío, *m*. **b. doll,** muñeco, *m*. **boy scout,** muchacho explorador, *m*
boycott /'bɔikɒt/ *vt* boicotear. *n* boicot, *m*
boyhood /'bɔihʊd/ *n* muchachez, mocedad, *f*; (childhood) niñez, *f*
boyish /'bɔiiʃ/ *a* muchachil; pueril; de niñez
brace /breis/ *n* (prop) puntal, barrote, *m*; abrazadera, *f*; berbiquí, *m*; viento, tirante, *m*; freno (for the teeth), *m*, (pair) par, *m*; *pl* **braces,** tirantes, *m pl*. *vt* apuntalar; asegurar; ensamblar; *Naut.* bracear; (trousers) tirar; *Fig.* fortalecer, refrescar
bracelet /'breislit/ *n* pulsera, *f*, brazalete, *m*, ajorca, *f*
bracing /'breisiŋ/ *a* (of air, etc.) fortificante, tónico; estimulador
bracken /'brækən/ *n* helecho, *m*
bracket /'brækit/ *n* consola, *f*; *Archit.* repisa, *f*; soporte, *m*; (on furniture, etc.) cantonera, *f*; *Print.* paréntesis angular, *m*; (for a light) brazo (de alumbrado), *m*. *vt Print.* poner entre paréntesis; juntar. **in brackets,** entre paréntesis. **They were bracketed equal,** Fueron juzgados iguales
brackish /'brækiʃ/ *a* salobre
brag /bræg/ *vi* jactarse, fanfarronear, *Lat. Am.* dragonear, *Argentina* faramallear. *n* jactancia, *f*. **to b. about,** hacer alarde de
braggart /'brægərt/ *a* baladrón, jactancioso. *n* jactancioso, fanfarrón, *m*
bragging /'brægiŋ/ *n* jactancia, *f*
Brahmin /'brɑmin/ *n* brahmán, *m*
Brahminism /'brɑmi,nizəm/ *n* brahmanismo, *m*
braid /breid/ *n* trencilla, *f*, cordoncillo, *m*; (for trimming) galón, *m*; (plait) trenza, *f*. *vt* (hair) trenzar; (trim) galonear; acordonar, trencillar
brain /brein/ *n* cerebro, *m*; entendimiento, *m*, inteligencia, *f*; talento, *m*; (common sense) sentido común, *m*; *pl* **brains,** sesos, *m pl*, (animal and human); cacumen, *m*. *vt* romper la crisma (a). **to blow one's brains out,** levantarse la tapa de los sesos. **to rack one's brains,** devanarse los sesos. **Brains Trust,** masa cefálica, *f*; consorcio de inteligencias, *m*. **b.-box,** cráneo, *m*. **b.-fever,** fiebre cerebral, *f*. **b.-storm,** torbellino de ideas, *m*. **b.-wave,** idea luminosa, *f*. **b.-work,** trabajo intelectual, *m*
brainchild /'brein,tʃaild/ *n* engendro, *m*
brain drain *n* fuga de cerebros, *f*
brained /breind/ *a* de cabeza, de cerebro
brainless /'breinlis/ *a* sin seso; tonto
brainy /'breini/ *a* sesudo, inteligente, talentudo
braise /breiz/ *vt Cul.* asar
brake /breik/ *n* (of vehicles and *Fig.*) freno, *m*, *Chile*, *Peru* alitranca *f* (flax and hemp) caballete, *m*; (car-

riage) break, *m*; (thicket) matorral, *m*. *vt* (vehicles) frenar; (hemp, etc.) rastrillar. **foot-b.,** freno de pedal, *m*. **hand-b.,** freno de mano, *m*. **to b. hard,** frenar de repente. **to release the b.,** quitar el freno
bramble /'bræmbəl/ *n* zarza, *f*. **b. patch,** breña, *f*, zarzal, *m*
brambly /'bræmbli/ *a* zarzoso
bran /bræn/ *n* salvado, *m*
branch /bræntʃ, brɑntʃ/ *n* (of a tree, a family) rama, *f*; (of flowers, of learning) ramo, *m*; (of a river) tributario, afluente, *m*; (of roads, railways) ramal, *m*; (of a firm) sucursal, dependencia, *f*. *a* sucursal, dependiente; (of roads, railways) secundario. *vi* echar ramas; bifurcarse, dividirse; ramificarse. **to b. off,** bifurcarse, ramificarse. **to b. out,** extenderse; emprender cosas nuevas
branched /bræntʃt/ *a* con ramas; *Bot.* ramoso; (of candlesticks) de... brazos
branchiness /'bræntʃinis/ *n* ramaje, *m*, frondosidad, *f*
branching /'bræntʃiŋ/ *n* ramificación, *f*; división, *f*. **b. off,** bifurcación, *f*
brand /brænd/ *n* tizón, *m*; (torch) tea, *f*; (on cattle, etc.) hierro, *m*; (trademark) marca de fábrica, *f*; marca, *f*; (stigma) estigma, *m*. *vt* marcar con el hierro, herrar; marcar; estigmatizar, tildar. **b.-new,** flamante
branding /'brændiŋ/ *n* (of livestock) herradero, *m*; (of slaves, criminals) estigmatización, *f*; difamación, *f*. **b.-iron,** hierro de marcar, *m*
brandish /'brændiʃ/ *vt* blandir
brandy /'brændi/ *n* coñac, *m*
brass /bræs/ *n* latón, *m*; *Mus.* metal, *m*; (tablet) placa conmemorativa, *f*; *Inf.* dinero, *m*. **the b.,** *Mus.* el metal. **b. band,** banda de instrumentos de viento, *f*. **b.-neck,** *Inf.* cara dura, *f*. **b. works** or **shop,** latonería, *f*
brassiere /brə'ziər/ *n* sostén, *m*
brat /bræt/ *n* crío, *m*
bravado /brə'vɑdou/ *n* bravata, *f*
brave /breiv/ *a* valiente, animoso, intrépido; espléndido, magnífico; bizarro. *n* valiente, *m*. *vt* desafiar, provocar; arrostrar
bravely /'breivli/ *adv* valientemente; espléndidamente; bizarramente
bravery /'breivəri/ *n* valentía, *f*, valor, *m*, intrepidez, *f*, coraje, *m*; esplendidez, suntuosidad, *f*; bizarría, *f*
bravo /'brɑvou/ *n* bandido, *m*; asesino pagado, *m*, *interj* ¡bravo! ¡olé!
bravura /brə'vyurə/ *n* bravura, *f*
brawl /brɔl/ *n* camorra, reyerta, pelotera, *Lat. Am.* follisca *f*. *vi* alborotar; (of streams) murmurar. **to start a b.,** armar camorra
brawler /'brɔlər/ *n* camorrista, *mf*
brawling /'brɔliŋ/ *n* alboroto, *m*, vocinglería, *f*; (of streams) murmullo, *m*
brawn /brɔn/ *n Cul.* embutido, *m*; músculo, *m*; (strength) fuerza, *f*
brawny /'brɔni/ *a* membrudo, musculoso, forzudo
bray /brei/ *n* rebuzno, *m*; (of trumpets) clangor, *m*, *vi* rebuznar; sonar
brazen /'breizən/ *a* de latón; (of voice) bronca; desvergonzado, descarado
brazier /'breizər/ *n* (fire) brasero, *m*; latonero, *m*
Brazil /brə'zil/ el Brasil, *m*
Brazilian /brə'zilyən/ *a* and *n* brasileño (-ña)
Brazil nut *n* nuez del Brasil, *f*
breach /britʃ/ *n* violación, contravención, *f*; (gap) abertura, *f*; *Mil.* brecha, *f*. *vt Mil.* hacer brecha (en); (in a line of defence) hacer mella (en). **b. of confidence,** abuso de confianza, *m*. **b. of promise,** incumplimiento de la palabra de casamiento, *m*. **b. of the peace,** alteración del orden público, *f*, quebrantamiento de la paz, *m*
bread /bred/ *n* pan, *m*. **to earn one's b. and butter,** ganarse el pan. **brown b.,** pan moreno, *m*. **unleavened b.,** pan ázimo, *m*. **b. and butter,** pan con mantequilla, *f*, *Fig.* sustento diario, *m*. **b.-basket,** cesta de pan, *f*, *Inf.* estómago, *m*. **b. bin,** caja del pan, *f*. **b.-crumb,** miga, *f*; migaja, *f*. **b.-knife,** cuchillo para cortar el pan, *m*. **b. poultice,** cataplasma de miga de

pan, f. **b.-winner,** ganador (-ra) de pan, trabajador (-ra)
breadfruit tree /'brɛd,frut/ n árbol del pan, m
breadth /brɛdθ/ n anchura, f; latitud, f; liberalidad, f; Sew. ancho de una tela, m
breadthways /'brɛdθ,weiz/ adv a lo ancho
break /breik/ n rotura, f; (opening) abertura, f; Geol. rajadura, f; (fissure) grieta, f; solución de continuidad, f; interrupción, f; (billiards) serie, f; (change) cambio, m; (in a boy's voice) muda (de la voz), f; (blank) vacío, m; (in the market) baja, f; intervalo, m; descanso, m; pausa, f; (truce) tregua, f; (clearing) clara, f; Mus. quiebra (de la voz), f; (carriage) break, m; (Fam. folly) disparate, m. **with a b. in one's voice,** con voz entrecortada. **b. of day,** aurora, alba, f. **at the b. of day,** al despuntar el alba
break /breik/ vt romper; quebrar; quebrantar, fracturar; (breach) abrir brecha en; (in two) partir, dividir; (into pieces) hacer pedazos, despedazar; (into small pieces) desmenuzar; (into crumbs) desmigajar; (destroy) destrozar; (a blow) parar; (a law) infringir, violar; (the bank in gambling) quebrar; (a journey, etc.) interrumpir; (of a habit) desacostumbrar, hacer perder el vicio de; (a promise) no cumplir, faltar a; (a record) superar; (plow ground) roturar; (spoil) estropear; arruinar; Com. ir a la quiebra; (an official) degradar; (an animal) domar, amansar; (Fig. crush) subyugar; (betray) traicionar; (Fig. of silence, a spell, a lance, peace, the ranks) romper; (cushion) amortiguar; (lessen) mitigar; (disclose) revelar; Elec. interrumpir. **to b. one's promise,** faltar a su palabra. **to b. the ice,** Fig. romper el hielo. **to b. asunder,** romper en dos (partes); dividir. **to b. down,** derribar; echar abajo; destruir; (suppress) suprimir; subyugar; abolir; disolver. **to b. in,** (animals) domar, amaestrar; (persons) disciplinar; (new shoes) ahormar, romper. **to b. in two,** partir; dividir en dos; (split) hender. **to b. off,** separar, quitar; (a branch) desgajar; Fig. romper; interrumpir; cesar. **to b. open,** forzar, abrir a la fuerza. **to b. up,** hacer pedazos; (scatter) poner en fuga, dispersar; hacer levantar la sesión; (the ground) roturar; (parliament) disolver; (a ship) desguazar, deshacer (un buque)
break /breik/ vi romperse; quebrarse; quebrantarse; (of beads) desgranarse; (burst) reventar, estallar; (of abscesses) abrirse; (of a boy's voice) mudar; (Fig. and of clouds, etc.) romperse; desaparecer; (of the dawn) despuntar (el alba), amanecer; (sprout) brotar; (of a ball) torcerse; (of fine weather) terminar; (change) cambiar; (of a storm) estallar. **to b. loose,** desasirse; Fig. desencadenarse. **to b. away,** escaparse, fugarse; (from a habit) romper con, independizarse de (another country); disiparse. **to b. down,** (of machinery, cars) averiarse; (fail) frustrarse, malograrse; (weep) deshacerse en lágrimas; (lose one's grip) perder la confianza en sí; (in health) sufrir una crisis de salud. **The car broke down,** El auto tuvo una avería. **to b. in,** (of burglars) forzar la entrada; irrumpir (en), penetrar (en); exclamar. **to b. in on,** sorprender; entrar de sopetón; invadir; interrumpir; caer sobre; molestar. **to b. into,** (force) forzar; (utter) romper a, prorrumpir en; empezar (a); pasar de repente a; (of time, etc.) ocupar; hacer perder. **to b. off,** (of speech) interrumpirse; cesar; (detach) desprenderse, separarse; (of branches) desgajarse. **to b. out,** huir, escaparse; Fig. estallar; aparecer; declararse; (of fire) tomar fuego; derramarse; (of an eruption) salir. **to b. over,** derramarse por; bañar. **to b. through,** abrirse paso (por); abrirse salida (por); atravesar; Fig. penetrar; (of the sun, etc.) romper (por). **to b. up,** (depart) separarse; (of meetings) levantarse la sesión; dispersarse; (smash) hacerse pedazos; disolverse; (of a school) cerrarse, empezar las vacaciones; (melt) fundir; desbandarse; (of a camp) levantar (el campo); (grow old) hacerse viejo; (be ill) estar agotado. **to b. with,** romper con; cesar; reñir con
breakable /'breikəbəl/ a quebradizo, frágil
breakage /'breikɪdʒ/ n rompimiento, quebrantamiento, m; cosa rota, f; fractura, f
breakdown /'breik,daun/ n accidente, m; (of a machine) avería, f; Auto. pane, f; (failure) fracaso, m,

falta de éxito, f; deterioración, f; (in health) crisis de salud, f
breaker /'breikər/ n oleada, f
breakfast /'brɛkfəst/ n desayuno, m. vi desayunar-(se), tomar el desayuno. **to have a good b.,** desayunar bien. **b.-cup,** tazón, m. **b.-time,** hora del desayuno, f
breaking /'breikɪŋ/ n rompimiento, m; quebrantamiento, m; fractura, f; ruptura, f; (in two) división, f; (into pieces) despedazamiento, m; (into small pieces) desmenuzamiento, m; (destruction) destrozo, m; (of a blow) parada, f; (of a law, etc.) violación, f; (of one's word) no cumplimiento, m; (of a journey, of sleep, etc.) interrupción, f; (escape) escape, m, huida, f; (of an animal) domadura, f; (of a boy's voice) muda (de la voz), f; (of news) revelación, f. **b. down,** demolición, f; (of negotiations) suspensión, f. **b. in,** irrupción, f; (of an animal) domadura, f; (training) entrenamiento, m. **b. open,** forzamiento, m; quebranto, m. **b. out,** huida, f, escape, m; Fig. estallido, m; aparición, f; declaración, f; (scattering) derramamiento, m; (of a rash) erupción, f. **b. up,** dispersión, f; disolución, f; fin, m; ruina, f; (of a school) cierre, m; (change in weather) cambio, m; (of a meeting) levantamiento (de una sesión), m; (of the earth) roturación, f
breakneck /'breik,nɛk/ a rápido, veloz, precipitado
breakwater /'breik,wɔtər/ n malecón, rompeolas, m
bream /brim/ n Ichth. sargo, m. **sea-b.,** besugo, m
breast /brɛst/ n pecho, m; (of birds) pechuga, f; (of female animals) teta, mama, f; (heart) corazón, m, vt (the waves) cortar (las olas); luchar con; Fig. arrostrar, hacer frente a. **b.-bone,** esternón, m. **b. high,** alto hasta el pecho. **b.-pin,** alfiler de pecho, m. **b.-pocket,** bolsillo de pecho, m. **b.-stroke,** estilo pecho, m
breast cancer n el cáncer del seno, m
breasted /'brɛstɪd/ a de pecho...; de pechuga...; de tetas... **a double-b. jacket,** una chaqueta cruzada. **a single-b. jacket,** una chaqueta
breastwork /'brɛst,wɜrk/ n Mil. parapeto, m
breath /brɛθ/ n aliento, m; suspiro, m; (phonetics) aspiración, f; (breeze) soplo (de aire), m; (of scandal, etc.) murmurio, m; (fragrance) perfume, m, fragancia, f; (life) vida, f. **in a b.,** de un aliento. **in the same b.,** sin respirar. **out of b.,** sin aliento. **under one's b.,** por lo bajo, entre dientes. **to draw b.,** tomar aliento. **to get one's b. back,** cobrar aliento. **to have bad b.,** tener mal aliento. **to hold one's b.,** contener el aliento. **to take one's b. away,** Fig. dejar consternado (a)
breathable /'briðəbəl/ a respirable
breathe /brið/ vi respirar; vivir; (of air, etc.) soplar; (take the air) tomar el fresco; (rest) tomar aliento. vt respirar; exhalar; dar aire (a); (whisper) murmurar; (convey) expresar, revelar; (infuse) infundir. **to b. forth fury,** echar rayos. **to b. hard,** jadear. **to b. one's last,** exhalar el último suspiro. **to b. in,** inspirar
breathing /'briðɪŋ/ n respiración, f; (of the air, etc.) soplo, m; (phonetics) aspiración, f. a que respira; viviente. **hard** and **heavy b.,** jadeo, resuello, resoplido, m. **b.-space,** Fig. respiro, m
breathless /'brɛθlɪs/ a jadeante, sin aliento; (dead) muerto; (sultry) sin un soplo de aire; intenso, profundo; (of haste) precipitado
breathlessly /'brɛθlɪsli/ adv anhelosamente; con expectación
breathlessness /'brɛθlɪsnɪs/ n falta de aliento, f; respiración difícil, f; (death) muerte, f; (of weather) falta de aire, f
bred /brɛd/ a criado. **ill (well) b.,** mal (bien) criado. **pure-b.,** de casta
breech /britʃ/ n Anat. trasero, m; (of fire-arms) recámara, f
breeches /'brɪtʃɪz/ n calzones, m pl; pantalones, m pl. **riding-b.,** pantalones de montar, m pl
breed /brid/ n casta, raza, f; tipo, m; clase, f, vt procrear; engendrar, crear; (bring up) educar; criar. vi reproducirse; sacar cría; multiplicarse. **to b. in-and-in,** procrear sin mezclar razas
breeder /'bridər/ n criador (-ra); animal reproductor, m

breeding /'bridɪŋ/ n reproducción, f; cría, f; (upbringing) crianza, f; educación, f; instrucción, f; producción, f; creación, f, a de cría; (of male animals) semental; prolífico. **bad b.,** mala crianza, f. **cross b.,** cruzamiento de razas, m. **good b.,** buena crianza, f. **b. farm,** criadero, m

breeze /briz/ n brisa, f, vientecillo, m, soplo de aire, m, Lat. Am. airecito m; (argument) altercación, f, argumento, m; (of coke) cisco de coque, m. **fresh b.,** brisa fresca, f. **light b.,** brisa floja, f. **strong b.,** viento fuerte, viento muy fresco, m

breezy /'brizi/ a con brisa, fresco; expuesto a la brisa; oreado; (of manner) animado, jovial

brethren /'brɛðrɪn/ n pl hermanos, m pl

Breton /'brɛtn/ a and n bretón (-ona). n (language) bretón, m

brevet /brə'vɛt/ n Mil. graduación honoraria, f; nombramiento honorario, m. vt Mil. graduar

breviary /'brivi,ɛri/ n breviario, m

brevity /'brɛvɪti/ n brevedad, f; concisión, f

brew /bru/ n mezcla, f; brebaje, m. vt hacer (cerveza, té, etc.); preparar, mezclar; Fig. urdir, tramar. vi prepararse; urdirse; (storm) gestarse.

brewer /'bruər/ n cervecero (-ra)

brewery /'bruəri/ n cervecería, fábrica de cerveza, f

brewing /'bruɪŋ/ n elaboración de cerveza, f

briar /'braiər/ n (wild rose) rosal silvestre, m; (heather) brezo, m. **b. pipe,** pipa de brezo, f

bribable /'braibəbəl/ a sobornable

bribe /braib/ n soborno, cohecho, m, Lat. Am. coima, f, Mexico mordida, f. vt sobornar, cohechar. **to take bribes,** dejarse sobornar

briber /'braibər/ n cohechador (-ra)

bribery /'braibəri/ n soborno, m

brick /brɪk/ n ladrillo, m; (for children) piedra de construcción, f; bloque, m; Inf. buen chico, m, joya, f, a de ladrillo. vt enladrillar. **b.-floor,** ladrillado, m; **b.-kiln,** horno de ladrillo, m. **b.-maker,** ladrillero, m. **b.-yard,** ladrillar, m

bricklayer /'brɪk,leiər/ n albañil, m

bricklaying /'brɪk,leiɪŋ/ n albañilería, f

brickwork /'brɪk,wɜrk/ n masonería, f

bridal /'braidl/ a nupcial; de la boda; de la novia. **b. bed,** tálamo, m. **b. cake,** torta de la boda, f. **b. shop,** tienda para novias, f. **b. shower,** despedida de soltera, despedida de soltería, f. **b. song,** epitalamio, m. **b. veil,** velo de la novia, velo nupcial, m. **b. wreath,** corona de azahar, f

bride /braid/ n novia, desposada, f; (after marriage) recién casada, f

bridegroom /'braid,grum/ n novio, m; (after marriage) recién casado, m

bridesmaid /'braidz,meid/ n madrina de boda, f; niña encargada de sostener la cola de la novia, f

bridge /brɪdʒ/ n (engineering, Mus. Naut.) puente, m; lomo (de la nariz), m; (game) bridge, m, vt construir un puente (sobre), pontear; (obstacles) salvar; evitar; (fill in) ocupar, llenar. **auction b.,** bridge por subasta, m. **contract b.,** bridge por contrato, m. **suspension-b.,** puente colgante, m. **b. toll,** pontazgo, m

bridgehead /'brɪdʒ,hɛd/ n cabeza de puente, f

bridle /'braidl/ n brida, f; freno, m. vt embridar, enfrenar; Fig. reprimir. vi (of horses) levantar la cabeza; (of persons) erguirse; hacer un gesto despreciativo. **snaffle b.,** bridón, m. **b. path,** camino de herradura, m

brief /brif/ a breve, corto; conciso; lacónico, seco; rápido; fugaz, pasajero. n (papal) breve, m; Law. relación, f; escrito, m. vt (a barrister) instruir. **to hold a b. for,** defender, abogar por. **b.-case,** portapapeles, m; cartera (grande), f

briefly /'brifli/ adv brevemente; en pocas palabras; sucintamente; (tersely) secamente

brier /'braiər/ n rosal silvestre, m; zarza, f

brigade /brɪ'geid/ n Mil. brigada, f; cuerpo, m; asociación, f

brigadier /,brɪgə'dɪər/ n brigadier, m

brigand /'brɪgənd/ n bandolero, bandido, m

brigandage /'brɪgəndɪdʒ/ n bandolerismo, m

bright /brait/ a brillante, reluciente; vivo; cristalino; subido; claro; optimista; sagaz; inteligente; (quick-witted) agudo; ilustre; (smiling) risueño; (of future,

etc.) halagüeño. **to be as b. as a new pin,** estar como una ascua de oro. **b. blue,** azul subido, m. **b.-eyed,** con ojos vivos, con ojos chispeantes, ojialegre

brighten /'braitn/ vt hacer brillar; (polish) pulir; (make happy) alegrar; (improve) mejorar. vi (of the weather) aclarar, despejarse (el cielo); sentirse más feliz; mejorar

brightly /'braitli/ adv brillantemente; alegremente

brightness /'braitnɪs/ n brillo, m; claridad, f; esplendor, m; (of colors) brillantez, f; vivacidad, f; inteligencia, f; agudeza de ingenio, f

Bright's disease /braits/ n enfermedad de Bright, glomerulonefritis, f

brilliance /'brɪlyəns/ n fulgor, brillo, m, refulgencia, f; esplendor, m; lustre, m; talento, m; brillantez, gloria, f

brilliant /'brɪlyənt/ a brillante. n (gem) brillante, m. **to be b.,** (in conversation, etc.) brillar; (be clever) ser brillante

brilliantine /'brɪlyən,tin/ n brillantina, f

brim /brɪm/ n (of a glass, etc.) borde, m; (of a hat) ala, f; margen, m, orilla, f. **to be full to the b.,** estar lleno hasta los bordes; Fig. rebosar. **eyes brimming with tears,** ojos arrasados de lágrimas

brimful /'brɪm'fʊl/ a hasta el borde (or los bordes); Fig. rebosante

brimless /'brɪmlɪs/ a (of hats) sin ala

brimmed /brɪmd/ a (of hats) con ala

brimstone /'brɪm,stoun/ n azufre, m

brindled /'brɪndld/ a atigrado, abigarrado

brine /brain/ n salmuera, f; mar, m; Poet. lágrimas, f pl

bring /brɪŋ/ vt traer; llevar; transportar; (take a person or drive a vehicle) conducir; Fig. acarrear, traer; causar, ocasionar; producir; crear; (induce) persuadir; hacer (ver, etc.); (be worth) valer; (sell for) vender por; Law. entablar (un pleito, etc.): (before a judge) hacer comparecer (ante); (present) presentar; (attract) atraer; (place) poner. **to b. home,** llevar a casa; Fig. hacer ver, hacer sentir; demostrar; (a crime) probar contra. **to b. near,** acercar. **to b. about,** efectuar, poner por obra; causar, ocasionar; (achieve) lograr, conseguir. **to b. again,** traer otra vez, llevar de nuevo. **to b. around,** traer; llevar; (from a swoon) sacar de un desmayo; curar; persuadir; conciliar. **to b. away,** llevarse. **to b. back,** devolver; traer; (of memories) recordar. **to b. down,** llevar abajo, bajar; (of persons) hacer bajar; (humble) humillar; hacer caer; (of prices) hacer bajar; arruinar; destruir. **to b. down the house,** Theat. hacer venirse el teatro abajo. **to b. forth,** (give birth to) dar a luz; producir; causar; sacar a luz. **to b. forward,** hacer adelantarse; empujar hacia adelante; Fig. avanzar; (allege) alegar; Com. llevar a nueva cuenta; presentar, producir. **brought forward,** Com. suma y sigue. **to b. in,** (things) llevar adentro; (persons) hacer entrar; introducir; aparecer con, presentarse con; (meals) servir; producir; declarar; (a verdict) dictar (sentencia de), fallar. **to b. into being,** hacer en práctica; dar origen (a). **to b. off,** (a ship) poner a flote; (rescue) salvar, rescatar; (carry out) efectuar, poner en práctica; (achieve) conseguir, lograr. **B. me the glass off the table,** Tráeme el vaso que hay en la mesa. **to b. on,** causar, inducir; acarrear; iniciar. **He brought a book on to the stage,** Entró en escena llevando un libro (or con un libro). **to b. out,** sacar; poner afuera; (a person) hacer salir; publicar; (a play) poner en escena; sacar a luz; (an idea, jewels, etc.) sacar a relucir; revelar; demostrar; hacer aparecer; (a girl in society) poner de largo (a). **to b. over,** llevar al otro lado; hacer venir; traer; conducir; hacer cruzar; (convert) convertir. **to b. through,** hacer atravesar; llevar a través de; ayudar a salir (de un apuro); (an illness) curar de. **to b. to,** traer a; llevar a; (from a swoon) hacer volver en sí; Naut. ponerse a la capa. **He cannot b. himself to,** No puede persuadirse a. **to b. together,** reunir; (things) juntar, amontonar; reconciliar, poner en paz. **to b. under,** someter; sojuzgar; incluir. **to b. up,** llevar arriba, subir; (a person) hacer subir; hacer avanzar; (a price) hacer subir; ir (a); andar; (breed) criar; (educate) educar, criar; (in a discussion) hacer presente; vomitar. **to b. up the rear,** ir al fin (de); Mil. ir a la retaguardia. **well** (or **badly**) **brought up,** bien (o mal) educado. **to b. upon oneself,** buscarse, incurrir (en). **to b. up-to-date,** poner al día; refrescar; rejuvenecer

bringing /'brɪŋɪŋ/ n acción de llevar o traer, f; conducción, f; transporte, m. **b. forth,** producción, f. **b. in,** introducción, f. **b. out,** producción, f; publicación, f; (of a girl in society) puesta de largo, f. **b. under,** reducción, f; subyugación, f. **b. up,** educación, crianza, f

brink /brɪŋk/ n borde, margen, m; (of water) orilla, f; Fig. margen, m. **on the b.,** al margen; a la orilla. **to be on the b. of,** (doing something) estar para, estar a punto de

briquette /brɪ'kɛt/ n briqueta, f, aglomerado de carbón, m

brisk /brɪsk/ a activo; vivo; animado; rápido, acelerado; enérgico

brisket /'brɪskɪt/ n falda, f

briskly /'brɪskli/ adv vivamente; enérgicamente; aprisa

briskness /'brɪsknɪs/ n actividad, f; viveza, f; animación, f; rapidez, f; energía, f

brisling /'brɪzlɪŋ/ n sardina noruega

bristle /'brɪsəl/ n cerda, seda, f, vi erizarse

bristly /'brɪsli/ a erizado, cerdoso; espinoso; hirsuto

Bristol board /'brɪstḷ/ n cartulina, f

British /'brɪtɪʃ/ a británico. **the B.,** el pueblo británico; los ingleses

British Commonwealth, the la Mancomunidad Británica, f

Briton /'brɪtṇ/ n inglés (-esa). **ancient B.,** britano (-na)

Brittany /'brɪtṇi/ Bretaña, f

brittle /'brɪtḷ/ a frágil, quebradizo, deleznable, friable

brittleness /'brɪtḷnɪs/ n fragilidad, friabilidad, f

broach /broutʃ/ n Cul. espetón, asador, m. vt espitar (un barril); abrir; Fig. introducir

broad /brɔd/ a ancho; grande; (extensive) vasto, extenso; **a b. confession,** una confesión amplia; (full) pleno; (of accents) marcado; (of words) lato; (clear) claro; (of the mind) liberal, tolerante; (of humor, etc.) grosero; (general) general, comprensivo. **in b. daylight,** en pleno día. **b.-brimmed,** de ala ancha. **b.-faced,** cariancho. **b.-mindedness,** tolerancia, liberalidad, f. **to be b.-minded,** ser tolerante, ser liberal, tener manga ancha. **b.-shouldered,** ancho de espaldas

broadcast /'brɔd,kæst/ n Agr. siembra al vuelo, f; Radio. radiodifusión, radiotransmisión, emisión, f, a radiado. adv por todas partes; extensamente. vt Agr. sembrar a vuelo; Radio. radiodifundir, radiar, transmitir por radio; (news, etc.) diseminar

broadcaster /'brɔd,kæstər/ n (lecturer) conferenciante, mf; radiodifusor (-ra); (announcer) locutor (-ra)

broadcasting /'brɔd,kæstɪŋ/ n radiación, radiodifución, f; radio, f. **b.-station,** estación de radio, emisora, f. **b.-studio,** estudio de emisión, m

broaden /'brɔdṇ/ vt ampliar, ensanchar. vi ampliarse, ensancharse

broad-leaved /'brɔd,livd/ a frondoso

broadly /'brɔdli/ adv anchamente; con marcado acento dialectal; de una manera general

broadness /'brɔdnɪs/ n anchura, f; extensión, vastedad, f; tolerancia, f; liberalidad, f; grosería, f; (of accent) acento marcado, m

broadside /'brɔd,said/ n (of a ship) costado, m; (of guns) andanada, f; Fig. batería, f; Print. cara de un pliego, f. **to be b. on,** dar el costado

brocade /brou'keid/ n brocado m. **imitation b.,** brocatel, m

brocaded /brou'keidɪd/ a decorado con brocado; de brocado

broccoli /'brɒkəli/ n bróculi, brécol, f

brochure /brou'ʃʊr/ n folleto, m

brogue /broug/ n acento, m; acento irlandés, m; (shoe) zapato grueso, m

broil /brɔil/ vt emparrillar, asar. vi asarse

broke /brouk/ a quebrado; (penniless) Peru calato

broken /'broukən/ a roto; quebrado; (spiritless) abatido, desalentado; (infirm) agotado, debilitado; (ru-

ined) arruinado; (of ground) desigual, escabroso; (of a language) chapucero; (spoiled) estropeado; imperfecto; incompleto; (loose) suelto; (of a horse, etc.) domado; (of the weather) variable; (of sleep) interrumpido; (of the heart, of shoes, etc.) roto; (of the voice, sobs, sighs) entrecortado; (of the voice through old age, etc.) cascada; (incoherent) incoherente. **b.-down,** (tired) rendido, agotado; arruinado; (not working) estropeado. **b.-hearted,** roto el corazón, angustiado. **b.-winged,** aliquebrado. **I speak broken Spanish,** Hablo el español chapuceramente

brokenly /'broukənli/ adv (of the voice) con voz entrecortada; a ratos; interrumpidamente

brokenness /'broukənnɪs/ n interrupción, f; (of the ground) desigualdad, f; (of speech) imperfección, f

broker /'broukər/ n corredor, m; (stock) corredor de bolsa, m

brokerage /'broukərɪdʒ/ n corretaje, m

bromide /'broumaid/ n bromuro, m

bromine /'broumin/ n bromo, m

bronchi /'brɒŋki/ n pl bronquios, m pl

bronchitis /brɒŋ'kaitɪs/ n bronquitis, f

broncopneumonia /'brɒŋkounʊ'mounyə/ n bronconeumonía, f

Brontosaurus /,brɒntə'sɔrəs/ n brontosauro, m

bronze /brɒnz/ n bronce, m; objeto de bronce, m, a de bronce. vt broncear. **B. Age,** Edad de Bronce, f

brooch /broutʃ/ n broche, m; alfiler de pecho, m

brood /brud/ n (of birds) nidada, f; (of chickens) pollada, f; (other animals) cría, f; prole, f, vi empollar. **to b. over,** meditar sobre, rumiar; (of mountains, etc.) dominar

brook /brʊk/ n arroyo, riachuelo, m

broom /brum/ n escoba, f; Bot. retama, f; hiniesta, f. **common b.,** retama de escobas, f. **Spanish b.,** retama común, retama de olor, hiniesta, f. **b.-handle,** palo de escoba, m

broomstick /'brum,stɪk/ n palo de escoba, m

broth /brɔθ/ n caldo, m

brothel /'brɒθəl/ n burdel, lupanar, m, casa de trato, f

brother /'brʌðər/ n hermano, m; (colleague) colega, m; Inf. compañero, m. **foster-b.,** hermano de leche, m. **half-b.,** medio hermano, m. **step-b.,** hermanastro, m. **b.-in-law,** hermano político, cuñado, m. **b.-officer,** compañero de promoción, m

brotherhood /'brʌðər,hʊd/ n fraternidad, f; Eccl. cofradía, f; hermandad, f

brotherliness /'brʌðərlinɪs/ n fraternidad, f

brotherly /'brʌðərli/ a fraterno

brow /brau/ n frente, f; ceja, f; (of a hill) cresta, cumbre, f; (edge) borde, m. **to knit one's b.,** fruncir el ceño

browbeat /'brau,bit/ vt intimidar, amenazar

browbeating /'brau,bitɪŋ/ n intimidación, f

brown /braun/ a castaño; (gallicism often used of shoes, etc.) marrón; pardo; (of complexion, eyes, hair) moreno; (dark brown) bruno; (blackish) negruzco; (toasted) tostado; (burnt) quemado. n color moreno, m; color pardo, m; castaño, m; (from the sun) bronce, m. vt (toast) tostar; (a person) volver moreno, broncear; (meat) asar. vi tostarse; volverse moreno, broncearse; asarse. **b. bear,** oso pardo, m. **b. owl,** autillo, m. **b. paper,** papel de estraza, m. **b. sugar,** azúcar moreno (or quebrado), m

brownie /'brauni/ n duende benévolo, m

brownish /'braunɪʃ/ a morenucho; que tira a castaño o a bruno; parduzco; trigueño

brownness /'braunnɪs/ n color moreno, m

browse /brauz/ vi pacer; (through a publication) hojear (un libro)

browsing /'brauzɪŋ/ n apacentamiento, m; hojeo (de un libro), m; lectura, f, estudio, m

Bruges /'brudʒɪz/ Brujas, f

bruise /bruz/ n cardenal, m. Lat. Am. magullón, m; abolladura, f; (in metal) bollo, m; (on fruit) maca, f. vt acardenalar, magullar; abollar; (fruit) macar

bruising /'bruzɪŋ/ n magullamiento, m; (of metal) abolladura, f; (crushing) machacadura, f; (boxing) boxeo, pugilato, m

brunette /bru'nɛt/ n trigueña, morena, f

brunt /brʌnt/ n peso, m; golpe, m; choque, m; esfuerzo, *m*. **to bear the b.,** soportar el peso; sufrir el choque; *Inf.* pagar el pato

brush /brʌʃ/ *n* cepillo, *m*; (broom) escoba, *f*; (for whitewashing, etc.) brocha, *f*; (for painting) pincel, *m*; (of a fox) cola (de zorro), *f*; (undergrowth) breñal, matorral, *m*; (fight) escaramuza, *f*; (argument) altercación, *f*. **scrubbing-b.,** cepillo para fregar, *m*. **shoe-b.,** cepillo para limpiar los zapatos, *m*. **stroke of the b.,** brochada, *f*; pincelada, *f*. **whitewash-b.,** brochón, *m*. **b. maker** or **seller,** escobero (-ra); pincelero (-ra)

brush /brʌʃ/ *vt* cepillar; (sweep) barrer; frotar; (touch) rozar; (touch lightly) acariciar. **to b.** against, rozar, tocar. **to b. aside,** echar a un lado; *Fig.* no hacer caso de; ignorar. **to b. off,** sacudir(se); quitar(se); (sweep) barrer. **to b. up,** cepillar; (wool) cardar; (tidy) asear; (a subject) refrescar, repasar

brushing /ˈbrʌʃɪŋ/ *n* acepilladura, *f*; (sweeping) barredura, *f*; (touching) roce, rozamiento, *m*; (of hair) peinadura, *f*

brushwood /ˈbrʌʃ.wʊd/ *n* enjutos, *m pl*, chamarasca, *f*; matorral, *m*

brusque /brʌsk/ *a* brusco, seco

brusquely /ˈbrʌskli/ *adv* secamente

brusqueness /ˈbrʌsknɪs/ *n* brusquedad, *f*

Brussels /ˈbrʌsəlz/ *a* bruselense; de Bruselas. **B. lace,** encaje de Bruselas, *m*

Brussels sprouts /sprauts/ *n pl* bretones, *m pl*

brutal /ˈbrutḷ/ *a* bestial, brutal; salvaje, inhumano

brutality /bruˈtælɪti/ *n* brutalidad, bestialidad, *f*; barbaridad, ferocidad, *f*

brutalize /ˈbrutḷ.aiz/ *vt* embrutecer

brutally /ˈbrutḷi/ *adv* brutalmente

brute /brut/ *n* bruto, animal, *m*; salvaje, bárbaro, *m*. **b. force,** la fuerza bruta

brutish /ˈbrutɪʃ/ *a* bruto; sensual, bestial; grosero; salvaje; estúpido; ignorante. **to become b.,** embrutecerse

bubble /ˈbʌbəl/ *n* burbuja, *f*; borbollón, *m*, *vi* burbujear; borbollar, bullir, hervir

bubbling /ˈbʌbəlɪŋ/ *n* burbujeo, *m*; hervidero, *m*; (of brooks) murmullo, *m*, a burbujeante; hirviente; (of brooks) parlero; (of wine) espumoso, efervescente

bubonic /byuˈbɒnɪk/ *a* bubónico. **b. plague,** peste bubónica, *f*

buccaneer /ˌbʌkəˈnɪər/ *n* corsario, *m*; aventurero, *m*

Bucharest /ˈbukəˌrɛst/ Bucarest, *m*

buck /bʌk/ *n* *Zool.* gamo, *m*; (male) macho, *m*; (fop) galán, petimetre, *m*, *vi* (of a horse) caracolear; fanfarronear. **to pass the b.,** *Inf.* echarle a uno el muerto. **b.-rabbit,** conejo, *m*. **to b. up,** hacer de tripas corazón

bucket /ˈbʌkɪt/ *n* cubo, balde, *m*, cubeta, *f*

buckle /ˈbʌkəl/ *n* hebilla, *f*. *vt* enhebillar, abrochar con hebilla. *vi* doblarse. **b. to,** ponerse a hacer algo con ahinco

buckled /ˈbʌkəld/ *a* con hebillas

buckler /ˈbʌklər/ *n* broquel, *m*, rodela, tarjeta, *f*

buckram /ˈbʌkrəm/ *n* bocací, *m*

buckshot /ˈbʌkˌʃɒt/ *n* perdigón, *m*

buckskin /ˈbʌkˌskɪn/ *n* ante, *m*

buckwheat /ˈbʌkˌwit/ *n* alforfón, trigo sarraceno, *m*

bucolic /byuˈkɒlɪk/ *a* bucólico, pastoril

bud /bʌd/ *n* brote, *m*; botón, capullo, *m*; (of vines) bollón, *m*; (of vegetables) gema, *f*. *vi* brotar, germinar. *vt* injertar de escudete

Buddhism /ˈbudɪzəm/ *n* budismo, *m*

Buddhist /ˈbudɪst/ *n* budista, *mf*

budding /ˈbʌdɪŋ/ *n* brotadura, *f*; (of roses, etc) injerto de escudete, *m*; *Fig.* germen, *m*

budge /bʌdʒ/ *vi* moverse, menearse. *vt* mover

budget /ˈbʌdʒɪt/ *n* presupuesto, *m*. *vi* presuponer

Buenos Aires /ˈbweiˈnəs aiˀrɪz/ (of or from the province of) *a* and *n* bonaerense, *mf*

buff /bʌf/ *n* color de ante, *m*; piel de ante, *f*. **b.-colored,** anteado. **in the buff = naked, nude**

buffalo /ˈbʌfəˌlou/ *n* búfalo, *f*

buffer /ˈbʌfər/ *n* (railway) parachoques, *m*. **b. state,** estado tapón, *m*

buffet /bəˈfei/ *n* bofetón, *m*; bofetada, *f*; bar, *m*. *vt* abofetear; golpear; luchar con las olas

buffoon /bəˈfun/ *n* bufón, *m*

buffoonery /bəˈfunəri/ *n* bufonería, *f*

bug /bʌg/ *n* chinche, *f*. **bugs,** *Lat. Am.* bicherío, *m*

bugbear /ˈbʌgˌbeər/ *n* pesadilla, *f*

bugle /ˈbyugəl/ *n* corneta, trompeta, *f*; (bead) abalorio, *m*. **b. blast,** trompetazo, *m*

bugler /ˈbyuglər/ *n* trompetero, *m*

build /bɪld/ *vt* edificar; (engines, ships, organs, etc.) construir; (a nest and *Fig.*) hacer; (have built) hacer, edificar; crear; formar; fundar. *n* estructura, *f*; (of the body) hechura, *f*; talle, *m*. **to b. castles in Spain,** hacer castillos en el aire. **built-up area,** zona urbana, *f*. **to b. up,** construir, levantar; (block) tapar; (business, reputation) establecer, crear. **to b. upon,** *Fig.* contar con, confiar en; esperar de

builder /ˈbɪldər/ *n* constructor, *m*; maestro de obras, *m*; (laborer) albañil, *m*; creador (-ra), fundador (-ra); arquitecto, *m*

building /ˈbɪldɪŋ/ *n* edificación, *f*; construcción, *f*; edificio, *m*; fundación, *f*; creación, *f*. **b. contractor,** maestro de obras, *m*. **b. material,** material de construcción, *m*. **b. site,** solar, terreno, *m*. **b. timber,** madera de construcción, *f*

built-in /ˈbɪlt ˌɪn/ *a* empotrado. **b. closet,** armario empotrado, *m*

bulb /bʌlb/ *n* *Bot.* bulbo, *m*; (*Elec. Phys.*) bombilla, *f*; (of an oil lamp) cebolla, *f*

bulbous /ˈbʌlbəs/ *a* bulboso

Bulgarian /bʌlˈgeəriən/ *a* and *n* búlgaro (-ra)

bulge /bʌldʒ/ *n* bulto, *m*; hinchazón, *f*; protuberancia, *f*; *Mil.* bolsa (en el frente), *f*. *vi* hincharse; estar lleno (de)

bulging /ˈbʌldʒɪŋ/ *a* lleno (de); con bultos; hinchado (de)

bulimia /buˈlimiə/ *n* bulimia, *f*

bulk /bʌlk/ *n* volumen, tamaño, *m*; bulto, *m*; (larger part) grueso, *m*; mayor parte, *f*; (of people) mayoría, *f*; (of a ship) capacidad, *f*. **in b.,** *Com.* en bruto, en grueso. **to b. large,** tener mucha importancia

bulkhead /ˈbʌlkˌhed/ *n* *Naut.* mamparo, *m*

bulkiness /ˈbʌlkinɪs/ *n* abultamiento, *m*; volumen, tamaño, *m*

bulky /ˈbʌlki/ *a* voluminoso, grande, grueso

bull /bul/ *n* toro, *m*; *Astron.* Tauro, *m*; (of some animals) macho, *m*; (Stock Exchange) alcista, *mf*; (of the Pope) bula (del Papa), *f*. **a b. in a china shop,** un caballo loco en una cacharrería. **to fight bulls,** torear. **b.-calf,** ternero, *m*. **bull's eye,** blanco, *m*; acierto, *m*. **b. fight,** corrida de toros, *f*. **b. fighter's gala uniform,** traje de luces, *m*. **b.-ring,** plaza de toros, *f*

bulldog /ˈbulˌdɔg/ *n* perro dogo, perro de presa, *m*

bulldozer /ˈbulˌdouzər/ *n* (excavator) topadora, *f*

bullet /ˈbulɪt/ *n* bala, *f*. **spent b.,** bala fría, *f*. **stray b.,** bala perdida, *f*. **b.-proof,** a prueba de bala, blindado

bulletin /ˈbulɪtɪn/ *n* boletín, *m*

bulletin board *n* tablero de anuncios, tablero de avisos, tablón, *m*

bulletproof vest /ˈbulɪtˌpruf/ *n* chaleco blindado, *m*

bullfighter /ˈbulˌfaitər/ *n* torero, *m* (on foot), toreador, *m* (on horseback)

bullfinch /ˈbulˌfɪntʃ/ *n* pinzón real, *m*

bullion /ˈbulyən/ *n* *Com.* metálico, *m*; oro (or plata) en barras, *m*, *f*

bullock /ˈbulək/ *n* becerro, *m*; buey, *m*

bullpen /ˈbulˌpen/ *n* toril, *m* (bullfighting); calentador, *m* (baseball)

bully /ˈbuli/ *n* valentón, perdonavidas, gallito, *m*; rufián, *Argentina* compadre *m*. *vt* intimidar; tratar mal. **b. beef,** vaca en lata, *f*

bulrush /ˈbulˌrʌʃ/ *n* anea, *f*

bulwark /ˈbulwərk/ *n* baluarte, *m*; *Naut.* antepecho, *m*

bumblebee /ˈbʌmbəlˌbi/ *n* abejorro, *m*

bump /bʌmp/ *n* golpe, *m*; ruido, *m*; choque, *m*; (bruise) chichón, *m*, roncha, *f*; *Aer.* sacudida, *f*, meneo, *m*. *vt* (into, against) tropezar con; (along) saltar en. *vt* chocar (contra)

bumper /'bʌmpər/ n (of a car) parachoques, m. **a b. harvest,** una cosecha abundante

bumpkin /'bʌmpkɪn/ n patán, villano, m

bumptious /'bʌmpʃəs/ a fatuo, presuntuoso, presumido

bumpy /'bʌmpi/ n (of surface) desigual, escabroso; (of a vehicle) incómodo, con mala suspensión

bun /bʌn/ n buñuelo, bollo, m; (hair) moño, m

bunch /bʌntʃ/ n (of fruit) racimo, m; manojo, m; (of flowers) ramo, m, Lat. Am. also maceta f; (tuft) penacho, m; (gang) pandilla, f, vi arracimarse, agruparse

bundle /'bʌndl/ n atado, lío, m; (of papers) legajo, m; (of sticks) haz, m; (sheaf) fajo, m; (package) paquete, m; fardo, hatillo, m; (roll) rollo, m, vt atar, liar; envolver; empaquetar; (stuff) meter, introducir. **to b. in,** meter dentro (de). **to b. out,** despachar sin ceremonia, poner de patitas en la calle

bungalow /'bʌŋgə,lou/ n casa de un solo piso, f

bungle /'bʌŋgəl/ vt estropear; hacer mal. n equivocación, f, yerro, m; cosa (o obra) mal hecha, f

bungling /'bʌŋglɪŋ/ a chapucero, torpe

bunion /'bʌnyən/ n juanete (del pie), m

bunk /bʌŋk/ n litera, f, vi Inf. poner pies en polvorosa, pirarse

bunker /'bʌŋkər/ n Naut. pañol, m; (for coal) carbonera, f; (golf) hoya de arena, f

bunkum /'bʌŋkəm/ n patrañas, f pl

bunting /'bʌntɪŋ/ n gallardete, m

buoy /'bui/ n boya, baliza, f, vt boyar; abalizar; Fig. sostener. **light b.,** boya luminosa, f

buoyancy /'bɔiənsi/ n flotación, f; Fig. optimismo, m, alegría, f

buoyant /'bɔiənt/ a boyante; ligero

burden /'bɜrdn/ n carga, f, peso, m; (of a ship) tonelaje, m, capacidad, f; (of a song) estribillo, m; (gist) quintaesencia, f. vt cargar. **to be a b. on,** pesar sobre

burdensome /'bɜrdnsəm/ a pesado, oneroso, gravoso; abrumador

burdensomeness /'bɜrdnsəmnɪs/ n pesadez, f; agobio, m

bureau /'byʊrou/ n buró, secreter, m; escritorio, m; (office) dirección, oficina, f; departamento, m

bureaucracy /byʊ'rɒkrəsi/ n burocracia, f

bureaucrat /'byʊrə,kræt/ n burócrata, mf; Inf. mandarín, m

bureaucratic /,byʊrə'krætɪk/ a burocrático

burgher /'bɜrgər/ n ciudadano (-na), vecino (-na)

burglar /'bɜrglər/ n ladrón de casas, escalador, m. **cat b.,** gato, m. **b. alarm,** alarma contra ladrones, f. **b. insurance,** seguro contra robo, m

burglary /'bɜrgləri/ n robo nocturno de una casa, m

burgle /'bɜrgəl/ vi robar una casa de noche. vt robar

burgundy /'bɜrgəndi/ n vino de Borgoña, borgoña, m

burial /'beriəl/ n entierro, m. **b.-ground,** campo santo, cementerio, m. **b. service,** misa de difuntos, f. **b. society,** sociedad de entierros, f

burlap /'bɜrlæp/ n arpillera, f

burlesque /bər'lɛsk/ a burlesco. n parodia. f. vt parodiar

burliness /'bɜrlinɪs/ n corpulencia, f

burly /'bɜrli/ a corpulento, fornido

burn /bɜrn/ vt quemar; calcinar; (bricks) cocer; cauterizar; (the tongue) picar; (dry up) secar; (the skin by sun or wind) tostar. vi quemar; arder; Fig. abrasarse (en). **b. at the stake,** vt quemar en la hoguera. **to b. to ashes,** reducir a cenizas. **to b. away,** consumir(se). **to b. oneself,** quemarse. **to b. the midnight oil,** Chile cranearse. **to b. up,** quemar del todo, consumir. **to b. with,** Fig. abrasarse en

burn /bɜrn/ n quemadura, f; (stream) arroyo, m

burnable /'bɜrnəbəl/ a combustible

burner /'bɜrnər/ n quemador (-ra); mechero, m

burning /'bɜrnɪŋ/ n quema, f; incendio, m; fuego, m; (inflammation) inflamación, f; (pain) quemazón, f; abrasamiento, m. a en llamas; ardiente; intenso; (notorious) notorio, escandaloso; abrasador; palpitante. **b. question,** cuestión palpitante, f

burnish /'bɜrnɪʃ/ n bruñido, m; lustre, brillo, m, vt

bruñir; pulir, pulimentar, dar brillo a; (weapons) acicalar. vi tomar lustre

burnisher /'bɜrnɪʃər/ n bruñidor, acicalador, m

burnishing /'bɜrnɪʃɪŋ/ n bruñido, m; pulimento, m; (of weapons) acicalado, m

burr /bɜr/ n Bot. cáliz de flor con espinas, m; Mech. rebaba, f; sonido fuerte de la erre, m

burrow /'bɜrou/ n madriguera, f, vivar, m; (for rabbits) conejera, f. vt amadrigar; minar

bursar /'bɜrsər/ n tesorero, m; becario, m

burst /bɜrst/ n estallido, m, explosión, f; (in a pipe) avería, f, (fit) acceso, m; transporte, m; (effort) esfuerzo, m; (expanse) extensión, f, panorama, m. **b. of applause,** salva de aplausos, f

burst /bɜrst/ vi estallar; reventar; quebrarse; romperse; (overflow) desbordar; (of seams) nacerse; derramarse (por); (into laughter) romper a; (into tears) deshacerse en. vt quebrar; romper; hacer estallar. **to b. into,** irrumpir en; (exclamations, etc.) prorrumpir en. **to b. into tears,** romper a llorar, deshacerse en lágrimas. **to b. on the scene,** aparecer de pronto. **to b. open,** abrir con violencia; forzar

bursting /'bɜrstɪŋ/ n estallido, m; quebrantamiento, m; (overflowing) desbordamiento, m

bury /'beri/ vt enterrar, sepultar; sumergir; (hide) esconder, ocultar; (forget) echar tierra a

bus /bʌs/ n (regular city bus) autobús m (Colombia, Spain, Venezuela), camión m (Mexico), camioneta f (Guatemala), casadoro m (Costa Rica), chiva f (Colombia, Panama, informal), colectivo m (Argentina, Bolivia), flota f (Colombia, informal), góndola f (Chile), guagua f (Canary Islands, Cuba), micro m (Chile), ómnibus m (Peru), omnibús m (Uruguay); (interurban bus), aerobús m (Venezuela), autobús (Argentina, Chile, Spain, Uruguay), camión, camión de primera clase m (Mexico), interprovincial m (Peru), pullmán m (Mexico; (interurban jitney bus) colectivo m (Colombia); (minibus) micro m (Colombia, Peru), liebre (Chile, informal) **double-decker bus,** ómnibus de dos pisos, m. **to travel by bus,** ir en autobús. **bus station,** estación de autobuses, Mexico camionera, f

busby /'bʌzbi/ n birretina, gorra de húsar, f

bush /bʊʃ/ n arbusto, matojo, m; (undergrowth) maleza, f; tierra virgen, f; Mech. manguito, m

bushel /'bʊʃəl/ n medida de áridos, f, (In England 8 gallons or 36.37 liters)

bushiness /'bʊʃɪnɪs/ n espesura, f; densidad, f

bushy /'bʊʃi/ a lleno de arbustos; denso; espeso; grueso; (eyebrows, etc.) poblado

busily /'bɪzəli/ adv diligentemente, solícitamente; afanosamente, laboriosamente. **He was b. occupied in...,** Estaba muy ocupado en...

business /'bɪznɪs/ n ocupación, f; quehaceres, m pl; (matter) asunto, m, cosa, f; empleo, oficio, m; Com. negocio(s), m, pl.; casa comercial, f; (trade) comercio, m; (clients, connection) clientela, f; (right) derecho, m; Theat. juego escénico, m, pantomima, f. **He had no b. to do that,** No tenía derecho a hacer eso. **Mind your own b.!** ¡No te metas donde no te llaman! **on b.,** por negocios. **to be in b. for oneself,** tener negocios por su propia cuenta. **to mean b.,** hacer algo en serio; estar resuelto. **to send about his b.,** mandar a paseo (a). **to set up in b.,** establecer un negocio. **b. affairs,** negocios, m pl. **b. agent,** agente de negocios, m. **b. hours,** horas de trabajo, f pl. **b.-like,** formal, práctico, sistemático. **b. man,** hombre de negocios, negociante, m

business administration n administración de empresas, f

bust /bʌst/ n Art. busto, bulto, m; pecho, m. **b. bodice,** sostén, m

bustard /'bʌstərd/ n avutarda, f

bustle /'bʌsəl/ n actividad, animación, f; confusión, f; (of a dress) polizón, tontillo, m. vi menearse, darse prisa. vt dar prisa (a)

bustling /'bʌslɪŋ/ a activo; ocupado, atareado; animado; bullicioso, ruidoso

busy /'bɪzi/ a ocupado; atareado; activo, diligente; (of places) animado, bullicioso; (of streets) de gran circulación; (officious) entremetido. **to b. oneself,**

ocuparse (en, con); dedicarse (a), entregarse (a); (interfere) entremeterse (con). **to be b.,** estar ocupado; estar atareado, tener mucho que hacer. **b.-body,** bullebulle, *mf.* entremetido (-da), chismoso (-sa), *Argentina* hurguete *mf*

busyness /'bɪzɪnɪs/ *n* ocupación, *f;* laboriosidad, *f;* actividad, *f*

but /bʌt/ *conjunc prep adv* pero; sino; (only) solamente; (except) menos; excepto; (almost) casi; que no; si no; (that) que; (nevertheless) sin embargo, empero, no obstante; (without) sin, sin que; (of time recently passed) no más que, tan recientemente. *n* pero, *m.* **He cannot choose but go,** No puede hacer otra cosa que marcharse. **to do nothing but...,** hacer únicamente..., no hacer más que... **but for,** a no ser por. **but yesterday,** solamente ayer. **but then (or but yet),** pero

butcher /'bʊtʃər/ *n* carnicero, *m. vt* matar reses; hacer una carnicería en. **butcher's boy,** mozo del carnicero, *m.* **butcher's shop,** carnicería, *f*

butchery /'bʊtʃəri/ *n* carnicería, *f;* matanza, *f*

butler /'bʌtlər/ *n* mayordomo, *m.* **butler's pantry,** despensa, repostería, *f*

butt /bʌt/ *n* (cask) tonel, *m,* pipa, *f;* (for water) barril, *m;* (of a cigarette, etc.) colilla, *f;* (of fire-arms) culata, *f;* (handle) mango, cabo, *m;* (billiards) mocho, *m;* (earthwork) terrero, *m;* (*Fig.* object) objeto (de), *m;* (of bulls, etc.) topetada, *f; pl* **butts,** campo de tiro, *m;* (target) blanco, *m. vt* (toss) topar, acornear; (meet) tropezar (con). **to b. in,** *Inf.* entremeterse, meter baza; encajarse

butter /'bʌtər/ *n* mantequilla, *f, vt* untar con mantequilla. **b.-dish,** mantequera, *f.* **b.-fingers,** torpe, *m.* **b.-knife,** cuchillo para mantequilla, *m.* **b.-milk,** suero de mantequilla, *m.* **b.-print,** molde para mantequilla, *m.* **b.-sauce,** mantequilla fundida, *f*

buttercup /'bʌtər,kʌp/ *n* ranúnculo, botón de oro, *m*

butterfly /'bʌtər,flaɪ/ *n* mariposa, *f*

butterscotch /'bʌtər,skɒtʃ/ *n* dulce de azúcar y mantequilla, *m*

buttocks /'bʌtəks/ *n pl* nalgas, posaderas, *f pl*

button /'bʌtn/ *n* botón, *m; pl* **buttons,** botones, paje, *m. vt* abotonar, abrochar. *vi* abotonarse, abrocharse. **to press the b.,** apretar el botón. **b.-hook,** abotonador, *m*

buttonhole /'bʌtn,hoʊl/ *n* ojal, *m;* flor que se lleva en el ojal, *f. vt Sew.* hacer ojales; (embroidery) hacer el festón; *Inf.* importunar

buttoning /'bʌtnɪŋ/ *n* abrochamiento, *m*

buttress /'bʌtrɪs/ *n* estribo, macho, contrafuerte, *m; Fig.* apoyo, sostén, *m. vt* afianzar, estribar; *Fig.* apoyar, sostener. **flying-b.,** arbotante, *m*

buxom /'bʌksəm/ *a* (of a woman) fresca, frescachona

buxomness /'bʌksəmnɪs/ *n* frescura, *f*

buy /baɪ/ *vt* comprar; obtener; (achieve) lograr; (bribe) sobornar. **to buy on credit,** comprar al fiado. **to buy back,** comprar de nuevo; redimir; (ransom) rescatar. **to buy for,** (a price) comprar por; (purpose or destination) comprar para. **to buy in,** (at an auction) comprar por cuenta del dueño. **to buy off,** librarse de uno con dinero. **to buy out,** (of a business) comprar la parte de un socio. **to buy up,** comprar todo, acaparar

buyable /'baɪəbəl/ *a* comprable, que se puede comprar

buyer /'baɪər/ *n* comprador (-ra)

buying /'baɪɪŋ/ *n* compra, *f.* **b. back,** rescate, *m.* **b. up,** acaparamiento, *m*

buying power *n* capacidad de compra, *f,* valor adquisitivo, *m*

buzz /bʌz/ *n* zumbido, *m;* (whisper) susurro, murmullo, *m;* (of a bell) sonido (del timbre), *m, vi* zumbar; susurrar

buzzer /'bʌzər/ *n* zumbador, *m;* sirena, *f;* (bell) timbre, *m*

buzzing /'bʌzɪŋ/ *a* zumbador, que zumba, *n.* See **buzz**

by /baɪ/ *prep* por; de; en; a; con; (of place) cerca de, al lado de; (according to) según, de acuerdo con; (in front of, past) delante (de); (at the latest) antes de, al más tardar; (expressing agency) por; (by means of) mediante; (through, along) por; (upon) sobre; (for) para; (under) bajo. **He will be here by Wednesday,** Estará aquí para el miércoles; (not later than) Estará aquí antes del miércoles (or el miércoles a lo más tardar). **How did he come by it?** ¿Cómo llegó a su poder? **He will come by train,** Vendrá en tren. **I know her by sight,** La conozco de vista. **There are three children by the first marriage,** Hay tres niños del primer matrimonio. **He goes by the name of Pérez,** Se le conoce por (or bajo) el nombre de Pérez. **six feet by eight,** seis pies por ocho. **They called her by her name,** La llamaron por su nombre. **two by two,** dos por dos. **The picture was painted by Cézanne,** El cuadro fue pintado por Cézanne. **drop by drop,** gota a gota. **by a great deal,** con mucho. **by all means,** naturalmente; de todos modos; cueste lo que cueste. **by chance,** por ventura. **by day (night),** de día (noche). **by daylight,** a la luz del día. **by doing it,** con hacerlo. **by myself,** solo; sin ayuda. **"By Appointment"** «Cita Previa». **by chance or by mischance,** por ventura o por desdicha. **an hour away by car,** a una hora de automóvil. **music by Brahms,** música de Brahms. **pull by the hair,** tirar por el pelo. **take by the hand,** llevar de la mano

by /baɪ/ *adv* (near) cerca; (before) delante; al lado; a un lado; aparte; (of time) pasado. **to put by,** (keep) guardar; (throw away) desechar; (accumulate) acumular; (put out of the way) arrinconar. **to pass by,** pasar; pasar delante (de). **by and by,** luego, pronto; más tarde. **by now,** ya, antes de ahora. **by the way,** entre paréntesis, a propósito; de paso; al lado del camino. **by-election,** elección parcial, *f.* **by-law,** reglamento, *m.* **by-pass,** ruta de evitación, *f,* desvío, *m;* (*Mech. Elec.*) derivación, *f. vi* desviarse de; *Mil.* rebasar. **by-product,** derivado, *m; Chem.* producto derivado, *m; Fig.* consecuencia, *f;* resultado, *m*

bye /baɪ/ *n* (in cricket) meta, *f.* **by the bye,** a propósito, entre paréntesis

bye! /baɪ/ *interj. Argentina, Chile* ¡chao!

bygone /'baɪ,gɒn/ *a* pasado. *f.* **Let bygones be bygones,** Lo pasado pasado

byplay /'baɪ,pleɪ/ *n* pantomima, *f,* gestos, *m pl; Theat.* juego escénico, *m,* escena muda, *f*

bystander /'baɪ,stændər/ *n* espectador (-ra) *pl* **bystanders,** los circunstantes

bystreet /'baɪ,strit/ *n* callejuela, *f;* calle pobre, *f*

byte /baɪt/ *n* octeto, byte, *m*

byway /'baɪ,weɪ/ *n* camino desviado, *m; Fig.* senda indirecta, *f; pl* **byways,** andurriales, *m pl*

byword /'baɪ,wɜrd/ *n* proverbio, *m;* objeto de burla o escándalo, *m*

Byzantine Empire, the /'bɪzən,tin/ el Imperio Bizantino, *m*

Byzantium /bɪ'zænʃəm/ *n* Bizancio, *m*

C

c /si/ *n* (letter) c, *f; Mus.* do, *m*

cab /kæb/ *n* (horse-drawn) simón, *m;* (taxi) coche de alquiler, *m;* (of a locomotive) cabina del conductor, *f.* **cab-rank,** punto de coches, *m*

cabala /'kæbələ/ *n* cábala, *f*

cabaret /,kæbə'reɪ/ *n* cabaret, *m;* taberna, *f*

buying power *n* capacidad de compra, *f,* valor adquisitivo, *m*

cabbage /'kæbɪdʒ/ *n* col, berza, *f.* **red c.,** lombarda, *f.* **c. butterfly,** mariposa de col, *f*

cabin /'kæbɪn/ *n* cabaña, choza, *f; Naut.* camarote, *m;* (railway) garita, *f; Aer.* cabina, *f.* **c. boy,** grumete, *m,* galopín, mozo de cámara, *m.* **c. trunk,** baúl mundo, *m*

cabinet /'kæbənɪt/ *n* (piece of furniture) vitrina, *f;* colección, exposición, *f; Polit.* gabinete, *m;* (of a radio) cónsola, *f.* **c.-maker,** ebanista, *m.* **c.-making,**

ebanistería, f. **c. meeting,** consejo de ministros, m. **c. minister,** ministro, m
cable /'keibəl/ n amarra, maroma, f; cable, m; cable- (grama), m, vt cablegrafiar. **electric c.,** cable eléctrico, m. **overhead c.,** cable aéreo, m
cabman /'kæbmən/ n cochero de punto, simón, m
caboose /kə'bus/ n Naut. cocina, f
cache /kæʃ/ n escondite, escondrijo, m
cackle /'kækəl/ vi (of a hen) cacarear; (of a goose) graznar; (of humans) chacharear. n cacareo, m; graznido, m; cháchara, f
cacophony /kə'kɒfəni/ n cacofonía, f
cactus /'kæktəs/ n cacto, m
cad /kæd/ n sinvergüenza, m; tipo de cuidado, m
cadaverous /kə'dævərəs/ a cadavérico
caddish /'kædıʃ/ a mal educado, grosero
caddy /'kædi/ n (for tea) cajita para té, f; (golf) cadi, mf
cadence /'keidns/ n cadencia, f
cadet /kə'dɛt/ n hermano menor, m; Mil. cadete, m
cadge /kædʒ/ vi sablear. vt dar un sablazo (a)
cadger /'kædʒər/ n sablista, mf; mendigo, m; (loafer) golfo, m
Cadiz /'kadis/ Cádiz, m
cadmium /'kædmiəm/ n cadmio, m
café /kæ'fei/ n café, m
cafeteria /ˌkæfı'tıəriə/ n bar automático, m
caffeine /kæ'fin/ n cafeína, f
cage /keidʒ/ n (animal's, bird's) jaula, f; (of a lift) camarín, m; (for transporting miners) jaula, f. vt enjaular; encerrar
Cain /kein/, **to raise** armar lo de Dios es Cristo
Cairo /'kairou/ el Cairo, m
cajole /kə'dʒoul/ vt lisonjear; engatusar, embromar; instar
cajolery /kə'dʒouləri/ n zalamerías, f pl; marrullería, f, engatusamiento, m
cake /keik/ n Cul. pastel, m, torta, f; (of chocolate, etc.) pastilla, f. vt and vi cuajar; formar costra; (with mud) enlodar. **to sell like hot cakes,** venderse como pan bendito. **to take the c.,** llevarse la palma. **c. of soap,** pastilla de jabón, f. **c.-shop,** pastelería, f
calamine /'kælə,main/ n calamina, f
calamitous /kə'læmıtəs/ a calamitoso, desastroso
calamity /kə'læmıti/ n calamidad, f; desastre, m, Mexico also funestidad f
calcium /'kælsiəm/ n calcio, m
calculate /'kælkyə,leit/ vt calcular; adaptar. **to c. on,** contar con
calculated /'kælkyə,leitıd/ a premeditado. **to be c. to,** conducir a; ser a propósito para
calculatedly /'kælkyə,leitıdli/ adv calculadamente
calculating /'kælkyə,leitıŋ/ n cálculo, m, a calculador; (of persons) interesado; (shrewd) perspicaz; atento. **c. machine,** máquina de calcular, f, calculador, m
calculation /ˌkælkyə'leifən/ n cálculo, m; calculación, f
calculator /'kælkyə,leitər/ n calculador, m
calculus /'kælkyələs/ n cálculo, m
calendar /'kæləndər/ n calendario, m; almanaque, m; (university, etc.) programa, m
calender /'kæləndər/ n calandria, f, vt calandrar, cilindrar
calf /kæf/ n becerro (-rra), ternero (-ra); (young of other animals) hijuelo, m; (of the leg) pantorrilla, f; (leather) cuero de becerro, m; piel, f. **calf's-foot,** pie de ternera, m. **c. love,** amor de muchachos, m
caliber /'kæləbər/ n calibre, m
calibrate /'kælə,breit/ vt calibrar
calico /'kælı,kou/ n indiana, f; percal, m. **c.-printer,** fabricante de estampados, m
Californian /ˌkælə'fɔrnyən/ a californio. n californio (-ia)
caliph /'keilıf/ n califa, m
calk. /kɔk/ See **caulk**
call /kɔl/ n llamada, f; (shout) grito, m; (of a bird) canto, m; (signal) señal, f; (visit) visita, f; (by a ship) escala, f; Mil. toque, m; (need) necesidad, f; (of religion, etc.) vocación, f; invitación, f; (demand) demanda, f; exigencia, f. **They came at my c.,** Acu-

dieron a mi llamada. **c. to arms,** llamada, llamada a filas, f. **port of c.,** puerto de escala, m. **telephone c.,** llamada telefónica, f. **to pay a c.,** hacer una visita. **within c.,** al alcance de la voz. **c.-box,** cabina del teléfono, f. **c.-boy,** ayudante del traspunte, m
call /kɔl/ vi llamar; gritar, dar voces; (visit) visitar, hacer una visita (a); venir; (stop) parar; (of a ship) hacer escala. vt llamar; (a meeting, etc.) convocar; (awaken) despertar, llamar; (say) decir; (appoint) nombrar; (at cards) declarar. **She is called Dorothy,** Se llama Dorotea. **Madrid calling!** ¡Aquí Madrid! **Will you c. me at eight o'clock, please?** Haga el favor de despertarme (llamarme) a las ocho. **to c. at a port,** hacer escala en un puerto. **to c. a halt,** hacer alto. **to c. a strike,** declarar una huelga. **to c. names,** vituperar, injuriar. **to c. to account,** pedir cuentas (a). **to c. to arms,** tocar el arma; alarmar. **to c. to mind,** acordarse (de), recordar. **to c. to witness,** hacer testigo (de). **to c. back,** vt llamar; hacer volver; (unsay) desdecir. vi (return) volver; venir a buscar; ir a buscar. **I called back for the parcel,** Volví a buscar el paquete. **to c. for,** pedir a gritos; llamar; (demand) pedir; exigir; (collect a person) pasar a buscar; (parcels, etc.) ir (or venir) a recoger. **He called for help,** Pidió socorro a gritos. **to c. forth,** producir; provocar; inspirar; revelar; (bring together) reunir. **to c. in,** hacer entrar; invitar; (a specialist, etc.) llamar; (worn coin) retirar de la circulación; recoger. **to c. in question,** poner en duda. **to c. off,** (dogs, etc.) llamar; (a strike) cancelar; parar; terminar; (a person) disuadir (de); (postpone) aplazar; suspender; (refrain) desistir (de). **to c. on,** (visit) hacer una visita (a), ir a ver, visitar; (of a doctor) visitar; (a person to do something) recurrir (a); (for a speech) invitar a hablar; (invoke) invocar. **I shall now c. on Mr. Martínez,** Doy la palabra al señor Martínez. **to c. out,** vt hacer salir; provocar; inspirar; (challenge) desafiar, retar. vi gritar. **c. the roll,** pasar lista. **to c. over,** (names) pasar lista (de). **to c. up,** hacer subir; (to the army) llamar a filas (a); (telephone) llamar por teléfono (a); (memories) evocar. **to c. upon.** See **to c. on**
caller /'kɔlər/ n visita, f; (telephone) la persona que llama, f
calligraphist /kə'lıgrəfıst/ n calígrafo, m
calligraphy /kə'lıgrəfi/ n caligrafía, f
calling /'kɔlıŋ/ n llamamiento, m; (occupation) profesión, f; empleo, m; vocación, f; (of a meeting) convocación, f
callipers /'kælıpərz/ n pl compás de puntas, pie de rey, m
callisthenics /ˌkæləs'θɛnıks/ n pl calistenia, f
callosity /kə'lɒsıti/ n callosidad, f
callous /'kæləs/ a (of skin) calloso; Fig. insensible, duro, inhumano
callously /'kæləsli/ adv sin piedad
callousness /'kæləsnıs/ n falta de piedad, inhumanidad, dureza, f
callow /'kælou/ a (of birds) implume; (inexperienced) bisoño, inexperto, novato
callus /'kæləs/ n callo, m
calm /kam/ n calma, f; paz, tranquilidad, f; sosiego, m; serenidad, f. a (of the sea) en calma; tranquilo; sereno; sosegado. vt calmar; tranquilizar; apaciguar. vi calmarse; tranquilizarse; sosegarse. **dead c.,** calma chicha, f
calming /'kamıŋ/ a calmante
calmly /'kamli/ adv tranquilamente, sosegadamente; con calma
calmness /'kamnıs/ n calma, tranquilidad, f; ecuanimidad, serenidad, f
caloric /kə'lɔrık/ a calórico
calorie /'kæləri/ n caloría, f
calumniation /kəˌlʌmni'eifən/ n calumnia, f
calumniator /kə'lʌmni,eitər/ n calumniador (-ra)
calumny /'kæləmni/ n calumnia, f
calvary /'kælvəri/ n calvario, m
calve /kæv/ vi (of a cow, etc.) parir
Calvinism /'kælvə,nızəm/ n calvinismo, m
Calvinist /'kælvənıst/ n calvinista, mf
Calvinistic /ˌkælvə'nıstık/ a calvinista
calyx /'keilıks/ n cáliz, m

cam /kæm/ n Mech. leva, f.

camshaft, árbol de levas, m

camaraderie /ˌkɑmə'rɑdəri/ n compañerismo, m

camber /'kæmbər/ n comba(dura), f

cambric /'keimbrik/ n batista, f

camcorder /'kæmˌkɔrdər/ n videocámara, m

camel /'kæməl/ n camello (-lla). **c.-driver,** camellero, m. **camel's hair,** pelo de camello, m

camellia /kə'milyə/ n camelia, f

cameo /'kæmiˌou/ n camafeo, m

camera /'kæmərə/ n Photo. máquina fotográfica, f. **folding c.,** máquina fotográfica plegable, f. **in c.,** a puerta cerrada. **c. obscura,** cámara obscura, f

Cameroon /ˌkæmə'run/ el Camerón, los Camerones, m

camouflage /'kæməˌflɑʒ/ n camuflaje, m, vt camuflar

camp /kæmp/ n campamento, m; campo, m; Fig. vida de cuartel, f; (for school children, etc.) colonia, f; (party) partido, m. vi acampar; vivir en tiendas de campaña. **to break c.,** levantar el campo. **c.-bed,** cama de campaña, f. **c.-stool,** silla de campaña, f

campaign /kæm'pein/ n campaña, f. vi hacer una campaña

campaigner /kæm'peinər/ n veterano, m; propagandista, mf

campaigning /kæm'peiniŋ/ n campañas, f pl

camphor /'kæmfər/ n alcanfor, m

camphorated /'kæmfəˌreitid/ a alcanforado

campus /'kæmpəs/ n Puerto Rico recinto, m, ciudad universitaria, f, campus, m

can /kæn/ v auxil poder; (know how to) saber. **You can go to the village when you like,** Puedes ir al pueblo cuando quieras. **I cannot allow that,** No puedo permitir eso. **What can they mean?** ¿Qué quieren decir? **If only things could have been different!** ¡Si solamente las cosas hubiesen sido distintas! **Can you come to dinner on Saturday?** ¿Puede Vd. venir a cenar el sábado? **I can come later if you like,** Puedo (or Podría) venir más tarde si Vd. quiere. **Mary can** (knows how to) **play the piano,** María sabe tocar el piano **You can't eat your cake and have it too.** No hay rosa sin espinas

can /kæn/ n lata, f. vt conservar en latas. **can-opener,** abrelatas, m

Canada /'kænədə/ el Canadá, m

Canadian /kə'neidiən/ a canadiense. n canadiense, mf

canaille /kə'nai/ n gentualla, gentuza, f

canal /kə'næl/ n canal, m

canalization /ˌkænələ'zeiʃən/ n canalización, f

canalize /'kænlˌaiz/ vt canalizar

canary /kə'neəri/ n canario (-ia); color de canario, m; vino de Canarias, m. **roller c.,** canario de raza flauta, m. **c.-seed,** alpiste, m

Canary Islands, the las Islas Canarias, f

cancel /'kænsəl/ vt cancelar; revocar; borrar; anular. **to c. out,** Math. anular

cancellation /ˌkænsə'leiʃən/ n cancelación, f; revocación, f; anulación, f

cancer /'kænsər/ n Med. cáncer, m; Astron. Cáncer, m

cancerous /'kænsərəs/ a canceroso. **to become c.,** cancerarse

candelabrum /ˌkændl'ɑbrəm/ n candelabro, m

candescent /kæn'dɛsənt/ a candente

candid /'kændid/ a franco; sincero. **If I am to be c.,** Si he de decir la verdad, Si he de ser franco

candidate /'kændɪˌdeit/ n candidato (-ta); aspirante, m

candidature /'kændidəˌtʃʊr/ n candidatura, f

candidly /'kændidli/ adv francamente; sinceramente

candidness /'kændidnis/ n franqueza, f; sinceridad, f

candied /'kændid/ a (of peel, etc.) almibarado, garapiñado

candle /'kændl/ n vela, candela, f. **wax c.,** cirio, m. **You cannot hold a c. to him,** No llegas a la suela de su zapato, Ni llegas a sus pies, Ni le llegas a los pies. **The game is not worth the c.,** La cosa no vale la pena. **to burn the c. at both ends,** consumir la vida. **c.-grease,** sebo, m. **c.-light,** luz de las velas, f; luz artificial, f. **c.-maker,** candelero, m. **c.-power,** Elec. potencia luminosa, bujía, f. **c.-snuffer,** apagavelas, matacandelas, m

Candlemas /'kændlˌməs/ n candelaria, f

candlestick /'kændlˌstik/ n candelero, m, palmatoria, f; (processional) cirial, m

candor /'kændər/ n franqueza, f; sinceridad, f; candor, m

candy /'kændi/ n caramelo, bombón, m, vt garapiñar, almibarar

cane /kein/ n Bot. caña, f; (for chair seats, etc.) rejilla, f; (walking stick) bastón, m; (for punishment) vara, f. vt apalear, pegar. **sugar-c.,** caña de azúcar, f. **c.-break,** cañaveral, m. **c. chair,** sillón de mimbres, m. **c.-sugar,** azúcar de caña, m. **c.-syrup,** miel de caña, f

canine /'keinain/ a canino. n (tooth) diente canino, m

caning /'keiniŋ/ n paliza, f

canister /'kænəstər/ n bote, m, cajita, f

canker /'kæŋkər/ n úlcera, f; (in trees) cancro, m; Fig. cáncer, m, vt roer; Fig. corromper

canned /kænd/ a en lata

cannibal /'kænəbəl/ n caníbal, mf antropófago (-ga). a caníbal, antropófago

cannibalism /'kænəbəˌlizəm/ n canibalismo, m, antropofagía, f

canning /'kæniŋ/ n conservación en latas, f. **c. factory,** fábrica de conservas alimenticias, f

cannon /'kænən/ n (fire-arm) cañón, m; (billiards) carambola, f, vi carambolear. **to c. into,** chocar con. **c.-ball,** bala de cañón, f. **c.-shot,** cañonazo, m

cannonade /ˌkænə'neid/ n cañoneo, m

canny /'kæni/ a cuerdo, sagaz

canoe /kə'nu/ n canoa, f; piragua, f, vi ir en canoa

canoeist /kə'nuist/ n canoero (-ra)

canon /'kænən/ n (Eccl. Mus. Print.) canón, m; (dignitary) canónigo, m; (criterion) criterio, m. **c. law,** derecho canónico, m

canonical /kə'nɒnikəl/ a canónico

canonization /ˌkænənə'zeiʃən/ n canonización, f

canonize /'kænəˌnaiz/ vt canonizar

canopy /'kænəpi/ n dosel, toldo, m; palio, m; Fig. capa, bóveda, f. **the c. of heaven,** la capa (or bóveda) del cielo

cant /kænt/ vt inclinar; ladear. vi inclinarse; (be a hypocrite) camandulear. n (slope) inclinación, f, sesgo, desplomo, m; (hypocrisy) gazmoñería, f

Cantabrian /kæn'teibriən/ a cantábrico

cantankerous /kæn'tæŋkərəs/ a irritable, intratable, malhumorado, Argentina cabrero

cantankerousness /kæn'tæŋkərəsnis/ n mal humor, m, irritabilidad, f

cantata /kən'tɑtə/ n cantata, f

canteen /kæn'tin/ n cantina, f; (water bottle) cantimplora, f. **c. of cutlery,** juego de cubiertos, m

canter /'kæntər/ n medio galope, m, vi andar a galope corto

canticle /'kæntikəl/ n cántico, m

canto /'kæntou/ n canto, m

canton /'kæntn/ n (province and Herald.) cantón, m, vt (of soldiers) acantonar

cantonment /kæn'tɒnmənt/ n acantonamiento, cantón, m

cantor /'kæntər/ n Eccl. chantre, m

canvas /'kænvəs/ n lona, f; Art. lienzo, m; Naut. vela, f, paño, m. **under c.,** en tiendas de campaña; (of ships) a toda vela

canvass /'kænvəs/ vt (votes, etc.) solicitar

canvasser /'kænvəsər/ n solicitador (-ra) (de votos, etc.)

canvassing /'kænvəsiŋ/ n solicitación (de votos, etc.), f

canyon /'kænyən/ n cañón, m

canzonet /ˌkænzə'nɛt/ n chanzoneta, f

cap /kæp/ n gorra, f; (with a peak) montera, f; (type of military headgear with brim at front) quépis, m; (cardinal's) birrete, m; Educ. bonete, m; (pointed) caperuza, f; (woman's old-fashioned) cofia, f; (jester's) gorro de bufón, m; (on a bottle) cápsula, tapa, f. vt Educ. conferir el grado (a). **cap and bells,** gorro de bufón, m. **cap and gown,** birrete y muceta, toga y bonete. **to throw one's cap over the windmill,** echar la casa por la ventana. **to cap it all,** ser el colmo

capability /ˌkeipə'biliti/ n capacidad, f; aptitud, f

capable /'keipəbəl/ a capaz; competente; (of improvement) susceptible; (full of initiative) emprendedor

capably /'keipəbli/ adv competentemente

capacious /kə'peiʃəs/ a espacioso; grande; extenso

capaciousness /kə'peiʃəsnis/ n capacidad, f; amplitud, f

capacitate /kə'pæsi,teit/ vt capacitar

capacity /kə'pæsiti/ n capacidad, f; calidad, f; aptitud, f. **in one's c. as,** en calidad de. **seating c.,** número de asientos, m; (in aircraft) número de plazas, m

caparison /kə'pærəsən/ n caparazón, m

cape /keip/ n (cloak) capa, f; (short) capotillo, m, capeta, f; (fur) cuello, m; Geog. cabo, promontorio, m. **c. coat,** capote, m

Cape Horn /'keip 'hɔrn/ Cabo de Hornos, m

caper /'keipər/ vi (gambol) brincar, saltar; cabriolar, corcovear; (play) juguetear. n travesura, f; zapateta, f; cabriola, f; (whim) capricho, m; Bot. alcaparra, f. **to c. about,** dar saltos, brincar; juguetear

capillarity /,kæpə'læriti/ n capilaridad, f

capillary /'kæpə,leri/ a capilar. n vaso capilar, m

capital /'kæpitl/ a capital; mortal; de muerte; de vida; principal; (of letters) mayúscula; (very good) excelente; (of the capital city) Lat. Am. capitalino n (city) capital, f; (letter) (letra) mayúscula, f; Com. capital, m; Archit. capitel, chapitel, m. **floating c.,** capital fluctuante, m. **idle c.,** fondos inactivos, m pl. **c. punishment,** pena de muerte, pena capital, pena de la vida, f. **C.!** ¡Estupendo! ¡Excelente! **to make c. out of,** aprovecharse de, sacar ventaja de

capitalism /'kæpitl,izəm/ n capitalismo, m

capitalist /'kæpitlist/ n capitalista, mf

capitalistic /,kæpitl'istik/ a capitalista

capitalization /,kæpitlə'zeiʃən/ n capitalización, f

capitalize /'kæpitl,aiz/ vt capitalizar, (letters) escribir con mayúsculas

capitally /'kæpitli/ adv estupendamente

capitation /,kæpi'teiʃən/ n capitación, f

Capitol /'kæpitl/ n Capitolio, m. **C. Hill,** el Congreso de los EEUU

capitulate /kə'pitʃə,leit/ vi capitular

capitulation /kə,pitʃə'leiʃən/ n capitulación, f

capon /'keipon/ n capón, m

caprice /kə'pris/ n capricho, m

capricious /kə'priʃəs/ a caprichoso

capriciousness /kə'priʃəsnis/ n carácter inconstante, m; lo caprichoso

Capricorn /'kæpri,kɔrn/ n Capricornio, m

capsize /'kæpsaiz/ vt Naut. hacer zozobrar. vi Naut. zozobrar; volcarse

capsizing /'kæp,saiziŋ/ n Naut. zozobra, f; vuelco, m

capsule /'kæpsəl/ n (Bot. Med. Chem. Zool.) cápsula, f

captain /'kæptən/ n (Mil. Nav. Aer. and Sports.) capitán, m, vt capitanear. **to c. a team,** ser el capitán de un equipo. **group c.,** Aer. capitán de aviación, m

captaincy /'kæptənsi/ n capitanía, f

caption /'kæpʃən/ n (arrest) arresto, m; (heading) encabezamiento, título, pie, m; (cinema) subtítulo, m

captious /'kæpʃəs/ a capcioso, caviloso

captivate /'kæptə,veit/ vt cautivar, seducir

captivating /'kæptə,veitiŋ/ a encantador, seductor

captive /'kæptiv/ a cautivo, n cautivo (-va), prisionero (-ra), preso (-sa). **c. balloon,** globo cautivo, globo de observación, m

captivity /kæp'tiviti/ n cautiverio, m

captor /'kæptər/ n el, m, (f, la) que hace prisionero (-ra), captor (-ra)

capture /'kæptʃər/ n captura, f; presa, toma, f; Law. captura, f. vt prender, capturar; tomar

car /kar/ n (chariot) carro, m; (tram) tranvía, m; (motor) automóvil, m, Lat. Am. carro m; (on a train) coche vagón, m. **sleeping car,** coche camas, m. **car park,** parque de automóviles, m

carafe /kə'ræf/ n garrafa, f

caramel /'kærəməl/ n caramelo, m; azúcar quemado, m

carat /'kærət/ n quilate, m

caravan /'kærə,væn/ n caravana, f; coche de gitanos, m; coche habitación, m

caraway /'kærə,wei/ n alcaravea, f

carbarn /'kar,barn/ n encierro, m (Mexico), cochera, cochera de tranvías, f, cobertizo, cobertizo para tranvías, m

carbide /'karbaid/ n carburo, m

carbine /'karbin/ n carabina, f

carbohydrate /,karbou'haidreit/ n hidrato de carbono, m

carbolic /kar'bɒlik/ a carbólico. **c. acid,** ácido fénico, m

carbon /'karbən/ n carbono, m. **c. copy,** copia en papel carbón, f. **c. dioxide,** anhídrido carbónico, m. **c. monoxide,** óxido de carbono, m. **c. paper,** papel carbón, papel de calcar, m

carbonate /'karbə,neit/ n carbonato, m

carbonated /'karbə,neitid/ a (beverage) carbónico (formal), con gas (informal)

carbonic /kar'bɒnik/ a carbónico

carbonization /,karbənə'zeiʃən/ n carbonización, f

carbonize /'karbə,naiz/ vt carbonizar

carbuncle /'karbʌŋkəl/ n Med. carbunco, m; (stone) carbúnculo, m

carburetor /'karbə,reitər/ n carburador, m

carcass /'karkəs/ n (animal) res muerta, f; (corpse) cadáver, m; (body) cuerpo, m; (of a ship) casco, m

carcinoma /,karsə'noumə/ n carcinoma, m

card /kard/ n (playing) naipe, m; (pasteboard) cartulina, f; (visiting, postal, etc.) tarjeta, f; (index) ficha, f; (for wool, etc.) carda, f. vt (wool, etc.) cardar. **I still have a c. up my sleeve,** Me queda todavía un recurso. **to lay one's cards on the table,** poner las cartas boca arriba. **to play one's cards well,** Fig. jugar el lance. **admission c.,** billete de entrada, m. **post c.,** tarjeta postal, f. **visiting c.,** tarjeta de visita, f. **c.-case,** tarjetero, m. **c.-index,** fichero, m. vt poner en el fichero. **c.-sharper,** fullero, m. **c.-table,** mesa de juego, f. **c. trick,** juego de manos con cartas, m

cardboard /'kard,bɔrd/ n cartón, m, a de cartón

cardiac /'kardi,æk/ a cardíaco. **c. arrest,** infarto, m

cardigan /'kardigən/ n rebeca, chaqueta de punto, f

cardinal /'kardnl/ a cardinal. n cardenal, m. **c. number,** número cardinal, m. **c. points,** puntos cardinales, m pl

cardinalate /'kardnl,eit/ n cardenalato, m

carding /'kardiŋ/ n (of wool, etc.) cardadura, f. **c. machine,** carda mecánica, f

cardiogram /'kardiə,græm/ n cardiograma, m

care /kɛər/ n cuidado, m; atención, f; inquietud, ansia, f; (charge) cargo, m. vi preocuparse; tener interés; (suffer) sufrir. **I couldn't c. less,** No se me da un bledo. **I don't c.,** Me es igual; No me importa. **They don't c. for eggs,** No les gustan los huevos. **We don't c. what his opinion is,** Su opinión nos tiene sin cuidado (or no nos importa). **to c. for,** cuidar, mirar por; (love) querer (a); (like) gustar. **Take c.!** ¡Cuidado! ¡Ojo! **Take c. not to spoil it!** ¡Ten cuidado que no lo estropees! **Would you c. to...?** ¿Le gustaría...? ¿Tendría inconveniente en...? **c. of,** (on a letter, etc.) en casa de. **c.-free,** a libre de cuidados

careen /kə'rin/ vt carenar. vi dar a la banda

careening /kə'riniŋ/ n carena, f

career /kə'riər/ n carrera, f; curso, m. vi correr a carrera tendida; galopar

careful /'kɛərfəl/ a cuidadoso; atento (a); prudente. **Careful!, Be careful!** ¡Cuidado! **to be c.,** tener cuidado

carefully /'kɛərfəli/ adv con cuidado. **drive c.,** manejar con cuidado; cuidadosamente; prudentemente; atentamente

carefulness /'kɛərfəlnis/ n cuidado, m; atención, f; prudencia, f

careless /'kɛərlis/ a sin cuidado; indiferente (a); insensible (a); negligente; (of mistakes, etc.) de poco; negligencia

carelessly /'kɛərlisli/ adv indiferentemente; negligentemente; descuidadamente

carelessness /'kɛərlisnis/ n descuido, m; negligencia, f; descuido, m; omisión, f

caress /kə'rɛs/ n caricia, f, vt acariciar

caressing /kə'resɪŋ/ a acariciador
caretaker /'kɛər,teikər/ n (of museums, etc.) guardián (-ana); (of apartments, etc.) portero (-ra)
careworn /'kɛər,wɔrn/ a devorado de inquietud, ansioso
cargo /'kargou/ n cargamento, m, carga, f. **c.-boat,** barco de carga, m
Caribbean /,kærə'biən, kə'rɪbi-/ a caribe
Caribbean Sea, the el Mar Caribe, m
caricature /'kærɪkətʃər/ n caricatura, f, vt caricaturizar
caricaturist /'kærɪkə,tʃʊrɪst/ n caricaturista, mf
carious /'kɛəriəs/ a cariado. **to become c.,** cariarse
Carmelite /'karmə,lait/ a carmelita. n carmelita, mf
carmine /'karmɪn/ n carmín, m, a de carmín
carnage /'karnɪdʒ/ n carnicería, f
carnal /'karnl̩/ a carnal; sensual
carnality /kar'nælɪti/ n carnalidad, f
carnally /'karnl̩i/ adv carnalmente
carnation /kar'neiʃən/ n clavel, m
carnival /'karnəvəl/ n carnaval, m, a de carnaval, carnavalesco
carnivore /'karnə,vɔr/ n carnívoro, m
carnivorous /kar'nɪvərəs/ a carnívoro
carol /'kærəl/ n villancico, m; canto, m. vi cantar alegremente; (of birds) trinar, gorjear
Carolingian /,kærə'lɪndʒiən/ a carolingio
carotid /kə'rɒtɪd/ n carótida, f
carousal /kə'rauzəl/ n borrachera, f; holgorio, m, jarana, f
carouse /kə'rauz/ vi emborracharse. n borrachera, orgía, f
carp /karp/ n carpa, f, vi criticar, censurar
Carpathian Mountains, the /kar'peiθiən/ los Montes Carpotes, m
carpel /'karpəl/ n carpelo, m
carpenter /'karpəntər/ n carpintero, m, vi carpintear. **carpenter's bench,** banco de carpintero, m. **carpenter's shop,** carpintería, f
carpentry /'karpəntri/ n carpintería, f
carpet /'karpɪt/ n alfombra, f; Fig. tapete, m. vt cubrir de una alfombra, alfombrar; entapizar. **to be on the c.,** estar sobre el tapete. **c.-beater,** sacudidor de alfombras, m. **c. merchant,** alfombrista, m. **c. slippers,** zapatillas de fieltro, f pl. **c.-sweeper,** aspirador de polvo, m
carpeting /'karpɪtɪŋ/ n alfombrado, m
carping /'karpɪŋ/ a capcioso, criticón
carriage /'kærɪdʒ/ n (carrying) transporte, porte, m; (deportment) porte, continente, m, presencia, f; (vehicle) carruaje, m; carroza, f; coche, m; (railway) departamento, m; (chassis) chasis, bastidor, m; (of a typewriter, etc.) carro, m. **c. door,** portezuela, f. **c.-forward,** porte debido. **c.-free,** franco de porte. **c.-paid,** porte pagado
carrier /'kæriər/ n el, m, (f, la) que lleva; portador (-ra); Com. mensajero, m; (on a car, bicycle) portaequipajes, m; (of a disease) vector, m; (aircraft) portaviones, m. **c.-pigeon,** paloma mensajera, f
carrion /'kæriən/ n carroña, f. **c.-crow,** chova, f
carrot /'kærət/ n zanahoria, f
carry /'kæri/ vt llevar; transportar; traer; conducir; (Mil. of arms) portar; (have with one) tener consigo; (an enemy position) tomar, ganar; (a motion) aprobar; (oneself) portarse; (one's point, etc.) ganar; (in the mind) retener; (conviction) convencer; (involve) implicar; (influence) influir; (send) despachar, enviar; (contain) incluir, comprender. vi (of the voice, etc.) alcanzar, llegar. **The noise of the guns carried a long way,** El ruido de los cañones se oía desde muy lejos. **to fetch and c.,** traer y llevar. **to c. into effect,** poner en efecto. **to c. one's audience with one,** captar (or cautivar) su auditorio. **to c. oneself well,** tener buena presencia. **to c. on one's back,** llevar a cuestas. **to c. the day,** quedar victorioso, quedar señor del campo. **to c. weight,** Fig. ser de peso. **to c. along,** llevar; (drag) arrastrar; conducir; acarrear. **to c. away,** llevar; llevarse, ·llevar consigo; (kidnap) robar, secuestrar; (of emotions) dominar; (by enthusiasm) entusiasmar; (inspire) inspirar. **to c. forward,** llevar a cabo; avanzar; fomentar; (bookkeeping) pasar a cuenta nueva. **to c. off,** (things) llevarse; (per-

sons) llevar consigo (a); (abduct or steal) robar; (kill) matar; (a prize) ganar. **to c. (a thing) off well,** llevar la mejor parte, salir vencedor. **to c. on,** vt (a discussion, etc.) seguir, continuar. **c. on a conversation,** llevar una conversación; mantener; (a business, etc.) tener; dirigir. vi ir tirando; seguir trabajando. **to c. out,** realizar, llevar a cabo; hacer, ejecutar, efectuar; (a promise) cumplir. **to c. through,** llevar a cabo
carrying /'kæriɪŋ/ n transporte, m; (of a motion) adopción, f
cart /kart/ n carro, m. vt acarrear; llevar. **c.-horse,** caballo de tiro, m. **c.-load,** carretada, f, carro, m. **c.-wheel,** rueda de carro, f; (somersault) voltereta, f
cartage /'kartɪdʒ/ n carretaje, transporte, porte, m
carte blanche /'kart 'blantʃ/ n carta blanca, f
cartel /kar'tɛl/ n cartel, m
carter /'kartər/ n carretero, m
Cartesian /kar'tiʒən/ a cartesiano. n cartesiano (-na)
Carthage /'karθɪdʒ/ Cartago, m
Carthaginian /,karθə'dʒɪniən/ a cartaginés. n cartaginés (-esa)
car thief n Lat. Am. autero (-ra)
cartilage /'kartl̩ɪdʒ/ n cartílago, m
cartilaginous /,kartl̩'ædʒənəs/ a cartilaginoso
cartographer /kar'tɒgrəfər/ n cartógrafo, m
cartography /kar'tɒgrəfi/ n cartografía, f
cartomancy /'kartəmənsi/ n cartomancia, f
carton /'kartn̩/ n caja de cartón, f
cartoon /kar'tun/ n (design for tapestry, etc.) cartón, m; caricatura, f
cartoonist /kar'tunɪst/ n caricaturista, mf
cartridge /'kartrɪdʒ/ n cartucho, m. **blank c.,** cartucho sin bala, m. **c.-belt,** cartuchera, canana, f. **c.-case,** cápsula de proyectil, f
carve /karv/ vt tallar, labrar; grabar; cortar; (meat, etc.) trinchar; (a career, etc.) hacer, forjarse
carver /'karvər/ n tallador, m; (at table) trinchador, m; (implement) trinchante, m
carving /'karvɪŋ/ n talla, f; (design) tallado, m. **c.-knife,** trinchante, m
cascade /kæs'keid/ n cascada, catarata, f, salto de agua, m; Fig. chorro, m. vi chorrear
case /keis/ n caso, m; Law. proceso, m, causa, f; Gram. caso, m; Med. caso, m; enfermo (-ma); (box) caja, f; (for scissors, etc.) vaina, f; (for a cushion, etc.) funda, f; (for jewels, manicure implements, etc.) estuche, m; (of a piano, watch and Print.) caja, f; (for documents) carpeta, f; (glass) vitrina, f; (for a book) sobrecubierta, f; (dressing) neceser, m. vt cubrir; forrar; resguardar. **packing-c.,** caja de embalaje, f. **c. of goods,** caja de mercancías, f; bulto, m. **in any c.,** en todo caso; venga lo que venga. **in c.,** por si acaso. **in c. of emergency,** en caso de urgencia. **in such a c.,** en tal caso. **in the c. of,** en el caso de; respecto a. **lower c.,** Print. caja baja, f. **upper c.,** Print. caja alta, f. **c.-hardened,** (of iron) templado, m; Fig. endurecido, indiferente
case closed! ¡asunto concluido!
casement window /'keismənt/ n ventana, f
cash /kæʃ/ n efectivo, metálico, m; dinero contante, m; Inf. dinero, m; Com. caja, f. vt cobrar; pagar, hacer efectivo. **hard or ready c.,** dinero contante, m. **to pay c.,** pagar al contado. **c. on delivery,** (C.O.D.) contra reembolso. **c. on hand,** efectivo en caja, m. **c.-book,** libro de caja, m. **c.-box,** caja, f. **c.-desk,** caja, f. **c. down,** pago al contado, m. **c. prize,** premio en metálico, m. **c.-register,** caja registradora, f. **petty c.,** caja chica, f
cashew /'kæʃu/ n anacardo, m
cashier /kæ'ʃiər/ n cajero (-ra). vt degradar. **cashier's desk,** caja, f
cash machine n cajera automática, f
cashmere /'kæʒmɪər/ n cachemira, f
casino /kə'sinou/ n casino, m
cask /kæsk/ n pipa, barrica, f, tonel, m; cuba, f
casket /'kæskɪt/ n cajita, arquilla, f, cofrecito, m
Caspian Sea, the /'kæspiən/ el (Mar) Caspio, m
casserole /'kæsə,roul/ n cacerola, f
cassock /'kæsək/ n sotana, f
cast /kæst/ vt arrojar, tirar; (in fishing, the anchor,

dice, darts, lots, a net, glances, blame, etc.) echar; (skin) mudar; (lose) perder; (a shadow, etc.) proyectar; (a vote) dar; (mold) vaciar; (accounts) echar, calcular; (a horoscope) hacer; (the parts in a play) repartir; (an actor for a part) dar el papel de; (metals) colar, fundir. **the shadow c. by the wall,** la sombra proyectada por el muro. **to c. anchor,** echar anclas, anclar. **to c. in one's lot with,** compartir la suerte de. **to c. something in a person's teeth,** echar en cara (a). **to c. lots,** echar suertes. **to c. about,** meditar, considerar; imaginar; (devise) inventar. **to c. aside,** desechar; poner a un lado; abandonar. **to c. away,** tirar lejos; desechar; (money) derrochar, malgastar. **to be c. away,** *Naut.* naufragar. **to c. down,** (overthrow) derribar, destruir; (eyes) bajar; (depress) desanimar, deprimir; (humiliate) humillar. **to be c. down,** estar deprimido. **c. iron,** *n* hierro colado, hierro fundido, *m*. **c.-iron,** *a* de hierro colado; *Fig.* inflexible. **to c. off,** quitarse; desechar; (a wife) repudiar; (desert) abandonar; (free oneself) librarse (de). **c.-off,** *n* desecho, *m*. **c.-off clothing,** ropa de desecho, *f*. **to c. out,** echar fuera; hacer salir; excluir. **to c. up,** echar; vomitar; (a sum) sumar; (something at a person) reprochar

cast /kæst/ *n* (of dice, fishing-line) echada, *f*; (of a net) redada, *f*; (worm) molde, *m*; (of a play) reparto, Lat. Am. elenco, *m*; (of mind) inclinación, *f*; (in the eye) defecto en la mirada, *m*; (of color) matiz, tinte, *m*. **c. of features,** facciones, *f pl,* fisonomía, *f*. **plaster c.,** vaciado, *m*

castanets /ˌkæstəˈnɛts/ *n pl* castañuelas, *f pl*

castaway /ˈkæstəˌwei/ *n* náufrago (-ga), *Fig.* perdido (-da)

caste /kæst/ *n* casta, *f*; clase social, *f*. **to lose c.,** desprestigiarse

castigate /ˈkæstɪˌgeit/ *vt* castigar

Castile /kæˈstil/ Castilla, *f*

Castilian /kæˈstɪlyən/ *a* castellano. *n* castellano (-na); (language) castellano, *m*

casting /ˈkæstɪŋ/ *n* lanzamiento, *m*; (of metals) fundición, colada, *f*; obra de fundición, *f*. **c.-net,** esparavel, *m*. **c.-vote,** voto de calidad, *m*

castle /ˈkæsəl/ *n* castillo, *m*; (in chess) torre, *f*, roque, *m*. **to build castles in Spain,** hacer castillos en el aire

castor /ˈkæstər/ *n* Zool. castor, *m*; (for sugar) azucarero, *m*; (cruet) convoy, *m*; (on chairs, etc.) ruedecilla, roldana, *f*. **c.-oil,** aceite de ricino, *m*. **c.-sugar,** azúcar en polvo, *m*

castrate /ˈkæstreit/ *vt* castrar, capar

castration /kæsˈtreiʃən/ *n* castración, capadura, *f*

casual /ˈkæʒuəl/ *a* fortuito, accidental; ligero, superficial; *Inf.* despreocupado. **c. clothing,** ropa de sport, *f*. **c. worker,** jornalero, *m*

casually /ˈkæʒuəli/ *adv* por casualidad; de paso; negligentemente

casualness /ˈkæʒuəlnɪs/ *n Inf.* negligencia, despreocupación, *f*

casualty /ˈkæʒuəlti/ *n* víctima, *f*; herido, *m*; *Mil.* baja, *f*; *pl* **casualties,** heridos, *m pl*; muertos, *m pl*. **c.-list,** lista de víctimas, *f*; *Mil.* lista de bajas, *f*

casuist /ˈkæʒuɪst/ *n* casuista, *mf*

casuistry /ˈkæʒuəstri/ *n* casuística, *f*

cat /kæt/ *n* gato (-ta). **She is an old cat,** Ella es una vieja chismosa. **to be like a cat on hot bricks,** estar como en brasas. **to let the cat out of the bag,** tirar de la manta. **to lead a cat-and-dog life,** vivir como perros y gatos. **cat's-cradle,** (game) cunas, *f pl.* **cat's paw,** (person) hombre de paja, *m*; *Naut.* bocanada de viento, *f*. **cat o' nine tails,** gato de siete colas, *m*, penca, *f*. **catwhisker,** Radio. detector, *m*

cataclysm /ˈkætəˌklɪzəm/ *n* cataclismo, *m*

catacombs /ˈkætəˌkoumz/ *n pl* catacumbas, *f pl*

catafalque /ˈkætəˌfɔk/ *n* catafalco, *m*

Catalan /ˈkætlˌæn/ *a* catalán (-ana). *n* catalán (language) catalán, *m*

catalepsy /ˈkætlˌɛpsi/ *n* catalepsia, *f*

catalogue /ˈkætlˌɔg/ *n* catálogo, *m*, *vt* catalogar

catalysis /kəˈtæləsɪs/ *n* catálisis, *f*

cat-and-mouse /ˈkæt ænd ˈmaus/ *n* el juego de ratón, *m*

catapult /ˈkætəˌpʌlt/ *n* Mil. catapulta, *f*; *Aer.* catapulta (para lanzar aviones), *f*; (toy) tirador de go-

mas, *m*. *vt* tirar con una catapulta (or con un tirador de gomas); (throw) lanzar

cataract /ˈkætəˌrækt/ *n* catarata, cascada, *f*, salto de agua, *m*; (of the eye) catarata, *f*

catarrh /kəˈtɑr/ *n* catarro, *m*; constipado, resfriado, *m*

catastrophe /kəˈtæstrəfi/ *n* catástrofe, *f*, desastre, *m*, *Mexico also* funestidad; (in drama) desenlace, *m*

catastrophic /ˌkætəˈstrɒfɪk/ *a* catastrófico

catcall /ˈkætˌkɔl/ *n* silbido, *m*

catch /kætʃ/ *vt* coger; agarrar, asir; (capture) prender, haber; (a disease) contraer; (habit) tomar; (on a hook, etc.) enganchar; (surprise) sorprender; (understand) comprender; (hear) oír; (with blows, etc.) dar. *vi* (of a lock) encajarse; (become entangled) engancharse; (of a fire) encenderse. **to c. a glimpse of,** ver por un instante (a); alcanzar a ver, entrever. **to c. at,** asir; agarrarse (a); echar mano de; procurar asir; alargar la mano hacia; (an idea, etc.) adoptar con entusiasmo. **to c. on,** (be popular) tener éxito; (understand) comprender. **to c. out,** coger en el acto; coger en un error; *Sports.* coger. **to c. up,** coger; interrumpir. **to c. up with,** (a person) alcanzar; (news) ponerse al corriente de

catch /kætʃ/ *n* presa, *f*; (of fish) redada, pesca, *f*; (of a window, etc.) cerradura, *f*; (latch) pestillo, *m*; (trick) trampa, *f*; *Mus.* canon, *m*. **a good c.,** (matrimonial) un buen partido. **to have a c. in one's voice,** hablar con voz entrecortada. **c.-as-c.-can,** lucha libre, *f*

catching /ˈkætʃɪŋ/ *a* contagioso

catchment /ˈkætʃmənt/ *n* desagüe, *m*

catchword /ˈkætʃˌwɜrd/ *n* reclamo, *m*; (theater cue) pie, apunte, *m*; (slogan) mote, *m*

catchy /ˈkætʃi/ *a* atractivo. **It's a c. tune,** Es una canción que se pega

catechism /ˈkætɪˌkɪzəm/ *n* catequismo, *m*

categorical /ˌkætɪˈgɒrɪkəl/ *a* categórico

category /ˈkætɪˌgɒri/ *n* categoría, *f*

cater /ˈkeitər/ *vi* proveer, abastecer. **to c. to all tastes,** atender a todos los gustos

caterer /ˈkeitərər/ *n* despensero (-ra)

catering /ˈkeitərɪŋ/ *n* provisión, *f*

caterpillar /ˈkætəˌpɪlər/ *n* oruga, *Argentina* isoca *f*. **c. tractor,** tractor de orugas, *m*

caterwaul /ˈkætərˌwɔl/ *vi* (of a cat) maullar

caterwauler /ˈkætərˌwɔlər/ *n* (violinist, etc.) rascatripas, *m*

caterwauling /ˈkætərˌwɔlɪŋ/ *n* maullidos, *m pl*; música ratonera, *f*

catfish /ˈkætˌfɪʃ/ *n* siluro, *m*

catgut /ˈkætˌgʌt/ *n Surg.* catgut, *m*; *Mus.* cuerda, *f*

catharsis /kəˈθɑrsɪs/ *n Med.* purga, *f*; *Fig.* catarsis, *f*

cathedral /kəˈθidrəl/ *n* catedral, *f*

Catherine wheel /ˈkæθrɪn/ *n Archit.* rosa, *f*; (firework) rueda de Santa Catalina, *f*; (somersault) tumba, *f*

catheter /ˈkæθɪtər/ *n* catéter, *m*

cathode /ˈkæθoud/ *n* cátodo, *m*. **c. rays,** rayos catódicos, *m pl.* **c. ray tube,** tubo de rayos catódicos, *m*

cathodic /kæˈθɒdɪk/ *a* catódico

catholic /ˈkæθəlɪk/ *a* católico

Catholicism /kəˈθɒlɪˌsɪzəm/ *n* catolicismo, *m*

catlike /ˈkætˌlaik/ *a* de gato; gatuno

cattle /ˈkætl/ *n* ganado vacuno, *m*; ganado, *m*; animales, *m pl.* **c.-dealer,** ganadero, *m*. **c.-lifter,** hurtador de ganado, *m*. **c.-pen,** corral, *m*. **c.-raiser,** criador de ganado, *m*. **c.-raising,** ganadería, *f*. **c.-ranch,** hacienda de ganado, estancia, *Argentina* cabaña *f*. **c.-show,** exposición de ganado, *f*. **c.-truck,** vagón de ferrocarril para ganado, *m*

cattle rustler /ˈrʌslər/ *n* abigeo, cuatrero, ladrón de ganado, *m*

cattle rustling *n* abigeato, *m*

catty /ˈkæti/ *a* gatuno; malicioso, chismoso

Caucasian /kɔˈkeiʒən/ *a* *n* caucáseo (-ea)

cauldron /ˈkɔldrən/ *n* caldera, *f*

cauliflower /ˈkɔliˌflauər/ *n* coliflor, *f*

caulk /kɔk/ *vt* calafatear

caulker /ˈkɔkər/ *n* calafate, *m*

causality /kɔˈzælɪti/ *n* causalidad, *f*

causative /ˈkɔzətɪv/ *a* causante

cause /kɔz/ *n* causa, *f*; (reason) motivo, *m*, razón, *f*; (lawsuit) proceso, *m*. *vt* causar; ocasionar, suscitar; (oblige) hacer, obligar (a). **final c.,** *Philos.* causa final, *f*. **to have good c. for,** tener buen motivo para
causeway /'kɔz,wei/ *n* dique, *m*; acera, *f*
caustic /'kɔstɪk/ *a* cáustico; *Fig.* mordaz. **c. soda,** sosa cáustica, *f*
caustically /'kɔstɪkli/ *adv* mordazmente, con sarcasmo
causticity /kɔ'stɪsɪti/ *n* causticidad, *f*
cauterization /,kɔtərə'zeiʃən/ *n* cauterización, *f*
cauterize /'kɔtə,raiz/ *vt* cauterizar
cautery /'kɔtəri/ *n* cauterio, *m*
caution /'kɔʃən/ *n* prudencia, cautela, *f*; (warning) amonestación, *f*; aviso, *m*. *vt* amonestar. **to proceed with c.,** ir con prudencia; ir despacio
"Caution" /'kɔʃən/ (road sign) «Atención»
cautionary /'kɔʃə,nɛri/ *a* (of tales) de escarmiento
cautious /'kɔʃəs/ *a* cauteloso, cauto; prudente, circunspecto
cautiously /'kɔʃəsli/ *adv* cautamente; prudentemente. **to go c.,** *Inf.* ir con pies de plomo
cavalcade /,kævəl'keid/ *n* cabalgata, *f*
cavalier /,kævə'lɪər/ *n* jinete, *m*; caballero, *m*; galán, *m*, *a* arrogante, altanero
cavalry /'kævəlri/ *n* caballería, *f*. **c.-man,** jinete, soldado de a caballo, *m*
cave /keiv/ *n* cueva, caverna, *f*. **to c. in,** hundirse; desplomarse; *Fig.* rendirse. **c.-man,** hombre cavernícola, *m*
caveat /'kævi,ɑt/ *n* aviso, *m;* advertencia, *f*
cavern /'kævərn/ *n* caverna, *f*
cavernous /'kævərnəs/ *a* cavernoso
caviar /'kævi,ɑr/ *n* caviar, *m*
cavil /'kævəl/ *vi* cavilar
cavity /'kævɪti/ *n* cavidad, *f*; hoyo, *m*; hueco, *m*; (in a lung) caverna, *f*; (in teeth) caries, *f*
cavy /'keivi/ *n* cobayo (-ya), conejillo (-lla) de las Indias
caw /kɔ/ *n* graznido, *m*, *vi* graznar, grajear
cawing /'kɔɪŋ/ *n* graznidos, *m pl*
cayenne /kai'ɛn/ *n* pimentón, *m*
cease /sis/ *vi* cesar (de), dejar de; parar. *vt* cesar de; parar de; (payments, etc.) suspender; discontinuar. **c. -fire,** tregua, *f*. **C. fire!** ¡Cesar fuego!
ceaseless /'sislɪs/ *a* incesante,continuo, sin cesar
ceaselessly /'sislɪsli/ *adv* sin cesar, incesantemente
ceasing /'sisɪŋ/ *n* cesación, *f*. **without c.,** sin cesar
cedar /'sidər/ *n* (tree and wood) cedro, *m*. **red c.,** cedro dulce, *m*
cede /sid/ *vt* ceder, traspasar; (admit) conceder
cedilla /sɪ'dɪlə/ *n* zedilla, *f*
ceiling /'silɪŋ/ *n* techo, *m*; *Aer.* altura máxima, *f*. **c. price,** máximo precio, *m*
celebrant /'sɛləbrənt/ *n* *Eccl.* celebrante, *m*
celebrate /'sɛlə,breit/ *vt* celebrar; solemnizar. **Their marriage was celebrated in the autumn,** Su casamiento se solemnizó en el otoño
celebrated /'sɛlə,breitɪd/ *a* célebre, famoso
celebration /,sɛlə'breiʃən/ *n* celebración, *f*; festividad, *f*
celebrity /sə'lɛbrɪti/ *n* celebridad, *f*
celerity /sə'lɛrɪti/ *n* celeridad, *f*
celery /'sɛləri/ *n* apio, *m*
celestial /sə'lɛstʃəl/ *a* celestial
celibacy /'sɛləbəsi/ *n* celibato, *m*
celibate /'sɛləbɪt/ *a* célibe. *n* célibe, *mf*
cell /sɛl/ *n* celda, *f*; (*Bot. Biol.*) célula, *f*; (bees, wasps) celdilla, *f*; *Elec.* elemento, *m*
cellar /'sɛlər/ *n* sótano, *m*; (wine) bodega, *f*
cellist /'tʃɛlɪst/ *n* violoncelista, *mf*
cello /'tʃɛlou/ *n* violoncelo, *m*
cellophane /'sɛlə,fein/ *n* (papel) celofán, *m*
cellular /'sɛlyələr/ *a* celular, celuloso
cellular phone *n* teléfono celular, *m*
cellule /'sɛlyul/ *n* célula, *f*
celluloid /'sɛlyə,lɔid/ *n* celuloide, *f*
cellulose /'sɛlyə,lous/ *n* celulosa, *f*
Celt /kɛlt, sɛlt/ *n* celta, *mf*
Celtic /'kɛltɪk, 'sɛl-/ *a* celta

cement /sɪ'mɛnt/ *n* cemento, *m*, *vt* cementar
cemetery /'sɛmɪ,tɛri/ *n* cementerio, *m*
cenotaph /'sɛnə,tæf/ *n* cenotafio, *m*
cenote /sə'nouti/ *n* cenote *m*
cense /sɛns/ *vt* incensar
censer /'sɛnsər/ *n* incensario, *m*, botafumeiro, *m*
censor /'sɛnsər/ *n* censor, *m*, *vt* censurar. **banned by the c.,** prohibido por la censura
censorious /sɛn'sɔriəs/ *a* severo; crítico
censoriousness /sɛn'sɔriəsnɪs/ *n* severidad, propensión a censurar, *f*
censorship /'sɛnsər,ʃɪp/ *n* censura, *f*
censure /'sɛnʃər/ *vt* censurar, culpar, criticar
census /'sɛnsəs/ *n* censo, *m*. **to take the c.,** formar el censo, levantar el censo, tomar el censo, empadronar
census-taking /'sɛnsəs ,teikɪŋ/ *n* la formación del censo, la formación de los censos, *f*, el levantamiento del censo, el levantamiento de los censos, *m*
cent /sɛnt/ *n* (coin) centavo, *Lat. Am.* cobre (of copper) *m*. **per c.,** por ciento. **not to have a c., not to have a c. to one's name,** no tener donde caer muerto
centaur /'sɛntɔr/ *n* centauro, *m*
centavo /sɛn'tɑvou/ *n* centavo, *Lat. Am.* cobre (of copper) *m*
centenarian /,sɛntn'ɛəriən/ *a* and *n* centenario (-ia)
centenary /sɛn'tɛnɛri/ *n* centenario, *m*, *a* centenario
center /'sɛntər/ *n* centro, *m*; medio, *m*. *a* central; centro. *vt* centrar; concentrar (en). **nervous centers,** centros nerviosos, *m pl.* **c.-forward,** *Sports.* delantero centro, *m.* **c.-half,** *Sports.* medio centro, *m.* **c. of gravity,** centro de gravedad, *m.* **c.-piece,** centro, *m*
centerfold /'sɛntər,fould/ *n* páginas centrales, *f pl*
centigrade /'sɛntɪ,greid/ *a* centígrado
centigram /'sɛntɪ,græm/ *n* centígramo, *m*
centiliter /'sɛntl,itər/ *n* centilitro, *m*
centime /'sɑntim/ *n* céntimo, *m*
centimeter /'sɛntə,mitər/ *n* centímetro, *m*. **cubic c.,** centímetro cúbico, *m*
centipede /'sɛntə,pid/ *n* ciempiés, *m*
central /'sɛntrəl/ *a* central; céntrico. **The house is very c.,** La casa es muy céntrica. **C. America** *n* Centroamérica *f* **C. American,** *a* and *n* centroamericano (-na). **c. depot,** central, *f*. **c. heating,** calefacción central, *f*
centralism /'sɛntrə,lɪzəm/ *n* centralismo, *m*
centralist /'sɛntrəlɪst/ *n* centralista, *mf*
centralization /,sɛntrələ'zeiʃən/ *n* centralización, *f*
centralize /'sɛntrə,laiz/ *vt* centralizar
centrally /'sɛntrəli/ *adv* centralmente; céntricamente
centric /'sɛntrɪk/ *a* céntrico; central
centrifugal /sɛn'trɪfyəgəl/ *a* centrífugo
centripetal /sɛn'trɪpɪtl/ *a* centrípeto
centuple /'sɛntupəl/ *a* céntuplo
centuplicate /sɛn'tupli,keit/ *vt* centuplicar
centurion /sɛn'tyuriən/ *n* centurión, *m*
century /'sɛntʃəri/ *n* siglo, *m*, centuria, *f*
ceramic /sə'ræmɪk/ *a* cerámico
ceramics /sə'ræmɪks/ *n* cerámica, *f*
cereal /'sɪəriəl/ *a* cereal. *n* cereal, *m*
cerebellum /,sɛrə'bɛləm/ *n* cerebelo, *m*
cerebral /sə'ribrəl/ *a* cerebral
cerebrospinal /sə,ribrou'spainl/ *a* cerebroespinal
cerebrum /sə'ribrəm/ *n* cerebro, *m*
ceremonial /,sɛrə'mouniəl/ *a* ceremonial; de ceremonia. *n* ceremonial, *m*
ceremonially /,sɛrə'mouniəli/ *adv* ceremonialmente; con ceremonia
ceremonious /,sɛrə'mouniəs/ *a* ceremonioso
ceremoniously /,sɛrə'mouniəsli/ *adv* ceremoniosamente
ceremoniousness /,sɛrə'mouniəsnɪs/ *n* ceremonia, formalidad, *f*
ceremony /'sɛrə,mouni/ *n* ceremonia, *f*. **to stand on c.,** gastar cumplidos. **without c.,** sin cumplidos
certain /'sɜrtn/ *a* (sure) seguro; cierto; (unerring) certero. **a c. man,** cierto hombre. **I am c. that...,** Estoy seguro de que... **to know for c.,** saber con toda seguridad, saber a ciencia cierta. **to make c. of,** asegurarse de
certainly /'sɜrtnli/ *adv* seguramente; ciertamente; (as

a reply) sin duda; naturalmente. **c. not,** no, por cierto; claro que no

certainty /'sɜrtņti/ n certidumbre, f; seguridad, f; convicción, f. **of a c.,** seguramente

certificate /n sər'tɪfɪkɪt/ v -ˌkeɪt/ n certificado, m; fe, f; partida, f; Com. bono, título, m; diploma, m. vt certificar. **birth c.,** partida de nacimiento, f. **death c.,** partida de defunción, f. **marriage c.,** partida de casamiento, f

certificated /sər'tɪfɪˌkeɪtɪd/ a (of teachers, etc.) con título

certify /'sɜrtəˌfaɪ/ vt certificar; atestiguar; declarar

certitude /'sɜrtɪˌtyud/ n certeza, certidumbre, f

cerulean /sə'ruliən/ a cerúleo

Cervantine /sər'væntin/ a cervantino

cervix /'sɜrvɪks/ n Anat. cerviz, f

Cesarean /sə'zɛəriən/ a cesáreo

cessation /sɛ'seɪʃən/ n cesación, f

cession /'sɛʃən/ n cesión, f

cessionary /'sɛʃənɛri/ n cesionario (-ia)

cesspool /'sɛsˌpul/ n sumidero, m

cetacean /sɪ'teɪʃən/ a cetáceo. n cetáceo, m

Ceylon /sɪ'lɒn/ Ceilán, m

cf. cfr.

chafe /tʃeɪf/ vt (rub) frotar; (make sore) escocer, rozar. vi raerse, desgastarse; escocerse; Fig. impacientarse; Fig. irritarse, enojarse

chaff /tʃæf/ n (of grain) ahechadura, f; (in a general sense and Fig.) paja, f; tomadura de pelo, burla, f. vt (a person) tomar el pelo (a), burlarse de

chaffinch /'tʃæfɪntʃ/ n pinzón, m

chafing /'tʃeɪfɪŋ/ n frotación, f; (soreness) excoriación, f; Fig. impaciencia, f. **c.-dish,** escalfador, m

chagrin /ʃə'grɪn/ n mortificación, decepción, f, disgusto, m, vt mortificar

chain /tʃeɪn/ n cadena, f, vt encadenar. **c. of mountains,** cadena de montañas, cordillera, f. **c.-gang,** cadena de presidiarios, f. **c.-mail,** cota de malla, f. **c.-stitch,** cadeneta, f. **c.-stores,** empresa con sucursales, f. **in chains,** cargado de cadenas (e.g., prisoners in chains, prisioneros cargado de cadenas)

chair /tʃɛər/ n silla, f; Educ. cátedra, f; (of a meeting) presidencia, f. vt llevar en hombros (a). **C.!** ¡Orden! **easy-c.,** (silla) poltrona, f. **to be in the c.,** ocupar la presidencia; presidir. **to take a c.,** sentarse, tomar asiento. **to take the c.,** presidir. **swivel-c.,** silla giratoria, f. **wheel-c.,** silla de ruedas, f. **c.-back,** respaldo de una silla, m

chairman /'tʃɛərmən/ n presidente (-ta). **to act as c.,** presidir

chairmanship /'tʃɛərmənˌʃɪp/ n presidencia, f

chaise longue /'ʃeɪz 'lɒŋ/ n meridiana, tumbona, f

Chaldea /kæl'diə/ Caldea, f

Chaldean /kæl'diən/ a caldeo

chalet /ʃæ'leɪ/ n chalet, m

chalice /'tʃælɪs/ n cáliz, m

chalk /tʃɔk/ n creta, f; (for writing, etc.) tiza, f, yeso, m. vt marcar con tiza; dibujar con tiza. **to c. up,** apuntar. **not by a long c.,** no con mucho

chalky /'tʃɔki/ a cretáceo; cubierto de yeso; (of the complexion) pálido

challenge /'tʃælɪndʒ/ n provocación, f; (of a sentry) quién vive, m; (to a duel, etc.) desafío, reto, m; Law. recusación, f; concurso, m. vt (of a sentry) dar el quién vive (a); desafiar; provocar; Law. recusar

challenger /'tʃælɪndʒər/ n desafiador (-ra)

challenging /'tʃælɪndʒɪŋ/ a desafiador, provocador

chamber /'tʃeɪmbər/ n cuarto, m; sala, f; (bed-) dormitorio, m, alcoba, f; cámara, f; Mech. cilindro, m; (in a gun) cámara, f. **c. concert,** concierto de música de cámara, m. **c.-maid,** camarera, f. **c. music,** música de cámara, f. **c. of commerce,** cámara de comercio, f. **c.-pot,** orinal, m

chamberlain /'tʃeɪmbərlɪn/ n camarero, m. **court c.,** chambelán, m. **Lord C.,** camarero mayor, m

chameleon /kə'miliən/ n camaleón, m

chamfer /'tʃæmfər/ n chaflán, bisel, m

chamois /'ʃæmi/ n gamuza, f, rebeco, m. **c. leather,** piel de gamuza, f

chamomile /'kæməˌmaɪl/ n camomila, manzanilla, f

champagne /ʃæm'peɪn/ n (vino de) champaña, m

champion /'tʃæmpiən/ n campeón, m; defensor (-ra)

championship /'tʃæmpiənˌʃɪp/ n campeonato, m; (of a cause) defensa, f

chance /tʃæns/ n casualidad, f; suerte, fortuna, f; posibilidad, f; probabilidad, f; esperanza, f; (opportunity) ocasión, oportunidad, f. a fortuito; accidental. vi impers suceder, acontecer. vt Inf. arriesgar; probar. **by c.,** por casualidad; por ventura. **if by c.,** si acaso. **If it chances that...,** Si sucede que; Si a mano viene que... **The chances are that...,** Las probabilidades son que... **There is no c.,** No hay posibilidad; No hay esperanza. **to let the c. slip,** perder la ocasión. **to take a c.,** aventurarse, arriesgarse. **to c. to do,** hacer algo por casualidad. **to c. upon,** encontrar por casualidad

chancel /'tʃænsəl/ n antealtar, entrecoro, m

chancellery /'tʃænsələri/ n cancillería, f

chancellor /'tʃænsələr/ n canciller, m; Educ. cancelario, m. **C. of the Exchequer,** Ministro de Hacienda, m

chancellorship /'tʃænsələrʃɪp/ n cancillería, f

chancery /'tʃænsəri, 'tʃɑn-/ n chancillería, f; (papal) cancelaría, f

chandelier /ˌʃændl̩'ɪər/ n araña de luces, f

chandler /'tʃændlər/ n velero, m

change /tʃeɪndʒ/ vt cambiar; transformar; modificar; (clothes) mudarse (de); (one thing for another) trocar; sustituir (por). vi cambiar; (clothes) mudarse. **All c.!** ¡Cambio de tren! **to c. a check,** cambiar un cheque. **to c. color,** cambiar de color; (of persons) mudar de color. **to c. countenance,** demudarse. **to c. front,** Fig. cambiar de frente. **to c. hands,** (of shops, etc.) cambiar de dueño. **to c. one's clothes,** cambiar de ropa, mudarse de ropa. **to c. one's mind,** cambiar de opinión. **to c. one's tune,** cambiar de tono. **to c. the subject,** cambiar de conversación. **to c. trains,** cambiar de trenes

change /tʃeɪndʒ/ n cambio, m; transformación, f; modificación, f; variedad, f; (of clothes, feathers) muda, f; (Theat. of scene) mutación, f; (money) cambio, m; (small coins) suelto, m; (stock) bolsa, f; lonja, f; vicisitud, f; (of bells) toque (de campanas), m. **for a c.,** para cambiar, como un cambio; para variar. **small c.,** suelto, m, moneda suelta, f. **c. for the better,** cambio para mejor, m. **c. for the worse,** cambio para peor, m. **c. of clothes,** cambio de ropa, m; **c. of front,** Fig. cambio de frente, m. **c. of heart,** cambio de sentimientos, m; conversión, f. **c. of life,** menopausia, f. **c.-over,** cambio, m

changeability /ˌtʃeɪndʒə'bɪlɪti/ n mutabilidad, f; inconstancia, volubilidad, f

changeable /'tʃeɪndʒəbəl/ a voluble; variable; cambiable

changeless /'tʃeɪndʒlɪs/ a immutable; constante

changeling /'tʃeɪndʒlɪŋ/ n niño (-ña) cambiado (-da) por otro

changing /'tʃeɪndʒɪŋ/ a cambiante. **c.-room,** vestuario, m

channel /'tʃænl̩/ n (of a river, etc.) cauce, m; canal, m; (irrigation) acequia, f; (strait) estrecho, m; Fig. conducto, m; (furrow) surco, m, estría, f; (of information, etc.) medio, m. vt acanalar; (furrow) surcar; (conduct) encauzar

chant /tʃænt/ n canto llano, m; salmo, m. vt salmodiar; cantar; recitar

chantey /'ʃænti/ n saloma, f

chaos /'keɪɒs/ n caos, m

chaotic /keɪ'ɒtɪk/ a caótico, desordenado

chaotically /keɪ'ɒtɪkli/ adv en desorden

chap /tʃæp/ vt agrietar. vi agrietarse. n Inf. chico, m

chapbook /'tʃæp,bʊk/ n librito de cordel, m

chapel /'tʃæpəl/ n capilla, f; templo disidente, m

chaperon /'tʃæpəˌroʊn/ n dama de compañía, señora de compañía, dueña, f, vt acompañar

chaplain /'tʃæplɪn/ n capellán, m

chaplaincy /'tʃæplɪnsi/ n capellanía, f

chaplet /'tʃæplɪt/ n guirnalda, f; rosario, m; (necklace) collar, m

chapter /'tʃæptər/ n (in a book) capítulo, m; Eccl. cabildo, capítulo, m. **a c. of accidents,** una serie de desgracias. **c. house,** sala capitular, f

char /tʃɑr/ vt (a house, etc.) fregar, hacer la limpieza de; (of fire) carbonizar. n Inf. fregona, asistenta, f

character /'kærɪktər/ n carácter, m; (of a play) personaje, m; (role) papel, m; (eccentric) tipo, m. **Gothic characters,** caracteres góticos, m pl. **in c.,** característico; apropiado. **in the c. of,** en el papel de. **out of c.,** nada característico; no apropiado. **principal c.,** protagonista, mf. **c. actor,** actor de carácter, m. **c. actress,** actriz de carácter

characteristic /ˌkærɪktə'rɪstɪk/ a característico, típico. n característica, peculiaridad, f, rasgo, m

characterization /ˌkærɪktərə'zeɪʃən/ n caracterización, f

characterize /'kærɪktəˌraiz/ vt caracterizar

characterless /'kærɪktərlɪs/ a sin carácter; insípido, soso

charade /ʃə'reid/ n charada, f

charcoal /'tʃɑrˌkoul/ n carbón de leña, m; (for blacking the face, etc.) tizne, m; Art. carboncillo, m. **c. burner,** carbonera, f. **c. crayon,** carboncillo, m. **c. drawing,** dibujo al carbón, m

charge /tʃɑrdʒ/ vt cargar; (enjoin) encargar; (accuse) acusar (de); (with price) cobrar; (with a mission, etc.) encomendar, confiar; Mil. acometer, atacar. vi Mil. atacar; (a price) cobrar, pedir. **How much do you c.?** ¿Cuánto cobra Vd.? **to c. with a crime,** acusar de un crimen

charge /tʃɑrdʒ/ n (load) carga, f; (price) precio, m; gasto, m; (on an estate, etc.) derechos, m pl; (task) encargo, m; (office or responsibility) cargo, m; (guardianship) tutela, f; (care) cuidado, m; exhortación, f; Law. acusación, f; Mil. ataque, m. **He is in c. of...,** Está encargado de...; Es responsable de... **The diamonds are in the c. of...,** Los diamantes están a cargo de. **depth c.,** carga de profundidad, f. **extra c.,** gasto suplementario, m; (on a train) suplemento, m. **free of c.,** gratis. **c. for admittance,** entrada, f. **to bring a c. against,** acusar de. **to give (someone) in c.,** entregar (una persona) a la policía. **to take c. of,** encargarse de

chargé d'affaires /ʃar'ʒei də'fɛər/ n encargado de negocios, m

charger /'tʃɑrdʒər/ n caballo de guerra, corcel, m

chariness /'tʃɛərɪnɪs/ n cautela, f

chariot /'tʃæriət/ n carro, m

charioteer /ˌtʃæriə'tɪər/ n auriga, m

charitable /'tʃærɪtəbəl/ a caritativo, limosnero; benéfico

charitableness /'tʃærɪtəbəlnɪs/ n caridad, f

charity /'tʃærɪti/ n caridad, f; beneficencia, f; (alms) limosna, f. **c. child,** niño (-ña) de la doctrina

charlatan /'ʃɑrlətn̩/ n charlatán (-ana); (quack) curandero, m

charlatanism /'ʃɑrlətn̩ˌɪzəm/ n charlatanismo, m; curanderismo, m

charm /tʃɑrm/ n hechizo, m; ensalmo, m; (amulet) amuleto, m; (trinket) dije, m; (general sense) encanto, atractivo, m. vt encantar, hechizar, fascinar

charming /'tʃɑrmɪŋ/ a encantador; atractivo, seductor, fascinador

charm school n academia de buenos modales, f

chart /tʃɑrt/ n Naut. carta de marear, f; (graph) gráfica, f, (table) tabla, f. vt poner en una carta

charter /'tʃɑrtər/ n carta, f; (of a city, etc.) fuero, m; cédula, f. vt (a ship) fletar; (hire) alquilar. **royal c.,** cédula real, f

Chartism /'tʃɑrtɪzəm/ n el cartismo, m

chartist /'tʃɑrtɪst/ n cartista, mf

charwoman /'tʃɑrˌwʊmən/ n fregona, asistenta; mujer de hacer faenas, Mexico fregandera f

chary /'tʃɛəri/ a cauteloso; desinclinado; frugal

chase /tʃeis/ n caza, f; seguimiento, m. vt cazar; dar caza (a); perseguir; (drive off) ahuyentar; Fig. disipar, hacer desaparecer; (engrave) cincelar. **to give c. to,** dar caza (a). **to go on a wild goose c.,** buscar pan de trastrigo

chasm /'kæzəm/ n sima, f, precipicio, m; Fig. abismo, m

chassis /'tʃæsi/ n chasis, m

chaste /tʃeist/ a casto

chasten /'tʃeisən/ vt castigar; corregir; humillar, mortificar

chastened /'tʃeisənd/ a sumiso, dócil

chastise /tʃæs'taiz/ vt castigar

chastisement /tʃæs'taizmənt/ n castigo, m

chastity /'tʃæstɪti/ n castidad, f

chat /tʃæt/ vi charlar, conversar. n conversación, f. **They are having a c.,** Están charlando, Están de palique

chattels /'tʃætəlz/ n pl bienes muebles, efectos, m pl

chatter /'tʃætər/ vi charlar; hablar por los codos, chacharear; (of water) murmurar; (of birds) piar; (of monkeys, etc.) chillar; (of teeth) rechinar; (of a person's teeth) dar diente con diente. n charla, f; cháchara, parla, f; (of water) murmurio, m; (of birds) gorjeo, m; (of monkeys, etc.) chillidos, m pl

chatterbox /'tʃætˌər bɒks/ n badajo, m, cotorra, f

chattering /'tʃætərɪŋ/ n charla, cháchara, f; (of teeth) rechinamiento, m, a gárrulo, chacharero, locuaz

chauffeur /'ʃoufər/ n chófer, m

cheap /tʃip/ a barato; (of works of art) cursi. adv barato. **dirt c.,** baratísimo. **to be dirt c.,** estar por los suelos. **to hold (something) c.,** tener en poco, estimar en poco

cheapen /'tʃipən/ vt disminuir el valor de; reducir el precio de

cheaply /'tʃipli/ adv barato; a bajo precio

cheapness /'tʃipnɪs/ n baratura, f; precio módico, m; mal gusto, m, vulgaridad, f

cheat /tʃit/ n engaño, fraude, m, estafa, f; (person) fullero (-ra), trampista, mf embustero (-ra). vt engañar; defraudar; (at cards) hacer trampas. **He cheated me out of my property,** Me defraudó de mi propiedad

cheating /'tʃitɪŋ/ n engaño, m; fraude, m; (at cards) fullerías, f pl

check /tʃɛk/ n (chess) jaque, m; revés, m; impedimento, m; contratiempo, m; (of a bridle) cama, f; (control) freno, m; control, m; (checking) verificación, f; (ticket) papeleta, f; (counterfoil) talón, m; (square) cuadro, m; (bill) cuenta, f, Argentina adición f; (bank) cheque, m. vt (chess) jaquear; (hamper) refrenar; detener; contrarrestar; (test) verificar. vi detenerse. **to c. off,** marcar. **to c. oneself,** detenerse; contenerse. **to c. up,** comprobar. **crossed c.,** cheque cruzado, m. **c. book,** libro de cheques, m

checked /tʃɛkt/ a (cloth) a cuadros

checker /'tʃɛkər/ vt escaquear; (variegate) motear, salpicar; diversificar. **a checkered career,** una vida accidentada

checkerboard /'tʃɛkərˌbɔrd/ n tablero de damas, m

checkers /'tʃɛkərz/ n pl damas, f pl

checking /'tʃɛkɪŋ/ n represión, f; control, m; verificación, f; comprobación, f

checkmate /'tʃɛkˌmeit/ n mate, jaque, mate, m. vt dar mate (a); (plans, etc.) frustrar

checks and balances n pl frenos y contrapesos, m pl

cheek /tʃik/ n mejilla, f; Inf. descaro, m; insolencia, Lat. Am. impavidez f. **They have plenty of c.,** Tienen mucha cara dura. **c. by jowl,** cara a cara; al lado de. **c.-bone,** pómulo, m

cheekiness /'tʃikɪnɪs/ n cara dura, insolencia, Lat. Am. impavidez f

cheeky /'tʃiki/ a insolente, descarado, Lat. Am. impávido, Peru lisurero; (pert) respondón

cheer /tʃiər/ n alegría, f; regocijo, m; vítor, m; aplauso, m. vt animar; alegrar, regocijar; vitorear, aplaudir. **to be of good c.,** estar alegre; ser feliz. **C. up!** ¡Ánimo! **to c. up,** animarse, cobrar ánimo

cheerful /'tʃiərfəl/ a alegre; jovial; de buen humor

cheerfully /'tʃiərfəli/ adv alegremente; (willingly) con mucho gusto, de buena gana

cheerfulness /'tʃiərfəlnɪs/ n alegría, f; jovialidad, f; buen humor, m

cheering /'tʃiərɪŋ/ n vítores, m pl, aclamaciones, f pl, a animador

cheerleader /'tʃiərˌlidər/ n porro, m

cheerless /'tʃiərlɪs/ a triste; sin alegría; (dank) obscuro, lóbrego

cheese /tʃiz/ n queso, m. **cream c.,** queso de nata, m. **grated c.,** queso rallado, m. **c.-dish,** quesera, f. **c.-**

mite, cresa, f. **c.-paring,** n corteza de queso, f. a Inf.
tacaño.

cheesecake /'tʃiz,keik/ n Lat. Am. alfandoque, m

cheesy /'tʃizi/ a caseoso

chemical /'kɛmɪkəl/ a químico. **c. warfare,** defensa química, f

chemicals /'kɛmɪkəlz/ n pl productos químicos, m pl

chemise /ʃə'miz/ n camisa (de mujer), f

chemist /'kɛmɪst/ n químico, m. **chemist's shop,** farmacia, f; droguería, f

chemistry /'kɛməstri/ n química, f

chemotherapy /,kimou'θɛrəpi/ n quimioterapia, f

cherish /'tʃɛrɪʃ/ vt amar, querer; (a hope, etc.) abrigar, acariciar

cherry /'tʃɛri/ n (fruit) cereza, f; (tree and wood) cerezo, m. **c. brandy,** aguardiente de cerezas, m. **c. orchard,** cerezal, m

cherub /'tʃɛrəb/ n querub(e), querubín, m

cherubic /tʃə'rubɪk/ a querúbico

chess /tʃɛs/ n ajedrez, m. **c.-board,** tablero de ajedrez, m

chessman /'tʃɛs,mæn/ n pieza de ajedrez, f

chest /tʃɛst/ n arca, f, cofre, m; cajón, m; Anat. pecho, m. **to throw out one's c.,** inflar el pecho. **c.-expander,** extensor, m. **c. of drawers,** cómoda, f

chested /'tʃɛstɪd/ a (in compounds) de pecho...

chestnut /'tʃɛs,nʌt/ n (tree) castaño, m; (fruit) castaña, f; (color) castaño, color castaño, m; (horse) caballo castaño, m; (joke) chiste del tiempo de Maricastaña, m, a canalesco. **horse-c. tree,** castaño de Indias, m

chevron /'ʃɛvrən/ n Herald. cabrio, m; (Mil. etc.) sardineta, f

chew /tʃu/ vt mascar, mascullar; (ponder) masticar

chewing /'tʃuɪŋ/ n masticación, f. **c.-gum,** chicle, m

chianti /ki'anti/ n (wine) quianti, m

chiaroscuro /ki,arə'skyʊrou/ n claroscuro, m

chic /ʃik/ n chic, m, elegancia, f

chicanery /ʃɪ'keinəri/ n sofistería, f

chicken /'tʃɪkən/ n pollo, m. **c.-hearted,** medroso, cobarde, timorato. **c.-pox,** varicela, f

chickenwire /'tʃɪkən,waiᵊr/ n alambrillo, m

chickpea /'tʃɪk,pi/ n garbanzo, m

chickweed /'tʃɪk,wid/ n pamplina, f

chicory /'tʃɪkəri/ n chicoria, f

chide /tʃaid/ vt reprender, reñir

chidingly /'tʃaidɪŋli/ adv en tono de reprensión

chief /tʃif/ n jefe, m, a principal; primero; en jefe; mayor. **c.-of-staff,** jefe de estado mayor, m

chiefly /'tʃifli/ adv principalmente; sobre todo

chieftain /'tʃiftən/ n caudillo, m; (of a clan) cabeza, jefe, m

chiffon /ʃɪ'fɒn/ n chifón, m, gasa, f

chiffonier /,ʃɪfə'niər/ n cómoda, f

chignon /'ʃinyɒn/ n moño, m

child /tʃaild/ n niño (-ña); hijo (-ja), Mexico escuincle mf. **from a c.,** desde niño, desde la niñez. **with c.,** encinta, embarazada. **How many children do you have?** ¿Cuántos hijos tiene Vd.? **child's play,** juegos infantiles, m pl; Fig. niñerías, f pl. **c. welfare,** puericultura, f

childbirth /'tʃaild,bɜrθ/ n parto, m

childhood /'tʃaildhʊd/ n niñez, infancia, f. **from his c.,** desde su niñez, desde niño

childish /'tʃaildɪʃ/ a de niño; aniñado; pueril; fútil. **to grow-c,** chochear

childishly /'tʃaildɪʃli/ adv como un niño

childishness /'tʃaildɪʃnɪs/ n puerilidad, f; futilidad, f

child labor n trabajo de menores, trabajo infantil, m

childless /'tʃaildlɪs/ a sin hijos; sin niños

childlike /'tʃaild,laik/ a de niño, aniñado; pueril

children. /'tʃɪldrən/ See **child**

Chilean /'tʃɪliən/ a and n chileno (-na)

chili /'tʃɪli/ n chile, pimento de cornetilla, Lat. Am. ají m. **c. sauce** Lat. Am. ají m

chill /tʃɪl/ n frío, m; (of fear, etc.) estremecimiento, m; (illness) resfriado, m; (unfriendliness) frialdad, frigidez, f, a frío; (unfriendly) frígido. vt enfriar; helar; (with fear, etc.) dar escalofríos (de). vi tener frío; tener escalofríos. **to take the c. off,** templar, calentar un poco

chilliness /'tʃɪlinɪs/ n frío, m; (unfriendliness) frialdad, frigidez, f

chilly /'tʃɪli/ a frío; (sensitive to cold) friolero; (of politeness, etc.) glacial, frígido

chime /tʃaim/ n juego de campanas, m; repique, campaneo, m; armonía, f. vi (of bells) repicar; Fig. armonizar. **to c. the hour,** dar la hora

chimera /kɪ'mɪərə/ n quimera, f

chimerical /kɪ'mɛrɪkəl/ a quimérico

chimney /'tʃɪmni/ n chimenea, f; (of a lamp) tubo (de lámpara), m. **c.-corner,** rincón de chimenea, m. **c.-pot,** sombrerete de chimenea, m. **c.-stack,** chimenea, f. **c.-sweep,** limpiador de chimeneas, deshollinador, m

chimpanzee /,tʃɪmpæn'zi, tʃɪm'pænzi/ n chimpancé, m

chin /tʃɪn/ n barbilla, barba, f, mentón, m. **c.-rest,** mentonera, f. **c.-strap,** barboquejo, m; venda para la barbilla, f

china /'tʃainə/ n china, porcelana, f; loza, f. a de porcelana; de loza. **China,** China, f. **c. cabinet,** chinero, m

chinchilla /tʃɪn'tʃɪlə/ n (animal and fur) chinchilla, f

Chinese /tʃai'niz/ a and n chino (-na); (language) chino, m. **C. lantern,** farolillo de papel, m. **C. white,** óxido blanco de cinc, m

chink /tʃɪŋk/ n resquicio, m, grieta, hendidura, f; (clink) retintín, tintineo, m. vi tintinar

chintz /tʃɪnts/ n zaraza, f

chip /tʃɪp/ n astilla, f; (counter) ficha, f. vt picar; cincelar. **a c. off the old block,** de tal palo tal astilla. **c. potatoes,** patatas fritas, f pl

chiromancy /'kairə,mænsi/ n quiromancia, f

chiropodist /kɪ'rɒpədɪst/ n pedicuro, m, callista, mf

chiropody /kɪ'rɒpədi/ n pedicura, f

chiropractor /'kairə,præktər/ n quiropráctico, m

chirp /tʃɜrp/ vi piar, gorjear. n pío, gorjeo, m

chirping /'tʃɜrpɪŋ/ n piada, f, a gárrulo, piante

chisel /'tʃɪzəl/ n escoplo, cincel, m, vt cincelar. **cold c.,** cortafrío, m

chitchat /'tʃɪt,tʃæt/ n charla, f

chitterlings /'tʃɪtlɪnz/ n asadura, f

chivalrous /'ʃɪvəlrəs/ a caballeroso

chivalry /'ʃɪvəlri/ n caballería, f; caballerosidad, f. **novel of c.,** novela de caballería, f

chive /tʃaiv/ n Bot. cebollana, f, cebollino, m

chloral /'klɔrəl/ n cloral, m

chlorate /'klɔreit/ n clorato, m

chloride /'klɔraid/ n cloruro, m

chlorine /'klɔrin/ n cloro, m

chloroform /'klɔrə,fɔrm/ n cloroformo, m, vt cloroformizar

chlorophyll /'klɔrəfɪl/ n clorófila, f

chock-full /'tʃɒk 'fʊl/ a lleno de bote en bote

chocolate /'tʃɒkəlɪt/ n chocolate, m, a de chocolate. **thick drinking-c.,** chocolate a la española, f. **thin drinking-c.,** chocolate a la francesa, m. **c. shop,** chocolatería, f

choice /tʃɔis/ n selección, f; preferencia, f; elección, f; opción, f; alternativa, f; lo más escogido. a escogido, selecto; excelente. **for c.,** con preferencia

choir /kwaiᵊr/ n coro, m. **c.-boy,** niño del coro, m. **c.-master,** maestro de capilla, m

choke /tʃouk/ vi ahogarse; atragantarse; obstruirse. vt ahogar; estrangular. **to c. with laughter,** ahogarse de risa. **to c. back,** (words) tragar. **to c. off,** (a person) disuadir (de); quitarse de encima(a). **to c. up,** obstruir, cerrar, obturar; (hide) cubrir, tapar

choking /'tʃoukɪŋ/ a asfixiante, sofocante. n ahogamiento, m, sofocación, f

cholera /'kɒlərə/ n cólera, m

choleric /'kɒlərɪk/ a colérico

cholesterol /kə'lɛstə,roul/ n colesterina, f

choline /'koulin/ n colina, f

choose /tʃuz/ vt escoger; elegir; optar por; (wish) querer, gustar. **They will do it when they c.,** Lo harán cuando les parezca bien. **If you c.,** Si Vd. quiere; Si Vd. gusta. **He was chosen as Mayor,** Fue elegido alcalde. **There is nothing to c. between them,** No hay diferencia entre ellos; Tanto vale el uno como el otro. **You cannot c. but love her,** No puedes menos de quererla

choosing /'tʃuzɪŋ/ n selección, f; (for an office, etc.) elección, f
chop /tʃɒp/ vt cortar; (mince) picar; (split) hender, partir. n (meat) chuleta, f; (jaw) quijada, f. **to c. about, round,** (of the wind) girar, virar. **to c. down,** (trees) talar. **to c. off,** separar; cortar; tajar. **to c. up,** cortar en pedazos
chopper /'tʃɒpər/ n hacha, f; (helicopter) helicóptero, m
choppy /'tʃɒpi/ a picado, agitado
chopstick /'tʃɒp,stɪk/ n palillo chino, m
choragus /kə'reigəs/ n corega, corego, m
choral /'kɔrəl/ a coral
chord /kɔrd/ n cuerda, f, lazo, m; Mus. acorde, m; **the right c.,** Fig. la cuerda sensible
choreographer /,kɔri'ɒgrəfər/ n coreógrafo, m
choreographic /,kɔriə'græfɪk/ a coreográfico
choreography /,kɔri'ɒgrəfi, ,kour-/ n coreografía, f
chorister /'kɔrəstər/ n corista, m
chorus /'kɔrəs/ n coro, m; (in revues) comparsa, f, acompañamiento, m; (of a song) refrán, m. **to sing in c.,** cantar a coro. **c. girl,** corista, f
chosen /'tʃouzən/ a escogido; elegido. **the c.,** los elegidos
chrestomathy /krɛs'tɒməθi/ n crestomatía, f
Christ /kraist/ n Cristo, Jesucristo, m
christen /'krɪsən/ vt bautizar
Christendom /'krɪsəndəm/ n cristianismo, m, cristiandad, f
christening /'krɪsənɪŋ/ n bautizo, m, a bautismal, de bautizo
Christian /'krɪstʃən/ a cristiano. n cristiano (-na). **C. name,** nombre de pila, m
christianity /,krɪstʃi'ænɪti/ n cristianismo, m
Christmas /'krɪsməs/ n Navidad, f. **A Merry C.!** ¡Felices Pascuas (de Navidad)! **Father C.,** Padre Noel, m; (Sp. equivalent) Los Reyes Magos. **C. box,** regalo de Navidad, m. **C. card,** felicitación de Navidad, f. **C. carol,** villancico de Navidad, m. **C. Day,** día de Navidad, m. **C. Eve,** Nochebuena, f. **C.-tide,** Navidades, f pl. **C. tree,** árbol de Navidad, m
Christopher Columbus /'krɪstəfər kə'lʌmbəs/ Cristóbal Colón, m
chromate /'kroumeit/ n cromato, m
chromatic /krou'mætɪk/ a cromático
chrome /kroum/ n cromo, m. **c. yellow,** amarillo de cromo, m
chromic /'kroumɪk/ a crómico
chromium /'kroumiəm/ n cromo, m. **c.-plated,** cromado
chromosome /'kroumə,soum/ n cromosoma, m
chronic /'krɒnɪk/ a crónico; inveterado
chronicle /'krɒnɪkəl/ n crónica, f, vt narrar
chronicler /'krɒnɪklər/ n cronista, mf
chronological /,krɒnl'ɒdʒɪkəl/ a cronológico. **in c. order,** por orden cronológico
chronology /krə'nɒlədʒi/ n cronología, f
chronometer /krə'nɒmɪtər/ n cronómetro, m
chrysalis /'krɪsəlɪs/ n crisálida, f
chrysanthemum /krɪ'sænθəməm/ n crisantemo, m
chubbiness /'tʃʌbɪnɪs/ n gordura, f
chubby /'tʃʌbi/ a regordete, gordito. **c.-cheeked,** mofletudo
chuck /tʃʌk/ vt (throw) lanzar, arrojar; (discontinue) abandonar, dejar. n (in a lathe) mandril, m. **to c. under the chin,** acariciar la barbilla (a). **to c. away,** derrochar; malgastar, perder. **to c. out,** echar, poner en la calle
chuckle /'tʃʌkəl/ vi reír entre dientes. n risa ahogada, f; risita, f
chum /tʃʌm/ n compinche, camarada, mf. **to c. up with,** ser camarada de
chunk /tʃʌŋk/ n pedazo, trozo, m
church /tʃɜrtʃ/ n iglesia, f; (Protestant) templo, m. vt (a woman) purificar. **poor as a c. mouse,** más pobre que las ratas. **the Roman Catholic C.,** la iglesia católica. **to go to c.,** ir a misa; ir al templo. **C. music,** música sagrada, f
churchyard /'tʃɜrtʃ,yard/ n cementerio, m
churl /tʃɜrl/ n patán, m

churlish /'tʃɜrlɪʃ/ a grosero, cazurro; (mean) tacaño, ruin
churn /tʃɜrn/ n mantequera, f. vt (cream) batir; Fig. azotar, agitar
chute /ʃut/ n (for grain, etc.) manga de tolva, f; vertedor, m; (in apartment buildings and amusement parks) tobogán, deslizadero, m
ciborium /sɪ'bɔriəm/ n (chalice) copón, m; (tabernacle) sagrario, m; Archit. ciborio, m
cicada /sɪ'keidə/ n cigarra, f
cicatrice /'sɪkətrɪs/ n cicatriz, f
cicatrization /,sɪkətrə'zeiʃən/ n cicatrización, f
cicatrize /'sɪkə,traiz/ vt cicatrizar. vi cicatrizarse
cider /'saidər/ n sidra, f
cigar /sɪ'gar/ n cigarro, m. **c.-box,** cigarrera, f. **c.-case,** petaca, cigarrera, f. **c.-cutter,** corta-puros, m
cigarette /,sɪgə'rɛt/ n cigarrillo, pitillo, Lat. Am. cigarro m. **c.-butt,** colilla, f. **c.-case,** pitillera, f. **c.-holder,** boquilla, f. **c.-lighter,** encendedor de cigarrillos, m. **c.-paper,** papel de fumar, m
cinch /sɪntʃ/ n (of a saddle) cincha, f; Inf. ganga, f; Inf. seguridad, f. **c.-strap,** látigo, m
cinchona /sɪŋ'kounə/ n quina, cinchona, f
cinder /'sɪndər/ n ceniza, f; carbonilla, f. **red-hot c.,** rescoldo, m. **c.-track,** pista de ceniza, f
cinema, cinematograph /'sɪnəmə/ n cine, cinematógrafo, m
cinematographic /,sɪnə,mætə'græfɪk/ a cinematográfico
cinematography /,sɪnəmə'tɒgrəfi/ n cinematografía, f
cinemogul /,sɪnə'mougəl/ n magnate del cine, mf
cinnamon /'sɪnəmən/ n (spice) canela, f; (tree) canelo, m; color de canela, m
cipher /'saifər/ n Math. cero, m; Fig. nulidad, f; (code) cifra, f; monograma, m. **to be a mere c.,** ser un cero
Circassian /sər'kæʃən/ a circasiano. n circasiano (-na)
circle /'sɜrkəl/ n círculo, m; (revolution) vuelta, f; (group) grupo; m; (club, etc.) centro, m; (cycle) ciclo, m. vt dar vueltas alrededor de; rodear; ceñir; (on an application, examination, etc.) encerrar en un círculo. vi dar vueltas; (aircraft) volar en círculo; (of a hawk, etc.) cernerse. **dress-c.,** Theat. anfiteatro, m. **the family c.,** el círculo de la familia. **to come full c.,** dar la vuelta. **upper c.,** Theat. segundo piso, m. **vicious c.,** círculo vicioso, m
circlet /'sɜrklɪt/ n (of flowers, etc.) corona, f; (ring) anillo, m
circuit /'sɜrkɪt/ n circuito, m; (tour) gira, f; (revolution) vuelta, f; (radius) radio, m. **short c.,** corto circuito, m. **c.-breaker,** corta-circuitos, m
circuit court of appeals /ə'pilz/ n tribunal colegial de circuito, m
circuitous /sər'kyuɪtəs/ a indirecto; tortuoso
circuitously /sər'kyuɪtəsli/ adv indirectamente
circular /'sɜrkyələr/ a circular; redondo. n carta circular, f; circular, f. **c. tour,** viaje redondo, m
circularize /'sɜrkyələ,raiz/ vt enviar circulares (a)
circulate /'sɜrkyə,leit/ vi circular. vt hacer circular; poner en circulación; (news, etc.) divulgar, diseminar
circulating library /'sɜrkyə,leitɪŋ/ n biblioteca por subscripción, f
circulation /,sɜrkyə'leiʃən/ n circulación, f; (of a newspaper, etc.) tirada, circulación, f. **c. of the blood,** circulación de la sangre, f
circulatory /'sɜrkyələ,tɔri/ a circulatorio
circumcise /'sɜrkəm,saiz/ vt circuncidar
circumcised /'sɜrkəm,saizd/ a circunciso
circumcision /,sɜrkəm'sɪʒən/ n circuncisión, f
circumference /sər'kʌmfərəns/ n circunferencia, f
circumflex /'sɜrkəm,flɛks/ a circunflejo. **c. accent,** acento circunflejo, m, (informal) capucha, f
circumlocution /,sɜrkəmlou'kyuʃən/ n circumlocución, f
circumnavigate /,sɜrkəm'nævɪ,geit/ vt circunnavegar
circumnavigation /'sɜrkəm,nævə'geiʃən/ n circunnavegación, f
circumscribe /'sɜrkəm,skraib/ vt circunscribir; Fig. limitar

circumscribed /'sɜrkəm,skraibd/ a circunscripto; *Fig.* limitado

circumscription /,sɜrkəm'skrɪpʃən/ n circunscripción, f; *Fig.* limitación, restricción, f

circumspect /'sɜrkəm,spɛkt/ a circunspecto; discreto, correcto; prudente

circumspection /,sɜrkəm'spɛkʃən/ n circunspección, f; prudencia, f

circumspectly /'sɜrkəm,spɛktli/ adv con circunspección; prudentemente

circumstance /'sɜrkəm,stæns/ n circunstancia, f; detalle, m. **aggravating c.,** circunstancia agravante, f. **attenuating c.,** circunstancia atenuante, f. **in the circumstances,** en las circunstancias. **in easy circumstances,** en buena posición, acomodado. **Do you know what his circumstances are?** ¿Sabes cuál es su situación económica? **under the circumstances,** bajo las circunstancias

circumstantial /,sɜrkəm'stænʃəl/ a circunstancial; detallado. **c. evidence,** prueba de indicios, f

circumvent /,sɜrkəm'vɛnt/ vt frustrar; impedir

circumvention /,sɜrkəm'vɛnʃən/ n frustración, f

circumvolution /,sɜrkəmvə'luʃən/ n circunvolución, f

circus /'sɜrkəs/ n circo, m; plaza redonda, f; (traffic) redondel, m

cirrhosis /sɪ'rousɪs/ n cirrosis, f

cirrus /'sɪrəs/ n (all meanings) cirro, m

cistern /'sɪstərn/ n tanque, m; cisterna, f, aljibe, m

citadel /'sɪtədl/ n ciudadela, f

citation /sai'teifən/ n Law. citación, f; cita, f

citation dictionary n diccionario de autoridades, m

cite /sait/ vt citar

citizen /'sɪtəzən/ n ciudadano (-na); vecino (-na); natural, mf. **fellow c.,** conciudadano, m; compatriota, mf

citizenship /'sɪtəzən,ʃɪp/ n ciudadanía, f

citrate /'sɪtreit/ n citrato, m

citric /'sɪtrɪk/ a cítrico

citrine /'sɪtrin/ a cetrino

citron /'sɪtrən/ n (fruit) cidra, f; (tree) cidro, m

city /'sɪti/ n ciudad, f, a municipal

city-state /'sɪti,steit/ n ciudad-estado, f, (plural: ciudades-estado)

civet /'sɪvɪt/ n algalia, f

civic /'sɪvɪk/ a cívico; municipal

civics /'sɪvɪks/ n civismo, m

civil /'sɪvəl/ a civil; doméstico; (polite) cortés, atento; (obliging) servicial. **c. defense,** defensa civil, f. **c. engineer,** ingeniero de caminos, canales y puertos, m. **C. Service,** cuerpo de empleados del Estado, m

civilian /sɪ'vɪlyən/ a civil. n ciudadano (-na). **c. dress,** traje paisano, m

civility /sɪ'vɪlti/ n civilidad, cortesía, f

civilization /,sɪvələ'zeiʃən/ n civilización, f

civilize /'sɪvə,laiz/ vt civilizar

civilized /'sɪvə,laizd/ a civilizado

civilizing /'sɪvə,laiziŋ/ a civilizador

civilly /'sɪvəli/ adv civilmente, cortésmente

clad /klæd/ a vestido

claim /kleim/ vt reclamar; pretender exigir; Law. demandar; (assert) afirmar. n Law. pedir en juicio. n reclamación, f; pretensión, f; Law. demanda, f; (in a gold-field, etc.) concesión, f; (right) derecho, m. **to lay c. to,** pretender a; exigir. **to put in a c. for,** reclamar

claimant /'kleimənt/ n Law. demandante, mf; pretendiente (-ta); Com. acreedor (-ra)

clairvoyance /klɛr'vɔiəns/ n doble vista, f, clarividencia, f

clairvoyant /klɛr'vɔiənt/ n vidente, m

clam /klæm/ n almeja, chirla, f

clamber /'klæmbər/ vi trepar, encaramarse. n subida difícil, f

clamminess /'klæmɪnɪs/ n viscosidad, humedad, f

clammy /'klæmi/ a viscoso; húmedo; mojado

clamor /'klæmər/ n clamor, estruendo, m; gritería, vocería, f. vi gritar, vociferar. **to c. against,** protestar contra. **to c. for,** pedir a voces

clamorous /'klæmərəs/ a clamoroso, ruidoso, estrepitoso

clamp /klæmp/ n grapa, f; abrazadera, f; tornillo, m; (pile) montón, m. vt empalmar; sujetar, lañar

clan /klæn/ n clan, m; familia, f; partido, grupo, m

clandestine /klæn'dɛstɪn/ a clandestino, furtivo

clandestinely /klæn'dɛstɪnli/ adv en secreto, clandestinamente

clang /klæŋ/ vi sonar; (of a gate, etc.) rechinar. vt hacer sonar. n sonido metálico, m; estruendo, m

clank /klæŋk/ vi dar un ruido metálico; crujir. vt hacer sonar; (glasses) hacer chocar. n ruido metálico, m; el crujir

clannish /'klænɪʃ/ a exclusivista

clansman /'klænzmən/ n miembro de un clan, m

clap /klæp/ vt (hands) batir; (spurs, etc.) poner rápidamente; (one's hat on) encasquetarse (el sombrero); (shut) cerrar apresuradamente. vi aplaudir. n (of the hands) palmada, f; (of thunder) trueno, m; (noise) ruido, m. **to c. eyes on,** echar la vista encima de. **to c. someone on the back,** dar una palmada en la espalda (a). **to c. the hands,** batir las palmas

clapper /'klæpər/ n (of a bell) badajo, m

clapping /'klæpɪŋ/ n aplausos, m pl

claque /klæk/ n claque, f

claret /'klærɪt/ n clarete, m

clarification /,klærəfə'keiʃən/ n clarificación, f; elucidación, f

clarify /'klærə,fai/ vt clarificar; elucidar, aclarar

clarinet /,klærə'nɛt/ n clarinete, m

clarinettist /,klærə'nɛtɪst/ n clarinete, m

clarion /'klæriən/ n clarín, m

clarity /'klærɪti/ n claridad, f; lucidez, f

clash /klæʃ/ vi chocar; encontrarse; (of events) coincidir; (of opinions, etc.) oponerse, estar en desacuerdo; (of colors) desentonar, chocar. n estruendo, fragor, m; choque, m; Mil. encuentro, m; (of opinions, etc.) desacuerdo, m; disputa, f

clasp /klæsp/ vt (a brooch, etc.) abrochar, enganchar; (embrace) abrazar; (of plants, etc.) ceñir. n (brooch) broche, m; (of a belt) hebilla, f; (of a necklace, handbag, book) cierre, m; (for the hair) pasador, m. **to c. someone in one's arms,** tomar en los brazos (a), abrazar. **c.-knife,** navaja, f

class /klæs/ n clase, f; (kind) especie, f; (of exhibits, etc.) categoría, f. vt clasificar. **in a c. by itself,** único en su línea. **the lower classes,** las clases bajas. **the middle classes,** la clase media. **the upper classes,** clase alta. **c.-mate,** condiscípulo (-la). **c.-room,** sala de clase, f, salón de clase, f. **c. war,** lucha de clases, f

classic /'klæsɪk/ a clásico. n clásico, m

classical /'klæsɪkəl/ a clásico

classicist /'klæsəsɪst/ a and n clasicista, mf

classifiable /'klæsə,faiəbəl/ a clasificable

classification /,klæsəfɪ'keiʃən/ n clasificación, f

classified /'klæsə,faid/ a (secreto) reservado, secreto; (advertisement) por palabras

classified advertisement n anuncio por palabras, m

classify /'klæsə,fai/ vt clasificar

clatter /'klætər/ vi hacer ruido; (knock) golpear; (of loose horseshoes) chacolotear. vt hacer ruido con; chocar (una cosa contra otra). n ruido, m; (hammering) martilleo, m; (of horseshoes) chacoloteo, m; (of a crowd) estruendo, m, bulla, f. **John clattered along the street,** Los pasos de Juan resonaban por la calle

clause /klɔz/ n Gram. cláusula, f; Law. condición, estipulación, cláusula, f

claustrophobia /,klɔstrə'foubiə/ n claustrofobia, f

clavichord /'klævɪ,kɔrd/ n clavicordio, m

clavicle /'klævɪkəl/ n clavícula, f

claw /klɔ/ n garra, f; (of a lobster, etc.) tenaza, f; (hook) garfio, gancho, m. vt arañar, clavar las uñas en; (tear) desgarrar. **c.-hammer,** martillo de orejas, m

clay /klei/ n arcilla, f; barro, m; (pipe) pipa de barro, f. **c.-pit,** barrizal, m

clayey /'kleii/ a arcilloso

clean /klin/ a limpio; puro, casto. adv limpio; completamente; exactamente. **to make a c. sweep (of),** no dejar títere con cabeza. **to make a c. breast of,** sincerarse sin tormento, no quedarse con nada en el pecho. **to show a c. pair of heels,** tomar las de Villadiego. **c. bill of health,** patente de sanidad, m. **c.-cut,**

bien definido; claro. **c.-limbed,** bien proporcionado, gallardo. **c.-shaven,** lampiño; sin barba, bien afeitado **clean** /klin/ *vt* limpiar; (streets) barrer; (a floor) fregar; (dryclean) lavar al seco. **to c. one's hands (teeth),** limpia=se las manos (los dientes). **to c. up,** limpiar; (tidy) asear; poner en orden
cleaner /'klinər/ *n* limpiador (-ra); (charwoman) fregona, *f*; (stain remover) sacamanchas, *m*; (drycleaner, person) tintorero (-ra)
cleaning /'klinɪŋ/ *n* limpieza, *f*, a de limpiar. **dry-c.,** lavado al seco, *m*. **c. rag,** trapo de limpiar, *m*. **c. woman** *Mexico* fregandera
cleanliness /'klɛnlinɪs/ *n* limpieza, *f*; aseo, *m*
cleanse /klɛnz/ *vt* limpiar; lavar; purgar; purificar
cleansing /'klɛnzɪŋ/ *n* limpieza, *f*; lavamiento, *m*; purgación, *f*; purificación, *f*
clear /klɪər/ *a* claro; (of the sky) sereno, despejado; transparente; (free (from)) libre (de); (open) abierto; (of profit, etc.) neto; (of thoughts, etc.) lúcido; (apparent) evidente; explícito; (of images) distinto; absoluto; (whole) entero, completo. **c. majority,** mayoría absoluta, *f*. **c. profit,** beneficio neto, *m*. **c.-cut,** bien definido. **c.-headed,** perspicaz; inteligente. **c.-sighted,** clarividente
clear /klɪər/ *vt* aclarar; despejar; limpiar; librar (de); quitar; (one's throat) carraspear; (*Com.* stock) liquidar; (of a charge) absolver; (one's character) vindicar; (avoid, miss) evitar; (jump) salvar, saltar; (a court, etc.) desocupar; (a debt) satisfacer; (an account) saldar; (a mortgage) cancelar; (win) ganar; hacer un beneficio de; (through customs) despachar en la aduana. *vi* (of sky, etc.) serenarse; escampar; (of wine, etc.) aclararse; despacharse en la aduana. **to c. the table,** levantar la mesa, levantar los manteles. **to c. the underbrush from** *Lat. Am.* desmalezar. **to c. the way,** abrir calle; *Fig.* abrir paso. **to c. away,** *vt* quitar; disipar. *vi* disiparse. **to c. off,** *vt* (finish) terminar; (debts) pagar; (discharge) despedir. *vi* (of rain) despejarse, escampar; marcharse. **to c. out,** *vt* limpiar; (a drain, etc.) desatascar; vaciar; echar. *vi* marcharse, escabullirse. **C. out!** ¡Fuera! **the decks,** hacer zafarrancho. **c. the decks for action,** hacer zafarrancho. **to c. up,** *vt* poner en orden; (a mystery, etc.) aclarar, resolver, *vi* (of weather) serenarse, escampar, despejarse
clearance /'klɪərəns/ *n* (of trees, etc.) desmonte, *m*; eliminación, *f*; expulsión, *f*; *Mech.* espacio muerto, *m*; despacho de aduana, *m*. **to make a c. of,** deshacerse de. **c. sale,** liquidación, venta de saldos, *f*
clearing /'klɪərɪŋ/ *n* (in a wood) claro, *m*, *Argentina* abra *f*; desmonte, *m*; (of one's character) vindicación, *f*. **c.-house,** casa de compensación, *f*
clearness /'klɪərnɪs/ *n* claridad, *f*
cleavage /'klivɪdʒ/ *n* hendimiento, *m*; (in views, etc.) escisión, *f*
cleave /kliv/ *vt* partir; abrir; (air, water, etc.) surcar, hender. *vi* (intranse: (stick) pegarse, adherirse
cleaver /'klivər/ *n* partidor, *m*; hacha, *f*
clef /klɛf/ *n* clave, *f*. **treble c.,** clave de sol, *f*
cleft /klɛft/ *n* hendidura, fisura, rendija, abertura, *f*. **c.-palate,** paladar hendido, *m*
clematis /'klɛmətɪs/ *n* clemátide, *f*
clemency /'klɛmənsi/ *n* (of weather) benignidad, *f*; (of character, etc.) clemencia, *f*
clement /'klɛmənt/ *a* (of weather) benigno; (of character, etc.) clemente, benévolo
clench /klɛntʃ/ *vt* agarrar; (teeth, etc.) apretar; (a bargain) cerrar, concluir
clergy /'klɜrdʒi/ *n* clero, *m*, clérigos, *m pl*
clergyman /'klɜrdʒimən/ *n* clérigo, *m*
cleric /'klɛrɪk/ *n* eclesiástico, *m*
clerical /'klɛrɪkəl/ *a* clerical; de oficina. **c. error,** error de oficina, *m*. **c. work,** trabajo de oficina, *m*
clericalism /'klɛrɪkə,lɪzəm/ *n* clericalismo, *m*
clerk /klɜrk/ *n* (clergyman) clérigo, *m*; (in an office) oficinista, escribiente, *m*; oficial, *m*; secretario, *m*
clerkship /'klɜrkʃɪp/ *n* puesto de oficinista, *m*; escribanía, *f*; secretaría, *f*
clever /'klɛvər/ *a* listo, inteligente; ingenioso; hábil; (dexterous) diestro

cleverly /'klɛvərli/ *adv* hábilmente; diestramente, con destreza
cleverness /'klɛvərnɪs/ *n* talento, *m*; inteligencia, *f*; habilidad, *f*; (dexterity) destreza, *f*
cliché /kli'ʃei/ *n* frase hecha, frase de cajón, *f*, cliché, *m*
click /klɪk/ *vi* (of the tongue) dar un chasquido; (of a bolt, etc.) cerrarse a golpe; hacer tictac. *vt* (one's tongue) chascar; (a bolt, etc.) cerrar a golpe. *n* golpe seco, *m*; tictac, *m*; (of the tongue) chasquido, *m*. **to c. one's heels together,** hacer chocar los talones
client /'klaiənt/ *n* cliente, *mf*; (customer) parroquiano (-na), *Lat. Am.* also marchante (-ta) *mf*
clientele /,klaiən'tɛl/ *n* clientela, *f*
cliff /klɪf/ *n* acantilado, *m*, roca, escarpa, *f*
cliff dweller *n* hombre de la roca, hombre de las rocas, *m*, mujer de la roca, mujer de las rocas, *f*
climate /'klaimɪt/ *n* clima, *m*
climatic /klai'mætɪk/ *a* climático
climatology /,klaimə'tɒlədʒi/ *n* climatología, *f*
climax /'klaimæks/ *n* culminación, *f*; (rhetoric) clímax, *m*; gradación, *f*; punto más alto, apogeo, cenit, *m*; (of a play, etc.) desenlace, *m*
climb /klaim/ *vt* and *vi* trepar; escalar; montar; subir; ascender. **rate of c.,** *Aer.* velocidad ascensional, *f*. **to c. down,** bajar; *Fig.* echar el pie atrás. **to c. over,** (obstacles) salvar. **to c. up,** encaramarse por; subir por; montar
climber /'klaimər/ *n* alpinista, *mf*; (plant) trepadera, enredadera, *f*; (social) arribista, *mf*
clinch /klɪntʃ/ *vt* (nails, etc.) remachar, rebotar; (a bargain, etc.) cerrar; (an argument, etc.) remachar. *n* (wrestling) cuerpo a cuerpo, *m*
cling /klɪŋ/ *vi* pegarse (a); agarrarse (a); (of scents) pegarse; (follow) seguir. **They clung together for an instant,** Quedaron abrazados un instante
clinging /'klɪŋɪŋ/ *a* tenaz; (of plants, etc.) trepador; (of persons) manso, dócil. **to be a c. vine,** *Inf.* ser una malva
clinic /'klɪnɪk/ *n* clínica, *f*
clinical /'klɪnɪkəl/ *a* clínico
clink /klɪŋk/ *vi* retiñir; (of glasses) chocarse. *vt* hacer sonar; (glasses) chocar. *n* retintín, *m*; (of a hammer) martilleo, *m*; sonido metálico, *m*; (of glasses) choque, *m*; (jail) *Argentina, Chile* capacha *f*
clip /klɪp/ *vt* (grasp) agarrar; (sheep, etc.) esquilar; (trim) recortar, cercenar; (prune) podar; (a ticket) taladrar. *n* pinza, *f*; (paper-clip) sujetapapeles, *Central America* ataché, *elsewhere in Lat. Am.* broche *m*; *Mech.* grapa, escarpia, *f*; (for ornament) sujetador, *m*. **to c. a person's wings,** *Fig.* cortar (or quebrar) las alas (a)
clipper /'klɪpər/ *n* (person) esquilador (-ra) (*Naut.* and *Aer.*) clíper, *m*; *pl* **clippers,** tenazas de cortar, *f pl*; (for pruning) podaderas, *f pl*; (punch) taladro, *m*
clipping /'klɪpɪŋ/ *n* (of sheep, etc.) esquileo, *m*; (of a newspaper, etc.) recorte, *m*
clique /klik/ *n* camarilla, *f*, grupito *m*
cliquish /'klikɪʃ/ *a* exclusivista
cliquishness /'klikɪʃnɪs/ *n* famiguismo, *m*
cloak /klouk/ *n* capa, *f*; manto, *m*; *Fig.* velo, *m*. *vt* encapotar; embozar; (conceal) ocultar, encubrir. **c. and sword play,** comedia de capa y espada, *f*. **c.-room,** guardarropa, *m*; (ladies') tocador, *m*; (on a station) consigna, *f*
clock /klɒk/ *n* reloj, *m*; (of a stocking) cuadrado, *m*. **It is six o'clock,** Son las seis. **c.-face,** esfera de reloj, *f*. **c.-maker,** relojero, *m*. **c.-making,** relojería, *f*. **c.-work,** aparato de relojería, *m*. **to go like c.-work,** ir como un reloj. **c.-work train,** tren de cuerda, *m*
clockwise /'klɒk,waiz/ *a* and *adv* en el sentido de las agujas del reloj; de derecha a izquierda
clod /klɒd/ *n* (of earth) terrón, *m*; (corpse) tierra, *f*; (person) zoquete, *m*. **c.-hopper,** patán, *m*
clog /klɒg/ *n* (shoe) zueco, zoclo, *m*; (obstacle) estorbo, obstáculo, *m*. *vt* estorbar; estorbar; impedir; (block) obturar, cerrar; *Fig.* paralizar
cloister /'klɔistər/ *n* claustro, *m*; convento, *m*. *vt* enclaustrar
cloistered /'klɔistərd/ *a* enclaustrado; retirado, aislado
close /klous/ *a* estrecho; (of a prisoner) incomuni-

cado; (reticent) reservado; (niggardly) tacaño, avaro; (scarce) escaso; (of friends) íntimo; (equal) igual; (lacking space) apretado; (dense) denso; (thick) tupido; compacto; (of a copy, etc.) fiel, exacto; (thorough) concienzudo; (careful) cuidadoso; (attentive) atento; (to the roots) a raíz; (of shaving) bueno; (of weather) pesado, sofocante; (of rooms) mal ventilado. **at c.** quarters, de cerca. **It is c.** to eight o'clock, Son casi las ocho. **to press c.,** perseguir de cerca; fatigar. **c. at hand, c. by,** cerca; al lado; a mano. **c.-cropped,** (of hair) al rape. **c. fight,** lucha igualada, f. **c.-fisted,** tacaño, apretado. **c.-fitting,** ajustado, ceñido al cuerpo; pequeño. **c. season,** veda, f. **c.-up,** n (cinema) primer plano, m

close /klouz/ n (end) fin, m, conclusión, f; (of day) caída, f; Mus. cadencia, f; (enclosure) cercado, m; (square) plazoleta, f; (alley) callejón, m; (of a cathedral) patio, m. **at the c. of day,** a la caída de la tarde. **to bring to a c.,** terminar; llevar a cabo. **to draw to a c.,** tocar a su fin; estar terminando

close /klouz/ vt cerrar; (end) concluir, terminar; poner fin a. vi cerrar(se); (of a wound) cicatrizarse, cerrarse; (end) terminar(se), acabar, concluir. **to c. the ranks,** cerrar filas. **to c. about,** (surround) rodear, cercar; (envelop) envolver. **to c. down,** vt cerrar. vi cerrar; Radio. cerrarse. **to c. halfway** entrecerrar **to c. in,** (surround) cercar; (of night) cerrar; caer; (envelop) envolver; (of length of days) acortarse. **to c. in on,** cercar. **to c. round,** envolver; (of water) tragar. **to c. up,** vt cerrar; cerrar completamente; obstruir. vi (of persons) acercarse; (of a wound) cicatrizarse; cerrarse

closed /klouzd/ a cerrado. **"Road C.,"** Paso Cerrado. **to have a c. mind,** ser cerrado de mollera; sufrir de estrechez de miras

closely /'klousli/ adv estrechamente; de cerca; (carefully) cuidadosamente; (exactly) exactamente; (attentively) con atención, atentamente

closeness /'klousnɪs/ n estrechez, f; densidad, f; (nearness) proximidad, f; (of a copy, etc.) fidelidad, exactitud, f; (stuffiness) falta de aire, f; (of friendship) intimidad, f; (stinginess) tacañería, f; (reserve) reserva, f

closet /'klɒzɪt/ n camarín, m; (cupboard) alacena, f; (water) excusado, m; (clothes) ropero, m

closing /'klouzɪŋ/ n cerramiento, m; (of an account) saldo, m. **c. time,** cierre, m, hora de cerrar, f

closure /'klouʒər/ n conclusión, f; Polit. clausura, f

clot /klɒt/ n coágulo, grumo, m. vt coagular. vi coagularse, cuajarse

cloth /klɔθ/ n tela, f; paño, m; (table) mantel, m; (clergy) clero, m. **She cleaned the books with a c.,** Ella limpió los libros con un paño. **in c.,** (of books) en tela

clothe /klouð/ vt vestir; cubrir; (with authority, etc.) revestir. **to c. oneself,** vestirse

clothes /klouz/ n pl vestidos, m pl, ropa, f. **a suit of c.,** un traje. **old c. shop,** ropavejería, f. **c.-basket,** cesta de la colada, f. **c.-brush,** cepillo para ropa, m. **c.-hanger,** percha, f. **c.-horse,** enjugador, m. **c.-line,** cuerda de la ropa, f. **c.-peg,** pinza de la ropa, f. **c.-prop,** palo para sostener la cuerda de la colada, m

clothier /'klouðiər/ n ropero, m. **clothier's shop,** ropería, f

clothing /'klouðɪŋ/ n vestidos, m pl, ropa, f. **article of c.,** prenda de vestir, f

clotted /'klɒtɪd/ a grumoso

cloud /klaud/ n nube, f. vt anublar, oscurecer; empañar; (blot out) borrar. vi anublarse. **to be under a c.,** estar bajo sospecha. **summer c.,** nube de verano, f. **storm-c.,** nubarrón, m. **c.-burst,** nubada, f, chaparrón, m. **c.-capped,** coronado de nubes

cloudiness /'klaudinɪs/ n nebulosidad, f; obscuridad, f; (of liquids) turbiedad, f

cloudless /'klaudlɪs/ a sin nubes, despejado; sereno, claro

cloudy /'klaudi/ a nublado, nubloso; obscuro; (of liquids) turbio

clout /klaut/ n Central America, Mexico arranque, m

clove /klouv/ n clavo de especia, m; (of garlic) diente de ajo, m. **c.-tree,** clavero, m

cloven /'klouvən/ a hendido. **to show the c. hoof,** enseñar la oreja. **c. hoof,** pezuña, f

clover /'klouvər/ n trébol, m. **to be in c.,** nadar en la abundancia

clown /klaun/ n patán, m; bufón, tonto, m; (in a circus) payaso, m. vi hacer el tonto, hacer el payaso

clowning /'klaunɪŋ/ n payasada, f

clownish /'klaunɪʃ/ a grosero; palurdo, zafio; bufón

cloy /klɔi/ vt empalagar

cloying /'klɔiɪŋ/ a empalagoso

club /klʌb/ n porra, cachiporra, clava, f; (gymnastic) maza, f; (hockey) bastón de hockey, m; (golf) palo de golf, m; (in cards) basto, m; (social) club, m. vt golpear. **to c. together,** asociarse, unirse. **We clubbed together to buy him a present,** Entre todos le compramos un regalo. **c.-house,** club, m

clubfoot /'klʌb,fʊt/ n pie calcáneo, pie contrahecho, pie de piña, pie equino, pie talo, pie zambo, m

club member n miembro de un club, m

cluck /klʌk/ vi cloquear. n cloqueo, m

clucking /'klʌkɪŋ/ n cloqueo, m

clue /klu/ n indicio, m; (to a problem) clave, f; (of a crossword) indicación, f; idea, f

clump /klʌmp/ n bloque, pedazo, m; (of trees) grupo, m; (of feet) ruido, m. vi caminar pisando fuerte

clumsily /'klʌmzəli/ adv torpemente; pesadamente

clumsiness /'klʌmzinɪs/ n torpeza, f; falta de maña, f; pesadez, f

clumsy /'klʌmzi/ a torpe; desmañado; chapucero, sin arte; (lumbering) pesado; (in shape) disforme

cluster /'klʌstər/ n (of currants, etc.) racimo, m; (of flowers) ramillete, m; grupo, m. vi arracimarse; agruparse. **They clustered around him,** Se agrupaban a su alrededor

clutch /klʌtʃ/ vt agarrar; sujetar, apretar. n Mech. embrague, m; (of eggs) nidada, f; Fig. garras, f pl. **to fall into the clutches of,** caer en las garras de. **to make a c. at,** procurar agarrar. **to throw in the c.,** Mech. embragar. **to throw out the c.,** Mech. desembragar. **c. pedal,** pedal de embrague, m

clutter /'klʌtər/ n desorden, m, confusión, f. vt desordenar

coach /koutʃ/ n carroza, f; charabán, m; Rail. vagón, coche, m; (hackney) coche de alquiler, m; Sports. entrenador, m; (tutor) profesor particular, m. vt Sports. entrenar; (teach) preparar, dar lecciones particulares (a). **through c.,** coche directo, m. **c.-box,** pescante, m. **c.-house,** cochera, f

coaching /'koutʃɪŋ/ n Sports. entrenamiento, m; lecciones particulares, f pl

coachman /'koutʃmən/ n cochero, m

coagulate /kou'ægyə,leit/ vi coagularse. vt coagular, cuajar

coagulation /kou,ægyə'leifən/ n coagulación, f

coal /koul/ n carbón, m; pedazo de carbón, m; (burning) brasa, f. vi carbonear, hacer carbón. vt proveer de carbón; carbonear. **to carry coals to Newcastle,** llevar leña al monte; elevar aqua al mar. **to rake a person over the coals,** reprender a alguien. **c.-barge,** (barco) carbonero, m. **c.-black,** negro como el azabache. **c.-cellar, house,** carbonera, f. **c.-dust,** cisco, m. **c.-field,** yacimiento de carbón, m. **c.-gas,** gas de hulla, m. **c.-heaver,** cargador de carbón, m. **c.-merchant,** carbonero, m. **c.-mine,** mina de carbón, f. **c.-miner,** minero de carbón, m. **c.-scuttle,** carbonera, f. **c.-tar,** alquitrán mineral, m

coalesce /,kouə'lɛs/ vi fundirse; unirse; incorporarse

coalescence /,kouə'lɛsəns/ n fusión, f; unión, f; incorporación, f

coalition /,kouə'lɪʃən/ n coalición, f

coarse /kɔrs/ a (in texture) basto, tosco; (gross) grosero; vulgar. **c.-grained,** de fibra gruesa; (of persons) vulgar, poco fino. **c. woolen cloth** Chile litro m

coarsen /'kɔrsən/ vt (of persons) embrutecer. vi embrutecerse; (of the skin) curtirse

coarseness /'kɔrsnɪs/ n basteza, f; tosquedad, f; (of persons) grosería, indelicadeza, f; vulgaridad, f

coast /koust/ n costa, f; litoral, m. vi costear; deslizarse en un tobogán; dejar muerto el motor. **The c. is**

not clear, Hay moros en la costa. **c.-guard,** guardacostas, *m*. **c.-line,** litoral, *m*
coastal /'koustļ/ *a* costanero, costero. **c. defences,** defensas costeras, *f pl*
coaster /'koustər/ *n Naut.* barco costanero, barco de cabotaje, *m*
coasting /'koustɪŋ/ *n Naut.* cabotaje, *m*
coat /kout/ *n* abrigo, *m*; gabán, *m*; chaqueta, *f*; (animal's) capa, *f*; (of paint) mano, *f. vt* recubrir; (with paint, etc.) dar una mano de. **fur c.,** abrigo de pieles, *m*. **sports c.,** Americana sport, *f*. **c. of arms,** escudo de armas, *m*. **c. of mail,** cota de malla, *f*. **c.-hanger,** percha, *f*
coating /'koutɪŋ/ *n* (of paint, etc.) capa, mano, *f*
co-author /ˌkou'ɔθər/ *n* coautor, *m*
coax /kouks/ *vt* instar; halagar, engatusar, *Lat. Am. also* engaratusar; persuadir (a)
coaxing /'kouksɪŋ/ *n* ruegos, *m pl*; mimos, *m pl*, caricias, *f pl*; persuasión, *f. a* mimoso, zalamero; persuasivo
cob /kɒb/ *n* (horse) jaca, *f*; (lump) pedazo, *m*; (swan) cisne macho, *m*
cobalt /'koubɔlt/ *n* cobalto, *m*. **c. blue,** azul cobalto, *m*
cobble /'kɒbəl/ *n* (stone) guijarro, *m*, *vt* (with stones) empedrar con guijarros; (shoes) remendar
cobbler /'kɒblər/ *n* zapatero remendón, *m*. **cobbler's last,** horma, *f*. **cobbler's wax,** cerote, *m*
cobblestone /'kɒbəlˌstoun/ *n* guijarro, *m*, piedra, *f*
cobelligerent /ˌkoubə'lɪdʒərənt/ *n* cobeligerante, *mf*
cobra /'koubrə/ *n* cobra, serpiente de anteojos, *f*
cobweb /'kɒbˌwɛb/ *n* telaraña, *f*
cobwebby /'kɒbˌwɛbi/ *a* cubierto de telarañas; transparente; de gasa
cocaine /kou'kein/ *n* cocaína, *f*
coccyx /'kɒksɪks/ *n* cóccix, *m*, *inf* rabadilla, *f*
cochlea /'kɒkliə/ *n* caracol (del oído), *m*
cock /kɒk/ *n* gallo, *m*; (male) macho, *m*; (tap) grifo, *m*, espita, *f*; (of a gun) martillo, *m*; (weather-vane) veleta, *f*; (of hay) montón, *m*. *vt* (a gun) amartillar; (a hat) ladear; (raise) erguir, enderezar. **a cocked hat,** un sombrero de tres picos. **at half c.,** (of a gun) desamartillada *f*. **He cocked his head,** Erguió la cabeza. **The dog cocked its ears,** El perro aguzó las orejas. **to c. one's eye at,** lanzar una mirada (a). **c.-a-doodle-doo,** quiquiriquí, *m*. **c.-a-hoop,** triunfante, jubiloso; arrogante. **c.-crow,** canto del gallo, *m*. **c.-fight,** riña de gallos, *f*. **c.-of-the-walk,** gallito, *m*. **c.-sure,** pagado de sí mismo; completamente convencido
cockerel /'kɒkərəl/ *n* gallo joven, gallito, *m*
cocker spaniel /ˌkɒkər 'spænyəl/ *n* cóquer, *m*
cockle /'kɒkəl/ *n* (bivalve) bucarda, *f. vi* arrugarse; (warp) torcerse; doblarse. **c.-shell,** (pilgrims') concha, *f*; (boat) cascarón de nuez, *m*
Cockney /'kɒkni/ *a* londinense, de Londres. *n* londinense, *mf*
cockpit /'kɒkˌpɪt/ *n* gallería, *f*; *Aer.* casilla del piloto, *f*; *Fig.* arena, *f*
cockroach /'kɒkˌroutʃ/ *n* cucaracha, *f*
cockscomb /'kɒksˌkoum/ *n* cresta de gallo, *f*
cocktail /'kɒkˌteil/ *n* (drink) cótel, coctel, *m*. **to shake a c.,** mezclar un coctel. **c. party,** coctel *m*. **c. shaker,** cotelera, *f*
cocky /'kɒki/ *a* fatuo, presuntuoso
cocoa /'koukou/ *n* cacao, *m*
coconut /'koukəˌnʌt/ *n* coco, *m*; *Inf.* cabeza, *f*. **c. milk,** agua de coco, *f*. **c. shy,** pim, pam, pum, *m*. **c. tree,** cocotero, *m*
cocoon /kə'kun/ *n* capullo, *m*
cod /kɒd/ *n* bacalao, *m*. **cod-liver oil,** aceite de hígado de bacalao, *m*
coddle /'kɒdļ/ *vt* criar con mimo, mimar, consentir
code /koud/ *n* código, *m*; clave, *f*; (secret) cifra, *f. vt* poner en cifra. **signal c.,** *Naut.* código de señales, *m*. **c. word,** palabra de clave, *f*
codeine /'koudin/ *n* codeína, *f*
codex /'koudɛks/ *n* códice, *m*
codicil /'kɒdəsəl/ *n* codicilio, *f*
codification /ˌkɒdəfɪ'keiʃən/ *n* codificación, *f*
codify /'kɒdəˌfai/ *vt* codificar

coeducation /ˌkouɛdʒu'keiʃən/ *n* coeducación, *f*
coefficient /ˌkouə'fɪʃənt/ *n* coeficiente, *m*
coequality /ˌkoui'kwɒlɪti/ *n* coigualdad, *f*
coerce /kou'ɜrs/ *vt* forzar, obligar; constreñir
coercion /kou'ɜrʃən/ *n* coerción, coacción, *f*
coercive /kou'ɜrsɪv/ *a* coercitivo, coactivo
coeval /kou'ivəl/ *a* coevo
coexist /ˌkouɪg'zɪst/ *vi* coexistir
coexistence /ˌkouɪg'zɪstəns/ *n* coexistencia, *f*
coffee /'kɔfi/ *n* café, *m*. **black c.,** café solo, *m*. **white c.,** café con leche, *m*. **c.-bean,** grano de café, *m*. **c.-cup,** taza para café, *f*. **c.-house,** café, *m*. **c.-mill,** molinillo de café, *m*. **c.-plantation,** cafetal, *m*. **c.-pot,** cafetera, *f*. **c.-set,** juego de café, *m*. **c.-tree,** cafeto, *m*
coffer /'kɔfər/ *n* cofre, *m*; arca, caja, *f*
coffin /'kɔfɪn/ *n* ataúd, féretro, *m*; caja, *f*
cog /kɒg/ *n Mech.* diente (de rueda), *m*
cogency /'koudʒənsi/ *n* fuerza, *f*
cogent /'koudʒənt/ *a* convincente, fuerte; urgente
cogitate /'kɒdʒɪˌteit/ *vi* pensar, considerar, meditar
cogitation /ˌkɒdʒɪ'teiʃən/ *n* reflexión, meditación, consideración, *f*
cognac /'kounyæk/ *n* coñac, *m*
cognate /'kɒgneit/ *a* (of stock) consanguíneo; afín; análogo; semejante
cognition /kɒg'nɪʃən/ *n* cognición, *f*
cognitive /'kɒgnɪtɪv/ *a* cognoscitivo. **c. science,** las ciencias cognoscitivas, *f pl*
cognizance /'kɒgnəzəns/ *n* conocimiento, *m*; jurisdicción, *f*
cognizant /'kɒgnɪzənt/ *a* conocedor
cogwheel /'kɒgˌwil/ *n* rueda dentada, *f*
cohabit /kou'hæbɪt/ *vi* cohabitar
cohabitation /kouˌhæbɪ'teiʃən/ *n* cohabitación, *f*
coheir /kou'ɛər/ *n* coheredero, *m*
coheiress /kou'ɛərɪs/ *n* coheredera, *f*
cohere /kou'hɪər/ *vi* pegarse, adherirse; unirse
coherent /kou'hɪərənt/ *a* coherente; consecuente
cohesion /kou'hiʒən/ *n* cohesión, *f*; coherencia, *f*
cohort /'kouhɔrt/ *n* cohorte, *f*
coif /kwɑf/ *n* cofia, *f*; toca, *f*
coiffure /kwɑ'fyʊr/ *n* peinado, *m*; tocado, *m*
coil /kɔil/ *vt* arrollar; (*Naut.* of ropes) adujar. *vi* arrollarse; enroscarse; serpentear. *n* rollo, *m*; (of a serpent and ropes) anillo, *m*; (of hair) trenza, *f*; *Elec.* carrete, *m*. **coil of smoke,** nube de humo, *f*. **to c. up,** hacerse un ovillo
coiling /'kɔilɪŋ/ *n* arrollamiento *m*; serpenteo, *m*
coin /kɔin/ *n* moneda, *f*; *Inf.* dinero, *m*. *vt* acuñar; (a new word) inventar. **to pay back in the same c.,** pagar en la misma moneda
coinage /'kɔinɪdʒ/ *n* acuñación, *f*; moneda, *f*; sistema monetario, *m*; invención, *f*; (new word) neologismo, *m*
coincide /ˌkouɪn'said/ *vi* coincidir (con); estar conforme, estar de acuerdo
coincidence /kou'ɪnsɪdəns/ *n* coincidencia, *f*; (chance) casualidad, *f*
coiner /'kɔinər/ *n* acuñador de moneda, *m*; monedero falso, *m*; (of phrases, etc.) inventor, *m*
coitus /'kouɪtəs/ *n* coito, *m*
coke /kouk/ *n* (carbón de) coque, *m*
colander /'kɒləndər/ *n* colador, *m*
cold /kould/ *a* frío. *n* frío, *m*; *Med.* catarro, constipado, *m*. **I am c.,** Tengo frío. **It is c.,** Está frío. (weather) Hace frío. **to catch a c.,** acatarrarse, resfriarse. **to grow c.,** enfriarse; (of the weather) empezar a hacer frío. **in c. blood,** a sangre fría. **c.-blooded,** (fishes, etc.) de sangre fría; (chilly, of persons) friolero; (pitiless) insensible, sin piedad; (of actions) a sangre fría, premeditado. **c.-chisel,** cortafrío, *m*. **c. cream,** crema (para el cutis), *f*. **c.-hearted,** seco, insensible. **c.-shoulder,** *n* frialdad, *f. vt* tratar con frialdad (a). **c.-storage,** conservación refrigerada, *f*
coldly /'kouldli/ *adv* fríamente
coldness /'kouldnɪs/ *n* frío, *m*; (of one's reception, etc.) frialdad, *f*; (of heart) inhumanidad, *f*
coleopterous /ˌkouli'ɒptərəs/ *a* coleóptero
colic /'kɒlɪk/ *n* cólico, *m*
coliseum /ˌkɒlɪ'siəm/ *n* coliseo, *m*
colitis /kə'laitɪs/ *n* colitis, *f*
collaborate /kə'læbəˌreit/ *vi* colaborar (con)

collaboration /kə‚læbə'reiʃən/ n colaboración, f
collaborationist /kə‚læbə'reiʃənist/ n colaboracionista, mf
collaborator /kə'læbə‚reitər/ n colaborador (-ra); (quisling) colaboracionista, mf
collapse /kə'læps/ n derrumbamiento, m; desplome, m; Med. colapso, m; (of buildings and Fig.) hundimiento, m; (of plans) frustración, f; (failure) fracaso, m. vi derrumbarse; (of buildings, etc.) hundirse, venirse abajo; (of persons, fall) desplomarse; Med. sufrir colapso; (of plans, etc.) frustrarse, venirse abajo. **George came to us after the c. of France,** Jorge vino a quedarse con nosotros después del hundimiento de Francia
collapsible /kə'læpsəbəl/ a plegable
collar /'kɒlər/ n (of a garment and of fur) cuello, m; (of a dog, etc., and necklace) collar, m. vt (seize) agarrar. **detachable c.,** cuello suelto, m. **high c.,** alzacuello, m. **c.-bone,** clavícula, f
collate /kou'leit/ vt cotejar; (to a benefice) colacionar
collateral /kə'lætərəl/ a colateral
collation /kə'leiʃən/ n colación, f
colleague /'kɒlig/ n colega, m; compañero (-ra)
collect /'kɒlekt/ vt (assemble) reunir; (catch) coger; acumular; (call for) pasar a buscar, ir (or venir) a buscar; (pick up) recoger; (taxes, etc.) recaudar; coleccionar; (one's strength, etc. and debts, etc.) cobrar; (letters) recoger. vi reunirse, congregarse; acumularse. n Eccl. colecta, f. **to c. oneself,** reponerse
collected /kə'lektid/ a (of persons) seguro de sí.
collection /kə'lekʃən/ n reunión, f; (of data, etc.) acumulación, f; (of pictures, stamps, etc.) colección, f; (of a debt, etc.) cobranza, f; (of taxes, etc.) recaudación, f; (from a mail box) recogida, f; (of laws, etc.) compilación, f; Eccl. ofertorio, m; (of donations) colecta, f
collection agency n agencia de cobros de cuentas, f
collective /kə'lektiv/ a colectivo. **c. bargaining,** regateo colectivo, trato colectivo, m
collectivism /kə'lektə‚vizəm/ n colectivismo, m
collector /kə'lektər/ n (of pictures, etc.) coleccionador (-ra), coleccionista, mf; cobrador, m; Elec. colector, m
college /'kɒlidʒ/ n colegio, m; escuela, f; universidad, f. **C. of Cardinals,** Colegio de Cardenales, m
collegiate /kə'lidʒit/ a colegial, colegiado. **c. church,** iglesia colegial, f
collide /kə'laid/ vi chocar (contra), topar (con); estar en conflicto (con). **c. head-on,** chocar frontalmente
collie /'kɒli/ n perro de pastor escocés, m
collier /'kɒlyər/ n minero de carbón, m; (barco) carbonero, m
collision /kə'liʒən/ n choque, m, colisión, f; (of interests, etc.) antagonismo, conflicto, m. **to come into c. with,** chocar con
colloid /'kɒlɔid/ a coloide, m
colloquial /kə'loukwiəl/ a familiar
colloquialism /kə'loukwiə‚lizəm/ n expresión familiar, f
colloquially /kə'loukwiəli/ adv en lenguaje familiar, familiarmente
colloquy /'kɒləkwi/ n coloquio, m
collusion /kə'luʒən/ n colusión, f. **to be in c.,** Law. coludir; conspirar, estar de manga
Colombia /kə'lʌmbiə/ Colombia, f
Colombian /kə'lʌmbiən/ a colombiano. n colombiano (-na)
colon /'koulən/ n Anat. colon, m; (punctuation) dos puntos, m pl
colonel /'kɜrnļ/ n coronel, m
colonial /kə'louniəl/ a colonial. n habitante de las colonias, m. **c. government,** Lat. Am. coloniaje, m. **C. Office,** Ministerio de Asuntos Coloniales, m. **c. period,** Lat. Am. coloniaje, m
colonist /'kɒlənist/ n colono, m; colonizador (-ra)
colonization /‚kɒlənə'zeiʃən/ n colonización, f
colonize /'kɒlə‚naiz/ vt colonizar. vi establecerse en una colonia
colonizer /'kɒlə‚naizər/ n colonizador (-ra)
colonizing /'kɒlə‚naizɪŋ/ n colonización, f, a colonizador

colonnade /‚kɒlə'neid/ n columnata, f
colony /'kɒləni/ n colonia, f
color /'kʌlər/ n color, m; colorido, m; tinta, f; materia colorante, f; pl **colors,** insignia, f; bandera, f, estandarte, m; Naut. pabellón, m. vt colorar; pintar; iluminar; (influence) influir, afectar. vi colorarse; ruborizarse; encenderse. **fast c.,** color estable, color sólido, m. **regimental colors,** bandera del regimiento, f. **with colors flying,** con tambor batiente, a banderas desplegadas. **to be off c.,** estar malucho, estar indispuesto. **to change c.,** (of persons) mudar de color, mudar de semblante. **to give c. to,** (a story, etc.) hacer verosímil. **to lay the colors on too thick,** recargar las tintas. **to pass with flying colors,** salir triunfante. **under c. of,** so color de, a pretexto de. **c.-blind,** daltoniano. **c.-blindness,** daltonismo, m
Colorado beetle /‚kɒlə'radou/ n escarabajo de la patata, m
colored /'kʌlərd/ a colorado; de color
coloring /'kʌlərɪŋ/ n (substance) colorante, m; (act of) coloración, f; Art. colorido, m; (of complexion) colores, m pl
colorist /'kʌlərist/ n colorista, mf
colorless /'kʌlərlis/ a sin color, incoloro; Fig. insípido
colossal /kə'lɒsəl/ a colosal, gigantesco; enorme; Inf. estupendo
colossus /kə'lɒsəs/ n coloso, m
colt /koult/ n potro, m; (boy) muchacho alegre, m
colt's-foot /'koults‚fʊt/ n Bot. fárfara, f
columbine /'kɒləm‚bain/ n Bot. aguileña, f; (in pantomime) Colombina, f
column /'kɒləm/ n columna, f. **Fifth c.,** quinta columna, f
columned /'kɒləmd/ a con columnas
columnist /'kɒləmnist/ n periodista, m
coma /'koumə/ n coma, m
comatose /'kɒmə‚tous/ a comatoso
comb /koum/ n peine, m; (for flax) carda, f; (curry) almohaza, f; (of cock) cresta, carúncula, f; (of a wave) cima, cresta, f; (honey) panal, m, vt (hair) peinar; (flax) rastrillar, cardar. **c. and brush,** cepillo y peine. **high c.,** peineta, f. **to c. one's hair,** peinarse
combat /v kəm'bæt; n 'kɒmbæt/ vt luchar contra, combatir, resistir. vi combatir, pelear. n combate, m; lucha, batalla, f. **in single c.,** cuerpo a cuerpo
combatant /kəm'bætņt/ n combatiente, m, a combatiente
combative /kəm'bætiv/ a belicoso, pugnaz
combination /‚kɒmbə'neiʃən/ n combinación, f; mezcla, f; unión, f; asociación, f; pl **combinations,** camisa pantalón, f. **c. lock,** cerradura de combinación, f
combine /v kəm'bain; n 'kɒmbain/ vt combinar; reunir, juntar; Chem. combinar. vi combinarse; asociarse (con), juntarse (con); Com. fusionarse. n asociación, f; Com. monopolio, m
combustible /kəm'bʌstəbəl/ a combustible. n combustible, m
combustion /kəm'bʌstʃən/ n combustión, f. **rapid c.,** combustión rápida, f. **spontaneous c.,** combustión espontánea, f
come /kʌm/ vi venir; llegar; avanzar; acercarse; (happen) suceder, acontecer; (result) resultar; (find oneself) encontrarse, hallarse; (become) llegar a ser; (begin to) ponerse (a), empezar (a). **Coming!** ¡Voy! ¡Allá voy! **C., c.!** ¡Vamos! ¡No es para tanto! ¡Ánimo! **I am ready whatever comes,** Estoy preparado venga lo que venga. **He comes of a good family,** Es (Viene) de buena familia. **I came to know him well,** Llegué a conocerle bien. **I don't know what came over me,** No sé lo que me pasó. **When I came to consider it,** Cuando me puse a considerarlo. **The bill comes to six thousand pesetas,** La cuenta sale a seis mil pesetas. **He comes up before the judge tomorrow,** Ha de comparecer ante el juez mañana. **What you say comes to this,** Lo que dice Vd. se reduce a esto. **What is the world coming to?** ¿A dónde va parar el mundo? **It does not c. within my scope,** No está dentro de mi alcance. **to c. apart,** deshacerse; romperse; dividirse. **to c. home to,** Fig. impresionar mucho, tocar en lo más íntimo; hacer comprender

(a). **to c. into bloom,** empezar a tener flores, florecer. **to c. into one's head,** venir a las mientes. **to c. into the world,** venir al mundo. **to c. near,** acercarse; aproximarse, estar próximo. **to c. next,** venir después; suceder luego. **to c. to an end,** terminar, acabarse. **to c. to blows,** venir a las manos. **to c. to grief,** salir mal parado; (of schemes, etc.) malograrse. **to c. to hand,** venir a mano; (of letters) llegar a las manos (de). **to c. to life,** despertar; animarse; resucitarse. **to c. to nothing,** frustrarse; no quedar en nada. **to c. to pass,** suceder; realizarse. **to c. to terms,** ponerse de acuerdo. **to c. true,** cumplirse, verificarse. **to c. about,** suceder, acontecer, tener lugar; (of the wind) girar. **to c. across,** dar con, encontrar por casualidad; tropezar con. **to c. after,** (a situation) solicitar; (follow) seguir (a); venir más tarde (que); (succeed) suceder. **to c. again,** volver. **to c. along,** caminar (por); andar (por); (arrive) llegar. **C. along!** ¡Ven! ¡Vamos! ¡Andamos! **to c. at,** alcanzar; (attack) embestir, atacar; (gain) obtener, adquirir. **to c. away,** irse, marcharse; (break) deshacerse. **to c. back,** volver, regresar, *Lat. Am.* devolverse **c.-back,** *n Inf.* respuesta, *f*; contraataque, *m*. **to c. before,** llegar antes; preceder (a). **to c. between,** interponerse (entre), intervenir. **to c. by,** pasar por, pasar junto a; (acquire) obtener, adquirir; (achieve) conseguir. **to c. down,** bajar, descender; (in the world) venir a menos; (be demolished) demolerse; (collapse) derrumbarse, hundirse; (of prices) bajar; (of traditions, etc.) llegar e.g. *This work has c. down to us in two fifteenth-century manuscripts* Esta obra nos ha llegado en dos manuscritos del siglo quince; (fall) caer. **c.-down,** *n* caída, *f*; frustración, *f*; desengaño, *m*; desprestigio, *m*; pérdida de posición, *f*. **to c. down on a person,** cantar la cartilla (a). **to c. down with altitude sickness** *Peru* asorocharse **to c. forward,** avanzar, adelantarse; (offer) ofrecerse; presentarse. **to c. in,** entrar; (of money) ingresar; (of trains, etc.) llegar; (of the tide) crecer; (of the new year) empezar; (of fashion) ponerse de moda; (be useful) servir (para). **C. in!** ¡Adelante! ¡Pase Vd.! **to c. into,** (a scheme) asociarse con; (property) heredar; (the mind) presentarse a la imaginación, ocurrirse (a). **to c. off,** (happen) tener lugar; realizarse, efectuarse; (be successful) tener éxito; (break off) separarse (de); romperse. **to c. off well,** tener éxito; (of persons) salir bien. **c. off the press,** salir de prensas. **to c. on,** avanzar; (of actors) salir a la escena; (progress) hacer progresos; (develop) desarrollarse; (of pain, etc.) acometer (a); (arrive) llegar; (of a lawsuit) verse. **C. on!** ¡Vamos! ¡En marcha! **to c. out,** salir; (of stars) nacer; (of buds, etc.) brotar; (of the moon, etc.) asomarse; (of stains) borrarse, salir; (of a book) ver la luz, publicarse; (of secrets) divulgarse, saberse; (of a girl, in society) ponerse de largo; (on strike) declararse en huelga; (of fashions, etc.) aparecer. **to c. out with,** (a remark) soltar; (oaths, etc.) prorrumpir (en); (disclose) revelar, hacer público. **to c. round,** (to see someone) venir a ver (a); (coax) engatusar; (after a faint, etc.) volver en sí; (after illness) reponerse; (to another's point of view) aceptar, compartir. **to c. through,** pasar por; (trials, etc.) subir; salir de; (of liquids) salirse. **to c. to,** volver en sí. **to c. together,** reunirse, juntarse; venir juntos; unirse. **to c. under,** venir (or estar) bajo la jurisdicción de; (the influence of) estar dominado por; (figure among) figurar entre, estar comprendido en. **to c. up,** subir; (of sun, moon) salir; (of plants) brotar; (of problems, etc.) surgir; (in conversation) discutirse; (before a court) comparecer. **to c. up to,** (equal) igualar, ser igual (a); rivalizar con; (in height) llegar hasta. **He came up to them in the street,** Les abordó (or se les acercó) en la calle. **We have c. up against many difficulties,** Hemos tropezado con muchas dificultades. **This novel does not c. up to his last,** Esta última novela no es tan buena como la anterior. **The party did not c. up to their expectations,** La reunión no fue tan divertida como esperaban. **to c. up with,** idear, (a person) alcanzar (a). **to c. upon,** encontrar, hallar; tropezar con; encontrar por casualidad. **to c. upon evil days,** venir a menos

comedian /kə'midiən/ *n* actor cómico, comediante, *m*

comedy /'kɒmɪdi/ *n* comedia, *f*. **c. of manners,** comedia de costumbres, *f*
comeliness /'kʌmlinɪs/ *n* hermosura, *f*
comely /'kʌmli/ *a* hermoso
comer /'kʌmər/ *n* el, *m*, (*f*, la) que viene. **all comers,** todo el mundo. **first c.,** primer (-ra) venido (-da)
comet /'kɒmɪt/ *n* cometa, *m*
comfort /'kʌmfərt/ *vt* consolar, confortar; (encourage) animar; (reassure) alegrar. *n* consuelo, *m*; satisfacción, *f*; comodidad, *f*; bienestar, *m*. **He lives in great c.,** Vive con mucha comodidad. **c.-loving,** comodón
comfortable /'kʌmftəbəl/ *a* cómodo; (with income) suficiente; (consoling) consolador. **to make oneself c.,** ponerse cómodo
comfortably /'kʌmftəbli/ *adv* cómodamente; suficientemente; fácilmente; con facilidad; (well) bien. **He is c. off,** Está bien de dinero
comforter /'kʌmfərtər/ *n* consolador (-ra); (scarf) bufanda, *f*
comforting /'kʌmfərtɪŋ/ *a* consolador
comfortless /'kʌmfərtlɪs/ *a* incómodo, sin comodidad; desconsolador; (of persons) inconsolable, desconsolado
comic /'kɒmɪk/ *a* cómico; bufo; satírico. *n* cómico, *m*; *pl* **comics,** (printed) historietas cómicas, *f pl.* **c. opera,** ópera cómicas, *f*
comical /'kɒmɪkəl/ *a* cómico; divertido, gracioso
coming /'kʌmɪŋ/ *a* (with year, etc.) próximo, que viene; (promising) de porvenir; (approaching) que se acerca. *n* venida, *f*; llegada, *f*; advenimiento, *m*. **c.-out party,** puesta de largo, *f.* **comings and goings,** entradas y salidas, *f pl*
comma /'kɒmə/ *n* coma, *f.* **inverted commas,** comillas, *f pl*
command /kə'mænd/ *vt* mandar, ordenar; (silence, respect, etc.) imponer; (an army, fleet, etc.) comandar; capitanear; (one's emotions) dominar; (have at one's disposal) disponer de; (a military position; view) dominar; (sympathy, etc.) despertar, merecer; (of price) venderse por. *vi* mandar. *n* orden, *f*; (*Mil. Nav.*) mando, *m*; (of an army, etc.) comandancia, *f*; (of one's emotions, etc.) dominio, *m*; (of a military position, etc.) dominación, *f*; disposición, *f.* **At your c.,** A sus órdenes. **By Royal C.,** Por Real Orden; (of shops, etc.) Proveedor de la Real Casa. **word of c.,** orden, *f*
commandant /ˌkɒmən'dænt/ *n* comandante, *m*
commandeer /ˌkɒmən'dɪər/ *vt* (conscript) reclutar; *Mil.* requisar; expropiar
commander /kə'mændər/ *n Mil.* comandante, *m*; *Nav.* capitán de fragata, *m*; (of order of Knighthood) comendador, *m.* **c.-in-chief,** generalísimo, *m.* **C. of the Faithful,** Comendador de los creyentes, *m*
commanding /kə'mændɪŋ/ *a Mil.* comandante; imponente; (of manner) imperioso; dominante. **c. officer,** comandante en jefe, *m*
commandment /kə'mændmənt/ *n* precepto, mandamiento, *m.* **the Ten Commandments,** los diez mandamientos
commando /kə'mændou/ *n Mil.* comando, *m*
commemorate /kə'memə,reit/ *vt* conmemorar
commemoration /kə,memə'reiʃən/ *n* conmemoración, *f*
commemorative /kə'memə,reitɪv/ *a* conmemorativo
commence /kə'mens/ *vt* comenzar, empezar, principiar. *vi* comenzar. **He commenced to eat,** Empezó a comer
commencement /kə'mensmənt/ *n* principio, comienzo, *m*
commend /kə'mend/ *vt* (entrust) encomendar; (recommend) recomendar; alabar
commendable /kə'mendəbəl/ *a* loable; recomendable
commendation /ˌkɒmən'deiʃən/ *n* aprobación, alabanza, *f*; aplauso, *m*
commendatory /kə'mendə,təri/ *a* (of letters) comendatorio
commensurable /kə'mensərəbəl/ *a* conmensurable
commensurate /kə'mensərɪt/ *a* proporcionado (a); conforme (a)
comment /'kɒment/ *n* observación, *f*; (on a work)

compel

comento, m; explicación, nota, f. vi hacer una observación (sobre); (a work) comentar, anotar. **to c. unfavorably on,** criticar
commentary /'kɒmən,teri/ n comentario, m; (on a person, etc.) comentos, m pl, observaciones, f pl
commentator /'kɒmən,teitər/ n comentador (-ra); (of a work) comentarista, mf
commerce /'kɒmərs/ n comercio, m; negocios, m pl; (social) trato, m
commercial /kə'mɜrʃəl/ a comercial; mercantil. **c. traveler,** viajante, mf
commercialism /kə'mɜrʃə,lɪzəm/ n mercantilismo, m
commercialize /kə'mɜrʃə,laiz/ vt hacer objeto de comercio
commercially /kə'mɜrʃəli/ adv comercialmente
commingle /kə'mɪŋgəl/ vt mezclar. vi mezclarse
commiserate /kə'mɪzə,reit/ vi compadecerse (de), apiadarse (de)
commiseration /kə,mɪzə'reiʃən/ n conmiseración, compasión, f
commissariat /,kɒmə'sɛəriət/ n comisaría, f; Inf. despensa, f
commissary /'kɒmə,sɛri/ n comisario, m
commission /kə'mɪʃən/ n comisión, f; Mil. graduación de oficial, f. vt comisionar; (a ship) poner en servicio activo, armar; (appoint) nombrar. **in c.,** en servicio, activo. **out of c.,** (of ships) inutilizado; inservible. **c. agent,** comisionista, mf **to gain one's c.,** Mil. graduarse de oficial. **to put out of c.,** retirar del servicio; poner fuera de combate; estropear
commissionaire /kə,mɪʃə'nɛər/ n portero, m
commissioned /kə'mɪʃənd/ a comisionado. **c. officer,** oficial, m
commissioner /kə'mɪʃənər/ n comisario, m. **High C.,** alto comisario, m. **c. for oaths,** notario, m. **c. of police,** jefe de policía, m
commit /kə'mɪt/ vt entregar (a); (a crime) cometer; (to prison) encarcelar; (for trial) remitir. **to c. oneself,** comprometerse. **to c. to memory,** aprender de memoria. **to c. to writing,** poner por escrito
commitment /kə'mɪtmənt/ n (financial, etc.) obligación, responsabilidad, f; compromiso, m
committal /kə'mɪtl/ n (of an offense) comisión, f; (placing, entrusting) entrega, f; (to prison) encarcelamiento, m; (legal procedure) auto de prisión, m
committee /kə'mɪti/ n comité, m; comisión, junta, f; consejo, m. **They decided in c.,** Tomaron la resolución en comité. **c. of management,** consejo de administración, m
commodious /kə'moudiəs/ a espacioso, grande
commodiousness /kə'moudiəsnɪs/ n espaciosidad, f
commodity /kə'mɒdɪti/ n artículo, m, mercancía, f
commodore /'kɒmə,dɔr/ n Nav. jefe de escuadra, m; comodoro, m
common /'kɒmən/ a común; general, corriente; universal; vulgar; (disparaging) cursi; (elementary) elemental. n pastos comunes, m pl. **He is not a c. man,** No es un hombre cualquiera; No es un hombre vulgar. **in c.,** en común. **the c. man,** el hombre medio. **the c. people,** el pueblo. **c. sense,** sentido común, m. **c. soldier,** soldado raso, m. **c. speech,** lenguaje vulgar, m. **c. usage,** uso corriente, m
commoner /'kɒmənər/ n plebeyo (-ya)
commonly /'kɒmənli/ adv comúnmente, por lo general
commonness /'kɒmənnɪs/ n frecuencia, f; vulgaridad, f
commonplace /'kɒmən,pleis/ n lugar común, m; trivialidad, f. a trivial
commons /'kɒmənz/ n el pueblo; (House of) Cámara de los Comunes, f; (food) provisiones, f pl. **to be on short c.,** comer mal, estar mal alimentado
Commonwealth /'kɒmən,wɛlθ/ n estado, m; república, f; comunidad (de naciones), f; mancomunidad, f. **the Commonwealth of Puerto Rico,** el Estado Libre Asociado de Puerto Rico, m
commotion /kə'mouʃən/ n confusión, f; conmoción, f; perturbación, f; tumulto, m
communal /kə'myunl/ a comunal
commune /'kɒmyun/ n comuna, f; comunión, f. vi conversar (con). **to c. with oneself,** hablar consigo

communicable /kə'myunɪkəbəl/ a comunicable
communicant /kə'myunɪkənt/ n Eccl. comulgante, mf; (of information) informante, mf
communicate /kə'myunɪ,keit/ vt comunicar; (diseases) transmitir. vi comunicarse (con); Eccl. comulgar
communication /kə,myunɪ'keiʃən/ n comunicación, f. **lines of c.,** comunicaciones, f pl. **to get into c. with,** ponerse en comunicación con. **c.-cord,** (in a railway carriage) timbre de alarma, m
communicative /kə'myunɪ,keitɪv/ a comunicativo; expansivo
communicativeness /kə'myunɪ,keitɪvnɪs/ n carácter expansivo, m; locuacidad, f
communion /kə'myunyən/ n comunión, f. **Holy C.,** comunión, f. **to take c.,** comulgar. **c. card,** cédula de comunión, f. **c. cup,** cáliz, f. **c. table,** sagrada mesa, f; altar, m
communiqué /kə,myunɪ'kei/ n comunicado, parte, f. **to issue a c.,** dar parte
communism /'kɒmyə,nɪzəm/ n comunismo, m
communist /'kɒmyənɪst/ n comunista, mf. a comunista
community /kə'myunɪti/ n comunidad, f. **the c.,** la nación; el público. **c. center,** centro social, m
commutation /,kɒmyə'teiʃən/ n conmutación, f; reducción, f
commute /kə'myut/ vt conmutar; reducir
compact /n 'kɒmpækt; a kəm'pækt/ n (pact) acuerdo, pacto, m; (powder) polvorera, f. a compacto; firme; sólido; apretado, cerrado; (of persons) bien hecho; (of style) conciso, sucinto
compact disc (CD) n disco compacto, m
compactness /kəm'pæktnɪs/ n compacidad, f; (of style) concisión, f
companion /kəm'pænyən/ n compañero (-ra); camarada, mf; (of an Order) caballero, m; dama, f. vt acompañar. **lady c.,** señora de compañía, f. **c.-hatch,** cubierta de escotilla, f. **c.-ladder,** escala de toldilla, f
companionable /kəm'pænyənəbəl/ a sociable, amistoso
companionably /kəm'pænyənəbli/ adv sociablemente, amistosamente
companionship /kəm'pænyən,ʃɪp/ n compañía, f; compañerismo, m
company /'kʌmpəni/ n (Com. Mil. etc.) compañía, f; (ship's) tripulación, f. **I will keep you c.,** Te haré compañía. **to part c. with,** separarse de. **Present c. excepted!** ¡Mejorando lo presente! **They are not very good c.,** No son muy divertidos
company store n tienda de raya, f (Mexico)
comparable /'kɒmpərəbəl/ a comparable
comparably /'kɒmpərəbli/ adv comparablemente
comparative /kəm'pærətɪv/ a comparativo; relativo
comparatively /kəm'pærətɪvli/ adv comparativamente; relativamente
compare /kəm'pɛər/ vt comparar. vi compararse; poder compararse. ser comparable. **beyond c.,** sin comparación; sin igual. **to c. favorably with,** no perder por comparación con. **to c. notes,** cambiar impresiones
comparison /kəm'pærəsən/ n comparación, f. **in c. with,** comparado con
compartment /kəm'partmənt/ n compartimiento, m; Rail. departamento, m
compass /'kʌmpəs/ n circuito, m; límites, m pl; alcance, m; (of a voice) gama, f; Naut. brújula, f; pl **compasses,** compás, m. vt (achieve) conseguir; (plan) idear, **mariner's c.,** compás de mar. m, rosa de los vientos, f. **pocket c.,** brújula de bolsillo, f. **to c. about,** cercar, rodear
compassion /kəm'pæʃən/ n compasión, f. **to have c. on,** apiadarse de, compadecerse de
compassionate /kəm'pæʃənɪt/ a compasivo, piadoso. **c. leave,** permiso, m
compassionately /kəm'pæʃənɪtli/ adv compasivamente, con piedad
compatibility /kəm,pætə'bɪlɪti/ n compatibilidad, f
compatible /kəm'pætəbəl/ a compatible, conciliable
compatriot /kəm'peitriət/ n compatriota, mf
compel /kəm'pɛl/ vt obligar (a), forzar (a); exigir;

imponer. **His attitude compels respect,** Su actitud impone el respeto

compelling /kəm'pɛlɪŋ/ a compulsivo

compendious /kəm'pɛndiəs/ a compendioso, sucinto

compendium /kəm'pɛndiəm/ n compendio, m; resumen, m

compensate /'kɒmpən,seit/ vt compensar; (reward) recompensar; (for loss, etc.) indemnizar. **to c. for,** compensar; indemnizar contra

compensation /,kɒmpən'seiʃən/ n compensación, f; (reward) recompensa, f; (for loss, etc.) indemnización, f

compensatory /kəm'pɛnsə,tɔri/ a compensatorio

compete /kəm'pit/ vi competir (con); rivalizar; ser rivales; (in a competition) concurrir

competence /'kɒmpɪtəns/ n aptitud, f; capacidad, f; competencia, f

competent /'kɒmpɪtənt/ a competente; capaz

competently /'kɒmpɪtəntli/ adv competentemente

competition /,kɒmpɪ'tɪʃən/ n competencia, competición, rivalidad, f; emulación, f; (contest, etc.) concurso, m. **spirit of c.,** espíritu de competencia, m

competitive /kəm'pɛtɪtɪv/ a competidor; de competición. **c. examination,** oposición, f

competitor /kəm'pɛtɪtər/ n competidor (-ra)

compilation /,kɒmpə'leiʃən/ n compilación, f

compile /kəm'pail/ vt compilar

compiler /kəm'pailər/ n compilador (-ra)

complacence /kəm'pleisəns/ n complacencia, satisfacción, f; contento de sí mismo, m

complacent /kəm'pleisənt/ a satisfecho; pagado de sí mismo

complacently /kəm'pleisəntli/ adv con satisfacción

complain /kəm'plein/ vi quejarse; lamentarse; Law. querellarse. **He complains about everything,** Se queja de todo

complainant /kəm'pleinənt/ n Law. demandante, mf

complaint /kəm'pleint/ n queja, f; lamento, m; Law. demanda, f; (illness) enfermedad, f. **to lodge a c. (against),** quejarse (de)

complaisance /kəm'pleisəns/ n afabilidad, cortesía, f

complaisant /kəm'pleisənt/ a complaciente, cortés, afable; (of husbands) consentido, sufrido

complement /n 'kɒmpləmənt/ v -,mɛnt/ n complemento, m; total, número completo, m. vt completar

complementary /,kɒmplə'mɛntəri/ a complementario

complete /kəm'plit/ a entero; completo; perfecto; acabado. v⁖ completar; acabar; (happiness, etc.) coronar, poner el último toque (a); (years) cumplir; (forms) llenar

completely /kəm'plitli/ adv completamente, enteramente

completeness /kəm'plitnɪs/ n entereza, f; totalidad, f

completion /kəm'pliʃən/ n terminación, f, fin, m

complex /a kəm'plɛks; n 'kɒmplɛks/ a complejo. n complejo, m. **inferiority c.,** complejo de inferioridad, m

complexion /kəm'plɛkʃən/ n tez, f, cutis, m; Fig. carácter, m

complexity /kəm'plɛksɪti/ n complejidad, f

compliance /kəm'plaiəns/ n condescendencia, f; (subservience) sumisión, f; obediencia, f. **in c. with,** de acuerdo con, en conformidad con

compliant /kəm'plaiənt/ a condescendiente; sumiso, dócil; obediente

complicate /'kɒmplɪ,keit/ vt complicar

complicated /'kɒmplɪ,keitɪd/ a complejo; complicado; enredado

complication /,kɒmplɪ'keiʃən/ n complicación, f

complicity /kəm'plɪsɪti/ n complicidad, f. **c. in a crime,** complicidad en un crimen

compliment /n 'kɒmpləmənt/ v -,mɛnt/ n cumplido, m, cortesía, f; requiebro, Inf. piropo, m; favor, m; honor, m; (greeting) saludo, m; (congratulation) felicitación, f. vt cumplimentar; requebrar; (flatter) adular, lisonjear; (congratulate) felicitar. **They did him the c. of reading his book,** Le hicieron el honor de leer su libro. **to pay compliments,** hacer cumplidos; Inf. echar piropos

complimentary /,kɒmplə'mɛntəri/ a lisonjero; galante. **c. ticket,** billete gratuito, m

comply /kəm'plai/ vi (with) cumplir, obedecer; conformarse (con); consentir

component /kəm'pounənt/ a componente. n componente, m

comport /kəm'pɔrt/ vt (oneself), comportarse

comportment /kəm'pɔrtmənt/ n comportamiento, m, conducta, f

compose /kəm'pouz/ vt (all meanings) componer. **to c. oneself,** serenarse, calmarse. **to c. one's features,** componer el semblante

composed /kəm'pouzd/ a sereno, tranquilo, sosegado

composer /kəm'pouzər/ n compositor (-ra)

composite /kəm'pɒzɪt/ a compuesto; mixto. n compuesto, m; Bot. planta compuesta, f

composition /,kɒmpə'zɪʃən/ n (all meanings) composición, f

compositor /kəm'pɒzɪtər/ n Print. cajista, mf

compost /'kɒmpoust/ n abono; estiércol, m

composure /kəm'pouʒər/ n tranquilidad, serenidad, calma, f; sangre fría, f, aplomo, m

compote /'kɒmpout/ n compota, f

compound /'kɒmpaund/ vt mezclar, componer; concertar. a compuesto. n compuesto, m; mixtura, f. **c. interest,** interés compuesto, m

comprehend /,kɒmprɪ'hɛnd/ vt comprender

comprehensible /,kɒmprɪ'hɛnsəbəl/ a comprensible

comprehensibly /,kɒmprɪ'hɛnsəbli/ adv comprensiblemente

comprehension /,kɒmprɪ'hɛnʃən/ n comprensión, f

comprehensive /,kɒmprɪ'hɛnsɪv/ a comprensivo

comprehensiveness /,kɒmprɪ'hɛnsɪvnɪs/ n alcance, m, extensión, f

compress /v kəm'prɛs; n 'kɒmprɛs/ vt comprimir; condensar; reducir, abreviar. n compresa, f

compression /kəm'prɛʃən/ n compresión, f

compressor /kəm'prɛsər/ n compresor, m

comprise /kəm'praiz/ vt comprender, abarcar, incluir

compromise /'kɒmprə,maiz/ n compromiso, m, transacción, f; concesión, f. vt (settle) componer; arreglar; (jeopardize) arriesgar; comprometer. vi transigir. **to c. oneself,** comprometerse

compromising /'kɒmprə,maizɪŋ/ a comprometedor

compulsion /kəm'pʌlʃən/ n compulsión, fuerza, f. **under c.,** a la fuerza

compulsory /kəm'pʌlsəri/ a obligatorio. **c. measures,** medidas obligatorias, f pl. **c. powers,** poderes absolutos, m pl

compunction /kəm'pʌŋkʃən/ n compunción, f, remordimiento, m; escrúpulo, m. **without c.,** sin escrúpulo

computable /kəm'pyutəbəl/ a calculable

computation /,kɒmpyu'teiʃən/ n computación, f, cómputo, m

compute /kəm'pyut/ vt computar, calcular

computer /kəm'pyutər/ m West. Hem. computador (-ra), Spain ordenador, m

computer center n centro calculador, centro de computación, m

comrade /'kɒmræd/ n camarada, mf compañero (-ra)

comradeship /'kɒmræd,ʃip/ n compañerismo, m

con /kɒn/ vt estudiar; leer con atención, Naut. gobernar (el buque)

concatenation /kɒn,kætn'eiʃən/ n concatenación, f

concave /kɒn'keiv/ a cóncavo

conceal /kən'sil/ vt esconder, ocultar; (the truth, etc.) encubrir, callar; disimular

concealed /kən'sild/ a oculto; escondido; disimulado. **c. lighting,** iluminación indirecta, f. **c. turning,** (on a road) viraje oculto, m

concealment /kən'silmənt/ n ocultación, f; encubrimiento, m; (place of) escondite, m; secreto, m

concede /kən'sid/ vt conceder

conceit /kən'sit/ n presunción, vanidad, fatuidad, f, envanecimiento, m

conceited /kən'sitɪd/ a presumido, fatuo, vanidoso. **to be c.,** estar pagado de sí mismo, ensimismarse. **to become c.** Lat. Am. ensimismarse

conceivable /kən'sivəbəl/ a concebible, imaginable

conceivably /kən'sivəbli/ *adv* posiblemente
conceive /kən'siv/ *vt* concebir; (affection, etc.) tomar; (an idea, etc.) formar; (plan) formular, idear. *vi* concebir; (understand) comprender; (suppose) imaginar, suponer
concentrate /'kɒnsən,treit/ *vt* concentrar. *vi* concentrarse; (on, upon) dedicarse (a), entregarse (a); prestar atención (a), concentrar atención (en)
concentrated /'kɒnsən,treitɪd/ *a* concentrado
concentration /,kɒnsən'treiʃən/ *n* concentración, *f*. **c. camp,** campo de concentración, *m*
concentric /kən'sɛntrɪk/ *a* concéntrico
concept /'kɒnsɛpt/ *n* concepto, *m*
conception /kən'sɛpʃən/ *n* concepción, *f*; conocimiento, *m*; idea, *f*, concepto, *m*. **to have not the remotest c. of,** no tener la menor idea de
conceptualism /kən'sɛptʃuə,lɪzəm/ *n* conceptualismo, *m*
concern /kən'sɜrn/ *vt* tocar, tener que vercon, importar, concernir; interesar; referirse (a); tratar (de); (trouble) preocupar, inquietar; (take part in) ocuparse (de or con). *n* asunto, *m*, cosa, *f*; (share) interés, *m*; (anxiety) inquietud, *f*; solicitud, *f*; (business) casa comercial, firma, *f*. **as concerns...,** en cuanto a..., respecto a... **It concerns the date of the next meeting,** Es cuestión de la fecha de la próxima reunión. **It is no c. of yours,** No tiene nada que ver contigo. **The book is concerned with the adventures of two boys,** El libro trata de las aventuras de dos muchachos
concerned /kən'sɜrnd/ *a* ocupado (en); afectado; (in a crime) implicado (en); (troubled) preocupado; inquieto, agitado
concerning /kən'sɜrnɪŋ/ *prep* tocante a, con respecto a, referente a, sobre
concert /'kɒnsɜrt/ *n* acuerdo, concierto, *m*, armonía, *f*; *Mus.* concierto, *m*, *vt* concertar, acordar. **in c. with,** de acuerdo con. **c. hall,** sala de conciertos, *f*
concerted /kən'sɜrtɪd/ *a* concertado
concertina /,kɒnsər'tinə/ *n* concertina, *f*
concerto /kən'tʃɛrtou/ *n* concierto, *m*
concession /kən'sɛʃən/ *n* concesión, *f*; privilegio, *m*
concessionaire /kən,sɛʃə'nɛər/ *n* concesionario, *m*
concierge /,kɒnsi'ɛərʒ/ *n* conserje, *m*
conciliate /kən'sɪli,eit/ *vt* conciliar
conciliation /kən,sɪli'eiʃən/ *n* conciliación, *f*
conciliatory /kən'sɪliə,tɔri/ *a* conciliador
concise /kən'sais/ *a* conciso, breve, sucinto
concisely /kən'saisli/ *adv* concisamente
concision /kən'sɪʒən/ *n* concisión, *f*
conclave /'kɒnkleiv/ *n* conciliábulo, *m*; (of cardinals) conclave, *m*
conclude /kən'klud/ *vt* concluir. *vi* concluirse
conclusion /kən'kluʒən/ *n* conclusión, *f*. **in c.,** en conclusión, para terminar. **to come to the c. that...,** concluir que...
conclusive /kən'klusɪv/ *a* conclusivo, concluyente, decisivo
conclusively /kən'klusɪvli/ *adv* concluyentemente
conclusiveness /kən'klusɪvnɪs/ *n* carácter decisivo, *m*, lo concluyente
concoct /kɒn'kɒkt/ *vt* confeccionar; inventar
concoction /kɒn'kɒkʃən/ *n* confección, *f*; mezcla, *f*; invención, *f*; (of a plot) maquinación, *f*
concomitant /kɒn'kɒmitənt/ *a* concomitante. *n* concomitante, *m*
concord /'kɒnkɔrd/ *n* concordia, buena inteligencia, armonía, *f*; (*Mus. Gram.*) concordancia, *f*; (of sounds) armonía, *f*
concordance /kɒn'kɔrdns/ *n* concordia, armonía, *f*; (book) concordancias, *f pl*
concordat /kɒn'kɔrdæt/ *n* concordato, *m*
concourse /'kɒnkɔrs/ *n* concurrencia, muchedumbre, *f*
concrete /'kɒnkrit/ *a* concreto; de hormigón. *n* hormigón, *m*, *vt* concretar; cubrir de hormigón. **reinforced c.,** hormigón armado, *m*
concretion /kɒn'kriʃən/ *n* concreción, *f*
concubine /'kɒŋkyə,bain/ *n* concubina, manceba, *f*
concur /kən'kɜr/ *vi* coincidir, concurrir; estar de acuerdo, convenir (en)

concurrence /kən'kɜrəns/ *n* (agreement) acuerdo, consentimiento, *m*, aprobación, *f*
concurrent /kən'kɜrənt/ *a* concurrente; unánime; coincidente
concurrently /kən'kɜrəntli/ *adv* concurrentemente
concussion /kən'kʌʃən/ *n* concusión, *f*; *Med.* concusión cerebral, *f*
condemn /kən'dɛm/ *vt* condenar; censurar, culpar; (forfeit) confiscar. **condemned cell,** celda de los condenados a muerte, *f*
condemnation /,kɒndɛm'neiʃən/ *n* condenación, *f*; censura, *f*
condensation /,kɒndɛn'seiʃən/ *n* condensación, *f*
condense /kən'dɛns/ *vt* condensar. *vi* condensarse
condenser /kən'dɛnsər/ *n* (*Elec. Mech. Chem.*) condensador, *m*
condescend /,kɒndə'sɛnd/ *vi* dignarse; (in a bad sense) consentir (en); (with affability) condescender
condescending /,kɒndə'sɛndɪŋ/ *a* condescendiente
condescendingly /,kɒndə'sɛndɪŋli/ *adv* con condescendencia
condescension /,kɒndə'sɛnʃən/ *n* condescendencia, *f*; afabilidad, *f*
condign /kən'dain/ *a* condigno
condiment /'kɒndəmənt/ *n* condimento, *m*
condition /kən'dɪʃən/ *n* condición, *f*; estado, *m*; *pl* **conditions,** condiciones, *f pl*; circunstancias, *f pl*. **on c. that,** con tal que; siempre que, dado que. **to be in no c. to,** no estar en condiciones de. **to change one's c.,** cambiar de estado. **to keep oneself in c.,** mantenerse en buena forma
conditional /kən'dɪʃənl/ *a* condicional. **to be c. on,** depender de
conditionally /kən'dɪʃənli/ *adv* condicionalmente
conditioned /kən'dɪʃənd/ *a* acondicionado. **c. reflex,** reflejo acondicionado, *m*
condole /kən'doul/ *vi* condolerse (de); (on a bereavement) dar el pésame
condolence /kən'douləns/ *n* condolencia, *f*. **to present one's condolences,** dar el pésame
condom /'kɒndəm/ *n* condón, *m*, *Argentina* forro, *m*
condone /kən'doun/ *vt* condonar, perdonar
conduce /kən'dus/ *vi* contribuir, conducir
conducive /kən'dusɪv/ *a* que contribuye, conducente; favorable
conduct /n 'kɒndʌkt; v kən'dʌkt/ *n* conducta, *f*. *vt* conducir; guiar; *Mus.* dirigir; (oneself) portarse, conducirse; *Phys.* conducir. *vi Mus.* dirigir (una orquesta, etc.); *Phys.* ser conductor. **conducted tour,** excursión acompañada, *f*; viaje acompañado, *m*
conduction /kən'dʌkʃən/ *n* conducción, *f*
conductive /kən'dʌktɪv/ *a* conductivo
conductivity /,kɒndʌk'tɪvɪti/ *n* conductibilidad, *f*
conductor /kən'dʌktər/ *n* (guide) guía, *mf*; (of an orchestra) director, *m*; (on a tram, etc.) cobrador, *m*; *Phys.* conductor, *m*
conduit /'kɒnduit/ *n* conducto, *m*; cañería, *f*; canal, *m*
cone /koun/ *n* (*Bot. Geom.* etc.) cono, *m*
confabulation /kən,fæbyə'leiʃən/ *n* confabulación, *f*
confection /kən'fɛkʃən/ *n* confección, *f*, *vt* confeccionar
confectioner /kən'fɛkʃənər/ *n* confitero (-ra); pastelero (-ra)
confectionery /kən'fɛkʃə,nɛri/ *n* confitería, pastelería, repostería, *f*
confederate /*a*, *n* kən'fɛdərɪt; *v* -'fɛdə,reit/ *a* confederado; aliado. *n* confederado, *m*; (in crime) cómplice, *mf*. *vt* confederar. *vi* confederarse; aliarse
confederation /kən,fɛdə'reiʃən/ *n* confederación, *f*
confer /kən'fɜr/ *vt* conceder, conferir; (an honor, etc.) otorgar, investir (con). *vi* consultar (con); deliberar, considerar
conference /'kɒnfərəns/ *n* conferencia, consulta, *f*; conversación, *f*
conferment /kən'fɜrmənt/ *n* otorgamiento, *m*; concesión, *f*
confess /kən'fɛs/ *vt* confesar, reconocer; *Inf.* admitir; (of a priest) confesar; (of a penitent) confesarse. *vi* hacer confesión; (one's sins) confesarse. **I c. that I was surprised,** No puedo negar que me sorprendió

confessed /kən'fɛst/ a confesado, declarado
confession /kən'fɛʃən/ n confesión, f; reconocimiento, m; declaración, f; religión, f; (creed) credo, m. **to go to c.,** confesarse. **to hear a c.,** confesar (a)
confessional /kən'fɛʃənl/ n confesionario, m
confessor /kən'fɛsər/ n confesor, m
confetti /kən'fɛti/ n pl confeti, papel picado m, serpentina, f
confidant /'kɒnfɪ,dænt/ n confidente, m
confidante /,kɒnfɪ'dænt/ n confidenta, f
confide /kən'faid/ vi confiar (a or en). vt confiar
confidence /'kɒnfɪdəns/ n confianza, f; seguridad, f; (revelation) confidencia, f. **in c.,** en confianza. **over-c.,** presunción, f. **to have c. in,** tener confianza en. **c. man,** caballero de industria, estafador, m. **c. trick,** timo, m
confident /'kɒnfɪdənt/ a confiado; seguro; (conceited) presumido
confidential /,kɒnfɪ'dɛnʃəl/ a confidencial; de confianza. **c. clerk,** empleado (-da) de confianza. **c. letter,** carta confidencial, f
confidentially /,kɒnfɪ'dɛnʃəli/ adv en confianza, confidencialmente
confidently /'kɒnfɪdəntli/ adv confiadamente
confiding /kən'faidɪŋ/ a confiado
confidingly /kən'faidɪŋli/ adv con confianza
configuration /kən,fɪgyə'reiʃən/ n configuración, f
confine /kən'fain/ vt limitar; (imprison) encerrar. **confined space,** espacio limitado, m. **to be confined,** (of a woman) estar de parto, parir. **to be confined to one's room,** no poder dejar su cuarto. **to c. oneself to,** limitarse a
confinement /kən'fainmənt/ n encierro, m, prisión, f; reclusión, f; (of a woman) parto, m. **to suffer solitary c.,** estar incomunicado
confines /'kɒnfainz/ n pl límites, m pl; confines, m pl; fronteras, f pl
confirm /kən'fɜrm/ vt confirmar; corroborar; Eccl. confirmar
confirmation /,kɒnfər'meiʃən/ n confirmación, f; (of a treaty) ratificación, f; Eccl. confirmación, f
confirmatory /kən'fɜrmə,tɔri/ a confirmatorio
confirmed /kən'fɜrmd/ a inveterado
confiscate /'kɒnfə,skeit/ vt confiscar
confiscation /,kɒnfə'skeiʃən/ n confiscación, f
conflagration /,kɒnflə'greiʃən/ n conflagración, f, incendio, m
conflict /'kɒnflɪkt/ v kən'flɪkt/ n conflicto, m; lucha, f. vⁱ estar opuesto (a), estar en contradicción (con)
conflicting /kən'flɪktɪŋ/ a opuesto; incompatible; (of evidence) contradictorio
confluence /'kɒnfluəns/ n confluencia, f
conform /kən'fɔrm/ vt ajustar, conformar. vi ajustarse (a), amoldarse (a); conformarse (a); adaptarse (a)
conformation /,kɒnfɔr'meiʃən/ n conformación, f
conformity /kən'fɔrmɪti/ n conformidad, f. **in c. with,** en conformidad con, con arreglo a
confound /kɒn'faund/ vt confundir. **C. it!** ¡Demonio!
confounded /kɒn'faundɪd/ a perplejo; Inf. maldito
confraternity /,kɒnfrə'tɜrnɪti/ n cofradía, hermandad, f
confront /kən'frʌnt/ vt hacer frente (a), afrontar; salir al paso; confrontar
Confucianism /kən'fyuʃə,nɪzəm/ n el confucianismo, m
confuse /kən'fyuz/ vt turbar, aturdir; confundir (con); (the issue) obscurecer; (disconcert) desconcertar, dejar confuso (a); dejar perplejo (a). **You have confused one thing with another,** Has confundido una cosa con otra. **My mind was confused,** Mis ideas eran confusas; Tenía la cabeza trastornada
confused /kən'fyuzd/ a confuso
confusing /kən'fyuzɪŋ/ a turbador; desconcertante. **It is all very c.,** Todo ello es muy difícil de comprender
confusion /kən'fyuʒən/ n confusión, f. **covered with c.,** confuso, avergonzado. **to be in c.,** estar confuso; estar en desorden

confute /kən'fyut/ vt (a person) confundir; (by evidence) refutar, confutar
congeal /kən'dʒil/ vt congelar; (blood) coagular. vi congelarse, helarse; coagularse
congealment /kən'dʒilmənt/ n congelación, f; (of blood) coagulación, f
congenial /kən'dʒinyəl/ a (of persons) simpático; propicio, favorable; agradable
congenital /kən'dʒɛnɪtl/ a congénito
congest /kən'dʒɛst/ vt atestar; amontonar; Med. congestionar
congested /kən'dʒɛstɪd/ a Med. congestionado; (of places) atestado de gente; de mayor población; concurrido. **c. area,** área de mayor densidad de población, f
congestion /kən'dʒɛstʃən/ n Med. congestión, f; densidad del tráfico, f; mayor densidad de población, f
conglomerate /kən'glɒmərɪt/ a conglomerado. n conglomerado, m
conglomeration /kən,glɒmə'reiʃən/ n conglomeración, f
congratulate /kən'grætʃə,leit/ vt felicitar, dar la enhorabuena (a); congratular
congratulation /kən,grætʃə'leiʃən/ n felicitación, enhorabuena, f; congratulación, f
congratulatory /kən'grætʃələ,tɔri/ a de felicitación, congratulatorio
congregate /'kɒŋgrɪ,geit/ vi congregarse, reunirse, juntarse
congregation /,kɒŋgrɪ'geiʃən/ n congregación, f; asamblea, reunión, f; (in a church) fieles, m pl; (parishioners) feligreses, m pl
congress /'kɒŋgrɪs/ n congreso, m. **C.-member,** miembro del Congreso, m, congresista, mf
conical /'kɒnɪkəl/ a cónico
conifer /'kounəfər/ n conífera, f
coniferous /kou'nɪfərəs/ a conífero
conjectural /kən'dʒɛktʃərəl/ a conjetural
conjecture /kən'dʒɛktʃər/ n conjetura, f, vt conjeturar
conjoint /kən'dʒɔint/ a asociado, conjunto
conjointly /kən'dʒɔintli/ adv juntamente, en común
conjugal /'kɒndʒəgəl/ a conyugal
conjugate /'kɒndʒə,geit/ vt conjugar. vi conjugarse
conjugation /,kɒndʒə'geiʃən/ n conjugación, f
conjunction /kən'dʒʌŋkʃən/ n conjunción, f. **in c. with,** de acuerdo con
conjunctive /kən'dʒʌŋktɪv/ a conjuntivo. n conjunción, f
conjunctivitis /kən,dʒʌŋktə'vaitɪs/ n conjuntivitis, f
conjure /'kʌndʒər/ vt (implore) rogar, suplicar. vi (juggle) hacer juegos de manos. **a name to c. with,** un nombre todopoderoso. **to c. up,** (spirits) conjurar; Fig. evocar
conjurer, conjuror /'kʌndʒərər/ n (magician) nigromante, m; prestidigitador, m. **conjuror's wand,** varilla de virtudes, f
conjuring /'kʌndʒərɪŋ/ n prestidigitación, f, juegos de manos, m pl. **c. trick,** juego de manos, m. **c. up,** evocación, f
connect /kə'nɛkt/ vt juntar, unir; (relate) relacionar; asociar; (Elec. and Mech.) conectar. vi juntarse, unirse; relacionarse; asociarse; (of events) encadenarse; (of trains) enlazar. **This train connects with the Madrid express,** Este tren enlaza con el expreso de Madrid. **They are connected with the Borgia family,** Están emparentados con los Borgia, Son parientes de los Borgia
connected /kə'nɛktɪd/ a conexo; (coherent) coherente; relacionado; asociado; (in a crime) implicado; (by marriage, etc.) emparentado
connectedly /kə'nɛktɪdli/ adv coherente
connecting /kə'nɛktɪŋ/ a que une; (Mech. and Elec.) conectivo; (of doors, etc.) comunicante. **c.-link,** Mech. varilla de conexión, f; Fig. lazo, m. **c.-rod,** biela, f
connection /kə'nɛkʃən/ n conexión, f; unión, f; (of ideas) relación, f; (junction) empalme, m; (of trains, boats) enlace, m; (intimacy) intimidad, f; (relative) pariente, m; (of a firm, etc.) clientela, f; Elec. conexión, f. **in c. with,** con referencia a, en asociación con. **in this c.,** respecto a esto

conning tower /'kɒnɪŋ/ n torre de mando, f
connivance /kə'naivəns/ n consentimiento, m; complicidad, f
connive (at) /kə'naiv/ vi hacer la vista gorda, ser cómplice (en)
connotation /ˌkɒnə'teiʃən/ n connotación, f
connote /kə'nout/ vt connotar
connubial /kə'nubiəl/ a conyugal
conquer /'kɒŋkər/ vt conquistar; vencer. vi triunfar
conquering /'kɒŋkərɪŋ/ a conquistador, vencedor; triunfante, victorioso
conqueror /'kɒŋkərər/ n conquistador, m; vencedor, m
conquest /'kɒnkwɛst/ n conquista, f. **to make a c. of,** conquistar
consanguineous /ˌkɒnsæŋ'gwiniəs/ a consanguíneo
consanguinity /ˌkɒnsæŋ'gwiniti/ n consanguinidad, f
conscience /'kɒnʃəns/ n conciencia, f. **in all c.,** en verdad. **with a clear c.,** con la conciencia limpia. **c.-stricken,** lleno de remordimientos
conscienceless /'kɒnʃənslis/ a desalmado, falto de conciencia, sin conciencia
conscientious /ˌkɒnʃi'ɛnʃəs/ a concienzudo; diligente. **c. objector,** objetor de conciencia, m
conscientiously /ˌkɒnʃi'ɛnʃəsli/ adv concienzudamente
conscientiousness /ˌkɒnʃi'ɛnʃəsnis/ n conciencia, diligencia, f; rectitud, f
conscious /'kɒnʃəs/ a consciente. n Psychol. consciente, m. **to become c.,** (after unconsciousness) volver en sí. **to become c. of,** darse cuenta de
consciously /'kɒnʃəsli/ adv conscientemente, a sabiendas
consciousness /'kɒnʃəsnis/ n conciencia, f; conocimiento, sentido, m. **to lose c.,** perder el conocimiento, perder el sentido. **to recover c.,** recobrar el sentido, volver en sí
conscript /n 'kɒnskript/ v kən'skript/ n conscripto, m, a conscripto. vt reclutar
conscription /kən'skripʃən/ n conscripción, f
consecrate /'kɒnsɪˌkreit/ vt consagrar; bendecir
consecration /ˌkɒnsɪ'kreiʃən/ n consagración, f; dedicación, f
consecutive /kən'sɛkyətiv/ a consecutivo
consecutively /kən'sɛkyətivli/ adv consecutivamente
consensus /kən'sɛnsəs/ n consenso, m, unanimidad, f. **c. of opinion,** opinión general, f
consent /kən'sɛnt/ vi consentir. n consentimiento, m; permiso, m, aquiescencia, f. **by common c.,** de común acuerdo
consequence /'kɒnsɪˌkwɛns/ n consecuencia, f; resultado, m; importancia, f, **in c.,** por consiguiente. **in c. of,** de resultas de. **of no c.,** sin importancia
consequences /'kɒnsɪˌkwɛnsiz/ n (game) cartas rusas, f pl
consequent /'kɒnsɪˌkwɛnt/ a consecuente, consiguiente
consequential /ˌkɒnsɪ'kwɛnʃəl/ a consecuente; (of persons) fatuo, engreído
consequently /'kɒnsɪˌkwɛntli/ adv por consiguiente, en consecuencia
conservation /ˌkɒnsər'veiʃən/ n conservación, f. **c. of energy,** conservación de energía, f
conservatism /kən'sɜrvəˌtizəm/ n conservadurismo, m
conservative /kən'sɜrvətiv/ a preservativo; conservador. n conservador (-ra). **c. party,** partido conservador, m
conservatoire /kən,sɜrvə'twɑr/ n conservatorio de música, m
conservatory /kən'sɜrvəˌtɔri/ n invernáculo, invernadero, m
conserve /kən'sɜrv/ vt conservar
consider /kən'sɪdər/ vt considerar, pensar meditar; tomar en cuenta; examinar; (deem) juzgar; (believe) creer, estar convencido de (que); (of persons) considerar. **all things considered,** considerando todos los puntos, después de considerarlo todo
considerable /kən'sɪdərəbəl/ a considerable
considerably /kən'sɪdərəbli/ adv considerablemente

considerate /kən'sɪdərɪt/ a considerado, solícito
considerately /kən'sɪdərɪtli/ adv con consideración, solícitamente
consideration /kən,sɪdə'reiʃən/ n consideración, f; reflexión, deliberación, f; remuneración, f. **out of c. for,** en consideración de; por consideración a. **to take into c.,** tomar en cuenta, tomar en consideración
considered /kən'sɪdərd/ a considerado
considering /kən'sɪdərɪŋ/ prep en consideración de, considerando, en vista de
consign /kən'sain/ vt consignar; Fig. enviar. **to c. to oblivion,** sepultar en el olvido
consignee /ˌkɒnsai'ni/ n consignatario, m
consignment /kən'sainmənt/ n consignación, f; envío, m
consignor /kən'sainər/ n consignador, m
consist /kən'sist/ vi consistir (en); ser compatible (con). **to c. of,** componerse de, consistir de
consistence, consistency /kən'sistəns; kən'sistənsi/ n consistencia, f; compatibilidad, f; lógica, f; (of persons) consecuencia, f
consistent /kən'sistənt/ a compatible; lógico; (of persons) consecuente
consistently /kən'sistəntli/ adv conformemente (a); consecuentemente
consolation /ˌkɒnsə'leiʃən/ n consuelo, m, consolación, f
console /v kən'soul; n 'kɒnsoul/ vt consolar; confortar. n Archit. cartela, f. **c. table,** consola, f
consolidate /kən'sɒlɪˌdeit/ vt consolidar. vi consolidarse
consolidation /kən,sɒlɪ'deiʃən/ n consolidación, f
consoling /kən'soulɪŋ/ a consolador; confortador
consols /'kɒnsɒlz, kən'sɒlz/ n pl (títulos) consolidados, m pl
consonance /'kɒnsənəns/ n consonancia, f
consonant /'kɒnsənənt/ a consonante
consort /n 'kɒnsɔrt; v kən'sɔrt/ n consorte, mf. **to c. with,** frecuentar la compañía de; ir con; acompañar (a). **prince c.,** príncipe consorte, m
conspicuous /kən'spɪkyuəs/ a conspicuo; prominente; notable. **to be c.,** destacarse; llamar la atención. **to make oneself c.,** ponerse en evidencia, llamar la atención
conspicuously /kən'spɪkyuəsli/ adv visiblemente; muy en evidencia
conspiracy /kən'spɪrəsi/ n conspiración, f; complot, m
conspirator /kən'spɪrətər/ n conspirador (-ra)
conspire /kən'spaiər/ vi conspirar
constable /'kɒnstəbəl/ n agente de policía, m; (historical) condestable, m. **chief c.,** jefe de policía, m
constabulary /kən'stæbyəˌleri/ n policía, f
constancy /'kɒnstənsi/ n constancia, f
constant /'kɒnstənt/ a constante; incesante. n constante, m
Constantinople /ˌkɒnstæntən'oupəl/ Constantinopla, f
constantly /'kɒnstəntli/ adv constantemente
constellation /ˌkɒnstə'leiʃən/ n constelación, f
consternation /ˌkɒnstər'neiʃən/ n consternación, f; espanto, terror, m
constipate /'kɒnstəˌpeit/ vt estreñir
constipation /ˌkɒnstə'peiʃən/ n estreñimiento, m, constipación de vientre, f
constituency /kən'stitʃuənsi/ n distrito electoral, m
constituent /kən'stitʃuənt/ a constituyente. n constituyente, m; componente, m; elector (-ra)
constitute /'kɒnstɪˌtut/ vt constituir; nombrar; autorizar
constitution /ˌkɒnstɪ'tuʃən/ n constitución, f
constitutional /ˌkɒnstɪ'tuʃənl/ a constitucional
constitutionally /ˌkɒnstɪ'tuʃənli/ adv constitucionalmente
constrain /kən'strein/ vt obligar, forzar. **I felt constrained to help them,** Me sentí obligado a ayudarles
constrained /kən'streind/ a (of smiles, etc.) forzado; (of silences) violento; (of persons) avergonzado
constraint /kən'streint/ n fuerza, compulsión, f; (of atmosphere) tensión, f; (reserve) reserva, f; vergüenza, f
constrict /kən'strikt/ vt apretar, estrechar

constriction /kən'strıkʃən/ n constricción, f
construct /kən'strʌkt/ vt edificar; construir
construction /kən'strʌkʃən/ n construcción, f; interpretación, f. **to put a wrong c. on,** interpretar mal
constructional /kən'strʌkʃənl/ a construccional
constructive /kən'strʌktıv/ a constructor
constructor /kən'strʌktər/ n constructor, m
construe /kən'stru/ vt construir; (translate) traducir; Fig. interpretar
consul /'kɒnsəl/ n cónsul, m
consular /'kɒnsələr/ a consular
consular fees n pl derechos consulares, m pl
consulate /'kɒnsəlıt/ n consulado, m. **c. general,** consulado general, m
consult /kən'sʌlt/ vt consultar. vi consultar (con), aconsejarse (con)
consultant /kən'sʌltənt/ n (Med. and other uses) especialista, m
consultation /ˌkɒnsəl'teıʃən/ n consulta, f
consultative /kən'sʌltətıv/ a consultativo
consulting /kən'sʌltıŋ/ a consultor. **c. hours,** horas de consulta, f pl. **c. rooms,** consultorio, m
consume /kən'sum/ vt consumir; (eat) comerse, tragarse. vi consumirse. **to be consumed by envy,** estar consumido por la envidia. **to be consumed by thirst,** estar muerto de sed
consumer /kən'sumər/ n consumidor (-ra)
consummate /a 'kɒnsəmıt; v -ˌmeıt/ a consumido, perfecto. vt consumar
consummation /ˌkɒnsə'meıʃən/ n consumación, f
consumption /kən'sʌmpʃən/ n consumo, m; gasto, m; Med. tuberculosis, f. **fuel c.,** consumo de combustible, m
consumptive /kən'sʌmptıv/ a destructivo; Med. tísico, hético. n tísico (-ca)
contact /'kɒntækt/ n contacto, m, vt ponerse en contacto con. **to be in c. with,** estar en contacto con
contact lens n lente de contacto, m
contagion /kən'teıdʒən/ n contagio, m
contagious /kən'teıdʒəs/ a contagioso
contain /kən'teın/ vt contener; incluir; Geom. encerrar; (arithmetic) ser divisible por; (oneself) dominarse. **I could not c. myself,** No pude dominarme
container /kən'teınər/ n recipiente, m; envase, m; (box) caja, f
contaminate /kən'tæmə,neıt/ vt contaminar; corromper
contamination /kən,tæmə'neıʃən/ n contaminación, f
contemplate /'kɒntəm,pleıt/ vt contemplar; meditar, considerar, (plan) tener intención de, pensar, proponerse
contemplation /ˌkɒntəm'pleıʃən/ n contemplación, f; meditación, f; expectación, f; (plan) proyecto, m. **to have something in c.,** proyectar algo
contemplative /kən'tɛmplətıv/ a contemplativo, meditabundo
contemplatively /kən'tɛmplətıvli/ adv contemplativamente; atentamente
contemporaneous /kən,tɛmpə'reıniəs/ a contemporáneo
contemporary /kən'tɛmpə,rɛri/ a contemporáneo; (of persons) coetáneo; (of events, etc.) actual. n contemporáneo (-ea)
contempt /kən'tɛmpt/ n desprecio, menosprecio, m; desdén, m. **c. of court,** falta de respeto a la sala, f
contemptible /kən'tɛmptəbəl/ a menospreciable, despreciable; vil
contemptibly /kən'tɛmptəbli/ adv vilmente
contempt of court n rebeldía a la corte, f
contempt of law n rebeldía a la ley, f
contemptuous /kən'tɛmptʃuəs/ a desdeñoso; despectivo; de desprecio. **to be c. of,** desdeñar; menospreciar, tener en poco (a)
contemptuously /kən'tɛmptʃuəsli/ adv con desprecio, desdeñosamente
contend /kən'tɛnd/ vi contender; (affirm) sostener, mantener. **He contended that...,** Sostuvo que...; **contending party,** Law. parte litigante, f
content /n 'kɒntɛnt; a, v kən'tɛnt/ n contenido, m; capacidad, f; (emotion) contento, m; satisfacción, f. a

contento; satisfecho (de). vt contentar; satisfacer. **to one's heart's c.,** a pedir de boca; a gusto de uno; cuanto quisiera
contented /kən'tɛntıd/ a satisfecho, contento
contentedly /kən'tɛntıdli/ adv con satisfacción, contentamente
contention /kən'tɛnʃən/ n disputa, controversia, discusión, f; argumento, m, opinión, f
contentious /kən'tɛnʃəs/ a contencioso
contentment /kən'tɛntmənt/ n contentamiento, m; contento, m
contest /v kən'tɛst; n 'kɒntɛst/ vt disputar; (a suit) defender; (a match, an election, etc.) disputar. n disputa, f; combate, m, lucha, f; (competition) concurso, m
contestant /kən'tɛstənt/ n contendiente, mf
context /'kɒntɛkst/ n contexto, m
contiguity /ˌkɒntı'gyuti/ n contigüidad, f
contiguous /kən'tıgyuəs/ a contiguo, lindero, adyacente
continence /'kɒntnəns/ n continencia, f
continent /'kɒntnənt/ a continente. n continente, m
continental /ˌkɒntn'ɛntl/ a continental
continental shelf n plataforma continental, f
contingency /kən'tındʒənsi/ n contingencia, f
contingent /kən'tındʒənt/ a contingente. n Mil. contingente, m. **to be c. on,** (of events) depender de
continual /kən'tınyuəl/ a continuo
continually /kən'tınyuəli/ adv continuamente
continuance /kən'tınyuəns/ n continuación, f
continuation /kən,tınyu'eıʃən/ n continuación, f; prolongación, f
continue /kən'tınyu/ vi continuar; seguir; prolongarse; durar. vt continuar; seguir; proseguir; perpetuar; (in an office) retener. **to be continued,** se continuará, continuará, seguirá
continuer /kən'tınyuər/ n continuador (-ra)
continuity /ˌkɒntn'uiti/ n continuidad, f
continuous /kən'tınyuəs/ a continuo. **c. performance,** sesión continua, f
continuously /kən'tınyuəsli/ adv de continuo, continuamente
contort /kən'tɔrt/ vt retorcer
contortion /kən'tɔrʃən/ n contorsión, f
contortionist /kən'tɔrʃənıst/ n contorsionista, mf
contour /'kɒntʊr/ n contorno, m; curva de nivel, f. **c. map,** mapa con curvas de nivel, m
contraband /'kɒntrə,bænd/ n contrabando, m
contrabandist /'kɒntrə,bændıst/ n contrabandista, mf
contrabass /'kɒntrə,beıs/ n contrabajo, m
contraception /ˌkɒntrə'sɛpʃən/ n anticoncepción, f
contraceptive /ˌkɒntrə'sɛptıv/ n anticonceptivo, m
contract /n 'kɒntrækt; v kən'trækt/ n pacto, m; (Com. and Law.) contrato, m; (betrothal) esponsales, m pl; (marriage) capitulaciones, f pl; (cards) "Bridge," m. vt contraer; (acquire) adquirir, contraer; (a marriage, etc.) contraer; (be betrothed to) desposarse con; (by formal contract) contratar; pactar. vi (shrink) contraerse, encogerse; comprometerse por contrato. **breach of c.,** no cumplimiento de contrato, m. **c. party,** (of matrimony) contrayente, mf
contractile /kən'træktl/ a contráctil
contraction /kən'trækʃən/ n contracción, f (act or process); forma contracta, f (like isn't or can't)
contractor /'kɒntræktər/ n contratista, m
contradict /ˌkɒntrə'dıkt/ vt contradecir; desmentir
contradiction /ˌkɒntrə'dıkʃən/ n contradicción, f; negación, f
contradictory /ˌkɒntrə'dıktəri/ a contradictorio; opuesto (a), contrario (a)
contralto /kən'træltou/ n (voice) contralto, m; (woman) contralto, f
contraption /kən'træpʃən/ n Inf. artefacto, m
contrapuntal /ˌkɒntrə'pʌntl/ a Mus. de contrapunto
contrariness /'kɒntrɛrinəs/ n Inf. testarudez, terquedad, f
contrariwise /'kɒntrɛri,waız/ adv al contrario; al revés
contrary /'kɒntrɛri/ a contrario; opuesto (a); desfavorable, poco propicio; (of persons) difícil, terco. n contraria, f; (logic) contrario, m, adv en contra, con-

trariamente. **on the c.,** al contrario. **to be c.,** (of persons) llevar la contraria
contrast /n 'kɒntræst; v kən'træst/ n contraste, m. vt contrastar (con). vi contrastar (con), hacer contraste (con)
contravene /ˌkɒntrə'vin/ vt contravenir; atacar, oponerse (a)
contravention /ˌkɒntrə'vɛnʃən/ n contravención, f
contribute /kən'trɪbyut/ vt contribuir; (an article) escribir
contribution /ˌkɒntrə'byuʃən/ n contribución, f; (to a review, etc.) artículo, m
contributor /kən'trɪbyətər/ n contribuyente, mf; (to a journal) colaborador (-ra)
contributory /kən'trɪbyəˌtɔri/ a contribuyente
contrite /kən'trait/ a penitente, arrepentido, contrito
contritely /kən'traitli/ adv contritamente
contrition /kən'trɪʃən/ n contrición, penitencia, f, arrepentimiento, m
contrivance /kən'traivəns/ n invención, f; (scheme) treta, idea, estratagema, f; (machine) aparato, mecanismo, artefacto, m
contrive /kən'traiv/ vt inventar; idear, proyectar. vi (succeed in) lograr, conseguir; (manage) arreglárselas
control /kən'troul/ n autoridad, f; dominio, m; gobierno, m; dirección, f; regulación, f; (restraint) freno, m; (Biol. and Spirit.) control, m; (of a vehicle) conducción, f; manejo, m; manipulación, f; pl **controls,** Mech. mando, m. vt dirigir, regir; regular; usar, manejar, manipular; controlar; (dominate) dominar; (curb) refrenar, reprimir; (command) mandar. **He lost c. of the car,** Perdió el mando (or control) del automóvil. **out of c.,** fuera de mando, fuera de control. **remote c.,** mando a distancia, m. **to c. oneself,** dominarse, contenerse. **to lose c. of oneself,** no lograr dominarse, perder el control. **c. stick,** Aer. palanca de mando, f. **c. tower,** Aer. torre de mando, f
controller /kən'troulər/ n interventor, m; (device) regulador, m
controlling /kən'troulɪŋ/ n See **control.** a regulador
controversial /ˌkɒntrə'vərʃəl/ a debatible, discutible
controversy /'kɒntrəˌvɜrsi/ n controversia, f; argumento, m; altercación, disputa, f
contumacious /ˌkɒntʊ'meiʃəs/ a contumaz
contumacy /'kɒntʊməsi/ n contumacia, f
contumely /'kɒntʊməli/ n contumelia, f
contusion /kən'tuʒən/ n herida contusa, f
conundrum /kə'nʌndrəm/ n acertijo, rompecabezas, m; problema, m
convalesce /ˌkɒnvə'lɛs/ vi convalecer, estar convaleciente
convalescence /ˌkɒnvə'lɛsəns/ n convalecencia, f
convalescent /ˌkɒnvə'lɛsənt/ a convaleciente. n convaleciente, mf. **c. home,** casa de convalecencia, f
convene /kən'vin/ vt (a meeting) convocar; (person) citar. vi reunirse
convenience /kən'vinyəns/ n conveniencia, f; (comfort) comodidad, f; utilidad, f; (advantage) ventaja, f; (public) retretes, m pl. **at one's c.,** cuando le sea conveniente a uno. **to make a c. of,** abusar de. **with all modern conveniences,** con todo el confort moderno
convenient /kən'vinyənt/ a conveniente; apropiado; cómodo. **I shall make it c. to see him at 6 p.m.,** Arreglaré mis asuntos para verle a las seis
conveniently /kən'vinyəntli/ adv cómodamente; oportunamente; sin inconveniente
convent /'kɒnvɛnt/ n convento, m
convention /kən'vɛnʃən/ n convención, f
conventional /kən'vɛnʃənl/ a convencional
conventual /kən'vɛntʃuəl/ a conventual. n conventual, m
converge /kən'vɜrdʒ/ vi convergir
convergence /kən'vɜrdʒəns/ n convergencia, f
convergent /kən'vɜrdʒənt/ a convergente
conversance /kən'vɜrsəns/ n familiaridad, f, conocimiento, m
conversant /kən'vɜrsənt/ a familiar, versado, conocedor. **c. with,** versado en
conversation /ˌkɒnvər'seiʃən/ n conversación, f. **to engage in c. with,** entablar conversación con

conversational /ˌkɒnvər'seiʃənl/ a de conversación; (talkative) locuaz
conversationally /ˌkɒnvər'seiʃənli/ adv en tono familiar; familiarmente; en conversación
converse /kən'vɜrs/ vi conversar. **to c. by signs,** hablar por señas
conversely /kən'vɜrsli/ adv recíprocamente
conversion /kən'vɜrʒən/ n conversión, f
convert /v kən'vɜrt; n 'kɒnvɜrt/ vt convertir; transformar. n converso (-sa). **to become a c.,** convertirse
convertible /kən'vɜrtəbəl/ a convertible; transformable
convex /kɒn'vɛks/ a convexo
convey /kən'vei/ vt transportar; conducir, llevar; (a meaning, etc.) comunicar, dar a entender; expresar; Law. traspasar
conveyance /kən'veiəns/ n transporte, m; conducción, f; medio de transporte, m; vehículo, m; carruaje, m; (of property) traspaso, m; (document) escritura de traspaso, f. **public c.,** coche de alquiler, m; ómnibus, m
convict /n 'kɒnvɪkt; v kən'vɪkt/ n convicto, m; presidiario, m. vt Law. condenar; culpar. **c. settlement,** colonia penal, f
conviction /kən'vɪkʃən/ n (of a prisoner) condenación, f; (belief) convencimiento, m, convicción, f
convince /kən'vɪns/ vt convencer
convincing /kən'vɪnsɪŋ/ a convincente
convivial /kən'vɪviəl/ a convivial
conviviality /kənˌvɪvi'ælɪti/ n jovialidad, f
convocation /ˌkɒnvə'keiʃən/ n convocación, f
convoke /kən'vouk/ vt convocar
convolution /ˌkɒnvə'luʃən/ n circunvolución, f; espira, f
convoy /'kɒnvɔi/ vt convoyar, escoltar. n convoy, m. **to sail in a c.,** navegar en convoy
convulse /kən'vʌls/ vt agitar; sacudir; estremecer. **to be convulsed with laughter,** desternillarse de risa, morirse de risa
convulsion /kən'vʌlʃən/ n convulsión, f; conmoción, f
convulsive /kən'vʌlsɪv/ a convulsivo
coo /ku/ vi arrullar; (of infants) gorjearse. n arrullo, m
cooing /'kuɪŋ/ n arrullo, m
cook /kʊk/ n cocinero (-ra). vt guisar, cocer, cocinar; (falsify) falsear
cookbook /'kʊkˌbʊk/ n libro de cocina, m.
cooker /'kʊkər/ n cocina, f. **gas c.,** cocina de gas, m
cookery /'kʊkəri/ n cocina, f
cookie /'kʊki/ n galleta, f
cooking /'kʊkɪŋ/ n arte de guisar, m, or f; cocina, f; (of accounts, etc.) falsificación, f. **c. range,** cocina económica, f. **c.-stove,** cocina, f. **c. utensils,** batería de cocina, f
cool /kul/ a fresco; bastante frío; (not ardent and of receptions, etc.) frío; (calm) sereno, imperturbable. n fresco, m. vi enfriarse; (of love, etc.) resfriarse; (of the weather) refrescar; (of persons) refrescarse. vt refrescar; enfriar. **to grow cooler,** (of weather) refrescarse; (of persons) tener menos calor. **It is c.,** Hace fresco. **to be as c. as a cucumber,** tener sangre fría. **c. drink,** bebida fría, f. **c.-headed,** sereno, imperturbable
coolie /'kuli/ n culí, m
cooling /'kulɪŋ/ n enfriamiento, m, a refrescante
coolly /'kuli/ adv frescamente; fríamente, con frialdad; imperturbablemente; (impudently) descaradamente
coolness /'kulnɪs/ n frescura, f; (of a welcome, etc.) frialdad, f; (sangfroid) sangre fría, serenidad, f; aplomo, m
coop /kup/ n gallinero, m; caponera, f, vt enjaular; encerrar. **to keep** (someone) **cooped up,** tener encerrado (a)
cooper /'kupər/ n tonelero, barrilero, m, vt hacer barriles
cooperate /kou'ɒpəˌreit/ vi cooperar; colaborar
cooperation /kouˌɒpə'reiʃən/ n cooperación, f
cooperative /kou'ɒpərətɪv/ a cooperativo. **c. society,** cooperativa, f

coopt /kou'ɒpt/ *vt* elegir por votación
coordinate /*v* kou'ɔrdn̩,eit; *n, a* kou'ɔrdn̩ɪt/ *vt* coordinar. *n Math.* coordenada, *f. a* coordenado
coordination /kou,ɔrdn̩'eiʃən/ *n* coordinación, *f*
coot /kut/ *n* fúlica, *f*
cop /kɒp/ *n* (police officer) polizonte, *mf, Ecuador,* chapa, *Mexico* cuico (-ca)
copartner /kou'pɑrtnər/ *n* copartícipe, *mf*; socio (-ia)
cope /koup/ *n Eccl.* capa, *f*; (of heaven) dosel, *m,* bóveda, *f.* **to c. with,** contender con; (a difficulty) hacer cara a, arrostrar
copeck /'koupɛk/ *n* copec, *m*
Copenhagen /,koupən'heigən, -'hɑgən/ Copenhague, *m*
copier /'kɒpiər/ *n* copiador (-ra)
coping /'koupɪŋ/ *n Archit.* albardilla, *f.* **c.-stone,** teja cumbrera, *f*; *Fig.* coronamiento, *m*
copious /'koupiəs/ *a* copioso, abundante
copiously /'koupiəsli/ *adv* en abundancia
copiousness /'koupiəsnɪs/ *n* abundancia, *f*
copper /'kɒpər/ *n* cobre, *m*; (coin) calderilla, *f*; (vessel) caldera, *f. a* de cobre. **c.-colored,** cobrizo. **c.-smith,** calderero, *m.* **c.-sulfate,** sulfato de cobre, *m*
copperplate /'kɒpər,pleit/ *n* lámina de cobre, *f*; grabado en cobre, *m*
coppery /'kɒpəri/ *a* cobrizo
coppice /'kɒpɪs/ *n* soto, bosquecillo, *m.* **c. with standards,** monte medio, *m*
coproprietor /,kouprə'praiɪtər/ *n* copropietario, *m*
copse /kɒps/ *n* arboleda, *f*, bosquecillo, *m*
copulate /'kɒpyə,leit/ *vi* copularse
copulation /,kɒpyə'leiʃən/ *n* cópula, *f*
copy /'kɒpi/ *n* copia, *f*; (of a book) ejemplar, *m*; (of a paper) número, *m*; manuscrito, *m*; (subject-matter) material, *m. vt* copiar; imitar; tomar como modelo (a). **rough c.,** borrador, *m.* **c.-book,** cuaderno de escritura, *m*
copy editor *n* redactor de textos, *m*
copying /'kɒpiɪŋ/ *n* imitación, *f*; transcripción, *f.* **c. ink,** tinta de copiar, *f*
copyist /'kɒpiɪst/ *n* copiador (-ra); (plagiarist) copiante, *mf*
copyright /'kɒpi,rait/ *n* derechos de autor, *m pl*; depósito legal, *m*; propiedad literaria, *f. a* protegido por los derechos de autor. *vt* registrar como propiedad literaria. **C. reserved,** Derechos reservados, Queda hecho el depósito que marca la ley
copywriter /'kɒpi,raitər/ *n* escritor de anuncios, *m*
coquet /kou'kɛt/ *vi* coquetear; *Fig.* jugar (con)
coquetry /'koukɪtri/ *n* coquetería, *f*
coquette /kou'kɛt/ *n* coqueta, *f*
coquettish /kou'kɛtɪʃ/ *a* coquetón; atractivo
coral /'kɔrəl/ *n* coral, *m*; (polyp) coralina, *f. a* de coral, coralino. **white c.,** madrépora, *f.* **c. beads,** corales, *m pl.* **c.-island,** atalón, *m.* **c.-reef,** escollo de coral, *m.* **c. snake,** coral, *f*
corbel /'kɔrbəl/ *n Archit.* ménsula, *f*
cord /kɔrd/ *n* cuerda, *f*; cordel, *m*; cordón, *m. vt* encordelar. **spinal c.,** médula espinal, *f.* **umbilical c.,** cordón umbilical, *m*
cordial /'kɔrdʒəl/ *a* cordial; sincero, fervoroso. *n* cordial, *m*
cordiality /kɔr'dʒælɪti/ *n* cordialidad, *f*
cordon /'kɔrdn̩/ *n* cordón, *m*; cinto, *m.* **to c. off,** acordonar
Cordova /'kɔrdəvə/ Córdoba, *f*
cordovan /'kɔrdəvən/ *a* cordobés. *n* (leather) cordobán, *m*
corduroy /'kɔrdə,rɔi/ *n* pana de cordoncillo, *f*
core /kɔr/ *n* (of a fruit) corazón, *m*; (of a rope) alma, *f*, centro, *m*; (of an abscess) foco, *m*; (of a corn) ojo, *m*; *Fig.* núcleo, *m*; esencia, *f*; lo esencial
corespondent /,kouɪ'spɒndənt/ *n* cómplice en un caso de divorcio, *mf*
Corinth /'kɔrɪnθ/ Corinto, *m*
Corinthian /kə'rɪnθiən/ *a* corintio. *n* corintio (-ia)
cork /kɔrk/ *n* corcho, *m*; (of a bottle) tapón, *m, a* de corcho. *vt* tapar con corcho, taponar; (wine) encorchar; (the face) tiznar con corcho quemado. **pop of a**

c., taponazo, *m.* **to draw a c.,** descorchar. **c.-jacket,** chaleco salvavidas, *m.* **c. tree,** alcornoque, *m*
corkscrew /'kɔrk,skru/ *n* sacacorchos, *m*
cormorant /'kɔrmərənt/ *n* cormorán, *m*
corn /kɔrn/ *n* grano, cereal, *m*; (wheat) trigo, *m*; (maize) maíz, *m*; (single seed) grano, *m*; (on the foot, etc.) callo, *m.* **Indian c.,** maíz, *m.* **c. cure,** callicida, *m.* **c.-exchange,** bolsa de granos, *f.* **c.-field,** campo de trigo, *m.* **c.-flower,** aciano, *m.* **c. liquor,** *Lat. Am.* chicha, *f*
cornea /'kɔrniə/ *n* córnea, *f*
corner /'kɔrnər/ *n* ángulo, *m*; (of a street or building) esquina, *f*; (of a room) rincón, *Mexico* ancón *m*; *Auto.* viraje, *m*; *Com.* monopolio, *m*; (of the eye) rabo, *m*; (soccer) "corner," *m. vt* arrinconar; acorralar; *Com.* acaparar. **the four corners of the earth,** los cuatro ángulos de la tierra. **a tight c.,** un lance apretado, un apuro. **to drive into a c.,** *Fig.* poner entre la espada y la pared. **to look out of the c. of the eye,** mirar de reojo. **to turn the c.,** doblar la esquina; *Fig.* pasar la crisis. **c.-cupboard,** rinconera, *f.* **c. seat,** asiento del rincón, *m.* **c. shop,** *Lat. Am.* esquina, *f.* **c.-stone,** piedra angular, *f*
cornered /'kɔrnərd/ *a* (of a person) acorralado, en aprieto; (of hats) de... picos. **three-c. hat,** sombrero de tres picos, *m*
cornet /'kɔr'nɛt/ *n* (musical instrument) corneta, *f*; *Mil.* corneta, *m*; (paper) cucurucho, *m.* **c. player,** cornetín, *m*
cornflour /'kɔrn,flauər/ *n* harina de maíz, *f*
cornice /'kɔrnɪs/ *n* cornisa, *f*
Cornish /'kɔrnɪʃ/ *a* de Cornualles
cornucopia /,kɔrnə'koupiə/ *n* cornucopia, *f*
corollary /'kɔrə,lɛri/ *n* corolario, *m*
corona /kə'rounə/ *n* (*Astron. Archit.*) corona, *f*
coronation /,kɔrə'neiʃən/ *n* coronación, *f*
coroner /'kɔrənər/ *n* juez de guardia, *mf*, médico forense, *m*
coronet /,kɔrə'nɛt/ *n* (of a peer, etc.) corona, *f*; tiara, *f*; guirnalda, *f*
corporal /'kɔrpərəl/ *a* corporal, *n Mil.* cabo, *m*; (altar-cloth) corporal, *m.* **c. punishment,** castigo corporal, *m*
corporate /'kɔrpərɪt/ *a* corporativo
corporation /,kɔrpə'reiʃən/ *n* corporación, *f*; concejo, cabildo municipal, *m*; *Com.* sociedad anónima, *f*
corporeal /kɔr'pɔriəl/ *a* corpóreo
corps /kɔr/ *n* cuerpo, *m*
corpse /kɔrps/ *n* cadáver, *m*
corpulence /'kɔrpyələns/ *n* gordura, obesidad, *f*
corpulent /'kɔrpyələnt/ *a* corpulento, grueso, gordo
corpus /'kɔrpəs/ *n* cuerpo, *m.* **C. Christi,** Corpus, *m.* **c. delicti,** cuerpo del delito, *m*
corpuscle /'kɔrpəsəl/ *n* corpúsculo, *m*
correct /kə'rɛkt/ *a* correcto; exacto, justo. *vt* corregir; rectificar; amonestar, reprender
correction /kə'rɛkʃən/ *n* corrección, *f*; rectificación, *f*
corrective /kə'rɛktɪv/ *a* correctivo. *n* correctivo, *m*
correctness /kə'rɛktnɪs/ *n* corrección, *f*; exactitud, *f*; justicia, *f*
correlate /'kɔrə,leit/ *vt* poner en correlación. *vi* tener correlación
correlation /,kɔrə'leiʃən/ *n* correlación, *f*
correspond /,kɔrə'spɒnd/ *vi* corresponder (a); (by letter) escribirse, corresponderse
correspondence /,kɔrə'spɒndəns/ *n* correspondencia, *f*; *Com.* correo, *m.* **c. course,** curso por correspondencia, *m*
correspondent /,kɔrə'spɒndənt/ *n* correspondiente, *mf*; (*Com.* and journalist) corresponsal, *mf.* **special c.,** corresponsal extraordinario, *m*
corresponding /,kɔrə'spɒndɪŋ/ *a* correspondiente. **c. member,** miembro correspondiente, *m*
corridor /'kɔrɪdər/ *n* corredor, pasillo, *m*; (railway) pasillo, *m*; *Polit.* corredor, *m.* **c. train,** tren con coches corridos, *m*
corroborate /kə'rɒbə,reit/ *vt* corroborar, confirmar
corroboration /kə,rɒbə'reiʃən/ *n* corroboración, confirmación, *f*

corroborative /kə'rɒbə,reitɪv/ *a* corroborativo, confirmatorio

corrode /kə'roud/ *vt* corroer, morder; *Fig.* roer

corrosion /kə'rouʒən/ *n* corrosión, *f*

corrosive /kə'rousɪv/ *a* corrosivo; mordaz

corrugate /'kɔrə,geit/ *vt* arrugar. *vi* arrugarse

corrugated /'kɔrə,geitɪd/ *a* arrugado; ondulado. **c. iron,** chapa canaleta, *f*

corrugation /,kɔrə'geiʃən/ *n* corrugación, *f*, arrugamiento, *m*

corrupt /kə'rʌpt/ *a* corrompido; vicioso, desmoralizado. *vt* corromper. *vi* corromperse

corrupter /kə'rʌptər/ *n* corruptor (-ra)

corruption /kə'rʌpʃən/ *n* corrupción, *f*

corsage /kɔr'saʒ/ *n* corpiño, *m*

corset /'kɔrsɪt/ *n* corsé, *m*, *vt* encorsetar. **c. shop,** corsetería, *f*

Corsica /'kɔrsɪkə/ Córcega, *f*

Corsican /'kɔrsɪkən/ *a* corso. *n* corso (-sa)

cortege /kɔr'tɛʒ/ *n* séquito, acompañamiento, *m*; desfile, *m*

cortex /'kɔrteks/ *n* *Bot. Anat.* corteza, *f*

cortisone /'kɔrtə,zoun/ *n* (drug) cortisona, *f*

Corunna /kə'runjə/ La Coruña, *f*

coruscation /,kɔrə'skeiʃən/ *n* brillo, *m*

corvette /kɔr'vet/ *n* corbeta, *f*

cosignatory /kou'sɪgnə,tɔri/ *n* cosignatario (-ia)

cosine /'kousain/ *n* coseno, *m*

cosiness /'kouzinɪs/ *n* comodidad, *f*

cosmetic /kɒz'metɪk/ *a* cosmético. *n* afeite, cosmético, *m*

cosmic /'kɒzmɪk/ *a* cósmico

cosmographer /kɒz'mɒgrəfər/ *n* cosmógrafo, *m*

cosmography /kɒz'mɒgrəfi/ *n* cosmografía, *f*

cosmopolitan /,kɒzmə'pɒlɪtṇ/ *a* cosmopolita. *n* cosmopolita, *mf*

cosmopolitanism /,kɒzmə'pɒlɪtṇ,ɪzəm/ *n* cosmopolitismo, *m*

cosmos /'kɒzməs/ *n* cosmos, universo, *m*

Cossack /'kɒsæk/ *a* cosaco. *n* cosaco (-ca)

cosset /'kɒsɪt/ *vt* mimar, consentir

cost /kɔst/ *vi* costar. *n* costa, *f*, coste, precio, *m*; *Fig.* costa, *f*; *pl* **costs,** *Law.* costas, *f pl.* **at all costs,** cueste lo que cueste, a toda costa. **to my c.,** a mi costa. **c. of living,** coste de la vida, *m*. **to c. a fortune,** costar un sentido

Costa Rican /'kɒstə 'rikən/ *a* and *n* costarricense, *mf*

coster /'kɔstər/ *n* vendedor (-ra) ambulante

costliness /'kɔstlinɪs/ *n* alto precio, *m*; suntuosidad, *f*

costly /'kɔstli/ *a* costoso; suntuoso, magnífico

costume /'kɒstum/ *n* traje, *m*; (fancy-dress) disfraz, *m*; (tailored) traje sastre, *m*; **"Costume,"** (among credits in films and plays) «Vestuario»

costumier /,kɒstu'mɪər/ *n* modista, *mf*; sastre, *m*

cot /kɒt/ *n* (hut) choza, cabaña, *f*; (child's) camita, *f*

coterie /'koutəri/ *n* círculo, grupo, *m*; (clique) camarilla, *f*

cotillion /kə'tɪljən/ *n* cotillón, *m*

cottage /'kɒtɪʒ/ *n* cabaña, choza, *f*; casita, *f*, hotelito, *m*; torre, villa, *f*. **c. cheese** *Mexico* asadero *m*

cotter /'kɒtər/ *n* chaveta, llave, *f*

cotton /'kɒtṇ/ *n* algodón, *m*, *a* de algodón. **I don't c. to the idea at all,** No me gusta nada la idea; La idea no me seduce. **sewing-c.,** hilo de coser, *m*. **c. goods,** géneros de algodón, *m pl.* **c. mill,** hilandería de algodón, algodonería, *f*. **c. plantation,** algodonal, *m*. **c.-seed oil,** aceite de semilla de algodón, *m*. **c.-spinner,** hilandero (-ra) de algodón. **c.-wool,** algodón en rama, *m*. **c.-yarn,** hilo de algodón, *m*

couch /kautʃ/ *n* sofá, canapé, *m*; (bed) lecho, *m*; (lair) cama, *f*. *vt* (lay down) acostar, echar; (a lance) enristrar; (express) expresar, redactar. *vi* acostarse; (crouch) agacharse; estar en acecho

cough /kɔf/ *vi* toser. *n* tos, *f*. **to c. up,** escupir, expectorar. **c.-drop,** pastilla para la tos, *f*

coughing /'kɔfɪŋ/ *n* tos, *f*

could. /kʊd/. See **can**

council /'kaunsəl/ *n* consejo, *m*; junta, *f*; *Eccl.* concilio, *m*. **Privy C.,** consejo privado, *m*. **to hold c.,** celebrar un consejo; aconsejarse (con); consultarse

town c., ayuntamiento, *m*. **c. chamber,** sala consistorial, *f*; sala de actos, *f*. **c. houses,** casas baratas, *f pl*. **c. of war,** consejo de guerra, *m*

councilor /'kaunsələr/ *n* concejal, *m*; miembro de la junta, *m*

counsel /'kaunsəl/ *n* consultación, *f*; deliberación, *f*; consejo, *m*; *Law.* abogado, *m*. *vt* aconsejar. **a c. of perfection,** un ideal imposible. **to keep one's own c.,** no decir nada, callarse, guardar silencio. **to take c. with,** consultar (a), aconsejarse con

counselor /'kaunsələr/ *n* consejero, *m*. **c. of state,** consejero de estado, *m*

count /kaunt/ *vt* contar; calcular; (consider) creer, considerar. *vi* contar. *n* cuenta, *f*; (of votes) escrutinio, *m*; *Law.* capítulo, *m*. **John simply doesn't c.,** Juan no cuenta para nada. **Erudition alone counts for very little,** La mera erudición sirve para muy poco. **to keep c. of,** tener cuenta de. **to lose c. of,** perder cuenta de. **to c. on,** contar con; (doing something) esperar. **to c. up,** contar

count /kaunt/ *n* (title) conde, *m*

countenance /'kauntṇəns/ *n* semblante, *m*; expresión de la cara, *f*; aspecto, *m*; (favor) apoyo, *m*, ayuda, *f*. *vt* autorizar, aprobar; apoyar, ayudar. **to put (a person) out of c.,** desconcertar (a)

counter /'kauntər/ *n* (in a bank) contador, *m*; (in a shop) mostrador, *m*; (in games) ficha, *f*, *adv* contra, al contrario; al revés. *a* opuesto (a), contrario (a). *vt* parar; contestar. **to run c. to my inclinations,** oponerse a mis deseos. **to c. with the left,** (boxing) contestar con la izquierda. **c.-attack,** contraataque, *m*. **c.-attraction,** atracción contraria, *f*. **c.-offensive,** contraofensiva, *f*. **c.-reformation,** contrarreforma, *f*. **c.-revolution,** contrarevolución, *f*

counteract /,kauntər'ækt/ *vt* neutralizar; frustrar

counterbalance /'kauntər,bæləns/ *n* contrapeso, *m*, *vt* contrabalancear; compensar, igualar

counterblast /'kauntər,blæst/ *n* denunciación, *f*; respuesta, *f*

countercharge /'kauntər,tʃɑrdʒ/ *n* recriminación, *f*. *vt* recriminar; *Law.* reconvenir

counterfeit /'kauntər,fit/ *a* falso, espurio; fingido. *n* falsificación, *f*; imitación, *f*; moneda falsa, *f*; (person) impostor (-ra). *vt* imitar; (pretend) fingir; (coins, handwriting, etc.) falsificar

counterfeiter /'kauntər,fitər/ *n* falsario (-ia)

counterfoil /'kauntər,fɔil/ *n* talón, *m*

countermand /*v* ,kauntər'mænd, *n* 'kauntər,mænd/ *vt* contramandar; (an order) revocar, cancelar. *n* contraorden, *f*; revocación, *f*

countermeasure /'kauntər,meʒər/ *n* contramedida, *f*

counterpane /'kauntər,pein/ *n* sobrecama, colcha, *f*

counterpart /'kauntər,pɑrt/ *n* contraparte, *f*; (of a document) duplicado, *m*

counterplot /'kauntər,plɒt/ *n* contratreta, *f*

counterpoint /'kauntər,pɔint/ *n* *Mus.* contrapunto, *m*

counterpoise /'kauntər,pɔiz/ *n* contrapeso, *m*; equilibrio, *m*, *vt* contrabalancear, contrapesar

countersign /'kauntər,sain/ *n* contraseña, *f*, *vt* refrendar

countess /'kauntɪs/ *n* condesa, *f*

counting /'kauntɪŋ/ *n* cuenta, *f*; numeración, *f*; (of votes) escrutinio, *m*. **c.-house,** contaduría, *f*

countless /'kauntlɪs/ *a* innumerable. **a c. number,** sinfín, *m*, sinnúmero

countrified /'kʌntrə,faid/ *a* rústico, campesino

country /'kʌntri/ *n* país, *m*; (fatherland) patria, *f*; región, campiña, tierra, *f*; (as opposed to town) campo, *m* . *a* del campo; campesino, campestre, rústico. **He lives in the c.,** Vive en el campo. **c. club,** club campestre, *m*. **c. cousin,** provinciano (-na). **c.-dance,** baile campestre, *m*. **c. gentleman,** hacendado, *m*. **c. girl,** campesina, *f*; aldeana, *f*. **c.-house,** finca, *f*; casa de campo, *f*. **c. life,** vida del campo, *f*. **c.-seat,** finca, *f*

countryman /'kʌntrimən/ *n* campesino, *m*; hombre del campo, *m*; compatriota, *m*

countryside /'kʌntri,said/ *n* campo, *m*; campiña, *f*

countrywoman /'kʌntri,wumən/ *n* campesina, *f*; compatriota, *f*

county /'kaunti/ *n* condado, *m*; provincia, *f*. **c. coun-**

cil, diputación provincial, *f.* **c. town,** cabeza de partido, *f;* ciudad provincial, *f*
county seat *n* cabecera municipal, cabeza de partido, *f*
coup /ku/ *n* golpe, *m.* **c. d'état,** golpe de estado, *m*
coupe /kup/ *n* cupé, *m*
couple /'kʌpəl/ *n* par, *m;* (in a dance, etc.) pareja, *f.* *vt* enganchar, acoplar; (in marriage) casar; (animals) aparear; (ideas) asociar; (names) juntar. **the young (married) c.,** el matrimonio joven
couplet /'kʌplɪt/ *n* copla, *f*
coupling /'kʌplɪŋ/ *n* enganche, acoplamiento, *m;* (of railway carriages) enganche, *m;* (of ideas) asociación, *f*
coupon /'kupɒn/ *n* talón, *m;* cupón, *m*
courage /'kɜrɪdʒ/ *n* valor, *m.* **C.!** ¡Ánimo! **to muster up c.,** cobrar ánimo
courageous /kə'reɪdʒəs/ *a* valiente
courageously /kə'reɪdʒəsli/ *adv* valientemente
courier /'kɜriər/ *n* correo, *m,* estafeta, *f;* (guide) guía, *m;* (newspaper) estafeta, *f*
course /kɔrs/ *n* curso, *m;* (of time) transcurso, *m;* (of events) marcha, *f;* (of a river, etc.) cauce, *m;* (of stars) carrera, *f,* curso, *m;* (of a ship) derrota, *f,* rumbo, *m;* (way) camino, *m,* ruta, *f;* (of conduct) línea de conducta, *f;* actitud, *f;* (of study) curso, *m;* (of a meal) plato, *m;* (of an illness) desarrollo, *m; Med.* tratamiento, *m.* **He took it as a matter of c.,** Lo tomó sin darle importancia. **in due c.,** a su tiempo debido. **in the c. of time,** andando el tiempo, en el transcurso de los años. **of c.,** claro está; naturalmente; por supuesto. **Are you coming tomorrow? Of c.!** ¿Vienes mañana? ¡Ya lo creo! **the best c. to take,** lo mejor que se puede hacer, el mejor plantamiento, *m*
course /kɔrs/ *vt* cazar, perseguir; *Poet.* correr por, cruzar. *vi* (of blood, etc.) correr; cazar
court /kɔrt/ *n* (yard) patio, *m;* (tennis) campo de tenis, *m;* (fives, racquets) cancha, *f;* (royal) corte, *f;* (of justice) tribunal, *m;* (following) séquito, acompañamiento, *m. vt* hacer la corte (a); cortejar, pretender; solicitar; (sleep) conciliar. **to c.,** (a woman) galantear, pretender; (a person) hacer la rueda (a), *Lat. Am.* afilar. **to respect the c.,** *Law.* guardar sala. **c. of appeal,** sala de apelación, *f.* **c. of justice,** sala de justicia, *f;* tribunal de justicia, *m.* **supreme c.,** tribunal supremo, *m.* **c. house,** palacio de justicia, *m.* **c. jester,** bufón, *m.* **c.-martial,** tribunal militar, *m.* **c.-room,** sala de justicia, *f*
courteous /'kɜrtiəs/ *a* cortés
courteousness /'kɜrtiəsnɪs/ *n* cortesía, *f*
courtesy /'kɜrtəsi/ *n* cortesía, *f;* favor, *m,* merced, *f;* permiso, *m*
courtier /'kɔrtiər/ *n* cortesano, palaciego, *m*
courtliness /'kɔrtlɪnɪs/ *n* cortesía, urbanidad, *f;* dignidad, *f;* elegancia, *f*
courtly /'kɔrtli/ *a* cortés, galante; digno; elegante
courtship /'kɔrtʃɪp/ *n* noviazgo, *m;* galanteo, *m*
courtyard /'kɔrt,yard/ *n* patio, *m*
cousin /'kʌzən/ *n* primo (-ma). **first c.,** primo (-ma) carnal. **second c.,** primo (-ma) segundo (-da)
cove /kouv/ *n* cala, abra, ensenada, *f,* ancón *m*
covenant /'kʌvənənt/ *n* contrato, *m;* estipulación, *f;* pacto, *m;* alianza, *f. vt* prometer; estipular
Coventry, to send to, /'kʌvəntri/ hacer el vacío (a)
cover /'kʌvər/ *vt* cubrir; abrigar; (dissemble) disimular; (a distance) recorrer; (comprise) comprender, abarcar; (with confusion, etc.) llenar (de); (with a revolver, etc.) amenazar (con); (an overdraft, etc.) garantizar; (of stallions) cubrir; (of a hen and eggs) empollar; (a story, journalism) investigar. *n* cubierta, *f;* (for a chair, umbrella, etc.) funda, *f;* (of a saucepan, jar, etc.) tapa, *f;* (dish-cover) tapadera, *f;* (of a book) cubierta, tapa, *f;* (of a letter) sobre, *m;* (shelter) abrigo, *m;* protección, *f;* (undergrowth) maleza, *f; Fig.* velo, manto, *m;* (pretence) pretexto, *m; Com.* garantía, *f.* **outer c.,** (of tire) cubierta de neumático, *f.* **to c. oneself with glory,** cubrirse de gloria. **to c. up,** cubrir completamente; (with clothes) arropar; (wrap up) envolver. **to c. with a revolver,** amenazar con un revólver. **to read a book from c. to c.,** leer un libro del principio al fin. **to take c.,** refugiarse, tomar abrigo. **under c.,** bajo tejado; al abrigo

cover charge *n* consumo mínimo, precio del cubierto, *m*
covering /'kʌvərɪŋ/ *n* cubrimiento, *m;* cubierta, *f;* envoltura, *f;* capa, *f,* abrigo, *m.* **c. letter,** carta adjunta, *f*
coverlet /'kʌvərlɪt/ *n* colcha, sobrecama, *f*
covert /a 'kouvərt; *n* 'kʌvərt/ *n* guarida, *f. a* oculto; furtivo
covertly /'kouvərtli/ *adv* secretamente, furtivamente
covet /'kʌvɪt/ *vt* codiciar; ambicionar, suspirar por
covetous /'kʌvɪtəs/ *a* codicioso; ávido; ambicioso
covetously /'kʌvɪtəsli/ *adv* codiciosamente; ávidamente
covetousness /'kʌvɪtəsnɪs/ *n* codicia, avaricia, *f;* avidez, *f;* ambición, *f*
cow /kau/ *vt* intimidar, acobardar
cow /kau/ *n* vaca, *Lat. Am.* also lechera *f;* (of other animals) hembra, *f.* **c.-bell,** cencerro, *m,* zumba, *f.* **c.-catcher,** *Auto.* salvavidas, *m.* **c.-hide,** cuero, cuero de vaca, zurriago, *m;* penca, *f.* **c.-house,** establo, *m,* boyera, *f.* **c.-pox,** vacuna, *f*
coward /'kauərd/ *n* cobarde, *m, a* cobarde
cowardice /'kauərdɪs/ *n* cobardía, *f, Argentina* canillera, *f*
cowardly /'kauərdli/ *a* cobarde, *Mexico, Venezuela* correlón
cowboy /'kau,bɔɪ/ *n* vaquero, *m;* gaucho, "cowboy," *m*
cower /'kauər/ *vi* temblar, acobardarse
cowherd /'kau,hɜrd/ *n* vaquero, boyero, *m*
cowl /kaul/ *n* capucha, *f;* (of a chimney) sombrerete, *m*
coworker /'kou,wɜrkər, kou'wɜr-/ *n* colaborador (-ra)
cowshed /'kau,ʃɛd/ *n* establo, *m*
cowslip /'kauslɪp/ *n* prímula, *f*
cox /kɒks/ *n* timonel, *m*
coxcomb /'kɒks,koum/ *n* (of a jester) gorra de bufón, *f;* mequetrefe, *m*
coxswain /'kɒksən/ *n* patrón, *m;* (of a rowboat) timonel, *m*
coy /kɔɪ/ *a* modoso, tímido; coquetón
coyly /'kɔɪli/ *adv* tímidamente; con coquetería
coyness /'kɔɪnɪs/ *n* timidez, modestia, *f;* coquetería, *f*
cozy /'kouzi/ *a* cómodo; agradable; caliente. **You are very c. here,** Estás muy bien aquí
crab /kræb/ *n* (sea) cangrejo de mar, cámbaro, *m, Lat. Am. also* jaiba *m;* (river) cangrejo, *m; Astron.* Cáncer, *m. vt* (thwart) frustrar. **hermit c.,** ermitaño, *m.* **c.-apple,** manzana silvestre, *f.* **c.-louse,** ladilla, *f*
crabbed /'kræbɪd/ *a* áspero, hosco, desabrido, arisco; (of handwriting) apretado, metido
crack /kræk/ *vt* hender; quebrantar, romper; (nuts) cascar; (a whip and fingers) chasquear; (a bottle of wine) abrir. *vi* (of earth, skin, etc.) agrietarse; romperse, quebrarse; (of the voice) romper; (of the male voice) mudar. *n* hendedura, rendija, *f;* quebraja, *f;* (of a whip) chasquido, *m;* (of a rifle) estallido, *m;* (blow) golpe, garrotazo, *m, a* excelente, de primera categoría; estupendo. **to c. a joke,** decir un chiste. **to c. up,** *vt* dar bombo (a), alabar. *vi* (in health) quebrantarse; (airplane) cuartearse, estrellarse. **c.-brained,** chiflado; estúpido, loco
cracked /krækt/ *a* agrietado; (of a bell, etc.) hendido; (of the voice) cascada; (of a person) chiflado
cracker /'krækər/ *n* (firework) petardo, *m;* buscapiés, *m*
crackle /'krækəl/ *vi* (of burning wood, etc.) crepitar; (rustle) crujir; (of rifle fire) tirotear. *n* crepitación, *f;* crujido, *m;* (of rifle fire) tiroteo, *m*
crackling /'kræklɪŋ/ *n.* See **crackle;** *Cul.* chicharrón, *m*
cradle /'kreɪdl/ *n* cuna, *f; Fig.* niñez, infancia, *f;* (for a limb) arco de protección, *m;* (for winebottle) cesta, *f. vt* mecer. **c.-song,** canción de cuna, *f*
craft /kræft/ *n* (guile) astucia, *f;* (skill) habilidad, *f;* arte, *mf;* (occupation) oficio manual, *m;* profesión, *f;* (guild) gremio, *m;* (ship, plane) nave, *f,* embarcación, *f*
crafty /'kræftli/ *adv* astutamente
craftiness /'kræftɪnɪs/ *n* astucia, *f*
craftsman /'kræftsmən/ *n* artífice, *m;* arte sano, *m;* artista, *m*

craftsmanship /'kræftsmən‚ʃɪp/ n arte, m, or f; habilidad, f; artificio, m

crafty /'kræfti/ a astuto, taimado, Lat. Am. macuco.

c. person Mexico fistol m

crag /kræg/ n peña, f, risco, despeñadero, m

cragginess /'kræginɪs/ n escabrosidad, aspereza, fragosidad, f

craggy /'krægi/ a escabroso, escarpado, peñascoso, riscoso

cram /kræm/ vt henchir; atestar; (one's mouth) llenar (de); (poultry) cebar; (a pupil) preparar para un examen; (a subject) empollar. vi (with food) atracarse. **The room was crammed with people,** La sala estaba atestada de gente

cramp /kræmp/ n Med. calambre, m; (numbness) entumecimiento, m; (rivet) grapa, f. vt dar calambre (a); (numb) entumecer; (fasten) lañar; (Fig. hamper) estorbar. **to c. someone's style,** cortar los vuelos (a). **writer's c.,** calambre del escribiente, m

cramped /kræmpt/ a (of space) apretado, estrecho; (of writing) menuda

cranberry /'kræn‚beri/ n arándano, m

crane /krein/ n Ornith. grulla, f; (machine) grúa, f. **jib c.,** grúa de pescante, f. **travelling c.,** grúa móvil, f. **to c. one's neck,** estirar el cuello. **crane's bill,** pico de cigüeña, m

cranium /'kreiniəm/ n cráneo, m

crank /kræŋk/ n (handle) manivela, f; (person) maniático (-ca). vt poner en marcha (un motor) con la manivela

crankiness /'kræŋkinɪs/ n (crossness) irritabilidad, f, mal humor, m; (eccentricity) excentricidad, f

cranky /'kræŋki/ a (cross) irritable, malhumorado; (eccentric) chiflado, maniático, excéntrico

cranny /'kræni/ n hendedura, grieta, f

crape /kreip/ n crespón, m

crash /kræʃ/ vi caer estrepitosamente; romperse; estallarse; (of aircraft, cars) estrellarse; Fig. hundirse, arruinarse. n estrépito, estruendo, m; estallido, m; (of aircraft) accidente de aviación, m; (car) accidente, m, (or choque, m) de automóviles; (financial) ruina, f; Fig. hundimiento, m. **to c. into,** estrellarse contra, chocar con. **c. helmet,** casco, m. **c.-landing,** aterrizaje violento, m

crass /kræs/ a craso

crassness /'kræsnɪs/ n estupidez, f

crate /kreit/ n (box) caja de embalaje, f; (basket) canasto, m, banasta, Mexico jaba f

crater /'kreitər/ n cráter, m

cravat /krə'væt/ n corbata, f

crave /kreiv/ vt suplicar, implorar. **to c. for,** perecer por, suspirar por, anhelar

craven /'kreivən/ a cobarde, pusilánime. n poltrón, cobarde, m

craving /'kreivɪŋ/ n deseo vehemente, m, sed, f

crawfish /'krɔ‚fɪʃ/ n cangrejo de río, m; cigala, f

crawl /krɔl/ vi arrastrarse; andar a gatas; andar a paso de tortuga; (abase oneself) humillarse; (be full of) abundar (en). n paso de tortuga, m; (swimming) arrastre m

crayfish /'krei‚fɪʃ/ n cangrejo de río, m; cigala, f

crayon /'kreiən/ n carbón, m; pastel, m; (pencil) lápiz de color, m. vt dibujar con pastel, etc. **c. drawing,** dibujo al carbón, m

craze /kreiz/ vt enloquecer, volver loco (a). n manía, f, capricho, entusiasmo, m; (fashion) moda, f

crazily /'kreizəli/ adv locamente

craziness /'kreizinɪs/ n locura, f

crazy /'kreizi/ a loco; chiflado; (of structure) dilapidado. **He is c. about music,** Está loco por la música. **to be completely c.,** (of persons) ser un loco de atar; ser completamente loco. **to drive c.,** volver loco (a)

creak /krik/ vi (of shoes, chairs, etc.) crujir; (of gates, etc.) rechinar, chirriar. n crujido, m; chirrido, m

creaking /'krikɪŋ/ n. See **creak**

creaky /'kriki/ a crujiente, que cruje; chirriador

cream /krim/ n crema, f; nata, f; Fig. flor, nata, f. a de nata. **whipped c.,** nata batida, f. **c. cake,** pastel de nata, m. **c.-cheese,** queso de nata, m. **c.-colored,** de color crema. **c.-jug,** jarro para crema, m. **c. of tartar,** cremor, tártaro, m

creamery /'krimɑri/ n lechería, f

creamy /'krimi/ a cremoso

crease /kris/ n (wrinkle) arruga, f; (fold) pliegue, m; (in trousers) raya, f; (in cricket) línea de la meta, f. vt (wrinkle) arrugar; (fold) plegar; (trousers) poner la raya en. vi arrugarse

create /kri'eit/ vt crear; (appoint) nombrar; (produce) suscitar, producir

creation /kri'eiʃən/ n creación, f; establecimiento, m; (appointment) nombramiento, m

creative /kri'eitɪv/ a creador; de la creación

creativeness /kri'eitɪvnɪs/ n facultad creativa, inventiva, f

creator /kri'eitər/ n creador (-ra)

creature /'kritʃər/ n criatura, f; animal, m. **c. comforts,** bienestar material, m

crèche /krɛʃ/ n casa cuna, f

credence /'kridns/ n crédito, m, fe, creencia, f; Eccl. credencia, f. **to give c. to,** dar crédito (a), creer

credentials /krɪ'dɛnʃəlz/ n pl credenciales, f pl

credibility /‚krɛdə'bɪlɪti/ n credibilidad, verosimilitud, f

credible /'krɛdəbəl/ a creíble, verosímil; (of persons) digno de confianza

credibly /'krɛdəbli/ adv creíblemente

credit /'krɛdɪt/ n crédito, m; reputación, f; honor, m; (Com. and banking) crédito, m; (in bookkeeping) data, f. vt dar fe (a), dar crédito (a); creer; atribuir; (bookkeeping) acreditar. **It does them c.,** Les hace honor. **on c.,** a crédito, al fiado. **open c.,** Com. letra abierta, f. **to give on c.,** dar fiado. **C. balance,** haber, m

creditable /'krɛdɪtəbəl/ a loable, honroso, digno de alabanza

creditably /'krɛdɪtəbli/ adv honrosamente

creditor /'krɛdɪtər/ n acreedor (-ra); (bookkeeping) haber, m

credulity /krə'dulɪti/ n credulidad, f

credulous /'krɛdʒələs/ a crédulo, Lat. Am. creído

credulously /'krɛdʒələsli/ adv con credulidad, crédulamente

creed /krid/ n credo, m

creek /krik/ n caleta, abra, f

creel /kril/ n (for fish) cesta de pescador, f

creep /krip/ vi arrastrarse; (of plants and birds) trepar; (of infants) andar a gatas; (totter) hacer pinitos; (slip) deslizarse; (cringe) lisonjear, rebajarse; (of one's flesh) sentir hormigueo. **to c. about on tiptoe,** andar de puntillas. **to c. into a person's favor,** insinuarse en el favor de. **to c. in,** entrar sin ser notado (en); deslizarse en. **to c. on,** (of time) avanzar lentamente; (of old age, etc.) acercarse insensiblemente. **to c. out,** salir sin hacer ruido; escurrirse. **to c. up,** trepar por; subir a gatas

creeper /'kripər/ n Bot. enredadera, f; Ornith. trepador, m; Zool. reptil, m

creeping /'kripɪŋ/ a Bot. trepante; Zool. trepador; (servile) rastrero

cremate /'krimeit/ vt incinerar

cremation /krɪ'meiʃən/ n cremación, f

crematorium /‚krimə'tɔriəm/ n crematorio, m; horno de incineración, m, inhumadora, f

creole /'krioul/ a criollo. n criollo (-lla)

creolize /'kriə‚laiz/ vt acriollar

crescent /'krɛsənt/ n media luna, f; Herald. creciente, m; calle en forma de semicírculo, f. a en forma de media luna; Poet. creciente

cress /krɛs/ n Bot. berro, m

crest /krɛst/ n (of a cock, etc.) cresta, f; (plume) penacho, m; (of a helmet) cimera, f; (of a hill) cumbre, cima, f; (of a wave) cresta, f. **family c.,** blasón, escudo, m

crested /'krɛstɪd/ a Lat. Am. copetudo (-da)

crestfallen /'krɛst‚fɔlən/ a cabizbajo, cariacontecido

cretan /'kritn/ a cretense. n cretense, mf

cretin /'kritn/ n cretino (-na)

crevasse /krə'væs/ n grieta en un ventisquero, f

crevice /'krɛvɪs/ n intersticio, m, rendija, grieta, f

crew /kru/ n (of ships, boats, aircraft) tripulación, f; (of a gun) servidores de una ametralladora, m pl; (gang) pandilla, cuadrilla, f

crib /krɪb/ n pesebre, m; (child's) camita de niño, f;

(plagiary) plagio, *m*. *vt* (plagiarize) plagiar; (steal) hurtar

crick /krɪk/ *n* (in the neck) tortícolis, *m*

cricket /'krɪkɪt/ *n Ent*. grillo, *m*; (game) cricquet, *m*. **c. ball,** pelota de cricquet, *f*. **c. bat,** paleta de cricquet, *f*. **c. ground,** campo de cricquet, *m*. **c. match,** partido de cricquet, *m*

cricketer /'krɪkɪtər/ *n* jugador de cricquet, *m*

crier /'kraɪər/ *n* (town) pregonero, *m*

crime /kraɪm/ *n* crimen, *m*; ofensa, *f*, delito, *m*

criminal /'krɪmən/ *a* criminal. *n* criminal, *m*; reo, *mf* **C. Investigation Department,** (nearest equivalent) policía secreta, *f*. **c. laws,** código penal, *m*

criminally /'krɪmənli/ *adv* criminalmente

criminologist /,krɪmə'nɒlədʒɪst/ *n* criminalista, *m*

criminology /,krɪmə'nɒlədʒi/ *n* criminología, *f*

crimson /'krɪmzən, -sən/ *n* carmesí, *m*. *a* de carmesí. *vt* teñir de carmesí. *vi* enrojecerse

cringe /krɪndʒ/ *vi* temblar; asustarse, acobardarse; inclinarse (ante)

cringing /'krɪndʒɪŋ/ *a* servil, humilde; adulador, *Mexico also* lambioche

crinkle /'krɪŋkəl/ *vi* arrugarse; rizarse. *vt* arrugar. *n* arruga, *f*

crinoline /'krɪnlɪn/ *n* crinolina, *f*, miriñaque, guardainfante, *m*

cripple /'krɪpəl/ *n* tullido (-da); cojo (-ja). *vt* lisiar, tullir, estropear; *Fig.* paralizar

crisis /'kraɪsɪs/ *n* crisis, *f*

crisp /krɪsp/ *a* (of hair and of leaves) crespo; (fresh) fresco; (stiff) tieso; (of style) nervioso, vigoroso; (of manner) decidido; (of repartee) chispeante; (of tone) incisivo

crisscross /'krɪs,krɔs/ *vt* entrecruzar

criterion /kraɪ'tɪərɪən/ *n* criterio, *m*

critic /'krɪtɪk/ *n* crítico, *m*; censor, *m*

critical /'krɪtɪkəl/ *a* crítico

criticism /'krɪtə,sɪzəm/ *n* crítica, *f*

criticize /'krɪtə,saɪz/ *vt* criticar; censurar

critique /krɪ'tik/ *n* crítica, *f*

croak /krouk/ *vi* (of frogs) croar; (of ravens) graznar; (of persons) lamentarse, gruñir

croaking /'kroukɪŋ/ *n* canto de la rana, *m*; graznido, *m*

Croat /'krouæt/ *a* croata. *n* croata, *mf*

Croatia /krou'eɪʃə/ Crocia, *f*

crochet /krou'ʃeɪ/ *n* ganchillo, *m*, *vi* hacer ganchillo. *vt* hacer (algo) de ganchillo. **c. hook,** aguja de gancho, *f*, ganchillo, *m*. **c. work,** croché, ganchillo, *m*

crockery /'krɒkəri/ *n* loza, *f*, cacharros, *m pl*. **c. store,** cacharrería, *f*

crocodile /'krɒkə,daɪl/ *n* cocodrilo, *m*. **c. tears,** lágrimas de cocodrilo, *f pl*

crocus /'kroukəs/ *n* azafrán de primavera, *m*

croft /krɔft/ *n* campillo, *m*; (farm) heredad, *f*

crony /'krouni/ *n* compinche, *mf*

crook /krʊk/ *n* curva, *f*; (staff) cayado, *m*; (swindler) caballero de industria, estafador, *m*, *vt* doblar, encorvar

crooked /'krʊkɪd/ *a* curvo; encorvado; torcido, *Mexico* chueco; ladeado; (deformed) contrahecho; (of paths, etc.) tortuoso; (dishonest) torcido, tortuoso

crookedly /'krʊkɪdli/ *adv* torcidamente; de través

crookedness /'krʊkɪdnɪs/ *n* encorvadura, *f*; tortuosidad, *f*; sinuosidad, *f*

croon /krun/ *vt and vi* canturrear; cantar

crooner /'krunər/ *n* cantante, *mf*

crop /krɒp/ *n* (of birds) buche, *m*; (whip) látigo, *m*, fusta, *f*; (handle) mango, *m*; (harvest) cosecha, *f*; (of the hair) cortadura, *f*. *vt* cortar; (nibble) rozar; (hair) rapar. **Eton c.,** pelo a la garçonne, *m*. **to c. up,** aparecer, surgir

crop rotation *n* la rotación de cultivos, *f*

croquet /krou'keɪ/ *n* juego de la argolla, juego de cro-quet, *m*

croquette /krou'ket/ *n Cul.* croqueta, *f*

crosier /'krouʒər/ *n* báculo, cayado del obispo, *m*; (Sew. bias) bies, *m*. **in the shape of a c.,** en cruz. **the Red C.,** la Cruz Roja. **c.-bearer,** *Eccl.* crucero, *m*

cross /krɔs/ *n* cruz, *f*; *Biol.* cruzamiento, *m*; (Sew. bias) bies, *m*. **in the shape of a c.,** en cruz. **the Red C.,** la Cruz Roja. **c.-bearer,** *Eccl.* crucero, *m*

cross /krɔs/ *vt* cruzar; atravesar; pasar por; (a check

and animals) cruzar; (thwart) contrariar. **It did not c. my mind,** No se me ocurrió. **Our letters must have crossed,** Nuestras cartas deben haberse cruzado. **to c. oneself,** *Eccl.* persignarse. **to c. out,** tachar, rayar. **to c. over,** *vt* atravesar, cruzar. *vi* ir al otro lado

cross /krɔs/ *a* transversal; cruzado; oblicuo; (contrary) opuesto (a); (bad-tempered) malhumorado. **c.-breed,** *a* mestizo, atravesado. **c.-country,** *a* a campo travieso. **c.-examination,** *Law.* repregunta, *f*, contrainterrogatorio, *m*. **c.-examine,** *vt Law.* repreguntar; interrogar. **c.-eyed,** bizco. **c.-fire,** *Mil.* fuego cruzado, *m sing* fuegos cruzados, *m pl*; *Fig.* tiroteo, *m*. **c.-grained,** (of wood) vetisesgado; (of persons) áspero, intratable, desabrido. **c.-legged,** con las piernas cruzadas. **c.-purpose,** despropósito, *m*. **at c.-purposes,** a despropósito. **c.-question,** *vt Law.* repreguntar; interrogar. **c. reference,** contrarreferencia, *f*. **c. section,** sección transversal, *f*. **c.-stitch,** punto cruzado, *m*. **c.-word puzzle,** crucigrama, *m*

crossbar /'krɔs,bar/ *n* travesaño, *m*

crossbeam /'krɔs,bim/ *n* viga transversal, *f*

crossbench /'krɔs,bentʃ/ *a* atravesado

crossbred /'krɔs,bred/ *a* cruzado, mestizo; híbrido

crossbreed /'krɔs,brid/ *n* mestizo (-za); híbrido, *m*

crossing /'krɔsɪŋ/ *n* cruzamiento, *m*; (of the sea) travesía, *f*; (intersection) cruce, *m*; paso, *m*. **level c.,** paso a nivel, *m*. **pedestrian c.,** paso para peatones, *m*. **c.-sweeper,** barrendero, *m*

crossly /'krɔsli/ *adv* con mal humor, con displicencia, irritablemente

crossness /'krɔsnɪs/ *n* irritabilidad, *f*, mal humor, *m*

crossroad /'krɔs,roud/ *n* travesía, *f*; cruce, *m*; *pl* **crossroads,** cruce, cruce de caminos, *m sing* encrucijada, *f sing*

crosswise /'krɔs,waɪz/ *adv* en cruz; a través

crotch /krɒtʃ/ *n* (of a tree) bifurcación, *f*; *Anat.* horcajadura, *f*; (of trousers) entrepiernas, *f pl*

crotchet /'krɒtʃɪt/ *n Mus.* semínima, *f*; (fad) capricho, *m*; extravagancia, excentricidad, *f*

crotchety /'krɒtʃɪti/ *a* caprichoso; raro, excéntrico; difícil

crouch /krautʃ/ *vi* acurrucarse, agacharse, acuclillarse

croup /krup/ *n* (disease) crup, garrotillo, *m*; (of a horse) grupa, anca, *f*

croupier /'krupiər/ *n* coime, crupié, *m*

crow /krou/ *n Ornith.* cuervo, *m*; *Ornith.* grajo, *m*; (of a cock) canto del gallo, cacareo, *m*; (of an infant) gorjeo, *m*. *vi* (of a cock) cantar, cacarear. **as the c. flies,** en línea recta. **to c. over,** gallear, cantar victoria. **crow's-foot,** pata de gallo, *f*. **crow's-nest,** *Naut.* gavias, *f pl*

crowbar /'krou,bar/ *n* alzaprima, palanca, *f*

crowd /kraud/ *n* multitud, muchedumbre, *f*; concurso, *m*; vulgo, *m*; (majority) mayoría, *f*; *Theat.* acompañamiento, *m*. *vi* reunirse, congregarse; agolparse, remolinarse, apiñarse. *vt* (fill) llenar; atestar. **in a c.,** en tropel. **So many ideas crowded in on me,** Se me ocurrieron tantas ideas a la vez. **to follow the c.,** seguir la multitud; *Fig.* ir con la mayoría. **to c. in,** entrar en tropel. **to c. round,** cercar, agruparse alrededor de. **to c. together,** apiñarse. **to c. up,** subir en masa, subir en tropel

crowded /'kraudɪd/ *a* lleno; atestado, apiñado; (weighed down) agobiado; (of hours, etc.) lleno

crowing /'krouɪŋ/ *n* cacareo, canto del gallo, *m*; (boasting) jactancia, *f*

crown /kraun/ *n* corona, *f*; (of the head) coronilla, corona, *f*; (of a hat) copa, *f*; *Archit.* coronamiento, *m*. *vt* coronar. **c. prince,** príncipe heredero, *m*

crowning /'kraunɪŋ/ *n* coronamiento, *m*; *Archit.* remate, *m*, *a* final; supremo

crozier /'krouʒər/ *n*. See **crosier**

crucial /'kruʃəl/ *a* decisivo, crítico; difícil

crucible /'krusəbəl/ *n* crisol, *m*

crucifix /'krusəfɪks/ *n* crucifijo, *m*

crucifixion /,krusə'fɪkʃən/ *n* crucifixión, *f*

cruciform /'krusə,fɔrm/ *a* cruciforme

crucify /'krusə,faɪ/ *vt* crucificar

crude /krud/ *a* crudo; (of colors) chillón, llamativo; (uncivilized) cerril, inculto; (vulgar) cursi; (of truth, etc.) desnudo

crudity /'kruditi/ n crudeza, f
cruel /'kruəl/ a cruel
cruelty /'kruəlti/ n crueldad, f
cruet /'kruit/ n ánfora, vinagrera, f; (stand) angarillas, f pl, convoy, m
cruise /kruz/ vi cruzar, navegar; (of cars) correr. n viaje por mar, m
cruiser /'kruzər/ n crucero, m
crumb /krʌm/ n miga, f; (spongy part of bread) migaja, f. vt (bread) desmigajar; desmenuzar. **c. brush,** recogemigas, m
crumble /'krʌmbəl/ vt desmigajar, desmenuzar. vi desmoronarse, desmigajarse; Fig. hundirse, derrumbarse; Fig. desaparecer
crumbling /'krʌmblɪŋ/ n (of buildings, etc.) desmoronamiento, m; Fig. destrucción, f
crumple /'krʌmpəl/ vt arrugar, ajar. vi arrugarse. **to c. up,** vt (crush) estrujar; (persons) dejar aplastado. vi (collapse) hundirse, derrumbarse; (of persons) desplomarse; (despair) desalentarse
crunch /krʌntʃ/ vt mascar; hacer crujir. vi crujir
crupper /'krʌpər/ n baticola, f
crusade /kru'seid/ n cruzada, f
crusader /kru'seidər/ n cruzado, m
crush /krʌʃ/ vt aplastar; (to powder) moler, triturar; (grapes, etc.) exprimir; (crease) arrugar; (opposition, etc.) vencer; (annihilate) aniquilar, destruir; (abash) humillar, confundir; (hope, etc.) matar; (of sorrow, etc.) agobiar. **We all crushed into his dining room,** Fuimos en tropel a su comedor. **to c. up,** machacar, moler; (paper, etc.) estrujar
crushing /'krʌʃɪŋ/ a (of defeats and replies) aplastante; (of sorrow, etc.) abrumador
crust /krʌst/ n (of bread, pie) corteza, f; (scab) costra, f; (of the earth, snow) capa, f. vt encostrar. vi encostrarse. **c. of bread,** mendrugo de pan, m
crustacean /krʌ'steiʃən/ a crustáceo. n crustáceo, m
crustily /'krʌstli/ adv irritablemente, malhumoradamente
crustiness /'krʌstinis/ n mal humor, m, aspereza, f
crusty /'krʌsti/ a costroso; (of persons) malhumorado, irritable; áspero
crutch /krʌtʃ/ n muleta, f; (fork) horquilla, f; (crotch) horcajadura, f
crux /krʌks/ n problema, m; (knotty point) nudo, m
cry /krai/ vi (weep) llorar; (shout) gritar; (exclaim) exclamar. vt (one's wares) pregonar. n grito, m. **to cry for help,** pedir socorro a voces. **to cry to high heaven,** poner el grito en el cielo. **to cry one's eyes out,** llorar a mares. **to cry down,** desacreditar. **to cry off,** desdecirse; volverse atrás. **to cry out,** vt gritar. vi dar gritos; gritar; Fig. clamar. **cry-baby,** niño (-ña) llorón (-ona)
crying /'kraiɪŋ/ a urgente; notorio. n gritos, m pl; (weeping) llanto, m, lamentaciones, f pl; (tears) lágrimas, f pl
crypt /kript/ n cripta, f
cryptic /'kriptik/ a secreto, oculto
cryptography /krip'tɒgrəfi/ n criptografía, f
crystal /'kristl/ n cristal, m. **c. set,** Radio. receptor de galena, m
crystal ball n bola de cristal, esfera de cristal, f
crystalline /'kristlin/ a cristalino
crystallization /ˌkristlə'zeiʃən/ n cristalización, f
crystallize /'kristl,aiz/ vt and vi cristalizar
crystallography /ˌkristl'ɒgrəfi/ n cristalografía, f
cub /kʌb/ n cachorro (-rra)
Cuba Cuba
Cuban /'kyubən/ a cubano. n cubano (-na)
cubbyhole /'kʌbi,houl/ n refugio, m; garita, f; cuarto pequeño, m; chiribitil, m
cube /kyub/ n cubo, m; (of sugar) terrón, m. vt cubicar. **c. root,** raíz cúbica, f
cubic /'kyubik/ a cúbico
cubicle /'kyubikəl/ n cubículo, m
cubism /'kyubizəm/ n cubismo, m
cuckold /'kʌkəld/ n cornudo, m
cuckoo /'kuku/ n cuclillo, m; (cry) cucú, m. **c.-clock,** reloj de cuclillo, m
cucumber /'kyukʌmbər/ n cohombro m

cud /kʌd/ n rumia, f. **to chew the cud,** rumiar
cuddle /'kʌdl/ vt abrazar. n abrazo, m. **to c. up together,** estar abrazados
cudgel /'kʌdʒəl/ n porra, estaca, tranca, f, vt aporrear, apalear
cue /kyu/ n Theat. pie, m; (lead) táctica, f; (hint) indicación, f; (of hair) coleta, f; (billiard) taco (de billar), m. **to take one's cue from,** tomar como modelo (a); seguir el ejemplo de
cueca /'kueka/ n cueca f
cuff /kʌf/ vt abofetear. n (blow) bofetón, m; (of sleeve) puño, m, bocamanga, valenciana, f.
cufflink /'kʌf,lɪŋk/ n gemelo m, Central America mancuerna, mancuernilla f, Chile collera f, Colombia mancorna f
cuisine /kwi'zin/ n cocina, f
cul-de-sac /'kʌldə'sæk/ n callejón sin salida, m
culinary /'kyulə,nɛri/ a culinario
cullender /'kʌləndər/ n colador, m
culminate /'kʌlmə,neit/ vi culminar (en), terminar (en). **culminating point,** punto culminante, m
culmination /ˌkʌlmə'neiʃən/ n culminación, f; Fig. apogeo, punto culminante, m
culpability /ˌkʌlpə'biliti/ n culpabilidad, f
culpable /'kʌlpəbəl/ a culpable
culpably /'kʌlpəbli/ adv culpablemente
culprit /'kʌlprit/ n culpado (-da)
cult /kʌlt/ n culto, m
cultivable /'kʌltəvəbəl/ a cultivable, labradero
cultivate /'kʌltə,veit/ vt cultivar
cultivated /'kʌltə,veitid/ a cultivado; (of persons) culto, fino
cultivation /ˌkʌltə'veiʃən/ n cultivación, f; (of the land) cultivo, m; (of persons, etc.) cultura, f
cultivator /'kʌltə,veitər/ n cultivador (-ra); (machine) cultivador, m
cultural /'kʌltʃərəl/ a cultural
culture /'kʌltʃər/ n cultura, f; (bacteriology) cultivo, m, vt (bacteriology) cultivar
cultured /'kʌltʃərd/ a culto
culvert /'kʌlvərt/ n alcantarilla, f
cumbersome /'kʌmbərsəm/ a pesado; incómodo
cumulative /'kyumyələtiv/ a cumulativo
cumulus /'kyumyələs/ n cúmulo, m
cuneiform /kyu'niə,fɔrm/ a cuneiforme
cunning /'kʌnɪŋ/ a astuto, taimado, Lat. Am. macuco n (skill) habilidad, f; astucia, f
cup /kʌp/ n taza, f; (Eccl. and Bot.) cáliz, m; Sports. copa, f; (hollow) hoyo, m, hondonada, f. **c.-final,** Sports. final de la copa, m. **c.-tie,** Sports. partido eliminatorio, m
cup-and-ball /'kʌpən'bɔl/ n boliche, m
cupboard /'kʌbərd/ n armario, m; (in the wall) alacena, f. **c. love,** amor interesado, m
cupful /'kʌpfʊl/ n taza, f
cupidity /kyu'piditi/ n avaricia, codicia, f
cup of sorrow n ramito de amargura, m
cupola /'kyupələ/ n cúpula, f
cur /kɜr/ n perro mestizo, m; canalla, m
curable /'kyurəbəl/ a curable
curableness /'kyurəbəlnis/ n curabilidad, f
curative /'kyurətiv/ a curativo, terapéutico
curator /kyu'reitər/ n (of a museum) director, m; (Scots law) curador, m
curb /kɜrb/ n (of a bridle) barbada, f; Fig. freno, m; (stone) bordillo, m, guarnición, f, vt (a horse) enfrenar; Fig. refrenar, reprimir; (limit) limitar
curd /kɜrd/ n requesón, m; cuajada, f
curdle /'kɜrdl/ vi coagularse; (of blood) helarse. vt coagular; (blood) helar
cure /kyur/ n cura, f; Eccl. curato, m. vt curar; (leather) zurrar; (salt) salar; Fig. remediar. **to take a c.,** tomar una cura. **c.-all,** panacea, f. **c. of souls,** cura de almas, f
curer /'kyurər/ n (of fish, etc.) salador, m; (of evils, etc.) remediador, m
curfew /'kɜrfyu/ n toque de queda, m
curing /'kyurɪŋ/ n curación, f; (salting) saladura, f
curio /'kyuri,ou/ n curiosidad, antigüedad, f
curiosity /ˌkyuri'ɒsiti/ n curiosidad, f

curious /'kyʊriəs/ *a* (all meanings) curioso
curiously /'kyʊriəsli/ *adv* curiosamente
curl /kɜrl/ *n* (of hair) rizo, bucle, *m*; (of smoke) penacho, *m*. *vt* rizar. *vi* rizarse; *Sports.* jugar al curling. **in c.**, rizado. **to c. one's lip**, hacer una mueca de desdén. **to c. up**, *vt* arrollar; *Fig.* dejar fuera de combate (a). *vi* hacerse un ovillo, enroscarse; (of leaves) abarquillarse; *Fig.* desplomarse; desanimarse. **c.-paper**, papillote, *m*
curlew /'kɜrlu/ *n Ornith.* zarapito, *m*
curling /'kɜrlɪŋ/ *n* (game) curling, *m*, a rizado. **c.-tongs**, encrespador, *m*
curly /'kɜrli/ *a* rizado, crespo
curmudgeon /kər'mʌdʒən/ *n* erizo, misántropo, cara de viernes, *m*
currant /'kɜrənt/ *n* (dry) pasa de Corinto, *f*; (fresh) grosella, *f*. **black c.**, grosella negra, *f*; (bush) grosellero negro, *m*. **c.-bush**, grosellero, *m*
currency /'kɜrənsi/ *n* uso corriente, *m*; moneda corriente, *f*, dinero, *m*; dinero en circulación, *m*; valor corriente, *m*; estimación, *f*
current /'kɜrənt/ *a* corriente; presente, de actualidad; (of money) en circulación. *n* (of water, etc., *Fig. Elec.*) corriente, *f*. **alternating c.**, *Elec.* corriente alterna, *f*. **direct c.**, *Elec.* corriente continua, *f*. **the c. number of a magazine**, el último número de una revista. **c. events**, actualidades, *f pl*
currently /'kɜrəntli/ *adv* actualmente, corrientemente, generalmente
curricle /'kɜrɪkəl/ *n* carriola, *f*
curriculum /kə'rɪkyələm/ *n* plan de estudios, *m*; curso, *m*
curriculum vitae /'vaiti/ *n* hoja de vida, *f*
curry /'kɜri/ *vt* (a horse) almohazar; *Cul.* condimentar con cari. **to c. favor with**, insinuarse en el favor de. **c.-comb**, almohaza, *f*
curse /kɜrs/ *n* maldición, *f*; blasfemia, *f*; (ruin) azote, castigo, *m*. *vt* maldecir; (afflict) castigar. *vi* blasfemar, echar pestes
cursed /'kɜrsɪd, kɜrst/ *a* maldito; abominable, odioso
cursing /'kɜrsɪŋ/ *n* maldición, *f*; blasfemias, *f pl*
cursorily /'kɜrsərəli/ *adv* rápidamente; de prisa; superficialmente
cursory /'kɜrsəri/ *a* rápido; apresurado; superficial
curt /kɜrt/ *a* seco, brusco; corto
curtail /kər'teil/ *vt* abreviar; reducir; disminuir
curtailment /kər'teilmənt/ *n* abreviación, *f*; reducción, *f*; disminución, *f*
curtain /'kɜrtn/ *n* cortina, *f*; *Theat.* telón, *m*. *vt* poner cortinas (a). **drop c.**, telón de boca, *m*. **iron c.**, *Polit.* telón de acero, *m*. **to c. off**, separar por cortinas. **c.-lecture**, reprimenda conyugal, *f*. **c.-raiser**, entremés, *m*. **c.-ring**, anilla, *f*
curtly /'kɜrtli/ *adv* secamente, bruscamente
curtness /'kɜrtnɪs/ *n* brusquedad, sequedad, *f*
curtsey /'kɜrtsi/ *n* reverencia, cortesía, *f*, *vi* hacer una reverencia
curvature /'kɜrvətʃər/ *n* curvatura, *f*
curve /kɜrv/ *n* curva, *f*; *Mech.* codo, *m*; (*Auto.* of a road) viraje, *m*. *vt* encorvar, torcer. *vi* encorvarse, torcerse; (of a road) hacer un viraje.
curved /kɜrvd/ *a* curvo
curvet /'kɜrvɪt/ *n* corveta, cabriola, *f*, *vi* corvetear, corcovear, cabriolar
curvilinear /,kɜrvə'lɪniər/ *a* curvilíneo
cushion /'kʊʃən/ *n* almohada, *f*; cojín, *m*; (billiards) banda, *f*; (of fingers, etc.) pulpejo, *m*. *vt* proveer de almohadas; (a shock) amortiguar; suavizar
custard /'kʌstərd/ *n* flan, *m*, natillas, *f pl*
custodian /kʌ'stoudiən/ *n* custodio, *m*; guardián, *m*; (of a museum, etc.) director, *m*
custody /'kʌstədi/ *n* custodia, *f*; guarda, *f*; prisión, *f*. **in safe c.**, en lugar seguro. **to take** (a person) **into c.**, arrestar
custom /'kʌstəm/ *n* costumbre, *f*; uso, *m*; *Com.* parroquia, clientela, *f*; (sales) ventas, *f pl*; *pl* **Customs**, aduana, *f*. **to go through the Customs**, pasar por la aduana. **Customs duty**, derechos de aduana, *m pl*. **Customs officer**, aduanero, *m*. **c.-house**, aduana, *f*

customarily /,kʌstə'mɛrəli/ *adv* habitualmente, por lo general
customary /'kʌstə,mɛri/ *a* acostumbrado, usual, habitual
customer /'kʌstəmər/ *n* cliente, *mf* parroquiano (-na), *Lat. Am. also* marchante (-ta)
customs barrier /'kʌstəmz/ *n* barrera aduanera, barrera arancelaria, *f*
cut /kʌt/ *vt* cortar; (diamonds) tallar; (hay, etc.) segar; (carve) labrar, tallar; (engrave) grabar; (a lecture, etc.) no asistir a; (cards) destajar, cortar; (*Fig.* wound) herir; (reduce) reducir; abreviar; (teeth) echar; (of lines) cruzar. *vi* cortar; cortar bien; (*Fam.* go) marcharse a prisa y corriendo. **I must get my hair cut**, He de hacerme cortar el pelo. **That cuts both ways**, Es una arma de dos filos. **His opinion cuts no ice**, Su opinión no cuenta. **Mary cut him dead**, María hizo como si no le reconociera. **to cut a caper**, dar saltos; hacer cabriolas. **to cut a person short**, echar el tablacho (a). **to cut and run**, poner los pies en polvorosa. **to cut for deal**, (cards) cortar para ver quién da las cartas. **to cut short**, (a career) terminar. **to cut to the quick**, herir en lo más vivo. **to cut across**, cortar al través; (fields, etc.) atravesar; tomar por un atajo. **to cut away**, *vt* quitar. *vi Inf.* poner pies en polvorosa. **to cut down**, derribar; (by the sword) acuchillar; (by death, etc.) segar, malograr; (expenses, etc.) reducir; (abbreviate) cortar, abreviar. **to cut off**, bloquear, cortar, separar; amputar; (on a telephone) cortar la comunicación; (gas, water, etc.) cortar; (supply of food, etc.) interrumpir; (of death) llevarse. **to cut out**, (dresses, etc.) cortar; (oust) suplantar. **He is not cut out for medicine**, No tiene la disposición para la medicina. **to cut up**, trinchar, cortar en pequeños trozos, *Lat. Am.* destajar; (afflict) entristecer, afligir. **to cut up rough**, *Inf.* ponerse furioso
cut /kʌt/ *a* cortado. **well-cut features**, facciones regulares, *f pl*. **cut and dried opinion**, opinión hecha, idea fija, *f*; ideas cerradas, *f pl*. **cut glass**, cristal tallado, *m*
cut /kʌt/ *n* corte, *m*; (with a whip) latigazo, *m*; (with a sword) cuchillada, *f*; (with a sharp instrument) tajo, *m*; cortadura, *f*; (in prices, etc.) reducción, *f*; (engraving) grabado, *m*; clisé, *m*; (of cards) corte, *m*. **short cut**, atajo, *m*. **the cut of a coat**, el corte de un abrigo. **to give** (someone) **the cut direct**, pasar cerca de (una persona) sin saludarle. **cut-out**, *n* (paper) recortado, *m*; *Elec.* cortacircuitos, *m*. **cut-throat**, *n* asesino, *m*
cutaneous /kyu'teiniəs/ *a* cutáneo
cute /kyut/ *a* guapo, cuco, listo; mono, *Mexico* chulo
cuteness /'kyutnɪs/ *n* cuquería, inteligencia, *f*; monería, *f*
cuticle /'kyutɪkəl/ *n* cutícula, *f*
cutlass /'kʌtləs/ *n* alfanje *m*
cutler /'kʌtlər/ *n* cuchillero, *m*
cutlery /'kʌtləri/ *n* cuchillería, *f*
cutlet /'kʌtlɪt/ *n* chuleta, *f*
cutter /'kʌtər/ *n* cortador, *m*; *Naut.* cúter, *m*; escampavía, *f*
cutting /'kʌtɪŋ/ *n* corte, *m*; (of diamonds) talla, *f*; (in a mountain, etc.) tajo, *m*; *Agr.* plantón, *m*; (of cloth) retazo, *m*; (newspaper) recorte, *m*. *a* cortante; (of remarks) mordaz. **newspaper c.**, recorte de periódico. **c. down**, (of trees) tala, *f*; reducción, *f*
cuttingly /'kʌtɪŋli/ *adv* mordazmente, con malicia
cuttlefish /'kʌtl,fɪʃ/ *n* jibia, *f*
cyanide /'saiə,naid/ *n* cianuro, *m*
cyberspace /'saibər,speis/ *n* ciberespacio, *m*
cycle /'saikəl/ *n* ciclo, *m*; período, *m*; (bicycle) bicicleta, *f*. *vi* ir en bicicleta
cyclic /'saiklɪk/ *a* cíclico
cycling /'saiklɪŋ/ *n* ciclismo, *m*
cyclist /'saiklɪst/ *n* ciclista, *mf*
cyclone /'saikloun/ *n* ciclón, *m*
cygnet /'sɪgnɪt/ *n* pollo del cisne, *m*
cylinder /'sɪlɪndər/ *n* cilindro, *m*; *Mech.* tambor, *m*. **c. head**, culata, *f*
cylindrical /sɪ'lɪndrɪkəl/ *a* cilíndrico
cymbal /'sɪmbəl/ *n* címbalo, platillo, *m*

cymbalist /'sɪmbəlɪst/ n cimbalero (-ra)
cynic /'sɪnɪk/ n cínico, m
cynical /'sɪnɪkəl/ a cínico
cynicism /'sɪnəˌsɪzəm/ n cinismo, m
cynosure /'saɪnəˌʃʊr/ n Astron. Osa Menor, f; blanco, m
cypress /'saiprəs/ n (tree and wood) ciprés, m. **c. grove,** cipresal, m

Cypriot /'sɪprɪət/ a chipriota. n chipriota, mf
Cyprus /'saiprəs/ Isla de Chipre, f
cyst /sɪst/ n quiste, m
cystic /'sɪstɪk/ a cístico
Czech /tʃɛk/ a checo. n checo (-ca); (language) checo, m
Czechoslovak /'tʃɛkə'slouvæk/ n checoslovaco (-ca)

D

d /di/ n (letter) de, f; Mus. re, m
dab /dæb/ vt golpear suavemente, tocar; (sponge) esponjar; (moisten) mojar. n golpecito, golpe blando, m; (small piece) pedazo pequeño, m; (blob) borrón, m; (peck) picotazo, m; Inf. experto (-ta). **to dab at one's eyes,** secarse los ojos
dabble /'dæbəl/ vt mojar (en). vi chapotear; (engage in) entretenerse en; (meddle in) meterse en; (speculate in) especular en. **to d. in politics,** meterse en política
dabbler /'dæblər/ n aficionado (-da)
dace /deis/ n dardo, albur, m
dachshund /'dɑks,hʊnt/ n perro pachón, m
daddy /'dædi/ n papaíto, m. **d.-longlegs,** típula, f
daffodil /'dæfədɪl/ n narciso trompón, m
daft /dæft/ a bobo, tonto, chiflado; loco
dagger /'dægər/ n daga, f, puñal, m; Print. cruz, f. **to be at daggers drawn,** estar a matar. **to look daggers (at),** lanzar miradas de odio (hacia), mirar echando chispas. **d. thrust,** puñalada, f
daguerreotype /də'gɛərəˌtaɪp/ n daguerrotipo, m
dahlia /'dælyə/ n dalia, f
daily /'deili/ a diario, de todos los días; cotidiano. adv diariamente, cada día, todos los días; cotidianamente. n (paper) diario, m. **d. bread,** pan cotidiano, pan de cada día, m. **d. help,** (person) asistenta, f. **d. pay,** jornal, m; Mil. pre, m
daintily /'deintli/ adv delicadamente; elegantemente; con primor
daintiness /'deintinɪs/ n delicadeza, f; elegancia, f; (beauty) primor, m
dainty /'deinti/ a delicado; elegante; primoroso, exquisito; (fastidious) melindroso, difícil. n bocado exquisito, m, golosina, f
dairy /'deəri/ n lechería, f. **d. cattle,** vacas lecheras, f pl. **d.-farm,** granja, f. **d.-farmer,** granjero (-ra). **d.-farming,** industria lechera, f
dairymaid /'deəri,meid/ n lechera, f
dairyman /'deərimən/ n lechero, m
dais /'deiɪs/ n estrado, m
daisy /'deizi/ n margarita, f
dale /deil/ n valle, m
dalliance /'dæliəns/ n (delay) tardanza, f; (play) jugueteo, m; diversiones, f pl; (caresses) caricias, f pl, abrazos, m pl
dally /'dæli/ vi tardar, perder el tiempo; entretenerse, divertirse; (make love) holgar (con); (with an idea) entretenerse con, jugar con
Dalmatian /dæl'meiʃən/ a dalmático, dálmata. n dálmata, mf. **D. dog,** perro dálmata, m
dalmatic /dæl'mætɪk/ n dalmática, f
daltonism /'dɔltn̩ˌɪzəm/ n daltonismo, m
dam /dæm/ n (of animals) madre, f; (of a river, etc.) presa, f, embalse, m; (mole) dique, m; pared de retención, f. vt represar, embalsar; cerrar; (restrain) contener, reprimir
damage /'dæmɪdʒ/ n daño, perjuicio, m; mal, m; (avería, f; pérdida, f; (Fam. price) precio, m; pl **damages,** Law. daños y perjuicios, m pl. vt dañar, perjudicar, Lat. Am. afectar; estropear; deteriorar; (reputation, etc.) comprometer
damageable /'dæmɪdʒəbəl/ a que puede ser dañado; frágil
damaging /'dæmɪdʒɪŋ/ a perjudicial; comprometedor
damascene /'dæməsɪn/ vt damasquinar
Damascus /də'mæskəs/ Damasio, m
damask /'dæməsk/ n (cloth) damasco, m; (steel)

acero damasquino, m. a de damasco; damasquino. vt (metals) damasquinar; (cloth) adamascar. **d.-like,** adamascado. **d. rose,** rosa de Damasco, f
dame /deim/ n dama, señora, f; Inf. madre, f; (schoolmistress) amiga, f. **to attend a d. school,** ir a la amiga
damming /'dæmɪŋ/ n embalse, m, represa, f; retención, f; represión, f
damn /dæm/ vt condenar al infierno; maldecir; vituperar. **D. it!** ¡Maldito sea!
damnable /'dæmnəbəl/ a detestable, infame; Inf. horrible
damnably /'dæmnəbli/ adv abominablemente; Inf. horriblemente
damnation /dæm'neiʃən/ n condenación, perdición, f; maldición, f; vituperación, f
damned /dæmd/ a condenado; maldito; detestable, odioso
damning /'dæmɪŋ/ a que condena; irresistible
damp /dæmp/ a húmedo. n humedad, f; (mist) niebla, f; exhalación, f; (gas) mofeta, f; Fig. tristeza, depresión, f. vt humedecer, mojar; apagar, amortiguar; (depress) deprimir, entristecer; (stifle) ahogar; (lessen) moderar; (trouble) turbar. **d.-proof,** impermeable
damper /'dæmpər/ n (of a chimney) registro de humos, m; (of a piano) batiente, m; (for stamps) mojador, m; (gloom) depresión, tristeza, f; (restraint) freno, m
dampish /'dæmpɪʃ/ a algo húmedo
dampness /'dæmpnɪs/ n humedad, f
damsel /'dæmzəl/ n chica, muchacha, f; damisela, f, Poet. doncella, f
damson /'dæmzən/ n ciruela damascena, f. **d. tree,** ciruelo damasceno, m
dance /dæns/ n danza, f; baile, m. vi bailar, danzar; saltar, brincar. vt bailar; hacer saltar. **to d. attendance on,** servir humildemente; hacer la rueda (a). **to lead someone a d.,** hacer bailar. **d. band,** orquestina, f; orquesta de jazz, f. **d. floor,** pista de baile, f. **d. hall,** salón de baile, m. **d. music,** música bailable, f. **d.-number,** (in a theater) bailable, m. **d. of death,** danza de la muerte, f
dancer /'dænsər/ n bailarín (-ina); danzador (-ra); pl **dancers,** (partners) parejas de baile, f pl
dancing /'dænsɪŋ/ n baile, m, danza, f. **d.-girl,** bailarina, f; (Indian) bayadera, f. **d.-master,** maestro de baile, m. **d. school,** academia de baile, f. **d. slipper,** zapatilla de baile, f
dandelion /'dændl̩ˌaɪən/ n diente de león, m
dandle /'dændl̩/ vt mecer, hacer saltar sobre las rodillas, hacer bailar
dandruff /'dændrəf/ n caspa, f
dandy /'dændi/ n dandi, petimetre, barbilindo, m
Dane /dein/ n danés (-esa). **Great D.,** perro danés, m
danger /'deindʒər/ n peligro, m; riesgo, m. **out of d.,** fuera de peligro. **to be in d.,** correr peligro, peligrar, estar en peligro
dangerous /'deindʒərəs/ a peligroso; arriesgado; nocivo
dangerously /'deindʒərəsli/ adv peligrosamente
dangerousness /'deindʒərəsnɪs/ n peligro, m
dangle /'dæŋgəl/ vi colgar, pender. vt dejar colgar; oscilar; (show) mostrar
Danish /'deinɪʃ/ a danés, de Dinamarca. n (language) danés, m

dank /dæŋk/ a húmedo
dankness /'dæŋknɪs/ n humedad, f
dapper /'dæpər/ a apuesto, aseado; activo, vivaz
dapple /'dæpəl/ vt motear, salpicar, manchar. **d.-grey,** a rucio
dappled /'dæpəld/ a (of horses) rodado, empedrado
Dardanelles, the /,dɑrdn̩'ɛlz/ los Dardanelos, m
dare /dɛər/ vi atreverse, osar. vt arriesgar; desafiar, provocar; hacer frente a, arrostrar. n reto, m. **I d. say!** ¡Ya lo creo! ¡No lo dudo! **I d. say that...,** No me sorprendería que...; Supongo que... **d.-devil,** calavera, m; atrevido (-da), valeroso (-sa)
daring /'dɛərɪŋ/ a intrépido, audaz; atrevido, Argentina agalludo (dangerous) arriesgado, peligroso. n audacia, osadia, f, atrevimiento, m; peligro, m
daringly /'dɛərɪŋli/ adv atrevidamente
dark /dɑrk/ a oscuro; (of complexion, etc.) moreno; negro; lóbrego; (of colors) oscuro; misterioso; enigmático; secreto, escondido; (sad) funesto, triste; (evil) malo, malévolo. n oscuridad, f; (shade) sombra, f; ignorancia, f. **after d.,** a nocturno. adv después del anochecer. **in the d.,** a oscuras; de noche; Fig. **be in the d.,** quedarse en la luna. **to become d.,** oscurecerse; (cloud over) anublarse; (become night) anochecer. **to keep d.,** vt tener secreto. vi esconderse. **d. ages,** los siglos de la ignorancia y de la superstición. **d.-eyed,** de ojos negros, ojinegro. **d. horse,** caballo desconocido, m; Polit. batacazo, m. **d. lantern,** linterna sorda, f. **d. room,** cuarto oscuro, m; Photo. laboratorio fotográfico, m; (optics) cámara oscura, f
darken /'dɑrkən/ vt obscurecer; sombrear; (of color) hacer más oscuro; (sadden) entristecer. vi obscurecerse; (of the sky) anublarse; (of the face with emotion) inmutarse.
darkening /'dɑrkənɪŋ/ n oscurecimiento, m
darkly /'dɑrkli/ adv oscuramente; misteriosamente; con malevolencia; secretamente; (archaic) indistintamente
darkness /'dɑrknɪs/ n oscuridad, f, tinieblas, f pl; sombra, f; (of color) oscuro, m; (of the complexion) color moreno, m; (of eyes, hair) negrura, f; (night) noche, f; (ignorance) ignorancia, f; (privacy) secreto, m. **Prince of d.,** el príncipe de las tinieblas
darling /'dɑrlɪŋ/ a querido, amado; (greatest) mayor. n querido (-da); (favorite) el predilecto, la predilecta, el favorito, la favorita. **My d.!** ¡Amor mío! ¡Vida mía! ¡Pichoncito mío!
darn /dɑrn/ vt zurcir, remendar. n zurcido, remiendo, m
darner /'dɑrnər/ n zurcidor (-ra); (implement) huevo de zurcir, m
darning /'dɑrnɪŋ/ n zurcidura, f; zurcido, recosido, m. **d.-needle,** aguja de zurcir, f. **d. wool,** lana de zurcir, f
dart /dɑrt/ n dardo, m; movimiento rápido, m; avance rápido, m; Sew. sisa, f. vi lanzarse, abalanzarse (sobre); volar; correr, avanzar rápidamente. vt lanzar, arrojar; dirigir. **to make darts in,** Sew. sisar
Darwinian /dɑr'wɪnɪən/ a darviniano. n darvinista, mf
Darwinism /'dɑrwə,nɪzəm/ n darvinismo, m
dash /dæʃ/ n (spirit) fogosidad, f, brío, m; energía, f; (impact) choque, golpe, m; (mixture) mezcla, f; (of a liquid) gota, f; (of the pen) rasgo, m; (attack) ataque, m; avance rápido, m; (a little) algo, un poco (de); Gram. raya, f; (show) ostentación, f. **He made a d. for the door,** Se precipitó a la puerta, Corrió hacia la puerta. **to cut a d.,** hacer gran papel. **d.-board,** tablero de instrumentos, m
dash /dæʃ/ vt arrojar con violencia; (break) quebrar, estrellar; (sprinkle) rociar (con), salpicar (con); (mix) mezclar; (knock) golpear; (disappoint) frustrar, destruir; (confound) confundir; (depress) desanimar. vi (rush) precipitarse; quebrarse, estrellarse; chocar (contra); (of waves) romperse. **to d. to pieces,** hacer añicos, estrellar. **to d. along,** avanzar rápidamente; correr. **to d. away,** vi marcharse apresuradamente. **to d. down,** vi bajar aprisa. vt derribar; (overturn) volcar; (throw) tirar. **to d. off,** vi marcharse apresuradamente; vt hacer apresuradamente; (a

letter, etc.) escribir de prisa; (sketch) bosquejar rápidamente. **to d. out,** vi salir precipitadamente; lanzarse a la calle. vt (erase) borrar; hacer saltar. **to d. through,** atravesar rápidamente; hacer de prisa. **to d. up,** llegar a prisa; (sprout) saltar
dashing /'dæʃɪŋ/ a valiente; (spirited) fogoso, gallardo; majo, brillante. n choque, m; (breaking) quebrantamiento, m; (of the waves) embate, m
dastardly /'dæstərdli/ a cobarde
data /'deitə/ n pl datos, m pl
database /'deitəbeis/ n base de datos, f
data entry n entrada de datos, f
data processing /'prɒsesɪŋ/ n elaboración electrónica de datos, f, recuento de datos, m
date /deit/ n fecha, f; (period) época, f; (term) plazo, m; (duration) duración, f; (appointment) cita, f; Bot. dátil, m. vt fechar, datar; poner fecha a; asignar. vi datar (de), remontar (a). **out of d.,** anticuado; pasado de moda; (of persons) atrasado de noticias. **to be up to d.,** ser nuevo; ser de última moda; (of persons) estar al día. **to bring up to d.,** renovar; (of persons) poner al corriente. **to fix the d.,** señalar el día; (chronologically) ajustar los tiempos. **to d.,** hasta la fecha. **under d. (of),** con fecha (de). **up to d.,** hasta hoy, hasta ahora. **What is the d.?** ¿Qué fecha es? ¿A cómo estamos hoy? ¿A cuántos estamos hoy? **d. palm,** datilera, f
date of expiration n fecha de vencimiento, f
daub /dɔb/ vt barrar, embadurnar; manchar, ensuciar; untar; (paint) pintorrear. n embadurnamiento, m; (picture) aleluya, f
dauber /'dɔbər/ n chafalmejas, pintamonas, mf pintor (-ra) de brocha gorda
daughter /'dɔtər/ n hija, f. **adopted d.,** hija adoptiva, f. **little d.,** hijita, f. **d.-in-law,** nuera, f
daughterly /'dɔtərli/ a de hija
daunt /dɔnt, dɑnt/ vt intimidar, acobardar; dar miedo (a), espantar; (dishearten) desanimar
dauntless /'dɔntlɪs/ a impávido, intrépido
dauphin /'dɔfɪn/ n delfín, m
dawdle /'dɔdl/ vi perder el tiempo; haraganear, gandulear
dawdler /'dɔdlər/ n gandul (-la)
dawdling /'dɔdlɪŋ/ a perezoso, lento
dawn /dɔn/ n alba, madrugada, primera luz, f; Fig. aurora, f. vi amanecer, alborear, romper el día; (appear) mostrarse, asomar. **at d.,** a primera luz, al amanecer, de madrugada, al alba. **It had not dawned on me,** No me había ocurrido
day /dei/ n día, m; luz del día, f; (day's work) jornada, f; (battle) batalla, f; (victory) victoria, f; pl **days,** (time) tiempos, m pl, época, f; (life) vida, f; (years) años, m pl, a (su) edad. **all day long,** durante todo el día. **any day,** cualquier día. **by day,** de día. **by the day,** al día. **every day,** todos los días, cada día. **every other day,** un día sí y otro no, cada dos días. **from this day forward,** desde hoy en adelante. **from day to day,** de día en día. **Good day!** ¡Buenos días! **in these days,** en estos días. **in olden days,** en la antigüedad, Inf. en tiempos de Maricastaña. **in the days of,** en los tiempos de; durante los años de; durante la vida de. **next day,** el día siguiente. **(on) the next day,** al día siguiente, al otro día. **one of these days,** un día de éstos. **some fine day,** el mejor día, de un día a otro. **the day after tomorrow,** pasado mañana. **the day before yesterday,** anteayer. **the day before,** la víspera. **to win the day,** ganar el día, salir victorioso. **day after day,** cada día, día tras día. **day by day,** día por día, día tras día, sin cesar, día tras día. **day-book,** Com. libro diario, m; **day's holiday,** día de asueto, m; día libre, m. **day laborer,** jornalero, m. **day nursery,** guardería de niños, f. **day-pupil,** alumno (-na) externo (-na). **day-school,** externado, m. **day shift,** turno de día, m. **day-star,** lucero del día, m. **day ticket,** billete de excursión, m. **daybreak** /'dei,breik/ n alba, f, amanecer, m. **at d.,** al romper el día, al amanecer
daydream /'dei,drim/ n ensueño, m; ilusión, f; fantasía, visión, f. vi Lit. soñar despierto, dejar volar sus pensamientos; Fig. hacerse ilusiones

daydreamer /'dei͜drimər/ n soñador (-ra); visionario (-ia)

daylight /'dei͜lait/ n luz del día, f, día, m; (contrasted with artificial light) luz natural, f. **in broad d.,** a plena calle, a plena luz, en plena luz del día. **It's d. robbery!** ¡Es un desuello! **d.-saving,** hora de verano, f

daytime /'dei͜taim/ n día, m. **in the d.,** durante el día

daze /deiz/ vt aturdir, confundir; (dazzle) deslumbrar. n aturdimiento, m, confusión, f; perplejidad, f

dazzle /'dæzəl/ vt (camouflage) disfrazar; deslumbrar, ofuscar. n deslumbramiento, m; brillo, m, refulgencia, f

dazzling /'dæzlɪŋ/ a deslumbrador; brillante

deacon /'dikən/ n diácono, m

deaconess /'dikənɪs/ n diaconisa, f

dead /dɛd/ a and past part muerto; inanimado; (withered) marchito; (deep) profundo; (unconscious) inerte; inmóvil; insensible; (numb) entumecido; (complete) absoluto, completo; (sure) certero, excelente; (useless) inútil; (of color and human character) apagado; sin espíritu; inactivo; (of eyes) mortecino; (of sound) sordo, opaco; (of villages, etc.) desierto, despoblado; (quiet) silencioso; (empty) vacío; (monotonous) monótono; (of fire) apagado; (with weight, language) muerto; Elec. interrumpido; Law. muerto civilmente. adv completamente, enteramente; del todo; directamente; exactamente; profundamente. **the d.,** los muertos. **in the d. of night,** en las altas horas de la noche. **to be d.,** estar muerto; haber muerto. **to be d. against,** estar completamente opuesto a. **to drop d.,** caer muerto; morir de repente. **to rise from the d.,** resucitar. **to sham d.,** hacer la mortecina, fingirse muerto. **to speak ill of the d.,** hablar mal de los muertos; Inf. desenterrar los muertos. **d. ball,** pelota fuera de juego, f. **d.-beat,** delincuente. **d. body,** cadáver, cuerpo muerto, m. **d. calm,** calma profunda, f; Naut. calma chicha, f. **d. certainty,** seguridad completa, f. **d.-drunk,** hecho una uva. **d. end,** callejón sin salida, m. **d. heat,** empate, m. **d. language,** lengua muerta, f. **d.-letter,** letra muerta, f; carta devuelta o no reclamada, f. **d.-lock,** punto muerto, m. **to reach a d.-lock,** llegar a un punto muerto. **d. march,** marcha fúnebre, f. **d. set,** empeñado (en). **d. shot,** (person) tirador (-ra) certero (-ra) (shot) tiro certero, m. **d. silence,** silencio profundo, m. **d. stop,** parada en seco, f. **d. tired,** rendido. **d. weight,** peso muerto, m. **d. wood,** leña seca, f; material inútil, m

deaden /'dɛdn̩/ vt amortiguar; (of pain) calmar; (remove) quitar; (of colors) apagar

deadening /'dɛdnɪŋ/ n amortiguamiento, m

deadliness /'dɛdlɪnɪs/ n carácter mortal, m; implacabilidad, f

deadly /'dɛdli/ a mortal; implacable; Inf. insoportable. adv mortalmente. **He was d. pale,** Estaba pálido como un muerto. **the seven d. sins,** los siete pecados capitales. **d. nightshade,** belladona, f

deadness /'dɛdnɪs/ n falta de vida, f; inercia, f; marchitez, f; (numbness) entumecimiento, m; desanimación, f; parálisis, f

Dead Sea, the el mar Muerto, m

Dead Sea Scrolls, the /skroulz/ los rollos del mar Muerto, m pl

deaf /dɛf/ a sordo. **d. people,** los sordos. **to be d.,** ser sordo; padecer sordera. **to be as d. as a post,** ser más sordo que una tapia. **to become d.,** ensordecer, volverse sordo. **to fall on d. ears,** caer en saco roto. **to turn a d. ear,** hacerse el sordo. **d. aid,** audífono, m. **d.-mute,** sordomudo (-da). **d.-mutism,** sordomudez, f

deafen /'dɛfən/ vt asordar, ensordecer

deafening /'dɛfənɪŋ/ a ensordecedor

deafly /'dɛfli/ adv sordamente

deafness /'dɛfnɪs/ n sordera, f

deal /dil/ n (transaction) negocio, trato, m; (at cards) reparto, m; (wood) pino, m; (plank) tablón de pino, m. **a d., a great d.,** mucho. **a very great d.,** muchísimo. **to conclude a d.,** cerrar un trato

deal /dil/ vt repartir; (a blow) asestar, dar; (cards) dar; (justice) dispensar. **to d. a blow at,** asestar un golpe; Fig. herir (en); Fig. destruir de un golpe. **to d. in,** comerciar en, traficar en; ocuparse en; meterse en. **to d. out,** dispensar. **to d. with,** (buy from) comprar de; tener relaciones con, tratar; entenderse con; portarse con; (of affairs) ocuparse en, arreglar, dirigir; (contend) luchar con; (discuss) discutir, tratar de; (of books) versar sobre. **d. regularly with,** Lat. Am. amarchantarse con. **to make a d.,** hacer un arreglo

dealer /'dilər/ n traficante, mf mercader, m, Lat. Am. marchante (-ta); (at cards) el que da las cartas

dealing /'dilɪŋ/ n conducta, f; proceder, m; trato, m; tráfico, m; pl **dealings,** relaciones, f pl; transacciones, f pl

dean /din/ n Eccl. deán, m; Educ. decano, m

dear /dɪər/ a (beloved) querido, amado; (charming) encantador, simpático; (in letters) estimado, querido; (favorite) predilecto; (expensive) caro. n querido (-da); persona querida, f, bien amado (-da). adv caro. **Oh d.!** ¡Dios mío! ¡Ay!

dearly /'dɪərli/ adv tiernamente, entrañablemente; caro

dearness /'dɪərnɪs/ n cariño, afecto, m, ternura, f; (of price) precio alto, m

dearth /dərθ/ n carestía, f; (of news, etc.) escasez, f

death /dɛθ/ n muerte, f; (Law. and in announcements) fallecimiento, m, defunción, f. **to be at death's door,** estar a la muerte. **to sentence to d.,** ajusticiar. **to the d.,** a muerte. **untimely d.,** muerte repentina, f; malogro, m. **death's head,** calavera, f. **d. certificate,** partida de defunción, f. **d.-duties,** derechos de herencia, m pl. **d.-like,** cadavérico. **d.-mask,** mascarilla, f. **d. penalty,** pena de muerte, f. **d.-rate,** mortalidad, f. **d.-trap,** lugar peligroso, m; Fig. trampa, f. **d.-warrant,** sentencia de muerte, f. **d.-watch beetle,** reloj de la muerte, m

deathbed /'dɛθ͜bɛd/ n lecho mortuorio, lecho de muerte, m. **on one's d.,** en su lecho de muerte

deathblow /'dɛθ͜blou/ n golpe mortal, m

deathly /'dɛθli/ a mortal

death toll n (of a bell) doble, toque de difuntos, m; (casualties) número de muertos, saldo de muertos, m

debacle /də'bakəl/ n Fig. ruina, f

debar /dɪ'bɑr/ vt excluir, privar

debase /dɪ'beis/ vt degradar, humillar, envilecer; (the coinage) alterar (la moneda)

debasement /dɪ'beismənt/ n degradación, humillación, f, envilecimiento, m; (of the coinage) alteración (de la moneda), f

debasing /dɪ'beisɪŋ/ a degradante, humillante

debatable /dɪ'beitəbəl/ a discutible

debate /dɪ'beit/ n debate, m; discusión, f; disputa, f. vt and vi debatir; discutir; disputar; considerar

debater /dɪ'beitər/ n discutidor (-ra); orador (-ra)

debating /dɪ'beitɪŋ/ n discusión, f; argumentación, f

debauch /dɪ'bɔtʃ/ vt corromper, pervertir; (a woman) seducir, violar. n libertinaje, m; borrachera, f

debauched /dɪ'bɔtʃt/ a vicioso, licencioso

debauchee /͜dɛbɔ'tʃi, -'ʃi/ n libertino, vicioso, m

debauchery /dɪ'bɔtʃəri/ n libertinaje, mal vivir, m, viciosidad, licencia, f

debenture /dɪ'bɛntʃər/ n obligación, f. **d. holder,** obligacionista, mf

debilitate /dɪ'bɪlɪ͜teit/ vt debilitar

debilitating /dɪ'bɪlɪ͜teitɪŋ/ a debilitante

debilitation /dɪ͜bɪlɪ'teiʃən/ n debilitación, f

debility /dɪ'bɪlɪti/ n debilidad, f

debit /'dɛbɪt/ n débito, cargo, m; saldo deudor, m; "debe" de una cuenta, m. vt adeudar. **d. and credit,** el cargo y la data. **d. balance,** saldo deudor, m

debonair /͜dɛbə'nɛər/ a gallardo, gentil, donairoso; alegre

debonairly /͜dɛbə'nɛərli/ adv gallardamente; alegremente

debris /də'bri/ n escombros, desechos, m pl; ruinas, f pl; Geol. despojos, m pl

debt /dɛt/ n deuda, f. Lat. Am. also dita f. **a bad d.,** una deuda incobrable. **to be in the d. of,** ser en cargo a; deber dinero a; Fig. sentirse bajo una obligación. **to get into d.,** adeudarse, contraer deudas, Lat. Am. enditarse

debtor /'dɛtər/ n deudor (-ra); Com. debe, m

debunk /dɪ'bʌŋk/ *vt* demoler
debut /dei'byu/ *n* (of a debutante) puesta de largo, *f*; (of a play, etc.) estreno, *m*. **to make one's d.**, ponerse de largo, presentarse en sociedad
debutante /'dɛbyʊˌtɑnt/ *n* debutante, *f*
decade /'dɛkeid/ *n* década, *f*, decenio, *m*; (of the rosary) decena, *f*
decadence /'dɛkədəns/ *n* decadencia, *f*
decadent /'dɛkədənt/ *a* decadente
decaffeinated /di'kæfəˌneitɪd/ *a* descafeinado
decagram /'dɛkəˌgræm/ *n* decagramo, *m*
decaliter /'dɛkəˌlitər/ *n* decalitro, *m*
decalogue /'dɛkəˌlɔg/ *n* decálogo, *m*
decameter /'dɛkəˌmitər/ *n* decámetro, *m*
decamp /dɪ'kæmp/ *vi* Mil. decampar; escaparse, fugarse
decant /dɪ'kænt/ *vt* decantar
decanter /dɪ'kæntər/ *n* garrafa, *f*
decapitate /dɪ'kæpɪˌteit/ *vt* decapitar, descabezar
decapitation /dɪˌkæpɪ'teiʃən/ *n* decapiˈación, *f*
decarbonization /diˌkɑrbənə'zeiʃən/ *n* descarburación, *f*
decarbonize /di'kɑrbəˌnaiz/ *vt* descarbonizar
decay /dɪ'kei/ *vi* (rot) pudrirse; degenerar; marchitarse; (of teeth) cariarse; (crumble) desmoronarse, caer en ruinas; decaer, declinar; (come down in the world) venir a menos, arruinarse. *n* pudrición, putrefacción, *f*; (of teeth) caries, *f*; (withering) marchitez, *f*; degeneración, *f*; desmoronamiento, *m*; ruina, *f*; (oldness) vejez, *f*; decadencia, declinación, *f*; (fall) caída, *f*
decease /dɪ'sis/ *n* fallecimiento, *m*, defunción, *f*, *vi* fallecer
deceased /dɪ'sist/ *n* finado (-da), difunto (-ta). *a* difunto
deceit /dɪ'sit/ *n* engaño, fraude, *m*; duplicidad, *f*
deceitful /dɪ'sitfəl/ *a* engañoso, falso; embustero, mentiroso; ilusorio
deceitfully /dɪ'sitfəli/ *adv* engañosamente
deceitfulness /dɪ'sitfəlnɪs/ *n* falsedad, duplicidad, *f*
deceivable /dɪ'sivəbəl/ *a* fácil a engañar, engañadizo
deceive /dɪ'siv/ *vt* engañar; (disappoint) decepcionar, desilusionar; frustrar. **If my memory does not d. me,** Si la memoria no me engaña, Si mal no me acuerdo
deceiver /dɪ'sivər/ *n* engañador (-ra); seductor, *m*
deceiving /dɪ'siviŋ/ *a* engañador
December /dɪ'sɛmbər/ *n* diciembre, *m*
decency /'disənsi/ *n* decoro, *m*, decencia, *f*; pudor, *m*, modestia, *f*; conveniencias, *f pl*; Inf. bondad, *f*; (manners) cortesía, *f*, buenos modales, *m pl*
decennial /dɪ'sɛniəl/ *a* decenal
decent /'disənt/ *a* decente; decoroso, honesto; púdico; (likable) simpático; (of things) bastante bueno; (honorable) honrado
decently /'disəntli/ *adv* decentemente
decentralization /diˌsɛntrələ'zeiʃən/ *n* descentralización, *f*
decentralize /di'sɛntrəˌlaiz/ *vt* descentralizar
deception /dɪ'sɛpʃən/ *n* engaño, *m*; ilusión, *f*
deceptive /dɪ'sɛptɪv/ *a* engañoso, mentiroso, ilusorio
deceptively /dɪ'sɛptɪvli/ *adv* engañosamente
decide /dɪ'said/ *vt* decidir; Law. determinar. *vi* decidir, resolver; acordar, quedar en; juzgar; Law. dictar sentencia, fallar
decided /dɪ'saidɪd/ *a* decidido; (downright) categórico, inequívoco; resuelto; positivo; definitivo
decidedly /dɪ'saidɪdli/ *adv* decididamente; categóricamente; definitivamente
deciduous /dɪ'sɪdʒuəs/ *a* Bot. caedizo
decigram /'dɛsɪˌgræm/ *n* decigramo, *m*
decimal /'dɛsəməl/ *a* decimal. **d. fraction,** fracción decimal, *f*. **d. point,** punto decimal, *m*. **d. system,** sistema métrico, *m*
decimate /'dɛsəˌmeit/ *vt* diezmar, asolar
decimation /ˌdɛsə'meiʃən/ *n* gran mortandad, *f*; matanza, *f*
decimeter /'dɛsəˌmitər/ *n* decímetro, *m*
decipher /dɪ'saifər/ *vt* descifrar; deletrear
decipherable /dɪ'saifərəbəl/ *a* descifrable

decipherer /dɪ'saifərər/ *n* descifrador, *m*
decipherment /dɪ'saifərmənt/ *n* el descifrar; deletreo, *m*
decision /dɪ'sɪʒən/ *n* decisión, determinación, *f*; Law. sentencia, *f*, fallo, *m*; (agreement) acuerdo, *m*; (of character) firmeza, resolución, *f*
decisive /dɪ'saisɪv/ *a* decisivo; terminante, conclusivo; crítico
decisively /dɪ'saisɪvli/ *adv* decisivamente
decisiveness /dɪ'saisɪvnɪs/ *n* carácter decisivo, *m*; firmeza, resolución, *f*; decisión, *f*
deck /dɛk/ *n* cubierta, *f*; (of cards) baraja (de naipes), *f*. *vt* adornar, ataviar; decorar. **between decks,** entrecubiertas, *f pl*. **lower d.,** cubierta, *f*. **promenade d.,** cubierta de paseo, *f*. **upper d.,** cubierta superior, *f*. **d.-cabin,** camarote de cubierta, *m*. **d.-chair,** silla de cubierta, silla de tijera, silla extensible, *f*. **d.-hand,** marinero, estibador, *m*
decked /dɛkt/ *a* ornado, ataviado; engalanado; Naut. de... puentes
declaim /dɪ'kleim/ *vt* recitar. *vi* perorar, declamar
declamation /ˌdɛklə'meiʃən/ *n* declamación, *f*
declamatory /dɪ'klæməˌtɔri/ *a* declamatorio
declaration /ˌdɛklə'reiʃən/ *n* declaración, *f*; manifiesto, *m*; proclamación, *f*
declarative /dɪ'klærətɪv/ *a* declaratorio, declarativo
declare /dɪ'klɛər/ *vt* declarar; proclamar; afirmar; manifestar; confesar. *vi* declarar; Law. deponer, testificar. **to d. war (on)** declarar la guerra (a)
declaredly /dɪ'klɛərɪdli/ *adv* declaradamente, explícitamente, abiertamente
declension /dɪ'klɛnʃən/ *n* declinación, *f*
declination /ˌdɛklə'neiʃən/ *n* declinación, *f*
decline /dɪ'klain/ *n* declinación, decadencia, *f*; disminución, *f*; debilitación, *f*; (of the day) caída, *f*; (of stocks, shares) depresión, *f*; (illness) consunción, *f*; (Fig. setting) ocaso, *m*, *vi* declinar; inclinarse; decaer; disminuir; debilitarse; (refuse) negarse (a). *vt* (refuse) rechazar, rehusar; Gram. declinar; (avoid) evitar
declining /dɪ'klainɪŋ/ *a* declinante. **in one's d. years,** en sus últimos años
declivity /dɪ'klɪvɪti/ *n* cuesta, pendiente, *f*, declive, *m*
declutch /dɪ'klʌtʃ/ *vi* desembragar
decoction /dɪ'kɒkʃən/ *n* decocción, *f*
decode /di'koud/ *vt* descifrar
decoder /di'koudər/ *n* descifrador, *m*
décolletee /ˌdeikɒlə'tei/ *a* escotado
decoloration /diˌkʌlə'reiʃən/ *n* decoloración, *f*
decompose /ˌdikəm'pouz/ *vt* descomponer. *vi* descomponerse
decomposition /diˌkɒmpə'zɪʃən/ *n* descomposición, *f*
decompressor /ˌdikəm'prɛsər/ *n* decompresor, *m*
decontaminate /ˌdikən'tæməˌneit/ *vt* descontaminar
decontamination /ˌdikɒnˌtæmə'neiʃən/ *n* descontaminación, *f*
decontrol /ˌdikən'troul/ *vt* suprimir las restricciones sobre
decorate /'dɛkəˌreit/ *vt* adornar (con), embellecer; (by painting, etc.) decorar, pintar; (honor) investir (con), condecorar
decoration /ˌdɛkə'reiʃən/ *n* decoración, *f*; Theat. decorado, *m*; (honor) condecoración, *f*; ornamento, *m*
decorative /'dɛkərətɪv/ *a* decorativo
decorator /'dɛkəˌreitər/ *n* decorador, *m*; (interior) adornista, *m*
decorous /'dɛkərəs/ *a* decoroso, decente; correcto
decorum /dɪ'kɔrəm/ *n* decoro, decencia, *f*; corrección, *f*
decoy /n 'dikɔi; *v* dɪ'kɔi/ *n* señuelo, *m*; añagaza, *f*; (trap) lazo, *m*, trampa, *f*; Fig. añagaza, *f*. *vt* (birds) reclamar, atraer con señuelo; Fig. tentar (con), seducir (con). **d. bird,** pájaro de reclamo, *m*
decrease /n 'dikris; *v* dɪ'kris/ *n* disminución, *f*; baja, *f*; reducción, *f*; (of the moon, waters) mengua, *f*. *vi* decrecer, disminuir; bajar; menguar. *vt* disminuir; reducir
decreasingly /dɪ'krisɪŋli/ *adv* de menos en menos
decree /dɪ'kri/ *n* decreto, *m*; edicto, *m*, *vt* decretar, mandar
decrepit /dɪ'krɛpɪt/ *a* decrépito

decry /dɪ'kraɪ/ vt desacreditar, rebajar
dedicate /'dɛdɪˌkeɪt/ vt dedicar; consagrar; destinar; aplicar; (a book, etc.) dedicar. **to d. oneself to,** dedicarse a, consagrarse a, entregarse a
dedication /ˌdɛdɪ'keɪʃən/ n dedicación, f; consagración, f; (of a book, etc.) dedicatoria, f
dedicatory /'dɛdɪkəˌtɔri/ a dedicatorio
deduce /dɪ'dus/ vt derivar; deducir, inferir
deduct /dɪ'dʌkt/ vt deducir; descontar
deduction /dɪ'dʌkʃən/ n deducción, f; descuento, m
deductive /dɪ'dʌktɪv/ a deductivo
deed /did/ n acción, f; hecho, acto, m; hazaña, f; (reality) realidad, f; Law. escritura, f; Law. contrato, m. **d. of gift,** escritura de donación, f
deem /dim/ vt juzgar, creer, estimar
deep /dip/ a profundo; (low) bajo; (of colors) subido; (of sounds) grave, profundo; (immersed (in)) absorto (en); (of the mind) penetrante; (secret) secreto; (intense) intenso, hondo; (cunning) astuto, artero; (dark) oscuro; (of mourning) riguroso. n Poet. piélago, mar, m; profundidad, f; abismo, m, adv profundamente; a una gran profundidad. **to be in d. waters,** Fig. estar con el agua al cuello. **to be three feet d.,** tener tres pies de profundidad. **to be d. in,** estar absorto en; (of debt) estar cargado de. **three d.,** tres de fondo. **d. into the night,** hasta las altas horas de la noche. **d.-felt,** hondamente sentido. **d. mourning,** luto riguroso, m. **d.-rooted,** arraigado. **d.-sea fishing,** pesca mayor, f. **d.-sea lead,** escandallo, m. **d.-seated,** íntimo, profundo; arraigado. **d.-set,** hundido
deepen /'dipən/ vt profundizar, ahondar; (broaden) ensanchar; (intensify) intensificar; (increase) aumentar; (of colors) aumentar el tono de, intensificar. vi hacerse más profundo, hacerse más hondo; intensificarse; aumentarse; (of sound) hacerse más grave
deeply /'dipli/ adv profundamente; intensamente; fuertemente
deepness /'dipnɪs/ n (cunning) astucia, f; see **depth**
deer /dɪər/ n ciervo (-va), venado, m, a cervuno. **d.-hound,** galgo de cazar venados, m. **d.-hunting,** caza del ciervo, f. **d.-skin,** piel de venado, f
deface /dɪ'feɪs/ vt desfigurar, mutilar; estropear; (erase) borrar
defacement /dɪ'feɪsmənt/ n desfiguración, mutilación, f; afeamiento, m; borradura, f
defamation /ˌdɛfə'meɪʃən/ n difamación, denigración, f
defamatory /dɪ'fæməˌtɔri/ a difamatorio, denigrante
defame /dɪ'feɪm/ vt difamar, denigrar, calumniar
default /dɪ'fɔlt/ n omisión, f, descuido, m; falta, f; ausencia, f; Law. rebeldía, f. vi dejar de cumplir; faltar; no pagar. vt Law. condenar en rebeldía. **in d. of,** en la ausencia de
defaulter /dɪ'fɔltər/ n el, m, (f, la) que no cumple sus obligaciones; delincuente, mf; desfalcador (-ra); Law. rebelde, mf
defeat /dɪ'fit/ vt vencer, derrotar; frustrar; (reject) rechazar; (elude) evitar; Fig. vencer, triunfar sobre. n derrota, f; vencimiento, m; frustración, f; rechazamiento, m. **to d. one's own ends,** defraudar sus intenciones
defeatism /dɪ'fitɪzəm/ n derrotismo, m
defeatist /dɪ'fitɪst/ n derrotista, mf
defecate /'dɛfɪˌkeɪt/ vt defecar
defecation /ˌdɛfɪ'keɪʃən/ n defecación, f
defect /'difɛkt/ n defecto, m; imperfección, f; falta, f
defection /dɪ'fɛkʃən/ n defección, f; deserción, f; (from a religion) apostasía, f
defective /dɪ'fɛktɪv/ a defectuoso; Gram. defectivo; falto; imperfecto; (mentally) anormal. n persona anormal, f, anormal, m
defectiveness /dɪ'fɛktɪvnɪs/ n imperfección, f; deficiencia, f; defecto, m
defend /dɪ'fɛnd/ vt defender; proteger; preservar; sostener; (a thesis) sustentar
defendant /dɪ'fɛndənt/ n Law. acusado (-da), procesado (-da), demandado (-da)
defender /dɪ'fɛndər/ n defensor (-ra); (of a thesis) sustentante, mf
defense /dɪ'fɛns/ n defensa, f; justificación, f; pl **defenses,** defensas, f pl; obras de fortificación, f pl. **for**

the d., (of witnesses) de descargo; (of counsel) para la defensa. **in d. of,** en defensa de. **in one's own d.,** en su propia defensa. **d. in depth,** Mil. defensa en fondo, f
defenseless /dɪ'fɛnslɪs/ a indefenso, sin defensa
defenselessness /dɪ'fɛnslɪsnɪs/ n incapacidad de defenderse, f; debilidad, f, desvalimiento, m
defensible /dɪ'fɛnsəbəl/ a defendible; justificable
defensive /dɪ'fɛnsɪv/ a defensivo. n defensiva, f. **to be on the d.,** estar a la defensiva
defensively /dɪ'fɛnsɪvli/ adv defensivamente
defer /dɪ'fɜr/ vt (postpone) diferir, aplazar; suspender. vi (yield) deferir, ceder; (delay) tardar, aguardar. **deferred payment,** pago a plazos, m
deference /'dɛfərəns/ n deferencia, f, respeto, m; consideración, f
deferential /ˌdɛfə'rɛnʃəl/ a deferente, respetuoso
deferment /dɪ'fɜrmənt/ n aplazamiento, m; suspensión, f
defiance /dɪ'faɪəns/ n desafío, m; provocación, f; oposición, f; insolencia, f. **in d. of,** en contra de
defiant /dɪ'faɪənt/ a provocativo; insolente
defiantly /dɪ'faɪəntli/ adv de un aire provocativo; insolentemente
deficiency /dɪ'fɪʃənsi/ n falta, deficiencia, f; imperfección, f; defecto, m; omisión, f; (scarcity) carestía, f; (in accounts) déficit, m
deficient /dɪ'fɪʃənt/ a deficiente; falto, incompleto; imperfecto; pobre; defectuoso; (not clever at) débil (en); (mentally) anormal. **to be d. in,** carecer de; ser pobre en
deficit /'dɛfəsɪt/ n déficit, m; descubierto, m
defile /dɪ'faɪl/ n desfiladero, m. vt contaminar; profanar; manchar; deshonrar. vi Mil. desfilar
defilement /dɪ'faɪlmənt/ n contaminación, f; corrupción, f; profanación, f
definable /dɪ'faɪnəbəl/ a definible
define /dɪ'faɪn/ vt definir; (throw into relief) destacar; fijar; Law. determinar
definite /'dɛfənɪt/ a definido; positivo; categórico; exacto; concreto. **d. article,** artículo definido, m
definitely /'dɛfənɪtli/ adv positivamente; claramente. **definitely not!** ¡definitivamente no!
definiteness /'dɛfənɪtnɪs/ n carácter definido, m; exactitud, f; lo categórico
definition /ˌdɛfə'nɪʃən/ n definición, f
definitive /dɪ'fɪnɪtɪv/ a definitivo
deflate /dɪ'fleɪt/ vt desinflar. vi desinflarse, deshincharse
deflation /dɪ'fleɪʃən/ n desinflación, f
deflect /dɪ'flɛkt/ vt desviar; apartar. vi desviarse, apartarse
deflection /dɪ'flɛkʃən/ n desviación, f; apartamiento, m
defloration /ˌdɛflə'reɪʃən/ n desfloración, f
deflower /dɪ'flaʊər/ vt desflorar
deforestation /dɪˌfɔrɪ'steɪʃən/ n desforestación, desmontadura, despoblación forestal, f
deform /dɪ'fɔrm/ vt deformar, desfigurar; afear
deformation /ˌdifɔr'meɪʃən/ n deformación, f
deformed /dɪ'fɔrmd/ a deformado; contrahecho
deformity /dɪ'fɔrmɪti/ n deformidad, f
defraud /dɪ'frɔd/ vt defraudar
defrauder /dɪ'frɔdər/ n defraudador (-ra)
defrauding /dɪ'frɔdɪŋ/ n defraudación, f
defray /dɪ'freɪ/ vt sufragar, costear, pagar
defrayal /dɪ'freɪəl/ n pago, m
defrost /dɪ'frɔst/ vt deshelar
deft /dɛft/ a diestro; hábil
deftly /'dɛftli/ adv con destreza; hábilmente
deftness /'dɛftnɪs/ n destreza, f; habilidad, f
defunct /dɪ'fʌŋkt/ a and n difunto (-ta)
defy /dɪ'faɪ/ vt desafiar; (face) arrostrar; (violate) contravenir
degeneracy /dɪ'dʒɛnərəsi/ n degeneración, f; depravación, degradación, f
degenerate /a, n dɪ'dʒɛnərɪt; v -ˌreɪt/ a and n degenerado (-da). vi degenerar
degeneration /dɪˌdʒɛnə'reɪʃən/ n degeneración, f

degradation /ˌdɛgrɪ'deiʃən/ n degradación, f; abyección, f

degrade /dɪ'greid/ vt degradar; envilecer, deshonrar

degrading /dɪ'greidɪŋ/ a degradante

degree /dɪ'gri/ n grado, m; (academic) título; punto, m; clase social, f. **by degrees**, poco a poco, gradualmente, **five degrees below zero**, cinco grados bajo cero. **in the highest d.**, en sumo grado, en grado superlativo. **to a certain d.**, hasta cierto punto. **to receive a d.**, graduarse

degree-granting institution /dɪ'gri ˌgræntɪŋ/ n plantel habilitado para expedir títulos, m

dehydrate /di'haidreit/ vt deshidratar

dehydration /ˌdihai'dreiʃən/ n deshidratación, f

de-ice /di'ais/ vt deshelar

deification /ˌdiəfɪ'keiʃən/ n deificación, f

deify /'diə,fai/ vt deificar, endiosar

deign /dein/ vi dignarse. vt conceder

deism /'diizəm/ n deísmo, m

deist /'diist/ n deísta, mf

deity /'diiti/ n deidad, divinidad, f; dios, m

dejected /dɪ'dʒɛktɪd/ a abatido, desanimado, deprimido

dejectedly /dɪ'dʒɛktɪdli/ adv tristemente, abatidamente

dejection /dɪ'dʒɛkʃən/ n abatimiento, desaliento, m; melancolía, f

delay /dɪ'lei/ n retraso, m, dilación, tardanza, demora, f. vt retrasar, demorar; (a person) entretener; (postpone) aplazar; (obstruct) impedir. vi tardar; entretenerse. **without more d.**, sin más tardar

delectable /dɪ'lɛktəbəl/ a deleitoso, delicioso

delectably /dɪ'lɛktəbli/ adv deliciosamente

delectation /ˌdilɛk'teiʃən/ n delectación, f, deleite, m

delegacy /'dɛlɪgəsi/ n delegación, f

delegate /n 'dɛlɪgɪt; v -ˌgeit/ n delegado (-da). vt delegar, diputar

delegation /ˌdɛlɪ'geiʃən/ n delegación, f

delete /dɪ'lit/ vt suprimir, borrar

deleterious /ˌdɛlɪ'tiəriəs/ a deletéreo

deletion /dɪ'liʃən/ n supresión, borradura, f

deliberate /a dɪ'lɪbərɪt; v -ə,reit/ a premeditado, intencionado; (slow) pausado, lento. vi and vt deliberar, discurrir, considerar

deliberately /dɪ'lɪbərɪtli/ adv (intentionally) con premeditación, a sabiendas, Central America adifés; (slowly) pausadamente, lentamente

deliberation /dɪ,lɪbə'reiʃən/ n reflexión, deliberación, consideración, f; (slowness) lentitud, pausa, f

deliberative /dɪ'lɪbərətɪv/ a deliberativo, de liberante

delicacy /'dɛlɪkəsi/ n delicadeza, f; fragilidad, f; suavidad, f; sensibilidad, f; escrupulosidad, f; (of health) debilidad, delicadez, f; (difficulty) dificultad, f; (food) manjar exquisito, m, golosina, f

delicate /'dɛlɪkɪt/ a delicado; fino; frágil; suave; exquisito; delicado (de salud); (of situations) difícil

delicatessen /ˌdɛlɪkə'tɛsən/ n (store) fiambrería, f

delicious /dɪ'lɪʃəs/ a delicioso

deliciously /dɪ'lɪʃəsli/ adv deliciosamente

deliciousness /dɪ'lɪʃəsnɪs/ n deleite, m, lo delicioso; excelencia, f; delicias, f pl

delict /dɪ'lɪkt/ n delito, m

delictive /dɪ'lɪktɪv/ a delictivo

delight /dɪ'lait/ n deleite, regocijo, m; encanto, m, delicia, f; placer, gozo, m. vt deleitar, encantar; halagar. vi deleitarse, complacerse. **to be delighted with**, estar encantado con. **to d. in**, deleitarse en, complacerse en; tomar placer en

delightful /dɪ'laitfəl/ a delicioso, precioso, encantador

delightfully /dɪ'laitfəli/ adv deliciosamente

delimit /dɪ'lɪmɪt/ vt delimitar

delimitation /dɪ,lɪmɪ'teiʃən/ n delimitación, f

delineate /dɪ'lɪni,eit/ vt delinear, diseñar; Fig. pintar, describir

delineation /dɪ,lɪni'eiʃən/ n delineación, f; retrato, m; Fig. descripción, f

delineator /dɪ'lɪnieitər/ n diseñador, m

delinquency /dɪ'lɪŋkwənsi/ n delincuencia, f; criminalidad, f; culpa, f; delito, m

delinquent /dɪ'lɪŋkwənt/ a delincuente. n delincuente, mf

deliquescence /ˌdɛlɪ'kwɛsəns/ n delicuescencia, f

deliquescent /ˌdɛlɪ'kwɛsənt/ a delicuescente

delirious /dɪ'lɪriəs/ a delirante; desvariado; Inf. loco. **to be d.**, delirar, desvariar

delirium /dɪ'lɪriəm/ n delirio, desvarío, m. **d. tremens**, delírium tremens, m

deliver /dɪ'lɪvər/ vt librar (de); salvar (de); (distribute) repartir; (hand over) entregar; (recite) recitar, decir; (a speech) pronunciar; comunicar; (send) despachar, expedir; (a blow) asestar; (give) dar; (bring) traer; (battle, a lecture) dar; (a woman, of a doctor) asistir en el parto (a); (a child) traer al mundo; (a judgment) pronunciar. **to be delivered (of a child)**, dar a luz. **to d. oneself up**, entregarse. **delivered free**, porte pagado.

deliverance /dɪ'lɪvərəns/ n libramiento, rescate, m; redención, salvación, f; (of a judgment) pronuncia, f

deliverer /dɪ'lɪvərər/ n libertador (-ra); salvador (-ra); (distributor) repartidor (-ra); entregador (-ra)

delivery /dɪ'lɪvəri/ n (distribution) reparto, m, distribución, f; entrega, f; Law. cesión, f; (of a judgment) pronuncia, f; (of a speech) pronunciación, f; (manner of speaking) declamación, f; dicción, f; (of a child) parto, m. **on d.**, al entregarse. **The letter came by the first d.**, La carta llegó en el primer reparto. **d. man**, mozo de reparto, m. **d. note**, nota de entrega, f. **d. van**, camión de reparto, m

delivery truck n camioneta de reparto, furgoneta, f, sedán de reparto, m

dell /dɛl/ n hondonada, f; pequeño valle, m

delouse /di'laus/ vt despiojar, espulgar

Delphi /'dɛlfai/ Delfos, m

delta /'dɛltə/ n (Greek letter) delta, f; (of a river) delta, m

delude /dɪ'lud/ vt engañar; ilusionar. **to d. oneself**, engañarse

deluded /dɪ'ludɪd/ a iluso, engañado, ciego

deluge /'dɛlyudʒ/ n diluvio, m. vt diluviar; inundar (con)

delusion /dɪ'luʒən/ n engaño, m, ceguedad, f; error, m; ilusión, f

delve /dɛlv/ vt and vi cavar; Fig. ahondar (en), penetrar (en), investigar

demagogic /ˌdɛmə'gɒdʒɪk/ a demagógico

demagogue /'dɛmə,gɒg/ n demagogo (-ga)

demagogy /'dɛmə,goudʒi/ n demagogia, f

demand /dɪ'mænd/ n exigencia, f; Com. demanda, f; petición, f; Polit. Econ. consumo, m. vt exigir; requerir; pedir; (claim) reclamar. **in d.**, en demanda. **on d.**, al solicitarse. **to be in d.**, ser popular. **d. note**, apremio, m

demanding /dɪ'mændɪŋ/ a exigente

demarcate /dɪ'mɑrkeit/ vt demarcar

demarcation /ˌdimɑr'keiʃən/ n demarcación, f

demean (oneself) /dɪ'min/ vr degradarse, rebajarse

demeanor /dɪ'minər/ n conducta, f; continente, porte, aire, m; (manners) modales, m pl

demented /dɪ'mɛntɪd/ a demente, loco

demerit /dɪ'mɛrɪt/ n demérito, f

demi- prefix semi; casi. **d.-tasse**, taza cafetera, jícara, f

demigod /'dɛmi,gɒd/ n semidios, m

demigoddess /'dɛmi,gɒdɪs/ n semidiosa, f

demijohn /'dɛmi,dʒɒn/ n damajuana, f

demilitarize /di'mɪlitə,raiz/ vt desmilitarizar

demise /dɪ'maiz/ n Law. traslación de dominio, f; sucesión de la corona, f; (death) óbito, fallecimiento, m

demisemiquaver /ˌdɛmi'sɛmi,kweivər/ n fusa, f

demobilization /di,moubələ'zeiʃən/ n desmovilización, f

demobilize /di'moubə,laiz/ vt desmovilizar

democracy /dɪ'mɒkrəsi/ n democracia, f

democrat /'dɛmə,kræt/ n demócrata, mf

democratic /ˌdɛmə'krætɪk/ a democrático. **to make d.**, democratizar

Democratic Party n Partido Democrático, m

demolish /dɪ'mɒlɪʃ/ vt demoler, derribar; Fig. destruir; (eat) engullir, devorar

demolisher /dɪ'mɒlɪʃər/ n demoledor, m; Fig. destructor (-ra)

demolition /,dɛmə'lɪʃən/ n demolición, f; derribo, m, a demoledor; de demolición. **d. squad,** pelotón de demolición, m

demon /'dimən/ n demonio, diablo, m

demonetization /di,mɒnɪtə'zeiʃən/ n desmonetización, f

demonetize /di'mɒnɪ,taiz/ vt desmonetizar

demoniacal /,dimə'naiɪkəl/ a demoníaco

demonology /,dimə'nɒlədʒi/ n demonología, f

demonstrable /dɪ'mɒnstrəbəl, 'dɛmən-/ a demonstrable

demonstrably /dɪ'mɒnstrəbli/ adv demostrablemente

demonstrate /'dɛmən,streit/ vt demostrar; mostrar, probar. vi hacer una demostración

demonstration /,dɛmən'streiʃən/ n demostración, f; manifestación, f

demonstrative /də'mɒnstrətɪv/ a demostrativo; (of persons) expresivo, mimoso. **d. pronoun,** pronombre demostrativo, m

demonstrator /'dɛmən,streitər/ n demostrador (-ra)

demoralization /dɪ,mɔrələ'zeiʃən/ n desmoralización, f

demoralize /dɪ'mɔrə,laiz, -'mɒr-/ vt desmoralizar

demoralizing /dɪ'mɔrə,laizɪŋ/ a desmoralizador

demur /dɪ'mɜr/ vi dudar, vacilar; objetar, protestar; poner dificultades. n objeción, protesta, f

demure /dɪ'myʊr/ a serio, modoso recatado; púdico; de una coquetería disimulada

demurely /dɪ'myʊrli/ adv modestamente; con recato; con coquetería disimulada

demureness /dɪ'myʊrnɪs/ n seriedad, f, recato, m; modestia fingida, coquetería disimulada, f

den /dɛn/ n madriguera, guardia, f; (of thieves) cueva, f; (in a zoo) cercado, recinto, m; (study) gabinete, m; (squalid room) cuartucho, m

denaturalization /di,nætʃərələ'zeiʃən/ n desnaturalización, f

denaturalize /di'nætʃərə,laiz/ vt desnaturalizar

denial /dɪ'naiəl/ n negación, f; rechazo, m; contradicción, f; negativa, f

denizen /'dɛnəzən/ n habitante, m; ciudadano (-na)

Denmark /'dɛnmɑrk/ Dinamarca, f

denominate /dɪ'nɒmə,neit/ vt denominar, nombrar

denomination /dɪ,nɒmə'neiʃən/ n denominación, f; secta, f; clase, f

denominational /dɪ,nɒmə'neiʃənl/ a sectario

denominator /dɪ'nɒmə,neitər/ n Math. denominador, m

denote /dɪ'nout/ vt denotar, indicar; significar

dénouement /,deinu'mɑ̃/ n desenlace, desenredo, m; solución, f

denounce /dɪ'nauns/ vt denunciar; delatar, acusar

denouncer /dɪ'naunsər/ n denunciante, mf delator (-ra)

dense /dɛns/ a denso; espeso, compacto; tupido; impenetrable; Inf. estúpido

densely /'dɛnsli/ adv densamente; espesamente. **d. populated,** con gran densidad de población

density /'dɛnsɪti/ n densidad, f; espesor, m; consistencia, f; Inf. estupidez, f

dent /dɛnt/ n mella, f; (in metal) abolladura, f, vt mellar; abollar

dental /'dɛntl/ a dental. n letra dental, f. **d. forceps,** gatillo, m. **d. mechanic,** mecánico dentista, m. **d. surgeon,** odontólogo, m

dental floss n seda dental, f

dentifrice /'dɛntəfrɪs/ n dentífrico, m

dentist /'dɛntɪst/ n dentista, mf; odontólogo, m

dentistry /'dɛntəstri/ n odontología, f

dentition /dɛn'tɪʃən/ n dentición, f

denture /'dɛntʃər/ n dentadura, f

denudation /,dinu'deiʃən/ n denudación, f

denude /dɪ'nud/ vt desnudar, despojar, privar (de)

denunciation /dɪ,nʌnsi'eiʃən/ n denuncia, f; acusación, delación, f

denunciatory /dɪ'nʌnsiə,tɔri/ a denunciatorio

Denver boot /'dɛnvər/ n cepo, m

deny /dɪ'nai/ vt negar; desmentir; rehusar; rechazar;

renegar (de); (give up) renunciar, sacrificar. **to d. oneself,** privarse (de); sacrificar; negarse

deodorant /di'oudərənt/ a and n desodorante m

deodorize /di'oudə,raiz/ vt desinfectar, destruir el olor de

depart /dɪ'pɑrt/ vi marcharse, irse, partir; (of trains, etc., and meaning go out) salir; (deviate) desviarse (de), apartarse (de); (go away) alejarse; (leave) dejar; (disappear) desaparecer; (alter) cambiar; (die) morir

departed /dɪ'pɑrtɪd/ a (past) pasado; desaparecido; (dead) difunto, muerto. n difunto (-ta)

department /dɪ'pɑrtmənt/ n departamento, m; sección, f; (of learning) ramo, m. **d. store,** grandes tiendas, f pl, (Argentina), grandes almacenes, m pl

departmental /dɪ,pɑrt'mɛntl/ a departamental

departure /dɪ'pɑrtʃər/ n partida, ida, f, Lat. Am. egreso, m; (going out, and of trains, etc.) salida, f; (deviation) desviación, el apartarse. **d. from the rules,** el apartarse de las reglas), f; (disappearance) desaparición, f; (change) cambio, m; (giving up) renuncia, f; (death) muerte, f. **to take one's d.,** marcharse

depend /dɪ'pɛnd/ vi depender. **to d. on,** depender de; (rest on) apoyarse en; (count on) contar con; (trust) fiarse de; tener confianza en, estar seguro de. **That depends!** ¡Eso depende!

dependable /dɪ'pɛndəbəl/ a digno de confianza; seguro

dependence, dependency /dɪ'pɛndəns; dɪ'pɛndənsi/ n dependencia, f; subordinación, f; (trust) confianza, f

dependent /dɪ'pɛndənt/ a dependiente; subordinado; condicional. n dependiente, m. **to be d. on,** depender de

depict /dɪ'pɪkt/ vt representar; pintar; dibujar; Fig. describir, retratar

depiction /dɪ'pɪkʃən/ n representación, f; pintura, f; dibujo, m; Fig. descripción, f

depilate /'dɛpə,leit/ vt depilar

depilatory /dɪ'pɪlə,tɔri, -,touri/ a and n depilatorio m

deplete /dɪ'plit/ vt agotar; disipar

depletion /dɪ'pliʃən/ n agotamiento, m

deplorable /dɪ'plɔrəbəl/ a lamentable, deplorable

deplorably /dɪ'plɔrəbli/ adv lamentablemente

deplore /dɪ'plɔr/ vt deplorar, lamentar

deploy /dɪ'plɔi/ vt desplegar. vi desplegarse. n despliegue, m

deployment /dɪ'plɔimənt/ n despliegue, m

deponent /dɪ'pounənt/ n Law. declarante, deponente, mf a deponente. **d. verb,** verbo deponente, m

depopulate /di'pɒpyə,leit/ vt despoblar

depopulation /di,pɒpyə'leiʃən/ n despoblación, f

deport /dɪ'pɔrt/ vt deportar

deportation /,dipɔr'teiʃən/ n deportación, f

deportment /dɪ'pɔrtmənt/ n comportamiento, m; porte, aire, m; conducta, f

depose /dɪ'pouz/ vt destronar; (give evidence) testificar, declarar

deposit /dɪ'pɒzɪt/ n depósito, m; Geol. yacimiento, filón, m; sedimento, m. vt depositar. **to leave a d.,** dejar un depósito. **d. account,** cuenta corriente, f

deposition /,depə'zɪʃən/ n deposición, f; Law. testimonio, m; declaración, Lat. Am. contancia f; (from the Cross) descendimiento, m, (de la Cruz)

depositor /dɪ'pɒzɪtər/ n depositador (-ra)

depository /dɪ'pɒzɪ,tɔri/ n depositaría, f, almacén, m; (of knowledge, etc.) pozo, m

depot /'dipou/ n almacén, m; (military headquarters) depósito, m; (for army vehicles, etc.) parque, m; (for buses, etc.) estación, f

depravation /,deprə'veiʃən/ n depravación, f

depraved /dɪ'preivd/ a pervertido, perverso, vicioso

depravity /dɪ'prævɪti/ n corrupción, maldad, perversión, f

deprecate /'dɛprɪ,keit/ vt desaprobar, criticar; lamentar, deplorar

deprecatingly /'dɛprɪ,keitɪŋli/ adv con desaprobación, críticamente

deprecation /,dɛprɪ'keiʃən/ n deprecación, f; desaprobación, crítica, f

deprecatory /'dɛprɪkə,tɔri/ a deprecativo; de desaprobación, de crítica
depreciate /dɪ'priʃi,eit/ vt depreciar, rebajar; Fig. tener en poco, menospreciar. vi depreciarse, deteriorarse; bajar de precio
depreciatingly /dɪ'priʃi,eitɪŋli/ adv con desprecio
depreciation /dɪ,priʃi'eiʃən/ n (in value) amortización, depreciación, f; Fig. desprecio, m
depreciatory /dɪ'priʃiə,tɔri/ a Fig. despectivo, despreciativo
depredation /,dɛprə'deiʃən/ n depredación, f
depress /dɪ'prɛs/ vt deprimir; (weaken) debilitar; (humble) humillar; (dispirit) abatir, entristecer; (trade) desanimar, paralizar
depressed /dɪ'prɛst/ a deprimido, desalentado, melancólico, triste; (of an area) necesitado
depressing /dɪ'prɛsɪŋ/ a melancólico, triste; pesimista
depressingly /dɪ'prɛsɪŋli/ adv con tristeza; con pesimismo
depression /dɪ'prɛʃən/ n depresión, f; (hollow) hoyo, m; (sadness) desaliento, abatimiento, m, melancolía, f; (in prices) baja, f; (in trade) desanimación, parálisis, f; Astron. depresión, f
deprivation /,dɛprə'veiʃən/ n privación, f; pérdida, f
deprive /dɪ'praiv/ vt privar (de), despojar (de); defraudar (de); Eccl. destituir (de)
depth /dɛpθ/ n profundidad, f; (thickness) espesor, m; fondo, m; (of night, winter, the country) medio, m; (of sound) gravedad, f; (of colour, feeling) intensidad, f; (abstruseness) dificultad, f; (sagacity) sagacidad, f; pl **depths**, profundidades, f pl; abismo, m; lo más hondo; lo más íntimo. **to be 4 feet in d.**, tener cuatro pies de profundidad. **to the depths of one's being,** hasta lo más íntimo de su ser; hasta los tuétanos. **d. charge,** carga de profundidad, f
deputation /,dɛpyə'teiʃən/ n deputación, delegación, f
deputize (for) /'dɛpyə,taiz/ vi desempeñar las funciones de, substituir
deputy /'dɛpyəti/ n (substitute) lugarteniente, m; (agent) representante, m; apoderado, m; (parliamentary) diputado, m; (in compounds) sub, vice. **d.-governor,** subgobernador, m. **d.-head,** subjefe, m; (of a school) subdirector (-ra)
derail /dɪ'reil/ vt (hacer) descarrilar, Lat. Am. desrielar
derailment /dɪ'reilmənt/ n descarrilamiento, m
derange /dɪ'reindʒ/ vt desordenar; desorganizar; turbar; (mentally) trastornar, hacer perder el juicio (a)
derangement /dɪ'reindʒmənt/ n desorden, m; turbación, f; (mental) trastorno, m, locura, f
derby /'dɜrbi/ n carrera del Derby, f; (hat) sombrero hongo, m
deregulate /di'rɛgyə,leit/ vt desregular
deregulation /di,rɛgyə'leiʃən/ n desregulación, f
derelict /'dɛrəlɪkt/ a abandonado, derrelicto. n derrelicto, m
dereliction /,dɛrə'lɪkʃən/ n abandono, m; omisión, negligencia, f; descuido, m
deride /dɪ'raid/ vt burlarse de, mofarse de; ridiculizar
derision /dɪ'rɪʒən/ n escarnio, f, menosprecio, m
derisive /dɪ'raisɪv/ a irrisorio; irónico
derisively /dɪ'raisɪvli/ adv irrisoriamente; con ironía, irónicamente
derivation /,dɛrə'veiʃən/ n derivación, f
derivative /dɪ'rɪvətɪv/ a derivativo. n derivado, m
derive /dɪ'raiv/ vt derivar; obtener; extraer; Fig. sacar, hallar. vi (from) derivar de; proceder de; remontar a
dermatitis /,dɜrmə'taitɪs/ n dermatitis, f
dermatologist /,dɜrmə'tɒlədʒɪst/ n dermatólogo, m
dermatology /,dɜrmə'tɒlədʒi/ n dermatología, f
derogatory /dɪ'rɒgə,tɔri/ a despectivo, despreciativo; deshonroso
derrick /'dɛrɪk/ n grúa, machina, f; abanico, m
descant /n 'dɛskænt; v dɛs'kænt/ n Mus. discante, m. vi Mus. discantar; v discurrir (sobre), disertar (sobre)
descend /dɪ'sɛnd/ vi descender, bajar; (be inherited) pasar a; (fall) caer; (of the sun) ponerse. vt bajar. **to d. from,** descender de. **to d. to,** (lower oneself) rebajarse; (consider) venir a, considerar. **to d. upon,** caer

sobre; (arrive unexpectedly) llegar inesperadamente, invadir
descendant /dɪ'sɛndənt/ n descendiente, mf; pl **descendants,** descendencia, f
descent /dɪ'sɛnt/ n descenso, m; bajada, f; (slope) pendiente, cuesta, f; (attack) invasión, f, ataque, m; (lineage) descendencia, alcurnia, procedencia, f; (inheritance) herencia, f; transmisión, f. **D. from the Cross,** Descendimiento de la Cruz, m
describable /dɪ'skraibəbəl/ a descriptible
describe /dɪ'skraib/ vt describir; pintar
description /dɪ'skrɪpʃən/ n descripción, f
descriptive /dɪ'skrɪptɪv/ a descriptivo
desecrate /'dɛsɪ,kreit/ vt profanar
desecration /,dɛsɪ'kreiʃən/ n profanación, f
desegregation /,disɛgrɪ'geiʃən/ n desegregación, f
desert /dɪ'zɜrt/ vt abandonar; dejar; (Mil. etc.) desertar. vi desertar
desert /'dɛzərt/ n desierto, m
desert /dɪ'zɜrt/ n (merit) mérito, m **to receive one's deserts,** llevar su merecido
deserted /dɪ'zɜrtɪd/ a abandonado; desierto; solitario; inhabitado, despoblado
deserter /dɪ'zɜrtər/ n desertor, m
desertion /dɪ'zɜrʃən/ n abandono, m, deserción, f; (Mil. etc.) deserción, f
deserve /dɪ'zɜrv/ vt and vi merecer
deservedly /dɪ'zɜrvɪdli/ adv merecidamente
deserving /dɪ'zɜrvɪŋ/ a merecedor; meritorio. **to be d. of,** merecer
desiccate /'dɛsɪ,keit/ vt desecar. vi desecarse
design /dɪ'zain/ n proyecto, m; plan, m; intención, f, propósito, m; objeto, m; modelo, m; (pattern) diseño, dibujo, m; arte del dibujo, mf. vt idear; proyectar; (destine) destinar, dedicar; diseñar, dibujar, delinear; planear. **by d.,** expresamente, intencionalmente
designate /v 'dɛzɪg,neit; a -nɪt/ vt señalar; designar; (appoint) nombrar. a electo
designation /,dɛzɪg'neiʃən/ n designación, f; nombramiento, m
designedly /dɪ'zainɪdli/ adv de propósito
designer /dɪ'zainər/ n inventor (-ra), autor (-ra); delineador (-ra); dibujante, mf; (of public works, etc.) proyectista, mf
designing /dɪ'zainɪŋ/ a intrigante, astuto
desirability /dɪ,zaiᵊrə'bɪliti/ n lo deseable; conveniencia, f; ventaja, f
desirable /dɪ'zaiᵊrəbəl/ a deseable; conveniente; ventajoso; agradable; apetecible
desire /dɪ'zaiᵊr/ vt desear; querer; ansiar, ambicionar; (request) rogar, pedir; (order) mandar. n deseo, m; ansia, aspiración, f; ambición, f; impulso, m; (will) voluntad, f. **to d. ardently,** perecerse por; suspirar por
desirous /dɪ'zaiᵊrəs/ a deseoso (de); ambicioso (de); ansioso (de); impaciente (a); curioso (de)
desist /dɪ'sɪst/ vi desistir; dejar (de)
desk /dɛsk/ n pupitre, m; escritorio, buró, m; mesa de trabajo, f; (cashier's) caja, f; (teacher's, lecturer's) pulpit) cátedra, f
desolate /a 'dɛsəlɪt; v -,leit/ a solitario; desierto; deshabitado; abandonado; arruinado; árido; (afflicted) desolado, angustiado. vt desolar; despoblar
desolation /,dɛsə'leiʃən/ n desolación, f; aflicción, angustia, f; desconsuelo, m
despair /dɪ'spɛər/ n desesperación, f. vi perder toda esperanza. **He despaired of life,** Se ha perdido la esperanza de salvarle (la vida). **to be in d.,** estar desesperado
despairing /dɪ'spɛərɪŋ/ a desesperado
despairingly /dɪ'spɛərɪŋli/ adv sin esperanza
desperate /'dɛspərɪt/ a desesperado; sin esperanza; irremediable; furioso; violento; (dangerous) arriesgado, peligroso; terrible
desperately /'dɛspərɪtli/ adv desesperadamente; furiosamente; terriblemente
desperation /,dɛspə'reiʃən/ n desesperación, f; furia, violencia, f
despicable /'dɛspɪkəbəl/ a vil, despreciable; insignificante

despise /dɪ'spaiz/ vt despreciar; desdeñar
despiser /dɪ'spaizər/ n menospreciador (-ra)
despite /dɪ'spait/ prep a pesar de
despoil /dɪ'spɔil/ vt despojar, desnudar
despoiler /dɪ'spɔilər/ n despojador (-ra)
despoliation /dɪˌspouli'eiʃən/ n despojo, m
despondency /dɪ'spɒndənsi/ n abatimiento, desaliento, m, desesperación, f
despondent /dɪ'spɒndənt/ a abatido, desanimado, deprimido
despondently /dɪ'spɒndəntli/ adv con desaliento
despot /'dɛspət/ n déspota, m
despotic /dɛs'pɒtɪk/ a despótico
despotism /'dɛspəˌtɪzəm/ n despotismo, m
dessert /dɪ'zɜrt/ n postre, m, a de postre. **d. plate,** plato para postre, m. **d.-spoon,** cuchara de postre, f
destination /ˌdɛstə'neiʃən/ n destinación, f
destine /'dɛstɪn/ vt destinar; dedicar; predestinar
destiny /'dɛstəni/ n destino, m
destitute /'dɛstɪˌtut/ a indigente, menesteroso; desnudo (de); privado (de); desprovisto (de), falto (de); desamparado
destitution /ˌdɛstɪ'tuʃən/ n destitución, indigencia, miseria, f; privación, falta, f; desamparo, m
destroy /dɪ'strɔi/ vt destruir; demoler; deshacer; (kill) matar; exterminar; (finish) acabar con
destroyer /dɪ'strɔiər/ n destructor (-ra); Nav. destructor, cazatorpedero, m
destructible /dɪ'strʌktəbəl/ a destructible, destruible
destruction /dɪ'strʌkʃən/ n destrucción, f; demolición, f; ruina, f; pérdida, f; muerte, f; exterminio, m; perdición, f
destructive /dɪ'strʌktɪv/ a destructivo, destructor; (of animals) dañino. **d. animal,** animal dañino, m, alimaña, f
destructiveness /dɪ'strʌktɪvnɪs/ n destructividad, f; instinto destructor, m
desultory /'dɛsəlˌtɔri/ a inconexo; sin método, descosido; irregular
detach /dɪ'tætʃ/ vt separar, desprender; (unstick) despegar; Mil. destacar
detachable /dɪ'tætʃəbəl/ a separable, de quita y pon
detached /dɪ'tætʃt/ a suelto, separado; (Fig. with outlook, etc.) imparcial; indiferente, despegado. **d. house,** hotelito, m
detachment /dɪ'tætʃmənt/ n separación, f; Mil. destacamento, m; (Fig. of mind) imparcialidad, f; independencia (de espíritu, etc.), f; indiferencia, f
detail /dɪ'teil/ n detalle, m; particularidad, f; circunstancia, f; Mil. destacamento, m. vt detallar; particularizar, referir con pormenores; Mil. destacar. **in d.,** detalladamente, f; Inf. ce por be. **to go into details,** entrar en detalles
detain /dɪ'tein/ vt detener; (arrest) arrestar, prender; (withhold) retener; (prevent) impedir
detect /dɪ'tɛkt/ vt descubrir; averiguar; (discern) discernir, percibir; Elec. detectar
detectable /dɪ'tɛktəbəl/ a perceptible
detection /dɪ'tɛkʃən/ n descubrimiento, m; averiguación, f; percepción, f
detective /dɪ'tɛktɪv/ n detective, m, a de detectives; policíaco. **d. novel,** novela policíaca, f
detector /dɪ'tɛktər/ n descubridor, m; Elec. detector, m; Mech. indicador, m
detention /dɪ'tɛnʃən/ n detención, f; (arrest) arresto, m; (confinement) encierro, m
deter /dɪ'tɜr/ vt desanimar, desalentar; acobardar; (dissuade) disuadir; (prevent) impedir
detergent /dɪ'tɜrdʒənt/ a detersorio. n detersorio, m
deteriorate /dɪ'tɪəriəˌreit/ vt deteriorar. vi deteriorarse; empeorar
deterioration /dɪˌtɪəriə'reiʃən/ n deterioración, f; empeoramiento, m
determinable /dɪ'tɜrmənəbəl/ a determinable
determination /dɪˌtɜrmə'neiʃən/ n determinación, f; definición, f; resolución, decisión, f; Law. fallo, m; Med. congestión, f
determine /dɪ'tɜrmɪn/ vt determinar; definir; decidir; resolver; concluir; (fix) señalar; Law. sentenciar. vi

resolverse, decidirse; (insist (on)) empeñarse en, insistir en
determined /dɪ'tɜrmɪnd/ a determinado; resuelto, decidido; (of price) fijo
determining /dɪ'tɜrmənɪŋ/ a determinante
determinism /dɪ'tɜrməˌnɪzəm/ n determinismo, m
deterministic /dɪˌtɜrmə'nɪstɪk/ a determinista
deterrent /dɪ'tɜrənt/ a disuasivo. n freno, m. **to act as a d.,** servir como un freno. **d. capability,** poder de disuasión, m
detest /dɪ'tɛst/ vt detestar, abominar, aborrecer
detestable /dɪ'tɛstəbəl/ a detestable, aborrecible, abominable
detestation /ˌditɛ'steiʃən/ n detestación, abominación, f, aborrecimiento, m
dethrone /dɪ'θroun/ vt destronar
detonate /'dɛtnˌeit/ vt hacer detonar. vi detonar, estallar
detonation /ˌdɛtn'eiʃən/ n detonación, f
detonator /'dɛtnˌeitər/ n detonador, m; señal detonante, f
detour /'ditur/ n rodeo, m; desvío, m, desviación, f
detract /dɪ'trækt/ vt quitar; (diminish) disminuir; (slander) detraer, denigrar
detraction /dɪ'trækʃən/ n detracción, denigración, f
detractor /dɪ'træktər/ n detractor (-ra); infamador (-ra)
detriment /'dɛtrəmənt/ n detrimento, m; perjuicio, m; daño, m
detrimental /ˌdɛtrə'mɛntl̩/ a perjudicial
deuce /dus/ n (dice, cards) dos, m; (tennis) "dos," m. **The d.!** ¡Diantre! **to be the d. of a row,** haber moros y cristianos. **D. take it!** ¡Demonios!
Deuteronomy /ˌdutə'rɒnəmi/ n Deuteronomio, m
devaluation /ˌdivælyu'eiʃən/ n desvalorización, f
devalue /di'vælyu/ vt rebajar el valor de
devastate /'dɛvəˌsteit/ vt devastar, asolar
devastation /ˌdɛvə'steiʃən/ n devastación, f
develop /dɪ'vɛləp/ vt desarrollar; (make progress) avanzar, fomentar; perfeccionar; Photo. revelar. vi desarrollarse; crecer; avanzar, progresar; evolucionar
developer /dɪ'vɛləpər/ n Photo. revelador, m
development /dɪ'vɛləpmənt/ n desarrollo, m; evolución, f; progreso, avance, m; (encouragement) fomento, m; (event) acontecimiento, suceso, m; (product) producto, m; (working) explotación, f; Photo. revelación, f
deviate /'diviˌeit/ vi desviarse (de); (disagree) disentir (de)
deviation /ˌdivi'eiʃən/ n desviación, f
device /dɪ'vais/ n (contrivance) aparato, artefacto, mecanismo, m; (invention) invento, m; (trick) expediente, artificio, m; (scheme) proyecto, m; (design) dibujo, emblema, m; (motto) divisa, leyenda, f; pl devices, placeres, caprichos, m pl
devil /'dɛvəl/ n diablo, Satanás, m; demonio, m; (printer's) aprendiz de impresor, m. **Go to the d.!** ¡Vete enhoramala! **He is a poor d.,** Es un pobre diablo. **little d.,** diablillo, m. **The devil's abroad,** Anda el diablo suelto. **The d. take it!** ¡Lléveselo el diablo! **to play the d. with,** arruinar por completo. **What the d.!** ¡Qué diablos! **d.-possessed,** endemoniado
devilish /'dɛvəlɪʃ/ a diabólico, demoníaco; infernal
devilry /'dɛvəlri/ n diablura, f; magia, f; demonología, f; (wickedness) maldad, f; crueldad, f
devious /'diviəs/ a desviado; tortuoso
deviousness /'diviəsnɪs/ n tortuosidad, f
devise /dɪ'vaiz/ vt idear, inventar; fabricar; Law. legar
deviser /dɪ'vaizər/ n inventor (-ra)
devitalize /di'vaitl̩ˌaiz/ vt restar vitalidad, privar de vitalidad
devoid /dɪ'vɔid/ a desprovisto (de), privado (de); libre (de), exento (de)
devolve /dɪ'vɒlv/ vt traspasar, transmitir. vi (on, upon) incumbir (a), corresponder (a), tocar (a)
devote /dɪ'vout/ vt dedicar; consagrar. **to d. oneself to,** darse a, dedicarse a; consagrarse a

devoted /dɪ'voutɪd/ *a* fervoroso, apasionado; (faithful) fiel, leal
devotedly /dɪ'voutɪdli/ *adv* con devoción
devotee /ˌdevə'ti/ *n* devoto (-ta), admirador (-ra); aficionado (-da)
devotion /dɪ'vouʃən/ *n* devoción, *f*; dedicación, *f*; (zeal) celo, *m*; afición, *f*; (loyalty) lealtad, *f*; *pl* **devotions,** rezos, *m pl*, oraciones, *f pl*
devotional /dɪ'vouʃənl/ *a* devoto, religioso, de devoción.
devotional literature, literatura de devoción, *f*
devour /dɪ'vaur/ *vt* devorar; consumir
devourer /dɪ'vaurər/ *n* devorador (-ra)
devouring /dɪ'vaurɪŋ/ *a* devorador; absorbente
devout /dɪ'vaut/ *a* devoto, piadoso, practicante (e.g., *a d.* Catholic, un católico practicante)
devoutly /dɪ'vautli/ *adv* piadosamente
devoutness /dɪ'vautnɪs/ *n* piedad, devoción, *f*
dew /du/ *n* rocío, sereno, relente, *m*; *Fig.* rocío, *m, vt* rociar; humedecer; (refresh) refrescar. **d.-drop,** aljófar, *m,* gota de rocío, *f*
dewlap /'du,læp/ *n* papada, *f,* papo, *m*
dewy /'dui/ *a* rociado, lleno de rocío; húmedo; (of eyes) lustroso
dexterity /dek'sterɪti/ *n* destreza, *f*
dextrine /'dekstrɪn/ *n* dextrina, *f*
dextrose /'dekstrous/ *n* dextrosa, glucosa, *f*
dextrous /'dekstrəs/ *a* diestro; hábil, listo
diabetes /ˌdaiə'bitɪs/ *n* diabetes, *f*
diabetic /ˌdaiə'betɪk/ *a* diabético
diabolical /ˌdaiə'bɒlɪkəl/ *a* diabólico
diadem /'daiə,dem/ *n* diadema, *f*
diagnose /'daiəg,nous/ *vt* diagnosticar
diagnosis /ˌdaiəg'nousɪs/ *n* diagnóstico, *m,* diagnosis, *f*
diagnostician /ˌdaiəgnɒ'stɪʃən/ *n* diagnóstico, *m*
diagonal /dai'ægənl/ *n* diagonal, *f*
diagram /'daiə,græm/ *n* diagrama, *m*; esquema, *f*; gráfico, *m*
diagrammatic /ˌdaiəgrə'mætɪk/ *a* esquemático
dial /'daiəl/ *n* (sundial) reloj de sol, *m*; (of clocks, gas-meter) esfera, *f*; (of machines) indicador, *m*; (of a wireless set) cuadrante graduado, *m*; (of a telephone) marcador, disco, *m. vt* (a telephone number) marcar. **d. telephone,** teléfono automático, *m*
dialect /'daiə,lekt/ *n* dialecto, *m,* habla, *f, a* dialectal
dialectic /ˌdaiə'lektɪk/ *a* dialéctico. *n* dialéctica, *f*
dialectics /ˌdaiə'lektɪks/ *n* dialéctica, *f*
dialogue /'daiə,lɔg/ *n* diálogo, *m*. **to hold a d.,** dialogar
dialysis /dai'æləsɪs/ *n* diálisis, *f*
diameter /dai'æmɪtər/ *n* diámetro, *m*
diametrical /ˌdaiə'metrɪkəl/ *a* diametral
diamond /'daimənd/ *n* diamante, *m*; brillante, *m*; (tool) cortavidrios, *m*; (cards) oros (de baraja), *m pl.* **rough d.,** diamante bruto, *m.* **d.-bearing,** diamantífero. **d. cutter,** diamantista, *mf* **d. cutting,** talla de diamantes, *f.* **d. edition,** edición diamante, *f.* **d.-like,** adiamantado. **d. wedding,** bodas de diamante, *f pl*
diapason /ˌdaiə'peizən/ *n* diapasón, *m*
diaper /'daipər/ *n* lienzo adamascado, *m*; (baby's) pañal, *m*; (woman's) servilleta higiénica, *f*
diaphanous /dai'æfənəs/ *a* diáfano, transparente
diaphragm /'daiə,fræm/ *n* diafragma, *m*
diarist /'daiərɪst/ *n* diarista, *mf*
diarrhea /ˌdaiə'riə/ *n* diarrea, *f*
diary /'daiəri/ *n* diario, *m*
diastase /'daiə,steis/ *n* diastasa, *f*
diastole /dai'æstl/ *n* diástole, *f*
diatribe /'daiə,traib/ *n* diatriba, denunciación violenta, *f*
dibble /'dɪbəl/ *n* plantador, *m, vt* and *vi* plantar con plantador
dice /dais/ *n pl* dados, *m pl.* **to load the d.,** cargar los dados
dicky /'dɪki/ *n* (front) pechera postiza, *f*; (seat) trasera, *f*; (apron) delantal, *m.* **d. seat,** *Inf.* ahí te pudras, *m*
dictaphone /'dɪktə,foun/ *n* dictáfono, *m*
dictate /'dɪkteit/ *vt* dictar; mandar, *n* (order) dictamen, *m*; *Fig.* dictado, *m*

dictation /dɪk'teiʃən/ *n* dictado, *m.* **to write from d.,** escribir al dictado
dictator /'dɪkteitər/ *n* dictador, *m*
dictatorial /ˌdɪktə'tɔriəl/ *a* dictatorial, dictatorio, imperioso
dictatorship /dɪk'teitərˌʃɪp/ *n* dictadura, *f*
diction /'dɪkʃən/ *n* dicción, *f*
dictionary /'dɪkʃə,neri/ *n* diccionario, *m*
dictum /'dɪktəm/ *n* dictamen, *m*; (saying) sentencia, *f*; *Law.* fallo, *m*
didactic /dai'dæktɪk/ *a* didáctico
die /dai/ *vi* morir; fallecer, finar; (wither) marchitarse; (disappear) desvanecerse, desaparecer; (of light) palidecer; extinguirse; (end) cesar; (desire) ansiar, perecerse (por). **Never say die!** ¡Mientras hay vida, hay esperanza! **to die early,** morir temprano; malograrse. **to die a violent death,** tener una muerte violenta, *Inf.* morir vestido. **to die from natural causes,** morir por causas naturales; *Inf.* morir en la cama. **to die hard,** luchar contra la muerte; tardar en morir; tardar en desaparecer. **to die of a broken heart,** morir con el corazón destrozado, morir de pena. **to die away,** desaparecer gradualmente; extinguirse poco a poco; dejar de oírse poco a poco; cesar; pasar. **to die down,** extinguirse gradualmente; palidecer; dejar de oírse; desaparecer; (of the wind) amainar; perder su fuerza. **to die out,** desaparecer; olvidarse; dejar de existir; pasarse de moda
die /dai/ *n* dado, *m*; *Fig.* suerte, *f*; (stamp) cuño, troquel, *m*; *Archit.* cubo, *m.* **The die is cast,** La suerte está echada. **die-sinker,** grabador en hueco, *m*
diehard /'dai,hɑrd/ *n* valiente, *m*; tradicionalista empedernido, *m*; partidario (-ia) entusiasta
dieresis /dai'erəsɪs/ *n* diéresis, crema, *f*
diesel /'dizəl, -səl/ *n* Diesel. **d. engine,** motor Diesel, *m*
diet /'daiɪt/ *n* dieta, *f,* régimen dietario, *m*; (assembly) dieta, *f. vi* estar a dieta, hacer régimen
dietetic /ˌdaiɪ'tetɪk/ *a* dietético
dietetics /ˌdaiɪ'tetɪks/ *n* dietética, *f*
dietician /ˌdaiɪ'tɪʃən/ *n* dietista, *mf*
differ /'dɪfər/ *vi* diferenciarse; (contradict) contradecir; (disagree) no estar de acuerdo; disentir
difference /'dɪfərəns/ *n* diferencia, *f*; disparidad, *f*; contraste, *m*; (of opinion) disensión, *f*; controversia, disputa, *f.* **to make no d.,** no hacer diferencia alguna; no afectar; dar lo mismo, no importar
different /'dɪfərənt/ *a* distinto; diferente; vario, diverso
differential /ˌdɪfə'renʃəl/ *a* diferencial. **d. calculus,** cálculo diferencial, *m*
differentiate /ˌdɪfə'renʃi,eit/ *vt* diferenciar, distinguir. *vi* diferenciarse, distinguirse
differentiation /ˌdɪfə,renʃi'eiʃən/ *n* diferenciación, *f*
differently /'dɪfərəntli/ *adv* diferentemente
difficult /'dɪfɪ,kʌlt/ *a* difícil. **to make d.,** hacer difícil, dificultar
difficulty /'dɪfɪ,kʌlti/ *n* dificultad, *f.* **d. in breathing,** opresión de pecho, *f*
diffidence /'dɪfɪdəns/ *n* modestia, timidez, *f*; huraña, *f*; falta de confianza en sí mismo, *f*
diffident /'dɪfɪdənt/ *a* modesto, tímido; huraño; sin confianza en sí mismo
diffidently /'dɪfɪdəntli/ *adv* tímidamente; vergonzosamente
diffract /dɪ'frækt/ *vt* difractar
diffraction /dɪ'frækʃən/ *n* difracción, *f*
diffractive /dɪ'fræktɪv/ *a* difrangente
diffuse /v dɪ'fyuz; *a* -'fyus/ *vt* difundir. *a* difuso; (long-winded) prolijo
diffuseness /dɪ'fyusnɪs/ *n* difusión, *f*; prolijidad, *f*
diffusion /dɪ'fyuʒən/ *n* difusión, *f*; esparcimiento, *m*; diseminación, *f*
diffusive /dɪ'fyusɪv/ *a* difusivo
dig /dɪg/ *vt* and *vi* cavar; excavar; (of animals) escarbar; (mine) zapar, minar; (into a subject) ahondar (en); (with the spurs) aguijonear, dar con las espuelas; (poke) clavar. **to dig one's heels in,** *Lat. Am.* encabestrarse. **to dig in,** enterrarse; *Mil.* abrir trincheras; *Inf.* arreglarse las cosas. **to dig out,** excavar; sacar cavando, sacar con azadón; extraer. **to dig up,** desenterrar; descubrir

digest /v dɪ'dʒɛst, dai-; n 'daidʒɛst/ vt (food, also *chem.* and *fig.* tolerate and think over) digerir; (of knowledge and territory) asimilar. vi digerir. n compendio, resumen, m; *Law.* digesto, m; recopilación, f. **This food is easy to d.,** Este alimento es fácil de digerir; Este alimento es muy ligero

digestibility /dɪˌdʒɛstə'bɪlɪti, dai-/ n digestibilidad, f

digestible /dɪ'dʒɛstəbəl, dai-/ a digerible, digestible

digestion /dɪ'dʒɛstʃən, dai-/ n digestión, f; (of ideas) asimilación, f; *Chem.* digestión, f

digestive /dɪ'dʒɛstɪv, dai-/ a digestivo

digger /'dɪgər/ n cavador (-ra)

digging /'dɪgɪŋ/ n cavadura, f; excavación, f; pl **diggings,** minas, f pl; excavaciones, f pl; *Inf.* alojamiento, m, posada, f

digit /'dɪdʒɪt/ n dígito, m, *Anat.* dedo.

digital /'dɪdʒɪtl̩/ a digital, dígito

digitalin /ˌdɪdʒɪ'tælɪn/ n digitalina, f

digitalis /ˌdɪdʒɪ'tælɪs/ n digital, f

dignified /'dɪgnəˌfaid/ a serio, grave; majestuoso; (worthy) digno; solemne; altivo; noble

dignify /'dɪgnəˌfai/ vt dignificar, honrar; exaltar; dar dignidad (a); ennoblecer

dignitary /'dɪgnɪˌtɛri/ n dignatario, m; dignidad, f

dignity /'dɪgnɪti/ n dignidad, f; (rank) rango, m; (post) cargo, puesto, m; (honor) honra, f; (stateliness) majestad, f; mesura, seriedad, f; (haughtiness) altivez, f; (nobility) nobleza, f. **to stand on one's d.,** darse importancia

digress /dɪ'grɛs, dai-/ vi divagar

digression /dɪ'grɛʃən, dai-/ n digresión, divagación, f

dike /daik/ n dique, m; (ditch) acequia, f; canal, m; (embankment) zanja, f, vt represar

dilapidated /dɪ'læpɪˌdeitɪd/ a arruinado, destartalado; (of fortune) dilapidado; (of persons, families) venido a menos; (shabby) raído

dilapidation /dɪˌlæpə'deiʃən/ n deterioración, f; ruina, f, estado ruinoso, m

dilatation /ˌdɪlə'teiʃən/ n dilatación, f; ensanche, m

dilate /dai'leit/ vt dilatar; ensanchar. vi dilatarse. **to d. upon,** extenderse sobre, dilatarse en

dilator /dai'leitər/ n dilatador, m

dilatoriness /'dɪlətərɪnɪs/ n tardanza, f; (slowness) lentitud, f

dilatory /'dɪləˌtɔri/ a dilatorio, tardo; (slow) lento

dilemma /dɪ'lɛmə/ n dilema, m

dilettante /'dɪlɪˌtɑnt/ n diletante, m; aficionado (-da)

dilettantism /'dɪlɪtɑnˌtɪzəm/ n diletantismo, m

diligence /'dɪlɪdʒəns/ n diligencia, f; asiduidad, f; (care) cuidado, m; (coach) diligencia, f

diligent /'dɪlɪdʒənt/ a diligente, asiduo, aplicado, industrioso; (painstaking) concienzudo

dilute /dɪ'lut, dai-/ vt diluir; *Fig.* adulterar. a diluido

dilution /dɪ'luʃən, dai-/ n dilución, f; *Fig.* adulteración, f

diluvian /dɪ'luviən/ a diluviano

dim /dɪm/ a (of light) apagado, débil, tenue; (of sight) turbio; (dark) sombrío, oscuro; (blurred, etc.) empañado; indistinto, confuso. vt obscurecer; empañar; (dazzle) ofuscar; (eclipse) eclipsar; reducir la intensidad (de una luz); (of memories) borrar. **dim intelligence,** de brumoso seso

dimension /dɪ'mɛnʃən/ n dimensión, f; (size) tamaño, m; (scope) extensión, f, alcance, m

dimensional /dɪ'mɛnʃənl/ a dimensional

diminish /dɪ'mɪnɪʃ/ vt disminuir; reducir; debilitar, atenuar. vi disminuir; reducirse; debilitarse, atenuarse

diminishing /dɪ'mɪnɪʃɪŋ/ a menguante

diminution /ˌdɪmə'nuʃən/ n disminución, f; reducción, f; atenuación, f

diminutive /dɪ'mɪnyətɪv/ a diminutivo. n diminutivo, m

diminutiveness /dɪ'mɪnyətɪvnɪs/ n pequeñez, f

dimly /'dɪmli/ adv obscuramente; vagamente; indistintamente. **dimly lit,** apenas alumbrado

dimness /'dɪmnɪs/ n oscuridad, f; deslustre, m; (of light) tenuidad (de la luz), f; confusión, f

dimple /'dɪmpəl/ n hoyuelo, m

dimpled /'dɪmpəld/ a con hoyuelos, que tiene hoyuelos

din /dɪn/ n estrépito, estruendo, ruido, m; algarabía, barahúnda, f, vt ensordecer

dine /dain/ vi (in the evening) cenar; (at midday) comer, almorzar. vt convidar a cenar or a comer. **to d. out,** cenar or comer fuera

diner /'dainər/ n (on a train) coche comedor, coche restaurante, m; cenador, m; comedor, m

ding-dong /'dɪŋˌdɔŋ/ n tintín, m

dinghy /'dɪŋgi/ n lancha, f; canoa, f, bote, m. **rubber d.,** canoa de goma, f

dinginess /'dɪndʒɪnɪs/ n deslustre, f; suciedad, f; oscuridad, f; (of a person) desaseo, m

dingy /'dɪndʒi/ a deslucido, empañado; sucio; oscuro; (of persons) desaseado

dining car /'dainɪŋ/ n coche comedor, vagón restaurante, m

dining room /'dainɪŋ/ n comedor, m; refectorio, m

dining table n mesa del comedor, f

dinner /'dɪnər/ n (in the evening) cena, f; (at midday) comida, f. **over the d. table,** de sobremesa. **d.-jacket,** smoking, m. **d. party,** cena, f. **d. plate,** plato, m. **d. roll,** panecillo, m. **d. service,** vajilla, f

dinosaur /'dainəˌsɔr/ n dinosauro, m

diocesan /dai'ɒsəsən/ a diocesano

diocese /'daiəsɪs/ n diócesis, f

Dionysus Thrax /ˌdaiə'naisəs 'θræks/ Dionisio el Tracio, m

dioxide /dai'ɒksaid, -sɪd/ n dióxido, m

dip /dɪp/ n inmersión, f; baño, m; (in the ground) declive, m; (in the road) columpio, m, depresión, f; (slope) pendiente, f; (candle) vela de sebo, f; (of the horizon) depresión (del horizonte), f; (of the needle) inclinación (de la aguja), f. vt sumergir; bañar; (put) poner. vi inclinarse hacia abajo. **to dip into a book,** hojear un libro. **to dip the colors,** saludar con la bandera

diphtheria /dɪf'θɪəriə/ n difteria, f

diphthong /'dɪfθɔŋ/ n diptongo, m

diploma /dɪ'ploumə/ n diploma, m

diplomacy /dɪ'plouməsi/ n diplomacia, f; tacto, m

diploma mill n fábrica de títulos académicos, f

diplomat /'dɪpləˌmæt/ n diplomático, m

diplomatic /ˌdɪplə'mætɪk/ a diplomático. **d. bag,** valija diplomática, f. **d. corps,** cuerpo diplomático, m

diplomatically /ˌdɪplə'mætɪkəli/ adv diplomáticamente

dipper /'dɪpər/ n (ladle) cazo, m. **Big Dipper,** Osa Mayor, f

dipsomania /ˌdɪpsə'meiniə/ n dipsomanía, f

dipsomaniac /ˌdɪpsə'meiniæk/ n dipsómano (-na)

diptych /'dɪptɪk/ n díptica, f

dire /daiər/ a espantoso, horrible; cruel; funesto

direct /dɪ'rɛkt, dai-/ a directo; claro, inequívoco; (of descent) recto; (of electric current) continuo; exacto. adv directamente. vt dirigir; (command) ordenar, encargar; dar instrucciones. **d. action,** acción directa, f. **d. current,** corriente continua, f. **d. line,** línea directa, f. **d. object,** acusativo, m. **d. speech,** oración directa, f

direct dialing /'daiəlɪŋ/ n discado directo, m

direction /dɪ'rɛkʃən, 'dai-/ n dirección, f; rumbo, m; instrucción, f; (on a letter) sobrescrito, m; señas, f pl. **in the d. of,** en la dirección de; hacia; *Naut.* con rumbo a. **in all directions,** por todas partes; a los cuatro vientos. **to go in the d. of,** ir en la dirección de; tomar por. **Directions for use,** Direcciones para el uso. **d. indicator, d. signal,** (on car) indicador de dirección, m

directive /dɪ'rɛktɪv, dai-/ a directivo, director. n orden, m

directly /dɪ'rɛktli, dai-/ adv directamente; inmediatamente, en seguida

directness /dɪ'rɛktnɪs, dai-/ n derechura, f

director /dɪ'rɛktər, dai-/ n director (-triz, -ora), **managing d.,** gerente, m

directorate /dɪ'rɛktərɪt, dai-/ n directorio, m, junta directiva, f; cargo de director, m

directory /dɪˈrɛktəri, dai-/ n directorio, m, guía, f.
telephone d., guía de teléfonos, f
dirge /dɜrdʒ/ n endecha, f, lamento, m; canto fúnebre, m
dirt /dɜrt/ n mugre, suciedad, f; (mud) lodo, m; (earth) tierra, f; (dust) polvo, m; Fig. inmundicia, f. **to be d. cheap,** (of goods) estar por los suelos. **d.-track,** pista de ceniza, f. **d.-track racing,** carreras en pista de ceniza, f pl
dirtiness /ˈdɜrtinɪs/ n suciedad, f; (untidiness) desaseo, m; sordidez, f; (meanness) bajeza, f
dirty /ˈdɜrti/ a sucio, Central America descacharrado; (untidy) desaseado; (muddy) enlodado; (dusty) polvoriento; (of weather) borrascoso; (sordid) sórdido; (base, mean) vil; (indecent) indecente, verde, obsceno. vt ensuciar. **d. trick,** mala pasada, Lat. Am. chancada f
disability /ˌdɪsəˈbɪlɪti/ n incapacidad, f; impotencia, f; desventaja, f
disable /dɪsˈeibəl/ vt (cripple) estropear, tullir; hacer incapaz (de), incapacitar; imposibilitar; (destroy) destruir; Law. incapacitar legalmente
disabled /dɪsˈeibəld/ a inválido; impedido, lisiado; (in the hand) manco; incapacitado; (of ships, etc.) fuera de servicio, estropeado. **d. soldier,** inválido, m
disablement /dɪsˈeibəlmənt/ n (physical) invalidez, f; inhabilitación, f; Law. impedimento, f
disabuse /ˌdɪsəˈbyuz/ vt desengañar, sacar de un error
disadvantage /ˌdɪsədˈvæntɪdʒ/ n desventaja, f. **to be under the d. of,** sufrir la desventaja de
disadvantaged /ˌdɪsədˈvæntɪdʒd/ a (financially) de escasos recursos
disadvantageous /dɪsˌædvənˈteidʒəs/ a desventajoso
disaffected /ˌdɪsəˈfɛktɪd/ a desafecto
disaffection /ˌdɪsəˈfɛkʃən/ n desafecto, descontento, m
disagree /ˌdɪsəˈgri/ vi no estar de acuerdo; diferir; (quarrel) reñir; (not share the opinion of) no estar de la opinión (de); (of food, etc.) sentar mal; no probar. **The meat disagreed with me,** La carne me sentó mal
disagreeable /ˌdɪsəˈgriəbəl/ a desagradable; repugnante; (of persons) antipático, displicente
disagreeableness /ˌdɪsəˈgriəbəlnɪs/ n lo desagradable; (of persons) displicencia, f
disagreeably /ˌdɪsəˈgriəbli/ adv desagradablemente; con displicencia
disagreement /ˌdɪsəˈgrimənt/ n desacuerdo, m; diferencia, f; desavenencia, f; discordia, f; (quarrel) riña, disputa, f; discrepancia, f
disallow /ˌdɪsəˈlau/ vt negar; rechazar
disappear /ˌdɪsəˈpɪər/ vi desaparecer. **to cause to d.,** hacer desaparecer
disappearance /ˌdɪsəˈpɪərəns/ n desaparición, f
disappoint /ˌdɪsəˈpoint/ vt desilusionar; frustrar; (hopes) defraudar; (deprive) privar de; (annoy) contrariar; (break a promise) faltar (a la palabra); Lat. Am. decepcionar
disappointedly /ˌdɪsəˈpointɪdli/ adv con desilusión, con desengaño
disappointing /ˌdɪsəˈpointɪŋ/ a desengañador; pobre; triste; poco halagüeño
disappointment /ˌdɪsəˈpointmənt/ n desengaño, m, decepción, f; frustración, f; desilusión, f; (vexation) contrariedad, f; contratiempo, m. **to suffer a d.,** sufrir un desengaño; Inf. llevarse un chasco
disapproval /ˌdɪsəˈpruvəl/ n desaprobación, f
disapprove /ˌdɪsəˈpruv/ vt desaprobar
disapproving /ˌdɪsəˈpruvɪŋ/ a de desaprobación, severo
disapprovingly /ˌdɪsəˈpruvɪŋli/ adv con desaprobación
disarm /dɪsˈarm/ vt desarmar. vi desarmarse; deponer las armas
disarmament /dɪsˈarməmənt/ n desarme, m
disarrange /ˌdɪsəˈreindʒ/ vt desarreglar; descomponer, desajustar; (hair) despeinar
disarrangement /ˌdɪsəˈreindʒmənt/ n desarreglo, m; desajuste, m; desorden, m
disarray /ˌdɪsəˈrei/ n desorden, desarreglo, m; confusión, f. vt desordenar, desarreglar

disarticulate /ˌdɪsarˈtɪkyəˌleit/ vt desarticular
disarticulation /ˌdɪsarˌtɪkyəˈleiʃən/ n desarticulación, f
disaster /dɪˈzæstər/ n desastre, m; catástrofe, m; infortunio, m
disastrous /dɪˈzæstrəs/ a desastroso; funesto, trágico
disastrously /dɪˈzæstrəsli/ adv desastrosamente
disastrousness /dɪˈzæstrəsnɪs/ n carácter desastroso, m
disavow /ˌdɪsəˈvau/ vt repudiar; retractar
disavowal /ˌdɪsəˈvauəl/ n repudiación, f
disband /dɪsˈbænd/ vt licenciar. vi desbandarse, dispersarse
disbelief /ˌdɪsbɪˈlif/ n incredulidad, f; desconfianza, f
disbelieve /ˌdɪsbɪˈliv/ vt and vi descreer, no creer; desconfiar (de)
disburse /dɪsˈbɜrs/ vt desembolsar, pagar
disbursement /dɪsˈbɜrsmənt/ n desembolso, m
disc /dɪsk/ n disco, m
discard /v dɪˈskard/ vt 'dɪskard/ vt desechar, arrinconar, Lat. Am. botar; despedir; (at cards) descartar. n (at cards) descarte, m
discern /dɪˈsɜrn/ vt discernir, distinguir, percibir
discerner /dɪˈsɜrnər/ n discernidor (-ra)
discernible /dɪˈsɜrnəbəl/ a distinguible, perceptible
discerning /dɪˈsɜrnɪŋ/ a perspicaz, discernidor
discernment /dɪˈsɜrnmənt/ n discernimiento, m
discharge /dɪsˈtʃardʒ/ vt descargar; (a gun) disparar; tirar; (an arrow) lanzar; Elec. descargar; emitir; (dismiss) destituir, despedir; arrojar; Mil. licenciar; (exempt) dispensar (de); (exonerate) absolver, exonerar; (free) dar libertad (a); (from hospital) dar de baja (a); Law. revocar; (perform) cumplir, ejecutar; (pay) pagar, saldar; (of an abscess, etc.) supurar
discharge /ˈdɪtʃardʒ/ n (of firearms) disparo, tiro, m; (of artillery) descarga, f; (of goods, cargo) descargue, m; Elec. descarga, f; (from a wound, etc.) pus, m, supuración, f; (from the intestine) flujo, m; (of a debt) pago, m.; Com. descargo, m; (receipt) carta de pago, quitanza, f; Mil. licencia absoluta, f; (dismissal) despedida, destitución, f; (exoneration) exoneración, f; (freeing) liberación, f; (from hospital) baja, f; (performance) cumplimiento, m; ejecución, f
disciple /dɪˈsaipəl/ n discípulo (-la)
disciplinarian /ˌdɪsəplɪˈneəriən/ n disciplinario (-ia)
disciplinary /ˈdɪsəpləˌneri/ a disciplinario
discipline /ˈdɪsəplɪn/ n disciplina, f. vt disciplinar
disclaim /dɪsˈkleim/ vt renunciar (a); (repudiate) rechazar, repudiar
disclaimer /dɪsˈkleimər/ n Law. renunciación, f; repudiación, f
disclose /dɪsˈklouz/ vt descubrir, revelar
disclosure /dɪsˈklouʒər/ n descubrimiento, f, revelación, f
discolor /dɪsˈkʌlər/ vt descolorar. vi descolorarse
discoloration /dɪsˌkʌləˈreiʃən/ n descoloramiento, f
discomfit /dɪsˈkʌmfɪt/ vt desconcertar
discomfiture /dɪsˈkʌmfɪtʃər/ n desconcierto, m
discomfort /dɪsˈkʌmfərt/ n falta de comodidades, f; incomodidad, f; malestar, m; molestia, f; inquietud, f; dolor, m
discomposure /ˌdɪskəmˈpouʒər/ n confusión, agitación, inquietud, f
disconcert /ˌdɪskənˈsɜrt/ vt desconcertar, turbar; (of plans, etc.) frustrar
disconnect /ˌdɪskəˈnɛkt/ vt separar; (of railway engines, etc.) desacoplar; desconectar; (of electric plugs) desenchufar
disconnected /ˌdɪskəˈnɛktɪd/ a inconexo; incoherente, deshilvanado
disconnectedness /ˌdɪskəˈnɛktɪdnɪs/ n inconexión, f; incoherencia, f
disconsolate /dɪsˈkɒnsəlɪt/ a desconsolado, triste
disconsolately /dɪsˈkɒnsəlɪtli/ adv desconsoladamente, tristemente
disconsolateness /dɪsˈkɒnsəlɪtnɪs/ n desconsuelo, f
discontent /ˌdɪskənˈtɛnt/ n descontento, disgusto, m, vt descontentar, desagradar
discontented /ˌdɪskənˈtɛntɪd/ a descontentadizo, descontento, disgustado

discontinuance /ˌdɪskən'tɪnyuəns/ n descontinuación, cesación, f; interrupción, f

discontinue /ˌdɪskən'tɪnyu/ vt descontinuar; cesar; interrumpir; (of payments, etc.) suspender. vi cesar

discontinuous /ˌdɪskən'tɪnyuəs/ a descontinuo; interrumpido; intermitente

discord /'dɪskɔrd/ n discordia, f; Mus. disonancia, f, desentono, m

discordant /dɪs'kɔrdənt/ a discorde, poco armonioso; incongruo; Mus. disonante, desentonado. **to be d.,** discordar; ser incongruo; Mus. disonar

discount /'dɪskaunt/ v also dɪs'kaunt/ n descuento, m; rebaja, f. vt descontar; rebajar; balancear; (disconsider) desechar. **at a d.,** al descuento; bajo la par; fácil de obtener; superfluo; Fig. en disfavor, en descrédito. **rate of d.,** tipo de descuento, m. **d. for cash,** descuento por venta al contado, m

discourage /dɪ'skɜrɪdʒ/ vt desalentar, desanimar; oponerse a; disuadir; frustrar

discouragement /dɪ'skɜrɪdʒmənt/ n desaliento, m; desaprobación, oposición, f; disuasión, f; (obstacle) estorbo, m

discouraging /dɪ'skɜrɪdʒɪŋ/ a poco animador, que ofrece pocas esperanzas; (with prospect, etc.) nada halagüeño

discourse /n 'dɪskɔrs; v dɪs'kɔrs/ n discurso, m; plática, f; (treatise) disertación, f. vi (converse) platicar, conversar; (with on, upon) disertar sobre, discurrir sobre; tratar de

discourteous /dɪs'kɜrtiəs/ a descortés, desconsiderado

discourtesy /dɪs'kɜrtəsi/ n descortesía, f

discover /dɪ'skʌvər/ vt descubrir; (see) ver; (realize) darse cuenta de; (show) manifestar; revelar

discoverable /dɪ'skʌvərəbəl/ a que se puede descubrir; averiguable; distinguible, perceptible

discoverer /dɪ'skʌvərər/ n descubridor (-ra); revelador (-ra)

discovery /dɪ'skʌvəri/ n descubrimiento, m; revelación, f

discredit /dɪs'krɛdɪt/ n descrédito, m; des honra, f; duda, f. vt dudar (de), no creer (en); desacreditar; deshonrar

discreditable /dɪs'krɛdɪtəbəl/ a deshonroso, ignominioso, vergonzoso

discreetly /dɪ'skritli/ adv discretamente; prudentemente

discrepancy /dɪ'skrɛpənsi/ n discrepancia, diferencia, f; contradicción, f

discrepant /dɪ'skrɛpənt/ a discrepante; contradictorio, inconsistente

discretion /dɪ'skrɛʃən/ n discreción, f; prudencia, circunspección, f; juicio, m; voluntad, f. **at one's own d.,** a voluntad (de uno). **years of d.,** edad de discreción, f

discriminate /dɪ'skrɪmɪˌneɪt/ vi distinguir (entre); hacer una distinción (en favor de or en perjuicio de). vt distinguir

discriminating /dɪ'skrɪməˌneɪtɪŋ/ a discerniente, que sabe distinguir, juicioso; culto; diferencial

discrimination /dɪˌskrɪmə'neɪʃən/ n discernimiento, m; gusto, m; distinción, f; discriminación, f

discursive /dɪ'skɜrsɪv/ a discursivo; digresivo

discus /'dɪskəs/ n disco, m. **d. thrower,** discóbolo, m

discuss /dɪ'skʌs/ vt discutir; hablar de; debatir; (deal with) tratar; (Fam. a dish) probar; (a bottle of wine) vaciar

discussion /dɪ'skʌʃən/ n discusión, f; debate, m

disdain /dɪs'deɪn/ n desdén, m; altivez, f. vt desdeñar, desairar, despreciar. **to d. to,** desdeñarse de

disdainful /dɪs'deɪnfəl/ a desdeñoso; altivo

disdainfully /dɪs'deɪnfəli/ adv desdeñosamente

disease /dɪ'ziz/ n enfermedad, f; Fig. mal, m. **infectious d.,** enfermedad contagiosa, f

diseased /dɪ'zizd/ a enfermo; (of fruit, etc.) malo

disembark /ˌdɪsɛm'bark/ vt and vi desembarcar

disembarkation /dɪsˌɛmbar'keɪʃən/ n desembarque, m; Mil. desembarco (de tropas), m

disembodied /ˌdɪsɛm'bɒdid/ a incorpóreo

disembowel /ˌdɪsɛm'bauəl/ vt desentrañar, destripar

disenchant /ˌdɪsɛn'tʃænt/ vt desencantar; deschechizar; desilusionar

disenchantment /ˌdɪsɛn'tʃæntmənt/ n desencanto, m; desilusión, f

disengage /ˌdɪsɛn'geɪdʒ/ vt desasir; soltar; (gears) desembragar; (uncouple) desacoplar; (free) librar

disengaged /ˌdɪsɛn'geɪdʒd/ a (free) libre

disentangle /ˌdɪsɛn'tæŋgəl/ vt (undo) desatar, desanudar; separar; (of threads, etc., and Fig.) desenredar, desenmarañar. vi desenredarse

disentanglement /ˌdɪsɛn'tæŋgəlmənt/ n desatadura, f; separación, f; desenredo, m

disestablish /ˌdɪsɪ'stæblɪʃ/ vt separar (la Iglesia del Estado)

disestablishment /ˌdɪsɪ'stæblɪʃmənt/ n separación (de la Iglesia del Estado), f

disfavor /dɪs'feɪvər/ n disfavor, m; (disapproval) desaprobación, f. vt desaprobar

disfigure /dɪs'fɪgyər/ vt desfigurar, afear; deformar; (mar) estropear

disfigurement /dɪs'fɪgyərmənt/ n desfiguración, f; deformidad, f; defecto, m

disfranchise /dɪs'fræntʃaiz/ vt privar de los derechos civiles (a)

disfranchisement /dɪs'fræntʃaizmənt/ n privación de los derechos civiles, privación del derecho de votar, f

disgrace /dɪs'greɪs/ n desgracia, vergüenza, ignominia, f; deshonra, f; (insult) afrenta, f; (scandal) escándalo, m; disfavor, m. vt deshonrar; despedir con ignominia. **in d.,** fuera de favor; desacreditado; (of children and animals) castigado

disgraceful /dɪs'greɪsfəl/ a deshonroso; ignominioso; escandaloso, desgraciado

disgracefully /dɪs'greɪsfəli/ adv escandalosamente

disgracefulness /dɪs'greɪsfəlnɪs/ n ignominia, vergüenza, f; deshonra, f

disgruntled /dɪs'grʌntl̩d/ a refunfuñador, enfurruñado, malhumorado

disguise /dɪs'gaiz/ n disfraz, m; (mask) máscara, f. vt disfrazar; cubrir, tapar; (Fig. conceal) ocultar. **in d.,** disfrazado

disgust /dɪs'gʌst/ n repugnancia, aversión, f; aborrecimiento, m; asco, m. vt repugnar, inspirar aversión; disgustar; dar asco (a)

disgusted /dɪs'gʌstɪd/ a asqueado; disgustado; furioso; (bored) aburrido

disgusting /dɪs'gʌstɪŋ/ a repugnante; odioso, horrible; asqueroso

dish /dɪʃ/ n (for meat, vegetables, fruit, etc.) fuente, f; (food) plato, m; pl **dishes,** platos, m pl, vajilla, f. vt servir; Inf. frustrar. **cooked d.,** guiso, m. **special d. for today,** plato del día, m. **to wash the dishes,** fregar los platos. **d.-cloth,** (for washing) fregajo, m; (for drying) paño de los platos, m. **d.-cover,** cubreplatos, m. **d.-rack,** escurre-platos, m. **d.-washer,** lavaplatos, lavavajillas, m. **d.-water,** agua de lavar los platos, f

disharmony /dɪs'harməni/ n falta de armonía, f; (disagreement) discordia, desavenencia, f; incongruencia, f; Mus. disonancia, f

dishearten /dɪs'hartn̩/ vt desalentar, desanimar; desesperar; disuadir (de)

disheveled /dɪ'ʃɛvəld/ a despeinado, desgreñado; (untidy) desaseado

dishonest /dɪs'ɒnɪst/ a deshonesto, falto de honradez, tramposo; fraudulento; falso, desleal, Lat. Am. also flequetero

dishonestly /dɪs'ɒnɪstli/ adv de mala fe, sin honradez; fraudulentamente; deslealmente

dishonesty /dɪs'ɒnəsti/ n deshonestidad, falta de honradez, falta de integridad, f; fraude, m; falsedad, deslealtad, f

dishonor /dɪs'ɒnər/ n deshonra, f. vt deshonrar; Com. no pagar, o no aceptar, un giro

dishonorable /dɪs'ɒnərəbəl/ a deshonroso

dishonorer /dɪs'ɒnərər/ n deshonrador (-ra); profanador (-ra)

disillusion /ˌdɪsɪ'luʒən/ vt desengañar, desilusionar

disillusionment /ˌdɪsɪ'luʒənmənt/ n desilusión, f, desengaño, desencanto, m

disinclination /ˌdɪsˌɪnklə'neɪʃən/ n aversión, f

disincline /ˌdɪsɪn'klaɪn/ vt desinclinar
disinfect /ˌdɪsɪn'fɛkt/ vt desinfectar
disinfectant /ˌdɪsɪn'fɛktənt/ a and n desinfectante m.
disinfection /ˌdɪsɪn'fɛkʃən/ n desinfección, f
disingenuous /ˌdɪsɪn'dʒɛnyuəs/ a tortuoso, doble, falso, insincero
disinherit /ˌdɪsɪn'hɛrɪt/ vt desheredar
disinheritance /ˌdɪsɪn'hɛrɪtəns/ n desheredación, f
disintegrate /dɪs'ɪntəˌgreɪt/ vt despedazar, disgregar. vi disgregarse; desmoronarse
disintegration /dɪsˌɪntə'greɪʃən/ n disgregración, f; disolución, f; desmoronamiento, m
disinter /ˌdɪsɪn'tɜr/ vt desenterrar
disinterested /dɪs'ɪntəˌrɛstɪd, -trɪstɪd/ a desinteresado
disinterestedness /dɪs'ɪntəˌrɛstɪdnɪs, -trɪstɪd-/ n desinterés, m
disinterment /ˌdɪsɪn'tɜrmənt/ n desenterramiento, m
disjointed /dɪs'dʒɔɪntɪd/ a dislocado; desarticulado; incoherente, inconexo; (of a speech, etc.) descosido
disjointedness /dɪs'dʒɔɪntɪdnɪs/ n descoyuntamiento, desencajamiento, m; incoherencia, f
disk /dɪsk/ n disco, m
diskette /dɪ'skɛt/ n disquete, m, disco flexible, m
dislike /dɪs'laɪk/ n aversión, f; antipatía, f; (hostility) animosidad, f. vt desagradar, no gustar; repugnar. **I d. the house,** No me gusta la casa. **I d. them,** No me gustan
dislocate /'dɪslouˌkeɪt/ vt dislocar, descoyuntar; Fig. interrumpir
dislocation /ˌdɪslou'keɪʃən/ n dislocación, f, descoyuntamiento, m; Fig. interrupción, f
dislodge /dɪs'lɒdʒ/ vt desalojar
dislodgement /dɪs'lɒdʒmənt/ n desalojamiento, m
disloyal /dɪs'lɔɪəl/ a desleal, infiel, falso
disloyalty /dɪs'lɔɪəlti/ n deslealtad, infidelidad, falsedad, f
dismal /'dɪzməl/ a lóbrego, sombrío; lúgubre; funesto; triste
dismantle /dɪs'mæntl̩/ vt (a ship or fort) desmantelar; (a machine) desmontar; (a house, etc.) desamueblar
dismantling /dɪs'mæntl̩ɪŋ/ n desmantelamiento, m
dismay /dɪs'meɪ/ n desmayo, desaliento, m; consternación, f; espanto, terror, m. vt desanimar; consternar; espantar, horrorizar
dismember /dɪs'mɛmbər/ vt desmembrar
dismemberment /dɪs'mɛmbərmənt/ n desmembración, f
dismiss /dɪs'mɪs/ vt (from a job) despedir (de); (from an official position) destituir (de) Chile desahuciar (de); (bid good-bye to) despedirse de; (after military parade) dar la orden de romper filas; (thoughts) apartar de sí; ahuyentar; (discard) desechar, descartar; (omit) pasar por alto de; (disregard) rechazar; (a parliament, etc.) disolver; (a law case) absolver de la instancia. **to d. in a few words,** tratar someramente; hablar brevemente de
dismissal /dɪs'mɪsəl/ n despedida, f; (from an official post) destitución, f, Chile desahúcio m; apartamiento, m; (discard) descarte, m; (of a parliament, etc.) disolución, f
dismount /dɪs'maunt/ vi apearse, desmontar, echar pie a tierra; bajar. vt desmontar; (dismantle) desarmar
disobedience /ˌdɪsə'bidiəns/ n desobediencia, f
disobedient /ˌdɪsə'bidiənt/ a desobediente
disobey /ˌdɪsə'beɪ/ vt and vi desobedecer
disobliging /ˌdɪsə'blaɪdʒɪŋ/ a poco servicial
disobligingly /ˌdɪsə'blaɪdʒɪŋli/ adv descortésmente
disorder /dɪs'ɔrdər/ n desorden, m; confusión, f; (unrest) perturbación del orden público, f, motín, m; (disease) enfermedad, f; (mental) enajenación mental, f; trastorno, m. vt desordenar, desarreglar; (of health) perjudicar; (the mind) trastornar. **in d.,** en desorden, desarreglado; (helter-skelter) atropelladamente
disordered /dɪs'ɔrdərd/ a en desorden; irregular, desordenado; (of the mind and bodily organs) trastornado; (ill) enfermo; (confused) confuso
disorganization /dɪsˌɔrgənə'zeɪʃən/ n desorganización, f
disorganize /dɪs'ɔrgəˌnaɪz/ vt desorganizar

disorientate /dɪs'ɔriənˌteɪt/ vt desorientar
disorientation /dɪsˌɔriən'teɪʃən/ n desorientación, f
disown /dɪs'oun/ vt repudiar; negar; renegar de
disparage /dɪ'spærɪdʒ/ vt menospreciar; desacreditar; denigrar; (spoil) perjudicar; (scorn) despreciar
disparagement /dɪ'spærɪdʒmənt/ n menosprecio, m; denigración, f; desprecio, m
disparagingly /dɪ'spærɪdʒɪŋli/ adv con desprecio
disparity /dɪ'spærɪti/ n disparidad, f
dispassionate /dɪs'pæʃənɪt/ a desapasionado, sereno; imparcial; moderado
dispassionately /dɪs'pæʃənɪtli/ adv con imparcialidad; serenamente; con moderación
dispatch /dɪ'spætʃ/ n despacho, m; Com. envío, m; (message) mensaje, m; (communiqué) parte, f; (cable) telegrama, m; (promptness) prontitud, presteza, f; (execution) ejecución, muerte, f. vt despachar; enviar, remitir; (Fam. kill) despachar. **f. d.-rider,** mensajero motociclista, m **d.-case,** cartera, f. **d.-rider,** mensajero motociclista, m
dispel /dɪ'spɛl/ vt disipar
dispensable /dɪ'spɛnsəbəl/ a dispensable
dispensary /dɪ'spɛnsəri/ n dispensario, m
dispensation /ˌdɪspən'seɪʃən/ n dispensación, f; (of the Pope, etc.) dispensa, f; (decree) ley, f, decreto, m; (of justice) administración, f
dispense /dɪ'spɛns/ vt dispensar; (of justice) administrar. **to d. with,** pasar sin, prescindir de
dispenser /dɪ'spɛnsər/ n dispensador (-ra); administrador (-ra)
dispersal /dɪ'spɜrsəl/ n dispersión, f; disipación, f; esparcimiento, m
disperse /dɪ'spɜrs/ vt dispersar; disipar; esparcir. vi dispersarse disiparse
dispirited /dɪ'spɪrɪtɪd/ a abatido, desanimado, deprimido; lánguido
dispiritedly /dɪ'spɪrɪtɪdli/ adv desanimadamente, con desaliento; lánguidamente
displace /dɪs'pleɪs/ vt desalojar; cambiar de situación; (of liquids) desplazar; (oust) quitar el puesto (a), destituir
displacement /dɪs'pleɪsmənt/ n desalojamiento, m; cambio de situación, m; (of liquid) desplazamiento, m; (from a post) destitución, f
display /dɪ'spleɪ/ n exhibición, f; ostentación, f; presentación, f; (development) desarrollo, m; manifestación, f; (naval or military) maniobras, f pl; espectáculo, m; (pomp) pompa, f; fausto, m. vt exhibir; mostrar, manifestar; ostentar; (unfold) desplegar, extender; (develop) desarrollar. **d. cabinet,** vitrina, f
displease /dɪs'pliz/ vt desagradar; ofender; enojar
displeasing /dɪs'plizɪŋ/ a desagradable
displeasure /dɪs'plɛʒər/ n desagrado, m; disgusto, m; disfavor, m; indignación, f; enojo, m; (grief) angustia, f
disposable /dɪ'spouzəbəl/ a desechable
disposal /dɪ'spouzəl/ n desalojamiento, m; (transfer) cesión, enajenación, f; (sale) venta, f; (gift) donación, f. **I am at your d.,** Estoy a la disposición de Vd. **the d. of the troops,** la disposición de las tropas
dispose /dɪ'spouz/ vt disponer; inclinar. vi disponer. **to d. of,** disponer de; (finish) terminar, concluir; (get rid of) deshacerse de, botar; (give away) regalar; (sell) vender; (transfer) ceder; (of houses, etc.) traspasar; (kill) matar; (send) enviar; (use) servirse de; (refute) refutar. **"To be disposed of,"** (a business, etc.) «Se traspasa»
disposed /dɪ'spouzd/ a (in compounds) intencionado, dispuesto. **well-d.,** bien intencionado
disposition /ˌdɪspə'zɪʃən/ n disposición, f; (temperament) naturaleza, índole, f, temperamento, carácter, m; (humor) humor, m
dispossess /ˌdɪspə'zɛs/ vt desposeer (de); privar (de); desahuciar
dispossession /ˌdɪspə'zɛʃən/ n desposeimiento, m; desahucio, m
disproportion /ˌdɪsprə'pɔrʃən/ n desproporción, f
disproportionate /ˌdɪsprə'pɔrʃənɪt/ a desproporcionado
disproportionately /ˌdɪsprə'pɔrʃənɪtli/ adv desproporcionadamente
disprovable /dɪs'pruvəbəl/ a refutable

distraction

disprove /dɪs'pruv/ vt refutar
disputable /dɪ'spyutəbəl/ a disputable; discutible
disputant /dɪ'spyutənt/ n disputador (-ra)
dispute /dɪ'spyut/ n disputa, controversia, f; altercación, f; discusión, f; debate, m. vt and vi disputar. **beyond d.,** a incontestable. adv incontestablemente; fuera de duda
disqualification /dɪs,kwɒləfɪ'keiʃən/ n incapacidad, f; inhabilitación, f; impedimento, m; Sports. descalificación, f
disqualify /dɪs'kwɒlə,fai/ vt incapacitar; inhabilitar; Sports. descalificar
disquiet /dɪs'kwaiɪt/ n desasosiego, m; intranquilidad, inquietud, agitación, f. vt desasosegar, intranquilizar, perturbar, agitar
disquieting /dɪs'kwaiɪtɪŋ/ a intranquilizador, perturbador
disquisition /,dɪskwə'zɪʃən/ n disquisición, f
disregard /,dɪsrɪ'gɑrd/ n indiferencia, f; omisión, f; descuido, m; (scorn) desdén, m. vt no hacer caso de, desatender; omitir; desconocer; descuidar; despreciar
disregardful /,dɪsrɪ'gɑrdfəl/ a indiferente; negligente; desatento; desdeñoso
disrepair /,dɪsrɪ'pɛər/ n deterioro, mal estado, m
disreputable /dɪs'rɛpyətəbəl/ a de mala fama; (shameful) vergonzoso, vil; (compromising) comprometedor; de mal aspecto, horrible; ruin
disreputably /dɪs'rɛpyətəbli/ adv ruinmente; vergonzosamente
disrepute /,dɪsrɪ'pyut/ n disfavor, m; mala fama, f; deshonra, f; descrédito, m. **to come into d.,** caer en disfavor; perder su reputación
disrespect /,dɪsrɪ'spɛkt/ n falta de respeto, f; irreverencia, f
disrespectful /,dɪsrɪ'spɛktfəl/ a irrespetuoso, irreverente
disrobe /dɪs'roub/ vt desnudar. vi desnudarse
disrupt /dɪs'rʌpt/ vt quebrar; desorganizar; interrumpir; separar
disruption /dɪs'rʌpʃən/ n quebrantamiento, m; desorganización, f; interrupción, f; separación, f
dissatisfaction /,dɪssætɪs'fækʃən/ n descontento, desagrado, disgusto, m
dissatisfied /dɪs'sætɪs,faid/ a descontentado, malcontento, no satisfecho
dissect /dɪ'sɛkt/ vt disecar; Fig. analizar
dissecting table /dɪ'sɛktɪŋ/ n mesa de disección, f
dissection /dɪ'sɛkʃən/ n disección, f; análisis, m
dissector /dɪ'sɛktər/ n disector, m; Fig. analizador (-ra)
dissemble /dɪ'sɛmbəl/ vt and vi disimular, fingir
dissembler /dɪ'sɛmblər/ n hipócrita, mf; disimulador (-ra)
disseminate /dɪ'sɛmə,neit/ vt diseminar; propagar, sembrar
dissemination /dɪ,sɛmə'neiʃən/ n diseminación, f; propagación, f
dissension /dɪ'sɛnʃən/ n disensión, f; disidencia, f
dissent /dɪ'sɛnt/ n disentimiento, m, vi disentir, disidir
dissenter /dɪ'sɛntər/ n disidente, mf
dissertation /,dɪsər'teiʃən/ n disertación, f, tesis, f
disservice /dɪs'sɜrvɪs/ n deservicio, m
dissimilar /dɪ'sɪmələr/ a disímil, desemejante, diferente
dissimilarity /dɪ,sɪmə'lærɪti/ n desemejanza, diferencia, disparidad, f
dissimulation /dɪ,sɪmyə'leiʃən/ n disimulación, f, disimulo, m
dissipate /'dɪsə,peit/ vt disipar; dispersar; (waste) derrochar, desperdiciar. vi disiparse; dispersarse; (vanish) desvanecerse; (of persons) ser disoluto
dissipated /'dɪsə,peitid/ a (of persons) disipado, disoluto, vicioso
dissipation /,dɪsə'peiʃən/ n disipación, f; (waste) derroche, m; libertinaje, m
dissociate /dɪ'souʃi,eit/ vt disociar
dissociation /dɪ,sousi'eiʃən/ n disociación, f
dissoluble /dɪ'sɒlyəbəl/ a disoluble
dissolute /'dɪsə,lut/ a disoluto, vicioso, licencioso

dissoluteness /'dɪsə,lutnɪs/ n disolución, inmoralidad, f
dissolution /,dɪsə'luʃən/ n disolución, f; separación, f; muerte, f
dissolvable /dɪ'zɒlvəbəl/ a soluble
dissolve /dɪ'zɒlv/ vt disolver; derretir; (of parliament) prorrogar; (a marriage, etc.) anular; Fig. disipar. vi disolverse; derretirse; (vanish) desvanecerse, disiparse, evaporarse. **to d. into tears,** deshacerse en lágrimas
dissolvent /dɪ'zɒlvənt/ a disolutivo. n disolvente, m
dissonance /'dɪsənəns/ n disonancia, f; Fig. discordia, falta de armonía, f
dissonant /'dɪsənənt/ n disonancia, f, a disonante
dissuade /dɪ'sweid/ vt disuadir (de), apartar (de)
dissuasion /dɪ'sweiʒən/ n disuasión, f
distaff /'dɪstæf/ n rueca, f
distance /'dɪstəns/ n distancia, f; lontananza, f; lejanía, f; trecho, m; (of time) intervalo, m; (difference) diferencia, f. **at a d.,** a alguna distancia; lejos; (from afar) desde lejos. **from a d.,** desde (or de) lejos. **in the d.,** a lo lejos, en lontananza. **to keep at a d.,** mantener lejos; guardar las distancias (con). **to keep one's d.,** mantenerse a distancia; no intimarse, guardar las distancias. **What is the d. from London to Madrid?** ¿Qué distancia hay desde Londres a Madrid?
distant /'dɪstənt/ a distante; lejano; remoto; (of manner) frío, reservado; (slight) ligero; (of references, etc.) indirecto. **He is a d. relation,** Es un pariente lejano. **They are always rather d. with her,** La tratan siempre con bastante frialdad
distantly /'dɪstəntli/ adv a distancia; a lo lejos; desde lejos; remotamente; (of manner) con frialdad; (slightly) ligeramente
distaste /dɪs'teist/ n aversión, repugnancia, f; disgusto, hastío, m
distasteful /dɪs'teistfəl/ a desagradable
distemper /dɪs'tɛmpər/ n enfermedad, f; (in animals) moquillo, m; Fig. mal, m; (for walls) pintura al temple, f. vt desordenar, perturbar; (walls) pintar al temple
distend /dɪ'stɛnd/ vt ensanchar; dilatar; inflar, henchir; Med. distender. vi ensancharse, etc.
distension /dɪs'tɛnʃən/ n dilatación, f; inflación, f; henchimiento, m; Med. distensión, f
distill /dɪ'stɪl/ vt destilar; extraer. vi destilar; exudar
distillation /,dɪstɪ'eiʃən/ n destilación, f; extracción, f; exudación, f
distiller /dɪ'stɪlər/ n destilador (-ra)
distillery /dɪ'stɪləri/ n destilería, f, destilatorio, m
distinct /dɪ'stɪŋkt/ a distinto; diferente; claro; notable, evidente
distinction /dɪ'stɪŋkʃən/ n distinción, f
distinctive /dɪ'stɪŋktɪv/ a distintivo; característico
distinctive feature n Ling. rasgo pertinente, m
distinctly /dɪ'stɪŋktli/ adv claramente; distintamente
distinctness /dɪ'stɪŋktnɪs/ n claridad, f; distinción, f; carácter distintivo, m
distinguish /dɪ'stɪŋgwɪʃ/ vt distinguir; discernir; caracterizar; (honor) honrar. vi distinguir, diferenciar
distinguishable /dɪ'stɪŋgwɪʃəbəl/ a distinguible; perceptible, discernible
distinguished /dɪ'stɪŋgwɪʃt/ a distinguido; eminente; famoso, ilustre, egregio
distinguishing /dɪ'stɪŋgwɪʃɪŋ/ a distintivo
distort /dɪ'stɔrt/ vt (twist) torcer; deformar; falsear; pervertir
distorting mirror /dɪ'stɔrtɪŋ/ n (at fairs) espejo de la risa, m; espejo deformador, m
distortion /dɪ'stɔrʃən/ n deformación, f; torcimiento, m; contorsión, f; perversión, f; Radio. deformación, f
distract /dɪ'strækt/ vt distraer; interrumpir; perturbar; (turn aside) desviar, apartar; (madden) enloquecer; volver loco (a)
distracted /dɪ'stræktid/ a aturdido; demente, loco
distractedly /dɪ'stræktidli/ adv locamente; perdidamente
distraction /dɪ'strækʃən/ n distracción, f; (amusement) diversión, f, pasatiempo, m; (bewilderment)

confusión, *f*, aturdimiento, *m*; (madness) locura, *f*; frenesí, *m*. **to drive to d.**, trastornar, sacar de quicio.

distraught /dɪ'strɔt/ *a* aturdido; desesperado; enloquecido

distress /dɪ'strɛs/ *n* dolor, *m*, aflicción, *f*; pena, *f*; miseria, penuria, *f*; (exhaustion) fatiga, *f*, cansancio, *m*; (pain) dolor, *m*; (misfortune) desdicha, *f*; apuro, *m*; (danger) peligro, *m*; *Law*. embargo, *m*. *vt* afligir, dar pena (a), llenar de angustia; cansar, fatigar; (pain) doler

distressed /dɪ'strɛst/ *a* afligido; necesitado, pobre

distressing /dɪ'strɛsɪŋ/ *a* congojoso, doloroso, penoso

distributable /dɪ'strɪbyʊtəbəl/ *a* repartible

distribute /dɪ'strɪbyut/ *vt* (of justice, etc.) administrar; distribuir; repartir

distribution /ˌdɪstrə'byuʃən/ *n* (of justice) administración, *f*; distribución, *f*; reparto, *m*

distributive /dɪ'strɪbyətɪv/ *a* distributivo

distributor /dɪ'strɪbyətər/ *n* distribuidor (-ra); repartidor (-ra). **d. of false money,** expendedor (-ra) de moneda falsa

district /'dɪstrɪkt/ *n* distrito, *m*; comarca, *f*; (of a town) barrio, *m*; (judicial) partido judicial, *m*, *Lat. Am*. comuna *f*; jurisdicción, *f*; región, zona, *f*

distrust /dɪs'trʌst/ *n* desconfianza, *f*; recelo, *m*, sospecha, *f*. *vt* desconfiar de, sospechar

distrustful /dɪs'trʌstfəl/ *a* desconfiado, receloso, suspicaz

distrustfully /dɪs'trʌstfəli/ *adv* desconfiadamente, con recelo

disturb /dɪ'stɜrb/ *vt* perturbar; interrumpir; incomodar; (make anxious) inquietar; (alter) cambiar; (disarrange) desordenar, desarreglar. **to d. the peace,** perturbar el orden público

disturbance /dɪ'stɜrbəns/ *n* perturbación, *f*; disturbio, *m*, conmoción, *f*; incomodidad, *f*; agitación, *f*; confusión, *f*; tumulto, *m*; desorden, *m*; *Radio*. parásitos, *m pl*

disturber /dɪ'stɜrbər/ *n* perturbador (-ra)

disturbing /dɪ'stɜrbɪŋ/ *a* perturbador; inquietador; conmovedor, impresionante, emocionante

disunion /dɪs'yunyən/ *n* desunión, *f*; discordia, *f*

disunite /ˌdɪsyu'nait/ *vt* desunir; separar, dividir. *vi* separarse

disuse /*n* dɪs'yus; *v* -'yuz/ *n* desuso, *m*. *vt* desusar; desacostumbrar. **to fall into d.,** caer en desuso

ditch /dɪtʃ/ *n* zanja, *f*; (for defense, etc.) foso, *m*; (irrigation) acequia, *f*. *vt* zanjar; abarrancar. **to die in the last d.,** morir en la brecha

ditto /'dɪtou/ *adv* ídem; también

ditty /'dɪti/ *n* canción, cantinela, *f*

diuretic /ˌdaiə'rɛtɪk/ *a* diurético

divan /dɪ'væn/ *n* diván, *m*

dive /daiv/ *n* buceo, *m*; *Aer*. picada, *f*; *Inf*. (bar) antro, *m*. *vi* bucear; sumergirse (en); *Aer*. volar en picado; penetrar (en); (into a book) enfrascarse in. **to d. out,** salir precipitadamente. **to d.-bomb,** bombardear en picado, *m*. **d.-bomber,** avión en picado, *m*. **d.-bombing,** bombardeo en picado, *m*

diver /'daivər/ *n* buceador, *m*; buzo, *m*; (bird) somorgujo, *m*

diverge /dɪ'vɜrdʒ/ *vi* divergir

divergence /dɪ'vɜrdʒəns/ *n* divergencia, *f*

divergent /dɪ'vɜrdʒənt/ *a* divergente

diverse /dɪ'vɜrs/ *a* diverso, vario

diversify /dɪ'vɜrsəˌfai/ *vt* diversificar

diversion /dɪ'vɜrʒən/ *n* diversión, *f*; entretenimiento, *m*, recreación, *f*; pasatiempo, *m*; placer, *m*; *Mil*. diversión, *f*

diversity /dɪ'vɜrsɪti/ *n* diversidad, variedad, *f*

divert /dɪ'vɜrt/ *vt* desviar; (amuse) divertir, entretener

divide /dɪ'vaid/ *vt* dividir; partir; separar; (cut) cortar; (share) repartir, distribuir; (hair) hacer la raya (del pelo); (of voting) provocar una votación. *vi* dividirse; separarse; (of roads, etc.) bifurcarse; (of voting) votar. **divided skirt,** *n* falda pantalón, *f*

dividend /'dɪvɪˌdɛnd/ *n* dividendo, *m*. **d. warrant,** cupón de dividendo, *m*

dividers /dɪ'vaidərz/ *n pl* compás de puntas, *m*

dividing /dɪ'vaidɪŋ/ *a* divisorio, divisor

divination /ˌdɪvə'neiʃən/ *n* adivinación, *f*

divine /dɪ'vain/ *a* divino; sublime; *Inf*. estupendo. *n* teólogo, *m*. *vt* (foretell) vaticinar, pronosticar; presentir; (guess) adivinar

diving /'daivɪŋ/ *n* buceo, *m*; *Aer*. picado, *m*. **d.-bell,** campana de bucear, *f*. **d.-board,** (low) trampolín, *m*; (high) palanca, *f*. **d.-suit,** escafandra, *f*. **scuba d.,** buceo, *m*

divining rod /dɪ'vainɪŋ/ *n* vara divinatoria, *f*

divinity /dɪ'vɪnɪti/ *n* divinidad, *f*; teología, *f*

divisibility /dɪˌvɪzə'bɪlɪti/ *n* divisibilidad, *f*

divisible /dɪ'vɪzəbəl/ *a* divisible

division /dɪ'vɪʒən/ *n* división, *f*; separación, *f*; (distribution) repartimiento, *m*; (*Mil. Math.*) división, *f*; sección, *f*; grupo, *m*; (voting) votación, *f*; (discord) discordia, desunión, *f*. **without a d.,** por unanimidad, sin votar

divisor /dɪ'vaizər/ *n Math*. divisor, *m*

divorce /dɪ'vɔrs/ *n* divorcio, *m*. *vt* divorciarse de; *Fig*. divorciar, separar. **to file a petition of d.,** poner una petición de divorcio

divorcee /dɪvɔr'sei/ *n* (wife) divorciada, *f*; (husband) divorciado, *m*

divulge /dɪ'vʌldʒ/ *vt* divulgar, revelar

dizzily /'dɪzəli/ *adv* vertiginosamente

dizziness /'dɪzɪnɪs/ *n* vértigo, *m*; mareo, *m*; (bewilderment) aturdimiento, *m*, confusión, *f*

dizzy /'dɪzi/ *a* vertiginoso; mareado; confuso, perplejo, aturdido

DNA *n* DNA, *m*

do /du/ *vt* hacer; ejecutar; (one's duty, etc.) cumplir con; concluir; (cause) causar; (homage) rendir; (commit) cometer; (arrange) arreglar; (cook) cocer, guisar; (roast) asar; (*Fam*. cheat) engañar; (suit) convenir; (suffice) bastar; (act) hacer el papel (de); (*Fam*. treat) tratar (bien o mal); (learn) aprender; (exhaust) agotar; (walk) andar; (travel, journey) recorrer; (translate) traducir; (prepare) preparar. *vi* hacer; (behave) conducirse; (of health) estar (bien o mal); (act) obrar; (get on) ir; (be suitable, suit) convenir; (suffice) bastar; (of plants) florecer; (cook) cocerse; (last) durar. **Don't!** ¡No lo hagas! ¡Quieto! ¡Calla! **How do you do?** ¿Cómo está Vd.? ¡Buenos días! **It will do you good,** Te conviene; Te hará bien; Te sentará bien. **It will do you no harm,** No te perjudicará; No te hará daño. **I could do with one,** Me gustaría (tener) uno; (of drinks) Me bebería uno con mucho gusto. **That is not done (customary),** Eso no se hace. **That will do,** Eso basta; Se puede advertir de eso; Está bien así; (leave it alone) ¡Déjate de eso! (be quiet!) ¡No digas más! ¡Cállate! **That won't do,** Eso no es bastante; Eso no sirve; Eso no se hace así. **That will never do,** Eso no servirá; Eso no puede ser. **This will do,** (when buying an article) Me quedaré con éste; Me serviré de esto; Esto basta; Esto será suficiente; (is all right) Está bien así. **Thy will be done!** ¡Hágase tu voluntad! **to be doing,** estar haciendo; estar ocupado en (o con) hacer; (of food) estar cocinando. **to be done for,** estar perdido; estar muerto. **to do better,** hacer mejor (que); (mend one's ways) enmendarse, corregirse; (improve) mejorar, hacer progresos; (in health) encontrarse mejor. **to do business with** *Lat*. amanchantarse con. **to do nothing,** no hacer nada. **to do reverence,** rendir homenaje; inclinarse. **to do violence to,** *Fig*. hacer fuerza a. **to do well,** hacer bien; obrar bien; (be successful) tener éxito; hacer buena impresión; (prosperous) tener una buena posición. **to do wonders,** hacer maravillas. **to have done with,** renunciar (a); dejar de usar; dejar de hacer, cesar; concluir, terminar; no tener más que ver con; (forsake) abandonar; (a person) romper con. **to have nothing to do,** no tener nada que hacer. **to have nothing to do with,** no tener nada que ver con; (of people) no tratar con; (end a friendship) romper su amistad con, dejar de ver. **well done,** bien hecho; (of food) bien guisado; (of meat) bien asado. **What is to be done?** ¿Qué hay que hacer? ¿Qué se puede hacer? **What is there to do?** ¿Qué pasa? ¿Qué hay? **When he had done speaking,** Cuando hubo terminado de hablar. **to do again,** hacer de nuevo, volver a hacer, rehacer; repetir. **He**

doomsday

will not do it again, No lo hará más. **to do away with,** quitar; eliminar; suprimir; hacer desaparecer; poner fin a; hacer cesar; destruir; matar. **to do by,** tratar (a), portarse con. **to do for,** arruinar; matar; (suffice) bastar para; ser a propósito para, servir para; (look after) cuidar; (as a housekeeper) dirigir la casa para. **to do out of,** quitar; privar de; (steal) robar.

to do up, (tie) atar; (fold) enrollar, plegar; envolver; (parcel) empaquetar; (arrange) arreglar; decorar; poner en orden; poner como nuevo; (iron) planchar; (launder) lavar y planchar; (tire) fatigar. **to do with,** (of people) tratar; (of things) tener que ver con; (put up with) poder con; poder sufrir. **to do without,** prescindir de; pasarse sin

do /duə/ as an auxiliary verb is not translated in Spanish, e.g. *I do believe,* creo. *Do not do that,* no hagas eso. *I did not know,* no sabía When it is used for emphasis, *do* is translated by *sí, ciertamente, claro* and similar words, e.g.: *She did not know, but he did,* Ella no lo sabía pero él sí *You do paint well,* Pintas muy bien por cierto *Do come this time,* No dejes de venir esta vez

docile /'dɒsəl/ *a* dócil

dock /dɒk/ *n* dique, *m*, dársena, *f*; (wharf) muelle, *m*; (in a law court) banquillo de los acusados, *m*; *Bot.* romaza, *f. vt* (a tail) descolar; cortar, cercenar; reducir; (money) descontar; (a ship) poner en dique. *vi* entrar en dársena, entrar en dique, entrar en muelle. **dry-d.,** dique seco, *m.* **floating-d.,** dique flotante, *m.* **d.-dues,** muellaje, *m.* **d. rat,** (thief) raquero, *m*

docker /'dɒkər/ *n* estibador, descargador del muelle, *m*

docket /'dɒkɪt/ *n* (bundle) legajo, *m*; extracto, *m*; minuta, *f*; (label) etiqueta, *f*, marbete, *m*

dockyard /'dɒk,yɑrd/ *n* arsenal, astillero, *m*

doctor /'dɒktər/ *n* doctor (-ra); (medical practitioner) médico (-ca), asistir; (repair) reparar, componer; adulterar; mezclar drogas con; falsificar. *vi* ejercer la medicina. **family d.,** médico de cabecera, *m.* **to graduate as a d.,** doctorarse. **d. of divinity, laws, medicine,** doctor (-ra) en teología, en derecho, en medicina, *m*

doctoral /'dɒktərəl/ *a* doctoral

doctorate /'dɒktərɪt/ *n* doctorado, *m*

doctrinaire /'dɒktrə'nɛər/ *a* and *n* doctrinario (-ia)

doctrinal /'dɒktrənl/ *a* doctrinal

doctrine /'dɒktrɪn/ *n* doctrina, *f*

document /*n* 'dɒkyəmənt/ *v* -,mɛnt/ *n* documento, *m. vt* documentar; probar con documentos. **d.-case,** carpeta, *f*

documentary /,dɒkyə'mɛntəri/ *a* documental; escrito, auténtico. **d. film,** película documental, *f*

documentation /,dɒkyəmɛn'teiʃən/ *n* documentación, *f*

Dodecanese, the /dou,dɛkə'nis, -'niz, ,doudɛkə-/ el Dodecaneso, *m*

dodge /dɒdʒ/ *n* esguince, regate, *m*; evasiva, *f*; (trick) estratagema, *m*, maniobra, *f*; artefacto, *m. vt* esquivar, evadir

doe /dou/ *n* gama, *f.* **doe rabbit,** coneja, *f*

doer /'duər/ *n* hacedor (-ra); autor (-ra)

doeskin /'dou,skɪn/ *n* ante, *m*, piel de gama, *f*

doff /dɒf/ *vt* quitar; (of hats, etc.) quitarse; desnudarse de

dog /dɒg/ *n* perro, *m*; (male) macho, *m*; (andiron) morillo, *m*; *Astron.* Can Mayor (or Menor), Sirio, *m. vt* perseguir; seguir los pasos de; espiar. **You can't deceive an old dog,** A perro viejo no hay tus tus. **to go to the dogs,** ir a las carreras de galgos; *Fig.* ir cuesta abajo. **mongrel dog,** perro mestizo, *m.* **thoroughbred dog,** perro de raza pura, *m.* **dog-collar,** collar de perro, *m*; *Eccl.* alzacuello, *m.* **dog-days,** días caniculares, *m pl*, canícula, *f.* **dog-eared** (of books) con las puntas de las hojas dobladas. **dog-fight,** lucha de perros, *f*; combate aéreo, *m.* **dog-fish,** lija, *f*, cazón, *m.* **dog in the manger,** el perro del hortelano. **dog-kennel,** perrera, *f.* **dog-latin,** bajo latín, *m.* **dog license,** matrícula de perros, *f.* **dog-racing,** carrera de galgos, *f.* **dog-rose,** escaramujo, *m.* **dog show,** exposición canina, *f.* **dog-tooth,** *Archit.* diente de perro, *m.* **dog-vane,** *Naut.* cataviento, *m*

doge /doudʒ/ *n* dux, *m*

dogged /'dɒgɪd/ *a* persistente, tenaz, pertinaz, obstinado

doggedly /'dɒgɪdli/ *adv* tenazmente

doggedness /'dɒgɪdnɪs/ *n* pertinacia, tenacidad, terquedad, persistencia, *f*

doggerel /'dɒgərəl/ *n* malos versos, *m pl*; aleluyas, coplas de ciego, *f pl*, *a* malo, irregular

dogma /'dɒgmə/ *n* dogma, *m*

dogmatic /dɒg'mætɪk/ *a* dogmático

dogmatize /'dɒgmə,taiz/ *vt* and *vi* dogmatizar; mostrarse dogmático

doh /dou/ *n Mus.* do, *m*

doily /'dɔili/ *n* carpeta, *f*, pañito de adorno, *m*

doings /'duɪŋz/ *n pl* acciones, *f pl*; (deeds) hechos, *m pl*; (behavior) conducta, *f*; (happenings) acontecimientos, *m pl*; (works) obras, *f pl*; (things) cosas, *f pl*

doldrums /'douldrəmz/ *n pl* calmas ecuatoriales, *f pl*

dole /doul/ *n* limosna, *f*; porción, *f.* **to d. out,** repartir; distribuir en porciones pequeñas; racionar; dar contra la voluntad de uno.

doleful /'doulfəl/ *a* triste, lúgubre, melancólico; doloroso

dolefulness /'doulfəlnɪs/ *n* tristeza, melancolía, *f*; dolor, *m*

doll /dɒl/ *n* muñeca, *f*

dollar /'dɒlər/ *n* dólar, *m*

dolly /'dɒli/ *n* muñeca, *f*; (trolley) carrito, (for clothes) moza, *f*

dolphin /'dɒlfɪn/ *n* delfín, *m*

dolt /doult/ *n* cabeza de alcornoque, *mf*, zamacuco, *m*

domain /dou'mein/ *n* territorio, *m*; heredad, posesión, propiedad, *f*; (empire) dominio, *m*

dome /doum/ *n* cúpula, *f*; bóveda, *f*; (palace) palacio, *m*

domestic /də'mɛstɪk/ *a* doméstico; familiar; (home-loving) casero, (of animals) doméstico; (national) interior, nacional. *n* doméstico, sirviente, *m*; criada, *f.* **d. economy,** economía doméstica, *f*

domesticate /də'mɛstɪ,keit/ *vt* domesticar

domesticated /də'mɛstɪ,keitɪd/ *a* (of animals) domesticado; (of persons) casero

domestication /də,mɛstɪ'keiʃən/ *n* domesticación, *f*

domesticity /,doumɛ'stɪstɪ/ *n* domesticidad, *f*

domicile /'dɒmə,sail/ *n* domicilio, *m*, *vt* domiciliar

domiciliary /,dɒmə'sɪli,ɛri/ *a* domiciliario

dominant /'dɒmənənt/ *a* dominante; imperante. *n Mus.* dominante, *f.* **to be d.,** prevalecer

dominate /'dɒmə,neit/ *vt* and *vi* dominar

domination /,dɒmə'neiʃən/ *n* dominación, *f*

domineer /,dɒmə'nɪər/ *vi* dominar, tiranizar. **to d. over,** mandar en

domineering /,dɒmə'nɪərɪŋ/ *a* dominante, mandón, tiránico. **d. person,** *Lat. Am.* mandarín *m*

Dominican /də'mɪnɪkən/ *a* dominicano. *n* dominicano, *m*

Dominican Republic, the la República Dominicana, *f*

dominion /də'mɪnyən/ *n* dominio, *m*; autoridad, soberanía, *f*; imperio, *m*; *pl* **dominions,** *Eccl.* dominaciones, *f pl*

Dominions, the /də'mɪnyənz/ los Dominios, *m*

domino /'dɒmə,nou/ *n* dominó, *m.* **to go d.,** nacer domino

don /dɒn/ *n* (Spanish and Italian title) don, *m*; señor, *m. vt* ponerse, vestirse

donation /dou'neiʃən/ *n* donación, dádiva, *f*; contribución, *f*

done /dʌn/ *a* and *past part* hecho; (of food) cocido; (roasted) asado; (tired) rendido; (*Fam.* deceived) engañado. **Well d.!** ¡Bien hecho! **d. for,** arruinado; muerto; perdido; vencido; (spoilt) estropeado

donkey /'dɒŋki/ *n* borrico (-ca), burro (-rra). **d.-engine,** máquina auxiliar, *f*

donor /'dounər/ *n* donador (-ra); dador (-ra)

doodle /'dudl/ *v* borrajear, garabatear, hacer garabatos

doom /dum/ *n* condena, *f*; (fate) suerte, *f*; (judgment) destino, *m*; ruina, *f*; juicio, *m. vt* sentenciar; condenar

doomsday /'dumz,dei/ *n* día del juicio final, *m*

door /dɔr/ *n* puerta, *f*; entrada, *f*. **front d.**, puerta de entrada, *f*. **next d.**, la casa vecina; la puerta de al lado, la puerta vecina. **next d. neighbor**, vecino (-na) de al lado. **out of doors**, al aire libre; en la calle. **to knock at the d.**, llamar a la puerta. **to slam the d.** in **a person's face**, dar con la puerta en las narices de alguien. **d.-bell**, timbre (non-electric, campanilla, *f*) de llamada, *m*. **d.-jamb**, quicial, *m*. **d. keeper**, portero, *m*. **d.-knob**, tirador, *m*. **d.-knocker**, manija, *f*; picaporte, *m*, aldaba, *f*. **d.-plate**, placa, *f*. **d.-shutter**, cierre metálico, *m*. **d.-step**, peldaño de la puerta, *m*; umbral, *m*. **d.-way**, portal, *m*
dope /doup/ *n* drogas, *f pl*, narcóticos, *m pl*; (news) información, *f*. **d. fiend**, morfinómano (-na)
dope-pusher /'doup ˌpʊʃər/ *n* narcotraficante, *mf*
Doric /'dɔrɪk/ *a* dórico
dormant /'dɔrmənt/ *a* durmiente; latente; secreto; inactivo. **to go d.**, dormirse
dormer window /'dɔrmər/ *n* lumbrera, *f*
dormitory /'dɔrmɪˌtɔri/ *n* dormitorio, *m*
dormouse /'dɔrˌmaus/ *n* lirón, *m*
dorsal /'dɔrsəl/ *a* dorsal
dory /'dɔri/ *n* (fish) dorado, *m*
dose, dosage /dous; 'dousɪdʒ/ *n*; dosis, *f*
dossier /'dɒsiˌei/ *n* documentación, *f*
dot /dɒt/ *n* punto, *m*; *pl* **dots**, *Gram.* puntos suspensivos, *m pl*. *vt* poner punto (a una letra); (scatter) salpicar. **on the dot**, (of time) en punto. **to dot one's i's**, poner los puntos sobre las íes
dotage /'doutɪdʒ/ *n* senectud, chochera, *f*
dotard /'doutərd/ *n* viejo chocho, *m*; vieja chocha, *f*; *Inf.* carcamal, *m*
dote /dout/ *vi* chochear. **to d. on**, adorar en, idolatrar
doting /'doutɪŋ/ *a* chocho
double /'dʌbəl/ *a* and *adv* doble; dos veces; (in a pair) en par; en dos; doblemente; (deceitful) doble, de dos caras, falso; ambiguo. *n* doble, *m*; duplicado, *m*; *Theat.* contrafigura, *f*; *pl* **doubles**, (tennis) dobles, *m pl*, juego doble, *m*. *vt* doblar; duplicar; (fold) doblegar; (the fist) cerrar (el puño); (*Theat.* and *Naut.*) doblar. *vi* doblarse; (dodge) volverse atrás, hacer un rodeo, dar una vuelta; esquivarse. **to d. up**, *vt* envolver; arrollar; (a person) doblar. *vi* doblegarse; arrollarse; (collapse) desplomarse. **on the d.,** corriendo. **He was doubled up with pain,** El dolor le hacía retorcerse. **mixed doubles**, parejas mixtas, *f pl*; dobles mixtos, *m pl*. **double two**, (telephone) dos dos. **with a d. meaning**, con segunda intención. **d.-barrelled**, de dos cañones. **d.-bass**, contrabajo, *m*. **d. bed**, cama de matrimonio, *f*. **d.-bedded**, con cama de matrimonio; con dos camas. **d.-breasted**, cruzado. **d.-chin**, papada, *f*. **d.-dealing**, duplicidad, *f*. **d.-edged**, de doble filo. **d.-entry**, *Com.* partida doble, *f*. **d.-faced**, de dos caras. **d.-jointed**, con articulaciones dobles
double room *Mexico* cuarto doble, *m*
double-spaced /'dʌbəl 'speist/ *a* a doble espacio, a dos espacios
doublet /'dʌblɪt/ *n* (garment) jubón, justillo, *m*; pareja, *f*, par, *m*
doubling /'dʌblɪŋ/ *n* doblamiento, *m*; doblez, plegadura, *f*; duplicación, *f*; (dodging) evasiva, *f*, esguince, *m*
doubloon /dʌ'blun/ *n* doblón, *m*
doubly /'dʌbli/ *adv* doblemente; con duplicidad
doubt /daut/ *n* duda, *f*; incertidumbre, *f*; sospecha, *f*. *vt* and *vi* dudar; sospechar; titubear, hesitar; temer. **beyond all d.,** fuera de duda. **no d.,** sin duda. **There is no d. that,** No hay duda de que, No cabe duda de que. **When in d.,...,** En caso de duda...
doubter /'dautər/ *n* incrédulo (-la)
doubtful /'dautfəl/ *a* dudoso; incierto; perplejo; ambiguo; (of places) sospechoso
doubtfully /'dautfəli/ *adv* dudosamente; inciertamente; irresolutamente; ambiguamente
doubtfulness /'dautfəlnɪs/ *n* duda, incertidumbre, *f*; ambigüedad, *f*
doubtless /'dautlɪs/ *adv* sin duda, por supuesto; probablemente
dough /dou/ *n* pasta, masa, *f*; (money) lana, *f*

dour /dʊr/ *a* huraño, adusto, austero
dourly /'dʊrli/ *adv* severamente
douse /daus/ *vt* zambullir; (a sail) recoger; *Inf.* apagar
dove /duv/ *n* paloma, *f*. **d.-cote**, palomar, *m*
dovetail /'dʌvˌteil/ *n* cola de milano, *f*, *vt* machihembrar, empalmar; *Fig.* encajar
dowager /'dauədʒər/ *n* viuda, *f*; matrona, *f*. **d. countess**, condesa viuda, *f*
dowager empress *n* emperatriz viuda, *f*
dowdiness /'daudinɪs/ *n* desaliño, desaseo, *m*; falta de elegancia, *f*
dowdy /'daudi/ *a* desaliñado, desaseado; poco elegante. *n* mujer poco elegante, *f*
dowel /'dauəl/ *n* espiga, clavija, *f*, zoquete, *m*, *vt* enclavijar
down /daun/ *n* (of a bird) plumón, *m*; (on a peach, etc.) pelusilla, *f*; (hair) vello, *m*; (before the beard) bozo, *m*; (of a thistle, etc.) vilano, *m*. **ups and downs**, vicisitudes, *f pl*
down /daun/ *a* pendiente; (of trains, etc.) descendente. *adv* abajo; hacia abajo; (lowered) bajado; (of the eyes) bajos; (on the ground) en tierra, por tierra; (stretched out) tendido a lo largo; (depressed) triste, abatido; (ill) enfermo; (fallen) caído; (of the wind) cesado; (closed) cerrado; (exhausted) agotado; *Com.* al contado; (of temperature) más bajo. *prep* abajo de; abajo; en la dirección de; (along) a lo largo de; por. **"Down"** (on elevators) «Para bajar». *interj* ¡Abajo!; ¡A tierra! **He went d. the hill,** Bajaba la colina. **He is d. now,** Ha bajado ahora; Está abajo ahora; Está derribado ahora. **The sun has gone d.,** Se ha puesto el sol. **His stock has gone d.,** *Fig. Inf.* Ha caído en disfavor. **Prices have come d.,** Los precios han bajado. **Their numbers have gone d.,** Sus números han disminuido. **to be d. and out,** estar completamente arruinado, ser pobre de solemnidad. **to boil d.,** reducir hirviendo. **to come d. in the world,** venir a menos. **while I was going d. the river,** mientras iba río abajo, mientras bajaba al río. **d. below,** allá abajo; abajo, en el piso de abajo. **D. on your knees!** ¡De rodillas! **to be d. spout,** tubo de bajada, *m*. **D. with!** ¡Abajo! ¡Muera! **d.-stream,** agua abajo. **d. train,** tren descendente, *m*
down /daun/ *vt* derribar; vencer. **to d. tools,** declararse en huelga
downcast /'daunˌkæst/ *a* bajo; cabizbajo, deprimido, abatido
downfall /'daunˌfɔl/ *n* caída, *f*; derrumbamiento, *m*; (failure) fracaso, *m*; (*Fig.* ruin) decadencia, ruina, *f*
downhearted /'daunˈhɑrtɪd/ *a* descorazonado, alicaído, desalentado
downhill /*adv* 'daun'hɪl; *a* 'daunˌhɪl/ *adv* cuesta abajo, hacia abajo. *a* en declive, inclinado. **to go d.,** ir cuesta abajo
downiness /'dauninɪs/ *n* vellosidad, *f*
download /'daunˌloud/ *vt* (computer) bajar, descargar
down payment *Mexico* enganche, *m*
downpour /'daunˌpɔr/ *n* chubasco (Mexico), aguacero, chaparrón, *m*
downright /'daunˌrait/ *a* franco, sincero; categórico, terminante; absoluto. *adv* muy; completamente
downstairs /'daun'stɛrz/ *adv* escalera abajo; en el piso de abajo; en el piso bajo; abajo. *a* del piso de abajo. *n* planta baja, *f*; piso de abajo, *m*. **to go d.,** bajar la escalera; ir al piso de abajo
downtrodden /'daunˌtrɒdn̩/ *a* oprimido, esclavizado
downward /'daunwərd/ *a* descendente; inclinado. *adv* hacia abajo
downy /'dauni/ *a* velloso; (*Fam.* of persons) con más conchas que un galápago
dowry /'dauri/ *n* dote, *mf*. **to give as d.,** dotar
dowse /dauz/ *vt*. See **douse**
doze /douz/ *vi* dormitar. *n* sueño ligero, *m*
dozen /'dʌzən/ *n* docena, *f*
drab /dræb/ *a* pardo, parduzco, grisáceo; *Fig.* gris, monótono. *n* (slut) pazpuerca, *f*; (prostitute) ramera, *f*
drachma /'drækmə/ *n* dracma, *f*
draft /dræft/ *n* (detachment) destacamento, *m*; *Com.* giro, *m*, letra de cambio, *f*; (for the army, navy) con-

scripción, leva, f; (outline) bosquejo, m; proyecto, m; borrador, m; (act of drawing) tiro, m; (of liquid) trago, m; (glass) vaso, m; (of a ship) calando, m; (of air) corriente de aire, f, Lat. Am. chiflón m; (party) destacamento, m. vt (detach) destacar; (recruit) reclutar; (outline) bosquejar, delinear; (draw up) redactar; proyectar. **on d.**, (of beer, etc.) por vaso. **d. horse,** caballo de tiro, m. **d. screen,** cancel, m

draft card n cartilla (Mexico), libreta de enrolamiento (Argentina), f

draft dodger /'dɒdʒər/ n emboscado, prófugo, m

drafting /'dræftɪŋ/ n (Mil. Nav.) reclutamiento, m; (of a bill, etc.) redacción, f; (wording) términos, m pl

draftsman /'dræftsmən/ n dibujante, m; delineante, m; redactor, m

draftsmanship /'dræftsmən,ʃɪp/ n arte del dibujo lineal, mf; redacción (de un proyecto de ley), f

drafty /'dræfti/ a que tiene corriente de aire; expuesto a los vientos. **This room is d.,** Hay corriente de aire en esta habitación

drag /dræg/ n (for dredging) draga, f; (harrow) rastrillo, m; (break) freno, m; (obstacle) estorbo, m; Aer. sonda, f. vt arrastrar; (fishing nets) rastrear; (harrow) rastrillar. vi (of the anchor) garrar; arrastrarse por el suelo; (of time) pasar lentamente; ir más despacio (que); (of interest) decaer, disminuir. **d.-hook,** garfio, m. **d.-net,** brancada, f

dragging /'drægɪŋ/ n arrastre, m; (of lakes, etc.) rastreo, m, a rastrero; cansado

draggled /'drægəld/ a mojado y sucio

dragon /'drægən/ n dragón, m. **d.-fly,** libélula, f, caballito de diablo, m

dragoon /drə'gun/ n Mil. dragón, m, vt someter a una disciplina rigurosa; obligar a la fuerza (a)

drain /drein/ n desaguadero, m; (sewer) cloaca, alcantarilla, f; sumidero, m; Agr. acequia, f. vt desaguar; sanear; (lakes, etc.) desangrar; secar; (bail) achicar; (empty and drink) vaciar; (swallow) tragar; (Fig. of sorrow, etc.) apurar; (despoil) despojar; (deprive) privar (de); (impoverish) empobrecer; (exhaust) agotar. vi desaguarse; vaciarse; (with off) escurrirse. **to be well drained,** tener buen drenaje. **to d. the sump,** vaciar la culata. **to d. away,** vaciar. **d.-pipe,** tubo de desagüe, m

drainage /'dreɪnɪdʒ/ n (of land) drenaje, m; desagüe, m; (of wounds) drenaje, m; (sewage) aguas del alcantarillado, f pl. **main d.,** drenaje municipal, m

draining /'dreɪnɪŋ/ a de desagüe; de drenaje. **d.-board,** escurridor, m

drake /dreik/ n ánade macho, m

drama /'drɑmə, 'dræmə/ n drama, m

dramatic /drə'mætɪk/ a dramático

dramatically /drə'mætɪkli/ adv dramáticamente

dramatis personae /'dræmətɪs pər'souni/ n pl personajes, m pl

dramatist /'dræmətɪst/ n dramaturgo, m

dramatization /,dræmətə'zeɪʃən, ,drɑmə-/ n versión escénica, f; descripción dramática, f; (of emotions) dramatización, f

dramatize /'dræmə,taiz, 'drɑmə-/ vt dramatizar

drape /dreip/ vt colgar, cubrir; vestir

draper /'dreipər/ n pañero (-ra)

drapery /'dreipəri/ n colgaduras, f pl; ropaje, m, ropas, f pl; pañería, f

drastic /'dræstɪk/ a drástico; enérgico, fuerte; **a drastic measure,** una medida avanzada, f

draw /drɔ/ vt tirar; arrastrar; traer; (pluck) arrancar; (attract) atraer; (extract) extraer; sacar; hacer salir; (unsheath) desenvainar; (a bow-string) tender; (cards, dominoes) tomar, robar; (threads) deshilar; (disembowel) destripar; (a check, etc.) girar, librar; (of a ship) calar; (of lines) hacer (rayas); (curtains) correr; (to draw curtains back) descorrer; (salt, money) cobrar, percibir; (obtain) obtener; (persuade) persuadir, inducir; (inhale) respirar; (a sigh) dar; (win) ganar; (a conclusion) deducir, inferir; (a distinction) hacer formular; Sports. empatar; (a number, etc.) sortear; (suck) chupar; (tighten) estirar; (lengthen) alargar; (comfort, etc.) tomar; (inspiration) inspirarse en; (obtain money) procurarse (recursos); (withdraw funds) retirar; (write) escribir; (draw) di-

bujar; (trace) trazar; (provoke) provocar. **to be drawn,** (of tickets in a lottery and cards) salir. **to d. lots,** echar suertes. **to d. water,** sacar agua. **to d. along,** arrastrar; conducir. **to d. aside,** tomar a un lado, tomar aparte; quitar de en medio, poner a un lado; (curtains) descorrer. **to d. away,** (remove) quitar; (a person) llevarse (a); apartar. **to d. back,** recular; hacer retirarse; hacer volverse atrás; (curtains) descorrer. **to d. down,** hacer bajar; tirar a lo largo de (or por); bajar; (attract) atraer. **to d. forth,** hacer salir; hacer avanzar; tirar hacia adelante; conducir; (develop) desarrollar; sacar; hacer aparecer; (comment, etc.) suscitar. **to d. in,** tirar hacia adentro; sacar; acercar; atraer. **to d. off,** sacar; retirar; quitar; (water from pipes, etc.) vaciar; Print. tirar; (turn aside) desviar. **to d. out,** sacar fuera; hacer salir; tirar (de); (extract) extraer; (trace) trazar; (a person) hacer hablar. **to d. over,** poner encima de; arrastrar por; hacer acercarse (a), tirar hacia; atraer; persuadir. **to d. prestige (from),** cobrar prestigio (de). **to d. round,** poner alrededor de. **to d. together,** reunir; acercar. **to d. up,** tirar hacia arriba; subir; sacar; extraer; (raise) levantar, alzar; (bring) traer; (bring near) acercar; (order) ordenar; Mil. formar; (a document) redactar; formular. **to d. oneself up,** erguirse

draw /drɔ/ vi tirar; (shrink) encogerse; (wrinkle) arrugarse; (of chimneys, etc.) tirar; (a picture) dibujar; Sports. empatar; (move) moverse; avanzar, adelantarse; (of a ship) calar; (a sword) desnudar (la espada); (lots) echar suertes; (attract people) atraer gente; Com. girar. **to d. aside,** ponerse a un lado; retirarse. **to d. back,** retroceder, recular; retirarse; vacilar. **to d. in,** retirarse; (of days) hacerse corto; (of dusk) caer. **to d. off,** alejarse; apartarse, retirarse. **to d. on,** (approach) acercarse; avanzar; Com. girar contra; inspirarse en. **to d. out,** hacerse largo; (of a vehicle) ponerse en marcha, empezar a andar. **to d. round,** ponerse alrededor; reunirse alrededor. **to d. together,** reunirse. **to d. up,** parar.

draw /drɔ/ n tirada, f; (of lotteries) sorteo, m; Sports. empate, m; atracción, f; (Fig. feeler) tanteo, m. **to be a big d.,** ser una gran atracción

drawback /'drɔ,bæk/ n desventaja, f, inconveniente, m

drawbridge /'drɔ,brɪdʒ/ n puente levadizo, m

drawee /drɔ'i/ n Com. girado, m

drawer /'drɔr/ n (receptacle) cajón, m; pl **drawers,** (men's) calzoncillos, m pl; (women's) pantalones, m pl

drawing /'drɔɪŋ/ n (pulling) tiro, m; atracción, f; (extraction) f; saca, f; (in raffles, etc. and of lots) sorteo, m; (of money) percibo, m; Com. giro, m; (sketch) dibujo, m; (plan) esquema, f. **free-hand d.,** dibujo a pulso, m. **d. from life,** dibujo del natural, m. **d.-board,** tablero de dibujo, m. **d.-paper,** papel para dibujar, m. **d.-pin,** chinche, f. **d.-room,** salón, m

drawl /drɔl/ vi hablar arrastrando las palabras

drawn /drɔn/ past part See **draw.** a (tired) ojeroso, con ojeras, con un aspecto de cansancio; (with pain) desencajado. **long d. out,** demasiado largo. **d. sword,** espada desnuda, f. **d.-thread work,** deshilados, m pl

dread /drɛd/ n pavor, temor, terror, espanto, m; trepidación, f, miedo, m. a temible, espantoso, terrible; augusto. vt temer. vi tener miedo, temer. **in d. of,** con miedo de, con terror de

dreader /'drɛdər/ n el, m, (f, la) que teme, temedor (-ra)

dreadful /'drɛdfəl/ a terrible, pavoroso, espantoso, horroroso; formidable; augusto

dreadfully /'drɛdfəli/ adv terriblemente, horriblemente

dreadfulness /'drɛdfəlnɪs/ n horror, m

dream /drim/ n sueño, m; ilusión, f; ensueño, m; fantasía, f. vt and vi soñar; imaginar. **He dreamed away the hours,** Pasaba las horas soñando. **I wouldn't d. of it!** ¡Ni por sueño! **in a d.,** en sueños; (waking) como en sueños; mecánicamente. **Sweet dreams!** ¡Duerme bien! **to d. of,** soñar con

dreamer /'drimər/ n soñador (-ra); visionario (-ia)

dreamily /'driməli/ adv como en sueños; soñolientamente; vagamente

dreaming /'drimɪŋ/ n sueños, m pl

dreamland /'drim,lænd/ n reino de los sueños, m

dreamy /'drimi/ a soñador; soñoliento; fantástico; (empty) vació

dreariness /'drɪərɪnɪs/ n tristeza, f; melancolía, f; lobreguez, f

dreary /'drɪəri/ a triste; melancólico; lóbrego

dredge /drɛdʒ/ vt dragar; (with sugar, etc.) espolvorear

dredger /'drɛdʒər/ n draga, f; (for sugar) azucarera, f; (for flour) harinero, m

dredging /'drɛdʒɪŋ/ n dragado, m; (sprinkling) salpicadura, f. **d. bucket,** cangilón, m

dregs /drɛgz/ n pl heces, f pl, posos, m pl, Lat. Am. concho m **to drain to the d.,** vaciar hasta las heces

drench /drɛntʃ/ vt mojar, calar. **He is drenched to the skin,** Está calado hasta los huesos

dress /drɛs/ vt (with clothes) vestir; (arrange) arreglar; (the hair) peinar(se); (a wound) curar; (hides); adobar; (cloth) aprestar; (flax) rastrillar; (stone) labrar; (wood) desbastar; (prune) podar; (a garden) cultivar; (manure) abonar; Cul. aderezar; preparar; (season) condimentar; (a table) poner; (adorn) ataviar, adornar; revestir; (a dead body) amortajar. vi vestirse; ataviarse; (of troops) alinearse. **all dressed up and nowhere to go,** compuesta y sin novio. **dress to kill, dress to the nines** Lat. Am. arriscarse, Central America empavonarse **dressed up to the nines,** vestido de veinticinco alfileres. **Left (Right) d.!** ¡A la izquierda (A la derecha) alinearse! **to d. down,** (scold) poner como un trapo (a), dar una calada (a). **to d. up,** vt ataviar; (disguise) disfrazar. vi ponerse muy elegante; disfrazarse

dress /drɛs/ n (in general) el vestir; (clothes) ropa, f; (frock) vestido, traje, m; (uniform) uniforme, m; (Fig. covering) hábitos, m pl; (appearance) aspecto, m; forma, f. **full d.,** (uniform) uniforme de gala, m; (civilian, man's) traje de etiqueta, m; (woman's) traje de gala, m. **morning d.,** (man's) traje de paisano, m; (woman's) vestido de todos los días, m; (man's formal dress) chaqué, m. **ready-made d.,** traje hecho, m. **d. allowance,** alfileres, m pl. **d.-circle,** anfiteatro, m. **d.-coat,** frac, m. **d. protector,** sobaquera, f. **d. rehearsal,** ensayo general, m. **d. shirt,** camisa de pechera dura, f. **d. suit,** (with white tie) traje de frac, m; (with black tie) smoking, m. **d. sword,** espada de gala, f. **d. tie,** corbata de smoking (or de frac), f

dresser /'drɛsər/ n el que adereza; (of wounds) practicante (de hospital), m; (valet) ayuda de cámara, m; (maid) doncella, f; (of skins) adobador de pieles, m; (furniture) aparador, m; (in the kitchen) armario de la cocina, rı

dressing /'drɛsɪŋ/ n el vestir(se); aderezamiento, m; (for cloth) apresto, m; (of leather) adobo, m; (of wood) desbaste, m; (of stone) labrado, m; (manuring) estercoladura, f; (sauce) salsa, f; (seasoning) condimentación, f; (of a wound) cura, f; (bandage) apósito, m, vendaje, m. **d.-case,** neceser, saco de noche, m. **d.-down,** Inf. rapapolvo, m. **d.-gown,** (woman's) salto de cama, quimono, m; (man's) batín, m. **d.-jacket,** chambra, f, peinador, m. **d.-room,** Theat. camarín, m; (in a house) trasalcoba, recámara, f. **d.-station,** puesto de socorro, m. **d.-table,** tocador, m, mesa de tocador, f

dressmaker /'drɛs,meikər/ n modista, mf

dressmaking /'drɛs,meikɪŋ/ n confección de vestidos, f; arte de la modista, m

dribble /'drɪbəl/ vi gotear; (slobber) babear. vt (in football) regatear. n (in football) regate, m

dried /draid/ a seco; (of fruit) paso. **d. up,** (withered) marchito; (of people) enjuto. **d. fish,** cecial, m. **d. meat,** cecina, f

drift /drɪft/ n (in a ship or airplane's course) deriva, f; (of a current) velocidad, f; (tendency) tendencia, f; (meaning) significación, f; (heap) montón, m; (aim) objeto, propósito, fin, m; Mineral. galería, f; (of dust, etc.) nube, f; (shower) lluvia, f; (impulsion) impulso, m; violencia, f. vi flotar, ir arrastrado por la corriente; amontonarse; Naut. derivar; Aer. abatir. vt llevar; amontonar. **continental d.,** deriva continental, f. **drifts of sand,** arena movediza, f. **to d. into,** (war, etc.) entrar sin querer en; (habits) dar su luna en la flor de; (a room, etc.) deslizarse en. **d.-wood,** madera de deriva, f

drill /drɪl/ n (instrument) taladro, perforador, m, barrena, f; ejercicio, m, educación física, f; Mil. instrucción militar, f; (cloth) dril, m; Agr. sembradora mecánica, f; (for seeds) hilera, f; (discipline) disciplina, f; (teaching) instrucción, f. vt taladrar, barrenar; enseñar el ejercicio (a); enseñar la instrucción; disciplinar; (seed) sembrar en hileras. vi hacer el ejercicio; hacer la instrucción militar. **d. ground,** (in a barracks) patio de un cuartel, m; (in a school) patio de recreo, m. **d.-sergeant,** sargento instructor, m

drilling /'drɪlɪŋ/ n (boring) perforación, f, barrenamiento, m; (of seeds) sembradura en hileras, f; ejercicios, m pl; (maneuvers) maniobras, f pl

drink /drɪŋk/ n bebida, f; (glass of wine, etc.) copita, f; (of water, etc.) vaso, m. vt beber; tomar; (empty) vaciar. vi beber. **to d. to,** beber a la salud de, brindar por. **to give someone a d.,** dar a beber. **Would you like a d.?** ¿Quieres tomar algo? **to d. in,** absorber. **to d. off, up,** beber de un trago

drinkable /'drɪŋkəbəl/ a potable, bebedero

drinker /'drɪŋkər/ n bebedor (-ra)

drinking /'drɪŋkɪŋ/ n acción de beber, f; el beber, m; (alcoholism) bebida, f. a que bebe; aficionado a la bebida; (of things) para beber; (drinkable) potable; (tavern) de taberna. **d.-fountain,** fuente pública para beber agua, f. **d. place,** bebedero, m; bar, m. **d.-song,** canción de taberna, f. **d.-trough,** abrevadero, m; **d.-water,** agua potable, f

drip /drɪp/ vi and vt chorrear, gotear; caer gota a gota; escurrir; destilar; chorrear. n gotec, m; gota, f; Archit. goterón, m

dripping /'drɪpɪŋ/ n goteo, m; chorreo, m; (fat) grasa, f, a que gotea; mojado; que chorrea agua. **d.-pan,** grasera, f

drive /draiv/ vt empujar; arrojar; conducir; (grouse, etc.) batir; (a ball) golpear; (a nail, etc.) clavar; (oblige) compeler, forzar a; (a horse, plow, car, etc.) manejar; (Mech. work) mover; (cause to work, of machines) hacer funcionar; (a tunnel, etc.) abrir, construir; (a bargain, etc.) hacer; (cause) impulsar, hacer; (mad, etc.) volver. vi lanzarse; (of rain) azotar; (a ball) devolver. vi volver (en auto, etc.); (arrive) llegar. **to d. crazy, d. insane,** enloquecer, Lat. Am. also idiotizar; **to d. down,** hacer bajar; arrojar hacia abajo; (in a vehicle) bajar (por). **to d. in, into,** vt hacer entrar; (of teeth, etc.) hincar; (nails) clavar; Fig. inculcar. vt entrar (en coche, carruaje); llegar (en coche, etc.). **to d. off,** See **away.** **to d. off the stage,** hacer dejar la escena, silbar. **to d. on,** vt empujar; hacer avanzar; (attack) atacar. vi seguir su marcha; seguir avanzando; emprender la marcha. **to d. out,** vt expulsar; hacer salir; (chase) cazar. vi salir (en coche, etc.). **to d. up,** vi illegar (en coche, etc.); parar. **to d. up to,** avanzar hasta, llegar hasta; conducir (el coche, etc.) hasta

drive /draiv/ n paseo (en coche, etc.), m; (avenue) avenida, f, camino, m; (distance) trayecto, m; (journey) viaje, m; Mech. acción, f; conducción, f, m; ataque, m; (a person) energía, f; campaña vigorosa, f; impulso, m. **left (right) hand d.,** conducción a la izquierda (derecha). **to take a d.,** dar un paseo en (auto, etc.). **to take for a d.,** llevar a paseo en (auto, etc.)

drive-in /'draiv,ɪn/ n autocine, autocinema, m

drivel /'drɪvəl/ n vaciedades, patrañas, f pl, disparates, m pl, a; decir disparates, chochear

driver /'draivər/ n conductor (-ra); chófer, m; (of an engine) maquinista, m; (of a cart) carretero, m; (of a coach, carriage) cochero, m; (of cattle, etc.) ganadero, m; (golf) conductor, m

driver's license /'draivərz/ Spain carné de chofer, Ar-

gentina carné de conductor, *m*, *elsewhere in Lat. Am.*
licencia de manejar, *f*
driveway /'draɪvˌweɪ/ *n* camino, *m*, entrada para coches *f*
driving /'draɪvɪŋ/ *n* conducción, *f*; modo de conducir, *m*; paseo (en coche, etc.), *m*; impulsión, *f*. *a* de conducir; de chófer; para choferes; motor; propulsor; impulsor; de transmisión; *Fig.* impulsor; (violent) violento, impetuoso. **to go d.**, ir de paseo (en auto o carruaje). **d. mirror,** espejo retrovisor, *m*. **d. seat,** asiento del conductor, *m*; (of an old-fashioned coach, etc.) pescante, *m*. **d.-shaft,** *Mech.* árbol motor, *m*. **d. test,** examen para choferes, *m*. **d.-wheel,** volante, *m*; rueda motriz, *f*
drizzle /'drɪzəl/ *n* llovizna, *f*, *vi* lloviznar, *Lat. Am.* briznar
droll /droul/ *a* chusco, gracioso. *n* bufón, *m*
drone /droun/ *n* abejón, *m*; *Fig.* zángano, *m*; (hum) zumbido, *m*; (of a song, voice) salmodia, *f*, *vt* and *vi* (hum) zumbar; (of a song, voice) salmodiar; (idle) zanganear
droop /drup/ *vi* inclinarse; colgar; caer; (wither) marchitarse; (fade) consumirse; (pine) desanimarse. *vt* bajar; dejar caer. *n* caída, *f*; inclinación, *f*
drooping /'drupɪŋ/ *a* caído; debilitado; lánguido; (of ears) gacho; (depressed) alicaído, deprimido
drop /drɒp/ *n* gota, *f*; (tear) lágrima, *f*; (for the ear) pendiente, *m*; (sweet) pastilla, *f*; (of a chandelier) almendra, *f*; (fall) caída, *f*; (in price, etc.) baja, *f*; (slope) pendiente, cuesta, *f*. **by drops,** a gotas. **d. bottle,** frasco cuentagotas, *m*. **d.-curtain,** telón de boca, *m*. **d.-hammer,** martinete, *m*. **d.-head coupé,** cupé descapotable, *m*. **d.-scene,** telón de foro, *m*
drop /drɒp/ *vt* verter a gotas; destilar; (sprinkle) salpicar, rociar; dejar caer; soltar; (lower) bajar; (of clothes, etc.) desprenderse de, quitar; (lose) perder; (a letter in a mailbox) echar; (leave) dejar; (give up) renunciar (a); desistir (de); abandonar; (kill) tumbar; (a hint) soltar; (a curtsey) hacer. *vi* gotear, caer en gotas, destilar; (descend) bajar, descender; caer muerto; caer desmayado; (sleep) dormirse; (fall) caer; (of the wind) amainar; (of prices, temperature) bajar. **to let the matter d.,** poner fin a una cuestión. **to d. a course,** bajar un curso. **to d. a line,** poner unas líneas. **to d. anchor,** anclar. **to d. behind,** quedarse atrás. **to d. down,** caer (a tierra). **to d. in,** entrar al pasar. **d. in on somebody,** pasarse por casa de fulano, pasarse por el despacho de (etc.). **to d. off,** separarse (de); disminuir; (sleep) quedar dormido; (die) morir de repente. **to d. out,** separarse; (from a race, etc.) retirarse (de); quedarse atrás; desaparecer; ausentarse, apartarse; (decrease) disminuir; decaer. **He has dropped out of my life,** Le he perdido de vista. **to d. through,** caer por; frustrarse; no dar resultado
dropping /'drɒpɪŋ/ *n* gotera, *f*; gotas, *f pl*; (fall) caída, *f*; *pl* **droppings** (of a candle) moco, *m*; (dung) cagadas, *f pl*. **Constant d. wears away the stone,** La gotera cava la piedra
dropsy /'drɒpsi/ *n* hidropesía, *f*
dross /drɔs/ *n* escoria, *f*; (rubbish) basura, *f*
drought /draut/ *n* aridez, *f*; (thirst) sed, *f*; (dry season) sequía, *f*
drove /drouv/ *n* manada, *f*, hato, *m*; (of sheep) rebaño, *m*; (crowd) muchedumbre, *f*
drown /draun/ *vi* ahogarse. *vt* ahogar; sumergir; inundar; (*Fig.* of cries, sorrow, etc.) ahogar
drowning /'draunɪŋ/ *n* ahogamiento, *m*; sumersión, *f*; inundación, *f*. *a* que se ahoga
drowse /drauz/ *vi* adormecerse
drowsily /'drauzəli/ *adv* soñolientamente
drowsiness /'drauzinɪs/ *n* somnolencia, *f*; sueño, *m*; (laziness) indolencia, pereza, *f*
drowsy /'drauzi/ *a* soñoliento; adormecedor, soporífero; (heavy) amodorrado. **to grow d.,** adormecerse. **to make d.,** adormecer
drudgery /'drʌdʒəri/ *n* trabajo arduo, *m*, faena monótona, *f*
drug /drʌg/ *n* droga, *f*; medicamento, *m*; narcótico, *m*. *vt* mezclar con drogas; administrar drogas (a); narcotizar. *vi* tomar drogas. **d. trade,** comercio de

drogas, *m*. **d. traffic,** contrabando de drogas, narcotráfico *m*
drug addict *n* drogadicto (-ta), *Lat. Am.* adicto *mf*
drug addiction *n* toxicomanía, *f*
druggist /'drʌgɪst/ *n* droguero (-ra)
drum /drʌm/ *n* tambor, *m*; (of the ear) tímpano (del oído), *m*; (cylinder) cilindro, *m*; (box) caja, *f*; *Archit.* cuerpo de columna, *m*. **drums,** batería, *f*. **bass d.,** bombo, *m*. **with drums beating,** con tambor batiente. **d.-head,** parche (del tambor), *m*. **d.-head service,** misa de campaña, *f*. **d.-major,** tambor mayor, *m*
drum /drʌm/ *vt* and *vi* tocar el tambor; (with the fingers) tabalear, teclear; (with the heels) zapatear; (into a person's head) machacar. **to d. out,** *Mil.* expulsar a tambor batiente
drummer /'drʌmər/ *n* tambor, *m*
drumming /'drʌmɪŋ/ *n* ruido del tambor, *m*; (of the heels) taconeo, *m*; (of the fingers) tabaleo, tecleo, *m*
drumstick /'drʌmˌstɪk/ *n* palillo (de tambor), *m*
drunk /drʌŋk/ *a* borracho, ebrio, *Lat. Am.* also iluminado, *Central America* azunumbaso *n* borracho, *m*. **to be d.,** estar borracho. **to get d.,** emborracharse, *Lat. Am.* also iluminarse; *Inf.* pillar un lobo, (on wine) *Mexico* envinarse. **to make d.,** emborrachar
drunkard /'drʌŋkərd/ *n* borracho (-cha)
drunken /'drʌŋkən/ *a* borracho, ebrio
drunkenness /'drʌŋkənnɪs/ *n* embriaguez, borrachera, ebriedad, *f*
dry /draɪ/ *vt* secarse. *vt* secar; desaguar; (wipe) enjugar. **to dry one's tears,** enjugarse las lágrimas; *Fig.* secarse las lágrimas. **to dry up,** secarse; (of persons) acecinarse; (with old age) apergaminarse; (of ideas, etc.) agotarse; (be quiet) callarse
dry /draɪ/ *a* seco; estéril; (thirsty) sediento; (of wine) seco; (U.S.A.) prohibicionista; (squeezed) exprimido; (of toast) sin mantequilla; (*Fig.* chilly) aburrido; (sarcastic) sarcástico; (of humor) agudo. **on dry land,** en seco. **dry battery,** pila seca, *f*. **to dry-clean,** lavar al seco, *m*. **dry-cleaner,** tintorero (-ra). **dry-cleaning,** lavado al seco, *m*. **dry-cleaning shop,** tintorería, *f*. **dry goods,** lencería, *f*. **dry land,** tierra firme, *f*. **dry measure,** medida para áridos, *f*. **dry-nurse,** ama seca, *f*. **dry-point,** punta seca, *f*. **dry-rot,** carcoma, *f*. **dry-shod,** con los pies secos
drying /'draɪɪŋ/ *n* secamiento, *m*; desecación, *f*, *a* secante; seco; para secar. **d. ground,** tendedero, *m*. **d. machine,** secadora, *f*; (for the hair) secadora de cabello, *f*. **d. room,** secadero, *m*
dryly /'draɪli/ *adv* secamente
dryness /'draɪnɪs/ *n* sequedad, *f*; aridez, *f*; (of humor) agudeza, *f*
dual /'duəl/ *a* doble; *Gram.* dual. **d. control,** mandos gemelos, *m pl*. **d. personality,** conciencia doble, *f*
dualism /'duəˌlɪzəm/ *n* dualismo, *m*
duality /du'ælɪti/ *n* dualidad, *f*
dub /dʌb/ *vt* (a knight) armar caballero; (call) apellidar; (nickname) motejar, apodar
dubbing /'dʌbɪŋ/ *n* (of films) doblaje, *m*
dubious /'dubiəs/ *a* dudoso, incierto; indeciso; problemático; ambiguo
dubiously /'dubiəsli/ *adv* dudosamente
dubiousness /'dubiəsnɪs/ *n* carácter dudoso, *m*; incertidumbre, *f*; ambigüedad, *f*
Dublin /'dʌblɪn/ Dublín, *f*
Dubliner /'dʌblənər/ *n* dublinés (-esa)
ducat /'dʌkət/ *n* ducado, *m*
duchess /'dʌtʃɪs/ *n* duquesa, *f*
duchy /'dʌtʃi/ *n* ducado, *m*
duck /dʌk/ *n* pato (-ta), ánade, *mf*; *Sports.* cero, *m*; (darling) vida mía, querida, *f*; (jerk) agachada, *f*; (under the water) chapuz, *m*; (material) dril, *m*; *Mil.* auto anfibio, *m*. *vi* agacharse; (under water) chapuzarse. *vt* zabullir, sumergir; bajar, inclinar
ducking /'dʌkɪŋ/ *n* chapuz, *m*. **d.-stool,** silla de chapuzar, *f*
duckling /'dʌklɪŋ/ *n* anadino (-na)
duct /dʌkt/ *n* conducto, canal, *m*; *Bot.* tubo, *m*
ductile /'dʌktl/ *a* dúctil
ductility /dʌk'tɪlɪti/ *n* ductilidad, *f*

ductless /'dʌktlɪs/ a sin tubos
due /du/ a debido; (payable) pagadero; (fallen due) vencido; (fitting) propio; (expected) esperado. n impuesto, m; derecho, m. **in due form,** en regla. **in its due time,** a su tiempo debido. **to fall due,** vencerse. **due bill,** Com. abonaré, m. **due west,** poniente derecho, m
duel /'duəl/ n duelo, lance de honor, m; Fig. lucha, f. **to fight a d.,** batirse en duelo
dueling /'duəlɪŋ/ n el (batirse en) duelo
duelist /'duəlɪst/ n duelista, m
duenna /du'ɛnə/ n dueña, f
duet /du'ɛt/ n dúo, m
duettist /du'ɛtɪst/ n duetista, mf
dug /dʌg/ n teta, f
dugout /'dʌg,aut/ n trinchera, f
duke /duk/ n duque, m
dukedom /'dukdəm/ n ducado, m
dulcet /'dʌlsɪt/ a dulce
dulcimer /'dʌlsəmər/ n dulcémele, m
dull /dʌl/ a (stupid) lerdo, estúpido, obtuso; (boring, tedious) aburrido; (of pain, sounds) sordo; (of colors and eyes) apagado; (of light, beams, etc.) sombrío; (not polished) mate; (pale) pálido; (insipid) insípido, insulso; (of people) soso, poco interesante; (dreary, sad) triste; (gray) gris; (of mirrors, etc.) empañado; (of weather) anublado; (of hearing) duro; (slow) lento; lánguido; insensible; (blunt) romo; Com. encalmado, inactivo. **to find life d.,** encontrar la vida aburrida. **d. of hearing,** duro de oído, algo sordo. **d. pain,** dolor sordo, m. **d.-witted,** lerdo
dull /dʌl/ a (make stupid) entontecer; (lessen) mitigar; (weaken) debilitar; (pain) calmar, aliviar; (sadden) entristecer; (blunt) embotar; (spoil) estropear; (a mirror, etc.) empañar; (a polished surface) hacer mate, deslustrar; (of enthusiasm, etc.) enfriar; (tire) fatigar; (obstruct) impedir
dullness /'dʌlnɪs/ n (stupidity) estupidez, f; (boredom) aburrimiento, m; (heaviness) pesadez, f; (drowsiness) somnolencia, f; (insipidity) insipidez, insulsez, f; (of literary style) prosaísmo, m; (of persons) sosería, f; (of a surface) deslustre, m; (laziness) pereza, languidez, f; (slowness) lentitud, f; (tiredness) cansancio, m; (sadness) tristeza, f; (bluntness) embotamiento, m; (of hearing) dureza, f; Com. desanimación, f
dully /'dʌli/ adv (stupidly) estúpidamente; sin comprender; (insipidly) insípidamente; (not brightly) sin brillo; (slowly) lentamente; (sadly) tristemente; (tiredly) con cansancio; (of sound) sordamente
duly /'duli/ adv debidamente; puntualmente
dumb /dʌm/ a mudo; callado; silencioso; Inf. tonto, estúpido, Lat. Am. also baboso, Central America azurumbado. **to become d.,** enmudecer. **to strike d.,** dejar sin habla. **d.-bell,** barra con pesas, f. **d. waiter,** bufete, m
dumbfound /dʌm'faund/ vt dejar sin habla; confundir; pasmar
dumbness /'dʌmnɪs/ n mudez, f, mutismo, m; silencio, m
dummy /'dʌmi/ n (tailor's, etc.) maniquí, m; (puppet) títere, m; (cabeza para pelucas, f; (figurehead) hombre de paja, testaferro, m; (baby's) chupador, m; (at cards) el muerto. a fingido. **to be d.,** (at cards) ser el muerto
dump /dʌmp/ n depósito, m; vaciadero, m. vt depositar; (goods on a market) inundar (con)
dumping /'dʌmpɪŋ/ n depósito, m; vaciamiento, m; (of goods on a market) inundación, f. **"D. prohibited,"** «Se prohíbe arrojar la basura»
dun /dʌn/ vt apremiar, importunar
dunce /dʌns/ n asno, bobo, zoquete, m. **dunce's cap,** coroza, f
dun-colored /'dʌn,kʌlərd/ a pardo
dune /dun/ n duna, f
dung /dʌŋ/ n estiércol, m; (of rabbits, mice, deer, sheep, goats) cagarruta, f; (of cows) boñiga, f; (of hens) gallinaza, f. **d.-cart,** carro de basura, m
dungarees /,dʌŋgə'riz/ n mono, m, pantalonesvaquero, m pl
dungeon /'dʌndʒən/ n mazmorra, f, calabozo, m

dunghill /'dʌŋ,hɪl/ n muladar, m
duodenum /,duə'dinəm/ n duodeno, m
dupe /dup/ n víctima, f; tonto (-ta). vt embelecar, engañar. **to be a d.,** Inf. hacer el primo
duplicate /a, n 'duplɪkɪt; v -,keit/ a duplicado, doble. n duplicado, m; copia, f. vt duplicar
duplication /,duplɪ'keiʃən/ n duplicación, f
duplicator /'duplɪ,keitər/ n copiador, m
duplicity /du'plɪsɪti/ n duplicidad, f
durability /,dʊrə'bɪlɪti/ n duración, f. **This is a cloth of great d.,** Este es un paño que dura mucho, Este es un paño muy duradero
durable /'dʊrəbəl/ a duradero
duration /dʊ'reiʃən/ n duración, f
duress /dʊ'rɛs/ n compulsión, f
during /'dʊrɪŋ/ prep durante
dusk /dʌsk/ n atardecer, anochecer, m; (twilight) crepúsculo, m; (darkness) oscuridad, f. **at d.,** al atardecer, a la caída de la tarde
dusky /'dʌski/ a (dim, dark) oscuro; (of colors) sucio
dust /dʌst/ n polvo, m; (cloud of dust) polvareda, f; (ashes) cenizas, f pl; (of coal) cisco, m; (sweepings) barreduras, f pl; (of grain) tamo, m. vt desempolvar, quitar (or sacudir) el polvo de; (cover with dust) polvorear; (scatter) salpicar; (sweep) barrer; (clean) limpiar. **d.-bin,** basurero, m. **d.-cart,** carro de la basura, m. **d. cloud,** polvareda, f. **d. jacket,** (books) sobrecubierta, f. **d.-pan,** recogedor de basura, m. **d.-sheet,** guardapolvo, m. **d. storm,** vendaval de polvo, m
duster /'dʌstər/ n el, m, que quita el polvo; paño (para quitar el polvo), m; (of feathers) plumero, m
dustiness /'dʌstɪnɪs/ n empolvoramiento, m; estado polvoriento, m
dusting /'dʌstɪŋ/ n limpieza, f; (sweeping) barredura, f; (powder) polvos antisépticos, m pl
dusty /'dʌsti/ a polvoriento, polvoroso, empolvado; del color del polvo; (of colors) sucio. **It is very d.,** Hay mucho polvo. **to get d.,** llenarse (or cubrirse) de polvo
Dutch /dʌtʃ/ a holandés. **the D.,** los holandeses. **double D.,** griego, galimatías, m. **D. cheese,** queso de bola, m. **D. courage,** coraje falso, m. **D. woman,** holandesa, f
Dutchman /'dʌtʃmən/ n holandés, m
dutiable /'dutiəbəl/ a sujeto a derechos de aduana
dutiful /'dutəful/ a que cumple con sus deberes; obediente, sumiso; respetuoso; excelente, muy bueno
dutifully /'dutəfəli/ adv obedientemente; respetuosamente
dutifulness /'dutəfəlnɪs/ n obediencia, docilidad, f; respeto, m
duty /'duti/ n deber, m; obligación, f; (greetings) respetos, m pl; (charge, burden) carga, f; (tax) derecho, impuesto, m; Mil. servicio, m; (guard) guardia, f. **off d.,** libre. **on d.,** de servicio. **to be on sentry d.,** estar de guardia. **to do d. as,** servir como. **to do one's d.,** hacer (or cumplir con) su deber. **to pay d. on,** pagar derechos de aduana sobre. **d.-free,** franco de derechos
dwarf /dwɔrf/ a enano. n enano (-na). vt impedir el crecimiento; empequeñecer
dwarfish /'dwɔrfɪʃ/ a enano
dwell /dwɛl/ vi vivir, habitar; (with on, upon) (think about) meditar sobre, pensar en; (deal with) tratar de; hablar largamente de; (insist on) insister en; apoyarse en, hacer hincapié en; (pause over) detenerse en
dweller /'dwɛlər/ n habitante, mf; (more poetic) morador (-ra)
dwelling /'dwɛlɪŋ/ n vivienda, f; (abode) morada, habitación, f; residencia, f; casa, f; (domicile) domicilio, m. **d.-house,** casa, f
dwindle /'dwɪndl/ vi disminuirse; consumirse; (decay) decaer; (degenerate) degenerar. **to d. to,** reducirse a
dwindling /'dwɪndlɪŋ/ n disminución, f
dye /dai/ vt teñir, colorar. vi teñirse. n tinte, m; (colour) color, m. **fast dye,** tinte estable, m. **dye-house,** tintorería, f. **dye-stuff,** materia colorante, f. **dyeworks,** tintorería, f
dyed-in-the-wool /'daid ən ðə 'wʊl/ a de pies a cabeza

dyeing /'daiiŋ/ n teñidura, tintura, f; (as a trade) tintorería, f. **d. and dry-cleaning shop,** tintorería, f
dyer /'daiər/ n tintorero (-ra)
dyestuff /'dai,stʌf/ n materia colorante, materia de tinte, materia tintórea, f
dying /'daiiŋ/ a moribundo, agonizante; de la muerte; (of light) mortecino; (last) último; supremo; (languishing) lánguido; (deathbed) hecho en su lecho mortuorio. **to be d.,** estar agonizando; (of light) fenecer. **to be d. for,** estar muerto por

dynamic /dai'næmɪk/ a dinámico
dynamics /dai'næmɪks/ n dinámica, f
dynamite /'dainə,mait/ n dinamita, f
dynamo /'dainə,mou/ n dinamo, f
dynastic /dai'næstɪk/ a dinástico
dynasty /'dainəsti/ n dinastía, f
dysentery /'dɪsən,tɛri/ n disentería, f
dyslexia /dɪs'lɛksiə/ n dislexia, f
dyspepsia /dɪs'pɛpʃə/ n dispepsia, f
dyspeptic /dɪs'pɛptɪk/ a dispéptico. n dispéptico (-ca)

E

e /i/ n (letter) e, f; Mus. mi, m
each /itʃ/ a cada (invariable), todo. pron cada uno, m; cada una, f. **e. other,** el uno al otro. **e. of them,** cada uno de ellos. **They help e. other,** Se ayudan mutuamente, Se ayudan entre sí. **to love e. other,** amarse
eager /'igər/ a impaciente; ansioso, deseoso; ambicioso
eagerly /'igərli/ adv con impaciencia; con ansia; ambiciosamente
eagerness /'igərnɪs/ n impaciencia, f; ansia, f, deseo, m; (promptness) alacridad, f; (zeal) fervor, m
eagle /'igəl/ n águila, f. **royal e.,** águila caudal, águila real, f. **e.-eyed,** con ojos de lince, de ojo avizor. **have the eyes of an e.,** tener ojos de lince, tener vista de lince
ear /iər/ n (outer ear) oreja, f; (inner ear and sense of hearing) oído, m; Bot. espiga, panoja, f. **to begin to show the ear,** (grain) espigar. **to be all ears,** ser todo oídos. **to give ear,** dar oído. **to have a good ear,** tener buen oído. **to play by ear,** tocar de oído. **to turn a deaf ear,** hacerse el sordo. **ear-ache,** dolor de oídos, m. **ear-drum,** tímpano (del oído), m. **ear-flap,** orejera, f. **ear-phone, ear-piece,** auricular, m. **ear-piercing,** penetrante, agudo. **ear-shot,** alcance del oído, m. **to be within ear-shot,** estar al alcance del oído. **ear-trumpet,** trompetilla, f. **ear wax,** cerilla, f
eared /iərd/ a con orejas; de orejas; Bot. con espigas
earl /ərl/ n conde, m
earldom /'ərldəm/ n condado, m
earlier, earliest /'ərliər; 'ərliist/ a comp and sup más temprano; más primitivo; más antiguo; (first, of time) primero. adv más temprano; más pronto; antes
earliness /'ərlinɪs/ n lo temprano; antigüedad, f, lo primitivo; (precocity) precocidad, f. **The e. of his arrival,** Su llegada de buena hora
early /'ərli/ a temprano; primitivo; (of fruit, etc.) temprano, adelantado; (movement) primero (e.g. early Romanticism, el primer romanticismo); (person) de la primera época (e.g. the early Cervantes, Cervantes de la primera época); (work) un primer (e.g. an early work of Unamuno's, una primera obra de Unamuno); (advanced) avanzado; (precocious) precoz; (first, of time) primero; (in the morning) matutino; (near) próximo; cercano; (premature) prematuro; (of child's age) tierno; joven. **in the e. hours,** en las primeras horas; en las altas horas (de la noche). **e. age,** edad temprana, tierna edad, f. **e.-fruiting,** Agr. trempanal. **e. riser,** madrugador (-ra). **e.-rising,** a madrugador. **e. years,** primeros años, años de la niñez, m pl
early /'ərli/ adv temprano; al principio (de); en los primeros días (de); desde los primeros días (de); (in the month, year) a principios (de); (in time) a tiempo; (in the day) de buena hora; (soon) pronto; (among the first) entre los primeros (de). **as e. as possible,** lo más temprano posible; lo más pronto posible. **to be e.,** llegar antes de tiempo; llegar de buena hora. **to get up e.,** madrugar. **to go to bed e.,** acostarse temprano. **too e.,** demasiado temprano, muy temprano. **e. in the morning,** de madrugada
earmark /'iər,mɑrk/ vt marcar; Fig. destinar, reservar
earn /ərn/ vt ganar; obtener, adquirir; (deserve) merecer
earnable /'ərnəbəl/ a ganable

earnest /'ərnɪst/ a serio; fervoroso; diligente; sincero. **to be in e. about something,** tomarlo en serio; ser sincero (en). **e. money,** arras, f pl
earnestly /'ərnɪstli/ adv seriamente; fervorosamente; con diligencia; sinceramente, de buena fe
earnestness /'ərnɪstnɪs/ n seriedad, f; fervor, celo, m; diligencia, f; sinceridad, buena fe, f
earnings /'ərnɪŋz/ n pl Com. ingresos, m pl; (salary) salario, m; estipendio, m; (of a workman) jornal, m
earring /'iər,rɪŋ/ n pendiente, arete, Lat. Am. also aro m
earth /ərθ/ n tierra, f; (of a badger, etc.) madriguera, f; Radio. tierra, f. **to cover con tierra;** Radio. conectar con tierra. **clod of e.,** terrón, m. **half the e.,** Inf. medio mundo, m. **on e.,** en este mundo, sobre la tierra
earthen /'ərθən/ a terrizo, terroso; (of mud) de barro
earthenware /'ərθən,wɛər/ n alfar, m, a de loza, de barro
earthiness /'ərθinɪs/ n terrosidad, f
earthly /'ərθli/ a terrestre, terrenal; de la tierra; (fleshly) carnal; (worldly) mundano; material. **There is not an e. chance,** No hay la más mínima posibilidad
earthquake /'ərθ,kweik/ n terremoto, temblor de tierra, m
earth tremor movimiento sísmico, m
earthwork /'ərθ,wɜrk/ n terraplén, m
earthworm /'ərθ,wɜrm/ n gusano de tierra, m
earthy /'ərθi/ a térreo, terroso
earwig /'iər,wig/ n tijereta, f
ease /iz/ n bienestar, m; tranquilidad, f; descanso, m; (leisure) ocio, m; (comfortableness) comodidad, f; (freedom from embarrassment) naturalidad, f, desembarazo, desenfado, m; (from pain) alivio, m; (simplicity) facilidad, f. vt (widen) ensanchar; aflojar; (pain) aliviar; (lighten) aligerar; (moderate) moderar; (soften) suavizar; (free) librar; (one's mind) tranquilizar. **in any moments of e.,** en mis ocios, en mis momentos de ocio. **Stand at e.!** Mil. ¡En su lugar descansen! **to be at e.,** estar a sus anchas; encontrarse bien; comportarse con toda naturalidad. **with e.,** fácilmente. **to e. off,** vt (Naut. cables, sails) arriar. vi sentirse menos, cesar
easel /'izəl/ n caballete (de pintor) m
easily /'izəli/ adv fácilmente. **The engine runs e.,** El motor marcha bien
easiness /'izinɪs/ n facilidad, f; sencillez, f; (of manner) desembarazo, m, naturalidad, f
east /ist/ n este, m; oriente, m, (of countries) Oriente, m; Levante, m. a del este; del oriente; (of countries) de Oriente, oriental; levantino. **e. North e.,** estenordeste, m. **e. South e.,** estesudeste, m. **e. wind,** viento del este, m
Easter /'istər/ n Pascua de Resurrección, f. **E. egg,** huevo de Pascua, m. **E. Saturday,** sábado de gloria, m. **E. Sunday,** domingo de Pascua, m
easterly /'istərli/ a del este; al este. adv hacia el este
eastern /'istərn/ a del este; de Oriente; oriental. n oriental, mf
easternmost /'istərn,moust/ a situado más al este
East Indies /'ɪndiz/ Indias Orientales, f pl
eastward /'istwərd/ adv hacia el este, hacia oriente
easy /'izi/ a fácil; sencillo; (comfortable) cómodo; (free from pain) aliviado; Com. flojo; (well-off) acomodado, holgado; (calm) tranquilo; tolerante; natu-

ral; afable, condescendiente; (of virtue, women) fácil. *adv* con calma; despacio. **to take it e.,** tomarlo con calma. **e.-chair,** (silla) poltrona, *f*. **easy come, easy go,** lo que por agua, agua (Mexico and Colombia), los dineros del sacristán cantando vienen y cantando se van (Spain). **e.-going,** acomodadizo; indolente; (morally) de manga ancha; (casual) descuidado

eat /it/ *vt* comer; (meals, soup, refreshments) tomar; (with a good, bad appetite) hacer; consumir; (corrode) corroer; desgastar. *vi* comer; (*Fam.* of food) ser de buen (or mal) comer. **to eat one's breakfast (lunch),** tomar el desayuno, desayunar (almorzar). **to eat one's words,** retractarse. **to eat away,** comer; consumir; corroer. **to eat into,** (of chemicals) morder; (a fortune) consumir; gastar. **eat out of s. b.'s hand,** comer de la mano de fulano, comer en la mano de fulano. **to eat up,** devorar (also *Fig.*)

eatable /'itəbəl/ *a* comestible, comedero. *n pl* **eatables,** comestibles, *m pl*

eater /'itər/ *n* el, *m*, (*f*, la) que come

eating /'itɪŋ/ *n* el comer; comida, *f*. **e. and drinking,** el comer y beber. **e.-house,** casa de comidas, *f*

eau de cologne /'ou də kə'loun/ *n* agua de Colonia, *f*

eaves /ivz/ *n* rafe, alero, *m*. **under the e.,** debajo del alero

eavesdrop /'ivz,drɒp/ *vi* escuchar a las puertas; fisgonear, espiar

eavesdropper /'ivz,drɒpər/ *n* fisgón (-ona)

eavesdropping /'ivz,drɒpɪŋ/ *n* fisgoneo, *m*

ebb /ɛb/ *n* (of the tide) reflujo, *m*; menguante, *f*; *Fig.* declinación, *f*; *Fig.* decadencia, *f*; (of life) vejez, *f*. *vi* (of tide) menguar; declinar; decaer. **to ebb and flow,** fluir y refluir. **to ebb away from,** dejar; dejar aislado. **ebb-tide,** marea menguante, *f*

ebonite /'ɛbə,nait/ *n* ebonita, *f*

ebony /'ɛbəni/ *n* ébano, *m*

ebullience /ɪ'bʌlyəns/ *n* efervescencia, exuberancia, *f*

ebullient /ɪ'bʌlyənt/ *a* efervescente, exuberante

ebullition /,ɛbə'lɪʃən/ *n* (boiling) ebullición, *f*, hervor, *m*; *Fig.* efervescencia, *f*, estallido, *m*

eccentric /ɪk'sɛntrɪk/ *a Geom.* excéntrico; raro, original; extravagante, excéntrico, *Lat. Am.* ideático. *n* persona excéntrica, *f*, original, *m*

eccentrically /ɪk'sɛntrɪkəli/ *adv* excéntricamente

eccentricity /,ɛksən'trɪsɪti/ *n Geom.* excentricidad, *f*; rareza, extravagancia, excentricidad, *f*

Ecclesiastes /ɪ,klizi'æstiz/ *n* Eclesiastés, *m*

ecclesiastic /ɪ,klizi'æstɪk/ *a* eclesiástico. *n* eclesiástico, clérigo, *m*

echo /'ɛkoʊ/ *n* eco, *m*; reverberación, resonancia, *f*. *vt* repercutir; *Fig.* repetir. *vi* resonar, retumbar, reverberar

echoing /'ɛkouɪŋ/ *a* retumbante. *n* eco, *m*

eclectic /ɪ'klɛktɪk/ *a* and *n* ecléctico (-ca)

eclecticism /ɪ'klɛktə,sɪzəm/ *n* eclecticismo, *m*

eclipse /ɪ'klɪps/ *n Astron.* eclipse, *m*, *vt* eclipsar; hacer eclipse. **to be in e.,** estar en eclipse

ecliptic /ɪ'klɪptɪk/ *n Astron.* eclíptica, *f*, a eclíptico

eclogue /'ɛklɒg/ *n* égloga, *f*

ecologist /ɪ'kɒlədʒɪst/ *n* ecólogo (-ga)

ecology /ɪ'kɒlədʒi/ *n* ecología, *f*

economic /,ɛkə'nɒmɪk, ,ikə-/ *a* económico

economical /,ɛkə'nɒmɪkəl, ,ikə-/ *a* económico

economics /,ɛkə'nɒmɪks, ,ikə-/ *n* economía política, *f*

economist /ɪ'kɒnəmɪst/ *n* economista, *mf*

economize /ɪ'kɒnə,maiz/ *vt* economizar, ahorrar. *vi* hacer economías

economy /ɪ'kɒnəmi/ *n* economía, *f*. **domestic e.,** economía doméstica, *f*. **political e.,** economía política, *f*

ecosystem /'ɛkou,sɪstəm/ *n* ecosistema, *m*

ecstasy /'ɛkstəsi/ *n* éxtasis, arrebato, *m*; transporte, *m*. **to be in e.,** estar en éxtasis

ecstatic /ɛk'stætɪk/ *a* extático

Ecuador /'ɛkwə,dɔr/ *el* Ecuador

Ecuadorian /,ɛkwə'dɔriən/ *a* and *n* ecuatoriano (-na)

ecumenical /'ɛkyʊ'mɛnɪkəl/ *a* ecuménico

eczema /'ɛksəmə/ *n* eczema, *f*

eddy /'ɛdi/ *n* remolino, *m*, *vi* remolinar; *Fig.* remolinear

edelweiss /'eidļ,wais/ *n* inmortal de las nieves, *f*

edema /ɪ'dimə/ *n* edema, *m*

Eden /'idņ/ *n* Edén, *m*

edge /ɛdʒ/ *n* (of sharp instruments) filo, *m*; (of a skate) cuchilla, *f*; margen, *mf*; (shore) orilla, *f*; (of two surfaces) arista, *f*; (of books) borde, *m*; (of a coin) canto, *m*; (of a chair, a precipice, a forest, a curb, etc.) borde, *m*; (extreme) extremidad, *f*. **on e.,** de canto; *Fig.* ansioso. **to be on e.,** *Fig.* tener los nervios en punta. **to set on e.,** poner de canto; (of teeth) dar dentera

edge /ɛdʒ/ *vt* (sharpen) afilar; *Sew.* ribetear; orlar; poner un borde (a); (cut) cortar. **to e. away,** escurrirse. **to e. into,** *vt* insinuarse. *vi* deslizarse en. **to e. out,** salir poco a poco

edged /ɛdʒd/ *a* afilado, cortante; (in compounds) de... filos; (bordered) bordeado; (of books) de bordes...

edgewise /'ɛdʒwaiz/ *adv* de lado; de canto. **He couldn't get a word in e.,** No pudo meter baza en la conversación

edging /'ɛdʒɪŋ/ *n* borde, *m*; ribete, *m*

edibility /,ɛdə'bɪlɪti/ *n* el ser comestible

edible /'ɛdəbəl/ *a* comestible

edict /'idɪkt/ *n* edicto, *m*

edification /,ɛdəfɪ'keiʃən/ *n* edificación, *f*

edifice /'ɛdəfɪs/ *n* edificio, *m*

edify /'ɛdə,fai/ *vt* edificar

edifying /'ɛdə,faiɪŋ/ *a* edificante, edificador, de edificación

Edinburgh /'ɛdņ,bərə/ Edimburgo, *m*

edit /'ɛdɪt/ *vt* editar; (a newspaper, journal) ser director de; (prepare for press) redactar; (correct) corregir

editing /'ɛdɪtɪŋ/ *n* trabajo editorial, *m*; redacción, *f*; dirección, *f*; corrección, *f*

edition /ɪ'dɪʃən/ *n* edición, *f*; *Print.* tirada, *f*. **first e.,** edición príncipe, *f*. **miniature e.,** edición diamante, *f*

editor /'ɛdɪtər/ *n* (of a book) editor (-ra); (of a newspaper, journal) director (-ra)

editorial /,ɛdɪ'tɔriəl/ *a* de redacción; editorial. *n* editorial, artículo de fondo, *m*. **e. staff,** redacción, *f*

editorial board consejo de redacción, *m*

editorship /'ɛdɪtər,ʃɪp/ *n* dirección (de un periódico, de una revista), *f*

educability /,ɛdʒəkə'bɪlɪti/ *n* educabilidad, *f*

educable /'ɛdʒəkəbəl/ *a* educable

educate /'ɛdʒʊ,keit/ *vt* educar; formar; (accustom) acostumbrar

educated /'ɛdʒʊ,keitɪd/ *a* culto

education /,ɛdʒʊ'keiʃən/ *n* educación, *f*; enseñanza, *f*; pedagogía, *f*. **chair of e.,** cátedra de pedagogía, *f*. **early e.,** primeras letras, *f pl*. **higher e.,** enseñanza superior, *f*

educational /,ɛdʒʊ'keiʃənl/ *a* educativo; pedagógico; instructivo

educationalist /,ɛdʒə'keiʃənļɪst/ *n* pedagogo, *m*

educative /'ɛdʒʊ,keitɪv/ *a* educativo

educator /'ɛdʒʊ,keitər/ *n* educador (-ra)

educe /ɪ'dus/ *vt* educir; deducir; *Chem.* extraer

eduction /ɪ'dʌkʃən/ *n* educción, *f*

eel /il/ *n* anguila, *f*. **electric eel,** gimnoto, *m*. **eel-basket,** nasa para anguilas, *f*

eerie /'ɪəri/ *a* misterioso, fantástico; sobrenatural; lúgubre

eerily /'ɪərəli/ *adv* fantásticamente; de modo sobrenatural

eeriness /'ɪərinɪs/ *n* ambiente de misterio, *m*; efecto misterioso, *m*

efface /ɪ'feis/ *vt* borrar, destruir; quitar. **to e. oneself,** retirarse; permanecer en el fondo

effacement /ɪ'feismənt/ *n* borradura, *f*

effect /ɪ'fɛkt/ *n* efecto, *m*; impresión, *f*; (result) resultado, *m*, consecuencia, *f*, (meaning) substancia, *f*, significado, *m*; *pl* **effects,** efectos, bienes, *m pl*. *vt* efectuar; producir. **in e.,** en efecto, efectivamente. **of no e.,** inútil. **striving after e.,** efectismo, *m*. **to feel the effects of,** sentir los efectos de; padecer las consecuencias de. **to put into e.,** poner en práctica; hacer efectivo. **to take e.,** producir efecto; ponerse en vigor

effective /ɪ'fɛktɪv/ a eficaz; (striking) de mucho efecto, poderoso, vistoso. **to make e.**, llevar a efecto

effectively /ɪ'fɛktɪvli/ adv eficazmente; (strikingly) con gran efecto; efectivamente, en efecto

effectiveness /ɪ'fɛktɪvnɪs/ n eficacia, f; efecto, m

effectuate /ɪ'fɛktʃu͵eit/ vt efectuar

effeminacy /ɪ'fɛmənəsi/ n afeminación, f

effeminate /ɪ'fɛmənɪt/ a afeminado, adamado. **to make e.**, afeminar

efferent /'ɛfərənt/ a eferente

effervesce /͵ɛfər'vɛs/ vi estar efervescente, hervir

effervescence /͵ɛfər'vɛsəns/ n efervescencia, f

effervescent /͵ɛfər'vɛsənt/ a efervescente

effete /ɪ'fit/ a gastado; estéril; decadente

effeteness /ɪ'fitnɪs/ n decadencia, f; esterilidad, f

efficacious /͵ɛfɪ'keiʃəs/ a eficaz

efficacy /'ɛfɪkəsi/ n eficacia, f

efficiency /ɪ'fɪʃənsi/ n eficiencia, f; buen estado, m; habilidad, f; Mech. rendimiento, m

efficient /ɪ'fɪʃənt/ a (e.g. medicine) eficaz; eficiente; (person) competente, capaz

efficiently /ɪ'fɪʃəntli/ adv eficientemente; eficazmente; competentemente

effigy /'ɛfɪdʒi/ n efigie, imagen, f

efflorescence /͵ɛflə'rɛsəns/ n Chem. eflorescencia, f; Bot. florescencia, f

effluvium /ɪ'fluviəm/ n efluvio, m

effort /'ɛfərt/ n esfuerzo, m. **to make an e.**, hacer un esfuerzo. **make every effort to**, hacer lo posible por + inf; empeñar sus máximos esfuerzos en el sentido de + inf

effortless /'ɛfərtlɪs/ a sin esfuerzo

effrontery /ɪ'frʌntəri/ n descaro, m, insolencia, f

effulgence /ɪ'fʌldʒəns/ n esplendor, fulgor, m

effulgent /ɪ'fʌldʒənt/ a fulgente, resplandeciente

effusion /ɪ'fyuʒən/ n efusión, f

effusive /ɪ'fyusɪv/ a efusivo, expansivo

egg /ɛg/ n huevo, m. **to egg on**, incitar (a). **boiled egg**, huevo cocido, m. **fried egg**, huevo frito, m. **hard egg**, huevo duro, m. **poached egg**, huevo escalfado, m. **scrambled egg**, huevos revueltos, m pl. **soft egg**, huevo pasado por agua, m. **to lay eggs**, poner huevos. **to put all one's eggs in one basket**, Fig. poner toda la carne en el asador. **egg-cup**, huevera, f. **egg dealer**, vendedor (-ra) de huevos. **egg flip**, huevo batido con ron, m. **eggplant**, berenjena, f. **egg-shaped**, aovado. **egg-shell**, cascarón, m, cáscara de huevo, f. **egg-shell china**, loza muy fina, f. **egg-spoon**, cucharita para comer huevos, f. **eggwhisk**, batidor de huevos, m

ego /'igou/ n (psychology) el yo, m

egoism /'igou͵izəm/ n egoísmo, m

egoist /'igouɪst/ n egoísta, mf

egoistic /͵igou'ɪstɪk/ a egoísta

egoistically /͵igou'ɪstɪkəli/ adv egoístamente

egotism /'igə͵tɪzəm/ n egotismo, m, egolatría, f

egotist /'igətɪst/ n egotista, mf

egotistic /͵igə'tɪstɪk/ a egotista

egregious /ɪ'gridʒəs/ a notorio, atroz

egress /'igrɛs/ n salida, f

Egypt /'idʒɪpt/ Egipto, m

Egyptian /ɪ'dʒɪpʃən/ a egipcio. n egipcio (-ia); cigarrillo egipcio, m

Egyptologist /͵idʒɪp'tɒlədʒɪst/ n egiptólogo (-ga)

Egyptology /͵idʒɪp'tɒlədʒi/ n egiptología, f

eh? /ei/ interj ¿eh? ¿qué?

eider /'aidər/ n Ornith. pato de flojel, m

eiderdown /'aidər͵daun/ edredón, m

eight /eit/ a and n ocho m. **He is e. years old,** Tiene ocho años. **It is e. o'clock,** Son las ocho. **e.-day clock,** reloj con cuerda para ocho días, m. **e. hundred,** a and n ochocientos m.. **e.-syllabled,** octosílabico

eighteen /'ei'tin/ a and n diez y ocho, m.

eighteenth /'ei'tinθ/ a décimoctavo; (of the month) (el) diez y ocho, dieciocho; (of monarchs) diez y ocho. n décimoctava parte, f. **e. century,** el siglo diez y ocho

eightfold /'eit͵fould/ a óctuple

eighth /eitθ, eiθ/ a octavo, m; (of the month) (el) ocho; (of monarchs) octavo. n octavo, m

eighthly /'eitθli/ adv en octavo lugar

eightieth /'eitiiθ/ a octogésimo

eighty /'eiti/ a and n ochenta, m.

either /'iðər/ a and pron uno u otro, cualquiera de los dos; ambos (-as). conjunc o (becomes **u** before words beginning with **o** or **ho**). adv tampoco. **I do not like e.,** No me gusta ni el uno ni el otro (ni la una ni la otra). **e.... or,** o... o

ejaculate /ɪ'dʒækyə͵leit/ vt exclamar, lanzar; Med. eyacular

ejaculation /ɪ͵dʒækyə'leiʃən/ n exclamación, f; Med. eyaculación, f

ejaculatory /ɪ'dʒækyələ͵tɔri/ a jaculatorio

eject /ɪ'dʒɛkt/ vt echar, expulsar; Law. desahuciar; (emit) despedir, emitir

ejection /ɪ'dʒɛkʃən/ n echamiento, m, expulsión, f; Law. desahucio, m; (emission) emisión, f

eke out /ik/ vt (make funds last) hacer alcanzar. **e. out a living,** ganarse la vida a duras penas.

elaborate /a ɪ'læbərɪt; v -ə͵reit/ a elaborado; primoroso; elegante; complicado; (detailed) detallado; (of meals) de muchos platos; (of courtesy, etc.) estudiado. vt elaborar; amplificar

elaborately /ɪ'læbərɪtli/ adv primorosamente; elegantemente; complicadamente; con muchos detalles

elaborateness /ɪ'læbərɪtnɪs/ n primor, m; elegancia, f; complicación, f; (care) cuidado, m; minuciosidad, f

elaboration /ɪ͵læbə'reiʃən/ n elaboración, f

elapse /ɪ'læps/ vi transcurrir, andar, pasar

elastic /ɪ'læstɪk/ a elástico. n elástico, m. **e. band,** anillo de goma, m; cinta de goma, f. **e. girdle,** faja elástica, f

elasticity /ɪlæ'stɪsɪti/ n elasticidad, f

elate /ɪ'leit/ vt alegrar; animar

elatedly /ɪ'leitɪdli/ adv alegremente; triunfalmente

elation /ɪ'leiʃən/ n alegría, f, júbilo, m; triunfo, m

elbow /'ɛlbou/ n codo, m; ángulo, m; (of a chair) brazo, m. vt codear, dar codazos (a). **at one's e.,** a la mano. **nudge with the e.,** codazo, m. **to be out at e.,** enseñar los codos, tener los codos raídos; ser harapiento. **to e. one's way,** abrirse paso a codazos. **e.-chair,** silla de brazos, f. **e.-grease,** jugo de muñeca, m. **e.-piece** or **patch,** codera, f. **e. room,** libertad de movimiento, f

elder /'ɛldər/ a comp mayor. n persona mayor, f; señor mayor, m; (among Jews and in Christian Church) anciano, m; Bot. saúco, m

elderly /'ɛldərli/ a mayor

eldest /'ɛldɪst/ a sup old (el, la, etc.) mayor. **e. daughter,** hija mayor, f. **e. son,** hijo mayor, m

elect /ɪ'lɛkt/ vt elegir. a elegido; predestinado. n electo, m; elegido, m

election /ɪ'lɛkʃən/ n Theol. predestinación, f; elección, f. **by-e.,** elección parcial, f

electioneer /ɪ͵lɛkʃə'nɪər/ vi solicitar votos; distribuir propaganda electoral

electioneering /ɪ͵lɛkʃə'nɪərɪŋ/ n solicitación de votos, f; propaganda electoral, f

elective /ɪ'dʒɛktɪv/ a electivo. n (subject at school) materia optativa, f

elector /ɪ'lɛktər/ n elector (-ra); (prince) elector, m

electoral /ɪ'lɛktərəl/ a electoral. **e. register,** lista electoral, f

electoral college colegio de compromisarios, m

electorate /ɪ'lɛktərɪt/ n electorado, m

electric, electrical /ɪ'lɛktrɪk, ɪ'lɛktrɪkəl/ a eléctrico; Fig. vivo, instantáneo. **e. arc,** arco voltaico, m. **e. engineer,** ingeniero electricista, m. **electric fan,** (Spain) ventilador, (Western Hemisphere) ventilador eléctrico, m. **e. fire,** estufa eléctrica, f. **e. immersion heater,** calentador de agua eléctrico, m. **e. light,** luz eléctrica, f. **e. pad,** alfombrilla eléctrica, f. **e. shock,** conmoción eléctrica, f. **e. washing-machine,** lavadora eléctrica, f. **e. wire** or **cable,** conductor eléctrico, m

electrically /ɪ'lɛktrɪkəli/ adv por electricidad

electrician /ɪlɛk'trɪʃən/ n electricista, mf

electricity /ɪlɛk'trɪsɪti/ n electricidad, f

electrification /ɪ͵lɛktrəfɪ'keiʃən/ n electrificación, f

electrify /ɪ'lɛktrə,fai/ vt electrificar; *Fig.* electrizar
electro- prefix (in compounds) electro. **e.-chemistry,**
electroquímica, f. **e.-dynamics,** electrodinámica, f. **e.-**
magnet, electroimán, m. **e.-magnetic,** electromagnético. **e.-plate,** vt galvanizar, platear. n artículo
galvanizado, m. **e.-therapy,** electroterapia, f
electrocute /ɪ'lɛktrə,kyut/ vt electrocutar
electrocution /ɪ,lɛktrə'kyuʃən/ n electrocución, f
electrode /ɪ'lɛktroud/ n electrodo, m
electrolysis /ɪlɛk'trɒləsɪs/ n electrólisis, f
electrolyte /ɪ'lɛktrə,lait/ n electrólito, m
electrolyze /ɪ'lɛktrə,laiz/ vt electrolizar
electrometer /ɪlɛk'trɒmɪtər/ n electrómetro, m
electromotive /ɪ,lɛktrə'moutɪv/ a electromotriz. **e.**
force, fuerza electromotriz, f
electron /ɪ'lɛktrɒn/ n electrón, m
electroscope /ɪ'lɛktrə,skoup/ n electroscopio, m
elegance /'ɛlɪɡəns/ n elegancia, f
elegant /'ɛlɪɡənt/ a elegante; bello
elegantly /'ɛlɪɡəntli/ adv elegantemente, con elegancia
elegiac /,ɛlɪ'dʒaiək/ a elegíaco
elegy /'ɛlɪdʒi/ n elegía, f
element /'ɛləmənt/ n elemento, m; factor, m; ingrediente, m; *Elec.* par, elemento, m; *Chem., Phys.*
cuerpo simple, m; pl **elements,** rudimentos, m pl,
nociones, f pl; (weather) intemperie, f; (Eucharist) el
pan y el vino. **to be in one's e.,** estar en su elemento
elemental /,ɛlə'mɛntl̩/ a elemental; rudimentario, lo
elemental
elementariness /,ɛlə'mɛntərinɪs/ n el carácter, elemental
elementary /,ɛlə'mɛntəri/ a elemental; rudimentario;
primario. **e. education,** enseñanza primaria, f
elephant /'ɛləfənt/ n elefante (-ta). **e. keeper** or
trainer, naire, m
elephantiasis /,ɛləfən'taiəsɪs/ n elefantíasis, f
elephantine /,ɛlə'fæntin/ a elefantino
elevate /'ɛlə,veit/ vt (the Host) alzar; elevar; (the
eyes, the voice) levantar; (honor) enaltecer
elevated /'ɛlə,veitɪd/ a noble, elevado, sublime; edificante; (drunk) achispado
elevation /,ɛlə'veiʃən/ n elevación, f; enaltecimiento,
m; (of style, thought) nobleza, sublimidad, f; (hill)
eminencia, altura, f
elevator /'ɛlə,veitər/ n (lift) ascensor, m; (for grain,
etc.) montacargas, m
elevator shaft caja, f, hueco pozo, m
eleven /ɪ'lɛvən/ a once. n once, m. **It is e. o'clock,**
Son las once
eleventh /ɪ'lɛvənθ/ a onceno, undécimo; (of month)
(el) once; (of monarchs) once. n onzavo, m; undé-
cima parte, f. **at the e. hour,** *Fig.* a última hora.
Louis the E., Luis once (XI)
elf /ɛlf/ n elfo, duende, m; (child) trasgo, m; (dwarf)
enano, m
elfin /'ɛlfɪn/ a de duendes; de hada
elicit /ɪ'lɪsɪt/ vt sacar; hacer contestar; hacer confesar;
descubrir
elicitation /ɪ,lɪsɪ'teiʃən/ n descubrimiento, m
elide /ɪ'laid/ vt elidir
eligibility /,ɛlɪdʒə'bɪlɪti/ n elegibilidad, f
eligible /'ɛlɪdʒəbəl/ a elegible; deseable
eliminate /ɪ'lɪmə,neit/ vt eliminar; quitar
elimination /ɪ,lɪmə'neiʃən/ n eliminación, f
eliminatory /ɪ'lɪmənə,tɔri/ a eliminador
elision /ɪ'lɪʒən/ n elisión, f
elite /ɪ'lit/ n élite, elite, f
elitism /ɪ'litɪzəm/ n elitismo, m
elixir /ɪ'lɪksər/ n elixir, m
Elizabethan /ɪ,lɪzə'biθən/ a de la época de la Reina
Isabel I de Inglaterra
elk /ɛlk/ n ante, m
ell /ɛl/ n (measure) ana, f
ellipse /ɪ'lɪps/ n *Geom.* elipse, f; óvalo, m
ellipsis /ɪ'lɪpsɪs/ n *Gram.* elipsis, f
elliptic /ɪ'lɪptɪk/ a *Geom., Gram.* elíptico
elm /ɛlm/ n olmo, m. **e. grove,** olmeda, f
elocution /,ɛlə'kyuʃən/ n elocución, f; (art of elocution) declamación, f

elocutionist /,ɛlə'kyuʃənɪst/ n recitador (-ra), declamador (-ra)
elongate /ɪ'lɔŋɡeit/ vt alargar; extender. vi alargarse;
extenderse. a alargado; (of face) perfilado
elongation /ɪlɔŋ'ɡeiʃən/ n alargamiento, m; prolongación, f; extensión, f
elope /ɪ'loup/ vi evadirse, huir; fugarse (con un
amante)
elopement /ɪ'loupmənt/ n fuga, f
eloquence /'ɛləkwəns/ n elocuencia, f
eloquent /'ɛləkwənt/ a elocuente
eloquently /'ɛləkwəntli/ adv elocuentemente
else /ɛls/ adv (besides) más; (instead) otra cosa, más;
(otherwise) si no, de otro modo. **anyone e.,** (cualquier) otra persona; alguien más. **Anything e.?** ¿Algo
más? **everyone e.,** todos los demás. **everything e.,**
todo lo demás. **nobody e.,** ningún otro, nadie más.
nothing e., nada más. **or e.,** o bien, de otro modo; si
no. **someone e.,** otra persona, otro. **somewhere e.,**
en otra parte. **There's nothing e. to do,** No hay nada
más que hacer; No hay más remedio
elsewhere /'ɛls,wɛər/ adv a, or en, otra parte
elucidate /ɪ'lusɪ,deit/ vt elucidar, aclarar
elucidation /ɪ,lusɪ'deiʃən/ n elucidación, aclaración, f
elucidatory /ɪ'lusɪdə,tɔri/ a aclaratorio
elude /ɪ'lud/ vt eludir, evitar
elusive /ɪ'lusɪv/ a (of persons) esquivo; fugaz; difícil
de comprender
elusiveness /ɪ'lusɪvnɪs/ n esquivez, f; fugacidad, f
Elysian /ɪ'lɪʒən/ a elíseo. **E. Fields,** campos elíseos, m
pl
Elysium /ɪ'lɪʒiəm/ n elíseo, m
emaciate /ɪ'meiʃi,eit/ vt extenuar, demacrar, enflaquecer
emaciated /ɪ'meiʃi,eitɪd/ a extenuado, demacrado. **to**
become e., demacrarse
emaciation /ɪ,meiʃi'eiʃən/ n demacración, emaciación, f; *Med.* depauperación, f
e-mail /'i,meil/ n correo electrónico, m. **e. message,**
mensaje de correo electrónico, m
emanate /'ɛmə,neit/ vi emanar (de), proceder (de)
emanation /,ɛmə'neiʃən/ n emanación, f; exhalación,
f
emancipate /ɪ'mænsə,peit/ vt emancipar
emancipated /ɪ'mænsə,peitɪd/ a emancipado
emancipation /ɪ,mænsə'peiʃən/ n emancipación, f
emancipator /ɪ'mænsə,peitər/ n emancipador (-ra),
libertador (-ra)
emancipatory /ɪ'mænsəpə,tɔri/ a emancipador
emasculate /a ɪ'mæskyəlɪt; v -,leit/ a afeminado. vt
emascular; *Fig.* afeminar; mutilar
emasculation /ɪ,mæskyə'leiʃən/ n emasculación, f
embalm /ɛm'bam/ vt embalsamar; *Fig.* conservar el
recuerdo de; perfumar
embalmer /ɛm'bamər/ n embalsamador, m
embalmment /ɛm'bammənt/ n embalsamamiento, m
embankment /ɛm'bæŋkmənt/ n declive, m; ribera, f;
terraplén, m; dique, m; (quay) muelle, m
embargo /ɛm'barɡou/ n embargo, m, al embargar.
to put an e. on, embargar. **to remove an e.,** sacar
de embargo
embark /ɛm'bark/ vi embarcarse; lanzarse (a). vt
embarcar
embarkation /,ɛmbar'keiʃən/ n (of persons) embarcación, f; (of goods) embarque, m
embarrass /ɛm'bærəs/ vt avergonzar, impedir; (financially) apurar; (perplex) tener perplejo; (worry) preocupar; (confuse) desconcertar, turbar; (annoy) molestar
embarrassed /ɛm'bærəst/ a avergonzado, turbado
embarrassing /ɛm'bærəsɪŋ/ a avergonzoso, embarazoso; desconcertante; molesto
embarrassingly /ɛm'bærəsɪŋli/ adv de un modo desconcertante; demasiado
embarrassment /ɛm'bærəsmənt/ n bochorno, m; vergüenza, f; pena, f; (financial) apuro, m; (obligation)
compromiso, m; (perplexity) perplejidad, f; (worry)
preocupación, f; (confusion) turbación, f
embassy /'ɛmbəsi/ n embajada, f

embattled /ɛm'bætḷd/ *a* en orden de batalla; *Herald.* almenado

embed /ɛm'bɛd/ *vt* empotrar, enclavar; fijar

embellish /ɛm'bɛlɪʃ/ *vt* embellecer; adornar

embellishment /ɛm'bɛlɪʃmənt/ *n* embellecimiento, *m*; adorno, *m*

ember /'ɛmbər/ *n* rescoldo, *m*. **E. days,** témporas, *f pl*

embezzle /ɛm'bɛzəl/ *vt* desfalcar

embezzlement /ɛm'bɛzəlmənt/ *n* desfalco, *m*

embezzler /ɛm'bɛzlər/ *n* desfalcador (-ra)

embitter /ɛm'bɪtər/ *vt Fig.* amargar; envenenar

embittering /ɛm'bɪtərɪŋ/ *a* amargo

embitterment /ɛm'bɪtərmənt/ *n* amargura, *f*

emblazon /ɛm'bleizən/ *vt* blasonar; *Fig.* ensalzar

emblem /'ɛmbləm/ *n* emblema, *m*

emblematic /ˌɛmblə'mætɪk/ *a* emblemático

embodiment /ɛm'bɒdimənt/ *n* incarnación, *f*; expresión, *f*; personificación, *f*; símbolo, *m*; síntesis, *f*

embody /ɛm'bɒdi/ *vt* encarnar; expresar; personificar; incorporar; contener; formular; sintetizar. **to be embodied in,** quedar plasmado en

embolden /ɛm'bouldən/ *vt* animar, dar valor (a)

embolism /'ɛmbəˌlɪzəm/ *n Med.* embolia, *f*

emboss /ɛm'bɔs/ *vt* repujar, abollonar; estampar en relieve

embossment /ɛm'bɔsmənt/ *n* abolladura, *f*; relieve, *m*

embrace /ɛm'breis/ *n* abrazo, *m*. *vt* abrazar, dar un abrazo (a); (*Fig..* seize) aprovechar; (accept) aceptar; adoptar; (engage in) dedicarse a; (comprise) incluir, abarcar; (comprehend) comprender. **They embraced,** Se abrazaron

embroider /ɛm'brɔidər/ *vt* bordar; embellecer; (a tale, etc.) exagerar; *vi* hacer bordado

embroiderer /ɛm'brɔidərər/ *n* bordador (-ra)

embroidery /ɛm'brɔidəri, -dri/ *n* bordado, *m*; labor, *f*. **e.-frame,** bastidor, *m*. **e. silk,** hilo de bordar, *m*

embroil /ɛm'brɔil/ *vt* enredar, embrollar; desordenar

embryo /'ɛmbriˌou/ *n* embrión, *m*; *Fig.* germen, *m. a* embrionario

embryology /ˌɛmbri'ɒlədʒi/ *n* embriología, *f*

embryonic /ˌɛmbri'ɒnɪk/ *a* embrionario

emend /ɪ'mɛnd/ *vt* enmendar; corregir

emendation /ˌimən'deiʃən/ *n* enmienda, *f*; corrección, *f*

emerald /'ɛmərəld/ *n* esmeralda, *f*, *a* de color de esmeralda. **e. green,** verde esmeralda, *m*

emerge /ɪ'mɜrdʒ/ *vt* emerger; surgir; *Fig.* salir; aparecer

emergence /ɪ'mɜrdʒəns/ *n* emergencia, *f*; salida, *f*; aparición, *f*

emergency /ɪ'mɜrdʒənsi/ *n* urgencia, *f*; necesidad, *f*; emergencia, *f*; aprieto, *m*. **e. exit,** salida de urgencia, *f*. **e. port,** *Naut.* puerto de arribada, *m*

emergent /ɪ'mɜrdʒənt/ *a* emergente; que sale; naciente

emery /'ɛməri/ *n* esmeril, *m*. **to polish with e.,** esmerilar. **e.-paper,** papel de lija, *m*

emetic /ɪ'mɛtɪk/ *a* and *n* emético, vomitivo, *m*.

emigrant /'ɛmɪgrənt/ *a* emigrante. *n* emigrante, *mf* emigrado, *m*

emigrate /'ɛmɪˌgreit/ *vi* emigrar; *Inf.* trasladarse

emigration /ˌɛmə'greiʃən/ *n* emigración, *f*. **e. officer,** oficial de emigración, *m*

eminence /'ɛmənəns/ *n* (hill) elevación, prominencia, *f*; eminencia (also as title), *f*; distinción, *f*

eminent /'ɛmənənt/ *a* distinguido, eminente; famoso, ilustre; notable; conspicuo

eminently /'ɛmənəntli/ *adv* eminentemente

emir /ə'mɪər/ *n* amir, *m*

emissary /'ɛməˌsɛri/ *n* emisario (-ia); embajador (-ra); agente, *m*

emission /ɪ'mɪʃən/ *n* emisión, *f*

emit /ɪ'mɪt/ *vt* despedir; exhalar; emitir

emollient /ɪ'mɒlyənt/ *a* emoliente, lenitivo. *n* emoliente, *m*

emolument /ɪ'mɒlyəmənt/ *n* emolumento, *m*

emotion /ɪ'mouʃən/ *n* emoción, *f*. **to cause e.,** emocionar

emotional /ɪ'mouʃənḷ/ *a* emocional, sentimental; emocionante

emotionalism /ɪ'mouʃənḷ'ɪzəm/ *n* sentimentalismo, *m*

emotionalize /ɪ'mouʃənḷˌaiz/ *vt* considerar bajo un punto de vista sentimental

emotionally /ɪ'mouʃənḷi/ *adv* con emoción, sentimentalmente

emotionless /ɪ'mouʃənlɪs/ *a* sin emoción

emotive /ɪ'moutɪv/ *a* emotivo

emperor /'ɛmpərər/ *n* emperador, *m*

emphasis (on) /'ɛmfəsɪs/ *n* énfasis (en), *mf*; insistencia especial (en), especial atención (a), *f*; accentuación, *f*

emphasize /'ɛmfəˌsaiz/ *vt* subrayar, dar énfasis a, poner de relieve, hacer resaltar, dar importancia a; acentuar; insistir en, hacer hincapié (en)

emphatic /ɛm'fætɪk/ *a* enfático

emphatically /ɛm'fætɪkəli/ *adv* con énfasis

empire /'ɛmpaiʳr/ *n* imperio, *m*

empirical /ɛm'pɪrɪkəl/ *a* empírico

empiricism /ɛm'pɪrəˌsɪzəm/ *n* empirismo, *m*

employ /ɛm'plɔi/ *n* empleo, *m*; servicio, *m. vt* emplear; ocupar; tomar; servirse de, usar. **How do you e. yourself?** ¿Cómo te ocupas? ¿Cómo pasas el tiempo?

employable /ɛm'plɔiəbəl/ *a* empleable; utilizable

employee /ɛm'plɔii/ *n* empleado (-da)

employer /ɛm'plɔiər/ *n* el, *m*, (*f*, la) que emplea; dueño (-ña), amo (-a); patrón (-ona)

employment /ɛm'plɔimənt/ *n* empleo, *m*; uso, *m*; ocupación, *f*; aprovechamiento, *m*; (post) puesto, cargo, *m*; (situation) colocación, *f*. **e. exchange,** bolsa de trabajo, *f*

emporium /ɛm'pɔriəm/ *n* emporio, *m*; (store) almacén, *m*

empower /ɛm'pauər/ *vt* autorizar; permitir; ayudar (a); dar el poder (para)

empress /'ɛmprɪs/ *n* emperatriz, *f*

emptiness /'ɛmptinɪs/ *n* vaciedad, *f*; futilidad, *f*; vacuidad, *f*; (verbosity) palabrería, *f*

empty /'ɛmpti/ *a* vacío; (of a house, etc.) deshabitado, desocupado; (deserted) desierto; (vain) vano, inútil; frívolo; (hungry) hambriento. *n* envase vacío, *m*. *vt* vaciar; descargar. *vi* vaciarse; (river, etc.) desembocar, venir a morir en. **e.-handed,** con las manos vacías. **e.-headed,** casquivano

emptying /'ɛmptiɪŋ/ *n* vaciamiento, *m*; abandono, *m*; *pl* **emptyings,** heces de la cerveza, *f pl*

emu /'imyu/ *n* emu, *m*

emulate /'ɛmyəˌleit/ *vt* emular

emulation /ˌɛmyə'leiʃən/ *n* emulación, *f*

emulative /'ɛmyəˌleitɪv/ *a* emulador

emulsify /ɪ'mʌlsɪfai/ *vt* emulsionar

emulsion /ɪ'mʌlʃən/ *n* emulsión, *f*

emulsive /ɪ'mʌlsɪv/ *a* emulsivo

enable /ɛn'eibəl/ *vt* (to) hacer capaz (de); ayudar (a); autorizar (para); permitir (de)

enact /ɛn'ækt/ *vt Law.* promulgar; decretar; (a part) hacer, desempeñar (un papel); (a play) representar; (happen) ocurrir, tener lugar

enaction /ɛn'ækʃən/ *n Law.* promulgación, *f*

enamel /ɪ'næməl/ *n* esmalte, *m*, *vt* esmaltar

enameler /ɪ'næmələr/ *n* esmaltador (-ra)

enameling /ɪ'næmelɪŋ/ *n* esmaltadura, *f*

enamor /ɪ'næmər/ *vt* enamorar. **to be enamored of,** estar enamorado de; estar aficionado a

encamp /ɛn'kæmp/ *vt* and *vi* acampar

encampment /ɛn'kæmpmənt/ *n* campamento, *m*

encase /ɛn'keis/ *vt* encajar; encerrar; (line) forrar

encasement /ɛn'keismənt/ *n* encaje, *m*; encierro, *m*

encephalitis /ɛnˌsefə'laitɪs/ *n* encefalitis, *f*. **e. lethargica,** encefalitis letárgica, *f*

enchant /ɛn'tʃænt/ *vt* encantar, hechizar; fascinar; embelesar, deleitar

enchanter /ɛn'tʃæntər/ *n* encantador, *m*

enchanting /ɛn'tʃæntɪŋ/ *a* encantador, fascinador

enchantment /ɛn'tʃæntmənt/ *n* encantamiento, *m*; fascinación, *f*; fascinación, deleite, *m*

enchantress /ɛn'tʃæntrɪs/ *n* bruja, *f*; *Fig.* mujer seductora, *f*

encircle /ɛn'sɜrkəl/ vt cercar; rodear; dar la vuelta (a)
enclose /ɛn'klouz/ vt cercar; meter dentro de; encerrar; (with a letter, etc.) incluir, adjuntar
enclosed /ɛn'klouzd/ a (of letters) adjunto
enclosure /ɛn'klouʒər/ n cercamiento, m; cercado, m; recinto, m; (wall) tapia, cerca, f; (with a letter) contenido adjunto, m
encomium /ɛn'koumiəm/ n encomio, m
encompass /ɛn'kʌmpəs/ vt cercar, rodear
encore /'aŋkɔr/ n repetición, f, interj ¡bis!
encounter /ɛn'kauntər/ n encuentro, m; combate, m; conflicto, m; lucha, f. vt encontrar; atacar; tropezar con
encourage /ɛn'kɜrɪdʒ/ vt animar; alentar; darle ánimo a; estimular; incitar; ayudar; (approve) aprobar; (foster) fomentar
encouragement /ɛn'kɜrɪdʒmənt/ n ánimos, m pl; estímulo, incentivo, m; ayuda, f; (approval) aprobación, f; (promotion) fomento, m
encourager /ɛn'kɜrɪdʒər/ n instigador (-ra); ayudador (-ra); aprobador (-ra); fomentador (-ra)
encouraging /ɛn'kɜrɪdʒɪŋ/ a alentador; estimulante; fomentador; (favorable) halagüeño, favorable
encouragingly /ɛn'kɜrɪdʒɪŋli/ adv de un modo alentador; con aprobación
encroach /ɛn'kroutʃ/ vi usurpar; abusar (de); invadir; robar; (of sea, river) hurtar
encroaching /ɛn'kroutʃɪŋ/ a usurpador; invadiente
encroachment /ɛn'kroutʃmənt/ n usurpación, f; abuso, m; invasión, f
encrust /ɛn'krʌst/ vt encostrar; incrustar
encumber /ɛn'kʌmbər/ vt impedir, estorbar; llenar; (burden) cargar; (mortgage) hipotecar; (overwhelm) agobiar
encumbrance /ɛn'kʌmbrəns/ n impedimento, estorbo, m; gravamen, m; carga, f; (mortgage) hipoteca, f
encyclical /ɛn'sɪklɪkəl/ n encíclica, f
encyclopedia /ɛn,saiklə'pidiə/ n enciclopedia, f
encyclopedic /ɛn,saiklə'pidɪk/ a enciclopédico
encyclopedist /ɛn,saiklə'pidɪst/ n enciclopedista, m
end /ɛnd/ n fin, m; extremidad, f; extremo, m; conclusión, f; (point) punta, f; cabo, m; (district) barrio, m; cabeza, f; (death) muerte, f; (aim) objeto, intento, m; (purpose) propósito, f; (issue) resultado, m; (bit) fragmento, pedazo, m; (of a word) terminación, f. vi terminar; acabar; concluir; cesar; (in) terminar en; resultar en; (with) terminar con. vt terminar; acabar, dar fin a. **at an end,** terminado. **at the end,** al cabo (de); al extremo (de). **end of quotation,** fin de cita, final de la cita, m. **from end to end,** de un extremo a otro; de un cabo a otro. **in the end,** por fin, finalmente. **on end,** de pie, de cabeza, derecho; de punta; (of hair) erizado. **no end of,** un sinnúmero de. **to make both ends meet,** pasar con lo que se tiene. **to make an end of,** acabar con. **to put an end to,** poner fin a. **to the end that,** a fin de que, para que; con objeto de. **toward the end of,** (months, years, etc.) a fines de, a últimos de; hacia el fin de. **two hours on end,** dos horas seguidas. **end-paper,** guarda, f
endanger /ɛn'deindʒər/ vt arriesgar, poner en peligro
endear /ɛn'dɪər/ vt hacer querer
endearing /ɛn'dɪərɪŋ/ a que inspira cariño; atrayente; cariñoso
endearment /ɛn'dɪərmənt/ n cariño, amor, m; caricia, terneza, f; palabra de cariño, f
endeavor /ɛn'dɛvər/ vi procurar, intentar, hacer un esfuerzo. n esfuerzo, m, tentativa, f
endemic /ɛn'dɛmɪk/ a Med. endémico
ending /'ɛndɪŋ/ n fin, m; conclusión, f; Gram. terminación, f; cesación, f; (climax) desenlace, m
endive /ɛn'daiv/ n Bot. escarola, f
endless /'ɛndlɪs/ a eterno; inacabable; infinito; sin fin; interminable; incesante
endlessly /'ɛndlɪsli/ adv sin fin; incesantemente; sin parar
endlessness /'ɛndlɪsnɪs/ n eternidad, f; infinidad, f; continuidad, f
endocrine /'ɛndəkrɪn/ a endocrino. n secreción interna, f

endocrinology /,ɛndoukrə'nɒlədʒi/ n endocrinología, f
end-of-season /'ɛnd əv 'sizən/ a por final de temporada (e.g., end-of-season reductions, rebajos por final de temporada, m pl. end-of-season sale, liquidación por final de temporada, f)
endogenous /ɛn'dɒdʒənəs/ a endógeno
endorse /ɛn'dɔrs/ vt Com. endosar; garantizar; (uphold) apoyar; confirmar
endorsee /ɛndɔr'si/ n endosatario (-ia)
endorsement /ɛn'dɔrsmənt/ n Com. endoso, m; aval, m, garantía, f; corroboración, confirmación, f
endorser /ɛn'dɔrsər/ n Com. endosante, m
endow /ɛn'dau/ vt dotar; fundar; crear
endowment /ɛn'daumənt/ n dotación, f; fundación, f; creación, f; (mental) inteligencia, f; cualidad, f, don, m. **e. policy,** póliza dotal, f
endurable /ɛn'dʊrəbəl/ a sufrible, soportable; tolerable
endurance /ɛn'dʊrəns/ n aguante, m; resistencia, f; sufrimiento, m; tolerancia, f; paciencia, f; (lastingness) duración, continuación, f. **beyond e.,** intolerable, inaguantable. **e. test,** prueba de resistencia, f
endure /ɛn'dʊr/ vt soportar; tolerar, aguantar; sufrir; resistir. vi sufrir; (last) durar, continuar
enduring /ɛn'dʊrɪŋ/ a permanente, perdurable; continuo; constante
enduringness /ɛn'dʊrɪŋnɪs/ n (lastingness) permanencia, f; paciencia, f; aguante, m
enema /'ɛnəmə/ n lavativa, enema, f
enemy /'ɛnəmi/ n enemigo (-ga); adversario (-ia) (in war) enemigo, m. a del enemigo, enemigo. **to be one's own e.,** ser enemigo de sí mismo. **to become an e. of,** enemistarse con; hacerse enemigo de, volverse hostil a
energetic /,ɛnər'dʒɛtɪk/ a enérgico
energy /'ɛnərdʒi/ n energía, fuerza, f, vigor, m
enervate /v 'ɛnər,veit/ a 'ɪnɜrvɪt/ vt enervar; debilitar. a enervado
enervation /,ɛnər'veiʃən/ n enervación, f; debilitación, f
enfeeble /ɛn'fibəl/ vt debilitar
enfeeblement /ɛn'fibəlmənt/ n debilitación, f, desfallecimiento, m
enfold /ɛn'fould/ vt envolver; abrazar
enforce /ɛn'fɔrs/ vt (a law) poner en vigor; (impose) imponer a la fuerza; hacer cumplir; conseguir por fuerza; (demonstrate) demostrar
enforcement /ɛn'fɔrsmənt/ n (of a law) ejecución (de una ley), f; imposición a la fuerza, f; observación forzosa, f
enfranchise /ɛn'fræntʃaiz/ vt emancipar; conceder derechos civiles (a)
enfranchisement /ɛn'fræntʃaizmənt/ n emancipación, f; concesión de derechos civiles, f
engage /ɛn'geidʒ/ vt empeñar; contratar; tomar en alquiler; tomar a su servicio; (seats, etc.) reservar; (occupy) ocupar; (attention) atraer; (in) aplicarse a, dedicarse a; Mil. combatir con, librar batalla con; atacar; (of wheels) endentar con. vi obligarse; dedicarse (a); tomar parte (en); (bet) apostar; Mil. librar batalla; (fight) venir a las manos. **to be engaged in,** traer entre manos, ocuparse en. **to become engaged,** comprometerse
engaged /ɛn'geidʒd/ a ocupado; (betrothed) prometido; reservado
engagement /ɛn'geidʒmənt/ n obligación, f; compromiso, m; (date) cita, f; (betrothal) palabra de casamiento, f; (battle) combate, m, batalla, f. **I have an e. at two o'clock.** Tengo una cita a las dos
engagement gift regalo de esponsales, m
engaging /ɛn'geidʒɪŋ/ a simpático, atractivo
engagingly /ɛn'geidʒɪŋli/ adv de un modo encantador
engender /ɛn'dʒɛndər/ vt Fig. engendrar; excitar
engine /'ɛndʒən/ n máquina, f; motor, m; (locomotive) locomotora, f; (pump) bomba, f. **to sit with one's back to the e.,** ir estar sentado de espaldas a la máquina (or locomotora). **e. builder,** constructor de máquinas, m. **e. driver,** maquinista, mf. **e. room,**

cuarto de máquinas, *m*. **e. works,** taller de maquinaria, *m*

engineer /ˌɛndʒə'nɪər/ *n* ingeniero, *m*; mecánico, *m*. *vt Fig.* gestionar, arreglar. **civil e.,** ingeniero de caminos, canales y puertos, *m*. **Royal Engineers,** Cuerpo de Ingenieros, *m*

engineering /ˌɛndʒə'nɪərɪŋ/ *n* ingeniería, *f*; *Fig.* manejo, *m*. **a de** ingeniería

England /'ɪŋglənd/ Inglaterra, *f*

English /'ɪŋglɪʃ/ *a* inglés. *n* (language) inglés, *m*. **in E. fashion,** a la inglesa. **to speak E.,** hablar inglés. **to speak plain E.,** hablar sin rodeos. **E.-speaking,** anglohablante. **E. Church,** iglesia anglicana, *f*. **E.-teacher,** maestro (-ra) de inglés. **English-translator,** traductor al inglés, *m*

English Channel, the el Canal de la Mancha

Englishman /'ɪŋglɪʃmən/ *n* inglés, *m*

Englishwoman /'ɪŋglɪʃˌwʊmən/ *n* inglesa, *f*

engrain /ɛn'greɪn/ *vt* inculcar

engrave /ɛn'greɪv/ *vt* grabar; esculpir, cincelar; *Fig.* grabar

engraver /ɛn'greɪvər/ *n* grabador (-ra); (tool) cincel, *m*

engraving /ɛn'greɪvɪŋ/ *n* grabadura, *f*; (picture) grabado, *m*. **e. needle,** punta seca, *f*

engross /ɛn'grous/ *vt* (a document) poner en limpio; redactar; (absorb) absorber

engrossing /ɛn'grousɪŋ/ *a* absorbente

engulf /ɛn'gʌlf/ *vt* hundir, sumir, sumergir

enhance /ɛn'hæns/ *vt* realzar; intensificar; aumentar; mejorar

enhancement /ɛn'hænsmənt/ *n* realce, *m*; intensificación, *f*; aumento, *m*; mejoría, *f*

enigma /ə'nɪgmə/ *n* enigma, *m*

enigmatic /ˌɛnɪg'mætɪk/ *a* enigmático

enjoin /ɛn'dʒɔɪn/ *vt* imponer; ordenar, mandar; encargar

enjoy /ɛn'dʒɔɪ/ *vt* disfrutar; gustar de; gozar de; poseer, tener. **to e. oneself,** recrearse, regocijarse; (amuse oneself) divertirse, entretenerse; pasarlo bien. **Did you e. yourself?** ¿Lo pasaste bien? **E. your meal,** Buen provecho

enjoyable /ɛn'dʒɔɪəbəl/ *a* agradable; divertido, entretenido

enjoyableness /ɛn'dʒɔɪəbəlnɪs/ *n* lo agradable; lo divertido

enjoyably /ɛn'dʒɔɪəbli/ *adv* de un modo muy agradable

enjoyer /ɛn'dʒɔɪər/ *n* el, *m*, (*f*, la) que disfruta; poseedor (-ra); (amateur) aficionado (-da)

enjoyment /ɛn'dʒɔɪmənt/ *n* posesión, *f*; goce, disfruto, *m*; (pleasure) placer, *m*; aprovechamiento, *m*; utilización, *f*; (satisfaction) satisfacción, *f*

enlarge /ɛn'lɑrdʒ/ *vt* agrandar; aumentar; ensanchar; extender; *Photo.* ampliar; dilatar; (the mind, etc.) ensanchar. *vi* agrandarse; ensancharse; aumentarse; extenderse. **an enlarged heart,** dilatación del corazón, *f*. **to e. upon,** tratar detalladamente, explayarse en

enlargement /ɛn'lɑrdʒmənt/ *n* engrandecimiento, *m*; ensanchamiento, *m*; *Photo.* ampliación, *f*; *Med.* dilatación, *f*; aumento, *m*; amplificación, *f*; (of a town, etc.) ensanche, *m*

enlarger /ɛn'lɑrdʒər/ *n* *Photo.* ampliadora, *f*

enlighten /ɛn'laɪtn̩/ *vt* iluminar; aclarar; informar

enlightened /ɛn'laɪtn̩d/ *a* culto; ilustrado; inteligente

enlightening /ɛn'laɪtn̩ɪŋ/ *a* instructivo

enlightenment /ɛn'laɪtn̩mənt/ *n* ilustración, *f*; cultura, civilización, *f*

enlist /ɛn'lɪst/ *vt* *Mil.* reclutar; alistar; obtener, conseguir. *vi* *Mil.* sentar plaza, sentar plaza de soldado; engancharse; alistarse

enlistment /ɛn'lɪstmənt/ *n* *Mil.* enganche, *m*; reclutamiento, *m*; alistamiento, *m*

enliven /ɛn'laɪvən/ *vt* animar; avivar; alegrar

enmity /'ɛnmɪti/ *n* enemistad, *f*; enemiga, hostilidad, *f*

ennoble /ɛn'noubəl/ *vt* ennoblecer; ilustrar

ennui /ɑn'wi/ *n* tedio, *m*; aburrimiento, *m*

enormity /ɪ'nɔrmɪti/ *n* enormidad, *f*; gravedad, *f*; atrocidad, *f*

enormous /ɪ'nɔrməs/ *a* enorme, colosal

enormously /ɪ'nɔrməsli/ *adv* enormemente

enormousness /ɪ'nɔrməsnɪs/ *n* enormidad, *f*

enough /ɪ'nʌf/ *a* bastante, suficiente. *n* lo bastante, lo suficiente. *adv* bastante; suficientemente. *interj* ¡bastante! ¡basta! **to be e.,** ser suficiente; bastar. **two are enough,** con dos tenemos bastante, con dos tengo bastante

enquire. /ɛn'kwaɪər/ See **inquire**

enrage /ɛn'reɪdʒ/ *vt* enfurecer, hacer furioso; *Inf.* hacer rabiar

enraged /ɛn'reɪdʒd/ *a* furioso

enrapture /ɛn'ræptʃər/ *vt* entusiasmar, extasiar; (intoxicate) embriagar; (charm) encantar, deleitar

enrich /ɛn'rɪtʃ/ *vt* enriquecer; (adorn) adornar, embellecer; (the land) fertilizar

enrichment /ɛn'rɪtʃmənt/ *n* enriquecimiento, *m*; embellecimiento, *m*; (of the land) abono, *m*

enroll /ɛn'roul/ *vt* alistar; matricular; inscribir; (perpetuate) inmortalizar

enrollment /ɛn'roulmənt/ *n* alistamiento, *m*; inscripción, *f*

ensconce /ɛn'skɒns/ *vt* acomodar, colocar; ocultar

ensemble /ɑn'sɑmbəl/ *n* conjunto, *m*

enshrine /ɛn'ʃraɪn/ *vt* poner en sagrario; guardar con cuidado; *Fig.* guardar como una reliquia

enshroud /ɛn'ʃraud/ *vt* amortajar; envolver; esconder

ensign /'ɛnsən/ *n* (badge) insignia, *f*; (flag) enseña, bandera, *f*; pabellón, *m*; bandera de popa, *f*; *Mil.* alférez, *m*; (U.S.A. navy) subteniente, *m*

enslave /ɛn'sleɪv/ *vt* esclavizar

enslavement /ɛn'sleɪvmənt/ *n* esclavitud, *f*

ensue /ɛn'su/ *vt* conseguir. *vi* resultar; suceder, sobrevenir

ensuing /ɛn'suɪŋ/ *a* (next) próximo; (resulting) resultante

ensure /ɛn'ʃʊr/ *vt* asegurar; estar seguro de que; garantizar

entail /ɛn'teil/ *vt* traer consigo, acarrear; *Law.* vincular; *n* *Law.* vinculación, *f*; herencia, *f*

entangle /ɛn'tæŋgəl/ *vt* enredar; coger; *Fig.* embrollar

entanglement /ɛn'tæŋgəlmənt/ *n* enredo, *m*; complicación, *f*; intriga, *f*; (of wire) alambrada, *f*

entangling /ɛn'tæŋglɪŋ/ *a* enmarañador (e.g., *entangling alliances,* alianzas enmarañadoras, *f pl*)

enter /'ɛntər/ *vt* entrar en; penetrar; (of thoughts) ocurrirse; (join) ingresar en; entrar en; (become a member of) hacerse miembro de; (enroll) alistarse; (a university) matricularse; (inscribe) inscribir, poner en la lista; (note) anotar, apuntar; (a protest) hacer constar; (make) hacer; formular. *vi* entrar; *Theat.* salir (a la escena); penetrar; *Com.* anotarse. **to e. for,** *vt* inscribir. *vi* inscribirse, tomar parte en. **to e. into,** entrar en; formar parte de; (conversation) entablar (conversación); (negotiations) iniciar; considerar; (another's emotion) acompañar en; (an agreement, etc.) hacer; (say) firmar; (bind oneself) obligarse a, comprometerse a; tomar parte en; (undertake) emprender; empezar; adoptar. **to e. up,** anotar; poner en la lista; registrar. **to e. upon,** comenzar, emprender; tomar posesión de; encargarse de, asumir; inaugurar; dar principio a

enteric /ɛn'tɛrɪk/ *a* entérico

enteritis /ˌɛntə'raɪtɪs/ *n* enteritis, *f*

enterprise /'ɛntər,praɪz/ *n* empresa, *f*; aventura, *f*; (spirit) iniciativa, *f*, empuje, *m*

enterprising /'ɛntər,praɪzɪŋ/ *a* emprendedor, acometedor; de mucha iniciativa

entertain /ˌɛntər'tein/ *vt* (an idea, etc.) acariciar, abrigar; considerar; (as a guest) agasajar, obsequiar; recibir en casa; (amuse) divertir, entretener. *vi* ser hospitalario; tener invitados en casa; dar fiestas

entertaining /ˌɛntər'teinɪŋ/ *a* entretenido, divertido

entertainingly /ˌɛntər'teinɪŋli/ *adv* entretenidamente; (witty) graciosamente

entertainment /ˌɛntər'teinmənt/ *n* convite, *m*; fiesta, *f*; reunión, *f*; banquete, *m*; (hospitality) hospitalidad, *f*; (amusement) diversión, *f*, entretenimiento, *m*; espectáculo, *m*; función, *f*; concierto, *m*

enthrall /ɛn'θrɔl/ *vt* seducir, atraer, encantar; absorber, captar la atención

enthralling /εn'θrɔlıŋ/ *a* absorbente; atrayente; halagüeño
enthrallment /εn'θrɔlmənt/ *n* absorción, *f*; atracción, *f*
enthrone /εn'θroun/ *vt* entronizar
enthronement /εn'θrounmənt/ *n* entronización, *f*
enthusiasm /εn'θuzi,æzəm/ *n* entusiasmo, *m*
enthusiast /εn'θuzi,æst, -ıst/ *n* entusiasta, *mf*
enthusiastic /εn,θuzi'æstık/ *a* entusiasta. **to make e.**, entusiasmar. **to be e.**, entusiasmarse
enthusiastically /εn,θuzi'æstıkəli/ *adv* con entusiasmo
entice /εn'tais/ *vt* tentar, inducir; atraer, seducir
enticement /εn'taismənt/ *n* tentación, *f*; atractivo, *m*
enticing /εn'taisıŋ/ *a* seduciente, atrayente; halagüeño
entire /εn'taiᵊr/ *a* entero; completo; intacto; absoluto; perfecto; íntegro; total
entirely /εn'taiᵊrli/ *adv* enteramente; completamente; integralmente; totalmente
entirety /εn'taiᵊrti/ *n* totalidad, *f*; integridad, *f*; todo, *m*
entitle /εn'taitl/ *vt* (designate) intitular; dar derecho (a); autorizar. **to be entitled to,** tener derecho a
entity /'εntıti/ *n* entidad, *f*; ente, ser, *m*
entombment /εn'tummənt/ *n* sepultura, *f*; entierro, *m*
entomological /,εntəmə'lɒdʒıkəl/ *a* entomológico
entomologist /,εntə'mɒlədʒıst/ *n* entomólogo, *m*
entomology /,εntə'mɒlədʒi/ *n* entomología, *f*
entourage /,ɑntu'raʒ/ *n* séquito, *m*; (environment) medio ambiente, *m*
entr'acte /ɑn'trækt/ *n* entreacto, *m*
entrails /'εntreilz/ *n* entrañas, tripas, *f pl*, intestinos, *m pl*
entrance /'εntrəns/ *n* entrada, *f*; *Theat.* salida (a la escena), *f*; (into a profession, etc.) ingreso, *m*; alistamiento, *m*; (beginning) principio, *m*; (door) puerta, *f*; (porch) portal, *m*; (of a cave) boca, *f*. **e. fee,** cuota de entrada, *f*. **e. hall,** zaguán, *m*. **e. money,** entrada, *f*
entrance /εn'træns/ *vt Fig.* encantar, fascinar; ecstasiar
entrancing /εn'trænsıŋ/ *a* encantador
entreat /εn'trit/ *vt* suplicar, implorar, rogar
entreating /εn'tritıŋ/ *a* suplicante, implorante
entreatingly /εn'tritıŋli/ *adv* de un modo suplicante; insistentemente
entreaty /εn'triti/ *n* súplica, instancia, *f*, ruego, *m*
entree /'ɑntrei/ *n* entrada, *f*
entrench /εn'trεntʃ/ *vt* atrincherar
entrenchment /εn'trεntʃmənt/ *n* atrincheramiento, *m*; *Mil.* parapeto, *m*; (encroachment) invasión, *f*
entresol /'εntər,sɒl/ *n* entresuelo, *m*
entrust /εn'trʌst/ *vt* confiar a (or en), encomendar a; encargar
entry /'εntri/ *n* entrada, *f*; (passage) callejuela, *f*; (note) inscripción, apuntación, *f*; *Com.* partida, *f*; (registration) registro, *m*. **double e.,** *Com.* partida doble, *f*. **single e.,** *Com.* partida simple, *f*
entwine /εn'twain/ *vt* entrelazar, entretejer
enumerate /ı'numə,reit/ *vt* enumerar
enumeration /ı,numə'reiʃən/ *n* enumeración, *f*
enumerative /ı'numə,reitıv/ *a* enumerativo
enunciate /ı'nʌnsi,eit/ *vt* enunciar; articular
enunciation /ı,nʌnsi'eiʃən/ *n* enunciación, *f*; articulación, *f*
envelop /εn'vεləp/ *vt* envolver, cubrir
envelope /'εnvə,loup/ *n* sobre, *m*
envelopment /εn'vεləpmənt/ *n* envolvimiento, *m*; cubierta, *f*
enviable /'εnviəbəl/ *a* envidiable
envious /'εnviəs/ *a* envidioso. **an e. look,** una mirada de envidia
enviously /'εnviəsli/ *adv* con envidia
environment /εn'vairənmənt/ *n* medio ambiente, *m*
environmental /εn,vairən'mεntl̩/ *a* ambiental
environs /εn'vairənz/ *n* inmediaciones, *f pl*, alrededores, *m pl*
envisage /εn'vızıdʒ/ *vt* hacer frente a; contemplar; imaginar
envoy /'εnvɔi/ *n* enviado, *m*; mensajero (-ra)

envy /'εnvi/ *n* envidia, *f*, *vt* envidiar
enzyme /'εnzaim/ *n* fermento, *m*, enzima, *f*
eon /'iən/ *n* eón, *m*
epaulette /'εpə,let/ *n* hombrera, *f*
ephemeral /ı'fεmərəl/ *a* efímero; *Fig.* fugaz, pasajero
Ephesus /'εfəsəs/ Efiso, *m*
Ephraim /'ifriəm/ Efraín, *m*
epic /'εpık/ *a* épico. *n* epopeya, *f*
epicenter /'εpə,sentər/ *n* epicentro, *m*
epicure /'εpı,kyʊr/ *n* epicúreo (-ea)
epicurean /,εpıkyʊ'riən/ *a* epicúreo
Epicureanism /,εpıkyʊ'riə,nızəm/ *n* epicureísmo, *m*
epidemic /,εpı'dεmık/ *n* epidemia, *f*; plaga, *f*, *a* epidémico
epidermis /,εpı'dɜrmıs/ *n* epidermis, *f*
epiglottis /,εpı'glɒtıs/ *n* epiglotis, *f*
epigram /'εpı,græm/ *n* epigrama, *m*
epigrammatic /,εpıgrə'mætık/ *a* epigramático
epigraph /'εpı,græf/ *n* epígrafe, *m*
epigraphy /ı'pıgrəfi/ *n* epigrafía, *f*
epilepsy /'εpə,lεpsi/ *n* epilepsia, alferecía, *f*
epileptic /,εpə'lεptık/ *a* and *n* epiléptico (-ca). **e. fit,** ataque epiléptico, *m*. **e. aura,** aura epiléptica, *f*
epilogue /'εpə,lɔg/ *n* epílogo, *m*
epiphany /ı'pıfəni/ *n* epifanía, *f*
episcopacy /ı'pıskəpəsi/ *n* episcopado, *m*
episcopal /ı'pıskəpəl/ *a* episcopal
Episcopalianism /ı,pıskə'peilyə,nızəm/ *n* episcopalismo, *m*
episode /'εpə,soud/ *n* suceso, incidente, *m*; *Lit.* episodio, *m*
episodic /,εpə'sɒdık/ *a* episódico
epistle /ı'pısəl/ *n* epístola, *f*
epistolary /ı'pıstl̩,εri/ *a* epistolar
epitaph /'εpı,tæf/ *n* epitafio, *m*
epithet /'εpə,θεt/ *n* epíteto, *m*
epitome /ı'pıtəmi/ *n* epítome, *m*
epitomize /ı'pıtə,maiz/ *vt* resumir, abreviar
epoch /'εpək/ *n* época, edad, *f*
epode /'εpoud/ *n* épodo, *m*
Epsom salts /'εpsəm/ *n* sal de la Higuera, *f*
equability /,εkwə'bılıti/ *n* igualdad (de ánimo), ecuanimidad, *f*; uniformidad, *f*
equable /'εkwəbəl/ *a* igual, ecuánime; uniforme
equably /'εkwəbli/ *adv* con ecuanimidad; igualmente; uniformemente
equal /'ikwəl/ *a* igual; uniforme; imparcial; equitativo, justo. *n* igual, *mf*. *vt* ser igual a; equivaler a; igualar; *Sports.* empatar. **to be e. to,** (of persons) ser capaz de; servir para; atreverse a; (circumstances) estar al nivel de; sentirse con fuerzas para. **without e.,** sin igual; (of beauty, etc.) sin par. **e. sign,** *Math.* igual, *m*
equality /ı'kwɒlıti/ *n* igualdad, *f*; uniformidad, *f*
equalization /,ikwələ'zeiʃən/ *n* igualación, *f*
equalize /'ikwə,laiz/ *vt* igualar
equalizing /'ikwə,laizıŋ/ *a* igualador; compensador
equally /'ikwəli/ *adv* igualmente; imparcialmente
equanimity /,ikwə'nımıti/ *n* ecuanimidad, *f*
equation /ı'kweiʒən/ *n* ecuación, *f*
equator /ı'kweitər/ *n* ecuador, *m*
equatorial /,ikwə'tɔriəl/ *a* ecuatorial
equestrian /ı'kwestriən/ *a* ecuestre
equiangular /,ikwi'æŋgyələr/ *a* equiángulo
equidistance /,ikwı'dıstəns/ *n* equidistancia, *f*
equidistant /,ikwı'dıstənt/ *a* equidistante
equilateral /,ikwə'lætərəl/ *a* equilátero
equilibrist /ı'kwılıbrıst/ *n* equilibrista, *mf*
equilibrium /,ikwə'lıbriəm/ *n* equilibrio, *m*
equine /'ikwain/ *a* equino; hípico; de caballo
equinoctial /,ikwə'nɒkʃəl/ *a* equinoccial. **e. gale,** tempestad equinoccial,
equinox /'ikwə,nɒks/ *n* equinoccio, *m*
equip /ı'kwıp/ *vt* proveer; pertrechar; equipar
equipage /'εkwəpıdʒ/ *n* (train) séquito, tren, *m*; (carriage) carruaje, *m*
equipment /ı'kwıpmənt/ *n* habilitación, *f*; equipo, *m*; pertrechos, *m pl*; material, *m*; aparatos, *m pl*; armamento, *m*

equitable /'ɛkwɪtəbəl/ a equitativo, justo
equitableness /'ɛkwɪtəbəlnɪs/ n equidad, justicia, f
equitably /'ɛkwɪtəbli/ adv equitativamente, con justicia
equity /'ɛkwɪti/ n equidad, f; imparcialidad, justicia, f
equivalence /ɪ'kwɪvələns/ n equivalencia, f
equivalent /ɪ'kwɪvələnt/ a and n equivalente, m. **to be e. to,** equivaler a
equivocal /ɪ'kwɪvəkəl/ a equívoco, ambiguo
equivocally /ɪ'kwɪvəkəli/ adv equivocadamente
equivocate /ɪ'kwɪvə,keit/ vi usar frases equívocas, emplear equívocos, tergiversar
equivocation /ɪ,kwɪvə'keiʃən/ n equívoco, m
era /'ɪərə, 'ɛrə/ n época, era, f
eradiation /ɪ,reidi'eiʃən/ n irradiación, f
eradicable /ɪ'rædɪkəbəl/ a erradicable
eradicate /ɪ'rædɪ,keit/ vt erradicar; destruir, extirpar; suprimir
eradication /ɪ,rædɪ'keiʃən/ n erradicación, f; destrucción, f; supresión, f
erasable /ɪ'reisəbəl/ a borrable
erase /ɪ'reis/ vt borrar; tachar
eraser /ɪ'reisər/ n goma de borrar, f. **ink e.,** goma para tinta, f
erasure /ɪ'reiʃər/ n borradura, f; tachón, m
ere /ɛər/ conjunc antes de (que), antes de. prep antes de
erect /ɪ'rɛkt/ a (upright) derecho; erguido; vertical; (uplifted) levantado; (standing) de pie; (firm) firme, resuelto; (alert) vigilante. vt (build) edificar, construir; instalar; (raise) alzar; convertir
erectile /ɪ'rɛktḷ/ a eréctil
erection /ɪ'rɛkʃən/ n erección, f; construcción, edificación, f; (building) edificio, m; (structure) estructura, f; instalación, f; (assembling) montaje, m
erectly /ɪ'rɛktli/ adv derecho
erectness /ɪ'rɛktnɪs/ n derechura, f
erg /ɜrg/ n Phys. ergio, m
ermine /'ɜrmɪn/ n armiño, m, a de armiño
erode /ɪ'roud/ vt corroer; comer; Geol. denudar
erosion /ɪ'rouʒən/ n erosión, f
erotic /ɪ'rɒtɪk/ a erótico
eroticism /ɪ'rɒtə,sɪzəm/ n erotismo, m
err /ɜr, ɛr/ vi desviarse; errar; desacertar; pecar
errand /'ɛrənd/ n mensaje, recado, m; encargo, m; misión, f. **e.-boy,** mandadero, mensajero, motril, mozo, recadero, m
errant /'ɛrənt/ a errante; (of knights) andante
erratic /ɪ'rætɪk/ a (of conduct) excéntrico, irresponsable; (of thoughts, etc.) errante; Med. errático
erratum /ɪ'rɑtəm/ n errata, f
erring /'ɛrɪŋ/ a extraviado; pecaminoso
erroneous /ə'rouniəs/ a erróneo; falso; injusto
erroneously /ə'rouniəsli/ adv erróneamente; falsamente; injustamente
erroneousness /ə'rouniəsnɪs/ n falsedad, f
error /'ɛrər/ n error, m; equivocación, f, desacierto, m; (sin) pecado, m. **in e.,** por equivocación
erudite /'ɛryʊ,dait/ a erudito; sabio
erudition /,ɛryʊ'dɪʃən/ n erudición, f
erupt /ɪ'rʌpt/ vi entrar en erupción, estar en erupción; Fig. salir con fuerza
eruption /ɪ'rʌpʃən/ n erupción, f
escalade /,ɛskə'leid/ n escalada, f, vt escalar
escalator /'ɛskə,leitər/ n escalera automática, escalera eléctrica, escalera mecánica, escalera móvil, escalera rodante, f
escapable /ɪ'skeipəbəl/ a evitable, eludible
escapade /'ɛskə,peid/ n escapada, f; aventura, f
escape /ɪ'skeip/ n huida, fuga, f; evasión, evitación, f; (leak) escape, m; Fig. salida, f. vt eludir, evitar; (of cries, groans, etc.) dar, salir de. vi huir, fugarse, escapar; (slip away) escurrirse; librarse; salvarse; (leak) escaparse. **His name escapes me,** Se me escapa (or se me olvida) su nombre. **to e. notice,** pasar inadvertido. **to have a narrow e.,** salvarse en una tabla. **to e. from,** escaparse de; librarse de; huir de
escape clause n cláusula de salvaguardia, f
escaping /ɪ'skeipɪŋ/ a fugitivo
escarpment /ɪ'skɑrpmənt/ n escarpa, f

eschew /ɛs'tʃu/ vt evitar
eschewal /ɛs'tʃuəl/ n evitación, f
escort /n 'ɛskɔrt; v ɪ'skɔrt/ n Mil. escolta, f; (of ships) convoy, m; acompañamiento, m; acompañante, m. vt Mil. escoltar; (of ships) convoyar; acompañar
escudo /ɛ'skudou/ n escudo, m
escutcheon /ɪ'skʌtʃən/ n escudo, blasón, m
Eskimo /'ɛskə,mou/ a and n esquimal mf
esoteric /,ɛsə'tɛrɪk/ a esotérico
esparto /ɪ'spɑrtou/ n esparto, m
especial /ɪ'spɛʃəl/ a especial; particular
especially /ɪ'spɛʃəli/ adv especialmente; ante todo; en particular
Esperantist /,ɛspə'rɑntɪst/ n esperantista, mf
Esperanto /,ɛspə'rɑntou/ n esperanto, m
espionage /'ɛspiə,nɑʒ/ n espionaje, m
esplanade /'ɛsplə,nɑd/ n Mil. explanada, f; bulevar, paseo, m
espousal /ɪ'spauzəl/ n desposorio, m; Fig. adhesión (a una causa), f
espouse /ɪ'spauz/ vt desposar; (a cause) abrazar; defender
espy /ɪ'spai/ vt divisar, ver, observar
esquire /'ɛskwaiᵊr/ n escudero, m; (landowner) hacendado, m; (as a title) don (before given name)
essay /n 'ɛsei; v ɛ'sei/ n tentativa, f; Lit. ensayo, m, vt probar; procurar; (on an examination) tema, m.
essay question, tema, m
essayist /'ɛseiɪst/ n ensayista, mf
essence /'ɛsəns/ n esencia, f
essential /ə'sɛntʃəl/ a esencial; indispensable, imprescindible; intrínseco. n artículo de primera necesidad, m; elemento necesario, m
essentially /ə'sɛntʃəli/ adv esencialmente
establish /ɪ'stæblɪʃ/ vt establecer; fundar; crear; erigir, Lat. Am. also instaurar; (constitute) constituir; (order) disponer; (prove) demostrar, probar; (take root, settle) arraigarse
established /ɪ'stæblɪʃt/ a establecido; arraigado; (proved) demostrado; bien conocido; (author) consagrado; (of churches) oficial
establishment /ɪ'stæblɪʃmənt/ n establecimiento, m; fundación, f; creación, f, Lat. Am. also instauración; institución, f; (building) erección, f; arraigo, m; (house) casa, f; (church) iglesia oficial, f; demostración, f; reconocimiento, m
estate /ɪ'steit/ n estado, m; clase, f; condición, f; (land) propiedad, finca, f; fortuna, f; (inheritance) heredad, f, patrimonio, m; Law. bienes, m pl. **personal e.,** bienes muebles, m pl; fortuna personal, f. **third e.,** estado llano, m. **e. agent,** agente de fincas, m; agente de casas, m
esteem /ɪ'stim/ n estima, f, aprecio, m; consideración, f, vt estimar, apreciar; creer, juzgar
ester /'ɛstər/ n Chem. éster, m
esthete /'ɛsθit/ n estético, m
esthetic /ɛs'θɛtɪk/ a estético
esthetically /ɛs'θɛtɪkli/ adv estéticamente
esthetics /ɛs'θɛtɪks/ n estética, f
estimable /'ɛstəməbəl/ a apreciable, estimable
estimableness /'ɛstəməbəlnɪs/ n estimabilidad, f
estimate /n 'ɛstəmɪt; v -,meit/ n estimación, tasa, f; cálculos, m pl; apreciación, f; opinión, f; pl **estimates,** presupuesto, m. vt (value) avalorar, tasar; calcular, computar; considerar. vi hacer un presupuesto
estimation /,ɛstə'meiʃən/ n opinión, f; cálculo, cómputo, m; (esteem) aprecio, m, estima, f
estrange /ɪ'streindʒ/ vt enajenar; ofender
estrangement /ɪ'streindʒmənt/ n enajenación, alienación, f
estuary /'ɛstʃu,ɛri/ n estuario, m, ría, f
etcetera /ɛt'sɛtərə/ etcétera. (Used as noun, f)
etch /ɛtʃ/ vt grabar al agua fuerte
etcher /'ɛtʃər/ n grabador (-ra) al agua fuerte
etching /'ɛtʃɪŋ/ n aguafuerte, f; grabado al agua fuerte, m. **e. needle,** punta seca, aguja de grabador, f
eternal /ɪ'tɜrnḷ/ a eterno; incesante. n (E.) el Eterno
eternally /ɪ'tɜrnḷi/ adv eternamente
eternity /ɪ'tɜrnɪti/ n eternidad, f

eternize /ɪ'tɜrnaiz/ vt eternizar
ether /'iðər/ n éter, m
ethereal /ɪ'θɪəriəl/ a etéreo; vaporoso, aéreo
etheric /ɪ'θɛrɪk/ a etéreo
etherize /'iðə,raiz/ vt eterizar
ethical /'ɛθɪkəl/ a ético, moral; n droga de ordenanza, f
ethics /'ɛθɪks/ n ética, f; (filosofía) moral, f
Ethiopia /,iθi'oupiə/ Etiopia, f
ethnic /'ɛθnɪk/ a étnico
ethnographic /,ɛθnou'græfɪk/ a etnográfico
ethnography /ɛθ'nɒgrəfi/ n etnografía, f
ethnologist /ɛθ'nɒlədʒɪst/ n etnólogo, m
ethnology /ɛθ'nɒlədʒi/ n etnología, f
ethyl /'ɛθəl/ n Chem. etilo, m
ethylene /'ɛθə,lin/ n Chem. etileno, m
etiquette /'ɛtɪkɪt/ n etiqueta, f
Etruscan /ɪ'trʌskən/ a and n etrusco (-ca)
etymological /,ɛtəmə'lɒdʒɪkəl/ a etimológico
etymologist /,ɛtə'mɒlədʒɪst/ n etimólogo, m, etimologista, mf
etymology /,ɛtə'mɒlədʒi/ n etimología, f
eucalyptus /,yukə'lɪptəs/ n eucalipto, m
Eucharist /'yukərɪst/ n Eucaristía, f
eucharistic /,yukə'rɪstɪk/ a eucarístico
eugenic /yu'dʒɛnɪk/ a eugenésico
eugenics /yu'dʒɛnɪks/ n eugenesia, f
eulogist /'yulədʒɪst/ n elogiador (-ra), loador (-ra)
eulogistic /,yulə'dʒɪstɪk/ a elogiador
eulogize /'yulə,dʒaiz/ vt elogiar, alabar, encomiar
eulogy /'yulədʒi/ n elogio, encomio, m; alabanza, f; panegírico, m
eunuch /'yunək/ n eunuco, m
euphemism /'yufə,mɪzəm/ n eufemismo, m
euphonious /yu'founiəs/ a eufónico
euphony /'yufəni/ n eufonía, f
euphuistic /,yufyu'ɪstɪk/ a alambicado, gongorino
Eurasian /yʊ'reiʒən/ a and n eurasio (-ia)
eurhythmic /yʊ'rɪðmɪk/ a eurítmico
eurhythmics /yʊ'rɪðmɪks/ n euritmia, f
European /,yʊrə'piən/ a and n europeo (-ea)
europeanize /,yʊrə'piə,naiz/ vt europeanizar
euthanasia /,yuθə'neiʒə, -ʒiə, -ziə/ n eutanasia, f
evacuate /ɪ'vækyu,eit/ vt evacuar
evacuation /ɪ,vækyu'eiʃən/ n evacuación, f
evade /ɪ'veid/ vt evadir, eludir; evitar, esquivar; rehuir
evaluate /ɪ'vælyu,eit/ vt evaluar, estimar; calcular
evaluation /ɪ,vælyu'eiʃən/ n evaluación, estimación, f
evanescent /,ɛvə'nɛsənt/ a transitorio, fugaz, pasajero
evangelical /,ivæn'dʒɛlɪkəl/ a evangélico
evangelicalism /,ivæn'dʒɛlɪkə,lɪzəm/ n evangelismo, m
evangelist /ɪ'vændʒəlɪst/ n evangelista, m
evangelize /ɪ'vændʒə,laiz/ vt evangelizar
evaporate /ɪ'væpə,reit/ vi evaporarse; desvanecerse. vt evaporar
evaporation /ɪ,væpə'reiʃən/ n evaporación, f; desvanecimiento, m
evaporative /ɪ'væpə,reitɪv/ a evaporatorio
evasion /ɪ'veiʒən/ n (escape) fuga, f; evasión, f; evasiva, f, efugio, m, Lat. Am. esquivada, f
evasive /ɪ'veisɪv/ a evasivo, ambiguo
evasively /ɪ'veisɪvli/ adv evasivamente
evasiveness /ɪ'veisɪvnɪs/ n carácter evasivo, m
eve /iv/ n víspera, f; Eccl. vigilia, f. **on the eve of,** la víspera de; Fig. en vísperas de
even /'ivən/ a (flat) llano; (smooth) liso; igual; (level with) al mismo nivel (de); uniforme; (of numbers) par; (approximate, of sums) redondo; rítmico; invariable, constante; (of temper) apacible; (just) imparcial; (monotonous) monótono, igual; (paid) pagado; (Com. of date) mismo. **to get e. with,** vengarse de. **to be e. (with...)** Lat. Am. estar a mano (con...)
even /'ivən/ adv siquiera; aun; hasta; (also) también. **not e.,** ni siquiera. **e. as,** así como, del mismo modo que. **e. if,** aun cuando, si bien. **e. now,** aun ahora;

ahora mismo. **e. so,** aun así; (nevertheless) sin embargo. **e. though,** aunque; suponiendo que
even /'ivən/ vt igualar; (level) allanar, nivelar; (accounts) desquitar; compensar; hacer uniforme
evening /'ivnɪŋ/ n tarde, f, atardecer, m; noche, f; Fig. fin, m, a vespertino, de la tarde. **Good e.!** ¡Buenas tardes! ¡Buenas noches! **in the e.,** al atardecer.
tomorrow e., mañana por la tarde. **yesterday e.,** ayer por la tarde. **e. class,** clase nocturna, f. **e. dress,** (women) traje de noche, m; (men) traje de etiqueta, m. **e. meal,** cena, f. **e. paper,** periódico (or diario) de la noche, m. **e. primrose,** hierba del asno, onagra, f.
e. star, estrella vespertina, estrella de la tarde, f; (Venus) lucero de la tarde, m
evenly /'ivənli/ adv igualmente; (on a level) a nivel; uniformemente; imparcialmente; (of speech) con suavidad
evenness /'ivənnɪs/ n igualdad, f; (smoothness) lisura, f; uniformidad, f; imparcialidad, f; (of temper) ecuanimidad, serenidad, f
evensong /'ivən,sɔŋ/ n vísperas, f pl
event /ɪ'vɛnt/ n incidente, suceso, acontecimiento, m; (result) consecuencia, f; resultado, m; caso, m; (athletics) prueba, f; (race) carrera, f. **at all events,** de todas maneras. **in such an e.,** en tal caso. **in the e. of,** en el caso de
eventful /ɪ'vɛntfəl/ a lleno de acontecimientos; accidentado; memorable
eventual /ɪ'vɛntʃuəl/ a eventual; final, último
eventuality /ɪ,vɛntʃu'ælɪti/ n eventualidad, f
eventually /ɪ'vɛntʃuəli/ adv a la larga, al fin
ever /'ɛvər/ adv siempre; (at any time) jamás; alguna vez; nunca; (even) siquiera; (very) muy; (in any way) en modo alguno. **As fast as e. he can,** Lo más aprisa que pueda. **Be it e. so big,** Por grande que sea. **Did you e.!** ¡Habráse visto! ¡Qué cosa! **for e.,** para siempre. **for e. and e.,** para siempre jamás; (mostly ecclesiastical) por los siglos de los siglos; eternamente. **He is e. so nice,** Es muy simpático. **Hardly e.,** casi nunca. **I don't think I have e. been there,** No creo que haya estado nunca allí. **if e.,** si alguna vez; (rarely) raramente. **nor... e.,** ni nunca. **not... e.,** nunca. **e. after,** desde entonces; (afterward) después. **e. and anon,** de vez en cuando. **e. so little,** siquiera un poco; muy poco
evergreen /'ɛvər,grin/ a siempre verde. n planta vivaz, f. **e. oak,** encina, f
everlasting /,ɛvər'læstɪŋ/ a eterno, perpetuo; (of colors) estable; incesante. **e. flower,** perpetua, f
evermore /,ɛvər'mɔr/ adv eternamente
every /'ɛvri/ a todo; cada (invariable); todos los, m pl; todas las, f pl. **e. day,** todos los días, cada día. **e. now and then,** de cuando en cuando. **e. other day,** cada dos días
everybody /'ɛvri,bɒdi, -,bʌdi/ n todo el mundo, m; todos, m pl; todas, f pl; todos una, m; cada una, f
everyday /'ɛvri,dei/ a diario, cotidiano; corriente, de cada día, usual
everything /'ɛvri,θɪŋ/ n todo, m; (e. that, which) todo lo (que). **e. possible,** todo lo posible
everywhere /'ɛvri,wɛər/ adv por todas partes
evict /ɪ'vɪkt/ vt desahuciar; expulsar
eviction /ɪ'vɪkʃən/ n evicción, f, desahúcio, m; expulsión, f
evidence /'ɛvɪdəns/ n Law. testimonio, m, deposición, f; indicios, m pl; evidencia, f; prueba, f; hecho, m, vt patentizar, probar. **to give e.,** dar testimonio, deponer
evident /'ɛvɪdənt/ a evidente, patente, manifiesto; claro. **to be e.,** ser patente, estar a la vista
evidently /'ɛvɪdəntli/ adv evidentemente; claramente
evil /'ivəl/ a malo; malvado, perverso; de maldad; (monotonous) aciago; de infortunio; (of spirits) diabólico, malo. n mal, m; maldad, perversidad, f; (misfortune) desgracia, f. **the E. one,** el Malo. **e.-doer,** malhechor (-ra). **e. eye,** mal de ojo, aojo, m. **e.-minded,** mal pensado; malintencionado. **e.-speaking,** maledicencia, calumnia, f. **e. spirit,** demonio, espíritu malo, m
evince /ɪ'vɪns/ vt evidenciar; mostrar
eviscerate /ɪ'vɪsə,reit/ vt destripar, desentrañar

evocation /ˌɛvəˈkeiʃən/ n evocación, f
evocative /ɪˈvɒkətɪv/ a evocador
evoke /ɪˈvouk/ vt evocar
evolution /ˌɛvəˈluʃən/ n evolución, f; desarrollo, m; (Nav., Mil.) maniobra, f; Math. extracción de una raíz, f; (revolution) revolución, vuelta, f
evolutionary /ˌɛvəˈluʃənˌɛri/ a evolucionario
evolve /ɪˈvɒlv/ vi evolucionar; desarrollarse. vt producir por evolución; desarrollar; pensar
ewe /yu/ n oveja, f. **ewe lamb,** cordera, f
ewer /ˈyuər/ n aguamanil, m
exacerbate /ɪgˈzæsərˌbeit/ vt exacerbar; agravar, empeorar
exacerbation /ɪgˌzæsərˈbeiʃən/ n exacerbación, f; agravación, f
exact /ɪgˈzækt/ a exacto; fiel; metódico; estricto. vt exigir
exacting /ɪgˈzæktɪŋ/ a exigente; severo, estricto; (hard) agotador, arduo
exaction /ɪgˈzækʃən/ n exigencia, f; extorsión, exacción, f
exactly /ɪgˈzæktli/ adv exactamente; precisamente
exactness /ɪgˈzæktnɪs/ n exactitud, f
exaggerate /ɪgˈzædʒəˌreit/ vt exagerar; acentuar. vi exagerar
exaggerated /ɪgˈzædʒəˌreitɪd/ a exagerado
exaggeration /ɪgˌzædʒəˈreiʃən/ n exageración, f
exaggerator /ɪgˈzædʒəˌreitər/ n exagerador (-ra)
exalt /ɪgˈzɔlt/ vt exaltar; enaltecer, elevar; (praise) glorificar, magnificar; (intensify) realzar; intensificar
exaltation /ˌɛgzɔlˈteiʃən/ n exaltación, elevación, f; alegría, f, júbilo, m; (ecstasy) éxtasis, arrobamiento, m; (of the Cross) exaltación, f
exalted /ɪgˈzɔltɪd/ a exaltado, eminente
exaltedness /ɪgˈzɔltɪdnɪs/ n exaltación, f
exam /ɪgˈzæm/ n examen, m
examination /ɪgˌzæməˈneiʃən/ n examen, m; inspección, f; investigación, f; Law. interrogatorio, m; prueba, f. **to sit an e.,** examinarse. **written e.,** prueba escrita, f
examine /ɪgˈzæmɪn/ vt examinar; inspeccionar; investigar; Law. interrogar; (search) reconocer; (by touch) tentar; observar; analizar. **to e. into,** examinar; considerar detenidamente; ahondar en
examinee /ɪgˌzæməˈni/ n examinando (-da)
examiner /ɪgˈzæmɪnər/ n examinador (-ra); inspector (-ra)
examinership /ɪgˈzæmɪnərˌʃɪp/ n cargo de examinador, m
examining /ɪgˈzæmɪnɪŋ/ a que examina; de examen; Law. interrogante
example /ɪgˈzæmpəl/ n ejemplo, m; ilustración, f; (parallel) ejemplar, m; (warning) escarmiento, m. **for e.,** por ejemplo. **to set an e.,** dar ejemplo, dar el ejemplo.
exasperate /ɪgˈzæspəˌreit/ vt exasperar, irritar; (increase) aumentar; (worsen) agravar
exasperating /ɪgˈzæspəˌreitɪŋ/ a exasperante, irritante, provocador
exasperation /ɪgˌzæspəˈreiʃən/ n exasperación, irritación, f; (worsening) agravación, f; enojo, m
excavate /ˈɛkskəˌveit/ vt excavar; (hollow) vaciar
excavation /ˌɛkskəˈveiʃən/ n excavación, f; Archit. vaciado, m
excavator /ˈɛkskəˌveitər/ n excavador (-ra); (machine) excavadora, f
exceed /ɪkˈsid/ vt exceder; (excel) superar, aventajar; (one's hopes, etc.) sobrepujar. vi excederse. **to e. all expectations,** exceder a toda ponderación. **to e. one's rights,** abusar de sus derechos, ir demasiado lejos
exceedingly /ɪkˈsidɪŋli/ adv sumamente, extremadamente; sobre manera
excel /ɪkˈsɛl/ vt aventajar, superar; vencer. vi sobresalir; distinguirse, señalarse; ser superior
excellence /ˈɛksələns/ n excelencia, f; superioridad, f; perfección, f; mérito, m; buena calidad, f
excellency /ˈɛksələnsi/ n (title) Excelencia, f. **Your E.,** Su Excelencia

excellent /ˈɛksələnt/ a excelente; superior; perfecto; magnífico; (in examinations) sobresaliente
excellently /ˈɛksələntli/ adv excelentemente; perfectamente; magníficamente
except /ɪkˈsɛpt/ vt exceptuar; omitir
except, excepting /ɪkˈsɛpt/ prep excepto, con excepción de; exceptuando; menos; salvo; fuera de. conjunc a menos que. **except for,** si no fuese por; con excepción de; fuera de
exception /ɪkˈsɛpʃən/ n excepción, f; objeción, protesta, f. **to make an e.,** hacer una excepción. **to take e. to,** protestar contra; tachar, criticar; desaprobar
exceptional /ɪkˈsɛpʃənl̩/ a excepcional
excerpt /n ˈɛksɜrpt; v ɪkˈsɜrpt/ n excerpta, f, extracto, m. vt extraer
excess /ɪkˈsɛs, ˈɛksɛs/ n exceso, m; superabundancia, f; demasía, f; Com. superávit, m. **in e.,** en exceso, de sobra. **in e. of,** en exceso de; arriba de. **to e.,** excesivamente, demasiado. **e. fare,** suplemento, m. **e. luggage,** exceso de equipaje, m; (overweight) exceso de peso, m
excessive /ɪkˈsɛsɪv/ a excesivo; superabundante; inmoderado, desmesurado; exagerado
excessively /ɪkˈsɛsɪvli/ adv excesivamente; exageradamente
excessiveness /ɪkˈsɛsɪvnɪs/ n exceso, m; superabundancia, f; exageración, f
exchange /ɪksˈtʃeindʒ/ n cambio, trueque, m; (of prisoners) canje, m; (financial) cambio, m; (building) bolsa, lonja, f; (telephone) oficina central de teléfonos, f. vt cambiar (for, por); trocar; (replace) reemplazar; (prisoners) canjear; (of blows) darse; (pass from, into) pasar de... a. vi hacer un cambio. **in e. for,** en cambio de, a trueque de; por. **to e. greetings,** saludarse; cambiar saludos. **They exchanged looks,** Se miraron. **What is the rate of e.?** ¿Cuál es el tipo de cambio? **e. of prisoners,** canje de prisioneros, m
exchangeable /ɪksˈtʃeindʒəbəl/ a cambiable; trocable
exchequer /ˈɛkstʃɛkər/ n (public finance) Hacienda pública, f; tesorería, f; (funds) fondos, m pl. **Chancellor of the E.,** Ministro de Hacienda, m
excise /n ˈɛksaiz; v ɪkˈsaiz/ n contribución indirecta, f; (customs and ex.) Aduana, f. vt (cut) cortar, extirpar; imponer una contribución indirecta. **e. duty,** derecho de aduana, m
excise tax arbitrios, m pl
excision /ɛkˈsɪʒən/ n excisión, f; extirpación, f
excitability /ɪkˌsaitəˈbɪlti/ n excitabilidad, f
excitable /ɪkˈsaitəbəl/ a excitable
excitation /ˌɛksaiˈteiʃən/ n excitación, f
excite /ɪkˈsait/ vt emocionar; conmover; agitar; excitar; suscitar, provocar; incitar, instigar; (attention, interest) despertar; estimular. **to become excited,** emocionarse; exaltarse; (annoyed) acalorarse; (upset) agitarse
excitedly /ɪkˈsaitɪdli/ adv con emoción; acaloradamente; agitadamente
excitement /ɪkˈsaitmənt/ n conmoción, f; agitación, f, Central America embullo m; (annoyance) acaloramiento, m; emoción, f; estímulo, m; instigación, f, fomento, m; (amusement) placer, m
exciting /ɪkˈsaitɪŋ/ a emocionante; conmovedor; agitador; muy interesante
exclaim /ɪkˈskleim/ vt and vi exclamar. **to e. against,** clamar contra
exclamation /ˌɛkskləˈmeiʃən/ n exclamación, f. **e. mark,** punto de exclamación, m
exclamatory /ɪkˈsklæməˌtɔri/ a exclamatorio
exclude /ɪkˈsklud/ vt excluir; exceptuar; evitar; (refuse) rechazar
exclusion /ɪkˈskluʒən/ n exclusión, f; exceptuación, f; eliminación, f
exclusive /ɪkˈsklusɪv/ a exclusivo; (snobbish) exclusivista. **e. of,** no incluido; aparte de
exclusively /ɪkˈsklusɪvli/ adv exclusivamente; únicamente
exclusiveness /ɪkˈsklusɪvnɪs/ n carácter exclusivo, m
exclusivism /ɪkˈsklusɪˌvɪzəm/ n exclusivismo, m
exclusivist /ɪkˈsklusəvɪst/ n exclusivista, mf
excommunicate /v ˌɛkskəˈmyunɪˌkeit; a -kɪt/ vt excomulgar. a excomulgado

excommunication /ˌɛkskə‚myunɪ'keiʃən/ n excomunión, f
excrement /'ɛkskrəmənt/ n excremento, m
excrescence /ɪk'skrɛsəns/ n excrecencia, f
excrescent /ɪk'skrɛsənt/ a que forma excrecencia; superfluo
excrete /ɪk'skrit/ vt excretar
excretion /ɪk'skriʃən/ n excreción, f
excretory /'ɛkskrɪ‚tɔri/ a excretorio
excruciating /ɪk'skruʃɪ‚eitɪŋ/ a atormentador, angustioso; (of pain) agudísimo
excursion /ɪk'skɜrʒən/ n excursión, f; expedición, f; (digression) digresión, f. **e. ticket,** billete de excursión, m. **e. train,** tren de excursionistas, m
excursionist /ɪk'skɜrʒənɪst/ n excursionista, mf; turista, mf
excusable /ɪk'skyuzəbəl/ a disculpable, excusable
excusably /ɪk'skyuzəbli/ adv excusablemente
excuse /ɪk'skyus/ n excusa, f; disculpa, f; pretexto, m; justificación, defensa, f. **to give as an e.,** pretextar
excuse /ɪk'skyuz/ vt disculpar, excusar; dispensar (de); librar (de); (forgive) perdonar; (defend) justificar, defender; (minimize) paiar; (oneself) disculparse. **E. me!** ¡Con permiso!; ¡Perdone Vd.!; ¡Dispense Vd.!
execrable /'ɛksɪkrəbəl/ a execrable, abominable
execrate /'ɛksɪ‚kreit/ vt execrar, abominar. vi maldecir
execration /ˌɛksɪ'kreiʃən/ n execración, abominación, f; maldición, f
execute /'ɛksɪ‚kyut/ vt (perform) ejecutar, poner en efecto, realizar; (Art., Mus.) ejecutar; (part in a play) hacer, desempeñar; (fulfil) cumplir; Law. otorgar (a document); (kill) ajusticiar
execution /ˌɛksɪ'kyuʃən/ n efectuación, realización, f; (Art., Mus.) ejecución, f; (of part in a play) desempeño (de un papel), m; (fulfilment) cumplimiento, m; Law. otorgamiento (de un documento), m; (killing) suplicio, m, ejecución de la pena de muerte, f; (Law. seizure) ejecución, f
executioner /ˌɛksɪ'kyuʃənər/ n verdugo, m
executive /ɪg'zɛkyətɪv/ a ejecutivo; administrativo. n poder ejecutivo, m
executor /ɪg'zɛkyətər/ n administrador testamentario, m
executrix /ɪg'zɛkyətrɪks/ n administradora testamentaria, f
exegesis /ˌɛksɪ'dʒisɪs/ n exégesis, f
exegetical /ˌɛksɪ'dʒɛtikəl/ a exegético
exemplary /ɪg'zɛmpləri/ a ejemplar
exemplification /ɪg‚zɛmpləfɪ'keiʃən/ n ejemplificación, ilustración, demostración, f
exemplify /ɪg'zɛmplə‚fai/ vt ejemplificar; ilustrar, demostrar
exempt /ɪg'zɛmpt/ vt exentar, eximir; librar; dispensar, excusar. a exento; libre; excusado; inmune
exemption /ɪg'zɛmpʃən/ n exención, f; libertad, f; inmunidad, f
exercise /'ɛksər‚saiz/ n ejercicio, m; uso, m; (essay) ensayo, m; pl **exercises,** (on land or sea) maniobras, f pl. vt ejercer; usar, emplear; (train) ejercitar, entrenar; adiestrar; pasear, dar un paseo; (worry) preocupar. vi hacer ejercicio; ejercitarse; adiestrarse. **spiritual exercises,** ejercicios espirituales, m pl. **to take e. in the open air,** tomar ejercicio al aire libre. **to write an e.,** escribir un ejercicio. **e. book,** cuaderno de ejercicios, m
exert /ɪg'zɜrt/ vt hacer uso de, emplear, ejercer, poner en juego; (deploy) desplegar. **to e. oneself,** hacer un esfuerzo (para); esforzarse (de); trabajar mucho; tratar (de); apurarse, tomarse mucha molestia; preocuparse
exertion /ɪg'zɜrʃən/ n esfuerzo, m; uso, m; (exercise) ejercicio, m; (good offices) diligencias, gestiones, f pl; buenos oficios, m pl
exhalation /ˌɛkshə'leiʃən/ n exhalación, f; efluvio, m; vapor, m; humo, m
exhale /ɛks'heil/ vt exhalar; emitir, despedir. vi evaporarse; disiparse
exhaust /ɪg'zɔst/ vt agotar; (empty) vaciar; (end) acabar; apurar; consumir; (tire) rendir, cansar mucho;

(weaken) debilitar; (a subject) tratar detalladamente. n Mech. escape, m; emisión de vapor, f; vapor de escape, m. **e. pipe,** tubo de escape, m
exhaustible /ɪg'zɔstəbəl/ a agotable
exhausting /ɪg'zɔstɪŋ/ a cansado, agotador
exhaustion /ɪg'zɔstʃən/ n agotamiento, m; rendimiento, cansancio, m; lasitud, f; postración, f
exhaustive /ɪg'zɔstɪv/ a completo; minucioso
exhaustively /ɪg'zɔstɪvli/ adv detenidamente; detalladamente; minuciosamente
exhaustiveness /ɪg'zɔstɪvnɪs/ n lo completo; minuciosidad, f
exhibit /ɪg'zɪbɪt/ vt exhibir; manifestar, ostentar; revelar, descubrir; presentar. vi exhibir, ser expositor. n exposición, f, objeto exhibido, m; Law. prueba, f
exhibition /ˌɛksə'bɪʃən/ n exposición, f; (performance) función, f; espectáculo, m; exhibición, f; (showing) manifestación, f; (grant) bolsa de estudio, beca, f
exhibitionism /ˌɛksə'bɪʃə‚nɪzəm/ n exhibicionismo, m
exhibitionist /ˌɛksə'bɪʃənɪst/ n exhibicionista, mf
exhibitor /ɪg'zɪbɪtər/ n expositor (-ra)
exhilarate /ɪg'zɪlə‚reit/ vt alegrar, alborozar
exhilarating /ɪg'zɪlə‚reitɪŋ/ a alegre; estimulador; vigorizador, tonificante
exhilaration /ɪg‚zɪlə'reiʃən/ n alegría, f, alborozo, regocijo, m
exhort /ɪg'zɔrt/ vt and vi exhortar
exhortation /ˌɛgzɔr'teiʃən/ n exhortación, f
exhumation /ˌɛkshyu'meiʃən/ n exhumación, f
exhume /ɪg'zum/ vt exhumar
exigence /'ɛksɪdʒəns/ n exigencia, f; urgencia, f; (need) necesidad, f
exigent /'ɛksɪdʒənt/ a exigente; urgente
exiguous /ɪg'zɪgyuəs/ a exiguo
exiguousness /ɪg'zɪgyuəsnɪs/ n exigüidad, f
exile /'ɛgzail/ n destierro, m; (person) desterrado (-da), Lat. Am. exiliado (-da) mf vt desterrar, Lat. Am. exiliar
exist /ɪg'zɪst/ vi existir
existence /ɪg'zɪstəns/ n existencia, f; (being) ser, m; (life) vida, f. **to bring into e.,** causar; producir
existentialism /ˌɛgzɪ'stɛnʃə‚lɪzəm/ n existencialismo, m
existing /ɪg'zɪstɪŋ/ a existente
exit /'ɛgzɪt/ n salida, f; partida, f; (death) muerte, f; Theat. mutis, m. vi Theat. hacer mutis. **to make one's e.,** salir; marcharse; irse; morir; Theat. hacer mutis
exodus /'ɛksədəs/ n éxodo, m; salida, f; emigración, f; **E.,** Éxodo, m
exonerate /ɪg'zɒnə‚reit/ vt exonerar
exoneration /ɪg‚zɒnə'reiʃən/ n exoneración, f
exorbitance /ɪg'zɔrbɪtəns/ n exorbitancia, f
exorbitant /ɪg'zɔrbɪtənt/ a exorbitante
exorcism /'ɛksɔr‚sɪzəm/ n exorcismo, m
exorcist /'ɛksɔrsɪst/ n exorcista, m
exorcize /'ɛksɔr‚saiz/ vt exorcizar, conjurar
exotic /ɪg'zɒtɪk/ a exótico. n planta exótica, f; Fig. flor de estufa, f
expand /ɪk'spænd/ vt extender; abrir; (wings, etc.) desplegar; (the chest, etc.) expandir; dilatar; (amplify) ampliar; (an edition) ampliar, aumentar; (develop) desarrollar; Fig. ensanchar; (increase) aumentar. vi dilatarse; hincharse; abrirse; extenderse; Fig. ensancharse; (increase) aumentarse
expanse /ɪk'spæns/ n extensión, f
expansibility /ɪk‚spænsə'bɪlɪti/ n Phys. expansibilidad, f; dilatabilidad, f
expansible /ɪk'spænsəbəl/ a Phys. expansible; dilatable
expansion /ɪk'spænʃən/ n expansión, f; extensión, f; dilatación, f; (amplification) ampliación, f; (development) desarrollo, m; Fig. ensanchamiento, m; (increase) aumento, m
expansionism /ɪk'spænʃə‚nɪzəm/ n expansionismo, m
expansive /ɪk'spænsɪv/ a expansivo; (of persons) efusivo, expresivo, comunicativo, afable
expansiveness /ɪk'spænsɪvnɪs/ n expansibilidad, f; (of persons) afabilidad, f

expatiate /ɪk'speiʃɪˌeit/ **(upon)** *vi* extenderse en

expatiation /ɪkˌspeiʃɪ'eiʃən/ *n* discurso, *m*; digresión, *f*

expatriation /ɛksˌpeitri'eiʃən/ *n* expatriación, *f*

expect /ɪk'spɛkt/ *vt* esperar; (await) aguardar; (suppose) suponer; (demand) exigir; (count on) contar con. *vi* creer

expectance /ɪk'spɛktəns/ *n* expectación, *f*; esperanza, *f*

expectant /ɪk'spɛktənt/ *a* expectante; (hopeful) esperanzudo; (pregnant) embarazada

expectantly /ɪk'spɛktəntli/ *adv* con expectación

expectation /ˌɛkspɛk'teiʃən/ *n* expectación, *f*; (hope) esperanza, *f*; expectativa, *f*; probabilidad, *f*

expectorate /ɪk'spɛktəˌreit/ *vt* expectorar. *vi* escupir

expectoration /ɪkˌspɛktə'reiʃən/ *n* expectoración, *f*

expedience /ɪk'spidiəns/ *n* conveniencia, *f*; oportunidad, *f*; aptitud, *f*; (self-interest) egoísmo, *m*

expedient /ɪk'spidiənt/ *a* conveniente; oportuno; apto; prudente; político. *n* expediente, recurso, medio, *m*

expedite /'ɛkspɪˌdait/ *vt* acelerar; facilitar; (send off) despachar

expedition /ˌɛkspɪ'diʃən/ *n* expedición, *f*; (haste) celeridad, diligencia, *f*

expeditionary /ˌɛkspɪ'diʃəˌnɛri/ *a* expedicionario. **e. force,** fuerza expedicionaria, *f*

expeditious /ˌɛkspɪ'diʃəs/ *a* expedito, pronto

expeditiously /ˌɛkspɪ'diʃəsli/ *adv* expeditamente, prontamente

expeditiousness /ˌɛkspɪ'diʃəsnɪs/ *n* prontitud, *f*

expel /ɪk'spɛl/ *vt* expeler, expulsar; echar, arrojar; despedir

expend /ɪk'spɛnd/ *vt* gastar, expender; (time) perder

expenditure /ɪk'spɛndɪtʃər/ *n* gasto, desembolso, *m*, *Lat. Am.* erogación *f*; (of time) pérdida, *f*

expense /ɪk'spɛns/ *n* gasto, *m*; pérdida, *f*; costa, *f*; *pl* **expenses,** expensas, *f pl,* gastos, *m pl.* **at the e. of,** a costa de. **e. account,** cuenta de gastos, *f.* **to be put to great e.,** tener que gastar mucho. **to pay one's expenses,** pagar sus gastos

expensive /ɪk'spɛnsɪv/ *a* costoso; caro

expensively /ɪk'spɛnsɪvli/ *adv* costosamente

expensiveness /ɪk'spɛnsɪvnɪs/ *n* lo costoso; costa, *f*

experience /ɪk'spɪəriəns/ *n* experiencia, *f. vt* experimentar; sentir; sufrir. **by e.,** por experiencia

experienced /ɪk'spɪəriənst/ *a* experimentado; experto; hábil; (lived) vivido

experiment /*n* ɪk'spɛrəmənt; *v* -ˌmɛnt/ *n* experimento, *m*; prueba, *f*; ensayo, *m*, tentativa, *f. vi* experimentar; hacer una prueba

experimental /ɪkˌspɛrə'mɛntl̩/ *a* experimental; tentativo

experimentally /ɪkˌspɛrə'mɛntl̩i/ *adv* experimentalmente; por experiencia

expert /'ɛkspərt/ *a* experto; perito; hábil; (finished) acabado. *n* experto, *m*, especialista, *mf*

expertise /ˌɛkspər'tiz/ *n* destreza, *f*

expertly /'ɛkspərtli/ *adv* expertamente; hábilmente

expertness /'ɛkspərtnɪs/ *n* pericia, *f*; maestría, *f*; habilidad, *f*; (knowledge) conocimiento, *m*

expiable /'ɛkspiəbəl/ *a* que se puede expiar

expiate /'ɛkspiˌeit/ *vt* expiar; reparar

expiation /ˌɛkspi'eiʃən/ *n* expiación, *f*

expiatory /'ɛkspiəˌtɔri/ *a* expiatorio

expiration /ˌɛkspə'reiʃən/ *n* (breathing out) espiración, *f*; (ending) expiración, *f*; terminación, *f*; *Com.* vencimiento, *m*; (death) muerte, *f*

expiration date fecha de vencimiento, *f*

expire /ɪk'spaiªr/ *vi* (exhale) espirar; (die) morir, dar el último suspiro; (of fire, light) extinguirse; (end) expirar; terminar; *Com.* vencer

expiry /ɪk'spaiªri/ *n* terminación, *f*; expiración, *f*; *Com.* vencimiento, *m*

explain /ɪk'splein/ *vt* explicar; aclarar; demostrar; exponer; (justify) justificar, defender. *vi* explicarse. **to e. away,** explicar; justificar

explainable /ɪk'spleinəbəl/ *a* explicable

explanation /ˌɛksplə'neiʃən/ *n* explicación, *f*; aclaración, *f*

explanatory /ɪk'splænəˌtɔri/ *a* explicativo; aclaratorio

expletive /'ɛksplitɪv/ *a* expletivo. *n* interjección, *f*

explicable /'ɛksplɪkəbəl/ *a* explicable

explicit /ɪk'splɪsɪt/ *a* explícito

explode /ɪk'sploud/ *vi* estallar; detonar; reventar. *vt* hacer estallar; (a mine) hacer saltar; (a belief, etc.) hacer abandonar; desechar

exploit /ɪk'splɔit/ *n* hazaña, proeza, *f*; aventura, *f. vt* explotar

exploitation /ˌɛksplɔi'teiʃən/ *n* explotación, *f*

exploiter /ɪk'splɔitər/ *n* explotador (-ra)

exploration /ˌɛksplə'reiʃən/ *n* exploración, *f*

exploratory /ɪk'splɔrəˌtɔri/ *a* exploratorio

explore /ɪk'splɔr/ *vt* explorar; examinar; averiguar; investigar; (*Med. Surg.*) explorar

explorer /ɪk'splɔrər/ *n* explorador (-ra)

explosion /ɪk'splouʒən/ *n* explosión, *f*; estallido, *m*, detonación, *f*

explosive /ɪk'splousɪv/ *a* and *n* explosivo, *m.* **high e.,** explosivo violento, *m.* **explosives chamber,** recámara, *f*

explosiveness /ɪk'splousɪvnɪs/ *n* propiedad explosiva, *f*; lo explosivo; violencia, *f*

exponent /ɪk'spounənt/ *a* and *n* exponente, *mf*

export /*n* 'ɛksport; *v* ɪk'sport/ *n* exportación, *f. vt* exportar. **e. license,** permiso de exportación, *m.* **e. trade,** comercio de exportación, *m*

exportation /ˌɛkspɔr'teiʃən/ *n* exportación, *f*

exporter /ɪk'spɔrtər/ *n* exportador (-ra)

expose /ɪk'spouz/ *vt* exponer; arriesgar; (exhibit) exhibir, (unmask) desenmascarar; descubrir; revelar; *Photo.* exponer; (ridicule) ridiculizar

exposed /ɪk'spouzd/ *a* descubierto; no abrigado; expuesto, peligroso

exposition /ˌɛkspə'zɪʃən/ *n* explicación, interpretación, *f*; declaración, *f*; (exhibition) exposición, *f*

expostulate /ɪk'spɒstʃəˌleit/ *vi* protestar, **to e. with,** reprochar; reconvenir

expostulation /ɪkˌspɒstʃə'leiʃən/ *n* protesta, *f*; reconvención, *f*

exposure /ɪk'spouʒər/ *n* exposición, *f*; (aspect) orientación, *f*; (scandal) revelación, *f*, escándalo, *m*; peligro, *m*; exposición al frío or al calor, *f*

expound /ɪk'spaund/ *vt* exponer, explicar; comentar

expounder /ɪk'spaundər/ *n* intérprete, *mf*; comentador (-ra)

express /ɪk'sprɛs/ *a* (clear) categórico, explícito, claro; expreso; (exact) exacto; (quick) rápido. *n* (messenger, post) expreso, *m*; (train) (tren) expreso, (tren) rápido, *m*; (goods) exprés, *m. vt* expresar; (a letter, etc.) mandar por expreso

expressible /ɪk'sprɛsəbəl/ *a* decible

expression /ɪk'sprɛʃən/ *n* expresión, *f*

expressionless /ɪk'sprɛʃənlɪs/ *a* sin expresión

expressive /ɪk'sprɛsɪv/ *a* expresivo; que expresa

expropriate /ɛks'proupriˌeit/ *vt* expropiar

expropriation /ɛksˌproupri'eiʃən/ *n* expropiación, *f*

expulsion /ɪk'spʌlʃən/ *n* expulsión, *f*

expunge /ɪk'spʌndʒ/ *vt* borrar; testar; omitir

expunging /ɪk'spʌndʒɪŋ/ *n* borradura, *f*; testación, *f*; omisión, *f*

expurgate /'ɛkspərˌgeit/ *vt* expurgar

expurgation /ˌɛkspər'geiʃən/ *n* expurgación, *f*

expurgator /'ɛkspərˌgeitər/ *n* expurgador, *m*

expurgatory /ɪk'spɜrgəˌtɔri/ *a* expurgatorio

exquisite /ɪk'skwɪzɪt/ *a* exquisito, precioso, primoroso; excelente; (acute) agudo, intenso; (keen) vivo. *n* elegante, petimetre, *m*

exquisitely /ɪk'skwɪzɪtli/ *adv* primorosamente, pulcramente; a la perfección

exquisiteness /ɪk'skwɪzɪtnɪs/ *n* primor, *m*; pulcritud, perfección, *f*; excelencia, *f*; (of pain) intensidad, *f*; (keenness) viveza, *f*

extant /'ɛkstənt/ *a* estante; existente; viviente

extemporize /ɪk'stɛmpəˌraiz/ *vt* and *vi* improvisar

extend /ɪk'stɛnd/ *vt* extender; (hold out) tender, alargar; (lengthen) prolongar; (a period of time) prorrogar, diferir; (make larger) ensanchar; (increase) aumentar; dilatar; ampliar; (offer) ofrecer; *vi* extenderse; dilatarse; continuar; (give) dar de sí, estirarse; (last) prolongarse, durar; (become known) propagarse

extensible /ɪk'stɛnsəbəl/ a extensible

extension /ɪk'stɛnʃən/ n extensión, f; expansión, f; (increase) aumento, m; prolongación, f; ampliación, f; Com. prórroga, f; (telephone number) extensión, f, interno, m

extension cord n cordón de extensión, m; ladrón m, (Mexico; slang)

extensive /ɪk'stɛnsɪv/ a extenso, ancho, vasto; grande, considerable; (comprehensive) comprensivo

extensively /ɪk'stɛnsɪvli/ adv extensamente; generalmente

extensiveness /ɪk'stɛnsɪvnɪs/ n extensión, f; amplitud, f

extensor /ɪk'stɛnsər, -sɔr/ n Anat. extensor, m

extent /ɪk'stɛnt/ n extensión, f; (degree) punto, m; (limit) límite, m. **to a great e.**, en gran parte; considerablemente. **to some e.**, hasta cierto punto. **to the full e.**, en toda su extensión; completamente. **to what e.?** ¿hasta qué punto?

extenuate /ɪk'stɛnyu,eit/ vt atenuar, desminuir, mitigar, paliar

extenuating /ɪk'stɛnyu,eitɪŋ/ a atenuante

extenuation /ɪk,stɛnyu'eiʃən/ n atenuación, mitigación, f

exterior /ɪk'stɪəriər/ a exterior, externo; de fuera; (foreign) extranjero. n exterior, m; aspecto, m; forma, f

exterminate /ɪk'stɜrmə,neit/ vt exterminar

extermination /ɪk,stɜrmə'neiʃən/ n exterminio, m

exterminator /ɪk'stɜrmə,neitər/ n exterminador (-ra)

exterminatory /ɪk'stɜrmənə,tɔri/ a exterminador

external /ɪk'stɜrnḷ/ a externo, exterior; (foreign) extranjero. n pl **externals**, apariencias, f pl; aspecto exterior, m; comportamiento, m

externally /ɪk'stɜrnḷi/ adv exteriormente

exterritorial /,ɛkstɛrɪ'tɔriəl/ a extraterritorial

exterritoriality /,ɛkstɛrɪtɔri'æliti/ n extraterritorialidad, f

extinct /ɪk'stɪŋkt/ a extinto; (of light, fire) extinguido; suprimido

extinction /ɪk'stɪŋkʃən/ n extinción, f

extinguish /ɪk'stɪŋgwɪʃ/ vt extinguir; apagar; Fig. eclipsar

extinguishable /ɪk'stɪŋgwɪʃəbəl/ a apagable

extinguisher /ɪk'stɪŋgwɪʃər/ n apagador (-ra); (for fires) extintor, m; (snuffer) matacandelas, m

extinguishment /ɪk'stɪŋgwɪʃmənt/ n apagamiento, m; extinción, f; abolición, f; (destruction) aniquilamiento, m

extirpate /'ɛkstər,peit/ vt extirpar

extirpation /,ɛkstər'peiʃən/ n extirpación, f

extol /ɪk'stoul/ vt elogiar, encomiar, alabar; cantar

extoller /ɪk'stoulər/ n alabador (-ra)

extort /ɪk'stɔrt/ vt arrancar, sacar por fuerza; exigir por amenazas

extortion /ɪk'stɔrʃən/ n extorsión, f; exacción, f

extortionate /ɪk'stɔrʃənɪt/ a injusto; opresivo; (of price) exorbitante, excesivo

extra /'ɛkstrə/ a and adv adicional; extraordinario; suplementario; (spare) de repuesto. prefix (in compounds) extra. n extra, m; suplemento, m; (of a paper) hoja extraordinaria, f; (actor) supernumerario (-ia). **e. charge,** gasto suplementario, m; (on the railway, etc.) suplemento, m. **e.-mural,** a de extramuros.

extract /v ɪk'strækt; n 'ɛkstrækt/ vt sacar; (Chem. Math.) extraer; extractar; (obtain) obtener. n Chem. extracto, m; (excerpt) cita, f

extraction /ɪk'strækʃən/ n saca, f; extracción, f; obtención, f

extradite /'ɛkstrə,dait/ vt entregar por extradición

extradition /,ɛkstrə'dɪʃən/ n extradición, f

extraneous /ɪk'streiniəs/ a extraño; (irrelevant) ajeno (a)

extraordinarily /ɪk,strɔrdṇ'ɛrəli/ adv extraordinariamente, singularmente

extraordinariness /ɪk'strɔrdṇ,ɛrinɪs/ n lo extraordinario; singularidad, f; (queerness) rareza, f

extraordinary /ɪk'strɔrdṇ,ɛri/ a extraordinario; singular; (queer) raro, excéntrico; (incredible) increíble

extraterrestrial /,ɛkstrətə'rɛstriəl/ a Lat. Am. extraterrenal

extravagance /ɪk'strævəgəns/ n (in spending) prodigalidad, f, derroche, m; (of dress, speech) extravagancia, f; (foolishness) disparate, m; (luxury) lujo, m

extravagant /ɪk'strævəgənt/ a extravagante; (queer) extraño, raro; (wasteful) pródigo; (of persons) gastador, manirroto; (of price) exorbitante; excesivo

extravagantly /ɪk'strævəgəntli/ adv extravagantemente; de un modo extraño; pródigamente; profusamente; excesivamente

extreme /ɪk'strim/ a extremo. n extremo, m. **in e.,** extremamente, en extremo, en sumo grado. **to carry to extremes,** llevar a extremos; **E. Unction,** Extremaunción, f

extremely /ɪk'strimli/ adv sumamente; Inf. muy

extremism /ɪk'stri,mɪzəm/ n extremismo, m

extremist /ɪk'strimɪst/ a and n extremista, mf

extremity /ɪk'strɛmɪti/ n extremidad, f; (point) punta, f; necesidad, f; pl **extremities,** Anat. extremidades, f pl; (measures) medidas extremas, f pl

extricate /'ɛkstrɪ,keit/ vt desenredar; librar; sacar

extrication /,ɛkstrɪ'keiʃən/ n liberación, f

extrinsic /ɪk'strɪnsɪk/ a extrínseco

extrovert /'ɛkstrə,vɜrt/ n Psychol. extravertido, n

exuberance /ɪg'zubərəns/ n exuberancia, f

exuberant /ɪg'zubərənt/ a exuberante

exudation /,ɛksyu'deiʃən/ n exudación, f

exude /ɪg'zud/ vt exudar; rezumar; sudar. vi exudar; rezumarse

exult /ɪg'zʌlt/ vi exultar; alegrarse

exultant /ɪg'zʌltṇt/ a exultante, triunfante

exultantly /ɪg'zʌltṇtli/ adv con exultación; triunfalmente

exultation /,ɛgzʌl'teiʃən/ n exultación, f; triunfo, m

eye /ai/ n ojo, m; (sight) vista, f; (look) mirada, f; atención, f; (opinion) opinión, f, juicio, m; (of a needle, of cheese) ojo, m; (of a hook) corcheta, f; Bot. yema, f; (of a potato) grillo, m. vt ojear; fijar los ojos en; examinar, mirar detenidamente. **bright eyes,** ojos vivos, m pl. **prominent eyes,** ojos saltones, m pl. **He couldn't keep his eyes off Mary,** Se le fueron los ojos tras María. **as far as the eye can reach,** hasta donde alcanza la vista. **before one's eyes,** a la vista de uno, ante los ojos de uno. **in my (etc.) eyes,** Fig. según creo yo, en mi opinión. **in the twinkling of an eye,** en un abrir y cerrar de ojos. **with an eye to,** pensando en. **with my own eyes,** con mis propios ojos. **with the naked eye,** con la simple vista. **To keep an eye on,** vigilar. **To make eyes at,** guiñar el ojo; mirar con ojos de enamorado. **To have one's eyes opened,** Fig. caérsele la venda. **eye-bath,** ojera, f. **eye-opener,** revelación, sorpresa, f. **eye-pencil,** pincel para las cejas, m. **eye-piece,** objetivo, ocular, m. **eye-shade,** visera, f. **eye-tooth,** colmillo, m. **eye-witness,** testigo ocular, testigo de vista, testigo presencial, mf

eyeball /'ai,bɔl/ n globo ocular, m

eyebrow /'ai,brau/ n ceja, f

eye care atención de la vista, f

eyed /aid/ a que tiene ojos; (in compounds) de ojos..., con ojos...; con los ojos; (of a needle) con el ojo... **She is a blue-eyed child,** Es una niña de ojos azules

eyeglass /'ai,glæs/ n ojera, f; **eyeglasses,** gafas, f pl, anteojos, m pl, Puerto Rico espejuelos, m pl

eyelash /'ai,læʃ/ n pestaña, f

eyeless /'ailɪs/ a sin ojos

eyelet /'ailɪt/ n ojete, m

eyelid /'ai,lɪd/ n párpado, m

eyesight /'ai,sait/ n vista, f

eyewash /'ai,wɒʃ/ n colirio, m; Inf. camelo, m. **That's all e.!** ¡Eso es un camelo!

eyrie /'ɛəri/ n nido (of any bird of prey), nido de águila (eagle's) m

F

f /ɛf/ n (letter) efe, f; Mus. fa, m. **f sharp,** fa sostenido, m

fa /fɑ/ n Mus. fa, m

fable /'feibəl/ n fábula, leyenda, historia, f, apólogo, cuento, m; (untruth) invención, mentira, f

fabled /'feibəld/ a celebrado, famoso

fabric /'fæbrɪk/ n obra, fábrica, f; estructura, construcción, f; (making) manufactura, f; (cloth) tejido, paño, m; textura, f

fabricate /'fæbrɪ,keit/ vt fabricar, construir; (invent) fingir, inventar

fabrication /,fæbrɪ'keiʃən/ n fabricación, manufactura, f; construcción, f; (lie) invención, ficción, f

fabulous /'fæbyələs/ a fabuloso

façade /fə'sɑd/ n fachada, frente, f

face /feis/ n superficie, f; (of persons) cara, f, rostro, m; (look) semblante, aire, m; (of coins) anverso, m; (grimace) mueca, f, gesto, m; (dial) esfera, f; (of gems) faceta, f; (of a wall) paramento, m; (front) fachada, frente, f; (effrontery) cara dura, f, descaro, m. **in the f. of,** ante; en presencia de. Mil. **Left f.!** ¡Izquierda! **on the f. of it,** juzgando por las apariencias. **to bring f. to f.,** confrontar (con). **to laugh in a person's f.,** reírse a la cara (de). **to make a f.,** hacer muecas. **to my f.,** en mi cara, en mis barbas. **to put a good f. on,** Fig. poner (or hacer) buena cara a. **to set one's f. against,** oponerse resueltamente a. **to straighten one's f.,** componer el semblante. **to wash one's f.,** lavarse la cara. **f. card,** figura (de la baraja), f. **f.-cloth,** paño para lavar la cara, m. **f. down,** boca abajo. **f. lift,** operación estética facial, f. **f. of the waters,** faz de las aguas, f. **f. powder,** polvos de arroz, m pl. **f. to f.,** cara a cara, de persona a persona; frente a frente. **f. value,** significado literal, m; Com. valor nominal, m

face /feis/ vt mirar hacia; confrontar, hacer cara (a); (of buildings, etc.) mirar a, caer a (or hacia); Fig. arrostrar, enfrentarse con; Sew. guarnecer, aforrar. vi estar orientado. **to f. the facts,** enfrentarse con la realidad. **to f. the music,** Fig. arrostrar las consecuencias. **to f. up to,** Fig. hacer cara a

faced /feist/ a con cara..., de cara...; Sew. forrado (de). **to be two-f.,** Fig. ser de dos haces

facer /'feisər/ n puñetazo en la cara, m; Fig. dificultad insuperable, f, problema muy grande, m

facet /'fæsɪt/ n faceta, f

facetious /fə'siʃəs/ a chancero, chistoso, jocoso

facetiousness /fə'siʃəsnɪs/ n jocosidad, festividad, f

facial /'feiʃəl/ a facial. **f. expression,** expresión de la cara, f, semblante, m

facile /'fæsɪl/ a (frivolous) ligero (e.g., a deduction or inference)

facilitate /fə'sɪlɪ,teit/ vt facilitar

facilitation /fə,sɪlɪ'teiʃən/ n facilitación, f

facility /fə'sɪlɪti/ n facilidad, f; habilidad, destreza, f

facing /'feisɪŋ/ n Sew. vuelta, f; (of a building) paramento, m; (of lumber) chapa f; encaramiento, m

facsimile /fæk'sɪməli/ n facsímile, m

fact /fækt/ n (event) hecho, suceso, m; (datum) dato, m; realidad, verdad, f. **as a matter of f.,** en realidad. **in f.,** en efecto, en realidad. **I know as a f.,** Tengo por cierto. **The f. is...,** La verdad es (que)... **the f. that,** el hecho de que

fact-finding /'fækt ,faindɪŋ/ informador (e.g. send s.b. on a fact-finding mission, enviar a fulano en misión informadora)

faction /'fækʃən/ n facción, f, partido, bando, m; (tumult) alboroto, m

factional /'fækʃənl/ a partidario

factious /'fækʃəs/ a faccioso, sedicioso

factiousness /'fækʃəsnɪs/ n espíritu de facción, m; rebeldía, f

factitious /fæk'tɪʃəs/ a falso; artificial

factor /'fæktər/ n (fact) factor, elemento, m; consideración, f; Math. factor, m; Com. agente, factor, m

factory /'fæktəri/ n fábrica, manufactura, f; taller, m. **F. Act,** ley de trabajadores industriales, f. **f. hand,** operario (-ia)

factual /'fæktʃuəl/ a basado en hechos, objetivo

faculty /'fækəlti/ n facultad, f; (talent) habilidad, f, talento, m; (university division) facultad, f; (teachers as a group) claustro de profesores, claustro, profesorado, m; (authorization) privilegio, m, autoridad, f

fad /fæd/ n capricho, m, chifladura, f, dengue, m

faddiness /'fædinɪs/ n manías, f pl, excentricidad, f

faddist /'fædɪst/ n chiflado (-da)

faddy /'fædi/ a caprichoso, dengoso, difícil, excéntrico

fade /feid/ vi (of plants) marchitarse, secarse; (of color) palidecer, descolorarse; (vanish) disiparse, desaparecer; (of persons) desmejorarse; (be lost) salir. vt descolorar. **to f. away,** desvanecer; (of persons) consumirse. **f.-out,** n (cinema) desaparecimiento gradual, m

faded /'feidɪd/ a (of plants) seco, marchito, mustio; (of colors) descolorido, pálido; (of people) desmejorado

fadeless /'feidlɪs/ a de colores resistentes; eterno, no olvidado; siempre joven

fading /'feidɪŋ/ a que palidece; (of flowers) medio marchito; (of light) mortecino, pálido; decadente. n desaparecimiento, m, marchitez, f; decadencia, f

faggot /'fægət/ n haz (de gavilla) or gavilla) de leña, f

faience /fai'ɑns/ n fayenza, f

fail /feil/ vi faltar; fracasar, malograrse; no tener éxito, salir mal; (of strength) decaer, acabarse; (be short of) carecer (de); Com. hacer bancarrota, suspender pagos. vt abandonar; (disappoint) decepcionar, engañar; (in exams) suspender. **Do not f. to see her,** No dejes de verla. **He failed to do his duty,** Faltó a su deber

fail /feil/ n without f., sin falta

failing /'feilɪŋ/ n falta, f; (shortcoming) vicio, flaco, m, debilidad, f; malogro, fracaso, m; decadencia, f

failure /'feilyər/ n fracaso, m; falta de éxito, f; (in exams) suspensión, f; (of power) no funcionamiento, m; omisión, f, descuido, m; Com. quiebra, bancarrota, f; (decay) decadencia, f. **on f. of,** al fracasar; bajo pena de

fain /fein/ a deseoso, muy contento. **He was f. to...,** Se sintió obligado a...; Quería

faint /feint/ a débil; (dim) indistinto, vago, borroso; (of colors) pálido, desmayado; (weak) lánguido, desfallecido; (slight) superficial, rudimentario. vi perder el sentido, desmayarse. n desmayo, m. **to be f. with hunger,** estar muerto de hambre. **to cause to f.,** hacer desmayar. **f.-hearted,** pusilánime, medroso. **f.-heartedness,** pusilanimidad, f

faintly /'feintli/ adv débilmente; en voz débil; indistintamente

faintness /'feintnɪs/ n languidez, debilidad, f; (swoon) desmayo, m; lo indistinto; lo borroso

fair /fɛər/ n feria, f; (sale) mercado, m; (exhibition) exposición, f

fair /fɛər/ a (beautiful) hermoso, lindo, bello; (of hair) rubio; (of skin) blanco; (clear, fresh) limpio, claro; (good) bueno; (favorable) favorable, propicio, próspero; (of weather) despejado, sereno; (just) imparcial; (straightforward) honrado, recto, justo; (passable) regular, mediano; (of writing) legible; (proper) conveniente. adv honradamente; (politely) cortésmente; exactamente. **by f. means,** por medios honrados. **It's not f.!** ¡No hay derecho! **to become f.,** (of weather) serenarse. **to give a f. trial,** juzgar imparcialmente; dar una buena oportunidad a. Law. procesar imparcialmente. **to make a f. copy,** poner en limpio. **f.-haired,** de pelo rubio, rubio. **f. one,** una beldad, f. **f. play,** Sports. juego limpio, m; proceder leal, m. **f.-skinned,** de tez blanca, rubio, güero. **f.-weather,** buen tiempo, m, bonanza, f. **f.-weather friends,** amigos de los días prósperos, m pl

fairing /'fɛərɪŋ/ *n Brit* regalo de feria, *m.* **to give fairings,** feriar

fairly /'fɛərli/ *adv* (justly) con imparcialidad; (moderately) bastante; totalmente, enteramente. **f. good,** bastante bueno; regular

fairness /'fɛərnɪs/ *n* belleza, hermosura, *f*; (of skin) blancura, *f*; (justness) imparcialidad, *f*; (reasonableness) justicia, equidad, *f*; (of hair) color rubio, oro, *m*

fairway /'fɛər,wei/ *n Naut.* canalizo, paso, *m*; (golf) terreno sin obstáculos, *m*

fairy /'fɛəri/ *n* hada, *f*, duende, *m, a* de hada, de duendes; *Fig.* delicado. **f.-gold,** tesoro de duendes, *m*; **f.-light,** lucecillo, *m*; luminaria, *f.* **f.-like,** aduendado, como una hada. **f.-ring,** círculo mágico, *m.* **f.-tale,** cuento de hadas, *m*; patraña, *f*, cuento de viejas, *m*

fairyland /'fɛəri,lænd/ *n* país de las hadas, *m*

faith /feiθ/ *n* fe, *f*; confianza, *f*; (doctrine) creencia, religión, filosofía, *f*; (honor) palabra, *f.* **in good f.,** de buena fe. **to break f.,** faltar a la palabra dada. **f.-healing,** curanderismo, *m*

faithful /'feiθfəl/ *a* fiel, leal; (accurate) exacto; (trustworthy) veraz. **the f.,** los creyentes

faithfully /'feiθfəli/ *adv* fielmente, lealmente; (accurately) con exactitud. **Yours f.,** Queda de Vd. su att. s.s.

faithfulness /'feiθfəlnɪs/ *n* fidelidad, lealtad, *f*; (accuracy) exactitud, *f*

faithless /'feiθlɪs/ *a* infiel, desleal, pérfido.

faithlessness /'feiθlɪsnɪs/ *n* infidelidad, deslealtad, traición, *f*

fake /feik/ *vt* imitar, falsificar. *n* imitación, falsificación, *f.* **to f. up,** inventar

Falangist /fei'lɑndʒɪst/ *a* and *n* falangista *mf*

falcon /'fɔlkən/ *n* halcón, *m*, (literary) azor, *m.* **f. gentle,** *Ornith.* neblí, *m*

falconry /'fɔlkənri/ *n* cetrería, *f*

Falkland Islands, the /'fɔklənd/ *pl* las Malvinas, *fpl*

fall /fɔl/ *n* caída, *f*; (of temperature, mercury) baja, *f*; (of water) salto de agua, *m*, catarata, cascada, *f*; (in value) depreciación, *f*; (in price and Stock Exchange) baja, *f*; (descent) bajada, *f*; (autumn) otoño, *m*; (declivity) declinación, *f*, declive, desnivel, *m*; (ruin) ruina, *f*; destrucción, *f*; (of night, etc.) caída (de la noche), *f*; (of snow) nevada, *f*; (of rain) golpe, *m*; (*Theat.* of curtain) caída, bajada, *f*; (surrender) capitulación, rendición, *f*; (of earth) desprendimiento de tierras, *m*; (of the tide) reflujo, *m*

fall /fɔl/ *vi* caer; (of mercury, temperature) bajar; (collapse) desplomarse, hundirse, derrumbarse; (die) caer muerto; (descend) descender; (*Theat.* of the curtain) bajar, caer; (of a river into the sea, etc.) desembocar, desaguar; (of hair, draperies) caer; (decrease) disminuir; (of spirits) ponerse triste, sentirse deprimido; (sin) caer; (come upon) sobrevenir; (of dusk, etc.) caer, llegar; (strike, touch) tocar; (as a share) tocar en suerte; (as a duty, responsibility) tocar, corresponder; (of seasons) caer en; (of words from the lips) caer de (los labios); (say) decir, pronunciar palabras; (of exclamations) escaparse; (become) venir a ser; (happen) suceder; (be) ser. **fallen upon evil days,** venido a menos. **His face fell,** Puso una cara de desengaño. **Christmas falls on a Thursday this year,** Navidad cae en jueves este año. **to let f.,** dejar caer. **to f. a-** (followed by verb) empezar a. **He fell a-crying,** Empezó a llorar. **to f. again,** volver a caer, recaer. **to f. among,** caer entre. **to f. away,** (leave) abandonar, dejar; (grow thin) enflaquecer; marchitarse; (crumble) desmoronarse. **to f. back,** retroceder, volver hacia atrás. **to f. back upon,** recurrir a; *Mil.* replegarse hacia. **to f. backward,** caer de espaldas, caer hacia atrás. **to f. behind,** quedarse atrás. **to f. down,** venirse a tierra; venirse abajo, dar consigo en el suelo, caer. **to f. due,** vencer. **to f. flat,** caer de bruces, (be unsuccessful) no tener éxito. **to f. in,** caer en; (collapse) desplomarse; *Mil.* alinearse; (expire) vencer. **to f. into,** caer en. **to f. in with,** tropezar con; reunirse con, juntarse con; (agree) convenir en; venir a ser. **to f. off,** caer de; (of leaves, etc.) desprenderse, separarse de; (abandon) abandonar; (diminish) disminuir. **to f. on,** caer de (e.g. *to f. on one's back,* caer de espaldas); (of seasons) caer en; (attack) echarse encima de, atacar. **to f. out,** (of a

window, etc.) caer por; (happen) acontecer, suceder; (quarrel) pelearse, reñir; *Mil.* romper filas. **to f. out with,** reñir con. **to f. over,** volcar, caer; (stumble) tropezar con. **to f. short,** faltar; carecer, ser deficiente; (fail) malograrse, no llegar a sus expectaciones; (of shooting) errar el tiro. **to f. through,** caer por; (fail) malograrse, fracasar. **to f. to,** empezar a, ponerse a; (be incumbent on) tocar a, corresponder a; (attack) atacar. **to f. under,** caer debajo; caer bajo; sucumbir, perecer; (incur) incurrir en, merecer. **to f. upon,** (attack) caer sobre, acometer; acaecer, tener lugar; (be incumbent) tocar a

fallacious /fə'leiʃəs/ *a* falaz, engañoso, ilusorio

fallaciousness /fə'leiʃəsnɪs/ *n* falacia, *f*, engaño, *m*

fallacy /'fæləsi/ *n* error, *m*, ilusión, *f*

fallen /'fɔlən/ *a* caído; arruinado; degradado. **f. angel,** ángel caído, *m.* **f. woman,** perdida, mujer caída, *f*

fallibility /,fælə'bɪlɪti/ *n* falibilidad, *f*

fallible /'fæləbəl/ *a* falible

falling /'fɔlɪŋ/ *a* que cae, cayente. *n* caída, *f*; (of mercury, temperature) baja, *f*; (crumbling) desmoronamiento, *m*; (collapse) hundimiento, derrumbamiento, *m*; (of tide) reflujo, *m*; (of water level) bajada, *f*; (in value) depreciación, *f*; (of prices and Stock Exchange) baja, *f*; (diminishment) disminución, *f*; (in level of earth) declinación, *f*; (*Com.* expiry) vencimiento, *m*; (*Theat.* of curtain) bajada, caída, *f.* **f. away,** (crumbling) desmoronamiento, *m*; desprendimiento de tierras, *m*; (desertion) deserción, *f*, abandono, *m.* **f. back,** retirada, *f*, retroceso, *m.* **f. down,** caída, *f*; derrumbamiento, *m.* **f. due,** vencimiento, *m.* **f. in,** hundimiento, *m*; (crumbling) desmoronamiento, *m.* **f. off,** (disappearance) desaparición, *f*; (diminution) disminución, *f*; (deterioration) deterioración, *f.* **f. out,** caída por, *f*, disensión, *f.* **f. short,** falta, *f*; carácter inferior, *m*; frustración, *f.* **f. star,** estrella fugaz, *f*

fallout /'fɔl,aut/ caída radiactiva, llovizna radiactiva, precipitación radiactiva, *f*

fallow /'fælou/ *a* (of color) leonado; *Agr.* barbechado; descuidado. *n* barbecho, *m. vt* barbechar. **to leave f.,** dejar en barbecho. **f. deer,** corzo (-za)

false /fɔls/ *a* incorrecto, erróneo, equivocado; falso; (unfounded) infundado; (disloyal) infiel, traidor, desleal; (not real) postizo; artificial; de imitación; *Mus.* desafinado; (pretended) fingido; engañoso, mentiroso. **to play a person f.,** traicionar (a). **f. bottom,** fondo doble, *m*; **f. claim,** pretensión infundada, *f.* **f. door,** surtida, *f.* **f.-hearted,** pérfido, desleal. **f. teeth,** dientes postizos, *m pl,* dentadura postiza, *f*

falsehood /'fɔlshʊd/ *n* mentira, *f*

falseness /'fɔlsnɪs/ *n* falsedad, *f*; (disloyalty) duplicidad, perfidia, traición, *f*

falsetto /fɔl'setou/ *n* falsete, *m*, voz de cabeza, *f*

falsification /,fɔlsəfɪ'keiʃən/ *n* falsificación, *f*; (of texts) corrupción, *f*

falsifier /'fɔlsəfaiər/ *n* falsificador (-ra)

falsify /'fɔlsəfai/ *vt* falsear, falsificar; (disappoint) defraudar, frustrar, contrariar

falter /'fɔltər/ *vi* (physically) titubear; (of speech) balbucir, tartamudear; (of action) vacilar. **to f. out,** balbucir; hablar con voz entrecortada; decir con vacilación

faltering /'fɔltərɪŋ/ *a* titubeante; (of speech) entrecortado; vacilante. *n* temblor, *m*; vacilación, *f*

falteringly /'fɔltərɪŋli/ *adv* (of speech) balbuciente, en una voz temblorosa; con dificultad, vacilantemente

fame /feim/ *n* fama, *f*; reputación, *f*; (renown) celebridad, *f*, renombre, *m.* **of ill f.,** de mala fama

famed /feimd/ *a* reputado; renombrado, célebre, famoso

familiar /fə'mɪlyər/ *a* íntimo, familiar; afable, amistoso; (ill-bred) insolente, demasiado familiar; (usual) corriente, usual, común; conocido. *n* amigo (-ga), íntimo (-ma); *Eccl.* familiar, *m*; demonio familiar, *m.* **to be f. with,** (a subject) estar versado en, conocer muy bien; (a person) tratar con familiaridad. **to become f. with,** acostumbrarse a; familiarizarse con; (a person) hacerse íntimo de

familiarity /fə,mɪli'ærɪti/ *n* intimidad, familiaridad, confianza, *f*; (friendliness) afabilidad, *f*; (over-familiarity) insolencia, demasiada familiaridad, *f*; (with a subject) conocimiento (de), *m*, experiencia (de), *f*

familiarize /fə'mɪlyə,raiz/ *vt* familiarizar, acostumbrar, habituar. *vr* familiarizarse

familiarly /fə'mɪlyərli/ *adv* familiarmente; amistosamente

family /'fæməli/ *n* familia, *f*; (lineage) linaje, abolengo, *m*; (*Bot. Zool.*) familia, *f*; (of languages) grupo, *m*. *a* de familia; familiar; casero. **f. doctor,** médico de cabecera, *m*. **f. life,** vida de familia, *f*; hogar, *m*. **f. man,** padre de familia, *m*. **f. name,** apellido, *m*. **f. seat,** casa solar, *f*. **f. tree,** árbol genealógico, *m*

family quarrel disputa de familia, *f*

famine /'fæmɪn/ *n* hambre, *f*; carestía, escasez, *f*

famish /'fæmɪʃ/ *vt* matar de hambre. *vi* morirse de hambre

famished /'fæmɪʃt/ *a* hambriento

famous /'feiməs/ *a* famoso, célebre, renombrado; insigne, distinguido; *Inf.* excelente

famously /'feiməsli/ *adv Inf.* muy bien, excelentemente

fan /fæn/ *n* abanico, *m*; *Agr.* aventador, *m*; *Mech.* ventilador, *m*; (on a windmill) volante, *m*; (amateur) aficionado (-da); (admirer) admirador (-ra); *Archit.* abanico, *m*. *vt* abanicar; *Agr.* aventar; ventilar. **fan oneself,** hacerse viento. **tap with a f.,** abanicazo, golpecito con el abanico, *m*. **f.-belt,** *Mech.* correa de transmisión del ventilador, *f*. **f.-light,** tragaluz, *m*. **f. maker** or **seller,** abaniquero (-ra). **f.-shaped,** en abanico, abanicado, en forma de abanico

fanatic /fə'nætɪk/ *a* and *n* fanático (-ca)

fanaticism /fə'nætə,sɪzəm/ *n* fanatismo, *m*

fanaticize /fə'nætə,saiz/ *vt* fanatizar

fancied /'fænsid/ *a* imaginario

fancier /'fænsiər/ *n* aficionado (-da); (of animals) criador (-ra)

fanciful /'fænsɪfəl/ *a* romántico, caprichoso; fantástico

fancifulness /'fænsɪfəlnɪs/ *n* extravagancia, *f*; romanticismo, *m*

fancy /'fænsi/ *n* fantasía, imaginación, *f*; (idea) idea, *f*, ensueño, *m*; (caprice) capricho, antojo, *m*; (liking) afecto, cariño, *m*; gusto, *m*, afición, *f*; (wish) deseo, *m*; (fantasy) quimera, *f*, *a* imaginario; elegante, ornado; *Com.* de capricho, de fantasía; fantástico, extravagante. *vt* imaginar, figurarse; (like) gustar de; aficionarse a; antojarse. **I have a f. for...,** Se me antoja.... **Just f.!** ¡Toma! ¡Quia! ¡Parece mentira! **to take a f. to,** (things) tomar afición a; (people) tomar cariño (a). **f.-dress,** disfraz, *m*. **f.-dress ball,** baile de trajes, *m*

fane /fein/ *n* templo, *m*

fanfare /'fænfeər/ *n* tocata de trompetas, *f*

fang /fæŋ/ *n* colmillo, *m*; raíz de un diente, *f*

fanged /fæŋd/ *a* que tiene colmillos; (of teeth) acolmillado

fangless /'fæŋlɪs/ *a* sin colmillos

fanner /'fænər/ *n* abanicador (-ra); *Agr.* aventador, *m*

fanning /'fænɪŋ/ *n* abaniqueo, *m*; *Agr.* avienta, *f*

fantastic /fæn'tæstɪk/ *a* fantástico; extravagante

fantastically /fæn'tæstɪkəli/ *adv* fantásticamente; extravagantemente

fantasy /'fæntəsi/ *n* imaginación, *f*; fantasía, quimera, visión, *f*; creación imaginativa, *f*

far /fɑr/ *adv* lejos; a lo lejos; (much, greatly) mucho, en alto grado; (very) muy; (mostly) en gran parte. *a* lejano, distante; (farther) ulterior. **as far as,** tan lejos como; (up to, until) hasta; en cuanto, por lo que, según que. (e.g. *As far as we reason,* En lo que razonemos. *As far as we are concerned,* En cuanto a nosotros toca). **by far,** con mucho. **from far and near,** de todas partes. **from far off,** desde lejos. **He read far into the night,** Leyó hasta las altas horas de la noche. **how far?** ¿a qué distancia? (to what extent) ¿hasta qué punto? ¿hasta dónde? **How far is it to...?** ¿Qué distancia hay a...? **in so far as,** en tanto que. **on the far side,** al lado opuesto; al otro extremo. **so far,** tan lejos; (till now) hasta ahora. **to go far,** ir lejos. **far away,** *a* distante, remoto, lejano; *Fig.*

abstraído. *adv* muy lejos. **far beyond,** mucho más allá. **far-fetched,** increíble, improbable. **far-off,** *a* distante. *adv* a lo lejos, en lontananza. **far-reaching,** de gran alcance. **far-sighted,** sagaz, presciente, previsor. **far-sightedness,** sagacidad, previsión, *f*

farce /fɑrs/ *n* farsa, *f*. *f. vt Cul.* embutir, rellenar

farcical /'fɑrsɪkəl/ *a* burlesco, cómico, sainetesco; absurdo, grotesco, ridículo

fare /feər/ *n* (price) pasaje, precio del billete, *m*; (traveler) viajero (-ra), pasajero (-ra); (food) comida, *f*. *vi* pasarlo (e.g. *to f. well,* pasarlo bien). **bill of f.,** menú, *m*. **full f.,** billete entero, *m*. **f. stage,** trayecto, *m*

farewell /,feər'wɛl/ *n* despedida, *f*, adiós, *m*. *a* de despedida. *interj* ¡adiós! ¡quede Vd. con Dios! **to bid f. to,** despedirse de

farewell address *n* discurso de despedida *m*

farflung /'fɑr'flʌŋ/ *a* de gran alcance, extenso, vasto; (empire) dilatado

farina /fə'rinə/ *n* harina (de cereales), *f*; *Chem.* fécula, *f*, almidón, *m*; *Bot.* polen, *m*

farm /fɑrm/ *n* granja, hacienda, quintería, finca, chacra, *f*, cortijo, *m*. *vt* cultivar, labrar (la tierra); (taxes) arrendar. *vi* ser granjero. **to f. out,** (taxes) dar en arriendo. **f. girl,** labradora, *f*. **f. house,** alquería, casa de labranza, granja, *f*. **f. laborer,** labriego, peón, *m*. **f. yard,** corral de una granja, *m*

farmer /'fɑrmər/ *n* granjero, hacendado, quintero, *m*, agrícola, *mf*; (small) colono, labrador, *m*; (of taxes) arrendatario, *m*

farmers' movement /'fɑrmərz/ *Mexico* agrarismo *m*

farmhand /'fɑrm,hænd/ *n* gañán, mozo, mozo de granja, peón *m*

farming /'fɑrmɪŋ/ *n* labranza, *f*, cultivo, *m*; agricultura, labor agrícola, *f*; (of taxes) arriendo, *m*. *a* de labranza, labradoril; agrícola

faro /'feərou/ *n* (card game) faraón, *m*

farouche /fə'ruʃ/ *a* huraño, esquivo

farrago /fə'rɑgou/ *n* fárrago, *m*, mezcla, *f*

farrier /'færiər/ *n* herrador, *m*

farther /'fɑrðər/ *adv* más lejos; (beyond) más adelante; (besides) además. *a* ulterior; más distante. **at the f. end,** al otro extremo; en el fondo. **f. on,** más adelante; más allá

farthest /'fɑrðɪst/ *adv* más lejos. *a* más lejano, más distante; extremo

farthing /'fɑrðɪŋ/ *n* cuarto, *m*; *Fig.* ardite, maravedí, *m*. **He hasn't a brass f.,** No tiene dos maravedís

fascinate /'fæsə,neit/ *vt* fascinar; encantar, hechizar, seducir

fascinating /'fæsə,neitɪŋ/ *a* fascinador; encantador, seduciente

fascination /,fæsə'neiʃən/ *n* fascinación, *f*; encanto, hechizo, *m*

Fascism /'fæʃ,ɪzəm/ *n* fascismo, *m*

Fascist /'fæʃɪst/ *a* and *n* fascista *mf*

fashion /'fæʃən/ *n* (form) forma, hechura, *f*; (way) modo, *m*; (custom) costumbre, *f*, uso, *m*; (vogue) moda, *f*; (high life) alta sociedad, *f*; (tone) buen tono, *m*. *vt* hacer, labrar; inventar. **in Spanish f.,** a la española, al uso de España. **the latest f.,** la última moda. **to be in f.,** estar de moda. **to go out of f.,** dejar de ser de moda, perder la popularidad. **f. book,** revista de modas, *f*. **f. plate,** figurín, *m*

fashionable /'fæʃənəbəl/ *a* de moda; elegante; de buen tono. **to be f.,** estar en boga, ser de moda. **f. world,** mundo elegante, mundo de sociedad, *m*

fashionableness /'fæʃənəbəlnɪs/ *n* buen tono, *m*; elegancia, *f*

fashionably /'fæʃənəbli/ *adv* a la moda, elegantemente

fashion show desfile de modas, *m*, exhibición de modas, *f*

fast /fæst/ *a* (firm) firme; (secure) seguro; (strong) fuerte; (fixed) fijo; (closed) cerrado; (of boats) amarrado; (tight) apretado; (of colors) estable; (of trains) rápido; (of sleep) profundo; (of friends) leal, seguro; (quick) rápido, veloz; (of a watch) adelantado; (dissipated) disoluto. *adv* firmemente, seguramente; (quickly) rápidamente; (of sleep) profundamente; (tightly) estrechamente, apretadamente; (of rain) (llover) a cántaros; (ceaselessly) continuamente; (of-

ten) frecuentemente; (entirely) completamente. **to be f.,** (clocks) adelantar. **to make f.,** *Naut.* amarrar, trincar. **f. asleep,** profundamente dormido. **f. color,** color estable, color sólido, *m*
fast /fæst/ *n* ayuno, *m*, *vi* ayunar. **to break one's f.,** romper el ayuno. **f.-day,** día de ayuno, día de vigilia, *m*
fasten /ˈfæsən/ *vt* (tie) atar; (fix) fijar; sujetar; (stick) pegar; (a door) cerrar; (bolt) echar el cerrojo; *Naut.* trincar; (together) juntar, unir; (with buttons, hooks, etc.) abrochar; (on, upon) fijar en; *Fig.* imputar (a). *vi* fijarse; pegarse; (upon) agarrarse a, asir. **to f. one's eyes on,** fijar los ojos en. **to f. up,** cerrar; atar; (nail) clavar
fastener /ˈfæsənər/ *n* (bolt) pasador, *m*; (for bags, jewelry, etc.) cierre, *m*; (buckle) hebilla, *f*; (of a coat, etc.) tiador, *m*; (of a book, file) sujetador, *m*; (lock) cerrojo, *m*. **paper-f.,** sujetador de papeles, *m*. **patent-f.,** botón automático, *m*
fastening /ˈfæsənɪŋ/ *n* atadura, *f*; sujeción, *f*, afianzamiento, *m*; (together) union, *f*; (of a garment) brochadura, *f*; (of a handbag) cierre, *m*
fastidious /fæˈstɪdiəs/ *a* dengoso, melindroso, desdeñoso; (sensitive) sensitivo, delicado; (critical) discerniente, crítico
fastidiously /fæˈstɪdiəsli/ *adv* melindrosamente
fastidiousness /fæˈstɪdiəsnɪs/ *n* dengues, melindres, *m pl*, nimiedad, *f*, desdén, *m*; sensibilidad, delicadeza, *f*; sentido crítico, *m*
fasting /ˈfæstɪŋ/ *n* ayuno, *m*. *a and part* de ayuno; en ayunas
fastness /ˈfæstnɪs/ *n* firmeza, solidez, *f*; (stronghold) fortaleza, *f*; (retreat) refugio, *m*; (speed) velocidad, rapidez, *f*; (dissipation) disipación, *f*, libertinaje, *m*
fat /fæt/ *a* (stout) gordo, grueso; mantecoso, graso, seboso; (greasy) grasiento; (rich) fértil, pingüe; (productive) lucrativo. *n* (stoutness) gordura, *f*; (for cooking) manteca, *f*; (lard) lardo, *m*; (of animal or meat) grasa, *f*; sebo, saín, *m*; *Fig.* riqueza, *f*; *Fig.* fertilidad, *f*. **to grow fat,** engordarse, ponerse grueso
fatal /ˈfeitl/ *a* fatal, mortal; funesto
fatalism /ˈfeitl̩ˌɪzəm/ *n* fatalismo, *m*
fatalist /ˈfeitl̩ɪst/ *n* fatalista, *mf*
fatalistic /ˌfeitl̩ˈɪstɪk/ *a* fatalista
fatality /feiˈtælɪti/ *n* fatalidad, *f*; infortunio, *m*, calamidad, *f*; muerte, *f*
fatally /ˈfeitl̩i/ *adv* mortalmente, fatalmente; inevitablemente
fate /feit/ *n* destino, sino, hado, *m*, providencia, *f*; fortuna, suerte, *f*; destrucción, ruina, *f*; muerte, *f*. **the Three Fates,** las Parcas
fated /ˈfeitɪd/ *a* fatal, destinado; predestinado
fateful /ˈfeitfəl/ *a* decisivo, fatal; aciago, ominoso
father /ˈfɑðər/ *n* padre, *m*. *vt* prohijar, adoptar; (on or upon) atribuir (a), imputar (a). **Eternal F.,** Padre Eterno, *m*. **Holy F.,** Padre Santo, *m*. **indulgent F.,** padre indulgente, padrazo, *m*. **Like f. like son,** De tal palo tal astilla. **f. confessor,** *Eccl.* director espiritual, *m*. **f.-in-law,** suegro, *m*
fatherhood /ˈfɑðərˌhʊd/ *n* paternidad, *f*
fatherland /ˈfɑðərˌlænd/ *n* patria, madre patria, *f*
fatherless /ˈfɑðərlɪs/ *a* sin padre, huérfano de padre
fatherliness /ˈfɑðərlɪnɪs/ *n* amor paternal, *m*; sentimiento paternal, *m*
fatherly /ˈfɑðərli/ *a* paternal, de padre
fathom /ˈfæðəm/ *n* *Naut.* braza, *f*. *vt* sondear; *Fig.* profundizar, tantear; (a mystery) desentrañar
fathomless /ˈfæðəmlɪs/ *a* insondable; *Fig.* incomprensible, impenetrable
fatigue /fəˈtig/ *n* fatiga, *f*, cansancio, *m*; *Mil.* faena, *f*; *Mech.* pérdida de resistencia, *f*. *vt* fatigar, cansar. **to be fatigued,** estar cansado, cansarse, fatigarse. **f. party,** *Mil.* pelotón de castigo, *m*
fatiguing /fəˈtigɪŋ/ *a* fatigoso
fatness /ˈfætnɪs/ *n* (stoutness) gordura, carnosidad, *f*; grasa, *f*, gordo, *m*; (richness) fertilidad, *f*; lo lucrativo
fatten /ˈfætn/ *vt* engordar; (animals) cebar, sainar; (land) abonar, fertilizar. *vi* ponerse grueso, echar carnes
fatty /ˈfæti/ *a* untoso, grasiento; *Chem.* graso. **f. acid,** ácido graso, *m*. **f. degeneration,** degeneración grasienta, *f*

fatuity /fəˈtuɪti/ *n* fatuidad, necedad, *f*
fatuous /ˈfætʃuəs/ *a* fatuo, necio, lelo
faucet /ˈfɔsɪt/ *n* canilla, llave, *f*, grifo, *m*
fault /fɔlt/ *n* defecto, *m*, imperfección, *f*; (blame) culpa, *f*; (mistake) falta, *f*, error, *m*; (in cloth) canilla, barra, *f*; *Geol.* falla, quiebra, *f*; *Elec.* avería, *f*; *Sports.* falta, *f*, *vi Sports.* cometer una falta. **to a f.,** excesivamente. **to be at f.,** (to blame) tener la culpa; (mistaken) estar equivocado; (puzzled) estar perplejo; (of dogs) perder el rastro. **to find f.,** tachar, culpar, criticar. **Whose f. is it?** ¿Quién tiene la culpa?
faultfinder /ˈfɔltˌfaɪndər/ *n* criticón (-ona)
faultiness /ˈfɔltɪnɪs/ *n* defectuosidad, imperfección, *f*
faultless /ˈfɔltlɪs/ *a* sin faltas; perfecto, sin tacha; impecable
faulty /ˈfɔlti/ *a* defectuoso, imperfecto
fauna /ˈfɔnə/ *n* fauna, *f*
favor /ˈfeivər/ *n* favor, *m*; (protection) amistad, protección, *f*, amparo, *m*; (permission) permiso, *m*, licencia, *f*; (kindness) merced, gracia, *f*; (gift) obsequio, *m*; (favoritism) favoritismo, *m*, preferencia, *f*; (benefit) beneficio, *m*; (badge) colores, *m pl*; *Com.* grata, atenta, *f*. *vt* favorecer, apoyar; mirar con favor, mostrar parcialidad (hacia); (suit) favorecer; (be advantageous) ser propicio (a); (contribute to) contribuir a, ayudar; (resemble) parecerse (a). **Circumstances f. the idea,** Las circunstancias son propicias a la idea, Las circunstancias militan en pro de la idea. **I f. the teaching of modern languages,** Soy partidario de la enseñanza de lenguas vivas. **in f. of,** a favor de, en pro de. **in the f. of,** en el favor de. **out of f.,** fuera de favor; (not fashionable) fuera de moda. **to count on the f. of,** tener de su parte (a), contar con el apoyo de. **to do a f.,** hacer un favor. **to enjoy the f. of,** gozar del favor de. **to fall out of f.,** caer en desgracia; (go out of fashion) pasar de moda. **to grow in f.,** aumentar en favor
favorable /ˈfeivərəbəl/ *a* favorable; propicio, próspero
favorableness /ˈfeivərəbəlnɪs/ *n* lo favorable; lo propicio; benignidad, benevolencia, *f*
favored /ˈfeivərd/ *a* favorecido; predilecto; (in compounds) parecido, encarado
favoring /ˈfeivərɪŋ/ *a* favorecedor, propicio
favorite /ˈfeivərɪt/ *a* favorito; predilecto, preferido. *n* favorito (-ta). **court f.,** valido, privado, *m*; (mistress) querida (de un rey), *f*; (lover) amante (de una reina), *m*. **to be a f.,** ser favorito
favoritism /ˈfeivərɪˌtɪzəm/ *n* favoritismo, *m*
fawn /fɔn/ *n Zool.* cervato, *m*; (color) color de cervato, color de ante, *m*. *a* de color de cervato, anteado, pardo; (of animals) rucio, pardo. *vt* and *vi* parir la cierva. *vi* acariciar; (on, upon) adular, lisonjear
fawning /ˈfɔnɪŋ/ *n* adulación, *f*, *Lat. Am.* adulonería *f*, *a* adulador, lisonjero, *Lat. Am. also* incondicional, *Mexico* lambioche
fax /fæks/ *n* facsimile, *m*, fax, *m*. **fax machine,** máquina fax, *f*. *vt* mandar un fax, pasar el tono
fear /fɪər/ *n* miedo, temor, *m*, *Argentina* canillera *f*; (apprehension) ansiedad, aprensión, *f*, recelo, *m*; (respect) veneración, *f*. *vt* temer; recelar; (respect) reverenciar. *vi* tener miedo; estar receloso, estar con cuidado. **for f. of,** por miedo de. **for f. that,** por temor de que, por miedo de que. **from f.,** por miedo. **There is no f. of...,** No hay miedo de (que)...
fearer /ˈfɪərər/ *n* temedor (-ra), el (la) que teme
fearful /ˈfɪərfəl/ *a* miedoso, aprensivo, receloso; (cowardly) tímido, pusilánime; (terrible) horrible, espantoso, pavoroso; *Inf.* tremendo, enorme
fearfully /ˈfɪərfəli/ *adv* con miedo; tímidamente; (terribly) horriblemente; *Inf.* enormemente
fearfulness /ˈfɪərfəlnɪs/ *n* temor, miedo, *m*; (horribleness) lo horrible
fearless /ˈfɪərlɪs/ *a* sin miedo, intrépido, audaz
fearlessness /ˈfɪərlɪsnɪs/ *n* intrepidez, valentía, *f*
fearsome /ˈfɪərsəm/ *a* temible, horrible, espantoso
feasibility /ˌfizəˈbɪlɪti/ *n* practicabilidad, posibilidad, *f*
feasible /ˈfizəbəl/ *a* factible, hacedero, practicable, ejecutable
feast /fist/ *n Eccl.* fiesta, *f*; banquete, *m*; *Fig.* abun-

dancia, *f*, *vi* regalarse. *vt* festejar, agasajar; (delight) recrear, deleitar. **immovable f.**, *Eccl.* fiesta fija, *f*.
movable f., fiesta movible, *f*. **f. day**, día de fiesta, *m*, festividad, *f*
feasting /'fistɪŋ/ *n* banquetes, *m pl*; fiestas, *f pl*
feat /fit/ *n* hazaña, proeza, *f*, hecho, *m*; (accomplishment) logro, *m*
feather /'fɛðər/ *n* pluma, *f*; (of the tail) pena, *f*; *pl* **feathers**, plumaje, *m*; plumas, *f pl*. *vt* emplumar; adornar con plumas; (rowing) poner casi horizontal la pala del remo. **to f. one's nest,** *Inf.* hacer su agosto. **f.-bed,** plumón, colchón de plumas, *m*. **f.-brained,** casquivano, alocado, aturdido. **f.-duster,** plumero, *m*. **f.-stitch,** *Sew.* diente de perro, *m*. **f. weight,** (boxing) peso pluma, *m*
feathered /'fɛðərd/ *a* plumado, plumoso; adornado con plumas; (winged) alado
feathery /'fɛðəri/ *a* plumoso; como plumas
feature /'fitʃər/ *n* rasgo, *m*, característica, *f*; (cinema) número de programa, *m*; *pl* **features** (of the face) facciones, *f pl*. *vt* dar importancia (a); (cinema) presentar. **f. film,** documentaria, *f*
febrile /'fibrəl/ *a* febril
February /'fɛbruˌɛri, 'fɛbyu-/ *n* febrero, *m*
fecal /'fikəl/ *a* fecal
feces /'fisiz/ *n* heces, *f pl*; excremento, *m*
fecund /'fikʌnd/ *a* fecundo, fértil
fecundate /'fikənˌdeit/ *vt* fecundar
fecundity /fɪ'kʌndɪti/ *n* fecundidad, fertilidad, *f*
federal /'fɛdərəl/ *a* federal, federalista
federalism /'fɛdərəˌlɪzəm/ *n* federalismo, *m*
federalist /'fɛdərəlɪst/ *n* federalista, federal, *mf*
federate /*v* 'fɛdəˌreit; *a* -ərɪt/ *vt* confederar. *vi* confederarse. *a* confederado
federation /ˌfɛdə'reiʃən/ *n* confederación, federación, *f*; liga, unión, asociación, *f*
fed up /fɛd/ *a Argentina, Chile* incomódo, *elsewhere in Lat. Am.* harto
fee /fi/ *n* (duty) derecho, *m*; (professional) honorario, estipendio, *m*; (to a servant) gratificación, *f*; (entrance, university, etc.) cuota, *f*; (payment) paga, *f*. **registration f.,** matrícula, *f*
feeble /'fibəl/ *a* débil; lánguido; enfermizo; (of light, etc.) tenue; *Fig.* flojo. **to grow f.,** debilitarse; disminuir. **f.-minded,** anormal
feebleness /'fibəlnɪs/ *n* debilidad, *f*; *Fig.* flojedad, *f*
feebly /'fibli/ *adv* débilmente; lánguidamente
feed /fid/ *n* alimento, *m*; (meal) comida, *f*; (of animals) pienso, forraje, *m*; *Mech.* alimentación, *f*. *vt* alimentar; dar de comer (a); (animals) cebar; *Mech.* alimentar; mantener; *Fig.* nutrir. *vi* comer, alimentarse; (graze) pastar. **to be fed up,** *Inf.* estar hasta la coronilla, estar harto. **to f. on,** alimentarse de; *Fig.* nutrirse de. **f. pipe,** tubo de alimentación, *m*
feedback /'fidˌbæk/ *n* retrocomunicación, *f*
feeder /'fidər/ *n* el, *m*, (*f*, la) que da de comer a; (eater) comedor (-ra); (of a river) tributario, afluente, *m*; (bib) babero, *m*; *Mech.* alimentador, *m*; (cup for invalids) pistero, *m*
feeding /'fidɪŋ/ *n* alimentación, *f*, *a* alimenticio, de alimentación. **f.-bottle,** biberón, *m*. **f.-cup,** pistero, *m*. **f.-trough,** pesebre, *m*
feel /fil/ *n* (touch) tacto, *m*; (feeling) sensación, *f*; (instinct) instinto, *m*, percepción innata, *f*
feel /fil/ *vt* (touch) tocar, tentar, palpar; (experience) sentir, experimentar; (understand) comprender; (believe) creer; (be conscious of) estar consciente de; (the pulse) tomar; examinar. *vi* sentir, ser sensible; sentirse, encontrarse; (to the touch) ser... al tacto, estar. **How do you f.?** ¿Cómo se siente Vd.? **I f. cold,** Tengo frío. **I f. for you,** Lo siento en el alma; Estoy muy consciente de ello. **I f. strongly that...,** Estoy convencido de que... **I f. that it is a difficult question,** Me parece una cuestión difícil. **It feels like rain,** Creo que va a llover. **to f. at home,** sentirse a sus anchas, sentirse como en su casa. **to f. hungry (thirsty),** tener hambre (sed). **to f. one's way,** andar a tientas; *Fig.* medir el terreno. **to f. soft,** ser blando al tacto. **to make itself felt,** hacerse sentir. **Your hands f. cold,** Tus manos están frías

feeler /'filər/ *n* (of insects) palpo, *m*, antena, *f*; tentáculo, *m*; *Fig.* tentativa, *f*, balón de ensayo, *m*
feeling /'filɪŋ/ *n* (touch) tacto, *m*; (sensation) sensación, *f*; (sentiment) sentimiento, *m*; emoción, *f*; (premonition) corazonada, intuición, premonición, *f*; (tenderness) ternura, *f*; (perception) sensibilidad, percepción, *f*; (passion) pasión, *f*; (belief) opinión, *f*, sentir, *m*. *a* sensible; tierno; (compassionate) compasivo; apasionado; (moving) conmovedor
feelingly /'filɪŋli/ *adv* con emoción, *f*; (strongly) enérgicamente, vivamente; (understandingly) comprensivamente
feign /fein/ *vt* fingir; (invent) inventar, imaginar; simular; (allege) pretextar; (dissemble) disimular. *vi* disimular
feint /feint/ *n* artificio, engaño, *m*; (in fencing) treta, finta, *f*. *vi* hacer finta
feldspar /'fɛldˌspɑr/ *n Mineral.* feldespato, *m*
felicitate /fɪ'lɪsɪˌteit/ *vt* felicitar, congratular, dar el parabién (a)
felicitation /fɪˌlɪsɪ'teiʃən/ *n* felicitación, *f*, parabién, *m*
felicitous /fɪ'lɪsɪtəs/ *a* feliz, dichoso, afortunado; (of phrases, etc.) feliz, acertado; oportuno
felicity /fɪ'lɪsɪti/ *n* felicidad, dicha, *f*
feline /'filain/ *a* felino, gatuno, de gato. *n* felino, *m*
fell /fɛl/ *n* (skin) piel, *f*; (upland) altura, cuesta de montaña, *f*. *a* cruel, feroz; (unhappy) aciago, funesto. *vt* talar, cortar; (knock down) derribar; *Sew.* sobrecoser
feller /'fɛlər/ *n* talador, leñador, *m*
felling /'fɛlɪŋ/ *n* corta, tala, *f*
fellow /'fɛlou/ *n* compañero (-ra); (equal) igual, *mf*; (in crime) cómplice, *mf*; (man) hombre, *m*; (boy, youth) chico, *m*; (colleague) colega, *m*; (of a society) miembro, *m*; (of a pair of objects) pareja, *f*, *Inf.* tipo, chico, *m*. **He's a good f.,** Es un buen chico. **How are you, old f.?** ¡Hombre! ¿Cómo estás? **f.-citizen,** conciudadano (-na). **f.-countryman,** compatriota, *m*; paisano (-na). **f.-creature,** semejante, *mf*. **f.-feeling,** simpatía, comprensión mutua, *f*. **f.-member,** compañero (-ra); colega, *m*. **f.-passenger,** compañero (-ra) de viaje. **f.-prisoner,** compañero (-ra) de prisión. **f.-student,** condiscípulo (-la). **f.-worker,** compañero (-ra) de trabajo; (collaborator) colaborador (-ra); (colleague) colega, *m*
fellowship /'fɛlouˌʃɪp/ *n* coparticipación, *f*; (companionship, religious) compañerismo, *m*; (brotherhood) comunidad, confraternidad, *f*; (society) asociación, *f*; (grant) beca, *f*; (of a university) colegiatura, *f*
felon /'fɛlən/ *n* reo, criminal, *m*; felón (-ona); malvado (-da); (swelling) panadizo, *m*
felonious /fə'louniəs/ *a* criminal; pérfido, traidor
felony /'fɛləni/ *n* felonía, *f*
felt /fɛlt/ *n* fieltro, *m*. **a f. hat,** un sombrero de fieltro
female /'fimeil/ *n* hembra, *f*, *a* femenino (**f.** is often rendered in Sp. by the feminine ending of the noun, e.g. *a f. cat,* una gata; *a f. friend,* una amiga.) **This is a f. animal,** Este animal es una hembra. **f. screw,** hembra de tornillo, tuerca, *f*
feminine /'fɛmənɪn/ *a* femenino; mujeril, afeminado. **in the f. gender,** en el género femenino
feminism /'fɛməˌnɪzəm/ *n* feminismo, *m*
feminist /'fɛmənɪst/ *n* feminista, *mf*
feministic /ˌfɛmə'nɪstɪk/ *a* feminista
femur /'fimər/ *n Anat.* fémur, *m*
fen /fɛn/ *n* marjal, pantano, *m*
fence /fɛns/ *n* cerca, *f*; (of stakes) estacada, palizada, *f*; (hedge) seto, *m*; (fencing) esgrima, *f*; *Mech.* guía, *f*; *Inf.* comprador (-ra) de efectos robados. *vi* cercar; *Fig.* defenderse; *Inf.* recibir efectos robados. *vt* cercar, estacar; *Fig.* defender; proteger. **to sit on the f.,** *Fig.* estar a ver venir
fencer /'fɛnsər/ *n* esgrimidor, *m*
fencesitter /'fɛnsˌsɪtər/ *n* bailarín de la cuerda flaja, *m*
fencing /'fɛnsɪŋ/ *n* cerca, *f*; palizada, empalizada, *f*. **f. mask,** careta, *f*. **f. master,** maestro de esgrima, maestro de armas, *m*. **f. match,** asalto de esgrima, *m*
fend /fɛnd/ (**off**) *vt* parar; defenderse de, guardarse de. *vi* (for) mantener, cuidar de. **to f. for oneself,** ganarse la vida; defenderse

fender /'fɛndər/ n (round hearth) guardafuegos, m; *Naut.* espolón, m, defensas, f pl; *Auto.* parachoques, m

fennel /'fɛnl/ n *Bot.* hinojo, m

ferment /n 'fɜrmɛnt; v fər'mɛnt/ n fermento, m; fermentación, f; *Fig.* agitación, conmoción, efervescencia f. vt hacer fermentar; *Fig.* agitar, excitar. vi fermentar, estar en fermentación; *Fig.* hervirse, agitarse, excitarse

fermentation /,fɜrmɛn'teiʃən/ n fermentación, f

fern /fɜrn/ n helecho, m

ferocious /fə'rouʃəs/ a feroz, bravo, salvaje

ferocity /fə'rɒsɪti/ n ferocidad, braveza, fiereza, f

ferreous /'fɛriəs/ a férreo

ferret /'fɛrɪt/ n *Zool.* hurón (-ona); **to f. out,** cazar con hurones; (discover) husmear, descubrir

Ferris wheel /'fɛrɪs/ n estrella giratoria, gran rueda, novia, rueda de feria, f

ferroconcrete /,fɛrou'kɒnkrit/ n hormigón armado, m

ferrous /'fɛrəs/ a ferroso

ferruginous /fə'rudʒənəs/ a ferruginoso; aherrumbrado, rojizo

ferrule /'fɛrəl/ n herrete, regatón, m, contera, f; garrucha de tornillos, f

ferry /'fɛri/ n barca de transporte, f; barca de pasaje, f, transbordador, m. vt transportar de una a otra orilla, llevar en barca. vi cruzar un río en barca. **ferry across** vt transbordar. **F.-Command,** servicio de entrega y transporte de aeroplanos, m

ferryman /'fɛrimən/ n barquero, m

fertile /'fɜrtl/ a fértil, fecundo; (rich) pingüe; *Fig.* prolífico, abundante

Fertile Crescent, the el Creciente Fértil m

fertility /fər'tɪlɪti/ n fertilidad, fecundidad, f

fertilization /,fɜrtlə'zeiʃən/ n *Biol.* fecundación, f; *Agr.* fertilización, f, abono, m

fertilize /'fɜrtl,aiz/ vt *Biol.* fecundar; *Agr.* fertilizar, abonar

fertilizer /'fɜrtl,aizər/ n abono, m

ferule /'fɛrəl/ n palmatoria, palmeta, férula, f

fervent /'fɜrvənt/ a ardiente; fervoroso, intenso; (enthusiastic) entusiasta, apasionado

fervently /'fɜrvəntli/ adv con fervor, con vehemencia

fervor /'fɜrvər/ n ardor, fervor, m, pasión, f; (enthusiasm) entusiasmo, celo, m; vehemencia, f

festal /'fɛstl/ a de fiesta; alegre, festivo, regocijado

fester /'fɛstər/ vi ulcerarse, enconarse; *Fig.* inflamarse, amargarse. vt ulcerar

festival /'fɛstəvəl/ a de fiesta. n festividad, f; *Eccl.* fiesta, f; (musical, etc.) festival, m

festive /'fɛstɪv/ a de fiesta; festivo, alegre

festivity /fɛ'stɪvɪti/ n festividad, fiesta, f; (merriment) alegría, f, júbilo, m

festoon /fɛ'stun/ n festón, m, guirnalda, f. vt festonear

festschrift /'fɛst,ʃrɪft/ n libro de homenaje, libro jubilar, m

fetal /'fitl/ a fetal

fetch /fɛtʃ/ vt traer; ir a buscar; ir por; llevar; (conduct) conducir; (of tears) hacer derramar lágrimas, hacer saltársele las lágrimas; (blood) hacer correr la sangre; (produce, draw) sacar; (a blow, a sigh) dar; (acquire) conseguir; (charm) fascinar; (of price) venderse por. **to go and f.,** ir a buscar

fetid /'fɛtɪd/ a fétido, hediondo

fetidness /'fɛtɪdnɪs/ n fetidez, f, hedor, m

fetish /'fɛtɪʃ/ n fetiche, m

fetishism /'fɛtɪ,ʃɪzəm/ n fetichismo, m

fetter /'fɛtər/ n grillete, m; pl **fetters,** grillos, m pl, cadenas, f pl; prisión, cárcel, f. vt encadenar, atar

fettle /'fɛtl/ n condición, f, estado, m

fetus /'fitəs/ n feto, m

feud /fyud/ n enemistad, riña, f; (feudal law) feudo, m

feudal /'fyudl/ a feudal. **f. lord,** señor feudal, señor de horca y cuchillo, m

feudalism /'fyudl,ɪzəm/ n feudalismo, m

feudatory /'fyudə,tɔri/ a and n feudatario (-ia)

fever /'fivər/ n fiebre, f; calentura, f; (enthusiasm) pasión, afición, f. **to be in a f.,** tener fiebre; (agitated) estar muy agitado. **to be in a f. to,** estar muy

impaciente de. **puerperal f.,** fiebre puerperal, f. **tertian f.,** fiebre terciana, f. **yellow f.,** fiebre amarilla, f

feverish /'fivərɪʃ/ a febril; *Fig.* ardiente, febril, vehemente. **to grow f.,** empezar a tener fiebre, acalenturarse

feverishness /'fivərɪʃnɪs/ n calentura, f; (impatience) impaciencia, f

few /fyu/ a and n pocos, m pl; pocas, f pl; algunos, m pl; algunas, f pl; (few in number) número pequeño (de), m. **a good f.,** bastantes, mf pl. **not a f.,** no pocos, m pl, (pocas, f pl). **the f.,** la minoría, f. **f. and far between,** raramente, en raras ocasiones; pocos y contados

fewer /'fyuər/ a comp menos. **The f. the better,** Cuantos menos mejor

fewest /'fyuɪst/ a sup (el) menos, m; el menor número (de), m; (el) menos posible de, m

fewness /'fyunɪs/ n corto número, m

fiancé(e) /,fian'sei/ n novio (-ia); desposado (-da), prometido (-da)

fiasco /fi'æskou/ n fiasco, mal éxito, fracaso, malogro, m

fiat /'fiat/ n fiat, mandato, m, orden, f

fib /fɪb/ n mentirilla, f, *Peru* bacho m vt, decir mentirillas, mentir

fibber /'fɪbər/ n embustero (-ra), mentiroso (-sa)

fiber /'faibər/ n fibra, f; filamento, m, hebra, f; (of grass, etc.) brizna, f; *Fig.* naturaleza, f

fibroid /'faibrɔid/ a fibroso. n fibroma, m

fibrous /'faibrəs/ a fibroso

fibula /'fɪbyələ/ n *Anat.* peroné, m

fichu /'fiʃu/ n pañoleta, f, fichú, m

fickle /'fɪkəl/ a inconstante; mudable; (of persons) liviano, ligero, voluble, falaz

fickleness /'fɪkəlnɪs/ n inconstancia, f; mudanza, f; liviandad, ligereza, veleidad, volubilidad, f

fiction /'fɪkʃən/ n ficción, f; invención, f; literatura narrativa, f; novelas, f pl. **legal f.,** ficción legal, ficción de derecho, m

fictitious /fɪk'tɪʃəs/ a ficticio; imaginario; fingido

fictitiousness /fɪk'tɪʃəsnɪs/ n carácter ficticio, m; falsedad, f

fiddle /'fɪdl/ n violín, m. vt tocar... en el violín. vi tocar el violín; (fidget) jugar; perder el tiempo. **to play second f.,** tocar el segundo violín; *Fig.* ser plato de segunda mesa

fiddler /'fɪdlər/ n violinista, mf

fiddling /'fɪdlɪŋ/ a insignificante, trivial, frívolo

fidelity /fɪ'dɛlɪti/ n fidelidad, f

fidget /'fɪdʒɪt/ vi estar nervioso, estar inquieto; impacientarse; trajinar; (with) jugar con. vt molestar; impacientar

fidgetiness /'fɪdʒɪtɪnɪs/ n inquietud, nerviosidad, f

fidgety /'fɪdʒɪti/ a inquieto, nervioso. **to be f.,** tener hormiguillo

fiduciary /fɪ'duʃi,ɛri/ a fiduciario. n fideicomisario (-ia)

fief /fif/ n feudo, m

field /fild/ n campo, m; (meadow) prado, m, pradera, f; (sown field) sembrado, m; (*Phys.*, *Herald.*) campo, m; (of ice) banco, m; *Mineral.* yacimiento, m; (background) fondo, m; (campaign) campaña, f; (battle) batalla, lucha, f; (space) espacio, m; (of knowledge, etc.) especialidad, esfera, f; (hunting) caza, f; *Sports.* campo, m; (competitors) todos los competidores en una carrera, etc.; (horses in a race) el campo. a campal, pradeño; de campo; de los campos. vt *Sports.* parar y devolver la pelota. **in the f.,** *Mil.* en el campo de batalla, en campaña. **magnetic f.,** campo magnético, m. **to take the f.,** entrar en campaña. **f.-artillery,** artillería ligera, artillería montada, f. **f.-day,** (holiday) día de asueto, m; (day out) día en el campo, m; *Mil.* día de maniobras, m. **f.-glasses,** anteojos, gemelos, m pl. **f.-hospital,** hospital de sangre, ambulancia fija, f. **f.-kitchen,** cocina de campaña, f. **f.-marshal,** capitán general de ejército, m. **f.-mouse,** ratón silvestre, m. **f. of battle,** campo de batalla, m. **f. of vision,** campo visual, m. **f.-telegraph,** telégrafo de campaña, m.

fielder /'fildər/ n (baseball) jardinero (-ra)

field work prácticas de campo, f pl

fiend /find/ *n* diablo, demonio, *m*; malvado (-da); (addict) adicto (-ta)

fiendish /'findɪʃ/ *a* diabólico, infernal; malvado, cruel, malévolo

fiendishness /'findɪʃnɪs/ *n* perversidad, crueldad, *f*

fierce /fɪərs/ *a* salvaje, feroz, cruel; (of the elements) violento, furioso; (intense) intenso, vehemente

fiercely /'fɪərsli/ *adv* ferozmente; violentamente, con furia; intensamente, con vehemencia

fierceness /'fɪərsnɪs/ *n* ferocidad, fiereza, *f*; violencia, furia, *f*; intensidad, vehemencia, *f*

fieriness /'faiᵊrinɪs/ *n* ardor, *m*; (flames) las llamas, *f pl*; (redness) rojez, *f*; (irritability) ferocidad, irritabilidad, *f*; (vehemence) pasión, vehemencia, *f*; (of horses) fogosidad, *f*

fiery /'faiᵊri/ *a* ardiente; (red) rojo; (irritable) feroz, colérico, irritable; (vehement) apasionado, vehemente; (of horses) fogoso

fife /faif/ *n Mus.* pífano, pito, *m*

fifteen /'fɪf'tin/ *a* and *n* quince *m*.; (of age) quince años, *m pl*

fifteenth /'fɪf'tinθ/ *a* and *n* décimoquinto *m*.; (part) quinzavo, *m*, décimoquinta parte, *f*; (of the month) (el) quince, *m*; (of monarchs) quince; *Mus.* quincena, *f*

fifth /fɪfθ/ *a* quinto; (of monarchs) quinto; (of the month) (el) cinco. *n* quinto, *m*; (part) quinto, *m*, quinta parte, *f*; *Mus.* quinta, *f*, **Charles V**, Carlos quinto. **f. column,** quinta columna, *f*

fifthly /'fɪfθli/ *adv* en quinto lugar

fiftieth /'fɪftiɪθ/ *a* quincuagésimo; (part) quincuagésima parte, *f*, cincuentavo, *m*

fifty /'fɪfti/ *a* and *n* cincuenta *m*.; (of age) cincuenta años, *m pl*

fiftyfold /'fɪfti,fould/ *a* and *adv* cincuenta veces

fig /fɪg/ *n* higo, *m*; (tree) higuera, *f*; *Fig.* bledo, ardite, *m*. **green fig,** higo, *m*, breva, *f*. **fig-leaf,** hoja de higuera, *f*; *Fig.* hoja de parra, *f*

fight /fait/ *n* lucha, pelea, *f*, combate, *m*; batalla, *f*; (struggle) lucha, *f*; (quarrel) riña, pelea, *Argentina* arenga *f*; (conflict) conflicto, *m*; (valor) coraje, brío, *m*. **hand-to-hand f.,** cachetina, *f*. **in fair f.,** en buena lid. **to have a f.,** tener una pelea. **to show f.,** mostrarse agresivo

fight /fait/ *vt* luchar contra, batirse con; (a battle) dar (batalla); (oppose) oponer, *Mexico* desafiar; (defend) defender, pelear por; hacer batirse. *vi* luchar, batirse, pelear; (with words) disputar; (struggle) luchar; (make war) hacer la guerra; (in a tournament) tornear. **to f. one's way,** abrirse paso con las armas. **to f. against,** luchar contra. **to f. off,** librarse de; sacudirse. **to f. with,** luchar con; pelear con; reñir con

fighter /'faitər/ *n* luchador (-ra); combatiente, *m*; guerrero, *m*; duelista, *m*; (boxer) boxeador, *m*; *Aer.* (avión de) caza, *m*. **night f.,** *Aer.* (avión de) caza nocturno, *m*. **f.-bomber,** *Aer.* caza bombardero, *m*. **F. Command,** *Aer.* servicio de aviones de caza, *m*

fighting /'faitɪŋ/ *n* lucha, *f*, combate, *m*; el pelear; (boxing) boxeo, *m*, a combatiente; (bellicose) agresivo, belicoso. **f.-man,** combatiente, guerrero, *m*

figment /'fɪgmənt/ *n* ficción, invención, *f*

figurative /'fɪgyərətɪv/ *a* figurado, metafórico; figurativo; simbólico

figuratively /'fɪgyərətɪvli/ *adv* en sentido figurativo; metafóricamente

figure /'fɪgyər/ *n* figura, *f*; forma, *f*; (statue) estatua, figura, *f*; (of a person) silueta, *f*; talle, *m*; (number) cifra, *f*, número, *m*; (quantity) cantidad, *f*; (price) precio, *m*; *Geom., Gram., Dance.* (skating) figura, *f*; (appearance) presencia, *f*, aire, *m*; (picture) imagen, *m*; (on fabric) diseño, *m*; *Mus.* cifra, *f*; *pl* **figures,** aritmética, *f*, matemáticas, *f pl*. *vt* figurar; (imagine) figurarse, imaginar; *Mus.* cifrar. *vi* figurar, hacer un papel; (calculate) calcular, hacer cuentas. **to f. out,** calcular; (a problem, etc.) resolver. **a fine f. of a woman,** *Inf.* una real hembra. **to be good at figures,** estar fuerte en matemáticas. **to cut a f.,** *Fig.* hacer figura. **to have a good f.,** tener buen talle. **f. of speech,** figura retórica, figura de dicción *f*; (manner of speaking) metáfora *f*. **f. dance,** baile de

figuras, *m*, contradanza, *f*. **f.-head,** *Naut.* mascarón, *m*, (or figura, *f*) de proa; *Fig.* figura decorativa, *f*

figured /'fɪgyərd/ *a* estampado, con diseños, labrado

figurine /,fɪgyə'rin/ *n* figurilla, *f*

filament /'fɪləmənt/ *n* filamento, *m*; hebra, *f*

filbert /'fɪlbərt/ *n* avellana, *f*; (tree) avellano, *m*

filch /fɪltʃ/ *vt* sisar, ratear

filching /'fɪltʃɪŋ/ *n* sisa, *f*

file /fail/ *n* (line) fila, hilera, sarta, línea, *f*; *Mil.* fila, *f*; (tool) lima, *f*; (rasp) escofina, *f*; (list) lista, *f*, catálogo, *m*; (for documents) carpeta, *f*, cartapacio, *m*; (bundle of papers) legajo, *m*; (for bills, letters, etc.) clasificador, *m*; archivo, *m*; (in an archives) expediente *m*. **in a f.,** en fila; en cola

file /fail/ *vt* hacer marchar en fila; (smooth) limar; (literary work) pulir; (classify) clasificar; (note particulars) fichar; (keep) guardar; (a petition, etc.) presentar, registrar. *vi* marchar en fila. **to f. in,** entrar en fila. **to f. off,** desfilar. **to file a brief,** presentar un escrito. **to f. letters,** clasificar correspondencia. **to f. past,** *Mil.* desfilar

filial /'fɪliəl/ *a* filial

filiation /,fɪli'eiʃən/ *n* filiación, *f*

filibuster /'fɪlə,bʌstər/ *n* filibustero, pirata, *m*

filigree /'fɪlə,gri/ *n* filigrana, *f*, *a* afiligranado

filing /'failɪŋ/ *n* (with a tool) limadura, *f*; clasificación, *f*; (of a petition, etc.) presentación, *f*, registro, *m*; *pl* **filings,** limaduras, *f pl*, retales, *m pl*. **f.-cabinet,** fichero, *m*. **f.-card,** ficha, *f*

fill /fɪl/ *vt* llenar; (stuff) rellenar; (appoint to a post) proveer; (occupy a post) desempeñar; (imbue) henchir; (saturate) saturar; (occupy) ocupar; (a tooth) empastar, *Argentina* emplomar; (fulfil) cumplir; (charge, fuel) cargar; (with food) hartar. *vi* llenarse. **fill an order,** servir un pedido. **fill a prescription,** surtir una receta. **to f. the chair,** ocupar la presidencia; (university) ocupar la cátedra. **to f. the place of,** ocupar el lugar de; substituir; suplir. **It will be difficult to find someone to f. his place,** Será difícil de encontrar uno que haga lo que hizo él. **to f. to the brim,** llenar hasta los bordes. **to f. in, f. out,** (a form) llenar (or completar) (una hoja); (insert) insertar, añadir; (a hollow) terraplenar. **to f. out,** *vt* hinchar. *vi* hincharse; echar carnes; (of the face) redondearse. **to f. up,** colmar, llenar hasta los bordes; (an office) proveer; (block) macizar; (a form) completar, llenar

fillet /'fɪlɪt/ *n* venda, cinta, *f*; (of meat or fish) filete, *m*; (of meat) solomillo, *m*; *Archit.* filete, *m*. *vt* atar con una venda o cinta; *Cul.* cortar en filetes

filling /'fɪlɪŋ/ *n* envase, *m*; (swelling) henchimiento, *m*; (of a tooth) empastadura, *f*; (in or up of forms, etc.) llenar, *m*. **f. station,** depósito de gasolina, *m*

filly /'fɪli/ *n* jaca, potra, *f*

film /fɪlm/ *n* (on liquids) tela, *f*; membrana, *f*; (coating) capa ligera, *f*; (on eyes) tela, *f*; (cinema) película, cinta, *f*; *Photo.* película, *f*; *Fig.* velo, *m*; nube, *f*, *vi* cubrirse de un velo, etc. *vt* cubrir de un velo, etc.; filmar, fotografiar para el cine. **roll f.,** película fotográfica, *f*. **silent f.,** película muda, *f*. **talking f.,** película sonora, *f*. **to shoot a f.,** hacer una película. **to take part in a f.,** actuar, o tomar parte, en una película. **f. pack,** película en paquetes *f*. **f. star,** estrella de la pantalla (or del cine), *f*

film industry industria fílmica, *f*

filminess /'fɪlmɪnɪs/ *n* transparencia, diafanidad, *f*

filmy /'fɪlmi/ *a* transparente, diáfano

filter /'fɪltər/ *n* filtro, *m*. *vt* filtrar. *vi* infiltrarse; (*Fig.* of news) trascender, divulgarse. **f.-bed,** filtro, *m*. **f.-paper,** papel filtro, *m*

filth /fɪlθ/ *n* inmundicia, suciedad, *f*; *Fig.* corrupción, *f*; *Fig.* obscenidad, *f*

filthiness /'fɪlθɪnɪs/ *n* suciedad, *f*; escualidez, *f*; *Fig.* asquerosidad, *f*; *Fig.* obscenidad, *f*

filthy /'fɪlθi/ *a* inmundo, sucio; escuálido, *Argentina* cascarriento, *Central America* descacharrado; *Fig.* asqueroso; *Fig.* obsceno

filtrate /'fɪltreit/ *n* filtrado, *m*, *vt* filtrar

filtration /fɪl'treiʃən/ *n* filtración, *f*

fin /fɪn/ *n* (of fish) aleta, *f*; (of whale) barba, *f*; *Aer.* aleta, *f*

final /'faɪn‖/ a último, final; (conclusive) conclusivo, decisivo, terminante. n Sports. finales, m pl; Educ. último examen, m. **f. blow,** Fig. golpe decisivo, m. **f. cause,** Philos. causa final, f
finale /fɪ'nælɪ/ n final, m
finalist /'faɪn‖ɪst/ n finalista, mf
finality /faɪ'nælɪti/ n finalidad, f; (decision) determinación, resolución, decisión, f
finally /'faɪn‖i/ adv por fin, finalmente, por último, a la postre; (irrevocably) irrevocablemente
finance /'faɪnæns/ n hacienda pública, f, asuntos económicos, m pl; finanzas, f pl. vt financiar
financial /fɪ'nænʃəl/ a financiero, monetario. **f. year,** año económico, m
financially /fɪ'nænʃəli/ adv del punto de vista financiero
financier /,fɪnən'sɪər, ,faɪnən-/ n financiero, m
find /faɪnd/ vt encontrar, hallar; (discover) descubrir, dar con; (invent) inventar, crear; (supply) facilitar, proporcionar; (provide) proveer; (instruct) instruir; Law. declarar. vi Law. fallar, dar sentencia. n hallazgo, m; descubrimiento, m. **I found him out a long time ago,** Fig. Hace tiempo que me di cuenta de cómo era él. **I found it possible to go out,** Me fue posible salir. **The judge found them guilty,** El juez les declaró culpables. **to f. a verdict,** Law. dar sentencia, fallar. **to f. one's way,** encontrar el camino. **to f. oneself,** hallarse, verse, encontrarse. **to f. out,** averiguar, descubrir, saber (especially in preterite). **to f. out about,** informarse sobre (or de)
finder /'faɪndər/ n hallador (-ra); (inventor) inventor (-ra), descubridor (-ra); (telescope, camera) buscador, m
finding /'faɪndɪŋ/ n hallazgo, m; (discovery) descubrimiento, m; Law. fallo, m, sentencia, f
fine /faɪn/ n multa, f; (end) fin, m. **in f.,** en fin, en resumen
fine /faɪn/ vt multar, cargar una multa de
fine /faɪn/ a (thin) delgado; (sharp) agudo; (delicate) fino, delicado; (minute) menudo; (refined) refinado, puro; (healthy) saludable; (of weather) bueno; magnífico; (beautiful) hermoso, lindo; excelente; (perfect) perfecto; (good) bueno; elegante; (showy) ostentoso, vistoso; (handsome) guapo; (subtle) sutil; (acute) agudo; (noble) noble; (eminent, accomplished) distinguido, eminente; (polished) pulido; (affected) afectado; (clear) claro; (transparent) transparente, diáfano. adv muy bien. **a f. upstanding young man,** un buen mozo. **a f. upstanding young woman,** una real moza. **He's a f. fellow,** (ironically) Es una buena pieza. **That is all very f. but...,** Todo eso está muy bien pero.... **to become f.,** (weather) mejorar
finely /'faɪnli/ adv finamente; menudamente; elegantemente; (ironically) lindamente
fineness /'faɪnnɪs/ n (thinness) delgadez, f; (excellence) excelencia, f; delicadeza, f; (softness) suavidad, f; elegancia, f; (subtlety) sutileza, f; (acuteness) agudeza, f; (perfection) perfección, f; (nobility) nobleza, f; (beauty) hermosura, f
finery /'faɪnəri/ n galas, f pl, atavíos magníficos, m pl; adornos, m pl; primor, m, belleza, f
finesse /fɪ'nɛs/ n sutileza, diplomacia, f; estratagema, artificio, m; (cunning) astucia, f, vi valerse de estratagemas y artificios
finger /'fɪŋgər/ n dedo, m; (of a clock, etc.) manecilla, f; (measurement) dedada, f; Fig. mano, f. vt manosear, tocar; (soil) ensuciar con los dedos; (steal) sisar; (Mus. a keyed instrument) teclear, (a stringed instrument) tocar. **first f.,** dedo índice, m. **fourth f.,** dedo anular, m. **little f.,** dedo meñique, m. **second f.,** dedo de en medio, dedo del corazón, m. **to burn one's fingers,** quemarse los dedos; Fig. cogerse los dedos. **to have at one's f.-tips,** Fig. saber al dedillo. **f.-board,** (of piano) teclado, m; (of stringed instruments) diapasón, m. **f.-bowl,** lavadedos, lavafrutas, m. finger's breadth, dedo, m. **f.-mark,** huella digital, f. **f.-nail,** uña del dedo, f. **f.-print,** impresión digital, f. **f.-stall,** dedil, m. **f.-tip,** punta del dedo, yema del dedo, f. **f.-wave,** peinado al agua, m
fingered /'fɪŋgərd/ a (in compounds) con dedos, que tiene los dedos...

fingering /'fɪŋgərɪŋ/ n (touching) manoseo, m; Mus. digitación, f; (Mus. the keys) tecleo, m; (wool) estambre, m
finial /'fɪniəl/ n pináculo, m
finicky /'fɪnɪki/ a (of persons) dengoso, remilgado; (of things) nimio
finish /'fɪnɪʃ/ n fin, m, conclusión, terminación, f; (final touch) última mano, f; perfección, f; (of an article) acabado, m; Sports. llegada, (horse race) meta, f. vt terminar, acabar, concluir; llevar a cabo, poner fin a; (perfect) perfeccionar; (put finishing touch to) dar la última mano a; (kill) matar; (exhaust) agotar, rendir; (overcome) vencer. vi acabar; concluirse. **to f. off,** acabar, terminar; (kill) matar, acabar con; (destroy) destruir. **to f. up,** acabar; (eat) comer; (drink) beber
finishable /'fɪnɪʃəbəl/ a acabable
finished /'fɪnɪʃt/ a acabado, terminado, completo; perfecto; (careful) cuidadoso
finished goods n pl bienes terminados, m pl
finisher /'fɪnɪʃər/ n terminador (-ra), acabador (-ra); pulidor (-ra); (final blow) golpe de gracia, m
finishing /'fɪnɪʃɪŋ/ a concluyente. n terminación, f, fin, m; perfección, f; (last touch) última mano, f. **to put the f. touch,** dar la última pincelada
finite /'faɪnaɪt/ a finito
Finland /'fɪnlənd/ Finlandia, f
Finn /fɪn/ n finlandés (-esa)
Finnish /'fɪnɪʃ/ a finlandés. n (language) finlandés, m
fir /fɜr/ n abeto, sapino, pino, m. **red fir,** pino silvestre, m. **fir-cone,** piña de abeto, f. **fir grove,** abetal, m
fire /faɪər/ n fuego, m; (conflagration) incendio, m; (on the hearth) lumbre, f, fuego, m; Fig. ardor, m, pasión, f; (shooting) fuego, tiro, m. **by f. and sword,** a sangre y fuego. **by the f.,** cerca del fuego; (in a house) al lado de la chimenea. **long-range f.,** Mil. fuego de largo alcance, m. **short-range f.,** Mil. fuego de corto alcance, m. **on f.,** en fuego, ardiendo, en llamas; Fig. impaciente; Fig. lleno de pasión. **to make a f.,** encender un fuego. **to miss f.,** no dar en el blanco, errar el tiro. **to open f.,** Mil. hacer una descarga. **to set on f.,** prender fuego a, incendiar. **to take f.,** encenderse. **under f.,** bajo fuego. **f.-alarm,** alarma de incendios, f. **f.-arm,** arma de fuego, f. **f.-box,** hogar, m. **f.-brand,** tea, f. **f.-damp,** aire detonante, grisú, m, mofeta, f. **f.-department,** cuerpo de bomberos, m. **f.-dog,** morillo, m. **f.-drill,** (firefighters') instrucción de bomberos, f, (others') simulacro de incendio, m. **f.-engine,** autobomba, bomba, de incendios, f. **f.-escape,** escalera de incendios, f. **f.-extinguisher,** apagador de incendio, extintor, matafuego, m. **f.-guard,** vigilante de incendios, m; (alambrera, f. **f.-hose,** manguera de incendios, f. **f.-insurance,** seguro contra incendios, m. **f.-irons,** badil m. y tenazas f pl. **f.-lighter,** encendedor, m. **f.-screen,** pantalla, f. **f.-shovel,** brulote, m. **f.-shovel,** badil, m, paleta, f. **f.-spotter,** vigilante de incendios, m. **f.-sprite,** salamandra, f. **f.-watching,** servicio de vigilancia de incendios, m
fire /faɪər/ vt incendiar, prender (or pegar) fuego a; quemar; (bricks) cocer; (fire-arms) disparar; (cauterize) cauterizar; (Fig. stimulate) estimular, excitar; (inspire) inspirar; (Inf. of questions) disparar; (Inf. sack) despedir. vi encenderse; (shoot) hacer fuego, disparar (un tiro); (Inf. away) disparar; (up) enojarse. **to f. a salute,** disparar un saludo. Mil. **F.!** ¡Fuego!
firecracker /'faɪər,krækər/ n buscapiés m
fire department n parque de bomberos, servicio de bomberos, servicio de incendios, parque de bombas (Puerto Rico), m
firefly /'faɪər,flaɪ/ n cocuyo, m, luciérnaga, f
fireman /'faɪərmən/ n bombero, m; (of an engine, etc.) fogonero, m. **fireman's lift,** silleta, f
fireplace /'faɪər,pleɪs/ n chimenea francesa, chimenea, f, Mexico brasero m; (hearth) hogar, m
fireproof /'faɪər,pruf/ a a prueba de incendios, f. incombustible
firer /'faɪərər/ n disparador, m
firewood /'faɪər,wʊd/ n leña, Lat. Am. charamusca f. **f. dealer,** leñador (-ra), vendedor (-ra) de leña

firework /'faiᵊr,wȝrk/ n fuego artificial, m

firing /'faiᵊrɪŋ/ n (of fire-arms) disparo, m; (burning) incendio, m, quema, f; (of bricks, etc.) cocimiento, m; (of pottery) cocción, f; (cauterization) cauterización, f; (fuel) combustible, m; (Inf. sacking) despedida, f. **within f. range,** a tiro. **f.-line,** línea de fuego, f. **f.-oven,** (pottery) horno alfarero, m. **f.-squad,** pelotón de ejecución, m

firm /fȝrm/ a firme; (strong) fuerte; (secure) seguro; sólido; (resolute) inflexible, resoluto; severo; (steady) constante; (persistent) tenaz. n Com. casa (de comercio), empresa, f; razón social, f

firmament /'fȝrmᵊmᵊnt/ n firmamento, m

firmly /'fȝrmli/ adv firmemente; inflexiblemente; constantemente

firmness /'fȝrmnɪs/ n firmeza, f; solidez, f; inflexibilidad, resolución, f; severidad, f; constancia, f; tenacidad, f

first /fȝrst/ a primero (primer before m sing nouns); (of monarchs) primero; (of dates) (el) primero. n primero, m; (beginning) principio, m. adv primero, en primer lugar; (before, of time) antes; (for the first time) por primera vez; (at the beginning) al principio; (ahead) adelante. **at f.,** al principio. **from the very f.,** desde el primer momento. **to appear for the f. time,** aparecer (or presentarse) por primera vez; Theat. debutar. **to go f.,** ir delante de todos, ir a la cabeza; ir adelante. **f. and foremost,** en primer lugar; ante todo. **f.-aid,** primera cura, f. **f.-aid post,** casa de socorro, f. **f.-aider,** practicante, m. **f.-born,** a and n primogénito (-ta). **f.-class,** a de primera clase; Fig. excelente. **f.-cousin,** primo (-ma) carnal, primo (-ma) hermano (-na). **f. edition,** edición príncipe, f. **f. floor,** primer piso, m. **f. fruits,** frutos primerizos, m pl; Fig. primicias, f pl. **f.-hand,** a original, de primera mano. **f. letters,** primeras letras, f pl. **f. night,** Theat. estreno, m. **f. of all,** primero, ante todo. **f.-rate,** a de primera clase

firstly /'fȝrstli/ adv en primer lugar, primero

firth /fȝrθ/ n ría, f

fiscal /'fɪskᵊl/ a and n fiscal m.. **f. year,** año económico, m

fish /fɪʃ/ n pez, m; (out of the water) pescado, m; Inf. tipo, indivíduo, m. vt pescar; (out) sacar. vi pescar; Fig. buscar. **fried f.,** pescado frito, m. **to be neither f. nor fowl,** no ser ni carne ni pescado. **to feel like a f. out of water,** sentirse fuera de su ambiente. **to f. in troubled waters,** A río revuelto ganancia de pescadores. **f.-eating,** a ictiófago. **f.-fork,** tenedor de pescado, m. **f.-glue,** cola de pescado, f. **f.-hook,** anzuelo, m. **f.-knife,** cuchillo de pescado, m. **f.-like,** de pez; como un pez, parecido a un pez. **f. roe,** hueva, f. **f.-server,** pala para pescado, f

fishbone /'fɪʃ,boun/ n espina de pescado, raspa de pescado, f

fisherman /'fɪʃᵊrmᵊn/ n pescador m

fishery /'fɪʃᵊri/ n pesquería, f

fishing /'fɪʃɪŋ/ n pesca, f, a de pescar. **to go f.,** ir de pesca. **f.-boat,** bote de pesca, m. **f.-floats,** levas, f pl. **f.-line,** sedal, m. **f.-net,** red de pesca, f. **f.-reel,** carretel, carrete, m. **f.-rod,** caña de pescar, f. **f.-tackle,** aparejo de pesca, m. **f.-village,** pueblo de pescadores, m

fishmeal /'fɪʃ,mil/ n harina de pescado, f

fishmonger /'fɪʃ,mʌŋgᵊr/ n pescadero (-ra).

fishpond /'fɪʃ,pɒnd/ n vivero, m, piscina, f

fishy /'fɪʃi/ a de pescado; (of eyes, etc.) de pez, como un pez; (in smell) que huele a pescado; Inf. sospechoso; (of stories) inverosímil

fissure /'fɪʃᵊr/ n grieta, hendidura, rendija, f; (Anat., Geol.) fisura, f

fissured /'fɪʃᵊrd/ a hendido

fist /fɪst/ n puño, m; Print. manecilla, f; (handwriting) letra, f. **with clenched fists,** a puño cerrado

fisticuff /'fɪstɪ,kʌf/ n puñetazo, m; pl **fisticuffs,** agarrada, riña, f

fit /fɪt/ n espasmo, paroxismo, m; ataque, m; (impulse) acceso, arranque, m; (whim) capricho, m; (of a garment) corte, m; (adjustment) ajuste, encaje, m. **by fits and starts,** a tropezones, espasmódicamente. **fit of fainting** Argentina, Venezuela insulto m

fit /fɪt/ a a propósito (para), bueno (para); (opportune) oportuno; (proper) conveniente; apto; (decent) decente; (worthy) digno; (ready) preparado, listo; (adequate) adecuado; (capable) capaz, en estado (de); (appropriate) apropiado; (just) justo. **It is not in a fit state to be used,** No está en condiciones para usarse. **to be not fit for,** no servir para; (through ill-health) no tener bastante salud para. **to think fit,** creer (or juzgar) conveniente. **fit for use,** usable. **fit to eat,** comestible

fit /fɪt/ vt ajustar, acomodar, encajar; adaptar (a); (furnish) proveer (de), surtir (con); (of tailor, dressmaker) entallar, probar; (of garments) calzar; (of garments, shoes) ir (bien o mal); (prepare) preparar; (go with) ser apropiado (a); (adapt itself to) adaptarse a. vi ajustarse, acomodarse, encajarse; adaptarse; (clothes) ir (bien o mal). **to fit in,** vt encajar; incluir. vi encajarse; caber; adaptarse. **to fit out, equipar;** proveer (de); preparar. **to fit up,** montar, instalar; proveer (de). **to fit with,** proveer de

fitful /'fɪtfᵊl/ a intermitente; espasmódico; caprichoso

fitfully /'fɪtfᵊli/ adv por intervalos, a ratos; caprichosamente

fitly /'fɪtli/ adv adecuadamente; justamente; apropiadamente

fitness /'fɪtnɪs/ n conveniencia, f; aptitud, capacidad, f; oportunidad, f; salud, f; (good health) vigor, m

fitted /'fɪtɪd/ a (of clothes) ajustado

fitter /'fɪtᵊr/ n ajustador, m; (mechanic) armador, mecánico, m; (tailoring) cortador, m; (dressmaking) probador (-ra)

fitting /'fɪtɪŋ/ n encaje, ajuste, m; adaptación, f; (of a garment) prueba, f; (size) medida, f; (installation) instalación, f; **pl. fittings,** guarniciones, f pl; instalaciones, f pl; accesorios, m pl. a conveniente, justo; apropiado; adecuado; (worthy) digno; (of coats, etc.) ajustado. **f. room,** cuarto de pruebas, m. **f. in,** encaje, m. **f. out,** equipo, m. **f. up,** arreglo, m; (of machines) montaje, m; (of a house) mueblaje, m

five /faiv/ a and n cinco m.; (of the clock) las cinco, f pl; (of age) cinco años, m pl. **to be f.,** tener cinco años. **f. feet deep,** de cinco pies de profundidad, f. **feet high,** cinco pies de altura. **f.-finger exercises,** ejercicios de piano, m pl. **F.-Year Plan,** Plan Quinquenal, m

fivefold /'faiv,fould/ a quíntuplo

fix /fɪks/ n aprieto, apuro, m; callejón sin salida, m. vt fijar; sujetar, afianzar; (bayonets) calar; (with nails) clavar; (Photo., Chem., Med.) fijar; (decide) establecer; (a date) señalar; (eyes, attention) clavar; (on the mind) grabar, estampar; (one's hopes) poner; (base) basar, fundar; (Inf. put right) arreglar, componer. vi fijarse; establecerse; determinarse. **to get in a fix,** hacer un lío. **to fix a price,** fijar un precio. **to fix on, upon,** elegir, escoger; decidir, determinar. **to fix up,** arreglar; decidir; organizar; (differences) olvidar (sus disensiones)

fixation /fɪk'seiʃᵊn/ n obsesión, idea fija, f; (scientific) fijación, f

fixative /'fɪksᵊtɪv/ n (Med., Photo.) fijador, m; (dyeing) mordiente, m. a que fija

fixed /fɪkst/ a fijo; inmóvil; permanente; (of ideas) inflexible. **f. bayonet,** bayoneta calada, f. **f. price,** precio fijo, m. **f. star,** estrella fija, f

fixedly /'fɪksɪdli/ adv fijamente; resueltamente; firmemente

fixing /'fɪksɪŋ/ n fijación, f; afianzamiento, m; arreglo, m; (of a date) señalamiento, m. **f. bath,** Photo. baño fijador, m

fixity /'fɪksɪti/ n permanencia, f; inmovilidad, f; invariabilidad, f; firmeza, f

fixture /'fɪkstʃᵊr/ n instalación, f; accesorio fijo, m; Sports. partido, m; Inf. permanencia, f. **f. card,** Sports. calendario deportivo, m

fizz /fɪz/ n espuma, f; chisporroteo, m. Inf. champaña, m. vi (liquids) espumear; (sputter) chisporrotear

fizzle /'fɪzᵊl/ n (failure) fiasco, fracaso, m. vi chisporrotear; (out) apagarse; (fail) fracasar, no tener éxito

fjord /fyᵊrd/ n fiordo, m

flabbergast /'flæbᵊr,gæst/ vt dejar con la boca abierta, dejar de una pieza

flabbiness, flaccidity /'flæbınıs; flæk'sıdıti/ *n* flaccidez, flojedad, *f; Med.* reblandecimiento, *m;* (of character) debilidad, flaqueza del ánimo, *f*
flabby, flaccid /'flæbi; 'flæksıd/ *a* fláccido, flojo; *Fig.* débil
flag /flæg/ *n* bandera, *f;* pabellón, estandarte, *m;* (small) banderola, *f;* (iris) (yellow) cala, *f,* (purple) lirio cárdeno, *m;* (stone) losa, *f.* **to dip the f.,** saludar con la bandera. **to hoist the f.,** izar la bandera. **to strike the f.,** bajar la bandera; (in defeat) rendir la bandera. **f. bearer,** portaestandarte, abanderado, *m.* **f.-day,** día de la banderita, *m;* día de la bandera, *m.* **f.-officer,** almirante, *m;* vicealmirante, *m;* jefe de escuadra, *m.* **f. of truce,** bandera blanca, bandera de paz, *f*
flag /flæg/ *vi* flaquear, debilitarse; languidecer; (wither) marchitarse; decaer, disminuir. *vt* adornar con banderas; (signal) hacer señales con una bandera; (for a race, etc.) marcar con banderas; (with stones) enlosar, embaldosar.
flagellant /'flædʒələnt/ *n* flagelante, *m*
flagellate /'flædʒəˌleit/ *vt* flagelar
flagellation /ˌflædʒə'leiʃən/ *n* flagelación, *f*
flageolet /ˌflædʒə'let/ *n Mus.* caramillo, *m,* chirimía, *f.* **f. player,** chirimía, *f*
flagging /'flægıŋ/ *n* pavimentación, *f;* (floor) enlosado, *m. a* lánguido, flojo
flagon /'flægən/ *n* frasco, *m;* botella, *f*
flagrancy /'fleigrənsi/ *n* escándalo, *m,* notoriedad, *f*
flagrant /'fleigrənt/ *a* escandaloso, notorio
flagship /'flæg,ʃıp/ *n* capitana, *f*
flagstaff /'flæg,stæf/ *n* asta de bandera, *f*
flagstone /'flæg,stoun/ *n* losa, lancha, *Lat. Am.* laja *f*
flail /fleil/ *n* mayal, *m*
flair /fleər/ *n* instinto natural, *m,* comprensión innata, *f;* habilidad natural, *f*
flak /flæk/ *n Aer.* cortina (or barrera) antiaérea, *f;* (criticism) críticas, *f pl*
flake /fleik/ *n* escama, *f;* laminilla, hojuela, *f;* (of snow) copo, *m;* (of fire) chispa, *f. vt* cubrir con escamas, etc.; exfoliar; (crumble) hacer migas de, desmigajar. *vi* escamarse; (off) exfoliarse; caer en copos
flaky /'fleiki/ *a* escamoso; en laminillas; (of pastry) hojaldrado. **f. pastry,** hojaldre, *f*
flamboyance /flæm'bɔiəns/ *n* extravagancia, *f, Lit.* ampulosidad, *f*
flamboyant /flæm'bɔiənt/ *a Archit.* flamígero; extravagante, llamativo, rimbombante; (of style) ampuloso. **f. gothic,** gótico florido, *m*
flame /fleim/ *n* llama, *f; Fig.* fuego, *m. Inf.* amorío, *m, vi* flamear, llamear; arder, abrasarse; (shine) brillar; (up, *Fig.*) inflamarse; acalorarse. **f.-colored,** de color de llama, anaranjado. **f.-thrower,** lanzallamas, *m*
flaming /'fleimıŋ/ *a* llameante; abrasador; (of colors) llamativo, chillón; (of feelings) ardiente, fervoroso, apasionado
flamingo /flə'mıŋgou/ *n Ornith.* flamenco, *m*
Flanders /'flændərz/ flandes, *m*
flange /flændʒ/ *n Mech.* reborde, *m, vt* rebordear
flank /flæŋk/ *n* (of animal) ijada, *f;* (human) costado, *m;* (of hill, etc.) lado, *m,* falda, *f; Mil.* flanco, *m. a* (*Mil. Nav.*) por el flanco. *vt* lindar con, estar contiguo a; (*Mil., Nav.*) flanquear. *vi* estar al lado de; tocar a, lindar con.
flannel /'flænl/ *n* franela, *f, a* de franela
flannelette /ˌflænl'ɛt/ *n* moletón, *m*
flap /flæp/ *n* golpe, *m;* (of a sail) zapatazo, *m,* sacudida, *f;* (of a pocket) cartera, tapa, *f;* (of skin) colgajo, *m;* (of a shoe, etc.) oreja, *f;* (of a shirt, etc.) falda, *f;* (of a hat) ala, *f;* (of trousers) bragueta, *f;* (rever) solapa, *f;* (of a counter) trampa, *f;* (of a table) hoja plegadiza, *f;* (of the wings) aletazo, *m; vt* sacudir, golpear, batir; agitar; (the tail) menear. *vi* agitarse; (of wings) volar con un batir de alas, aletear; (of sails) zapatear, sacudirse; colgar. **f.-eared,** de orejas grandes y gachas
flapjack /'flæp,dʒæk/ *n Cul.* torta de sartén, *f;* (for powder) polvorera, *f*
flapper /'flæpər/ *n Inf.* polla, tobillera, chica "topolino,'' *f*

flapping /'flæpıŋ/ *n* batimiento, *m;* (waving) ondulación, *f;* (of sails) zapatazo, *m;* (of wings) aleteo, *m*
flare /fleər/ *n* fulgor, *m,* llama, *f;* hacha, *f; Aer.* cohete de señales, *m; Sew.* vuelo, *m. vi* relampaguear, fulgurar; brillar; (of a lamp) llamear; (up) encolerizarse, salirse de tino; (of epidemic) declararse; (war, etc.) desencadenarse
flash /flæʃ/ *n* relámpago, centelleo, *m;* ráfaga de luz, *f;* brillo, *m;* (from a gun) fuego, fogonazo, *m;* (of wit, genius) rasgo, *m;* (of joy, etc.) acceso, *m. vi* relampaguear, fulgurar, centellear; brillar; cruzar rápidamente, pasar como un relámpago. *vt* hacer relampaguear; hacer brillar; (a look, etc.) dar; lanzar; (light) encender; (powder) quemar; transmitir señales por heliógrafo; *Inf.* sacar a relucir, enseñar. **shoulder-f.,** *Mil.* emblema, *m.* **to be gone like a f.,** desaparecer como un relámpago. **to f. out,** brillar, centellear. **f. of lightning,** relámpago, rayo, *m.* **f. of wit,** agudeza, *f,* rasgo de ingenio, *m*
flashback /'flæʃ,bæk/ *n* episodio intercalado, *m,* retrospección, *f*
flashily /'flæʃəli/ *adv* llamativamente, ostentosamente
flashing /'flæʃıŋ/ *n* centelleo, *m,* llamarada, *f. a* centellador, relampagueante; brillante; chispeante
flashlight /'flæʃ,lait/ *n* luz de magnesio, *f;* (torch) lamparilla eléctrica, *f, Mexico* rayo, *m;* **f. photograph,** magnesio, *m*
flashy /'flæʃi/ *a* llamativo, charro, *Lat. Am.* figuroso; frívolo, superficial
flask /flæsk/ *n* frasco, *m,* redoma, botella, *f;* (for powder) frasco, *m;* (vacuum) termos, *m*
flat /flæt/ *a* llano; (smooth) liso; (lying) tendido, tumbado; (flattened) aplastado; (destroyed) arrasado; (stretched out) extendido; (of nose, face) chato, romo; (of tire) desinflado; (uniform) uniforme; (depressed) desanimado; (uninteresting) monótono; (boring) aburrido; *Com.* paralizado; (downright) categórico; absoluto; (net) neto; *Mus.* bemol; (of boats) de fondo plano. *adv* See **flatly.** *n* planicie, *f;* (of a sword) hoja, *f;* (of the hand) palma, *f;* (land) llanura, *f;* (apartment) piso, *m; Mus.* bemol, *m.* **to fall f.,** caer de bruces, *Fig.* no tener éxito. **to make f.,** allanar. **to sing f.,** desafinar. **f. boat,** barco de fondo plano, *m.* **f.-footed,** de pies achatados; *Fig.* pedestre. **f.-iron,** plancha, *f.* **f. roof,** azotea, *f*
flatly /'flætli/ *adv* de plano; a nivel; (plainly) llanamente, netamente; (dully) indiferentemente; (categorically) categóricamente
flatness /'flætnıs/ *n* planicie, *f;* llanura, *f;* (smoothness) lisura, *f;* (evenness) igualdad, *f;* (uninterestingness) insulsez, insipidez, *f;* aburrimiento, *m;* (depression) desaliento, abatimiento, *m*
flatten /'flætn/ *vt* aplanar, allanar; aplastar; (smooth) alisar; (even) igualar; (destroy) derribar, arrasar, destruir; (dismay) desconcertar; (out) extender. *vi* aplanarse, allanarse; aplastarse
flattening /'flætnıŋ/ *n* achatamiento, *m,* allanamiento, *m;* aplastamiento, *m;* igualación, *f*
flatter /'flætər/ *vt* adular, lisonjear, halagar, engatusar, *Lat. Am. also* adular, engaratusar; (of a dress, photograph, etc.) favorecer; (please the senses) regalar, deleitar; (oneself) felicitarse
flatterer /'flætərər/ *n* adulador (-ra), lisonjero (-ra), *Guatemala* barbero (-ra) *mf*
flattering /'flætərıŋ/ *a* adulador, lisonjero; (promising) halagüeño; favoreciente; deleitoso
flattery /'flætəri/ *n* adulación, *f, Lat. Am.* adulonería *f*
flat tire llanta deshinchada, *f*
flatulence /'flætʃələns/ *n* flatulencia, *f*
flatulent /'flætʃələnt/ *a* flatulento
flaunt /flɔnt/ *vi* (flutter) ondear; (boast) pavonearse. *vt* desplegar; ostentar, sacar a relucir; enseñar
flaunting /'flɔntıŋ/ *n* ostentación, *f;* alarde, *m. a* ostentoso; magnífico; (fluttering) ondeante
flautist /'flɔtıst/ *n* flautista, *mf*
flavor /'fleivər/ *n* sabor, gusto, *m; Cul.* condimento, *m; Fig.* dejo, *m. vt Cul.* sazonar, condimentar; dar un gusto (de), hacer saborear (a); *Fig.* dar un dejo (de)
flavored /'fleivərd/ *a* (in compounds) de sabor...; sazonado; que tiene sabor de...

flavoring /'fleivəriŋ/ n Cul. condimento, m; Fig. sabor, dejo, m

flavorless /'fleivərlis/ a insípido, soso, sin sabor

flaw /flɔ/ n desperfecto, m, imperfección, f; (crack) grieta, hendedura, f; (in wood, metals) quebraja, f; (in gems) pelo, m; (in fruit) maca, f; (in cloth) gabarro, m; Fig. defecto, error, m; (wind) ráfaga de viento, f

flawless /'flɔlis/ a sin defecto; perfecto; impecable

flax /flæks/ n lino, m. **to dress f.,** rastrillar lino. **f.-comb,** rastrillo, m. **f. field,** linar, m

flaxen /'flæksən/ a de lino; (fair) rubio, blondo. **f.-haired,** de pelo rubio

flay /flei/ vt desollar; (criticize) despellejar

flaying /'fleiiŋ/ n desuello, m, desolladura, f

flea /fli/ n pulga, f. **f. bite,** picada de pulga, f

fleck /flɛk/ n pinta, mancha, f, lunar, m; (of sun) mota, f; (speck) partícula, f; (freckle) peca, f. vt abigarrar; manchar; (dapple) salpicar, motear

fledged /flɛdʒd/ a emplumecido, plumado; alado; Fig. maduro

fledgling /'flɛdʒliŋ/ n volantón, m; Fig. niño (-ña); Fig. novato (-ta)

flee /fli/ vi huir, fugarse, escapar; (vanish) desaparecer; (avoid) evitar, huir de. vt abandonar

fleece /flis/ n vellón, m; lana, f; toisón, m. vt esquilar; Fig. Inf. pelar. **Order of the Golden F.,** Orden del Toisón de Oro, f

fleecy /'flisi/ a lanudo, lanar; (white) blanquecino; (of clouds) borreguero. **f. clouds,** borregos, m pl

fleet /flit/ n (navy) armada, f; escuadra, flota, f; Fig. serie, f, a alado, rápido, veloz. **f.-footed,** ligero de pies

fleeting /'flitiŋ/ a fugaz, momentáneo, efímero, pasajero

flesh /flɛʃ/ n carne, f; (mankind) género humano, m, humanidad, f; (of fruit) pulpa, f. **a man of f. and blood,** un hombre de carne y hueso. **of one's own f. and blood,** de la misma sangre de uno. **to make one's f. creep,** dar carne de gallina (a). **f.-colored,** encarnado, de color de carne. **f.-eating,** carnívoro. **f. wound,** herida superficial, f

fleshiness /'flɛʃinis/ n carnosidad, gordura, f

fleshpot /'flɛʃˌpɒt/ n marmita, f; Fig. olla, f. **the fleshpots of Egypt,** las ollas de Egipto

fleshy /'flɛʃi/ a carnoso, grueso; (of fruit) pulposo; suculento

fleur-de-lis /ˌflɜrdl'i/ n flor de lis, f

flex /flɛks/ n Elec. flexible, m, vt doblar. vi doblarse

flexibility /ˌflɛksə'biliti/ n flexibilidad, f; (of style) plasticidad, f; docilidad, f

flexible /'flɛksəbəl/ a flexible; dúctil, maleable; (of style) plástico; (of voice) quebradizo; adaptable; dócil

flexion /'flɛkʃən/ n flexión, f; Gram. inflexión, f; Gram. flexión, f

flexor /'flɛksər/ n Anat. músculo flexor, m

flick /flik/ n golpecito, toque, m; (of the finger) capirotazo, m; Inf. cine, m, vt dar un golpecito a; dar ligeramente con un látigo; sacudir. **f. one's wrist,** hacer girar la muñeca. **to f. over the pages of,** hojear

flicker /'flikər/ n estremecimiento, temblor, m; fluctuación, f; (of bird) aleteo, m; (of flame) onda (de una llama), f; (of eyelashes) pestañeo, m; (of a smile) indicio, f, vi agitarse; (of flags) ondear; vacilar

flickering /'flikəriŋ/ a tenue; vacilante

flier /'flaiər/ n volador (-ra); aviador (-ra); piloto, m; fugitivo (-va)

flight /flait/ n vuelo, m; (of bird of prey) colada, f; (flock of birds) bandada, f; (migration) migración, f; (of time) transcurso, m; (of imagination, etc.) arranque, m; (volley) lluvia, f; (of airplanes) escuadrilla (de aviones), f; (of stairs) tramo, tiro, m; (staircase) escalera, f; (of locks on canal, etc.) ramal, m; (escape) huida, fuga, f. **long-distance f.,** Aer. vuelo de distancia, m. **non-stop f.,** Aer. vuelo sin parar, m. **reconnaissance f.,** Aer. vuelo de reconocimiento, vuelo de patrulla, m. **test f.,** Aer. vuelo de pruebas, m. **to put to f.,** ahuyentar, poner en fuga. **to take f.,** alzar el vuelo. **f.-lieutenant,** teniente aviador, m. **f.-sergeant,** sargento aviador, m

flight attendant sobrecarbo, Lat. Am. aeromozo (-za), cabinero (-ra) mf

flightiness /'flaitinis/ n frivolidad, veleidad, ligereza, f

flighty /'flaiti/ a frívolo, inconstante, veleidoso

flimsiness /'flimzinis/ n falta de solidez, endeblez, f; fragilidad, f; (of arguments) futilidad, f

flimsy /'flimzi/ a endeble; frágil; fútil, insubstancial

flinch /flintʃ/ vi echarse atrás, retirarse (ante); vacilar, titubear. **without flinching,** sin vacilar; sin quejarse

fling /fliŋ/ vt arrojar, echar, tirar; lanzar; (scatter) derramar; (oneself) echarse; (oneself upon) echarse encima; Fig. confiar en. vi lanzarse; marcharse precipitadamente; saltar. n tiro, m; (of dice, etc.) echada, f; (gibe) sarcasmo, m, burla, chufleta, f; (of horse) respingo, brinco, m; baile escocés, m. **in full f.,** en plena operación; en progreso. **to have a f.,** darse un verde amorío, correrla. **to f. away,** vt desechar; (waste) desperdiciar, malgastar, perder. vi marcharse enfadado; marcharse rápidamente. **to f. back,** (a ball) devolver; (the head) echar atrás. **to f. down,** tirar al suelo; arrojar; derribar. **to f. off,** vt rechazar; apartar; (a garment, etc.) quitar. vi marcharse sin más ni más. **to f. oneself down,** tumbarse, echarse; despeñarse (por). **to f. oneself headlong,** despeñarse. **to f. open,** abrir violentamente, abrir de repente. **to f. out,** vt echar a la fuerza; (a hand) alargar, extender. vi salir apresuradamente. **to f. over,** (upset) volcar; arrojar por; abandonar. **to f. up,** lanzar al aire; levantar, erguir; renunciar (a), abandonar; dejar

flint /flint/ n pedernal, m; (for producing fire) piedra de encendedor, f

flinty /'flinti/ a pedernalino; Fig. endurecido

flippancy /'flipənsi/ n levedad, ligereza, f; frivolidad, f; impertinencia, f

flippant /'flipənt/ a poco serio, ligero; frívolo; impertinente

flipper /'flipər/ n aleta, f

flirt /flɜrt/ n (man) coquetón, castigador, m; (woman) coqueta, castigadora, f. vi (shake) sacudir; (move) agitar; (wave) menear. vi flirtear, coquetear; (toy with) jugar con; divertirse con

flirtation /flɜr'teiʃən/ n flirteo, amorío, m

flirtatious /flɜr'teiʃəs/ a (of men) galanteador, castigador; (of women) coqueta

flit /flit/ vi revolotear, mariposear; (move silently) deslizarse, pasar silenciosamente; (depart) irse, marcharse; mudarse por los aires. **to f. about,** ir y venir silenciosamente. **to f. past,** pasar como una sombra

float /flout/ n masa flotante, f; (raft) balsa, f; Mech. flotador, m; (of fishing rod or reel) corcho, m; (of fish) vejiga natatoria, f; (for swimming) nadadera, calabaza, f; (for tableaux) carroza, f; pl **floats,** Theat. candilejas, f pl. vi flotar; (flags, hair, etc.) ondear; (wander) vagar; Naut. boyar. vt poner a flote; hacer flotar; (a grounded ship) desencallar; (Com. a company) fundar; (a loan, etc.) emitir, poner en circulación; (launch a ship) botar; (flood) inundar

floating /'floutiŋ/ n flotación, f, flote, m; Com. fundación (de una compañía), f; (of a loan) emisión, f; (of a ship) botadura, f. a flotante; boyante; Com. en circulación, flotante; fluctuante, variable. **f. capital,** capital fluctuante, m. **f. debt,** deuda flotante, f. **f. dock,** dique flotante, m. **f. light,** buque faro, m. **f. population,** población flotante, f. **f. rib,** costilla flotante, f

flock /flɒk/ n rebaño, m, manada, f; (of birds) bandada, f; Fig. grey, f; (crowd) multitud, muchedumbre, f; (parishioners) congregación, f; (of wool or cotton) vedija (de lana or de algodón), f; pl **flocks,** (for stuffing) borra, f. vi concurrirse, reunirse, congregarse; ir en tropel, acudir; (birds) volar en bandada. **f.-bed,** colchón de borra, m

floe /flou/ n banco de hielo, m

flog /flɒg/ vt azotar; castigar

flogging /'flɒgiŋ/ n azotamiento, vapuleo, m

flood /flʌd/ n inundación, f; (Bible) diluvio, m; (of the tide) flujo, m; Fig. torrente, m; (abundance) copia, abundancia, f; (fit) paroxismo, m. vt inundar; sumergir; (of tears) mojar. vi desbordar. **f. lighting,** iluminación intensiva, f

floodgate /'flʌd,geit/ n compuerta (de esclusa), f

flooding /'flʌdɪŋ/ n inundación, f; desbordamiento, m; Med. hemorragia uterina, f

floodtide /'flʌd,taid/ n marea creciente, f

floor /flɔr/ n suelo, piso, m; (wooden) entarimado, m; (story) piso, m; (of a cart) cama, f; Agr. era, f. vt entablar; echar al suelo, derribar; Fig. desconcertar, confundir. **on the f.,** en el suelo. **on the ground f.,** en el piso bajo. **to take the f.,** Fig. tener la palabra. **f. mop** Lat. Am. lampazo m. **f.-polisher,** lustrador de piso, m

flooring /'flɔrɪŋ/ n tablado, m, tablazón, f; piso, m

flop /flɒp/ n golpe, m; ruido sordo, m; (splash) chapoteo, m; Inf. fiasco, m. vi dejarse caer

flora /'flɔrə/ n flora, f

floral /'flɔrəl/ a floral. **f. games,** juegos florales, m pl

Florence /'flɔrəns/ Florencia, f

Florentine /'flɔrən,tin/ a and n florentino (-na)

florescence /flɔ'rɛsəns/ n florescencia, f

florid /'flɒrɪd/ a florido; demasiado ornado, cursi, llamativo; (of complexion) rubicundo

floridness /'flɒrɪdnɪs/ n floridez, f, estilo florido, m; demasiada ornamentación, vulgaridad, f, mal gusto, m; (of complexion) rubicundez, f

florin /'flɔrɪn/ n florín, m

florist /'flɔrɪst/ n florista, mf

floss /flɒs/ n seda floja, filoseda, f; (of maize) penacho, m; (of a cocoon) cadarzo, m. **f. silk,** seda floja, f

flotilla /flou'tɪlə/ n flotilla, f

flotsam /'flɒtsəm/ n pecio, m

flounce /flauns/ n volante, m, vi saltar de impaciencia. **to f. out,** salir airadamente

flounder /'flaundər/ n (nearest equivalent) Ichth. platija, f; tumbo, m. vi tropezar; revolcarse; andar dificultosamente; (wander) errar, vagar

flour /flauʳr/ n harina, f, vt enharinar. **f.-bin,** tina, f, harinero, m. **f. merchant,** harinero, m

flourish /'flɔrɪʃ/ n movimiento, m; gesto, saludo, m; (of a pen) plumada, f; (on the guitar, in fencing) floreo, m; preludio, m; (fanfare) tocata (de trompetas), f; (of a signature) rúbrica, f; (in rhetoric) floreo, m. vi (of plants) vegetar; (prosper) prosperar, medrar; florecer; (of the guitar, in fencing) florear; Mus. preludiar; (with a pen) hacer plumadas (or rasgos de pluma); (of a signature) firmar con rúbrica; (sound a fanfare) hacer una tocata (de trompetas). vt agitar en el aire, blandir

flourishing /'flɔrɪʃɪŋ/ a (of plants) lozano; floreciente; (prosperous) próspero; (happy) feliz

flourmill /'flauʳr,mɪl/ n molino de harina, m, fábrica de harina, f, molina harinero, m

floury /'flauʳri, 'flauəri/ a harinoso

flout /flaut/ vt burlarse de; despreciar, no hacer caso de

flow /flou/ n flujo, m; corriente, f; chorro, m; (of water) caudal, m; (output) producción total, cantidad, f; (of the tide) flujo (de la marea), m; (of words) facilidad, f. vi fluir, manar; correr; (of the tide) crecer (la marea); (pass) pasar, correr; (result) resultar (de), provenir (de); (of hair, drapery) caer, ondular; (abound) abundar (en). **to f. away,** escaparse, salir. **to f. back,** refluir. **to f. down,** descender, fluir hacia abajo; (of tears) correr por. **to f. from,** dimanar de; manar de; provenir de. **to f. in,** llegar en abundancia. **to f. into,** (rivers) desaguar en, desembocar en. **to f. over,** derramarse por. **to f. through,** fluir por; atravesar; (water) regar. **to f. together,** (rivers) confluir

flower /'flauər/ n flor, f; (best) flor y nata, crema, f. vi florecer. **in f.,** en flor. **No flowers by request,** (for a funeral) No flores por deseo del finado. **f.-bud,** capullo, m. **f.-garden,** jardín, m. **f. girl,** florista, vendedora de flores, f. **f. market,** mercado de flores, m. **f.-piece,** florero, m. **f. pot,** tiesto, m, maceta, f, Lat. Am. macetero m. **f. show,** exposición de flores, f. **f. vase,** florero, m

flowerbed /'flauər,bɛd/ n cuadro, macizo, m

flower car coche portacoronas, m

flowered /'flauərd/ a (in compounds) con flores; con dibujos de flores

floweriness /'flauərɪnɪs/ n abundancia de flores, f; (of style) floridez, f, estilo florido, m

flowering /'flauərɪŋ/ n florecimiento, m. a floreciente; con flores; (of shrubs) de adorno. **f. season,** época de la floración, f

flowery /'flauəri/ a florido

flowing /'flouɪŋ/ n flujo, m; derrame, f. a fluente, corriente; (of tide) creciente; (waving) ondeante; suelto; (of style) flúido

flow of capital corriente de capital, f

fluctuate /'flʌktʃu,eit/ vi fluctuar, vacilar; variar

fluctuating /'flʌktʃu,eitɪŋ/ a fluctuante, vacilante; variable; (hesitating) irresoluto, dudoso

fluctuation /,flʌktʃu'eiʃən/ n fluctuación, f; cambio, m, variación, f; (hesitancy) indecisión, vacilación, f

flue /flu/ n (of a chimney) cañón, m; (of a boiler) tubo, m

fluency /'fluənsi/ n fluidez, f

fluent /'fluənt/ a flúido; fácil

fluently /'fluəntli/ adv corrientemente, con facilidad, de corrido

fluff /flʌf/ n borra, pelusa, f, tamo, m

fluffy /'flʌfi/ a velloso; (feathered) plumoso; (woolly) lanudo; (of hair) encrespado

fluid /'fluɪd/ n flúido, líquido, m, a flúido

fluidity /flu'ɪditi/ n fluidez, f

fluke /fluk/ n (in billiards) chiripa, f; Naut. uña, f; Inf. carambola, chiripa, chambonada, f. **by a f.,** de carambola, por suerte. **f.-worm,** duela del hígado, f

flunkey /'flʌŋki/ n lacayo, m; Fig. adulador, m

fluorescence /flʊ'rɛsəns/ n fluorescencia, f

fluorescent /flʊ'rɛsənt/ a fluorescente

fluorine /'flʊrin/ n Chem. flúor, m

fluorite /'flʊrait/ n fluorita, f

flurry /'flʌri/ n (of wind) ráfaga, f; (squall) chubasco, m; agitación, f; conmoción, f. vt agitar

flush /flʌʃ/ n rubor, m; (in the sky) arrebol, rojo, color de rosa, m; emoción, f, acceso, m; sensación, f; (at cards) flux, m; vigor, m; (flowering) floración, f; abundancia, f; (of youth, etc.) frescura, f. a (level) igual, parejo; abundante; (generous) pródigo, liberal; (rich) adinerado. vi ruborizarse, enrojecerse, ponerse colorado; (flood) inundarse, llenarse (de agua, etc.); (of sky) arrebolarse. vt inundar, limpiar con un chorro de agua, etc., lavar; (of blood) circular por; (redden) enrojecer; (make blush) hacer ruborizarse; (exhilarate) excitar, animar, (inflame) inflamar, encender; (make level) igualar, nivelar. **f. with,** a ras de

flushing /'flʌʃɪŋ/ n rojez, f; (cleansing) limpieza, lavadura, f; (flooding) inundación, f

fluster /'flʌstər/ n agitación, confusión, f, aturdimiento, m. vt agitar, poner nervioso (a), aturdir; (oneself) preocuparse. vi agitarse; estar nervioso, estar perplejo; (with drink) estar entre dos velas

flute /flut/ n flauta, f; Archit. estría, f; (organ-stop) flautado, m. vi tocar la flauta; flautear; tener la voz flauteada. vt tocar (una pieza) en la flauta; (groove) encanutar, acanalar, estriar. **f. player,** flautista, mf

fluted /'flutɪd/ a (grooved) acanalado

fluting /'flutɪŋ/ n Mus. sonido de la flauta, m; (of birds) trinado, m; Archit. estría, f; Sew. rizado, m

flutter /'flʌtər/ n (of wings) aleteo, m; (of leaves, etc.) murmurio, m; (of eyelashes) pestañeo, m; (of flags, etc.) ondulación, f; (excitement) agitación, f; (stir) sensación, f; (gamble) jugada, f. vi (of birds) aletear; revolotear; (of butterflies) mariposear; (of flags) ondear; palpitar; (of persons) estar agitado. vt agitar; (the eyelashes) pestañear; (agitate) agitar, alarmar, azorar

fluttering /'flʌtərɪŋ/ n mariposeo, m; revoloteo, m; (of birds) aleteo, m; (of leaves, etc.) murmurio, m; (of flags, etc.) ondeo, m, ondulación, f; (of eyelashes) pestañeo, m

fluvial /'fluviəl/ a fluvial

flux /flʌks/ n flujo, m

fly /flai/ n (insect) mosca, f; (on a fishhook) mosca artificial, f; (carriage) calesín, m; (of trousers) bragueta, *f*; *Theat.* bambalina, *f*; (of a tent) toldo, *m*; (flight) vuelo, *m*; (of a flag) vuelo, *m*. **fly-blown,** manchado por las moscas. **fly-by-night,** trasnochador (-ra). **fly-catcher,** *Ornith.* papamoscas, *m*; matamoscas, *m*. **fly-fishing,** pesca con moscas artificiales, *f*. **fly-leaf,** guarda (de un libro), *f*. **fly-paper,** papel matamoscas, *m*. **fly-swatter,** matamoscas, *m*. **fly-wheel,** *Mech.* volante, *m*

fly /flai/ *vi* volar; (flutter) ondear; (jump) saltar; (rush) lanzarse, precipitarse; (pass away) pasar volando, volar; (run off) marcharse a todo correr; (escape) huir, escapar; (seek refuge) refugiarse; (to the head, of intoxicants) subirse; (vanish) desaparecer. *vt* hacer volar; hacer ondear, enarbolar; (an airplane) pilotar, dirigir; (flee from) huir de; evitar. **to let fly (at),** descargar, tirar; *Fig.* saltar la sinhueso. **to fly about,** volar en torno de; revolotear. **to fly at,** lanzarse sobre; acometer, asaltar. **to fly away,** emprender el vuelo. **to fly back,** volar hacia el punto de partida; (of doors, etc.) abrir, o cerrar, de repente. **to fly down,** volar abajo. **to fly in,** volar dentro de; volar adentro; (of airplanes) llegar (el avión). **to fly into a rage,** montarse en cólera. **to fly low,** rastrear; *Aer.* volar a poca altura. **to fly off,** emprender el vuelo; (hasten) marcharse volando; (of buttons, etc.) saltar (de), separarse (de). **to fly open,** abrirse de repente. **to fly over,** volar por, volar por encima de. **to fly to pieces,** hacerse pedazos. **to fly upwards,** volar hacia arriba; subir

flying /'flaiiŋ/ *n* vuelo, *m. a* volante, volador; que vuela; de volar; volátil; (hasty) rápido; (flowing) ondeante, ondulante. **to shoot f.,** tirar al vuelo. **with f. colors,** con banderas desplegadas, triunfante. **f.-boat,** hidroavión, *m*. **f.-buttress,** botarel, arbotante, *m*. **f.-column,** *Mil.* cuerpo volante, *m*. **f.-fish,** (pez) volador, *m*. **f.-fortress,** *Aer.* fortaleza volante, *f*. **f.-officer,** oficial de aviación, *m*. **f.-sickness,** mal de altura, *m*. **f.-squad,** escuadra ligera, *f*. **f.-test,** *Aer.* examen de pilotaje, *m*

foal /foul/ *n* potro (-ra). *vi* and *vt* parir una yegua

foam /foum/ *n* espuma, *f*. *vi* espumar; (of horses, etc.) echar espumarajos. **to f. and froth,** (of the sea) hervir. **f. at the mouth,** echar espuma por la boca.

foam rubber *n* caucho esponjoso, *m*, espuma de caucho, *f*, espuma sintética, *f*

foamy /'foumi/ *a* espumoso

fob /fɒb/ *n* bolsillo del reloj, *m*; faltriquera pequeña, *f*. *vt* (off) engañar con

focal /'foukəl/ *a* focal

focus /'foukəs/ *n* foco, *m*; centro, *m*. *vt* enfocar; concentrar. *vi* convergir. **in f.,** en foco

fodder /'fɒdər/ *n* *Agr.* pienso, forraje, *m*. *vt* dar forraje (a)

foe /fou/ *n* enemigo, *m*

fog /fɒg/ *n* neblina, niebla, *f*; *Fig.* confusión, *f*; *Fig.* perplejidad, *f*, *vt* obscurecer; *Photo.* velar; *Fig.* ofuscar. *vi* hacerse nebuloso; *Photo.* velarse. **fog-signal,** señal de niebla, *f*

fogbound /'fɒg,baund/ *a* rodeado de niebla; detenido por la niebla

fogey /'fougi/ *n* obscurantista, *m*. **He is an old f.,** Es un señor chapado a la antigua

fogginess /'fɒginis/ *n* oscuridad, neblina, *f*

foggy /'fɒgi/ *a* nebuloso; *Photo.* velado. **It is f.,** Hay niebla

foghorn /'fɒg,hɔrn/ *n* sirena, *f*; bocina, *f*

foible /'fɔibəl/ *n* flaco, *m*, debilidad, *f*

foil /fɔil/ *n* (sword) florete, *m*; (coat) hoja, *f*; (of a mirror) azogado, *m*. *vt* frustrar. **f. a plot,** desbaratar un complot

foiling /'fɔiliŋ/ *n* frustración, *f*

foist /fɔist/ *vt* imponer; insertar, incluir; engañar (con)

fold /fould/ *n* doblez, *f*, pliegue, *m*; arruga, *f*; *Sew.* cogido, *m*; (for sheep) redil, aprisco, *m*; *Fig.* iglesia, congregación de los fieles, *f*; (in compounds) vez, *f*. *vt* doblar, plegar, doblegar; (the arms) cruzar (los brazos); (embrace) abrazar; (wrap) envolver; (clasp) entrelazar; (sheep) meter en redil, encerrar. *vi* doblarse, plegarse; cerrarse

folder /'fouldər/ *n* doblador (-ra); plegadera, *f*

folding /'fouldiŋ/ *n* plegadura, *f*, doblamiento, *m*; (of sheep) encerramiento, *m*, *a* plegadizo. **f.-door,** puerta plegadiza, *f*. **f.-machine,** plegador, *m*. **f.-seat,** *Auto.* traspuntín, *m*. **f.-table,** mesa de tijeras, *f*; mesa plegadiza, *f*

foliage /'fouliidʒ/ *n* follaje, *m*, frondas, *f pl*. **thick f.,** frondosidad, *f*

folio /'fouli,ou/ *n* folio, *m*; (a volume) infolio, *m. a* de infolio. *vt* foliar

folk /fouk/ *n* (nation) pueblo, *m*, nación, *f*; gente, *f*; *pl* **folks,** *Inf.* familia, *f*; parientes, *m pl*. **f.-dance,** danza popular, *f*

folklore /'fouk,lɔr/ *n* folclore, *m*, tradiciones folclóricas, *f pl*

folklorist /'fouk,lɔrist/ *n* folclorista, *mf*

folksong /'fouk,sɔŋ/ *n* canción popular, *f*; romance, *m*; copla, *f*

folktale /'fouk,teil/ *n* conseja, *f*, cuento popular, *m*

follicle /'fɒlikəl/ *n* (*Anat.*, *Bot.*) folículo, *m*

follow /'fɒlou/ *vt* seguir; (pursue) perseguir; (hunt) cazar; (adopt) adoptar; (understand) comprender; (notice) observar. *vi* ir, o venir, detrás; (of time) venir después; (gen. impers.) seguir, resultar; seguirse. as follows, como sigue. **I shall f. your advice,** Seguiré tus consejos. **to f. on the heels of,** *Fig.* pisar los talones (a). **to f. suit,** (at cards) asistir, jugar al mismo palo; *Fig.* imitar. **to f. up,** proseguir; continuar; (pursue) perseguir; (enhance) reforzar. **f.-me-lads,** *Inf.* siguemepollo, *m*

follower /'fɒlouər/ *n* seguidor (-ra); adherente, secuaz, *mf*; (imitator) imitador (-ra); (lover) novio, *m*; *pl* **followers,** acompañamiento, séquito, *m*

following /'fɒlouiŋ/ *n* séquito, acompañamiento, *m*, comitiva, *f*; partidarios, *m pl*, adherentes, *mf pl*. *a* siguiente; próximo. **f. wind,** viento en popa, *m*

folly /'fɒli/ *n* locura, extravagancia, absurdidad, tontería, *f*, disparate, *m*

foment /fou'mɛnt/ *vt* (poultice) fomentar; provocar, incitar, instigar; (assist) fomentar, proteger, promover

fomentation /,foumɛn'teiʃən/ *n* *Med.* fomentación, *f*; provocación, instigación, *f*; fomento, *m*, protección, *f*

fomenter /'foumɛntər/ *n* fomentador (-ra), instigador (-ra)

fond /fɒnd/ *a* (doting) demasiado indulgente; (loving) cariñoso, tierno, afectuoso; (addicted to) aficionado a, adicto a, amigo de. **to be f. of,** (things) tener afición a, estar aficionado de; (people) tener cariño (a). **to grow f. of,** (things) aficionarse a; (people) tomar cariño (a)

fondle /'fɒndl/ *vt* mimar, acariciar; jugar (con.)

fondly /'fɒndli/ *adv* cariñosamente, tiernamente

fondness /'fɒndnis/ *n* cariño, afecto, *m*; (for things) afición, inclinación, *f*; gusto, *m*

font /fɒnt/ *n* pila bautismal, *f*; *Poet.* fuente, *f*; *Print.* fundición, *f*

food /fud/ *n* alimento, *m*; comida, *f*, el comer, *m* (of animals) pasto, *m*; *Fig.* pábulo, *m*; materia, *f*. **She gave him f.** Le dio de comer. **You have given me f. for thought,** Me has dado en qué pensar. **f.-card,** cartilla de racionamiento, *f*. **food, clothing, and shelter** comida, abrigo y vivienda, *f*. **F. Ministry,** Ministerio de Alimentación, *m*. **f. value,** valor nutritivo, *m*.

food poisoning, intoxicación alimenticia, *f*

foodstuffs /'fud,stʌfs/ *n pl* comestibles, víveres, *m pl*

fool /ful/ *n* tonto (-ta), mentecato (-ta), majadero (ra) necio (-ia); (jester) bufón, *m*; (butt of jest) hazmerreír, *m*; víctima, *f*; *Cul.* compota de frutas con crema, *f*, *vi* tontear, hacer tonterías. *vt* poner en ridículo (a); (deceive) engañar, embaucar; (with) jugar con. **to make a f. of oneself,** ponerse en ridículo. **to f. about,** *vi* perder el tiempo, vagabundear. **to f. away,** malgastar, malbaratar. **fool's bauble,** cetro de bufón, *m*. **fool's cap,** gorro de bufón, *m*

foolhardiness /'ful,hardinis/ *n* temeridad, *f*

foolhardy /'ful,hardi/ *a* temerario, atrevido

fooling /'fuliŋ/ *n* payasada, bufonada, *f*; (deceiving) engaño, *m*, burla, *f*

foolish /'fuliʃ/ *a* imprudente; estúpido, tonto; ridículo, absurdo; imbécil

foolishly /'fuliʃli/ *adv* imprudentemente; tontamente; imbécilmente

foolishness /'fulɪʃnɪs/ n imprudencia, f; estupidez, tontería, f, disparate, m; ridiculez, f; imbecilidad, f
foolproof /'ful,pruf/ a (of utensils, etc.) con garantía absoluta
fool's gold /fulz/ n pirita amarilla, f, sulfuro de hierro m
foot /fʊt/ n pie, m; (of animals, furniture) pata, f; (of bed, sofa, grave, ladder, page, etc.) pie, m; (hoof) pezuña, f; (metric unit and measure) pie, m; Mil. infantería, f; (base) base, f; (step) paso, m. a Mil. de a pie; a pie. vi ir a pie; venir a pie; bailar. vt hollar; (account) pagar (una cuenta); (stockings) poner pie (a). **on f.**, a pie; (of soldiers) de a pie; (in progress) en marcha. **to go on f.**, ir a pie, andar. **to put one's best f. forward**, apretar el paso; Fig. hacer de su mejor. **to put one's f. down**, poner pies en pared, pararle fulano el alto. **to put one's f. in it**, meter la pata. **to rise to one's feet**, ponerse de pie. **to set f. on**, pisar, hollar. **to set on f.**, poner en pie; Fig. poner en marcha. **to trample under f.**, pisotear. **f.-and-mouth disease**, glosopeda, f. **f.-brake**, freno de pedal, m. **f.-pump**, fuelle de pie, m. **f.-rule**, (nearest equivalent) doble decímetro, m. **f.-soldier**, soldado de a pie, infante, m
football /'fʊt,bɔl/ n (game) fútbol americano, m; (ball) pelota de fútbol, f. **f. field**, campo de fútbol, m. **f. match**, partida de fútbol, f. **f. pools**, apuestas de fútbol, f pl; (in Spain) apuestas benéficas de fútbol, f pl
football player n fútbolista, m
footbath /'fʊt,bæθ/ n baño de pies, m
footbridge /'fʊt,brɪdʒ/ n puente para peatones, m
footed /'fʊtɪd/ a con pies; de pies...; de patas...
footfall /'fʊt,fɔl/ n pisada, f, paso, m
foothills /'fʊt,hɪlz/ n pl faldas de la montaña, f pl
foothold /'fʊt,hould/ n hincapié, m; posición establecida, f
footing /'fʊtɪŋ/ n hincapié, m; posición firme, f; condiciones, f pl; relaciones, f pl. **on a peacetime f.**, en pie de paz. **to be on an equal f.**, estar en pie de igualdad, estar en iguales condiciones. **to miss one's f.**, resbalar
footlights /'fʊt,laits/ n pl canilejas, candilejas, f pl. **to get across the f.**, hacer contacto con el público
footman /'fʊtmən/ n lacayo, m
footnote /'fʊt,nout/ n llamada a pie de página, nota a pie de página, f, cita, f
footpath /'fʊt,pæθ/ n senda, vereda, f, sendero, m
footprint /'fʊt,prɪnt/ n huella, pisada, f, vestigio, m
footsore /'fʊt,sɔr/ a con los pies lastimados
footstep /'fʊt,stɛp/ n paso, m; (trace) pisada, huella, f. **to follow in the footsteps of**, Fig. seguir las pisadas de
footstool /'fʊt,stul/ n escabel, banquito, m
footwarmer /'fʊt,wɔrmər/ n calientapiés, m
footwear /'fʊt,wɛar/ n calzado, m
for /fɔr; unstressed fər/ prep (expressing exchange, price or penalty of, instead of, in support or favor of, on account of) por; (expressing destination, purpose, result) para; (during) durante, por; (for the sake of) para; (because of) a causa de; (in spite of) a pesar de; (as) como; (with) de; (in favor of) en favor de; (in election campaign) con (e.g., "Ecuadorians for Martínez!" ¡Ecuatorianos con Martínez!) (toward) hacia; (that) que, para que (with subjunc); a, (before) antes de; (searching for) en busca de; (bound for) con rumbo a; (regarding) en cuanto a; (until) hasta. What's for dinner? ¿Qué hay de comida? **center for...** centro de... (e.g., Center for Applied Linguistics, Centro de Lingüística Aplicada). **He is in business for himself**, Tiene negocios por su propia cuenta. **It is raining too hard for you to go there**, Llueve demasiado para que vayas allí. **It is not for him to decide**, No le toca a él decidirlo. **Were it not for...**, Si no fuese por... **She has not been to see me for a week**, Hace una semana que no viene a verme. **It is impossible for them to go out**, Les es imposible salir. **but for all that**, pero con todo. **for ever**, por (or para) siempre. **for fear that**, por miedo de que. **for myself**, en cuanto a mí, personalmente. **for the present**, por ahora. **for what reason?** ¿para qué? ¿por cuál motivo? **for brevity's sake, for the sake of brevity**, por causa de la brevedad. **For such a young girl, she plays the piano well**, Para una niña tan joven toca bien el piano
for /fɔr; unstressed fər/ conjunc porque; visto que, pues, puesto que, en efecto, ya que
forage /'fɔrɪdʒ/ n forraje, m. vt and vi forrajear. **to f. for**, buscar. **f. cap**, gorra de cuartel, f
forager /'fɔrɪdʒər/ n forrajeador, m
foraging /'fɔrɪdʒɪŋ/ n forraje, m
forasmuch as /,fɔrəz'mʌtʃ ,æz/ conjunc puesto que, como que, ya que, por tanto que
foray /'fɔrei/ n correría, cabalgada, f; saqueo, m
forbear /'fɔr,bɛar/ vt and vi dejar (de), guardarse (de); abstenerse de; evitar; reprimirse (de); rehusarse (de); (cease) cesar (de); (be patient) ser paciente; ser tolerante
forbearance /fɔr'bɛarəns/ n abstención, f; tolerancia, transigencia, f; indulgencia, f; paciencia, f
forbearing /fɔr'bɛarɪŋ/ a tolerance, transigente; generoso, magnánimo; paciente
forbid /fər'bɪd/ vt prohibir, defender (de); impedir. **I f. you to do it**, Te prohibo hacerlo. **The game is forbidden**, El juego está prohibido. **They have forbidden me to...**, Me han defendido de... **Heaven f.!** ¡Dios no lo quiera!
forbidden /fər'bɪdn/ a prohibido; ilícito. **f. fruit**, fruto prohibido, m
forbidding /fər'bɪdɪŋ/ a repugnante, horrible; antipático, desagradable; (dismal) lúgubre; (threatening) amenazador. n prohibición, f
force /fɔrs/ n fuerza, f; violencia, f; vigor, m; (efficacy) eficacia, f; (validity) validez, f; (power) poder, m; (motive) motivo, m, razón, f; (weight) peso, m, importancia, f; (police) policía, f; pl forces, Mil. fuerzas, tropas, f pl. **by main f.**, por fuerza mayor. **in f.**, vigente, en vigor. **to be in f.**, estar vigente
force /fɔrs/ vt forzar; (compel) obligar, constreñir, precisar; (ravish) violar; Cul. rellenar; (impose) imponer; (plants) forzar; (the pace) apresurar; (cause) hacer; (a lock, etc.) forzar. **to f. oneself into**, entrar a la fuerza en; (a garment) ponerse con dificultad; imponerse a la fuerza. **to f. oneself to**, esforzarse a. **to f. the pace**, forzar el paso. **to f. away**, ahuyentar. **to f. back**, hacer retroceder; rechazar; (a sigh, etc.) ahogar. **to f. down**, hacer bajar, obligar a bajar; (make swallow) hacer tragar; (of airplanes) hacer tomar tierra. **to f. in**, introducir a la fuerza; obligar a entrar. **to f. into**, meter a la fuerza; obligar a entrar (en). **to f. on, upon**, imponer. **to f. open**, abrir a la fuerza; (a lock) romper, forzar. **to f. out**, hacer salir; empujar hacia fuera; (words) pronunciar con dificultad. **to f. up**, obligar a subir; hacer subir; hacer vomitar
forced /fɔrst/ a forzado; forzoso; afectado. **f. landing**, Aer. aterrizaje forzoso, m. **f. march**, Mil. marcha forzada, f
forceful /'fɔrsfəl/ a See **forcible**
forceps /'fɔrsəps/ n pl fórceps, m pl; pinzas, f pl. **arterial f.**, pinzas hemostáticas, f pl
forcible /'fɔrsəbəl/ a fuerte; a la fuerza; violento; enérgico, vigoroso; poderoso; Lit. vívido, gráfico, vehemente. **f. feeding**, alimentación forzosa, f
forcibleness /'fɔrsəbəlnɪs/ n fuerza, f; vigor, m, energía, f; vehemencia, f
forcibly /'fɔrsəbli/ adv a la fuerza
forcing /'fɔrsɪŋ/ n forzamiento, m; compulsión, f. **f. frame**, semillero, m, especie de invernadero, f
ford /fɔrd/ n esguazo, vado, m. vt esguazar, vadear
fordable /'fɔrdəbəl/ a esguazable, vadeable
fore /fɔr/ a delantero; Naut. de proa adv delante; Naut. de proa. **f.-and-aft**, Naut. de popa a proa.
forearm /fɔr'ɑrm/ n antebrazo, m. vt armar de antemano; preparar
forebear /'fɔr,bɛar/ n antecesor, m, ascendiente, mf
forebode /fɔr'boud/ vt presagiar, augurar, anunciar; presentir
foreboding /fɔr'boudɪŋ/ n presagio, augurio, m; presentimiento, m, corazonada, f
forecast /'fɔr,kæst/ n pronóstico, m; proyecto, plan, m, vt pronosticar; proyectar. **weather f.**, pronóstico del tiempo, m

forecastle /'fouksəl/ n Naut. castillo de proa, m
foreclose /fɔr'klouz/ vt excluir; impedir; vender por orden judicial; anticipar el resultado de; decidir de antemano
foreclosure /fɔr'klouʒər/ n venta por orden judicial, f; juicio hipotecario, m
foredoom /fɔr'dum/ vt predestinar
forefather /'fɔr,faðər/ n antepasado, antecesor, m
forefinger /'fɔr,fɪŋgər/ n índice, dedo índice, m
forefoot /'fɔr,fʊt/ n pata delantera, f
forefront /'fɔr,frʌnt/ n delantera, primera línea, f; frente, m; vanguardia, f. **in the f.,** en la vanguardia; en el frente
foregoing /fɔr'gouɪŋ/ a precedente, anterior
foregone /fɔr'gɔn/ a decidido de antemano; previsto
foreground /'fɔr,graund/ n primer plano, primer término, frente, m. **in the f.,** Art. en primer término
forehand /'fɔr,hænd/ a derecho. **f. stroke,** golpe derecho, m
forehead /'fɔrɪd/ n frente, f
foreign /'fɔrɪn/ a extranjero; extraño; exótico; exterior; (alien) ajeno. **f. affairs,** asuntos extranjeros, m pl. **f. body,** cuerpo extraño, m. **f. debt,** deuda exterior, f. **F. Legion,** tercio extranjero, m. **F. Office,** Ministerio de Relaciones Extranjeras, m. **f. parts,** extranjero, m. **f. policy,** política internacional, f. **F. Secretary,** Secretario de Asuntos Extranjeros, Secretario de Asuntos Exteriores, Ministro de Relaciones Extranjeras, m. **f. trade,** comercio con el extranjero, m
foreigner /'fɔrənər/ n extranjero (-ra), Argentina, Chile also cuico (-ca), Mexico also fuereño (-ña) mf
foreignness /'fɔrənnɪs/ n extranjerismo, m; (strangeness) extrañeza, f; lo exótico
foreknowledge /'fɔr,nɒlɪdʒ/ n presciencia, precognición, f
foreland /'fɔr,lænd/ n promontorio, cabo, m
forelock /'fɔr,lɒk/ n guedeja, vedeja, f; (of a horse) copete, tupé, m. **to take time by the f.,** asir la ocasión por la melena
foreman /'fɔrmən/ n (of jury) presidente (del jurado), m; (of a farm) mayoral, m; (in a works) capataz, m
foremost /'fɔr,moust/ a delantero; de primera fila; más importante. adv en primer lugar; en primera fila
forensic /fə'rɛnsɪk/ a forense, legal. **f. medicine,** medicina legal, f
foreordained /,fɔrɔr'deind/ a predestinado
forerunner /'fɔr,rʌnər/ n precursor (-ra), predecessor (-ra); (presage) anuncio, presagio, m
foresee /fɔr'si/ vt prever, anticipar
foreseeing /fɔr'siɪŋ/ a presciente, sagaz
foreseer /fɔr'siər/ n previsor (-ra)
foreshadow /fɔr'ʃædou/ vt anunciar, prefigurar; simbolizar; hacer sentir.
foresight /'fɔr,sait/ n presciencia, f; previsión, prudencia, f; (of gun) punto de mira, m; (optical) croquis de nivel, m
forest /'fɔrɪst/ n bosque, m, selva, f. vt arbolar
forestall /fɔr'stɔl/ vt anticipar, saltear; prevenir; Com. acaparar
forestalling /fɔr'stɔlɪŋ/ n anticipación, f
forestation /,fɔrə'steifən/ n repoblación forestal, f
forester /'fɔrəstər/ n silvicultor, guardamonte, ingeniero forestal, m; habitante de los bosques, m
forest fire incendio forestal, m
forestry /'fɔrəstri/ n silvicultura, f
foresworn /fɔr'swɔrn/ a perjuro
foretaste /n 'fɔr,teist/ v fɔr'teist/ n muestra, f; presagio, m. vt gustar con anticipación
foretell /fɔr'tɛl/ vt predecir, profetizar; anunciar, presagiar
foreteller /fɔr'tɛlər/ n profeta, m; presagio, m
foretelling /fɔr'tɛlɪŋ/ n profecía, predicción, f
forethought /'fɔr,θɔt/ n presciencia, previsión, f; prevención, f
forewarn /fɔr'wɔrn/ vt prevenir, advertir
forewarning /fɔr'wɔrnɪŋ/ n presagio, m
forewoman /'fɔr,wʊmən/ n encargada, f; primera oficiala, f
foreword /'fɔr,wɜrd/ n prefacio, m, introducción, f

forfeit /'fɔrfɪt/ n pérdida, f; (fine) multa, f; (in games) prenda, f; (of rights, goods, etc.) confiscación, f. a confiscado. vt perder; perder el derecho o el título de
forfeiture /'fɔrfɪtʃər/ n pérdida, f; confiscación, f; secuestro, m
forge /fɔrdʒ/ n fragua, f; (smithy) herrería, f. vt and vi fraguar, forjar; (fabricate) inventar, fabricar; falsificar; (advance) avanzar lentamente. **to f. ahead,** abrirse camino; avanzar
forged /fɔrdʒd/ a (of iron) forjado; (of checks, etc.) falso, falsificado
forger /'fɔrdʒər/ n falsificador (-ra), falsario (-ia); (creator) artífice, mf
forgery /'fɔrdʒəri/ n falsificación, f
forget /fər'gɛt/ vt olvidar; descuidar. vi olvidarse. **to f. about,** olvidarse de, desacordarse de. **to f. oneself,** olvidarse de sí mismo; propasarse; (in anger) perder los estribos. **I forgot my key,** Se me olvidó la llave
forgetful /fər'gɛtfəl/ a olvidadizo; descuidado, negligente
forgetfulness /fər'gɛtfəlnɪs/ n olvido, m; descuido, m; falta de memoria, f
forging /'fɔrdʒɪŋ/ n fraguado, m; falsificación, f
forgivable /fər'gɪvəbəl/ a perdonable, excusable
forgive /fər'gɪv/ vt perdonar, disculpar, condonar; (debts) remitir
forgiveness /fər'gɪvnɪs/ n perdón, m; condonación, f; (remission) remisión, f
forgiving /fər'gɪvɪŋ/ a misericordioso, clemente, dispuesto a perdonar
forgo /fɔr'gou/ vt renunciar, sacrificar, privarse de; abandonar, ceder
forgoing /fɔr'gouɪŋ/ n renunciación, f, sacrificio, m; cesión, f
"For Immediate Occupancy" «De Ocupación Inmediata»
fork /fɔrk/ n Agr. horca, horquilla, f; (table fork) tenedor, m; bifurcación, f; (of rivers) confluencia, f; (of branches) horcadura, f; (of legs) horcajadura, f; (for supporting trees, etc.) horca, f; Mus. diapasón normal, m. vt hacinar con horca. vi bifurcarse; ramificarse
forked /fɔrkt/ a bifurcado, hendido, ahorquillado. **f. lightning,** relámpago, m. **f. tail,** cola hendida, f
forlorn /fɔr'lɔrn/ a abandonado, desamparado, desesperado. **f. hope,** aventura desesperada, f
forlornness /fɔr'lɔrnnɪs/ n desamparo, m, miseria, f; desolación, f, desconsuelo, m
form /fɔrm/ n forma, f, figura, f; (shadowy) bulto, m; (formality) formalidad, f, ceremonia, f; Eccl. rito, m; método, m; regla, f; (in a school) clase, f; (lair) cama, f; (seat) banco, m; (system) sistema, m; (ghost) espectro, m; aparición, f; (to fill out) documento, m; hoja, f, Mexico esqueleto m; (state) condición, f; Lit. construcción, forma, f. **It is a matter of f.,** Es una pura formalidad. **in due f.,** en debida forma, en regla. **in the usual f.,** Com. al usado. **It is not good f.,** No es de buena educación
form /fɔrm/ vt formar; (a habit) contraer; (an idea) hacerse (una idea). vi formarse. **to f. fours,** Mil. formar a cuatro
formal /'fɔrməl/ a esencial; formal; ceremonioso, solemne; (of person) etiquetero, formalista. **f. call,** visita de cumplido, f
formaldehyde /fɔr'mældə,haid/ n formaldehído. m
formalism /'fɔrmə,lɪzəm/ n formalismo, m
formality /fɔr'mælɪti/ n formalidad, f; ceremonia, solemnidad, f
formally /'fɔrməli/ adv formalmente
format /'fɔrmæt/ n formato, m.
formation /fɔr'meifən/ n formación, f; disposición, f, arreglo, m; organización, f; (Mil., Geol.) formación, f
formative /'fɔrmətɪv/ a formativo
former /'fɔrmər/ a primero; antiguo; anterior; pasado. **in f. times,** antes, antiguamente. **the f.,** ése, aquél, etc.; ésa, aquélla, f; aquéllos, m pl; aquéllas, f pl
former /'fɔrmər/ n formador (-ra); creador (-ra), autor (-ra)
formerly /'fɔrmərli/ adv antiguamente, antes

formidable /'fɔrmɪdəbəl/ *a* formidable; terrible, espantoso

formless /'fɔrmlɪs/ *a* informe

formlessness /'fɔrmlɪsnɪs/ *n* falta de forma, *f*

formula /'fɔrmyələ/ *n* fórmula, *f*. **standard f.**, (*Math.*, *Chem.*) fórmula clásica, *f*

formulate /'fɔrmyə,leit/ *vt* formular

fornicate /'fɔrnɪ,keit/ *vi* fornicar

fornication /,fɔrnɪ'keiʃən/ *n* fornicación, *f*

fornicator /'fɔrnɪ,keitər/ *n* fornicador (-ra)

forsake /fɔr'seik/ *vt* dejar, desertar; abandonar, desamparar; separarse de; (of birds, the nest) aborrecer; (one's faith) renegar de

forsaker /fɔr'seikər/ *n* el, *m*, (la, *f*) que abandona; desertor, *m*; renegado (-da)

"For Sale" «Se Vende»

forsooth /fɔr'suθ/ *adv* ciertamente, claro está

forswear /fɔr'swɛər/ *vt* abjurar; renunciar a. **to f. oneself**, perjurarse

forswearing /fɔr'swɛərɪŋ/ *n* abjuración, *f*; renuncia, *f*; perjurio, *m*

fort /fɔrt/ *n* fortaleza, *f*, fuerte, *m*

forte /'fɔrtei/ *n* fuerte, *m*. *a Mus.* fuerte

forth /fɔrθ/ *adv* (on) adelante, hacia adelante; (out) fuera; (in time) en adelante, en lo consecutivo; (show) a la vista. **and so f.**, y así en lo sucesivo; etcétera

forthcoming /'fɔrθ'kʌmɪŋ/ *a* próximo; futuro; en preparación

forthwith /,fɔrθ'wɪθ/ *adv* en seguida, sin tardanza

fortieth /'fɔrtiɪθ/ *a* cuadragésimo; cuarenta. *n* cuarentavo, *m*

fortifiable /'fɔrtə,faiəbəl/ *a* fortificable

fortification /,fɔrtəfɪ'keiʃən/ *n* fortificación, *f*

fortify /'fɔrtə,fai/ *vt* fortificar; fortalecer; confirmar; *Fig.* proveer (de)

fortitude /'fɔrtɪ,tud/ *n* aguante, *m*, fortaleza, *f*, estoicismo, *m*

fortnight /'fɔrt,nait/ *n* quince días, *m pl*, dos semanas, *f pl*; quincena, *f*. **a f. ago**, hace quince días. **a f. tomorrow**, mañana en quince. **in a f.**, dentro de quince días; al cabo de quince días. **once a f.**, cada quince días

fortress /'fɔrtrɪs/ *n* fortaleza, plaza fuerte, *f*

fortuitous /fɔr'tuɪtəs/ *a* fortuito, accidental

fortuitously /fɔr'tuɪtəsli/ *adv* accidentalmente

fortuity /fɔr'tuɪti/ *n* casualidad, *f*; accidente, *m*

fortunate /'fɔrtʃənɪt/ *a* dichoso, feliz; afortunado; próspero. **to be f.**, (of persons) tener suerte

fortunately /'fɔrtʃənɪtli/ *adv* afortunadamente, por dicha, felizmente

fortune /'fɔrtʃən/ *n* suerte, fortuna, *f*, destino, *m*; (money) caudal, *m*, fortuna, *f*; bienes, *m pl*; buena ventura, *f*. **good f.**, buena fortuna, dicha, *f*. **ill f.**, mala suerte, *f*. **to cost a f.**, costar un sentido. **to make one's f.**, enriquecerse; *Inf.* hacer su pacotilla. **to tell fortunes**, echar las cartas. **f. hunter**, buscador de dotes, cazador de dotes, cazador de fortunas, aventurero, *m*. **f.-teller**, adivinadora, *f*; echadora de cartas, *f*. **f.-telling**, buenaventura, *f*

forty /'fɔrti/ *a* and *n* cuarenta, *m*. **He is turned f.**, Ha cumplido los cuarenta. **person of f.**, cuarentón (-ona). **She is f.**, Tiene cuarenta años. **She's over f.**, Ella pasó los cuarenta años

forum /'fɔrəm/ *n* foro, tribuna *f*, (e.g., *to serve as a forum for discussion*, servir de tribuna de discusión)

forward /'fɔrwərd/ *a* avanzado; adelantado; (of position) delantero; (ready) preparado; (eager) pronto, listo, impaciente; activo, emprendedor; (of persons, fruit, etc.) precoz; (pert) insolente, desenvuelto, atrevido. *adv* adelante; hacia adelante; (of time) en adelante; (farther on) más allá; hacia el frente; en primera línea. *vt* ayudar, promover; adelantar; (letters) hacer seguir; *Com.* expedir, remitir; (a parcel) despachar; (hasten) apresurar; (plants) hacer crecer. *n Sports.* delantero, *m*. **center-f.**, *Sports.* delantero centro, *m*. **from this time f.**, de hoy en adelante. **Please f.**, ¡Haga seguir! **putting f. of the clock**, el adelanto de la hora. **to carry f.**, *Com.* pasar a cuenta nueva. **to go f.**, adelantarse; estar en marcha,

estar en preparación. **f. line**, *Sports.* delantera, *f*. **F.!** ¡Adelante!

forwarder /'fɔrwərdər/ *n* promotor (-ra); *Com.* remitente, *m*

forwarding /'fɔrwərdɪŋ/ *n* fomento, *m*, promoción, *f*; *Com.* expedición, *f*, envío, *m*

forwardness /'fɔrwərdnɪs/ *n* progreso, adelantamiento, *m*; (haste) apresuramiento, *m*; (of persons, fruit, etc.) precocidad, *f*; (pertness) desenvoltura, insolencia, frescura, *f*, descaro, *m*; (eagerness) impaciencia, *f*

fossil /'fɒsəl/ *a* and *n* fósil, *m*

fossilization /,fɒsələ'zeiʃən/ *n* fosilización, *f*

fossilize /'fɒsə,laiz/ *vt* fosilizar; petrificar. *vi* fosilizarse

foster /'fɒstər/ *vt* provocar, promover, suscitar; (favor) favorecer, ser propicio a. **f.-brother**, hermano de leche, *m*. **f.-child**, hijo (-ja) de leche. **f.-father**, padre adoptivo, *m*. **f.-mother**, ama de leche, *f*. **f.-sister**, hermana de leche, *f*

foul /faul/ *a* sucio, asqueroso, puerco; (evil-smelling) hediondo, fétido; (of air) viciado; impuro; (language) ofensivo; (coarse) indecente, obsceno; (harmful) nocivo, dañino; (wicked) malvado; infame; vil; (unfair) injusto; *Sports.* sucio; (ugly) feo; (entangled) enredado; (with corrections) lleno de erratas; (choked) atascado; (of weather) borrascoso, tempestuoso; malo, desagradable; (repulsive) repugnante. *n Sports.* juego sucio, *Lat. Am.* faul *m*. *vt* ensuciar; *Naut.* chocar, abordar; (block) atascar; (the anchor) enredar; *Sports, Lat. Am.* faulear; (dishonor) deshonrar. *vi* atascarse; (anchor) enredarse; *Naut.* chocar. **to fall f. of**, *Naut.* abordar (un buque); *Fig.* habérselas con. **by fair means or f.**, a las buenas o a las malas. **f. breath**, aliento fétido, aliento corrompido, *m*. **f. brood**, peste de las abejas, *f*. **f. language**, palabras ofensivas, *f pl*; lenguaje obsceno, *m*. **f. play**, juego sucio, *m*. **f. weather**, mal tiempo, tiempo borrascoso, *m*

found /faund/ *vt* fundar; (metal, glass) fundir; (create, etc.) establecer

foundation /faun'deiʃən/ *n* fundación, *f*; establecimiento, *m*; creación, *f*; *Archit.* cimiento, embasamiento, *m*; (basis) base, *f*; (cause) causa, *f*, origen, principio, *m*; (endowment) dotación, *f*; *Sew.* refuerzo, *m*. **to lay the f.**, poner las fundaciones. **f. stone**, piedra angular, *f*; *Fig.* primera piedra, *f*. **to lay the f. stone**, poner la piedra angular

founder /'faundər/ *n* fundador (-ra); (of metals) fundidor, *m*. *vi* (a ship) hacer zozobrar, irse a pique; *Fig.* fracasar

foundering /'faundərɪŋ/ *n Naut.* zozobra, *f*

founding /'faundɪŋ/ *n* fundación, *f*; establecimiento, *m*; (of metals) fundición, *f*

foundling /'faundlɪŋ/ *n* hijo (-ja) de la cuna, expósito (-ta). **f. hospital** or **home**, casa de cuna, casa de expósitos, inclusa, *f*

foundry /'faundri/ *n* fundición, *f*

fountain /'fauntɪn/ *n* fuente, *f*; (spring) manantial, *m*; (jet) chorro, *m*; (artificial) fuente, *f*, surtidero, *m*; (source) origen, principio, *m*. **f.-head**, fuente, *f*. **Fountain of Youth**, Fuente de la juventud, Fuente de Juvencio, *f*. **f. pen**, pluma estilográfica, *f*

four /fɔr/ *a* and *n* cuatro, *m*. **It is f. o'clock**, Son las cuatro. **She is f.**, Tiene cuatro años. **on all fours**, a gatas. **f.-course**, (of meals) de cuatro platos. **f.-engined**, cuadrimotor. **f.-engined plane**, cuadrimotor, *m*. **f.-footed**, cuadrúpedo. **f.-horse**, de cuatro caballos. **f. hundred**, cuatrocientos. **f.-inhand**, tiro par, *m*. **f.-part**, (of a song) a cuatro voces. **f.-wheel brakes**, freno de las cuatro ruedas, *m*

fourfold /'fɔr,fould/ *a* cuádruple

fourscore /'fɔr'skɔr/ *a* and *n* ochenta, *m*

foursome /'fɔrsəm/ *n* partido de cuatro personas, *m*

fourteen /'fɔr'tin/ *a* and *n* catorce, *m*. **He is f.**, Tiene catorce años

fourteenth /'fɔr'tinθ/ *a* and *n* décimocuarto *m*.; (of the month) (el) catorce, *m*; (of monarchs) catorce. **April f.**, El 14 (catorce) de abril

fourth /fɔrθ/ *a* cuarto; (of the month) el cuatro; (of monarchs) cuarto. *n* (fourth part) cuarta parte, *f*;

Mus. cuarta, *f*. **f. dimension,** cuarta dimensión, *f*. **f. term,** *Polit.* cuarto mandato, *m*

fourthly /'fɔrθli/ *adv* en cuarto lugar

fowl /faul/ *n* gallo. *m*; gallina, *f*; (chicken) pollo, *m*; (bird) ave, *f*; (barndoor f.) ave de corral, *f*. *vi* cazar aves. **f.-house or run,** gallinero, *m*

fox /fɒks/ *n* zorro, *m*; (vixen) zorra, raposa, *Argentina* chilla *f*; *Fig.* zorro, taimado, *m*. *vi* disimular. *vt* (books) descolorar. **f.-brush,** cola de raposa, *f*. **f.-earth,** zorrera, *f*. **f.-hunting,** caza de zorras, *f*. **f. terrier,** fox-térrier, *m*

foxhound /'fɒks,haund/ *n* perro zorrero, *m*

foxiness /'fɒksinis/ *n* zorrería, astucia, *f*

foxtrot /'fɒks,trɒt/ *n* foxtrot, *m*

foxy /'fɒksi/ *a* de zorro; zorrero, astuto

foyer /'fɔiər/ *n* foyer, salón de descanso, *m*

fraction /'frækʃən/ *n* *Math.* fracción, *f*, número quebrado, *m*; pequeña parte, *f*; fragmento, *m*. **improper f.,** *Math.* fracción impropia, *f*. **proper f.,** *Math.* fracción propia, *f*

fractional /'frækʃənl/ *a* fraccionario

fractious /'frækʃəs/ *a* malhumorado, enojadizo

fractiousness /'frækʃəsnis/ *n* mal humor, *m*

fracture /'fræktʃər/ *n* *Surg.* fractura, *f*. *vt* fracturar. **compound f.,** fractura conminuta, *f*

fragile /'frædʒəl/ *a* frágil, quebradizo; (of persons) delicado

fragility /frə'dʒɪliti/ *n* fragilidad, *f*

fragment /'frægmənt/ *n* fragmento, *m*; trozo, pedazo, *m*. **to break into fragments,** hacer pedazos, hacer añicos

fragmentary /'frægmən,tɛri/ *a* fragmentario

fragrance /'freigrəns/ *n* fragancia, *f*, buen olor, perfume, aroma, *m*

fragrant /'freigrənt/ *a* fragante, oloroso. **to make f.,** perfumar

frail /freil/ *a* frágil, quebradizo; débil, endeble. *n* capacho, *m*, espuerta, *f*

frailty /'freilti/ *n* fragilidad, *f*; debilidad, *f*

frame /freim/ *n* constitución, *f*; sistema, *m*; organización, *f*; (of the body) figura, *f*, talle, *m*; (of window, picture) marco, *m*; (of machine, building) armadura, *f*; (of a bicycle) cuadro (de bicicleta), *m*; *Agr.* cajonera, *f*; (embroidery) bastidor (para bordar), *m*; (skeleton) esqueleto, *m*; *Lit.* composición, construcción, *f*; (of eyeglasses) armadura, *f*; (of mind) disposición (de ánimo), *f*; humor, *m*. *vt* formar; construir; arreglar; ajustar; (a picture) enmarcar; componer, hacer; (draw up) redactar; (think up) idear, inventar; (words) articular, pronunciar. **f. a constitution,** elaborar una constitución

framer /'freimər/ *n* fabricante de marcos, *m*; autor (-ra), creador (-ra), inventor (-ra)

framework /'freim,wɜrk/ *n* armadura, armazón, *f*, esqueleto, *m*; organización, *f*; (basis) base, *f*

franc /fræŋk/ *n* (coin) franco, *m*

France /fræns/ Francia, *f*

Franche-Comté /frɑ̃ʃ kɔ̃'tei/ Franco-Condado, *m*

franchise /'fræntʃaiz/ *n* (retail) franquicia, *f*, concesión, *f*; privilegio, *m*; (vote) derecho de sufragio, *m*; (citizenship) derecho político, *m*

Franciscan /fræn'sɪskən/ *a* and *n* franciscano (-na)

Franco- (in compounds) franco-... *a* (referring to General Franco) franquista

Francophile /'fræŋkə,fail/ *a* and *n* afrancesado (-da)

frank /fræŋk/ *a* franco, cándido, sincero; abierto. *vt* franquear

frankincense /'fræŋkɪn,sɛns/ *n* incienso, *m*

frankly /'fræŋkli/ *adv* francamente; sinceramente; cara a cara; sin rodeos, claramente; abiertamente. **to speak f.,** hablar claro, hablar sin rodeos

frankness /'fræŋknis/ *n* franqueza, *f*; sinceridad, *f*; candor, *m*

frantic /'fræntik/ *a* frenético, furioso, loco. **He drives me f.,** Me vuelve loco

fraternal /frə'tɜrnl/ *a* fraterno, fraternal

fraternity /frə'tɜrniti/ *n* fraternidad, hermandad, *f*

fraternization /,frætərnə'zeiʃən/ *n* fraternización, *f*

fraternize /'frætər,naiz/ *vi* fraternizar

fratricidal /,frætrɪ'saidl/ *a* fratricida

fratricide /'frætrɪ,said/ *n* (person) fratricida, *mf*; (action) fratricidio, *m*

fraud /frɔd/ *n* fraude, *m*; engaño, embuste, *Argentina* *also* forro *m*; (person) farsante, *m*, embustero (-ra)

fraudulence /'frɔdʒələns/ *n* fraudulencia, fraude, *f*

fraudulent /'frɔdʒələnt/ *a* fraudulento

fraught /frɔt/ *a* (with) cargado de; lleno de, preñado de

fray /frei/ *n* refriega, riña, *f*; combate, *m*, batalla, *f*; (rubbing) raedura, *f*. *vt* raer, tazar. *vi* tazarse, deshilarse

frayed /freid/ *a* raído

fraying /'freiiŋ/ *n* raedura, deshiladura, *f*

freak /frik/ *n* monstruo, *m*; fenómeno, *m*; (whim) capricho, *m*

freakish /'frikɪʃ/ *a* monstruoso; caprichoso; extravagante; raro, singular

freakishness /'frikɪʃnis/ *n* carácter raro, *m*; extravagancia, *f*; rareza, extrañeza, *f*

freckle /'frɛkəl/ *n* peca, *f*. *vi* tener pecas; salir pecas (a la cara, etc.)

freckled /'frɛkəld/ *a* pecoso, con pecas

free /fri/ *a* (in most senses) libre; independiente; emancipado; desembarazado; abierto; limpio (de); franco; (voluntary) voluntario; (self-governing) autónomo, independiente; accesible; (disengaged) desocupado; (vacant) vacío; (exempt) exento (de); (immune) immune (de); ajeno; gratuito; (loose) suelto; (generous) generoso, liberal; (vicious) disoluto, licencioso; (bold) atrevido; (impudent) insolente, demasiado familiar. *adv* gratis, gratuitamente. **There are two f. seats in the train,** Hay dos asientos libres en el tren. **to get f.,** libertarse. **to make f. with,** tomarse libertades con; usar como si fuera suyo. **to set f.,** poner en libertad. **f. agent,** libre albedrío, *m*. **f. and easy,** familiar, sin ceremonia. **f. gift,** *Com.* objeto de reclamo, *m*. **f.-hand drawing,** dibujo a pulso, *m*. **f. kick,** *Sports.* golpe franco, *m*. **f. love,** amor libre, *m*. **f. port,** puerto franco, *m*. **f. rein,** rienda suelta, *f*; *Mech.* holgura, *f*. **f. speech,** libertad de palabra, *f*. **f. thought,** libre pensamiento, *m*. **f. ticket,** *Theat.* billete de favor, *m*. **f. trade,** a librecambista. *n* librecambio, *m*. **f. trader,** librecambista, *mf*. **North American Free Trade Agreement (NAFTA),** Tratado libre de comercio (TLC), *m*. **f. verse,** verso libre, verso suelto, *m*. **f.-wheeling,** desenfrenado, libre. **f. will,** propia voluntad, *f*; (theology) libre albedrío, *m*

free /fri/ *vt* libertar, poner en libertad (a); librar (de); (slave) salvar; emancipar; exentar; (of obstacles, difficulties) desembarazar; **to f. from,** libertar de; librar de; (clean) limpiar de

freebooter /'fri,butər/ *n* pirata, filibustero, *m*

freeborn /'fri,bɔrn/ *a* nacido libre, libre por herencia

freedman /'fridmən/ *n* liberto, *m*

freedom /'fridəm/ *n* libertad, *f*; independencia, *f*; exención, *f*; inmunidad, *f*; soltura, facilidad, *f*, franqueza, *f*; (over-familiarity) insolencia, *f*; (boldness) audacia, intrepidez, *f*; (of customs) licencia, *f*. **to receive the f. of a city,** ser recibido como ciudadano de honor. **f. of speech,** libertad de palabra, *f*. **f. of the press,** libertad de la prensa, *f*. **f. of worship,** libertad de cultos, *f*

freehold /'fri,hould/ *n* feudo franco, *m*

freeing /'friiŋ/ *n* liberación, *f*; emancipación, *f*; salvación, *f*; (from obstruction) desembarazo, *m*; limpieza, *f*

freelance /'fri,læns/ *n* *Mil.* soldado libre, *m*; *Polit.* independiente, *m*; aventurero (-ra). **f. journalist,** periodista libre, *m*

freely /'frili/ *adv* libremente; francamente; generosamente; sin reserva

freeman /'frimən/ *n* hombre libre, *m*; (of a city) ciudadano de honor, *m*

freemason /'fri,meisən/ *n* francmasón, *m*. **freemason's lodge,** logia masónica, *f*

freemasonry /'fri,meisənri/ *n* francmasonería, masonería, *f*

freethinker /'fri'θiŋkər/ *n* librepensador (-ra)

freeze /friz/ *vt* helar; (meat, etc.) congelar; *Fig.* helar. *vi* helarse; congelarse; (impers, of the weather) helar. **to f. to death,** morir de frío

freezing /'frizɪŋ/ *n* hielo, *m*; congelación, *f*. *a* glacial;

congelante, frigorífico. **f. mixture,** mezcla frigorífica, *f.* **f. of assets,** bloqueo de los depósitos bancarios, *m.* **f.-point,** punto de congelación, *m.* **above f.-point,** sobre cero. **below f.-point,** bajo cero

freight /freit/ *n* flete, *m*; porte, *m. vt* fletar

freighter /'freitər/ *n* fletador, *m*; (ship) buque de carga, *m*

French /frɛntʃ/ *a* francés. *n* (language) francés, *m*; (people) los franceses, *m pl.* **in F. fashion,** a la francesa. **to take F. leave,** despedirse a la inglesa. **What is the F. for "hat"?** ¿Cómo se dice «sombrero» en francés? **F. spoken,** Se habla francés. **F. bean,** judía, *f.* **F. chalk,** jabón de sastre, *m.* **F. horn,** trompa, *f.* **F. lesson,** lección de francés, *f.* **F. marigold,** flor del estudiante, *f.* **F. polish,** barniz de muebles, *m.* **F. poodle,** perro (-rra) de aguas. **F. roll,** panecillo, *m.* **F. window,** puerta ventana, *f*

Frenchify /'frɛntʃə,fai/ *vt* afrancesar

Frenchman /'frɛntʃmən/ *n* francés, *m.* **a young F.,** un joven francés

Frenchwoman /'frɛntʃ,wʊmən/ *n* francesa, mujer francesa, *f.* **a young F.,** una joven francesa, una muchacha francesa, *f*

frenzied /'frɛnzid/ *a* frenético

frenzy /'frɛnzi/ *n* frenesí, delirio, paroxismo, *m*

frequency /'frikwənsi/ *n* frecuencia, *f.* **high f.,** alta frecuencia, *f.* **low f.,** baja frecuencia, *f*

frequent /'frikwənt; *v* fri'kwɛnt/ *a* frecuente; (usual) común, corriente. *vt* frecuentar

frequentation /,frikwən'teiʃən/ *n* frecuentación, *f*

frequenter /'frikwəntər/ *n* frecuentador (-ra)

frequently /'frikwəntli/ *adv* frecuentemente, con frecuencia, muchas veces; comúnmente

fresco /'frɛskou/ *n Art.* fresco, *m*, pintura al fresco, *f. vt* pintar al fresco

fresh /frɛʃ/ *a* fresco; nuevo; reciente; (newly arrived) recién llegado; (inexperienced) inexperto, bisoño; (of water, not salt) dulce; puro; (healthy) sano; (brisk) vigoroso, enérgico; (vivid) vivo, vívido; (bright) brillante; (cheeky) fresco, *Lat. Am.* impávido. *adv* neuvamente, recién (with past participle). **He came to us f. from school,** Vino a nosotros recién salido de su colegio. **We are going to get some f. air,** Vamos a tomar el fresco. **The milk is not f.,** La leche no está fresca. **f.-complexioned,** de buenos colores. **f. news,** noticias nuevas, *f pl.* **f. troops,** tropas nuevas, *f pl,* (reinforcements) tropas de refuerzo, *f pl.* **f. water,** agua fresca, *f;* (not salt) agua dulce, *f.* **f.-water shrimp** *Mexico* acocil *m.* **f. wind,** viento fresco, *m*

freshen /'frɛʃən/ *vt* refrescar; (remove salt) desalar. *vi* (wind) refrescar. **to f. up,** renovar; refrescar; (of dress, etc.) arreglar

freshly /'frɛʃli/ *adv* nuevamente; recientemente

freshness /'frɛʃnɪs/ *n* frescura, *f;* (newness) novedad, *f;* (vividness, brightness) intensidad, *f;* pureza, *f;* (beauty) lozanía, hermosura, *f;* (cheek) frescura, *f,* descaro, *m*

freshwater /'frɛʃ,wɔtər/ *n* agua dulce, *f.* **f. sailor,** marinero de agua dulce, *m*

fret /frɛt/ *n* agitación, *f;* ansiedad, preocupación, *f;* *Archit.* greca, *f;* (of stringed instrument) traste, *m. vt* roer; (of a horse) bocezar; (corrode) desgastar, corroer; (of the wind, etc.) rizar; (worry) tener preocupado (a); irritar, enojar; (lose) perder; (oneself) apurarse, consumirse; *Archit.* calar. *vi* torturarse, preocuparse, inquietarse; (complain) quejarse; (mourn) lamentarse, estar triste

fretful /'frɛtfəl/ *a* mal humorado, mohíno, quejoso, irritable

fretfully /'frɛtfəli/ *adv* irritablemente, con mal humor

fretwork /'frɛt,wɜrk/ *n* calado, *m*

Freudian /'frɔidiən/ *a* freudiano

friar /'fraiər/ *n* fraile, *m.* **Black F.,** dominicano, *m.* **Gray f.,** franciscano, *m.* **White f.,** carmelita, *m.* **f.-like,** frailesco

friction /'frikʃən/ *n* frote, frotamiento, roce, *m;* *Phys.* rozamiento, *m;* fricción, *f.* **to make f.,** friccionar, dar fricciones (a). **f. gearing,** engranaje de fricción, *m.* **f. glove,** guante de fricciones, *m*

Friday /'fraidei/ *n* viernes, *m.* **Good F.,** Viernes Santo, *m*

fried /fraid/ *a* frito. **f. egg,** huevo frito, *m*

friend /frɛnd/ *n* amigo (-ga); (acquaintance) conocido (-da); (Quaker) cuáquero (-ra); (follower) adherente, *m*; partidario (-ia); (ally) aliado (-da); *pl* **friends,** amistades, *f pl*; amigos, *m pl.* **a f. of yours,** un amigo tuyo, uno de tus amigos. **to make friends,** hacer amigos; (become friends) hacerse amigos; (after a quarrel) hacer las paces. **Friends!** (to sentinel) ¡Gente de paz!

friendless /'frɛndlɪs/ *a* sin amigos; desamparado

friendliness /'frɛndlinɪs/ *n* amabilidad, afabilidad, cordialidad, amigabilidad, *f*

friendly /'frɛndli/ *a* amistoso, amigable, amigo; afable, acogedor, simpático; propicio, favorable. **to be f. with,** ser amigo de. **f. society,** sociedad de socorros, *f*

friendship /'frɛndʃip/ *n* amistad, intimidad, *f*

frieze /friz/ *n* friso, *m;* (cloth) frisa, jerga, *f*

frigate /'frigit/ *n Nav.* fragata, *f*

fright /frait/ *n* terror, susto, *m;* (guy) espantajo, *m. vt* asustar. **to have a f.,** tener un susto. **to take f.,** asustarse

frighten /'fraitn/ *vt* espantar, dar un susto (a), alarmar, asustar; horrorizar; (overawe) acobardar. **to be frightened out of one's wits,** estar muerto de miedo. **to f. away,** ahuyentar, espantar

frightened /'fraitnd/ *a* miedoso, tímido, medroso, nervioso

frightening /'fraitnɪŋ/ *a* que da miedo; alarmante, amedrentador; horrible

frightful /'fraitfəl/ *a* horrible, espantoso, horroroso; *Inf.* tremendo, enorme

frightfully /'fraitfəli/ *adv* horrorosamente; *Inf.* enormemente

frigid /'fridʒid/ *a* frío; helado; *Med.* impotente

frigidity /fri'dʒiditi/ *n* frialdad, frigidez, *f; Med.* impotencia, *f*

frigidly /'fridʒidli/ *adv* fríamente

frill /fril/ *n Sew.* volante, *m;* (jabot) chorrera, *f;* (round a bird's neck) collarín de plumas, *m;* (of paper) frunce, *m. vt* alechugar; fruncir

fringe /frindʒ/ *n* fleco, *m,* franja, *f, Lat. Am.* cerquillo *f;* (of hair) flequillo, *m;* (edge) borde, *m,* margen, *mf. vt* guarnecer con fleco, franjar; adornar; (grow by) crecer al margen (de)

Frisian /'friʒən/ *a* and *n* frisón (-ona); (language) frisón, *m*

frisk /frisk/ *vi* retozar, brincar

friskiness /'friskinɪs/ *n* viveza, agilidad, *f*

frisky /'friski/ *a* retozón, juguetón

fritter /'fritər/ *n Cul.* fruta de sartén, *f. vt* (away) malgastar, desperdiciar; perder

frivolity /fri'vɒliti/ *n* frivolidad, ligereza, *f;* futilidad, *f*

frivolous /'frivələs/ *a* frívolo, ligero, liviano; (futile) trivial, fútil

frizz /friz/ *vt* (cloth) frisar; (hair) rizar

frizzy /'frizi/ *a* (of hair) crespo, rizado

fro /frou/ *adv* hacia atrás. **movement to and fro,** vaivén, *m.* **to and fro,** de un lado a otro. **to go to and fro,** ir y venir

frock /frɒk/ *n* vestido, *m;* (of a monk) hábito, *m;* (of priest) sotana, *f.* **f.-coat,** levita, *f*

frog /frɒg/ *n* rana, *f.* **to have a f. in the throat,** padecer carraspera

frolic /'frɒlik/ *n* (play) juego, *m;* (mischief) travesura, *f;* (folly) locura, extravagancia, *f;* (joke) chanza, *f;* (amusement) diversión, *f;* (wild party) holgorio, *m,* parranda, *f. vi* retozar, juguetear; divertirse

frolicsome /'frɒliksəm/ *a* retozón, juguetón

from /frʌm, frɒm; *unstressed* frəm/ *prep* de; desde; (according to) según; (in the name of, on behalf of) de parte de; (through, by) por; (beginning on) a contar de; (with) con; **F.** (on envelope) Remite, Remitente. **He is coming here from the dentist's,** Vendrá aquí desde casa del dentista. **Give him this message f. me,** Dale este recado de mi parte. **Judging f. his appearance,** Juzgando por su apariencia. **prices f. five hundred pesetas upward,** precios desde quinientas pesetas en adelante. **f. what I hear,** según mi información, según lo que oigo. **f. above,** desde arriba. **f. among,** de entre. **f. afar,** de lejos, desde lejos. **f. time to time,** de cuando en cuando, de vez en cuando

frond /frɒnd/ n Bot. fronda, f

front /frʌnt/ n frente, f; cara, f; Mil. frente, m; (battle line) línea de combate, f; (of a building) fachada, f; (of shirt) pechera, f; (at the seaside) playa, f; (promenade) paseo de la playa, m; (forefront) primera línea, f; (forepart) parte delantera, f; Theat. auditorio, m; (organization) organización de fachada, f; (impudence) descaro, m, a delantero; anterior; de frente; primero. adv hacia delante. vi mirar a, dar a; hacer frente a. **in f.,** en frente. **in f. of,** en frente de; (in the presence of) delante de, en la presencia de. **to face f.,** hacer frente. **to put on a bold f.,** hacer de tripas corazón. **f. door,** puerta de entrada, puerta principal, f. **f. line,** Mil. línea del frente, f; primera línea, f. **f. seat,** (at an entertainment, etc.) delantera, f. **f. organization,** organización de fachada f. **f. tooth,** diente incisivo, m. **f. view,** vista de frente, f; vista de cerca, f

frontage /ˈfrʌntɪdʒ/ n (of a building) fachada, f; (site) terreno de... metros de fachada, m

frontal /ˈfrʌnt]/ a Mil. de frente; Anat. frontal

frontier /frʌnˈtɪər/ n frontera, f; Fig. límite, m. a fronterizo

frontispiece /ˈfrʌntɪsˌpis/ n (of a building) frontispicio, m, fachada, f; (of a book) portada, f

frost /frɔst/ n escarcha, f; helada, f. vt helar; Cul. escarchar; (glass) deslustrar; Fig. escarchar. vi helar. **f.-bitten,** helado

frostbite /ˈfrɔstˌbaɪt/ n efectos del frío, m pl

frosted /ˈfrɔstɪd/ a escarchado; helado; (of glass) deslustrado, opaco; Cul. escarchado

frostily /ˈfrɔstəli/ adv Fig. glacialmente, con frialdad

frostiness /ˈfrɔstɪnɪs/ n; frío glacial, m

frosting /ˈfrɔstɪŋ/ n escarcha, f; (of glass) deslustre, m; Cul. cobertura, escarcha, f

frosty /ˈfrɔsti/ a helado; de hielo; (of hair) canoso; Fig. glacial, frío. **It was f. last night,** Anoche heló

froth /frɔθ/ n espuma, f; Fig. frivolidad, vanidad, f, vi espumar, hacer espuma; echar espuma. vt hacer espumar; hacer echar espuma

frothiness /ˈfrɔθɪnɪs/ n espumosidad, f; Fig. frivolidad, superficialidad, vaciedad, f

frothy /ˈfrɔθi/ a espumoso, espumajoso; Fig. frívolo, superficial

frown /fraun/ n ceño, m; cara de juez, expresión severa, f; desaprobación, f; (of fortune) revés, golpe, m. vi fruncir el ceño. **to f. at, on, upon,** mirar con desaprobación, ver con malos ojos; ser enemigo de; desaprobar

frowning /ˈfraunɪŋ/ a ceñudo; severo; amenazador

frowningly /ˈfraunɪŋli/ adv severamente

frozen /ˈfrouzən/ a helado; cubierto de hielo; congelado; (Geog. and Fig.) glacial. **to be f. up,** estar helado. **f. meat,** carne congelada, f

frugal /ˈfrugəl/ a económico; frugal; sobrio

frugality /fruˈɡælɪti/ n economía, f; frugalidad, sobriedad, f

fruit /frut/ n (in general sense) fruto, m; (off a tree or bush) fruta, f; Fig. fruto, m; resultado, m, consecuencia, f. vi frutar, dar fruto. **bottled f.,** fruta en almíbar, f. **candied f.,** fruta azucarada, f. **dried f.,** fruta seca, f. **first fruits,** primicias, f pl. **soft f.,** frutas blandas, f pl. **stone f.,** fruta de hueso, f. **f.-bearing,** frutal. **f.-cake,** pastel de fruta, m. **f.-dish,** frutero, m. **f. farming,** fruticultura, f. **f.-knife,** cuchillo de postres, m. **f. shop,** frutería, f. **f. tree,** frutal, m

fruitful /ˈfrutfəl/ a fructuoso, fértil; prolífico, fecundo; provechoso

fruitfulness /ˈfrutfəlnɪs/ n fertilidad, f; fecundidad, f; provecho, m

fruition /fruˈɪʃən/ n fruición, f

fruitless /ˈfrutlɪs/ a infructuoso, estéril; inútil

fruitlessness /ˈfrutlɪsnɪs/ n infructuosidad, esterilidad, f; inutilidad, f

fruity /ˈfruti/ a de fruta; (wines) vinoso; (of voice) melodioso

frump /frʌmp/ n estantigua, f

frumpish /ˈfrʌmpɪʃ/ a estrafalario; fuera de moda

frustrate /ˈfrʌstreit/ vt frustrar; defraudar; malograr; destruir; anular

frustration /frʌˈstreiʃən/ n frustración, f; defraudación, f; malogro, m; destrucción, f; desengaño, m

fry /frai/ n Cul. fritada, f, vt freír. vi freírse. **small fry,** Inf. gente menuda, f

frying /ˈfraiɪŋ/ n fritura, f, el freír. **to fall out of the f.-pan into the fire,** ir de mal en peor, andar de zocos en colodros; ir de Guatemala en Guatepeor. **f.-pan,** sartén, f

fuchsia /ˈfyuʃə/ n fuscia, Lat. Am. aljaba f

fuddle /ˈfʌdl/ vt atontar, aturdir; embriagar, emborrachar

fudge /fʌdʒ/ n patraña, tontería, f, disparate, m; (food) Lat. Am. manjar m. interj ¡qué disparate! ¡qué va!

fuel /ˈfyuəl/ n combustible, m; Fig. cebo, pábulo, m. vt cebar, echar combustible en. vi tomar combustible. **to add f. to the flame,** echar leña al fuego. **f. consumption,** consumo de combustible, m. **f.-oil,** aceite combustible, aceite de quemar, m. **f.-tank,** depósito de combustible, m

fueling /ˈfyuəlɪŋ/ n aprovisionamiento de combustible, m

fugitive /ˈfyudʒɪtɪv/ a fugitivo; pasajero, perecedero; transitorio, efímero, fugaz. n fugitivo (-va); (from justice) prófugo (-ga); Mil. desertor, m; (refugee) refugiado (-da)

fugue /fyug/ n Mus. fuga, f

fulcrum /ˈfulkrəm/ n Mech. fulcro, m

fulfill /fulˈfil/ vt cumplir; (satisfy) satisfacer; (observe) observar; guardar. **to be fulfilled,** cumplirse, realizarse

fulfillment /fulˈfilmənt/ n cumplimiento, m; desempeño, ejercicio, m; (satisfaction) satisfacción, realización, f; (observance) observancia, f

full /ful/ a lleno; colmado; todo; pleno; (crowded) atestado; (replete) harto; abundante; (intent on) preocupado con, pensando en; (loose) amplio; (plentiful) copioso; (occupied) ocupado; completo; (resonant) sonoro; (mature) maduro; puro; perfecto; (satiated) saciado (de); (of the moon, sails) lleno; (weighed down) agobiado, abrumado, f; (detailed) detallado; (with uniform, etc.) de gala; (with years, etc.) cumplido. n colmo, m; totalidad, f. adv muy; completamente, totalmente. **at f. gallop,** a galope tendido. **at f. speed,** a todo correr; a toda velocidad. **His hands are f.,** Sus manos están llenas. **The moon was f.,** La luna estaba llena. **in f.,** por completo; sin abreviaciones; integralmente. **in f. swing,** en plena actividad. **in f. vigor,** en pleno vigor. **to the f.,** completamente; hasta la última gota; a la perfección. **to be f. to the brim,** estar lleno hasta el tope. **f.-blooded,** sanguíneo; de pura raza; Fig. viril, vigoroso; Fig. apasionado. **f.-blown,** en plena flor, abierto. **f. dress,** a de gala. n traje de etiqueta, traje de ceremonia, m. **f.-face,** de cara. **f.-flavored,** (wine) abocado. **f.-grown,** adulto; completamente desarrollado. **f.-length,** de cuerpo entero. **f. moon,** luna llena, f; plenilunio, m. **f. name,** nombre y apellidos, m. **f. powers,** plenos poderes, m pl. **f. scale,** tamaño natural, m. **f. scope,** carta blanca, f; toda clase de facilidades. **f. steam ahead,** a todo vapor. **f. stop,** Gram. punto final, m

full-color /ˈful ˈkʌlər/ a a todo color. **full-color plates,** láminas a todo color

fuller /ˈfulər/ n batanero, m. **fuller's earth,** tierra de batán, galactita, f

fulling /ˈfulɪŋ/ n abatanadura, f. **f.-mill,** batán, m

fullness /ˈfulnɪs/ n abundancia, f; plenitud, f; (repletion) hartura, f; (of clothes) amplitud, f; (stoutness) gordura, f; (swelling) hinchazón, f. **She wrote with great f. of all that she had seen,** Describía muy detalladamente todo lo que había visto. **in the f. of time,** andando el tiempo

full-page /ˈful ˈpeidʒ/ a a toda plana. **full-page advertisement,** anuncio a toda plana.

full-time /ˈful ˈtaim/ a de tiempo completo

fully /ˈfuli/ adv plenamente; enteramente. **It is f. six years since...,** Hace seis años bien cumplidos que... **It is f. 9 o'clock,** Son las nueve bien sonadas. **f. dressed,** completamente vestido

fulminant /ˈfʌlmənənt/ a fulminante

fulminate /'fʌlmə,neit/ *n Chem.* fulminato, *m.* *vi* estallar; fulminar. *vt* volar; fulminar

fulminous /'fʌlmənəs/ *a* fulmíneo, fulminoso

fulsome /'fʊlsəm/ *a* servil; insincero, hipócrita; asqueroso, repugnante

fumble /'fʌmbəl/ *vi* (grope) ir a tientas; procurar hacer algo; chapucear (con); (for a word) titubear

fumbling /'fʌmblɪŋ/ *n* hesitación, *f*; tacto incierto, *m.* *a* incierto; vacilante

fumblingly /'fʌmblɪŋli/ *adv* de manera incierta; a tientas

fume /fyum/ *n* vaho, humo, gas, *m*; emanación, *f*; mal olor, *m*, fetidez, *f*; *Fig.* vapor, *m*; (state of mind) agitación, *f*; frenesí, *m.* *vi* humear; refunfuñar, echar pestes, *Lat. Am.* estar hecho un ají

fumigate /'fyumɪ,geit/ *vt* fumigar, *Lat. Am.* also humear; sahumar, perfumar; desinfectar

fumigation /,fyumə'geiʃən/ *n* fumigación, *f*; sahumerio, *m*

fumigator /'fyumɪ,geitər/ *n* fumigador (-ra); (apparatus) fumigador, *m*

fumigatory /'fyuməgə,tɔri/ *a* fumigatorio

fuming /'fyumɪŋ/ *n* refunfuño, *m.* *a* refunfuñador

fumy /'fyumi/ *a* humoso

fun /fʌn/ *n* diversión, *f*, entretenimiento, *m*; (joke) chanza, broma, *f.* **for fun,** para divertirse; en chanza. **in fun,** de burlas. **to have fun,** divertirse. **to poke fun at,** burlarse de, mofarse de, ridiculizar

function /'fʌŋkʃən/ *n* función, *f.* *vi* funcionar

functional /'fʌŋkʃənl/ *a* funcional

functionary /'fʌŋkʃə,nɛri/ *n* funcionario, *m.* *a* funcional

functioning /'fʌŋkʃənɪŋ/ *n* funcionamiento, *m*

fund /fʌnd/ *n* fondo, *m*; *pl* **funds,** fondos, *m pl*; *Inf.* dinero, *m.* **public funds,** fondos públicos, *m pl.* **sinking f.,** fondo de amortización, *m*

fundamental /,fʌndə'mɛntl/ *a* fundamental, básico; esencial. *n* fundamento, *m*

fundamentally /,fʌndə'mɛntli/ *adv* fundamentalmente, básicamente; esencialmente

funeral /'fyunərəl/ *a* funeral, fúnebre, funerario. *n* funerales, *m pl*; entierro, *m.* **to attend the f.** (of), asistir a los funerales (de). **f. feast,** banquetes fúnebres, *m pl.* **f. director, f. furnisher,** director de pompas fúnebres, *m.* **f. procession,** cortejo fúnebre, *m.* **f. pyre,** pira funeraria, *f.* **f. service,** misa de difuntos, *f*

funereal /fyu'nɪəriəl/ *a* fúnebre, lúgubre

fungicide /'fʌndʒə,said/ *n* anticriptógamo, *m*

fungous /'fʌŋgəs/ *a* fungoso

fungus /'fʌŋgəs/ *n* hongo, *m*

funicular /fyu'nɪkyələr/ *a* funicular. **f. railway,** ferrocarril funicular, *m*

funnel /'fʌnl/ *n Chem.* embudo, *m*; *Naut.* chimenea, *f*; (of a chimney) cañón (de chimenea), *m.* **f.-shaped,** en forma de embudo

funnily /'fʌnli/ *adv* de un modo raro, curiosamente

funniness /'fʌninɪs/ *n* lo divertido; rareza, extrañeza, *f*

funny /'fʌni/ *a* cómico, gracioso; divertido; (strange) curioso, extraño, raro; (mysterious) misterioso. **It struck me as f.,** (amused me) Me hizo gracia; (seemed strange) Me pareció raro. **f.-bone,** hueso de la alegría, *m*

fur /fɜr/ *n* piel, *f*; depósito, sarro, *m*; (on tongue) saburra, *f.* *a* hecho de pieles. *vt* forrar, or adornar, or cubrir, con pieles; depositar sarro sobre; (the tongue) ensuciarse la lengua. *vi* estar forrado, or adornado, or cubierto, con pieles; formarse incrustaciones; (of the tongue) tener la lengua sucia. **fur cap,** gorra de pieles, *f.* **fur cape,** cuello de piel, *m*; capa de pieles, *f.* **fur trade,** peletería, *f*

furbish /'fɜrbɪʃ/ *vt* pulir; renovar; limpiar

furious /'fyʊriəs/ *a* furioso. **to become f.,** ponerse furioso, enfurecerse

furiously /'fyʊriəsli/ *adv* furiosamente, con furia

furiousness /'fyʊriəsnɪs/ *n* furia, *f*

furl /fɜrl/ *vt* plegar; enrollar; *Naut.* aferrar

furlong /'fɜrlɔŋ/ *n* estadio, *m*

furlough /'fɜrlou/ *n Mil.* permiso, *m.* *vt* conceder un permiso (a). **on f.,** de permiso

furnace /'fɜrnɪs/ *n* horno, *m*; (of steam boiler) fogón,

m; (for central heating) caldera de calefacción central, *f*; (for smelting) cubilote, *m*

furnish /'fɜrnɪʃ/ *vt* proveer (de), equipar (de), suplir (de); amueblar; (an opportunity) proporcionar; producir

furnished /'fɜrnɪʃt/ *a* amueblado, con muebles. **f. house,** casa amueblada, *f*

furnisher /'fɜrnɪʃər/ *n* decorador, *m*; proveedor (-ra)

furnishing /'fɜrnɪʃɪŋ/ *n* provisión, *f*, equipo, *m*; *pl* **furnishings,** accesorios, *m pl*; mobiliario, mueblaje, *m*

furniture /'fɜrnɪtʃər/ *n* muebles, *m pl*, mobiliario, mueblaje, *Central America, Mexico* amoblado *m*; ajuar, equipo, *m*; avíos, *m pl*; *Naut.* aparejo, *m.* **a piece of f.,** un mueble. **to empty of f.,** desamueblar, quitar los muebles (de). **f. dealer** or **maker,** mueblista, *mf.* **f. factory,** mueblería, *f.* **f. polish,** crema para muebles, *f.* **f. mover,** transportador de muebles, *m*; (packer) embalador, *m.* **f. repository,** guardamuebles, *m.* **f. van,** carro de mudanzas, *m*

furor /'fyʊrɔr/ *n* furor, *m*

furred /fɜrd/ *a* forrado or cubierto or adornado de piel; (of the tongue) sucia

furrier /'fɜriər/ *n* peletero, *m.* **furrier's shop,** peletería, *f*

furrow /'fɜrou/ *n* surco, *m*; muesca, *f*; *Archit.* estría, *f*; (wrinkle) arruga, *f.* *vt* surcar

furry /'fɜri/ *a* cubierto de piel; parecido a una piel; hecho de pieles

further /'fɜrðər/ *a* ulterior, más distante; (other) otro; opuesto; adicional, más. *adv* más lejos; más allá; además; también; por añadidura. *vt* promover, fomentar; ayudar. **on the f. side,** al otro lado. **till f. orders,** hasta nueva orden. **f. on,** más adelante; más allá

furtherance /'fɜrðərəns/ *n* fomento, *f*, promoción, *f*; progreso, avance, *m*

furthermore /'fɜrðər,mɔr/ *adv* además, por añadidura

furthest /'fɜrðɪst/ *a* (el, la, lo) más lejano or más distante; extremo. *adv* más lejos

furtive /'fɜrtɪv/ *a* furtivo

furtively /'fɜrtɪvli/ *adv* furtivamente, a hurtadillas. **to look at f.,** mirar de reojo

fury /'fyʊri/ *n* furor, enfurecimiento, *m*, rabia, *f*; violencia, *f*; frenesí, arrebato, *m*; furia, *f.* **like a f.,** hecho una furia. **to breathe forth f.,** echar rayos

fuse /fyuz/ *n* (of explosives) espoleta, mecha, *f*; *Elec.* fusible, *m.* *vt* (metals) fundir; fusionar, mezclar. *vi* (metals) fundirse; mezclarse. **safety-f.,** espoleta de seguridad, *f.* **time-f.,** espoleta de tiempo, *f.* **to blow a f.,** fundir un fusible, *f.* **f. box,** caja de fusibles, *f.* **f. wire,** fusible, *m*

fuselage /'fyusə,laʒ/ *n Aer.* fuselaje, *m*

fusible /'fyuzəbəl/ *a* fusible

fusillade /'fyusə,lad/ *n* descarga cerrada, *f*

fusion /'fyuʒən/ *n* fusión, *f*; unión, *f*; (melting) fundición, *f*

fuss /fʌs/ *n* agitación, *f*; (bustle) conmoción, bulla, *f*; bullicio, *m.* *vi* agitarse, preocuparse. *vt* poner nervioso. **There's no need to make such a f.,** No es para tanto. **to make a f. of,** (a person) hacer la rueda (a), ser muy atento (a); (spoil) mimar mucho (a). **to f. about,** andar de acá para allá

fussily /'fʌsəli/ *adv* nerviosamente; de un aire importante

fussy /'fʌsi/ *a* meticuloso, nimio; nervioso; (of style) florido, hinchado; (of dress) demasiado adornado

fusty /'fʌsti/ *a* (moldy) mohoso; mal ventilado; mal oliente; (of views, etc.) pasado de moda

futile /'fyutl/ *a* fútil, superficial, frívolo; inútil

futility /fyu'tɪləti/ *n* futilidad, superficialidad, frivolidad, *f*; (action) tontería, estupidez, *f*

future /'fyutʃər/ *a* futuro, venidero. *n* futuro, porvenir, *m*; en adelante, en lo venidero, en lo sucesivo. **for f. reference,** para información futura. **f. perfect tense,** *Gram.* futuro perfecto, *m.* **f. tense,** *Gram.* futuro, *m*

futurism /'fyutʃə,rɪzəm/ *n* futurismo, *m*

futurist /'fyutʃərɪst/ *n* futurista, *mf*

futuristic /,fyutʃə'rɪstɪk/ *a* futurístico

fuzz /fʌz/ *n* vello, *m*, pelusa, *f.* **f.-ball,** *Bot.* bejín, *m*

fuzzy /'fʌzi/ *a* crespo rizado; velloso

G

g /dʒi/ n (letter) ge, f; Mus. sol, m. **G clef,** clave de sol, f

gab /gæb/ n Inf. labia, f. **to have the gift of the gab,** tener mucha labia

gabardine /'gæbər,din/ n gabardina, f

gabble /'gæbəl/ vi chacharear, garlar; hablar indistintamente; (of goose and some birds) graznar. vt decir indistintamente; decir rápidamente; (a language) chapurrear; mascullar. n cháchara, f; vocerío, m; (of goose and some birds) graznido, m

gabbler /'gæblər/ n charlatán (-ana), chacharero (-ra)

gabbling /'gæblɪŋ/ n See **gabble**

gable /'geibəl/ n Archit. gablete, hastial, m. **g.-end,** alero, m

gad /gæd/ vi corretear, callejear. **to gad about,** correr por todos lados; divertirse.

gadabout /'gædə,baut/ n azotacalles, mf; gandul (-la), vagabundo (-da)

gadding /'gædɪŋ/ a callejero; vagabundo. n vagancia, f; vida errante, f; gandulería, f

gadfly /'gæd,flai/ n Ent. tábano, m; Inf. moscardón, m

gadget /'gædʒɪt/ n accesorio, m; aparato, m; chuchería, f

Gael /geil/ n escocés (-esa) del norte; celta, mf

Gaelic /'geilɪk/ a gaélico. n gaélico, m

gaff /gæf/ n (hook) garfio, m; Naut. pico de cangrejo, m; Theat. teatrucho, m

gaffer /'gæfər/ n viejo, tío, abuelo, m

gag /gæg/ n mordaza, f; Theat. morcilla, f. vt amordazar; Fig. hacer callar. vi Theat. meter morcillas

gage /geidʒ/ n prenda, fianza, f; (symbol of challenge) guante, m; (challenge) desafío, m. See **gauge**

gagging /'gægɪŋ/ n amordazamiento, m

gaggle /'gægəl/ n (cry) graznido, m; (of geese) manada (de ocas), f. vi graznar; cacarear

gaiety /'geiɪti/ n alegría, f; animación, vivacidad, f; (entertainment) diversión, festividad, f

gaily /'geili/ adv alegremente

gain /gein/ n ganancia, f; provecho, beneficio, m; (increase) aumento, m; (riches) riqueza, f. vt ganar; (acquire) conseguir; adquirir; obtener; conquistar, captar; (friends) hacerse; (reach) llegar a, alcanzar. vi ganar; (improve) mejorar; (of a watch) adelantarse. **What have they gained by going to Canada?** ¿Qué han logrado con marcharse al Canadá? **to g. ground,** Fig. ganar terreno. **to g. momentum** adquirir velocidad **to g. time,** ganar tiempo. **to g. on, upon,** acercarse a; (overtake) alcanzar; (outstrip) dejar atrás, pasar; (of sea) invadir; (of habits) imponerse

gainful /'geinfəl/ a gananciero, lucrativo; ventajoso

gainfully /'geinfəli/ adv ventajosamente; lucrativamente

gainsay /gein,sei/ vt contradecir; oponer; negar

gainsaying /gein,seiɪŋ/ n contradicción, f; oposición, f; negación, f

gait /geit/ n porte, andar, m; paso, m, andadura, f

gaiter /'geitər/ n polaina, f; (spat) botín, m

gala /'geilə/ n gala, fiesta, f. **g.-day,** día de fiesta, m. **g.-dress,** traje de gala, m

galaxy /'gæləksi/ n Astron. vía láctea, f; Fig. constelación, f; grupo brillante, m

gale /geil/ n vendaval, ventarrón, m; (storm) temporal, m; tempestad, f

Galician /gə'lɪʃən/ a and n gallego (-ga).

Galilean /,gælə'leiən/ a and n galileo (-ea)

Galilee /'gælə,li/ Galilea, f

gall /gɔl/ n (on horses) matadura, f; (abrasion) rozadura, f; hiel, bilis, f; Fig. hiel, amargura, f; rencor, m; (impudence) descaro, m, impertinencia, f; Bot. agalla, f. vt rozar; Fig. mortificar, herir. **g.-bladder,** vejiga de la hiel, f. **g.-stone,** cálculo hepático, m

gallant /'gælənt/ a hermoso; (imposing) imponente, majestuoso; (brave) valiente, gallardo, valeroso, intrépido; (chivalrous) caballeroso; noble; (attentive to ladies, or amorous) galante. n galán, m. vt galantear, cortejar

gallantly /'gæləntli/ adv (bravely) valientemente; caballerosamente; cortésmente; galantemente

gallantry /'gæləntri/ n (bravery) valentía, f, valor, m; heroísmo, m, proeza, f; (chivalry) gallantería, cortesía, f; (toward women, or amorousness) galantería, f

galleon /'gæliən/ n galeón, m

gallery /'gæləri/ n galería, f; pasillo, m; (of a cloister) tránsito, m; (cloister) claustro, m; (for spectators) tribuna, f; Theat. paraíso, gallinero, m; (theater audience) galería, f; (of portraits, etc.) galería, colección, f; (Mineral., Mil.) galería, f; (building) museo, m. **art g.,** museo de pinturas, m

galley /'gæli/ n (Naut. Print.) galera, f; (kitchen) cocina, f; (rowboat) falúa de capitán, f. **to condemn to the galleys,** echar a galeras. **wooden g.,** Print. galerín, m. **g.-proof,** galerada, f. **g.-slave,** galeote, m

Gallic /'gælɪk/ a gálico, galicano; francés

gallicism /'gælɪsɪzəm/ n galicismo, m

galling /'gɔlɪŋ/ a Fig. irritante; mortificante

gallivant /'gælə,vænt/ vi callejear, corretear; divertirse; ir de parranda

gallon /'gælən/ n galón, m

gallop /'gæləp/ n galope, m. vi galopar; ir aprisa. vt hacer galopar, **at full g.,** a rienda suelta, a galope tendido. **to g. back,** volver a galope. **to g. down,** bajar a galope. **to g. off,** marcharse galopando; alejarse corriendo. **to g. past,** desfilar a galope ante. **to g. through,** cruzar a galope. **to g. up,** vt subir a galope. vi llegar a galope

gallopade /,gælə'peid/ n (dance) galop, m

galloping /'gæləpɪŋ/ n galope, m; galopada, f. a que va a galope; Med. galopante. **g. consumption,** tisis galopante, f

gallows /'gælouz/ n patíbulo, m, horca, f; (framework) montante, m. **g.-bird,** criminal digno de la horca, m

galop /'gæləp/ n galop, m

galore /gə'lɔr/ adv a granel, en abundancia (e.g. sunshine galore, sol a granel)

galosh /gə'lɒʃ/ n chanclo, m

galvanic /gæl'vænɪk/ a Elec. galvánico; espasmódico

galvanize /'gælvə,naiz/ vt galvanizar

gambit /'gæmbɪt/ n (chess) gambito, m; Fig. táctica, f

gamble /'gæmbəl/ n juego de azar, m; jugada, f; aventura, f; Com. especulación, f. vi jugar por dinero; especular; (with) Fig. aventurar, arriesgar. **to g. on the Stock Exchange,** jugar en la bolsa. **to g. away,** perder al juego

gambler /'gæmblər/ n jugador (-ra), Mexico dadista mf

gambling /'gæmblɪŋ/ n juego, m. a jugador de juego. **g.-den,** casa de juego, f, garito, m

gambol /'gæmbəl/ n salto, brinco, retozo, m; cabriola, f; juego, m. vi saltar, brincar, retozar; juguetear

game /geim/ n juego, m; (match) partido, m; (jest) chanza, f; (trick) trampa, f; (birds, hares, etc.) caza menor, f; (tigers, lions, etc.) caza mayor, f; (flesh of game) caza, f; pl **games,** deportes, m pl. a de caza; (courageous) valiente, animoso, brioso; resuelto. vi jugar por dinero. **He is g. for anything,** Se atreve a todo. **big g. hunting,** caza mayor, f. **head of g.,** pieza de caza, f. **It is a g. at which two can play,** Donde las dan las toman. **The g. is not worth the candle,** La cosa no vale la pena. **The g. is up,** Fig. El proyecto se ha frustrado. **to make g. of,** (things) burlarse de; (persons) tomar el pelo a; mofarse de. **to play the g.,** Fig. jugar limpio. **to g. away,** perder al juego. **g. of cards,** juego de naipes, m. **g. of chance,** juego de azar, m. **g.-bag,** morral, m. **g.-drive,** batida de caza, f. **g.-laws,** leyes de caza, f pl. **g.-license,** licencia de caza, f. **g.-pie,** tortada, f. **g. preserve,** coto de caza, m

gamekeeper /'geim,kipər/ n guardabosque, m

gamely /'geimli/ adv valientemente
gameness /'geimnıs/ n valentía, resolución, fortaleza, f
gamete /'gæmit/ n gameto, m
gaming /'geimıŋ/ n juego, m, a de juego. **g.-house,** garito, m. **g.-table,** mesa de juego, f; Fig. juego, m
gamut /'gæmət/ n gama, f
gander /'gændər/ n ganso, m
gang /gæŋ/ n cuadrilla, pandilla, banda, Mexico carpanta f; (squad) pelotón, m; (of workers) brigada, cuadrilla, f; group, m. **g.-plank,** plancha, f
ganglion /'gæŋgliən/ n ganglio, m; Fig. centro, m
gangrene /'gæŋgrin/ n gangrena, f. vt gangrenar. vi gangrenarse
gangrenous /'gæŋgrınəs/ a gangrenoso
gangster /'gæŋstər/ n pistolero, gángster, bandito, m
gangway /'gæŋ,wei/ n pasillo, m; Naut. plancha, f, pasamano, m; (opening in ship's side) portalón, m. **midship g.,** crujía, f
gap /gæp/ n brecha, f; abertura, f; (hole) boquete, m; (pass) desfiladero, paso, m; (ravine) hondonada, barranca, f; (blank) laguna, f, vacío, m; (crack) intersticio, m, hendedura, f, resquicio, m. **to fill a gap,** llenar un boquete; llenar un vacío
gape /geip/ vi estar con la boca abierta, papar moscas. **to g. at,** mirar con la boca abierta
gaping /'geipıŋ/ n huelgo, m; abertura, f, a que bosteza; boquiabierto; abierto
garage /gə'raʒ/ n garaje, m. vt poner (un coche, etc.) en un garaje. **g. owner,** garajista, mf
garb /garb/ n traje, vestido, m, ropa f; uniforme, m; Herald. espiga, f. vt vestir, ataviar
garbage /'garbıdʒ/ n basura, inmundicia, f
garbage can basurero, tarro de la basura, m
garbage dump Lat. Am. basural m
garble /'garbəl/ vt falsear, mutilar, pervertir
garden /'gardṇ/ n jardín, m; huerto, m; (fertile region) huerta, f. a de jardín. vi trabajar en el jardín, cultivar un huerto. **g. city,** ciudad jardín, f. **g.-frame,** semillero, m. **g. mold,** tierra vegetal, f. **g.-party,** fiesta de jardín, m. **g.-plot,** terraza, f. **g. produce,** hortalizas, legumbres, f pl. **g. roller,** rodillo, m. **g.-seat,** banco de jardín, m. **g. urn,** jarrón, m
gardener /'gardnər/ n jardinero, m
gardenia /gar'dinyə/ n gardenia, f, jazmín de la India, m
gardening /'gardnıŋ/ n jardinería, f; horticultura, f. a de jardinería
gargantuan /gar'gæntʃuən/ a gargantuesco; tremendo, enorme
gargle /'gargəl/ n (liquid) gargarismo, m; gárgaras, f pl. vi hacer gárgaras, gargarizar
gargling /'garglıŋ/ n gargarismo, m
gargoyle /'gargɔil/ n gárgola, f
garish /'geərıʃ/ a cursi, llamativo, charro, chillón
garishness /'geərıʃnıs/ n cursería, ostentación, f, lo llamativo
garland /'garlənd/ n guirnalda, f; corona, f; (anthology) florilegio, m; Archit. festón, m. vt enguirnaldar
garlic /'garlık/ n ajo, m
garment /'garmənt/ n prenda de vestir, f; traje, vestido, m; Fig. vestidura, f; (Fig. cloak) capa, f
garner /'garnər/ n granero, m; tesoro, m; colección, f. vt atesorar, guardar
garnet /'garnıt/ n granate, m
garnish /'garnıʃ/ n Cul. aderezo, m; adorno, m. vt Cul. aderezar; embellecer, adornar
garnishing /'garnıʃıŋ/ n. See **garnish**
garret /'gærıt/ n guardilla, buhardilla, f, desván, m
garrison /'gærəsən/ n guarnición, f, presidio, m. vt guarnecer, presidiar. **g. town,** plaza de armas, f
garrote /gə'rɒt/ n garrote, m. vt agarrotar, dar garrote (a)
garrulity /gə'rulıti/ n garrulidad, locuacidad, charlatanería, f
garrulous /'gærələs/ a gárrulo, locuaz, charlatán
garter /'gartər/ n liga, f; (G.) Jarretera, f, vt atar con liga; investir con la Jarretera
gas /gæs/ n gas, m; Fig., Inf. palabrería, f; (fuel) gasolina, f, a de gas; con gas; para gases. vt asfixiar

con gas; Mil. atacar con gas; saturar de gas. **gas attack,** ataque con gases asfixiantes, m. **gas-bag,** bolsa de gas, f; Inf. charlatán (-ana). **gas-burner,** mechero de gas, m. **gas-chamber,** cámara de gas, f. **gas detector,** detector de gases, m. **gas-fire,** estufa de gas, f. **gas-fitter,** gasista, m. **gas-fittings,** lámparas de gas, f pl. **gas-light,** luz de gas, f; mechero de gas, m. **gas-main,** cañería maestra de gas, f **gas-man,** gasista, m. **gas-mantle,** camiseta incandescente, f. **gas-mask,** máscara para gases, f. **gas-meter,** contador de gas, m. **gas-pipes,** cañerías (or tuberías) de gas, f pl. **gas-ring,** fogón de gas, m. **gas-shell,** obús de gases asfixiantes, m. **gas-stove,** cocina de gas, f. **gas warfare,** guerra química, f. **gas-works,** fábrica de gas, f
gaseous /'gæsiəs/ a gaseoso
gash /gæʃ/ n cuchillada, f; herida extensa, f. vt acuchillar; herir extensamente
gasket /'gæskıt/ n aro de empaquetadura, m
gasoline /,gæsə'lin/ n gasolina, f; bencina, f
gasp /gæsp/ n boqueada, f. vi boquear. **to be at the last g.,** estar agonizando, m. **to g. for breath,** luchar por respirar. **to g. out,** decir anhelante, decir con voz entrecortada
gastric /'gæstrık/ a gástrico
gastritis /gæ'straitıs/ n gastritis, f
gastronome /'gæstrə,noum/ n gastrónomo (-ma)
gastronomic /,gæstrə'namık/ a gastronómico
gastronomy /gæ'strɒnəmi/ n gastronomía, f
gate /geit/ n puerta, f; cancela, verja, f; entrada, f; (of a lock, etc.) compuerta, f; (across a road, etc.) barrera, f; (money) entrada, f; Fig. puerta, f. **automatic g.,** (at level crossings, etc.) barrera de golpe, f. **g.-keeper,** portero, m; guardabarrera, mf **g.-money,** entrada, f. **g.-post,** soporte de la puerta, m
gateway /'geit,wei/ n entrada, f; puerta, f; paso, m; vestíbulo, m; Fig. puerta, f
gather /'gæðər/ vt (assemble) reunir; (amass) acumular, amontonar; (acquire) obtener, adquirir; hacer una colección (de); cobrar; (harvest) cosechar, recolectar; (pick up) recoger; (pluck) coger; (infer) sacar en limpio, aprender; Sew. fruncir; (the brows) fruncir (el ceño). vi reunirse, congregarse; amontonarse; (threaten) amenazar; (sadden) amargar; (Fig. hover over) cernerse (sobre); (increase) aumentar, crecer; (be covered) cubrirse; (fester) supurar. n Sew. frunce, pliegue, m. **to g. breath,** tomar aliento. **to g. speed,** ganar velocidad. **to g. strength,** cobrar fuerzas. **I g. from Mary that they are going abroad,** Según lo que me ha dicho María, van al extranjero. **to g. in,** juntar; reunir; (harvest) cosechar; coger. **to g. together,** vt reunir. vi reunirse. **to g. up,** recoger; coger; tomar; (one's limbs) encoger. **to g. up the threads,** Fig. recoger los hilos.
gatherer /'gæðərər/ n (of gas) cogedor, colector, m; (harvester) segador, m; (of grapes) vendimiador (-ra); (of taxes) recaudador, m
gathering /'gæðərıŋ/ n cogedura, f; (fruit, etc.) recolección, f; (of taxes) recaudación, f; amontonamiento, m; colección, f; Med. absceso, m; Sew. fruncimiento, m; (assembly) reunión, asamblea, f; (crowd) concurrencia, muchedumbre, f
gathers /'gæðərz/ n Sew. fruncidos, pliegues, m pl
gauche /gouʃ/ a torpe, huraño
gaudily /'gɔdəli/ adv ostentosamente; brillantemente
gaudiness /'gɔdinıs/ n ostentación, f; brillantez, f
gaudy /'gɔdi/ a llamativo, vistoso, brillante, ostentoso
gauge /geidʒ/ n (of gun) calibre, m; (railway) entrevía, f; (for measuring) indicator, m; regla de medir, f; Naut. calado, m; Fig. medida, f; (test) indicación, f; (model) norma, f. vt calibrar; medir; estimar; (ship's capacity) arquear; (judge) juzgar; (size up) tomar la medida (de); Fig. interpretar; Sew. fruncir; (liquor) aforar. **broad (narrow) g. railway,** ferrocarril de vía ancha (estrecha), m. **pressure g.,** manómetro, m. **water g.,** indicador del nivel de agua, m
gauging /'geidʒıŋ/ n medida, f; (of ship's capacity) arqueo, m; (of liquor) aforamiento, m; Fig. apreciación, f; interpretación, f
gaunt /gɔnt/ a anguloso, huesudo, desvaído; (of houses, etc.) lúgubre
gauntlet /'gɔntlıt/ n guante de manopla, m; (part of

armor) manopla, *f*, guantelete, *m*. **to throw down the g.**, echar el guante, desafiar
gauntness /'gɔntnɪs/ *n* angulosidad, flaqueza, *f*
gauze /gɔz/ *n* gasa, *f*; (mist) bruma, *f*. **wire-g.**, tela metálica, *f*
gauziness /'gɔzinɪs/ *n* diafanidad, *f*
gauzy /'gɔzi/ *a* diáfano; de gasa
gavotte /gə'vɒt/ *n* gavota, *f*
gawkiness /'gɔkinɪs/ *n* torpeza, desmaña, *f*
gawky /'gɔki/ *a* anguloso, desgarbado, torpe
gay /gei/ *a* alegre; festivo, animado; ligero de cascos, disipado; homosexual; (of colors) brillante, llamativo
Gaza Strip /'gɑzə/ la franja de Gaza, *f*
gaze /geiz/ *n* mirada, *f*; mirada fija, *f*. *vi* mirar; mirar fijamente, contemplar
gazelle /gə'zɛl/ *n* gacel (-la)
gazer /'geizər/ *n* espectador (-ra)
gazette /gə'zɛt/ *n* gaceta, *f*. *vt* publicar en la gaceta.
gazing /'geizɪŋ/ *n* contemplación, *f*, *a* contemplador; que presencia, que asiste a
gear /gɪər/ *n* (apparel) atavíos, *m pl*; (harness) guarniciones, *f pl*, arneses, *m pl*; (tackle) utensilios, *m pl*, herramientas, *f pl*; *Naut.* aparejo, *m*; *Mech.* engranaje, *m*; juego, *m*, marcha, *f*. *vt* aparejar, enjaezar; *Mech.* poner en marcha, hacer funcionar. *vi Mech.* engranar, endentar. **low g.**, pimera velocidad, *f*. **neutral g.**, punto muerto, *m*. **reverse g.**, marcha atrás, *f*. **second g.**, segunda velocidad, *f*. **three-speed g.**, cambio de marchas de tres velocidades, *m*. **top g.**, tercera (or cuarta--according to gear-box) velocidad, *f*. **to change g.**, cambiar de marcha, cambiar de velocidad. **to throw out of g.**, *Fig.* desquiciar. **g.-box**, caja de velocidades, *f*. **g.-changing**, cambio de velocidad, *m*. **g.-changing lever**, palanca de cambio de velocidad, palanca de cambio de marchas, *f*
gearing /'gɪərɪŋ/ *n* engranaje, *m*
gehenna /gɪ'hɛnə/ *n* gehena, *m*
geisha /'geiʃə/ *n* geisha, *f*
gelatin /'dʒɛlətɪn/ *n* gelatina, *f*. **cooking g.**, gelatina seca, *f*
gelatinous /dʒə'lætɲəs/ *a* gelatinoso
geld /gɛld/ *vt* capar, castrar
gelder /'gɛldər/ *n* castrador, *m*
gelding /'gɛldɪŋ/ *n* castración, capadura, *f*; caballo castrado, *m*; animal castrado, *m*
gem /dʒɛm/ *n* piedra preciosa, *f*; joya, alhaja, *f*; *Fig.* joya, *f*. *vt* adornar con piedras preciosos; enjoyar
Gemini /'dʒɛmə,nai/ *n* (los) Gemelos
gender /'dʒɛndər/ *n Gram.* género, *m*; sexo, *m*
gene /dʒin/ *n Biol.* gene, *m*
genealogical /,dʒiniə'lɒdʒɪkəl/ *a* genealógico. **g. tree**, árbol genealógico, *m*
genealogist /,dʒini'ɒlədʒɪst/ *n* genealogista, *mf*
genealogy /,dʒini'ɒlədʒi/ *n* genealogía, *f*
general /'dʒɛnərəl/ *a* general; universal; común; corriente; (usual) acostumbrado, usual; del público, público. *n* lo general; (*Mil.*, *Eccl.*) general, *m*; *Inf.* criada para todo, *f*. **in g.**, por lo general, en general, generalmente. **to become g.**, generalizarse. **to make g.**, generalizar, hacer general. **g. average**, (marine insurance) avería gruesa, *f*. **g. election**, elección general, *f*. **g. meeting**, pleno, mitin general, *m*. **g. opinion**, voz común, opinión general, *f*. **G. Post Office**, Oficina Central de Correos, *f*. **g. practitioner**, médico (-ca) general. **g. public**, público, *m*. **the general reader**, el lector de tipo general *m*
generalissimo /,dʒɛnərə'lɪsə,mou/ *n* generalísimo, *m*
generality /,dʒɛnə'rælɪti/ *n* generalidad, *f*
generalization /,dʒɛnərələ'zeiʃən/ *n* generalización, *f*
generalize /'dʒɛnərə,laiz/ *vt* and *vi* generalizar
generally /'dʒɛnərəli/ *adv* en general, por regla general, por lo general, generalmente; comúnmente, por lo común
generalship /'dʒɛnərəl,ʃɪp/ *n Mil.* generalato, *m*; (strategy) táctica, estrategia, *f*; dirección, jefatura, *f*
generate /'dʒɛnə,reit/ *vt* (beget) engendrar, procrear; (*Phys.*, *Chem.*) generar; *Fig.* producir, crear
generation /,dʒɛnə'reiʃən/ *n* procreación, *f*; generación, *f*; *Fig.* producción, creación, *f*. **the younger g.**, los jóvenes

generative /'dʒɛnərətɪv/ *a* generador
generator /'dʒɛnə,reitər/ *n Mech.* generador, *m*; dínamo, *f*
generic /dʒə'nɛrɪk/ *a* genérico
generosity /,dʒɛnə'rɒsɪti/ *n* generosidad, *f*; liberalidad, *f*
generous /'dʒɛnərəs/ *a* generoso; liberal, dadivoso, limosnero, *Lat. Am.* maniabierto; magnánimo; (plentiful) abundante; (of wines) generoso
generously /'dʒɛnərəsli/ *adv* generosamente; abundantemente
genesis /'dʒɛnəsɪs/ *n* principio, origen, *m*; (G.) Génesis, *m*
genetic /dʒə'nɛtɪk/ *a* genético
genetics /dʒə'nɛtɪks/ *n* genética, *f*
Geneva /dʒə'nivə/ Ginebra, *f*
genial /'dʒinyəl/ *a* (of climate) agradable, bueno; (of persons) afable, bondadoso; de buen humor, bonachón
geniality /,dʒini'ælɪti/ *n* afabilidad, bondad, *f*; buen humor, *m*
genially /'dʒinyəli/ *adv* afablemente
genie /'dʒini/ *n* genio, *m*
genital /'dʒɛnɪtl/ *a* genital, sexual. *n pl* **genitals**, genitales, *m pl*
genitive /'dʒɛnɪtɪv/ *a* and *n Gram.* genitivo *m*.
genius /'dʒinyəs/ *n* genio, *m*; carácter, *m*, índole, *f*; ingenio, *m*; *Inf.* talento, *m*
Genoa /'dʒɛnouə/ Genova, *f*
Genoese /,dʒɛnou'iz/ *a* and *n* genovés (-esa)
genre /'ʒɑnrə/ *n* género, *m*. **g. painting**, cuadro de género, *m*
genteel /dʒɛn'til/ *a* fino; (affected) remilgado, melindroso; de buen tono; de buena educación
gentile /'dʒɛntail/ *a* and *n* gentil, *mf*
gentility /dʒɛn'tɪlɪti/ *n* aristocracia, *f*; respetabilidad, *f*
gentle /'dʒɛntl/ *a* noble, bien nacido, de buena familia; amable; suave; ligero; dulce; (docile) manso, dócil; (affectionate) cariñoso; bondadoso; sufrido, paciente; cortés; pacífico, tolerante. **He was a man of g. birth**, Era un hombre bien nacido. **"G. reader,"** «Querido lector». **g. wind**, *Lat. Am.* airecito, *m*
gentlefolk /'dʒɛntl,fouk/ *n* gente de bien, gente fina, *f*; gente de buena familia, *f*
gentleman /'dʒɛntlmən/ *n* caballero, señor, *m*; gentilhombre, *m*. **Ladies and gentlemen,** Señoras y caballeros, Señores. **young g.**, señorito, *m*. **to be a perfect g.**, ser un caballero perfecto. **g.-inwaiting**, gentilhombre de la cámara, *m*
gentlemanliness /'dʒɛntl,mənlinɪs/ *n* caballerosidad, *f*
gentlemanly /'dʒɛntl,mənli/ *a* caballeroso
gentleness /'dʒɛntl,nɪs/ *n* amabilidad, *f*; suavidad, *f*; dulzura, *f*; mansedumbre, docilidad, *f*; bondad, *f*; paciencia, *f*; cortesía, *f*; tolerancia, *f*
gentlewoman /'dʒɛntl,wumən/ *n* dama, *f*; dama de servicio, *f*
gently /'dʒɛntli/ *adv* suavemente; dulcemente; silenciosamente, sin ruido; (slowly) despacio, poco a poco. **g. born**, bien nacido
gentry /'dʒɛntri/ *n* pequeña aristocracia, alta clase media, *f*; (disparaging) gente, *f*
genuflect /'dʒɛnyʊ,flɛkt/ *vi* doblar la rodilla
genuflection /,dʒɛnyʊ'flɛkʃən/ *n* genuflexión, *f*
genuine /'dʒɛnyuin/ *a* puro; genuino; verdadero; real; sincero; auténtico
genuinely /'dʒɛnyuinli/ *adv* genuinamente; verdaderamente; realmente; sinceramente
genuineness /'dʒɛnyuinnɪs/ *n* pureza, *f*; autenticidad, *f*; verdad, *f*; sinceridad, *f*
genus /'dʒinəs/ *n* género, *m*
geodesic /,dʒiə'dɛsɪk/ *a* geodésico
geodesy /dʒi'ɒdəsi/ *n* geodesia, *f*
geographer /dʒi'ɒgrəfər/ *n* geógrafo, *m*
geographical /,dʒiə'græfɪkəl/ *a* geográfico
geographically /,dʒiə'græfɪkəli/ *adv* geográficamente; desde el punto de vista geográfico
geography /dʒi'ɒgrəfi/ *n* geografía, *f*
geological /,dʒiə'lɒdʒəkəl/ *a* geológico
geologically /,dʒiə'lɒdʒɪkəli/ *adv* geológicamente; desde el punto de vista geológico

geologist /dʒi'ɒlədʒɪst/ n geólogo, m
geologize /dʒi'ɒlə,dʒaiz/ vi estudiar la geología. vt
estudiar desde un punto de vista geológico
geology /dʒi'ɒlədʒi/ n geología, f
geometric /,dʒiə'metrɪk/ a geométrico
geometry /dʒi'ɒmɪtri/ n geometría, f
geophysics /,dʒiou'fɪzɪks/ n geofísica, f
Georgian /'dʒɔrdʒən/ a Geog. georgiano; Lit. del
principio del siglo diez y nueve
georgic /'dʒɔrdʒɪk/ n geórgica, f
geotropism /dʒi'ɒtrə,pɪzəm/ n geotropismo, m
geranium /dʒə'reiniəm/ n geranio, m
germ /dʒɜrm/ n embrión, germen, m; microbio, bacilo, m; Fig. germen, m. **g.-cell**, célula germinal, f
German /'dʒɜrmən/ a alemán; germánico. n alemán
(-ana); (language) alemán, m; germano (-na), germánico (-ca). **Sudeten G.**, alemán (-ana) sudete. **G.
measles**, rubeola, f. **G. silver**, alpaca, f, melchor m,
plata alemana f
germander /dʒər'mændər/ n Bot. camedrio, m
germane /dʒər'mein/ a pertinente (a), a propósito
(a)
Germanic /dʒər'mænɪk/ a germánico. n (language)
germánico, m
Germanization /,dʒɜrmənɪ'zeiʃən/ n germanización, f
Germanize /'dʒɜrmə,naiz/ vt germanizar. vi germani-
zarse
Germanophile /dʒər'mænə,fail/ n germanófilo (-la)
Germany /'dʒɜrməni/ Alemania, f
germicidal /,dʒɜrmə'saidl/ a bactericida
germicide /'dʒɜrmə,said/ n desinfectante, m
germinal /'dʒɜrmənḷ/ a germinal. n (G.) germinal, m
germinate /'dʒɜrmə,neit/ vi germinar, brotar. vt
hacer germinar
germination /,dʒɜrmə'neiʃən/ n germinación, f
germinative /'dʒɜrmə,neitɪv/ a germinativo
gerund /'dʒɛrənd/ n gerundio, m
gerundive /dʒə'rʌndɪv/ n gerundio adjetivado, m
Gestapo /gə'stɑpou/ n Gestapo, f
gestation /dʒɛ'steiʃən/ n gestación, f
gesticulate /dʒɛ'stɪkyə,leit/ vi gesticular, hacer gestos; accionar. vt expresar por gestos
gesticulation /dʒɛ,stɪkyə'leiʃən/ n gesticulación, f
gesticulatory /dʒɛ'stɪkyələ,tɔri/ a gesticular
gesture /'dʒɛstʃər/ n movimiento, m; gesticulación, f;
(of the face) gesto, m, mueca, f; ademán, m, acción,
f. vi gesticular. vt decir por gestos; acompañar con
gestos
get /gɛt/ vt (obtain) obtener; (acquire) adquirir;
(buy) comprar; (take) tomar; (receive) recibir; (gain,
win) ganar; (hit) acertar, dar; (place) poner;
(achieve) alcanzar, lograr; (make) hacer; (call) llamar; (understand) comprender; (catch) coger; (procreate) procrear, engendrar; (induce) persuadir; (invite) convidar, invitar; (cause) hacer; (with have and
past part.) tener; (with have and past part. followed
by infin.) tener que; (followed by noun and past
part.) hacer; (fetch) buscar, ir a buscar; (order) mandar, disponer; (procure) procurar; (bring) traer;
(money) hacer; (a reputation, etc.) hacerse; (a prize,
an advantage) llevar; (learn) aprender; (be) ser. vi
(become) hacerse; ponerse; venir a ser; (old) enve-
jecerse; (angry) montar (en cólera), enojarse; (arrive)
llegar a; (attain) alcanzar; (accomplish) conseguir, lograr; (drunk) emborracharse; (hurt) hacerse daño;
(wet) mojarse; (cool) enfriarse; (money) hacer (dinero); (of health) ponerse; (find oneself) hallarse, encontrarse; (late) hacerse (tarde); (dark) empezar a
caer (la noche), empezar a caer (la noche), empezar a
oscurecer; (put oneself) meterse; (grow, be) estar;
(on to or on top of) montar sobre, subir a. **He has
got run over**, Ha sido atropellado. **It gets on my
nerves**, Se me pone los nervios en punta. **Let's get it
over!** ¡Vamos a concluir de una vez! **How do you
get on with her?** ¿Cómo te va con ella? **She must be
getting on for twenty**, Tendrá alrededor de veinte
años. **to get a suit made**, mandar hacerse un traje.
to get altitude sickness, Peru asorocharse. **to get
better**, (in health) mejorar de salud; hacer progresos
adelantar. **to get dark**, obscurecer. **to get depressed**, Lat. Am. amurrarse. **to get into conversa-**

tion with, trabar conversación con. **to get into bad
company**, frecuentar malas compañías. **to get into
the habit of**, acostumbrarse a. **to get married**, casarse. **to get near**, acercarse. **to get one's own
way**, salir con la suya. **to get oneself up as**, disfrazarse de. **to get out in a hurry**, salir apresuradamente; marcharse rápidamente, Inf. salir pitando. **to
get out of the way**, quitarse de en medio, apartarse.
to get rid of, desembarazarse de, librarse de; salir
de; perder. tener; padecer. **Get on!** ¡Adelante!; (to a
horse) ¡Arre!; (continue) ¡Sigue! **Get out!** ¡Fuera!
¡Largo de aquí! ¡Sal! **to get the blues = to get depressed**, **Get up!** ¡Levántate!; (to a horse) ¡Arre!
get about, moverse mucho; andar mucho; (attend to
business affairs) ir a sus negocios; (travel) viajar; (get
up from sick bed) levantarse; (go out) salir; (be
known) saberse, divulgarse, hacerse público. **to get
above**, subir a un nivel más alto (de). **to get across**,
vi cruzar, atravesar. vt hacer cruzar. **to get along**, vi
(depart) marcharse; (continue) seguir, vivir; (manage) ir y tirando. vt llevar; traer; hacer andar por.
How are you getting along? ¿Cómo le va? **I am getting along all right, thank you**, Voy tirando, gracias.
to get along without, pasarse sin. **to get angry** vi
Central America empurrarse. **to get at**, (remove) sacar; (find) encontrar; (reach) llegar a; alcanzar; (discover) descubrir; (allude to) aludir a; (understand)
comprender. **to get away**, vi dejar (un lugar); marcharse, irse; (escape) escaparse. vt ayudar a marcharse; ayudar a escaparse. **to get away with**, llevarse, marcharse con; Inf. salir con la suya. **to get
back**, vi regresar, volver; (get home) volver a casa;
(be back) estar de vuelta. vt (recover) recobrar; (receive) recibir; (find again) hallar de nuevo. **to get
depressed**, Central America acuilmarse. **to get down**,
vi bajar, descender. vt bajar; (take off a hook) descolgar; (swallow) tragar; (note) anotar; escribir. **to get
down on all fours**, ponerse en cuatro patas. **to get
down to**, ponerse a (estudiar, trabajar, etc.). **to get
in**, vi entrar en; lograr entrar en; (slip in) colarse en;
(of political party) entrar en el poder; (of a club)
hacerse socio de; (return) regresar; (home) volver a
casa; (find oneself) hallarse, estar; (a habit) adquirir.
vt hacer entrar en; (a club, etc.) hacer socio de; (a
word) decir. **to get in line**, Mexico formarse. **to get
into**. See **to get off**, vt apearse de; bajar
de; (send) enviar; (from punishment) librar; (bid
goodbye) despedirse de; (remove) quitar, sacar. vi
apearse; bajar; (from punishment) librarse; (leave)
ponerse en camino, marcharse. **to get on**, vi (wear)
tener puesto; (progress) hacer progresos, adelantar;
(prosper) medrar, prosperar; (succeed) tener éxito;
avanzar; seguir el camino; (agree) avenirse. vt (push)
empujar; (place) poner; (cause) hacer; (clothes)
ponerse; (mount) subir a. **to get open**, abrir. **to get
out**, vi hacer salir; sacar; (publish) publicar; divulgar. vi salir; escapar; **to get out of a jam**, salir de
un paso; (descend) bajar (de). **to get over**, (cross)
atravesar, cruzar; (an illness, grief, etc.) reponerse
reponerse de; (excuse) perdonar; (surmount) superar;
(ground) recorrer. **to get round**, (a person) persuadir; (surround) rodear; (avoid) evitar; (difficulties) superar, vencer. **to get one's degree**, Lat. Am.
diplomarse. **to get through**, pasar por; (time) pasar,
entretener; (money) gastar; (finish) terminar, acabar;
(pierce or enter) penetrar; (communicate) comunicar
(con); (difficulties) vencer; (an exam) aprobar. **to get
the blues**, Central America acuilmarse. **to get to**, vi
llegar a; encontrar; (begin) empezar. **to get together**, vt reunir, juntar. vi reunirse, juntarse. **to get
under**, ponerse debajo de; (control) dominar. **to get
up**, vt (raise) alzar, levantar; (carry up things) subir;
(out of bed) levantarse; (dress) vestir; (learn) aprender;
(linen) blanquear, colar; (ascend) subir; hacer;
(dress) ataviar; (steam) generar; (a play) ensayar,
poner en escena. vi levantarse; (on a horse) montar a
caballo; (of the wind) refrescarse; (of the fire) avi-
varse; (of the sea) embravecerse. **to get up to**, llegar
a; alcanzar

getting /'gɛtɪŋ/ n adquisición, f; (of money) ganancia, f. **g. up**, preparación, f; organización, f; (of a
play) representación (de una comedia), puesta en escena, f

get-up /'gɛt ˌʌp/ *n* atavío, *m*; (of a book, etc.) aspecto, *m*

geyser /'gaizər/ *n* géiser, *m*; (for heating water) calentador (de agua), *m*

ghastliness /'gæstlinis/ *n* horror, *m*; palidez mortal, *f*; aspecto miserable, *m*; (boringness) tedio, aburrimiento, *m*; lo desagradable

ghastly /'gæstli/ *a* horrible; de una palidez mortal; cadavérico; (boring) aburrido; muy desagradable

ghetto /'gɛtou/ *n* gueto *m*

ghost /goust/ *n* fantasma, espectro, aparecido, *m*; (spirit) alma, *f*, espíritu, *m*; (shadow) sombra. *f*; (writer) mercenario, *m*. **Holy G.,** Espíritu Santo, *m*. **to give up the g.,** entregar el alma; perder la esperanza, desesperarse. **to look like a g.,** parecer un fantasma

ghostliness /'goustlinis/ *n* espiritualidad, *f*; lo misterioso; palidez, *f*; tenuidad, *f*

ghostly /'goustli/ *a* espiritual; espectral; misterioso; pálido; vaporoso, tenue; indistinto

ghost town *n* pueblo-fantasma, *m*

ghost word *n* palabra-fantasma, *f*

ghoul /gul/ *n* vampiro, *m*

ghoulish /'guliʃ/ *a* insano; cruel; sádico

giant /'dʒaiənt/ *n* gigante, *m*; *Fig.* coloso, *m*, *a* gigantesco; de gigantes; de los gigantes. **g.-killer,** matador de gigantes, *m*. **g.-stride,** (gymnastics) paso volante, *m*

gibber /'dʒibər/ *vi* hablar incoherentemente, hablar entre dientes; farfullar, hablar atropelladamente; decir disparates

gibberish /'dʒibəriʃ/ *n* galimatías, *m*; jerigonza, *f*, griego, *m*

gibbet /'dʒibit/ *n* horca, *f*, patíbulo, *m*. **to die on the g.,** morir ahorcado

gibbon /'gibən/ *n Zool.* gibón, *m*

gibe /dʒaib/ *n* improperio, escarnio, *m*, burla, mofa, *f*. *vi* criticar. **to g. at,** burlarse de, ridiculizar, mofarse de

gibing /'dʒaibiŋ/ *a* burlón, mofador. *n* mofas, burlas, *f pl*

gibingly /'dʒaibiŋli/ *adv* burlonamente, con sorna

giblets /'dʒiblits/ *n* menudillos, *m pl*

giddily /'gidli/ *adv* vertiginosamente; frívolamente, atolondradamente

giddiness /'gidinis/ *n* vértigo, *m*; atolondramiento, *m*; inconstancia, *f*; frivolidad, ligereza de cascos, *f*

giddy /'gidi/ *a* vertiginoso; mareado; atolondrado, casquivano, frívolo; inconstante. **She felt very g.,** Se sintió muy mareada. **to make g.,** dar vértigo (a), marear

gift /gift/ *n* regalo, *m*, dádiva, *f*; (quality) don, talento, *m*; prenda, *f*; poder, *m*; *Law.* donación, *f*; (offering) ofrenda, oblación, *f*. *vt* dotar. **deed of g.,** *Law.* escritura de donación, *f*. **in the g. of,** en el poder de, en las manos de. **I wouldn't have it as a g.,** No lo tomaría ni regalado. **Never look a g. horse in the mouth,** A caballo regalado no se le mira el diente. **g. of tongues,** don de las lenguas, genio de las lenguas, *m*

gifted /'giftid/ *a* talentoso

gig /gig/ *n* (carriage) carrocín, *m*; (boat) falúa, lancha, *f*; (for wool) máquina de cardar paño, *f*; (harpoon) arpón, *m*, (performance) actuación, *f*

gigantic /dʒai'gæntik/ *a* gigantesco; colosal, enorme

giggle /'gigəl/ *vi* reírse sin motivo; reírse disimuladamente. *n* risa disimulada, *f*

giggling /'gigliŋ/ *n* risa estúpida, *f*; risa nerviosa, *f*

gigolo /'dʒigəˌlou/ *n* gigolo, mantenido, jinetero (Cuba), *m*

gild /gild/ *vt* dorar; (metals) sobredorar; embellecer. **to g. the pill,** dorar la píldora

gilder /'gildər/ *n* dorador, *m*

gilding /'gildiŋ/ *n* dorado, *m*, doradura, *f*; embellecimiento, *m*

Gileadite /'giliəˌdait/ *n* and *a* galaadita, *mf*

gill /gil/ *n* (of fish) agalla, branquia, *f*; (ravine) barranco, *m*;

gill /dʒil/ *n* (measure) cierta medida de líquidos, *f*, (⅛ litro)

gilt /gilt/ *n* dorado, *m*; pan de oro, *m*; relumbrón, *m*;

Fig. encanto, *m*, *a* dorado, áureo. **g.-edged,** (of books) con los bordes dorados. **g.-edged security,** papel del Estado, *m*; valores de toda confianza, *m pl*

gimcrack /'dʒimˌkræk/ *n* chuchería, *f*. *a* de baratillo, cursi; mal hecho

gimlet /'gimlit/ *n* barrena, *f*, taladro, *m*

gin /dʒin/ *n* (drink) ginebra, *f*; (snare) trampa, *f*. *vt* (snare) coger con trampa. **g. block,** *Mech.* garrucha, *f*

ginger /'dʒindʒər/ *n* jengibre, *m*; *Inf.* energía, *f*, brío, *m*, *a* rojo. *vt* sazonar con jengibre; *Inf.* animar, estimular. **g.-beer,** gaseosa, *f*

gingerly /'dʒindʒərli/ *adv* con gran cuidado; delicadamente

gingham /'giŋəm/ *n* guinga, *f*

gingivitis /ˌdʒindʒə'vaitis/ *n* gingivitis, *f*

gipsy /'dʒipsi/ *n*. See **gypsy**

giraffe /dʒə'ræf/ *n* jirafa, *f*

gird /gard/ *vt* ceñir; (invest) investir; (surround) cercar, rodear; (put on) revestir. **to g. oneself for the fray,** prepararse para la lucha

girder /'gardər/ *n* viga, jácena, *f*. **main g.,** viga maestra, *f*

girdle /'gardl/ *n* (belt) cinturón, *m*; (corset) faja, *f*; circunferencia, *f*; zona, *f*. *vt* ceñir; *Fig.* cercar, rodear

girl /garl/ *n* niña, *f*; chica, muchacha, *f*; (maidservant) criada, muchacha, *f*; (young lady) señorita, *f*. **a young g.,** una jovencita; (a little older) una joven. **old g.,** (of a school) antigua alumna, *f*; *Inf.* vieja, *f*; (*Inf.* affectionate) chica, *f*. **g. friend,** amiguita, *f*. **g. guide, girl scout,** exploradora, *f*. **girls' school,** colegio de niñas, colegio de señoritas, *m*

girlhood /'garlhud/ *n* niñez, *f*; juventud, *f*

girlish /'garliʃ/ *a* de niña, de muchacha; (of boys) afeminado; joven

girth /garθ/ *n* (of horse, etc.) cincha, *f*; circunferencia, *f*; (of person) talle, *m*; (obesity) corpulencia, obesidad, *f*

gist /dʒist/ *n* esencia, substancia, *f*, importe, *m*

give /giv/ *vt* dar; (a present) regalar; (infect) contagiar; (impart) comunicar; (grant) otorgar; (allow, concede) conceder; (assign) asignar, señalar; (appoint) nombrar; (a toast) brindar (a la salud de); (a party, ball, etc.) dar; (a bill) presentar; (wish) desear; (punish) castigar; (pay) pagar; (hand over) entregar; (names at baptism) imponer; (produce) producir; dar; (cause) causar; (of judicial sentences) condenar a; (evoke) proporcionar; (provoke) provocar; (devote) dedicar, consagrar; (sacrifice) sacrificar; (evidence, an account, orders, a lesson, a performance, a concert) dar; (a cry, shout) lanzar, proferir; (a laugh) soltar; (describe) describir; (paint) pintar; (write) escribir; (offer) ofrecer; (show) mostrar; (transmit) transmitir; (heed, pain) hacer; (a speech) pronunciar, hacer; (award, adjudge) adjudicar; (ear) prestar (oído (a)). *vi* dar; ser dadivoso, mostrarse generoso; (give in) ceder; (be elastic) dar de sí; ablandarse; (collapse) hundirse. **G. them my best wishes!** ¡Dales mis mejores recuerdos! **G. us a song!** ¡Cántanos algo! **I can g. him a lift in my car,** Puedo ofrecerle un asiento en mi auto. **I g. you my word,** Os doy mi palabra. **to g. a good account of oneself,** defenderse bien; hacer bien; salir bien. **to g. a person a piece of one's mind,** contarle cuatro verdades. **to g. chase,** dar caza (a). **to g. it to a person,** poner a uno como nuevo; reprender; (beat) pegar, dar de palos. **to g. of itself,** dar de sí. **to g. rise to,** dar lugar a, ocasionar, causar. **to g. way,** no poder resistir; (break) romperse; (yield) ceder; (collapse) hundirse; (retreat) retroceder. **to g. way to,** (retreat before) retirarse ante; (abandon oneself to) entregarse a, abandonarse a. **to g. away,** enajenar; dar; regalar; (sell cheaply) vender a un precio muy bajo; (get rid of) deshacerse de; (sacrifice) sacrificar; (a secret) revelar; (betray) traicionar; (expose) descubrir; (tell) contar; (a bride) conducir al altar. **He gave himself away,** Reveló su pensamiento sin querer. **to g. back,** *vt* devolver; restituir. *vi* retirarse, cejar. **to g. forth,** divulgar, publicar; (scatter) derramar; (emit) emitir, despedir; (smoke, rays) echar. **to g. in,** *vt* entregar; presentar. *vi* darse por vencido. **to g. in to,** (agree with) asentir en, consentir en; rendirse ante. **Mary always gives in to George,** María hace siempre lo que Jorge quiere. **to g. off,** (of odors, etc.) emitir, exhalar, despedir. **to g. out,** *vt* (distribute) distribuir, repartir; (allocate) asignar; (publish) publicar; (announce) anunciar; (reveal) divulgar; (allege) afirmar, hacer saber; (emit) emitir. *vi* (be exhausted) agotarse; (end) acabarse; (be lacking) faltar. **to g. over,** *vt* entregar; (transfer) traspasar; cesar de. *vi* cesar. **to g. up,** entregar; ceder; (renounce) renunciar (a); (sacrifice) sacrificar; (abandon) abandonar; (cease) dejar de; (as lost) dar por perdido; (of a patient) desahuciar; (a post) dimitir de; (return) devolver, restituir; (a problem) renunciar (a resolver un problema); (lose hope) perder la esperanza; (give in) darse por vencido. **I had given up on you,** (didn't expect you), Creí que no ibas a venir. **to g. oneself up to,** entregarse a; dedicarse a; *Mil.* rendirse a. **to g. up one's seat,** ceder su sitio (or asiento). **to g. upon,** (overlook) dar sobre

give /gɪv/ *n* elasticidad, *f*; el dar de sí; (concession) concesión, *f*. **g. and take,** concesiones mutuas, *f pl.*
g. away, *Inf.* revelación indiscreta, *f*
given /'gɪvən/ *a* dado; especificado; convenido; (with to) dado a, adicto a. **in a g. time,** en un tiempo dado. **g. that,** dado que
giver /'gɪvər/ *n* dador (-ra); donador (-ra)
giving /'gɪvɪŋ/ *a* = **generous**
gizzard /'gɪzərd/ *n* molleja, *f*. **It sticks in my g.,** *Inf.* No lo puedo tragar
glacial /'gleɪʃəl/ *a* glacial
glacier /'gleɪʃər/ *n* glaciar, *m*
glad /glæd/ *a* feliz, alegre; contento, satisfecho; *Inf.* elegante. **to be g.,** alegrarse, estar contento; estar satisfecho. **to give the g. eye,** hacer ojos
gladden /'glædn/ *vt* alegrar, regocijar
glade /gleɪd/ *n* claro, *m*; rasa, *f*
gladiator /'glædiˌeɪtər/ *n* gladiador, *m*
gladiolus /ˌglædi'oʊləs/ *n* *Bot.* gladíolo, gladio, *m*; espadaña, *f*
gladly /'glædli/ *adv* alegremente; con mucho gusto, gustoso, de buena gana
gladness /'glædnɪs/ *n* alegría, felicidad, *f*, contento, *m*; placer, *m*
glamorous /'glæmərəs/ *a* exótico; garboso
glamour /'glæmər/ *n* encanto, *m*, fascinación, *f*; garbo, *m*. **g. girl,** belleza exótica, *f*
glance /glæns/ *n* (of a projectile) desviación, *f*; (of light) vislumbre, *m*; relumbrón, centelleo, *m*; (look) vistazo, *m*, ojeada, *f*; mirada, *f*, *vi* desviarse; relumbrar, centellear, brillar; (with at) ojear, echar un vistazo a, lanzar miradas a; (a book) hojear; mirar; mirar de reojo; *Fig.* indicar brevemente. **at a g.,** de un vistazo; en seguida. **at the first g.,** a primera vista. **to g. off,** desviarse (al chocar). **to g. over,** repasar, echar un vistazo a; (a book) hojear
glancing /'glænsɪŋ/ *a* (of a blow) que roza
gland /glænd/ *n* (*Anat., Bot.*) glándula, *f*; (in the neck) ganglio, *m*. **to have swollen glands,** tener inflamación de los ganglios
glandular /'glændʒələr/ *a* glandular
glare /glɛər/ *n* brillo, fulgor, *m*; luminosidad, *f*; reflejo, *m*; (look) mirada feroz, *f*. *vi* relumbrar, centellear; (stare) mirar con ferocidad, mirar fijamente
glaring /'glɛərɪŋ/ *a* deslumbrante, brillante; (of colors) chillón, llamativo; (of looks) de mirada feroz; (flagrant) notorio, evidente
glaringly /'glɛərɪŋli/ *adv* brillantemente; con mirada feroz; notoriamente
glass /glæs/ *n* vidrio, *m*; cristal, *m*; (glassware) artículos de vidrio, *m pl*; cristalería, *f*; (for drinking) vaso, *m*, copa, *f*; (pane) cristal, *m*; (mirror) espejo, *m*; (telescope) telescopio, *m*; catalejo, *m*; (barometer) barómetro, *m*; (hour-glass) reloj de arena, *m*; (of a watch) vidrio (de reloj), *m*; *pl* **glasses,** (binoculars) anteojos, *m pl*; (eyeglasses) gafas, lentes, *m, f*; (opera glasses) gemelos de teatro, *m pl*, *a* de vidrio; de cristal. *vt* vidriar. **John wears glasses,** Juan lleva gafas. **The g. is falling (rising),** El barómetro baja (sube). **to clink glasses,** trincar las copas. **to look in the g.,** mirarse en el espejo. **clear g.,** vidrio trasparente, *m*. **cut g.,** cristal tallado, *m*. **frosted g.,** vidrio jaspeado, *m*. **plate-g.,** vidrio plano, *m*; **safety g.,** vidrio inastillable, *m*. **stained**

g., vidrio de color, vidrio pintado, *m*. **under g.,** bajo vidrio; en invernáculo. **g. bead,** abalorio, *m*; cuenta de vidrio, *f*. **g.-blower,** soplador de vidrio, *m*. **g.-blowing,** el soplar de vidrio. **g. case,** escaparate, *m*. **g.-cloth,** paño para vasos, *m*. **g. eye,** ojo de cristal, *m*. **g. paper,** papel de vidrio, *m*. **g. roof,** techo de cristal, *m*. **g. window,** vidriera, *f*
glasscutter /'glæsˌkʌtər/ *n* cortador de vidrio, *m*
glassful /'glæsfʊl/ *n* contenido de un vaso, *m*; vaso, vaso lleno, *m*, copa, *f*
glasshouse /'glæsˌhaʊs/ *n* fábrica de vidrio, *f*; vidriería, *f*; invernáculo, invernadero, *m*, estufa, *f*
glassware /'glæsˌwɛər/ *n* cristalería, *f*
glassy /'glæsi/ *a* vitreo; (of eyes) vidrioso; *Fig.* cristalino; (smooth) liso, raso
glaze /gleɪz/ *n* barniz, *m*: luster, brillo, *m*. *vt* poner vidrios (a); vidriar; barnizar; (paper, leather, etc.) satinar. *vi* (of eyes) vidriarse, ponerse vidrioso
glazier /'gleɪʒər/ *n* vidriero, *m*
glazing /'gleɪzɪŋ/ *n* vidriado, *m*; barnizado, *m*; satinado, *m*; (material) barniz, *m*
gleam /glim/ *n* rayo, destello, *m*; (of color) viso, *m*, mancha, *f*; *Fig.* rayo, *m*; (in the eye) chispa, *f*. *vi* relucir, centellear, resplandecer; brillar; reflejar la luz; *Fig.* brillar. **g. of hope,** rayo de esperanza, *m*
gleaming /'glimɪŋ/ *a* reluciente, centelleante; brillante. *n* see **gleam**
glean /glin/ *vt* espigar, rebuscar; recoger. *vi* espigar
gleaner /'glinər/ *n* espigador, *m*; recogedor (-ra)
gleaning /'glinɪŋ/ *n* espigueo, *m*; rebusca, recolección, *f*; *pl* **gleanings,** fragmentos, *m pl*
glee /gli/ *n* alegría, *f*, júbilo, alborozo, *m*; *Mus.* canción para voces solas, *f*
gleeful /'glifəl/ *a* alegre, jubiloso, gozoso
gleefully /'glifəli/ *adv* alegremente, con júbilo
glen /glɛn/ *n* cañada, *f*, cañón, *m*, hondonada, *f*
glib /glɪb/ *a* locuaz, voluble; (easy) fácil
glibness /'glɪbnɪs/ *n* locuacidad, volubilidad, *f*; (easiness) facilidad, *f*
glide /glaɪd/ *n* deslizamiento, *m*; *Aer.* planeo, *m. vi* deslizarse; resbalar; *Aer.* planear. **to g. away,** escurrirse; desaparecer silenciosamente
glider /'glaɪdər/ *n* *Aer.* deslizador, planeador, *m*
gliding /'glaɪdɪŋ/ *n* *Aer.* vuelo sin motor, *m*
glimmer /'glɪmər/ *n* luz trémula, luz débil, *f*, tenue resplandor, *m*; vislumbre, *m. vi* brillar con luz trémula, rielar *Fig.*; tener vislumbres (de)
glimpse /glɪmps/ *n* vistazo, *m*; vislumbre, *m*; indicio, *m*; impresión, *f*; vista, *f. vt* entrever, divisar; tener una vista (de); ver por un instante; vislumbrar
glint /glɪnt/ *n* tenue resplandor, *m*; lustre, *m*; centelleo, *m*; reflejo, *m*; (in the eye) chispa, *f. vi* relucir, destellar, rutilar; reflejar
glisten /'glɪsən/ *vi* brillar, relucir
glistening /'glɪsənɪŋ/ *a* coruscante; brillante, reluciente
glitter /'glɪtər/ *n* brillo, resplandor, *m*, rutilación, *f. vi* brillar, resplandecer, relucir; rutilar. **All that glitters is not gold,** Todo lo que reluce no es oro
glittering /'glɪtərɪŋ/ *a* reluciente, resplandeciente; *Fig.* brillante
gloat (over) /gloʊt/ *vi* recrearse en, gozarse en, deleitarse en
globe /gloʊb/ *n* globo, *m*; esfera, *f*; (for fish) pecera, *f*; (for gas, electric light) globo, *m*. **geographical g.,** globo terráqueo, *m*; globo mapamundi, *m*. **g.-trotter,** trotamundos, *mf*
globular /'glɒbyələr/ *a* globular, esférico
globule /'glɒbyul/ *n* glóbulo, *m*
gloom /glum/ *n* obscuridad, *f*; lobreguez, *f*, tinieblas, *f pl*; *Fig.* melancolía, tristeza, *f*; taciturnidad, *f. vi* *Fig.* ponerse melancólico; ser taciturno
gloomily /'glumli/ *adv* obscuramente; *Fig.* tristemente; taciturnamente
gloomy /'glumi/ *a* obscuro; sombrío, lóbrego; melancólico, triste; taciturno; (of prospects, etc.) poco halagüeño, nada atrayente
glorification /ˌglɔrəfɪ'keɪʃən/ *n* glorificación, *f*
glorify /'glɔrəˌfaɪ/ *vt* glorificar; exaltar; alabar

glorious /ˈglɔːriəs/ *a* glorioso; espléndido, magnífico; insigne; *Inf.* estupendo

glory /ˈglɔːri/ *n* gloria, *f*; esplendor, *m*, magnificencia, *f*; *Art.* gloria, *f*. *vi* recrearse, gozarse; glorificarse, jactarse. **to be in one's g.**, estar en la gloria. **to g. in,** hacer gala de, glorificarse en

gloss /glɒs/ *n* (sheen) lustre, brillo, *m*; *Fig.* apariencia, *f*; (note) glose, *m*; (excuse) disculpa, *f*. *vt* pulir; glosar. **to g. over,** (faults) disculpar, excusar

glossary /ˈglɒsəri/ *n* glosario, *m*

glossiness /ˈglɒsɪnɪs/ *n* lustre, *m*, tersura, *f*; brillo, *m*

glossy /ˈglɒsi/ *a* lustroso, terso; brillante; (of hair) liso

glottal stop /ˈglɒtl/ *n* choque glótica, golpe de glotis, *m*

glottis /ˈglɒtɪs/ *n Anat.* glotis, *f*

glove /glʌv/ *n* guante. **evening gloves,** guantes largos, *m pl.* **to be hand in g. with,** juntar diestra con diestra. **to fit like a g.**, sentar como un guante. **to put on one's gloves,** ponerse los guantes. **g. shop,** guantería, *f*. **g.-stretcher,** ensanchador (-ra) de guantes, abridor (-ra) de guantes *mf*

glove compartment gaveta, guantera, *f*, guantero, portaguantes *m*

glove-compartment light /glʌv kəmˈpɑːtmənt/ luz de portaguantes, *f*

glover /ˈglʌvər/ *n* guantero (-ra)

glow /glou/ *n* incandescencia, *f*; claridad, *f*; luz difusa, *f*; (heat) calor, *m*; (of color) intensidad, *f*; color vivo, *m*; (enthusiasm) ardor, entusiasmo, *m*; (redness) rojez, *f*; (in the sky) arrebol, *m*; (of pleasure, etc.) sentimiento de placer, *m*; sensación de bienestar, *f*. *vi* estar incandescente; arder; abrasarse; sentir entusiasmo; mostrarse rojo; experimentar un sentimiento de placer o una sensación de bienestar. **to g. with health,** estar rebosando de salud. **g.-worm,** luciérnaga, *f*

glower /ˈglauər/ *n* ceño, *m*; mirada amenazadora, *f*. *vi* poner cara de pocos amigos, mirar airadamente; tener los ojos puestos (en)

glowing /ˈglouɪŋ/ *a* candente, incandescente; ardiente; entusiasta; satisfecho; intenso; (bright) vivo; (red) encendido; (with health) rebosante de salud. *n* see **glow**

glowingly /ˈglouɪŋli/ *adv* encendidamente; *Fig.* con entusiasmo

glucose /ˈglukous/ *n* glucosa, *f*

glue /glu/ *n* engrudo, *m*, cola, *f*. *vt* encolar, engrudar; pegar; *Fig.* fijar, poner. **He kept his eyes glued on them,** Tenía los ojos fijados (or pegados) en ellos. **g.-pot,** pote de cola, *m*

gluey /ˈglui/ *a* gomoso; pegajoso, viscoso

glueyness /ˈgluinɪs/ *n* viscosidad, *f*

gluing /ˈgluiŋ/ *n* encoladura, *f*

glum /glʌm/ *a* deprimido, taciturno, sombrío

glumly /ˈglʌmli/ *adv* taciturnamente

glut /glʌt/ *n* superabundancia, *f*, exceso, *m*. *vt* (satiate) hartar; *Fig.* saciar; (the market) inundar

gluteal /ˈglutiəl/ *a* glúteo

glutinous /ˈglutnəs/ *a* glutinoso, pegajoso, viscoso

glutton /ˈglʌtn/ *n* glotón (-ona); *Fig.* ávido (-da)

gluttonous /ˈglʌtnəs/ *a* glotón, comilón

gluttony /ˈglʌtni/ *n* glotonería, gula, *f*

glycerin /ˈglɪsərɪn/ *n* glicerina, *f*

gnarled /nɑːld/ *a* nudoso; (of human beings) curtido

gnash /næʃ/ *vt* rechinar, crujir (los dientes)

gnashing /ˈnæʃɪŋ/ *n* rechinamiento (de dientes), *m*

gnat /næt/ *n* mosquito, *m*

gnaw /nɔ/ *vt* roer; morder; (of wood by worms) carcomer; *Fig.* roer

gnawing /ˈnɔɪŋ/ *n* roedura, *f*; mordedura, *f*, *a* roedor; mordedor

gnome /noum/ *n* nomo, *m*

gnostic /ˈnɒstɪk/ *a* and *n* nóstico (-ca)

gnosticism /ˈnɒstɪsɪzəm/ *n* nosticismo, *m*

go /gou/ *vi* ir; (depart) irse, marcharse; (go toward) dirigirse a, encaminarse a; (lead to, of roads, etc.) conducir a, ir a; (vanish) desaparecer; (leave) dejar, salir de; (lose) perder; (pass) pasar; (of time) transcurrir, pasar; (be removed) quitarse; (be prohibited) prohibirse; (fall) caer; (collapse) hundirse; (be torn off) desprenderse; desgajarse; *Mech.* funcionar, trabajar, andar; (sound) sonar; (of the heart) palpitar, latir; (follow) seguir; (gesture) hacer un gesto; (be stated) decirse, afirmarse; (live) vivir; (wear) llevar; (turn out) salir, resultar; (improve) mejorar; (prosper) prosperar; (turn, become) ponerse; volverse; (to sleep) dormirse; (into a faint) desmayarse; (decay) echarse a perder, estropearse; (turn sour) agriarse; (become, adopt views, etc.) hacerse; (be sold) venderse; (be decided) decidirse, ser decidido; (have) tener; (by will) pasar; (belong) pertenecer; (receive) recibir; (have its place) estar; (put) ponerse; (going plus infin.) ir a; (die) morir, irse; (do a journey, a given distance) hacer; (a pace, step) dar; (take) tomar; (escape) escaparse, (contribute) contribuir (a); (harmonize) armonizar (con); (be current) ser válido; (be) ser; (of a document, etc., run) rezar, decir; (attend) asistir a; (be broken) estar roto; (be worn) estar raído; (be granted) darse, otorgarse. **It's gone five,** Ya dieron las cinco. **It's time to be going,** Es hora de marcharse. **Let's go!** ¡Vamos! **These two colors go well together,** Estos colores armonizan bien. **Well, how goes it?** Bueno, ¿qué tal? ¿Cómo te va? **Who goes there?** *Mil.* ¿Quién va? **to go and fetch,** ir a buscar. **to let go,** soltar; dejar ir. **to go one's way,** seguir su camino. **to go wrong,** salir mal, fracasar; (sin) descarriarse. **"Go!"** (traffic sign) «¡Siga!» **Go on!** ¡Adelante!; (continue) ¡Siga!; *Inf.* ¡Qué va! **to go about,** dar la vuelta a; rodear; recorrer; (undertake) emprender, hacer; intentar; (of news, etc.) circular; *Naut.* virar de bordo. **Go about your business!** ¡Métete en lo que te importa! **to go abroad,** ir al extranjero; salir a la calle; publicarse, divulgarse. **to go across,** cruzar, atravesar; pasar. **to go after,** andar tras; seguir; (seek) ir a buscar; (persecute) perseguir. **to go again,** ir de nuevo; (be present) asistir otra vez; volver. **to go against,** ir contra; militar contra; oponerse a; ser desfavorable a. **to go ahead,** adelantar, avanzar; progresar; prosperar; (lead) ir a la cabeza (de), conducir; *Naut.* marchar hacia adelante. **to go along,** andar por; recorrer; (depart) irse, marcharse. **go apartment-hunting,** ir en busca de piso. **to go along with,** acompañar (a). **to go aside,** quitarse de en medio; apartarse, retirarse. **to go astray,** perderse; extraviarse, descarriarse. **to go at,** atacar, acometer; (undertake) emprender; empezar a. **to go at it again,** *Inf.* volver a la carga. **to go away,** irse, marcharse; ausentarse; alejarse; desaparecer. **to go away with,** marcharse con; (an object) llevarse. **to go back,** volver, regresar, *Lat. Am.* devolverse; (retreat) retroceder, volverse atrás; (in history) remontarse a. **to go back on,** (a promise, etc.) faltar a; (retract) retractarse; (betray) traicionar. **to go backwards,** retroceder, cejar; desandar lo andado; *Fig.* deteriorar, empeorar. **to go backwards and forwards,** ir y venir; oscilar. **to go before,** (lead) ir a la cabeza de, conducir; anteceder; proceder; (a judge, etc.) comparecer ante. **to go behind,** ir detrás de; esconderse detrás de; seguir; (evidence, etc.) mirar más allá de. **to go between,** ponerse entre; interponerse; (as a mediator) mediar; (insert) intercalarse; (travel) ir entre; llevar cartas entre, ser mensajero de. **to go beyond,** ir más allá; exceder. **to go by,** pasar por; pasar cerca de, pasar junto a; ir por; (of time) transcurrir, pasar; (follow) seguir; guiarse por, atenerse a; (judge by) juzgar por; (a name) pasar por; tomar el nombre de. **to go down,** bajar, descender; (of the sun) ponerse; (sink) hundirse; sumergirse; (fall) caer; (be remembered) ser recordado; (believe) tragar; ser creído. **to go down again,** bajar de nuevo; volver a caer. **to go Dutch,** ir a escote, ir a la gringa, ir a la par, ir a limón. **to go far,** ir lejos; influir mucho (en); impresionar mucho; (contribute) contribuir (a). **to go for,** (seek) ir en busca de; procurar tener; (attack) echarse encima de, atacar. **to go for a ride (by car, bicycle, on horseback),** dar un paseo (en coche, en bicicleta, a caballo). **to go forth,** salir; publicarse. **to go forward,** adelantar, avanzar; progresar; continuar; (happen) tener lugar. **to go from,** dejar, abandonar; separarse de, apartarse de; marcharse de. **to go in,** entrar en; (a railway carriage, etc.) subir a; (compete) concurrir. **to go in again,** volver a entrar en, entrar de nuevo en. **to go in and out,** entrar y salir; ir y venir. **to go in for,** entrar a buscar; dedicarse a, entregarse a; (buy) comprarse; tomar parte en; (an examination) tomar (un examen); (for a competition) entrar en (un concurso); (try) ensayar; arriesgar. **to go into,** entrar en; examinar; investigar; ocuparse con. **to go native,** *Lat. Am.* acriollarse. **to go near,** acercarse a. **to go off,** marcharse; (explode) estallar; (of fire-arms) dispararse; (of the voice, etc.) perder (la voz, etc.); (run away) huir, fugarse. **to go off badly,** salir mal, fracasar, no tener éxito. **to go off well,** salir bien, tener éxito. **to go on,** subirse a; continuar; durar; avanzar; proseguir su marcha; progresar; prosperar; *Theat.* entrar en escena; (of clothes) ponerse; (rely on) apoyarse en. **to go on an excursion, go on an outing, go on a trip,** *Lat. Am.* excursionarse. **Don't go on like that,** No seas así, No te pongas así. **This glove will not go on me,** No puedo ponerme este guante. **to be gone on a person,** *Inf.* estar loco por. **I went on to say...,** Después dije; Continuando mi discurso dije... **It was going on six o'clock when...** Serían alrededor de las seis cuando... **He is going on fifty,** Raya en los cincuenta años. **to go on foot,** ir a pie. **to go on with,** continuar con; empezar. **to go out,** salir; (descend) bajar; (of fires, lights) extinguirse, apagarse; (of fashion, etc.) pasar (de); (the tide) menguar; (retire) retirarse; (in society) frecuentar la alta sociedad; (die) morir; (arouse) excitar. **to go out of** salir de, *Lat. Am. also* egresar de. **to go out of fashion,** pasar de moda. **to go out of one's way (to),** dejar su camino (para); (lose oneself) perder el camino, extraviarse; (take trouble) desvivirse (por), tomarse molestia (para). **to go over,** cruzar; pasar por encima; (to another party or to the other side) pasarse a; (read) repasar; examinar. **to go past,** pasar; pasar en frente de. **to go round,** dar la vuelta a; (revolve) girar; (surround) rodear; (of news, etc.) divulgarse; (be enough) ser suficiente para todos. **to go through,** ir por, pasar por; recorrer; (pierce) penetrar, atravesar; (examine) examinar; (suffer) padecer, sufrir; (experience) experimentar; (live) vivir; (of time) pasar; (of money) malgastar, derrochar. **to go to,** ir a, encaminarse a; (a person) acercarse a, dirigirse a; (help, be useful) servir para; (be meant for) destinarse a; (rise of price) subir a; (find) encontrar; (of a bid) subir una apuesta hasta. **to go to war,** declarar la guerra. **to go together,** ir juntos (juntas). **to go toward,** encaminarse hacia; ir hacia; (help) ayudar a. **to go under,** pasar por debajo de; (sink) hundirse; (fail) fracasar; (be bankrupt) arruinarse, declararse en quiebra; (the name of) hacerse pasar por. **to go up,** subir; ir arriba; (a tree) trepar; (a ladder, etc.) subir; (a river) ir río arriba; (to town) ir a; (explode) estallar. **to go up and down,** subir y bajar; oscilar; ir de una parte a otra. **to go upon,** subirse a; (rely on) apoyarse en; obrar según; emprender. **to go upstairs,** ir arriba; (to another story, as in an apartment) subir al otro piso; subir la escalera. **to go up to,** acercarse a; (of a bid) subir una apuesta hasta. **to go with,** acompañar; (agree with) estar de acuerdo con; (of principles) seguir, ser fiel a; (harmonize) armonizar con; (be suitable to) ir bien con; convenir a; (*Inf.* get along) ir. **to go without,** marcharse sin; (lack) pasarse sin. **It goes without saying that...,** Huelga decir que.... **Where are you going with this?** (What do you mean?) ¿A dónde quieres llegar con esto?

go /gou/ *n* (fashion) moda, boga, *f*; (happening) suceso, *m*; (fix) apuro, *m*; (energy) energía, *f*, empuje, brío, *m*; (turn) turno, *m*; (attempt) tentativa, *f*; (action) movimiento, *m*, acción, *f*; (bargain) acuerdo, *m*. **It's a go!** (agreed) ¡Trato hecho! ¡Acordado! ¡Entendidos! ¡Entendidas! **It is all the go,** Hace furor, Es la gran moda. **It is no go,** No puede ser, Es imposible. **Now it's my go,** Ahora me toca a mí, Ahora es mi turno. **on the go,** en movimiento; entre manos; ocupado. **to have a go,** probar suerte; procurar, tratar de; tener un turno

goad /goud/ *n* garrocha, aguijada, *f*, aguijón, *m*, *Lat. Am.* lanceta *f*; *Fig.* acicate, estímulo, *m.* *vt* aguijar, picar; *Fig.* incitar, estimular, empujar. **prick with a g.,** aguijonazo, *m*

go-ahead /'gou ə,hɛd/ *a* emprendedor: progresivo **goal** /goul/ *n* (posts in football, etc.) meta, portería, *f*, *Lat. Am.* arco, *m*; (score) gol, *m*; (in racing) meta, *f*; (destination) destinación, *f*; *Fig.* ambición, *f*; (purpose, objective) fin, objeto, *m*. **to score a g.,** marcar un gol. **g.-keeper,** guardameta, *m*, portero (-ra). **g.-post,** palo de la portería, *m*

goat /gout/ *n* cabra, *f*; *Astron.* capricornio, *m*. **he-g.,** cabrón, *m*. **young g.,** cabrito, *m*, chivo (-va). **g.-herd,** cabrero, *m*. **g. skin,** piel de cabra, *f*; (wineskin) odre, *m*

goatee /gou'ti/ *n* pera, perilla, *f*

goatish /'goutɪʃ/ *a* cabruno; de cabra; lascivo

gobble /'gɒbəl/ *vt* and *vi* engullir, tragar. *vi* (of turkey) gluglutear. *n* glugluteo, *m*, voz del pavo, *f*

go-between /'gou bɪ,twin/ *n* trotaconventos, *f*; alcahuete, *m*; (mediator) medianero (-ra)

goblet /'gɒblɪt/ *n* copa, *f*

goblin /'gɒblɪn/ *n* trasgo, duende, *m*

go-cart /'gou ,kɑrt/ *n* andaderas, *f pl*; pollera, *f*; cochecito de niño, *m*

god /gɒd/ *n* dios, *m*; *pl* **gods,** dioses, *m pl*; (in a theater) público del paraíso, *m*; paraíso, *m*. **By God!** ¡Vive Dios! **For God's sake,** ¡Por el amor de Dios!; ¡Por Dios! **Please God,** ¡Plegue a Dios! **Thank God!** ¡Gracias a Dios! **God Bless You!** (to someone who has sneezed) ¡Salud! **God forbid!** ¡No lo quiera Dios! **God grant it!** ¡Dios lo quiera! **God keep you!** ¡Dios le guarde! ¡Vaya Vd. con Dios! **God willing,** Dios mediante. **My father, God rest his soul, was...,** Mi padre, que Dios perdone, era...

godchild /'gɒd,tʃaild/ *n* ahijado (-da)

goddess /'gɒdɪs/ *n* diosa, *f*; *Poet.* dea, *f*

godfather /'gɒd,faðər/ *n* padrino, *m*. **to be a g. to,** ser padrino de, sacar de pila (a)

godfearing /'gɒd,fiərɪŋ/ *a* timorato, temeroso de Dios; religioso

godforsaken /'gɒdfɔr,seikən/ *a* dejado de la mano de Dios; (of places) remoto, solitario

Godhead /'gɒd,hɛd/ *n* divinidad, *f*

godless /'gɒdlɪs/ *a* impío, irreligioso; sin Dios

godlessness /'gɒdlɪsnɪs/ *n* impiedad, irreligiosidad, *f*

godlike /'gɒd,laik/ *a* divino

godliness /'gɒdlinɪs/ *n* piedad, *f*; santidad, *f*

godling /'gɒdlɪŋ/ *n* diosecillo, *m*

godly /'gɒdli/ *a* devoto, piadoso, religioso

godmother /'gɒd,mʌðər/ *n* madrina, *f*. **fairy g.,** hada madrina, *f*. **to be a g. to,** ser madrina de

godparent /'gɒd,pɛərənt/ *n* padrino, *m*; madrina, *f*, *pl.* **godparents,** padrinos, *m pl*

godsend /'gɒd,sɛnd/ *n* bien, *m*; buena suerte, *f*; fortuna, *f*

go-getter /'gou ,gɛtər/ *n* buscavidas, *mf*

goggle /'gɒgəl/ *n* mirada fija, *f*; *pl* **goggles,** anteojos, *m pl*, gafas, *f pl*; (of a horse) anteojeras, *f pl*. *vi* mirar fijamente; salirse a uno los ojos de la cabeza. **g.-eyed,** de ojos saltones. **g.-eyes,** ojos saltones, *m pl*

going /'gouɪŋ/ *n* ida, *f*; (departure) partida, marcha, *f*; salida, *f*; (pace) paso, *m*; (speed) velocidad, *f*. **It was heavy g.,** El avance era lento; El progreso era lento; (of parties, etc.) Era aburrido. **The g. was difficult on those mountainous roads,** El conducir (or el ir or el andar) era difícil en aquellos caminos de montaña. **g. back,** vuelta, *f*, regreso, *m*. **g. down,** bajada, *f*, descenso, *m*; (of the sun, etc.) puesta, *f*. **g. forward,** avance, *m*; progreso, *m*. **g. in,** entrada, *f*. **g. in and out,** idas y venidas, *f pl*. **g. out,** salida, *f*; (of a fire, light) apagamiento, *m*

going /'gouɪŋ/ *a* and *pres part* que va, yendo; que funciona. **G., g.,** gone (at an auction) A la una, a las dos, a las tres. **goings-on,** (tricks) trapujos, *m pl*; (conduct) conducta, *f*. **g. concern,** empresa próspera, *f*. **g. to,** con destino a

going-away present /'gouɪŋ ə,wei/ *n* regalo de despedida, *m*

goiter /'gɔitər/ *n* bocio, *m*

gold /gould/ *n* oro, *m*; color de oro, *m. a* de oro; áureo. **All that glitters is not g.,** No es oro todo lo que reluce. **cloth of g.,** tela de oro, *f*. **dull g.,** oro cchecito de niño, *m*. **light g.,** oro pálido, *m*. **old g.,** oro viejo, *m*. **g.-beater,** batidor de oro, *m*. **g.-digger,** minero de oro, *m*; (woman) aventurera, *f*. **g. dust**, oro en polvo, *m*. **g.-fever**, fiebre de oro, *f*. **g. lace**, galón de oro, *m*. **g. lacquer**, sisa dorada, *f*. **g. leaf**, pan de oro, oro batido, *m*. **g.-mine**, mina de oro, *f*. **g. piece**, moneda de oro, *f*. **g. plate**, vajilla de oro, *f*. **g. standard**, patrón oro, *m*. **g.-thread**, hilo de oro, *m*. **g.-yielding**, *a* aurífero

golden /'gouldən/ *a* de oro; dorado; áureo; amarillo; *Fig.* feliz; excelente. **to become g.**, dorarse. **g. age**, edad de oro, *f*. **G. Age**, (Spanish literature) El Siglo de Oro, *m*. **g.-crested wren**, abadejo, *m*. **g. hair**, cabellos dorados (or de oro), *m pl*. **G. Legend**, leyenda áurea, *f*. **g. mean**, justo medio, *m*. **g. rose**, rosa de oro, *f*. **g. rule**, regla áurea, *f*. **g. syrup**, jarabe de arce, *m*. **g. voice**, voz de oro, *f*. **g. wedding anniversary**, bodas de oro, *f pl*

goldfinch /'gould,fıntʃ/ *n* jilguero, *m*

goldfish /'gould,fıʃ/ *n* carpa dorada, *f*. **g. bowl**, pecera, *f*

goldrush /'gould,rʌʃ/ carrera de oro, *f*

goldsmith /'gould,smıθ/ *n* orfebre, oribe, orífice, *m*

golf /gɒlf/ *n* golf, *m*. **g.-club**, (stick) palo de golf, *m*; (organization) club de golf, *m*

golfer /'gɒlfər/ *n* jugador (-ra) de golf

gonad /'gounæd/ *n* gonada, *f*

gondola /'gɒndlə/ *n* góndola, *f*

gondolier /,gɒndl'ıər/ *n* gondolero, *m*

gone /gɒn/ *a* and *past part* ido; (lost) perdido; (ruined) arruinado; (dead) muerto; (past) pasado; (disappeared) desaparecido; (fainted) desmayado; (suppressed) suprimido; (drunk) borracho; (ended) terminado; (exhausted) agotado; (ill) enfermo. **far g.**, avanzado; (in years) de edad avanzada; (of illness) cerca de la muerte, muy enfermo; (in love) loco de amor; (drunk) muy borracho. **It is all g.**, No hay más. **It is g. seven o'clock**, Son las siete y pico, Son las siete ya

gong /gɒŋ/ *n* gong, *m*; (Chinese) batintín, *m*

gonorrhea /,gɒnə'riə/ *n* gonorrea, *f*

good /gʊd/ *a* bueno (before *m sing* nouns) buen; agradable; afortunado; (appropriate) apropiado, oportuno; (beneficial) provechoso, ventajoso; (wholesome) sano, saludable; (suitable) apto; (useful) útil; (kind) bondadoso; (much) mucho; (obliging) amable; (virtuous) virtuoso; (skilled) experto; (fresh) fresco; (genuine) genuino, legítimo; verdadero. *adv* bien. *interj* ¡bueno! ¡bien! **a g. deal**, mucho. **a g. many**, bastantes. **a g. turn**, un favor. **a g. way**, (distance) un buen trecho; mucho. **a g. while**, un buen rato. **as g. as**, tan bueno como. **Be so g. as to...!** Haga el favor de, Tenga Vd. la bondad de (followed by infin.). **fairly g.**, *a* bastante bueno. *adv* bastante bien. **g. for another five miles**, Tengo fuerzas para cinco millas más. **It was g. of you to do it**, Vd. fue muy amable de hacerlo, Vd. tuvo mucha bondad de hacerlo. **to be no g. at this sort of thing**, no servir para tales cosas. **to have a g. time**, pasarlo bien. **to make g.**, reparar; indemnizar; (accomplish) llevar a cabo, poner en práctica; justificar; (a promise) cumplir. **very g.**, *a* muy bueno. *adv* muy bien. **g.-feeling**, buena voluntad, *f*. **g.-fellowship**, compañerismo, *m*; buena compañía, *f*. **g.-for-nothing**, *n* papanatas, badulaque, *m*. **to be g.-for-nothing**, no servir para nada. **g. luck**, buena suerte, *Lat. Am. also* derechura, leche *f*. **g. manners**, buenos modales, *m pl*; buena crianza, educación, *f*. **g. nature**, buen humor, *m*. **g.-natured**, de buen natural; de buen humor, bonachón. **g.-step**, paso de oca, *m*. **g. offices**, buenos oficios, *m pl*. **g.-tempered**, de buen humor

good /gʊd/ *n* bien, *m*; provecho, *m*; utilidad, *f*; *pl* **goods.** See separate entry. **I am saying this for your g.**, Lo digo para tu bien. **Much g. may it do you!** ¡Buen provecho le haga! **for g. and all**, para siempre jamás. **It is no g.**, Es inútil; No vale la pena. **the g.**, el bien; (people) los buenos. **They have gone to the g.**, Se han marchado para no volver. **to do one g.**, hacer bien a uno; mejorar; ser provechoso a (uno); (suit) sentar bien (a uno). **What is the g. of...?** ¿Para qué sirve...?; ¿Qué vale...? **g. and evil**, el bien y el mal

good-bye /gʊd 'baı/ *interj* ¡adiós! *n* adiós, *m*, despedida, *f*. **to bid g.-b.**, decir adiós. **G.-b. for the**

present! ¡Hasta la vista! ¡Hasta luego! **G.-b. until tomorrow, then**, Hasta mañana pues, adiós, Hasta mañana entonces

goodness /'gʊdnıs/ *n* bondad, *f*; (of quality) buena calidad, *f*; (of persons) amabilidad, benevolencia, *f*; (essence) esencia, substancia, *f*; bien, *m*: excelencia, *f*; *interj* ¡Jesús! ¡Dios mío! **For g. sake!** ¡Por Dios! **I wish to g. that**, ¡Ojalá que...!

goods /gʊdz/ *n pl* bienes, efectos, *m pl*; artículos, *m pl*; *Com.* mercancías, *f pl*, géneros, *m pl*. **by g.-train**, en pequeña velocidad. **stolen g.**, objetos robados, *m pl*. **g. lift**, montacargas, *m*. **g. office**, depósito de mercancías, *m*. **g. station**, estación de carga, *f*. **g.-train**, tren de mercancías, *m*. **g. van**, furgón, *m*. **g. wagon**, vagon de mercancías, *m*

good-smelling /'gʊd ,smɛlıŋ/ *a* oloroso

goodwill /'gʊd'wıl/ *n* benevolencia, *f*; buena voluntad, *f*; (of a business) clientela, *f*

goose /gus/ *n* oca, *f*, ganso (-sa); plancha de sastre, *f*. *a* de oca. **g.-flesh**, *Fig.* carne de gallina, *f*. **g. girl**, ansarera, *f*. **g.-step**, paso de oca, *m*

gooseberry /'gus,bɛri/ *n* uva espina, *f*

Gordian /'gɔrdiən/ *a* gordiano. **G. knot**, nudo gordiano, *m*

gore /gɔr/ *n* sangre, *f*; *Sew.* sesga, nesga, *f*. *vt* acornear; desgarrar; herir (con arma blanca)

gorge /gɔrdʒ/ *n* (valley) cañón, barranco, *m*; (heavy meal) comilona, *f*, atracón, *m*. *vt* engullir, tragar. *vi* hartarse, atracarse

gorgeous /'gɔrdʒəs/ *a* magnífico; espléndido, suntuoso; *Inf.* maravilloso, estupendo

gorgeously /'gɔrdʒəsli/ *adv* magníficamente

gorgeousness /'gɔrdʒəsnıs/ *n* magnificencia, *f*; suntuosidad, *f*, esplendor, *m*

gorilla /gə'rılə/ *n* gorila, *m*

gormandize /'gɔrmən,daiz/ *vi* glotonear

gormandizer /'gɔrmən,daizər/ *n* glotón (-ona)

gory /'gɔri/ *a* ensangrentado; sangriento

gosh /gɒʃ/ *interj* ¡caray! ¡caramba!

goshawk /'gɒs,hɔk/ *n* *Ornith.* azor, *m*

gosling /'gɒzlıŋ/ *n* ansarino, *m*

gospel /'gɒspəl/ *n* evangelio, *m*; doctrina, *f*. **The G. according to St. Mark**, El Evangelio según San Marcos. **to believe as g. truth**, creer como si fuese el evangelio. **to preach the G.**, predicar el evangelio

gossamer /'gɒsəmər/ *n* hilo de araña, *m*, red de araña, telaraña, *f*; (filmy material) gasa, *f*; hilo finísimo, *m*, *a* de gasa; sutil, delgado, fino

gossip /'gɒsəp/ *n* murmurador (-ra), chismoso (-sa), hablador (-ra); (scandal) chisme, *m*, *Lat. Am. also* lengüeterías *fpl*; habladuría, murmuración, *f*; (obsolete; of a woman) comadre, *f*; (talk) charla, *f*. *vi* charlar, conversar; (in bad sense) murmurar, chismear; criticar. **to g. about**, charlar de; poner lenguas en; cortar un sayo (a); hablar mal de (uno). **g. column**, gacetilla, *f*

gossiping /'gɒsəpıŋ/ *a* charlatán, hablador; chismoso, murmurador. *n* See **gossip**

Goth /gɒθ/ *n* godo (-da); bárbaro (-ra)

Gothic /'gɒθık/ *a* *Art.* gótico; (of race) godo, bárbaro. *n* (language) gótico, *m*; arquitectura gótica, *f*. **G. characters**, letra gótica, *f*

gouge /gaudʒ/ *n* gubia, *f*. *vt* escoplear. **to g. out**, vaciar; sacar

gourd /gɔrd/ *n* calabaza, *f*

gourmand /gʊr'mɑnd/ *n* glotón, *m*

gourmet /gʊr'mei/ *n* gastrónomo, *m*

gout /gaut/ *n* *Med.* gota, *f*

gouty /'gauti/ *a* gotoso

govern /'gʌvərn/ *vt* gobernar; regir; (guide) guiar; dominar; domar, refrenar; *Gram.* regir; (regulate) regular

governable /'gʌvərnəbəl/ *a* gobernable; manejable; dócil

governess /'gʌvərnıs/ *n* institutriz, *f*; (in a school) maestra, *f*

governing /'gʌvərnıŋ/ *a* gubernante; director; (with principle, etc.) directivo. *n* See **government**

government /'gʌvərnmənt, -ərmənt/ *n* gobierno, *m*; dirección, *f*; autoridad, *f*. **g. bond**, bono del gobierno,

m. **g. house,** palacio del gobernador, *m.* **g. office,** oficina del gobierno, *f.* **g. stock,** papel del Estado, *m*
governmental /ˌgʌvərn'mentl̩, ˌgʌvər-/ *a* gubernamental, gubernativo.

Government Printing Office Talleres Gráficos de la Nación, *m pl*

governor /'gʌvərnər/ *n* gobernador (-ra); vocal de la junta de gobierno, *mf;* (of a prison) director (-ra) (de una prisión); *Mech.* regulador, *m.* **g.-general,** gobernador general, *m*

governorship /'gʌvərnərˌʃɪp/ *n* gobierno, *m;* dirección, *f*

gown /gaun/ *n* toga, *f;* (cassock) sotana, *f;* (dressing-g.) bata, *f;* (for sleeping) camisa de noche, *f;* (bathing-wrap) albornoz, *m;* (dress) vestido, traje, *m*

Goyesque /gɔi'esk/ *a* goyesco

grab /græb/ *n* asimiento, *m,* presa, *f; Mech.* gancho, *m. vt* arrebatar, asir, agarrar; *Fig.* alzarse con, tomar

grabber /'græbər/ *n* cogedor (-ra); codicioso (-sa)

grace /greis/ *n* elegancia, *f;* simetría, armonía, *f;* gracia, gentileza, *f,* donaire, *m;* encanto, *m;* (goodness) bondad, *f;* gracia, *f;* merced, *f,* favor, *m;* (period of time) plazo, *m;* (privilege) privilegio, *m; Theol.* gracia divina, *f;* (at table) bendición de la mesa, *f;* (as a title) excelentísimo, (to an archbishop) ilustrísimo. *vt* adornar; favorecer; honrar. **airs and graces,** humos, *m pl.* **the Three Graces,** las Gracias. **three days' g.,** plazo de tres días, *m.* **to get into a person's good graces,** congraciarse con; caer en gracia con. **to say g.,** bendecir la mesa. **with a bad g.,** a regañadientes. **with a good g.,** de buena gana. **g.-note,** *Mus.* nota de adorno, *f*

graceful /'greisfəl/ *a* airoso, gentil, gracioso; elegante; bonito

gracefully /'greisfəli/ *adv* airosamente, gentilmente; con gracia; elegantemente

gracefulness /'greisfəlnɪs/ See **grace**

graceless /'greislɪs/ *a* réprobo; dejado de la mano de Dios; sin gracia

gracious /'greiʃəs/ *a* (merciful) piadoso, clemente; (urbane) afable, condescendiente, agradable. **Good g.!** ¡Vamos!, ¡Dios mío!

graciously /'greiʃəsli/ *adv* afablemente; con benevolencia. **to be g. pleased,** tener a bien

graciousness /'greiʃəsnɪs/ *n* amabilidad, afabilidad, condescendencia, *f*

gradation /grei'deiʃən/ *n* graduación, *f; Mus.* gradación, *f;* paso gradual, *m;* serie, *f*

grade /greid/ *n* grado, *m;* (quality) calidad, clase, *f;* (class in school) clase, *f,* (evaluation of coursework) nota, *f;* (gradient) pendiente, *f,* declive, *m. vt* graduar, clasificar; (cattle breeding) cruzar. **down g.,** cuesta abajo. **up g.,** cuesta arriba. **highest g.,** *n* primera clase, *f. a* de primera clase; de calidad excelente

gradient /'greidiənt/ *n* declive, *m.* cuesta, pendiente, *f*

gradual /'grædʒuəl/ *a* gradual. *n Eccl.* gradual, *m*

gradually /'grædʒuəli/ *adv* gradualmente; poco a poco

graduate /n, a 'grædʒuɪt; v -ˌeit/ *n* licenciado (-da), *Lat. Am.* exalumno (na) *mf a* graduado. *vt* graduar. *vi* graduarse; (as a doctor) doctorarse. **to g. as,** recibirse de. **be graduated from.—** *Lat. Am.* egresar de...

graduation /ˌgrædʒu'eiʃən/ *n* graduación, *f, Lat. Am.* egreso *m*

graft /græft/ *n Bot.* injerto, *m; Surg.* injerto de piel, *m;* (swindle) estafa, *f;* (bribery) soborno, *m. vt Bot.* injertar; *Surg.* injertar un trozo de piel; *Fig.* inferir

grafting /'græftɪŋ/ *n Bot.* injerto, *m; Surg.* injerto de piel, *m; Fig.* inserción, *f*

grain /grein/ *n* (corn) grano, *m;* (cereal) cereal, *m,* or *f;* (seed, weight) grano, *m;* (trace) pizca, *f;* (of wood, etc.) hila, *m,* fibra, hebra, veta, *f;* (of leather) flor, *f;* (texture) textura, *f. vt* granear; granular; (wood, marble, etc.) vetear. **against the g.,** a contrapelo. **g. lands,** mieses, *f pl*

gram /græm/ *n* graino, *m*

grammar /'græmər/ *n* gramática, *f.* **g. school,** instituto de segunda enseñanza, *m*

grammarian /grə'meəriən/ *n* gramático, *m*

grammatical /grə'mætikəl/ *a* gramático

grammatically /grə'mætikəli/ *adv* gramaticalmente, como la gramática lo quiere. (e.g., *She now speaks Catalan g.,* Ahora habla el catalán como la gramática lo quiere)

grammaticalness /grə'mætikəlnɪs/ *n* corrección gramatical, *f*

gramophone /'græməˌfoun/ *n* gramófono, *m.*

granary /'greinəri/ *n* granero, hórreo, *m,* troj, *f, Mexico* espiguero *m.* **g. keeper,** trojero, *m*

grand /grænd/ *a* magnífico, soberbio; imponente; (of dress) espléndido, vistoso; (of people) distinguido, importante; aristocrático; (proud) orgulloso; (of style) elevado, sublime; (morally) noble; augusto; (main) principal; (full) completo; *Inf.* estupendo, magnífico; (with duke, etc.) gran. *n* piano de cola, *m.* **g.-aunt,** tía abuela, *f.* **g. cross,** gran cruz, *f.* **g. duchess,** gran duquesa. *f.* **g. duke,** gran duque, *m.* **g. lodge,** (of freemasons) Gran Oriente, *m.* **g. master,** gran maestre, *m.* **g.-nephew,** resobrino, *m.* **g.-niece,** resobrina, *f.* **g. opera,** ópera, *f.* **g. piano,** piano de cola, *m.* **g.-stand,** tribuna, *f.* **g.-uncle,** tío abuelo, *m.* **g. vizier,** gran visir, *m*

grandchild /'grænˌtʃaild/ *n* nieto (-ta). **great-g.,** bisnieto (-ta). **great-great-g.,** tataranieto (-ta)

granddaughter /'grænˌdɔtər/ *n* nieta, *f.* **great-g.,** bisnieta, *f.* **great-great-g.,** tataranieta, *f*

grandee /græn'di/ *n* grande (de España, grande de Portugal), *m*

grandeur /'grændʒər/ *n* magnificencia, *f;* grandiosidad, *f;* magnitud, grandeza, *f;* (pomp) pompa, *f,* fausto, *m*

grandfather /'grænˌfɑðər/ *n* abuelo, *m.* **great-g.,** bisabuelo, *m.* **great-great-g.,** tatarabuelo, *m*

grandfather clock reloj de péndulo, *m*

grandfatherly /'grænˌfɑðərli/ *a* de abuelo

grandiloquence /græn'dɪləkwəns/ *n* grandilocuencia, *f*

grandiloquent /græn'dɪləkwənt/ *a* grandílocuo

grandiose /'grændiˌous/ *a* grandioso, sublime; impresionante; imponente; (in a bad sense) extravagante; (of style) bombástico, hinchado

grand jury *n* jurado de acusación, jurado de juicio, *m*

grandmother /'grænˌmʌðər/ *n* abuela, *f.* **great-g.,** bisabuela, *f.* **great-great-g.,** tatarabuela, *f*

grandness /'grændnɪs/ *n* magnificencia, *f;* aristocracia, *f;* (pride) orgullo, *m;* grandiosidad, *f;* (of style) sublimidad, *f;* (of character) nobleza, *f*

grandparent /'grænˌpeərənt/ *n* abuelo, *m;* abuela, *f; pl* **grandparents,** abuelos, *m pl.* **great-great-grandparents,** bisabuelos, *m pl.* **great-great-grandparents,** tatarabuelos, *m pl*

grandson /'grænˌsʌn/ *n* nieto, *m.* **great-g.,** bisnieto, *m.* **great-great-g.,** tataranieto, *m*

grange /greindʒ/ *n* granja, *f;* casa de campo, *f*

granite /'grænɪt/ *n* granito, *m*

granny /'græni/ *n* abuelita, nana, *f;* abuela, *f.* **g. knot,** nudo al revés, *m*

grant /grænt/ *n* concesión, *f;* otorgamiento, *m;* donación, *f;* privilegio, *m;* (for study) beca, bolsa de estudio, *f;* (transfer) traspaso, *m,* cesión, *f. vt* conceder; (bestow) otorgar, dar; donar; (agree to) acceder a, asentir en; permitir; (transfer) traspasar; (assume) suponer. **to g. a degree,** expedir un título. **to g. a motion,** dar por entrada a una moción. **to take for granted,** descontar, dar por hecho, dar por sentado. **God g. it!** ¡Dios lo quiera! **granted that,** dado que, *f*

grantee /græn'ti/ *n* cesionario (-ia), adjudicatorio (-ia)

grantor /'græntər/ *n* cesionista, *mf;* otorgador (-ra)

granulated /'grænyəˌleitid/ *a* granulado

granule /'grænyul/ *n* gránulo, *m*

granulous /'grænyələs/ *a* granuloso

grape /greip/ *n* uva, *f.* **bunch of grapes,** racimo de uvas, *m.* **muscatel g.,** uva moscatel, *f.* **sour grapes,** uvas agrias, *f pl;* (phrase) ¡están verdes! **g.-fruit,** toronja, *f.* **g. gatherer,** vendimiador (-ra). **g. harvest,** vendimia, *f.* **g. juice,** mosto, *m.* **g.-shot,** metralla, *f.* **g. stone,** granuja, *f.* **g.-sugar,** glucosa, *f.* **g.-vine,** vid, parra, *f*

graph /græf/ *n* gráfica, *f;* diagrama, *m*

graphic /'græfik/ *a* gráfico

graphite /'græfait/ n grafito, m

graphology /græ'fɒlədʒi/ n grafología, f

grapple /'græpəl/ n Naut. rezón, arpeo, m; lucha a brazo partido, f. vt Naut. aferrar; asir, agarrar. vi Naut. aferrarse. **to g. with,** luchar a brazo partido (con); Fig. luchar con

grappling /'græpliŋ/ n Naut. aferramiento, m; lucha cuerpo a cuerpo, f; (with a problem) lucha con, f

grasp /græsp/ n agarro, m; (reach) alcance, m; (of a hand) apretón, m; (power) garras, f pl, poder, m; (understanding) comprensión, f; inteligencia, capacidad intelectual, f. vt agarrar, asir; empuñar; abrazar; Fig. comprender, alcanzar; (a hand) estrechar. vi agarrarse. **within one's g.,** al alcance de uno. **to g. at,** asirse de

grasping /'græspiŋ/ n asimiento, m; (understanding) comprensión, f, a codicioso, tacaño, mezquino

graspingness /'græspiŋnis/ n codicia, f

grass /græs/ n hierba, f; (pasture) pasto, herbaje, m; (sward) césped, m. vt cubrir de hierba; sembrar de hierba; apacentar. **to hear the g. grow,** sentir crecer la hierba. **to let the g. grow,** Fig. dejar crecer la hierba. **to turn out to g.,** echar al pasto. **g.-blade,** brizna de hierba, f. **g.-green,** a and n verde como la hierba m.. **g.-grown,** cubierto de hierba. **g.-land,** pradera, f. **g.-snake,** culebra f. **g. widow,** mujer cuyo marido está ausente

grasshopper /'græs,hɒpər/ n saltamontes, m. **grasshopper's chirp,** chirrido (del saltamontes), m

grassy /'græsi/ a parecido a la hierba, como la hierba; cubierto de hierba; de hierba

grate /greit/ n parrilla, f; (grating) reja, f. vt raspar, raer; Cul. rallar; (make a noise) hacer rechinar. vi rozar; rechinar, chirriar. **to g. on, upon,** (of sounds) irritar, molestar; chocar con. **to g. on the ear,** herir el oído

grateful /'greitfəl/ a agradecido, reconocido; (pleasant) agradable, grato

gratefully /'greitfəli/ adv agradecidamente; gratamente

gratefulness /'greitfəlnis/ n agradecimiento, m, gratitud, f; (pleasantness) agrado, m

grater /'greitər/ n Cul. rallador, m

gratification /,grætəfɪ'keiʃən/ n satisfacción, f; (pleasure) placer, gusto, m

gratified /'grætə,faid/ a satisfecho, contento

gratify /'grætə,fai/ vt satisfacer; (please) gratificar, agradar

gratifying /'grætə,faiiŋ/ a satisfactorio, agradable

grating /'greitiŋ/ n reja, f; rejilla, f; Naut. jareta, f; (optics) retículo, m; (sound) rechinamiento, chirrido, m. a rechinante, chirriador; áspero

gratis /'grætis/ a and adv gratis

gratitude /'græti,tud/ n agradecimiento, m, gratitud, f

gratuitous /grə'tuitəs/ a gratuito

gratuitousness /grə'tuitəsnis/ n gratuidad, f

gratuity /grə'tuiti/ n gratificación, propina, f

grave /greiv/ n (hole) sepultura, fosa, f; (monument) tumba, f, sepulcro, m; Fig. muerte, f. **g.-digger,** enterrador, sepulturero, m

grave /greiv/ a grave; importante; serio; sobrio; (anxious) preocupado; (of accent) grave. n (grave accent) acento grave, m

gravel /'grævəl/ n grava, f; cascajo, casquijo, m; Med. arenillas, f pl, cálculo, m

gravely /'greivli/ adv gravemente; seriamente

Graves' disease /greivz/ n bocio exoftálmico, m

gravestone /'greiv,stoun/ n lápida mortuoria, f

graveyard /'greiv,yard/ n camposanto, cementerio, m

gravitate /'grævi,teit/ vi gravitar; tender

gravitation /,grævi'teiʃən/ n gravitación, f; tendencia, f

gravitational /,grævi'teiʃənl/ a de gravitación, gravitacional, gravitatorio

gravitational pull n atracción gravitatoria, f

gravity /'græviti/ n Phys. gravedad, f; seriedad, f; solemnidad, f; gravedad, f; (weight) peso, m; importancia, f; (enormity) enormidad, f; (danger) peligro, m. **center of g.,** centro de gravedad, m. **law of g.,** ley de la gravedad, f. **specific g.,** peso específico, m

gravy /'greivi/ n salsa, f; jugo (de la carne), m. **g.-boat,** salsera, f

gray /grei/ a gris; (of animals) rucio. n color gris, gris, m; caballo gris, m. **g. hairs,** canas, f. **His hair is turning g.,** Se le está saliendo canas. **g.-haired,** de pelo gris. **g. matter,** materia gris, f; cacumen, m. **g. mullet,** Ichth. mújol, m. **g. squirrel,** gris, m. **g. wolf,** lobo gris, m

grayish /'greiiʃ/ a grisáceo, agrisado; (of hair) entrecano

grayness /'greinis/ n color gris, gris, m; Fig. monotonía, f

graze /greiz/ n abrasión, f; (brush) roce, m, vi pacer, apacentarse. vt pastorear, apacentar; (brush) rozar

grazing /'greiziŋ/ n Agr. apacentamiento, pastoreo, m; (brushing) rozadura, f. a que pace, herbívoro; (of land) pacedero. **g. land,** pasto, m

grease /gris/ n grasa, f; (dirt) mugre, f; (of a candle) sebo, m, cera, f. vt engrasar; manchar con grasa; Fig. Inf. untar. **to g. the wheels,** Fig. untar el carro. **g.-box,** Mech. caja de sebo, f. **g.-gun,** engrasador de compresión, m. **g.-paint,** afeites de actor (or de actriz), m pl. **g.-proof paper,** papel impermeable, m. **g. spot,** lámpara, mancha de grasa, f, saín, m

greaser /'grisər/ n engrasador, m

greasiness /'grisinis/ n graseza, f; lo aceitoso; untuosidad, f

greasing /'grisiŋ/ n engrasado, m

greasy /'grisi/ a grasiento; (oily) aceitoso; (grubby) mugriento, bisunto, Argentina cascarriento; Fig. lisonjero. **g. pole,** cucaña, f

great /greit/ a gran; grande; enorme; vasto; (much) mucho; (famous) famoso, ilustre; noble, sublime; (intimate) íntimo; importante; principal; poderoso; magnífico, impresionante; Inf. famoso, estupendo; (of time) largo; (clever) fuerte. **Alexander the G.,** Alejandro Magno. **the G. Mogul,** el Gran Mogul. **a g. deal,** mucho. **a g. man,** un grande hombre, un hombre famoso. **a g. many,** muchos (muchas). **He lived to a g. age,** Vivió hasta una edad avanzada. **so g.,** tan grande, tamaño. **the g.,** los grandes hombres. **g. on,** aficionado a. **g.-aunt,** tía abuela, f. **g.-grandchild,** etc. See **grandchild,** etc. **g.-hearted,** valeroso; magnánimo, generoso. **g. power,** gran poder, m. **G. Britain,** Gran Bretaña, f **G. War,** Gran Guerra, f. **the Great Schism,** el Gran Cisma, m

greater /'greitər/ a comp. of **great,** mayor; más grande. **to make g.,** agrandar

greatest /'greitist/ a sup. of **great,** más grande; mayor; máximo; más famoso; sumo

greatly /'greitli/ adv mucho; con mucho; (very) muy; noblemente

greatness /'greitnis/ n grandeza, f; grandiosidad, f; extensión, vastedad, f; importancia, f; poder, m; majestad, f; esplendor, m; (intensity) intensidad, f; (enormity) enormidad, f

Greco- prefix (in compounds) greco-, greco

Greece /gris/ Grecia, f

greed /grid/ n (cupidity) codicia, rapacidad, avaricia, f; avidez, ansia, f; (of food) gula, glotonería, f

greedily /'gridəli/ adv codiciosamente; con avidez; (of eating) vorazmente

greedy /'gridi/ a (for food) glotón; codicioso; ambicioso; ávido; deseoso

Greek /grik/ a griego. n griego, m, griega f; (language) griego, m. **It's all G. to me,** Para mí es como si fuese en latín, Me es chino. **G. tunic,** peplo, m

green /grin/ a verde; (inexpert) inexperto, bisoño; (recent) nuevo, reciente; (fresh) fresco; (of complexion) pálido, descolorido; (flowery) floreciente; (vigorous) lozano; (young) joven; (unripe) verde; (credulous) crédulo; (raw) crudo; (of wood, vegetables) verde. n verde, color verde, m; (vegetables) verdura, f; (meadow) prado, m; (turf) césped, m; (grass) hierba, f; (bowling) campo de juego, m. vt teñir (or pintar) de verde. **dark g.,** n verdinegro, m. **light g.,** n verde pálido, m. **to grow** or **look g.,** verdear. **g.-eyed,** de ojos verdes. **g. peas,** guisantes, m pl. **g. table,** tapete verde, m

greenery /'grinəri/ n follaje, m; verdura, f

greengrocery /'griŋ͵grousəri/ n verduleria, f
greenhorn /'griŋ͵hɔrn/ n bisoño (-ña); papanatas, m
greenhouse /'griŋ͵haus/ n invernáculo, invernadero, Lat. Am. conservatorio m
greenish /'griniʃ/ a verdoso. **g.-yellow,** cetrino
Greenland /'grinlənd/ Groenlandia, f
Greenlander /'grinləndər/ n groenlandés (-esa)
greenness /'grinnis/ a lo verde; verdor, m, verdura, f; (inexperience) falta de experiencia, f; (vigor) vigor, m, lozanía, f; (newness) novedad, f; (of wood, fruit) falta de madurez, f
greenroom /'grin͵rum/ n Theat. saloncillo, m
greenstuff /'grin͵stʌf/ n hortalizas, legumbres, f pl
greet /grit/ vt saludar; recibir; (express pleasure) dar la bienvenida (a)
greeting /'gritiŋ/ n salutación, f, saludo, m; recepción, f; (welcome) bienvenida, f; pl **greetings,** recuerdos, m pl
gregarious /gri'gɛəriəs/ a gregario
gregariousness /gri'gɛəriəsnis/ n gregarismo, m
Gregorian /gri'gɔriən/ a gregoriano
grenade /gri'neid/ n granada, bomba, f. **hand-g.,** bomba de mano, f
grey /grei/ See **gray**
greyhound /'grei͵haund/ n galgo, lebrel, m. **g. bitch,** galga, f; **g. racing,** carreras de galgos, f pl
grid /grid/ n (of electric power) red, f; rejilla, f; (for water, etc.) alcantarilla, f
gridiron /'grid͵aiərn/ n Cul. parrilla, f; (of electric power) red, f; Theat. telar, m
grief /grif/ n angustia, pena, aflicción, f; dolor, suplicio, m. **to come to g.,** pasarlo mal, tener un desastre
grievance /'grivəns/ n injusticia, f; motivo de queja, m
grieve /griv/ vt entristecer, afligir, angustiar; atormentar. vi entristecerse, afligirse, acongojarse. **to g. for,** lamentar; echar de menos
grievous /'grivəs/ a (heavy) oneroso, gravoso; opresivo; doloroso, penoso; lamentable; cruel. **g. error,** error lamentable
grievousness /'grivəsnis/ n (weight) peso, m; carácter opresivo, m; dolor, m, aflicción, f; enormidad, f; crueldad, f
griffin /'grifin/ n grifo, m; (Fig. chaperon) carabina, f; (dog) grifón, m
grill /gril/ n Cul. parrilla, f; (grating) rejilla, f; (before a window) reja, f; (food) asado a la parrilla, m. vt Cul. asar a la parrilla; (burn) quemar; (question) interrogar; (torture) torturar. vi Cul. asarse a la parrilla; (be burnt) quemarse. **g.-room,** parrilla, f
grille /gril/ n reja, f; rejilla, f; (screen) verja, f
grilled /grild/ a Cul. a la parrilla; con rejilla
griller /'grilər/ n Cul. parrilla, f
grim /grim/ a (fierce) feroz, salvaje; (severe) severo, ceñudo, adusto; inflexible; (frightful) horrible
grimace /'griməs/ n mueca, f, gesto, mohín, visaje, m, vi hacer muecas
grime /graim/ n mugre, f; suciedad, f. **to cover with g.,** enmugrecer
grimly /'grimli/ adv severamente; sin sonreír; inflexiblemente; (without retreating) sin cejar; (frightfully) horriblemente; de un modo espantoso
grimness /'grimnis/ n (ferocity) ferocidad, f; (severity) severidad, f; inflexibilidad, f; (frightfulness) horror, m, lo espantoso
grimy /'graimi/ a mugriento, sucio
grin /grin/ n sonrisa grande, f; sonrisa burlona, f; (grimace) mueca, f. vi sonreír mostrando los dientes; sonreír bonachonamente; sonreír de un modo burlón
grind /graind/ vt (to powder) pulverizar; moler; (break up) quebrantar; (oppress) agobiar, oprimir; (sharpen) afilar, amolar; (a barrel-organ) tocar (un manubrio); (the teeth) crujir, rechinar (los dientes); (into) reducir a; (Inf. teach) empollar. vi moler; Inf. trabajar laboriosamente. n Inf. trabajo pesado, m; Inf. estudiantón, m
grinder /'graindər/ n (of scissors, etc.) afilador, m; (of an organ) organillero; (mill-stone) piedra de moler, f; (molar) muela, f
grinding /'graindiŋ/ a (tedious) cansado, aburrido; opresivo; (of pain) incesante. n pulverización, f;

amoladura, f; (of grain) molienda, f; (polishing) pulimento, bruñido, m; (oppression) opresión, f; (of teeth) rechinamiento, m
grindstone /'graind͵stoun/ n amoladera, afiladera, f, piedra de amolar, f. **to have one's nose to the g.,** batir el yunque
grinning /'griniŋ/ a sonriente; riente; (mocking) burlón
grip /grip/ n asimiento, agarro, m; (claws, clutches) garras, f pl; (hand) mano, f; (of shaking hands) apretón de manos, m; (of a weapon, etc.) empuñadura, f; (reach) alcance, m; (understanding) comprensión, f; (control) dominio, m; (bag) portamanteo, m; maleta, f. vt asir, agarrar; (of wheels) agarrarse; Mech. morder; (a sword, etc.) empuñar; (pinch) pellizcar; (surround) cercar; (understand) comprender; (press; to grip the hand and Fig. the heart) apretar; (fill) llenar; (the attention) atraer, llamar; (sway, hold) dominar
gripe /graip/ n (Inf. pain) retortijón (de tripas), m. vi quejarse (de)
grisly /'grizli/ a espantoso; repugnante
grist /grist/ n molienda, f. **Everything is g. to their mill,** Sacan partido de todo
gristle /'grisəl/ n cartílago, m, ternilla, f
gristly /'grisli/ a cartilaginoso
grit /grit/ n cascajo, m; polvo, m; Fig. firmeza (de carácter), f; (courage) valor, m; (endurance) aguante, m
gritty /'griti/ a arenoso, arenisco
grizzled /'grizəld/ a (of hair, etc.) gris; canoso; grisáceo
grizzly bear /'grizli/ n oso (-sa) pardo (-da)
groan /groun/ n gemido, m. vi gemir; (creak) crujir. **to g. out,** decir (o contar) entre gemidos. **to g. under,** sufrir bajo, gemir bajo; (of weight) crujir bajo
groaning /'grouniŋ/ n gemidos, m pl. a que gime, gemidor; (under a weight) crujiente
grocer /'grousər/ n abacero (-ra) vendedor (-ra) de comestibles, Lat. Am. abarrotero (-ra). **grocer's shop,** tienda de comestibles, bodega, f, Mexico abarrotería, f
grocery /'grousəri/ n tienda de comestibles, tienda de ultramarinos, abarrotería, lonja, bodega, f, negocio de comestibles, m; pl **groceries,** provisiones, f pl, comestibles, m pl, Lat. Am. abarrotes mpl
groin /grɔin/ n Anat. ingle, f
groom /grum/ n (in a royal household) gentilhombre, m; lacayo, m; mozo de caballos, m; (of a bride) novio, m. vt (a horse) cuidar; (oneself) arreglarse. **She is always well groomed,** Está siempre muy bien arreglada
groomsman /'grumzmən/ n padrino de boda, m
groove /gruv/ n ranura, muesca, f; estría, f; surco, m; Fig. rutina, f. vt entallar; estriar
grooved /gruvd/ a con ranura; estriado
grope /group/ vi andar a tientas; (with for) buscar a tientas; procurar, encontrar, buscar. **to g. one's way toward,** avanzar a tientas hacia; Fig. avanzar poco a poco hacia
gropingly /'groupiŋli/ adv a tientas; irresolutamente
gross /grous/ n Com. gruesa, f; totalidad, f, a grueso; denso, espeso; (unrefined) grosero; (great) grande; (crass) craso; total; Com. bruto; (tremendous) enorme. **in g.,** en grueso. **g. amount,** total, m; Com. importe bruto, m. **g. weight,** peso bruto, m
grossly /'grousli/ adv groseramente; (much) enormemente
grossness /'grousnis/ n gordura, f; (vulgarity) grosería, f; obscenidad, f; (enormity) enormidad, f
grotesque /grou'tesk/ a grotesco; extravagante, estrambótico; ridículo. n grotesco, m
grotesqueness /grou'tesknis/ n lo grotesco; ridiculez, f
grotto /'grɒtou/ n gruta, f
ground /graund/ n suelo, m; (of water and Naut.) fondo, m; (earth) tierra, f; Fig. terreno, m; (strata) capa, f; Sports. campo, m; (parade) plaza (de armas), f; (background) fondo, m; (basis) base, f, fundamento, m; (reason) causa, f; motivo, m; (excuse) pretexto, m; pl **grounds,** jardines, m pl, parque, m; (sediment) sedimento, m, heces, f pl; (reason) causa, f. vi Naut. varar, encallar. vt poner en tierra; Naut.

hacer varar; *Elec.* conectar con tierra; (base) fundar (en), basar (en); (teach) enseñar los rudimentos (de). *a* molido; en polvo; (of floors, stories) bajo; (of glass) deslustrado; *Bot.* terrestre. **common g.,** tierra comunal, *f*; *Fig.* tierra común, *f*. **He is on his own g.,** Está en terreno propio. **It fell to the g.,** Cayó al suelo; *Fig.* Fracasó. **It is on the g.,** Está en el suelo. **It suits me to the g.,** Me viene de perilla. **to break fresh g.,** *Fig.* tratar problemas nuevos. **to be well grounded in,** conocer bien los elementos (or rudimentos) de. **to cover g.,** cubrir terreno; recorrer; (in discussion) tocar muchos puntos. **to cut the g. from beneath one's feet,** hacer perder la iniciativa (a). **to give g.,** retroceder; perder terreno. **to raze to the g.,** echar por tierra, arrasar. **to stand one's g.,** resistir el ataque; no darse por vencido; *Fig.* mantenerse firme, mantenerse en sus trece. **to win g.,** ganar terreno. **g. coffee,** café molido, *m*. **g.-color,** (of paint) primera capa, *f*; (color de) fondo, *m*; **g.-floor,** piso bajo, *m*. **g. glass,** vidrio deslustrado, *m*. **g.-ivy,** hiedra terrestre, *f*. **g. nut,** cacahuete, *m*. **g.-plan,** *Archit.* planta, *f*. **g.-rent,** censo, *m*. **g.-sheet,** tela impermeable, *f*; **g. staff,** *Aer.* personal del aeropuerto, *m*. **g.-swell,** mar de fondo, *m*

grounded /'graundɪd/ *a* fundado. **The airplanes are g.,** Los aviones están sin vuelo. **His suspicions are well g.,** Tiene motivos para sus sospechas

grounding /'graundɪŋ/ *n Naut.* encalladura, *f*; (teaching) instrucción en los rudimentos, *f*

groundless /'graundlɪs/ *a* sin fundamento, inmotivado, sin causa, sin motivo

groundwork /'graund,wɜrk/ *n* fundamento, *m*; base, *f*; principio, *m*

group /grup/ *n* grupo, *m*. *vt* agrupar. *vi* agruparse. **g. captain,** coronel de aviación, *m*

grouping /'grupɪŋ/ *n* agrupación, *f*

grouse /graus/ *n Ornith.* ortega, *f*. *vi* rezongar, refunfuñar

grove /grouv/ *n* soto, boscaje, *m*; arboleda, *f*

grovel /'grɒvəl/ *vi* arrastrarse; *Fig.* humillarse

groveling /'grɒvəlɪŋ/ *a Fig.* servil; ruin

grow /grou/ *vi* crecer; (increase) aumentar; (become) hacerse; empezar a; llegar a; (turn) volverse, ponerse; (flourish) progresar, adelantar; (develop) desarrollarse; (extend) extenderse. *vt* cultivar; dejar crecer. **I grew to fear it,** Llegué a temerlo. **to g. cold,** ponerse frío; enfriarse; (of weather) empezar a hacer frío. **to g. fat,** engordar. **to g. hard,** ponerse duro; *Fig.* endurecerse. **to g. hot,** ponerse caliente; calentarse; (of weather) empezar a hacer calor. **to g. like Topsy,** crecer a la buena de Dios. **to g. old,** envejecer. **to g. tall,** crecer mucho; ser alto. **to g. again,** crecer de nuevo. **to g. into,** hacerse, llegar a ser; venir a ser. **to g. out of,** brotar de; originarse en; (a habit) desacostumbrarse poco a poco. **He is growing out of his clothes,** La ropa se le hace pequeña. **to g. up,** (of persons) hacerse hombre (mujer); desarrollarse; (of a custom, etc.) imponerse. **to g. on, upon,** crecer sobre; llegar a dominar; (make think) hacer creer, empezar a pensar; (of a habit) arraigar en

grower /'grouər/ *n* cultivador (-ra)

growing /'grouɪŋ/ *n* crecimiento, *m*; desarrollo, *m*; (increase) aumento, *m*; (of flowers, etc.) cultivación, *f*, *a* creciente

growing pains /peinz/ *n pl* crisis de desarrollo, *f*

growl /graul/ *n* gruñido, *m*; reverberación, *f*; trueno, *m*. *vi* gruñir; (of guns) tronar; (of thunder) reverberar. **to g. out,** decir gruñendo

grown /groun/ *a* crecido; maduro; adulto. **a g. up,** una persona mayor. **to be full-g.,** estar completamente desarrollado; haber llegado a la madurez. **g. over with,** cubierto de

growth /grouθ/ *n* crecimiento, *m*; (development) desarrollo, *m*; (progress) progreso, adelanto, *m*; (increase) aumento, *m*; (cultivation) cultivo, *m*; (vegetation) vegetación, *f*; *Med.* tumor, *m*. **He has a week's g. on his chin,** Tiene una barba de una semana

grub /grʌb/ *n* larva, *f*, gusano, *m*; *Inf. Argentina* (food) morfe, papeo, *m*. *vt* (with up, out) desarraigar; cavar; desmalezar; *Fig. Inf.* buscar

grubbiness /'grʌbinɪs/ *n* suciedad, *f*; (untidiness) desaliño, *m*

grubby /'grʌbi/ *a* lleno de gusanos; sucio; bisunto; desaliñado

grudge /grʌdʒ/ *n* motivo de rencor, *m*; rencor, resentimiento, *m*, ojeriza, *f*; mala voluntad, *f*; aversión, *f*. *vt* envidiar. **to bear a g.,** tener ojeriza

grudging /'grʌdʒɪŋ/ *a* (niggardly) mezquino; envidioso; poco afable; de mala gana; nada afable

grudgingly /'grʌdʒɪŋli/ *adv* de mala gana, contra su voluntad; con rencor; a regañadientes

gruel /'gruəl/ *n* gachas, *f pl*

gruesome /'grusəm/ *a* pavoroso, horrible; macabro

gruff /grʌf/ *a* (of the voice) bronco, grave, áspero; (of manner) brusco, malhumorado

gruffly /'grʌfli/ *adv* en una voz bronca (or áspera); bruscamente, con impaciencia, malhumoradamente

gruffness /'grʌfnɪs/ *n* aspereza, bronquedad, *f*; brusquedad, sequedad, impaciencia, *f*, mal humor, *m*

grumble /'grʌmbəl/ *n* ruido sordo, trueno, *m*; estruendo, *m*; (complaint) refunfuño, rezongo, *m*. *vi* tronar; refunfuñar, rezongar; hablar entre dientes; quejarse; protestar (contra). *vt* decir refunfuñando

grumbler /'grʌmblər/ *n* murmurador (-ra), refunfuñador (-ra)

grumbling /'grʌmblɪŋ/ *a* gruñón, refunfuñador; regañón; descontento. *n* See **grumble**

grumblingly /'grʌmblɪŋli/ *adv* a regañadientes, refunfuñando

grumpiness /'grʌmpinɪs/ *n* mal humor, *m*, irritabilidad, *f*

grumpy /'grʌmpi/ *a* malhumorado, irritable

grunt /grʌnt/ *n* gruñido, *m*. *vi* gruñir

grunting /'grʌntɪŋ/ *a* gruñidor

guarantee /,gærən'ti/ *n Law.* persona de quien otra sale fiadora, *f*; garantía, *f*; abono, *m*. *vt* garantizar; responder de; abonar; (assure) asegurar, acreditar

guarantor /'gærən,tɔr/ *n* garante, *mf*

guard /gard/ *n* (watchfulness) vigilancia, *f*; (in fencing) guardia, *f*; (of a sword) guarnición, *f*; (sentry) centinela, *m*; (soldier) guardia, *m*; (body of soldiers) guardia, *f*; (escort) escolta, *f*; (keeper) guardián, *m*; (protection) protección, defensa, *f*; (of a train) jefe de tren, *m*. *vt* guardar; proteger, defender; vigilar; (escort) escoltar. **to g. against,** guardarse de. **the changing of the g.,** el relevo de la guardia. **to be on g.,** *Mil.* estar de guardia; (in fencing) estar en guardia. **to be on one's g.,** estar prevenido, estar alerta. **to be off one's g.,** estar desprevenido. **to mount g.,** *Mil.* montar la guardia; vigilar. **guard's van,** furgón de equipajes, *m*. **g.-house,** cuerpo de guardia, *m*; prisión militar, *f*

guarded /'gardɪd/ *a* (reticent) reservado, circunspecto, prudente, discreto

guardedly /'gardɪdli/ *adv* prudentemente, con circunspección, discretamente

guardian /'gardiən/ *n* protector (-ra); guardián (-ana); *Law.* tutor, *m*. *a* que guarda; tutelar. **g. angel,** ángel de la guarda, ángel custodio, *m*; deidad tutelar, *f*

guardianship /'gardiən,ʃip/ *n* protección, *f*; patronato, *m*; *Law.* curaduría, tutela, *f*

guardsman /'gardzmən/ *n* guardia, *m*

Guatemalan /,gwatə'malən/ *a* and *n* guatemalteco (-ca)

guava /'gwavə/ *n Bot.* guayaba, *f*

guerrilla /gə'rɪlə/ *n* guerrilla, *f*; (soldier) guerrillero, *m*. *a* de guerrilla. **g. warfare,** guerra de guerrillas, *f*

guess /gɛs/ *n* adivinación, *f*; estimación, *f*; conjetura, *f*; sospecha, *f*. *vt* and *vi* adivinar; conjeturar; sospechar; imaginar; (suppose) suponer, creer; calcular. **to g. at,** formar una opinión sobre; imaginar. **a rough g.,** estimación aproximada, *f*. **at a g.,** a poco más o menos, a ojo de buen cubero. **g.-work,** conjeturas, suposiciones, *f pl*

guest /gɛst/ *n* (at a meal) convidado (-da), invitado (-da); (at a hotel, etc.) cliente (-da); *Lat. Am.* (house guest) alojado (-da); *Biol.* parásito, *m*. **g.-room,** alcoba de respeto, alcoba de honor, alcoba de huéspedes, *f*, cuarto de amigos, cuarto para invitados, *m*

guffaw /gʌ'fɔ/ n carcajada, f. vi reírse a carcajadas, soltar el trapo

Guiana /gi'ænə/ Guayana, f

guidance /'gaidn̥s/ n dirección, f; gobierno, m; (advice) consejos, m pl; inspiración, f

guide /gaid/ n (person) guía, mf; (girl g.) exploradora, f; (book and Fig.) guía, f; mentor, m; modelo, m; (inspiration) norte, m; Mech. guía, f. vt guiar; conducir; encaminar; dirigir; (govern) gobernar. **g.-book,** guía (de turistas), f. **g.-post,** poste indicador, m

guided tour /'gaidıd/ n visita explicada, visita programada, f

guideline /'gaid,lain/ Lit. falsarregla, falsilla, f; Fig. pauta, f

guiding /'gaidıŋ/ a que guía; directivo; decisivo. n See **guidance**

guild /gıld/ n gremio, m. a gremial. **g. member,** gremial, m

guilder /'gıldər/ n (coin) florín holandés, m

guile /gail/ n astucia, superchería, maña, f

guileful /'gailfəl/ a astuto

guileless /'gaillıs/ a cándido, sin malicia, inocente

guilelessly /'gaillısli/ adv inocentemente

guilelessness /'gaillısnıs/ n inocencia, candidez, f

guillotine /'gılə,tin/ n guillotina, f. vt guillotinar

guilt /gılt/ n culpabilidad, f; crimen, m; (sin) pecado, m

guilt complex complejo de culpa, m

guiltily /'gıltəli/ adv culpablemente; como si fuese culpable

guiltless /'gıltlıs/ a libre de culpa, inocente; puro; ignorante

guilty /'gılti/ a culpable; delincuente; criminal. **to find g.,** encontrar culpable. **to plead g.,** confesarse culpable. **g. party,** culpable, m

Guinea /'gıni/ Guinea, f

guinea /'gıni/ n guinea, f. **g.-fowl,** gallina de Guinea, f. **g.-pig,** conejillo de Indias, cobayo, m

guise /gaiz/ n manera, guisa, f; (garb) traje, m; máscara, f; Fig. pretexto, m. **under the g. of,** bajo el pretexto de; bajo la apariencia de

guitar /gı'tar/ n guitarra, f

guitarist /gı'tarıst/ n guitarrista, mf

gulf /gʌlf/ n golfo, m; abismo, m

Gulf Stream, the la Corriente del Golfo

gull /gʌl/ n Ornith. gaviota, f; (dupe) primo, m. vt engañar, timar, defraudar

gullet /'gʌlıt/ n esófago, m; garganta, f

gullibility /,gʌlə'bılıti/ n credulidad, f

gullible /'gʌləbəl/ a crédulo

gully /'gʌli/ n hondonada, barranca, f; (gutter) arroyo, m

gulp /gʌlp/ n trago, sorbo, m. vt engullir, tragar; (repress) ahogar; (believe) tragar. **to g. up,** vomitar

gum /gʌm/ n (of the mouth) encía, f; goma, f. vt engomar; pegar con goma. **gum arabic,** goma arábiga, f. **gum boots,** botas de goma, f. **gum-resin,** gomorresina, f. **gum starch,** aderezo, m. **gum tree,** eucalipto, m

gummy /'gʌmi/ a gomoso

gumption /'gʌmpʃən/ n sentido común, seso, m

gun /gʌn/ n arma de fuego, f; (handgun) fusil, m; (sporting g.) escopeta, f; (pistol) pistola, f, revólver, m; (cannon) cañón, m; (firing) cañonazo, m. **big gun,** Inf. pájaro gordo, m. **heavy gun,** cañón de grueso calibre, m. **gun-barrel,** cañón de escopeta, m. **gun-carriage,** cureña, f. **gun-cotton,** pólvora de algodón, f. **gun-fire,** cañonazos, m pl, fuego, m. **gun-metal,** bronce de cañón, m; pavón, m. **gun-room,** ar-

mería, f; (on a ship) polvorín, m. **gun-running,** contrabanda de armas, f. **gun-turret,** torre, f. **gun wound,** balazo, m

gunboat /'gʌn,bout/ n cañonero, m, lancha bombardera, f

gunflint /'gʌn,flınt/ n piedra de escopeta, f

gunman /'gʌnmən/ n escopetero, armero, m; bandido armado, m; gángster, apache, m

gunner /'gʌnər/ n artillero, m; escopetero, m

gun permit n licencia de armas, f, permiso de armas, m

gunpowder /'gʌn,paudər/ n pólvora, f

gunshot /'gʌn,ʃɒt/ n escopetazo, m; tiro de fusil, m

gunsmith /'gʌn,smıθ/ n escopetero, m

gunwale /'gʌnl̩/ n Naut. regala, borda, f

gurgle /'gɜrgəl/ n murmullo, murmurio, gorgoteo, m; gluglú, m; (of a baby) gorjeo, m. vi murmurar; hacer gluglú; (of babies) gorjear

gurgling /'gɜrglıŋ/ a murmurante; (of babies) gorjeador. n See **gurgle**

gush /gʌʃ/ n chorro, m; (of words) torrente, m; (of emotion) efusión, f. vi chorrear, borbotar; surtir, surgir. **to g. out,** saltar, brotar a borbotones, salir a borbollones, salira borbotones. **to g. over,** Fig. hablar con efusión de

gushing /'gʌʃıŋ/ a hirviente; (of people) efusivo, extremoso, empalagoso

gusset /'gʌsıt/ n Sew. escudete, m

gust /gʌst/ n (of wind) ráfaga, bocanada (de aire), f; Fig. arrebato, acceso, m

gusto /'gʌstou/ n brío, m; entusiasmo, m

gusty /'gʌsti/ a borrascoso

gut /gʌt/ n intestino, m, tripa, f; (catgut) cuerda de tripa, f; Naut. estrecho, m; pl **guts,** tripas, f pl; (content) meollo, m, substancia, f; (stamina) aguante, espíritu, m. vt (of fish, etc.) destripar; (plunder) saquear; destruir por completo; quemar completamente

gutter /'gʌtər/ n canal, m; (of a street) arroyo (de la calle), m; (ditch) zanja, f; Fig. hampa, f. vt surcar. vi gotear; (of a candle) cerotear, gotear la cera. **g. spout,** canalón, m

guttersnipe /'gʌtər,snaip/ n golfillo, m; niño (-ña) del hampa

guttural /'gʌtərəl/ a gutural. n letra gutural, f

guy /gai/ n (rope) viento, m; Naut. guía, f; (effigy) mamarracho, m; (scarecrow) espantajo, m; Inf. (fellow) tipo, m, Mexico chavo. vt sujetar con vientos o guías; burlarse de

guzzle /'gʌzəl/ vt tragar, engullir. vi atracarse, engullir; emborracharse. n comilón, m; borrachera, f

guzzler /'gʌzlər/ n tragador (-ra); borracho (-cha)

gymnasium /dʒɪm'naziəm/ n gimnasio, m

gymnast /'dʒɪmnæst/ n gimnasta, mf

gymnastic /dʒɪm'næstɪk/ a gimnástico. **g. rings,** anillas, f pl

gymnastics /dʒɪm'næstıks/ n gimnasia, f

gynecological /,gainıkə'lɒdʒıkəl/ a ginecológico

gynecologist /,gainı'kɒlədʒıst/ n ginecólogo (-ga)

gynecology /,gainı'kɒlədʒi/ n ginecología, f

gypsum /'dʒıpsəm/ n yeso, m

gypsy /'dʒıpsi/ n gitano (-na); gitanesco (-ca); (music) flamenco

gyrate /'dʒaireit/ vi girar, rodar

gyration /dʒai'reiʃən/ n giro, m, vuelta, f

gyratory /'dʒairə,tɔri/ a giratorio

gyro-compass /'dʒairou ,kʌmpəs/ n brújula giroscópica, f

gyroscope /'dʒairə,skoup/ n Phys. giroscopio, m

H

h /eitʃ/ n (letter) hache, f
ha /hɑ/ interj ¡ah!
ha, ha! /hɑ/ interj ¡ja, ja!
haberdasher /'hæbər,dæʃər/ n mercero, m
haberdashery /'hæbər,dæʃəri/ n mercería, f
habiliment /hə'bɪləmənt/ n vestidura, f; pl **habiliments,** indumentaria, f
habilitate /hə'bɪlɪ,teit/ vt habilitar
habilitation /hə,bɪlɪ'teiʃən/ n habilitación, f
habit /'hæbɪt/ n costumbre, f, hábito, m; (temperament) temperamento, carácter, m; (use) uso, m; (of body) complexión, constitución, f; Eccl. hábito, m. **to be in the h. of,** soler, acostumbrar, estar acostumbrado a. **to have bad habits,** estar malacostumbrado. **to have the bad h. of,** tener el vicio (or la mala costumbre) de. **to contract the h. of,** contraer la costumbre de. **h. maker,** sastre de trajes de montar, m
habitable /'hæbɪtəbəl/ a habitable, vividero
habitat /'hæbɪ,tæt/ n (Bot., Zool.) medio, m, habitación, f
habitation /,hæbɪ'teiʃən/ n habitación, f
habit-forming /'hæbɪt,fɔrmɪŋ/ a enviciador, que crea vicio
habitual /hə'bɪtʃuəl/ a habitual, acostumbrado, usual; constante; común
habitually /hə'bɪtʃuəli/ adv habitualmente; constantemente; comúnmente
habituate /hə'bɪtʃu,eit/ vt habituar, acostumbrar
habituation /hə,bɪtʃu'eiʃən/ n habituación, f
habitué /hə'bɪtʃu,ei/ n parroquiano (-na); veterano (-na)
hack /hæk/ n caballo de alquiler, m; rocín, jaco, m; (writer) escritor mercenario, m. vt acuchillar; tajar, cortar. vi cortar. **to h. to pieces,** cortar en pedazos; pasar a cuchillo
hacker /'hækər/ n (computer) violador de seguridades, m
hacking /'hækɪŋ/ a (of coughs) seco
hackle /'hækəl/ n (for flax, hemp) rastrillo, m
hackney carriage /'hækni/ n coche de plaza, coche de alquiler, m
hackneyed /'hæknid/ a gastado, trillado, muy usado, repetido, resobado
hacksaw /'hæk,sɔ/ n sierra de cerrajero, sierra para metal, f
hackwork /'hæk,wɜrk/ n trabajo de rutina, m
haddock /'hædək/ n merlango, m, pescadilla, f
Hades /'heidiz/ n Hades, m; Inf. el infierno, m
haft /hæft/ n mango, tomadero, m, manija, f; puño, m
hag /hæg, hɑg/ n bruja, f
haggard /'hægərd/ a ojeroso, trasnochado, trasojado
haggardly /'hægərdli/ adv ansiosamente
haggardness /'hægərdnɪs/ n aspecto ojeroso, m
haggle /'hægəl/ vi regatear; vacilar
haggling /'hæglɪŋ/ n regateo, m, a regatón
hagiographer /,hægi'ɒgrəfər/ n hagiógrafo, m
hagiography /,hægi'ɒgrəfi/ n hagiografía, f
hail /heil/ n (salutation) saludo, m; (shout) grito, m; aclamación, f; (frozen rain) granizo, m; (of blows) lluvia, f. interj ¡salve! vt saludar; llamar; aclamar; Fig. lanzar, echar. vi (hailstones) granizar; (blows, etc.) llover. **to h. from,** proceder de, ser natural de. **within h.,** al habla. **H. Mary,** Salve Regina, Avemaría, f
hailstone /'heil,stoun/ n granizo, pedrisco, m
hailstorm /'heil,stɔrm/ n granizada, f
hair /hɛər/ n (single h.) cabello, m; (Zool., Bot.) pelo, m; (of horse's mane) crin, f; (head of h.) cabellera, mata de pelo, f, pelo, m; (superfluous) vello, m; (fiber) fibra, f, filamento, m; (on the pen) raspa, f, pelo, m; Fig. pelo, m. **lock of h.,** bucle, rizo, m; mecha, f. **to dress one's h.,** peinarse. **to have one's h. cut,** hacerse el pelo. **to part the h.,** hacer(se) la raya del pelo. **to put up one's h.,** hacerse el moño; (to "come out") ponerse de largo. **to tear one's h.,** mesarse los cabellos.

h. combings, peinaduras, f pl. **h.-curler,** tirabuzón, m. **h. dryer,** secadora de cabello, f. **h. dye,** tinte para el pelo, m. **h.-net,** redecilla, f, Mexico invisible m. **h.-oil,** brillantina, f. **h.-raising,** horripilante, espeluznante. **h.-ribbon,** cinta para el pelo, f. **h.-shirt,** cilicio, m. **h. slide,** pasador, m. **h.-splitting,** sofistería, argucia, f; mez quinas argucias, quis quillas, f pl. **h.-spring,** muelle del volante, m. **h.-switch,** añadido, m. **h.-trigger,** pelo de una pistola, m
hairband /'hɛər,bænd/ m Lat. Am. bincha, f
hairbrush /'hɛər,brʌʃ/ n cepillo para el cabello, m
hairdresser /'hɛər,drɛsər/ n peluquero (-ra), peinadora, f
hairdressing /'hɛər,drɛsɪŋ/ n peinado, m. **h. establishment** or **trade,** peluquería, f
haired /hɛərd/ a peludo, con pelo; (in compounds) de pelo...
hairless /'hɛərlɪs/ a sin pelo; calvo
hairlike /'hɛər,laik/ a filiforme
hairpin /'hɛər,pɪn/ n horquilla, f, Argentina invisible m. **h. bend,** viraje en horquilla, m
hairsbreadth /'hɛərz,brɛdθ/ n pelo, m. **to have a h. escape,** escapar por un pelo.
hairsplitting arguments /'hɛər,splɪtɪŋ 'ɑrgyəmənts/ Lat. Am. abogaderas, abogaderías fpl
hairy /'hɛəri/ a peludo; velloso; Bot. hirsuto
Haiti /'heiti/ Haití, m
Haitian /'heiʃən/ a and n haitiano (-na)
hake /heik/ n merluza, f
halcyon /'hælsiən/ n alción, martín pescador, m. a Fig. feliz, sereno, tranquilo
hale /heil/ a fuerte, sano, robusto. vt hacer comparecer
half /hæf/ n mitad, f; (school term) trimestre, semestre, m; a medio; semi. adv a medias; mitad; (almost) casi; insuficientemente; imperfectamente. **It is h.-past two,** Son las dos y media. **an hour and a h.,** una hora y media. **better h.,** Inf. media naranja, cara mitad, f. **by halves,** a medias. **in h.,** en dos mitades. **one h.,** la mitad. **to go halves,** ir a medias. **to h. close,** entreabrir. **to h. open,** entreabrir. **h. a bottle,** media botella, f. **h. a crown,** media corona, f. **h.-alive,** semivivo. **h. an hour,** media hora, f. **h.-and-h.,** mitad y mitad; en partes iguales. **h.-asleep,** semidormido, medio dormido. **h.-awake,** medio despierto, entre duerme y vela. **h.-back,** Sports. medio, m. **h.-baked,** medio cocido, crudo; Fig. poco maduro. **h.-binding,** encuadernación en media pasta, f. **h.-breed,** a mestizo. n cruce, m. **h.-brother,** hermanastro, hermano de padre, hermano de madre, m. **h. circle,** semicírculo, m. **h.-closed,** entreabierto; medio cerrado. **h.-dead,** medio muerto; más muerto que vivo. **h.-done,** hecho a medias, sin acabar. **h.-dozen,** media docena, f. **h.-dressed,** medio desnudo. **h. fare,** medio billete, m. **h.-full,** medio lleno. **h.-hearted,** débil, poco eficaz, lánguido; indiferente, sin entusiasmo. **h.-heartedness,** debilidad, f; indiferencia, f. **h.-hourly,** cada media hora. **h.-length,** (portrait) de medio cuerpo. **h.-length coat,** abrigo de tres cuartos, m. **h.-light,** media luz, f. **h.-mast,** a media asta. **h.-measure,** medida poco eficaz, f. **h.-moon,** n media luna, f; Astron. semilunio, m; (of a nail) blanco (de la uña), m. **h.-mourning,** medio luto, m. **h.-pay,** media paga, f. **h.-price,** a mitad de precio. **h.-seas-over,** Inf. entre dos velas. **h.-sister,** hermanastra, hermana de padre, hermana de madre, f. **h.-time,** Sports. media parte, f, medio tiempo, m. **h.-tone,** medio tono. **h.-truth,** verdad a medias, f. **h.-turn,** media vuelta, f. **h.-way,** a medio camino; medio. **h.-witted,** medio loco, tonto, imbécil. **h.-year,** medio año, m. **h.-yearly,** semestral
half close vt entrecerrar
half title anteportada, falsa portada, portadilla, preportada, f
halibut /'hæləbət/ n halibut, m; (genus) hipogloso, m
halitosis /,hælɪ'tousɪs/ n halitosis, f

hall /hɔl/ n (mansion) mansión, casa de campo, f, caserón, m; (public building) edificio, m, casa (de); (town h.) casa del ayuntamiento, f; (room) sala, f; (entrance) vestíbulo, m; (dining room) comedor, m; (of residence for students) residencia, f. **h. door**, portón, m, puerta del vestíbulo, f. **h. porter**, conserje, m. **h.-stand**, perchero, m

hallelujah /ˌhælə'luyə/ n aleluya, f

hallmark /'hɔlˌmɑrk/ n marca de ley, f; Fig. señal, f; indicio, m. vt poner la marca de ley sobre; Fig. sellar

halloo /hə'lu/ vt (hounds) azuzar; perseguir dando voces; (call) llamar

hallow /'hælou/ vt santificar; reverenciar; (consecrate) consagrar

Halloween /ˌhælə'win/ n la víspera de Todos los Santos, f

hallucination /həˌlusə'neiʃən/ n alucinación, ilusión, f; visión, f; fantasma, m

hallucinatory /hə'lusənəˌtɔri/ a alucinador

halo /'heilou/ n halo, nimbo, m

halogen /'hælədʒən/ n halógeno, m

halt /hɔlt/ n Mil. alto, m; cesación, f; interrupción, f; (on a railway) apeadero, m; (for trams, buses) parada, f. vt parar, detener. vi pararse, detenerse; Mil. hacer alto; cesar; interrumpirse; (in speech) titubear; (of verse) estar cojo; (doubt) dudar; (limp) cojear. **H.!** Mil. ¡Alto!

halter /'hɔltər/ n ronzal, cabestro, m; (for hanging) dogal, m. vt encabestrar, cabestrar

halting /'hɔltɪŋ/ n parada, f; interrupción, f. a (of gait) cojo; incierto; vacilante; (of speech) titubeante

halve /hæv/ vt partir (or dividir) en dos mitades

ham /hæm/ n jamón, m; Anat. pernil, m; (radio-operator) radioaficionado, m

hamburger /'hæmˌbɜrgər/ n hamburguesa, f

hamlet /'hæmlɪt/ n aldea, f, pueblecito, m

hammer /'hæmər/ n martillo, m; (stone cutter's) maceta, f; (mason's) piqueta, f; (of fire-arms) percusor, m; (of piano) macillo, m. vt amartillar, martillar, batir. **to throw the h.**, lanzar el martillo. **under the h.**, en subasta, al remate. **h. blow**, martillazo, m

hammering /'hæmərɪŋ/ n martilleo, martillazo, m. **by h.**, a martillo

hammock /'hæmək/ n hamaca, f; Naut. coy, m

hamper /'hæmpər/ n banasta, canasta, f, cesto grande, m. vt estorbar, dificultar, impedir; Fig. embarazar

hamster /'hæmstər/ n Zool. hámster, m, marmota de Alemania, rata del trigo, f

hand /hænd/ n mano, f; (of animal) pata, mano, f; (worker) operario (-ia); obrero (-ra); (skill) habilidad, f; (side) mano, f, lado, m; (measure) palmo, m; (of a clock) manecilla, f; (of instruments) aguja, f; (applause) aplauso, m; (power) poder, m; las manos; (at cards) mano, f; (card player) jugador, m; (signature) firma, f; (handwriting) letra, escritura, f; (influence) influencia, parte, mano, f. **old h.**, veterano; perro viejo. **at h.**, a mano, al lado, cerca. **have at hand,** tener a la mano. **at the hands of,** de manos de. **by h.,** a mano; (on the bottle) con biberón. **from h. to h.,** de mano a mano. **in h.,** entre manos; (of money) de contado. **in the hands of,** Fig. en el poder de. **"Hands wanted,"** «Se desean trabajadores.» **h. over h.,** mano sobre mano. **hand's breadth,** palmo, m. **Hands off!** ¡Fuera las manos! **Hands up!** ¡Manos arriba! **lost with all hands,** (of a ship) perdido con toda su tripulación. **off one's hands,** despachado; (of a daughter) casada. **on all hands,** por todas partes. **on h.,** entre manos; (of goods) existente; (present) presente. **on one's hands,** a cargo de uno. **on the one h.,** por un lado; a un lado. **on the other h.,** por otra parte; en cambio. **out of h.,** luego, inmediatamente; revoltoso. **to get one's h. in,** ejercitarse. **to have a h. in,** tener parte en; intervenir en. **to have no h. in,** no tener arte ni parte en. **to have on h.,** traer entre manos. **to have the upper h.,** tener la sartén por el mango, llevar la ventaja. **to hoid one's h.,** abstenerse; detenerse. **to hold hands,** cogerse de las manos. **to lay hands on,** tocar; poner mano en; echar manos a. **to set one's h. to,** emprender; (sign) firmar. **to shake hands,** estrechar la mano. **to**

stretch out one's hands, tender las manos. **to take one's hands off,** no tocar. **with folded hands,** mano sobre mano. **with his hands behind his back,** con las manos en la espalda. **h.-in-h.,** cogidos (cogidas) de las manos. **h.-lever,** manija, f. **h.-loom,** telar de mano, m. **h. luggage,** equipaje de mano, m. **h.-made,** hecho a mano. **h.-mill,** molinillo, m. **h.-pump,** n Naut. sacabuche, m. **h. rail,** pasamano, m, baranda, balustrada, f. **h.-sewn,** cosido a mano. **h.-to-h.,** de mano en mano; (of a fight) a brazo partido, cuerpo a cuerpo. **h.-to-h. fight,** cachetina, f. **h.-to-mouth,** precario. **to live from h.-to-mouth,** vivir de día en día **hand** /hænd/ vt dar; entregar; alargar. **to h. down,** bajar; (a person) ayudar a bajar; transmitir. **to h. in,** entregar; (a person) ayudar a entrar; (one's resignation) dimitir; (send) mandar, enviar. **to h. on,** transmitir. **to h. out,** vt distribuir; (a person) ayudar a salir; (from a vehicle) ayudar a bajar. vi Inf. pagar. **to h. over,** vt entregar. vi Mil. traspasar los poderes (a). **to h. around,** pasar de mano en mano; pasar; ofrecer. **to h. up,** subir; (a person) ayudar a subir

handbag /'hændˌbæg/ n bolso, saco, monedero, m, cartera, Mexico bolsa, f

handbill /'hændˌbɪl/ n anuncio, m

handbook /'hændˌbʊk/ n manual, compendio, tratado, m; anuario, m; (guide) guía, f

handcart /'hændˌkɑrt/ n carretilla de mano, f, carretón, m

handcuff /'hændˌkʌf/ n esposa, f, grillo, m, (gen. pl). vt poner las esposas (a), maniatar

handed /'hændɪd/ a (in compounds) que tiene manos; de manos...; con las manos... **four-h.,** Sports. de cuatro personas. **one-h.,** manco

handful /'hændfʊl/ n puño, puñado, manojo, m. **to be a h.,** Inf. tener el diablo en el cuerpo. **in handfuls,** a manojos

handgrip /'hændˌgrɪp/ n apretón de manos, f

handicap /'hændiˌkæp/ n desventaja, f; obstáculo, m; Sports. handicap, m; ventaja, f. vt Fig. perjudicar, impedir, dificultar. **the handicapped,** los lisiados, m pl

handicraft /'hændiˌkræft/ n mano de obra, f; (skill) destreza manual, f,

handiwork /'hændiˌwɜrk/ n mano de obra, f; trabajo manual, m; obra, f; (deed) acción, f, hecho, m

handkerchief /'hæŋkərtʃif/ n pañuelo, m

handle /'hændl/ n mango, puño, m, Lat. Am. also manivela f; (lever) palanca, f; (of baskets, dishes, jugs) asa, f; (of doors, windows, drawers) pomo, m, (of a car door) picaporte m; (to one's name) designación, f; título, m; (excuse) pretexto, m. vt (touch) tocar; manejar, manipular; (treat) tratar; **h. with kid gloves,** tratar con guantes de seda; (deal in) comerciar en; tomar; (paw) manosear; (direct) dirigir; (control) gobernar; (pilot) pilotar; (a theme) explicar, tratar de. **h.-bar grip,** puño de un manillar, m

handlebars /'hændlˌbɑrz/ npl Spain guia, f sing, manillar, f sing, Lat. Am. manubrio, m sing

handless /'hændlɪs/ a sin manos; manco; Fig. torpe

handling /'hændlɪŋ/ n manejo, m; manipulación, f; (treatment) trato, m, relaciones (con), f pl; (thumbing) manoseo, m; interpretación, f; Art. tratamiento, m, técnica, f

handmaid /'hændˌmeid/ n sirvienta, criada, f; Fig. mayordomo, m

handsaw /'hændˌsɔ/ n sierra de mano, f, serrucho, m

handsbreadth /'hændzˌbrɛdθ/ n palmo, m

handshake /'hændˌʃeik/ n apretón de manos, m

handsome /'hænsəm/ a (generous) generoso; magnánimo; considerable; hermoso, bello; elegante; (of people) guapo, distinguido; excelente; (flattering) halagüeño, Lat. Am. buen mozo. **He was a very h. man,** Era un hombre muy guapo

handsomely /'hænsəmli/ adv generosamente; con magnanimidad; elegantemente; bien

handsomeness /'hænsəmnɪs/ n generosidad, f; magnanimidad, f; hermosura, f; elegancia, f; distinción, f

handspring /'hændˌsprɪŋ/ n voltereta de las manos, f

handwork /'hændˌwɜrk/ n obra hecha a mano, f, trabajo manual, m; (needlework) labor de aguja, f

handworked /'hænd,wɜrkt/ *a* hecho a mano; (embroidered) bordado

handwriting /'hænd,raitiŋ/ *n* caligrafía, letra, escritura, *f*. **the h. on the wall,** la mano que escribía en la pared, *f*

handy /'hændi/ *a* (of persons) diestro, manoso, hábil; (of things) conveniente; útil; (near) cercano, a mano. *adv* cerca. **h.-man,** hombre de muchos oficios, *m*; factótum, *m*

hang /hæŋ/ *vt* colgar; suspender; (execute) ahorcar; (the head) bajar; dejar caer; (upholster) entapizar; (with wallpaper) empapelar; (drape) poner colgaduras en; (place) poner; (cover) cubrir. *vi* colgar, pender; estar suspendido; (be executed) ser ahorcado; (of garments) caer. *n* (of garments) caída, *f*; (of a machine) mecanismo, *m*; (meaning) sentido, *m*, significación, *f*. **to h. by a thread,** pender de un hilo. **to h. in the balance,** estar en la balanza. **to h. fire,** estar (una cosa) en suspenso. **to h. loose,** caer suelto; (clothes) venir ancho. **to h. about,** (surround) rodear, pegarse a; (frequent) frecuentar; (haunt) rondar; (be imminent) ser inminente, amenazar; (embrace) abrazar. **to h. back,** retroceder; quedarse atrás; *Fig.* vacilar, titubear. **to h. down,** colgar, pender; estar caído; caerse. **to h. on,** seguir agarrado (a); apoyarse en; *Fig.* persistir; (a person's words) estar pendiente de, beber; (remain) quedarse. **to h. out,** *vt* tender. *vi* (lean out) asomarse (por); (*Inf.* live) habitar. **to h. over,** colgar por encima; (brood) cernerse sobre; (lean over) inclinarse sobre; quedarse cerca de; (overhang) sobresalir; (overarch) abovedar; (threaten) amenazar. **to h. together,** (of persons) permanecer unidos; (of things) tener cohesión; (be consistent) ser lógico, ser consistente. **to h. up,** colgar; suspender; *Fig.* dejar pendiente, interrumpir. **to h. upon,** apoyarse en; (a person's words) beber las palabras de uno

hangar /'hæŋər/ *n* cobertizo; *aer* hangar, *m*

hanger /'hæŋər/ *n* colgadero, *m*; percha *f*. **h.-on,** parásito, *m*; dependiente, *m*

hanging /'hæŋiŋ/ *n* colgamiento, *m*; (killing) ahorcamiento, *m*; *pl* **hangings,** colgaduras, *f pl*, cortinajes, *m pl*. *a* pendiente colgante; péndulo; (of gardens) pensil. **It's not a h. matter,** No es una cuestión de vida y muerte. **h. bridge,** puente colgante, *m*. **h. committee,** junta (de una exposición,) *f*. **h. lamp,** lámpara de techo, *f*

hangman /'hæŋmən/ *n* verdugo, *m*

hangnail /'hæŋ,neil/ *n* padrastro, *m*

hangover /'hæŋ,ouvər/ *n* (after drinking) resaca, *f*; cruda (Mexico), *f*

hank /hæŋk/ *n* madeja, *f*

hanker /'hæŋkər/ *vi* (with after) ansiar, ambicionar; (with for) anhelar, suspirar por, desear con vehemencia

hankering /'hæŋkəriŋ/ *n* ambición, *f*; deseo vehemente, *m*

hanky-panky /'hæŋki 'pæŋki/ *n* superchería, *f*; engaño, *m*

hap /hæp/ *n* casualidad, suerte, *f*; suceso fortuito, *m*

haphazard /*n* 'hæp,hæzərd/ *a* hæp'hæzərd/ *n* casualidad, *f*. *a* fortuito, casual

hapless /'hæplɪs/ *a* desgraciado, desdichado

haplessness /'hæplɪsnɪs/ *n* desgracia, desdicha, *f*

happen /'hæpən/ *vi* suceder, acontecer, ocurrir, pasar; (to be found, be) hallarse por casualidad; (take place) tener lugar, verificarse; (arise) sobrevenir. **Do you know what has happened to...?** ¿Sabes qué se ha hecho de...? **as if nothing had happened,** como si no hubiese pasado nada. **He turned up as if nothing had happened,** Se presentó como si tal cosa. **How did it h.?** ¿Cómo fue esto? **If they h. to see you,** Si acaso te vean. **I happened to be in London,** Me hallaba por casualidad en Londres. **It won't h. again,** No volverá a suceder. **whatever happens,** venga lo que venga. *Inf.* **What's happening?** ¿Qué pasa?

happening /'hæpəniŋ/ *n* suceso, acontecimiento, hecho, *m*, ocurrencia, *f*

happily /'hæpəli/ *adv* felizmente; por suerte

happiness /'hæpinɪs/ *n* felicidad, dicha, *f*; alegría, *f*; regocijo, *m*

happy /'hæpi/ *a* (lucky) afortunado; (felicitous) feliz,

oportuno; feliz, dichoso; alegre, regocijado. **to be h.,** estar contento, ser feliz. **to be h. about,** alegrarse de. **to make h.,** hacer feliz, alegrar. **h.-go-lucky,** irresponsable, descuidado

harangue /həˈræŋ/ *n* arenga, *f*. *vt* arengar. *vi* pronunciar una arenga

harass /həˈræs/ *vt* hostigar, acosar; atormentar; preocupar; *Mil.* picar. **to h. the rear-guard,** picar la retaguardia

harbinger /'hɑrbɪndʒər/ *n Fig.* precursor, heraldo, *m*; presagio, anuncio, *m*. *vt* anunciar, presagiar

harbor /'hɑrbər/ *n* puerto, *m*; (bay) bahía, *f*; (haven) asilo, refugio, *m*. *vt* dar refugio (a), albergar, acoger; (cherish) abrigar, acariciar; (conceal) esconder. **inner h.,** puerto interior, *m*. **outer h.,** rada del puerto, *f*. **to put into h.,** entrar en el puerto. **h. bar,** barra del puerto, *f*. **h.-dues,** derechos de puerto, *m pl*. **h.-master,** capitán de puerto, contramaestre de puerto, *m*

harborer /'hɑrbərər/ *n* amparador (-ra), protector (-ra); (criminal) encubridor (-ra)

hard /hɑrd/ *a* duro; (firm) firme; difícil; laborioso, agotador; violento; poderoso; arduo; fuerte, recio; vigoroso, robusto; insensible, inflexible; cruel; (of weather) inclemente, severo; (unjust) injusto, opresivo; (stiff) tieso; (of water) cruda; (of wood) brava. *adv* duro; duramente; con ahínco; con fuerza; de firme; difícilmente; (of gazing) fijamente; severamente; (firmly) firmemente; vigorosamente; (of raining) a cántaros, mucho; (quickly) rápidamente; excesivamente; (much) mucho; (of bearing misfortune) a pechos; (attentively) atentamente; (heavily) pesadamente; (badly) mal; (closely) de cerca, inmediatamente. **It was a h. blow,** Fue un golpe recio. **to be h. put to,** encontrar difícil. **to go h.,** endurecerse. **to go h. with,** irle mal a uno. **to have a h. time,** pasar apuros, pasarlo mal. **to look h. at,** mirar atentamente, examinar detenidamente; mirar fijamente. **to be a h. drinker,** ser un bebedor empedernido. **h. and fast rule,** regla inalterable, *f*. **h.-bitten,** de carácter duro. **a h.-boiled egg,** un huevo duro. **h. breathing,** resuello, *m*. **h. cash,** efectivo, *m*. **h.-earned,** difícilmente conseguido; ganado con el sudor de la frente. **h.-featured,** de facciones duras. **h.-fisted,** tacaño. **h.-fought,** arduo, reñido. **h.-headed,** práctico, perspicaz. **h.-hearted,** duro de corazón, insensible. **h.-heartedness,** insensibilidad, *f*. **h. labor,** *Law.* trabajos forzados, *m pl*, presidio, *m*. **h.-mouthed,** (of horses) boquiduro. **h. of hearing,** duro de oído. **h.-up,** apurado. **to be very h.-up,** ser muy pobre; *Inf.* estar a la cuarta pregunta. **h.-wearing,** duradero; sufrido. **h.-won,** See **h.-earned. h.-working,** trabajador, hacendoso, diligente

harden /'hɑrdṇ/ *vt* endurecer; (metal) templar; robustecer; (to war) aguerrir; (make callous) hacer insensible. *vi* endurecerse; hacerse duro; templarse; robustecerse; (of shares) entonarse

hardening /'hɑrdṇiŋ/ *n* endurecimiento, *m*; (of metal) temple, *m*. **h. of the arteries,** arteriosclerosis, *f*

hardiness /'hɑrdinɪs/ *n* vigor, *m*, fuerza, robustez, *f*; audacia, *f*

hardly /'hɑrdli/ *adv* duramente; difícilmente; (badly) mal; severamente; (scarcely) apenas, casi. **h. ever,** casi nunca

hardness /'hɑrdnɪs/ *n* dureza, *f*; severidad, *f*; inhumanidad, insensibilidad, *f*; (stiffness) tiesura, *f*; (difficulty) dificultad, *f*; (of water) crudeza, *f*; (of hearing) dureza de oído, *f*

hardship /'hɑrdʃɪp/ *n* penas, *f pl*, trabajos, *m pl*; infortunio, *m*, desdicha, *f*; (suffering) sufrimiento, *m*; (affliction) aflicción, *f*; (privation) privación, *f*. **to undergo h.,** pasar trabajos

hardware /'hɑrd,wɛr/ *n* ferretería, *f*

hardwood /'hɑrd,wʊd/ *n* madera brava, *f*

hardy /'hɑrdi/ *a* audaz, intrépido; (strong) fuerte, robusto; *Bot.* resistente

hare /hɛr/ *n* liebre, *f*. **young h.,** lebrato, *m*. **h. and hounds,** rally paper, *m*, caza de papelitos, *f*. **h.-brained,** casquivano, atronado, con cabeza de chorlito. **hare's foot,** mano de gato, *f*. **h.-lip,** labio leporino, *m*. **h.-lipped,** labihendido

harebell /'hɛr,bɛl/ *n* campanilla, campánula, *f*

harem /'hɛərəm/ *n* harén, serrallo, *m*

haricot /'hærə,kou/ n (green bean) judia, f; (dried bean) alubia, f

hark /hɑrk/ vt escuchar; oír. **to h. back,** volver al punto de partida; volver a la misma canción

harlequin /'hɑrləkwɪn/ n arlequín, m

harlequinade /,hɑrləkwɪ'neid/ n arlequinada, f

harlot /'hɑrlət/ n ramera, prostituta, meretriz, f

harlotry /'hɑrlətri/ n prostitución, f

harm /hɑrm/ n mal, m; daño, m; perjuicio, m; (danger) peligro, m; (detriment) menoscabo, m; (misfortune) desgracia, f, vt hacer mal (a); dañar, hacer daño (a); perjudicar. **And there's no h. in that,** Y en eso no hay mal. **to keep out of harm's way,** evitar el peligro; guardarse del mal

harmful /'hɑrmfəl/ a malo; dañino, perjudicial, nocivo; (dangerous) peligroso. **to be h.,** (of food, etc.) hacer mal (a); (of pests) ser dañino; (of behavior, etc.) perjudicar

harmfulness /'hɑrmfəlnɪs/ n lo malo; perniciosidad, f; daño, m; peligro, m

harmless /'hɑrmlɪs/ a innocuo; inofensivo; inocente

harmlessness /'hɑrmlɪsnɪs/ n innocuidad, f; inocencia, f

harmonic /hɑr'mɒnɪk/ n (Phys. Math.) harmónica, f; Mus. armónico, m, a Mus. armónico

harmonica /hɑr'mɒnɪkə/ n armónica, f

harmonics /hɑr'mɒnɪks/ n armonía, f; (tones) armónicos, m pl

harmonious /hɑr'mouniəs/ a armonioso

harmoniously /hɑr'mouniəsli/ adv armoniosamente; Fig. en armonía

harmoniousness /hɑr'mouniəsnɪs/ n armonía, f

harmonium /hɑr'mouniəm/ n armonio, m

harmonization /,hɑrmənɪ'zeiʃən/ n armonización, f

harmonize /'hɑrmə,naiz/ vt armonizar. vi armonizarse, estar en armonía

harmony /'hɑrməni/ n armonía, f; Fig. paz, f, buenas relaciones, f pl; música, f. **to live in h.,** vivir en paz

harness /'hɑrnɪs/ n guarniciones, f pl, jaeces, m pl; (armor) arnés, m. vt enjaezar; (yoke) enganchar; (water) represar. **to die in h.,** Fig. morir en la brecha. **h. maker,** guarnicionero, m. **h. room,** guadarnés, m

harp /hɑrp/ n arpa, f. **to h. on,** volver a la misma canción, volver a repetir

harpist /'hɑrpɪst/ n arpista, mf

harpoon /hɑr'pun/ n arpón, m. vt arponear

harpooner /hɑr'punər/ n arponero, m

harpsichord /'hɑrpsɪ,kɔrd/ n arpicordio, m

harpy /'hɑrpi/ n arpía, f

harridan /'hærədn/ n bruja, f

harrow /'hærou/ n Agr. rastra, f, escarificador, m. vt Agr. escarificar; Fig. lastimar, atormentar

harrowing /'hærouɪŋ/ a patibulario, conmovedor, atormentador, angustioso

harry /'hæri/ vt devastar, asolar; (persons) robar; perseguir; (worry) atormentar; (annoy) molestar

harsh /hɑrʃ/ a áspero; (of voice) ronco; (of sound) discordante; (of colors) áspero; duro; chillón; severo, duro; (of features) duro; (of taste) ácido, acerbo

harshly /'hɑrʃli/ adv severamente

harshness /'hɑrʃnɪs/ n (roughness) aspereza, f; (of voice) ronquedad, aspereza, f; (of sound) disonancia, f; (of colors) aspereza, f; severidad, f; dureza, f; (of taste) acidez, f

harum-scarum /'hɛərəm 'skɛərəm/ n tronera, saltabarrancos, mf molino, m, a irresponsable

harvest /'hɑrvɪst/ n cosecha, siega, f; recolección, f; Fig. producto, fruto, m. vt cosechar; recoger. **h. festival,** fiesta de la cosecha, f

harvester /'hɑrvəstər/ n segador, m, cosechero (-ra); (machine) segadora, f

hash /hæʃ/ n Cul. picado, m. vt Cul. picar

hashish /'hæʃɪʃ/ n hachich, hachís, quif, m

hasp /hæsp/ n pasador, m; sujetador, m

hassle /'hæsəl/ n Lat. Am. fregada, f

hassock /'hæsək/ n cojín, m

haste /heist/ n prisa, rapidez, f; precipitación, f; urgencia, f. vt dar prisa (a); acelerar; precipitar. vi darse prisa; acelerarse; precipitarse. **in h.,** de prisa,

aprisa. **to be in h.,** estar de prisa, llevar prisa. **in great h.,** muy aprisa, aprisa y corriendo, precipitadamente; con mucha prisa. **More h. less speed,** (Spanish equivalent. Words said by Charles III of Spain to his valet) ¡Vísteme despacio que voy de prisa!

hasten /'heisən/ vt acelerar, apresurar; precipitar. vi darse prisa, apresurarse; moverse con rapidez; correr. **to h. one's steps,** apretar el paso. **to h. away,** marcharse rápidamente. **to h. back,** regresar apresuradamente. **to h. down,** bajar rápidamente. **to h. on,** seguir el camino sin descansar; seguir rápidamente. **to h. out,** salir rápidamente. **to h. towards,** ir rápidamente hacia; correr hacia. **to h. up,** subir aprisa, correr hacia arriba; darse prisa

hastily /'heistḷi/ adv de prisa, rápidamente; con precipitación, precipitadamente; (angrily) impacientemente, airadamente; (thoughtlessly) sin reflexión

hastiness /'heistinɪs/ n rapidez, f; precipitación, f; (anger) impaciencia, irritación, f

hasty /'heisti/ a rápido, apresurado; precipitado; (superficial) superficial, ligero; (ill-considered) desconsiderado, imprudente; (angry) impaciente, irritable; violento, apasionado

hat /hæt/ n sombrero, m. **to pass round the h.,** pasar el platillo. **Andalusian h.,** sombrero calañés, m. **bowler h.,** sombrero hongo, m. **broad-brimmed h.,** sombrero chambergo, m. **Panama h.,** sombrero de jipijapa, m. **picture h.,** pamela, f. **shovel h.,** sombrero de teja, m. **soft felt h.,** sombrero flexible, m. **straw h.,** sombrero de paja, m. **three-cornered h.,** sombrero de tres picos, m. **top-h.,** sombrero de copa, m. **h. shop** or **trade,** sombrerería, f

hatband /'hæt,bænd/ n cinta de sombrero, f, cintillo, m

hatbox /'hæt,bɒks/ n sombrerera, f

hatbrush /'hæt,brʌʃ/ n cepillo para sombreros, m

hatch /hætʃ/ n (wicket) compuerta, f; (trap-door) puerta caediza, f; Naut. escotilla, f; compuerta de esclusa, f; (of chickens) pollada, f; (of birds) nidada, f. vt (birds) empollar; incubar, encobar; Fig. tramar, urdir. vi empollarse, salir del cascarón; incubarse; Fig. madurarse. **to h. a plot,** urdir un complot, conspirar. **to h. chickens,** sacar pollos

hatchet /'hætʃɪt/ n hacha pequeña, f, machado, m. **to bury the h.,** hacer la paz. **h.-faced,** de cara de cuchillo

hatching /'hætʃɪŋ/ n incubación, f; (of a plot) maquinación, f

hatchway /'hætʃ,wei/ n Naut. escotilla, f

hate /heit/ n odio, aborrecimiento, m, aversión, f; abominación, f. vt odiar, aborrecer, detestar; repugnar; saber mal, sentir. **I h. to trouble you,** Me sabe mal molestarle, Siento mucho molestarle. **to h. the sight of,** Inf. no poder ver (a)

hateful /'heitfəl/ a odioso, aborrecible; repugnante

hatefulness /'heitfəlnɪs/ n odiosidad, f, lo odioso; maldad, f

hater /'heitər/ n aborrecedor (-ra)

hatful /'hætfəl/ n un sombrero lleno (de)

hatless /'hætlɪs/ a sin sombrero, descubierto

hatpin /'hæt,pɪn/ n horquilla de sombrero, f

hatred /'heitrɪd/ n odio, aborrecimiento, m, detestación, f; aversión, enemistad, f

hatstand /'hæt,stænd/ n perchera, f

hatter /'hætər/ n sombrerero, m. **as mad as a h.,** loco como una cabra

haughtiness /'hɔtinɪs/ n altanería, arrogancia, altivez, soberbia, f, orgullo, m

haughty /'hɔti/ a altanero, arrogante, altivo, orgulloso, Lat. Am. copetudo, Mexico also alzado

haul /hɔl/ n (pull) tirón, m; (of fish) redada, f; (booty) botín, m. vt arrastrar, tirar de; Naut. halar. **to h. at, upon,** (ropes, etc.) aflojar, soltar, arriar. **to h. down,** (flags, sails) arriar

haulage /'hɔlɪdʒ/ n transporte, acarreo, m; coste de transporte, m. **h. contractor,** contratista de transporte, m

haunch /hɔntʃ/ n anca, culata, f; (of meat) pierna, f, hueso ilíaco, m

haunt /hɔnt/ n punto de reunión, lugar frecuentado (por), m; (lair) cubil, nido, m, guarida, f. vt frecuentar; rondar; (of ideas) perseguir; (of ghosts) aparecer, visitar. **It is a h.** of thieves, Es una cueva de ladrones

haunted /'hɔntɪd/ a (by spirits) encantado

haunter /'hɔntər/ n frecuentador (-ra); (ghost) fantasma, espectro, m

haunting /'hɔntɪŋ/ n frecuentación, f; aparición de un espectro, f. a persistente

hautboy /'houbɔi, 'oubɔi/ n oboe, m

hauteur /hou'tɜr/ n altivez, f

Havana /hə'vænə/ la Habana, f. n (cigar) habano, m. (native) habanero (-ra), habano (-na)

have /hæv; unstressed həv, əv/ vt tener; poseer; (suffer) padecer; (spend) pasar; (eat or drink) tomar; (eat) comer; (a cigarette) fumar; (a bath, etc.) tomar; (a walk, a ride) dar; (cause to be done) mandar (hacer), hacer (hacer); (deceive) engañar; (defeat) vencer; (catch) coger; (say) decir; (allow) permitir; (tolerate) tolerar, sufrir; (obtain) lograr, conseguir; (wish) querer; (know) saber; (realize) realizar; (buy) comprar; (acquire) adquirir. As an auxiliary verb, haber (e.g. I h. done it, Lo he hecho, etc.). **As fate would h. it,** Según quiso la suerte. **Do you h. to go?** ¿Tiene Vd. que marcharse? **H. him come here,** Hazle venir aquí. **I h. been had,** Me han engañado. **I h. a good mind to...,** Tengo ganas de... **I had all my books stolen,** Me robaron todos los libros. **You had better go,** Es mejor que te vayas. **I had rather,** Preferiría, Me gustaría más bien. **I h. had a suit made,** Mandé hacerme un traje, Hice hacerme un traje. **I would not h. had it otherwise,** No lo hubiese querido de otra manera. **I will not h. it,** No lo quiero; No quiero tomarlo; (object) No lo permitiré. **If we had known,** Si lo hubiésemos sabido. **It has to do with the sun,** Está relacionado con el sol, Tiene que ver con el sol. **Have a good trip!** ¡Buen viaje!, ¡Feliz viaje! **What are you going to h.?** ¿Qué quiere Vd. tomar? **Will you h. some jam?** ¿Quiere Vd. mermelada? **to h. breakfast,** desayunar. **to h. dinner, supper,** cenar. **to h. lunch,** almorzar. **to h. four tea,** invitar a tomar el té; (of food) merendar. **to h. tea,** tomar el té. **to h. it out with,** habérselas con. **to h. just,** acabar de. **I h. just done it,** Acabo de hacerlo. **to h. on hand,** traer entre manos. **to h. one's eye on,** no perder de vista (a), vigilar. **to h. one's tail between one's legs,** ir rabo entre piernas. **to h. to,** tener que; deber. **It has to be so,** Tiene que ser así. **to h. too much of,** sobrar, tener demasiado de. **He has too much time,** Le sobra tiempo. **to h. back,** aceptar; recibir. **to h. down,** hacer bajar. **She had her hair down,** El pelo le caía por las espaldas. **to h. in,** hacer entrar. **to h. on,** vestir, llevar puesto; (engagements) tener (compromisos). **to h. out,** hacer salir; llevar a paseo; llevar fuera; (have removed) hacerse sacar; quitar. **to h. up,** (persons) hacer subir; (things) subir; Law. llevar a (ante) los tribunales. **to h. with one,** tener consigo. **I h. her with me,** La tengo conmigo, Ella me acompaña

haven /'heivən/ n puerto, m, abra, f; Fig. oasis, abrigo, refugio, m

haversack /'hævər,sæk/ n mochila, f, morral, m

havoc /'hævək/ n destrucción, ruina, f; Fig. estrago, m. **to wreak h. among,** destruir; Fig. hacer estragos entre (o en)

Hawaii /hə'waii/ Hawai, m

Hawaiian /hə'waiən/ a and n hawaiano; n (language) hawaiano, m

hawk /hɔk/ n halcón, m; gavilán, milano, m. vi cazar con halcón. vt vender mercancías por las calles; Fig. difundir. **h.-eyed,** de ojos de lince. **h.-nosed,** de nariz aguileña

hawker /'hɔkər/ n halconero, m; (vendor) buhonero, m, vendedor (-ra) ambulante

hawking /'hɔkɪŋ/ n caza con halcones, cetrería, f; (expectorating) gargajeo, m; (selling) buhonería, f

hawser /'hɔzər/ n maroma, f, calabrote, m

hawthorn /'hɔ,θɔrn/ n espino, m. **white h.,** espino blanco, m

hay /hei/ n heno, m. **to make hay while the sun shines,** hacer su agosto. **hay fever,** fiebre del heno, f. **hay-fork,** horca, f

hayloft /'hei,lɔft/ n henil, m

haymaker /'hei,meikər/ n segador (-ra); (machine) segadora, f

haymaking /'hei,meikɪŋ/ n recolección del heno, f

haystack /'hei,stæk/ n almiar, m, niara, f

hazard /'hæzərd/ n peligro, azar, m, suerte, f; riesgo, peligro, m; (game) juego de azar, m. vt arriesgar, aventurar. **at all hazards,** a todo riesgo

hazardous /'hæzərdəs/ a azaroso, arriesgado, peligroso

haze /heiz/ n bruma, f; confusión, f

hazel /'heizəl/ n avellano, m. **h.-nut,** avellana, f

hazy /'heizi/ a brumoso, calinoso; confuso

he /hi/ pers. pron él. n (of humans) varón, m; (of animals) macho, m. **he who,** el que, quien. **he-goat,** macho cabrío, m. **he-man,** todo un hombre, hombre cabal, m

head /hɛd/ vt golpear con la cabeza; encabezar; (lead) capitanear; (direct) dirigir, guiar; (wine) cabecear. vi irse a, estar a la cabeza de; dirigirse a. **headed for,** con rumbo a, en dirección a. **to h. off,** interceptar; desviar; Fig. distraer

head /hɛd/ n Anat. cabeza, f; (upper portion) parte superior, f; (of a coin) cara, f; (hair) cabellera, f; (individual) persona, f; (of cattle) res, f; (of a mountain) cumbre, f; (of a ladder) último peldaño, m; (of toadstools) sombrero, m; (of trees) copa, f; (of a stick) puño, m; (of a cylinder) culata, f; (of a river, etc.) manantial, origen, m; (of a bed) cabecera, f; (of nails, pins) cabeza, f; (froth) espuma, f; (flower) flor, f; (leaves) hojas, f pl; (first place) primer puesto, m; (of game, fish) pieza, f; (of a page, column) cabeza, f; (cape) cabo, m; (of an arrow, dart, lance) punta, f; (front) frente, m; (leader) jefe, cabeza, m; (chief) director (-ra), superior (-ta); presidente (-ta); (of a school) director (-ra); (of a cask) fondo, m; Mech. cabezal, m; (of an ax) filo, m; (of a bridge) cabeza, f; (of a jetty, pier) punta, f; (of a ship) proa, f; (of a flower) cabezuela, f; (of asparagus) punta, f; (of a table) cabeza, f; (of family) jefe, cabeza, m; (seat of honor) cabecera, f; (title) título, m; (aspect) punto de vista, m; (division) capítulo, m; (management, direction) dirección, f; (talent) talento, m, cabeza, f; (intelligence) inteligencia, f. a principal; primero; en jefe. **at the h. of,** a la cabeza de. **crowned h.,** testa coronada, f. **from h. to foot,** de pies a cabeza; de hito en hito; de arriba abajo. **He took it into his h. to...,** Se le ocurrió de... **This story has neither h. nor tail,** Este cuento no tiene pies ni cabeza. **with h. held high,** con la frente levantada. **to come to a h.,** llegar a la crisis; llegar al punto decisivo. **to get an idea out of a person's h.,** quitar una idea a uno de la cabeza. **to keep one's h.,** conservar la sangre fría, no perder la cabeza. **to lose one's h.,** Fig. perder la cabeza. **to put into a person's h.,** Fig. meter (a uno) en la cabeza. **to run one's h. against,** golpear la cabeza contra. **h. first,** de cabeza. **h. of cattle,** res, f. **h. office,** central, f. **h. of hair,** cabellera, f; mata de pelo, f. **h.-on,** de cabeza. **h.-on collision,** choque de frente, m. **h. opening,** (of a garment) cabezón, m. **heads or tails,** cara o cruz (Spain), águila o sol (Mexico), cruz o sello (Argentina, Chile). **h. over heels,** de patas arriba. **h. over heels in love,** calado hasta los huesos. **h.-dress,** tocado, m; peinado, m; sombrero, m. **h. voice,** voz de cabeza, f. **h. waiter,** encargado de comedor, jefe de camareros, m

headache /'hɛd,eik/ n dolor de cabeza, m; Fig. quebradero de cabeza, m

headboard /'hɛd,bɔrd/ n cabecera (de una cama), f

headed /'hɛdɪd/ a con cabeza...; que tiene la cabeza...; de cabeza...; (of an article) intitulado. **large h.,** cabezudo

header /'hɛdər/ n caída de cabeza, f; salto de cabeza, m

headgear /'hɛd,gɪər/ n tocado, m; sombrero, gorro, m

head-hunting /'hɛd,hʌntɪŋ/ n la caza de cabezas, f

heading /'hɛdɪŋ/ n Naut. el poner la proa en dirección (a); el guiar en dirección (a); (of a book, etc.) título, encabezamiento, m; (soccer) golpe de cabeza, m. **to come under the h. of,** estar incluido entre; clasificarse bajo

headland /'hɛdlənd/ n cabo, promontorio, m

headlight /'hɛd,lait/ n Auto. faro, m; (Rail., Naut.) farol, m. **to dim the headlights,** bajar los faros. **to switch on the headlights,** encender los faros (or los faroles)

headline /'hɛd,lain/ n (of a newspaper) titular, m; (to a chapter) título de la columna, m

headlong /'hɛd,lɔŋ/ a precipitado; despeñado. adv de cabeza; precipitadamente. **to fall h.,** caer de cabeza

headman /'hɛd'mæn/ n cacique, cabecilla, m; (foreman) capataz, contramaestre, m

headmaster /'hɛd'mæstər/ n director de colegio, rector, m

headmistress /'hɛd'mɪstrɪs/ n directora de colegio, rectora, f

head nurse enfermero-jefe, m

head-on collision /'hɛd ,ɒn/ n choque frontal, m

headphones /'hɛd,founz/ n pl auriculares, m pl

headquarters /'hɛd,kwɔrtərz/ n Mil. cuartel general, m; oficina central, f; jefatura, f; centro, m

headrest /'hɛd,rɛst/ n respaldo, m; apoyo para la cabeza, m

headstone /'hɛd,stoun/ n piedra mortuoria, f

headstrong /'hɛd,strɔŋ/ a impetuoso, terco, testarudo

headway /'hɛd,wei/ n marcha, f; Fig. progreso, avance, m. **to make h.,** avanzar; Fig. hacer progresos; Fig. prosperar

headwind /'hɛd,wɪnd/ n viento en contra, m

heady /'hɛdi/ a apasionado, violento; impetuoso, precipitado; (obstinate) terco; (of alcohol) encabezado; Fig. embriagador

heal /hil/ vt curar, sanar; (flesh) cicatrizar. vi curar, sanar; cicatrizarse; (superficially) sobresanar

healable /'hiləbəl/ a curable

healer /'hilər/ n sanador (-ra), curador (-ra); curandero, m

healing /'hiliŋ/ a curador, sanador; médico. n curación, f; cura, f, remedio, m

health /hɛlθ/ n salud, f; higiene, sanidad, f. **Here's to your very good h.!** ¡Salud y pesetas! **He is in good h.,** Disfruta de buena salud. **to drink a person's h.,** beber a la salud de. **to enjoy good h.,** gozar de buena salud. **to look full of h.,** vender salud. **h.-giving,** saludable. **h. inspection,** visita de sanidad, f. **h. officer,** inspector de sanidad, m. **h. resort,** balneario, m

healthiness /'hɛlθinɪs/ n buena salud, f; sanidad, salubridad, f

healthy /'hɛlθi/ a sano; con buena salud; (healthful) saludable. **to be h.,** tener buena salud

heap /hip/ n montón, m; rima, pila, f, acervo, m; (of people) muchedumbre, f, tropel, m. vt amontonar; apilar; colmar. **in heaps,** a montones. **We have heaps of time,** Nos sobra tiempo, Tenemos tiempo de sobra. **to h. together,** juntar, mezclar. **to h. up, upon,** colmar; amontonar; Agr. hacinar; Fig. acumular

hear /hiər/ vt oír; (listen) escuchar; (attend) asistir a; (give audience) dar audiencia (a); (a lawsuit) ver (un pleito); (speak) hablar; (be aware of, feel) sentir. vi oír; tener noticias; (learn) enterarse de; (allow) permitir. **H.! H.!** ¡Muy bien! **I have heard it said that...** he oído decir que... **Let me h. from you!** ¡Mándame noticias tuyas! **They were never heard of again,** No se volvió a saber de ellos, No se supo más de ellos. **to h. about,** oír de; (know) saber de, tener noticias de; recibir información sobre. **to h. from,** ser informado por; tener noticias de: recibir carta de. **to h. of,** enterarse de, saber; recibir información sobre; (allow) permitir

hearer /'hiərər/ n oyente, mf

hearing /'hiəriŋ/ n (sense of) oído, m; alcance del oído, m; presencia, f; audición, f; Law. vista (de una causa) f. **It was said in my h.,** Fue dicho en mi presencia. **out of h.,** fuera del alcance del oído. **within h.,** al alcance del oído. **have a h. problem,** ser parcialmente sordo

hearing aid acústica, aparato auditivo, aparato acústico, m

hearsay /'hiər,sei/ n fama, f, rumor, m. **by h.,** de oídas

hearse /hɜrs/ n coche fúnebre, m

heart /hɑrt/ n corazón, m; (feelings) entrañas, f pl; (of the earth, etc.) seno, corazón, m; (of lettuce, etc.) cogollo, repollo, m; (suit in cards) copas, f pl; Bot. médula, f; (soul) alma, f; (courage) valor, m; ánimo, m. **at h.,** en el fondo, esencialmente. **by h.,** de memoria. **from the h.,** con toda sinceridad, de todo corazón. **He is a man after my own h.,** Es un hombre de los que me gustan. **I have no h. to do it,** No tengo valor de hacerlo. **in the h. of the country,** en medio del campo. **to break one's h.,** partirse el corazón. **to have one's h. in one's mouth,** tener el alma en un hilo, estar muerto de miedo. **to have no h.,** Fig. no tener entrañas. **to lose h.,** desanimarse, descorazonarse. **to set one's h. on,** poner el corazón en. **to take h.,** cobrar ánimo; Inf. hacer de tripas corazón. **to take to h.,** tomar a pechos. **to wear one's h. on one's sleeve,** tener el corazón en la mano. **with all my h.,** con toda el alma. **h.-ache,** angustia, pena, f; **h.-beat,** latido del corazón, m. **h.-breaker,** (woman) coqueta, f; (man) ladrón de corazones, m. **h. disease,** enfermedad del corazón, enfermedad cardíaca, f. **h. failure,** colapso cardíaco, m. **h.-rending,** desgarrador, angustioso. **h.-searching,** examen de conciencia, m. **h.-shaped,** acorazonado, en forma de corazón. **h.-strings,** fibras del corazón, f pl. **h.-to-h. talk,** conversación íntima, f

heartbreaking /'hɑrt,breikiŋ/ a desgarrador, angustioso, doloroso, lastimoso

heartbroken /'hɑrt,broukən/ a acongojado, afligido, transido de dolor

heartburn /'hɑrt,bɜrn/ n acidez del estómago, acedía, pirosis, rescoldera, f

heartburning /'hɑrt,bɜrniŋ/ n rencor, m, animosidad, envidia, f

hearted /'hɑrtid/ a de corazón... que tiene el corazón... **kind-h.,** de buen corazón, bondadoso

hearten /'hɑrtn/ vt alentar, animar

heartfelt /'hɑrt,fɛlt/ a hondo; de todo corazón, sincero; más expresivo

hearth /hɑrθ/ n hogar, m; chimenea, f; Fig. hogar, m

heartily /'hɑrtḷi/ adv cordialmente; sinceramente; enérgicamente; con entusiasmo; (of eating) con buen apetito; (very) muy, completamente. **I am h. sick of it all,** Inf. Estoy harto hasta los dientes

heartiness /'hɑrtinɪs/ n cordialidad, f; sinceridad, f; energía, f, vigor, m; vehemencia, f; entusiasmo, m; (of appetite) buen diente, buen apetito, m

heartless /'hɑrtlɪs/ a sin corazón, sin piedad, despiadado, inhumano, cruel

heartlessness /'hɑrtlɪsnɪs/ n falta de corazón, inhumanidad, crueldad, f

hearty /'hɑrti/ a cordial; sincero; enérgico; vigoroso; robusto; (frank) campechano; (of appetite) voraz; bueno; (big) grande

heat /hit/ n calor, m; (in animals) celo, m; (of an action) calor, m; Fig. vehemencia, fogosidad, f; Fig. fuego, m; (passion) ardor, m, pasión, f; (of a race) carrera eliminatoria, f. vt calentar; (excite) conmover, acalorar, excitar; (annoy) irritar. vi calentarse. **dead h.,** empate, m. **in h.,** en celo. **in the h. of the moment,** en el calor del momento. **to become heated,** Fig. acalorarse, exaltarse. **white h.,** candencia, incandescencia, f. **h. lightning,** fucilazo, m. **h. spot,** pápula, f; terminación sensible, f. **h. stroke,** insolación, f. **h. wave,** onda de calor, f

heated /'hitid/ a calentado; caliente; excitado; apasionado

heatedly /'hitidli/ adv con vehemencia, con pasión

heater /'hitər/ n calentador, m; calorífero, m; (stove) estufa, f; (for plates) calientaplatos, m. **water-h.,** calentador de agua, m

heath /hiθ/ n brezal, m; yermo, páramo, m; Bot. brezo, m

heathen /'hiðən/ n pagano (-na); idólatra, mf; ateo (-ea), descreído (-da). a pagano; ateo; bárbaro

heathenism /'hiðə,nizəm/ n paganismo, m; idolatría, f; ateísmo, m

heather /'hɛðər/ n brezo, m

heating /'hitiŋ/ n calefacción, f, a calentador; (of drinks) fortificante. **central h.,** calefacción central, f

heave /hiv/ *vt* alzar, levantar; *Naut.* izar; (the anchor, etc.) virar; (throw) arrojar, lanzar; elevar; (extract) extraer; (emit) dar, exhalar. *vi* subir y bajar; palpitar; agitarse. *n* tirón, *m*; (of the sea) vaivén, *m*. **to h. in sight,** aparecer, surgir. **to h. out sail,** *Naut.* desenvergar. **to h. the lead,** *Naut.* escandallar. **to h. to,** *Naut.* estarse a la capa

heaven /'hɛvən/ *n* cielo, *m*; firmamento, *m*; paraíso, *m*. **Heavens!** ¡Cielos! ¡Por Dios! **Thank H.!** ¡Gracias a Dios! **h.-born,** celeste. **h.-sent,** *Fig.* providencial

heavenliness /'hɛvənlinɪs/ *n* carácter celestial, *m*; delicia, *f*

heavenly /'hɛvənli/ *a* celeste, celestial; divino; *Fig.* delicioso. **h. body,** astro, *m*

heavily /'hɛvəli/ *adv* pesadamente; torpemente; penosamente; (slowly) lentamente; severamente; excesivamente; (of sighing) hondamente; (sadly) tristemente; (of rain, etc.) reciamente, fuertemente; (of wind) con violencia. **He fell h.,** Cayó de plomo. **to lie h. upon,** pesar mucho sobre. **to rain h.,** llover mucho, diluviar

heaviness /'hɛvɪnɪs/ *n* peso, *m*; (lethargy) torpor, letargo, *m*; sueño, *m*, languidez, *f*; (clumsiness) torpeza, *f*; (severity) severidad, *f*; importancia, responsabilidad, *f*; dificultad, *f*; (gravity) gravedad, *f*; tristeza, melancolía, *f*; (boredom) sosería, insulsez, *f*; (of style) monotonía, ponderosidad, *f*

heavy /'hɛvi/ *a* pesado; torpe; sin gracia; (slow) lento; (thick) grueso; (strong) fuerte; (hard) duro; grave; difícil; oneroso; responsable, importante; (oppressive) opresivo; penoso; grande; (sad) triste, melancólico; (of the sky) anublado; (of food) indigesto; (tedious) aburrido, soso; (pompous) pomposo; (of roads) malo; (of scents) fuerte, penetrante; (of sleep, weather) pesado; (weary) rendido; (charged with) cargado de; (of a meal) grande, abundante; (violent) violento; (of a cold, etc.) malo; (drowsy) soñoliento; (torpid) tórpido; (of rain, snow, hail) fuerte, recio; (of firing) intenso; (of sighs) profundo; (of soil) recio, de mucha miga; (*Phys. Chem.*) pesado. **to be h.,** pesar mucho. **How h. are you?** ¿Cuánto pesa Vd.? **h.-armed,** pesado; armado hasta los dientes. **h.-eyed,** con ojeras. **h. guns,** artillería pesada, *f*. **h.-handed,** de manos torpes; *Fig.* tiránico, opresivo. **h.-hearted,** triste, apesadumbrado. **h. industry,** la gran industria, la industria pesada, *f*. **h.-laden,** muy cargado. **h. losses,** *Mil.* pérdidas cuantiosas, *f pl.* **h.weight,** *Sports.* peso pesado, *m*

Hebraic /hɪ'breiɪk/ *a* hebraico, hebreo, judaico

Hebraist /'hibreiɪst/ *n* hebraísta, *m*

Hebrew /'hibru/ *n* hebreo (-ea), judío (-ía): (language) hebreo, *m*

Hebrides, the /'hɛbrɪ.diz/ las Hébridas

heckle /'hɛkəl/ *vt* *Fig.* interrumpir, importunar con preguntas

heckler /'hɛklər/ *n* perturbador (-ra)

heckling /'hɛklɪŋ/ *n* interrupción, *f*

hectare /'hɛktɛər/ *n* hectárea, *f*

hectic /'hɛktɪk/ *a* (consumptive) hético; (feverish) febril; *Fig. Inf.* agitado

hector /'hɛktər/ *vt* intimidar, amenazar

hectoring /'hɛktərɪŋ/ *a* imperioso; amenazador

hectowatt /'hɛktə.wɑt/ *n* *Elec.* hectovatio, *m*

hedge /hɛdʒ/ *n* seto, *m*; barrera, *f*. *vt* cercar con un seto; rodear. *vi* *Fig.* vacilar. **h.-hopping,** *Aer.* vuelo a ras de tierra, *m*. **h.-sparrow,** acentor de bosque, *m*

hedgehog /'hɛdʒ.hɒg/ *n* erizo, *m*. **h. position,** *Mil.* puesto fuerte, *m*

hedonism /'hidn.ɪzəm/ *n* hedonismo, *m*

hedonist /'hidnɪst/ *n* hedonista, *mf*

heed /hid/ *n* atención, *f*, cuidado, *m*. *vt* atender; observar, considerar; escuchar. *vi* hacer caso

heedful /'hidfəl/ *a* atento; cuidadoso

heedless /'hidlɪs/ *a* desatento; descuidado, negligente; distraído

heedlessly /'hidlɪsli/ *adv* sin hacer caso; negligentemente; distraídamente

heedlessness /'hidlɪsnɪs/ *n* desatención, distracción, *f*; descuido, *m*; negligencia, *f*; inconsideración, *f*

heel /hil/ *n* *Anat.* talón, calcañar, *m*; (of shoe) tacón,

m; (of a violin, etc., bow) talón, *m*; (remains) restos, *m pl*. *vt* poner tacón a; poner talón a; *Naut.* hacer zozobrar. *vi* *Naut.* zozobrar. **rubber h.,** tacón de goma, *m*. **She let him cool his heels for half an hour,** le dio un plantón de media hora. **to follow on a person's heels,** pisarle (a uno) los talones. **to be down at h.,** (of shoes) estar gastados los tacones; estar desaseado. **to take to one's heels,** apretar a correr, poner pies en polvorosa. **to turn on one's h.,** dar media vuelta. **h.-bone,** zancajo, *m*. **h.-piece,** talón, *m*

heeltap /'hil.tæp/ *n* tapa de tacón, *f*; escurridura, *f*

heft /hɛft/ *vt* sopesar, tomar al peso

hegemony /hɪ'dʒɛməni/ *n* hegemonía, *f*

heifer /'hɛfər/ *n* ternera, vaquilla, *f*

heigh /hei/ *interj* (calling attention) ¡oye! ¡oiga! **h.-ho!** ¡ay!

height /hait/ *n* altura, *f*; elevación, *f*; altitud, *f*; (stature) estatura, *f*; (high ground) cerro, *m*, colina, *f*; (sublimity) sublimidad, excelencia, *f*; colmo, *m*; (zenith) auge, *m*, cumbre, *f*

heighten /'haitn/ *vt* hacer más alto; (enhance) realzar; (exaggerate) exagerar; (perfect) perfeccionar; (intensify) intensificar

heightening /'haitnɪŋ/ *n* elevación, *f*; (enhancement) realce, *m*; (exaggeration) exageración, *f*; (perfection) perfección, *f*; (intensification) intensificación, *f*

heinous /'heinəs/ *a* atroz, nefando, horrible.

heinousness /'heinəsnɪs/ *n* atrocidad, enormidad, *f*

heir /ɛər/ *n* heredero, *m*. *Lat. Am.* asignatario *m*. **h. apparent,** heredero aparente, *m*. **h.-at-law,** heredero forzoso, *m*. **h. presumptive,** presunto heredero, *m*

heiress /'ɛərɪs/ *n* heredera, *Lat. Am.* asignataria *f*

heirloom /'ɛər.lum/ *n* reliquia de familia, *f*; *Fig.* herencia, *f*

helicopter /'hɛlɪ.kɒptər/ *n* helicóptero, *m*

helium /'hiliəm/ *n* *Chem.* helio, *m*

helix /'hilɪks/ *n* *Geom.* hélice, *m*; (*Archit. Geom.*) espira, *f*

hell /hɛl/ *n* infierno, *m*. **h.-fire,** fuego del infierno, *m*, llamas del infierno, *f pl*

Hellenic /hɛ'lɛnɪk/ *a* helénico

Hellenism /'hɛlə.nɪzəm/ *n* helenismo, *m*

Hellenist /'hɛlənɪst/ *n* helenista, *mf*

Hellenize /'hɛlə.naiz/ *vt* helenizar

hellish /'hɛlɪʃ/ *a* infernal; *Inf.* horrible, detestable

hello /hɛ'lou/ *interj* ¡hola!; (on telephoning someone) ¡oiga! ¡alo!; (answering telephone) *Spain* ¡diga!, ¡alo!, *Colombia* ¡a ver!, *Mexico* ¡bueno!

helm /hɛlm/ *n* caña del timón, *f*; timón, gobernalle, *m*. **to obey the h.,** obedecer el timón. **to take the h.,** gobernar el timón; ponerse a pilotar

helmet /'hɛlmɪt/ *n* casco, *m*; (in olden days) yelmo, capacete, *m*; (sun) casco colonial, *m*

helmsman /'hɛlmzmən/ *n* timonero, *m*

help /hɛlp/ *n* ayuda, *f*; auxilio, socorro, *m*; (protection) favor, *m*, protección, *f*; (remedy) remedio, *m*; (cooperation) cooperación, *f*, concurso, *m*; (domestic) criada, *f*. **A little h. is worth a lot of sympathy,** Más vale un toma que dos te daré. **There's no h. for it,** No hay más remedio. **to call for h.,** pedir socorro a gritos. **without h.,** a solas, sin la ayuda de nadie

help /hɛlp/ *vt* ayudar; socorrer, auxiliar; (favor) favorecer; (mitigate) aliviar; (contribute to) contribuir a, facilitar; (avoid) evitar. *vi* ayudar. **He cannot h. worrying,** No puede menos de preocuparse. **God h. you!** ¡Dios te ampare! **So h. me God!** ¡Así Dios me salve! **to h. one another,** ayudarse mutuamente, ayudarse los unos a los otros. **to h. oneself,** (to food) servirse. **to h. down, off,** ayudar a bajar; ayudar a apearse. **to h. in,** ayudar a entrar. **to h. along, forward, on,** avanzar, fomentar, promover; contribuir a. **Shall I h. you on with the dress?** ¿Quieres que te ayude a ponerte el vestido? **to h. out,** ayudar a salir; (from a vehicle) ayudar a bajar; (of a difficulty, etc.) sacar; suplir la falta de; ayudar. **to h. over,** ayudar a cruzar; (a difficulty) ayudar a salir (de un apuro); ayudar a vencer (un obstáculo, etc.); (a period) ayudar a pasar. **to h. to,** contribuir a, ayudar en; (food) servir. **to h. up,** ayudar a subir; ayudar a levantarse, levantar

helper /'hɛlpər/ n auxiliador (-ra); asistente (-ta); (protector) favorecedor (-ra); bienhechor (-ra), *Argentina also* ladero m; (colleague) colega, m; (coworker) colaborador (-ra). **He thanked all his helpers,** Dio las gracias a todos los que le habían ayudado
helpful /'hɛlpfəl/ a útil, provechoso; (obliging) servicial, atento, *Lat. Am.* acomedido; (favorable) favorable; (healthy) saludable
helpfulness /'hɛlpfəlnɪs/ n utilidad, f; bondad, f
helping /'hɛlpɪŋ/ n ayuda, f; (of food) porción, ración, f, plato, m. **Won't you have a second h.?** ¿No quiere usted servirse más (or otra vez)? ¿No quiere usted repetir? **to lend a h. hand (to),** prestar ayuda (a)
helpless /'hɛlplɪs/ a desamparado, abandonado; (through infirmity) imposibilitado; impotente, sin fuerzas (para); (shiftless) incompetente, inútil
helplessness /'hɛlplɪsnɪs/ n desamparo, m; invalidez, debilidad, f; impotencia, f; incompetencia, f
helter-skelter /'hɛltər 'skɛltər/ adv atropelladamente; en desorden. n barahunda, f
hem /hɛm/ n *Sew.* dobladillo, filete, m; bastilla, f; (edge) orilla, f. *interj* ¡ejem! *vt* hacer dobladillo en, dobladillar. *vi* (cough) fingir toser. **false hem,** *Sew.* dobladillo falso, m. **running hem,** *Sew.* jareta, f. **to hem and haw,** tartamudear; vacilar. **to hem in,** cercar, sitiar
hematology /,himə'tɔlədʒi/ n hematología, f
hemisphere /'hɛmɪ,sfɪər/ n hemisferio, m
hemispherical /,hɛmɪ'sfɛrɪkəl/ a hemisférico, semiesférico
hemlock /'hɛm,lɒk/ n *Bot.* cicuta, f
hemoglobin /'himə,gloubɪn/ n *Chem.* hemoglobina, f
hemophilia /,himə'fɪliə/ n *Med.* hemofilia, f
hemorrhage /'hɛmərɪdʒ/ n hemorragia, f, flujo de sangre, m
hemorrhoids /'hɛmə,rɔidz/ n pl *Med.* hemorroides, f
hemp /hɛmp/ n cáñamo, m. **h. cloth,** lienzo, m. **h.-seed,** cañamón, m
hemstitch /'hɛm,stɪtʃ/ n vainica, f. *vt* hacer vainica en
hen /hɛn/ n gallina, f; (female bird) hembra, f. **the hen pheasant,** la hembra del faisán. **hen bird,** pájara, f. **hen-coop** or **house,** gallinero, m. **hen party,** *Inf.* reunión de mujeres, f. **hen-roost,** nidal, ponedero, m
hence /hɛns/ adv (of place) de aquí; (of time) de ahora, de aquí a, al cabo de, en; (therefore) por eso, por lo tanto, por consiguiente. *interj* ¡fuera! ¡fuera de aquí! **I shall come to see you a month h.,** Vendré a verte en un mes (or al cabo de un mes). **ten years h.,** de aquí a diez años. **h. the fact that...,** de aquí que.... **H. it happens that...,** Por eso sucede que...
henceforth /,hɛns'fɔrθ/ adv desde aquí en adelante, de hoy en adelante
henchman /'hɛntʃmən/ n escudero, m; satélite, secuaz, m
henna /'hɛnə/ n alheña, f
henpecked /'hɛn,pɛkt/ a gobernado por su mujer, que se deja mandar por su mujer
hepatitis /,hɛpə'taitɪs/ n hepatitis, m
her /hɜr/ unstressed hər, ər/ pers pron direct object la; (with prepositions) ella. pers. pron indirect object le, a ella. poss a su, mf; sus, mf pl, de ella. **I saw her on Wednesday,** La vi el miércoles. **The message is for her,** El recado es para ella. **It is her book,** Es su libro, Es el libro de ella
herald /'hɛrəld/ n heraldo, m; presagio, anuncio, m. *vt* anunciar; presagiar
heraldic /hɛ'rældɪk/ a heráldico
heraldry /'hɛrəldri/ n heráldica, f
herb /ɜrb; esp. Brit. hɜrb/ n hierba, f
herbaceous /hɜr'beiʃəs, ɜr-/ a herbáceo
herbage /'ɜrbɪdʒ, 'hɜr-/ n herbaje, m; pasto, m
herbal /'ɜrbəl, 'hɜr-/ a herbario. n herbolaria, f
herbalist /'hɜrbəlɪst, 'ɜr-/ n herbario, m, simplista, mf
herbarium /hɜr'bɛəriəm, ɜr-/ n herbario, m
herbivorous /hɜr'bɪvərəs, ɜr-/ a herbívoro
herby /'ɜrbi, 'hɜr-/ a herbáceo
Herculean /,hɜrkyə'liən/ a hercúleo
herd /hɜrd/ n manada, f; (of cattle) hato, m; (race)

raza, f; (*Fig.* contemptuous) populacho, m, masa, f. *vt* reunir en manadas; reunir en hatos; (sheep) reunir en rebaños; guiar las manadas, etc. *vi* ir en manadas, hatos o rebaños; asociarse, reunirse. **h.-instinct,** instinto gregario, m; instinto de las masas, m
herdsman /'hɜrdzmən/ n ganadero, pastor, manadero, m; (head herdsman) rabadán, m
here /hɪər/ adv aquí; (at roll-call) ¡presente!; acá; en este punto; ahora. n presente, m. **And h. he looked at me,** Y a este punto me miró. **Come h.!** ¡Ven acá! **in h.,** aquí dentro. **h. below,** aquí abajo, en la tierra. **h. and there,** aquí y allá. **h., there and everywhere,** en todas partes. **H. I am,** Heme aquí. **h. is...,** he aquí.... **H. they are,** Aquí los tienes, Aquí están. **Here's to you!** (on drinking) ¡Salud y pesetas! ¡A tu salud!
hereabouts /'hɪərə,bauts/ adv por aquí cerca
hereafter /hɪər'æftər/ adv en lo futuro; desde ahora; en adelante. n futuro, m. **the H.,** la otra vida, la vida venidera
hereat /hɪər'æt/ adv en esto
hereby /hɪər'bai/ adv por esto, por las presentes
hereditarily /hə,rɛdɪ'tɛrəli/ adv hereditariamente, por herencia
hereditary /hə'rɛdɪ,tɛri/ a hereditario
heredity /hə'rɛdɪti/ n herencia, f
herein /hɪər'ɪn/ adv en esto; aquí dentro; incluso
hereinafter /,hɪərɪn'æftər/ adv después, más abajo, más adelante, en adelante, en lo sucesivo
hereinbefore /,hɪərɪnbɪ'fɔr/ adv en lo anterior, en lo arriba citado, en lo antes mencionado, en lo precedente
hereof /hɪər'ʌv/ adv de esto
heresy /'hɛrəsi/ n herejía, f
heretic /'hɛrɪtɪk/ n hereje, mf
heretical /hə'rɛtɪkəl/ a herético
hereupon /,hɪərə'pɒn/ adv en esto, en seguida
herewith /hɪər'wɪθ/ adv junto con esto, con esto; ahora, en esta ocasión
heritage /'hɛrɪtɪdʒ/ n herencia, f
hermaphrodite /hɜr'mæfrə,dait/ a and n hermafrodita, mf
hermetic /hɜr'mɛtɪk/ a hermético
hermit /'hɜrmɪt/ n ermitaño, m. **h. crab,** paguro, cangrejo ermitaño, m
hernia /'hɜrniə/ n hernia, f
hero /'hɪərou/ n héroe, m. **h.-worship,** culto a los héroes, m
heroic /hɪ'rouɪk/ a heroico, épico
heroin /'hɛrouɪn/ n *Chem.* heroína, f
heroine /'hɛrouɪn/ n heroína, f
heroism /'hɛrou,ɪzəm/ n heroísmo, m
heron /'hɛrən/ n garza, f
herpes /'hɜrpiz/ n pl herpes, mf pl
herring /'hɛrɪŋ/ n arenque, m
hers /hɜrz/ poss pron 3rd sing (el) suyo, m; (la) suya, f; (los) suyos, m pl; (las) suyas, f pl; de ella. **This book is h.,** Este libro es el suyo de ella. **This book is h., not mine,** Este libro es el suyo no el mío. **a sister of h.,** una de sus hermanas, una hermana suya
herself /hər'sɛlf/ pron sí misma, sí; ella misma; (with reflexive verb) se. **She has done it by h.,** Lo ha hecho por sí misma. **She h. told me so,** Ella misma me lo dijo. **She is by h.,** Está a solas, Está sola
hesitancy /'hɛzɪtənsi/ n. See **hesitation**
hesitant /'hɛzɪtənt/ a indeciso, vacilante, irresoluto. **to be h.,** mostrarse irresoluto
hesitate /'hɛzɪ,teit/ vi vacilar, dudar; titubear. **I do not h. to say...,** No vacilo en decir... **He hesitated over his reply,** Tardaba en dar su respuesta
hesitatingly /'hɛzɪ,teitɪŋli/ adv irresolutamente, titubeando
hesitation /,hɛzɪ'teiʃən/ n vacilación, hesitación, f; irresolución, indecisión, f; (reluctance) aversión, repugnancia, f; titubeo, m
heterodox /'hɛtərə,dɒks/ a heterodoxo
heterodoxy /'hɛtərə,dɒksi/ n heterodoxia, f
heterogeneity /,hɛtəroudʒə'niiti/ n heterogeneidad, f
heterogeneous /,hɛtərə'dʒiniəs/ a heterogéneo

heterosexual /ˌhɛtərə'sɛkʃuəl/ n and a heterosexual, mf

hew /hyu/ vt cortar, tajar; (trees) talar; (a career, etc.) hacerse

hewer /'hyuər/ n partidor, talador, m

hexagon /'hɛksəˌgɒn/ n hexágono, m

hey /hei/ interj ¡he! ¡oye!

heyday /'hei,dei/ n apogeo, colmo, m; buenos tiempos, m pl; reinado, m; pleno vigor, m

hi /hai/ interj ¡oye! ¡hola!

hiatus /hai'eitəs/ n hiato, m; laguna, f, vacío, m

hibernate /'haibərˌneit/ vi invernar

hibernation /ˌhaibər'neiʃən/ n invernada, f

hibiscus /hai'bɪskəs/ n Bot. hibisco, m

hiccup /'hɪkʌp/ n hipo, m. vi hipar. vt decir con hipo

hidden /'hɪdn/ a escondido, secreto, oculto

hide /haid/ n piel, f; pellejo, cuero, m

hide /haid/ vt esconder, ocultar; (cover) cubrir, tapar; (dissemble) disimular; (meaning) obscurecer. vi esconderse; ocultarse, Mexico atejonarse; refugiarse. **to h. from each other,** esconderse el uno del otro. **h.-and-seek,** escondite, dormirlas, m

hidebound /'haid,baund/ a Fig. muy conservador, reaccionario, de ideas muy tradicionales

hideous /'hɪdiəs/ a horrible, repulsivo, horroroso; repugnante, odioso

hideously /'hɪdiəsli/ adv horriblemente. **to be h. ugly,** (of people) ser más feo que Picio

hideousness /'hɪdiəsnɪs/ n fealdad, horribilidad, f; repugnancia, f

hiding /'haidɪŋ/ n ocultación, f; encubrimiento, m; refugio, m; Inf. paliza, tunda, f. **h.-place,** escondite, escondrijo, m

hierarchical /ˌhaiə'rɑrkɪkəl/ a jerárquico

hierarchy /'haiəˌrɑrki/ n jerarquía, f

hieroglyph /'haiərəˌglɪf/ n jeroglífico, m

higgledy-piggledy /'hɪgəldi 'pɪgəldi/ adv revueltamente, en confusión; en montón, en desorden

high /hai/ a alto; elevado; (with altar, Mass, street, festival) mayor; grande; eminente; aristocrático; (of shooting) fijante; (of quality) superior; excelente; (haughty) orgulloso; (solemn) solemne; (good) bueno; noble; supremo; sumo; (of price) subido, m Mus. agudo; (of the sea) tempestuoso, borrascoso; (of wind and explosives) violento, fuerte; (of polish) brillante; (with speed) grande; (with tension, frequency) alto; (with number, etc.) importante, grande; (with colors) subido; (of food) pasado; (angry) enojado, airado; (of cheek bones) saliente, prominente; (well-seasoned) picante; (flattering) lisonjero. adv alto; hacia arriba; arriba; (deeply) profundamente; fuertemente; con violencia; (of price) a un precio elevado; (luxuriously) lujosamente; Mus. agudo. **a room 12 ft. h.,** un cuarto de doce pies de altura. **I knew her when she was so h.,** La conocí tamaña. **It is h. time he came,** Ya es hora de que viniese. **on h.,** en alto, arriba; en los cielos. **h. altar,** altar mayor, m. **h. and dry,** en la playa, varado, Fig. en seco. **h. and low,** arriba abajo; por todas partes. **h.-born,** aristocrático, de alta alcurnia. **h.-bred,** (of people) de buena familia; (of animals) de buena raza. **h.-class,** de buena clase, de alta calidad. **h. collar,** alzacuello, m. **h. colored,** de colores vivos; Fig. exagerado. **h. command,** (Mil., Nav.) alto mando, m. **h. court,** tribunal supremo, m. **h. day,** día festivo, m. **h. explosive,** explosivo violento, m. **h.-flown,** hinchado, retumbante, altisonante. **h. frequency,** alta frecuencia, f. **h.-handed,** arbitrario, dominador, despótico. **h.-heeled,** a de tacón alto. **h. jump,** salto de altura, m. **h. land,** tierras altas, f pl; eminencia, f. **h. life** Lat. Am. calidad m. **h. light,** Art. realce, m; acontecimiento de más interés, m; momento culminante, m. **h. mass,** misa mayor, f. **h.-minded,** de nobles pensamientos; arrogante. **h.-necked,** con cuello alto. **h.-pitched,** de tono alto, agudo. **h.-powered,** de alta potencia. **h.-powered car,** coche de muchos caballos, m. **h. precision,** suma precisión, f. **h. pressure,** n alta presión, f; Fig. urgencia, f; de alta presión, f; Fig. urgente. **h.-priced,** caro. **h. priest,** sumo pontífice, sumo sacerdote, alto sacerdote, m. **h. relief,** alto relieve, m. **h. road,** carretera mayor, f. **h. school,** instituto de

segunda enseñanza, instituto, colegio, liceo, m; colegio, liceo, instituto, m, escuela secundaria, secundaria, f. **h. sea,** marejada, f. **h. seas,** alta mar, f. **h.-seasoned,** picante. **h. society,** alta sociedad, f. **h.-sounding,** altisonante, bombástico. **h.-speed,** de alta velocidad. **h.-spirited,** brioso; alegre. **h.-strung,** nervioso, excitable, sensitivo. **h. tension,** alta tensión, f. **h. tide,** marea alta, f. **h.-toned,** Mus. agudo; Inf. de alto calibre; aristocrático. **h. treason,** alta traición, f. **h. water,** marea alta, pleamar, f. **h.-water mark,** límite de la marea, m; Fig. colmo, m; apogeo, m

High Andes, the el Altiplano m

highball /'hai,bɔl/ m Spain qüisquisoda, f, Lat. Am. jáibol, m

highbrow /'hai,brau/ a and n intelectual, mf

high-ceilinged /'hai 'silɪŋd/ a alto de techo

higher /'haiər/ a comp of **high,** más alto; más elevado; superior. **on a h. plane,** en un nivel más alto. **h. education,** enseñanza superior, f. **h. mathematics,** la alta matemática, f. **h. criticism,** la alta crítica, f. **h. up,** más arriba. **h. up the river,** río arriba

highest /'haiɪst/ a superl of **high,** el más alto; la más alta; los más altos; la más alta; sumo, supremo; excelente. **h. common factor,** Math. máximo común divisor, m. **h. references,** (of cook, gardener, etc.) informes inmejorables, m pl; Com. referencias excelentes, f pl

highland /'hailənd/ n altiplanicie, f; montañas, f pl, distrito montañoso, m. a montañoso

highlight /'hai,lait/ vtr dar relieve a, destacar

highly /'haili/ adv altamente; mucho; muy; extremadamente; grandemente; bien; favorablemente; con lisonja, lisonjeramente. **h. seasoned,** picante. **h. strung,** nervioso, excitable

highness /'hainɪs/ n altura, f; elevación, f; excelencia, f; nobleza, f; (title) Alteza, f. **His Royal H., Her Royal Highness,** Su Alteza Real

high-ranking /'hai 'ræŋkɪŋ/ a de alta jerarquía, de alto rango

highway /'hai,wei/ n camino real, m, carretera, f. **h. code,** código de la vía pública (o de la circulación), m. **h. robbery,** salteamiento de caminos, atraco, m

highwayman /'hai,weimən/ n salteador de caminos, m

highways and byways /'hai,weiz ən 'bai,weiz/ caminos y veredas

hike /haik/ vi ir de excursión. n marcha con equipo, f

hiker /'haikər/ n excursionista, mf

hiking /'haikɪŋ/ n excursionismo, m; marcha con equipo, f

hilarious /hɪ'lɛəriəs/ a alegre

hilarity /hɪ'lærɪti/ n hilaridad, f

hill /hɪl/ n colina, f, cerro, otero, m; monte, m, montaña, f; (pile) montón, m. **h.-side,** falda de montaña, ladera de una colina, f. **h.-top,** cumbre de una colina, f

hilliness /'hɪlinɪs/ n montuosidad, f, lo montañoso

hillman /'hɪl,mæn/ n montañés, m

hillock /'hɪlək/ n altozano, montículo, collado, m

hilly /'hɪli/ a montañoso

hilt /hɪlt/ n puño, m, empuñadura, f

him /hɪm/ pers pron 3rd sing direct object le, lo; (with prep.) él; indirect object le, a él; (with a direct obj. in 3rd person) se. **I gave him the magazine,** Le di la revista. **I gave it to him,** Se lo di a él. **This is for him,** Esto es para él

Himalayan /ˌhɪmə'leiən/ a himalayo

Himalayas, the /ˌhɪmə'leiəz, hɪ'mɑlyəz/ los Himalayas, m pl

himself /hɪm'sɛlf/ pron sí, sí mismo; él mismo; (reflexive) se. **He did it by h.,** Lo hizo por sí mismo. For more examples see **herself**

hind /haind/ n corza, cierva, f. a trasero, posterior. **h.-quarters,** cuarto trasero, m; (of a horse) ancas, f pl

hinder /'haindər/ a trasero, posterior

hinder /'hɪndər/ vt impedir, estorbar; embarazar, dificultar; interrumpir. vi ser un obstáculo; formar un obstáculo

hinderer /'hɪndərər/ n estorbador (-ra); interruptor (-ra)

hindmost /'haind,moust/ a posterior, postrero, último

hindrance /'hɪndrəns/ *n* obstáculo, estorbo, impedimento, *m*; perjuicio, *m*; interrupción, *f*
Hindu /'hɪndu/ *a* hindú, *mf*
Hinduism /'hɪndu,ɪzəm/ *n* indoísmo, *m*
Hindustani /,hɪndu'stɑni/ *a* indostanés. *n* (language) indostani, *m*
hinge /hɪndʒ/ *n* gozne, pernio, *m*, bisagra, *f*; articulación, *f*; *Fig.* eje, *m.* *vi* moverse (or abrirse) sobre goznes; *Fig.* depender (de). *vt* engoznar
hinged /hɪndʒd/ *a* con goznes
hint /hɪnt/ *n* indirecta, insinuación, sugestión, *f*; (advice) consejo, *m.* *vt* dar a entender, decir con medias palabras, insinuar, sugerir. *vi* insinuar. **to take the h.,** darse por aludido
hinterland /'hɪntər,lænd/ *n* interior (de un país), *m*
hip /hɪp/ *n* *Anat.* cadera, *f*; *Bot.* fruto del rosal silvestre, *m.* **h.-bath,** baño de asiento, *m.* **h.-bone,** hueso ilíaco, *m.* **h.-joint,** articulación de la cadera, *f.* **h.-pocket,** faltriquera, *f*
hipped /hɪpt/ *a* de caderas
hippodrome /'hɪpə,droum/ *n* hipódromo, *m*
hippopotamus /,hɪpə'pɒtəməs/ *n* hipopótamo, *m*
hire /haiᵊr/ *n* (employee) empleado (-da); salario, *m.* *vt* emplear; (person) contratar; tomar a su servicio. **to h. out,** alquilar. **for** or **on h.,** de alquiler.
hireling /'haiᵊrlɪŋ/ *n* mercenario, *m*
hirer /'haiᵊrər/ *n* alquilador (-ra), arrendador (-ra)
hirsute /'hɜrsut/ *a* hirsuto. **non-h.** *Bot.* lampiño
his /hɪz/ *unstressed* ɪz/ *poss pron 3rd sing* (el) suyo, *m*; (la) suya, *f*; (los) suyos, *m pl*; (las) suyas, *f pl*; de él. *poss a* su, *mf*; sus, *mf pl*; de él. **his handkerchiefs,** sus pañuelos. **his mother,** su madre, la madre de él. **a sister of his,** una de sus hermanas, una hermana suya. See **hers** for more examples.
Hispanic /hɪ'spænɪk/ *n* and *a* hispano (-na)
Hispanism /'hɪspə,nɪzəm/ *n* hispanismo, *m*
Hispanist /'hɪspənɪst/ *n* hispanista, *mf*
hispanize /'hɪspə,naiz/ *vt* españolizar
Hispano-American /hɪs'pænou ə'mɛrɪkən/ *a* hispano-americano
hiss /hɪs/ *n* silbido, *m*; (sputter) chisporroteo, *m.* *vi* silbar
hissing /'hɪsɪŋ/ *n* silbido, *m*; chisporroteo, *m.* *a* silbante
hist /hɪst/ *interj* ¡chist!
histologist /hɪs'tɒlədʒɪst/ *n* histólogo, *m*
histology /hɪ'stɒlədʒi/ *n* histología, *f*
historian /hɪ'stɔriən/ *n* historiador (-ra)
historic /hɪ'stɔrɪk/ *a* histórico
historical /hɪ'stɔrɪkəl/ *a* histórico. **h. truth,** verdad histórica, *f*
historically /hɪs'tɔrɪkəli/ *adv* históricamente
historiographer /hɪ,stɔri'ɒgrəfər/ *n* historiógrafo, *m*
historiography /hɪ,stɔri'ɒgrəfi/ *n* historiografía, *f*
history /'hɪstəri/ *n* historia, *f*. **Biblical h.,** historia sagrada, *f*. **natural h.,** historia natural, *f*
histrionic /,hɪstri'ɒnɪk/ *a* histriónico
hit /hɪt/ *n* golpe, *m*; *Aer.* impacto, *m*; (success) éxito, *m*; (piece of luck) buena suerte, *f*; (satire) sátira, *f.* *vt* golpear; (buffet) abofetear, pegar; (find) dar con, tropezar con; (attain) acertar; (guess) adivinar; (attract) atraer; (deal) lanzar, dar; (wound) herir, hacer daño (a). **The sun hits me right in the eyes,** El sol me da en la cabeza. **direct hit,** *Aer.* impacto de lleno, *m*. **lucky hit,** acierto, *m.* **to hit a straight left,** (boxing) lanzar un directo con la izquierda. **to hit the mark,** dar en el blanco; *Fig.* dar en el clavo. **hit or miss,** acierto o error. **to hit against,** dar contra, estrellar contra. **to hit back,** defenderse; devolver golpe por golpe. **to hit off,** imitar; (a likeness) coger. **to hit out,** abofetear; *Fig.* atacar; golpear (la pelota) fuera. **to hit upon,** dar con; tropezar con; encontrar por casualidad; (remember) acordarse de
hitch /hɪtʃ/ *n* tirón fácil de soltar, *m*; *Fig.* obstáculo, *m*; *Fig.* dificultad, *f*; (lift, ride) *Mexico* aventón *m.* *vt* sacudir; (a chair, etc.) arrastrar, empujar; amarrar, enganchar; atar. *vi* (along a seat, etc.) correrse (en); (get entangled) enredarse, cogerse; (rub) rascarse. **without a h.,** sin dificultad alguna, viento en popa; (smoothly) a pedir de boca

hitchhike /'hɪtʃ,haik/ *vi* ir a dedo (Argentina), pedir aventón (Mexico), pedir botella (Cuba), hacer autostop, ir por autostop (Spain)
hither /'hɪðər/ *adv* acá, hacia acá; *a* citerior, más cercano. **h. and thither,** acá y aculla allá
hitherto /'hɪðər,tu/ *adv* hasta ahora, hasta el presente
Hitlerian /hɪt'lɛəriən/ *a* hitleriano, nacista
Hitlerism /'hɪtlə,rɪzəm/ *n* hitlerismo, nacismo, *m*
hive /haiv/ *n* (for bees) colmena, *f*; (swarm) enjambre, *m*; *Fig.* centro, *m.* *vt* (bees) enjambrar. **h. of industry,** centro de industria
hoard /hɔrd/ *n* acumulación, *f*; provisión, *f*; tesoro, *f.* *vt* acumular, amasar, amontonar; guardar
hoarder /'hɔrdər/ *n* acaparador (-ra)
hoarding /'hɔrdɪŋ/ *n* amontonamiento, *m*; acaparamiento, *m*; (fence) empalizada, cerca, *f*; palizada de tablas, *f*
hoarfrost /'hɔr,frɔst/ *n* escarcha, helada blanca, *f*
hoariness /'hɔrinɪs/ *n* (of the hair) canicie, *f*; blancura, *f*; (antiquity) vejez, vetustez, *f*
hoarse /hɔrs/ *a* ronco; discordante. **to be h.,** tener la voz ronca. **to grow h.,** enronquecerse
hoarsely /'hɔrsli/ *adv* roncamente
hoarseness /'hɔrsnɪs/ *n* ronquera, *f*; *Inf.* carraspera, *f*
hoary /'hɔri/ *a* (of the hair) canoso; blanco; (old) vetusto, antiguo, viejo
hoax /houks/ *n* estafa, *f*, engaño, *m*; broma pesada, *f*; burla, *f.* *vt* estafar, engañar; burlar
hoaxer /'houksər/ *n* burlador (-ra); estafador (-ra)
hobble /'hɒbəl/ *n* (gait) cojera, *f*; traba, maniota, *f.* *vi* cojear. *vt* manear. **h. skirt,** falda muy estrecha, *f*
hobby /'hɒbi/ *n* pasatiempo, *m*, recreación, *f*; manía, afición, *f.* **h.-horse,** caballo de cartón, *m*; *Fig.* caballo de batalla, *m*
hobgoblin /'hɒb,gɒblɪn/ *n* trasgo, duende, *m*
hobnail /'hɒb,neil/ *n* clavo de herradura, clavo de botas, *m*
hobnailed /'hɒb,neild/ *a* (of boots) con clavos
hobnob /'hɒb,nɒb/ *vi* codearse, tratar con familiaridad
hock /hɒk/ *n* *Anat.* pernil, *m*; (wine) vino del Rin, *m*
hockey /'hɒki/ *n* hockey, chueca, *m.* **h. ball,** bola, pelota de chueca, *f.* **h. stick,** bastón de chueca, *m*
hocus-pocus /'houkəs 'poukəs/ *n* juego de pasa pasa, *m*; engaño, *m*, treta, *f*
hod /hɒd/ *n* cuezo, *m*
hodgepodge /'hɒdʒ,pɒdʒ/ *n* mezcolanza, *f*, fárrago, *m*
hoe /hou/ *n* azadón, *m*, *Chile, Peru* lampa *f.* *vt* azadonar; sachar
hoeing /'houɪŋ/ *n* cavadura con azadón, *f*; sachadura, *f*
hog /hɔg/ *n* cerdo, puerco, *Peru* cuchí *m.* **to go the whole hog,** ir al extremo. **hogskin,** piel de cerdo, *f*
hoggish /'hɔgɪʃ/ *a* porcuno; (greedy) comilón, tragón; (selfish) egoísta
hoist /hɔist/ *n* levantamiento, *m*; (lift) montacargas, *m*; (winch) cabria, *f*; (crane) grúa, *f.* *vt* levantar, alzar; (flags) enarbolar; suspender; *Naut.* izar
hoity-toity /'hɔiti 'tɔiti/ *a* picajoso, quisquilloso; presuntuoso
hold /hould/ *n* asimiento, agarro, *m*, presa, *f*; asidero, *m*; *Fig.* autoridad, *f*, poder, *m*; *Fig.* comprensión, *f*; (of a ship) cala, bodega, *f.* **to loose one's h.,** aflojar su presa. **to lose one's h.,** perder su presa. **to seize h. of,** asirse de, echar mano de. **h.-all,** funda, *f.* **h.-up,** (robbery) atraco, robo a mano armada, *m*; (in traffic) atasco (or detención) en el tráfico, *m*; (in work) parada, cesación de (trabajo), *f*
hold /hould/ *vt* tener; asir, agarrar; coger; retener; (embrace) abrazar; (a post) ocupar; (a meeting, etc.) celebrar; (bear weight of) aguantar, soportar; (own) poseer; *Mil.* ocupar, defender; (contain) contener; (have in store) reservar; tener capacidad para; (retain) retener; (believe) creer, sostener; (consider) opinar, tener para (mi, etc.); juzgar; (restrain) detener; contener; (of attention, etc.) mantener; (maneuvers) hacer; (observe) guardar. *vi* resistir, aguantar; (be valid) ser válido; regir; (apply) aplicarse; (continue) seguir, continuar. *interj* ¡tente! ¡para! **The room won't h. more,** En este cuarto no caben más. **They h. him in

great respect, Le tienen mucho respeto. **The theory does not h. water,** La teoría es falsa, La teoría no es lógica. **to h.** one's own, defenderse, mantenerse en sus trece. **to h.** one's breath, contener la respiración. **to h.** one's tongue, callarse. **to h.** sway, mandar; reinar. **to h.** tightly, agarrar fuertemente; (clasp) estrechar. **H. the line!** (telephone) ¡Aguarde un momento! **to h.** back, *vt* detener; contener; retener; esconder; abstenerse de entregar. *vi* quedarse atrás; vacilar, dudar; tardar en. **to h.** by, seguir; basarse en, apoyarse en. **to h.** down, sujetar; (oppress) oprimir. **to h.** fast, *vt* sujetar fuertemente. *vi* mantenerse firme; *Fig.* estar agarrado (a). **to h.** forth, *vt* ofrecer; expresar. *vi* hacer un discurso, perorar. **to h.** in, *vt* contener; retener. *vi* contenerse. **to h.** off, *vt* apartar, alejar. *vi* apartarse, alejarse, mantenerse alejado. **to h.** on, seguir, persistir en; aguantar. **to h.** out, *vt* alargar, extender; ofrecer. *vi* aguantar; durar; resistir. **to h.** over, tener suspendido sobre; (postpone) aplazar; *Fig.* amenazar con. **to h.** to, agarrarse a; atenerse a. **to h.** together, *vt* unir; juntar. *vi* mantenerse juntos. **to h.** up, *vt* (display) mostrar, enseñar; levantar; sostener, soportar; (rob) atracar, saltear; (delay) atrasar; (stop) interrumpir, parar. *vi* mantenerse en pie; (of weather) seguir bueno. **The train has been held up by fog,** El tren viene con retraso a causa de la niebla
holder /'houldər/ *n* tenedor *m*, (*f*, la) que tiene; poseedor (-ra); *Com.* tenedor (-ra); inquilino (-na); propietario (-ia); (support) soporte, *m*; mango, *m*; asa, *f*; (in compounds) porta...
holding /'houldɪŋ/ *n* tención, *f*; posesión, *f*; propiedad, *f*; (leasing) arrendamiento, *m*; (celebration) solemnización, *f*; (of a meeting) el celebrar, the tener; *pl* **holdings,** *Com.* valores habidos, *m pl*
holding company *n* compañía de cartera, *f*
hole /houl/ *n* hoyo, *m*, *Lat. Am. also* foramen *m*; boquete, *m*; agujero, *m*; cavidad, *f*; (hollow) depresión, *f*, hueco, *m*; orificio, *m*; (tear) roto, desgarro, *m*; (eyelet) punto, *m*; (in cheese) ojo, *m*; (in stocking) rotura, *f*, punto, *m*; (lair) madriguera, *f*; (nest) nido, *m*; (golf) hoyo, *m*; (fix) aprieto, *m*. *vt* agujerear; excavar; (bore) taladrar; *Sports.* meter la pelota (en). **to h. out,** (golf) meter la pelota en el hoyo. **h.-and-corner,** *a Inf.* bajo mano, secreto
hole-puncher /'houl ,pʌntʃər/ *n* agujereadora, *f*
holiday /'hɒlɪˌdei/ *n* día feriado, *m*; día de fiesta, día festivo, *m*; *a* festivo, alegre; hacer fiesta.
holiness /'houlɪnɪs/ *n* santidad, *f*
Holland /'hɒlənd/ *n* Holanda, *f*
holland /'hɒlənd/ *n* lienzo crudo. *a* holandés. **H. gin,** ginebra holandesa, *f*
hollow /'hɒlou/ *a* hueco; cóncavo; (empty) vacío; (of eyes, etc.) hundido; (of sound) sordo; (of a cough) cavernoso; (echoing) retumbante; (*Fig.* unreal) vacío, falso; insincero. *adv* vacío; *Inf.* completamente. *n* hueco, *m*; concavidad, *f*; (hole) hoyo, *m*; cavidad, *f*; (valley) hondonada, *f*, barranco, *m*; (groove) ranura, *f*; (depression) depresión, *f*; (in the back) curvadura, *f*. *vt* excavar, ahuecar; vaciar. **h.-cheeked,** con las mejillas hundidas. **h.-eyed,** con los ojos hundidos, de ojos hundidos
hollowness /'hɒlounɪs/ *n* concavidad, *f*; (falseness) falsedad, *f*; insinceridad, *f*
holly /'hɒli/ *n* acebo, agrifolio, *m*
holocaust /'hɒlə,kɔst/ *n* holocausto, *m*
holograph /'hɒlə,græf/ *n* hológrafo, *m*
holster /'houlstər/ *n* pistolera, *f*
holy /'houli/ *a* santo; sagrado; (blessed) bendito. **most h.,** *a* santísimo. **to make h.,** santificar. **H. Father,** Padre Santo, el Papa, *m*. **H. Ghost,** Espíritu Santo, *m*. **H. Office,** Santo Oficio, *m*, Inquisición, *f*. **H. Orders,** órdenes sagradas, *f pl*. **h. places,** santos lugares, *m pl*. **H. Scripture,** Sagrada Escritura, *f*. **H. See,** Cátedra de San Pedro, *f*. **h. water,** agua bendita, *f*. **H. Souls,** las Ánimas Benditas. **h. water stoup,** acetre, *m*. **H. Week,** Semana Santa, *f*
Holy Land, the la Tierra Santa, *f*.
homage /'hɒmɪdʒ/ *n* homenaje, *m*; culto, *m*; reverencia, *f*. **to pay h.,** rendir homenaje
home /houm/ *n* casa, *f*; hogar, *m*; domicilio, *m*, residencia, *f*; (institution) asilo, *m*; (haven) refugio, *m*;

(habitation) morada, *f*; (country of origin) país de origen, *m*; (native land) patria, *f*; (environment) ambiente natural, *m*; *Sports.* meta, *f*. *a* casero, doméstico; nativo; nacional, del país; indígena. *adv* a casa, hacia casa; (in one's country) en su patria; (returned) de vuelta; (of the feelings) al corazón, al alma; (to the limit) al límite. **at h.,** en casa; *Fig.* en su elemento; (of games) en campo propio; de recibo. **at-h. day,** día de recibo, *m*. **He shot the bolt h.,** Echó el cerrojo. **one's long h.,** su última morada. **to be at h.,** estar en casa; estar de recibo. **to be away from h.,** estar fuera de casa; estar ausente. **to bring h.,** traer (or llevar) a casa; hacer ver; convencer; llegar al alma; (a crime) probar (contra). **to go h.,** volver a casa; volver a la patria; (be effective) hacer su efecto; (move) herir en lo más vivo. **to make oneself at h.,** ponerse a sus anchas, sentirse como en casa de uno. **Please make yourself at home!** ¡Ha tomado posesión de su casa! **to strike h.,** dar en el blanco; herir; (hit) golpear; herir en lo más vivo; hacerse sentir. **h. affairs,** asuntos domésticos, *m pl*, (Ministry of) Gobernación, *f*. **h.-bred,** criado en el país. **h.-brewed,** fermentado en el país; fermentado en casa. **h.-coming,** regreso al hogar, *m*. **h. farm,** residencia del propietario de una finca, *f*. **h. for the aged,** asilo de ancianos, *m*. **h. front,** frente doméstico, *m*. **h. life,** vida de familia, *f*. **h.-made,** casero, de fabricación casera, hecho en casa. **H. Rule,** autonomía, *f*. **h. stretch,** último trecho (de una carrera), *m*. **h. truth,** verdad, *f*, *Inf.* fresca, *f*. **to tell someone a few h. truths,** contarle cuatro verdades
homeless /'houmlɪs/ *a* sin casa; sin hogar. **the h.,** los sin techo
homeliness /'houmlɪnɪs/ *n* comodidad, *f*; sencillez, *f*; (ugliness) fealdad, *f*
homely /'houmli/ *a* doméstico; familiar; (unpretentious) sencillo; llano; (ugly) feo; desabrido
homemaker /'houm,meikər/ *n* ama de casa, *f*
homeopath /'houmiə,pæθ/ *n* homeópata, *mf*
homeopathic /,houmiə'pæθɪk/ *a* homeópata
homeopathy /,houmi'ɒpəθi/ *n* homeopatía, *f*
home page *n* página web, *f*
Homeric /hou'mɛrɪk/ *a* homérico
home run *n* (sports) jonrón, *m*
homesick /'houm,sɪk/ *a* nostálgico. **to be h.,** tener morriña
homesickness /'houm,sɪknɪs/ *n* nostalgia, añoranza, morriña, *f*
homespun /'houm,spʌn/ *a* tejido en casa; hecho en casa; basto, grueso
homestead /'houmstɛd/ *n* hacienda, *f*; casa solariega, *f*; casa, *f*
homeward /'houmwərd/ *adv* hacia casa, en dirección al hogar; de vuelta; hacia la patria. **h.-bound,** en dirección a casa; (of ships) con rumbo al puerto de origen; (of other traffic) de vuelta
homicidal /,hɒmə'saidl/ *a* homicida
homicide /'hɒmə,said/ *n* (act) homicidio, *m*; (person) homicida, *mf*
homily /'hɒməli/ *n* *Eccl.* homilía, *f*; sermón, *m*
homing pigeon /'houmɪŋ/ *n* palomo (-ma) mensajero (-ra)
homogeneity /,houmədʒə'niiti/ *n* homogeneidad, *f*
homogeneous /,houmə'dʒiniəs/ *a* homogéneo
homologous /hə'mɒləgəs/ *a* homólogo
homonym /'hɒmənɪm/ *n* homónimo, *f*
homonymous /hə'mɒnəməs/ *a* homónimo
homosexual /,houmə'sɛkʃuəl/ *a* and *n* homosexual, *mf*
Honduran /hɒn'durən/ *a* and *n* hondureño (-ña)
Honduras /hɒn'durəs/ Honduras *f*
hone /houn/ *n* piedra de afilar, *f*. *vt* afilar, vaciar
honest /'ɒnɪst/ *a* honrado; decente, honesto; (chaste) casto; (loyal) sincero, leal; (frank) franco; imparcial. **an h. man,** un hombre de buena fe, un hombre honrado, un hombre decente
honesty /'ɒnəsti/ *n* honradez, *f*; honestidad, *f*; (chastity) castidad, *f*; sinceridad, *f*; rectitud, imparcialidad, *f*
honey /'hʌni/ *n* miel, *f*. **h.-bee,** abeja obrera, *f*. **h.-colored,** melado. **h.-pot,** jarro de miel, *m*. **h.-tongued,** melifluo; de pico de oro

honeycomb /'hʌni,koum/ n panal, m
honeycombed /'hʌni,koumd/ a apanalado
honeydew /'hʌni,du/ n mielada, f; Fig. ambrosia, f
honeyed /'hʌnid/ a de miel; Fig. meloso, adulador
honeymoon /'hʌni,mun/ n luna de miel, f; viaje de novios, viaje nupcial, m. vi hacer un viaje nupcial
honeysuckle /'hʌni,sʌkəl/ n madreselva, f
honor /'ɒnər/ n honor, m; honra, f; honradez, rectitud, integridad, f; pl **honors**, honores, m pl; condecoraciones, f pl; (last h.) honras, pompas fúnebres, f pl. vt honrar; (God) glorificar; (decorate) condecorar, laurear; (respect) respetar; reverenciar; Com. aceptar; (a toast) beber. **On my h.,** A fe mía. **point of h.,** punto de honor, pundonor, m. **word of h.,** palabra de honor, f. **Your H.,** (to a judge) Excelentísimo Señor Juez
honorable /'ɒnərəbəl/ a honorable; glorioso; digno; ilustre; (sensitive of honor) pundonoroso
honorable mention n accésit, m
honorableness /'ɒnərəbəlnıs/ n honradez, f
honorably /'ɒnərəbli/ adv honorablemente; dignamente
honorarium /,ɒnə'rɛəriəm/ n honorario, m
honorary /'ɒnə,rɛri/ a honorario, honorífico. **h. member,** socio (-ia) honorario (-ia). **h. mention,** mención honorífica, f
hood /hʊd/ n capucha, caperuza, f; (folding, of vehicles) capota, cubierta, cubierta del motor f; (of a carriage) caparazón, fuelle, m; (of a car) capó, m, (university) muceta, f; (of a fireplace) campana (de hogar), f; (cowl of chimney) sombrerete (de chimenea), m. vt cubrir con capucha; cubrir; (the eyes) ocultar, cubrir, velar
hooded /'hʊdıd/ a con capucha
hoodwink /'hʊd,wıŋk/ vt vendar (los ojos); Fig. engañar, embaucar, burlar
hoof /hʊf/ n casco, m; (cloven) pezuña, f
hoofed /hʊft/ a ungulado
hoof it ir a golpe de calcetín
hook /hʊk/ n gancho, garfio, m; (boat-) bichero, m; (fish-) anzuelo, m; (on a dress) corchete, m; (hanger) colgadero, m; (claw) garra, f. vt enganchar; (a dress) abrochar; (fish) pescar, coger; (nab) atrapar, pescar. **by h. or by crook,** a tuertas o a derechas. **left h.,** (boxing) izquierdo, m. **right h.,** (boxing) derecho, m. **to catch oneself on a h.,** engancharse. **h. and eye,** los corchetes. **h.-nosed,** con nariz de gancho, con nariz aguileña. **h.-up,** Radio. circuito, m; transmisión en circuito, f
hooked /hʊkt/ a con ganchos; corvo, ganchoso
hooking /'hʊkıŋ/ n enganche, m; (of a dress) abrochamiento, m; (of fish and Inf.) pesca, f
hookworm /'hʊk,wɜrm/ n anquilostoma, m
hooligan /'hulıgən/ n rufián, m
hoop /hup/ n aro, arco, m; (of a skirt) miriñaque, m; (croquet) argolla, f; (toy) aro, m; círculo, m. vt poner aros a; Fig. rodear
hoot /hut/ n (of owls) ululación, f, grito, m; (whistle) silbido, m; ruido, clamor, m. vi (of owls) ulular; gritar; silbar; Auto. avisar con la bocina. **to h. off the stage,** hacer abandonar la escena. **to h. down,** silbar
hooting /'hutıŋ/ n See **hoot**
hop /hɒp/ n salto, brinco, m; Bot. lúpulo, m; Bot. flores de oblón, f pl; (dance) baile, m. vi saltar con un pie; andar dando brincos; saltar; (limp) cojear; recoger lúpulo; (of plant) dar lúpulo. vt saltar. **hopgarden,** huerto de lúpulo, m. **hop-kiln,** horno para secar lúpulo, m. **hop-picker,** recolector (-ra) de lúpulo. **hop-picking,** recolección de lúpulos, f
hope /houp/ n esperanza, f; (faith) confianza, f; (expectation) anticipación, expectación, f; (probability) probabilidad, f; (illusion) ilusión, f; sueño, m. vi esperar. **to live in h. that,** vivir con la esperanza de que. **to lose h.,** desesperarse. **to h. against h.,** esperar sin motivo, esperar lo imposible. **to h. for,** desear. **to h. in,** confiar en
hopeful /'houpfəl/ a lleno de esperanzas, confiado; optimista; (Fig.) risueño. n Inf. la esperanza de la casa. **to look h.,** Fig. prometer bien
hopefully /'houpfəli/ adv con esperanza

hopefulness /'houpfəlnıs/ n optimismo, m; Fig. aspecto prometedor, m
hopeless /'houplıs/ a desesperado, sin esperanza; irremediable; (of situations) imposible; (of disease) incurable. **to be h.,** (lose hope) desesperarse; (have no remedy) ser irremediable; (of disease) no tener cura. **to make h.,** hacer perder la esperanza, desesperar; dejar sin remedio; (a situation) hacer imposible; (an illness) hacer imposible de curar
hopelessly /'houplısli/ adv sin esperanza; sin remedio; imposiblemente; incurablemente
hopelessness /'houplısnıs/ n desesperación, f; (of an illness) imposibilidad de curar, f; lo irremediable; imposibilidad, f
hopscotch /'hɒp,skɒtʃ/ n infernáculo, m, rayuela, f
horde /hɔrd/ n horda, f
horizon /hə'raizən/ n horizonte, m
horizontal /,hɔrə'zɒntl/ a horizontal. **h. suspension,** (gymnastics) plancha, f
horizontality /,hɔrəzɒn'tælıti/ n horizontalidad, f
horizontally /,hɔrə'zɒntļi/ adv horizontalmente
hormone /'hɔrmoun/ n hormona, f
horn /hɔrn/ n (of bull, etc.) cuerno, m; (antler) asta, f; (of an insect) antena, f; (of a snail) tentáculo, m; Mus. cuerno, m; trompa, f; (of motor and phonograph) bocina, f, Mexico kláxon m; (of moon) cuerno (de la luna), m. **article made of h.,** objeto de cuerno, m. **on the horns of a dilemma,** entre la espada y la pared. **h. of plenty,** cuerno de abundancia, m; cornucopia, f. **h.-rimmed spectacles,** anteojos de concha, m pl. **h. thrust,** cornada, f
horned /hɔrnd/ a cornudo; (antlered) enastado
hornet /'hɔrnıt/ n avispón, abejón, m
horny /'hɔrni/ a córneo; calloso; duro; Inf. (sexually excited) caliente
horoscope /'hɔrə,skoup/ n horóscopo, m
horrible /'hɔrəbəl/ a horrible, repugnante, espantoso; (of price) enorme; Inf. horrible
horribleness /'hɔrəbəlnıs/ n horribilidad, f, horror, m, lo espantoso
horribly /'hɔrəbli/ adv horriblemente
horrid /'hɔrıd/ a horroroso; desagradable
horridness /'hɔrıdnıs/ n horror, m; lo desagradable
horrific /hɔ'rıfık/ a horrífico, horrendo
horrify /'hɔrə,fai/ vt horrorizar; escandalizar
horrifying /'hɔrə,faiıŋ/ a horroroso, horripilante
horror /'hɔrər/ n horror, m. **h.-stricken,** horrorizado
hors d'oeuvres /'ɔr dɜrvz/ n pl entremeses, m pl
horse /hɔrs/ n caballo, m; (frame) caballete, m; (gymnastics and as punishment) potro, m. a caballar, caballuno. vt montar a caballo. **pack of horses,** caballada, f. **to ride a h.,** cabalgar, montar a caballo. **h. blanket,** manta para caballos, f; sudadero m, Lat. Am. mandil m. **h.-block,** montador, m. **h.-box,** vagón para caballos, m. **h.-breaker,** domador de caballos, m. **h.-cab,** simón, m. **h.-chestnut,** castaña pilonga, f. **h.-chestnut flower,** candela, f. **h.-collar,** collera, f, collerón m. **h.-dealer,** chalán m. **h.-doctor,** veterinario, m. **h.-flesh,** carne de caballo, f. **h.-fly,** tábano, m. **h.-latitudes,** calmas de Cáncer, f pl. **h.-laugh,** carcajada, f. **h.-master,** maestro de equitación, m. **h. meat,** carne de caballo, f. **h. pistol,** pistola de arzón, f. **h.-play,** payasada, f. **h.-power,** caballo de vapor, m; potencia, f. **a twelve-h.p. car,** un coche de doce caballos, m. **h.-race,** carrera de caballos, f. **h.-radish,** rábano picante, raíz amarga, m. **h.-sense,** sentido común, m, gramática parda, f. **h. show,** exposición de caballos, feria equina f; concurso de caballos, m. **h.-trainer,** entrenador de caballos, m. **h. tram,** tranvía de sangre, m. **h. trappings,** monturas, f pl. **That's a horse of a different color** Es harina de otro costal, Argentina, Peru Esas son otras cuarenta
horseback /'hɔrs,bæk/ n lomo de caballo, m. **on h.,** a caballo. **to ride on h.,** ir a caballo
horseman /'hɔrsmən/ n jinete, cabalgador, m
horsemanship /'hɔrsmən,ʃıp/ n equitación, f, manejo del caballo, m
horseshoe /'hɔrs,ʃu/ n herradura, f. **h. arch,** arco de herradura, arco morisco, m
horsewoman /'hɔrs,wʊmən/ n amazona, f

horticultural /ˌhɔrtɪ'kʌltʃərəl/ *a* horticultural. **h. show,** exposición de flores, *f*
horticulturalist /ˌhɔrtɪ'kʌltʃərɪst/ *n* horticultor (-ra)
horticulture /'hɔrtɪˌkʌltʃər/ *n* horticultura, *f*
hosanna /hou'zænə/ *n* hosanna, *m*
hose /houz/ *n* (tube) manga, *f*; (breeches) calzón, *m*; (stockings) medias, *f pl*; (socks) calcetines, *m pl*. **h. man,** manguero, *m*. **h.-pipe,** manga de riego, manguera, *f*
hosier /'houʒər/ *n* calcetero (-ra)
hosiery /'houʒəri/ *n* calcetería, *f*. **h. trade,** calcetería, *f*
hospice /'hɒspɪs/ *n* hospicio, *m*; asilo, refugio, *m*
hospitable /'hɒspɪtəbəl/ *a* hospitalario
hospitableness /'hɒspɪtəbəlnɪs/ *n* hospitalidad, *f*
hospital /'hɒspɪtl̩/ *n* hospital, *m*; (school) colegio, *m*. **h. nurse,** enfermera, *f*. **h. ship,** buque hospital, *m*
hospital bed cama hospitalaria, *f*
hospitality /ˌhɒspɪ'tælɪti/ *n* hospitalidad, *f*
host /houst/ *n* huésped, convidador, (of radio or tv program) presentador, *m*; (at an inn) patrón, mesonero, *m*; (army) ejército, *m*; (crowd) multitud, muchedumbre, *f*; *Eccl.* hostia, *f*; *pl* **hosts,** huestes, *f pl*. **h.-plant,** planta huésped, *f*
hostage /'hɒstɪdʒ/ *n* rehén, *m*; *Fig.* prenda, *f*
host country *n* (of an organization) país-sede, *m*
hostel /'hɒstl̩/ *n* hostería, *f*; club, *m*; residencia de estudiantes, *f*
hostelry /'hɒstl̩ri/ *n* hospedería, *f*; parador, mesón, *m*
hostess /'houstɪs/ *n* ama de la casa, *f*; la que recibe a los invitados; la que convída; (of an inn) patrona, mesonera, *f*
hostile /'hɒstl̩/ *a* enemigo; hostil, contrario (a); (of circumstances, etc.) desfavorable
hostility /hɒ'stɪlɪti/ *n* enemistad, *f*, antagonismo, *m*, mala voluntad, *f*; hostilidad, guerra, *f*. **suspension of hostilities,** suspensión de hostilidades, *f*
hot /hɒt/ *a* caliente; (of a day, etc.) caluroso; (piquant) picante; ardiente, vehemente, impetuoso; violento; impaciente; colérico; entusiasta; lleno de deseo; *Art.* intenso; (great) grande, mucho; (vigorous) enérgico. **It is hot,** Está caliente; (of weather) Hace calor. **to grow hot,** calentarse; *Fig.* acalorarse; (of weather) empezar a hacer calor. **to make hot,** calentar; dar calor (a); *Inf.* dar vergüenza. **hot-blooded,** de sangre caliente; apasionado; colérico. **hot-foot,** aprisa, apresuradamente. **hot-headed,** impetuoso. **hot-plate,** *Elec.* calientaplatos, *m*. **hot springs,** termas, *f pl*. **hot-tempered,** colérico, irascible. **hot water,** agua caliente, *f*. **hot-water bottle,** bolsa de goma, *f*. **hot-water pipes,** las cañerías del agua caliente
hotbed /'hɒtˌbɛd/ *n* semillero, vivero, *m*; *Fig.* semillero, foco, *m*
hotchpotch /'hɒtʃˌpɒtʃ/ *n* potaje, *m*
hotel /hou'tɛl/ *n* hotel, *m*. **h.-keeper,** hotelero (-ra)
hothead /'hɒtˌhɛd/ *n* exaltado (-da), fanático (-ca)
hothouse /'hɒtˌhaus/ *n* invernáculo, *m*, estufa, *f*. **h. plant,** *Fig.* planta de estufa, *f*
hotly /'hɒtli/ *adv* calurosamente; con vehemencia; coléricamente
hough /hɒk/ *n* *Zool.* pernil, *m*; (in man) corva, *f*
hound /haund/ *n* perro de caza, sabueso de artois, *m*; perro, *m*; *Inf.* canalla, *m*. *vt* cazar con perros; *Fig.* perseguir; *Fig.* incitar. **master of hounds,** montero, *m*. **pack of hounds,** jauría, *f*
hour /auər/ *n* hora, *f*; momento, *m*; ocasión, oportunidad, *f pl*. **hours,** horas, *f pl*. **after hours,** fuera de horas. **at the eleventh h.,** en el último minuto. **by the h.,** por horas; horas enteras. **small hours,** altas horas de la noche, *Inf.* las tantas, *f pl*. **to keep late hours,** acostarse tarde. **to strike the h.,** dar la hora. **h.-glass,** reloj de arena, *m*. **h.-hand,** horario, *m*. **h. of death,** hora suprema, hora de la muerte, *f*. **till all hours,** hasta la madrugada
hourly /'auərli/ *a* cada hora; por hora; continuo. *adv* a cada hora; de un momento a otro
house /*n* haus; *v* hauz/ *n* casa, *f*; (home) hogar, *m*; (lineage) familia, *f*, abolengo, *m*; *Theat.* sala, *f*, teatro, *m*; *Com.* casa comercial, *f*; (takings) entrada, *f*; (audience) público, *m*; (of Lords, Commons) cámara, *f*; (college) colegio, *m*; (parliament) parla-

mento, *m*; (building) edificio, *m*. *a* de casa; de la casa; doméstico. *vt* dar vivienda (a); alojar, recibir (or tener) en casa de uno; (store) poner, guardar. **The cottage will not h. them all,** No habrá bastante lugar para todos ellos en la cabaña, No cabrán todos en la cabaña. **country-h.,** finca, *f*; casa de campo, *f*. **full h.,** casa llena, *f*; *Theat.* lleno, *m*. **to bring down the h.,** *Theat.* hacer venirse el teatro abajo. **to keep h.,** llevar la casa; ser ama de casa. **to keep open h.,** tener mesa puesta, ser hospitalario. **to set up h.,** poner casa. **h. of cards,** castillo de naipes, *m*. **H. of Commons,** Cámara de los Comunes, *f*. **H. of Lords,** Cámara de los Lores, *f*. **H. of Representatives,** Cámara de Representantes/de Diputados. **h.-agent,** agente de casas, *m*. **h.-boat,** barco-habitación, *m*, casa flotante, *f*. **h.-dog,** perro de guardia, *m*; perro de casa, *m*. **h.-fly,** mosca doméstica, *f*. **h. furnisher,** mueblista, *mf*. **h. painter,** pintor de brocha gorda, *m*. **h. party,** reunión en una casa de campo, *f*. **h.-physician,** médico (-ca) interno (-na). **h. porter,** portero, *m*. **h. property,** propiedad inmueble, *f*. **h.-room,** capacidad de una casa, *f*. **h. slipper,** zapatilla, *f*, pantuflo, *m*. **h.-surgeon,** cirujano interno, *m*. **h.-to-h.,** de casa en casa. **h.-warming,** reunión para colgar la cremallera, *f*. **publishing h.,** editorial, *f*
housebreaker /'hausˌbreikər/ *n* ladrón de casas, *m*
housebreaking /'hausˌbreikɪŋ/ *n* robo de una casa, *m*
houseful /'hausfʊl/ *n* casa, *f*
house furnishings /'fərnɪʃɪŋz/ *n pl* artefactos para el hogar, accesorios caseros, aparatos electrodomésticos, *m pl*
household /'hausˌhould/ *n* casa, *f*; familia, *f*; hogar, *m*. *a* de la casa; doméstico; del hogar. **to be a h. word,** andar en lenguas. **h. accounts,** cuentas de la casa, *f pl*. **h. duties,** labores de la casa, *f pl*. **h. gods,** penates, *m pl*. **h. goods,** ajuar, mobiliario, *m*. **h. management,** gobierno de la casa, *m*
householder /'hausˌhouldər/ *n* padre de familia, *m*; dueño (-ña) (or inquilino (-na)) de una casa
housekeeper /'hausˌkipər/ *n* ama de llaves, *f*; mujer de su casa, *f*
housekeeping /'hausˌkipɪŋ/ *n* gobierno de la casa, *m*; economía doméstica, *f*. *a* doméstico. **to set up h.,** poner casa
housemaid /'hausˌmeid/ *n* camarera, sirvienta, *f*. **housemaid's knee,** rodilla de fregona, *f*
house of ill repute /rɪ'pyut/ *n* burdel, *m*, casa de citas, casa de zorras, casa pública, *f*; lupanar, *m*
housetops /'hausˌtɒps/ *n* tejado, *m*; (flat roof) azotea, *f*. **to shout from the h.,** pregonar a los cuatro vientos
housewife /'hausˌwaif/ *n* madre de familia, mujer de su casa, *f*; (sewing-bag) neceser de costura, *m*
housewifely /'hausˌwaifli/ *a* propio de una mujer de su casa; doméstico; (of a woman) hacendosa
housing /'hauzɪŋ/ *n* provisión de vivienda, *f*; (storage) almacenaje, *m*; alojamiento, *m*; *Inf.* casa, vivienda, *f*. **h. scheme,** urbanización, *f*. **h. shortage,** crisis de vivienda, *f*, déficit habitacional, *m*
hovel /'hʌvəl/ *n* casucha, *f*
hover /'hʌvər/ *vi* revolotear; (of hawks, etc.) cernerse; estar suspendido; rondar; seguir de cerca, estar al lado (de); *Fig.* vacilar, dudar
hovering /'hʌvərɪŋ/ *n* revoloteo, *m*; (of birds of prey) calada, *f*; *Fig.* vacilación, *f*. *a* revolante, que revolotea; que se cierne (sobre); (menacing) que amenaza, inminente
how /hau/ *adv* cómo; (by what means, in what manner) de qué modo; (at what price) a qué precio; qué; cuánto. *n* el cómo. **to know how,** saber. **For how long?** ¿Por cuánto tiempo? **How are you?** ¿Cómo está Vd.? *Inf.* ¿Qué tal? **How do you do!** ¡Mucho gusto (en conocerlo/conocerla/conocerlos/conocerlas)! **How old are you?** ¿Qué edad tiene Vd.? **How beautiful!** ¡Qué hermoso! **How big!** ¡Cuán grande! **How early?** ¿Cuán temprano? ¿Cuándo a más tardar? **How far?** ¿A qué distancia? ¿Hasta qué punto? ¿Hasta dónde? **How fast?** ¿A qué velocidad? **How few!** ¡Qué pocos! **How little!** ¡Qué pequeño!; **How!;** ¡cuánto tiempo? **How many?** ¿Cuántos? *m pl*; ¿Cuántas? *f pl*. **How much is it?** ¿Cuánto vale? **How much cloth do you want?** ¿Cuánta tela quieres? **How**

often? ¿Cuán a menudo? ¿Cuántas veces? **How would you like to go for a walk?** ¿Te gustaría pasearte? **How are you going to Lisbon?** ¿En qué vas a Lisboa?

however /hau'ɛvər/ *adv* como quiera (que) (followed by subjunctive); por más que (followed by subjunctive); por... que (followed by subjunctive). *conjunc* (nevertheless) sin embargo, no obstante. **h. good it is,** por bueno que sea. **h. he does it,** como quiera que lo haga. **h. it may be,** sea como sea. **h. much,** por mucho que

howl /haul/ *n* aullido, *m*; (groan) gemido, *m*; (cry) grito, *m*; (roar) rugido, bramido, *m*; lamento, *m*. *vi* aullar; gemir; gritar; rugir, bramar. *vt* chillar. **Each time he opened his mouth he was howled down,** Cada vez que abrió la boca se armó una bronca

howler /'haulər/ *n* aullador (-ra); *Zool.* mono (-na) chillón (-ona); (blunder) coladura, plancha, *f*. **h. monkey** *Lat. Am.* araguato *m*

howling /'haulɪŋ/ *a* aullante; gemidor; (crying) que llora; bramante, rugiente. *n* los aullidos; (groaning) el gemir, los gemidos; (crying) los gritos; (weeping) el lloro; (roaring) los bramidos, el rugir; los lamentos

hub /hʌb/ *n* (of a wheel) cubo (de rueda) *m*; *Fig.* centro, *m*. **hub cap,** tapa de cubo, *f*

hubbub /'hʌbʌb/ *n* algarada, barahúnda, *f*

huckster /'hʌkstər/ *n* revendedor (-ra). *vi* revender; (haggle) regatear

huddle /'hʌdl/ *n* (heap) montón, *m*; colección, *f*; (group) corrillo, grupo, *m*; (mixture) mezcla, *f*. *vt* arrebujar, amontonar; acurrucar, arrebujar; (throw on) echarse. *vi* amontonarse; apiñarse; acurrucarse, arrebujarse

hue /hyu/ *n* color, *m*; matiz, tono, *m*; (of opinion) matiz, *m*; (clamor) clamor, *m*, gritería, *f*. **hue and cry,** alarma, *f*

huff /hʌf/ *n* acceso de cólera, *m*

huffily /'hʌfəli/ *adv* malhumoradamente; petulantemente

huffiness /'hʌfinɪs/ *n* mal humor, *m*; petulancia, *f*; arrogancia, *f*

hug /hʌg/ *n* abrazo, *m*. *vt* abrazar, apretujar; *Fig.* acariciar; *Naut.* navegar muy cerca de. **to hug oneself,** *Fig.* congratularse

huge /hyudʒ/ *a* enorme, inmenso; gigante; vasto

hugely /'hyudʒli/ *adv* inmensamente, enormemente

hugeness /'hyudʒnɪs/ *n* inmensidad, enormidad, *f*; vastedad, *f*

Huguenot /'hyugə,nɒt/ *a* and *n* hugonote (-ta)

hulk /hʌlk/ *n* barco viejo, *m*; pontón, *m*

hulking /'hʌlkɪŋ/ *a* pesado, desgarbado

hull /hʌl/ *n Naut.* casco (de un buque), *m*; (shell) cáscara, *f*; (pod) vaina, *f*, *vt* mondar

hullabaloo /'hʌləbə,lu/ *n* alboroto, tumulto, *m*; vocerío, *m*

hum /hʌm/ *n* zumbido, *m*; ruido confuso, *m*. *vi* (sing) canturrear; zumbar; (confused sound) zurrir; (hesitate) vacilar. *vt* (a tune) tararear

human /'hyumən/ *a* humano. **the h. touch,** el don de gentes. **h. being,** ser humano, hombre, *m*

humane /hyu'mein/ *a* humanitario, humano

humanely /hyu'meinli/ *adv* humanitariamente

humaneness /hyu'meinnɪs/ *n* humanidad, *f*

humanism /'hyumə,nɪzəm/ *n* humanismo, *m*

humanist /'hyumənɪst/ *n* humanista, *mf*

humanistic /,hyumə'nɪstɪk/ *a* humanista

humanitarian /hyu,mænɪ'tɛəriən/ *a* humanitario

humanitarianism /hyu,mænɪ'tɛəriə,nɪzəm/ *n* humanitarismo, *m*

humanity /hyu'mænɪti/ *n* humanidad, *f*; raza humana, *f*. **the humanities,** las humanidades

humanize /'hyumə,naiz/ *vt* humanizar; (milk) maternizar. *vi* humanizarse

humanly /'hyumənli/ *adv* humanamente

humble /'hʌmbəl/ *a* humilde; modesto; (cringing) servil; sumiso; pobre. *vt* humillar; mortificar. **to h. oneself,** humillarse

humbleness /'hʌmbəlnɪs/ *n* humildad, *f*; modestia, *f*; (abjectness) servilismo, *m*; sumisión, *f*; pobreza, *f*; (of birth, etc.) obscuridad, *f*

humbling /'hʌmblɪŋ/ *n* humillación, *f*; mortificación, *f*

humbly /'hʌmbli/ *adv* humildemente; modestamente; servilmente

humbug /'hʌm,bʌg/ *n* (fraud) embuste, engaño, *m*; (nonsense) disparate, *m*, tontería, *f*; mentira, *f*; (person) farsante, charlatán, *m*; (sweetmeat) caramelo de menta, *m*. *vt* engañar, embaucar; burlarse de

humdrum /'hʌm,drʌm/ *a* monótono; aburrido

humeral /'hyumərəl/ *a* humeral. *n Eccl.* velo humeral, *m*

humerus /'hyumərəs/ *n Anat.* húmero, *m*

humid /'hyumɪd/ *a* húmedo

humidity /hyu'mɪdɪti/ *n* humedad, *f*

humiliate /hyu'mɪli,eit/ *vt* humillar, mortificar. **to h. oneself,** humillarse

humiliating /hyu'mɪli,eitɪŋ/ *a* humillante; degradante

humiliation /hyu,mɪli'eiʃən/ *n* humillación, mortificación, *f*; degradación, *f*

humility /hyu'mɪlɪti/ *n* humildad, *f*; modestia, *f*

humming /'hʌmɪŋ/ *n* zumbido, *m*; (of a tune) tarareo, *m*. *a* zumbador. **h.-bird,** pájaro mosca, colibrí, *m*. **h.-top,** trompa, *f*

humor /'hyumər/ *n* humor, *m*; humorismo, *m*; (temperament) disposición, *f*, carácter, *m*; (whim) capricho, *m*. *vt* seguir el humor (a), complacer; satisfacer, consentir en; (a lock, etc.) manejar. **in a good (bad) h.,** de buen (mal) humor. **I am not in the h. to...** No estoy de humor para... **sense of h.,** sentido de humor, *m*

humored /'hyumərd/ *a* (in compounds) de humor... **good-h.,** de buen humor. **ill-h.,** malhumorado, de mal humor

humoresque /,hyumə'rɛsk/ *n Mus.* capricho musical, *m*

humorist /'hyumərɪst/ *n* humorista, *mf*

humorless /'hyumərlɪs/ *a* sin sentido humorístico, sin sentido de humor

humorous /'hyumərəs/ *a* humorístico; cómico, risible

humorously /'hyumərəsli/ *adv* humorísticamente; cómicamente

humorousness /'hyumərəsnɪs/ *n* humorismo, *m*; lo cómico

hump /hʌmp/ *n* joroba, giba, *f*; (hillock) montecillo, *m*; *Inf.* depresión, *f*

humpback /'hʌmp,bæk/ *n* giba, joroba, *f*; (person) jorobado (-da), giboso (-sa)

humpbacked /'hʌmp,bækt/ *a* jorobado, giboso, corcovado

humph /*an inarticulate expression resembling a snort or grunt; spelling pron.* hʌmf/ *interj* ¡qué va!; ¡patrañas!

humus /'hyuməs/ *n* humus, mantillo, *m*

hunch /hʌntʃ/ *n:* **I have a hunch that...** *Mexico* Me cque va...

hunchback /'hʌntʃ,bæk/ *n* joroba, giba, *f*; (person) jorobado (-da), corcovado (-da), giboso (-sa)

hunchbacked /'hʌntʃ,bækt/ *a* jorobado, giboso, corcovado

hundred /'hʌndrɪd/ *n* ciento, *m*; centenar, *m*, centena, *f*. *a* ciento; (before nouns and adjectives, excluding numerals, with the exception of mil and millón) cien. **a h. thousand,** cien mil. **one h. and one,** ciento uno. **by the h.,** a centenares. **hundreds of people,** centenares de personas, *m pl.* **h.-millionth,** *a* and *n* cienmillonésimo *m* **h.-thousandth,** *a* and *n* cienmilésimo *m*

hundredfold /'hʌndrɪd,fould/ *adv* cien veces. *n* céntuplo, *m*

hundredth /'hʌndrɪdθ/ *a* centésimo, céntimo. *n* centésimo, *m*, centésima parte, *f*

Hungarian /hʌŋ'gɛəriən/ *a* and *n* húngaro (-ra) (language) húngaro, *m*

Hungary /'hʌŋgəri/ Hungría, *f*

hunger /'hʌŋgər/ *n* hambre, *f*; apetito, *m*; (craving) deseo, *m*, ansia, *f*. *vi* estar hambriento, tener hambre. **to h. for,** desear, ansiar. **h.-strike,** huelga de hambre, *f*

hungrily /'hʌŋgrəli/ *adv* hambrientamente, con hambre; ansiosamente

hungry /'hʌŋgri/ *a* hambriento; (of land) pobre;

(anxious) deseoso. **to be h.,** tener hambre. **to make h.,** dar hambre

hunk /hʌŋk/ n rebanada, f, pedazo, m

hunt /hʌnt/ n caza, cacería, montería, f; grupo de cazadores, m; (search) busca, f; (pursuit) persecución, f. vt cazar; cazar a caballo; (search) buscar; rebuscar, explorar; (pursue) perseguir. **to h. down,** perseguir. **to h. for,** buscar. **to h. out,** buscar; descubrir, desenterrar

hunter /'hʌntər/ n cazador, m; caballo de caza, m; (watch) saboneta, f

hunting /'hʌntɪŋ/ n caza, f; caza a caballo, f; persecución, f. a cazador, de caza. **to go h.,** ir a cazar. **h.-box,** pabellón de caza, m. **h.-cap,** gorra de montar, f. **h.-crop,** látigo para cazar, m. **h.-ground,** coto de caza, terreno de caza, m. **h.-horn,** cuerno de caza, m; corneta de monte, f. **h. party,** partido de caza, m, cacería, f

huntsman /'hʌntsmən/ n cazador, montero, m

huntsmanship /'hʌntsmənˌʃɪp/ n montería, arte de cazar, f

hurdle /'hɜrdl/ n valla, f; zarzo, m. **h.-race,** carrera de obstáculos, f; carrera de vallas, f

hurdy-gurdy /'hɜrdi'gɜrdi/ n organillo, m

hurl /hɜrl/ vt lanzar, tirar, arrojar, echar. **to h. oneself,** lanzarse. **to h. oneself against,** arrojarse a (o contra). **to h. oneself upon,** abalanzarse sobre

hurly-burly /'hɜrli'bɜrli/ n alboroto, tumulto, m

hurrah /hə'rɑ/ interj ¡hurra! ¡viva! n vítor, m. **H. for...!** ¡Viva...!, ¡Vivan...! **to shout h.,** vitorear

hurricane /'hɜrɪˌkein/ n huracán, m. **h.-lamp,** lámpara sorda, f

hurried /'hɜrid/ a apresurado, precipitado; hecho a prisa; superficial

hurriedly /'hɜridli/ adv apresuradamente, precipitadamente, con prisa; superficialmente; (of writing) a vuela pluma

hurry /'hɜri/ n prisa, f; precipitación, f; urgencia, f; confusión, f; alboroto, m. **in a h.,** aprisa. **in a great h.,** aprisa y corriendo. **to be in a h.,** llevar prisa, estar de prisa. **There is no h.,** No corre prisa, No hay prisa

hurry /'hɜri/ vt apresurar, dar prisa, Lat. Am. apurar (a); llevar aprisa; hacer andar aprisa; enviar apresuradamente; precipitar; acelerar. vi darse prisa; apresurarse. **to h. after,** correr detrás de, seguir apresuradamente. **to h. away,** vi marcharse aprisa, marcharse corriendo; huir; salir precipitadamente. vt hacer marcharse aprisa; llevar con prisa. **to h. back,** vi volver aprisa, apresurarse a volver. vt hacer volver aprisa. **to h. in,** vi entrar aprisa, entrar corriendo. vt hacer entrar aprisa. **to h. off.** See **to h. away. to h. on,** vi apresurarse. vt apresurar, precipitar. **to h. out,** salir rápidamente. **to h. over,** hacer rápidamente; concluir aprisa; despachar rápidamente; (travel over) atravesar aprisa; pasar rápidamente por. **to h. toward,** llevar rápidamente hacia; arrastrar hacia; impeler hacia. **to h. up,** vi darse prisa. vt apresurar, precipitar, Lat. Am. apurar; estimular

hurt /hɜrt/ n herida, f; (harm) daño, mal, m; perjuicio, m. vt (wound) herir; (cause pain) doler; hacer daño (a); hacer mal (a); (damage) perjudicar, estropear, Lat. Am. afectar; (offend) ofender; (the feelings) mortificar, lastimar, herir. vi doler; hacer mal; perjudicarse, estropearse. **I haven't h. myself,** No me he hecho daño. **Does it still h. you?** ¿Te duele todavía? **to h. deeply,** Fig. herir en el alma. **to h. a person's feelings,** herirle (a uno) el amor propio, lastimar, ofender

hurtful /'hɜrtfəl/ a nocivo, dañino; injurioso, pernicioso

hurtfulness /'hɜrtfəlnɪs/ n nocividad, f; perniciosidad, f

hurtle /'hɜrtl/ vt lanzar. vi lanzarse; volar; caer

husband /'hʌzbənd/ n esposo, marido, m. vt economizar, ahorrar. **h. and wife,** los esposos, los cónyuges

husbandry /'hʌzbəndri/ n labor de los campos, agricultura, f; (thrift) frugalidad, parsimonia, f

hush /hʌʃ/ n silencio, m, tranquilidad, f. interj ¡chitón! ¡calla! ¡silencio! vt silenciar, hacer callar, imponer silencio (a); (a baby) adormecer; Fig. sosegar, calmar. vi callarse, enmudecer. **to h. up,** mantener secreto, ocultar. **h.-h.,** secreto. **h. money,** soborno, chantaje, m

hushaby /'hʌʃəˌbai/ interj ¡duerme!

husk /hʌsk/ n (of grain) cascabillo, m; zurrón, m; cáscara, f; (of chestnut) erizo, m; vt Lat. Am. deshojar (corn)

huskily /'hʌskəli/ adv roncamente

huskiness /'hʌskinɪs/ n ronquera, f; Inf. robustez, f

husky /'hʌski/ a (of voice) ronco; Bot. cascarudo; (Eskimo) esquimal; Inf. robusto, fuerte. n perro esquimal, m

hussy /'hʌsi/ n pícara, bribona, f

hustle /'hʌsəl/ vt empujar, codear; Fig. precipitar; Inf. acelerar. vi codearse; andarse de prisa

hut /hʌt/ n choza, cabaña, barraca, f, Mexico jacal, elsewhere in Lat. Am. bohío m

hutch /hʌtʃ/ n (chest) arca, f, cofre, m; (cage) jaula, f; (for rabbits) conejera, f; (for rats) ratonera, f; Inf. choza, f

hyacinth /'haiəsɪnθ/ n jacinto, m

hybrid /'haibrɪd/ a híbrido; mestizo, mixto. n híbrido, m

hybridism /'haibrɪˌdɪzəm/ n hibridismo, m

hybridization /ˌhaibrɪdə'zeiʃən/ n hibridación, f

hybridize /'haibrɪˌdaiz/ vt cruzar. vi producir (o generar) híbridos

hydrangea /hai'dreindʒə/ n Bot. hortensia, f

hydrant /'haidrənt/ n boca de riego, f

hydrate /'haidreit/ n Chem. hidrato, m. vt hidratar

hydraulic /hai'drɔlɪk/ a hidráulico. **h. engineering,** hidrotecnia, f

hydraulics /hai'drɔlɪks/ n hidráulica, f

hydrocarbon /ˌhaidrə'karbən/ n Chem. hidrocarburo, m

hydrochloric /ˌhaidrə'klɔrɪk/ a clorhídrico. **h. acid,** ácido clorhídrico, m

hydrogen /'haidrədʒən/ n hidrógeno, m. **h. peroxide,** agua oxigenada, f

hydrogenation /ˌhaidrədʒə'neiʃən/ n hidrogenación, f

hydrogenize /'haidrədʒəˌnaiz/ vt hidrogenizar

hydrolysis /hai'drɒləsɪs/ n hidrólisis, f

hydromel /'haidrəˌmel/ n aguamiel, f, hidromel, m

hydropathic /ˌhaidrə'pæθɪk/ a hidropático. **h. establishment,** balneario, m

hydrophobia /ˌhaidrə'foubiə/ n hidrofobia, rabia, f

hydrophobic /ˌhaidrə'foubɪk/ a hidrofóbico, rabioso

hydroplane /'haidrəˌplein/ n hidroplano, m

hydrotherapic /ˌhaidrouθə'ræpɪk/ a hidroterápico

hydrotherapy /ˌhaidrə'θerəpi/ n hidroterapia, f

hyena /hai'inə/ n hiena, f

hygiene /'haidʒin/ n higiene, f. **personal h.,** higiene privada, f

hygienic /ˌhaidʒi'ɛnɪk/ a higiénico

hymen /'haimən/ n Anat. himen, m; himeneo, m

hymeneal /ˌhaimə'niəl/ a nupcial

hymn /hɪm/ n himno, m. **h.-book,** himnario, m

hyperbole /hai'pɜrbəli/ n hipérbole, f

hyperbolical /ˌhaipər'bɒlɪkəl/ a hiperbólico

hypercorrection /ˌhaipərkə'rɛkʃən/ n seudocultismo, supercultismo, m, ultracorrección, f

hypercritic /ˌhaipər'krɪtɪk/ n hipercrítico, m

hypercritical /ˌhaipər'krɪtɪkəl/ a hipercrítico, criticón, f

hypersensitive /ˌhaipər'sɛnsɪtɪv/ a vidrioso, quisquilloso

hypertension /ˌhaipər'tɛnʃən/ n hipertensión, f

hypertrophy /hai'pɜrtrəfi/ n hipertrofia, f. vi hipertrofiarse

hyphen /'haifən/ n guión, m

hypnosis /hɪp'nousɪs/ n hipnosis, f

hypnotic /hɪp'nɒtɪk/ a hipnótico. n (person) hipnótico (-ca); (drug) hipnótico, narcótico, m

hypnotism /'hɪpnəˌtɪzəm/ n hipnotismo, m

hypnotist /'hɪpnətɪst/ n hipnotizador (-ra)

hypnotization /ˌhɪpnətə'zeiʃən/ n hipnotización, f

hypnotize /'hɪpnəˌtaiz/ vt hipnotizar

hypo /'haipou/ *n* (sodium hyposulfite) hiposulfito sólido, *m*

hypochondria /,haipə'kɒndriə/ *n* hipocondria, *f*

hypochondriac /,haipə'kɒndri,æk/ *n* hipocondríaco (-ca)

hypochondriacal /,haipoukən'draiəkəl/ *a* hipocondríaco

hypocrisy /hɪ'pɒkrəsi/ *n* hipocresía, *f*; mojigatería, gazmoñería, *f*

hypocrite /'hɪpəkrɪt/ *n* hipócrita, *mf*; mojigato (-ta). **to be a h.,** ser hipócrita

hypocritical /,hɪpə'krɪtɪkəl/ *a* hipócrita; mojigato, gazmoño

hypocritically /,hɪpə'krɪtɪkəli/ *adv* hipócritamente, con hipocresía

hypodermic /,haipə'dɜrmɪk/ *a* hipodérmico. **h. syringe,** jeringa de inyecciones, *f*

hypotenuse /hai'pɒtṇ,us/ *n Geom.* hipotenusa, *f*

hypothesis /hai'pɒθəsɪs/ *n* hipótesis, *f*

hypothetical /,haipə'θetɪkəl/ *a* hipotético

hysterectomy /,hɪstə'rektəmi/ *n Surg.* histerectomía, *f*

hysteria /hɪ'steriə/ *n Med.* histerismo, *m*; histeria, *f*, ataque de nervios, *m*

hysterical /hɪ'sterɪkəl/ *a* histérico. **to become h.,** tener un ataque de nervios. **hysterics,** *n pl* ataque de nervios, *m*

I

i /ai/ *n* (letter) i. *1st pers pron* yo. **It is I,** Soy yo. Normally omitted, the verb alone being used except when **yo** is needed for emphasis, e.g. *Hablo a María,* I speak to Mary, *but Yo toco el violín, pero Juan toca el piano, I* play the violin, but *John* plays the piano

Iberia /ai'biriə/ Iberia

Iberian /ai'biəriən/ *a* ibero, ibérico. *n* ibero (-ra)

Iberian Peninsula, the la Península Ibérica

ibex /'aibeks/ *n Zool.* íbice, *m*

ice /ais/ *n* hielo, *m*; (ice cream) helado, *m. vt* helar; cubrir de hielo; congelar, cuajar; (a cake, etc.) garapiñar, escarchar, alcorzar. **to ice up,** (*Aer., Auto.*) helarse. **to be as cold as ice,** *Inf.* estar hecho un hielo. **His words cut no ice,** Sus palabras ni pinchan ni cortan. **ice-age,** edad del hielo, *f.* **ice-ax,** piolet, *m.* **icebox,** nevera, *f.* **ice-cream,** helado, mantecado, *m.* **ice-cream cone,** cucurucho de helado, *m.* **ice-cream freezer,** heladora, *f.* **ice-cream vendor,** mantequero (-ra). **ice-field,** campo de hielo, *m.* **ice hockey,** hockey sobre patines, *m.* **ice-pack,** bolsa para hielo, *f.* **ice-skates,** patines de cuchilla, *m pl.* **ice water,** agua helada, *f*

iceberg /'aisbɜrg/ *n* iceberg, témpano de hielo, banco de hielo, *m*

icebound /'ais,baund/ *a* aprisionado por el hielo; atascado en el hielo; (of roads, etc.) helado

iced /aist/ *a* helado; congelado, cuajado; (cakes) garapiñado, escarchado; (of drinks) con hielo. **i. drink,** sorbete, *m*

Iceland /'aislənd/ Islandia, *f*

Icelander /'ais,lændər/ *n* islandés (-esa)

icelandic /ais'lændɪk/ *a* islandes, islándico. *n* (language) islandés, *m*

icicle /'aisikəl/ *n* carámbano, canelón, cerrión, *m*

icily /'aisəli/ *adv* fríamente; *Fig.* frígidamente, con indiferencia, con frialdad

iciness /'aisinɪs/ *n* frialdad, frigidez, *f*; *Fig.* indiferencia, frigidez, *f*

icing /'aisɪŋ/ *n* helada, *f*, hielo, *m*; (on a cake, etc.) alcorza, capa de azúcar, *f*

icon /'aɪkɒn/ *n* icono, *m*

iconocl /ai'kɒnə,klæst/ *n* iconoclasta, *mf*

iconoclasuc /ai,kɒnə'klæstɪk/ *a* iconoclasta

iconography /,aikə'nɒgrəfi/ *n* iconografía, *f*

iconology /,aikə'nɒlədʒi/ *n* iconología, *f*

icy /'aisi/ *a* helado; glacial, frío; *Med.* álgido; *Fig.* indiferente, desabrido; *Poet.* frígido, gélido

idea /ai'diə/ *n* idea, *f*, concepto, *m*; (opinion) juicio, *m*, opinión, *f*; (notion) impresión, noción, *f*; (plan) proyecto, plan, designio, *m*. **to form an i. of,** hacerse una idea de, formar un concepto de. **to have an i. of,** tener una idea de; tener nociones de. **An i. struck me,** Se me ocurrió una idea. **full of ideas,** preñado (or lleno) de ideas. **I had no i. that...** No tenía la menor idea de que... No sabía que... **What an i.!** ¡Qué idea!

ideal /ai'diəl/ *a* ideal; excelente, perfecto; (utopian) utópico; (imaginary) imaginario, irreal, ficticio. *n* ideal, *m*; modelo, prototipo, *m*

idealism /ai'diə,lɪzəm/ *n* idealismo, *m*

idealist /ai'diəlɪst/ *n* idealista, *mf*

idealistic /ai,diə'lɪstɪk/ *a* idealista

idealization /ai,diəlɪ'zeiʃən/ *n* idealización, *f*

idealize /ai'diə,laiz/ *vt* idealizar

ideally /ai'diəli/ *adv* idealmente

ideation /,aidi'eiʃən/ *n Philos.* ideación, *f*

idem /'aidɛm/ *adv* ídem

identical /ai'dɛntɪkəl/ *a* idéntico, mismo, igual; muy parecido, semejante

identically /ai'dɛntɪkəli/ *adv* idénticamente

identifiable /ai,dɛntɪ'faiəbəl/ *a* identificable

identification /ai,dɛntəfɪ'keiʃən/ *n* identificación, *f*. **i. number,** placa de identidad, *f*

identify /ai'dɛntə,fai/ *vt* identificar. **to i. oneself with,** identificarse con

identity /ai'dɛntɪti/ *n* identidad, *f*. **i. card,** cédula personal, *f*; carnet de identidad, *m*. **i. disc,** disco de identidad, *m*

ideogram, ideograph /'ɪdiə,græm; 'ɪdiə,græf/ *n* ideograma, *m*

ideography /,ɪdi'ɒgrəfi/ *n* ideografía, *f*

ideological /,aidiə'lɒdʒɪkəl/ *a* ideológico

ideologist /,aidi'ɒlədʒɪst/ *n* ideólogo (-ga)

ideology /,aidi'ɒlədʒi/ *n* ideología, *f*

Ides /aidz/ *n pl* idus, *m pl*

idiocy /'ɪdiəsi/ *n* idiotez, imbecilidad, *f*; (foolishness) necedad, tontería, sandez, *f*

idiom /'ɪdiəm/ *n* idiotismo, *m*; modismo, *m*, locución, *f*; (language) habla, *f*; lenguaje, *m*

idiomatic /,ɪdiə'mætɪk/ *a* idiomático

idiopathy /,ɪdi'ɒpəθi/ *n Med.* idiopatía, *f*

idiosyncrasy /,ɪdiə'sɪŋkrəsi/ *n* idiosincrasia, *f*

idiosyncratic /,ɪdiousɪn'krætɪk/ *a* idiosincrásico

idiot /'ɪdiət/ *n* idiota, imbécil, *mf*; (fool) necio (-ia), tonto (-ta), mentecato (-ta)

idiotic /,ɪdi'ɒtɪk/ *a* idiota, imbécil; (foolish) necio, tonto, sandio

idle /'aidḷ/ *a* desocupado; indolente, ocioso; (unemployed) cesante, sin empleo; (lazy) perezoso, holgazán; (of machines) parado, inactivo; (useless) vano, inútil, sin efecto; (false) falso, mentiroso, infundado; (stupid) fútil, frívolo. *vi* holgar, estar ocioso; holgazanear, haraganear, gandulear. **to i. away,** malgastar, perder. **to i. away the time,** pasar el rato, matar el tiempo. **i. efforts,** vanos esfuerzos, *m pl.* **i. fancies,** ilusiones, fantasías, *f pl,* sueños, *m pl.* **i. hours,** horas desocupadas, *f pl,* ratos perdidos, *m pl.* **i. question,** pregunta ociosa, *f.* **i. tale,** cuento de viejas, *m.* **i. threat,** reto vacuo, *m*

idleness /'aidḷnɪs/ *n* ociosidad, indolencia, inacción, *f*; pereza, holgazanería, gandulería, *f*; (uselessness) inutilidad, futilidad, *f*

idler /'aidlər/ *n* ocioso (-sa), haragán (-ana); perezoso (-sa), holgazán (-ana), gandul (-la), *Lat. Am.* aplanacalles *mf*

idly /'aidli/ *adv* ociosamente, perezosamente; (uselessly) vanamente

idol /'aidḷ/ *n* ídolo, *m*. **a popular i.,** el ídolo de las masas, *m*

idolater /ai'dɒlətər/ *n* idólatra, *mf*; (admirer) amante, *mf* esclavo (-va), admirador (-ra)

idolatrous /ai'dɒlətrəs/ *a* idólatra, idolátrico

idolatrously /ai'dɒlətrəsli/ *adv* idolatradamente, con idolatría
idolatry /ai'dɒlətri/ *n* idolatría, *f*; (devotion) adoración, pasión, *f*
idolization /ˌaidl̩ə'zeiʃən/ *n* idolatría, *f*
idolize /'aidl̩ˌaiz/ *vt* idolatrar, adorar
idyll /'aidl̩/ *n* idilio, *m*
idyllic /ai'dilik/ *a* idílico
if /if/ *conjunc* si; (even if) aunque, aun cuando; (whenever) cuando, en caso de que; (whether) si. **as if,** como si (foll. by subjunc.). **If he comes, we shall tell him,** Si viene se lo diremos. **If he had not killed the tiger, she would be dead,** Si él no hubiera matado al tigre, ella estaría muerta. **If ever there was one,** Si alguna vez lo hubiera. **if necessary,** si fuese necesario. **if not,** si no, si no es que (e.g., *Poet and philosopher are twins, if not one and the same,* Poeta y filósofo son hermanos gemelos, si no es que la misma cosa). **If only!** ¡Ojalá que! (foll. by subjunc.)
igloo /'iglu/ *n* iglú, *m*
igneous /'igniəs/ *a* ígneo
ignite /ig'nait/ *vt* encender, pegar fuego (a), incendiar. *vi* prender fuego, incendiarse; arder
ignition /ig'niʃən/ *n* ignición, *f*; *Auto.* encendido, *m*. **i. coil,** *Auto.* carrete de inducción del encendido, *m*. **i. key,** *Auto.* llave del contacto, *f*
ignoble /ig'noubəl/ *a* innoble, vil, indigno
ignobly /ig'noubli/ *adv* bajamente, vilmente
ignominious /ˌignə'miniəs/ *a* ignominioso
ignominiously /ˌignə'miniəsli/ *adv* ignominiosamente
ignominy /'ignəˌmini/ *n* ignominia, deshonra, afrenta, *f*
ignoramus /ˌignə'reiməs/ *n* ignorante, *mf*
ignorance /'ignərəns/ *n* ignorancia, *f*; (unawareness) desconocimiento, *m*. **to plead i.,** pretender ignorancia
ignorant /'ignərənt/ *a* ignorante; inculto. **He is an i. fellow,** Es un ignorante. **to be i. of,** no saber, ignorar. **to be very i.,** ser muy ignorante, *Inf.* ser muy burro
ignorantly /'ignərəntli/ *adv* ignorantemente, por ignorancia; neciamente
ignore /ig'nɔr/ *vt* no hacer caso de, desatender; (omit) pasar por alto de, ignorar; *Law.* rechazar; (pretend not to recognize) hacer semblante de no reconocer; (not recognize) no reconocer
iguana /i'gwanə/ *n Zool.* iguana, *f*
ileac /'iliæk/ *a Anat.* ilíaco
ileum /'iliəm/ *n Anat.* íleon, *m*
Iliad /'iliəd/ *n* Ilíada, *f*
ilium /'iliəm/ *n Anat.* ilion, *m*
ill /il/ *n* mal, *m*. *a* (sick) enfermo, malo; (bad) malo; (unfortunate) desdichado, funesto. *adv* mal. **to be ill,** estar malo, **to be taken ill,** caer enfermo. **ill-advised,** mal aconsejado; desacertado, imprudente. **ill-advisedly,** imprudentemente. **ill at ease,** incómodo. **ill-bred,** mal criado, mal educado, mal nacido. **ill-breeding,** mala crianza, mala educación, *f*. **ill-disposed,** malintencionado. **ill fame,** mala fama, *f*. **ill-fated,** malhadado, malaventurado, aciago, fatal. **ill-favored,** mal parecido, feúcho. **ill-feeling,** hostilidad, *f*, rencor, *m*. **ill-gotten,** maladquirido. **ill-humor,** mal humor, *m*. **ill-humored,** de mal humor, malhumorado. **ill-luck,** desdicha, mala suerte, malaventura, *f*; infortunio, *m*. **ill-mannered,** mal educado. **ill-natured,** malévolo, perverso. **ill-naturedly,** malignamente. **ill-omened,** nefasto. **ill-spent,** malgastado, perdido. **ill-spoken,** mal hablado. **ill-suited,** malavenido. **ill-timed,** inoportuno, intempestivo. **ill-treat,** maltratar, malparar, tratar mal. **ill-treated,** que ha sido tratado mal; maltrecho. **ill-treatment,** maltratamiento, *m*, crueldad, *f*. **ill-turn,** mala jugada, *f*. **to do an ill-turn,** hacer un flaco servicio. **ill will,** mala voluntad, *f*; rencor, *m*, ojeriza, *f*. **to bear a person ill will,** guardarle rencor
illegal /i'ligəl/ *a* ilegal; indebido, ilícito
illegality /ˌili'gæliti/ *n* ilegalidad, *f*
illegally /i'ligəli/ *adv* ilegalmente
illegibility /iˌledʒə'biliti/ *n* ilegibilidad, *f*
illegible /i'ledʒəbəl/ *a* ilegible, indescifrable
illegibly /i'ledʒəbli/ *adv* de un modo ilegible

illegitimacy /ˌili'dʒitəməsi/ *n* ilegitimidad, *f*; falsedad, *f*
illegitimate /ˌili'dʒitəmit/ *a* ilegítimo, bastardo; falso; ilícito, desautorizado
illegitimately /ˌili'dʒitəmitli/ *adv* ilegítimamente
illiberal /i'libərəl/ *a* iliberal; intolerante, estrecho de miras; (mean) avaro, tacaño, ruin
illiberally /i'libərəli/ *adv* avariciosamente, ruinmente
illicit /i'lisit/ *a* ilícito, indebido, ilegal
illicitly /i'lisitli/ *adv* ilícitamente, ilegalmente
illicitness /i'lisitnis/ *n* ilicitud, ilegalidad, *f*
illimitable /i'limitəbəl/ *a* ilimitado, sin límites, infinito
illiteracy /i'litərəsi/ *n* analfabetismo, *m*
illiterate /i'litərit/ *a and n* analfabeto (-ta), iliterato (-ta)
illness /'ilnis/ *n* enfermedad, dolencia, *f*, mal, *m*
illogical /i'lɒdʒikəl/ *a* ilógico; absurdo, irracional
illogicality /iˌlɒdʒi'kæliti/ *n* falta de lógica, *f*; absurdo, *m*, irracionalidad, *f*
illuminant /i'lumənənt/ *a* iluminador, alumbrador
illuminate /i'luməˌneit/ *vt* iluminar, alumbrar; *Art.* iluminar; (explain) aclarar, ilustrar
illuminated /i'luməˌneitid/ *a* iluminado, encendido; *Art.* iluminado. **i. sign,** letrero luminoso, *m*
illuminati /iˌlumə'nati/ *n pl* secta de los alumbrados, *f*
illuminating /i'luməˌneitiŋ/ *a* iluminador; (explanatory) aclaratorio. *n Art.* iluminación, *f*
illumination /iˌlumə'neiʃən/ *n* iluminación, *f*, alumbrado, *m*; (for decoration) luminaria, *f*; *Art.* iluminación, *f*; *Fig.* inspiración, *f*
illuminator /i'luməˌneitər/ *n Art.* iluminador (-ra)
illumine /i'lumin/ *vt* encender, alumbrar; *Fig.* inspirar
illusion /i'luʒən/ *n* ilusión, *f*, engaño, *m*; (dream) esperanza, ilusión, *f*, ensueño, *m*. **to harbor illusions,** tener ilusiones
illusive /i'lusiv/ *a* ilusivo, engañoso, falso
illusively /i'lusivli/ *adv* falsamente, aparentemente
illusoriness /i'lusərinis/ *n* ilusión, falsedad, *f*, engaño, *m*
illusory /i'lusəri/ *a* ilusorio, deceptivo, falso, irreal
illustrate /'iləˌstreit/ *vt* ilustrar, aclarar, explicar, elucidar; *Art.* ilustrar; (prove) probar, demostrar
illustration /ˌilə'streiʃən/ *n* ejemplo, *m*; ilustración, *f*; *Art.* grabado, *m*; estampa, *f*; (explanation) elucidación, aclaración, *f*
illustrative /i'lʌstrətiv/ *a* ilustrativo, ilustrador, explicativo, aclaratorio
illustrator /'iləˌstreitər/ *n* ilustrador (-ra), grabador (-ra)
illustrious /i'lʌstriəs/ *a* ilustre, famoso, renombrado, distinguido
illustriously /i'lʌstriəsli/ *adv* ilustremente, noblemente
illustriousness /i'lʌstriəsnis/ *n* eminencia, *f*, renombre, *m*, grandeza, *f*
image /'imidʒ/ *n* (optics) imagen, *f*; efigie, imagen, *f*; (religious) imagen, estatua, *f*; *Art.* figura, *f*; (metaphor) metáfora, expresión, *f*; (of a person) retrato, *m*. **to be the i. of,** ser el retrato de. **sharp i.,** imagen nítida, *f*. **i. breaker,** iconoclasta, *mf*. **i. vendor,** vendedor (-ra) de imágenes
imagery /'imidʒri/ *n Art.* imaginería, *f*; (style) metáforas, *f pl*
imaginable /i'mædʒənəbəl/ *a* imaginable
imaginary /i'mædʒəˌneri/ *a* imaginario; fantástico, de ensueño
imagination /iˌmædʒə'neiʃən/ *n* imaginación, *f*; imaginativa, fantasía, inventiva, *f*, ingenio, *m*
imaginative /i'mædʒənətiv/ *a* imaginativo; fantástico
imagine /i'mædʒin/ *vt* imaginar, concebir; idear, proyectar, inventar; figurarse, suponer. **Just i.!** ¡Imagínese usted!
imam /i'mɑm/ *n* imán, *m*
imbecile /'imbəsil/ *a* imbécil; (foolish) necio, estúpido, tonto. *n* imbécil, *mf*; (fool) necio (-ia), tonto (-ta), estúpido (-da)
imbecility /ˌimbə'siliti/ *n* imbecilidad, *f*; (folly) necedad, sandez, *f*

imbibe /ɪm'baib/ vt embeber, absorber; (drink) sorber, chupar; empaparse de
imbibing /ɪm'baibɪŋ/ n imbibición, absorción, f
imbroglio /ɪm'brouljou/ n embrollo, lío, m
imbue /ɪm'byu/ vt imbuir, calar, empapar; teñir. **to i. with,** infundir de
imitable /'ɪmɪtəbəl/ a imitable
imitate /'ɪmɪˌteit/ vt imitar; copiar, reproducir; (counterfeit) contrahacer
imitation /ˌɪmɪ'teiʃən/ n imitación, f; copia, f; remedo, traslado, m. a imitado; falso, artificial
imitative /'ɪmɪˌteitɪv/ a imitativo; imitador
imitativeness /'ɪmɪˌteitɪvnɪs/ n facultad imitativa (or de imitacion), f
imitator /'ɪmɪˌteitər/ n imitador (-ra); contrahacedor (-ra), falsificador (-ra)
immaculate /ɪ'mækyəlɪt/ a inmaculado, puro; (of dress) elegante. **I. Conception,** la Purísima Concepción
immaculately /ɪ'mækyəlɪtli/ adv inmaculadamente; elegantemente
immaculateness /ɪ'mækyəlɪtnɪs/ n pureza, f; (of dress) elegancia, f
immanence /'ɪmənəns/ n inmanencia, inherencia, f
immanent /'ɪmənənt/ a inmanente; inherente
immaterial /ˌɪmə'tɪəriəl/ a inmaterial, incorpóreo; sin importancia. **It is i. to me,** Me es indiferente, No me importa, Me da lo mismo, Me da igual
immateriality /ˌɪməˌtɪəri'ælɪti/ n inmaterialidad, f
immature /'ɪmə'tʃʊr/ a inmaduro; precoz; (of fruit) verde
immaturity /ˌɪmə'tʃʊrɪti/ n falta de madurez, f; precocidad, f
immeasurability /ɪˌmɛʒərə'bɪlɪti/ n inmensurabilidad, inmensidad, f
immeasurable /ɪ'mɛʒərəbəl/ a inmensurable, inmenso, imponderable
immeasurably /ɪ'mɛʒərəbli/ adv inmensamente, enormemente
immediate /ɪ'midiɪt/ a (of place) inmediato, cercano, contiguo; (of time) próximo, inmediato, directo; (of action) inmediato, perentorio; (on letters) urgente. **to take i. action,** tomar acción inmediata
immediately /ɪ'midiɪtli/ adv inmediatamente, (of place) próximamente, contiguamente; (of time) luego, seguidamente, en el acto, ahora mismo, enseguida; directamente; (as soon as) así que
immemorial /ˌɪmə'mɔriəl/ a inmemorial, inmemorable
immemoria.ly /ˌɪmə'mɔriəli/ adv desde tiempo inmemorial
immense /ɪ'mɛns/ a inmenso, enorme; vasto, extenso; infinito
immensely /ɪ'mɛnsli/ adv inmensamente, enormemente
immensity /ɪ'mɛnsɪti/ n inmensidad, f; extensión, vastedad, f
immerse /ɪ'mɜrs/ vt sumergir, hundir en, zambullir; bautizar por sumersión. Fig. **to be immersed in,** estar absorto en
immersion /ɪ'mɜrʒən/ n sumersión, f, hundimiento, m; Astron. inmersión, f
immigrant /'ɪmɪgrənt/ a and n inmigrante, mf
immigrate /'ɪmɪˌgreit/ vi inmigrar
immigration /ˌɪmɪ'greiʃən/ n inmigración, f, (US Immigration and Naturalization Service) Inf. La Migra
imminence /'ɪmənəns/ n inminencia, f
imminent /'ɪmənənt/ a inminente
immobile /ɪ'moubəl/ a inmóvil, inmoble; impasible, imperturbable
immobility /ˌɪmou'bɪlɪti/ n inmovilidad, f; impasibilidad, imperturbabilidad, f
immobilization /ɪˌmoubələ'zeiʃən/ n inmovilización, f
immobilize /ɪ'moubəˌlaiz/ vt inmovilizar
immoderate /ɪ'mɒdərɪt/ a inmoderado, excesivo, indebido
immoderately /ɪ'mɒdərɪtli/ adv inmoderadamente, excesivamente
immoderateness /ɪ'mɒdərɪtnɪs/ n inmoderación, f, exceso, m

immodest /ɪ'mɒdɪst/ a inmodesto; indecente, deshonesto; (pert) atrevido, descarado
immodestly /ɪ'mɒdɪstli/ adv impúdicamente, inmodestamente
immodesty /ɪ'mɒdɪsti/ n inmodestia, impudicia, f; deshonestidad, licencia, f; (forwardness) descaro, atrevimiento, m
immolate /'ɪməˌleit/ vt inmolar, sacrificar
immolation /ˌɪmə'leiʃən/ n inmolación, f, sacrificio, m
immolator /'ɪməˌleitər/ n inmolador (-ra)
immoral /ɪ'mɔrəl/ a inmoral; licencioso, vicioso; incontinente
immorality /ˌɪmə'rælɪti/ n inmoralidad, f
immortal /ɪ'mɔrtl/ a inmortal; perenne, eterno, imperecedero. n inmortal, mf
immortality /ˌɪmɔr'tælɪti/ n inmortalidad, f; fama inmortal, f
immortalize /ɪ'mɔrtlˌaiz/ vt inmortalizar, perpetuar
immortally /ɪ'mɔrtli/ adv inmortalmente, eternamente, para siempre
immovability /ɪˌmuvə'bɪlɪti/ n inamovilidad, inmovilidad, f; (of purpose) inflexibilidad, tenacidad, constancia, f
immovable /ɪ'muvəbəl/ a inmoble, fijo, inmóvil; (of purpose) inconmovible, inalterable, constante. n pl. immovables, Law. bienes inmuebles, m pl. **i. feast,** Eccl. fiesta fija, f
immovably /ɪ'muvəbli/ adv inmóvilmente, fijamente
immune /ɪ'myun/ a inmune, libre; Med. inmune. **i. from,** exento de; libre de
immunity /ɪ'myunɪti/ n inmunidad, libertad, f; exención, f; Med. inmunidad, f
immunization /ɪˌmyunə'zeiʃən/ n Med. inmunización, f
immunize /'ɪmyəˌnaiz/ vt inmunizar
immure /ɪ'myʊr/ vt emparedar, recluir, encerrar
immutability /ɪˌmyutə'bɪlɪti/ n inmutabilidad, inalterabilidad, f
immutable /ɪ'myutəbəl/ a inmutable, inalterable, constante
immutably /ɪ'myutəbli/ adv inmutablemente
imp /ɪmp/ n trasgo, diablillo, duende, m; (child) picaruelo (-la)
impact /'ɪmpækt/ n impacto, m, impacción, f; choque, m, colisión, f
impair /ɪm'pɛər/ vt perjudicar, echar a perder, deteriorar, empeorar, desmejorar. **to be impaired,** deteriorarse, perjudicarse
impairment /ɪm'pɛərmənt/ n deterioración, perjuicio, empeoramiento, m
impale /ɪm'peil/ vt (punishment) empalar; (with a sword) atravesar, espetar
impalement /ɪm'peilmənt/ n (punishment) empalamiento, m; atravesamiento, m, transfixión, f
impalpability /ɪmˌpælpə'bɪlɪti/ n impalpabilidad, intangibilidad, f
impalpable /ɪm'pælpəbəl/ a impalpable, intangible; incorpóreo
impart /ɪm'part/ vt comunicar, dar parte (de); conferir
impartial /ɪm'parʃəl/ a imparcial, ecuánime
impartiality /ɪmˌparʃi'ælɪti/ n imparcialidad, ecuanimidad, entereza, f, desinterés, m
impartially /ɪm'parʃəli/ adv imparcialmente, con desinterés
impassability /ɪm,pæsə'bɪlɪti/ n impracticabilidad, f
impassable /ɪm'pæsəbəl/ a intransitable, impracticable; (of water) invadeable
impasse /'ɪmpæs/ n callejón sin salida, m
impassibility /ɪmˌpæsə'bɪlɪti/ n impasibilidad, imperturbabilidad, indiferencia, f
impassible /ɪm'pæsəbəl/ a impasible, insensible; indiferente, imperturbable
impassion /ɪm'pæʃən/ vt apasionar, conmover
impassioned /ɪm'pæʃənd/ a apasionado, vehemente, ardiente
impassive /ɪm'pæsɪv/ a impasible, insensible; indiferente, imperturbable; apático
impassively /ɪm'pæsɪvli/ adv indiferentemente

impassivity /ˌɪmpæˈsɪvɪti/ n impasibilidad, f; indiferencia, f; apatía, f
impatience /ɪmˈpeiʃəns/ n impaciencia, f
impatient /ɪmˈpeiʃənt/ a impaciente; intolerante. **to make i.,** impacientar. **to grow i.,** impacientarse, perder la paciencia. **to grow i. at,** impacientarse ante. **to grow i. to,** impacientarse a or por. **to grow i. under,** impacientarse bajo
impatiently /ɪmˈpeiʃəntli/ adv con impaciencia, impacientemente
impeach /ɪmˈpitʃ/ vt Law. denunciar, delatar, acusar, hacer juicio político (Argentina); censurar, criticar, tachar
impeachable /ɪmˈpitʃəbəl/ a Law. delatable, denunciable, acusable; censurable
impeacher /ɪmˈpitʃər/ n acusador (-ra), denunciador (-ra), delator (-ra)
impeachment /ɪmˈpitʃmənt/ n Law. acusación, denuncia, f; reproche, m, queja, f
impeccability /ɪmˌpɛkəˈbɪlɪti/ n (perfection) impecabilidad, perfección, f; elegancia, f
impeccable /ɪmˈpɛkəbəl/ a impecable, intachable, perfecto; elegante
impeccably /ɪmˈpɛkəbli/ adv perfectamente; elegantemente
impecuniosity /ˌɪmpəˌkyuniˈɒsɪti/ n indigencia, pobreza, f
impecunious /ˌɪmpəˈkyuniəs/ a indigente, pobre
impede /ɪmˈpid/ vt impedir, obstruir, estorbar; Fig. dificultar, embarazar
impediment /ɪmˈpedəmənt/ n obstáculo, estorbo, m; Fig. dificultad, f; Law. impedimento, m. **to have an i. in one's speech,** tener una dificultad en el hablar
impel /ɪmˈpɛl/ vt impulsar, impeler; Fig. estimular, obligar, mover, constreñir. **I felt impelled (to),** Me sentí obligado (a)
impend /ɪmˈpɛnd/ vi ser inminente, amenazar
impending /ɪmˈpɛndɪŋ/ a inminente, pendiente
impenetrability /ɪmˌpɛnɪtrəˈbɪlɪti/ n impenetrabilidad, f; Fig. enigma, secreto, misterio, m
impenetrable /ɪmˈpɛnɪtrəbəl/ a impenetrable; intransitable; denso, espeso; Fig. enigmático, insondable, secreto
impenetrably /ɪmˌpɛnɪtrəˈbɪlɪti/ adv impenetrablemente, densamente
impenitence /ɪmˈpɛnɪtəns/ n impenitencia, f
impenitent /ɪmˈpɛnɪtənt/ a impenitente, incorregible
impenitently /ɪmˈpɛnɪtəntli/ adv sin penitencia
imperative /ɪmˈpɛrətɪv/ a imperioso, perentorio; Gram. imperativo; (necessary) esencial, urgente. n mandato, m, orden, f; Gram. imperativo, m. **in the i.,** en el imperativo
imperatively /ɪmˈpɛrətɪvli/ adv imperativamente
imperativeness /ɪmˈpɛrətɪvnɪs/ n perentoriedad, f; urgencia, importancia, f
imperceptible /ˌɪmpərˈsɛptəbəl/ a imperceptible, insensible
imperceptibly /ˌɪmpərˈsɛptəbli/ adv imperceptiblemente
imperceptive /ˌɪmpərˈsɛptɪv/ a insensible
imperfect /ɪmˈpərfɪkt/ a imperfecto; incompleto, defectuoso. a and n Gram. imperfecto m
imperfection /ˌɪmpərˈfɛkʃən/ n imperfección, f; defecto, desperfecto, m; falta, tacha, f
imperfectly /ɪmˈpərfɪktli/ adv imperfectamente
imperial /ɪmˈpɪəriəl/ a imperial, imperatorio. n (beard) pera, f. **i. preference,** preferencia dentro del Imperio, f
imperial /ɪmˈpɪəriəl/ vt arriesgar, poner en peligro, aventurar
imperialism /ɪmˈpɪəriəˌlɪzəm/ n imperialismo, m
imperialist /ɪmˈpɪəriəlɪst/ n imperialista, mf
imperialistic /ɪmˌpɪəriəˈlɪstɪk/ a imperialista
imperious /ɪmˈpɪəriəs/ a imperioso, altivo, arrogante; (pressing) urgente, apremiante
imperiously /ɪmˈpɪəriəsli/ adv imperiosamente, con arrogancia
imperiousness /ɪmˈpɪəriəsnɪs/ n autoridad, arrogancia, altivez, f; necesidad, urgencia, f, apremio, m

imperishability /ɪmˌpɛrɪʃəˈbɪlɪti/ n (immortality) inmortalidad, perennidad, f
imperishable /ɪmˈpɛrɪʃəbəl/ a imperecedero, inmarchitable, perenne, eterno
impermanence /ɪmˈpɜrmənəns/ n inestabilidad, interinidad, f; brevedad, fugacidad, f
impermanent /ɪmˈpɜrmənənt/ a interino, no permanente
impermeability /ɪmˌpɜrmiəˈbɪlɪti/ n impermeabilidad, f
impermeable /ɪmˈpɜrmiəbəl/ a impermeable
impersonal /ɪmˈpɜrsənl/ a impersonal, objetivo; Gram. impersonal
impersonality /ɪmˌpɜrsəˈnælɪti/ n objetividad, f
impersonally /ɪmˈpɜrsənli/ adv impersonalmente
impersonate /ɪmˈpɜrsəˌneit/ vt personificar, simbolizar; Theat. representar
impersonation /ɪmˌpɜrsəˈneiʃən/ n personificación, simbolización, f; Theat. representación, f
impertinence /ɪmˈpɜrtnəns/ n impertinencia, majadería, insolencia, f; inoportunidad, f; despropósito, m
impertinent /ɪmˈpɜrtnənt/ a impertinente, insolente; (unseasonable) intempestivo, inoportuno; (irrelevant) fuera de propósito
impertinently /ɪmˈpɜrtnəntli/ adv con insolencia, impertinentemente
imperturbability /ˌɪmpərtɜrbəˈbɪlɪti/ n imperturbabilidad, serenidad, impasibilidad, f; impavidez, f
imperturbable /ˌɪmpərˈtɜrbəbəl/ a imperturbable, impasible, sereno; impávido
imperturbably /ˌɪmpərˈtɜrbəbli/ adv con serenidad, imperturbablemente
impervious /ɪmˈpɜrviəs/ a impermeable, impenetrable; Fig. insensible. **He is i. to arguments,** No hace caso de argumentos
imperviousness /ɪmˈpɜrviəsnɪs/ n impermeabilidad, impenetrabilidad, f; Fig. insensibilidad, f
impetigo /ˌɪmpɪˈtaigou/ n Med. impétigo, m
impetuosity /ɪmˌpɛtʃuˈɒsɪti/ n impetuosidad, temeridad, irreflexión, f
impetuous /ɪmˈpɛtʃuəs/ a impetuoso, temerario, irreflexivo; violento, vehemente
impetuously /ɪmˈpɛtʃuəsli/ adv impetuosamente; con vehemencia
impetus /ˈɪmpɪtəs/ n Mech. ímpetu, m, impulsión, f; Fig. incentivo, estímulo, impulso, m
impiety /ɪmˈpaiɪti/ n impiedad, irreligión, irreligiosidad, f
impinge (upon) /ɪmˈpɪndʒ/ vi chocar con, tropezar con
impious /ˈɪmpiəs/ a impío, irreligioso, sacrílego; (wicked) malvado, perverso, malo
impish /ˈɪmpɪʃ/ a travieso, revoltoso, enredador
implacability /ɪmˌplækəˈbɪlɪti/ n implacabilidad, f
implacable /ɪmˈplækəbəl/ a implacable, inexorable, inflexible, riguroso
implacably /ɪmˈplækəbli/ adv implacablemente
implant /ɪmˈplænt/ vt Fig. implantar, inculcar, instilar
implantation /ˌɪmplænˈteiʃən/ n Fig. implantación, instilación, inculcación, f
implement /n ˈɪmpləmənt; v also -ˌmɛnt/ n instrumento, utensilio, m, herramienta, f; (of war) elemento, m. vt cumplir, hacer efectivo; llevar a cabo
implicate /ˈɪmplɪˌkeit/ vt enredar, envolver; (imply) implicar, contener, llevar en sí; (in a crime) comprometer. **to be implicated in a crime,** estar implicado en un crimen
implication /ˌɪmplɪˈkeiʃən/ n implicación, inferencia, repercusión, sugestión, f; (in a crime) complicidad, f
implicit /ɪmˈplɪsɪt/ a implícito, virtual, tácito; (absolute) ciego, absoluto, implícito. **with i. faith,** con fe ciega
implicitness /ɪmˈplɪsɪtnɪs/ n carácter implícito, m, lo implícito
implied /ɪmˈplaid/ a tácito, implícito
implore /ɪmˈplɔr/ vt implorar, suplicar
imploring /ɪmˈplɔrɪŋ/ a suplicante, implorante
imploringly /ɪmˈplɔrɪŋli/ adv con encarecimiento, a súplica, de un modo suplicante
imply /ɪmˈplai/ vt implicar, indicar, presuponer;

impolite

(mean) querer decir, significar; (hint) insinuar, sugerir

impolite /ˌɪmpə'laɪt/ a descortés, mal educado

impolitely /ˌɪmpə'laɪtlɪ/ adv con descortesía

impoliteness /ˌɪmpə'laɪtnɪs/ n descortesía, falta de urbanidad, f

impolitic /ɪm'pɒlɪtɪk/ a impolítico

imponderability /ɪmˌpɒndərə'bɪlɪtɪ/ n imponderabilidad, f

imponderable /ɪm'pɒndərəbəl/ a imponderable

import /v ɪm'pɔːt; a, n 'ɪmpɔːt/ vt Com. importar; (mean) significar, querer decir. a Com. importado, de importación. n Com. importación, f; (meaning) significado, sentido, m; (value) importe, valor, m; (contents) contenido, tenor, m; importancia, f. **i. duty,** derechos de importación derechos de entrada, m pl, gravamen a la importación, m. **i. licence,** permiso de importación, m. **i. trade,** negocios de importación, m pl

importable /ɪm'pɔːtəbəl/ a importable, que se puede importar

importance /ɪm'pɔːtn̩s/ n importancia, f; valor, alcance, m, magnitud, f; consideración, eminencia, f. **to be fully conscious of one's i.,** tener plena conciencia de su importancia

important /ɪm'pɔːtn̩t/ a importante; distinguido; presuntuoso, vanidoso. **to be i.,** importar, ser importante. **i. person,** personaje, m, persona importante, f

importantly /ɪm'pɔːtn̩tlɪ/ adv importantemente, con importancia

importation /ˌɪmpɔː'teɪʃən/ n importación, f; Com. introducción (or importación) de géneros extranjeros, f

importer /ɪm'pɔːtər/ n importador (-ra)

importunate /ɪm'pɔːtʃənɪt/ a (of a demand) insistente, importuno; (of persons) impertinente, pesado

importunately /ɪm'pɔːtʃənɪtlɪ/ adv importunadamente

importune /ˌɪmpɔː'tuːn/ vt importunar, asediar, perseguir

importuning /ˌɪmpɔː'tuːnɪŋ/ n persecución, importunación, f

importunity /ˌɪmpɔː'tuːnɪtɪ/ n importunidad, insistencia, impertinencia, f

impose /ɪm'pouz/ vt (on, upon) imponer, infligir, cargar; Print. imponer. vi (on, upon) (deceive) engañar, embaucar

imposing /ɪm'pouzɪŋ/ a imponente, impresionante; (of persons) majestuoso, importante

imposition /ˌɪmpə'zɪʃən/ n imposición, f; (burden) impuesto, tributo, m, carga, f; (Print., etc.) imposición, f; (trick) fraude, engaño, m, decepción, f

impossibility /ɪmˌpɒsə'bɪlɪtɪ/ n imposibilidad, f

impossible /ɪm'pɒsəbəl/ a imposible. **Nothing is i.,** No hay nada imposible, Inf. De menos nos hizo Dios. **to do the i.,** hacer lo imposible

impostor /ɪm'pɒstər/ n impostor (-ra), bribón (-ona), embustero (-ra)

imposture /ɪm'pɒstʃər/ n impostura, f, engaño, fraude, m

impotence /'ɪmpətəns/ n impotencia, f

impotent /'ɪmpətənt/ a impotente

impound /ɪm'paund/ vt acorralar; (water) embalsar; (goods) confiscar

impoverish /ɪm'pɒvərɪʃ/ vt empobrecer, depauperar, arruinar; (health) debilitar; (land) agotar

impoverished /ɪm'pɒvərɪʃt/ a indigente, necesitado; (of land) agotado

impoverishment /ɪm'pɒvərɪʃmənt/ n empobrecimiento, m, ruina, f; (of land) agotamiento, m

impracticability /ɪmˌpræktɪkə'bɪlɪtɪ/ n impracticabilidad, imposibilidad, f

impracticable /ɪm'præktɪkəbəl/ a impracticable, no factible, imposible

imprecation /ˌɪmprɪ'keɪʃən/ n imprecación, maldición, f

imprecatory /'ɪmprɪkə,tɔrɪ/ a imprecatorio, maldiciente

impregnable /ɪm'pregnəbəl/ a inexpugnable, inconquistable

impregnate /ɪm'pregneɪt/ vt impregnar, empapar; Biol. fecundar. **to become impregnated,** impregnarse

impregnation /ˌɪmpreg'neɪʃən/ n impregnación, f; Biol. fecundación, fertilización, f; Fig. inculcación, f

impresario /ˌɪmprə'sɑrɪ,ou/ n empresario, m

imprescriptible /ˌɪmprə'skrɪptəbəl/ a imprescriptible, inalienable

impress /v ɪm'pres; n 'ɪmpres/ vt imprimir; (on the mind) impresionar; inculcar, imbuir; (with respect) imponer; Mil. reclutar; (of goods) confiscar. n impresión, marca, señal, huella, f

impression /ɪm'preʃən/ n impresión, f; marca, señal, huella, f; Print. impresión, f; efecto, m; idea, noción, f. **He has the i. that they do not like him,** Sospecha que no les es simpático. **to be under the i.,** tener la impresión

impressionability /ɪmˌpreʃənə'bɪlɪtɪ/ n susceptibilidad, sensibilidad, f

impressionable /ɪm'preʃənəbəl/ a susceptible, impresionable, sensitivo

impressionism /ɪm'preʃə,nɪzəm/ n impresionismo, m

impressionist /ɪm'preʃənɪst/ n impresionista, mf

impressionistic /ɪmˌpreʃə'nɪstɪk/ a impresionista

impressive /ɪm'presɪv/ a impresionante; emocionante; imponente, majestuoso; enfático

impressively /ɪm'presɪvlɪ/ adv solemnemente, de modo impresionante; enfáticamente

impressiveness /ɪm'presɪvnɪs/ n efecto impresionante, m, Lat. Am. imponencia f; grandiosidad, pompa, f; majestuosidad, f; fuerza, f

imprint /n 'ɪmprɪnt; v ɪm'prɪnt/ n impresión, señal, marca, huella, f; Print. pie de imprenta, m. vt imprimir; (on the mind) grabar, fijar

imprison /ɪm'prɪzən/ vt encerrar, encarcelar, aprisionar

imprisonment /ɪm'prɪzənmənt/ n encarcelación, prisión, f, encierro, m

improbability /ɪmˌprɒbə'bɪlɪtɪ/ n improbabilidad, f; inverosimilitud, f

improbable /ɪm'prɒbəbəl/ a improbable; inverosímil

improbity /ɪm'proubɪtɪ/ n improbidad, f

impromptu /ɪm'prɒmptu/ a indeliberado, impremeditado, espontáneo. adv de improviso, in promptu. n improvisación, f

improper /ɪm'prɒpər/ a impropio, inadecuado; incorrecto; indebido; indecente, indecoroso. **i. fraction,** Math. quebrado impropio, m

improperly /ɪm'prɒpərlɪ/ adv impropiamente, incorrectamente; indecorosamente

impropriety /ˌɪmprə'praɪtɪ/ n inconveniencia, f; incorrección, f; (style) impropiedad, f; falta de decoro, f

improvable /ɪm'pruvəbəl/ a mejorable, perfectible

improve /ɪm'pruv/ vt mejorar; perfeccionar; (beautify) embellecer, hermosear; (land) bonificar; Lit. corregir, enmendar; (cultivate) cultivar; (increase) aumentar; (an opportunity) aprovechar; (strengthen) fortificar; (business) sacar provecho de, explotar. vi mejorar; perfeccionarse; (progress) hacer progresos, progresar, adelantarse; Com. subir; (become beautiful) hacerse hermoso, embellecerse; (increase) aumentarse. **to i. upon,** mejorar, perfeccionar; pulir

improvement /ɪm'pruvmənt/ n mejora, f; perfeccionamiento, m; aumento, m; adelantamiento, progreso, m; (in health) mejoría, f; mejoría, f; embellecimiento, m; cultivación, f; (of land) abono, m, f

improver /ɪm'pruvər/ n aprendiz (-za)

improvidence /ɪm'prɒvɪdəns/ n imprevisión, f; improvidencia, f

improvident /ɪm'prɒvɪdənt/ a impróvido, desprevenido

improvidently /ɪm'prɒvɪdəntlɪ/ adv impróvidamente

improvisation /ˌɪmprɒvə'zeɪʃən/ n improvisación, f

improvise /'ɪmprə,vaɪz/ vt improvisar

improviser /'ɪmprə,vaɪzər/ n improvisador (-ra)

imprudence /ɪm'prudn̩s/ n imprudencia, f; desacierto, m, indiscreción, f

imprudent /ɪm'prudn̩t/ a imprudente; desacertado, indiscreto, mal avisado, irreflexivo

imprudently /ɪm'prudn̩tlɪ/ adv imprudentemente; sin pensar

impudence /'ɪmpyədəns/ n impudencia, f, descaro, m, insolencia, desvergüenza, f, atrevimiento, m
impudent /'ɪmpyədənt/ a impudente, descarado, insolente, desvergonzado, atrevido, Peru lisurero
impudently /'ɪmpyədəntli/ adv descaradamente, con insolencia
impugn /ɪm'pyun/ vt impugnar, contradecir, atacar
impugnable /ɪm'pyunəbəl/ a impugnable, atacable
impugnment /ɪm'pyunmənt/ n impugnación, f
impulse /'ɪmpʌls/ n ímpetu, m, impulsión, f; impulso, estímulo, m; incitación, instigación, f; motivo, m; (fit) arranque, arrebato, acceso, m
impulsion /ɪm'pʌlʃən/ n ímpetu, m, impulsión, f; empuje, m, arranque, m
impulsive /ɪm'pʌlsɪv/ a impelente; irreflexivo, impulsivo
impulsively /ɪm'pʌlsɪvli/ adv por impulso
impulsiveness /ɪm'pʌlsɪvnɪs/ n irreflexión, f; carácter impulsivo, m
impunity /ɪm'pyunɪti/ n impunidad, f. **with i.**, impunemente
impure /ɪm'pyʊr/ a impuro; adulterado, mezclado; (indecent) deshonesto, indecente; (dirty) turbio, sucio
impurity /ɪm'pyʊrɪti/ n impureza, f; adulteración, mezcla, f; deshonestidad, liviandad, f; suciedad, turbiedad, f
imputable /ɪm'pyutəbəl/ a imputable, atribuible
imputation /ˌɪmpyʊ'teiʃən/ n imputación, atribución, f; (in a bad sense) acusación, f, reproche, m
impute /ɪm'pyut/ vt imputar, achacar, atribuir; acusar, reprochar
in /ɪn/ prep en; a; (of duration) durante, mientras; (with) con; (through) por; dentro de; (under) bajo; (following a superlative) de; (of specified time) dentro de, de aquí a; (with afternoon, etc.) por; (out of) sobre. **course in medieval Catalan literature**, curso de literatura catalana medioeval. **dressed in black**, vestido de negro. **in New York**, en Nueva York. **in the morning**, por la mañana; (in the course of) durante la mañana. **in time**, a tiempo; dentro de algún tiempo. **in a week**, dentro de una semana. **in the best way**, del mejor modo. **in writing**, por escrito. **in anger**, con enojo. **in one's hand**, en la mano. **in addition to**, además de, a más de. **in case**, por si acaso, en caso de que. **in order to**, a fin de, para (foll. by infin.). **in order that**, para que (foll. by subjunc.). **in so far as**, en cuanto. **in spite of**, a pesar de. **in the distance**, a lo lejos, en lontananza. **in the meantime**, entre tanto. **in the middle of**, en el medio de; a la mitad de. **in the style of**, al modo de; a la manera de, a la (francesa, etc.)
in /ɪn/ adv adentro, dentro; (at home) en casa; (of sun) escondido; (of fire) alumbrado; (in power) en el poder; (of harvest) cosechado; (of boats) entrado (with haber); (of trains) llegado (with haber). **to be in**, estar dentro; haber llegado; estar en casa. **to be in for**, estar expuesto a, correr el riesgo de. **to be in with a person**, ser muy amigo de, estar muy metido con. **Come in!** ¡Adelante!; ¡Pase usted! **ins and outs**, sinuosidades, f pl; (of river) meandros, m pl; (of an affair) pormenores, detalles, m pl. **in less time than you can say Jack Robinson**, en menos de Jesús, en un credo, en menos que canta un gallo, en menos que se persigna un cura loco. **in the middle of nowhere**, donde Cristo dio las tres voces, (Western Hemisphere) donde el diablo perdió el poncho.
in /ɪn/ a interno. **in-law** (of relations) político. **in-patient**, enfermo (-ma) de hospital
inability /ˌɪnə'bɪlɪti/ n incapacidad, inhabilidad, ineptitud, incompetencia, f; impotencia, f
inaccessibility /ˌɪnəkˌsesə'bɪlɪti/ n inaccesibilidad, f
inaccessible /ˌɪnək'sesəbəl/ a inaccesible
inaccuracy /ɪn'ækyərəsi/ n inexactitud, incorrección, f
inaccurate /ɪn'ækyərɪt/ a inexacto, incorrecto
inaccurately /ɪn'ækyərɪtli/ adv inexactamente, erróneamente
inaction /ɪn'ækʃən/ n inacción, f
inactive /ɪn'æktɪv/ a inactivo, pasivo; (of things) inerte, (lazy) perezoso, indolente; (machinery) parado; (motionless) inmóvil; (at leisure) desocupado, sin empleo

inactivity /ˌɪnæk'tɪvɪti/ n inactividad, pasividad, f; (of things) inercia, f; pereza, indolencia, f; (of machinery) paro, m; inmovilidad, f; (leisure) desocupación, f
inadaptable /ˌɪnə'dæptəbəl/ a inadaptable, no adaptable
inadequacy /ɪn'ædɪkwəsi/ n insuficiencia, escasez, f; imperfección, f, defecto, m
inadequate /ɪn'ædɪkwɪt/ a inadecuado, insuficiente, escaso; imperfecto, defectuoso
inadequately /ɪn'ædɪkwɪtli/ adv inadecuadamente
inadmissible /ˌɪnəd'mɪsəbəl/ a inadmisible, no admisible
inadvertence /ˌɪnəd'vɜrtn̩s/ n inadvertencia, f; equivocación, f, descuido, m
inadvertent /ˌɪnəd'vɜrtn̩t/ a inadvertido, accidental, casual; negligente
inadvertently /ˌɪnəd'vɜrtn̩tli/ adv inadvertidamente, sin querer
inalienability /ɪnˌeilyənə'bɪlɪti/ n inalienabilidad, f
inalienable /ɪn'eilyənəbəl/ a inajenable, inalienable
inalterability /ɪnˌɔltərə'bɪlɪti/ n inalterabilidad, f
inalterable /ɪn'ɔltərəbəl/ a inalterable
inalterably /ɪn'ɔltərəbli/ adv inalterablemente, sin alteración
inane /ɪ'nein/ a lelo, fatuo, vacío, necio
inanimate /ɪn'ænəmɪt/ a (of matter) inanimado; sin vida, exánime, muerto
inanity /ɪ'nænɪti/ n vacuidad, fatuidad, necedad, f
inappeasable /ˌɪnə'pizəbəl/ a implacable, riguroso
inapplicability /ɪnˌæplɪkə'bɪlɪti/ n no aplicabilidad, f
inapplicable /ɪn'æplɪkəbəl/ a inaplicable
inapposite /ɪn'æpəzɪt/ a fuera de propósito, no pertinente, inoportuno
inappreciable /ˌɪnə'priʃəbəl/ a inapreciable, imperceptible
inappreciation /ˌɪnəpriʃi'eiʃən/ n falta de apreciación, f
inappreciative /ˌɪnə'priʃiətɪv/ a desagradecido, ingrato. **i. of**, insensible a, indiferente a
inapproachable /ˌɪnə'proutʃəbəl/ a inaccesible, huraño, adusto
inappropriate /ˌɪnə'proupriɪt/ a impropio, inconveniente, inadecuado, incongruente; inoportuno
inappropriately /ˌɪnə'proupriɪtli/ adv impropiamente; inoportunamente
inappropriateness /ˌɪnə'proupriɪtnɪs/ n impropiedad, inconveniencia, incongruencia, f; inoportunidad, f
inapt /ɪn'æpt/ a inepto, inhábil; impropio
inaptitude /ɪn'æptɪˌtud/ n ineptitud, inhabilidad, f; impropiedad, f
inarticulate /ˌɪnɑr'tɪkyəlɪt/ a (of speech) inarticulado; (reticent) inexpresivo, reservado; indistinto; Anat. inarticulado
inarticulately /ˌɪnɑr'tɪkyəlɪtli/ adv indistintamente, de un modo inarticulado
inarticulateness /ˌɪnɑr'tɪkyəlɪtnɪs/ n inexpresión, reserva, f; silencio, m
inartistic /ˌɪnɑr'tɪstɪk/ a antiartístico, antiestético
inartistically /ˌɪnɑr'tɪstɪkli/ adv sin gusto (estético)
inasmuch (as) /ˌɪnəz'mʌtʃ/ adv puesto que, visto que, dado que
inattention /ˌɪnə'tenʃən/ n desatención, inaplicación, abstracción, f; falta de solicitud, f
inattentive /ˌɪnə'tentɪv/ a desatento, distraído; poco solícito, no atento
inattentively /ˌɪnə'tentɪvli/ adv sin atención, distraídamente
inaudibility /ɪnˌɔdə'bɪlɪti/ n imposibilidad de oír, f
inaudible /ɪn'ɔdəbəl/ a inaudible, no audible, ininteligible
inaudibly /ɪn'ɔdəbli/ adv indistintamente, de modo inaudible
inaugurate /ɪn'ɔgyəˌreit/ vt inaugurar; (open) estrenar, abrir, dedicar; (install) investir, instalar; (initiate) originar, iniciar, dar lugar (a)
inauguration /ɪnˌɔgyə'reiʃən/ n inauguración, f; (opening) estreno, m, apertura, f; (investiture) instalación, investidura, f
inauspicious /ˌɪnɔ'spiʃəs/ a poco propicio, desfavorable; ominoso, triste, infeliz

inauspiciously /ˌɪnɔ'spɪʃəsli/ adv en condiciones desfavorables, desfavorablemente; infelizmente, bajo malos auspicios

inauspiciousness /ˌɪnɔ'spɪʃəsnɪs/ n condiciones desfavorables, f pl; infelicidad, f; malos auspicios, m pl

inborn /'ɪn'bɔrn/ a innato, instintivo, inherente

inbred /'ɪn'brɛd/ a innato, inherente, instintivo

Inca /'ɪŋkə/ a incaico, de los incas, Lat. Am. also incásico. n inca, m

incalculability /ɪn,kælkyələ'bɪlɪti/ n imposibilidad de calcular, f; (of persons) volubilidad, veleidad, f; infinidad, immensidad, f

incalculable /ɪn'kælkyələbəl/ a incalculable, innumerable; (of persons) voluble, veleidoso, caprichoso; infinito, immenso

incalculably /ɪn'kælkyələbli/ adv enormemente, infinitamente; caprichosamente

incandescence /ˌɪnkən'dɛsəns/ n incandescencia, candencia, f

incandescent /ˌɪnkən'dɛsənt/ a incandescente, candente. **i. light,** luz incandescente, f. **to make i.,** encandecer

incantation /ˌɪnkæn'teɪʃən/ n hechizo, m, encantación, f, ensalmo, m

incapability /ɪn,keɪpə'bɪlɪti/ n incapacidad, f; inhabilidad, ineptitud, incompetencia, f

incapable /ɪn'keɪpəbəl/ a incapaz; inhábil, incompetente; (physically) imposibilitado

incapacitate /ˌɪnkə'pæsɪˌteɪt/ vt imposibilitar, incapacitar, inutilizar; (disqualify) inhabilitar, incapacitar

incapacitation /ˌɪnkə,pæsɪ'teɪʃən/ n inhabilitación, f

incapacity /ˌɪnkə'pæsɪti/ n incapacidad, inhabilidad, f

incarcerate /ɪn'kɑrsə,reɪt/ vt encarcelar

incarceration /ɪn,kɑrsə'reɪʃən/ n encarcelación, prisión, f

incarnate /a ɪn'kɑrnɪt; v -neit/ a encarnado. vt encarnar

incarnation /ˌɪnkɑr'neɪʃən/ n encarnación, f

incautious /ɪn'kɔʃəs/ a incauto, imprudente

incautiously /ɪn'kɔʃəsli/ adv incautamente

incautiousness /ɪn'kɔʃəsnɪs/ n imprudencia, negligencia, falta de cautela, f

incendiary /ɪn'sɛndi,ɛri/ a incendiario. **i. bomb,** incendiaria, f

incense /ɪn'sɛns/ n incienso, m; Fig. adulación, f. vt Eccl. incensar; (annoy) irritar, exasperar, enojar. **i. burner,** incensario, m

incentive /ɪn'sɛntɪv/ n incentivo, estímulo, motivo, m. a estimulador, incitativo

inception /ɪn'sɛpʃən/ n comienzo, principio, m; inauguración, f

incertitude /ɪn'sɜrtɪˌtud/ n incertidumbre, f

incessant /ɪn'sɛsənt/ a incesante, continuo, constante

incessantly /ɪn'sɛsəntli/ adv incesantemente, sin cesar

incest /'ɪnsɛst/ n incesto, m

incestuous /ɪn'sɛstʃuəs/ a incestuoso

inch /ɪntʃ/ n pulgada, f. **every i. a man,** hombre hecho y derecho. **Not an i.!** ¡Ni pizca! **within an i. of,** a dos dedos de. **i. by i.,** palmo a palmo, paso a paso. **i. tape,** cinta métrica, f

inchoate /ɪn'kout/ a rudimentario; imperfecto, incompleto

incidence /'ɪnsɪdəns/ n incidencia, f

incident /'ɪnsɪdənt/ a propio, característico, incidental. n incidente, acontecimiento, m, ocurrencia, f

incidental /ˌɪnsɪ'dɛntl/ a incidente, incidental; accidental, accesorio, no esencial. **i. expense,** gasto imprevisto, m

incidentally /ˌɪnsɪ'dɛntli/ adv (secondarily) incidentalmente; (by the way) de propósito

incident of navigation n accidente de navegación, m

incinerate /ɪn'sɪnəˌreɪt/ vt incinerar

incineration /ɪn,sɪnə'reɪʃən/ n incineración, cremación, f

incinerator /ɪn'sɪnəˌreɪtər/ n incinerador, m

incipient /ɪn'sɪpiənt/ a incipiente, naciente, rudimentario

incision /ɪn'sɪʒən/ n incisión, f; corte, tajo, m; Med. abscisión, f

incisive /ɪn'saisɪv/ a (of mind) agudo, penetrante; (of words) mordaz, incisivo, punzante

incisively /ɪn'saisɪvli/ adv en pocas palabras; mordazmente, incisivamente

incisiveness /ɪn'saisɪvnɪs/ n (of mind) agudeza, penetración, f; (of words) mordacidad, f, sarcasmo, m

incisor /ɪn'saizər/ n diente incisivo, m

incite /ɪn'sait/ vt incitar, estimular, animar; provocar, tentar. **to i. to,** mover a, incitar a

incitement /ɪn'saitmənt/ n incitación, instigación, f; estímulo, m; tentación, f; aliciente, m

incivility /ˌɪnsə'vɪlɪti/ n incivilidad, descortesía, f

inclemency /ɪn'klɛmənsi/ n inclemencia, f, rigor, m

inclement /ɪn'klɛmənt/ a inclemente, riguroso, borrascoso

inclination /ˌɪnklə'neɪʃən/ n inclinación, f; (slope) declive, m, pendiente, cuesta, f; (tendency) propensión, tendencia, f; (liking) afición, f; amor, m; (bow) reverencia, f; Geom. inclinación, f

incline /v ɪn'klain; n 'ɪnklain/ vt inclinar, torcer; doblar; (cause) inclinar (a), hacer. vi inclinarse, torcerse; (tend) tender, propender, inclinarse; (colors) tirar (a). n declive, m, pendiente, cuesta, inclinación, f. **I am inclined to believe it,** Me inclino a creerlo. **I am inclined to do it,** Estoy por hacerlo, Creo que lo haré

inclined /ɪn'klaind/ a torcido, inclinado, doblado; Fig. propenso, adicto. **i. plane,** plano inclinado, m

include /ɪn'klud/ vt incluir, contener, encerrar; comprender, abrazar

including /ɪn'kludɪŋ/ present part incluso, inclusive. **not i.,** no comprendido

inclusion /ɪn'kluʒən/ n inclusión, f

inclusive /ɪn'klusɪv/ a inclusivo. **January 2 to January 12 i.,** del 2 al 12 de enero, ambos inclusivos. **not i. of,** sin contar, exclusivo de. **i. of,** que incluye. **i. terms,** todo incluido, todos los gastos incluidos

incognito /ˌɪnkɒg'nitou/ a and adv and n incógnito, m.

incoherence /ˌɪnkou'hɪərəns/ n incoherencia, inconsecuencia, f

incoherent /ˌɪnkou'hɪərənt/ a incoherente, inconexo, inconsecuente. **an i. piece of writing,** un escrito sin pies ni cabeza

incoherently /ˌɪnkou'hɪərəntli/ adv con incoherencia

incombustibility /ˌɪnkəm,bʌstə'bɪlɪti/ n incombustibilidad, f

incombustible /ˌɪnkəm'bʌstəbəl/ a incombustible

income /ɪn'kʌm/ n renta, f, ingreso, m; Com. rédito, m. **i.-tax,** impuesto sobre la renta, m. **i.-tax agents,** inspectores de impuestos de utilidades, m pl. **i.-tax return,** declaración de utilidades, f

incoming /'ɪn,kʌmɪŋ/ a entrante; nuevo. n entrada, llegada, f. n pl **incomings,** ingresos, m pl

incommensurability /ˌɪnkə,mɛnsərə'bɪlɪti/ n inconmensurabilidad, f

incommensurable /ˌɪnkə'mɛnsərəbəl/ a inconmensurable, no conmensurable

incommensurate /ˌɪnkə'mɛnsərɪt/ a desproporcionado, desmedido

incommodious /ˌɪnkə'moudiəs/ a estrecho; incómodo, inconveniente

incommodiousness /ˌɪnkə'moudiəsnɪs/ n estrechez, f; incomodidad, f

incommunicable /ˌɪnkə'myunɪkəbəl/ a incomunicable, indecible, inexplicable

incommunicative /ˌɪnkə'myunɪkətɪv/ a insociable, intratable, adusto, huraño

incomparable /ɪn'kɒmpərəbəl/ a incomparable; sin par, sin igual, excelente

incomparableness /ɪn'kɒmpərəbəlnɪs/ n excelencia, perfección, f

incomparably /ɪn'kɒmpərəbli/ adv incomparablemente, con mucho

incompatibility /ˌɪnkəm,pætə'bɪlɪti/ n incompatibilidad, f

incompatible /ˌɪnkəm'pætəbəl/ a incompatible

incompetence /ɪn'kɒmpɪtəns/ n incompetencia, ineptitud, inhabilidad, f; Law. incapacidad, f

incompetent /ɪn'kɒmpɪtənt/ a incompetente, inepto, incapaz, inepto, inhábil; Law. incapaz

incompetently /ɪn'kɒmpɪtəntli/ adv inhábilmente

incomplete /ˌɪnkəm'plit/ *a* incompleto; imperfecto, defectuoso; (unfinished) sin terminar, inacabado, inconcluso. **incomplete sentence,** frase que queda colgando, *f*

incompletely /ˌɪnkəm'plitli/ *adv* incompletamente; imperfectamente

incompleteness /ˌɪnkəm'plitnɪs/ *n* estado incompleto, *m*; imperfección, *f*; inconclusión, *f*

incomprehensibility /ˌɪnkɒmprɪˌhɛnsə'bɪlɪti/ *n* incomprensibilidad, *f*

incomprehensible /ˌɪnkɒmprɪ'hɛnsəbəl/ *a* incomprensible

incomprehension /ˌɪnkɒmprɪ'hɛnʃən/ *n* incomprensión, falta de comprensión, *f*

inconceivable /ˌɪnkən'sivəbəl/ *a* inconcebible, inimaginable

inconclusive /ˌɪnkən'klusɪv/ *a* inconcluyente, cuestionable, dudoso, no convincente

inconclusiveness /ˌɪnkən'klusɪvnɪs/ *n* carácter inconcluso, *m*, falta de conclusiones, *f*

incongruity /ˌɪnkən'gruɪti/ *n* incongruencia, desproporción, disonancia, *f*

incongruous /ɪn'kɒŋɡruəs/ *a* incongruente, incongruo; chocante, desproporcionado, disonante

incongruously /ɪn'kɒŋɡruəsli/ *adv* incongruentemente, incongruamente

inconsequence /ɪn'kɒnsɪˌkwɛns/ *n* inconsecuencia, *f*

inconsequent, inconsequential /ɪn'kɒnsɪˌkwɛnt; ɪnˌkɒnsɪ'kwɛnʃəl/ *a* inconsecuente, ilógico; inconsistente

inconsiderable /ˌɪnkən'sɪdərəbəl/ *a* insignificante

inconsiderate /ˌɪnkən'sɪdərɪt/ *a* desconsiderado, irreflexivo, irrespetuoso

inconsiderately /ˌɪnkən'sɪdərɪtli/ *adv* sin consideración, desconsideradamente

inconsiderateness /ˌɪnkən'sɪdərɪtnɪs/ *n* desconsideración, falta de respeto, *f*

inconsistency /ˌɪnkən'sɪstənsi/ *n* inconsistencia, inconsecuencia, incompatibilidad, contradicción, anomalía, *f*

inconsistent /ˌɪnkən'sɪstənt/ *a* inconsistente, inconsiguiente, incompatible, contradictorio, anómalo

inconsistently /ˌɪnkən'sɪstəntli/ *adv* contradictoriamente

inconsolable /ˌɪnkən'souləbəl/ *a* inconsolable, desconsolado. **to be i.,** estar inconsolable, (*Inf.* of a woman) estar hecha una Magdalena

inconsolably /ˌɪnkən'souləbli/ *adv* desconsoladamente

inconspicuous /ˌɪnkən'spɪkyuəs/ *a* que no llama la atención; insignificante, humilde, modesto

inconspicuously /ˌɪnkən'spɪkyuəsli/ *adv* humildemente, modestamente

inconspicuousness /ˌɪnkən'spɪkyuəsnɪs/ *n* modestia, humildad, *f*

inconstancy /ɪn'kɒnstənsi/ *n* inconstancia, movilidad, *f*; mudanza, veleidad, *f*

inconstant /ɪn'kɒnstənt/ *a* inconstante, mudable, variable; veleidoso, volátil, voluble

incontestable /ˌɪnkən'tɛstəbəl/ *a* incontestable, evidente, indisputable

incontinence /ɪn'kɒntɪnəns/ *n* incontinencia, *f*

incontinent /ɪn'kɒntɪnənt/ *a* incontinente

incontrollable /ˌɪnkən'trouləbəl/ *a* ingobernable, indomable

incontrovertible /ˌɪnkɒntrə'vɜrtəbəl/ *a* incontrovertible, incontrastable

inconvenience /ˌɪnkən'vinyəns/ *n* incomodidad, inconveniencia, *f*; (of time) inoportunidad, *f*. *vt* incomodar, causar inconvenientes (a)

inconvenient /ˌɪnkən'vinyənt/ *a* incómodo, inconveniente, molesto, embarazoso; (of time) inoportuno. **at an i. time,** a deshora

inconveniently /ˌɪnkən'vinyəntli/ *adv* incómodamente; (of time) inoportunamente

incorporate /*v* ɪn'kɔrpəˌreit; *a* -pərɪt/ *vt* incorporar, agregar; comprender, incluir, encerrar. *vi* asociarse, incorporarse. *a* incorpóreo, inmaterial; asociado, asociado

incorporation /ɪnˌkɔrpə'reiʃən/ *n* incorporación, agregación, *f*; asociación, *f*

incorporeal /ˌɪnkɔr'pɔriəl/ *a* incorpóreo, inmaterial

incorporeity /ɪnˌkɔrpə'riɪti/ *n* incorporeidad, inmaterialidad, *f*

incorrect /ˌɪnkə'rɛkt/ *a* incorrecto; inexacto, erróneo, falso

incorrectness /ˌɪnkə'rɛktnɪs/ *n* incorrección, *f*

incorrigibility /ɪnˌkɔrɪdʒə'bɪlɪti/ *n* incorregibilidad, *f*

incorrigible /ɪn'kɔrɪdʒəbəl/ *a* incorregible, empecatado

incorrigibly /ɪn'kɔrɪdʒəbli/ *adv* incorregiblemente, obstinadamente

incorrupt /ˌɪnkə'rʌpt/ *a* incorrupto; recto, honrado

incorruptibility /ˌɪnkəˌrʌptə'bɪlɪti/ *n* incorruptibilidad, *f*; honradez, probidad, *f*

incorruptible /ˌɪnkə'rʌptəbəl/ *a* incorrupto; honrado, incorruptible

incorruption /ˌɪnkə'rʌpʃən/ *n* incorrupción, *f*

increase /*v* ɪn'kris; *n* 'ɪnkris/ *vt* aumentar, acrecentar; (in numbers) multiplicar; (extend) ampliar, extender; (of price) encarecer, aumentar. *vi* aumentar, crecer; multiplicarse; extenderse; encarecerse, aumentar. *n* aumento, crecimiento, *m*; multiplicación, *f*; (in price) encarecimiento, *m*, alza, *f*; (of water) crecida, *f*; (of moon) creciente, *f*. **It is on the i.,** Va en aumento. **to i. and multiply,** crecer y multiplicar

increasingly /ɪn'krisɪŋli/ *adv* más y más; en creciente, en aumento

incredibility /ɪnˌkrɛdə'bɪlɪti/ *n* incredibilidad, *f*

incredible /ɪn'krɛdəbəl/ *a* increíble; fabuloso, extraordinario. **It seems i.,** Es increíble, *Inf.* Parece mentira

incredibly /ɪn'krɛdəbli/ *adv* increíblemente

incredulity /ˌɪnkrɪ'dulɪti/ *n* incredulidad, *f*, escepticismo, *m*

incredulous /ɪn'krɛdʒələs/ *a* incrédulo, escéptico

incredulously /ɪn'krɛdʒələsli/ *adv* con incredulidad, escépticamente

increment /'ɪnkrəmənt/ *n* aumento, incremento, *m*; adición, añadidura, *f*; *Math.* incremento, *m*. **unearned i.,** plusvalía, mayor valía, *f*

incriminate /ɪn'krɪməˌneit/ *vt* incriminar

incriminating /ɪn'krɪməˌneitɪŋ/ *a* incriminante, acriminador

incrust /ɪn'krʌst/ *vt* incrustar, encostrar

incrustation /ˌɪnkrʌ'steiʃən/ *n* incrustación, *f*; (scab) costra, *f*

incubate /'ɪnkyəˌbeit/ *vt* empollar; *Med.* incubar

incubation /ˌɪnkyə'beiʃən/ *n* empolladura, incubación, *f*; *Med.* incubación, *f*

incubator /'ɪnkyəˌbeitər/ *n* incubadora, *f*

incubus /'ɪnkyəbəs/ *n* íncubo, *m*; (burden) carga, *f*

inculcate /ɪn'kʌlkeit/ *vt* inculcar, implantar, instilar

inculcation /ˌɪnkʌl'keiʃən/ *n* inculcación, implantación, instilación, *f*

incumbency /ɪn'kʌmbənsi/ *n* posesión, duración de, posesión, duración (de cualquier puesto), *f*

incumbent /ɪn'kʌmbənt/ *a* obligatorio. *n* *Eccl.* beneficiado, *m*. **to be i. on,** incumbir a, ser de su obligación

incur /ɪn'kɜr/ *vt* incurrir (en), incidir (en). **to i. an obligation,** contraer una obligación

incurability /ɪnˌkyʊrə'bɪlɪti/ *n* incurabilidad, *f*

incurable /ɪn'kyʊrəbəl/ *a* incurable, insanable; *Fig.* sin solución, irremediable. *n* incurable, *mf*

incurably /ɪn'kyʊrəbli/ *adv* incurablemente, irremediablemente

incurious /ɪn'kyʊriəs/ *a* indiferente, sin interés; incurioso, negligente, descuidado

incursion /ɪn'kɜrʒən/ *n* incursión, invasión, irrupción, *f*, acometimiento, *m*

indebted /ɪn'dɛtɪd/ *a* empeñado, adeudado; (obliged) reconocido

indebtedness /ɪn'dɛtɪdnɪs/ *n* deuda, *f*; (gratitude) obligación, *f*; agradecimiento, *m*

indecency /ɪn'disənsi/ *n* indecencia, *f*

indecent /ɪn'disənt/ *a* indecente; obsceno, deshonesto

indecently /ɪn'disəntli/ adv torpemente, indecentemente

indecision /ˌɪndɪ'sɪʒən/ n indecisión, vacilación, irresolución, f

indecisive /ˌɪndɪ'saɪsɪv/ a indeciso, irresoluto, vacilante

indeclinable /ˌɪndɪ'klaɪnəbəl/ a indeclinable

indecorous /ɪn'dɛkərəs/ a indecoroso, indecente, indigno

indecorum /ˌɪndɪ'kɔrəm/ n indecoro, m, indecencia, f; incorrección, f

indeed /ɪn'did/ adv en efecto, de veras, a la verdad, realmente, por cierto, claro está. *interr* ¿de veras? ¿es posible? **I shall be very glad i.,** Estaré contento de veras. **It is i. an excellent book,** Es en efecto un libro excelente. **There are differences i. between this house and the other,** Hay diferencias, claro está, entre esta casa y la otra

indefatigability /ˌɪndɪˌfætɪgə'bɪlɪti/ n resistencia, f, aguante, m, tenacidad, f

indefatigable /ˌɪndɪ'fætɪgəbəl/ a incansable, infatigable, resistente

indefatigably /ˌɪndɪ'fætɪgəbli/ adv infatigablemente

indefensible /ˌɪndɪ'fɛnsəbəl/ a indefendible, insostenible

indefinable /ˌɪndɪ'faɪnəbəl/ a indefinible

indefinite /ɪn'dɛfənɪt/ a indefinido, incierto; (delicate) sutil, delicado; *Gram.* indefinido; (vague) vago. *Gram.* **i. article,** artículo indefinido, m

indefinitely /ɪn'dɛfənɪtli/ adv indefinidamente

indefiniteness /ɪn'dɛfənɪtnɪs/ n lo indefinido, el carácter indefinido, m; vaguedad, f

indelibility /ɪnˌdɛlə'bɪlɪti/ n resistencia, f, lo indeleble; *Fig.* duración, tenacidad, f

indelible /ɪn'dɛləbəl/ a indeleble, imborrable; *Fig.* inolvidable

indelibly /ɪn'dɛləbli/ adv indeleblemente

indelicacy /ɪn'dɛlɪkəsi/ n falta de buen gusto, grosería, f; (tactlessness) indiscreción, falta de tacto, f

indelicate /ɪn'dɛlɪkɪt/ a grosero, descortés; indecoroso, inmodesto; (tactless) inoportuno, indiscreto

indemnification /ɪnˌdɛmnəfɪ'keɪʃən/ n indemnización, compensación, f

indemnify /ɪn'dɛmnəˌfaɪ/ vt indemnizar, compensar

indemnity /ɪn'dɛmnɪti/ n indemnización, reparación, f

indent /ɪn'dɛnt/ vt endentar, mellar; *Print.* sangrar

indentation /ˌɪndɛn'teɪʃən/ n impresión, depresión, f; corte, m, mella, f; línea quebrada, f, zigzag, m

indenture /ɪn'dɛntʃər/ n escritura, f, instrumento, m. vt escriturar

independence /ˌɪndɪ'pɛndəns/ n independencia, libertad, f; (autonomy) autonomía, f. **I. Day,** El Día de la Independencia, m. **i. movement,** movimiento en favor de la independencia, m

independent /ˌɪndɪ'pɛndənt/ a independiente; libre; (autonomous) autónomo; **i. of,** libre de; aparte de. **a person of i. means,** una persona acomodada

independently /ˌɪndɪ'pɛndəntli/ adv independientemente

indescribability /ˌɪndɪˌskraɪbə'bɪlɪti/ n imposibilidad de describir, f, lo indescriptible

indescribable /ˌɪndɪ'skraɪbəbəl/ a indescriptible; indefinible, indecible, inexplicable; incalificable

indestructibility /ˌɪndɪˌstrʌktə'bɪlɪti/ n indestructibilidad, f

indestructible /ˌɪndɪ'strʌktəbəl/ a indestructible

indeterminable /ˌɪndɪ'tɜrmənəbəl/ a indeterminable

indeterminate /ˌɪndɪ'tɜrmənɪt/ a indeterminado, indefinido, vago; *Math.* indeterminado

indetermination /ˌɪndɪˌtɜrmə'neɪʃən/ n irresolución, indecisión, duda, vacilación, f

index /'ɪndɛks/ n (forefinger) dedo índice, m; (of book) tabla de materias, f, índice, m; (on instruments) manecilla, aguja, f; *Math.* índice, m; (sign) señal, indicación, f. vt poner índice (a); poner en el índice. **i. card,** ficha, f. **I. expurgatorius,** Índice expurgatorio, m

India /'ɪndiə/ n la India, f. **I. paper,** papel de China, m. **i.-rubber,** *Bot.* caucho, m; (eraser) goma de borrar, f. **i.-rubber tree,** yacio, m

Indian /'ɪndiən/ a and n indio (-ia). **I. chief,** cacique, m. **I. club,** maza, f. **I. corn,** maíz, m. **I. ink,** tinta china, f. **I. summer,** veranillo, veranillo de San Martín, m

Indian Ocean, the el Océano Indico, m

indicate /'ɪndɪˌkeɪt/ vt indicar, señalar; (show) denotar, mostrar, anunciar

indication /ˌɪndɪ'keɪʃən/ n indicación, f; señal, f, indicio, síntoma, m; prueba, f

indicative /ɪn'dɪkətɪv/ a indicador, indicativo, demostrativo; *Gram.* indicativo. n *Gram.* indicativo, m. **to be i. of,** indicar, señalar

indicator /'ɪndɪˌkeɪtər/ n indicador, señalador, m

indict /ɪn'daɪt/ vt acusar; *Law.* demandar, enjuiciar

indictable /ɪn'daɪtəbəl/ a procesable, denunciable, enjuiciable

indictment /ɪn'daɪtmənt/ n acusación, f; *Law.* procesamiento, m

indifference /ɪn'dɪfərəns/ n indiferencia, apatía, f, desinterés, desapego, m; imparcialidad, neutralidad, f; (coldness) frialdad, tibieza, f

indifferent /ɪn'dɪfərənt/ a indiferente, apático; imparcial, neutral; frío; (ordinary) regular, ordinario, ni bien ni mal

indifferently /ɪn'dɪfərəntli/ adv con indiferencia; imparcialmente; friamente

indigence /'ɪndɪdʒəns/ n indigencia, necesidad, penuria, f

indigenous /ɪn'dɪdʒənəs/ a indígena, nativo, natural

indigent /'ɪndɪdʒənt/ a indigente, necesitado, menesteroso

indigestible /ˌɪndɪ'dʒɛstəbəl/ a indigesto

indigestion /ˌɪndɪ'dʒɛstʃən/ n indigestión, f, *Mexico* insulto m; *Fig.* empacho, ahíto, m

indignant /ɪn'dɪgnənt/ a indignado. **to make i.,** indignar

indignantly /ɪn'dɪgnəntli/ adv con indignación

indignation /ˌɪndɪg'neɪʃən/ n indignación, cólera, f

indignity /ɪn'dɪgnɪti/ n indignidad, f; ultraje, m

indigo /'ɪndɪˌgoʊ/ n añil, índigo, m

indirect /ˌɪndə'rɛkt/ a indirecto; oblicuo; tortuoso; *Gram.* **i. case,** caso oblicuo, m

indirectness /ˌɪndə'rɛktnɪs/ n (of route) rodeo, m, desviación, f; oblicuidad, f; (falsity) tortuosidad, f

indiscernible /ˌɪndɪ'sɜrnəbəl/ a imperceptible

indiscipline /ɪn'dɪsəplɪn/ n indisciplina, falta de disciplina, f

indiscreet /ˌɪndɪ'skrit/ a indiscreto, imprudente, impolítico

indiscretion /ˌɪndɪ'skrɛʃən/ n indiscreción, imprudencia, f; (slip) desliz, m

indiscriminate /ˌɪndɪ'skrɪmənɪt/ a general, universal; indistinto, promiscuo

indiscriminately /ˌɪndɪ'skrɪmənɪtli/ adv promiscuamente

indiscrimination /ˌɪndɪˌskrɪmə'neɪʃən/ n universalidad, indistinción, f

indispensability /ˌɪndɪˌspɛnsə'bɪlɪti/ n indispensabilidad, precisión, necesidad, f

indispensable /ˌɪndɪ'spɛnsəbəl/ a imprescindible, indispensable, insustituible

indispensably /ˌɪndɪ'spɛnsəbli/ adv forzosamente, indispensablemente

indispose /ˌɪndɪ'spoʊz/ vt indisponer. **to be indisposed,** estar indispuesto, indisponerse

indisposed /ˌɪndɪ'spoʊzd/ a indispuesto, enfermo, destemplado; (reluctant) maldispuesto

indisposition /ˌɪndɪspə'zɪʃən/ n indisposición, enfermedad, f

indisputability /ˌɪndɪˌspyutə'bɪlɪti/ n verdad manifiesta, certeza, evidencia, f

indisputable /ˌɪndɪ'spyutəbəl/ a innegable, incontestable; irrefutable, evidente

indisputably /ˌɪndɪ'spyutəbli/ adv indisputablemente

indissoluble /ˌɪndɪ'sɒlyəbəl/ a indisoluble

indistinct /ˌɪndɪ'stɪŋkt/ a indistinto, indeterminado, confuso, vago

indistinctly /ˌɪndɪ'stɪŋktli/ adv indistintamente; confusamente, vagamente

indistinctness /ˌɪndɪ'stɪŋktnɪs/ *n* incertidumbre, vaguedad, indistinción, indeterminación, *f*
indistinguishable /ˌɪndɪ'stɪŋgwɪʃəbəl/ *a* indistinguible
individual /ˌɪndə'vɪdʒuəl/ *a* (single) solo, único; individual, individuo, particular, propio; personal. *n* individuo, *m*, particular, *mf*
individualism /ˌɪndə'vɪdʒuəˌlɪzəm/ *n* individualismo, *m*
individualist /ˌɪndə'vɪdʒuəlɪst/ *n* individualist, *mf*
individualistic /ˌɪndə,vɪdʒuə'lɪstɪk/ *a* individualista
individuality /ˌɪndə,vɪdʒu'ælɪti/ *n* individualidad, personalidad, *f*; carácter, *m*, naturaleza, *f*
individualize /ˌɪndə'vɪdʒuəˌlaɪz/ *vt* particularizar, individuar
individually /ˌɪndə'vɪdʒuəli/ *adv* individualmente, particularmente
indivisibility /ˌɪndəˌvɪzə'bɪlɪti/ *n* indivisibilidad, *f*
indivisible /ˌɪndə'vɪzəbəl/ *a* incompartible, impartible, indivisible
indivisibly /ˌɪndə'vɪzəbli/ *adv* indivisiblemente
Indo /'ɪndou/ (in compounds) indo. **I.-China,** *n* indochina. **I.-European,** indoeuropeo
indocile /ɪn'dɒsɪl/ *a* indócil, desobediente, rebelde
indocility /ˌɪndɒ'sɪlɪti/ *n* indocilidad, desobediencia, falta de docilidad, *f*
indolence /'ɪndləns/ *n* indolencia, pereza, desidia, *f*
indolent /'ɪndlənt/ *a* indolente, perezoso, holgazán; *Med.* indoloro
indolently /'ɪndləntli/ *adv* perezosamente
indomitable /ɪn'dɒmɪtəbəl/ *a* indomable, indómito
indoor /'ɪnˌdɔr/ *a* de casa; de puertas adentro, interno. **i. swimming pool,** piscina bajo techo, *f*. **i. tennis,** tenis en pistas cubiertas, tenis bajo techo, *m*
indoors /ɪn'dɔrz/ *adv* en casa; adentro, bajo techo
indorsee /ˌɪndɔr'si/ *n* endosatario (-ia)
indubitable /ɪn'dubɪtəbəl/ *a* indudable
indubitably /ɪn'dubɪtəbli/ *adv* indudablemente, sin duda
induce /ɪn'dus/ *vt* inducir, mover; instigar, incitar; producir, ocasionar; *Elec.* inducir. **Nothing would i. me to do it,** Nada me induciría a hacerlo
inducement /ɪn'dusmənt/ *n* incitamiento, *m*; estímulo, *m*; aliciente, atractivo, *m*; tentación, *f*
induct /ɪn'dʌkt/ *vt* instalar; introducir, iniciar
induction /ɪn'dʌkʃən/ *n* instalación, *f*; iniciación, introducción, *f*; *Phys.* inducción, *f*. **i. coil,** carrete de inducción, *m*
inductive /ɪn'dʌktɪv/ *a* (of reasoning) inductivo; *Phys.* inductor
indulge /ɪn'dʌldʒ/ *vt* (children) consentir, mimar; (a desire) satisfacer, dar rienda suelta a; (with a gift) agasajar (con), dar gusto (con). **to i. in,** *vt* consentir en. *vi* entregarse a, permitirse, gustar de
indulgence /ɪn'dʌldʒəns/ *n* (of children) mimo, cariño excesivo, *m*; (of a desire) propensión (a), afición (a), *f*; (toward others) tolerancia, transigencia, *f*; *Eccl.* indulgencia, *f*
indulgent /ɪn'dʌldʒənt/ *a* indulgente; tolerante, transigente
indult /ɪn'dʌlt/ *n* *Eccl.* indulto, *m*
industrial /ɪn'dʌstriəl/ *a* industrial. **i. alcohol,** alcohol desnaturalizado, *m*. **i. school,** escuela de artes y oficios, *f*, *Com.* **i. shares,** valores industriales, *m pl*
industrialism /ɪn'dʌstriəˌlɪzəm/ *n* industrialismo, *m*
industrialist /ɪn'dʌstriəlɪst/ *n* industrial, *m*
industrialization /ɪnˌdʌstriəlɪ'zeɪʃən/ *n* industrialización, *f*
industrialize /ɪn'dʌstriəˌlaɪz/ *vt* industrializar
industrious /ɪn'dʌstriəs/ *a* industrioso, aplicado, diligente
industriously /ɪn'dʌstriəsli/ *adv* industriosamente, diligentemente
industriousness /ɪn'dʌstriəsnɪs/ *n* industria, laboriosidad, *f*
industry /'ɪndəstri/ *n* diligencia, aplicación, *f*; (work) trabajo, *m*, labor, *f*; *Com.* industria, *f*
inebriate /*a*, *n* ɪ'nibriɪt; *v* -briˌeɪt/ *a* borracho, ebrio. *n* borracho (-cha). *vt* embriagar, emborrachar
inebriation /ɪˌnibri'eɪʃən/ *n* embriaguez, borrachera, *f*
inedible /ɪn'ɛdəbəl/ *a* incomible, no comestible

inedited /ɪn'ɛdɪtɪd/ *a* inédito
ineffable /ɪn'ɛfəbəl/ *a* indecible, inefable
ineffaceable /ˌɪnɪ'feɪsəbəl/ *a* imborrable, indeleble
ineffective /ˌɪnɪ'fɛktɪv/ *a* ineficaz; vano, fútil. **to be i.,** (of persons) no pinchar ni cortar. **to prove i.,** quedar sin efecto; no tener influencia
ineffectiveness /ˌɪnɪ'fɛktɪvnɪs/ *n* ineficacia, *f*; futilidad, *f*
inefficiency /ˌɪnɪ'fɪʃənsi/ *n* ineficacia, incompetencia, ineptitud, *f*
inefficient /ˌɪnɪ'fɪʃənt/ *a* ineficaz, incapaz
inefficiently /ˌɪnɪ'fɪʃəntli/ *adv* ineficazmente
inelastic /ˌɪnɪ'læstɪk/ *a* inelástico
inelegance /ɪn'ɛlɪgəns/ *n* inelegancia, fealdad, vulgaridad, *f*
inelegant /ɪn'ɛlɪgənt/ *a* inelegante, ordinario, de mal gusto
inelegantly /ɪn'ɛlɪgəntli/ *adv* sin elegancia
ineligibility /ɪnˌɛlɪdʒə'bɪlɪti/ *n* ineligibilidad, *f*
ineligible /ɪn'ɛlɪdʒəbəl/ *a* inelegible
inept /ɪn'ɛpt/ *a* inepto, inoportuno; absurdo, ridículo; (of persons) incompetente, ineficaz
ineptitude /ɪn'ɛptɪˌtud/ *n* ineptitud, *f*; necedad, *f*; (of persons) incapacidad, incompetencia, *f*
ineptly /ɪn'ɛptli/ *adv* ineptamente, neciamente
inequality /ˌɪnɪ'kwɒlɪti/ *n* desigualdad, desemejanza, disparidad, *f*; (of surface) escabrosidad, aspereza, *f*; *Fig.* injusticia, *f*; (of opportunity) diferencia, *f*
inequitable /ɪn'ɛkwɪtəbəl/ *a* desigual, injusto
inequity /ɪn'ɛkwɪti/ *n* injusticia, desigualdad, *f*
ineradicable /ˌɪnɪ'rædɪkəbəl/ *a* indeleble, imborrable
ineradicably /ˌɪnɪ'rædɪkəbli/ *adv* indeleblemente
inert /ɪn'ɜrt/ *a* inerte, inactivo, pasivo; ocioso, flojo, perezoso
inertia /ɪn'ɜrʃə/ *n* inercia, inacción, *f*; abulia, pereza, *f*; *Phys.* inercia, *f*
inertly /ɪn'ɜrtli/ *adv* indolentemente, sin mover, pasivamente
inescapable /ˌɪnə'skeɪpəbəl/ *a* ineludible, inevitable
inessential /ˌɪnɪ'sɛnʃəl/ *a* no esencial
inestimable /ɪn'ɛstəməbəl/ *a* inestimable
inevitability /ɪnˌɛvɪtə'bɪlɪti/ *n* fatalidad, necesidad, *f*; lo inevitable
inevitable /ɪn'ɛvɪtəbəl/ *a* inevitable, necesario, fatal, forzoso, ineludible
inevitably /ɪn'ɛvɪtəbli/ *adv* inevitablemente, necesariamente, forzosamente
inexact /ˌɪnɪg'zækt/ *a* inexacto, incorrecto
inexactitude /ˌɪnɪg'zæktɪˌtud/ *n* inexactitud, *f*
inexcusable /ˌɪnɪk'skyuzəbəl/ *a* imperdonable, inexcusable, irremisible
inexcusableness /ˌɪnɪk'skyuzəbəlnɪs/ *n* enormidad, *f*; lo inexcusable
inexcusably /ˌɪnɪk'skyuzəbli/ *adv* inexcusablemente
inexhaustible /ˌɪnɪg'zɔstəbəl/ *a* inagotable, inexhausto
inexorability /ɪnˌɛksərə'bɪlɪti/ *n* inflexibilidad, inexorabilidad, *f*
inexorable /ɪn'ɛksərəbəl/ *a* inexorable, inflexible, duro
inexorably /ɪn'ɛksərəbli/ *adv* inexorablemente, implacablemente
inexpediency /ˌɪnɪk'spidiənsi/ *n* inoportunidad, inconveniencia, imprudencia, *f*
inexpedient /ˌɪnɪk'spidiənt/ *a* inoportuno; inconveniente; impolítico, imprudente. **to deem i.,** creer inoportuno
inexpensive /ˌɪnɪk'spɛnsɪv/ *a* poco costoso, barato
inexpensiveness /ˌɪnɪk'spɛnsɪvnɪs/ *n* baratura, *f*, bajo precio, *m*
inexperience /ˌɪnɪk'spɪriəns/ *n* inexperiencia, falta de experiencia, *f*
inexperienced /ˌɪnɪk'spɪriənst/ *a* inexperto, novato
inexpert /ɪn'ɛkspərt/ *a* inexperto, imperito
inexpertly /ɪn'ɛkspərtli/ *adv* sin habilidad
inexpertness /ɪn'ɛkspərtnɪs/ *n* impericia, torpeza, *f*
inexpiable /ɪn'ɛkspiəbəl/ *a* inexpiable
inexplicable /ɪn'ɛksplɪkəbəl/ *a* inexplicable
inexplicably /ɪn'ɛksplɪkəbli/ *adv* inexplicablemente
inexplicit /ˌɪnɪk'splɪsɪt/ *a* no explícito
inexplosive /ˌɪnɪk'splousɪv/ *a* inexplosible

inexpressible /ˌɪnɪk'spresəbəl/ a inexplicable, indecible, inefable

inexpressive /ˌɪnɪk'spresɪv/ a inexpresivo; (of persons) reservado, callado, poco expresivo, retraído

inexpressiveness /ˌɪnɪk'spresɪvnɪs/ n falta de expresión, f; (of persons) reserva, f, silencio, retraimiento, m

inexpugnable /ˌɪnɪk'spʌgnəbəl/ a inexpugnable

inextinguishable /ˌɪnɪk'stɪŋgwɪʃəbəl/ a inapagable, inextinguible

inextricable /ɪn'ekstrɪkəbəl/ a inextricable, intrincado, enmarañado

inextricably /ɪn'ekstrɪkəbli/ adv intrincadamente

infallibility /ɪnˌfælə'bɪlɪti/ n infalibilidad, f

infallible /ɪn'fæləbəl/ a infalible

infamous /'ɪnfəməs/ a infame, torpe, vil, ignominioso; odioso, repugnante

infamously /'ɪnfəməsli/ adv infamemente

infamy /'ɪnfəmi/ n infamia, torpeza, vileza, ignominia, f; deshonra, f

infancy /'ɪnfənsi/ n infancia, niñez, f; Law. minoridad, f

infant /'ɪnfənt/ n criatura, f; crío (-ía), niño (-ña); Law. menor, mf. **i. school,** escuela de párvulos, f

infanticidal /ɪnˌfæntə'saidl/ a infanticida

infanticide /ɪn'fæntə,said/ n (act) infanticidio, m; (person) infanticida, mf

infantile /'ɪnfən,tail/ a infantil. **i. paralysis,** parálisis infantil, f

infantry /'ɪnfəntri/ n Mil. infantería de la guerra, f

infantryman /'ɪnfəntrimən/ n Mil. infante, soldado, peón, m

infatuate /ɪn'fætʃu,eit/ vt infatuar, embobar

infatuation /ɪnˌfætʃu'eiʃən/ n infatuación, f, encaprichamiento, m

infect /ɪn'fekt/ vt infectar, contagiar; Fig. pegar, influir; (Fig. in a bad sense) corromper, pervertir, inficionar. **to become infected,** infectarse

infected /ɪn'fektɪd/ a infecto

infection /ɪn'fekʃən/ n infección, f, contagio, m; Fig. influencia, f; (Fig. in a bad sense) corrupción, perversión, f

infectious /ɪn'fekʃəs/ a infeccioso, contagioso; (Fig. in a bad sense) corruptor; Fig. contagioso

infectiousness /ɪn'fekʃəsnɪs/ n contagiosidad, f

infelicitous /ˌɪnfə'lɪsɪtəs/ a poco apropiado, desacertado

infelicity /ˌɪnfə'lɪsɪti/ n infelicidad, desdicha, f, infortunio, m; desacierto, m, inoportunidad, f

infer /ɪn'fɜr/ vt inferir, concluir, educir, deducir, implicar

inferable /ɪn'fɜrəbəl/ a deducible, demostrable

inference /'ɪnfərəns/ n inferencia, deducción, conclusión, f

inferential /ˌɪnfə'renʃəl/ a ilativo, deductivo

inferior /ɪn'fɪəriər/ a inferior; (in rank) subordinado, subalterno; (of position) secundario. n inferior, mf subordinado (-da). **to be not i.,** no ser inferior, Inf. no quedarse en zaga

inferiority /ɪnˌfɪəri'ɔrɪti/ n inferioridad, f. **i. complex,** complejo de inferioridad, m

infernal /ɪn'fɜrnl/ a infernal; Poet. inferno, tartáreo

infernally /ɪn'fɜrnli/ adv infernalmente

inferno /ɪn'fɜrnou/ n infierno, m

infertile /ɪn'fɜrtl/ a infértil, infecundo, estéril

infertility /ˌɪnfər'tɪlɪti/ n infertilidad, infecundidad, esterilidad, f

infest /ɪn'fest/ vt infestar. **to be infested with,** plagarse de

infestation /ˌɪnfes'teiʃən/ n infestación, f

infidel /'ɪnfɪdl/ n infiel, gentil, mf pagano (-na); (atheist) descreído (-da), ateo (-ea). a pagano; infiel, descreído, ateo

infidelity /ˌɪnfɪ'delɪti/ n infidelidad, alevosía, perfidia, f

infiltrate /ɪn'fɪltreit/ vt infiltrar. vi infiltrarse

infiltration /ˌɪnfɪl'treiʃən/ n infiltración, f

infinite /'ɪnfənɪt/ a infinito, ilimitado; inmenso, enorme; (of number) innumerable, infinito. n infinito, m

infinitely /'ɪnfənɪtli/ adv infinitamente

infinitesimal /ˌɪnfɪnɪ'tesəməl/ a infinitesimal. **i. calculus,** cálculo infinitesimal, m

infinitive /ɪn'fɪnɪtɪv/ a and n Gram. infinitivo, m.

infinitude, infinity /ɪn'fɪnɪtud; ɪn'fɪnɪti/ n infinidad, infinitud, f; (extent) inmensidad, f; (of number) sinfín, m; Math. infinito, m

infirm /ɪn'fɜrm/ a achacoso, enfermizo, enclenque; (shaky) inestable, inseguro; (of purpose) irresoluto, vacilante

infirmary /ɪn'fɜrməri/ n enfermería, f, hospital, m

infirmity /ɪn'fɜrmɪti/ n achaque, m, enfermedad, dolencia, f; (fault) flaqueza, falta, f

inflame /ɪn'fleim/ vt encender; (excite) acalorar, irritar, provocar; Med. inflamar. vi encenderse, arder; acalorarse, irritarse; Med. inflamarse

inflammability /ɪnˌflæmə'bɪlɪti/ n inflamabilidad, f

inflammable /ɪn'flæməbəl/ a inflamable

inflammation /ˌɪnflə'meiʃən/ n inflamación, f

inflammatory /ɪn'flæmə,tɔri/ a inflamador; Med. inflamatorio

inflate /ɪn'fleit/ vt inflar, hinchar; (with pride) engreír, ensoberbecer

inflation /ɪn'fleiʃən/ n inflación, hinchazón, f; Com. inflación, f

inflationism /ɪn'fleiʃə,nɪzəm/ n inflacionismo, m

inflator /ɪn'fleitər/ n Mech. bomba para inflar, f

inflect /ɪn'flekt/ vt torcer; (voice) modular; Gram. conjugar, declinar

inflection /ɪn'flekʃən/ n dobladura, f; (of voice) tono, acento, m, modulación, f; Gram. conjugación, declinación, f

inflexibility /ɪnˌfleksə'bɪlɪti/ n inflexibilidad, dureza, rigidez, f

inflexible /ɪn'fleksəbəl/ a inflexible, rígido; Fig. inexorable, inalterable

inflexibly /ɪn'fleksəbli/ adv inflexiblemente

inflict /ɪn'flɪkt/ vt infligir, imponer

infliction /ɪn'flɪkʃən/ n imposición, f; castigo, m

inflorescence /ˌɪnflɔ'resəns/ n Bot. inflorescencia, f

inflow /'ɪn,flou/ n afluencia, f, flujo, m

influence /'ɪnfluəns/ n influencia, f, influjo, m; ascendiente, m; (importance) influencia, importancia, f. vt influir, afectar; persuadir, inducir. **to have i. over,** (a person) tener ascendiente sobre. Law. **undue i.,** influencia indebida, f

influential /ˌɪnflu'enʃəl/ a influyente; (of person) prestigioso, importante

influenza /ˌɪnflu'enzə/ n Med. gripe, f, trancazo, m

influx /'ɪn,flʌks/ n influjo, m; (of rivers) desembocadura, afluencia, f

inform /ɪn'fɔrm/ vt (fill) infundir, llenar; (tell) informar, enterar, advertir; instruir; (with about) poner al corriente de, participar. vi (with against) delatar (a), denunciar. **to i. oneself,** informarse, enterarse. **to be informed about,** estar al corriente de

informal /ɪn'fɔrməl/ a irregular; sin ceremonia, de confianza; (meeting) no oficial, extraoficial

informality /ˌɪnfɔr'mælɪti/ n irregularidad, f; falta de ceremonia, sencillez, f; intimidad, f

informally /ɪn'fɔrməli/ adv sin ceremonia

informant /ɪn'fɔrmənt/ n informante, mf; informador (-ra)

information /ˌɪnfɔr'meiʃən/ n información, instrucción, f; noticia, f, aviso, m; Law. denuncia, delación, f. **piece of i.,** información, f. **i. bureau,** oficina de información, f

informative /ɪn'fɔrmətɪv/ a informativo

informer /ɪn'fɔrmər/ n delator (-ra), denunciador (-ra)

infraction /ɪn'frækʃən/ n contravención, infracción, transgresión, f

infrared /ˌɪnfrə'red/ a Phys. infrarrojo, ultrarrojo

infrequency /ɪn'frikwənsi/ n infrecuencia, rareza, irregularidad, f

infrequent /ɪn'frikwənt/ a infrecuente, raro, irregular

infrequently /ɪn'frikwəntli/ adv rara vez, infrecuentemente

infringe /ɪn'frɪndʒ/ vt infringir, violar, contravenir, quebrantar

infringement /ɪn'frɪndʒmənt/ n contravención, violación, infracción, f

infringer /ɪn'frɪndʒər/ n infractor (-ra), contraventor (-ra), violador (-ra), transgresor (-ra)

infuriate /ɪn'fyʊri,eit/ vt enfurecer, enloquecer, enojar. **to be infuriated,** estar furioso

infuse /ɪn'fyuz/ vt vaciar, infiltrar; Fig. infundir, inculcar, instilar

infusible /ɪn'fyuzəbəl/ a infundible

infusion /ɪn'fyuʒən/ n infusión, f; Fig. instilación, inculcación, f

ingathering /ɪn'gæðərɪŋ/ n cosecha, recolección, f

ingenious /ɪn'dʒinyəs/ a ingenioso; mañoso, hábil

ingeniously /ɪn'dʒinyəsli/ adv ingeniosamente, hábilmente

ingenuity /,ɪndʒə'nuiti/ n ingeniosidad, inventiva, listeza, habilidad, f

ingenuous /ɪn'dʒɛnyuəs/ a ingenuo, franco, sincero, cándido, sencillo, inocente

ingenuousness /ɪn'dʒɛnyuəsnɪs/ n ingenuidad, franqueza, sinceridad, f; candor, m

ingest /ɪn'dʒest/ vt ingerir

ingestion /ɪn'dʒestʃən/ n ingestión, f

ingoing /'ɪn,gouɪŋ/ a entrante, que entra. n ingreso, m, entrada, f; Com. **i. and outgoing,** entradas y salidas, f pl

ingot /'ɪŋgət/ n pepita, f, lingote, m; (of any metal) barra, f

ingrained /ɪn'greind, 'ɪn,greind/ a innato, natural

ingratiate /ɪn'greiʃi,eit/ vt (oneself with) congraciarse con, captarse la buena voluntad de, insinuarse en el favor de

ingratiating /ɪn'greiʃi,eitɪŋ/ a obsequioso

ingratitude /ɪn'græti,tud/ n ingratitud, f, desagradecimiento, m

ingredient /ɪn'gridiənt/ n ingrediente, m

ingress /'ɪngrɛs/ n ingreso, m; derecho de entrada, m

ingrowing /'ɪn,grouɪŋ/ a que crece hacia adentro. **i. nail,** uñero, m

inhabit /ɪn'hæbɪt/ vt habitar, ocupar, vivir en, residir en

inhabitable /ɪn'hæbɪtəbəl/ a habitable, vividero

inhabitant /ɪn'hæbɪtənt/ n habitante, residente, m; vecino (-na)

inhabited /ɪn'hæbɪtɪd/ a habitado, poblado

inhalation /,ɪnhə'leiʃən/ n inspiración, f; Med. inhalación, f

inhale /ɪn'heil/ vt aspirar; Med. inhalar

inharmonious /,ɪnhɑr'mouniəs/ a Mus. disonante, inarmónico; desavenido, discorde, desconforme. **to be i.,** disonar; (of people) llevarse mal

inhere /ɪn'hɪər/ vi ser inherente; pertenecer (a), residir (en)

inherence /ɪn'hɪərəns/ n inherencia, f

inherent /ɪn'hɪərənt/ a inherente; innato, intrínseco, natural

inherently /ɪn'hɪərəntli/ adv intrínsecamente

inherit /ɪn'hɛrɪt/ vt heredar

inheritance /ɪn'hɛrɪtəns/ n herencia, f; patrimonio, abolengo, m

inheritor /ɪn'hɛrɪtər/ n heredero (-ra)

inhibit /ɪn'hɪbɪt/ vt inhibir, impedir; Eccl. prohibir. **be inhibited, became inhibited,** cohibirse

inhibition /,ɪnɪ'bɪʃən/ n inhibición, f

inhibitory /ɪn'hɪbɪ,tɔri/ a inhibitorio

inhospitable /ɪn'hɒspɪtəbəl/ a inhospitalario

inhospitably /ɪn'hɒspɪtəbli/ adv desabridamente

inhuman /ɪn'hyumən/ a inhumano; cruel, bárbaro

inhumanity /,ɪnhyu'mænɪti/ n inhumanidad, crueldad, f

inhumanly /ɪn'hyumənli/ adv inhumanamente, cruelmente

inhume /ɪn'hyum/ vt inhumar, sepultar

inimical /ɪ'nɪmɪkəl/ a enemigo, hostil, opuesto, contrario

inimically /ɪ'nɪmɪkəli/ adv hostilmente

inimitable /ɪ'nɪmɪtəbəl/ a inimitable

inimitably /ɪ'nɪmɪtəbli/ adv inimitablemente

iniquitous /ɪ'nɪkwɪtəs/ a inicuo, malvado, perverso, nefando; Inf. diabólico

iniquity /ɪ'nɪkwɪti/ n iniquidad, maldad, injusticia, f

initial /ɪ'nɪʃəl/ a inicial. n inicial, letra inicial, f. vt firmar con las iniciales

initially /ɪ'nɪʃəli/ adv al principio, en primer lugar

initiate /a ɪ'nɪʃit; v ɪ'nɪʃi,eit/ a iniciado. vt iniciar, poner en pie, empezar, entablar; (a person) admitir

initiation /ɪ,nɪʃi'eiʃən/ n principio, m; (of a person) iniciación, admisión, f

initiative /ɪ'nɪʃiətɪv/ n iniciativa, f. **to take the i.,** tomar la iniciativa

initiator /ɪ'nɪʃi,eitər/ n iniciador (-ra)

inject /ɪn'dʒɛkt/ vt inyectar

injection /ɪn'dʒɛkʃən/ n inyección, f. **i. syringe,** jeringa de inyecciones, f

injudicious /,ɪndʒu'dɪʃəs/ a imprudente, indiscreto

injudiciously /,ɪndʒu'dɪʃəsli/ adv imprudentemente

injudiciousness /,ɪndʒu'dɪʃəsnɪs/ n imprudencia, indiscreción, f

injunction /ɪn'dʒʌŋkʃən/ n precepto, mandato, m; Law. embargo, m

injure /'ɪndʒər/ vt perjudicar, dañar, Lat. Am. afectar; menoscabar, deteriorar; (hurt) lastimar, lisiar. **to i. oneself,** hacerse daño

injured /'ɪndʒərd/ a (physically) lisiado; (morally) ofendido

injurer /'ɪndʒərər/ n perjudicador (-ra)

injurious /ɪn'dʒʊriəs/ a dañoso, perjudicial, malo; ofensivo, injurioso

injuriously /ɪn'dʒʊriəsli/ adv perjudicialmente

injury /'ɪndʒəri/ n perjuicio, daño, m; (physical) lesión, Lat. Am. also lastimadura, f; (insult) agravio, insulto, m

injustice /ɪn'dʒʌstɪs/ n injusticia, desigualdad, f. **You do him an i.,** Le juzgas mal

ink /ɪŋk/ n tinta, f. vt entintar. **copying-ink,** tinta de copiar, f. **marking-ink,** tinta indeleble, f. **printer's ink,** tinta de imprenta, f. **ink-stand** or **ink-well,** tintero, m

inker /'ɪŋkər/ n Print. rodillo, m

inkling /'ɪŋklɪŋ/ n sospecha, noción, f

inky /'ɪŋki/ a manchado de tinta

inland /'ɪnlænd/ n el interior de un país, a interior, mediterráneo; del país, regional. adv tierra adentro. **to go i.,** internarse en un país. **I. Revenue,** delegación de contribuciones, f. **i. town,** ciudad del interior, f

inlay /'ɪn,lei/ vt taracear, ataracear, embutir; incrustar. n taracea, f, embutido, m

inlet /'ɪnlɛt/ n entrada, admisión, f; Geog. ensenada, f. **i. valve,** válvula de admisión, f

inmate /'ɪn,meit/ n residente, habitante, m; (of hospital) paciente, mf; enfermo (-ma); (of prison) prisionero

inmost /'ɪnmoust/. See **innermost**

inn /ɪn/ n posada, fonda, venta, f, mesón, m

innate /ɪ'neit/ a innato, inherente, instintivo, nativo

innately /ɪ'neitli/ adv naturalmente, instintivamente

innavigable /ɪ'nævɪgəbəl/ a innavegable

inner /'ɪnər/ a interior, interno. **i. tube** Auto. cámara de neumatico, cámara de aire, f

innermost /'ɪnər,moust/ a más adentro; Fig. más íntimo, más hondo

innings /'ɪnɪŋz/ n (sport) turno, m

innkeeper /'ɪn,kipər/ n fondista, mf; tabernero (-ra), mesonero (-ra), posadero (-ra)

innocence /'ɪnəsəns/ n inocencia, f; pureza, f; (guilelessness) simplicidad, f, candor, m

innocent /'ɪnəsənt/ a inocente, puro; (guiltless) inocente, inculpable; (foolish) simple, tonto, candoroso, inocentón; (harmless) innocuo. n inocente, mf **Holy Innocents,** Santos Inocentes, m pl

innocuous /ɪ'nɒkyuəs/ a innocuo, inofensivo

innocuousness /ɪ'nɒkyuəsnɪs/ n inocuidad, f

innovate /'ɪnə,veit/ vt innovar

innovation /,ɪnə'veiʃən/ n innovación, f

innovative /'ɪnə,veitɪv/ a innovador

innovator /'ɪnə,veitər/ n innovador (-ra)

innuendo /,ɪnyu'ɛndou/ n indirecta, insinuación, f

innumerable /ɪ'numərəbəl/ a innumerable, incalculable. **i. things,** un sinfín de cosas

inobservance /ˌɪnəb'zɜrvəns/ n inobservancia, f, incumplimiento, m
inoculate /ɪ'nɒkyə,leit/ vt inocular
inoculation /ɪ,nɒkyə'leiʃən/ n inoculación, f
inoculator /ɪ'nɒkyə,leitər/ n inoculador, m
inodorous /ɪn'oudərəs/ a inodoro
inoffensive /ˌɪnə'fensɪv/ a inofensivo, innocuo; (of people) pacífico, apacible, manso
inoffensively /ˌɪnə'fensɪvli/ adv inofensivamente
inoffensiveness /ˌɪnə'fensɪvnɪs/ n inocuidad, f; (of people) mansedumbre, f
inoperable /ɪn'ɒpərəbəl/ a inoperable
inoperative /ɪn'ɒpərətɪv/ a ineficaz, impracticable, inútil
inopportune /ɪn,ɒpər'tun/ a inoportuno, intempestivo, inconveniente
inopportunely /ɪn,ɒpər'tunli/ adv inoportunamente, a destiempo
inopportuneness /ɪn,ɒpər'tunnɪs/ n inoportunidad, inconveniencia, f
inordinate /ɪn'ɔrdn̩ɪt/ a desordenado, excesivo
inordinately /ɪn'ɔrdn̩ɪtli/ adv desmedidamente
inorganic /ˌɪnɔr'gænɪk/ a inorgánico
inoxidizable /ɪn'ɒksɪ,daizəbəl/ a inoxidable
input /'ɪn,pʊt/ n capacidad instalada, f, insumo, m
inquest /'ɪnkwest/ n Law. indagación, investigación, f
inquietude /ɪn'kwaiɪ,tud/ n inquietud, f, desasosiego, m, agitación, preocupación, f
inquire /ɪn'kwaiªr/ vt and vi preguntar, averiguar, indagar. **to i. about,** (persons) preguntar por; (things) hacer preguntas sobre. **to i. into,** investigar, examinar, averiguar. **to i. of,** preguntar a. **"I. within,"** «Se dan informaciones»
inquirer /ɪn'kwaiªrər/ n indagador (-ra), inquiridor (-ra)
inquiring /ɪn'kwaiªrɪŋ/ a indagador, inquiridor
inquiringly /ɪn'kwaiªrɪŋli/ adv interrogativamente
inquiry /ɪn'kwaiªri/ n interrogación, pregunta, f; indagación, pesquisa, investigación, f; examen, m. **i. office,** oficina de informaciones, f. **on i.,** al preguntar
inquisition /ˌɪnkwə'zɪʃən/ n investigación, indagación, f; inquisición, f. **Holy I.,** Santo Oficio, m, Inquisición, f
inquisitive /ɪn'kwɪzɪtɪv/ a curioso, inquiridor; preguntador, impertinente, mirón
inquisitively /ɪn'kwɪzɪtɪvli/ adv con curiosidad, impertinentemente
inquisitiveness /ɪn'kwɪzɪtɪvnɪs/ n curiosidad, f; impertinencia, f
Inquisitor /ɪn'kwɪzɪtər/ n Eccl. inquisidor, m
inquisitorial /ɪn,kwɪzɪ'tɔriəl/ a inquisitorial, inquisidor
inroad /'ɪn,roud/ n incursión, f
insalubrious /ˌɪnsə'lubriəs/ a malsano, insalubre
insane /ɪn'sein/ a loco, demente, insano; (senseless) insensato, ridículo. **to become i.,** enloquecer, volverse loco, perder la razón. **to drive i.,** volver a uno el juicio, enloquecer, trastornar. **i. person,** demente, mf. loco (-ca)
insanely /ɪn'seinli/ adv locamente
insanitary /ɪn'sænɪ,teri/ a antihigiénico, malsano
insanity /ɪn'sænɪti/ n demencia, locura, f; enloquecimiento, m; (folly) insensatez, ridiculez, f
insatiability /ɪn,seiʃə'bɪlɪti/ n insaciabilidad, f
insatiable /ɪn'seiʃəbəl/ a insaciable
insatiably /ɪn'seiʃəbli/ adv insaciablemente
inscribe /ɪn'skraib/ vt inscribir
inscription /ɪn'skrɪpʃən/ n inscripción, f; letrero, m; (of a book) dedicatoria, f; Com. inscripción, anotación, f, asiento, m
inscrutability /ɪn,skrutə'bɪlɪti/ n enigma, misterio, m; incomprensibilidad, f
inscrutable /ɪn'skrutəbəl/ a enigmático, insondable, incomprensible, inescrutable
inscrutably /ɪn'skrutəbli/ adv incomprensiblemente, enigmáticamente
insect /'ɪnsekt/ n insecto, m. **i. powder,** polvos insecticidas, m pl
insecticide /ɪn'sektə,said/ a and n insecticida m.
insecure /ˌɪnsɪ'kyʊr/ a inseguro, precario

insecurely /ˌɪnsɪ'kyʊrli/ adv inseguramente
insecurity /ˌɪnsɪ'kyʊrɪti/ n inseguridad, f; incertidumbre, inestabilidad, f
inseminate /ɪn'semə,neit/ vt Fig. implantar; Med. fecundar
insemination /ɪn,semə'neiʃən/ n Fig. implantación, f; Med. fecundación, f
insensate /ɪn'senseit/ a (unfeeling) insensible, insensitivo; (stupid) insensato, sin sentido, necio
insensibility /ɪn,sensə'bɪlɪti/ n insensibilidad, inconsciencia, f; (stupor) sopor, letargo, m; impasibilidad, indiferencia, f
insensible /ɪn'sensəbəl/ a insensible, inconsciente; indiferente, impasible, duro de corazón; (scarcely noticeable) imperceptible. **to make i.,** (to sensations) hacer indiferente (a); insensibilizar
insensibly /ɪn'sensəbli/ adv insensiblemente, imperceptiblemente
insensitive /ɪn'sensɪtɪv/ a insensible, insensitivo; (person) hecho un tronco, hecho un leño
insensitiveness /ɪn'sensɪtɪvnɪs/ n insensibilidad, f
insentient /ɪn'senʃiənt/ a insensible
inseparability /ɪn,sepərə'bɪlɪti/ n inseparabilidad, f
inseparable /ɪn'sepərəbəl/ a inseparable
insert /ɪn'sɜrt/ vt insertar, intercalar; (introduce) meter dentro, introducir, encajar; (in a newspaper) publicar
insertion /ɪn'sɜrʃən/ n inserción, intercalación, f; (introduction) introducción, f; metimiento, encaje, m; Sew. entredós, m; (in a newspaper) publicación, f
inshore /'ɪn'ʃɔr/ a cercano a la orilla. adv cerca de la orilla. **i. fishing,** pesca de arrastre, f
inside /ɪn'said/ a interior, interno. adv adentro, dentro. n interior, m; (contents) contenido, m; (lining) forro, m; (Inf. stomach) entrañas, f pl. **to turn i. out,** volver al revés. **to walk on the i. of the pavement,** andar a la derecha de la acera. **from the i.,** desde el interior; por dentro. **on the i.,** por dentro, en el interior. **i. information,** información confidencial, f. **i. out,** al revés, de dentro afuera
insidious /ɪn'sɪdiəs/ a insidioso, enganoso, traidor
insidiously /ɪn'sɪdiəsli/ adv insidiosamente
insidiousness /ɪn'sɪdiəsnɪs/ n insidia, f; engaño, m, traición, f
insight /'ɪn,sait/ n percepción, perspicacia, intuición, f. atisbo, m
insignia /ɪn'sɪgniə/ n pl insignias, f pl
insignificance /ˌɪnsɪg'nɪfɪkəns/ n insignificancia, futilidad, pequeñez, f
insignificant /ˌɪnsɪg'nɪfɪkənt/ a insignificante, fútil, trivial
insincere /ˌɪnsɪn'sɪr/ a insincero, hipócrita, falso
insincerely /ˌɪnsɪn'sɪrli/ adv falsamente, hipócritamente
insincerity /ˌɪnsɪn'serɪti/ n insinceridad, hipocresía, falsedad, falta de sinceridad, doblez, f
insinuate /ɪn'sɪnyu,eit/ vt insinuar, introducir; (hint) soltar una indirecta, sugerir; (oneself) insinuarse, introducirse con habilidad
insinuation /ɪn,sɪnyu'eiʃən/ n insinuación, introducción, f; (hint) indirecta, f
insipid /ɪn'sɪpɪd/ a insípido, insulso; (dull) soso
insipidity /ˌɪnsə'pɪdɪti/ n insipidez, insulsez, f, desabor, m; (dullness) sosería, f
insist /ɪn'sɪst/ vi insistir; persistir, obstinarse. **to i. on,** insistir en; obstinarse en, hacer hincapié en, aferrarse en (or a)
insistence /ɪn'sɪstəns/ n insistencia, f; obstinación, pertinacia, f
insistent /ɪn'sɪstənt/ a insistente; porfiado, obstinaz
insistently /ɪn'sɪstəntli/ adv insistentemente; porfiadamente
insobriety /ˌɪnsə'braiɪti/ n falta de sobriedad, f; embriaguez, ebriedad, f
insole /'ɪn,soul/ n (of shoes) plantilla, f
insolence /'ɪnsələns/ n insolencia, altanería, majadería, frescura, f, atrevimiento, descaro, m
insolent /'ɪnsələnt/ a insolente, arrogante, atrevido, descarado, desmesurado, fresco

insolently /'ɪnsələntli/ adv insolentemente, con descaro
insolubility /ɪn,sɒljə'bɪlɪti/ n insolubilidad, f
insoluble /ɪn'sɒljəbəl/ a insoluble
insolvency /ɪn'sɒlvənsi/ n in olvencia, f
insolvent /ɪn'sɒlvənt/ a insolvente
insomnia /ɪn'sɒmniə/ n insomnio, m
insomuch /,ɪnsə'mʌtʃ/ adv (gen. with as or that) de modo (que), así (que), de suerte (que)
inspect /ɪn'spɛkt/ vt examinar, investigar, inspeccionar; (officially) registrar, reconocer
inspection /ɪn'spɛkʃən/ n inspección, investigación, f; examen, m; (official) reconocimiento, registro, m
inspector /ɪn'spɛktər/ n inspector, m, veedor, interventor, m
inspectorate /ɪn'spɛktərɪt/ n inspectorado, m; cargo de inspector, m
inspiration /,ɪnspə'reɪʃən/ n (of breath) inspiración, aspiración, f; numen, m, inspiración, vena, f. **to find i. in,** inspirarse en.
inspire /ɪn'spaɪ*ər*/ vt (inhale) aspirar, inspirar; (stimulate) animar, alentar, iluminar; (suggest) sugerir, inspirar; infundir. **to i. enthusiasm,** entusiasmar. **to i. hope,** dar esperanza, esperanzar
inspired /ɪn'spaɪ*ər*d/ a inspirado, intuitivo, iluminado; (of genius) genial
inspirer /ɪn'spaɪ*ər*ər/ n inspirador (-ra)
inspiring /ɪn'spaɪ*ər*ɪŋ/ a alentador, animador; inspirador
inspirit /ɪn'spɪrɪt/ vt alentar, inspirar, estimular, animar
inspiriting /ɪn'spɪrɪtɪŋ/ a alentador, estimulador
instability /,ɪnstə'bɪlɪti/ n inestabilidad, mutabilidad, inconstancia, f
install /ɪn'stɔl/ vt (all meanings) instalar. **to i. oneself,** instalarse, establecerse
installation /,ɪnstə'leɪʃən/ n (all meanings) instalación, f
installment /ɪn'stɔlmənt/ n (of a story) entrega, f; Com. plazo, m, cuota, f. **by installments,** Com. a plazos. **i. plan,** pago a plazos, pago por cuotas, m
instance /'ɪnstəns/ n ejemplo, caso, m; (request) solicitación, f, ruego, m; Law. instancia, f. vt citar como ejemplo, mencionar; demostrar, probar. **for i.,** por ejemplo, verbigracia. **in that i....,** en el caso... **in the first i.,** en primer lugar, primero
instant /'ɪnstənt/ a immediato, urgente; Com. corriente, actual. n instante, momento, m; Inf. tris, santiamén, m. Com. **the 2nd i.,** el 2° (segundo) del corriente. **this i.,** (immediately) en seguida
instantaneous /,ɪnstən'teɪniəs/ a instantáneo. Photo. **i. exposure,** instantánea, f
instantaneously /,ɪnstən'teɪniəsli/ adv instantáneamente
instantaneousness /,ɪnstən'teɪniəsnɪs/ n instantaneidad, f
instantly /'ɪnstəntli/ adv en seguida, al instante, inmediatamente
instead /ɪn'stɛd/ adv en cambio; (with of) en vez de, en lugar de
instep /'ɪn,stɛp/ n empeine, m
instigate /'ɪnstɪ,geɪt/ vt instigar, incitar, aguijar, animar, provocar; fomentar
instigating /'ɪnstɪ,geɪtɪŋ/ a instigador, provocador, fomentador
instigation /,ɪnstɪ'geɪʃən/ n instigación, incitación, f; estímulo, m
instigator /'ɪnstɪ,geɪtər/ n instigador (-ra), provocador (-ra), fomentador (-ra)
instill /ɪn'stɪl/ vt instilar; (ideas) inculcar, infundir
instillment /ɪn'stɪlmənt/ n inculcación, implantación, insinuación, f
instinct /ɪn'stɪŋkt/ n instinto, m. **i. with,** imbuido de, lleno de. **by i.,** por instinto, movido por instinto
instinctive /ɪn'stɪŋktɪv/ a instintivo, espontáneo
instinctively /ɪn'stɪŋktɪvli/ adv por instinto
institute /'ɪnstɪ,tut/ vt instituir, fundar, establecer; (an inquiry) iniciar, empezar. n instituto, m; pl **institutes,** Law. instituta, f
institution /,ɪnstɪ'tuʃən/ n (creation) fundación, crea-

ción, f; institución, f, instituto, m; (beginning) comienzo, m, iniciación, f; (charitable) asilo, m; (custom) uso, m, costumbre, tradición, f
institutional /,ɪnstɪ'tuʃənl/ a institucional
instruct /ɪn'strʌkt/ vt (teach) instruir, enseñar; (order) mandar, dar orden (a)
instruction /ɪn'strʌkʃən/ n (teaching) instrucción, enseñanza, f; pl **instructions,** (orders) instrucciones, f pl orden, f, mandato, m
instructive /ɪn'strʌktɪv/ a instructivo, instructor, informativo
instructively /ɪn'strʌktɪvli/ adv instructivamente
instructiveness /ɪn'strʌktɪvnɪs/ n el carácter informativo, lo instructivo
instructor /ɪn'strʌktər/ n instructor, preceptor, m
instrument /'ɪnstrəmənt/ n instrumento, m; (tool) herramienta, f, utensilio, aparato, m; (agent) órgano, agente, medio, m; Law. instrumento, m, escritura, f. vt Mus. instrumentar. **percussion i.,** instrumento de percusión, m. **scientific i.,** instrumento científico, m. **stringed i.,** instrumento de cuerda, m. **wind i.,** instrumento de viento, m
instrumental /,ɪnstrə'mɛntl/ a instrumental; influyente. **to be i. in,** contribuir a
instrumentalist /,ɪnstrə'mɛntlɪst/ n Mus. instrumentista, m
instrumentality /,ɪnstrəmɛn'tælɪti/ n mediación, intervención, agencia, f, buenos oficios, m pl
instrumentation /,ɪnstrəmɛn'teɪʃən/ n Mus. instrumentación, f; mediación, f
insubordinate /,ɪnsə'bɔrdnɪt/ a insubordinado, rebelde, desobediente, refractario
insubordination /,ɪnsə,bɔrdn'eɪʃən/ n insubordinación, rebeldía, desobediencia, f
insubstantial /,ɪnsəb'stænʃəl/ a irreal; insubstancial
insubstantiality /,ɪnsəb,stænʃi'ælɪti/ n irrealidad, f; insubstancialidad, f
insufferable. /ɪn'sʌfərəbəl/. See **intolerable**
insufficiency /,ɪnsə'fɪʃənsi/ n insuficiencia, falta, carestía, f
insufficient /,ɪnsə'fɪʃənt/ a insuficiente, falto. **"I. Postage,"** «Falta de franqueo»
insufficiently /,ɪnsə'fɪʃəntli/ adv insuficientemente
insular /'ɪnsələr/ a isleño, insular; (narrow-minded) intolerante, liberal
insularity /,ɪnsə'lɛərɪti/ n carácter isleño, m; (narrowmindedness) iliberalidad, intolerancia, f
insulate /'ɪnsə,leɪt/ vt aislar
insulating /'ɪnsə,leɪtɪŋ/ a aislador. **i. tape,** Elec. cinta aisladora, f
insulation /,ɪnsə'leɪʃən/ n aislamiento, f
insulator /'ɪnsə,leɪtər/ n Elec. aislador, m
insulin /'ɪnsəlɪn/ n Med. insulina, f
insult /n. 'ɪnsʌlt; v. ɪn'sʌlt/ n insulto, agravio, ultraje, m, afrenta, ofensa, f. vt insultar, ofender, afrentar. **He was insulted,** Fue insultado; Se mostró ofendido
insulter /ɪn'sʌltər/ n insultador (-ra)
insulting /ɪn'sʌltɪŋ/ a insultante, injurioso, ofensivo. **He was very i. to them,** Les insultó, Les trató con menosprecio
insultingly /ɪn'sʌltɪŋli/ adv con insolencia, ofensivamente
insuperability /ɪn,supərə'bɪlɪti/ n dificultades insuperables, f pl, imposibilidad, f, lo insuperable
insuperable /ɪn'supərəbəl/ a insuperable, invencible
insuperably /ɪn'supərəbli/ adv invenciblemente
insupportable /,ɪnsə'pɔrtəbəl/ a insoportable, inaguantable, intolerable, insufrible
insupportably /,ɪnsə'pɔrtəbli/ adv insufriblemente, insoportablemente
insurable /ɪn'ʃurəbəl/ a asegurable
insurance /ɪn'ʃurəns/ n aseguramiento, m; Com. seguro, m; aseguración, f. **accident i.,** seguro contra accidentes, m. **fire-i.,** seguro contra incendio, m. **life i.,** seguro sobre la vida, m. **maritime i.,** seguro marítimo, m. **National I. Act,** Ley del Seguro Nacional Obligatorio, f. **i. broker,** corredor de seguros, m. **i. company,** compañía de seguros, f. **i. policy,** póliza de seguros, f. **i. premium,** prima de seguros, f

insure /ɪn'ʃʊr, -'ʃɜr/ vt Com. asegurar. **to i. oneself,** asegurarse. **the insured,** (person) el asegurado
insurer /ɪn'ʃʊrər/ n asegurador (-ra)
insurgent /ɪn'sɜrdʒənt/ a insurgente, rebelde; (of sea) invasor. n rebelde, mf, insurrecto (-ta)
insurmountable /ˌɪnsər'maʊntəbəl/ a insalvable, insuperable, invencible, intransitable
insurrection /ˌɪnsə'rɛkʃən/ n insurrección, sublevación, f, levantamiento, m
insurrectionary /ˌɪnsə'rɛkʃəˌnɛri/ a rebelde, amotinado, insurgente
insusceptible /ˌɪnsə'sɛptəbəl/ a no susceptible, indiferente, insensible
intact /ɪn'tækt/ a intacto, íntegro, indemne
intake /'ɪnˌteik/ n (of a stocking) menguado, m; Mech. aspiración, f; válvula de admisión, f; Aer. admisión, toma, f; orificio de entrada, m
intangibility /ɪnˌtændʒə'bɪlɪti/ n intangibilidad, f
intangible /ɪn'tændʒəbəl/ a intangible; incomprensible
integer /'ɪntɪdʒər/ n Math. número entero, m
integral /'ɪntɪgrəl/ a íntegro, intrínseco, inherente; Math. entero. n Math. integral, f. **i. calculus,** cálculo integral, m
integrate /'ɪntɪˌgreit/ vt integrar, completar; formar en un todo; Math. integrar
integrity /ɪn'tɛgrɪti/ n integridad, honradez, rectitud, entereza, f
intellect /'ɪntḷˌɛkt/ n intelecto, entendimiento, m
intellectual /ˌɪntḷ'ɛktʃuəl/ a intelectual, mental. n intelectual
intellectualism /ˌɪntḷ'ɛktʃuəˌlɪzəm/ n intelectualismo, m, intelectualidad, f
intellectually /ˌɪntḷ'ɛktʃuəli/ adv intelectualmente, mentalmente
intelligence /ɪn'tɛlɪdʒəns/ n inteligencia, comprensión, mente, f; (quickness of mind) agudeza, perspicacia, f; (news) noticia, f, conocimiento, informe, m. **the latest i.,** las últimas noticias. **i. quotient,** cociente de inteligencia, m. **I. Service,** Inteligencia, f; policía secreta, f. **i. test,** prueba de inteligencia, f
intelligent /ɪn'tɛlɪdʒənt/ a inteligente
intelligentsia /ɪnˌtɛlɪ'dʒɛntsiə/ n clase intelectual, intelectualidad, f, Inf. masa cefálica, f
intelligibility /ɪnˌtɛlɪdʒə'bɪlɪti/ n comprensibilidad, inteligibilidad, f
intelligible /ɪn'tɛlɪdʒəbəl/ a inteligible, comprensible
intelligibly /ɪn'tɛlɪdʒəbəl/ adv inteligiblemente
intemperance /ɪn'tɛmpərəns/ n intemperancia, inmoderación, f; exceso en la bebida, m
intemperate /ɪn'tɛmpərɪt/ a intemperante, destemplado, descomedido; inmoderado; bebedor en exceso
intemperately /ɪn'tɛmpərɪtli/ adv inmoderadamente
intend /ɪn'tɛnd/ vt intentar, proponerse, pensar; destinar, dedicar; (mean) querer decir. **to be intended,** estar destinado; tener por fin; querer decir
intendant /ɪn'tɛndənt/ n intendente, m
intended /ɪn'tɛndɪd/ a pensado, deseado. n Inf. novio (-ia), futuro (-ra), prometido (-da)
intense /ɪn'tɛns/ a intenso, vivo, fuerte; (of emotions) profundo, hondo, vehemente; (of colors) subido, intenso; (great) extremado, sumo, muy grande
intensification /ɪnˌtɛnsəfɪ'keiʃən/ n intensificación, f; aumento, m
intensify /ɪn'tɛnsəˌfai/ vt intensar, intensificar; aumentar
intensity /ɪn'tɛnsɪti/ n intensidad, fuerza, f; (of emotions) profundidad, vehemencia, violencia, f; (of colors) intensidad, f
intensive /ɪn'tɛnsɪv/ a intensivo
intensive-care unit /ɪn'tɛnsɪv'kɛər/ n sala de terapia intensiva, unidad de cuidados intensivos, unidad de vigilancia intensiva, f
intent /ɪn'tɛnt/ n intento, propósito, deseo, m. a atento; (absorbed) absorto, interesado; (on doing) resuelto a, decidido a. **to all intents and purposes,** en efecto, en realidad. **to be i. on,** (reading, etc.) estar absorto en, entregarse a. **with i. to defraud,** con el propósito deliberado de defraudar

intention /ɪn'tɛnʃən/ n intención, voluntad, f, propósito, pensamiento, proyecto, m
intentional /ɪn'tɛnʃənḷ/ a intencional, deliberado, premeditado
intentionally /ɪn'tɛnʃənḷi/ adv a propósito, intencionalmente, de pensado
intentioned /ɪn'tɛnʃənd/ a intencionado
intently /ɪn'tɛntli/ adv atentamente
inter /ɪn'tɜr/ vt enterrar, sepultar
inter- prefix inter, entre. **i.-allied,** interaliado, de los aliados. **i.-denominational,** intersectario. **i.-university,** interuniversitario. **i.-urban,** interurbano
interaction /ˌɪntər'ækʃən/ n interacción, acción recíproca, acción mutua, f
intercalate /ɪn'tɜrkəˌleit/ vt intercalar, interpolar
intercede /ˌɪntər'sid/ vi interceder, mediar. **to i. for,** hablar por
intercept /ˌɪntər'sɛpt/ vt interceptar, detener; entrecoger, atajar
interception /ˌɪntər'sɛpʃən/ n interceptación, detención, f
intercession /ˌɪntər'sɛʃən/ n mediación, intercesión, f
intercessor /ˌɪntər'sɛsər/ n intercesor (-ra), mediador (-ra)
interchange /n. 'ɪntərˌtʃeindʒ; v. ˌɪntər'tʃɛndʒ/ n intercambio, m; (of goods) comercio, tráfico, m. vt cambiar, trocar; alternar
interchangeable /ˌɪntər'tʃeindʒəbəl/ a intercambiable
intercom /'ɪntərˌkɒm/ n teléfono interior, m
intercommunicate /ˌɪntərkə'myunɪˌkeit/ vi comunicarse
intercommunication /ˌɪntərkəˌmyunɪ'keiʃən/ n comunicación mutua, f; comercio, m
intercostal /ˌɪntər'kɒstḷ/ a Anat. intercostal
intercourse /'ɪntərˌkɔrs/ n (social) trato, m, relaciones, f pl; Com. comercio, tráfico, m; (of ideas) intercambio, m; (sexual) coito, trato sexual, m
interdependence /ˌɪntərdɪ'pɛndəns/ n dependencia mutua, mutualidad, f
interdependent /ˌɪntərdɪ'pɛndənt/ a mutuo
interdict /n. 'ɪntərˌdɪkt; v. ˌɪntər'dɪkt/ n interdicto, veto, m, prohibición, f; Eccl. entredicho, m. vt interdecir, prohibir, privar; Eccl. poner entredicho
interdiction /ˌɪntər'dɪkʃən/ n interdicción, prohibición, f
interest /'ɪntərɪst/ n interés, m; provecho, m; Com. premio, rédito, interés, m; (in a firm) participación, f; (curiosity) interés, m; curiosidad, f; simpatía, f; (influence) influencia, f. n pl **interests,** (commercial undertakings) empresas, f pl, intereses, negocios, m pl. vt interesar. **to be interested in,** interesarse en, (on behalf of) por. **to be in one's own i.,** ser en provecho de uno, ser en su propio interés. **to bear eight per cent. i.,** dar interés del ocho por ciento. **to pay with i.,** pagar con creces. **to put out at i.,** dar a interés. **in the interests of,** en interés de. **compound i.,** interés compuesto, m. **simple i.,** interés sencillo, m. **vested interests,** intereses creados, m pl
interesting /'ɪntərəstɪŋ/ a interesante, curioso, atractivo
interestingly /'ɪntərəstɪŋli/ adv amenamente, de modo interesante
interfere /ˌɪntər'fɪər/ vi intervenir, meterse, entremeterse, mezclarse; Inf. mangonear, meter las narices; (with) meterse con; (impede) estorbar, impedir
interference /ˌɪntər'fɪərəns/ n intervención, f, entrometimiento, m; (obstacle) estorbo, obstáculo, m; Phys. interferencia, f; Radio. parásitos, m pl
interfering /ˌɪntər'fɪərɪŋ/ a entremetido, oficioso; Inf. mangoneador
interim /'ɪntərəm/ n ínterin, intermedio, Lat. Am. also interregno /n a interino, provisional. **in the i.,** entre tanto, en el ínterin, intermedio, m
interino, m
interior /ɪn'tɪəriər/ a interior, interno; doméstico. n interior, m
interject /ˌɪntər'dʒɛkt/ vt interponer
interjection /ˌɪntər'dʒɛkʃən/ n exclamación, interjección, f; interposición, f
interlace /ˌɪntər'leis/ vt entrelazar, entretejer
interleave /ˌɪntər'liv/ vt interfoliar, interpaginar

interline /'ɪntər,laɪn/ *vt* entrerrenglonar, interlinear

interlinear /,ɪntər'lɪniər/ *a* interlineal

interlineation /,ɪntər,lɪni'eɪʃən/ *n* interlineación, *f*

interlining /'ɪntər,laɪnɪŋ/ *n* entretela, *f*

interlock /,ɪntər'lɒk/ *vt* (of wheels, etc.). endentar; trabar; cerrar. *vi* endentarse; entrelazarse, unirse; cerrar

interlocutor /,ɪntər'lɒkyətər/ *n* interlocutor (-ra)

interloper /'ɪntər,loupər/ *n* intruso (-sa); *Com.* intérlope, *m*

interloping /,ɪntər'loupɪŋ/ *a* intérlope

interlude /'ɪntər,lud/ *n* intervalo, intermedio, *m*; *Mus.* interludio, *m*; *Theat.* entremés, *m*

intermarriage /,ɪntər'mærɪdʒ/ *n* casamiento entre parientes próximos, entre razas distintas, o entre grupos étnicos distintos, *m*

intermarry /,ɪntər'mæri/ *vi* contraer matrimonio entre parientes próximos, entre personas de razas distintas, o entre grupos étnicos distintos

intermediary /,ɪntər'midi,ɛri/ *a* and *n* intermediario (-ia)

intermediate /,ɪntər'midi,eit/ *a* intermedio, medio, medianero. *n* sustancia intermedia, *f*. *vi* intervenir, mediar

interment /ɪn'tɜrmənt/ *n* entierro, *m*

intermezzo /,ɪntər'mɛtsou/ *n* *Theat.* intermedio, *m*; *Mus.* intermezzo, *m*

interminable /ɪn'tɜrmənəbəl/ *a* interminable, inacabable

interminably /ɪn'tɜrmənəbli/ *adv* interminablemente, sin fin, sin cesar

intermingle /,ɪntər'mɪŋgəl/ *vt* entremezclar, entreverar. *vi* mezclarse

intermission /,ɪntər'mɪʃən/ *n* intermisión, interrupción, pausa, *f*; *Theat.* entreacto, *m*. **without i.,** sin pausa, sin tregua

intermittence /,ɪntər'mɪtns/ *n* intermitencia, alternación, *f*

intermittent /,ɪntər'mɪtn̩t/ *a* intermitente, discontinuo; (of fever) intermitente

intermittently /,ɪntər'mɪtn̩tli/ *adv* a intervalos, a ratos, a pausas

intern /ɪn'tɜrn/ *n* *Med.* practicante de hospital *m*, interino (-na), interno (-na), interno de hospital, alumno interno, *m*. *vt* confinar, encerrar

internal /ɪn'tɜrn̩/ *a* interno, interior; (of affairs) doméstico, civil; intrínseco; íntimo. **i.-combustion engine,** motor de combustión interna, *m*

internally /ɪn'tɜrn̩li/ *adv* interiormente

international /,ɪntər'næʃən̩/ *a* internacional. *n* *Sports.* un partido internacional. **i. law,** derecho internacional, *m*. **i. studies,** estudios internacionales

internationalism /,ɪntər'næʃən̩,ɪzəm/ *n* internacionalismo, *m*

internationalist /,ɪntər'næʃən̩ɪst/ *n* internacionalista, *mf*

internationalization /,ɪntər,næʃən̩ə'zeɪʃən/ *n* internacionalización, *f*

internationalize /,ɪntər'næʃən̩,aɪz/ *vt* hacer internacional, poner bajo un control internacional

internecine /,ɪntər'nisin/ *a* sanguinario, feroz

internee /,ɪntɜr'ni/ *n* internado (-da)

Internet /'ɪntər,nɛt/ *n* Internet, *m*

internment /ɪn'tɜrnmənt/ *n* internamiento, *m*. **i. camp,** campo de internamiento, *m*

internship /'ɪntɜrn,ʃɪp/ *n* interino, *m*

interoceanic /,ɪntər,ouʃi'ænɪk/ *a* interoceánico

interpolate /ɪn'tɜrpə,leit/ *vt* interpolar, intercalar, interponer

interpolation /ɪn,tɜrpə'leiʃən/ *n* interpolación, inserción, añadidura, *f*

interpolator /ɪn'tɜrpə,leitər/ *n* interpolador (-ra)

interpose /,ɪntər'pouz/ *vt* interponer; (a remark) interpolar. *vi* interponerse, intervenir; (interfere) entrometerse; interrumpir

interposition /,ɪntərpə'zɪʃən/ *n* interposición, *f*; entrometimiento, *m*

interpret /ɪn'tɜrprɪt/ *vt* interpretar; (translate) traducir; (explain) explicar, descifrar. *vi* interpretar.

interpretation /ɪn,tɜrprɪ'teiʃən/ *n* interpretación, *f*; (translation) traducción, *f*; (explanation) explicación, *f*

interpretative /ɪn'tɜrprɪ,teitɪv/ *a* interpretativo, interpretador

interpreter /ɪn'tɜrprɪtər/ *n* intérprete, *mf*

interregnum /,ɪntər'rɛgnəm/ *n* interregno, *m*

interrelation /,ɪntərrɪ'leiʃən/ *n* relación mutua, *f*

interrogate /ɪn'tɛrə,geit/ *vt* interrogar, examinar, preguntar

interrogating /ɪn'tɛrə,geitɪŋ/ *a* interrogante

interrogation /ɪn,tɛrə'geiʃən/ *n* interrogación, *f*, examen, *m*; pregunta, *f*. **mark of i.,** punto de interrogación, *m*

interrogative /,ɪntə'rɒgətɪv/ *a* interrogativo. *n* palabra interrogativa, *f*

interrogatively /,ɪntə'rɒgətɪvli/ *adv* interrogativamente

interrogator /ɪn'tɛrə'geitər/ *n* examinador (-ra), interrogador (-ra)

interrogatory /,ɪntə'rɒgə,tɔri/ *a* interrogativo. *n* interrogatorio, *m*

interrupt /,ɪntə'rʌpt/ *vt* interrumpir

interruptedly /,ɪntə'rʌptɪdli/ *adv* interrumpidamente

interrupter /,ɪntə'rʌptər/ *n* interruptor (-ra); *Elec.* interruptor, *m*

interruption /,ɪntə'rʌpʃən/ *n* interrupción, *f*

intersect /,ɪntər'sɛkt/ *vt* cruzar. *vi* cruzarse, intersecarse

intersection /,ɪntər'sɛkʃən/ *n* intersección, *f*; cruce, *m*, (of streets) bocacalle, *Lat. Am.* cruza *f*

intersperse /,ɪntər'spɜrs/ *vt* diseminar, esparcir; interpolar, entremezclar

interstice /ɪn'tɜrstɪs/ *n* intervalo, intermedio, *m*; (chink) intersticio, *m*, hendedura, *f*

intertwine /,ɪntər'twain/ *vt* entretejer, entrelazar. *vi* entretwinarse

interval /'ɪntərvəl/ *n* intervalo, intermedio, *m*, pausa, *f*; *Theat.* entreacto, *m*, intermisión, *f*; (in schools) recreo, *m*. **at intervals,** a trechos, de vez en cuando. **lucid i.,** intervalo claro, intervalo lúcido, *m*

intervene /,ɪntər'vin/ *vi* intervenir, tomar parte (en); mediar; (occur) sobrevenir, acaecer; *Law.* interponerse

intervening /,ɪntər'vinɪŋ/ *a* intermedio; interventor

intervention /,ɪntər'vɛnʃən/ *n* intervención, mediación, *f*

interventionist /,ɪntər'vɛnʃənɪst/ *n* *Polit.* partidario (-ia) de la intervención

interview /'ɪntər,vyu/ *n* entrevista, *f*, interviev, *m*. *vt* entrevistarse con

interviewer /'ɪntər,vyuər/ *n* interrogador (-ra); (reporter) reportero, periodista, *m*

interweave /,ɪntər'wiv/ *vt* entretejer, entrelazar

interweaving /,ɪntər'wivɪŋ/ *n* entretejimiento, *m*

intestacy /ɪn'tɛstəsi/ *n* ausencia de un testamento, *f*

intestate /ɪn'tɛsteit/ *a* and *n* intestado (-da)

intestinal /ɪn'tɛstən̩/ *a* intestinal, intestino. **i. worm,** lombriz intestinal, *f*

intestine /ɪn'tɛstɪn/ *n* intestino, *m*. **large i.,** intestino grueso, *m*. **small i.,** intestino delgado, *m*

intimacy /'ɪntəməsi/ *n* intimidad, *f*, familiaridad, *f*; (of nobility and others) privanza, *f*

intimate /'ɪntəmɪt/ *a* íntimo; (of relations) entrañable, estrecho; intrínseco, esencial; (of knowledge) profundo, completo, detallado. *n* amigo (-ga) de confianza. *vt* intimar, dar a entender, indicar; **to become i.,** intimarse. **to be on i. terms with,** tratar de tú (a), ser amigo íntimo de

intimately /'ɪntəmɪtli/ *adv* íntimamente, al fondo

intimation /,ɪntə'meiʃən/ *n* intimación, indicación, *f*; (hint) insinuación, indirecta, *f*

intimidate /ɪn'tɪmɪ,deit/ *vt* intimidar, aterrar, infundir miedo (a), espantar, acobardar, amedrentar

intimidation /ɪn,tɪmɪ'deiʃən/ *n* intimidación, *f*

intimidatory /ɪn'tɪmɪdə,tɔri/ *a* aterrador, amenazador

into /'ɪntu; *unstressed* -tʊ, -tə/ *prep* en; a, al, a la; dentro, adentro; (of transforming, forming, etc.) en. **Throw it i. the fire,** Échalo al (o en el) fuego. **She went i. the house,** Entró en la casa. **to look i.,** mirar dentro de; mirar hacia el interior (de); investigar

intolerable /ɪn'tɒlərəbəl/ a intolerable, insufrible, inaguantable, insoportable, inllevable
intolerableness /ɪn'tɒlərəbəlnɪs/ n intolerabilidad, f
intolerably /ɪn'tɒlərəbli/ adv intolerablemente, insufriblemente
intolerance /ɪn'tɒlərəns/ n intolerancia, intransigencia, f
intolerant /ɪn'tɒlərənt/ a intolerante, intransigente; Med. intolerante
intonation /ˌɪntou'neiʃən/ n entonación, f
intone /ɪn'toun/ vt entonar; Eccl. salmodiar
intoxicant /ɪn'tɒksɪkənt/ a embriagador. n bebida alcohólica, f
intoxicate /ɪn'tɒksɪˌkeit/ vt emborrachar, embriagar; Med. intoxicar, envenenar; (excite) embriagar, embelesar
intoxicated /ɪn'tɒksɪˌkeitɪd/ a borracho; (excited) ebrio, embriagado; Med. intoxicado
intoxicating /ɪn'tɒksɪˌkeitɪŋ/ a embriagador
intoxication /ɪnˌtɒksɪ'keiʃən/ n borrachera, embriaguez, f; Med. intoxicación, f, envenenamiento, m; (excitement) entusiasmo, m, ebriedad, f
intractability /ɪnˌtræktə'bɪlɪti/ n insociabilidad, hurañería, f
intractable /ɪn'træktəbəl/ a intratable, insociable, huraño
intramural /ˌɪntrə'myʊrəl/ adv intramuros
intransigence /ɪn'trænsɪdʒəns/ n intransigencia, intolerancia, f
intransigent /ɪn'trænsɪdʒənt/ a intransigente, intolerante
intransitive /ɪn'trænsɪtɪv/ a intransitivo, neutro
intrauterine /ˌɪntrə'yutərɪn/ a Med. intrauterino
intravenous /ˌɪntrə'vinəs/ a Med. intravenoso
intrepid /ɪn'trepɪd/ a intrépido, osado, audaz
intrepidity /ˌɪntrə'pɪdɪti/ n intrepidez, osadía, audacia, f
intrepidly /ɪn'trepɪdli/ adv intrépidamente, audazmente
intricacy /'ɪntrɪkəsi/ n intrincación, complejidad, f
intricate /'ɪntrɪkɪt/ a intrincado, complejo
intricately /'ɪntrɪkɪtli/ adv intrincadamente
intrigue /ɪn'trig/ n. also 'ɪntrig/ n intriga, maquinación, f, enredo, m; (amorous) lío, m. vi intrigar, enredar; (amorous) tener un lío. vt (interest) atraer, interesar; (with) intrigar con. **to be intrigued** Lat. Am. intrigarse
intriguer /ɪn'trigər/ n intrigante, mf. urdemalas, m, enredador (-ra)
intriguing /ɪn'trigɪŋ/ a enredador; (attractive) atrayente, interesante, seductor
intrinsic /ɪn'trɪnsɪk/ a intrínseco, innato, inherente, esencial
intrinsically /ɪn'trɪnsɪkli/ adv intrínsecamente, esencialmente
introduce /ˌɪntrə'dus/ vt introducir; hacer entrar; insertar, injerir; (a person) presentar; poner de moda, introducir; (a bill) presentar; (a person to a thing) llamar la atención sobre. **Allow me to i. my friend,** Permítame que le presente mi amigo
introduction /ˌɪntrə'dʌkʃən/ n introducción, f; (of a book) prefacio, prólogo, m, advertencia, f; (of a person) presentación, f; inserción, f
introductory /ˌɪntrə'dʌktəri/ a introductor, preliminar, preparatorio
intromission /ˌɪntrə'mɪʃən/ n intromisión, f
introspection /ˌɪntrə'spekʃən/ n introspección, f
introspective /ˌɪntrə'spektɪv/ a introspectivo
introversion /ˌɪntrə'vɜrʒən/ n Psychol. introversión, f
introvert /'ɪntrəˌvɜrt/ a and n Psychol. introverso (-sa)
intrude /ɪn'trud/ vt introducir, imponer. vi entremeterse, inmiscuirse. **Do I i.?** ¿Estorbo?
intruder /ɪn'trudər/ n intruso (-sa)
intrusion /ɪn'truʒən/ n intrusión, f; Geol. intromisión, f
intrusive /ɪn'trusɪv/ a intruso
intuition /ˌɪntu'ɪʃən/ n intuición, f. **to know by i.,** intuir, saber por intuición
intuitive /ɪn'tuɪtɪv/ a intuitivo

inundate /'ɪnənˌdeit/ vt inundar, anegar; Fig. abrumar
inundation /ˌɪnən'deiʃən/ n inundación, anegación, f; Fig. diluvio, m, abundancia, f
inure /ɪn'yʊr/ vt endurecer, habituar
inurement /ɪn'yʊrmənt/ n habituación, f
invade /ɪn'veid/ vt invadir, irrumpir, asaltar; Med. invadir
invader /ɪn'veidər/ n invasor (-ra), acometedor (-ra), agresor (-ra)
invading /ɪn'veidɪŋ/ a invasor, irruptor
invalid /ɪn'vælɪd/ a inválido, nulo. **to become i.,** caducar
invalid /ɪn'vælɪd/ n inválido (-da), enfermo (-ma). **to become an i.,** quedarse inválido. **to i. out of the army,** licenciar por invalidez. **i. carriage,** cochecillo de inválido, m
invalidate /ɪn'vælɪˌdeit/ vt invalidar, anular
invalidation /ɪnˌvælɪ'deiʃən/ n invalidación, f
invalidity /ˌɪnvə'lɪdɪti/ n invalidez, nulidad, f
invaluable /ɪn'vælyuəbəl/ a inestimable
invariability /ɪnˌveəriə'bɪlɪti/ n invariabilidad, invariación, inalterabilidad, inmutabilidad, f
invariable /ɪn'veəriəbəl/ a invariable, inmutable, inalterable
invariably /ɪn'veəriəbli/ adv invariablemente, inmutablemente
invariant /ɪn'veəriənt/ n Math. invariante, m
invasion /ɪn'veiʒən/ n invasión, irrupción, f; Med. invasión, f
invective /ɪn'vektɪv/ n invectiva, diatriba, f
inveigh (against) /ɪn'vei/ vi desencadenarse (contra), prorrumpir en invectivas (contra)
inveigle /ɪn'veigəl/ vt seducir, engatusar, persuadir
invent /ɪn'vent/ vt inventar, descubrir, originar; (a falsehood) fingir; (create) idear, componer
invention /ɪn'venʃən/ n invención, f, invento, descubrimiento, m; (imagination) ingeniosidad, inventiva, f; (falsehood) ficción, mentira, f; (finding) invención, f, hallazgo, m
inventive /ɪn'ventɪv/ a inventor, inventivo; ingenioso, despejado
inventiveness /ɪn'ventɪvnɪs/ n inventiva, f
inventor /ɪn'ventər/ n inventor (-ra), autor (-ra)
inventory /'ɪnvənˌtɔri/ n inventario, m; descripción, f. vt inventariar
inverse /ɪn'vɜrs/ a inverso. **i. proportion,** razón inversa, f
inversely /ɪn'vɜrsli/ adv inversamente, a la inversa
inversion /ɪn'vɜrʒən/ n inversión, f, trastrocamiento, m; Gram. hipérbaton, m
invert /ɪn'vɜrt/ vt invertir, trastornar, trastrocar. **inverted commas,** comilla, f
invertebrate /ɪn'vɜrtəbrɪt/ a and n invertebrado m.
invest /ɪn'vest/ vt Com. invertir; Mil. sitiar, cercar; (foll. by with) poner, cubrir con; (of qualities) conferir, otorgar, dar. vi (with in) poner dinero en, echar caudal en; Inf. comprar
investigable /ɪn'vestɪgəbəl/ a averiguable
investigate /ɪn'vestɪˌgeit/ vt investigar, estudiar; examinar, averiguar; explorar; **to i. closely** Lat. Am. interiorizar
investigation /ɪnˌvestɪ'geiʃən/ n investigación, f, estudio, m; examen, m, averiguación, f; encuesta, pesquisa, f
investigator /ɪn'vestɪˌgeitər/ n investigador (-ra); averiguador (-ra)
investigatory /ɪn'vestɪɡəˌtɔri/ a investigador
investiture /ɪn'vestɪtʃər/ n investidura, instalación, f
investment /ɪn'vestmənt/ n (Com. of money) inversión, f, empleo, m; Mil. cerco, m; (investiture) instalación, f; pl **investments,** Com. acciones, f pl, fondos, m pl
investor /ɪn'vestər/ n inversionista, m; accionista, mf, Lat. Am. inversor (-ra) mf
inveteracy /ɪn'vetərəsi/ n antigüedad, f, lo arraigado
inveterate /ɪn'vetərɪt/ a inveterado, antiguo, arraigado, incurable
invidious /ɪn'vɪdiəs/ a odioso, repugnante, injusto
invidiousness /ɪn'vɪdiəsnɪs/ n injusticia, f, lo odioso

invigorate /ɪn'vɪgə,reɪt/ *vt* vigorizar, dar fuerza (a), avivar

invigorating /ɪn'vɪgə,reɪtɪŋ/ *a* fortaleciente, fortificador, vigorizador

invincibility /ɪn,vɪnsə'bɪlɪti/ *n* invencibilidad, *f*

invincible /ɪn'vɪnsəbəl/ *a* invencible, indomable; *Fig.* insuperable

inviolability /ɪn,vaɪələ'bɪlɪti/ *n* inviolabilidad, *f*

inviolable /ɪn'vaɪələbəl/ *a* inviolable

inviolate /ɪn'vaɪəlɪt/ *a* inviolado

invisibility /ɪn,vɪzə'bɪlɪti/ *n* invisibilidad, *f*

invisible /ɪn'vɪzəbəl/ *a* invisible. **i. ink**, tinta simpática, *f*. **i. mending**, zurcido invisible, *m*

invitation /,ɪnvɪ'teɪʃən/ *n* invitación, *f*; convite, *m*; (card) tarjeta de invitación, *f*

invite /ɪn'vaɪt/ *vt* invitar, convidar; (request) pedir, rogar; (of things) incitar, tentar.

inviting /ɪn'vaɪtɪŋ/ *a* atrayente, incitante; (of food) apetitoso; (of looks) provocativo

invocation /,ɪnvə'keɪʃən/ *n* invocación, *f*

invocatory /ɪn'vɒkətɔri/ *a* invocatorio, invocador

invoice /'ɪnvɔɪs/ *n* *Com.* factura, *f*. *vt* facturar. **proforma i.**, factura simulada, *f*. **shipping i.**, factura de expedición, *f*. **i. book**, libro de facturas, *m*

invoke /ɪn'voʊk/ *vt* invocar; suplicar, implorar; (*Law*) acogerse (a)

involuntarily /ɪn,vɒlən'tɛərəli/ *adv* sin querer, involuntariamente

involuntariness /ɪn'vɒlən,tɛrɪnɪs/ *n* involuntariedad, *f*

involuntary /ɪn'vɒlən,tɛri/ *a* involuntario; instintivo, inconsciente

involve /ɪn'vɒlv/ *vt* (entangle) enredar, embrollar, enmarañar; (implicate) comprometer; (imply) implicar, ocasionar, suponer, traer consigo

involved /ɪn'vɒlvd/ *a* complejo, intrincado; (of style) confuso, obscuro

invulnerability /ɪn,vʌlnərə'bɪlɪti/ *n* invulnerabilidad, *f*

invulnerable /ɪn'vʌlnərəbəl/ *a* invulnerable

inward /'ɪnwərd/ *a* interior, interno; íntimo, espiritual. *adv* adentro

inwardly /'ɪnwərdli/ *adv* interiormente; para sí, entre sí

inwards /'ɪnw'ərdz/ *adv* hacia dentro; adentro

iodine /'aɪə,daɪn/ *n* yodo, *m*. **i. poisoning**, yodismo, *m*

ion /'aɪən/ *n Chem.* ion, *m*

Ionian /aɪ'oʊniən/ *a* and *n* jónico (-ca)

Ionic /aɪ'ɒnɪk/ *a* jónico. **i. foot** *Poet.* jónico, *m*

iota /aɪ'oʊtə/ *n* (letter) iota, *f*; jota, pizca, *f*, ápice, *m*. **not an i.**, ni pizca

I.O.U. *n Com.* abonaré, *m*

ipecacuanha /,ɪpɪ,kækyə'wany'ə/ *n* ipecacuana, *f*

Iranian /ɪ'reɪniən/ *a* and *n* iranio (-ia)

irascibility /ɪ,ræsə'bɪlɪti/ *n* irascibilidad, iracundia, irritabilidad, *f*

irascible /ɪ'ræsəbəl/ *a* irascible, iracundo, irritable

irate /aɪ'reɪt/ *a* airado, colérico, enojado

ire /aɪər/ *n* ira, cólera, furia, *f*

Ireland /'aɪərlənd/ Irlanda, *f*

iridescence /,ɪrɪ'dɛsəns/ *n* iridiscencia, *f*

iridescent /,ɪrɪ'dɛsənt/ *a* iridiscente. **to look i.**, irisar, tornasolarse

iridium /ɪ'rɪdiəm/ *n Chem.* iridio, *m*

iris /'aɪrɪs/ *n Anat.* iris, *m*; *Bot.* irídea, *f*

Irish /'aɪrɪʃ/ *a* and *n* irlandés (-esa). **the I.**, los irlandeses

Irish Sea Mar de Irlanda, *f*

irksome /'ɜrksəm/ *a* fastidioso, tedioso, aburrido

irksomeness /'ɜrksəmnɪs/ *n* tedio, fastidio, aburrimiento, *m*

iron /'aɪərn/ *n* hierro, *m*; (for clothes) plancha, *f*; (tool) utensilio, *m*, herramienta, *f*; (golf) hierro, *m*; *pl* **irons,** grillos, *m pl*, cadenas, *f pl*. *a* de hierro, férreo; *Fig.* duro, severo. *vt* (linen) planchar; (with out) allanar. **to have too many irons in the fire**, tener demasiados asuntos entre manos. **to put in irons**, echar grillos (a). **to strike while the i. is hot,** A hierro caliente batir de repente. **cast-i.**, hierro colado, *m*. **scrap i.,** hierro viejo, *m*. **sheet i.,** hierro en planchas, *m*. **wrought i.**, hierro dulce, *m*. **i. age,** edad de hierro, *f*. **i.-foundry,** fundición de hierro, *f*. **i. lung,**

Med. pulmón de hierro, pulmón de acero, *m*. **i.-mold,** mancha de orín, *f*. **i. smelting furnace,** alto horno, *m*. **i. tonic,** *Med.* reconstituyente ferruginoso, *m*. **i. will,** voluntad de hierro, *f*

ironclad /a 'aɪərn'klæd; *n* -,klæd/ *a* blindado, acorazado. *n* buque de guerra blindado, acorazado, *m*

ironer /'aɪərnər/ *n* planchador (-ra)

ironical /aɪ'rɒnɪkəl/ *a* irónico

ironically /aɪ'rɒnɪkli/ *adv* con ironía, irónicamente

ironing /'aɪərnɪŋ/ *n* planchado, *m*; ropa por planchar, *f*. *a* de planchar. **i. board,** tabla de planchar, *f*

ironist /'aɪərnɪst/ *n* ironista, *mf*

ironmonger /'aɪərn,mʌŋgər/ *n* ferretero (-ra). **ironmonger's shop,** ferretería, *f*

ironmongery /'aɪərn,mʌŋgəri/ *n* ferretería, quincallería, *f*

iron sulphide /'sʌlfaɪd/ sulfuro de hierro, *m*

ironwork /'aɪərn,wɜrk/ *n* herraje, *m*; obra de hierro, *f*

ironworks /'aɪərn,wɜrks/ *n* herrería, *f*

irony /'aɪrəni/ *n* ironía, *f*. *a* (like iron) ferruginoso

Iroquois /'ɪrə,kwɔɪ/ *a* and *n* iroqués (-esa)

irradiate /ɪ'reɪdi,eɪt/ *vt* irradiar; *Fig.* iluminar, aclarar

irradiation /ɪ,reɪdi'eɪʃən/ *n* irradiación, *f*; *Fig.* iluminación, *f*

irrational /ɪ'ræʃənl/ *a* ilógico, ridículo, irracional

irrationality /ɪ,ræʃə'nælɪti/ *n* irracionalidad, *f*

irreclaimable /,ɪrɪ'kleɪməbəl/ *a* irrecuperable, irredimible; (of land) inservible, improductivo; irreformable

irreconcilable /ɪ'rɛkən,saɪləbəl/ *a* irreconciliable

irreconcilably /ɪ'rɛkən,saɪləbli/ *adv* irremediablemente

irrecoverable /,ɪrɪ'kʌvərəbəl/ *a* irrecuperable, incobrable

irredeemable /,ɪrɪ'diməbəl/ *a* irredimible, perdido. **i. government loan,** deuda perpetua, *f*

irredeemably /,ɪrɪ'diməbli/ *adv* perdidamente

irreducible /,ɪrɪ'dusəbəl/ *a* irreducible

irrefutability /ɪ,rɛfyətə'bɪlɪti/ *n* verdad, *f*

irrefutable /ɪ'rɛfyətəbəl/ *a* irrefutable, indisputable, innegable, irrebatible

irregular /ɪ'rɛgyələr/ *a* irregular; anormal; (of shape) disforme; desordenado; *Gram.* irregular; (of surface) desigual, escabroso

irregularity /ɪ,rɛgyə'lærɪti/ *n* irregularidad, *f*; anormalidad, *f*; (of shape) desproporción, irregularidad, *f*; (of surface) escabrosidad, desigualdad, *f*; exceso, *m*, demasía, *f*

irrelevance /ɪ'rɛləvəns/ *n* inconexión, *f*; inoportunidad, *f*; futilidad, poca importancia, *f*; (stupidity) desatino, *m*, impertinencia, *f*

irrelevant /ɪ'rɛləvənt/ *a* inaplicable, fuera de propósito; inoportuno; sin importancia, fútil; (stupid) impertinente

irreligion /,ɪrɪ'lɪdʒən/ *n* irreligión, impiedad, *f*

irreligious /,ɪrɪ'lɪdʒəs/ *a* irreligioso, impío

irremediable /,ɪrɪ'midiəbəl/ *a* irremediable, irreparable

irremediably /,ɪrɪ'midiəbli/ *adv* sin remedio, irremediablemente

irreparable /ɪ'rɛpərəbəl/ *a* irreparable

irreplaceable /,ɪrɪ'pleɪsəbəl/ *a* irreemplazable

irrepressible /,ɪrɪ'prɛsəbəl/ *a* incontrolable, indomable

irreproachable /,ɪrɪ'proutʃəbəl/ *a* irreprochable, intachable

irresistible /,ɪrɪ'zɪstəbəl/ *a* irresistible

irresistibleness /,ɪrɪ'zɪstəbəlnɪs/ *n* superioridad, *f*

irresolute /ɪ'rɛzə,lut/ *a* irresoluto, indeciso, vacilante

irresoluteness /ɪ'rɛzə,lutnɪs/ *n* irresolución, indecisión, *f*

irrespective /,ɪrɪ'spɛktɪv/ *a* (with of) independiente de, aparte de, sin contar

irresponsibility /,ɪrɪ,spɒnsə'bɪlɪti;/ *n* irresponsabilidad, *f*

irresponsible /,ɪrɪ'spɒnsəbəl/ *a* irresponsable

irretrievable /,ɪrɪ'trivəbəl/ *a* irrecuperable

irretrievably /,ɪrɪ'trivbli/ *adv* irreparablemente, sin remedio

irreverence /ɪ'rɛvərəns/ *n* irreverencia, *f*

irreverent /ɪ'rɛvərənt/ *a* irreverente, irrespetuoso

irrevocability /ɪˌrevəkə'bɪlɪti/ n irrevocabilidad, f
irrevocable /ɪ'revəkəbəl/ a irrevocable; inquebrantable
irrigable /'ɪrɪgəbəl/ a regadío
irrigate /'ɪrɪˌgeit/ vt Agr. poner en regadío, regar; Med. irrigar
irrigation /ˌɪrɪ'geiʃən/ n Agr. riego, m; Med. irrigación, f. i. channel, cacera, acequia, f, canal de riego, m
irritability /ˌɪrɪtə'bɪlɪti/ n irritabilidad, iracundia, f
irritable /'ɪrɪtəbəl/ a irritable, irascible, iracundo
irritably /'ɪrɪtəbli/ adv con irritación, airadamente
irritant /'ɪrɪtn̩t/ a irritante, irritador. n irritador, m; Med. medicamento irritante, m
irritate /'ɪrɪˌteit/ vt provocar, estimular; irritar, molestar, exasperar; Med. irritar
irritating /'ɪrɪˌteitɪŋ/ a irritador, irritante
irritatingly /'ɪrɪˌteitɪŋli/ adv de un modo irritante
irritation /ˌɪrɪ'teiʃən/ n irritación, f, enojo, m; Physiol. picazón, f, picor, m
irruption /ɪ'rʌpʃən/ n irrupción, invasión, f
isinglass /'aizənˌglæs/ n cola de pescado, f
Islamic /ɪs'læmɪk/ a islámico
Islamism /ɪs'lɑmɪzəm/ n islamismo, m
Islamite /ɪs'læmait/ a and n islamita mf
island /'ailənd/ n isla, f, a isleño
islander /'ailəndər/ n isleño (-ña)
islet /'ailɪt/ n isleta, f; isolote, m
isobaric /ˌaisə'bærɪk/ a isobárico
isolate /'aisəˌleit/ vt aislar, apartar
isolated /'aisəˌleitɪd/ a aislado, apartado, solitario; único, solo
isolation /ˌaisə'leiʃən/ n aislamiento, apartamiento, m, soledad, f
isolationism /ˌaisə'leiʃəˌnɪzəm/ n Polit. aislacionismo, aislamientismo, m
isolationist /ˌaisə'leiʃənɪst/ a and n Polit. aislacionista, aislamientista, mf
isomerism /ai'somə,rɪzəm/ n Chem. isomería, f
isometric /ˌaisə'metrɪk/ a isométrico
isosceles /ai'sosəˌliz/ a isósceles
isotope /'aisəˌtoup/ n isotope, isotopo, m
Israelite /'ɪzriəˌlait/ a and n israelita mf
issue /'ɪʃu/ n salida, f; (result) resultado, m, consecuencia, f; (of a periodical) número, m; Print. edición, tirada, f; (offspring) prole, sucesión, f; (of notes, bonds) emisión, f; Med. flujo, m; cuestión, f, problema, m. vi salir, fluir, manar; nacer, originarse; resultar, terminarse. vt (an order) expedir, emitir, dictar; publicar, dar a luz; (of notes, bonds) poner en

circulación, librar. **at i.,** en disputa, en cuestión. **to join i.,** llevar la contraria, oponer
isthmian /'ɪsmiən/ a ístmico
isthmus /'ɪsməs/ n istmo, m
it /ɪt/ pron (as subject) él, m; ella, f; (gen. omitted with all verbs in Sp.); (as object) lo, m; la, f; (as indirect object) le (se with an object in 3rd pers.); (meaning that thing, that affair) eso, ello. Sometimes omitted in other cases, e.g. He has thought it necessary to stay at home, Ha creído necesario de quedarse en casa. We heard it said that..., Oímos decir que... to make it perfectly clear that..., dejar bien claro que... n (slang) garbo, aquél, m; atractivos, m pl. **Is it not so?** ¿No es así? **That is it,** Eso es. **It's me,** Soy yo
Italian /ɪ'tælyən/ a and n italiano (-na) (language) italiano, m. Art. **I. School,** escuela italiana, f
italic /ɪ'tælɪk/ a (of Italy) itálico; Print. itálico, bastardillo. n letra bastardilla, bastardilla, letra itálica, f.
italics mine, el subrayado es mío, los subrayados son míos
italicize /ɪ'tælə,saiz/ vt imprimir en bastardilla; dar énfasis (a)
Italy /'ɪtl̩i/ Italia, f
itch /ɪtʃ/ n sarna, f; Fig. picazón, f; prurito, capricho, m. vi picar; Fig. sentir picazón; (with to) rabiar por, suspirar por.
itching /'ɪtʃɪŋ/ n picazón, f, picor, m. a sarnoso, picante; Med. pruriginoso. **to have an i. palm,** Fig. ser de la virgen del puño
item /n 'aitəm; adv 'aitɛm/ n ítem, artículo, m; Com. partida, f; punto, detalle, m; (of a program) número, m; asunto, m. adv ítem
iterative /'ɪtəˌreitɪv/ a iterativo
Ithaca /'ɪθəkə/ Ítaca, f
itinerant /ai'tɪnərənt/ a nómada, errante
itinerary /ai'tɪnəˌreri/ n itinerario, m, ruta, f
its /ɪts/ poss a su (with pl. obj.) sus. **a book and its pages,** un libro y sus páginas.
itself /ɪt'self/ pron él mismo, m; ella misma, f; (with prep.) sí; (with reflex. verb) se; (with noun) mismo, la, misma; (meaning alone) solo. **in i.,** en sí
ivied /'aivid/ a cubierto de hiedra
ivory /'aivəri/ n marfil, m. a ebúrneo, de marfil, marfileño. **vegetable i.,** marfil vegetal, m. **i. carving,** talla de marfil, f
ivory tower /'aivəri 'tauər/ n torre de marfil, f
ivory-tower /'aivəri 'tauər/ a de torre de marfil
ivy /'aivi/ n hiedra, f

J

j /dʒei/ n (letter) jota, f
jab /dʒæb/ vt (with a hypodermic needle, etc.) pinchar; introducir (en); clavar (con); (scrape) hurgar; (place) poner. n pinchazo, m; golpe, m. **He jabbed his pistol in my ribs,** Me puso la pistola en las costillas
jabber /'dʒæbər/ vt and vi chapurrear; (of monkeys) chillar
jabbering /'dʒæbərɪŋ/ n chapurreo, m; (of monkeys) chillidos, m pl
Jack /dʒæk/ n Juan, m; (man) hombre, m; (sailor) marinero, m; (in cards) sota, f; (for raising weights) gato, m; (of a spit) torno, m; (of some animals) macho, m; (bowls) boliche, m. vt (with up) solevantar con gatos. **Union J.,** pabellón británico, m. **j.-boot,** bota de montar, f. **J.-in-office,** mandarín, funcionario impertinente, m. **J.-in-the-box,** faca, f. **j.-knife,** navaja, f. **J. of all trades,** hombre de muchos oficios, m. **jack of all trades, master of none,** aprendiz de todo, oficial de nada. **J.-rabbit,** liebre americana, f. **J.-tar,** marinero, m
jackal /'dʒækəl/ n chacal, adive, m
jackass /'dʒæk,æs/ n asno, m; (fool) tonto, asno, m. **laughing j.,** martín pescador, m
jacket /'dʒækɪt/ n chaqueta, f; americana, f; (for boil-

ers, etc.) camisa, f; (of a book) forro, m, sobrecubierta, f. **strait j.,** camisa de fuerza, f
jacks /dʒæks/ n (game) matatenas, f pl, cantillos, m pl
jade /dʒeid/ n Mineral. jade, m; (horse) rocín, m; (woman) mala pécora, f; (saucy wench) mozuela, picaruela, f
jaded /'dʒeidɪd/ a fatigado, agotado, rendido; (of the palate) saciado
jagged /'dʒægɪd/ a dentado
jaguar /'dʒægwɑr/ n jaguar, m
jai alai /'hai ˌlai/ n Mexico frontón, m
jail /dʒeil/ n cárcel, prisión, f; encierro, m. vt encarcelar. a carcelario, carcelero.
jailbird /'dʒeil,bɜrd/ n malhechor; presidiario, m
jailer /'dʒeilər/ n carcelero (-ra)
jalopy /dʒə'lɒpi/ n carcacho, m, (Mexico), cafetera rusa, f, (Spain)
jalousie /'dʒælə,si/ n celosía, f
jam /dʒæm/ vt (press) apretar; apiñar; estrujar; (a machine) atascar; (radio) causar interferencia (a); (preserve) hacer confitura de. vi atascarse. n (of people) aglolpamiento, m; (traffic) atasco, m; (preserve) confitura, mermelada, compota, f. **He jammed his hat on,** Se encasquetó el sombrero. **She suddenly jammed**

down on the brakes, Frenó de repente. **jam-dish,** compotera, *f.* **jam-jar,** pote para confitura, *m.*

Jamaican /dʒə'meikən/ *a* jamaicano, *n* jamaicano (-na)

jamboree /,dʒæmbə'ri/ campamento, *m* .

jamming /'dʒæmɪŋ/ *n Radio.* interferencias, *f pl*

jangle /'dʒæŋgəl/ *vi* cencerrear; chocar; rechinar. *n* cencerreo, *m;* choque, *m;* rechinamiento, *m*

janissary /'dʒænə,sɛri/ *n* jenízaro, *m*

janitor /'dʒænɪtər/ *n* portero, *m;* (in a university, etc.) bedel, *m*

January /'dʒænyu,ɛri/ *n* enero, *m*

Japan /dʒə'pæn/ el Japón, *m*

Japanese /,dʒæpə'niz/ *a* japonés. *n* japonés (-esa); (language) japonés, *m*

jar /dʒɑr/ *n* chirrido, *m;* choque, *m;* sacudida, *f;* vibración, trepidación, *f;* (quarrel) riña, *f;* (receptacle) jarra, *f;* (for tobacco, honey, cosmetics, etc.) pote, *m;* (Leyden) botella (de Leyden), *f. vi* chirriar; vibrar, trepidar; chocar; (of sounds) ser discorde; (of colors) chillar. *vt* sacudir; hacer vibrar. **It jarred on my nerves,** Me atacaba los nervios. **It gave me a nasty jar,** *Fig.* Me hizo una impresión desagradable. **on the jar,** entreabierto

jardiniere /,dʒɑrdn̩'ɪər/ *n* jardinera, *f*

jargon /'dʒɑrgən/ *n* jerga, jerigonza, *f;* monserga, *f;* (technical) lenguaje especial, *m*

jarring /'dʒɑrɪŋ/ *a* discorde, disonante; en conflicto, opuesto; (to the nerves) que ataca a los nervios

jasmine /'dʒæzmɪn/ *n* jazmín, *m.* **yellow j.,** jazmín amarillo, *m*

jasper /'dʒæspər/ *n Mineral.* jaspe, *m*

jaundice /'dʒɔndɪs/ *n* ictericia, *f*

jaundiced /'dʒɔndɪst/ *a* envidioso; desengañado, desilusionado

jaunt /dʒɔnt/ *n* excursión, *f, vi* ir de excursión

jauntily /'dʒɔntl̩i/ *adv* airosamente, con garbo

jauntiness /'dʒɔntinɪs/ *n* garbo, *m,* gentileza, ligereza, *f*

jaunty /'dʒɔnti/ *a* garboso, airoso

Javanese /,dʒævə'niz/ *a* javanés. *n* javanés (-esa)

javelin /'dʒævlɪn/ *n* jabalina, *f.* **j. throwing,** lanzamiento de la jabalina, *m*

jaw /dʒɔ/ *n* quijada, *f;* maxilar, *m;* *pl* **jaws,** boca, *f;* (of death, etc.) garras, *f pl;* *Mech.* quijada, *f;* (narrow entrance) boca, abertura, *f.* **jaw-bone,** mandíbula, *f, Anat.* hueso maxilar, *m*

jay /dʒei/ *n* arrendajo, *m*

jazz /dʒæz/ *n* jazz, *m. vi* bailar el jazz. **j. band,** orquesta de jazz, *f*

jealous /'dʒɛləs/ *a* celoso; envidioso. **to be j. of,** tener celos de. **to make j.,** dar celos (a)

jealously /'dʒɛləsli/ *adv* celosamente

jealousy /'dʒɛləsi/ *n* celos, *m pl*

jeans /dʒinz/ *n* vaqueros, *m pl*

jeep /dʒip/ *n Mil.* yip, *m*

jeer /dʒɪər/ *n* burla, mofa, *f;* insulto, *m, vi* burlarse; (with at) mofarse de

jeerer /'dʒɪərər/ *n* mofador (-ra)

jeering /'dʒɪərɪŋ/ *a* mofador. *n* burlas, *f pl;* insultos, *m pl*

jeeringly /'dʒɪərɪŋli/ *adv* burlonamente

jellied /'dʒɛlid/ *a* en gelatina

jelly /'dʒɛli/ *n* jalea, *f;* gelatina, *f, vi* solidificarse. **j.-bag,** manga, *f.* **j.-fish,** aguamala, aguaviva, malagna, medusa, *f*

jeopardize /'dʒɛpər,daiz/ *vt* arriesgar, poner en juego; comprometer

jeopardy /'dʒɛpərdi/ *n* peligro, *m*

jeremiad /,dʒɛrə'maiəd/ *n* jeremiada, *f*

jerk /dʒɜrk/ *n* sacudida, *f. vt* sacudir, dar una sacudida (a); lanzar bruscamente; (pull) tirar de; (push) empujar. *vi* moverse a sacudidas. **I jerked myself free,** Me libré de una sacudida

jerkily /'dʒɜrkɪli/ *adv* con sacudidas; espasmódicamente; nerviosamente

jerkin /'dʒɜrkɪn/ *n* justillo, *m*

jerky /'dʒɜrki/ *a* espasmódico; nervioso (also of style)

jerry-built /'dʒɛri,bɪlt/ *a* mal construido, de pacotilla

jersey /'dʒɜrzi/ *n* jersey, *m. a* de jersey; de Jersey.

football j., camiseta de fútbol, *f,* jersey de fútbol, *m.* **J. cow,** vaca jerseysa, *f*

Jerusalem /dʒɪ'rusələm/ Jerusalén, *m*

jest /dʒɛst/ *n* broma, chanza, *f;* (joke) chiste, *m;* (laughingstock) hazmerreír, *m. vi* bromear; burlarse (de). **in j.,** en broma, de guasa

jester /'dʒɛstər/ *n* burlón (-ona); (practical joker, etc.) bromista, *mf;* (at a royal court) bufón, *m*

jesting /'dʒɛstɪŋ/ *n* bromas, *f pl;* chistes, *m pl;* burlas, *f pl. a* de broma; burlón

jestingly /'dʒɛstɪŋli/ *adv* en broma

Jesuit /'dʒɛʒuɪt/ *n* Jesuita, *m*

Jesuitical /,dʒɛʒu'ɪtɪkəl/ *a* jesuítico

jet /dʒɛt/ *n Mineral.* azabache, *m;* (stream) chorro, *m;* (pipe) surtidero, *m;* (burner) mechero, *m, vi* chorrear. **jet-black,** negro como el azabache, de azabache. **jet-propelled engine,** motor de retroacción, *m.* **jet-propelled plane,** aeroplano de reacción, *m*

jetsam /'dʒɛtsəm/ *n* echazón, *f. Fig.* víctima, *f*

jettison /'dʒɛtəsən/ *n* echazón, *f. vt* echar (mercancías) al mar; *Fig.* librarse de, abandonar

jetty /'dʒɛti/ *n* dique, malecón, *m;* (landing pier) embarcadero, muelle, *m*

Jew /dʒu/ *n* judío (-ía). **Jew's harp,** birimbao, *m*

jewel /'dʒuəl/ *n* joya, alhaja, *f;* (of a watch) rubí, *m; Fig.* alhaja, *f. vt* enjoyar, adornar con piedras preciosas. **j.-box, -case,** joyero, *m*

jeweled /'dʒuəld/ *a* adornado con piedras preciosas, enjoyado; (of a watch) con rubíes

jeweler /'dʒuələr/ *n* joyero (-ra). **jeweler's shop,** joyería, *f*

jewelry /'dʒuəlri/ *n* joyas, *f pl;* artículos de joyería, *m pl*

Jewish /'dʒuɪʃ/ *a* judío

Jewry /'dʒuri/ *n* judería, *f*

jib /dʒɪb/ *n Naut.* foque, *m. vi* (of a horse) plantarse; (refuse) rehusar. **to jib at,** vacilar en; mostrarse desinclinado. **jib-boom,** *Naut.* botalón de foque, *m*

jiffy /'dʒɪfi/ *n* instante, credo, *m.* **in a j.,** en un decir Jesús, en un credo, en un santiamén

jig /dʒɪg/ *n* (dance) jiga, *f. vi* bailar una jiga; bailar, agitarse, sacudirse. *vt* agitar, sacudir; (sieve) cribar

jigger /'dʒɪgər/ *n Naut.* cangreja de mesana, *f;* aparejo de mano, *m;* jigger, *m*

jigsaw puzzle /'dʒɪg,sɔ/ *n* rompecabezas, *m*

jilt /dʒɪlt/ *vt* dar calabazas (a)

jingle /'dʒɪŋgəl/ *n* tintineo, *m;* ruido, *m;* verso, *m;* estribillo, *m. vi* tintinar; sonar; rimar

jingoism /'dʒɪŋgou,ɪzəm/ *n* jingoísmo, *m*

jitters, to have the /'dʒɪtərz/ no tenerlas todas consigo, no saber dónde meterse

job /dʒɒb/ *n* tarea, *f;* trabajo, *m;* empleo, *m;* (affair) asunto, *m;* (thing) cosa, *f;* (unscrupulous transaction) intriga, *f.* **It is a good (bad) job that...,** Es una buena (mala) cosa que... **He has done a good job,** Ha hecho un buen trabajo. **He has lost his job,** Ha perdido su empleo, Le han declarado cesante. **odd-job man,** factótum, *m;* **job-lot,** colección miscelánea, *f; Com.* saldo de mercancías, *m*

jobber /'dʒɒbər/ *n* (workman) destajista, *m;* (in stocks) agiotista, *m; Com.* corredor, *m*

jobless /'dʒɒblɪs/ *a* sin trabajo

jockey /'dʒɒki/ *n* jockey, *m. vt* engañar; (with into) persuadir, hacer; (with out of) quitar, robar. **j. cap,** gorra de jockey, *f.* **J. Club,** jockey-club, *m*

jocose /dʒou'kous/ *a* jocoso, gracioso, guasón

jocosity /dʒou'kɒsɪti/ *n* jocosidad, *f*

jocular /'dʒɒkyələr/ *a* gracioso, alegre; chistoso, zumbón

jocularity /,dʒɒkyə'lærɪti/ *n* alegría, jocosidad, *f*

jocularly /'dʒɒkyələrli/ *adv* en broma; alegremente

jocund /'dʒɒkənd/ *a* alegre, jovial; jocundo

jocundity /dʒou'kʌndɪti/ *n* alegría, *f;* jocundidad, *f*

jog /dʒɒg/ *vt* empujar; (the memory) refrescar. *vi Sport.* correr, ir despacio; andar a trote corto. *n* empujón, *m.* **He jogged me with his elbow,** Me dio con el codo. **jog-trot,** trote corto, *m*

joie de vivre /ʒwad'vivrə/ *n* goce de vivir, arreg … :o de vivir, *m*

join /dʒɔin/ *vt* juntar; unir; añadir; (railway lines)

empalmar; juntarse con; (meet) encontrarse (con); reunirse (con); (a club, etc.) hacerse miembro (de); (share) acompañar; (regiments, ships) volver (a). *vi* juntarse; unirse; asociarse. *n* unión, *f*; (railway) empalme, *m*; (roads) bifurcación, *f*. **At what time will you j. me?** ¿A qué hora me vendrás a buscar? **He has joined his ship,** Ha vuelto a su buque. **Will you j. me in a drink?** ¿Me quieres acompañar en una bebida? **to j. battle,** librar batalla. **to j. forces,** combinar; *Inf.* juntar meriendas. **to j. in,** tomar parte en, participar en. **to j. together,** *vt* unir, juntar. *vi* juntarse; asociarse. **to j. up,** alistarse

joiner /'dʒɔɪnər/ *n* carpintero, ensamblador, *m*,

joinery /'dʒɔɪnəri/ *n* ensambladuría, *f*; carpintería, *f*

joining /'dʒɔɪnɪŋ/ *n* juntura, conjunción, *f*; (etc.) ensambladura, *f*; *Fig.* unión, *f*

joint /dʒɔɪnt/ *n* juntura, junta, *f*; *Anat.* coyuntura, articulación, *f*; (knuckle) nudillo, *m*; (of meat) cuarto, *m*; (hinge) bisagra, *f*; *Bot.* nudo, *m*, *a* unido; combinado; colectivo; mixto; mutuo; (in compounds) co. *vt* juntar; (meat) descuartizar. **out of j.,** dislocado; (of the times) fuera de compás. **j. account,** cuenta corriente mutua, *f*. **j.-heir,** coheredero, *m*. **j. stock company,** compañía por acciones, sociedad anónima, *f*

jointed /'dʒɔɪntɪd/ *a* articulado; (foldable) plegadizo

jointly /'dʒɔɪntli/ *adv* juntamente, en común, colectivamente

joist /dʒɔɪst/ *n* sopanda, viga, *f*

joke /dʒouk/ *n* chiste, *m*; burla, broma, *f*. *vi* bromear, chancearse. *vt* burlarse (de). **Can he take a j.?** ¿Sabe aguantar una broma? **practical j.,** broma pesada, *f*. **to play a j.,** gastar una broma, hacer una burla

joker /'dʒoukər/ *n* bromista, *Argentina also* fomista, *mf*; (in cards) comodín, *m*

joking /'dʒoukɪŋ/ *n* chistes, *m pl*, bromas, *f pl. a* chistoso; cómico

jokingly /'dʒoukɪŋli/ *adv* en broma, de guasa

jollification /,dʒɒləfɪ'keɪʃən/ *n* regocijo, *m*; festividades, fiestas, *f pl*

jollity /'dʒɒlɪti/ *n* alegría, *f*, regocijo, *m*

jolly /'dʒɒli/ *a* alegre, jovial; (tipsy) achispado; (amusing) divertido; (nice) agradable. *adv* muy. **He is a j. good fellow,** Es un hombre estupendo. **I am j. glad,** Estoy contentísimo, Me alegro mucho

jolt /dʒoult/ *n* sacudida, *f*. *vt* sacudir. *vi* (of a vehicle) traquetear

jolting /'dʒoultɪŋ/ *n* sacudidas, *f pl*, sacudimiento, *m*; (of a vehicle) traqueteo, *m*

jonquil /'dʒɒŋkwɪl/ *n* *Bot.* junquillo, *m*

Jordan /'dʒɔrdn/ Jordania, *f*

jostle /'dʒɒsəl/ *vt* empujar, empellar. *vi* dar empujones, codear

jot /dʒɒt/ *n* jota, pizca, *f*. *vt* (down) apuntar. **not a jot,** ni jota, ni pizca. **to be not worth a jot,** no valer un comino

jotter /'dʒɒtər/ *n* taco para notas, *m*; (exercise book) cuaderno, *m*

jotting /'dʒɒtɪŋ/ *n* apunte, *m*; observación, *f*

journal /'dʒɜrnl/ *n* (diary) diario, *m*; (ship's) diario de navegación, *m*; (newspaper) periódico, *m*; (review) revista, *f*

journalese /,dʒɜrnl'iz/ *n* lenguaje periodístico, *m*

journalism /'dʒɜrnl,ɪzəm/ *n* periodismo, *Lat. Am. also* diarismo, *m*

journalist /'dʒɜrnlɪst/ *n* periodista, *mf*

journalistic /,dʒɜrnl'ɪstɪk/ *a* periodístico

journey /'dʒɜrni/ *n* viaje, *m*; expedición, *f*; trayecto, *m*; camino, *m*. *vi* viajar. **j. by sea,** viaje por mar. **Pleasant j.!** ¡Buen viaje! ¡Feliz viaje! **outward j.,** viaje de ida, *m*. **return j.,** viaje de regreso, *m*

Jove /dʒouv/ *n* Júpiter, *m*. **By J.!** ¡Pardiez! ¡Caramba!

jovial /'dʒouviəl/ *a* jovial

joviality /,dʒouvi'ælɪti/ *n* jovialidad, *f*

jowl /dʒaul/ *n* (cheek) carrillo, *m*; (of cattle, etc.) papada, *f*; (jaw) quijada, *f*

joy /dʒɔɪ/ *n* alegría, *f*; felicidad, *f*; deleite, placer, *m*, *vi* alegrarse. **I wish you joy,** Te deseo la felicidad.

joy-ride, excursión en coche, *f*; vuelo en avión, *m*.

joy-stick /(of an airplane) palanca de gobierno, *f*

joyful /'dʒɔɪfəl/ *a* alegre

joyfulness /'dʒɔɪfəlnɪs/ *n* alegría, *f*

joyless /'dʒɔɪlɪs/ *a* sin alegría, triste

joylessness /'dʒɔɪlɪsnɪs/ *n* falta de alegría, tristeza, *f*

joyous /'dʒɔɪəs/. See **joyful**

jubilant /'dʒubələnt/ *a* jubiloso; triunfante

jubilantly /'dʒubələntli/ *adv* con júbilo, alegremente; triunfalmente

jubilation /,dʒubə'leɪʃən/ *n* júbilo, *m*, alegría, *f*; ruido triunfal, *m*

jubilee /'dʒubə,li/ *n* jubileo, *m*

jubilee volume *n* libro de homenaje, libro jubilar, *m*

Judaic /dʒu'deɪk/ *a* judaico

Judaism /'dʒudi,ɪzəm/ *n* judaísmo, *m*

Judas /'dʒudəs/ *n* (traitor and hole) judas, *m*

Judezmo /dʒu'dɛzmou/ el judesmo, el ladino, *m*

judge /dʒʌdʒ/ *n* juez, *m*; (connoisseur) conocedor (-ra) (de); (umpire) arbitrio, *m*. *vt* juzgar; considerar, tener por. *vi* servir como juez; juzgar. **judging by,** a juzgar por. **to be a good j. of,** ser buen juez de. **to j. for oneself,** formar su propia opinión

judgment /'dʒʌdʒmənt/ *n* *Law.* fallo, *m*; sentencia, *f*; juicio, *m*; (understanding) entendimiento, discernimiento, *m*; (opinion) opinión, *f*, parecer, *m*. **In my j....,** Según mi parecer,... Según creo yo... **Last J.,** Juicio Final, *m*. **to pass j. on,** *Law.* pronunciar sentencia (en or sobre); dictaminar sobre; juzgar. **to sit in j. seat,** tribunal, *m*

judicature /'dʒudɪ,keɪtʃər/ *n* judicatura, *f*; (court) juzgado, *m*

judicial /dʒu'dɪʃəl/ *a* judicial; legal; (of the mind) juicioso. **j. inquiry,** investigación judicial, *f*. **j. separation,** separación legal, *f*

judiciary /dʒu'dɪʃi,ɛri/ *a* judicial. *n* judicatura, *f*

judicious /dʒu'dɪʃəs/ *a* juicioso, prudente

judiciously /dʒu'dɪʃəsli/ *adv* prudentemente, juiciosamente

judiciousness /dʒu'dɪʃəsnɪs/ *n* juicio, *m*, prudencia, sensatez, *f*

judo /'dʒudou/ *n* yudo, *m*

judoka /'dʒudou,ka/ *n* yudoca, *mf*

jug /dʒʌg/ *n* jarro, *m*; cántaro, *m*; pote, *m*; (jail) *Argentina, Chile* capacha *f*. *vt* *Cul.* estofar. *vi* (of nightingale) trinar, cantar. **jugged hare,** *n* liebre en estofado, *f*

juggle /'dʒʌgəl/ *vi* hacer juegos malabares. *vt* **to j. out of,** (money, etc.) quitar con engaño, estafar. **to j. with,** *Fig.* (facts, etc.) tergiversar, falsificar; (person) engañar

juggler /'dʒʌglər/ *n* malabarista, *mf*; (deceiver) estafador (-ra)

jugglery /dʒʌgləri/ *n* prestidigitación, *f*; juegos malabares, *m pl*; (imposture) engaño, *m*, estafa, *f*; trampas, *f pl*

jugular /'dʒʌgyələr/ *a* *Anat.* yugular. **j. vein,** yugular, *m*

juice /dʒus/ *n* jugo, *m*; *Fig.* zumo, *m*. **digestive j.,** jugo digestivo, *m*

juiciness /'dʒusɪnɪs/ *n* jugosidad, *f*; suculencia, *f*

juicy /'dʒusi/ *a* jugoso; suculento

jukebox /'dʒuk,bɒks/ *n* tocadiscos, vitrola, sinfonola, *f*

July /dʒu'laɪ/ *n* julio, *m*

jumble /'dʒʌmbəl/ *vt* mezclar, confundir. *n* mezcla confusa, colección miscelánea, confusión, *f*. **j. sale,** tómbola, *f*

jump /dʒʌmp/ *n* salto, *m*; (in prices, etc.) aumento, *m*. **at one j.,** de un salto. **high j.,** salto de altura, *m*. **long j.,** salto de longitud, *m*. **to be nervous,** *Inf.* estar nervioso, tener los nervios en punta

jump /dʒʌmp/ *vi* saltar; dar un salto; brincar; (of tea-cups, etc.) saltar; (throb) pulsar. *vt* saltar; hacer saltar; (a child) brincar; (omit) pasar por alto de, omitir. **The train jumped the rails,** El tren se descarriló. **to j. out of bed,** saltar de la cama. **to j. to the conclusion that...,** darse prisa a concluir que... **to j. about,** dar saltos, brincar; revolverse, moverse de un lado para otro. **to j. at,** saltar sobre; precipitarse sobre; (seize) coger con entusiasmo. **to j. down,** bajar de un salto. **to j. over,** saltar; saltar por encima de. **to j. up,** saltar; (on to a horse, etc.) montar rápida-

mente; levantarse apresuradamente. **to j. with,** (agree) convenir en, estar conforme con
jumper /'dʒʌmpər/ n saltador (-ra); (sailor's) blusa, f; jersey, suéter m, Lat. Am. chompa, f
jumpiness /'dʒʌmpinɪs/ n nerviosidad, f
jumping /'dʒʌmpɪŋ/ n saltos, m pl. a saltador. **j.-off place,** base avanzada, f; Fig. trampolín, m. **j.-pole,** pértiga, f
jumpy /'dʒʌmpi/ a nervioso, agitado
junction /'dʒʌŋkʃən/ n unión, f; (of roads) bifurcación, f; (railway) empalme, m; (connection) conexión, f
juncture /'dʒʌŋktʃər/ n coyuntura, f; momento, m; crisis, f, momento crítico, m; (joint) junta, f
June /dʒun/ n junio, m
jungle /'dʒʌŋgəl/ n selva, f. **j.-fever,** fiebre de los grandes bosques, f
junior /'dʒunyər/ a joven; hijo; más joven; menos antiguo; subordinado, segundo. n joven, mf **Carmen is my j. by three years,** Carmen es tres años más joven que yo. **James Thomson, Jr.,** James Thomson, hijo. **the j. school,** los pequeños. **j. partner,** socio menor, m
juniper /'dʒunəpər/ n Bot. enebro, m
junk /dʒʌŋk/ n trastos viejos, m pl; (nonsense) patrañas, f pl; Naut. junco, m; (salt meat) tasajo, m. **j.-shop,** tienda de trastos viejos, f
junk bond bono-basura, m
junketing /'dʒʌŋkɪtɪŋ/ n festividades, f pl
junk mail n correo basura, m
juridical /dʒʊ'rɪdɪkəl/ a jurídico
jurisconsult /,dʒʊrɪskən'sʌlt/ n jurisconsulto, m
jurisdiction /,dʒʊrɪs'dɪkʃən/ n jurisdicción, f; competencia, f
jurisprudence /,dʒʊrɪs'prudns/ n jurisprudencia, f
jurist /'dʒʊrɪst/ n jurista, legista, mf
juror /'dʒʊrər/ n (miembro del) jurado, m
jury /'dʒʊri/ n jurado, m. **to be on the j.,** formar parte del jurado. **j.-box,** tribuna del jurado, f
juryman /'dʒʊrimən/ n miembro del jurado, m
just /dʒʌst/ a justo; justiciero; exacto; fiel. **Peter the J.,** Pedro el justiciero

just /dʒʌst/ adv justamente, exactamente; precisamente; (scarcely) apenas; (almost) casi; (entirely) completamente; (simply) meramente, solamente, tan sólo; nada más; Mexico no más; (newly) recién (followed by past part.), recientemente. **He only j. missed being run over,** Por poco le atropellan. **It is j. near,** Está muy cerca. **It is j. the same to me,** Me es completamente igual. **J. as he was leaving,** Cuando estaba a punto de marcharse, En el momento de marcharse. **Just as you arrive in Spain, you must...** Nada más llegar a España, tienes que... **That's j. it!** ¡Eso es! ¡Exactamente! **to have j.,** acabar de. **They have j. dined,** Acaban de cenar. **J. as you wish,** Como Vd. quiera. **j. at that moment,** precisamente en aquel momento. **j. by,** muy cerca; al lado. **j. now,** ahora mismo; hace poco; pronto, dentro de poco. **j. yet,** todavía. **They will not come j. yet,** No vendrán todavía. **Just looking** (browser to shopkeeper) Estoy viendo, Estamos viendo
justice /'dʒʌstɪs/ n justicia, f; (judge) juez, m; (magistrate) juez municipal, m. **to bring to j.,** llevar ante el juez (a). **to do j. to,** (a person) hacer justicia (a); (a meal) hacer honor (a). **to do oneself j.,** quedar bien
justifiable /'dʒʌstə,faiəbəl/ a justificable
justifiably /'dʒʌstə,faiəbli/ adv con justicia, justificadamente
justification /,dʒʌstəfɪ'keiʃən/ n justificación, f
justify /'dʒʌstə,fai/ vt justificar, vindicar; (excuse) disculpar; Print. justificar. **to be justified (in),** tener derecho (a), tener motivo (para), tener razón (en)
justly /'dʒʌstli/ adv justamente; con justicia; con derecho; con razón; exactamente; debidamente
justness /'dʒʌstnɪs/ n justicia, f; exactitud, f
jute /dʒut/ n yute, m
jut (out) /dʒʌt/ vi salir, proyectar; sobresalir
juvenile /'dʒuvənl/ a juvenil; de la juventud; para la juventud; joven; de niños; para niños. n joven, mf. **j. court,** tribunal de menores, m. **j. lead,** Theat. galancete, galán joven, m. **j. offender,** delincuente infantil, m
juxtapose /'dʒʌkstə,pouz/ vt yuxtaponer
juxtaposition /,dʒʌkstəpə'zɪʃən/ n yuxtaposición, f

K

k /kei/ n (letter) ka, f
kaiser /'kaizər/ n káiser, emperador, m. **the K.** el emperador alemán, m
kaleidoscope /kə'laidə,skoup/ n calidoscopio, m
kaleidoscopic /kə,laidə'skɒpɪk/ a calidoscópico
kangaroo /,kæŋgə'ru/ n canguro, m
kaolin /'keiəlɪn/ n caolín, m
kapok /'keipɒk/ n miraguano, m
keel /kil/ n quilla, f. vt carenar. **to k. over,** volcar; caer; Naut. zozobrar
keelson /'kɛlsən/ n sobrequilla, f
keen /kin/ a (of edges) afilado; agudo; penetrante; vivo; sutil; ardiente; celoso, entusiasta; mordaz; (desirous) ansioso; (of appetite) grande, bueno. **He is a k. tennis player,** Es tenista entusiasta. **Joan has a very k. ear,** Juana tiene un oído muy agudo. **I'm not very k. on apples,** No me gustan mucho las manzanas
keenly /'kinli/ adv agudamente; vivamente; (of feeling) hondamente; (of looking) atentamente
keenness /'kinnɪs/ n (of a blade) afiladura, f; agudeza, f; viveza, f; sutileza, f; perspicacia, f; (enthusiasm) entusiasmo, m, afición, f; (desire) ansia, f
keep /kip/ vt guardar; tener; quedarse con; retener; conservar; mantener; (a shop, hotel, etc.) dirigir, tener; (a school) ser director de; (a promise, etc.) cumplir; (the law, etc.) observar, guardar; (celebrate) solemnizar; (a secret) guardar; (books, accounts, a house, in step) llevar; (sheep, etc., one's bed) guardar; (a city, etc.) defender; (domestic animals, cars, etc.) tener; (lodge) alojar; (detain) detener; (reserve) reservar; (cause) hacer. **They had kept this room for me,** Me habían reservado este cuarto. **Dorothy**

has kept the blue dress, Dorotea se ha quedado con el vestido azul. **The government could not k. order,** El gobierno no sabía mantener el orden. **I did not know how to k. their attention,** No sabía retener su atención. **Carmen kept quiet,** Carmen guardó silencio, Carmen se calló. **Can you k. a secret?** ¿Sabes guardar un secreto? **to k. an appointment,** acudir a una cita. **to k. in repair,** conservar en buen estado. **to k. someone from doing something,** evitar que uno haga algo. **to k. someone waiting,** hacer que espere uno. **to k. something from someone,** ocultar algo de uno. **We were kept at it night and day,** Nos hacían trabajar día y noche. **I always k. it by me,** Lo tengo siempre a mi lado (or conmigo). **to k. away,** alejar; mantener a distancia; no dejar venir. **to k. back,** (a crowd, etc.) detener; cortar el paso (a); no dejar avanzar; (retain) guardar, retener; reservar; (tears, words) reprimir, contener; (evidence, etc.) callar, suprimir. **to k. down,** no dejar subir (a); sujetar; (a nation, etc.) oprimir, subyugar; (emotions) dominar; (prices, expenses) mantener bajo; (check) moderar; reprimir. **to k. in,** (feelings) contener; reprimir; (the house) hacer quedarse en casa, no dejar salir; (imprison) encerrar; (school) hacer quedar en la escuela (a). **to k. off,** alejar; tener a distancia (a); cerrar el paso (a), no dejar avanzar; no andar sobre; no tocar; (a subject) no tratar de, no discutir, no tocar. **K. your hands off!** ¡No toques! **to k. on,** guardar; tener; (eyes) fijar en, poner en. **to k. out,** no dejar entrar; excluir. **It is difficult to k. him out of trouble,** Es difícil de evitar que se meta en líos. **to k. to,** seguir; limitarse a; adherirse a; **K. to the Left,** «Tome su izquierda», **K. to the right,** «Tome su derecha»; (a path, etc.) seguir por; (one's bed) guardar; (fulfil) cumplir; (oblige) hacer, obligar. **to k. under,** subyugar, oprimir; dominar; controlar. **to k. up,** mantener; (appearances) guardar; conservar; persistir en; (prices) sostener; (in good repair) conservar en buen estado; (go on doing) continuar. **He kept me up late last night,** Anoche me entretuvo hasta muy tarde; Ayer me hizo trasnochar; Anoche me hizo velar. **to k. one's end up,** volver por sí, hacerse fuerte. **to k. up one's spirits,** no desanimarse

keep /kip/ *vi* quedar; (be) estar; (continue) seguir, continuar; mantenerse; (at home, etc.) quedarse, permanecer; (be accustomed) acostumbrar, soler; (persist) perseverar; (of food) conservarse fresco. **How is he keeping?** ¿Cómo está? **to k. in with someone,** cultivar a alguien. **to k. up with the times,** mantenerse al corriente. **to k. at,** seguir; persistir; perseverar; (pester) importunar. **John keeps at it,** Juan trabaja sin descansar. **to k. away,** mantenerse apartado; mantenerse a distancia; no acudir. **to k. back,** hacerse a un lado, apartarse, alejarse. **to k. down,** quedarse tumbado; seguir acurrucado; no levantarse; esconderse. **to k. from,** (doing something) guardarse de. **to k. off,** mantenerse a distancia. **If the storm keeps off,** Si no estalla una tempestad. **If the rain keeps off,** Si no empieza a llover, Si no hay lluvia. **to k. on,** continuar; seguir. **to k. straight on,** seguir derecho. **I'm tired, but I still k. on,** Estoy cansado, pero sigo trabajando. **to k. out,** quedarse fuera. **to k. out of,** (quarrels, trouble, etc.) no meterse en, evitar. **to k. out of sight,** no dejarse ver, no mostrarse, mantenerse oculto. **to k. together,** quedarse juntos; reunirse

keep /kip/ *n* (of a castle) mazmorra, *f*; (maintenance) subsistencia, *f*; comida, *f*. **for keeps,** para siempre jamás

keeper /'kipər/ *n* guarda, *mf*; (in a park, zoo, of a lunatic) guardián, *m*; (of a museum, etc.) director, *m*; (of animals) criador (-ra); (gamekeeper) guardabosque, *m*; (of a boardinghouse, shop, etc.) dueño (-ña); (of accounts, books) tenedor, *m*. **Am I my brother's k.?** ¿Soy yo responsable por mi hermano?

keeping /'kipɪŋ/ *n* guarda, *f*; conservación, *f*; protección, *f*; (of a rule) observación, *f*; (of an anniversary, etc.) celebración, *f*; (of a person) mantenimiento, *m*. **in k. with,** en armonía con; de acuerdo con. **out of k. with,** en desacuerdo con. **to be in safe k.,** estar en buenas manos; estar en un lugar seguro. **k. back,** retención, *f*

keepsake /'kip,seik/ *n* recuerdo, *m*

keg /kɛg/ *n* barrilete, *m*

ken /kɛn/ *n* alcance de la vista, *m*; vista, *f*; comprensión, *f*

kennel /'kɛnl/ *n* (of a dog) perrera, *f*; (of hounds) jauría, *f*; (dwelling) cuchitril, *m*; (gutter) arroyo, *m*. **k. man,** perrero, *m*

kepi /'keipi/ *n* quepis, *m*

Kepler /'kɛplər/ Keplero

kerchief /'kɜrtʃif/ *n* pañuelo, *m*; pañoleta, *f*. **brightly-colored k.,** pañuelo de hierbas, *m*

kernel /'kɜrnl/ *n* almendra, semilla, *f*; *Fig.* meollo, *m*, esencia, *f*

kerosene /'kɛrə,sin/ *n* petróleo de lámpara, *m*; kerosén, *m*

ketchup /'kɛtʃəp/ *n* salsa de tomate y setas, *f*

kettle /'kɛtl/ *n* caldero, *m*, *Mexico* marmita, *f*. **pretty k. of fish,** olla de grillos, *f*. **k.-drum,** timbal, *m*. **k.-drum player,** timbalero, *m*

key /ki/ *n* llave, *f*; (*Fig. Archit., Mus.*) clave, *f*; (tone) tono, *m*; (of a piano, typewriter, etc.) tecla, *f*; *Mech.* chaveta, *f*; (of a wind instrument) pistón, *m*; (winged fruit) sámara, *f*; *Elec.* conmutador, *m*. **major (minor) key,** tono mayor (menor), *m*. **latch-key,** llave de la puerta, *f*; (Yale) llavín, *m*. **master key,** llave maestra, *f*. **skeleton key,** ganzúa, *f*. **He is all keyed up,** Tiene los nervios en punta. **key industry,** industria clave, *f*. **key man,** hombre indispensable, *m*. **key point,** punto estratégico, *m*. **key-ring,** llavero, *m*. **key signature,** *Mus.* clave, *f*. **key word,** palabra clave, *f*

keyboard /'ki,bɔrd/ *n* teclado, *m*

keyhole /'ki,houl/ *n* ojo de la cerradura, *m*. **through the k.,** por el ojo de la cerradura

keynote /'ki,nout/ *n Mus.* tónica, *f*; *Fig.* piedra clave, idea fundamental, *f*

keystone /'ki,stoun/ *n* piedra clave, *f*

khaki /'kæki/ *n* caqui, *m*

kick /kɪk/ *vt* dar un puntapié (a); golpear; (a goal) chutar. *vi* (of horses, etc.) dar coces, cocear; (of guns) recular. **to k. one's heels,** hacer tiempo. **to k. the bucket,** palmarla, *Lat. Am.* arrancarse. **to k. up a row,** hacer un ruido de mil diablos; (quarrel) armar camorra. **to k. about,** dar patadas (a). **to k. away,** quitar con el pie; lanzar con el pie. **to k. off,** quitar con el pie; lanzar; sacudirse. **k.-off,** *n* golpe de salida, puntapié inicial, saque, *m*. **to k. out,** echar a puntapiés

kick /kɪk/ *n* puntapié, *m*; golpe, *m*; coz, *f*; (of guns) culatazo, *m*. **free k.,** golpe franco, *m*

kicking /'kɪkɪŋ/ *n* coces, *f pl*; acoceamiento, *m*; pataleo, *m*; golpeamiento, *m*

kid /kɪd/ *n* cabrito, *m*, chivo (-va); carne de cabrito, *f*; (leather) cabritilla, *f*; *Inf.* crío, *m*. **kid gloves,** guantes de cabritilla, *m pl*

kidnap /'kɪdnæp/ *vt* secuestrar

kidnapper /'kɪdnæpər/ *n* secuestrador (-ra); ladrón (-ona) de niños

kidnapping /'kɪdnæpɪŋ/ *n* secuestro, *m*

kidney /'kɪdni/ *n* riñón, *m*; *Fig.* especie, índole, *f*. **k.-bean,** (plant) judía, *f*; (fruit) habichuela, judía, *f*, fréjol, *Mexico* calamaco, *m*

kill /kɪl/ *vt* matar; destruir; suprimir. **to k. off,** exterminar. **to k. time,** entretener el tiempo, pasarse las horas muertas. **to k. two birds with one stone,** matar dos pájaros de un tiro. **k.-joy,** aguafiestas, *mf*

killer /'kɪlər/ *n* matador (-ra); (murderer) asesino, *mf*

killing /'kɪlɪŋ/ *n* matanza, *f*; (murder) asesinato, *m*. *a* matador; destructivo; (comic) cómico; ridículo, absurdo; (ravishing) irresistible

kiln /kɪl/ *n* horno de cerámica, horno, *m*

kilo /'kilou/ *n* kilo, *m*

kilocycle /'kɪlə,saikəl/ *n Elec.* kilociclo, *m*

kilogram /'kɪlə,græm/ *n* kilogramo, *m*

kiloliter /'kɪlə,litər/ *n* kilolitro, *m*

kilometer /kɪ'lɒmɪtər/ *n* kilómetro, *m*

kilometric /,kɪlə'mɛtrɪk/ *a* kilométrico

kilowatt /'kɪlə,wɒt/ *n Elec.* kilovatio, *m*

kin /kɪn/ *n* parientes, *m pl*; familia, *f*; clase, especie, *f*. **the next of kin,** los parientes próximos, la familia

kind /kaind/ *n* género, *m*, clase, *f*; especie, *f*; *Inf.* tipo, *m*. **He is a queer k. of person,** Es un tipo muy raro. **What k. of cloth is it?** ¿Qué clase de tela es? **Nothing of the k!** ¡Nada de eso! **payment in k.,** pago en especie, *m*

kind /kaind/ *a* bondadoso, bueno; cariñoso, tierno; amable; favorable, propicio. **Will you be so k. as to...** Tenga Vd. la bondad de... **With k. regards,** Con un saludo afectuoso. **You have been very k. to her,** Vd. ha sido muy bueno para ella. **k.-hearted,** bondadoso. **k.-heartedness,** bondad, benevolencia, *f*

kindergarten /'kɪndər,gɑrtn/ *n* jardín de la infancia, kindergarten, *m*

kindle /'kɪndl/ *vt* encender; hacer arder; *Fig.* avivar. *vi* prender, empezar a arder; encenderse; *Fig.* inflamarse

kindliness /'kaindlɪnɪs/ *n* bondad, *f*

kindling /'kɪndlɪŋ/ *n* encendimiento del (fuego), *m*; (wood) leña menuda, *Lat. Am.* charamusca, *f*

kindly /'kaindli/ *a* bondadoso; bueno; benévolo; propicio, favorable; (of climate) benigno. *adv* con bondad, bondadosamente; fácilmente. **K. sit down,** Haga el favor de sentarse

kindness /'kaindnɪs/ *n* bondad, *f*; benevolencia, *f*; amabilidad, *f*; cariño, *m*; favor, *m*, atención, *f*

kindred /'kɪndrɪd/ *n* parentesco, *m*; parientes, *m pl*; familia, *f*; afinidad, *f*, *a* emparentado; hermano

king /kɪŋ/ *n* (ruler, important person, chess, cards) rey, *m*; (in checkers) dama, *f*. **king's evil,** escrófula, *f*. **k.-bolt,** perno real, *m*. **k.-craft,** arte de gobernar, *m*, or *f*. **k.-cup,** *Bot.* botón de oro, *m*. **K.-of-Arms,** rey de armas, *m*. **k.-post,** pendolón, *m*

kingdom /'kɪŋdəm/ *n* reino, *m*. **animal k.,** reino animal, *m*

kingfisher /'kɪŋ,fɪʃər/ *n* martín pescador, alción, *m*

kink /kɪŋk/ n nudo, m; pliegue, m; (curl) rizo, m; Fig. peculiaridad, f

kinsfolk /ˈkɪnz,fouk/ n parientes, m pl, familia, f

kinship /ˈkɪnʃɪp/ n parentesco, m; afinidad, f

kinsman /ˈkɪnzmən/ n pariente, deudo, m

kinswoman /ˈkɪnz,wumən/ n parienta, f

kiosk /ˈkiɒsk/ n quiosco, m

kipper /ˈkɪpər/ n arenque ahumado, m. vt ahumar

kiss /kɪs/ n beso, m; (in billiards) pelo, m. vt besar; dar un beso (a); (of billiard balls) tocar. **to k. each other**, besarse. **k.-curl**, rizo de la sien, m, sortijilla, f

kit /kɪt/ n (tub) cubo, m; (for tools, etc.) cajita, caja, f; (soldier's) equipo, m. **kit-bag**, mochila, f

kitchen /ˈkɪtʃən/ n cocina, f. **k.-boy**, pinche (de cocina), m. **k.-garden**, huerta, f. **k.-maid**, fregona, f. **k.-range**, cocina económica, f. **k.-sink**, fregadero, Chile, Mexico, also lavaplatos, m. **k.-stove**, horno de cocina, m. **k. utensils**, batería de cocina, f

kitchenette /ˌkɪtʃəˈnɛt/ n cocinilla, f

kite /kait/ n Ornith. milano, m; cometa, pájara, f. **to fly a k.**, hacer volar una cometa. **box-k.**, cometa celular, f

kith and kin /kɪθ/ n pl parientes y amigos, m pl

kitten /ˈkɪtṇ/ n gatito (-ta). vi (of a cat) parir

kittenish /ˈkɪtṇɪʃ/ a de gatito; juguetón

kitty /ˈkɪti/ n michito, m; (in card games) platillo, m

kleptomania /ˌklɛptəˈmeiniə/ n cleptomanía, f

kleptomaniac /ˌklɛptəˈmeiniæk/ a cleptómano. n cleptómano (-na)

knack /næk/ n destreza, f; talento, m; (trick) truco, m

knapsack /ˈnæp,sæk/ n mochila, f; Mil. alforja, f

knave /neiv/ n bellaco, truhán, tunante, m; (at cards) sota, f

knavery /ˈneivəri/ n bellaquería, truhanería, f

knavish /ˈneiviʃ/ a de bribón; taimado, truhanesco

knead /nid/ vt amasar; (massage) sobar; Fig. formar

kneading /ˈnidɪŋ/ n amasijo, m; (massaging) soba, f. **k.-trough**, amasadera artesa f

knee /ni/ n rodilla, f; Fig. ángulo, codillo, m. **on bended k.**, de hinojos. **on one's knees**, de rodillas, arrodillado. **to go down on one's knees**, arrodillarse, ponerse de rodillas. **k.-cap**, rótula, f. **k.-deep**, hasta las rodillas. **k.-joint**, articulación de la rodilla, f; Mech. junta de codillo, f. **k.-pad**, rodillera, f

kneel (down) /nil/ vi arrodillarse, hincarse de rodillas, ponerse de rodillas

kneeling /ˈnilɪŋ/ a arrodillado, de rodillas

knell /nɛl/ n toque de difuntos, tañido fúnebre, m; toque de campanas, m; Fig. muerte, f. vi tocar a muerto. vt Fig. anunciar, presagiar

knickerbockers /ˈnɪkər,bɒkərz/ n pl bragas, f pl; calzón corto, m; (women's) pantalones, m pl

knickknack /ˈnɪk,næk/ n chuchería, f

knife /naif/ n cuchillo, m. **to have one's k. in someone**, tener enemiga (a), querer mal (a). **war to the k.**, guerra a muerte, f. **k.-edge**, filo de cuchillo, m; fiel de soporte, m. **k. grinder**, amolador, m. **k.-handle**, mango de cuchillo, m. **k. thrust**, cuchillada, f

knife, fork, and spoon /naif/ cuchara, tenedor, y cuchillo

knight /nait/ n caballero, m; (chess) caballo, m. vt armar caballero, calzar la espuela; (in modern usage) dar el título de caballero. **untried k.**, caballero novel, m. **k. commander**, comendador, m. **k.-errant**, caballero andante, m. **k.-errantry**, caballería andante, f. **Knight of Labor**, Caballero del Trabajo m. **k. of the rueful countenance**, el caballero de la triste figura

knighthood /ˈnaithʊd/ n caballería, f; (in modern usage) título de caballero, m

knightly /ˈnaitli/ a caballeresco; de caballero; de caballería

knit /nɪt/ vt and vi hacer calceta, hacer de punto, hacer media; juntar, ligar; unir. **Isabel is knitting me a jumper**, Isabel me hace un jersey de punto de media. **to k. one's brows**, fruncir el ceño

knitted /ˈnɪtɪd/ a de punto. **k. goods**, géneros de punto, m pl

knitter /ˈnɪtər/ n calcetero (-ra); (machine) máquina de hacer calceta, f

knitting /ˈnɪtɪŋ/ n acción de hacer calceta, f; trabajo de punto, m, labor de calceta, f; unión, f. **k.-**

machine, máquina de hacer calceta, f. **k.-needle**, aguja de media, aguja de hacer calceta, f

knob /nɒb/ n protuberancia, f; (of a door, etc.) perilla, borlita, f; (ornamental) bellota, f; (of sugar) terrón, m; (of a stick) puño, m

knock /nɒk/ n golpe, m; choque, m; (with a knocker) aldabada, f

knock /nɒk/ vt golpear; chocar (contra). vi llamar a la puerta; (of an engine) picar. **to k. one's head against**, chocar con la cabeza contra, dar con la cabeza contra. **to k. about**, vt pegar; aporrear. vi viajar; vagar, rodar; callejear. **to k. against**, golpear contra; chocar contra. **to k. down**, derribar; (of vehicles) atropellar, Mexico antellevar; (houses, etc.) demoler; (an argument, etc.) destruir; (a tender, etc.) rebajar; (of an auctioneer) rematar al mejor postor. **to k. in**, (nails, etc.) clavar. **to k. into one another**, toparse. **to k. off**, hacer caer; sacudir; quitar; (from price) descontar; (from speed, etc.) reducir; (finish) terminar pronto; (runs in cricket) hacer. **to k. on or at the door**, tocar (a) la puerta. **to k. out**, (remove) quitar; (boxing) dejar fuera de combate, noquear; (Fig. stun) atontar; (an idea, etc.) bosquejar. **to k. over**, volcar. **to k. up against**, chocar contra; tropezar con. **k.-kneed**, a patiabierto. **k.-out**, "knockout," m

knocker /ˈnɒkər/ n (on a door) aldaba, f. **k.-up**, despertador, m

knocking /ˈnɒkɪŋ/ n golpes, m pl, golpeo, m; (with a knocker) aldabeo, m. **k. over**, vuelco, m; (by a vehicle) atropello, m

knoll /noul/ n altillo, otero, m

knot /nɒt/ n nudo, m; (bow) lazo, m; (of hair) moño, m; Naut. nudo, m, milla náutica, f; (of people) corrillo, grupo, m; (on timber) nudo, m. vt anudar. vi hacer nudos; enmarañarse. **to tie a k.**, hacer un nudo

knotted /ˈnɒtɪd/ a nudoso

knotty /ˈnɒti/ a nudoso; Fig. intrincado, difícil, complicado. **a k. problem**, problema espinoso

know /nou/ vt conocer; saber; (understand) comprender; (recognize) reconocer. **I k. her very well by sight**, La conozco muy bien de vista. **John knows Latin**, Juan sabe latín. **How can I k.?** ¿Cómo lo voy a saber yo? **I knew you at once**, Te reconocí en seguida. **They always k. best**, Siempre tienen razón. **Did you k. about Philip?** ¿Has oído lo de Felipe? **to be in the k.**, estar bien informado, saber de buena tinta. **to get to k.**, (a person) llegar a conocer, trabar amistad con. **to make known**, dar a conocer; manifestar. **Who knows?** ¿Quién sabe? **to k. by heart**, saber de coro. **to k. how**, (to do something) saber. **to k. oneself**, conocerse a sí mismo. **k.-it-all**, sabelotodo, mf, marisabidilla, f

knowing /ˈnouɪŋ/ a inteligente; malicioso; (of animals) sabio. **There is no k.**, No hay modo de saberlo

knowingly /ˈnouɪŋli/ adv a sabiendas, de intento; conscientemente; (cleverly) hábilmente; (with look, etc.) de un aire malicioso

knowledge /ˈnɒlɪdʒ/ n conocimiento, m. **To the best of my k. the book does not exist**, El libro no existe que yo sepa. **He has a thorough k. of...**, Conoce a fondo... **lack of k.**, ignorancia, f. **He did it without my k.**, Lo hizo sin que lo supiera yo. **It is a matter of common k. that...** Es notorio que...

knowledgeable /ˈnɒlɪdʒəbəl/ a sabedor

known /noun/ a conocido

knuckle /ˈnʌkəl/ n (of a finger) nudillo, m, articulación del dedo, f; (of meat) jarrete, m. **He knuckled down to his work**, Se puso a trabajar con ahínco. **to k. under**, someterse. **k.-duster**, rompecabezas, m

kopeck /ˈkoupɛk/ n copec, f

Koran /kəˈrɑn/ n Corán, Alcorán, m

Korea /kəˈriə/ Corea, f

kosher /ˈkouʃər/ a cosher; (slang) genuino

kowtow /ˈkau'tau/ vi saludar humildemente, m; Fig. bajar la cerviz

Kremlin /ˈkrɛmlɪn/ n Kremlín, m

kudos /ˈkudouz/ n prestigio, m, gloria, f

Kurdish /ˈkərdɪʃ/ a curdo

kyrie eleison /ˈkɪəri,ei ɛ'leiə,sɔn/ n kirieleisón, m

L

l /ɛl/ n (letter) ele, f
la /lɑ/ n Mus. la, m
label /'leibəl/ n etiqueta, (on a garment), rótula, m, (on a can), f; (on a museum specimen, etc.) letrero, m; Fig. calificación, f. vt poner etiqueta en; marcar, rotular; Fig. calificar, designar, clasificar
labial /'leibiəl/ a labial. n letra labial, f
labor /'leibər/ n trabajo, m; labor, f; fatiga, pena, f; clase obrera, f; (manual workers) mano de obra, f; (effort) esfuerzo, m; (of childbirth) dolores de parto, m pl. vi trabajar; (strive) esforzarse, afanarse; (struggle) forcejar, luchar; (try) procurar, tratar de; avanzar con dificultad; (in childbirth) estar de parto. vt elaborar; pulir, perfeccionar. **to l. under,** sufrir; tener que luchar contra. **hard l.,** trabajo arduo, m; Law. trabajos forzosos, m pl, presidio, m. **Ministry of L.,** Ministerio de Trabajo, m. **to be in l.,** estar de parto. **to l. in vain,** trabajar en balde, arar en el mar. **to l. under a delusion,** estar en el error, estar equivocado. **L. Exchange,** Bolsa de Trabajo, f. **l. leader,** dirigente sindical, m. **L. party,** partido laborista, partido obrero, m. **l. question,** cuestión obrera, f; (domestic) problema del servicio, m. **l.-saving,** a que ahorra trabajo. **l. union,** sindicato, m
laboratory /'læbrə,tɔri/ n laboratorio, m
labored /'leibərd/ a (of style) premioso, artificial; forzado; (of breathing) fatigoso; (slow) torpe, lento
laborer /'leibərər/ n obrero, m; (on the land) labrador, labriego, m; (on the roads, etc.) peón, m; (by the day) jornalero, m
laborious /lə'bɔriəs/ a laborioso; arduo, difícil, penoso
laboriously /lə'bɔriəsli/ adv laboriosamente; con dificultad, penosamente
laboriousness /lə'bɔriəsnɪs/ n laboriosidad, f; dificultad, f
Labrador dog /'læbrə,dɔr/ n perro de Labrador, m
labyrinth /'læbərɪnθ/ n laberinto, m
labyrinthine /,læbə'rɪnθɪn/ a laberíntico; intrincado
lace /leis/ n (of shoes, corsets, etc.) cordón, m; (tape) cinta, f; encaje, m; (narrow, for trimming) puntilla, f; (of gold or silver) galón, m. vt and vi (shoes, etc.) atarse los cordones; (trim) guarnecer con encajes, etc.; Fig. ornar; (a drink) echar (coñac, etc.) en. **blond l.,** blonda, f. **gold l.,** galón de oro, m. **point l.,** encaje de aguja, m. **l. curtain,** cortina de encaje, f; (of net) visillo, m. **l. maker** or **seller,** encajero (-ra), mf. **l. making,** obra de encaje, f. **l.-pillow,** almohadilla para encajes, f. **l. shoes,** zapatos con cordones, m pl
lacerate /'læsə,reit/ vt lacerar
laceration /,læsə'reifən/ n laceración, f
lachrymal /'lækrəməl/ a lagrimal, lacrimal
lachrymose /'lækrə,mous/ a lacrimoso
lack /læk/ n falta, f. **l. of evidence,** falta de pruebas, f; carestía, escasez, f; (absence) ausencia, f; (need) necesidad, f. vt carecer de; no tener; necesitar. vi hacer falta; necesitarse. **to l. confidence in oneself,** no tener confianza en sí mismo, carecer de confianza en sí mismo. **l.-luster,** a (of eyes) apagado, mortecino. **l. of evidence,** falta de pruebas, f
lackadaisical /,lækə'deizikəl/ a lánguido; indiferente; (dreamy) ensimismado, distraído
lackey /'læki/ n lacayo, m
laconic /lə'kɒnɪk/ a lacónico
lacquer /'lækər/ n laca, f, vt dar laca (a), barnizar con laca. **gold l.,** sisa dorada, f. **l. work,** laca, f
lacquering /'lækərɪŋ/ n barnizado de laca, m; laca, capa de barniz de laca, f
lactate /'lækteit/ n lactato, m, vi lactar
lactation /læk'teifən/ n lactancia, f
lacteal /'læktiəl/ a lácteo
lactic /'læktɪk/ a láctico
lactose /'læktous/ n lactosa, f
lacuna /lə'kyunə/ n laguna, f

lacy /'leisi/ a de encaje; parecido a encaje; Fig. transparente, etéreo
lad /læd/ n muchacho, joven, mozalbete, m; zagal, m; (stable, etc.) mozo, m. **He's some l.!** ¡Qué tío que es! **l. of the village,** chulo, m
ladder /'lædər/ n escalera de mano, f; Naut. escala, f; (in a stocking, etc.) carrera, f. **companion l.,** escala de toldilla, f. **to l. one's stocking,** escurrirse un punto de las medias
Ladies and gentlemen /'leidiz/ n. pl Señoras y señores, Damas y caballeros. **ladies' man,** hombre de salón, Perico entre ellas, mujeriego, m
lading /'leidɪŋ/ n flete, m, carga, f
ladle /'leidl/ n cucharón, cazo, m. vt servir con cucharón; (a boat) achicar; Inf. distribuir, repartir
lady /'leidi/ n dama, f; señora, f; (English title) milady, f; (woman) mujer, f. **to be a l.,** ser una señora. **leading l.,** Theat. dama primera, f. **Our L.,** Nuestra Señora. **young l.,** señorita, f; Inf. novia, f. **lady's maid,** doncella, f. **l. of the house,** señora de la casa, f. **l. bug,** Ent. catalina mariquita, vaca de San Antonio, f. **L. Chapel,** capilla de la Virgen, f. **L. Day,** día de la Anunciación (de Nuestra Señora), m. **l.-help,** asistenta, f. **l.-in-waiting,** dama de servicio, f. **l.-killer,** ladrón de corazones, castigador, tenorio, m. **l.-love,** querida, amada, f. **ladies' room,** baño para damas, m
ladylike /'leidi,laik/ a de dama; elegante; distinguido; bien educado; delicado; (of men) afeminado
ladyship /'leidi,ʃɪp/ n señoría, f. **Your L.,** Su Señoría
lag /læg/ vt recubrir; aislar. vi retrasarse; quedarse atrás; ir (or andar) despacio; rezagarse; Naut. roncear. n retraso, m; Mech. retardación de movimiento, f
laggard /'lægərd/ n holgazán (-ana), haragán (-ana)
lagoon /lə'gun/ n laguna, f
laid /leid/ past part of verb **to lay. l. up,** (ill) enfermo; Naut. inactivo; (of cars, etc.) fuera de circulación
lair /leər/ n cubil, m; guarida, madriguera, f
laity /'leiiti/ n legos, m pl
lake /leik/ n lago, m; (pigment) laca, f. **small l.,** laguna, f. **l. dwelling,** vivienda palustre, f
lama /'lɑmə/ n lama, m
lamb /læm/ n cordero (-ra), m. vi parir corderos. **lamb's wool,** lana de cordero, f
lambent /'læmbənt/ a ondulante, vacilante; centelleante
lamblike /'læm,laik/ a manso como un cordero; inocente
lambskin /'læm,skɪn/ n corderina, piel de cordero, f
lame /leim/ a estropeado, lisiado; (in the feet) cojo; (of meter) que cojea, malo; (of arguments) poco convincente; frívolo, flojo. vt lisiar; hacer cojo. **to be l.,** (in the feet) (permanently) ser cojo; (temporarily) estar cojo
lamely /'leimli/ adv cojeando, con cojera; Fig. sin convicción; mal
lameness /'leimnɪs/ n cojera, f; falta de convicción, f. Fig. falta de elegancia, f
lament /lə'ment/ n lamento, m; queja, lamentación, f. vi lamentarse; quejarse. vt lamentar, deplorar, llorar
lamentable /lə'mɛntəbəl/ a lamentable, deplorable; lastimero
lamentation /,læmən'teifən/ n lamentación, f, lamento, m. **Book of Lamentations,** Libro de los Lamentos, m
lamenting /lə'mɛntɪŋ/ n lamentación, f
lamina /'læmənə/ n lámina, f
laminate /'læmə,neit/ a laminado, laminar. vt laminar
lamp /læmp/ n lámpara, f; (on vehicles, trains, ships and in the street) farol, m; luz, f; (oil) candil, m, lámpara de aceite, f. **safety-l.,** lámpara de seguridad, lámpara de los mineros, f. **street l.,** farol (de las calles), m. **l.-black,** negro de humo, m. **l.-chimney,**

tubo de una lámpara, *m.* **l. factory** or **shop,** lamparería, *f.* **l.-holder,** portalámpara, *f.* **l.-lighter,** farolero, lamparero, *m.* **l.-post,** farola, *f.* **l.-shade,** pantalla (de lámpara,) *f.* **l. stand,** pie de lámpara, *m*
lamplight /'læmp‚lait/ *n* luz de la lámpara, *f;* luz artificial, *f.* **in the l.,** a la luz de la lámpara; en luz artificial
lampoon /læm'pun/ *n* pasquinada, *f*, pasquín, *m*, *vt* pasquinar, satirizar
lampooner /læm'punər/ *n* escritor (-ra) de pasquinadas, libelista, *m*
lamprey /'læmpri/ *n* lamprea, *f*
lance /læns/ *n* lanza, *f;* (soldier) lancero, *m.* *vt* alancear; *Med.* lancinar. **l. in rest,** lanza en ristre, *f.* **l. thrust,** lanzada, *f.* **l.-corporal,** soldado de primera clase, *m*
lancer /'lænsər/ *n Mil.* lancero, *m; pl* lancers, (dance and music) lanceros, *m pl*
lancet /'lænsɪt/ *n* apostemero, *m*, lanceta, *f.* **l. arch,** arco puntiagudo, *m*
land /lænd/ *n* tierra, *f;* terreno, *m;* (country) país, *m;* (region) región, *f;* territorio, *m;* (estate) bienes raíces, *m pl*, tierras, fincas, *f pl. vt* desembarcar; echar en tierra; *(Fig.* place) poner; *Inf.* dejar plantado (con); (obtain) obtener; (a fish) sacar del agua; (a blow) dar (un golpe); (leave) dejar. *vi* desembarcar; saltar en tierra; (of a plane) aterrizar; (arrive) llegar; (fall) caer. **to l. on water** *Lat. Am.* acuatizar. **cultivated l.,** tierras cultivadas, *f pl.* **dry l.,** (not sea) tierra firme, *f.* **native l.,** patria, *f;* suelo natal, *m.* **on l.,** en tierra. **Promised Land,** la tierra prometida. **to see how the l. lies,** *Fig.* tantear el terreno. **l. of milk and honey,** jauja, *f*, paraíso, *m.* **l. agent,** procurador de fincas, *m.* **l. breeze,** brisa de tierra, *f.* **l. forces,** fuerzas terrestres, *f pl.* **l. law,** leyes agrarias, *f pl.* **l.-locked,** cercado de tierra, mediterráneo **l.-lubber,** marinero de agua dulce, *m.* **l. mine,** mina terrestre, *f.* **l. surveying,** agrimensura, *f.* **l. surveyor,** agrimensor, *m.* **l. tax,** contribución territorial, *f*
landau /'lændɔ/ *n* landó, *m*
landed /'lændɪd/ *a* hacendado. **l. gentry,** hacendados, terratenientes, *m pl.* **l. property,** bienes raíces, *m pl*
landfall /'lænd‚fɔl/ *n* derrumbamiento de tierras, *m*
landing /'lændɪŋ/ *n* desembarque, desembarco, *m;* (landing place) desembarcadero, *m; Aer.* aterrizaje, *m;* (of steps) descanso, rellano, *m*, mesa, mesilla, *f.* **forced l.,** aterrizaje forzoso, *m.* **l. certificate,** *Com.* tornaguía, *f.* **l. craft,** barcaza de desembarco, *f.* **l. field,** campo de aterrizaje, *m*, pista de vuelo, *f.* **l.-net,** salabardo, *m.* **l. party,** trozo de abordaje, *m.* **l. signal,** *Aer.* señal de aterrizaje, *f.* **l.-stage,** desembarcadero, *m;* (jetty) atracadero, *m*
landlady /'lænd‚leidi/ *n* patrona, huéspeda, *f*
landlord /'lænd‚lɔrd/ *n* (of houses, land) propietario, *m;* hotelero, patrón, *m*
landmark /'lænd‚mɑrk/ *n* (of a hill or mountain) punto destacado, *m;* lugar conocido, *m;* característica, *f; Fig.* monumento, *m*
landmass /'lænd‚mæs/ *n* unidad territorial, *f*
landowner /'lænd‚ounər/ *n* hacendado, terrateniente, *m*
landscape /'lænd‚skeip/ *n* paisaje, *m;* perspectiva, *f.* **l. gardener,** arquitecto de jardines, *m.* **l. painter,** paisajista, *mf*
landslide /'lænd‚slaid/ *n* desprendimiento de tierras, *m; Fig.* cambio brusco de la opinión pública, *m*
landward /'lændwərd/ *adv* hacia tierra
lane /lein/ *n* vereda, senda, *f;* (of traffic) carril, *m, Argentina, Spain,* línea, *f*
language /'læŋgwɪdʒ/ *n* lenguaje, *m;* lengua, *f,* idioma, *m.* **modern l.,** lengua viva, *f.* **strong l.,** palabras mayores, *f pl*
languid /'læŋgwɪd/ *a* lánguido
languidness /'læŋgwɪdnɪs/ *n* languidez, *f*
languish /'læŋgwɪʃ/ *vi* languidecer
languishing /'læŋgwɪʃɪŋ/ *a* lánguido; amoroso, sentimental
languishingly /'læŋgwɪʃɪŋli/ *adv* lánguidamente; amorosamente
languor /'læŋgər/ *n* languidez, *f*

languorous /'læŋgərəs/ *a* lánguido
languorously /'læŋgərəsli/ *adv* con langor
lank /læŋk/ *a* flaco, descarnado, alto y delgado; (of hair) lacio
lankiness /'læŋkinɪs/ *n* flacura, *f*
lanky /'læŋki/ *a* larguirucho, descarnado, *Lat. Am.* largucho
lanolin /'lænlɪn/ *n* lanolina, *f*
lantern /'læntərn/ *n* linterna, *f;* (Naut. and of a lighthouse) farol, *m; Archit.* linterna, *f;* (small) farolillo, *m.* **dark l.,** linterna sorda, *f.* **magic l.,** linterna mágica, *f.* **l.-jawed,** carilargo. **l. maker,** farolero, *m.* **l. slide,** diapositiva, *f*
lap /læp/ *n* regazo, *m;* falda, *f;* (knees) rodillas, *f pl;* (lick) lamedura, *f;* (of water) murmurio, susurro, *m;* (in a race) vuelta, *f;* (stage) etapa, *f. vt* (wrap) envolver; (cover) cubrir; (fold) plegar; (lick) lamer; (swallow) tragar. *vi* (overlap) traslaparse; estar replegado; (lick) lamer; (of water) murmurar, susurrar, besar. **l.-dog,** perro de faldas, perro faldero, *m*
lapel /lə'pɛl/ *n* solapa, *f*
lapidary /'læpɪ‚dɛri/ *a* lapidario
lapidate /'læpɪ‚deit/ *vt* lapidar
lapis lazuli /'læp'ɪs læzuli/ *n* lapislázuli, *m*
Laplander /'læp‚lændər/ *n* lapón (-ona)
lapping /'læpɪŋ/ *n* (licking) lamedura, *f;* (of water) murmurio, susurro, chapaleteo, *m*
lapse /læps/ *n* lapso, *m;* (fault) desliz, *m*, falta, *f;* (of time) transcurso, intervalo, *m;* (fall) caída, *f; (Law.* termination) caducidad, *f.* **lapse (into),** *vi* caer (en), recaer (en), reincidir (en); volver a, caer de nuevo (en); (*Law.* cease) caducar; (*Law.* pass to) pasar (a); dejar de existir, desaparecer. **after the l. of three days,** después de tres días, al cabo de tres días. **with the l. of years,** en el transcurso de los años
laptop /'læp‚tɒp/ *n* laptop, *m*, ordenador portátil, *m*
larceny /'lɑrsəni/ *n* latrocinio, *m*
lard /lɑrd/ *n* manteca, *f;* lardo, *m. vt Cul.* lardear, mechar; *Fig.* sembrar (con), adornar (con)
larder /'lɑrdər/ *n* despensa, *f*
large /lɑrdʒ/ *a* grande; grueso; amplio; vasto, extenso; (wide) ancho; considerable; (in number) numeroso; (main, chief) principal; liberal; magnánimo. **at l.,** en libertad, suelto. **on the l. side,** algo grande. **l.-headed,** cabezudo. **l.-hearted,** que tiene un gran corazón, magnánimo. **l. mouth,** boca grande, boca rasgada, *f.* **l.-nosed,** narigudo. **l. scale,** en gran escala. **l.-sized,** de gran tamaño. **l.-toothed,** dentudo, que tiene dientes grandes. **l. type,** letras grandes, *f pl*
largely /'lɑrdʒli/ *adv* grandemente; en gran manera; en su mayor parte, considerablemente; muy; ampliamente; liberalmente; extensamente
largeness /'lɑrdʒnɪs/ *n* gran tamaño, *m;* (of persons) gran talle, *m;* amplitud, *f;* vastedad, extensión, *f;* (width) anchura, *f;* liberalidad, *f;* (generosity) magnanimidad, *f;* grandeza de ánimo, *f*
larger /'lɑrdʒər/ *a comp* más grande, etc. See **large.** **to grow l.,** crecer, aumentarse. **to make l.,** hacer más grande; aumentar
largesse /lɑr'dʒɛs/ *n* liberalidad, prodigalidad, *f*
largo /'lɑrgou/ *n* and *adv Mus.* largo, *m*
lariat /'læriət/ *n* lazo, *m*
lark /lɑrk/ *n* alondra, *f;* (spree) juerga, *f;* (joke) risa, *f.* **to rise with the l.,** levantarse con las gallinas
larva /'lɑrvə/ *n* larva, *f*
laryngeal /lə'rɪndʒiəl/ *a* laríngeo
laryngitis /‚lærən'dʒaitɪs/ *n* laringitis, *f*
larynx /'lærɪŋks/ *n* laringe, *f*
lascivious /lə'sɪviəs/ *a* lascivo, lujurioso
lasciviousness /lə'sɪviəsnɪs/ *n* lujuria, lascivia, *f*
lash /læʃ/ *n* (thong) tralla, *f;* (whip) látigo, *m;* (blow) latigazo, *m;* azote, *m;* (of the eye) pestaña, *f. vt* dar latigazos (a); azotar; (of waves) romper contra; (of hail, rain) azotar; (excite) provocar; (the tail) agitar (la cola); (scold) fustigar; (fasten) sujetar, atar; *Naut.* trincar. **to l. out,** (of horses, etc.) dar coces; (in words) prorrumpir (en)
lashing /'læʃɪŋ/ *n* (whipping) azotamiento, *m;* (tying) ligadura, atadura, *f;* amarradura, *f*
lass /læs/ *n* muchacha, chica, mozuela, *f;* zagala, *f;* niña, *f*

lassitude /'læsɪ‚tud/ *n* lasitud, *f*
lasso /'læsou/ *n* lazo, *m*, mangana, *Argentina* armada, *f*, *vt* lazar, manganear, *Lat. Am.* lacear
last /læst/ *vi* durar; subsistir, conservarse; continuar
last /læst/ *a* último; (with month, week, etc.) pasado; (supreme) extremo, (el) mayor. *adv* al fin; finalmente; por último; después de todos; por última vez; la última vez. *n* el, *m*, (*f*, la) último (-ma); los últimos, *m pl*, (*f pl*, las últimas); (end) fin, *m*; (for shoes) horma, *f*. **at l.**, en fin; por fin, a la postre. **at the l. moment,** a última hora. **I have not been there these l. five years,** Hace cinco años que no voy allá. **John spoke l.,** Juan habló el último. **She came at l.,** Por fin llegó. **to the l.,** hasta el fin. **l. but one,** penúltimo (-ma). **l. hope,** última esperanza, *f*; último recurso, *m*. **l. kick,** *Inf.* último suspiro, *m*. **l. night,** anoche. **l. week,** la semana pasada
lasting /'læstɪŋ/ *a* permanente, perdurable; duradero; constante; (of colours) sólido
lastly /'læstli/ *adv* en conclusión, por fin, finalmente, por último
latch /lætʃ/ *n* pestillo, *m*, *vt* cerrar con pestillo. **l.-key,** llave de la puerta, *f*; (Yale) llavín, *m*
late /leit/ *a* tarde; tardío; (advanced) avanzado; (last) último; reciente; (dead) difunto; (former) antiguo, ex…; (new) nuevo. *adv* tarde. **Better l. than never,** Más vale tarde que nunca. **Helen arrived l.,** Elena llegó tarde. **The train arrived five minutes l.,** El tren llegó con cinco minutos de retraso. **He keeps l. hours,** Se acuesta muy tarde, Se acuesta a las altas horas de la noche (*Inf.* a las tantas). **of l.,** últimamente. **to grow l.,** hacerse tarde. **l.-eighteenth-century poetry,** la poesía de fines del siglo diez y ocho; llorado, malogrado (e.g. *the l. Mrs. Smith,* la llorada Sra. Smith, la malograda Sra. Smith)
lateen /læ'tin/ *a* latino. **l. sail,** vela latina, *f*
lately /'leitli/ *adv* recientemente; últimamente, hace poco
latency /'leitṇsi/ *n* estado latente, *m*
lateness /'leitnɪs/ *n* lo tarde; lo avanzado; retraso, *m*. **the l. of the hour,** la hora avanzada
latent /'leitṇt/ *a* latente
later /'leitər/ *a* más tarde; posterior; más reciente. *adv* más tarde; (afterwards) luego, después; posteriormente. **sooner or l.,** tarde o temprano. **l. on,** más tarde
lateral /'lætərəl/ *a* lateral, ladero
late registration *n* matrícula tardía, *f*
latest /'leitɪst/ *a* and *adv sup* último; más reciente, etc. See **late. at the l.,** a lo más tarde, a más tardar. **l. fashion,** última moda, *f*. **l. news,** últimas noticias, *f pl*; novedad, *f*
latex /'leitɛks/ *n* (*Bot. Chem.*) látex, *m*
lath /læθ/ *n* listón, *m*. **to be as thin as a l.,** no tener más que el pellejo, estar en los huesos
lathe /leiθ/ *n* torno, *m*
lather /'læðər/ *n* espuma de jabón, *f*, jabonaduras, *f pl*; (of sweat) espuma, *f*. *vt* enjabonar; *Inf.* zurrar. *vi* hacer espuma
lathering /'læðərɪŋ/ *n* jabonadura, *f*; *Inf.* tunda, zurra, *f*
Latin /'lætṇ/ *n* latín, *m*, *a* latino. **Low L.,** bajo latín, *m*. **L.-American,** *a* latinoamericano. *n* latinoamericano (-na)
Latin America Latinoamérica
Latinism /'lætṇ‚ɪzəm/ *n* latinismo, *m*
Latinist /'lætṇɪst/ *n* latinista, *mf*
latitude /'lætɪ‚tud/ *n* latitud, *f*; libertad, *f*
latitudinal /‚lætɪ'tudṇl/ *a* latitudinal
latrine /lə'trin/ *n* letrina, *f*
latter /'lætər/ *a* más reciente; último, posterior; moderno. **the l.,** éste, *m*; ésta, *f*; esto, *neut*; éstos, *m pl*; éstas, *f pl*. **the l. half,** la segunda mitad. **toward the l. end of the year,** hacia fines del año. **L.-Day Saint,** santo de los últimos días *m*, santa de los últimos días, *f*
latterly /'lætərli/ *adv* recientemente, últimamente; en los últimos tiempos; hacia el fin
lattice /'lætɪs/ *n* rejilla, *f*; celosía, reja, *f*. *vt* poner celosía (a); entrelazar. **l.-work,** enrejado, *m*
latticed /'lætɪst/ *a* (of windows, etc.) con reja
Latvia /'lætviə/ Latvia, Letonia, *f*

Latvian /'lætviən/ *a* latvio. *n* latvio (-ia)
laud /lɔd/ *n* alabanza, *f*; *pl.* **lauds,** *Eccl.* laudes, *f pl.* *vt* alabar, elogiar
laudability /‚lɔdə'bɪlɪti/ *n* mérito, *m*, lo meritorio
laudable /'lɔdəbəl/ *a* loable, meritorio
laudably /'lɔdəbli/ *adv* laudablemente
laudatory /'lɔdə‚tɔri/ *a* laudatorio
laugh /læf/ *n* risa, *f*; carcajada, *f*. *vi* reír; (smile) sonreír; reírse. **loud l.,** risa estrepitosa, *f*. **to l. in a person's face,** reírsele a uno en las barbas. **to l. loudly,** reírse a carcajadas. **to l. to oneself,** reírse interiormente. **to l. to scorn,** poner en ridículo. **to l. at,** reírse de; burlarse de, ridiculizar
laughable /'læfəbəl/ *a* risible, irrisible, ridículo, absurdo
laughing /'læfɪŋ/ *a* risueño, alegre; (absurd) risible, *n* risa, *f*. **to burst out l.,** reírse a carcajadas. **l.-gas,** gas hilarante, *m*. **l.-stock,** hazmerreír, *m*
laughingly /'læfɪŋli/ *adv* riendo
laughter /'læftər/ *n* risa, *f*; (in a report) risas, *f pl*. **burst of l.,** carcajada, *f*. **to burst into l.,** soltar el trapo, reírse a carcajadas, desternillarse de risa
launch /lɔntʃ/ *n* botadura (de un buque), *f*; lancha, *f*; bote, *m*; canoa, *f*. *vt* (throw) lanzar; (a blow) asestar; (a vessel) botar, echar al agua; (begin) iniciar, dar principio a; (make) hacer. **to l. an offensive,** *Mil.* emprender una ofensiva. **to l. into,** arrojarse en; entregarse a. **motor l.,** canoa automóvil, *f*. **steam l.,** bote de vapor, *m*
launching /'lɔntʃɪŋ/ *n* botadura (de un buque), *f*; (throwing) lanzamiento, *m*; (beginning) iniciación, *f*; inauguración, *f*; (of a loan, etc.) emisión, *f*. **l. site,** rampa, *f*
launder /'lɔndər/ *vt* lavar y planchar (ropa)
laundress /'lɔndrɪs/ *n* lavandera, *f*
laundromat /'lɔndrə‚mæt/ *n* lavandería automática, *f*
laundry /'lɔndri/ *n* lavadero, *m*, lavandería, *f*; (washing) colada, *f*; *Inf.* ropa lavada or ropa para lavar, *f*. **l.-man,** lavandero, *m*
laureate /'lɔriit/ *a* laureado. *n* poeta laureado, *m*
laurel /'lɔrəl/ *n* laurel, cerezo, *m*, *a* láureo. **to crown with l.,** laurear. **l. wreath,** laureola, *f*
Lausanne /lou'zæn/ Lausana, Losana, *f*
lava /'lavə/ *n* lava, *f*
lavabo /lə'veibou/ *n* lavabo, *m*; *Eccl.* lavatorio, *m*
lavatory /'lævə‚tɔri/ *n* lavabo, *m*; retrete, excusado, *m*
lavender /'lævəndər/ *n* espliego, *m*, lavanda, *f*. **l.-water,** agua de lavanda, *f*
lavish /'lævɪʃ/ *a* pródigo; profuso, abundante; (spender) *Mexico* disparador. *vt* prodigar
lavishly /'lævɪʃli/ *adv* pródigamente; en profusión
lavishness /'lævɪʃnɪs/ *n* prodigalidad, *f*; profusión, abundancia, *f*
law /lɔ/ *n* ley, *f*; derecho, *m*; jurisprudencia, *f*; código de leyes, *m*. **according to law,** según derecho. **canon law,** derecho civil, *m*. **constitutional law,** derecho político, *m*. **criminal law,** derecho penal, *m*. **in law,** por derecho, de acuerdo con la ley; desde el punto de vista legal. **international law,** derecho internacional, *m*. **maritime law,** código marítimo, *m*. **statutary law,** ley suntuaria, *f*. **to go to law,** pleitear (sobre). **to sue at law,** pedir en juicio, poner pleito. **to take the law into one's own hands,** tomar la ley por su propia mano. **law-abiding,** observante de la ley; amigo del orden. **law-breaker,** transgresor (-ra). **law court,** tribunal de justicia, *m*; palacio de justicia, *m*. **law of nature,** ley natural, *f*. **law report,** revista de tribunales, *f*. **law school,** escuela de derecho, *f*. **law student,** estudiante de derecho, *mf*
lawful /'lɔfəl/ *a* legal; legal; lícito; válido
lawfully /'lɔfəli/ *adv* legalmente, legítimamente, lícitamente
lawfulness /'lɔfəlnɪs/ *n* legalidad, *f*; legitimidad, *f*
lawgiver /'lɔ‚gɪvər/ *n* legislador (-ra)
lawless /'lɔlɪs/ *a* ilegal; desordenado; ingobernable, rebelde
lawlessness /'lɔlɪsnɪs/ *n* ilegalidad, *f*; desorden, *m*; rebeldía, *f*
lawn /lɔn/ *n* césped, prado, *m*; (cloth) estopilla, *f*. **l.-**

mower, cortacésped *m*, tundidora de césped, *f*, máquina segadora del césped, *f*. **l.-tennis,** tenis (en pista de hierba), *m*

lawsuit /'lɔˌsut/ *n* pleito, litigio, *m*, causa, acción, *f*, *Lat. Am.* demanda, *f*

lawyer /'lɔyər/ *n* abogado (-da). **lawyer's office** or **practice,** bufete, *m*

lax /læks/ *a* laxo; indisciplinado; vago; descuidado

laxative /'læksətɪv/ *n* laxante, *m*, purga, *f*, *a* laxativo

laxity /'læksɪti/ *n* laxitud, *f*; descuido, *m*; indiferencia, *f*

lay /lei/ *a* laico, seglar, lego; profano. *n* poema, *m*, trova, *f*; romance, *m*; (song) canción, *f*. **the lay of the land,** la configuración del terreno. **lay brother,** confeso, monigote, *m*. **lay figure,** maniquí, *m*. **lay sister,** (hermana) lega, *f*

lay /lei/ *vt* and *vi* poner; colocar; dejar; (strike) tumbar; (demolish) derribar; (the dust) matar; (pipes, etc.) instalar; (hands on) asentar (la mano en); (deposit) depositar; (beat down corn, etc.) encamar, abatir; (eggs, keel) poner; (the table) cubrir, poner; (stretch) extender(se); (bury) depositar en el sepulcro; (a bet) hacer; (wager) apostar; (an accusation) acusar; (the wind, etc.) sosegar, amainar; (a ghost) exorcizar; (impute) atribuir, imputar; (impose) imponer; (prepare) prepara; (make) hacer; (open) abrir; (blame, etc.) echar; (claim) reclamar; (reveal) revelar. **Don't lay the blame on me!** ¡No me eches la culpa! **We laid our plans,** Hicimos nuestros planes; Hicimos nuestros preparativos. **to lay siege to,** asediar. **to lay the colors on too thick,** *Fig.* recargar las tintas. **to lay the foundations,** abrir los cimientos; *Fig.* crear, establecer; fundar. **to lay about one,** dar garrotazos de ciego. **to lay aside,** poner a un lado; arrinconar; (save) ahorrar; (cast away) desechar; abandonar; (reserve) reservar; (a person) apartar de sí; (incapacitate) incapacitar. **lay something at somebody's feet,** embutir algo en el guante de fulano. **to lay before,** mostrar; presentar; poner a la vista; revelar. **to lay by,** See **to lay aside. to lay down,** acostar; depositar; (a burden) posar; (arms) rendir; (one's life); (give up) renunciar (a); (sketch out) trazar, dibujar; (plan) proyectar; (keep) guardar; (as a principle) establecer, sentar; (the law) dictar. **to lay oneself down,** echarse, tumbarse. **to lay in,** (a stock) proveerse de, hacer provisión de; (hoard) ahorrar; (buy) compara. **to lay off,** *Naut.* virar de bordo; *Inf.* quitarse de encima. **to lay on,** *vt* colocar sobre; (thrash) pegar; (blows) descargar; (paint, etc.) dar; (water, etc.) instalar; (impose) imponer; (exaggerate) exagerar. *vi* atacar. **to lay open,** abrir; descubrir, revelar; manifestar; exponer. **to lay oneself open to attack,** exponerse a ser atacado. **to lay out,** poner; arreglar; (the dead) amortajar; (one's money) invertir, emplear; (at interest) poner a rédito; (plan) planear; (knock down) derribar. **to lay oneself out to,** esforzarse a; tomarse la molestia de. **to lay over,** cubrir; sobreponer; extender sobre. **to lay to,** *vi Naut.* estar a la capa. **to lay up,** guardar, acumular, atesorar; poner a un lado; (a ship) desarmar; (a car) poner fuera de circulación; (a person) obligar a guardar cama, incapacitar

layabout /'leiəˌbaut/ *n* = **lazybones**

layer /'leiər/ *n* capa, *f*; *Geol.* estrato, *m*; *Mineral.* manto, *m*; (bird) gallina (pata, etc.) ponedera, *f*; (one who bets) apostador (-ra); *Agr.* acodo, *m*. *vt* (of plants) acodar

laying /'leiɪŋ/ *n* colocación, *f*; puesta, *f*; (of an egg) postura, *f*. **l. down,** depósito, *m*; conservación, *f*; (explanation) exposición, *f*. **l. on of hands,** imposición de manos, *f*. **l. out,** tendedura, *f*; (of money) empleo, *m*; inversión, *f*; (arrangement) arreglo, *m*

layman /'leimən/ *n* seglar, *mf*; profano (-na)

layout /'leiˌaut/ *n* plan, *m*; diagramación, disposición, *f*; distribución, *f*; esquema, *m*

laze /leiz/ *vi* holgazanear, gandulear, no hacer nada; encontrarse a sus anchas

lazily /'leizəli/ *adv* perezosamente; indolentemente; lentamente

laziness /'leizinɪs/ *n* pereza, holgazanería, *f*; indolencia, *f*; lentitud, *f*

lazy /'leizi/ *a* perezoso, holgazán; indolente. **l.bones,** gandul (-la), *Lat. Am.* aplanacalles, *Mexico* flojo, *mf*

lead /lɛd/ *n* (metal) plomo, *m*; (in a pencil) mina, *f*; (plummet) sonda, *f*; *Print.* interlínea, *f*; *pl* **leads,** (roofs) tejados, *m pl*. *vt* emplomar; guarnecer con plomo; *Print.* interlinear. **black-l.,** grafito, *m*. **deep-sea l.,** *Naut.* escandallo, *m*. **white l.,** albayalde, *m*. **to heave the l.,** echar el escandallo, sondar. **l.-colored,** de color de plomo, plomizo. **l.-footed,** pesado; lento. **l. mine,** mina de plomo, *f*. **l. poisoning,** saturnismo, *m*

lead /lid/ *n* delantera, *f*; primer lugar, *m*; dirección, *f*, mando, *m*; (suggestion) indicación, *f*; (influence) influencia, *f*; (dog's) traílla, *f*; *Theat.* protagonista, *mf*; *Theat.* papel principal, *m*; (at cards) mano, *f*

lead /lid/ *vt* and *vi* (conduct) conducir, llevar; guiar; (induce) mover, persuadir, inducir; inclinar; (cause) hacer, causar; (captain) capitanear, encabezar; dirigir; (channel) encauzar; (with life) llevar; (give) dar; (head) ir a la cabeza de; *Mil.* mandar; (at cards) salir; (at games) jugar en primer lugar; tomar la delantera; tomar la iniciativa. **to l. one to think,** hacer pensar. **to l. the way,** mostrar el camino; ir adelante. **to l. along,** llevar (por la mano, etc.), conducir; conducir por; guiar. **to l. astray,** descarriar; desviar (de), seducir (de). **to l. away,** conducir (a otra parte); llevarse (a). **to l. back,** conducir de nuevo; hacer volver. **This path leads back to the village,** Por esta senda se vuelve al pueblo. **to l. in, into,** conducir a (or ante); introducir en, hacer entrar en; invitar a entrar en; (of rooms) comunicarse con; (sin, etc.) inducir a. **to l. off,** *vi* ir adelante; (begin) empezar; (of rooms) comunicarse con. *vt* hacer marcharse, llevarse (a). **to l. on,** *vt* conducir; guiar; hacer pensar en; (make talk) dar cuerda (a). *vi* ir a la cabeza; tomar la delantera. **to l. out,** conducir afuera; (to dance) sacar. **to l. to,** conducir a; desembocar en, salir a; (cause) dar lugar a, causar; (make) hacer; (incline) inclinar. **This street leads to the square,** Por esta calle se va a la plaza, Esta calle conduce a la plaza. **to l. up to,** conducir a; (in conversation, etc.) preparar el terreno a; preparar; tener lugar antes de, ocurrir antes de

leaden /'lɛdn/ *a* hecho de plomo, plúmbeo; (of skies, etc.) plomizo, de color de plomo, aplomado

leader /'lidər/ *n* conductor (-ra); guía, *mf*; jefe (-fa); general, *m*; director (-ra); (in a journal) artículo de fondo, *m*; (of an orchestra) primer violín, *m*. **follow-the-l.,** (game) juego de seguir la fila, *m*

leadership /'lidərˌʃɪp/ *n* dirección, *f*; jefatura, *f*; *Mil.* mando, *m*

lead-in /'lid ˌɪn/ *a* Radio. de entrada. *n* Radio. conductor de entrada, *m*

leading /'lɛdɪŋ/ *n* (leadwork) emplomadura, *f*

leading /'lidɪŋ/ *n* (guidance) dirección, *f*. *a* principal; primero; importante; eminente. **l. article,** artículo de fondo, *m*; editorial, *m*. **l. card,** primer naipe, *m*. **l. counsel,** abogado (-da) principal, *m*. **l. lady,** *Theat.* dama primera, primera actriz, *f*; (cinema) estrella (de la pantalla), *f*. **l. man,** *Theat.* primer galán, *m*. **l. question,** pregunta que sugiere la respuesta, *f*; cuestión importante, *f*. **l. strings,** andadores, *m pl*; *Fig.* tutelaje, *m*

leaf /lif/ *n* (*Bot.* and of a page, door, window, table, screen, etc.) hoja, *f*; (petal) pétalo, *m*, *v* echar hojas. **gold l.,** pan de oro, *m*. **to turn over a new l.,** volver la hoja, hacer libro nuevo, hacer vida nueva. **to turn over the leaves of a book,** hojear (un libro). **l.-bud,** yema, *f*. **l.-mold,** abono verde, *m*. **l. tobacco,** tabaco en hoja, *m*

leafiness /'lifinɪs/ *n* frondosidad, *f*

leafless /'liflɪs/ *a* sin hojas

leaflet /'liflɪt/ *n* hojuela, *f*; (pamphlet) folleto, *m*

leafy /'lifi/ *a* frondoso

league /lig/ *n* (measure) legua, *f*; liga, federación, sociedad, *f*; (football) liga, *f*. *vt* aliar; asociar. *vi* aliarse; asociarse, confederarse. **to be in l.,** *Inf.* estar de manga. **L. of Nations,** Sociedad de las Naciones, *f*. **the Ivy L.,** las universidades prestigiosas, *f pl*

leak /lik/ *n* (hole) agujero, *m*, grieta, *f*; *Naut.* vía de agua, *f*; (of gas, liquids, etc.) escape, *m*; (in a roof, etc.) gotera, *f*; *Elec.* resistencia de escape, *f*. *vi Naut.* hacer agua; (gas, liquids, etc.) escaparse, salirse; (drip) gotear. **to l. out,** (of news, etc.) trascender, saberse. **to spring a l.,** aparecer una vía de agua, hacer agua

leakage /'likɪdʒ/ *n* (of gas, liquids) escape, *m*, fuga, *f*; derrame, *m*; pérdida, *f*; (of information) revelación, *f*
leaky /'liki/ *a Naut.* que hace agua; agujereado; poroso; que tiene goteras
lean /lin/ *a* magro, seco, enjuto, delgado; (of meat) magro; *Fig.* pobre, estéril. *n* carne magra, *f*, magro, *m*. **to grow l.,** enflaquecer
lean /lin/ *vi* inclinarse; apoyarse (en). *vt* apoyar (en); dejar arrimado (en). **to l. out of the window,** asomarse a la ventana. **to l. against,** apoyarse en, recostarse en (or contra). **to l. back,** echarse hacia atrás; recostarse. **to l. over,** inclinarse. **to l. upon,** apoyarse en; descansar sobre
leaning /'linɪŋ/ *n* inclinación, tendencia, *f*; predilección, afición, *f*
leanness /'linnɪs/ *n* magrura, flaqueza, *f*; (of meat) magrez, *f*; *Fig.* pobreza, *f*
leap /lip/ *n* salto, *m*; brinco, *m*; (caper) zapateta, *f*; *Fig.* salto, *m*. *vi* saltar, dar un salto; brincar. *vt* saltar; hacer saltar. **at one l.,** en un salto. **by leaps and bounds,** en saltos. **My heart leaped,** Mi corazón dio un salto. **to l. to the conclusion that...,** saltar a la conclusión de que... **to l. to the eye,** saltar a la vista. **l. frog,** salto, salto de la muerte, *m*, pídola *f*. **l. year,** año bisiesto, *m*, salta cabrillas, *f pl*
leaping /'lipɪŋ/ *a* saltador. *n* saltos, *m pl*
learn /lɜrn/ *vt* and *vi* aprender; instruirse; enterarse de. **to l. by heart,** aprender de memoria. **to l. from a reliable source,** saber de buena tinta. **to l. from experience,** aprender por experiencia
learned /'lɜrnɪd/ *a* sabio, docto; erudito; (of professions) liberal; versado (en), entendido (en). **a l. society,** una sociedad erudita
learner /'lɜrnər/ *n* aprendedor (-ra)
learning /'lɜrnɪŋ/ *n* saber, *m*; conocimientos, *m pl*; erudición, *f*; estudio, *m*; (literature) literatura, *f*
lease /lis/ *n* arrendamiento, arriendo, *m*; contrato de arrendamiento, *m*. *vt* dar en arriendo, arrendar. **on l.,** en arriendo. **to take a new l. on life,** recobrar su vigor. **Lend L. Act,** ley de préstamo y arriendo, *f*
leaseholder /'lis,houldər/ *n* concesionario, *m*; arrendatario (-ia)
leash /liʃ/ *n* (of a dog) traílla, *f*
least /list/ *a sup little,* mínimo; el (la, etc.) menor; más pequeño. *adv* menos. *n* lo menos. **at l.,** siquiera; por lo menos, al menos. **at the very l.,** a lo menos. **not in the l.,** de ninguna manera, nada. **to say the l. of,** sin exagerar, para no decir más
leather /'lɛðər/ *n* cuero, *m*; piel, *f*, a de cuero; de piel. **patent l.,** charol, *m*. **Spanish l.,** cordobán, *m*. **tanned l.,** curtido, *m*. **l. apron,** mandil, *m*. **l. bag,** saco de cuero, *m*. **l. bottle,** bota, *f*. **l. breeches,** pantalón de montar, *m*. **l. jerkin,** coleto, *m*. **l. shield,** adarga, *f*. **l. strap,** correa, *f*. **l. trade,** comercio en cueros, *m*
leatherette /,lɛðə'rɛt/ *n* cartón cuero, *m*
leathery /'lɛðəri/ *a* de cuero; (of the skin) curtido por la intemperie; (tough) correoso
leave /liv/ *n* (permission) permiso, *m*; (*Mil.* etc.) licencia, *f*; (farewell) despedida, *f*. *vt* and *vi* dejar; abandonar; salir (de), quitar, marcharse (de), partir. *Am.* egresar (de...); (as surety) empeñar; (by will) legar, mandar; (an employment) darse de baja (de), dejar; (give into the keeping of) entregar; (bid farewell) despedirse (de). **By your l.,** Con permiso de Vd. (Vds.). Con la venia de Vd. (Vds.) **on l.,** de permiso. **l.-taking,** despedidas, *f pl*. **to be left,** quedar. **to be left over,** quedar; sobrar. **Two from four leaves two,** De cuatro a dos van dos. **to take French l.,** despedirse a la inglesa. **to take l. of,** despedirse de. **to take one's l.,** marcharse; despedirse. **to l. a deep impression,** *Fig.* impresionar mucho; quedar grabado (en). **to l. undone,** dejar de hacer, no hacer; dejar sin terminar. **to l. about,** *vt* dejar por todas partes. *vi* (of time) marcharse a eso de... **to l. ajar,** entreabrir, (when opening), entrecerrar (when closing), entornar. **to l. alone,** dejar a solas; dejar en paz; no molestar,

no meterse con. **to l. aside,** omitir; prescindir de; olvidar. **to l. behind,** dejar atrás; olvidar. **l. much to be desired,** tener mucho que desear. **to l. off,** *vt* dejar de; abandonar; (garments) no ponerse, quitarse. *vi* terminar. **to l. out,** dejar fuera; dejar a un lado, descontar; omitir; pasar por; (be silent about) callar; suprimir. **to l. to,** dejar para; dejar hacer
leaven /'lɛvən/ *n* levadura, *f*, fermento, *m*, *vt* fermentar; (*Fig.* permeate) penetrar (en), infiltrar en, imbuir; (a speech) salpimentar (con)
leaving /'livɪŋ/ *n* salida, partida, marcha, *f*, *Lat. Am.* egreso, *m*; *pl* **leavings,** sobras, *f pl*; desechos, *m pl*
lecherous /'lɛtʃərəs/ *a* lascivo, lujurioso
lechery /'lɛtʃəri/ *n* lascivia, lujuria, *f*
lectern /'lɛktərn/ *n* atril, *m*; (in a church) facistol, *m*
lecture /'lɛktʃər/ *n* conferencia, *f*; (in a university) lección, clase, *f*; discurso, *m*; (*Inf.* scolding) sermoneo, *m*. *vi* dar una conferencia; (in a university) dar clase. *vt* (*Inf.* scold) predicar, sermonear. **l. room,** sala de conferencias, *f*; (in a university) sala de clase, aula, *f*
lecturer /'lɛktʃərər/ *n* conferenciante, *Lat. Am.* conferencista, *mf*; (university rank) auxiliar, *m*; (professor) catedrático (-ca), profesor (-ra)
lectureship /'lɛktʃər,ʃɪp/ *n* auxiliaría, *f*
ledge /lɛdʒ/ *n* borde, *m*; capa, *f*; (of a window) alféizar, *m*; (shelf) anaquel, *m*
ledger /'lɛdʒər/ *n* libro mayor, *m*
leech /litʃ/ *n* sanguijuela, *f*
leek /lik/ *n* puerro, *m*
leer /lɪər/ *vi* mirar de soslayo; guiñar el ojo; mirar con los ojos llenos de deseo. *n* mirada de soslayo, *f*; mirada de lascivia, *f*
lees /liz/ *n pl* heces, *f pl*; sedimento, *m*
leeward /'liwərd/ *n* sotavento, *m*. **on the l. side,** a sotavento
leeway /'li,wei/ *n Naut.* deriva, *f*; *Fig.* amplitud, margen de holgura, márgenes de maniobra, *f pl.* **to give someone l.,** darle espacio a alguien
left /lɛft/ *past part* dejado, etc. See **leave.** *a* izquierda. *adv* a la izquierda; hacia la izquierda. *n* izquierda, *f*. **on the l.,** a la izquierda, *Lat. Am., Polit.* las izquierdas. **the Left Bank (of Paris)** la Ribera izquierda, la Orilla izquierda **L. face!** ¡Izquierda! **l.-hand,** mano izquierda, *f*; izquierda, *f*. **l.-hand drive,** conducción a la izquierda, *f*. **l.-handed,** zurdo. **l. luggage office,** consigna, *f*. **l.-overs,** sobras, *f pl*, desperdicios, *m pl*
leg /lɛg/ *n* pierna, *f*; (of animals, birds, furniture) pata, *f*; (of a triangle) cateto, *m*; (of a pair of compasses, trousers, lamb, veal) pierna, *f*; (of boots, stockings) caña, *f*; (of pork) pernil, *m*; (support) pie, *m*; (stage) etapa, *f*. **to be on one's last legs,** estar en las últimas; estar acabándose; estar sin recursos. **to pull a person's leg,** tomar el pelo (a). **leg-pull,** tomadura de pelo, *f*. **leg-of-mutton sleeve,** manga de pernil, *f*
legacy /'lɛgəsi/ *n* legado, *m*, manda, *f*; herencia, *f*
legal /'ligəl/ *a* legal; de derecho; jurídico; (lawful, permissible) legítimo, lícito; (of a lawyer) de abogado. **l. expenses,** litisexpensas, *f pl*. **l. inquiry,** investigación jurídica, *f*
legalistics /,ligə'lɪstɪks/ *n. Lat. Am.* abogaderas, abogaderías, *f pl*
legality /li'gælɪti/ *n* legalidad, *f*
legalization /,ligələ'zeiʃən/ *n* legalización, *f*
legalize /'ligə,laiz/ *vt* legalizar; autorizar, legitimar
legally /'ligəli/ *adv* según la ley; según derecho; legalmente
legal tender *n* moneda de curso liberatorio, *f*
legate /'lɛgɪt/ *n* legado, *m*; **papal l.,** legado papal, *m*
legatee /,lɛgə'ti/ *n* legatario (-ia), *Lat. Am.* asignatario (-ia)
legation /lɪ'geiʃən/ *n* legación, *f*
legend /'lɛdʒənd/ *n* leyenda, *f*
legendary /'lɛdʒənderi/ *a* legendario
legerdemain /,lɛdʒərdə'mein/ *n* juegos de manos, *m pl*
legged /lɛgɪd/ *a* con piernas; de piernas...; de patas... **a three-l. stool,** un taburete de tres patas. **long l.,** zancudo
leggings /'lɛgɪŋz/ *n pl* polainas, *f pl*

legibility /ˌlɛdʒə'bɪlɪti/ n legibilidad, f
legible /'lɛdʒəbəl/ a legible
legion /'lidʒən/ n legión, f. **L.** of Honor, Legión de Honor, f
legionary /'lidʒə,nɛri/ a legionario. n legionario, m
legislate /'lɛdʒɪs,leit/ vt legislar
legislation /ˌlɛdʒɪs'leifən/ n legislación, f
legislative /'lɛdʒɪs,leitɪv/ a legislativo, legislador
legislator /'lɛdʒɪs,leitər/ n legislador (-ra)
legislature /'lɛdʒɪs,leitʃər/ n legislatura, f
legitimacy /lɪ'dʒɪtəməsi/ n legitimidad, f; justicia, f
legitimate /lɪ'dʒɪtəmɪt/ a legítimo; justo
legitimation /lɪ,dʒɪtə'meifən/ n legitimación, f
leisure /'liʒər/ n ocio, m, desocupación, f; tiempo libre, m. **at one's l.,** con sosiego, despacio. **You can do it at your l.,** Puedes hacerlo cuando tengas tiempo. **to be at l.,** estar desocupado, no tener nada que hacer. **l. moments,** ratos perdidos, momentos de ocio, m pl
leisured /'liʒərd/ a desocupado, libre; sin ocupación; (wealthy) acomodado
leisurely /'liʒərli/ a pausado, lento, deliberado; tardo
lemon /'lɛmən/ n limón, m; (tree) limonero, m, a limonado, de color de limón; hecho o sazonado con limón. **l. drop,** pastilla de limón, f. **l.-grove,** limonar, m. **l.-squash,** limonada natural, f. **l.-squeezer,** exprime limones, m, exprimidera, f
lemonade /ˌlɛmə'neid/ n limonada, f. **l. powder,** limonada seca, f
lemur /'limər/ n lemur, m
lend /lɛnd/ vt prestar. **to l. an ear to,** prestar atención a. **It does not l. itself to...,** No se presta a... **to l. a hand,** echar una mano, dar una mano
lender /'lɛndər/ n el, m, (f, la) que presta; prestador (-ra); (of money) prestamista, mf; *Com.* mutuante, mf
lending /'lɛndɪŋ/ n prestación, f, préstamo, m. **l.-library,** biblioteca circulante, f
length /lɛŋθ/ n largo, m; longitud, f; (of fabric) corte, m; (of a ship) eslora, f; (in racing) largo, m; distancia, f; (in time) duración, f; alcance, m. **at l.,** por fin, finalmente; (in full) extensamente, largamente. **by a l.,** por un largo. **full-l.,** de cuerpo entero. **three feet in l.,** tres pies de largo. **to go the l. of...,** llegar al extremo de...
lengthen /'lɛŋkθən/ vt alargar; prolongar; extender. vi alargarse; prolongarse; extenderse; (of days) crecer
lengthening /'lɛŋkθənɪŋ/ n alargamiento, m; prolongación, f; crecimiento, m
lengthily /'lɛŋkθəli/ adv largamente
lengthiness /'lɛŋkθɪnɪs/ n largueza, f; prolijidad, f
lengthy /'lɛŋkθi/ a largo; demasiado largo, larguísimo; (of speech) prolijo; verboso
leniency /'liniənsi/ n lenidad, f; indulgencia, f
lenient /'liniənt/ a indulgente; poco severo
leniently /'liniəntli/ adv con indulgencia
Leningrad /'lɛnɪn,græd/ Leningrado, m
lenitive /'lɛnɪtɪv/ a lenitivo. n lenitivo, m
lens /lɛnz/ n lente, m; (of the eye) cristalino, m
Lent /lɛnt/ n Cuaresma, f
Lenten /'lɛntn̩/ a de Cuaresma, cuaresmal
lentil /'lɛntɪl/ n lenteja, f
lentitude /'lɛntɪ,tud/ n lentitud, f
Leo /'liou/ n León, m
leonine /'liə,nain/ a leonino
leopard /'lɛpərd/ n leopardo, m
leper /'lɛpər/ n leproso (-sa). **l. colony,** colonia de leprosos, f
leprosy /'lɛprəsi/ n lepra, f
leprous /'lɛprəs/ a leproso
lesbian /'lɛzbiən/ a and n lesbiana
lesion /'liʒən/ n lesión, f
less /lɛs/ a menor; más pequeño; menos; inferior. adv menos; sin. **l. than,** menos de (que). **more or l.,** poco más o menos. **no l.,** nada menos. **none the l.,** sin embargo. **to grow l.,** disminuir. **l. and l.,** cada vez menos
lessee /lɛ'si/ n arrendador (-ia); inquilino (-na)
lessen /'lɛsən/ vi disminuir; reducirse. vt disminuir; reducir; (lower) rebajar; (disparage) menospreciar
lessening /'lɛsənɪŋ/ n disminución, f; reducción, f

lesser /'lɛsər/ a comp menor; más pequeño. See **little**
lesson /'lɛsən/ n lección, f. **to give a l.,** dar lección, dar clase; *Fig.* dar una lección (a). **to hear a l.,** tomar la lección
lessor /'lɛsɔr/ n arrendador (-ra)
lest /lɛst/ conjunc para que no; por miedo de (que), no sea que. **I did not do it l. they should not like it,** No lo hice por miedo de que no les gustase
let /lɛt/ vt dejar, permitir; (lease) arrendar. vi alquilarse, ser alquilado. **Let** as an expression of the imperative is rendered in Spanish by the subjunctive or the imperative, e.g. *Let them go!* ¡Que se vayan! ¡Déjalos marchar! *He let them go,* Les dejó marchar. **to let fall,** dejar caer. **to let go,** dejar marchar; soltar; poner en libertad (a). **to let loose,** dar suelta a; *Fig.* desencadenar. **to let one know,** hacer saber, comunicar. **to let the cat out of the bag,** tirar de la manta. **to let th chance slip,** perder la ocasión. **to let alone,** (a thing) no tocar; (a person) dejar en paz, dejar tranquilo; (an affair) no meterse (en or con); (omit) no mencionar, omitir toda mención de. **to let down,** bajar; (by a rope) descolgar; (hair, etc.) dejar caer; (a dress, etc.) alargar; *Naut.* calar; (disappoint) dejar plantado. **to let in,** dejar entrar; hacer entrar; invitar a entrar; recibir; (insert) insertar. **to let into,** (initiate) iniciar en, admitir en; (a secret) revelar. Other meanings, see **to let in. to let off,** dejar salir; dejar en libertad; exonerar; perdonar; (a gun) disparar; (fireworks, etc.) hacer estallar. **to let out,** dejar salir; poner en libertad; (from a house) acompañar a la puerta; abrir la puerta; *Sew.* ensanchar; (hire) alquilar; (the fire, etc.) dejar extinguirse. **to let up,** dejar subir; (decrease) disminuir; (end) terminar
let /lɛt/ n estorbo, impedimento, obstáculo, m. **without let or hindrance,** sin estorbo ni obstáculo
lethal /'liθəl/ a letal. **l. weapon,** instrumento de muerte, m
lethargic /lə'θɑrdʒɪk/ a aletargado; letárgico
lethargy /'lɛθərdʒi/ n letargo, m; *Med.* letargía, f
letter /'lɛtər/ n (of the alphabet) letra, f; (epistle) carta, f; *Print.* carácter, m; (lessor) arrendador (-ra); pl **letters,** letras, f pl; (correspondence) correo, m; (literature) letras, f. vt inscribir; imprimir. **capital l.,** letra mayúscula, f. **first letters,** *Fig.* primeras letras, f pl. **registered l.,** carta certificada, f, certificado, m. **small l.,** letra minúscula, f. **the l. of the law,** la ley escrita. **to be l.-perfect,** saber de memoria. **to the l.,** *Fig.* a la letra. **letters patent,** patente, f; título de privilegio, m. **l.-balance,** pesacartas, m. **l.-book,** *Com.* libro copiador, m. **l.-box,** buzón de correos, m. **l.-card,** tarjeta postal del gobierno, f. **l. of credit,** carta de crédito, f. **l. of introduction,** carta de presentación, f. **l.-writer,** escritor (-ra) de cartas
lettered /'lɛtərd/ a culto, instruido; (printed) impreso
lettering /'lɛtərɪŋ/ n inscripción, f; letrero, rótulo, m
letterpress /'lɛtər,prɛs/ n imprenta, f; (not illustrations) texto, m
letting /'lɛtɪŋ/ n (hiring) arrendamiento, m
lettuce /'lɛtɪs/ n lechuga, f. **l. plant,** lechuguino, m. **l. seller,** lechuguero (-ra)
Leuven /'luvən/ Lovaina, f
Levant, the /lɪ'vænt/ el Levante, m
Levantine /'lɛvən,tain/ a and n levantino (-na)
levee /'lɛvi/ n besamanos, m, recepción, f, dique, m
level /'lɛvəl/ n nivel, m; ras, m, flor, f, llano, m; (plain) llanura, f; (instrument) nivel, m, a llano; igual; al nivel (de); uniforme; imparcial. adv a nivel; igualmente. vt nivelar; igualar; allanar; (a blow) asestar; (a gun) apuntar; (raze) arrasar, derribar; adaptar; hacer uniforme. **on the l.,** a nivel; *Fig.* de buena fe. **spirit l.,** nivel de burbuja, m. **to make l. again,** rellanar. **l. country,** campaña, llanura, f. **l. with the ground,** a ras de la tierra. **l. with the water,** a flor de agua. **l. crossing,** paso a nivel, m. **l.-headed,** sensato, cuerdo. **l. stretch,** rellano, m; llanura, f
leveler /'lɛvələr/ n nivelador (-ra)
leveling /'lɛvəlɪŋ/ a nivelador; de nivelación; igualador. n nivelación, f; allanamiento, m; (to the ground) arrasamiento, m; igualación, f
levelness /'lɛvəlnɪs/ n nivel, m; planicie, f; igualdad, f

lever /'lɛvər/ n palanca, f; (handle) manivela, f; escape de reloj, m; (excuse) pretexto, m; (means) modo, m. vt sopalancar. **control l.,** Aer. palanca de mando, f. **hand-l.,** palanca de mano, f
leverage /'lɛvərɪdʒ/ n sistema de palancas, m; acción de palanca, f; Fig. influencia, fuerza, f, poder, m
Leviathan /lɪ'vaiəθən/ n leviatán, m
levitation /ˌlɛvɪ'teiʃən/ n levitación, f
Levite /'livait/ n levita, m
Levitical /lɪ'vɪtɪkəl/ a levítico
Leviticus /lɪ'vɪtɪkəs/ n Levítico, m
levity /'lɛvɪti/ n levedad, frivolidad, ligereza, f
levy /'lɛvi/ n exacción (de tributos), f; impuesto, m; (of a fine) imposición, f; Mil. leva, f. vt (taxes) exigir; (a fine) imponer; (troops) reclutar, enganchar
levying /'lɛviɪŋ/ n (of a tax) exacción (de tributos), f; (of a fine) imposición, f; (of troops) leva, f
lewd /lud/ a lascivo, lujurioso, impúdico
lewdness /'ludnɪs/ n lascivia, lujuria, impudicia, f
lexicographer /ˌlɛksɪ'kɒgrəfər/ n lexicógrafo, m
lexicography /ˌlɛksɪ'kɒgrəfi/ n lexicografía, f
lexicon /'lɛksɪˌkɒn/ n léxico, m
liability /ˌlaiə'bɪlɪti/ n responsabilidad, obligación, f; tendencia, f; riesgo, m; pl **liabilities,** obligaciones, f pl; Com. pasivo, m
liable /'laiəbəl/ a responsable; propenso (a); expuesto (a); sujeto (a)
liaison /li'eizən/ n lío, m; coordinación, f. **l. officer,** oficial de coordinación, m
liar /'laiər/ n mentiroso (-sa)
libation /lai'beiʃən/ n libación, f
libel /'laibəl/ n libelo, m; difamación, f, vt difamar, calumniar
libeler /'laibələr/ n libelista, mf difamador (-ra)
libelous /'laibələs/ a difamatorio
liberal /'lɪbərəl/ a liberal; generoso; abundante. n liberal, mf **l. profession,** carrera liberal, f. **l.-minded,** tolerante. **l.-mindedness,** tolerancia, f
liberalism /'lɪbərəˌlɪzəm/ n liberalismo, m
liberality /ˌlɪbə'rælɪti/ n liberalidad, f; generosidad, f
liberalize /'lɪbərəˌlaiz/ vt liberalizar
liberate /'lɪbəˌreit/ vt (a prisoner) poner en libertad; librar (de); (a gas, etc.) dejar escapar
liberation /ˌlɪbə'reiʃən/ n liberación, f; (of a captive) redención, f; (of a slave) manumisión, f
liberator /'lɪbəˌreitər/ n libertador (-ra)
libertinage /'lɪbərˌtinɪdʒ/ n libertinaje, m
libertine /'lɪbərˌtin/ n libertino, m
libertinism /'lɪbərtiˌnɪzəm/ n libertinaje, m
liberty /'lɪbərti/ n libertad, f; (familiarity) familiaridad, f; (right) privilegio, m, prerrogativa, f; (leave) permiso, m. **at l.,** en libertad; desocupado, libre. **I have taken the l. of giving them your name,** Me he tomado la libertad de darles su nombre. **to set at l.,** poner en libertad (a). **to take liberties with,** tratar con familiaridad; (a text) tergiversar. **l. of speech,** libertad de palabra, libertad de expresión, f. **l. of thought,** libertad de pensamiento, f
libidinous /lɪ'bɪdnəs/ a libidinoso
Libra /'librə/ n Libra, f
librarian /lai'brɛəriən/ n bibliotecario (-ia)
librarianship /lai'brɛəriənˌʃip/ n carrera f, o empleo m, de bibliotecario
library /'laiˌbrɛri/ n biblioteca, f; (book shop) librería, f. **l. catalog,** catálogo de la biblioteca, m
librettist /lɪ'brɛtɪst/ n libretista, mf
libretto /lɪ'brɛtou/ n libreto, m
Libya /'lɪbiə/ Libia, f
Libyan /'lɪbiən/ a and n libio (-ia)
license /'laisəns/ n licencia, f, permiso, m; autorización, f; (driving) carnet de chófer, permiso de conducción, m; (of a car) permiso de circulación, m; (for a wireless, etc.) licencia, f; (marriage) licencia de casamiento, f; (excess) libertinaje, desenfreno, m. **import l.,** permiso de importación, m. **poetic l.,** licencia poética, f. **l. number,** (of a car) número de matrícula, m. vt licenciar; autorizar; (a car) sacar la licencia del automóvil
licensee /ˌlaisən'si/ n concesionario (-ia)
licentiate /lai'sɛnʃiɪt/ n licenciado (-da)

licentious /lai'sɛnʃəs/ a licencioso, disoluto
licentiousness /lai'sɛnʃəsnɪs/ n libertinaje, m, disipación, f
lichen /'laikən/ n liquen, m
licit /'lɪsɪt/ a lícito
lick /lɪk/ vt lamer; (of waves) besar; (of flames) bailar; (thrash) azotar; (defeat) vencer. **to l. one's lips,** relamerse los labios, chuparse los dedos. **to l. the dust,** morder el polvo
licking /'lɪkɪŋ/ n lamedura, f; (beating) paliza, tunda, f; (defeat) derrota, f
licorice /'lɪkərɪʃ, -rɪs/ n regaliz, m
lid /lɪd/ n cobertera, f; tapa, f; (of the eye) párpado, m
lie /lai/ n mentira, f; invención, falsedad, f; mentís, m, vi mentir. **to tell a barefaced lie,** mentir por la mitad de la barba. **white lie,** mentira oficiosa, f
lie /lai/ vi estar tumbado, estar echado; estar recostado; descansar, reposar; (in the grave) yacer; (be) estar; (be situated) hallarse, estar situado; (stretch) extenderse; (sleep) dormir; (depend) depender; (consist) consistir, estribar; (as an obligation) incumbir. **Here lies...,** Aquí descansa..., Aquí yace... **It does not lie in my power,** No depende de mí. **to let lie,** dejar; dejar en paz. **to lie at anchor,** estar anclado. **to lie fallow,** estar en barbecho; Fig. descansar. **to lie about,** estar esparcido por todas partes; estar en desorden. **to lie along,** estar tendido a lo largo de; Naut. dar a la banda. **to lie back,** recostarse; apoyarse (en). **to lie by,** estar acostado al lado de; (of things, places) estar cerca (de); descansar. **to lie down,** tenderse, tumbarse, echarse, acostarse; reposar. **Lie down!** (to a dog) ¡Échate! **to lie down under,** tenderse bajo; (an insult) tragar, sufrir. **to lie in,** consistir en; depender de; (of childbirth) estar de parto. **to lie open,** estar abierto; estar expuesto (a); estar al descubierto, estar a la vista. **to lie over,** (be postponed) quedar aplazado. **to lie under,** Naut. estarse a la capa, ponerse en facha. **to lie under,** estar bajo, hallarse bajo; estar bajo el peso de; (be exposed to) estar expuesto a. **to lie with,** (concern) tocar (a); corresponder (a)
lie /lai/ n configuración, f; disposición, f; posición, f. **the lie of the land,** la configuración del terreno
lieu /lu/ n lugar, m. **in l. of,** en lugar de, en vez de
lieutenant /lu'tɛnənt/ n teniente, lugarteniente, m; (naval) alférez, m. **first l.,** (in the army) primer teniente, teniente, m; (in the navy) alférez de navío, m. **naval l.,** teniente de navío, m. **second l.,** (in the army) segundo teniente, m; (in the navy) alférez de fragata, m. **l.-colonel,** teniente coronel
life /laif/ n vida, f; (being) ser, m; (society) mundo, m, sociedad, f; (vitality) vitalidad, f; vigor, m, a de vida; (of annuities, etc.) vitalicio; (life-saving) de salvamento. **for l.,** de por vida. **from l.,** del natural. **high l.,** gran mundo, m, alta sociedad, f. **low l.,** vida del hampa, vida de los barrios bajos, f. **to the l.,** al vivo. **to lay down one's l.,** entregar la vida. **to take one's l. in one's hands,** jugarse la vida. **l. annuity,** fondo vitalicio, m. **l.-belt,** (cinturón) salvavidas, m. **l.-blood,** sangre vital, f; Fig. nervio, m; vigor, m. **l.-boat,** (on a ship) bote salvavidas, m; (on the coast) lancha de salvamento, f. **l.-boat station,** estación de salvamento, f. **l.-giving,** vivificante, que da vida; tonificante. **l.-guard,** (soldier) guardia militar, f; Guardia de Corps, f; (at beach or swimming pool) guardavidas, mf. **l.-insurance,** seguro sobre la vida, m. **l.-interest,** usufructo, m. **l.-jacket,** chaleco salvavidas, m. **l.-like,** natural, m. **l.-line,** cable de salvamento, m. **l.-saving,** a de salvamento; curativo. **l.-saving apparatus,** aparato salvavidas, m. **l.-sized,** de tamaño natural
life cycle n ciclo vital, m
life imprisonment n reclusión perpetua, f
life jacket n chaleco salvavidas, f
lifeless /'laiflɪs/ a sin vida, muerto; inanimado; Fig. desanimado
lifelessness /'laiflɪsnɪs/ n falta de animación; inercia
lifelong /'laifˌlɔŋ/ a de toda la vida
lifetime /'laifˌtaim/ n vida, f
lift /lɪft/ n esfuerzo para levantar, m; acción de levantar, f; alza, f; (blow) golpe, m; (help) ayuda, f;

(hitch, ride) *Mexico* aventón; *m,* (elevator) ascensor, *m;* (for goods) montacargas, *m; pl* **lifts,** *Naut.* balancines, *m pl.* **to give a l. to,** (help) ayudar; (hitchhiker etc.) dar un aventón.

lift /lɪft/ *vt* levantar; alzar, elevar; (pick up) coger; (one's hat) quitarse; (steal) hurtar; exaltar. *vi* (of mist) disiparse; desaparecer. **to l. the elbow,** empinar el codo. **to l. down,** quitar (de); (a person) bajar en brazos. **to l. up,** alzar; erguir, levantar; levantar en brazos

lifting /'lɪftɪŋ/ *n* acción de levantar, *f;* levantamiento, alzamiento, *m*

ligament /'lɪɡəmənt/ *n* ligamento, *m*

ligature /'lɪɡətʃər/ *n* (*Surg. Mus.*) ligadura, *f*

light /lait/ *a* (not dark) claro, con mucha luz, bañado de luz; (of colors) claro; (not heavy, and of sleep, food, troops, movements) ligero; (of reading) de entretenimiento; (irresponsible) frívolo; (easy) fácil; (slight) leve; (of hair) rubio; (happy) alegre; (fickle) inconstante, liviano; (of complexion) blanco. *adv* ligero. **to be l.,** no pesar mucho; estar de día. **to grow l.,** (dawn) clarear; iluminarse. **to make l. of,** no tomar en serio; no preocuparse de; (suffering) sufrir sin quejarse. **l.-colored,** (of color) claro. **l.-fingeredness,** sutileza de manos, *f.* **l.-footed,** ligero de pies. **l.-haired,** de pelo rubio. **l.-headed,** casquivano, ligero de cascos; delirante. **l.-headedness,** ligereza de cascos, frivolidad, *f;* delirio, *m.* **l.-hearted,** alegre (de corazón). **l.-heartedness,** alegría, *f.* **l. horse,** *Mil.* caballería ligera, *f.* **l. troops,** tropas ligeras, *f pl.* **l.-weight,** *n* (*Box.*) peso ligero, *m,* *a* de peso ligero

light /lait/ *n* luz., *f;* (day) día, *m;* (match) cerilla, *f;* (of a cigarette, etc.) fuego, *m;* (of a window) cristal, vidrio, *m;* (point of view) punto de vista, *m;* (in a picture) toque de luz, *m; pl* **lights,** (offal) bofes, *m pl.* **against the l.,** al trasluz. **by the l. of,** a la luz de; según. **half-l.,** media luz, *f.* **high light (s),** *Art.* claros, *m pl; Fig.* momento culminante, *m;* acontecimiento de más interés, *m.* **to come to l.,** descubrirse. **to put a l. to the fire,** encender el fuego. **l.-year,** año de luz, *m*

light /lait/ *vt* (a lamp, fire, etc.) encender; iluminar. *vi* encenderse; iluminarse; *Fig.* animarse; brillar. **to l. upon,** encontrar por casualidad; tropezar con

lighten /'laitn/ *vt* (illuminate) iluminar; (of weight) aligerar; (cheer) alegrar; (mitigate) aliviar. *vi* (grow light) clarear; (of lightning) relampaguear; (become less heavy) disminuir de peso, aligerarse; volverse más alegre

lightening /'laitnɪŋ/ *n* aligeramiento, *m;* (easing) alivio, *m;* luz, *f*

lighter /'laitər/ *n* (boat) lancha, barcaza, gabarra, *f;* (device) encendedor, *m.* **l. man,** gabarrero, *m*

light-fingered /'lait 'fɪŋɡərd/ *a* ligero de manos

lighthouse /'lait,haus/ *n* faro, *m.* **l.-keeper,** guardafaro, *m*

lighting /'laitɪŋ/ *n* iluminación, *f;* alumbrado, *m.* **flood l.,** iluminación intensiva, *f.* **l.-up time,** hora de encender los faros, *f*

lightly /'laitli/ *adv* ligeramente; fácilmente; (slightly) levemente; ágilmente; sin seriedad. **l. wounded,** levemente herido

lightness /'laitnɪs/ *n* ligereza, *f;* poco peso, *m;* agilidad, *f;* (brightness) claridad, *f;* (inconstancy) liviandad, inconstancia, *f;* frivolidad, *f*

lightning /'laitnɪŋ/ *n* relámpago, rayo, *m.* **as quick as l.,** como un relámpago. **to be struck by l.,** ser herido por un relámpago. **l.-rod,** pararrayos, *m*

lightship /'lait,ʃɪp/ *n* buque faro, *m*

ligneous /'lɪɡniəs/ *a* leñoso

lignite /'lɪɡnait/ *n* lignito, *m*

likable /'laikəbəl/ *a* simpático

like /laik/ *a* semejante; parecido; igual, mismo; (characteristic) típico, característico; (likely) probable; (equivalent) equivalente. *adv* como; igual (que); del mismo modo (que). *n* semejante, igual, *mf;* tal cosa, *f;* cosas semejantes, *f pl.* **Don't speak to me l. that,** No me hables así. **He was l. a fury,** Estaba hecho una furia. **They are very l. each other,** Se parecen

mucho. **to be l.,** parecerse (a), semejar. **to look l.,** parecer ser (que); tener el aspecto de; (of persons) parecerse (a). **to return l. for l.,** pagar en la misma moneda

like /laik/ *vt* gustar, agradar; estar aficionado (a), gustar de; (wish) querer. **I l. coffee and Adam likes tea,** A mí me gusta café y a Adán le gusta té. **Do you l. coffee?** ¿Te gusta café? **I don't like hot drinks,** No me gustan las bebidas calientes. **As you l.,** Como te parezca bien, Como quieras. **If you l.,** Si quieres. **James likes painting,** Jaime está aficionado a la pintura. **Judith does not l. the north of England,** A Judit no le gusta el norte de Inglaterra. **I don't l. to do it,** No me gusta hacerlo. **I should l. him to go to Madrid,** Me gustaría que fuera a Madrid

likelihood /'laikli,hʊd/ *n* posibilidad, *f;* probabilidad, *f*

likely /'laikli/ *a* probable; verosímil, creíble, plausible; posible; (suitable) satisfactorio, apropiado; (handsome) bien parecido. *adv* probablemente. **They are not l. to come,** No es probable que vengan

liken /'laikən/ *vt* comparar

likeness /'laiknɪs/ *n* parecido, *m,* semejanza, *f;* (portrait) retrato, *m*

likewise /'laik,waiz/ *adv* igualmente, asimismo, también. *conjunc* además

liking /'laikɪŋ/ *n* (for persons) simpatía, *f,* cariño, *m;* (for things) gusto, *m,* afición, *f;* (appreciation) aprecio, *m.* **I have a l. for old cities,** Me gustan (or me atraen) las viejas ciudades. **to take a l. to,** (things) aficionarse a; (persons) prendarse de, tomar cariño (a)

lilac /'lailək/ *n* lila, *f.* **l. color,** color de lila, *m*

Lilliputian /,lɪlɪ'pyuʃən/ *a* liliputiense. *n* liliputiense, *mf*

lilt /lɪlt/ *n* canción, *f;* ritmo, *m;* armonía, *f*

lily /'lɪli/ *n* lirio, *m,* azucena, *f;* (of France) flor de lis, *f.* **l. of the valley,** lirio de los valles, muguete, *m.* **l.-white,** blanco como la azucena

limb /lɪm/ *n* Anat. miembro, *m;* (of a tree) rama, *f*

limbless /'lɪmlɪs/ *a* mutilado

limbo /'lɪmbou/ *n* limbo, *m*

lime /laim/ *n* Chem. cal, *f;* (for catching birds) liga, hisca, *f;* (linden tree) tilo, *m;* (tree like a lemon) limero, *m;* (fruit) lima, *f. vt* (whiten) encalar; Agr. abonar con cal. **slaked l.,** cal muerta, *f.* **l.-flower,** flor del tilo, lila, *f;* flor del limero, *f.* **l.-juice,** jugo de lima, *m.* **l.-kiln,** calera, *f.* **l.-pit,** pozo de cal, *m.* **l. tree** Lat. Am. limo, *m*

limelight /'laim,lait/ *n* luz de calcio, *f; Fig.* centro de atención, *m;* publicidad, *f.* **to be in the l.,** ser el centro de atención, estar a la vista (de público)

limestone /'laim,stoun/ *n* piedra caliza, *f.* **l. deposit,** calar, *m*

limit /'lɪmɪt/ *n* límite, *m;* confín, *m;* linde, *m,* or *f;* limitación, *f, vt* limitar; fijar; (restrict) restringir. **This is the l.!** ¡Este es el colmo! ¡No faltaba más!

limitation /,lɪmɪ'teiʃən/ *n* limitación, *f;* restricción, *f*

limitative /'lɪmɪ,teitɪv/ *a* restrictivo, limitativo

limited /'lɪmɪtɪd/ *a* limitado; restringido; escaso; (of persons) de cortos alcances; Com. anónimo. **l. company,** sociedad anónima, *f*

limited monarchy *n* monarquía moderada, *f*

limiting adjective /'lɪmɪtɪŋ/ *n* adjetivo determinativo, *m*

limitless /'lɪmɪtlɪs/ *a* sin límites; ilimitado, inmenso

limousine /'lɪmə,zin/ *n* limousina, *f,* coche cerrado, *m*

limp /lɪmp/ *a* flojo; débil; fláccido; lánguido. *n* cojera, *f. vi* cojear. **to l. off,** marcharse cojeando. **to l. up,** acercarse cojeando; subir cojeando

limpid /'lɪmpɪd/ *a* límpido, cristalino, puro

limpidity /lɪm'pɪdɪti/ *n* limpidez, *f*

limping /'lɪmpɪŋ/ *a* cojo

limply /'lɪmpli/ *adv* flojamente; débilmente; lánguidamente

limpness /'lɪmpnɪs/ *n* flojedad, *f;* debilidad, *f;* languidez, *f*

linchpin /'lɪntʃ,pɪn/ *n* pezonera, *f*

linden /'lɪndən/ *n* tilo, *m,* (tea) tilia americana, *f*

line /lain/ *vt* (furrow) surcar; (troops, etc.) poner en fila; alinear; (clothes, nests, etc.) forrar; (building)

revestir; (one's pocket) llenar. *vi* estar en línea, alinearse
line /lain/ *n* (most meanings) línea, *f*; (cord) cuerda, *f*; *Naut.* cordel, *m*; (fishing) sedal, *m*; (railway) vía, *f*; (wrinkle) surco, *m*; arruga, *f*; (row) hilera, ringlera, fila, *f*; (of verse) verso, *m*; *Print.* renglón, *m*; (of business) ramo, *m*; profesión, *f*; (interest) especialidad, *f*. **bowling** or **serving l.**, línea de saque, *f*; **hard lines,** mala suerte, *f*; apuro, *m*, situación difícil, *f*. **in a l.,** en fila; en cola. **in direct l.,** (of descent) en línea recta. **It is not in my l.,** No es una especialidad mía; No es uno de mis intereses. **on the lines of,** conforme a; parecido a. **to cross the l.,** (equator) pasar la línea; (railway) cruzar la vía. **to drop a l.,** escribir unas líneas, poner unas líneas. **to read between the lines,** leer entre líneas. **l.-drawing,** dibujo de líneas, *m*. **l. of battle,** línea de batalla, *f*
lineage /'lɪnɪdʒ/ *n* linaje, *m*, familia, raza, *f*
lineal /'lɪnɪəl/ *a* lineal
lineament /'lɪnɪəmənt/ *n* lineamento, *m*; (of the face) facciones, *f pl*
linear /'lɪnɪər/ *a* lineal. **l. equation,** ecuación de primer grado, *f*
lined /laind/ *a* rayado, con líneas; (of the face) surcado, arrugado; (of gloves, etc.) forrado. **lined paper,** papel rayado, *m*
linen /'lɪnən/ *n* lino, *m*; *Inf.* ropa blanca, *f*; *a* de lino. **clean l.,** ropa limpia, *f*. **dirty l.,** ropa sucia, *f*; ropa para lavar, *f*. **table-l.,** mantelería, *f*. **l. cupboard,** armario para ropa blanca, *m*. **l. draper,** lencero (-ra). **l.-draper's shop,** lencería, *f*. **l. room,** lencería, *f*. **l. tape,** trenzadera, *f*. **l. thread,** hilo de lino, *m*
liner /'lainər/ *n* (ship) transatlántico, *m*; buque de vapor, *m*; *Aer.* avión de pasaje, *m*
linesman /'lainzmən/ *n* soldado de línea, *m*; *Sports.* juez de línea, *m*
ling /lɪŋ/ *n* *Bot.* brezo, *m*; *Ichth.* especie de abadejo, *f*
linger /'lɪŋgər/ *vi* (remain) quedarse; tardar en marcharse; ir lentamente; hacer algo despacio
lingerie /,lɒnʒə'reɪ/ *n* ropa blanca, *f*
lingering /'lɪŋgərɪŋ/ *a* lento; largo, prolongado; melancólico, triste
lingeringly /'lɪŋgərɪŋli/ *adv* lentamente; largamente; melancólicamente
linguist /'lɪŋgwɪst/ *n* lingüista, *mf*
linguistic /lɪŋ'gwɪstɪk/ *a* lingüístico
linguistics /lɪŋ'gwɪstɪks/ *n* lingüística, *f*
liniment /'lɪnəmənt/ *n* linimento, *m*
lining /'lainɪŋ/ *n* (of a garment, etc.) forro, *m*; (building) revestimiento, *m*
link /lɪŋk/ *n* (in a chain) eslabón, *m*; (of beads) sarta, *f*; *Fig.* enlace, *m*, cadena, *f*; conección, *f*; *Mech.* corredera, *f*; (torch) hacha de viento, *f*. *vt* enlazar, unir; *Fig.* encadenar. **missing l.,** *Fig.* eslabón perdido, *m*. **to l. arms,** cogerse del brazo
linking /'lɪŋkɪŋ/ *n* encadenamiento, *m*; *Fig.* conección, *f*
links /lɪŋks/ *n pl* campo de golf, *m*
linoleum /lɪ'nouliəm/ *n* linóleo, *m*
linotype /'lainə,taip/ *n* linotipia, *f*
linseed /'lɪn,sid/ *n* linaza, *f*. **l. cake,** bagazo, *m*. **l.-oil,** aceite de linaza, *m*
lint /lɪnt/ *n* *Med.* hilas, *f pl*; (fluff) borra, *f*
lintel /'lɪntl/ *n* dintel, *m*; (threshold) umbral, *m*
lion /'laiən/ *n* león, *m*; *Fig.* celebridad, *f*. **l. cage** or **den,** leonera, *f*. **l.-hearted,** valeroso. **l.-hunter,** cazador (-ra) de leones. **l.-keeper,** leonero (-ra). **lion's mane,** melena, *f*. **l.-tamer,** domador (-ra) de leones
lioness /'laiənɪs/ *n* leona, *f*
lionize /'laiə,naiz/ *vt* dar bombo (a), hacer la rueda (a), tratar como una celebridad (a)
lion's share *n* parte del león, tajada del león, *f*
lip /lɪp/ *n* labio, *m*; (of a vessel) pico, *m*; (of a crater) borde, *m*; *Fig.* boca, *f*. **to open one's lips,** abrir la boca. **to smack one's lips,** chuparse los dedos. **lip reading,** lectura labial, *f*. **lip-service,** amor fingido, *m*; promesas hipócritas, *f pl*. **lip stick,** lápiz para los labios, *m*
liposuction /'lɪpə,sʌkʃən, 'laipə-/ *n* liposucción, *f*
lipped /lɪpt/ *a* (in compounds) con labios..., que tiene labios; (of vessels in compounds) con... picos

liquefaction /,lɪkwə'fækʃən/ *n* licuefacción, *f*
liquefiable /'lɪkwə,faiəbəl/ *a* liquidable
liquefy /'lɪkwə,fai/ *vt* liquidar. *vi* liquidarse
liqueur /lɪ'kɜr/ *n* licor, *m*. **l.-glass,** copita de licor, *f*. **l.-set,** licorera, *f*
liquid /'lɪkwɪd/ *n* líquido, *m*, *a* líquido; límpido. **l. air,** aire líquido, *m*. **l. measure,** medida para líquidos, *f*
liquidate /'lɪkwɪ,deit/ *vt* liquidar; saldar (cuentas); *Mil.* soldar
liquidation /,lɪkwɪ'deiʃən/ *n* liquidación, *f*
liquidness /'lɪkwɪdnɪs/ *n* liquidez, *f*; fluidez, *f*
liquor /'lɪkər/ *n* licor, *m*. **l. shop,** aguardentería, *f*. **l. traffic,** negocio de vinos y licores, *m*; contrabando, *m*
lira /'lɪərə/ *n* lira, *f*
Lisbon /'lɪzbən/ Lisboa, *f*
lisp /lɪsp/ *n* ceceo, *m*; balbuceo, *m*, *vi* cecear; balbucir
lisping /'lɪspɪŋ/ *a* ceceoso; balbuciente. *n* ceceo, *m*; (of a child, etc.) balbuceo, *m*
lissom /'lɪsəm/ *a* flexible; ágil
list /lɪst/ *n* lista, *f*; catálogo, *m*; matrícula, *f*; *Naut.* recalcada, *f*; inclinación, *f*; (tournament) liza, *f*. *vt* hacer una lista de; catalogar; matricular, inscribir. *vi* *Naut.* recalcar; inclinarse a un lado. **to enter the lists,** entrar en liza. **l. of wines,** lista de vinos, *f*
listen /'lɪsən/ *vi* escuchar; (attend) atender. **Don't you want to l. to the music?** ¿No quieres escuchar la música? **to l. in,** (to the radio) escuchar la radio; (eavesdrop) escuchar a hurtadillas
listener /'lɪsənər/ *n* oyente, *mf*; (to radio) radioyente, *mf*
listless /'lɪstlɪs/ *a* lánguido, apático, indiferente
listlessly /'lɪstlɪsli/ *adv* lánguidamente, indiferentemente
listlessness /'lɪstlɪsnɪs/ *n* apatía, languidez, indiferencia, inercia, *f*
litany /'lɪtni/ *n* letanía, *f*
liter /'lɪtər/ *n* litro, *m*
literal /'lɪtərəl/ *a* literal. **l.-minded,** sin imaginación
literalness /'lɪtərəlnɪs/ *n* literalidad, *f*
literary /'lɪtə,reri/ *a* literario
literary executor *n* depositario de la obra literaria, *m*
literate /'lɪtərɪt/ *a* and *n* literato (-ta)
literature /'lɪtərətʃər/ *n* literatura, *f*
lithe /laið/ *a* flexible; sinuoso y delgado; ágil
litheness /'laiðnɪs/ *n* flexibilidad, *f*; sinuosidad, *f*; delgadez, *f*; agilidad, *f*
lithograph /'lɪθə,græf/ *n* litografía, *f*, *vt* litografiar
lithographer /lɪ'θɒgrəfər/ *n* litógrafo, *m*
lithographic /,lɪθə'græfɪk/ *a* litográfico
lithography /lɪ'θɒgrəfi/ *n* litografía, *f*
Lithuania /,lɪθu'einiə/ Lituania, *f*
Lithuanian /,lɪθu'einiən/ *a* lituano, *n* lituano (-na); (language) lituano, *m*
litigant /'lɪtɪgənt/ *n* litigante, *mf*
litigate /'lɪtɪ,geit/ *vi* and *vt* litigar, pleitear
litigation /,lɪtɪ'geiʃən/ *n* litigación, *f*
litigious /lɪ'tɪdʒəs/ *a* litigioso
litmus /'lɪtməs/ *n* tornasol, *m*. **l. paper,** papel de tornasol, *m*
litter /'lɪtər/ *n* litera, *f*; (stretcher) camilla, *f*; (bed) lecho, *m*; cama de paja, *f*; (brood) camada, cría, *f*; (rubbish) cosas en desorden, *f pl*; (papers) papeletas, *f pl*; (untidiness) desarreglo, desorden, *m*, confusión, *f*, *vt* poner en desorden
little /'lɪtl/ *a* pequeño; poco; (scanty) escaso; insignificante; bajo, mezquino. *adv* poco. **a l.,** un poco (de); un tanto. **in l.,** en pequeño. **not a l.,** no poco; bastante. **l. by l.,** poco a poco. **l. or no,** poco o nada. **however l.,** por pequeño que sea. **as l. as possible,** lo menos posible. **to make l. of,** no dar importancia a; sacar poco en claro de, no comprender bien; no hacer caso de; (persons) acoger mal. **l. by l.,** poco a poco. **l. finger,** dedo meñique, *m*. **l. one,** pequeñuela, *f*, pequeñito, *m*
littleness /'lɪtlnɪs/ *n* pequeñez, *f*; poquedad, *f*; mezquindad, *f*; trivialidad, *f*
littoral /'lɪtərəl/ *a* and *n* litoral, *m*
liturgical /lɪ'tɜrdʒɪkəl/ *a* litúrgico. **l. calendar,** calendario litúrgico, *m*

liturgical vestment n paramento litúrgico, m
liturgy /'lɪtərdʒi/ n liturgia, f
live /laɪv/ a vivo, viviente; (alight) encendido; (of a wire, etc.) cargado de electricidad. **l. cartridge,** cartucho con bala, m. **l. coal,** ascua, f. **l.-stock,** ganadería, f. **l. wire,** conductor eléctrico, m; Fig. fuerza viva, f
live /lɪv/ vi vivir; residir, habitar; (of ships) mantenerse a flote; salvarse; subsistir. vt (one's life) llevar, pasar. **Long l.!** ¡Viva! **to have enough to l. on,** tener de que vivir. **to l. together,** convivir. **to l. again,** volver a vivir. **to l. at,** vivir en, habitar. **to l. down,** sobrevivir a; (a fault) lograr borrar. **to l. on,** vivir de. **to l. up to,** vivir con arreglo a, vivir en conformidad con; estar al nivel de, merecer. **to l. up to one's income,** vivir al día, gastarse toda la renta
live broadcast n emisión en directo, f
livelihood /'laɪvli,hʊd/ n vida, subsistencia, f. **to make a l.,** ganarse la vida
liveliness /'laɪvlinɪs/ n vivacidad, vida, f; animación, f; alegría, f
livelong /'lɪv,lɔŋ/ a entero, todo; eterno. **all the l. day,** todo el santo día
lively /'laɪvli/ a vivo; vivaracho; brioso, enérgico; alegre; bullicioso; animado; (fresh) fresco; (of colours) brilliante; intenso
liver /'lɪvər/ n vividor (-ra), el, m, (f, la) que vive; habitante, m; Anat. hígado, m. **l. cancer,** cáncer del hígado, m. **l. complaint,** mal de hígado, m. **l. extract,** extracto de hígado, m
livery /'lɪvəri/ n librea, f; uniforme, m; Poet. vestiduras, f pl. **l. stables,** pensión de caballos, f; cochería de alquiler, f
livid /'lɪvɪd/ a lívido; cárdeno, amoratado
lividness /'lɪvɪdnɪs/ n lividez, f
living /'lɪvɪŋ/ a viviente; vivo, vital. n vida, f; modo de vivir, m; beneficio eclesiástico, m. **the l.,** los vivos. **to make one's l.,** ganarse la vida. **l. memory,** memoria de personas vivientes, memoria de los que aún viven, f. **l.-room,** sala de estar, f. **l. soul,** ser viviente; Inf. bicho viviente, m. **l. wage,** jornal básico, m
lizard /'lɪzərd/ n lagarto (-ta). **giant l.,** dragón, m. **wall l.,** lagartija, f. **l. hole,** lagartera, f
llama /'lɑmə/ n llama, f
load /loud/ n carga, f; peso, m; (cart) carretada, f; Elec. carga, f; (quantity) cantidad, f. vt cargar (con); (with honors) llenar (de); (Fig. weigh down) agobiar (con); (a stick with lead) emplomar; (Elec. and of dice) cargar; (wine) mezclar vino con un narcótico. **to be loaded with fruit,** estar cargado de fruta. **to l. oneself with,** cargarse de. **to l. the dice,** cargar los dados. **to l. again,** recargar
loader /'loudər/ n cargador, m
loading /'loudɪŋ/ n carga, f. **l. depot,** cargadero, m
loaf /louf/ n pan, m; (French) barra de pan, f. vi golfear, vagabundear, gandulear. **l. sugar,** azúcar de pilón, m
loafer /'loufər/ n vago (-ga); azotacalles, mf; gandul (-la); golfo (-fa)
loafing /'loufɪŋ/ n gandulería, f, vagabundeo, m
loam /loum/ n marga, f
loamy /'loumi/ a margoso
loan /loun/ n empréstito, m; (lending) prestación, f; préstamo, m. vt prestar. **l. fund,** caja de empréstitos, f. **l. company office,** casa de préstamos, f
loath /louθ/ a desinclinado, poco dispuesto
loathe /louð/ vt abominar, detestar, odiar, aborrecer; repugnar
loather /'louðər/ n el, m, (f, la) que odia; aborrecedor (-ra)
loathing /'louðɪŋ/ n aborrecimiento, odio, m; repugnancia, aversión, f
loathsome /'louðsəm/ a odioso, aborrecible; asqueroso; repugnante
loathsomeness /'louðsəmnɪs/ n carácter repugnante, m; asquerosidad, f
lobby /'lɒbi/ n pasillo, m; antecámara, f; (in a hotel, house) vestíbulo, recibidor, m; (waiting-room) sala de espera, f; (in Parliament) sala de los pasos perdidos, f. vt and vi cabildear

lobe /loub/ n Bot. lobo, m; (Anat. Archit.) lóbulo, m
lobster /'lɒbstər/ n langosta, f; bogavante, m. **l.-pot,** cambín, m, nasa, f
local /'loukəl/ a local; de la localidad. **l. anesthetic,** anestésico local, m. **l. color,** color local, m
locale /lou'kæl/ n local, m
locality /lou'kælɪti/ n localidad, f; situación, f
localization /,loukələ'zeɪʃən/ n localización, f
localize /'loukə,laɪz/ vt localizar
locate /'loukeɪt/ vt situar; colocar; localizar. **to be located,** situarse; hallarse
location /lou'keɪʃən/ n colocación, f; emplazamiento, m; localidad, f; situación, posición, f
loch /lɒk/ n lago, m
lock /lɒk/ n cerradura (of a door, including a vehicle) f; (of a gun) cerrojo, m; (in wrestling) llave, f; (on rivers, canals) presa, f; (at a dock) esclusa, f; (of hair) mechón, m, guedeja, f; (ringlet) bucle, m; pl **locks,** (hair) cabellos, m pl, pelo, m. **spring l.,** cerradura de golpe, f. **to put a l. on,** poner cerradura a. **under l. and key,** bajo cuatro llaves. **l.-jaw,** trismo, m. **l. keeper,** esclusero (-ra) mf. **l.-out strike,** huelga patronal, f
lock /lɒk/ vt cerrar con llave; Fig. encerrar; (embrace) abrazar estrechamente; (of wheels, etc.) trabar; (twine) entrelazar. vi cerrarse con llave. **to l. in,** cerrar con llave; encerrar. **to l. out,** cerrar la puerta (a); dejar en la calle (a). **to l. up,** encerrar; (imprison) encarcelar
locker /'lɒkər/ n (drawer) cajón, m; (cupboard) armario, m; Naut. cajonada, f
locket /'lɒkɪt/ n guardapelo, m; medallón, m
locksmith /'lɒk,smɪθ/ n cerrajero, m. **locksmith's trade,** cerrajería, f
locomotion /,loukə'mouʃən/ n locomoción, f
locomotive /,loukə'moutɪv/ a locomotor. n locomotora, f
locum tenens /'loukəm 'tinɛnz/ n interino (-na)
locust /'loukəst/ n langosta migratoria, f
locution /lou'kyuʃən/ n locución, f
lode /loud/ n filón, m
lodestar /'loud,stɑr/ n estrella polar, f; Fig. norte, m
lodge /lɒdʒ/ n casita, garita, f; casa de guarda, f; (freemason's) logia, f; (porter's) portería, f; vi hospedarse, alojarse, vivir, parar; penetrar; entrar (en); fijarse (en). vt hospedar, alojar; albergar; (a blow) asestar; (a complaint) hacer, dar; (money, etc.) depositar. **to l. an accusation against,** querellarse contra, quejarse de. **l.-keeper,** conserje, m
lodger /'lɒdʒər/ n huésped (-eda) f; Lat. Am. alojado (-da)
lodging /'lɒdʒɪŋ/ n hospedaje, alojamiento, m; (inn) posada, f; residencia, f; casa, f. **l.-house,** casa de huéspedes, f
loft /lɒft/ n desván, sotabanco, m; pajar, m
loftily /'lɔftli/ adv en alto; (proudly) con arrogancia, con altanería
loftiness /'lɔftinɪs/ n altura, f; sublimidad, f; nobleza, f; dignidad, f; (haughtiness) altanería, soberbia, f
lofty /'lɔfti/ a alto; sublime; noble; eminente; (haughty) altanero, soberbio
log /lɔg/ n madero, tronco, m; palo, m; leño, m; Naut., diario de a bordo m, barquilla, f. **to lie like a log,** estar hecho un tronco. **log-book,** Naut. cuaderno de bitácora, m. **log-cabin,** cabañas de troncos, f. **log-wood,** palo campeche, m
logarithm /'lɔgə,rɪðəm/ n logaritmo, m
logarithmic /,lɔgə'rɪðmɪk/ a logarítmico
logic /'lɒdʒɪk/ n lógica, f
logical /'lɒdʒɪkəl/ a lógico
logician /lou'dʒɪʃən/ n lógico (-ca)
loin /lɔɪn/ n (of meat) falda, f; pl **loins,** lomos, riñones m pl. **to gird up one's loins,** Fig. arremangarse los faldones. **l.-cloth,** taparrabo, m
loiter /'lɔɪtər/ vi vagabundear, vagar, errar; haraganear; rezagarse
loiterer /'lɔɪtərər/ n haragán (-ana); vago (-ga); rezagado (-da)
loll /lɒl/ vi recostarse (en), apoyarse (en). vt (the tongue) sacar

London /'lʌndən/ Londres, *m*
Londoner /'lʌndənər/ *n* londinense, *mf*
lone /loun/ *a* solitario, (only) único
loneliness /'lounlinis/ *n* soledad, *f*; aislamiento, *m*
lonely /'lounli/ *a* solitario; solo; aislado, remoto; desierto
lonesome /'lounsəm/ *a* solo, solitario
long /lɔŋ/ *a* largo; prolongado; de largo; (extensive) extenso; (big) grande; (much) mucho. **a l. time,** mucho tiempo. **It is five feet l.,** Tiene cinco pies de largo. **l.-armed,** que tiene los brazos largos. **l.-boat,** falúa, *f*. **l. clothes,** (infant's) mantillas, *f pl*. **l.-distance call,** conferencia telefónica, *f*. **l.-distance race,** carrera de fondo, *f*. **l.-eared,** de orejas largas. **l.-faced,** de cara larga, carilargo. **l.-forgotten,** olvidado hace mucho tiempo. **l.-haired,** que tiene el pelo largo. **l.-headed,** dolicocéfalo; *Fig.* astuto, sagaz. **l.-legged,** zanquilargo, zancudo. **l.-lived,** que vive hasta una edad avanzada; longevo; duradero. **l.-lost,** perdido hace mucho tiempo. **l.-sighted,** présbita; previsor; sagaz. **l.-standing,** viejo, de muchos años. **l.-suffering,** sufrido, paciente. **l.-tailed,** de cola larga. **l.-waisted,** de talle largo. **l.-winded,** prolijo
long /lɔŋ/ *adv* mucho tiempo; mucho; durante mucho tiempo. **as l. as,** mientras (que). **before l.,** dentro de poco. **the l. and the short of it,** en resumidas cuentas. **How l. has she been here?** ¿Cuánto tiempo hace que está aquí? **not l. before,** poco tiempo antes. **l. ago,** tiempo ha, muchos años ha
long /lɔŋ/ *vi* anhelar, suspirar (por), desear con vehemencia
longanimity /,lɔŋgə'nimiti/ *n* longanimidad, *f*
longer /'lɔŋgər/ *a comp* más largo. *adv comp* más tiempo. **How much l. must we wait?** ¿Cuánto tiempo más hemos de esperar? **He can no l. walk as he used,** Ya no puede andar como antes
longevity /lɒn'dʒɛviti/ *n* longevidad, *f*
longing /'lɔŋiŋ/ *a* anheloso, ansioso; de envidia. *n* anhelo, *m*, ansia, *f*; deseo vehemente, *m*; envidia, *f*
longingly /'lɔŋiŋli/ *adv* con ansia; impacientemente; con envidia
longish /'lɔŋiʃ/ *a* algo largo
longitude /'lɒndʒi,tud/ *n* longitud, *f*
longitudinal /,lɒndʒi'tudn̩l/ *a* longitudinal
loofah /'lufə/ *n* esponja vegetal, *f*
look /lʊk/ *n* mirada, *f*; (glance) vistazo, *m*, ojeada, *f*; (air) semblante, aire, porte, *m*; (appearance) aspecto, *m*; apariencia, *f*. **good looks,** buen parecer, *m*; guapeza, *f*. **the new l.,** la nueva línea, la nueva silueta, la nueva moda. **to be on the l.-out,** andar a la mira
look /lʊk/ *vi* and *vt* mirar; considerar, contemplar; (appear, seem) parecer; tener aire (de); tener aspecto (de); hacer el efecto (de); (show oneself) mostrarse; (of buildings, etc.) caer (a), dar (a); mirar (a); (seem to be) revelar (e.g., *You don't l. thirty*, No revelas treinta años) **to l. alike,** parecerse. **to l. hopeful,** *Fig.* prometer bien. **to l. out of the corner of the eye,** mirar de reojo. **to l.** (**a person**) **up and down,** mirar de hito en hito. **to l. about one,** mirar a su alrededor; observar. **to l. after,** tener la mirada puesta en, mirar; (care for) cuidar; (watch) vigilar; mirar por. **to l. at,** mirar; considerar; examinar. **He looked at his watch,** Miró su reloj. **He looked at her,** La miró. **to l. away,** desviar los ojos, apartar la mirada. **to l. back,** mirar hacia atrás, volver la cabeza; (in thought) pensar en el pasado. **to l. down,** bajar los ojos; mirar el suelo; mirar hacia abajo. **to l. down upon,** dominar, mirar a (sobre) despreciar; mirar de arriba para abajo. **to l. for,** buscar; buscar con los ojos; (await) aguardar; (expect) esperar. **to l. forward,** mirar hacia el porvenir; pensar en el futuro; esperar con ilusión. **to l. in,** entrar por un instante, hacer una visita corta. **to l. into,** mirar dentro de; mirar hacia el interior de; estudiar, investigar, *Lat. Am. also* interiorizar. **to l. on,** *vt* mirar; considerar; (of buildings, etc.) dar a. *vi* ser espectador. **to l. on to,** dar a, mirar a. **to l. out,** *vi* (be careful) tener cuidado; (look through) mirar por; asomarse a. *vt* (search) buscar; (find) hallar; (choose) escoger, elegir. **L. out!** ¡Atención! ¡Ojo!, *Mexico* ¡abusado! **to l. out for,** buscar; (await) aguardar, esperar; (be careful) tener cuidado con. **to l. out**

of, mirar por; asomarse a. **to l. over,** mirar bien; (persons) mirar de hito en hito; examinar; visitar; (a house) inspeccionar; (a book) hojear; mirar superficialmente. **to l. around,** *vt* (a place) visitar. *vi* volver la cabeza, volverse; mirar hacia atrás. **to l. around for,** buscar con los ojos; buscar por todas partes. **to l. through,** mirar por; mirar a través de; examinar; (search) registrar; (understand) registrar. **to l. to,** (be careful of) tener cuidado de; (attend to) atender a; (care for) cuidar de; (count on) contar con; (resort to) acudir a; (await) esperar. **to l. toward,** mirar hacia, mirar en la dirección de; caer a. **to l. up,** *vi* mirar hacia arriba; (aspire) aspirar; (improve) mejorar. *vt* visitar, ir (o venir) a ver; (turn up) buscar; averiguar. **to l. upon,** mirar. Other meanings see **to l. on.** **They l. upon her as their daughter,** La miran como una hija suya. **to l. up to,** *Fig.* respetar
looking /'lʊkiŋ/ *a* (in compounds) de... aspecto, de... apariencia. **dirty-l.,** de aspecto sucio. **l.-glass,** espejo, *m*
lookout /'lʊk,aut/ *n* vigilancia, observación, *f*; (view) vista, *f*, panorama, *m*; (viewpoint) miradero, *m*; *Mil.* atalaya, *m*; *Naut.* gaviero, *m*; (*Fig.* prospect) perspectiva, *f*
loom /lum/ *n* telar, *m*, *vi* asomar, aparecer
loop /lup/ *n* (turn) vuelta, *f*; (in rivers, etc.) recodo, *m*, curva, *f*; (fold) pliegue, *m*; bucle, *m*; (fastening) fiador, *m*, presilla, *f*; *Aer.* rizo, *m*; (knot) nudo corredizo, *m*. **to l. the l.,** *Aer.* hacer el rizo, hacer rizos. **l.-line,** empalme de ferrocarril, *m*
loophole /'lup,houl/ *n* saetera, aspillera, *f*; *Fig.* escapatoria, *f*; pretexto, *m*, excusa, *f*
loose /lus/ *a* suelto; (free) libre; (slack) flojo; (of garments) holgado; (untied) desatado; (unfastened) desprendido; movible; (unchained) desencadenado; en libertad; (of the bowels) suelto (de vientre); (pendulous) colgante; (of a nail, tooth, etc.) inseguro; poco firme; que se mueve; (of knots, etc.) flojo; (of the mind, etc.) incoherente, ilógico; poco exacto; (of style, etc.) vago, impreciso; (of conduct) disoluto, vicioso; (careless) negligente, descuidado. *vt* (untie) desatar; desprender; soltar; aflojar; (of a priest) absolver; *Fig.* desencadenar. **to break l.,** desprenderse; soltarse; libertarse; escapar; *Fig.* desencadenarse. **to let l.,** desatar; aflojar; poner en libertad; soltar; *Fig.* desencadenar; (interject) lanzar. **to turn l.,** poner en libertad; dar salida (a); echar de casa, poner en la calle. **to give someone l. reins,** darle reinda suelta. **to work l.,** desprenderse; aflojarse; desvencijarse. **l.-box,** caballeriza, *f*. **l. change,** suelto, *m*. **l.-leaf notebook,** libreta de hojas sueltas, *f*
loosely /'lusli/ *adv* flojamente; sueltamente; (vaguely) vagamente; incorrectamente; incoherentemente; (carelessly) negligentemente; (viciously) disolutamente
loosen /'lusən/ *vt* (untie) desatar; aflojar; soltar; desasir; (the tongue) desatar; *Fig.* hacer menos riguroso, ablandar
looseness /'lusnis/ *n* flojedad, *f*; (of clothing) holgura, *f*; soltura, *f*; relajación, *f*; (of the bowels) diarrea, *f*; (viciousness) licencia, *f*, libertinaje, *m*; (vagueness) vaguedad, *f*; incoherencia, *f*
loosening /'lusəniŋ/ *n* desprendimiento, *m*; desasimiento, *m*; aflojamiento, *m*
loot /lut/ *n* botín, *m*, *vt* saquear
looter /'lutər/ *n* saqueador (-ra)
looting /'lutiŋ/ *n* saqueo, pillaje, *m*, *a* saqueador
lop /lɒp/ *vt* mochar; podar; destroncar; cortar de un golpe. *a* (of ears) gacho. **to lop off the ends,** cercenar. **to lop off the top,** desmochar. **lop-sided,** *a* desproporcionado; desequilibrado
lopping /'lɒpiŋ/ *n* desmoche, *m*; poda, *f*
loquacious /lou'kweiʃəs/ *a* locuaz, gárrulo
loquacity /lou'kwæsiti/ *n* locuacidad, garrulidad, *f*
lord /lɔrd/ *n* señor, *m*; (husband) esposo, *m*; (English title) lord, *m*, (pl lores); (Christ) Señor, *m*. **feudal l.,** señor de horca y cuchillo, *m*. **my l.,** milord. **my lords,** milores. **Our L.,** Nuestro Señor. **the Lord's Prayer,** el Padrenuestro. **to lord it over,** mandar a la baqueta
lordliness /'lɔrdlinis/ *n* suntuosidad, *f*; liberalidad,

munificencia, *f*; dignidad, *f*; (haughtiness) altivez, arrogancia, *f*

lordly /'lɔrdli/ *a* señorial, señoril; altivo, arrogante

lordship /'lɔrdʃɪp/ *n* señoría, *f*; señorío, poder, *m*. **his l.,** su señoría

lore /lɔr/ *n* saber, *m*; erudición, *f*; tradiciones, *f pl*

lose /luz/ *vt* perder; hacer perder, quitar; (forget) olvidar. *vi* perder; (of clocks) atrasar. **to be lost in thought,** estar ensimismado, estar absorto. **to l. oneself (in)** perderse (en); abstraerse (en); entregarse (a). **to l. one's footing,** resbalar. **to l. one's way,** extraviarse, perder el camino. **to l. one's self-control,** perder el tino. **to l. one's head,** perder la cabeza. **to l. ground,** perder terreno. **to l. one's voice,** perder la voz. **to l. patience,** perder la paciencia, perder los estribos

loser /'luzər/ *n* perdedor (-ra), *Inf.* desdichado (-da)

losing /'luzɪŋ/ *a* perdedor. *n* pérdida, *f*

loss /lɔs/ *n* pérdida, *f*. **at a l.,** *Com.* con pérdida; perplejo, dudoso. **heavy losses,** *Mil.* pérdidas cuantiosas, *f pl.* **loss of blood** *Lat. Am.* desangre *m*. **We are at a l. for words...,** No tenemos palabras para...

lot /lɒt/ *n* suerte, *f*; fortuna, *f*; lote, *m*; parte, porción, cuota, *f*; (for building) solar, *m*. **a lot of people,** muchas personas. **Our lot would have been very different,** Nuestra suerte hubiera sido muy distinta, Otro gallo nos cantara. **to draw lots,** echar suertes, sortear. **to take the lot,** *Inf.* alzarse con el santo y la limosna

lotion /'louʃən/ *n* loción, *f*

lottery /'lɒtəri/ *n* lotería, *f*. **l. ticket,** billete de la lotería, *m*

lotus /'loutəs/ *n* loto, *m*. **l.-eating,** lotofagía, *f*; *Fig.* indolencia, pereza, *f*

loud /laud/ *a* fuerte; (noisy) ruidoso, estrepitoso; alto; (gaudy) chillón, llamativo, cursi, *Lat. Am. also* figuroso. *adv* ruidosamente. **l.-speaker,** *Radio.* altavoz, *Mexico* magnavoz. *m*

loudly /'laudli/ *adv* en alta voz; fuertemente; ruidosamente, con estrépito

loudness /'laudnɪs/ *n* (noise) ruido, *m*; sonoridad, *f*; (force) fuerza, *f*; (of colors, etc.) mal gusto, *m*, vulgaridad, *f*

lounge /laundʒ/ *n* sala de estar, *f*; salón, *m*, *vi* reclinarse, ponerse a sus anchas; apoyarse (en); gandulear; vagar. **l. chair,** poltrona, *f*. **l.-lizard,** *Inf.* pollo pera, *m*. **l.-suit,** traje americano, *m*

lounger /'laundʒər/ *n* holgazán (-ana); golfo (-fa), azotacalles, *mf*

louse /laus/ *n* piojo, *m*

lousy /'lauzi/ *a* piojoso

lout /laut/ *n* patán, zamacuco, *m*

loutish /'lautɪʃ/ *a* rústico

lovable /'lʌvəbəl/ *a* amable; simpático

lovableness /'lʌvəbəlnɪs/ *n* amabilidad, *f*

love /lʌv/ *n* amor, *m*; (friendship) amistad, *f*; (enthusiasm, liking) afición, *f*; (in tennis) cero, *m*, *vt* querer; amar; gustar mucho; tener afición (a). *vi* estar enamorado. **I should l. to dine with you,** Me gustaría mucho cenar con Vds. **to be in l. with,** estar enamorado de. **to fall in l. with,** enamorarse de. **They l. each other,** Se quieren. **to make l. to,** hacer el amor (a), galantear. **l. affair,** amorío, lance de amor, *m*. **l.-bird,** periquito, *m*. **l.-letter,** carta amatoria, carta de amor, *f*. **l.-making,** galanteo, *m*. **l.-philtre,** filtro, *m*. **l.-song,** canción de amor, *f*. **l.-story,** historia de amor, *f*. **l.-token,** prenda de amor, *f*

loveless /'lʌvlɪs/ *a* sin amor

loveliness /'lʌvlinɪs/ *n* hermosura, belleza, *f*; encanto, *m*; amabilidad, *f*

lovely /'lʌvli/ *a* hermoso, bello; delicioso; amable; *Inf.* estupendo

lover /'lʌvər/ *n* amante, *mf*; aficionado (-da)

lovesick /'lʌv,sɪk/ *a* enfermo de amor, enamorado

loving /'lʌvɪŋ/ *a* amoroso; cariñoso; (friendly) amistoso; de amor

low /lou/ *a* bajo; de poca altura; (of dresses, etc.) escotado; (of musical notes) grave; (soft) suave; (feeble) débil; (depressed) deprimido, triste, abatido; (plain) sencillo; (of a fever) lento; (of a bow) profundo; pequeño; inferior; humilde; (ill) enfermo;

(vile) vil, ruin; obsceno, escabroso. *adv* bajo; cerca de la tierra; en voz baja; (cheaply) barato, a bajo precio. **in a low voice,** en voz baja, paso. **to lay low,** (kill) tumbar; (knock down) derribar; incapacitar. **to lie low,** descansar; estar muerto; esconderse, agacharse; callar. **to run low,** escasear. **low-born,** de humilde cuna. **low-brow,** nada intelectual. **low comedy,** farsa, *f*. **low flying,** *n* bajo vuelo, *m*, *a* que vuela bajo; terrero, rastrero; que vuela a ras de tierra. **low frequency,** baja frecuencia, *f*. **low Latin,** bajo latín, *m*. **Low Mass,** misa rezada, *f*. **low neck,** escote, *m*. **low-necked,** escotado. **low-pitched,** grave. **low-spirited,** deprimido. **Low Sunday,** domingo de Cuasimodo, *m*. **low tension,** baja tensión, *f*. **low trick,** mala pasada, *f*. **low water,** marea baja, bajamar, *f*; (of rivers) estiaje, *m*

low /lou/ *vi* berrear, mugir. *n* berrido, mugido, *m*

low-ceiling /'lou 'silɪŋ/ *a* bajo de techo.

lower /'louər/ *vt* bajar; descolgar; disminuir; (price) rebajar; (a boat, sails) arriar. *vi* (of persons) fruncir el ceño, mostrarse malhumorado; (of the sky) encapotarse, cargarse; (menace) amenazar. **to l. a boat,** arriar un bote. **to l. oneself,** (by a rope, etc.) descolgarse. **to l. the flag,** abatir la bandera

lower /'louər/ *a comp* más bajo; menos alto; bajo; inferior. **l. classes,** clase obrera, *f*, clases bajas, *f pl*. **l. down,** más abajo. cámara baja, *f*. **l. jaw,** mandíbula inferior, *f*. **l. story,** piso bajo, *m*; piso de abajo, *m*

lowering /'louərɪŋ/ *n* abajamiento, *m*; descenso, *m*; (of prices) baja, *f*; (of a boat) arriada, *f*; (of the flag) abatimiento, *m*, *a* (of persons) ceñudo; (of the sky) anublado, encapotado; (threatening) amenazador

lowest /'louɪst/ *a sup* el (la, etc.) más bajo; el (la, etc.) más profundo; ínfimo

lowing /'louɪŋ/ *n* berrido, mugido, *m*

lowland /'loulənd/ *n* tierra baja, *f*. **the Lowlands,** las tierras bajas de Escocia

lowliness /'loulinɪs/ *n* humildad, *f*; modestia, *f*

lowly /'louli/ *a* humilde

lowness /'lounɪs/ *n* poca altura, *f*; situación poco elevada, *f*; pequeñez, *f*; (of musical notes) gravedad, *f*; (softness) suavidad, *f*; (feebleness) debilidad, *f*; (sadness) tristeza, *f*, abatimiento, *m*; (of price) baratura, *f*; inferioridad, *f*; humildad, *f*; (vileness) bajeza, *f*; obscenidad, *f*

loyal /'lɔiəl/ *a* leal, fiel

loyalist /'lɔiəlɪst/ *n* realista, *mf*; defensor (-ra) del gobierno legítimo

loyalty /'lɔiəlti/ *n* lealtad, fidelidad, *f*

loyalty oath *n* (approximate equivalent) certificado de adhesión, *m*

lozenge /'lɒzɪndʒ/ *n* pastilla, *f*

lubricant /'lubrɪkənt/ *a and n* lubricante *m*

lubricate /'lubrɪ,keit/ *vt* lubricar, engrasar

lubricating oil /'lubrɪ,keitɪŋ/ *n* aceite lubricante, *m*

lubrication /,lubrɪ'keiʃən/ *n* lubricación, *f*, engrasado, *m*

lubricator /'lubrɪ,keitər/ *n* lubricador, *m*; engrasador, *m*

Lucerne /lu'sɜrn/ Lucerna, *f*

lucid /'lusɪd/ *a* lúcido; claro

lucidity /lu'sɪdɪti/ *n* lucidez, *f*; claridad, *f*

lucidly /'lusɪdli/ *adv* claramente

luck /lʌk/ *n* destino, azar, *m*; (good) buenaventura, suerte, *f*. **to bring bad l.,** traer mala suerte. **to try one's l.,** probar fortuna

luckily /'lʌkəli/ *adv* por fortuna, afortunadamente, felizmente

luckless /'lʌklɪs/ *a* desdichado

lucky /'lʌki/ *a* afortunado; dichoso, venturoso, *Lat. Am. also* lechudo; feliz. **to be l.,** tener buena suerte

lucrative /'lukrətɪv/ *a* lucrativo

lucre /'lukər/ *n* lucro, *m*

lucubration /,lukyu'breiʃən/ *n* lucubración, *f*

ludicrous /'ludɪkrəs/ *a* absurdo, risible, ridículo

ludicrousness /'ludɪkrəsnɪs/ *n* ridiculez, *f*

lug /lʌg/ *n* tirón, *m*; (ear and projection) oreja, *f*, *vt* tirar (de); arrastrar. **to lug about,** arrastrar (por); llevar con dificultad. **to lug in,** arrastrar adentro; introducir; hacer entrar. **to lug out,** arrastrar afuera; hacer salir

luggage /'lʌgɪdʒ/ n equipaje, m. **excess l.**, exceso de equipaje, m. **piece of l.**, bulto, m. **to register one's l.**, facturar el equipaje. **l. carrier**, (on buses, etc.) baca, f; (on a car) portaequipajes, m. **l. porter**, mozo de equipajes, m. **l. rack**, (on a car) portaequipajes, m; (in a train) rejilla para el equipaje, f. **l. receipt**, talón de equipaje, m. **l. room**, consigna, f. **l. van**, furgón de equipajes, m

lugubrious /lʊ'gubriəs/ a lúgubre

lukewarm /'luk'wɔrm/ a tibio, templado; Fig. indiferente, frío

lukewarmness /'luk'wɔrmnɪs/ n tibieza, f; Fig. indiferencia, frialdad, f

lull /lʌl/ n momento de calma, m; tregua, f; silencio, m, vt (a child) arrullar, adormecer; (soothe) sosegar, calmar; disminuir, mitigar

lullaby /'lʌlə,bai/ n canción de cuna, f

lumbago /lʌm'beigou/ n lumbago, m

lumbar /'lʌmbər/ a lumbar

lumber /'lʌmbər/ n (wood) maderas de sierra, f pl; (rubbish) trastos viejos, m pl. vt amontonar trastos viejos; obstruir. vi andar pesadamente; avanzar ruidosamente, avanzar con ruido sordo. **l.-jack**, maderero, ganchero, m. **l.-room**, leonera, f. **l.-yard**, maderería, f, depósito de maderas, m

lumbering /'lʌmbərɪŋ/ a pesado

luminary /'lumə,nɛri/ n lumbrera, f

luminosity /,lumə'nɒsɪti/ n luminosidad, f

luminous /'lumənəs/ a luminoso

lump /lʌmp/ n masa, f; bulto, m; pedazo, m; (of sugar) terrón, m; (swelling) hinchazón, f; protuberancia, f. vt amontonar. **to l. together**, mezclar; incluir. **in the l.**, en la masa; en grueso. **Let him l. it!** ¡Que se rasque! **l. in one's throat**, nudo en la garganta, m. **l. of sugar**, terrón de azúcar, m. **l. sum**, cantidad gruesa, f

lumpishness /'lʌmpɪʃnɪs/ n hobachonería, f

lunacy /'lunəsi/ n locura, f

lunar /'lunər/ a lunar

lunatic /'lunətɪk/ n loco (-ca); demente, mf a de locos; loco. **l. asylum**, manicomio, m

lunch, luncheon /lʌntʃ; lʌntʃən/ n almuerzo, m, Mexico fajina, f; (snack) merienda, f. vi almorzar. **l. basket** or **pail**, fiambrera, f

lunch counter, luncheonette Mexico almuercería, elsewhere in Lat. Am. lonchería, f

lunette /lu'nɛt/ n (Archit. Mil.) luneta, f

lung /lʌŋ/ n pulmón, m

lunge /lʌndʒ/ n (fencing) estocada, f; embestida, f, vi dar una estocada; abalanzarse sobre

lurch /lɜrtʃ/ n sacudida, f; Naut. guiñada, f; tambaleo, m; movimiento brusco, m. vi Naut. guiñar; tambalearse; andar haciendo eses. **to leave in the l.**, dejar plantado

lure /lʊr/ n añagaza, f; reclamo, m; aliciente, atractivo, m; seducción, f. vt atraer, tentar

lurid /'lʊrɪd/ a misterioso, fantástico; cárdeno; ominoso; funesto, triste; (orange) anaranjado; (vicissitudinous) accidentado

lurk /lɜrk/ vi acechar, espiar; esconderse

lurking /'lɜrkɪŋ/ a (in ambush) en acecho; (of fear, etc.) vago

luscious /'lʌʃəs/ a delicioso; suculento; meloso; atractivo, apetitoso; sensual

lusciousness /'lʌʃəsnɪs/ n suculencia, f; melosidad, f; atractivo, m; sensualidad, f

lush /lʌʃ/ a jugoso; fresco y lozano; maduro

lust /lʌst/ n lujuria, lascivia, f; codicia, f; deseo, m. **l. for revenge**, deseo de venganza, m

luster /'lʌstər/ n lustre, brillo, m; brillantez, f

lusterless /'lʌstərlɪs/ a sin brillo; mate, deslustrado; (of eyes) apagado

lustful /'lʌstfəl/ a lujurioso, lúbrico, lascivo

lustrous /'lʌstrəs/ a lustroso

lusty /'lʌsti/ a vigoroso, fuerte, lozano

lute /lut/ n laúd, m, vihuela, f. **l.-player**, vihuelista, mf

Lutheran /'luθərən/ a luterano. n luterano (-na)

Lutheranism /'luθərə,nɪzəm/ n luteranismo, m

luxation /lʌk'seiʃən/ n luxación, f

luxuriance /lʌg'ʒʊriəns/ n lozanía, f; exuberancia, superabundancia, f

luxuriant /lʌg'ʒʊriənt/ a lozano; fértil; exuberante

luxuriate /lʌg'ʒʊri,eit/ vi crecer con exuberancia; complacerse (en); disfrutar (de), gozar (de)

luxurious /lʌg'ʒʊriəs/ a lujoso

luxuriously /lʌg'ʒʊriəsli/ adv lujosamente, con lujo

luxury /'lʌkʃəri/ n lujo, m. **l. goods**, artículos de lujo, m pl

lyceum /lai'siəm/ n liceo, m

lye /lai/ n lejía, f

lying /'laiɪŋ/ a (recumbent) recostado; (untrue) mentiroso, falso. n mentiras, f pl. **l.-in**, parto, m

lymph /lɪmf/ n linfa, f; vacuna, f

lymphatic /lɪm'fætɪk/ a linfático; flemático

lynch /lɪntʃ/ vt linchar

lynching /'lɪntʃɪŋ/ n linchamiento, m

lynx /lɪŋks/ n lince, m. **l.-eyed**, de ojos de lince

lyre /laiᵊr/ n lira, f. **l.-bird**, pájaro lira, m

lyric /'lɪrɪk/ n poesía lírica, f; poema lírico, m; letra (de una canción), f

lyrical /'lɪrɪkəl/ a lírico

lyricism /'lɪrə,sɪzəm/ n lirismo, m

M

m /ɛm/ n (letter) eme, f

ma'am /mæm/ n señora, f

macabre /mə'kɑbrə/ a macabro

macadam /mə'kædəm/ n macadán, m, a de macadán

macadamize /mə'kædə,maiz/ vt macadanizar

macaroni /,mækə'rouni/ n macarrones, m pl

macaronic /,mækə'rɒnɪk/ a macarrónico

macaroon /,mækə'run/ n macarrón de almendras, m

macaw /mə'kɔ/ n macagua, f, guacamayo, m

mace /meis/ n maza, f; Cul. macis, f. **m.-bearer**, macero, m

Macedonian /,mæsɪ'douniən/ a macedón, macedonio. n macedonio (-ia)

macerate /'mæsə,reit/ vt macerar. vi macerarse

machete /mə'ʃɛti/ n Mexico alfanje, elsewhere machete, m

Machiavellian /,mækiə'vɛliən/ a maquiavélico

Machiavellism /,mækiə'vɛlɪzəm/ n maquiavelismo, m

machination /,mækə'neiʃən/ n maquinación, f

machine /mə'ʃin/ n máquina, f; mecanismo, m; aparato, m; instrumento, m; organización, f, vt trabajar a máquina; Sew. coser a máquina. **m.-gun**, n

ametralladora, f. vt ametrallar. **m.-gun carrier**, portametralladoras, m. **m.-gunner**, ametrallador, m. **m.-made**, hecho a máquina. **m.-oil**, aceite de motores, m. **m.-shop**, taller de maquinaria, m, Lat. Am. maestranza, f. **m.-tool**, máquina herramienta, f

machinery /mə'ʃinəri/ n maquinaria, f; mecanismo, m; organización, f; sistema, m

machinist /mə'ʃinɪst/ n maquinista, mf; Sew. costurera a máquina, f

mackerel /'mækərəl/ n caballa, f. **m. sky**, cielo aborregado, m

mackintosh /'mækɪn,tɒʃ/ n impermeable, m

macrocosm /'mækrə,kɒzəm/ n macrocosmo, m

mad /mæd/ a loco; fuera de sí; (of a dog, etc.) rabioso; furioso. **as mad as a hatter**, loco como una cabra. **to drive mad**, volver loco (a). **to go mad**, volverse loco, enloquecer, perder el seso. **mad with joy (pain)**, loco de alegría (dolor). **mad dog**, perro rabioso, m

madam /'mædəm/ n señora, f; (French form) madama, f. **Yes, m.**, Sí señora

madcap /'mæd,kæp/ n locuelo (-la), f, botarate, m; tarambana, mf

madden /'mædn̩/ *vt* enloquecer; enfurecer, exasperar

maddening /'mædn̩ɪŋ/ *a* exasperante, irritador

madder /'mædər/ *n* Bot. rubia, *f*

made /meid/ *past part* and *a* hecho; formado. **self-m. man,** un hombre hecho y derecho. **m.-to-measure,** hecho a la medida. **m.-up,** compuesto; (of clothes) confeccionado, ya hecho; (of the face) pintado; (fictitious) inventado, ficticio; artificial

Madeira /mə'dɪərə/ *n* vino de Madera, *m*, *a* de Madera

madhouse /'mæd,haus/ *n* casa de locos, *f*, manicomio, *m*

madly /'mædli/ *adv* locamente; furiosamente

madman /'mæd,mæn/ *n* loco, *m*

madness /'mædnɪs/ *n* locura, *f*; (of a dog, etc.) rabia, *f*; furia, *f*

Madonna /mə'dɒnə/ *n* Madona, *f*

madrigal /'mædrɪgəl/ *n* madrigal, *m*

Madrilenian /,mædrə'liniən/ *a* madrileño, matritense. *n* madrileño (-ña)

madwoman /'mæd,wumən/ *n* loca, *f*

Maecenas /mi'sinəs/ *n* mecenas, *f*

maelstrom /'meilstrəm/ *n* remolino, vórtice, *m*

magazine /,mægə'zin/ *n* (store) almacén, *m*; (for explosives) polvorín, *m*, santabárbara, *f*; (periodical) revista, *f*. **m. rifle,** rifle de repetición, *m*

Magdalen /'mægdə,lin/ *n* magdalena, *f*

magenta /mə'dʒɛntə/ *n* color magenta, *m*

maggot /'mægət/ *n* gusano, *m*, cresa, *f*; Fig. manía, *f*, capricho, *m*

maggoty /'mægəti/ *a* gusanoso

Magi, the /'meidʒai/ *n pl* los reyes magos

magic /'mædʒɪk/ *n* magia, *f*; mágica, *f*; Fig. encanto, *m*, *a* mágico. **as if by m.,** por ensalmo. **m. lantern,** linterna mágica, *f*

magically /'mædʒɪkli/ *adv* por encanto

magician /mə'dʒɪʃən/ *n* mago, mágico, brujo, *m*; (conjurer) jugador de manos, *m*

magisterial /,mædʒə'stɪərɪəl/ *a* magistral

magistracy /'mædʒəstrəsi/ *n* magistratura, *f*

magistrate /'mædʒə,streit/ *n* magistrado, *m*; juez municipal, *m*

Magna Charta /'mægnə 'kartə/ *n* Carta Magna, *f*

magnanimity /,mægnə'nɪmɪti/ *n* magnanimidad, generosidad, *f*

magnanimous /mæg'nænəməs/ *a* magnánimo, generoso

magnanimously /mæg'nænəməsli/ *adv* magnánimamente

magnate /'mægneit/ *n* magnate, *m*

magnesia /mæg'niʒə/ *n* magnesia, *f*

magnesium /mæg'niziəm/ *n* magnesio, *m*. **m. light,** luz de magnesio, *f*

magnet /'mægnɪt/ *n* imán, *m*

magnetic /mæg'nɛtɪk/ *a* magnético; Fig. atractivo. **m. field,** campo magnético, *m*. **m. needle,** brújula, *f*

magnetics /mæg'nɛtɪks/ *n* la ciencia del magnetismo, *f*

magnetism /'mægnɪ,tɪzəm/ *n* magnetismo, *m*

magnetization /,mægɪtɪ'zeiʃən/ *n* imanación, magnetización, *f*

magnetize /'mægnɪ,taiz/ *vt* magnetizar, imanar; (hypnotize) magnetizar; Fig. atraer

magnification /,mægnəfɪ'keiʃən/ *n* (by a lens, etc.) aumento, *m*; exageración, *f*

magnificence /mæg'nɪfəsəns/ *n* magnificencia, *f*

magnificent /mæg'nɪfəsənt/ *a* magnífico

magnify /'mægnə,fai/ *vt* (by lens) aumentar; exagerar; (praise) magnificar

magnifying /'mægnə,faiŋ/ *a* de aumento, vidrio de aumento. **m. glass,** lente de aumento, *m*

magniloquence /mæg'nɪləkwəns/ *n* grandilocuencia, *f*

magniloquent /mæg'nɪləkwənt/ *a* grandílocuo

magnitude /'mægnɪ,tud/ *n* magnitud, *f*

magnolia /mæg'noulyə/ *n* magnolia, *f*

magnum /'mægnəm/ *n* botella de dos litros, *f*

magpie /'mæg,pai/ *n* marica, picaza, *f*

maharaja /,mahə'radʒə/ *n* maharajá, *m*

mahogany /mə'hɒgəni/ *n* caoba, *f*, *a* de caoba

maid /meid/ *n* doncella, muchacha, *f*; virgen, *f*; soltera, *f*; (servant) criada, *f*; (daily) asistenta, *f*. **old m.,** solterona, *f*. **m.-of-all-work,** criada para todo, *f*. **m.-of-honor,** dama de honor, *f*

maiden /'meidn̩/ *n* doncella, joven, soltera, *f*; virgen, *f*; zagala, *f*. *a* de soltera; soltera *f*; virginal; (of speeches, voyages, etc.) primero. **m. lady,** dama soltera, *f*. **m.-name,** apellido de soltera, *m*. **m. speech,** primer discurso, *m*

maidenhood /'meidn̩,hud/ *n* doncellez, virginidad, *f*

maidenly /'meidn̩li/ *a* virginal; modesto, modoso; tímido

maidservant /'meid,sɜrvənt/ *n* criada, sirvienta, *f*

mail /meil/ *n* correo, *m*; correspondencia, *f*; (armor) cota de malla, *f*. *vt* mandar por correo, enviar por correo; armar con cota de malla. **coat of m.,** cota de malla, *f*. **royal m.,** malla real, *f*. **m.-bag,** valija de correo, *f*; portacartas, *m*. **m.-boat,** buque correo, *m*. **m.-cart,** ambulancia de correos, *f*. **m.-clad,** vestido de cota de malla; armado. **m.-coach,** coche correo, *m*, diligencia, *f*. **m.-order,** pedido postal, *m*. **m.-order business,** negocio de ventas por correo, *m*. **m.-plane,** avión postal, *m*. **m. service,** servicio de correos, *m*. **m. steamer,** vapor correo, *m*. **m. train,** tren correo, *m*. **m. van,** (on a train) furgón postal, *m*

mailed /meild/ *a* de malla; armado. **m. fist,** Fig. puño de hierro, *m*

maim /meim/ *vt* mancar; mutilar, tullir; estropear

maimed /meimd/ *a* manco; tullido, mutilado

main /mein/ *a* mayor; principal; más importante, esencial; maestro. *n* (mainland) continente, *m*; (sea) océano, *m*; (pipe) cañería maestra, *f*. **by m. force,** por fuerza mayor. **in the m.,** en general, generalmente; en su mayoría. **m. beam,** viga maestra, *f*. **m. body,** (of a building) ala principal, *f*; (of a church) cuerpo (de iglesia), *m*; (of an army) cuerpo (del ejército), *m*; mayor parte, mayoría, *f*. **m. line,** línea principal, *f*. **m. mast,** palo mayor, *m*. **m. thing,** cosa principal, *f*, lo más importante. **m. wall,** pared maestra, *f*

mainland /'mein,lænd/ *n* continente, *m*; tierra firme, *f*

mainly /'meinli/ *adv* principalmente; en su mayoría; generalmente

mainsail /'mein,seil/ *n* vela mayor, *f*

mainspring /'mein,sprɪŋ/ *n* (of a watch) muelle real, *m*; motivo principal, *m*; origen, *m*

mainstay /'mein,stei/ *n* estay mayor, *m*; Fig. sostén principal, *m*

maintain /mein'tein/ *vt* mantener; sostener; tener; guardar; afirmar

maintainable /mein'teinəbəl/ *a* sostenible; defendible

maintenance /'meintənəns/ *n* mantenimiento, *m*; manutención, *f*, sustento, *m*; conservación, *f*, subsistencia, *f*

maize /meiz/ *n* maíz, *m*. **m. field,** maizal, *m*

majestic /mə'dʒɛstɪk/ *a* majestuoso

majesty /'mædʒəsti/ *n* majestad, *f*; majestuosidad, *f*. **His or Her M.,** Su Majestad

majolica /mə'dʒɒlɪkə/ *n* mayólica, *f*

major /'meidʒər/ *a* mayor; principal. *n* mayor de edad, *m*; Mil. comandante. **anthropology major,** alumno con la especialidad en antropología *m*. **m.-domo,** mayordomo, *m*. **m.-general,** general de división, *m*. **m. road,** carretera, *f*; ruta de prioridad, *f*. **m. scale,** escala mayor, *f*

Majorca /mə'dʒɔrkə/ Mallorca, *f*

majority /mə'dʒɔrɪti/ *n* mayoría, *f*; mayor número, *m*; generalidad, *f*. **to have attained one's m.,** ser mayor de edad

make /meik/ *vt* hacer; crear, formar; (manufacture) fabricar, confeccionar; construir; (produce) producir; causar; (prepare) preparar; (a bed, a fire, a remark, poetry, friends, enemies, war, a curtsey) hacer; (earn, win) ganar; (a speech) pronunciar; (compel) obligar (a), forzar (a); inclinar (a); (arrive at) alcanzar, llegar (a); (calculate) calcular; (arrange) arreglar; deducir; (be) ser; (equal) ser igual a; (think) creer; (appoint as) constituir (en), hacer; (behave) portarse (como). *vi* (begin) ir (a), empezar (a); (make as though) hacer (como si); (of the tide) crecer; contribuir (a); tender (a). **He made as if to go,** Hizo como si de marchara. **to m. as though...,** aparentar, fingir. **It made me ill,** Me hizo sentir mal. **They have made up,** Han hecho las paces. **They m.** a great deal of **money,** Hacen (or ganan) mucho dinero. **You cannot m.** me believe it, No puedes hacerme creerlo. **He is making himself ridiculous,** Se está poniendo en ridículo. **to m. ready,** preparar. **to m. the tea,** hacer el té; preparar el té. **Two and two m. four,** Dos y dos son cuatro. **to m. oneself known,** darse a conocer. **to m. one of...,** ser uno de... **to m. after,** seguir; correr detrás de. **to m. again,** hacer de nuevo, rehacer. **to m. angry,** *Mexico.* amuinar. **to m. away with,** quitar; suprimir; destruir; (kill) matar; (squander) derrochar; (steal) llevarse; hurtar. **to m. away with oneself,** quitarse la vida, suicidarse. **to m. for,** encaminarse a, dirigirse a; (attack) abalanzarse sobre, atacar; (tend to) contribuir a, tender a. **to m. off,** marcharse corriendo, largarse; huir, escaparse. **to m. out,** (discern) distinguir; descifrar; (understand) comprender; (prove) probar, justificar; (draw up) redactar; (fill in a form) completar, llenar; (a check, etc.) extender; (an account) hacer; (get on, succeed or otherwise) ir (with bien or mal); (convey) dar la impresión de que; sugerir. **I cannot m. it out,** No lo puedo comprender. **How did you m. out** (get on)**?** ¿Cómo te fue? **to m. over,** hacer de nuevo, rehacer; (transfer) ceder, traspasar. **to m. up,** hacer; acabar; concluir; (clothes) confeccionar; fabricar; (the face) pintarse, maquillarse; (the fire) echar carbón, etc. a; *Print.* compaginar; (invent) inventar; (lies) fabricar; (compose) formar; (package) empaquetar; reparar; indemnizar; compensar; (an account) ajustar; preparar; arreglar; (conciliate) conciliar; enumerar; *Theat.* caracterizarse. **to m. up for,** reemplazar; compensar; (lost time, etc.) recobrar. **to m. up to,** compensar; indemnizar; (flatter) adular, halagar; procurar congraciarse con, procurar obtener el favor de; (court) galantear (con). **m. an impression (on),** dejar(le a fulano) una impresión

make /meik/ *n* forma, *f*; hechura, *f*; estructura, *f*; confección, *f*; manufactura, *f*; producto, *m*; (trade name) marca, *f*; (character) carácter, temperamento, *m*. **m.-believe,** *m* artificio, pretexto, *m*, *a* fingido, *vi* fingir. **land of m.-believe,** reino de los sueños, *m*. **m.-up,** (for the face, etc.) maquillaje, *m*; *Theat.* caracterización, *f*; *Print.* imposición, *f*; (whole) conjunto, *m*; (character) carácter, modo de ser, *m*

maker /'meikər/ *n* creador, *m*; autor (-ra); artífice, *mf*; (manufacturer) fabricante, *m*; constructor, *m*; (of clothes, etc.) confeccionador (-ra); (worker) obrero (-ra)

makeshift /'meik,ʃift/ *n* expediente, *m*, *a* provisional

makeweight /'meik,weit/ *n* añadidura (de peso), *f*, contrapeso, *m*; *Fig.* suplente, *m*

making /'meikiŋ/ *n* creación, *f*; hechura, *f*; (manufacture) fabricación, *f*; construcción, *f*; (of clothes, etc.) confección, *f*; formación, *f*; preparación, *f*; estructura, *f*; composición, *f*; *pl* **makings,** (profits) ganancias, *f pl*; (elements) elementos, *m pl*; germen, *m*; rasgos esenciales, *m pl*, características, *f. pl.* **m.-up,** (of clothes) confección, *f*; *Print.* ajuste, *m*; (of the face) maquillaje, *m*; (invention) invención, *f*; fabricación, *f*

maladjustment /,mælə'dʒʌstmənt/ *n* mal ajuste, *m*; inadaptación, *f*

maladministration /,mæləd,mɪnə'streiʃən/ *n* desgobierno, *m*, mala administración, *f*; (of funds) malversación, *f*

maladroit /,mælə'drɔit/ *a* torpe

maladroitness /,mælə'drɔitnɪs/ *n* torpeza, *f*

malady /'mælədi/ *n* enfermedad, *f*; mal, *m*

Malaga /'mæləgə/ *n* Málaga, *f* (wine) vino de Málaga, *m*

malaria /mə'lɛəriə/ *n* paludismo, *m*

malarial /mə'lɛəriəl/ *a* palúdico. **m. fever,** fiebre palúdica, *f*

Malaya /mə'leiə/ *n* Malasia, *f*, Archipiélago Malayo, *m*

Malayan /mə'leiən/ *a* malayo. *n* malayo (-ya)

malcontent /,mælkən'tɛnt/ *n* malcontento (-ta). *a* descontento

Maldives /'mɔldivz/ *n* Maldivas, *f pl*

male /meil/ *a* macho; masculino. *n* macho, *m*;

varón, *m*. **m. child,** niño, *m*; niño varón, *m*; (son) hijo varón, *m*. **m. flower,** flor masculina, *f*. **m. issue,** sucesión masculina, *f*. **m. nurse,** enfermero, *m*. **m. sex,** sexo masculino, *m*

malediction /,mælɪ'dɪkʃən/ *n* maldición, *f*

malefactor /'mælə,fæktər/ *n* malhechor (-ra)

malefic /mə'lefɪk/ *a* maléfico

malevolence /mə'lɛvələns/ *n* malevolencia, *f*

malevolent /mə'lɛvələnt/ *a* malévolo, maligno

malformation /,mælfɔr'meiʃən/ *n* formación anormal, deformidad, deformación congénita, *f*

malice /'mælɪs/ *n* malicia, *f*; *Law.* alevosía, *f*. **to bear m.,** guardar rencor

malicious /mə'lɪʃəs/ *a* malicioso; maligno, rencoroso

maliciousness /mə'lɪʃəsnɪs/ *n* malicia, mala intención, *f*

malign /mə'lain/ *vt* calumniar, difamar. *a* maligno; malévolo

malignancy /mə'lɪgnənsi/ *n* malignidad, *f*; malevolencia, *f*

malignant /mə'lɪgnənt/ *a* maligno; malévolo; *Med.* maligno

malinger /mə'lɪŋgər/ *vi* fingirse enfermo

malingerer /mə'lɪŋgərər/ *n* enfermo (-ma) fingido (-da)

malingering /mə'lɪŋgərɪŋ/ *n* enfermedad fingida, *f*

mallard /'mælərd/ *n* pato (-ta), silvestre

malleability /,mæliə'bɪliti/ *n* maleabilidad, *f*

malleable /'mæliəbəl/ *a* maleable

mallet /'mælɪt/ *n* mazo, *m*; (in croquet) pala, *f*, mazo, *m*; (in polo) maza (de polo), *f*

mallow /'mælou/ *n* malva, *f*

malmsey /'mɑmzi/ *n* (wine) malvasía, *f*

malnutrition /,mælnu'trɪʃən/ *n* desnutrición, alimentación deficiente, *f*

malodorous /mæl'oudərəs/ *a* de mal olor, hediondo, fétido

malpractice /mæl'præktɪs/ *n* (wrongdoing) maleficencia, *f*; (by a doctor) tratamiento equivocado, perjudicial o ilegal, *m*; (malversation) malversación, *f*; inmoralidad, *f*

malt /mɔlt/ *n* malta, *f*, *vt* preparar el malta. **m.-house,** fábrica de malta, *f*. **m. vinegar,** vinagre de malta, *m*

malted milk /'mɔltɪd/ *n* leche malteada, *f*

Maltese /mɔl'tiz/ *a* maltés. *n* maltés (-esa). **M. cat,** gato maltés, *m*. **M. cross,** cruz de Malta, *f*. **M. dog,** perro maltés, *m*

Malthusian /mæl'θuʒən/ *a* maltusiano

Malthusianism /mæl'θuʒə,nizəm/ *n* maltusianismo, *m*

maltose /'mɔltous/ *n* maltosa, *f*

maltreat /mæl'trit/ *vt* maltratar

maltreatment /mæl'tritmənt/ *n* maltrato, *m*,

malt shop *n* café-nevería, *m*

mamma /'mæmə *for 1;* 'mɑmə *for 2/ n Anat.* mama, *f*; (mother) mamá, *f*

mammal /'mæməl/ *n* mamífero, *m*

mammalian /mə'meiliən/ *a* mamífero

mammary /'mæməri/ *a* mamario. **m. gland,** mama, teta, *f*

mammon /'mæmən/ *n* becerro de oro, *m*

mammoth /'mæməθ/ *n* mamut, *m*, *a* gigantesco, enorme

man /mæn/ *n* hombre, *m*; varón, *m*; persona, *f*; (servant) criado, *m*; (workman) obrero, *m*; (soldier) soldado, *m*; (sailor) marinero, *m*; (humanity) raza humana, *f*; (husband) marido, *m*; (chess) peón, *m*; (checkers) dama, *f*; (a ship) buque, *m*. **no man,** nadie; ningún hombre. **young man,** joven, *m*. **to a man,** como un solo hombre. **to come to man's estate,** llegar a la edad viril. **Man overboard!** ¡Hombre al agua! **man and wife,** marido y mujer, *m*, cónyuges, esposos, *m pl.* **man about town,** hombre de mundo, señorito, *m*. **man-at-arms,** hombre de armas, *m*. **man-eater,** caníbal, *mf*; tigre, *m*. **man-eating,** *a* antropófago. **man hater,** misántropo, *m*; mujer que odia a los hombres, *f*. **man-hole,** pozo, *m*. **man-hunter,** caníbal, *mf*; (woman) castigadora, *f*. **man in charge,** encargado, *m*. **man in the moon,** mujer de la luna, f. **man in the street,** hombre de la calle, hombre medio, m. **man of letters,** hombre de letras, literato, m; **man of straw,** bausán, m; (figure-head) testaferro, m. **man of the world,** hombre del mundo, m. **man of war,** buque de guerra, m. **man-power,** mano de obra, f, brazos, m pl, (e.g. lack of manpower, falta de brazos, f). **man servant,** criado, m **man** /mæn/ vt armar; Mil. poner guarnición (a); ocupar; Naut. tripular; dirigir; Fig. fortificar

manacle /'mænəkəl/ n manilla, f; pl **manacles,** esposas, f pl; grillos, m pl. vt poner esposas (a)

manage /'mænɪdʒ/ vt manejar; (animals) domar; dirigir; gobernar; administrar; (arrange) agenciar, arreglar; (work) explotar; (do) hacer; (eat) comer. vi arreglárselas (para); (get along) ir tirando; (know how) saber hacer; (succeed in) lograr; (do) hacer

manageability /ˌmænɪdʒəˈbɪlɪti/ n lo manejable; flexibilidad, f; (of animals, persons) docilidad, mansedumbre, f

manageable /'mænɪdʒəbəl/ a manejable; flexible; (of persons, animals) dócil

management /'mænɪdʒmənt/ n manejo, m; dirección, f; gobierno, m; administración, f; arreglo, m; (working) explotación, f; Com. gerencia, f; Theat. empresa, f; conducta, f; (economy) economía, f; (skill) habilidad, f; prudencia, f. **the m.,** la dirección, el cuerpo de directores. **domestic m.,** economía doméstica, f

manager /'mænɪdʒər/ n director (-ra); administrador (-ra); jefe (-fa); Theat. empresario (-ria); Com. gerente, mf; regente, mf. **She is not much of a m.,** No es muy mujer de su casa. **manager's office,** dirección, f

managerial /ˌmænɪˈdʒɪəriəl/ a directivo; administrativo. **m. board,** junta directiva, f

managership /'mænɪdʒərˌʃɪp/ n puesto de director, m; jefatura, f

managing /'mænɪdʒɪŋ/ a directivo; (officious) mandón, dominante; (niggardly) tacaño

manatee /'mænəˌti/ n manatí, m

mandarin /'mændərɪn/ n mandarín, m; (language) mandarina, f. **m. orange,** mandarina, f

mandate /'mændeit/ n mandato, m. **mandated territory,** territorios bajo mandato, m pl

mandatory /'mændəˌtɔri/ a obligatorio

mandible /'mændəbəl/ n mandíbula, f

mandolin /'mændl̩ɪn/ n bandolín, m, bandurria, f

mandrake /'mændreik, -drɪk/ n mandrágora, f

mandrill /'mændrɪl/ n mandril, m

mane /mein/ n melena, f; (of a horse) crines, f pl

maned /meind/ a (in compounds) con melena...; con crines...

maneuver /məˈnuvər/ n maniobra, f. vi maniobrar, hacer maniobras. vt hacer maniobrar; manipular

maneuvering /məˈnuvərɪŋ/ n maniobras, f pl; maquinaciones, intrigas, f pl

manfully /'mænfəli/ adv valientemente; vigorosamente

manganate /'mæŋgəneit/ n manganato, m

manganese /'mæŋgəˌnis, -ˌniz/ n manganeso, m

mange /meindʒ/ n sarna, f; (in sheep) roña, f

manger /'meindʒər/ n pesebre, m

manginess /'meindʒɪnɪs/ n estado sarnoso, m

mangle /'mæŋgəl/ n (for clothes) exprimidor de la ropa, m. vt pasar por el exprimidor; (mutilate) mutilar, lacerar, magullar; (a text) mutilar

mangling /'mæŋglɪŋ/ n (mutilation) mutilación, laceración, f

mango /'mæŋgou/ n mango, m

mangy /'meindʒi/ a sarnoso

manhandle /'mænˌhændl̩/ vt maltratar

manhood /'mænhʊd/ n virilidad, f; edad viril, f; masculinidad, f; los hombres; (manliness) hombradía, f, valor, m

mania /'meiniə/ n manía, f; obsesión, f; capricho, m; chifladura, f, Lat. Am. barreno, m

maniac /'meiniˌæk/ n maníaco (-ca). a maníaco, maniático

manicure /'mænɪˌkyʊr/ n manicura, f. vt arreglar las uñas. **m.-set,** estuche de manicura, m

manicurist /'mænɪˌkyʊrɪst/ n manicuro (-ra)

manifest /'mænəˌfest/ n Naut. manifiesto, m. vt mostrar; hacer patente, probar; manifestarse. vi publicar un manifiesto; (of spirits) manifestarse. a manifiesto, evidente, claro, patente. **to make m.,** poner de manifiesto

manifestation /ˌmænəfəˈsteiʃən/ n manifestación, f

manifestly /'mænəˌfestli/ adv evidentemente, manifiestamente

manifesto /ˌmænəˈfestou/ n manifiesto, m

manifold /'mænəˌfould/ a múltiple; numeroso; diverso, vario

manikin /'mænɪkɪn/ n enano, m; muñeco, m; Art. maniquí, m

Manilla /məˈnɪlə/ n Manila, f; cigarro filipino, m. **M. hemp,** cáñamo de Manila, m

maniple /'mænəpəl/ n manípulo, m

manipulate /məˈnɪpyəˌleit/ vt manipular

manipulation /məˌnɪpyəˈleiʃən/ n manipulación, f

manipulative /məˈnɪpyəˌleitɪv/ a manipulador

mankind /'mænˈkaind/ n humanidad, raza humana, f, género humano, m

manlike /'mænˌlaik/ a de hombre, masculino; varonil; (of a woman) hombruno

manliness /'mænlinɪs/ n masculinidad, hombradía, f; virilidad, f; valor, m; (of a woman) aire hombruno, m

manly /'mænli/ a masculino, de hombre; varonil, viril; valiente; fuerte. **to be very m.,** ser muy hombre, ser todo un hombre

manna /'mænə/ n maná, m

mannequin /'mænɪkɪn/ n manequín, modelo, f. **m. parade,** exposición de modelos, f

manner /'mænər/ n manera, f, modo, m; aire, porte, m; conducta, f; (style) estilo, m; (sort) clase, f; Gram. modo, m; pl **manners,** modales, m pl, crianza, educación, f; (customs) costumbres, f pl. **after the m. of,** en (or según) el estilo de. **in a m. of speaking,** en cierto modo, para decirlo así. **in this m.,** de este modo. **to have bad (good) manners,** tener malos (buenos) modales, ser mal (bien) criado. **the novel of manners,** la novela de costumbres

mannered /'mænərd/ a amanerado; (in compounds)... educado, de... modales; de costumbres... **well-m.,** bien educado, de buenos modales

mannerism /'mænəˌrɪzəm/ n amaneramiento, m; afectación, f; Theat. latiguillo, m. **to acquire mannerisms,** amanerarse

mannerliness /'mænərlinɪs/ n cortesía, buena educación, urbanidad, f

mannerly /'mænərli/ a cortés, bien educado, atento

mannish /'mænɪʃ/ a (of a woman) hombruno; de hombre, masculino

manor /'mænər/ n feudo, m; finca, hacienda, f; casa solariega, f; señorío, m

manorial /məˈnɔriəl/ a señorial

mansion /'mænʃən/ n mansión, f; casa solariega, f; hotel, m. **m.-house,** casa solariega, f; residencia del alcalde de Londres, f

manslaughter /'mænˌslɔtər/ n homicidio, m; Law. homicidio sin premeditación, m

mantelpiece /'mæntl̩ˌpis/ n repisa de chimenea, f

mantilla /mænˈtɪlə/ n mantilla, f

mantle /'mæntl̩/ n capa, f, manto, m; Fig. cobertura, f; (gas) camiseta, f, manguito, mf; Zool. manto, m. vt cubrir; envolver; ocultar. vi extenderse; (of blushes) inundar, subirse (a las mejillas)

Mantuan /'mæntʃuən/ a mantuano

manual /'mænyuəl/ a manual, m; Mus. teclado de órgano, m. **m. work,** trabajo manual, m

manufactory /ˌmænyəˈfæktəri/ n fábrica, f, taller, m

manufacture /ˌmænyəˈfæktʃər/ n fabricación, f; manufactura, f. vt manufacturar, fabricar

manufacturer /ˌmænyəˈfæktʃərər/ n fabricante, industrial, m. **manufacturer's price,** precio de fábrica, m

manufacturing /ˌmænyəˈfæktʃərɪŋ/ n manufacturero, fabril. n fabricación, f

manure /məˈnʊr/ n estiércol, abono, m. vt estercolar, abonar. **m. heap,** estercolero, m

manuring /məˈnʊrɪŋ/ n estercoladura, f

manuscript /'mænyə‚skrɪpt/ n manuscrito, m, a manuscrito

many /'mɛni/ a muchos (-as); numeroso; diversos (-as); varios (-as). n muchos (-as); la mayoría; las masas; muchedumbre, multitud, f. **a great m.**, muchísimos, m pl, muchísimas, f pl; un gran número. **as m. as...**, tantos como... **How m. are there?** ¿Cuántos hay? ¿Cuántas hay? **m. a time**, muchas veces. **three too m.**, tres de más. **for m.** long years, por largos años. **m.-colored**, multicolor. **m.-headed**, con muchas cabezas. **m.-sided**, multilátero; polifacético; complicado

Maori /'mauri/ n maorí, m, (pl maoríes)

map /mæp/ n mapa, m; plano, m; (chart) carta, f. vt hacer un mapa (or plano) de. **to map out**, Surv. apear; trazar; (plan) proyectar. **ordnance map,** mapa del estado mayor, m. **map of the world,** mapamundi, mapa del mundo, m. **map-making,** cartografía, f

maple /'meipəl/ n (tree) arce, m; (wood) madera de arce, f. **m.-syrup,** jarabe de arce, m

mapping /'mæpɪŋ/ n cartografía, f

maquiladora /mə‚kilə'dɔrə/ n maquiladora, f

mar /mɑr/ vt estropear; desfigurar; (happiness) destruir, aguar; frustrar

maraca /mə'rɑkə/ n Lat. Am. alfandoque, m

maraschino /‚mærə'skinou/ n marrasquino, m. **m. cherry,** cerezas en marrasquino, f pl

maraud /mə'rɔd/ vi merodear

marauder /mə'rɔdər/ n merodeador, m

marauding /mə'rɔdɪŋ/ a merodeador, n merodeo, m

marble /'mɑrbl/ n mármol, m; (for playing with) canica, f, a de marmol, marmóreo; Fig. insensible; (of paper, etc.) jaspeado. vt jaspear. **m. cutter,** marmolista, m. **m. works,** marmolería, f

marbled /'mɑrbəld/ a jaspeado

March /mɑrtʃ/ n marzo, m. **as mad as a M. hare,** loco como una cabra, loco de atar

march /mɑrtʃ/ n marcha, f; (step) paso, m; Fig. marcha, f, progreso, m. **forced m.,** marcha forzada, f. **quick m.,** paso doble, m. **to steal a m. on,** tomar la delantera (a), ganar por la mano (a). **to strike up a m.,** batir la marcha. **m.-past,** desfile, m

march /mɑrtʃ/ vi marchar; (of properties) lindar (con). vt hacer marchar, poner en marcha (a). **to m. back,** vi regresar (or volver) a pie. vt hacer volver a pie. **to m. in,** entrar (a pie) en. **to m. off,** marcharse. **to m. on,** seguir marchando; seguir adelante; avanzar. **to m. past,** desfilar ante

marching /'mɑrtʃɪŋ/ n marcha, f. a en marcha; de marcha. **to receive one's m. orders,** recibir la orden de marchar; Inf. ser despedido. **m. order,** orden de marcha, m. **m. song,** canción de marcha, f

mardi gras /'mardi ‚gra/ n martes de carnaval, m

mare /mɛər/ n yegua, f

margarine /'mɑrdʒərin/ n margarina, f

margin /'mɑrdʒɪn/ n borde, lado, m, orilla, f; (of a page) margen, mf; reserva, f; sobrante, m. **in the m.**, al margen

marginal /'mɑrdʒənl/ a marginal. **m. note,** acotación, nota marginal, f

marigold /'mæri‚gould/ n caléndula, maravilla, f

marijuana /‚mærə'wanə/ n marijuana, f. Lat. Am. cáñamo m

marine /mə'rin/ a marino, de mar; marítimo; naval. n (fleet) marina, f; (soldier) soldado de marina, m. **Tell that to the marines!** ¡Cuéntaselo a tu tía! **mercantile m.,** marina mercante, f. **m. forces,** infantería de marina, f. **m. insurance,** seguro marítimo, m

mariner /'mærənər/ n marinero, marino, m. **mariner's compass,** aguja de marear, brújula, f

marionette /‚mæriə'nɛt/ n marioneta, f, títere, m

marital /'mærɪtl/ a marital

maritime /'mærɪ‚taim/ a marítimo

mark /mɑrk/ n marca, f; señal, f; mancha, f; impresión, f; (target) blanco, m; (standard) norma, f; (level) nivel, m; (distinction) importancia, distinción, f; (in examinations) nota, f; calificación, f; (signature) cruz, f; (coin) marco, m. vt marcar; señalar; (price) poner precio (a); (notice) observar, darse cuenta (de); (characterize) caracterizar. **trade-m.,**

marca de fábrica, f. **to be beside the m.**, no dar en el blanco; errar el tiro; Fig. no tener nada que ver con; equivocarse. **to hit the m.**, dar en el blanco; Fig. dar en el clavo. **to make one's m.**, firmar con una cruz; distinguirse. **to m. time,** marcar el paso; Fig. hacer tiempo. **to m. down,** (a person) señalar; escoger; (in price) rebajar. **to m. out,** marcar; trazar; definir; (erase) borrar; (a person) escoger; destinar. **m. somebody absent,** ponerle a alguien su ausencia. **m. somebody present,** ponerle a alguien su asistencia.

Mark /mɑrk/ n Marcos. **the Gospel according to St. M.,** el Evangelio de San Marcos

marked /mɑrkt/ a marcado; señalado; notable; acentuado; particular, especial. **He speaks with a m. Galician accent,** Habla con marcado acento gallego

markedly /'mɑrkɪdli/ adv marcadamente; notablemente; especialmente, particularmente

marker /'mɑrkər/ n (billiards) marcador, m; (football etc.) tanteador, m

market /'mɑrkɪt/ n mercado, m; tráfico, m; venta, f; (price) precio, m; (shop) bazar, emporio, m. vt and vi comprar en un mercado; vender en un mercado. **black m.,** mercado negro, estraperlo, m. **open m.,** mercado al aire libre, m; Fig. mercado libre, m. **m. day,** día de mercado, m. **m. garden,** huerto, m, huerta, f. **m. gardener,** hortelano, m. **m.-place,** plaza de mercado, f; Fig. mercado, m. **m. price,** precio corriente, m. **m. stall,** tabanco, puesto de mercado, m. **m.-woman,** verdulera, f

marketable /'mɑrkɪtəbl/ a comerciable, vendible; corriente

marketing /'mɑrkɪtɪŋ/ n venta, f; compra en un mercado, f; mercado, m. **to go m.,** ir al mercado

marking /'mɑrkɪŋ/ n marca, f; (spot on animals, etc.) pinta, f. **m.-ink,** tinta de marcar, f. **m.-iron,** ferrete, hierro de marcar, m

marksman /'mɑrksmən/ n tirador (-ra)

marksmanship /'mɑrksmən‚ʃɪp/ n puntería, f

marl /mɑrl/ n marga, f

marmalade /'mɑrmə‚leid/ n mermelada de naranjas amargas, f

marmoset /'mɑrmə‚zɛt/ n tití, m

marmot /'mɑrmət/ n Zool. marmota, f

maroon /mə'run/ n (color) marrón, m; (slave) cimarrón (-ona); (firework) petardo, m. a de marrón. vt abandonar, dejar

marquee /mɑr'ki/ n marquesina, f

marqueterie /'mɑrkɪtri/ n marquetería, f

marquis /'mɑrkwɪs/ n marqués, m

marriage /'mærɪdʒ/ n matrimonio, m; unión, f; (wedding) boda, f, casamiento, m. **by m.,** (of relationship) político. **She is an aunt by m.,** tía política. **m. articles,** capitulaciones (matrimoniales), f pl. **m. contract,** contrato matrimonial, m. **m. license,** licencia de casamiento, f. **m. portion,** dote, mf. **m. rate,** nupcialidad, f. **m. register,** acta matrimonial, f. **m. song,** epitalamio, m

marriageable /'mærɪdʒəbl/ a casadero

married /'mærid/ past part and a casado; matrimonial, conyugal. **newly-m. couple,** los recién casados. **to get m. to,** casarse con. **m. couple,** matrimonio, m, cónyuges m pl. **m. life,** vida conyugal, f

married name n nombre de casada, f

marrow /'mærou/ n tuétano, m, médula, f; Fig. meollo, m. **to the m. of one's bones,** hasta los tuétanos.

marrowbone /'mærou‚boun/ n hueso medular, m. **on one's marrowbones,** de rodillas

marry /'mæri/ vt casarse con, contraer matrimonio con; casar; (of a priest) unir a personas en matrimonio. Fig. juntar, unir. vi casarse. **to m. again,** volver a casarse

Marseillaise /‚mɑrsei'ɛz/ n marsellesa, f

Marseilles /mɑr'sei/ Marsella, f

marsh /mɑrʃ/ n marjal, pantano, Central America chagüe, m. **m.-mallow,** Bot. malvavisco, m. **m. marigold,** calta, f

marshal /'mɑrʃəl/ n mariscal, m; vt poner en orden, arreglar; dirigir. Milit. mariscal, m; capitán general de ejército, m

marshaling /'mɑrʃəlɪŋ/ n ordenación, f; dirección, f. **m.-yard,** (railway) apartadero ferroviario, m

marshy /'marʃi/ *a* pantanoso
mart /mart/ *n* Poet. plaza de mercado, *f*; mercado, *m*; emporio, *m*; (auction rooms) martillo, *m*
marten /'martn/ *n* marta, *f*
martial /'marʃəl/ *a* militar; marcial, belicoso. **m. array,** orden de batalla, *m*. **m. law,** derecho militar, *m*; estado de guerra, *m*. **m. spirit,** marcialidad, *f*, espíritu belicoso, *m*
martially /'marʃəli/ *adv* militarmente; marcialmente
Martian /'marʃən/ *a* marciano
martinet /ˌmartn̩'ɛt/ *n* Mil. ordenancista, *m*; rigorista, *mf*
Martinique /ˌmartn̩'ik/ Martinica, *f*
Martinmas /'martn̩məs/ *n* día de San Martín, *m*
martyr /'martər/ *n* mártir, *mf vt* martirizar
martyrdom /'martərdəm/ *n* martirio, *m*
martyrize /'martəˌraiz/ *vt* martirizar
marvel /'marvəl/ *n* maravilla, *f*. **to m. at,** maravillarse de, admirarse de
marvelous /'marvələs/ *a* maravilloso
marvelousness /'marvələsnis/ *n* maravilla, *f*, carácter maravilloso, *m*, lo maravilloso
Marxism /'marksɪzəm/ *n* marxismo, *m*
Marxist /'marksɪst/ *a* and *n* marxista, *mf*
marzipan /'marzəˌpæn/ *n* mazapán, *m*
mascot /'mæskɒt/ *n* mascota, *f*
masculine /'mæskyəlɪn/ *a* masculino; varonil, macho; de hombre; (of a woman) hombruno. *n* masculino, *m*
masculinity /ˌmæskyə'lɪnɪti/ *n* masculinidad, *f*
mash /mæʃ/ *n* mezcla, *f*; amasijo, *m*; pasta, *f*, puré, *m*. *vt* mezclar; amasar. **mashed potatoes,** puré de patatas (de papas), *m*
mask /mæsk/ *n* máscara, *f*; antifaz, *m*; (death) mascarilla, *f*; (person) máscara, *mf*. *vt* enmascarar; Fig. encubrir, disimular. *vi* ponerse una máscara; disfrazarse. **masked ball,** *n* baile de máscaras, *m*
masker /'mæskər/ *n* máscara, *m*
masochism /'mæsəˌkɪzəm/ *n* masoquismo, *m*
mason /'meisən/ *n* albañil, *m*; (freemason) francmasón, masón, *m*
masonic /mə'sɒnɪk/ *a* masónico. **m. lodge,** logia de francmasones, *f*
masonry /'meisənri/ *n* (trade) albañilería, *f*; mampostería, *f*
masque /mæsk/ *n* mascarada, *f*
masquerade /ˌmæskə'reid/ *n* mascarada, *f*
masquerader /ˌmæskə'reidər/ *n* máscara, *mf*
mass /mæs/ *n* misa, *f*. **to hear m.,** oír misa. **to say m.,** celebrar misa. **high m.,** misa mayor, *f*. **low m.,** misa rezada, *f*. **m. book,** libro de misa, *m*
mass /mæs/ *n* masa, *f*; (shape) bulto, *m*; (heap) montón, *m*; (great number) muchedumbre, *f*; (cloud of steam, etc.) nube, *f*. *vt* amasar; Mil. concentrar. *vi* congregarse en masa. **in a m.,** en masa; en conjunto. **the m.** (of)..., la mayoría (de)... **the masses,** las masas, el vulgo, el pueblo. **m. formation,** columna cerrada, *f*. **m.-meeting,** mitin, mitin popular, *m*. **m.-production,** fabricación en serie, *f*
massacre /'mæsəkər/ *n* matanza, carnicería, *f*, *vt* hacer una carnicería (de)
massage /mə'saʒ/ *n* masaje, *m*; (friction) fricción, *f*. *vt* dar un masaje (a)
masseur, masseuse /mə'sɜr; mə'sus/ *n* masajista, *mf*
massive /'mæsɪv/ *a* macizo; sólido
massively /'mæsɪvli/ *adv* macizamente; sólidamente
massiveness /'mæsɪvnɪs/ *n* macicez, *f*; solidez, *f*
mast /mæst/ *n* Naut. palo, árbol, *m*; (for wireless) mástil, *m*; poste, *m*; (beech) hayuco, *m*; (oak) bellota, *f*. *vt* Naut. arbolar. **at half-m.,** a media asta. **m.-head,** calcés, tope, *m*
masted /'mæstɪd/ *a* arbolado; (in compounds) de... palos
master /'mæstər/ *n* (of the house, etc.) señor, amo, *m*; maestro, *m*; Naut. patrón, *m*; (owner) dueño, *m*; (teacher) profesor, maestro, *m*; (young master and as address) señorito, *m*; director, *m*; jefe, *m*; (expert) perito, *m*; (of a military order) maestre, *m*, *a* maestro; superior. *vt* dominar; ser maestro en; dominar, conocer a fondo. **This picture is by an old m.,** Este cuadro es de un gran maestro antiguo. **to be m. of**

oneself, ser dueño de sí. **to be one's own m.,** ser dueño de sí mismo; trabajar por su propia cuenta; ser independiente; estar libre. **m. builder,** maestro de obras, *m*. **m. hand,** mano maestra, *f*. **M. of Arts,** (academic degree) maestría en artes. **master's degree,** la maestría. **M. of Ceremonies,** maestro de ceremonias, *m*. **m.-key,** llave maestra, *f*. **m. mind,** águila, *f*, ingenio, *m*. **m. stroke,** golpe maestro, *m*
masterful /'mæstərfəl/ *a* imperioso, dominante; autoritario, arbitrario
masterfulness /'mæstərfəlnɪs/ *n* imperiosidad, *f*; arbitrariedad, *f*
masterless /'mæstərlɪs/ *a* sin amo
masterliness /'mæstərlɪnɪs/ *n* maestría, *f*; excelencia, *f*; perfección, *f*
masterly /'mæstərli/ *a* maestro; excelente; perfecto. **m. performance,** obra maestra, *f*; Theat. representación perfecta, *f*; ejecución excelente, *f*
masterpiece /'mæstərˌpis/ *n* obra maestra, *f*
master plan *n* plan regulador, *m*
masterstroke /'mæstərˌstrouk/ *n* golpe magistral, *m*; golpe de maestro, *m*
mastery /'mæstəri/ *n* dominio, *m*; autoridad, *f*; poder, *m*; ventaja, *f*; superioridad, maestría, *f*; conocimiento profundo, *m*. **to gain the m. of,** hacerse el señor de; llegar a dominar
mastic /'mæstɪk/ *n* masilla, almáciga, *f*
masticate /'mæstɪˌkeit/ *vt* masticar, mascar
mastication /ˌmæstɪ'keiʃən/ *n* masticación, *f*
mastiff /'mæstɪf/ *n* mastín, alano, *m*
mastodon /'mæstəˌdɒn/ *n* mastodonte, *m*
mastoid /'mæstɔid/ *a* mastoides. *n* apófisis mastoides, *f*
masturbate /'mæstərˌbeit/ *vi* masturbarse
masturbation /ˌmæstər'beiʃən/ *n* masturbación, *f*
mat /mæt/ *n* esterilla, *f*; alfombrilla, *f*; (on the table) tapete individual, *m*. *vt* (tangle) enmarañar, desgreñar. *vi* enmarañarse
match /mætʃ/ *n* Sports. partido, *m*; (wrestling, boxing) lucha, *f*; (fencing) asalto, *m*; (race) carrera, *f*; (contest) concurso, *m*; (equal) igual, *mf*; (pair) pareja, *f*; compañero (-ra); (marriage) boda, *f*, casamiento, *m*; (for lighting) cerilla, *f*, fósforo, Mexico cerillo, *m*; (for guns) mecha, *f*. *vt* competir con; (equal) igualar; ser igual (a); hacer juego con; emparejar, aparear; armonizar. *vi* ser igual; hacer juego; armonizarse. **good m.,** Inf. buen partido, *m*. **as thin as a m.,** más delgado que una cerilla. **to meet one's m.,** dar con la horma de su zapato. **to play a m.,** jugar un partido. **m.-box,** cajita de cerillas, fosforera, *f*. **m.-seller,** fosforero (-ra)
matchless /'mætʃlɪs/ *a* incomparable, sin igual, sin par
matchwood /'mætʃˌwʊd/ *n* madera para cerillas, *f*
mate /meit/ *n* compañero, camarada, *m*; (spouse) compañero (-ra); pareja, *f*; (on merchant ships) piloto, *m*; (assistant) ayudante, *m*; (at chess) mate, *m*. *vt* (marry) casar, desposar; (animals, birds) aparear, acoplar; (chess) dar jaque mate (a). *vi* casarse; aparearse, acoplarse
maté /'matei/ *n* maté, té del Paraguay, *m*
materfamilias /ˌmeitərfə'mɪliəs/ *n* madre de familia, *f*
material /mə'tɪəriəl/ *a* material; importante, esencial; considerable, sensible, notable; grave. *n* material, *m*; materia, *f*; (fabric) tela, *f*; tejido, *m*. **raw materials,** materias primas, *f pl*. **writing materials,** utensilios de escritorio, *m pl*; papel de escribir, *m*
materialism /mə'tɪəriəˌlɪzəm/ *n* materialismo, *m*
materialist /mə'tɪəriəlɪst/ *n* materialista, *mf*
materialistic /məˌtɪəriə'lɪstɪk/ *a* materialista
materiality /məˌtɪəri'ælɪti/ *n* materialidad, *f*; importancia, *f*
materialization /məˌtɪəriəlɪ'zeiʃən/ *n* materialización, *f*
materialize /mə'tɪəriəˌlaiz/ *vt* materializar
maternal /mə'tɜrnl/ *a* materno, maternal. **m. grandparents,** abuelos maternos, *m pl*
maternity /mə'tɜrnɪti/ *n* maternidad, *f*. **m. center,** centro de maternidad, *m*. **m. hospital,** casa de maternidad, *f*
mathematical /ˌmæθə'mætɪkəl/ *a* matemático

mathematician /ˌmæθəmə'tɪʃən/ n matemático, m
mathematics /ˌmæθə'mætɪks/ n pl; matemáticas, f pl.
applied m., matemáticas prácticas, f pl. **higher m.**,
matemáticas superiores, f pl. **pure m.**, matemáticas
teóricas, f pl
matinee /ˌmætɪn'ei/ n función de tarde, f
mating /'meitɪŋ/ n (of animals) apareamiento, acoplamiento, m; unión, f; casamiento, m
matins /'mætɪnz/ n pl Eccl. maitines, m pl
matriarch /'meitri,ɑrk/ n matriarca, f
matriarchal /ˌmeitri'ɑrkəl/ a matriarcal
matriarchy /'meitri,ɑrki/ n matriarcado, m
matricide /'mætrɪ,said/ n (crime) matricidio, m; (person) matricida, mf
matriculate /mə'trɪkyə,leit/ vt matricular. vi matricularse
matriculation /mə,trɪkyə'leiʃən/ n matriculación, f
matrimonial /ˌmætrə'mouniəl/ a matrimonial, de
matrimonio; marital. **m. agency**, agencia de matri-
monios, f
matrimony /'mætrə,mouni/ n matrimonio, m
matrix /'meitrɪks/ n matriz, f
matron /'meitrən/ n matrona, mujer casada, madre
de familia, f; (of a hospital) matrona, f; (of a school)
ama de llaves, f; directora, f. **m. of honor**, (at a wedding) madrina, f
matronly /'meitrənli/ a de matrona, matronal; respetable; serio
matte /mæt/ a mate
matted /'mætɪd/ a enmarañado, enredado
matter /'mætər/ n materia, f; substancia, f; caso, m;
cuestión, f; asunto, m; causa, f; (distance) distancia,
f; (amount) cantidad, f; (duration) espacio de tiempo,
m; (importance) importancia, f; Med. pus, m; pl
matters, asuntos, m pl, etc.; situación, f. **as if nothing were the m.**, como si no hubiese pasado nada.
for that m., en cuanto a eso. **gray m.**, substancia
gris, f. **in the m. of**, en el caso de. **It is a m. of
taste**, Es cuestión de gusto. **printed m.**, impresos, m
pl. **What is the m.?** ¿Qué pasa? ¿Qué hay? **What is
the m. with him?** ¿Qué tiene? ¿Qué le pasa? **m.-of-
course**, cosa natural, f. **m.-of-fact**, práctico; sin
imaginación; positivista. **m. of fact**, n hecho positivo,
m, realidad, f. **As a m. of fact...**, En realidad..., El
caso es que... **m. of form**, cuestión de fórmula, f;
pura formalidad, f
matter /'mætər/ vi importar; (discharge) supurar.
What does it m.? ¿Qué importa? **It doesn't m.**, Es
igual, No importa, Da lo mismo
Matterhorn, the /'mætər,hɔrn/ el Matterhorn, m
matting /'mætɪŋ/ n estera, f
mattress /'mætrɪs/ n colchón, m. **spring-m.**, colchón
de muelles, m. **m.-maker**, colchonero, m
mature /mə'tʃʊr/ a maduro; Com. vencido. vt madurar. vi madurarse; Com. vencer
maturity /mə'tʃʊriti/ n madurez, f; edad madura, f;
(Com. of a bill) vencimiento, m
matutinal /mə'tutn̩l/ a matutino
maudlin /'mɔdlɪn/ a sensiblero; lacrimoso; (tipsy)
calamocano
maul /mɔl/ vt maltratar; herir
Maundy Thursday /'mɔndi/ n Jueves Santo, m
Mauritius /mɔ'rɪʃəs/ Mauricio, m, Isla de Francia, f
mausoleum /ˌmɔsə'liəm/ n mausoleo, m
mauve /mouv/ n color purpúreo delicado, color de
malva, m, a de color de malva
maw /mɔ/ n (of a ruminant) cuajar, m; (of a bird)
buche, m; Fig. abismo, m
mawkish /'mɔkɪʃ/ a insípido, insulso; sensiblero; asqueroso
mawkishness /'mɔkɪʃnɪs/ n insipidez, insulsez, f;
sensiblería, f; asquerosidad, f
maxilla /mæk'sɪlə/ n hueso maxilar, maxilar, m
maxillary /'mæksə,leri/ a maxilar
maxim /'mæksɪm/ n máxima, f
maximum /'mæksəməm/ a máximo. n máximo, m
may /mei/ v aux poder; ser posible; (expressing
wish, hope) ojalá que..., y Dios quiera que..., or the
present subjunctive may be used, e.g. *May you live
many years!* ¡(qué) Viva Vd. muchos años! (to denote

uncertainty, the future tense of the verb is often used,
e.g. *You may perhaps remember the date*, Vd. quizás
se acordará de la fecha. *Who may he be?* ¿Quién
será?) **May God grant it!** ¡(que) Dios lo quiera! **It
may be that...**, Puede ser que..., Es posible que...,
Quizás... **He may come on Saturday**, Es posible que
venga el sábado; Puede venir el sábado. **May I come
in?** ¿Puedo entrar? ¿Se puede entrar? **May I come and
see you?** ¿Me das permiso para hacerte una visita?
¿Me dejas venir a verte? **May I go then?** ¿Puedo irme
pues? ¿Tengo permiso para marcharme entonces?
May /mei/ n mayo, m; Fig. abril, m; Bot. espina
blanca, f. **May Day**, primero de mayo, m. **mayflower**, flor del cuclillo, f. **mayfly**, cachipolla, f. **May
queen**, maya, f
maybe /'meibi/ adv quizás, tal vez
mayonnaise /ˌmeiə'neiz/ n mayonesa, f. **m. sauce**,
salsa mayonesa, f
mayor /'meiər/ n alcalde, m, alcaldesa, f, Argentina
intendente, m
mayoral /'meiərəl/ a de alcalde
mayoralty /'meiərəlti/ n Argentina intendencia, f
maypole /'mei,poul/ n mayo, m. **m. dance**, danza de
cintas, f
maze /meiz/ n laberinto, m; Fig. perplejidad, f. vt dejar perplejo, aturdir
mazurka /mə'zɜrkə/ n mazurca, f
me /mi/ pron me; (after a preposition only) mí. **They
sent it for me**, Lo mandaron para mí. **Dear me!** ¡Ay
de mí!
meadow /'mɛdou/ n prado, m, pradera, f. **m.-sweet**,
reina de los prados, f
meager /'migər/ a magro, enjuto, flaco; (scanty) exiguo, escaso, insuficiente; pobre; Fig. árido
meagerness /'migərnɪs/ n exigüidad, escasez, f; pobreza, f; Fig. aridez, f
meal /mil/ n comida, f; (flour) harina, f. **to have a
good m.**, comer bien. **test m.**, Med. comida de
prueba, f. **m.-time**, hora de comida, f
mealy /'mili/ a harinoso; (of the complexion) pastoso
mean /min/ a (middle) mediano; (average) mediano; (humble) humilde; pobre; inferior; bajo, vil,
ruin; (avaricious) tacaño, mezquino, Argentina agalludo, Chile, Peru coñete, m. **m.-spirited**, vil, de alma
ruin
mean /min/ n medio, m; medianía, f; pl **means** medio, m; expediente, m; medios, m pl; (financial) recursos, m pl; modo, m, manera, f. **by all means**, por
todos los medios; (certainly) ¡ya lo creo! ¡no faltaba
más! ¡naturalmente! **by means of**, mediante, por medio de; con la ayuda de. **by no means**, de ningún
modo; nada. **by some means**, de algún modo, de alguna manera
mean /min/ vt destinar (para); pretender, proponerse; intentar, pensar; querer decir, significar; importar; (wish) querer; (concern, speak about) tratarse
(de). vi tener el propósito, tener la intención. **I did
not m. to do it**, Lo hice sin querer. **What does this
word m.?** ¿Qué significa esta palabra? **What do you
m. by that?** ¿Qué quieres decir con eso? **This portrait
is meant to be Joan**, Este retrato quiere ser Juana.
What do they m. to do? ¿Qué piensan (or se pro-
ponen) hacer? **Do you really m. it?** ¿Lo dices en
serio? **Charles always means well**, Carlos siempre
tiene buenas intenciones
meander /mi'ændər/ n meandro, serpenteo, m;
camino tortuoso, m, vi serpentear; errar, vagar; (in
talk) divagar
meandering /mi'ændərɪŋ/ n meandros, m pl, serpenteo, m; (in talk) divagaciones, f pl, a serpentino,
tortuoso
meaning /'minɪŋ/ n intención, voluntad, f; significación, f, significado, m; (of words) acepción, f; (sense)
sentido, m; (thought) pensamiento, m. a significante.
double m., doble intención, f. **He gave me a m.
look**, Me miró con intención. **What is the m. of it?**
¿Qué significa? ¿Qué quiere decir?
meaningful /'minɪŋfʊl/ a significante
meaningless /'minɪŋlɪs/ a sin sentido; insensato; insignificante
meanness /'minnɪs/ n pobreza, f; inferioridad, f; me-

diocridad, *f*; bajeza, ruindad, *f*; (stinginess) mezquindad, tacañería, *Lat. Am. also* lechería, *f*
meantime, meanwhile /'min,taim/; 'min,wail/ *n* ínterin, *m, adv* entre tanto, mientras tanto, a todo esto. **in the m.,** mientras tanto, en el ínterin
measles /'mizəlz/ *n* sarampión, *m*. **German m.,** rubéola, *f*
measurable /'mɛʒərəbəl/ *a* mensurable
measure /'mɛʒər/ *n* medida, *f*; capacidad, *f*; (for measuring) regla, *f*; número, *m*; proporción, *f*; (limit) límite, *m*; (*Fig.* step) medida, *f*; (meter) metro, *m*; *Mus.* compás, *m*; (degree) grado, *m*; manera, *f*; (parliamentary) proyecto (de ley), *m*. *vt* medir; proporcionar, distribuir; (water) aforar; (land) apear; (height of persons) tallar; (for clothes) tomar las medidas (a); (judge) juzgar; (test) probar; (*Poet.* traverse) recorrer. **a suit made to m.,** un traje hecho a medida. **in great m.,** en gran manera, en alto grado. **in some m.,** hasta cierto punto. **to m. one's length,** caer tendido. **to take a person's m.,** *Fig.* tomar las medidas (a). **to m. up to,** *Fig.* estar al nivel de, ser igual a
measured /'mɛʒərd/ *a* mesurado, moderado; uniforme; limitado. **to walk with m. tread,** andar a pasos contados
measurement /'mɛʒərmənt/ *n* medición, *f*; medida, *f*; dimensión, *f*
meat /mit/ *n* carne, *f*; (food) alimento, *m*; (meal) comida, *f*; *Fig.* substancia, *f*. **to sit at m.,** estar a la mesa. **cold meats,** fiambres, *m pl.* **m.-ball,** albóndiga, *f*. **m.-chopper,** picador, *m*. **m.-dish,** fuente, *f*. **m.-eater,** comedor (-ra) de carne. **m. extract,** carne concentrada, *f*. **m.-market,** carnicería, *f*. **m.-pie,** pastel de carne, *m*. **m.-safe,** fresquera, *f*
meaty /'miti/ *a* carnoso; *Fig.* substancial
Mecca /'mɛkə/ la Meca, *f*
mechanic /mə'kænɪk/ *n* mecánico, *m*
mechanical /mə'kænɪkəl/ *a* mecánico; maquinal
mechanically /mə'kænɪkli/ *adv* mecánicamente; maquinalmente
mechanical pencil *n* lapicero, *m*
mechanics /mə'kænɪks/ *n* mecánica, *f*
mechanism /'mɛkə,nɪzəm/ *n* mecanismo, *m*; (philosophy) mecanicismo, *m*
mechanize /'mɛkə,naiz/ *vt* convertir en máquina; (gen. *Mil.*) mecanizar; motorizar
medal /'mɛdḷ/ *n* medalla, *f*
medallion /mə'dælyən/ *n* medallón, *m*
medallist /'mɛdḷɪst/ *n* grabador de medallas, *m*; el, *m*, (*f*, la) que recibe una medalla
meddle /'mɛdḷ/ *vi* tocar; meterse (con or en); entremeterse, inmiscuirse; intrigar
meddler /'mɛdlər/ *n* entremetido (-da); intrigante, *mf*
meddlesome /'mɛdḷsəm/ *a* entremetido; oficioso; impertinente; enredador, intrigante. **to be very m.,** meterse en todo
meddlesomeness /'mɛdḷsəmnɪs/ *n* entremetimiento, *m*; oficiosidad, *f*; impertinencia, *f*; intrigas, *f pl*
media, the /'midiə/ los medios informativos, *m pl*
median /'midiən/ *a* del medio
mediate /*v* 'midi,eit; *a* -ɪt/ *vi* intervenir, mediar, arbitrar; abogar (por). *a* medio; interpuesto
mediation /,midi'eifən/ *n* mediación, intervención, *f*; intercesión, *f*; interposición, *f*
mediator /'midi,eitər/ *n* mediador (-ra); arbitrador (-ra); intercesor (-ra)
mediatory /'midiə,tɔri/ *a* de mediador; intercesor
medical /'mɛdɪkəl/ *a* médico; de medicina; de médico. *n Inf.* estudiante de medicina, *m*. **Army M. Service,** Servicio de Sanidad Militar, *m*. **m. books,** libros de medicina, *m pl.* **m. examination,** examen médico, *m*, exploración médica, *f*. **m. jurisprudence,** medicina legal, *f*. **m. knowledge,** conocimientos médicos, *m pl.* **m. practitioner,** médico (-ca). **m. school,** escuela de medicina, *f*
medicate /'mɛdɪ,keit/ *vt* medicar; medicinar
medicated /'mɛdɪ,keitɪd/ *a* medicado
medication /,mɛdɪ'keifən/ *n* medicación, *f*, *Lat. Am.* medicamentos, *m pl*
medicinal /mə'dɪsənḷ/ *a* medicinal
medicine /'mɛdəsɪn/ *n* medicina, *f*; medicamento, *m*; (charm) ensalmo, hechizo, *m*. **patent m.,** específico

farmacéutico, *m*. **m. ball,** balón medical, *m*. **m. chest,** botiquín, *m*. **m. man,** hechizador, *m*
medico- *prefix* médico-. **m.-legal,** médicolegal
medieval /,midi'ivəl/ *a* medieval
medievalism /,midi'ivə,lɪzəm/ *n* afición a la edad media, *f*; espíritu medieval, *m*
mediocre /,midi'oukər/ *a* mediocre
mediocrity /,midi'ɒkrɪti/ *n* mediocridad, *f*; medianía, *f*
meditate /'mɛdɪ,teit/ *vt* idear, proyectar, meditar. *vi* meditar, reflexionar; pensar, intentar
meditation /,mɛdɪ'teifən/ *n* meditación, *f*
meditative /'mɛdɪ,teitɪv/ *a* meditabundo, contemplativo; de meditación
meditatively /'mɛdɪ,teitɪvli/ *adv* reflexivamente
Mediterranean /,mɛdɪtə'reiniən/ *a* mediterráneo. *n* Mar Mediterráneo, *m*
medium /'midiəm/ *n* medio, *m*; (cooking) término medio, a medio cocer, a medio asar, *m*; (environment) medio ambiente, *m*; (agency) intermediario, *m*; (spiritualism) médium, *m*; *Art.* medio, *m*, *a* mediano; regular; mediocre. **through the m. of,** por medio de. **m.-sized,** de tamaño regular
medlar /'mɛdlər/ *n* (fruit) níspola, *f*; (tree) níspero, *m*
medley /'mɛdli/ *n* mezcla, *f*; miscelánea, *f*, *a* mezclado, mixto
medulla /mə'dʌlə/ *n* medula, *f*
meek /mik/ *a* dulce, manso; humilde; modesto; pacífico
meekly /'mikli/ *adv* mansamente; humildemente; modestamente
meekness /'miknɪs/ *n* mansedumbre, *f*; humildad, *f*; modestia, *f*
meet /mit/ *vt* encontrar; encontrarse con; tropezar con; (by arrangement) reunirse con; (make the acquaintance of) conocer (a); (satisfy) satisfacer; cumplir (con); (a bill) pagar, saldar; (refute) refutar; (fight) batirse (con); (confront) hacer frente (a). *vi* juntarse; encontrarse; reunirse; verse; (of rivers) confluir. *n* montería, *f*, *a* conveniente. **I shall m. you at the station,** Te esperaré en la estación. **Until we m. again!** ¡Hasta la vista! **to go to m.,** ir al encuentro de. **to m. half-way,** encontrar a la mitad del camino; partir la diferencia con; hacer concesiones (a). **to m. the eye,** saltar a la vista. **to m. with,** encontrar; experimentar; sufrir
meeting /'mitɪŋ/ *n* encuentro, *m*; reunión, *f*; (interview) entrevista, *f*; (of rivers) confluencia, *f*; (public, etc.) mitin, *m*; (council) concilio, *m*; concurso, *m*; (race) concurso de carreras de caballos, *m*. **creditors' m.,** concurso de acreedores, *m*. **m.-house,** templo de los Cuáqueros, *m*. **m.-place,** lugar de reunión, *m*; lugar de cita, *m*; centro, *m*. **to adjourn the m.,** levantar la sesión. **to call a m.,** convocar una sesión. **to open the m.,** abrir la sesión
megalomania /,mɛgəlou'meiniə/ *n* megalomanía, monomanía de grandezas, *f*
megalomaniac /,mɛgəlou'meiniæk/ *n* megalómano (-na)
megaphone /'mɛgə,foun/ *n* megáfono, portavoz, *m*
Meknès /mɛk'nɛs/ Mequínez, *f*
melancholy /'mɛlən,kɒli/ *a* melancólico. *n* melancolía, *f*
mellifluence /mə'lɪfluəns/ *n* melifluidad, *f*
mellifluous /mə'lɪfluəs/ *a* melifluo; dulce
mellow /'mɛlou/ *a* maduro; dulce; (of wine) rancio; blando; suave; (of sound) melodioso, (slang) alegre; (tipsy) entre dos luces. *vt* madurar; ablandar; suavizar. *vi* madurarse
mellowing /'mɛlouɪŋ/ *n* maduración, *f*
mellowness /'mɛlounɪs/ *n* madurez, *f*; dulzura, *f*; (of wine) ranciedad, *f*; blandura, *f*; suavidad, *f*; melodía, *f*
melodic /mə'lɒdɪk/ *a* melódico
melodious /mə'loudiəs/ *a* melodioso
melodiously /mə'loudiəsli/ *adv* melodiosamente
melodiousness /mə'loudiəsnɪs/ *n* melodía, *f*
melodrama /'mɛlə,dramə/ *n* melodrama, *m*
melodramatic /,mɛlədrə'mætɪk/ *a* melodramático
melody /'mɛlədi/ *n* melodía, *f*
melon /'mɛlən/ *n* melón, *m*; sandía, *f*. **slice of m.,**

raja de melón, f. **m. bed,** sandiar, m. **m.-shaped,** amelonado

melt /mɛlt/ vi derretirse; deshacerse; disolverse; evaporarse; desaparecer; (of money, etc.) hacerse sal y agua; (relent) enternecerse, ablandarse. vt fundir; (snow, etc.) derretir; (Fig. soften) ablandar. **He melted away,** Inf. Se escurrió. **to m. into tears,** deshacerse en lágrimas. **to m. down,** fundir

melting /'mɛltɪŋ/ a fundente; (forgiving) indulgente; (tender) de ternura; lánguido; dulce. n fusión, f; derretimiento, m. **m. point,** punto de fusión, m. **m. pot,** Metall. crisol, m; Fig. caldera de razas, f, m

member /'mɛmbər/ n miembro, m; (of a club, etc.) socio (-ia). **M. of Congress,** representante del Congreso de los Estados Unidos, congresista, mf

membership /'mɛmbərˌʃɪp/ n calidad de miembro, socio(-ia); número de miembros (or socios), m, composición, integración, f

membrane /'mɛmbrein/ n membrana, f

membranous /'mɛmbrənəs/ a membranoso

memento /mə'mɛntou/ n recuerdo, m

memoir /'mɛmwɑr/ n memoria, f

memorable /'mɛmərəbəl/ a memorable

memorably /'mɛmərəbli/ adv memorablemente

memorandum /ˌmɛmə'rændəm/ n memorándum, m

memorial /mə'mɔriəl/ a conmemorativo. n monumento conmemorativo, m; memorial, m

memorize /'mɛməˌraiz/ vt aprender de memoria

memory /'mɛməri/ n memoria, f; recuerdo, m. **from m.,** de memoria. **If my m. does not deceive me,** Si mal no me acuerdo. **in m. of,** en conmemoración de; en recuerdo de

memory span n retentiva memorística, f

menace /'mɛnɪs/ n amenaza, f, vt amenazar

menacing /'mɛnəsɪŋ/ a amenazador

menacingly /'mɛnəsɪŋli/ adv con amenazas

menagerie /mə'nædʒəri/ n colección de fieras, f; casa de fieras, f

mend /mɛnd/ vt remendar; componer; reparar; (darn) zurcir; (rectify) remediar; reformar; enmendar; (a fire) echar carbón (or leña, etc.) a; (one's pace) avivar. vi (in health and of the weather) mejorar. n remiendo, m; (darn) zurcido, m. **to be on the m.,** ir mejorando. **to m. one's ways,** reformarse, enmendarse

mendacious /mɛn'deiʃəs/ a mendaz

mendacity /mɛn'dæsɪti/ n mendacidad, f

Mendelism /'mɛndlˌɪzəm/ n mendelismo, m

mender /'mɛndər/ n componedor (-ra); (darner) zurcidor (-ra); reparador (-ra); (cobbler and tailor) remendón, m

mendicancy /'mɛndɪkənsi/ n mendicidad, f

mendicant /'mɛndɪkənt/ a mendicante. n mendicante, mf. **m. friar,** fraile mendicante, m

mending /'mɛndɪŋ/ n compostura, f; reparación, f; (darning) zurcidura, f; ropa por zurcir, f

menial /'miniəl/ a doméstico; servil; bajo, ruin. n criado (-da); lacayo, m

meningeal /ˌmɛnɪn'dʒiəl/ a meningeo

meningitis /ˌmɛnɪn'dʒaitɪs/ n meningitis, f

menopause /'mɛnəˌpɔz/ n menopausia, f

menses /'mɛnsiz/ n menstruación, f

menstrual /'mɛnstruəl/ a menstrual

menstruate /'mɛnstruˌeit/ vi menstruar

menstruation /ˌmɛnstru'eiʃən/ n menstruación, f,

mental /'mɛntl/ a mental; intelectual. **m. derangement,** enajenación mental, f. **m. hospital,** manicomio, m

mentality /mɛn'tælɪti/ n mentalidad, f

mentally /'mɛntli/ adv mentalmente. **m. deficient,** anormal

menthol /'mɛnθɔl/ n mentol, m

mention /'mɛnʃən/ n mención, f; alusión, f. vt hacer mención (de), mencionar, mentar, hablar (de); aludir (a); (quote) citar; (in dispatches) nombrar. **Don't m. it!** (keep silent) ¡No digas nada!; (you're welcome) ¡No hay de que!

mentor /'mɛntɔr/ n mentor, m

menu /'mɛnyu/ n menú, m; lista de platos, f

meow /mi'au/ vi maullar. n maullido, m

Mephistophelean /ˌmɛfəstə'filiən/ a mefistofélico

mercantile /'mɜrkən,til/ a mercantil; mercante. **m. law,** derecho mercantil, m. **m. marine,** marina mercante, f

mercantilism /'mɜrkəntiˌlizəm/ n mercantilismo, m

mercenariness /'mɜrsəˌnɛrinɪs/ n lo mercenario

mercenary /'mɜrsəˌnɛri/ a mercenario. n (soldier) mercenario, m

mercer /'mɜrsər/ n mercero, m

mercerize /'mɜrsəˌraiz/ vt mercerizar

mercery /'mɜrsəri/ n mercería, f

merchandise /'mɜrtʃənˌdaiz/ n mercancía, f

merchant /'mɜrtʃənt/ n traficante (en), mf, negociante (en), m; comerciante, Lat. Am. marchante (-ta), mf mercader, m. a mercante. **The M. of Venice,** El Mercader de Venecia. **m. navy, service,** marina mercante, f. **m. ship,** buque mercante, m

merchantman /'mɜrtʃəntmən/ n buque mercante, m

merciful /'mɜrsifəl/ a misericordioso, piadoso; compasivo; clemente; indulgente

mercifully /'mɜrsifəli/ adv misericordiosamente; compasivamente; con indulgencia

mercifulness /'mɜrsifəlnɪs/ n misericordia, f; compasión, f; indulgencia, f

merciless /'mɜrsilɪs/ a despiadado, inhumano

mercilessly /'mɜrsilɪsli/ adv sin piedad

mercilessness /'mɜrsilɪsnɪs/ n inhumanidad, f; falta de compasión, f

mercurial /mər'kyuriəl/ a mercurial; (changeable) volátil; (lively) vivo

mercury /'mɜrkyəri/ n mercurio, m; (Astron. and Myth.) Mercurio, m. **Mercury's wand,** caduceo, m

mercy /'mɜrsi/ n misericordia, f; compasión, f; clemencia, f; indulgencia, f; merced, f. **at the m. of the elements,** a la intemperie. **to be at the m. of,** estar a la merced de

mere /mɪər/ a mero; simple; no más que, solo. n lago, m

merely /'mɪərli/ adv meramente, solamente; simplemente, sencillamente

meretricious /ˌmɛri'triʃəs/ a (archaic) meretricio; (flashy) de oropel; llamativo, charro

meretriciousness /ˌmɛri'triʃəsnɪs/ n mal gusto, m

merge /mɜrdʒ/ vt fundir; Com. fusionar; mezclar. vi fundirse; Com. fusionarse; mezclarse

merger /'mɜrdʒər/ n combinación, f; Com. fusión, f

meridian /mə'rɪdiən/ n (Geog. Astron.) meridiano, m; (noon) mediodía, m; (peak) apogeo, m

meringue /mə'ræŋ/ n merengue, m, Lat. Am. espumilla, f

merino /mə'rinou/ a de merino; merino. n (fabric and sheep) merino, m

merit /'mɛrit/ n mérito, m, vt merecer, ser digno de

meritorious /ˌmɛri'tɔriəs/ a meritorio

meritoriously /ˌmɛri'tɔriəsli/ adv merecidamente

meritoriousness /ˌmɛri'tɔriəsnɪs/ n mérito, m

merlon /'mɜrlən/ n merlón, m, almena, f

mermaid /'mɜrˌmeid/ n sirena, f

merrily /'mɛrili/ adv alegremente

merriment /'mɛrimənt/ n alegría, f; júbilo, m; regocijo, m; diversión, f; juego, m

merry /'mɛri/ a alegre; jovial; feliz; regocijado, divertido; (tipsy) calamocano. **to make m.,** divertirse. **to make m. over,** reírse de. **M. Christmas!** ¡Felices Navidades! **m.-go-round,** caballitos, m pl, tiovivo, m, Lat. Am. calesita, f. **m.-making,** festividades, fiestas, f pl

meseta /me'seta/ n meseta, f

mesh /mɛʃ/ n malla, f; Mech. engranaje, m; (network) red, f; (snare) lazo, m. vt coger con red; Mech. endentar

mesmerism /'mɛzməˌrizəm/ n mesmerismo, m

mesmerize /'mɛzməˌraiz/ vt hipnotizar

mess /mɛs/ n (of food) plato de comida, m; porción, ración, f; rancho, m; (mixture) mezcla, f; (disorder) desorden, m; suciedad, f; Inf. reguero, m; (failure) fracaso, m. vt (dirty) ensuciar; desordenar; (mismanage) echar a perder. **to be in a m.,** Inf. estar aviado. **to get in a m.,** Inf. hacerse un lío. **to make a m. of,** ensuciar; desordenar; (spoil) echarlo todo a rodar

message /'mɛsidʒ/ n mensaje, m; recado, m; (tele-

graphic) parte, *m*. **I have to take a m.**, Tengo que hacer un recado
messenger /'mɛsəndʒər/ *n* mensajero (-ra); (of telegrams) repartidor, *m*; heraldo, *m*; anuncio, *m*
Messiah /mɪ'saiə/ *n* Mesías, *m*
Messianic /ˌmɛsi'ænɪk/ *a* mesiánico
messrs. /'mɛsərz/ *n pl* (abbreviation) sres. (from señores), *m pl*
metabolism /mə'tæbə,lɪzəm/ *n* metabolismo, *m*
metabolize /mə'tæbə,laiz/ *va* metabolizar
metal /'mɛtl̩/ *n* metal, *m*; vidrio en fusión, *m*; (road) grava, *f*; *Herald.* metal, *m*; (mettle) temple, temperamento, *m*; brío, fuego, *m*; *pl* metals, (of a railway) rieles, *m pl*. **m. engraver,** grabador en metal, *m*. **m. polish,** limpiametales, *m*. **m. shavings,** cizallas, *f pl*. **m. work,** metalistería, *f*. **m. worker,** metalario, *m*
metallic /mə'tælɪk/ *a* metálico
metalloid /'mɛtl̩,ɔid/ *n* metaloide, *m*
metallurgic /ˌmɛtl̩'ɜrdʒɪk/ *a* metalúrgico
metallurgist /'mɛtl̩,ɜrdʒɪst/ *n* metalúrgico, *m*
metallurgy /'mɛtl̩,ɜrdʒi/ *n* metalurgia, *f*
metamorphosis /ˌmɛtə'mɔrfəsɪs/ *n* metamorfosis, *f*
metaphor /'mɛtə,fɔr/ *n* metáfora, *f*
metaphorical /ˌmɛtə'fɔrɪkəl/ *a* metafórico
metaphysical /ˌmɛtə'fɪzɪkəl/ *a* metafísico
metaphysician /ˌmɛtəfə'zɪʃən/ *n* metafísico, *m*
metaphysics /ˌmɛtə'fɪzɪks/ *n* metafísica, *f*
metathesis /mə'tæθəsɪs/ *n* metátesis, *f*
mete /mit/ *vt* repartir, distribuir
metempsychosis /mə,tɛmsə'kousɪs/ *n* metempsicosis, *f*
meteor /'mitiər/ *n* meteoro, *m*
meteoric /ˌmiti'ɔrɪk/ *a* meteórico
meteorite /'mitiə,rait/ *n* meteorito, *m*
meteorological /ˌmitiərə'lɒdʒɪkəl/ *a* meteorológico
meteorologist /ˌmitiə'rɒlədʒɪst/ *n* meteorologista, *mf*
meteorology /ˌmitiə'rɒlədʒi/ *n* meteorología, *f*
meter /'mitər/ *n* (for gas, etc.) contador, *m*; (verse and measure) metro, *m*
methane /'mɛθein/ *n* metano, *m*
method /'mɛθəd/ *n* método, *m*; técnica, *f*; táctica, *f*
methodical /mə'θɒdɪkəl/ *a* metódico; ordenado, sistemático
Methodism /'mɛθə,dɪzəm/ *n* metodismo, *m*
Methodist /'mɛθədɪst/ *n* metodista, *mf*
methyl /'mɛθəl/ *n* metilo, *m*. **m. alcohol,** alcohol metílico, *m*
methylated spirit /'mɛθə,leitid/ *n* alcohol desnaturalizado, *m*
meticulous /mə'tɪkyələs/ *a* meticuloso; minucioso
meticulously /mə'tɪkyələsli/ *adv* con meticulosidad
meticulousness /mə'tɪkyələsnɪs/ *n* meticulosidad, *f*; minuciosidad, *f*
metric /'mɛtrɪk/ *a* métrico. **m. system,** sistema métrico, *m*
metrics /'mɛtrɪks/ *n* métrica, *f*
metronome /'mɛtrə,noum/ *n* metrónomo, *m*
metropolis /mɪ'trɒpəlɪs/ *n* metrópoli, *f*; capital, *f*
metropolitan /ˌmɛtrə'pɒlɪtn̩/ *a* metropolitano; de la capital. *n Eccl.* metropolitano, *m*
mettle /'mɛtl̩/ *n* temple, temperamento, *m*; fuego, brío, *m*; valor, *m*
mew /myu/ *n* (gull) gaviota, *f*; (of a cat) maullido, *m*; (of sea-birds) alarido, *m*. *vi* (of a cat) maullar; (of sea-birds) dar alaridos. **to mew up,** encerrar
mews /myuz/ *n* establos, *m pl*, caballeriza, *f*
Mexican /'mɛksɪkən/ *a* mexicano, mejicano. *n* mexicano (-na), mejicano (-na)
Mexico /'mɛksɪ,kou/ México, Méjico, *m*
mezzanine /'mɛzə,nin/ *n* entresuelo, *m*
mezzosoprano /'mɛtsou sə'prænou/ *n* mezzosoprano
mi /mi/ *n Mus.* mi, *m*
miaow /mi'au/ *n* miau, *m*, *vi* maullar
miasma /mai'æzmə/ *n* miasma, *m*
miasmatic /ˌmaiəz'mætɪk/ *a* miasmático
mica /'maikə/ *n* mica, *f*
microbe /'maikroub/ *n* microbio, *m*
microbial /mai'kroubiəl/ *a* microbiano

microbiologist /ˌmaikroubai'plədʒɪst/ *n* microbiólogo, *m*
microbiology /ˌmaikroubai'plədʒi/ *n* microbiología, *f*
microchip /'maikrou,tʃɪp/ *n* microchip *m*, microplaqueta, *f*
microcosm /'maikrə,kɒzəm/ *n* microcosmo, *m*
microphone /'maikrə,foun/ *n* micrófono, *m*
microscope /'maikrə,skoup/ *n* microscopio, *m*
microscopic /ˌmaikrə'skɒpɪk/ *a* microscópico
microwave /'maikrou,weiv/ *n* microonda, *f*
mid /mɪd/ *a* medio. *prep* entre; en medio de; a mediados de. **from mid May to August,** desde mediados de mayo hasta agosto. **a mid-fourteenth century castle,** un castillo de mediados del siglo catorce. **in mid air,** en medio del aire. **in mid channel,** en medio del canal. **in mid winter,** en medio del invierno
midday /'mɪd'dei/ *n* mediodía, *m*, *a* del mediodía, meridional. **at m.,** a mediodía
middle /'mɪdl̩/ *a* medio; en medio de; del centro; intermedio; (average) mediano. *n* medio, *m*; mitad, *f*; centro, *m*; (waist) cintura, *f*. **in the m. of,** en medio de. **in the m. of nowhere,** donde Cristo dio las tres voces. **toward the m. of the month,** a mediados del mes. **m. age,** edad madura, *f*. **m.-aged,** de edad madura, de cierta edad. **M. Ages,** edad media, *f*. **m. class,** clase media, burguesía, *f*, *a* de la clase media, burgués. **m. distance,** término medio, *m*. **m. ear,** oído medio, *m*. **m. finger,** dedo de en medio (or del corazón), *m*. **m. way,** *Fig.* término medio, *m*. **m. weight,** peso medio, *m*
Middle East, the el Medio Oriente, el Oriente Medio, el Levante, *m*
middleman /'mɪdl̩,mæn/ *n* agente de negocios, *m*; (retailer) revendedor, *m*; intermediario, *m*
middling /'mɪdlɪŋ/ *a* mediano; mediocre; regular, así, así
midge /mɪdʒ/ *n* mosquito, *m*, mosca de agua, *f*
midget /'mɪdʒɪt/ *n* enano (-na). **m. submarine,** submarino de bolsillo, *m*
midnight /'mɪd,nait/ *n* medianoche, *f*. *a* de medianoche; nocturno. **at m.,** a medianoche. **to burn the m. oil,** quemar las cejas. **m. mass,** misa del gallo, *f*
midriff /'mɪdrɪf/ *n* diafragma, *m*
midship /'mɪdʃɪp/ *a* maestro. *n* medio del buque, *m*. **m. beam,** bao maestro, *m*. **m. gangway,** crujía, *f*
midshipman /'mɪd,ʃɪpmən/ *n* guardiamarina, *m*
midst /mɪdst/ *n* medio, *m*; seno, *m*, *prep* entre. **in the m. of,** en medio de. **There is a traitor in our m.,** Hay un traidor entre nosotros (or en nuestra compañía)
midstream /'mɪd'strim/ *n* **in m.,** en medio de la corriente, *m*
midsummer /'mɪd'sʌmər/ *n* pleno verano, *m*; solsticio estival, *m*; fiesta de San Juan, *f*. **A M. Night's Dream,** El Sueño de la Noche de San Juan
midway /adv, a 'mɪd'wei; *n* -,wei/ *a* and *adv* situado a medio camino; a medio camino, a la mitad del camino; entre. *n* mitad del camino, *f*; medio, *m*. **m. between...,** equidistante de..., entre
midwife /'mɪd,waif/ *n* comadrona, partera, *f*
midwifery /mɪd'wɪfəri/ *n* obstetricia, *f*
midwinter /'mɪd'wɪntər/ *n* medio del invierno, *m*
mien /min/ *n* aire, *m*; porte, semblante, *m*
might /mait/ *vi* poder. **It m. or m. not be true,** Podría o no podría ser verdad. **How happy Mary might have been!** ¡Qué feliz pudo haber sido María! **I thought that you m. have seen him in the theater,** Creí que pudieras haberle visto en el teatro. **That I m....!** ¡Que yo pudiese...! **This m. have been avoided if...,** Esto podría haberse evitado si...
might /mait/ *n* fuerza, *f*; poder, *m*. **with m. and main,** con todas sus fuerzas
mightily /'maitl̩i/ *adv* fuertemente; poderosamente; *Inf.* muchísimo, sumamente
mightiness /'maitinɪs/ *n* fuerza, *f*; poder, *m*; grandeza, *f*
mighty /'maiti/ *a* fuerte, vigoroso; poderoso; grande; *Inf.* enorme; (proud) arrogante. *adv Inf.* enormemente, muy
migraine /'maigrein/ *n* migraña, jaqueca, *f*

migrant /'maigrənt/ a migratorio, de paso. n ave migratoria, ave de paso, f
migrate /'maigreit/ vi emigrar
migration /mai'greiʃən/ n migración, f
migratory /'maigrə,tɔri/ a migratorio, de paso; (of people) nómada, pasajero
migratory worker n trabajador golondrino, m
Milanese /,milə'niz/ a milanés. n milanés (-esa)
milch /miltʃ/ a f, (of cows) lechera
mild /maild/ a apacible, pacífico; manso; dulce; suave; (of the weather) blando; Med. benigno; (light) leve; (of drinks) ligero; (weak) débil
mildew /'mil,du/ n mildiu, añublo, m; moho, m. vt anublar; enmohecer. vi anublarse; enmohecerse
mildly /'maildli/ adv suavemente; dulcemente; con indulgencia
mildness /'maildnɪs/ n apacibilidad, f; mansedumbre, f; suavidad, f; (of weather) blandura, f; dulzura, f; indulgencia, f; (weakness) debilidad, f
mile /mail/ n milla, f
mileage /'mailidʒ/ n distancia en millas, f; kilometraje, m
milestone /'mail,stoun/ n hito, m, piedra miliaria, f; mojón kilométrico, m
milfoil /'mil,fɔil/ n Bot. milenrama, f
militancy /'militənsi/ n carácter militante, m; belicosidad, f
militant /'militənt/ a militante, combatiente; belicoso; agresivo. n combatiente, mf
militarily /,mili'terəli/ adv militarmente
militariness /'mili,terinɪs/ n lo militar, el carácter militar
militarism /'militə,rizəm/ n militarismo, m
militarist /'militərist/ n militarista, mf
militaristic /,militə'ristik/ a militarista
militarization /,militəri'zeiʃən/ n militarización, f
militarize /'militə,raiz/ vt militarizar
military /'mili,teri/ a militar; de guerra. **the m.**, los militares. **m. academy**, colegio militar, m. **m. camp**, campo militar, m. **m. law**, código militar, m. **m. man**, militar, m. **m. police**, policía militar, f. **m. service**, servicio militar, m
militate (against) /'mili,teit/ vi militar contra
militia /mi'liʃə/ n milicia, f
militiaman /mi'liʃəmən/ n miliciano, m
milk /milk/ n leche, f. a de leche; lácteo. vt ordeñar. vi dar leche. **to have m. and water in one's veins**, tener sangre de horchata. **condensed m.**, leche condensada, leche en lata, f. **m.-can**, lechera, f. **m.-cart**, carro de la leche, m. **m. chocolate**, chocolate con leche, m. **m. of magnesia**, leche de magnesia, f. **m.-pail**, ordeñadero, m. **m.-tooth**, diente de leche, m. **m.-white**, blanco como la leche
milkiness /'milkinɪs/ n lactescencia, f; carácter lechoso, m; (whiteness) blancura, f
milking /'milkiŋ/ n ordeño, m. **m.-machine**, máquina ordeñadora, f. **m.-stool**, taburete, banquillo, m
milkmaid /'milk,meid/ n lechera, f
milkman /'milk,mæn/ n lechero, m
milky /'milki/ a lechero; de leche; lechoso, como leche; Astron. lácteo. **the Milky Way** la Vía láctea f
mill /mil/ n molino, m; (for coffee, etc.) molinillo, m; (factory) fábrica, f; taller, m; (textile) hilandería, f; fábrica de tejidos, f; (fight) riña a puñetazos, f; pugilato, m. vt (grind) moler; (coins) acordonar; (cloth) abatanar; (chocolate) batir. **cotton m.**, hilandería de algodón, f. **hand-m.**, molinillo, m. **paper-m.**, fábrica de papel, f. **saw-m.**, serrería, f. **spinning m.**, hilandería, f. **water m.**, molino de agua, m. **m.-course**, saetín, canal de molino, m. **m.-dam**, esclusa de molino, f. **m.-hand**, obrero (-ra). **m.-pond**, cubo, m. **m.-race**, caz, m. **m.-wheel**, rueda de molino, f
millennial /mi'leniəl/ a milenario
millennium /mi'leniəm/ n milenario, m
miller /'milər/ n molinero, m. **miller's wife**, molinera
millet /'milit/ n mijo, m
milligram /'mili,græm/ n miligramo, m
milliliter /'mili,litər/ n mililitro, m
millimeter /'mili,mitər/ n milímetro, m

milliner /'milənər/ n sombrerero (-ra), modista, mf
milliner's shop, sombrerería, tienda de modista, f
millinery /'mili,neri/ n sombreros, m pl; modas, f pl; tienda de modista, f
milling /'miliŋ/ n molienda, f; acuñación, f; (edge of coin) cordoncillo, m. **m. machine**, fresadora, f
million /'milyən/ n millón, m. **the m.**, las masas
millionaire /,milyə'nɛər/ a millonario. n millonario, m
millionairess /,milyə'nɛəris/ n millonaria, f
millionth /'milyənθ/ a millonésimo
millstone /'mil,stoun/ n piedra de moler, muela, f
mime /maim/ n (Greek farce and actor) mimo, m; (mimicry) mímica, f; pantomima, f. vi hacer en pantomima
mimetic /mi'metik/ a mímico, imitativo
mimic /'mimik/ a mímico; (pretended) fingido. n imitador (-ra). vt imitar, contrahacer; Biol. imitar, adaptarse a
mimicry /'mimikri/ n mímica, imitación, f; Biol. mimetismo, m
minaret /,minə'ret/ n minarete, m; (of a mosque) alminar, m
minatory /'minə,tɔri, -,touri/ a amenazador
mince /mins/ vt desmenuzar; (meat) picar; (words) medir (las palabras). vi andar con pasos menuditos; andar o moverse con afectación; hacer remilgos. **m.-meat**, carne picada, f; (sweet) conserva de fruta y especias, f
mincing /'minsiŋ/ a afectado. n acción de picar carne, f. **m. machine**, máquina de picar carne, f
mincingly /'minsiŋli/ adv con afectación; con pasos menuditos
mind /maind/ n inteligencia, f; espíritu ánimo, m; imaginación, f; alma, f; (memory) memoria, f, recuerdo, m; (understanding) entendimiento, m; (genius) ingenio, m; (cast of mind) mentalidad, f; (opinion) opinión, f; (liking) gusto, m; (thoughts) pensamiento, m; (intention) propósito, m, intención, f; (tendency) propensión, inclinación, f. **I have a good m. to go away**, Por poco me marcho; Tengo ganas de marcharme. **I have changed my m.**, He cambiado de opinión. **out of m.**, olvidado. **I shall give him a piece of my m.**, Le diré cuatro verdades. It had quite gone out of my m., Lo había olvidado completamente. **I can see it in my mind's eye**, Está presente a mi imaginación. **I shall bear it in m.**, Lo tendré en cuenta. **I thought in my own m. that...**, Pensé por mis adentros que... **We are both of the same m.**, Ambos somos de la misma opinión. **to be out of one's m.**, estar fuera de juicio. **to call to m.**, acordarse de. **to have something on one's m.**, estar preocupado. **to make up one's m.** (to), resolverse (a), decidirse (a), determinar; animarse (a). **m.-reader**, adivinador (-ra) del pensamiento
mind /maind/ vt (remember) recordar, no olvidar; (heed) atender a; hacer caso de; tener cuidado de; (fear) tener miedo de; (obey) obedecer; preocuparse de; (object to) molestar; importar; (care for) cuidar. vi tener cuidado; molestar; (feel) sentir; (fear) tener miedo; (be the same thing) ser igual, lo mismo; (be bothered by) molestar. **Do you m. being quiet a moment?** ¿Quieres hacer el favor de callarte un momento? **Do you m. if I smoke?** ¿Le molesta si fumo? **They don't m.**, No les importa, Les da igual. **Never m.!** ¡No se moleste!; ¡No se preocupe!; ¡No importa! ¡Vaya! **M. what you are doing!** ¡Cuidado con lo que haces! **M. your own business!** ¡No te metas donde no te llaman!
minded /'maindid/ a dispuesto, inclinado; de... pensamientos; de... disposición
mindful /'maindfəl/ a atento a (a), cuidadoso (de); que se acuerda (de)
mine /main/ a poss mío, m, (mía, f; míos, m pl; mías, f pl); el mío, m, (la mía, f); lo mío, neut; los míos, m pl; las mías, f pl); mi (pl mis). **a friend of m.**, un amigo mío; uno de mis amigos
mine /main/ n mina, f. vt minar; extraer; sembrar minas en, colocar minas en. vi minar; hacer una mina; dedicarse a la minería. **drifting m.**, mina a la deriva, f. **land m.**, mina terrestre, f. **magnetic m.**, mina magnética, f. **to lay mines**, colocar (or sembrar)

minas. **m.-sweeper,** dragaminas, buque barreminas, *m*

minefield /'main,fild/ *n* campo de minas, *m*; barrera de minas, *f*

minelayer /'main,leiər/ *n* barca plantaminas, *f*, barco siembraminas, lanzaminas, *m*

miner /'mainər/ *n* minero, *m*; *Mil.* zapador minador, *m*

mineral /'minərəl/ *n* mineral, *m*, *a* mineral. **m. baths,** baños, *m pl.* **m. water,** agua mineral, *f*; gaseosa, *f*

mineralogical /,minərə'lɒdʒıkəl/ *a* mineralógico

mineralogist /,minə'ɒlədʒıst/ *n* mineralogista, *m*

mineralogy /,minə'rɒlədʒi/ *n* mineralogía, *f*

mingle /'miŋgəl/ *vt* mezclar; confundir. *vi* mezclarse; confundirse

mingling /'miŋgliŋ/ *n* mezcla, *f*

miniature /'miniətʃər/ *n* miniatura, *f. a* en miniatura. **m. edition,** edición diamante, *f*

miniature golf *n* minigolf, *m*

miniaturist /'miniətʃərist/ *n* miniaturista, *mf*

minibus /'mini,bʌs/ *n* micro, microbús, *Mexico* combi, *m*

minimize /'minə,maiz/ *vt* aminorar, reducir al mínimo; mitigar; (underrate) tener en menos, despreciar

minimum /'minəməm/ *n* mínimo, *m*, *a* mínimo

mining /'mainiŋ/ *n* minería, *f*, *a* minero; de mina; de minas; de minero. **m. engineer,** ingeniero de minas, *m*

minion /'minyən/ *n* favorito (-ta); satélite, *m*; *Print.* miñona, *f*

minister /'minəstər/ *n* ministro, *m. vi* servir; suministrar, proveer de; (contribute) contribuir (a). **m. of health,** ministro de sanidad, *m.* **m. of war,** ministro de la guerra, *m*

ministration /,minə'streiʃən/ *n Eccl.* ministerio, *m*; servicio, *m*; agencia, *f*

ministry /'minəstri/ *n* ministerio, *m.* **m. of food,** Ministerio de Abastecimientos, *m*

mink /miŋk/ *n* visón, *m*

minnow /'minou/ *n* pez pequeño de agua dulce, *m*

minor /'mainər/ *a* menor. *n* menor de edad, *m*; (logic) menor, *f*; *Mus.* tono menor, *m*; *Eccl.* menor, *m.* **to be a m.,** ser menor de edad. **m. key,** tono menor, *m.* **m. orders,** *Eccl.* órdenes menores, *f pl.* **m. scale,** escala menor, *f*

Minorca /mi'nɔrkə/ Menorca, *f*

minority /mi'nɔriti/ *a* minoritario. *n* minoría, *f*; (of age) minoridad, *f.* **in the m.,** en la minoría

minster /'minstər/ *n* catedral, *f*; monasterio, *m*

minstrel /'minstrəl/ *n* trovador, juglar, *m*; músico, *m*; cantante, *m*

minstrelsy /'minstrəlsi/ *n* música, *f*; canto, *m*; arte del trovador, *m*, or *f*; gaya ciencia, *f*

mint /mint/ *n Bot.* menta, hierbabuena, *f*; casa de moneda, casa de la moneda, ceca, *f*; *Fig.* mina, *f*; (source) origen, *m. vt* (money) acuñar; *Fig.* inventar, *a* (postage stamp) en estado nuevo

minter /'mintər/ *n* acuñador, *m*; *Fig.* inventor (-ra)

minting /'mintiŋ/ *n* (of coins) acuñación, *f*; *Fig.* invención, *f*

minuet /,minyu'ɛt/ *n* minué, *m*

minus /'mainəs/ *a* menos; negativo; desprovisto de; sin. *n* signo menos, *m*; cantidad negativa, *f*

minute /mai'nut/ *a* menudo, diminuto; insignificante; minucioso

minute /'minit/ *n* minuto, *m*; momento, *m*; instante, *m*; (note) minuta, *f*; *pl* **minutes,** actas, *f pl.* **in a m.,** en un instante. **m.-book,** libro de actas, minutario *m*; **m.-hand,** minutero, *m*

minutely /mai'nutli/ *adv* minuciosamente; en detalle; exactamente

minuteness /mai'nutnis/ *n* suma pequeñez, *f*; minuciosidad, *f*

minx /miŋks/ *n* picaruela, *f*; coqueta, *f*

miracle /'mirəkəl/ *n* milagro, *m.* **m.-monger,** milagrero (-ra). **m. play,** milagro, *m*

miraculous /mi'rækyələs/ *a* milagroso

miraculously /mi'rækyələsli/ *adv* milagrosamente, por milagro

miraculousness /mi'rækyələsnis/ *n* carácter milagroso, *m*, lo milagroso

mirage /mi'rɑʒ/ *n* espejismo, *m*

mire /mai°r/ *n* fango, lodo, *m*; (miry place) lodazal, *m*

mirror /'mirər/ *n* espejo, *m. vt* reflejar. **to look in the m.,** mirarse al espejo. **full-length m.,** espejo de cuerpo entero, *m.* **small m.,** espejuelo, *m*

mirth /mərθ/ *n* alegría, *f*, júbilo, *m*; risa, *f*; hilaridad, *f*

mirthful /'mɛrθfəl/ *a* alegre

mirthless /'mɛrθlis/ *a* sin alegría, triste

miry /'mai°ri/ *a* lodoso, fangoso, cenagoso

misadventure /,misəd'vɛntʃər/ *n* desgracia, *f*; accidente, *m*

misanthrope /'misən,θroup/ *n* misántropo, *m*

misanthropic /,misən'θrɒpik/ *a* misantrópico

misanthropy /mis'ænθrəpi/ *n* misantropía, *f*

misapplication /,misæpli'keiʃən/ *n* mala aplicación, *f*; mal uso, *m*; abuso, *m*

misapply /,misə'plai/ *vt* aplicar mal; hacer mal uso de; abusar de

misapprehend /,misæpri'hɛnd/ *vt* comprender mal; equivocarse sobre

misapprehension /,misæprə'hɛnʃən/ *n* concepto erróneo, *m*; equivocación, *f*, error, *m*

misappropriate /,misə'proupri,eit/ *vt* malversar

misappropriation /,misəproupri'eiʃən/ *n* malversación, *f*

misbehave /,misbi'heiv/ *vi* portarse mal; (of a child) ser malo

misbehavior /,misbi'heivyər/ *n* mala conducta, *f*

miscalculate /mis'kælkyəleit/ *vt* calcular mal; engañarse (sobre)

miscalculation /,miskælkyə'leiʃən/ *n* mal cálculo, error, *m*; desacierto, *m*

miscall /mis'kɔl/ *vt* mal nombrar; llamar equivocadamente; (abuse) insultar

miscarriage /mis'kæridʒ/ *n Med.* aborto, *m*; (failure) malogro, fracaso, *m*; (of goods) extravío, *m*

miscarriage of justice *n* yerro en la administración de la justicia, *m*

miscarry /mis'kæri/ *vi Med.* abortar, malparir; (fail) malograrse, frustrarse; (of goods) extraviarse

miscellaneous /,misə'leiniəs/ *a* misceláneo; vario, diverso

miscellany /'misə,leini/ *n* miscelánea, *f*

mischance /mis'tʃæns/ *n* mala suerte, *f*; infortunio, *m*, desgracia, *f*; accidente, *m*

mischief /'mistʃif/ *n* daño, *m*; mal, *m*; (wilfulness) travesura, *f*; (person) diablillo, *m.* **m.-maker,** enredador (-ra), chismoso (-sa); alborotador, *m*; malicioso (-sa). **m.-making,** *a* enredador; chismoso; malicioso; alborotador

mischievous /'mistʃəvəs/ *a* dañino, perjudicial, malo; malicioso; chismoso; (wilful) travieso; juguetón; (of glances, etc.) malicioso

mischievously /'mistʃəvəsli/ *adv* maliciosamente; con (or por) travesura

mischievousness /'mistʃəvəsnis/ *n* mal, *m*; malicia, *f*; maleficencia, *f*; travesura, *f*

misconceive /,miskən'siv/ *vt* formar un concepto erróneo de; concebir mal; juzgar mal

misconception /,miskən'sepʃən/ *n* concepto erróneo, *m*, idea falsa, *f*; error, *m*, equivocación, *f*; engaño, *m*

misconduct /*n* mis'kɒndʌkt/ *v* ,miskən'dʌkt/ *n* mala conducta, *f.* **to m. oneself,** portarse mal

misconstruction /,miskən'strakʃən/ *n* mala interpretación, *f*; falsa interpretación, *f*; tergiversación, *f*; mala traducción, *f*

misconstrue /,miskən'stru/ *vt* interpretar mal; entender mal; tergiversar; traducir mal

miscount /*v* mis'kaunt; *n* 'mis,kaunt/ *vt* contar mal, equivocarse en la cuenta de; calcular mal. *n* error, *m*; yerro de cuenta, *m*

miscreant /'miskriənt/ *n* malandrín, *m*; bribón, *m*, *a* vil, malandrín

misdeed /mis'did/ *n* delito, malhecho, crimen, *m*

misdemeanor /,misdi'minər/ *n* mala conducta, *f*; *Law.* delito, *m*; ofensa, *f*, malhecho, *m*

misdirect /,misdi'rɛkt/ *vt* informar mal (acerca del

camino); (a letter) dirigir mal, poner unas señas incorrectas en

miser /'maizər/ n avaro (-ra)

miserable /'mɪzərəbəl/ a infeliz, desgraciado; miserable; despreciable; sin valor

miserably /'mɪzərəbli/ adv miserablemente

miserliness /'maizərlinis/ n avaricia, tacañería, f

miserly /'maizərli/ a avaro, tacaño

misery /'mɪzəri/ n miseria, f; sufrimiento, m; dolor, tormento, m

misfire /mɪs'fɪᵊr/ vi no dar fuego; (of a car, etc.) hacer falsas explosiones, errar el encendido

misfit /mɪs'fɪt; 'mɪs,fɪt for person/ n traje que no cae bien, m; zapato que no va bien, m; (person) inadaptado, m

misfortune /mɪs'fɔrtʃən/ n infortunio, m, mala suerte, adversidad, f; desdicha, desgracia, f; mal, m

misgive /mɪs'gɪv/ vt hacer temer; llenar de duda; hacer recelar; hacer presentir

misgiving /mɪs'gɪvɪŋ/ n temor, m; duda, f; recelo, m; presentimiento, m

misgovern /mɪs'gʌvərn/ vt gobernar mal; administrar mal; dirigir mal

misgovernment /mɪs'gʌvərnmənt/ n desgobierno, m; mala administración, f

misguided /mɪs'gaidɪd/ a mal dirigido; extraviado; engañado; (blind) ciego

misguidedly /mɪs'gaidɪdli/ adv equivocadamente

mishap /'mɪshæp/ n desgracia, f; contratiempo, accidente, m. **to have a m.,** sufrir una desgracia; tener un accidente

misinform /ˌmɪsɪn'fɔrm/ vt informar mal; dar informes erróneos (a)

misinformation /ˌmɪsɪnfər'meiʃən/ n noticia falsa, f; información errónea, f

misinterpret /ˌmɪsɪn'tɜrprɪt/ vt interpretar mal; entender mal; torcer; tergiversar; traducir mal

misinterpretation /ˌmɪsɪn,tɜrprɪ'teiʃən/ n mala interpretación, f; interpretación falsa, f; tergiversación, f; mala traducción, f

misjudge /mɪs'dʒʌdʒ/ vt juzgar mal; equivocarse (en or sobre); tener una idea falsa de

misjudgment /mɪs'dʒʌdʒmənt/ n juicio errado, m; idea falsa, f; juicio injusto, m

mislay /mɪs'lei/ vt extraviar, perder

mislead /mɪs'lid/ vt extraviar; llevar a conclusiones erróneas, despistar; engañar

misleading /mɪs'lidɪŋ/ a de falsas apariencias; erróneo, falso; engañoso

mismanage /mɪs'mænɪdʒ/ vt administrar mal; dirigir mal; echar a perder

mismanagement /mɪs'mænɪdʒmənt/ n mala administración, f; desgobierno, m

misname /mɪs'neim/ vt mal nombrar; llamar equivocadamente

misnomer /mɪs'noumər/ n nombre equivocado, m; nombre inapropiado, m

misogynist /mɪ'sɒdʒənɪst/ n misógino, m

misogyny /mɪ'sɒdʒəni/ n misoginia, f

misplace /mɪs'pleis/ vt colocar mal; poner fuera de lugar

misplaced /mɪs'pleist/ a mal puesto; inoportuno; equivocado

misprint /n. 'mɪs,prɪnt; v. mɪs'prɪnt/ n error de imprenta, m, errata, f, vt imprimir con erratas

mispronounce /ˌmɪsprə'nouns/ vt pronunciar mal

mispronunciation /ˌmɪsprənʌnsi'eiʃən/ n mala pronunciación, f

misquotation /ˌmɪskwou'teiʃən/ n cita errónea, f

misquote /mɪs'kwout/ vt citar mal, citar erróneamente

misrepresent /ˌmɪsreprɪ'zɛnt/ vt desfigurar; tergiversar; falsificar

misrepresentation /ˌmɪs,reprɪzɛn'teiʃən/ n desfiguración, f; tergiversación, f; falsificación, f

misrule /mɪs'rul/ vt gobernar mal. n mal gobierno, desgobierno, m; confusión, f

miss /mɪs/ n señorita, f

miss /mɪs/ vt (one's aim) errar (el tiro, etc.); no acertar (a); (let fall) dejar caer; (lose a train, the post,

etc., one's footing, an opportunity, etc.) perder; (fall short of) dejar de; no ver; no notar; pasar por alto de, omitir; echar de menos; notar la falta de; no encontrar. vi errar; (fail) salir mal, fracasar. **I m. you,** Te echo de menos. **to be missing,** faltar; estar ausente; haberse marchado; haber desaparecido. **to m. one's mark,** errar el blanco. **to m. out,** omitir, pasar por alto de. **She doesn't miss a beat,** (fig.) No se le escapa nada

missal /'mɪsəl/ n misal, m

misshapen /mɪs'ʃeipən/ a deforme

missile /'mɪsəl/ n arma arrojadiza, f; proyectil, m

missing /'mɪsɪŋ/ a que falta; perdido; ausente; Mil. desaparecido

mission /'mɪʃən/ n misión, f

missionary /'mɪʃə,nɛri/ n misionero, m

missionize /'mɪʃə,naiz/ vi misionar

missis /'mɪsəz/ n señora, f; Inf. mujer, f

Mississippi /ˌmɪsə'sɪpi/ el Misisipí, m

missive /'mɪsɪv/ n misiva, f

Missouri /mɪ'zʊri/ el Misuri, m

misspend /mɪs'spɛnd/ vt malgastar; desperdiciar; perder

mist /mɪst/ n bruma, neblina, f; vapor, m; (drizzle) llovizna, f; Fig. nube, f. vt anublar, empañar. vi llovizna

mistakable /mɪ'steikəbəl/ a confundible

mistake /mɪ'steik/ vt comprender mal; equivocarse sobre; errar; (with for) confundir con, equivocarse con. n equivocación, f; error, m; inadvertencia, f; (in an exercise, etc.) falta, f. **And no m.!** Inf. Sin duda alguna. **by m.,** por equivocación (involuntarily) sin querer. **If I am not mistaken,** Si no me engaño, Si no estoy equivocado. **to make a m.,** equivocarse

mistaken /mɪ'steikən/ a (of persons and things) equivocado; (of things) erróneo; incorrecto

mistakenly /mɪ'steikənli/ adv equivocadamente; injustamente, falsamente

mister /'mɪstər/ n señor, m

mistily /'mɪstəli/ adv a través de la neblina; obscuramente; indistintamente, vagamente

mistimed /mɪs'taimd/ a intempestivo; inoportuno

mistiness /'mɪstinɪs/ n neblina, bruma, f; vaporosidad, f; obscuridad, f

mistletoe /'mɪsəl,tou/ n muérdago, m

mistranslate /ˌmɪstrænz'leit/ vt traducir mal; interpretar mal

mistranslation /ˌmɪstrænz'leiʃən/ n mala traducción, f; traducción inexacta, f

mistress /'mɪstrɪs/ n señora, f; maestra, f; (fiancée) prometida, f; (beloved) amada, dulce dueña, f; (concubine) amiga, querida, f. **M. (Mrs.) Gómez,** Sra Gómez. **m. of the robes,** camarera mayor, f

mistrust /mɪs'trʌst/ vt desconfiar de, no tener confianza en; dudar de. n desconfianza, f; recelo, m; suspicacia, f; aprensión, f

mistrustful /mɪs'trʌstfəl/ a desconfiado; receloso, suspicaz. **to be m. of,** recelarse de

misty /'mɪsti/ a brumoso, nebuloso; vaporoso; (of the eyes) anublado; (of windows, etc.) empañado

misunderstand /ˌmɪsʌndər'stænd/ vt comprender mal; tomar en sentido erróneo; interpretar mal

misunderstanding /ˌmɪsʌndər'stændɪŋ/ n concepto erróneo, error, m; equivocación, f; (disagreement) desavenencia, f

misuse /n mɪs'yus; v -'yuz/ vt emplear mal; abusar de; (funds) malversar; (ill-treat) tratar mal. n m. abuso, m; (of funds) malversación, f

mite /mait/ n (coin) ardite, m; (trifle) pizca, f; óbolo, m; Ent. ácaro, m

miter /'maitər/ n mitra, f; inglete, m, vt cortar ingletes en

mitigate /'mɪti,geit/ vt (pain) aliviar; mitigar; suavizar

mitigation /ˌmɪti'geiʃən/ n (of pain) alivio, m; mitigación, f

mitten /'mɪtn̩/ n mitón, f

mix /mɪks/ vt mezclar; (salad) aderezar; (concrete, etc.) amasar; combinar, unir; (sociably) alternar (con) (confuse) confundir. vi mezclarse; frecuentar la compañía (de); frecuentar; (get on well) llevarse bien

mixed /mɪkst/ a mezclado; vario, surtido; mixto; (confused) confuso. **m. doubles,** parejas mixtas, f pl. **m. up,** (in disorder) revuelto; confuso. **m. up with,** implicado en; asociado con

mixer /'mɪksər/ n mezclador, m; (person) mezclador (-ra); Inf. persona sociable, f. **electric m.,** mezclador eléctrico, m

mixture /'mɪkstʃər/ n mezcla, f; (medicine) poción, medicina, f

mizzen /'mɪzən/ n mesana, f. **m.-mast,** palo de mesana, m. **m.-sail,** vela de mesana, f. **m.-topsail,** sobremesana, f

mnemonics /nɪ'mɒnɪks/ n mnemotecnia, f

moan /moun/ vt lamentar; llorar. vi gemir; quejarse, lamentarse. n gemido, m; lamento, m; quejido, m

moaning /'mounɪŋ/ n gemidos, m pl

moat /mout/ n foso, m

mob /mɒb/ n (crowd) muchedumbre, multitud, f; (rabble) populacho, m, gentuza, f. vt atropellar; atacar. **mob-cap,** cofia, f

mobile /'moubil/ a móvil; ambulante; (fickle) voluble. **m. canteen,** cantina ambulante, f

mobility /mou'bɪlɪti/ n movilidad, f

mobilization /,moubələ'zeiʃən/ n movilización, f

mobilize /'moubə,laiz/ vt movilizar. vi movilizarse

moccasin /'mɒkəsɪn, -zən/ n mocasín, m

mocha /'moukə/ n café de Moca, m

mock /mɒk/ vt ridiculizar; burlarse (de), mofarse (de); (cause to fail) frustrar; (mimic) imitar; (delude) engañar. vi mofarse, burlarse, reírse. a cómico, burlesco; falso; fingido; imitado. **to make a m. of,** poner en ridículo; hacer absurdo; burlarse de. **m.-heroic,** heroico-cómico. **m.-orange,** Bot. jeringuilla, f. **m.-turtle soup,** sopa hecha con cabeza de ternera a imitación de tortuga, f

mocker /'mɒkər/ n mofador (-ra); el, m, (f, la) que se burla de

mockery /'mɒkəri/ n mofa, burla, f; ridículo, m; ilusión, apariencia, f. **to make a m. of,** mofarse de; hacer ridículo

mocking /'mɒkɪŋ/ a burlón. **m. bird,** pájaro burlón, m

mockingly /'mɒkɪŋli/ adv burlonamente

modality /mou'dælɪti/ n modalidad, f

mode /moud/ n modo, m; manera, f; (fashion) moda, f; uso, m, costumbre, f

model /'mɒdl/ n modelo, m; (artist's) modelo vivo, m, a modelo; en miniatura. vt modelar; moldear; formar; hacer; planear. **m. display,** (hats, etc.) exposición de modelos, f. **m. railway,** ferrocarril en miniatura, m

modeler /'mɒdlər/ n modelador (-ra); disenador, m

modeling /'mɒdlɪŋ/ n modelado, m; modelo, m. **m. wax,** cera para moldear, f

modem /'moudəm/ n módem, m

moderate /a, n. 'mɒdərɪt v. -ə,reit/ a moderado; (of prices, etc.) módico; (fair, medium) regular, mediano; razonable; mediocre. n moderado, m. vt moderar; modificar; calmar. vi moderarse; calmarse

moderately /'mɒdərɪtli/ adv moderadamente; módicamente; medianamente; bastante; razonablemente; mediocremente

moderation /,mɒdə'reiʃən/ n moderación, f. **in m.,** en moderación

moderator /'mɒdə,reitər/ n moderador, m; (Church of Scotland) presidente, m; Educ. examinador, m; Educ. inspector de exámenes, m. **m. lamp,** lámpara de regulador, f

modern /'mɒdərn/ a moderno. n modernista, mf. **in the m. way,** a la moderna. **m. language,** lengua viva, f

modernism /'mɒdər,nɪzəm/ n modernismo, m

modernist /'mɒdərnɪst/ n modernista, mf

modernistic /,mɒdər'nɪstɪk/ a modernista

modernity /mɒ'dərnɪti/ n modernidad, f

modernization /,mɒdərnə'zeiʃən/ n modernización, f

modernize /'mɒdər,naiz/ vt modernizar

modernness /'mɒdərnnɪs/ n modernidad, f

modest /'mɒdɪst/ a modesto; (of a woman) púdico

modesty /'mɒdəsti/ n modestia, f; (of a woman) pudor, m

modicum /'mɒdɪkəm/ n porción pequeña, f; poco, m

modifiable /,mɒdə'faiəbəl/ a modificable

modification /,mɒdəfɪ'keiʃən/ n modificación, f

modify /'mɒdə,fai/ vt modificar. **It has been much modified,** Se ha modificado mucho; Se han hecho muchas modificaciones

modifying /'mɒdə,faiɪŋ/ a modificante, modificador

modish /'moudiʃ/ a de moda en boga; elegante

modishness /'moudiʃnɪs/ n elegancia, f

modiste /mou'dist/ n modista, mf

modulate /'mɒdʒə,leit/ vt and vi modular

modulation /,mɒdʒə'leiʃən/ n modulación, f

modus vivendi /'moudəs vɪ'vɛndi, -dai/ n modo de conveniencia, m

Mogul /'mougəl/ a mogol. n mogol (-la). **the Great M.,** el Gran Mogol

Mohammedan /mʊ'hæmɪdn̩, mou-/ a mahometano, agareno

Mohican /mou'hikən/ a mohican, m

moiety /'mɔiɪti/ n mitad, f

moiré /mwɑ'rei, mɔ-/ n muaré, m

moist /mɔist/ a húmedo

moisten /'mɔisən/ vt humedecer, mojar

moisture /'mɔistʃər/ n humedad, f

molar /'moulər/ n muela, f, a molar

molasses /mə'læsɪz/ n pl melaza, f

mold /mould/ n (fungus) moho, m; (humus) mantillo, m; (iron-mold) mancha de orín, f; (matrix) molde, m, matriz, f; Cul. cubilete, m; Naut. gálibo, m; (for jelly, etc.) molde, m; Archit. moldura, f; (temperament) temple, m, disposición, f. vt moldear; (cast) vaciar; moldurar; Naut. galibar; Fig. amoldar, formar; Agr. cubrir con mantillo. **to m. oneself on,** modelarse sobre. **m.-board,** (of a plow) orejera, f

Moldavian /moul'deiviən/ a moldavo. n moldavo (-va)

molder /'mouldər/ n moldeador, m; Fig. amolador (-ra); creador (-ra). vi desmoronarse, convertirse en polvo; Fig. decaer, desmoronarse; vegetar

moldiness /'mouldinɪs/ n moho, m

molding /'mouldɪŋ/ n amoldamiento, m; vaciado, m; Archit. moldura, f; Fig. formación, f

moldy /'mouldi/ a mohoso, enmohecido; Fig. anticuado

mole /moul/ n (animal) topo, m; (spot) lunar, m; (breakwater) dique, malecón, m; muelle, m

molecular /mə'lɛkyələr/ a molecular

molecule /'mɒlɪ,kyul/ n molécula, f

molehill /'moul,hil/ n topera, f

moleskin /'moul,skɪn/ n piel de topo, f

molest /mə'lɛst/ vt molestar; perseguir, importunar; faltar al respeto (a)

molestation /,moulə'steiʃən/ n importunidad, persecución, f; molestia, incomodidad, f

mollification /,mɒləfɪ'keiʃən/ n apaciguamiento, m; mitigación, f

mollify /'mɒlə,fai/ vt apaciguar, calmar; mitigar

mollusk /'mɒləsk/ n molusco, m

mollycoddle /'mɒli,kɒdl/ n alfeñique, mírame y no me toques, m; niño (-ña), mimado (-da)

Moloch /'moulɒk/ n Moloch, Moloc, m

molt /moult/ vi mudar. n muda, f

molten /'moultn̩/ a fundido; derretido

Moluccas, the /mə'lʌkəz/ las Malucas, f pl

moment /'moumənt/ n momento, m; instante m; (importance) importancia, f. **at this m.,** en este momento. **Do it this m.!** ¡Hazlo al instante (or en seguida)!

momentarily /,moumən'tɛərəli, 'moumən,tɛr-/ adv momentáneamente; por un momento

momentariness /'moumən,tɛrinɪs/ n momentaneidad, f

momentary /'moumən,tɛri/ a momentáneo

momentous /mou'mɛntəs/ a de suma importancia; crítico; grave

momentousness /mou'mɛntəsnɪs/ n importancia, f; gravedad, f

momentum /mou'mɛntəm/ n momento, m, veloci-

dad adquirida *f*; *Fig.* ímpetu, *m.* **to gather m.**, cobrar velocidad, acelerar
monarch /'mɒnərk/ *n* monarca, *m*
monarchic /mə'nɑrkɪk/ *a* monárquico
monarchism /'mɒnər,kɪzəm/ *n* monarquismo, *m*
monarchist /'mɒnərkɪst/ *n* monárquico (-ca)
monarchy /'mɒnərki/ *n* monarquía, *f*
monastery /'mɒnə,steri/ *n* monasterio, *m*
monastic /mə'næstɪk/ *a* monástico. **m. life,** vida de clausura, *f*
monasticism /mə'næstə,sɪzəm/ *n* vida monástica, *f*
Monday /'mʌndei, -di/ *n* lunes, *m*
monetary /'mɒnɪ,teri/ *a* monetario
monetization /,mɒnɪtɪ'zeiʃən/ *n* monetización, *f*
money /'mʌni/ *n* dinero, *m*; (coin) moneda, *f*; sistema monetario, *m.* **paper m.,** papel moneda, *m.* **ready m.,** dinero contante, *m.* **to make m.,** ganar (or hacer) dinero; enriquecerse. **M. talks,** Poderoso caballero es Don Dinero. **m.-bag,** talega, *f*; (person) ricacho (-cha). **m.-bags,** riqueza, *f.* **m.-box,** alcancía, hucha, *f.* **m.-changer,** cambista, *mf* **m.-lender,** prestamista, *mf* **m.-making,** *n* el hacer dinero; prosperidad, ganancia, *f. a* lucrativo, *Lat. Am.* libranza de correos, libranza postal, *f.* **m.-order,** giro postal, *m* (postal)
moneyed /'mʌnid/ *a* adinerado; acomodado
mongoose /'mɒŋ,gus/ *n* mangosta, *f*
mongrel /'mʌŋgrəl/ *a* mestizo, atravesado. *n* perro mestizo, *m*; (in contempt) bastardo, *m*
monitor /'mɒnɪtər/ *n* monitor, *m*
monitory /'mɒnɪ,tɔri/ *a* monitorio. *n Eccl.* monitorio, *m*
monk /mʌŋk/ *n* monje, *m.* **to become a m.,** hacerse monje, tomar el hábito. **monk's-hood,** acónito, *m*
monkey /'mʌŋki/ *n* mono (-na); (imp) diablillo, *m*; (of a pile-driver) pilón de martinete, *m*; (in glassmaking) crisol, *m.* **m. business,** disparates, *m pl*, tretas, *f pl.* **to m. with,** meterse con; entremeterse. **m. nut,** cacahuete, *m.* **m.-puzzle,** (tree) araucaria, *f.* **m. tricks,** monadas, travesuras, diabluras, *f pl.* **m.-wrench,** llave inglesa, *f*
monkish /'mʌŋkɪʃ/ *a* monacal, de monje; monástico
monochromatic /,mɒnəkrou'mætɪk/ *a* monocromo
monochrome /'mɒnə,kroum/ *n* monocromo, *m*
monocle /'mɒnəkəl/ *n* monóculo, *m*
monogamist /mə'nɒgəmɪst/ *n* monógamo (-ma)
monogamous /mə'nɒgəməs/ *a* monógamo
monogamy /mə'nɒgəmi/ *n* monogamia, *f*
monogram /'mɒnə,græm/ *n* monograma, *m*
monograph /'mɒnə,græf/ *n* monografía, *f*, opúsculo, *m*
monolith /'mɒnəlɪθ/ *n* monolito, *m*
monolithic /,mɒnə'lɪθɪk/ *a* monolítico
monologue /'mɒnə,lɔg/ *n* monólogo, *m*
monomania /,mɒnə'meiniə/ *n* monomanía, *f*
monomaniac /,mɒnə'meini,æk/ *n* monomaníaco (-ca)
monomial /mou'noumiəl/ *n* monomio, *m*, *a* de un solo término
monoplane /'mɒnə,plein/ *n* monoplano, *m*
monopolist /mə'nɒpəlɪst/ *n* monopolista, *mf*; acaparador (-ra)
monopolization /mə,nɒpələ'zeiʃən/ *n* monopolio, *m*
monopolize /mə'nɒpə,laiz/ *vt* monopolizar
monopoly /mə'nɒpəli/ *n* monopolio, *m*
monotheism /'mɒnəθi,ɪzəm/ *n* monoteísmo, *m*
monotheist /'mɒnə,θiɪst/ *n* monoteísta, *mf*
monotone /'mɒnə,toun/ *n* monotonía, *f*
monotonous /mə'nɒtnəs/ *a* monótono
monotony /mə'nɒtn̩i/ *n* monotonía, *f*
monoxide /mɒn'ɒksaid/ *n* monóxido, *m*
Monroe doctrine /mən'rou/ *n* monroísmo, *m*
monsignor /mɒn'sinyər/ *n* monseñor, *m*
monsoon /mɒn'sun/ *n* monzón, *mf*
monster /'mɒnstər/ *n* monstruo, *m*
monstrosity /mɒn'strɒsɪti/ *n* monstruosidad, *f*
monstrous /'mɒnstrəs/ *a* monstruoso; horrible, atroz; enorme
montage /mɒn'tɑʒ/ *n* montaje, *m*

month /mʌnθ/ *n* mes, *m.* **He arrived a m. ago,** Llegó hace un mes. **a m. later** *Lat. Am.* al mes
monthly /'mʌnθli/ *a* mensual. *adv* mensualmente, cada mes. *n* revista (or publicación) mensual, *f*; *pl* **monthlies,** menstruación, regla, *f.* **m. salary** or **payment,** mensualidad, *f*
monument /'mɒnyəmənt/ *n* monumento, *m*
monumental /,mɒnyə'mɛntl̩/ *a* monumental
moo /mu/ *vi* (of cattle) mugir. *n* mugido, *m*
mood /mud/ *n* humor, *m*; espíritu, *m*; *Gram.* modo, *m*
moodily /'mudli/ *adv* taciturnamente; tristemente, pensativamente
moodiness /'mudinɪs/ *n* mal humor, *m*, taciturnidad, *f*; melancolía, tristeza, *f*
moody /'mudi/ *a* taciturno, de mal humor; triste, melancólico, pensativo
mooing /'muɪŋ/ *n* (of cattle) mugido, *m*
moon /mun/ *n* luna, *f*; satélite, *m*; mes lunar, *m*; luz de la luna, *f.* **full m.,** plenilunio, *m*; luna llena, *f.* **new m.,** novilunio, *m*, luna nueva, *f*
moonbeam /'mun,bim/ *n* rayo de luna, *m*
moonless /'munlɪs/ *a* sin luna
moonlight /'mun,lait/ *n* luz de la luna, *f.* **in the m.,** a la luz de la luna. **to do a m. flit,** *Inf.* mudarse por el aire
moonlighting /'mun,laitɪŋ/ *n* el pluriempleo, *m*
moonlit /'mun,lɪt/ *a* iluminado por la luna. **moonlit night,** noche de luna, *f*
moonshine /'mun,ʃain/ *n* claridad de la luna, *f*; *Fig.* música celestial, ilusión, *f*
moonstone /'mun,stoun/ *n* adularia, *f*
moonstruck /'mun,strʌk/ *a* lunático
Moor /mʊr/ *n* moro (-ra)
moor /mʊr/ *n* páramo, brezal, *m*; (marsh) pantano, *m*; (for game) coto, *m. vt* amarrar, aferrar; afirmar con anclas o cables. **m.-hen,** polla de agua, *f*
mooring /'mʊrɪŋ/ *n* amarre, *m.* **m.-mast,** *Aer.* poste de amarre, *m*
moorings /'mʊrɪŋz/ *n pl* amarradero, *m*
Moorish /'mʊrɪʃ/ *a* moro; árabe. **M. architecture,** arquitectura árabe, *f.* **M. girl,** mora, *f*
moorland /'mʊrlənd/ *n* páramo, brezal, *m*
moose /mus/ *n* anta, *f*
moot /mut/ *n* junta, *f*; ayuntamiento, *m. a* discutible. *vt* (bring up) suscitar; (discuss) discutir, debatir
mop /mɒp/ *n* (implement) trapeador, *m*, *Ecuador*, escoba con fleco, *f*, *elsewhere in Lat. Am.* lampazo, *m*; (of hair) mata (de pelo), *f. vt* trapear *Ecuador*; (dry) enjugar, secar. **to mop up,** *Inf.* limpiar; *Mil.* acabar con (el enemigo)
mope /moup/ *vi* replace by tristear. **to m. about,** vagar tristemente
moquette /mou'kɛt/ *n* moqueta, *f*
moral /'mɔrəl/ *a* moral; (chaste) casto, virtuoso; honrado. *n* (maxim) moraleja, *f*; *pl* **morals,** moralidad, *f*; ética, *f*; moral, *f*; (conduct) costumbres, *f pl.* **m. philosophy,** filosofía moral, *f.* **m. support,** apoyo moral, *m.* **m. tale,** apólogo, *m*
morale /mə'ræl/ *n* moral, *f*
moralist /'mɔrəlɪst/ *n* moralista, *m*
morality /mə'rælɪti/ *n* moralidad, *f*; virtud, *f*; castidad, *f.* **m. play,** moralidad, *f*, drama alegórico, *m*
moralization /,mɔrələ'zeiʃən/ *n* moralización, *f*
moralize /'mɔrə,laiz/ *vt* and *vi* moralizar
moralizer /'mɔrə,laizər/ *n* moralizador (-ra)
moralizing /'mɔrə,laizɪŋ/ *a* moralizador
morally /'mɔrəli/ *adv* moralmente
morals /'mɔrəlz/. See **moral**
morass /mə'ræs/ *n* marisma, ciénaga, *f*
moratorium /,mɔrə'tɔriəm/ *n* moratoria, *f*
Moravian /mə'reiviən/ *a* moravo. *n* moravo (-va)
morbid /'mɔrbɪd/ *a* mórbido *a* mórbido, mórboso; (of the mind, etc.) insano
morbidezza /,mɔrbɪ'dɛtsə/ *n* (*Art.* and *Lit.*) morbidez, *f*
morbidity /mɔr'bɪdɪti/ *n* morbidez, *f*
mordacity /mɔr'dæsɪti/ *n* mordacidad, *f*
mordant /'mɔrdn̩t/ *a* mordaz; (of acid) mordiente. *n* mordiente, *m*
more /mɔr/ *a* and *adv* más. **The m. he earns, the**

less he saves, Cuanto más gana, menos ahorra. **the m. the better,** cuanto más, tanto mejor. **without m. ado,** sin más ni más; sin decir nada. **Would you like some m.?** ¿Quiere Vd. más? (of food) ¿Quiere Vd. repetir? **no m.,** no más; (never) nunca más; (finished) se acabó. **once m.,** otra vez, una vez más. **m. and m.,** cada vez más, más y más. **m. or less,** más o menos; (about) poco más o menos

moreover /mɔr'ouvər/ *adv* además, también; por otra parte

morganatic /ˌmɔrgə'nætɪk/ *a* morganático

morgue /mɔrg/ *n* depósito de cadáveres, *m*

moribund /'mɔrəˌbʌnd/ *a* moribundo

Mormon /'mɔrmən/ *a* mormónico. *n* mormón (-ona)

Mormonism /'mɔrmə,nɪzəm/ *n* mormonismo, *m*

morning /'mɔrnɪŋ/ *n* mañana, *f*, *a* matutino, de la mañana. **Good m.!** ¡Buenos días! **the next m.,** la mañana siguiente. **very early in the m.,** muy de mañana. **m. coat,** chaqué, *m*. **m. dew,** rocío de la mañana, *m*. **m. paper,** periódico de la mañana, *m*. **m. star,** lucero del alba, *m*. **m. suit,** chaqué, *m*

Moroccan /mə'rɒkən/ *a* marroquí, marrueco. *n* marrueco (-ca), marroquí, *mf*

Morocco /mə'rɒkou/ Marruecos, *m*

morocco /mə'rɒkou/ *n* (leather) marroquí, tafilete, *m*

morose /mə'rous/ *a* sombrío, taciturno, malhumorado

morosely /mə'rousli/ *adv* taciturnamente

moroseness /mə'rousnɪs/ *n* taciturnidad, *f*; mal humor, *m*

morpheme /'mɔrfim/ *n* morfema, *f*

morphine /'mɔrfin/ *n* morfina, *f*. **m. addict,** morfinómano (-na)

morphology /mɔr'fɒlədʒi/ *n* morfología, *f*

morrow /'mɔrou/ *n* mañana, *f*; día siguiente, *m*

Morse code /mɔrs/ *n* la clave telegráfica de Morse, *f*, el alfabeto de Morse, *m*

morsel /'mɔrsəl/ *n* pedazo, *m*; (mouthful) bocado, *m*

mortal /'mɔrtl̩/ *a* mortal. *n* mortal, *mf*. **m. sin,** pecado mortal, pecado capital, *m*

mortality /mɔr'tælɪti/ *n* mortalidad, *f*

mortally wounded /'mɔrtl̩i/ *adv* herido de muerte

mortar /'mɔrtər/ *n* (for building) argamasa, *f*; (for mixing and *Mil.*) mortero, *m*. **m. and pestle,** mortero y majador, *m*. **m.-board,** (in building) cuezo, *m*; (academic cap) birrete, *m*

mortgage /'mɔrgɪdʒ/ *n* hipoteca, *f*. *vt* hipotecar. *a* hipotecario. **to pay off a m.,** redimir una hipoteca

mortgageable /'mɔrgɪdʒəbəl/ *a* hipotecable

mortgaged debt /'mɔrgɪdʒd/ *n* deuda garantizada con una hipoteca, *f*

mortgagee /ˌmɔrgə'dʒi/ *n* acreedor (-ra) hipotecario (-ia)

mortgagor /'mɔrgədʒər/ *n* deudor (-ra) hipotecario (-ia)

mortification /ˌmɔrtəfɪ'keɪʃən/ *n* mortificación, *f*; humillación, *f*; *Med.* gangrena, *f*

mortify /'mɔrtəˌfaɪ/ *vt* mortificar; humillar. *vi Med.* gangrenarse

mortifying /'mɔrtəˌfaɪɪŋ/ *a* humillante

mortise /'mɔrtɪs/ *n* muesca, *f*. *vt* hacer muescas (en); ensamblar

mortuary /'mɔrtʃuˌɛri/ *a* mortuorio. *n* depósito de cadáveres, *m*

Mosaic /mou'zeɪɪk/ *n* mosaico

mosaic /mou'zeɪɪk/ *n* mosaico, *m*

Moscow /'mɒskou,-kau/ Moscú, *m*

mosque /mɒsk/ *n* mezquita, *f*

mosquito /mə'skitou/ *n* mosquito, *m*. **m. net,** mosquitero, *m*

moss /mɔs/ *n* musgo, *m*; moho, *m*; (swamp) marjal, *m*

mossgrown /'mɔs,groun/ *a* musgoso, cubierto de musgo; *Fig.* anticuado

mossiness /'mɔsɪnɪs/ *n* estado musgoso, *m*

mossy /'mɔsi/ *a* musgoso

most /moust/ *a* el (la, los, etc.) más; la mayor parte de; la mayoría de; (el, etc.) mayor. *adv* más; el (la, etc.) más; (extremely) sumamente; (very) muy; (before adjectives sometimes expressed by superlative, e.g. m. *reverend*, reverendísimo; m. *holy*, santísimo,

etc.). *n* (highest price) el mayor precio; la mayor parte; el mayor número; lo más. **m. of all,** sobre todo. **m. people,** la mayoría de la gente. **at the m.,** a lo más, a lo sumo. **for the m. part,** en su mayor parte; casi todos; generalmente, casi siempre. **to make the m. of,** sacar el mayor partido posible de; aprovechar bien; exagerar

mostly /'moustli/ *adv* principalmente; en su mayoría; en su mayor parte; casi siempre; en general, generalmente

mote /mout/ *n* átomo, *m*; mota, *f*. **to see the m. in our neighbor's eye and not the beam in our own,** ver la paja en el ojo del vecino y no la viga en el nuestro

moth /mɔθ/ *n* mariposa nocturna, *f*; polilla, *f*. **m.ball,** bola de naftalina, *f*. **m.-eaten,** apolillado

mother /'mʌðər/ *n* madre, *f*; madre de familia, *f*; (of alcoholic beverages) madre, *f*. *vt* cuidar como una madre (a); servir de madre (a); (animals) ahijar. **M. Church,** madre iglesia, *f*; iglesia metropolitana, *f*. **m.-in-law,** suegra, *f*. **m. land,** (madre) patria, *f*. **m.-of-pearl,** *n* madreperla, *f*; nácar, *m*. *a* nacarado, nacáreo. **M. Superior,** (madre) superiora, *f*. **m. tongue,** lengua materna, *f*

motherhood /'mʌðər,hʊd/ *n* maternidad, *f*

motherless /'mʌðərlɪs/ *a* huérfano de madre, sin madre

motherlike /'mʌðər,laɪk/ *a* de madre, como una madre

motherliness /'mʌðərlinɪs/ *n* cariño maternal, *m*

motherly /'mʌðərli/ *a* maternal

motif /mou'tif/ *n* motivo, *m*; tema, *m*; *Sew.* adorno, *m*

motion /'mouʃən/ *n* movimiento, *m*; Mech. marcha, operación, *f*; mecanismo, *m*; (sign) seña, señal, *f*; (gesture) ademán, gesto, *m*; (carriage) aire, porte, *m*; (of the bowels) movimiento del vientre, *m*, deyección, *f*; (will) voluntad, *f*, deseo, *m*; (proposal in an assembly or debate) proposición, moción, *f*; *Law.* pedimento, *m*. *vt* hacer una señal (a). *vi* hacer señas. **to set in m.,** poner en marcha. **m. picture,** fotografía cinematográfica, película, *f*. **m.-picture theater,** cine, *m*

motionless /'mouʃənlɪs/ *a* inmóvil

motivate /'moutə,veɪt/ *vt* motivar

motive /'moutɪv/ *n* motivo, *m*. *a* motor; motivo. **with no m.,** sin motivo. **m. power,** fuerza motriz, *f*

motley /'mɒtli/ *a* abigarrado, multicolor; (mixed) diverso, vario. *n* traje de colores, *m*, botarga, *f*

motor /'moutər/ *n* motor, *m*; automóvil, *m*, *a* motor; movido por motor; con motor; (traveling) de viaje. *vi* ir en automóvil. *vt* llevar en automóvil (a). **m.boat,** lancha automóvil, *f*. **m.bus,** autobús, ómnibus, *m*. **m. car,** automóvil, *m*. **m.-coach,** autobús, *m*. **m.cycle,** motocicleta, *f*. **m.cyclist,** motociclista, *mf* **m.-launch,** canoa automóvil, *f*. **m.oil,** aceite para motores, *m*. **m.-road,** autopista, *f*. **m.-rug,** manta de viaje, *f*. **m.-scooter,** bicicleta con motor, *f*. **m.-spirit,** bencina, *f*

motoring /'moutərɪŋ/ *n* automovilismo, *m*

motorist /'moutərɪst/ *n* automovilista, motorista, *mf*

mottled /'mɒtl̩d/ *a* abigarrado; (of marble, etc.) jaspeado, esquizado; manchado (con), con manchas (de); pintado (con)

motto /'mɒtou/ *n Herald.* divisa, *f*; mote, *m*; (in a book, etc.) lema, *m*

mound /maund/ *n* montón, *m*; (knoll) altozano, *m*; (for defence) baluarte, *m*; (for burial) túmulo, *m*

mount /maunt/ *n* (hill, and in palmistry) monte, *m*; (for riding) caballería, *f*; montadura, *f*; (for a picture) borde, *m*. *vt* subir; (machines, etc.) montar; (jewels) engastar; (a picture) poner un borde a; (a play) poner en escena; poner a caballo; proveer de caballo. *vi* montar; subir; (increase) aumentar. **to m. a horse,** subir a caballo, montar a caballo. **to m. guard,** *Mil.* montar la guardia. **to m. the throne,** subir al trono

mountain /'mauntn̩/ *n* montaña, *f*; (mound) montón, *m*; *a* de montaña(s); montañés; alpino, alpestre. **to make a m. out of a molehill,** convertir un grano de arena en una montaña. hacer de una pulga un camello, hacer de una pulga un elefante. **m.-chain,** cadena de montañas, *f*. **m. climber,** *Lat. Am.* andinista, *mf*. **m. climbing,** *Lat. Am.* andinismo, *m*. **m.**

dweller, montañés (-esa). **m. railway,** ferrocárril de cremallera, *m*. **m.-side,** falda de una montaña, *f*

mountaineer /ˌmauntn̩'ɪər/ *n* (inhabitant) montañés (-esa); (climber) alpinista, *mf*. *vi* hacer alpinismo

mountaineering /ˌmauntn̩'ɪərɪŋ/ *n* alpinismo, *m*

mountainous /'mauntn̩əs/ *a* montañoso; (huge) enorme

mountebank /'mauntə,bæŋk/ *n* saltabanco, *m*; charlatán, *m*

mounting /'mauntɪŋ/ *n* (ascent) subida, *f*; ascensión, *f*; (of machinery, etc.) armadura, *f*; montadura, *f*; (of a precious stone) engaste, *m*. **m.-block,** subidero, *m*

mourn /mɔrn/ *vi* afligirse, lamentarse; (wear mourning) estar de luto. *vt* llorar; lamentar; llevar luto por

mourner /'mɔrnər/ *n* lamentador (-ra); (paid) plañidera, *f*; el, *m*, (f, la) que acompaña al féretro

mournful /'mɔrnfəl/ *a* triste, acongojado; funesto, lúgubre; fúnebre; lamentable

mournfully /'mɔrnfəli/ *adv* tristemente

mournfulness /'mɔrnfəlnɪs/ *n* tristeza, *f*; melancolía, aflicción, *f*, pesar, *m*

mourning /'mɔrnɪŋ/ *n* aflicción, *f*; lamentación, *f*; luto, *m*. **deep m.,** luto riguroso, *m*. **half m.,** medio luto, *m*. **to be in m.,** estar de luto. **to be in m. for,** llevar luto por. **to come out of m.,** dejar el luto. **m.-band,** (on the hat) tira de gasa, *f*; (on the arm) brazal de luto, *m*. **m.-coach,** coche fúnebre, *m*

mouse /maus/ *n* ratón (-na); *Naut.* barrilete, *m*. *vi* cazar ratones. **m.-colored,** de color de rata. **m.-hole, m.-trap,** ratonera, *f*

mouser /'mauzər/ *n* gato ratonero, *m*

mousing /'mausɪŋ/ *n* caza de ratones, *f*

mousy /'mausi/ *a* ratonesco, ratonil

mouth /*n.* mauθ; *v.* mauð/ *n* (*Anat.* human being, of a bottle, cave) boca, *f*; entrada, *f*; (of a river) desembocadura, *f*; (of a channel) embocadero, *m*; (of a wind-instrument) boquilla, *f*. *vt* pronunciar con afectación; (chew) mascar. *vi* clamar a gritos, vociferar. **It makes my m. water,** Se me hace la boca agua. **large m.,** boca rasgada, *f*. **m.-gag,** abrebocas, *m*. **m.-organ,** armónica, *f*. **m.-wash,** antiséptico bucal, *m* (Argentina), enjuague, *m*

mouthed /mauðd, mauθt/ *a* que tiene boca...; de boca... **open-m.,** boquiabierto

mouthful /'mauθ,fʊl/ *n* bocado, *m*; (of smoke, air) bocanada, *f*

mouthpiece /'mauθ,pis/ *n* (of wind-instruments, tobacco-pipe, waterpipe) boquilla, *f*; (of a wineskin) brocal, *m*; (spokesman) portavoz, *m*; intérprete, *mf*

movable /'muvəbəl/ *a* movible; (of goods) mobiliario. **m. feast,** fiesta movible, *f*

movables /'muvəbəlz/ *n pl* bienes muebles, efectos, *m pl*

movable type *n* tipos sueltos, *m pl*

move /muv/ *n* movimiento, *m*; (of household effects) mudanza, *f*; (motion) marcha, *f*; (in a game) jugada, *f*; (*Fig.* step) paso, *m*; (device) maniobra, *f*. **Whose m. is it?** ¿A quién le toca jugar? **to be on the m.,** estar en movimiento; estar de viaje. **to be always on the m.,** *Inf.* parecer una lanzadera

move /muv/ *vt* mover; poner en marcha; (furniture) trasladar; cambiar de lugar; (stir) remover; (shake) agitar, hacer temblar; (transport) transportar; (a piece in chess, etc.) jugar; (pull) arrancar; (impel) impulsar; (incline) inclinar, disponer; (affect emotionally) conmover, emocionar, enternecer; impresionar. *vi* moverse; ponerse en marcha; (walk) andar; ir; avanzar; (a step forward, etc.) dar; (move house) trasladarse; (act) entrar en acción; (in games) hacer una jugada; (progress) progresar; (shake) agitarse, temblar; remverse; (propose in an assembly) hacer una proposición; (in a court of law) hacer un pedimento; (grow) crecer. **to m. about,** pasearse; ir y venir; (of traffic) circular; (remove) trasladarse; (stir, tremble) agitarse. **to m. along,** caminar por; avanzar por. **to m. aside,** *vt* apartar; poner a un lado; (curtains) descorrer. *vi* ponerse a un lado; quitarse de en medio. **to m. away,** *vt* alejar. *vi* alejarse; marcharse; trasladarse; mudar de casa. **to m. back,** retroceder, volver hacia atrás. **to m. down,** bajar, descender. **to m. forward,** adelantarse; avanzar; progresar. **to m. in,** en-

trar (en); tomar posesión de una casa. **to m. off,** *vt* quitar. *vi* marcharse; ponerse en marcha; alejarse, apartarse. **to m. on,** avanzar; ponerse en marcha; circular; (of time) pasar, correr. **to m. out,** *vt* sacar, quitar. *vi* salir; (from a house) mudarse, abandonar (una casa, etc.). **to m. round,** dar vueltas, girar; (turn round) volverse. **to m. to,** (make) hacer, animar (a); causar. **to m. up,** *vt* montar, subir. *vi* montar; avanzar

movement /'muvmənt/ *n* movimiento, *m*; *Mech.* mecanismo, *m*; (Stock Exchange) actividad, *f*. **encircling m.,** *Mil.* movimiento envolvente, *m*

mover /'muvər/ *n* motor, *m*; móvil, *m*; promotor (-ra); (of a motion, proposer) autor (-ra) de una moción

movie /'muvi/ *n Inf.* cine, *m*. **m. camera,** máquina de impresionar, *f*. **m. star,** estrella de la pantalla, *f*

moving /'muvɪŋ/ *a* móvil; motor; (affecting) emocionante, conmovedor; impresionante; patético. *n* movimiento, *m*; traslado, *m*; cambio de domicilio, *m*. **m. picture,** fotografía cinematográfica, *f*. **m. staircase,** escalera móvil, *f*

movingly /'muvɪŋli/ *adv* con emoción; patéticamente

mow /mou/ *vt* segar. *vi* (grimace) hacer muecas

mowing /'mouɪŋ/ *n* siega, *f*. **m.-machine,** segadora, *f*

Mr. /'mɪstər/ See **mister**

Mrs. /'mɪsəz/ See **mistress**

much /mʌtʃ/ *a* mucho. *adv* mucho; (by far) con mucho; (with past part.) muy; (pretty nearly) casi, más o menos. **m. of a size,** más o menos del mismo tamaño. **I was m.** angered, Estuve muy enfadado. **as m. as,** tanto como. **as m. more,** otro tanto. **How m. is it?** ¿Cuánto es? ¿Cuánto cuesta? **however m....,** por mucho que.... **not m.,** no mucho. **not to think m. of,** tener en poco (a). **so m. so that,** tanto que. **too m., demasiado. to make m. of,** dar grande importancia a; (a person) apreciar, querer; agasajar; (a child) mimar, acariciar

mucilage /'myusəlɪdʒ/ *n* mucílago, *m*

muck /mʌk/ *n* (dung) estiércol, *m*; (filth) porquería, inmundicia, *f*; suciedad, *f*; (rubbish, of a literary work, etc.) porquería, *n*. **to m. up,** ensuciar; (spoil) estropear por completo

mucky /'mʌki/ *a* muy sucio; puerco; asqueroso, repugnante

mucosity /mu'kɒsɪti/ *n* mucosidad, *f*

mucous /'myukəs/ *a* mucoso. **m. membrane,** mucosa, *f*

mucus /'myukəs/ *n* mucosidad, *f*; (from the nose) moco, *m*

mud /mʌd/ *n* lodo, barro, fango, *m*. **to stick in the mud,** (of a ship, etc.) embarrancarse. **mudbath,** baño de barro, *m*. **mud wall,** tapia, *f*

muddiness /'mʌdɪnɪs/ *n* estado fangoso, *m*; (of liquids) turbiedad, *f*; oscuridad, *f*

muddle /'mʌdl̩/ *vt* (bewilder) dejar perplejo, aturdir; (intoxicate) emborrachar; (stupefy) entontecer; (spoil) estropear; embarullar, dejar en desorden; hacer un lío de. *n* desorden, *m*; confusión, *f*; lío, embrollo, *m*. **in a m.,** en desorden; en confusión. **to make a m.,** armar un lío. **to m. away,** derrochar sin ton ni son

muddled /'mʌdl̩d/ *a* desordenado; confuso; estúpido; torpe; (drunk) borracho

muddy /'mʌdi/ *a* fangoso, lodoso, barroso; cubierto de lodo; (of liquids, etc.) turbio; (of the complexion) cetrino. *vt* enlodar, cubrir de lodo; ensuciar; (liquids) enturbiar

muezzin /myu'ɛzɪn, mu-/ *n* almuecín, almuédano, *m*

muff /mʌf/ *n* manguito, *m*; (for a car radiator) cubierta para radiador, *f*; (*Inf.* at games, etc.) maleta, *m*. *vt* dejar escapar (una pelota); (an opportunity) perder

muffin /'mʌfɪn/ *n* mollete, *m*

muffle /'mʌfəl/ *vt* embozar, arrebozar; envolver; encubrir, ocultar, tapar; (stifle sound of) apagar; (oars, bells) envolver con tela para no hacer ruido; *Fig.* ahogar. **to m. oneself up,** embozarse

muffled /'mʌfəld/ *a* (of sound) sordo; confuso; apagado. **m. drum,** tambor enlutado, *m*

muffler /'mʌflər/ *n* (furnace) mufla, *f*; (of a car radiator) mofle, *m*, cubierta para radiador, *f*; (silencer) silencioso, *m*

mufti /'mʌfti/ *n* mufti, *m*

mug /mʌg/ *n* vaso, *m*; (tankard) pichel, tarro, *m*; (face) jeta, *f*; (dupe) primo, *m*; (at games, etc.) maleta, *m*

mulatto /mə'lætou/ *a* mulato. *n* mulato (-ta). **m.-like,** amulatado

mulberry /'mʌl,beri/ *n* (fruit) mora, *f*; (bush) morera, *f*. **m. plantation,** moreral, *m*

mule /myul/ *n* mulo (-la); (slipper) mula, chinela, *f*; (spinning-jenny) huso mecánico, *m*

mulish /'myuliʃ/ *a* mular; terco como una mula

mulishness /'myuliʃnis/ *n* terquedad de mula, *f*

mullet /'mʌlit/ *n* (red) salmonete, *m*, trilla, *f*; (grey) mújol, *m*

multicolored /'mʌlti,kʌlərd/ *a* multicolor

multifarious /,mʌltə'feəriəs/ *a* numeroso, mucho; diverso, vario

multiform /'mʌltə,fɔrm/ *a* multiforme

multilateral /,mʌlti'lætərəl/ *a* multilátero

multimillionaire /,mʌlti'milyə,neər/ *a* archimillonario, multimillonario, *n* multimillonario, *m*

multiple /'mʌltəpəl/ *a* múltiple, múltiplo. *n* múltiplo, *m*

multiple-choice question /'mʌltəpəl 'tʃɔis/ *n* pregunta optativa, *f*

multiplicand /,mʌltəpli'kænd/ *n* multiplicando, *m*

multiplication /,mʌltəpli'keiʃən/ *n* multiplicación, *f*. **m. table,** tabla de multiplicación, *f*

multiplicity /,mʌltə'plisiti/ *n* multiplicidad, *f*

multiplier /'mʌltə,plaiər/ *n* Math. multiplicador, *m*; máquina de multiplicar, *f*

multiply /'mʌltəpli/ *vt* multiplicar. *vi* multiplicarse

multitude /'mʌlti,tud/ *n* multitud, *f*. **the m.,** las masas

multitudinous /,mʌlti'tudnəs/ *a* muy numeroso

mumble /'mʌmbəl/ *vi* and *vt* musitar, hablar entre dientes; refunfuñar; (chew) mascullar

mummer /'mʌmər/ *n* momero (-ra); máscara, *mf*

mummery /'mʌməri/ *n* momería, *f*; mascarada, *f*

mummification /,mʌməfi'keiʃən/ *n* momificación, *f*

mummify /'mʌmə,fai/ *vt* momificar. *vi* momificarse

mummy /'mʌmi/ *n* momia, *f*; carne de momia, *f*; **m. case,** sarcófago, *m*

mumps /mʌmps/ *n pl* parotiditis, papera, *f*

munch /mʌntʃ/ *vt* masticar, mascullar, mascar

mundane /mʌn'dein/ *a* mundano

municipal /myu'nisəpəl/ *a* municipal. **m. charter,** fuero municipal, *m*. **m. government,** gobierno municipal, *m*

municipality /myu,nisə'pæliti/ *n* municipio, *m*

munificence /myu'nifəsəns/ *n* munificencia, *f*

munificent /myu'nifəsənt/ *a* munífico, generoso

munition /myu'niʃən/ *n* munición, *f*. *vt* municionar. **m. dump,** depósito de municiones, *m*. **m. factory,** fábrica de municiones, *f*. **m. worker,** obrero (-ra) de una fábrica de municiones

mural /'myurəl/ *a* mural. *n* pintura mural, *f*

murder /'mʌrdər/ *n* asesinato, *m*. *vt* asesinar; dar muerte (a), matar; (a work, etc.) degollar. **He was murdered,** Fue asesinado. **willful m.,** homicidio premeditado, *m*

murderer /'mʌrdərər/ *n* asesino, *m*

murderess /'mʌrdəris/ *n* asesina, *f*

murderous /'mʌrdərəs/ *a* homicida; cruel, sanguinario; fatal; imposible, intolerable

murderously /'mʌrdərəsli/ *adv* con intento de asesinar; (with look) con ojos asesinos; cruelmente

murkiness /'mʌrkinis/ *n* obscuridad, lobreguez, *f*, tinieblas, *f pl*

murky /'mʌrki/ *a* lóbrego, negro, obscuro; (of one's past, etc.) negro, accidentado

murmur /'mʌrmər/ *n* murmullo, *m*; rumor, *m*; susurro, *m*; (grumble) murmurio, *m*. *vi* murmurar, susurrar; (complain) murmurar, quejarse. *vt* murmurar, decir en voz baja

murmuring /'mʌrmərɪŋ/ *n* murmurio, *m*, *a* que murmura, susurrante

muscatel /,mʌskə'tɛl/ *a* moscatel. *n* moscatel, *m*. **m. grape,** uva moscatel, *f*

muscle /'mʌsəl/ *n* músculo, *m*

Muscovite /'mʌskə,vait/ *a* moscovita. *n* moscovita, *mf*

muscular /'mʌskyələr/ *a* muscular, musculoso; (brawny) membrudo, fornido. **m. pains,** (in the legs, etc.) agujetas, *f pl*

muscularity /,mʌskyə'læriti/ *n* fuerza muscular, *f*

musculature /'mʌskyələtʃər/ *n* musculatura, *f*

Muse /myuz/ *n* musa, *f*

muse /myuz/ *n* meditación, *f*. *vi* meditar, reflexionar, rumiar; mirar las musarañas, estar distraído. **to m. on,** meditar en (or sobre)

museum /myu'ziəm/ *n* museo, *m*

museum of arms *n* museo de armas, *m*, aploteca, *f*

mushroom /'mʌʃrum/ *n* Bot. seta, *f*, hongo, *m*. *a* de setas; de forma de seta; (upstart) advenedizo; (ephemeral) efímero, de un día. **m.-bed,** setal, *m*. **m.-spawn,** esporas de setas, *f pl*

music /'myuzik/ *n* música, *f*; armonía, *f*; melodía, *f*. *a* de música. **to set to m.,** poner en música. **m.-hall,** teatro de variedades, *m*; salón de conciertos, *m*. **m. master,** profesor de música, *m*. **m. publisher,** editor de obras musicales, *m*. **m. stand,** atril, *m*; tablado para una orquesta, *m*. **m. stool,** taburete de piano, *m*

musical /'myuzikəl/ *a* musical; de música; armonioso, melodioso. **She is very m.,** Es muy aficionada a la música; Tiene mucho talento para la música. **m.-box,** caja de música, *f*. **m. comedy,** zarzuela, *f*. **m. instrument,** instrumento de música, *m*

musical chairs *n* escobas, *f pl*, el juego de sillas, *m sg*

musically /'myuzikli/ *adv* musicalmente; melodiosamente

musician /myu'ziʃən/ *n* músico (-ca)

musing /'myuzɪŋ/ *n* meditación, *f*; ensueños, *m pl*, *a* pensativo, meditabundo

musingly /'myuzɪŋli/ *adv* reflexivamente

musk /mʌsk/ *n* (substance) almizcle, *m*; perfume de almizcle, *m*. *a* de almizcle; almizclero; (of scents) almizcleño. **m.-deer,** almizclero, *m*. **m.-rat,** rata almizclera, *f*

musket /'mʌskit/ *n* mosquete, *m*

musketeer /,mʌski'tiər/ *n* mosquetero, *m*

Muslim /'mʌzlim/ *a* musulmán, mahometano. *n* musulmán (-ana)

muslin /'mʌzlin/ *n* muselina, *f*, *a* de muselina

mussel /'mʌsəl/ *n* mejillón, *m*. **m.-bed,** criadero de mejillones, *m*

must /mʌst/ *vi* haber de; tener que; deber; (expressing probability) deber de, ser. **This question m. be settled without delay,** Esta cuestión m. ser resuelta sin demora. **You m. do it at once,** Tienes que hacerlo en seguida. **I m. have seen him in the street sometime,** Debo haberle visto en la calle alguna vez. **One m. eat to live,** Se ha de comer para vivir. **Well, go if you m.,** Bueno, vete si no hay más remedio. **It m. be a difficult decision for him,** Debe ser una decisión difícil para él. **It m. have been about twelve o'clock when...,** Serían las doce cuando...

must /mʌst/ *n* mosto, zumo de la uva, *m*; (mould) moho, *m*

mustache /'mʌstæf, mə'stæʃ/ *n* bigote, mostacho, *m*

mustang /'mʌstæŋ/ *n* potro mesteño, *m*

mustard /'mʌstərd/ *n* mostaza, *f*. **m. gas,** iperita, *f*. **m. plaster,** sinapismo, *m*. **m. pot,** mostacera, *f*. **m. spoon,** cucharita para la mostaza, *f*

muster /'mʌstər/ *n* lista, *f*, rol, *m*; revista, *f*; reunión, *f*, *vt* pasar lista (de); pasar revista (a); reunir. *vi* juntarse, reunirse. **to m. out,** (from the army) dar de baja (a). **to m. up sufficient courage,** cobrar ánimos suficientes. **to pass m.,** pasar revista; ser aceptado. **m.-roll,** Mil. revista, *f*; Naut. rol de la tripulación, *m*

mustiness /'mʌstinis/ *n* moho, *m*; ranciedad, *f*; (of a room, etc.) olor de humedad, *m*

musty /'mʌsti/ *a* mohoso; rancio; que huele a humedad. **to go m.,** enmohecerse

mutability /,myutə'biliti/ *n* mutabilidad, *f*; inconstancia, inestabilidad, *f*

mutable /'myutəbəl/ *a* mudable; inconstante, inestable

mutation /myu'teiʃən/ n mutación, f
mute /myut/ a mudo; silencioso. n mudo (-da); *Mus.* sordina, f; (phonetics) letra muda, f. **deaf m.**, sordomudo (-da)
muted /'myutɪd/ a (of sounds) sordo, apagado
mutely /'myutli/ adv mudamente; en silencio
muteness /'myutnɪs/ n mudez, f; silencio, m
mutilate /'myutl̩,eit/ vt mutilar; estropear
mutilation /,myutl̩'eiʃən/ n mutilación, f
mutineer /,myutn'ɪər/ n amotinador, rebelde, m
mutinous /'myutn̩əs/ a amotinado; rebelde, sedicioso; turbulento
mutiny /'myutn̩i/ n motín, m; sublevación, insurrección, f, vi amotinarse, sublevarse
mutt /mʌt/ n chucho, m
mutter /'mʌtər/ vt and vi murmurar, musitar; mascullar, decir (or hablar) entre dientes; gruñir, refunfuñar; (of thunder, etc.) tronar, retumbar. n murmurio, m; rumor, m; retumbo, m
mutton /'mʌtn̩/ n carnero, m, a de carnero. **m.-chop,** chuleta, f
mutual /'myutʃuəl/ a mutuo, recíproco; común. **by m. consent,** de común acuerdo. **m. aid society,** sociedad de socorros mutuos, f. **m. insurance company,** sociedad de seguros mutuos, f
mutual fund n fondo de inversiones rentables, m
mutualism /'myutʃuə,lɪzəm/ n mutualismo, m
mutuality /,myutʃu'ælɪti/ n mutualidad, f
mutually /'myutʃuəli/ adv mutuamente, recíprocamente
muzzle /'mʌzəl/ n (snout) hocico, m; (for a dog) bozal, m; (of a gun) boca, f. vt abozalar, poner un bozal (a); *(Fig.* gag) amordazar, imponer silencio (a)
muzzling /'mʌzlɪŋ/ n acción de abozalar, f; *(Fig.* gagging) amordazamiento, m
my /mai/ a poss mi, mf; mis, mf pl **my relatives,** mis parientes. **My goodness!** ¡Dios mío!
myelitis /,maiə'laitɪs/ n mielitis, f
myopia /mai'oupiə/ n miopía, f
myopic /mai'ɒpɪk/ a miope
myriad /'mɪriəd/ n miríada, f
myrmidon /'mɜrmɪ,dɒn/ n rufián, m; asesino, m; secuaz, m
myrrh /mɜr/ n mirra, f
myrtle /'mɜrtl̩/ n mirto, arrayán, m
myself /mai'sɛlf/ pron yo mismo; (as a reflexive with a preposition) mí; (with a reflexive verb) me. **I m. sent it,** yo mismo (-ma) lo mandé
mysterious /mɪ'stɪəriəs/ a misterioso
mysteriousness /mɪ'stɪəriəsnɪs/ n misterio, m, lo misterioso
mystery /'mɪstəri/ n misterio, m. **m. play,** (religious) misterio, drama litúrgico, m; (thriller) comedia de detectives, f. **m. story,** novela policíaca, f; novela de aventuras, f
mystic /'mɪstɪk/ a místico
mysticism /'mɪstə,sɪzəm/ n misticismo, m
mystification /,mɪstəfɪ'keiʃən/ n mistificación, f
mystify /'mɪstə,fai/ vt mistificar
myth /mɪθ/ n mito, m
mythical /'mɪθɪkəl/ a mítico
mythologist /mɪ'θɒlədʒɪst/ n mitólogo, f
mythology /mɪ'θɒlədʒi/ n mitología, f

N

n /ɛn/ n (letter) ene, f
nab /næb/ vt *Inf.* atrapar, apresar, agazapar
nabob /'neibɒb/ n nabab, m; ricacho, m
nacre /'neikər/ n nácar, m, madreperla, f
nadir /'neidər/ n nadir, m
nag /næg/ n jaca, f; (wretched hack) rocín, jamelgo, penco, m. vt zaherir, echar en cara, regañar; (of one's conscience) remorder; *Lat. Am.* majaderear (pester) vi criticar, regañar
nagging /'nægɪŋ/ n zaherimiento, m. a zaheridor, criticón; (pain) continuo, incesante, constante
naiad /'neiæd/ n *Myth.* náyade, f
nail /neil/ vt clavar, enclavar; (for ornament) clavetear, tachonar, adornar con clavos. n uña, f; *Mech.* clavo, m; (animal's) garra, f. **to n. down,** sujetar (or cerrar) con clavos. **to n. to (on to),** clavar en. **to n. together,** fijar con clavos. *Inf.* **on the n.,** en el acto, en seguida. *Inf.* **to hit the n. on the head,** dar en el clavo. **brass-headed n.,** tachón, m. **French n.,** punta de París, f. **headless n.,** puntilla, f. **hob-n.,** clavo de herradura, m. **hook n.,** gancho, m. **round-headed n.,** bellota, f. **n.-brush,** cepillo para las (or de) uñas, m. **n.-file,** lima para las uñas, f. **n. head,** cabeza de un clavo, f. **n. polish,** barniz para las uñas, m. **n.-puller,** sacaclavos, arrancaclavos, botador, m. **n.-scissors,** tijeras para las uñas, f pl. **n. trade,** ferretería, f
nailed /neild/ a adornado con clavos, claveteado
nailer /'neilər/ n fabricante de clavos, chapucero, f
nailing /'neilɪŋ/ n enclavación, f
naive /nɑ'iv/ a ingenuo, candoroso, espontáneo
naively /nɑ'ivli/ adv ingenuamente, espontáneamente
naiveté /nɑiv'tei, -'ivtei, -'ivə-/ n ingenuidad, naturalidad, franqueza, f; candor, m
naked /'neikɪd/ a desnudo, nudo, *Peru* calato, *elsewhere in Lat. Am.* encuerado; desabrigado, indefenso, desamparado; (birds) implume; calvo; (truth) simple, sencillo, puro; evidente, patente. **stark n.,** en cueros vivos, tal como le parió su madre. **with the n. sword,** con la espada desnuda. **n. eye,** simple vista, f. **n. light,** llama descubierta, f
nakedly /'neikɪdli/ adv nudamente; desabrigadamente; abiertamente, claramente
nakedness /'neikɪdnɪs/ n desnudez, f; *Fig.* desabrigo,
m, aridez, f; *Fig.* claridad, f. **the truth in all its n.,** la verdad desnuda
namby-pamby /'næmbi'pæmbi/ a soso, insípido, ñoño
name /neim/ n nombre, m; título, m; fama, opinión, f; renombre, crédito, m; autoridad, f; apodo, mal nombre, m. vt nombrar, llamar, imponer el nombre de, apellidar; mencionar, señalar; (appoint) designar, elegir; (ships) bautizar. **by n.,** por nombre. **Christian n.,** nombre de pila, m. **in his n.,** en nombre de él, en nombre suyo; de parte de él. **in n. only,** nada más que en nombre. **to be named,** llamarse. **to call** (a person) **names,** poner como un trapo (a). **to go under the n. of,** vivir bajo el nombre de. **to have a good n.,** tener buena fama. **What is her n.?** ¿Cómo se llama? **n. day,** santo, m. **n. plate,** (machinery) placa de fábrica, f; (streets) rótulo, m; (professional) placa profesional, f
nameless /'neimlɪs/ a anónimo; desconocido; (inexpressible) vago, indecible
namely /'neimli/ adv a saber, es decir
namesake /'neim,seik/ n tocayo (-ya)
naming /'neimɪŋ/ n bautizo, m; nombramiento, m; designación, f
nannygoat /'næni,gout/ n cabra, f
nap /næp/ n (cloth) pelusa, f, pelo, tamo, m; (plants) vello, m, pelusilla, f; (sleep) siesta, f, sueño, m; (cards) napolitana, f. **to take a nap,** vi dormitar, echar un sueño, echar una siesta. **to take an afternoon nap,** dormir la siesta. **to be caught napping,** estar desprevenido
nape /neip/ n nuca, f, cogote, m; (animal's) testuz, m
naphtha /'næfθə, 'næp-/ n *Chem.* nafta, f. **wood n.,** alcohol metílico, m
naphthalene /'næfθə,lin, 'næp-/ n *Chem.* naftalina, f
napkin /'næpkɪn/ n (table) servilleta, f; (babies') pañal, m. **n.-ring,** servilletero, m
Naples /'neipəlz/ Nápoles, m
Napoleonic /nə,pouli'ɒnɪk/ a napoleónico
narcissism /'nɑrsə,sɪzəm/ n narcisismo, m
narcissus /nɑr'sɪsəs/ n narciso, f
narcosis /nɑr'kousɪs/ n *Med.* narcosis, f

narcotic /nɑr'kɒtɪk/ *a Med.* narcótico, calmante, soporífero. *n Med.* narcótico, *m*, opiata, *f*

nard /nɑrd/ *n Bot.* nardo, *m*, tuberosa, *f*

narrate /'næreit/ *vt* narrar, contar; referir, relatar

narration /næ'reiʃən/ *n* narración, narrativa; relación, descripción, *f*, relato, *m*

narrative /'nærətɪv/ *a* narrador, narrativo, narratorio. *n* narrativa, *f*; descripción, *f*

narrator /'næreitər/ *n* narrador (-ra), relator (-ra), descriptor (-ra)

narrow /'nærou/ *vt* estrechar, angostar; reducir, limitar. *vi* reducirse, hacerse más estrecho; (eyes) entornarse; (knitting) menguar. *a* estrecho, angosto; limitado, restringido, reducido, corto; (avaricious) ruin, avaro, mezquino; (ideas) intolerante, intransigente. **"Narrow Road,"** «Camino Estrecho». *n pl* **narrows,** *Naut.* estrecho, *m*; desfiladero, paso estrecho, *m.* **to have a n. escape,** escapar en una tabla. **n.-brimmed** (hats), de ala estrecha. **n. circumstances,** estrechez, escasez de medios, *f.* **n.-gauge railway,** ferrocarril de vía estrecha (or de vía angosta), *m.* **n. life,** vida de horizontes estrechos, *f.* **n. majority,** escasa mayoría, *f.* **n.-minded,** cerrado al mundo, intolerante, intransigente. **n.-mindedness,** intolerancia, intransigencia, estrechez de miras, *f*

narrowing /'nærouɪŋ/ *n* estrechez, *f*, estrechamiento, *m*; reducción, limitación, *f*; (in knitting) menguado, *m*

narrowly /'nærouli/ *adv* estrechamente; por poco, con dificultad; atentamente, cuidadosamente. **I n. escaped being run over,** Por poco me atropellan

narrowness /'nærounɪs/ *n* estrechez, angostura, *f*; (of means) pobreza, miseria, *f*; (of ideas) intolerancia, intransigencia, *f*

nasal /'neizəl/ *a* nasal, gangoso. *n* letra nasal, *f*

nasally /'neizəli/ *adv* nasalmente. **to speak n.,** hablar por las narices, ganguear

nascent /'næsənt, 'neisənt/ *a* naciente

nastily /'næstəli/ *adv* suciamente; ofensivamente, de un modo insultante; maliciosamente, con malignidad

nastiness /'næstɪnɪs/ *n* suciedad, inmundicia, porquería, *f*; (indecency) obscenidad, indecencia, *f*; (rudeness) insolencia, impertinencia, grosería, *f*; (difficulty) dificultad, *f*, lo malo

nasturtium /nə'stɜrʃəm/ *n* mastuerzo, *m*, capuchina, *f*

nasty /'næsti/ *a* nauseabundo, repugnante; asqueroso, inmundo, sucio; (obscene) indecente, obsceno; desagradable, malo; (malicious) rencoroso, malicioso; violento; malévolo, amenazador; peligroso; difícil. *Fig.* **to be in a n. mess,** tener el agua al cuello. **to turn n.,** *Inf.* ponerse desagradable

nation /'neiʃən/ *n* nación, *f*, estado, país, *m*; (people) pueblo, *m*

national /'næʃən̩/ *a* nacional; público; patriótico. *n* nacional, *mf.* **n. anthem,** himno nacional, *m.* **n. debt,** deuda pública, *f.* **n. schools,** escuelas públicas, *f pl.* **n. socialism,** nacionalsocialismo, *m.* **n. socialist,** *a* and *n* nacionalsocialista *mf.* **n. syndicalism,** *Polit.* nacionalsindicalista, *m.* **n. syndicalist,** *a* and *n Polit.* nacionalsindicalista, *m*

nationalism /'næʃən̩ˌɪzəm/ *n* nacionalismo, patriotismo, *m*

nationalist /'næʃən̩ɪst/ *a* and *n* nacionalista, *mf*

nationality /ˌnæʃ ə'nælɪti/ *n* nacionalidad, *f*; nación, *f*

nationalization /ˌnæʃən̩ə'zeiʃən/ *n* nacionalización, *f*

nationalize /'næʃən̩ˌaiz, 'næʃnəˌlaiz/ *vt* nacionalizar, *Lat. Am. also* estatizar

National Labor Relations Board *n* Junta Nacional de Relaciones Laborales

nationally /'næʃən̩li/ *adv* nacionalmente, como nación; del punto de vista nacional

native /'neitɪv/ *a* (of a place) nativo, natal, oriundo; indígena; nacional, típico, del país; (vocabulary) patrimonial (as opposed to borrowed vocabulary); (of genius) natural, innato, instintivo; *Mineral.* nativo; (language) vernáculo. *n* nacional, *mf*; natural, *mf*; ciudadano (-na) indígena, aborigen (gen. pl.), *mf*; producto nacional, *m.* **He is a n. of Madrid,** Nació en Madrid, Es natural de Madrid, Es madrileño. **Native American commune** (in Peru) ayllu, *m.* **native informant,** sujeto, *m.* **n. land,** patria, tierra. **n. of the capital** *Lat. Am.* capitalino, n. of Rio de Janeiro ca-

rioca, *mf.* **n. place,** lugar natal, *m.* **n. region,** patria chica, *f.* **n. soil,** terruño, *m.* **n. tongue,** lengua materna, *f*

Native American *n* (Indian) indígena, *mf*

Native American movement *n Lat. Am.* indigenismo, *m*

nativity /nə'tɪvɪti/ *n* navidad, natividad, *f*; (manger) nacimiento, *m*

natty /'næti/ *a Inf.* chulo, majo; coquetón

natural /'nætʃərəl/ *a* natural; (wild) virgen, salvaje; nativo; (of products) crudo; normal; (usual) acostumbrado, corriente, natural; (of likeness) fiel, verdadero; (illegitimate) ilegítimo, bastardo; (of qualities) innato, instintivo; físico; característico, propio; (of people) inafectado, sencillo, genuino; *Mus.* natural. *n Mus.* becuadro, *m*; *Mus.* nota natural, *f*; imbécil, *mf* **n. features,** geografía física, *f.* **n. history,** historia natural, *f.* **n. philosophy,** filosofía natural, *f.* **n. science,** ciencias naturales, *f pl.* **n. selection,** selección natural, *f.* **n. state,** estado virgen, *m*

natural child *n* hijo natural, *m*

naturalism /'nætʃərəˌlɪzəm/ *n* naturalismo, *m*

naturalist /'nætʃərəlɪst/ *n* (*Lit.* and *Science.*) naturalista, *mf*

naturalistic /ˌnætʃərə'lɪstɪk/ *a* naturalista

naturalization /ˌnætʃərələ'zeiʃən/ *n* naturalización, *f*; aclimatación, *f.* **n. papers,** carta de naturaleza, *f*

naturalize /'nætʃərəˌlaiz/ *vt* naturalizar; aclimatar. **to become naturalized,** naturalizarse

naturally /'nætʃərəli/ *adv* naturalmente, por naturaleza; normalmente; sin afectación; instintivamente, por instinto; (without art) al natural. **n. curly hair,** *Guatemala* colocho, *m*

naturalness /ˌnætʃərəlnɪs/ *n* naturalidad, *f*; sencillez, desenvoltura, *f*; desembarazo, *m*

nature /'neitʃər/ *n* naturaleza, *f*; (of people) carácter, fondo, temperamento, genio, natural, modo de ser, *m*; (kind) género, *m*, especie, *f*; (essence) condición, esencia, cualidad, *f*, *Art.* **from n.,** del natural. **good n.,** bondad natural, afabilidad, *f.* **ill n.,** mala índole, *f.* **nature cure,** naturismo, *m.* **n. curist,** naturista, *mf.* **n. study,** historia natural, *f.* **n. worship,** panteísmo, culto de la naturaleza, *m*

natured /'neitʃərd/ *a* de carácter, de índole, con un modo de ser, de condición

naught /nɔt/ *n* nada, *f*; cero, *m. a* inútil, sin valor. **all for n.,** todo en balde. **to come to n.,** malograrse. **to set at n.,** tener en menos; despreciar

naughtily /'nɔtli/ *adv* traviesamente; con picardía, con malicia

naughtiness /'nɔtɪnɪs/ *n* travesura, picardía, mala conducta, *f*; malicia, *f*

naughty /'nɔti/ *a* travieso, pícaro, revoltoso, malo; salado, escabroso, verde (stories, etc.). **to be n.,** (children) ser malo

nausea /'nɔziə, -ʒə/ *n* náusea, *f*, bascas, *f pl*, mareo, *m*; *Fig.* asco, *m*; repugnancia, *f*

nauseate /'nɔziˌeit, -ʒi-/ *vt* dar náuseas, *Fig.* repugnar, dar asco

nauseating /'nɔziˌeitɪŋ, -ʒi-/ *a* repugnante, horrible; asqueroso

nauseous /'nɔʃəs/ *a* nauseabundo, asqueroso; *Fig.* repugnante

nauseousness /'nɔʃəsnɪs/ *n* náusea, asquerosidad, *f*; *Fig.* repugnancia, *f*, asco, *m*

nautical /'nɔtɪkəl/ *a* náutico, marítimo. **n. day, twenty-four hours,** singladura, *f*

naval /'neivəl/ *a* naval; de marina, marítimo. **n. base,** base naval, *f.* **n. engagement,** batalla naval, *f.* **n. hospital,** hospital de marina, *m.* **n. law,** código naval, *m.* **n. officer,** oficial de marina, *m.* **n. power,** poder marítimo, *m.* **n. reservist,** marinero de reserva, *m.* **n. yard,** arsenal, *m*

Navarre /nə'vɑr/ Navarra, *f*

nave /neiv/ *n Archit.* nave, *f*; (of wheels) cubo, *m*

navel /'neivəl/ *n* ombligo, *m.* **n. string,** cordón umbilical, *m*

navigability /ˌnævɪgə'bɪlɪti/ *n* navegación, practicabilidad de navegar, *f*

navigable /'nævɪgəbəl/ *a* navegable, practicable

navigate /'nævɪ,geit/ *vt* navegar, marear, dirigir (unbuque); *Fig.* conducir, guiar. *vi* navegar

navigation /,nævɪ'geiʃən/ *n* navegación, *f*; (science of) náutica, marina, *f*. **n. company,** empresa naviera, *f*. **n. laws,** derecho marítimo, *m*. **n. lights,** luces de navegación, *f pl*

navigator /'nævɪ,geitər/ *n* navegador, navegante, *m*; piloto, *m*

navvy /'nævi/ *n* peón, bracero, jornalero, *m*; *Mech.* máquina, excavadora, *f*. **road n.,** peón caminero, *m*. **to work like a n.,** estar hecho un azacán, sudar la gota gorda

navy /'neivi/ *n* marina, *f*; armada, *f*; (color) azul marino, *m*. **n. board,** consejo de la armada, *m*. **n. department** ministerio de marina, *m*. **n. estimates,** presupuesto de marina, *m*. **n. list,** escalafón de marina, *m*

nay /nei/ *adv* no; al contrario, más bien, mejor dicho. *n* negativa, *f*, voto contrario, *m*

Nazarene /,næzə'rin/ *a* and *n* nazareno (-na)

Nazareth /'næzərəθ/ Nazaret, *m*

Nazi /'nɑtsi/ *a* and *n* nacionalsocialista, naci, *mf*

Nazism /'natsɪzəm/ *n* nacismo, *m*

n.d. (no date) *s.f.* (sin fecha)

Neapolitan /,niə'pɒlitn̩/ *a* and *n* neapolitano (-na)

near /nɪər/ *vi* acercarse, aproximarse. *a* cercano, inmediato, contiguo; (of time) inminente, próximo; (relationship) cercano, consanguíneo; (of friends) íntimo, entrañable; (mean) tacaño, avariento

near /nɪər/ *prep* cerca de, junto a; hacia, en la dirección de; (of time) cerca de, casi. *adv* cerca, *Central America, Chile, Mexico* lueguito; (time) cerca, próximamente. **to be n. to,** estar cerca de. **to bring n.,** acercar, aproximar. **It was a N. thing,** Escapamos por un pelo. **n. at hand,** a la mano; (time) cerca, inminente. **n.-by,** *a* cercano, inmediato, *Central America, Chile, Mexico* lueguito. *adv* cerca. **n. side,** (of vehicles) lado de la acera, *m*. **n.-sighted,** corto de vista, miope. **n.-sightedness,** miopía, cortedad de vista, *f*

nearest /'nɪərɪst/ *a comp* and *sup* más cercano, más cerca; más corto. **the n. way,** el camino más corto, el camino directo

nearly /'nɪərli/ *adv* casi; cerca de, aproximadamente; estrechamente; íntimamente. **It touches me n.,** Me toca de cerca, Es de sumo interés para mí. **They n. killed me,** Por poco me matan. **to be n.,** (of age) frisar en, rayar en

nearness /'nɪərnɪs/ *n* (of place) cercanía, proximidad, contigüidad, *Argentina* adyacencia, *f*; (of time) inminencia, proximidad, *f*; (relationship) consanguinidad, *f*; (avarice) avaricia, tacañería, *f*; (dearness) intimidad, amistad estrecha, *f*

neat /nit/ *a* limpio, ordenado, sencillo, de buen gusto; (of the body) bien hecho, airoso, esbelto; aseado; (of handwriting) legible, bien proporcionado; pulido, esmerado, acabado; hábil, astuto, diestro; *Zool.* vacuno; (of liquor, spirits) puro, solo. **to make a n. job of,** hacer (algo) bien

neatly /'nitli/ *adv* sencillamente, con elegancia, con primor; con aseo, limpiamente; bien (proporcionado); diestramente, hábilmente

neatness /'nitnɪs/ *n* aseo, *m*, limpieza, *f*; elegancia, sencillez, *f*; buen gusto, *m*; destreza, habilidad, *f*; (aptness) pertinencia, *f*

nebula /'nɛbyələ/ *n* *Astron.* nebulosa, *f*

nebulosity /,nɛbyə'lɒsɪti/ *n* nebulosidad, *f*; *Astron.* nebulosa, *f*; vaguedad, imprecisión, *f*

nebulous /'nɛbyələs/ *a* nebuloso; vago, impreciso, confuso

necessarily /,nɛsə'sɛərəli/ *adv* necesariamente; inevitablemente, sin duda

necessary /'nɛsə,sɛri/ *a* necesario, inevitable; imprescindible, preciso, indispensable, esencial; obligatorio, debido, forzoso. *n* requisito esencial, *m*. **if n.,** en caso de necesidad; si fuera necesario. **to be n.,** hacer falta; necesitarse

necessitate /nə'sɛsɪ,teit/ *vt* necesitar, exigir, requerir, obligar

necessitous /nə'sɛsɪtəs/ *a* pobre, indigente, miserable, necesitado

necessity /nə'sɛsɪti/ *n* necesidad, *f*; menester, *m*; (e.g., *an indispensable n.,* un menester imprescin-

dible); consecuencia, *f*, resultado, efecto, *m*; inevitabilidad, fatalidad, *f*; (poverty) indigencia, pobreza, *f*. **Fire and clothing are necessities,** El fuego y el vestir son cosas necesarias. **from n.,** por necesidad. **in case of n.,** si fuese necesario, en caso de necesidad. **of n.,** de necesidad, sin remedio. **physical necessities,** menesteres físicos, *m pl.* **prime n.,** artículo de primera necesidad, *m*. **to be under the n. of,** tener que, tener la necesidad de

Necessity is the mother of invention La necesidad es una gran inventora, La necesidad aguza el ingenio

neck /nɛk/ *n* cuello, *m*, garganta, *f*; (of bottles) gollete, cuello, *m*; (of animals) pescuezo, *m*; *Geog.* istmo, *m*, lengua de tierra, *f*; (of musical instruments) clavijero, mástil, *m*; *Sew.* escote, *m*. **low-necked,** (of dresses) escotado. **She fell on his n.,** Se colgó de su cuello. **He won by a n.,** Ganó por un cuello; *Fig.* Ganó por un tris. **to break anyone's n.,** romperle el pescuezo. **to wring the n. of,** torcer el pescuezo (a). **n. and n.,** parejos. **n. or nothing,** todo o nada, perdiz o no comerla. **n. stock,** alzacuello, *m*

neckband /'nɛk,bænd/ *n* tirilla de camisa, *f*

necklace /'nɛklɪs/ *n* collar, *m*

necklet /'nɛklɪt/ *n* collar, *m*; (of fur) cuello, *m*

necktie /'nɛk,tai/ *n* corbata, *f*

necrological /,nɛkrə'lɒdʒɪkəl/ *a* necrológico

necrology /nə'krɒlədʒi/ *n* necrología, *f*

necropolis /nə'krɒpəlɪs/ *n* necrópolis, *f*

nectar /'nɛktər/ *n* néctar, *m*

nectarine /,nɛktə'rin/ *n* *Bot.* variedad de melocotón, *f*

need /nid/ *vt* necesitar, haber menester, requerir, exigir. *vi* ser necesario, hacer falta, carecer; haber (de). **N. I obey?** ¿He de obedecer? **You need to write carefully,** Hay que escribir con cuidado. **The work n. not be done for tomorrow,** No es preciso hacer el trabajo para mañana

need /nid/ *n* necesidad, *f*; cosa necesaria, *f*; falta; (poverty) indigencia, pobreza, *f*; urgencia, *f*; (shortage) escasez, carestía, *f*. **in case of n.,** en caso de necesidad, en caso de urgencia. **I have n. of two more books,** Me hacen falta dos libros más

needful /'nidfəl/ *a* necesario, preciso; indispensable, esencial. **the n.,** lo necesario

needfulness /'nidfəlnɪs/ *n* necesidad, falta, *f*

neediness /'nidinɪs/ *n* pobreza, penuria, miseria, estrechez, *f*

needle /'nidl̩/ *n* *Sew.* aguja, *f*; (of compass) brújula, aguja imanada, *f*; (monument) obelisco, *m*; (of scales) fiel, *m*, lengüeta, *f*; (of phonograph) púa, *f*, (of measuring instruments) índice, *m*; *Med.* aguja de inyecciones, *f*. *Inf.* **to be as sharp as a n.,** no tener pelo de tonto. **pack n.,** aguja espartera, *f*. **n.-case,** alfiletero, agujero, *m*. **n. maker,** fabricante de agujas, *m*. **n.-shaped,** en forma de aguja, acicular. *vt Lat. Am.* engorrar

needle and thread hilo y aguja

needless /'nidlɪs/ *a* innecesario, superfluo. **n. to say,** claro está que..., huelga decir que...

needlessly /'nidlɪsli/ *adv* innecesariamente, inútilmente; en vano, de balde

needlessness /'nidlɪsnɪs/ *n* superfluidad, *f*, lo innecesario

needlewoman /'nidl̩,wʊmən/ *n* (professional) cosedora, *f*; costurera, *f*. **She is a good n.,** Cose bien (or es una buena cosedora)

needlework /'nidl̩,wɜrk/ *n* labor de aguja, labor blanca, costura, *f*; bordado, *m*. **to do n.,** hacer costura

needs /nidz/ *adv* necesariamente, sin remedio *n pl* necesidades, *f pl.* **if must n.,** si hace falta

needy /'nidi/ *a* necesitado, menesteroso, corto de medios, pobre, apurado

ne'er-do-well /'nɛərdu,wɛl/ *n* calavera, perdido, *m*. **to be a n.,** ser de mala madera

nefarious /nɪ'fɛəriəs/ *a* nefario, vil, nefando

nefariously /nɪ'fɛəriəsli/ *adv* vilmente, nefariamente

negation /nɪ'geiʃən/ *n* negación, *f*

negative /'nɛgətɪv/ *vt* negar, denegar; votar en contra (de), oponerse (a); (prevent) impedir, imposibilitar. *a* negativo. *n* negativa, negación, *f*; repulsa, denegación, *f*; *Photo.* negativo, *m*, prueba negativa, *f*; *Elec.*

electricidad negativa, *f.* **to reply in the n.**, dar una respuesta negativa
negativeness /'nɛɡətɪvnɪs/ *n* el carácter negativo, *m*
neglect /nɪ'ɡlɛkt/ *vt* descuidar, desatender; abandonar, dejar; (ignore) despreciar, no hacer caso (de); omitir, olvidar. *n* descuido, *m*, desatención, *f*; inobservancia, *f*; abandono, olvido, *m*; desdén, *m*, frialdad, *f.* **to fall into n.**, caer en desuso. **to n. one's obligations**, descuidar sus obligaciones
neglectful /nɪ'ɡlɛktfəl/ *a* negligente, descuidado, omiso
negligee /ˌnɛɡlɪ'ʒei/ *n* salto de cama, quimono, *m*, bata, *f*
negligence /'nɛɡlɪdʒəns/ *n* negligencia, *f*, descuido, *m*; flojedad, pereza, *f*; (of dress) desaliño, *m*
negligent /'nɛɡlɪdʒənt/ *a* negligente, descuidado; remiso, flojo, perezoso
negligently /'nɛɡlɪdʒəntli/ *adv* negligentemente; con indiferencia
negligible /'nɛɡlɪdʒəbəl/ *a* insignificante, escaso, insuficiente; sin importancia, desdeñable
negotiable /nɪ'ɡouʃiəbəl, -ʃəbəl/ *a* negociable; (of a road) practicable, transitable
negotiate /nɪ'ɡouʃi,eit/ *vt* gestionar, agenciar, tratar; (a bend) tomar; (an obstacle) salvar, franquear; *vi* negociar. **to n. a bill of exchange,** descontar una letra de cambio. **to n. for a contract,** tratar un contrato
negotiation /nɪ,ɡouʃi'eiʃən/ *n* negociación, *f*; *Com.* gestión, transacción, *f*; (of a bend) toma, *f*; (of an obstacle) salto, *m*
negotiator /nɪ'ɡouʃi,eitər/ *n* negociador (-ra)
neigh /nei/ *vi* relinchar. *n* relincho, relinchido, *m*
neighbor /'neibər/ *n* vecino (-na); (biblical) prójimo (-ma)
neighborhood /'neibər,hʊd/ *n* vecindad, *f*, vecindario, *m*; cercanía, *f*, afueras, *f pl*, alrededores, *m pl*; *a* de barrio (e.g. *neighborhood moviehouse,* cine del barrio)
neighboring /'neibərɪŋ/ *a* vecino; cercano, inmediato, adyacente
neighborliness /'neibərlɪnɪs/ *n* buena vecindad, *f*
neighborly /'neibərli/ *a* amistoso, sociable, bondadoso. **to be n.,** ser de buena vecindad.
neither /'niðər, 'nai-/ *a* ningún; ninguno de los dos, e.g. *N. explanation is right,* Ninguna de las dos explicaciones es correcta. *conjunc* ni, tampoco, e.g. *N. Mary nor John,* Ni María ni Juan. *N. will he give it to her,* Tampoco se lo dará. *pron* ni uno ni otro, ninguno, e.g. *N. of them heard it,* Ni uno ni otro lo oyó.
nemesis /'nɛməsɪs/ *n* némesis, *f*; justicia, *f*
neo- *prefix* neo. **neo-Catholic,** *a* and *n* neo-católico (-ca). **neo-Platonic,** neoplatónico. **neo-Platonism,** neoplatonismo, *m*
neolithic /ˌniə'lɪθɪk/ *a* neolítico
neologism /ni'ɒlə,dʒɪzəm/ *n* neologismo, *m*
neon /'niɒn/ *n Chem.* neón, *m*
neon sign anuncio luminoso, *m*
neophyte /'niə,fait/ *n* neófito (-ta); aspirante, *mf*
nephew /'nɛfyu/ *n* sobrino, *m*
nephritis /nə'fraitɪs/ *n Med.* nefritis, *f*
nepotism /'nɛpə,tɪzəm/ *n* nepotismo, *m*
nerve /nɜrv/ *n* (*Anat. Bot.*) nervio, *m*; valor, ánimo, *m*; vitalidad, *f*; *Inf.* descaro, *m*, desvergüenza, frescura, *f. vt* animar, alentar, envalentonar; esforzar; dar fuerza (a). *vi* animarse, esforzarse (a). **My nerves are all on edge,** Se me crispan los nervios. **n.-cell,** neurona, *f.* **to lose one's n.,** perder la cabeza; perder los nervios. **to strain every n.,** hacer un esfuerzo supremo. **n. center,** centro nervioso, *m*. **n.-racking,** espantoso, horripilante. **n. strain,** tensión nerviosa, *f*
nerveless /'nɜrvlɪs/ *a* sin nervio; enervado
nerviness /'nɜrvinɪs/ *n* nervosidad, *f*
nervous /'nɜrvəs/ *a* nervioso, asustadizo, tímido; agitado, excitado; (of style) vigoroso. **n. breakdown,** crisis nerviosa, *f.* **n. system,** sistema nervioso, *m*
nervously /'nɜrvəsli/ *adv* nerviosamente; tímidamente

nervousness /'nɜrvəsnɪs/ *n* nervosidad, timidez, *f*; agitación, *f*; (of style) vigor, *m*; energía, *f*
nervy /'nɜrvi/ *a* valeroso; *Inf.* descarado
nest /nɛst/ *vi* anidar, hacerse un nido. *n* (bird's) nido, *m*; (animal's) madriguera, *f*; (of drawers) juego, *m*, serie, *f*; (of thieves) cueva, guarida, *f*; *Inf.* casita, *f*, hogar, *m.* **to feather one's n.,** hacer su agosto. **n.-egg,** *Fig.* nidal, *m.* **n. of eggs,** nidada de huevos, *f*
nestle /'nɛsəl/ *vt* apoyar. *vi* apiñarse, hacerse un ovillo. **to n. up to a person,** apretarse contra
nestling /'nɛstlɪŋ/ *n* pichón, pollo, *m*; pajarito, *m*
net /nɛt/ *vt* coger con redes; obtener, coger; cubrir con redes. *vi* hacer redes. *n* red, *f*; (mesh) malla, *f*; (fabric) tul, *m.* **net making,** manufactura de redes, *f*
net /nɛt/ *a Com.* líquido, neto, limpio; (of fabric) de tul. **net amount,** importe líquido, importe neto, *m.* **net balance,** saldo líquido, *m.* **net cost,** precio neto, *m.* **net profit,** beneficio neto (or líquido), *m*
nether /'nɛðər/ *a* inferior, bajero, más bajo. **n. regions,** infierno, *m*
Netherland /'nɛðərlənd/ *a* neerlandés, holandés
Netherlander /'nɛðər,lændər/ *n* neerlandés (-esa), holandés (-esa)
Netherlands, the /'nɛðərləndz/ los Países Bajos *m pl*
nethermost /'nɛðər,moust/ *a* lo más bajo, ínfimo, más hondo
netting /'nɛtɪŋ/ *n* red, (obra de) malla, *f; Naut.* jareta, *f*; manufactura de redes, *f*; pesca con redes, *f.* **wire-n.,** tela metálica, malla de alambre, *f*
nettle /'nɛtl/ *vt* picar; *Fig.* irritar, picar, fastidiar, disgustar. *n* ortiga, *f.* **n.-rash,** urticaria, *f*
network /'nɛt,wɜrk/ *n* red, malla, randa, *f*; (of communications) sistema, *m*, red, *f*
neuralgia /nʊ'rældʒə/ *n* neuralgia, *f*
neuralgic /nʊ'rældʒɪk/ *a* neurálgico
neurasthenia /ˌnʊrəs'θiniə/ *n* neurastenia, *f*
neurasthenic /ˌnʊrəs'θɛnɪk/ *a* and *n* neurasténico (-ca)
neuritis /nʊ'raitɪs/ *n* neuritis, *f*
neurologist /nʊ'rɒlədʒɪst/ *n* neurólogo, *m*
neurology /nʊ'rɒlədʒi/ *n* neurología, *f*
neuropath /'nʊrə,pæθ/ *n* neurópata, *m*
neuropathic /ˌnʊrə'pæθɪk/ *a* neuropático
neurosis /nʊ'rousɪs/ *n* neurosis, *f*
neurosurgeon /'nʊrou,sɜrdʒən/ *n* neurocirujano, *m*
neurotic /nʊ'rɒtɪk/ *a* and *n* neurótico (-ca)
neuter /'nʊtər/ *a* neutro; (of verbs) intransitivo; (*Zool. Bot.*) sin sexo
neutral /'nutrəl/ *a* neutral; (*Chem. Mech.*) neutro; (of colors) indeciso, indeterminado; (of persons) imparcial, indiferente. *n* neutral, *mf Mech.* **to go into n.,** pasar a marcha neutra
neutrality /nu'trælɪti/ *n* neutralidad, *f*; indiferencia, *f*; imparcialidad, *f*
neutralization /ˌnutrələ'zeiʃən/ *n* neutralización, *f*
neutralize /'nutrə,laiz/ *vt* neutralizar
never /'nɛvər/ *adv* nunca, jamás; de ningún modo; no; ni aun, ni siquiera. **Better late than n.,** Más vale tarde que nunca. **Never look a gift horse in the mouth,** A caballo regalado no se le mira el diente. **Were the hour n. so late,** Por más tarde que fuese la hora. **n. again,** nunca jamás. **n. a one,** ni siquiera uno. **n. a whit,** ni pizca. **N. mind!** ¡No importa! ¡No te preocupes! ¡No hagas caso! ¡Olvídatelo! **n.-ceasing,** continuo, incesante. **n.-ending,** inacabable, eterno, sin fin. **n.-failing,** infalible. **n.-to-be-forgotten,** inolvidable
nevermore /ˌnɛvər'mɔr/ *adv* nunca jamás
nevertheless /ˌnɛvərðə'lɛs/ *adv* sin embargo, no obstante, con todo
new /nu/ *a* nuevo; novel, fresco; distinto, diferente; (inexperienced) novato, no habituado; reciente. *adv* (in compounds) recién. **as good as new,** como nuevo. **brand-new,** flamante, nuevecito. **new-born,** recién nacido. **new-comer,** recién llegado (-da). **new-fashioned,** de última moda. **new-found,** recién hallado. **new moon,** luna nueva, *f*, novilunio, *m*. **new rich,** ricacho (-cha); indio, *m*. **new student,** alumno de nuevo ingreso. **New Testament,** Nuevo Testamento, *m.* **New World,** Nuevo Mundo, *m.* **New**

York (er), *a* and *n* neoyorquino (-na). **New Zealand** (er), *a* and *n* neozelandés (-esa)

newel /'nuəl/ *n* (of stair) alma, *f*, árbol, nabo, *m*. **n.-post,** pilarote (de escalera), *m*

newest /'nuɪst/ *a sup* novísimo; más reciente

Newfoundland /'nufənlənd/ Terranova, *f*. **N. dog,** perro de Terranova, *m*

newish /'nuɪʃ/ *a* bastante nuevo

newly /'nuli/ *adv* nuevamente; hace poco, recientemente. The abb. form **recién** is used only with past part, e.g. *the n. painted door,* la puerta recién pintada. *the n.-weds,* los desposados, los recién casados

newness /'nunɪs/ *n* novedad, *f*; inexperiencia, falta de práctica, *f*; innovación, *f*

New Orleans /'ɔrliənz, ɔr'linz/ Nueva Orleans, *f*

news /nuz/ *n pl* noticias, *f pl*; nueva, *f*; reporte, aviso, *m*; novedad, *f*. **No n. is good n.,** Falta de noticias, buena señal. **piece of n.,** noticia, *f*. **What's the n.?** ¿Qué hay de nuevo? **n. agency,** agencia de noticias, agencia periodística, *f*. **n.-agent,** agente de la prensa, *m*; vendedor (-ra) de periódicos. **n. bulletin,** *Radio.* boletín de noticias, *m*. *Inf.* **n.-hound,** gacetillero (-ra). **n. item,** noticia de actualidad, *f*. **n.-print,** papel para periódicos, *m*. **n.-room,** gabinete de lectura, *m*. **n. reel,** película noticiera, revista cinematográfica, *f*, noticiario cinematográfico, noticiero *m*, de tualidades, *f pl*. **n.-stand,** puesto de periódicos, quiosco de periódicos, *m*

newsboy /'nuz,bɔi/ *n Lat. Am.* canillito, *m*

newscast /'nuz,kæst/ *n* noticiario, *m*

newsgirl /'nuz,gɜrl/ *n Lat. Am.* canillita, *f*

newsletter circular /'nuz,lɛtər/ noticiera, relación de sucesos, *f*

newspaper /'nuz,peipər/ *n* periódico, diario, noticiero, *m*. **n. clipping, n. cutting,** recorte de periódico, *m*. **n. paragraph,** suelto, *m*. **n. reporter,** reportero (-ra); periodista, *mf* **n. reporting,** reporterismo, *m*. **n. serial,** folletín, *m*, novela por entregas, *f*. **n. vendor,** vendedor (-ra) de periódicos, *n*

news report *n* reportaje, *m*

newsy /'nuzi/ *a Inf.* lleno de noticias, noticioso

newt /nut/ *n* tritón, *m*

Newtonian /nu'touniən/ *a* neutoniano

New York /yɔrk/ Nueva York, *f*

New Zealand /'zilənd/ Nueva Zelandia, *f*

next /nɛkst/ *a* (of place) siguiente, vecino, contiguo; (of time) próximo, siguiente. **on the n. page,** en la página siguiente. **the n. day,** el día siguiente. **the n.-door house,** la casa vecina. **the n. life,** la otra vida. **n. month** (yesar), el mes (año) próximo (or que viene). **the n. time,** otra vez, la próxima vez

next /nɛkst/ *adv* (of time) luego, en seguida; (of place) inmediatamente después. **I come n.,** Ahora me toca a mí. **It is n. to a certainty that...,** Es casi seguro que... **the n. best,** el segundo. **the n. of kin,** los pariente más cercaror, *m*, parientes más cercanos, *m pl*. **to wear n. to the skin,** llevar sobre la piel. **n. to,** al lado de, junto a; primero después de; casi. **n. to nothing,** casi nada, muy poco. **What n.?** ¿Qué más?; ¿Y ahora qué?

nib /nɪb/ *n* punto, tajo (de una pluma), *m*

nibble /'nɪbəl/ *vt* mordiscar, mordisquear, roer; (horses) rozar; (fish) picar; *Fig.* considerar, tantear; *vi* picar. *n* mordisco, *m*; roedura, *f*

Nicaragua /ˌnɪkə'rɑgwə/ Nicaragua

Nicaraguan /ˌnɪkə'ragwən/ *a* and *n* nicaragüeño (-ña)

Nice /nis/ Niza, *f*

nice /nais/ *a* escrupuloso, minucioso, exacto; (of persons) simpático, afable, amable; fino; (of things) agradable, bonito; bueno; sutil, delicado; (*Inf. Ironic.*) bonito. **a n. point,** un punto delicado. **a n. view,** una vista agradable (or bonita). **n.-looking,** guapo. **n. people,** gente fina, *f*; gente simpática, *f*

nicely /'naisli/ *adv* muy bien; con elegancia; primorosamente; con amabilidad, gentilmente; agradablemente

Nicene /nai'sin/ *a* niceno

niceness /'naisnɪs/ *n* exactitud, minuciosidad, *f*; (of persons) bondad, amabilidad, *f*; amenidad, hermosura, *f*; lo bonito; sutileza, *f*; refinamiento, *m*

nicety /'naisɪti/ *n* exactitud, *f*; sutileza, *f*; refina-

miento, *m*. **niceties,** *n pl* detalles, *m pl*. **to a n.,** con la mayor precisión; a la perfección

niche /nɪtʃ/ *n* nicho, templete, *m*; (vaulted) hornacina, *f*, *Fig.* **to find a n. for oneself,** encontrarse una buena posición; situarse

nick /nɪk/ *vt* cortar en muescas, mellar, tarjar. *n* mella, muesca, *f*. **in the n. of time,** en el momento oportuno, a tiempo

nickel /'nɪkəl/ *n* níquel, *m*; *Com.* moneda de níquel, *f*. **n.-plated,** niquelado

nickname /'nɪk,neim/ *vt* apodar, motejar, apellidar. *n* apodo, sobrenombre, mote, mal nombre, *m*

nicotine /'nɪkə,tin/ *n* nicotina, *f*

nictitating membrane /'nɪktɪ,teitɪŋ/ *n Anat.* membrana nictitante, *f*

niece /nis/ *n* sobrina, *f*

niggardliness /'nɪgərdlinɪs/ *n* tacañería, avaricia, parsimonia, mezquindad, *f*

niggardly /'nɪgərdli/ *a* tacaño, avaricioso, mezquino, ruin, miserable

niggling /'nɪglɪŋ/ *a* nimio, meticuloso; escrupuloso, minucioso

nigh /nai/ See **near**

night /nait/ *n* noche, *f*; *Fig.* oscuridad, *f*, tinieblas, *f pl*. **all n.,** toda la noche, la noche entera. **all n. service,** servicio nocturno permanente, *m*. **at** or **by n.,** de noche. **every n.,** todas las noches, cada noche. **Good n.!** ¡Buenas noches! **last n.,** ayer por la noche, anoche, la noche pasada. **restless n.,** noche mala, noche toledana, *f*. **the n. before last,** anteayer por la noche, *m*. **to-n.,** esta noche. **tomorrow n.,** mañana por la noche. **to be n.,** ser de noche. **to spend the n.,** pernoctar, pasar la noche. **n.-bird,** pájaro nocturno, *m*; *Inf.* trasnochador (-ra). **n.-blindness,** nictalopia, *f*. **n.-cap,** gorro de dormir, *m*. **n. clothes,** traje de dormir, *m*. **n. club,** cabaré *m*. **n. dew,** relente, sereno, *m*. **n. flying,** vuelo nocturno, *m*. **n.-jar,** *Ornith.* chotacabras, *m*. **n.-light,** mariposa, lamparilla, *f*. **n. mail,** último correo, *m*; tren correo de la noche, *m*. **n. school,** escuela nocturna, *f*. **n. shift,** turno de noche, *m*. **n. table** *Mexico* buró, *m*. **n. watch,** ronda de noche, *f*; *Naut.* sonochada, *f*. **n. watchman,** (in the street) sereno, *m*; (of a building) vigilante nocturno, *m*

nightfall /'nait,fɔl/ *n* anochecer, crepúsculo, atardecer, *m*

nightgown /'nait,gaun/ *n* camisa de noche, *f*

nightingale /'naitŋ,geil, 'naitɪŋ-/ *n* ruiseñor, *m*

nightly /'naitli/ *a* de noche; nocturno, nocturnal. *adv* todas las noches, cada noche

nightmare /'nait,mɛər/ *n* pesadilla, *f*

nightmarish /'nait,mɛərɪʃ/ *a* de pesadilla, horrible

nightshade /'nait,ʃeid/ *n Bot.* hierba mora, *f*, solano, *m*

nihilism /'naiə,lɪzəm, 'ni-/ *n* nihilismo, *m*

nihilist /'naiəlɪst, 'ni-/ *n* nihilista, *mf*

Nile, the /nail/ el Nilo, *m*

nimble /'nɪmbəl/ *a* ágil, activo, *Mexico* alacre; vivo, listo. **n.-fingered,** ligero de dedos. **n.-witted,** despierto, vivo

nimbleness /'nɪmbəlnɪs/ *n* agilidad, actividad, *Mexico* alacridad, *f*; viveza, habilidad, *f*

nimbly /'nɪmbli/ *adv* ágilmente, ligeramente

nimbus /'nɪmbəs/ *n* nimbo, *m*, aureola, *f*

nincompoop /'nɪnkəm,pup, 'nɪŋ-/ *n* papirote, *m*, papanatas, *mf* tonto (-ta)

nine /nain/ *a* and *n* nueve, *m*. **He is n.,** Tiene nueve años. **the N.,** las nueve Musas. **n. o'clock,** las nueve. **to be dressed up to the nines,** estar hecho un brazo de mar

ninefold /a 'nain,fould; *adv.* 'nain'fould/ *a* and *a* and *adv* nueve veces

ninepins /'nain,pɪnz/ *n* juego de bolos, *m*

nineteen /'nain'tin/ *a* and *n* diez y nueve, diecinueve *m*

nineteenth /'nain'tinθ/ *a* décimonono. *n* (of month) el diez y nueve; (of monarchs) diez y nueve. **the n. century,** el siglo diez y nueve

ninetieth /'naintiəθ/ *a* nonagésimo, noventa

ninety /'nainti/ *a* and *n* noventa *m*. **n.-one,** noventa y uno. **n.-two,** noventa y dos. **the n.-first chapter,** el capítulo noventa y uno

ninny /'nɪni/ *n* parapoco, chancleta, *mf*; mentecato (-ta)

ninth /nainθ/ a noveno, nono. n nueve, m; (of the month) el nueve (of sovereigns) nono. **one n.,** un noveno

ninthly /'nainθli/ adv en noveno (or nono) lugar

nip /nɪp/ vt pellizcar, pinchar; mordiscar, morder; (wither) marchitar; (freeze) helar; (run) correr. vi pinchar; picar (el viento). n pellizco, pinchazo, m; mordisco, m; (of spirits) trago, m; copita, f; (in the air) viento frío, hielo, m. **to nip in,** colarse dentro, deslizarse en. **to nip off,** pirarse, mudarse. *Fig.* **to nip in the bud,** cortar en flor

nippers /'nɪpərz/ n pl alicates, m pl; tenacillas, pinzas, f pl

nipping /'nɪpɪŋ/ n pinchadura, f; mordedura, f. a punzante; helado, glacial, mordiente. **n. off,** (of a point) despuntadura, f

nipple /'nɪpəl/ n pezón, m; pezón artificial, m

nit /nɪt/ n. *Ent.* liendre, f

niter /'naitər/ n salitre, m

nitrate /'naitreit/ n *Chem.* nitrato, m

nitric /'naitrɪk/ a nítrico

nitrite /'naitrait/ n *Chem.* nitrito, m

nitro- prefix *Chem.* nitro. **n.-cellulose,** algodón pólvora, m. **n.-glycerine,** nitroglicerina, f

nitrogen /'naitrədʒən/ n *Chem.* nitrógeno, m

no /nou/ a ningún, ninguno, ninguna, e.g. *by no means,* de ningún modo. *No* is often not translated in Sp., e.g. *I have no time,* No tengo tiempo. adv no. n voto negativo, no, m. *to be of no account,* no tener importancia; no significar nada. *to be no good for,* no servir para. *to be of no use,* ser inútil. *to have no connection with,* no tener nada que ver con. *for no reason,* sin motivo alguno. *"No Admittance,"* «Entrada Prohibida.» *no, indeed,* Cierto que no. *no-man's land,* tierra de nadie, f. *no more,* no más. *No more of this!* ¡No hablemos más de eso! *no one,* nadie, ninguno. *no sooner,* no bien, tan pronto (como). **no such thing,** no tal. **"No Thoroughfare,"** «Prohibido el Paso.» **whether or not,** sea o no sea

Noah's Ark /'nouəz/ n arca de Noé, f

nobility /nou'bɪlɪti/ n nobleza, f; (of rank) aristocracia, nobleza, f; (of conduct) caballerosidad, hidalguía, generosidad, bondad, f; (grandeur) grandeza, sublimidad, f. **the higher n.,** los nobles de primera clase

noble /'noubəl/ a noble; (in rank) aristocrático, noble, linajudo; (of conduct) caballeroso, generoso; (of buildings) sublime, magnífico. n noble, m, aristócrata, mf **to make n.,** ennoblecer. **n.-mindedness,** generosidad, grandeza de alma, f. **n. title,** título de nobleza, título del reino, m

noblewoman /'noubəl,wʊmən/ n dama noble, mujer noble, aristócrata, f

nobly /'noubli/ adv noblemente, generosamente. **n. born,** noble de nacimiento

nobody /'nou,bɒdi/ n nadie, ninguno. **There was n. there,** No había nadie allí. *Inf.* **a n.,** un (una) cualquiera, una persona insignificante. **n. else,** nadie más, ningún otro

nocturnal /nɒk'tɜrnḷ/ a nocturno, nocherniego, nocturnal

nocturne /'nɒktɜrn/ n *Mus.* nocturno, m

nod /nɒd/ vt inclinar la cabeza; hacer una señal (or señas) con la cabeza; vi dar cabezadas; cabecear; (of trees) mecerse, inclinarse; inclinar la cabeza. n señal (or seña) con la cabeza, f; inclinación de la cabeza, f; cabeceo, m, cabezada, *Lat. Am.* cabeceada, f. **A nod is as good as a wink,** A buen entendedor pocas palabras. **He nodded to me as he passed,** Me saludó con la cabeza al pasar. **He signed to me with a nod,** Me hizo una señal con la cabeza

nodding /'nɒdɪŋ/ a que cabecea; *Bot.* colgante, inclinado; temblante. n cabeceo, m; saludo con la cabeza, m

noddle /'nɒdḷ/ n mollera, f

node /noud/ n (*Bot. Med.*) nudo, m

nodule /'nɒdʒul/ n nódulo, m; nudillo, m

noise /nɔiz/ n ruido, son, m; tumulto, clamor, estruendo, alboroto, *Central America* embullo, m. **to make a n.,** hacer ruido. **to n. abroad,** divulgar, publicar

noiseless /'nɔizlɪs/ a silencioso, callado, sin ruido

noiselessness /'nɔizlɪsnɪs/ n silencio, m, falta de ruido, f

noisily /'nɔizəli/ adv ruidosamente

noisiness /'nɔizinɪs/ n ruido, estrépito, tumulto, clamor, m; (of voices) gritería, f

noisome /'nɔisəm/ a ofensivo; fétido, apestoso

noisy /'nɔizi/ a ruidoso; estruendoso; estrepitoso, clamoroso

nomad /'noumæd/ a nómada, errante; (of flocks) trashumante. n nómada, mf

nomadism /'noumædɪzəm/ n nomadismo, m

nomenclature /'noumən,kleitʃər/ n nomenclatura, f

nominal /'nɒmənḷ/ a nominal; titular; insignificante, de poca importancia. **the n. head,** el director en nombre

nominalism /'nɒmənḷ,ɪzəm/ n nominalismo, m

nominally /'nɒmənḷi/ adv nominalmente, en nombre

nominate /'nɒmə,neit/ vt nombrar, designar, elegir; fijar, señalar

nominating /'nɒmə,neitɪŋ/ a nominador

nomination /,nɒmə'neiʃən/ n nombramiento, m, nominación, f; señalamiento, m

nominator /'nɒmə,neitər/ n nominador (-ra)

nominee /,nɒmə'ni/ n nómino propuesto, m

non /nɒn/ adv non; des-; in-; falta de. **non-acceptance,** rechazo, m. **non-acquaintance,** ignorancia, f. **non-admission,** no admisión, f; denegación, f, rechazo, m. **non-aggression,** no agresión, f. **non-alcoholic,** no alcohólico. **non-appearance,** ausencia, f; *Law.* no comparecencia, contumacia, f. **non-arrival,** ausencia, f; falta de recibo, f. **non-attendance,** falta de asistencia, ausencia, f. **non-carbonated,** sin gas. **non-combatant,** no combatiente. **non-commissioned officer,** oficial subalterno, m. **non-committal,** evasivo, equívoco, ambiguo. **non-compliance,** falta de obediencia, f. **non-concurrence,** falta de acuerdo, f. **non-conducting,** no conductivo. **non-conductor,** mal conductor, m; *Elec.* aislador, m. **non-contagious,** no contagioso. **non-cooperation,** *Polit.* resistencia pasiva, f; no cooperación, f. **non-delivery,** falta de entrega, f. **non-essential,** no esencial, prescindible. **non-execution,** no cumplimiento, m. **non-existence,** no existencia, f. **non-existent,** inexistente, no existente. **non-intervention,** no intervención, f. **non-manufacturing,** no industrial. **non-member,** visitante, mf **non-observance,** incumplimiento, m; violación, f. **non-payment,** falta de pago, f. **non-performance,** falta de ejecución, f. **non-poisonous,** no venenoso, innocuo. **non-resistance,** falta de resistencia, f; obediencia pasiva, f. **non-skid,** antideslizante, antirresbaladizo. **non-smoking,** que no fuma; (of a railway compartment, etc.) para no fumadores. **non-stop,** continuo, incesante; directo, sin parar; *Aer.* sin escalas

nonagenarian /,nɒnədʒə'nɛəriən/ a and n nonagenario (-ia)

non-aligned /,nɒn ə'laind/ a no abanderado

non-alignment /,nɒn ə'lainmənt/ n no abanderamiento m

nonce word /nɒns/ n palabra ocasional, f

nonchalance /,nɒnʃə'lɑns/ n aplomo, m, indiferencia, frialdad, calma, f

nonchalant /,nɒnʃə'lɑnt/ a indiferente, frío, impasible

nonchalantly /,nɒnʃə'lɑntli/ adv con indiferencia

nonconformist /,nɒnkən'fɔrmɪst/ a and n disidente mf; a inconforme, m, inconformista, mf

nonconformity /,nɒnkən'fɔrmɪti/ n disidencia, f

nondescript /,nɒndɪ'skrɪpt/ a indeterminado, indefinido, indeciso, mediocre

none /nʌn/ pron nadie, ninguno; nada. a and n ninguno (-na). adv no; de ningún modo, de ninguna manera. **I have n.,** No lo tengo, No tengo ninguno. **We have n. of your things,** No tenemos ninguna de tus cosas. **I was n. the worse,** No me hallaba peor. **N. can read his account with pleasure,** Nadie puede leer su narración con gusto. **n. the less,** no menos, sin embargo

nonentity /nɒn'ɛntɪti/ n persona sin importancia, medianía, f, cero, m

nones /nounz/ *n pl Eccl.* nona, *f*; (Roman Calendar) nonas, *f pl*,

nonplussed /nɒn'plʌst/ *a* cortado, perplejo, confuso

non-profit /nɒn 'prɒfɪt/ *a* sin fines de lucro, sin fines lucrativos

non-self-governing /'nɒn sɛlf'gʌvərnɪŋ/ *a* no autónomo

nonsense /'nɒnsɛns/ *n* disparate, despropósito, desatino, *m*, absurdidad, *f*; *Inf.* galimatías, *m*; pamplina, patraña, *f.* **to talk n.,** hablar sin ton ni son. **N.!** ¡A otro perro con este hueso! ¡Patrañas!

nonsensical /nɒn'sɛnsɪkəl/ *a* absurdo, ridículo, disparatado

noodle /'nudl/ *n Cul.* tallarín, *m*; *Inf.* mentecato (-ta), bobo (-ba)

nook /nʊk/ *n* escondrijo, lugar retirado, rincón, *m*

noon /nun/ *n* mediodía, *m*; *Fig.* punto culminante, apogeo, *m*, *a* de mediodía, meridional. **at n.,** a mediodía

noose /nus/ *vt* coger con lazos. *n* lazo corredizo, dogal, *m*

nopal /'noupəl/ *n Bot.* nopal, *m*

No Parking «Se Prohibe Estacionar,» «Estacionarse Prohibido»

nor /nɔr/ *unstressed* nər/ *conjunc* ni, no, tampoco. **He** removed neither his coat nor his hat, No se quitó ni el gabán ni el sombrero. **Nor was this the first time,** Y no fue ésta la primera vez. **Nor I,** Ni yo tampoco

Nordic /'nɔrdɪk/ *a* and *n* nórdico (-ca)

norm /nɔrm/ *n* modelo, *m*, norma, regla, pauta, *f*; (of size) marca, *f*; (*Bot. Zool.*) tipo, *m*

normal /'nɔrməl/ *a* normal; común, natural, corriente, regular; *Math.* perpendicular, normal. *n* condición normal, *f*, estado normal, *m*; *Math.* normal, *f.* **to become n.,** normalizarse, hacerse normal. **to make n.,** normalizar. **n. school,** escuela normal, *f*

normality /nɔr'mælɪti/ *n* normalidad, *f*

normalization /ˌnɔrmələ'zeiʃən/ *n* normalización, *f*

normalize /'nɔrmə,laiz/ *vt* normalizar

normally /'nɔrməli/ *adv* normalmente

Norman /'nɔrmən/ *a* and *n* normando (-da)

Normandy /'nɔrməndi/ Normandía, *f*

Norse /nɔrs/ *n* noruego (language), *m*, *a* escandinavo

Norseman /'nɔrsmən/ *n* normando, viking (*pl* -os), hombre del norte, *m*

north /nɔrθ/ *n* norte, *m*. *a* del norte, septentrional. **n. by west,** norte, cuarta noroeste. **n. of the city,** al norte de la ciudad. **N.-American,** *a* and *n* norteamericano (-na). **n.-east,** *a* and *n* nordeste *m*. **n.-easter,** viento del nordeste, *m*. **n.-easterly,** del nordeste (winds). **n.-eastern,** del nordeste (places). **n.-eastward,** hacia el nordeste. **n.-n.-east,** nornordeste, *m*. **n.-n.-west,** nornorueste, *m*. **n.-polar,** árctico. **N. Star,** estrella del norte, estrella polar, *f.* **n.-west,** noroeste, *m*. **n.-wester,** viento del noroeste, *m*. **n.-westerly,** del noroeste (winds). **n.-westerly gale,** temporal del noroeste, *m*. **n.-western,** del noroeste; situado al noroeste. **n.-westwards,** hacia el noroeste. **n. wind,** el viento del norte, el cierzo

North America Norteamérica, América del Norte, *f*

northern /'nɔrðərn/ *a* del norte, septentrional, norteño; (of races) nórdico. **N. Cross,** crucero, *m*. **n. lights,** aurora boreal, *f*

northerner /'nɔrðərnər/ *n* hombre del norte, *m*, habitante del norte, *mf*

northernmost /'nɔrðərn,moust/ *a sup* al extremo norte, más septentrional

northwards /'nɔrθwɜrdz/ *adv* hacia el norte

Norway /'nɔrwei/ Noruega, *f*

Norwegian /nɔr'widʒən/ *a* and *n* noruego (-ga); (language) noruego, *m*

nose /nouz/ *n* nariz, *f*; (of animals) hocico, *m*; (sense of smell) olfato, *m*; (of ships) proa, *f*; (of jug) pico, *m*, boca, *f*; (projecting piece) cuerno, *m*, nariz, *f*; (of airplane) cabeza, *f*, *vt* acariciar con la nariz; avanzar lentamente. *vi* husmear, olfatear. **to n. into,** *Inf.* meter las narices, poner baza. **to n. out,** descubrir, averiguar. **to bleed at the n.,** echar sangre por las narices. **to blow one's n.,** sonar (or limpiarse) las narices. **to keep one's n. to the grindstone,** estar sobre el yunque, batir el cobre. *Fig.* **to lead by the**

n., tener a uno agarrado por las narices. **to pay through the n.,** costar un ojo de la cara. **to speak through the n.,** ganguear. **to turn up one's n.,** *Fig.* hacer gestos (a), volver la cara. **flat n.,** nariz chata, *f*. **snub n.,** nariz respingona, *f*. **well-shaped n.,** nariz perfilada, *f*. **under one's n.,** bajo las narices de uno. **n.-bag,** cebadera, mochila, *f*; morral, *m*. **n.-bleeding,** *Med.* epistaxis, *f*; hemorragia de las narices, *f*. **n.-dive,** *Aer.* descenso de cabeza, picado, *m*. *vi* picar. **n.-piece,** (of microscope) ocular, *m*. **n.-ring,** (of a bull, etc.) narigón, *m*

-nosed /nouzd/ *a* de nariz..., con la nariz...

nosegay /'nouz,gei/ *n* ramillete, *m*

nosey Parker /'nouzi 'parkər/ *n Inf.* mequetrefe, *m*; cócora, *Lat. Am.* averigüetas, *mf*

No Smoking «Prohibido Fumar», Se Prohibe Fumar

nostalgia /nɒ'stældʒə/ *n* nostalgia, añoranza, *f*

nostalgic /nɒ'stældʒɪk/ *a* nostálgico

nostril /'nɒstrəl/ *n* ventana de la nariz, *f*, *n pl* **nostrils,** narices, *f pl*

nostrum /'nɒstrəm/ *n* panacea, *f*, curalotodo, *m*; medicina patentada, *f*

not /nɒt/ *adv* no; sin; ni, ni siquiera. **Is it not true? We think not,** ¿No es verdad? No lo creemos. **You have seen Mary, have you not?** Vd. ha visto a María, ¿verdad? **not caring whether he came or not,** sin preocuparse de que viniese o no. **not that he will come,** no es decir que venga. **not at all,** de ningún modo; (courtesy) ¡de nada! **not even,** ni siquiera. **not guilty,** no culpable. **not one,** ni uno. **not so much as,** no tanto como; ni siquiera. **It is not so much that, as it is...** No es tanto eso, cuanto que... **not to say,** por no decir

notability /ˌnoutə'bɪlɪti/ *n* notabilidad, *f*; (person) notable, *mf* persona de importancia, *f*

notable /'noutəbəl/ *a* notable, señalado, memorable; digno de atención. *n* persona eminente, *f*, notable, *mf*

notably /'noutəbli/ *adv* notablemente, señaladamente

notary /'noutəri/ *n* notario, escribano, *m*

notation /nou'teiʃən/ *n* notación, *f*

notch /nɒtʃ/ *vt* cortar muescas (en); mellar, ranurar, entallar. *n* muesca, mella, ranura, entalladura, *f*

note /nout/ *vt* notar, observar; anotar, apuntar; advertir, hacerse cuenta de. *n Mus.* nota, *f*; son, acento, *m*; (letter) recado, billete, *m*; anotación, glosa, *f*; apuntación, *f*, apunte, *m*, nota, *f*; (importance) importancia, distinción, *f*; *Com.* vale, abonaré, *m*; (sign) marca, señal, *f.* **to n. down,** anotar, **worthy of note,** digno de atención. **n.-book,** libro de apuntes, cuaderno, *m*, libreta, *f.* **n.-case,** cartera, *f*, *Com.* **n. of hand,** pagaré, *m*. **n.-paper,** papel de escribir, *m*. **n.-taker,** apuntador (-ra)

noted /'noutɪd/ *a* célebre, famoso, ilustre, eminente, insigne

noteworthy /'nout,wɜrði/ *a* digno de nota, notable, digno de atención

nothing /'nʌθɪŋ/ *n* nada, *f*; la nada; cero, *m*. *adv* en nada. **to do n.,** anonadarse, fracasar. **to do n.,** no hacer nada. **to do n. but,** no hacer más que. **to have n. to do with,** no tener nada que ver con; *Inf.* no tener arte ni parte en. **There is n. else to do,** No hay nada más que hacer; No hay más remedio. **There is n. to fear,** No hay de que tener miedo. **We could make n. of the book,** No llegamos a comprender el libro. **for n.,** de balde, en vano; gratis. **next to n.,** casi nada. **n. else or more,** nada más. **n. like,** ni con mucho. **n. much,** poca cosa. **n. new,** nada nuevo. **n. similar,** nada semejante. **n. to speak of,** poca cosa

nothingness /'nʌθɪŋnɪs/ *n* nada, *f*

notice /'noutɪs/ *vt* observar, reparar en, darse cuenta (de), marcar, caer en la cuenta (de), fijarse (en). *n* observación, atención, *f*; aviso, *m*, notificación, *f*; anuncio, *m*; (term) plazo, *m*; (review) crítica, *f*. **at short n.,** a corto aviso. **until further n.,** hasta nuevo aviso (or orden). **to attract n.,** atraer la atención. **I hadn't noticed,** No me había fijado. **to be beneath one's n.,** no merecer su atención. **to be under n.,** estar dimitido. **to bring to the n. of,** dar noticia de. **to escape n.,** pasar desapercibido. **to give n.,** hacer saber, informar; (of employer) despedir (a); (of employee) dimitir, dar la dimisión. **to take n. of,** notar, darse cuenta de; hacer caso, atender (a). **n. board,** letrero, tablero de anuncios, *m*. **n. to quit,** desahúcio, *m*

noticeable /'noutɪsəbəl/ *a* perceptible, evidente; digno de observación, notable

noticeably /'noutɪsəbli/ *adv* perceptiblemente; notablemente

notifiable /ˌnoutə'faiəbəl/ *a* declarable, notificable

notification /ˌnoutəfɪ'keiʃən/ *n* notificación, intimación, advertencia, *f*, aviso, *m*

notify /'noutəˌfai/ *vt* notificar, comunicar, avisar, intimar, hacer saber

notion /'nouʃən/ *n* noción, idea, *f*, concepto, *m*; (view) opinión, *f*, parecer, *m*; (novelty) novedad, *f*; artículo de fantasía, *m*. **I have a n. that...,** Tengo la idea de que..., Sospecho que... **I haven't a n.,** No tengo idea

No Tipping /'tɪpɪŋ/ «No Se Admiten Propinas»

notoriety /ˌnoutə'raiɪti/ *n* notoriedad, publicidad, *f*; escándalo, *m*; persona notoria, *f*

notorious /nou'tɔriəs/ *a* notorio, famoso, conocido; escandaloso, sensacional

notoriously /nou'tɔriəsli/ *adv* notoriamente

notwithstanding /ˌnɒtwɪð'stændɪŋ/ *prep* a pesar de. *adv* sin embargo, no obstante. *conjunc* aunque, bien que, por más que

nougat /'nugət/ *n* turrón, *m*

nought /nɔt/ *n Math.* cero, *m*; nada, *f*

noun /naun/ *n* substantivo, nombre, *m*

nourish /'nɜrɪʃ/ *vt* sustentar, alimentar, nutrir; *Fig.* fomentar, favorecer

nourishing /'nɜrɪʃɪŋ/ *a* nutritivo, alimenticio, nutricio

nourishment /'nɜrɪʃmənt/ *n* nutrición, *f*; sustento, *m*; alimento, *m*; *Fig.* fomento, pasto, *m*

Nova Scotia /'nouvə 'skouʃə/ Nueva Escocia, *f*

novel /'nɒvəl/ *a* nuevo, original, inacostumbrado. *n* novela, *f*. **n. of roguery,** novela picaresca, *f*

novelette /ˌnɒvə'lɛt/ *n* novela corta, *f*

novelist /'nɒvəlɪst/ *n* novelista, *mf*

novelty /'nɒvəlti/ *n* novedad, *f*; innovación, *f*; cambio, *m*

November /nou'vɛmbər/ *n* noviembre, *m*

novice /'nɒvɪs/ *n Eccl.* novicio (-ia); comenzante, principiante, *mf*, aspirante, *m*, *Lat. Am.* advenedizo (-za)

novocain /'nouvəˌkein/ *n Med.* novocaína, *f*

now /nau/ *adv* ahora, actualmente, al presente, a la fecha; en seguida, ahora, inmediatamente; poco ha, hace poco; pues bien. *interj* ¡A ver! ¡Vamos! *conjunc* pero, mas. *n* presente, *m*, actualidad, *f*. **before now,** antes, en otras ocasiones, ya, previamente. **just now,** ahora mismo, hace poco. **now... now,** ya... ya; sucesivamente, en turno. **now and then,** de vez en cuando, de tarde en tarde. **now that,** ya que, ahora que, dado que. **until now,** hasta el presente, hasta aquí, hasta ahora

nowadays /'nauəˌdeiz/ *adv* hoy en día, actualmente, en nuestros días

nowhere /'nouˌwɛər/ *adv* en ninguna parte. **in the middle of n.,** en tierra de nadie. **n. else,** en ninguna otra parte. *Inf.* **n. near,** ni con mucho; muy lejos (de)

nowise /'nouˌwaiz/ *adv* de ningún modo, en modo alguno, de ninguna manera

noxious /'nɒkʃəs/ *a* dañoso, nocivo; pestífero

noxiousness /'nɒkʃəsnɪs/ *n* nocividad, *f*

nozzle /'nɒzəl/ *n* (of a hose-pipe) boquilla, *f*; *Mech.* gollete, *m*; tubo de salida, *m*, tobera, *f*; inyector, *m*

n.p. (no place) s.l. (sin lugar)

nuance /'nuans/ *n* matiz, *m*, gradación, sombra, *f*

nubile /'nubɪl, -bail/ *a* núbil

nuclear /'nukliər/ *a* nuclear

nucleus /'nukliəs/ *n* núcleo, *m*; centro, foco, *m*

nude /nud/ *a* desnudo, nudo, *Peru* calato, *elsewhere in Lat. Am.* encuerado

nudge /nʌdʒ/ *vt* dar un codazo (a). *n* codazo, *m*

nudism /'nudɪzəm/ *n* nudismo, *m*

nudist /'nudɪst/ *n* nudista, *mf*

nudity /'nudɪti/ *n* desnudez, *f*

nugget /'nʌgɪt/ *n Mineral.* pepita, *f*

nuisance /'nusəns/ *n* molestia, incomodidad, *f*, fastidio, *m*; *Inf.* tostón, *m*, lata, *f*; *Lat. Am.* fregada, *Colom-*

bia vaina, *f*. **to make a n. of oneself,** meterse donde no le llaman, ser un pelmazo. **What a n.!** ¡Qué lata! ¡Qué fastidio!, *Colombia* ¡Qué vaina!

null /nʌl/ *a* nulo, inválido, sin fuerza legal. **n. and void,** nulo, írrito

nullification /ˌnʌləfɪ'keiʃən/ *n* anulación, invalidación, *f*

nullity /'nʌlɪti/ *n* nulidad, *f*

numb /nʌm/ *vt* entumecer, entorpecer. *a* entumecido; torpe, dormido; paralizado; *Fig.* insensible, pasmado. **n. with cold,** entumecido de frío

number /'nʌmbər/ *vt* numerar, contar; poner número (a); (pages of a book) foliar; ascender a. *n* número, *m*; (figure) cifra, *f*; (crowd) multitud, muchedumbre, *f*; cantidad, *f*; (of a periodical) ejemplar, *m*; *Gram.* número, *m*; pl versos, *m pl*. **Numbers,** (Bible) Números, *m pl*; **to be numbered among,** figurar entre. **among the n. of,** entre la muchedumbre de. **a n. of,** varios, muchos, una cantidad de. **in great n.,** en gran número; en su mayoría. **6 Peace Street,** Calle de la Paz nº (número) 6. **one of their n.,** uno entre ellos. **n. board,** (racing) indicador, *m*. **n. plate,** *Auto.* chapa de identidad, placa de número, *f*

numbering /'nʌmbərɪŋ/ *n* numeración, *f*

numberless /'nʌmbərlɪs/ *a* innumerable, sin número, sin fin, infinito

numbness /'nʌmnɪs/ *n* entumecimiento, entorpecimiento, *m*; *Fig.* insensibilidad, *f*

numeral /'numərəl/ *a* numeral. *n* número, *m*, cifra, *f*; *Gram.* nombre o adjetivo numeral, *m*

numerator /'numəˌreitər/ *n* numerador

numerical /nu'mɛrɪkəl/ *a* numérico

numerous /'numərəs/ *a* numeroso; nutrido, grande; muchos (-as)

numerousness /'numərəsnɪs/ *n* numerosidad, multitud, muchedumbre, *f*

numismatic /ˌnumɪz'mætɪk/ *a* numismático. *n pl* **numismatics,** numismática, *f*

numismatist /nu'mɪzmətɪst/ *n* numismático, *m*

numskull /'nʌmˌskʌl/ *n* zote, topo, *m*

nun /nun/ *n* monja, religiosa, *f*. **to become a nun,** profesar, tomar el hábito, meterse monja, hacer los votos

nuncio /'nʌnʃiˌou/ *n* nuncio, *m*. **acting n.,** pronuncio, *m*

nunnery /'nʌnəri/ *n* convento de monjas, *m*

nuptial /'nʌpʃəl/ *a* nupcial. *n pl* **nuptials,** nupcias, *f pl*, enlace, *m*. **n. mass,** *Eccl.* misa de velaciones, *f*. **n. song,** epitalamio, *m*

nurse /nɜrs/ *vt* criar; dar de mamar (a), amamantar; (the sick) cuidar, asistir; (fondle) acariciar, mecer; *Fig.* fomentar, promover. *vi* trabajar como enfermera. *n* (of the sick) enfermera, *f*; (wet) nodriza, ama de leche, *f*; *Am.* criandera, *f*; (children's) niñera, *f*; *Gram.* fomentador, *m*. **male n.,** enfermero, *m*

nursery /'nɜrsəri/ *n Agr.* plantel, vivero semillero, criadero, *m*; (children's room) cuarto de los niños, *m*; *Fig.* sementera, *f*; semillero, *m*. **n. governess,** aya, *f*. **n. rhyme,** canción infantil, *f*

nurseryman /'nɜrsərimən/ *n* horticultor, *m*; jardinero, *m*

nursing /'nɜrsɪŋ/ *n* lactancia, crianza, *f*; (of the sick) asistencia, *f*, cuido, *m*. **n. home,** clínica, *f*. **n. mother,** madre lactante, *f*

nurture /'nɜrtʃər/ *vt* alimentar; criar, educar. *n* nutrición, alimentación, *f*; crianza, educación, *f*

nut /nʌt/ *n Bot.* nuez, *f*; *Mech.* tuerca, hembra de tornillo, *f*, *Inf.* lo de nuez **to crack,** ser un tío de cuidado. **to crack nuts,** cascar nueces. **to go nutting,** coger nueces. **cashew nut,** anacardo, *m*. **loose nut,** *Mech.* tuerca aflojada, *f*. **nut-brown,** castaño. **nut tree,** nogal, *m*

nutcrackers /'nʌtˌkrækərz/ *n pl* cascanueces, quebrantanueces, *m*

nutmeg /'nʌtmɛg/ *n* nuez moscada, nuez de especia, *f*

nutria /'nutriə/ *n Zool.* nutria, *f*

nutriment /'nutrəmənt/ *n* nutrimento, alimento, *m*

nutrition /nu'trɪʃən/ *n* nutrición, alimentación, *f*

nutritious, nutritive /nu'trɪʃəs; 'nutrɪtɪv/ *a* nutritivo, alimenticio, alible

nutshell /'nʌt‚ʃɛl/ n cáscara de nuez, f. **to put in a n.,** decir en resumidas cuentas, decir en forma apastillada

nutty /'nʌti/ a de nuez

nuzzle /'nʌzəl/ vt acariciar con la nariz

nylon /'nailɒn/ n nilón, nylon, m. **n. stockings,** medias de cristal (or de nilón), f pl

nymph /nɪmf/ n ninfa, f; Ent. crisálida, f. **n.-like,** como una ninfa; de ninfa

nymphomania /‚nɪmfə'meiniə/ n ninfomanía, f, furor uterino, m

O

o /ou/ n (letter) o, f, interj ¡o! **O that…!** ¡Ojalá que!

oaf /ouf/ n zoquete, zamacuco, m

oafish /'oufɪʃ/ a lerdo, torpe

oafishness /'oufɪʃnɪs/ n torpeza, estupidez, f

oak /ouk/ n (tree and wood) roble, m, a de roble. **carved oak,** roble tallado, m. **holm-oak,** encina, f. **oak-apple,** agalla, f. **oak grove,** robledo, m

oakum /'oukəm/ n estopa, f

oar /ɔr/ n remo, m. **to lie on the oars,** cesar de remar. **to pull at the oars,** bogar, remar. **to put in one's oar,** Inf. meter baza. **to ship the oars,** armar los remos. **to unship the oars,** desarmar los remos. **oar-stroke,** palada, f

oarsman /'ɔrzmən/ n remero, bogador, m

oarsmanship /'ɔrzmən‚ʃɪp/ n arte de remar, m, or f

oasis /ou'eisɪs/ n oasis, m

OAS (Organization of American States) OEA (Organización de los Estados Americanos)

oast /oust/ n horno para secar el lúpulo, m

oat /out/ n Bot. avena, f. **wild oat,** avena silvestre, f. **to sow one's wild oats,** correrla, andarse a la flor del berro. **oat field,** avenal, m

oath /ouθ/ n juramento, m; (curse) blasfemia, f, reniego, m. **on o.,** bajo juramento. **to break an o.,** violar el juramento. **to put on o.,** tomar juramento, hacer prestar juramento. **to take an o.,** prestar (or hacer) juramento. **to take the o. of allegiance,** jurar la bandera

oatmeal /'out‚mil/ n harina de avena, f

obduracy /'ɒbdurəsi/ n obduración, obstinación, terquedad, f

obdurate /'ɒbdurɪt/ a obstinado, terco, porfiado. **He is o. to our requests,** Es sordo a nuestros ruegos

obedience /ou'bidiəns/ n obediencia, sumisión, docilidad, f. **blind o.,** obediencia ciega, f. **in o. to,** conforme a, de acuerdo con

obedient /ou'bidiənt/ a obediente, sumiso, dócil. **to be o. to,** ser obediente (a), obedecer (a)

obediently /ou'bidiəntli/ adv obedientemente, dócilmente. **Yours o.,** Su atento servidor (su att. s.)

obeisance /ou'beisəns, ou'bi-/ n reverencia, cortesía, f, saludo, m; (homage) homenaje, m

obelisk /'ɒbəlɪsk/ n obelisco, m

obese /ou'bis/ a obeso, corpulento, grueso, gordo

obesity /ou'bisɪti/ n obesidad, gordura, corpulencia, f

obey /ou'bei/ vt and vi obedecer. vt (carry out) cumplir, observar. **to be obeyed,** ser obedecido

obfuscate /'ɒbfə‚skeit/ vt ofuscar, cegar

obfuscation /‚ɒbfə'skeiʃən/ n ofuscamiento, m, confusión, f

obituary /ou'bɪtʃu‚ɛri/ a mortuorio, necrológico. n obituario, m, necrología, f. **o. column,** (in newspaper) sección necrológica, f. **o. notice,** esquela de defunción, f

object /n. 'ɒbdʒɪkt; v. əb'dʒɛkt/ n objeto, artículo, m, cosa, f; (purpose) propósito, intento, m; (aim) fin, término, m; Gram. complemento, m; Inf. individuo, m. vt objetar, poner reparos (a). vi oponerse, poner objeciones. **I o. to that remark,** Protesto contra esa observación. **If you don't o.,** Si Vd. no tiene inconveniente. **o. finder,** objetivo, m. **o. lesson,** lección de cosas, f; lección práctica, f. **direct o.,** complemento directo, m; **indirect o.,** complemento indirecto, **o. of the preposition,** complemento circunstancial

objection /əb'dʒɛkʃən/ n objeción, protesta, f, reparo, m; (obstacle) dificultad, f, inconveniente, m. **to have no o.,** no tener inconveniente. **to raise an o.,** hacer constar una protesta, poner una objeción

objectionable /əb'dʒɛkʃənəbəl/ a censurable, reprensible; desagradable, molesto

objective /əb'dʒɛktɪv/ a objetivo; Gram. acusativo. n objeto, propósito, m; destinación, f; Mil. objetivo, m, Gram. **o. case,** caso acusativo, m,

objectivism /əb'dʒɛktə‚vɪzəm/ n Philos. objetivismo, m

objectivity /‚ɒbdʒɪk'tɪvɪti/ n objetividad, f

objector /ɒb'dʒɛktər/ n objetante, mf, impugnador (-ra). **conscientious o.,** (dissident) el, m, (f, la) que protesta contra; (pacifist) pacifista, mf

oblation /ɒ'bleiʃən/ n oblación, ofrenda, f

obligation /‚ɒblɪ'geiʃən/ n obligación, f; deber, m, precisión, f; compromiso, m. **of o.,** de deber; de precepto. **to be under an o.,** estar bajo una obligación; deber un favor. **to place under an o.,** poner bajo una obligación

obligatory /ə'blɪgə‚tɔri/ a obligatorio, forzoso

oblige /ə'blaidʒ/ vt (insist on) obligar, hacer, forzar; (gratify) hacer un favor (a), complacer. **He obliged me with a match,** Me hizo el favor de una cerilla. **They are much obliged to you,** Le están muy reconocidos. **Much obliged!** ¡Se agradece!

obliging /ə'blaidʒɪŋ/ a atento, condescendiente, complaciente, servicial, Lat. Am. acomedido

obligingly /ə'blaidʒɪŋli/ adv cortésmente

obligingness /ə'blaidʒɪŋnɪs/ n cortesía, amabilidad, bondad, f

oblique /ə'blik/ a oblicuo, sesgado; (indirect) indirecto, evasivo; Gram. oblicuo

obliquely /ə'blikli/ adv oblicuamente, al sesgo, sesgadamente; indirectamente. **to place o.,** poner al sesgo

obliquity /ə'blɪkwɪti/ n oblicuidad, f, sesgo, m; (of conduct, etc.) tortuosidad, f

obliterate /ə'blɪtə‚reit/ vt borrar; destruir, aniquilar. **to be obliterated,** borrarse; quedar destruido

obliteration /ə‚blɪtə'reiʃən/ n testación, f; destrucción, f. **o. raid,** bombardeo de saturación, m

oblivion /ə'blɪviən/ n olvido, m. **to cast into o.,** echar al olvido

oblivious /ə'blɪviəs/ a olvidadizo, descuidago

oblong /'ɒb‚lɔŋ/ a oblongo, cuadrilongo, rectangular. n rectángulo, cuadrilongo, m

obloquy /'ɒbləkwi/ n infamia, maledicencia, deshonra, f

obnoxious /əb'nɒkʃəs/ a odioso, ofensivo, aborrecible

obnoxiously /əb'nɒkʃəsli/ adv odiosamente

obnoxiousness /əb'nɒkʃəsnɪs/ n odiosidad, f

oboe /'oubou/ n Mus. oboe, m. **o. player,** oboe, m

obol /'ɒbəl/ n óbolo, m

obscene /əb'sin/ a indecente, obsceno, escabroso

obscenely /əb'sinli/ adv obscenamente, escabrosamente

obscenity /əb'sɛnɪti/ n indecencia, obscenidad, f

obscurantism /əb'skyurən‚tɪzəm/ n obscurantismo, m

obscurantist /əb'skyurəntɪst/ a and n obscurantista mf

obscure /əb'skyur/ a (indistinct) obscuro, indistinto; (dark) lóbrego, tenebroso; (remote) retirado, apartado; (puzzling) confuso; (unknown) desconocido; humilde; (difficult to understand) abstruso, obscuro; (vague) vago. vt obscurecer; (hide) esconder; (eclipse) eclipsar. **to o. the issue,** hacer perder de vista el problema

obscurely /əb'skyurli/ adv obscuramente; humildemente, retiradamente; confusamente; vagamente

obscurity /əb'skyurɪti/ n (darkness) obscuridad, lobreguez, f; (difficulty of meaning) ambigüedad, confusión, vaguedad, f; humildad, f

obsequies /'ɒbsɪkwiz/ n pl exequias, f pl, ritos fúnebres, m pl

obsequious /əb'sikwiəs/ a servil, empalagoso, zalamero

obsequiously /əb'sikwiəsli/ adv servilmente

obsequiousness /əb'sikwiəsnɪs/ n servilismo, m, sumisión, f

observable /əb'zɜrvəbəl/ a observable, perceptible, visible; notable

observably /əb'zɜrvəbli/ adv notablemente

observance /əb'zɜrvəns/ n observancia, f, cumplimiento, m; práctica, costumbre, f; (religious) rito, m

observant /əb'zɜrvənt/ a observador; obediente, atento. **o. of,** observador de; atento a

observation /,ɒbzɜr'veiʃən/ n observación, f, examen, escrutinio, m; (experience) experiencia, f; (remark) advertencia, f, comento, m. **to escape o.,** no ser advertido. **o. car.,** vagón-mirador, m, **o. post,** puesto de observación, m

observatory /əb'zɜrvə,tɔri/ n observatorio, m

observe /əb'zɜrv/ vt (laws) cumplir; (holy days, etc.) guardar; (notice) observar, mirar, notar, ver, reparar en; (remark) decir, advertir; (examine) vigilar, atisbar, examinar; Astron. observar. vi ser observador. **to o. silence,** guardar silencio

observer /əb'zɜrvər/ n observador (-ra)

obsess /əb'sɛs/ vt obsesionar, obcecar

obsessed /əb'sɛst/ a obseso

obsession /əb'sɛʃən/ n obsesión, obcecación, idea fija, manía, f

obsidian /əb'sɪdiən/ n Mineral. obsidiana, f

obsolescent /,ɒbsə'lɛsənt/ a que se hace antiguo, que cae en desuso

obsolete /,ɒbsə'lit/ a obsoleto, anticuado; Biol. rudimentario, atrofiado

obstacle /'ɒbstəkəl/ n obstáculo, impedimento, m; dificultad, f, inconveniente, m. **to put obstacles in the way of,** Fig. dificultar, hacer difícil. **o. race,** carrera de obstáculos, f

obstetric /əb'stɛtrɪk/ a obstétrico

obstetrician /,ɒbstɪ'trɪʃən/ n obstétrico (-ea), médico (-ca) partero (-ra)

obstetrics /əb'stɛtrɪks/ n obstetricia, tocología, f

obstinacy /'ɒbstənəsi/ n obstinación, terquedad, tenacidad, porfía, f, tesón, m; persistencia, f

obstinate /'ɒbstənɪt/ a terco, porfiado, obstinado, tenaz; refractario; persistente, pertinaz. **to be o.,** ser terco; porfiar. **to be o. about,** obstinarse en.

obstinately /'ɒbstənɪtli/ adv tercamente

obstreperous /əb'strɛpərəs/ a turbulento, ruidoso

obstruct /əb'strʌkt/ vt obstruir: impedir; cerrar; (thwart) estorbar; (hinder) dificultar, embarazar; (the traffic) obstruir, atascar. vi estorbar. **to become obstructed,** obstruirse, cerrarse

obstruction /əb'strʌkʃən/ n obstrucción, f; estorbo, obstáculo, m. **to cause a street o.,** obstruir el tráfico

obstructionism /əb'strʌkʃə,nɪzəm/ n obstruccionismo, m

obstructionist /əb'strʌkʃənɪst/ n obstruccionista, mf

obstructive /əb'strʌktɪv/ a estorbador, obstructor

obtain /əb'tein/ vt obtener, conseguir, lograr; recibir; (by threats) arrancar. vi estar en boga, estar en vigor, predominar. **to o. on false pretenses,** conseguir por engaño

obtainable /əb'teinəbəl/ a asequible, alcanzable. **easily o.,** fácil a obtener

obtainer /əb'teinər/ n conseguidor (-ra), adquisidor (-ra)

obtainment /əb'teinmənt/ n obtención, f, logro, m

obtrude /əb'trud/ vt imponer

obtrusion /əb'truʒən/ n imposición, f; importunidad, f

obtrusive /əb'trusɪv/ a importuno; entremetido; pretencioso

obtrusiveness /əb'trusɪvnɪs/ n importunidad, f; entremetimiento, m

obtuse /əb'tus/ a (blunt) obtuso, romo; (stupid) estúpido, torpe, lerdo. **o. angle,** obtusángulo, m

obtuseness /əb'tusnɪs/ n (bluntness) embotamiento, m; (stupidity) estupidez, torpeza, f

obverse / a. ɒb'vɜrs; n. 'ɒbvɜrs/ a del anverso. n anverso, m

obviate /'ɒbvi,eit/ vt obviar, evitar

obvious /'ɒbviəs/ a evidente, manifiesto, patente, obvio, aparente, transparente; poco sutil

obviously /'ɒbviəsli/ adv evidentemente, patentemente

obviousness /'ɒbviəsnɪs/ n evidencia, transparencia, f

occasion /ə'keiʒən/ n ocasión, f; oportunidad, f, momento oportuno, tiempo propicio, m; (reason) motivo, origen, m, causa, razón, f; (need) necesidad, f. vt ocasionar, causar, producir. **as o. demands,** cuando las circunstancias lo exigen, en caso necesario. **for the o.,** para la ocasión. **on one o.,** una vez. **on the o. of,** en la ocasión de. **on that o.,** en tal ocasión, en aquella ocasión. **He has given me no o. to say so,** No me ha dado motivos de decirlo. **There is no o. for it,** No hay necesidad para ello. **to have o. to,** haber de, tener que, necesitar. **to lose no o.,** no perder ripio (or oportunidad). **to rise to the o.,** estar al nivel de las circunstancias. **to take this o.,** aprovechar esta oportunidad

occasional /ə'keiʒənl/ a (occurring at times) de vez en cuando, intermitente; poco frecuente, infrecuente; (of verse) de ocasión. **o. table,** mesilla, f

occasionally /ə'keiʒənļi/ adv de vez en cuando, de cuando en cuando

occiput /'ɒksə,pʌt/ n Anat. occipucio, m

occlude /ə'klud/ vt obstruir, cerrar; Med. ocluir; Chem. absorber

occlusion /ə'kluʒən/ n cerramiento, m; Med. oclusión, f; Chem. absorción de gases, f

occlusive /ə'klusɪv/ a oclusivo

occult /ə'kʌlt/ a oculto, escondido, misterioso; mágico. **o. sciences,** creencias ocultas, f pl

occultation /,ɒkʌl'teiʃən/ n Astron. ocultación, f, eclipse, m

occultism /ə'kʌltɪzəm/ n ocultismo, m

occultist /ə'kʌltɪst/ n ocultista, mf

occupancy /'ɒkyəpənsi/ n ocupación, posesión, f; (tenancy) tenencia, f

occupant /'ɒkyəpənt/ n habitante, mf; ocupante, mf; (tenant) inquilino (-na)

occupation /,ɒkyə'peiʃən/ n ocupación f; (tenure) inquilinato, m, tenencia, f; (work) trabajo, quehacer, m, labor, m; (employment) empleo, oficio, m; profesión, f

occupational /,ɒkyə'peiʃənļ/ a de oficio. **o. disease,** enfermedad profesional, f

occupier /'ɒkyə,paiər/ n ocupante, mf, inquilino (-na)

occupy /'ɒkyə,pai/ vt ocupar; (live in) vivir en, habitar; (time) emplear, pasar; (take over) apoderarse de, ocupar. **to o. oneself in or with,** ocuparse en, ocuparse con. **to be occupied in or with,** estar ocupado con, ocuparse en

occur /ə'kɜr/ vi (happen) suceder, tener lugar, acaecer; (exist) encontrarse, existir; (of ideas) ocurrirse, venirse. **to o. to one's mind,** venírsele a las mientes. **to o. again,** volver a suceder, ocurrir de nuevo. **An idea occurred to her,** Se le ocurrió una idea

occurrence /ə'kɜrəns/ n ocurrencia, f; incidente, suceso, acontecimiento, m. **to be of frequent o.,** ocurrir con frecuencia, acontecer a menudo

ocean /'ouʃən/ n océano, m; Fig. mar, abundancia, f. **o.-going vessel,** buque de alta mar, m

Oceania /,ouʃi'æniə/ el Mundo Novísmo, m

oceanic /,ouʃi'ænɪk/ a oceánico

oceanography /,ouʃə'nɒgrəfi/ n oceanografía, f

ocelot /'ɒsə,lɒt/ n Zool. ocelote, m

ocher /'oukər/ n ocre, m

octagon /'ɒktə,gɒn/ n octágono, m

octagonal /ɒk'tægən/ a octagonal

octave /'ɒktɪv/ n (Eccl. metrics, Mus.) octava, f

octavo /ɒk'teivou, -'ta-/ n Print. libro, etc. en octavo (8°), m. **in o.,** en octavo. **large o.,** octavo mayor, m. **small o.,** octavo menor, m

octet /ɒk'tɛt/ n Mus. octeto, m

October /ɒk'toubər/ n octubre, m. **October 2, 1996,** el segundo (2°) de octubre de mil novecientos noventa y seis, **October 2, 2000,** el segundo de octubre del dos mil

octogenarian /ˌɒktədʒəˈnɛəriən/ a and n octogenario (-ia)

octopus /ˈɒktəpəs/ n pulpo, m

ocular /ˈɒkyələr/ a ocular, visual. n ocular, m

oculist /ˈɒkyəlɪst/ n oculista, mf

odd /ɒd/ a (of numbers) impar; (of volumes, etc.) suelto; (strange) raro, curioso, extraño, extravagante; (casual) casual, accidental; (extra) y pico, y tantos, sobrante; (of gloves, etc.) sin pareja. **at odd moments,** en momentos de ocio. **at odd times,** de vez en cuando. **thirty odd,** treinta y pico. **odd number,** número impare, m. **odd or even,** pares o impares.

odd trick, (at cards) una baza más

oddity /ˈɒdɪti/ n excentricidad, rareza, extravagancia, f; (person) ente singular, m; (curio) objeto curioso, m, antigüedad, f

oddly /ˈɒdli/ adv singularmente, curiosamente

oddment /ˈɒdmənt/ n bagatela, baratija, f

oddness /ˈɒdnɪs/ n singularidad, rareza, extravagancia, f

odds /ɒdz/ n pl diferencia, desigualdad, f; (superiority) ventaja, superioridad, f; (quarrel) disputa, riña, f. **The o. are that...,** Lo más probable es que... **to fight against dreadful o.,** luchar contra fuerzas muy superiores. **o. and ends,** (remains) sobras y picos, f pl; (trifles) ñaques, m pl, chucherías, f pl

Odessa /ouˈdɛsə/ Odesa, f

odious /ˈoudiəs/ a odioso, detestable, aborrecible, repugnante

odiousness /ˈoudiəsnɪs/ n odiosidad, f

odium /ˈoudiəm/ n odio, m

odor /ˈoudər/ n olor, m, (fragrance) perfume, aroma, m, fragancia, f; Fig. sospecha, f. **in bad o.,** Fig. en disfavor. **o. of sanctity,** olor de santidad, m

odoriferous /ˌoudəˈrɪfərəs/ a odorífero; (perfumed) oloroso, perfumado

odorless /ˈoudərlɪs/ a inodoro

odorous /ˈoudərəs/ a fragante, oloroso

odyssey /ˈɒdəsi/ n odisea, f

Oedipus complex /ˈɛdəpəs/ n complejo de Edipo, m

of /əv/ prep de. **of** has many idiomatic translations which are given as far as possible under the heading of the word concerned. It is also not translated. **I robbed him of his reward,** Le robé su recompensa. **I was thinking of you,** Pensaba en tí. **It was very good of you to...,** Vd. ha tenido mucha bondad de... **Your naming of the child Mary,** El que Vd. haya dado el nombre de María al niño. **29th of Sept., 1936,** el 2ᵒ de septiembre de 1936. **Of course!** ¡Claro está! ¡Ya lo creo! ¡Naturalmente! **of late,** últimamente. **of the** (before m, sing) del; (before f, sing) de la; (before m pl) de los; (before f pl) de las. **to dream of,** soñar con. **to smell of,** oler a tener olor de. **to taste of, etc.,** saber a, tener gusto de.

off /ɒf/ prep de; fuera de; cerca de; desde; Naut. a la altura de. **from off,** de. **Take your gloves off the table!** ¡Quítate los guantes de la mesa! **The wheel was off the car,** La rueda se había desprendido del coche. **to be off duty,** no estar de servicio; Mil. no estar de guardia. **to lunch off cold meat,** almorzar de carne fría. **off one's head,** chiflado

off /ɒf/ a (contrasted with near) de la derecha, derecho; (unlikely) improbable, remoto. adv (with intransitive verbs of motion) se (e.g. He has gone off, Se ha marchado); (contrasted with on) de (e.g. He has fallen off the horse, Ha caído del caballo); (of place at a distance) lejos, a distancia de; (of time) generally a verb is used (e.g. The wedding is three months off, Faltan tres meses para la boda); (completely) enteramente. **Off** is often not translated in Sp. (e.g. to put off, aplazar, to cut off, cortar). **day off,** día libre, día de asueto, m. **How far off is the house from here? The house is five miles off.** ¿Cuántas millas está la casa de aquí? La casa está a cinco millas de aquí. **His hat is off,** Está sin sombrero, Se ha quitado el sombrero. **The cover is off,** La cubierta está quitada. **The party is off,** Se ha anulado la reunión. **6% off,** un descuento de seis por ciento. interj **Off with you!** ¡Márchate! ¡Fuera! **off and on,** de vez en cuando, espasmódicamente. **off color,** (ill) malucho; (of jokes)

verde. **off season,** estación muerta, f. **off-shore,** a vista de tierra. **off-stage,** entre bastidores

offal /ˈɒfəl/ n (butchers') menudencias, f pl, asadura, f, menudos, despojos, m pl; desperdicio, m

offend /əˈfɛnd/ vt ofender; agraviar, insultar; herir; desagradar, disgustar; vi ofender, pecar. **to be offended,** resentirse, insultarse. **This offends my sense of justice,** Esto ofende mi sentimiento de justicia. **to o. against,** pecar contra; violar

offender /əˈfɛndər/ n delincuente, mf; agraviador (-ra), pecador (-ra), transgresor (-ra). **old o.,** Law. criminal inveterado, m

offense /əˈfɛns/ n ofensa, transgresión, violación, f; pecado, m; Law. delito, crimen, m; (insult) agravio, m, afrenta, f. **the first o.,** el primer delito, m. **fresh o.,** nuevo delito, m. **political o.,** crimen político, m. **technical o.,** Law. cuasidelito, m. **to commit an o. against,** ofender contra. **to take o.,** resentirse, darse por ofendido

offensive /əˈfɛnsɪv/ a ofensivo, desagradable, repugnante; (insulting) injurioso, agraviador, agresivo. n Mil. ofensiva, f. **to take the o.,** tomar la ofensiva

offensiveness /əˈfɛnsɪvnɪs/ n lo desagradable; (insult) ofensa, f; lo injurioso

offer /ˈɒfər/ n oferta, f; ofrecimiento, m; (of help) promesa, f; proposición, f; Com. oferta, f. vt ofrecer; prometer; (opportunities, etc.) deparar, brindar; tributar. vi ofrecerse, ocurrir, surgir. **to o. up,** ofrecer; inmolar, sacrificar. **He did not offer to go,** No hizo además de marcharse. **to o. resistance,** oponer resistencia. **o. of marriage,** oferta de matrimonio, f

offerer /ˈɒfərər/ n ofrecedor (-ra)

offering /ˈɒfərɪŋ/ n ofrecimiento, m; Eccl. ofrenda, oblación, f, sacrificio, m; regalo, don, m, dádiva, f

offhand /ˈɒfˈhænd/ a sin preparación, de repente; (casual) casual, despreocupado; (discourteous) brusco, descortés

offhandedly /ˈɒfˈhændɪdli/ adv sin preparación, espontáneamente; negligentemente; bruscamente

office /ˈɒfɪs/ n oficina, m; (post) cargo, puesto, destino, m; (state department) ministerio, m; (of a Cabinet minister) cartera, f; (room) oficina, f; despacho, escritorio, m; (of a newspaper) redacción, f; (lawyer's) bufete, m; departamento, m; Eccl. oficio, m pl; Eccl. oficios, m pl. **domestic offices,** dependencias, f pl. **good offices,** Fig. buenos oficios, m pl. **head o.,** casa central, oficina principal, f. **private o.,** despacho particular, m. **to be in o.,** estar en el poder. **o.-bearer,** miembro de la junta, m; funcionario, m. **o.-boy,** mozo de oficina, m. **o. employee,** oficinista, mf. **o. hours,** horas de oficina, f pl; (professions) horas de consulta, f pl. **o.-seeker,** aspirante, m; pretendiente, m. **o. work,** trabajo de oficina, m

officer /ˈɒfəsər/ n oficial, funcionario, m; (police) agente de policía, m; (of the Church) dignatario, m; (Mil. Nav. Aer.) oficial, m. vt mandar. **commissioned o.,** oficial, m. **non-commissioned o.,** oficial subalterno, m. **to be well officered,** tener buena oficialidad. **Officers' Training Corps,** Escuela de Oficiales, f

office worker n oficinista, mf

official /əˈfɪʃəl/ a oficial; autorizado; ceremonioso, grave. n funcionario, m; oficial público, m. **high o.,** funcionario importante, m. **o. mourning,** duelo oficial, m. **o. receiver,** fiscal de quiebras, m

officialdom /əˈfɪʃəldəm/ n funcionarismo, m; círculos oficiales, m pl

officiant /əˈfɪʃiənt/ n oficiante, m

officiate /əˈfɪʃiˌeit/ vi celebrar; oficiar, funcionar

officiating /əˈfɪʃiˌeitɪŋ/ a oficiante; celebrante. **o. priest,** sacerdote oficiante, celebrante, m

officious /əˈfɪʃəs/ a oficioso, entremetido

officiousness /əˈfɪʃəsnɪs/ n oficiosidad, f

off season fuera de temporada

offset /n. ˈɒfˌsɛt; v. ˌɒfˈsɛt/ n compensación, f, vt compensar, neutralizar

offshoot /ˈɒfˌʃut/ n renuevo, vástago, m

offside /ˈɒfˈsaid/ a (of a car) del lado derecho (or izquierda); Sports. fuera de juego

offspring /'ɔf,sprɪŋ/ n vástago, m; descendiente, mf; prole, f; hijos, m pl
often /'ɔfən/ adv a menudo, mucho, con frecuencia, frecuentemente, muchas veces. **as o. as**, tan a menudo como, siempre que. **as o. as not**, no pocas veces. **How o.?** ¿Cuántas veces? **It is not o. that...**, No ocurre con frecuencia que... **so o.**, tantas veces, con frecuencia. **Do you go there o.?** ¿Va Vd. allí con frecuencia (or frecuentemente)? **Not o.**, Voy rara vez allá
ogival /'oudʒaivəl/ a Archit. ojival
ogive /'oudʒaiv/ n Archit. ojiva, f
ogle /'ougəl/ vt and vi comer(se) con los ojos (a), ojear, guiñar el ojo (a). n ojeada, f, guiño, m
ogling /'ouglɪŋ/ n guiño, m, ojeada, f
ogre /'ougər/ n ogro, m
oh! /ou/ interj ¡o! **O no!** ¡Ca! ¡Claro que no!
ohm /oum/ n Elec. ohmio, m
oil /ɔil/ n aceite, m; petróleo, m; óleo, m. vt aceitar, engrasar, Argentina enaceitar; olear, ungir, untar; (bribe) sobornar, untar la mano; Fig. suavizar. a aceitero; petrolero. **to pour oil on troubled waters,** echar aceite sobre aguas turbulentas. **to strike oil,** encontrar un pozo de petróleo; Fig. encontrar un filón. **crude oil,** petróleo bruto, m. **heavy oil,** aceite pesado, m. **thin oil,** aceite ligero, m. Art. **in oils,** al óleo. **oil-bearing,** petrolífero. **oil-box,** engrasador, m. **oil-burner,** quemador de petróleo, m. **oil-can,** aceitera, f. **oil-colors,** pinturas al óleo, f pl. **oil field,** yacimiento petrolífero, campo de petróleo, m. **oil-filter,** separador de aceite, m. **oil-gauge,** nivel de aceite, m. **oil lamp,** velón, candil, quinqué, m. **oil of turpentine,** aceite de trementina, aguarrás, m. esencia de trementina, f. **oil-painting,** pintura al óleo, f. **oil pipeline,** oleoducto, m. **oil shop,** aceitería, f. **oil-silk,** encerado, m. **oil stove,** estufa de petróleo, f. **oil tanker,** Naut. petrolero, m. **oil-well,** pozo de petróleo, m
oilcake /'ɔil,keik/ n bagazo, m
oilcloth /'ɔil,klɔθ/ n hule, m; linóleo, m
oiler /'ɔilər/ n (can) aceitera, f; Naut. petrolero, m; lubricador, m
oiliness /'ɔilinɪs/ n oleaginosidad, untuosidad, f
oiling /'ɔilɪŋ/ n engrasado, m
oil seed n semilla oleaginosa, f
oilskin /'ɔil,skɪn/ n encerado, m
oily /'ɔili/ a aceitoso, grasiento
ointment /'ɔintmənt/ n ungüento, m, pomada, f
old /ould/ a viejo; antiguo, anciano; (of wines, etc.) añejo; (worn out) usado, gastado; (inveterate) arraigado, inveterado. **How old are you?** ¿Cuántos años tiene usted? **to be sixteen years old,** tener dieciséis años. **He is old enough to know his own mind,** Tiene bastante edad para saber lo que quiere. **to grow old,** envejecer. **of old,** antiguamente. **prematurely old,** revejido averiado. **old age,** vejez, senectud, f. **old bachelor,** solterón, m. **old clothes,** ropa vieja (or usada), ropa de segunda mano, f. **old-clothes dealer,** ropavejero (-ra). **old-clothes shop,** ropavejería, f. **old-established,** viejo. **old-fashioned,** pasado de moda, viejo; (of people) chapado a la antigua. **old lady,** anciana, dama vieja, f. **old-looking,** de aspecto viejo, avejentado. **old maid,** solterona, f. **old-maidish,** remilgado. **old man,** viejo, m; Theat. barba, m. **old salt,** lobo de mar, m. **Old Testament,** Antiguo Testamento, m. **old wives' tale,** cuento de viejas, m. **old woman,** vieja, f. **Old World,** Viejo Mundo, mundo antiguo, m.
old-age home /'ould 'eidʒ/ n asilo de ancianos, m
olden /'ouldən/ a antiguo. **o. days,** días pasados, m pl
older /'ouldər/ a comp más viejo, mayor. **The older the madder,** A la vejez viruelas
old hat n viejo conocido
oldish /'ouldɪʃ/ a bastante viejo, de cierta edad
oldness /'ouldnɪs/ n antigüedad, ancianidad, edad, f
oleaginous /,ouli'ædʒənəs/ a oleaginoso
oleander /'ouli,ændər/ n Bot. adelfa, f, baladre, m
olfactory /ɒl'fæktəri/ a olfactorio, olfativo
oligarchic /,ɒlɪ'gɑrkɪk/ a oligárquico
oligarchy /'ɒlɪ,gɑrki/ n oligarquía, f
olive /'ɒlɪv/ n (tree) olivo, m; (fruit) aceituna, oliva,

f, a aceitunado, Lat. Am. aceituno. **wild o. tree,** acebuche, m. **o.-complected,** con tez aceitunada. **o. green,** verde oliva, m. **o. grove,** olivar, m. **o. oil,** aceite de oliva, m
olympiad /ə'lɪmpi,æd/ n olimpíada, f
olympian /ə'lɪmpiən/ a olímpico
olympic /ə'lɪmpɪk/ a olímpico. **o. games,** juegos olímpicos, m pl
olympus /ə'lɪmpəs/ n olimpo, m
omasum /ou'meisəm/ n Zool. librillo, libro, m
omber /'ɒmbər/ n tresillo, hombre, m
omega /ou'migə, ou'mei-/ n omega, f
omelet /'ɒmlɪt/ n tortilla, f. **sweet o.,** tortilla dulce, f
omen /'oumən/ n pronóstico, presagio, agüero, m, vt agorar, anunciar
ominous /'ɒmənəs/ a ominoso, azaroso, siniestro, amenazante
ominously /'ɒmənəsli/ adv ominosamente, con amenazas
omission /ou'mɪʃən/ n omisión, f; olvido, descuido, m; supresión, f
omit /ou'mɪt/ vt omitir; olvidar; descuidar; (suppress) suprimir, excluir, callar, dejar a un lado
omitting /ou'mɪtɪŋ/ pres part salvo, excepto
omnibus /'ɒmnə,bʌs/ n ómnibus, autobús, m. **o. conductor,** cobrador de autobús, m. **o. driver,** conductor de autobús, m. **o. route,** trayecto de autobús, m. **o. service,** servicio de autobuses, m. **o. volume,** volumen de obras coleccionadas, m
omnipotence /ɒm'nɪpətəns/ n omnipotencia, f
omnipotent /ɒm'nɪpətənt/ a omnipotente, todopoderoso
omnipresence /,ɒmnə'prɛzəns/ n omnipresencia, ubicuidad, f
omnipresent /,ɒmnə'prɛzənt/ a ubicuo
omniscience /ɒm'nɪʃəns/ n omnisciencia, f
omniscient /ɒm'nɪʃənt/ a omniscio, omnisciente
omnivorous /ɒm'nɪvərəs/ a omnívoro
on /ɒn/ prep (upon) sobre, en, encima de; (concerning) de, acerca de, sobre; (against) contra; (after) después; (according to) según; (with gerund) en; (with infin.) al; (at) a; (connected with, employed in) de; (by means of) por, mediante; (near to) cerca de, sobre; (into) en. Untranslated before days of week, dates of month or time of day (e.g. on Monday, el lunes. on Friday afternoons, los viernes por la tarde). **She has a bracelet on her wrist,** Tiene una pulsera en la muñeca. **He will retire on a good income,** Se jubilará con una buena renta. **on my uncle's death,** después de la muerte (or a la muerte) de mi tío, al morir. **on leave,** con licencia, en uso de licencia. **on the next page,** en la página siguiente. **on this occasion,** en esta ocasión. **on the other hand,** en cambio. **on second thoughts,** luego de pensarlo bien. **on the way,** en camino. **on one side,** a un lado. **on the left,** a la izquierda. **on time,** a tiempo. **on my honor,** bajo palabra de honor. **on pain of death,** so pena de muerte, bajo pena de muerte. **on an average,** por término medio. **on his part,** por su parte. **on and after,** desde, a partir de. **on credit,** de fiado. **on fire,** ardiendo, en llamas. **on foot,** a pie. **on purpose,** a propósito. **on,** adv puesto (e.g. She has her gloves on, Tiene los guantes puestos); (forward) adelante, hacia adelante; (continue, with a verb) seguir, continuar (e.g. He went on talking, Siguió hablando). Often **on** is included in Sp. verb (e.g. The new play is on, Se ha estrenado la nueva comedia. The fight is on, Ya ha empezado la lucha). **On!** interj ¡Adelante! **and so on,** y así sucesivamente. **to have on,** llevar puesto. **on and off,** de vez en cuando. **on and on,** sin cesar
onanism /'ounə,nɪzəm/ n onanismo, m
once /wʌns/ adv una vez; (formerly) en otro tiempo, antiguamente; conjunc si (e.g. O. you give him the opportunity, Si le das la oportunidad). **all at o.,** todo junto, a un mismo tiempo; simultáneamente; (suddenly) súbitamente, de repente. **at o.,** en seguida, inmediatamente, Lat. Am. también lueguito. **for o.,** por una vez. **more than o.,** más de una vez. **not o.,** ni siquiera una vez. **o. before,** una vez antes. **o. and for**

all, una vez para siempre; por última vez. **o. in a while,** de vez en cuando. **o. more,** otra vez. **o. or twice,** una vez o dos, algunas veces. **o. too often,** una vez demasiado. **O. upon a time,** En tiempos pasados, En tiempos de Maricastaña; (as beginning of a story) Érase una vez, Había una vez, Hubo una vez **once in a blue moon** a cada muerte de un obispo

one /wʌn/ *a* un, uno, una; (first) primero; (single) único, solo; (indifferent) igual, indiferente; (some, certain) algún, cierto, un (e.g. *one day,* cierto día). *n* uno; (hour) la una; (of age) un año. Often not translated in Sp. (e.g. *I shall take the blue one,* Tomaré el azul). *pron* se; uno. **one's,** su, de uno (e.g. *one's work,* el trabajo de uno). **I for one do not think so,** Yo por uno no lo creo. **It is all one,** Es igual, No hace diferencia alguna. **only one,** un solo. **that one,** ése, *m,* ésa, *f,* eso, *neut.* **this one,** éste, *m,* ésta, *f,* esto, *neut.* **these ones,** éstos, etc. **those ones,** ésos, etc. **the one,** el (que), *m,* la (que), *f.* **with one accord,** unánimemente. **one and all,** todos. **one another,** se, uno a otro, mutuamente. **one by one,** uno a uno. **one day,** un día; un día de éstos, algún día. **one-eyed,** tuerto. **one-handed,** manco. **one-sided,** parcial. **one-way street,** *Spain* calle de dirección única, *Argentina* calle de una sola mano, *Mexico* calle de un sentido, calle de una corrida, *f.* **one-way traffic,** tráfico en una sola dirección, *m*

oneiric /ouˈnairik/ *a* onírico

oneness /ˈwʌnnis/ *n* unidad, *f*

onerous /ˈɒnərəs/ *a* oneroso, pesado, molesto, gravoso

onerousness /ˈɒnərəsnɪs/ *n* pesadez, molestia, dificultad, inconveniencia, *f*

one-seater /ˈwʌn ˈsitər/ *n* avión de una plaza, *m*

oneself /wʌnˈsɛlf/ *pron* se, uno mismo (una misma); (after prep.) sí mismo, sí. **It must be done by o.,** Uno mismo ha de hacerlo

onion /ˈʌnyən/ *n* cebolla, *f.* **string of onions,** ristra de cebollas, *f.* **young o.,** babosa, *f.* **o. bed,** cebollar, *m.* **o. seed,** cebolino, *m.* **o. seller,** cebollero (-ra)

on-line /ˈɒnˈlain, ˈɒn-/ *a* conectado, en línea

onlooker /ˈɒnˌlʊkər/ *n* espectado (-ra), observador (-ra); testigo, *mf*

only /ˈounli/ *a* único, solo. *adv* únicamente, sólo; no... más (que), tan sólo; con la excepción de, salvo. *conjunc* pero, salvo (que), si no fuera (que). **I shall o. give you three,** No te daré más de tres. **The o. thing one can do,** Lo único que se puede hacer. **I o. wished to see her,** Quería verla nada más. **if o.,** ¡ojalá (que)! **not o....,** no sólo... **o.-begotten,** *a* unigénito. **o. child,** hijo (-ja) único (-ca)

onomatopoeia /ˌɒnəˌmætəˈpiə/ *n* onomatopeya, *f*

onomatopoeic /ˌɒnəˌmætəˈpiik/ *a* onomatopéyico

onrush /ˈɒnˌrʌʃ/ *n* asalto, ataque, acometimiento, *m,* acometida, embestida, *f;* (of water, etc.) acceso, *m;* torrente, *m,* corriente, *f*

onset /ˈɒnˌsɛt/ *n* ataque, *m,* acometida, *f;* (beginning) principio, *m.* **at the first o.,** al primer ímpetu

onslaught /ˈɒnˌslɔt/ *n* asalto, ataque, *m*

onus /ˈounəs/ *n* responsabilidad, *f.* **o. of proof,** obligación de probar, *f*

onward /ˈɒnwərd/ *a* progresivo. *adv* adelante, hacia adelante; (as a command) ¡Adelante!

onyx /ˈɒnɪks/ *n* ónice, *m*

ooze /uz/ *n* légamo, limo, fango, *m,* lama, *f. vi* exudar, rezumarse; manar; *vt* sudar. **to o. satisfaction,** caérsele (a uno) la baba. **to o. away,** (of money, etc.) desaparecer, volar. **to o. out,** (news) divulgarse

oozing /ˈuzɪŋ/ *a* fangoso, legamoso, lamoso

opacity /ouˈpæsɪti/ *n* opacidad, *f*

opal /ˈoupəl/ *n* ópalo, *m*

opalescence /ˌoupəˈlɛsəns/ *n* opalescencia, *f*

opalescent /ˌoupəˈlɛsənt/ *a* opalescente, iridiscente

opaline /ˈoupəlin/ *a* opalino

opaque /ouˈpeik/ *a* opaco

opaqueness /ouˈpeiknɪs/ *n* opacidad, *f*

op. cit. /ˈɒpˈsit/ (opere citato) obra cit. (obra citada)

open /ˈoupən/ *vt* abrir; (a package) desempaquetar, desenvolver; (remove lid) destapar; *Lat. Am.* desenlatar (canned food); (unfold) desplegar; (inaugurate)

inaugurar; iniciar, empezar; establecer; (an abscess) cortar; (with arms, heart, eyes) abrir; (with mind, thought) descubrir, revelar; (make accessible) franquear, hacer accesible; (tear) romper; *vi* abrirse; empezar, comenzar; (of a view, etc.) aparecer, extenderse; inaugurarse; (of a career, etc.) prepararse. **to o. fire against,** abrir el fuego contra. **to o. into,** comunicar con, salir a. **to o. into each other,** (of rooms) comunicarse. **to o. on,** mirar a, dar a, caer a. **to o. out,** *vt* abrir; desplegar; revelar. *vi* extenderse; revelarse. **to o. the eyes of,** *Fig.* desengañar, desilusionar. **to o. up,** abrir; explorar, hacer accesible; revelar; *Fig. Inf.* desabrocharse. **to o. with** or **by,** empezar con

open /ˈoupən/ *a* abierto; descubierto; expuesto; (unfenced) descercado; (not private) público; libre; (unfolded) desplegado, extendido; (persuasible) receptivo; no resuelto, pendiente; (frank) franco, candoroso; (with sea) alto; (liberal) generoso, hospitalario; sin prejuicios; *Com.* abierto, pendiente; sin defensa; (of weather) despejado; (of a letter) sin sellar; (without a lid) destapado; (well-known) manifiesto, bien conocido. *n* aire libre, *m.* **in the o.,** al descubierto. **in the o. air,** al aire libre, al raso, a cielo abierto. **to break o.,** forzar. **to cut o.,** abrir de un tajo, cortar. **to leave o.,** dejar abierto. **wide o.,** muy abierto; (of doors) de par en par. **half o.,** entreabierto. **o. boat,** barco descubierto. **o. car,** coche abierto, *m.* **o. carriage,** carruaje descubierto, *m.* **o. cast,** *Mineral.* roza abierta, *f.* **o.-eyed,** con los ojos abiertos. **o.-handed,** generoso, dadivoso, *Lat. Am. also* maniabierto. **o. letter,** carta abierta, *f.* **o.-minded,** imparcial. **o.-mouthed,** con la boca abierta, boquiabierto. **o. question,** cuestión por decidir, cuestión discutible, *f.* **o. secret,** secreto a voces, *m.* **o. sea,** alta mar, *f.* **o. town,** ciudad abierta, *f.* **o. tramcar,** jardinera, *f.* **o. truck,** vagoneta, *f.* **o.-work,** *Sew.* calado, enrejado, *m*

opener /ˈoupənər/ *n* abridor, *m*

opening /ˈoupənɪŋ/ *n* abertura, brecha, *f;* orificio, *m;* inauguración, apertura, *f;* principio, *m;* (chance) oportunidad, *f;* (employment) puesto, *m.* **o. price,** *Com.* (on Exchange) precio de apertura, *m,* primer curso *m*

openly /ˈoupənli/ *adv* abiertamente, francamente; públicamente

openness /ˈoupənnɪs/ *n* situación expuesta, *f;* espaciosidad, *f;* franqueza, *f,* candor, *m;* imparcialidad, *f*

opera /ˈɒpərə/ *n* ópera, *f.* **comic o.,** zarzuela, *f.* **o.-cloak,** abrigo de noche, *m.* **o.-glasses,** gemelos de teatro, *m pl.* **o.-hat,** clac, *m.* **o.-house,** teatro de la ópera, *m.* **o. singer,** cantante de ópera, operista, *mf*

operate /ˈɒpəˌreit/ *vi* funcionar, trabajar; obrar; (with o. upon) producir efecto sobre; influir; *Surg.* operar; (on Exchange) especular, jugar a la bolsa; *vt* hacer funcionar, manejar; mover, impulsar; dirigir

operatic /ˌɒpəˈrætɪk/ *a* de ópera, operístico

operating /ˈɒpəˌreitɪŋ/ *a* (of surgeons) operante; de operación. **o. table,** mesa de operaciones, *f.* **o. theater,** anfiteatro, *m;* sala de operaciones, *f*

operation /ˌɒpəˈreiʃən/ *n* funcionamiento, *m,* acción, *f;* *Surg.* intervención quirúrgica, operación, *f;* (*Mil. Naut.*) maniobra, *f;* manipulación, *f.* **to come into o.,** ponerse en práctica; hacerse efectivo. **to continue in o.,** (*Law*) seguir en vigor. **to perform an o.,** *Surg.* operar, praticar una intervención quirúrgica; hacer una maniobra. **to put into o.,** poner en práctica

operative /ˈɒpərətɪv/ *a* operativo, activo. *n* operario (-ia), obrero (-ra). **to become o.,** tener efecto

operator /ˈɒpəˌreitər/ *n* operario (-ia); (telephone) telefonista, *mf;* (machines, engines) maquinista, *mf;* *Surg.* operador, *m*

operetta /ˌɒpəˈrɛtə/ *n* opereta, *f*

ophthalmologist /ˌɒfθælˈmɒlədʒɪst/ *n* oftalmólogo, *m*

ophthalmology /ˌɒfθælˈmɒlədʒi/ *n* oftalmología, *f*

opiate /ˈoupiɪt/ *n* opiata, *f,* narcótico, *m,* *a* opiado

opinion /əˈpɪnyən/ *n* opinión, *f,* parecer, juicio, *m;* concepto, *m,* idea, *f.* **in my o.,** según mi parecer. **to be of the o. that,** ser de la opinión que, opinar que. **to be of the same o.,** estar de acuerdo, concurrir. **public o.,** opinión (or voz) pública, *f*

opinionated /əˈpɪnyəˌneitɪd/ *a* terco, obstinado

opium /'oupiəm/ n opio, m. **o. addict,** opiónamo (-ma). **o. den,** fumadero de opio, m. **o. eater,** mascador de opio, opiófago, m. **o. smoker,** fumador (-ra) de opio

Oporto /ou'pɔrtou/ Oporto, Porto, m

opponent /ə'pounənt/ n antagonista, mf, enemigo (-ga); contrario (-ia), adversario (-ia), competidor (-ra)

opportune /,ɒpər'tun/ a oportuno, tempestivo, conveniente, a propósito. **to be o.,** venir al caso. **o. moment,** momento oportuno, m; hora propicia, f

opportunely /,ɒpər'tunli/ adv oportunamente. **to come o.,** venir a pelo

opportuneness /,ɒpər'tunnɪs/ n oportunidad, tempestividad, conveniencia, f

opportunism /,ɒpər'tunɪzəm/ n oportunismo, m

opportunist /,ɒpər'tunɪst/ n oportunista, Lat. Am. also maromero (-ra), mf

opportunity /,ɒpər'tunɪti/ n oportunidad, ocasión, posibilidad, f. **to give an o. for,** dar margen para. **to open new opportunities,** abrir nuevos horizontes. **to take the o.,** tomar la oportunidad

opposable /ə'pouzəbəl/ a oponible

oppose /ə'pouz/ vt (counterbalance) oponer, contrarrestar; combatir; hacer frente (a), contrariar, pugnar contra, oponerse (a)

opposed (to) /ə'pouzd/ a opuesto a, enemigo de, contra

opposing /ə'pouzɪŋ/ a opuesto; enemigo, contrario

opposite /'ɒpəzɪt/ a (facing) de cara a, frente a, del otro lado de; opuesto; (antagonistic) contrario, antagónico; otro, diferente. n contraria, f, lo opuesto; antagonista, mf; adversario (-ia). **the o. sex,** el otro sexo. **o. leaves,** Bot. hojas opuestas, f pl. **o. to,** frente a; distinto de

opposition /,ɒpə'zɪʃən/ n oposición, f; (obstacle) estorbo, impedimento, m, dificultad, f; resistencia, hostilidad, f; (Astron. Polit.) oposición, f; (difference) contraste, m, diferencia, f. a de la oposición. **in o.,** en oposición; Polit. en la oposición. **to be in o.,** estar en oposición; Polit. ser de la oposición, estar en la oposición

oppress /ə'prɛs/ vt oprimir, tiranizar, sojuzgar, apremiar; (of moral causes) abrumar, agobiar, desanimar; (of heat, etc.) ahogar

oppression /ə'prɛʃən/ n opresión, tiranía, crueldad, f; (moral) agobio, sufrimiento, m, ansia, f; (difficulty in breathing) sofocación, f, ahogo, m

oppressive /ə'prɛsɪv/ a opresivo, tiránico, cruel; (taxes, etc.) gravoso; (of heat) sofocante, asfixiante; agobiador, abrumador

oppressor /ə'prɛsər/ n opresor (-ra), sojuzgador (-ra), tirano (-na)

opprobrious /ə'proubriəs/ a oprobioso, vituperioso; infame

opprobrium /ə'proubriəm/ n oprobio, m, ignominia, f

opt /ɒpt/ vi optar, escoger, elegir

optic, optical /'ɒptɪk; 'ɒptɪkəl/ a óptico. **o. illusion,** ilusión óptica, f; engaño a la vista, trampantojo, m. **o. nerve,** nervio óptico, m

optician /ɒp'tɪʃən/ n óptico, m

optics /'ɒptɪks/ n óptica, f

optimism /'ɒptə,mɪzəm/ n optimismo, m

optimist /'ɒptəmɪst/ n optimista, mf

optimistic /,ɒptə'mɪstɪk/ a optimista

optimum /'ɒptəməm/ n lo óptimo, m. (used as adjective) óptimo

option /'ɒpʃən/ n opción, f, (all meanings)

optional /'ɒpʃənl/ a discrecional, facultativo

opulence /'ɒpyələns/ n opulencia, riqueza, magnificencia, f; (abundance) abundancia, copia, f

opulent /'ɒpyələnt/ a opulento, rico, acaudalado; abundante

opus /'oupəs/ n obra, composición, f

opuscule /ou'pʌskyul/ n opúsculo, m

or /ɔr/ conjunc o; (before a word beginning with o or ho) u; (negative) ni. n Herald. oro, m. **an hour or so,** una hora más o menos, alrededor de una hora. **either... or,** o... o. **or else,** o bien. **whether... or,** que... que, siquiera... siquiera, ya... ya. **without... or,** sin... ni

oracle /'ɔrəkəl/ n oráculo, m

oracular /ɔ'rækyələr/ a profético, vatídico; ambiguo, misterioso, sibilino; dogmático, magistral

oral /'ɔrəl/ a verbal, hablado; Anat. oral, bucal

oral cavity n cavidad bucal, f

orange /'ɒrɪndʒ/ n (tree) naranjo, m; (fruit) naranja, f; **bitter o.,** naranja amarga, f. **blood o.,** naranja dulce, f. **tangerine o.,** naranja mandarina, f. **o. blossom,** azahar, m. **o. color,** color de naranja, m. **o.-colored,** de color de naranja, anaranjado. **o.-flower water,** agua de azahar, f. **o. grove,** naranjal, m. **o. grower** (or **seller**), naranjero (-ra). **o. peel,** piel de naranja, f. **o.-stick,** (for nails) limpiauñas, m

orangeade /,ɒrɪndʒ'eid/ n naranjada, f; (mineral water) gaseosa, f

orangery /'ɒrɪndʒri/ n naranjal, m

orangutan /ɔ'ræŋʊ,tæn/ n Zool. orangután, m

oration /ɔ'reiʃən/ n oración, declamación, f, discurso, m

orator /'ɔrətər/ n orador (-ra), declamador (-ra)

oratorical /,ɔrə'tɔrɪkəl/ a oratorio, declamatorio, retórico

oratorio /,ɔrə'tɔri,ou/ n Mus. oratorio, m

oratory /'ɔrə,tɔri/ n oratoria, elocuencia, f; Eccl. oratorio, m, capilla, f

orb /ɔrb/ n orbe, m; esfera, f, globo, m; astro, m; Poet. ojo, m

orbit /'ɔrbɪt/ n Astron. órbita, f; Anat. órbita, cuenca del ojo, f

orbital /'ɔrbɪtl/ a Anat. orbital

orchard /'ɔrtʃərd/ n huerto, vergel, m; (especially of apples) pomar, m

orchestra /'ɔrkəstrə/ n orquesta, f. **with full o.,** con gran orquesta. Theat. **o. seat,** butaca de platea, f

orchestral /ɔr'kɛstrəl/ a orquestal, instrumental

orchestrate /'ɔrkə,streit/ vt orquestar, instrumentar

orchestration /,ɔrkə'streiʃən/ n orquestración, instrumentación, f

orchid /'ɔrkɪd/ n orquídea, f

orchitis /ɔr'kaitɪs/ n Med. orquitis, f

ordain /ɔr'dein/ vt mandar, disponer, decretar; Eccl. ordenar. **to be ordained as,** Eccl. ordenarse de

ordeal /ɔr'dil/ n Hist. ordalías, f pl; prueba severa, f

order /'ɔrdər/ n (most meanings) orden, m; (command) precepto, mandamiento, decreto, m; orden, f; (rule) regla, f; (for money) libranza postal, f; (for goods) pedido, encargo, m; (arrangement) método, arreglo, m, clasificación, f; (condition) estado, m; Archit. estilo, m; (Zool. Bot.) orden, m; (sort) clase, especie, f; (rank) clase social, f; Eccl. orden, f; (badge) condecoración, insignia, f; (association) sociedad, asociación, compañía, f; (to view a house, etc.) permiso, m; (series) serie, f. **His liver is out of o.,** No está bién del hígado. **in good o.,** en buen estado; arreglado. **in o.,** (alphabetical, etc.) en orden; arreglado; (parliamentary) en regla. **in o. that,** para que, a fin de que. **in o. to,** a fin de, para. **out of o.,** estropeado, descompuesto; (on a notice) No funciona; (parliamentary) fuera del orden del día. **till further o.,** hasta nueva orden, m, Com. por encargo especial. **to give an o.,** dar una orden; Com. poner un pedido. **to go out of o.,** descomponerse. **to keep in o.,** mantener en orden. **to put in o.,** poner en orden, ordenar. **to take holy orders,** tomar órdenes sagradas. **O.!** ¡Orden! **O. in Council,** orden real, m. **O. of knighthood,** orden de caballería, f. **o. of the day,** orden del día, f; reglamento, m

order /'ɔrdər/ vt disponer; arreglar; (command) mandar, ordenar; (request) rogar, pedir; (direct) dirigir, gobernar; Com. encargar, cometer; (a meal, a taxi) encargar. **I ordered them to do it,** Les mandé hacerlo. **to o. about,** mandar. **to o. back,** hacer volver, mandar que vuelva. **to o. down,** hacer bajar, pedir (a uno) que baje. **to o. in,** mandar entrar. **to o. off,** despedir, decir (a uno) que se vaya. **to o. out,** mandar salir; (the troops) hacer salir la tropa; echar. **to o. up,** mandar subir, hacer subir

orderliness /'ɔrdərlinɪs/ n orden, aseo, método, m; limpieza, f; buena conducta, formalidad, f; buena administración, f

orderly /'ɔrdərli/ a bien arreglado, metódico; aseado, en orden; (of behaviour) formal, bien disciplinado. n *Mil.* ordenanza, m; ayudante de hospital m

ordinal /'ɔrdn̩əl/ a and n ordinal m

ordinance /'ɔrdn̩əns/ n ordenanza, f, reglamento, m; *Archit.* ordenación, f; *Eccl.* rito, m

ordinarily /ˌɔrdn̩'eərəli/ adv de ordinario, ordinariamente, comúnmente

ordinary /'ɔrdn̩ˌɛri/ a (usual) corriente, común, usual, ordinario, normal; (average) mediano, mediocre; (somewhat vulgar) ordinario, vulgar. n *Eccl.* ordinario, m. **out of the o.,** excepcional; poco común. **o. seaman,** marinero, m. **o. share,** *Com.* acción ordinaria, f

ordination /ˌɔrdn̩'eiʃən/ n *Eccl.* ordenación, f

ordnance /'ɔrdnəns/ n artillería, f, cañones, m pl; pertrechos de guerra, m pl. **o. survey map,** mapa del estado mayor, m. **o. survey number,** acotación, f

ore /ɔr/ n *Mineral.* mena, f, quijo, *Lat. Am.* llampo, m

organ /'ɔrgən/ n (all meanings) órgano, m. **barrel-o.,** organillo, órgano de manubrio, m. **o.-blower,** entonador (-ra). **o.-grinder,** organillero (-ra). **o.-loft,** tribuna del órgano, f. **o.-pipe,** cañón de órgano, m. **o.-stop,** registro de órgano, m

organdy /'ɔrgəndi/ n organdí, m

organic /ɔr'gænɪk/ a orgánico. **o. chemistry,** química orgánica, f

organism /'ɔrgəˌnɪzəm/ n organismo, m

organist /'ɔrgənɪst/ n organista, mf

organization /ˌɔrgənə'zeiʃən/ n organización, f; grupo, m, asociación, sociedad, f; organismo, m

organize /'ɔrgəˌnaiz/ vt organizar; arreglar. vi organizarse; asociarse, constituirse

organizer /'ɔrgəˌnaizər/ n organizador (-ra)

organizing /'ɔrgəˌnaizɪŋ/ a organizador

orgasm /'ɔrgæzəm/ n *Med.* orgasmo, m

orgiastic /ˌɔrdʒi'æstɪk/ a orgiástico

orgy /'ɔrdʒi/ n orgía, f

oriel /'ɔriəl/ n *Archit.* mirador, m

orient /'ɔriənt/ a *Poet.* naciente, oriental. n Oriente, Este, m. **pearl of fine o.,** perla de hermoso oriente, f

oriental /ˌɔri'ɛntl̩/ a and n oriental, mf

orientalism /ˌɔri'ɛntlˌɪzəm/ n orientalismo, m

orientalist /ˌɔri'ɛntlɪst/ n orientalista, mf

orientate /'ɔriənˌteit/ vt orientar; dirigir, guiar. vi mirar (or caer) hacia el este; orientarse

orientation /ˌɔriən'teiʃən/ n orientación, f

orifice /'ɔrəfɪs/ n orificio, m; abertura, boca, f

origin /'ɔrɪdʒɪn/ n origen, génesis, m; raíz, causa, f; principio, comienzo, m; (extraction) descendencia, procedencia, familia, f, nacimiento, m

original /ə'rɪdʒən̩l/ a original; primitivo, primero; ingenioso. n original, m; prototipo, modelo, m. **o. sin,** pecado original, m

originality /əˌrɪdʒə'nælɪti/ n originalidad, f

originally /ə'rɪdʒən̩li/ adv originalmente; al principio; antiguamente

originate /ə'rɪdʒəˌneit/ vt (produce) ocasionar, producir, suscitar, iniciar, engendrar; (create) inventar, crear. vi originarse, surgir, nacer. **to o. in,** tener su origen en, surgir de, emanar de, venir de

origination /əˌrɪdʒə'neiʃən/ n origen, principio, génesis, m

originator /ə'rɪdʒəˌneitər/ n iniciador (-ra), fundador (-ra); autor (-ra), creador (-ra)

oriole /'ɔriˌoul/ n *Ornith.* oropéndola, f

Orion /ə'raiən/ n *Astron.* Orión, m

Orkneys, the /'ɔrkniz/ las Orcades, f pl

ornament /n. 'ɔrnəmənt/ v. -ˌmɛnt/ n adorno, m; decoración, f; *Fig.* ornamento, m; (trinket) chuchería, f, n pl. **ornaments,** *Eccl.* ornamentos, m pl. vt ornar, adornar, decorar, embellecer

ornamental /ˌɔrnə'mɛntl̩/ a ornamental, decorativo

ornamentation /ˌɔrnəmɛn'teiʃən/ n ornamentación, decoración, f

ornate /ɔr'neit/ a vistoso, ornado en demasía, barroco

ornateness /ɔr'neitnɪs/ n elegancia, vistosidad, magnificencia, f

ornithological /ˌɔrnəθə'lɒdʒɪkəl/ a ornitológico

ornithologist /ˌɔrnə'θɒlədʒɪst/ n ornitólogo, m

ornithology /ˌɔrnə'θɒlədʒi/ n ornitología, f

orphan /'ɔrfən/ a and n huérfano (-na)

orphanage /'ɔrfənɪdʒ/ n orfanato, hospicio, m

orphanhood /'ɔrfənˌhʊd/ n orfandad, f

Orphean /ɔr'fiən/ a órfico

orthodox /'ɔrθəˌdɒks/ a ortodoxo

orthodoxy /'ɔrθəˌdɒksi/ n ortodoxia, f

orthographic /ˌɔrθə'græfɪk/ a ortográfico

orthography /ɔr'θɒgrəfi/ n ortografía, f

orthopedic /ˌɔrθə'pidɪk/ a ortopédico

orthopedics /ˌɔrθə'pidɪks/ n ortopedia, f

orthopedist /ˌɔrθə'pidɪst/ n ortopedista, mf ortopédico (-ca)

oscillate /'ɒsəˌleit/ vi oscilar, fluctuar; (hesitate) dudar, vacilar. vt hacer oscilar

oscillation /ˌɒsə'leiʃən/ n oscilación, fluctuación, vibración, f; *Elec.* oscilación, f

oscillator /'ɒsəˌleitər/ n oscilador, m

oscillatory /'ɒsələˌtɔri/ a oscilante

osculation /ˌɒskyə'leiʃən/ n ósculo, m

osier /'ouʒər/ n *Bot.* mimbre, m, or f. **o. bed,** mimbrera, f

osmic /'ɒzmɪk/ a *Chem.* ósmico

osmosis /ɒz'mousɪs/ n (*Phys. Chem.*) ósmosis, f

osprey /'ɒspri, -prei/ n *Ornith.* quebrantahuesos, m

osseous /'ɒsiəs/ a óseo

ossification /ˌɒsəfɪ'keiʃən/ n osificación, f

ossify /'ɒsəˌfai/ vt osificar; vi osificarse

ossuary /'ɒʃuˌɛri/ n osario, m

osteitis /ˌɒsti'aitɪs/ n *Med.* osteítis, f

Ostend /ɒs'tɛnd/ Ostende, m

ostensible /ɒ'stɛnsəbəl/ a ostensible; aparente, engañoso, ilusorio

ostensibly /ɒ'stɛnsəbli/ adv en apariencia, ostensiblemente

ostentation /ˌɒstɛn'teiʃən/ n ostentación, f; aparato, fausto, boato, alarde, m, soberbia, f

ostentatious /ˌɒstɛn'teiʃəs/ a ostentoso; aparatoso, fastuoso, rumboso

ostentatiously /ˌɒstɛn'teiʃəsli/ adv con ostentación

osteology /ˌɒsti'ɒlədʒi/ n osteología, f

osteomyelitis /ˌɒstiouˌmaiə'laitɪs/ n *Med.* osteomielitis, f

osteopath /'ɒstiəˌpæθ/ n osteópata, m

osteopathy /ˌɒsti'ɒpəθi/ n osteopatía, f

osteoplasty /'ɒstiəˌplæsti/ n *Surg.* osteoplastia, f

ostler /'ɒslər/ n mozo de cuadras, establero, m

ostracism /'ɒstrəˌsɪzəm/ n ostracismo, m

ostracize /'ɒstrəˌsaiz/ vt desterrar; excluir del trato, echar de la sociedad

ostrich /'ɔstrɪtʃ/ n avestruz, m. **o. farm,** criadero de avestruces, m

otalgia /ou'tældʒiə/ n *Med.* otalgia, f, dolor de oídos, m

other /'ʌðər/ a otro. pron el otro, m; la otra, f; lo otro, neut adv (with than) de otra manera que, de otro modo que; otra cosa que. **this hand, not the o.,** esta mano, no la otra. **every o. day,** un día sí y otro no, cada dos días. **no o.,** ninguno otro, m; otra ninguna, f; ningún otro, m pl; las otras, f pl. **someone or o.,** alguien. **the others,** los (las) demás, m, f pl; los otros, m pl; las otras, f pl. **o. people,** otros, m pl, los demás

otherwise /'ʌðərˌwaiz/ adv de otra manera, de otro modo, otramente; (in other respects) por lo demás, por otra parte; (if not) si no

otitis /ou'taitɪs/ n *Med.* otitis, f

otologist /ou'tɒlədʒɪst/ n otólogo, m

otology /ou'tɒlədʒi/ n otología, f

otter /'ɒtər/ n *Zool.* nutria, f. **o. hound,** perro para cazar la nutria

ottoman /'ɒtəmən/ a otomano, turco. n otomana, f

ouch! /autʃ/ interj ¡ax!, ¡huy!

ought /ɔt/ v aux deber, tener la obligación (de); ser conveniente, convenir; ser necesario (que), tener que. **I o. to have done it yesterday,** Debía haberlo hecho ayer. **She o. not to come,** No debe (debiera, debería) venir. **He o. to see them tomorrow,** (should) Conviene que los vea mañana; Tiene la obligación de verles mañana; (must) Es necesario que les vea mañana, Tiene que verles mañana.

ounce /auns/ *n* (animal and weight) onza, *f*. **He hasn't an o. of common sense,** No tiene pizca de sentido común

our /auᵊr *unstressed* ɑr/ *a* nuestro.

ours /auᵊrz/ *pron* nuestro, *m*; nuestra, *f*; nuestros, *m pl*; nuestras, *f pl*; de nosotros, *m pl*; de nosotras, *f pl*; el nuestro, *m*; la nuestra, *f*; lo nuestro, *neut*; los nuestros, *m pl*; las nuestras, *f pl*. **This book is ours,** Este libro es nuestro (or el nuestro)

ourselves /ɑr'sɛlvz/ *pron pl* nosotros mismos, *m pl*; nosotras mismas, *f pl*

oust /aust/ *vt* despedir, desahuciar, expulsar, echar

out /aut/ *adv* afuera; hacia fuera; (gone out) fuera, salido, ausente; (invested) puesto; (published) publicado, salido; (discovered) conocido, descubierto; (on strike) en huelga; (mistaken) en error, equivocado; (of journeys) de ida, (on ships) de navegación (e.g. *on the second day out*, al segundo día de navegación); (of fire, etc.) extinguido; (at sea) en el mar; (of girls in society) puesta de largo, que ha entrado en sociedad; (of fashion) fuera de moda; (of office) fuera del poder; (in holes) roto, agujereado, andrajoso; (exhausted) agotado; (expired) vencido; (of a watch) llevar... minutos (horas) de atraso or de adelanto; (unfriendly) reñido; (way out) salida, *f*; (sport) fuera de juego; (of flowers) abierto; (of chickens) empollado. **a scene out of one of Shakespeare's plays,** una escena de una de las comedias de Shakespeare. **I am out $6,** He perdido seis dólares. **I am out of tea,** Se me ha acabado el té. **to drink out of a glass,** beber de un vaso. **to read out of a book,** leer en un libro. **to speak out,** hablar claro. **Murder will out,** El asesinato se descubrirá. **out-and-out,** completo; (with rogue, etc.) redomado. **out of,** fuera de; (beyond) más allá de; (through, by) por; (with) con; (without) sin; (from among) entre; (in) en; (with a negative sense) no. **out of breath,** jadeante, sin aliento. **out of character,** impropio. **out of commission,** fuera de servicio. **out of danger,** fuera de peligro. **out of date,** anticuado. **out of hand,** en seguida; indisciplinado. **out of money,** sin dinero. **out of necessity,** por necesidad. **out of one's mind,** loco, demente. **out of order.** See **order.** **out of print,** agotado. **out of reach,** fuera de alcance, inasequible. **out of season,** fuera de temporada. **out of sight,** fuera del alcance de la vista; invisible. **Out of sight, out of mind,** Ojos que no ven, corazón que no siente. **out of sorts,** indispuesto. **out of temper,** de mal genio. **out of the question,** imposible. **out of the way,** *adv* (of work) terminado, hecho; (remote) fuera del camino; (put aside) arrinconado; donde no estorbe. **out-of-the-way,** *a* remoto, aislado; (unusual) extraordinario, singular. **out of this world,** lo máximo, lo último. **out of touch with,** alejado de; sin relaciones con; sin simpatía con. **out of work,** sin empleo, sin trabajo, en paro forzoso. **out-patient,** enfermo (-ma) de un dispensario. **Out!** *interj* ¡Fuera! ¡Fuera de aquí! ¡Márchate! **Out with it!** ¡Hable Vd.! sin rodeos! ¡Hablen claro!

outbalance /ˌaut'bæləns/ *vt* exceder, sobrepujar

outbid /ˌaut'bɪd/ *vt* pujar, mejorar, ofrecer más dinero

outbidding /ˌaut'bɪdɪŋ/ *n* puja, mejora, *f*

outbreak /'aut,breik/ *n* (of war) declaración, *f*; comienzo, *m*; (of disease) epidemia, *f*; (of crimes, etc.) serie, *f*

outbuilding /'aut,bɪldɪŋ/ *n* dependencia, *f*, edificio accesorio, anexo, *m*

outburst /'aut,bɜrst/ *n* acceso, arranque, *m*, explosión, *f*

outcast /'aut,kæst/ *n* paria, *mf*; desterrado (-da), proscripto (-ta)

outclass /ˌaut'klæs/ *vt* aventajar, ser superior (a), exceder

outcome /'aut,kʌm/ *n* consecuencia, *f*, resultado, *m*

outcry /'aut,krai/ *n* clamor, grito, *m*; protesta, *f*

outdistance /ˌaut'dɪstəns/ *vt* dejar atrás

outdo /ˌaut'du/ *vt* eclipsar, aventajar, sobrepujar

outdoor /'aut,dɔr/ *a* externo; (of activities) al aire libre; fuera de casa

outdoors /ˌaut'dɔrz/ *adv* fuera de casa; al aire libre

outer /'autər/ *a* externo, exterior

outermost /'autər,moust/ *a* *sup* (el, etc.) más externo; más exterior; extremo, de más allá

outer space *n* espacio extraatmosférico, espacio extraterrestre, espacio exterior, espacio sideral, espacio sidéreo, espacio ultraterrestre, *m*

outfit /'aut,fɪt/ *n* equipo, *m*; (of clothes) traje, *m*; (of furniture or trousseau) ajuar, *m*; (gear) pertrechos, avíos, *m pl*. *vt* aviar equipar

outfitter /'aut,fɪtər/ *n* proveedor (-ra), abastecedor (-ra)

outflank /ˌaut'flæŋk/ *vt* *Mil.* flanquear; ser más listo (que)

outgoing /'aut,gouɪŋ/ *a* saliente, que sale; cesante. **outgoings,** *n pl* gastos, *m pl*

outgrow /ˌaut'grou/ *vt* hacerse demasiado grande para; crecer más que; (ideas) perder; (illness) curarse de, curarse con la edad; pasar de la edad de, ser ya viejo para. **to o. one's clothes,** quedársele a uno chica la ropa. **to o. one's strength,** estar demasiado crecido para su edad

outgrowth /'aut,grouθ/ *n* excrecencia, *f*; resultado, fruto, *m*, consecuencia, *f*

outhouse /'aut,haus/ *n* edificio accesorio, *m*

outing /'autɪŋ/ *n* excursión, vuelta, *f*, paseo, *m*

outlandish /aut'lændɪʃ/ *a* extraño, singular, raro; absurdo, ridículo

outlast /ˌaut'læst/ *vt* durar más que; (outlive) sobrevivir a

outlaw /'aut,lɔ/ *n* bandido, proscrito, *m*, *vt* proscribir

outlay /'aut,lei/ *n* gasto, desembolso, *m*

outlet /'autlɛt/ *n* salida, *f*; orificio de salida, *m*; (of drains, etc.) desagüe, *m*; (of streets, rivers) desembocadura, *f*; *Fig.* escape, *m*, válvula de seguridad, *f*

outline /'aut,lain/ *n* perfil, contorno, *m*; (drawing) esbozo, bosquejo, *m*; idea general, *f*; plan general, *m*, *vt* esbozar, bosquejar. **in o.,** en esbozo; en perfil. **to be outlined** (against), dibujarse (contra), destacarse (contra)

outlive /ˌaut'lɪv/ *vt* sobrevivir (a); (live down) hacer olvidar

outlook /'aut,lʊk/ *n* (view) perspectiva, vista, *f*; (opinion) actitud, *f*, punto de vista, *m*; aspecto, *m*, apariencia, *f*; (for trade, etc.) perspectiva, *f*, posibilidades, *f pl*. **o. tower,** atalaya, *f*

outlying /'aut,laiɪŋ/ *a* remoto, lejano, distante. **o. areas,** los alrededores, *m pl.*

outmaneuver /ˌautmə'nuvər/ *vt* superar en estrategia

outmatch /ˌaut'mætʃ/ *vt* aventajar, superar

outmoded /ˌaut'moudɪd/ *a* anticuado, pasado de moda

outnumber /ˌaut'nʌmbər/ *vt* ser más numerosos que, exceder en número

out-of-court settlement /'aut əv ˌkɔrt/ *n* arreglo pacífico, *m*

out-of-town /'aut əv 'taun/ *a* de las provincias

outpost /'aut,poust/ *n* *Mil.* avanzada, *f*, puesto avanzado, *m*

outpouring /'aut,pɔrɪŋ/ *n* derramamiento, *m*; efusión, *f*

output /'aut,pʊt/ *n* producción, *f*. **o. capacity,** capacidad de producción, *f*

outrage /'autreidʒ/ *n* barbaridad infamia, atrocidad, *f*; rapto, *m*, violación, *f*. *vt* ultrajar; violar; violentar

outrageous /aut'reidʒəs/ *a* atroz, terrible; desaforado, monstruoso; injurioso; ridiculo

outrageousness /aut'reidʒəsnɪs/ *n* lo atroz; violencia, furia, *f*; escándalo, *m*; enormidad, *f*; lo excesivo; lo horrible

outré /u'trei/ *a* cursi, extravagante

outride /ˌaut'raid/ *vt* cabalgar más a prisa que

outright /*adv.* 'aut'rait/ *a.* 'aut,rait/ *adv* (frankly) de plano (e.g. *to reject outright,* rechazar de plano), francamente, sin reserva; (immediately) en seguida, inmediatamente. *a* categórico; completo; franco

outrival /'aut,raivəl/ *vt* vencer, superar

outrun /ˌaut'rʌn/ *vt* correr más que

outset /'aut,sɛt/ *n* principio, comienzo, *m*

outshine /ˌaut'ʃain/ *vt* brillar más que, eclipsar en brillantez; superar, eclipsar

outside /*adv., prep., a.* ˌaut'said/ *n.* 'aut'said/ *adv* afuera, fuera. *prep* fuera de, al otro lado de, al exterior de; (besides) aparte de, fuera de. *a* externo, exterior; (of labor, etc.) desde fuera; máximo; ajeno. *n* exterior, *m*; superficie, *f*; aspecto, *m*, apariencia, *f*. **at the o.,** a lo sumo, cuando más. **from the o.,** de (or desde) fuera. **on the o.,** (externally) por fuera. **o. the door,** a la puerta

outsider /ˌaut'saidər/ *n* forastero (-ra); desconocido (-da), *Argentina, Chile also* cuico (-ca); caballo desconocido, *m*; persona poco deseable, *f*

outsize /'autˌsaiz/ *n* artículo de talla mayor que las corrientes, *m*

outskirts /'aut'skɜrts/ *n pl* alrededores, *m pl*, afueras, immediaciones, cercanías, *f pl*

outspoken /'aut'spoukən/ *a* franco. **to be o.,** decir lo que se piensa, no tener pelos en la lengua

outspokenness /'aut'spoukənnɪs/ *n* franqueza, *f*,

outspread /'autˌsprɛd/ *a* extendido; (of wings) desplegadas

outstanding /ˌaut'stændɪŋ/ *a* excelente; sobresaliente, conspicuo; *Com.* pendiente, sin pagar. **to be o.,** *Com.* estar pendiente; *Fig.* sobresalir. **o. account,** *Com.* cuenta pendiente, *f*

outstay /ˌaut'stei/ *vt* quedarse más tiempo que. **to o. one's welcome,** pegársele la silla

outstretched /ˌaut'strɛtʃt/ *a* extendido

outstrip /ˌaut'strɪp/ *vt* dejar atrás, pasar; aventajar, superar

outvote /ˌaut'vout/ *vt* emitir más votos que; rechazar por votación

outward /'autwərd/ *a* exterior, externo; aparente, visible. *adv* exteriormente; hacia fuera; superficialmente. **o. bound,** con rumbo a... **o. voyage,** el viaje de ida

outwardly /'autwərdli/ *adv* exteriormente; hacia fuera; en apariencia

outwear /ˌaut'wɛər/ *vt* durar más que; gastar

outweigh /ˌaut'wei/ *vt* exceder, valer más que

outwit /ˌaut'wɪt/ *vt* ser más listo que; vencer

outworn /'aut'wɔrn/ *a* anticuado, ya viejo

oval /'ouvəl/ *a* óvalo, *m*, *a* oval, ovalado, aovado

ovarian /ou'vɛəriən/ *a* (*Bot. Zool.*) ovárico

ovary /'ouvəri/ *n* ovario, *m*

ovation /ou'veiʃən/ *n* ovación, recepción entusiasta, *f*

oven /'ʌvən/ *n* horno, *m*. **o. peel,** pala de horno, *f*. **o. rake,** hurgón, *m*

over /'ouvər/ *prep* (above, upon, over) sobre, encima de; (on the other side) al otro lado de; (across) allende, a través de; (more than) más de; (beyond) más allá de; (of rank) superior a; (during) durante; (in addition) además de; (through) por. *n* (cricket) serie de saques, *f*, *adv* encima; en; por encima; al otro lado; de un lado a otro; enfrente; al lado contrario; de un extremo a otro; (finished) terminado; (ruined) arruinado, perdido; (more) más; (excessively) demasiado, excesivamente; (covered) cubierto (de); (extra) en exceso; (completely) enteramente; (from head to foot) de pies a cabeza, de hito en hito; (of time) pasado. **over** is also used as a prefix. Indicating excess, it is generally translated by demasiado or excesivamente. In other meanings, it is either not translated or its meaning forms part of the verb, being translated as re-, super-, trans-, ultra. Very often a less literal translation is more successful than the employment of the above prefixes. **all o.,** (everywhere) en todas partes; (finished) todo acabado; (covered) cubierto (de); (up and down) de pies a cabeza. **all the world o.,** en todo el mundo. **embroidered all o.,** todo bordado. **He is o. in Germany,** Está en Alemania. **He trembled all o.,** Estaba todo tembloroso. **that which is o.,** el exceso, lo que queda. **to read o.,** leer, repasar. **o. again,** de nuevo. **o. and above,** por encima de, fuera de, en exceso de. **o. and o.,** repetidamente, muchas veces. **o. my signature,** bajo mi firma. **o. six months since...,** más de seis meses desde que...

overabundance /ˌouvərə'bʌndəns/ *n* sobreabundancia, *f*

overabundant /ˌouvərə'bʌndənt/ *a* sobreabundante

overact /ˌouvər'ækt/ *vt* exagerar (un papel)

overall /'ouvərˌɔl/ *n* bata, *f*; guardapolvo, *m*; de-

conjunto (e.g., *overall assessment*, evaluación de conjunto) *pl* **overalls,** mono, *m*

overanxious /ˌouvər'æŋkʃəs/ *a* demasiado ansioso; demasiado inquieto. **to be o.-a.,** preocuparse demasiado

overarch /ˌouvər'artʃ/ *vt* abovedar

overawe /ˌouvər'ɔ/ *vt* intimidar, acobardar

overbalance /ˌouvər'bæləns/ *vt* hacer perder el equilibrio. hacer caer; preponderar. *vi* perder el equilibrio, caer

overbalancing /'ouvərˌbæslənsɪŋ/ *n* pérdida del equilibrio, caída, *f*; preponderancia, *f*

overbearing /ˌouvər'bɛərɪŋ/ *a* dominante, autoritario, imperioso

overboard /'ouvərˌbɔrd/ *adv* al agua, al mar, *Fig.* en exceso

overburden /ˌouvər'bɜrdn̩/ *vt* sobrecargar, agobiar

overcast /*a.* 'ouvər'kæst; *v.* ˌouvər'kæst/ *a* anublado, cerrado, encapotado. *vt Sew.* sobrehilar. **to become o.,** anublarse

overcharge /*n.* 'ouvərˌtʃardʒ; *v.* ˌouvər'tʃardʒ/ *n* recargo, *m*; (price) recargo de precio, precio excesivo, *m*. *vt* recargar, cobrar un precio excesivo; *Elec.* sobrecargar. *vi* cobrar demasiado

overcloud /ˌouvər'klaud/ *vt* anublar; *Fig.* entristecer

overcoat /'ouvərˌkout/ *n* abrigo, sobretodo, gabán, *m*

overcome /ˌouvər'kʌm/ *vt* vencer, rendir, subyugar; (difficulties) triunfar de, allanar, dominar. *vi* saber vencer. *a* (by sleep, etc.) rendido; (at a loss) turbado, confundido; (by kindness) agradecidísimo

overconfidence /ˌouvər'kɒnfɪdəns/ *n* confianza excesiva, *f*

overcooked /'ouvərˌkʊkt/ *a* recocido, demasiado cocido

overcrowd /ˌouvər'kraud/ *vt* atestar, llenar de bote en bote; (over-populate) sobrepoblar

overcrowding /'ouvərˌkraudɪŋ/ *n* sobrepoblación, *f*

overdo /ˌouvər'du/ *vt* exagerar; ir demasiado lejos, hacer demasiado; *Cul.* recocer; (overtire) fatigarse demasiado

overdose /'ouvərˌdous/ *n* dosis excesiva, *f*

overdraft /'ouvərˌdræft/ *n Com.* giro en descubierto, *m*

overdraw /ˌouvər'drɔ/ *vt* and *vi Com.* girar en descubierto

over-dressed /'ouvər 'drɛst/ *a* que viste demasiado; cursi

overdue /ˌouvər'du/ *a* atrasado; *Com.* vencido y no pagado

overeat /ˌouvər'it/ *vi* comer demasiado, atracarse, *Lat. Am.* jambarse

overestimate /ˌouvər'ɛstəˌmeit/ *vt* estimar en valor excesivo; exagerar, sobreestimar, *n* presupuesto excesivo, *m*; estimación excesiva, *f*

overexcite /ˌouvərɪk'sait/ *vt* sobreexcitar

overexposure /ˌouvərɪk'spouʒər/ *n Photo.* exceso de exposición, *f*

overfatigue /ˌouvərfə'tig/ *vt* fatigar demasiado, *n* cansancio excesivo, *m*

overfeeding /'ouvərˌfidɪŋ/ *n* sobrealimentación, *f*

overflow /*v.* ˌouvər'flou; *n.* 'ouvərˌflou/ *vt* inundar, derramarse por; *Fig.* cubrir, llenar; desbordarse. *vi* (with) rebosar de. *n* inundación, *f*, desbordamiento, derrame, *m*; *Fig.* residuo, resto, exceso, *m*; (plumbing) sumidero, vertedero, *m*, descarga, *f*. **The river overflowed its banks,** El río se desbordó, El río salió de cauce

overflowing /ˌouvər'flouɪŋ/ *a* rebosante; superabundante; (its banks) *Lat. Am.* desbordado. **filled to o.,** lleno hasta los bordes. **o. with health,** rebosante de salud, vendiendo salud

overgrown /ˌouvər'groun/ *a* (gawky) talludo; (plants) exuberante, vicioso; frondoso, cubierto de verdura

overhang /ˌouvər'hæŋ/ *vt* caer a, mirar a; colgar; *Fig.* amenazar. *vi* colgar, sobresalir; *Fig.* amenazar

overhanging /'ouvərˌhæŋɪŋ/ *a* saledizo, sobresaliente; colgante, pendiente

overhaul /*v.* ˌouvər'hɔl; *n.* 'ouvərˌhɔl/ *vt* examinar, investigar; comprar, hacer una inspección general de; (of boats overtaking) alcanzar. *n* examen, *m*, revisión, *f*; *Med.* exploración general, *f*

overhead /'ouvər'hɛd/ *adv* arriba, en lo alto, encima de la cabeza. *a* aéreo, elevado; general, fijo. **o. cable,** cable eléctrico, *m*. **o. expenses,** gastos generales, *m pl*. **o. railway,** ferrocarril aéreo (or elevado), *m*

overhear /,ouvər'hɪər/ *vt* (accidentally) oír por casualidad, oír sin querer; (on purpose) alcanzar a oír, lograr oír

overheat /,ouvər'hit/ *vt* acalorar, hacer demasiado caliente, recalentar. *vi* (in argument) acalorarse; hacerse demasiado caliente

overheating /,ouvər'hitɪŋ/ *n* recalentramiento, *m*

overindulge /,ouvərɪn'dʌldʒ/ *vt* mimar demasiado; dedicarse a algo con exceso; tomar algo con exceso. *vi* darse demasiada buena vida

overjoyed /'ouvər,dʒɔid/ *a* contentísimo, lleno de alegría, encantado

overland /'ouvər,lænd/ *adv* por tierra. *a* terrestre, trascontinental

overlap /*v*. ,ouvər'læp; *n*. 'ouvər,læp/ *vi* traslaparse; coincidir. *n* traslapo, *m*

overlay /,ouvər'lei/ *vt* cubrir, dar una capa; (with silver) platear; (with gold) dorar. *n* capa, *f*; cubierta, *f*

overleaf /'ouvər,lif/ *adv* a la vuelta

overload /*v*. ,ouvər'loud; *n*. 'ouvər,loud/ *vt* sobrecargar, recargar. *n* sobrecarga, *f*

overlook /,ouvər'lʊk/ *vt* (face) dar a, mirar a, dominar; (supervise) vigilar, examinar, inspeccionar; (not notice) no notar, pasar por alto, no hacer, caso de, no fijarse en; (neglect) desdeñar; (ignore) no darse cuenta de, ignorar; (excuse) perdonar, tolerar, hacer la vista gorda

overlord /'ouvər,lɔrd/ *n* señor de horca y cuchillo, señor, jefe, *m*

overmuch /'ouvər'mʌtʃ/ *adv* demasiado, en exceso

overnight /*adv*. 'ouvər'nait; *a*. 'ouvər,nait/ *adv* la noche pasada, durante la noche; toda la noche. *a* de la víspera, nocturno. **to stay o. with,** pasar la noche con

overpass /'ouvər,pæs/ *n* pasaje elevado, viaducto, *m*

overpay /,ouvər'pei/ *vt* pagar demasiado

overpayment /'ouvər,peimənt/ *n* pago excesivo, *m*

overpopulate /,ouvər'pɒpyə,leit/ *vt* sobrepoblar, become overpopulated recargarse de habitantes (with people), recargarse de animales (with animals)

overpower /,ouvər'pauər/ *vt* vencer, subyugar; (of scents, etc.) trastornar; rendir, dominar

overpowering /,ouvər'pauərɪŋ/ *a* irresistible

overpraise /,ouvər'preiz/ *vt* encarecer, alabar mucho

overproduce /,ouvərprə'dus/ *vt* and *vi* sobreproducir

overproduction /,ouvərprə'dʌkʃən/ *n* sobreproducción, *f*

overrate /,ouvər'reit/ *vt* exagerar el valor de; (of property) sobrevalorar

overreach /,ouvər'ritʃ/ *vt* sobrealcanzar. **to o. oneself,** sobrepasarse, ir demasiado lejos

override /,ouvər'raid/ *vt* (trample) pasar por encima (de); *Fig*. rechazar, poner a un lado; (bully) dominar; (a horse) fatigar, reventar

overripe /'ouvər'raip/ *a* demasiado maduro

overrule /,ouvər'rul/ *vt* *Law*. denegar, no admitir; vencer

overrun /,ouvər'rʌn/ *vt* (flood) inundar; (ravage) invadir; (infest) plagar, infestar; desbordarse, derramarse

overseas /*a*. 'ouvər'siz; *adv*. ,ouvər'siz/ *a* ultramarino, de ultramar. *adv* en ultramar, allende los mares

oversee /,ouvər'si/ *vt* vigilar, inspeccionar

overseer /'ouvər,siər/ *n* capataz, mayoral, sobrestante, contramaestre, *m*; inspector (-ra), veedor (-ra)

oversell /,ouvər'sɛl/ *vt* and *vi* vender en exceso

oversensitive /,ouvər'sɛnsɪtɪv/ *a* demasiado sensitivo; vidrioso; susceptible

oversew /'ouvər,sou/ *vt* sobrecoser

overshadow /,ouvər'ʃædou/ *vt* sombrear; *Fig*. eclipsar, obscurecer; (sadden) entristecer

overshoe /'ouvər,ʃu/ *n* chanclo, *m*; (for snow) galocha, *f*

overshoot /,ouvər'ʃut/ *vt* tirar más allá del blanco; *Fig*. exceder, rebasar el límite conveniente, **overshoot**

the target (fig.) ir más allá del blanco, ir más allá de lo razonable. **to o. oneself,** exagerar; propasarse, descomedirse

oversight /'ouvər,sait/ *n* inadvertencia, omisión, equivocación, *f*; descuido, *m*

oversimplify /,ouvər'sɪmplə,fai/ *vt* simplificar en exceso

oversleep /,ouvər'slip/ *vi* dormir demasiado; *Inf*. pegársele a uno las sábanas, levantarse demasiado tarde

overspend /,ouvər'spɛnd/ *vt* and *vi* gastar demasiado

overspread /,ouvər'sprɛd/ *vt* desparramar, salpicar, esparcir, sembrar; cubrir

overstate /,ouvər'steit/ *vt* exagerar, encarecer, ponderar

overstatement /,ouvər'steitmənt/ *n* exageración, ponderación, *f*

overstep /,ouvər'stɛp/ *vt* exceder, pasar, violar; rebasar, pasar más allá (de)

overstrain /,ouvər'strein/ *vt* fatigar demasiado, agotar. *n* fatiga, *f*. **to o. oneself,** esforzarse demasiado, cansarse demasiado

overstrung /,ouvər'strʌŋ/ *a* nervioso, excitable; (piano) de cuerdas cruzadas

oversubscribe /,ouvərsəb'skraib/ *vt* subscribir en exceso

overt /ou'vɜrt/ *a* abierto, público; manifiesto, evidente

overtake /,ouvər'teik/ *vt* alcanzar, pasar, dejar atrás; adelantarse (a); (surprise) coger, sorprender; (overwhelm) vencer, dominar

overtax /,ouvər'tæks/ *vt* oprimir de tributos; agobiar, cansar demasiado

overthrow /*v*. ,ouvər'θrou; *n*. 'ouvər,θrou/ *vt* volcar, echar por tierra, derribar; *Fig*. vencer, destruir, destronar. *n* vuelco, derribo, *m*; *Fig*. destrucción, ruina, *f*

overtime /'ouvər,taim/ *adv* fuera de las horas estipuladas. *n* horas extraordinarias de trabajo, *f pl*. **to work o.,** trabajar horas extraordinarias

overtone /'ouvər,toun/ *n* *Mus*. armónico, *m*

overtop /,ouvər'tɒp/ *vt* dominar, sobresalir, elevarse encima de

overture /'ouvərtʃər/ *n* *Mus*. obertura, *f*

overturn /,ouvər'tɜrn/ *vt* volcar, derribar, echar a rodar, echar abajo; (upset) revolver, desordenar. *vi* volcar, venirse abajo, allanarse; estar revuelto

overturning /,ouvər'tɜrnɪŋ/ *n* vuelco, salto de campana, *m*

overweening /'ouvər'winɪŋ/ *a* arrogante, insolente, altivo

overweight /'ouvər,weit/ *n* sobrepeso, exceso en el peso, *m*. **to be o.,** pesar más de lo debido

overwhelm /,ouvər'wɛlm/ *vt* (conquer) vencer, aplastar, derrotar; (of waves, etc.) sumergir, hundir, inundar, engolfar; (in argument) confundir, dejar confuso, avergonzar; (of grief, etc.) vencer, postrar, dominar; (of work) inundar

overwhelming /,ouvər'wɛlmɪŋ/ *a* irresistible, invencible, abrumador, apabullante

overwind /,ouvər'waind/ *vt* (a watch) dar demasiada cuerda a; romper la cuerda de

overwork /*v*. ,ouvər'wɜrk; *n*. 'ouvər,wɜrk/ *vt* hacer trabajar demasiado (or con exceso); esclavizar. *vi* trabajar demasiado. *n* exceso de trabajo, demasiado trabajo, *m*

overwrought /'ouvər'rɔt/ *a* (overworked) agotado por el trabajo, rendido, muy cansado; nerviosísimo, sobreexcitado, exaltado, muy agitado

ovine /'ouvain/ *a* ovejuno

ovoid /'ouvɔid/ *a* ovoide

ovulation /,ɒvyə'leiʃən/ *n* *Med*. ovulación, *f*

owe /ou/ *vt* deber, tener deudas (de); deber, estar agradecido (por), estar obligado (a). *vi* estar en deuda, estar endeudado, tener deudas. **He owes his tailor \$30,** Le debe treinta dólares a su sastre. **I owe him thanks for his help,** Le estoy agradecido por su ayuda (or Le debo las gracias por...). **He owes his success to good fortune,** Su éxito se debe a la suerte

owing /'ouɪŋ/ *a* sin pagar. **o. to,** debido a, a causa de, por. **We had to stay in o. to the rain,** Tuvimos que quedarnos en casa a causa de la lluvia. **What is o. to you now?** ¿Cuánto se le debe ahora?

owl /aul/ *n* búho, mochuelo, *Peru* carancho, *m*. **barn or screech owl,** lechuza, *f*. **brown owl,** autillo, *m*
owlish /'aulıʃ/ *a* parecido a un búho, de búho
own /oun/ *a* propio. *n* (dearest) bien, *m*. *vt* poseer, tener, ser dueño de; (recognize) reconocer; (admit) confesar. *vi* confesar. **my (thy, his, our, your) own,** mi (tu, su, nuestro, vuestro) propio, *m*, (*f*, propia); mis (tus, sus, nuestros, vuestros) propios, *m pl*, (*f pl*, propias); (when not placed before a noun) el mío (tuyo, suyo, nuestro, vuestro), la mía (tuya, etc.), los míos (tuyos, etc.), las mías (tuyas, etc.); (relations) los suyos. **in his own house,** en su propia casa. **my (thy, his, etc.) own self,** yo (tú, él) mismo, *m*, (*f*, misma, *m pl*, mismos, *f pl*, mismas). **a room of one's own,** un cuarto para sí (or para uno mismo). **to be on one's own,** ser independiente; estar a solas. **to hold one's own,** mantenerse en sus trece. **to own up,** confesar

owner /'ounər/ *n* dueño (-ña), propietario (-ia), posesor (-ra)
ownerless /'ounərlıs/ *a* sin dueño, sin amo
ownership /'ounərʃıp/ *n* posesión, *f*, dominio, *m*; propiedad, *f*
ox /ɒks/ *n* buey (*pl* bueyes), *m*. **oxeye daisy,** margarita, *f*. **oxstall,** boyera, *f*
oxidation /,ɒksı'deıʃən/ *n Chem.* oxidación, *f*
oxide /'ɒksaid/ *n Chem.* óxido, *m*
oxidization /,ɒksədı'zeıʃən, -,daı-/ *n* oxidación, *f*
oxidize /'ɒksı,daız/ *vt Chem.* oxidar; *vi* oxidarse
oxygen /'ɒksıdʒən/ *n* oxígeno, *m*. **o. mask,** máscara de oxígeno, *f*. **o. tent,** tienda de oxígeno, *f*
oxygenate /'ɒksıdʒə,neıt/ *vt Chem.* oxigenar
oxygenation /,ɒksədʒə'neıʃən/ *n Chem.* oxigenación, *f*
oyster /'ɔıstər/ *n* ostra, *f*, *Lat. Am.* ostión, *m*. **o. bed,** pescadero (or criadero) de ostras, *m*. **o. culture,** ostricultura, *f*
ozone /'ouzoun/ *n* ozono, *m*

P

p /pi/ *n* (letter) pe, *f*. **to mind one's p's and q's,** poner los puntos sobre las íes; ir con pies de plomo
pabulum /'pæbyələm/ *n* pábulo, *m*; sustento, *m*
pace /peıs/ *n* paso, *m*; (gait) andar, *m*, marcha, *f*; (of a horse) andadura, *f*; (speed) velocidad, *f*. *vi* pasear(se), andar; (of a horse) amblar. *vt* recorrer, andar por; marcar el paso para; (with out) medir a pasos. **at a good p.,** a un buen paso. **to keep p. with,** ajustarse al paso de, ir al mismo paso que; andar al paso de; (events) mantenerse al corriente de. **to p. up and down,** pasearse, dar vueltas. **p.-maker,** el que marca el paso
paced /peıst/ *a* de andar...; (of a horse) de andadura...; de paso...
pachyderm /'pækı,dərm/ *n* paquidermo, *m*
Pacific, the /pə'sıfık/ el (Océano) Pacífico, *m*
pacific /pə'sıfık/ *a Geog.* pacífico; sosegado, tranquilo, pacífico. **He is of a p. disposition,** Es amigo de la paz
pacification /,pæsəfı'keıʃən/ *n* pacificación, *f*
pacificatory /pə'sıfıkə,tɔri/ *a* pacificador
pacifier /'pæsə,faıər/ *n* pacificador (-ra)
pacifism /'pæsə,fızəm/ *n* pacifismo, *m*
pacifist /'pæsəfıst/ *a* pacifista. *n* pacifista, *mf*
pacify /'pæsə,faı/ *vt* pacificar; calmar, tranquilizar; aplacar, conciliar
pack /pæk/ *n* (bundle) fardo, lío, *m*; paquete, *m*; (load) carga, *f*; (of hounds) jauría, *f*; (herd) hato, *m*; (of seals) manada, *f*; (of cards) baraja (de naipes), *f*; (of rogues) cuadrilla, *f*; (of lies, etc.) colección, *f*; masa, *f*; (of ice) témpanos flotantes, *m pl*; (Rugby football) delanteros, *m pl*; (for the face) compresa, *f*. **p.-horse,** caballo de carga, *m*. **p.-needle,** aguja espartera, *f*. **p.-saddle,** albarda, *f*. **p.-thread,** bramante, *m*
pack /pæk/ *vt* embalar; empaquetar; envasar; encajonar; (a suit-case, etc.) hacer; (cram) apretar; (crowd) atestar, llenar; (a pipe joint, etc.) empaquetar; (an animal) cargar. *vi* llenar; (one's luggage) hacer el equipaje, hacer el baúl, arreglar el equipaje. **packed like sardines,** como sardinas en banasta. **The train was packed,** El tren estaba lleno de bote en bote. **to p. off,** (a person) despachar; poner de partitas en la calle. **to p. up,** hacer el equipaje; empaquetar; embalar; *Inf.* liar el hato
package /'pækıdʒ/ *n* paquete, *m*; bulto, *m*; (bundle) fardo, *m*
packer /'pækər/ *n* embalador, *m*; envasador (-ra)
packet /'pækıt/ *n* paquete, *m*; (of cigarettes, etc.) cajetilla, *f*; (boat) paquebote, *m*. **to make one's p.,** *Inf.* hacer su pacotilla
packing /'pækıŋ/ *n* embalaje, *m*; envoltura, *f*; envase, *m*; (on a pipe, etc.) guarnición, *f*. **I must do my p.,** Tengo que hacer las maletas. **p.-case,** caja de embalaje, *f*. **p.-needle,** aguja espartera, *f*
pact /pækt/ *n* pacto, convenio, *m*. **to make a p.,** pactar

pad /pæd/ *n* almohadilla, *f*, cojinete, *m*; (on a bed, chair) colchoneta, *f*; (on a wound) cabezal, *m*; (for polishing) muñeca, *f*; (hockey) defensa, *f*; (cricket) espinillera, *f*; (writing) bloque, *m*; (of a calendar) taco, *m*; (blotting) secafirmas, *m*; (of a quadruped's foot) pulpejo, *m*; (of fox, hare) pata, *f*; (leaf) hoja grande, *f*, *vt* almohadillar; acolchar; rellenar, forrar; (out, a book, etc.) meter paja en. **inking-pad,** almohadilla de entintar, *f*. **padded cell,** celda acolchonada, *f*. **shoulder-pad,** (in a garment) hombrera, *f*
padding /'pædıŋ/ *n* relleno, *m*, almohadilla, *f*; (material) borra, *f*, algodón, *m*; *Fig.* paja, *f*, ripio, *m*,
paddle /'pædl/ *n* (oar) canalete, zagual, *m*; paleta, *f*; (flipper) aleta, *f*, *vt* and *vi* remar con canalete; (dabble) chapotear. **double p.,** remo doble, *m*. **p.-steamer,** vapor de ruedas, vapor de paleta, *m*. **p.-wheel,** rueda de paletas, *f*
paddler /'pædlər/ *n* remero (-ra); el, *m*, (*f*, la) que chapotea
paddling /'pædlıŋ/ *n* chapoteo, chapaleo, *m*
paddock /'pædək/ *n* prado, *m*, dehesa, *f*; parque, *m*; (near a racecourse) en silla dero, picadero, *m*; (toad) sapo, *m*
padlock /'pæd,lɒk/ *n* candado, *m*, *vt* cerrar con candado, acerrojar
paean /'piən/ *n* himno de alegría, *m*
pagan /'peigən/ *a* and *n* pagano (-na)
paganism /'peigənızəm/ *n* paganismo, *m*
page /peidʒ/ *n* (boy) paje, *m*; (squire) escudero, *m*; (of a book, etc.) página, *f*; *Fig.* hoja, *f*. *vt* compaginar; (a person) vocear. **on p. nine,** en la página nueve. **to turn the p.,** *Fig.* volver la hoja
pageant /'pædʒənt/ *n* espectáculo, *m*; (procession) desfile, *m*; representación teatral, *f*; fiesta, *f*; *Fig.* pompa, *f*, aparato, *m*
pageantry /'pædʒəntri/ *n* pompa, *f*, aparato, *m*, magnificencia, *f*
paginate /'pædʒə,neıt/ *vt* paginar
pagination /,pædʒə'neıʃən/ *n* paginación, *f*
pagoda /pə'goudə/ *n* pagoda, *f*
paid /peid/ *a* pagado; (on a parcel) porte pagado. **p. mourner,** plañidera, *f*. **p.-up share,** acción liberada, *f*
pail /peil/ *n* cubo, pozal, *m*, cubeta, *f*
pailful /'peil,ful/ *n* cubo (de agua, etc.), *m*
pain /pein/ *n* dolor, *m*; sufrimiento, *m*; (mental) tormento, *m*, angustia, *f*; *Law.* pena, *f*; *pl* **pains,** (effort) trabajo, esfuerzo, *m*. *vt* doler; atormentar, afligir. **dull p.,** dolor sordo, *m*. **I have a p. in my head,** Me duele la cabeza. **on p. of death,** so pena de muerte. **to be in great p.,** sufrir mucho. **to take pains,** tomarse trabajo, esforzarse, esmerarse
pained /peind/ *a* dolorido; afligido; de angustia
painful /'peinfəl/ *a* doloroso; angustioso; fatigoso; (troublesome) molesto; (embarrassing) embarazoso; difícil; (laborious) arduo

painfully /'peinfəli/ adv dolorosamente; penosamente; fatigosamente; con angustia; laboriosamente
painfulness /'peinfəlnıs/ n dolor, m; angustia, aflicción, f; tormento, m; dificultad, f
painless /'peinlıs/ a sin dolor, indoloro
painlessly /'peinlısli/ adv sin dolor; sin sufrir
painlessness /'peinlısnıs/ n falta de dolor, f
painstaking /'peinz,teikıŋ, 'pein,stei-/ a concienzudo; diligente, industrioso; cuidadoso. n trabajo, m; diligencia, industria, f; cuidado, m
paint /peint/ n pintura, f; (for preserving metal) pavón, m; (rouge) colorete, m. vt pintar. vi pintar; pintarse. **The door is painted blue,** La puerta está pintada de azul. **p.-box,** caja de pinturas, f. **p.-brush,** pincel, m; (for house painting) brocha, f
painter /'peintər/ n pintor (-ra); (house) pintor de brocha gorda, pintor de casas, m; (of a boat) boza, f. **sign-p.,** pintor de muestras, m
painting /'peintıŋ/ n pintura, f; (picture) cuadro, m, pintura, f
pair /pɛər/ n par, m; (of people) pareja, f; (of oxen) yunta, f. vt parear, emparejar; (persons) unir, casar; (animals) aparear. vi parearse; casarse; aparearse. **a carriage and p.,** un landó con dos caballos. **a p. of steps,** una escalera de mano. **a p. of pants, a p. of trousers,** unos pantalones. **in pairs,** de dos en dos; por parejas. **to p. off,** vi formar pareja; Inf. casarse
pal /pæl/ n camarada, compinche, mf; amigote, m, Carribean pana, mf
palace /'pælıs/ n palacio, m
paladin /'pælədın/ n paladín, m
palatable /'pælətəbəl/ a sabroso, apetitoso; Fig. agradable, aceptable
palatableness /'pælıtəbəlnıs/ n buen sabor, gusto agradable, m; Fig. lo agradable
palatably /'pælıtəbli/ adv agradablemente
palatal /'pælətḷ/ a paladial. n letra paladial, f
palatalize /'pælətḷ,aiz/ vt palatizar
palate /'pælıt/ n paladar, m. **hard p.,** paladar, m. **soft p.,** velo del paladar, m
palatial /pə'leiʃəl/ a (of a palace) palaciego; (sumptuous) magnífico, suntuoso
pale /peil/ n (stake) estaca, f; límite, m; Herald. palo, m, a pálido; (wan) descolorido, Lat. Am. also lívido; (of colors) claro, desmayado; (of light) tenue, mortecino; (lusterless) sin brillo, muerto. vi palidecer, perder el color; Fig. suceder
palely /'peilli/ adv pálidamente; vagamente, indistintamente
paleness /'peilnıs/ n palidez, f; (wanness) descoloramiento, m, amarillez, f; (of light) tenuidad, f
paleographer /,peili'ngrəfər/ n paleógrafo, m
paleography /,peili'ngrəfi/ n paleografía, f
paleolithic /,peiliə'lıθık/ a paleolítico
paleology /,peili'nlədʒi/ n paleología, f
paleontology /,peiliən'tnlədʒi/ n paleontología, f
palette /'pælıt/ n paleta, f. **p.-knife,** espátula, f
palimpsest /'pælımp,sest/ n palimpsesto, m
palindrome /'pælın,droum/ n capicúa f, (of numbers), palíndromo m
paling /'peilıŋ/ n palizada, estacada, valla, f
palisade /,pælə'seid/ n palenque, m, tranquera, palizada, f; Mil. estacada, f
palish /'peilıʃ/ a algo pálido; paliducho
pall /pɔl/ n (on a coffin) paño mortuorio, m; (Fig. covering) manto, m, capa, f; Eccl. palio, m; (over a chalice) palia, f. vi perder el sabor, hacerse insípido; saciarse (de); aburrirse (de), cansarse (de). **The music of Bach never palls on me,** No me canso nunca de la música de Bach
palladium /pə'leidiəm/ n Mineral. paladio, m; (safeguard) paladión, m
pallet /'pælıt/ n jergón, m; camilla, f; Mech. fiador de rueda, m; torno de alfarero, m

pallid /'pælıd/ a pálido, Lat. Am. also lívido
pallidness /'pælıdnıs/ n palidez, f
pallor /'pælər/ n palidez, f
palm /pɑm/ n (of the hand, and Fig., victory) palma, f; (measurement) ancho de la mano, m; (tree) palmera, f. vt (a card, etc.) empalmar; (with off) defraudar (con); dar gato por liebre (a). **to bear away the p.,** llevar la palma. **p. branch,** palma, f. **p. grove,** palmar, m. **p.-oil,** aceite de palma, m; (bribe) soborno, m. **P. Sunday,** Domingo de Ramos, m. **p. tree,** palmera, Lat. Am. chonta, f
palmate /'pælmeit, -mıt, 'pɑl-, 'pɑmeit/ a palmeado
palmer /'pælmər, 'pɑl-/ n peregrino, m; (caterpillar) oruga velluda, f
palming /'pɑmıŋ/ n (in conjuring, etc.) empalme, m
palmist /'pɑmıst/ n quiromántico (-ca)
palmistry /'pɑməstri/ n quiromancía, f
palmy /'pɑmi/ a palmar; (flourishing) floreciente; (happy) dichoso, feliz; (prosperous) próspero; triunfante
Palmyra /pæl'mairə/ Palmira, f
palp /pælp/ n palpo, m
palpability /,pælpə'bılıti/ n palpabilidad, f
palpable /'pælpəbəl/ a palpable
palpate /'pælpeit/ vt palpar
palpation /pæl'peiʃən/ n palpación, f
palpitate /'pælpı,teit/ vi palpitar
palpitating /'pælpı,teitıŋ/ a palpitante
palpitation /,pælpı'teiʃən/ n palpitación, f
palsied /'pɔlzid/ a paralítico
palsy /'pɔlzi/ n parálisis, perlesía, f. vt paralizar. **cerebral p.,** perlesía cerebral
paltriness /'pɔltrinıs/ n mezquindad, pequeñez, f
paltry /'pɔltri/ a mezquino, insignificante, pobre
paludism /'pælyə,dizəm/ n Med. paludismo, m
pampas /'pæmpəz/ attributively 'pæmpəs/ n pampa, f
pamper /'pæmpər/ vt mimar, consentir demasiado; criar con mimos, regalar; alimentar demasiado bien
pampered /'pæmpərd/ a mimado, consentido; demasiado bien alimentado
pamphlet /'pæmflıt/ n folleto, m
pamphleteer /,pæmflı'tıər/ n folletinista, mf
pan /pæn/ n (vessel) cazuela, f; cacerola, f; (brain) cráneo, m; (of a balance) platillo, m; (of a firelock) cazoleta, f, Cinema. toma panorámica f, prefix pan-. **to pan off,** separar el oro en una gamella. **to pan out,** dar oro; Fig. suceder. **Pan-Americanism,** panamericanismo, m. **Pan-American Highway,** la carretera panamericana, f
Pan /pæn/ n Pan, m. **pipes of Pan,** flauta de Pan, f
panacea /,pænə'siə/ n panacea, f
panache /pə'næʃ/ n penacho, m
panada /pənə'dɑ/ n Cul. panetela, f
Panama /'pænə,mɑ/ el Panamá, m
Panama /'pænə,mɑ/ a panameño. (-ña). **P. hat,** sombrero de jipijapa, panamá m
pancake /'pæn,keik/ n fruta de sartén, hojuela, f. **p. landing,** Aer. aterrizaje brusco, m. **P. Tuesday,** martes de Carnaval, m
panchromatic /,pænkrou'mætık, -krə-/ a pancromático
pancreas /'pænkriəs, 'pæŋ-/ n páncreas, m
pancreatic /,pænkri'ætık/ a pancreático
panda /'pændə/ n Zool. panda, mf
pandemic /pæn'demık/ a pandémico
pandemonium /,pændə'mouniəm/ n pandemonio
pander /'pændər/ n alcahuete, m, vi alcahuetear. **to p. to,** prestarse a; favorecer, ayudar
pandore /pæn'dɔr/ n Mus. bandola, f
pane /pein/ n hoja de vidrio, hoja de cristal, f; cuadro, m
panegyric /,pænı'dʒırık/ a panegírico. n panegírico, m
panel /'pænḷ/ n panel, entrepaño, m; Art. tabla, f; (in a dress) paño, m; (list) lista, f, registro, m; (jury) jurado, m; lista de jurados, f, vt labrar a entrepaños; artesonar. **p. doctor,** médico (-ca) de seguros
paneled /'pænḷd/ a entrepañado; (of ceilings) artesonado. **p. ceiling,** artesonado, m
paneling /'pænḷıŋ/ n entrepaños, m pl; artesonado, m
panful /'pæn,fʊl/ n cazolada, f

pang /pæŋ/ n punzada (de dolor), f, dolor agudo, m; dolor, m; (anguish of mind) angustia, f, tormento, m; (of conscience) remordimiento, m
panic /'pænɪk/ n pánico, m; pavor, espanto, m; terror súbito, m, a pánico. vi espantarse. **p.-monger,** alarmista, mf **p.-stricken,** aterrorizado, despavorido
panicky /'pænɪki/ a Inf. lleno de pánico; nervioso
pannier /'pænyər/ n (basket) alforja, f; cesto, m; (bustle) caderillas, f pl
panoply /'pænəpli/ n panoplia, f
panorama /ˌpænə'ræmə, -'rɑmə/ n panorama, m
panoramic /ˌpænə'ræmɪk/ a panorámico
pansy /'pænzi/ n pensamiento, m, trinitaria, f
pant /pænt/ vi jadear; (of dogs) hipar; resollar; (of the heart) palpitar. n jadeo, m; palpitación, f. **to p. after,** suspirar por
pantaloon /ˌpænt'lun/ n (trouser) pantalón, m; (Pantaloon) Pantalón, m
pantheism /'pænθiˌɪzəm/ n panteísmo, m
pantheist /'pænθiɪst/ n panteísta, mf
pantheistic /ˌpænθi'ɪstɪk/ a panteísta
pantheon /'pænθiˌɒn, -ən/ n panteón, m
panther /'pænθər/ n pantera, f
panties /'pæntiz/ n pl pantalones, m pl
panting /'pæntɪŋ/ a jadeante, sin aliento. n jadeo, m; resuello, m, respiración difícil, f; palpitación, f
pantomime /'pæntəˌmaɪm/ n pantomima, f; revista, f. **in p.,** en pantomima; por gestos
pantry /'pæntri/ n despensa, f
pants /pænts/ n pl calzoncillos, m pl; (trousers) pantalones, m pl. **p. buttoned down the sides** Mexico calzoneras, f pl
panzer division /'pænzər/ n división motorizada, f
pap /pæp/ n (nipple) pezón, m; (soft food) papilla, f
papa /'pɑpə, pə'pɑ/ n papá, m
papacy /'peɪpəsi/ n papado, pontificado, m
papal /'peɪpəl/ a papal, pontificio. **p. bull,** bula pontificia, f. **p. nuncio,** nuncio del Papa, nuncio apostólico, m. **p. see,** sede apostólica, f
papaya /pə'paɪə/ n Cuba fruta bomba, f
paper /'peɪpər/ n papel, m; hoja de papel, f; documento, m; (lecture) comunicación, f; (newspaper) periódico, m; (journal) revista, f; (exam.) examen escrito, trabajo, m; ejercicio, m; pl **papers,** (credentials) documentación, f, credenciales, f pl; Com. valores negociables, m pl; (packet) paquete, m, a de papel; para papeles; parecido al papel. vt (a room) empapelar; (a parcel) envolver. **daily p.,** diario, m. **in p. covers,** (of books) en rústica. **slip of p.,** papeleta. f. **to send in one's papers,** entregar su dimisión. **p. bag,** saco de papel, m. **p.-chase,** rally-paper, m. **p.-clip,** prendedero de oficina, sujetapapeles, Central America ataché, elsewhere in Lat. Am. broche, m. **p.-cutting machine,** guillotina, f. **p. folder,** plegadera, f. **p.-hanger,** empapelador, m. **p.-hanging,** empapelado, m. **p.-knife,** cortapapel, m. **p.-maker,** fabricante de papel, m. **p.-making,** manufactura de papel, f. **p.-mill,** fábrica de papel, f. **p.-money,** papel moneda, m. **p.-pulp,** pasta, f. **p.-streamer,** serpentina, f. **p.-weight,** pisapapeles, m
papering /'peɪpərɪŋ/ n (of a room) empapelado, m
papery /'peɪpəri/ a semejante al papel
papier-mâché /ˌpeɪpərmə'ʃeɪ, pɑˌpyei-/ n cartón piedra, m
papillary /'pæpəˌlɛri/ a papilar
paprika /pæ'prikə, pə-, pɑ-, 'pæprɪkə/ n pimienta húngara, f
papyrus /pə'paɪrəs/ n papiro, m
par /pɑr/ n par, f. **at par,** Com. a la par. **above (below) par,** Com. por encima (or debajo) de la par. **He is a little below par,** No está muy bien de salud. **to be on par with,** ser el equivalente de; ser igual a. **par excellence,** por excelencia
parable /'pærəbəl/ n parábola, f
parabola /pə'ræbələ/ n Geom. parábola, f
parachute /'pærəˌʃut/ n paracaídas, m; Bot. vilano, m. **to p. down,** lanzarse en paracaídas. **p. troops,** cuerpo de paracaidistas, m
parachutist /'pærəˌʃutɪst/ n paracaidista, mf
parade /pə'reɪd/ n alarde, m; Mil. parada, revista, f;

(procession) desfile, m, procesión, f; (promenade) paseo, m. vt (display) hacer alarde de, hacer gala de, ostentar; (troops) formar en parada; pasar revista (a); (patrol) recorrer. vi Mil. tomar parte en una parada; desfilar. **to p. up and down,** pasearse. **p.-ground,** campo de instrucción, m; plaza de armas, f
paradigm /'pærəˌdaɪm/ n paradigma, m
paradise /'pærəˌdaɪs/ n paraíso, edén, m; Fig. jauja, f. **bird of p.,** ave del paraíso, f
paradisiac /ˌpærə'dɪziˌæk/ a paradisíaco
paradox /'pærəˌdɒks/ n paradoja, f
paradoxical /ˌpærə'dɒksɪkəl/ a paradójico
paradoxicality /ˌpærəˌdɒksɪ'kælɪti/ n lo paradójico
paraffin /'pærəfɪn/ n parafina, f. vt parafinar. **p.-oil,** parafina líquida, f
paragon /'pærəˌgɒn/ n modelo perfecto, dechado, m
paragraph /'pærəˌgræf/ n párrafo, m; (in a newspaper) suelto, m, vt dividir en párrafos; escribir un suelto sobre. **new p.,** párrafo aparte, m
Paraguay /'pærəˌgwaɪ, -ˌgwei/ el Paraguay, m
Paraguayan /ˌpærə'gwaɪən/ a and n paraguayo (-ya)
parakeet /'pærəˌkit/ n Ornith. perico, m
parallel /'pærəˌlɛl/ a paralelo; igual; semejante, análogo. n línea paralela, f; paralelo, m; Mil. paralela, f; Geog. paralelo, m; Print. pleca, f. vt poner en paralelo; cotejar, comparar; igualar. **to run p. to,** ser paralelo a; ser conforme a. **p. bars,** paralelas, f pl
parallelism /'pærəlɛˌlɪzəm/ n paralelismo, m
parallelogram /ˌpærə'lɛləˌgræm/ n paralelogramo, m
paralysis /pə'ræləsɪs/ n parálisis, f
paralytic /ˌpærə'lɪtɪk/ a and n paralítico (-ca)
paralyze /'pærəˌlaɪz/ vt paralizar
paramount /'pærəˌmaʊnt/ a supremo, sumo
paramour /'pærəˌmʊr/ n amante, querido, m; querida, amiga, f
paranoia /ˌpærə'nɔɪə/ n paranoia, f
paranoiac /ˌpærə'nɔɪæk/ n paranoico, m
parapet /'pærəpɪt, -ˌpɛt/ n (Archit. and Mil.) parapeto, m
paraphernalia /ˌpærəfər'neɪlyə, -fə'neil-/ n Law. bienes parafernales, m, p; (finery) atavíos, adornos, m pl; equipo, m; arreos, m pl; insignias, f pl
paraphrase /'pærəˌfreɪz/ n paráfrasis, f, vt parafrasear
parasite /'pærəˌsaɪt/ n parásito, m; Inf. zángano, m, gorrista, mf, Mexico arrimado, m
parasitic /ˌpærə'sɪtɪk/ a parásito, parasitario; Med. parasítico
parasitology /ˌpærəsaɪ'tɒlədʒi, -sɪ-/ n parasitología, f
parasol /'pærəˌsɔl, -ˌsɒl/ n parasol, quitasol, m
parathyroid /ˌpærə'θaɪrɔɪd/ a paratiroides. n paratiroides, f pl
paratroops /'pærəˌtrups/ n pl paracaidistas, m pl
paratyphoid /ˌpærə'taɪfɔɪd/ n paratifoidea, f
parboil /'pɑrˌbɔɪl/ vt sancochar
parcel /'pɑrsəl/ n paquete, m; fardo, m; (of land) parcela, f. **to p. out,** repartir, distribuir; dividir. **to p. up,** envolver, empaquetar. **p. post,** servicio de paquetes, m
parceling /'pɑrsəlɪŋ/ n empaque, m; (out) reparto, m, distribución, f; división, f
parch /pɑrtʃ/ vt secar; abrasar, quemar; (roast) tostar. vi secarse; quemarse, abrasarse
parched /pɑrtʃt/ a seco, sediento. **p. with thirst,** muerto de sed
parchedness /'pɑrtʃɪdnɪs/ n sequedad, aridez, f
parchment /'pɑrtʃmənt/ n pergamino, m; (of a drum) parche, m. **p.-like,** apergaminado
pardon /'pɑrdn/ n perdón, m; Eccl. indulgencia, f. vt perdonar; indultar, amnistiar. **a general p.,** una amnistía. **I beg your p.!** ¡Vd. dispense!; ¡Perdone Vd.! **to beg p.,** pedir perdón; disculparse. **P.?** ¿Cómo?
pardonable /'pɑrdnəbəl/ a perdonable, disculpable, excusable
pardonableness /'pɑrdnəbəlnɪs/ n disculpabilidad, f
pardonably /'pɑrdnəbli/ adv disculpablemente, excusablemente
pardoner /'pɑrdnər/ n vendedor de indulgencias, m; perdonador (-ra)
pardoning /'pɑrdnɪŋ/ n perdón, m; remisión, f
pare /pɛər/ vt (one's nails) cortar; (fruit) mondar;

(potatoes, etc.) pelar; (remove) quitar; (reduce) reducir

parent /'pɛərənt, 'pær-/ *n* padre, *m*; madre, *f*; (ancestor) antepasado, *m*; (origin) origen, *m*, fuente, *f*; (cause) causa, *f*; (author) autor, *m*; autora, *f*; *pl* **parents,** padres, *m pl.*

parentage /'pɛərəntɪdʒ, 'pær-/ *n* parentela, *f*; linaje, *m*, familia, alcurnia, *f*; procedencia, *f*, nacimiento, origen, *m*

parental /pə'rɛntļ/ *a* paternal; maternal, de madre

parentally /pə'rɛntļi/ *adv* como un padre; como una madre

parenthesis /pə'rɛnθəsɪs/ *n* paréntesis, *m*

parenthetical /ˌpɛərən'θətɪkəl/ *a* entre paréntesis; de paréntesis

parenthood /'pɛərənt,hʊd, 'pær-/ *n* paternidad, *f*; maternidad, *f*

pariah /pə'raiə/ *n* paria, *mf*

parietal /pə'raiɪtļ/ *a* parietal

paring /'pɛərɪŋ/ *n* (act) raedura, *f*; peladura, mondadura, *f*; (shred) brizna, *f*; (refuse) desecho, desperdicio, *m.* **p.-knife,** trinchete, *m*

Paris /'pærɪs/ París, *m*

parish /'pærɪʃ/ *n* parroquia, *f*; feligresía, *f*, a parroquial. **p. church,** parroquia, *f.* **p. clerk,** sacristán de parroquia, *m.* **p. priest,** párroco, *m.* **p. register,** registro de la parroquia, *m*

parishioner /pə'rɪʃənər/ *n* parroquiano (-na); feligrés (-esa)

Parisian /pə'rɪʒən, -'riʒən, -'rɪziən/ *a* parisiense. *n* parisiense, *mf*

parity /'pærɪti/ *n* paridad, *f*

park /pɑrk/ *n* parque, *m*; jardín, *m. vt* (vehicles) estacionar; (dump) depositar. **car p.,** parque de automóviles, *m.* **p.-keeper,** guardián del parque, *m*

parking /'pɑrkɪŋ/ *n* (of vehicles) estacionamiento, *m*; (dumping) depósito, *m.* **p. lights,** Auto. luces de estacionamiento, *f pl.* **p. place,** parque de estacionamiento, *m*

parking meter *n Mexico* estacionómetro, *m, Argentina, Spain* parquímetro, *m, elsewhere in Lat. Am.* parcómetro, *m, Spain* reloj de estacionamiento, *m*

parlance /'pɑrləns/ *n* lenguaje, *m.* **in common p.,** en lenguaje vulgar

parley /'pɑrli/ *n* plática, conversación, *f*; discusión, *f*; Mil. parlamento, *m. vi* Mil. parlamentar; discutir; conversar. *vt* hablar

parliament /'pɑrləmənt/ *n* parlamento, *m*; cortes, *f pl*; cuerpo legislativo, *m*

parliamentarian /ˌpɑrləmɛn'tɛəriən/ *a* and *n* parlamentario; (of an academy) censor, *m*

parliamentarianism /ˌpɑrləmɛn'tɛəriənɪzəm/ *n* parlamentarismo, *m*,

parliamentary /ˌpɑrlə'mɛntəri, -tri/ *a* parlamentario. **p. immunity,** inviolabilidad parlamentaria, *f*

parlor /'pɑrlər/ *n* salón, gabinete, *m*; sala de recibo, *f*; (in a convent) locutorio, *m.* **p. games,** diversión de salón, *f*, juego de sociedad, *m.* **p.-maid,** camarera, *f*

parlous /'pɑrləs/ *a* crítico, malo. *adv* sumamente, muy

Parmesan /'pɑrmə,zɑn, ˌpɑrmə'zɑn/ *a* parmesano, de Parma. *n* parmesano (-na). **P. cheese,** queso de Parma, *m*

Parnassian /pɑr'næsiən/ *a* del parnaso; parnasiano. *n* parnasiano, *m*

Parnassus /pɑr'næsəs/ *n* Parnaso, *m*

parochial /pə'roukiəl/ *a* parroquial, parroquiano; Fig. provincial

parochialism /pə'roukiə,lɪzəm/ *n* provincialismo, *m*

parochially /pə'roukiəli/ *adv* por parroquias

parodist /'pærədɪst/ *n* parodista, *mf*

parody /'pærədi/ *n* parodia, *f*, *vt* parodiar

parole /pə'roul/ *n* (of convict) libertad vigilada, *f*

paroxysm /'pærək,sɪzəm/ *n* paroxismo, *m*; ataque, acceso, *m*

parquet /pɑr'kei/ (floor) entarimado *m*; (of theater) platea, *f*

parquetry /'pɑrkɪtri/ *n* taracea, *f*

parricide /'pærə,said/ *n* (act) parricidio, *m*; (person) parricida, *mf*

parrot /'pærət/ *n* papagayo, loro, *m, Lat. Am.* cata, *f*

parry /'pæri/ *vt* (a blow, and in fencing) parar; rechazar; evitar. *n* parada, *f*; (in fencing) quite, *m*, parada, *f*

parse /pɑrs, pɑrz/ *vt* analizar

Parsee /'pɑrsi, pɑr'si/ *n* parsi, *m*

parsimonious /ˌpɑrsə'mouniəs/ *a* parsimonioso

parsimoniously /ˌpɑrsə'mouniəsli/ *adv* con parsimonia

parsimony /'pɑrsə,mouni/ *n* parsimonia, *f*

parsley /'pɑrsli/ *n* perejil, *m*

parsnip /'pɑrsnɪp/ *n* chirivía, *f*

parson /'pɑrsən/ *n* párroco, cura, *m*; (clergyman) clérigo, *m*

parsonage /'pɑrsənɪdʒ/ *n* rectoría, *f*

part /pɑrt/ *n* parte, *f*; porción, *f*; trozo, *m*; Mech. pieza, *f*; (Gram. and of a literary work) parte, *f*; (of a living organism) miembro, *m*; (duty) deber, *m*, obligación, *f*; Theat. papel, *m*; Mus. voz, *f*; *pl* **parts,** (region) partes, *f pl*, lugar, *m*; (talents) partes, dotes, *f pl.* **foreign parts,** países extranjeros, *m pl*, el extranjero. **For my p....,** Por lo que a mí toca, Por mi parte. **for the most p.,** en su mayoría. **from all parts,** de todas partes. **in p.,** en parte; parcialmente. **spare p.,** pieza de recambio, *f.* **The funny p. of it is...,** Lo cómico del asunto es... **the latter p. of the month,** los últimos días del mes, la segunda quincena del mes. **to form p. of,** formar parte de. **to play a p.,** hacer un papel; desempeñar un papel. **to take a person's p.,** apoyar a alguien, ser partidario de alguien. **to take in good p.,** tomar bien. **to take p. in,** tomar parte en, participar en. **p. of speech,** parte de la oración, *f.* **p.-owner,** copropietario (-ia). **p.-time job,** trabajo de unas cuantas horas, *m*, trabajo de medio-tiempo, *m*

part /pɑrt/ *vt* distribuir, repartir; dividir; separar (de); (open) abrir. *vi* partir, marcharse; despedirse; (of roads, etc.) bifurcarse; dividirse; (open) abrirse. **to p. one's hair,** hacerse la raya. **to p. from,** (things) separarse de; (people) despedirse de. **to p. with,** separarse de; deshacerse de; perder; (dismiss) despedir (a)

partake /pɑr'teik/ *vt* participar de, compartir; tomar parte en. *vi* tomar algo (de comer, de beber). **to p. of,** comer (beber) de; tener rasgos de

partaker /pɑr'teikər/ *n* partícipe, *mf*

Parthian /'pɑrθiən/ *a* parto. *n* parto (-ta). **P. shot,** la flecha del parto

partial /'pɑrʃəl/ *a* parcial; (fond of) aficionado (a). **p. eclipse,** eclipse parcial, *m*

partiality /ˌpɑrʃi'ælɪti, pɑr'ʃæl-/ *n* parcialidad, *f*; preferencia, predilección, *f*

partially /'pɑrʃəli/ *adv* en parte, parcialmente; (with bias) con parcialidad

participant /pɑr'tɪsəpənt/ *a* participante. *n* partícipe, *mf*

participate /pɑr'tɪsə,peit/ *vi* participar (de), compartir; tomar parte (en)

participation /pɑr,tɪsə'peiʃən/ *n* participación, *f*

participial /ˌpɑrtə'sɪpiəl/ *a* Gram. participial

participle /'pɑrtə,sɪpəl, -səpəl/ *n* Gram. participio, *m.* **past p.,** participio pasado (or pretérito or pasivo), *m.* **present p.,** participio activo (or presente), *m*

particle /'pɑrtɪkəl/ *n* partícula, *f*; Fig. átomo, grano, *m*, pizca, *f*; Gram. partícula, *f*

parti-colored /'pɑrti,kʌlərd/ *a* bicolor

particular /pər'tɪkyələr/ *a* particular; especial; individual; singular; cierto; exacto; escrupuloso; difícil, exigente. *n* detalle, pormenor, *m*; circunstancia, *f*; caso particular, *m*; *pl* **particulars,** informes, detalles, *m pl.* **further particulars,** más detalles. **in p.,** en particular; sobre todo. **He is very p. about...,** Es muy exigente en cuanto a...; Le es muy importante..., Le importa mucho...

particularize /pər'tɪkyələ,raiz/ *vt* particularizar, detallar; especificar

particularly /pər'tɪkyələrli/ *adv* en particular; particularmente; sobre todo

parting /'pɑrtɪŋ/ *n* despedida, *f*; partida, *f*; separación, *f*; (of the hair) raya, crencha, *f*; (cross roads) bifurcación, *f. a* de despedida. **at p.,** al despedirse. **to reach the p. of the ways,** Fig. llegar al punto decisivo

partisan /'pɑrtəzən, -sən/ n partidario (-ia); (fighter) guerrillero, m, a partidario; de guerrilleros
partisanship /'pɑrtə,zənʃɪp/ n partidarismo, m
partition /pɑr'tɪʃən, pər-/ n partición, f; división, f; (wall) pared, f, tabique, m. **the p. of Ireland,** la división de Irlanda. vt **to p. off,** Lat. Am. entabicar
partly /'pɑrtli/ adv en parte
partner /'pɑrtnər/ n asociado (-da); Com. socio (-ia); (dancing) pareja, f; (in games, and companion) compañero (-ra); (spouse) consorte, mf; (in crime) codelincuente, mf **sleeping p.,** socio comanditario, m. **working p.,** socio industrial, m
partnership /'pɑrtnər,ʃɪp/ n asociación, f; Com. sociedad, compañía, f. **deed of p.,** artículos de sociedad, m pl. **to take into p.,** tomar como socio (a). **to form a p.,** asociarse
partridge /'pɑrtrɪdʒ/ n Ornith. perdiz, f. **young p.,** perdigón, m
parturient /pɑr'tʊriənt/ a f, parturienta. n parturienta, f
parturition /,pɑrtʊ'rɪʃən, -tʃʊ-/ n parto, m
party /'pɑrti/ n partido, m; grupo, m; (of pleasure, etc.) partida, f; reunión, fiesta, f; Mil. pelotón, destacamento, m; Law. parte, f; (person) interesado (-da); (accessory) cómplice, mf. **rescue p.,** pelotón de salvamento, m. **to be a p. to,** prestarse a; ser cómplice en. **to give a p.,** dar una fiesta, dar una reunión. **p.-spirit,** espíritu del partido, m. **p.-wall,** pared medianera, f
parvenu /'pɑrvə,nu/ n advenedizo (-za)
parvis /'pɑrvɪs/ n Archit. atrio, m
Paschal /'pæ'skæl/ a pascual
pass /pæs/ n (in an exam.) aprobación, f; (crisis) crisis, situación crítica, f; estado, m; (with the hands) pase, m; (permit) permiso, m; Mil. licencia, f; (safeconduct) salvoconducto, m; (in football, etc.) pase, m; (membership card) carnet, m; (defile) desfiladero, paso, puerto, m; Naut. rebasadero, m; (fencing) estocada, f. **free p.,** billete de favor, m. **p.-book,** libreta de banco, f. **p. certificate,** (in exams.) aprobado, m. **p.-key,** llave maestra, f
pass /pæs/ vi pasar; (of time) correr, pasar, transcurrir; (happen) occurrir, tomar lugar; (end) cesar, desaparecer; (die) morir. vt pasar; hacer pasar; (the butter, etc.) dar, alargar; (in football, hockey) pasar; (excel) aventajar, exceder; (a bill, an examination) aprobar; (sentence) fallar, pronunciar; (a remark) hacer; (transfer) traspasar; (tolerate) sufrir, tolerar; evacuar. **He passed in psychology,** Aprobó sicología. **to allow to p.,** ceder el paso (a). **to bring to p.,** ocasionar. **to come to p.,** suceder. **to let p.,** (put up with) dejar pasar; no hacer caso de; (forgive) perdonar. **to p. a vote of confidence,** votar una proposición de confianza. **to p. the buck,** Inf. echarle a uno el muerto. **p. the hat, p. the plate,** pasar la gorra. **to p. along,** pasar por; pasar. **to p. away,** pasar; desaparecer; (die) morir, fallecer; (of time) transcurrir. **to p. by,** pasar por, pasar delante de, pasar al lado de; (omit) pasar por alto de, omitir; (ignore) pasar sin hacer caso de. **to p. for,** pasar por. **to p. in,** entrar. **to p. in and out,** entrar y salir. **to p. off,** vi pasar; cesar, acabarse; desaparecer; evaporarse, disiparse; (of events) tener lugar. vt (oneself) darse por; dar por, hacer pasar por. **to p. a cat off as hare,** dar gato por liebre. **to p. on,** vi pasar; seguir su camino, continuar su marcha. vt pasar algo de uno a otro. **to p. out,** salir. **to p. over,** pasar por encima de; pasar; cruzar, atravesar; (transfer) traspasar; (disregard) pasar por alto de, dejar a un lado; omitir. **to p. over in silence,** pasar en silencio (por). **to p. around,** circular. **to p. through,** cruzar, atravesar, pasar por; (pierce) traspasar; Fig. experimentar
passable /'pæsəbəl/ a transitable, pasadero; (fairly good) regular, mediano; tolerable
passably /'pæsəbli/ adv medianamente, pasaderamente, tolerablemente
passage /'pæsɪdʒ/ n pasaje, m; paso, tránsito, m; (voyage) viaje, m, travesía, f; (corridor) pasillo, m; (entrance) entrada, f; (way) camino, m; (alley) callejón, m; (in a mine) galería, f; (of time) transcurso, m; (of birds) pasa, f; (in a book, and Mus.) pasaje, m; (occurrence) episodio, incidente, m; (of a bill) apro-

bación, f. **p. money,** pasaje, m. **p. of arms,** lucha, f, combate, m; disputa, f
passementerie /pæs'mɛntri/ n pasamanería, f
passenger /'pæsəndʒər/ n viajero (-ra); (on foot) peatón, m. **by p. train,** en gran velocidad
passerby /'pæsər'bai/ n transeúnte, paseante, mf
passing /'pæsɪŋ/ a pasajero; fugitivo; momentáneo. adv sumamente, extremadamente. n pasada, f; paso, m; (death) muerte, f; (disappearance) desaparición, f; (of a law) aprobación, f. **in p.,** de paso. **p.-bell,** toque de difuntos, m. **p. grade,** calificación mínima aprobatoria, f
passion /'pæʃən/ n pasión, f; (Christ's) Pasión, f; (anger) cólera, f. **to fly into a p.,** montar en cólera. **p.-flower,** pasionaria, granadilla, f. **P. play,** drama de la Pasión, f. **P. Sunday,** Domingo de Pasión, m. **P. Week,** Semana Santa, f
passionate /'pæʃənɪt/ a apasionado; (quick-tempered) irascible, colérico; (fervid) vehemente, intenso, ardiente
passionately /'pæʃənɪtli/ adv con pasión, apasionadamente; (irascibly) coléricamente; (fervidly) con vehemencia, ardientemente
passionless /'pæʃənlɪs/ a sin pasión, frío; impasible; imparcial
passive /'pæsɪv/ a pasivo. n Gram. pasiva, f. **p. resistance,** resistencia pasiva, f
passivity /pæ'sɪvɪti/ n pasividad, f
Passover /'pæs,ouvər/ n Pascua de los judíos, f
passport /'pæspɔrt/ n pasaporte, m
password /'pæs,wɜrd/ n contraseña, f
past /pæst/ a pasado; último; (expert) consumado; (former) antiguo, ex-. n pasado, m; historia, f, antecedentes, m pl, prep después de; (in front of) delante de; (next to) al lado de; (beyond) más allá de; (without) sin; fuera de; (of age) más de; (no longer able to) incapaz de. adv más allá. (The translation of **past** as an adverb is often either omitted, or included in the verb, e.g. The years flew p., Los años transcurrieron. for centuries p., durante siglos.) **I am p. caring,** Nada me importa ya. **It is a quarter p. ten,** Son las diez y cuarto. **It is p. four o'clock,** Son las siete pasadas, Son después de las cuatro. **what's p. is p.,** lo pasado, pasado. **p. doubt,** fuera de duda. **p. endurance,** insoportable. **p. help,** sin remedio, irremediable. **p. hope,** sin esperanza. **p.-master,** maestro, consumado, experto, m. **p. participle,** participio pasado, m. **p. president,** ex-presidente, m. **p. tense,** (tiempo) pasado, m
paste /peist/ n pasta, f; (gloy) engrudo, m. vt (affix) pegar; (glue) engomar, engrudar
pasteboard /'peist,bɔrd/ n cartón, m, cartulina, f, a de cartón, de cartulina
pastel /pæ'stɛl/ n Art. pastel, f. **p. drawing,** pintura al pastel, f
pastelist /pæ'stɛlɪst/ n pastelista, mf
pasteurization /,pæstʃərə'zeiʃən/ n pasteurización, f
pasteurize /'pæstʃə,raiz/ vt pasteurizar
pastille /pæ'stil/ n pastilla, f
pastime /'pæs,taim/ n pasatiempo, entretenimiento, m, diversión, recreación, f
pastor /'pæstər/ n pastor, m
pastoral /'pæstərəl/ a pastoril; Eccl. pastoral. n Eccl. pastoral, f; (Poet. Mus.) pastorela, f
pastorate /'pæstərɪt/ n pastorado, m
pastry /'peistri/ n (dough) pasta, f; pastel, m, torta, f; pastelería, f. **p.-cook,** repostero, m, pastelero (-ra)
pasturage /'pæstʃərɪdʒ/ n (grass, etc.) pasto, m; pasturaje, m; pastoreo, m
pasture /'pæstʃər/ n (grass, etc.) pasto, herbaje, m; pasturaje, m; (field) prado, m; pradera, dehesa, f. vi pacer; pastar. vt apacentar, pastar, Argentina costear
pasty /'pæsti/ a pastoso; (pale) pálido. n empanada, f
pat /pæt/ n toque, m; caricia, f; (for butter) molde (de mantequilla), m. vt tocar; acariciar; pasar la mano (sobre). adv a propósito; oportunamente; fácilmente. **pat of butter,** pedacito de mantequilla, m. **pat on the back,** golpe en la espalda, m; Fig. elogio, m
Patagonian /,pætə'gouniən/ a and n patagón (-ona)
patch /pætʃ/ n (mend) remiendo, m; (piece) pedazo, m; (plaster and Auto., etc.) parche, m; (beauty spot)

lunar postizo, *m*; (of ground) parcela, *f*; (of flowers, etc.) masa, *f*; (stain, and *Fig.*) mancha, *f*. *vt* (mend) remendar; poner remiendo (a); pegar; (roughly) chafallar; (the face) ponerse lunares postizos. **p. of blue sky,** pedazo de cielo azul. **patch of green grass,** mancha de hierba verde. **to be not a p. on,** no ser de la misma clase que; (of persons) no llegarle a los zancajos de. **to p. up a quarrel,** hacer las paces
patchwork /ˈpætʃˌwɜrk/ *n* labor de retazos, obra de retacitos, *f*; *Fig.* mezcla, mezcolanza, *f*. **p. quilt,** centón, *m*
patchy /ˈpætʃi/ *a* desigual; manchado
patella /pəˈtɛlə/ *n Anat.* rótula, *f*
patency /ˈpeɪtṇsi/ *n* evidencia, claridad, *f*
patent /ˈpætṇt/ *a* evidente, patente; patentado. *n* patente, *f*. *vt* patentar. **p. of nobility,** carta de hidalguía, ejecutoria, *f*. **"P. Applied For,"** «Patente Solicitada.» **Patent Pending** marca en trámite. **p. leather,** *n* charol, *m*. *a* de charol. **p. medicine,** específico farmacéutico, *m*
patentee /ˌpætṇˈti/ *n* el, *m*, (*f*, la) que obtiene una patente; inventor (-ra)
patently /ˈpætṇtli/ *adv* evidentemente, claramente
paterfamilias /ˌpeɪtərfəˈmɪliəs, ˌpɑ-, ˌpætər-/ *n* padre de familia, *m*
paternal /pəˈtɜrnḷ/ *a* paterno, paternal
paternally /pəˈtɜrnḷi/ *adv* paternalmente
paternity /pəˈtɜrnɪti/ *n* paternidad, *f*
path /pæθ/ *n* senda, vereda, *f*, sendero, *m*; camino, *m*; (track) pista, *f*; (trajectory) trayectoria, *f*. **the beaten p.,** el camino trillado
pathetic /pəˈθɛtɪk/ *a* patético, desgraciado, desafortunado
pathless /ˈpæθlɪs/ *a* sin senda
pathogenic /ˌpæθəˈdʒɛnɪk/ *a Med.* patógeno
pathological /ˌpæθəˈlɒdʒɪkəl/ *a* patológico
pathologist /pəˈθɒlədʒɪst/ *n* patólogo, *m*
pathology /pəˈθɒlədʒi/ *n* patología, *f*
pathos /ˈpeɪθɒs/ *n* lo patético
patience /ˈpeɪʃəns/ *n* paciencia, *f*. **He tries my p. very much,** Me cuesta mucho no impacientarme con él. **to lose p.,** perder la paciencia; (grow angry) perder los estribos. **to play p.,** hacer solitarios
patient /ˈpeɪʃənt/ *n* paciente. *n* paciente, *mf*; (ill person) enfermo (-ma); (of a physician) cliente, *mf*
patiently /ˈpeɪʃəntli/ *adv* con paciencia, pacientemente
patina /ˈpætṇə, pəˈtinə/ *n* pátina, *f*
patriarch /ˈpeɪtriˌɑrk/ *n* patriarca, *m*
patriarchal /ˌpeɪtriˈɑrkəl/ *a* patriarcal
patriarchy /ˈpeɪtriˌɑrki/ *n* patriarcado, *m*
patrician /pəˈtrɪʃən/ *a* and *n* patricio (-ia)
patrimonial /ˌpætrəˈmouniəl/ *a* patrimonial
patrimony /ˈpætrəˌmouni/ *n* patrimonio, *m*
patriot /ˈpeɪtriət/ *n* patriota, *mf*
patriotic /ˌpeɪtriˈɒtɪk/ *a* patriótico
patriotism /ˈpeɪtriəˌtɪzəm/ *n* patriotismo, *m*
patrol /pəˈtroul/ *n* patrulla, *f*; ronda, *f*, *vi* and *vt* patrullar; rondar; recorrer. **p. boat,** lancha escampavía, *f*. **p. flight,** vuelo de patrulla, *m*
patron /ˈpeɪtrən/ *n* (of a freed slave) patrono, *m*; (of the arts, etc.) mecenas, protector, *m*; (customer) parroquiano (-na), cliente, *mf*. **p. saint,** santo (-ta) patrón (-ona)
patronage /ˈpeɪtrənɪdʒ/ *n* (protection) patrocinio, *m*; protección, *f*; *Eccl.* patronato, *m*; (regular custom) clientela, *f*; (of manner) superioridad, *f*
patroness /ˈpeɪtrənɪs/ *n* patrona, *f*; protectora, *f*; (of a charity, etc.) patrocinadora, *f*; (of a regiment, etc.) madrina, *f*
patronize /ˈpeɪtrəˌnaɪz/ *vt* patrocinar; proteger, favorecer; (a shop) ser parroquiano de; (treat arrogantly) tratar con superioridad
patronizing /ˈpeɪtrəˌnaɪzɪŋ/ *a* (with air, behavior, etc.) de superioridad, de altivez
patten /ˈpætṇ/ *n* zueco, chanclo, *m*
patter /ˈpætər/ *n* (jargon) jerga, *f*; charla, *f*; (of rain) azotes, *m pl*; (of feet) son, *m*; golpecitos, *m pl*. *vt* (repeat) decir mecánicamente. *vi* (chatter) charlar; (of rain) azotar, bailar; correr ligeramente

pattern /ˈpætərn/ *n* modelo, *m*; (*Sew.* and dressmaking) patrón, *m*; (in founding) molde, *m*; (templet) escantillón, *m*; (of cloth, etc.) muestra, *f*; (design) dibujo, diseño, *m*; (example) ejemplar, *m*. *vt* diseñar; estampar. **p. book,** libro de muestras, *m*
patty /ˈpæti/ *n* empanada, *f*, pastelillo, *m*
paucity /ˈpɔsɪti/ *n* poquedad, *f*; corto número, *m*; insuficiencia, escasez, *f*
paunch /pɔntʃ/ *n* panza, barriga, *f*
pauper /ˈpɔpər/ *n* pobre, *mf*
pauperism /ˈpɔpəˌrɪzəm/ *n* pauperismo, *m*
pauperization /ˌpɔpərəˈzeɪʃən/ *n* empobrecimiento, *m*
pauperize /ˈpɔpəˌraɪz/ *vt* empobrecer, reducir a la miseria
pause /pɔz/ *n* pausa, *f*; intervalo, *m*; silencio, *m*; interrupción, *f*; *Mus.* pausa, *f*. *vi* pausar, hacer una pausa; detenerse, interrumpirse; vacilar. **to give p. to,** hacer vacilar (a)
pave /peɪv/ *vt* empedrar, enlosar. **to p. the way for,** facilitar el paso de, preparar el terreno para, abrir el camino de
pavement /ˈpeɪvmənt/ *n* pavimento, *m*, *Mexico* escarpa, *f*; (sidewalk) acera, *f*. **p.-artist,** pintor callejero, *m*
pavilion /pəˈvɪlyən/ *n* pabellón, *m*; (for a band, etc.) quiosco, *m*; (tent) tienda de campaña, *f*
paving /ˈpeɪvɪŋ/ *n* pavimentación, *f*; empedrado, *m*; see **pavement. p.-stone,** losa, *f*
paw /pɔ/ *n* pata, *f*; (with claws) garra, *f*; *Inf.* manaza, *f*. *vt* tocar con la pata; (scratch) arañar; (handle) manosear. *vi* (of a horse) piafar
pawing /ˈpɔɪŋ/ *n* (of a horse) el piafar; (handling) manoseo, *m*
pawn /pɔn/ *n* (chess) peón (de ajedrez), *m*; empeño, *m*; *Fig.* prenda, *f*. *vt* empeñar, pignorar; dar en prenda. **p.-ticket,** papeleta de empeño, *f*
pawnbroker /ˈpɔnˌbroukər/ *n* prestamista, *mf*
pawnshop /ˈpɔnˌʃɒp/ *n* casa de préstamos, casa de empeño, *f*, monte de piedad, *m*
pay /peɪ/ *n* paga, *f*; (*Mil. Nav.*) soldada, *f*; salario, *m*; (of a workman) jornal, *m*; (reward) recompensa, compensación, *f*; (profit) beneficio, provecho, *m*. **pay-day,** día de paga, *m*. **pay-office,** pagaduría, *f*. **pay list, pay-sheet,** nómina, *Mexico* lista de raya, *f*
pay /peɪ/ *vt* pagar; (a debt) satisfacer; (spend) gastar; (recompense) remunerar, recompensar; (hand over) entregar; (yield) producir; (a visit) hacer; (attention) prestar; (homage) rendir; (one's respects) presentar. *vi* pagar; producir ganancia; sacar provecho; ser una ventaja, ser provechoso. **It would not pay him to do it,** No le saldría a cuenta hacerlo. **This job doesn't pay,** Este trabajo no da dinero. **to pay a compliment (to),** cumplimentar, decir alabanzas (a), echar una flor (a). **to pay attention,** prestar atención; hacer caso. **to pay cash,** pagar al contado. **to pay in advance,** pagar adelantado, *Lat. Am.* aprontar. **to pay in full,** saldar. **to pay off old scores,** ajustar cuentas viejas. **to pay one's addresses to,** hacer la corte (a), pretender en matrimonio (a). **to pay the penalty,** sufrir el castigo, hacer penitencia. **to pay with interest,** *Fig.* pagar con creces. **to pay again,** volver a pagar, pagar de nuevo. **to pay back,** devolver, restituir; (money only) reembolsar; *Fig.* pagar en la misma moneda, vengarse (de). **to pay down,** pagar al contado. **to pay for,** pagar, costear; satisfacer. **to pay in,** ingresar. **to pay off,** (persons) despedir; (a debt) saldar; (a mortgage) cancelar, redimir. **to pay out,** (persons) vengarse de; (money) pagar; (ropes, etc.) arriar. **to pay up,** pagar; pagar por completo; (shares, etc.) redimir
payable /ˈpeɪəbəl/ *a* pagadero; a pagar; que puede ser pagado
payee /peɪˈi/ *n* tenedor, *m*
payer /ˈpeɪər/ *n* pagador (-ra)
paying /ˈpeɪɪŋ/ *n* See **payment**
paymaster /ˈpeɪˌmæstər/ *n* pagador, *m*; tesorero, *m*. **P.-General,** ordenador general de pagos, *m*
payment /ˈpeɪmənt/ *n* pago, *m*, paga, *f*, *Lat. Am.* also entero, *m*; remuneración, *f*, *Fig.* recompensa, satisfacción, *f*; *Fig.* premio, *m*. **in p. of,** en pago de. **on**

p. of, mediante el pago de. **p. in advance,** pago adelantado, anticipo, *m*
pea /pi/ *n* guisante, *m*, *Lat. Am.* alverjana, arveja, *f*.
dry or split pea, guisante seco, *m*. **sweet pea,** guisante de olor, *m*. **pea-flour,** harina de guisantes, *f*.
pea-green, verde claro, *m*. **pea-jacket,** chaquetón de piloto, *m*. **pea-shooter,** cerbatana, *f*
peace /pis/ *n* paz, *f*; tranquilidad, quietud, *f*, sosiego, *m*; *Law.* orden público, *m*. **P.!** ¡Silencio! **to hold one's p.,** callarse, guardar silencio. **to make p.,** hacer las paces. **P. be upon this house!** ¡Paz sea en esta casa! **p.-footing,** pie de paz, *m*. **p.-loving,** pacífico. **p.-offering,** sacrificio propiciatorio, *m*; satisfacción, oferta de paz, *f*
peaceable /'pisəbəl/ *a* pacífico; apacible; tranquilo, sosegado
peaceableness /'pisəbəlnıs/ *n* paz, *f*; apacibilidad, *f*; tranquilidad, quietud, *f*, sosiego, *m*
peaceably /'pisəbli/ *adv* pacíficamente; tranquilamente
peaceful /'pisfəl/ *a* pacífico; tranquilo; silencioso. **to come with p. intentions,** venir de paz
peacefully /'pisfəli/ *adv* en paz; pacíficamente; tranquilamente
peacefulness /'pisfəlnıs/ *n* paz, *f*; tranquilidad, calma, quietud, *f*; silencio, *m*; carácter pacífico, *m*
peacemaker /'pis,meikər/ *n* pacificador (-ra); conciliador (-ra)
peach /pitʃ/ *n* (fruit) melocotón, *m*; (tree) melocotonero, melocotón, *m*; (girl) breva, *f*. **p.-colour,** color de melocotón, *m*
peacock /'pi,kɒk/ *n* pavo real, pavón, *m*. *vi* pavonearse; darse humos. **The p. spread its tail,** El pavo real hizo la rueda
peahen /'pi,hɛn/ *n* pava real, *f*
peak /pik/ *n* punta, *f*; (of a cap) visera, *f*; (of a mountain) peñasco, *m*, cumbre, cima, *f*; (mountain itself) pico, *m*; (*Naut.* of a hull) pico, *m*; *Fig.* auge, apogeo, *m*; punto más alto, *m*. *vi* consumirse, enflaquecer. **p. hours,** horas de mayor tráfico, *f pl*
peaked /'pikıd/ *a* en punta; puntiagudo; picudo; (of a cap) con visera; (wan) ojeroso; (thin) delgaducho, macilento, consumido
peal /pil/ *n* toque (or repique) de campanas, *m*; campanillazo, *m*; carillón, *m*; (noise) estruendo, ruido, *m*; (of thunder) trueno, *m*; (of an organ) sonido, *m*. *vi* repicar; sonar. *vt* tañer, echar a vuelo (las campanas); (of a bell that one presses) hacer sonar, tocar. **a p. of laughter,** una carcajada
peanut /'pi,nʌt/ *n* cacahuete, *m*, *Dominican Republic* maní, *m*. **p. butter,** mantequilla de cacahuete, *f*
pear /pɛər/ *n* pera, *f*. **p.-shaped,** piriforme, de figura de pera. **p. tree,** peral, *m*
pearl /pɜrl/ *n* perla, *f*; (mother-of-pearl) nácar, *m*, *a* de perla; perlero. *vt* (dew) rociar, aljofarar. *vi* pescar perlas; formar perlas. **seed p.,** aljófar, *m*. **p.-ash,** carbonato potásico, *m*. **p.-barley,** cebada perlada, *f*. **p.-button,** botón de nácar, *m*. **p.-fisher,** pescador de perlas, *m*. **p.-fishery,** pescaduría de perlas, *f*. **p.-gray,** gris de perla, *m*
pearly /'pɜrli/ *a* perlino; de perla; nacarado; (dewy) aljofarado
peasant /'pɛzənt/ *n* campesino (-na), labrador (-ra). *a* campesino
peasant movement *n Mexico* agrarismo, *m*
peasantry /'pɛzəntri/ *n* campesinos, *m pl*, gente del campo, *f*
peat /pit/ *n* turba, *f*. **p.-bog,** turbera, *f*
pebble /'pɛbəl/ *n* guijarro, *m*, pedrezuela, guija, *f*; (gravel) guijo, *m*; cristal de roca, *m*; lente de cristal de roca, *m*
pebbled, pebbly /'pɛbəld; 'pɛbli/ *a* guijarroso, enguijarrado
peccadillo /,pɛkə'dılou/ *n* pecadillo, *m*
peck /pɛk/ *n* (of a bird) picotazo, *m*, picada, *f*; (kiss) besito, *m*; (large amount) montón, *m*; multitud, *f*. *vt* (of a bird) picotear; sacar (or coger) con el pico; (kiss) besar rápidamente. *vi* (with al) picotear; picar
pectoral /'pɛktərəl/ *a* pectoral
peculiar /pı'kyulyər/ *a* particular, peculiar, individual;

propio, característico; (marked) especial; (unusual) extraño, raro, extraordinario
peculiarity /pı,kyuli'ærıti/ *n* peculiaridad, particularidad, *f*; singularidad, *f*; (eccentricity) excentricidad, rareza, *f*
peculiarly /pı'kyulyərli/ *adv* particularmente, peculiarmente; especialmente; extrañamente
pecuniarily /pı,kyuni'ɛərəli/ *adv* pecuniariamente
pecuniary /pı'kyuni,ɛri/ *a* pecuniario
pedagogic /,pɛdə'gɒdʒık/ *a* pedagógico
pedagogy /'pɛdə,goudʒi, -,gɒdʒi/ *n* pedagogía, *f*
pedal /'pɛdl/ *a Zool.* del pie. *n* pedal, *m*. *vi* pedalear
pedant /'pɛdn̩t/ *n* pedante, *mf*
pedantic /pə'dæntık/ *a* pedante
pedantically /pə'dæntıkli/ *adv* con pedantería, pedantescamente
pedantry /'pɛdn̩tri/ *n* pedantería, *f*
peddle /'pɛdl/ *vi* ser buhonero. *vt* revender
peddling /'pɛdlıŋ/ *n* buhonería, *f*. *a* trivial, insignificante; mezquino
pedestal /'pɛdəstl̩/ *n* pedestal, *m*; *Fig.* fundamento, *m*, base, *f*. **to put on a p.,** *Fig.* poner sobre un pedestal
pedestrian /pə'dɛstriən/ *n* peatón, peón, *m*, *a* pedestre; *Fig.* patoso. **p. traffic,** circulación de los peatones, *f*
pedestrian crosswalk /'krɔs,wɔk/ *n* cruce peatonal, *Argentina* cruce de peatones, *m*
pediatrician /,pidiə'trıʃən/ *n* pediatra, *mf*
pedigree /'pɛdı,gri/ *n* genealogía, *f*; raza, *f*; (of words) etimología, *f*. *a* (of animals) de raza, de casta. **p. dog,** perro de casta, *m*
pediment /'pɛdəmənt/ *n Archit.* frontón, *m*
pedlar /'pɛdlər/ *n* buhonero (-ra), *Lat. Am.* marchante (-ta), *mf*
pedometer /pə'dɒmıtər/ *n* pedómetro, cuentapasos, *m*
peel /pil/ *n* (baker's) pala, *f*; (of fruit, etc.) piel, *f*, hollejo, *m*; (bark) descortezar; *Lat. Am.* deshojar (fruit). *vi* descascararse, desconcharse; (of the bark of a tree) descortezarse
peeling /'pilıŋ/ *n* (of fruit, etc.) peladura, monda, *f*; (of bark) descortezadura, *f*; (of paint, etc.) desconchadura, *f*
peep /pip/ *vi* (of birds) piar; (of mice) chillar; (peer) atisbar, mirar a hurtadillas; (appear) asomar; mostrarse; (of the dawn) despuntar. *n* (of birds) pío, *m*; (of mice) chillido, *m*; (glimpse) vista, *f*; (glance) ojeada, mirada furtiva, *f*; **at the p. of day,** al despuntar el día. **p.-hole,** mirilla, *f*, atisbadero, *m*; escucha, *f*. **p.-show,** óptica, *f*
peeper /'pipər/ *n* (eye) avizón *m*
peer /pıər/ *n* par, *m*; igual, *mf*. *vi* atisbar; escudriñar; *Fig.* asomar, aparecer
peerage /'pıərıdʒ/ *n* nobleza, aristocracia, *f*; dignidad de par, *f*
peeress /'pıərıs/ *n* paresa, *f*
peerless /'pıərlıs/ *a* sin par, incomparable, sin igual
peevish /'pivıʃ/ *a* displicente, malhumorado; picajoso, vidrioso, enojadizo
peevishness /'pivıʃnıs/ *n* displicencia, *f*, mal humor, *m*; impaciencia, *f*
peg /pɛg/ *n* clavija, *f*; (of a tent) estaca, *f*; (of a barrel) estaquilla, *f*; (of a violin, etc.) clavija, *f*; (for coats, etc.) colgadero, *m*; (of whisky, etc.) trago, *m*; *Fig.* pretexto, *m*. *vt* clavar, enclavijar, empernar. **to take down a peg,** bajar los humos (a). **to peg away,** batirse el cobre. **to peg down,** fijar con clavijas; (a tent) sujetar con estacas; (prices) fijar
peignoir /pein'wɑr/ *n* peinador, salto de cama, *m*, bata, *f*
pekinese /,pikə'niz/ *n* perro (-rra) pequinés (-esa)
pelican /'pɛlıkən/ *n* pelícano, *m*
pellagra /pə'lægrə/ *n Med.* pelagra, *f*
pellet /'pɛlıt/ *n* bolita, *f*; (pill) píldora, *f*; (shot) perdigón, *m*
pellmell /'pɛl'mɛl/ *adv* a trochemoche; atropelladamente
pellucid /pə'lusıd/ *a* diáfano
Peloponnesian /,pɛləpə'niʒən/ *a* and *n* peloponense, *mf*

pelota /pə'loutə/ n pelota vasca, f. **p. player,** pelotari, m

pelt /pɛlt/ n pellejo, m; cuero, m; (fur) piel, f; (blow) golpe, m. vt llover (piedras, etc.) sobre, arrojar... sobre; (questions) disparar; (throw) tirar. vi (of rain) azotar, diluviar

pelvic /'pɛlvɪk/ a pélvico, pelviano

pelvis /'pɛlvɪs/ n pelvis, f

pen /pɛn/ n (for sheep, etc.) aprisco, m; corral, m; (paddock) parque, m; (for hens) pollera, f; (for writing and Fig., author, etc.) pluma, f. vt (shut up) acorralar; encerrar; (write) escribir (con pluma). **pen-and-ink drawing,** dibujo a la pluma, m. **pen-holder,** portaplumas, m. **pen-name,** seudónimo, m. **pen-wiper,** limpiaplumas, m

penal /'pinl/ a penal. **p. code,** código penal, m. **p. colony,** colonia penal, f. **p. servitude,** trabajos forzados (or forzosos), m pl. **p. servitude for life,** cadena perpetua, f

penalization /,pinlə'zeiʃən/ n castigo, m

penalize /'pinl,aiz/ vt penar, imponer pena (a); castigar

penalty /'pɛnlti/ n Law. penalidad, f; castigo, m; (fine) multa, f; (risk) riesgo, m; Sports. sanción, m. **the p. of,** la desventaja de. **under p. of,** so pena de. **p. kick,** (football) penalty, m

penance /'pɛnəns/ n penitencia, f. **to do p.,** hacer penitencia

penchant /'pɛntʃənt/ n tendencia, f; inclinación, f

pencil /'pɛnsəl/ n lápiz, m; (automatic) lapicero, m. vt escribir (or dibujar or marcar) con lápiz. **p.-case,** estuche para lápices, m. **p.-holder,** lapicero, m. **p.-sharpener,** cortalápices, afilalápices, m

pendant /'pɛndənt/ n (jewel) pendiente, m; Archit. culo de lámpara, m; (Naut. rope) amantillo, m; (flag) gallardete, m

pending /'pɛndɪŋ/ a pendiente. prep durante. **to be p.,** pender; amenazar

pendulous /'pɛndʒələs/ a péndulo; colgante; oscilante

pendulum /'pɛndʒələm/ n péndola, f, péndulo, m

penetrability /,pɛnɪtrə'bɪlɪti/ n penetrabilidad, f

penetrable /'pɛnɪtrəbəl/ a penetrable

penetrate /'pɛnɪ,treit/ vt and vi penetrar

penetrating /'pɛnɪ,treitɪŋ/ a penetrante

penetration /,pɛnɪ'treiʃən/ n penetración, f

penguin /'pɛŋgwɪn/ n pingüino, pájaro bobo, m

penicillin /,pɛnə'sɪlɪn/ n penicilina, f

peninsula /pə'nɪnsələ, -'nɪnsyələ/ n península, f

peninsular /pə'nɪnsələr, -'nɪnsyələr/ a peninsular. **P. War,** Guerra de la Independencia, f

penis /'pinɪs/ n pene, m

penitence /'pɛnɪtəns/ n penitencia, f

penitent /'pɛnɪtənt/ a penitente. n penitente, mf

penitential /,pɛnɪ'tɛnʃəl/ a penitencial

penitentiary /,pɛnɪ'tɛnʃəri/ n Eccl. penitenciaria, f; casa de corrección, f; penitenciaria, f, presidio, m; cárcel modelo, f, a penitenciario

penknife /'pɛn,naif/ n cortaplumas, m

penmanship /'pɛnmən,ʃɪp/ n caligrafía, f

pennant /'pɛnənt/ n Naut. gallardete, m; banderola, f; (ensign) insignia, bandera, f

penniless /'pɛnɪlɪs/ a sin un penique, sin blanca; indigente, pobre de solemnidad, Peru calato. **to leave p.,** dejar en la miseria; Inf. dejar sin camisa

pennilessness /'pɛnɪlɪsnɪs/ n falta de dinero, extrema pobreza, f

penning /'pɛnɪŋ/ n escritura, f; (drawing up) redacción, f; (of bulls, etc.) acorralamiento, m

pennon /'pɛnən/ n pendón, m, banderola, f; (ensign) bandera, insignia, f

Pennsylvanian /,pɛnsəl'veinyən/ a and n pensilvano (-na)

penny /'pɛni/ n de un centavo, penique, m; perra gorda, f. a de un penique. **p.-a-liner,** gacetillero, m. **p. dreadful,** folletín, m, novela por entregas, f. **p.-in-the-slot machine,** tragaperras, m

pennyworth /'pɛni,wɜrθ/ n penique, valor de un penique, m

pension /'pɛnʃən/ n pensión, f; Mil. retiro, m; (grant) beca, f; (boardinghouse) pensión de familia, f. vt pensionar, dar una pensión (a); (with off) jubilar. **old age p.,** pensión para la vejez, f. **retirement p.,** pensión vitalicia, f

pensioner /'pɛnʃənər/ n pensionista, mf; (Mil. and Nav.) inválido, m

pensive /'pɛnsɪv/ a pensativo, meditabundo; cabizbajo, triste

pensively /'pɛnsɪvli/ adv pensativamente; tristemente

pensiveness /'pɛnsɪvnɪs/ n reflexión, meditación profunda, f; tristeza, melancolía, f

pentagon /'pɛntə,gɒn/ n pentágono, m

Pentateuch /'pɛntə,tuk/ n pentateuco, m

Pentecost /'pɛntɪ,kɔst/ n Pentecostés, m

pentecostal /,pɛntɪ'kɔstl/ a de Pentecostés, pascual. n (religious movement) pentecostal, mf

penthouse /'pɛnt,haus/ n cobertizo, tinglado, m, tejavana, f

pent-up /pɛnt 'ʌp/ a encerrado; enjaulado; (of emotion) reprimido

penultimate /pɪ'nʌltəmɪt/ a penúltimo. n penúltimo, m

penurious /pə'nʊriəs/ a pobre; escaso; (stingy) tacaño, avaro

penury /'pɛnyəri/ n penuria, f

peony /'piəni/ n peonía, f, saltaojos, m; rosa albardera, rosa montés, f

people /'pipəl/ n pueblo, m; nación, f; gente, f; personas, f pl; (used disparagingly, mob) populacho, vulgo, m; (inhabitants) habitantes, m pl; (subjects) súbditos, m pl; (relations) parientes, m pl; familia, f. vt poblar. **little p.,** (children) gente menuda, f. **respectable p.,** gente de bien, f. **the p. of Burgos,** los habitantes de Burgos. **P. say,** Se dice, La gente dice. **Very few p. think as you do,** Hay muy pocas personas que opinan como Vd. **How are your p.** (family)? ¿Cómo están los de tu casa? ¿Cómo está tu familia? **"People Working"** «Trabajadores»

peopling /'piplɪŋ/ n población, f; colonización, f

pep /pɛp/ n Inf. energía, f, ánimo, m. **p. talk,** discurso estimulante, m. **p. up,** animar

peplum /'pɛpləm/ n peplo, m

pepper /'pɛpər/ n pimienta, f; (plant) pimentero, pimiento, m, vt sazonar con pimienta; (pelt) acribillar; (with questions) disparar; (a literary work with quotations, etc.) salpimentar. **black p.,** pimienta negra, f. **red p.,** pimiento, m; (cayenne) pimentón, m. **p.-castor,** pimentero, m

peppercorn /'pɛpər,kɔrn/ n grano de pimienta, m

peppermint /'pɛpər,mɪnt/ n menta, f. **p. drop,** pastilla de menta, f

peppery /'pɛpəri/ a picante; (irascible) colérico, irascible

pepsin /'pɛpsɪn/ n Chem. pepsina, f

peptic /'pɛptɪk/ a péptico

per /pɜr; unstressed pər/ prep por. **ninety miles per hour,** noventa millas por hora. **ten pesetas per dozen,** diez pesetas la docena. **$60 per annum,** sesenta dólares al año. **per cent.,** por ciento

perambulate /pər'æmbyə,leit/ vt recorrer

perambulator /pər'æmbyə,leitər/ n cochecito para niños, m

percale /pər'keil/ n percal, m

percaline /,pɜrkə'lin/ n percalina, f

perceive /pər'siv/ vt percibir, comprender, darse cuenta de; percibir, discernir

percentage /pər'sɛntɪdʒ/ n tanto por ciento, m; porcentaje, m

perceptible /pər'sɛptəbəl/ a perceptible, visible; sensible

perceptibly /pər'sɛptəbli/ adv visiblemente; sensiblemente

perception /pər'sɛpʃən/ n percepción, f; sensibilidad, f

perceptive /pər'sɛptɪv/ a perceptivo

perch /pɜrtʃ/ n Ichth. perca, f; (for birds) percha, f; (measure) pértiga, f. vi posarse (en or sobre). vt posar (en or sobre)

percolate /'pɜrkə,leit/ vi filtrar; Fig. penetrar. vt filtrar, colar

percolation /,pɜrkə'leiʃən/ n filtración, f

percolator /'pɜrkə,leitər/ n filtro, m. **coffee p.**, colador de café, m
percussion /pər'kʌʃən/ n percusión, f; choque, m. **p. cap,** fulminante, m. **p. instrument,** instrumento de percusión, m
perdition /pər'dɪʃən/ n perdición, f; ruina, f
peregrination /,perɪgrə'neiʃən/ n peregrinación, f
peremptorily /pə'rɛmptərəli/ adv perentoriamente
peremptoriness /pə'rɛmptərɪnɪs/ n perentoriedad, f
peremptory /pə'rɛmptəri/ a perentorio; (of manner, etc.) imperioso, autoritario
perennial /pə'rɛniəl/ a Bot. vivaz; perenne; eterno, perpetuo. n planta vivaz, f
perennially /pə'rɛniəli/ adv perennemente
perfect /a., n. 'pɜrfɪkt; v. pər'fɛkt/ a perfecto; (of a work) acabado; completo. n Gram. (tiempo) perfecto, m. vt perfeccionar; (oneself) perfeccionarse. **to have a p. knowledge of...,** conocer a fondo... **They are p. strangers to me,** Me son completamente desconocidos
perfectible /pər'fɛktəbəl/ a perfectible
perfecting /pər'fɛktɪŋ/ n perfeccionamiento, m; terminación, f
perfection /pər'fɛkʃən/ n perfección, f; excelencia, f. **to p.,** a la perfección, a las mil maravillas
perfectionist /pər'fɛkʃənɪst/ n perfeccionista, mf
perfidious /pər'fɪdiəs/ a pérfido
perfidy /'pɜrfɪdi/ n perfidia, f
perforate /'pɜrfə,reit/ vt perforar, agujerear
perforating /'pɜrfə,reitɪŋ/ a perforador
perforation /,pɜrfə'reiʃən/ n perforación, f; agujero, m
perform /pər'fɔrm/ vt hacer; poner por obra, llevar a cabo; desempeñar, cumplir; ejercer; (a piece of music, etc.) ejecutar; realizar; (a play) representar, dar; (a part in a play) desempeñar (el papel de...); (Divine Service) oficiar. vi Theat. trabajar, representar un papel; (a musical instrument) tocar; (sing) cantar; (of animals) hacer trucos
performable /pər'fɔrməbəl/ a hacedero, practicable, ejecutable; Theat. que puede representarse; Mus. tocable
performance /pər'fɔrməns/ n ejecución, realización, f; desempeño, ejercicio, m; cumplimiento, m; acción, f; hazaña, f; (work) obra, f; Theat. función, representación, f; (Theat. acting of a part) interpretación, f; Mus. ejecución, f; Mech. potencia, f. **first p.,** Theat. estreno, m
performer /pər'fɔrmər/ n Mus. ejecutante, mf, músico, m; Theat. actor (-triz), representante, mf; artista, mf
performing /pər'fɔrmɪŋ/ a (of animals) sabio. **p. dog,** perro sabio, m
perfume /n. 'pɜrfyum; v. pər'fyum/ n perfume, m; fragancia, f; aroma, m. vt perfumar; embalsamar, aromatizar, llenar con fragancia. **p. burner,** perfumador, m
perfumer /pər'fyumər/ n perfumista, mf
perfumery /pər'fyuməri/ n perfumería, f
perfuming /'pɜrfyumɪŋ/ n acción de perfumar, f, a que perfuma
perfunctorily /pər'fʌŋktərəli/ adv perfunctoriamente, sin cuidado; superficialmente
perfunctoriness /pər'fʌŋktərɪnɪs/ n descuido, m, negligencia, f; superficialidad, f
perfunctory /pər'fʌŋktəri/ a perfunctorio, negligente; superficial; ligero, de cumplido
pergola /'pɜrgələ/ n emparrado, cenador, m
perhaps /pər'hæps/ adv quizá, quizás(s), tal vez
peril /'perəl/ n peligro, m; riesgo, m. vt poner en peligro; arriesgar. **at one's p.,** a su riesgo. **in p.,** en peligro
perilous /'perələs/ a peligroso, arriesgado
perimeter /pə'rɪmɪtər/ n perímetro, m
perineum /,perə'niəm/ n Anat. perineo, m
period /'pɪəriəd/ n período, m; época, f; edad, f, tiempo, m; duración, f; término, plazo, m; Gram. período, m; (full stop) punto final, m; Med. menstruación, regla, f. **p. furniture,** muebles de época, m pl
periodic /,pɪəri'ɒdɪk/ a periódico

periodical /,pɪəri'ɒdɪkəl/ a periódico. n publicación periódica, revista, f
periodicity /,pɪəriə'dɪsɪti/ n periodicidad, f
peripatetic /,perəpə'tɛtɪk/ a peripatético
peripheral /pə'rɪfərəl/ a periférico
periphery /pə'rɪfəri/ n periferia, f
periphrastic /,perə'fræstɪk/ a perifrástico
periscope /'perə,skoup/ n periscopio, m
perish /'perɪʃ/ vi perecer; marchitarse; desaparecer, acabar. **to be perished with cold,** estar muerto de frío
perishable /'perɪʃəbəl/ a perecedero, frágil
peritoneum /,perɪtn̩'iəm/ n peritoneo, m
peritonitis /,perɪtn̩'aitɪs/ n peritonitis, f
periwig /'perɪ,wɪg/ n peluca, f
periwinkle /'perɪ,wɪŋkəl/ n Zool. caracol marino, m; Bot. vincapervinca, f
perjure /'pɜrdʒər/ vt perjurar. **to p. oneself,** perjurarse
perjurer /'pɜrdʒərər/ n perjuro (-ra); perjurador (-ra)
perjury /'pɜrdʒəri/ n perjurio, m. **to commit p.,** jurar en falso, perjurar
perkiness /'pɜrkinɪs/ n desenvoltura, gallardía, f, despejo, m
perk (up) /pɜrk/ vi levantar la cabeza; recobrar sus bríos, alzar la cabeza; sacar la cabeza
perky /'pɜrki/ a desenvuelto, gallardo; coquetón, atrevido; (gay) alegre
permanence /'pɜrmənəns/ n permanencia, f; estabilidad, f
permanent /'pɜrmənənt/ a permanente; estable; (of posts, etc.) fijo. **p. wave,** ondulación permanente, f. **p. way,** Rail. vía, f
permanganate /pər'mæŋgə,neit/ n permanganato, m
permeability /,pɜrmiə'bɪlɪti/ n permeabilidad, f
permeable /'pɜrmiəbəl/ a permeable
permeate /'pɜrmi,eit/ vt penetrar; impregnar; Fig. infiltrar (en)
permeation /,pɜrmi'eiʃən/ n penetración, f; impregnación, f; Fig. infiltración, f
permissible /pər'mɪsəbəl/ a permisible, admisible; lícito
permission /pər'mɪʃən/ n permiso, m, licencia, f
permissive /pər'mɪsɪv/ a permisivo, tolerado; (optional) facultativo
permit /v pər'mɪt; n 'pɜrmɪt/ vt permitir; dar permiso (a), dejar; tolerar, sufrir; admitir. n permiso, m; licencia, f; pase, m. **Will you p. me to smoke?** ¿Me permites fumar?
permutation /,pɜrmyʊ'teiʃən/ n permutación, f
permute /pər'myut/ vt permutar
pernicious /pər'nɪʃəs/ a pernicioso. **p. anemia,** anemia perniciosa, f
perniciousness /pər'nɪʃəsnɪs/ n perniciosidad, f
peroration /,perə'reiʃən/ n peroración, f
peroxide /pə'rɒksaid/ n peróxido, m
perpendicular /,pɜrpən'dɪkyələr/ a perpendicular. n perpendicular, f
perpendicularity /,pɜrpən,dɪkyə'lærɪti/ n perpendicularidad, f
perpendicularly /,pɜrpən'dɪkyələrli/ adv perpendicularmente
perpetrate /'pɜrpɪ,treit/ vt Law. perpetrar; cometer
perpetration /,pɜrpɪ'treiʃən/ n Law. perpetración, f; comisión, f
perpetrator /'pɜrpɪ,treitər/ n el, m, (f, la) que comete; Law. autor (-ra); perpetrador (-ra)
perpetual /pər'pɛtʃuəl/ a perpetuo, perdurable, eterno; incesante, constante; (life-long) perpetuo
perpetually /pər'pɛtʃuəli/ adv perpetuamente; sin cesar; continuamente; constantemente
perpetuate /pər'pɛtʃu,eit/ vt perpetuar, eternizar; inmortalizar
perpetuation /pər,pɛtʃu'eiʃən/ n perpetuación, f
perpetuity /,pɜrpɪ'tuɪti/ n perpetuidad, f. **in p.,** para siempre
perplex /pər'plɛks/ vt dejar perplejo, aturdir, confundir; embrollar
perplexed /pər'plɛkst/ a perplejo, irresoluto; confuso; (of questions, etc.) complicado, intrincado

perplexedly /pər'plɛksɪdli/ *adv* perplejamente
perplexing /pər'plɛksɪŋ/ *a* difícil; complicado; confuso
perplexity /pər'plɛksɪti/ *n* perplejidad, *f*; confusión, *f*
perquisites /'pɜrkwəzɪts/ *n pl* emolumentos, *m pl*; gajes, percances, *m pl*; (tips) propinas, *f pl*
persecute /'pɜrsɪ,kyut/ *vt* perseguir; importunar, molestar
persecution /,pɜrsɪ'kyuʃən/ *n* persecución, *f*
persecutor /'pɜrsɪ,kyutər/ *n* perseguidor (-ra)
perseverance /,pɜrsə'vɪərəns/ *n* perseverancia, *f*
persevere /,pɜrsə'vɪər/ *vi* perseverar
persevering /,pɜrsə'vɪərɪŋ/ *a* perseverante
perseveringly /,pɜrsə'vɪərɪŋli/ *adv* con perseverancia, perseverantemente
Persia /'pɜrʒə/ (la) Persia, *f*
Persian /'pɜrʒən/ *a* persa; de Persia; pérsico. *n* persa, *mf*; (language) persa, *m*. **P. blinds,** persianas, *f pl*. **P. cat,** gato (-ta) de Angora
persist /pər'sɪst/ *vi* persistir; persistir (en), empeñarse (en), obstinarse (en)
persistence /pər'sɪstəns/ *n* persistencia, *f*
persistent /pər'sɪstənt/ *a* persistente
persistently /pər'sɪstəntli/ *adv* con persistencia, persistentemente
person /'pɜrsən/ *n* persona, *f*. **first p.,** *Gram.* primera persona, *f*. **in p.,** en persona. **no p.,** nadie
personable /'pɜrsənəbəl/ *a* bien parecido
personage /'pɜrsənɪdʒ/ *n* personaje, *m*
personal /'pɜrsən/ *a* personal; íntimo; particular; en persona; (movable) mueble. **He is to make a p. appearance,** Va a estar presente en persona. **p. column,** (in a newspaper) columna de los suspiros, *f*. **p. equation,** ecuación personal, *f*. **p. estate,** (goods) bienes muebles, *m pl*
personality /,pɜrsə'nælɪti/ *n* personalidad, *f*; (insult) personalismo, *m*. **dual p.,** conciencia doble, *f*
personification /pər,sɒnəfɪ'keiʃən/ *n* personificación, *f*
personify /pər'sɒnə,fai/ *vt* personificar
personnel /,pɜrsə'nɛl/ *n* personal, *m*
perspective /pər'spɛktɪv/ *n* perspectiva, *f*, *a* en perspectiva
perspicacious /,pɜrspɪ'keiʃəs/ *a* perspicaz, clarividente, sagaz
perspicacity /,pɜrspɪ'kæsɪti/ *n* perspicacia, clarividencia, sagacidad, *f*
perspicuity /,pɜrspɪ'kyuɪti/ *n* perspicuidad, claridad, lucidez, *f*
perspicuous /pər'spɪkyuəs/ *a* perspicuo, claro
perspiration /'pɜrspə'reiʃən/ *n* sudor, *m*
perspire /pər'spaiər/ *vi* sudar, transpirar
persuadable /pər'sweidəbəl/ *a* persuasible
persuade /pər'sweid/ *vt* persuadir; inducir (a), instar (a), mover (a), inclinar (a)
persuasion /pər'sweiʒən/ *n* persuasión, *f*; persuasiva, *f*; opinión, *f*; creencia, *f*; religión, *f*; secta, *f*
persuasive /pər'sweisɪv/ *a* persuasivo. *n* persuasión, *f*; aliciente, atractivo, *m*
persuasively /pər'sweisɪvli/ *adv* de un modo persuasivo, persuasivamente
persuasiveness /pər'sweisɪvnɪs/ *n* persuasiva, *f*
pert /pɜrt/ *a* petulante; respondón, desparpajado
pertain /pər'tein/ *vi* pertenecer (a); tocar (a), incumbir (a), convenir (a); estar relacionado (con)
pertinacious /,pɜrtn'eiʃəs/ *a* pertinaz
pertinaciously /,pɜrtn'eiʃəsli/ *adv* con pertinacia
pertinacity /,pɜrtn'æsɪti/ *n* pertinacia, *f*
pertinence /'pɜrtnəns/ *n* pertinencia, *f*
pertinent /'pɜrtnənt/ *a* pertinente, atinado
pertinently /'pɜrtnəntli/ *adv* atinadamente
pertly /'pɜrtli/ *adv* con petulancia; con descaro
pertness /'pɜrtnɪs/ *n* petulancia, *f*; desparpajo, descaro, *m*
perturb /pər'tɜrb/ *vt* perturbar, agitar, turbar, inquietar
perturbation /,pɜrtər'beiʃən/ *n* perturbación, agitación, inquietud, *f*; confusión, *f*; desorden, *m*
perturbed /pər'tɜrbd/ *a* perturbado, agitado, ansioso, intranquilo

perturbing /pər'tɜrbɪŋ/ *a* perturbador, inquietador
Peru /pə'ru/ el Perú
peruke /pə'ruk/ *n* peluca, *f*
perusal /pə'ruzəl/ *n* lectura, *f*; examen, *m*
peruse /pə'ruz/ *vt* leer con cuidado, estudiar, examinar
Peruvian /pə'ruviən/ *a and n* peruano (-na)
pervade /pər'veid/ *vt* penetrar; llenar, saturar; difundirse por; reinar en
pervasion /pər'veiʒən/ *n* penetración, *f*
pervasive /pər'veisɪv/ *a* penetrante
perverse /pər'vɜrs/ *a* (wicked) perverso, depravado; obstinado; travieso; intratable
perversion /pər'vɜrʒən/ *n* perversión, *f*
perversity /pər'vɜrsɪti/ *n* (wickedness) perversidad, *f*; obstinaca, *f*; travesura, *f*
perversive /pər'vɜrsɪv/ *a* perversivo
pervert /pər'vɜrt/ *vt* pervertir; (words, etc.) torcer, tergiversar
pervious /'pɜrviəs/ *a* penetrable; permeable
pessimism /'pɛsə,mɪzəm/ *n* pesimismo, *m*
pessimist /'pɛsəmɪst/ *n* pesimista, *mf*
pessimistic /,pɛsə'mɪstɪk/ *a* pesimista
pessimistically /,pɛsə'mɪstɪkli/ *adv* con pesimismo
pest /pɛst/ *n* insecto nocivo, *m*; animal dañino, *m*; parásito, *m*; (pestilence) peste, *f*; *Fig.* plaga, *f*; (person) mosca, *f*
pester /'pɛstər/ *vt* importunar, molestar, incomodar, *Lat. Am.* acatorrar, cargosear, majaderear. **to p. constantly,** *Inf.* no dejar a sol ni a sombra
pestering /'pɛstərɪŋ/ *n* importunaciones, *f pl*; *a* = annoying
pestilence /'pɛstləns/ *n* pestilencia, peste, *f*; plaga, *f*
pestilential /,pɛstl'ɛnʃəl/ *a* pestilente, pestífero; pernicioso
pestle /'pɛsəl/ *n* mano de mortero, *f*, *vt* pistar, machacar, majar
pet /pɛt/ *n* animal doméstico, *m*; niño (-ña) mimado (-da); favorito (-ta); (dear) querido (-da); (peevishness) despecho, malhumor, *m*. *vt* acariciar; (spoil) mimar. **to be a great pet,** ser un gran favorito
petal /'pɛtl/ *n* pétalo, *m*, hoja, *f*
peter (out) *vi* desaparecer; agotarse
petition /pə'tɪʃən/ *n* petición, *f*; súplica, *f*; instancia, solicitud, *f*; memorial, *m*. *vt* suplicar; pedir, demandar; dirigir un memorial (a). **to file a p.,** elevar una instancia
petitioner /pə'tɪʃənər/ *n* peticionario (-ia)
pet peeve /piv/ *Lat. Am.* barreno, *m*
Petrarchan /pɪ'trɑrkən/ *a* petrarquista
petrifaction /,pɛtrə'fækʃən/ *n* petrificación, *f*
petrify /'pɛtrə,fai/ *vt* petrificar; *Inf.* dejar seco. **to become petrified,** petrificarse
petrol /'pɛtrəl/ *n* bencina, gasolina, *f*. *a* de gasolina, de bencina.
petroleum /pə'trouliəm/ *n* petróleo, *m*. *a* petrolero; de petróleo. **p. works,** refinería de petróleo, *f*
petrology /pɪ'trɒlədʒi/ *n* petrografía, *f*
petrous /'pɛtrəs/ *a* pétreo
petticoat /'pɛti,kout/ *n* enagua, *f*; *pl* **petticoats,** (slang) faldas, *f pl*. *a* de faldas, de mujeres; de mujer
pettifogger /'pɛti,fɒgər/ *n* (lawyer) picapleitos, *m*, rábula, *mf*; (quibbler) sofista, *mf*
pettifogging /'pɛti,fɒgɪŋ/ *a* charlatán, mezquino, trivial
pettiness /'pɛtinɪs/ *n* trivialidad, insignificancia, *f*; pequeñez, *f*; mezquindad, *f*; ruindad, bajeza, *f*
petty /'pɛti/ *a* trivial, sin importancia, insignificante; inferior; pequeño; mezquino; ruin; bajo. **p. cash,** gastos menores de caja, *m pl*. **p. expense,** gasto menudo, *m*. **p. officer,** suboficial, *m*. **p. thief,** ratero (-ra)
petulance /'pɛtʃələns/ *n* mal humor, *m*, displicencia, irritabilidad, *f*
petulant /'pɛtʃələnt/ *a* malhumorado, displicente, enojadizo, irritable
petulantly /'pɛtʃələntli/ *adv* displicentemente, con mal humor
petunia /pɪ'tunyə/ *n* petunia, *f*

pew /pyu/ *n* banco (de iglesia), *m*. **p.-opener,** sacristán, *m*
pewter /'pyutər/ *n* peltre, *m*, *a* de peltre
phalange /'fæləndʒ/ *n* falange, *f*
phalanx /'feilæŋks/ *n* falange, *f*
phallic /'fælɪk/ *a* fálico
phallus /'fæləs/ *n* falo, *m*
phantasmagoria /fæn,tæzmə'gɔriə/ *n* fantasmagoría, *f*
phantasmagoric /fæn,tæzmə'gɔrɪk/ *a* fantasmagórico
phantom /'fæntəm/ *n* fantasma, espectro, *m*; sombra, ficción, *f*; visión, *f*
Pharisaical /,færə'seɪɪkəl/ *a* farisaico
Pharisee /'færə,si/ *n* fariseo, *m*
pharmaceutical /,farmə'sutɪkəl/ *a* farmacéutico; *n* producto farmacéutico, *m*
pharmacist /'farməsɪst/ *n* farmacéutico, *m*
pharmacological /,farməkə'lɒdʒɪkəl/ *a* farmacológico
pharmacologist /,farmə'kɒlədʒɪst/ *n* farmacólogo, *m*
pharmacology /,farmə'kɒlədʒi/ *n* farmacología, *f*
pharmacopoeia /,farmə'koupiə/ *n* farmacopea, *f*
pharmacy /'farməsi/ *n* farmacia, *f*
pharyngeal /fə'rɪndʒiəl/ *a* faríngeo
pharyngitis /,færɪn'dʒaitɪs/ *n* faringitis, *f*
pharynx /'færɪŋks/ *n* faringe, *f*
phase /feiz/ *n* fase, *f*; aspecto, *m*; *Astron.* fase, *f*
pheasant /'fezənt/ *n* faisán, *m*. **hen p.,** faisana, *f*. **p. shooting,** caza de faisanes, *f*
phenic /'finɪk/ *a* fénico
phenol /'finɔl/ *n* fenol, *m*
phenomenal /fɪ'nɒmənḷ/ *a* fenomenal
phenomenon /fɪ'nɒmə,nɒn/ *n* fenómeno, *m*
phial /'faiəl/ *n* redoma, *f*
philander /fɪ'lændər/ *vi* galantear
philanderer /fɪ'lændərər/ *n* Tenorio, galanteador, *m*
philandering /fɪ'lændərɪŋ/ *n* galanteo, *m*
philanthropic /,fɪlən'θrɒpɪk/ *a* filantrópico
philanthropist /fɪ'lænθrəpɪst/ *n* filántropo, *m*
philanthropy /fɪ'lænθrəpi/ *n* filantropía, *f*
philatelic /,fɪlə'telɪk/ *a* filatélico
philatelist /fɪ'lætḷɪst/ *n* filatelista, *mf*
philately /fɪ'lætḷi/ *n* filatelia, *f*
philharmonic /,fɪlhɑr'mɒnɪk/ *a* filarmónico
Philippine /'fɪlə,pin/ *a* and *n* filipino (-na)
Philippines, the /'fɪlə,pinz/ las (Islas) Filipinas, *f pl*
Philistine /'fɪlə,stin/ *a* and *n* filisteo (-ea)
philological /,fɪlə'lɒdʒɪkəl/ *a* filológico
philologist /fɪ'lɒlədʒɪst/ *n* filólogo, *m*
philology /fɪ'lɒlədʒi/ *n* filología, *f*
philosopher /fɪ'lɒsəfər/ *n* filósofo, *m*. **philosopher's stone,** piedra filosofal, *f*
philosophical /,fɪlə'sɒfɪkəl/ *a* filosófico
philosophize /fɪ'lɒsə,faiz/ *vi* filosofar
philosophy /fɪ'lɒsəfi/ *n* filosofía, *f*. **moral p.,** filosofía moral, *f*. **natural p.,** filosofía natural, *f*
phlebitis /flə'baitɪs/ *n* flebitis, *f*
phlebotomist /flə'bɒtəmɪst/ *n* sangrador, flebotomiano, *m*
phlebotomy /flə'bɒtəmi/ *n* flebotomía, *f*
phlegm /flɛm/ *n* flema, *f*, *Lat. Am.* desgarro, *m*
phlegmatic /flɛg'mætɪk/ *a* flemático
phlox /flɒks/ *n* flox, *m*
Phoenician /fɪ'nɪʃən/ *a* and *n* fenicio (-ia)
phoenix /'finɪks/ *n* fénix, *f*
phonetic /fə'nɛtɪk/ *a* fonético
phoneticist /fe'nɛtəsɪst/ *n* fonetista, *mf*
phonetics /fə'nɛtɪks, fou-/ *n* fonética, *f*
phonograph /'founə,græf/ *n* fonógrafo, *m*
phonological /,fɒnḷɒdʒɪkəl/ *a* fonológico
phonology /fə'nɒlədʒi/ *n* fonología, *f*
phony /'founi/ *a* falso; espurio. **p. war,** guerra tonta, guerra falsa, *f*
pyorrhea /,paiə'riə/ *n* piorrea, *f*
phosphate /'fosfeit/ *n* fosfato, *m*
phosphoresce /,fosfə'rɛs/ *vi* fosforecer, ser fosforescente
phosphorescence /,fosfə'rɛsəns/ *n* fosforescencia, *f*
phosphorescent /,fosfə'rɛsənt/ *a* fosforescente
phosphoric /fɒs'fɔrɪk/ *a* fosfórico

phosphorus /'fosfərəs/ *n* fósforo, *m*
photo /'foutou/ *n* foto, *f*
photochemistry /,foutou'kɛməstri/ *n* fotoquímica, *f*
photocopy /'foutə,kɒpi/ *n* fotocopia, *f*. *vt* fotocopiar, sacar copias
photogenic /,foutə'dʒɛnɪk/ *a* fotogénico
photograph /'foutə,græf/ *n* fotografía, *f*. *vt* fotografiar, retratar. **to have one's p. taken,** hacerse retratar
photographer /fə'tɒgrəfər/ *n* fotógrafo, *m*
photographic /,foutə'græfɪk/ *a* fotográfico
photography /fə'tɒgrəfi/ *n* fotografía, *f*
photogravure /,foutəgrə'vyʊr/ *n* fotograbado, *m*
photostat /'foutə,stæt/ *n* fotostato, *m*
photosynthesis /,foutə'sɪnθəsɪs/ *n* fotosíntesis, *f*
phrase /freiz/ *n* frase, *f*; *Mus.* frase musical, *f*. *vt* expresar, frasear; redactar. **p.-book,** libro de frases, *m*
phraseology /,freizi'ɒlədʒi/ *n* fraseología, *f*
phrasing /'freizɪŋ/ *n* (drawing up) redacción, *f*; (style) estilo, *m*; *Mus.* frases, *f pl*
phrenetic /frɪ'nɛtɪk/ *a* frenético
Phrygian /'frɪdʒiən/ *a* and *n* frigio (-ia)
Phrygian cap *n* gorro frigio, *m*
phthisis /'θaisɪs/ *n* tisis, *f*
phylactery /fɪ'læktəri/ *n* filactria, *f*
phylloxera /fɪ'lɒksərə/ *n* filoxera, *f*
physical /'fɪzɪkəl/ *a* físico. **p. fitness,** buen estado físico, *m*. **p. geography,** geografía física, *f*. **p. jerks,** ejercicios físicos, *m pl*. **p. sciences,** ciencias físicas, *f pl*. **p. training,** educación física, *f*
physician /fɪ'zɪʃən/ *n* médico (-ca)
physicist /'fɪzəsɪst/ *n* físico, *m*
physics /'fɪzɪks/ *n* física, *f*
physiognomist /,fɪzi'ɒgnəmɪst/ *n* fisonomista, *mf*
physiognomy /,fɪzi'ɒgnəmi/ *n* fisonomía, *f*
physiological /,fɪziə'lɒdʒɪkəl/ *a* fisiológico
physiologist /,fɪzi'ɒlədʒɪst/ *n* fisiólogo, *m*
physiology /,fɪzi'ɒlədʒi/ *n* fisiología, *f*
physiotherapy /,fɪziou'θerəpi/ *n* fisioterapia, *f*
physique /fɪ'zik/ *n* físico, *m*
pianist /pi'ænɪst, 'piənɪst/ *n* pianista, *mf*
piano /pi'ænou/ *n* piano, *m*. **baby grand p.,** piano de media cola, *m*. **grand p.,** piano de cola, *m*. **upright p.,** piano vertical, *m*. **p. maker,** fabricante de pianos, *m*. **p. stool,** taburete de piano, *m*. **p. tuner,** afinador de pianos, *m*
pianola /,piə'noulə/ *n* piano mecánico, *m*
picaresque /,pɪkə'rɛsk/ *a* picaresco
piccolo /'pɪkə,lou/ *n* flautín, *m*
pick /pɪk/ *n* (tool) pico, zapapico, *m*; (mattock) piqueta, *f*; (choice) selección, *f*; derecho de elección, *m*; (best) lo mejor, lo más escogido; (*Fig.* cream) flor, nata, *f*. **tooth-p.,** mondadientes, *m*. **p.-a-back,** sobre los hombros a cuestas. **p.-ax,** zapapico, *m*, alcotana, *f*. **p.-me-up,** tónico, *m*; trago, *m*
pick /pɪk/ *vt* (with a pick-ax, make a hole) picar; (pluck, pick up) coger; (remove) sacar; (clean) limpiar; (one's teeth) mondarse (los dientes); (one's nose) hurgarse (las narices); (a bone) roer; (a lock) abrir con ganzúa; (a pocket) bolsear, robar del bolsillo; (peck) picotear; (choose) escoger; (a quarrel) buscar. *vi* (steal) hurtar, robar; (nibble) picar. **I have a bone to p. with you,** Tengo que ajustar unas cuentas contigo. **Take your p.!** ¡Escoja! **to p. and choose,** mostrarse difícil. **to p. to pieces,** *Fig.* criticar severamente. **to p. one's way through,** abrirse camino entre; andar con precaución por; andar a tientas por. **to p. off,** coger; arrancar; quitar; (shoot) disparar; fusilar. **to p. out,** entresacar; escoger; (recognize) reconocer; (understand) llegar a comprender; (a tune) sacar de oídas; (a song) cantar de oídas; (colors) contrastar, resaltar. **to p. up,** *vt* (ground, etc.) romper con pico; coger; tomar; recoger; (raise) levantar, alzar; (information, etc.) cobrar, adquirir; (a living) ganar; (make friends with) trabar amistad con; (recover) recobrar; (find) encontrar, hallar; (buy) comprar; (learn) aprender; (a wireless message) interceptar; (a radio station) oír, tener. *vi* recobrar la salud; reponerse; mejorar. *n Mech.* recobro, *m*
picket /'pɪkɪt/ *n* estaca, *f*; (*Mil.* and during strikes) pi-

quete, *m*. *vt* cercar con estacas; poner piquetes ante (or alrededor de); poner de guardia; estacionar

picking /'pɪkɪŋ/ *n* (gathering) recolección, *f*; (choosing) selección, *f*; (pilfering) robo, *m*; *pl* **pickings**, desperdicios, *m pl*; (perquisites) gajes, *m pl*; ganancias, *f pl*

pickle /'pɪkəl/ *n* (solution) escabeche, *m*; (vegetable, etc.) encurtido, *m*; (plight) apuro, *m*; (child) diablillo, *m*. *vt* encurtir, escabechar

picklock /'pɪk,lɒk/ *n* (thief and instrument) ganzúa, *f*

pickpocket /'pɪk,pɒkɪt/ *n* carterista, *mf* ratero (-ra)

picnic /'pɪknɪk/ *n* partida de campo, jira, *f*, picnic, *m*. *vi* llevar la merienda al campo, hacer un picnic

picnicker /'pɪknɪkər/ *n* excursionista, *mf*

pictorial /pɪk'tɔriəl/ *a* pictórico; ilustrado. *n* revista ilustrada, *f*

pictorially /pɪk'tɔriəli/ *adv* pictóricamente; en grabados; por imágenes

picture /'pɪktʃər/ *n* cuadro, *m*; (of a person) retrato, *m*; imagen, *f*; (illustration) grabado, *m*, lámina, *f*; fotografía, *f*; (outlook) perspectiva, *f*; idea, *f*. *vt* pintar; describir; imaginar. **to go to the pictures,** ir al cine. **motion p.,** película, *f*. **talking p.,** película sonora, *f*. **p. book,** libro con láminas, *m*. **p. frame,** marco, *m*. **p. gallery,** museo de pinturas, *m*; galería de pinturas, *f*. **p. hat,** pamela, *f*. **p. postcard,** tarjeta postal, *f*. **p. restorer,** restaurador de cuadros, *m*. **p. writing,** pictografía, *f*

picturesque /,pɪktʃə'rɛsk/ *a* pintoresco

picturesqueness /,pɪktʃə'rɛsknɪs/ *n* carácter pintoresco, *m*, lo pintoresco; pintoresquismo, *m*

pie /pai/ *n* (savory) empanada, *f*; (sweet) pastel, *m*, torta, *f*; (of meat) pastelón, *m*; *Print*. pastel, *m*. **apple pie,** torta de manzanas, *f*. **to eat humble pie,** bajar las orejas. **to have a finger in the pie,** meter baza

piebald /'pai,bɔld/ *a* pío; tordo

piece /pis/ *n* pedazo, *m*; trozo, *m*; parte, porción, *f*; (literary, artistic work, coin, of fabric, at chess, etc. and slang) pieza, *f*; (of luggage) bulto, *m*; (of paper) hoja, *f*; (of ground) parcela, *f*; (of money) moneda, *f*, *vt* remendar; unir, juntar. **a p. of advice,** un consejo. **a p. of bread,** un pedazo de pan; una rebanada de pan. **a p. of folly,** un acto de locura. **a p. of furniture,** un mueble. **a p. of insolence,** una insolencia. **a p. of news,** una noticia. **a p. of paper,** un papel, una hoja de papel, una cuartilla. **a p. of poetry,** una poesía. **to break in pieces,** *vt* hacer pedazos, romper. *vi* hacerse pedazos, romperse. **to come or fall to pieces,** deshacerse; (of machines) desarmarse. **to cut in pieces,** cortar en pedazos; (an army) destrozar. **to give a p. of one's mind (to),** decir cuatro verdades (a), decir cuántas son cinco (a). **to go to pieces,** (of persons) hacerse pedazos. **to take to pieces,** (a machine) desmontar; deshacer. **to tear or pull to pieces,** hacer pedazos, despedazar; desgarrar. **p. goods,** géneros en piezas, *m pl*. **p.-work,** trabajo a destajo, *m*. **to do p.-work,** trabajar a destajo. **p.-worker,** destajista, *mf*

piecemeal /'pis,mil/ *adv* en pedazos; a remiendos; en detalle; poco a poco

piecrust /'pai,krʌst/ *n* pasta, *f*

pied /paid/ *a* bicolor; abigarrado, de varios colores

pier /pɪər/ *n* (jetty) dique, *m*; embarcadero, *m*; malecón, *m*; (of a bridge) pila, *f*; (pillar) columna, *f*; (between windows, etc.) entrepaño, *m*. **p.-glass,** espejo de cuerpo entero, *m*. **p. head,** punta del dique, *f*. **p. table,** consola, *f*

pierce /pɪərs/ *vt* penetrar; (of sorrow, etc.) traspasar, herir; (bore) agujerear, taladrar. *vi* penetrar

pierced ear /pɪərst/ *n* oreja perforada, *f*

piercing /'pɪərsɪŋ/ *a* penetrante; (of the wind, etc.) cortante; (of the voice, etc.) agudo. *n* penetración, *f*

piercingly /'pɪərsɪŋli/ *adv* de un modo penetrante, agudamente

pietism /'paiɪ,tɪzəm/ *n* pietismo, *m*

pietist /'paiɪtɪst/ *n* pietista, *mf*

pietistic /,paiɪ'tɪstɪk/ *a* pietista

piety /'paiɪti/ *n* piedad, devoción, *f*

piezometer /,paiə'zɒmɪtər/ *n* piezómetro, *m*

piffle /'pɪfəl/ *n* patrañas, tonterías, *f pl*

pig /pɪg/ *n* puerco, cerdo, *Lat. Am.* chancho, *m*; *Inf.*

cochino, *m*; (metal) lingote, *m*. **to buy a p. in a poke,** cerrar un trato a ciegas. **p.-eyed,** de ojos de cerdo. **p.-iron,** arrabio; hierro colado en barras, lingote de fundición, *m*

pigeon /'pɪdʒən/ *n* paloma, *f*, palomo, *m*; *Inf.* primo, *m*. *vt* embaucar, engañar. **carrier p.,** paloma mensajera, *f*. **clay p.,** pichón de barro, platillo de arcilla, *m*. **male p.,** pichón, *m*. **pouter p.,** paloma buchona, *f*. **young p.,** palomino, *m*. **p. fancier,** palomero, *m*. **p.-hole,** casilla, *f*. *vt* encasillar. **set of p.-holes,** encasillado, *m*. **p.-shooting,** tiro de pichón, *m*. **p.-toed,** patituerto

piggy bank /'pɪgi/ *n* alcancía, *f*

pigheaded /'pɪg,hɛdɪd/ *a* terco, testarudo, *Lat. Am.* empecinado

pigheadedness /'pɪg,hɛdɪdnɪs/ *n* terquedad, testarudez, *f*

piglet /'pɪglɪt/ *n* cerdito, *m*

pigment /'pɪgmənt/ *n* pigmento, *m*

pigmentation /,pɪgmən'teɪʃən/ *n* pigmentación, *f*

pigskin /'pɪg,skɪn/ *n* piel de cerdo, *f*

pigsty /'pɪg,stai/ *n* pocilga, *f*

pigtail /'pɪg,teil/ *n* coleta, *f*

pike /paik/ *n Mil.* pica, *f*, chuzo, *m*; (peak) pico, *m*

pilaster /pɪ'læstər/ *n* pilastra, *f*

pile /pail/ *n* estaca, *f*; poste, *m*; (engineering) pilote, *m*; (heap) pila, *f*, montón, *m*; (pyre) pira, *f*; (building) edificio grande, *m*; *Elec.* pila, *f*; (hair) pelo, *m*; (nap) pelusa, *f*; *pl* **piles,** *Med.* almorranas, *f pl*. *vt* clavar pilotes en; apoyar con pilotes; (heap) amontonar; (load) cargar. **to make one's p.,** *Inf.* hacer su pacotilla. **to p. arms,** poner los fusiles en pabellón. **to p. on,** (coal, etc.) echar; (increase) aumentar. **to p. it on,** exagerar, intensificar; (a table) cargar. **to p. up,** *vi* amontonarse; acumularse; *vt Lat. Am.* empilonar; (of a ship) encallar. **p.-driver,** machina, *f*; martinete, *m*. **p. dwelling,** vivienda palustre, sostenida por pilares, *f*

pilfer /'pɪlfər/ *vt* sisar, sonsacar, hurtar, ratear, *Mexico* chalequear

pilferer /'pɪlfərər/ *n* sisador (-ra), ratero (-ra)

pilfering /'pɪlfərɪŋ/ *n* sisa, ratería, *f*

pilgrim /'pɪlgrɪm/ *n* peregrino (-na). **pilgrim's staff,** bordón, *m*

pilgrimage /'pɪlgrəmɪdʒ/ *n* peregrinación, *f*; romería, *f*. **to make a p.,** hacer una peregrinación, peregrinar; ir en romería

piling /'pailɪŋ/ *n* amontonamiento, *m*; (of buildings) pilotaje, *m*

pill /pɪl/ *n* píldora, *f*. **to gild the p.,** *Fig.* dorar la píldora. **p.-box,** caja de píldoras, *f*; casamata, *f*, *Mil.* nido de ametralladoras, *m*

pillage /'pɪlɪdʒ/ *vt* pillar, saquear. *n* saqueo, *m*

pillager /'pɪlɪdʒər/ *n* saqueador (-ra)

pillaging /'pɪlɪdʒɪŋ/ *n* pillaje, *m*, *a* pillador, saqueador

pillar /'pɪlər/ *n* pilar, *m*, columna, *f*; (person) sostén, soporte, *m*. **from p. to post,** de Ceca en Meca. **p. of salt,** estatua de sal, *f*. **the Pillars of Hercules,** las Columnas de Hércules. **to be a p. of strength,** *Inf.* ser una roca. **p.-box,** buzón, *m*

pillared /'pɪlərd/ *a* con columnas, sostenido por columnas; en columnas

pillion /'pɪlyən/ *n* (on a horse, etc.) grupera, *f*; (on a motor-cycle) grupa, *f*. **to ride p.,** ir a la grupa

pillory /'pɪləri/ *n* picota, argolla, *f*. *vt* empicotar; *Fig.* poner en ridículo; censurar duramente

pillow /'pɪlou/ *n* almohada, *f*; (for lace-making) cojín, *m*; (of a machine) cojinete, *m*. *vt* apoyar; reposar; servir como almohada. **to take counsel of one's p.,** consultar con la almohada. **p.-case,** funda de almohada, *f*

pilot /'pailət/ *n* piloto, *m*; *Naut.* práctico, piloto (de puerto), *m*. *vt* guiar, conducir; (*Naut. Aer.*) pilotar, pilotear. **p. boat,** vaporcito del práctico, *m*. **p. jacket,** chaquetón de piloto, *m*. **p. officer,** oficial de aviación, *m*

pilotage /'pailətɪdʒ/ *n* pilotaje, *m*; *Naut.* practicaje, *m*

pilotless /'pailətlɪs/ *a* sin piloto

pimento /pɪ'mɛntou/ *n* pimiento, *m*

pimp /pɪmp/ *n* rufián, alcahuete, *m*, *vi* alcahuetear

pimple /'pɪmpəl/ n grano, m

pimply /'pɪmpli/ a con granos

pin /pɪn/ n alfiler, m; prendedor, m; clavija, f; clavo, m, chaveta, f; (bolt) perno, m. vt prender con alfileres; (with a peg) enclavijar; fijar; sujetar. **to pin up,** sujetar con alfileres; (the hair) sujetar con horquillas. **to be on pins,** estar en ascuas. **to suffer from pins and needles,** tener aguijones. **pin-head,** cabeza de alfiler, f. **pin-money,** alfileres, m pl. **pin-oak,** Bot. pincarrasco, m, carrasca, f. **pin point,** punta de alfiler, f. **pin-prick,** alfilerazo, m

pinafore /'pɪnəˌfɔr/ n delantal de niño, m

pince-nez /'pæns,nei/ n quevedos, m pl

pincers /'pɪnsərz/ n pl pinzas, tenazas, f pl, alicates, m pl; (of crustaceans) pinzas, f pl. **p. movement,** movimiento de pinzas, m

pinch /pɪntʃ/ vt pellizcar; (crush) estrujar; aplastar; apretar; (of the cold) helar; (steal) hurtar, birlar; (arrest) coger, prender. n pellizco, torniscón, m; pulgarada, f; (of snuff) polvo, m; (distress) miseria, f; (pain) dolor, m, angustia. f. **at a p.,** en caso de apuro. **to know where the shoe pinches,** saber dónde le aprieta el zapato

pinched /pɪntʃt/ a (by the cold) helado; (wan) marchito, descolorido

pincushion /'pɪn,kʊʃən/ n acerico, m

Pindaric /pɪn'dærɪk/ a pindárico

pine /pain/ n Bot. pino, m. vi languidecer, marchitarse, consumirse. **to p. for,** anhelar, suspirar por, perecer por. **pitch-p.,** pino de tea, m. **p.-apple,** piña de las Indias, f, ananás, m. **p. cone,** piña, f. **p. kernel,** piñón, m. **p. needle,** pinocha, f. **p. wood,** pinar, m, pineda, f

pineal /'pɪnial/ a en figura de piña; Anat. pineal

ping /pɪŋ/ n silbido de una bala, m; zumbido, m. **p. pong,** tenis de mesa, pingpong, m

pinion /'pɪnyən/ n (wing) ala, f; (small feather) piñón, m; (in carving) alón, m; (wheel) piñón, m. vt atar las alas de; cortar un piñón de; (a person) atar; (the arms of) trincar, asegurar

pink /pɪŋk/ n Bot. clavel, m; color de rosa, m; (perfection) modelo, m; colmo, m; (hunting) color rojo, m; levitón rojo de caza, m. a de color de rosa, rosado. vt Sew. picar; (pierce) penecrar, atravesar. vi (of an engine) picar

pinking /'pɪŋkɪŋ/ n Sew. picadura, f

pinkish /'pɪŋkɪʃ/ a rosáceo

pinky /'pɪŋki/ n (finger) meñique, m

pinnacle /'pɪnəkəl/ n Naut. pinaza, f

pinnacle /'pɪnəkəl/ n pináculo, m

pinpoint /'pɪn,pɔint/ vt precisar

pint /paint/ n (measure) pinta, f

pintle /'pɪntḷ/ n (pin) perno, m

pioneer /ˌpaiə'nɪər/ n pionero, explorador, m; introductor, m. **to be a p. in...,** ser el primero en (or a)...

pioneering role, papel de iniciador (e.g. *She played a pioneering role,* jugó un papel de iniciador)

pious /'paiəs/ a pío, devoto, piadoso

piously /'paiəsli/ adv piadosamente, devotamente

pip /pɪp/ n (of fruit) pepita, f; (on cards, dice) punto, m; (disease) moquillo, m; (of an army, etc., officer) insignia, f

pipe /paip/ n (for tobacco) pipa (de fumar), *Argentina* cachimba, f; Mus. caramillo, m; (boatswain's) pito, m; (of a bird) trino, m; (voice) voz aguda, f; tubo, m; (for water, etc.) cañería, f; (of a hose) manga, f; (of an organ) cañón, m; (of wine) pipa, f; pl **pipes,** Mus. gaita, f. vi tocar el caramillo (or la gaita); empezar a cantar; silbar; (of birds) trinar. vt (a tune) tocar; (sing) cantar; (whistle) llamar con pito; conducir con cañerías; instalar cañerías en. **He smokes a p.,** Fuma una pipa. **I smoked a p.** (of tobacco) **before I went to bed,** Fumé una pipa antes de acostarme. **Put that in your p. and smoke it!** ¡Chúpate eso! **p. clay,** blanquizal, m. **p. cleaner,** limpiapipas, m. **p. layer,** cañero, fontanero, m. **p. laying,** instalación de cañerías, f. **p.-line,** cañería, f; (oil) oleoducto, m. **p. tobacco,** tabaco de pipa, m

pipeful /'paipfʊl/ n pipa, f

piper /'paipər/ n (bagpiper) gaitero, m; flautista, mf

pipette /pai'pɛt/ n Chem. pipeta, f

piping /'paipɪŋ/ n sonido del caramillo, m; música de la flauta, etc., f; (of birds) trinos, m pl; voz aguda, f; (for water, etc.) cañería, tubería, f; Sew. cordoncillo, m. **p.-hot,** hirviente

pipkin /'pɪpkɪn/ n ollita de barro, f

piquant /'pikənt/ a picante

pique /pik/ n (resentment, and score in game) pique, m. **to p. oneself upon,** preciarse de, jactarse de. **to be piqued,** estar enojado; *Inf.* amoscarse

piquet /pɪ'kei/ n juego de los cientos, m

piracy /'pairəsi/ n piratería, f

pirate /'pairət/ n pirata, mf. vi piratear. vt publicar una edición furtiva de, f

pirouette /ˌpiru'ɛt/ n pirueta, f

Pisces /'paisiz/ n pl peces, m pl

pisciculture /'pɪsɪ,kʌltʃər/ n piscicultura, f

Pisgah /'pɪzgə/ Fasga, f

pistachio /pɪ'stæʃi,ou/ n pistacho, m

pistil /'pɪstḷ/ n Bot. pistilo, m

pistol /'pɪstḷ/ n pistola, f. **p. belt,** charpa, f, cinto de pistolas, m. **p. case,** pistolera, f. **p. shot,** pistoletazo, m

piston /'pɪstən/ n Mech. émbolo, pistón, m; Mus. pistón, m, llave, f. **p. ring,** anillo de émbolo, segmento de émbolo, m. **p. rod,** biela, f. **p. stroke,** carrera del émbolo, f

pit /pɪt/ n hoyo, m; foso, m; (in a garage) foso de reparación, m; Theat. platea, f; (trap) trampa, f; (scar) hoyo, m; precipicio, m; (hell) infierno, m. vt (with smallpox) marcar con viruelas; (against) competir con. **pithead,** boca de mina, f. **pit of the stomach,** boca del estómago, f. **pit stall,** butaca de platea, f

pitch /pɪtʃ/ n Chem. pez, brea, f, alquitrán, m; (place) puesto, m; (throwing) lanzamiento, m; (distance thrown) alcance, m; (for cricket) cancha, f; (bowling) saque, m; (slope) pendiente, inclinación, f; (height) elevación, f; Mus. tono, m; (Fig. degree) grado, extremo, m; (Naut. Aer.) cabeceo, m; (of threads of a screw, etc.) paso, m. vt (camp) asentar; (a tent, etc.) colocar, poner; (throw) lanzar, arrojar, tirar; (cricket, etc.) lanzar; (fix in) clavar; Mus. graduar el tono de; (tell) narrar. vi (fall) caer; Naut. cabecear, zozobrar; Aer. cabecear. **to paint with p.,** embrear. **p. into,** (attack) acometer, atacar; (scold) desatarse contra; (food) engullir. **p.-black,** negro como la pez; oscuro como boca de lobo. **p.-pine,** pino de tea, m. **p.-pipe,** diapasón vocal, m

pitched battle /pɪtʃt/ n batalla campal, f

pitcher /'pɪtʃər/ n jarro, cántaro, m; (in baseball) lanzador de pelota, m

pitcherful /'pɪtʃər,fʌl/ n jarro (de), m

pitchfork /'pɪtʃ,fɔrk/ n horquilla, f, aventador, m. vt levantar con horquilla; Fig. lanzar

pitching /'pɪtʃɪŋ/ n (pavement) adoquinado, m; (of a ship) socollada, f; cabeceo, m

piteous /'pɪtiəs/ a lastimero; triste; plañidero; compasivo, tierno

piteousness /'pɪtiəsnɪs/ n estado lastimero, m; tristeza, f; compasión, ternura, f

pitfall /'pɪt,fɔl/ n trampa, f; Fig. añagaza, f, lazo, peligro, m

pith /pɪθ/ n Bot. médula, f; médula espinal, f; Fig. meollo, m; fuerza, f, vigor, m; substancia, f; quinta esencia, f; importancia, f

pithiness /'pɪθinɪs/ n jugosidad, f; fuerza, f, vigor, m

pithy /'pɪθi/ a meduloso; Fig. jugoso; enérgico, vigoroso

pitiable /'pɪtiəbəl/ a lastimoso, digno de compasión; (paltry) despreciable

pitiful /'pɪtifəl/ a piadoso, compasivo; conmovedor, doloroso, lastimero; (contemptible) miserable

pitifully /'pɪtifəli/ adv lastimosamente

pitiless /'pɪtilɪs/ a sin piedad, despiadado

pitilessness /'pɪtilɪsnɪs/ n crueldad, inhumanidad, f

pitman /'pɪtmən/ n minero, m; aserrador de foso, m

pittance /'pɪtns/ n pitanza, f; pequeña porción, f; ración de hambre, f

pitted /'pɪtɪd/ a picoso

pituitary /pɪ'tui,teri/ a pituitario

pity /'pɪti/ n piedad, compasión, f; lástima. f. vt compadecerse de, tener lástima (a); compadecer. **It is a p.**

that..., Es lástima que... **Have p.!** ¡Ten piedad! **to take p. on,** tener lástima (de). **to move to p.,** dar lástima (a), enternecer

pityingly /'pɪtiɪŋli/ *adv* con lástima

pivot /'pɪvət/ *n* pivote, *m*; eje, *m*; *Fig.* punto de partida, *m*, *vi* girar sobre un pivote o eje

pivotal /'pɪvətl̩/ *a Fig.* cardinal, principal, fundamental

pixy /'pɪksi/ *n* duende, *m*. **p. hood,** caperuza, *f*

pizzicato /,pɪtsɪ'katou/ *a* pichigato

placability /,plækə'bɪlɪti/ *n* placabilidad, *f*

placable /'plækəbəl/ *a* aplacable, placable

placard /'plækɑrd/ *n* cartel, *m*. *vt* fijar carteles (en); publicar por carteles

placate /'pleikeit/ *vt* aplacar, ablandar, apaciguar

placatory /'pleikə,tɔri/ *a* placativo

place /pleis/ *n* lugar, *m*; sitio, *m*; (position) puesto, *m*; (seat) asiento, *m*; (laid at table) cubierto, *m*; (square) plaza, *f*; (house) residencia, *f*; (in the country) casa de campo, finca, *f*; (in a book) pasaje, *m*; (in an examination) calificación, *f*; (rank) posición, *f*, rango, *m*; situación, *f*; (employment) empleo, *m*, colocación, *f*. *vt* poner; colocar; (in employment) dar empleo (a); (appoint) nombrar; (an order) dar; (money) invertir; (remember) recordar, traer a la memoria; (size up) fijar; (confidence) poner. **in p.,** en su lugar; apropiado. **in p. of,** en vez de, en lugar de. **in the first p.,** en primer lugar, primero. **in the next p.,** luego, después. **out of p.,** fuera de lugar; inoportuno. **It is not my p. to...,** No me toca a mí de... **to give p. to,** ceder el paso (a); ceder (a). **to take p.,** verificarse, tener lugar, ocurrir. **p. of business,** establecimiento, local de negocios, *m*. **p. of worship,** edificio de culto, *m*

placenta /plə'sɛntə/ *n* placenta, *f*

placid /'plæsɪd/ *a* plácido, apacible; calmoso; sereno, sosegado; dulce

placidity /plə'sɪdɪti/ *n* placidez, *f*; serenidad, tranquilidad, *f*, sosiego, *m*

placidly /'plæsɪdli/ *adv* plácidamente

placing /'pleisɪŋ/ *n* colocación, *f*; posición, *f*; localización, *f*

placket /'plækɪt/ *n* abertura (en una falda), *f*

plagiarism /'pleidʒə,rɪzəm/ *n* plagio, *m*

plagiarist /'pleidʒərɪst/ *n* plagiario (-ia)

plagiarize /'pleidʒə,raiz/ *vt* plagiar, hurtar

plague /pleig/ *n* plaga, *f*; peste, pestilencia, *f*. *vt* importunar, atormentar; plagar

plaid /plæd/ *n* manta escocesa, *f*; género de cuadros, *m*, *a* a cuadros

plain /plein/ *a* claro; evidente; (simple) sencillo; llano; sin adorno; (flat) liso, igual; (candid) franco; (with truth, etc.) desnudo; mero; puro, sin mezcla; (of words) redondo; (ugly) feo. *adv* claramente, *n* llanura, *f*, llano, *m*. **the p. truth,** la pura verdad. **p. clothes,** traje de paisano, *m*. **p. clothes man,** detective, *m*. **p. cooking,** cocina sencilla, cocina casera, *f*. **p. dealing,** buena fe, sinceridad, *f*. **p. dweller,** llanero (-ra). **p. living,** vida sencilla, *f*. **p. people,** gente sencilla, *f*. **p. sailing,** camino fácil, *m*. **p. sewing,** costura, *f*. **p.-song,** canto llano, *m*. **p. speaking,** franqueza, *f*. **p.-spoken,** franco. **in p. English,** sin rodeos, en cristiano (e.g. *Speak in p. English!* Habla sin rodeos! Habla en cristiano!)

plainly /'pleinli/ *adv* claramente; sencillamente; llanamente; francamente; rotundamente

plainness /'pleinnɪs/ *n* claridad, *f*; sencillez, *f*; llaneza, *f*; franqueza, *f*; (ugliness) fealdad, *f*

plainsman /'pleinzmən/ *n* hombre de las llanuras, *m*

plaintiff /'pleintɪf/ *n* demandante, *mf*; actor, *m*, parte actora, actora, *f*

plaintive /'pleintɪv/ *a* quejumbroso, dolorido; patético

plaintively /'pleintɪvli/ *adv* quejumbrosamente

plaintiveness /'pleintɪvnɪs/ *n* melancolía, tristeza, *f*; voz quejumbrosa, *f*

plait /pleit/ *n* trenza, *f*. *vt* trenzar; tejer. **in plaits,** (of hair) en trenzas

plan /plæn/ *n* plan, *m*; (map) plano, *m*; proyecto, *m*. *vt* planear; proyectar; proponerse. **the Marshall P.,** el

Plan Marshall. **to make a p. of,** trazar un plano de. **to make plans,** hacer planes

planchette /plæn'ʃɛt/ *n* mesa giratoria, *f*

plane /plein/ *n* (tree) plátano, *m*; (tool) cepillo, *m*; *Geom.* plano, *m*; (level) nivel, *m*; *Aer.* avión, *m*, plano. *vt* acepillar, alisar. *vi Aer.* planear

planet /'plænɪt/ *n* planeta, *m*

planetarium /,plænɪ'tɛəriəm/ *n* planetario, *m*

planetary /'plænɪ,tɛri/ *a* planetario

planing /'pleinɪŋ/ *n* acepilladura, alisadura, *f*,

plank /plæŋk/ *n* tabla, *f*; *Fig.* fundamento, principio, *m*; *pl* **planks,** tablazón, *f*. *vt* entablar, enmaderar

planking /'plæŋkɪŋ/ *n* entablado, *m*, tablazón, *f*

plankton /'plæŋktən/ *n* plancton, *m*

planned /plænd/ *a* proyectado, planeado; dirigido. **p. economy,** economía dirigida, *f*

planner /'plænər/ *n* proyectista, *mf*; autor (-ra) de un plan; (appointment book) agenda, *f*

planning /'plænɪŋ/ *n* proyecto, *m*; concepción, *f*

plant /plænt/ *n Bot.* planta, *f*; instalación, *f*, material, *m*. *vt* plantar; (place) colocar; fijar; (a blow) asestar; (people) establecer; (instill) inculcar, imbuir (con); (conceal) esconder. **p. pot,** florero, *m*. **p. stand,** jardinera, *f*

plantain /'plæntɪn/ *n Bot.* llantén, plátano, *m*

plantation /plæn'teiʃən/ *n* plantación, *f*; plantío, *m*; *Fig.* colonia, *f*; introducción, *f*, establecimiento, *m*

planter /'plæntər/ *n* plantador, cultivador, *m*

planting /'plæntɪŋ/ *n* plantación, *f*; *Fig.* colonia, *f*; introducción, *f*. **p. out,** trasplante, *m*

plantlike /'plænt,laik/ *a* como una planta; de planta

plaque /plæk/ *n* placa, *f*; medalla, *f*

plash /plæʃ/ *n* (puddle) charco, *m*; (sound) chapaleteo, *m*. *vt* and *vi* chapotear, chapalear

plasma /'plæzmə/ *n* plasma, *m*

plaster /'plæstər/ *n* (for walls, etc.) argamasa, *f*, yeso, *m*; *Med.* parche, emplasto, *m*. *vt* (walls, etc.) enlucir, enyesar; poner emplastos (a or en); (daub) embadurnar manchar; (cover) cubrir. **p. cast,** vaciado, yeso, *m*. **p. of Paris,** escayola, *f*

plasterer /'plæstərər/ *n* yesero, *m*

plastering /'plæstərɪŋ/ *n* revoque, enyesado, guarnecido, *m*. **p. trowel,** fratás, *m*

plastic /'plæstɪk/ *a* plástico. *n* plástica, *f*; *pl* **plastics,** materias plásticas, *f pl.* **p. surgery,** cirugía plástica, cirugía estética, *f*

plasticine /'plæstə,sin/ *n* plasticina, *f*

plasticity /plæ'stɪsɪti/ *n* plasticidad, *f*

plate /pleit/ *n* plancha, chapa, *f*; (engraving and *Phot.,* of a doctor, etc.) placa, *f*; (illustration) lámina, *f*; (cutlery, etc.) vajilla, *f*; (for eating) plato, *m*; (for money) platillo, *m*; electrotipo, *m*; (dental) dentadura postiza, *f*. *vt* (with armor) blindar; (with metal) planchear; (silver) platear; (electro-plate) niquelar. **silver p.,** vajilla de plata, plata, *f*. **p.-armor,** armadura, *f*; (of a ship) blindaje, *m*. **p.-draining rack,** escurreplatos, *m*. **p.-glass,** vidrio plano, *m*. **p.-rack,** escurridero para platos, *m*. **p. warmer,** calientaplatos, *m*

plateau /plæ'tou/ *n* meseta, altiplanicie, *f*, *Lat. Am.* altiplano, *m*

plateful /'pleit,fʌl/ *n* plato (de), *m*

plater /'pleitər/ *n* plateador, *m*; platero, *m*

plateresque /,plætə'rɛsk/ *a Archit.* plateresco

platform /'plætfɔrm/ *n* plataforma, *f*; (railway) andén, *m*. **p. ticket,** billete de andén, *m*

plating /'pleitɪŋ/ *n* niquelado, *m*; electrogalvanización, *f*; (with armor) blindaje, *m*

platinum /'plætnəm/ *n* platino, *m*. **p. blonde,** rubia platino, *f*

platitude /'plætɪ,tud/ *n* perogrullada, *f*, lugar común, *m*; trivialidad, vulgaridad, *f*

platitudinous /,plætɪ'tudnəs/ *a* lleno de perogrulladas; trivial

platonic /plə'tɒnɪk/ *a* platónico

Platonism /'pleitn̩,ɪzəm/ *n* platonismo, *m*

Platonist /'pleitnɪst/ *n* platonista, *mf*

platoon /plə'tun/ *n Mil.* pelotón, *m*

platter /'plætər/ *n* fuente, *f*, trinchero, *m*; plato, *m*

plaudit /'plɔdɪt/ *n* aplauso, *m*, aclamación, *f*; (praise) elogio, *m*, alabanza, *f*

plausibility /ˌplɔːzəˈbɪlɪti/ n plausibilidad, f
plausible /ˈplɔːzəbəl/ a plausible
plausibly /ˈplɔːzəbli/ adv plausiblemente
play /plei/ vi jugar; (frolic) juguetear, retozar; recrearse, divertirse; *Mech.* moverse; (on a musical instrument) tocar; (wave) ondear, flotar; *Theat.* representar; (behave) conducirse. vt jugar; (of a searchlight, etc.) enfocar; (direct) dirigir; (a fish) agotar; (a joke, etc.) hacer; (a piece in a game) mover; (a musical instrument or music) tocar; (a string instrument) tañer; (a character in a play) hacer el papel de; (a drama, etc.) representar, poner en escena. **to p. a joke,** gastar una broma, hacer una burla. **to p. fair,** jugar limpio. **to p. false,** jugar sucio, engañar. **to p. the fool,** hacerse el tonto, hacerse el payaso. **to p. at,** jugar a; (pretend) fingir; hacer sin entusiasmo. **to p. off,** confrontar, contraponer. **to p. for,** (a person) tocar para. **to p. upon,** tocar; (a person's fears, etc.) explotar. **to p. up to,** (a person) adular, hacer la rueda (a). **to p. with,** jugar con; burlarse de; (an idea) acariciar play, n juego, m; diversión, f, recreo, m; (reflection) reflejo, m; movimiento libre, m; (to the imagination, etc.) rienda suelta, f; *Mech.* holgura, f; *Lit.* pieza dramática, comedia, f; (performance) función, representación, f; (*Theat.*) teatro, m. **fair p.,** juego limpio, m. **foul p.,** juego sucio, m; traición, perfidia, f. **to bring into p.,** poner en juego. **to come into p.,** entrar en juego. **to give p. to,** dar rienda a. **p. on words,** juego de palabras, m. **p.-pen,** cuadro enrejado, m
playact /ˈpleiˌækt/ vi hacer la comedia
playbill /ˈpleiˌbɪl/ n cartel, m; programa, m
played-out /ˌpleid ˈaut/ a agotado; viejo
player /ˈpleiər/ n jugador (-ra); *Theat.* actor (-triz), representante, mf; *Mus.* músico (-ca), tocador (-ra)
playfellow /ˈpleiˌfɛlou/ n camarada, mf; compañero (-ra) de juego, compañero de juegos
playful /ˈpleifəl/ a juguetón; travieso; alegre
playfully /ˈpleifəli/ adv en juego, de broma; alegremente
playfulness /ˈpleifəlnɪs/ n carácter juguetón, m; travesuras, f pl; alegría, f
playgoer /ˈpleiˌgouər/ n persona que frecuenta los teatros, f; espectador de comedias, m
playground /ˈpleiˌgraund/ n patio de recreo, m
playing /ˈpleiɪŋ/ n juego, m. **p.-cards,** naipes, m pl, cartas, f pl. **p.-field,** campo de deportes, m
playlet /ˈpleilɪt/ n comedia corta, f
playmate /ˈpleiˌmeit/. See **playfellow**
plaything /ˈpleiˌθɪŋ/ n juguete, m
playtime /ˈpleiˌtaim/ n recreación, f; (in schools) hora de recreo, f, recreo, m
playwright /ˈpleiˌrait/ n dramaturgo, m, autor (-ra) de comedias
plea /pliː/ n *Law.* informe, m; declaración, f; *Law.* acción, f, proceso, m; (excuse) pretexto, m, excusa, f; (entreaty) súplica, f. **under p. of,** bajo pretexto de, con excusa de
plead /pliːd/ vi *Law.* pleitear; suplicar; (of counsel, etc.) abogar (por); interceder (por). vt defender en juicio; aducir, alegar; pretender. **to p. guilty,** confesarse culpable. **to p. not guilty,** negar la acusación. **to p. ignorance,** pretender ignorancia
pleading /ˈpliːdɪŋ/ n súplicas, f pl; *Law.* defensa, f; pl **pleadings,** alegatos, m pl, a implorante
pleasant /ˈplɛzənt/ a agradable; placentero; ameno; encantador; dulce; alegre; (of persons) simpático, amable; bueno; divertido
pleasantly /ˈplɛzəntli/ adv agradablemente; de un modo muy amable; alegremente
pleasantness /ˈplɛzəntnɪs/ n agrado, m; placer, m; amabilidad, f; alegría, f
pleasantry /ˈplɛzəntri/ n jocosidad, f; broma, chanza, f
please /pliːz/ vi dar placer, gustar, dar gusto, agradar; parecer bien, querer, servirse; tener a bien, placer. vt deleitar, agradar, gustar; halagar; contentar, satisfacer; (polite request) por favor. **I will do what I p.,** Haré lo que me parezca bien. **If you p.,** Si te parece bien; Con tu permiso. **She is very easy to p.,** Es muy fácil de darle placer. **When you p.,** Cuando Vd. quiera, Cuando a Vd.

le venga bien Cuando Vd. guste. **"Please Do Not Disturb,"** «No Molesten.» **P. sit down!** ¡Haga el favor de sentarse! ¡Sírvase de sentarse! **P. God!** ¡Plegue a Dios!
pleased /pliːzd/ a contento (de or con); encantado (de); alegre (de); satisfecho (de or con). **I am p. with my new house,** Estoy contento con mi nueva casa. **I'm p. to meet you,** Mucho gusto (en conocerle), Mucho gusto (en conocerla). **to be p.,** estar contento; complacerse en
pleasing /ˈpliːzɪŋ/ a agradable, grato; placentero; halagüeño
pleasurable /ˈplɛʒərəbəl/ a agradable; divertido, entretenido
pleasure /ˈplɛʒər/ n placer, m; gusto, m; satisfacción, f; (will) voluntad, f; recreo, m; diversión, distracción, f. **to give p. (to),** dar placer (a); deleitar, agradar; complacer. **to take p. in,** gustar de, disfrutar de; complacerse en. **I shall do it with great p.,** Lo haré con mucho gusto, Lo haré con mucho placer. **p.-boat,** barco de recreo, m. **p.-ground,** parque de atracciones, m. **p.-seeking,** amigo de placeres, frívolo. **p. trip,** viaje de recreo, m; excursión, f
pleasure craft n barco de recreo, m, (one vessel); barcas de recreo (collectively), m pl
pleat /pliːt/ n pliegue, m, vt plegar, hacer pliegues en
pleating /ˈpliːtɪŋ/ n plegado, m
plebeian /plɪˈbiːən/ a plebeyo. n plebeyo (-ya)
plebiscite /ˈplɛbəˌsait/ n plebiscito, m. **to take a p.,** hacer un plebiscito
plectrum /ˈplɛktrəm/ n plectro, m
pledge /plɛdʒ/ n prenda, f; empeño, m; garantía, f; (hostage) rehén, m; (toast) brindis, m. vt empeñar; dar en prenda; garantizar; brindar por; prometer. **to p. oneself,** comprometerse. **to p. support for,** prometer apoyo para
Pleiades /ˈpliːəˌdiz/ n pl pléyades, f pl
plenary /ˈpliːnəri/ a pleno; plenario. **p. indulgence,** indulgencia plenaria, f. **p. session,** sesión plenaria, f
plenipotentiary /ˌplɛnəpəˈtɛnʃiˌɛri/ a plenipotenciario. n plenipotenciario, m
plenitude /ˈplɛnɪˌtud/ n plenitud, f
plentiful /ˈplɛntəfəl/ a copioso, abundante. **to be p.,** abundar
plentifully /ˈplɛntəfəli/ adv en abundancia
plenty /ˈplɛnti/ n abundancia, f; en abundancia; de sobra; mucho. adv *Inf.* bastante. **There is p. of food,** Hay comida en abundancia. **We have p. of time,** Tenemos tiempo de sobra
pleonasm /ˈpliːəˌnæzəm/ n pleonasmo, m
plethora /ˈplɛθərə/ n plétora, f
pleurisy /ˈplʊrəsi/ n pleuresía, f
plexus /ˈplɛksəs/ n plexo, m
pliability /ˌplaiəˈbɪliti/ n flexibilidad, f; docilidad, f
pliable, pliant /ˈplaiəbəl; ˈplaiənt/ a flexible; dócil
pliers /ˈplaiərz/ n pinzas, f pl, alicates, m pl, tenazas, f pl
plight /plait/ n (fix) aprieto, apuro, m. **the p. of the poor,** la situación de los pobres
plinth /plɪnθ/ n *Archit.* plinto, m
Pliny the Elder /ˈplɪni/ Plinio el Antiguo, Plinio el Mayor
Pliny the Younger /ˈplɪni/ Plinio el Menor
plod /plɒd/ vi andar despacio, caminar con trabajo; *Fig.* trabajar con ahínco
plodder /ˈplɒdər/ n trabajador lento y concienzudo, m; (student) empollón (-ona)
plot /plɒt/ n (of land) parcela, f; terreno, solar, m; (plan) proyecto, m; estratagema, m; (literary) intriga, trama, f; (story) argumento, m; (conspiracy) conjuración, f, complot, m. vt trazar (un plano, etc.); urdir, tramar. vi conspirar, intrigar
plotter /ˈplɒtər/ n conspirador (-ra conjurado (-da)
plotting /ˈplɒtiŋ/ n trazado (de un plano, una gráfica), m; (conspiracy) conspiración, f; maquinaciones, f pl; (hatching) trama, f
plover /ˈplʌvər, ˈplouvər/ n ave fría, f, chorlito, m
plow /plau/ n arado, m; *Astron.* el Carro, la Osa Mayor; (in an examination) escabechina, f. vt and vi arar; *Fig.* surcar; (in examinations) escabechar, dar calabazas a; suspender. **plow the sands,** arar en el mar. **p. handle,** esteva, f. **to p. up,** roturar

plowman /'plaumən/ *n* arador, surcador, *m*; (peasant) labrador, *m*

plowshare /'plau‚ʃɛər/ *n* reja de arado, *f*

pluck /plʌk/ *vt* (pick) coger; (a bird) desplumar; *Mus.* puntear; (in an examination) calabacear escabechar. *vi* tirar (de). *n* (tug) tirón, *m*; (of an animal) asadura, *f*; (courage) coraje, *m*. **to p.** up courage, tomar coraje, sacar ánimos. **to p. off,** quitar. **to p. out,** arrancar; quitar

pluckily /'plʌkɪli/ *adv* valientemente

pluckiness /'plʌkɪnɪs/ *n* coraje, valor, *m*

plucky /'plʌki/ *a* valiente, esforzado, resuelto, animoso

plug /plʌg/ *n* tapón, tarugo, *m*; (in building) nudillo, *m*; (of a switchboard) clave, *f*; *Elec.* enchufe, *m*; (of a w.c.) tirador, *m*; (of a bath, etc.) tapón, *m*; (of tobacco) rollo, *m*. *vt* atarugar, taponar, obturar; (in building) rellenar. *vi* (with away) batirse el cobre, sudar la gota gorda. **to p. in,** enchufar

plum /plʌm/ *n* (tree) ciruelo, *m*; (fruit) ciruela, *f*; (raisin) pasa, *f*; (*Inf.* prize) breva, golosina, *f*. **p. cake,** pastel de fruta, *m*

plumage /'plumɪdʒ/ *n* plumaje, *m*

plumb /plʌm/ *n* plomada, *f*; (sounding-lead) escandallo, *m*. *a* perpendiculo; recto; completo. *adv* a plomo, verticalmente; exactamente. *vt* aplomar; *Naut.* sondar; (*Fig.* pierce) penetrar; (understand) comprender. *vi* trabajar como plomero. **p.-line,** plomada, *f*

plumbago /plʌm'beigou/ *n* plombagina, *f*

plumber /'plʌmər/ *n* plomero, fontanero, *m*; instalador de cañerías, *m*

plumbic /'plʌmbɪk/ *a* *Chem.* plúmbico

plumbing /'plʌmɪŋ/ *n* plomería, fontanería, *f*; instalación de cañerías, *f*

plumbless /'plʌmlɪs/ *a* *Poet.* insondable

plume /plum/ *n* pluma, *f*; penacho, *m*. *vt* adornar con plumas; desplumar; **to p. itself,** (of a bird) limpiarse las plumas. **to p. oneself on,** echárselas de, hacer alarde de; jactarse de

plumed /plumd/ *a* plumado; con plumas; empenachado

plumelet /'plumlɪt/ *n* agujas, *f pl*

plummet /'plʌmɪt/ *n* plomada, *f*; (weight) plomo, *m*; (sounding-lead) sonda, *f*. *vi* sondear

plump /plʌmp/ *a* gordito, llenito; rollizo; hinchado. *adv* de golpe; claramente. *vt* (swell) hinchar, rellenar; (make fall) hacer (or dejar) caer. *vi* (swell) hincharse; engordar; (fall) caer a plomo; dejarse caer. **to p. for,** escoger, dar apoyo (a); votar por. **p.-cheeked,** mofletudo

plumpness /'plʌmpnɪs/ *n* gordura, *f*; lo rollizo

plumy /'plumi/ *a* como una pluma; plumado

plunder /'plʌndər/ *vt* saquear; pillar; despojar. *n* saqueo, pillaje, *m*; (booty) botín, despojo, *m*

plunderer /'plʌndərər/ *n* saqueador (-ra); ladrón (-ona)

plundering /'plʌndərɪŋ/ *n* saqueo, *m*; despojo, *m*. *a* saqueador

plunge /plʌndʒ/ *vt* chapuzar; sumergir; hundir; meter. *vi* sumergirse; (into water) zambullirse; (rush) precipitarse, lanzarse; *Naut.* zozobrar; (of a horse) encabritarse; (gamble) jugarse el todo. *n* sumersión, *f*; zambullida, *f*; chapuz, *m*; (rush) salto, *m*; (*Fig.* step) paso, *m*

plunger /'plʌndʒər/ *n* *Mech.* émbolo, *m*

plunging /'plʌndʒɪŋ/ *n* (of a ship) zozobra, *f*; (of a horse) cabriolas, *f pl*; saltos, *m pl*, For other meanings, see **plunge**

plural /'plʊrəl/ *a* plural. *n* plural, *m*. **in the p.,** en el plural. **to make p.,** poner en plural

plurality /plʊ'rælɪti/ *n* pluralidad, *f*

pluralize /'plʊrə‚laiz/ *vt* pluralizar

plus /plʌs/ *prep* and *a* más; (*Math. Elec.*) positivo. *n* signo más, *m*; *Math.* cantidad positiva, *f*. **p. fours,** pantalones de golf, *m pl*

plush /plʌʃ/ *n* felpa, *f*; velludo, *m*

plushy /'plʌʃi/ *a* felpudo; de felpa

Pluto /'plutou/ *n* Plutón, *m*; (pipe-line) oleoducto, *m*

plutocracy /plu'tɒkrəsi/ *n* plutocracia, *f*

plutocrat /'plutə‚kræt/ *n* plutócrata, *mf*

plutocratic /‚plutə'krætɪk/ *a* plutocrático

pluviometer /‚pluvi'ɒmɪtər/ *n* pluviómetro, *m*

ply /plai/ *n* cabo, *m*. *vt* emplear, usar; manejar; ejercer; ofrecer, servir (con); importunar (con). *vi* hacer el trayecto; hacer el servicio; ir y venir; hacer viajes. **to ply for hire,** tomar viajeros; ofrecerse para ser alquilado

plywood /'plai‚wʊd/ *n* madera contrachapada, *f*

pneumatic /nʊ'mætɪk/ *a* neumático. *n* (tire) neumático, *m*. **p. drill,** barreno neumático, *m*

pneumococcus /‚numə'kɒkəs/ *n* neumococo, *m*

pneumonia /nʊ'mounyə/ *n* pulmonía, *f*. **double p.,** pulmonía doble, *f*

poach /poutʃ/ *vi* cazar (or pescar) en vedado. *vt* robar caza de un vedado; *Fig.* invadir; (*Fig.* steal) hurtar; (eggs) escalfar. **to p. upon another's preserves,** meterse en los asuntos de otro

poacher /'poutʃər/ *n* cazador furtivo, *m*

poaching /'poutʃɪŋ/ *n* caza (or pesca) furtiva, *f*

pock /pɒk/ *n* pústula, *f*. **p.-mark,** hoyo, *m*. **p.-marked,** picado de viruelas

pocket /'pɒkɪt/ *n* bolsillo, *m*; bolsillo del reloj, *m*; faltriquera, *f*; *Mineral.* bolsa, *f*, depósito, *m*; *Fig.* bolsa, *f*; (in billiards) tronera, *f*. *vt* meter (or poner) en el bolsillo; (an insult) tragarse; (in billiards) entronerar; (a profit) ganar; apropiarse. **air-p.,** bolsa de aire, *f*. **to be out of p.,** haber perdido, tener una pérdida. **to have a person in one's p.,** calzarse a una persona. **to p. one's pride,** olvidarse de su orgullo. **p. battleship,** acorazado de bolsillo, *m*. **p.-book,** cartera, *f*. **p. dictionary,** diccionario de bolsillo, *m*. **p.-flap,** portezuela, *f*. **p.-handkerchief,** pañuelo (de bolsillo), *m*. **p.-knife,** cortaplumas, *m*. **p.-lighter,** encendedor de bolsillo, *m*. **p.-money,** alfileres, *m pl*, dinero del bolsillo, *m*. **p. picking,** ratería de carterista, *f*

pocketful /'pɒkɪt‚fʊl/ *n* bolsillo lleno (de), *m*; lo que cabe en un bolsillo

pocket of resistance *n* foco de resistencia, *m*

pod /pɒd/ *n* *Bot.* vaina, *f*; (of a silkworm) capullo, *m*. *vt* desvainar; mondar. *vi* hincharse, llenarse

podgy /'pɒdʒi/ *a* gordo, grueso

poem /'pouəm/ *n* poema, *m*; *pl* **poems,** poesías, *f pl*, versos, *m pl*

poet /'pouɪt/ *n* poeta, *m*. **p. laureate,** poeta laureado, *m*

poetaster /'pouɪt‚æstər/ *n* poetastro, *m*

poetess /'pouɪtɪs/ *n* poetisa, *f*

poetic /pou'etɪk/ *a* poético. **p. license,** licencia poética, *f*

poeticize /pou'etə‚saiz/ *vt* poetizar; hacer un poema (de)

poetics /pou'etɪks/ *n* poética, *f*

poetry /'pouɪtri/ *n* poesía, *f*; versos, poemas, *m pl*

pogrom /pə'grʌm/ *n* pogrom, *m*

poignancy /'pɔinyənsi/ *n* (of emotions) profundidad, violencia, *f*, lo patético; (of a retort, etc.) mordacidad, acerbidad, *f*

poignant /'pɔinyənt/ *a* (moving) conmovedor, hondo, agudo; patético; (mordant) mordaz, agudo

poignantly /'pɔinyəntli/ *adv* de un modo conmovedor, patéticamente; mordazmente

poinsettia /pɔin'setiə/ *n* flor de nochebuena, *f*

point /pɔint/ *n* (usual meanings and *ast.*, *math.*, in cards, in a speech, etc.) punto, *m*; característica, *f*; cualidad, *f*; (purpose) motivo, fin, *m*; (question) cuestión, *f*; asunto, *m*; (wit) agudeza, *f*; (significance) significación, *f*; (detail) detalle, *m*; (in rationing) cupón, *m*; (sharp end) punta, *f*; (of a shawl, etc.) pico, *m*; (of land) promontorio, cabo, *m*; (engraving) buril, *m*; (railway) aguja, *f*; (of horses) cabo, *m*. **Mary has many good points,** María tiene muchas cualidades buenas. **There is no p. in being angry,** No hay caso que enfadarse. **in p.,** en cuestión; a propósito. **in p. of fact,** en efecto, en verdad. **on the p. of,** a punto de. **to be in a serious case; ser apropiado. to carry one's p.,** salir con la suya. **to come to the p.,** ir al grano, ir al caso, ir al mollo del asunto. **to make a p. of,** insistir en; tener por principio. **to win on points,** (boxing) ganar por puntos. **p. at issue,** cuestión bajo consideración, *f*, punto en cuestión, *m*. **p.-blank,** a boca de jarro. **p.-duty,** re-

point

gulación de tráfico, f. **p. lace,** encaje de aguja, m. **p. of honor,** punto de honor, m; cuestión de honor, f. **p. or order,** cuestión de orden, f. **p. of view,** punto de vista, m. **What's your p.?** ¿A dónde quieres llegar con esto?

point /pɔint/ vt sacar punta (a), afilar; (a moral, etc.) inculcar; (in building) rejuntar; Gram. puntuar; (of dogs) mostrar la caza. **He pointed his gun at them,** Les apuntó con su fusil. **The hands of the clock pointed to seven o'clock,** Las agujas del reloj marcaban las siete. **to p. with the finger,** señalar con el dedo. **to p. at,** señalar, indicar; (with a gun) apuntar; dirigir. **to p. out,** señalar, indicar; enseñar, mostrar; advertir

pointed /'pɔintid/ a (sharpened) afilado; (in shape) puntiagudo; picudo; Archit. ojival; Fig. mordaz; satírico; (of a remark, etc.) directo; personal; aparente, evidente

pointedly /'pɔintidli/ adv explícitamente, categóricamente; mordazmente; directamente; satíricamente

pointedness /'pɔintidnis/ n forma puntiaguda, f; (incisiveness) mordacidad, aspereza, f; claridad, f

pointer /'pɔintər/ n (of a clock, weighing-machine, etc.) aguja, f; (of a balance) fiel, m; (wand) puntero, m; Fig. índice, m; (dog) perro de muestra, m

pointillism /'pwantl,izem/ n Art. puntillismo, m

pointing /'pɔintiŋ/ n (in building) rejuntado, m; (of a gun) puntería, f

pointless /'pɔintlis/ a sin motivo, innecesario; fútil; sin importancia

pointlessly /'pɔintlisli/ adv sin motivo, sin necesidad; fútilmente

pointsman /'pɔintsmən/ n (railway) guardaagujas, m; (policeman) guardia del tráfico, m

poise /pɔiz/ vt balancear; pesar. vi balancearse; posar, estar suspendido. n equilibrio, m; (of mind) serenidad de ánimo, sangre fría, f; aplomo, m; (bearing) porte, aire, m

poison /'pɔizən/ n veneno, m; Fig. ponzoña, f, veneno, m. vt envenenar; intoxicar; Fig. emponzoñar. **p. gas,** gas asfixiante, m

poisoner /'pɔizənər/ n envenenador (-ra); Fig. corruptor (-ra)

poisoning /'pɔizəniŋ/ n envenenamiento, m; intoxicación, f

poisonous /'pɔizənəs/ a venenoso; tóxico; Fig. ponzoñoso, pernicioso. **p. snake,** serpiente venenosa

poisonousness /'pɔizənsnis/ n venenosidad, f; toxicidad, f; Fig. veneno, m, ponzoña, f

poke /pouk/ vt (thrust) clavar; (make) hacer; (the fire) atizar; hurgar; (push) empujar; (put away) arrinconar. vi andar a tientas; meterse. **Don't p. your nose into other people's business!** ¡No te metas donde no te llaman! **They poked his eyes out,** Le saltaron los ojos. **to p. fun at,** burlarse de, mofarse de. **to p. the fire,** atizar la lumbre (or el fuego). **to p. about for,** buscar a tientas

poker /'poukər/ n (game) póker, m; (for the fire) hurgón, atizador, m. **p. work,** pirograbado, m

poky /'pouki/ a estrecho, ahogado, pequeño; miserable

Poland /'poulənd/ Polonia, f

polar /'poulər/ a polar. **p. bear,** oso (-sa) blanco (-ca). **p. lights,** aurora boreal, f

polarimeter /,poulə'rimitər/ n polarímetro, m

polarity /pou'læriti/ n polaridad, f

polarization /,poulərə'zeifən/ n polarización, f

polarize /'poulə,raiz/ vt polarizar

pole /poul/ n palo largo, m; poste, m; (of a tent) mástil, m; (of a cart) pértiga, f; Sports. pértiga, garrocha, f; (measurement) percha, f; (Astron. Geog. Biol. Math. Elec.) polo, m. vt (a punt) impeler con pértiga. **from p. to p.,** de polo a polo. **greasy p.,** cucaña, f. **under bare poles,** Naut. a palo seco. **p.-ax,** hachuela de mano, f; hacha de marinero, f; (butcher's) mazo, m. **p. jumping,** salto de pértiga, salto a la garrocha, m. **p.-star,** estrella polar, f

Pole /poul/ n polaco (-ca)

polemic /pə'lɛmik/ n polémica, f

polemical /pə'lɛmikəl/ a polémico

police /pə'lis/ n policía, f. vt mantener servicio de

policía en; mantener el orden público en; administrar, regular. **mounted p.,** policía montada, f. **p. constable,** (agente de) policía, guardia urbano, m. **p. court,** tribunal de la policía, m. **p. dog,** perro de policía, m. **p. force,** cuerpo de policía, m, policía, f. **p. magistrate,** juez municipal, m. **p. station,** comisaría de policía, f. **p. trap,** puesto oculto de la policía del tráfico, m. **p. woman,** policía, f

policeman /pə'lismən/ n policía, guardia, Lat. Am. cívico, m

policy /'pɒləsi/ n política, f; táctica, f; sistema, m; norma de conducta, f; ideas, f pl, principios, m pl; prudencia, f; (insurance) póliza, f. **fixed premium p.,** póliza a prima fija, f. **p.-holder,** asegurado (-da), tenedor de una póliza), m

poliomyelitis /,pouliou,maiə'laitis/ n poliomielitis, f

polish /'pɒlif/ vt (metals and wood) pulir; (furniture and shoes) dar brillo (a); (Lit. works) limar; (persons) descortezar, civilizar. n (shine) brillo, m; (furniture) cera para los muebles, f; (metal, silver) líquido para limpiar metales, m; (for shoes) betún para zapatos, m; (varnish) barniz, m; (of lit. works) pulidez, elegancia, f; (of persons) urbanidad, cultura, f. **to p. off,** terminar a prisa; (a person) acabar con; (food) engullir

Polish /'poulif/ a polaco, polonés. n (language) polaco, m

polished /'pɒlift/ a (of verses, etc.) pulido, elegante; (of person) culto, distinguido; (of manners) fino, cortés, (shined) brillante

polisher /'pɒlifər/ n (machine) pulidor, m; lustrador, m. **floor-p.,** lustrador de piso, m. **French p.,** barnizador, m

polite /pə'lait/ a cortés, bien educado; atento; elegante

politely /pə'laitli/ adv cortésmente; atentamente

politeness /pə'laitnis/ n cortesía, f. **for p. sake,** por cortesía

politic /'pɒlitik/ a político

political /pə'litikəl/ a político. **p. agent,** agente político, m. **p. economist,** hacendista, mf **p. economy,** economía política, f

politically /pə'litikli/ adv políticamente

politician /,pɒli'tifən/ n político (-ca)

politics /'pɒlitiks/ n política, f. **to dabble in p.,** meterse en política

polity /'pɒliti/ n forma de gobierno, constitución política, f

polka /'poulkə/ n polca, f

polka-dot /'poukə,dɒt/ a con puntos

poll /poul/ n (head of person) cabeza, f; (voters' register) lista electoral, f; (voting) votación, f; (counting of votes) escrutinio, m. vt (trees) desmochar; (vote) votar, dar su voto (a); (obtain votes) obtener, recibir; (count votes) escrutar. **p.-tax,** capitación, f

pollard /'pɒlərd/ vt desmochar. n (tree) árbol desmochado, m

pollen /'pɒlən/ n polen, m

pollinate /'pɒlə,neit/ vt fecundar con polen

pollination /,pɒlə'neifən/ n polinización, f

polling /'pouliŋ/ n votación, f. **p. booth,** colegio electoral, m

pollute /pə'lut/ vt contaminar; ensuciar; profanar; (corrupt morally) corromper

polluter /pə'lutər/ n profanador (-ra), corruptor (-ra)

pollution /pə'lufən/ n contaminación, f; profanación, f; corrupción, f

polo /'poulou/ n polo, m. **p. mallet,** maza de polo, f. **p. player,** jugador de polo, m, polista, mf

polonaise /,pɒlə'neiz/ n polonesa, f

poltroon /pɒl'trun/ n cobarde, m

polychrome /'pɒli,kroum/ a policromo

polygamist /pə'ligəmist/ n polígamo (-ma)

polygamous /pə'ligəməs/ a polígamo

polygamy /pə'ligəmi/ n poligamia, f

polygenesis /,pɒli'dʒɛnəsis/ n poligenismo, m

polyglot /'pɒli,glɒt/ n poligloto (-ta). **p. Bible,** poliglota, f

polygon /'pɒli,gɒn/ n polígono, m

Polynesia /,pɒlə'niʒə/ Polinesia, f

polyp /'pɒlɪp/ n pólipo, m
polyphonic /ˌpɒliˈfɒnɪk/ a polifónico
polyphony /pəˈlɪfəni/ n polifonía, f
polytechnic /ˌpɒliˈteknɪk/ a politécnico
polytheism /ˈpɒliθiˌɪzəm/ n politeísmo, m
polytheistic /ˌpɒliθiˈɪstɪk/ a politeísta
pomade /pɒˈmeid/ n pomada, f
pomegranate /ˈpɒmˌɡrænɪt/ n granada, f
Pomeranian /ˌpɒməˈreiniən/ a pomerano. **P. dog,** perro pomerano, m
pommel /ˈpʌməl/ n pomo, m, vt aporrear
pomp /pɒmp/ n pompa, magnificencia, f, fausto, aparato, m; ostentación, f
Pompeii /pɒmˈpei/ Pompeya, f
pompom /ˈpɒmˌpɒm/ n pompón, m
pomposity /pɒmˈpɒsɪti/ n pomposidad, presunción, f; (of language) ampulosidad, f
pompous /ˈpɒmpəs/ a pomposo, ostentoso; (of style) ampuloso, hinchado; importante. **to be p.,** (of persons) darse tono
pond /pɒnd/ n charca, f, estanque, m
ponder /ˈpɒndər/ vt ponderar, estudiar, considerar. vi meditar (sobre), reflexionar (sobre)
ponderable /ˈpɒndərəbəl/ a ponderable
ponderous /ˈpɒndərəs/ a pesado; macizo, abultado; grave; (dull) pesado, aburrido
ponderously /ˈpɒndərəsli/ adv pesadamente; gravemente
ponderousness /ˈpɒndərəsnɪs/ n pesadez, f; gravedad, importancia, f
pontiff /ˈpɒntɪf/ n pontífice, m
pontifical /pɒnˈtɪfɪkəl/ a pontificio
pontificate /pɒnˈtɪfɪˌkɪt/ n pontificado, m
pontonier /ˌpɒntnˈɪər/ n pontonero, m
pontoon /pɒnˈtun/ n pontón, m. **p. bridge,** puente de pontones, m
pony /ˈpouni/ n jaca, f
poodle /ˈpudl/ n perro (-rra) de aguas, perro de lanas, perro lanudo
pooh-pooh /ˈpuˈpu/ vt despreciar, desdeñar. **Pooh!** ¡Bah!
pool /pul/ n (in a river) rebalsa, f; charca, f, estanque, m; (of blood, etc.) charco, m; (swimming) Spain piscina, Lat. Am. alberca, f; (in cards) baceta, f; Com. asociación, f; Fig. fuente, f; pl **pools,** (football) apuestas benéficas de fútbol, f pl. vt (resources, etc.) combinar; juntar
poop /pup/ n Naut. popa, f. **p. lantern,** fanal, m
poor /pur/ a pobre; malo; (insignificant or unfortunate) infeliz, desgraciado. **the p.,** los pobres. **to be in p. health,** estar mal de salud. **to be p. stuff,** ser de pacotilla. **to be poorer than a church mouse,** ser más pobre que las ratas. **to have a p. opinion of,** tener en poco (a). **P. me!** ¡Ay de mí! ¡Pecador de mí! **p.-box,** cepillo, m. **p.-law,** ley de asistencia pública, f. **p.-spirited,** apocado
poorhouse /ˈpurˌhaus/ n asilo, m
poorly /ˈpurli/ adv pobremente; mal. a indispuesto, malo
poorness /ˈpurnɪs/ n pobreza, f; mala calidad, f; (lack) carestía, f; (of soil) infertilidad, f; (of character) mezquindad, f
pop /pɒp/ n (of a cork) taponazo, m; (of a gun) detonación, f; (drink) gaseosa, f, adv ¡pum! vi (of a cork) saltar; (of guns) detonar. vt (corks) hacer saltar; (a gun, a question, etc.) disparar. **popgun,** escopeta de aire comprimido, f. **to pop down,** bajar a presuradamente. **to pop in,** (visit) dejarse caer; entrar rápidamente. **to pop off,** marcharse a prisa; (die) estirar la pata, Lat. Am. arrancarse. **to pop up,** subir corriendo; aparecer de pronto
popcorn /ˈpɒpˌkɔrn/ nsg palomitas (de maíz), rosetas (de maíz) fpl (Spain), cabritos mpl (Chile), alborotos mpl (Argentina, Central America, Peru), cabritas fpl (elsewhere)
pope /poup/ n Papa, m
poplar /ˈpɒplər/ n (black) chopo, álamo, m; (white) álamo blanco, m. **p. grove,** alameda, f
poplin /ˈpɒplɪn/ n popelina, f
poppy /ˈpɒpi/ n amapola, adormidera, f

populace /ˈpɒpyələs/ n pueblo, m; (scornful) populacho, m
popular /ˈpɒpyələr/ a popular; en boga, de moda; cómun. **He is a p. hero,** Es un héroe popular
popularity /ˌpɒpyəˈlærɪti/ n popularidad, f
popularization /ˌpɒpyələrəˈzeiʃən/ n vulgarización, f
popularize /ˈpɒpyələˌraiz/ vt popularizar, vulgarizar
popularly /ˈpɒpyələrli/ adv popularmente
populate /ˈpɒpyəˌleit/ vt poblar
population /ˌpɒpyəˈleiʃən/ n población, f
populous /ˈpɒpyələs/ a populoso; muy poblado
porcelain /ˈpɔrsəlɪn/ n porcelana, f
porch /pɔrtʃ/ n pórtico, m; (of a house) portal, m
porcine /ˈpɔrsain/ a porcino, porcuno
porcupine /ˈpɔrkyəˌpain/ n puerco espín, m
pore /pɔr/ n poro, m. **to p. over,** estar absorto en; examinar cuidadosamente
pork /pɔrk/ n carne de cerdo, f. **salt p.,** tocino, m. **p. butcher,** tocinero, m. **p. pie,** pastel de carne de cerdo, m
pornographic /ˌpɔrnəˈɡræfɪk/ a pornográfico
pornography /pɔrˈnɒɡrəfi/ n pornografía, f
porosity /pɔˈrɒsɪti/ n porosidad, f
porous /ˈpɔrəs/ a poroso
porphyry /ˈpɔrfəri/ n pórfido, m
porpoise /ˈpɔrpəs/ n marsopa, f, puerco marino, m
porridge /ˈpɒrɪdʒ/ n gachas, f pl, m
port /pɔrt/ n puerto, m; (in a ship) porta, f; (larboard) babor, m; (wine) vino de Oporto, m; (mien) porte, m, presencia, f. vt (the helm) poner a babor; Mil. llevar un fusil terciado. **to put into p.,** tomar puerto. **to stop at a p.,** hacer escala en un puerto. **p. dues,** derechos de puerto, m pl
portable /ˈpɔrtəbəl/ a portátil; móvil. **p. typewriter,** máquina de escribir portátil (or de viaje), f. **p. wireless,** radio portátil, f
portal /ˈpɔrtl/ n portal, m
portcullis /pɔrtˈkʌlɪs/ n rastrillo, m
portend /pɔrˈtend/ vt presagiar, anunciar
portent /ˈpɔrtent/ n augurio, presagio, m; portento, m
portentous /pɔrˈtentəs/ a ominoso; portentoso; importante
porter /ˈpɔrtər/ n (messenger) mozo de cordel, m; (of a university, hotel) portero, m; (of apartments) conserje, m; (railway) mozo de estación, Argentina changador, m; (drink) cerveza negra, f. **porter's lodge,** portería, f; conserjería, f
porterage /ˈpɔrtərɪdʒ/ n porte, m
portfolio /pɔrtˈfouliˌou/ n carpeta, f; (Polit. of a minister) cartera, f; (Polit. ministry) ministerio, m
porthole /ˈpɔrtˌhoul/ n tronera, f
portico /ˈpɔrtɪˌkou/ n pórtico, m
portion /ˈpɔrʃən/ n porción, f; parte, f; (marriage) dote, mf; (piece) pedazo, m; (in a restaurant) ración, f; (in life) fortuna, f. vt dividir; repartir; (dower) dotar
portliness /ˈpɔrtlinɪs/ n corpulencia, f
portly /ˈpɔrtli/ a corpulento, grueso
portmanteau /pɔrtˈmæntou/ n maleta, f
portmanteau word n palabra de acarreo, f
portrait /ˈpɔrtrɪt/ n retrato, m. **p. painter,** pintor (-ra) de retratos
portraiture /ˈpɔrtrɪtʃər/ n retratos, m pl; descripción, pintura, f
portray /pɔrˈtrei/ vt retratar; pintar, representar; (in words) describir, pintar
portrayal /pɔrˈtreiəl/ n pintura, f; retrato, m; (in words) descripción, f
portrayer /pɔrˈtreiər/ n retratista, mf, pintor (-ra)
portress /ˈpɔrtrɪs/ n portera, f; (in a convent) tornera, f
Portugal /ˈpɔrtʃəɡəl/ Portugal
Portuguese /ˌpɔrtʃəˈɡiz/ a portugués. n portugués (-esa); (language) portugués, m
pose /pouz/ vt colocar; (a problem, etc.) plantear; (a question) hacer; vi colocarse; (with as) echárselas de, dárselas de, fingir ser; hacerse pasar por. n actitud, postura, f; (affected) pose, f; (deception) engaño, m
poser /ˈpouzər/ n problema difícil, m; (in an examination) pega, f; pregunta embarazosa, f
position /pəˈzɪʃən/ n posición, f; situación, f; actitud,

postura, *f*; condición, *f*, estado, *m*; (post) puesto, empleo, *m*. **He is not in a p. to...**, No está en condiciones de..., No está para... **to place in p.**, poner en posición, colocar

positive /'pɒzɪtɪv/ *a* positivo; absoluto; (convinced) convencido, seguro; (downright) categórico; *Inf.* completo. *n* realidad, *f*; *Photo.* (prueba) positiva, *f*

positively /'pɒzɪtɪvli/ *adv* positivamente; categóricamente

positiveness /'pɒzɪtɪvnɪs/ *n* certitud, seguridad, *f*; terquedad, obstinacia, *f*

positivism /'pɒzɪtə,vɪzəm/ *n* positivismo, *m*

posse /'pɒsi/ *n* pelotón, *m*; multitud, muchedumbre, *f*

possess /pə'zɛs/ *vt* poseer; gozar (de); (of ideas, etc.) dominar. **to p. oneself of,** apoderarse de, apropiarse. **What possessed you to do it?** ¿Qué te hizo hacerlo?

possession /pə'zɛʃən/ *n* posesión, *f*. **to take p. of,** tomar posesión de; hacerse dueño de, apoderarse de; (a house, etc.) entrar en, ocupar

possessive /pə'zɛsɪv/ *a* posesivo. *n* posesivo, *m*

possessor /pə'zɛsər/ *n* poseedor (-ra); dueño (-ña); propietario (-ia)

possibility /,pɒsə'bɪlɪti/ *n* posibilidad, *f*

possible /'pɒsəbəl/ *a* posible. **as soon as p.,** cuanto antes, lo más pronto posible. **to make p.,** hacer posible, posibilitar

possibly /'pɒsəbli/ *adv* posiblemente; (perhaps) quizás. **I shall come as soon as I p. can,** Vendré lo más pronto posible

post /poust/ *n* (pole) poste, *m*; (of a sentry, etc.) puesto, *m*; (employment) empleo, *m*; (mail) correo, *m*; *Mil.* toque, *m*. *vt* (a notice) fijar; anunciar; (to an appointment) destinar; (letters, etc.) echar al correo; *Com.* pasar al libro mayor; (inform) tener al corriente. *vi* viajar en posta. **"P. no bills!"** «Se prohibe fijar carteles.» **registered p.,** correo certificado, *m*. **p. card,** tarjeta postal, *f*. **p.-chaise,** silla de posta, *f*. **p.-date,** posfecha, *f*. **p.-free,** franco de porte. **p.-haste,** con gran celeridad. **p.-horse,** caballo de posta, *m*. **p.-impressionism,** post-impresionismo, *m*. **p.-mortem,** *n* autopsia, *f*. **p.-natal,** post-natal. **p.-nuptial,** postnupcial. **p. office,** correo, *m*, correos, *m pl*; (on a train) ambulancia de correos, *m*. **p. office box,** *Spain* apartado de correos, *m*, *Lat. Am.* casilla, *f*. **p. office savings bank,** caja postal de ahorros, *f*. **p.-paid,** porte pagado; franco. **p.-war,** *n* postguerra, *f*. *a* de la postguerra

postage /'poustɪdʒ/ *n* porte de correos, franqueo, *m*. **p. stamp,** sello postal, *m*, *Mexico* timbre, m, *elsewhere in Lat. Am.* estampilla, *f*

postage meter *n* franqueadora, *f*

postal /'poustl/ *a* postal. **p. money order** *Spain* giro postal, *m*, *Lat. Am.* libranza de correos, libranza postal, *f*. **p. order,** orden postal de pago, *f*. **p. packet,** paquete postal, *m*

poster /'poustər/ *n* cartel, *m*. *vt* fijar carteles (a or en); anunciar por carteles. **bill-p.,** fijador de carteles, *m*

poste restante /,poust rɛ'stɑnt/ *n* lista de correos, *f*

posterior /pɒ'stɪəriər/ *a* posterior. *n* trasero, *m*, asentaderas, *f pl*

posteriority /pɒ,stɪəri'ɒrɪti/ *n* posterioridad, *f*

posterity /pɒ'stɛrɪti/ *n* posteridad, *f*

postgraduate /poust'grædʒuɪt/ *n* posgraduado (-da), estudiante graduado que hace estudios avanzados, *m*. *a* avanzado; para estudiantes graduados

posthumous /'pɒstʃəməs/ *a* póstumo

posthumously /'pɒstʃəməsli/ *adv* después de la muerte

postman /'poustmən/ *n* cartero, *m*

postmark /'poust,mɑrk/ *n* matasellos, *m*, *vt* poner matasellos (a)

postmaster /'poust,mæstər/ *n* administrador de correos, *m*

postmistress /'poust,mɪstrɪs/ *n* administradora de correos, *f*

postpone /poust'poun/ *vt* aplazar, diferir; retrasar; (subordinate) postergar

postponement /poust'pounmənt/ *n* aplazamiento, *m*; tardanza, *f*

postscript /'poust,skrɪpt/ *n* posdata, *f*, *Mexico* aumento, *m*

postulate /*n.* 'pɒstʃəlɪt; *v.* -,leit/ *n* postulado, *m*, *vt* postular

posture /'pɒstʃər/ *n* postura, actitud, *f*; (of affairs) estado, *m*, situación, *f*. *vi* tomar una postura

posy /'pouzi/ *n* (nosegay) ramillete de flores, *m*; flor, *f*; (motto) mote, *m*

pot /pɒt/ *n* pote, *m*; tarro, *m*; (flower-) tiesto, *m*; (for cooking) olla marmita, *f*; jarro, *m*. *vt* plantar en tiestos; conservar en potes. **pot-bellied,** panzudo. **pot-boiler,** obra literaria escrita con el sólo propósito de ganar dinero, *f*. **pot-herb,** hierba que se emplea para sazonar, hortaliza, *f*. **pot-hole,** bache, *m*. **pot-luck,** comida ordinaria, *f*. **pot-shot,** tiro fácil, *m*; tiro al azar, *m*

potage /pou'tɑʒ/ *n* potaje, *m*

potash /'pɒt,æʃ/ *n* potasa, *f*. **caustic p.,** potasa cáustica, *f*

potassium /pə'tæsiəm/ *n* potasio, *m*

potato /pə'teitou/ *n* patata, *f*. **sweet p.,** batata, *f*. **p. beetle,** coleóptero de la patata, *m*. **p. omelet,** tortilla a la española, *f*. **p. patch,** patatal, *m*. **p. peeler,** pelapatatas, *m*

potency /'poutnsi/ *n* potencia, *f*; fuerza, eficacia, *f*

potent /'poutnt/ *a* potente, fuerte; eficaz

potentate /'poutn,teit/ *n* potentado, *m*

potential /pə'tɛnʃəl/ *a* potencial; virtual; (*Phys.* *Gram.*) potencial, *n* poder, *m*; *Gram.* modo potencial, *m*; *Phys.* energía potencial, *f*; *Elec.* tensión potencial, *f*

potentiality /pə,tɛnʃi'ælɪti/ *n* potencialidad, *f*

pothook /'pɒt,hʊk/ *n* garabato de cocina, *m*; palote, *m*; (scrawl) garabato, *m*

potion /'pouʃən/ *n* poción, *f*,

potpourri /,poupʊ'ri/ *n* popurrí, *m*

potter /'pɒtər/ *n* alfarero, *m*. *vi* gandulear. *vt* perder. **potter's clay,** barro de alfarero, *m*. **potter's wheel,** tabanque, *m*. **potter's workshop,** alfar, *m*

pottery /'pɒtəri/ *n* alfarería, *f*; (china) loza, porcelana, *f*

pouch /pautʃ/ *n* bolsa, *f*; *Zool.* bolsa marsupial, *f*; (for tobacco) tabaquera, *f*; (for cartridges) cartuchera, *f*. *vt* embolsar. *vi* bolsear

poulterer /'poultərər/ *n* pollero (-ra)

poultice /'poultɪs/ *n* apósito, emplasto, *m*, *vt* poner emplastos (a or en)

poultry /'poultri/ *n* volatería, *f*. **p. dealer,** gallinero (-ra) vendedor (-ra) de volatería. **p. manure** *Mexico* cuitla, *f*. **p. yard,** gallinero, *m*

poultry farming *n* avicultura, *f*

pounce /pauns/ *n* (swoop) calada, *f*. *vi* (swoop) calarse; saltar (sobre); agarrar, hacer presa (en); *Fig.* atacar; descubrir, hacer patente

pound /paund/ *n* (weight and currency) libra, *f*; (for cattle) corral de concejo, *m*; (thump) golpe, *m*. *vt* (break up) machacar, pistar; (beat) batir; (thump) golpear, aporrear. **p. sterling,** libra esterlina, *f*. **p. troy,** libra medicinal, *f*

pounding /'paundɪŋ/ *n* machucamiento, *m*; batimiento, *m*

pour /pɔr/ *vt* vaciar, verter; derramar. *vi* correr; (of rain) diluviar, llover a cántaros; (fill) llenar; (of crowds, words, etc.) derramarse. **to p. out the tea,** servir el té. **The crowd poured in,** La multitud entró en tropel

pouring /'pɔrɪŋ/ *a* (of rain) torrencial

pout /paut/ *vi* torcer el gesto; hacer pucheritos

poverty /'pɒvərti/ *n* pobreza, *f*. **p.-stricken,** menesteroso, indigente, necesitado

powder /'paudər/ *n* polvo, *m*; (face) polvos de arroz, *m pl*; (gun) pólvora, *f*. *vt* polvorear; (crush) reducir a polvo, pulverizar. *vi* ponerse polvos. **p.-flash,** fogonazo, *m*. **p.-flask,** polvorín, *m*. **p.-magazine,** santabárbara, *f*. **p.-mill,** fábrica de pólvora, *f*. **p.-puff,** polvera, borla de empolvarse, *f*

powdered /'paudərd/ *a* en polvo

powdery /'paudəri/ *a* polvoriento; friable

power /'pauər/ *n* poder, *m*; facultad, capacidad, *f*; vigor, *m*, fuerza, *f*; (*Polit.* and *Math.*) potencia, *f*; *Mech.* fuerza, *f*; influencia, *f*. **as far as lies within my p.,** en cuanto me sea posible. **It does not lie within my p.,** No está dentro de mis posibilidades, No está en mi poder. **the Great Powers,** las grandes potencias. **the powers that be,** los que mandan. **to be in p.,** estar en el poder. **p.-house, p.-station,** central eléctrica, f. **p. of attorney,** poderes, m pl, procuración, f. **to grant p.** of attorney (to), dar poderes (a)

powerful /'pauərfəl/ a poderoso; fuerte; eficaz; potente; (of arguments, etc.) convincente

powerfully /'pauərfəli/ adv poderosamente; fuertemente

powerless /'pauərlıs/ a impotente

power steering n dirección asistida f (Spain), servo dirección f

powwow /'pau,wau/ n conferencia, f; conversación, f

pox /poks/ n sífilis, f; (smallpox) viruelas, f pl; (chicken-pox) viruelas falsas, f pl

practicability /,præktıkə'bılıti/ n factibilidad, f

practicable /'præktıkəbəl/ a practicable, factible, posible; viable, transitable

practical /'præktıkəl/ a (doable) factible; práctico; virtual. **p. joke,** burla de consecuencias

practically /'præktıkli/ adv prácticamente; en práctica; virtualmente; (in fact) en efecto. **p. nothing,** casi nada

practicalness /'præktıkəlnıs/ n carácter práctico, m

practice /'præktıs/ n (custom) costumbre, f; práctica, f; ejercicio, m; (of a doctor, etc.) clientela, f; profesión, f; (religious) rito, m, ceremonias, f pl; (experience) experiencia, f. **It is not his p. to...,** No es su costumbre de... **to be out of p.,** estar desentrenado. **to put into p.,** poner en práctica. **P. makes perfect,** El ejercicio hace maestro. vt tener la costumbre de; practicar; (a profession) ejercer; (a game) entrenarse en; (work at) estudiar; (a musical instrument) tocar; (accustom) acostumbrar. **to p. what one preaches,** predicar con el ejemplo

practiced /'præktıst/ a experimentado; experto

practitioner /præk'tıʃənər/ n médico (-ca). **general p.,** médico (-ca) general

pragmatic /præg'mætık/ a pragmatista; (historical) pragmático; práctico

pragmatism /'prægmə,tızəm/ n pragmatismo, m

pragmatist /'prægmətıst/ n pragmatista, mf

Prague /prɑg/ Praga, f

prairie /'preəri/ n pradera, sabana, pampa, f, a de la pradera, etc.

praise /preiz/ vt alabar; ensalzar, glorificar; elogiar. n alabanza, f; elogio, m; glorificación, f, ensalzamiento, m. **to p. to the skies,** poner en los cuernos de la luna poner por las nubes, poner sobre las estrellas hacerse lenguas de

praiseworthiness /'preiz,wɜrðinıs/ n mérito, m

praiseworthy /'preiz,wɜrði/ a digno de alabanza, laudable

prance /præns/ vi (of a horse) caracolear, encabritarse, cabriolar; saltar; andar airosamente. n corveta, cabriola, f; salto, m

prank /præŋk/ n travesura, diablura, f. **to play pranks,** hacer diabluras

prankster /'præŋstər/ n juguetón (-ona), burlón (-ona)

prate, prattle /preit; 'prætl/ vi charlar, chacharear; (lisp) balbucir; (of brooks, etc.) murmurar, susurrar. vt divulgar. n charla, cháchara, f; balbuceo, m

prattler /'prætlər/ n parlanchín (-ina) (gossip) chismoso (-sa); (child) niño (-ña)

prattling /'prætlıŋ/ n charla, f; (lisping) balbuceo, m; (of brooks, etc.) murmullo, susurro, ruido armonioso, m. a charlatán, gárrulo; balbuciente; (of brooks, etc.) parlero

prawn /prɔn/ n camarón, m

pray /prei/ vt and vi suplicar; implorar; rezar, orar. **P. be seated,** Haga el favor de sentarse

prayer /'preiər/ n rezo, m, plegaria, oración, f; súplica, f; Law. petición, f. **p. book,** libro de devociones, devocionario, m. **p.-meeting,** reunión para rezar, f. **p.-rug,** alfombra de rezo, f

praying /'preiıŋ/ n rezo, m; suplicación, f

pre- prefix de antes de (e.g. pre-World-War-1 publications, publicaciones de antes de la Primera Guerra Mundial)

preach /pritʃ/ vt and vi predicar

preacher /'pritʃər/ n predicador (-ra). **to turn p.,** meterse a predicar

preaching /'pritʃıŋ/ n predicación, f, a predicador

preamble /'pri,æmbəl/ n preámbulo, m

prearrange /,priə'reindʒ/ vt preparar de antemano, predisponer

precarious /prı'kɛəriəs/ a precario; inseguro; incierto, arriesgado

precariousness /prı'kɛəriəsnıs/ n condición precaria, f; inseguridad, f; incertidumbre, f

precaution /prı'kɔʃən/ n precaución, f. **to take precautions,** tomar precauciones

precautionary /prı'kɔʃə,nɛri/ a de precaución; preventivo

precede /prı'sid/ vt preceder (a), anteceder (a); tomar precedencia (a), exceder en importancia (a). vi ir delante; tener la precedencia

precedence /'prɛsıdəns/ n precedencia, f; prioridad, f; superioridad, f. **to take p. over,** tomar precedencia (a), preceder (a)

precedent /n. 'prɛsıdənt; a. prı'sidnt/ n precedente, m, a precedente. **without p.,** sin precedente

preceding /prı'sidıŋ/ a anterior, precedente

precept /'prisɛpt/ n precepto, m

preceptor /prı'sɛptər/ n preceptor, m

precinct /'prisıŋkt/ n (police station) Argentina comisaría de sección, Mexico delegación, f

precincts /'prisıŋkts/ n pl recinto, m; ámbito, m; distrito, barrio, m

preciosity /,prɛʃi'ɒsıti/ n afectación, f

precious /'prɛʃəs/ a precioso; de gran valor; hermoso; amado; muy querido; (with rogue, etc.) redomado; completo. **p. little,** muy poco. **p. stone,** piedra preciosa, f

preciousness /'prɛʃəsnıs/ n preciosidad, f; gran valor, m

precipice /'prɛsəpıs/ n precipicio, m

precipitancy /prı'sıpıtənsi/ n precipitación, f

precipitant /prı'sıpıtənt/ n precipitante, m

precipitate /v. prı'sıpı,teit; n., a. -tıt/ vt precipitar; despeñar, arrojar; acelerar; Chem. precipitar. vi precipitarse. n precipitado, m. a precipitado, súbito. **to p. oneself,** tirarse, lanzarse

precipitately /prı'sıpıtıtli/ adv precipitadamente

precipitation /prı,sıpı'teiʃən/ n Chem. precipitación, f; Chem. precipitado, m; (rain, etc.) precipitación pluvial, f

precipitous /prı'sıpıtəs/ a precipitoso, escarpado, acantilado

precipitously /prı'sıpıtəsli/ adv en precipicio

precise /prı'sais/ a preciso; exacto; justo; puntual; escrupuloso; formal; claro; pedante, afectado; ceremonioso

precisely /prı'saisli/ adv precisamente; exactamente; puntualmente; escrupulosamente; claramente; con afectación; ceremoniosamente. **at six o'clock p.,** a las seis en punto

precision /prı'sıʒən/ n precisión, f; exactitud, f; puntualidad, f; escrupulosidad, f; claridad, f; afectación, f; ceremonia, f

preclude /prı'klud/ vt excluir; impedir, hacer imposible

preclusion /prı'kluʒən/ n exclusión, f; imposibilidad, f

precocious /prı'kouʃəs/ a precoz

precocity /prı'kɒsıti/ n precocidad, f

preconceived /,prikən'sivd/ a preconcebido

preconception /,prikən'sɛpʃən/ n idea preconcebida, f; (prejudice) prejuicio, m

preconcerted /,prikən'sɜrtıd/ a concertado de antemano

precursor /prı'kɜrsər/ n precursor (-ra)

precursory /prı'kɜrsəri/ a precursor

predatory /'prɛdə,tɔri/ a rapaz; de rapiña; voraz

predecease /,pridı'sis/ vt morir antes (de or que); Law. premorir. n Law. premuerto, m

predecessor /'prɛdə,sɛsər/ n predecesor (-ra); (ancestor) antepasado, m

predestination /prı,dɛstə'neiʃən/ n predestinación, f

predestine /prı'dɛstın/ vt predestinar

predetermination /ˌpridɪˌtɜrmɪˈneɪʃən/ n predeterminación, f
predetermine /ˌpridɪˈtɜrmɪn/ vt predeterminar
predicament /prɪˈdɪkəmənt/ n /ˈprɛdɪkəmənt/ (logic) predicamento, m; situación, f; (fix) apuro, m; pl **predicaments**, categorías, f pl
predicate /v. ˈprɛdɪˌkeit; n. -kɪt/ vt afirmar. n (logic, Gram.) predicado, m
predict /prɪˈdɪkt/ vt predecir, pronosticar, profetizar
prediction /prɪˈdɪkʃən/ n predicción, f; pronóstico, vaticinio, m, profecía, f
predilection /ˌprɛdlˈɛkʃən/ n predilección, f
predispose /ˌpridɪˈspouz/ vt predisponer
predisposition /ˌpridɪspəˈzɪʃən/ n predisposición, f
predominance /prɪˈdɒmənəns/ n predominio, m
predominant /prɪˈdɒmənənt/ a predominante
predominate /prɪˈdɒməˌneit/ vi predominar
preeminence /priˈɛmənəns/ n preeminencia, f; primacia, superioridad, f
preeminent /priˈɛmənənt/ a preeminente; superior; extraordinario
preeminently /priˈɛmənəntli/ adv preeminentemente; extraordinariamente; por excelencia; entre todos
preen /prin/ vt (of birds) limpiarse; (of people) darse humos, jactarse
preexist /ˌpriɪgˈzɪst/ vi preexistir
preexistence /ˌpriɪgˈzɪstəns/ n preexistencia, f
prefabricated /priˈfæbrɪˌkeitɪd/ a prefabricado
preface /ˈprɛfɪs/ n prólogo, m; Eccl. prefacio, m; introducción, f. vt dar principio (a), empezar. **He prefaced his remarks by...,** Dijo a modo de introducción
prefatory /ˈprɛfəˌtɔri/ a preliminar, introductorio; a manera de prólogo
prefect /ˈprifɛkt/ n prefecto, m
prefecture /ˈprifɛktʃər/ n prefectura, f
prefer /prɪˈfɜr/ vt preferir, gustar más (a); (promote) ascender, elevar; (a charge, etc.) presentar. **to p. a charge against,** pedir en juicio (a). **I p. oranges to apples,** Me gustan más las naranjas que las manzanas, Prefiero las naranjas a las manzanas
preferability /ˌprɛfərəˈbɪliti/ n preferencia, ventaja, f
preferable /ˈprɛfərəbəl/ a preferible
preferably /ˈprɛfərəbli/ adv preferiblemente, con preferencia
preference /ˈprɛfərəns/ n preferencia, f; privilegio, m. **p. share,** acción privilegiada, acción preferente, f
preferential /ˌprɛfəˈrɛnʃəl/ a preferente
preferment /prɪˈfɜrmənt/ n promoción, f, ascenso, m; puesto eminente, m
preferred ˈprɪˈfɜrd/ a preferente; favorito, predilecto. **p. share,** acción preferente, f
prefix /ˈprifɪks/ vt anteponer, prefijar; (to a word) poner prefijo (a). n prefijo, m
pregnancy /ˈprɛgnənsi/ n embarazo, m, preñez, f
pregnant /ˈprɛgnənt/ a embarazada, encinta, preñada, f; Fig. fértil; Fig. preñado
prehensile /prɪˈhɛnsɪl/ a prensil
prehistoric /ˌprihɪˈstɔrɪk/ a prehistórico
prehistory /priˈhɪstəri/ n prehistoria, f
prejudge /priˈdʒʌdʒ/ vt prejuzgar
prejudice /ˈprɛdʒədɪs/ n prejuicio, m; Law. perjuicio, m. vt influir, predisponer; (damage) perjudicar. **without p.,** sin perjuicio
prejudiced /ˈprɛdʒədɪst/ a parcial; con prejuicios
prejudicial /ˌprɛdʒəˈdɪʃəl/ a perjudicial
prelacy /ˈprɛləsi/ n prelacía, f; episcopado, m
prelate /ˈprɛlɪt/ n prelado, m
preliminarily /prɪˌlɪməˈnɛərəli/ adv preliminarmente
preliminary /prɪˈlɪməˌnɛri/ a preliminar. n preliminar, f
prelude (to) /ˈprɛlyud/ n preludio (de) m; presagio (de) m, vt and vi preludiar
premature /ˌpriməˈtʃʊr/ a prematuro
prematurely /ˌpriməˈtʃʊrli/ adv prematuramente
prematureness /ˌpriməˈtʃʊrnɪs/ n lo prematuro
premeditate /priˈmɛdɪˌteit/ vt premeditar
premeditatedly /priˈmɛdɪˌteitɪdli/ adv premeditadamente, con premeditación
premeditation /prɪˌmɛdɪˈteiʃən/ n premeditación, f
premier /prɪˈmɪər/ a primero, principal. n primer

minístro, m; (in Spain) presidente del Consejo de Ministros, m
premiere /prɪˈmɪər/ n estreno, m
premiership /prɪˈmɪərʃɪp/ n puesto de primer ministro, m; in Spain presidencia del Consejo de Ministros, f
premise /ˈprɛmɪs/ n (logic) premisa, f; pl **premises,** local, m; recinto, m; establecimiento, m; propiedad, f; tierras, f pl. **on the premises,** en el local; en el establecimiento
premium /ˈprimiəm/ n (prize) premio, m, recompensa, f; Com. prima, f; precio, m. **at a p.,** a premio; a una prima; (of shares) sobre la par; Fig. en boga, muy solicitado, en gran demanda
premonition /ˌpriməˈnɪʃən/ n presentimiento, presagio, m
premonitory /prɪˈmɒnɪˌtɔri/ a premonitorio
prenatal /priˈneitl/ a prenatal, antenatal
preoccupation /priˌɒkyəˈpeiʃən/ n preocupación, f
preoccupied /priˈɒkyəˌpaid/ a preocupado; abstraído, absorto
preoccupy /priˈɒkyəˌpai/ vt preocupar
prepaid /priˈpeid/ a porte pagado, franco de porte
preparation /ˌprɛpəˈreiʃən/ n preparación, f; preparativo, m, disposición, f; (patent food) preparado, m. **I have made all my preparations,** He hecho todos mis preparativos. **The book is in p.,** El libro está en preparación
preparative /prɪˈpærətɪv/ a preparativo. n preparativo, m
preparatory /prɪˈpærəˌtɔri/ a preparatorio, preparativo; preliminar. **p. school,** escuela preparatoria, f, m. **p. to,** como preparación para; antes de
prepare /prɪˈpɛər/ vt preparar; aparejar, aviar; equipar; (cloth) aprestar. vi prepararse; hacer preparativos
preparedness /prɪˈpɛərɪdnɪs/ n estado de preparación, m; preparación, f, apercibimiento, m
prepay /priˈpei/ vt pagar adelantado, Lat. Am. aprontar; (a letter, etc.) franquear
prepayment /priˈpeimənt/ n pago adelantado, m; (of a letter, etc.) franqueo, m
preponderance /prɪˈpɒndərəns/ n preponderancia, f
preponderant /prɪˈpɒndərənt/ a preponderante, predominante
preponderantly /prɪˈpɒndərəntli/ adv predominantemente; en su mayoría
preponderate /prɪˈpɒndəˌreit/ vi preponderar; prevalecer (sobre), predominar (sobre)
preposition /ˌprɛpəˈzɪʃən/ n preposición, f
prepossess /ˌpriˈpɒˈzɛs/ vt predisponer; causar buena impresión (a)
prepossessing /ˌpripəˈzɛsɪŋ/ a atractivo
preposterous /prɪˈpɒstərəs/ a ridículo, absurdo
preposterously /prɪˈpɒstərəsli/ adv absurdamente
preposterousness /prɪˈpɒstərəsnɪs/ n ridiculez, f
Prep School /prɛp/ n preparatoria, f
prepuce /ˈpripyus/ n prepucio, m
prerequisite /priˈrɛkwəzɪt/ n requisito necesario, esencial, m, a previamente necesario, esencial
prerogative /prɪˈrɒgətɪv/ n prerrogativa, f
presage /ˈprɛsɪdʒ/ n presagio, m; anuncio, m. vt presagiar; anunciar
Presbyterian /ˌprɛzbɪˈtɪəriən/ a and n presbiteriano (-na)
prescience /ˈprɛʃəns/ n presciencia, previsión, f
prescient /ˈprɛʃənt/ a presciente
prescind /prɪˈsɪnd/ vt prescindir (de); separar (de). vi separarse
prescribe /prɪˈskraib/ vt and vi prescribir; Med. recetar; dar leyes, Law. prescribir
prescription /prɪˈskrɪpʃən/ n prescripción, f; Med. receta, f
presence /ˈprɛzəns/ n presencia, f; (ghost) aparición, f. **in the p. of,** en presencia de; delante; a vista de. **p. of mind,** presencia de ánimo, serenidad de ánimo, f
present /ˈprɛzənt/ a presente; actual; (with month) corriente; Gram. presente. **at p.,** al presente, actualmente. **at the p. day,** a la fecha, en la actualidad, hoy día. **P. company excluded!** ¡Mejorando lo presente! **the present writer,** el que suscribe, el que

esto escribe, el que estas líneas traza. **to be p. at,** presenciar, ser testigo de; asistir a, acudir a; hallarse en. **p.-day,** de hoy, actual. **p. tense,** *Gram.* tiempo presente, *m*

present /'prɛzənt/ *n* (time) presente, *m*; actualidad, *f*; *Gram.* tiempo presente, *m*; (gift) regalo, *m*, dádiva, *f*. **By these presents...,** *Law.* Por estas presentes... **to make a p. of,** regalar. **Jane made me a p. of a watch,** Juana me regaló un reloj

present /prɪ'zɛnt/ *vt* presentar; ofrecer; manifestar; (a gift) regalar, dar; (*Eccl. Mil.*) presentar. **New problems presented themselves,** Nuevos problemas surgieron. **to p. arms,** presentar las armas. **He presented himself in the office,** Se presentó en la oficina. **He presented his friend Mr. Moreno to me,** Me presentó a su amigo el Sr. Moreno

presentable /prɪ'zɛntəbəl/ *a* presentable

presentation /,prɛzən'teɪʃən/ *n* presentación, *f*; homenaje, *m*; (exhibition) exposición, *f*. **on p.,** *Com.* a presentación

presentiment /prɪ'zɛntəmənt/ *n* presentimiento, *m*, corazonada, *f*. **I had a p. that...,** Tuve el presentimiento de que..., Tuve una corazonada que... **to have a p. about,** presentir

presently /'prɛzəntli/ *adv* pronto; en seguida; dentro de poco

preservation /,prɛzər'veɪʃən/ *n* conservación, *f*; (from harm) preservación, *f*

preservative /prɪ'zɜrvətɪv/ *a* preservativo. *n* preservativo, *m*

preserve /prɪ'zɜrv/ *vt* preservar (de); guardar; proteger; conservar; *Cul.* hacer conservas de; (in syrup) almibarar. *n Cul.* conserva, *f*; (of fruit) compota, confitura, *f*; (covert) coto, *m*. **preserved fruit,** dulce de almíbar, *m*. **p. dish,** compotera, *f*

preserver /prɪ'zɜrvər/ *n* conservador (-ra); (savior) salvador (-ra); (benefactor) bienhechor (-ra)

preserving /prɪ'zɜrvɪŋ/ *n* (from harm) preservación, *f*; conservación, *f*. **p. pan,** cazuela para conservas, *f*

preside /prɪ'zaɪd/ *vi* (over) presidir; dirigir, gobernar. **He presided at the meeting,** Presidió la reunión

presidency /'prɛzɪdənsi/ *n* presidencia, *f*

president /'prɛzɪdənt/ *n* presidente (-ta); (of a college) rector (-ra)

presidential /,prɛzɪ'dɛnʃəl/ *a* presidencial

presidentship /'prɛzɪdənt,ʃɪp/ *n* presidencia, *f*

press /prɛs/ *vt* prensar; (juice out of) exprimir; (clothes) planchar; (a bell, a hand, and of a shoe, etc.) apretar, *Mexico* apachurrar; (embrace) dar un abrazo (a); (a stamp, a kiss, etc.) imprimir; (an enemy) hostigar, acosar; (in a game) apretar; (crowd upon) oprimir; (emphasize) insistir en; (urge) instar, instigar; (compel) obligar; apremiar; (oppress) abrumar, agobiar; (paper) satinar; (an advantage) aprovecharse de. **Lola pressed his hand,** Lola le apretó la mano. **Time presses,** El tiempo es breve. **I did not p. the point,** No insistí. **to p. against,** pegar(se) contra. **to p. down,** comprimir; *Fig.* agobiar. **to p. for,** exigir, reclamar. **to p. forward, on,** avanzar; seguir el camino, continuar la marcha; (hurry) apretar el paso

press /prɛs/ *n* (pressure) apretón, *m*; (push) golpe, *m*; (throng) muchedumbre, *f*; (of business, etc.) urgencia, *f*; (apparatus) prensa, *f*; (printing press and publishing firm) imprenta, *f*; (cupboard) armario, *m*. **Associated P.,** Prensa Asociada, *f*. **freedom of the p.,** libertad de la prensa, *f*. **in p., in the p.,** en prensa. **in the p. of battle,** en lo más reñido de la batalla. **to go to p.,** entrar en prensa. **p.-agent,** agente de publicidad, *m*. **p.-box,** tribuna de la prensa, *f*. **p. clipping, p.-cutting,** recorte de prensa, *m*. **p.-gallery,** tribuna de la prensa, *f*. **p.-gang,** ronda de enganche, *f*. **p.-mark,** número de catálogo, *m*. **p. proof,** prueba de imprenta, *f*. **p.-room,** taller de imprenta, *m*. **p. conference,** rueda de prensa, entrevista de prensa, conferencia de prensa, *f*

pressing /'prɛsɪŋ/ *a* urgente, apremiante; importuno. *n* prensado, *m*, prensadura, *f*; expresión, *f*; (of a garment) planchado, *m*

pressingly /'prɛsɪŋli/ *adv* urgentemente, con urgencia; importunamente

pressman /'prɛsmən/ *n* tirador, *m*; (journalist) periodista, *m*

pressure /'prɛʃər/ *n* presión, *f*; (of the hand) apretón, *m*; apremio, *m*; opresión, *f*; (weight) peso, *m*; (force) fuerza, *f*; urgencia, *f*. **p.-cooker,** cazuela de presión, olla de presión, *f*, presto, *m*. **p.-gauge,** manómetro, *m*

prestidigitation /,prɛstɪ,dɪdʒɪ'teɪʃən/ *n* prestidigitación, *f*, juegos de manos, *m pl*

prestige /prɛ'stiʒ/ *n* prestigio, *m*

prestigious /prɛ'stɪdʒəs/ *a* prestigiado

presumable /prɪ'zuməbəl/ *a* presumible

presume /prɪ'zum/ *vt* presumir; suponer, sospechar; (attempt) pretender. *vi* presumir; tomarse libertades; abusar (de)

presumption /prɪ'zʌmpʃən/ *n* presunción, *f*; suposición, *f*; (effrontery) atrevimiento, *m*; insolencia, *f*

presumptive /prɪ'zʌmptɪv/ *a* presuntivo; (with heir, etc.) presunto

presumptuous /prɪ'zʌmptʃuəs/ *a* presumido, insolente, presuntuoso; atrevido

presumptuously /prɪ'zʌmptʃuəsli/ *adv* presuntuosamente

presumptuousness /prɪ'zʌmptʃuəsnɪs/ *n* presunción, presuntuosidad, *f*; atrevimiento, *m*

presuppose /,prisə'pouz/ *vt* presuponer

presupposition /,prisʌpə'zɪʃən/ *n* presuposición, *f*

pretence /prɪ'tɛns/ *n* (claim) pretensión, *f*; afectación, *f*; (simulation) fingimiento, *m*; pretexto, *m*. **false pretences,** apariencias fingidas, *f pl*; engaño, *m*, estafa, *f*. **to make a p. of,** fingir. **under p. of,** bajo pretexto de

pretend /prɪ'tɛnd/ *vt* dar como pretexto de; aparentar, fingir, simular, hacer el papel (de). *vi* pretender (a); tener pretensiones (de); ser pretendiente (a); fingir

pretended /prɪ'tɛndɪd/ *a* supuesto, fingido; falso

pretender /prɪ'tɛndər/ *n* pretendiente, *m*; hipócrita, *mf*

pretension /prɪ'tɛnʃən/ *n* pretensión, *f*; afectación, simulación, *f*

pretentious /prɪ'tɛnʃəs/ *a* pretencioso; (of persons) presumido

pretentiousness /prɪ'tɛnʃəsnɪs/ *n* pretensiones, *f pl*, lo pretencioso

preterite /'prɛtərɪt/ *n* (tiempo) pretérito, *m*, *a* pretérito, pasado

pretext /'pritɛkst/ *n* pretexto, *m*. *vt* pretextar. **under p. of,** bajo pretexto de, so color de

prettily /'prɪtli/ *adv* lindamente; con gracia; agradablemente

prettiness /'prɪtɪnɪs/ *n* lo bonito; elegancia, *f*; gracia, *f*

pretty /'prɪti/ *a* bonito; (of women, children) guapo, mono; (of men) lindo; elegante; excelente; *Ironic.* bueno. *adv* bastante; medianamente; (very) muy; (almost) casi. **p. good,** bastante bueno. **p. ways,** monerías, *f pl*

prevail /prɪ'veɪl/ *vi* prevalecer, predominar; ser la costumbre. **to p. against or over,** triunfar de, vencer (a). **to p. on, upon,** inducir, convencer, persuadir. **to be prevailed upon to,** dejarse persuadir a

prevailing /prɪ'veɪlɪŋ/ *a* prevaleciente; dominante; predominante, reinante; general; común; (fashionable) en boga

prevalence /'prɛvələns/ *n* predominio, *m*; existencia, *f*; (habit) costumbre, *f*; (fashion) boga, *f*

prevalent /'prɛvələnt/ *a* prevaleciente; predominante; general; común; corriente; (fashionable) en boga

prevaricate /prɪ'værɪ,keɪt/ *vi* tergiversar; *Law.* prevaricar

prevarication /prɪ,værɪ'keɪʃən/ *n* tergiversación, *f*, equívoco, *m*

prevaricator /prɪ'værɪ,keɪtər/ *n* tergiversador (-ra)

prevent /prɪ'vɛnt/ *vt* evitar; (hinder) impedir (a)

preventable /prɪ'vɛntəbəl/ *a* evitable

prevention /prɪ'vɛnʃən/ *n* prevención, *f*; (preventive) estorbo, obstáculo, *m*

preventive /prɪ'vɛntɪv/ *a* preventivo. *n* preservativo, *m*

preview /'pri,vyu/ *n* vista de antemano, *f*; (of a film) avances, *m pl* (Cuba, Mexico), colas, *f pl* (Argentina),

previous

cortos *m pl* (Venezuela), sinopsis, *f* (Uruguay), tráiler, *m* (Spain)
previous /'priviəs/ *a* previo, anterior. **p. to,** antes de
previously /'priviəsli/ *adv* anteriormente, antes, previamente
previousness /'priviəsnıs/ *n* anterioridad, *f*; inoportunidad, *f*
prevision /prı'vıʒən/ *n* previsión, *f*
prewar /'pri'wɔr/ *a* de antes de la guerra
prey /prei/ *n* presa, *f*; *Fig.* víctima, *f*; (booty) botín, *m*. *vi* (of animals) devorar; (plunder) robar, pillar; (of sorrow, etc.) hacer presa (de); agobiar, consumir; (sponge on) vivir a costa de. **to fall p. to,** ser víctima de
price /prais/ *n* precio, *m*; valor, *m*; costa, *f*. *vt* evaluar, tasar; poner precio a; preguntar el precio de; fijar el precio de. **at any p.,** a cualquier precio; (whatever the cost) cueste lo que cueste. **at a reduced p.,** a precio reducido. **fixed p.,** precio fijo, *m*. **p. ceiling,** precio máximo, precio tope, *m*. **p. control,** control de precios, *m*. **price list,** lista de precios, *f*; tarifa, *f*; (of shares, etc.) boletín de cotización, *m*. **Prices are subject to change without notice,** Los precios están sujetos a variación sin previo aviso.
priceless /'praislıs/ *a* sin precio; (amusing) divertidísimo. **These jewels are p.,** Estas joyas no tienen precio
prick /prık/ *n* pinchazo, *m*; picadura, *f*; punzada, *f*; (prickle) espina, *f*; (with a goad) aguijonazo, *m*; (with a pin) alfilerazo, *m*; (with a spur) espolada, *f*; (of conscience) remordimiento, escrúpulo, *m*. *vt* pinchar, punzar; picar; (with remorse) atormentar, causar remordimiento (a); (urge on) incitar. **to p. the ears,** aguzar las orejas
pricking /'prıkıŋ/ *n* picadura, *f*; punzada, *f*. **prickings of conscience,** remordimientos, *m pl*
prickle /'prıkəl/ *n* espina, *f*; (irritation) escozor, *m*
prickly /'prıkli/ *a* espinoso; erizado. **p. heat,** salpullido causado por exceso de calor, *m*. **p. pear,** higo chumbo, *m*, chumbera, *f*
pride /praid/ *n* orgullo, *m*; arrogancia, *f*; (splendour) pompa, *f*, fausto, aparato, *m*; belleza, *f*; vigor, *m*; (of lions) manada, *f*. **to take p. in,** estar orgulloso de. **to p. oneself,** sentirse orgulloso, ufanarse. **to p. oneself upon,** jactarse de, preciarse de
prie-dieu /'pri'dyʊ/ *n* reclinatorio, *m*
prier /'praiər/ *n* espía, *mf*; curioso (-sa)
priest /prist/ *n* sacerdote, *m*; cura, *m*. **high-p.,** sumo sacerdote, *m*. **p.-ridden,** dominado por el clero
priestess /'pristıs/ *n* sacerdotisa, *f*
priesthood /'pristhʊd/ *n* sacerdocio, *m*
priestly /'pristli/ *a* sacerdotal
prig /prıg/ *n* fatuo (-ua), mojigato (-ta)
priggish /'prıgıʃ/ *a* fatuo, gazmoño
priggishness /'prıgıʃnıs/ *n* gazmoñería, fatuidad, *f*
prim /prım/ *a* almidonado, etiquetero; peripuesto; afectado
primacy /'praiməsi/ *n* primacía, *f*
prima donna /,primə 'dɒnə/ *n* cantatriz, *f*
primarily /prai'mɛərəli/ *adv* en primer lugar principalmente
primary /'praimɛri/ *a* primario; primitivo; principal. **p. education,** enseñanza primaria, *f*. **p. color,** color primario, *m*. **p. school,** escuela primaria, *f*. **p. election,** elección interna (dentro de un partido), *f*
primate /'praimeit/ *n* primado, *m*
prime /praim/ *a* primero; principal; excelente; de primera calidad; de primera clase. *n* (spring) primavera, *f*; (of life, etc.) flor, *f*, vigor, *m*; (best) nata, crema, *f*; *Eccl.* prima, *f*; (number) número primo, *m*. *vt* preparar, aprestar; (fire-arms) cebar. **p. the pump,** cebar la bomba; (with paint, etc.) imprimar; (instruct) dar instrucciones (a), informar. **in his p.,** en la flor de su edad. **of p. quality,** de primera calidad. **P. Minister,** Primer Ministro, *m*. **p. necessity,** artículo de primera necesidad, *m*
primer /'praimər/ *n* cartilla, *f*, abecedario, *m*; libro de lectura, *m*; (prayer book) devocionario, *m*
primeval /prai'mivəl/ *a* primevo, primitivo
priming /'praimıŋ/ *n* preparación, *f*; (of fire-arms) cebo, *m*; (of paint, etc.) imprimación, *f*; instrución, *f*

primitive /'prımıtıv/ *a* primitivo; anticuado. *n* primitivo, *m*
primitiveness /'prımıtıvnıs/ *n* lo primitivo; carácter primitivo, *m*
primly /'prımli/ *adv* afectadamente, con afectación; gravemente
primness /'prımnıs/ *n* afectación, *f*; gravedad, *f*
primogeniture /,praimə'dʒɛnıtʃər/ *n* primogenitura, *f*
primordial /prai'mɔrdiəl/ *a* primordial
primrose /'prım,rouz/ *n* *Bot.* vellorita, primavera, *f*; color amarillo pálido, *m*
prince /prıns/ *n* príncipe, *m*. **P. Consort,** príncipe consorte, *m*. **P. of Wales,** (Britain) príncipe heredero, *m*; (Spanish equivalent) Príncipe de Asturias, *m*. **p. regent,** príncipe regente, *m*. **P. Charming,** el Príncipe Azul, *m*
princeliness /'prınslınıs/ *n* magnificencia, *f*; nobleza, *f*
princely /'prınsli/ *a* principesco; magnífico; noble
princess /'prınsıs/ *n* princesa, *f*
principal /'prınsəpəl/ *a* principal; fundamental; mayor. *n* principal, jefe, *m*; (of a university) rector, *m*; (of a school) director (-ra). *Law.* causante, *m*; *Com.* capital, *m*
principality /,prınsə'pælıti/ *n* principado, *m*
principally /'prınsəpli/ *adv* principalmente
principle /'prınsəpəl/ *n* principio, *m*. **in p.,** en principio
principled /'prınsəpəld/ *a* de principios...
print /prınt/ *n* (mark) impresión, marca, *f*; (type) letra de molde, *f*, tipo, *m*; (of books) imprenta, *f*; (fabric) estampado, *m*; (picture) grabado, *m*; (photograph) positiva impresa, *f*; (mold) molde, *m*. *vt* marcar; imprimir; (on the mind) grabar; *Print.* tirar, hacer una tirada (de); (in photography) tirar una prueba (de); (publish) sacar a luz, publicar; (fabrics) estampar. **in p.,** impreso; publicado; **He likes to see his name in print,** Le gusta ver su nombre en letras de molde; (available) existente. **to be out of p.,** estar agotado, *m*
printed /'prıntıd/ *a* impreso. **p. fabric,** estampado, *m*. **p. matter,** impresos, *m pl*
printer /'prıntər/ *n* impresor, *m*; tipógrafo, *m*. **printer's devil,** aprendiz de impresor, *m*. **printer's ink,** tinta de imprenta, tinta tipográfica, *f*. **printer's mark,** pie de imprenta, *m*
printing /'prıntıŋ/ *n* imprenta, *f*; impresión, *f*; (of fabrics) estampación, *f*; (art of) tipografía, *f*. **p. house,** imprenta, *f*. **p. machine,** máquina de imprimir, *f*. **p. press,** prensa tipográfica, *f*. **p. types,** caracteres de imprenta, *m pl*
prior /'praiər/ *n* prior, *m*, *a* anterior, previo. **p. to,** anterior a, antes de
prioress /'praiərıs/ *n* priora, *f*
priority /prai'ɔrıti/ *n* prioridad, *f*
prism /'prızəm/ *n* prisma, *m*; espectro solar, *m*
prismatic /prız'mætık/ *a* prismático
prison /'prızən/ *n* prisión, cárcel, *f*. **p. camp,** campo de prisioneros, *m*. **p. van,** coche celular, *m*. **p. yard,** patio de la prisión, *m*
prisoner /'prızənər/ *n* prisionero (-ra), preso (-sa). **to take p.,** prender, hacer prisionero (a)
pristine /'prıstın/ *a* pristino, original
privacy /'praivəsi/ *n* privacidad, soledad, *f*, aislamiento, retiro, *m*; intimidad, *f*; secreto, *m*
private /'praivıt/ *a* particular; privado; secreto; confidencial; reservado; íntimo; personal; doméstico; (of hearings, etc.) a puertas cerradas, secreto; (own) propio. *n* (soldier) soldado raso, *m*. **in p.,** en secreto; confidencialmente; de persona a persona. **They wish to be p.,** Quieren estar a solas. **p. company,** sociedad en comandita, *f*. **p. hotel,** pensión, *f*. **p. house,** casa particular, *f*. **p. individual,** particular, *mf*. **p. interview,** entrevista privada, *f*. **p. life,** vida privada, *f*. **p. office,** despacho particular, *m*. **p. secretary,** secretario (-ia) particular. **p. viewing, (of a film)** función privada, *f*; **(of an exhibition)** día de inauguración, *m*
privateer /,praivə'tıər/ *n* corsario, *m*
privately /'praivıtli/ *adv* privadamente, en secreto; personalmente; confidencialmente; (of hearings) a puertas cerradas

privation /prai'veiʃən/ n privación, f; carencia, escasez, f
privet /'prɪvɪt/ n alheña, f
privilege /'prɪvəlɪdʒ/ n privilegio, m; derecho, m; inmunidad, f. vt privilegiar
privileged /'prɪvəlɪdʒd/ a privilegiado; confidencial
privy /'prɪvi/ a privado; cómplice; enterado; personal, particular. n (latrine) retrete, m. **p. council,** consejo privado, m
prize /praiz/ n premio, m; recompensa, f, galardón, m; (capture) presa, f. a que ha ganado un premio; premiado; (huge) enorme; (complete) de primer orden. vt estimar, apreciar. **to p. open,** abrir con una palanca. **to carry off the p.,** ganar el premio. **cash p.,** premio en metálico, m. **first p.,** primer premio, m; (in a lottery) premio gordo, m. **p. court,** tribunal de presas, m. **p. fight,** partido de boxeo, m. **p. fighter,** boxeador, m. **p. giving,** distribución de premios, f. **p. money,** premio en metálico, m; (boxing) bolsa, f
pro /prou/ prep pro. **pro forma invoice,** factura simulada, f
probability /,prɒbə'bɪlɪti/ n probabilidad, f
probable /'prɒbəbəl/ a probable
probably /'prɒbəbli/ adv probablemente
probate /'proubeit/ n verificación de un testamento, f
probation /prou'beiʃən/ n probación, f; Law. libertad vigilada, f
probationary /prou'beiʃə,nɛri/ a de probación; de prueba
probationer /prou'beiʃənər/ n novicio, m; estudiante de enfermera, f; candidato, m; aspirante, m
probe /proub/ n Surg. sonda, cala, tienta, f. vt Surg. tentar; escudriñar
probing /'proubɪŋ/ n sondeo, m
probity /'proubiti/ n probidad, integridad, f
problem /'prɒbləm/ n problema, m; cuestión, f. **p. play,** drama de tesis, m
problematic /,prɒblə'mætɪk/ a problemático
problem child n niño problemático, m (male), niña problemática, f (female)
proboscis /prou'bɒsɪs/ n (of an elephant) trompa, f; (of an insect) trompetilla, f
Probus /'proubəs/ Probo, m
procedure /prə'sidʒər/ n procedimiento, m
proceed /prə'sid/ vi seguir el camino, continuar la marcha; avanzar, seguir adelante; ir; proceder; ponerse (a); empezar (a); (say) proseguir; (come to) llegar a, ir a; (of a play, etc.) desarrollarse. **Before we p. any further...** Antes de ir más lejos... **to p. to blows,** llegar a las manos. **to p. against,** proceder contra, procesar. **to p. from,** venir de. **to p. with,** proseguir; poner por obra; usar
proceeding /prə'sidɪŋ/ n modo de obrar, m; conducta, f; procedimiento, m; transacción, f; pl **proceedings,** (measures) medidas, f pl, actos, m pl; (of a learned society or a conference) actas, f pl. **to take proceedings against,** Law. procesar
proceeds /'prousidz/ n pl producto, m; ganancias, f pl; beneficios, m pl. **net p.,** producto neto, m
process /'prɒsɛs/ n proceso, m; (method) procedimiento, m; (course) curso, m; marcha, f; (Law., Zool.) proceso, m. vt beneficiar (ore), trasformar, elaborar. **in p. of,** en curso de. **in the p. of time,** con el tiempo marchando el tiempo
processing industry /'prɒsesɪŋ/ n industria de trasformación, industria de elaboración, f
procession /prə'sɛʃən/ n desfile, m; cortejo, m; (religious) procesión, f. **funeral p.,** cortejo fúnebre, m. **to walk in p.,** desfilar
processional /prə'sɛʃənl/ a procesional
proclaim /prou'kleim/ vt proclamar; publicar, pregonar; anunciar; (reveal) revelar; (outlaw) denunciar
proclamation /,prɒklə'meiʃən/ n proclamación, f; proclama, f, anuncio, m; declaración, f
proclivity /prou'klɪvɪti/ n proclividad, propensión, f
procrastinate /prou'kræstə,neit/ vi tardar (en decidirse), aplazar su decisión; vacilar; perder el tiempo
procrastination /prou,kræstə'neiʃən/ n dilación, tardanza, f; vacilación, f; pereza, f
procrastinator /prou'kræstə,neitər/ n perezoso (-sa)
procreate /'proukri,eit/ vt procrear

procreation /,proukri'eiʃən/ n procreación, f
procreator /'proukri,eitər/ n procreador (-ra)
proctor /'prɒktər/ n procurador, m; Educ. censor, m
procurable /prou'kyʊrəbəl/ a procurable; asequible
procure /prou'kyʊr/ vt obtener, conseguir, lograr
procurement /prou'kyʊrmənt/ n obtención, f, logro, m
procurer /prou'kyʊrər/ n alcahuete, m
procuress /prou'kyʊrɪs/ n alcahueta, celestina, trotaconventos, f
prod /prɒd/ n (with a bayonet, etc.) punzada, f; Fig. pinchazo, m. vt punzar; (in the ribs, etc.) clavar; Fig. pinchar
prodigal /'prɒdɪgəl/ a and n pródigo (-ga)
prodigality /,prɒdɪ'gælɪti/ n prodigalidad, f
prodigally /'prɒdɪgəli/ adv pródigamente
prodigious /prə'dɪdʒəs/ a prodigioso
prodigiousness /prə'dɪdʒəsnɪs/ n prodigiosidad, f; enormidad, f
prodigy /'prɒdɪdʒi/ n prodigio, m; portento, m. **child p.,** niño prodigio, m
produce /v. prə'dus; n. 'prɒdus, 'proudus/ vt producir; dar frutos; (show) mostrar, presentar; (take out) sacar; (occasion) causar, traer consigo, ocasionar; (goods) fabricar, manufacturar; (of shares, etc.) rendir; Geom. prolongar; (a play) poner en escena. n producto, m; víveres, comestibles, m pl
producer /prə'dusər/ n productor (-ra); Theat. director de escena, m
product /'prɒdʌkt/ n producto, m; (result) fruto, resultado, m, consecuencia, f; Math. producto, m
production /prə'dʌkʃən/ n producción, f; producto, m; Geom. prolongación, f; (of a play) dirección escénica, f; (performance) producción, f. **p. cost,** coste de producción, m
productive /prə'dʌktɪv/ a productivo
productivity /,proudʌk'tɪvɪti/ n productividad, f
profanation /,prɒfə'neiʃən/ n profanación, f
profane /prə'fein/ a profano; sacrílego, blasfemo. vt profanar
profaner /prə'feinər/ n profanador (-ra)
profanity /prə'fænɪti/ n profanidad, f; blasfemia, f
profess /prə'fes/ vt (assert) afirmar, manifestar; declarar; (a faith, a profession, teach) profesar; (feign) fingir; (pretend) tener pretensiones de. vi (as a monk or nun) tomar estado, entrar en religión. **He professed himself surprised,** Se declaró sorprendido
professed /prə'fest/ a declarado; Eccl. profeso; ostensible, fingido
profession /prə'feʃən/ n profesión, f; carrera, f; declaración, f. **p. of faith,** profesión de fe, f. **the learned professions,** las carreras liberales
professional /prə'feʃənl/ a profesional; de la profesión; de profesión; de carrera. **p. diplomat,** diplomático (-ca) de carrera. **p. etiquette,** etiqueta profesional, f. **p. man,** hombre profesional, m; hombre de carrera liberal, m
professor /prə'fesər/ n catedrático (-ca), profesor (-ra)
professorate /prə'fesərɪt/ n profesorado, m
professorial /,proufə'sɔriəl/ a de catedrático; de profesor
professorship /prə'fesər,ʃɪp/ n cátedra, f
proffer /'prɒfər/ vt proponer; ofrecer. n oferta, f
proficiency /prə'fɪʃənsi/ n pericia, habilidad, f
proficient /prə'fɪʃənt/ a proficiente, experto, adepto, perito
profile /'proufail/ n perfil, m. vt perfilar. **in p.,** de perfil
profit /'prɒfɪt/ n provecho, m; utilidad, f; ventaja, f; Com. ganancia, f, lucro, m, vt aprovechar. vi ganar; Com. sacar ganancia. **to p. by,** aprovechar. **gross p.,** ganancia total, f. **p. and loss,** lucros y daños, f pl. **p. sharing,** participación en las ganancias, participación de utilidades, f. **non-p. organization,** compañía sin fines de lucro
profitable /'prɒfɪtəbəl/ a provechoso, útil, ventajoso; lucrativo. **p. use,** aprovechamiento, m
profitably /'prɒfɪtəbli/ adv con provecho, provechosamente; lucrativamente
profiteer /,prɒfɪ'tɪər/ n estraperlista, mf

profit incentive *n* acicate del lucro, *m*
profitless /'prɒfɪtlɪs/ *a* sin provecho, infructuoso, inútil
profligacy /'prɒflɪgəsi/ *n* libertinaje, *m*
profligate /'prɒflɪgɪt/ *a* licencioso, disoluto. *n* libertino, *m*
profound /prə'faund/ *a* profundo
profundity /prə'fʌndɪti/ *n* profundidad, *f*
profuse /prə'fyus/ *a* profuso; pródigo; lujoso
profusely /prə'fyusli/ *adv* profusamente; pródigamente; lujosamente
profusion /prə'fyuʒən/ *n* profusión, abundancia, *f*; prodigalidad, *f*; exceso, *m*
progenitor /prou'dʒɛnɪtər/ *n* progenitor, *m*; (ancestor) antepasado, *m*
progeny /'prɒdʒəni/ *n* prole, *f*
prognosis /prɒg'nousɪs/ *n* prognosis, *f*; presagio, *m*; *Med.* pronóstico, *m*
prognosticate /prɒg'nɒstɪ,keit/ *vt* pronosticar, presagiar
prognostication /prɒg,nɒstɪ'keiʃən/ *n* pronosticación, *f*; pronóstico, presagio, augurio, *m*
program /'prougræm/ *n* programa, *m*
programmer /'prougræmər/ *n* programador (-ra)
progress /*n.* 'prɒgrɛs; *v.* prə'grɛs/ *n* progreso, *m*; avance, *m*; (betterment) mejora, *f*; (of events) marcha, *f*. *vi* avanzar, marchar; (improve) progresar, adelantar; mejorar. **to make p.,** adelantarse; hacer progresos
progression /prə'grɛʃən/ *n* progresión, *f*
progressive /prə'grɛsɪv/ *a* progresivo; avanzado; *Polit.* progresista. *n* *Polit.* progresista, *mf*
progressiveness /prə'grɛsɪvnɪs/ *n* carácter progresivo, *m*
prohibit /prou'hɪbɪt/ *vt* prohibir; defender; (prevent) impedir, privar. **His health prohibited him from doing it,** Su salud le impidió hacerlo
prohibition /,prouə'bɪʃən/ *n* prohibición, *f*; interdicción, *f*; (of alcohol) prohibicionismo, *m*
prohibitionist /,prouə'bɪʃənɪst/ *n* prohibicionista, *mf*
prohibitive /prou'hɪbɪtɪv/ *a* prohibitivo, prohibitorio
project /*v.* prə'dʒɛkt; *n.* 'prɒdʒɛkt/ *vt* (all meanings) proyectar. *vi* sobresalir; destacarse. *n* proyectil, plan, *m*
projectile /prə'dʒɛktɪl/ *n* proyectil, *m*, *a* arrojadizo
projecting /prə'dʒɛktɪŋ/ *a* saliente; (of teeth) saltón
projection /prə'dʒɛkʃən/ *n* (hurling) lanzamiento, *m*; prominencia, protuberancia, *f*; (other meanings) proyección, *f*
projector /prə'dʒɛktər/ *n* proyectista, *mf*; proyector, *m*
proletarian /,proulɪ'tɛəriən/ *a* proletario
proletariate /,proulɪ'tɛəriit/ *n* proletariado, *m*
prolific /prə'lɪfɪk/ *a* prolífico; fecundo, fértil
prolix /prou'lɪks/ *a* prolijo
prolixity /prou'lɪksɪti/ *n* prolijidad, *f*
prolog /'prou,lɔg/ *n* prólogo, *m*, *vt* prologar
prolong /prə'lɔŋ/ *vt* prolongar
prolongation /,proulɔŋ'geiʃən/ *n* prolongación, *f*
promenade /,prɒmə'neid, -'nɑd/ *n* paseo, *m*; bulevar, *m*; avenida, *f*. *vi* pasearse. *vt* recorrer, andar por, pasearse por. **p. deck,** cubierta de paseo, *f*
Promethean /prə'miθiən/ *a* de Prometeo
prominence /'prɒmənəns/ *n* prominencia, *f*; protuberancia, *f*; eminencia, *f*; importancia, *f*
prominent /'prɒmənənt/ *a* prominente, saliente; (of eyes, teeth) saltón; (distinguished) eminente, distinguido. **They placed the vase in a p. position,** Pusieron el florero muy a la vista. **to play a p. part,** desempeñar un papel importante. **p. eyes,** ojos saltones, *m pl*
promiscuous /prə'mɪskyuəs/ *a* promiscuo
promiscuousness /prə'mɪskyuəsnɪs/ *n* promiscuidad, *f*
promise /'prɒmɪs/ *n* promesa, *f*; (hope) esperanza, *f*; (word) palabra, *f*; (future) porvenir, *m*. *vt* and *vi* prometer. **a young man of p.,** un joven de porvenir. **to break one's p.,** faltar a su palabra; no cumplir una promesa. **to keep one's p.,** guardar su palabra; cumplir su promesa. **to p. and do nothing,** apuntar y no

dar. **under p. of,** bajo palabra de. **p. of marriage,** palabra de matrimonio, *f*
promised /'prɒmɪst/ *a* prometido. **P. Land,** Tierra de promisión, *f*
promising /'prɒməsɪŋ/ *a* que promete bien, que promete mucho; prometedor; (of the future, etc.) halagüeño; (of persons) que llegará
promissory /'prɒmə,sɔri/ *a* promisorio. **p. note,** pagaré, abonaré, *m*
promontory /'prɒmən,tɔri/ *n* promontorio, *m*
promote /prə'mout/ *vt* fomentar, promover; provocar; (aid) favorecer, proteger; avanzar; estimular; (to a post) ascender; (an act bill) promover; *Com.* negociar
promoter /prə'moutər/ *n* promotor (-ra); instigador (-ra); (*Theat.* etc.) empresario, *m*
promotion /prə'mouʃən/ *n* (encouragement) fomento, *m*; (furtherance) adelanto, *m*; protección, *f*, favorecimiento, *m*; (in employment, etc.) promoción, *f*, ascenso, *m*; (of a company, etc.) creación, *f*
prompt /prɒmpt/ *a* pronto; diligente; presuroso; puntual; rápido; *Com.* inmediato. *vt* impulsar, incitar, mover; dictar; insinuar; *Theat.* apuntar; (remind) recordar. **He came at five o'clock p.,** Vino a las cinco en punto. **p. book,** libro del traspunte, *m*. **p. box,** concha (del apuntador), *f*
prompter /'prɒmptər/ *n* *Theat.* apuntador, (in the wings) traspunte, *m*
prompting /'prɒmptɪŋ/ *n* sugestión, *f*; instigación, *f*; *pl* **promptings,** impulso, *m*; (of the heart, etc.) dictados, *m pl*
promptitude /'prɒmptɪ,tud/ *n* prontitud, presteza, *f*; prisa, expedición, *f*; puntualidad, *f*
promptly /'prɒmptli/ *adv* inmediatamente, en seguida; con prontitud, con celeridad; puntualmente
promptness /'prɒmptnɪs/ *n* See **promptitude**
promulgate /'prɒməl,geit/ *vt* promulgar; divulgar, diseminar
promulgation /'prɒməl'geiʃən/ *n* promulgación, *f*; divulgación, diseminación, *f*
prone /proun/ *a* postrado; inclinado, propenso
proneness /'prounɪs/ *n* postración, *f*; inclinación, tendencia, propensión, *f*
prong /prɔŋ/ *n* (pitchfork) horquilla, *f*; (of a fork) diente, *m*, púa, *f*
pronged /prɔŋd/ *a* dentado, con púas
pronoun /'prou,naun/ *n* pronombre, *m*
pronounce /prə'nauns/ *vt* pronunciar; declarar; articular
pronounced /prə'naunst/ *a* marcado, perceptible; bien definido
pronouncement /prə'naunsmənt/ *n* pronunciamiento, *m*
pronunciation /prə,nʌnsi'eiʃən/ *n* pronunciación, *f*; articulación, *f*
proof /pruf/ *n* prueba, *f*; demostración, *f*; ensayo, *m*; *Law.* testimonio, *m*; (*Photo. Print.*) prueba, *f*; *Math.* comprobación, *f*, a hecho a prueba (de); impenetrable (a), *Fig.* insensible (a). *vt* (raincoats, etc.) impermeabilizar. **p. whereof,** en fe de lo cual. **p. against bombs,** a prueba de bombas. **p. reading,** corrección de pruebas, *f*
prop /prɒp/ *n* apoyo, puntal, estribadero, *m*; (for a tree) horca, *f*, rodrigón, *m*; *Naut.* escora, *f*; *Fig.* báculo, *m*, columna, *f*, apoyo, *m*. *vt* apoyar; apuntalar; (a tree) ahorquillar; (a building) acodalar; *Naut.* escorar; *Fig.* sostener. **He propped himself against the wall,** Se apoyó en el muro, Se arrimó al muro
propaganda /,prɒpə'gændə/ *n* propaganda, *f*
propagandist /,prɒpə'gændɪst/ *n* propagandista, *mf*
propagate /'prɒpə,geit/ *vt* propagar. *vi* propagarse
propagation /,prɒpə'geiʃən/ *n* propagación, *f*
propagator /'prɒpə,geitər/ *n* propagador (-ra)
propel /prə'pɛl/ *vt* propulsar, empujar, mover
propeller /prə'pɛlər/ *n* propulsor, *m*; *Mech.* hélice, *f*
propelling /prə'pɛlɪŋ/ *n* propulsión, *f*. **p. pencil,** lapicero, *m*
propensity /prə'pɛnsɪti/ *n* propensión, tendencia, inclinación, *f*
proper /'prɒpər/ *a* propio; apropiado; correcto; decente; (prim) afectado; serio, formal; (exact) justo,

exacto; (suitable (for)) bueno (para), apto (para); (true) verdadero; (characteristic) peculiar; *Herald.* natural; (with rascal, etc.) redomado; (handsome) guapo. **If you think it p.,** Si te parece bien. **p. noun,** nombre propio, *m*
properly /'prɒpərli/ *adv* decentemente; correctamente; propiamente; bien. **to do (a thing) p.,** hacer algo bien. **p. speaking,** propiamente dicho, hablando con propiedad
propertied /'prɒpərtid/ *a* propietario, hacendado; (rich) pudiente, adinerado
property /'prɒpərti/ *n* propiedad, *f;* (belongings) bienes, *m pl;* posesiones, *f pl;* (estate) hacienda, *f;* (quality) cualidad, *f; pl* **properties,** *Theat.* accesorios, *m pl.* **personal p.,** bienes muebles, *m pl;* cosas personales, *f pl.* **real p.,** bienes raíces, *m pl.* **p. man,** *Theat.* encargado de los accesorios, *m.* **p. owner,** propietario (-ia). **p. tax,** contribución sobre la propiedad, *f*
prophecy /'prɒfəsi/ *n* profecía, *f;* predicción, *f*
prophesier /'prɒfə,siər/ *n* See **prophet**
prophesy /'prɒfə,sai/ *vt* profetizar; presagiar, predecir. *vi* hacer profecías
prophet /'prɒfit/ *n* profeta, *m*
prophetess /'prɒfitis/ *n* profetisa, *f*
prophetic /prə'fɛtik/ *a* profético
prophylactic /,proufə'læktik/ *a* and *n* profiláctico, *m*
propinquity /prou'piŋkwiti/ *n* propincuidad, proximidad, *f;* (relationship) parentesco, *m*
propitiate /prə'piʃi,eit/ *vt* propiciar; apaciguar, conciliar
propitiation /prə,piʃi'eiʃən/ *n* propiciación, *f*
propitiator /prə'piʃi,eitər/ *n* propiciador (-ra)
propitiatory /prə'piʃiə,tɔri/ *a* propiciador
propitious /prə'piʃəs/ *a* propicio, favorable
propitiousness /prə'piʃəsnis/ *n* lo propicio
proportion /prə'pɔrʃən/ *n* proporción, *f;* parte, *f;* porción, *f; pl* **proportions,** proporciones, *f pl;* dimensiones, *f pl. vt* proporcionar; repartir, distribuir. **in p.,** en proporción; conforme (a), según; *Com.* a prorrata. **in p. as,** a medida que. **out of p.,** desproporcionado. **He has lost all sense of p.,** Ha perdido su equilibrio (mental)
proportional /prə'pɔrʃənl/ *a* proporcional; en proporción (a); proporcionado (a). **p. representation,** representación proporcional, *f*
proportionally /prə'pɔrʃənli/ *adv* proporcionalmente, en proporción
proportionate /a. prə'pɔrʃənit; v. -,neit/ *a* proporcionado; proporcional. *vt* proporcionar
proportionately /prə'pɔrʃənitli/ *adv* See **proportionally**
proposal /prə'pouzəl/ *n* proposición, *f;* oferta, *f;* (plan) propósito, proyecto, *m.* **p. of marriage,** oferta de matrimonio, *f*
propose /prə'pouz/ *vt* proponer; ofrecer; (a toast) dar, brindar. *vi* pretender, intentar, tener la intención de; pensar; (marriage) declararse
proposer /prə'pouzər/ *n* proponente, *m;* (of a motion) autor (-ra) de una proposición
proposition /,prɒpə'ziʃən/ *n* proposición, *f;* (plan) proyecto, propósito, *m*
propound /prə'paund/ *vt* proponer; plantear, presentar
proprietary /prə'praii,tɛri/ *a* propietario; de propiedad
proprietor /prə'praiitər/ *n* propietario, *m;* dueño, *m*
proprietorship /prə'praiitər,ʃip/ *n* propiedad, pertenencia, *f*
proprietress /prə'praiitris/ *n* propietaria, *f;* dueña, *f*
propriety /prə'praiiti/ *n* decoro, *m;* conveniencia, *f;* corrección, *f*
propulsion /prə'pʌlʃən/ *n* propulsión, *f*
propulsive /prə'pʌlsiv/ *a* propulsor
prorogation /,prourou'geiʃən/ *n* prorrogación, *f*
prorogue /prou'roug/ *vt* prorrogar, suspender (la sesión de una asamblea legislativa)
prosaic /prou'zeiik/ *a* prosaico
pros and cons /'prouz ən 'kɒnz/ el pro y el contra
proscenium /prou'siniəm/ *n* proscenio, *m*

proscribe /prou'skraib/ *vt* proscribir
proscription /prou'skripʃən/ *n* proscripción, *f*
prose /prouz/ *n* prosa, *f. f.* **p. writer,** prosista, *mf*
prosecute /'prɒsi,kyut/ *vt* proseguir, llevar adelante; (*Law.* a person) procesar; (*Law.* a claim) pedir en juicio
prosecution /,prɒsi'kyuʃən/ *n* prosecución, *f;* cumplimiento, *m; Law.* acusación, *f;* (*Law.* party) parte actora, *f.* **p. in the p. of his duty,** en el cumplimiento de su deber
prosecutor /'prɒsi,kyutər/ *n* demandante, actor, *m.* **public p.,** fiscal, *m*
proselyte /'prɒsə,lait/ *n* prosélito, *m*
proselytism /'prɒsəli,tizəm/ *n* proselitismo, *m*
prose writer *n* prosador, *m*
prosody /'prɒsədi/ *n* prosodia, *f*
prospect /'prɒspɛkt/ *n* perspectiva, *f;* esperanza, *f;* probabilidad, *f;* (in mining) indicio de filón, *m;* criadero (de oro, etc.), *m. vi* explorar; (of a mine) prometer (bien), dar buenas esperanzas. *vt* explorar, inspeccionar; examinar. **He is a man with good prospects,** Es un hombre de porvenir
prospecting /'prɒspɛktiŋ/ *n* la prospección, *f*
prospective /prə'spɛktiv/ *a* en expectativa, futuro; previsor
prospector /'prɒspɛktər/ *n* explorador, operador, *m*
prospectus /prə'spɛktəs/ *n* prospecto, programa, *m*
prosper /'prɒspər/ *vi* prosperar. *vt* favorecer, prosperar
prosperity /prɒ'spɛriti/ *n* prosperidad, *f*
prosperous /'prɒspərəs/ *a* próspero; favorable
prostate /'prɒsteit/ *n* próstata, *f*
prostitute /'prɒsti,tut/ *n* prostituta, *f, vt* prostituir
prostitution /,prɒsti'tuʃən/ *n* prostitución, *f*
prostrate /'prɒstreit/ *a* tendido; postrado; abatido. *vt* derribar; arruinar; (by grief, etc.) postrar; (oneself) postrarse
prostration /prɒ'streiʃən/ *n* postración, *f;* abatimiento, *m.* **nervous p.,** neurastenia, *f*
protagonist /prou'tægənist/ *n* protagonista, *mf*
protean /'proutiən/ *a* proteico
protect /prə'tɛkt/ *vt* proteger
protection /prə'tɛkʃən/ *n* protección, *f;* defensa, *f;* garantía, *f;* abrigo, *m;* refugio, *m;* (passport) salvoconducto, *m; Polit.* proteccionismo, *m*
protectionism /prə'tɛkʃə,nizəm/ *n* proteccionismo, *m*
protectionist /prə'tɛkʃənist/ *n* proteccionista, *mf*
protective /prə'tɛktiv/ *a* protector; *Polit.* proteccionista
protector /prə'tɛktər/ *n* protector, *m*
protectorate /prə'tɛktərit/ *n* protectorado, *m*
protectress /prou 'tɛktris/ *n* protectriz, *f*
protégé /'proutə,ʒei/ *n* protegido (-da)
protein /'proutin, -tiin/ *n* proteína, *f*
protest /v. prə'tɛst, 'proutɛst; n. 'proutɛst/ *vt* protestar; *Law.* hacer el protesto de una letra de cambio. *vi* declarar; insistir (en); hacer una protesta. *n* protesta, *f; Law.* protesto, *m.* **under p.,** bajo protesta. **to p. against,** protestar contra
Protestant /'prɒtəstənt/ *a* and *n* protestante, *mf*
Protestantism /'prɒtəstən,tizəm/ *n* protestantismo, *m*
protestation /,prɒtə'steiʃən/ *n* protesta, *f*
protester /'proutɛstər/ *n* el, *m,* (*f,* la) que protesta
protest literature *n* literatura de denuncia, *f*
protocol /'proutə,kɒl/ *n* protocolo, *m, vt* protocolizar
protoplasm /'proutə,plæzəm/ *n* protoplasma, *f*
prototype /'proutə,taip/ *n* prototipo, *m*
protract /prou'trækt/ *vt* prolongar; dilatar
protracted /prou'træktid/ *a* prolongado; largo
protraction /prou'trækʃən/ *n* prolongación, *f*
protractor /prou'træktər/ *n* (*Geom.* and *Surv.*) transportador, *m.* **p. muscle,** músculo extensor, *m*
protrude /prou'trud/ *vt* sacar fuera. *vi* salir fuera; sobresalir
protuberance /prou'tubərəns/ *n* protuberancia, *f*
protuberant /prou'tubərənt/ *a* protuberante, prominente
proud /praud/ *a* orgulloso; arrogante; noble; glorioso; magnífico; soberbio, *Mexico* alzado. **to be p.,** enorgullecerse. **to make p.,** enorgullecer; hacer

orgulloso. **to be p. of,** ser orgulloso de, pagarse de, gloriarse en

proudly /'praudli/ *adv* con orgullo, orgullosamente

provable /'pruvəbəl/ *a* demostrable

prove /pruv/ *vt* probar; demostrar; (experience) experimentar, sufrir; poner a prueba; (a will) verificar; (show) mostrar; confirmar. *vi* resultar, salir (bien o mal)

provenance /'prɒvənəns/ *n* origen, *m*

Provençal /,prouvən'sɑl, ,prɒvɑ̃-/ *a* provenzal. *n* provenzal, *mf*; (language) provenzal, *m*

Provence /prə'vɑns/ Provenza, *f*

provender /'prɒvəndər/ *n* forraje, *m*; *Inf.* provisiones, *f pl*

proverb /'prɒvɜrb/ *n* refrán, *m*; proverbio, *m*. **collection of proverbs,** refranero, *m*. **Book of Proverbs,** Proverbios, *m pl*

proverbial /prə'vɜrbiəl/ *a* proverbial

proverbially /prə'vɜrbiəli/ *adv* proverbialmente

provide /prə'vaid/ *vt* proporcionar, dar; proveer, surtir, suplir; (stipulate) estipular; preparar (por); tomar precauciones (contra); sufragar los gastos (de); proporcionar medios de vida (a); señalar una pensión (a). **to p. oneself with,** proveerse de

provided (that) /prə'vaidɪd/ *conjunc* si; a condición de que, siempre que, con tal que

providence /'prɒvɪdəns/ *n* providencia, *f*

provident /'prɒvɪdənt/ *a* próvido, previsor, prudente; económico

providential /,prɒvɪ'dɛnʃəl/ *a* providencial

providentially /,prɒvɪ'dɛnʃəli/ *adv* providencialmente

providently /'prɒvɪdəntli/ *adv* próvidamente, prudentemente

provider /prə'vaidər/ *n* proveedor (-ra)

province /'prɒvɪns/ *n* provincia, *f*; esfera, *f*; función, incumbencia, *f*

provincial /prə'vɪnʃəl/ *a* provincial, de provincia; provinciano. *n* provinciano (-na); *Eccl.* provincial, *m*

provincialism /prə'vɪnʃə,lɪzəm/ *n* provincialismo, *m*

provision /prə'vɪʒən/ *n* provisión, *f*; (stipulation) estipulación, *f*; *pl* **provisions,** provisiones, *f pl*; víveres, comestibles, *m pl. vt* abastecer, aprovisionar. **to make p. for,** hacer provisión para, proveer de. **to make p. for one's family,** asegurar el porvenir de su familia. **p. merchant,** vendedor (-ra) de comestibles

provisional /prə'vɪʒənḷ/ *a* provisional, interino

provisioning /prə'vɪʒənɪŋ/ *n* aprovisionamiento, abastecimiento, *m*

proviso /prə'vaizou/ *n* condición, estipulación, disposición, *f*

provisory /prə'vaizəri/ *a* provisional; condicional

provocation /,prɒvə'keiʃən/ *n* provocación, *f*

provocative /prə'vɒkətɪv/ *a* provocativo, provocador

provocatively /prə'vɒkətɪvli/ *adv* de un modo provocativo

provoke /prə'vouk/ *vt* provocar; suscitar; incitar, excitar; (irritate) sacar de madre (a), indignar

provoker /prə'voukər/ *n* provocador (-ra); instigador (-ra)

provoking /prə'voukɪŋ/ *a* provocativo; (irritating) enojoso, irritante

provost /'prouvoust *or, esp. in military usage,* 'prouvou/ *n* preboste, *m*; (of a college) director, *m*; (in Scotland) alcalde, *m*. **p.-marshal,** capitán preboste, *m*

prow /prau/ *n* proa, *f*

prowess /'prauɪs/ *n* valor, *m*, destreza, *f*; proeza, *f*

prowl /praul/ *vi* and *vt* rondar; cazar al acecho

prowler /'praulər/ *n* rondador (-ra); ladrón (-ona)

proximity /prɒk'sɪmɪti/ *n* proximidad, *Argentina* adyacencia, *f*

proxy /'prɒksi/ *n* poder, *m*; delegación, *f*; apoderado, *m*; delegado (-da); substituto (-ta). **to be married by p.,** casarse por poderes

prude /prud/ *n* mojigata, beata, *f*

prudence /'prudṇs/ *n* prudencia, *f*

prudent /'prudṇt/ *a* prudente

prudently /'prudṇtli/ *adv* con prudencia

prudery /'prudəri/ *n* mojigatería, beatería, damería, *f*; gazmoñería, *f*

prudish /'prudɪʃ/ *a* mojigato, gazmoño, remilgado

prune /prun/ *n* ciruela pasa, *f*; color de ciruela, *m*, *vt* podar; (cut) cortar; reducir

pruning /'prunɪŋ/ *n* poda, *f*; reducción, *f*. **p. knife,** podadera, *f*

prurient /'pruriənt/ *a* lascivo, lujurioso, salaz

prussic acid /'prʌsɪk/ *n* acido prúsico, *m*

pry /prai/ *vi* escudriñar; acechar, espiar, fisgonear; (meddle) entremeterse, meterse donde no le llaman. *vt* See **prize**

prying /'praiɪŋ/ *n* fisgoneo, *m*; curiosidad, *f*, *a* fisgón, curioso

psalm /sɑm/ *n* salmo, *m*. **to sing psalms,** salmodiar

psalmist /'sɑmɪst/ *n* salmista, *m*

psaltery /'sɔltəri/ *n* salterio, *m*

pseudo- *a* seudo. **p.-learned,** erudito a la violeta

pseudonym /'sudnɪm/ *n* seudónimo, *m*

psychiatrist /sɪ'kaiətrɪst, sai-/ *n* siquiatra, *m*

psychiatry /sɪ'kaiətri, sai-/ *n* siquiatría, *f*

psychic /'saikɪk/ *a* síquico

psychoanalysis /,saikouə'næləsɪs/ *n* sicoanálisis, *mf*

psychoanalyst /,saikou'ænḷɪst/ *n* sicoanalista, *mf*

psychoanalyze /,saikou'ænḷ,aiz/ *vt* sicoanalizar

psychological /,saikə'lɒdʒɪkəl/ *a* sicológico

psychologist /sai'kɒlədʒɪst/ *n* sicólogo (-ga)

psychology /sai'kɒlədʒi/ *n* sicología, *f*

psychopathic /,saikə'pæθɪk/ *a* sicopático

psychosis /sai'kousɪs/ *n* sicosis, *f*

psychotherapy /,saikou'θɛrəpi/ *n* sicoterapia, *f*

ptomaine poisoning /'toumein/ *n* intoxicación por tomaínas, *f*

puberty /'pyubərti/ *n* pubertad, *f*

pubescent /pyu'bɛsənt/ *a* púber

pubic /'pyubɪk/ *a* púbico

pubis /'pyubɪs/ *n* pubis, *m*

public /'pʌblɪk/ *a* and *n* público *m*. **in p.,** en público. **p. assistance,** asistencia pública, *f*. **p. funds,** hacienda pública, *f*. **p. health,** higiene pública, *f*. **p.-house,** taberna, *f*. **p. opinion,** opinión pública, *f*. *Inf.* el qué dirán. **p.-spirited,** patriótico. **p. thoroughfare,** vía pública, *f*. **p. works,** obras públicas, *f pl*

publican /'pʌblɪkən/ *n* tabernero, *m*

publication /,pʌblɪ'keiʃən/ *n* publicación, *f*

publicist /'pʌbləsɪst/ *n* publicista, *mf*

publicity /pʌ'blɪsɪti/ *n* publicidad, *f*

publicity agent *n* publicista, *mf*

publish /'pʌblɪʃ/ *vt* publicar, divulgar, difundir; (a book, etc.) dar a luz, dar a la prensa, publicar; (of a publisher) editar. **to p. abroad,** pregonar a los cuatro vientos. **to p. banns of marriage,** correr las amonestaciones

publisher /'pʌblɪʃər/ *n* publicador (-ra); (of books) editor (-ra)

publishing /'pʌblɪʃɪŋ/ *n* publicación, *f*. **p. house,** casa editorial, *f*. **the p. world,** el mundo de la edición, *m*

puck /pʌk/ *n* trasgo, *m*; diablillo, picaruelo, *m*

pucker /'pʌkər/ *vt* (one's brow, etc.) fruncir; (crease) arrugar. *vi* arrugarse. *n* frunce, *m*; arruga, *f*; (fold) bolsa, *f*

puckering /'pʌkərɪŋ/ *n* fruncido, *m*; arrugas, *f pl*

puckish /'pʌkɪʃ/ *a* travieso

pudding /'pudɪŋ/ *n* pudín, budín, *m*. **black p.,** morcilla, *f*

puddle /'pʌdḷ/ *n* charco, *m*

puerile /'pyuərɪl/ *a* pueril

puerperal /pyu'ɜrpərəl/ *a* puerperal. **p. fever,** fiebre puerperal, *f*

Puerto Rican /'pwɛrtə 'rikən, 'pɔr-/ *a* and *n* puertorriqueño (-ña), a boricua, *n* brindueño (-ña)

Puerto Rico /'pwɛrtə 'rikou/ Puerto Rico

puff /pʌf/ *vt* and *vi* (blow) soplar; (at a pipe, etc.) chupar; (smoke) lanzar bocanadas de humo; (make pant) hacer jadear; (advertise) dar bombo (a); (distend) hinchar; (make conceited) envanecerse; (of a train, etc.) bufar; resoplar. *n* soplo, *m*; (of smoke, etc.) bocanada, *f*; (of an engine, etc.) resoplido, bufido, *m*; (for powder) borla (para polvos), *f*; (pastry) bollo, *m*; (advertisement) bombo, *m*. **to be puffed up,** *Fig.* hincharse, inflarse. **p. of wind,** ráfaga de

aire, *f.* **p.-ball,** bejín, *m.* **p.-pastry,** hojaldre, *m,* or *f.*
p.-sleeve, manga de bullón, *f*
puffiness /'pʌfinɪs/ *n* hinchazón, *f*
puffy /'pʌfi/ *a* (of the wind) a ráfagas; (panting) jadeante; (swollen) hinchado
pug /pʌg/ *n* (dog) doguino, *m.* **p.-nosed,** de nariz
respingona
pugilism /'pyudʒə,lɪzəm/ *n* boxeo, pugilato, *m*
pugilist /'pyudʒəlɪst/ *n* pugilista, *mf,* boxeador, *m*
pugnacious /pʌg'neiʃəs/ *a* pugnaz, belicoso
pugnacity /pʌg'næsɪti/ *n* pugnacidad, belicosidad, *f*
pull /pʊl/ *n* tirón, *m;* sacudida, *f;* golpe, *m;* (row) paseo en barco, *m;* (with the oars) golpe (de remos), *m;*
(at a bell) tirón, *m;* (bell-rope) tirador, *m;* (at a bottle) trago, *m;* (strain) fuerza, *f;* atracción, *f;* (struggle) lucha, *f;* (advantage) ventaja, *f;* (influence) influencia, *f, Central America, Mexico* arranque *m.* **to
give a p.,** tirar (de), dar un tirón (a). **to have plenty
of p.,** *Inf.* tener buenas aldabas
pull /pʊl/ *vt* tirar (de); (drag) arrastrar; (extract) sacar; (a boat) remar; (gather) coger; *Print.* imprimir.
He pulled the trigger (of his gun), Apretó el gatillo.
to p. a person's leg, tomar el pelo (a). **to p. oneself
together,** componer el semblante, serenarse; recobrar
el aplomo; (tidy oneself) arreglarse. **to p. apart,** *vt*
separar; romper en dos. *vi* separarse; romperse en
dos. **to p. away,** *vt* arrancar; quitar. *vi* tirar con esfuerzo. **to p. back,** tirar hacia atrás; hacer retroceder
(a); retener. **to p. down,** hacer bajar, obligar a bajar;
(objects) bajar; (buildings) derribar, demoler; (humble) humillar; degradar; (weaken) debilitar. **to p. in,**
tirar hacia dentro; hacer entrar; (a horse) enfrenar;
(expenditure) reducir. **to p. off,** arrancar; (clothes)
quitarse; (a deal) cerrar (un trato), concluir con éxito;
(win) ganar. **to p. on,** *vt* (gloves, etc.) meterse,
ponerse. *vi* seguir remando. **to p. open,** abrir; abrir
rápidamente. **to p. out,** hacer salir; obligar a salir;
(teeth, daggers, etc.) sacar; (hair) arrancar. **to p.
round, through,** *vt* ayudar a reponerse (a); sacar de
un aprieto. *vi* restablecerse; reponerse, cobrar la salud, sanar. **to p. together,** obrar de acuerdo; (get on)
llevarse (bien o mal). **He pulled himself together
very quickly,** Se repuso muy pronto. **to p. up,** *vt*
montar, subir; (a horse) sofrenar; (stop) parar; (by
the root) desarraigar, extirpar; (interrupt) interrumpir;
(scold) reñir. *vi* parar(se); (restrain oneself) reprimirse, contenerse
pullet /'pʊlɪt/ *n* polla, *f*
pulley /'pʊli/ *n* polea, *f; Naut.* garrucha, *f.* **p. wheel,**
roldana, *f*
pulling /'pʊlɪŋ/ *n* tracción, *f;* tirada, *f;* arranque, *m*
pullover /'pʊl,ouvər/ *n* jersey, *m, Lat. Am.* chompa, *f*
pullulate /'pʌlyə,leit/ *vi* pulular
pulmonary /'pʌlmə,nɛri/ *a* pulmonar
pulp /pʌlp/ *n* pulpa, *f;* (of fruit) carne, *f;* (paper)
pasta, *f;* (of teeth) bulbo dentario, *m. vt* reducir a
pulpa; deshacer (el papel). **to beat to a p.,** *Inf.*
poner como un pulpo
pulpit /'pʊlpɪt, 'pʌl-/ *n* púlpito, *m*
pulpy /'pʌlpi/ *a* pulposo; *Bot.* carnoso
pulsate /'pʌlseit/ *vi* pulsar, latir
pulsation /pʌl'seiʃən/ *n* pulsación, *f,* latido, *m*
pulsatory /'pʊlsə,tɔri/ *a* pulsante, pulsativo, latiente
pulse /pʌls/ *n* pulso, *m;* pulsación, *f,* latido, *m;* vibración, *f;* (vegetable) legumbre, *f, vi* pulsar, latir; vibrar. **to take a person's p.,** tomar el pulso (a)
pulverization /,pʊlvərə'zeiʃən/ *n* pulverización, *f*
pulverize /'pʌlvə,raiz/ *vt* pulverizar
puma /'pyumə, 'pu-/ *n* puma, *f, Lat. Am.* león, *m*
pumice /'pʌmɪs/ *n* piedra pómez, *f*
pummel /'pʌməl/ *vt* aporrear
pump /pʌmp/ *n Mech.* bomba, *f;* (for water, etc.)
aguatocha, *f; Naut.* pompa, *f;* (slipper) escarpín, *m,*
vt bombear, extraer por medio de una bomba; (inflate) inflar; (for information) sondear, sonsacar.
hand-p., bomba de mano, *f.* **to work a p.,** darle a la
bomba
pumpkin /'pʌmpkɪn/ *n* calabaza, *f, Central America*
ayote, *m, Chile* zapallo, *m;* (plant) calabacera, *f*
pun /pʌn/ *n* retruécano, *m*
punch /pʌntʃ/ *n* (drink) ponche, *m;* (blow) puñetazo,

golpe, *m; Mech.* punzón, *m;* (for tickets, etc.) taladro,
m; Inf. fuerza, *f. vt* (perforate) taladrar, punzar; estampar; (hit) dar un puñetazo (a). **p.-ball,** pelota de
boxeo, *f.* **p.-bowl,** ponchera, *f*
punctilious /pʌŋk'tɪliəs/ *a* formal, puntual, puntilloso
punctiliousness /pʌŋk'tɪliəsnɪs/ *n* formalidad, punc-
tualidad, *f*
punctual /'pʌŋktʃuəl/ *a* puntual
punctually /'pʌŋktʃuəli/ *adv* puntualmente
punctuate /'pʌŋktʃu,eit/ *vt* puntuar
punctuation /,pʌŋktʃu'eiʃən/ *n* puntuación, *f*
puncture /'pʌŋktʃər/ *n* pinchazo, *m;* perforación, *f;*
Surg. punción, *f. vt* pinchar; perforar; punzar. **We
have a p. in the right tire,** Tenemos un pinchazo en
el neumático derecho
pungency /'pʌndʒənsi/ *n* picante, *m;* acerbidad, *f,*
mordacidad, *f*
pungent /'pʌndʒənt/ *a* picante; acerbo, mordaz
Punic /'pyunɪk/ *a* púnico, cartaginés
punish /'pʌnɪʃ/ *vt* castigar; maltratar
punishable /'pʌnɪʃəbəl/ *a* punible
punishment /'pʌnɪʃmənt/ *n* castigo, *m;* pena, *f;*
maltrato, *m*
punitive /'pyunɪtɪv/ *a* punitivo
punt /pʊnt/ *n* batea, *f. vt* impeler una batea con una
pértiga; ir en batea; (a ball) golpear, dar un puntapié
(a)
puny /'pyuni/ *a* débil, encanijado; insignificante; pequeño
pup /pʌp/ *n* cachorro (-rra). *vi* parir la perra
pupa /'pyupə/ *n* crisálida, *f*
pupil /'pyupəl/ *n* alumno (-na), discípulo (-la); (of
the eye) pupila, niña (del ojo), *f; Law.* pupilo (-la). *a*
escolar. **day p.,** alumno (-na) externo (-na). **p.
teacher,** maestro (-tra) alumno (-na)
puppet /'pʌpɪt/ *n* títere, *m,* marioneta, *f;* muñeca, *f;*
(person) maniquí, *m.* **p. show,** función de títeres, *f.*
p. showman, titiritero, titerero, *m*
puppy /'pʌpi/ *n* perrito (-ta), cachorro (-rra)
purblind /'pɜr,blaind/ *a* ciego; (short-sighted and
Fig.) miope
purchasable /'pɜrtʃəsəbəl/ *a* comprable, que puede
comprarse, *Fig.* sobornable
purchase /'pɜrtʃəs/ *vt* comprar; adquirir; *Fig.* lograr,
conseguir. *n* compra, *f;* adquisición, *f; Mech.* apalan-
camiento, *m;* fuerza, *f;* (lever) palanca, *f,* aparejo, *m;*
Fig. influencia, *f.* **p. tax,** impuesto de lujo, *m*
purchaser /'pɜrtʃəsər/ *n* comprador (-ra)
purchasing /'pɜrtʃəsɪŋ/ *n* See **purchase. p. power,**
poder de adquisición, *m*
pure /pyʊr/ *a* puro. **p.-bred,** de raza
purgation /pɜr'geiʃən/ *n* purgación, *f*
purgative /'pɜrgətɪv/ *a* purgativo. *n* purga, *f*
purgatorial /,pɜrgə'tɔriəl/ *a* del purgatorio; (expiatory) purgatorio
purgatory /'pɜrgə,tɔri/ *n* purgatorio, *m*
purge /pɜrdʒ/ *n* purgación, *f;* (laxative) purga, *f;*
Polit. depuración, *f;* purificación, *f. vt* purgar; *Polit.*
depurar; purificar; expurgar
purging /'pɜrdʒɪŋ/ *n* purgación, *f; Polit.* depuración,
f; Fig. purificación, *f*
purification /,pyʊrəfɪ'keiʃən/ *n* purificación, *f*
purificatory /pyu'rɪfɪkə,tɔri/ *a* purificador, purificatorio, que purifica
purifier /'pyʊrə,faiər/ *n* purificador (-ra)
purify /'pyʊrə,fai/ *vt* purificar; (metals) acrisolar; refinar; depurar; (purge) purgar
purist /'pyʊrɪst/ *n* purista, *mf*
puritan /'pyʊrɪtn̩/ *a* and *n* puritano (-na)
Puritanism /'pyʊrɪtn̩,ɪzəm/ *n* puritanismo, *m*
purity /'pyʊriti/ *n* pureza, *f*
purl /pɜrl/ *vi* (of a stream, etc.) murmurar, susurrar.
n (of a stream, etc.) susurro, murmullo, *m*
purling /'pɜrlɪŋ/ *a* murmurante, que susurra, parlero.
n murmullo, susurro, *m*
purloin /pər'lɔin/ *vt* hurtar, robar
purple /'pɜrpəl/ *n* púrpura, *f, a* purpúreo. *vt* purpu-
rar, teñir de púrpura; purpurear
purplish /'pɜrplɪʃ/ *a* purpurino, algo purpúreo
purport /v. pər'pɔrt; n. 'pɜrpɔrt/ *vt* dar a entender,

querer decir; significar; indicar; parecer; tener el objeto de; pretender. *n* importe, *m*; sentido, significado, *m*; objeto, *m*

purpose /'pɜrpəs/ *n* objeto, *m*; propósito, fin, *m*; intención, *f*; proyecto, *m*; designio, *m*; determinación, voluntad, *f*; efecto, *m*; ventaja, utilidad, *f*, *vi* and *vt* proponerse; pensar, tener el propósito (de), intentar. **It will serve my p.,** Servirá para lo que yo quiero. **for the p. of...,** con el propósito de..., con el fin de... for purposes of... para efectos de... **on p.,** de propósito, expresamente, *Central America* adifés. **to no p.,** inútilmente; en vano

purposeful /'pɜrpəsfəl/ *a* resuelto; de substancia

purposeless /'pɜrpəslɪs/ *a* irresoluto, vacilante, vago; sin objeto; inútil

purposely /'pɜrpəsli/ *adv* expresamente, de intento

purr /pɜr/ *vi* ronronear. *n* ronroneo, *m*

purse /pɜrs/ *n* bolsa, *f*; monedero, portamonedas, *m*. **to p.** one's lips, apretar los labios

purser /'pɜrsər/ *n* Naut. contador, sobrecargo, *Argentina* comisario, *m*. **purser's office,** contaduría, *f*

pursuance /pər'suəns/ *n* cumplimiento, desempeño, *m*, prosecución, *f*. **in p. of,** en cumplimiento de; en consecuencia de

pursuant /pər'suənt/ *a* and *adv* según; conforme (a), de acuerdo (con); en consecuencia (de)

pursue /pər'su/ *vt* perseguir; seguir; (search) buscar; (hunt) cazar; (a submarine, etc.) dar caza (a); (continue) proseguir, continuar; (an occupation) dedicarse (a), ejercer

pursuer /pər'suər/ *n* perseguidor (-ra)

pursuit /pər'sut/ *n* perseguimiento, *m*; (search) busca, *f*; (hunt) caza, *f*; (performance) prosecución, *f*, desempeño, *m*; (employment) ocupación, *f*. **in p. of,** en busca de. **p. plane,** avión de caza, *m*

purulence /'pyʊrələns/ *n* purulencia, *f*

purulent /'pyʊrələnt/ *a* purulento

purvey /pər'vei/ *vt* proveer, surtir, suministrar; abastecer; procurar

purveyance /pər'veiəns/ *n* suministro, abastecimiento, *m*; provisión, *f*

purveyor /pər'veiər/ *n* suministrador (-ra), proveedor (-ra), bastecedor (-ra)

pus /pʌs/ *n* pus, *m*

push /pʊʃ/ *n* empujón, *m*; empellón, *m*; impulso, *m*; (of a person) empuje, *m*, energía, *f*; (attack) ataque, *m*; ofensiva, *f*; (effort) esfuerzo, *m*; crisis, *f*, momento crítico, *m*. **at a push,** *Inf.* en caso de necesidad; en un aprieto, si llegara el caso. **to give the p. to,** *Inf.* despedir (a). **p.-bicycle,** bicicleta, *f*. **p.-button,** botón, *m*; botón de llamada, *m*. **p.-cart,** carretilla de mano, *f*; (child's) cochecito de niño, *m*

push /pʊʃ/ *vt* empujar; (jostle) empellar, dar empellones (a); (a finger in one's eye, etc.) clavar; (a button) apretar; (*Fig.* a person) proteger, ayudar; dar publicidad (a); (a claim, etc.) insistir en; (compel) obligar. *vi* empujar; dar empujones, empellar. **I have pushed my finger in my eye,** Me he clavado el dedo en el ojo. **to p. against,** empujar contra; lanzarse contra; empellar, dar empellones (a). **to p. aside, away,** apartar con la mano; rechazar, alejar. **to p. back,** (hair, etc.) echar hacia atrás; (people) hacer retroceder; rechazar. **to p. by,** pasar. **to p. down,** hacer bajar; hacer caer; (demolish) derribar. **to p. forward,** *vt* empujar hacia delante, hacer avanzar; (a plan, etc.) llevar adelante. **to p.** adelantarse a empujones; avanzar; seguir su camino. **to p. oneself forward,** *Fig.* abrirse camino; entremeterse; darse importancia. **to p. in,** *vt* empujar; hacer entrar; clavar, hincar. *vi* entrar a la fuerza; entremeterse. **to p. off,** *vt* apartar con la mano (a); *Inf.* quitar de encima (a). *vi* Naut. desatracar; *Inf.* ponerse en camino. **to p. open,** empujar, abrir. **to p. out,** *vt* empujar hacia fuera; hacer salir; echar. *vi* Naut. zarpar. **to p. through,** *vt* (business, etc.) despachar rápidamente; (a crowd) abrirse camino por. *vi* aparecer, mostrarse. **to p. to,** cerrar. **to p. up,** empujar; hacer subir; (windows, etc.) levantar.

pushing /'pʊʃɪŋ/ *a* enérgico, emprendedor; ambicioso; agresivo. **by p. and shoving,** a empellones, a empujones

pusillanimity /ˌpyusələ'nɪmɪti/ *n* pusilanimidad, *f*

pusillanimous /ˌpyusə'lænəməs/ *a* pusilánime

puss /pʊs/ *n* micho (-cha). **P.! P.!** ¡Miz, Miz!

pustule /'pʌstʃʊl/ *n* pústula, *f*

put /pʊt/ *vt* poner; colocar; (pour out) echar; aplicar; emplear; (estimate) calcular; presentar; (ask) preguntar; (say) decir; (express) expresar; (a question) hacer; (a problem) plantear; (the weight) lanzar; (rank) estimar. **As the Spanish put it,** Como dicen los españoles. **If I may put it so,** Si puedo expresarlo así, Por así decirlo. **hard put to it,** en dificultades, apurado. **How will you put it to her?** ¿Cómo se lo vas a explicar a ella? **to put ashore,** echar en tierra (a). **to put a child to bed,** acostar a un niño. **to put in order,** arreglar; ordenar, *Lat. Am.* acotejar. **to put out of joint,** dislocar. **to put out of order,** estropear. **to put to death,** matar; (judicially) ajusticiar. **to put about,** *vt* (a rumor) diseminar, divulgar; (worry) preocupar. *vi* Naut. virar, cambiar de rumbo **to put a roof on** = **roof** *vt.* **to put aside,** poner a un lado; descartar; (omit) omitir, pasar por alto de; (fears, etc.) desechar. **to put away,** quitar; guardar; poner en salvo; arrinconar; (thoughts) desechar, ahuyentar; (save) ahorrar; (banish) despedir, alejar; (a wife) repudiar, divorciar; (food) tragar. **to put back,** *vt* echar hacia atrás; hacer retroceder; (replace) devolver, restituir; (the clock) retrasar; (retard) retardar, atrasar. *vi* volver; Naut. volver a puerto. **to put down,** depositar; poner en el suelo; (the blinds) bajar; (an umbrella) cerrar; (a rebellion) sofocar; (gambling, etc.) suprimir; (humble) abatir, humillar; degradar; (silence) hacer callar; (reduce) reducir, disminuir; (write) apuntar, anotar; (a name) inscribir; (to an account) poner a la cuenta de; (estimate) juzgar, creer; (impute) atribuir. **The book is so interesting that it's hard to put down,** El libro es tan interesante que es difícil dejarlo. **to put forth,** (leaves, flowers, sun's rays) echar; (a book) publicar, dar a luz; (a hand) alargar; (an arm) extender; (show) manifestar, mostrar; (strength, etc.) desplegar; (use) emplear. **to put forward,** avanzar; (a clock) adelantar; (a suggestion, etc.) hacer; (propose) proponer; (a case) presentar. **to put oneself forward,** ponerse en evidencia. **to put in,** (room) poner dentro; (a hand, etc.) introducir; (liquids) echar en; (a government) poner en el poder; (an employment) nombrar, colocar; (insert) insertar; (a claim) presentar; (say) decir. **I shall put in two hours' work before bedtime,** Trabajaré por dos horas antes de acostarme. **He put in a good word for you,** Habló en tu favor. **to put in writing,** poner por escrito. **to put in for,** (an employment) solicitar (un empleo); (as a candidate) presentarse como candidato para. **to put into,** meter dentro de; (words) expresar; (port) arribar, hacer escala en (un puerto). **to put off,** desechar; (garments) quitarse, despojarse (de); (postpone) diferir, aplazar; (evade) evadir, entretener; quitarse de encima (a), desembarazarse de; (confuse) desconcertar; (discourage) desanimar; quitar el apetito (a). **to put on,** poner sobre; (clothes) ponerse; (pretend) fingir, afectar; poner; (a play) poner en escena; (the hands of a clock) adelantar; (weight) engordar; poner carnes; (add) añadir; (*Sports.* score) hacer; (bet) apostar; (the light) encender; (assume) tomar; (the brake) frenar; (abuse) abusar (de). engañar. **He put the kettle on the fire,** Puso la tetera en el fuego. **to put on airs and graces,** darse humos. **to put on probation,** dar el azul a, poner a prueba a. **to put on more trains,** poner más trenes. **to put one's foot down,** ponerle a fulano el alto. **to put one's foot in it,** (eject) echar, expulsar; hacer salir; poner en la calle; (a tenant) desahuciar; (one's hand) alargar; (one's arm) extender; (one's tongue) sacar; (eyes) saltar; (fire, light) apagar, extinguir; (leaves, etc.) echar; (horns) sacar; (head) asomar; sacar; (use) emplear; (give) entregar, dar; (at interest) dar a interés; (finish) terminar; (dislocate) dislocar; (worry) desconcertar; turbar; poner los nervios en punta (a); (anger) enojar; (inconvenience) incomodar; (a book) publicar; (a boat) echar al mar. *vi* (of a ship) hacerse a la vela, zarpar. **to put out to grass,** mandar a pacer. **We put out to sea,** Nos hicimos a la mar. **to put the cart before the horse,** poner la carreta por delante de los bueyes. **to put through,**

(perform) desempeñar; concluir, terminar; (thrust) meter; (subject to) someter a; (exercise) ejercitar; (on the telephone) poner en comunicación (con). **to put together,** juntar; (a machine, etc.) montar, armar. **to put two and two together,** atar cabos. **to put up,** *vt* (sails, a flag) izar; (raise a window) levantar, cerrar; (open a window, or an umbrella) abrir; (one's hands, etc.) poner en alto; (one's fists) alzar; (a prayer) ofrecer, hacer; (as a candidate) nombrar; (for sale) poner (a la venta); (the price) aumentar; (a prescription) preparar; (food) conservar; (pack) empaquetar; (a sword) envainar; (lodge) alojar; (a petition) presentar; (build) construir; *Mech.* montar; (*Inf.* plan) arreglar. *vi* alojarse. **to put upon,** abusar (de); oprimir; (accuse) imputar, acusar (de). **to put up to,** incitar (a), instigar (a); dar informaciones sobre; poner al corriente (de). **to put up with,** tolerar, soportar, aguantar; resignarse a; contentarse con, conformarse con

putative /'pyutətɪv/ *a* supuesto; (of relationship) putativo

putrefaction /ˌpyutrə'fækʃən/ *n* putrefacción, *f*

putrefy /'pyutrəˌfai/ *vt* pudrir. *vt* pudrirse, descomponerse

putrid /'pyutrɪd/ *a* pútrido; *Inf.* apestoso

putt /pʌt/ *vt* and *vi* patear.

putting /'pʊtɪŋ/ *n* acción de poner, *f*; colocación, *f*. **p. forward of the clock,** adelanto de la hora, *m*. **p. off,** tardanza, dilación, *f*. **p. the weight,** lanzamiento

del peso, *m*. **p. up,** (for office) candidatura, *f*. **p. green,** pista de golf en miniatura, *f*

putty /'pʌti/ *n* masilla, *f*, *vt* enmasillar, rellenar con masilla

puzzle /'pʌzəl/ *vt* dejar perplejo; desconcertar; confundir; embrollar. *n* problema, *m*; dificultad, *f*; enigma, *m*; (perplexity) perplejidad, *f*; (game) rompecabezas, *m*. **to p. out,** procurar resolver; encontrar la solución de. **to p. over,** pensar en, meditar sobre. **I am puzzled by...,** Me trae (or tiene) perplejo.... **to be puzzled** Lat. Am. intrigarse

pygmy /'pɪgmi/ *a* and *n* pigmeo (-ea)

pyjamas /pə'dʒɑməz, -'dʒæməz/ *n* pijama, *m*

pylon /'pailɒn/ *n* pilón, *m*; poste, *m*; (at an airport) poste de señales, *m*

pylorus /pai'lɔrəs/ *n* píloro, *m*

pyramid /'pɪrəmɪd/ *n* pirámide, *f*

pyramidal /pɪ'ræmɪdḷ/ *a* piramidal

pyre /paiər/ *n* pira, *f*

Pyrenean /ˌpɪərə'niən/ *a* pirineo, pirenaico

Pyrenees, the /'pɪrəˌniz/ los Pirineos, *m pl*

pyromancy /'pairəˌmænsi/ *n* piromancia, *f*

pyrotechnic /ˌpairə'tɛknɪk/ *a* pirotécnico

pyrotechnics /ˌpairə'tɛknɪks/ *n* pirotecnia, *f*

pyrotechnist /ˌpairə'tɛknɪst/ *n* pirotécnico, *m*

Pyrrhic /'pɪrɪk/ *a* pírrico

Pythagorean /pɪˌθægə'riən/ *a* and *n* pitagórico (-ca)

Pythian /'pɪθiən/ *a* pitio

python /'paiθɒn/ *n* pitón, *m*

pythoness /'paiθənɪs/ *n* pitonisa, *f*

Q

q /kyu/ *n* (letter) cu, *f*

quack /kwæk/ *vi* (of a duck) graznar. *n* (of a duck) graznido, *m*; (charlatan) charlatán, farsante, *m*; curandero, *m*. **q. doctor,** matasanos, medicastro, curandero, *m*. **q. medicine,** curanderismo, *m*

quackery /'kwækəri/ *n* charlatanería, *f*, charlatanismo, *m*

quadrangle /'kwɒdˌræŋgəl/ *n* cuadrángulo, *m*; (courtyard) patio, *m*

quadrangular /kwɒd'ræŋgələr/ *a* cuadrangular

quadratic /kwɒ'drætɪk/ *a* cuadrático. **q. equation,** cuadrática, ecuación de segundo grado, *f*

quadrature /'kwɒdrətʃər/ *n* (*Math. Astron.*) cuadratura, *f*

quadrennial /kwɒ'drɛniəl/ *a* cuadrienal

quadrilateral /ˌkwɒdrə'lætərəl/ *a* and *n* cuadrilátero *m*

quadrille /kwɒ'drɪl/ *n* cuadrilla, *f*; (card game) cuatrillo, *m*

quadruped /'kwɒdrʊˌpɛd/ *a* and *n* cuadrúpedo, *m*

quadruple /kwɒ'drupəl/ *a* cuádruple. *vt* cuadruplicar. *n* cuádruplo, *m*

quadruplet /kwɒ'drʌplɪt/ *n* serie de cuatro cosas, *f*; bicicleta de cuatro asientos, *f*; uno (una) de cuatro niños (-as) gemelos (-as)

quadruplication /kwɒˌdrupli'keiʃən/ *n* cuadruplicación, *f*

quagmire /'kwægˌmaiər/ *n* tremedal, pantano, *m*; *Fig.* cenagal, *m*

quail /kweil/ *n* codorniz, *f*; parpayuela, *f*. *vi* cejar, retroceder; temblar, acobardarse

quaint /kweint/ *a* pintoresco; curioso, raro; (eccentric) excéntrico, extravagante

quaintly /'kweintli/ *adv* de un modo pintoresco; curiosamente; con extravagancia

quaintness /'kweintnɪs/ *n* lo pintoresco; rareza, singularidad, *f*; (eccentricity) extravagancia, *f*

quake /kweik/ *vi* estremecerse, vibrar; temblar. *n* estremecimiento, *m*; (of the earth) terremoto, *m*. **to q. with fear,** temblar de miedo

Quaker /'kweikər/ *n* cuáquero (-ra)

quaking /'kweikɪŋ/ *a* temblón; tembloroso. *n* temblor, *m*; estremecimiento, *m*. **q. ash,** álamo temblón, *m*

qualifiable /'kwɒləˌfaiəbəl/ *a* calificable

qualification /ˌkwɒləfɪ'keiʃən/ *n* calificación, *f*; requi-

sito, *m*; capacidad, aptitud, *f*; (reservation) reservación, salvedad, *f*

qualified /'kwɒləˌfaid/ *a* apto, competente; (of professions) con título universitario; habilitado; limitado

qualify /'kwɒləˌfai/ *vt* habilitar, calificar; modificar; suavizar; *vi* habilitarse; prepararse; llenar los requisitos

qualifying /'kwɒləˌfaiɪŋ/ *a* *Gram.* calificativo

qualitative /'kwɒlɪˌteitɪv/ *a* cualitativo

quality /'kwɒlɪti/ *n* cualidad, *f*; calidad, *f*; propiedad, *f*. **This cloth is of good q.,** Esta tela es de buena calidad. **the q.,** la alta sociedad, la aristocracia

qualm /kwɑm/ *n* náusea, *f*; mareo, desmayo, *m*; (of conscience) escrúpulo, remordimiento, *m*

quandary /'kwɒndəri/ *n* incertidumbre, perplejidad, *f*; dilema, apuro, *m*. **to be in a q.,** estar perplejo

quantitative /'kwɒntɪˌteitɪv/ *a* cuantitativo

quantity /'kwɒntɪti/ *n* cantidad, *f*; gran cantidad, *f*. **unknown q.,** incógnita, *f*

quantum /'kwɒntəm/ *n* cantidad, *f*; tanto, *m*. **q. theory,** teoría de la quanta, *f*

quarantine /'kwɔrənˌtin/ *n* cuarentena, *f*, *vt* someter a cuarentena

quarrel /'kwɔrəl/ *vi* pelear, disputar; (scold) reñir; (find fault) criticar. *n* pelea, disputa, *Argentina* arenga, *f*; (glazier's) diamante de vidriero, *m*. **to pick a q. with,** armar pleito con, reñir con, *Chile, Peru* cruzar. **to q. with,** reñir con, romper con; quejarse de

quarreller /'kwɔrələr/ *n* reñidor (-ra)

quarrelling /'kwɔrəlɪŋ/ *n* disputas, altercaciones, *f pl*

quarrelsome /'kwɔrəlsəm/ *a* pendenciero, peleador, belicoso

quarrelsomeness /'kwɔrəlsəmnɪs/ *n* belicosidad, pugnacidad, *f*

quarry /'kwɔri/ *n* cantera, *f*, pedrera *f*; *Fig.* mina, *f*; (prey) presa, *f*; víctima, *f*. *vt* explotar una cantera; examinar

quarrying /'kwɔriɪŋ/ *n* explotación de canteras, *f*; cantería, *f*

quarryman /'kwɔrimən/ *n* cantero, *m*, picapedrero, *m*

quart /kwɔrt/ *n* cuarto de galón, *m*

quartan /'kwɔrtṇ/ *a* cuartanal. *n* (fever) cuartana, *f*

quarter /'kwɔrtər/ *n* (fourth part) cuarta parte, *f*, cuarto, *m*; (of a year) trimestre, *m*; (of an hour, the moon, a ton, an animal, etc.) cuarto, *m*; (of the compass) cuarta, *f; Naut.* cuartelada, *f;* (of a town) barrio, *m;* (mercy) cuartel, *m; Herald.* cuartel, *m;* dirección, *f;* origen, *m,* fuente, *f; pl* **quarters,** vivienda, *f;* alojamiento, *m;* (barracks) cuartel, *m. vt* cuartear; (a body) descuartizar, hacer cuartos (a); (troops) alojar; (in barracks) acuartelar; *Herald.* cuartelar. **a q. of an hour,** un cuarto de hora. **at close quarters,** de cerca. **hind quarters,** cuartos traseros, *m pl.* **It is a q. to four,** Son las cuatro menos cuarto. **It is a q. past four,** Son las cuatro y cuarto. **q.-day,** primer día de un trimestre, *m.* **q.-deck,** alcázar, *m;* cuerpo de oficiales de un buque, *m.* **q.-mile,** cuarto de milla, *m.* **q.-plate,** cuarto de placa, *m.* **q.-sessions,** sesión trimestral de los juzgados municipales, *f.* **q.-staff,** barra, *f.* **q.-tone,** cuarto de tono, *m*

quartering /'kwɔrtərɪŋ/ *n* (punishment) descuartizamiento, *m; Herald.* cantón, *m*

quarterly /'kwɔrtərli/ *a* trimestral, trimestre. *n* publicación trimestral, *f, adv* trimestralmente

quartermaster /'kwɔrtər,mæstər/ *n Mil.* cabo furriel, *m; Nav.* maestre de víveres, cabo de mar, *m.* **q.-general,** intendente de ejército, *m*

quartet /kwɔr'tɛt/ *n* cuarteto, *m*

quarto /'kwɔrtou/ *n* papel en cuarto, *m;* libro en cuarto, *m.* **in q.,** en cuarto

quartz /kwɔrts/ *n* cuarzo, *m*

quash /kwɒʃ/ *vt Law.* anular, derogar; *Inf.* sofocar, reprimir

quasi /'kweizai, 'kwɑsi/ *a* and *adv* cuasi

quasimodo /,kwɑsə'moudou/ *n* cuasimodo, *m*

quatrain /'kwɒtrein/ *n* cuarteta, *f*

quaver /'kweivər/ *vi* vibrar; temblar; (trill) trinar, hacer quiebros. *vt* decir con voz temblorosa. *n* vibración, *f;* trémolo, *m;* (trill) trino, *m;* (musical note) corchea, *f*

quaveringly /'kweivərɪŋli/ *adv* con voz temblorosa

quavery /'kweivəri/ *a* trémulo, tembloroso

quay /ki, kei/ *n* muelle, *m*

queasiness /'kwizinɪs/ *n* náusea, *f;* escrupulosidad, *f*

queasy /'kwizi/ *a* propenso a la náusea; nauseabundo; delicado, escrupuloso

Quechua /'kɛtʃwa/ *n* and *a* quechua, *mf*

queen /kwin/ *n* reina, *f;* (in a Spanish pack of cards) caballo, *m;* (in a French or English pack and in chess) reina, *f.* **to q. it,** conducirse como una reina; mandar. **q. bee,** maestra, abeja reina, *f.* **q. cell,** maestril, *m.* **q. mother,** reina madre, *f.* **q. regent,** reina regente, *f*

queenliness /'kwinlinɪs/ *n* majestad de reina, *f*

queenly /'kwinli/ *a* de reina; regio

queer /kwɪər/ *a* raro; extraño, singular; ridículo; (shady) sospechoso; (ill) malucho, algo enfermo; (mad) chiflado

queerly /'kwɪərli/ *adv* extrañamente; ridículamente

queerness /'kwɪərnɪs/ *n* rareza, extrañeza, singularidad, *f;* ridiculez, *f*

quell /kwɛl/ *vt* subyugar; reprimir; apaciguar, calmar

quench /kwɛntʃ/ *vt* apagar; calmar; satisfacer. **to q. one's thirst,** apagar la sed

quenching /'kwɛntʃɪŋ/ *n* apagamiento, *m;* satisfacción, *f*

querulous /'kwɛrələs/ *a* quejumbroso

querulousness /'kwɛrələsnɪs/ *n* hábito de quejarse, *m;* quejumbre, *f*

query /'kwɪəri/ *n* pregunta, *f;* duda, *f;* punto de interrogación, *m. vt* preguntar; dudar (de); poner en duda. *vi* hacer una pregunta; expresar una duda

quest /kwɛst/ *n* busca, *f;* (adventure) demanda, *f.* **in q. of,** en busca de

question /'kwɛstʃən/ *n* pregunta, *f;* problema, *m;* asunto, *m;* cuestión, *f;* (discussion) debate, *m,* discusión, *f. vt* and *vi* interrogar; examinar; poner en duda, dudar de; preguntarse; hacer preguntas. **beyond q.,** fuera de duda. **to ask a q.,** hacer una pregunta. **without q.,** sin duda. **It is out of the q.,** Es completamente imposible. **It is a q. of whether...,** Se trata de si... **q.-mark,** punto interrogante, *m*

questionable /'kwɛstʃənəbəl/ *a* cuestionable, discutible, dudoso; equívoco, sospechoso

questionableness /'kwɛstʃənəbəlnɪs/ *n* lo discutible; carácter dudoso, *m;* carácter sospechoso, *m*

questioner /'kwɛstʃənər/ *n* preguntador (-ra); interrogador (-ra)

questioning /'kwɒstʃənɪŋ/ *n* preguntas, *f pl;* interrogatorio, *m*

questioningly /kwɛstʃənɪŋli/ *adv* interrogativamente

questionnaire /,kwɛstʃə'nɛər/ *n* cuestionario, *m*

quetzal /kɛt'sɑl/ *n* (money and *Ornith.*) quetzal, *m*

queue /kyu/ *n* coleta, *f;* cola, *f, vi* formar cola; hacer cola

quibble /'kwɪbəl/ *n* equívoco, subterfugio, *m;* sutileza, *f;* (pun) retruécano, *m. vi* hacer uso de subterfugios; sutilizar

quibbler /'kwɪblər/ *n* sofista, *mf*

quibbling /'kwɪblɪŋ/ *n* sofistería, *f,* sofismas, *m pl,* sutilezas, *f pl*

quick /kwɪk/ *a* vivo; agudo; penetrante; sagaz; rápido, veloz; (ready) pronto; ágil, activo; (light) ligero. *adv* rápidamente; (soon) pronto. *n* carne viva, *f; Fig.* lo vivo. **Be q.!** ¡Date prisa! **He was very q.,** Lo hizo muy aprisa; Volvió (or Fue, according to sense) rápidamente. **the q. and the dead,** los vivos y los muertos. **to cut to the q.,** herir en lo más vivo. **q. march,** paso doble, *m.* **q.-sighted,** de vista aguda; perspicaz. **q. step,** paso rápido, *m.* **q.-tempered,** de genio vivo, colérico. **q. time,** compás rápido, *m; Mil.* paso doble, *m.* **q.-witted,** de ingenio agudo

quicken /'kwɪkən/ *vt* vivificar; animar; acelerar; excitar, avivar. *vi* vivificarse; despertarse; renovarse; acelerarse; (stir) moverse. **to q. one's step,** acelerar el paso

quicklime /'kwɪk,laim/ *n* cal viva, *f*

quickly /'kwɪkli/ *adv* rápidamente; (soon) pronto; (immediately) en seguida; (promptly) con presteza; vivamente

quickness /'kwɪknɪs/ *n* viveza, *f;* (of wit, etc.) agudeza, *f;* rapidez, velocidad, *f;* (promptness) prontitud, *f;* agilidad, *f;* (lightness) ligereza, *f;* (understanding) penetración, sagacidad, *f*

quicksand /'kwɪk,sænd/ *n* arena movediza, *f; Fig.* cenagal, *m*

quicksilver /'kwɪk,sɪlvər/ *n* azogue, mercurio, *m, vt* azogar

quiescence /kwi'ɛsəns/ *n* reposo, *m;* quietud, tranquilidad, *f;* inactividad, *f;* pasividad, *f*

quiescent /kwi'ɛsənt/ *a* quieto; inactivo; pasivo

quiet /'kwaiət/ *a* tranquilo; quieto; silencioso; quedo; monótono; inactivo; (informal) sin ceremonia; (simple) sencillo; (of the mind) sereno; (of colours, etc.) suave. *n* tranquilidad, quietud, *f;* silencio, *m;* paz, *f;* (of mind) serenidad, *f. vt* tranquilizar, sosegar; calmar. **to be q.,** callarse; no hacer ruido. **Be q.!** ¡Estate quieto! ¡A callar!

quietism /'kwaiɪ,tɪzəm/ *n* quietismo, *m*

quietist /'kwaiɪtɪst/ *n* quietista, *mf*

quietistic /,kwaiɪ'tɪstɪk/ *a* quietista

quietly /'kwaiɪtli/ *adv* tranquilamente; en silencio; sin ruido; en calma; (simply) sencillamente; dulcemente

quietness /'kwaiɪtnɪs/ *n* tranquilidad, quietud, *f;* calma, *f;* paz, *f;* silencio, *m*

quietus /kwai'itəs/ *n* (quittance) quitanza, *f,* finiquito, *m;* golpe de gracia, *m;* muerte, *f*

quill /kwɪl/ *n* pluma de ave, *f;* (of a feather) cañón, *m;* (pen) pluma, *f;* (of a porcupine) púa, *f.* **q.-driver,** cagatintas, *mf*

quilt /kwɪlt/ *n* colcha, *f,* edredón, *m. vt* acolchar. **q. maker,** colchero, *m*

quilting /'kwɪltɪŋ/ *n* acolchamiento, *m;* colchadura, *f*

quince /kwɪns/ *n* (tree and fruit) membrillo, *m.* **q. cheese,** carne de membrillo, *f.* **q. jelly,** jalea de membrillo, *f*

quincentenary /,kwɪnsɛn'tɛnəri/ *n* quinto centenario, *m*

quinine /'kwainain/ *n* quinina, *f*

quinsy /'kwɪnzi/ *n* angina, *f*

quintessence /kwɪn'tɛsəns/ *n* quinta esencia, *f*

quintessential /,kwɪntə'sɛnʃəl/ *a* quintaesenciado

quintet /kwɪn'tɛt/ *n* quinteto, *m*

quintuple /kwɪn'tupəl/ *a* quíntuplo

quintuplet /kwɪn'tʌplɪt/ *n* quintupleto, *m;* uno (una) de cinco niños (-as) gemelos (-as)

quip /kwɪp/ *n* agudeza, salida, *f*; (hint) indirecta, *f*; donaire, *m*, chanza, burla, *f*

quire /kwaiªr/ *n* (of paper) mano (de papel), *f*

quirk /kwɜrk/ *n* (quip) agudeza, salida, *f*; (quibble) sutileza, evasiva, *f*, (gesture) gesto, *m*

quit /kwɪt/ *vt* abandonar; dejar; renunciar (a). *vi* marcharse, *Inf.* tomar las de Villadiego, poner pies en polvorosa; (slang) dejar de, cesar de. **notice to q.,** aviso de desahúcio, *m*

quite /kwait/ *adv* completamente, enteramente; totalmente; del todo; (very) muy; (fairly) bastante. **It is not q. the thing to do,** Esto es algo que no se hace. **Q. so!** ¡Claro!; ¡Eso es! Se comprende. **It is not q. so good as we hoped,** No es tan bueno como esperábamos. **Peter is q. grown-up,** Pedro está hecho un hombre (*or* es todo un hombre)

quits /kwɪts/ *adv* quito, descargado

quittance /'kwɪtns/ *n* quitanza, *f*; recibo, *m*; recompensa, *f*

quitter /'kwɪtər/ *n* desertor (-ra); cobarde, *mf*

quiver /'kwɪvər/ *vi* temblar; vibrar; estremecerse; palpitar; (of light) titilar. *n* (for arrows) aljaba, *f*, carcaj, *m*. See also **quivering**

quivering /'kwɪvərɪŋ/ *a* tremulante; vibrante; palpitante. *n* temblor, *m*; estremecimiento, *m*

quixotic /kwɪk'sɒtɪk/ *a* quijotesco

quixotism /'kwɪksə,tɪzəm/ *n* quijotismo, *m*

quiz /kwɪz/ *n* examen parcial, *m*. *vt* tomar el pelo (a); burlarse (de); (stare) mirar de hito en hito (a)

quizzical /'kwɪzɪkəl/ *a* burlón; cómico; estrafalario

quizzically /'kwɪzɪkli/ *adv* burlonamente; cómicamente

quoin /kɔin, kwɔin/ *n* piedra angular, *f*; ángulo, *m*; (wedge) cuña, *f*. *vt* meter cuñas (a)

quoit /kwɔit/ *n* tejo, *m*; *pl* **quoits,** juego de tejos, *m*

quondam /'kwɒndəm/ *a* antiguo

quorum /'kwɔrəm/ *n* quórum, *m*. **to form a q.,** hacer un quórum

quota /'kwoutə/ *n* cuota, *f*

quotable /'kwoutəbəl/ *a* citable; (Stock Exchange) cotizable

quota system *n* tablas diferenciales, *f pl*

quotation /kwou'teiʃən/ *n* citación, *f*; cita, *f*; *Com.* cotización, *f*. **q. mark,** comilla, *f*

quote /kwout/ *vt* citar; *Com.* cotizar. *n Inf.* comilla, *f*

quoth /kwouθ/ *vt* **q. I,** dije yo. **q. he,** dijo él

quotient /'kwouʃənt/ *n* cociente, *m*. **intelligence q.,** cociente intelectual, *m*

R

r /ɑr/ *n* (letter) erre, *f*

rabbet /'ræbɪt/ *n* ranura, *f*, rebajo, *m*. *vt* ensamblar a rebajo. **r.-joint,** junta a rebajo, *f*

rabbi /'ræbai/ *n* rabí, rabino, *m*. **grand r.,** gran rabino, *m*

rabbinical /rə'bɪnɪkəl/ *a* rabínico

rabbinism /'ræbə,nɪzəm/ *n* rabinismo, *m*

rabbit /'ræbɪt/ *n* conejo (-ja). *a* conejuno, de conejo. *vi* cazar conejos. **young r.,** gazapo, *m*. **r.-hutch,** jaula para conejos, *f*. **r.-warren,** conejera, *f*

rabble /'ræbəl/ *n* populacho, vulgo, *m*, plebe, *f*

rabid /'ræbɪd/ *a* rabioso; fanático; furioso, violento

rabies /'reibiz/ *n* rabia, hidrofobia, *f*

raccoon /ræ'kun/ *n* mapache, *m*

race /reis/ *n* carrera, *f*; (current) corriente, *f*; (prize) premio, *m*; (breed) raza, *f*; casta, estirpe, *f*; (family) linaje, *m*, familia, *f*; (scornful) ralea, *f*; (struggle) lucha, *f*. *vi* tomar parte en una carrera; correr de prisa; asistir a concursos de carreras de caballos; (of a machine) dispararse. *vt* (hacer) correr; competir en una carrera (con); desafiar a una carrera. **flat r.,** carrera llana, *f*. **mill-r.,** caz, *m*. **to run a r.,** tomar parte en una carrera; *Fig.* hacer una carrera. **r.-card,** programa de carreras de caballos, *m*. **r. hatred,** odio de razas, *m*. **r.-meeting,** concurso de carreras de caballos, *m*. **r. suicide,** suicidio de la raza, *m*. **r.-track,** pista, *f*

racecourse /'reis,kɔrs/ *n* hipódromo, *m*; estadio, *m*

racehorse /'reis,hɔrs/ *n* caballo de carreras, *m*

racer /'reisər/ *n* (horse) caballo de carreras, *m*; (person) carrerista, *mf*; (car) coche de carreras, *m*; (boat) yate de carreras, *m*; (bicycle) bicicleta de carreras, *f*

rachitic /rə'kɪtɪk/ *a* raquítico

racial /'reiʃəl/ *a* racial, de raza

racialism /'reiʃə,lɪzəm/ *n* rivalidad de razas, *f*

raciness /'reisɪnɪs/ *n* sabor, *m*; savia, *f*, picante, *m*

racing /'reisɪŋ/ *n* carreras, *f pl*; *Mech.* disparo, *m*, *a* de carreras; hípico. **r. calendar,** calendario de concursos de carreras de caballos, *m*. **r. car,** coche de carreras, *m*. **r. cycle,** bicicleta de carreras, *f*

racism /'reisɪzəm/ *n* racismo, *m*

racist /'reisɪst/ *n* racista, *mf*

rack /ræk/ *n* (for hay) percha (del pesebre), *f*; (in a railway compartment) rejilla, *f*; (for billiard cues) taquera, *f*; (for clothes) percha, *f*; (for torture) potro, *m*; *Mech.* cremallera, *f*. *vt* poner en el potro, torturar; atormentar. **to be on the r.,** estar en el potro **to r. one's brains,** devanarse los sesos, quebrarse la cabeza. **r. and ruin,** ruina total, *f*. **r. railway,** ferrocarril de cremallera, *m*,

racket /'rækɪt/ *n Sports.* raqueta, *f*; (din) barahúnda, *f*; ruido, estrépito, *m*; confusión, *f*; (bustle) bullicio, *m*, agitación, *f*; (swindle) estafa, *f*; (binge) parranda, *f*. **to play rackets,** jugar a la raqueta

racking /'rækɪŋ/ *n* tortura, *f*; (of wine) trasiego, *m*, *a* torturante; (of a pain or cough) persistente

racoon /ræ'kun/ *n* mapache, *m*

racquet /'rækɪt/ *n* See **racket**

racy /'reisi/ *a* picante; sabroso

radar /'reidɑr/ *n* radar, *m*

raddled /'rædld/ *a* pintado de almagre; mal pintado

radial /'reidiəl/ *a* radial

radiance /'reidiəns/ *n* resplandor, brillo, *m*, luminosidad, *f*

radiant /'reidiənt/ *a* radiante; brillante, luminoso. *n Geom.* línea radial, *f*. **r. heat,** calor radiante, *m*

radiantly /'reidiəntli/ *adv* con resplandor; brillantemente; con alegría

radiate /'reidi,eit/ *vi* radiar. *vt* irradiar

radiation /,reidi'eiʃən/ *n* irradiación, *f*; *Geom.* radiación, *f*

radiator /'reidi,eitər/ *n* (for central heating and of a car) radiador, *m*; (stove) calorífero, *m*

radical /'rædɪkəl/ *a* radical. *n* (*Math. Chem.*) radical, *m*; *Polit.* radical, *mf*

radicalism /'rædɪkə,lɪzəm/ *n* radicalismo, *m*

radio /'reidi,ou/ *n* radio, *f*; radiocomunicación, *f*. **r. amateur, r. enthusiast,** radioaficionado (-da). **r. announcer,** locutor (-ra). **r. broadcast,** radioemisión, radiodifusión, *f*. **r. listener,** radiooyente, *mf* **r. receiver,** (technical) radiorreceptor, *m*; (usual word) aparato de radio, *m*. **r. transmitter,** radiotransmisor, *m*

radioactive /,reidiou'æktɪv/ *a* radiactivo

radioactive fallout *n* caída radiactiva, llovizna radiactiva, precipitación radiactiva, *f*

radioactivity /,reidiouæk'tɪvɪti/ *n* radiactividad, *f*

radiofrequency /,reidiou'frikwənsi/ *n* radiofrecuencia, *f*

radiolocation /,reidioulou'keiʃən/ *n* radiolocación, *f*

radiologist /,reidi'ɒlədʒɪst/ *n* radiólogo, *m*

radiology /reidi'ɒlədʒi/ *n* radiología, *f*

radiometer /,reidi'ɒmɪtər/ *n* radiómetro, *m*

radiometry /,reidi'ɒmɪtri/ *n* radiometría, *f*

radioscopy /,reidi'ɒskəpi/ *n* radioscopia, *f*

radiotherapy /,reidiou'θerəpi/ *n* radioterapia, *f*

radish /'rædɪʃ/ *n* rábano, *m*. **horse-r.,** rábano picante, *m*

radium /'reidiəm/ *n* radio, *m*

radius /'reidiəs/ *n* (*Geom. Anat.*) radio, *m*; (of a wheel) rayo, *m*; (scope) alcance, *m*

raffia /'ræfiə/ *n* rafia, *f*

raffish /'ræfɪʃ/ *a* disoluto, libertino

raffle /'ræfəl/ *n* rifa, *f*, sorteo, *m*; lotería, *f*. *vt* rifar, sortear

raffling /'ræflɪŋ/ *n* sorteo, *m*, rifa, *f*

raft /ræft/ *n* balsa, *f*; (timber) armadía, *f*. *vt* transportar en balsa; cruzar en balsa

rafter /'ræftər/ *n* (of a roof) viga, traviesa, *f*; (raftsman) balsero, *m*

raftered /'ræftərd/ *a* con vigas

rag /ræg/ *n* jirón, guiñapo, *m*; (for cleaning) paño, trapo, *m*; (for papermaking) estraza, *f*; (of smoke, etc.) penacho, *m*; (newspaper) papelucho, *m*; *pl* **rags**, harapos, *m pl*; *Inf.* viejos hábitos, *m pl. vt* (tease) tomar el pelo (a); burlarse de; hacer una broma pesada (a). **r.-and-bone-man**, **ragpicker**, andrajero, trapero (Mexico), pepinador, *m*. **r. doll**, muñeca de trapo, *f*

ragamuffin /'rægə,mʌfɪn/ *n* galopín, *m*

rage /reidʒ/ *n* (anger) cólera, rabia, ira, *f*; (of the elements) furia, violencia, *f*; (ardor) entusiasmo, ardor, *m*; (fashion) boga, moda, *f*; (craze) manía, *f*; (of the poet) furor, *m. vi* (be angry) rabiar, estar furioso; (of the sea) encresparse, alborotarse, enfurecerse; (of wind, fire, animals) bramar, rugir; (of pain) rabiar; (be prevalent) prevalecer, desencadenarse. **to r. against**, protestar furiosamente contra; culpar amargamente (de). **to be all the r.**, *Inf.* ser la ultima moda. **to fly into a r.**, montar en cólera. **to put into a r.**, hacer rabiar

ragged /'rægɪd/ *a* harapiento, andrajoso; roto; (uneven) desigual; (rugged) peñascoso, áspero, escabroso; (serrated) serrado; dentellado; (of a coastline) accidentado; (unfinished) inacabado, sin terminar; (of style) descuidado, sin pulir

raggedness /'rægɪdnɪs/ *n* harapos, *m pl*; estado andrajoso, *m*; aspereza, escabrosidad, *f*; lo serrado; lo accidentado; (of style) falta de elegancia, tosquedad, *f*

raging /'reidʒɪŋ/ *a* furioso, rabioso; violento; (roaring) bramante; (of the sea) bravío; intenso. *n* furia, *f*; violencia, *f*; intensidad, *f*

raglan /'ræglən/ *n* raglán, *m*. **r. sleeve**, manga raglán, *f*

ragout /ræ'gu/ *n* estofado, *m*

ragpicker /'ræg,pɪkər/ *n* trapero (-ra)

ragtime /'ræg,taim/ *n* música sincopada, *f*

raid /reid/ *n* incursión, correría, *f*; asalto, ataque, *m*; (by the police) razzia, *f*; (by aircraft) bombardeo, *m*, *vt* invadir; atacar, asaltar; apoderarse de; hacer una razzia en; (by aircraft) bombear, bombardear; (pillage) pillar, saquear. **obliteration r.**, hombardeo de saturación, *m*

raider /'reidər/ *n* corsario, *m*; atacador, asaltador, *m*; (aircraft) avión enemigo, *m*

rail /reil/ *n* barra, *f*; antepecho, *m*; (of a staircase) barandilla, *f*, pasamano, *m*; (track) riel, *m*; (railway) ferrocarril, *m*; (of a ship) barandilla, *f*; (of a chair) travesaño, *m pl*. **rails**, (fence) cerca, barrera, palizada, *f. vt* cercar con una palizada, poner cerca a; mandar por ferrocarril. **by r.**, por ferrocarril. **to run off the rails**, descarrilar. **to r. at**, protestar contra; prorrumpir en invectivas contra, injuriar de palabra (a)

railing /'reilɪŋ/ *n* barandilla, *f*; antepecho, *m*, enrejado, *m*; (grille) reja, *f*; (jeers) burlas, *f pl*; insultos, *m pl*, injurias, *f pl*; quejas, *f pl*

raillery /'reiləri/ *n* jocosidad, tomadura de pelo, *f*; sátiras, *f pl*

railway /'reil,wei/ *n* ferrocarril, *m*; vía férrea, *f*, camino de hierro, *m*, *a* de ferrocarril, ferroviario. **elevated r.**, ferrocarril aéreo, *m*. **narrow gauge r.**, ferrocarril de vía estrecha, *m*. **r. buffet**, fonda, *f*, (or restaurante, *m*) de estación. **r. carriage**, departamento de tren, *m*. **r. company**, compañia de ferrocarriles, *f*. **r. crossing**, paso a nivel, *m*. **r. engine**, locomotora, *f*. **r. guard**, jefe del tren, *m*. **r. guide**, guía de ferrocarriles, *f*. **r. line**, vía férrea, *f*. **r. marshalling yard**, apartadero ferroviario, *m*. **r. passenger**, viajero (-ra) en un tren. **r. platform**, andén, *m*. **r. porter**, mozo de estación, *m*. **r. siding**, vía muerta, *f*. **r. signal**, disco de señales, *m*. **r. station**, estación (de ferrocarril), *f*. **r. system**, sistema ferroviario, *m*. **r. ticket**, billete de tren, *m*

railwayman /'reil,weimən/ *n* ferroviario, empleado de los ferrocarriles, *m*

raiment /'reimənt/ *n* ropa, *f*; *Poet.* hábitos, *m pl*

rain /rein/ *n* lluvia, *f. vi* and *vt* llover. **a r. of arrows**, una lluvia de flechas. **fine r.**, llovizna, *f*. **to r. cats and dogs**, llover a cántaros. **to r. hard**, diluviar. **r. cloud**, nubarrón, *m*. **r.-gauge**, pluviómetro, *m*

rainbow /'rein,bou/ *n* arco iris, arco de San Martín, *m*

raincoat /'rein,kout/ *n* abrigo impermeable, *m*

raindrop /'rein,drop/ *n* gota de lluvia, *f*

rainfall /'rein,fɔl/ *n* cantidad llovida, *f*; (shower) aguacero, *m*

rainless /'reinlɪs/ *a* sin lluvia, seco

rainstorm /'rein,stɔrm/ *n* chaparrón, *m*, tempestad de lluvia, *f*

rainwater /'rein,wɔtər/ *n* lluvia, *f*; agua lluvia, *f*

rainy /'reini/ *a* lluvioso. **r. day**, día de lluvia, *m*; *Fig.* tiempo de escasez, *m*

raise /reiz/ *vt* levantar; alzar; (the hat) quitar; solevantar; (dough) fermentar; (erect) erigir, edificar; (dust) levantar; elevar; (promote) ascender; (increase) aumentar; hacer subir; (spirits, memories) evocar; (the dead) resucitar; (cause) causar; dar lugar (a); hacer concebir; (a question, a point) hacer; plantear; (breed or educate) criar; (a crop) cultivar; (an army) alistar; (gather together) juntar; (a subscription) hacer; (money, etc.) obtener, hallar; (a siege, etc.) levantar, alzar; (a laugh, a protest, etc.) suscitar, provocar; (utter) poner, dar; (a fund) abrir. **to r. oneself**, incorporarse. **To he succeeded in raising himself**, Logró alzarse; Logró mejorar su posición. **He raised their hopes unduly**, Les hizo concebir esperanzas desmesuradas. **to r. an objection (to)**, poner objeción (a). **to r. an outcry**, armar un alboroto. **to r. a point**, hacer una observación; plantear una cuestión. **to r. a siege**, levantar un sitio. **to r. Cain**, armar un alboroto. **to r. one's voice**, alzar la voz

raised /reizd/ *a* (in relief) en relieve; (embossed) de realce

raiser /'reizər/ *n* (breeder) criador (-ra); (cultivator) cultivador (-ra); (educator) educador (-ra); autor (-ra); fundador (-ra); (of objections, etc.) suscitador (-ra)

raisin /'reizɪn/ *n* pasa, *f*

raising /'reizɪŋ/ *n* levantamiento, *m*; alzamiento, *m*; (of a building, monument) erección, *f*; elevación, *f*; (increase) aumento, *m*; provocación, *f*; fundación, *f*; (breeding or education) crianza, *f*; (of spirits) evocación, *f*; (of the dead) resucitación, *f*; producción, *f*; (of crops) cultivo, *m*

rake /reik/ *n Agr.* rastrillo, *m*, rastra, *f*; (for the fire) hurgón, *m*; (croupier's) raqueta, *f*; (of a mast, funnel) inclinación, *f*; (person) tenorio, calavera, *m. vt Agr.* rastrillar; (a fire, etc.) hurgar; (sweep) barrer; recoger; (ransack) buscar (en); (with fire) enfilar, tirar a lo largo de; (scan) escudriñar. *vi* trabajar con el rastrillo; (slope) inclinarse. **r. off**, tajada, *f*. **to r. together**, juntar con el rastrillo; amontonar; ahorrar. **to r. up**, (revive) resucitar, desenterrar

raking /'reikɪŋ/ *n* rastrillaje, *m*; (the fire, etc.) hurgonada, *f*

rakish /'reikɪʃ/ *a* (of a ship) de palos muy inclinados, (dissolute) disoluto, libertino; (dashing) elegante

rakishly /'reikɪʃli/ *adv* disolutamente; elegantemente

rakishness /'reikɪʃnɪs/ *n* (licentiousness) libertinaje, *m*, disipación, disolución, *f*; (elegance) elegancia, *f*

rally /'ræli/ *vt* reunir; *Mil.* rehacer; (faculties) concentrar; (tease) tomar el pelo (a). *vi* reunirse; *Mil.* rehacerse; (revive) mejorar, recobrar las fuerzas; (of markets, etc.) mejorar *n* reunión, *f*

rallying /'ræliɪŋ/ *n* reunión, *f*; (of faculties, etc.) concentración, *f*; (recovery) mejora, *f*. **r. point**, punto de reunión, *m*

ram /ræm/ *n Zool.* carnero, morueco, *m*; *Astron.* Aries, Carnero, *m*; (*Mil.* etc.) ariete, *m*; (tool) pisón, *m*; *Nav.* espolón, *m. vt* golpear con ariete o espolón; (of a gun) atacar; apisonar; meter a la fuerza; hacer tragar a la fuerza; (squeeze) apretar; (crowd) atestar

Ramadan /,ræmə'dan/ *n* ramadán, *m*

ramble /'ræmbəl/ *vi* vagar, vagabundear; hacer una excursión. *vt* errar por

rambler /'ræmblər/ n excursionista, mf; paseante, mf; Bot. rosa trepante, f

rambling /'ræmblɪŋ/ a (of houses) encantado; laberíntico; (straggly) disperso; (of thought, etc.) incoherente, inconexo. n vagabundeo, m; excursiones, f pl; paseo, m; (digression) digresiones, f pl; (delirium) desvaríos, m pl

ramification /ˌræməfɪ'keiʃən/ n ramificación, f

ramify /'ræməˌfai/ vi ramificarse, tener ramificaciones. vt ramificar; dividir en ramales

rammer /'ræmər/ n pisón de empedrador, m; baqueta (de fusil), f; (of a ship) espolón, m

ramp /ræmp/ n rampa, f; (swindle) estafa, f; (storm, commotion) tormenta, f

rampage /'ræmpeidʒ/ n alboroto, m. vi alborotarse; bramar

rampant /'ræmpənt/ a salvaje; Herald. rampante; (of persons) impaciente, furioso; (of plants, growth) lozano, exuberante; desenfrenado; (rife) prevaleciente, predominante

rampart /'ræmpɑrt/ n muralla, f; terraplén, m; Fig. baluarte, m. vt abaluartar, abastionar

ramrod /'ræmˌrɒd/ n baqueta, f

ramshackle /'ræmˌʃækəl/ a destartalado, ruinoso; desvencijado; (badly made) mal hecho

ranch /ræntʃ/ n rancho, m, hacienda (de ganado), Lat. Am. estancia, f

rancher /'ræntʃər/ n ranchero (-ra), Lat. Am. estanciero (-ra) mf

rancid /'rænsɪd/ a rancio

rancor /'ræŋkər/ n rencor, encono, m

rancorous /'ræŋkərəs/ a rencoroso

random /'rændəm/ n azar, m, a fortuito, al azar; sin orden ni concierto. **at r.,** a la ventura, al azar; sin pensar; (of shooting) sin apuntar. **to talk at r.,** hablar a trochemoche

randomly /'rændəmli/ adv al azar, por casualidad

range /reindʒ/ n línea, hilera, f; (of mountains) cadena, f; serie, f; clase, f; variedad, f; (of goods) surtido, m; (of a gun, voice, vision, etc.) alcance, m; (area) extensión, área, f; esfera de actividad, f; (scope) alcance, m; (of voice, musical instrument) compás, m; (of colors) gama, f; (for shooting) campo de tiro, m; (for cooking) cocina económica, f. **at close r.,** de cerca. **out of r.,** fuera de alcance. **within r.,** al alcance. **r.-finder,** (of guns, cameras) telémetro, m. **r. of mountains,** cadena de montañas, f; sierra, f

range /reindʒ/ vt clasificar; (a gun, etc.) apuntar; (place oneself) ponerse; sumarse (a); (roam) recorrer; (scan) escudriñar. vi extenderse; (roam) vagar; (of plants) crecer (en); variar, fluctuar; oscilar, vacilar; (of guns, etc.) alcanzar; (of the mind) pasar (por); (include) incluir

ranger /'reindʒər/ n (wanderer) vagabundo, m; (keeper) guardabosque, m; Mil. batidor, m

ranging /'reindʒɪŋ/ n clasificación, f; (roving) vida errante, f

rank /ræŋk/ n línea, f; fila, f; grado, m; clase, f; rango, m; categoría, f; posición, f; calidad, f; distinción, f. vt ordenar; clasificar; (estimate) estimar; poner (entre). vi ocupar un puesto; tener un grado, rango, etc.; estar al nivel (de); ser igual (a); contarse (entre). a (luxuriant) lozano, exuberante; fértil; (thick) espeso; (rancid) rancio; (complete) consumado; completo; (foul-smelling) fétido; Fig. repugnante, aborrecible; (very) muy. **of the first r.,** de primera calidad; de primera clase; de distinción. **the r. and file,** los soldados, la tropa; las masas, hombres de filas, m pl, mujeres de fila, f pl, la mayoría; los socios ordinarios (de un club, etc.). **to break ranks,** Mil. romper filas. **to rise from the ranks,** ascender de las filas. **to r. high,** ocupar alta posición; ser de los mejores (de). **to r. with,** estar al nivel de; (be numbered among) contarse entre, figurar entre

rankle /'ræŋkəl/ vi Fig. irritar, molestar; envenenarse la vida, hacerse odioso

rankly /'ræŋkli/ adv ranciamente; lozanamente; con exuberancia; abundantemente; groseramente

rankness /'ræŋknɪs/ n rancidez, f; olor rancio, m; fertilidad, lozanía, f; exuberancia, f; vigor, m; enormidad, f

ransack /'rænsæk/ vt (search) registrar; (pillage) saquear; Fig. buscar en

ransacking /'rænsækɪŋ/ n (searching) registro, m; (sacking) saqueo, m

ransom /'rænsəm/ n rescate, m, redención, f; liberación, f. vt rescatar, redimir

ransomer /'rænsəmər/ n rescatador (-ra)

ransoming /'rænsəmɪŋ/ n redención, f; liberación, f

rant /rænt/ vi declamar a gritos, vociferar; despotricar (contra); desvariar; hablar por hablar, hablar sin ton ni son. n declamación, vociferación, f; desvarío, m

ranter /'ræntər/ n declamador (-ra); agitador populachero, m; predicador chillón, m

rap /ræp/ n golpecito, m; toque, m; (with the knocker) aldabada, f; (worthless trifle) ardite, maravedí, m. vt and vi golpear; tocar. **He doesn't care a rap,** No le importa un ardite. **to rap at the door,** tocar a la puerta. **to rap with the knuckles,** golpear con los nudillos. **to rap out an oath,** proferir una blasfemia

rapacious /rə'peiʃəs/ a rapaz

rapacity /rə'pæsɪti/ n rapacidad, f

rape /reip/ n violación, f, (carrying off) rapto, m. **the Rape of the Sabine Women,** el Rapto de las Sabinas, m; Law. estupro, m; violación, f; Bot. nabo silvestre, m. vt (carry off) raptar, robar; violar, forzar

rapid /'ræpɪd/ a rápido. n rápido, m. **r. combustion,** combustión activa, f

rapidity /rə'pɪdɪti/ n rapidez, f

rapidly /'ræpɪdli/ adv rápidamente, con rapidez

rapids /'ræpɪdz/ npl Argentina correntada, f sg

rapier /'reipiər/ n estoque, m; espadín, m

rapine /'ræpɪn/ n rapiña, f

rapist /'reipɪst/ n violador (-ra)

rapping /'ræpɪŋ/ n golpecitos, m pl; golpeo, m; toques, m pl; (of the knocker) aldabeo, m

rapscallion /ræp'skælyən/ n bribón, m

rapt /ræpt/ past part and a arrebatado; absorto; extático, extasiado

rapture /'ræptʃər/ n arrebato, m; éxtasis, m; transporte, m; embriaguez, f; entusiasmo, m; Eccl. El Retorno de Cristo

rapturous /'ræptʃərəs/ a embelesado; extático; entusiasta

rapturously /'ræptʃərəsli/ adv extáticamente; con entusiasmo

rare /rɛər/ a raro; extraordinario; exótico; infrecuente

raree show /'rɛəri/ n barracón de los fenómenos, barracón de las atracciones, m

rarefaction /ˌrɛərə'fækʃən/ n rarefacción, f

rarefy /'rɛərəˌfai/ vt rarefacer. vi rarefacerse

rareness /'rɛərnɪs/ n rareza, f; singularidad, f; infrecuencia, f

rarity /'rɛərɪti/ n raridad, f; (uncommonness and rare object) rareza, f

rascal /'ræskəl/ n sinvergüenza, m; truhán, bribón, pícaro, m; (affectionately) picaruelo, m

rascality /ræ'skælɪti/ n bellaquería, truhanería, f

rascally /'ræskəli/ a redomado; vil, ruin, canallesco

rash /ræʃ/ a temerario, precipitado; imprudente. n erupción, m, salpullido, m

rasher /'ræʃər/ n magra, f; (of bacon) torrezno, m

rashly /'ræʃli/ adv temerariamente, precipitadamente; imprudentemente, con imprudencia

rashness /'ræʃnɪs/ n temeridad, precipitación, f; imprudencia, f

rasp /ræsp/ n escofina, f, rallo, m; sonido áspero, m. vt raspar, escofinar; (get on one's nerves) poner los nervios en punta (a)

raspberry /'ræz,bɛri/ n frambuesa, f. **r.-cane,** frambueso, m. **r. jam,** mermelada de frambuesa, f

rasping /'ræspɪŋ/ a (of the voice) áspero, estridente

rat /ræt/ n rata, f; desertor, m; (black leg) esquirol, m. vi cazar ratas; ser desertor; ser esquirol. **ratcatcher,** cazador de ratas, m. **rat poison,** matarratas, m, raticida, f. **rat-trap,** ratonera, f

ratable /'reitəbəl/ a sujeto a contribución; imponible; valuable

ratafia /ˌrætə'fiə/ n ratafía, f

rataplan /ˌrætə'plæn/ n rataplán, m

ratchet /'rætʃɪt/ n Mech. trinquete, m; (of a watch) disparador, m. **r.-drill,** carraca, f. **r.-wheel,** rueda dentada con trinquete, f

rate /reit/ n velocidad, f; razón, proporción, f; (of exchange) tipo, m; tanto, m; precio, m; clase, f; modo, m, manera, f; Naut. clasificación, f; (tax) contribución, f, impuesto, m; pl **rates,** (of a house) inquilinato, m. vt tasar; estimar; fijar el precio (a); Naut. clasificar; imponer una contribución (de); (scold) reñir. **at a great r.,** rápidamente, velozmente. **at a r. of,** a razón de; a una velocidad de. **at any r.,** de todos modos; por lo menos; sea como fuere. **at this r.,** de este modo; a este paso; a esa cuenta; en esta proporción; (with seguir) así. **first-r.,** de primera clase. **rates and taxes,** contribuciones e impuestos, f pl. **r. of climb,** Aer. velocidad ascensional, f. **r. of exchange,** tipo de cambio, m. **r.-payer,** contribuyente, mf

rather /'ræðər/ adv más bien; antes; (more willingly) de mejor gana; (somewhat) algo, un poco; (perhaps) quizás; mejor dicho; (fairly) bastante; (very) muy; mucho; al contrario. **or r.,** o más bien. **anything r. than...,** todo menos... **He had r.,** Preferiría. **r. than,** antes que, en vez de

ratification /ˌrætəfɪ'keiʃən/ n ratificación, f; (of a bill) aprobación, f

ratifier /'rætəˌfaiər/ n ratificador (-ra)

ratify /'rætəˌfai/ vt ratificar

ratifying /'rætəˌfaiɪŋ/ n ratificación, f, a ratificatorio

rating /'reitɪŋ/ n tasación, f; valuación, f; clasificación, f; impuesto, m, contribución, f; repartición de impuestos, f; (of a ship's company) graduación, f; (scolding) represión, f

ratio /'reiʃou/ n razón, f; proporción, f. **in direct r.,** en razón directa

ratiocinate /ˌræʃi'ɒsəˌneit/ vi raciocinar

ratiocination /ˌræʃiˌɒsə'neiʃən/ n raciocinación, f

ration /'ræʃən, 'reiʃən/ n ración, f. vt racionar. **r.-book,** cartilla de racionamiento, f

rational /'ræʃənḷ/ a racional; razonable, juicioso. n ser racional, m

rationalism /'ræʃənḷˌɪzəm/ n racionalismo, m

rationalist /'ræʃənḷɪst/ n racionalista, mf

rationalistic /ˌræʃənḷ'ɪstɪk/ a racionalista

rationality /ˌræʃə'nælɪti/ n racionalidad, f; justicia, f

rationalization /ˌræʃənḷə'zeiʃən/ n racionalización, f; justificación, f

rationalize /'ræʃənḷˌaiz/ vt hacer racional; concebir racionalmente; Math. quitar los radicales (a); justificar

rationing /'ræʃənɪŋ, 'rei-/ n racionamiento, m

rattan /ræ'tæn/ n rota, f, bejuco, m; junquillo, m

ratteen /ræ'tin/ n ratina, f

ratter /'rætər/ n perro ratonero, m; gato que caza ratas, m

ratting /'rætɪŋ/ n caza de ratas, f; deserción, f

rattle /'rætḷ/ vi hacer ruido; rechinar, crujir; (of loose windows, etc.) zangolotearse; (knock) golpear; tocar; (patter) bailar; sonar; (of the dying) dar un estertor. vt (shake) sacudir; hacer vibrar; (jolt) traquetear; (do rapidly) acabar rápidamente; (confuse) aturdir, hacer perder la cabeza (a); desconcertar. **to r. along,** deslizarse (or correr) rápidamente. **to r. off,** (repeat) decir rápidamente; terminar apresuradamente. **to r. on about,** charlar mucho de, hablar sin cesar sobre

rattle /'rætḷ/ n rechinamiento, crujido, m; zangoloteo, m; ruido, m; son (de la lluvia, etc.), m; (in the throat) estertor, m; (of a rattlesnake) cascabel, m; (child's) sonajero, m; matraca, f; carraca, f; (chatter) charla, f. **r.-headed,** de cabeza de chorlito, casquivano

rattlesnake /'rætḷˌsneik/ n serpiente de cascabel, f, crótalo, m

rattling /'rætlɪŋ/ n See **rattle**

raucous /'rɔkəs/ a ronco, estridente

raucousness /'rɔkəsnɪs/ n ronquedad, f, estridor, m

ravage /'rævɪdʒ/ vt devastar; (pillage) saquear; destruir; (spoil) estropear. n devastación, f; destrucción, f; estrago, m

ravager /'rævɪdʒər/ n devastador (-ra); saqueador (-ra)

rave /reiv/ vi desvariar, delirar; (of the elements) bra-

mar, rugir. **to r. about,** hablar con entusiasmo de; delirar por. **to r. against,** vociferar contra, despotricarse contra

ravel /'rævəl/ vt deshilar, destejer; Fig. enredar. **to r. out,** deshilarse; Fig. desenredarse, desenmarañarse

raven /'reivən/ n cuervo, m, a negro como el azabache

ravening /'rævənɪŋ/ a rapaz, salvaje

ravenous /'rævənəs/ a voraz

ravenously /'rævənəsli/ adv vorazmente

ravenousness /'rævənəsnɪs/ n voracidad, f

ravine /rə'vin/ n cañada, f, barranco, cañón, m

raving /'reivɪŋ/ n delirio, m, desvaríos, m pl. a delirante; violento; bravío

ravioli /ˌrævi'ouli/ n pl ravioles, m pl

ravish /'rævɪʃ/ vt (carry off) arrebatar, raptar; extasiar, encantar; (rape) violar, forzar

ravisher /'rævɪʃər/ n raptador, m; violador, m

ravishing /'rævɪʃɪŋ/ n violación, f, a encantador

ravishment /'rævɪʃmənt/ n violación, f; arrobamiento, m; transporte, éxstasis, m

raw /rɔ/ a (of meat, etc., silk, leather, weather) crudo; bruto; (inexpert) bisoño; (of flesh) vivo; Com. en bruto. **raw-boned,** huesudo. **raw hand,** novato (-ta). **raw material,** primera materia, f. **raw materials,** materias primas, f pl. **raw score,** puntuación bruta, f. **raw silk,** seda cruda, seda en rama, f. **raw sugar,** azúcar bruto, m

rawhide /'rɔˌhaid/ a de cuero crudo

rawness /'rɔnɪs/ n crudeza, f; inexperiencia, f; (of weather) humedad, f

ray /rei/ n rayo, m; (line) raya, f; (radius) radio, m; (fish) raya, f. **cathode rays,** rayos catódicos, m pl

rayon /'reiɒn/ n rayón, m

raze /reiz/ vt arrasar, asolar; demoler; (erase) borrar, tachar

razor /'reizər/ n navaja, f. **electric r.,** máquina de afeitar eléctrica, f. **safety r.,** máquina de afeitar, f. **slash with a r.,** navajada, f. **r. blade,** hoja de afeitar, f. **r. case,** navajero, m. **r. strop,** suavizador, m

re /ri, rei/ n Mus. re, m; prep Law. causa, f; Com. concerniente a

re prefix (attached to verb) re-; (after the verb) de nuevo; (followed by infin.) volver a... **to re-count,** volver a contar, contar de nuevo, recontar

reabsorb /ˌriəb'sɔrb, -'zɔrb/ vt resorber

reabsorption /ˌriəb'sɔrpʃən, -'zɔrp-/ n reabsorción, resorción, f

reach /ritʃ/ vt (stretch out) alargar; extender; alcanzar; llegar hasta; (arrive at) llegar a; (achieve) lograr, obtener. vi extenderse; alcanzar; penetrar. n alcance, m; extensión, f; poder, m; capacidad, f; (of a river) tabla, f. **as far as the eye could r.,** hasta donde alcanzaba la vista. **He reached home very soon,** Llegó muy pronto a casa. **out of r.,** fuera de alcance. **to r. a deadlock,** llegar a un punto muerto. **within r.,** al alcance. **within easy r.,** de fácil acceso; a corta distancia. **to r. after,** procurar alcanzar; hacer esfuerzos para obtener. **to r. back,** (of time) remontarse. **to r. down,** bajar.

react /ri'ækt/ vi reaccionar. vt hacer de nuevo; Theat. volver a representar

reaction /ri'ækʃən/ n reacción, f

reactionary /ri'ækʃəˌnɛri/ a and n reaccionario (-ia)

reactive /ri'æktɪv/ a reactivo

read /rid/ vt leer; (a riddle, etc.) adivinar; descifrar; interpretar; (study) estudiar; (the Burial Service, etc.) decir; (correct) corregir; (of thermometers, etc.) marcar. vi leer; estudiar; (be written) estar escrito, decir. **The play acts better than it reads,** La comedia es mejor representada que leída. **to r. aloud,** leer en voz alta. **to r. between the lines,** leer entre líneas. **to r. proofs,** corregir pruebas. **to r. to oneself,** leer para sí. **to r. about,** leer; (learn) enterarse de. **to r. again,** volver a leer, leer otra vez. **to r. on,** continuar leyendo. **to r. out,** leer en alta voz. **to r. over,** leer; leerlo todo. **to r. over and over again,** leer muchas veces, leer y releer.

read /rɛd/ past part leído, etc. **well-r.,** releído; instruido, culto

readability /ˌridəˈbɪlɪti/ n legibilidad, f; interés, m, amenidad, f

readable /ˈridəbəl/ a legible; interesante

readdress /ˌriəˈdrɛs/ vt dirigir de nuevo (una carta, etc.); poner la nueva dirección en (una carta, etc.)

reader /ˈridər/ n lector (-ra); Eccl. lector, m; (proof) corrector de pruebas, m; (citation collector for a dictionary) cedulista, mf; (university) profesor (-ra) auxiliar a cátedra; (book) libro de lectura, m. **to be a great r.**, leer mucho. **the Spanish r.** (reader of Spanish books) el lector de español

readily /ˈrɛdli/ adv fácilmente; en seguida, inmediatamente; de buena gana, con placer

readiness /ˈrɛdinɪs/ n prontitud, expedición, f; buena voluntad, f; (of speech, etc.) facilidad, f. **in r.**, preparado. **r. of wit**, viveza de ingenio, f

reading /ˈridɪŋ/ n lectura, Lat. Am. also leída, f; (erudition) conocimientos, m pl; (recital) declamación, f; (lecture) conferencia, f; (study) estudio, m; interpretación, f; (of a thermometer, etc.) registro, m; (of a will) apertura, f. **at one reading**, Lat. Am. de una leída. **r.-book**, libro de lectura, m. **r.-desk**, atril, m. **r.-glass**, lente para leer, m, carlita, f. **r.-lamp**, lámpara de sobremesa, f. **r.-matter**, material de lectura, m. **r.-room**, gabinete de lectura, m, sala de lectura, f

readjourn /ˌriəˈdʒɜrn/ vt (a meeting) suspender (la sesión) de nuevo

readjust /ˌriəˈdʒʌst/ vt reajustar, reacomdar; vi reacomodarse

readjustment /ˌriəˈdʒʌstmənt/ n reajuste, m, reacomodación, f

readmission /ˌriədˈmɪʃən/ n readmisión, f

ready /ˈrɛdi/ a listo, preparado; dispuesto; pronto; (on the point of) a punto de; (easy) fácil; (near at hand) a la mano; (with money) contante; (with wit, etc.) vivo; (available) disponible; (nimble) ágil, ligero. **I am r. to do it**, Estoy dispuesto a hacerlo. **in r. cash**, en dinero contante. **to get r.**, prepararse; (dress) vestirse. **to make r.**, vt preparar; aprestar; Print. imponer. vi prepararse, disponerse. **r.-made**, hecho; confeccionado. **r.-made clothing**, ropa hecha, f. **r. money**, dinero contante, m. **r.-witted**, de ingenio vivo

reaffirm /ˌriəˈfɜrm/ vt afirmar de nuevo; reiterar, volver a repetir

reaffirmation /ˌriæfərˈmeɪʃən/ n reiteración, f

reagent /riˈeɪdʒənt/ n reactivo, m

real /ˈreiˈɑl/ a real; verdadero; efectivo; (with silk, etc.) puro; sincero. **r. estate, r. property**, bienes raíces, m pl

realism /ˈriəˌlɪzəm/ n realismo, m

realist /ˈriəlɪst/ n realista, mf

realistic /ˌriəˈlɪstɪk/ a realista

reality /riˈælɪti/ n realidad, f; verdad, f

realizable /ˌriəˈlaizəbəl/ a realizable; factible

realization /ˌriələˈzeɪʃən/ n realización, f; comprensión, f

realize /ˈriəˌlaiz/ vt (understand) darse cuenta de, hacerse cargo de; realizar; (make real) dar vida (a); (accomplish) llevar a cabo; Com. realizar; (gain) adquirir

really /ˈriəli/ adv realmente; en verdad; en realidad; en efecto; (frankly) francamente. **R.?** ¿De veras?

realm /rɛlm/ n reino, m, dominios, m pl; Fig. esfera, f

realty /ˈriəlti/ n bienes raíces, m pl

ream /rim/ n resma, f

reanimate /ˌriˈænəˌmeit/ vt reanimar

reap /rip/ vt segar; Fig. cosechar, recoger

reaper /ˈripər/ n segador (-ra); (machine) segadora mecánica, f

reaping /ˈripɪŋ/ n siega, f; Fig. cosecha, f. **r.-machine**, segadora mecánica, f

reappear /ˌriəˈpɪər/ vi reaparecer

reappearance /ˌriəˈpɪərəns/ n reaparición, f

reapplication /ˌriæplɪˈkeɪʃən/ n nueva aplicación, f; (of paint, etc.) otra capa, f; (for a post, etc.) neuva solicitud, f

reapply /ˌriəˈplai/ vt aplicar de nuevo; (paint, etc.) dar otra capa (de); (for a post, etc.) mandar una nueva solicitud

reappoint /ˌriəˈpɔint/ vt designar de nuevo

rear /riər/ vt (lift) alzar, levantar; (breed, educate) criar; (build) erigir, construir. vi (of horses) encabritarse, corcovear

rear /riər/ n cola, f; parte de atrás, f; parte posterior, f; última fila, f; (background) fondo, m; Inf. trasera, f; Mil. retaguardia, f. a de atrás; trasero; último; posterior; de última fila; Mil. de retaguardia. **in the r.**, por detrás; a la cola; a retaguardia. **to bring up the r.**, cerrar la marcha. **r.-admiral**, contra almirante, m. **r.-axle**, eje trasero, m. **r.-guard**, retaguardia, f. **r. lamp**, faro trasero, m. **r. rank**, última fila, f. **r. view**, vista por detrás, f; vista posterior, f

rearing /ˈriərɪŋ/ n (breeding) cría, f; (education) crianza, f

rearm /riˈɑrm/ vt rearmar. vi rearmarse

rearmament /riˈɑrməmənt/ n rearmamento, m

rearrange /ˌriəˈreindʒ/ vt volver a arreglar; arreglar de otra manera; (a literary work) refundir, adaptar

rearrangement /ˌriəˈreindʒmənt/ n nuevo arroglo, m; (of a literary work) refundición, adaptación, f

reascend /ˌriəˈsɛnd/ vi and vt subir de nuevo, subir otra vez; montar de nuevo (sobre)

reason /ˈrizən/ n razón, f. **I have plenty of r. to...** No me faltarían motivos para... vi and vt razonar. **to r. out of**, disuadir de. **by r. of**, a causa de, con motivo de; en virtud de. **for this r.**, por esto, por esta razón. **out of all r.**, fuera de razón. **to stand to r.**, ser lógico, estar puesto en razón. **with r.**, con razón. **r. of state**, razón de estado, f

reasonable /ˈrizənəbəl/ a razonable; racional

reasonableness /ˈrizənəbəlnɪs/ n lo razonable; moderación, f; justicia, f; racionalidad, f

reasonably /ˈrizənəbli/ adv razonablemente; con razón; bastante

reasoning /ˈrizənɪŋ/ n razonamiento, m

reassemble /ˌriəˈsɛmbəl/ vt reunir otra vez. vi juntarse de nuevo

reassert /ˌriəˈsɜrt/ vt afirmar de nuevo, reiterar

reassertion /ˌriəˈsɜrʃən/ n reiteración, f

reassess /ˌriəˈsɛs/ vt tasar de nuevo; repartir de nuevo; (a work of art) hacer una nueva apreciación (de)

reassessment /ˌriəˈsɛsmənt/ n nueva tasación, f; nuevo repartimiento, m; (of a work of art) nueva estimación, f

reassume /ˌriəˈsum/ vt reasumir

reassumption /ˌriəˈsʌmpʃən/ n reasunción, f

reassurance /ˌriəˈsʊrəns/ n afirmación repetida, f; confianza restablecida, f

reassure /ˌriəˈʃʊr/ vt asegurar de nuevo; tranquilizar, confortar

reassuring /ˌriəˈʃʊrɪŋ/ a tranquilizador, consolador

rebate /ˈribeit/ n rebaja, f, descuento, m; reducción, f. vt rebajar, descontar; reducir. **to r. pro rata**, ratear

rebec /ˈribɛk/ n Mus. rabel, m

rebel / n. ˈrɛbəl; v. rɪˈbɛl/ n rebelde, mf, insurrecto (-ta). vi rebelarse, sublevarse. **r. leader**, cabecilla, m

rebellion /rɪˈbɛlyən/ n rebelión, f

rebellious /rɪˈbɛlyəs/ a rebelde; revoltoso; refractario

rebelliousness /rɪˈbɛlyəsnɪs/ n rebeldía, f

rebind /riˈbaind/ vt atar de nuevo; (a book) reencuadernar

rebirth /riˈbɜrθ/ n renacimiento, m

rebore /riˈbɔr/ vt (an engine) descarbonizar

reboring /riˈbɔrɪŋ/ n (of an engine) descarburación, f

reborn, to be /riˈbɔrn/ vi renacer; ser reincarnado, m; (Christianity) ser naciado (-da) de nuevo

rebound /v. rɪˈbaund; n. ˈri,baund/ a (of books) reencuadernado, m. vi rebotar; repercutir; (revive) reavivarse. n rebote, resalto, m; reacción, f, rechazo, m

rebuff /rɪˈbʌf/ n repulsa, f, desaire, m; contrariedad, f. vt rechazar; contrariar

rebuild /riˈbɪld/ vt reedificar

rebuilding /riˈbɪldɪŋ/ n reedificación, f

rebuke /rɪˈbyuk/ n reconvención, reprensión, censura, f, reproche, m, vt reprender, censurar, reprochar

rebukingly /rɪˈbyukɪŋli/ adv en tono de censura; con reprensión, con reprobación

rebut /rɪˈbʌt/ vt refutar

rebuttal /rɪˈbʌtl/ n refutación, f

recalcitrance /rɪ'kælsɪtrəns/ n terquedad, obstinacia, f; rebeldía, f
recalcitrant /rɪ'kælsɪtrənt/ a reacio, recalcitrante
recall / v. rɪ'kɔl; n. also 'rikɔl/ vt llamar; hacer volver; (dismiss) destituir; (ambassador, etc.) retirar; (remind or remember) recordar; (revoke) revocar. n llamada, f; Mil. toque de llamada, m; (of ambassadors, etc.) retirada, f; (dismissal) destitución, f. **beyond r.**, irrevocable; (forgotten) olvidado
recant /rɪ'kænt/ vt retractar, retirar. vi desdecirse (de), retractarse
recantation /ˌrikæn'teɪʃən/ n recantación, f
recapitulate /ˌrikə'pɪtʃə,leɪt/ vt recapitular, resumir
recapitulation /ˌrikə,pɪtʃə'leɪʃən/ n recapitulación, f
recapture /ri'kæptʃər/ vt volver a prender, hacer prisionero nuevamente; (a place) volver a tomar; (a ship) represar
recast /ri'kæst/ vt (metals, a literary work) refundir; (alter) cambiar; (reckon) volver a calcular
recasting /ri'kæstɪŋ/ n (metals, a literary work) refundición, f
recede /ri'sid/ vi retroceder; alejarse (de), separarse (de); desviarse (de); retirarse; desaparecer; (diminish) disminuir; (of prices) bajar
receding /ri'sidɪŋ/ a que retrocede, etc.
receipt /rɪ'sit/ n recibo, m; (for money) recibí, m; (recipe) receta, f; pl **receipts**, ingresos, m pl. vt firmar (or extender) recibo. **on r. of**, al recibir. **to acknowledge the r. of**, acusar recibo de. **r. book**, libro talonario, m
receive /rɪ'siv/ vt and vi recibir; admitir, aceptar; acoger; (money) percibir, cobrar; (lodge) hospedar, alojar; (contain) contener. **to r. one's degree,** Lat. Am. diplomarse. **to be well received,** tener buena acogida
receiver /rɪ'sivər/ n recibidor (-ra); (of stolen goods) receptador (-ra); (in bankruptcies) síndico, m; (for other legal business) receptor, m; (of a telephone) auricular, m; Elec. receptor, m; Radio. radiorreceptor, m. **to hang up (the r.),** colgar (el auricular)
receivership /rɪ'sivər,ʃip/ n sindicatura, f; receptoría, f
receiving /rɪ'sivɪŋ/ n recibimiento, m; (of money, etc.) cobranza, f, percibo, m; (of stolen goods) encubrimiento, m. a que recibe; recipiente; de recepción. **r. set,** aparato de radio, m
recency /'risənsi/ n lo reciente; novedad, f
recent /'risənt/ a reciente; nuevo. **in r. years,** en estos últimos años
recently /'risəntli/ adv recientemente; (before past participles) recién. **until r.,** hasta hace poco. **r. painted,** recién pintado
receptacle /rɪ'sɛptəkəl/ n receptáculo, recipiente, m; Bot. receptáculo, m
reception /rɪ'sɛpʃən/ n recepción, f; recibo, m; (welcome) acogida, f; (of evidence) recepción, f. **r. room,** pieza de recibo, f, gabinete, m
receptive /rɪ'sɛptɪv/ a receptivo; susceptible
receptiveness /rɪ'sɛptɪvnɛs/ n sensibilidad, susceptibilidad, f
recess /rɪ'sɛs, 'risɛs/ n (holiday) vacaciones, f pl; (during school hours) hora de recreo, f; (Fig. heart) seno, m, entrañas, f pl; (of the soul, heart) hondón, m; (in a coastline, etc.) depresión, f; (in a wall) nicho, m; (alcove) alcoba, f. **parliamentary r.,** interregno parlamentario, m
recessional /rɪ'sɛʃənl/ n himno que se canta mientras se retiran los eclesiásticos y el coro, m
recharge /ri'tʃɑrdʒ/ vt (a gun, etc.) recargar; acusar de nuevo
recipe /'rɛsəpi/ n receta, f
recipient /rɪ'sɪpiənt/ n recibidor (-ra); el, m, (f, la) que recibe. a recipiente; receptivo
reciprocal /rɪ'sɪprəkəl/ a recíproco
reciprocate /rɪ'sɪprə,keɪt/ vt reciprocar; Mech. producir movimiento de vaivén. vi Mech. oscilar, tener movimiento alternativo; corresponder; ser recíproco
reciprocation /rɪ,sɪprə'keɪʃən/ n reciprocación, f; reciprocidad, correspondencia, f
reciprocity /ˌrɛsə'prɒsɪti/ n reciprocidad, f
recital /rɪ'saɪtl/ n narración, relación, f; enumeración, f; recitación, f; Mus. recital, m

recitation /ˌrɛsɪ'teɪʃən/ n recitación, f
recitative /ˌrɛsɪtə'tiv/ n recitado, m
recite /rɪ'saɪt/ vt recitar, repetir; narrar; declamar. vi decir una recitación
reciter /rɪ,saɪtər/ n recitador (-ra); declamador (-ra)
reckless /'rɛklɪs/ a temerario, audaz; precipitado; descuidado (de); indiferente (a); excesivo; imprudente
recklessly /'rɛklɪsli/ adv temerariamente; descuidadamente; imprudentemente
recklessness /'rɛklɪsnɪs/ n temeridad, audacia, f; descuido, m; imprudencia, f; indiferencia, f
reckon /'rɛkən/ vt calcular, computar; contar; enumerar; (believe) considerar, juzgar; (attribute) atribuir; (think) creer (que). **to r. up,** echar cuentas, calcular. **to r. with,** contar; tomar en serio
reckoner /'rɛkənər/ n calculador (-ra). **ready r.,** tablas matemáticas, f pl
reckoning /'rɛkənɪŋ/ n cálculo, m, calculación, f; cuenta, f; Fig. retribución, f, castigo, m; Naut. estima, f. **the day of r.,** el día de ajuste de cuentas; el día del juicio final. **to be out in one's r.,** equivocarse en el cálculo; engañarse en el juicio
reclaim /rɪ'kleɪm/ vt (land) entarquinar; (reform) reformar; (tame) domesticar; (claim) reclamar; (restore) restaurar
reclamation /ˌrɛklə'meɪʃən/ n (of land) entarquinamiento, m; cultivo, m; (reform) reformación, f; (restoration) restauración, f; (claiming) reclamación, f
recline /rɪ'klaɪn/ vt apoyar; recostar; reclinar; descansar, reposar. vi recostarse, reclinarse; estar tumbado; apoyarse; descansar
reclining /rɪ'klaɪnɪŋ/ n reclinación, f. a inclinado; acostado; (of statues) yacente
recluse /'rɛklus, rɪ'klus/ a solitario, n recluso (-sa); solitario (-ia); ermitaño, m, anacoreta, mf
recognition /ˌrɛkəg'nɪʃən/ n reconocimiento, m
recognizable /ˌrɛkəg'naɪzəbəl/ a que puede reconocerse; identificable
recognizance /rɪ'kɒgnəzəns, -'kɒnə-/ n reconocimiento, m; Law. obligación, f
recognize /'rɛkəg,naɪz/ vt reconocer; confesar
recoil /n. 'ri,kɔɪl; v. rɪ'kɔɪl/ n reculada, f; (of a gun) culatazo, m; (refusal) rechazo, m; (result) repercusión, f; (repugnance) aversión, repugnancia, f. vi recular; retroceder; repercutir; sentir repugnancia
recoin /ri'kɔɪn/ vt acuñar de nuevo
recollect /ˌrɛkə'lɛkt/ vt acordarse de, recordar. **to r. oneself,** reponerse, recobrarse
recollection /ˌrɛkə'lɛkʃən/ n recuerdo, m, memoria, f
recommence /ˌrikə'mɛns/ vt and vi empezar de nuevo
recommend /ˌrɛkə'mɛnd/ vt recomendar; aconsejar; encargar
recommendable /ˌrɛkə'mɛndəbəl/ a recomendable
recommendation /ˌrɛkəmɛn'deɪʃən/ n recomendación, f
recommendatory /ˌrɛkə'mɛndə,tɔri/ a recomendatario
recommender /ˌrɛkə'mɛndər/ n el, m, (f, la) que recomienda
recompense /'rɛkəm,pɛns/ n recompensa, f, vt recompensar
recomposition /ˌrikɒmpə'zɪʃən/ n recomposición, f
reconcilability /ˌrɛkən,saɪlə'bɪlɪti/ n posibilidad de conciliación, f; compatibilidad, f
reconcilable /ˌrɛkən'saɪləbəl/ a reconciliable; compatible; conciliable
reconcile /'rɛkən,saɪl/ vt reconciliar; (quarrels) componer, ajustar; (opposing theories, etc.) conciliar; (accounts) ajustar. **to r. oneself (to),** aceptar; acostumbrarse (a); resignarse (a)
reconciler /'rɛkən,saɪlər/ n reconciliador (-ra)
reconciliation /ˌrɛkən,sɪli'eɪʃən/ n reconciliación, f; (of theories, etc.) conciliación, f; (of accounts) ajuste, m
reconciliatory /ˌrɛkən'sɪliə,tɔri/ a reconciliador
recondite /'rɛkən,daɪt/ a recóndito
recondition /ˌrikən'dɪʃən/ vt reacondicionar
reconnaissance /rɪ'kɒnəsəns, -zəns/ n reconoci-

redoubt

miento, *m*; exploración, *f*. **r. flight,** vuelo de reconocimiento, *m*. **r. plane,** avión de reconocimiento, *m*
reconnoiter /ˌrikəˈnɔitər/ *vt Mil.* reconocer; explorar. *vi Mil.* practicar un reconocimiento; correr la campaña
reconnoitering /ˌrikəˈnɔitəriŋ/ *n* reconocimiento, *m*, *a* de reconocimiento
reconquer /riˈkɒŋkər/ *vt* reconquistar
reconquest /ˈrikɒŋkwɛst/ *n* reconquista, *f*
reconsecrate /riˈkɒnsɪˌkreit/ *vt* consagrar de nuevo
reconsider /ˌrikənˈsɪdər/ *vt* considerar de nuevo, volver a considerar; volver a discutir
reconsideration /ˌrikənˌsɪdəˈreiʃən/ *n* nueva consideración, *f*; nueva discusión, *f*
reconstitute /riˈkɒnstɪˌtut/ *vt* reconstituir
reconstitution /riˌkɒnstɪˈtuʃən/ *n* reconstitución, *f*
reconstruct /ˌrikənˈstrʌkt/ *vt* reconstruir
reconstruction /ˌrikənˈstrʌkʃən/ *n* reconstrucción, *f*
reconversion /ˌrikənˈvɜrʒən/ *n* reconversión, *f*
recopy /riˈkɒpi/ *vt* copiar de nuevo
record /v. rɪˈkɔrd; *n.* ˈrɛkərd/ *vt* apuntar; inscribir; (recount) contar, escribir; recordar; registrar; (of thermometers, etc.) marcar, registrar; hacer un disco de gramófono de; (radio, cinema) impresionar. *n* relación, *f*; crónica, *f*; historia, *f*; (soldier's) hoja de servicios, *f*; (past) antecedentes, *m pl*; documento, *m*; inscripción, *f*; (entry) partida, *f*; testimonio, *m*; (memory) recuerdo, *m*; registro, *m*; (phonograph) disco, *m*; *Sports.* record, *m*, plusmarca, *f*; *pl* **records,** *m pl*; (notes) notas, *f pl*; (facts) datos, *m pl*; anales, *m pl*. **keeper of the records,** archivero, *m*. **off the r.,** confidencialmente. **on r.,** escrito; registrado; inscrito en los anales de la historia. **to break a r.,** supremar precedentes. **r.-holder,** plusmarquista, *mf*
recorder /rɪˈkɔrdər/ *n* registrador, *m*; archivero, *m*; *Law.* juez, *m*; (historian) historiador, *m*; *Mus.* caramillo, *m*; *Mech.* contador, indicador, *m*; (scientific) aparato registrador, *m*
recording /rɪˈkɔrdiŋ/ *a* registrador. **r. apparatus,** (cinema, radio, record player) máquina de impresionar, *f*; (scientific) aparato registrador, *m*. **r. van,** carro de sonido, *m*
recount /rɪˈkaunt/ *vt* contar de nuevo; (tell) referir, narrar, contar
recoup /rɪˈkup/ *vt* compensar, indemnizar; recobrar, desquitarse de
recourse /ˈrikɔrs/ *n* recurso, *m*. **to have r. to,** recurrir a
recover /rɪˈkʌvər/ *vt* (regain) recobrar; *Fig.* reconquistar; (retrieve) rescatar; *Law.* reivindicar. *vi* reponerse; (in health) recuperarse, recobrar la salud, sanar, curarse; *Law.* ganar un pleito. **to r. consciousness,** volver en sí
recoverable /rɪˈkʌvərəbəl/ *a* recuperable
recovery /rɪˈkʌvəri/ *n* (regaining) recobro, *m*, recuperación, *f*; (of money) cobranza, *f*; (retrieval) rescate, *m*; *Fig.* reconquista, *f*; (from illness) mejoría, convalecencia, *f*; restablecimiento, *m*; *Law.* reivindicación, *f*
recreant /ˈrɛkriənt/ *a* traidor, falso, desleal. *n* apóstata, *mf* traidor (-ra)
recreate /ˈrikriˌeit/ *vt* recrear
recreation /ˌrɛkriˈeiʃən/ *n* recreación, *f*; (break in schools) recreo, *m*. **r. hall,** sala de recreo, *f*
recreative /ˈrɛkriˌeitiv/ *a* recreativo
recriminate /rɪˈkrɪməˌneit/ *vi* recriminar
recrimination /rɪˌkrɪməˈneiʃən/ *n* recriminación, reconvención, *f*
recriminator /rɪˈkrɪməˌneitər/ *n* recriminador (-ra)
recriminatory /rɪˈkrɪmənəˌtɔri/ *a* recriminador
recross /riˈkrɔs/ *vt* volver a cruzar, cruzar de nuevo
recrudesce /ˌrikruˈdɛs/ *vi* recrudecer
recrudescence /ˌrikruˈdɛsəns/ *n* recrudescencia, *f*
recrudescent /ˌrikruˈdɛsənt/ *a* recrudescente
recruit /rɪˈkrut/ *n* recluta, *m*. *vt* reclutar; (restore) reponer
recruiting /rɪˈkrutiŋ/ *n* reclutamiento, *m*. **r. office,** caja de reclutamiento, *f*
rectal /ˈrɛktl̩/ *a* rectal
rectangle /ˈrɛkˌtæŋɡəl/ *n* rectángulo, *m*
rectangular /rɛkˈtæŋɡyələr/ *a* rectangular

rectifiable /ˈrɛktəˌfaiəbəl/ *a* rectificable
rectification /ˌrɛktəfɪˈkeiʃən/ *n* rectificación, *f*
rectifier /ˈrɛktəˌfaiər/ *n* rectificador, *m*
rectify /ˈrɛktəˌfai/ *vt* rectificar
rectilinear /ˌrɛktl̩ˈɪniər/ *a* rectilíneo
rectitude /ˈrɛktɪˌtud/ *n* rectitud, *f*
rector /ˈrɛktər/ *n* (of a university or school) rector, *m*; (priest) párroco, *m*
rectorship /ˈrɛktərˌʃip/ *n* rectorado, *m*
rectory /ˈrɛktəri/ *n* rectoral, rectoría, *f*
rectum /ˈrɛktəm/ *n* recto, *m*
recumbent /rɪˈkʌmbənt/ *a* recostado, reclinado; (of a statue) yacente
recuperable /rɪˈkupərəbəl/ *a* recuperable
recuperate /rɪˈkupəˌreit/ *vt* recuperar, recobrar. *vi* restablecerse, reponerse; recuperarse
recuperation /rɪkupəˈreiʃən/ *n* recuperación, *f*
recuperative /rɪˈkupərətiv/ *a* recuperativo
recur /rɪˈkɜr/ *vi* presentarse a la imaginación; volver (sobre); presentarse de nuevo, aparecer otra vez; repetirse; reproducirse
recurrence /rɪˈkɜrəns/ *n* reaparición, *f*; repetición, *f*
recurrent /rɪˈkɜrənt/ *a* periódico; *Med.* recurrente
recycle /riˈsaikəl/ *vt* reciclar
red /rɛd/ *a* rojo; (of wine) tinto. *n* color rojo, *m*; (in billiards) mingo, *m*, bola roja, *f*; *Polit.* rojo, *m*. **to catch red-handed,** coger con el hurto en las manos; coger con las manos en la masa, coger en el acto. **to grow red,** enrojecerse, ponerse rojo; volverse rojo. **red-berried,** con bayas rojas. **red cabbage,** lombarda, *f*. **red cedar,** cedro dulce, *m*. **red corpuscle,** glóbulo rojo, *m*. **Red Cross,** Cruz Roja, *f*. **red currant,** grosella, *f*. **red currant bush,** grosellero, *m*. **red-eyed,** con los ojos inyectados. **red fir,** pino silvestre, *m*. **red flush,** (in the sky) arrebol, *m*. **red-gold,** bermejo; (of hair, etc.) rojo. **red-haired,** pelirrojo, de pelo rojo. **red-handed,** con las manos ensangrentadas; *Fig.* en el acto. **red-head** (person) pelirrojo (-ja). **red-heat,** incandescencia, *f*. **red-hot,** candente. *m*. **red-lead,** minio, *m*. **red-letter,** de fiesta; extraordinario. **red-letter day,** día de fiesta, *m*; día extraordinario, *m*. **red mullet,** salmonete, *m*, trilla, *f*. **red ocher,** almagre, *m*. **red pepper,** pimiento, *m*; (cayenne) pimentón, *Lat. Am.* ají, *m*, **Red Sea,** mar Rojo, mar Bermejo, *m*. **red tape,** balduque, *m*; formulismo, *m*; burocracia, *f*. **red wine,** vino tinto, *m*
redbreast /ˈrɛdˌbrɛst/ *n* petirrojo, *m*
redden /ˈrɛdn̩/ *vt* rojear, enrojecer; pintar de rojo. *vi* enrojecerse, ponerse rojo; volverse rojo
reddish /ˈrɛdɪʃ/ *a* rojizo
redeem /rɪˈdim/ *vt* (a mortgage, bonds, etc.) amortizar; (from pawn) desempeñar; (a promise, etc.) cumplir; libertar; redimir; compensar; (a fault) expiar; (reform) reformar; (rescue) rescatar
redeemable /rɪˈdiməbəl/ *a* redimible; amortizable
redeemer /rɪˈdimər/ *n* rescatador (-ra); salvador (-ra); *Theol.* Redentor, *m*
redeeming /rɪˈdimiŋ/ *a* redentor; compensatorio. **r. feature,** compensación, *f*; rasgo bueno, *m*. **There is no r. feature in his work,** No hay nada bueno en su obra
redemption /rɪˈdɛmpʃən/ *n* (of a mortgage, etc.) amortización, *f*; (from pawn) desempeño, *m*; (of a promise, etc.) cumplimiento, *m*; (ransom, etc.) rescate, *m*; *Theol.* redención, *f*; compensación, *f*; (of a fault) expiación, *f*; reformación, *f*
redemptive /rɪˈdɛmptiv/ *a* redentor
redescend /ˌridɪˈsɛnd/ *vi* bajar de nuevo
rediscovery /ˌridɪˈskʌvəri/ *n* nuevo descubrimiento, *m*
redistribute /ˌridɪˈstribyut/ *vt* distribuir de nuevo, volver a distribuir
redistribution /ˌridɪstrəˈbyuʃən/ *n* nueva distribución, *f*
redness /ˈrɛdnɪs/ *n* rojez, *f*, color rojo, *m*
redolent /ˈrɛdl̩ənt/ *a* fragante, oloroso; *Fig.* evocador (de)
redouble /riˈdʌbəl/ *vt* redoblar. *vi* redoblarse
redoubling /riˈdʌbliŋ/ *n* redoblamiento, *m*
redoubt /rɪˈdaut/ *n* reducto, *m*

redoubtable /rɪ'dautəbəl/ a formidable, terrible; valiente

redound /rɪ'daund/ vi redundar (en)

redress /rɪ'drɛs/ vt rectificar; reparar; remediar; hacer justicia (a); corregir

reduce /rɪ'dus/ vt reducir; disminuir; (in price) rebajar; abreviar; (exhaust, weaken) agotar; (impoverish) empobrecer; (degrade) degradar. **to r. to the ranks,** *Mil.* volver a las filas; degradar. **to be in reduced circumstances,** estar en la indigencia

reducible /rɪ'dusəbəl/ a reducible

reduction /rɪ'dʌkʃən/ n reducción, f; (in price) rebaja, f

redundance /rɪ'dʌndəns/ n redundancia, f

redundant /rɪ'dʌndənt/ a redundante; superfluo, excesivo

reduplicate /rɪ'dupli,keit/ vt reduplicar

reduplication /rɪ,dupli'keiʃən/ n reduplicación, f

reecho /ri'ɛkou/ vt repetir; devolver el son de, hacer reverberar. vi repercutirse, reverberar

reed /rid/ n Bot. caña, f; (arrow) saeta, f; (pipe) caramillo, m; (in wind-instruments) lengüeta, f; Archit. junquillo, m; (in a loom) peine, m; (pastoral poetry) poesía bucólica, f. vt (thatch) bardar con cañas

reedit /ri'ɛdɪt/ vt reeditar, volver a editar

reedy /'ridi/ a juncoso, lleno de cañas; (of the voice) silbante

reef /rif/ n arrecife, escollo, encalladero, m; Mineral. filón, m; Naut. rizo, m. vt Naut. arrizar. **to take in reefs,** Naut. hacer el rizo. **r.-knot,** nudo de marino, m

reek /rik/ n humo, m; olor, m. vi humear; oler (de); Fig. recordar, hacer pensar (en)

reeky /'riki/ a humoso

reel /ril/ n carrete, m; devanadera, f; (of a fishing rod) carrete, carretel, m; (cinema) cinta, f; (dance) baile escocés, m. vt devanar. vi tambalear, titubear; (of ships, etc.) cabecear; temblar; oscilar. **to r. about drunkenly,** (of persons) andar haciendo eses, arrimarse a las paredes. **to r. off,** recitar; enumerar; decir rápidamente

reelect /,rii'lɛkt/ vt reelegir

reelection /,rii'lɛkʃən/ n reelección, f

reeligible /ri'ɛlidʒəbəl/ a reelegible

reeling /'rilɪŋ/ n tambaleo, m; andar vacilante, m; (of a ship, etc.) cabeceo, m; oscilación, f

reembarcation /,riembar'keiʃən/ n reembarque, m

reembark /,riem'bark/ vt reembarcar. vi reembarcarse

reemerge /,rii'mɜrdʒ/ vi reaparecer

reemergence /,rii'mɜrdʒəns/ n reaparición, f

reenact /,rii'nækt/ vt revalidar (una ley); decretar de nuevo

reenactment /,rii'næktmənt/ n revalidación (de una ley), f; nuevo decreto, m

reengage /,riin'geidʒ/ vt contratar de nuevo

reengagement /,riin'geidʒmənt/ n nuevo contrato, m

reenlist /,riin'lɪst/ vt and vi alistar(se) de nuevo

reenlistment /,riin'lɪstmənt/ n reenganche, m

reenter /ri'ɛntər/ vt volver a entrar (en); reingresar (en)

reentry /ri'ɛntri/ n segunda entrada, f, reingreso, m

reequip /,rii'kwɪp/ vt equipar de nuevo

reestablish /,rii'stæblɪʃ/ vt restablecer; restaurar

reestablishment /,rii'stæblɪʃmənt/ n restablecimiento, m; restauración, f

reexamination /,riig,zæmi'neiʃən/ n reexaminación, f; nuevo examen, m; Law. nuevo interrogatorio, m

reexamine /,riig'zæmɪn/ vt reexaminar; Law. interrogar de nuevo

refashion /ri'fæʃən/ vt volver a hacer; formar de nuevo

refection /rɪ'fɛkʃən/ n refección, f

refectory /rɪ'fɛktəri/ n refectorio, m

refer /rɪ'fɜr/ vt atribuir (a); (send) enviar, remitir; (assign) referir (a), relacionar (con). vi referirse (a); aludir (a); hablar (de)

referee /,rɛfə'ri/ n árbitro, m; Law. juez arbitrador, m; (reference) garante, mf fiador (-ra). vi servir de árbitro

reference /'rɛfərəns/ n referencia, f; consulta, f; mención, f; alusión, f; (relation) relación, f; pl **references,** Com. referencias, f pl. **for r.,** para consulta. **in r. to,** con referencia a, respecto a, en cuanto a. **terms of r.,** puntos de consulta, m pl. **work of r.,** libro de consulta, m

reference book n libro de consulta, m

referendum /,rɛfə'rɛndəm/ n referéndum, m

refill /v. ri'fɪl; n. 'ri,fɪl/ vt rellenar; rehenchir; (pen) llenar de nuevo con tinta. n (for a pencil) mina de recambio, f

refine /rɪ'fain/ vt refinar; (metals) acrisolar; (fats) clarificar; Fig. perfeccionar, pulir, refinar

refined /rɪ'faind/ a refinado; fino; culto; cortés; elegante; delicado; (subtle) sutil; (affected) afectado

refinement /rɪ'fainmənt/ n refinamiento, f; finura, f; cultura, f; cortesía, f; elegancia, f; delicadeza, f; (subtlety) sutileza, f; (affectation) afectación, f

refiner /rɪ'fainər/ n refinador, m

refinery /rɪ'fainəri/ n refinería, f

refining /rɪ'fainɪŋ/ n refinación, f; Fig. refinamiento, m

refit /ri'fɪt/ vt reparar; Naut. embonar

refitting /ri'fɪtɪŋ/ n reparación, f; Naut. embonada, f

reflect /rɪ'flɛkt/ vt reflejar; reflexionar. vi reflejar; reflexionar (sobre), pensar (en), meditar (sobre). **This offer reflects credit on him,** Esta oferta le hace honor. **to r. on, upon,** reflexionar sobre; (disparage) desacreditar; (affect unfavorably) perjudicar

reflecting /rɪ'flɛktɪŋ/ a reflector

reflection /rɪ'flɛkʃən/ n Phys. reflexión, f; reflejo, m; consideración, f, pensamiento, m; (aspersion) censura, f, reproche, m. **upon mature r.,** después de pensarlo bien

reflective /rɪ'flɛktɪv/ a Phys. reflector; reflexivo, pensativo, meditabundo

reflectively /rɪ'flɛktɪvli/ adv reflexivamente

reflector /rɪ'flɛktər/ n reflector, m; (shade) pantalla, f

reflex /'riflɛks/ a reflejo. n reflejo, m; acción refleja, f. **r. action,** acción refleja, f

refloat /ri'flout/ vt (a ship) poner otra vex a flote, desvarar

reflux /'ri,flʌks/ n reflujo, m

reforestation /ri,fɔrə'steiʃən/ n nuevas plantaciones, f pl

reform /rɪ'fɔrm/ n reforma, f. a de reforma; reformista. vt reformar; formar de nuevo. vi reformarse

reformation /,rɛfər'meiʃən/ n reformación, f; **Reformation,** Reforma, f

reformatory /rɪ'fɔrmə,tɔri/ a reformatorio, reformador. n reformatorio, m, casa de corrección, f

reformer /rɪ'fɔrmər/ n reformador (-ra), reformista, mf

refract /rɪ'frækt/ vt refractar

refraction /rɪ'frækʃən/ n refracción, f

refractive /rɪ'fræktɪv/ a refringente

refractoriness /rɪ'fræktərinɪs/ n terquedad, obstinacia, f; rebeldía, indocilidad, f

refractory /rɪ'fræktəri/ a (of substances) refractario; recalcitrante, intratable, rebelde

refrain /rɪ'frein/ n estribillo, estrambote, m

refrain /rɪ'frein/ vi abstenerse (de), evitar

refresh /rɪ'frɛʃ/ vt refrescar

refreshing /rɪ'frɛʃɪŋ/ a refrescante; atractivo; estimulante; interesante

refreshment /rɪ'frɛʃmənt/ n (solace) solaz, reposo, m; recreación, f, deleite, m; (food and (or) drink) refresco, m. **r.-room,** (at a station) fonda, f. **r. stand,** Mexico fresquería, f

refrigerate /rɪ'frɪdʒə,reit/ vt refrigerar; enfriar; refrescar

refrigeration /rɪ,frɪdʒə'reiʃən/ n refrigeración, f; enfriamiento, m. **r. chamber,** cámara frigorífica, f

refrigerative /rɪ'frɪdʒərətɪv/ a refrigerante, frigorífico

refrigerator /rɪ'frɪdʒə,reitər/ n refrigerador, m, nevera, f

refringent /rɪ'frɪndʒənt/ a refringente

refuel /ri'fyuəl/ vt (a furnace) cargar con carbón, etc.; (of a ship) tomar carbón; (of an airplane, motor vehicle) tomar bencina

refuge /'rɛfyudʒ/ n refugio, m; asilo, m; (resort) recurso, m; subterfugio, m; (traffic island) refugio para peatones, m. **to take r.,** refugiarse; resguardarse (de)

refugee /ˌrɛfyʊ'dʒi/ a refugiado. n refugiado (-da)
refulgence /rɪ'fʌldʒəns/ n refulgencia, f
refulgent /rɪ'fʌldʒənt/ a refulgente
refund /ri'fʌnd/ n reembolso, m; devolución, f. vt reembolsar; devolver
refurbish /ri'fɜrbɪʃ/ vt restaurar; renovar; (a literary work) refundir
refurnish /ri'fɜrnɪʃ/ vt amueblar de nuevo
refusal /rɪ'fyuzəl/ n negativa, f; (rejection) rechazo, m; (option) opción, f; preferencia, f
refuse /rɪ'fyuz/ vt negar; (reject) rechazar. vi negarse (a), rehusar; (of a horse) resistirse a saltar
refuse /'rɛfyus/ n desecho, m; desperdicios, m pl; residuo, m; basura, f. a de desecho. **r. dump,** muladar, m
refutable /rɪ'fyutəbəl/ a refutable
refutation /ˌrɛfyʊ'teɪʃən/ n refutación, f
refute /rɪ'fyut/ vt refutar
regain /ri'geɪn/ vt recobrar, recuperar; cobrar; ganar de nuevo; Fig. reconquistar. **to r. one's breath,** cobrar aliento. **to r. consciousness,** volver en sí
regal /'rigəl/ a regio, real
regale /rɪ'geɪl/ vt regalar, agasajar; recrear, deleitar
regalia /rɪ'geɪliə/ n regalía, f; insignias reales, f pl; distintivos, m pl, insignias, f pl
regally /'rigəli/ adv regiamente
regard /rɪ'gɑrd/ vt mirar; observar; considerar; (respect) respetar; (concern) importar, concernir; relacionarse con. n mirada, f; atención, f; (esteem) aprecio, m, estimación, f; respeto, m; veneración, f; (relation) referencia, f; pl **regards,** recuerdos, saludos, m pl. **He has little r. for their feelings,** Le importan poco sus susceptibilidades. **With kindest regards,** Con mis saludos más afectuosos. **as regards, with r. to,** con referencia a, respecto a, en cuanto a
regardful /rɪ'gɑrdfəl/ a atento (a), cuidadoso (de); que se preocupa (de)
regarding /rɪ'gɑrdɪŋ/ prep tocante a, en cuanto a, respecto de
regardless /rɪ'gɑrdlɪs/ a negligente (de); indiferente (a), insensible (a); que no se interesa (en); que no se inqueta (por); sin preocuparse (de)
regatta /rɪ'gætə, -'gɑtə/ n regata, f
regency /'ridʒənsi/ n regencia, f
regeneracy /rɪ'dʒɛnərəsi/ n regeneración, f
regenerate /rɪ'dʒɛnə,reɪt/ vt regenerar. a regenerado
regeneration /rɪ,dʒɛnə'reɪʃən/ n regeneración, f
regenerative /rɪ'dʒɛnərətɪv/ a regenerador
regenerator /rɪ'dʒɛnə,reɪtər/ n regenerador (-ra)
regent /'ridʒənt/ n regente, mf
regime /rei'ʒim/ n régimen, m
regimen /'rɛdʒəmən/ n (Gram. Med.) régimen, m,
regiment /n. 'rɛdʒəmənt; v. -ˌmɛnt/ n regimiento, m. vt regimentar. **r. of the line,** tropa de línea, f
regimental /ˌrɛdʒə'mɛntl/ a de (un) regimiento, perteneciente a un regimiento
regimentation /ˌrɛdʒəmən'teɪʃən/ n regimentación, f
region /'ridʒən/ n región, f
regional /'ridʒənl/ a regional
regionalism /'ridʒənl,ɪzəm/ n regionalismo, m
regionalist /'ridʒənlɪst/ n regionalista, mf
regionalistic /'ridʒənlɪstɪk/ a regionalista
register /'rɛdʒəstər/ n (record and Mech. Mus. Print.) registro, m; (of ships, etc.) matrícula, f; lista, f. vt registrar; matricular; (a ship) abanderar; inscribir; (one's child in a school) anotar (Argentina); inscribir; (of thermometers, etc.) marcar; (letters) certificar; (luggage) facturar; (in one's mind) grabar; (emotion) mostrar, manifestar. vi (at a hotel, etc.) registrarse; Print. estar en registro. **cash r.,** caja registradora, f. **r. of births, marriages and deaths,** registro civil, m
registered letter /'rɛdʒəstərd/ n carta certificada, f
registrar /'rɛdʒə,strɑr/ n registrador, m; archivero, m; secretario, m; (of a school) jefe de inscripciones, secretario general (the latter has many more duties) **r. of births, marriages and deaths,** secretario del registro civil, m. **registrar's office,** oficina del registro civil, f
registration /ˌrɛdʒə'streɪʃən/ n registro, m; inscrip-

ción, f; (of a vehicle, etc.) matrícula, f; Naut. abanderamiento, m; (of a letter, etc.) certificación, f. **r. number,** número de matrícula, m
registry /'rɛdʒəstri/ n registro, m; inscripción, f; matrícula, f. **r. office,** oficina del registro civil, f; (for servants) agencia doméstica, f
regression /rɪ'grɛʃən/ n regresión, f, retroceso, m
regret /rɪ'grɛt/ vt sentir; lamentar, pesar; arrepentirse (de); (miss) echar de menos (a). n sentimiento, pesar, m; (remorse) remordimiento, m. **I r. very much that...,** Me pesa mucho que..., Siento mucho que... **to send one's regrets,** mandar sus excusas
regretful /rɪ'grɛtfəl/ a lleno de pesar; arrepentido; lamentable, deplorable. **He was most r. that...,** Lamentaba mucho que...
regretfully /rɪ'grɛtfəli/ adv con pesar
regrettable /rɪ'grɛtəbəl/ a lamentable, deplorable; doloroso; (with loss, etc.) sensible
regrettably /rɪ'grɛtəbli/ adv lamentablemente; sensiblemente
regroup /ri'grup/ vt arreglar de nuevo; formar de nuevo; reorganizar
regular /'rɛgyələr/ a regular; normal; (ordinary) corriente, común; (in order) en regla; (Gram. Bot. Eccl. Mil. Geom.) regular. n Eccl. regular, m; (soldier) soldado de línea, m; (officer) militar de carrera, m; (client) parroquiano habitual, m
regularity /ˌrɛgyə'lærɪti/ n regularidad,
regularization /ˌrɛgyələrə'zeɪʃən/ n regularización, f
regularize /'rɛgyələ,raiz/ vt regularizar
regularly /'rɛgyələrli/ adv regularmente
regulate /'rɛgyə,leɪt/ vt regular; ajustar, arreglar; (direct) dirigir; reglamentar
regulation /ˌrɛgyə'leɪʃən/ n regulación, f; arreglo, m; (rule) reglamento, m, a de reglamento; normal
regulative /'rɛgyə,leɪtɪv/ a regulador
regulator /'rɛgyə,leɪtər/ n Mech. regulador, m
regurgitate /rɪ'gɜrdʒɪ,teɪt/ vt and vi regurgitar
regurgitation /rɪ,gɜrdʒɪ'teɪʃən/ n regurgitación, f
rehabilitate /ˌrihə'bɪlɪ,teɪt/ vt rehabilitar
rehabilitation /ˌrihə,bɪlɪ'teɪʃən/ n rehabilitación, f
rehash /ri'hæʃ/ vt (a literary work, etc.) refundir; Inf. hacer un refrito de
rehearing /ri'hɪərɪŋ/ n nueva audición, f, (of a case) revisión, f
rehearsal /rɪ'hɜrsəl/ n Theat. ensayo, m; recitación, f; relación, narración, f. **dress r.,** ensayo general, m
rehearse /rɪ'hɜrs/ vt Theat. ensayar; recitar; (narrate) narrar; enumerar
reheat /ri'hit/ vt recalentar
reign /rein/ n reinado, m. vi reinar; predominar
reigning /'reinɪŋ/ a reinante; predominante
reimburse /ˌriɪm'bɜrs/ vt reembolsar
reimbursement /ˌriɪm'bɜrsmənt/ n reembolso, m
reimport /ri'ɪmpɔrt/ vt importar de nuevo, reimportar, n reimporte, m
reimportation /ˌriɪmpɔr'teɪʃən/ n reimportación, f
reimpose /ˌriɪm'pouz/ vt reimponer
reimposition /ˌriɪmpə'zɪʃən/ n reimposición, f
reimprison /ˌriɪm'prɪzən/ vt encarcelar de nuevo, reencarcelar
reimprisonment /ˌriɪm'prɪzənmənt/ n reencarcelamiento, m
rein /rein/ n rienda, f. vt llevar las riendas (de); (hold back) refrenar. **to give r. to,** Fig. dar rienda suelta (a)
reincarnation /ˌriɪnkɑr'neɪʃən/ n reencarnación, f
reincorporate /ˌriɪn'kɔrpə,reɪt/ vt reincorporar
reincorporation /ˌriɪn,kɔrpə'reɪʃən/ n reincorporación, f
reindeer /'rein,dɪər/ n reno, m
reinforce /ˌriɪn'fɔrs/ vt reforzar; (concrete) armar; fortalecer. **reinforced concrete,** n hormigón armado, m
reinforcement /ˌriɪn'fɔrsmənt/ n reforzamiento, m; (Mil. Nav. Fig.) refuerzo, m
reins n See **rein**
reinsert /ˌriɪn'sɜrt/ vt volver a insertar
reinstall /ˌriɪn'stɔl/ vt reinstalar; rehabilitar
reinstallment /ˌriɪn'stɔlmənt/ n reinstalación, f; rehabilitación, f; restablecimiento, m

reinstate /ˌriːɪnˈsteit/ vt reponer, restablecer; reinstalar; rehabilitar

reinstatement /ˌriːɪnˈsteitmənt/ n restablecimiento, m; rehabilitación, f

reinsurance /ˌriːɪnˈʃʊrəns/ n reaseguro, m

reinsure /ˌriːɪnˈʃʊr, -ˈʃɜr/ vt reasegurar

reintegrate /riˈɪntəˌgreit/ vt reintegrar

reintegration /ˌriːɪntəˈgreiʃən/ n reintegración, f

reinter /ˌriːɪnˈtɜr/ vt enterrar de nuevo

reinvest /ˌriːɪnˈvest/ vt reinvertir

reinvestment /ˌriːɪnˈvestmənt/ n reinversión, f

reinvigorate /ˌriːɪnˈvɪgəˌreit/ vt reanimar, dar nuevo vigor (a)

reinvite /ˌriːɪnˈvait/ vt invitar de nuevo (a)

reissue /riˈɪʃu/ n nueva emisión, f; (of a book, etc.) nueva edición, reimpresión, f. vt hacer una nueva emisión (de); reeditar, publicar de nuevo

reiterate /riˈɪtəˌreit/ vt reiterar, repetir

reiteration /riˌɪtəˈreiʃən/ n reiteración, f

reiterative /riˈɪtəˌreitiv/ a reiterativo

reject /rɪˈdʒekt/ vt rechazar, rehusar; repudiar; repulsar; desechar

rejection /rɪˈdʒekʃən/ n rechazamiento, m; repudiación, refutación, f; repulsa, f

rejoice /rɪˈdʒɔis/ vt alegrar, regocijar. vi alegrarse (de), regocijarse (de), gloriarse (en)

rejoicing /rɪˈdʒɔisɪŋ/ n regocijo, júbilo, m, alegría, f; algazara, f, fiestas, f pl

rejoin /rɪˈdʒɔin/ vt and vi juntar de nuevo; volver a; reunirse con; (reply) contestar, replicar

rejoinder /rɪˈdʒɔindər/ n contestación, respuesta, f

rejuvenate /rɪˈdʒuvəˌneit/ vt rejuvenecer

rejuvenation /rɪˌdʒuvəˈneiʃən/ n rejuvenecimiento, m

rekindle /riˈkɪndl/ vt encender de nuevo; despertar, reavivar. vi encenderse de nuevo; reavivarse

relapse /rɪˈlæps/ n. also 'rilæps/ n reincidencia, recaída, f; Med. recidiva, f. vi reincidir (en); Med. recaer

relapsed /rɪˈlæpst/ a relapso

relate /rɪˈleit/ vt (recount) relatar, narrar; relacionar; unir; (of kinship) emparentar. vi ajustarse (a); referirse a (a). **The first fact is not related to the second,** El primer hecho no tiene nada que ver con el segundo

related /rɪˈleitɪd/ a relacionado; (by kinship) emparentado. **John is well-r.,** Juan es de buena familia; Juan es de familia influyente; Juan tiene buenas relaciones

relater /rɪˌleitər/ n narrador (-ra)

relation /rɪˈleiʃən/ n (narrative) relación, narración, f; conexión, f; relación, f; (kinship) parentesco, m; (person) pariente (-ta). **in r. to,** con relación a, en cuanto a

relationship /rɪˈleiʃənˌʃɪp/ n parentesco, m; conexión, relación, Lat. Am. atingencia, f

relative /ˈrelətɪv/ a relativo. n pariente (-ta); pl **relatives,** parientes, m pl, parentela, f

relativism /ˈrelətəˌvɪzəm/ n relativismo, m

relativity /ˌreləˈtɪvɪti/ n relatividad, f

relax /rɪˈlæks/ vt relajar; aflojar; soltar; (make less severe) ablandar; (decrease) mitigar. vi relajarse; aflojar; (rest) descansar

relaxation /ˌrilækˈseiʃən/ n relajación, f; aflojamiento, m; ablandamiento, m; mitigación, f; (rest) descanso, reposo, m; (pastime) pasatiempo, m; (amusement) diversión, f

relaxing /rɪˈlæksɪŋ/ a relajante; (of climate) enervante

relay /n. 'rilei; v. also ri'lei/ n (of horses) parada, f; (shift) tanda, f; relevo, m; Elec. relais, m; Radio. redifusión, f. vt enviar por posta; Elec. reemitir; Radio. retransmitir; (lay again) colocar de nuevo. **r. race,** carrera de equipo, carrera de relevos, f

release /rɪˈlis/ vt soltar; (hurl) lanzar; (set free) poner en libertad (a); librar (de); absolver; (surrender) renunciar (a); dar al público, poner en circulación; (lease again) realquilar. n soltura, f; lanzamiento, m; liberación, f; (from pain) alivio, m; remisión, f; exoneración, f; publicación, f; (of films) representación, f; Law. soltura, f

relegate /ˈreliˌgeit/ vt relegar

relegation /ˌreliˈgeiʃən/ n relegación, f

relent /rɪˈlent/ vi ablandarse, enternecerse; ceder

relenting /rɪˈlentɪŋ/ n enternecimiento, desenojo, m

relentless /rɪˈlentlɪs/ a implacable, inexorable; despiadado

relentlessly /rɪˈlentlɪsli/ adv inexorablemente; sin piedad

relentlessness /rɪˈlentlɪsnɪs/ n inexorabilidad, f; falta de piedad, f

relevance /ˈreləvəns/ n conexión, f; pertinencia, f; aplicabilidad, f

relevant /ˈreləvənt/ a relativo; pertinente, a propósito, oportuno; aplicable

reliability /rɪˌlaiəˈbɪlɪti/ n seguridad, f; formalidad, f; confianza, f; exactitud, f; veracidad, f

reliable /rɪˈlaiəbəl/ a seguro; formal; digno de crédito, de confianza, solvente digno de confianza; exacto; veraz

reliably /rɪˈlaiəbli/ adv seguramente; de una manera digna de confianza; exactamente

reliance /rɪˈlaiəns/ n confianza, f. **to place r. on,** tener confianza en

reliant /rɪˈlaiənt/ a confiado

relic /ˈrelɪk/ n vestigio, rastro, m; Eccl. reliquia, f

relief /rɪˈlif/ n (alleviation) alivio, m; desahogo, m; (help) socorro, m, ayuda, f; beneficencia, f; Mil. relevo, m; (pleasure) placer, m, satisfacción, f; (consolation) consuelo, m; Law. remisión, f; Art. relieve, m. **high r.,** alto relieve, m. **low r.,** bajo relieve, m. **r. map,** mapa en relieve, m. **r. train,** tren de socorro, m

relieve /rɪˈliv/ vt aliviar; aligerar, suavizar; mitigar; (one's feelings, etc.) desahogar; Mil. and to take the place of) relevar; (free) librar; (dismiss) destituir; (remove) quitar; (rob) robar; (help) socorrer, remediar; (redeem) redimir; (ornament) adornar; (from a wrong) hacer justicia (a)

relieving /rɪˈlivɪŋ/ n alivio, m; aligeramiento, m; mitigación, f; (of the feelings) desahogo, m; Mil. relevo, m; (help) socorro, m. **r. arch,** sobrearco, m

relight /rɪˈlait/ vt volver a encender. vi encenderse de nuevo

religion /rɪˈlɪdʒən/ n religión, f

religiosity /rɪˌlɪdʒiˈɒsɪti/ n religiosidad, f

religious /rɪˈlɪdʒəs/ a religioso; en religión; piadoso, crevente; devoto. n religioso (-sa). **r. orders,** órdenes religiosas, f pl. **r. toleration,** libertad de cultos, f

religiousness /rɪˈlɪdʒəsnɪs/ n religiosidad, f

relinquish /rɪˈlɪŋkwɪʃ/ vt abandonar; (one's grip) soltar; renunciar; desistir (de), dejar (de); (a post) dimitir (de)

relinquishment /rɪˈlɪŋkwɪʃmənt/ n abandono, m; renuncia, f; dejamiento, m; (of a post) dimisión, f

reliquary /ˈreliˌkweri/ n relicario, m

relish /ˈrelɪʃ/ n gusto, m; sabor, m; (touch, smack) dejo, m; condimento, m; apetito, m, gana, f. vt gustar de; comer con apetito; saborear; paladear; Fig. seducir, atraer, gustar. vi tener gusto (de). **I do not much r. the idea,** No me seduce la idea

relishing /ˈrelɪʃɪŋ/ n saboreo, m; (enjoyment) goce, m, fruición, f; consideración, f

relive /riˈlɪv/ vt vivir de nuevo, volver a vivir

reload /riˈloud/ vt recargar

reluctance /rɪˈlʌktəns/ n repugnancia, desgana, f. **with r.,** a regañadientes, de mala gana

reluctant /rɪˈlʌktənt/ a poco dispuesto (a), que tiene repugnancia a (hacer algo), sin gana; (forced) forzado; artificial; (hesitating) vacilante

reluctantly /rɪˈlʌktəntli/ adv de mala gana, con repugnancia, a disgusto

rely on /rɪˈlai/ vi contar con, confiar en, depender de

remain /rɪˈmein/ vi quedar; permanecer; (be left over) sobrar; continuar. **I r. yours faithfully...,** (in a letter) Queda de Vd. su att. s.s.... **It remains to be written,** Queda por escribir

remainder /rɪˈmeindər/ n (math) resto, m; restos, m pl, sobras, f pl; residuo, m. **The r. of the people went away,** Los demás se marcharon

remaining /rɪˈmeinɪŋ/ pres. part and a que queda; sobrante. **r. to be paid,** Lat. Am. impago

remains /rɪˈmeinz/ n pl restos, m pl; sobras, f pl, desperdicios, m pl; ruinas, f pl

remake /ri'meik/ *vt* rehacer; reformar
remand /ri'mænd/ *vt Law.* reencarcelar. *n Law.* reencarcelamiento, *m*
remark /ri'mɑrk/ *n* observación, *f*; nota, *f*; comentario, *m*. *vt* and *vi* observar; notar. **to r. on,** comentar, hacer una observación sobre
remarkable /ri'mɑrkəbəl/ *a* notable, singular, extraordinario
remarkably /ri'mɑrkəbli/ *adv* singularmente
remarriage /'ri,mærɪdʒ/ *n* segundas nupcias, *f pl,* segundo casamiento, *m*
remarry /ri'mæri/ *vt* volver a casar (a). *vi* casarse en segundas nupcias; volver a casarse
remediable /ri'midiəbəl/ *a* remediable
remedial /ri'midiəl/ *a* remediador; curativo, terapéutico
remedy /'rɛmɪdi/ *n* remedio, *m*; recurso, *m*, *vt* remediar; curar
remember /ri'mɛmbər/ *vt* recordar; tener presente; acordarse de. *vi* acordarse; no olvidarse. **R. me to your mother,** Dale recuerdos míos a tu madre. **If I r. rightly...,** Si bien me acuerdo... **And r. that I shall do no more!** ¡Y no olvides que no haré más!
remembrance /ri'mɛmbrəns/ *n* recuerdo, *m*; memoria, *f*; *pl* **remembrances,** recuerdos, *m pl*
remind /ri'maind/ *vt* recordar
reminder /ri'maindər/ *n* recuerdo, *m*; (warning) advertencia, *f*. **a gentle r.,** una indirecta, una insinuación
reminisce /,rɛmə'nɪs/ *vi Inf.* recordar viejas historias
reminiscence /,rɛmə'nɪsəns/ *n* reminiscencia, *f*, recuerdo, *m*
reminiscent /,rɛmə'nɪsənt/ *a* evocador, que recuerda; de reminiscencia; que piensa en el pasado. **to be r. of,** recordar; *Inf.* oler a
reminiscently /,rɛmə'nɪsəntli/ *adv* evocadoramente, como si recordara
remiss /ri'mɪs/ *a* negligente, descuidado
remission /ri'mɪʃən/ *n* remisión, *f*
remissly /ri'mɪsli/ *adv* negligentemente
remissness /ri'mɪsnɪs/ *n* negligencia, *f*, descuido, *m*
remit /ri'mɪt/ *vt* remitir; *Com.* remesar, enviar. *vi* (pay) pagar
remittance /ri'mɪtns/ *n* remesa, *f*, envío, *m*
remitter /ri'mɪtər/ *n* remitente, *mf*
remnant /'rɛmnənt/ *n* resto, *m*; (of fabric) retal, retazo, *m*; (relic) vestigio, *m*, reliquia, *f*. **r. sale,** saldo, *m*
remodel /ri'mɒdl/ *vt* rehacer; reformar; modelar de nuevo; (a play, etc.) refundir
remodeling /ri'mɒdlɪŋ/ *n* reformación, *f*; (of a play, etc.) refundición, *f*
remonstrance /ri'mɒnstrəns/ *n* protesta, *f*; reconvención, *f*
remonstrate /ri'mɒnstreit/ *vi* protestar, objetar. **to r. with,** reprochar, reconvenir
remorse /ri'mɔrs/ *n* remordimiento, *m*
remorseful /ri'mɔrsfəl/ *a* lleno de remordimientos; penitente, arrepentido
remorsefully /ri'mɔrsfəli/ *adv* con remordimiento
remorseless /ri'mɔrslɪs/ *a* sin conciencia, sin remordimientos; despiadado, inflexible
remorselessness /ri'mɔrslɪsnɪs/ *n* inexorabilidad, crueldad, dureza, *f*
remote /ri'mout/ *a* distante, lejano; remoto; aislado; ajeno; (slight) leve, vago. **r. control,** mando a distancia, *m*; (for a television) remoto, *m*
remotely /ri'moutli/ *adv* remotamente
remoteness /ri'moutnɪs/ *n* distancia, *f*; aislamiento, *m*; alejamiento, *m*; (vagueness) vaguedad, *f*
remount /*v.* ri'maunt; *n.* 'ri,maunt/ *vt* subir de nuevo, montar de nuevo; *Mil.* remontar. *vi* (go back to) remontar (a), derivarse (de). *n Mil.* remonta, *f*
removable /ri'muvəbəl/ *a* que puede quitarse; (of collars, etc.) de quita y pon; transportable; (of officials, etc.) amovible
removal /ri'muvəl/ *n* acción de quitar o levantar, *f*; sacamiento, *m*; separación, *f*; eliminación, *f*; alejamiento, *m*; traslado, *m*; (from office, etc.) deposición, *f*; supresión, *f*; asesinato, *m*. **r. van,** carro de mudanzas, *m*

remove /ri'muv/ *vt* quitar; retirar; levantar; sacar; apartar; separar; eliminar; trasladar; (from office) destituir; suprimir; asesinar. *vi* trasladarse. *n* grado, *m*; distancia, *f*; (departure) partida, *f*. **to r. oneself,** quitarse de en medio. **to r. one's hat,** descubrirse. **first cousin once removed,** hijo de primo carnal, primo hermano del padre, primo hermano de la madre, *m*
remunerate /ri'myunə,reit/ *vt* remunerar
remuneration /ri,myunə'reiʃən/ *n* remuneración, *f*
remunerative /ri'myunərətɪv/ *a* remunerador
renaissance /'rɛnə,sans/ *n* renacimiento, *m*, *a* renacentista
Renaissance man /'rɛnə,sans/ *n* hombre del Renacimiento, *m*
Renaissance woman *n* mujer del Renacimiento, *f*
renal /'rinl/ *a* renal
rename /ri'neim/ *vt* poner otro nombre (a)
renascent /ri'næsənt, -'neisənt/ *a* renaciente, que renace
rend /rɛnd/ *vt* desgarrar, rasgar; *Fig.* lacerar; (split) hender; *Fig.* dividir. **to r. from,** arrancar (a). **to r. the air,** (with cries, etc.) llenar el aire
render /'rɛndər/ *vt* (return) devolver; dar; rendir; (make) hacer; (help, service) prestar; interpretar; (translate) traducir; (fat) derretir y clarificar
rendering /'rɛndərɪŋ/ *n* versión, *f*; interpretación, *f*
rendezvous /'randə,vu, -dei-/ *n* cita, *f*; lugar de cita, *m*; reunión, *f*. *vi* reunirse
rending /'rɛndɪŋ/ *n* desgarro, *m*; hendimiento, *m*
renegade /'rɛni,geid/ *a* renegado. *n* renegado (-da)
renew /ri'nu/ *vt* renovar; (resume) reanudar; (a lease, etc.) prorrogar
renewable /ri'nuəbəl/ *a* renovable
renewal /ri'nuəl/ *n* renovación, *f*; (resumption) reanudación, *f*; (of a lease, etc.) prorrogación, *f*
renewed /ri'nud/ *a* renovado; nuevo
rennet /'rɛnɪt/ *n* cuajo, *m*
renounce /ri'nauns/ *vt* renunciar; (a throne) abdicar; renegar (de), repudiar; abandonar. *vi Law.* desistir; (cards) renunciar
renouncement /ri'naunsmənt/ *n* renuncia, *f*; (of a throne) abdicación, *f*; repudiación, *f*
renovate /'rɛnə,veit/ *vt* renovar; limpiar; restaurar
renovation /,rɛnə'veiʃən/ *n* renovación, *f*; limpiadura, *f*; restauración, *f*
renovator /'rɛnə,veitər/ *n* renovador (-ra)
renown /ri'naun/ *n* renombre, *m*, fama, *f*
renowned /ri'naund/ *a* renombrado, famoso
rent /rɛnt/ *n* (tear) rasgadura, *f*; desgarro, *m*; abertura, *f*; raja hendedura, *f*; (discord) división, *f*; (hire) alquiler, *m*; arrendamiento, *m*. *vt* arrendar, alquilar. **r.-free,** sin pagar alquiler
rentable /'rɛntəbəl/ *a* alquilable, arrendable
rental /'rɛntl/ *See* **rent**
renter /'rɛntər/ *n* arrendador (-ra)
rentier /ʀɑn'tyei/ *n* rentista, *mf*
renting /'rɛntɪŋ/ *n* alquiler, *m*; arrendamiento, *m*
renumber /ri'nʌmbər/ *vt* numerar de nuevo
renunciation /ri,nʌnsi'eiʃən/ *n* renunciación, renuncia, *f*
reoccupy /ri'ɒkyu,pai/ *vt* volver a ocupar, ocupar otra vez
reopen /ri'oupən/ *vt* abrir de nuevo, volver a abrir. *vi* abrirse nuevamente, abrirse otra vez
reopening /ri'oupənɪŋ/ *n* reapertura, *f*
reorder /ri'ɔrdər/ *vt* ordenar de nuevo, *Com.* volver a pedir. *n Com.* nuevo pedido, *m*
reorganization /ri,ɔrgənə'zeiʃən/ *n* reorganización, *f*
reorganize /ri'ɔrgə,naiz/ *vt* reorganizar
reorganizing /ri'ɔrgə,naizɪŋ/ *a* reorganizador
repack /ri'pæk/ *vt* reembalar; reenvasar; volver a hacer (una maleta)
repaint /ri'peint/ *vt* pintar de nuevo
repainting /ri'peintɪŋ/ *n* nueva pintura, *f*
repair /ri'pɛər/ *vt* arreglar (e.g. a machine) componer; remendar; reparar; restaurar; rehacer. *vi* (with to) dirigirse a, ir a; acudir a. *n* arreglo *m*, reparación, *f*; compostura, *f*; restauración, *f*. **to keep in r.,** conservar en buen estado

repairable /rɪ'pɛərəbəl/ *a* que se puede componer

repairer /rɪ'pɛərər/ *n* componedor (-ra); restaurador (-ra)

repairing /rɪ'pɛərɪŋ/ *a* reparador

reparable /'rɛpərəbəl/ *a* reparable; remediable

reparation /ˌrɛpə'reɪʃən/ *n* reparación, *f*

repartee /ˌrɛpər'ti, -'teɪ, -ɑr-/ *n* respuestas, agudezas, *f pl; Inf.* dimes y diretes, *m pl*

repast /rɪ'pæst/ *n* comida, *f*; (light) colación, *f*

repatriate /ri'peitri,eit/ *vt* repatriar

repatriation /ri,peitri'eiʃən/ *n* repatriación, *f*

repay /rɪ'pei/ *vt* reembolsar; recompensar, pagar; pagar en la misma moneda. *vi* pagar. **It well repays a visit,** Vale la pena de visitarse

repayable /rɪ'peiəbəl/ *a* reembolsable

repayment /rɪ'peiməənt/ *n* reembolso, *m*; pago, retorno, *m*

repeal /rɪ'pil/ *n* abrogación, revocación, *f, vt* abrogar, rescindir, revocar

repeat /rɪ'pit/ *vt* repetir; reiterar; (renew) renovar; duplicar. *n* repetición, *f*

repeated /rɪ'pitɪd/ *a* reiterado; redoblado

repeatedly /rɪ'pitɪdli/ *adv* reiteradamente, repetidamente

repeater /rɪ'pitər/ *n* repetidor (-ra); reloj de repetición, *m*; arma de repetición, *f*

repel /rɪ'pel/ *vt* repeler; ahuyentar; (spurn) rechazar; *Phys.* resistir; repugnar

repellent /rɪ'pɛlənt/ *a* repulsivo. *n* (insect) repelente para insectos, *m*

repent /rɪ'pɛnt/ *vt* arrepentirse de. *vi* arrepentirse

repentance /rɪ'pɛntn̩s/ *n* arrepentimiento, *m*, penitencia, *f*

repentant /rɪ'pɛntn̩t/ *a* arrepentido, penitente, contrito

repentantly /rɪ'pɛntn̩tli/ *adv* arrepentidamente, con contrición

repercuss /ˌripər'kʌs/ *vt* repercutir (en)

repercussion /ˌripər'kʌʃən/ *n* repercusión, *f*

repercussive /ˌripər'kʌsɪv/ *a* repercusivo

repertory /'rɛpərˌtɔri/ *n* repertorio, *m*

repetition /ˌrɛpɪ'tɪʃən/ *n* repetición, *f*; recitación, *f*

repetitive /rɪ'pɛtɪtɪv/ *a* iterativo

repine /rɪ'pain/ *vi* afligirse (de); quejarse (de); padecer nostalgia

repining /rɪ'painɪŋ/ *n* pesares, *m pl*; quejas, *f pl*, descontento, *m*; nostalgia, *f*

replace /rɪ'pleis/ *vt* (put back) reponer, colocar de nuevo; restituir, devolver; (renew) renovar; (in a post, etc.) reemplazar, substituir

replaceable /rɪ'pleisəbəl/ *a* restituible; renovable; reemplazable

replacement /rɪ'pleismənt/ *n* reposición, *f*; restitución, devolución, *f*; renovación, *f*; reemplazo, *m*

replant /ri'plænt/ *vt* replantar

replanting /ri'plæntɪŋ/ *n* replantación, *f*

replenish /rɪ'plɛnɪʃ/ *vt* rellenar

replenishment /ri'plɛnɪʃmənt/ *n* relleno, *m*

replete /rɪ'plit/ *a* repleto

repletion /rɪ'pliʃən/ *n* repleción, *f*

replica /'rɛplɪkə/ *n* réplica, *f*

reply /rɪ'plai/ *n* respuesta, contestación, *f, vi* responder, contestar. **Awaiting your r.,** En espera de sus noticias. **in his r.,** en su respuesta

repolish /ri'pɒlɪʃ/ *vt* repulir

repopulate /ri'pɒpyəˌleit/ *vt* repoblar

repopulation /ri,pɒpyə'leiʃən/ *n* repoblación, *f*

report /rɪ'pɔrt/ *n* (rumor) voz, *f*, rumor, *m*; (reputation) fama, *f*; (news) noticia, *f*; (journalistic) reportaje, *m*; (*Mil. Nav.* and from school) parte, *f*; (weather) boletín, *m*; (proceedings) actas, *f pl*; (statement) informe, *m*; relación, *f*; (of a gun, etc.) detonación, *f*; explosión, *f*. *vt* dar cuenta de, relatar; informar; (measure) registrar; (*Mil. Nav.*) dar parte de; comunicar; (journalistic) hacer un reportaje de; (transcribe) transcribir; (accuse) denunciar; quejarse de. *vi* presentar informe; ser reportero; (present oneself) presentarse, comparecer. **It is reported that...,** Se informa que...

report card *n* boletín de calificaciones, *m*

reporter /rɪ'pɔrtər/ *n* reportero (-ra); *Law.* relator, *m*

reporting /rɪ'pɔrtɪŋ/ *n* reporterismo, *m*

repose /rɪ'pouz/ *n* reposo, *m*; quietud, *f*; tranquilidad, serenidad, *f. vt* reposar, descansar; reclinar; (place) poner. *vi* reposar; tener confianza (en); basarse (en)

repository /rɪ'pɒzɪˌtɔri/ *n* repositorio, depósito, *m*; almacén, *m*; (furniture) guardamuebles, *m*; (person) depositario (-ia)

reprehend /ˌrɛprɪ'hɛnd/ *vt* reprender, reprobar

reprehensible /ˌrɛprɪ'hɛnsəbəl/ *a* reprensible

reprehension /ˌrɛprɪ'hɛnʃən/ *n* reprensión, *f*

represent /ˌrɛprɪ'zɛnt/ *vt* representar; significar

representation /ˌrɛprɪzɛn'teiʃən/ *n* representación, *f*

representational /ˌrɛprɪzɛn'teiʃənl/ *a* Art. realista

representative /ˌrɛprɪ'zɛntətɪv/ *a* que representa; representativo. *n* representante, *mf*

repress /rɪ'prɛs/ *vt* reprimir

repression /rɪ'prɛʃən/ *n* represión, *f*

repressive /rɪ'prɛsɪv/ *a* represivo

reprieve /rɪ'priv/ *vt* Law. aplazar la ejecución (de); *Fig.* dar una tregua (a)

reprimand /'rɛprəˌmænd/ *n* reprimenda, *f, vt* reprender

reprint /*n*. 'riˌprɪnt; *v.* ri'prɪnt/ *n* reimpresión, tirada aparte, separata, *f, vt* reimprimir

reprinting /'ri,prɪntɪŋ/ *n* reimpresión, *f*

reprisal /rɪ'praizəl/ *n* represalia, *f*. **to take reprisals,** tomar represalias

reproach /rɪ'proutʃ/ *n* reproche, *m*; censura, *f*; (shame) vergüenza, *f. vt* reprochar; censurar, echar en cara, afear

reproachful /rɪ'proutʃfəl/ *a* severo; lleno de reproches; de censura; (shameful) vergonzoso

reproachfully /rɪ'proutʃfəli/ *adv* con reprobación, con reprensión, severamente

reproachfulness /rɪ'proutʃfəlnɪs/ *n* severidad, *f*. **the r. of my gaze,** mi mirada llena de reproches

reprobate /'rɛprə,beit/ *v* réprobo (-ba)

reproduce /ˌriprə'dus/ *vt* reproducir. *vi* reproducirse

reproducible /ˌriprə'dusəbəl/ *a* reproductible

reproduction /ˌriprə'dʌkʃən/ *n* reproducción, *f*

reproductive /ˌriprə'dʌktɪv/ *a* reproductor; de reproducción

reproof /rɪ'pruf/ *n* reconvención, *f*

reprove /rɪ'pruv/ *vt* censurar, culpar; reprender

reprovingly /rɪ'pruvɪŋli/. See **rebukingly**

reptile /'rɛptɪl, -tail/ *a* and *n* reptil, *m*

republic /rɪ'pʌblɪk/ *n* república, *f*

republican /rɪ'pʌblɪkən/ *a* and *n* republicano (-na)

republicanism /rɪ'pʌblɪkəˌnɪzəm/ *n* republicanismo, *m*

Republican Party *n* Partido Republicano, *m*

republish /ri'pʌblɪʃ/ *vt* publicar de nuevo; volver a editar

repudiate /rɪ'pyudiˌeit/ *vt* repudiar; negar, rechazar

repudiation /ri,pyudi'eiʃən/ *n* repudiación, *f*

repugnance /rɪ'pʌgnəns/ *n* repugnacia, *f*

repugnant /rɪ'pʌgnənt/ *a* repugnante; contrario; opuesto. **to be r. to,** repugnar (a)

repulse /rɪ'pʌls/ *n* rechazar, repeler; rebatir, refutar; (refuse) rechazar. *n* repulsa, *f*; refutación, *f*; rechazo, *m*

repulsion /rɪ'pʌlʃən/ *n Phys.* repulsión, *f*; repugnancia, aversión, *f*

repulsive /rɪ'pʌlsɪv/ *a* repulsivo, repugnante, repelente

repulsiveness /rɪ'pʌlsɪvnɪs/ *n* carácter repulsivo, *m*; aspecto repugnante, *m*

reputable /'rɛpyətəbəl/ *a* honrado, respetable, formal

reputation /ˌrɛpyə'teiʃən/ *n* reputación, *f*; fama, *f*, renombre, *m*. **to have the r. of,** ser reputado como, pasar por

reputed /rɪ'pyutɪd/ *a* supuesto; putativo

reputedly /rɪ'pyutɪdli/ *adv* según la opinión común, según dice la gente

request /rɪ'kwɛst/ *n* ruego, *m*, petición, *f*; instancia, *f*; solicitud, *f*; Com. demanda, *f. vt* pedir, rogar; suplicar. **in r.,** en boga; solicitado; en demanda, **on r.,** a solicitud. **r. stop,** (for buses) parada discrecional, *f*

requiem /'rɛkwiəm/ n réquiem, m. **r. mass,** misa de difuntos, f

require /rɪ'kwaiᵊr/ vt exigir, requerir; necesitar; (wish) desear; invitar. vi ser necesario

required /rɪ'kwaiərd/ a necesario; obligatorio

requirement /rɪ'kwaiᵊrmənt/ n deseo, m; requisito, m; formalidad, f; estipulación, f; necesidad, f

requisite /'rɛkwəzɪt/ n requisito, m. a necesario, requisito, preciso. **to be r.,** ser necesario, ser menester hacer falta

requisition /ˌrɛkwə'zɪʃən/ n pedida, solicitud, f. vt Mil. requisar

requisitioning /ˌrɛkwə'zɪʃənɪŋ/ n requisa, f

requital /rɪ'kwaitl/ n recompensa, f; compensación, satisfacción, f

requite /rɪ'kwait/ vt pagar, recompensar; (affection) corresponder a

reread /ri'rid/ vt releer

resale /'ri,seil/ n reventa, f

rescind /rɪ'sɪnd/ vt rescindir

rescue /'rɛskyu/ vt salvar; librar; Mil. rescatar. n socorro, m; salvamento, m; Mil. rescate, m. **to go to the r. of,** ir al socorro de. **r. party,** expedición de salvamento, f; Mil. expedición de rescate, f

rescuer /'rɛskyuər/ n salvador (-ra)

reseal /ri'sil/ vt resellar

research /rɪ'sɜrtʃ, 'risɜrtʃ/ n investigación, f, vt investigar

researcher /rɪsɜrtʃər, 'risɜrtʃər/ n investigador (-ra)

reseda /rɪ'sidə/ n Bot. reseda, f

resell /ri'sɛl/ vt revender

resemblance /rɪ'zɛmbləns/ n parecido, m, semejanza, f. **The two sisters bear a strong r. to each other,** Las dos hermanas se parecen mucho

resemble /rɪ'zɛmbəl/ vt parecerse (a). **Mary doesn't r. her mother,** María no se parece a su madre

resent /rɪ'zɛnt/ vt resentirse de; ofenderse por, indignarse por; tomar a mal

resentful /rɪ'zɛntfəl/ a resentido; ofendido, indignado, agraviado; vengativo

resentfully /rɪ'zɛntfəli/ adv con resentimiento; con indignación

resentment /rɪ'zɛntmənt/ n resentimiento, m

reservation /ˌrɛzər'veiʃən/ n reservación, f; reserva, f; territorio reservado, m; santuario, m. **mental r.,** reserva mental, f

reserve /rɪ'zɜrv/ n reserva, f. vt reservar. a de reserva. **without r.,** sin reserva

reserved /rɪ'zɜrvd/ a reservado; callado, taciturno. **r. compartment,** reservado, m. **r. list,** (Mil. Nav.) sección de reserva, f

reservedly /rɪ'zɜrvɪdli/ adv con reserva

reservist /rɪ'zɜrvɪst/ n reservista, mf

reservoir /'rɛzər,vwɑr/ n depósito, m; cisterna, f, aljibe, tanque, m

reset /ri'sɛt/ vt montar de nuevo

resettle /ri'sɛtl/ vt repoblar; rehabilitar; (a dispute) llegar a un nuevo acuerdo sobre

resettlement /ri'sɛtlmənt/ n repoblación, f; rehabilitación, f; (of a dispute) nuevo acuerdo, m

reshape /ri'ʃeip/ vt reformar

reship /ri'ʃɪp/ vt reembarcar

reshipment /ri'ʃɪpmənt/ n reembarque, m

reshuffle /ri'ʃʌfəl/ vt volver a barajar; Fig. cambiar

reside /rɪ'zaid/ vi residir, habitar; vivir

residence /'rɛzɪdəns/ n residencia, f; permanencia, estada, f; domicilio, m

resident /'rɛzɪdənt/ a residente; (of a servant) que duerme en casa; interno. n residente, mf; (diplomacy) residente, m. **r. of the capital,** Lat. Am. capitalino (-na). **r. of Rio de Janeiro,** carioca, mf

residential /ˌrɛzɪ'dɛnʃəl/ a residencial

residue /'rɛzɪ,du/ n resto, m; (Law., Chem.) residuo, m

residuum /rɪ'zɪdʒuəm/ n residuo, m

resign /rɪ'zain/ vt renunciar (a); ceder; resignar. vi dimitir. **to r. oneself,** resignarse

resignation /ˌrɛzɪg'neiʃən/ n resignación, f; (from a post) dimisión, f. **to send in one's r.,** dimitir

resigned /rɪ'zaind/ a resignado

resignedly /rɪ'zainɪdli/ adv con resignación

resilience /rɪ'zɪlyəns/ n elasticidad, f

resilient /rɪ'zɪlyənt/ a elástico

resin /'rɛzɪn/ n resina, f, Central America, Mexico copal, m; (solid, for violin bows, etc.) colofonia, f

resinous /'rɛzənəs/ a resinoso

resist /rɪ'zɪst/ vt and vi (bear) aguantar; (impede) impedir; (repel, ward off) resistir; rechazar; hacer frente (a); oponerse (a); negarse (a)

resistance /rɪ'zɪstəns/ n resistencia, f; aguante, m, tenacidad, f; oposición, f; repugnancia, f. **passive r.,** resistencia pasiva, f. **r. coil,** Elec. resistencia, f. **r. movement,** movimiento de resistencia, m

resistant /rɪ'zɪstənt/ a resistente

resister /rɪ'zɪstər/ n el, m, (f, la) que resiste

resole /ri'soul/ vt remontar

resolute /'rɛzə,lut/ a resuelto, decidido

resolutely /ˌrɛzə'lutli/ adv resueltamente

resolution /ˌrɛzə'luʃən/ n resolución, f; (proposal placed before a legislative body, etc.) proposición, f; propósito, m

resolve /rɪ'zɒlv/ vt resolver; desarrollar, deshacer (an abbreviation, acronym, or initialism). vi resolverse. n propósito, m; (of character) resolución, firmeza, f

resonance /'rɛzənəns/ n resonancia, f; sonoridad, f

resonant /'rɛzənənt/ a resonante; reverberante, sonoro

resort /rɪ'zɔrt/ n recurso, m; punto de reunión, m; (frequentation) frecuentación, f; (gathering) concurrencia, f; reunión, f. vi acudir (a), acogerse (a); hacer uso (de); pasar (a); (frequent) frecuentar, concurrir. **health r.,** balneario, m. **holiday r.,** playa de verano, f; pueblo de veraneo, m. **in the last r.,** en último recurso

resound /rɪ'zaund/ vi resonar, retumbar, retronar; Fig. tener fama, ser celebrado; vt hacer reverberar; Fig. celebrar

resounding /rɪ'zaundɪŋ/ a retumbante, resonante

resource /'risɔrs/ n recurso, m; (of character) inventiva, f; pl **resources;** recursos, fondos, m pl

resourceful /rɪ'sɔrsfəl/ a ingenioso

resourcefulness /rɪ'sɔrsfəlnɪs/ n ingeniosidad, f

respect /rɪ'spɛkt/ n respeto, m; consideración, f; (reference, regard) respecto, m; pl **respects,** (greetings) saludos, m pl; homenaje, m. vt respetar; honrar; (concern, regard) concernir, tocar (a). **in other respects,** por lo demás. **in r. of,** tocante a, respecto a. **in some respects,** desde algunos puntos de vista. **out of r. for,** por consideración a

respectability /rɪ,spɛktə'bɪlɪti/ n respetabilidad, f

respectable /rɪ'spɛktəbəl/ a respetable; pasable; considerable

respectably /rɪ'spɛktəbli/ adv respetablemente

respected /rɪ'spɛktɪd/ a and part respetado; apreciado, estimado; digno de respeto, honrado

respectful /rɪ'spɛktfəl/ a respetuoso

respectfully /rɪ'spɛktfəli/ adv respetuosamente

respectfulness /rɪ'spɛktfəlnɪs/ n aire respetuoso, m; conducta respetuosa, f

respecting /rɪ'spɛktɪŋ/ prep con respecto a, en cuanto a, tocante a, a propósito de

respective /rɪ'spɛktɪv/ a respectivo; relativo

respectively /rɪ'spɛktɪvli/ adv respectivamente

respiration /ˌrɛspə'reiʃən/ n respiración, f

respirator /'rɛspə,reitər/ n respirador, m

respiratory /'rɛspərə,tɔri/ a respiratorio

respire /rɪ'spaiᵊr/ vt and vi respirar; exhalar; descansar

respite /'rɛspɪt/ n tregua, pausa, f; respiro, m; Law. espera, f. vt dar tregua (a); (postpone) aplazar; (relieve) aliviar

resplendence /rɪ'splɛndəns/ n resplandor, m, refulgencia, f, esplendor, fulgor, m

resplendent /rɪ'splɛndənt/ a resplandeciente, refulgente, relumbrante. **He was r. in a new uniform,** Lucía (or Ostentaba) un nuevo uniforme. **to be r.,** ser resplandeciente; relumbrar, refulgir

resplendently /rɪ'splɛndntli/ adv esplendorosamente

respond /rɪ'spɒnd/ vi responder; contestar; (obey) obedecer; reaccionar

respondent /rɪˈspɒndənt/ n (in a suit) demandado (-da)

response /rɪˈspɒns/ n respuesta, f; Eccl. responso, m

responsibility /rɪˌspɒnsəˈbɪlɪti/ n responsabilidad, f

responsible /rɪˈspɒnsəbəl/ a responsable

responsive /rɪˈspɒnsɪv/ a simpático; sensible, sensitivo

responsiveness /rɪˈspɒnsɪvnɪs/ n simpatía, f; sensibilidad, f

rest /rest/ n descanso, m; reposo, m; (the grave) última morada, f; tranquilidad, paz, f; inacción, f; (prop) soporte, apoyo, m; base, f; (for a lance) ristre, m; (for a rifle) apoyo, m; Mus. silencio, m, pausa, f; (in verse) cesura, f. **in r.**, en ristre. **the r.**, el resto; los demás, los otros. **to set at r.**, calmar, tranquilizar; (remove) quitar. **r.-cure**, cura de reposo, f. **r.-house**, hospedería, f; refugio, m. **r.-room, lounge**, sala de descanso, f; (toilet) excusado, retrete, m; (in theaters) saloncillo, m

rest /rest/ vi reposar, descansar; (lie down) acostarse, echarse; (stop) cesar, parar; estar en paz; apoyarse (en); descansar (sobre); posar; depender (de); (remain) quedar. vt descansar; dar un descanso (a); (lean) apoyar; basar (en). **It rests with them**, Depende de ellos. **These valuable documents now rest in the Library of Congress**, Estos valiosos documentos han parado en la Biblioteca del Congresso. **May he r. in peace!** ¡Que en paz descanse! **to r. assured**, estar seguro. **to r. on one's oars**, cesar de remar; descansar

restate /riˈsteit/ vt repetir, afirmar de nuevo

restatement /riˈsteitmənt/ n repetición, f

restaurant /ˈrestərənt/ n restaurante, restorán, m. **r.-car**, coche-comedor, m

restful /ˈrestfəl/ a descansado; tranquilo, sosegado

resting /ˈrestɪŋ/ n reposo, m. **last r.-place**, última morada, f. **r.-place**, descansadero, m; refugio, m

restitution /ˌrestɪˈtuʃən/ n restitución, f

restive /ˈrestɪv/ a (of a horse) repropio, ingobernable; inquieto, agitado; impaciente

restiveness /ˈrestɪvnɪs/ n inquietud, agitación, f; impaciencia, f

restless /ˈrestlɪs/ a agitado; inquieto, intranquilo; turbulento; sin reposo; (wakeful) desvelado; (ceaseless) incesante. **r. night**, noche desvelada, noche intranquila, Inf. noche toledana, f

restlessly /ˈrestlɪsli/ adv agitadamente; con inquietud; turbulentamente; incesantemente

restlessness /ˈrestlɪsnɪs/ n agitación, f; inquietud, intranquilidad, f; turbulencia, f; falta de reposo, f; (wakefulness) desvelo, m; movimiento incesante, m

restock /riˈstɒk/ vt (with goods) surtir de nuevo; proveer de nuevo; restablecer; repoblar

restoration /ˌrestəˈreiʃən/ n restauración, f; renovación, f; restablecimiento, m; (returning) restitución, f

restorative /rɪˈstɒrətɪv/ a and n restaurativo m

restore /rɪˈstɔr/ vt restaurar; restituir; devolver; restablecer; reponer; (repair) reformar, reparar; reconstruir; (to former rank, etc.) rehabilitar. **He restored the book to its place**, Devolvió el libro a su sitio

restorer /rɪˈstɔrər/ n restaurador (-ra)

restrain /rɪˈstrein/ vt refrenar; reprimir; (restrict) limitar, restringir; (prevent) impedir; desviar; (detain) recluir. **to r. oneself**, contenerse

restrained /rɪˈstreind/ a moderado, mesurado; sobrio; (of emotion) contenido

restraining /rɪˈstreinɪŋ/ a restrictivo; moderador, calmante

restraint /rɪˈstreint/ n freno, m; restricción, f; limitación, f; prohibición, f; compulsión, f; (reserve) reserva, f; moderación, f

restrict /rɪˈstrɪkt/ vt restringir; limitar

restriction /rɪˈstrɪkʃən/ n restricción, f; limitación, f

restrictive /rɪˈstrɪktɪv/ a restrictivo

result /rɪˈzʌlt/ n resultado, m; consecuencia, resulta, f; solución, f. vi resultar. **as the r. of**, de resultas de

resultant /rɪˈzʌltnt/ a resultante; consecuente. n resultado, m; Mech. resultante, f

resume /rɪˈzum/ vt reasumir; (continue) reanudar, continuar; (summarize) resumir

résumé /ˈrezuˌmei/ n resumen, m, recapitulación, f

resummon /riˈsʌmən/ vt convocar de nuevo (a); citar de nuevo (a)

resumption /rɪˈzʌmpʃən/ n (renewal) reanudación, f; reasunción, f

resurgence /rɪˈsɜrdʒəns/ n resurgimiento, m

resurrect /ˌrezəˈrekt/ vt Inf. desenterrar; resucitar

resurrection /ˌrezəˈrekʃən/ n resurrección, f

resuscitate /rɪˈsʌsɪˌteit/ vt and vi resucitar

resuscitation /rɪˌsʌsɪˈteiʃən/ n resurrección, f; renovación, f; renacimiento, m

retail /ˈriteil/ n venta al por menor, reventa, f. adv al por menor. vt (goods) vender al por menor, revender; (tell) contar; repetir. **r. trade**, comercio al por menor, m

retailer /ˈriteilər/ n vendedor (-ra) al por menor; (of a story) narrador (-ra); el, m, (f, la) que cuenta algo

retain /rɪˈtein/ vt retener; guardar; conservar; (a barrister) ajustar; (hire) contratar

retainer /rɪˈteinər/ n (dependent) criado, dependiente, m; partidario, adherente, m; (fee) honorario, m; pl **retainers**, séquito, m, adherentes, m pl, gente, f

retaining wall /rɪˈteinɪŋ/ n muro de contención, m

retake /n ˈriteik; v riˈteik/ n (cinema) nueva toma, f. vt volver a tomar; reconquistar

retaking /ˈriˌteikɪŋ/ n reconquista, f

retaliate /rɪˈtæliˌeit/ vt vengarse de, desquitarse de. vi vengarse, tomar represalias

retaliation /rɪˌtæliˈeiʃən/ n represalias, f pl; desquite, m, satisfacción, f. **law of r.**, talión, m,

retaliatory /rɪˈtæliə, a de represalias; de desquite

retard /rɪˈtɑrd/ vt retardar

retch /retʃ/ vi tener náuseas, procurar vomitar

retching /ˈretʃɪŋ/ n náusea, basca, f

retell /riˈtel/ vt repetir, volver a contar

retention /rɪˈtenʃən/ n retención, f; conservación, f

retentive /rɪˈtentɪv/ a retentivo

retentiveness /rɪˈtentɪvnɪs/ n poder de retención, m; (memory) retentiva, f

reticence /ˈretəsəns/ n reticencia, reserva, f

reticent /ˈretəsənt/ a reservado, inexpresivo, taciturno

retina /ˈretnə/ n retina, f

retinue /ˈretnˌu, -ˌyu/ n séquito, acompañamiento, m, comitiva, f

retire /rɪˈtaiər/ vi retirarse; (to bed) recogerse, acostarse; (from a post) jubilarse. vt retirar; jubilar. **to r. from a post**, Mil. rendir el puesto

retired /rɪˈtaiərd/ a retirado; (remote) apartado, aislado; (hidden) escondido; (former) antiguo; (from employment, etc.) jubilado; (of an officer) retirado. **to place on the r. list**, jubilar; (Mil. Nav.) dar el retiro (a)

retirement /rɪˈtaiərmənt/ n retirada, f; (solitude) apartamiento, aislamiento, m; retiro, m; (superannuation) jubilación, f

retiring /rɪˈtaiərɪŋ/ a que se retira; (from a post) dimitente; (with pension, etc.) de jubilación; (reserved) reservado; modesto

retort /rɪˈtɔrt/ vi replicar. vt retorcer; devolver (una acusación, etc.). n réplica, f; contestación, f; Chem. retorta, f

retouch /riˈtʌtʃ/ vt retocar

retrace /rɪˈtreis/ vt volver a trazar; volver a andar (un camino); (one's steps) volver sobre sus pasos, volver atrás; (in memory) rememorar, recordar; buscar el origen (de); (recount) narrar, contar

retract /rɪˈtrækt/ vt retractar, retirar; (draw back) retraer. vi retractarse

retraction /rɪˈtrækʃən/ n retracción, f

retranslate /riˈtrænsleit/ vt hacer una nueva traducción (de)

retransmission /ˌritrænsmˈmɪʃən/ n retransmisión, f

retread /riˈtred/ vt pisar de nuevo; (tires) recauchetear

retreat /rɪˈtrit/ n retirada, f; (Mil. signal) retreta, f; (refuge and Eccl.) retiro, m. vi retirarse; retroceder; refugiarse

retreat house n casa de ejercicios, f

retreating /rɪˈtritɪŋ/ a que se retira; que retrocede; Mil. que se bate en retirada

retrench /rɪ'trentʃ/ vt reducir; disminuir; vi economizar, hacer economías

retrenchment /rɪ'trentʃmənt/ n disminución, reducción, f; economías, f pl

retrial /'rɪtraɪl/ n (of a person) nuevo proceso, m; (of a case) revisión, f

retribution /,retrə'byuʃən/ n retribución, f; justo castigo, m, pena merecida, f

retrievable /rɪ'trivəbəl/ a recuperable, que puede recobrarse; reparable

retrieval /rɪ'trivəl/ n recuperación, f; reparación, f; (of game) cobra, f; (of one's character) rehabilitación, f

retrieve /rɪ'triv/ vt (game, of dogs) cobrar; (regain) recobrar, recuperar; restaurar; reparar; restablecer; (one's character) rehabilitar. vi cobrar la caza

retriever /rɪ'trivər/ n (dog) perdiguero (-ra)

retroactive /,retrou'æktɪv/ a retroactivo

retrocede /,retrə'sid/ vi retroceder

retrograde /'retrə,greid/ a retrógrado

retrogression /,retrə'grɛʃən/ n retrogradación, regresión, f; Med. retroceso, m

retrogressive /,retrə'grɛsɪv/ a retrógrado

retrospect /'retrə,spɛkt/ n mirada retrospectiva, f, examen del pasado, m. **in r.,** retrospectivamente

retrospection /,retrə'spɛkʃən/ n retrospección, f

retrospective /,retrə'spɛktɪv/ a retrospectivo

retrospectively /,retrə'spɛktɪvli/ adv retrospectivamente

retry /ri'trai/ vt (a case) rever; (a person) procesar de nuevo

return /rɪ'tɜrn/ vi regresar, Lat. Am. devolverse; volver; reaparecer; presentarse de nuevo; Law. revertir; (answer) contestar, responder. vt (give back or put back) devolver; (a ball) restar; (a kindness, visit) pagar; restituir; (reciprocate) corresponder (a); recompensar; contestar (a); dar; rendir; (yield) producir; (a verdict) fallar, pronunciar; (report) dar parte de; anunciar; (exchange) cambiar; (elect) elegir. n regreso, m; vuelta, f; (giving or putting back) devolución, f; pago, m; restitución, f; correspondencia, f; recompensa, f; (reply) respuesta, f; (reappearance) reaparición, f; reinstalación, f; repetición, f; (gain) ganancia, f; provecho, m; rendimiento, m; (exchange) cambio, m; (report) parte oficial, f; informe, m; lista, f; (election) elección, f; pl **returns,** tablas estadísticas, f pl; (of an election) resultados, m pl. **Many happy returns!** ¡Feliz cumpleaños! **by return mail,** a vuelta de correo. **on my (his, etc.) r.,** a la vuelta, cuando vuelva. **to r. like for like,** pagar en la misma moneda. **r. journey, r. trip,** viaje de vuelta, m. **r. match,** partido de vuelta, m. **r. ticket,** billete de ida y vuelta, m; billete de vuelta, m

returnable /rɪ'tɜrnəbəl/ a restituible; susceptible a ser devuelto; (on approval) a prueba; Law. devolutivo

returning /rɪ'tɜrnɪŋ/ a que vuelve. n See **return**

"Return to Sender" «Al remitente»

reunion /ri'yunyən/ n reunión, f

reunite /,riyu'nait/ vt reunir. vi reunirse

revaccinate /ri'væksə,neit/ vt revacunar

revaccination /ri,væksə'neiʃən/ n revacunación, f

reveal /rɪ'vil/ vt revelar; descubrir

revealer /rɪ'vilər/ n revelador (-ra)

revealing /rɪ'vilɪŋ/ a revelador. n revelación, f; descubrimiento, m

reveille /'revəli/ n Mil. diana, f, toque de la diana, m

revel /'revəl/ vi divertirse; regocijarse (en), gozarse (en); entregarse (a); (carouse) ir de parranda; emborracharse. n algazara, jarana, f; pl **revels,** fiestas, festividades, f pl

revelation /,revə'leiʃən/ n revelación, f; descubrimiento, m; **Revelation,** (in the Bible) Apocalipsis, m

reveler /'revələr/ n convidado alegre, m; (at night) trasnochador (-ra); (drunk) borracho (-cha); (masked) máscara, mf

revelry /'revəlri/ n festividades, f pl, regocijo, m; orgías, f pl, Central America embullo, m

revenge /rɪ'vendʒ/ n venganza, f. vt vengarse de; desquitarse de

revengeful /rɪ'vendʒfəl/ a vengativo

revengefully /rɪ'vendʒfəli/ adv vengativamente

revengefulness /rɪ'vendʒfəlnɪs/ n deseo de venganza, m; carácter vengativo, m

revenger /rɪ'vendʒər/ n vengador (-ra)

revenue /'revən,yu, -ə,nu/ n rentas públicas, f pl; (treasury) fisco, m; Com. rédito, m, ingresos, m pl; beneficio, m. **Inland R.,** delegación de contribuciones, f. **r. officer,** agente fiscal, m

reverberate /rɪ'vɜrbə,reit/ vt and vi (of sound) retumbar, resonar; (of light, etc.) reverberar

reverberation /rɪ,vɜrbə'reiʃən/ n (reflection) reverberación, f; (of sound) retumbo, eco, m

revere /rɪ'vɪər/ vt reverenciar, venerar, honrar

reverence /'revərəns/ n reverencia, f, vt reverenciar

reverend /'revərənd/ a reverendo

reverent /'revərənt/ a reverente

reverie /'revəri/ n ensueño, m

reversal /rɪ'vɜrsəl/ n inversión, f; (of a verdict) revocación, f

reverse /rɪ'vɜrs/ vt invertir; (a steam engine) dar contra vapor (a); (a vehicle) poner en marcha atrás; (arms) llevar a la funerala; (a judgment, etc.) revocar, derogar. vi (dancing) dar vueltas al revés. n lo contrario, lo opuesto; (back) dorso, revés, m; (change) cambio, m; (check) revés, m, vicisitud, f; (loss) pérdida, f; (defeat) derrota, f; Mech. marcha atrás, f, a inverso; contrario, opuesto. **quite the r.,** todo el contrario. **r. turn,** (of an engine) cambio de dirección, m; (in dancing) vuelta al revés, f

reversible /rɪ'vɜrsəbəl/ a reversible

reversion /rɪ'vɜrʒən, -ʃən/ n reversión, f; Biol. atavismo, m; (of offices) futura, f; (of property) reversión, f

revert /rɪ'vɜrt/ vi Law. revertir; volver (a)

review /rɪ'vyu/ n examen, análisis, m; juicio crítico, m; (journal and Mil.) revista, f; (criticism) revista, reseña, f; Law. revisión, f. vt examinar, analizar; (Mil. etc.) pasar revista (a); revisar; repasar; (a book, etc.) reseñar; Law. revisar. vi escribir revistas

review article n artículo de reseña, m

reviewer /rɪ'vyuər/ n revistero (-ra), crítico, m

revile /rɪ'vail/ vt injuriar, maldecir, difamar

reviler /rɪ'vailər/ n maldiciente, m, insultador (-ra)

reviling /rɪ'vailɪŋ/ n insultos, m pl, injurias, f pl

revisal /rɪ'vaizəl/ n revisión, f

revise /rɪ'vaiz/ vt revisar; repasar; corregir; (change) cambiar

reviser /rɪ'vaizər/ n revisor, m; corrector de pruebas, m

revision /rɪ'vɪʒən/ n revisión, f; repaso, m; corrección de pruebas, f

revisit /rɪ'vɪzɪt/ vt volver a visitar, visitar de nuevo

revival /rɪ'vaivəl/ n resurgimiento, m; renovación, f; (awakening) despertamiento, m; restablecimiento, m; resurrección, f; (of learning) renacimiento, m; Theat. reposición, f; (religious) despertar religioso, m

revive /rɪ'vaiv/ vi reponerse; restablecerse; resucitar; renovarse; renacer; cobrar fuerzas; (recover consciousness) volver en sí. vt hacer revivir; resucitar; restablecer; renovar; restaurar; despertar; (fire, colors) avivar

reviver /rɪ'vaivər/ n resucitador (-ra)

revivification /rɪ,vɪvəfi'keiʃən/ n revivificación, f

revivify /rɪ'vɪvə,fai/ vt revivificar

revocable /'revəkabəl, rɪ'vou-/ a revocable

revocation /,revə'keiʃən/ n revocación, f

revoke /rɪ'vouk/ vt revocar, anular, derogar; (wills) quebrantar. vi revocar, anular; (at cards) renunciar. n (cards) renuncio, m

revolt /rɪ'voult/ n rebelión, f, vi rebelarse, sublevarse. vt repugnar, indignar, dar asco (a)

revolting /rɪ'voultɪŋ/ a repugnante, asqueroso; (rebellious) rebelde

revolution /,revə'luʃən/ n revolución, f; (turn) vuelta, f, giro, m

revolutionary /,revə'luʃə,nɛri/ a and n revolucionario (-ia)

revolutionize /,revə'luʃə,naiz/ vt revolucionar

revolve /rɪ'volv/ vi dar vueltas, girar; suceder periódicamente. vt hacer girar; (ponder) revolver, discurrir

revolver /rɪ'volvər/ n revólver, m

revolving /rɪ'volvɪŋ/ a giratorio; que vuelve; peri-

ódico. **r. chair,** silla giratoria, *f.* **r. door,** puerta giratoria, *f.* **r. stage,** escenario giratorio, *m*
revue /rɪ'vyu/ *n Theat.* revista, *f*
revulsion /rɪ'vʌlʃən/ *n* revulsión, *f*
revulsive /rɪ'vʌlsɪv/ *a Med.* revulsivo
rev up /rɛv/ *vt* (an engine) calentar
reward /rɪ'wɔrd/ *n* recompensa, *f*; retribución, *f. vt* recompensar; satisfacer, premiar
rewarding /rɪ'wɔrdɪŋ/ *a* premiador; que recompensa. *n* recompensación, *f.* **a rewarding experience,** una experiencia compensadora, *f*
rewrite /ri'rait/ *vt* escribir de nuevo; volver a escribir; redactar otra vez
rhapsody /'ræpsədi/ *n* rapsodia, *f*
rheostat /'riə,stæt/ *n* reóstato, *m*
rhetoric /'rɛtərɪk/ *n* retórica, *f*
rhetorical /rɪ'tɔrɪkəl/ *a* retórico; declamatorio
rhetorician /,rɛtə'rɪʃən/ *n* retórico (-ca)
rheumatic /rʊ'mætɪk/ *a* reumático. **r. fever,** reumatismo poliarticular agudo, *m*
rheumatism /'rumə,tɪzəm/ *n* reumatismo, reuma, *m*
rheumy /'rumi/ *a* catarroso; (of the eyes) legañoso
Rhine, the /rain/ el Rin, *m*
rhinestone /'rain,stoun/ circón, *m*
rhinoceros /rai'nɒsərəs/ *n* rinoceronte, *m*
Rhodes /roudz/ Rodas, *f*
rhododendron /,roudə'dɛndrən/ *n* rododendro, *m*
rhubarb /'rubɑrb/ *n* ruibarbo, *m*
rhyme /raim/ *n* rima, *f*; verso, *m. vi* and *vt* rimar. **without r. or reason,** sin ton ni son; a tontas y a locas
rhymer /'raimər/ *n* rimador (-ra)
rhyming /'raimɪŋ/ *a* rimador
rhythm /'rɪðəm/ *n* ritmo, *m*
rhythmic /'rɪðmɪk/ *a* rítmico
rib /rɪb/ *n* (*Anat., Bot., Aer., Naut., Archit.*) costilla, *f*; (of an umbrella or fan) varilla, *f*; (in cloth) cordoncillo, *m*, lista, *f*
ribald /'rɪbɑld/ *a* escabroso, ribaldo, indecente
ribaldry /'rɪbəldri/ *n* ribaldería, escabrosidad, indecencia, *f*
ribbed /rɪbd/ *a* con costillas; (of cloth) listado, con listas
ribbon /'rɪbən/ *n* cinta, *f*; tira, *f*; (tatter) jirón, *m*. **to tear to ribbons,** hacer jirones
rice /rais/ *n* arroz, *m. a* de arroz; con arroz. **r. field,** arrozal, *m*. **r.-paper,** papel de paja de arroz, *m*. **r.-pudding,** arroz con leche, *m*
rich /rɪtʃ/ *a* rico; opulento; (happy) dichoso; (of land, etc.) fértil; abundante; (of objects) magnífico, suntuoso, hermoso; precioso; (of food) exquisito; suculento; (highly seasoned) muy sazonado; (creamy) con mucha nata; (of colors) brillante, vivo. **new r.,** ricacho (-cha). **newly-r.,** advenedizo. **to grow r.,** enriquecerse, *Lat. Am. also* fondearse
riches /'rɪtʃɪz/ *n* riqueza, *f*
richly /'rɪtʃli/ *adv* ricamente; abundantemente; magníficamente; bien
richness /'rɪtʃnɪs/ *n* riqueza, *f*; opulencia, *f*; (of land, etc.) fertilidad, *f*; abundancia, *f*; (of objects) magnificencia, suntuosidad, hermosura, *f*; preciosidad, *f*; (of food) gusto exquisito, *m*; suculencia, *f*; (piquancy) gusto picante, *m*; (of colors) viveza, *f*
rickets /'rɪkɪts/ *n* raquitismo, *m*
rickety /'rɪkɪti/ *a Med.* raquítico; destartalado, desvencijado; (unsteady) tambaleante; cojo
rickshaw /'rɪkʃɔ/ *n* riksha, *m*
ricochet /,rɪkə'ʃei/ *n* rebote, *m*, *vi* rebotar
rid /rɪd/ *vt* librar (de). **to get rid of,** librarse de; quitarse de encima (a); perder, quitarse; (dismiss) despedir. **to rid oneself of,** librarse de, deshacerse de
riddance /'rɪdns/ *n* libramiento, *m*
riddle /'rɪdl/ *n* acertijo, *m*; enigma, problema, *m*; misterio, *m*; (sieve) tamiz de alambre, *m*; *vt* (guess) adivinar; (sift) cribar; (with holes) acribillar
ride /raid/ *vi* (a horse) montar a caballo, cabalgar; pasear a caballo; (a mule, a bicycle) montar en, pasear en; (a vehicle, train) ir en; (a carriage, car) andar en, pasear en; (float) flotar; (on the wind) dejarse llevar por el viento; ser llevado por el viento; (go) ir;

(come) venir; (a distance) hacer... a caballo, en coche, etc.; *Naut.* estar al ancla; *Mech.* tener juego. *vt* (a horse, mule, bicycle) montar; ir montado sobre; manejar; (a race) hacer; (float) flotar en; (cleave, the sea, etc.) surcar. *n* paseo (a caballo, en bicicleta, en coche, etc.), *m*; viaje (en un autobús, de tren, etc.), *m*; (bridle path) camino de herradura, *m*; cabalgata, *f*, desfile a caballo, *m*; (hitch, lift) *Mexico* aventón, *m*. **a r. on horseback,** un paseo a caballo. **They gave me a r. in their car,** (e.g. to see the sights) Me llevaron a paseo en su auto, (a lift to a certain place) Me dieron un aventón. **ride at anchor,** estar fondeado. **to r. a bicycle,** montar en bicicleta. **to r. rough-shod over,** mandar a la baqueta (a), mandar a puntapiés (a). **to r. sidesaddle,** cabalgar a mujeriegas. **to r. at,** embestir con. **to r. away,** marcharse, alejarse; marcharse a caballo, etc. **to r. back,** volver; volver a caballo, en bicicleta, etc. **to r. behind,** seguir a caballo; ir inmediatamente detrás (de); (on the back seat) ocupar el asiento de atrás; (on the same animal) cabalgar en la grupa. **to r. down,** atropellar; (trample) pisotear, pasar por encima de. **to r. on,** seguir su camino. **to r. out,** salir a paseo en caballo, etc.; irse a paseo en coche, etc.; (a storm) hacer frente a, luchar con. **to r. over,** pasar por encima de; recorrer. **to r. up,** *vi* llegar, acercarse; (of a tie, etc.) subir. *vt* montar
rider /'raidər/ *n* cabalgador (-ra); jinete, *m*; persona que va en coche, etc., *f*; (on a bicycle) ciclista, *mf*; (on a motorcycle) motociclista, *mf*; (horsebreaker) domador de caballos, *m*; (clause) añadidura, *f*; corolario, *m*
ridge /rɪdʒ/ *n* cumbre, cima, *f*; (of mountains) cordillera, sierra, *f*; (of a roof, of a nose) caballete, *m*; *Agr.* lomo, caballón, *m*; (wrinkle) arruga, *f*; (on coins) cordoncillo, *m. vt* surcar; formar lomos (en); (wrinkle) arrugar
ridicule /'rɪdɪ,kyul/ *n* ridículo, *m*, *vt* poner en ridículo, ridiculizar, burlarse (de), mofarse (de)
ridiculous /rɪ'dɪkyələs/ *a* ridículo, absurdo
riding /'raidɪŋ/ *a* cabalgante; que va a caballo; montado (a, en, sobre); *Naut.* al ancla; (in compounds) de equitación; de montar. *n* equitación, *f*; paseo a caballo; en bicicleta, etc., *m*; acción de ir a caballo, etc., *f*; (district) comarca, *f*. **r.-boots,** botas de montar, *f pl*. **r.-habit,** traje de montar, *m*; (woman's) amazona, *f*. **r.-master,** profesor de equitación, *m. ***r.-saddle,** silla de montar, *f*. **r.-school,** escuela de equitación, *f*
rife /raif/ *a* común: corriente; frecuente; prevalente; abundante; general. **r. with,** abundante en; lleno de
riffraff /'rɪf,ræf/ *n* desperdicios, *m pl*; (rabble) gentuza, canalla, *f*
rifle /'raifəl/ *n* rifle, fusil rayado, *m. vt* robar; (a suitcase, etc.) desvalijar; (a gun) rayar. **r.-case,** *Mexico* carcaj, *m*. **r.-range,** campo de tiro, *m*. **r.-shot,** fusilazo, *m*
rifleman /'raifəlmən/ *n* fusilero, *m*
rifler /'raiflər/ *n* saqueador (-ra)
rifling /'raiflɪŋ/ *n* (robbing) saqueo, robo, *m*; (of a suitcase, etc.) desvalijamiento, *m*
rift /rɪft/ *n* hendedura, abertura, *f*; grieta, *f*
rig /rɪg/ *n Naut.* aparejo, *m*; *Inf.* atavío, *m. vt* (a ship) aparejar; equipar; (elections) falsificar. **to rig out,** proveer de; equipar con; ataviar. **to rig up,** arreglar; armar, construir
rigging /'rɪgɪŋ/ *n* (of a ship) aparejo, *m*
right /rait/ *a* recto; correcto; conveniente, debido; apropiado; exacto; (opposite of left hand) derecho; (straight) directo; en línea recta; razonable; (true) verdadero, genuino, legítimo; (just) justo; (prudent) prudente; (in health) sano. **All r.!** ¡Está bien! **I feel all r.,** Me siento perfectamente bien, Estoy bien. **He is the r. man for the job,** Él es el hombre que hace falta para el puesto. **It is the r. word,** Es la palabra apropiada. **on the r.,** a la derecha. **to be r.,** (of persons) tener razón. **to make r.,** poner en orden; arreglar. **r.-angle,** ángulo recto, *m*. **r.-angled,** rectangular. **r.-angled triangle,** triángulo rectángulo, *m*. **the R. Bank (of Paris),** la Orilla derecha, la Ribera derecha, *f*. **r. hand,** *n* (mano) derecha, diestra, *f*; derecha, *f*; (person) brazo derecho, *m*. *a* de la mano de-

recha; de la derecha; a la derecha. **r.-handed,** derecho; diestro, hábil. **r. mind,** entero juicio, *m.* **r.-minded,** juicioso, prudente; honrado. **r.-of-way,** derecho a la vía, *m.*

right /rait/ *adv* directamente; inmediatamente; derechamente; correctamente; debidamente; exactamente; bien; (quite, thoroughly) completamente; honradamente; (very) muy. **r. on,** adelante; en frente. **R. about face!** ¡Media vuelta a la derecha! **r. at the bottom,** al fondo; al final; el último (de la clase, etc.). **r. at the end of his speech,** al fin de su discurso. **r. away,** **r. now** en seguida, inmediatamente, *Mexico* ahorita, *elsewhere in Lat. Am.* lueguito

right /rait/ *n* razón, *f;* verdad, *f;* justicia, *f;* (good) bien, *m;* derecho, *m;* (not left side) derecha, *f;* (of political parties) derechas, *f pl.* **r. and wrong,** el bien y el mal. **"All rights reserved,"** «Derechos reservados.» **by rights,** por derecho. **It is on the r.,** Está a la derecha. **to exercise one's r.,** usar de su derecho. **r. of association,** derecho de asociación, *m.* **r. of way,** derecho de paso, *m.* **to be in the r.,** tener razón; estar en su derecho

right /rait/ *vt* enderezar; rectificar; corregir; poner en orden; *Naut.* enderezar; hacer justicia (a). **to r. wrongs,** deshacer agravios

righteous /'raitʃəs/ *a* recto, virtuoso, justo; justificado

righteously /'raitʃəsli/ *adv* virtuosamente; justamente

righteousness /'raitʃəsnɪs/ *n* rectitud, integridad, virtud, *f;* justicia, *f*

rightful /'raitfəl/ *a* justo; legítimo; verdadero

rightfully /'raitfəli/ *adv* justamente; legitimamente; verdaderamente

rightfulness /'raitfəlnɪs/ *n* justicia, *f;* legitimidad, *f;* verdad, *f*

rightly /'raitli/ *adv* justamente; debidamente; correctamente; bien. **r. or wrongly,** mal que bien

rightness /'raitnɪs/ *n* rectitud, *f;* derechura, *f;* justicia, *f;* exactitud, *f*

rigid /'rɪdʒɪd/ *a* rígido; inflexible; severo, riguroso

rigidity /rɪ'dʒɪdɪti/ *n* rigidez, *f;* inflexibilidad, *f;* severidad, *f*

rigmarole /'rɪgməˌroul/ *n* monserga, *f,* galimatías, *m,* jerigonza, *f*

rigor /'rɪgər/ *n* rigor, *m*

rigorous /'rɪgərəs/ *a* riguroso

rile /rail/ *vt Inf.* irritar, sacar de tino (a)

rim /rɪm/ *n* borde, *m;* orilla, *f;* (of a wheel) llanta, *f,* aro, *m*

rime /raim/ *n* escarcha, *f, vt* cubrir con escarcha. See also **rhyme**

rind /raind/ *n* (of fruit) cáscara, corteza, *f;* (of cheese) costra, *f;* (of bacon) piel, *f*

ring /rɪŋ/ *n* círculo, *m;* (round the eyes) ojera, *f;* (for curtains, etc.) anilla, *f;* (for the finger) anillo, *m,* sortija, *f;* (for children's games, etc.) corro, *m;* (for the ears) arete, *m;* (of smoke and for the nose) anillo, *m;* (for hitching, etc.) argolla, *f;* (for boxing) cuadrilátero, *m;* (on a racecourse) picadero, *m;* (at a circus, bull-fight) ruedo, redondel, *m; Fig.* arena, *f;* (group) camarilla, *f,* grupo, *m;* (metallic sound) sonido metálico, *m;* resonancia, *f;* (tinkle) tintín, *m;* (of a bell) repique, tañido, son (de la campana), *m;* (of bells) juego de campanas, *m;* (of laughter, etc.) ruido, *m;* (of truth, etc.) apariencia, *f.* **r.-bolt,** *Naut.* cáncamo, *m.* **r. finger,** dedo anular, *m.* **r.-master,** director de circo, *m*

ring /rɪŋ/ *vt* (surround) cercar, rodear; (a bull, etc.) poner un anillo (a); (sound) hacer sonar; sonar; (a door bell, etc.) tocar, apretar; (bells) echar a vuelo; (announce by pealing the bells) anunciar, proclamar; sonar, tañer. *vi* (of bells) sonar; (re-echo) resonar; (of the ears) zumbar; (tinkle) tintinar. **to r. the bell,** tocar la campana; tocar el timbre. **to r. off,** colgar el teléfono. **to r. up,** llamar por teléfono, telefonear

ringing /'rɪŋɪŋ/ *n* acción de tocar las campanas o el timbre, *f;* toque, *m;* repique, *m;* campanilleo, *m;* (in the ears) zumbido, *m. a* resonante, sonoro. **r. signal,** señal de llamada, *f.* **the r. of the bells,** el son de las campanas

ringleader /'rɪŋˌlidər/ *n* cabecilla, *m*

ringlet /'rɪŋlɪt/ *n* rizo, bucle, *m*

ringworm /'rɪŋˌwɜrm/ *n* tiña, *f*

rink /rɪŋk/ *n* pista, *f.* **skating-r.,** sala de patinar, *f;* pista de patinar, *f*

rinse /rɪns/ *n* enjuague, *m;* enjuagadura, *f;* (of clothes) aclarado, *m. vt* enjuagar; (clothes) aclarar; lavar

rinsing /'rɪnsɪŋ/ *n* See **rinse;** *pl* **rinsings,** lavazas, *f pl. a* de aclarar

Rio de Janeiro /'riou dei ʒə'nɛərou/ *n* Rio de Janeiro, *f; a* carioca, *formal* fluminense, *mf*

riot /'raiət/ *n* motín, *m;* tumulto, *m;* desorden, *m;* exceso, *m;* orgía, *f;* disipación, *f. vi* amotinarse; alborotarse; entregarse a la disipación (or al placer); (enjoy) gozar, disfrutar. **to run r.,** hacer excesos; perder el freno; desmandarse; *Fig.* extenderse por todas partes; crecer en abundancia, cubrir todo

rioter /'raiətər/ *n* amotinador (-ra); alborotador (-ra)

riotous /'raiətəs/ *a* sedicioso; bullicioso; disoluto; desordenado; desenfrenado

riotousness /'raiətəsnɪs/ *n* sedición, *f;* disolución, *f;* excesos, *m pl,* desenfreno, *m;* desorden, *m*

rip /rɪp/ *vt* rasgar; (unsew) descoser; (wood, etc.) partir; (make) hacer. *vi* rasgarse. *n* rasgón, *m;* rasgadura, *f;* desgarro, *m;* (libertine) calavera, *m.* **to rip off,** arrancar; quitar. **to rip open,** abrir; (an animal) abrir en canal

riparian /rɪ'pɛəriən/ *a* and *n* ribereño (-ña)

ripe /raip/ *a* maduro; preparado; perfecto, acabado

ripen /'raipən/ *vt* and *vi* madurar

ripeness /'raipənɪs/ *n* madurez, *f*

ripening /'raipənɪŋ/ *n* maduración, *f*

ripping /'rɪpɪŋ/ *n* rasgadura, *f;* (unstitching) deshiladura, *f. a Inf.* estupendo

ripple /'rɪpəl/ *n* rizo, *m;* onda, *f;* (of sound) murmullo, *m. vt* rizar. *vi* rizarse; murmurar

rippling /'rɪplɪŋ/ *n* rizado, *m;* murmullo, *m*

rise /raiz/ *vi* ascender; subir; levantarse; ponerse de pie; (of a meeting) suspenderse; (from the dead) resucitar; (grow) crecer; (swell) hincharse; (of sun, moon) salir; (of sound, gradient, price, stock exchange quotations) subir; (of river source) nacer; (in revolt) sublevarse, rebelarse; (to the mind) presentarse, surgir; (appear) aparecer; (of buildings, etc.) elevarse, alzarse; (in the world) mejorar de posición; (originate) originarse (en), proceder (de); (of mercury) alzarse; (of fish) picar. **He has risen in my estimation,** Ha ganado en mi estimación. **She rose early,** Se levantó temprano. **The color rose in her cheeks,** Se le subieron los colores a la cara. **to r. to the occasion,** estar al nivel de las circunstancias. **to r. to one's feet,** ponerse de pie. **to r. to the bait,** morder el anzuelo. **to r. again,** levantarse de nuevo; resucitar; renovarse; suscitarse otra vez. **to r. above,** alzarse por encima de; mostrarse superior a

rise /raiz/ *n* ascensión, *f;* subida, *f;* levantamiento, *m;* (in price, temperature) alza, *f;* (increase) aumento, *m;* (of the sun, moon) salida, *f;* (of a river) nacimiento, *m;* (origin) origen, *m;* (growth, development) desarrollo, crecimiento, *m;* (promotion) ascenso, *m;* (slope) cuesta, *f;* pendiente, *f;* (high ground) eminencia, altura, *f.* **to give r. to,** dar lugar a, causar. **r. and fall,** subida y baja, *f;* (of the voice) ritmo, *m;* (of music) cadencia, *f;* (of institutions) grandeza y decadencia, *f.* **r. to power,** subida al poder, *f*

riser /'raizər/ *n* el, *m,* (*f,* la) que se levanta; (of a step) contrahuella, *f.* **early r.,** madrugador (-ra). **late r.,** el, *m,* (*f,* la) que se levanta tarde

risibility /ˌrɪzə'bɪlɪti/ *n* risibilidad, *f*

risible /'rɪzəbəl/ *a* risible

rising /'raizɪŋ/ *n* subida, *f;* (of the source of rivers) nacimiento, *m;* (overflowing of rivers) crecimiento, *m;* (of sun, moon) salida, *f;* (from the dead) resurrección, *f;* (rebellion) sublevación, insurrección, *f;* (of the tide) crecida, *f;* (of bread) levadura, *f;* (of an assembly) suspensión, *f;* (of a theater curtain) subida, *f;* (literary) renacimiento, *m, a* creciente; naciente; saliente; (promising) de porvenir; (young) joven. **the r. generation,** los jóvenes, la generación joven. **He likes r. early,** Le gusta madrugar. **On the r. of the curtain...,** Al levantarse el telón... **the r. of the**

moon, la salida de la luna, *f.* **the r. tide,** la marea creciente

risk /rɪsk/ *n* riesgo, *m*; peligro, *m*. *vt* arriesgar; atreverse (a), osar. **at the r. of,** al riesgo de. **to take a r.,** tomar un riesgo; correr peligro. **to r. everything on the outcome,** jugar el todo por el todo

risk capital *n* capital-riesgo, *m*

riskiness /'rɪskɪnɪs/ *n* peligro, *m*

risky /'rɪski/ *a* arriesgado, peligroso

rissole /rɪ'soul/ *n* risol, *m*, (*pl* risoles)

rite /raɪt/ *n* rito, *m*

rite of passage *n* rito de tránsito, *m*

ritual /'rɪtʃuəl/ *a* ritual. *n* rito, *m*, ceremonia, *f*

ritualist /'rɪtʃuəlɪst/ *n* ritualista, *mf*

ritualistic /ˌrɪtʃuə'lɪstɪk/ *a* ritualista

rival /'raɪvəl/ *n* rival, *mf a* competidor; rival. *vt* rivalizar con, competir con

rivalry /'raɪvəlri/ *n* rivalidad, *f*

river /'rɪvər/ *n* río, *m*. *a* del río; fluvial. **r.-basin,** cuenca de un río, *f*. **r.-bed,** lecho, cauce (de un río), *m*. **r.** civilization, civilización fluvial, *f.* **r.-god,** dios de los ríos, *m*. **r.-mouth,** ría, *f*. **r.** port, puerto fluvial, *m*

riverside /'rɪvərˌsaɪd/ *n* ribera, orilla de un río, *f. a* de la(s) orilla(s) de un río; situado a la orilla de un río; ribereño

rivet /'rɪvɪt/ *n* remache, roblón, *m*. *vt* remachar; clavar; *Fig.* fijar, concentrar; *Fig.* cautivar, absorber

riveter /'rɪvɪtər/ *n* remachador, *m*

riveting /'rɪvɪtɪŋ/ *n* remachado, remache, *m*; *Fig.* fijación, concentración, *f*; *Fig.* absorción, *f*. **r. machine,** remachadora, *f*

Riviera, the /ˌrɪvi'ɛərə/ la Riviera, *f*

rivulet /'rɪvyəlɪt/ *n* riachuelo, arroyo, *m*

road /roud/ *n* camino, *m*; carretera, *f*; ruta, *f*; *pl* **roads,** *Naut.* rada, *f*. **high r.,** camino real, *m*. **main r.,** carretera, *f*. **secondary r.,** carretera de segunda clase, *f.* **on the r. to...,** en el camino de... **to get out of the r.,** *Inf.* quitarse de en medio. **to go by r.,** ir por carretera. **"R. work ahead!"** «Carretera en reparaciones.» **r.-book,** guía de carreteras, *f.* **r. house,** albergue de carretera, *m*. **r. maker,** constructor de caminos, *m*; (navvy) peón caminero, *m*. **r. making,** construcción de caminos, *f*. **r. map,** mapa de carreteras, *m*. **r. sign,** señal de carretera, señal de tránsito, señal vial, *f*, poste indicador, *m*. **The r. to hell is paved with good intentions,** El camino del infierno está empedrado de buenas intenciones. **"R. Repairs,"** «Camino en Reparación»

roadmender /'roudˌmɛndər/ *n* peón caminero, *m*

roadside /'roudˌsaɪd/ *n* borde del camino, *m, a* al lado del camino

roadstead /'roudˌstɛd/ *n* rada, *f*

roadster /'roudstər/ *n* automóvil de turismo, *m*; bicicleta de carreras, *f*; caballo de aguante, *m*; buque fondeado en rada, *m*

roadway /'roudˌwei/ *n* calzada, carretera, *f*

roam /roum/ *vi* vagar, vagabundear, andar errante. *vt* errar por

roamer /'roumər/ *n* vagabundo (-da), hombre errante, *m*

roaming /'roumɪŋ/ *n* vagabundeo, *m*; excursiones, *f pl*, paseos, *m pl*; *a* errante, vagabundo; nómada

roan /roun/ *a* roano, sabino. *n* caballo roano, *m*

roar /rɔr/ *vi* rugir; (of a bull, of the wind, of a person in anger) bramar; dar voces; (of the fire) crepitar; (of cannon) retumbar; (of thunder) estallar. *vt* gritar. *n* rugido, bramido, *m*; (shout) grito, *m*; (of the fire) crepitación, *f*; (of cannon, thunder) estallido, *m*; (noise) ruido, *m*. **to r. with laughter,** reírse a carcajadas

roaring /'rɔrɪŋ/ *n* (of horses) asma de los caballos, *f*, For other meanings, see under **roar.** *a* rugiente, bramante; *Inf.* magnífico. **to do a r. trade,** hacer un buen negocio

roast /roust/ *n* asado, *m*, carne asada, *f. a* asado; tostado. *vt* asar; (coffee and to warm one's feet, etc.) tostar; (metals) calcinar; (scold) desollar vivo (a). *vi* asarse; tostarse. **r. beef,** rosbif, *m*

roaster /'roustər/ *n* asador, *m*; (for coffee or peanuts) tostador, *m*; (for chestnuts, etc.) tambor, *m*

roasting /'roustɪŋ/ *n* asación, *f*; (of coffee) tostado, *m*; (of metals) calcinación, *f*. **r. spit,** asador, *m*

rob /rɒb/ *vt* robar; quitar, privar (de). **They have robbed her of her pocketbook,** Le han robado la cartera

robber /'rɒbər/ *n* ladrón (-ona); (footpad) salteador de caminos, *m*; (brigand) bandido, *m*

robbery /'rɒbəri/ *n* robo, *m*. **It's daylight r.!** ¡Es un desuello! **to commit a r.,** cometer un robo. **r. with violence,** robo armado, *m*

robe /roub/ *n* traje talar, *m*, toga, *f*; (of a monk, nun) hábito, *m*; (of a priest, etc.) sotana, *f*; *Poet.* manto, *m*; (infant's) mantillas, *f pl*; *pl* **robes,** traje de ceremonia, *m*. *vt* vestir; cubrir, revestir (de). *vi* vestirse. **bath r.,**

robin /'rɒbɪn/ *n* petirrojo, *m*

robot /'roubət, -bɒt/ *n* hombre mecánico, *m*; *Aer.* piloto mecánico, *m*. **traffic r.,** torre del tráfico, *f*, aparato automático, *m*. **r. plane,** avión sin piloto, *m*

robust /rou'bʌst/ *a* robusto; fuerte, vigoroso. **to make r.,** robustecer

robustness /rou'bʌstnɪs/ *n* robustez, *f*; vigor, *m*, fuerza, *f*

rock /rɒk/ *n* roca, *f*; (in the sea) abrojo, escollo, *m*; peña, *f*, peñasco, *m*. **as firm as a r.,** como una roca. **to be on the rocks,** *Inf.* estar a la cuarta pregunta. **r. bottom,** *n* fondo, *m. a* mínimo, más bajo. **r. crystal,** cuarzo, *m*. **r.-garden,** jardincito rocoso, jardín alpestre, *m*. **r.-plant,** planta alpestre, *f*. **r.-rose,** heliantemo, *m*. **r.-salt,** sal gema, *f*

rock /rɒk/ *vt* mecer; (shake) hacer temblar, sacudir; (to sleep) arrullar. *vi* mecerse, balancearse; tambalearse; agitarse; temblar

rocker /'rɒkər/ *n* (of a chair, cradle) balancín, *m*; (chair) mecedora, *f*

rocket /'rɒkɪt/ *n* cohete, volador, *m. vi* lanzarse. **r.-launching aircraft,** caza lanzacohetes, *f*

rockiness /'rɒkɪnɪs/ *f* abundancia de rocas, *f*; fragosidad, escabrosidad, *f*

rocking /'rɒkɪŋ/ *n* balanceo, *m*; (staggering) tambaleo, *m*; oscilación, *f*; (of an infant) arrullo, *m*. **r.-chair,** mecedora, *f*. **r.-horse,** caballo balancín, caballo mecedor, *m*

rocky /'rɒki/ *a* rocoso; de roca; roqueño; (rough) fragoso, escabroso; (rugged) peñascoso, escarpado. **the R. Mountains,** las Montañas Rocosas, *f pl*

rococo /rə'koukou/ *n* rococó, *m*

rod /rɒd/ *n* vara, *f*; bastón de mando, *m*; (for fishing) caña, *f*; (measure) pértiga, *f*; (surveying) jalón, *m*; palo, *m*; (of punishment) vergajo, *m*; *Mech.* vástago, *m*. **connecting rod,** biela, *f*. **to fish with rod and line,** pescar con caña

rodent /'roudnt/ *a* and *n* roedor, *m*

roe /rou/ *n* (deer) corzo (-za); (of fish) hueva, *f.* **soft roes,** lechas, *f*

rogue /roug/ *n* bribón (-ona), pícaro (-ra), pillo (-lla), *Argentina* farabute, *mf*; *Law.* vago, *m*; (affectionate) picaruelo (-la)

roguery /'rougəri/ *n* truhanería, picardía, *f*; (knaves) pícaros, *m pl*; (mischief) travesuras, *f pl*. **novel of r.,** novela picaresca, *f*

roguish /'rougɪʃ/ *a* picaresco, bellaco; (mischievous) travieso, juguetón; malicioso

roguishly /'rougɪʃli/ *adv* como un pícaro; con malicia

roguishness /'rougɪʃnɪs/ *n* picardía, bribonería, bellaquería, *f*; (mischievousness) travesuras, *f pl*; malicia, *f*

role /roul/ *n* papel, *m*

roll /roul/ *n* rollo, *m*; (list) rol, *m*, lista, *f*; (of bread) panecillo, *Mexico* bolillo, *m*; (of a drum) redoble, *m*; (of thunder) tronido, *m*; (of cloth) pieza, *f*; (of ship) balanceo, rollo, *m*; (of meat, etc.) pastel, *m*; (of a ship) balanceo, *m*; *pl* **rolls,** (records) archivos, *m pl.* **He has a nautical r.,** Tiene un andar de marinero. **to call the r.,** pasar lista. **r. film,** película fotográfica, *f.* **r. of honor,** lista de honor, *f.* **r.-on corset,** faja elástica, *f*, corsé de goma, *m*. **r.-top desk,** buró de cierre enrollable, *m*

roll /roul/ *vt* rodar; dar vueltas; (wallow) revolcarse; (of a ship) balancearse, bambolearse; (in money, etc.) nadar; (flow) correr, fluir; (*Fig.* of time) pasar tranquilamente; (of vehicle) rodar; pasar rodando; (of country) ondular; (of the sea) ondear; (of drums) redoblar; (of thunder) retumbar. *vt* hacer rodar; arrollar; (a cigarette) liar; (metals) laminar; (move) mover; (the eyes) guiñar (los ojos); (the ground) apisonar; (pastry) aplanar; (of an organ) sonar; (a drum) redoblar. **Mary rolled her eyes heavenwards,** María puso los ojos en blanco. **to r. away,** alejarse; desaparecer; (of time) pasar. **to r. back,** volver, retirarse; desaparecer. **to r. by,** pasar rodando; desaparecer. **to r. down,** bajar rodando, rodar por. **to r. in,** llegar en gran cantidad (or en gran número). **to r. off,** caer de. **to r. on,** seguir su marcha; fluir sin cesar; seguir su curso; (of time) avanzar. **to r. out,** (metal) laminar; (pastry) aplanar; (bring out) sacar; desenrollar. **to r. over,** *vt* volcar; tumbar; dar la vuelta (a). *vi* dar la vuelta; volverse al otro lado. **to r. up,** arrollar; envolver; (of hedgehogs, etc.) enroscarse, hacerse un ovillo

roll-call vote /'roul,kɔl/ *n* votación nominal, *f*

roller /'roulər/ *n* rodillo, *m*; cilindro, *m*; (wheel, castor) rueda, *f*; (for flattening the ground) apisonadora, *f*; *Print.* rodillo, *m*; (wave) ola grande, *f*. **r.-bandage,** venda, *f*. **r. canary,** canario de raza flauta, *m*. **r.-skate,** patín de ruedas, *m*. **r.-skating,** patinaje de ruedas, *m*. **r.-towel,** toalla continua, *f*

rollicking /'rɒlɪkɪŋ/ *a* alegre, jovial; juguetón

rolling /'roulɪŋ/ *a* rodante; (of landscape) ondulante, quebrado. *n* rodadura, *f*; (wallowing) revuelco, *m*; (of metals) laminación, *f*; (of a ship) balanceo, *m*; (rolling up) enrollamiento, *m*. **r.-pin,** rollo, rodillo de pastelero, *m*. **r.-stock,** material móvil ferroviario, *m*

Roman /'roumən/ *a* romano, de los romanos; (of noses and *Print.*) romano. *n* romano (-na). **in R. fashion,** a la romana. **R. Catholic,** *a* católico; católico apostólico romano. *n* el católico (-ca). **R. Catholicism,** catolicismo, *m*. **R. figures,** números romanos, *m pl*. **R. nose,** nariz romana, *f*. **R. road,** vía romana, *f*. **R. type,** *Print.* tipo romano, *m*

Romance /'roumæns/ *a* (of languages) romance. *n* (language) romance, *m*

romance /'roumæns/ *n* novela de caballería, *f*; romance, *m*; aventura, *f*; cuento, *m*, novela, *f*; romanticismo, *m*; *Mus.* romanza, *f*. *vi* inventar ficciones; exagerar

romancer /rou'mænsər/ *n* romancerista, *mf*; mentiroso (-sa), embustero (-ra)

Romanesque /,roumə'nɛsk/ *a* románico; romanesco

Romania /rou'meiniə/ Romania

Romanian /rʊ'meiniən/ *a* rumano. *n* rumano (-na); (language) rumano, *m*

romantic /rou'mæntɪk/ *a* and *n* romántico (-ca)

romantically /rou'mæntɪkli/ *adv* románticamente; de un modo romántico

romanticism /rou'mæntə,sɪzəm/ *n* romanticismo, *m*

romanticist /rou'mæntəsɪst/ *n* romántico (-ca)

Rome /roum/ Roma, *f*

romp /rɒmp/ *vi* juguetear, brincar, retozar; loquear; correr rápidamente. *n* locuelo (-la), saltaparedes, *mf*; (game) retozo, *m*. **The horse romped home easily,** El caballo ganó la carrera fácilmente

romping /'rɒmpɪŋ/ *n* juegos, *m pl*, travesuras, *f pl*

rondo /'rɒndou/ *n* rondó, *m*

rood /rud/ *n* cruz, *f*; crucifijo, *m*; cuarto de acre, *m*. **By the r.!** ¡Por mi santiguada!

roof /ruf/ *n* tejado, techado, *m*; (of a motor-car, bus) tejadillo, *m*; (of coaches, etc.) imperial, *f*; cubierta, *f*; (of the mouth) paladar, *m*; (bower) enramada, *f*; (of heaven) bóveda (del cielo), *f*. *vt* techar, tejar, *Lat. Am.* entechar; (shelter) abrigar. **r.-garden,** azotea, *f*. **r.-gutter,** canalera, *f*

roofer /'rufər/ *n* techador, *m*; constructor de tejados, *m*

rook /rʊk/ *n* chova, *f*, grajo, *m*; (chess) torre, *f*. *vt* engañar, estafar; (overcharge) desollar vivo (a)

room /rum/ *n* (in a house) habitación, *f*, cuarto, *m*; sala, *f*; cámara, *f*; (behind a shop) trastienda, *f*; (space) sitio, espacio, *m*; lugar, *m*; (opportunity) oportunidad, *f*; (cause) motivo, *m*, causa, *f*. *vi* alojarse. **bath-r.,** cuarto de baño, *m*. **dining-r.,** comedor, *m*. **drawing-r.,** salón, *m*. **There is no r. for us in this car,** No cabemos en este coche. **There is still r. for improvement,** Se puede mejorar todavía. **There**

isn't r. for anything else, No cabe más. **to be r.,** caber, haber sitio. **to make r.,** hacer sitio

roomed /rumd/ *a* (in compounds) de... habitaciones; de... salas

roominess /'ruminɪs/ *n* espaciosidad, amplitud, amplitud de habitación, *f*; (of garments) holgura, *f*

rooming house /'rutɪd/ *n* casa de huéspedes, *f*

roommate /'rum,meit, 'rʊm-/ *n* compañero de cuarto, compañero de pieza, *m*

roomy /'rumi, 'romi/ *a* espacioso, amplio; (of garments) holgado

roost /rust/ *n* percha de gallinero, *f*, *Lat. Am.* dormidero, *m*. *vi* dormir en una percha; recogerse. **to rule the r.,** ser el amo del cotarro

rooster /'rustər/ *n* gallo, *m*,

root /rut *or, sometimes,* rʊt/ *n* raíz, *f*; *Gram.* radical, *m*; *Mus.* base, *f*; origen, *m*; explicación, *f*. *vt* arraigar; *Fig.* fijar, clavar. *vi* echar raíces; *Fig.* arraigarse; (of pigs, etc.) hozar, escarbar; revolver. **to r. out,** arrancar de raíz; *Fig.* desarraigar; (destroy) extirpar. **cubed r.,** raíz cúbica, *f*. **from the r.,** (entirely) de raíz. **square r.,** raíz cuadrada, *f*. **to cut close to the r.,** cortar a raíz

rooted /'rutɪd/ *a* (in compounds) de raíces...; arraigado

rope /roup/ *n* soga, cuerda, *f*; (hawser) maroma, *f*; *Naut.* cabo, *m*; (tight-rope) cable, *m*, cuerda de volatinero, *f*; (string) ristra, sarta, *f*; hilo, *m*; *pl* **ropes,** (boxing) cuerdas del cuadrilátero, *f pl*. *vt* encordelar, atar con cuerdas. **to r. in,** encerrar; (a person) enganchar, coger. **to give a person plenty of r.,** dar mucha latitud (a). **to know the ropes,** conocer todos los trucos. **r.-ladder,** escala de cuerda, *f*. **r.-maker,** cordelero (-ra), soguero, *m*. **r.-making,** cordelería, soguería, *f*. **r.-trick,** truco de la cuerda, *m*. **r.-walk,** cordelería, *f*. **r.-yarn,** *Naut.* filástica, *f*

rosary /'rouzəri/ *n* rosario, *m*. **to pray the r.,** rezar el rosario

rose /rouz/ *n* rosa, *f*; color de rosa, *m*; (rosette) roseta, *f*; *Archit.* rosetón, *m*; (of watering-can) pomo, *m*, roseta, *f*. *a* de rosa, rosado. **to see the world through r.-colored glasses,** ver las cosas en color de rosa. **to turn to r.,** volverse color de rosa, rosear. **r.-bay,** *Bot.* rododafne, adelfa, *f*. **r.-bush,** rosal, *m*. **r.-color,** color de rosa, rosa, *m*. **r.-colored,** de color de rosa, rosado. **r.-garden,** rosalera, rosaleda, *f*. **r. grower,** cultivador (-ra) de rosas. **r. hip,** escaramujo, *m*. **r. leaf,** hoja de rosa, *f*; pétalo de rosa, *m*. **r.-like,** como una rosa, de color de rosa; de color de rosa; como una rosa. **climbing r.-tree,** rosal trepador, *m*. **dwarf r.-tree,** rosal bajo, *m*. **standard r.-tree,** rosal de tallo, *m*. **r.-water,** agua de rosas, *f*. **r.-window,** rosetón, *m*, rosa, *f*. **r.-wood,** palo de rosa, *m*

rosé /rou'zei/ *a* (of wines) rosado

rosebud /'rouz,bʌd/ *n* capullo de rosa, *m*

rosemary /'rouz,mɛəri/ *n* romero, *m*

rosin /'rɒzɪn/ *n* (solid, for violin-bows, etc.) colofonia, *f*; resina, *f*. *vt* dar con colofonia; dar con resina

rosiness /'rouzinɪs/ *n* color de rosa, *m*

roster /'rɒstər/ *n* lista, *f*; registro, *m*, matrícula, *f*

rostrum /'rɒstrəm/ *n* tribuna, *f*, podio, *m*; *Zool.* pico, *m*; (of a ship) espolón, *m*

rosy /'rouzi/ *a* róseo, rosado; sonrosado; *Fig.* de color de rosa, halagüeño; optimista. **r.-cheeked,** con (de) mejillas sonrosadas

rot /rɒt/ *n* putrefacción, podredumbre, *f*; (in trees) caries, *f*; (in sheep) comalía, *f*; (slang) patrañas, *f pl*, disparates, *m pl*, *vi* pudrirse; descomponerse; *Fig.* echarse a perder; (slang) decir disparates. *vt* pudrir; *Fig.* corromper; (slang) tomar el pelo (a)

rota /'routə/ *n* lista, *f*; orden del día, *m*

rotary /'routəri/ *a* rotativo. **r. printing press,** rotativa, *f*

rotary telephone *n* teléfono de discado, *m*

rotate /'routeit/ *vi* girar, dar vueltas; alternarse. *vt* hacer girar

rotating /'routeitɪŋ/ *a* rotativo; giratorio

rotation /rou'teiʃən/ *n* rotación, *f*; turno, *m*. **in r.,** por turnos. **r. of crops,** rotación de cultivos, *f*

rotatory /'routə,tɔri/ *a* rotatorio

rote, to learn by /rout/ *vt* aprender de memoria, aprender por repetición, aprender de cotorra

rotogravure /ˌroutəgrə'vyʊr/ *n* rotograbado, *m*

rotten /'rɒtn̩/ *a* putrefacto; podrido; (of bones, teeth) cariado; dañado, echado a perder; *Fig.* corrompido; (slang) pésimo. **to smell r.,** oler a podredumbre; apestar

rottenness /'rɒtn̩nɪs/ *n* putrefacción, podredumbre, *f*; *Fig.* corrupción, *f*

rotter /'rɒtər/ *n Slang.* perdido, *m*

rotting /'rɒtɪŋ/ *n* pudrición, *f*, *a* que se pudre

rotund /rou'tʌnd/ *a* rotundo

rotunda /rou'tʌndə/ *n* rotonda, *f*

rotundity /rou'tʌndɪti/ *n* redondez, *f*; rotundidad, *f*

rouge /ruʒ/ *n* colorete, *m*, *vt* and *vi* pintar de rojo, poner(se) colorete

rough /rʌf/ *a* áspero; duro; (of country) fragoso, escabroso; (uneven) desigual; (stormy) borrascoso, tempestuoso; (of the sea) encrespado, bravo; (of movement) violento; (bristling) erizado; (of the hair) despeinado; (unpolished) tosco; basto; (unskilled, clumsy) torpe; (of sounds, tastes) áspero; (of persons) rudo, inculto; (severe) severo; (of behavior) brutal; (of manners) brusco; (rude) grosero; (approximate) aproximado. *adv* duramente, mal. *n* estado tosco, *m*; (person) matón, *m*. **in the r.,** en bruto; (roughed out) bosquejado. **to grow r.,** (of the sea) encresparse, embravecerse. **to take the r. with the smooth,** *Fig.* aceptar la realidad; tomar lo bueno con lo malo. **to r. it,** luchar contra las dificultades, pasar apuros; llevar una vida sencilla; vivir mal. **to r. out,** bosquejar. **r. and ready,** improvisado; provisional. **r. and tumble,** *n* camorra, pendencia, *f*. **r.-cast,** *vt* dar una primera capa de mezcla gruesa (a); bosquejar. **r. diamond,** diamante bruto (or en bruto), *m*. **r.-draft,** borrador, *m*; bosquejo, *m*. **r.-haired,** (of a dog) de pelo crespo. **r.-hewn,** modelado toscamente; desbastado; *Fig.* cerril, tosco. **r.-house,** jarana, *f*. **r.-rider,** domador (de caballos), *m*. **r. sketch,** bosquejo, esbozo, *m*. **r.-spoken,** malhablado

roughen /'rʌfən/ *vt* poner áspero. *vi* ponerse áspero

roughly /'rʌfli/ *adv* rudamente, toscamente; duramente; brutalmente; bruscamente; (of tastes, sounds) ásperamente; (approximately) aproximadamente, más o menos

roughness /'rʌfnɪs/ *n* aspereza, *f*; dureza, *f*; tosquedad, *f*; rudeza, *f*; (of the sea, wind) braveza, *f*; violencia, *f*; (of manner) brusquedad, *f*; brutalidad, *f*; (vulgarity) grosería, *f*. **the r. of the way,** la aspereza del camino

roulette /ru'let/ *n* ruleta, *f*

round /raund/ *a* redondo; (plump) rollizo; rotundo, categórico; sonoro. **a r. sum,** una cantidad redonda; un número redondo. **to walk at a r. pace,** andar a un buen paso. **r. dance,** baile en ruedo, *m*. **r.-faced,** carilleno, de cara redonda. **r.-house,** cuerpo de guardia, *m*; *Naut.* tumbadillo, *m*. **r.-shouldered,** cargado de espaldas. **r. table,** mesa redonda, *f*; (of King Arthur) Tabla Redonda, *f*. **r. trip,** viaje redondo, viaje de ida y vuelta, *m*. **r.-up,** rodeo de ganado, *m*; arresto, *m*

round /raund/ *n* círculo, *m*; esfera, *f*; redondez, *f*; (slice) rodaja, *f*; (of a ladder) peldaño, *m*; (patrol and *Mil.*) ronda, *f*; circuito, *m*; vuelta, *f*, giro, *m*; serie, *f*; rutina, *f*; (of ammunition) andanada, descarga, *f*; (of cartridge) cartucho con bala, *m*; (of applause, etc.) salva, *f*; (of golf) partido, *m*; (in a fight) asalto, *m*; *Sports.* vuelta, *f*; (of drinks) ronda, *f*; (doctor's) visitas, *f pl*

round /raund/ *vt* redondear; (*Fig.* complete) acabar, perfeccionar; (go round, e.g. a corner) dar vuelta (a), doblar, trasponer; rodear, cercar; (of a ship) doblar. *vi* redondearse. **to r. off,** redondear; terminar; coronar. **to r. up,** (cattle) rodear. **to r. upon,** volverse contra

round /raund/ *adv* alrededor, en derredor; por todos lados; a la redonda, en torno; en circunferencia; en conjunto (**r.** is not translated in Spanish, e.g. *I shall come r. to your house,* Vendré a tu casa). *prep* alrededor de. **all the year r.,** todo el año, el año entero. **r. about,** a la redonda de, al derredor de; (nearly) cerca de; (of time by the clock) a eso de. **The road is**

closed and we shall have to go r., El camino está cerrado y tendremos que dar una vuelta. **to come r.,** volver; dejarse persuadir; recobrar su buen humor. **to go r.,** (spin) dar vueltas; (of the wind) cambiar. **There is enough to go r.,** Hay bastante para todos

roundabout /a ˌraundə'baut, *n* 'raundə,baut/ *a* indirecto; desviado; vago. *n* tiovivo, *m*; (traffic) redondel, *m*. **He spoke in a r. way,** Hablaba con circunloquios. **We went there by a r. way,** Fuimos dando un rodeo

roundly /'raundli/ *adv* en redondo; rotundamente, claramente

roundness /'raundnɪs/ *n* redondez, *f*; rotundidad, *f*

rouse /rauz/ *vt* despertar; animar; excitar; suscitar; provocar. **to r. oneself,** despertarse; animarse (a hacer algo)

rousing /'rauzɪŋ/ *a* que despierta; (moving) emocionante; (enthusiastic) entusiasta; grande, bueno

rout /raut/ *n* (rabble) chusma, *f*; (party) sarao, *m*; (defeat) derrota, *f*; (meeting) reunión, *f*. *vt* derrotar, poner en fuga; vencer

route /rut, raut/ *n* ruta, *f*; camino, *m*; itinerario, *m*. **r. march,** marcha de maniobras, *f*

routine /ru'tin/ *n* rutina, *f*, *a* rutinario, de rutina

rove /rouv/ *vi* vagar, errar

rover /'rouvər/ *n* vagabundo (-da); pirata, *m*

roving /'rouvɪŋ/ *a* vagabundo, errante; ambulante

row /rou, rau/ *n* (line) hilera, fila, hila, *f*; (in a theater, etc.) fila, *f*; (string) ristra, *f*; (in a boat) paseo en bote, *m*; (commotion) alboroto, *m*; (noise) ruido, *m*; (altercation) gresca, camorra, *f*; (scolding) regaño, *m*. *vi* (a boat) remar, bogar. *vt* conducir remando; (scold) regañar. **to be a row,** (altercation) haber la de San Quintín. **to start a row,** (altercation) armar camorra.

rowboat /'rou,bout/ *n* bote de remos, *m*

rowdiness /'raudinɪs/ *n* alboroto, *m*

rowdy /'raudi/ *a* alborotador. *n* trafalmejas, *mf* rufián, *m*. **rowdy party** *Lat. Am.* fandango, *m*

rower /'rouər/ *n* remero (-ra), bogador (-ra)

rowing /'rouɪŋ/ *n* que rema; de remos. *n* deporte del remo, *m*; paseo en bote, *m*. **r.-boat,** bote de remos, *m*. **r.-club,** club náutico, *m*. **r.-seat,** bancada, *f*. **r.-stroke,** bogada, *f*

royal /'rɔiəl/ *a* real; regio. *n Naut.* sobrejuanete, *m*. **r. academy,** real academia, *f*. **r. eagle,** águila real, *f*. **R. Highness,** Alteza Real, *f*. **r. letters patent,** cédula real, *f*. **R. Mail,** mala real, *f*. **R. Standard,** estandarte real, *m*

royalist /'rɔiəlɪst/ *a* and *n* realista, *mf*

royally /'rɔiəli/ *adv* realmente; regiamente

royalty /'rɔiəlti/ *n* realeza, *f*; miembro de la familia real, *m*; tanto por ciento de los ingresos, *m*; derechos de autor, *m pl*

R.R. (abbrev. of railroad) F.R. (abbrev. of *ferrocarril*)

rub /rʌb/ *vt* frotar, estregar; fregar; rozar; friccionar; (make sore) raspar. **to rub one's hands together,** frotarse las manos. **to rub the wrong way,** frotar a contrapelo. **to rub against,** rozar. **to rub along,** *Inf.* ir tirando. **to rub down,** (a horse) bruzar; limpiar; (dry) secar; (wear down) desgastar. **to rub in,** dar fricciones con; frotar con; (an idea, etc.) machacar. **to rub off,** *vt* quitar (frotando); borrar. *vi* borrarse; separarse (de). **to rub out,** *vt* borrar. *vi* borrarse. **to rub up,** (polish) limpiar; *Fig.* refrescar

rub /rʌb/ *n* frotación, *f*; roce, *m*; fricción, *f*; *Fig.* obstáculo, *m*; dificultad, *f*. **to give a rub,** frotar, etc.

rub-a-dub, rataplán, *m*

rubber /'rʌbər/ *n* de caucho, de goma. *n* caucho, *m*, goma, *f*; (for erasing) goma de borrar, *f*; (masseur) masajista, *mf*; (at whist, etc.) partida, *f*; *pl* **rubbers,** zapatos de goma, chanclos, *m pl*. **synthetic r.,** caucho artificial, *m*. **r. band,** goma, banda de goma, *f*. **r. belt,** *Mech.* correa de transmisión de caucho, *f*. **r.-plant, tree,** cauchera, *f*, *Central America, Mexico* hule, *m*. **r. plantation,** cauchal, *m*. **r.-plantation worker** cauchero (-a) *mf*. **r. planter,** cauchero, *m*. **r. stamp,** estampilla, *f*

rubbing /'rʌbɪŋ/ *n* frotación, *f*; fricción, *f*; roce, *m*; (of floors, dishes, etc.) fregado, *m*

rubbish /'rʌbɪʃ/ *n* basura, *f*; desperdicios, *m pl*, desecho, *m*; (of goods) pacotilla, *f*; (nonsense) pamplinas, patrañas, *f pl*, disparates, *m pl*. **r. cart,** carro del basurero, *m*

rubbishy /'rʌbɪʃi/ *a* sin valor, malo; (of goods) de pacotilla, de calidad inferior

rubble /'rʌbəl/ *n* escombros, *m pl*; cascote, *m*; piedra bruta, *f*

rubicund /'rubɪ,kʌnd/ *a* rubicundo

ruble /'roublei/ *n* rublo, *m*

rubric /'rubrɪk/ *n* rúbrica, *f*

ruby /'rubi/ *n* rubí, *m*. *a* de rubíes; de rubí. **r. lips,** labios de rubí, *m pl*

rucksack /'rʌk,sæk, 'rʊk-/ *n* mochila, *f*

rudder /'rʌdər/ *n* timón, gobernalle, *m*

ruddiness /'rʌdinɪs/ *n* rubicundez, *f*; rojez, *f*; frescura, *f*

ruddy /'rʌdi/ *a* rubicundo; rojo; frescote; (of animals) barcino

rude /rud/ *a* rudo; tosco; vigoroso; grosero, descortés

rudely /'rudli/ *adv* toscamente; groseramente

rudeness /'rudnɪs/ *n* rudeza, *f*; tosquedad, *f*; grosería, incivilidad, descortesía, *f*

rudiment /'rudəmənt/ *n* rudimento, *m*

rudimentary /,rudə'mɛntəri/ *a* rudimentario

rue /ru/ *vt* lamentar, llorar. *n Bot.* ruda, *f*

rueful /'rufəl/ *a* triste, melancólico; lamentable

ruefulness /'rufəlnɪs/ *n* tristeza, *f*

ruff /rʌf/ *n* golilla, lechuguilla, *f*; (of a bird) collarín de plumas, *m*; (of an animal) collarín de pelo, *m*

ruffian /'rʌfiən/ *n* rufián, *m*

ruffle /'rʌfəl/ *n Sew.* volante fruncido, *m*; (of a bird) collarin de plumas, *m*; (of an animal) collarín de pelo, *m*; (ripple) rizo, *m*; (annoyance) irritación, *f*. *vt* (ripple) rizar; (pleat) fruncir; (feathers) erizar; (hair) despeinar; agitar; (annoy) irritar, incomodar

ruffling /'rʌflɪŋ/ *n* (rippling) rizado, *m*; (pleating) fruncido, *m*; (of the temper) irritación, *f*

rug /rʌg/ *n* (floor) alfombra, *f*; manta de viaje, *f*. **rug strap,** portamantas, *m*

rugged /'rʌgɪd/ *a* áspero, escabroso; escarpado, abrupto; (wrinkled) arrugado; tosco; (harsh) duro, severo; inculto; mal acabado; vigoroso

ruggedness /'rʌgɪdnɪs/ *n* aspereza, escabrosidad, *f*; lo escarpado; dureza, severidad, *f*; rudeza, *f*; vigor, *m*

ruin /'ruɪn/ *n* ruina, *f*. *vt* arruinar; echar a perder, estropear por completo; (a woman) perder

ruination /,ruə'neiʃən/ *n* ruina, perdición, *f*

ruined /'ruɪnd/ *a* arruinado; en ruinas

ruinous /'ruənəs/ *a* ruinoso; en ruinas

rule /rul/ *n* regla, *f*; gobierno, *m*; autoridad, *f*, mando, *m*; administración, *f*; (reign) reinado, *m*; (of a court, etc.) orden, *f*; (for measuring) regla, *f*; *Print.* regleta, *f*; *pl* **rules,** reglas, *f pl*; reglamento, *m*. *vt* gobernar; regentar, regir; (control) dominar; (of a chairman, etc.) disponer, decidir; (guide) guiar; (lines) reglar. *vi* gobernar; (of a monarch) reinar; (of prices) mantenerse; estar en boga, prevalecer. **as a r.,** por regla general, en general. **slide-r.,** regla de cálculo, *f*. **to make it a r.,** tener por regla; tener por costumbre; tener por máxima. **to r. out,** excluir; *Law.* no admitir. **to r. over,** (of a king, etc.) reinar sobre. **r. of the road,** reglamento del tráfico, *m*. **r. of thumb,** regla empírica, *f*; rutina, *f*

ruler /'rulər/ *n* gobernador (-ra); soberano (-na); (master) amo (ama); (for ruling lines) regla, *f*

ruling /'rulɪŋ/ *a* regente; dominante; (current) vigente. *n* gobierno, *m*; *Law.* decisión, *f*, fallo, *m*; (with lines) rayado, *m*. **r. pen,** tiralíneas, *m*

rum /rʌm/ *n* ron, *m*

rumble /'rʌmbəl/ *vi* retumbar, tronar; (of vehicles) rugir; crujir. *n* retumbo, trueno, *m*; rugido, *m*; ruido sordo, *m*; rumor, *m*; crujido, *m*

rumbling /'rʌmblɪŋ/ *a* que retumba, etc. *n* ruido sordo, *m*; retumbo, *m*; crujido, *m*; (in the bowels) rugido, *m*

ruminant /'rumənənt/ *a* and *n* rumiante, *mf*

ruminate /'rumə,neit/ *vi* and *vt* rumiar

rumination /,rumə'neiʃən/ *n* rumia, *f*; meditación, reflexión, *f*

rummage /'rʌmɪdʒ/ *vt* revolver, desordenar, trastornar; explorar. **to r. out,** desenterrar

rumor /'rumər/ *n* rumor, *m*, fama, *f*. **It is rumored that...,** Hay rumores de que..., La voz corre que..., Se dice que...

rump /rʌmp/ *n* (of an animal) nalgas, ancas, *f pl*; cuarto trasero, *m*; (of a bird) rabadilla, *f*; (scornful) culo, *m*, posaderas, *f pl*. **r.-steak,** solomillo, *m*

rumple /'rʌmpəl/ *vt* arrugar; desordenar

run /rʌn/ *vi* correr; acudir; (flee) huir; (rush) precipitarse, lanzarse; (in a race) tomar parte en una carrera; competir; (pass over) deslizarse (por); (of machines) andar, marchar; (of traffic) circular; (leave, of trains, ships, etc.) salir; (ply between) hacer el trayecto entre... y...; (flow) fluir, correr; (into the sea, of rivers) desembocar (en); (spurt) chorrear, manar; (drip) gotear; (leak) dejar fugar (el agua, etc.); (of colors) correrse; caer; (of tears) correr; derramarse; (of eyes) llorar; (melt) derretirse; (of a sore) supurar; (travel or go) ir; moverse; (work) trabajar; funcionar; (of editions of a book) agotarse; (of a play) representarse; (cross) cruzar; (elapse) correr; transcurrir, pasar; (become) hacerse; (of wording) decir; (be current) correr; (for office, etc.) hacerse candidato; (navigate) navegar; (spread) extenderse; (be) estar; ser; (of thoughts) pasar; (last) durar; (tend) tender (a). *vt* (a race, a horse) correr; (drive) conducir; (a business, etc.) administrar; dirigir; (govern) gobernar, regir; (hunt) cazar; perseguir; (water, etc.) hacer correr; (pierce) clavar; introducir; (push) empujar; (one's hand, eye, etc.) pasar; (risks, etc.) correr; (possess) tener; establecer un servicio de (autobuses, etc.); (smuggle) hacer contrabando de. **The ship ran aground,** El barco encalló. **to run dry,** secarse; agotarse. **to run in the family,** estar en la familia. **to run into debt,** endeudarse, contraer deudas. **to run to seed,** granar; agotarse. **Steamers run daily between Barcelona and Mallorca,** Hay servicio diario de vapores entre Barcelona y Mallorca. **A stab of pain ran up his leg,** Sintió un dolor agudo en la pierna. **Feeling was running high,** Los ánimos estaban excitados. **My arrangements ran smoothly,** Mis planes marchaban bien. **Funds are running low,** El dinero escasea. **The tune runs in my head,** Tengo la canción metida en la cabeza. **The message runs like this,** El mensaje reza así, El mensaje dice así. **He ran his fingers through his hair,** Se mesaba los cabellos. **to run about,** andar de un lado a otro, correr por todas partes; (gad) corretear. **to run across,** cruzar corriendo; (meet) topar con, tropezar con. **to run after,** correr detrás (de); perseguir; buscar. **to run against,** (collide with) dar contra; (meet) tropezar con. **to run at,** abalanzarse hacia, precipitarse sobre; atacar. **to run away,** huir, escaparse; (slip away) escurrirse; (of a horse) dispararse, desbocarse. **to run away with,** huir con, fugarse con; (carry off) arrebatar; (steal) llevarse; (imagine) imaginarse, figurarse; (of temper, etc.) dominar, poseer. **to run back,** volver corriendo; llegar corriendo; retroceder rápidamente, correr hacia atrás. **to run backwards,** correr hacia atrás; **to run backwards and forwards,** ir y venir. **to run behind,** correr detrás (de); quedarse atrás; (be late) estar atrasado. **to run down,** *vi* bajar corriendo; descender; bajar; (of a clock) parar; (of a battery) gastarse; (of liquids) correr; fluir; (drop by drop) destilar. *vt* (capture) coger; alcanzar; (a person by a vehicle) atropellar; (a ship) echar a pique; (disparage) hablar mal de. **run-down,** (in health) agotado; (of a clock) parado. **to run for,** buscar corriendo; correr para coger (el autobús, etc.); (president, etc.) ser candidato para. **to run in,** *vi* entrar corriendo. *vt* arrestar; hacer prisionero; *Print.* recorrer. **to run into,** tropezar con; chocar con; (plunge into) meterse de cabeza en; (of sums of money, etc.) ascender a; (of streets, rivers, etc.) desembocar en. **to run off,** *vi* escaparse corriendo; marcharse corriendo. *vt* deslizarse por; (drain) vaciar; *Print.* imprimir; (compose) componer. **to run off with,** huir con. **to run on,** correr delante; continuar; (of the mind) pensar en, entregarse a; hablar sin cesar; *Print.* recorrer. **to run out,** *vi* salir corriendo; (of liquids) derramarse; salir; (end) acabarse; agotarse; (project) sobresalir. *vt* (cricket) coger al lanzador fuera de la línea de saque. **to run out of,**

no tener más de, haber terminado. **to run over,** *vi* rebosar; derramarse. *vt* (of a vehicle) atropellar, pasar por encima de, *Mexico* antellevar; (peruse) repasar; revisar. **to run pell-mell,** salir pitando, salir volando, salvarse por pies. **to run through,** correr por; pasar por; recorrer; (go directly) ir directamente (a); (pierce) traspasar, pasar de parte a parte; (squander) derrochar, malbaratar; (read) hojear, leer por encima. **to run up,** *vt* (hoist) izar; hacer de prisa; construir rápidamente; (incur) incurrir. *vi* subir corriendo; (of plants) trepar (por); (shrink) encogerse; (of expenses) aumentar. **to run up to time,** llegar a su hora. **to run up against,** tropezar con; (opposition, etc.) encontrar.

run /rʌn/ *n* carrera, corrida, *f*; (excursion) visita, excursión, *f*; (cricket) carrera, *f*; (walk) paseo, *m*; (by train or sea) viaje, *m*; (by bus, tram) trayecto, *m*; (sea crossing) travesía, *f*; (distance run) recorrido, *m*; (of events, etc.) curso, *m*; marcha, *f*; (of markets, etc.) tendencia, *f*; (rhythm) ritmo, *m*; dirección, *f*; distancia, *f*; *Mus.* serie de notas, *f*; serie, *f*; duración, *f*; *Theat.* serie de representaciones, *f*; (freedom to use) libre uso, *m*; (majority) mayoría, *f*; (on a bank) asedio, *m*; (on a book, etc.) demanda, *f*; (for sheep, etc.) terreno de pasto, *m*; (for fowls) gallinero, *m* (in a stocking) *Lat. Am.* acarraladura, *f*, *m*. **a run of bad luck,** una temporada de mala suerte. **at a run,** corriendo. **in the long run,** a la larga, al fin y al cabo. **on the run,** en fuga; ocupado. **Prices came down with a run,** Los precios bajaron de golpe. **take-off run,** *Aer.* recorrido de despegue, *m*

runaway /'rʌnə,wei/ *a* fugitivo; (of a horse) desbocado

rung /rʌŋ/ *n* (of a ladder) peldaño, *m*; (of a chair) travesaño, *m*; (lath) listón, *m*

runner /'rʌnər/ *n* corredor (-ra); (carrier of sedan chair, etc.) silletero, *mf*; (smuggler) contrabandista, *m*; (courier) estafeta, *f*; (messenger) mensajero, *m*; (ring) anillo movible, pasador corredizo, *m*; rueda móvil, *f*; (of a sledge) patín, *m*; *Bot.* tallo rastrero, *m*. **r.-up,** el segundo

running /'rʌnɪŋ/ *a* corredor; (of water, bank accounts) corriente; (of a knot) corredizo; (of a sore) supurante; (continuous) continuo; (consecutive) consecutivo. *n* carrera, *f*; marcha, *f*; funcionamiento, *m*; administración, *f*; gobierno, *m*; dirección, *f*; (flowing) derrame, *m*; (of trains, buses, etc.) servicio, *m*; (smuggling) contrabando, *m*; (of a sore) supuración, *f*. **six times r.,** seis veces consecutivas. **The car is in r. order,** El auto está en buen estado. **r. away,** fuga, *f*. **r.-boarc',** (of a car, etc.) estribo, *m*; (of a locomotive) plataforma, *f*. **r. costs,** gastos de mantenimiento, *m pl*; (railway) gastos de explotación, *m pl*. **r. fight,** acción de retirada, *f*. **r.-knot,** lazo corredizo, *m*. **r. title,** *Print.* título de la columna, *m*

run-off match /'rʌnɒf/ *n* desempate, *m*

runway /'rʌn,wei/ *n* (for launching a ship) grada, *f*; (of an airfield) pista de aterrizaje, *f*

rupee /ru'pi, 'rupi/ *n* (Indian currency) rupia, *f*

rupestrian /ru'pɛstriən/ *a* rupestre

rupture /'rʌptʃər/ *n* rompimiento, *m*, rotura, *f*; ruptura, *f*; *Med.* hernia, *f*

ruptured /'rʌptʃərd/ *a Med.* herniado, quebrado

rupturing /'rʌptʃərɪŋ/ *n* ruptura, *f*

rural /'rʊrəl/ *a* rural, campestre, del campo; agrario

ruse /ruz/ *n* artimaña, treta, ardid, *f*

rush /rʌʃ/ *n Bot.* junco, *m*; acometida, *f*; ataque, *m*; (of water) torrente, *m*; (bustle) bullicio, *m*; (speed) prisa, *f*; precipitación, *f*; acceso, *m*; (crowd) tropel, *m*, masa, *f*; (struggle) lucha, *f*; furia, *f*. *vi* precipitarse, lanzarse; agolparse. *vt* llevar rápidamente (a); despachar rápidamente; precipitar; (attack) asaltar, atacar; (capture) tomar, capturar; hacer de prisa; (a bill) hacer aprobar de prisa. **to r. upon,** abalanzarse hacia; embestir. **in a r.,** en tropel, en masa; de prisa. **to r. to a conclusion,** precipitarse a una conclusión. **r.-bottomed,** con asiento de enea. **r. hour,** hora de mayor circulación, *f*, hora de aglomeración, hora-pico (Argentina), hora brava (Argentina, informal). **r. order,** pedido urgente, *m*

Russia /'rʌʃə/ Rusia, *f*

Russian /'rʌʃən/ *a* ruso. *n* ruso (-sa); (language) ruso, *m*. **R. leather,** piel de Rusia, *f*

rust /rʌst/ *n* herrumbre, *f*, orín, *m*; moho, *m*; (disease) añublo, tizón, *m*. *vt* aherrumbrar; enmohecer. *vi* aherrumbrarse; enmohecerse

rustic /'rʌstɪk/ *a* rústico; campesino, aldeano; (scornful) palurdo, grosero. *n* aldeano, *m*; (scornful) patán, *m*

rusticate /'rʌstɪ,keit/ *vi* rusticar, vivir en el campo. *vt* enviar al campo

rustication /,rʌstɪ'keiʃən/ *n* rusticación, *f*

rusticity /rʌ'stɪsɪti/ *n* rusticidad, *f*

rustiness /'rʌstinɪs/ *n* herrumbre, *f*; enmohecimiento, *m*; color rojizo, *m*; *Fig.* falta de práctica, *f*

rustle /'rʌsəl/ *n* susurro, *m*; murmurio, *m*; (of silk, a dress, etc.) frufru, *m*; (of paper, etc.) crujido, *m*. *vi* susurrar; murmurar; crujir. *vt* (a paper) hacer crujir

rustless /'rʌstlɪs/ *a* inoxidable

rustling /'rʌstlɪŋ/ *n* see **rustle**

rusty /'rʌsti/ *a* herrumbroso; enmohecido, mohoso; (red) rojizo, (worn out) usado, viejo; (out of practice) desacostumbrado; (forgotten) empolvorado, oxidado (e.g. *My Portuguese is rusty,* Mi portugués está empolvorado)

rut /rʌt/ *n* rodera, *f*, bache, surco, *m*; *Fig.* sendero trillado, *m*; *Fig.* rutina, *f*

ruthless /'ruθlɪs/ *a* inhumano, insensible, despiadado; inexorable, inflexible

ruthlessly /'ruθlɪsnɪs/ *adv* inhumanamente; inflexiblemente, inexorablemente

ruthlessness /'ruθlɪsnɪs/ *n* inhumanidad, *f*; inflexibilidad, inexorabilidad, *f*

rye /rai/ *n* centeno, *m*. **rye field,** centenar, *m*

S

---

s /ɛs/ *n* (letter) ese, *f*

sabbatarian /,sæbə'tɛəriən/ *a* sabatario

Sabbath /'sæbəθ/ *n* (Jewish) sábado, *m*; (Christian) domingo, *m*

sabbatical /sə'bætɪkəl/ *a* sabático

saber /'seibər/ *n* sable, *m*; (soldier) jinete, *m*. *vt* dar sablazos (a), acuchillar. **s. cut, thrust,** sablazo, *m*

sable /'seibəl/ *n* (animal and fur) marta, *f*; *Herald.* sable, *m*. *a Herald.* sable; *Poet.* negro

sabotage /'sæbə,taʒ/ *n* sabotaje, *m*, *vt* cometer un acto de sabotaje en

saboteur /,sæbə'tɜr/ *n* saboteador, *m*

sac /sæk/ *n Biol.* saco, *m*

saccharin /'sækərɪn/ *n* sacarina, *f*

sachet /sæ'ʃei/ *n* sachet, *m*; bolsa, *f*. **handkerchief s.,** bolsa para pañuelos, *f*

sack /sæk/ *n* (bag) saco, *m*; *Mil.* saqueo, saquea-

miento, saco, *m*. *vt* meter en sacos; (dismiss) dar pasaporte (a), despedir; *Mil.* saquear. **to get the s.,** recibir el pasaporte. **to give the s.,** dar el pasaporte (a), poner de patitas en la calle (a). **s. coat,** saco, *m*

sackcloth /'sæk,klɔθ/ *n* harpillera, *f*. **to repent in s. and ashes,** ponerse cenizas en la cabeza

sacking /'sækɪŋ/ *n* harpillera, *f*; *Mil.* saqueo, *m*

sacrament /'sækrəmənt/ *n* sacramento, *m*; Eucaristía, *f*. **the Blessed S.,** el Santísimo Sacramento. **to receive the Holy S.,** comulgar. **to receive the last sacraments,** recibir los sacramentos

sacramental /,sækrə'mɛntl/ *a* sacramental

sacramentalist /,sækrə'mɛntlɪst/ *n* sacramentario (-ia)

sacred /'seikrɪd/ *a* sagrado; sacro, santo; consagrado. **Nothing is s. to them,** No hay nada sagrado para ellos, No respetan nada. **the S. Heart of Jesus,** el Sagrado Corazón de Jesús). **S. to the memory of...**

Consagrado a la memoria de... **s. music,** música sagrada, f
sacredness /'seikrɪdnɪs/ n carácter sagrado, m; santidad, f; inviolabilidad, f
sacrifice /'sækrə,fais/ n sacrificio, m. vt and vi sacrificar. **s. of the mass,** sacrificio del altar, m
sacrificial /ˌsækrə'fɪʃəl/ a sacrificador; del sacrificio
sacrilege /'sækrəlɪdʒ/ n sacrilegio, m
sacrilegious /ˌsækrə'lɪdʒəs/ a sacrílego
sacristan /'sækrɪstən/ n sacristán, m
sacristy /'sækrɪsti/ n sacristía, f
sacrosanct /'sækrou,sæŋkt/ a sacrosanto
sacrum /'sækrəm, 'seikrəm/ n Anat. sacro, m
sad /sæd/ a triste; melancólico; (of a mistake) deplorable, funesto; Inf. redomado; (pensive) pensativo. **How s.!** ¡Qué lástima! ¡Qué triste! **It made me s.,** Me entristeció
sadden /'sædn̩/ vt entristecer, acongojar, afligir
saddle /'sædl̩/ n (riding) silla de montar, Lat. Am. albarda, f; (of a bicycle, etc.) sillín, m; Mech. silla, f; Anat. espalda, f. vt ensillar. **to s. with the responsibility of,** echar la responsabilidad de (a). **s. of mutton,** lomo de carnero, m. **s.-bag,** alforja, Lat. Am. buchaca, f. **s.-cloth,** mantilla de silla, f. **s.-tree,** arzón, m
saddler /'sædlər/ n sillero, guarnicionero, f
Sadducee /'sædʒə,si/ n saduceo (-ea)
sadism /'seidɪzəm/ n sadismo, m
sadist /'seidɪst/ n sadista, mf
sadistic /sə'dɪstɪk/ a sadístico
sadly /'sædli/ adv tristemente; (very) muy
sadness /'sædnɪs/ n tristeza, melancolía, f
safe /seif/ a al abrigo (de); seguro; salvo; (certain) cierto; prudente; digno de confianza. n caja de caudales, f; (for food) alacena, f. **I stood beneath a tree s. from the rain,** Estaba de pie bajo un árbol, al abrigo de la lluvia. **to put something in a s. place,** poner algo en lugar seguro; poner algo en un lugar seguro. **s. and sound,** sano y salvo. **s.-conduct,** salvoconducto, m. **s.-keeping,** lugar seguro, m; (of a person) buenas manos, f pl
safeguard /'seif,gɑrd/ n protección, garantía, f; precaución, f. vt proteger, guardar; tomar precauciones (contra)
safely /'seifli/ adv seguramente; sin accidente, sin novedad, sano y salvo; sin peligro. **You may s. tell him,** Puedes decírselo con toda seguridad. **to put (something) away s.,** poner (algo) en un lugar seguro
safety /'seifti/ n seguridad, f. a de seguridad; (of locks) de golpe. **a place of s.,** un lugar seguro. **in s.,** en salvo, en seguro; con seguridad. **to believe in s. first,** poner la seguridad en primer lugar. **to play for s.,** jugar seguro. **with complete s.,** con toda seguridad. **s.-belt,** (cinto) salvavidas, m. **s.-catch,** fiador, m. **s.-curtain,** telón de seguridad, telón contra incendios, m. **s.-fuse,** espoleta de seguridad, f. **s.-glass,** vidrio inastillable, m. **s.-island,** refugio para peatones, m. **s.-lamp,** lámpara de seguridad, f. **s.-latch,** pestillo de golpe, m. **s.-lock,** (of fire-arms) seguro, m; (of doors, etc.) cerradura de seguridad, f. **s.-pin,** imperdible, m; Mexico seguro, m. **s.-razor,** máquina de afeitar, f. **s.-valve,** válvula de seguridad, f
saffron /'sæfrən/ n azafrán, m, a azafranado, de color de azafrán.
sag /sæg/ vi doblegarse, ceder; inclinarse; Naut. caer a sotavento; (of prices) bajar; (of spirits, etc.) flaquear
saga /'sɑgə/ n saga, f; epopeya, f
sagacious /sə'geiʃəs/ a sagaz, perspicaz; (of animals) sabio
sagacity /sə'gæsɪti/ n sagacidad, perspicacia, f; (of animals) sagacidad, f
sage /seidʒ/ n sabio, m; Bot. salvia, f. a sabio; sagaz; cuerdo
Sagittarius /ˌsædʒɪ'tɛəriəs/ n Sagitario, m
Sahara, the /sə'hærə/ el Sáhara, m
said /sɛd/ a antedicho; tal dicho. **No sooner s. than done,** Dicho y hecho. **the s. Mr. Martínez,** el tal Sr. Martínez
sail /seil/ n (of a ship) vela, f; (sailing-ship) velero, m; (of a windmill) aspa, f; Mech. ala, f; (trip) paseo

en barco, m. vi navegar; ir en barco; dar un paseo en barco; (leave) salir en barco; zarpar; (of swans, etc.) deslizarse; (of clouds, etc.) flotar. vt (a ship) gobernar; (the sea) navegar por. **She sailed into the room,** Entró majestuosamente en la sala. **The ship sailed at eight knots,** El buque navegaba a ocho nudos. **to go for a s.,** dar un paseo en barco. **to s. around the world,** dar la vuelta al mundo. **to s. the seas,** navegar por los mares. **to set s.,** darse a la vela, zarpar. **to take in the sails,** amainar. **s.-maker,** velero, m. **to s. into,** entrar en. **to s. around,** (the Cape, etc.) doblar. **to s. up,** subir en barco; (of a boat) ir río arriba
sailcloth /'seil,klɔθ/ n lona, f
sailing /'seilɪŋ/ n navegación, f; (departure) salida, f. **It's all plain s.,** Todo va viento en popa. **s.-boat,** bote de vela, m. **s.-ship,** buque de vela, velero, m
sailor /'seilər/ n marinero, m. **s.-blouse,** marinera, f. **s.-suit,** traje de marinero, m
saint /seint/ n santo (-ta); (before masculine names of Sts., excluding Sts. Dominic and Thomas) San; Inf. ángel, m. **All Saints' Day,** el día de Todos los Santos. **saint's day,** fiesta de un santo (or de una santa), f; (of a person) santo, m. **St. Bernard dog,** perro de San Bernardo, m. **St. John the Baptist,** San Juan Bautista. **St. Martin's summer,** el veranillo de San Martín. **St. Vitus's dance,** el baile de San Vito
sainthood /'seinthʊd/ n santidad, f
saintliness /'seintlinɪs/ n santidad, f
saintly /'seintli/ a de santo; de santa; santo; Inf. angelical
Saint Petersburg /seint 'pitərz,bɜrg/ San Petersburgo, m
sake /seik/ n amor, m; causa, f. **for God's s.,** por el amor de Dios. **for the s. of,** para; por amor de. **to talk for talking's s.,** hablar por hablar
salable /'seiləbəl/ a vendible
salaciousness /sə'leiʃəsnɪs/ n salacidad, f
salad /'sæləd/ n ensalada, f; (lettuce) lechuga, f. **fruit s.,** macedonia de frutas, f. **s.-bowl,** ensaladera, f. **s.-dressing,** aderezo, aliño, m, salsa para ensalada, f. **s.-oil,** aceite para ensaladas, m
salamander /'sælə,mændər/ n salamandra, f
salaried /'sælərid/ a a sueldo; (of posts) retribuido
salary /'sæləri/ n sueldo, salario, m
sale /seil/ n venta, f; (auction) almoneda, subasta pública, f. **(clearance) s.,** liquidación, f, saldo, m, Mexico barata, f. **to be on s.,** estar de venta. "Piano for s.," «Se vende un piano.» **s. price,** precio de venta, m; precio de saldo, m
sales contract /seilz/ n contrato de compraventa, m
salesman /'seilzmən/ n dependiente de tienda, m; (traveller) viajante, m
salesmanship /'seilzmən,ʃɪp/ n arte de vender, mf
salesroom /'seilz,rum/ n salón de ventas, m
saleswoman /'seilz,wʊmən/ n dependiente de tienda, vendedera, f
salient /'seiliənt/ a saliente; Fig. prominente, conspicuo, notable, n saliente, m. **s. angle,** ángulo saliente, m
saline /'seilin/ a salino (marsh) saladar, m; Med. salino, m
saliva /sə'laivə/ n saliva, f
salivary /'sælə,vɛri/ a salival
salivate /'sælə,veit/ vi salivar
salivation /ˌsælə'veiʃən/ n salivación, f
sallow /'sælou/ a cetrino, olivác, lívido
sallowness /'sælounɪs/ n amarillez, lividez, f; palidez, f
sally /'sæli/ n (Mil. etc.) salida, f; (quip) ocurrencia, salida, f. vi hacer una salida, salir. **to s. forth,** ponerse en camino
salmon /'sæmən/ n salmón, m; color de salmón, m. **s.-net,** salmonera, f. **s. trout,** trucha asalmonada, f
salon /sə'lɒn/ n salón, m
Salonika /sə'lɒnɪkə/ Salónica, f
saloon /sə'lun/ n sala, f; (of a steamer) cámara, f, salón, m; (on train, for sleeping) departamento de coche cama, m; (on train, for dining) coche comedor, m; Auto. coche cerrado, m. **billiard s.,** salón de billa-

res, *m*. **dancing s.,** salón de baile, *m*. **hair-dresser's s.,** salón de peluquero, *m*. **s. bar,** bar, *m*

salsify /'sælsəfi/ *n Bot.* salsifí, *m*

salt /sɔlt/ *n* sal, *f*; (spice) sabor, *m*; (wit) sal, agudeza, *f. a* salobre, salino; salado; (of land) salitroso. *vt* (season) poner sal en; (cure) salar. **kitchen s.,** sal de cocina, *f. old s., Inf.* lobo de mar, *m*. **rock s.,** sal gema, *f.* **sea s.,** sal marina, *f.* **to be not worth one's s.,** no merecer el pan que se come. **to take with a pinch of s.,** tomar con su grano de sal. **s.-cellar,** salero, *m*. **s. lagoon,** albufera, *f.* **s. lake,** lago salado, *m*. **s. marsh,** saladar, *m*. **s. meat,** carne salada, cecina, *f.* **s. merchant,** salinero, *m*. **s.-mine,** mina de sal, *f.* **s.-spoon,** cucharita de sal, *f.* **s. water,** agua salada, *f*; agua de mar, *f.* **s.-water fish,** pez de mar, *m*. **s.-works,** salinas, *f pl*

saltiness /'sɔltɪnɪs/ *n* sabor de sal, *m*; salobridad, *f*

salting /'sɔltɪŋ/ *n* saladura, *f*; (salt marsh) saladar, *m*

saltless /'sɔltlɪs/ *a* sin sal, soso, insípido; *Fig.* soso

saltpeter /,sɔlt'pitər/ *n* salitre, *m*. **s. bed,** salitral, *m*. **s. works,** salitrería, *f*

salty /'sɔlti/ *a* salado; salobre

salubrious /sə'lubriəs/ *a* salubre, saludable, sano

salubriousness /sə'lubriəsnɪs/ *n* salubridad, *f*

salutary /'sælyə,teri/ *a* saludable, beneficioso

salutation /,sælyə'teiʃən/ *n* salutación, *f*, saludo, *m*

salute /sə'lut/ *vt* and *vi* saludar. *n* saludo, *m*; (of guns) salva, *f.* **to fire a s.,** hacer salvas, saludar con... salvas. **The soldier saluted them,** El soldado les saludó. **to take the s.,** tomar el saludo. **saluting base,** puesto de mando, *m*

Salvadoran, Salvadorian /,sælvə'dɔrən; -'dɔriən/ *a* and *n* salvadoreño (-ña)

salvage /'sælvɪdʒ/ *n* salvamento, *m*, *vt* salvar

salvation /sæl'veiʃən/ *n* salvación, *f.* **to find the s. of one's soul,** salvar el alma. **the S. Army,** el Ejército de la Salvación, *m*

salve /sæv/ *n* pomada, *f*; *Fig.* bálsamo, *m*. *vt* curar; (overcome) vencer; (soothe) tranquilizar; *Naut.* salvar. **to s. one's conscience,** tranquilizar la conciencia

salver /'sælvər/ *n* salva, bandeja, *f*

salvo /'sælvou/ *n* (of guns or applause) salva, *f*; (reservation) salvedad, reservación, *f.* **s. of applause,** salva de aplausos, *f*

Samaritan /sə'mærɪtn/ *a* and *n* samaritano (-na)

same /seim/ *a* mismo; igual; parecido; idéntico. *adv* lo mismo; del mismo modo. **all the s.,** sin embargo; con todo, a pesar de eso. **at the s. time,** al mismo tiempo; a la vez. **just the s.,** igual; (nevertheless) sin embargo. ῾le bowed deeply and I did the s.,** El hizo una profunda reverencia y yo hice lo mismo. **They do not look at things the s. as we do,** No ven las cosas del mismo modo que nosotros. **If it is the s. to her,** Si le da igual. **It's all the s.,** Es igual, Lo mismo da, Es todo uno. **Ávila, capital of the province of the s. name,** Ávila, capital de la provincia de su nombre **"Same-Day Service"** /'seimdei/ «En el día» (Argentina)

sameness /'seimnɪs/ *n* identidad, *f*; semejanza, *f*, parecido, *m*; monotonía, *f*

samovar /'sæmə,var/ *n* samovar, *m*

sampan /'sæmpæn/ *n* (boat) champán, *m*

sample /'sæmpəl/ *n* muestra, *f*; prueba, *f*; ejemplo, *m*. *vt* sacar una muestra de; (try) probar. **s. book,** muestrario, *m*

sampler /'sæmplər/ *n* probador, *m*; (of wines) catador, *m*; *Sew.* dechado, *m*

sanatorium /,sænə'tɔriəm/ *n* sanatorio, *m*

sanctification /,sæŋktəfɪ'keiʃən/ *n* santificación, *f*; consagración, *f*

sanctify /'sæŋktə,fai/ *vt* santificar; consagrar

sanctimonious /,sæŋktə'mouniəs/ *a* santurrón, mojigato, beato

sanctimoniousness /,sæŋktə'mouniəsnɪs/ *n* beatería, mojigatería, santurronería, *f*

sanction /'sæŋkʃən/ *n* sanción, *f. vt* sancionar; autorizar. **to apply sanctions,** *Polit.* aplicar sanciones

sanctity /'sæŋktɪti/ *n* santidad, *f*; lo sagrado; inviolabilidad, *f.* **odor of s.,** olor de santidad, *f*

sanctuary /'sæŋktʃu,ɛri/ *n* santuario, *m*; (historical)

sagrado, sagrado asilo, *m*; refugio, asilo, *m*. **to take s.,** acogerse a sagrado; refugiarse

sand /sænd/ *n* arena, *f*; (for drying writing) arenilla, *f*; granos de arena, *m pl*; *pl* **sands,** playa, *f*; (of life) horas de la vida, *f pl. vt* arenar. **to plow the s.,** arar en el mar. **s.-bag,** *n* saco de arena, *m*. *vt* (a building) proteger con sacos de arena; (a person) golpear con un saco de arena. **s.-bank,** banco de arena, *m*, barra, *f.* **to run on a s.-bank,** encallar. **s.-colored,** de color de arena. **s.-dune,** médano, *m*. **s.-paper,** *n* papel de lija, *m. vt* pulir con papel de lija, lijar. **s.-pit,** arenal, *m*. **s. shoes,** alpargatas, *f pl*

sandal /'sændl/ *n* sandalia, *f*, *Central America* caite, *m*; (rope-soled) alpargata, *f.* **s.-wood,** sándalo, *m*

sandiness /'sændɪnɪs/ *n* naturaleza arenosa, *f*; (of hair) color bermejo, *m*

sandstone /'sænd,stoun/ *n* arenisca, *f*

sandstorm /'sænd,stɔrm/ *n* tempestad de arena, *f*; simún, *m*

sandwich /'sændwitʃ, 'sæn-/ *n* emparedado, bocadillo, *m. vt* insertar. **I found myself sandwiched between two fat men,** Me encontré aplastado entre dos hombres gordos. **s.-man,** hombre sándwich, *m*

sandy /'sændi/ *a* arenoso; sabuloso; (of hair) rojo, rufo, bermejo. **a s. beach,** una playa arenosa

sane /sein/ *a* de juicio sano; razonable, prudente; sensato. **He is a very s. person,** Es un hombre con mucho sentido común. **to be s.,** estar en su juicio; (of a policy, etc.) ser prudente, ser razonable

sangfroid /san'frwa/ *n* sangre fría, *f*; aplomo, *m*

sanguinary /'sæŋgwə,nɛri/ *a* sanguinario

sanguine /'sæŋgwɪn/ *a* (of complexion) rubicundo; sanguíneo; optimista, confiado. *n* (drawing) sanguina, *f.* **to be s. about the future,** ser optimista acerca del porvenir, tener confianza en el porvenir

sanhedrin /sæn'hɛdrɪn/ *n* sanedrín, *m*

sanitary /'sænɪ,tɛri/ *a* sanitario; higiénico, **s. inspector,** inspector de sanidad, *m*. **s. napkin, s. towel,** servilleta higiénica, toalla sanitaria, *mf*, paño higiénico, *m*

sanitation /,sænɪ'teiʃən/ *n* higiene, *f*; sanidad pública, *f*; (apparatus) instalación sanitaria, *f*

sanity /'sænɪti/ *n* juicio sano, *m*; prudencia, *f*; (common sense) sentido común, *m*, sensatez, *f*

Santa Claus /'sæntə klɔz/ *n* (Spanish equivalent) los Reyes Magos, *m pl*

São Paulo /'sau 'paulou, -lʊ/ San Pablo, *m*

sap /sæp/ *n* (*Bot.* and *Fig.*) savia, *f*; *Mil.* zapa, *f. vt* (undermine) debilitar, agotar; *Mil.* zapar

sapidity /sæ'pɪdɪti/ *n* sabor, *m*

sapling /'sæplɪŋ/ *n* arbolillo, *m*

sapper /'sæpər/ *n* *Mil.* zapador, *m*

Sapphic /'sæfɪk/ *a* sáfico, **S. verse,** verso sáfico, *m*

sapphire /'sæfaiᵊr/ *n* zafiro, *m. a* de zafiros; cerúleo, de zafiro

Saracen /'særəsən/ *a* and *n* sarraceno (-na)

Saragossa /,særə'gɒsə/ Zaragoza, *f*

sarcasm /'sarkæzəm/ *n* sarcasmo, *m*

sarcastic /sar'kæstɪk/ *a* sarcástico

sarcastically /sar'kæstɪkli/ *adv* con sarcasmo, sarcásticamente

sarcophagus /sar'kɒfəgəs/ *n* sarcófago, *m*

sardine /sar'din/ *n* sardina, *f.* **packed like sardines,** como sardinas en banasta. **s.-net,** sardinal, *m*

Sardinia /sar'dɪniə/ Cerdeña, *f*

Sardinian /sar'dɪniən/ *a* and *n* sardo (-da)

sardonic /sar'dɒnɪk/ *a* sardónico

sarsaparilla /,sæspə'rɪl, ,sarspə-/ *n* zarzaparrilla, *f*

sash /sæʃ/ *n* (with uniform) faja, *f*; (belt) cinto, cinturón, *m*; (of a window) cerco, *m*. **s. window,** ventana de guillotina, *f*

Satan /'seitn/ *n* Satanás, *m*

satanic /sə'tænɪk, sei-/ *a* satánico

satchel /'sætʃəl/ *n* saquito de mano, *m*, bolsa, *f*; (school) vademécum, *m*; cartapacio, *m*, cartera, *f*

sate /seit/ *vt* saciar, hartar; satisfacer

sateen /sæ'tin/ *n* satén, *m*

satellite /'sætl,ait/ *n* satélite, *m*

satiable /'seiʃəbəl/ *a* saciable

satiate /*v.* 'seiʃi,eit; *a.* -ɪt, -,eit/ *vt* saciar, hartar; satisfacer. *a* harto; repleto

scamper

satiety /sə'taiiti/ n saciedad, f
satin /'sætn̩/ n raso, m. a de raso; (glossy) lustroso, terso. vt (paper) satinar
satiny /'sætn̩i/ a arrasado; lustroso, brillante
satire /'sætaɪ³r/ n sátira, f
satiric /sə'tɪərɪk/ a satírico
satirist /'sætərɪst/ n escritor (-ra) satírico (-ca)
satirize /'sætə,raiz/ vt satirizar
satisfaction /,sætɪs'fækʃən/ n satisfacción, f; (contentment) contento, m, satisfacción, f; (for sin) expiación, f; (of a debt) pago, m; desquite, m; recompensa, f. **to demand s.,** pedir satisfacción. **to give** (someone) **s.,** dar contento (a), alegrar
satisfactorily /,sætɪs'fæktərəli/ adv satisfactoriamente
satisfactoriness /,sætɪs'fæktərɪnɪs/ n carácter satisfactorio, m, lo satisfactorio
satisfactory /,sætɪs'fæktəri/ a satisfactorio; (for sin) expiatorio
satisfy /'sætɪs,fai/ vt satisfacer; (convince) convencer; (allay) tranquilizar, apaciguar. **I am satisfied with him,** Estoy satisfecho (Estoy contento) con él. **The explanation did not s. me,** La explicación no me convenció. **to s. oneself that...,** asegurarse de que... **to s. one's thirst,** apagar la sed
satisfying /'sætɪs,faiɪŋ/ a que satisface; satisfactorio; (of food) nutritivo
satrap /'seitræp, 'sæ-/ n sátrapa, m
saturate /'sætʃə,reit/ vt saturar (de), empapar (de); Chem. saturar; Fig. imbuir; Fig. empapar. **to s. oneself in,** (a subject) empaparse en
saturation /,sætʃə'reiʃən/ n saturación, f. **s. point,** (Chem. etc.) punto de saturación, m
Saturday /'sætər,dei/ n sábado, f
Saturn /'sætərn/ n Saturno, m
saturnine /'sætər,nain/ a saturnino, taciturno
satyr /'seitər, 'sætər/ n sátiro, m
sauce /sɔs/ n salsa, f; (thick fruit) compota, f; Inf. insolencia, f. **s.-boat,** salsera, f
saucepan /'sɔs,pæn/ n cazuela, cacerola, f. **double s.,** baño de María, m
saucer /'sɔsər/ n platillo, m. **flying s.,** platillo volante, m. **s.-eyed,** con ojos redondos
sauciness /'sɔsinɪs/ n impertinencia, insolencia, f
saucy /'sɔsi/ a respondón, descarado; (cheerful) alegre; (of hats, etc.) coquetón, majo
sauerkraut /'sauᵊr,kraut/ n chucruta, f
saunter /'sɔntər/ vi pasearse, vagar, n paseo, m, vuelta, f
sausage /'sɔsɪdʒ/ n chorizo, m; salchicha, f. **s.-balloon,** globo cautivo, m. **s.-curl,** bucle, m. **s.-machine,** choricera, f. **s.-maker,** choricero (-ra)
savage /'sævɪdʒ/ a salvaje; feroz; (cruel) inhumano, cruel; (furious) furioso. n salvaje, mf
savagely /'sævɪdʒli/ adv bárbaramente; ferozmente; furiosamente
savagery /'sævɪdʒri/ n salvajismo, m; ferocidad, f; brutalidad, crueldad, f
savannah /sə'vænə/ n sabana, f. **s. dweller,** sabanero (-ra)
save /seiv/ vt salvar; (keep) guardar; conservar; reservar; (money, one's clothes, etc.) ahorrar; (time) ganar; (avoid) evitar. vi salvar, (evangelized) ser salvado (-da); hacer economías; ahorrar. **He saved my life,** Me salvó la vida. **They have saved a room for me,** Me han reservado una habitación. **to s. appearances,** guardar las apariencias. **to s. oneself trouble,** ahorrarse molestias. **to s. the situation,** estar al nivel de las circunstancias. **to s. one's soul,** salvar el alma
save /seiv/ prep salvo, excepto, menos. conjunc sino, a menos que; con la excepción de. **all s. one,** todos menos uno. **all the conspirators s. he,** todos los conspiradores con la excepción de él
saving /'seiviŋ/ a frugal, económico; (stingy) tacaño, avaricioso; (clause) condicional. n salvación, f; (of money, time, etc.) ahorro, m, economía, f; pl **savings,** ahorros, m pl. prep salvo, excepto, fuera de. conjunc con excepción de que, fuera de que. **s. grace,** único mérito, m. **savings bank,** caja de ahorros, f
savings fund, montepío, m

savior /'seivyər/ n salvador (-ra). **the S.,** el Salvador, el Redentor
savor /'seivər/ n sabor, gusto, m; (aftertaste) dejo, m; (zest) salsa, f. vi saber (a), tener sabor (de); Fig. oler (a). vt saborear, paladear; (flavor) sazonar
savoriness /'seivərinɪs/ n buen sabor, m; (of a district) respetabilidad, f
savory /'seivəri/ a sabroso, apetitoso; (not sweet) no dulce; (of places) respetable; (of reputation, etc.) bueno. n entremés salado, m. **s. omelette,** tortilla, f
Savoy /sə'vɔi/ Saboya, f
saw /sɔ/ n (maxim) sentencia, f; (proverb) refrán, decir, m; (tool) sierra, f. vt aserrar, Lat. Am. aserruchar; (the air) cortar. vi usar una sierra. **two-handled saw,** tronzador, m. **saw-fish,** pez sierra, m. **saw-mill,** molino de aserrar, m. **saw-pit,** aserradero, m
sawdust /'sɔ,dʌst/ n aserrín, m
sawhorse /'sɔ,hɔrs/ n caballete de aserrar, m
sawyer /'sɔyər/ n aserrador, m
Saxon /'sæksən/ a and n sajón (-ona)
Saxony /'sæksəni/ Sajonia, f
saxophone /'sæksə,foun/ n saxófono, saxofón m
say /sei/ vt decir; recitar. vi decir. **Let us say that the house is worth $100,000,** Digamos que la casa vale cien mil dólares. **He has no say in the matter,** No entra ni sale en el asunto. **I have said my say,** He dicho lo que quería. **They say,** Se dice, Dicen, La gente dice. **You don't say!** ¡Calle! ¿De veras? ¡Imposible! **that is to say...,** es decir...; esto es..., a saber... **to say one's prayers,** rezar, decir sus oraciones. **to say again,** volver a decir; decir otra vez, repetir. **to say over and over again,** repetir muchas veces, decir repetidamente. **What do you say to that?** ¿Qué dices a esto?
saying /'seiiŋ/ n decir, m; (proverb) refrán, m; (maxim) sentencia, f. **As the s. is,** Como suele decirse; Según el refrán. **It goes without s.,** Eso no tiene discusión, Huelga decir. **It's only a s.,** Es un decir, nada más
scab /skæb/ n (of a wound) costra, f; (disease) escabro, m; (blackleg) esquirol, m
scabbard /'skæbərd/ n vaina (de espada), f
scabby /'skæbi/ a costroso; (diseased) roñoso, sarnoso
scabies /'skeibiz/ n sarna, f. **s. mite,** arador de la sarna, m
scaffold /'skæfəld/ n (in building) andamio, m; (for execution) cadalso, patíbulo, m. **to go to the s.,** ir al patíbulo; acabar en el patíbulo
scaffolding /'skæfəldɪŋ/ n andamiada, f; (building, scaffold) andamio, m
scald /skɔld/ vt escaldar; quemar; (instruments) esterilizar. n quemadura, escaldadura, f. **to s. oneself,** escaldarse. **scalding hot,** hirviendo
scale /skeil/ n (of a balance) platillo, m; Zool. escama, f; Bot. bráctea, f; Bot. hojuela, f; (flake) laminita, f; (Mus., Math.) escala, f; (of charges, etc.) tarifa, f; (of salaries) escalafón, m; (of a thermometer) escala, f. vt escalar; (fish) escamar. **major s.,** escala mayor, f. **minor s.,** escala menor, f. **on a grand s.,** en gran escala. **on a small s.,** en pequeña escala. **pair of scales,** balanza, f; (for heavy weights) báscula, f; (scale) escala social, f. **The Scales,** Astron. Libra, f. **to draw to s.,** dibujar a escala. **to turn the scales,** pesar; Fig. inclinar la balanza. **to s. down,** (Art. and of charges) reducir
scaling /'skeilɪŋ/ n (of fish) escamadura, f; (of buildings) desconchadura, f; (ascent) escalamiento, m
scallop /'skɒləp, 'skæl-/ n (Ichth. and badge) venera, f; concha, f; Sew. onda, f, festón, m. vt Cul. guisar en conchas; Sew. ondear, festonear
scalp /skælp/ n Anat. pericráneo, m; cuero cabelludo, m; Fig. trofeo, m. vt escalpar. **s.-hunter,** cazador de cabelleras, m
scalpel /'skælpəl/ n escalpelo, m
scaly /'skeili/ a escamoso, conchado; (of boilers) incrustado
scamp /skæmp/ n bribón, granuja, m, vt (work) frangollar
scamper /'skæmpər/ vi retozar, brincar; correr. n ca-

rrerita, *f.* **to s. off,** salvarse por los pies, huir; marcharse corriendo

scan /skæn/ *vt* (verse) medir, escandir; (examine) escudriñar, examinar; (glance at) dar un vistazo (a)

scandal /'skændḷ/ *n* escándalo, *m*; maledicencia, *f*; (slander) calumnia, *f.* **to talk s.,** murmurar

scandalize /'skændḷ͵aiz/ *vt* escandalizar

scandalous /'skændḷəs/ *a* escandaloso; infame; calumnioso

scandalously /'skændḷəsli/ *adv* escandalosamente

scandalousness /'skændḷəsnıs/ *n* carácter escandaloso, *m*

Scandinavia /͵skændə'neiviə/ Escandinavia, *f*

Scandinavian /͵skændə'neiviən/ *a* escandinavo. *n* escandinavo (-va)

scant /skænt/ *a* escaso; insuficiente

scantily /'skæntḷi/ *adv* insuficientemente

scantiness /'skæntinıs/ *n* escasez, *f*; insuficiencia, *f*

scanty /'skænti/ *a* insuficiente; escaso; (of hair) ralo; (of crops, etc.) pobre

scapegoat /'skeip͵gout/ *n* chivo expiatorio, *m*, víctima propiciatoria, *f*; cabeza de turco, *f.* **to be a s. for,** pagar el pato por

scapegrace /'skeip͵greis/ *n* bribón, *m*

scapula /'skæpyələ/ *n Anat.* escápula, *f*

scapulary /'skæpyə͵leri// *n Eccl.* escapulario, *m*

scar /skɑr/ *n* cicatriz, *f*; *Fig.* señal, *f. vt* marcar con una cicatriz. **to s. over,** cicatrizarse

scarab /'skærəb/ *n* escarabajo, *m*; escarabajo sagrado, *m*

scarce /skɛərs/ *a* escaso; insuficiente; raro. *adv Poet.* apenas. **to make oneself s.,** largarse, pirarse, escabullirse; ausentarse, esconderse

scarcely /'skɛərsli/ *adv* apenas; no bien; casi; (with difficulty) a duras penas, con dificultad. **It is s. likely he said that,** No es muy probable que lo hubiese dicho. **There were s. twenty people in the building,** Había apenas veinte personas en el edificio. **S. anyone likes his pictures,** Sus cuadros no le gustan a casi nadie

scarcity /'skɛərsıti/ *n* escasez, insuficiencia, *f*; (famine) carestía, *f*; (rarity) rareza, *f*

scare /skɛər/ *vt* asustar, espantar, llenar de miedo (a), *Lat. Am. also* julepear; intimidar. *n* susto, pánico, *m*; alarma, *f.* **What a s. I got!** ¡Qué susto me ha llevado! **to s. away,** ahuyentar. **to be scared,** *Lat. Am.* julepearse

scarecrow /'skɛər͵krou/ *n* espantapájaros, *m*; *Inf.* estantigua, *f*, mamarracho, espantajo, *m*

scaremonger /'skɛər͵mʌŋgər/ *n* alarmista, *mf*

scarf /skɑrf/ *n* bufanda, *f*; (tie) corbata, *f*; *Mil.* faja, *f*

scarlatina /͵skɑrlə'tinə/ *n Med.* escarlatina, *f*

scarlet /'skɑrlıt/ *n* escarlata, *f. a* de color escarlata. **to turn s.,** (of persons) enrojecerse. **s. fever,** escarlatina, *f.* **s. hat,** *Eccl.* capelo (cardenalicio), *m.* **s. runner,** *Bot.* judía verde, *f*

scatheless /'skeiðlıs/ *a* ileso, sano y salvo

scathing /'skeiðıŋ/ *a* mordaz, cáustico

scatter /'skætər/ *vt* esparcir, sembrar con; (benefits, etc.) derramar; (put to flight) derrotar; dispersar; disipar; *Fig.* frustrar; (squander) derrochar, desparramar. *vi* dispersarse. **The crowd scattered,** La muchedumbre se dispersó. **s.-brained,** de cabeza de chorlito, atolondrado

scattered /'skætərd/ *a* disperso; esparcido

scattered showers /'ʃauərz/ *n* lluvias aisladas, *f pl*

scattering /'skætərıŋ/ *n* dispersión, *f*; (defeat) derrota, *f*; esparcimiento, *m*; (small number) número pequeño, *m*

scavenge /'skævındʒ/ *vt* (streets) recoger la basura de, barrer

scavenger /'skævındʒər/ *n* (of the streets) barrendero, *m*; *Zool.* animal que se alimenta de carne muerta, *m*; insecto que se alimenta de estiércol, *m. vt* See **scavenge**

scenario /sı'nɛəri͵ou, -'nɑr-/ *n* escenario, *m*

scene /sin/ *n* escena, *f*; teatro, lugar, *m*; espectáculo, *m*; (*Theat.* décor) decoración, *f*; (of a play) escena, *f*; (view) vista, perspectiva, *f.* **behind the scenes,** entre bastidores. **The s. is laid...,** La acción pasa... **to come**

---

on the s., entrar en escena. **to make a s.,** hacer una escena. **s.-painter,** *n* escenógrafo (-fa). **s.-shifter,** tramoyista, *mf*

scenery /'sinəri/ *n Theat.* decorado, *m*; (landscape) paisaje, *m*

scenic /'sinık/ *a* dramático; escénico; pintoresco. **s. railway,** montaña rusa, *f*

scenography /si'nɒgrəfi/ *n* escenografía, *f*

scent /sɛnt/ *vt* perfumar; (smell) oler; (out) husmear, olfatear; (suspect) sospechar. *n* perfume, *m*; fragancia, *f*, aroma, *rı*; (smell) olor, *m*; (of hounds) viento, *m*; (of game, etc.) rastro, viento, *m*; (*Fig.* of person) nariz, *f*; (trail) pista, *f.* **to lose the s.,** perder la pista. **to s. danger,** oler el peligro. **to throw off the s.,** despistar. **s.-bottle,** frasco de perfume, *m.* **s.-spray,** pulverizador, *m*

scented /'sɛntıd/ *a* perfumado; (of roses, etc.) de olor, oloroso; (in compounds) de... olfato. **s. sweet pea,** guisante de olor, *m*

scentless /'sɛntlıs/ *a* sin olor; inodoro

scepter /'sɛptər/ *n* cetro, *m*

sceptic /'skɛptık/ *n* escéptico (-ca)

sceptical /'skɛptıkəl/ *a* escéptico

scepticism /'skɛptə͵sızəm/ *n* escepticismo, *m*

schedule /'skɛdʒul/ *n* lista, *m*; programa, *m*; (of taxes) clase, *f*; (of trains, etc.) horario, *m. vt* poner en una lista; inventariar

scheme /skim/ *n* plan, *m*; proyecto, *m*; diagrama, esquema, *m*; (summary) resumen, *m*; (of colors, etc.) combinación, *f*; (plot) intriga, maquinación, *f. vt* proyectar. *vi* planear, formar planes; (intrigue) intrigar, conspirar. **color s.,** combinación de colores, *f*

schemer /'skimər/ *n* (plotter) intrigante, *mf*

scheming /'skimıŋ/ *a* intrigante; astuto. *n* planes, proyectos, *m pl*; intrigas, maquinaciones, *f pl*

schism /'sızəm, 'skız-/ *n* cisma, *mf*

schismatic /sız'mætık, skız-/ *a* cismático. *n* cismático (-ca)

scholar /'skɒlər/ *n* (at school) colegial (-la); (disciple) alumno (-na); (student) estudiante, *mf*; (learned person) erudito (-ta), hombre de letras, *m*; (scholarship holder) becario, *m*

scholarly /'skɒlərli/ *a* de sabio, de hombre de letras; erudito

scholarship /'skɒlər͵ʃıp/ *n* erudición, (research) investigación, *f*; saber, *m*; (tuition grant) beca, *f. s.* **holder,** becario, *m*

scholastic /skə'læstık/ *a* escolar, escolástico; pedante; (medieval) escolástico. *n* escolástico, *m.* **the s. profession,** el magisterio

school /skul/ *n* escuela, *f*; colegio, *m*; academia, *f*; *Educ.* departamento, *m*; (faculty) facultad, *f*; (of fish) banco, *m. vt* enseñar, instruir; formar; disciplinar. **in s.,** en clase. **day s.,** escuela, *f*, colegio, *m.* **the Florentine s.,** (of painting) la escuela florentina. **the lower s.,** los alumnos del preparatorio. **private s.,** colegio particular, *m.* **s.-bag,** vademécum, *m.* **s.-book,** libro escolar, *m.* **s.-days,** los días de escuela; los años de colegio. **in his s.-days,** cuando él iba a la escuela. **s.-fees,** gastos de la enseñanza, *m pl*, cuota escolar, *f*

schoolboy /'skul͵bɔi/ *n* muchacho de escuela, colegial, *m*

school district *n* sector escolar, *m*

schoolfellow /'skul͵fɛlou/ *n* compañero de colegio, condiscípulo, *m*

schoolgirl /'skul͵gɜrl/ *n* colegiala, *f*

schooling /'skulıŋ/ *n* educación, enseñanza, *f*

schoolmaster /'skul͵mæstər/ *n* maestro de escuela, professor, *Mexico* escuelante, *m*

schoolmistress /'skul͵mıstrıs/ *n* maestra de escuela, profesora, *f*

school of hard knocks *n* universidad sin tejados, *f*

schoolroom /'skul͵rum/ *n* aula, sala de clase, salón de clase, *m*

sciatic /sai'ætık/ *a* ciático

sciatica /sai'ætıkə/ *n* ciática, *f*

science /'saiəns/ *n* ciencia, *f.* **social s.,** las ciencias sociales, *f pl*

scientific /͵saiən'tıfık/ *a* científico; exacto, sistemático

scientist /'saiəntıst/ *n* hombre de ciencia, *m*, científico (-ca)

scimitar /'sɪmɪtər, -,tɑr/ n cimitarra, f
scintilla /sɪn'tɪlə/ n Fig. átomo, vestigio, m
scintillate /'sɪntl,eit/ vi centellear, lucir, chispear; (of persons) brillar
scion /'saiən/ n (sucker) acodo, m; (shoot) vástago, renuevo, m; (human) descendiente, mf. **s. of a noble race,** vástago de una raza noble, m
scissors /'sɪzərz/ n pl tijeras, f pl, Argentina cortante, msg. **s.-sharpener,** amolador, m
sclerosis /sklɪ'rousɪs/ n Med. esclerosis, f
sclerotic /sklɪ'rɒtɪk/ n Anat. esclerótica, f
scoff /skɔf, skɒf/ n burla, mofa, f. vi burlarse. **to s. at,** burlarse de, mofarse de
scoffer /'skɔfər, 'skɒf-/ n mofador (-ra); (at religion, etc.) incrédulo (-la)
scoffing /'skɔfɪŋ, 'skɒf-/ a burlón. n mofas, burlas, f pl
scold /skould/ n virago, f, vt reñir, reprender, regañar
scolding /'skouldɪŋ/ n reprensión, increpación, f
sconce /skɒns/ n cubo de candelero, m; candelabro de pared, m; cornucopia, f
scone /skoun, skɒn/ n bollo, m
scoop /skup/ n pala de mano, f; cuchara de draga, f; (boat) achicador, m; (financial) golpe, m; (journalistic) éxito periodistico, m. vt sacar con pala (de); sacar con cuchara (de); (shares, etc.) comprar, obtener. **to s. out,** vaciar; excavar; (bail) achicar
scooter /'skutər/ n (child's) patinete, patín del diablo, m; monopatín, m
scope /skoup/ n alcance, m; esfera de acción, f; lugar, m. **to give full s. to,** dar rienda suelta a. **to have full s.,** tener plena oportunidad; tener todas las facilidades. **within the s. of,** dentro del alcance de
scorbutic /skɔr'byutɪk/ a Med. escorbútico
scorch /skɔrtʃ/ vt chamuscar; (the skin) tostar; (of the sun) abrasar, quemar; (wither) agostar. **to s. along,** ir como un relámpago. **scorching,** a abrasador, ardiente; Fig. mordaz
score /skɔr/ n (scratch) rasguño, m; señal, f; (crossing out) raya, f; (reckoning) cuenta, f, escote, m; (notch) muesca, f; Sports. tanteo, m, puntuación, Lat. Am. anotación, f; (point) punto, tanto, m; (twenty) veintena, f; (reason) motivo, m, causa, f; respecto, m; Mus. partitura, f. vt marcar; rayar; (erase) tachar, borrar; (cricket runs, etc.) hacer; (goals) marcar; (points) ganar; (reckon) apuntar. **s. a triumph,** apuntarse un triunfo; Mus. instrumentar; (for orchestra) orquestar. vi (be fortunate) llevar la ventaja. **to pay off old scores,** ajustar cuentas viejas. **to s. off someone,** ganar un punto (a), triunfar de. **on that s.,** a ese respecto; por esa causa. **On what s.?** ¿Con qué motivo? **s.-board,** marcador, m
scorer /'skɔrər/ n (of a goal, etc.) tanteador, m; (keeper of score) marcador, m
scoria /'skɔriə/ n escoria, f
scorn /skɔrn/ n desprecio, desdén, m. vt despreciar, desdeñar; reírse de. **to s. to do,** no dignarse hacer
scornful /'skɔrnfəl/ a desdeñoso, despreciativo
scornfully /'skɔrnfəli/ adv desdeñosamente, con desprecio
Scorpion /'skɔrpiən/ n Escorpión, m
scorpion /'skɔrpiən/ n escorpión, alacrán, m; Astron. Escorpión, m
Scot /skɒt/ n escocés, m
scotch /skɒtʃ/ vt (kill) matar; (thwart) frustrar; (a wheel) calzar
Scotland /'skɒtlənd/ Escocia, f
Scotswoman /'skɒts,wumən/ n escocesa, f
Scottish /'skɒtɪʃ/ a escocés
scoundrel /'skaundrəl/ n canalla, sinvergüenza, mf
scour /skauər/ vt (traverse) recorrer, batir; (pans, etc.) fregar, estregar; (free from) limpiar (de); (of water) arrastrar
scourge /skɜrdʒ/ vt azotar, flagelar; castigar, mortificar. n disciplinas, f pl; Fig. verdugo, m, plaga, f
scout /skaut/ n Mil. batidor, explorador, m. vi Mil. explorar, reconocer. vt (flout) rechazar a mano airada, rechazar con desdén. **boy s.,** muchacho explorador, m
scowl /skaul/ vi fruncir el ceño. n ceño, m. **to s. at,** mirar con ceño

scowling /'skaulɪŋ/ a amenazador
scragginess /'skrægɪnɪs/ n magrez, flaqueza, f
scraggy /'skrægi/ a flaco, magro, descarnado
scramble /'skræmbəl/ vi trepar. vt (throw) arrojar; (eggs) revolver. **scrambled eggs,** huevos revueltos, m pl. **to s. for,** andar a la rebatiña por; (for coins, etc.) luchar para. **to s. up,** escalar; subir a gatas
scrap /skræp/ n pedazo, m; fragmento, m; pizca, brizna, f; (shindy) suiza, camorra, f; (boxing) combate de boxeo, m; pl **scraps,** desperdicios, m pl; (food) restos de la comida, m pl. vt desechar; (expunge) borrar; vi (fight) armar camorra. **a few scraps of news,** algunas noticias. **Do you mind not coming? Not a s.,** ¿Te importa no venir? Ni pizca. **s.-book,** álbum de recortes, m; **s.-heap,** depósito de basura, m; Fig. olvido, m. **s. iron,** chatarra, f, hierro viejo, m
scrape /skreip/ vt raspar, rascar, raer; (one's shoes) restregar; (a musical instrument) rascar. n rasguño, m; ruido de raspar, m; (predicament) lío, apuro, m; dificultad, f. **to s. acquaintance with,** trabar amistad con. **to s. along,** Inf. ir tirando. **to s. away,** rascar; quitar. **to s. through,** (an examination) aprobar justo. **to s. together,** amontonar poco a poco
scrappy /'skræpi/ a escaso; fragmentario; (incoherent) descosido. **a s. meal,** una comida escasa
scratch /skrætʃ/ vt arañar; (the earth) escarbar; (rub) rascar; (a hole) hacer; (sketch) dibujar, trazar; (a horse) retirar de una carrera. vi arañar; rascar; escarbar; (of a pen) rasguear; (back out) retirarse. n arañazo, m; (of a pen) rasgueo, m; (in a race) línea de salida, f; (in games) cero, m. a improvisado. **The dog scratched at the door,** El perro arañó la puerta. **to come up to s.,** estar al nivel de las circunstancias. **to s. one's head,** rascarse la cabeza. **to s. a person's eyes out,** sacar los ojos con las uñas (a). **to s. the surface of,** (a subject) tratar superficialmente. **to s. out,** tachar
scrawl /skrɔl/ vi hacer garabatos. vt garabatear, garrapatear. n garabato, m
scream /skrim/ vt and vi chillar. n chillido, m. **It was a perfect s.** Era para morirse de risa. **to s. with laughter,** reírse a carcajadas, morirse de risa
screaming /'skrimɪŋ/ n chillidos, m pl. a chillador; (piercing) penetrante, agudo; (funny) divertidísimo
screech /skritʃ/ vi chillar; (of owls, etc.) ulular; graznar. n chillido, m, ululación, f; graznido, m. **s.-owl,** úlula, f
screen /skrin/ n biombo, m; (wire) tela metálica, f; (nonfolding) mampara, f; (eco) cancel, m; (cinema, television) pantalla, f; (of trees, etc., and Mil.) cortina, f; (Fig. protection) abrigo, m. vt proteger; (shelter) abrigar; (hide) esconder, ocultar; (a light) proteger con pantalla; (a film) proyectar; (sieve) cribar, cerner; (examine) investigar. **to s. from view,** ocultar la vista (de), esconder. **s.-play,** guión, m. **s. star,** estrella de la pantalla, f. **s. test,** prueba, m. **s.-writer,** guionista, mf
screw /skru/ n tornillo, m; (propeller) hélice, f; vuelta de tornillo, f; presión, f; (miser) tacaño, m; (salary) salario, m. vt atornillar; torcer; apretar, oprimir. **He has a s. loose,** Le falta un tornillo. **to s. down,** sujetar con tornillos. **to s. up,** cerrar con tornillos; Inf. meter la pata. **to s. up one's eyes,** desojarse, entornar los ojos; **s.-driver,** destornillador, Mexico desarmador, m
scribble /'skrɪbəl/ vt escribir de prisa, vi garabatear, garrapatear; escribir, ser autor. n garabato, garrapato, m; mala letra, letra ilegible, f; (note) billete, m
scribbler /'skrɪblər/ n el, m, (f, la) que tiene mala letra; (author) autor (-ra) malo (-la)
scribbling /'skrɪblɪŋ/ n garabateo, m. **s.-block,** bloque de papel, m
scribe /skraib/ n escribiente, copista, mf; (Jewish history) escriba, m
scrimmage /'skrɪmɪdʒ/ n reyerta, pelea, camorra, f; (Rugby) mêlée, f
script /skrɪpt/ n letra cursiva, f; Print. plumilla, f; manuscrito, m; Law. escritura, f; examen escrito, m; (film) escenario, m; (screen-play) guión, m
scriptural /'skrɪptʃərəl/ a bíblico

Scripture /'skrɪptʃər/ n Sagrada Escritura, f.

Scriptures, Escrituras, f pl; (of non-Christian religions) los libros sagrados

scrofula /'skrɒfyələ/ n escrófula, f

scrofulous /'skrɒfyələs/ a escrofuloso

scroll /skroul/ n (of paper, etc.) rollo, m; pergamino, m; (flourish) rúbrica, f; (of an Ionic capital) voluta, f. **s. of fame,** lista de la fama, f

scrotum /'skroutəm/ n Anat. escroto, m

scrounge /skraundʒ/ vi sablear. vt dar un sablazo (a); hurtar

scrounger /'skraundʒər/ n sablista, mf, Mexico lapa, f

scrub /skrʌb/ vt fregar; limpiar; restregar. n fregado, m; limpieza, f; fricción, f; (brushwood) matorral, breñal, m, maleza, f

scrubbing /'skrʌbɪŋ/ n fregado, m. **s.-brush,** cepillo para el suelo, m

scrubby /'skrʌbi/ a (of plants) anémico; (of persons) insignificante, pobre; (of land) cubierto de maleza

scruff /skrʌf/ n nuca, f, pescuezo, m

scruple /'skrupəl/ n escrúpulo, m. vi tener escrúpulos. **to have no scruples,** no tener escrúpulos

scrupulous /'skrupyələs/ a escrupuloso; exacto, meticuloso

scrupulously /'skrupyələsli/ adv escrupulosamente; meticulosamente

scrupulousness /'skrupyələsnɪs/ n escrupulosidad, f; meticulosidad, f

scrutinize /'skrutnˌaiz/ vt escudriñar, examinar, Lat. Am. also interiorizar; (votes) escrutar

scrutinizer /'skrutnˌaiˀər/ n escudriñador (-ra); (of votes) escrutador (-ra)

scrutinizing /'skrutnˌaizɪŋ/ a escrutador

scrutiny /'skrutni/ n escrutinio, m

scud /skʌd/ vi correr; deslizarse; flotar. **to s. before the wind,** ir viento en popa

scuffle /'skʌfəl/ vi pelear, forcejear, andar a la rebatiña. n refriega, pelea, sarracina, arrebatiña, f

scull /skʌl/ n remo, m, vi remar

scullery /'skʌləri/ n fregadero, m. **s. maid,** fregona, f

sculptor /'skʌlptər/ n escultor, m, escultora, f

sculptural /'skʌlptʃərəl/ a escultural, escultórico

sculpture /'skʌlptʃər/ n escultura, f, vt esculpir

scum /skʌm/ n espuma, f; (dregs) heces, f pl. vt espumar. **s. of the earth,** las heces de la sociedad

scupper /'skʌpər/ n Naut. clava, f. vt abrir las clavas (de); (frustrate) frustrar, destruir

scurrility /skə'rɪliti/ n grosería, indecencia, f

scurrilous /'skərələs/ a grosero, indecente

scurry /'skɜˑri/ vi echar a correr. n fuga precipitada, f; (of rain) chaparrón, m; (of snow) remolino, m. **to s. off,** escabullirse. **to s. through,** hacer de prisa, terminar rápidamente

scurvy /'skɜrvi/ a tiñoso, vil, ruin. n escorbuto, Mexico berbén, m. **a s. trick,** una mala pasada

scuttle /'skʌtl/ n (trap-door) escotillón, m; Naut. escotilla, f; (for coal) carbonera, f; (flight) huida precipitada, f. vt (a boat) echar a pique, vi (run away) escabullirse, apretar a correr

scythe /saið/ n dalle, m, guadaña, f, vt dallar, segar

sea /si/ n mar, m, or f; ola, f; multitud, f. **Black Sea,** Mar Negro. **Mediterranean Sea,** (Mar) Mediterráneo, m. **at sea,** en el mar; perplejo. **beyond the seas,** allende los mares. **by sea,** por mar. **by the sea,** a la orilla del mar. **high seas,** alta mar, f. **the seven seas,** todos los mares del mundo. **to go to sea,** hacerse marinero. **to put to sea,** hacerse a la mar, hacerse a la vela. **sea-anemone,** anémone de mar. f. **sea-bathing,** baños de mar, m pl. **sea-breeze,** brisa de mar, f. **sea captain,** capitán de mar, m. **sea chart,** carta de marear, f. **sea-coast,** litoral, m, costa marítima, f. **sea-cow,** manatí, m. **sea dog,** lobo de mar, m. **sea-fight,** combate naval, m. **sea-foam,** espuma de mar, f. **sea-girt,** rodeado por el mar. **sea-going,** de altura; navegante. **sea-going craft,** embarcación de alta mar, f. **sea-green,** verdemar, m. **sea-gull,** gaviota, f. **sea-horse,** caballo marino, m. **sea-legs,** piernas de marino, f pl. **sea-level,** nivel del mar, m. **sea-lion,** león marino, m. **sea-mist,** bruma, f. **sea-nymph,** nereida, f. **sea-power,** potencia naval, f. **sea-serpent,** serpiente de mar, f. **sea-sick,** mareado.

to be sea-sick, marearse. **sea-sickness,** mal de mar, m. **sea-trip,** viaje por mar, m. **sea-urchin,** erizo de mar, m. **sea-wall,** dique de mar, m

seafarer /'siˌfeərər/ n (traveler) viajero (-ra) por mar; (sailor) marinero, m

seafaring /'siˌfeərɪŋ/ a marinero, marino. n viajes por mar, m pl; vida del marinero, f

seal /sil/ n Zool. foca, f, lobo marino, m; piel de foca, f; sello, m; (stamp) estampillo, timbre, m; vt sellar; (stamp) estampar; (letters, etc.) cerrar; vi cazar focas. **His fate is sealed,** Su suerte está determinada. **His lips were sealed,** Sus labios estaban cerrados. **under my hand and s.,** firmado y sellado por mí. **s.-ring,** sortija de sello, f

sealing wax /'silɪŋ/ n lacre, m

sealskin /'silˌskɪn/ n piel de foca, f

seam /sim/ n Sew. costura, f; Naut. costura de los tablones, f; Anat. sutura, f; Surg. cicatriz, f; (wrinkle) arruga, f, surco, m; Geol. capa, f, yacimiento, m; Mineral. vena, f, filón, m. vt coser; juntar; (a face) surcar, arrugar

seaman /'simən/ n marinero, m; hombre de mar, m; navegante, m. **able-bodied s.,** marinero práctico, m

seamanlike /'simənˌlaik/ a de marinero, marino; de buen marinero

seamanship /'simənˌʃip/ n marinería, f; náutica, f

seamstress /'simstrɪs/ n costurera, f

seamy /'simi/ a con costuras. **the s. side of life,** el lado peor de la vida

seance /'seians/ n sesión, junta, f; sesión de espiritistas, f

seaplane /'siˌplein/ n hidroavión, hidroplano, m

seaport /'siˌpɔrt/ n puerto de mar, m

sear /sɪər/ a marchito. vt agostar, secar; (a wound) cauterizar; marchitar, ajar; (a conscience) endurecer

search /sɜrtʃ/ vt registrar; (a wound) explorar; examinar; escudriñar; investigar. vi buscar. n busca, f; (of luggage, etc.) reconocimiento, m. **in s. of,** en busca de. **to s. after, for,** buscar; ir al encuentro de. **to s. out,** ir en busca de; preguntar por. **right of s.,** (international law) derecho de visita, m. **s.-party,** pelotón de salvamento, m. **s.-warrant,** auto de reconocimiento, auto de registro domiciliario, orden de allanamiento, orden de cateo, m

searching /'sɜrtʃɪŋ/ a escrutador; penetrante; minucioso. **a s. look,** una mirada penetrante. **a s. wind,** un viento penetrante. **a s. question,** una pregunta perspicaz

searchlight /'sɜrtʃˌlait/ n reflector, proyector, m

seashore /'siˌʃɔr/ n playa, f; orilla del mar, f

seaside /'siˌsaid/ n orilla del mar, f; playa, f. **to go to the s.,** ir al mar, ir a la playa

season /'sizən/ n estación, f; sazón, f; temporada, f; tiempo, m. vt (food) sazonar; (wood, wine) madurar; (accustom) acostumbrar, aclimatar; (with wit, etc.) salpimentar; (temper) templar, moderar. vi madurarse. **at that s.,** a la sazón. **close s.,** veda, f. **in s.,** en sazón; a su tiempo. **out of s.,** fuera de sazón; fuera de tiempo, inoportuno. **the dead s.,** la estación muerta. **the autumn s.,** el otoño; (for social functions, etc.) la temporada de otoño. **s.-ticket,** billete de abono, m

seasonable /'sizənəbəl/ a de estación; tempestivo, oportuno

seasonably /'sizənəbli/ adv en sazón; oportunamente

seasonal /'sizənl/ a estacional; de temporada

seasonal worker n trabajador por temporada, m

seasoned /'sizənd/ a (of food) sazonado; (of wood, etc.) maduro. **highly-s.,** (of a dish) picante, con muchas especies

seasoning /'sizənɪŋ/ n Cul. condimento, m; madurez, f; aclimatación, f; Fig. salsa, sal, f

seat /sit/ n asiento, m; (bench) banco, m; (chair) silla, f; (in a cinema, etc.) localidad, f; (Theat. etc., ticket) entrada, f; (of a person) trasero, m, asentaderas, f pl; (of trousers) fondillos, m pl; (of government, etc.) sede, capital, f; (of war, etc.) teatro, m; (place) sitio, lugar, m; (house) casa solar, f. vt sentar; poner en una silla (a); encontrar sitio; (of buildings) tener… asientos; (a chair) poner asiento (a). **The hall seats a thousand,** La sala tiene mil asientos, Hay mil

asientos en la sala. **Please be seated!** ¡Haga el favor de sentarse! **to be seated,** estar sentado; sentarse. **to have a good s.,** (on a horse) caer bien a caballo. **to hold a s.** in parliament, ser diputado a Cortes. **to keep one's s.,** permanecer sentado. **to take a s.,** tomar asiento, sentarse. **s.-back,** respaldo, *m*; **s. belt,** cinturón de seguridad, *m*
seater /'sitər/ *n* de... asientos. **four-s.,** automóvil de cuatro asientos, *m*
seaweed /'si,wid/ *n* alga marina, *f*; (edible) *Lat. Am.* cochayuyo, *m*
seaworthy /'si,wɜrði/ *a* (of a ship) en buen estado; marinero
sebaceous /sɪ'beiʃəs/ *a* sebáceo
secede /sɪ'sid/ *vi* retirarse (de); separarse (de)
secessionist /sɪ'sɛʃənɪst/ *n* secesionista, *mf*; *Polit.* separatista, *mf*. *a* secesionista; *Polit.* separatista
secluded /sɪ'kludɪd/ *a* apartado, retirado; solitario
seclusion /sɪ'kluʒən/ *n* reclusión, *f*; apartamiento, retiro, *m*; soledad, *f*
second /sɪ'kɒnd/ *a* segundo; otro; igual. *adv* en segundo lugar; después. *n* segundo, *m*; (in a duel) padrino, *m*; (helper) ayudante, *m*; (boxing) segundo, *m*; (railway compartment) departamento de segunda (clase), *m*; *Mus.* segunda, *f*; (of time) segundo, *m*; (moment) instante, momento, *m*. *vt* secundar; (a motion) apoyar; *Mil.* ayudar. **the s. of May,** el dos de mayo. **James the S.,** Jaime el segundo. **on s. thoughts,** después de pensarlo bien. **every s. day,** cada dos días. **They live on the s. floor,** Viven en el primer piso (since the ground floor is not counted separately in Spanish speaking areas, the American second floor = the Spanish **primer piso**). **the s. largest,** el más grande menos uno. **to be s. to none,** no ser inferior a ninguno; (of persons) no ser inferior a nadie; no ceder a nadie. **to come off s.,** llegar el segundo; ser vencido. **seconds hand,** (of watch) segundero, *m*. **s.-in-command,** segundo, *m*; subjefe, *m*. **s.-best,** segundo. **My s.-best hat,** Mi sombrero número dos. **to come off s.-best,** salir mal parado, ser vencido. **s. class,** segunda clase, *f*. **s.-class,** de segunda clase; de calidad inferior; mediocre. **s. cousin,** primo (-ma) segundo (-a). **s. gear,** segunda velocidad, *f*. **s.-hand,** *a* usado; de ocasión; no nuevo. *adv* de segunda mano. **s.-hand car,** un coche de segunda mano. **s.-hand clothing,** ropa usada, *f*. **s.-hand shop,** *Lat. Am.* cambalache *m*. **s. lieutenant,** *Mil.* subteniente, segundo teniente, *m*; *Nav.* alférez de fragata, *m*. **s.-rate,** *a* inferior, mediocre. **s. sight,** doble vista, *f*
secondary /'sɛkən,dɛri/ *a* secundario; subordinado; accesorio; poco importante. **s. school** colegio, liceo. **s. education,** enseñanza secundaria, *f*
seconder /'sɛkəndər/ *n* ayudante, *m*; el, *m*, (*f*, la) que apoya una proposición
secondly /'sɛkəndli/ *adv* en segundo lugar
secrecy /'sikrəsi/ *n* secreto, *m*; reserva, *f*, silencio, *m*. **in the s. of one's own heart,** en lo más íntimo de su corazón
secret /'sikrɪt/ *a* secreto; clandestino; (of persons) reservado, taciturno; (secluded) remoto, apartado; oculto; misterioso. *n* secreto, *m*; (key) clave, *f*. **a s. code,** un código secreto. **in s.,** en secreto, secretamente. **open s.,** secreto a voces. **to keep a s.,** guardar un secreto. **to keep s.,** tener secreto, ocultar. **s. drawer,** secreto, *m*
secretarial /,sɛkrɪ'tɛəriəl/ *a* de secretario. **s. college,** academia comercial, *f*
secretariat /,sɛkrɪ'tɛəriət/ *n* secretaría, *f*
secretary /'sɛkrɪ,tɛri/ *n* secretario (-ia). **private s.,** secretario (-ia) particular. **S. of State,** ministro, *m*; Ministro de Estado, *m*
secrete /sɪ'krit/ *vt* esconder, ocultar; *Med.* secretar
secretion /sɪ'kriʃən/ *n* escondimiento, *m*; *Med.* secreción, *f*
secretive /'sikrɪtɪv/ *a* reservado, callado
secretly /'sikrɪtli/ *adv* en secreto, secretamente; ocultamente, a escondidas
sect /sɛkt/ *n* secta, *f*
sectarian /sɛk'tɛəriən/ *a* and *n* sectario (-ia)
section /'sɛkʃən/ *n* sección, *f*; porción, *f*; subdivisión,

f; (of a law) artículo, *m*. *vt* seccionar. **conic s.,** sección cónica, *f*
sectional /'sɛkʃənl/ *a* en secciones. **s. bookcase,** biblioteca desmontable, *f*
sector /'sɛktər/ *n* sector, *m*
secular /'sɛkyələr/ *a* (very old) secular; (lay) seglar; laico; profano. **s. music,** música profana, *f*. **s. school,** escuela laica, *f*
secularization /,sɛkyələrə'zeiʃən/ *n* secularización, *f*
secularize /'sɛkyələ,raiz/ *vt* secularizar
secure /sɪ'kyʊr/ *a* seguro; (certain) asegurado; (safe) en seguridad; sano y salvo; (firm) firme; fijo; (confident (in)) confiado (en). *vt* asegurar; (insure) garantizar; (lock) cerrar; (confine) prender; (acquire) adquirir, obtener; lograr, conseguir
securely /sɪ'kyʊrli/ *adv* seguramente; en seguridad, sin peligro; con confianza; (firmly) firmemente
security /sɪ'kyʊrɪti/ *n* seguridad, *f*; protección, defensa, *f*; garantía, *f*; (faith) confianza, *f*; *Com.* fianza, *f*; (person) fiador, *m*; *pl* **securities,** valores, títulos, *m pl*. **government securities,** papel del Estado, *m*. **to give s.,** *Com.* dar fianza. **to stand s. for,** *Com.* salir fiador de. **S. Council (United Nations),** El Consejo de Seguridad (de las Naciones Unidas), *m*
sedan-chair /sɪ'dæn,tʃɛər/ *n* silla de manos, *f*
sedate /sɪ'deit/ *a* tranquilo, sosegado; formal, serio, grave
sedately /sɪ'deitli/ *adv* sosegadamente; seriamente
sedateness /sɪ'deitnɪs/ *n* sosiego, *m*, tranquilidad, *f*; formalidad, compostura, *f*
sedative /'sɛdətɪv/ *a* and *n* sedativo, calmante *m*
sedentary /'sɛdn,tɛri/ *a* sedentario
sediment /'sɛdəmənt/ *n* sedimento, *m*; *Lat. Am.* concho, *m*
sedimentation /,sɛdəmən'teiʃən/ *n* sedimentación, *f*
sedition /sɪ'dɪʃən/ *n* sedición, *f*
seditious /sɪ'dɪʃəs/ *a* sedicioso
seduce /sɪ'dus/ *vt* seducir
seducer /sɪ'dusər/ *n* seductor, *m*
seduction /sɪ'dʌkʃən/ *n* seducción, *f*
seductive /sɪ'dʌktɪv/ *a* seductivo, atractivo; persuasivo
sedulous /'sɛdʒələs/ *a* asiduo, diligente
see /si/ *n* sede, *f*. **The Holy S.,** La Santa Sede, *f*
see /si/ *vt* and *vi* ver; mirar; (understand) comprender; (visit) visitar; (attend to) atender a; ocuparse de. **He sees the matter quite differently,** Él mira el asunto de un modo completamente distinto, Su punto de vista sobre el asunto es completamente distinto. **You are not fit to be seen,** No eres nada presentable. **See you next Tuesday!** ¡Hasta el miércoles que viene! **I see!** ¡Ya! ¡Ahora comprendo! **Let's see!** ¡Vamos a ver! **Shall I see you home?** ¿Quiere que te acompañe a casa? **to go and see,** ir a ver. **to see red,** echar chispas. **to see the sights,** visitar los monumentos. **to see life,** ver mundo. **to see service,** servir (en el ejército, etc.). **to see about,** atender a; pensar en; ocuparse de. **to see after,** cuidar de; atender (a); ocuparse de. **to see again,** volver a ver. **to see into,** investigar, examinar. **to see off,** (at the station, etc.) ir a despedir; acompañar. **to see out,** (a person) acompañar a la puerta; (a play, etc.) quedarse hasta el fin (de); no dejar el puesto. **to see over,** inspeccionar. **to see through,** (a house, etc.) inspeccionar; (a person) calarle las intenciones; (a mystery) penetrar; (a person through trouble) ayudar. **to see it through,** llevarlo al cabo; quedarse hasta el fin. **to see to,** atender a; ocuparse de; encargarse de. **to see to everything,** encargarse de todo
seed /sid/ *n* semilla, *f*; simiente, *f*; (of fruit) pepita, *f*, grano, *m*; *Fig.* germen, *m*; (offspring) prole, descendencia, *f*. *vi* granar. *vt* sembrar. **s.-bed,** almáciga, *f*, semillero, *m*. **s.-pearl,** aljófar, *m*. **s.-plot,** sementera, *f*; *Fig.* semillero, *m*. **s.-time,** tiempo de sembrar, *m*
seedling /'sidlɪŋ/ *n* planta de semilla, *f*
seedsman /'sidzmən/ *n* tratante en semillas, *m*
seedy /'sidi/ *a* granado; (of clothes) raído, roto; (of persons) andrajoso, desharrapado; infeliz, desgraciado; (ill) indispuesto, malucho
seeing /'siɪŋ/ *n* vista, *f*; visión, *f*. **It is worth s.,** Vale

la pena de verse. **s.** that..., visto que, dado que, como que. **S.** is believing, Ver es creer

seek /sik/ *vt* buscar; solicitar, pretender; (demand) pedir; (investigate) investigar; (to do something) procurar, tratar de. **They are much sought after,** Son muy populares, Están en demanda. **to s.** after, buscar; perseguir. **to s. for,** buscar

seeker /'sikər/ *n* el, *m*, (*f*, la) que busca; investigador (-ra)

seem /sim/ *vi* parecer. **He seemed honest,** Parecía honrado. **It seemed to me,** Me pareció a mí. **It seems that they were both at home last night,** Parece ser que ambos estaban en casa anoche

seeming /'simɪŋ/ *a* aparente; supuesto

seemingly /'simɪŋli/ *adv* aparentemente; en apariencia

seemliness /'simlinɪs/ *n* decoro, *m*

seemly /'simli/ *a* decoroso, decente

seep /sip/ *vi* filtrar; rezumarse

seer /sɪər/ *n* profeta, *m*

seesaw /'si,sɔ/ *n* columpio, *m*; vaivén, *m*. *vi* columpiarse; balancearse, oscilar. *a* de vaivén, oscilante

seethe /sɪð/ *vi* hervir; *Fig.* bullir

segment /'sɛgmənt/ *n* segmento, *m*

segregate /'sɛgrɪ,geit/ *vt* segregar. *vi* segregarse.

segregation /,sɛgrɪ'geiʃən/ *n* segregación, *f*

Seine, the /sein/ el Sena, *m*

seismic /'saizmɪk/ *a* sísmico

seismograph /'saizmə,græf/ *n* sismógrafo, *m*

seismological /,saizmə'lɒdʒɪkəl/ *a* sismológico

seismology /saiz'mɒlədʒi/ *n* sismología, *f*

seize /siz/ *vt Law.* embargar; apoderarse de; asir; (a person) prender; coger; (a meaning) comprender; (an occasion, etc.) aprovecharse de; (of emotions) dominar; (of illnesses) atacar. *vi Mech.* atascarse. **He was seized by fear,** Le dominó el miedo. **to s. the opportunity,** aprovecharse de la oportunidad. **to s. upon a pretext,** valerse de un pretexto

seizure /'siʒər/ *n* asimiento, *m*; (of property) embargo, secuestro, *m*; (of a person) captura, *f*; arresto, *m*; *Med.* ataque, *m*

seldom /'sɛldəm/ *adv* rara vez, raramente; pocas veces

select /sɪ'lɛkt/ *a* escogido, selecto; exclusivista. *vt* escoger

selection /sɪ'lɛkʃən/ *n* selección, *f*. **selections from Cervantes,** trozos escogidos de Cervantes, *m pl.* **to make a s. from,** escoger entre. **s. committee,** comité de selección, *m*

selective /sɪ'lɛktɪv/ *a* selectivo

self /sɛlf/ *n* mismo (-a), propio (-a); sí mismo (-a), se; personalidad, *f*; ser, *m*. **all by one's s.,** sin ayuda de nadie; solo; *Inf.* solito. **my other s.,** mi otro yo. **my better s.,** mi mejor parte. **the s.,** el yo. **s.-abasement,** humillación de sí mismo, *f*. **s.-acting,** automático. **s.-apparent,** evidente, patente. **s.-appointed,** nombrado por uno mismo. **s.-assertion,** presunción, *f*. **s.-assertive,** presumido. **s.-assurance,** confianza en sí mismo, *f*; aplomo, *m*; (impertinence) cara dura, frescura, *f*. **s.-centered,** egocéntrico. **s.-colored,** del mismo color; de su color natural. **s.-command,** dominio de sí mismo, *m*; sangre fría, ecuanimidad, *f*. **s.-complacent,** satisfecho de sí mismo. **s.-conceit,** vanidad, arrogancia, petulancia, *f*. **s.-confidence,** confianza en sí mismo, *f*; aplomo, *m*. **s.-confident,** seguro de sí mismo, lleno de confianza en sí mismo. **s.-conscious,** turbado, confuso, apocado. **s.-consciousness,** turbación, confusión, *f*, apocamiento, azoramiento, *m*. **s.-contained,** (of a person) reservado, poco comunicativo; dueño de sí mismo; (of things) completo; (of flats, etc.) independiente; con entrada independiente. **s.-contradictory,** contradictorio. **s.-control,** dominio de sí mismo, *m*; ecuanimidad, serenidad, sangre fría, *f*. **s.-controlled,** dueño de sí mismo; ecuánime, sereno. **s.-deception,** engaño de sí mismo, *m*; ilusiones, *f pl*. **s.-defense,** defensa propia, *f*. **s.-denial,** abnegación, *f*; renunciación, *f*; frugalidad, *f*. **s.-destruction,** suicidio, *m*. **s.-determination,** libre albedrío, *m*; (of peoples) autonomía, *f*; independencia, *f*. **s.-educating,** autodidacto. **s.-esteem,** respeto a uno mismo, *m*; amor

propio, *m*. **s.-evident,** aparente, que salta a la vista. **s.-explanatory,** que se explica a sí mismo; evidente. **s.-generating,** autógeno. **s.-government,** (of a person) dominio de sí mismo, *m*; (of a state) autonomía, *f*. **s.-importance,** presunción, petulancia, *f*. **s.-important,** pagado de sí mismo. **to be s.-important,** darse importancia, darse tono. **s.-indulgence,** indulgencia con sí mismo, *f*; (of food, drink, etc.) excesos, *m pl*, falta de moderación, *f*. **s.-indulgent,** indulgente con sí mismo; dado a los placeres, sibarita. **s.-interest,** propio interés, *m*. **s.-knowledge,** conocimiento de sí mismo, *m*. **s.-love,** egolatría, *f*. **s.-made man,** hombre que ha llegado a su posición actual por sus propios esfuerzos, *m*. **self-medication,** automedicación, *f*. **s.-opinionated,** terco, obstinaz. **s.-portrait,** autorretrato, *m*. **s.-possessed,** dueño de sí mismo; reservado; de sangre fría. **s.-possession,** aplomo, *m*, sangre fría, serenidad, *f*. **s.-preservation,** protección de sí mismo, *f*. **s.-reliance,** independencia, *f*; confianza en sí mismo, *f*. **s.-reliant,** independiente; confiado en sí mismo. **s.-reproach,** remordimiento, *m*. **s.-respect,** respeto de sí mismo, *m*; amor propio, *m*, dignidad, *f*. **s.-respecting,** que se respeta; que tiene amor propio. **s.-restraint,** dominio de sí mismo, *m*; moderación, *f*. **s.-righteous,** farisaico. **s.-sacrifice,** abnegación, *f*. **s.-sacrificing,** abnegado. **s.-same,** mismo, idéntico. **s.-satisfaction,** satisfacción de sí mismo, *f*; vanidad, *f*; (of desires, etc.) satisfacción, indulgencia, *f*. **s.-satisfied,** satisfecho de sí mismo, pagado de sí mismo. **s.-seeking,** egoísta, interesado. *n* egoísmo, *m*. **s.-starter,** *Mech.* arranque automático, *m*. **s.-styled,** autodenominado, autotitulado, llamado por sí mismo. **s.-sufficiency,** suficiencia, *f*; presunción, *f*. **s.-sufficient,** que basta a sí mismo; contento de sí mismo. **s.-supporting,** que vive de su propio trabajo; (of an institution, business) independiente. **s.-taught,** autodidacto. **s.-willed,** voluntarioso

selfish /'sɛlfɪʃ/ *a* egoísta, interesado

selfishly /'sɛlfɪʃli/ *adv* interesadamente; por egoísmo

selfishness /'sɛlfɪʃnɪs/ *n* egoísmo, *m*

sell /sɛl/ *vt* vender. *vi* vender; venderse. **They sold him to his enemies,** Le vendieron a sus enemigos. **House to s.,** «Se vende una casa.» **to s. at a loss,** malvender, vender con pérdida. **to s. for cash,** vender al contado. **to s. retail,** vender por menor. **to s. wholesale,** vender al por mayor. **to s. one's life dearly,** vender cara la vida. **They sold the chair for $10,** Vendieron la silla por diez dólares. **to s. off,** (goods) liquidar, saldar. **to s. out,** vender; agotar. **The best edition is sold out,** La mejor edición está agotada. **All the nylons have been sold out,** Se han vendido todas las medias de nilón (de cristal). **to s. up,** vender

seller /'sɛlər/ *n* vendedor (-ra); comerciante (en), *m*

selling /'sɛlɪŋ/ *n* venta, *f*. **s. off,** liquidación, *f*. **s. price,** precio de venta, *m*

selvage /'sɛlvɪdʒ/ *n* (in cloth) orillo, *m*

semantic /sɪ'mæntɪk/ *a* semántico

semantics /sɪ'mæntɪks/ *n* semántica, *f*

semaphore /'sɛmə,fɔr/ *n* semáforo, *m*, *vt* and *vi* hacer señales semafóricas (a)

semaphoric /,sɛmə'fɔrɪk/ *a* semafórico

semblance /'sɛmbləns/ *n* apariencia, *f*. **to put on a s. of woe,** aparentar ser triste

semen /'simən/ *n* semen, *m*, esperma, *f*

semester /sɪ'mɛstər/ *n* semestre, *m*

semi- *prefix* semi; medio. **s.-conscious,** medio consciente. **s.-detached house,** casa doble, *f*

semicircle /'sɛmɪ,sɜrkəl/ *n* semicírculo, *m*

semicircular /,sɛmɪ'sɜrkyələr/ *a* semicircular

semicolon /'sɛmɪ,koulən/ *n* punto y coma, *m*

semidetached /,sɛmɪdɪ'tætʃt/, ,sɛmai-/ *a* (house) apartado

semiformal /,sɛmɪ'fɔrməl/, ,sɛmai-/ *a* de media ceremonia

seminarist /'sɛmɪnərɪst/ *n* seminarista, *mf*

seminary /'sɛmə,nɛri/ *n* seminario, *m*; (for girls) colegio interno, *m*

Semite /'sɛmait/ *n* semita, *mf*

Semitic /sə'mɪtɪk/ *a* semítico, semita

Semitism /'sɛmɪ,tɪzəm/ *n* semitismo, *m*

semolina /ˌsɛməˈlinə/ n sémola, f
senate /ˈsɛnɪt/ n senado, m
senator /ˈsɛnətər/ n senador, m
senatorial /ˌsɛnəˈtɔriəl/ a senatorio
send /sɛnd/ vt enviar, mandar; Com. remitir; (a ball) lanzar; (grant) conceder; permitir; (inflict) afligir (con). **I sent Jane for it,** Envié a Juana a buscarlo. **He sent us word that he could not come,** Nos mandó un recado diciéndonos que no podía venir. **to s. mad,** hacer enloquecer. **to s. packing,** mandar a paseo. **to s. again,** volver a mandar. **to s. away,** vt enviar; (dismiss) destituir; despedir; (scare off) ahuyentar, vi enviar a otra parte. **to s. back,** (goods) devolver; (persons) volver. **to s. down,** hacer bajar; (rain, etc.) mandar, derramar; (a student) suspender, expulsar. **to s. in,** mandar; (persons) hacer entrar, introducir; (food) servir; (a bill) presentar; (one's name) dar. **Please s. him in!** ¡Sírvase de invitarle a entrar! **to s. in one's resignation,** mandar su dimisión. **to s. off,** enviar, mandar; (goods) despachar; (persons) destituir; (scare) ahuyentar. **s.-off,** n despedida, f. **a good s.-off,** una despedida afectuosa. **to s. on,** (a letter) hacer seguir; (instructions) trasmitir. **to s. out,** hacer salir; mandar; (emit) despedir, dar; (new shoots, etc.) echar. **to s. round,** (the hat, etc.) hacer circular. **to s. up,** enviar arriba; mandar subir, hacer subir; mandar, enviar; (a ball) lanzar
sender /ˈsɛndər/ n remitente, mf; Elec. transmisor, m
sending /ˈsɛndɪŋ/ n envío, m
Senegal /ˌsɛnɪˈgɔl, -ˈgɑl/ Senegal, m
Senegalese /ˌsɛnəgəˈliz/ a and n senegalés (-esa)
senile /ˈsinail/ a senil
senility /sɪˈnɪlɪti/ n senilidad, f
senior /ˈsinyər/ a mayor, de mayor edad; más antiguo. **Martínez s.,** Martínez padre. **Charles is Mary's s. by five years,** Carlos es cinco años mayor que María. **s. member,** decano, m
seniority /sinˈyɔrɪti/ n ancianidad, f; antigüedad, f
senna /ˈsɛnə/ n Bot. sena, f
sensation /sɛnˈseiʃən/ n sensación, f; sentimiento, m; impresión, f. **to create a s.,** causar una sensación
sensational /sɛnˈseiʃənl/ a sensacional
sensationalism /sɛnˈseiʃənlˌɪzəm/ n Philos. sensualismo, m; efectismo, m
sensationalist /sɛnˈseiʃənlɪst/ n Philos. sensualista, mf; efectista, mf
sense /sɛns/ n sentido, m. vt sentir. **in a s.,** hasta cierto punto; desde un punto de vista. **in the full s. of the word,** en toda la extensión de la palabra. **common s.,** sentido común, m. **He has no s. of smell,** No tiene olfato. **the five senses,** los cinco sentidos. **to be out of one's senses,** estar fuera de sí, estar trastornado. **You must be out of your senses!** ¡Debes de haber perdido el juicio! ¡Estás loco! **to come to one's senses,** (after unconsciousness) volver en sí; (after folly) recobrar el sentido común. **to talk s.,** hablar con sentido común, hablar razonablemente. **s. organ,** órgano de los sentidos, m. **have a good s. of direction,** saber orientarse, tener buena orientación. **have no s. of smell,** ser incapaz de percibir olores. **have no s. of taste,** ser incapaz de distinguir gustos
senseless /ˈsɛnslɪs/ a (unconscious) sin sentido, insensible; desmayado; (silly) necio, estúpido. **to knock s.,** derribar, tumbar
senselessness /ˈsɛnslɪsnɪs/ n falta de sentido común, f; locura, absurdidad, f
sensibility /ˌsɛnsəˈbɪlɪti/ n sensibilidad, f
sensible /ˈsɛnsəbəl/ a sensible; (conscious) consciente (de); sesudo. **to be s. of,** estar consciente de; estar persuadido de
sensibly /ˈsɛnsəbli/ adv sensiblemente; sesudamente, cuerdamente
sensitive /ˈsɛnsɪtɪv/ a sensitivo; susceptible (a); impresionable. **s. plant,** sensitiva, f
sensitivity /ˌsɛnsɪˈtɪvɪti/ n sensibilidad, f; susceptibilidad, f; delicadeza, f
sensitize /ˈsɛnsɪˌtaiz/ vt Photo. sensibilizar
sensory /ˈsɛnsəri/ a sensorio
sensual /ˈsɛnʃuəl/ a sensual; voluptuoso
sensualism /ˈsɛnʃuəˌlɪzəm/ n sensualismo, m

sensualist /ˈsɛnʃuəlɪst/ n sensualista, mf
sensuality /ˌsɛnʃuˈælɪti/ n sensualidad, f
sensually /ˈsɛnʃuəli/ adv sensualmente
sensuous /ˈsɛnʃuəs/ a sensorio
sensuousness /ˈsɛnʃuəsnɪs/ n sensualidad, f
sentence /ˈsɛntns/ n Law. sentencia, f; (penalty) pena, f; Gram. frase, oración, f; (maxim) máxima, sentencia, f. vt sentenciar, condenar. **to pass s.,** pronunciar sentencia, fallar. **under s. of,** bajo pena de
sententious /sɛnˈtɛnʃəs/ a sentencioso
sentient /ˈsɛnʃənt/ a sensible
sentiment /ˈsɛntəmənt/ n sentimiento, m; (sentimentality) sentimentalismo, m; opinión, f
sentimental /ˌsɛntəˈmɛntl/ a sentimental; (mawkish) sensiblero
sentimentalist /ˌsɛntəˈmɛntlɪst/ n romántico (-ca), persona sentimental, f
sentimentality /ˌsɛntəmɛnˈtælɪti/ n sentimentalismo, m, sensiblería, f
sentimentalize /ˌsɛntəˈmɛntlˌaiz/ vt idealizar
sentimentally /ˌsɛntəˈmɛntli/ adv sentimentalmente
sentinel /ˈsɛntnl/ n centinela, mf
sentry /ˈsɛntri/ n centinela, m. **to be on s. duty,** estar de guardia. **s.-box,** garita de centinela, f
separable /ˈsɛpərəbəl/ a separable
separate /a. ˈsɛpərɪt; v. -ˌreit/ a separado; distinto; independiente. vt separar; dividir. vi separarse; (of husband and wife) separarse de bienes y de cuerpos
separately /ˈsɛpərɪtli/ adv separadamente; aparte
separation /ˌsɛpəˈreiʃən/ n separación, f; Law. separación de bienes y de cuerpos, f
separatism /ˈsɛpərəˌtɪzəm/ n separatismo, m
separatist /ˈsɛpərətɪst/ a and n separatista mf
Sephardic /səˈfardɪk/ a Sefaradí
sepia /ˈsipiə/ n (color and fish) sepia, f
September /sɛpˈtɛmbər/ n setiembre, septiembre, m
septic /ˈsɛptɪk/ a séptico
septicemia /ˌsɛptəˈsimiə/ n septicemia, f
septuagenarian /ˌsɛptʃuədʒəˈnɛəriən/ n setentón (-ona); septuagenario (-ia)
septum /ˈsɛptəm/ septo, tabique, m
sepulcher /ˈsɛpəlkər/ n sepulcro, m
sepulchral /səˈpʌlkrəl/ a sepulcral
sequel /ˈsikwəl/ n (of a story, etc.) continuación, f; consecuencia, f; resultado, m
sequence /ˈsikwəns/ n sucesión, f; serie, f; orden, mf; (at cards) serie, f; Gram. correspondencia, f; (Eccl. and cinema) secuencia, f. **s. of tenses,** correspondencia de los tiempos, f
sequestered /sɪˈkwɛstərd/ a aislado, remoto
sequestrate /sɪˈkwɛstreit/ vt secuestrar
sequestration /ˌsikwɛsˈtreiʃən/ n secuestro, m,
sequin /ˈsikwɪn/ n lentejuela, f
seraglio /sɪˈrælyou/ n serrallo, m
seraph /ˈsɛrəf/ n serafín, m
seraphic /sɪˈræfɪk/ a seráfico
seraphim /ˈsɛrəfɪm/ n serafín, m
Serbia /ˈsɜrbiə/ Servia, f
Serbian /ˈsɜrbiən/ a servio. n servio (-ia); (language) servio, m
serenade /ˌsɛrəˈneid/ n serenata, f, vt dar una serenata (a)
serene /səˈrin/ a sereno. **His S. Highness,** Su Alteza Serenísima
serenity /səˈrɛnɪti/ n serenidad, f; tranquilidad, f
serf /sɜrf/ n siervo (-va)
serfdom /ˈsɜrfdəm/ n servidumbre, f
serge /sɜrdʒ/ n estameña, f; (silk) sarga, f
sergeant /ˈsardʒənt/ n Mil. sargento, m; (police) sargento de policía, m. **s.-at-arms,** macero, m. **s.-major,** sargento instructor, m
serial /ˈsiəriəl/ a en serie; (of a story) por entregas. n novela por entregas, f. **s. number,** número de serie, m
sericulture /ˈsɜrɪˌkʌltʃər/ n sericultura, f
series /ˈsiəriz/ n serie, f; cadena, f; Math. serie, progresión, f. **in s.,** en serie
serious /ˈsiəriəs/ a serio; sincero; verdadero; (of illness, etc.) grave; importante. **He was s.** (not laughing) **when he said it,** Lo dijo en serio. **He is very s.**

about it, Lo toma muy en serio. **to grow s.,** (of persons) ponerse serio; (of events) hacerse grave
seriously /'sɪərɪəsli/ *adv* seriamente; en serio; gravemente. **to take** (something) **s.,** tomar (algo) en serio.
to take oneself s., tomarse muy en serio
seriousness /'sɪərɪəsnɪs/ *n* seriedad, *f*; gravedad, *f*. **in all s.,** en serio, seriamente
sermon /'sɜːrmən/ *n* sermón, *m*
sermonize /'sɜːrmə,naɪz/ *vt* and *vi* sermonear
serpent /'sɜːrpənt/ *n* serpiente, *f*; *Mus.* serpentón, *m*
serpentine /'sɜːrpən,tin, -,taɪn/ *a* serpentino; (of character) tortuoso. *n Mineral.* serpentina, *f*
serrated /'sɛreitɪd/ *a* serrado; dentellado
serried /'sɛrɪd/ *a* apretado, apiñado
serum /'sɪərəm/ *n* suero, *m*
servant /'sɜːrvənt/ *n* servidor (-ra); (domestic) criado (-da); (employee) empleado (-da); (slave and *Fig.*) siervo (-va); *pl* (domestic) servidumbre, *f*, servicio, *m*. **I remain your obedient s.,** Quedo de Vd. atento y seguro servidor (att. y s.s.). **civil s.,** empleado del estado, *m*. **general s.,** criada para todo, *f*. **man s.,** criado, *m*. **the s. problem,** el problema del servicio. **Your s., sir,** Servidor de Vd., señor. **s.-girl,** criada, *f*
serve /sɜːrv/ *vt* servir (a); ser útil (a); satisfacer; (in a shop) despachar; (an apprenticeship, etc.) hacer; (a prison sentence) cumplir; (treat) tratar; (of stallion) cubrir; (a warrant, etc.) ejecutar; (a notice) entregar; (a ball) servir; (on a jury, etc.) formar parte de; *Naut.* aforrar. *vi* servir; (*Mil., Nav.*) hacer el servicio. *n Sports.* saque, *m*. **It serves you right!** ¡Lo tienes merecido! **to s. at table,** servir a la mesa. **to s. as,** servir de. **to s. out,** distribuir; servir. **Serves 8,** (recipe) Da 8 porciones
server /'sɜːrvər/ *n Eccl.* acólito, *m*; *Sports.* saque, *m*; (tray) bandeja, *f*; (for fish, etc.) pala, *f*
service /'sɜːrvɪs/ *n* servicio, *m*; *Eccl.* oficio, *m*; servicio de mesa, *m*; (of a writ) entrega, *f*; *Sports.* saque, *m*. **coffee s.,** juego de café, *m*. **diplomatic s.,** cuerpo diplomático, *m*. **at your s.,** Para servir a Vd., A su disposición. **on active s.,** en acto de servicio; en el campo de batalla. **to go into s.,** (of servants) ir a servir. **to render s.,** prestar servicios. **s. tree,** serbal, *m*
serviceable /'sɜːrvəsəbəl/ *a* (of persons) servicial; (of things) servible, utilizable; útil; práctico; (lasting) duradero
service road *n* vía de servicio, *f*
servile /'sɜːrvɪl/ *a* servil, *Lat. Am. also* incondicional
servility /sər'vɪlɪti/ *n* servilismo, *m*
serving /'sɜːrvɪŋ/ *a* sirviente; al servicio (de). **s. maid,** criada, *f*. **s. table,** trinchero, *m*
servitude /'sɜːrvɪ,tud/ *n* servidumbre, esclavitud, *f*. **penal s.,** cadena perpetua, *f*
session /'sɛʃən/ *n* sesión, *f*; junta, *f*. **petty sessions,** tribunal de primera instancia, *m*
set /sɛt/ *vt* poner; colocar; fijar; (seeds, etc.) plantar; (bones) reducir, componer; (gems) engastar, montar; (a clock) regular; (sails) desplegar; (the teeth of a saw) trabar, triscar; (congeal) hacer coagular; (a trap) armar; (a snare) tender; (a razor) afilar; (made ready) preparar; (type) componer; (cause) hacer; *Mus.* poner en música; *Mus.* adaptar; (order) mandar; (prescribe) dar, asignar; (estimate) estimar, evaluar; (an example, etc.) dar; (establish) establecer, crear. *vi* (of the sun, etc.) ponerse; (solidify) coagularse; solidificarse; (of tides) fluir; (of the wind) soplar; (of dogs) hacer punta. **The joke set him laughing,** El chiste le hizo reír. **set an example,** dar ejemplo, dar el ejemplo. **to set a precedent,** sentar precedente. **to set a person's mind at rest,** tranquilizar, sosegar. **to set a trap,** armar lazo. **to set at ease,** poner a sus anchas (a), hacer cómodo (a). **to set at naught,** despreciar. **to set eyes on,** poner los ojos en. **to set fire to,** pegar fuego a, incendiar. **to set free,** poner en libertad, librar (de). **to set in motion,** poner en marcha. **to set one's teeth,** apretar los dientes. **to set people talking,** dar que hablar a la gente. **to set the fashion,** fijar la moda; poner de moda. **to set the alarm at seven o'clock,** poner el despertador a las siete. **to set the table,** poner la mesa. **to set to work,** ponerse a trabajar. **to set about,** *vi* (begin)

ponerse (a); empezar; (undertake) emprender. *vt* (a rumour, etc.) divulgar. **They set about each other,** Empezaron a golpearse, Vinieron a las manos. **to set against,** indisponer (con), enemistar (con); hacer el enemigo (de), ser hostil (a); (balance) oponer, balancear. **to set oneself against,** oponerse a; atacar; luchar contra. **to set aside,** poner a un lado; apartar; (discard) desechar; (omit) omitir, pasar por alto de; dejar aparte, excluir; (keep) reservar; (money, etc.) ahorrar; (reject) rechazar; (quash) anular. **to set back,** retrasar; hacer retroceder. **set-back,** *n* revés, *m*; contrariedad, *f*. **to set before,** poner ante; (facts) exponer; (introduce) presentar. **to set down,** poner en tierra; depositar; (of a bus, etc.) dejar; (in writing) poner por escrito; anotar, apuntar; narrar, contar; (attribute) atribuir; (fix) fijar, formular; (believe to be) creer. **Passengers are set down at...,** Los viajeros pueden apearse en... **to set forth,** *vt* (one's opinions, etc.) exponer; publicar; (display) exhibir, mostrar; (make) hacer. *vi* ponerse en camino. **to set going,** poner en marcha; echar a andar. **to set in,** empezar; (of the tide) fluir. **A reaction has set in,** Se ha hecho sentir una reacción. **to set off,** *vt* (explode) hacer estallar; (cause) hacer; (heighten) realzar; hacer resaltar; (counterbalance) contraponer. *vi* partir; ponerse en camino. **set-off,** *n* contraste, *m*, contraposición, *f*. **to set off against,** contraponer. **to set on,** *vt* (a dog) azuzar; (incite) instigar, incitar. *vi* atacar. **to set out,** *vt* (state) exponer, manifestar; (embellish) realzar; (display) arreglar, disponer. *vi* ponerse en camino, partir. **to set over,** (rule) tener autoridad sobre, gobernar. **to set to,** (begin to) ponerse a, empezar a; (work) ponerse a trabajar. **set-to,** *n* lucha, *f*; (boxing) asalto, *m*; (quarrel) pelea, riña, *f*. **to set up,** (a monument, etc.) erigir, levantar; (fix) fijar; (apparatus, machinery) montar; (exalt) exaltar; (found) establecer, *Lat. Am. also* instaurar; crear; (propound) exponer; (a howl, etc.) dar; (equip with) proveer de; instalar; (make strong) robustecer; fortificar; (type) componer; (raise) alzar. *vi* establecerse; dárselas de. **He sets himself up as a painter,** Se las da de pintor. **to set** (a person) **up as a model,** poner como modelo (a). **to set up house,** poner casa. **to set up a business,** establecer un comercio. **set-up,** *n* establecimiento, *m*; arreglo, *m*. **to set upon,** atacar
set /sɛt/ *n* (of sun, etc.) puesta, *f*, ocaso, *m*; (of the head, etc.) porte, *m*; (of a garment) corte, *m*; (of the tide, etc.) dirección, *f*; (slant) inclinación, *f*; (*Fig.* drift) tendencia, *f*, movimiento, *m*; (of the teeth of a saw) triscamiento, *m*; (of men, houses, etc.) grupo, *m*; (of tools, golf clubs, china, etc.) juego, *m*; (gang) pandilla, camarilla, *f*; clase, *f*; (*Dance.*) tanda, *f*; (tennis) partido, *f*; *Theat.* decoración, *f*; *Radio.* aparato de radio, *m*, radio, *f*. **coffee set,** juego de café, *m*. **all-mains set,** radio de corriente eléctrica, *f*. **battery set,** radio de batería, *f*. **portable set,** radio portátil, *f*. **the smart set,** el mundo elegante. **to have a shampoo and set,** hacerse lavar y marcar (el pelo). **to make a set,** hacer juego. **to make a dead set at,** hacer un ataque vigoroso (a), atacar resueltamente; procurar insinuarse en el favor de. **set of teeth,** dentadura, *f*
set /sɛt/ *a* fijo; inmóvil; (of a smile) forzado; (of a task) asignado; (of times) señalado, fijo; (prescribed) prescrito, establecido; (firm) firme; (resolved) resuelto; (well-known) consabido; (obstinate) terco, nada adaptable. **well set-up,** apuesto, bien plantado. **He is set on doing it,** Se empeña en hacerlo. **to be dead set against,** estar completamente opuesto a. **set phrase,** frase hecha, *f*. **set-square,** cartabón, *m*
setter /'sɛtər/ *n* (perro) séter, perdiguero, *m*. **s.-on,** instigador (-ra)
setting /'sɛtɪŋ/ *n* (of the sun, etc.) puesta, *f*; (of mortar, etc.) fraguado, *m*; (of a jelly) solidificación, *f*; (of jewels) engaste, *m*, montadura, *f*; (of bones) aliño, *m*; (of teeth of saw) traba, *f*; (of razor) afiladura, *f*; (of a trap) armadura, *f*; (of a machine, etc.) ajuste, *m*; (frame) marco, *m*; *Mus.* arreglo, *m*; *Theat.* decorado, *m*; (emplacement) lecho, *m*. **the s. sun,** el sol poniente. **s. free,** liberación, *f*. **s. off,** partida, salida, *f*. **s. out,** ida, marcha, *f*; principio, *m*; **s.-up,** creación, institución, *f*; establecimiento, *m*; (of a machine) montaje, *m*; *Print.* composición, *f*

settle /'sɛtl/ *vt* colocar; asegurar, afirmar; (a country) colonizar; (live in) establecer (en); (populate) poblar; (in a profession, etc.) dar; (install) instalar; (the imagination, etc.) sosegar, calmar; (resolve) resolver; (arrange) disponer, arreglar; (differences) componer, concertar; (an opponent, etc.) confundir; (a bill) saldar, pagar; (a claim) satisfacer; (clarify) depositar, clarificar; (end) poner fin (a). *vi* establecerse; (of weather) serenarse; (to work, etc.) empezar a, ponerse a; aplicarse a; (decide) decidirse; (alight) posarse; (of foundations, etc.) asentarse; (of a ship) zozobrar; (of sediment) depositarse; (of liquid) clarificarse. **to s. accounts with,** *Fig.* ajustar cuentas con. **to s. down,** establecerse, arraigarse; adaptarse (a); (become calm) sosegarse, calmarse; sentar el juicio; (of foundations) asentarse; (of a ship) zozobrar; (of sediment) depositarse. **to s. in,** *vt* instalar. *vi* instalarse. **to s. on,** (choose) escoger; (decide on) decidirse (a). **to s. a pension on,** señalar pensión (a). **to s. up,** *vt* (one's affairs) poner en orden; (bill) pagar, saldar. *vi* llegar a un acuerdo; pagar cuentas

settled /'sɛtld/ *a* fijo; permanente; invariable; (of countries) colonizado; (of weather) sereno

settlement /'sɛtlmənt/ *n* (of a country) colonización, *f*; (of a dispute) arreglo, ajuste, *m*; (of a question) solución, *f*; decisión, *f*; (of a bill) saldo, pago, *m*, liquidación, *f*; (of an obligation) satisfacción, *f*; (colony) colonia, *f*; (creation) creación, institución, *f*; establecimiento, arraigo, *m*. **deed of s.,** escritura de donación, *f*. **marriage s.,** contrato matrimonial, *m*; **s. out of court,** arreglo pacífico, *m*

settler /'sɛtlər/ *n* colono, *m*; colonizador (-ra)

seven /'sɛvən/ *a* and *n* siete *m*. **It is s. o'clock,** Son las siete. **the s. deadly sins,** los siete pecados capitales

seventeen /'sɛvən'tin/ *a* diecisiete, diez y siete. *n* diecisiete, *m*. **She is just s.,** Acaba de cumplir los diez y siete años

seventeenth /'sɛvən'tinθ/ *a* décimoséptimo; (of monarchs and of the month) diez y siete. *n* décimoséptimo, *m*. **Louis the S.,** Luis diez y siete. **the s. of June,** el diez y siete de junio

seventh /'sɛvənθ/ *a* séptimo; (of the month) siete. *n* séptimo, *m*; séptima parte, *f*; *Mus.* séptima, *f*. **Edward the S.,** Eduardo séptimo. **the s. of August,** el siete de agosto

seventieth /'sɛvəntiiθ/ *a* septuagésimo, setentavo. *n* setentavo, *m*

seventy /'sɛvənti/ *a* and *n* setenta, *m*

sever /'sɛvər/ *vt* separar; romper; dividir

several /'sɛvərəl/ *a* distinto, diferente; respectivo; varios, *m pl*, (*f pl*, varias); algunos, *m pl*, (*f pl*, algunas)

severally /'sɛvərəli/ *adv* separadamente; individualmente; independientemente

severance /'sɛvərəns/ *n* separación, *f*; (of friendship, etc.) ruptura, *f*

severe /sə'vɪər/ *a* severo; riguroso; fuerte; duro; (of style) austero; (of pain) agudo; (of illness) grave

severely /sə'vɪərli/ *adv* severamente; intensamente; gravemente

severity /sə'vɛrɪti/ *n* severidad, *f*; intensidad, *f*; (of weather) inclemencia, *f*; (of illness) gravedad, *f*

sew /sou/ *vt* and *vi* coser, *Lat. Am.* costurar, costurear. **to sew on,** coser

sewage /'suɪdʒ/ *n* aguas residuales, *f pl.* **s. system,** alcantarillado, *m*

sewer /'suər/ *n* alcantarilla, cloaca, *f*, albañal, *m*

sewing /'souɪŋ/ *n* costura, *f.* **s. bag,** costurero, *m.* **s. cotton,** hilo de coser, *m.* **s.-machine,** máquina de coser, *f.* **s. silk,** torzal, *m*

sex /sɛks/ *n* sexo, *m.* **the fair sex,** el bello sexo. **the weaker sex,** el sexo débil. **sex appeal,** atractivo, *m*

sexagenarian /ˌsɛksədʒə'nɛəriən/ *n* sexagenario (-ia)

sexless /'sɛkslɪs/ *a* neutro; frígido

sexologist /sɛk'splədʒɪst/ *n* sexólogo (-ga)

sexology /sɛk'splədʒi/ *n* sexología, *f*

sextant /'sɛkstənt/ *n* sextante, *m*

sexton /'sɛkstən/ *n* sacristán, *m*; sepulturero, *m*; (bell-ringer) campanero, *m*

sexual /'sɛkʃuəl/ *a* sexual

sexuality /ˌsɛkʃu'ælɪti/ *n* sexualidad, *f*

sh! /ʃ/ *interj* ¡Chitón! ¡Chis!

shabbily /'ʃæbəli/ *adv* (of dressing) pobremente; (of treatment) mezquinamente

shabbiness /'ʃæbinɪs/ *n* pobreza, *f*; estado andrajoso, *m*; (of behavior) mezquindad, ruindad, *f*

shabby /'ʃæbi/ *a* (of persons) desharrapado, andrajoso, *Lat. Am.* maltraído; (of garments) raído, roto; (of a neighborhood, etc.) pobre; (mean) ruin, mezquino

shack /ʃæk/ *n* choza, *f*, *Mexico* jacal, *elsewhere in Lat. Am.* bohío, *m*

shackle /'ʃækəl/ *n* traba, *f*; *pl* **shackles,** grillos, *m pl*, esposas, *f pl*; *Fig.* cadenas, *f pl.* *vt* poner esposas (a), encadenar; (a horse) apear; *Fig.* atar; (impede) estorbar

shade /ʃeid/ *n* sombra, *f*; (in a picture) toque de obscuro, *m*; (for the eyes) visera, *f*; (of a lamp) pantalla, *f*; (ghost) espectro, fantasma, *m*; (of color) matiz, *m*; (tinge) dejo, *m.* *vt* sombrear, dar sombra (a); (the face, etc.) proteger, resguardar; (a drawing) esfumar. **in the s.,** a la sombra. **80° in the s.,** ochenta grados a la sombra. **to put** (a person) **in the s.,** eclipsar

shadiness /'ʃeidɪnɪs/ *n* sombra, *f*

shading /'ʃeidɪŋ/ *n* sombra, *f*; *Art.* degradación, *f*

shadow /'ʃædou/ *n* sombra, *f*; obscuridad, *f*; (in a picture) toque de obscuro, *m.* *vt* sombrear; obscurecer; (a person) seguir **to cast a s.,** proyectar una sombra. **to s. forth,** indicar; simbolizar. **s. show,** sombras chinescas, *f pl*

shadowy /'ʃædoui/ *a* umbroso; vago, indistinto, indefinido

shady /'ʃeidi/ *a* sombreado, umbrío; sombrío; (of persons, etc.) sospechoso. **It was s. in the wood,** Hacía sombra en el bosque

shaft /ʃæft/ *n* fuste, *m*; (arrow) flecha, saeta, *f*, dardo, *m*; (of a golf club, etc.) mango, *m*; (of a cart) vara, *f*; *Mech.* árbol, eje, *m*; (of a column and a feather) cañón, *m*; (of light) rayo, *m*; (of a mine) pozo, tiro, *m*; (air-shaft) conducto de aire, ventilador, *m.* **cam-s.,** árbol de levas, *m.* **driving s.,** árbol motor, *m*

shaggy /'ʃægi/ *a* peludo; lanudo

shah /ʃɑ, ʃɔ/ *n* cha, *m*

shake /ʃeik/ *vt* sacudir; agitar; hacer temblar; (weaken) debilitar, hacer flaquear. *vi* estremecerse; temblar; (trill) trinar. **He managed to s. himself free,** Consiguió librarse por una sacudida. **to s. hands,** darse la mano, estrecharse la mano. **to s. one's finger at,** señalar con el dedo (a). **to s. one's fist at,** amenazar con el puño (a). **to s. one's head,** mover la cabeza; negar con la cabeza. **to s. one's sides,** (with laughter) reírse a carcajadas. **to s. with fear,** temblar de miedo. **to s. down,** sacudir, hacer caer. **s.-down,** *n* cama improvisada, *f.* **to s. off,** sacudirse; librarse (de), perder; quitar de encima (a). **to s. out,** (unfurl) desplegar; sacudir. **to s. up,** agitar; sacudir, remover

shake /ʃeik/ *n* sacudida, *f*; (of the head) movimiento (de la cabeza), *m*; (of the hand) apretón (de manos), *m*; temblor, *m*; *Mus.* trino, gorjeo, *m.* **in two shakes,** *Inf.* en un periquete. **to give a person a good s.,** sacudir violentamente (a)

Shakespearean /ʃeik'spɪəriən/ *a* shakespeariano

shakiness /'ʃeikinɪs/ *n* inestabilidad, *f*; poca firmeza, *f*; temblor, *m*; lo dudoso. **the s. of his voice,** su voz trémula

shaking /'ʃeikɪŋ/ *n* sacudimiento, *m*; temblor, *m*; (of windows, etc.) zangoloteo, *m*

shaky /'ʃeiki/ *a* inestable; poco firme; (of hands, etc.) tembloroso; (of the voice) trémulo; (of gait) vacilante; dudoso

shale /ʃeil/ *n* esquisto, *m*

shall /ʃæl/ *unstressed* ʃəl/ *v aux* (expressing simple future) **I s. arrive tomorrow,** Llegaré mañana. **S. we go to the sea next week?** ¿Iremos al mar la semana próxima? (expressing obligation, compulsion) **You s. not go out,** No has de salir, No quiero que salgas. **He s. see her immediately,** Tiene que verla en seguida; (as a polite formula) **S. I go?** ¿Quiere Vd.

que vaya? **S. we buy the soap?** ¿Quiere Vd. que compremos el jabón? ¿Compraremos el jabón?

shallot /'ʃælət, ʃə'lɒt/ *n Bot.* chalote, *m*, ascalonia, *f*

shallow /'ʃælou/ *a* poco profundo; (of a receptacle) llano; (of persons) superficial, frívolo; (of knowledge, etc.) superficial, ligero, somero. *n* bajío, *m*

shallowness /'ʃælounɪs/ *n* poca profundidad, *f*; superficialidad, *f*

sham /ʃæm/ *vt* fingir, simular. *n* farsa, *f*; imitación, *f*; engaño, *m*; (person) farsante, *m. a* fingido; falso; espurio. **to s. illness,** fingirse enfermo. **to s. dead,** hacer la mortecina. **You're just a s.,** Eres un farsante **sham battle** *n Mil.* imulacro de combate, simulacro guerrero, *m*

shamble /'ʃæmbəl/ *vi* andar arrastrándose. *n* andar pesado, *m*; *pl* **shambles,** matadero, *m*; *Fig.* carnicería, *f*

shambling /'ʃæmblɪŋ/ *a* pesado, lento

shame /ʃeim/ *n* vergüenza, *f*; ignominia, *f*; deshonra, *f. vt* avergonzar; deshonrar. **For s.!** ¡Qué vergüenza! **What a s.!** ¡Qué lástima! **to put to s.,** avergonzar

shamefaced /'ʃeim,feist/ *a* (bashful) vergonzoso, tímido; (ashamed) avergonzado

shamefacedly /,ʃeim'feisɪdli/ *adv* vergonzosamente, tímidamente; con vergüenza

shameful /'ʃeimfəl/ *a* vergonzoso, escandaloso; indecente

shamefully /'ʃeimfəli/ *adv* escandalosamente

shameless /'ʃeimlɪs/ *a* desvergonzado; impúdico, indecente

shamelessly /'ʃeimlɪsli/ *adv* desvergonzadamente

shamelessness /'ʃeimlɪsnɪs/ *n* desvergüenza, poca vergüenza, *f*; impudicia, deshonestidad, *f*

shampoo /ʃæm'pu/ *n* champú, *m. vt* dar un champú (a); dar un masaje (a). **dry s.,** champú seco, *m*

shank /ʃæŋk/ *n* zanca, *f*; *Mech.* pierna, *f*; (handle) mango, *m*; (of a button) rabo, *m*, cola, *f.* **go on Shank's mare, ride on Shank's mare,** caminar en coche de San Francisco, ir en boricua de Villadiego

shanty /'ʃænti/ *n* choza, *f*

shanty town *n* barriada (Peru), callampa, población, población, callampa (Chile), *f.* rancho (Venezuela), *m*, villa-miseria (Argentina), *f*

shape /ʃeip/ *n* forma, *f*; bulto, *m*; fantasma, *m*; (of a garment) corte, *m*; (of a person) talle, *m*; *Cul.* molde, *m*; (of a hat) forma, *f. vt* formar; (a garment) cortar; (ideas) dar forma (a); adaptar; (stone, etc.) labrar; (one's life) dominar. *vi* (of events) desarrollarse. **to go out of s.,** perder la forma. **to take s.,** tomar forma. **to s. one's course,** dirigirse (hacia, a); *Naut.* dar el rumbo. **to s. well,** prometer bien

shaped /ʃeipt/ *a* de forma de..., que tiene figura de... **pear-s.,** piriforme

shapeless /'ʃeiplɪs/ *a* informe; disforme, sin forma

shapelessness /'ʃeiplɪsnɪs/ *n* informidad, *f*; deformidad, *f*

shapeliness /'ʃeiplɪnɪs/ *n* belleza de forma, *f*; simetría, *f*

shapely /'ʃeipli/ *a* bien formado; simétrico

share /ʃɛər/ *n* porción, *f*; parte, *f*; cuota, *f*; contribución, *f*; (part ownership) interés, *m*; (in a company) acción, *f. vt* distribuir; compartir; dividir; tomar parte en. *vi* participar (de); tomar parte (en). **to fall to one's s.,** tocar, corresponder. **to go shares with,** dividir con, compartir con. **to take a s. in the conversation,** tomar parte en la conversación. **paid-up s.,** *Com.* acción liberada, *f.* **to s. out,** repartir, distribuir

sharecropper /'ʃɛər,krɒpər/ *Lat. Am.* agregado (-da)

shareholder /'ʃɛər,houldər/ *n* accionista, *mf*

sharer /'ʃɛərər/ *n* partícipe, *mf*

shark /ʃɑrk/ *n Ichth.* tiburón, *m*; *Inf.* caimán, *m*

sharp /ʃɑrp/ *a* (of edges) afilado, cortante, *Lat. Am. also* filoso, filudo; (of points) punzante, puntiagudo; (of features, etc.) anguloso; (of bends, etc.) brusco; (of outlines, etc.) definido, distinto, (of pain, sound) agudo; (marked) marcado; (intense) intenso; (of winds, glance, etc.) penetrante; (of hearing) fino; (of appetite) bueno; (of showers) fuerte; (quick) rápido; (clever, etc.) vivo, listo; perspicaz; (of children) despierto, precoz; (unscrupulous) astuto, sin escrúpulos;

(of criticism, remarks) mordaz; (of rebukes, sentences, etc.) severo; (of winters, etc.) riguroso; (of fighting) encarnizado; (of taste) picante; (sour) ácido; *Mus.* sostenido. *adv* en punto; puntualmente. *n Mus.* sostenido, *m.* **at five o'clock s.,** a las cinco en punto. **Look s.!** ¡Date prisa! **s.-edged,** afilado. **s.-eyed,** con ojos de lince; de mirada penetrante. **s.-featured,** de facciones angulosas. **s.-nosed,** de nariz puntiaguda. **s.-pointed,** puntiagudo. **s. practice,** procedimientos poco honrados, *m pl.* **s.-tongued,** de lengua áspera. **s. turn,** curva brusca, curva cerrada, *f.* **s.-witted,** de inteligencia viva, listo

sharpen /'ʃɑrpən/ *vt* (knives) afilar, amolar; (pencils, etc.) sacar punta (a); (wits, etc.) despabilar; (appetite) abrir. **This walk has sharpened my appetite,** Este paseo me ha abierto el apetito. **to s. one's claws,** afilarse las uñas

sharper /'ʃɑrpər/ *n Inf.* caballero de industria, timador, *m*; (at cards) fullero, *m*

sharply /'ʃɑrpli/ *adv* claramente; bruscamente; severamente; ásperamente

sharpness /'ʃɑrpnɪs/ *n* (of cold, etc.) intensidad, *f*; severidad, *f*; (cleverness) agudeza, perspicacia, *f*; (of a child) precocidad, *f*; (sarcasm, etc.) mordacidad, *f*; aspereza, *f*; brusquedad, *f*

sharpshooter /'ʃɑrp,ʃutər/ *n* franco tirador, *m*

sharpsighted /'ʃɑrp,saitɪd/ *a* de vista penetrante, listo, perspicaz

shatter /'ʃætər/ *vt* romper, quebrantar; hacer añicos; *Fig.* destrozar. **You have shattered my illusions,** Has destrozado todas mis ilusiones

shave /ʃeiv/ *vt* afeitar, rasurar; (wood, etc.) acepillar. *vi* afeitarse; (of razors) afeitar. *n* afeitada, *f.* **to have a s.,** hacerse afeitar. **to have a close s.,** *Inf.* escapar por un pelo

shaving /'ʃeivɪŋ/ *n* afeitada, *f*; (of wood, etc.) viruta, acepilladura, *f.* **s.-bowl,** bacía, *f.* **s.-brush,** brocha de afeitar, *f.* **s.-glass,** espejo de afeitar, *m.* **s.-soap,** jabón de afeitar, *m.* **s.-stick,** barra de jabón de afeitar, *f*

shawl /ʃɔl/ *n* chal, mantón, rebozo, *m*

she /ʃi/ *pers pron* ella; la; (female) hembra, *f*; (translated by fem. ending in the case of animals, etc., e.g. *she bear,* osa, *she cat,* gata). **It is her,** Es ella. **she who is dancing,** la que baila

sheaf /ʃif/ *n* (of corn, etc.) gavilla, garba, *f*; (of arrows) haz, *m*; (of papers, etc.) paquete, atado, *m.* **to bind in sheaves,** agavillar

shear /ʃiər/ *vt* (sheep) esquilar, trasquilar; tonsurar; cortar; (cloth) tundir

shearer /'ʃiərər/ *n* (of sheep) esquilador, *m*

shearing /'ʃiərɪŋ/ *n* (of sheep) esquileo, *m*, tonsura, *f*; (of cloth) tunda, *f.* **s. machine,** esquiladora, *f.* **s. season,** esquileo, *m*

shears /ʃiərz/ *n pl* tijeras grandes, *f pl*, cizalla, *f*

sheath /ʃiθ/ *n* vaina, *f.* **s.-knife,** cuchillo de monte, *m*

sheathe /ʃið/ *vt* envainar; *Naut.* aforrar

shed /ʃɛd/ *vt* derramar; (skin, etc.) mudar; perder; (remove) quitarse, desprenderse de; (get rid of) deshacerse de. *n* cobertizo, sotechado, *m*; cabaña, *f.* **to s. light on,** echar luz sobre, iluminar

sheen /ʃin/ *n* lustre, *m*; brillo, *m*

sheep /ʃip/ *n* oveja, *f*; carnero, *m*; ganado lanar, *m.* **to cast sheep's eyes at,** lanzar miradas de carnero degollado. **s. breeder,** ganadero, *m.* **s.-dip,** desinfectante para ganado, *m.* **s.-dog,** perro de pastor, *m.* **s.-like,** ovejuno, de oveja. **s.-shearing,** esquileo, *m*

sheepfold /'ʃip,fould/ *n* aprisco, redil, *m*

sheepish /'ʃipɪʃ/ *a* tímido, vergonzoso; estúpido

sheepishly /'ʃipɪʃli/ *adv* tímidamente

sheepishness /'ʃipɪʃnɪs/ *n* timidez, cortedad, *f*; estupidez, *f*

sheepskin /'ʃip,skɪn/ *n* piel de carnero, *f.* **s. jacket,** zamarra, *f*

sheer /ʃiər/ *a* puro; completo, absoluto; (steep) escarpado, acantilado; a pico; (of fabrics) transparente; ligero, fino. *adv* completamente; de un golpe; (perpendicularly) a pico. **to s. off,** desviarse; largarse, marcharse

sheet /ʃit/ *n* (bed) sábana, *f*; (shroud) mortaja, *f*; (of paper) hoja, *f*; cuartilla, *f*; (pamphlet) folleto, *m*; (news) periódico, *m*, hoja, *f*; (of metal, etc.) lámina, plancha, f; (of water, etc.) extensión, f; *Naut.* escota, f. *vt* poner sábanas en; envolver en sábanas; (a corpse) amortajar. **to be as white as a s.,** estar pálido como un muerto. **s. bend,** (knot) nudo de tejedor, m. **s. glass,** vidrio en lámina, m. **s. iron,** hierro en planchas, m

sheik /ʃīk/ n jeque, m

shekel /ˈʃekəl/ n (coin) siclo, m; pl **shekels,** dinero, m

shelf /ʃelf/ n estante, anaquel, m; (reef) banco de arena, bajío, m; (of rock) escalón, m. **to be on the s.,** *Inf.* quedarse para tía, quedarse para vestir imágenes

shell /ʃel/ n (of small shellfish) concha, f; (of tortoise) coraza, f; (of insects, lobsters, etc.) caparazón, m; (of a nut) cáscara, f; (of an egg) cascarón, m; (of peas, beans) vaina, f; (*Com.* and *Mus.*) concha, f; (of a building) casco, m; (outside) exterior, m; (empty form) apariencia, f; *Mil.* granada, f. *vt* pelar; (nuts) descascarar; (beans, etc.) desvainar; *Mil.* bombardear. **to be under s.-fire,** sufrir un bombardeo. **s. shock,** neurosis de guerra, f

shellfish /ˈʃel.fɪʃ/ n crustáceo, m; (as food) marisco, m

shelling /ˈʃelɪŋ/ n *Mil.* bombardeo, m

shelter /ˈʃeltər/ n abrigo, amparo, m; refugio, m; asilo, m. *vt* dar asilo (a); abrigar; (defend) amparar, proteger; (hide) esconder. *vi* refugiarse; resguardarse; esconderse

sheltered /ˈʃeltərd/ a abrigado

sheltering /ˈʃeltərɪŋ/ a protector

shelve /ʃelv/ *vt* (books) poner en un estante; (persons) destituir; (questions, etc.) aplazar, arrinconar; proveer de estantes, *vi* (slope) inclinarse, formar declive; (of sea bed) formar escalones

shelving /ˈʃelvɪŋ/ a inclinado; (of ocean bed) acantilado

shepherd /ˈʃepərd/ n pastor, m. *vt* guardar; guiar, conducir. **s. boy,** zagal, m. **shepherd's pouch,** zurrón, m

shepherdess /ˈʃepərdɪs/ n pastora, f

sherbet /ˈʃɑrbɪt/ n sorbete, m

sheriff /ˈʃerɪf/ n (in U.K.) sheriff, m; (U.S.A.) jefe de la policía, m

sherry /ˈʃeri/ n (vino de) jerez, m. **dry s.,** jerez seco, m

shield /ʃild/ n escudo, m; (round) rodela, f; *Herald.* escudo de armas, m; *Fig.* defensa, f, amparo, m. *vt* proteger, amparar. **to s. a person,** proteger a una persona. **to s. one's eyes from the sun,** proteger los ojos del sol. **s.-bearer,** escudero, m

shift /ʃɪft/ *vt* mover; trasladar; quitar, librarse de; cambiar. *vi* moverse; (of the wind) girar; cambiar. n cambio, m; (expedient) recurso, expediente, m; (dodge) artificio, m, trampa, f; (of workers) tanda, f, turno, m. **to make s.,** arreglárselas (para hacer algo); procurar (hacer algo); (manage) ir tirando. **to s. for oneself,** componérselas, arreglárselas. **to s. the scenes,** *Theat.* cambiar de decoración. **to s. the helm,** *Naut.* cambiar el timón. **to work in shifts,** trabajar por turnos

shiftiness /ˈʃɪftɪnɪs/ n falta de honradez, informalidad, f; astucia, f

shifting /ˈʃɪftɪŋ/ a (of light, etc.) cambiante; (of sand, etc.) movedizo; (of wind) mudable; (of moods) voluble. **s. sand,** arena movediza, f

shiftless /ˈʃɪftlɪs/ a perezoso; sin energía, ineficaz

shiftlessness /ˈʃɪftlɪsnɪs/ n pereza, f; falta de energía, f

shifty /ˈʃɪfti/ a (tricky) tramposo, astuto; (dishonest) informal, falso; (of gaze) furtivo. **s.-eyed,** a de mirada furtiva

Shiite /ˈʃiaɪt/ a and n chiita

shilling /ˈʃɪlɪŋ/ n chelín, m. **nine shillings in the £,** nueve chelines por libra. **to cut off with a s.,** desheredar

shilly shally /ˈʃɪli ˌʃæli/ n irresolución, vacilación, f, *vi* estar irresoluto, titubear, no saber qué hacer

shimmer /ˈʃɪmər/ *vi* rielar; relucir. n luz trémula, f, resplandor, m; viso, m

shin /ʃɪn/ n espinilla, f; (of beef) corvejón, m. **to s. up,** trepar

shine /ʃaɪn/ *vi* brillar; resplandecer, relucir, relumbrar. *vt* (shoes) dar lustre (a). n brillo, f; lustre, m; (shoeshine) *Mexico* bola, f. **in rain or s.,** en buen o

mal tiempo. **to s. with happiness,** radiar felicidad. **to take the s. out of,** eclipsar

shingle /ˈʃɪŋɡəl/ n (pebbles) guijarros, m pl; cascajo, m; barda, f; (hair) pelo a la garçonne, m; pl **shingles,** *Med.* zona, f, herpe zóster, m. *vt* (the hair) cortar a la garçonne

shining /ˈʃaɪnɪŋ/ a resplandeciente, brillante, reluciente; radiante. **s. with happiness,** radiante de felicidad. **s. example,** ejemplo notable, m

Shintoism /ˈʃɪntouˌɪzəm/ n sintoísmo, m

shiny /ˈʃaɪni/ a brillante; lustroso, terso; (of trousers, etc.) reluciente; (of paper) glaseado

ship /ʃɪp/ n buque, barco, m; (sailing) velero, m. *vt* embarcar; (oars) armar. *vi* embarcar; (as a member of crew) embarcarse. **on board s.,** a bordo. **to s. a sea,** embarcar agua. **to take s.,** embarcar. **to s. off,** mandar. **ship's boat,** lancha, f. **ship's boy,** grumete, m. **ship's carpenter,** carpintero de ribera, m. **ship's company,** tripulación, f. **s.-breaker,** desguazador, m. **s.-canal,** canal de navegación, m. **s.-load,** cargamento, m

shipbuilder /ˈʃɪpˌbɪldər/ n constructor de buques, arquitecto naval, m

shipbuilding /ˈʃɪpˌbɪldɪŋ/ n construcción naval, f

shipment /ˈʃɪpmənt/ n embarque, m; despacho por mar, m; (consignment) remesa, f

shipowner /ˈʃɪpˌounər/ n naviero, m

shipper /ˈʃɪpər/ n naviero, m; importador, m; exportador, m

shipping /ˈʃɪpɪŋ/ n embarque, m; buques, barcos, m pl; (of a country) marina, f. **s. agent,** consignatario de buques, m. **s. company,** compañía de navegación, f. **s. offices,** oficinas de una compañía de navegación, f pl

shipshape /ˈʃɪpˌʃeip/ a en buen orden; bien arreglado

shipwreck /ˈʃɪpˌrek/ n naufragio, m, *vt* hacer naufragar, echar a pique

shipwrecked person /ˈʃɪpˌrekt/ n náufrago (-ga). **to be shipwrecked,** naufragar

shipyard /ˈʃɪpˌyɑrd/ n astillero, varadero, m

shire /ʃaɪr/ n condado, m

shirk /ʃɑrk/ *vt* eludir, esquivar; desentenderse de. *vi* faltar al deber

shirker /ˈʃɑrkər/ n gandul (-la); persona que no cumple con su deber, f

shirt /ʃɑrt/ n camisa, f. **dress s.,** camisa de pechera dura, f. **hair-s.,** cilicio, m. **in one's s.-sleeves,** en mangas de camisa. **s.-blouse,** blusa sencilla, f. **s.-collar,** cuello de camisa, m. **s. factory** or **shop,** camisería, f. **shirt-front,** pechera, f. **s.-maker,** camisero (-ra)

shirting /ˈʃɑrtɪŋ/ n tela para camisas, f

shiver /ˈʃɪvər/ *vi* temblar, tiritar; dar diente con diente; (of a boat) zozobrar. *vt* (break) hacer añicos, romper; (sails) sacudir. n temblor, estremecimiento, m; escalofrío, m; (of glass, etc.) fragmento, m, astilla, f. **You give me the shivers,** Me das escalofríos

shivery /ˈʃɪvəri/ a tembloroso; friolero. **I feel s.,** Tengo escalofríos

shoal /ʃoul/ n (of fish) banco, m; gran cantidad, f; (of people) multitud, muchedumbre, f; (water) bajo fondo, m; (sand-bank) banco, bajío, m, a poco profundo

shock /ʃɒk/ n choque, m; *Elec.* conmoción, f; *Med.* shock, m; (*Med.* stroke) conmoción cerebral, f; (fright) sobresalto, susto, m. *vt* sacudir, dar una sacudida (a); chocar; escandalizar, horrorizar. *vi* chocar. **electric s.,** conmoción eléctrica, f. **She is easily shocked,** Ella se escandaliza fácilmente. **s. of hair,** mata de pelo, f. **s. absorber,** *Mech.* amortiguador, m; *Auto.* amortiguador (de las muelles), m. **s. troops,** tropas de asalto, f pl, elementos de choque, m pl

shocking /ˈʃɒkɪŋ/ a escandaloso; repugnante, horrible; espantoso. **How s.!** ¡Qué horror! **s. bad,** malísimo

shockingly /ˈʃɒkɪŋli/ adv horriblemente

shod /ʃɒd/ a calzado; (of horses) herrado

shoddy /ˈʃɒdi/ n pacotilla, f. a de pacotilla; espurio, falso

shoe /ʃu/ n zapato, m; (horse) herradura, f; (*Naut. Mech.*) zapata, f. *vt* (horses) herrar. **I should not like**

to be in his shoes, No me gustaría estar en su pellejo. **That is quite another pair of shoes,** Eso es harina de otro costal. **to cast a s.,** (of horses) desherrarse, perder una herradura. **to put on one's shoes,** ponerse los zapatos, calzarse. **to remove one's shoes,** quitarse los zapatos, descalzarse. **wooden shoes,** zuecos, *m pl.* **s.-buckle,** hebilla de zapato, *f.* **s.-lace,** cordón de zapato, *m.* **s.-leather,** cuero para zapatos, *m*; calzado, *m.* **s.-scraper,** limpiabarros, *m*, estregadera, *f.* **s.-shop,** zapatería, *f*

shoeblack /'ʃu,blæk/ *n* betún, *m*; (person) limpiabotas, *m*

shoehorn /'ʃu,hɔrn/ *n* calzador, *m*

shoemaker /'ʃu,meikər/ *n* zapatero (-ra)

shoemaking /'ʃu,meikɪŋ/ *n* fabricación de calzado, zapatería, *f*

shoeshine /'ʃu,ʃain/ *n Mexico* bola, *f*

shoo! /ʃu/ *interj* ¡fuera!; ¡zape! *vt* ahuyentar

shoot /ʃut/ *vt* (throw) lanzar; precipitar; (empty) vaciar; (a rapid) salvar; (rays, etc.) echar; (an arrow, a gun, etc.) disparar; (a person, etc.) pegar un tiro (a); *Sports.* tirar; *Mil.* fusilar, pasar por las armas, *Lat. Am.* afusilar; (a film) hacer, impresionar. *vi* lanzarse, precipitarse; (of pain) latir; (sprout) brotar; disparar; tirar; (at football) tirar a gol, chutar. **s.-out,** tiroteo, *m.* **to s. a glance at,** lanzar una mirada (a). **I was shot in the foot,** Una bala me hirió en el pie. **to s. the sun,** *Naut.* tomar el sol. **to s. ahead,** tomar la delantera. **to s. at,** tirar a, *Lat. Am.* abalear. **to s. at** *Central America, Mexico* balacear. **to s. by,** pasar como una bala. **to s. down,** *Aer.* derribar; matar de un tiro. **to s. up,** (of children) espigarse; (of prices) subir mucho; (of cliffs, etc.) elevarse

shoot /ʃut/ *n* partida de caza, *f*; tiro, *m*; *Bot.* renuevo, retoño, *m*

shooting /'ʃutɪŋ/ *n* tiro, *m*; caza con escopeta, *f*; (of guns) tiroteo, *m*; (of an arrow) disparo, *m*; (of a film) rodaje, *m.* **to go s.,** ir a cazar con escopeta. **s.-box,** pabellón de caza, *m.* **s. butts,** tiradero, *m.* **s. dog,** perro de caza, *m.* **s.-gallery,** tiro al blanco, *m.* **s. match,** concurso de tiro, *m.* **s. pain,** punzada de dolor, *f.* **s. party,** partida de caza, *f.* **s. practice,** ejercicios de tiro, *m pl.* **s.-range,** campo de tiro, *m.* **s. star,** estrella fugaz, *f*

shop /ʃɒp/ *n* tienda, *f*; (workshop) taller, *m. vi* ir de compras, ir de tiendas; comprar. **to talk s.,** hablar de negocios. **s.-assistant,** dependiente (-ta). **s.-soiled,** deslucido. **s.-steward,** representante de los obreros de una fábrica o taller, *m.* **s. window,** escaparate, *Mexico* aparador, *m*

shopkeeper /'ʃɒp,kipər/ *n* tendero (-ra), *Chile* despachero (-ra)

shoplifter /'ʃɒp,lɪftər/ *n* ladrón (-ona) de tiendas, ratero (-ra) de las tiendas

shoplifting /'ʃɒp,lɪftɪŋ/ *n* ratería en las tiendas, *f*

shopper /'ʃɒpər/ *n* comprador (-ra)

shopping /'ʃɒpɪŋ/ *n* compra, *f*; compras, *f pl.* **to go s.,** ir de compras. **s. basket,** cesta para compras, *f.* **s. center,** centro comercial, *m*

shopwalker /'ʃɒp,wɔkər/ *n* jefe de recepción, *m*

shore /ʃɔr/ *n* orilla, ribera, *f*; costa, *f*; (sands) playa, *f.* **off s.,** en alta mar. **on s.,** en tierra. **to come on s.,** desembarcar. **to s. up,** apuntalar, acodalar; *Fig.* apoyar

short /ʃɔrt/ *a* corto; (of persons) bajo; breve; (of temper) vivo; insuficiente; distante (de); (brusque) seco; (of money) alcanzado. *adv* súbitamente; brevemente. *n* (vowel) vocal breve, *m*; *pl* **shorts,** calzones cortos, *m pl.* **for s.,** para mayor brevedad. **for a s. time,** por poco tiempo. **in a s. time,** dentro de poco. **in s.,** en breve, en resumen, en pocas palabras. **on s. notice,** con poco tiempo de aviso. **to s. of,** con la excepción de, menos. **to be s.,** faltar, ser escaso. **to be s. with someone,** tratar con sequedad (a). **to fall s. of expectations,** no cumplir las esperanzas. **to go s. of,** pasarse sin. **to grow s.,** escasear. **s.-circuit,** corto circuito, *m.* **s. cut,** atajo, *Lat. Am.* desecho, *m.* **s.-haired,** pelicorto. **s.-handed,** falto de mano de obra. **s.-lived,** de vida corta; efímero, fugaz. **to be shortlived,** tener vida corta. **s.-sighted,** corto de vista. **s. sightedness,** miopía, cortedad de vista, *f.* **s. story,** cuento, *m.* **s.-tempered,** irascible, irritable, de genio

vivo. **s.-waisted,** corto de talle. **s.-winded,** corto de resuello; asmático

shortage /'ʃɔrtɪdʒ/ *n* falta, escasez, *f*; carestía, *f.* **water s.,** carestía de agua, *f*

shortcoming /'ʃɔrt,kʌmɪŋ/ *n* defecto, *m*; imperfección, *f*

shorten /'ʃɔrtṇ/ *vt* acortar; reducir, disminuir; abreviar. *vi* acortarse

shorthand /'ʃɔrt,hænd/ *n* taquigrafía, estenografía, *f. a* taquigráfico, estenográfico

shortly /'ʃɔrtli/ *adv* dentro de poco, pronto; brevemente, en resumen, en pocas palabras; (curtly) bruscamente, secamente

shortness /'ʃɔrtnɪs/ *n* cortedad, *f*; brevedad, *f*; (of a person) pequeñez, *f*; (lack) falta, *f*; (of memory, sight) cortedad, *f*; (brusqueness) sequedad, brusquedad, *f.* **s. of breath,** falta de aliento, respiración difícil, *f*

shot /ʃɒt/ *n* perdigón, *m*; *Inf.* perdigones, *m pl*; bala, *f*; (firing) tiro, *m*; (person) tirador (-ra); (stroke, etc.) golpe, *m*, tirada, *f*; (cinema) fotograma, *m. a* (of silk) tornasolado. **at one s.,** de un tiro. **like a s.,** *Fig.* como una bala. **to exchange shots,** tirotearse. **to fire a s.,** disparar un tiro. **to have a s. at,** probar suerte. **s.-gun,** escopeta, *f.* **s. silk,** seda tornasolada, *f*

should /ʃʊd/ *v aux* (expressing future) **I s. like to go to the sea,** Me gustaría ir al mar; (expressing conditional) **I s. like to see them if I could,** Me gustaría verlos si pudiera; (expressing obligation) **You s. go at once,** Debes ir en seguida; (expressing probability) **They s. arrive tomorrow,** Seguramente llegarán mañana; (expressing doubt) **If the moment s. be opportune,** Si el momento fuera oportuno. **I s. just think so!** ¡Ya lo creo! ¡No lo dudo!

shoulder /'ʃoʊldər/ *n* hombro, *m*; (of mutton) espalda, *f*; (of a hill) falda, *f. vt* echar al hombro, echar sobre sí; (a responsibility) cargar con, hacerse responsable para; (jostle) dar codazos (a). **s. to s.,** hombro a hombro. **S. arms!** ¡Armas al hombro! **s.-blade,** omoplato, *m.* **s.-knot,** charretera, *f.* **s.-pad,** hombrera, *f.* **s.-strap,** *Mil.* dragona, *f*; (of a dress, etc.) tirante, *m*; (of a naval carrier, etc.) correón, *m*

shouldered /'ʃoʊldərd/ *a* de hombros..., de espaldas... **round-s.,** cargado de espaldas

shout /ʃaʊt/ *vi* gritar, hablar a gritos. *vt* gritar. *n* grito, *m.* **shouts of applause,** aclamaciones, *f pl*, aplausos, *m pl.* **to s. from the housetops,** pregonar a los cuatro vientos. **to s. with laughter,** reírse a carcajadas. **to s. down,** silbar. **to s. out,** gritar

shouting /'ʃaʊtɪŋ/ *n* gritos, *m pl*, vocerío, clamor, *m*; (applause) aclamaciones, *f pl*

shove /ʃʌv/ *vt* empujar; poner. *n* empujón, *m.* **to s. along,** empujar. **to s. aside,** empujar a un lado; apartar a codazos. **to s. away,** rechazar. **to s. back,** hacer retroceder. **to s. forward,** hacer avanzar, empujar hacia adelante. **to s. off,** (a boat) echar afuera. **to s. out,** empujar hacia fuera

shovel /'ʃʌvəl/ *n* pala, *f. vt* traspalar. **s. hat,** sombrero de teja, *m*

show /ʃoʊ/ *vt* mostrar; hacer ver; (disclose) descubrir; revelar; (exhibit) exhibir; (indicate) indicar; (prove) demostrar, probar; (conduct) conducir, llevar, guiar; (explain) explicar; (oneself) presentarse. *vi* mostrarse; verse; parecer. **to s. cause,** mostrar causa. **to s. fight,** ofrecer resistencia. **s. signs of,** dar señales de. **to s. itself,** declararse, asomarse, surgir. **to s. the door,** acompañar a la puerta. **to s. in,** (a person) hacer entrar, introducir (en). **to s. off,** *vt* exhibir; realzar; (new clothes, etc.) lucir. *vi* darse importancia; pavonearse. **to s. out,** (a person) acompañar a la puerta; (in anger) poner de patitas en la calle. **to s. through,** *vi* transparentarse. *vt* conducir por. **to s. up,** *vt* invitar a subir; (a fraud, etc.) descubrir; (a swindler) desenmascarar; (defects) revelar. *vi* (stand out) destacarse; (be present) asomarse, asistir

show /ʃoʊ/ *n* (exhibition) exposición, *f*; espectáculo, *m*; (sign) indicio, *m*, señal, *f*; (ostentation) pompa, *f*, aparato, *m*, ostentación, *f*; (appearance) apariencia, *f*; (affair) negocio, *m.* **to give the s. away,** echar los títeres a rodar. **to make a s. of,** hacer gala de. **s.-case,** escaparate, *m*, vitrina, *f.* **s. of hands,** votación por manos levantadas, *f.* **s.-room,** salón de muestras, *m*

showdown /'ʃou‚daun/ n cartas boca arriba, m

shower /'ʃauər/ n chaparrón, chubasco, m; (of spray, etc.) chorro, m; (of stones, arrows, etc.) lluvia, f; (of honors) cosecha, f, (bridal) despedida de soltera, despedida de soltería, f. vt derramar; rociar; mojar; llover. vi chaparrear, llover. **shower (bath)** ducha, f, Argentina baño de China, f

shower cap n gorro de ducha, m

showery /'ʃauəri/ a lluvioso

showily /'ʃouəli/ adv aparatosamente, con ostentación

showiness /'ʃouinis/ n ostentación, f; esplendor, m, magnificencia, f

showman /'ʃoumən/ n director de un espectáculo de feria, m; titiritero, m; pregonero, m

showy /'ʃoui/ a vistoso; ostentoso, Lat. Am. also figuroso

shrapnel /'ʃræpnl/ n granada, m, granada de metralla, f

shred /ʃred/ n fragmento, m; (of cloth) jirón, m; brizna, f; Fig. pizca, f. vt desmenuzar. **to tear in shreds,** hacer pedazos

shrew /ʃru/ n Zool. musaraña, f; (woman) fiera, f

shrewd /ʃrud/ a sagaz, perspicaz; prudente; (of the wind) penetrante; (pain) punzante. **to have a s. idea of,** tener una buena idea de. **as. diplomat,** un fino diplomático

shrewdly /'ʃrudli/ adv sagazmente, con perspicacia; prudentemente

shrewdness /'ʃrudnis/ n sagacidad, perspicacia, f; prudencia, f

shrewish /'ʃruiʃ/ a regañón

shrewishness /'ʃruiʃnis/ n mal genio, m

shriek /ʃrik/ vi chillar, gritar. vt decir a voces, gritar. n chillido, m; grito agudo, m. **shrieks of laughter,** carcajadas, f pl

shrieking /'ʃrikɪŋ/ n gritos, chillidos, m pl

shrift /ʃrɪft/ **to give short,** enviar normala (a), enviar a paseo (a)

shrill /ʃrɪl/ a estridente, agudo

shrillness /'ʃrɪlnis/ n estridencia, f

shrimp /ʃrɪmp/ n camarón, m, gamba, f; (small person) Inf. renacuajo. vi pescar camarones

shrine /ʃrain/ n relicario, m; sepulcro de santo, m; templete, m, capilla, f; santuario, m

shrink /ʃrɪŋk/ vi encogerse; contraerse; disminuir, reducirse. vt encoger; reducir, disminuir; desaparecer; disiparse. **I shrank from doing it,** Me repugnaba hacerlo. **to s. away from,** retroceder ante; recular ante; huir de. **to s. back,** recular (ante)

shrinkage /'ʃrɪŋkɪdʒ/ n encogimiento, m; contracción, f; reducción, disminución, f

shrinking /'ʃrɪŋkɪŋ/ a tímido

shrive /ʃraiv/ vt confesar

shrivel /'ʃrɪvəl/ vi avellanarse; (of persons, through old age) acartonarse, apergaminarse; (wither) marchitarse; arrugarse. vt arrugar; secar, marchitar

shroud /ʃraud/ n sudario, m, mortaja, m; Naut. obenque, m. **to wrap in a s.,** amortajar

Shrove Tuesday /'ʃrouv/ n martes de carnaval, m

shrub /ʃrʌb/ n arbusto, m; matajo, m

shrubbery /'ʃrʌbəri/ n arbustos, m pl, maleza, f; bosquecillo, m

shrug /ʃrʌg/ vi encogerse de hombros. n encogimiento de hombros, m

shrunken /'ʃrʌŋkən/ a contraído; acartonado, apergaminado; seco, marchito. **shrunken head,** cabeza reducida, f

shudder /'ʃʌdər/ vi estremecerse; vibrar. n estremecimiento, m; escalofrío, m; (of an engine, etc.) vibración, f

shuffle /'ʃʌfəl/ vt (the feet) arrastrar; (scrape) restregar; (cards) barajar; (papers) mezclar. vi arrastrar los pies, arrastrarse; (cards) barajar; Fig. tergiversar. n (of the cards) barajadura, f; Fig. evasiva, f; embuste, m. **to s. along,** andar arrastrando los pies

shuffling /'ʃʌflɪŋ/ n el arrastrar, m, (e.g. the shuffling of chairs, el arrastrar de sillas)

shun /ʃʌn/ vt evitar, rehuir, esquivar

shunt /ʃʌnt/ vt Rail. apartar; Elec. shuntar. vi Rail. hacer maniobras

shunting /'ʃʌntɪŋ/ n (of trains) maniobras, f pl

shut /ʃʌt/ vt and vi cerrar. **to s. again,** volver a cerrar. **to s. down,** vt cerrar; (a machine) parar. vi (of factories, etc.) cerrar. **to s. in,** encerrar; (surround) cercar, rodear. **to s. off,** (water, etc.) cortar; (isolate) aislar (de). **to s. out,** excluir; obstruir, impedir; negar la entrada (a). **to s. up,** vt cerrar; encerrar; Inf. hacer callar (a); vi Inf. callarse, cerrar la boca. **to s. oneself up,** encerrarse

shutter /'ʃʌtər/ n (window) contraventana, f, postigo, m; (of a camera) obturador, m; (of a fireplace) campana (de hogar), f. vt poner contraventanas (a); cerrar los postigos de

shuttle /'ʃʌtl/ n (weaver's, and sewing-machine) lanzadera, f, (airplane service) puente aéreo, m. **s.-cock,** volante, gallito, m

shy /ʃai/ a (of animals) tímido, salvaje; (of persons) huraño, tímido; vergonzoso. vi (of a horse) respingar; (of persons) asustarse (de). vt (a ball, etc.) lanzar. n (of a horse) respingo, m; (of a ball) lanzamiento, m; (try) prueba, tentativa, f. **to fight shy of,** procurar evitar. **to have a shy at,** probar

shyly /'ʃaili/ adv tímidamente; con vergüenza, vergonzosamente

shyness /'ʃainis/ n timidez, f; huraña, f; vergüenza, f

Siamese /‚saiə'miz/ a siamés. n siamés (-esa); (language) siamés, m. **S. cat,** gato siamés, m

sic /sɪk/ vt atacar; abijar, azuzar (a dog); adv así (in academic prose)

Sicilian /sɪ'sɪlyən/ a and n siciliano (-na)

Sicily /'sɪsəli/ Sicilia, f

sick /sɪk/ a enfermo; mareado. **the s.,** los enfermos. **to be s.,** vomitar; estar enfermo. **to be s. of,** estar harto de. **to feel s.,** sentirse mareado. **to be on the s.-list,** estar enfermo. **s.-bed,** lecho de dolor, m. **s.-headache,** jaqueca, con náuseas, f. **s.-leave,** Mil. permiso por enfermedad, m. **s.-nurse,** enfermera, f

sicken /'sɪkən/ vi caer enfermo, enfermar; (feel sick) marearse; (recoil from) repugnar; (weary of) cansarse (de), aburrirse (de). vt marear; dar asco (a), repugnar; cansar, aburrir. **It sickens me,** Me da asco. **He is sickening for measles,** Muestra síntomas de sarampión

sickening /'sɪkənɪŋ/ a nauseabundo; repugnante; (tedious) fastidioso

sickle /'sɪkəl/ n hoz, segadera, f

sickliness /'sɪklɪnis/ n falta de salud, f; náusea, f; (paleness) palidez, f

sickly /'sɪkli/ a enfermizo, achacoso, malucho, Lat. Am. farruto, Central America, Mexico fifiriche; (of places, etc.) malsano; (pale) pálido; débil; (of a smell) nauseabundo; (mawkish) empalagoso

sickness /'sɪknis/ n enfermedad, f; mal, m; náusea, f, mareo, m

side /said/ n lado, m; (hand) mano, f; (of a river, etc.) orilla, f, margen, m; (of a person) costado, m; (of an animal) ijada, f; (of a hill) falda, pendiente, ladera, f; (of a ship) banda, f, costado, m; (aspect) aspecto, m; punto de vista, m; (party) partido, grupo, m; (team) equipo, m; (of descent) lado, m. a lateral, de lado; oblicuo. **on all sides,** por todas partes. **on both sides,** por ambos lados. **s. by s.,** lado a lado. **the other s. of the picture,** el revés de la medalla. **to change sides,** cambiar de partido. **to pick sides,** escoger el equipo. **to put on s.,** darse tono, alzar el gallo. **to split one's sides,** desternillarse de risa, reírse a carcajadas. **to s. with,** declararse por, ponerse al lado de. **to turn el partido de. wrong s. out,** al revés. **s.-car,** sidecar, asiento lateral, m. **s.-chain,** Chem. cadena lateral, f. **s.-dish,** entremés, m. **s. door,** puerta lateral, f. **s.-face,** a de perfil. m. perfil, m. **s.-glance,** mirada de soslayo, f. **s.-issue,** cuestión secundaria, f. **s.-line,** negocio accesorio, m; ocupación secundaria, f; Rail. vía secundaria, f. **s.-saddle,** silla de señora, silla de montar de lado, f. **s.-show,** (at a fair) barraca, f, puesto de feria, m; exhibición secundaria, f; función secundaria, f. **s.-track,** n Rail. apartadero, m. vt desviar (de), apartar (de). **s.-view,** perfil, m. **s.-walk,** acera, f, Mexico banqueta, f, elsewhere in Lat. Am. andén, m, vereda f. **s.-whiskers,** patillas, f pl

sidelight /'said,lait/ *n* luz lateral, *f*; (on a ship) ojo de buey, *m*; *Fig.* información incidental, *f*

sidelong /'said,lɔŋ/ *adv* de lado, lateralmente; (of glances) de soslayo. *a* oblicuo

side road *n* camino lateral, *m*

sideways /'said,weiz/ *adv* oblicuamente, de lado; (edgewise) de soslayo. *a* de soslayo

siding /'saidiŋ/ *n* *Rail.* apartadero, *m*

sidle /'saidl/ *vi* andar (or ir) de lado. **to s. up to,** acercarse servilmente a; arrimarse (a)

siege /sidʒ/ *n* asedio, sitio, cerco, *m*. **to lay s. to,** poner cerco (a), sitiar, asediar cercar. **to raise a s.,** levantar un sitio

sienna /si'enə/ *n* tierra de siena natural, *f*. **burnt s.,** tierra de siena tostada, *f*

sieve /siv/ *n* cedazo, tamiz, *m*, criba, *f*, *Lat. Am.* arnero, *m*, *vt* tamizar, cerner, cribar

sift /sift/ *vt* (sieve) cerner, cribar; (sugar, etc.) salpicar (con); (a question) escudriñar, examinar minuciosamente

sifting /ʃiftiŋ/ *n* cribado, *m*; (of a question) investigación minuciosa, *f*; *pl* **siftings,** cerniduras, *f pl*

sigh /sai/ *vi* suspirar; (of the wind) susurrar. *n* suspiro, *m*; (of the wind) susurro, *m*. **to s. for,** suspirar por; lamentar

sighing /'saiiŋ/ *n* suspiros, *m pl*; (of the wind) susurro, *m*

sight /sait/ *n* vista, *f*; visión, *f*; espectáculo, *m*; (fright) estantigua, *f*. *vt* ver, divisar; (aim) apuntar. **front s.,** (of guns) alza, *f*. **short s.,** (of eyes) vista corta, *f*. **at first s.,** a primera vista. **in s.,** a la vista. **in s. of,** a vista de. **out of s.,** que no está a la vista; perdido de vista. **Out of s., out of mind,** Ojos que no ven, corazón que no siente. **to be lost to s.,** perderse de vista. **to lose s. of,** perder de vista (a). **to catch a s. of,** vislumbrar. **to come in s.,** aparecer, asomarse. **to know by s.,** conocer de vista (a). **s.-reading,** lectura a primera vista, *f*

sightly /'saitli/ *a* hermoso; deleitable

sightseeing /'sait,siiŋ/ *n* turismo, *m*. **to go s.,** visitar los monumentos, ver los puntos de interés

sightseer /'sait,siər/ *n* curioso (-sa); turista, *mf*

sign /sain/ *n* señal, *f*; seña, *f*; indicio, *m*; (of the zodiac and *Mus.*) signo, *m*; marca, *f*; *Eccl.* símbolo, *m*; (of a shop, etc.) muestra, *f*, rótulo, *m*; (symptom) síntoma, *m*. *vt* firmar; indicar; *Eccl.* persignar. **as a s. of,** en señal de. **to converse by signs,** hablar por señas. **to make the s. of the cross over,** santiguar. **to show signs (of),** dar señas (de); indicar. **s.-painter,** pintor de muestras, *m*

signal /'signl/ *n* señal, *f*. *vt* señalar; hacer señas (a). *vi* hacer señales. *a* insigne, notable. **fog-s.,** señal de niebla, *f*. **landing s.,** *Aer.* señal de aterrizaje, *f*. **to give the s. for,** dar la señal para. **s.-box,** garita de señales, *f*. **s. code,** *Naut.* código de señales, *m*

signaler /'signlər/ *n* señalador, *m*

signalize /'signl,aiz/ *vt* señalar, distinguir

signalman /'signlmən/ *n* *Rail.* guardavía, *m*

signatory /'signə,tɔri/ *a* and *n* signatario (-ia)

signature /'signətʃər/ *n* firma, *f*; (*Mus.* and *Print.*) signatura, *f*

signboard /'sain,bɔrd/ *n* letrero, *m*, muestra, *f*

signet /'signit/ *n* sello, *m*. **s.-ring,** anillo de sello, *m*

significance /sig'nifikəns/ *n* significación, *f*, significado, *m*; importancia, *f*

significant /sig'nifikənt/ *a* significativo, significante; expresivo; importante

significantly /sig'nifikəntli/ *adv* significativamente; expresivamente

signify /'signə,fai/ *vt* significar; querer decir; importar. *vi* significar, tener importancia; importar

signpost /'sain,poust/ *n* indicador de dirección, *m*

silage /'sailidʒ/ *n* forraje conservado en silo, *m*

silence /'sailəns/ *n* silencio, *m*, *interj* ¡silencio! *vt* hacer callar, imponer silencio (a); silenciar. **to keep s.,** guardar silencio, callarse. **to pass over in s.,** pasar en silencio (por), pasar por alto de. **S. gives consent,** Quien calla otorga

silencer /'sailənsər/ *n* (of fire-arms) silencioso, *m*; *Auto.* silenciador, silencioso, *m*

silent /'sailənt/ *a* silencioso. **to become s.,** enmu-

decer; callar. **to remain s.,** callarse, guardar silencio; permanecer silencioso. **s. partner,** *n* socio (-ia) comanditario (-ia)

silent film, silent movie *n* película muda, *f*

silently /'sailəntli/ *adv* silenciosamente, en silencio

silhouette /,silu'et/ *n* silueta, *f*. *vt* representar en silueta; destacar. **in s.,** en silueta. **to be silhouetted against the sky,** destacarse contra el sielo

silica /'silikə/ *n* sílice, *f*

silk /silk/ *n* seda, *f*, *a* de seda. **artificial s.,** seda artificial, *f*. **floss s.,** seda ocal, *f*. **sewing s.,** seda de coser, *f*. **twist s.,** seda cordelada, *f*. **as smooth as s.,** como una seda. **s. growing,** sericultura, *f*. **s. hat,** sombrero de copa, *m*. **s. merchandise,** sedería, *f*. **s. stocking,** media de seda, *f*

silken /'silkən/ *a* de seda; sedoso

silkiness /'silkinis/ *n* carácter sedoso, *m*; suavidad, *f*

silk-screen process /'silk,skrin/ *n* imprenta por tamiz, imprenta serigráfica, imprenta tamigráfica, impresión con estarcido de seda, *f*, proceso tamigráfico, *m*, serigrafía, tamigrafía, *f*

silkworm /'silk,wɜrm/ *n* gusano de seda, *m*

silky /'silki/ *a* sedoso; (of wine) suave

sill /sil/ *n* (of a window) alféizar, antepecho, *m*; (of a door) umbral, *m*

silliness /'silinis/ *n* tontería, estupidez, *f*

silly /'sili/ *a* tonto, estúpido; imbécil, *Central America also* azurumbado. *n* tonto (-ta)

silo /'sailou/ *n* silo, *m*

silt /silt/ *n* aluvión, *m*, sedimentación, *f*. **to s. up,** *vt* cegar (or obstruir) con aluvión. *vi* cegarse con aluvión

silver /'silvər/ *n* plata, *f*. *a* de plata; argénteo; (of the voice, etc.) argentino. *vt* platear; (mirrors) azogar; (hair) blanquear. **s. birch,** abedul, *m*. **s. fox,** zorro plateado, *m*. **s.-gray,** gris perla, *m*. **s.-haired,** de pelo entrecano. **s.-paper,** papel de estaño, *m*. **s.-plate,** *n* vajilla de plata, *f*. *vt* platear. **s.-tongued,** de pico de oro; de voz argentina. **s. wedding,** bodas de plata, *f pl*

silversmith /'silvər,smiθ/ *n* platero, *m*. **silversmith's shop,** platería, *f*

silvery /'silvəri/ *a* plateado, argentado; (of sounds) argentino

simian /'simiən/ *a* símico

similar /'simələr/ *a* parecido (a), semejante (a); similar; *Geom.* semejante. **to be s. to,** asemejarse (a), parecerse (a)

similarity /,simə'læriti/ *n* parecido, *m*, semejanza, similitud, *f*

similarly /'simələrli/ *adv* de un modo parecido, asimismo

simile /'siməli/ *n* símil, *m*

simmer /'simər/ *vi* hervir a fuego lento; *Fig.* estar a punto de estallar. **to s. down,** *Fig.* moderarse poco a poco. **to s. over,** *Fig.* estallar

simper /'simpər/ *vi* sonreírse bobamente

simpering /'simpəriŋ/ *n* sonrisilla tonta, *f*

simperingly /'simpəriŋli/ *adv* con sonrisa necia

simple /'simpəl/ *a* sencillo; simple; ingenuo, inocente; crédulo; (humble) humilde; (mere) mero. **s.-hearted,** inocente, cándido, sin malicia. **s.-minded,** ingenuo; crédulo. **s.-mindedness,** ingenuidad, *f*; credulidad, *f*

simpleton /'simpəltən/ *n* primo (-ma); papanatas, *m*, tonto (-ta)

simplicity /sim'plisiti/ *n* sencillez, *f*; simplicidad, candidez, *f*

simplifiable /,simplə'faiəbəl/ *a* simplificable

simplification /,simpləfi'keiʃən/ *n* simplificación, *f*

simplify /'simplə,fai/ *vt* simplificar

simply /'simpli/ *adv* sencillamente; simplemente, meramente; absolutamente

simulacrum /,simyə'leikrəm/ *n* simulacro, *m*

simulate /'simyə,leit/ *vt* fingir, aparentar, simular

simulation /,simyə'leiʃən/ *n* simulación, *f*, fingimiento, *m*

simultaneous /,saiməl'teiniəs/ *a* simultáneo

simultaneously /,saiməl'teiniəsli/ *adv* simultáneamente; al mismo tiempo (que)

simultaneousness /ˌsaiməl'teiniəsnɪs/ n simultaneidad, f

sin /sɪn/ n pecado, m, vi pecar; faltar (a)

since /sɪns/ adv desde entonces, desde (que). prep desde. conjunc desde que; ya que, puesto que. **a long time s.,** hace mucho. **not long s.,** hace poco. **How long is it s....?** ¿Cuánto tiempo hace que...? **s. then,** desde entonces

sincere /sɪn'sɪər/ a sincero

sincerely /sɪn'sɪərli/ adv sinceramente. **Yours s.,** Su afectísimo...

sincerity /sɪn'sɛrɪti/ n sinceridad, f

sine /sain/ n Math. seno, m

sinecure /'sainɪˌkyʊr/ n canonjía, sinecura, f, empleo de aviador (Mexican slang), m

sinew /'sɪnyu/ n tendón, m; pl **sinews,** nervio, m, fuerza, f

sinewy /'sɪnyui/ a (stringy) fibroso; musculoso, nervudo

sinful /'sɪnfəl/ a (of persons) pecador; (of thoughts, acts) pecaminoso

sinfulness /'sɪnfəlnɪs/ n pecado, m; culpabilidad, perversidad, maldad, f

sing /sɪŋ/ vi cantar; (of the ears) zumbar; (of wind, water) murmurar, susurrar; (of a cat) ronronear. vt cantar. **to s. a child to sleep,** dormir a un niño cantando. **to s. another song,** Inf. bajar el tono. **to s. small,** hacerse el chiquito. **to s. the praises of,** hacer las alabanzas de. **to s. out,** vocear, gritar. **s.-song,** n canturía, f; concierto improvisado, m. a monótono

Singapore /'sɪŋgəˌpɔr/ Singapur, m

singe /sɪndʒ/ vt chamuscar; (a fowl) aperdigar; (hair) quemar las puntas de los cabellos

singer /'sɪŋər/ n cantor (-ra); (professional) cantante, mf; (bird) ave cantora, f

singing /'sɪŋɪŋ/ n canto, m; (of the ears) zumbido, m. a cantante. **s.-bird,** ave cantora, f. **s.-master,** maestro de cantar, m

single /'sɪŋgəl/ a único; sencillo; solo; simple; (individual) particular; individual; (unmarried) soltero. n (tennis) juego sencillo, individual, m. **in s. file,** de reata. **to s. out,** escoger; singularizar. **s. bed,** cama de monja, f. **s. bedroom,** habitación individual, habitación con una sola cama, f. **s.-breasted,** (of coats) recto. **s. combat,** combate singular, m. **s. entry,** Com. partida simple, f. **s.-handed,** de una mano; para una sola persona; sin ayuda, solo, en solitario. **s.-minded,** sin doblez, sincero de una sola idea. **s. ticket,** billete sencillo, m

singleness /'sɪŋgəlnɪs/ n celibato, m, soltería, f. **with s. of purpose,** con un solo objeto

single room n Mexico cuarto sencillo, m

singlet /'sɪŋglɪt/ n camiseta, f

singly /'sɪŋgli/ adv separadamente, uno a uno; a solas, solo; sin ayuda

singular /'sɪŋgyələr/ a and n singular, m

singularity /ˌsɪŋgyə'lærɪti/ n singularidad, f

singularly /'sɪŋgyələrli/ adv singularmente

sinister /'sɪnəstər/ a siniestro

sink /sɪŋk/ vi ir al fondo; bajar; hundirse; (of ships) irse a pique, naufragar; sumergirse; disminuir; caer (en); penetrar; (of persons, fires) morir; (of the sun, etc.) ponerse. vt (a ship) echar a pique; sumergir; hundir; dejar caer; bajar; (wells) cavar; reducir, disminuir; (invest) invertir; (one's identity, etc.) tener secreto; (differences) olvidar; (engrave) grabar. **My heart sank,** Se me cayeron las alas del corazón. **He sank to his knees,** Cayó de rodillas. **He is sinking fast,** Está en las últimas. **Their words began to s. in,** Sus palabras empezaban a tener efecto (or hacer mella). **I found her sunk in thought,** La encontré ensimismada. **to s. one's voice,** bajar la voz. **to s. down on a chair,** dejarse caer en una silla. **to s. into misery,** caer en la miseria. **to s. under,** (a responsibility, etc.) estar agobiado bajo

sink /sɪŋk/ n (kitchen) fregadero, Chile, Mexico also lavaplatos, m; sumidero, m, sentina, f. **s. of iniquity,** sentina, f

sinker /'sɪŋkər/ n (engraver) grabador (-ra); (of a fishing line) plomada, f

sinking /'sɪŋkɪŋ/ n hundimiento, m; (of the sun)

puesta, f; (of wells) cavadura, f; sumergimiento, m. **the s. of a boat,** el hundimiento de un buque. **with s. heart,** con la muerte en el alma. **s. fund,** fondo de amortización, m

sinless /'sɪnlɪs/ a sin pecado, inocente, puro

sinner /'sɪnər/ n pecador (-ra)

sinuous /'sɪnyuəs/ a sinuoso, tortuoso; flexible, ágil

sinus /'sainəs/ n (Anat. etc.) seno, m

sip /sɪp/ vt sorber; (wine) saborear, paladear. n sorbo, m

siphon /'saifən/ n sifón, m, vt sacar con sifón

sir /sɜr/ n señor, m; (British title) sir. **Dear s.,** Muy Señor mío

sire /saiər/ n (to a monarch) Señor, m; (father) padre, m; (stallion) semental, m. vt procrear, engendrar

siren /'sairən/ n sirena, f. **s. suit,** mono, m

sirloin /'sɜrlɔin/ n solomillo, Mexico diezmillo, m

sirocco /sə'rɒkou/ n siroco, m

sister /'sɪstər/ n hermana, f; (before nun's christian name) Sor; (hospital) hermana del hospital, f; enfermera, f. **s. language,** lengua hermana, f. **s. ship,** buque gemelo, m. **s.-in-law,** cuñada, hermana política, f. **S. of Mercy,** Hermana de la Caridad, f

sisterhood /'sɪstərˌhʊd/ n hermandad, f; comunidad de monjas, f

sisterly /'sɪstərli/ a de hermana

sit /sɪt/ vi sentarse; estar sentado; (of birds) posarse; (of hens) empollar; (in Parliament, etc.) ser diputado; (of a committee, etc.) celebrar sesión; (on a committee, etc.) formar parte de; (function) funcionar; (of garments, food, and Fig.) sentar. **to sit a horse,** mantenerse a caballo; montar a caballo. **to sit oneself,** sentarse, tomar asiento. **to sit by,** (or estar sentado) al lado de. **to sit for** (a portrait) servir de modelo para; hacerse retratar. **to sit tight,** no moverse. **to sit down,** sentarse; (besiege) sitiar. **to sit on,** sentarse (on or sobre); (eggs) empollar; (a committee, etc.) formar parte de; (investigate) investigar; (snub) dejar aplastado (a). **to sit out,** quedarse hasta el fin (de). **to sit out a dance,** conversar un baile. **to sit up,** incorporarse en la cama; tenerse derecho; (at night) velar; (of dogs, etc.) pedir. **to sit up and take notice,** abrir los ojos. **to sit up in bed,** incorporarse en la cama. **to sit up late,** estar de pie hasta muy tarde

sit-down strike /'sɪtˌdaun/ n huelga de brazos caídos, huelga de sentados, f

site /sait/ n sitio, local, m; (for building) solar, m

sitting /'sɪtɪŋ/ n asentada, f; (of Parliament, etc.) sesión, f; (for a portrait) estadía, f; (of eggs) nidada, f. **at a s.,** de una asentada. **s.-room,** sala de estar, f

situated /'sɪtʃuˌeitid/ a situado. **How is he s.?** ¿Cómo está situado? ¿Cuál es su situación?

situation /ˌsɪtʃu'eifən/ n situación, f; (job) empleo, m

six /sɪks/ a and n seis, m. **It is six o'clock,** Son las seis. **Everything is at sixes and sevens,** Todo está en desorden. **six-foot,** de seis pies. **six hundred,** seiscientos (-as)

sixfold /'sɪksˌfould/ a séxtuplo

sixteen /'sɪks'tin/ a and n diez y seis, dieciséis, m. **John is s.,** Juan tiene dieciséis años

sixteenth /'sɪks'tinθ/ a décimosexto, m; (of the month) (el) diez y seis; (of monarch) diez y seis. n dieciseisavo, m

sixth /sɪksθ/ a sexto, m; (of the month) (el) seis; (of monarchs) sexto. n seisavo, m; sexta parte, f; Mus. sexta, f. **Henry the S.,** Enrique sexto. **May the s.,** el seis de mayo

sixtieth /'sɪkstiiθ/ a sexagésimo. n sesentavo, m; sexagésima parte, f

sixty /'sɪksti/ a and n sesenta m. **John has turned s.,** Juan ha pasado los sesenta

sizable /'saizəbəl/ a bastante grande

size /saiz/ n tamaño, m; dimensión, f; (height) altura, f; (measurement) medida, f; talle, m; (in gloves, etc.) número, m; (glue) cola, f. vt clasificar por tamaños; (glaze, etc.) encolar. **to s. up,** tomar las medidas (a)

sizzle /'sɪzəl/ vi chisporrotear, chirriar. n chisporroteo, chirrido, m

skate /skeit/ n patín, m; Ichth. raya, f, vi patinar

skateboard /'skeitˌbɔrd/ n patín, m

skater /'skeitər/ n patinador (-ra)

skating /'skeitɪŋ/ n patinaje, m. **s. rink,** sala de patinar, f; pista de hielo, pista de patinar, f, patinadero, m

skein /skein/ n madeja, f

skeleton /'skɛlɪtn/ n esqueleto, m; (of a building) armadura, f; (of a literary work) esquema, m. **s. key,** ganzúa, f

sketch /skɛtʃ/ n croquis, apunte, m; (for a literary work) esbozo, esquema, m; (article) cuadro, artículo, m; descripción, f; Theat. entremés, sainete, m. vt dibujar; esbozar, bosquejar; trazar; describir. **s.-book,** álbum de croquis, m

sketchily /'skɛtʃəli/ adv incompletamente

sketching /'skɛtʃɪŋ/ n arte de dibujar, mf. **He likes s.,** Le gusta dibujar

sketchy /'skɛtʃi/ a bosquejado; incompleto; escaso

skewer /'skyuər/ n broqueta, f, vt espetar

ski /ski/ n esquí, m, vi esquiar

skid /skɪd/ n (of a vehicle) patinazo, m, vi patinar

skidding /'skɪdɪŋ/ n patinaje, m

skier /'skiər/ n esquiador (-ra), mf

skiff /skɪf/ n esquife, m

skiing /'skiɪŋ/ n patinaje sobre la nieve, m, el esquiar. **to go s.,** ir a esquiar

skill /skɪl/ n habilidad, f

skilled /skɪld/ a hábil; experto

skilled worker n obrero calificado, m

skillful /'skɪlfəl/ a hábil

skim /skɪm/ vt espumar; (milk) desnatar, Lat. Am. descremar; (touch lightly) deslizarse sobre, rozar; (a book) hojear

skimp /skɪmp/ vt escatimar; escasear; (work) frangollar. vi ser parsimonioso

skimpy /'skɪmpi/ a escaso

skin /skɪn/ n tez, f, cutis, m; piel, f; (of fruit) pellejo, m, piel, f; (for wine) odre, pellejo, m; (on milk) espuma, f. vt despellejar; pelar, mondar; (graze) hacerse daño (a); Inf. desollar. **next to one's s.,** sobre la piel. **to s. over,** cicatrizarse. **to have a thin s.,** Fig. ser muy susceptible. **to save one's s.,** salvar el pellejo. **s.-deep,** superficial. **s.-tight,** escurrido, muy ajustado

skinflint /'skɪn,flɪnt/ n avaro (-ra)

skinny /'skɪni/ a flaco, descarnado, magro

skip /skɪp/ vi retozar, brincar, saltar; saltar a la comba; (bolt) largarse, escaparse. vt saltar; (a book) hojear; (omit) omitir; pasar por alto de. n brinco, pequeño salto, m

skipper /'skɪpər/ n Naut. patrón, m; (Inf. and Sports.) capitán, m

skirmish /'skɜrmɪʃ/ vi escaramuzar. n escaramuza, f

skirt /skɜrt/ n falda, f; (edge) margen, borde, m, orilla, f; (of a jacket, etc.) faldón, m. vt ladear; (hug) rodear, ceñir

skit /skɪt/ n sátira, f; parodia, f

skittish /'skɪtɪʃ/ a (of a horse) retozón; (of persons) frívolo; caprichoso

skittle /'skɪtl/ n bolo, m; pl **skittles,** juego de bolos, m. **s. alley,** pista de bolos, bolera, f

skulk /skʌlk/ vi estar en acecho; esconderse; rondar

skull /skʌl/ n cráneo, m; calavera, f. **s.-cap,** gorro, casquete, m; (for ecclesiastics) solideo, m

skunk /skʌŋk/ n Zool. mofeta, f, chingue, mapurite, yaguré, zorrillo, zorrino, zorro hediondo, m

sky /skai/ n cielo, m. **to praise the skies,** poner en los cuernos de la luna. **s.-blue,** n azul celeste, m. a de color azul celeste, cerúleo. **s.-high,** hasta las nubes, hasta el cielo. **s.-line,** horizonte, m. **s.-scraper,** rascacielos, m. **s.-sign,** anuncio luminoso, m

skylight /'skai,lait/ n claraboya, f, tragaluz, m

slab /slæb/ n bloque, m; losa, f, Lat. Am. also laja; plancha, f

slack /slæk/ a lento; flojo; (lazy) perezoso; negligente, descuidado; Com. encalmado; débil. vi ser perezoso. **the s. season,** la estación muerta. **to be s. in one's work,** ser negligente en el trabajo. **to s. off,** disminuir sus esfuerzos; dejar de trabajar

slacken /'slækən/ vt and vi aflojar; disminuir, reducir. **The wind slackened,** El viento amainaba, El viento

aflojaba. **to s. one's efforts,** disminuir sus esfuerzos. **to s. speed,** disminuir la velocidad

slackening /'slækənɪŋ/ n aflojamiento, m; disminución, f

slacker /'slækər/ n gandul (-la)

slackness /'slæknɪs/ n flojedad, f; pereza, falta de energía, f; negligencia, f; Com. desanimación, f

slacks /slæks/ n pl pantalones, m pl

slake /sleik/ vt (one's thirst and lime) apagar; satisfacer

slam /slæm/ vt cerrar de golpe; golpear. n (of a door) portazo, m; golpe, m; (cards) capote, m. **He went out and slammed the door,** Salió dando un portazo

slander /'slændər/ n calumnia, f, vt calumniar

slanderer /'slændərər/ n calumniador (-ra)

slanderous /'slændərəs/ a calumnioso

slang /slæŋ/ n argot, m, jerga, f, vt poner como un trapo (a), llenar de insultos

slant /slænt/ vi estar al sesgo; inclinarse; ser oblicuo. vt inclinar. n inclinación, f; oblicuidad, f. **on the s.,** inclinado; oblicuo

slanting /'slæntɪŋ/ a al sesgo, inclinado; oblicuo

slap /slæp/ vt pegar con la mano. n bofetada, f; palmada, Lat. Am. cachetada, f. **to s. on the back,** golpear en la espalda. **s.-dash,** (of persons) irresponsable, descuidado; (of work) chapucero, sin cuidado

slash /slæʃ/ vt (gash, also sleeves, etc.) acuchillar; cortar; (with a whip) dar latigazos (a). n cuchillada, f; corte, m; latigazo, m

slashing /'slæʃɪŋ/ a mordaz, severo

slat /slæt/ n tablilla, f, vi (of sails) dar zapatazos, zapatear

slate /sleit/ n pizarra, f, esquisto, m; (for roofs and for writing) pizarra, f, vt (a roof) empizarrar; (censure) criticar severamente, censurar. **s.-colored,** apizarrado. **s. pencil,** pizarrín, m. **s. quarry,** pizarrería, f, pizarral, m

slater /'sleitər/ n pizarrero, m

slating /'sleitɪŋ/ n empizarrado, m; (criticism) crítica severa, censura, f; (scolding) peluca, f

slattern /'slætərn/ n pazpuerca, f

slatternly /'slætərnli/ a desgarbado, desaliñado

slaughter /'slɔtər/ n matanza, f; carnicería, f. vt (animals) sacrificar, matar; matar, hacer una carnicería de. **s.-house,** matadero, m

slaughterer /'slɔtərər/ n jifero, carnicero, m

Slav /slav, slæv/ a and n eslavo (-va)

slave /sleiv/ n esclavo (-va). vi trabajar mucho. **white s. traffic,** trata de blancas, f. **s.-bangle,** esclava, f. **s.-driver,** capataz de esclavos, m; sayón de esclavos, m. **s.-trade,** trata de esclavos, f

slaver /'sleivər/ n negrero, m

slaver /'slævər/ vi babear. n baba, f

slavering /'slævərɪŋ/ a baboso

slavery /'sleivəri/ n esclavitud, f; trabajo muy arduo, m

slavish /'sleivɪʃ/ a de esclavo; servil

slavishly /'sleivɪʃli/ adv como esclava; servilmente

Slavonic /slə'vɒnɪk/ a eslavo. n (language) eslavo, m, lengua eslava, f

slay /slei/ vt matar; asesinar

slayer /'sleiər/ n matador (-ra); asesino, m

slaying /'sleiɪŋ/ n matanza, f; asesinato, m

sled /slɛd/ n trineo m, rastra, f

sledge /slɛdʒ/ n trineo, m. vi ir en trineo. vt transportar por trineo. **s.-hammer,** acotillo, m

sleek /slik/ a liso, lustroso; (of general appearance) pulcro, bien aseado, elegante; (of manner) obsequioso

sleekness /'sliknɪs/ n lustre, m, lisura, f; (of an animal) gordura, f; elegancia, f

sleep /slip/ n sueño, m. vi dormir; reposar, descansar. vt dormir. **s. a deep s.,** un sueño pesado. **He walks in his s.,** Es un sonámbulo. **to court s.,** conciliar el sueño. **to go to s.,** dormirse; entumecerse. **My foot has gone to s.,** Se me ha dormido (or Se me ha entumecido) el pie. **to send a person to s.,** adormecer. **to s. like a top,** dormir como un lirón. **to s. oneself sober,** dormir la mona. **to s. in,** dormir tarde; dormir en casa. **to s. off,** (a cold, etc.) curarse... durmiendo; (drunkenness) dormirla. **to s. on,** *vt* (consider) dormir sobre, consultar con la almohada. *vi* seguir durmiendo. **to s. out,** dormir fuera de casa; dormir al aire libre

sleeper /'slipər/ *n* durmiente, *mf*; *Rail.* traviesa, *f*; (on a train) coche cama, *m*. **to be a bad s.,** dormir mal. **to be a good s.,** dormir bien.

sleepily /'slipəli/ *adv* soñolientamente

sleepiness /'slipınıs/ *n* somnolencia, *f*; letargo, *m*

sleeping /'slipıŋ/ *a* durmiente. *n* el dormir. **between s. and waking,** entre duerme y vela. **s.-bag,** saco-cama, *m*. **s.-car,** coche camas, *m*. **s.-draft,** narcótico, *m*. **s. partner,** *n* socio (-ia) comanditario (-ia). **s. sickness,** enfermedad del sueño, *f*

sleepless /'sliplıs/ *a* (of persons) insomne, desvelado; (unremitting) incansable; (of the sea, etc.) en perpetuo movimiento. **to spend a s. night,** pasar una noche en vela, pasar una noche toledana, pasar una noche sin dormir

sleeplessness /'sliplısnıs/ *n* insomnio, *m*

sleepwalker /'slip‚wɔkər/ *n* sonámbulo (-la)

sleepwalking /'slip‚wɔkıŋ/ *n* sonambulismo, *m*

sleepy /'slipi/ *a* soñoliento; letárgico. **to be s.,** tener sueño. **s.-head,** lirón, *m*, marmota, *f*

sleet /slit/ *n* aguanieve, cellisca, nevisca, *f*, *vi* caer aguanieve, cellisquear, neviscar

sleeve /sliv/ *n* manga, *f*; (of a hose pipe, etc.) manguera, *f*; *Mech.* manguito, *m*. **to have something up one's s.,** traer algo en la manga

sleeved /slivd/ *a* con mangas...; de... manga(s)

sleeveless /'slivlıs/ *a* sin manga. **s. shirt** *Lat. Am.* cusma, *f*

sleigh /slei/ *n* trineo, *m*, *vi* ir en trineo

sleight of hand /sleit/ *n* prestidigitación, *f*; juego de manos, *m*

slender /'slɛndər/ *a* delgado; esbelto; tenue; escaso; pequeño; ligero. **Their means are very s.,** Sus recursos son muy escasos. **It is a very s. hope,** Es una esperanza muy remota

slenderness /'slɛndərnıs/ *n* delgadez, *f*; esbeltez, *f*; tenuidad, *f*; escasez, *f*

sleuth /sluθ/ *n* (dog) sabueso, *m*; *Inf.* detective, *m*

slice /slais/ *n* lonja, tajada, *f*; (of fruit) raja, *f*; (of bread, etc.) rebanada, *f*; (share) parte, porción, *f*; (for fish, etc.) pala, *f*. *vt* cortar en tajadas, etc.; rajar; cortar

slick /slık/ *a* hábil, diestro

slide /slaid/ *vi* deslizarse, resbalar; (over a question) pasar por alto de; (into a habit, etc.) caer (en). *n* resbalón, *m*; pista de hielo, *f*; (chute) tobogán, *m*; (of a microscope) portaobjetos, *m*; (lantern) diapositiva, *f*; (for the hair) pasador, *m*; (of rock, etc.) desprendimiento, *m*; *Mech.* guía, *f*. **to let things s.,** dejar rodar la bola. **s.-rule,** regla de cálculo, *f*

sliding /'slaidıŋ/ *a* resbaladizo, corredizo; movible. **s.-door,** puerta corrediza, puerta de corradera, *f*. **s.-roof,** techo corredizo, *m*. **s.-scale,** escala graduada, *f*. **s.-seat,** asiento movible, *m*; (in a rowing-boat) bancada corrediza, *f*

slight /slait/ *a* delgado; débil, frágil; ligero; (small) pequeño; escaso; (trivial) insignificante, poco importante. *vt* desairar, despreciar, *Mexico* descolar. *n* desaire, desprecio, *m*; falta de respeto, *f*

slighting /'slaitıŋ/ *a* despreciativo, de desprecio

slightingly /'slaitıŋli/ *adv* con desprecio

slightly /'slaitli/ *adv* ligeramente; poco. **I only know her s.,** La conozco muy poco. **s. built,** de talle delgado

slightness /'slaitnıs/ *n* (slimness) delgadez, *f*; ligereza, *f*; (triviality) poca importancia, insignificancia, *f*

slim /slım/ *a* delgado; escaso. *vi* adelgazarse. **He has very s. chances of success,** Tiene muy pocas posibilidades de conseguir el éxito

slime /slaim/ *n* légamo, limo, lodo, cieno, *m*; (of a snail) limazo, *m*; *Fig.* cieno, *m*

sliminess /'slaiminıs/ *n* limosidad, *f*; viscosidad, *f*

slimness /'slımnıs/ *n* delgadez, *f*; escasez, *f*

slimy /'slaimi/ *a* limoso, legamoso; pecinoso, viscoso; (of persons) rastrero, servil

sling /slıŋ/ *vt* arrojar, lanzar; tirar con honda; (a

---

sword, etc.) suspender; (lift) embragar; (a limb) poner en cabestrillo. *n* (for missiles) honda, *f*; *Naut.* balso, *m*; (for a limb) cabestrillo, *m*, charpa, *f*

slink /slıŋk/ *vi* (away, off) escurrirse, escabullirse

slip /slıp/ *vi* resbalar, deslizar; (stumble) resbalar, tropezar; (fall) caer; (out of place) salirse; (become untied) desatarse; (steal away) escabullirse; (glide) deslizarse; (of years) correr, pasar; (skid) patinar. *vt* deslizar; (garments, shoes) ponerse; (dogs, cables) soltar; (an arm around, etc.) pasar; *Rail.* desacoplar; (escape) escaparse de; (free oneself of) librarse de. *n* resbalón, *m*; (skid) patinazo, *m*; (stumble) tropezón, traspié, *m*; (oversight) inadvertencia, *f*; (mistake) falta, equivocación, *f*; (moral lapse) desliz, *m*; (petticoat) combinación, *f*; (cover) funda, *f*; *Bot.* vástago, *m*; *Print.* galerada, *f*; (of paper) papeleta, *f*; *pl* **slips,** *Naut.* anguilas, *f pl.* **It slipped my memory,** Se me fue de la memoria. **There's many a s. 'twixt the cup and the lip,** Del dicho al hecho hay muy gran trecho, De la mano a la boca desaparece la sopa. **to give (someone) the slip,** escaparse de. **You ought not to let the opportunity s.,** No debes perder la oportunidad. **to let s. a secret,** revelar un secreto. **to let s. an exclamation,** soltar (dar) una exclamación. **to s. into,** colarse en, deslizarse en. **to s. into,** colarse en, deslizarse en. **to s. into one's clothes,** vestirse rápidamente. **to s. on,** (a garment) ponerse. **to s. out,** salir a hurtadillas; escaparse; (of information) divulgarse. **s. of a boy,** mozalbete, joven imberbe, *m*. **s. of the tongue,** error de lengua, *m*. **s.-knot,** nudo corredizo, *m*

slipcover /'slıp‚kʌvər/ *n* cubierta, cubierta para muebles, funda para muebles, *f*

slipper /'slıpər/ *n* babucha, chinela, *f*, pantuflo, *m*; (heelless) chancleta, *f*; (dancing) zapatilla de baile, *m*. **s.-shaped,** achinelado

slippered /'slıpərd/ *a* en zapatillas

slippery /'slıpəri/ *a* resbaladizo; poco firme, inestable; (of persons) informal, sin escrúpulos

slipshod /'slıp‚ʃod/ *a* descuidado, negligente; poco correcto

slit /slıt/ *vt* cortar; hender, rajar; (the throat) degollar. *n* cortadura, *f*; resquicio, *m*. **to s. open,** abrir de un tajo

slither /'slıðər/ *vi* resbalar; deslizarse

sliver /'slıvər/ *n* raja, *f*; (of wood) astilla, *f*; (of cloth) tira, *f*

slobber /'slobər/ *vi* babear; (blubber) gimotear, *n* baba, *f*

sloe /slou/ *n* (fruit) endrina, *f*; (tree) endrino, *m*. **s.-colored,** endrina, *f*. **s.-eyed,** con ojos de mora

slog /slog/ *vt* golpear duramente. **to s. away,** batirse el cobre, trabajar como un negro

slogan /'slougan/ *n* grito de batalla, *m*; reclamo, *m*; frase hecha, *f*; mote, *m*

slop /slop/ *n* charco, *m*; *pl* **slops,** agua sucia, *f*; alimentos líquidos, *m pl.* *vi* derramarse, verterse. *vt* verter, derramar

slope /sloup/ *n* inclinación, *f*; pendiente, *f*; (of a mountain, etc.) falda, ladera, cuesta, *f*; vertiente, *mf*. *vi* inclinarse; estar en declive; bajar (hacia). **to s. down,** declinar

sloping /'sloupıŋ/ *a* inclinado; en declive; (of shoulders) caídos, *m pl*

sloppy /'slopi/ *a* casi líquido; (muddy) lodoso, lleno de barro; (of work) chapucero; (of persons) baboso, sobón. **s. sentiment,** sensiblería, *f*

slot /slot/ *n* ranura, muesca, *f*. **s.-machine,** máquina expendedora, *f*, expendedor, *m*; (in amusement arcades, etc.) tragaperras, *m*

sloth /sloθ *or, esp. for 2,* slouθ/ *n* pereza, indolencia, *f*; *Zool.* perezoso, *m*

slothful /'sloθfəl, 'slouθ-/ *a* perezoso, indolente

slouch /slautʃ/ *n* inclinación del cuerpo, *f*. *vi* andar cabizbajo, andar arrastrando los pies. **to s. about,** vagar, golfear. **s.-hat,** sombrero gacho, *m*

slough /slʌf/ *n* (bog) cenagal, pantano, *m*, marisma, *f*; (of a snake) camisa, *f*. *vt* (a skin) mudar; (prejudices, etc.) desechar

Slovak /'slouvak/ *n* eslovaco (-ca)

Slovakian /slou'vakiən/ *a* eslovaco

sloven /'slʌvən/ n puerco, m; (at work) chapucero, m
Slovene /slou'vin/ a and n esloveno (-na)
slovenliness /'slʌvənlinıs/ n desaseo, desaliño, m; (carelessness) descuido, m, negligencia, f; (of work) chapucería, f
slovenly /'slʌvənli/ a desgarbado, desaseado, Central America descacharrado, Lat. Am. distraído; (careless) descuidado, negligente; (of work) chapucero
slow /slou/ a despacio; lento, Lat. Am. demorón; (stupid) torpe; tardo; (of clocks) atrasado; (boring) aburrido; (inactive) flojo. adv despacio, lentamente. **I was not s. to...,** No tardé en..., Lat. Am. No dilaté en... **The clock is ten minutes s.,** El reloj lleva diez minutos de atraso. **to s. down,** aflojar el paso; ir más despacio. **s.-motion,** velocidad reducida, f. **s. train,** tren ómnibus, m. **s.-witted,** lerdo tardo
"Slow Down" «Moderar Su Velocidad»
slow learner n alumno de lento aprendizaje, m
slowly /'slouli/ adv despacio, lentamente; poco a poco
slowness /'slounıs/ n lentitud, f; (delay) tardanza, f; (stupidity) torpeza, estupidez, f
slug /slʌg/ n babosa, f
sluggard /'slʌgərd/ n gandul (-la), perezoso (-a)
sluggish /'slʌgıʃ/ a perezoso; (of the market) flojo; (of temperament, etc.) calmoso, flemático; (slow) lento
sluggishness /'slʌgıʃnıs/ n pereza, f; (of the market) flojedad, f; (slowness) lentitud, f
sluice /slus/ n esclusa, f; canal, m, acequia, f. **to s. down,** lavar; echar agua sobre; (a person) dar una ducha (a), dar un baño (a). **s.-gate,** compuerta de esclusa, f; tajaderas, f pl, tablacho, m
slum /slʌm/ nsg (inner-city slum) barrio bajo (understood everywhere), arrabales mpl (Argentina, Uruguay), banda de miseria fsg (Argentina), barracas fpl (Mexico), barriada fsg (Peru), callampa fsg (Chile), cantegriles mpl (Spain, Uruguay), chabolas fpl (Spain), clandestinos mpl (Colombia), morenales mpl (Honduras), orillas fpl (Mexico), población fsg (Chile), pueblo joven msg (Peru), ranchos mpl (Venezuela), tugurios mpl (Colombia), villa-miseria fsg (Argentina), rancherío msg, ribera fpl, villorio msg (elsewhere in Lat. Am.); (in Brazil) favelas fpl; (slum on the outskirts of an urban area) suburbio msg
slumber /'slʌmbər/ vi dormir; (go to sleep) dormirse, caer dormido; (be latent) estar latente. n sueño, m
slump /slʌmp/ n Com. baja repentina, f; Fig. baja, racha mala, f. vi Com. bajar repentinamente. **the s.,** la crisis económica. **to s. into an armchair,** dejarse caer en un sillón
slur /slɜr/ vt (words) comerse sílabas o letras (de); (in writing) unir (las palabras); (Mus. of notes) ligar. **to cast a s. on,** difamar, manchar. **to s. over,** pasar por alto de, omitir, suprimir
slush /slʌʃ/ n lodo, m; agua nieve, f; (sentimentality) ñoñería, f
slushy /'slʌʃi/ a lodoso, fangoso
sly /slai/ a astuto, taimado, socarrón, Lat. Am. macuco; disimulado; (arch) malicioso. **on the sly,** a hurtadillas. **sly person,** Mexico fistol, m
slyness /'slainıs/ n astucia, socarronería, f; disimulo, m; malicia, f
smack /smæk/ n (taste) sabor, gusto, m; (tinge) dejo, m; (blow) golpe, m; (with the hand) bofetada, palmada, f; (with a whip) latigazo, m; (crack of whip) restallido, chasquido, m; (kiss) beso sonado, m; (boat) lancha de pescar, f. vi (taste of) tener gusto de, saber a; (be tinged with) oler a. vt (a whip) hacer restallar; (slap) pegar con la mano. **to s. one's lips over,** chuparse los dedos
small /smɔl/ a pequeño; menudo; menor; poco; (petty) mezquino, vulgar. n parte estrecha, f. **a s. number,** un pequeño número. **to make a person look s.,** humillar. **to make oneself s.,** hacerse chiquito. **s.-arms,** armas portátiles, f pl. **s. change,** suelto, m. **s. craft,** embarcaciones menores, f pl. **s. farm,** Lat. Am. chacra, Central America labor, f. **s. fry,** pececillos, m pl; (children) gente menuda, f; gente sin importancia, f. **s. hours,** altas horas de la

noche, f pl. **s.-minded,** adocenado, de cortos alcances. **s.-talk,** trivialidades, f pl, charla frívola, f
small holding n Lat. Am. chacra, f
smallish /'smɔlıʃ/ a bastante pequeño; más bien pequeño que grande
smallpox /'smɔl,pɒks/ n viruelas, f pl
smart /smɑrt/ vi picar; dolerse (de). n escozor, m; dolor, m. a severo; vivo; rápido; pronto; (competent) hábil; (clever) listo; (unscrupulous) cuco, astuto; (of personal appearance) majo; elegante, distinguido, Lat. Am. also fachoso; (neat) aseado; (fashionable, etc.) de moda; de buen tono. **to s. for,** ser castigado por. **to s. under,** sufrir
smarten /'smɑrtn̩/ vt embellecer. vi (up) ponerse elegante; mejorar. **I must go and s. myself up a little,** Tengo que arreglarme un poco
smartness /'smɑrtnıs/ n viveza, f; prontitud, rapidez, f; (cleverness) despejo, m, habilidad, f; (wittiness) agudeza, f; (astuteness) cuquería, astucia, f; (of dress, etc.) elegancia, f; buen tono, m
smash /smæʃ/ vt romper, quebrar; (a ball, etc.) golpear; (annihilate) destruir; (an opponent) aplastar. vi romperse, quebrarse; hacerse pedazos; (collide) chocar (con, contra); estallarse (contra); (financially) hacer bancarrota. n rotura, f; quebrantamiento, m; estruendo, m; (financial) quiebra, ruina, f; (car, etc.) accidente, m; desastre, m, catástrofe, f. **to s. to atoms,** hacer trizas. **to s. up,** hacer pedazos. **s. and grab raid,** atraco a mano armada, m
smash hit n éxito arrollador, éxito rotundo, m
smattering /'smætərıŋ/ n conocimiento superficial, m, tintura, f, barniz, m
smear /smıər/ n mancha, f; Biol. frotis, m. vt embadurnar (de); manchar (con), ensuciar (con); (oneself) untarse; (blur) borrar
smell /smɛl/ n (sense of) olfato, m; (odor) olor, m. vt oler. vi oler; tener olor; (disagreeably) oler mal, tener mal olor; (stink) apestar. **How good it smells!** ¡Qué bien huele! **to s. of,** oler a. **to s. out,** husmear
smelling /'smɛlıŋ/ n olfateo, m. **s.-bottle,** frasco de sales, m. **s.-salts,** sales (inglesas), f pl
smelt /smɛlt/ vt fundir. n Ichth. eperlano, m
smelter /'smɛltər/ n fundidor, m
smelting /'smɛltıŋ/ n fundición, f. **s. furnace,** horno de fundición, m
smile /smail/ vi sonreír; reírse. vt expresar con una sonrisa. n sonrisa, f. **Mary smiled her thanks,** María dio las gracias con una sonrisa. **smile at adversity,** ponerse buena cara a mal tiempo. **to s. at threats,** reírse de las amenazas
smiling /'smailıŋ/ a sonriente, risueño
smilingly /'smailıŋli/ adv sonriendo, con una sonrisa, con cara risueña
smirch /smɜrtʃ/ vt manchar. n mancha, f
smirk /smɜrk/ vi sonreír con afectación; hacer visajes. n sonrisa afectada, f
smirking /'smɜrkıŋ/ a afectado; sonriente
smite /smait/ vt golpear; (kill) matar; (punish) castigar; (pain) doler; (of bright lights, sounds, etc.) herir; (cause remorse) remorder. **My conscience smites me,** Tengo remordimientos de conciencia. **to be smitten by,** Inf. estar prendado de. **I was smitten by a desire to smoke,** Me entraron deseos de fumar
smith /smıθ/ n herrero, m. **smith's hammer,** destajador, m
smithereens /,smıðə'rinz/ n pl añicos, m pl
smithy /'smıθi, 'smıði/ n herrería, f
smock /smɒk/ n blusa, f; (child's) delantal, m
smoke /smouk/ n humo, m. vi humear, echar humo; (tobacco) fumar. vt ahumar; ennegrecer; (tobacco) fumar. **smoked glasses,** gafas ahumadas, f pl. **s. helmet,** casco respiratorio, m. **s.-screen,** cortina de humo, f. **s. signal,** ahumada, f. **s.-stack,** chimenea, f
smokeless /'smouklıs/ a sin humo
smoker /'smoukər/ n fumador (-ra)
smoking /'smoukıŋ/ a humeante. n el fumar, m. **"S. Prohibited,"** «Se prohíbe fumar.» **non-s. compartment,** Rail. departamento de no fumadores, m. **s.-carriage,** Rail. departamento para fumadores, m. **s.-room,** fumadero, m

smoky /'smouki/ *a* humeante; lleno de humo; (black) ahumado

smooth /smuð/ *a* liso; igual; (of the skin, etc.) suave; (of water) calmo, tranquilo; (flattering, etc.) lisonjero; obsequioso; afable. *vt* allanar; (hair, etc.) alisar; (paths, etc.) igualar. **to s. down,** (a person) tranquilizar, calmar. **to s. over,** (faults) exculpar. **to s. the way for,** allanar el camino para. **s.-faced,** barbilampiño, lampiño, bien afeitado, todo afeitado; *Fig.* obsequioso, untuoso. **s.-haired,** de pelo liso. **s.-spoken,** de palabras lisonjeras; obsequioso

smoothly /'smuðli/ *adv* lisamente; (of speech) afablemente; con lisonjeras. **Everything was going s.,** Todo iba viento en popa

smoothness /'smuðnɪs/ *n* igualdad, *f*; lisura, *f*; (of skin, etc.) suavidad, *f*; (of water) calma, tranquilidad, *f*; (of manner, etc.) afabilidad, *f*

smother /'smʌðər/ *vt* ahogar, sofocar; (a fire) apagar; (cover) envolver, cubrir

smoulder /'smouldər/ *vi* arder sin llama, arder lentamente; (of passions, etc.) arder; estar latente

smouldering /'smouldərɪŋ/ *a* que arde lentamente; *Fig.* latente

smudge /smʌdʒ/ *vt* manchar, ensuciar; (blur) borrar. *n* mancha, *f*

smug /smʌg/ *a* satisfecho de sí mismo, pagado de sí mismo; farisaico

smuggle /'smʌgəl/ *vt* pasar de contrabando. *vi* hacer contrabando

smuggler /'smʌglər/ *n* contrabandista, *mf*

smuggling /'smʌglɪŋ/ *n* contrabando, *m*

smugly /'smʌgli/ *adv* con presunción, de un aire satisfecho

smugness /'smʌgnɪs/ *n* satisfacción de sí mismo, *f*; fariseísmo, *m*

smut /smʌt/ *n* copo de hollín, *m*; mancha, *f*; (disease) tizón, *m*

smutty /'smʌti/ *a* tiznado; ahumado; *Inf.* verde

snack /snæk/ *n* tentempié, piscolabis, bocado, *Lat. Am.* botana, *f.* **to take a s.,** tomar un piscolabis

snack bar *n* merendero, *m*, *Lat. Am.* lonchería, *f*

snaffle /'snæfəl/ *n* filete, *m. vt* (a horse) refrenar. **s.-bridle,** bridón, *m*

snag /snæg/ *n* (of a tree) tocón, *m*; (of a tooth) raigón, *m*; (problem) busilis, *m*; obstáculo inesperado, *m*

snail /sneil/ *n* caracol, *m.* **at a snail's pace,** a paso de tortuga

snake /sneik/ *n* serpiente, *f.* **s.-charmer,** encantador de serpientes, *m*

snakelike /'sneik,laik/ *a* de serpiente; serpentino

snap /snæp/ *vt* morder; (break) romper; (one's fingers) castañetear; (a whip) chasquear; (down a lid, etc.) cerrar de golpe; (beaks, etc.) cerrar ruidosamente; *Photo.* sacar una instantánea de. *vi* partirse; quebrarse; hablar bruscamente. *n* (bite) mordedura, *f*; golpe seco, *m*; chasquido, *m*; rotura, *f*; (clasp) cierre, *m*; (of weather) temporada, *f*; (spirit) vigor, brío, *m*; *Photo.* instantánea, *f.* **to s. at,** procurar morder; (an invitation, etc.) aceptar gustoso. **to s. one's fingers at,** *Fig.* burlarse de. **to s. up,** coger, agarrar; (a person) cortar la palabra (a), interrumpir. **s.-fastener,** botón de presión, *m*

snapdragon /'snæp,drægən/ *n* dragón, *m*, becerra, boca de dragón, *f*

snappily /'snæpəli/ *adv* irritablemente

snappishness /'snæpɪʃnɪs/ *n* irritabilidad, *f*

snappy /'snæpi/ *a* irritable; vigoroso

snapshot /'snæpʃɒt/ *n* instantánea, foto, *f*

snare /snɛər/ *n* cepo, lazo, *m*, trampa, *f*; *Fig.* red, *f. vt* coger en el lazo; *Fig.* enredar

snarl /snɑrl/ *vi* (of dogs) regañar; (cats, etc.) gruñir. *n* regañamiento, *m*; gruñido, *m*

snarling /'snɑrlɪŋ/ *n* regañamiento, *m*; gruñidos, *m pl. a* gruñidor

snatch /snætʃ/ *vt* asir; agarrar; (enjoy) disfrutar; (an opportunity) tomar, aprovecharse de. *n* asimiento, agarro, *m*; (of time) rato, *m*; instante, *m*; (of song) fragmento, *m.* **to make a s. at,** procurar agarrar; alargar la mano hacia. **to s. a hurried meal,** comer aprisa. **to s. away,** arrebatar, quitar; (carry off) robar. **to s. up,** coger rápidamente; coger en brazos

sneak /snik/ *vi* deslizarse (en), colarse (en); (lurk) rondar; (inform) acusar. *n* mandilón, *m*; (accuser) acusón (-ona). **to s. off,** escabullirse, irse a hurtadillas. **s.-thief,** *n* garduño (-ña)

sneaker /'snikər/ *n* (shoe) zapatilla de tenis, *f*

sneaking /'snikɪŋ/ *a* furtivo, ruin, mezquino; secreto

sneer /snɪər/ *vi* sonreír irónicamente; burlarse, mofarse. *n* sonrisa sardónica, sonrisa de desprecio, *f*; burla, mofa, *f.* **to s. at,** mofarse de, burlarse de; hablar con desprecio de

sneering /'snɪərɪŋ/ *a* mofador, burlón

sneeringly /'snɪərɪŋli/ *adv* con una sonrisa sardónica; burlonamente

sneeze /sniz/ *vi* estornudar. *n* estornudo, *m.* **It's not to be sneezed at,** No es moco de pavo

sniff /snɪf/ *vi* respirar fuertemente; resollar. *vt* oler, olfatear; aspirar. **to s. at,** oler. **to s. out,** *Inf.* husmear

sniffle /'snɪfəl/ *n* sorbo, *m. vi* olfatear

snigger /'snɪgər/ *vi* reírse por lo bajo, reírse disimuladamente. *n* risa disimulada, *f*

snip /snɪp/ *vt* cortar con tijeras; cortar, quitar. *n* tijeretada, *f*; (of cloth, etc.) recorte, pedacito, *m*

sniper /'snaipər/ *n Mil.* paco, *m*

snippet /'snɪpɪt/ *n* pedacito, fragmento, *m*; (of prose, etc.) trocito, *m*; (of news) noticia, *f*

snivel /'snɪvəl/ *vi* lloriquear, gimotear

sniveling /'snɪvəlɪŋ/ *n* lloriqueo, gimoteo, *m. a* llorón; mocoso

snob /snɒb/ *n* esnob, *mf*

snobbery /'snɒbəri/ *n* snobismo, *m*

snobbish /'snɒbɪʃ/ *a* esnob

snood /snud/ *n* (for the hair) redecilla, *f*; (turkey's) moco (de pavo), *m*; (fishing) cendal, *m*

snoop /snup/ *vi* espiar; entremeterse

snooper /'snupər/ *n Lat. Am.* averigüetas, *mf*

snooze /snuz/ *vi* dormitar, echar un sueño. *n* sueñecito, *m*; (afternoon) siesta, *f*

snore /snɔr/ *vi* roncar. *n* ronquido, *m*

snoring /'snɔrɪŋ/ *n* ronquidos, *m pl*

snort /snɔrt/ *vi* bufar; resoplar. *n* bufido, *m*; resoplido, *m*

snout /snaut/ *n* hocico, *m*; (of a pig) jeta, *f*

snow /snou/ *n* nieve, *f. vi* nevar. *vt* nevar; *Fig.* inundar. **to s. under** (with), inundar con. **to be snowed up,** estar aprisionado por la nieve. **s.-blindness,** deslumbramiento causado por la nieve, *m.* **s.-boot,** bota para la nieve, *f.* **s.-bound,** aprisionado por la nieve; bloqueado por la nieve. **s.-capped,** coronado de nieve. **s.-clad,** cubierto de nieve. **s.-drift,** acumulación de nieve. **s.-field,** ventisquero, *m.* **s.-goggles,** gafas ahumadas, *f pl.* **s.-line,** límite de las nieves perpetuas, *m.* **s.-man,** figura de nieve, *f.* **s.-plow,** quitanieve, *m.* **s.-shoe,** raqueta de nieve, *f.* **s.-white,** blanco como la nieve

snowball /'snou,bɔl/ *n* bola de nieves, *f*; *Bot.* bola de nieve, *f*

snowdrop /'snou,drɒp/ *n* campanilla de invierno, violeta de febrero, *f*

snowfall /'snou,fɔl/ *n* nevada, *f*

snowflake /'snou,fleik/ *n* copo de nieve, *m*

snowstorm /'snou,stɔrm/ *n* ventisca, *f*

snowy /'snoui/ *a* nevoso; de nieve

snub /snʌb/ *vt* repulsar; desairar, tratar con desdén, *Mexico* descolar. *n* repulsa, *f*, desaire, *m*; (nose) nariz respingona, *f.* **s.-nosed,** de nariz respingona

snuff /snʌf/ *vt* (breathe) oler, olfatear; inhalar; (a candle) atizar; despabilar. *n* (of a candle) moco, *m*, despabiladura, *f*; (tobacco) rapé, *m.* **to take s.,** tomar rapé. **to s. out,** extinguir. **s.-box,** caja de rapé, tabaquera, *f*

snuffling /'snʌflɪŋ/ *a* mocoso; (of the voice) gangoso

snug /snʌg/ *a* caliente; cómodo; (hidden) escondido, acomodado. **to have a s. income,** tener el riñón bien cubierto, ser acomodado

snuggle /'snʌgəl/ *vi* hacerse un ovillo; acomodarse; ponerse cómodo. **to s. up to,** arrimarse a, apretarse contra

snugly /'snʌgli/ *adv* cómodamente

snugness /'snʌgnɪs/ *n* comodidad, *f*

so /sou/ *adv* así; de este modo, de esta manera; por lo tanto; tanto; (before adjs. and advs. but not before **más, mejor, menos, peor,** where tanto is used) tan; (in the same way) del mismo modo, de igual modo; (therefore) de modo que, de manera que; (also) también; (approximately) más o menos, aproximadamente. **Is that so?** ¿De veras? **if so...,** si así es... **He has not yet done so,** no lo ha hecho todavía. **I told you so!** ¡Ya te lo dije yo! **So be it!** ¡Así sea! **so far,** hasta aquí; hasta ahora. **so forth,** etcétera. **So long!** ¡Nos vemos! **so much,** tanto. **So much the worse for them,** Tanto peor para ellos. **so to speak...,** por decirlo así. **so as to,** a fin de, para. **so long as,** con tal que, a condición de que. **so on,** etcétera. **so soon as,** tan pronto como. **so that,** de suerte que, de modo que, para que; con que. **so-and-so,** *n* fulano (-na); mengano (-na). **so-called,** así llamado, supuesto. **so-so,** así-así, regular

soak /souk/ *vt* remojar; empapar; (skins) abrevar. *vi* estar en remojo. *n* remojo, *m*; (rain) diluvio, *m*; (booze) borrachera, *f.* **to s. into,** filtrar en; penetrar. **to s. through,** penetrar; filtrar **so-called,** así llamado, supuesto. **so-so,** así, regular

soaked /soukt/ *a* remojado. **He is s. to the skin,** Está calado hasta los huesos

soaking /'soukɪŋ/ *n* remojo, *m*; empapamiento, *m*,

soap /soup/ *n* jabón, *m. vt* jabonar; (flatter) enjabonar. **a tablet of s.,** una pastilla de jabón. **soft s.,** jabón blando, *m.* **toilet s.,** jabón de tocador, jaboncillo, *m.* **s.-bubble,** burbuja de jabón, *f.* **s. dish,** jabonera, *f.* **s. factory,** jabonería, *f.* **s.-flakes,** copos de jabón, *m pl*

soapbark tree /'soup,bark/ *n* quillay, palo de jabón, *m*

soap box *n Lit.* caja de jabón, *f; Fig.* tribuna callejera, *f*

soap opera /'ɒpərə/ *n* radionovela (on radio), telenovela (on television), *f*, serial lacrimógeno (derogatory), *m*

soapsuds /'soup,sʌdz/ *n pl* jabonaduras, *f pl*

soapy /'soupi/ *a* cubierto de jabón; jabonoso

soar /sɔr/ *vi* remontarse; *Fig.* elevarse; (of prices, etc.) subir de golpe

soaring /'sɔrɪŋ/ *n* remonte, vuelo, *m; Fig.* aspiración, *f*; (of prices, etc.) subida repentina, *f*

sob /sɒb/ *vi* sollozar. *n* sollozo, *m.* **to sob one's heart out,** llorar a lágrima viva. **to sob out,** decir sollozando, decir entre sollozos

s.o.b. /sɒb/ *n* (son of a bitch) hache de pe (hijo de puta)

sobbing /'sɒbɪŋ/ *n* sollozos, *m pl, a* sollozante

sober /'soubər/ *a* sobrio; moderado; (of colors) obscuro. **s.-minded,** serio; reflexivo

sobriety /sə'braiiti/ *n* sobriedad, *f*; moderación, *f*; seriedad, *f*; calma, tranquilidad, *f*

sobriquet /'soubrɪˌkei, -,kɛt/ *n* apodo, *m*

soccer /'sɒkər/ *n* fútbol (Asociación), *m*

sociability /ˌsoufə'bɪlɪti/ *n* sociabilidad, *f*

sociable /'soufəbəl/ *a* sociable; amistoso

sociably /'soufəbli/ *adv* sociablemente; amistosamente

social /'soufəl/ *a* social; sociable. *n* reunión, velada, *f.* **s.-democrat,** *a* and *n* socialdemócrata, *mf.* **s. event,** acontecimiento social, *m.* **s. insurance,** previsión social, *f.* **s. services,** servicios sociales, *m pl.* **s. work,** asistencia social, *f*

socialism /'soufə,lɪzəm/ *n* socialismo, *m*

socialist /'soufəlɪst/ *a* socialista, laborista. *n* socialista, *mf*

socialization /ˌsoufələ'zeiʃən/ *n* socialización, *f*

socialize /'soufə,laiz/ *vt* socializar

socially /'soufəli/ *adv* socialmente

society /sə'saiiti/ *n* sociedad, *f*; (fashionable) mundo elegante, *m*, alta sociedad, *f*; compañía, *f.* **to go into s.,** (of girls) ponerse de largo; entrar en el mundo elegante. **s. hostess,** dama de sociedad, *f.* **society for the prevention of cruelty to animals,** sociedad protectora de animales, *f.* **s. news,** noticias de sociedad, *f pl*

sociological /ˌsousiə'lɒdʒɪkəl/ *a* sociológico

sociologist /ˌsousi,ɒlədʒɪst/ *n* sociólogo (-ga)

sociology /ˌsousi'ɒlədʒi/ *n* sociología, *f*

sock /sɒk/ *n* calcetín, *m*; (for a shoe) plantilla, *f*

socket /'sɒkɪt/ *n Mech.* encaje, cubo, ojo, *m*; (of a lamp, and *Elec.*) enchufe, *m*; (of the eye) órbita, cuenca, *f*; (of a tooth) alvéolo, *m*; (of a joint) fosa, *f.* **His eyes started out of their sockets,** Sus ojos estaban fuera de su órbita

Socratic /sə'krætɪk/ *a* socrático

sod /sɒd/ *n* césped, *m*; (cut) tepe, *m*

soda /'soudə/ *n* sosa, *f.* **caustic s.,** sosa cáustica, *f.* **s.-ash,** carbonato sódico, *m.* **s.-fountain,** aparato de aguas gaseosas, *m.* **s.-water,** sifón, *m*

sodden /'sɒdn̩/ *a* saturado, empapado

sodium /'soudiəm/ *n* sodio, *m*

Sodomite /'sɒdə,mait/ *n* sodomita, *mf*

sodomy /'sɒdəmi/ *n* sodomía, *f*

sofa /'soufə/ *n* sofá, *m*

soft /sɔft/ *a* blando; suave; muelle; (flabby) flojo; (of disposition, etc.) dulce; (effeminate) muelle, afeminado; (lenient) indulgente; (easy) fácil; (silly) tonto. **to have a s. spot for,** (a person) tener una debilidad para. **s. coal,** carbón bituminoso, *m.* **s. drink,** bebida no alcohólica, *f.* **s. felt hat,** sombrero flexible, *m.* **s. fruit,** fruta blanda, *f.* **s.-boiled,** (of eggs) pasado por agua; (of persons) inocente, ingenuo. **s.-hearted,** de buen corazón; compasivo, bondadoso. **s.-heartedness,** buen corazón, *m*, bondad, *f.* **s.-spoken,** de voz suave; que habla con dulzura, meloso. **s. water,** agua blanda, *f*

soften /'sɔfən/ *vt* ablandar, reblandecer) (weaken) debilitar; (mitigate) mitigar, suavizar; (the heart, etc.) enternecer. *vi* reblandecerse; enternecerse

softening /'sɔfənɪŋ/ *n* reblandecimiento, *m*; (relenting) enternecimiento, *m*

softly /'sɔftli/ *adv* suavemente; dulcemente, tiernamente; sin ruido, silenciosamente

softness /'sɔftnɪs/ *n* blandura, *f*; suavidad, *f*; (sweetness, etc.) dulzura, *f*; (of character) debilidad de carácter, *f*; (silliness) necedad, estupidez, *f*

software /'sɔft,wɛər/ *n* programas de computo, *mpl*; software, *m*

soggy /'sɒgi/ *a* empapado de agua; saturado

soil /sɔil/ *n* tierra, *f*; (country) país, *m*, tierra, *f. vt* ensuciar; *Fig.* manchar. **my native s.,** mi tierra, mi patria

soiled /sɔild/ *a* sucio. **s. linen,** ropa sucia, *f*

soiree /swa'rei/ *n* velada, *f*

sojourn /'soudʒɜrn/ *vi* morar, residir, permanecer. *n* residencia, permanencia, *f*

sojourner /'soudʒɜrnər/ *n* morador (-ra), residente, *mf*

sol /sɔl/ *n Mus.* sol, *m.* **sol-fa,** *n* solfa, *f*, solfeo, *m. vt* solfear

solace /'sɒlɪs/ *n* consuelo, solaz, *m. vt* consolar; solazar

solar /'soulər/ *a* solar. **s. plexus,** *Anat.* plexo solar, *m.* **s. system,** sistema solar, *m*

solder /'sɒdər/ *n* soldadura, *f*, *vt* soldar

soldering /'sɒdərɪŋ/ *n* soldadura, *f*

soldier /'souldʒər/ *n* soldado, *m*; militar, *m.* **He wants to be a s.,** Quiere ser militar

soldierly /'souldʒərli/ *a* militar; marcial

soldiery /'souldʒəri/ *n* soldadesca, *f*

sole /soul/ *n* (of a foot) planta, *f*; (of a shoe) suela, *f*; (of a plow) cepa, *f; Ichth.* lenguado, *m*, suela, *f. vt* (shoes) solar; poner suela (a). *a* solo, único; exclusivo. **s. right,** exclusiva, *f*, derecho exclusivo, *m*

solecism /'sɒlə,sɪzəm/ *n* solecismo, *m*

solely /'soulli/ *adv* sólo; únicamente, puramente; meramente

solemn /'sɒləm/ *a* solemne; grave; serio; (sacred) sagrado. **Why do you look so s.?** ¿Por qué estás tan serio?

solemnity /sə'lɛmnɪti/ *n* solemnidad, *f*

solemnization /ˌsɒlɛmnə'zeiʃən/ *n* solemnización, celebración, *f*

solemnize /'sɒləm,naiz/ *vt* solemnizar

solemnly /'sɒləmli/ *adv* solemnemente; gravemente

solicit /sə'lɪsɪt/ *vt* solicitar; implorar, rogar encarecidamente

solicitation /sə,lɪsɪ'teiʃən/ *n* solicitación, *f*

solicitor /sə'lɪsɪtər/ *n* abogado (-da)

solicitous /sə'lɪsɪtəs/ a ansioso (de), deseoso (de); solícito, atento; (worried) preocupado

solicitude /sə'lɪsɪ,tud/ n solicitud, f, cuidado, m; (anxiety) preocupación, f

solid /'sɒlɪd/ a sólido; macizo; (of persons) serio, formal; (unanimous) unánime. n sólido, m. **a s. meal,** una comida fuerte. **He slept for ten s. hours,** Durmió por diez horas seguidas. **solid-colored material,** tela lisa, f. **s. food,** alimentos sólidos, m pl. **s. geometry,** geometría del espacio, f. **solid gold,** oro de ley, m. **s. tire,** llanta de goma maciza, f

solidarity /,sɒlɪ'dærɪti/ n solidaridad, f

solidification /sə,lɪdəfɪ'keɪʃən/ n solidificación, f

solidify /sə'lɪdə,faɪ/ vt solidificar. vi solidificarse; congelarse

solidity /sə'lɪdɪti/ n solidez, f; unanimidad, f

solidly /'sɒlɪdli/ adv sólidamente

soliloquize /sə'lɪlə,kwaɪz/ vi soliloquiar, hablar a solas

soliloquy /sə'lɪləkwi/ n soliloquio, m

solitaire /'sɒlɪ,teər/ n (diamond and game) solitario, m

solitary /'sɒlɪ,teri/ a solitario; solo, aislado, único. **He was in s. confinement for three months,** Estuvo incomunicado durante tres meses. **There is not a s. one,** No hay ni uno

solitude /'sɒlɪ,tud/ n soledad, f

solo /'soʊloʊ/ n (performance and cards) solo, m. **to sing a s.,** cantar un solo. **It was his first s. flight,** Era su primer vuelo a solas

soloist /'soʊloʊɪst/ n solista, mf

solstice /'sɒlstɪs, 'soʊl-/ n solsticio, m. **summer s.,** solsticio vernal, m. **winter s.,** solsticio hiemal, m

solubility /,sɒlyə'bɪlɪti/ n solubilidad, f

soluble /'sɒlyəbəl/ a soluble

solution /sə'luʃən/ n solución, f

solvable /'sɒlvəbəl/ a que se puede resolver, soluble

solve /sɒlv/ vt resolver, hallar la solución de

solvency /'sɒlvənsi/ n solvencia, f

solvent /'sɒlvənt/ a Com. solvente; (Chem. and Fig.) disolvente. n disolvente, m

somatic /soʊ'mætɪk/ a somático

somber /'sɒmbər/ a sombrío

somberly /'sɒmbərli/ adv sombríamente

somberness /'sɒmbərnɪs/ n lo sombrío; sobriedad, f; melancolía, f

some /sʌm; unstressed səm/ a alguno (-a), algunos (-as); (before a masculine sing. noun) algún; unos (-as); un poco de, algo de; (as a partitive, often not translated, e.g. Give me s. wine, Dame vino); (approximately) aproximadamente, unos (-as). pron algunos (-as), unos (-as); algo, un poco. **I should like s. strawberries,** Me gustaría comer unas fresas. **s. day,** algún día. **S. say yes, others no,** Algunos dicen que sí, otros que no. **There are s. sixty people in the garden,** Hay unas sesenta personas en el jardín

somebody, someone /'sʌm,bɒdi; 'sʌm,wʌn/ n alguien, mf. **s. else,** otro (-a), otra persona, f. **S. or other said that the book is worth reading,** No sé quién dijo que el libro vale la pena de leerse. **to be s.,** Inf. ser un personaje

somehow /'sʌm,haʊ/ adv de un modo u otro, de alguna manera. **S. I don't like them,** No sé por qué, pero no me gustan

somersault /'sʌmər,sɔlt/ n salto mortal, m, vi dar un salto mortal

something /'sʌm,θɪŋ/ n algo, m, alguna cosa, f. adv algún tanto. **Would you like s. else?** ¿Quiere Vd. otra cosa? **He left s. like fifty thousand pounds,** Dejó algo así como cincuenta mil libras. **He has s. to live for,** Tiene para que vivir

sometime /'sʌm,taɪm/ adv algún día, alguna vez; en algún tiempo. a ex-. **Come and see me s. soon,** Ven a verme algún día de estos. **He will have to go abroad s. or another,** Tarde o temprano, tiene que ir al extranjero. **s. last month,** durante el mes pasado

sometimes /'sʌm,taɪmz/ adv algunas veces, a veces. **s. happy, s. sad,** algunas veces feliz y otras triste, ora feliz ora triste

somewhat /'sʌm,wʌt/ adv algo; algún tanto, un tanto; un poco. **I am s. busy,** Estoy algo ocupado. **He**

is s. of a lady-killer, Tiene sus puntos de castigador, Tiene algo de castigador

somewhere /'sʌm,weər/ adv en alguna parte. **s. about,** por ahí. **s. else,** en otra parte

somnambulism /sɒm'næmbyə,lɪzəm/ n somnambulismo, m

somnambulist /sɒm'næmbyəlɪst/ n somnámbulo (-la)

somnolence /'sɒmnələns/ n somnolencia, f

somnolent /'sɒmnələnt/ a soñoliento; soporífero

son /sʌn/ n hijo, m. **son-in-law,** yerno, hijo político, m

sonata /sə'nɑtə/ n sonata, f

song /sɔŋ/ n canto, m; canción, f; (poem) poema, f, verso, m. **It's nothing to make a s. about,** No es para tanto. **to break into s.,** ponerse a cantar. **to be not worth an old s.,** no valer un pito. **the S. of Songs,** Cantar de los Cantares, m. **s.-bird,** ave canora, f. **s.-book,** libro de canciones, m. **s.-writer,** compositor (-ra) de canciones

sonic /'sɒnɪk/ adj sónico. **sonic boom,** estampido sónico, m

sonnet /'sɒnɪt/ n soneto, m

sonorous /sə'nɔrəs/ a sonoro

sonorousness /sə'nɔrəsnɪs/ n sonoridad, f

soon /sun/ adv pronto; dentro de poco, luego. **as s. as,** así que, en cuanto, luego que, no bien... **as s. as possible,** lo antes posible, lo más pronto posible, con la mayor antelación posible, cuanto antes. **s. after,** poco después (de). **See you s.!** ¡Hasta pronto! **sooner or later,** tarde o temprano. **the sooner the better,** cuanto antes mejor. **No sooner had he left the house, when...** Apenas hubo dejado la casa, cuando... **Emily would sooner go to London,** Emilia preferiría ir a Londres (A Emilia le gustaría más ir a Londres)

soot /sʊt/ n hollín, m, vt cubrir de hollín

soothe /suð/ vt tranquilizar, calmar, (pain) aliviar, mitigar

soothing /'suðɪŋ/ a calmante, tranquilizador, sosegador; (of powders, etc.) calmante

soothingly /'suðɪŋli/ adv con dulzura; suavemente; como un consuelo

soothsayer /'suθ,seɪər/ n adivino (-na), adivinador (-ra)

soothsaying /'suθ,seɪɪŋ/ n adivinanza, f

sooty /'sʊti/ a cubierto de hollín; negro como el hollín

sop /sɒp/ n sopa, f; (bribe) soborno, m

sophism /'sɒfɪzəm/ n sofisma, m

sophist /'sɒfɪst/ n Hist. sofista, m; (quibbler) sofista, mf

sophistic /sə'fɪstɪk/ a Philos. sofista; (of persons, arguments) sofístico

sophisticated /sə'fɪstɪ,keɪtɪd/ a nada ingenuo; mundano; (cultured) culto

sophistication /sə,fɪstɪ'keɪʃən/ n falta de simplicidad, f; mundanería, f; cultura, f

sophistry /'sɒfəstri/ n sofistería, f

Sophoclean /,sɒfə'kliən/ a sofocleo

soporific /,sɒpə'rɪfɪk/ a soporífico

sopping /'sɒpɪŋ/ a muy mojado. **s. wet,** hecho una sopa

soprano /sə'prænoʊ/ n (voice and part) soprano, m; (singer) soprano, tiple, mf

sorcerer /'sɔrsərər/ n encantador, mago, brujo, m

sorceress /'sɔrsərɪs/ n hechicera, bruja, f

sorcery /'sɔrsəri/ n sortilegio, m, hechicería, brujería, f; encanto, m

sordid /'sɔrdɪd/ a sórdido; (of motives, etc.) ruin, vil

sordidness /'sɔrdɪdnɪs/ n sordidez, f; (of motives, etc.) vileza, bajeza, f

sordine /'sɔrdɛn/ n Mus. sordina, f

sore /sɔr/ a doloroso, malo; (sad) triste; (annoyed) enojado; (with need, etc.) extremo. n llaga, Lat. Am. also lacra, f; (on horses, etc., caused by girths) matadura, f; Fig. herida, f; recuerdo doloroso, m. **to open an old s.,** Fig. renovar la herida. **running s.,** úlcera, f. **s. throat,** dolor de garganta, m

sorely /'sɔrli/ adv grandemente; muy; urgentemente. **He was s. tempted,** Tuvo grandes tentaciones

soreness /'sɔrnɪs/ n dolor, m; (resentment) amargura, f, resentimiento, m; (ill-feeling) rencor, m
sorrel /'sɔrəl, 'sɒr-/ a alazán. n (horse) alazán, m; Bot. acedera, f
sorrow /'sɒrou/ n pesar, m, aflicción, pesadumbre, f; tristeza, f. vi afligirse; entristecerse. **To my great s.,** Con gran pesar mío. **s.-stricken,** afligido, agobiado de pena
sorrowful /'sɒrəfəl/ a afligido, angustiado; triste
sorrowfully /'sɒrəfəli/ adv con pena, tristemente
sorrowing /'sɒrouɪŋ/ a afligido. n aflicción, f; lamentación, f
sorry, to be /'sɒri/ vi sentir. **I'm s.,** Lo siento.
sort /sɔrt/ n especie, f; clase, f; tipo, m. vt separar (de); clasificar. **a s. of hat,** una especie de sombrero. **all sorts of,** toda clase de. **He is a good s.,** Es buen chico. **He is a queer s.,** Es un tipo raro. **in some s.,** hasta cierto punto. **I am out of sorts,** Estoy destemplado. **Nothing of the s.!** ¡Nada de eso!
sorter /'sɔrtər/ n oficial de correos, m; clasificador (-ra)
sorting /'sɔrtɪŋ/ n clasificación, f
sotto voce /'sɒt'ou voutʃi/ adv a sovoz, en voz baja
soul /soul/ n alma, f; espíritu, m; (departed) ánima, f; (being) ser, m; (life) vida, f; (heart) corazón, m. **All Souls' Day,** Día de los Difuntos, m. **He is a good s.!** ¡Es un bendito! **She is a simple s.,** Ella es una alma de Dios. **without seeing a living s.,** sin ver un bicho viviente. **Upon my s.!** ¡Por mi vida! **s. in purgatory,** alma en pena, f. **s.-stirring,** emocionante
soulful /'soulfəl/ a sentimental, emocional; espiritual; romántico
soulless /'soullɪs/ a sin alma; mecánico
sound /saund/ n sonido, m; son, m; ruido, m; (strait) estrecho, m. vi sonar; hacer ruido; resonar; (seem) parecer. vt sonar; (the horn, the alarm, musical instrument) tocar; (express) expresar; proclamar; (praise) celebrar; Naut. hondear; Med. tentar; (the chest) auscultar; (try to discover) tentar, sondar; (experience) experimentar. **to the s. of,** al son de. **s.-box,** (of a gramophone) diafragma, m. **s.-detector,** fonolocalización de aviones, f. **s.-film,** película sonora, f. **s.-proof,** (of radio studios, etc.) aislado de todo sonido. **s.-track,** guía sonora, banda sonora, f. **s.-wave,** onda sonora, f
sound /saund/ a sano; (of a person) perspicaz; (reasonable) lógico, razonable; (of a policy, etc.) prudente; (of an argument, etc.) válido; (of an investment) seguro; (solvent) solvente; (good) bueno; (deep) profundo. adv profundamente, bien
sounding /'saundɪŋ/ n Naut. sondeo, m; pl **soundings,** sondas, f pl. a sonoro. **to take soundings,** sondar, echar la plomada. **s.-board,** tabla de armonía, f
soundless /'saundlɪs/ a sin ruido, silencioso
soundly /'saundli/ adv sanamente; juiciosamente, prudentemente; bien; (deeply) profundamente
soundness /'saundnɪs/ n (of a person) perspicacia, f; (of a policy, etc.) prudencia, f; (of an argument, etc.) validez, fuerza, f; (financial) solvencia, f
soup /sup/ n sopa, f. **clear s.,** consommé, m. **thick s.,** puré, m. **to be in the s.,** Inf. estar aviado. **s.-ladle,** cucharón, m. **s.-plate,** plato sopero, m. **s.-tureen,** sopera, f
sour /sauºr/ a ácido, agrio; (of milk) agrio; (of persons, etc.) agrio, desabrido. vt agriar. **to go s.,** volverse agrio. **S. grapes!** ¡Están verdes!
source /sɔrs/ n (of a river, etc.) nacimiento, m; fuente, f; (of infection) foco, m. **to know from a good s.,** saber de buena tinta
sourly /'sauºrli/ adv agriamente
sourness /'sauºrnɪs/ n acidez, agrura, f; acrimonia, f
south /sauθ/ n sur, m; mediodía, m. a del sur. adv hacia el sur. **S. African,** a and n sudafricano (-na). **S. American,** a and n sudamericano (-na). **s.-east,** n sudeste, m. a del sudeste. adv hacia el sudeste. **s.-easter,** viento del sudeste, m. **s.-easterly,** a del sudeste; al sudeste. adv hacia el sudeste. **s.-eastern,** del sudeste. **s.-s.-east,** n sudsudeste, m. **s.-s.-west,** sudsudoeste, m. **s.-west,** n sudoeste, m. a del sudoeste. adv hacia el sudoeste. **s.-west wind,** viento su-

doeste, ábrego, m. **s.-westerly,** a del sudoeste. adv hacia el sudoeste. **s.-western,** a del sudoeste
South Africa /'æfrɪkə/ República Sudafricana, f
South America América del Sur, f
southerly /'sʌðərli/ a del sur; hacia el sur. **The house has a s. aspect,** La casa está orientada al sur
southern /'sʌðərn/ a del sur; del mediodía; meridional. **S. Cross,** Cruz, f, Crucero, m. **s. express,** sudexpreso, m
southerner /'sʌðərnər/ n habitante del sur, m
South Sea Mar del Sur, Mar del Pacífico, m
southward /'sauθwərd/ Naut. 'sʌðərd/ a del sur; al sur. adv hacia el sur
souvenir /,suvə'nɪər/ n recuerdo, m
sovereign /'sɒvrɪn/ a soberano. n soberano (-na); (coin) soberano, m
sovereignty /'sɒvrɪnti/ n soberanía, f
soviet /'souvi,ɛt/ n soviet, m, a soviético
Soviet Union, the la Unión Soviética, f
sow /sau/ n cerda, puerca, marrana, f; (of a wild boar) jabalina, f; (of iron) galápago, m
sow /sou/ vt sembrar; esparcir; diseminar
sower /'souər/ n sembrador (-ra)
sowing /'souɪŋ/ n sembradura, siembra, f. **s. machine,** sembradera, f. **s. time,** tiempo de la siembra, m
soya bean /'sɔiə/ n soja, f
spa /spɑ/ n balneario, m; (spring) manantial mineral, m, caldas, f pl
space /speis/ n espacio, m; (of time) temporada, f; intervalo, m; (Print., Mus.) espacio, m. vt espaciar. **blank s.,** blanco, m. **s.-bar,** tecla de espacios, f, espaciador, m
spacious /'speiʃəs/ a espacioso; amplio
spaciousness /'speiʃəsnɪs/ n espaciosidad, f; amplitud, f
spade /speid/ n pala, azada, f; (cards) espada, f. **to call a s. a s.,** llamar al pan pan y al vino vino, llamar a las cosas por su nombre. **s.-work,** trabajo preparatorio, m, labor de pala, f
spaghetti /spə'gɛti/ n fideos, macarrones, m pl, espagueti, m
Spain /spein/ España, f
span /spæn/ vt medir a palmos; rodear; medir; (cross) atravesar, cruzar. n palmo, m; espacio, m, duración, f; (of a bridge) vano, m; (of wing, Aer., Zool.) envergadura, f; (distance) distancia, f. **single-s. bridge,** puente de vano único. **the brief s. of human life,** la corta duración de la vida humana
spangle /'spæŋgəl/ n lentejuela, f; (tinsel) oropel, m. vt adornar con lentejuelas; sembrar (de), esparcir (de). **spangled with stars,** sembrado de estrellas
Spaniard /'spænyərd/ n español (-la). **a young S.,** un joven español
spaniel /'spænyəl/ n perro de aguas, perro sabueso español, m; (cocker) sabueso, m
Spanish /'spænɪʃ/ a español. n (language) español, castellano, m. **a S. girl,** una muchacha española. **in S. fashion,** a la española. **S. American,** a and n hispanoamericano (-na). **S. broom,** retama de olor, f. **S. fly,** cantárida, f
Spanish America Hispanoamérica, f
spank /spæŋk/ vt pegar con la mano, azotar. n azotazo, m. **to s. along,** correr rápidamente; (of a horse) galopar
spanking /'spæŋkɪŋ/ n azotamiento, vapuleo, m
spanner /'spænər/ n llave inglesa, llave de tuercas, f
spar /spɑr/ n Naut. mastel, m; Mineral. espato, m; (boxing) boxeo, m; (quarrel) disputa, f. vi boxear; (argue) disputar
spare /spɛər/ a (meager) frugal, escaso; (of persons) enjuto, flaco; (available) disponible; (extra) de repuesto. n recambio, m. **s. part,** pieza de recambio, pieza de repuesto, f. **s. room,** cuarto de amigos, m. **s. time,** ratos de ocio, m pl, tiempo disponible, m. **s. tire,** Mexico llanta de refación, f. **s. wheel,** rueda de repuesto, f
spare /spɛər/ vt (expense, etc.) escatimar; ahorrar; (do without) pasarse sin; (give) dar; (a life, etc.) perdonar; (avoid) evitar; dispensar de; (grant) hacer gracia de; (time) dedicar. **I cannot s. her,** No puedo es-

tar sin ella. **They have no money to s.,** No tienen dinero de sobra. **to be sparing of,** ser avaro de
sparingly /'spɛərɪŋli/ adv frugalmente; escasamente. **to eat s.,** comer con frugalidad
spark /spɑrk/ n chispa, f; (gallant) pisaverde, m. vi chispear, echar chispas
sparking /'spɒrkɪŋ/ a chispeante. n emisión de chispas, f. **s.-plug,** bujía de encendido, f
sparkle /'spɑrkəl/ vi centellear, rutilar, destellar; Fig. brillar; (of wines) ser espumoso. n centelleo, destello, m; Fig. brillo, m
sparkling /'spɒrklɪŋ/ a rutilante, centelleante, reluciente; Fig. brillante, chispeante; (of wines) espumante
sparring match /'spɒrɪŋ/ n combate de boxeo amistoso, m
sparrow /'spærou/ n gorrión, m. **s.-hawk,** gavilán, esparaván, m
sparse /spɑrs/ a claro, ralo; esparcido
sparsely /'spɑrsli/ adv escasamente
Sparta /'spɑrtə/ Esparta, f
Spartan /'spɑrtn̩/ a and n espartano (-na)
spasm /'spæzəm/ n espasmo, m; ataque, m; acceso, m
spasmodic /spæz'mɒdɪk/ a espasmódico; intermitente
spasmodically /spæz'mɒdɪkli/ adv espasmódicamente
spat /spæt/ n (gaiter) polaina de tela, f
spate /speit/ n crecida, f; Fig. torrente, m. **in s.,** crecido
spatter /'spætər/ vt salpicar; (Fig. smirch) manchar. vi rociar. n salpicadura, f; rociada, f
spatula /'spætʃələ/ n espátula, f
spawn /spɒn/ vt and vi desovar; engendrar. n huevas, f pl, freza, f; (offspring) producto, m
speak /spik/ vi hablar; pronunciar un discurso; (sound) sonar. vt decir; (French, etc.) hablar. **She never spoke to him again,** Nunca volvió a dirigirle la palabra. **roughly speaking,** aproximadamente, más o menos. **Speaking for myself,** En cuanto a mí, Por mi parte. **without speaking,** sin decir nada, sin hablar. **to s. for,** (a person) hablar por. **to s. for itself,** hablar por sí mismo, ser evidente. **to s. one's mind,** decir lo que se piensa. **to s. of,** hablar de. **to s. out,** hablar claro; hablar alto. **to s. up for,** (a person) hablar en favor de (alguien)
speaker /'spikər/ n el, m, (f, la) que habla; (public) orador (-ra). **the S.,** el Presidente de la Cámara de los Comunes
speaking /'spikɪŋ/ a hablante; para hablar; elocuente, expresivo. n habla, f, discurso, m. **They are not on s. terms,** No se hablan. **within s. distance,** al habla. **s.-trumpet,** portavoz, m. **s.-tube,** tubo acústico, m
spear /spɪər/ n lanza, f; (javelin) venablo, m; (harpoon) arpón, m. vt herir con lanza, alancear; (fish) arponear. **s.-head,** punta de la lanza, f. **s.-thrust,** lanzada, f
special /'spɛʃəl/ a especial; particular; extraordinario. n (train) tren extraordinario, m. **s. correspondent,** corresponsal extraordinario, m. **s. friend,** amigo (-ga) del alma, amigo íntimo
specialist /'spɛʃəlɪst/ n especialista, mf
specialization /ˌspɛʃələ'zeɪʃən/ n especialización, f
specialize /'spɛʃəˌlaɪz/ vt especializar. vi especializarse
specially /'spɛʃəli/ adv especialmente; particularmente; sobre todo
specialty /'spɛʃəlti/ n particularidad, f; especialidad, f
species /'spiʃiz, -siz/ n especie, f; raza, f
specific /spɪ'sɪfɪk/ a específico; explícito. n específico, m. **s. gravity,** peso específico, m, densidad, f
specifically /spɪ'sɪfɪkli/ adv específicamente; explícitamente
specification /ˌspɛsəfɪ'keɪʃən/ n especificación, f
specify /'spɛsəˌfaɪ/ vt especificar
specimen /'spɛsəmən/ n espécimen, m; ejemplo, m; Inf. tipo, m
specious /'spiʃəs/ a especioso. **s. arguments** Lat. Am. abogaderas, abogaderías, fpl
speciousness /'spiʃəsnɪs/ n plausibilidad, f; apariencia engañosa, f

speck /spɛk/ n pequeña mancha, f; punto, m; átomo, m; (on fruit) maca, f
speckle /'spɛkəl/ vt motear, manchar
speckled /'spɛkəld/ a abigarrado; con manchas...
spectacle /'spɛktəkəl/ n espectáculo, m; escena, f; pl **spectacles,** gafas, f pl, anteojos, m pl. **s.-case,** cajita para las gafas, f
spectacled /'spɛktəkəld/ a con gafas, que lleva gafas
spectacular /spɛk'tækələr/ a espectacular
spectator /'spɛkteɪtər/ n espectador (-ra)
specter /'spɛktər/ n espectro, fantasma, m
spectral /'spɛktrəl/ a espectral
spectrum /'spɛktrəm/ n Phys. espectro, m
speculate /'spɛkyəˌleɪt/ vi especular (sobre, acerca de); Com. especular (en)
speculation /ˌspɛkyə'leɪʃən/ n especulación, f
speculative /'spɛkyəˌlɑtɪv/ a especulativo
speculator /'spɛkyəˌleɪtər/ n especulador (-ra)
speech /spitʃ/ n habla, f; palabra, f; (idiom) lenguaje, m; (language) idioma, m; Gram. oración, f; (address) discurso, m; disertación, f. **part of s.,** parte de la oración, f. **to make a s.,** pronunciar un discurso. **s. maker,** orador (-ra)
speechless /'spitʃlɪs/ a mudo; sin habla; desconcertado, turbado
speed /spid/ n prisa, rapidez, f; velocidad, f. vt dar la bienvenida (a); conceder éxito (a); (accelerate) acelerar. vi darse prisa; correr a toda prisa; (of arrows) volar. **at full s.,** a toda prisa; a toda velocidad; a todo correr. **maximum s.,** velocidad máxima, f. **with all s.,** a toda prisa. **s. of impact,** velocidad del choque, f. **s.-boat,** lancha de carrera, f. **s.-limit,** velocidad máxima, f, límite de velocidad, m
speedily /'spidli/ adv aprisa, rápidamente; prontamente
speediness /'spidɪnɪs/ n rapidez, prisa, celeridad, f; prontitud, f
speeding /'spidɪŋ/ n exceso de velocidad, m. **s. up,** aceleración, f
speedometer /spi'dɒmɪtər/ n cuentakilómetros, m
speedway /'spidˌweɪ/ n autódromo, m, pista de ceniza, f
speedy /'spidi/ a rápido; pronto
spell /spɛl/ n ensalmo, hechizo, m; encanto, m; (bout) turno, m; (interval) rato, m; temporada, f. vt (a word) deletrear; (a word in writing) escribir; (mean) significar; (be) ser. **a s. of good weather,** una temporada de buen tiempo. **by spells,** a ratos. **to learn to s.,** aprender la ortografía. **s.-bound,** encantado, fascinado; asombrado. **How do you spell "hinchado"?** &iquest:Cómo se escribe "hinchado"?
spelling /'spɛlɪŋ/ n deletreo, m; ortografía, f. **s.-book,** silabario, m. **s. mistake,** falta de ortografía, f
spelling bee n certamen de deletreo, m
spend /spɛnd/ vt gastar; (time, etc.) pasar; perder; consumir, agotar. vi gastar, hacer gastos. **to s. lavishly,** Mexico disparar. **to s. oneself,** agotarse
spendthrift /'spɛnd,θrɪft/ n derrochador (-ra), maniroto (-ta). a despilfarrado, pródigo
spent /spɛnt/ a agotado, rendido. **The night is far s.,** La noche está avanzada. **s. bullet,** bala fría, f
sperm /spɜrm/ n Biol. esperma, f; (whale) cachalote, m
spermaceti /ˌspɜrmə'sɛti/ n esperma de ballena, f
sphere /sfɪər/ n esfera, f. **s. of influence,** zona de influencia, f
spherical /'sfɛrɪkəl, 'sfɪər-/ a esférico
sphinx /sfɪŋks/ n esfinge, f. **s.-like,** de esfinge
spice /spaɪs/ n especia, f; Fig. sabor, m; (trace) dejo, m. vt especiar. **s. cupboard,** especiero, m
spick and span /'spɪk ən 'spæn/ a limpio como una patena; (brand-new) flamante; (of persons) muy compuesto
spicy /'spaɪsi/ a especiado; aromático; Fig. picante
spider /'spaɪdər/ n araña, f. **spider's web,** telaraña, f
spidery /'spaɪdəri/ a de araña; lleno de arañas. **s. writing,** letra de patas de araña, f
spigot /'spɪgət/ n espiche, m, llave, f
spike /spaɪk/ n punta (de hierro, etc.), f; escarpia, f;

spill 604

(for boots) clavo, *m*; *Bot.* espiga, *f*. *vt* clavetear; (a cannon) clavar

spill /spɪl/ *vt* derramar. *n* (fall) caída, *f*

spilling /'spɪlɪŋ/ *n* derramamiento, derrame, *m*

spin /spɪn/ *vt* hilar; (a cocoon) tejer; (a top) bailar; (a ball) tornear; (a coin) lanzar. *vi* hilar; girar, bailar. *n* vuelta, *f*; paseo, *m*. **to send spinning downstairs,** hacer rodar por la escalera (a). **to s. a yarn,** contar un cuento. **to s. out,** prolongar

spinach /'spɪnɪtʃ/ *n* espinaca, *f*

spinal /'spaɪnl/ *a* espinal. **s. anaesthesia,** raquianestesia, *f*. **s. column,** columna vertebral, *f*

spindle /'spɪndl/ *n* huso, *m*; *Mech.* eje, *m*. **s.-shaped,** ahusado

spine /spaɪn/ *n Anat.* espinazo, *m*, columna vertebral, *f*; *Bot.* espina, *f*; (of a porcupine, etc.) púa, *f*

spineless /'spaɪnlɪs/ *a Zool.* invertebrado; *Fig.* débil

spinet /'spɪnɪt/ *n* espineta, *f*

spinner /'spɪnər/ *n* hilandero (-ra); máquina de hilar, *f*

spinney /'spɪni/ *n* arboleda, *f*; bosquecillo, *m*

spinning /'spɪnɪŋ/ *n* hilado, *m*; hilandería, *f*. **s.-machine,** máquina de hilar, *f*. **s.-top,** trompo, *m*, peonza, *f*. **s.-wheel,** rueca, *f*

spinster /'spɪnstər/ *n* soltera, *f*. **confirmed s.,** solterona, *f*

spiny /'spaɪni/ *a* con púas; espinoso

spiral /'spaɪrəl/ *a* espiral; en espiral. *n* espiral, *f*

spirally /'spaɪrəli/ *adv* en espiral

spire /spaɪər/ *n* (of a church) aguja, *f*; espira, *f*

spirit /'spɪrɪt/ *n* espíritu, *m*; alma, *f*; (ghost) aparecido, fantasma, *m*; (outstanding person) ingenio, *m*, inteligencia, *f*; (disposition) ánimo, *m*; (courage) valor, espíritu, *m*; (for a lamp, etc.) alcohol, *m*. **the Holy S.,** El Espíritu Santo. **to be in high spirits,** no caber de contento, saltar de alegría. **to be in low spirits,** estar desalentado, estar deprimido. **to be full of spirits,** ser bullicioso, tener mucha energía. **to keep up one's spirits,** sostener el valor. **to s. away,** quitar secretamente, hacer desaparecer; (kidnap) secuestrar. **s.-level,** nivel de burbuja, *m*. **s.-stove,** cocinilla, *f*

spirited /'spɪrɪtɪd/ *a* animado, vigoroso; fogoso, animoso, brioso

spiritless /'spɪrɪtlɪs/ *a* sin espíritu, apático; flojo, débil; (depressed) abatido, desalentado; (cowardly) sin valor, cobarde

spiritual /'spɪrɪtʃuəl/ *a* espiritual

spiritualism /'spɪrɪtʃuə,lɪzəm/ *n* espiritismo, *m*; *Philos.* espiritualismo, *m*

spiritualist /'spɪrɪtʃuəlɪst/ *n* espiritista, *mf*; *Philos.* espiritualista, *mf*

spiritualistic /,spɪrɪtʃuə'lɪstɪk/ *a* espiritista; *Philos.* espiritualista, *m*

spirituality /,spɪrɪtʃu'ælɪti/ *n* espiritualidad, *f*

spiritually /'spɪrɪtʃuəli/ *adv* espiritualmente

spirituous /'spɪrɪtʃuəs/ *a* espirituoso

spirt /spɜrt/ *vi, vt, n.* See **spurt**

spit /spɪt/ *n* (for roasting) espetón, asador, *m*; (sandbank) banco de arena, *m*; (of land) lengua de tierra, *f*; (spittle) saliva, *f*. **the spit of, the spit and image of, the spitting image of,** la imagen viva de, la segunda edición de, *f*. *vt* (skewer) espetar; (saliva, etc.) escupir; (curses, etc.) vomitar. *vi* escupir, expectorar; (of a cat) fufear, decir fu; (sputter) chisporrotear; (rain) lloviznar

spite /spaɪt/ *n* malevolencia, mala voluntad, hostilidad, *f*; rencor, *m*, ojeriza, *f*. *vt* contrariar, hacer daño (a). **He has a s. against them,** Les tiene rencor. **in s. of,** a pesar de, a despecho de

spiteful /'spaɪtfəl/ *a* rencoroso, malévolo

spitefully /'spaɪtfəli/ *adv* malévolamente; con rencor; por maldad; por venganza

spitefulness /'spaɪtfəlnɪs/ *n* malevolencia, *f*; rencor, *m*

spitfire /'spɪt,faɪ³r/ *n* cascarrabias, *mf*, furia, *f*

spittle /'spɪtl/ *n* saliva, *f*

splash /splæʃ/ *vt* salpicar (de); manchar (con). *vi* derramarse, esparcirse; chapotear, chapalear. *n* chapoteo, *m*; (of rain, etc.) chapaleteo, *m*; (stain or patch) mancha, *f*. **John was splashing about in the sea,** Juan chapoteaba en el mar. **to make a s.,** *Fig.* causar una sensación. **s.-board,** alero, *m*

spleen /splin/ *n Anat.* bazo, *m*; esplín, *m*

splendid /'splɛndɪd/ *a* espléndido; magnífico; glorioso; excelente

splendidly /'splɛndɪdli/ *adv* espléndidamente; magníficamente; excelentemente

splendor /'splɛndər/ *n* resplandor, *m*; magnificencia, *f*; (of exploits, etc.) esplendor, brillo, *m*

splice /splaɪs/ *vt* (ropes, timbers) empalmar; (marry) unir, casar. *n* empalme, *m*

splint /splɪnt/ *n Surg.* férula, *f*. **to put in a s.,** entablar

splinter /'splɪntər/ *vt* astillar, hacer astillas. *vi* hacerse astillas

splintery /'splɪntəri/ *a* astilloso

split /splɪt/ *vi* henderse; resquebrajarse; (of seams) nacerse; abrirse; dividirse. *vt* hender; partir; dividir; abrir; (the atom) escindir. *n* hendedura, *f*; grieta, *f*; división, *f*; (in fabric) rasgón, *m*; (quarrel) ruptura, *f*. **to s. hairs,** andar en quisquillas, pararse en pelillos, sutilizar. **I have a splitting headache,** Tengo un dolor de cabeza que me trae loco. **to s. one's sides,** reírse a carcajadas, desternillarse de risa. **to s. on a rock,** estrellarse contra una roca. **to s. the difference,** partir la diferencia. **The blow s. his head open,** El golpe le abrió la cabeza. **to s. on,** *Inf.* delatar, denunciar

splodge /splɒdʒ/ *n* mancha, *f*, borrón, *m*

splutter /'splʌtər/ *vi* chisporrotear; (of a person) balbucir. *n* chisporroteo, *m*. **to s. out,** decir tartamudeando

spoil /spɔɪl/ *n* botín, despojo, *m*; (of war) trofeo, *m*. *vt* estropear; echar a perder; (diminish) mitigar; (a child) mimar; (injure) dañar; (destroy) arruinar, destruir. *vi* estropearse; echarse a perder. **to be spoiling for a fight,** tener ganas de pelearse. **You have spoiled my fun,** Me has aguado la fiesta. **s.-sport,** aguafiestas, *mf*

spoiled /spɔɪld/ *a* (of a child, etc.) mimado, consentido, malacostumbrado

spoke /spouk/ *n* (of a wheel) rayo, *m*; (of a ladder) travesaño, peldaño, *m*; *Naut.* cabilla (de la rueda del timón), *f*

spoken /'spoukən/ *a* hablado. **well-s.,** bien hablado; cortés

spokesman /'spouksmən/ *n* portavoz, *m*. **to be s.,** llevar la palabra

spoliation /,spouli'eɪʃən/ *n* expoliación, *f*; despojo, *m*

sponge /spʌndʒ/ *n* esponja, *f*; (cadger) gorrón (-ona); (cake) bizcocho, *m*. *vt* limpiar con esponja. **to s.,** *Inf.* vivir de gorra. **s.-holder,** esponjera, *f*

sponginess /'spʌndʒɪnɪs/ *n* esponjosidad, *f*

sponging /'spʌndʒɪŋ/ *n* esponjadura, *f*; *Inf.* sablazo, *m*

spongy /'spʌndʒi/ *a* esponjoso

sponsor /'spɒnsər/ *n* garante, *mf*; valedor (-ra), patron (-na); (godfather) padrino, *m*; (godmother) madrina, *f*, (radio and TV) auspiciador, patrocinador, *m*

spontaneity /,spɒntə'niɪti, -'neɪ-/ *n* espontaneidad, *f*

spontaneous /spɒn'teɪniəs/ *a* espontáneo. **s. combustion,** combustión espontánea, *f*

spontaneously /spɒn'teɪniəsli/ *adv* espontáneamente

spook /spuk/ *n* fantasma, espectro, *m*

spool /spul/ *n* (for thread) bobina, *f*, carrete, *m*; (in a sewing machine) canilla, *f*; (of a fishing rod) carrete, *m*

spoon /spun/ *n* cuchara, *f*. *vt* sacar con cuchara. *vi* (slang) besuquearse. **to s.-feed,** dar de comer con cuchara (a); tratar como un niño (a)

spoonful /'spunfʊl/ *n* cucharada, *f*

spoor /spʊr, spɔr/ *n* pista, huella de animal, *f*; rastro, *m*

sporadic /spə'rædɪk/ *a* esporádico

spore /spɔr/ *n Bot.* espora, *f*; *Zool.* germen, *m*

sport /spɔrt/ *n* deporte, sport, *m*; deportismo, *m*; (jest) broma, *f*; (game) juego, *m*; (plaything) juguete, *m*; (pastime) pasatiempo, *m*. *vi* jugar; recrearse, divertirse. *vt* llevar; ostentar, lucir. **He is a s.,** Es un buen chico. **to make s. of,** burlarse de. **sports car,** coche de deporte, *m*. **sports ground,** campo de recreo, *m*. **sports jacket,** chaqueta de deporte, americana, *f*. **sports shirt,** camisa corta, *f*

sporting /'spɔrtɪŋ/ *a* deportista; caballeroso. **I think**

there is a s. chance, Me parece que hay una posibilidad de éxito

sporting goods n artículos de deporte, efectos de deportes, m pl

sportive /'spɔrtɪv/ a juguetón; bromista

sportsman /'spɔrtsmən/ n deportista, m; aficionado al sport, m; Fig. caballero, señor, m; buen chico, m

sportsmanlike /'spɔrtsmən,laik/ a de deportista; caballeroso

sportsmanship /'spɔrtsmən,ʃɪp/ n deportividad, f

spot /spɒt/ n mancha, f; pinta, f; (on the face, etc.) peca, f; grano, m; (place) sitio, m; lugar, m; (of liquor) trago, m; (of food) bocado, m; (of rain) gota, f. vt manchar; motear; (recognize) reconocer; (understand) darse cuenta de, comprender. **a tender s.,** Fig. debilidad, f. **on the s.,** en el acto. **s. ball,** (billiards) pinta, f. **s. cash,** dinero contante, m

spotless /'spɒtlɪs/ a saltando de limpio; sin mancha; inmaculado; puro; virgen

spotlight /'spɒt,lait/ n luz del proyector, f; proyector, m

spotted /'spɒtɪd/ a (stained) manchado; (of animals, etc.) con manchas; (of garments, etc.) con pintas

spotty /'spɒti/ a lleno de manchas; moteado; (pimply) con granos

spouse /spaus/ n esposo, m; esposa, f

spout /spaut/ vi chorrear; Inf. hablar incesantemente. vt arrojar; vomitar; Inf. declamar, recitar. n (of a jug, etc.) pico, m; (for water, etc.) tubo, m, cañería, f; canalón, m; (gust) ráfaga, nube, f. **down s.,** tubo de bajada, m

spouting /'spautɪŋ/ n chorreo, m; Inf. declamación, f

sprain /sprein/ vt dislocar, torcer. n dislocación, f, esguince, m. **Victoria has sprained her foot,** Victoria se ha torcido el pie

sprawl /sprɔl/ vi recostarse (en); extenderse; (of plants) trepar. **He went sprawling,** Cayó cuan largo era

spray /sprei/ n (branch) ramo, m; (of water, etc.) rocío, m; (of the sea) espuma, f; (mechanical device) pulverizador, m. vt pulverizar; rociar; regar; (the throat) jeringar

spread /spred/ vt tender; cubrir (de); poner; (stretch out) extender; (open out) desplegar; (of disease, etc.) propagar; diseminar; divulgar, difundir. vi extenderse; propagarse; difundirse; divulgarse; (become general) generalizarse. n extensión, f; expansión, f; propagación, f; divulgación, f; (Aer. and of birds) envergadura, f. **Carmen s. her hands to the fire,** Carmen extendió las manos al fuego. **The peacock s. its tail,** El pavo real hizo la rueda. **The dove s. its wings,** La paloma desplegó sus alas. **to s. out,** vt extender; desplegar; (scatter) esparcir, vi extenderse. **spread like wildfire,** correr como pólvora en reguero, propagarse como un reguero de pólvora, ser un reguero de pólvora

spreading /'spredɪŋ/ n (of a disease) propagación, f; (of knowledge, etc.) divulgación, f; expansión, f; extensión, f

spreadsheet /'spred,ʃit/ n hoja de cálculo, f

spree /spri/ n juerga, parranda, f; excursión, f. **to go on the s.,** ir de juerga, ir de picos pardos

sprig /sprɪg/ n ramita, f; (of heather, etc.) espiga, f; (scion) vástago, m

sprightliness /'spraitlɪnɪs/ n vivacidad, f, despejo, m; energía, f

sprightly /'spraitli/ a vivaracho, despierto; enérgico

spring /sprɪŋ/ vi saltar, brincar; (become) hacerse; (seek) buscar; (of plants, water) brotar; (of tears) arrasar, llenar; (from) originarse (en), ser causado (por); inspirarse (en). vt (a mine) volar; (a trap) soltar. **to s. a surprise,** dar una sorpresa. **to s. a surprise on a person,** coger a la imprevista (a). **to s. at a person,** precipitarse sobre. **to s. to one's feet,** ponerse de pie de un salto. **to s. back,** saltar hacia atrás; recular; volver a su sitio. **to s. open,** abrirse súbitamente. **to s. up,** (of plants) brotar, crecer; (of difficulties, etc.) surgir, asomarse

spring /sprɪŋ/ n (jump) salto, brinco, m; (of water) fuente, f, manantial, m; (season) primavera, f; (of a watch, etc.) resorte, m; (of a mattress, etc.) muelle, m;

m. a primaveral. vi saltar, brincar. **at one s.,** en un salto. **to give a s.,** dar un salto. **s.-board,** trampolín, m. **s.-mattress,** colchón de muelles, m. **s.-tide,** marea viva, f

springiness /'sprɪŋinɪs/ n elasticidad, f

springlike /'sprɪŋ,laik/ a primaveral

springtime /'sprɪŋ,taim/ n primavera, f

sprinkle /'sprɪŋkəl/ vt esparcir; salpicar; rociar

sprinkling /'sprɪŋklɪŋ/ n salpicadura, f; rociadura, f; pequeño número, m. **a s. of snow,** una nevada ligera

sprint /sprɪnt/ vi sprintar. n sprint, m

sprite /sprait/ n trasgo, m; hada, f

sprout /spraut/ vi brotar, despuntar, retoñar, tallecer; germinar. vt salir. n brote, retoño, pimpollo, m; germen, m. **Brussels sprouts,** coles de Bruselas, f pl

spruce /sprus/ a peripuesto, muy aseado, pulido; elegante, n Bot. pícea, f. **to s. oneself up,** arreglarse, ponerse elegante

spruceness /'sprusnɪs/ n aseo, buen parecer, m, elegancia, f

spry /sprai/ a activo, ágil

spur /spɜr/ n espuela, f; aguijada, f; (of a bird) espolón, m; Bot. espuela, f; (of a mountain range) espolón, estribo, m; Fig. estímulo, m. vt espolear, picar con la espuela; calzarse las espuelas; Fig. estimular, incitar, Lat. Am. espuelar. **on the s. of the moment,** bajo el impulso del momento

spurious /'spyʊriəs/ a espurio; falso

spurn /spɜrn/ vt rechazar; tratar con desprecio; menospreciar

spurt /spɜrt/ vi (gush) chorrear, borbotar; brotar, surgir; (in racing, etc.) hacer un esfuerzo supremo. vt hacer chorrear; lanzar. n (jet) chorro, m; esfuerzo supremo, m

sputter /'spʌtər/ vi chisporrotear; crepitar; (of a pen) escupir; (of a person) balbucir

sputtering /'spʌtərɪŋ/ n chisporroteo, m; crepitación, f; (of a person) balbuceo, m

sputum /'spyutəm/ n esputo, m

spy /spai/ vt observar, discernir. vi espiar, ser espía. n espía, mf. **to spy out the land,** explorar el terreno. **to spy upon,** espiar; seguir los pasos (a). **spy-glass,** catalejo, m

spying /'spaiɪŋ/ n espionaje, m

squabble /'skwɒbəl/ n disputa, f; riña, f. vi pelearse; disputar

squabbling /'skwɒblɪŋ/ n riñas, querellas, f pl; disputas, f pl

squad /skwɒd/ n escuadra, f; pelotón, m

squadron /'skwɒdrən/ n Mil. escuadrón, m; Nav. escuadra, f; Aer. escuadrilla, f; (of persons) pelotón, m. **s.-leader,** comandante, m

squalid /'skwɒlɪd/ a escuálido; (of quarrels, etc.) sórdido, mezquino

squall /skwɔl/ vi berrear, chillar. n berrido, m; chillido, m; (storm) chubasco, turbión, f; (storm) chubasco, turbión, m; Fig. tormenta, tempestad, f

squalor /'skwɒlər/ n escualidez, f; sordidez, mezquindad, f

squander /'skwɒndər/ vt derrochar, tirar, desperdiciar; (time, etc.) malgastar

squanderer /'skwɒndərər/ n derrochador (-ra)

squandering /'skwɒndərɪŋ/ n derroche, desperdicio, dispendio, m; (of time, etc.) pérdida, f, desperdicio, m

square /skwɛər/ n Math. cuadrado, m; rectángulo, m; (of a chessboard) escaque, m; (of a draftboard and of graph paper) casilla, f; (in a town) plaza, f; (of troops) cuadro, m, a cuadrado; justo; igual; (honest) honrado, formal; (unambiguous) redondo, categórico; Math. cuadrado, m. **She wore a silk s. on her head,** Llevaba un pañuelo de seda en la cabeza. **five s. feet,** cinco pies cuadrados. **nine feet s.,** nueve pies en cuadro. adv. honradamente. **a s. dance,** contradanza, f. **a s. meal,** una buena comida. **s. dealing,** trato limpio, m. **The account is s.,** La cuenta está justa. **to get s. with,** desquitarse (de), vengarse de. **s. measure,** medida de superficie, f. **s. root,** raíz cuadrada, f. **s.-shouldered,** de hombros cuadrados

square /skwɛər/ vt cuadrar; escuadrar; (arrange) arreglar; (bribe) sobornar; (reconcile) acomodar; Math. cuadrar. vi conformarse (con), cuadrar (con). **to s.**

the circle, cuadrar el círculo. **to s. one's shoulders,** enderezarse. **to s. accounts with,** saldar cuentas con. **to s. up to,** (a person) avanzar belicosamente hacia
squarely /'skwɛərli/ *adv* en cuadro; directamente; sin ambigüedades, rotundamente; (honestly) de buena fe, honradamente
squareness /'skwɛərnɪs/ *n* cuadratura, *f*; (honesty) honradez, buena fe, *f*
squash /skwɒʃ/ *vt* aplastar. *vi* aplastarse; apretarse. *n* aplastamiento, *m*; (of fruit, etc.) pulpa, *f*; (of people) agolpamiento, *m*; muchedumbre, *f*; (drink) refresco (de limón, etc.), *m*, (sport) frontón con raqueta, *m*
squashy /'skwɒʃi/ *a* blando y húmedo
squat /skwɒt/ *vi* acuclillarse, agacharse, agazaparse ponerse en cuclillas; estar en cuclillas; (on land, etc.) apropiarse sin derecho. *a* rechoncho
squatter /'skwɒtər/ *n* intruso (-sa); colono usurpador, *m*
squatter town *n*. See **shanty town**
squawk /skwɔk/ *vi* graznar; lanzar gritos agudos. *n* graznido, *m*; grito agudo, *m*
squeak /skwik/ *vi* (of carts, etc.) chirriar, rechinar; (of shoes) crujir; (of persons, mice, etc.) chillar; (slang) cantar. *n* chirrido, crujido, *m*; chillido, *m*. **to have a narrow s.,** escapar por un pelo
squeaking /'skwikɪŋ/ *n* chirrido, rechinamiento, *m*; crujido, *m*; (of humans, mice, etc.) chillidos, *m pl*
squeal /skwil/ *vi* lanzar gritos agudos, chillar; (complain) quejarse; (slang) cantar. *n* grito agudo, chillido, *m*
squealing /'skwilɪŋ/ *n* gritos agudos, chillidos, *m pl*
squeamish /'skwimɪʃ/ *a* que se marea fácilmente; mareado; (nauseated) asqueado; delicado; remilgado
squeamishness /'skwimɪʃnɪs/ *n* tendencia a marearse, *f*; delicadeza, *f*; remilgos, *m pl*
squeeze /skwiz/ *vt* apretar; estrujar; (fruit) exprimir; (extort) arrancar; (money from) sangrar. *n* (of the hand, etc.) apretón, *m*; estrujón, *m*; (of fruit juice) algunas gotas (de). **It was a tight s. in the car,** Íbamos muy apretados en el coche. **He was in a tight s.,** Se encontraba en un aprieto. **to s. one's way through the crowd,** abrirse camino a codazos por la muchedumbre. **to s. in,** *vt* hacer sitio para. *vi* introducirse con dificultad (en)
squelch /skwɛltʃ/ *vi* gorgotear, chapotear. *vt* aplastar
squib /skwɪb/ *n* (firework) rapapiés, buscapiés, *m*; (lampoon) pasquinada, *f*
squid /skwɪd/ *n* calamar, *m*
squiggle /'skwɪgəl/ *vi* cimbrearse, menear
squint /skwɪnt/ *n* estrabismo, *m*; mirada furtiva, *f*; *Inf.* vistazo, *m*, mirada, *f*. *vi* ser bizco; bizcar. **to s. at,** mirar de soslayo. **s.-eyed,** bizco. **to be s.-eyed,** mirar contra el gobierno
squire /skwaɪər/ *n* escudero, *m*; hacendado, *m*. *vt* escoltar, acompañar
squirm /skwɜrm/ *vi* retorcerse; (with embarrassment) no saber dónde meterse. *n* retorcimiento, *m*. **to s. along the ground,** arrastrarse por el suelo
squirrel /'skwɜrəl// *n* ardilla, *f*
squirt /skwɜrt/ *vt* (liquids) lanzar. *vi* chorrear, salir a chorros. *n* chorro, *m*; (syringe) jeringa, *f*
stab /stæb/ *vt* apuñalar, dar de puñaladas (a); herir. *n* puñalada, *f*; herida, *f*; (of pain, and *Fig.*) pinchzo, *m*. **a s. in the back,** una puñalada por la espalda
stability /stə'bɪliti/ *n* estabilidad, *f*; solidez, firmeza, *f*
stabilize /'steibə,laiz/ *vt* estabilizar
stable /'steibəl/ *a* estable; fijo, firme. *n* cuadra, caballeriza, *f*; (for cows, etc.) establo, *m*. *vt* poner en la cuadra; alojar. **s.-boy,** mozo de cuadra, *m*
stack /stæk/ *n* (of hay) niara, *f*, almiar, *m*; (heap) montón, *m*; (of rifles) pabellón, *m*; (of a chimney) cañón, *m*. *vt Agr.* hacinar; amontonar; *Mil.* poner (las armas) en pabellón
stacked /stækt/ *a* (woman) abultada de pechera
stadium /'steidiəm/ *n* estadio, *m*
staff /stæf/ *n* vara, *f*; (bishop's, and *Fig.*) báculo, *m*; (pilgrim's) bordón, *m*; (pole) palo, *m*; (flagstaff) asta, *f*; (of an office, etc.) personal, *m*; (editorial) redacción, *f*; (corps) cuerpo, *m*; *Mil.* plana mayor, *f*, estado mayor, *m*; *Mus.* pentagrama, *m*. *vt* proveer de

personal. **general s.,** estado mayor general, *m*. **s. officer,** *Mil.* oficial de estado mayor, *m*
stag /stæg/ *n* ciervo, *m*. **s.-beetle,** ciervo volante, *m*. **s.-hunting,** caza del ciervo, *f*
stage /steidʒ/ *n* (for workmen) andamio, *m*; (of a microscope) portaobjetos, *m*; *Theat.* escena, *f*, tablas, *f pl*; teatro, *m*; (of development, etc.) etapa, *f*; fase, *f*. *vt Theat.* escenificar, poner en escena; *Theat.* representar; (a demonstration, etc.) arreglar. **by easy stages,** poco a poco; (of a journey) a pequeñas etapas. **to come on the s.,** salir a la escena. **to go on the s.,** hacerse actor (actriz), dedicarse al teatro. **s. carpenter,** tramoyista, *m*. **s.-coach,** diligencia, *f*. **s.-craft,** arte de escribir para el teatro, *f*; arte escénica, *f*. **s.-direction,** acotación, *f*. **s.-door,** entrada de los artistas, *f*. **s.-effect,** efecto escénico, *m*. **s.-fright,** miedo al público, *m*. **s.-hand,** tramoyista, sacasillas, metesillas y sacamuertos, *m*. **s. manager,** director de escena, *m*. **s.-whisper,** aparte, *m*
stagger /'stægər/ *vi* tambalear; andar haciendo eses; (hesitate) titubear, vacilar. *vt* desconcertar. *n* titubeo, tambaleo, *m*; *Aer.* decalaje, *m*. **staggered working hours,** horas de trabajo escalonadas, *f pl*
staggering /'stægərɪŋ/ *a* tambaleante; (surprising) asombroso, sorprendente; (dreadful) espantoso. **a s. blow,** un golpe que derriba
staging /'steidʒɪŋ/ *n* (scaffolding) andamio, *m*; *Theat.* producción, *f*; representación, *f*; decorado, *m*
stagnancy /'stægnənsi/ *n* (of water) estancación, *f*; (inactivity) estancación, *f*; paralización, *f*
stagnant /'stægnənt/ *a* estancado; paralizado. **to be s.,** estar estancado. **s. water,** agua estancada, *f*
stagnate /'stægneit/ *vi* estancarse; (of persons) vegetar
stagnation /stæg'neiʃən/ *n* (of water) estancación, *f*; estagnación, *f*; parálisis, *f*
staid /steid/ *a* serio, formal, juicioso
staidness /'steidnɪs/ *n* seriedad, formalidad, *f*
stain /stein/ *vt* manchar; (dye) teñir. *n* mancha, *f*; colorante, *m*. **without a s.,** *Fig.* sin mancha. **stained glass,** vidrio de color, *m*. **s.-remover,** quitamanchas, *m*
stainless /'steinlis/ *a* sin mancha; inmaculado, puro
stair /stɛər/ *n* escalón, peldaño, *m*; escalera, *f*; *pl* **stairs,** escalera, *f*. **a flight of stairs,** una escalera, un tramo de escaleras. **below stairs,** escalera abajo. **s.-carpet,** alfombra de escalera, *f*. **s.-rod,** varilla para alfombra de escalera, *f*
staircase /'stɛər,keis/ *n* escalera, *f*. **spiral s.,** escalera de caracol, *f*
stake /steik/ *n* estaca, *f*; (for plants) rodrigón, *m*; (gaming) envite, *m*, apuesta, *f*; (in an undertaking) interés, *m*; *pl* **stakes,** (prize) premio, *m*; (race) carrera, *f*. *vt* estacar; (plants) rodrigar; (bet) jugar. **at s.,** en juego; en peligro. **to be burnt at the s.,** morir en la hoguera. **to s. one's all,** jugarse el todo por el todo. **to s. a claim,** hacer una reclamación. **to s. out,** jalonar
stalactite /stə'læktait/ *n* estalactita, *f*
stalagmite /stə'lægmait/ *n* estalagmita, *f*
stale /steil/ *a* no fresco; (of bread, etc.) duro, seco; (of air) viciado; viejo; pasado de moda; (tired) cansado
stalemate /'steil,meit/ *n* (chess, checkers) tablas, *f pl*; *Fig.* punto muerto, *m*. **to reach a s.,** llegar a un punto muerto
staleness /'steilnɪs/ *n* rancidez, *f*; (of bread, etc.) dureza, *f*; (of news, etc.) falta de novedad, *f*
stalk /stɔk/ *n Bot.* tallo, *m*; *Bot.* pedúnculo, *m*; (of a glass) pie, *m*. *vi* andar majestuosamente; *Fig.* rondar. *vt* (game) cazar al acecho; (a person) seguir los pasos (a)
stalking horse /'stɔkɪŋ/ *n* boezuelo, *m*; *Fig.* pretexto, disfraz, *m*
stall /stɔl/ *n* (in a stable) puesto (individual), *m*; (stable) establo, *m*; (choir) silla de coro, *f*; (in a fair, etc.) barraca, *f*, puesto, *m*; *Theat.* butaca, *f*; (finger-stall) dedal, *m*. *vt* (an engine) cortar accidentalmente. *vi Auto.* pararse de pronto; *Aer.* perder velocidad. *vi* atascarse. **pit s.,** *Theat.* butaca de platea, *f*
stalling /'stɔlɪŋ/ *n Auto.* parada accidental, *f*; *Aer.* pérdida de velocidad, *f*. **Stop s.!** ¡Déjate de rodeos!

stallion /'stælyən/ *n* semental, *m*

stalwart /'stɔlwərt/ *a* robusto, fornido; leal; valiente

stalwartness /'stɔlwərtnɪs/ *n* robustez, *f*; lealtad, *f*; valor, *m*

stamina /'stæmənə/ *n* resistencia, *f*

stammer /'stæmər/ *vi* tartamudear; (hesitate in speaking) titubear, balbucir. *n* tartamudez, *f*; titubeo, balbuceo, *m*

stammerer /'stæmərər/ *n* tartamudo (-da)

stammering /'stæmərɪŋ/ *a* tartamudo; balbuciente. *n* tartamudeo, *m*; balbuceo, *m*

stamp /stæmp/ *vt* estampar; imprimir; (documents) timbrar; pegar el sello de correo (a); (characterize) sellar; (*Fig.* engrave) grabar; (coins) acuñar; (press) apisonar; (with the foot) golpear con los pies, patear; (in dancing) zapatear. *n* (with the foot) patada, *f*, golpe con los pies, *m*; (mark, etc.) marca, *f*; (rubber, etc.) estampilla, *f*; matasellos, *m*; cuño, *m*; (for documents) póliza, *f*; timbre, *m*; (for letters) sello, *m*; *Mexico* timbre, *m*, *elsewhere in Lat. Am.* estampilla, *f*, (machine) punzón, *m*; mano de mortero, *f*; (*Fig.* sign) sello, *m*; (kind) temple, *m*, clase, *f.* **The events of that day are stamped on my memory,** Los acontecimientos de aquel día están grabados en mi memoria. **to s. out,** (a fire, etc.) extinguir, apagar; (resistance, etc.) vencer; destruir. **postage-s.,** sello de correos, *m.* **s.-album,** álbum de sellos, *m.* **s.-duty,** impuesto del timbre, *m.* **s.-machine,** expendedor automático de sellos de correo, *m*

stampede /stæm'pid/ *n* fuga precipitada, *f*; pánico, *m. vi* huir precipitadamente; (of animals) salir de estampía; huir en desorden. *vt* hacer perder la cabeza (a), sembrar el pánico entre

stamping /'stæmpɪŋ/ *n* selladura, *f*; (of documents) timbrado, *m*; (of fabrics, etc.) estampado, *m*; (with the feet) pataleo, *m*; (in dancing) zapateo, *m*

stance /stæns/ *n* posición de los pies, *f*; postura, *f*

stanch /stɔntʃ/ *vt* restañar

stand /stænd/ *vi* estar de pie; ponerse de pie, incorporarse; estar; hallarse; sostenerse; ser; ponerse; (halt) parar; (remain) permanecer, quedar. *vt* poner; (endure) resistir; tolerar; sufrir; (entertain) convidar. **S.!** ¡Alto! **S. up!** ¡Ponte de pie! **as things s.,** tal como están las cosas. **I cannot s. any more,** No puedo más. **I cannot s. him,** No le puedo ver. **Nothing stands between them and ruin,** No hay nada entre ellos y la ruina. **I stood him a drink,** Le convidé a un trago. **How do we s.?** ¿Cómo estamos? **It stands to reason that...,** Es lógico que... **Edward stands six feet,** Eduardo tiene seis pies de altura. **to s. accused of,** ser acusado de. **to s. godfather (or godmother) to,** sacar de pila (a). **to s. in need (of),** necesitar, tener necesidad (de). **to s. on end,** (of hair) ponerse de punta, despeluzarse. **to s. one in good stead,** ser útil, ser ventajoso. **to s. one's ground,** no ceder, tenerse fuerte. **to s. to attention,** cuadrarse, permanecer en posición de firmes. **to s. well with,** tener buenas relaciones con, ser estimado de. **to s. aside,** tenerse a un lado; apartarse; (in favor of someone) retirarse. **to s. back,** quedarse atrás; recular, retroceder. **to s. by,** estar de pie cerca de; estar al lado de; estar presente (sin intervenir); ser espectador; estar preparado; (one's friends) ayudar, proteger; (a promise, etc.) atenerse (a); ser fiel (a); (of a ship) mantenerse listo. **s.-by,** *n* recurso, *m.* **to s. for,** representar; simbolizar; (mean) significar; (Parliament, etc.) presentar como candidato; (put up with) tolerar, sufrir. **to s. in,** colaborar. **to s. in with,** estar de acuerdo con, ser partidario de; compartir. **to s. off,** mantenerse a distancia. **to s. out,** (in relief, and *Fig.* of persons) destacarse; (be firm) resistir, mantenerse firme; *Naut.* gobernar más afuera. **S. out of the way!** ¡Quítate del medio! **to s. over,** (be postponed) quedar aplazado. **to s. up,** estar de pie; ponerse de pie, incorporarse; tenerse derecho. **to s. up against,** resistir; oponerse a. **to s. up for,** defender. **to s. up to,** hacer cara a

stand /stænd/ *n* puesto, *m*; posición, actitud, *f*; (for taxis, etc.) punto, *m*; (in a market, etc.) puesto, *m*; *Sports.* tribuna, *f*; (for a band) quiosco, *m*; (of a dish, etc.) pie, *m*; *Mech.* sostén, *f*; (opposition) resistencia, oposición, *f.* **to make a s. against,** oponerse re-

sueltamente (a); ofrecer resistencia (a). **to take one's s.,** fundarse (en), apoyarse (en). **to take up one's s. by the fire,** ponerse cerca del fuego

standard /'stændərd/ *n* (flag) estandarte, *m*, bandera, *f*; (for gold, weights, etc.) marco, *m*; norma, *f*; convención, regla, *f*; (of a lamp) pie, *m*; (pole) poste, *m*; columna, *f*; (level) nivel, *m. a* corriente; normal; típico; clásico. **It is a s. type,** Es un tipo corriente. **gold s.,** patrón de oro, *m.* **s. author,** autor clásico, *m.* **s. formula,** fórmula clásica, *f.* **s. of living,** nivel de vida, *m.* **s.-bearer,** abanderado, *m.* **s.-lamp,** lámpara vertical, *f*

standardization /ˌstændərdə'zeifən/ *n* (of armaments, etc.) unificación de tipos, *f*; (of dyestuffs, medicinals, etc.) control, *m*, estandardización, *f*

standardize /'stændərˌdaiz/ *vt* hacer uniforme; controlar

standing /'stændɪŋ/ *a* de pie, derecho; permanente, fijo; constante. *n* posición, *f*; reputación, *f*; importancia, *f*; antigüedad, *f.* **It is a quarrel of long s.,** Es una riña antigua. **s. committee,** comisión permanente, *f.* **s. room,** sitio para estar de pie, *m.* **s. water,** agua estancada, *f.* **standoffish,** frío, etiquetero; altanero. **stand-offishness,** frialdad, *f*; altanería, *f.* **standpoint,** punto de vista, *m*

standstill /'stændˌstɪl/ *n* parada, *f*; pausa, *f.* **at a s.,** parado; (of industry) paralizado

stanza /'stænzə/ *n* estrofa, estancia, *f*

staple /'steipəl/ *n* (fastener) grapa, *f*; (of wool, etc.) hebra, fibra, *f*; producto principal (de un país), *m*; (raw material) materia prima, *f*; *a* principal; más importante; corriente

stapler /'steiplər/, (device) cosepapeles, engrapador, *m*, atrochadora (Argentina), *f*

star /star/ *n* (all meanings) estrella, *f*; (asterisk) asterisco, *m. vt* estrellar, sembrar de estrellas; marcar con asterisco. *vi* (*Theat.* cinema) presentarse como estrella, ser estrella. **stars and stripes,** las barras y las estrellas. **to be born under a lucky s.,** tener estrella. **to see stars,** ver estrellas. **s.-gazing,** observación de las estrellas, *f*; ensimismamiento, *m.* **s.-spangled,** estrellado, tachonado de estrellas, sembrado de estrellas. **s.-turn,** gran atracción, *f*

starboard /'starbərd/ *n Naut.* estribor, *m*

starch /startʃ/ *n* almidón, *m*, las harinas, *f pl, vt* almidonar

starchy /'startʃi/ *a* almidonado, *f*; (of food) feculento; *Fig.* tieso, entonado, etiquetero

stare /steər/ *vi* mirar fijamente; abrir mucho los ojos. *n* mirada fija, *f.* **stony s.,** mirada dura, *f.* **to s. at,** (a person) clavar la mirada en; mirar de hito en hito (a). **The explanation stares one in the face,** La explicación salta a la vista (or está evidente). **to s. into space,** mirar las telarañas. **to s. out of countenance,** avergonzar con la mirada

starfish /'starˌfiʃ/ *n* estrella de mar, *f*

staring /'steərɪŋ/ *a* (of colors) chillón, llamativo, encendido. **s. eyes,** ojos saltones, *m pl*; ojos espantados, *m pl*

stark /stark/ *a* rígido; *Poet.* poderoso; absoluto. **s. staring mad,** loco de atar. **s.-naked,** en cueros vivos, en pelota

starless /'starlɪs/ *a* sin estrellas

starlight /'starˌlait/ *n* luz de las estrellas, *f*, *a* estrellado

starry /'stari/ *a* estrellado, sembrado de estrellas

start /start/ *vi* (begin) empezar, comenzar; (upset) estremecerse, asustarse; saltar; (set out) salir; ponerse en camino; (of a train, a race) arrancar; ponerse en marcha; *Aer.* despegar; (of timbers) combarse. *vt* empezar; (a car, etc.) poner en marcha; (a race) dar la señal de partida; (a hare, etc.) levantar; (cause) provocar, causar; (a discussion, etc.) abrir; iniciar. *n* (fright) susto, *m*; (setting out) partida, salida, *f*; (beginning) principio, comienzo, *m*; (starting-point of a race) arrancadero, *m*; -*Aer.* despegue, *m*; (advantage) ventaja, *f.* **at the s.,** al principio. **for a s.,** para empezar. **from s. to finish,** desde el principio hasta el fin. **She started to cry,** Se puso a llorar. **He has started his journey to Canada,** Ha empezado su viaje al Canadá. **I started up the engine,** Puse el motor en marcha. **to get a s.,** asustarse; tomar la delantera. **to give** (a person) **a s.,** asustar, dar un susto (a); dar la ventaja (a). **to give** (a person) **a s. in life,** ayudar a alguien a situarse en la vida. **to make a fresh s. (in life),** hacer vida nueva, empezar la vida de nuevo. **to s. after,** lanzarse en busca de; salir tras. **to s. back,** retroceder; emprender el viaje de regreso; marcharse. **to s. off,** salir, partir; ponerse en camino. **to s. up,** *vi* incorporarse bruscamente, ponerse de pie de un salto; (appear) surgir, aparecer. *vt* (an engine) poner en marcha

starter /'stɑrtər/ *n* iniciador (-ra); (for a race) starter, juez de salida, *m*; (competitor in a race) corredor, *m*; (of a car, etc.) arranque, *m*

starting /'stɑrtɪŋ/ *n* (setting out) salida, partida, *f*; (beginning) principio, *m*; (fear) estremecimiento, *m*; susto, *m*. **s.-gear,** palanca de arranque, *f*. **s.-handle,** manivela de arranque, *f*. **s.-point,** punto de partida, *m*; *Fig.* arrancadero, punto de arranque, *m*. **s.-post,** puesto de salida, *m*

startle /'stɑrtl/ *vt* asustar, sobresaltar, alarmar. **The news startled him out of his indifference,** Las noticias le hicieron salir de su indiferencia

startling /'stɑrtlɪŋ/ *a* alarmante; (of dress, etc.) exagerado; (of colors) chillón

starvation /stɑr'veɪʃən/ *n* hambre, *f*; *Med.* inanición, *f*. **s. diet,** régimen de hambre, *m*. **s. wage,** ración de hambre, *f*

starve /stɑrv/ *vi* morir de hambre; pasar hambre, no tener bastante que comer; no comer. *vt* matar de hambre; privar de alimentos (a). **I am simply starving,** Tengo una hambre canina, Me muero de hambre. **to s. with cold,** *vi* morir de frío. *vt* matar de frío

starved /stɑrvd/ *a* muerto de hambre, hambriento. **s. of affection,** hambriento de cariño

starving /'stɑrvɪŋ/ *a* que muere de hambre, hambriento

state /steɪt/ *n* estado, *m*; condición, *f*; (anxiety) agitación, ansiedad, *f*; (social) rango, *m*; (pomp) magnificencia, pompa, *f*; (government, etc.) Estado, *m*; nación, *f*. *a* de Estado; de gala, de ceremonia. **the married s.,** el estado matrimonial. **s. of war,** estado de guerra. **in s.,** con gran pompa. **to lie in s.,** (of a body) estar expuesto. **s. apartments,** habitaciones de gala, *f pl.* **s. banquet,** comida de gala, *f.* **s. coach,** coche de gala, *m.* **s. control,** control por el Estado, *m.* **S. Department,** Departamento de Estado, *m.* **s. education,** instrucción pública, *f.* **State of the Union message,** Mensaje al Congreso, *m.* **s. papers,** documentos de Estado, *m pl*

state /steɪt/ *vt* decir (que), afirmar (que); declarar; (one's case, etc.) exponer; explicar; *Math.* proponer

statecraft /'steɪt,kræft/ *n* arte de gobernar, *m*

stated /'steɪtɪd/ *a* arreglado, indicado; fijo. **the s. date,** la fecha indicada. **at s. intervals,** a intervalos fijos

statehood /'steɪthʊd/ *n* estadidad, *f*

stateliness /'steɪtlɪnɪs/ *n* dignidad, *f*; majestad, *f*

stately /'steɪtli/ *a* majestuoso; imponente; noble; digno

statement /'steɪtmənt/ *n* afirmación, declaración, *f*; resumen, *m*; exposición, *f*; *Law.* deposición, *f*; *Com.* estado de cuenta, *m*. **to make a s.,** hacer una declaración

stateroom /'steɪt,rum/ *n* sala de recepción, *f*; (on a ship) camarote, *m*

statesman /'steɪtsmən/ *n* hombre de estado, *m*

statesmanlike /'steɪtsmən,laɪk/ *a* de hombre de estado

statesmanship /'steɪtsmən,ʃɪp/ *n* arte de gobernar, *m*

static /'stætɪk/ *a* estático

statics /'stætɪks/ *n* estática, *f*

station /'steɪʃən/ *n* (place) puesto, sitio, *m*; (*Rail.* and *Eccl.*) estación, *f*; (social) posición social, *f*; *Naut.* apostadero, *m*; *Surv.* punto de marca, *m*. *vt* estacionar, colocar, poner. **to s. oneself,** colocarse. **Stations of the Cross,** Estaciones, *f pl.* **s.-master,** jefe de la estación, *m*

stationary /'steɪʃə,nɛri/ *a* estacionario; inmóvil; *Astron.* estacional

stationer /'steɪʃənər/ *n* papelero (-ra). **stationer's shop,** papelería, *f*

stationery /'steɪʃə,nɛri/ *n* (shop) papelería, *f*, efectos de escritorio, *m pl*; (paper) papel de escribir, *m*

station wagon *n* pisicorre, coche camioneta, coche rural, *m*

statistical /stə'tɪstɪkəl/ *a* estadístico

statistician /,stætɪ'stɪʃən/ *n* estadista, *m*

statistics /stə'tɪstɪks/ *n* estadística, *f*

statuary /'stætʃu,ɛri/ *a* estatuario. *n* estatuaria, *f*; estatuas, *f pl*; (sculptor) estatuario, *m*

statue /'stætʃu/ *n* estatua, *f*; imagen, *f*

statuesque /,stætʃu'ɛsk/ *a* escultural

statuette /,stætʃu'ɛt/ *n* figurilla, *f*

stature /'stætʃər/ *n* estatura, *f*; (moral, etc.) valor, *m*

status /'steɪtəs, 'stætəs/ *n* (*Law.* etc.) estado, *m*; posición, *f*; rango, *m*. **What is his s. as a physicist?** ¿Cómo se le considera entre los físicos? **social s.,** posición social, *f*; rango social, *m*

statute /'stætʃut/ *n* ley, *f*; acto legislativo, *m*; estatuto, *m*; regla, *f*. **s. book,** código legal, *m*

statutory /'stætʃʊ,tɔri/ *a* establecido; reglamentario; estatutario

staunch /stɔntʃ/ *a* leal, fiel; firme, constante. *vt* restañar

staunchness /'stɔntʃnɪs/ *n* lealtad, fidelidad, *f*; firmeza, *f*

stave /steɪv/ *n* (of a barrel, etc.) duela, *f*; (of a ladder) peldaño, *m*; (stanza) estrofa, *f*; *Mus.* pentagrama, *m*. **to s. in,** abrir boquete en; romper a golpes; quebrar. **to s. off,** apartar, alejar; (delay) aplazar, diferir; (avoid) evitar; (thirst, etc.) dominar

stay /steɪ/ *vt* detener; (a judgment, etc.) suspender. *vi* permanecer; quedarse; detenerse; (of weather, etc.) durar; (lodge) hospedarse, vivir. **to come to s.,** venir a ser permanente. **to s. a person's hand,** detenerle a fulano el brazo. **to s. at home,** quedarse en casa. **s.-at-home,** *a* casero. *n* persona casera, *f.* **to s. the course,** terminar la carrera. **S.! Say no more!** ¡Calle! ¡No diga más! **to s. away,** ausontarse. **to s. up,** no acostarse; velar. **to s. with,** quedarse con; alojarse con; quedarse en casa de, vivir con

stay /steɪ/ *n* estancia, permanencia, *f*; residencia, *f*; (restraint) freno, *m*; *Law.* suspensión, *f*; (endurance) aguante, *m*, resistencia, *f*; *Naut.* estay, *m*; (prop) puntal, *m*; *Fig.* apoyo, soporte, *m*; *pl* **stays,** corsé, *m*

stead /stɛd/ *n* lugar, *m*. **in the s. of,** en el lugar de, como substituto de. **It has stood me in good s.,** Me ha sido muy útil

steadfast /'stɛd,fæst/ *a* fijo; constante; firme; tenaz. **s. gaze,** mirada fija, *f*

steadfastly /'stɛd,fæstli/ *adv* fijamente; con constancia; firmemente; tenazmente

steadfastness /'stɛd,fæstnɪs/ *n* fijeza, *f*; constancia, *f*; firmeza, *f*; tenacidad, *f*

steadily /'stɛdɪli/ *adv* firmemente; (without stopping) sin parar; continuamente; (assiduously) diligentemente; (uniformly) uniformemente. **Prices have gone up s.,** Los precios no han dejado de subir. **He looked at it s.,** Lo miraba sin pestañear (or fijamente)

steadiness /'stɛdinɪs/ *n* estabilidad, *f*; firmeza, *f*; constancia, *f*; (of persons) seriedad, formalidad, *f*; (of workers) diligencia, asiduidad, *f*

steady /'stɛdi/ *a* firme; seguro; fijo; constante; uniforme; continuo; estacionario; (of persons) serio, formal, juicioso; (of workers) diligente, asiduo. *vt* afirmar; (persons) hacer más serio (a); (nerves, etc.) calmar, fortificar. **a s. job,** un empleo seguro. **S.!** ¡Calma!; *Naut.* ¡Seguro! **He steadied himself against the table,** Se apoyó en la mesa

steak /steɪk/ *n* tajada, *f*; biftec, *Argentina* bife, *m*

steal /stil/ *vt* robar, hurtar; tomar. *vi* robar, ser ladrón; (glide) deslizarse; (overwhelm) dominar, ganar insensiblemente. **to s. a kiss,** robar un beso. **to s. a look at,** mirar de soslayo (or de lado). **to s. away,** escurrirse, escabullirse; marcharse a hurtadillas. **to s. in,** deslizarse en, colarse en

stealthily /'stɛlθəli/ *adv* a hurtadillas; a escondidas, furtivamente

stealthiness /'stɛlθinɪs/ *n* carácter furtivo, *m*

stealthy /'stɛlθi/ *a* furtivo; cauteloso

steam /stim/ *n* vapor, *m*. *a* de vapor. *vi* echar vapor. *vt Cul.* cocer al vapor; (clothes) mojar; (windows, etc.) empañar. **to have the s. up,** estar bajo presión. **The windows are steamed,** Los cristales están empañados. **s.-boiler,** caldera de vapor, *f.* **s.-engine,** máquina de vapor, *f.* **s.-hammer,** maza de fragua, *f.* **s.-heat,** calefacción por vapor, *f.* **s.-roller,** *Lit.* apisonadora, *Fig.* fuerza arrolladora, *f*

steamboat /'stim₁bout/ *n* vapor, *m*

steamer /'stimər/ *n Cul.* marmita al vacío, *f; Naut.* buque de vapor, *m*

steamship /'stim₁ʃip/ *n* buque de vapor, piróscafo, *m*

steamy /'stimi/ *a* lleno de vapor

steed /stid/ *n* corcel, *m*

steel /stil/ *n* (metal, and *Poet.* sword) acero, *m*; (for sharpening) afilón, *m. a* de acero; acerado. *vt* acerar; *Fig.* endurecer. **to be made of s.,** *Fig.* ser de bronce. **He cannot s. himself to do it,** No puede persuadirse a hacerlo. **to s. one's heart,** hacerse duro de corazón. **cold s.,** arma blanca, *f.* **stainless s.,** acero inoxidable, *m.* **s.-engraving,** grabado en acero, *m*

steel mill *n* fábrica de acero, *f*

steep /stip/ *a* acantilado, escarpado; precipitoso; (of stairs, etc.) empinado; (of price) exorbitante. *vt* (soak) remojar, empapar; *Fig.* absorber; (in a subject) empaparse (en). *n* remojo, *m.* **It's a bit s.!** *Inf.* ¡Es un poco demasiado!

steeping /'stipiŋ/ *n* remojo, *m,* maceración, *f*

steeple /'stipəl/ *n* campanario, *m,* torre, *f;* aguja, *f*

steeplechase /'stipəl₁tʃeis/ *n* steeplechase, *m,* carrera de obstáculos, *f*

steepness /'stipnis/ *n* carácter escarpado, *m,* lo precipitoso

steer /stiər/ *vt Naut.* gobernar; (a car, etc.) conducir; *Fig.* guiar, conducir. *vi Naut.* timonear; *Naut.* navegar; *Auto.* conducir. *n Zool.* novillo, *m.* **to s. clear of,** evitar. **to s. one's way through the crowd,** abrirse paso entre la muchedumbre

steerage /'stiəridʒ/ *n* gobierno, *m;* (stern) popa, *f;* (quarters) entrepuente, *m.* **to go s.,** viajar en tercera clase

steering /'stiriŋ/ *n Naut.* gobierno, *m;* (tiller, etc.) gobernalle, timón, *m;* (of a vehicle) conducción, *f.* **s.-column,** barra de dirección, *f;* **s.-wheel,** *Auto.* volante de dirección, *m; Naut.* rueda del timón, *f*

stellar /'stelər/ *a* estelar

stem /stem/ *n* (of a tree) tronco, *m;* (of a plant) tallo, *m;* (of a glass, etc.) pie, *m;* (*Mus.* of a note) rabo, *m;* (of a pipe) tubo, *m;* (of a word) radical, *m. vt* (check) contener; (the tide) ir contra; (the current) vencer; (dam) estancar. **from s. to stern,** de proa a popa

stench /stentʃ/ *n* tufo, hedor, *m,* hediondez, *Lat. Am. also* fortaleza, *f*

stencil /'stensəl/ *n* patrón para estarcir, *m;* estarcido, *m. vt* estarcir

stenographer /stə'nɒgrəfər/ *n* estenógrafo (-fa), taquígrafo (-fa)

stenography /stə'nɒgrəfi/ *n* estenografía, taquigrafía, *f*

stentorian /sten'tɔriən/ *a* estentóreo

step /step/ *n* paso, *m;* (footprint) huella, *f;* (measure) medida, *f;* (of a stair, etc.) escalón, peldaño, *m,* grada, *f;* (of a ladder) peldaño, *m;* (of vehicles) estribo, *m;* (grade) escalón, *m; Mus.* intervalo, *m.* **at every s.,** a cada paso. **flight of steps,** escalera, *f;* (before a building, etc.) escalinata, *f.* **in steps,** en escalones. **to bend one's steps towards,** dirigirse hacia. **to keep in s.,** llevar el paso. **to take a s.,** dar un paso. **to take steps,** tomar medidas. **s. by s.,** paso a paso; poco a poco. **s.-dance,** baile típico, *m.* **s.-ladder,** escalera de tijera, *f*

step /step/ *vi* dar un paso; pisar; andar. **Please s. in!** Sírvase de entrar. **Will you s. this way, please?** ¡Haga el favor de venir por aquí! **to s. aside,** ponerse a un lado; desviarse; *Fig.* retirarse (en favor de). **to s. in,** entrar; intervenir (en); (meddle) entrometerse. **He stepped into the train,** Subió al tren. **to s. on,** pisar. **to s. on board,** *Naut.* ir a bordo. **to s. out,** salir; (from a vehicle) bajar; (a dance) bailar. **He stepped out a moment ago,** Salió hace un instante

stepbrother /'step₁brʌðər/ *n* hermanastro, medio hermano, *m*

stepchild /'step₁tʃaild/ *n* hijastro (-ra)

stepdaughter /'step₁dɔtər/ *n* hijastra, *f*

stepfather /'step₁faðər/ *n* padrastro, *m*

stepmother /'step₁mʌðər/ *n* madrastra, *f*

steppingstone /'stepiŋ₁stoun/ *n* pasadera, *f; Fig.* escabel, escalón, *m*

stepsister /'step₁sistər/ *n* hermanastra, media hermana, *f*

stepson /'step₁sʌn/ *n* hijastro, *m*

stereotype /'steriə₁taip/ *n* estereotipia, *f,* clisé, *m, vt* (*Print.* and *Fig.*) estereotipar

sterile /'steril/ *a* estéril; árido

sterility /stə'riliti/ *n* esterilidad, *f;* aridez, *f*

sterilization /₁sterələ'zeiʃən/ *n* esterilización, *f*

sterilize /'sterə₁laiz/ *vt* esterilizar

sterilizer /'sterə₁laizər/ *n* esterilizador, *m*

sterling /'stɜrliŋ/ *a* esterlina *f; Fig.* genuino. **pound s.,** libra esterlina, *f*

stern /stɜrn/ *a* severo, austero; duro. *n Naut.* popa, *f*

sternly /'stɜrnli/ *adv* con severidad, severamente, duramente

sternness /'stɜrnnis/ *n* severidad, *f;* dureza, *f*

sternum /'stɜrnəm/ *n Anat.* esternón, *m*

stethoscope /'steθə₁skoup/ *n* estetoscopio, *m*

stevedore /'stivi₁dɔr/ *n* estibador, *m*

stew /stu/ *vt* guisar a la cazuela, estofar; (mutton, etc.) hervir; (fruit) cocer. *n* estofado, *m; Inf.* agitación, *f.* **to be in a s.,** *Inf.* sudar la gota gorda. **stewed fruit,** compota de frutas, *f.* **s.-pot,** cazuela, olla, *f,* puchero, *m*

steward /'stuərd/ *n* administrador, *m;* mayordomo, *m;* (provision) despensero, *m; Naut.* camarero, *m*

stewardess /'stuərdis/ *n Naut.* camarera, *f*

stick /stik/ *vt* clavar (en), hundir (en); (put) poner; sacar; (stamps, etc.) pegar; fijar; (endure) resistir; tolerar. *vi* clavarse, hundirse; estar clavado; pegarse; (remain) quedar; (in the mud, etc.) atascarse, embarrancarse, (on a reef) encallarse; (in the throat, etc.) atravesarse; (stop) detenerse. **It sticks in my throat,** *Inf.* No lo puedo tragar. **Friends always s. together,** Los amigos no se abandonan. **The nickname stuck to him,** El apodo se le quedó. **to s. at,** persistir en; desistir (ante); pararse (ante); tener escrúpulos sobre. **to s. at nothing,** no tener escrúpulos. **He stuck at his work,** Siguió trabajando. **to s. down,** pegar. **to s. one's nose into other people's business** *Mexico* entrucharse. **to s. out,** *vi* proyectar; sobresalir. *vt* (one's chest) inflar; (one's tongue) sacar. **His ears s. out,** Tiene las orejas salientes. **to s. to,** (one's job) no dejar; (one's plans) adherirse (a); (one's principles) ser fiel (a); (one's friends) no abandonar; (one's word, etc.) cumplir; atenerse a. **to s. up,** *vi* (of hair) erizarse, ponerse de punta; salirse. *vt* clavar; (a notice) fijar. **to s. up for,** (a person) defender

stick /stik/ *n* estaca, *f;* (for the fire) leña, *f;* (walking-s.) bastón, *m;* (of office) vara, *f;* (of sealing-wax, etc.) barra, *f;* palo, *m;* (baton) batuta, *f;* (of celery) tallo, *m.* **in a cleft s.,** entre la espada y la pared. **to give** (a person) **the s.,** dar palo a

stickiness /'stikinis/ *n* viscosidad, *f*

sticking plaster /'stikiŋ/ *n* esparadrapo, *m*

stick-in-the-mud /'stikinðə₁mʌd/ *n* chapado a la antigua, *m*

stickler /'stiklər/ *n* rigorista, *mf.* **to be a s. for etiquette,** ser etiquetero

sticky /'stiki/ *a* pegajoso, viscoso; *Fig.* difícil

stiff /stif/ *a* rígido; inflexible; tieso; (of paste, etc.) espeso; (of manner) distante; (of a bow, etc.) frío; (of a person) almidonado, etiquetero; severo; (of examinations, etc.) difícil; (strong) fuerte; (of price, etc.) alto, exorbitante; (of a shirt front, etc.) duro. **s. with cold,** aterido de frío. **s. neck,** torticolis, *m.* **s.-necked,** terco, obstinaz

stiffen /'stifən/ *vt* reforzar; atiesar; (paste, etc.) hacer más espeso; (*Fig.* strengthen) robustecer; (make more obstinate) hacer más tenaz. *vi* atiesarse; endurecerse; (straighten oneself) enderezarse; (of manner) volverse menos cordial; (become firmer) robustecerse; (become more obstinate) hacerse más tenaz. **The breeze stiffened,** Refrescó el viento

stiffly /'stɪfli/ *adv* tiesamente; rígidamente; obstinadamente

stiffness /'stɪfnɪs/ *n* rigidez, *f*; tiesura, *f*; dureza, *f*; (of manner) frialdad, *f*; (obstinacy) terquedad, obstinación, *f*; (of an examination, etc.) dificultad, *f*

stifle /'staɪfəl/ *vt* ahogar, sofocar; apagar; suprimir

stifling /'staɪflɪŋ/ *a* sofocante, bochornoso

stigma /'stɪɡmə/ *n* estigma, *m*

stigmatize /'stɪɡmə,taɪz/ *vt* estigmatizar

stile /staɪl/ *n* (nearest equivalent) portilla con escalones, *f*

still /stɪl/ *a* tranquilo; inmóvil; quedo; silencioso; (of wine) no espumoso. *n* silencio, *m*. **in the s. of the night,** en el silencio de la noche. **Keep s.!** ¡Estate quieto! **to keep s.,** quedarse inmóvil, no moverse. **s.-birth,** nacimiento de un niño muerto, *m*. **s.-born,** nacido muerto. **s. life,** *Art.* bodegón, *m*, naturaleza muerta, *f*

still /stɪl/ *vt* hacer callar, acallar; calmar, tranquilizar; apaciguar; (pain) aliviar

still /stɪl/ *adv* todavía, aún; (nevertheless) sin embargo, no obstante; (always) siempre. **I think she s. visits them every week,** Me parece que sigue visitándoles cada semana. **s. and all,** con todo y eso. **s. more,** aún más. **s. to be paid,** *Lat. Am.* impago

still /stɪl/ *n* alambique, *m*. **salt water s.,** adrazo, *m*

stillness /'stɪlnɪs/ *n* quietud, tranquilidad, *f*; silencio, *m*. **in the s. of the night,** en el silencio de la noche

stilt /stɪlt/ *n* zanco, *m*

stilted /'stɪltɪd/ *a* ampuloso, campanudo, hinchado

stimulant /'stɪmyələnt/ *a* and *n* estimulante, *m*

stimulate /'stɪmyə,leɪt/ *vt* estimular; incitar (a), excitar (a)

stimulating /'stɪmyə,leɪtɪŋ/ *a* estimulante; (encouraging) alentador; (inspiring) sugestivo, inspirador

stimulation /,stɪmyə'leɪʃən/ *n* excitación, *f*; (stimulus) estímulo, *m*

stimulus /'stɪmyələs/ *n* estímulo, *m*; *Med.* estimulante, *m*; (incentive) impulso, incentivo, *m*; acicate, aguijón, *m*

sting /stɪŋ/ *vt* picar, pinchar; (of snakes, etc.) morder; (of hot dishes) resquemar; (of hail, etc.) azotar; (pain) atormentar; (provoke) provocar (a), incitar (a). *n* (*Zool.* organ) aguijón, *m*; *Bot.* púa, *f*; (of a scorpion) uña, *f*; (of a serpent) colmillo, *m*; (pain and wound) pinchazo, *m*; (serpent's) mordedura, *f*; (stimulus) acicate, estímulo, *m*; (torment) tormento, dolor, *m*

stingily /'stɪndʒəli/ *adv* avaramente, tacañamente

stinginess /'stɪndʒɪnɪs/ *n* tacañería, avaricia, *f*

stinging /'stɪŋɪŋ/ *a* picante; *Fig.* mordaz; (of blows) que duele

stingy /'stɪndʒi/ *a* tacaño, avaro, mezquino, *Argentina* agallado, *Chile, Peru* coñete

stink /stɪŋk/ *vi* apestar, heder, oler mal. *n* tufo, *m*, hediondez, *Lat. Am. also* fortaleza, *f*

stinking /'stɪŋkɪŋ/ *a* apestoso, hediondo, fétido, mal oliente

stint /stɪnt/ *vt* escatimar; limitar. *n* límite, *m*, restricción, *f*. **without s.,** sin límite; sin restricción

stipend /'staɪpɛnd/ *n* estipendio, salario, *m*

stipple /'stɪpəl/ *vt* *Art.* puntear. *n* punteado, *m*

stipulate /'stɪpyə,leɪt/ *vi* estipular, poner como condición. *vt* estipular, especificar. **They stipulated for a five-day week,** Pusieron como condición (*or* Estipularon) que trabajasen cinco días por semana

stipulation /,stɪpyə'leɪʃən/ *n* estipulación, *f*; condición, *f*

stir /stɜr/ *vt* agitar; revolver; (the fire) atizar; (move) mover; (emotionally) conmover, impresionar; (the imagination) estimular. *vi* moverse. *n* movimiento, *m*; conmoción, *f*; (bustle) bullicio, *m*; sensación, *f*. **to make a s.,** causar una sensación. **to s. one's coffee,** revolver el café. **to s. up discontent,** fomentar el descontento

stirring /'stɜrɪŋ/ *a* conmovedor, emocionante, impresionante; (of times, etc.) turbulento, agitado

stirrup /'stɜrəp/ 'stɪr-/ *n* estribo, *m*. **s.-cup,** última copa, *f*. **s.-pump,** bomba de mano (para líquidos), *f*

stitch /stɪtʃ/ *n* (action) puntada, *f*; (result) punto, *m*; *Surg.* punto de sutura, *m*; (pain) punzada, *f*, pinchazo, *m*. *vt* coser; *Surg.* suturar

stock /stɒk/ *n* (of a tree) tronco, *m*; (of a rifle) culata, *f*; (handle) mango, *m*; (of a horse's tail) nabo, *m*; (stem for grafting etc.) injerto, *m*; (race) raza, *f*; (lineage) linaje, *m*, estirpe, *f*; (supply) provisión, *f*; reserva, *f*; (of merchandise) surtido, *m*; *Cul.* caldo, *m*; (collar) alzacuello, *m*; *Bot.* alhelí, *m*; (government) papel del estado, *m*, valores públicos, *m pl*; (financial) valores, *m pl*, (of a company) capital, *m*; *pl* **stocks,** *Hist.* cepo, *m*; (of goods) existencias, *f pl*, stock, *m*, a corriente; del repertorio. **in s.** en existencia. **lives.,** ganado *m*. **rolling-s.,** *Rail.* materia móvil ferroviario, *m*. **s. phrase,** frase hecha, *f*. **s. size,** talla corriente, *f*. **to lay in a s. of,** hacer provisión de, almacenar, **to stand s.-still,** quedarse completamente inmóvil. **to take s.,** hacer inventario. **to take s. of,** inventariar; examinar, considerar. **s.-breeder,** ganadero, *m*. **s.-broker,** corredor de bolsa, bolsista, *m*. **s. exchange,** bolsa, *f*. **s.-in-hand,** *Com.* existencias, *f pl*. **s.-in-trade** (*Com.* etc.) capital, *m*. **s.-raising,** cría de ganados, ganadería, *f*. **s.-taking,** *Com.* inventario, *m*

stock /stɒk/ *vt* proveer (de), abastecer (de); (of shops) tener existencia de

stockade /stɒ'keɪd/ *n* estacada, empalizada, *f*, *vt* empalizar

stocking /'stɒkɪŋ/ *n* media, *f*. **nylon stockings,** medias de cristal (*or* de nilón), *f pl*

stocky /'stɒki/ *a* rechoncho, doblado, achaparrado

stodgy /'stɒdʒi/ *a* (of food) indigesto; (of style, etc.) pesado, amazacotado

stoic /'stouɪk/ *a* and *n* estoico (-ca)

stoical /'stouɪkəl/ *a* estoico

stoke /stouk/ *vt* (a furnace, etc.) cargar, alimentar; (a fire) echar carbón, etc., en. **s.-hole,** cuarto de fogoneros, *m*; *Naut.* cámara de calderas, *f*

stoker /'stoukər/ *n* fogonero, *m*; (mechanical) cargador, *m*

stole /stoul/ *n* (*Eccl.* and of fur, etc.) estola, *f*

stolid /'stɒlɪd/ *a* impasible, imperturbable

stolidly /'stɒlɪdli/ *adv* imperturbablemente

stomach /'stʌmək/ *n* estómago, vientre, *m*; apetito, estómago, *m*; (courage) corazón, valor, *m*. *vt* digerir; (tolerate) tragar, sufrir. **s.ache,** dolor de estómago, *m*

stone /stoun/ *n* piedra, *f*; (gem) piedra preciosa, *f*; *Med.* cálculo, *m. a.* de piedra. *vt* apedrear; (a wall, etc.) revestir de piedra; (fruit) deshuesar. **to pave with stones,** empedrar. **to leave no s. unturned,** no dejar piedra sin remover. **within a stone's throw,** a corta distancia, a un paso. **S. Age,** edad de piedra, *f*. **s.-breaker,** cantero, picapedrero, *m*. **s.-cold,** muy frío, completamente frío. **s.-deaf,** completamente sordo. **s.-fruit,** fruta de hueso, *f*. **s.-mason,** mazonero, albañil, *m*; picapedrero, *m*. **s.-quarry,** pedrera, cantera, *f*

stonily /'stounli/ *adv* fríamente; fijamente, sin pestañear

stoniness /'stounɪnɪs/ *n* lo pedregoso; (of hearts, etc.) dureza, *f*; (of stares, etc.) fijeza, inmovilidad, *f*

stoning /'stounɪŋ/ *n* apedreamiento, *m*, lapidación, *f*

stony /'stouni/ *a* pedregoso; (of hearts, etc.) duro, insensible, empedernido; (of a stare, etc.) fijo, duro

stool /stul/ *n* banquillo, taburete, *m*; (feces) excremento, *m*

stoop /stup/ *vi* inclinarse, doblarse; encorvarse; ser cargado de espaldas; andar encorvado; (demean oneself) rebajarse (a). *vt* inclinar, doblar. *n* inclinación, *f*; cargazón de espaldas, *f*

stooping /'stupɪŋ/ *a* inclinado, doblado; (of shoulders) cargado

stop /stɒp/ *vt* (a hole) obstruir, atascar; (a leak) cegar, tapar; (a tooth) empastar; (stanch) restañar; (the traffic, etc.) parar; detener; (prevent) evitar; (discontinue) cesar (de); dejarse de; (cut off) cortar; (end) poner fin (a), acabar con; (payment) suspender. *vi* parar; detenerse; cesar; terminar; (stay) quedarse, permanecer. **I stopped myself from saying what I thought,** Me abstuve de decir lo que pensaba, Me mordí la lengua. **They stopped the food-supply,** Cortaron las provisiones. **to s. beating about the bush,** dejarse de historias. **to s. one's ears,** *Fig.* taparse los oídos. **to s. payments,** suspender pagos

stop /stɒp/ n parada, f; pausa, f; interrupción, f; cesación, f; (of an organ) registro, m. **"Stop,"** (road sign) «Alto.» **full s.**, Gram. punto, m. **tram s.**, parada de tranvía, f. **to come to a full s.**, pararse de golpe; cesar súbitamente. **to put a s. to,** poner fin a, poner coto a, acabar con. f pl. **s.-watch,** cronógrafo, m

stopgap /'stɒp‚gæp/ n (person) tapagujeros, m; substituto, m

stoppage /'stɒpɪdʒ/ n parada, f; cesación, f; suspensión, f; interrupción, f; pausa, f; (obstruction) impedimento, m; obstrucción, f. **s. of work,** suspensión de trabajo, f

stopper /'stɒpər/ n tapón, m; obturador, m, vt cerrar con tapón, taponar

stopping /'stɒpɪŋ/ n parada, f; cesación, f; suspensión, f; (of a tooth) empaste, m. **without s.,** sin parar. **without s. to draw breath,** de un aliento. **s.-place,** paradero, m; (of buses, etc.) parada, f. **s. train,** tren ómnibus, m. **s. up,** obturación, f

storage /'stɔrɪdʒ/ n almacenamiento, m; (charge) almacenaje, m; (place) depósito, m. **cold s.,** cámara frigorífica, f. **s. battery,** acumulador, m

store /stɔr/ n provisión, f; abundancia, f; reserva, f; (of knowledge, etc.) tesoro, m; (for furniture, etc.) depósito, almacén, m; pl **stores,** (shop) almacenes, m pl; (food) provisiones, f pl; (Mil. etc.) pertrechos, m pl. vt proveer; guardar, acumular; tener en reserva; (furniture, etc.) almacenar; (hold) caber en, tomar. **in s.,** en reserva; en depósito, en almacén. **to set s. by,** estimar en mucho; dar importancia a. **to set little s. by,** estimar en poco; conceder poca importancia a. **s.-room,** despensa, f

storehouse /'stɔr‚haus/ n almacén, m; Fig. mina, f, tesoro, m

storekeeper /'stɔr‚kipər/ = **shopkeeper**

storied /'stɔrid/ a de... pisos. **two-s.,** de dos pisos

stork /stɔrk/ n cigüeña, f

storm /stɔrm/ n tempestad, tormenta, f, temporal, m; Fig. tempestad, f; Mil. asalto, m. vt Mil. tomar por asalto, asaltar. vi (of persons) bramar de cólera. **to take by s.,** tomar por asalto; Fig. cautivar, conquistar. **s. cloud,** nubarrón, m. **s.-signal,** señal de temporal, f. **s.-tossed,** a sacudido por la tempestad. **s. troops,** tropas de asalto, f pl. **s. window,** contravidriera, f

stormily /'stɔrməli/ adv tempestuosamente; con tormenta

storming /'stɔrmɪŋ/ n (Mil. etc.) asalto, m; violencia, f. **s.-party,** pelotón de asalto, m

stormy /'stɔrmi/ a tempestuoso; de tormenta; (of life, etc.) borrascoso; (of meetings, etc.) tempestuoso

story /'stɔri/ n historia, f; cuento, m; anécdota, f; (funny) chiste, m; (plot) argumento, enredo, m; (fib) mentira, f; (floor) piso m. **It's always the same old s.,** Es siempre la misma canción (or historia). **That is quite another s.,** Eso es harina de otro costal, Argentina, Peru esas son otras cuarenta. **short s.,** cuento, m. **s. book,** libro de cuentos, m. **s. teller,** cuentista, mf; (fibber) mentiroso (-sa)

stout /staut/ a fuerte; (brave) intrépido, indómito; (fat) gordo, grueso; (firm) sólido, firme; (decided) resuelto; vigoroso. n (drink) cerveza negra, f. **s.-hearted,** valiente, intrépido

stove /stouv/ n estufa, f; (open, for cooking) cocina económica, f; (gas, etc., for cooking) cocina, f, fogón, m. **s. maker,** Argentina fumista, mf; **s. pipe,** tubo de la chimenea, m

stow /stou/ vt meter, poner; colocar; (hide) esconder; (cargo) estibar, arrimar

stowaway /'stouə‚wei/ n polizón, llovido, m, vi embarcarse secretamente

straddle /'strædl/ vi (Nav. etc.) graduar el tiro. vt montar a horcajadas en. **s.-legged,** patiabierto

strafe /streif/ vt bombardear concentradamente; castigar; reñir

straggle /'strægəl/ vi rezagarse; vagar en desorden; dispersarse; estar esparcido; extenderse

straggler /'stræglər/ n rezagado (-da)

straight /streit/ a derecho; recto; (of hair) lacio; directo; (tidy) en orden; (frank) franco; (honest) honrado. adv derecho; en línea recta; directamente. **Keep s. on!** ¡Siga Vd. derecho! **to go s. to the point,**

---

dejarse de rodeos, ir al grano. **to look s. in the eyes,** mirar derecho en los ojos. **s. away,** inmediatamente, en seguida. **s. out,** sin rodeos

straighten /'streitn/ vt enderezar; poner derecho; poner en orden; arreglar. vi ponerse derecho; enderezarse. **to s. one's face,** componer el semblante. **to s. the line,** Mil. rectificar el frente. **to s. out,** poner en orden; Fig. desenredar. **to s. oneself up,** erguirse

straightforward /‚streit'fɔrwərd/ a honrado, sincero; franco; (simple) sencillo. **s. answer,** respuesta directa, f

straightforwardly /‚streit‚fɔrwərdli/ adv honradamente; francamente

straightforwardness /‚streit'fɔrwərdnɪs/ n honradez, integridad, f; franqueza, f; (simplicity) sencillez, f

straightness /'streitnɪs/ n derechura, rectitud, f; (of persons) honradez, probidad, f

straightway /'streit'wei, -‚wei/ adv al instante, inmediatamente

strain /strein/ vt estirar; forzar; esforzar; (one's eyes) quebrarse; (one's ears) aguzar (el oído); (a muscle, etc.) torcer; (a friendship) pedir demasiado (a), exigir demasiado (de); (a person's patience, etc.) abusar (de); (words) tergiversar; (embrace) abrazar estrechamente (a); (filter) filtrar; Cul. colar. vi hacer un gran esfuerzo, esforzarse (para). n tirantez, f; tensión, f; (effort) esfuerzo, m; (sprain) torcedura, f; (nervous) tensión nerviosa, f; Mech. esfuerzo, m; (breed) raza, f; Biol. cepa, f; (tendency) tendencia, f; (heredity) herencia, f; rasgo, m, vena, f; (style) estilo, m; Mus. melodía, f; (of mirth, etc.) son, ruido, m; (poetry) poesía, f. **to s. a point,** hacer una excepción, m. **to s. after effect,** buscar demasiado el efecto

strained /streind/ a tenso; (of muscles, etc.) torcido; (of smiles, etc.) forzado. **s. relations,** Polit. estado de tirantez, m

strainer /'streinər/ n filtro, m; colador, m

strait /streit/ n Geog. estrecho, m. **to be in great straits,** estar en un apuro. **s. laced,** Fig. de manga estrecha

straiten /'streitn/ vt estrechar; limitar, **in straitened circumstances,** en la necesidad

Strait of Magellan /mə'dʒɛlən/ Estrecho de Magallanes, m

Straits Settlements /'streits 'sɛtlmənts/ Establecimientos del Estrecho, m pl

strand /strænd/ n (shore) playa, f; (of a river) ribera, orilla, f; (of rope) cabo, ramal, m; (of thread, etc.) hebra, f; (of hair) trenza, f. vt and vi (a ship) encallar, varar. **to be stranded,** hallarse abandonado; (by missing a train, etc.) quedarse colgado. **to leave stranded,** abandonar, dejar plantado (a)

strange /streindʒ/ a (unknown) desconocido; nuevo; (exotic, etc.) extraño, singular; extraordinario; raro; exótico. **I felt very s. in a s. country,** Me sentía muy solo en un país desconocido. **He is a very s. person,** Es una persona muy rara

strangely /'streindʒli/ adv extrañamente, singularmente; de un modo raro

strangeness /'streindʒnɪs/ n novedad, f; singularidad, f; rareza, f

stranger /'streindʒər/ n desconocido (-da); (from a foreign country) extranjero (-ra); (from another region, etc.) forastero (-ra).

strangle /'stræŋgəl/ vt estrangular; (a sob, etc.) ahogar

stranglehold /'stræŋgəl‚hould/ n collar de fuerza, m. **to have a s. (on),** tener asido por la garganta; paralizar

strap /stræp/ n correa, f; tirante de botas, m, vt atar con correas

strapping /'stræpɪŋ/ a rozagante, robusto

stratagem /'strætədʒəm/ n estratagema, f, ardid, m

strategic /strə'tidʒɪk/ a estratégico

strategist /'strætɪdʒɪst/ n estratego, m

strategy /'strætɪdʒi/ n estrategia, f

stratification /‚strætəfɪ'keiʃən/ n estratificación, f

stratosphere /'strætə‚sfɪər/ n estratosfera, f

stratum /'streitəm, 'strætəm/ n Geol. estrato, m, capa, f; (social, etc.) estrato, m

straw /strɔ/ n paja, f. **I don't care a s.,** No se me da un bledo. **to be not worth a s.,** no valer un ardite. **to be the last s.,** ser el colmo. **to drink through a s.,** sorber con una paja. **s. hat,** sombrero de paja, *m.* **s.-colored,** pajizo

strawberry /'strɔˌbɛri/ *n* (plant and fruit, especially small or wild) fresa, *f*; (large cultivated) fresón, *m.* **s. bed,** fresal, *m.* **s. ice,** helado de fresa, *m*

stray /strei/ *vi* errar, vagar; perderse; (from a path, etc., also *Fig.*) descarriarse. *n* animal perdido, *m*; niño (-ña) sin hogar. *a* descarriado, perdido; errante; (sporadic) esporádico

stray bullet *n* bala perdida, *f*

streak /strik/ *n* raya, *f*; (in wood and stone) vena, *f*; (of light) rayo, *m*; (of humor, etc.) rasgo, *m. vt* rayar. **like a s. of lightning,** como un relámpago

streaky /'striki/ *a* rayado; (of bacon) entreverado

stream /strim/ *n* arroyo, riachuelo, *m*; río, *m*; (current) corriente, *f*; (of words, etc.) torrente, *m. vi* correr, fluir; manar, brotar; (float) flotar, ondear. *vt* (blood, etc.) manar, echar. **The tears streamed down Jean's cheeks,** Las lágrimas corrían por las mejillas de Juana. **s.-lined,** fuselado

streamer /'strimər/ *n* gallardete, *m*, serpentina, *f*; (on a hat, etc.) cinta colgante, *f*, siguemepollo, *m*

stream-of-consciousness /'strim əv 'kɒnʃəsnɪs/ *n* escritura automática, *f*, fluir de la conciencia, *m*, flujo de la subconciencia, monólogo interior, *m*

street /strit/ *n* calle, *f.* **the man in the s.,** el hombre medio. **at s. level,** a ras de suelo. **s. arab,** golfo, *m.* **s. cries,** gritos de vendedores ambulantes, *m pl.* **s. entertainer,** saltabanco, *m.* **s. brawl, s. fight,** algarada callejera, *f.* **s. fighting,** luchas en las calles, *f pl.* **s. musician,** músico ambulante, *m.* **s.-sweeper,** barrendero, *m.* **s.-walker,** buscona, prostituta, *f*

strength /strɛŋkθ, strɛnθ/ *n* fuerza, *f*; (of colors, etc.) intensidad, *f*; (of character) firmeza (de carácter), *f*; (of will) resolución, decisión, *f*; *Mil.* complemento, *m.* **The enemy is in s.,** El enemigo está presente en gran número. **by sheer s.,** a viva fuerza. **on the s. of,** confiando en, en razón de

strengthen /'strɛŋkθən, 'strɛn-/ *vt* fortificar; consolidar; reforzar. *vi* fortificarse; consolidarse; reforzarse

strengthening /'strɛŋkθənɪŋ, 'strɛn-/ *a* fortificante; tonificante. *n* refuerzo, *m*; fortificación, *f*; consolidación, *f*

strenuous /'strɛnyuəs/ *a* activo, enérgico; vigoroso; (arduous) arduo

strenuously /'strɛnyuəsli/ *adv* enérgicamente, vigorosamente

strenuousness /'strɛnyuəsnɪs/ *n* energía, *f*; vigor, *m*; (arduousness) arduidad, *f*

streptococcus /ˌstrɛptə'kɒkəs/ *n Med.* estreptococo, *m*

streptomycin /ˌstrɛptə'maisɪn/ *n Med.* estreptomicina, *f*

stress /strɛs/ *n* tensión, *f*; impulso, *m*; importancia, *f*; énfasis, *m*; *Gram.* acento (tónico), *m*; acentuación, *f*; *Mech.* esfuerzo, *m. vt* acentuar; poner énfasis en, insistir en. **under s. of circumstance,** impulsado por las circunstancias. **times of s.,** tiempos turbulentos, *m pl.* **to lay great s. on,** insistir mucho en; dar gran importancia a

stretch /strɛtʃ/ *vt* (make bigger) ensanchar; (pull) estirar; (one's hand, etc.) alargar, extender; (knock down) tumbar. *vi* ensancharse; dar de sí; ceder; extenderse. **to s. oneself,** estirarse, desperezarse. **to s. as far as,** llegar hasta, extenderse hasta. **to s. a point,** hacer una concesión. **to s. one's legs,** estirar las piernas

stretch /strɛtʃ/ *n* estirón, *m*; tensión, *f*; (of country, etc.) extensión, *f*; (scope) alcance, *m.* **by a s. of the imagination,** con un esfuerzo de imaginación. **He can sleep for hours at a s.,** Puede dormir durante horas enteras

stretcher /'strɛtʃər/ *n* (for gloves) ensanchador, *m*; dilatador, *m*; (for canvas) bastidor, *m*; (for wounded, etc.) camilla, *f.* **s.-bearer,** camillero, *m*

strew /stru/ *vt* esparcir; derramar

stricken /'strɪkən/ *a* (wounded) herido; (ill) enfermo; (with grief) afligido, agobiado de dolor. **s. in years,** entrado en años

strict /strɪkt/ *a* exacto; estricto; escrupuloso; severo

strictly /'strɪktli/ *adv* exactamente; estrictamente; severamente, con severidad. **s. speaking,** en rigor, en realidad

strictness /'strɪktnɪs/ *n* exactitud, *f*; escrupulosidad, *f*; rigor, *m*; severidad, *f*

stricture /'strɪktʃər/ *n Fig.* crítica severa, censura, *f.* **to pass strictures on,** criticar severamente

stride /straid/ *vi* andar a pasos largos, dar zancadas; cruzar a grandes trancos. *vt* cruzar de un tranco; poner una pierna en cada lado de. *n* zancada, *f*, paso largo, tranco, *m.* **to s. up and down,** dar zancadas

strident /'straidnt/ *a* estridente; (of colors) chillón

strife /straif/ *n* lucha, *f*, conflicto, *m*

strike /straik/ *vt* golpear; pegar, dar una bofetada (a); (wound) herir; (a coin) acuñar; (a light) encender; (of a snake) morder; (a blow) asestar, dar; (of ships, a rock, etc.) chocar contra; estrellarse contra; (flags) bajar, arriar; (a tent) desmontar; (camp) levantar; (come upon) llegar a; (discover) encontrar por casualidad, tropezar con; hallar, descubrir; (seem) parecer; (impress) impresionar; (of ideas) ocurrirse; (an attitude) tomar, adoptar; (of a clock) dar; (a balance) hacer; (a bargain) cerrar, llegar a; (level) nivelar; (cuttings) enraciar. *vi* golpear; (of a clock) dar la hora; (of a ship) encallar; (go) ir; (penetrate) penetrar; (of a cutting) arraigar; (sound) sonar. **He struck the table with his fist,** Golpeó la mesa con el puño. **I was very much struck by the city's beauty,** La belleza de la ciudad me impresionó mucho. **The news struck fear into their hearts,** La noticia les llenó el corazón de miedo. **The clock struck three,** El reloj dio las tres. **The hour has struck,** *Fig.* Ha llegado la hora. **How did the house s. you?** ¿Qué te pareció la casa? **to s. a bargain,** cerrar un trato. **to s. a blow,** asestar un golpe. **to s. an attitude,** tomar una actitud. **to s. home,** dar en el blanco; herir; herir en lo más vivo; hacerse sentir. **to s. at,** asestar un golpe (a); acometer, embestir; atacar. **to s. down,** derribar; (of illness) acometer. **to s. off,** (a head, etc.) cortar; (a name) borrar, tachar; (print) imprimir. **to s. out,** *vi* asestar un golpe (a); (a swimmer) nadar; echarse, lanzarse. *vt* (a word, etc.) borrar, rayar; (begin) iniciar. **to s. through,** (cross out) rayar, tachar; (of the sun's rays, etc.) penetrar. **to s. up,** *vt* tocar; empezar a cantar; (a friendship) trabar. *vi* empezar a tocar. **to s. up a march,** *Mil.* batir la marcha

strike /straik/ *n* huelga, *f. vi* declararse en huelga. **go-slow s.,** tortuguismo, *m.* **lock-out s.,** huelga patronal, *f.* **sit-down s.,** huelga de brazos caídos, *f.* **to go on s.,** declararse en huelga. **s.-breaker,** esquirol, *m.* **s.-pay,** subsidio de huelga, *m*

striker /'straikər/ *n* huelguista, *mf*

striking /'straikɪŋ/ *a* notable, sorprendente; (impressive) impresionante; que llama la atención; llamativo

string /strɪŋ/ *n* bramante, *m*; cuerda, *f*; (ribbon) cinta, *f*; (of beads, etc.) sarta, *f*; (of onions) ristra, *f*; (of horses, etc.) reata, *f*; hilera, *f*; (of a bridge) cable, *m*; (of oaths, lies) sarta, serie, *f*; (of beans) fibra, *f. vt* encordar; (beads, etc.) ensartar; (beans) quitar las fibras (de). **He is all strung up,** Se le crispan los nervios. **the strings,** los instrumentos de cuerda. **a s. of pearls,** un collar de perlas. **for strings,** *Mus.* para arco. **to pull strings,** *Fig.* manejar los hilos. **to s. up,** (an instrument) templar; (a person) pender, ahorcar. **s. bean,** judía verde, *f, Central America, Mexico* ejote, *m*

stringed /strɪŋd/ *a* (of musical instruments) de cuerda. **s. instrument,** instrumento de cuerda, *m*

stringent /'strɪndʒənt/ *a* estricto; severo

stringy /'strɪŋi/ *a* fibroso; filamentoso; correoso; arrugado

strip /strɪp/ *vt* desnudar; despojar (de); quitar; robar; (a cow) ordeñar hasta agotar la leche. *vi* desnudarse. *n* (tatter) jirón, *m*; tira, lista, *f*; (of wood) listón, *m*; (of earth) pedazo, *m*; (*Geog.* of land) zona, *f.* **to s. off,** *vt* quitar; (bark from a tree) descortezar; (one's clothes) despojarse de. *vi* desprenderse, separarse. **to s. the leaves from, to s. the petals from,** *Lat. Am.* deshojar

stripe /straip/ *n* raya, lista, *f*; (*Mil.* etc.) galón, *m*; (lash) azote, *m. vt* rayar. **the stripes of the tiger,** las rayas del tigre

striped /straipt, 'straipɪd/ *a* listado, a rayas; con rayas. **s. trousers,** pantalón de corte, *m*

stripling /'strɪplɪŋ/ *n* joven imberbe, pollo, mancebo, *m*

strive /straiv/ *vi* esforzarse (a); pugnar (por, para); trabajar (por); (fight against) luchar contra; pelear con. **He was striving to understand,** Pugnaba por (or Se esforzaba a) comprender

stroke /strouk/ *n* (blow) golpe, *m*; (of the oars) golpe del remo, *m*, remada, *f*; (at billards) tacada, *f*; (in golf) tirada, *f*; (in swimming) braza, *f*; (of a clock) campanada, *f*; (of a pen) rasgo de la pluma, *m*; (of a brush) pincelada, *f*; *Mech.* golpe de émbolo, *m*; (caress) caricia con la mano, *f*. *vt* acariciar con la mano. **on the s. of six,** al acabar de dar las seis. **to have a s.,** tener un ataque de apoplejía. **s. of genius,** rasgo de ingenio, *m*. **s. of good luck,** racha de buena suerte, *f*

stroll /stroul/ *vi* pasearse, vagar. *n* vuelta, *f*, paseo, *m*. **to go for a s.,** dar una vuelta

stroller /'stroulər/ *n* paseante, *mf*

strolling /'stroulɪŋ/ *a* errante; ambulante. **s. player,** *n* cómico (-ca) ambulante

strong /strɔŋ/ *a* fuerte; vigoroso; robusto; *Argentina* alentado; enérgico; firme; poderoso; (of colors) intenso, vivo; (of tea, coffee) cargado; *Gram.* fuerte. **The government took s. measures,** El gobierno tomó medidas enérgicas. **They gave very s. reasons,** Alegaron unas razones muy poderosas. **Grammar is not his s. point,** La gramática no es su punto fuerte. **The enemy is s. in numbers,** El enemigo es numéricamente fuerte. **The society is four thousand s.,** La sociedad tiene cuatro mil miembros. **s. box,** caja de caudales, *f*. **s. man,** hombre fuerte, *m*; (in a circus) hércules, *m*. **s.-minded,** de espíritu fuerte; independiente. **s. room,** cámara acorazada, *f*

stronghold /'strɔŋˌhould/ *n* fortaleza, *f*; refugio, *m*

strongly /'strɔŋli/ *adv* vigorosamente; fuertemente; firmemente

structural /'strʌktʃərəl/ *a* estructural

structurally /'strʌktʃərəli/ *adv* estructuralmente, desde el punto de vista de la estructura

structure /'strʌktʃər/ *n* estructura, *f*; edificio, *m*; construcción, *f*

struggle /'strʌgəl/ *vi* luchar; pelear; disputarse, *Lat. Am.* abrocharse (con...); *n* lucha, *f*; combate, *m*; conflicto, *m*. **to s. to one's feet,** luchar por levantarse. **without a s.,** sin luchar

struggling /'strʌglɪŋ/ *a* pobre, indigente, que lucha para vivir

strum /strʌm/ *vt* (a stringed instrument) rascar; tocar mal

strut /strʌt/ *vi* pavonearse. *vt* (prop) apuntalar. *n* pavonada, *f*; (prop) puntal, *m*. **to s. out,** salir de un paso majestuoso

stub /stʌb/ *n* (of a tree) tocón, *m*; (of a pencil, candle, etc.) cabo, *m*; pedazo, fragmento, *m*; (of a cigarette or cigar) colilla, *f*. **s.-book,** talonario, *m*

stubborn /'stʌbərn/ *a* inquebrantable, tenaz; persistente; (pig-headed) terco, testarudo, *Lat. Am.* empecinado

stubbornness /'stʌbərnɪs/ *n* tenacidad, *f*; terquedad, testarudez, *f*

stucco /'stʌkou/ *n* estuco, *m*, *vt* estucar

stuck /stʌk/ past part. of **stick. be stuck** (for an answer) = **be stumped**

stuck-up /'stʌk 'ʌp/ *a* = **haughty**

stud /stʌd/ *n* (of horses) caballeriza, *f*; (nail) tachón, *m*; (for collars) pasador para camisas, *m*. *vt* tachonar; sembrar. **dress s.,** botón de la pechera, *m*. **s.-farm,** potrero, *m*

student /'studnt/ *n* estudiante, *mf*. *a* estudiantil. **students** (as a body) *Lat. Am.* estudiantado, *msg*.

student body *n Lat. Am.* estudiantado, *m*

studied /'stʌdid/ *a* estudiado; calculado; (of style) cerebral, reflexivo; (intentional) deliberado

studio /'studi,ou/ *n* estudio, *m*. **broadcasting s.,** estudio de emisión, *m*

studious /'studiəs/ *a* estudioso, aplicado; (deliberate) intencional, deliberate; (eager) solícito, ansioso

studiously /'studiəsli/ *adv* estudiosamente; con intención, deliberadamente; solícitamente

study /'stʌdi/ *n* estudio, *m*; solicitud, *f*, cuidado, *m*; investigación, *f*; (room) gabinete, cuarto de trabajo, *m*. *vt* ocuparse de, cuidar de, atender a; considerar; estudiar; examinar; (the stars) observar; (try) procurar. *vi* estudiar. **in a brown s.,** en Babia. **to make a s. of,** hacer un estudio de, estudiar. **to s. for an examination,** prepararse para un examen

stuff /stʌf/ *n* substancia, materia, *f*; (fabric) tela, *f*, paño, *m*; (rubbish) cachivaches, *m pl*, cosas, *f pl*. *a* de estofa. *vt* henchir; llenar; *Cul.* rellenar; (with food) ahitar (de); (cram) atestar, apretar; (furniture) rehenchir; (an animal, bird) disecar; (put) meter, poner. **S. and nonsense!** ¡Patrañas! **to be poor s.,** ser de pacotilla; no valer para nada

stuffed animal /stʌft/ *n* animal disecado, *m*

stuffiness /'stʌfinɪs/ *n* mala ventilación, *f*; falta de aire, *f*; calor, *m*

stuffing /'stʌfɪŋ/ *n* (of furniture) rehenchimiento, *m*; *Cul.* relleno, *m*

stuffy /'stʌfi/ *a* mal ventilado, poco aireado, ahogado

stumble /'stʌmbəl/ *vi* tropezar; dar un traspié; (in speaking) tartamudear. *n* tropezón, *m*; traspié, *m*. **to s. through a speech,** pronunciar un discurso a tropezones. **to s. against,** tropezar contra. **to s. upon, across,** tropezar con; encontrar por casualidad

stumbling block /'stʌmblɪŋ/ *n* tropiezo, impedimento, *m*

stump /stʌmp/ *n* (of a tree) tocón, *m*; (of an arm, leg) muñón, *m*; (of a pencil, candle) cabo, *m*; (of a tooth) raigón, *m*; (of a cigar) colilla, *f*; (cricket) poste, montante, *m*; *Art.* esfumino, *m*; (leg) pata, *f*. *vt* (disconcert) desconcertar; *Art.* esfumar; recorrer. **to s. up,** *Inf.* pagar. **be stumped** (for an answer) *Mexico* atrojarse

stun /stʌn/ *vt* dejar sin sentido (a); aturdir de un golpe (a); (astound) pasmar

stunning /'stʌnɪŋ/ *a* aturdidor; que pasma; *Inf.* estupendo

stunt /stʌnt/ *vt* impedir el crecimiento de; encanijar. *n* (advertising) anuncio de reclamo, *m*; recurso (para conseguir algo), *m*; proeza, *f*

stunted /'stʌntid/ *a* (of trees, etc.) enano; (of children) encanijado; (of intelligence) inmaduro

stupefy /'stupə,fai/ *vt* atontar, embrutecer; causar estupor (a), asombrar

stupendous /stu'pɛndəs/ *a* asombroso; enorme

stupid /'stupid/ *a* (with sleep, etc.) atontado; (silly) estúpido, tonto, *Lat. Am.* baboso, *Central America* azurumbado. *n* tonto (-ta)

stupidity /stu'pɪditi/ *n* estupidez, *f*; tontería, *f*

stupor /'stupər/ *n* estupor, *m*

sturdiness /'stərdinɪs/ *n* robustez, *f*, vigor, *m*; firmeza, tenacidad, *f*

sturdy /'stərdi/ *a* robusto, vigoroso, fuerte; firme, tenaz

sturgeon /'stərdʒən/ *n Ichth.* esturión, *m*

stutter /'stʌtər/ *vi* tartamudear. *vt* balbucir. *n* tartamudeo, *m*

stutterer /'stʌtərər/ *n* tartamudo (-da)

stuttering /'stʌtərɪŋ/ *a* tartamudo; balbuciente. *n* tartamudeo, *m*

sty /stai/ *n* (pig) pocilga, *f*; *Med.* orzuelo, *m*

style /stail/ *n* (for etching) buril, *m*; (Lit., Art., Archit., etc.) estilo, *m*; (fashion) moda, *f*; (model) modelo, *m*; (behavior, etc.) tono, *m*; elegancia, *f*; (kind) especie, clase, *f*; (designation) tratamiento, *m*; *vt* llamar, nombrar. **the latest styles from Madrid,** los últimos modelos de Madrid. **He has a very individual s.,** Su estilo es muy personal. **They live in great s.,** Viven en gran lujo

stylet /'stailɪt/ *n* estilete, *m*

stylish /'stailɪʃ/ *a* elegante

stylishness /'stailɪʃnɪs/ *n* elegancia, *f*

stylist /'stailɪst/ *n* estilista, *mf*

stylize /'stailaiz/ *vt* estilizar

suasion /'sweiʒən/ *n* persuasión, *f*

suasive /'sweisɪv/ *a* suasorio, persuasivo

suave /swɑv/ *a* afable, cortés, urbano; (of wine) suave

suavity /'swɒvɪti/ n afabilidad, urbanidad, f
subaltern /sʌb'ɔltərn/ n Mil. subalterno, m, a subalterno, subordinado
subcommittee /'sʌbkə,mɪti/ n subcomisión, f
subconscious /sʌb'kɒnʃəs/ a subconsciente. **the s.,** la subconsciencia
subconsciously /sʌb'kɒnʃəsli/ adv subconscientemente
subcutaneous /,sʌbkyu'teiniəs/ a subcutáneo
subdivide /,sʌbdɪ'vaid/ vt subdividir. vi subdividirse
subdivision /'sʌbdɪ,vɪʒən/ n subdivisión, f
subdominant /sʌb'dɒmənənt/ n Mus. subdominante, f
subdue /səb'du/ vt subyugar, sojuzgar, vencer; (one's passions) dominar; (colors, voices) suavizar; (lessen) mitigar; apagar
subdued /səb'dud/ a (of colors) apagado; (of persons) sumiso; (depressed) deprimido, melancólico. **in a s. voice,** en voz baja
subheading /'sʌb,hɛdɪŋ/ n subtítulo, m
subhuman /sʌb'hyumən/ a subhumano
subject /n., a. 'sʌbdʒɪkt; v. səb'dʒɛkt/ a sujeto; sometido (a); expuesto (a). n (of a country) súbdito (-ta); sujeto, m; (of study) asignatura, materia, f; (theme) tema, m; (Gram., Philos.) sujeto, m. vt subyugar; someter. **It can only be done s. to his consent,** Podrá hacerse únicamente si él lo consiente. **to change the s.,** cambiar de conversación. **to s. to criticism,** criticar (a). **s.-matter,** materia, f; (of a letter) contenido, m
subjection /səb'dʒɛkʃən/ n sujeción, f; sometimiento, m. **He was in a state of complete s.,** Estaba completamente sumiso. **to bring into s.,** subyugar
subjective /səb'dʒɛktɪv/ a subjetivo
subjectiveness /səb'dʒɛktɪvnɪs/ n subjetividad, f
subjectivism /səb'dʒɛktə,vɪzəm/ n subjetivismo, m
subjoin /səb'dʒɔin/ vt añadir, adjuntar
subjugate /'sʌbdʒə,geit/ vt subyugar, someter
subjugation /,sʌbdʒə'geiʃən/ n subyugación, f
subjunctive /səb'dʒʌŋktɪv/ a and n subjuntivo m
sublet /v. sʌb'lɛt; n. 'sʌb,lɛt/ vt subarrendar. n subarriendo, m
sublimate /v. 'sʌblə,meit; n. -mɪt/ vt sublimar. n sublimado, m
sublimation /,sʌblɪ'meiʃən/ n sublimación, f
sublime /sə'blaim/ a sublime; absoluto, completo; extremo. **the s.,** lo sublime
sublimely /sə'blaimli/ adv sublimemente; completamente
submachine gun /,sʌbmə'ʃin/ n metralleta, f, subfusil ametrallador, m
submarine /,sʌbmə'rin/ a submarino. n submarino, m. **midget s.,** submarino enano, submarino de bolsillo, m. **s. chaser,** cazasubmarino, m
submerge /səb'mɜrdʒ/ vt sumergir; inundar. vi sumergirse. **The submarine submerged,** El submarino se sumergió
submergence /səb'mɜrdʒəns/ n sumergimiento, m, sumersión, f; hundimiento, m
submersible /səb'mɜrsəbəl/ a sumergible
submersion /səb'mɜrʒən/ n sumersión, f; hundimiento, m
submission /səb'mɪʃən/ n sometimiento, m; sumisión, resignación, f; docilidad, f
submissive /səb'mɪsɪv/ a sumiso, dócil, manso
submissively /səb'mɪsɪvli/ adv sumisamente, con docilidad
submissiveness /səb'mɪsɪvnɪs/ n sumisión, docilidad, f
submit /səb'mɪt/ vt someterse (a); doblarse ante; (a scheme, etc.) someter; presentar; (urge) proponer. vi someterse; resignarse; (surrender) rendirse, entregarse. **to s. to arbitration,** someter a arbitraje
subordinate /adj., n. sə'bɔrdnɪt; v. -dŋ,eit/ a subordinado; subalterno, inferior; secundario. n subordinado (-da). vt subordinar
subordination /sə,bɔrdŋ'eiʃən/ n subordinación, f
suborn /sə'bɔrn/ vt sobornar, cohechar
subplot /'sʌb,plɒt/ n intriga secundaria, trama secundaria, f
subpoena /sə'pinə/ n citación, f. vt citar

subscribe /səb'skraib/ vt and vi subscribir; (to a periodical, etc.) abonarse (a)
subscriber /səb'skraibər/ n subscriptor (-ra); abonado (-da)
subscription /səb'skrɪpʃən/ n subscripción, f; (to a periodical, series of concerts, etc.) abono, m; (to a club) cuota, f
subsection /'sʌb,sɛkʃən/ n subsección, f
subsequent /'sʌbsikwənt/ a subsiguiente, subsecuente; posterior. **s. to,** después de, posterior a. **s. upon,** de resultas de
subsequently /'sʌbsikwəntli/ adv más tarde; subsiguientemente; luego
subservience /səb'sɜrviens/ n servilidad, f; utilidad, f
subservient /səb'sɜrviənt/ a servil; subordinado; útil
subside /səb'said/ vi (of water) bajar; (of ground) hundirse; (of foundations) asentarse; disminuir; calmarse; (be quiet) callarse. **to s. into a chair,** dejarse caer en un sillón
subsidence /səb'saidns/ n hundimiento, m; desplome, derrumbamiento, m; (of floods) bajada, f; (of anger, etc.) apaciguamiento, m
subsidiary /səb'sɪdi,ɛri/ a subsidiario
subsidize /'sʌbsi,daiz/ vt subvencionar
subsidy /'sʌbsidi/ n subvención, f, subsidio, m; prima, f
subsist /səb'sɪst/ vi subsistir
subsistence /səb'sɪstəns/ n subsistencia, f
subsoil /'sʌb,sɔil/ n subsuelo, m
substance /'sʌbstəns/ n substancia, f
substantial /səb'stænʃəl/ a substancial; sólido; importante
substantially /səb,stænʃəli/ adv substancialmente; sólidamente
substantiate /səb'stænʃi,eit/ vt establecer, verificar; justificar
substantiation /səb,stænʃi'eiʃən/ n comprobación, verificación, f; justificación, f
substantive /'sʌbstəntɪv/ a real, independiente; Gram. substantivo. n Gram. substantivo, m
substitute /'sʌbstɪ,tut/ n substituto (-ta); (material) substituto, m. vt substituir, reemplazar. **to be a s. for,** hacer las veces de
substitution /,sʌbstɪ'tuʃən/ n substitución, f, reemplazo, m
substratum /'sʌb,streitəm, -,strætəm/ n substrato, m
subterfuge /'sʌbtər,fyudʒ/ n subterfugio, m; evasiva, f
subterranean /,sʌbtə'reiniən/ a subterráneo
subtitle /'sʌb,taitl/ n subtítulo, m; (on films) guión, m
subtle /'sʌtl/ a sutil; delicado; penetrante; (crafty) astuto
subtlety /'sʌtlti/ n sutileza, f; delicadeza, f; (craftiness) astucia, f
subtly /'sʌtli/ adv sutilmente; con delicadeza
subtract /səb'trækt/ vt restar, substraer
subtraction /səb'trækʃən/ n resta, substracción, f
suburb /'sʌbɜrb/ n suburbio, m; pl **suburbs,** las afueras, f pl los arrabales, m pl
suburban /sə'bɜrbən/ a suburbano
subvention /səb'vɛnʃən/ n subvención, f
subversion /səb'vɜrʒən/ n subversión, f
subversive /səb'vɜrsɪv/ a subversivo
subvert /səb'vɜrt/ vt subvertir
subway /'sʌb,wei/ n (passageway) pasaje subterráneo, m; (underground railway) metro (Spain, Puerto Rico), m; subte (Argentina), m
succeed /sək'sid/ vt seguir (a); suceder (a); heredar. vi seguir (a); suceder (a); (be successful) tener éxito. **I did not s. in doing it,** No logré hacerlo. **to s. to the throne,** subir al trono
succeeding /sək'sidɪŋ/ a subsiguiente; futuro; consecutivo; sucesivo
success /sək'sɛs/ n éxito, m; triunfo, m. **to be a s.,** tener éxito. **The film was a great s.,** La película tuvo mucho éxito
successful /sək'sɛsfəl/ a que tiene éxito; afortunado, venturoso; próspero, Lat. Am. exitoso
successfully /sək'sɛsfəli/ adv con éxito; prósperamente

succession /sək'sɛʃən/ n sucesión, f; (series) serie, f; (inheritance) herencia, f; (descendants) descendencia, f. **in s.,** sucesivamente

successive /sək'sɛsɪv/ a sucesivo

successor /sək'sɛsər/ n sucesor (-ra)

succinct /sək'sɪŋkt/ a sucinto, conciso

succinctly /sək'sɪŋktli/ adv sucintamente, brevemente, en pocas palabras

succor /'sʌkər/ vt socorrer, auxiliar. n socorro, m, ayuda, f

succulence /'sʌkyələns/ n suculencia, f

succulent /'sʌkyələnt/ a suculento

succumb /sə'kʌm/ vi sucumbir; someterse, ceder

such /sʌtʃ/ a tal; parecido, semejante; así; tanto; (before an adjective, adverb) tan. n el, m, (f, la) que, los, m pl, (f pl, las) que; tal. **s. men,** tales hombres. **I have never seen s. magnificence,** Nunca he visto tanta magnificencia. **s. an important man,** un hombre tan importante. **s. pictures as these,** cuadros como estos. **S. is life!** ¡Así es la vida! **science as s.,** la ciencia como tal. **s.-and-s.,** tal y tal

suchlike /'sʌtʃ,laik/ a parecido, semejante; de esta clase

suck /sʌk/ vt chupar; (the breast) mamar; sorber; (of a vacuum cleaner, etc.) aspirar. n chupada, f; succión, f. **to s. down,** tragar. **to s. up,** aspirar; absorber

sucker /'sʌkər/ n Zool. ventosa, f; Bot. acodo, mugrón, m; (greenhorn) primo, m; (pig) lechón, m

suckle /'sʌkəl/ vt amamantar, dar el pecho (a)

suckling pig /'sʌklɪŋ/ n lechón, cochinillo, m

suction /'sʌkʃən/ n succión, f; aspiración, f. **s.-pump,** bomba aspirante, f

Sudan, the /su'dæn/ el Sudán, m

Sudanese /,sudn'iz/ a and n sudanés (-esa)

sudden /'sʌdn/ a súbito; (unexpected) inesperado, impensado; (of bends) brusco. **all of a s.,** de repente; súbitamente

suddenly /'sʌdnli/ adv súbitamente; de pronto, de repente

suddenness /'sʌdnnɪs/ n carácter repentino, m; (of a bend, etc.) brusquedad, f

suds /sʌdz/ n pl jabonaduras, f pl; espuma, f

sue /su/ vt Law. proceder contra, pedir en juicio; Law. demandar; litigar; (beg) suplicar. **to sue for peace,** pedir la paz

suede /sweid/ n ante, m. **s. glove,** guante de ante, m

suet /'suɪt/ n sebo, m

Suez Canal, the /su'ɛz/ el Canal de Suez, m

suffer /'sʌfər/ vt sufrir, padecer; pasar, experimentar; (tolerate) tolerar, sufrir; (allow) permitir. vi sufrir. **She suffers from her environment,** es la víctima de su medio ambiente

sufferance /'sʌfərəns/ n tolerancia, f. **on s.,** por tolerancia

sufferer /'sʌfərər/ n enfermo (-ma); víctima, f

suffering /'sʌfərɪŋ/ n sufrimiento, m; dolor, m. a sufriente

suffice /sə'fais/ vi ser suficiente, bastar. vt satisfacer

sufficiency /sə'fɪʃənsi/ n suficiencia, f; (of money) subsistencia, f

sufficient /sə'fɪʃənt/ a suficiente, bastante. **to be s.,** bastar, ser suficiente

sufficiently /sə'fɪʃəntli/ adv suficientemente, bastante

suffix /'sʌfɪks/ n Gram. sufijo, m

suffocate /'sʌfə,keit/ vt ahogar, sofocar, asfixiar. vi sofocarse, asfixiarse

suffocating /'sʌfə,keitɪŋ/ a sofocante, asfixiante

suffocation /,sʌfə'keiʃən/ n sofocación, asfixia, f; ahogo, m

suffrage /'sʌfrɪdʒ/ n sufragio, m; voto, m. **universal s.,** sufragio universal, m

suffragette /,sʌfrə'dʒɛt/ n sufragista, f

suffuse /sə'fyuz/ vt bañar, inundar, cubrir

sugar /'ʃʊgər/ n azúcar, m. vt azucarar. **brown s.,** azúcar moreno, m. **loaf s.,** azúcar de pilón, m. **white s.,** azúcar blanco, m. **to s. the pill,** dorar la píldora. **s.-almond,** peladilla, f. **s.-basin,** azucarera, f. **s.-beet,** remolacha, f. **s.-candy,** azúcar candi, m. **s.-cane,** caña de azúcar, f. **s.-cane syrup,** miel de caña, f. **s.-**

paste, alfeñique, m, alcorza, f. **s.-refinery,** fábrica de azúcar, f. **s.-tongs,** tenacillas para azúcar, f pl

sugary /'ʃʊgəri/ a azucarado; Fig. meloso, almibarado

suggest /səg'dʒɛst/ vt implicar; indicar, dar a entender; sugerir; (advise) aconsejar; (hint) insinuar; (evoke) evocar. **I suggested they should go to London,** Les aconsejé que fueran a Londres. **An idea suggested itself to him,** Se le ocurrió una idea

suggestion /səg'dʒɛstʃən/ n sugestión, f; insinuación, f

suggestive /səg'dʒɛstɪv/ a sugestivo; estimulante

suicidal /,suə'saidl/ a suicida. **s. tendency,** tendencia suicida, tendencia al suicidio, f

suicide /'suə,said/ n (act) suicidio, m; (person) suicida, mf. **to commit s.,** darse la muerte, quitarse la vida suicidarse

suit /sut/ n (request) petición, súplica, f; oferta de matrimonio, f; Law. pleito, m, demanda, f; (of clothes) traje, Colombia, Venezuela flus, m; (cards) palo, m; (of cards held) serie, f, vt convenir; sentar; ir bien (a); venir bien (a); (adapt) adaptar. **S. yourself!** ¡Haz lo que quieras! **The arrangement suits me very well,** El arreglo me viene muy bien. **The climate doesn't s. me,** El clima no me sienta bien. **The color does not s. you,** El color no te va bien. **to follow s.,** seguir el ejemplo (de); (cards) jugar el mismo palo. **s.-case,** maleta, f

suitability /,sutə'bɪliti/ n conveniencia, f; aptitud, f

suitable /'sutəbəl/ a conveniente; apropiado; apto; a propósito. **Not s. for children,** No apto para menores. **to make s. for,** adaptar a las necesidades de

suitably /'sutəbli/ adv convenientemente; apropiadamente

suite /swit/ n (of retainers, etc.) séquito, acompañamiento, m; (of furniture, etc.) juego, m; Mus. suite, f. **private s.,** habitaciones particulares, f pl. **s. of rooms,** apartamiento, m

suitor /'sutər/ n Law. demandante, m; pretendiente, m

sulk /sʌlk/ vi ponerse malhumorado, ser mohíno

sulkiness /'sʌlkinɪs/ n mohína, f, mal humor, m

sulky /'sʌlki/ a mohíno, malhumorado

sullen /'sʌlən/ a taciturno, hosco; malhumorado, sombrío; (of a landscape, etc.) triste, sombrío

sullenly /'sʌlənli/ adv taciturnamente, hoscamente

sullenness /'sʌlənnɪs/ n taciturnidad, f, hosquedad, f, mal humor, m

sully /'sʌli/ vt desdorar, empañar; manchar

sulphur /'sʌlfər/ n azufre, m

sulphuric /sʌl'fyʊrɪk/ a sulfúrico

sulphurous /'sʌlfərəs/ a sulfuroso

sultan /'sʌltn/ n sultán, m

sultriness /'sʌltrinɪs/ n bochorno, calor sofocante, m

sultry /'sʌltri/ a bochornoso, sofocante; (seductive) seductivo

sum /sʌm/ n suma, f; total, m; cantidad, f; (in arithmetic) problema (de aritmética), m. vt sumar, calcular. **in sum,** en suma; en resumen. **to sum up,** recapitular; resumir; (a person) tomar las medidas (a)

summarily /sə'mɛərəli/ adv someramente; Law. sumariamente

summarize /'sʌmə,raiz/ vt resumir brevemente; compendiar

summary /'sʌməri/ a somero; Law. sumario. n resumen, sumario, compendio, m. **summary records,** actas resumidas, f pl

summer /'sʌmər/ n verano, estío, m. **to spend the s.,** veranear. **s.-house,** cenador, m. **s.-time,** verano, m; hora de verano, f. **s. wheat,** trigo tremesino, m

summing-up /'sʌmɪŋ ,ʌp/ n recapitulación, f

summit /'sʌmɪt/ n cima, cumbre, f; Fig. apogeo, m

summitry /'sʌmɪtri/ n diplomacia en la cumbre, f

summon /'sʌmən/ vt llamar, hacer venir; mandar, requerir; Law. citar. **to s. up one's courage,** cobrar ánimos

summons /'sʌmənz/ n llamamiento, m; Mil. intimación, f; Law. citación, f. vt Law. citar

summon /'sʌmən/ vt llamar, hacer venir; mandar, requerir; Law. citar. **to s. up one's courage,** cobrar ánimos

sump /sʌmp/ n Mineral. sumidero, m

sumptuous /'sʌmptʃuəs/ a suntuoso, lujoso, magnífico

sumptuousness /'sʌmptʃuəsnɪs/ n suntuosidad, magnificencia, f

sun /sʌn/ n sol, m. **The sun was shining,** Hacía sol, El sol brillaba. **to bask in the sun,** tomar el sol. **sunbathing,** baños de sol, m pl. **sun-blind,** toldo para el sol, m. **sun-bonnet,** capelina, f. **sun-glasses,** gafas ahumadas, f pl. **sun-helmet,** casco colonial, m. **sunspot,** Astron. mancha del sol, f; (freckle) peca, f.

sun-worship, adoración del sol, f

sunbeam /'sʌn,bim/ n rayo de sol, m

sunburn /'sʌn,bɜrn/ n quemadura del sol, f; bronceado, m

sunburned /'sʌn,bɜrnd/ a quemado por el sol; bronceado, tostado por el sol

sundae /'sʌndei/ n helado de frutas, m

Sunday /'sʌndei/ n domingo, m. **in his S. best,** en su traje dominguero, endomingado. **S. school,** escuela dominical, f

Sunday's child /'sʌndeiz/ n niño nacido de pies, niño nacido un domingo, niño mimado de la fortuna

sunder /'sʌndər/ vt dividir en dos, hender; separar

sundial /'sʌn,daiəl/ n reloj de sol, reloj solar, m

sundown /'sʌn,daun/ n puesta del sol, f

sundry /'sʌndri/ a varios (-as). n pl **sundries,** artículos diversos, m pl; Com. varios, m pl. **all and s.,** todo el mundo, todos y cada uno

sunflower /'sʌn,flauər/ n girasol, tornasol, m, trompeta de amor, f

sunken /'sʌŋkən/ a (of eyes, etc.) hundido

sunless /'sʌnlɪs/ a sin sol

sun letter n letra solar, f

sunlight /'sʌn,lait/ n luz del sol, f, rayos del sol, m pl. **artificial s.,** sol artificial, m. **in the s.,** al sol

sunny /'sʌni/ a de sol; bañado de sol; asoleado; expuesto al sol; (face) risueño; (of disposition, etc.) alegre. **to be s.,** hacer sol

sunrise /'sʌn,raiz/ n salida del sol, f. **from s. to sunset,** de sol a sol

sunset /'sʌn,sɛt/ n puesta del sol, f. **at s.,** a la caída (or puesta) del sol

sunshade /'sʌn,ʃeid/ n parasol, quitasol, m, sombrilla, f

sunshine /'sʌn,ʃain/ n luz del sol, f. **in the s.,** al sol

sunstroke /'sʌn,strouk/ n insolación, f

sup /sʌp/ vt sorber. vi cenar. n sorbo, m

super /'supər/ n (actor) comparsa, mf; (film) superproducción, f; (of a beehive) alza, f

superabun lance /,supərə'bʌndəns/ n superabundancia, sobreabundancia, f

superabundant /,supərə'bʌndənt/ a superabundante, sobreabundante. **to be s.,** sobreabundar

superannuate /,supər'ænyu,eit/ vt (retire) jubilar

superannuated /,supər'ænyu,eitid/ a (retired) jubilado; (out-of-date) anticuado

superannuation /,supər,ænyu'eiʃən/ n (retirement and pension) jubilación, f

superb /su'pɜrb/ a magnífico, espléndido

superbly /su'pɜrbli/ adv magníficamente

supercargo /'supər,kɑrgou/ n Naut. sobrecargo, m

supercharger /'supər,tʃɑrdʒər/ n (Auto., Aer.) compresor, m

supercilious /,supər'siliəs/ a altanero, altivo, orgulloso; desdeñoso

superciliousness /,supər'siliəsnɪs/ n altanería, altivez, f, orgullo, m; desdén, m

superficial /,supər'fiʃəl/ a superficial

superficiality /,supər,fiʃi'ælɪti/ n superficialidad, f

superficially /,supər'fiʃəli/ adv superficialmente

superfine /,supər'fain/ a superfino

superfluity /,supər'fluiti/ n superfluidad, f

superfluous /su'pɜrfluəs/ a superfluo. **to be s.,** sobrar

superfortress /'supər,fɔrtrɪs/ n Aer. superfortaleza volante, f

superhuman /,supər'hyumən/ a sobrehumano

superimpose /,supərɪm'pouz/ vt sobreponer

superintend /,supərɪn'tɛnd/ vt superentender, dirigir

superintendent /,supərɪn'tɛndənt/ n superinten-

dente, mf; director (-ra); (school) inspector; (police) subjefe de la policía, m

superior /sə'pɪəriər/ a superior; (in number) mayor; (smug) desdeñoso. n superior (-ra). **Mother S.,** (madre) superiora, f. **s. to,** superior a; encima de

superiority /sə,pɪəri'ɔrɪti/ n superioridad, f

superlative /sə'pɜrlətɪv/ a extremo, supremo; Gram. superlativo. n Gram. superlativo, m

superlatively /sə'pɜrlətɪvli/ adv en sumo grado, superlativamente

superman /'supər,mæn/ n superhombre, m

supermarket /'supər,mɑrkɪt/ n supermercado, m

supernatural /,supər'nætʃərəl/ a sobrenatural

superposition /,supərpə'zɪʃən/ n superposición, f

superscribe /'supər,skraib/ vt sobrescribir; poner el sobrescrito (a)

superscription /,supər'skrɪpʃən/ n (on letters, documents) sobrescrito, m; (superscription)

supersede /,supər'sid/ vt reemplazar; suplantar

supersensible /,supər'sɛnsəbəl/ a suprasensible

superstition /,supər'stɪʃən/ n superstición, f

superstitious /,supər'stɪʃəs/ a supersticioso

supertax /'supər,tæks/ n impuesto suplementario, m

supervene /,supər'vin/ vi sobrevenir

supervise /'supər,vaiz/ vt superentender, vigilar; dirigir

supervision /,supər'vɪʒən/ n superintendencia, f; dirección, f

supervisor /'supər,vaizər/ n superintendente, mf; inspector (-ra); director (-ra)

supine /a. su'pain; n. 'supain/ a supino; indolente, negligente. n Gram. supino, m

supper /'supər/ n cena, f. **the Last S.,** la Última Cena. **to have s.,** cenar. **s.-time,** hora de cenar, f

supplant /sə'plænt/ vt suplantar; usurpar; reemplazar

supplanter /sə'plæntər/ n suplantador (-ra)

supple /'sʌpəl/ a flexible; dócil, manso; (fawning) adulador, servil, lisonjero

supplement /'sʌpləmənt/ n suplemento, m; (of a book) apéndice, m

supplementary /,sʌplə'mɛntəri/ a suplementario; adicional

suppleness /'sʌpəlnɪs/ n flexibilidad, f; docilidad, f; servilidad, f

suppliant /'sʌpliənt/ a and n suplicante, mf

supplicate /'sʌpli,keit/ vt and vi suplicar

supplication /,sʌpli'keiʃən/ n suplicación, f; súplica, f

supply /sə'plai/ vt proveer (de); suministrar; proporcionar, dar; (a deficiency) suplir; (a post) llenar; (a post temporarily) reemplazar. n suministro, surtimiento, m; provisión, f; (of electricity, etc.) suministro, m; Com. oferta, f; (person) substituto (-ta); pl **supplies,** Com. existencias, f pl; Mil. pertrechos, m pl; víveres, m pl, provisiones, f pl. **s. and demand,** oferta y demanda, f

support /sə'pɔrt/ vt apoyar, sostener; mantener; (endure) soportar; (a cause) apoyar, defender; (corroborate) confirmar, vindicar. n apoyo, m; sostén, m; soporte, m. **to speak in s. of,** defender, abogar por. **to s. oneself,** ganarse la vida, mantenerse

supporter /sə'pɔrtər/ n apoyo, m; defensor (-ra), partidario (-ia)

suppose /sə'pouz/ vt suponer; imaginar(se); creer. **always supposing,** dado que, en el caso de que. **Supposing he had gone out?** ¿Y si hubiera salido? **I don't s. they will go to Spain,** No creo que vayan a España. **He is supposed to be clever,** Tiene fama de listo

supposed /sə'pouzd, -'pouzɪd/ a supuesto; que se llama a sí mismo

supposition /,sʌpə'zɪʃən/ n suposición, hipótesis, f

suppress /sə'prɛs/ vt reprimir; (yawns, etc.) ahogar; contener; (heresies, rebellions, books, etc.) suprimir; (dissemble) disimular, esconder; (a heckler, etc.) hacer callar

suppressed /sə'prɛst/ a reprimido; contenido; disimulado

suppression /sə'prɛʃən/ n represión, f; supresión, f; disimulación, f

suppurate /'sʌpyə,reit/ vi supurar

suppuration /ˌsʌpyəˈreiʃən/ n supuración, f
supremacy /səˈprɛməsi/ n supremacía, f
supreme /səˈprim/ a supremo; sumo. **with s. indifference,** con suma indiferencia. **s. court,** tribunal supremo, m
surcharge /ˈsɜr.tʃɑrdʒ/ n sobrecarga, f
sure /ʃʊr/ a seguro; cierto. adv seguramente. **Be s. to...!** ¡Ten cuidado de...! ¡No dejes de...! **to be s.,** seguramente, sin duda; ¡claro!; (fancy!) ¡no me digas!; ¡qué sorpresa! **I am not so s. of that,** No diría yo tanto. **Come on Thursday for s.,** Venga el jueves sin falta. **It is s. to rain tomorrow,** Seguramente va a llover mañana. **to make s. of,** asegurarse de. **to be (or feel) s.,** estar seguro. **s.-footed,** de pie firme, seguro
surely /ˈʃʊrli/ adv seguramente; sin duda, ciertamente; por supuesto
sureness /ˈʃʊrnɛs/ n seguridad, f; certeza, f
surety /ˈʃʊriti/ n garantía, fianza, f; (person) garante, mf
surf /sɜrf/ n resaca, f; rompiente, m; oleaje, m. **s.-board,** aquaplano, m. **s.-riding,** patinaje sobre las olas, m
surface /ˈsɜrfis/ n superficie, f; exterior, m. a superficial. vi (of a submarine) salir a la superficie. **on the s.,** en apariencia
surface mail n correo por vía ordinaria, servicio ordinario, servicio per vía de superficie, m
surfeit /ˈsɜrfit/ n exceso, m, superabundancia, f; saciedad, f. vt hartar; saciar
surge /sɜrdʒ/ vi (of waves) embravecerse, hincharse; (of crowds) agitarse, bullir; (of emotions) despertarse. n (of sea, crowd, blood) oleada, f; (of anger) ola, f. **The blood surged into his face,** La sangre se le subió a las mejillas
surgeon /ˈsɜrdʒən/ n cirujano, m; (Nav., Mil.) médico, m
surgery /ˈsɜrdʒəri/ n cirugía, f; (doctor's) consultorio, m; (dispensary) dispensario, m
surgical /ˈsɜrdʒɪkəl/ a quirúrgico
surliness /ˈsɜrlinɪs/ n mal genio, m, taciturnidad, f; brusquedad, f
surly /ˈsɜrli/ a taciturno, huraño, malhumorado; brusco
surmise /sərˈmaiz/ n conjetura, suposición, f. vt conjeturar, adivinar; imaginar, suponer. vi hacer conjeturas
surmount /sərˈmaunt/ vt superar, vencer; coronar
surname /ˈsɜr.neim/ n apellido, m. vt denominar, nombrar
surpass /sərˈpæs/ vt superar, exceder; aventajarse (a); eclipsar
surpassing /sərˈpæsɪŋ/ a sin par, incomparable
surplus /ˈsɜrplʌs/ n exceso, sobrante, m; (Com.) of accounts) superávit, m. **sale of s. stock,** liquidación de saldos, f
surplusage /ˈsɜrplʌsɪdʒ/ n material de desecho, m
surprise /sərˈpraiz, sə-/ n sorpresa, f; asombro, m. vt sorprender; asombrar. **to s. (someone) in the act,** coger en el acto. **to take (a person) by s.,** sorprender (a). **He was surprised into admitting it,** Cogido a la imprevista, lo confesó
surprising /sərˈpraizɪŋ, sə-/ a sorprendente
surrealism /səˈriə,lɪzəm/ n surrealismo, m
surrealist /səˈriəlɪst/ a and n surrealista, mf
surrender /səˈrɛndər/ vt rendir, entregar; (goods) ceder, renunciar (a). vi rendirse, entregarse; abandonarse. n rendición, capitulación, f; entrega, f; (of goods) cesión, f; (of an insurance policy) rescate, m. **to s. oneself to remorse,** abandonarse (or entregarse) al remordimiento. **to s. unconditionally,** entregarse a discreción
surreptitious /ˌsɜrəpˈtiʃəs/ a subrepticio
surreptitiously /ˌsɜrəpˈtiʃəsli/ adv subrepticiamente, a hurtadillas
surround /səˈraund/ vt rodear; cercar; Mil. asediar, sitiar. n borde, m. **Peter was surrounded by his friends,** Pedro estaba rodeado por sus amigos
surrounding /səˈraundɪŋ/ a (que está) alrededor de; vecino. **the s. country,** los alrededores

surroundings /səˈraundɪŋz/ n pl cercanías, f pl, alrededores, m pl; (environment) medio, m; ambiente, m
surtax /ˈsɜr.tæks/ n impuesto suplementario, m
surveillance /sərˈveiləns/ n vigilancia, f
survey /v. sərˈvei; n. ˈsɜrvei/ vt contemplar, mirar; (events, etc.) pasar en revista; estudiar; (land, etc.) apear; (a house, etc.) inspeccionar. n vista general, f; inspección, f; (of facts, etc.) examen, m; estudio, m; (of land, etc.) apeo, m; (of literature, etc.) bosquejo, breve panorama, m
surveying /sərˈveiɪŋ/ n agrimensura, f
surveyor /sərˈveiər/ n agrimensor, m; (superintendent) inspector, m; superintendente, m
survival /sərˈvaivəl/ n supervivencia, f. **s. of the fittest,** supervivencia de los más aptos, f
survive /sərˈvaiv/ vt sobrevivir a. vi sobrevivir; (of customs) subsistir, durar
survivor /sərˈvaivər/ n sobreviviente, mf
susceptibility /səˌsɛptəˈbɪliti/ n susceptibilidad, f; tendencia, f; pl susceptibilities, sensibilidad, f
susceptible /səˈsɛptəbəl/ a susceptible; impresionable; sensible; (to love) enamoradizo. **He is s. to bronchitis,** Es susceptible a la bronquitis
suspect /a., n. ˈsʌspɛkt; v. səˈspɛkt/ a and n sospechoso (-sa). vt sospechar; dudar; imaginar, suponer. vi tener sospechas
suspend /səˈspɛnd/ vt suspender. **suspended animation,** muerte aparente, f
suspender /səˈspɛndər/ n liga, f; pl **suspenders,** (braces) tirantes del pantalón, m pl. **s.-belt,** faja, f
suspense /səˈspɛns/ n incertidumbre, f. **to keep (a person) in s.,** dejar en la incertidumbre (a)
suspension /səˈspɛnʃən/ n suspensión, f. **s.-bridge,** puente colgante, m. **s. of payments,** suspensión de pagos, f
suspicion /səˈspiʃən/ n sospecha, f; (touch) dejo, m; cantidad muy pequeña, f. **to be above s.,** estar por encima de toda sospecha. **I had no suspicions...,** No sospechaba...
suspicious /səˈspiʃəs/ a (by nature) suspicaz; sospechoso. **to make s.,** hacer sospechar
suspiciously /səˈspiʃəsli/ adv suspicazmente, desconfiadamente; de un modo sospechoso. **It seems s. like...,** Tiene toda la apariencia de...
suspiciousness /səˈspiʃəsnɪs/ n carácter sospechoso, m, lo sospechoso; suspicacia, f
sustain /səˈstein/ vt sostener; mantener; sustentar; apoyar; corroborar, confirmar; (a note) prolongar. **to s. injuries,** recibir heridas
sustenance /ˈsʌstənəns/ n mantenimiento, m; sustento, m, alimentos, m pl
suture /ˈsutʃər/ n sutura, f
svelte /svɛlt/ a esbelto, gentil
swab /swɒb/ vt Naut. lampacear; limpiar con lampazo; Surg. tamponar. n lampazo, m; Surg. torunda, f, tampón, m
swaddle /ˈswɒdl/ vt envolver; (infants) fajar
swaddling clothes /ˈswɒdlɪŋ/ n pl pañales, m pl. **to be still in s. clothes,** Fig. estar en mantillas, estar en pañales
swagger /ˈswægər/ vi fanfarronear, pavonearse; darse importancia. n pavoneo, m; aire importante, m; (coat) tonto, m. a majo; de última moda
swaggering /ˈswægərɪŋ/ a fanfarrón, jactancioso; importante
Swahili /swɑˈhili/ suaili; n suaili, m
swain /swein/ n zagal, m; enamorado, m; pretendiente, amante, m
swallow /ˈswɒlou/ vt tragar; engullir. n trago, m; sorbo, m; Ornith. golondrina, f. **to s. an insult (a story),** tragar un insulto (una historia). **to s. one's words,** retractarse. **to s. one's pride,** bajar la cerviz, humillarse. **to s. up,** tragar; absorber. **s.-tailed coat,** frac, m
swamp /swɒmp/ n pantano, m, marisma, f, Argentina fachinal, f, Central America chagüe, m. vt sumergir; (a boat) echar a pique, hundir; (inundate) inundar
swampy /ˈswɒmpi/ a pantanoso
swan /swɒn/ n cisne, m. **swan's down,** plumón de cisne, m. **s.-song,** canto del cisne, m

swank /swæŋk/ n pretensiones, f pl, vi darse humos
sward /swɔrd/ n césped, m, hierba, f
swarm /swɔrm/ n enjambre, m; (of people) muchedumbre, multitud, f; tropel, m. vi (of bees) enjambrar; (of other insects) pulular; (of people) hormiguear, bullir, pulular. vt (climb) trepar. **to s. with,** estar infestado de
swarthiness /'swɔrðɪnɪs/ n tez morena, f; color moreno, m
swarthy /'swɔrði/ a moreno
swashbuckler /'swɒʃ,bʌklər, 'swɔʃ-/ n perdonavidas, matasiete, m
swashbuckling /'swɒʃ,bʌklɪŋ/ a de capa y espada, valentón, fanfarrón
swastika /'swɒstɪkə/ n esvástica, cruz gamada, f
swathe /swɒð/ vt envolver; fajar; (with bandages) vendar
swathing /'swɒðɪŋ/ n envoltura, f; (bandages) vendas, f pl
sway /swei/ vi balancearse; oscilar; (stagger, of persons) bambolearse; (totter, of things) tambalearse; (of carriages) cabecear; (gracefully, in walking) cimbrarse. vt balancear, mecer; oscilar; hacer tambalear; (influence) influir, inclinar; (govern) regir, gobernar. n balanceo, m; oscilación, f; vaivén, m; tambaleo, m; (influence) ascendiente, dominio, m, influencia, f; (rule) imperio, poder, m. **to hold s. over,** gobernar, regir
swear /swɛər/ vt jurar; (Law. etc.) declarar bajo juramento. vi jurar; (curse) echar pestes, blasfemar. **to s. at,** maldecir. **to s. by,** jurar por; poner fe implícita en. **to be sworn in,** prestar juramento. **to s. in,** tomar juramento (a). **to s. to,** atestiguar
sweat /swɛt/ n sudor, m; Inf. trabajo arduo, m. vi sudar. vt sudar; hacer sudar; (workers) explotar. **by the s. of one's brow,** con el sudor de la frente, con el sudor del rostro. **s.-gland,** glándula sudorípara, f
sweated /'swɛtɪd/ a (of persons) explotado; (of labor) mal retribuido
sweater /'swɛtər/ n suéter, jersey, m
sweating /'swɛtɪŋ/ n transpiración, f; (of workers) explotación, f
sweaty /'swɛti/ a sudoroso
Swede /swid/ n sueco (-ca); (vegetable) naba, f
Sweden /'swidn/ Suecia, f
sweep /swip/ vi extenderse (por); (cleave) surcar; pasar rápidamente (por); invadir; dominar; andar majestuosamente; (with a brush) barrer. vt barrer; pasar (por); (the strings of a musical instrument) rasguear; (the sea) navegar por; (mines) barrer; (the horizon, etc.) examinar; (a chimney) deshollinar; (with a brush) barrer; (remove) arrebatar; quitar; llevarse; (abolish) suprimir. **to s. along,** vt (of the current, crowds, etc.) arrastrar. vi barrer majestuosamente; correr rápidamente (por). **to s. aside,** apartar con la mano; abandonar; (a protest) desoír, no hacer caso de. **to s. away,** barrer; (remove) llevarse; destruir; suprimir. **to s. down,** vt barrer; (carry) arrastrar. vi (of cliffs, etc.) bajar; (of an enemy) abalanzarse (sobre); lanzarse (por). **to s. off,** barrer; (a person) llevarse sin perder tiempo; arrebatar con violencia (a). **to be swept off one's feet,** ser arrastrado (por); perder el balance; (of emotion) ser dominado por. **to s. on,** seguir su avance inexorable; seguir su marcha. **to s. up,** recoger, barrer
sweep /swip/ n barredura, f; (of a chimney) deshollinador, m; (of the tide) curso, m; (of a scythe, etc.) golpe, m; (range) alcance, m; (fold) pliegue, m; (curve) curva, f; (of water, etc.) extensión, f; (of wings) envergadura, f. **with a s. of the arm,** con un gesto del brazo. **to make a clean s. of,** hacer tabla rasa de
sweeping /'swipɪŋ/ a completo; comprensivo; demasiado general; radical. **a s. judgment,** un juicio demasiado general. **s. change,** cambio radicale, m pl. **s. brush,** escoba, f
sweepings /'swipɪŋz/ n pl barreduras, f pl; residuos, m pl; (of society) heces, f pl
sweepstakes /'swip,steiks/ n lotería, f
sweet /swit/ a dulce; (of scents) oloroso, fragante; (of sounds) melodioso, dulce; (charming) encantador;

amable; (pretty) bonito. n bombón, m; golosina, f; (at a meal) (plato) dulce, m; dulzura, f; (beloved) amor, m, querido (-da). **How s. it smells!** ¡Qué buen olor tiene! **the sweets of life,** las dulzuras de la vida. **s.-pea,** guisante de olor, m, haba de las Indias, f. **s.-potato,** batata, f, Lat. Am. boniato, camote, m. **s.-scented,** perfumado, fragante. **s.-tempered,** amable, de carácter dulce. **s.-toothed,** goloso. **s.-william,** Bot. clavel de la China, clavel de ramillete, clavel de San Isidro, ramillete de Constantinopla, m, minutisa, f
sweetbread /'swit,brɛd/ n lechecillas, f pl
sweeten /'switn/ vt azucarar; endulzar. **Cervantes sweetens one's bitter moments,** Cervantes endulza los momentos ásperos
sweetheart /'swit,hɑrt/ n amante, mf, amado (-da); (as address) querido (-da)
sweetish /'switɪʃ/ a algo dulce
sweetly /'switli/ adv dulcemente; (of scents) olorosamente; (of sounds) melodiosamente; (of behavior, etc.) amablemente
sweetness /'switnɪs/ n dulzura, f; (of scents) buen olor, m, fragancia, f; (of sounds) melodía, dulzura, f; (of character) bondad, amabilidad, f
sweet potato n batata, f, boniato, buniato, Mexico camote, m
sweet sixteen n (age) los dieciséis abriles, m pl; (party) quinceañera (at age fifteen) f
sweet turnip n Central America jícama, f
swell /swɛl/ vi hincharse; (of the sea) entumecerse; crecer; aumentarse. vt hinchar; aumentar. n (of the sea) oleada, f, oleaje, m; (of the ground) ondulación, f; (of sound) crescendo, m; (increase) aumento, m; (dandy) pisaverde, elegante, m; (important person) pájaro gordo, m; (at games, etc.) espada, m. a estupendo; elegantísimo; de primera, excelente. **to suffer from swelled head,** tener humos, darse importancia. **This foot is swollen,** Este pie está hinchado (or tumefacto). **The refugees have swelled the population,** Los refugiados han aumentado la población. **eyes swollen with tears,** ojos arrasados de lágrimas. **to s. with pride,** hincharse de orgullo
swelling /'swɛlɪŋ/ n hinchazón, f; Med. tumefacción, f; (bruise, etc.) chichón, m
swelter /'swɛltər/ vi abrasarse; arder. n bochorno, calor sofocante, m
swerve /swɜrv/ vi desviarse; apartarse (de); torcerse. n desvío, m
swift /swɪft/ a rápido, veloz; pronto. adv velozmente, rápidamente. n Ornith. vencejo, m. **s.-flowing,** (of rivers, etc.) de corriente rápida. **s.-footed,** de pies ligeros
swiftly /'swɪftli/ adv rápidamente, velozmente
swiftness /'swɪftnɪs/ n rapidez, velocidad, f; prontitud, f
swim /swɪm/ vi nadar; flotar; (glide) deslizarse; (fill) inundarse. vt (a horse) hacer nadar; pasar a nado; nadar. n natación, f. **eyes swimming with tears,** ojos inundados de lágrimas. **He enjoys a s.,** Le gusta nadar. **My head swims,** Se me va la cabeza. **Everything swam before my eyes,** Todo parecía bailar ante mis ojos. **to be in the s.,** formar parte (de), ser (de); (be up to date) estar al corriente. **to s. the Channel,** atravesar el canal de la Mancha a nado. **to s. with the tide,** ir con la corriente
swimmer /'swɪmər/ n nadador (-ra). **He is a bad s.,** Nada mal
swimming /'swɪmɪŋ/ n natación, f; (of the head) vértigo, m. **s.-bath,** piscina, f. **s.-pool,** piscina, Lat. Am. alberca, f
swindle /'swɪndl/ vt engañar, estafar; defraudar (de). n estafa, f, timo, m; engaño, m; impostura, f, Lat. Am. cambullón, Argentina forro, m
swindler /'swɪndlər/ n estafador (-ra), trampeador (-ra); engañador (-ra)
swine /swain/ n cerdo, puerco, m; (person) cochino (-na). **a herd of s.,** una manada de cerdos
swineherd /'swain,hɜrd/ n porquero, m
swing /swɪŋ/ vi balancearse; oscilar; (hang) colgar, pender; columpiarse; girar; dar la vuelta; (of a boat) bornear. vt balancear; (hang) colgar; (rock) mecer; (in a swing, etc.) columpiar; hacer oscilar; (raise)

subir. *n* oscilación, *f*; vaivén, *m*; balanceo, *m*; (rhythm) ritmo, *m*; (seat, etc.) columpio, *m*; (reach) alcance, *m*. **The door swung open**, La puerta se abrió silenciosamente. **He swung the car around**, Dio la vuelta al auto. **He swung himself into the saddle**, Montó de un salto. **to be in full s.**, estar a toda marcha. **to go with a s.**, tener mucho éxito. **s.-boat**, columpio, *m*. **s.-bridge**, puente giratorio, *m*. **s.-door**, puerta giratoria, *f*

swinging /'swɪŋɪŋ/ *a* oscilante; pendiente; rítmico. *n* balanceo, *m*; oscilación, *f*; vaivén, *m*; ritmo, *m*. **s. stride**, andar rítmico, *m*

swinish /'swaɪnɪʃ/ *a* porcuno, de cerdo; cochino, sucio

swipe /swaip/ *vt* golpear duro; aplastar; (steal) *Mexico* chalequear. *n* golpe fuerte, *m*

swirl /swɜrl/ *vi* arremolinarse. *n* remolino, *m*

swish /swɪʃ/ *vt* (of an animal's tail) agitar, mover, menear; (of a cane) blandir; (thrash) azotar. *vi* silbar; (of water) susurrar; (of a dress, etc.) crujir. *n* silbo, *m*; (of water) susurro, murmullo, *m*; (of a dress, etc.) crujido, *m*

Swiss /swɪs/ *a* and *n* suizo (-za)

switch /swɪtʃ/ *n* vara, *f*; (riding) látigo, *m*; (of hair) trenza, *f*; *Elec.* interruptor, *m*; *Rail.* aguja, *f*; (*Rail.* siding) desviadero, *m*. *vt* azotar; (a train) desviar; *Elec.* interrumpir; (transfer) trasladar; (of an animal, its tail) remover, mover rápidamente. **to s. off**, (*Elec.* and telephone) cortar; (*Radio.* and *Auto.*) desconectar. **to s. on**, conectar; (a light) poner (la luz); (a radio) encender

switchboard /'swɪtʃ,bɔrd/ *n* cuadro de distribución, *m*

Switzerland /'swɪtsərlənd/ Suiza, *f*

swivel /'swɪvəl/ *n* torniquete, *m*; anillo móvil, *m*; pivote, *m*. *vi* girar sobre un eje; dar una vuelta. **s.-chair**, silla giratoria, *f*. **s.-door**, puerta giratoria, *f*

swoon /swun/ *vi* desvanecerse, desmayarse. *n* desmayo, desvanecimiento, *m*

swoop /swup/ *vi* calarse, abatirse; (of robbers, etc.) abalanzarse (sobre). *n* calada, *f*. **at one fell s.**, de un solo golpe

sword /sɔrd/ *n* espada, *f*; sable, *m*. **to measure swords with**, cruzar espadas con. **to put to the s.**, pasar a cuchillo (a). **s.-arm**, brazo derecho, *m*. **s.-belt**, talabarte, *m*. **s.-cut**, sablazo, *m*. **s.-dance**, danza de espadas, *f*. **s.-fish**, pez espada, pez sierra, espadarte, *m*, jifia, *f*. **s.-play**, esgrima, *f*; manejo de la espada, *m*. **s.-stick**, bastón de estoque, *m*. **s.-thrust**, golpe de espada, *m*; estocada, *f*

swordsman /'sɔrdzmən/ *n* espadachín, *m*; esgrimidor, *m*

swordsmanship /'sɔrdzmən,ʃɪp/ *n* manejo de la espada, *m*; esgrima, *f*

sybarite /'sɪbə,rait/ *a* and *n* sibarita, *mf*

sybaritic /,sɪbə'rɪtɪk/ *a* sibarítico, sibarita

sycamore /'sɪkə,mɔr/ *n* sicomoro, *m*; falso plátano, *m*

sycophancy /'sɪkəfənsi/ *n* servilismo, *m*

sycophant /'sɪkəfənt/ *n* sicofanta, *m*

syllabic /sɪ'læbɪk/ *a* silábico

syllable /'sɪləbəl/ *n* sílaba, *f*

syllabus /'sɪləbəs/ *n* programa, *m*; compendio, *f*

syllogism /'sɪlə,dʒɪzəm/ *n* silogismo, *m*

sylph /sɪlf/ *n* sílfide, *f*, silfo, *m*; (woman) sílfide, *f*; (hummingbird) colibrí, *m*. **s.-like**, de sílfide; como una sílfide

sylvan /'sɪlvən/ *a* selvático, silvestre; rústico

symbiosis /,sɪmbi'ousɪs/ *n* simbiosis, *f*

symbol /'sɪmbəl/ *n* símbolo, emblema, *m*; *Math.* símbolo, *m*; (of rank, etc.) insignia, *f*

symbolical /sɪm'bɒlɪkəl/ *a* simbólico

symbolism /'sɪmbə,lɪzəm/ *n* simbolismo, *m*

symbolist /'sɪmbəlɪst/ *n* simbolista, *mf*

symbolize /'sɪmbə,laɪz/ *vt* simbolizar

symmetrical /sɪ'mɛtrɪkəl/ *a* simétrico

symmetry /'sɪmɪtri/ *n* simetría, *f*

sympathetic /,sɪmpə'θɛtɪk/ *a* simpático; compasivo; (of the public, etc.) bien dispuesto. *n Anat.* gran simpático, *m*. **s. words**, palabras de simpatía, *f pl*. **s. ink**, tinta simpática, *f*

sympathetically /,sɪmpə'θɛtɪkli/ *adv* simpáticamente; con compasión

sympathize /'sɪmpə,θaɪz/ *vi* simpatizar (con); (understand) comprender; (condole) compadecerse (de), condolerse (de); dar el pésame

sympathizer /'sɪmpə,θaɪzər/ *n* partidario (-ia)

sympathy /'sɪmpəθi/ *n* simpatía, *f*; compasión, *f*. **Paul is in s. with their aims**, Pablo está de acuerdo con sus objetos. **Please accept my s.**, (on a bereavement) Le acompaño a Vd. en su sentimiento

symphonic /sɪm'fɒnɪk/ *a* sinfónico

symphony /'sɪmfəni/ *n* sinfonía, *f*

symposium /sɪm'pouziəm/ *n* colección de artículos, *f*

symptom /'sɪmptəm/ *n* síntoma, *m*; señal, *f*, indicio, *m*. **to show symptoms of**, dar indicios de

symptomatic /,sɪmptə'mætɪk/ *a* sintomático

synagogue /'sɪnə,gɒg/ *n* sinagoga, *f*

synchronization /,sɪŋkrənə'zeɪʃən/ *n* sincronización, *f*

synchronize /'sɪŋkrə,naɪz/ *vi* coincidir, tener lugar simultáneamente; sincronizarse. *vt* sincronizar

synchronous /'sɪŋkrənəs/ *a* sincrónico

syncopate /'sɪŋkə,peɪt/ *vt* (*Gram. Mus.*) sincopar

syncopation /,sɪŋkə'peɪʃən/ *n Mus.* síncopa, *f*

syncope /'sɪŋkə,pi/ *n* (*Med. Gram.*) síncope, *m*

syndical /'sɪndɪkəl/ *a* sindical

syndicalism /'sɪndɪkə,lɪzəm/ *n* sindicalismo, *m*

syndicalist /'sɪndɪkəlɪst/ *n* sindicalista, *mf*

syndicate /*n.* 'sɪndɪkɪt; *v.* -,keit/ *n* sindicato, *m*, *f*. *vt* sindicar

syndication /,sɪndɪ'keɪʃən/ *n* sindicación, *f*

synod /'sɪnəd/ *n Eccl.* sínodo, *m*

synonym /'sɪnənɪm/ *n* sinónimo, *m*

synonymous /sɪ'nɒnəməs/ *a* sinónimo

synopsis /sɪ'nɒpsɪs/ *n* sinopsis, *f*

synoptic /sɪ'nɒptɪk/ *a* sinóptico

syntax /'sɪntæks/ *n* sintaxis, *f*

synthesis /'sɪnθəsɪs/ *n* síntesis, *f*

synthetic /sɪn'θɛtɪk/ *a* sintético

synthetize /'sɪnθə,taɪz/ *vt* sintetizar

syphilis /'sɪfəlɪs/ *n* sífilis, *f*

syphilitic /,sɪfə'lɪtɪk/ *a* and *n* sifilítico (-ca)

Syracuse /'sɪrə,kyus, -,kyuz/ Siracusa, *f*

syren /'sairən/ *n*. See **siren**

Syria /'sɪəriə/ Siria, *f*

Syrian /'sɪəriə/ *a* and *n* siríaco (-ca), sirio (-ia)

syringe /sə'rɪndʒ/ *n* jeringa, *f*, *vt* jeringar

syrup /'sɪrəp, 'sɜr-/ *n* (for coughs) jarabe, sirope, *m*; (for bottling fruit, etc.) almíbar, *m*

syrup cake *n Argentina* chancaca, *f*

syrupy /'sɪrəpi, 'sɜr-/ *a* siroposo

system /'sɪstəm/ *n* sistema, *m*; régimen, *m*; método, *m*; (body) organismo, *m*. **He has no s. in his work**, No tiene método en su trabajo. **the nervous s.**, el sistema nervioso. **the feudal s.**, el feudalismo, el sistema feudal

systematic /,sɪstə'mætɪk/ *a* sistemático, metódico

systematically /,sɪstə'mætɪkli/ *adv* sistemáticamente, metódicamente

systematization /,sɪstəmətə'zeɪʃən/ *n* sistematización, *f*

systematize /'sɪstəmə,taɪz/ *vt* sistematizar

T

t /ti/ *n* (letter) te, *f. a* en T, en forma de T. **T band-age**, vendaje en T, *m*. **T square**, regla T, *f*
tab /tæb/ *n* oreja, *f*
tabby /'tæbɪ/ *n* gato romano, *m*; (female) gata, *f*; *Inf.* vieja chismosa, *f*
tabernacle /'tæbər,nækəl/ *n* tabernáculo, *m*; templo, *m*; *Archit.* templete, *m*; *Eccl.* custodia, *f*
tabes /'teibiz/ *n Med.* tabes, *f*
table /'teibəl/ *n* mesa, *f*; (food) comida, mesa, *f*; (of the law, weights, measures, contents, etc.) tabla, *f*; (of land) meseta, *f*; (of prices) lista, tarifa, *f. vt* (parliament) poner sobre la mesa; enumerar, apuntar, hacer una lista de. **to clear the t.**, alzar (or levantar) la mesa. **to lay the t.**, cubrir (or poner) la mesa. **to have a t.-d'hôte meal**, tomar el menú. **to rise from t.**, levantarse de la mesa. **to sit down to t.**, ponerse a la mesa. **The tables are turned**, Se volvió la tortilla. **side t.**, aparador, trinchero, *m*. **small t.**, mesilla, *f. t. of contents**, tabla de materias, *f*, índice, índice de materias, índice general, *m*. **t.-centerpiece**, centro de mesa, *m*. **t.-cloth**, mantel, *m*. **t.-companion**, comensal, *mf* **t.-knife**, cuchillo de mesa, *m*. **t.-lamp**, quinqué, *m*; lampara de mesa, *f*. **t.-land**, meseta, *f. t. -leg**, pata de una mesa, *f. t.-linen**, mantelería, *f. t.-napkin**, servilleta, *f. t.-runner**, camino de mesa, *m*. **t. -spoon**, cuchara para los legumbres, *f. t.-talk**, conversación de sobremesa, *f. t.-turning**, mesas que dan vueltas, *f pl.* **t.-ware**, artículos para la mesa, *m pl*
tableau /'tæ'blou/ *n* cuadro, *m*. **tableaux vivants**, cuadros vivos, *m pl*
table d'hôte /'tɑbəl 'dout/ *n Spain* el menú, *m*, *Mexico* comida corrida, *f*
tablespoonful /'teibəlspun,fʊl/ *n* cucharada, *f*
tablet /'tæblɪt/ *n* tabla, *f*; (with inscription) tarjeta, losa, lápida, *f*; *Med.* comprimido, *m*, tableta, *f*; (of soap, chocolate) pastilla, *f. writing t.**, taco de papel, *m*
tabloid /'tæblɔid/ *n* comprimido, *m*, pastilla, *f*
taboo /tɔ'bu, tæ-/ *n* tabú, *m. a* prohibido, tabú. *vt* declarar tabú, prohibir
tabor /'teibər/ *n Mus.* tamboril, tamborín, *m. t. player*, tamborilero, *m*
tabouret /,tæbə'rɛt/ *n* (stool) taburete, *m*; (for embroidery) tambor de bordar, *m*; *Mus.* tamborilete, *m*
tabulate /'tæbyə,leit/ *vt* resumir en tablas; hacer una lista de, catalogar
tabulation /,tæbyə'leiʃən/ *n* distribución en tablas, *f*
tacit /'tæsɪt/ *a* tácito
taciturn /'tæsɪ,tɜrn/ *a* taciturno, sombrío, reservado, de pocas palabras
tack /tæk/ *n* (nail) tachuela, puntilla, *f*; *Sew.* hilván, embaste, *m*; *Naut.* amura, *f*; *Naut.* puño de amura, *m*; *Naut.* bordada, *f*; *Fig.* cambio de política, *m. vt* clavar con tachuelas; *Sew.* hilvanar, embastar; *Fig.* añadir. *vi Naut.* virar; *Fig.* cambiar de política, adoptar un nuevo plan de acción. **t. puller**, sacabrocas, *m*
tackle /'tækəl/ *n* aparejo, *m*; maniobra, *f*; *Naut.* cuadernal, *m*, jarcia, *f*; (gear) aparejos, avíos, *m pl*; (football) carga, *f. vt* agarrar, asir; *Fig.* atacar, abordar; (football) cargar; (undertake) emprender; (a problem) luchar con. **t.-block**, polea, *f*
tacky /'tæki/ *a* pegajoso, viscoso
tact /tækt/ *n* tacto, *m*, discreción, diplomacia, delicadeza, *f*
tactful /'tæktfəl/ *a* lleno de tacto, diplomático, discreto
tactfully /'tæktfəli/ *adv* discretamente, diplomáticamente
tactical /'tæktɪkəl/ *a* táctico
tactically /'tæktɪkli/ *adv* según la táctica; del punto de vista táctico
tactician /tæk'tɪʃən/ *n* táctico, *m*
tactics /'tæktɪks/ *n pl* táctica, *f*
tactile /'tæktɪl/ *a* táctil; tangible
tactless /'tæktlɪs/ *a* que no tiene tacto, sin tacto alguno, indiscreto

tactlessly /'tæktlɪsli/ *adv* impolíticamente, indiscretamente
tactlessness /'tæktlɪsnɪs/ *n* falta de tacto, *f*
tadpole /'tædpoul/ *n* renacuajo, *m*
taffeta /'tæfɪtə/ *n* tafetán, *m*
tag /tæg/ *n* herrete, *m*; (label) marbete, *m*, etiqueta, *f*; (of tail) punta del rabo, *f*; (of boot) tirador de bota, *m*; (game) marro, *m*; (rag) arrapiezo, *m*; (quotation) cita bien conocida, *f*; (of song, poem) refrán, *m*. **to play t.**, jugar al marro
Tagus /'teigəs/ el Tajo, *m*
tail /teil/ *n* cola, *f*, rabo, *m*; (plait) trenza, *f*; (wisp of hair) mechón, *m*; (of a comet) cola, cabellera, *f*; (of a note in music) rabito, *m*; (of a coat) faldon, *m*; (of a kite) cola, *f*; (of the eye), rabo, *m*; (retinue) séquito, *m*, banda, *f*; (of an airplane) cola, *f*; (end) fin, *m*; (of coin) cruz, *f*; (line) fila, cola, *f. vt* seguir de cerca, pisarle (a uno) los talones. **to t. after**, seguir de cerca. **to t. away**, disminuir; desaparecer, perderse de vista. **to t. on**, unir, juntar. **to turn t.**, volver la espalda, poner los pies en polvorosa. **with the t. between the legs**, con el rabo entre piernas. **t.-board**, (of a cart) escalera, *f. t.-coat**, frac, *m. t.-end**, extremo, *m*; fin, *m*; lo último. **t.-feather**, pena, *f. t.-fin**, aleta caudal, *f*; *Aer.* timón de dirección, *m. t.-light**, farol trasero, *m*, *Mexico* calavera, *f. t.-piece**, (of a violin, etc.) cola, *f*; *Print.* marmosete, culo de lámpara, *m. t. spin**, *Aer.* barrena de cola, *f. t. wind**, viento de cola, *m*
tailed /teild/ *a* de rabo. **big-t.**, rabudo, de cola grande. **long-t.**, rabilargo. **short-t.**, rabicorto
tailless /'teillɪs/ *a* rabón, sin rabo
tailor /'teilər/ *n* sastre (-ra). **t.-made**, *n* traje sastre, *m, a* de hechura de sastre. **tailor's shop**, sastrería, *f*
tailoring /'teilərɪŋ/ *n* sastrería, *f*; (work) corte, *m*
taint /teint/ *n* corrupción, *f*; infección, *f*; (blemish) mancha, *f*; (tinge) dejo, *m. vt* corromper, pervertir; inficionar; (meat) corromper. *vi* corromperse, inficionarse; (meat) corromperse
take /teik/ *vt* tomar; (receive) aceptar; (remove) quitar; (pick up) coger; (grab) asir, agarrar; *Math.* restar; (carry) llevar; (a person) traer, llevar; (guide) conducir, guiar; (win) ganar; (earn) cobrar, percibir; obtener; (make prisoner) hacer prisionero, prender; (a town, etc.) tomar, rendir, conquistar; (appropriate) apoderarse de, apropiarse; (steal) robar, hurtar; (ensnare) coger, cazar con trampas; (fish) pescar, coger; (a trick, in cards) hacer (una baza); (an illness) contraer, coger; (by surprise) sorprender, coger desprevenido (a); (attract) atraer; (drink) beber; (a meal) tomar; (select) escoger; (hire) alquilar; (suppose) suponer; (a journal) estar abonado a; (use) emplear, usar; (impers., require) necesitarse, hacer falta; (purchase) comprar; (assume) adoptar, asumir; (a leap) dar (un salto); (a walk) dar (un paseo); (a look) echar (un vistazo); (measures) tomar (medidas); (the chair) presidir; (understand) comprender; (a photograph) sacar (una fotografía); (believe) creer; (consider) considerar; (a note) apuntar; (jump over) saltar; (time) tomar, emplear. **I t. size three in shoes**, Calzo el número tres. **to t. to be**, (believe) suponer; (mistake) creer quivocadamente (a). **to t. (a thing) badly**, tomarlo (or llevarlo) a mal. **The book took me two hours to read**, Necesité dos horas para leer el libro, Leí el libro en dos horas. **And this, I t. it, is Mary?** ¿Y supongo que ésta será María? **to be taken with**, ser entusiasta de; (of persons) estar prendado de. **to t. aback**, desconcertar, coger desprevenido (a). **to t. again**, volver a tomar; llevar otra vez; (a photograph) retratar otra vez. **to t. along**, llevar; traer. **to t. a long time**, tardar, *Lat. Am.* dilatar. **to t. away**, quitar; llevarse. **to t. back**, devolver; (retract) retractar; (receive) recibir (algo) devuelto. **to t. down**, bajar; (a building) derribar; (machinery) desmontar; (hair) deshacerse (el cabello); (swallow) tragar; (in writing) apuntar; (humble) quitar los humos (a), humillar. **to t. for**, creer, imaginar; (a walk, etc.) lle-

var a; (mistake) creer erróneamente; tomar por. **Whom do you t. me for?** ¿Por quién me tomas? **to. t. for granted (assume),** dar por descontado, dar por lecho, dar por sentado, dar por supuesto; (underestimate) no hacer caso de, tratar con indiferencia. **t. the lion's share (of),** llevarse la parte del león (de), llevarse la tajada del león (de). **t. shape,** cobrar perfiles más nítidos, estructurarse con más nitidez, ir adquiriendo consistencia, tomar forma. **t. the law into one's own hands,** tomar la justicia por la mano. **to t. from,** privar, quitar de; (subtract) restar; substraer de. **to t. in,** (believe) tragar, creer; (sail) acortar las velas; (deceive) engañar; (lead in) hacer entrar; (accept) recibir, aceptar. **to t. it from somebody,** llevarse de alguien. **to t. off,** quitar; (surgically) amputar; (one's hat, etc.) quitarse (el sombrero); (eyes) sacar; (take away) llevarse; (mimic) imitar; (ridicule) ridiculizar; (unstick) despegar; (discount) descontar. **to t. on,** emprender; aceptar; (at sports) jugar. **to t. on oneself,** encargarse de, tomar por su cuenta, asumir. **to t. out,** sacar; extraer; (remove) quitar; (outside) llevar fuera; (for a walk) llevar a paseo; (obtain) obtener, sacar; (tire) agotar, rendir. **to t. over,** tomar posesión de; asumir; (show) mostrar, conducir por. **t. the bull by the horns,** ir al toro por los cuernos. **take seriously,** tomar en serio. **to t. up,** subir; (pick up) recoger; tomar; (a challenge, etc.) aceptar; (a dress, etc.) acortar; (absorb) absorber; (of space) ocupar; (of time) ocupar, hacer perder; (buy) comprar; (adopt) dedicarse a; (arrest) arrestar, prender; (criticize) censurar, criticar; (begin) empezar; (resume) continuar

take /teik/ *vi* tomar; (be successful) tener éxito; (of vaccination, etc.) prender; (a good (bad) photograph) salir bien (mal). **to t. after,** salir a, parecerse a; (of conduct) seguir el ejemplo de; **to t. off,** salir; *Aer.* despegar. **to t. on,** *Inf.* lamentarse de. **to t. to,** dedicarse a; darse a; (of persons) tomar cariño a; (grow accustomed) acostumbrarse a. **to t. up with,** hacerse amigo de

take /teik/ *n* toma, *f*; cogida, *f*; *Print.* tomada, *f*; *Theat.* taquilla, *f.* **t.-in,** engaño, *m.* **t.-off,** *Aer.* (recorrido de) despegue, *m*; caricatura, *f*; sátira, *f*

taking /'teikiŋ/ *n* toma, *f*; secuestro, *m*, *n pl* **takings,** ingresos, *m pl*; *Theat.* taquilla, entrada, *f. a* atractivo, encantador; simpático; (of disease) contagioso

talc /tælk/ *n Mineral.* talco, *m*

talcum powder /'tælkəm/ *n* talco, polvo de talco, *m*

tale /teil/ *n* (recital) narración, historia, *f*; relato, *m*; cuento, *m*; leyenda, historia, fábula, *f*; (number) cuenta, *f*, número, *m*; (gossip) chisme, *m.* **old wives' t.,** cuento de viejas, *m.* **to tell a t.,** contar una historia. **to tell tales,** contar cuentos; revelar secretos, chismear

talebearer /'teil,bɛərər/ *n* correveidile, *mf*; chismoso (-sa), soplón (-ona)

talebearing /'teil,bɛəriŋ/ *n* el chismear, *m*

talent /'tælənt/ *n* (coin) talento, *m*; (ability) ingenio, *m*; habilidad, *f.* **the best t. in Spain,** la flor de la cultura española

talented /'tæləntid/ *a* talentoso, ingenioso

talisman /'tælismən/ *n* talismán, *m*

talit /'talis, talit/ *n* taled, *m*

talk /tɔk/ *vi* and *vt* hablar, decir. **to t. business,** hablar de negocios. **to t. for talking's sake,** hablar por hablar. **to t. French,** hablar francés. **to t. nonsense,** decir disparates. **to t. too much,** hablar demasiado; *Inf.* hablar por los codos, irse (a uno) la lengua. **to t. about,** hablar de; conversar sobre. **to t. at,** decir algo a alguien para que le entienda otro. **Are you talking at me?** ¿Lo dices por mí? **to t. away,** seguir hablando; disipar. **to t. into,** persuadir, inducir (a). **to t. of,** hablar de; charlar sobre. **to t. on,** hablar acerca de (or sobre); (continue) seguir hablando. **to t. out of,** disuadir de. **to t. out of turn,** meterse donde no le llaman, meter la pata. **to t. over,** hablar de; discutir, considerar. **to t. to,** (address) hablar a; (consult) hablar con; (scold) reprender. **to t. to each other,** hablarse. **to t. up,** hablar claro

talk /tɔk/ *n* conversación, *f*; (informal lecture) charla, *f*; (empty words) palabras, *f pl*; (notoriety) escándalo, *m*; rumor, *m.* **There is t. of...,** Se dice que...; Se

habla de que. **to give a t.,** dar una charla. **to indulge in small t.,** hablar de cosas sin importancia, hablar de naderías

talkative /'tɔkətɪv/ *a* locuaz, gárrulo, hablador, decidor. **to be very t.,** ser muy locuaz; *Inf.* tener mucha lengua

talkativeness /'tɔkətɪvnɪs/ *n* locuacidad, garrulidad, *f*

talker /'tɔkər/ *n* hablador (-ra), conversador (-ra); (lecturer) orador (-ra); (in a derogatory sense) fanfarrón (-ona), charlatán (-ana). **to be a good t.,** hablar bien, ser buen conversacionista

talking /'tɔkiŋ/ *a* que habla, hablante; (of birds, dolls, etc.) parlero. **to give a good t. to,** dar una peluca (a). **t.-film,** película sonora, *f.* **t.-machine,** fonógrafo, *m*

talk show *n* programa de entrevistas, *m*

tall /tɔl/ *a* alto; (of stories) exagerado. **five feet tall,** de cinco pies de altura

tallboy /'tɔl,bɔi/ *n* cómoda alta, *f*

tallness /'tɔlnɪs/ *n* altura, *f*; estatura, talla, *f*; (of stories) lo exagerado

tallow /'tælou/ *n* sebo, *m.* **t. candle,** vela de sebo, *f.* **t. chandler,** velero (-ra). **t.-faced,** con cara de color de cera

tallowy /'tæloui/ *a* seboso

tall tale *n Peru* bacho, *m*

tally /'tæli/ *n* tarja, tara, *f*; cuenta, *f.* *vt* llevar la cuenta (de). *vi* estar conforme, cuadrar

Talmud /'talmʊd/ *n* Talmud, *m*

Talmudic /tal'mʊdɪk/ *a* talmúdico

talon /'tælən/ *n* garra, *f*

tamable /'teiməbəl/ *a* domable, domesticable

tambour /'tæmbʊr, tæm'bʊr/ *n Mus.* tambor, *m*; (for embroidery) tambor (or bastidor) para bordar, *m*

tambourine /,tæmbə'rin/ *n* pandereta, *f*

tame /teim/ *a* domesticado, manso; (spiritless) sumiso; (dull) aburrido, soso. *vt* domar, domesticar; (curb) reprimir, gobernar, domar, suavizar. **to grow t.,** domesticarse

tamer /'teimər/ *n* domador (-ra)

taming /'teimiŋ/ *n* domadura, *f.* **The T. of the Shrew,** La Fierecilla Domada

tamp /tæmp/ *vt* apisonar; (in blasting) atacar (un barreno)

tamper /'tæmpər/ *vi* (with) descomponer, estropear; (meddle with) meterse con; (witnesses) sobornar; (documents) falsificar

tampon /'tæmpon/ *n Surg.* tampón, tapón, *m*, *vt* taponar

tan /tæn/ *vt* curtir, adobar; (of sun) tostar, quemar; (slang) zurrar. *vi* tostarse por el sol. *n* color café claro, *m*; bronceado, cutis tostado, *m. a* de color café claro

tandem /'tændəm/ *n* tándem, *m*

tang /tæŋ/ *n* (of sword, etc.) espiga, *f*; (flavor) fuerte sabor, *m*; (sound) retintín, *m*

tangent /'tændʒənt/ *a* and *n* tangente *f.* **to fly off at a t.,** *Fig.* salir por la tangente

tangerine /,tændʒə'rin/ *a* and *n* tangerino (-na). **t. orange,** naranja mandarina, *f*

tangible /'tændʒəbəl/ *a* tangible; *Fig.* real

Tangier /tæn'dʒir/ *n* Tánger, *m*

tangle /'tæŋgəl/ *n* embrollo, enredo, nudo, *m*; (of streets) laberinto, *m*; *Fig.* confusión, *f. vt* embrollar, enmarañar; (entangle) enredar; *Fig.* poner en confusión, complicar. *vi* enmarañarse

tank /tæŋk/ *n* tanque, depósito (de agua, etc.), *m*; cisterna, *f*; (as a reservoir) aljibe, estanque, *m*; *Mil.* tanque, carro de asalto, *m.* **t. up** (get drunk) *Argentina* acatarrarse

tankard /'tæŋkərd/ *n* pichel, bock, *m*

tanker /'tæŋkər/ *n* petrolero, *m*

tanned /tænd/ *a* bronceado, quemado por el sol, dorado por el sol

tanner /'tænər/ *n* curtidor, *m*; (slang) medio chelín, *m.* **tanner's scraper,** descarnador, *m.* **tanner's vat,** noque, *m*

tannery /'tænəri/ *n* curtiduría, *f*

tannic /'wsmintænik/ *a Chem.* tánico. **t. acid,** ácido tánico, *m*

tannin /'tænɪn/ n Chem. tanino, m
tanning /'tænɪŋ/ n curtido, adobamiento, m
tantalize /'tæntḷ,aiz/ vt tentar, atormentar, provocar
tantalizing /'tæntḷ,aizɪŋ/ a tentador, atormentador; provocativo
tantamount /'tæntə,maunt/ a equivalente, igual. **to be t.** to, ser equivalente a
tantrum /'tæntrəm/ n pataleta, rabieta, f, berrinche, m
taoism /'dauizəm/ n taoísmo, m
taoist /'dauist/ n taoísta, mf
tap /tæp/ n (blow) pequeño golpe, toque ligero, m; palmadita, f; (for drawing water, etc.) grifo, m, llave, f; (of a barrel) canilla, f; (brew of liquor) clase de vino, f; (tap-room) bar con mostrador, m; (tool) macho de terraja, m; (piece of leather on shoe) tapa, f; pl **taps,** Mil. toque de apagar las luces, m. vt (strike) golpear ligeramente, dar una palmadita a; (pierce) horadar; (a barrel) decentar; Surg. hacer una puntura en; (trees) sangrar; Elec. derivar (una corriente); (of water, current) tomar; (information) descubrir; (telephone) escuchar las conversaciones telefónicas. vi golpear ligeramente. **to tap at the door,** llamar suavemente a la puerta. **on tap,** en tonel. **screw-tap,** terraja, f. **tap-dance,** claqué, m. **tap-root,** raíz pivotante, f
tape /teip/ n (linen) cinta de hilo, f; (cotton) cinta de algodón, f; (telegraph machine) cinta de papel, f; (surveying) cinta para medir, f. **adhesive t.,** cinta adhesiva, f. **red t.,** balduque, m; Fig. burocracia, f; formulismo, m. **t.-machine,** telégrafo de cotizaciones, bancarias, m. **t.-measure,** cinta métrica, f
taper /'teipər/ n bujía, cerilla, f; Eccl. cirio, m. vi ahusarse, rematar en punta. vt afilar
tapering /'teipərɪŋ/ a cónico, piramidal; (of fingers) afilado
tapestried /'tæpəstrid/ a cubierto de tapices, tapizado
tapestry /'tæpəstri/ n tapiz, m. **t. weaver,** tapicero, m
tapeworm /'teip,wɜrm/ n tenia, lombriz solitaria, f
tapioca /,tæpi'oukə/ n tapioca, f
tapir /'teipər/ n Zool. danta, f
tar /tɑr/ n alquitrán, m, brea, f; vt embrear, alquitranar. **to tar and feather,** emplumar. **coal t.,** alquitrán mineral, m
tarantella /,tærən'tɛlə/ n tarantela, f
tarantula /tə'ræntʃələ/ n tarántula, f
tardily /'tardḷi/ adv tardíamente; lentamente
tardiness /'tardinɪs/ n tardanza, lentitud, f
tardy /'tardi/ a (late) tardío; (slow) lento; (reluctant) desinclinado
tare /tɛər/ n Bot. yero, m; (in the Bible) cizaña, f; Com. tara, f; (of a vehicle) peso en vacío, m
target /'targɪt/ n blanco (de tiro), m; (shield) rodela, tarja, f. **t. practice,** tiro al blanco, m
tariff /'tærɪf/ n tarifa, f. **to put a t. on,** tarifar
tarlatan /'tarlətṇ/ n tarlatana, f
tarmac /'tarmæk/ n alquitranado, m
tarn /tarn/ n lago de montaña, m
tarnish /'tarnɪʃ/ n deslustre, m. vt deslustrar, empañar; Fig. obscurecer, manchar. vi deslustrarse
tarpaulin /tar'pɔlin, 'tarpəlɪn/ n alquitranado, encerado, m
tarred /tard/ a alquitranado, embreado
tarring /'tarɪŋ/ n embreadura, f
tarry /'tari/ vi tardar, detenerse
tart /tart/ a ácido, acerbo, agridulce; Fig. áspero. n tarta, f; pastelillo de fruta, m
tartan /'tartṇ/ n Naut. tartana, f; (plaid) tartán, m
tartar /'tartər/ n Chem. tártaro, m; (in teeth) sarro, tártaro, m; **cream of t.,** (cremor) tártaro, m. **t. emetic,** tártaro emético, m. **Tartar,** a and n tártaro (-ra)
tartly /'tartli/ adv ásperamente, agriamente
tartness /'tartnɪs/ n acidez, f; Fig. aspereza, f
task /tæsk/ n tarea, labor, f; empresa, f; misión, f. **to take to t.,** regañar, censurar. **t.-force,** (naval or military) contingente, m
taskmaster /'tæsk,mæstər/ n el que señala una tarea; amo, m
tassel /'tæsəl/ n borla, f; (of corn) panoja, espiga, f
taste /teist/ n gusto, m; (flavor) sabor, m; (speci-

men) ejemplo, m, idea, f; (small quantity) un poco, muy poco; (liking) afición, inclinación, f; (of drink) sorbo, trago, m; (tinge) dejo, m. vt (appraise) probar; gustar, percibir el gusto de; (experience) experimentar, conocer. vi tener gusto, tener sabor. **a matter of t.,** cuestión de gusto. **Each to his own t.,** Entre gustos no hay disputa. **He had not tasted a bite,** No había probado bocado. **in bad (good) t.,** de mal (buen) gusto; de mal (buen) tono. **to have a t. for,** ser aficionado a, gustar de. **to t.,** Cul. a gusto, a sabor. **to t. of,** tener gusto de, saber a
tasted /'teistɪd/ a (in compounds) de sabor...
tasteful /'teistfəl/ a de buen gusto
tastefully /'teistfəli/ adv con buen gusto
tastefulness /'teistfəlnɪs/ n buen gusto, m
tasteless /'teistlɪs/ a insípido, soso, insulso; de mal gusto
tastelessness /'teistlɪsnɪs/ n insipidez, insulsez, f; mal gusto, m
taster /'teistər/ n catador, m; (vessel) catavino, m
tasting /'teistɪŋ/ n saboreo, m, gustación, f, a (in compounds) de sabor...
tasty /'teisti/ a apetitoso, sabroso
tatter /'tætər/ n andrajo, harapo, m; jirón, m. **to tear in tatters,** hacer jirones
tattered /'tætərd/ a andrajoso, haraposo
tatting /'tætɪŋ/ n frivolité, m
tattoo /tæ'tu/ n tatuaje, m; Mil. retreta, f; (display) parada militar, f. vt tatuar
tattooing /tæ'tuɪŋ/ n tatuaje, m; tamboreo, m
taunt /tɔnt/ n mofa, f, insulto, escarnio, m. vt insultar, atormentar. **to t. with,** echar en cara
taunting /'tɔntɪŋ/ a insultante, burlón, insolente
tauntingly /'tɔntɪŋli/ adv burlonamente, insolentemente
Taurus /'tɔrəs/ n tauro, toro, m
taut /tɔt/ a tieso, tirante, tenso; en regla; Naut. **to make t.,** tesar
tauten /'tɔtṇ/ vt tesar; poner tieso
tautness /'tɔtnɪs/ n tensión, f
tautological /,tɔtḷ'ɒdʒɪkəl/ a tautológico
tautology /tɔ'tɒlədʒi/ n tautología, f
tavern /'tævərn/ n taberna, f; (inn) mesón, m, posada, f. **t.-keeper,** tabernero, m
tawdrily /'tɔdrɪli/ adv llamativamente, de un modo cursi
tawdriness /'tɔdrɪnɪs/ n charrería, f
tawdry /'tɔdri/ a chillón, charro, cursi
tawny /'tɔni/ a leonado
tax /tæks/ n contribución, gabela, imposición, f; Fig. carga, f; vt imponer contribuciones (a); Law. tasar; Fig. cargar, abrumar. **to tax with,** tachar (de), acusar (de). **direct (indirect) tax,** contribución directa (indirecta), f. **tax-collector,** recaudador de contribuciones, m. **tax-free,** libre de impuestos. **tax-rate,** tarifa de impuestos, f, cupo, m. **tax-register,** lista de contribuyentes, f
taxable /'tæksəbəl/ a imponible, sujeto a impuestos
taxation /tæk'seiʃən/ n imposición de contribuciones (or impuestos), f
tax evasion n evasión tributaria, f
taxi /'tæksi/ n taxi, Mexico libre, m. vi ir en un taxi; Aer. correr por tierra. **t. driver,** chófer de un taxi, taxista, m. **t. rank, taxi stand,** parada de taxis, f
taxidermist /'tæksɪ,dɜrmɪst/ n taxidermista, f
taxidermy /'tæksɪ,dɜrmi/ n taxidermia, f
taximeter /'tæksi,mitər/ n taxímetro, m
taxpayer /'tæks,peiər/ n contribuyente, mf
taxpaying /'tæks,peiɪŋ/ a tributario, que paga contribuciones
tax reform n reforma impositiva, reforma tributaria, f
tea /ti/ n (liquid) té, m; (meal) merienda, f. **to have tea,** tomar el té, merendar. **tea-caddy,** bote para té, m. **tea-chest,** caja para té, f. **tea-cosy,** cubretetera, f. **tea-cup,** taza para té, f. **tea-dance,** té baile, m. **tea-kettle** or **tea-pot,** tetera, f. **tea-leaf,** hoja de té, f. **tea-party,** reunión para tomar té, f. **tea-room,** salón de té, m. **tea-rose,** rosa de té, f. **tea-set,** juego de té, m. **tea-strainer,** colador de té, m. **tea-time,** hora

de té, f. **tea-urn,** samowar, m, tetera para hacer té, f.

tea-wagon, carrito para el té, m

teach /titʃ/ vt (a person) enseñar, instruir; (a subject) enseñar; (to lecture on) ser profesor de; (a lesson) dar una lección (de). vi (be a teacher) dedicarse a la enseñanza. **to teach at...,** desempeñor una cátedra en... **to t. a person Spanish,** enseñar el castellano a alguien. **to t. how to,** enseñar a (followed by infin.)

teachability /ˌtitʃəˈbɪlɪti/ n docilidad, f

teachable /ˈtitʃəbəl/ a educable; dócil

teacher /ˈtitʃər/ n preceptor, m; profesor, maestro, m. **woman t.,** profesora, maestra, f

teaching /ˈtitʃɪŋ/ n enseñanza, f; (belief) doctrina, f, a docente. **t. profession,** magisterio, m

teaching method n método didáctico, f

teak /tik/ n Bot. teca, f; (wood) madera de teca, f

team /tim/ n (of horses) tiro, m; (of oxen, mules) par, m, pareja, yunta, f; Sports. partido, equipo, m; compañía, f, grupo, m. vt enganchar, uncir. **t.-work,** cooperación, f

teamster /ˈtimstər/ n gañán, m

tear /tɛər/ vt rasgar; romper; lacerar; (in pieces) hacer pedazos, despedazar; (scratch) arañar; Fig. atormentar. **to t. asunder,** romper; desmembrar. **to t. away,** arrancar, quitar violentamente. **to t. down,** derribar, echar abajo. **to t. off,** arrancar; desgajar. **to t. oneself away,** arrancarse, desgarrarse. **to t. one's hair,** arrancarse los pelos, mesarse. **to t. open,** abrir apresuradamente. **to t. up,** hacer pedazos; (uproot) arrancar, desarraigar.

tear /tɛər/ vi rasgarse; romper; correr precipitadamente. **to t. along,** correr rápidamente (por). **to t. away,** marcharse corriendo. **to t. down,** bajar corriendo. **to t. into,** entrar corriendo en. **to t. off,** irse precipitadamente, marcharse corriendo. **to t. up,** subir corriendo; llegar corriendo; atravesar rápidamente

tear /tɪər/ n lágrima, f; (drop) gota, f. **with tears in one's eyes,** con lágrimas en los ojos. **to shed tears,** llorar, lagrimear. **to wipe away one's tears,** secarse las lágrimas. **t.-drop,** lágrima, f. **t.-duct,** conductor lacrimal, m. **t.-gas,** gas lacrimante, m. **t.-stained,** mojado de lágrimas

tear /tɛər/ n (rent) rasgón, m

tearful /ˈtɪərfəl/ a lloroso, lacrimoso

tearfully /ˈtɪərfəli/ adv con lágrimas en los ojos

tearing /ˈtɛərɪŋ/ n rasgadura, f, desgarro, m

tearjerker /ˈtɪərˌdʒɜrkər/ n drama lacrimón, m

tease /tiz/ vt (card) cardar; (annoy) fastidiar, irritar, molestar; (chaff) tomar el pelo (a), embromar; (pester) importunar. n bromista, mf

teasel /ˈtizəl/ n Bot. cardencha, f, cardo, m

teaser /ˈtizər/ n (problem) rompecabezas, m; (person) bromista, mf

teaspoon /ˈtiˌspun/ n cucharita, f

teaspoonful /ˈtispunˌfʊl/ n cucharadita, f

teat /tit, tɪt/ n pezón, m; (of animals) teta, f

technical /ˈtɛknɪkəl/ a técnico. **t. offense,** Law. cuasidelito, m. **t. school,** escuela industrial, f

technicality /ˌtɛknɪˈkælɪti/ n carácter técnico, m; tecnicismo, m; detalle técnico, m

technician /tɛkˈnɪʃən/ n técnico, m

technicolor /ˈtɛknɪˌkʌlər/ n tecnicolor, m

technique /tɛkˈnik/ n técnica, f; ejecución, f; mecanismo, m

technological /ˌtɛknəˈlɒdʒɪkəl/ a tecnológico

technologist /tɛkˈnɒlədʒɪst/ n tecnólogo, m

technology /tɛkˈnɒlədʒi/ n tecnología, f

teddy bear /ˈtɛdi/ n osito de trapo, m

tedious /ˈtidiəs/ a aburrido, tedioso, pesado

tediously /ˈtidiəsli/ adv aburridamente

tediousness /ˈtidiəsnəs/ n aburrimiento, m, pesadez, f

tedium /ˈtidiəm/ n tedio, m, monotonía, f

tee /ti/ n Sports. meta, f; (golf) tee, m; (letter) te, f; cosa en forma de te, f. vt (golf) colocar la pelota en el tee

teem /tim/ vi rebosar (de), abundar (en); pulular, hormiguear, estar lleno (de); (with rain) diluviar

teeming /ˈtimɪŋ/ a prolífico, fecundo. **t. with,** abundante en, lleno de

teens /tinz/ n pl números y años desde trece hasta diez y nueve; edad de trece a diez y nueve años de edad. **to be still in one's t.,** no haber cumplido aún los veinte

teeter /ˈtitər/ vi balancearse, columpiarse

teethe /tið/ vi endentecer, echar los dientes

teething /ˈtiðɪŋ/ n dentición, f. **t.-ring,** chupador, m

teetotal /ˈtiˈtoutl/ a abstemio

teetotalism /ˈtiˈtoutlˌɪzəm/ n abstinencia completa de bebidas alcohólicas, f

teetotaller /ˈtiˌtoutlər/ n abstemio (-ia)

teetotum /ˈtiˈtoutəm/ n perinola, f

telecast /ˈtɛlɪˌkæst/ vt telefundir

telecommunication /ˌtɛlɪkəˌmyunɪˈkeɪʃən/ n telecomunicación, f

telegram /ˈtɛlɪˌgræm/ n telegrama, m

telegraph /ˈtɛlɪˌgræf/ n telégrafo, m. vi telegrafiar; Fig. hacer señas. vt telegrafiar, enviar por telégrafo. **t. line,** línea telegráfica, f. **t. office,** central de telégrafos, f. **t. pole,** poste telegráfico, m. **t. wire,** hilo telegráfico, m

telegraphic /ˌtɛlɪˈgræfɪk/ a telegráfico

telegraphist /təˈlɛgrəfɪst/ n telegrafista, mf

telegraphy /təˈlɛgrəfi/ n telegrafía, f. **wireless t.,** telegrafía sin hilos, f

telemetry /təˈlɛmɪtri/ n telemetría, f

teleology /ˌtɛliˈɒlədʒi/ n teleología, f

telepathic /ˌtɛləˈpæθɪk/ a telepático

telepathy /təˈlɛpəθi/ n telepatía, f

telephone /ˈtɛləˌfoun/ n teléfono, m. vi telefonear, vt telefonear, llamar por teléfono. **to be on the t.,** (speaking) estar communicando; (of subscribers) tener teléfono. **dial t.,** teléfono automático, m. **t. call,** comunicación telefónica, f; conversación telefónica, f. **t. call box,** teléfono público, m. **t. directory,** guía de teléfonos, f. **t. exchange,** central telefónica, f. **t. number,** número de teléfono, m. **t. operator,** telefonista, mf **t. receiver,** receptor telefónico, m. **t. wire,** hilo telefónico, m

telephonic /ˌtɛləˈfɒnɪk/ a telefónico

telephonist /təˈlɛfənɪst/ n telefonista, mf

telephony /təˈlɛfəni/ n telefonía, f. **wireless t.,** telefonía sin hilos, f

teleprinter /ˈtɛləˌprɪntər/ n teletipo, m

telescope /ˈtɛləˌskoup/ n telescopio, catalejo, m vt enchufar. vi enchufarse, meterse una cosa dentro de otra

telescopic /ˌtɛləˈskɒpɪk/ a telescópico; de enchufe

televise /ˈtɛləˌvaɪz/ vt trasmitir por televisión

television /ˈtɛləˌvɪʒən/ n televisión, f. **on television,** por televisión. **I saw her on television,** La vi por televisión

television series n serie televisiva, f

tell /tɛl/ vt contar, narrar; decir; revelar; expresar; (the time, of clocks) marcar; (inform) comunicar, informar; (show) indicar, manifestar; (explain) explicar; distinguir; (order) mandar; (compute) contar. vi decir; (have effect) producir efecto. **We cannot t.,** No sabemos. **Who can t.?** ¿Quién sabe? **T. that to the marines!,** ¡Cuéntaselo a tu tía! **to t. its own tale,** hacer ver por sí mismo lo que hay. **to t. again,** volver a decir; contar otra vez. **to t. off,** regañar, reñir; (on a mission) despachar, mandar. **to t. on,** delatar. **to t. upon,** afectar

teller /ˈtɛlər/ n narrador (-ra); (of votes) escrutador (-ra) de votos; (payer) pagador, (bank) cajero (-ra), m

telling /ˈtɛlɪŋ/ a notable, significante. n narración, f

telltale /ˈtɛlˌteil/ n chismoso (-sa), soplón (-ona); (informer) acusón (-ona); Fig. indicio, m, señal, f, a revelador

temerity /təˈmɛrɪti/ n temeridad, f

temper /ˈtɛmpər/ n (of metals) temple, m; (nature) naturaleza, f, carácter, m; espíritu, m; (mood) humor, m; (anger) mal genio, m. vt (of metals) templar; moderar, mitigar; mezclar. vi templarse. **bad (good) t.,** mal (buen) humor. **to keep one's t.,** no enojarse, no impacientarse. **to lose one's t.,** enojarse, perder la paciencia

tempera /ˈtɛmpərə/ n Art. templa, f. **in t.,** al temple, m

temperament /ˈtɛmpərəmənt, -prəmənt/ n temperamento, *m*; modo de ser, natural, *m*, naturaleza, índole, *f*; *Mus.* temple, *m*

temperamental /ˌtɛmpərə'mɛntḷ, -prə'mɛn-/ *a* natural, innato; caprichoso

temperamentally /ˌtɛmpərə'mɛntḷi, -prə'mɛn-/ *adv* por naturaleza

temperance /'tɛmpərəns/ *n* moderación, templanza, *f*; sobriedad, abstinencia, *f*

temperate /'tɛmpərɪt/ *a* moderado; sobrio; (of regions) templado. **t. zone,** zona templada, *f*

temperately /'tɛmpərɪtli/ *adv* sobriamente

temperateness /'tɛmpərɪtnɪs/ *n* moderación, sobriedad, mesura, *f*; (of regions) templanza, *f*

temperature /'tɛmpərətʃər/ *n* temperatura, *f*. **to have a t.,** tener fiebre

tempered /'tɛmpərd/ *a* de humor..., de genio... **to be good (bad) t.,** ser de buen (mal) humor

tempering /'tɛmpərɪŋ/ *n* temperación, *f*

tempest /'tɛmpɪst/ *n* tempestad, borrasca, *f*, temporal, *m*; *Fig.* tormenta, *f*

tempest in a teapot /'ti,pɒt/ borrasca en un vaso de agua, *m*

tempestuous /tɛm'pɛstʃuəs/ *a* tempestuoso, borrascoso; *Fig.* impetuoso, violento

tempestuousness /tɛm'pɛstʃuəsnɪs/ *n* lo tempestuoso; *Fig.* impetuosidad, violencia, *f*

temple /'tɛmpəl/ *n* templo, *m*; *Anat.* sien, *f*

tempo /'tɛmpou/ *n* *Mus.* tiempo, *m*

temporal /'tɛmpərəl/ *a* temporal; (transient) transitorio, fugaz; *Anat.* temporal. *n* *Anat.* hueso temporal, *m*

temporality /ˌtɛmpə'rælɪti/ *n* temporalidad, *f*

temporarily /ˌtɛmpə'rɛərəli/ *adv* provisionalmente

temporariness /'tɛmpə,rɛrɪnɪs/ *n* interinidad, *f*

temporary /'tɛmpə,rɛri/ *a* provisional, interino

temporize /'tɛmpə,raiz/ *vi* ganar tiempo; contemporizar

temporizing /'tɛmpə,raizɪŋ/ *n* contemporización, *f*, *a* contemporizador

tempt /tɛmpt/ *vt* tentar; atraer, seducir

temptation /tɛmp'teiʃən/ *n* tentación, *f*; aliciente, atractivo, *m*

tempter /'tɛmptər/ *n* tentador (-ra)

tempting /'tɛmptɪŋ/ *a* tentador, atrayente; seductor

ten /tɛn/ *a* diez; (of the clock) las diez, *f pl*; (of age) diez años, *m pl*, diez, *m*; (a round number) decena, *f*; **ten-millionth,** *a* and *n* diezmillonésimo *m*. **ten months old,** diezmesino. **ten syllable,** decasílabo. **ten thousand,** *a* and *n* diez mil *m*. **There are ten thousand soldiers,** Hay diez mil soldados. **ten-thousandth,** *a* and *n* diezmilésimo *m*

tenable /'tɛnəbəl/ *a* sostenible, defendible

tenacious /tə'neiʃəs/ *a* tenaz; (stubborn) porfiado, obstinaz, terco; (sticky) adhesivo. **to be t. of life,** estar muy apegado a la vida

tenaciously /tə'neiʃəsli/ *adv* tenazmente; porfiadamente

tenacity /tə'næsɪti/ *n* tenacidad, *f*; porfía, *f*, tesón, *m*

tenancy /'tɛnənsi/ *n* inquilinato, *m*; tenencia, *f*

tenant /'tɛnənt/ *n* arrendatario (-ia), inquilino (-na); habitante, *m*; morador (-ra). **t. farmer,** *Chile* inquilino (-na), *mf*

tench /tɛntʃ/ *n* *Ichth.* tenca, *f*

tend /tɛnd/ *vt* cuidar, atender; guardar; vigilar. *vi* tender; inclinarse (a), propender (a)

tendency /'tɛndənsi/ *n* tendencia, inclinación, propensión, *f*; proclividad, *f*

tendentious /tɛn'dɛnʃəs/ *a* tendencioso

tender /'tɛndər/ *n* guardián, *m*; *Com.* oferta, propuesta, *f*; *Naut.* falúa, *f*; (of a railway engine) ténder, *m*. **legal t.,** moneda corriente, *f*

tender /'tɛndər/ *a* tierno; delicado; (of conscience) escrupuloso; (of a subject) espinoso; compasivo, afectuoso, sensible; muelle, blando. **t.-hearted,** compasivo, tierno de corazón

tender /'tɛndər/ *vt* ofrecer; dar; presentar. *vi* hacer una oferta. **to t. condolences,** dar el pésame. **to t. one's resignation,** presentar la dimisión. **to t. thanks,** dar las gracias

tenderly /'tɛndərli/ *adv* tiernamente

tenderness /'tɛndərnɪs/ *n* ternura, *f*; sensibilidad, *f*; delicadeza, *f*; dulzura, *f*; indulgencia, *f*; compasividad, *f*; benevolencia, *f*; escrupulosidad, *f*; mimo, cariño, *m*

tendon /'tɛndən/ *n* *Anat.* tendón, *m*. **t. of Achilles,** tendón de Aquiles, *m*

tenement /'tɛnəmənt/ *n* casa de vecindad, *f*; vivienda, *f*, *Lat. Am.* conventillo, *m*; *Poet.* morada, *f*

Teneriffe /ˌtɛnə'rif/ Tenerife, *f*

tenet /'tɛnɪt/ *n* principio, dogma, *m*, doctrina, *f*

tenfold /a.'tɛn,fould; adv. -'fould/ *a* décuplo. *adv* diez veces

tennis /'tɛnɪs/ *n* tenis, *m*. **to play t.,** jugar al tenis. **t. ball,** pelota de tenis, *f*. **t. court,** campo de tenis, *m*, cancha de tenis, pista de tenis, *f*. **tennis club,** club de tenis, *m*. **t. racket,** raqueta de tenis, *f*; **tennis shoe,** zapatilla de tenis, *f*

tenon /'tɛnən/ *n* espiga, *f*, *vt* espigar

tenor /'tɛnər/ *n* curso, *m*; tenor, contenido, *m*; *Mus.* tenor, *m*; *Mus.* alto, *m*; (mus. instrument) viola, *f*. *a* *Mus.* de tenor

tense /tɛns/ *n* *Gram.* tiempo, *m*. *a* tirante, estirado, tieso; tenso

tenseness /'tɛnsnɪs/ *n* tirantez, *f*; tensión, *f*

tensile /'tɛnsəl/ *a* tensor; extensible

tension /'tɛnʃən/ *n* tensión, *f*; *Elec.* voltaje, *m*, tensión, *f*; (of sewing-machine) tensahílo, *m*. **state of t.,** (diplomatic) estado de tirantez, *m*

tent /tɛnt/ *n* tienda (de campaña), *Lat. Am.* carpa, *f*; (bell) pabellón, *m*; *Surg.* tienda, *f*. **oxygen t.,** tienda oxígena, *f*. **to pitch tents,** armar las tiendas de campaña; acamparse. **to strike tents,** plegar tiendas. **t. fly,** toldo de tienda, *m*. **t. maker,** tendero, *m*. **t. peg,** clave que sujeta las cuerdas de una tienda, *f*. **t. pole,** mástil (or montante) de tienda, *m*

tentacle /'tɛntəkəl/ *n* tentáculo, *m*

tentative /'tɛntətɪv/ *a* tentativo, interino, provisional, de prueba, *n* tentativa, *f*, ensayo, *m*

tentatively /'tɛntətɪvli/ *adv* por vía de ensayo, experimentalmente

tenth /tɛnθ/ *a* décimo; (of monarchs) diez; (of the month) (el) diez. *n* décimo, *m*; (part) décima parte, *f*; *Mus.* decena, *f*

tenthly /'tɛnθli/ *adv* en décimo lugar

tenuity /tə'nuiti/ *n* tenuidad, *f*; sutilidad, *f*; delgadez, *f*

tenuous /'tɛnyuəs/ *a* tenue; sutil; delgado; fino

tenure /'tɛnyər/ *n* tenencia, posesión, *f*; (duration) duración, *f*; (of office) administración, *f*

tepid /'tɛpɪd/ *a* tibio

tepidity /tə'pɪdɪti/ *n* tibieza, *f*

tercentenary /ˌtɜrsɛn'tɛnəri/ *n* tercer centenario, *m*

tercet /'tɜrsɪt/ *n* terceto, *m*

term /tɜrm/ *n* (limit) límite, fin, *m*; (period) plazo, tiempo, período, *m*; (schools, universities) trimestre, *m*; (*Math., Law., Logic.*) término, *m*; (word) expresión, palabra, *f pl.* **terms,** (conditions) condiciones, *f pl*; (charges) precios, *m pl*, tarifa, *f*; (words) términos, *m pl*, palabras, *f pl. vt* llamar, calificar. **for a t. of years,** por un plazo de años. **in plain terms,** en palabras claras. **on equal terms,** en condiciones iguales. **to be on bad (good) terms with,** estar en (or tener) malas (buenas) relaciones con. **to come to terms,** llegar a un acuerdo; hacer las paces. **What are your terms?** ¿Cuáles son sus condiciones? (price) ¿Cuáles son sus precios? **terms of sale,** condiciones de venta, *f pl*

termagant /'tɜrməgənt/ *n* arpía, fiera, *f*

terminable /'tɜrmənəbəl/ *a* terminable

terminal /'tɜrmənl/ *a* terminal, final; (of schools, universities) trimestre. *n* término, *m*; *Elec.* borne, *m*; (schools, universities) examen de fin de trimestre, *m*; (railway) estación terminal, *f*; (*Archit.* and figure) término, *m*; *Archit.* remate, *m*

terminate /'tɜrmə,neit/ *vt* limitar; terminar, concluir; poner fin (a). *vi* terminarse, concluirse (por); cesar

termination /ˌtɜrmə'neiʃən/ *n* terminación, conclusión, *f*; fin, *m*; *Gram.* terminación, *f*; cabo, remate, *m*

terminology /ˌtɜrmə'nɒlədʒi/ *n* nomenclatura, terminología, *f*

terminus /'tɜrmənəs/ *n* (railway) estación terminal, *f*;

(*Archit.* and figure) término, *m*; *Archit.* remate, *m*; *Myth.* Término

termite /'tɜrmait/ *n Ent.* termita, *m*

term paper *n* trabajo de examen, *m*

terms of trade *n* relación de los precios de intercambio, *f*

terrace /'tɛrəs/ *n* terraza, *f*, *vt* terraplenar

terraced /'tɛrəst/ *a* en terrazas; con terrazas

terracotta /ˌtɛrə'kɒtə/ *n* terracota, *f*

terrain /tə'rein/ *n* terreno, campo, *m*, región, *f*

terrapin /'tɛrəpin/ *n* tortuga de agua dulce, *f*

terrestrial /tə'rɛstriəl/ *a* terrestre, terrenal

terrible /'tɛrəbəl/ *a* terrible, pavoroso, espantoso; *Inf.* tremendo

terribleness /'tɛrəbəlnɪs/ *n* terribilidad, *f*, lo horrible

terrier /'tɛriər/ *n* terrier, *m*; *Inf.* soldado del ejército territorial, *m*

terrific /tə'rɪfɪk/ *a* espantoso, terrible; *Inf.* atroz, tremendo

terrify /'tɛrəˌfai/ *vt* aterrorizar, espantar, horrorizar, *Lat. Am. also* julepear. **to be terrified,** *Lat. Am.* julepearse

terrifying /'tɛrəˌfaiiŋ/ *a* aterrador, espantoso

territorial /ˌtɛri'tɔriəl/ *a* territorial. *n* soldado del ejército territorial, *m*

territoriality /ˌtɛriˌtɔri'ælɪti/ *n* territorialidad, *f*

territory /'tɛriˌtɔri/ *n* región, comarca, *f*; (state) territorio, *m*; jurisdicción, *f*. **mandated territory,** territorio bajo mandato, *m pl*

terror /'tɛrər/ *n* terror, pavor, espanto, *m*. **the Reign of T.,** el Reinado del Terror, *m*. **t.-stricken,** espantado, muerto de miedo

terrorism /'tɛrəˌrɪzəm/ *n* terrorismo, *m*

terrorist /'tɛrərɪst/ *n* terrorista, *m*

terrorization /ˌtɛrərə'zeiʃən/ *n* aterramiento, *m*

terrorize /'tɛrəˌraiz/ *vt* aterrorizar

terse /tɜrs/ *a* conciso, sucinto; seco, brusco

tersely /'tɜrsli/ *adv* concisamente; secamente

terseness /'tɜrsnɪs/ *n* concisión, *f*; brusquedad, *f*

tertiary /'tɜrʃiˌɛri, -ʃəri/ *a* tercero; *Geol.* terciario. *n Eccl.* terciario, *m*

tessera /'tɛsərə/ *n* tesela, *f*

test /tɛst/ *n* (proof) prueba, *f*; examen, *m*; investigación, *f*; (standard) criterio, *m*, piedra de toque, *f*; *Chem.* análisis, *m*; (trial) ensayo, *m*; *Zool.* concha, *f*. *vt Chem.* ensayar; probar, poner a prueba; examinar; (eyes) graduar (la vista). **to put to the t.,** poner a prueba. **to stand the t.,** soportar la prueba. **t. match,** partido internacional de cricket, *m*. **t. meal,** *Med.* comida de prueba, *f*. **t. pilot,** *Aer.* piloto de pruebas, *m*. **t. tube,** tubo de ensayo, *m*

testament /'tɛstəmənt/ *n* testamento, *m*. **the New T.,** el Nuevo Testamento, *m*. **the Old T.,** el Antiguo Testamento, *m*

testamentary /ˌtɛstə'mɛntəri/ *a* testamentario

testate /'tɛsteit/ *a* testado

testator /'tɛsteitər/ *n* testador, *m*, (**testatrix,** testadora, *f*)

testicle /'tɛstɪkəl/ *n* testículo, *m*

testification /ˌtɛstəfɪ'keiʃən/ *n* testificación, *f*

testify /'tɛstəˌfai/ *vt* and *vi* declarar, atestar; *Law.* atestiguar, testificar, dar fe

testily /'tɛstəli/ *adv* malhumoradamente

testimonial /ˌtɛstə'mouniəl/ *n* recomendación, *f*; certificado, *m*; (tribute) homenaje, *m*

testimony /'tɛstəˌmouni/ *n* testimonio, *m*, declaración, *f*; (proof) prueba, *f*. **in t. whereof,** en fe de lo cual. **to bear t.,** atestar

testiness /'tɛstinɪs/ *n* mal humor, *m*, irritación, *f*

testing grounds /'tɛstiŋ/ *n* campo de experimentación, campo de pruebas, *m*

testy /'tɛsti/ *a* enojadizo, irritable, irascible, quisquilloso

tetanus /'tɛtnəs/ *n* tétano, *m*

tether /'tɛðər/ *n* traba, atadura, maniota, *f*. *vt* atar con una correa. **to be at the end of one's t.,** acabarse la resistencia; acabarse la paciencia

Teutonic /tu'tɒnɪk/ *a* teutónico

text /tɛkst/ *n* texto, *m*; (subject) tema, *m*; (motto)

lema, *m*; (of a musical composition) letra, *f*. **t.-book,** libro de texto, *m*

textile /'tɛkstail/ *a* textil, de tejer. *n* textil, *m*, materia textil, *f*; tejido, *m*

textual /'tɛkstʃuəl/ *a* textual

texture /'tɛkstʃər/ *n* (material and *Biol.*) tejido, *m*; textura. *f*

Thailand /'tai,lænd/ Tailandia, *f*

thalamus /'θæləməs/ *n* (*Anat.*, *Bot.*) tálamo, *m*

Thames, the /tɛmz/ *n* el Támesis, *m*. **to set the T. on fire,** descubrir la pólvora

than /ðæn, ðɛn; *unstressed* ðən, ən/ *conjunc* que; (between **more, less,** or **fewer** and a number) de; (in comparisons of inequality) que, but que becomes *a* del (de la, de los, de las) que if the point of comparison is a noun in the principal clause, which has to be supplied mentally to fill up the ellipsis; (b) de lo que if there is no noun to act as a point of comparison, e.g. *He was older than I thought,* Era más viejo de lo que yo pensaba. *They have less than they deserve,* Tienen menos de lo que merecen. *They lose more money than* (*the money*) **they earn,** Pierden más dinero del que ganan. **He will meet with more opposition than he thought,** Va a encontrar más oposición de la que pensaba. **I have more books than you,** Tengo más libros que tú. **She has fewer than nine and more than five,** Ella tiene menos de nueve y más de cinco

thank /θæŋk/ *vt* agradecer, dar las gracias (a). **to t. for,** agradecer. **I will t. you to be more polite,** Le agradecería que fuese más cortés. **He has himself to t. for it,** Él mismo tiene la culpa de ello. **No, t. you,** No, muchas gracias. **T. goodness!** ¡Gracias a Dios!

thankful /'θæŋkfəl/ *a* agradecido. **I am t. to see,** Me alegro de ver, Me es grato ver

thankfully /'θæŋkfəli/ *adv* con gratitud, agradecido

thankfulness /'θæŋkfəlnɪs/ *n* agradecimiento, *m*; gratitud, *f*

thankless /'θæŋklɪs/ *a* ingrato; desagradecido; desagradable

thanks /θæŋks/ *n* gracias, *f pl*. **a vote of thanks,** un voto de gracias. **Many thanks!** ¡Muchas gracias! **to return thanks,** dar las gracias. **thanks to,** merced a, debido a. **thanks to you,** gracias a tí. **t.-offering,** ofrecimiento en acción de gracias, *m*

thanksgiving /ˌθæŋks'givɪŋ/ *n* acción de gracias, *f*. **t. service,** servicio de acción de gracias, *m*. **Thanksgiving (Day),** *n* día de acción de dar gracias, día de gracias, *m*

that /ðæt; *unstressed* ðət/ *dem a* ese, *m*; esa, *f*; aquel, *m*; aquella, *f*. *dem. pron* ése, *m*; ésa, *f*; eso, *neut*; aquél, *m*; aquélla, *f*; aquello, *neut*; (standing for a noun) el, *m*; la, *f*; lo, *neut* **All t. there is,** Todo lo que hay. **His temperament is t. of his mother,** Su temperamento es de el de su madre. **We have not come to t. yet,** Todavía no hemos llegado a ese punto. **T. is what I want to know,** Eso es lo que quiero saber. **with t.,** con eso; (thereupon) en eso. **Go t. way,** Vaya Vd. por allí; Tome Vd. aquel camino. **T. is to say...,** Es decir... **What do you mean by t.?** ¿Qué quieres decir con eso? **The novel is not as bad as all t.,** La novela no es tan mala como tú piensas (*or* como dicen, etc.)

that /ðæt; *unstressed* ðət/ *pron. rel* que; el cual, *m*; la cual, *f*; lo cual, *neut*; (of persons) a quien, *mf*; a quienes, *mf pl*; (with from) de quien, *mf*; de quienes, *mf pl*; (of place) donde. **The letter t. I sent you,** la carta que te mandé. **The box t. John put them in,** la caja en la cual los puso Juan. **The last time t. I saw her,** La última vez que la vi

that /ðæt; *unstressed* ðət/ *conjunc* que; (of purpose) para que; afin de que; (before infin.) para; (because) porque. **O t. he would come!** ¡Ojalá que viniese! **so t.,** para que; (before infin.) para; (as a result) de manera que; de modo que. **It is better t. he should not come,** Es mejor que no venga. **now t.,** ahora que

thatch /θætʃ/ *n* barda, *f*, *vt* bardar

thaw /θɔ/ *n* deshielo, *m*. *vt* deshelar; derretir. *vi* deshelarse; derretirse

the /*stressed* ði; *unstressed* ðə, *unstressed before a consonant* ðə, *unstressed before a vowel* ði/ *def art.* el, *m*; la, *f*; lo, *neut*; los, *m pl*; las, *f pl*; (before feminine sing. noun beginning with stressed a or ha) el; (untranslated between the name and number of a monarch, pope, ruler, e.g. *Charles the Fifth,* Carlos quinto). *adv* (before a comparative) cuanto, tanto más. **at the** or **to the,** al, *m,* (also before feminine sing. noun beginning with a or ha); **a la,** *f;* **a lo,** *neut;* **a los,** *m pl;* **a las,** *f pl.* **from the** or **of the,** del, *m,* (also before feminine sing. noun beginning with stressed a or ha); de la, *f;* de lo, *neut;* de los, *m pl;* de las, *f pl.* **the one,** see **one. The sooner the better,** Cuanto antes mejor. **The room will be all the warmer,** El cuarto estará tanto más caliente

theater /'θiətər/ *n* teatro, *m;* (lecture) anfiteatro, *m;* (drama) teatro, *m,* obra dramática, *f;* (scene) teatro, *m,* escena, *f.* **t. attendant,** acomodador (-ra)

theater-in-the-round /'θiətərɪnðə'raund/ *n* teatro circular, teatro en círculo, *m*

Theatine /'θiətɪn/ *a* and *n Eccl.* teatino *m*

theatrical /θi'ætrɪkəl/ *a* teatral. *n pl* **theatricals,** funciones teatrales, *f pl.* **amateur theatricals,** función de aficionados, *f.* **t. company,** compañía de teatro, *f.* **t. costumier,** mascarero (-ra), alquilador (-ra) de disfraces. **t. manager,** empresario de teatro, *m*

theatricality /θi,ætrɪ'kælɪti/ *n* teatralidad, *f*

Theban /'θibən/ *a* and *n* tebeo (-ea), tebano (-na)

Thebes /θibz/ Tebas, *f*

thee /ði/ *pers pron* te; (after prep.) tí. **with t.,** contigo

theft /θɛft/ *n* robo, hurto, *m*

their /ðɛər/ *unstressed* ðər/ *poss a* su, *mf sing;* sus, *pl;* de ellos, *m pl;* de ellas, *f pl.* **They have t. books,** Tienen sus libros. **I have t. books,** Tengo los libros de ellos

theirs /ðɛərz/ *poss pron* (el) suyo, *m;* (la) suya, *f;* (los) suyos, *m pl;* (las) suyas, *f pl;* de ellos, *m pl;* de ellas, *f pl.* **These hats are t.,** Estos sombreros son los suyos

them /ðɛm; *unstressed* ðəm, əm/ *pers pron* ellos, *m pl;* ellas, *f pl;* (as object of a verb) los, *m pl;* las, *f pl;* (to them) les

thematic /θi'mætɪk/ *a* temático

theme /θim/ *n* tema, asunto, *m;* tesis, *f; Mus.* tema, motivo, *m*

themselves /ðəm'sɛlvz, ,ðɛm-/ *pers pron pl* ellos mismos, *m pl;* ellas mismas, *f pl, reflexive pron* sí; sí mismos; (with a reflexive verb) se. **They t. told me about it,** Ellos mismos me lo dijeron. **They left it for t.,** Lo dejaron para sí (mismos)

then /ðɛn/ *adv* (of future time) entonces; (of past time) a la sazón, en aquella época, entonces; (next, afterwards) luego, después, en seguida; (in that case) en este caso, entonces; (therefore) por consiguiente. *a* de entonces. *n* entonces, *m. conjunc* (moreover) además; pues. **And what t.?** ¿Y qué pasó después?; ¿Y qué pasará ahora?; ¿Y qué más? **by t.,** por entonces. **now and t.,** de vez en cuando. **now... t.,** ya... ya, ora... ora. **since t.,** desde aquel tiempo; desde entonces; desde aquella ocasión. **until t.,** hasta entonces; hasta aquella época. **well t.,** bien, pues. **t. and there,** en el acto, en seguida; allí mismo

thence /ðɛns/ *adv* desde allí, de allí; (therefore) por eso, por esa razón, por consiguiente

thenceforth /,ðɛns'fɔrθ/ *adv* de allí en adelante, desde entonces

theocracy /θi'ɒkrəsi/ *n* teocracia, *f*

theocratic /,θiə'krætɪk/ *a* teocrático

theologian /,θiə'loudʒən/ *n* teólogo, *m*

theological /,θiə'lɒdʒɪkəl/ *a* teológico, teologal

theologize /θi'ɒlə,dʒaiz/ *vi* teologizar

theology /θi'ɒlədʒi/ *n* teología, *f*

theorem /'θiərəm/ *n* teorema, *m*

theoretical /,θiə'rɛtɪkəl/ *a* teórico

theoretically /,θiə'rɛtɪkli/ *adv* teóricamente, en teoría

theorist /'θiərɪst/ *n* teórico, *m*

theorize /'θiə,raiz/ *vi* teorizar

theory /'θiəri/ *n* teoría, *f*

theosophical /,θiə'sɒfɪkəl/ *a* teosófico

theosophist /θi'ɒsəfɪst/ *n* teósofo, *m*

theosophy /θi'ɒsəfi/ *n* teosofía, *f*

therapeutic /,θɛrə'pyutɪk/ *a* terapéutico. *n* **therapeutics,** terapéutica, *f*

therapeutist /,θɛrə'pyutɪst/ *n* terapeuta, *mf*

therapy /'θɛrəpi/ *suffix* terapia, *f*

there /ðɛər; *unstressed* ðər/ *adv* allí; ahí, allá; (at that point) en eso; (used pronominally as subject of verb) haber, e.g. *T. was once a king,* Hubo una vez un rey; *What is t. to do here?* ¿Qué hay que hacer aquí? *interj* ¡vaya!; (I told you so!) ¡ya ves! ¡ya te lo dije yo!; (in surprise) ¡toma! **about t.,** cerca de allí. **down t.,** allí abajo. **in t.,** allí dentro. **out t.,** allí fuera. **over t.,** ahí; allá a lo lejos. **up t.,** allí arriba. **T. came a time when...,** Llegó la hora cuando... **T. it is!** ¡Allí está! **t. is** or **t. are,** hay. **t. was** or **t. were,** había, hubo. **t. may be,** puede haber, quizás habrá. **t. must be,** tiene que haber. **t. will be,** habrá. **T., t.!** (to a child, etc.) ¡Vamos!

thereabouts /'ðɛrə,bauts/ *adv* (near to a place) cerca de allí, por ahí, allí cerca; (approximately) aproximadamente, cerca de

thereafter /,ðɛr'æftər/ *adv* después, después de eso

thereby /,ðɛr'bai/ *adv* (near to that place) por allí cerca; (by that means) con lo cual, de este modo

therefore /'ðɛr,fɔr/ *adv* por lo tanto, por eso, así, por consiguiente; por esta razón

therein /,ðɛr'ɪn/ *adv* (inside) allí dentro; (in this, that particular) en estre, en eso, en ese particular

thereinafter /,ðɛrɪn'æftər/ *adv* posteriormente, más adelante

thereupon /,ðɛərə,pɒn/ *adv* (in consequence) por consiguiente, por lo tanto; (at that point) luego, en eso; (immediately afterwards) inmediatamente después, en seguida

thermal /'θɜrməl/ *a* termal. **t. springs,** aguas termales, termas, *f pl*

thermodynamics /,θɜrmoudai'næmɪks/ *n* termodinámica, *f*

thermoelectric /,θɜrmoui'lɛktrɪk/ *a* termoeléctrico

thermometer /θər'mɒmɪtər/ *n* termómetro, *m*

thermos flask /'θɜrməs/ *n* termos, *m*

thermostat /'θɜrmə,stæt/ *n* termostato, *m*

thermostatic /,θɜrmə'stætɪk/ *a* termostático

thesaurus /θi'sɔrəs/ *n* tesoro, tesauro, *m*

these /ðiz/ *dem pron* of **this,** éstos, *m pl;* éstas, *f pl, dem a* estos, *m pl;* estas, *f pl.* **Are not t. your flowers?** ¿No son éstas tus flores? **T. pictures have been sold,** Estos cuadros han se han vendido

thesis /'θisɪs/ *n* tesis, *f*

Thespian /'θɛspiən/ *a* dramático

they /ðei/ *pers pron* ellos, *m pl;* ellas, *f pl;* (people) se (followed by sing. verb). **T. say,** Dicen, Se dice

thick /θɪk/ *a* espeso; (big) grueso, (wall) grueso, (string, cord) gordo; (vapors) denso; (muddy) turbio; (dense, close) tupido apretado; (numerous) numeroso, repetido, continuo; (full of) lleno (de); (of voice) velado, indistinto; (obtuse) estúpido, lerdo; (friendly) íntimo. *adv* densamente, continuamente, sin cesar. **three feet t.,** de tres pies de espesor. **That's a bit t.!** ¡Eso es un poco demasiado! **to be as t. as thieves,** estar unidos como los dedos de la mano. **t.-lipped,** con labios gruesos, bezudo. **t.-headed,** estúpido, lerdo. **t.-skinned,** de piel gruesa; *Zool.* paquidermo; *Fig.* sin vergüenza, insensible. **t. stroke,** (of letters) grueso, *m*

thick /θɪk/ *n* espesor, *m;* parte gruesa, *f;* lo más denso; (of a fight) lo más reñido; centro, *m,* en medio de. **in the t. of,** en el centro (de), en medio de

thicken /'θɪkən/ *vt* espesar; (increase) aumentar, multiplicar; *Cul.* espesar. *vi* espesarse; condensar; aumentar, multiplicarse; (of a mystery, etc.) complicarse; hacerse más denso; *Cul.* espesarse

thickening /'θɪkənɪŋ/ *n* hinchamiento, *m;* gordura, *f;* (Cul. and of paints) espesante, *m*

thicket /'θɪkɪt/ *n* matorral, soto, *m,* maleza, *f;* (grove) boscaje, *m*

thickly /'θɪkli/ *adv* densamente; espesamente; continuamente, sin cesar; (of speech) indistintamente

thickness /'θɪknɪs/ *n* espesor, *m;* grueso, *m;* densidad, *f;* (of liquids) consistencia, *f;* (layer) capa, *f;* (of speech) dificultad (en el hablar), *f*

thickset /'θɪk'sɛt/ *a* doblado

thief /θif/ *n* ladrón (-ona); (in a candle) moco de

vela, *m*. **Stop t.!** ¡Ladrones! **thieves' den,** *Fig.* cueva de ladrones, *f*
thieve /θiv/ *vi* hurtar, robar. *vt* robar
thievish /'θivɪʃ/ *a* ladrón
thigh /θai/ *n* muslo, *m*. **t.-bone,** fémur, *m*
thimble /'θɪmbəl/ *n* dedal, *m*
thimbleful /'θɪmbəl,fʊl/ *n* lo que cabe en un dedal; *Fig.* dedada, *f*
thin /θɪn/ *a* delgado; (lean) flaco; (small) pequeño; delicado; fino; (of air, light) tenue, sutil; (clothes) ligero; (sparse) escaso; transparente; (watery) aguado; (of wine) bautizado; (not close) claro; (of arguments) flojo. *vt* adelgazar; aclarar; *Agr.* limpiar; reducir. *vi* adelgazarse; afilarse; reducirse. **somewhat t.,** (of persons) delgaducho, algo flaco. **to grow t.,** enflaquecer; afilarse. **to make t.,** hacer adelgazar volver flaco. **t.-clad,** ligero de ropa; mal vestido. **t.-faced,** de cara delgada. **t.-lipped,** de labios apretados. **t.-skinned,** de piel fina; *Fig.* sensitivo, sensible
thine /ðain/ See **theirs.** *poss pron* (el) tuyo, *m*; (la) tuya, *f*; (los) tuyos, *m pl*; (las) tuyas, *f pl*; tu, *mf*; tus, *mf pl*; de tí. **The fault is t.,** La culpa es tuya, La culpa es de tí
thing /θɪŋ/ *n* cosa, *f*; objeto, artículo, *m*; (affair) asunto, *m*; (contemptuous) sujeto, tipo, *m*; (creature) ser, *m*, criatura, *f*; *pl* **things,** (belongings) efectos, trastos, *m pl*; (luggage) equipaje, *m*; (clothes) trapitos, *m pl*; (circumstances) circunstancias, condiciones, *f pl*. **above all things,** ante todo, sobre todo. **a very pretty little t.,** (child) una pequeña muy mona. **as things are,** tal como están las cosas. **for one t.,** en primer lugar. **Her behavior is not quite the t.,** La conducta de ella no está bien vista. **It is a bad t. that...,** Lo malo es que... **It is a good t. that...,** Menos mal que...; Lo bueno es que... **No such t.!** ¡No hay tal!; ¡Nada de eso! **Poor t.!** ¡Pobrecito!; (woman) ¡Pobre mujer!; (man) ¡Pobre hombre! **to be just the t.,** venir al pelo. **with one t. and another,** entre unas cosas y otras. **I like things Spanish,** Me gusta lo español
think /θɪŋk/ *vt* and *vi* pensar; (believe) creer; (deem) considerar, juzgar; imaginar; (suspect) sospechar; (opine) ser de opinión (que). **And to t. that...!** ¡Y pensar que...! **As you t. fit,** Como usted quiera, Como a usted le parezca bien. **He thought as much,** Se lo figuraba. **He little thought that...!** ¡Cuán lejos estaba de pensar que...! **He thinks nothing of...,** No le importa...; Desprecia, Tiene una opinión bastante mala de. **I don't t. so,** No lo creo. **I should just t. not!** ¡Claro que no! ¡Eso sí que no! **I should just t. so!** ¡Claro! ¡Ya lo creo! **It makes me t. of...,** Me hace pensar en... **One might t.,** Podría creerse... **to t. better of something,** cambiar de opinión, considerar mejor. **to t. highly (badly) of,** tener buen (mal) concepto sobre. **to t. over carefully,** pensarlo bien, considerar detenidamente; *Inf.* consultar con la almohada. **to t. proper,** pensar conveniente. **to t. to oneself,** pensar para sí (or entre sí). **to t. too much of oneself,** pensar demasiado en sí; tener amasiada buena opinión de sí mismc; tener humos. **What do you t. about it?** ¿Qué te parece? **to t. about,** (of persons) pensar en; (of things) pensar de (or sobre); meditar, considerar, reflexionar sobre. **to t. for,** pensar por. **to t. of,** pensar en; pensar de (or sobre). **What do you t. of this?** ¿Qué te parece esto? **to t. out,** idear, proyectar, hacer planes para; (a problem) resolver. **to t. over,** pensar; reflexionar sobre, meditar sobre. **I shall t. it over,** Lo pensaré.
thinker /'θɪŋkər/ *n* pensador, *m*
thinking /'θɪŋkɪŋ/ *n* pensamiento, *m*, reflexión, meditación, *f*; juicio, *m*; opinión, *f*, parecer, *m*. *a* pensador; inteligente; racional; serio. **To my way of t.,** Según pienso yo, A mi parecer. **way of t.,** modo de pensar, *m*
thinly /'θɪnli/ *adv* delgadamente; esparcidamente; (lightly) ligeramente; poco numeroso
thinness /'θɪnnɪs/ *n* delgadez, *f*; (leanness) flaqueza, *f*; sutileza, tenuidad, *f*; (lack) escasez, *f*; pequeño número, *m*; poca consistencia, *f*
third /θɜrd/ *a* tercero (tercer before *m*, *sing* noun) (of monarchs) tercero; (of the month) (el) tres. *n* tercio, *m*, tercera parte, *f*; *Mus.* tercera, *f*. **T. time lucky!**

¡A la tercera va la vencida! **t. class,** *n* tercera clase, *f*. *a* de tercera clase. **t. party,** tercera persona, *f*. **t.-party insurance,** seguro contra tercera persona, *m*. **t. person,** tercero (-ra); *Gram.* tercera persona, *f*. **t.-rate,** de tercera clase
thirdly /'θɜrdli/ *adv* en tercer lugar
thirst /θɜrst/ *n* sed, *f*; *Fig.* deseo, *m*, ansia, *f*; entusiasmo, *m*. **to satisfy one's t.,** apagar (or matar) la sed
thirsty /'θɜrsti/ *a* sediento. **to be t.,** tener sed. **to make t.,** dar sed.
thirteen /'θɜr'tin/ *a* and *n* trece *m*. **t. hundred,** *a* and *n* mil trescientos *m*
thirteenth /θɜr'tinθ/ *a* décimotercio; (of monarchs) trece; (of month) (el) trece, *m*, *n* décimotercio, trezavo, *m*
thirtieth /'θɜrtiəθ/ *a* trigésimo; (of month) (el) treinta, *m*. *n* treintavo, *m*
thirty /'θɜrti/ *a* and *n* treinta, *m*. **t.-first,** treinta y uno
this /ðɪs/ *dem a* este, *m*; esta, *f*, *dem pron* éste, *m*; ésta, *f*; esto, *neut* by **t. time,** a esta hora, ya. **like t.,** de este modo, así. **T. is Wednesday,** Hoy es miércoles. **What is all t.?** ¿Qué es todo esto?
thistle /'θɪsəl/ *n* cardo, *m*. **t.-down,** papo de cardo, vilano de cardo, *m*
thither /'θɪðər, 'ðɪð-/ *adv* allá, hacia allá; a ese fin. *a* más remoto
thong /θɔŋ/ *n* correa, tira, *f*
thoracic /θɔ'ræsɪk/ *a* torácico
thorax /'θɔræks/ *n* tórax, *m*
thorn /θɔrn/ *n* espina, *f*; (tree) espino, *m*; *Fig.* abrojo, *m*, espina, *f*. **to be a t. in the flesh of,** ser una espina en el costado de. **t. brake,** espinar, *m*
thornless /'θɔrnlɪs/ *a* sin espinas
thorny /'θɔrni/ *a* espinoso; *Fig.* difícil, arduo
thorough /'θɜrou/ *a* completo; perfecto; (conscientious) concienzudo; (careful) cuidadoso. **t.-bred,** (of animals) de pura raza, de casta; (of persons) bien nacido. **t.-paced,** cabal, consumado
thoroughfare /'θɜrə,fɛər/ *n* vía pública, *f*. **"No t.,"** «Prohibido el paso», Calle cerrada
thoroughly /'θɜrəli/ *adv* completamente; (of knowing a subject) a fondo; concienzudamente
thoroughness /'θɜrənɪs/ *n* perfección, *f*; minuciosidad, *f*
those /ðouz/ *dem a pl* of **that,** esos, *m pl*; esas, *f pl*; aquellos, *m pl*; aquellas, *f pl*, *dem pron* ésos, *m pl*; ésas, *f pl*; aquéllos, *m pl*; aquéllas, *f pl*; (standing for) los que, *m pl*; las que, *f pl*. **t. who,** quienes, *mf pl*; los que, *m pl*; las que, *f pl*. **t. that** or **which,** los que, *m pl*; las que, *f pl*. **Your eyes are t. of your mother,** Tus ojos son los de tu madre
thou /ðau/ *pers pron* tú
though /ðou/ *conjunc* (followed by subjunc. when doubt is implied or uncertain future time) aunque, bien que; (nevertheless) sin embargo, no obstante; (in spite of) a pesar de que; (but) pero. **as t.,** como si (followed by subjunc.). **even t.,** aunque (followed by subjunc.)
thought /θɔt/ *n* pensamiento, *m*; meditación, reflexión, *f*. **some thoughts on...** algunas reflexiones sobre...; opinión, *f*; consideración, *f*; idea, *f*, propósito, *m*; (care) cuidado, *m*, solicitud, *f*; *Inf.* pizca, *f*. **on second thought,** después de pensarlo bien. **The t. struck him,** Se le ocurrió la idea. **to collect one's thoughts,** orientarse; informarse (de). **t.-reading,** adivinación del pensamiento, *f*. **t.-transference,** telepatía, transmisión del pensamiento, *f*
thoughtful /'θɔtfəl/ *a* pensativo, meditabundo; serio; especulativo; (provident) previsor; (kind) atento, solícito; cuidadoso; (anxious) inquieto, intranquilo
thoughtfully /'θɔtfəli/ *adv* pensativamente; seriamente; (providently) con previsión; (kindly) atentamente, solícitamente
thoughtfulness /'θɔtfəlnɪs/ *n* natural reflexivo, *m*, seriedad, *f*; (kindness) solicitud, atención, *f*; (forethought) previsión, *f*
thoughtless /'θɔtlɪs/ *a* irreflexivo; (careless) descuidado, negligente; (unkind) inconsiderado; (silly) necio, estúpido

thoughtlessly /'θɔtlɪsli/ *adv* sin pensar, irreflexivamente; negligentemente

thoughtlessness /'θɔtlɪsnɪs/ *n* irreflexión, *f*; descuido, *m*, negligencia, *f*; (unkindness) inconsideración, *f*; (silliness) neciedad, *f*

thousand /'θauzənd/ *a* mil. *n* mil, *m*; millar, *m*. **one t.,** mil, *m*. **one t. three hundred,** *a* mil trescientos, *m pl*; mil trescientas, *f pl*. *n* mil trescientos, *m pl*. **two (three) t.,** dos (tres) mil. **by thousands,** por millares; por miles. **t.-fold,** mil veces más

thousandth /'θauzəndθ/ *a* and *n* milésimo *m*

Thrace /θreis/ Tracia, *f*

thrall /θrɔl/ *n* esclavo (-va); esclavitud, *f*

thrash /θræʃ/ *vt* azotar, apalear *Mexico* festejar, *Lat. Am.* humear; *Agr.* trillar, desgranar; *Inf.* triunfar sobre, derrotar. *vi* , *agr* trillar el grano; arrojarse, agitarse. *Fig.* **to t. out,** ventilar

thrashing /'θræʃɪŋ/ *n* apaleamiento, *m*, paliza, *Lat. Am. also* azotera, *f*; *Agr.* See **threshing**

thread /θrɛd/ *n* hilo, *m*; (fiber) hebra, fibra, *f*, filamento, *m*; (of a screw) filete, *m*; *Fig.* hilo, *m*, *a* de hilo. *vt* (a needle) enhebrar; (beads) ensartar; (make one's way) colarse a través de, atravesar; pasar por. **to hang by a t.,** pender de un hilo. **to lose the t. of,** *Fig.* perder el hilo de

threadbare /'θrɛd,bɛər/ *a* raído; muy usado; *Fig.* trivial, viejo

threadlike /'θrɛd,laik/ *a* como un hilo, filiforme

threadworm /'θrɛd,wɜrm/ *n m*, lombriz intestinal, *f*

threat /θrɛt/ *n* amenaza, *f*

threaten /'θrɛtn/ *vt* and *vi* amenazar. **to t. with,** amenazar con

threatening /'θrɛtnɪŋ/ *a* amenazador. *n* amenazas, *f pl*

threateningly /'θrɛtnɪŋli/ *adv* con amenazas

three /θri/ *a* and *n* tres *m*; (of the clock) las tres, *f pl*; (of one's age) tres años, *m pl*. **t.-color process,** tricromía, *f*. **t.-colored,** tricolor. **t.-cornered,** triangular; (of hats) de tres picos, tricornio. **t.-cornered hat,** sombrero de tres picos, tricornio, *m*. **t. decker,** *Naut.* navío de tres puentes, *m*; novela larga, *f*. **t. deep,** en tres hileras. **t. hundred,** *a* and *n* trescientos *m*. **t.-hundredth,** *a* and *n* tricentésimo *m*. **t.-legged,** de tres patas. **t.-legged stool,** banqueta, *f*. **t.-per-cents,** accion al tres por ciento (3%), *f*. **t.-phase,** *Elec.* trifásico. **t.-ply,** (of yarn) triple; (of wood) de tres capas. **t.-quarter,** de tres cuartos. **t. quarters of an hour,** tres cuartos de hora, *m pl*. **t.-sided,** trilátero. **t. speed gear box,** cambio de marcha de tres velocidades, *m*. **t.-stringed,** *Mus.* de tres cuerdos. **t. thousand,** *a* tres mil, *mf pl*; *n* tres mil, *m*

threefold /'θri,fould/ *a* triple

threescore /'θri'skɔr/ *a* and *n* sesenta, *m pl*

threesome /'θrisəm/ *n* partido de tres, *m*

thresh /θrɛʃ/ *vt* trillar, desgranar. *vi* trillar el grano. **to t. out,** ventilar

threshing /'θrɛʃɪŋ/ *n* trilla, *f*. **t. floor,** era, *f*. **t. machine,** trilladora, *f*

threshold /'θrɛʃould/ *n* umbral, *m*, *Lat. Am. also* dintel, *m*; *Psychol.* limen, *m*; *Fig.* comienzo, principio, *m*; (entrance) entrada, *f*. **to cross the t.,** atravesar (or pisar) los umbrales

thrice /θrais/ *adv* tres veces

thrift /θrɪft/ *n* frugalidad, parsimonia, *f*

thriftless /'θrɪftlɪs/ *a* malgastador, manirroto

thrifty /'θrɪfti/ *a* frugal, económico

thrill /θrɪl/ *n* estremecimiento, *m*; emoción, *f*. *vt* conmover, emocionar; penetrar. *vi* estremecerse, emocionarse

thriller /'θrɪlər/ *n* libro, *m*, (or comedia, *f*) sensacional; (detective novel) novela policíaca, *f*

thrilling /'θrɪlɪŋ/ *a* sensacional, espeluznante; (moving) emocionante, conmovedor

thrive /θraiv/ *vi* prosperar, medrar; enriquecerse, tener éxito; (grow) desarrollarse, robustecerse; florecer; (of plants) acertar

thriving /'θraivɪŋ/ *a* próspero; floreciente; robusto, vigoroso

throat /θrout/ *n* garganta, *f*; orificio, *m*; (narrow entry) paso, *m*. **sore t.,** dolor de garganta, *m*. **to cut**

one's t., cortarse la garganta. **to take by the t.,** asir (or agarrar) por la garganta

throat cancer *n* cáncer de la garganta, *m*

throaty /'θrouti/ *a* indistinto, ronco

throb /θrɒb/ *n* latido, *m*; pulsación, *f*; vibración, *f*; *Fig.* estremecimiento, *m*. *vi* palpitar, latir; vibrar

throbbing /'θrɒbɪŋ/ *n* pulsación, *f*; vibración, *f*. *a* palpitante; vibrante. **t. pain,** dolor pungente, *m*

throe /θrou/ *n* dolor, *m*, agonía, angustia, *f*. **in the throes of,** en medio de; luchando con; en las garras de. **throes of childbirth,** dolores de parto, *m pl*. **throes of death,** agonía de la muerte, *f*

thrombosis /θrɒm'bousɪs/ *n Med.* trombosis, *f*

throne /θroun/ *n* trono, *m*; (royal power) corona, *f*, poder real, *m*. *vt* elevar al trono. **speech from the t.,** el discurso de la corona, *m*

throng /θrɒŋ/ *n* muchedumbre, multitud, *f*. *vi* apiñarse remolinarse, acudir. *vt* atestar, llenar de bote en bote

throttle /'θrɒtl/ *n Mech.* regulador, *m*; *Auto.* estrangulador, *m*; *Inf.* garganta, *f*. *vt* estrangular; *Fig.* ahogar, suprimir. **to open (close) the t.,** abrir (cerrar) el estrangulador

throttling /'θrɒtlɪŋ/ *n* estrangulación, *f*

through /θru/ *prep* por; al través de; de un lado a otro de; por medio de; (between) entre; por causa de; gracias a. *adv* al través; de un lado a otro; (whole) entero, todo; (from beginning to end) desde el principio hasta el fin; (to the end) hasta el fin. *a* (of passages, etc.) que va desde... hasta...; (of trains) directo. **to look t. the window,** mirar por la ventana, asomarse a la ventana. **to be wet t.,** estar calado hasta los huesos; estar muy mojado. **to carry t.,** llevar a cabo. **to fall t.,** caer por; (fail) fracasar. **to sleep the whole night t.,** dormir durante toda la noche, dormir la noche entera. **t. and t.,** completamente. **through the length and breadth of,** a lo largo y a lo ancho de, hasta los últimos rincones de. **t. traffic,** tráfico directo, *m*. **t. train,** tren directo, *m*

throughout /θru'aut/ *prep* por todo; durante todo. *adv* completamente; (from beginning to end) desde el principio hasta el fin; (everywhere) en todas partes

throw /θrou/ *vt* arrojar, lanzar, echar; (fire) disparar; (pottery) plasmar; (knock down) derribar; (slough) mudar (la piel); (cast off) despojarse de; (a rider) desmontar; (a glance) echar, dirigir (una mirada, etc.); (silk) torcer; (dice) echar; (light) dirigir, enfocar. **to t. oneself at the head of,** echarse a la cabeza de. **to t. open,** abrir de par en par; abrir. **to t. overboard,** *Naut.* echar al mar; desechar; (desert) abandonar. **to t. about,** esparcir, desparramar; derrochar. **to t. aside,** echar a un lado, desechar; abandonar, dejar. **to t. away,** tirar; desechar, *Lat. Am.* botar; (spend) malgastar, derrochar; (waste) sacrificar; (of opportunities) malograr, perder. **to t. back,** devolver; echar hacia atrás. **to t. down,** derribar, dar en el suelo con; echar abajo; (arms) rendir. **to t. down the glove,** arrojar el guante. **to t. oneself down,** tumbarse, echarse; (descend) echarse abajo. **to t. oneself down from,** arrojarse de. **to t. in,** echar dentro; (give extra) añadir; (the clutch) embragar; insertar; (a remark) hacer (una observación). **to t. off,** despojarse de; quitarse; (refuse) rechazar; sacudirse; (get rid of) despedir; (renounce) renunciar; (exhale) emitir, despedir; (verses) improvisar. **to t. on,** echar sobre; (garments) ponerse. **to t. oneself upon,** lanzarse sobre. **to t. out,** expeler; hacer salir; plantar en la calle; (utter) proferir, soltar; (one's chest) inflar; (discard) tirar, desechar, *Lat. Am.* botar. **to t. over,** (desert) abandonar, dejar. **to t. up,** (build) levantar; lanzar en el aire; (a post, etc.) renunciar (a), abandonar; vomitar, *Central America, Mexico* deponer

throw /θrou/ *n* echada, *f*; tiro, *m*; (at dice) lance, *m*; jugada, *f*; (wrestling) derribo, *m*. **within a stone's t.,** a tiro de piedra. **t.-back,** retroceso, *m*; *Biol.* atavismo, *m*

thrower /'θrouər/ *n* tirador (-ra), lanzador (-ra)

throwing /'θrouɪŋ/ *n* lanzamiento, *m*, lanzada, *f*. **t. the hammer,** lanzamiento del martillo, *m*

thrust /θrʌst/ *n* empujón, *m*; (with a sword) estocada, *f*; (fencing) golpe, *m*; (with a lance) bote, *m*; ataque, *m*; asalto, *m*. *vt* empujar; (put) meter; (insert) introducir; (pierce) atravesar; (out, through, of the head, etc.) asomar. *vi* acometer, atacar, embestir; meterse, introducirse; (intrude) entrometerse; (fencing) dar un golpe. **to t. aside,** empujar a un lado; (proposals) rechazar. **to t. back,** hacer retroceder, empujar hacia atrás; (words) tragarse; (thoughts) apartar, rechazar. **to t. down,** empujar hacia abajo; hacer bajar; *Fig.* reprimir. **to t. forward,** empujar hacia delante; hacer seguir. **to t. oneself forward,** adelantarse; *Fig.* ponerse delante de los otros, darse importancia. **to t. in,** introducir; (stick) hincar; (insert) intercalar. **to t. on,** hacer seguir; empujar sobre; (garments) ponerse rápidamente. **to t. oneself in,** introducirse; entrometerse. **to t. out,** echar fuera; hacer salir, echar; expulsar; (the tongue) sacar (la lengua); (the head, etc.) asomar. **to t. through,** atravesar; (pierce) traspasar. **to t. one's way through,** abrirse paso por. **to t. upon,** imponer, hacer aceptar

thud /θʌd/ *n* sonido sordo, *m*; golpe sordo, *m*

thug /θʌg/ *n* asesino, criminal, *m*

thumb /θʌm/ *n* pulgar, *m*. *vt* hojear; ensuciar con los dedos. **under the t. of,** *Fig.* en el poder de. **t. index,** índice pulgar, *m*. **t.-mark,** huella del dedo, *f*. **t.-screw,** tornillo de orejas, *m*, **t.-stall,** dedil, *m*. **t.-tack,** chinche, *m*

thump /θʌmp/ *n* golpe, porrazo, *m*. *vt* and *vi* golpear, aporrear; (the ground, of rabbits) zapatear

thunder /'θʌndər/ *n* trueno, *m*; (of hooves, etc.) estampido, *m*; estruendo, *m*. *vi* tronar; retumbar; *Fig.* fulminar. *vt* gritar en una voz de trueno, rugir. **to t. along,** avanzar como el trueno; galopar ruidosamente. **t.-clap,** trueno, *m*. **t.-cloud,** nube de tormenta, *f*, nubarrón, *m*. **t.-storm,** tronada, *f*. **t. struck,** muerto, estupefacto. **to be thunderstruck,** quedarse frío

thunderbolt /'θʌndər,boult/ *n* rayo, *m*

thunderer /'θʌndərər/ *n* fulminador, *m*. **the Thunderer,** Júpiter tonante, Júpiter tronante, *m*; el «Times» londinense, *m*

Thursday /'θɜrzdei/ *n* jueves, *m*. **Holy T.,** Jueves Santo, *m*

thus /ðʌs/ *adv* así; de este modo; en estos términos; hasta este punto. **t. far,** hasta ahora; hasta este punto; hasta aquí. **Thus it is that...,** Así es que...

thwack /θwæk/ *n* golpe, *m*; *vt* golpear

thwart /θwɔrt/ *vt* frustrar, impedir

thy /ðai/ *poss a* tu, *mf*; tus, *m pl*, and *f pl*

thyme /taim/ *n Bot.* tomillo, *m*

thymus /'θaiməs/ *n Anat.* timo, *m*

thyroid /'θairɔid/ *a* tiroideo. **t. gland,** tiroides, *f*

thyself /ðai'sɛlf/ *poss pron* tu mismo, *m*; tu misma, *f*; (with prep.) tí mismo, *m*; tí misma, *f*; (in a reflexive verb) te

tiara /ti'ærə, -'ɑrə/ *n* tiara, *f*

Tiberias /tai'biəriəs/ Tiberíades, *f*

Tibetan /tɪ'bɛtn/ *a* and *n* tibetano (-na); (language) tibetano, *m*

tibia /'tɪbiə/ *n Anat.* tibia, *f*

tic /tɪk/ *n* (twitch) tic nervioso, *m*

tick /tɪk/ *n Ent.* ácaro, *m*; (sound) tictac, *m*; (cover) funda de colchón, *f*; *Inf.* fiado, crédito, *m*; (mark) marca, *f vi* hacer tictac. *vt* poner una marca contra. **on t.,** *Inf.* al fiado. **to t. off,** poner una marca contra; *Inf.* reñir. **to t. over,** *Auto.* andar, marchar

ticket /'tɪkɪt/ *n* billete, *Lat. Am.* boleto, *m*; (for an entertainment) entrada, localidad, *f*; (label) etiqueta, *f*; (pawn) papeleta de empeño, *f*; (for luggage) talón, *m*; *Polit.* candidatura, *f*, *vt* marcar. **to take one's t.,** sacar el billete (or for entertainment) la entrada, *f*). **excursion t.,** billete de excursión, *m*. **return t.,** billete de ida y vuelta, *m*. **season t.,** billete de abono, *m*. **single t.,** billete sencillo, *m*. **t. agency,** (for travel) agencia de viajes, *f*; (for entertainments) agencia de teatros, *f*. **t. collector or inspector,** revisor, *m*. **t. holder,** tenedor de billete, *m*; abonado (-da). **t. office,** (railway) despacho de billetes, *m*; taquilla, *Lat. Am.* boletería, *f*. **t.-of-leave,** libertad condicional, *f*. **t. punch,** sacabocados, *m*; (on tramcars) clasificador de billetes, *m*

ticking /'tɪkɪŋ/ *n* (sound) tictac, *m*; (cloth) cotí, *m*

tickle /'tɪkəl/ *vt* hacer cosquillas (a), cosquillear; irri-

tar; (gratify) halagar; (amuse) divertir. *vi* tener cosquillas; hacer cosquillas; ser irritante

ticklish /'tɪklɪʃ/ *a* cosquilloso; (of persons) difícil, vidrioso; (of affairs) espinoso, delicado

tidal /'taidl/ *a* de marea. **t. wave,** marejada, *f*; *Fig.* ola popular, *f*

tidbit /'tɪd,bɪt/ *n* See **titbit**

tiddlywinks /'tɪdli,wɪŋks/ *n* juego de la pulga, *m*

tide /taid/ *n* marea, *f*; (season) tiempo, *m*, estación, *f*; (trend) corriente, *f*; (progress) curso, *m*; marcha, *f*. *vi* (with over) vencer, superar; aguardar la ocasión. **to go against the t.,** ir contra la corriente. **to go with the t.,** seguir la corriente. **high t.,** marea alta, *f*. **low t.,** marea baja, *f*, bajamar, *m*. **neap t.,** marea muerta, *f*. **t. mark,** lengua del agua, *f*

tidily /'taidḷi/ *adv* aseadamente; en orden, metódicamente

tidiness /'taidnɪs/ *n* aseo, *m*; buen orden, *m*

tidings /'taidɪŋz/ *n pl* noticias, nuevas, *f pl*

tidy /'taidi/ *a* aseado; metódico, en orden; pulcro; *Inf.* considerable. *vt* poner en orden, asear; limpiar; (oneself) arreglarse

tie /tai/ *n* lazo, *m*, atadura, *f*; (knot) nudo, *m*; (for the neck) corbata, *f*; *Sports.* empate, *m*; *Mus.* ligado, *m*; *Archit.* tirante, *m*; (spiritual bond) lazo, *m*; (burden) carga, responsabilidad, *f*, **tie clasp,** pisa corbata, *mf*. **tie-pin,** alfiler de corbata, *Mexico* fistol, *m*. **tie seller,** corbatero (-ra)

tie /tai/ *vt* atar; (bind) ligar; (lace) lacear; (a knot) hacer; (with a knot) anudar; (unite) unir; (*Fig.* bind) constreñir, obligar; (limit) limitar, restringir; (occupy) ocupar, entretener; (hamper) estorbar, impedir. *vi* atarse; *Sports.* empatar. **to tie one's tie,** hacer la corbata. **to tie down,** atar a; limitar; obligar. **They tied him down to a chair,** Le ataron a una silla. **to tie together,** enlazar, ligar; unir. **to tie up,** liar, atar; (wrap) envolver; recoger; *Naut.* amarrar, atracar; (restrict) limitar, restringir; (invest) invertir

tie-breaker /'tai,breikər/ *n* desempate, *m*

tier /'tɪər/ *n* fila, hilera, *f*. **in tiers,** en gradas; (of a dress) en volantes

tiff /tɪf/ *n* riña, *m*, disgusto, *m*

tiger /'taigər/ *n* tigre, *m*. **t.-cat,** gato (-ta) atigrado (-da). **t.-lily,** tigridia, *f*

tigerish /'taigərɪʃ/ *a* atigrado, de tigre; salvaje, feroz

tight /tait/ *a* apretado; (not leaky) hermético, impermeable; (taut) tieso, tirante; (narrow) estrecho; (trim) compacto; (of clothes) muy ajustado; (shut) bien cerrado; *Naut.* estanco; (risky) peligroso, difícil; (miserly) tacaño, *Argentina* agalludo; (of money, goods) escaso; (tipsy) borracho, *Mexico* abombado. **become t.,** get t.** (get tipsy) *Mexico* abombarse. **to be t.-fisted,** ser como un puño. **to hold t.,** agarrar fuerte. **t. corner,** *Fig.* aprieto, lance apretado, *m*. **t.-rope,** cuerda de volatinero, cuerda floja, *Lat. Am.* maroma, *f*. **t.-rope walker,** alambrista, equilibrista, *mf*; volatinero (-ra), bailarín de la cuerda floja, *m*, *Lat. Am.* maromero (-ra), *mf*. **t.-rope walker's pole,** balancín, *m*

tighten /'taitn/ *vt* estrechar, apretar, *Lat. Am.* atesar; (stretch) estirar; (of saddle girths) cinchar. *vi* estrecharse; estirarse. **t. up** *Lat. Am.* atesar

tightly /'taitli/ *adv* estrechamente

tightness /'taitnɪs/ *n* estrechez, *f*; tirantez, tensión, *f*; (feeling of constriction) opresión, *f*; (drunkenness) emborrachamiento, *m*

tights /taits/ *n pl* mallas, *f pl*

tile /tail/ *n* teja, *f*; (for flooring) baldosa, losa, *f* (ornamental) azulejo, *m*; (hat) chistera, *f*. *vt* tejar; embaldosar. **t. floor,** enlosado, embaldosado, *m*. **t. manufacturer,** tejero, *m*. **t. works** or **yard,** tejar, *m*, (Colombia) galpón *m*

tiler /'tailər/ *n* solador, *m*; tejero, *m*

till /tɪl/ *n* (for money) cajón, *m*. *vt Agr.* cultivar, labrar. *prep* hasta. *conjunc* hasta que

tillable /'tɪləbəl/ *a* laborable

tiller /'tɪlər/ *n Agr.* labrador, *m*; *Bot.* mugrón, renuevo, vástago, *m*; *Naut.* caña del timón, *f*

tilling /'tɪlɪŋ/ *n Agr.* cultivo, laboreo, *m*

tilt /tɪlt/ *n* inclinación, *f*; ladeo, *m*; (fight) torneo, *m*, justa, *f*. *vt* inclinar; ladear; (a drinking vessel) empinar. *vi* inclinarse; ladearse; (fight) justar. **to t. against,** *Fig.* arremeter contra, atacar. **at full t.,** a todo correr. **t. hammer,** martinete de báscula, *m*. **t.-yard,** palestra, *f*

tilting /'tɪltɪŋ/ *n* incinación, *f*; (fighting) justas, *f pl. a* inclinado

timber /'tɪmbər/ *n* madera de construcción, *f*; (trees) árboles de monte, *m pl*; bosque, *m*; (beam) viga, *f*; *Naut.* cuaderna, *f*. *vt* enmaderar. **t. line,** límite del bosque maderable, *m*. **t. merchant,** maderero, *m*. **t. wolf,** lobo gris, *m*. **t. work,** maderaje, *m*. **t. yard,** maderería, *f*, corral de madera, *m*

timbered /'tɪmbərd/ *a* enmaderado; (with trees) arbolado

timbre /'tæmbər, 'tɪm-/ *n Mus.* timbre, *m*

timbrel /'tɪmbrəl/ *n Mus.* tamborete, tamboril, *m*

time /taim/ *n* (in general) tiempo, *m*; (epoch) época, edad, *f*; tiempos, *m pl*; (of the year) estación, *f*; (by the clock) hora, *f*; (lifetime) vida, *f*; (particular moment of time) momento, *m*; (occasion) sazón, ocasión, *f*; (day) día, *m*; (time allowed) plazo, *m*; (in repetition) vez, *f*; *Mus.* compás, *m*; *Mil.* paso, *m*. *vt* ajustar al tiempo; hacer con oportunidad; (regulate) regular; calcular el tiempo que se emplea en hacer una cosa; (a blow) calcular. **all the t.,** todo el tiempo; continuamente, sin cesar. **a long t.,** mucho tiempo. **a long t. ago,** mucho tiempo ha, hace mucho tiempo. **at a t.,** a la vez, al mismo tiempo; (of period) en una época. **at any t.,** a cualquier hora; en cualquier momento; (when you like) cuando gustes. **at no t.,** jamás, nunca. **at some t.,** alguna vez; en alguna época. **at some t. or another,** un día u otro; en una u otra ocasión; en alguna época. **at that t.,** en aquella época; en la sazón; en aquel instante. **at the one t.,** de una vez. **at the present t.,** en la actualidad, al presente. **at the proper t.,** a su debido tiempo; a la hora señalada; a la hora conveniente. **at the same t.,** al mismo tiempo. **at the same t. as,** mientras, a medida que; al mismo instante que, **at times,** a veces, en ocasiones. **behind the times,** *Fig.* atrasado de noticias; pasado de moda. **behind t.,** atrasado. **by that t.,** para entonces. **every t.,** cada vez; siempre. **for some t.,** durante algún tiempo. **for some t. past,** de algún tiempo a esta parte. **for the t. being,** de momento, por ahora, por lo pronto. **from this t.,** desde hoy; desde esta fecha. **from this t. forward,** de hoy en adelante. **from t. to t.,** de vez en cuando, de cuando en cuando, de tarde en tarde. **in a month's t.,** en un mes. **in a short t.,** en breve, dentro de poco. **in good t.,** puntualmente; temprano. **in my t.,** en mis días, en mis tiempos. **in olden times,** antiguamente, en otros tiempos. **in the course of t.,** andando el tiempo, en el transcurso de los años. **in the t. of,** en la época de. **in t.,** (promptly) a tiempo; con el tiempo. **in t. to come,** en el porvenir. **It is t. to...,** Es hora de.... **many times,** frecuentemente, muchas veces. **Once upon a t.,** Érase una vez, Una vez había, Érase que érase. Érase que se era. **Since t. out of mind,** Desde tiempo inmemorial. **the last (next) t.,** la última (próxima) vez. **this t. of year,** esta estación del año. **T. hangs heavy on his hands,** El tiempo se le hace interminable. **T. flies,** El tiempo vuela. **T. will tell!** ¡El tiempo lo dirá! ¡Veremos lo que veremos! **What t. is it?** ¿Qué hora es? **The t. is...,** La hora es... **within a given t.,** dentro de un plazo dado. **to be out of t.,** estar fuera de compás. **to gain t.,** ganar tiempo. **to have a good t.,** pasarlo bien, divertirse. **to have a bad t.,** pasarlo mal; *Inf.* tener un mal cuarto de hora. **to have no t. to,** no tener tiempo para + noun or pronoun, no tener tiempo de + infinitive. **to keep t.,** guardar el compás. **to kill t.,** engañar (or entretener) el tiempo. **to mark t.,** marcar el paso; *Fig.* hacer tiempo. **to pass the t.,** pasar el rato; pasar el tiempo. **to pass the t. of day,** saludar. **to serve one's t.,** (to a trade) servir el aprendizaje; (in prison) cumplir su condena; *Mil.* hacer el servicio militar. **to take t. to,** tomar tiempo para. **to take t. by the forelock,** asir la ocasión por la melena. **to waste t.,** perder el tiempo. **t. exposure,** pose, *f*. **t. fuse,** espoleta de tiempo, espoleta graduada, *f*. **t.-honored,** tradicional, consagrado por el tiempo. **t.-keeper,** capataz, *m*; reloj, *m*. **t.-saving,** que ahorra el

tiempo. **t.-server,** lameculos, *mf* **t.-signal,** señales horarias, *f pl.* **t.-table,** horario, *m*; itinerario, programa, *m*; (railway) guía de ferrocarriles, *f*. **t. to come,** porvenir, *m*, lo venidero

timed /taimd/ *a* calculado; (ill-) intempestivo; (well-) oportuno

timeless /'taimlɪs/ *a* eterno

timeliness /'taimlinɪs/ *n* tempestividad, oportunidad, *f*

timely /'taimli/ *a* oportuno

timepiece /'taim,pis/ *n* reloj, *m*

time zone *n* huso esférico, huso horario, *m*

timid /'tɪmɪd/ *a* tímido, asustadizo, medroso; (shy) vergonzoso

timidity /tɪ'mɪdɪti/ *n* timidez, *f*; vergüenza, *f*

timing /'taimɪŋ/ *n* medida del tiempo, *f*; *Mech.* regulación, *f*; (timetable) horario, *m*

timorous /'tɪmərəs/ *a* timorato, apocado, asustadizo

timorousness /'tɪmərəsnɪs/ *n* encogimiento, *m*, timidez, *f*

tin /tɪn/ *n* (metal) estaño, *m*; (container) lata, *f*; (sheet) hojalata, *f*; (money) plata, *f*. *vt* estañar; (place in tins) envasar en lata; cubrir con hojalata, hoja de aluminio, *f*. **tin-foil,** papel de estaño, *m*. **tin hat,** casco de acero, *m*. **tin-plate,** hojalata, *f*. **tin soldier,** soldado de plomo, *m*. **tin ware,** hojalatería, *f*

tincture /'tɪŋktʃər/ *n* tintura, *f*, tinte, *m*; *Med.* tintura, *f*; (trace) dejo, *m*; (veneer) capa, *f*. *vt* teñir, tinturar

tinder /'tɪndər/ *n* yesca, *f*. **t. box,** yescas, lumbres, *f pl*

tinge /tɪndʒ/ *n* tinte, matiz, *m*; *Fig.* dejo, toque, *m*. *vt* matizar, tinturar; *Fig.* tocar

tingle /'tɪŋgəl/ *n* picazón, comezón, *f*; (thrill) estremecimiento, *m*. *vi* picar; (of ears) zumbar; (thrill) estremecerse (de); vibrar

tingling /'tɪŋglɪŋ/ *n* picazón, *f*; (of the ears) zumbido, *m*; (thrill) estremecimiento, *m*

tinker /'tɪŋkər/ *n* calderero remendón, *m*. *vt* remendar. *vi* chafallar. **to t. with,** jugar con

tinkle /'tɪŋkəl/ *n* tilín, retintín, *m*; campanilleo, *m*; cencerreo, *m*. *vi* tintinar. *vt* hacer tintinar

tinkling /'tɪŋklɪŋ/ *n* retintín, tintineo, *m*; campanilleo, *m*

tinned /tɪnd/ *a* (of food) en lata, en conserva

tinsel /'tɪnsəl/ *n* oropel, *m*; (cloth) lama de oro o plata, *f*, brocadillo, *m*; *Fig.* oropel, *m. a* de oropel; de brocadillo; *Fig.* charro. *vt* adornar con oropel

tinsmith /'tɪn,smɪθ/ *n* hojalatero, estañador, *m*

tint /tɪnt/ *n* tinta, *f*, color, *m*; matiz, *m*; tinte, *m*. *vt* colorar, teñir; matizar

tinting /'tɪntɪŋ/ *n* tintura, *f*, teñido, *m*

tiny /'taini/ *a* diminuto, minúsculo, menudo, chiquito

tip /tɪp/ *n* punta, *f*; cabo, *m*, extremidad, *f*; (of an umbrella, etc.) regatón, *m*; (of a lance) borne, *m*; (of a cigarette) boquilla, *f*; (of a shoe) puntera, *f*; (of a finger) yema, *f*; (for rubbish) depósito de basura, *m*; (gratuity) propina, *f*; (information) informe oportuno, *m*; (tap) golpecito, *m*. **to have on the tip of one's tongue,** tener en la punta de la lengua. **tip-cart,** volquete, *m*. **tip-up seat,** asiento plegable, *m*

tip /tɪp/ *vt* inclinar; volcar, voltear; (drinking vessel) empinar; poner regatón, etc. (a); *Poet.* tocar, golpear ligeramente; (reward) dar propina (a). *vi* inclinarse; (topple) tambalearse; (reward) dar propina. **to tip the wink,** guiñar el ojo (a). **to tip off,** (liquids) echar; hacer caer; (inform) decir en secreto; informar oportunamente. **to tip over,** *vt* volcar; hacer caer. *vi* volcarse; caer; (of a boat) zozobrar. **to tip up,** *vt* (a seat) levantar; (money) proporcionar (el dinero); (upset) volcar; hacer perder el equilibrio. *vi* volcarse; (of a seat) levantarse; (lose the balance) perder el equilibrio

tippler /'tɪplər/ *n* borracho (-cha)

tipsily /'tɪpsəli/ *adv* como borracho

tipsy /'tɪpsi/ *a* achispado, algo borracho, *Lat. Am.* mamado. **to be t.,** estar entre dos luces, estar entre dos velas

tiptoe /'tɪp,tou/ (on) *adv* de puntillas; *Fig.* excitado, ansioso. **to stand on t.,** ponerse de puntillas, empinarse

tirade /'taireid/ *n* diatriba, *f*

tire /taiᵊr/ n (of a cart, etc.) llanta, f; *Auto.* neumático, *Lat. Am.* caucho, m; (of baby carriage, etc.) rueda de goma, f. **balloon t.,** neumático balón, m. **pneumatic t.,** neumático, m. **slack t.,** neumático desinflado, m. **solid t.,** neumático macizo, m. **spare t.,** neumático de recambio (or de repuesto), m. **t. burst,** estallido de un neumático, m. **t. valve,** válvula de cámara (del neumático), f

tire /taiᵊr/ vt cansar, fatigar; (bore) aburrir. vi cansarse, fatigarse; aburrirse. **to be tired of,** estar cansado de. **to grow tired,** empezar a cansarse. **to t. out,** rendir de cansancio

tired /taiᵊrd/ a cansado, fatigado. **to be sick and t. of,** estar hasta la coronilla (de), (of persons) con. **t. of,** cansado de; disgustado de

tiredness /'taiᵊrdnis/ n cansancio, m, fatiga, f; aburrimiento, m

tireless /'taiᵊrlis/ a infatigable, incansable

tiresome /'taiᵊrsəm/ a fastidioso, molesto, pesado; (dull) aburrido

tiresomeness /'taiᵊrsəmnis/ n pesadez, f, fastidio, m; tedio, aburrimiento, m

tiring /'taiᵊrɪŋ/ a fatigoso

tissue /'tɪʃu/ n (cloth) tisú, m, lama, f; (paper) pañuelito m; *Biol.* tejido, m; (series) serie, sarta, f. **t. paper,** papel de seda, m

tit /tɪt/ n *Ornith.* paro, m. **tit for tat,** tal para cual

Titan /'taitn/ n titán, m

titanic /tai'tænɪk/ a titánico

titbit /'tɪt,bɪt/ n golosina, f

tithe /taið/ n décima, f; fracción, pequeña parte, f, vt diezmar. **t. gatherer,** diezmero (-ra)

titillate /'tɪtl,eit/ vt titilar, estimular

titivate /'tɪtə,veit/ vi arreglarse

title /'taitl/ n título, m; (right) derecho, m; documento, m. **to give a t. to,** intitular; ennoblecer. **t. deed,** títulos de propiedad, m. **t. page,** portada, f. **t. role,** papel principal, m

titter /'tɪtər/ vi reírse disimuladamente. n risa disimulada, f

tittle /'tɪtl/ n adarme, tilde, ápice, m

titular /'tɪtʃələr/ a titular; nominal

to /tu/ *unstressed* tʊ, tə/ *prep* a; (as far as) hasta; (in the direction of) en dirección a, hacia; (with indirect object) a; (until) hasta; (compared with) en comparación con, comparado con; (against) contra; (according to) según; (as) como; (in) en; (so that, in order to, for the purpose of) para; (indicating possession) a, de; (of time by the clock) menos; (by) por; (before verbs of motion or which imply motion) a (sometimes para); (before some other verbs) de; en; (before verbs of beginning, inviting, exhorting, obliging) a; (indicating indirect object) a; (before a subjunctive or infinitive indicating future action or obligation) que. **To** is often not translated. With most Spanish infinitives no separate translation is necessary, e.g. leer, decir, to read, to speak. Some verbs are always followed by a preposition (e.g. *to begin to speak,* empezar a hablar, etc.). adv (shut) cerrado. **to come to,** volver en sí. **to lie to,** *Naut.* ponerse a la capa. **to and from,** de un lado a otro. **face to face,** cara a cara. **He has been a good friend to them,** Ha sido un buen amigo para ellos. **That is new to me,** Eso es nuevo para mí. **He went to London,** Se fue a Londres. **to go to France (Canada),** ir a Francia (al Canadá). **the road to Madrid,** la carretera de Madrid. **She kept the secret to herself,** Guardó el secreto para sí. **to go to the dentist,** ir al dentista. **We give it to them,** Se lo damos a ellos. **It belongs to me,** Pertenece a mí. **What does it matter to you?** ¿Qué te importa a tí? **I wish to see him,** Quiero verle. **They did it to help us,** Lo hicieron para ayudarnos. **I have to go to see her,** Tengo que ir a verla. **to this day,** hasta hoy, hasta el presente. **It is a quarter to six,** Son las seis menos cuarto. **to the house of...,** to...'s a casa de, *Lat. Am. also* donde (e.g. *My wife went to her friend's house* Mi mujer fue a casa de su amiga, Mi mujer fue donde su amiga). **to the last shilling,** hasta el último chelín. **the next to me,** el que me sigue. **closed to the public,** cerrado para el público

toad /toud/ n sapo, m

toady /'toudi/ n lameculos, mf adulador (-ra). vt lamer el culo (a), adular

toast /toust/ n *Cul.* tostada, f; (drink) brindis, m. vt tostar; brindar, beber a la salud de. vi brindar. **buttered t.,** mantecada, f. **t.-rack,** portatostadas, m

toaster /'toustər/ n (device) tostador, m; (person) brindador, m

toasting /'toustɪŋ/ n tostadura, f, tueste, m, a de tostar. **t.-fork,** tostadera, f

tobacco /tə'bækou/ n tabaco, m. a tabacalero. **black** or **cut t.,** picadura, f. **leaf t.,** tabaco de hoja, m. **mild t.,** tobaco flojo, m. **pipe t.,** tabaco de pipa, m. **plug t.,** tabaco para mascar, m. **strong t.,** tabaco fuerte, m. **Turkish t.,** tabaco turco, m. **Virginian t.,** tabaco rubio, m. **t.-pipe,** pipa (de tabaco), f. **t.-pipe cleaner,** escobillón para limpiar pipas, m. **t. plantation,** tabacal, m. **t. planter,** tabacalero (-ra). **t. poisoning,** tabaquismo, m. **t.-pouch** or **jar,** tabaquera, f

tobacconist /tə'bækənɪst/ n tabaquero (-ra). **tobacconist's shop,** tabaquería, f, *Lat. Am.* cigarrería, f, expendio, m

toboggan /tə'bɒgən/ n tobogán, m. vi ir en tobogán. **t. run,** pista de tobogán, f

tocsin /'tɒksɪn/ n rebato, m

today /tə'dei/ adv hoy; ahora, actualmente, al presente, hoy día. n el día de hoy. **from t.,** desde hoy. **from t. forward,** de hoy en adelante

toddle /'tɒdl/ vi hacer pinos, empezar a andar; (stroll) dar una vuelta; (leave) marcharse

toddy /'tɒdi/ n ponche, m

toe /tou/ n dedo del pie, m; (cloven) pezuña, f; uña, f; (of furniture) base, f, pie, m; (of stockings, shoes) punta, f. **He stepped on my toe,** Me pisó el dedo del pie. **big toe,** dedo pulgar del pie, dedo gordo del pie, m. **little toe,** dedo pequeño del pie, m. **to toe the line,** ponerse en la raya, *Fig.* cumplir con su deber. **toe-cap,** puntera, f. **toe-dancing,** baile de puntillas, m. **toe-nail,** uña del dedo del pie, f

toffee /'tɔfi/ n caramelo, m

toga /'tougə/ n toga, f

together /tə'gɛðər/ adv junto; (uninterruptedly) sin interrupción; (in concert) simultáneamente, a la vez, al mismo tiempo; (consecutively) seguido, m. **t. with,** con; junto con; en compañía de; (simultaneously) a la vez que

toil /tɔil/ n labor, f, trabajo, m pl. **toils,** lazos, m pl; *Fig.* redes, f pl. vi trabajar, afanarse. **to t. along,** caminar penosamente (por); adelantar con dificultad. **to t. up,** subir penosamente

toiler /'tɔilər/ n trabajador (-ra)

toilet /'tɔilit/ n atavío, m; vestido, m; (lavatory) retrete, excusado, m; (for ladies) tocador, m. **to make one's t.,** arreglarse. **t. case,** neceser, m. **t.-paper,** papel higiénico, m. **t.-powder,** polvos de arroz, m pl. **t. roll,** rollo de papel higiénico, m. **t.-set,** juego de tocador, m. **t. soap,** jabón de olor, jabón de tocador, m

toiling /'tɔilɪŋ/ n trabajo duro, m, a laborioso, trabajador

token /'toukən/ n señal, muestra, f; prueba, f; (presage) síntoma, indicio, m; (remembrance) recuerdo, m. **as a t. of,** en señal de; como recuerdo de

Tokyo /'toukiou/ Tokio, m

tolerable /'tɒlərəbəl/ a tolerable, soportable, llevadero; (fairly good) mediano, mediocre, regular

tolerably /'tɒlərəbli/ adv bastante

tolerance /'tɒlərəns/ n tolerancia, f; paciencia, indulgencia, f

tolerant /'tɒlərənt/ a tolerante; indulgente

tolerate /'tɒlə,reit/ vt tolerar, sufrir, soportar; permitir

toleration /,tɒlə'reiʃən/ n tolerancia, f; indulgencia, paciencia, f. **religious t.,** libertad de cultos, f

toll /toul/ n (of a bell) tañido, doble, m; (for passage) peaje, portazgo, m; (for grinding) derecho de molienda, m. vt and vi doblar, tañer. **to t. the hour,** dar la hora. **t. call,** conferencia telefónica interurbana, llamada a larga distancia, f. **t. gate,** barrera de peaje, f. **t. house,** oficina de portazgos, f

toll booth n caseta de pago, f

tolling /'toulɪŋ/ n tañido, clamor (de las campanas), m

tomahawk /'tɒmə‚hɔk/ n hacha de guerra de los indios, f

tomato /tə'meitou/ n tomate, jitomate (Mexico) m. **t. plant**, tomatera, f. **t. sauce**, salsa de tomate, f

tomb /tum/ n tumba, f, sepulcro, m

tombac /'tɒmbæk/ n tombac, m, tumbaga, f

tomboy /'tɒm‚bɔi/ n muchachote, torbellino, m

tombstone /'tum‚stoun/ n piedra mortuoria, f, monumento funerario, m

tome /toum/ n tomo, volumen, m

tomfoolery /‚tɒm'fuləri/ n necedad, tontería, f; payasada, f

tomorrow /tə'mɔrou/ adv and n mañana, f. **a fortnight t.**, mañana en quince. **the day after t.**, pasado mañana. **t. afternoon** (**morning**), mañana por la tarde (mañana). **T. is Friday**, Mañana es viernes

ton /tʌn/ n tonelada, f

tonality /tou'nælɪti/ n tonalidad, f

tone /toun/ n tono, m; (Mus., Med., Art.) tono, m; (of the voice) acento, m, entonación, f; (of musical instruments) sonido, m; (shade) matiz, m. (of tone) Photo. virar. **to t. down**, vt (Art., Mus.) amortiguar; Fig. suavizar, modificar. vi (Art., Mus.) amortiguarse; Fig. suavizarse, modificarse. **to t. in with**, (of colors) vt armonizar con. vi armonizarse, corresponder en tono o matiz. **to t. up**, vt subir de color, intensificar el color de; Med. entonar, robustecer. **t. poem**, poema sinfónico, m

tonelessly /'tounlisli/ adv sin tono; apáticamente

tongs /tɒŋz/ n pl tenazas, f pl; tenacillas, f pl. **curling t.**, tenacillas para el pelo, f pl. **sugar t.**, tenacillas para azúcar, f pl

tongue /tʌŋ/ n Anat. lengua, f; (language) idioma, m, lengua, f; (speech) modo de hablar, m, habla, f; Mus. lengüeta, f; (of buckle) diente, m; (of shoe) oreja, f; (of land) lengua, f; (of a bell) badajo, m; (flame) lengua, f. **My t. ran away with me,** Inf. Se me fue la mula. **to give t.,** ladrar. **to hold one's t.,** cerrar el pico, tener la boca. **t. of fire**, lengua de fuego, f. **t. tied,** con impedimento en el habla; turbado, confuso; mudo. **t.-twister,** trabalenguas, m

-tongued /tʌŋd/ a de voz...

tonic /'tɒnɪk/ a tónico. n Med. tónico, reconstituyente, m; Mus. tónica, f

tonight /tə'nait/ adv and n esta noche

tonnage /'tʌnɪdʒ/ n tonelaje, porte, m; (duty) derecho de tonelaje, m

tonner /'tʌnər/ n Naut. de... toneladas

tonsil /'tɒnsəl/ n amígdala, tonsila, f

tonsillitis /‚tɒnsə'laitɪs/ n amigdalitis, f

tonsure /'tɒnʃər/ n Eccl. tonsura, f, vt tonsurar

tonsured /'tɒnʃərd/ a tonsurado

too /tu/ adv demasiado; (very) muy; también; además. **too hard**, demasiado difícil, demasiado rígido; (of persons) demasiado duro. **too much**, demasiado. **too often**, con demasiada frecuencia

tool /tul/ n herramienta, f; utensilio, m; instrumento, m; (person) criatura, f. vt labrar con herramienta; (a book) estampar en seco. **t.-bag**, capacho, m. **t. box**, caja de herramientas, f

tooling /'tulɪŋ/ n (of books) estampación en seco, f

toot /tut/ n sonido de bocina, m, vi sonar una bocina

tooth /tuθ/ n diente, m; muela, f; (of comb) púa, f; (taste) gusto, paladar, m; (cog) diente de rueda, m; (of saw) diente, m. vt dentar; mellar. vi Mech. engranar. **armed to the teeth**, armado hasta los dientes. **double t.**, muela, f. **false teeth**, dentadura postiza, f. **set of teeth**, dentadura, f. **to cut one's teeth**, echar los dientes. **to have a sweet t.**, ser muy goloso. **to show one's teeth**, enseñar los dientes. **t.-brush**, cepillo para los dientes, m. **t. drawing**, extracción de un diente, f. **t.-paste**, pasta dentífrica, f

toothache /'tuθ‚eik/ n dolor de muelas, m

toothed /tuθt/ a con dientes; dentado

toothless /'tuθlɪs/ a desdentado, sin dientes; (of combs) sin púas

toothpick /'tuθ‚pɪk/ n mondadientes, m, Mexico palillo, m

top /tɒp/ n (summit) cima, cumbre, f; (of a tree) copa, f; (of the head) coronilla, f; (of a page) cabeza, f; (crest) copete, m, cresta, f; (surface) superficie, f;

(of a wall) coronamiento, m; (tip) punta, f; (point) ápice, m; (of a tram, bus) imperial, baca, f; (of a wave) cresta, f; (acme) auge, m; (of a class) primero (de la clase), m; (highest rank) último grado, m; (of a plant) hojas, f pl; (of a piano) cima, f; Naut. cofa, f; (head of a bed, etc.) cabeza, f; (lid) tapadera, f; (toy) trompo, peón, m; (humming) trompa, f, a más alto; máximo; (chief) principal, primero. vt (cover) cubrir de; (cut off) desmochar; (come level with) llegar a la cima de; (rise above) elevarse por encima (de), coronar, dominar; (be superior to) exceder, aventajar; (golf) topear. **at the top**, a la cabeza; a la cumbre. **from top to bottom**, de arriba abajo. **on top of**, encima de; (besides) en adición a, además de. **to be top-dog**, ser un gallito. **to sleep like a top**, dormir como un lirón. **top boots**, botas de campaña, f pl. **top-dog**, vencedor, m; poderoso, m. **top-hat**, sombrero de copa, m. **top-heavy**, más pesado por arriba que por abajo

topaz /'toupæz/ n topacio, jacinto occidental, m

topcoat /'tɒp‚kout/ n sobretodo, gabán, m

top floor n piso alto, m

topic /'tɒpɪk/ n asunto, tema, m

topical /'tɒpɪkəl/ a tópico; actual

topknot /'tɒp‚nɒt/ n cresta, f, penacho, m; (of birds) moño, m; copete, m

topmast /'tɒp‚mæst/ Naut. -məst/ n mastelero, m

topmost /'tɒp‚moust/ a más alto; más importante

topographer /tə'pɒgrəfər/ n topógrafo, m

topographical /‚tɒpə'græfɪkəl/ a topográfico

topography /tə'pɒgrəfi/ n topografía, f

topple /'tɒpəl/ vi tambalearse, estar al punto de caer. **to t. down**, volcarse; derribarse; caer. **to t. over**, vi venirse abajo; perder el equilibrio. vt derribar, hacer caer

topsail /'tɒp‚seil; Naut. -səl/ n gavia, f

topsyturvy /'tɒpsi'tɜrvi/ a desordenado. adv en desorden, patas arriba, de arriba abajo

toque /touk/ n toca, f

torch /tɔrtʃ/ n antorcha, hacha, tea, f. **electric t.**, lamparilla eléctrica, f. **t.-bearer**, hachero, m

torchlight /'tɔrtʃ‚lait/ n luz de antorcha, f. **by t.**, a la luz de las antorchas

torment /v. tɔr'mɛnt, n. 'tɔrmɛnt/ n tormento, m, angustia, f; (torture) tortura, f; suplicio, m; mortificación, f; disgusto, m. m. vt atormentar, martirizar; (torture) torturar; molestar

tormentor /tɔr'mɛntər/ n atormentador (-ra)

tornado /tɔr'neidou/ n tornado, m

torpedo /tɔr'pidou/ n torpedo, m; Ichth. pez torpedo, m. vt torpedear. **self-propelling t.**, torpedo automóvil, m. **t.-boat**, torpedero, m. **t.-boat destroyer**, cazatorpedero, contratorpedero, m. **t. netting**, red contra torpedos, f. **t. station**, base de torpederos, f. **t. tube**, tubo lanzatorpedos, m

torpedoing /tɔr'pidouɪŋ/ n torpedeamiento, torpedeo, m

torpid /'tɔrpɪd/ a aletargado, entorpecido; (of the mind) torpe, tardo, apático

torpidity, torpor /tɔr'pɪdɪti, 'tɔrpər/ n letargo, m; apatía, f

torrent /'tɔrənt/ n torrente, m

torrential /tɔ'rɛnʃəl/ a torrencial

torrid /'tɔrɪd/ a tórrido. **t. zone**, zona tórrida, f

torsion /'tɔrʃən/ n torsión, f

torso /'tɔrsou/ n torso, m

tort /tɔrt/ n Law. tuerto, m

tortoise /'tɔrtəs/ n tortuga, f. **t.-shell**, carey, m. a de carey

tortuous /'tɔrtʃuəs/ a tortuoso

tortuousness /'tɔrtʃuəsnɪs/ n tortuosidad, f

torture /'tɔrtʃər/ n tortura, f, tormento, m; angustia, f. vt torturar, dar tormento (a); martirizar

torturer /'tɔrtʃərər/ n atormentador (-ra)

torturing /'tɔrtʃərɪŋ/ a torturador, atormentador; angustioso

toss /tɔs/ n sacudimiento, m, sacudidad, f; (of the head) movimiento (de cabeza), m; (bull fighting) cogida, f; (from a horse) caída de caballo, f. vt echar, lanzar; agitar, sacudir; (of bulls) acornear. vi agitarse; (of plumes, etc.) ondear; (in a boat) balancearse a la merced de las olas; jugar a cara o cruz. **to t. a coin** *Mexico* echar un volado. **to t. in a blanket,** mantear, dar una manta (a). **to t. aside,** echar a un lado; abandonar. **to t. off,** beber de un trago. **to t. up,** jugar a cara o cruz

tot /tɒt/ *n* (child) nene (-na), crío (-ía); (of drink) vaso pequeño, *m.* **to tot up,** sumar

total /'toutl/ *a* total; absoluto, completo, entero. *n* total, *m,* suma, *f. vt* sumar. *vi* ascender (a). **t. employment,** ocupación total, *f.* **t. war,** guerra total, *f*

totalitarian /tou,tælɪ'teəriən/ *a* totalitario

totality /tou'tælɪti/ *n* totalidad, *f*

totally /'toutli/ *adv* totalmente, completamente

totem /'toutəm/ *n* tótem, *m*

totemism /'toutə,mɪzəm/ *n* totemismo, *m*

totter /'tɒtər/ *vi* (of persons) bambolearse; tambalear, estar al punto de caer; *Fig.* aproximarse a su fin

tottering /'tɒtərɪŋ/ *a* vacilante; tambaleante. *n* bamboleo, *m;* tambaleo, *m*

toucan /'tukæn/ *n Ornith.* tucán, *m*

touch /tʌtʃ/ *vt* tocar; (brush against) rozar; (reach) alcanzar; (musical instruments) tocar; (move) emocionar, enternecer; (spur on) aguijar; (food) tomar; (affect) influir, afectar; (arouse) despertar, estimular; (equal) compararse con, igualar; (consider) tratar ligeramente (de); (money) dar un sablazo (a). *vi* tocarse; imponer las manos para curar. **I have not touched a bite,** No he probado un bocado. **This touches me nearly,** Esto me toca de cerca. **to t. at,** hacer escala en, tocar en (un puerto). **to t. off,** descargar. **to t. up,** retocar; corregir. **to t. upon,** (a subject) tratar superficialmente de, tratar ligeramente de; hablar de; considerar

touch /tʌtʃ/ *n* (sense of) tacto, *m;* (contact) toque, contacto, *m;* (brushing) roce, *m;* (tap) golpe ligero, *m;* palmadita, *f;* (of an illness) ataque ligero, *m; Mus.* dedeo, *m;* (little) dejo, *m;* (test) prueba, *f,* toque, *m; Art.* toque, *m,* pincelada, *f.* **by the t.,** a tiento. **in t. with,** en relaciones con; en comunicación con; al corriente de. **to give the finishing t.,** dar la última pincelada; dar el último toque. **t.-line,** (football) línea de toque, línea lateral, *f.* **t.-me-not,** *Inf.* erizo, *m.* **t.-stone,** piedra de toque, *f*

touched /tʌtʃt/ *a* emocionado, conmovido

touchiness /'tʌtʃɪnɪs/ *n* susceptibilidad, *f, Argentina* acometividad, *f*

touching /'tʌtʃɪŋ/ *a* patético, conmovedor. *prep* tocante a, acerca de. *n* tocamiento, *m*

touchy /'tʌtʃi/ *a* susceptible, quisquilloso, vidrioso

tough /tʌf/ *a* (hard) duro; vigoroso, fuerte, robusto; resistente; (of character) tenaz, firme; (of a job) difícil; espinoso. *n* chulo, *m*

toughen /'tʌfən/ *vt* endurecer. *vi* endurecerse

toughness /'tʌfnɪs/ *n* dureza, *f;* vigor, *m,* fuerza, *f;* resistencia, *f;* tenacidad, firmeza, *f;* dificultad, *f*

toupee /tu'pei/ *n* tupé, *m*

tour /tʊr/ *n* viaje, *m,* excursión, *f. vi* viajar. *vt* viajar por. **circular t.,** viaje redondo, *m.* **on t.,** *Theat.* en tour, de gira

touring /'tʊrɪŋ/ *a* de turismo. *n* turismo, *m;* viaje, *m.* **t. car,** coche de turismo, *m*

tourist /'tʊrɪst/ *n* turista, *mf;* viajero (-ra). **t. agency,** agencia de turismo, *f,* patronato de turismo, *m.* **t. ticket,** billete kilométrico, *m*

tournament /'tʊrnəmənt/ *n* torneo, *m,* justa, *f;* (of games) concurso, *m*

tourniquet /'tɜrnɪkət, 'tʊr-/ *n* torniquete, *m*

tousle /'tauzəl, -səl/ *vt* despeinar; desordenar el pelo

tout /taut/ *n* buhonero, *m.* **t. for,** pescar, solicitar

tow /tou/ *n* remolque, *m;* (rope) estopa, *f. vt* (*Naut., Auto.*) remolcar. **on tow,** a remolque. **tow-path,** camino de sirga, *m.* **tow rope,** cable de remolque, *m*

towage /'touɪdʒ/ *n* remolque, *m;* (fee) derechos de remolque, *m pl*

towards /tɔrdʒ/ *prep* hacia, en dirección a; (of time) sobre, cerca de; (concerning) tocante a; (with persons) para, con

towel /'tauəl/ *n* toalla, *f. Lat. Am. also* limpiamanos, *m.* **roller t.,** toalla continua, *f.* **t. rail,** toallero, *m*

tower /'tauər/ *n* torre, *f;* (fortress) fortaleza, *f;* (bel-

fry) campanario, *m;* (large) torreón, *m. vi* elevarse. **to t. above,** destacarse sobre, sobresalir; *Fig.* sobrepujar, superar

towered /'tauərd/ *a* torreado; de las... torres. **high t.,** de las altas torres

towering /'tauərɪŋ/ *a* elevado; dominante; orgulloso; *Fig.* violento, terrible

town /taun/ *n* población, *f,* pueblo, *m;* ciudad, *f.* **t. clerk,** secretario de ayuntamiento, *m.* **t. council,** concejo municipal, *m.* **t. councilor,** concejero municipal, *m.* **t. crier,** pregonero, *m.* **t. hall,** (casa de) ayuntamiento, casa consistorial, *f.* **t. house,** casa de ciudad, *f.* **t. planning,** urbanismo, *m;* reforma urbana, *f.* **t. wall,** muralla, *f*

"Town Ahead" «Poblado Próximo»

townsman /'taunzmən/ *n* ciudadano, *m*

town worthy *n* persona principal de la ciudad, *f*

toxic /'tɒksɪk/ *a* tóxico

toxicological /,tɒksɪkə'lɒdʒɪkəl/ *a* toxicológico

toxicologist /,tɒksɪ'kɒlədʒɪst/ *n* toxicólogo, *m*

toxicology /,tɒksɪ'kɒlədʒi/ *n* toxicología, *f*

toxin /'tɒksɪn/ *n* toxina, *f*

toy /tɔi/ *n* juguete, *m. vi* (with) jugar con; acariciar. **toy maker,** fabricante de juguetes, *m*

toyshop /'tɔi,ʃɒp/ *n* juguetería, tienda de juguetes, *f*

trace /treis/ *n* huella, pista, *f,* rastro, *m;* vestigio, *m;* indicio, *m,* evidencia, *f;* (of a harness) tirante, *m;* (touch) dejo, *m;* (of fear, etc.) sombra, *f. vt* trazar; (through transparent paper) calcar; seguir la pista (de); (write) escribir; (discern) distinguir; investigar; descubrir; determinar; (walk) atravesar, recorrer. **to t. back,** (of ancestry, etc.) hacer remontar (a)

traceable /'treisəbəl/ *a* que se puede trazar; atribuible

tracer /'treisər/ *n* trazador (-ra). **t. bullet,** bala luminosa, *f*

trachea /'treikiə/ *n Anat.* tráquea, *f*

trachoma /trə'koumə/ *n Med.* tracoma, *f*

tracing /'treisɪŋ/ *n* calco, *m;* trazo, *m;* seguimiento, *m.* **t.-paper,** papel de calcar, *m*

track /træk/ *n* huella, *f,* rastro, *m;* (for racing, etc.) pista, *f;* (of wheels) rodada, *f;* (railway) vía, *f;* (of a boat) estela, *f;* (path) senda, vereda, *f;* (sign) señal, evidencia, *f;* (course) ruta, *f. vt* rastrear, seguir la pista (de); *Naut.* sirgar. **to t. down,** seguir y capturar. **double t.,** vía doble, *f.* **off the t.,** extraviado; (of a train) descarrilado; *Fig.* por los cerros de Úbeda. **side t.,** desviadero, *m.* **to keep t. of,** *Inf.* no perder de vista (a); seguir las fortunas de

trackless /'træklɪs/ *a* sin camino; sin huella; (of trams, etc.) sin rieles; (untrodden) no pisado

tract /trækt/ *n* tracto, *m;* región, *f; Anat.* vía, *f;* (written) tratado, *m*

tractability /,træktə'bɪlɪti/ *n* docilidad, *f*

tractable /'træktəbəl/ *a* dócil

traction /'trækʃən/ *n* tracción, *f.* **t.-engine,** máquina de arrastre (or de tracción), *f*

tractor /'træktər/ *n* máquina de arrastre, *f;* tractor, *m*

trade /treid/ *n* comercio, *m;* tráfico, *m;* negocio, *m;* industria, *f;* (calling) oficio, *m,* profesión, *f;* (dealers) comerciantes, *mf pl. vi* comerciar, traficar. *vt* cambiar. **to t. on,** explotar, aprovecharse de. **by t.,** de oficio, por profesión. **t.-mark,** marca de fábrica, *f.* **t.-name,** razón social, *f.* **t. price,** precio para el comerciante, *m.* **t. union,** sindicato, *m.* **t. unionism,** sistema de sindicatos obreros, *m.* **t.-winds,** vientos alisios, *m pl*

trader /'treidər/ *n* comerciante, traficante, *mf;* mercader, *m;* (boat) buque mercante, *m*

tradesman /'treidzmən/ *n* tendero, *m.* **tradesmen's entrance,** puerta de servicio, *f*

trading /'treidɪŋ/ *n* comercio, tráfico, *m. a* mercantil, comerciante, mercante. **t. ship,** buque mercante, *m.* **t. station,** factoría, *f*

tradition /trə'dɪʃən/ *n* tradición, *f*

traditional /trə'dɪʃənl/ *a* tradicional; del lugar

traditionalism /trə'dɪʃənl,ɪzəm/ *n* tradicionalismo, *m*

traditionalist /trə'dɪʃənlɪst/ *n* tradicionalista, *mf*

traditionally /trə'dɪʃənli/ *adv* según la tradición, tradicionalmente

traduce /trə'dus/ *vt* calumniar, denigrar, vituperar

traducer /trə'dusər/ n calumniador (-ra)

traffic /'træfɪk/ n comercio, negocio, tráfico, m; (in transit) transporte, m; (in movement) circulación, f. vi comerciar, traficar, negociar. **to cause a block in the t.**, interrumpir la circulación. **t. block**, obstrución del tráfico, f, atasco en la circulación, m. **t. indicator**, (on a car) indicador de dirección, m. **t. island**, refugio para peatones, salvavidas, m. **t. light**, disco, m, luz (de tráfico), f, semáforo, m. **t. roundabout**, redondel, m

trafficker /'træfɪkər/ n traficante, mf

tragedian /trə'dʒidiən/ n trágico, m

tragedy /'trædʒɪdi/ n tragedia, f

tragic /'trædʒɪk/ a trágico

tragicomedy /,trædʒɪ'kɒmɪdi/ n tragicomedia, f

tragicomic /,trædʒɪ'kɒmɪk/ a tragicómico

trail /treil/ n rastro, m, pista, huella, f; (path) sendero, m; (of a comet) cola, cabellera, f. vt rastrear, seguir el rastro de; (drag) arrastrar; (the anchor) garrar. vi arrastrar; (of plants) trepar. **on the t. of**, en busca de; siguiendo el rastro de; **put somebody on the t. of...** darle a fulano la pista de...

trailer /'treilər/ n cazador (-ra); perseguidor (-ra); Auto. remolque, m; (cinema) anuncio de próximas atracciones, m; Bot. talle rastrero, m

train /trein/ n (railway) tren, m; (of a dress) cola, f; (retinue) séquito, m; (procession) desfile, m, comitiva, f; (series) serie, sucesión, f; (of gunpowder) reguero de pólvora, m. **down t.**, tren descendente, m. **excursion t.**, tren de excursionistas, m. **express t.**, exprés, tren expreso, m. **fast t.**, rápido, m. **goods t.**, tren de mercancías, m. **mail t.**, tren correo, m. **next t.**, próximo tren, m. **passenger t.**, tren de pasajeros, m. **stopping t.**, tren ómnibus, m. **through t.**, tren directo, m. **up t.**, tren ascendente, m. **t.-bearer**, paje que lleva la cola, m; dama de honor, f; (of a cardinal, etc.) caudatario, m. **t.-ferry**, buque transbordador, m. **t.-oil**, aceite de ballena, m. **t. service**, servicio de trenes, m

train /trein/ vt educar; adiestrar; enseñar; Sports. entrenar; (firearms) apuntar; (plants) guiar; (accustom) habituar, acostumbrar; (a horse for racing) entrenar; (circus) amaestrar. vi educarse; adiestrarse; Sports. entrenarse

trainer /'treinər/ n (of men and racehorses) entrenador, m; (of performing animals) domador, m

training /'treinɪŋ/ n educación, f; enseñanza, instrucción, f; Sports. entrenamiento, m. **t.-college**, escuela normal, f. **t.-ship**, buque escuela, m

trait /treit/ n rasgo, m, característica, f

traitor /'treitər/ n traidor (-ra)

trajectory /trə'dʒɛktəri/ n trayectoria, f

tram /træm/ n tranvía, m. a tranviario. **t. conductor**, cobrador de tranvía, m. **t. depot**, cochera de tranvías, f. **t. stop**, parada de tranvía, f

trammel /'træməl/ n (of a horse) traba, f; Fig. obstáculo, estorbo, m. vt travar, Fig. estorbar, impedir

tramp /træmp/ n (person) vagabundo (-da); vago (-ga); (walk) caminata, f, paseo largo, m; ruido de pasos, m; Naut. vapor volandero, m. vi ir a pie; patear; vagabundear. vt vagar por

trample /'træmpəl/ n pisoteo, m; (of feet) ruido de pasos, m. vt pisotear, pisar, hollar. vi pisar fuerte. **to t. on**, Fig. atropellar humillar

trance /træns/ n rapto, arrobamiento, m; Med. catalepsia, f

tranquil /'træŋkwɪl/ a tranquilo, apacible; sereno, sosegado

tranquility /træŋ'kwɪlɪti/ n tranquilidad, paz, quietud, f; serenidad, f, sosiego, m; calma, f

tranquilize /'træŋkwə,laiz/ vt tranquilizar, sosegar, calmar

tranquilizer /'træŋkwə,laizər/ n calmante, m

tranquilizing /'træŋkwə,laizɪŋ/ a sosegador, tranquilizador

trans- prefix tras-. **t.-Pyrenean**, a traspirenaico. **to t.-ship**, trasbordar. **t.-shipment**, trasbordo, m. **t.-Siberian**, trasiberiano

transact /træn'sækt/ vt despachar, hacer. vi despachar un negocio

transaction /træn'sækʃən/ n desempeño, m; negocio,

m; transacción, operación, f; pl **transactions** (of a society) actas, f pl

transatlantic /,trænsət'læntɪk/ a transatlántico. **t. liner**, transatlántico, m

transcend /træn'sɛnd/ vt exceder, superar, rebasar. vi trascender

transcendence /træn'sɛndəns/ n superioridad, f; trascendencia, f

transcendental /,trænsɛn'dɛntl/ a trascendental

transcontinental /,trænskɒntn̩'ɛntl/ a transcontinental

transcribe /træn'skraib/ vt transcribir, copiar; Mus. transcribir, adaptar

transcriber /træn'skraibər/ n copiador (-ra); Mus. adaptador (-ra)

transcript /'trænskrɪpt/ n traslado, trasunto, m; (student's) certificado de estudios, certificado de materias aprobadas, m, constancia de estudios, copia del expediente académico, hoja de estudios, f

transcription /træn'skrɪpʃən/ n transcripción, copia, f, trasunto, m; Mus. transcripción, adaptación, f, arreglo, m. **phonetic t.**, transcripción fonética, f

transept /'trænsɛpt/ n Archit. transepto, crucero, m

transfer /v. træns'fər, n. 'trænsfər/ n traslado, m; trasferencia, f, traspaso, m; Law. cesión, enajenación, f; (picture) calcomanía, f. vt trasladar; trasferir; pasar; Law. enajenar, ceder; estampar; calcografiar. vi trasbordarse. **deed of t.**, escritura de cesión, f. **t.-paper**, papel de calcar, m

transferable /træns'fərəbəl/ a trasferible

transferee /,trænsfə'ri/ n cesionario (-ia)

transference /træns'fərəns/ n traslado, m; transferencia, f; Law. cesión, enajenación, f

transferor /træns'fərər/ n cesionista, mf

transfiguration /,trænsfɪgyə'reiʃən/ n trasfiguración, f

transfigure /træns'fɪgyər/ vt trasfigurar, trasformar

transfix /træns'fɪks/ vt traspasar; Fig. paralizar

transfixion /træns'fɪkʃən/ n trasfixión, f

transform /træns'fɔrm/ vt trasformar; convertir, cambiar. **It is completely transformed**, Está completamente trasformado

transformation /,trænsfər'meiʃən/ n trasformación, f; conversión, f, cambio, m

transformative /træns'fɔrmətɪv/ a trasformador

transformer /træns'fɔrmər/ n Elec. trasformador, m

transfuse /træns'fyuz/ vt trasfundir

transfusion /træns'fyuʒən/ n trasfusión, f. **blood t.**, trasfusión de sangre, f

transgress /træns'grɛs/ vt exceder, sobrepasar; (violate) contravenir, violar, pecar contra. vi pecar

transgression /træns'grɛʃən/ n contravención, trasgresión, f; pecado, m

transgressor /træns'grɛsər/ n trasgresor (-ra); pecador (-ra)

transient /'trænʃənt, -ʒənt/ a transitorio, fugaz, pasajero; perecedero

transiently /'trænʃəntli, -ʒənt-/ adv pasajeramente

transistor /træn'zistər/ n transistor, m

transit /'trænsɪt/ n tránsito, paso, m; trasporte, m; Astron. tránsito, m. **in t.**, de tránsito

transition /træn'zɪʃən/ n transición, f; cambio, m; tránsito, paso, m

transitional /træn'zɪʃənl/ a de transición, transitorio

transitive /'trænsɪtɪv/ a Gram. transitivo, activo. **t. verb**, verbo transitivo, verbo activo, m

transitively /'trænsɪtɪvli/ adv transitivamente

transitorily /,trænsɪ'tɔrəli/ adv transitoriamente; provisionalmente

transitoriness /'trænsɪ,tɔrinɪs/ n brevedad, f, lo fugaz

transitory /'trænsɪ,tɔri/ a transitorio, fugaz, pasajero, breve

translatable /træns'leitəbəl/ a traducible

translate /træns'leit/ vt traducir; interpretar; (transfer) trasladar

translation /træns'leiʃən/ n traducción, f; versión, f; traslado, m

translator /træns'leitər/ n traductor (-ra)

translucence /træns'lusəns/ n traslucidez, f

translucent /træns'lusənt/ a traslúcido, trasparente

transmigrate /træns'maigreit/ vi trasmigrar

transmigration /ˌtrænsmaiˈgreiʃən/ n trasmigración, f
transmissibility /trænsˌmisəˈbiliti/ n trasmisibilidad, f
transmissible /trænsˈmisəbəl/ a trasmisible
transmission /trænsˈmiʃən/ n trasmisión, f
transmit /trænsˈmit/ vt trasmitir; remitir, dar
transmitter /trænsˈmitər/ n trasmisor (-ra); *Radio.* radiotrasmisor, m; *Elec.* trasmisor, m
transmutable /trænsˈmyutəbəl/ a trasmutable
transmutation /ˌtrænsmyuˈteiʃən/ n trasmutación, f
transmute /trænsˈmyut/ vt trasmutar
transoceanic /ˌtrænsouʃiˈænik/ a transoceánico
transom /ˈtrænsəm/ n travesaño, m; *Naut.* yugo de popa, m
transpacific /ˌtrænspəˈsifik/ a traspacífico
transparency /trænsˈpɛərənsi/ n trasparencia; diafanidad, f; (picture) trasparente, m
transparent /trænsˈpɛərənt/ a trasparente; diáfano; (of style) claro, limpio
transpire /trænˈspaiər/ vi traspirar; rezumarse; hacerse público; *Inf.* acontecer. vt exhalar
transplant /trænsˈplænt/ vt trasplantar
transplantation /ˌtrænsplænˈteiʃən/ n trasplante, m, trasplantación, f
transport /v. trænsˈpɔrt, n. ˈtrænspɔrt/ n trasporte, m; *Naut.* navío de trasporte, m; *Aer.* avión de trasporte, m; (fit) acceso, paroxismo, m. vt trasportar; (convicts) deportar; *Fig.* (joy) colmar; (rage) llenar
transportable /trænsˈpɔrtəbəl/ a trasportable
transportation /ˌtrænspərˈteiʃən/ n trasporte, m; (convicts) deportación, f
transporter /trænsˌpɔrtər/ n trasportador (-ra)
transpose /trænsˈpouz/ vt trasponer; *Mus.* trasportar
transposition /ˌtrænspəˈziʃən/ n trasposición, f
transversal /trænsˈvɜrsəl/ a and n trasversal, m
transverse /trænsˈvɜrs/ a trasverso, trasversal
transversely /trænsˈvɜrsli/ adv trasversalmente
transvestite /trænsˈvɛstait/ n travestido, m
trap /træp/ n trampa, f; cepo, m; (net) lazo, m, red, f; (for mice, rats) ratonera, f; *Mech.* sifón de depósito, m; pequeño carruaje de dos ruedas, m; (door) puerta caediza, f; *Theat.* escotillón, m; pl **traps**, trastos, m pl; equipaje, m. vt coger con trampa; hacer caer en el lazo; *Fig.* tender el lazo. vi armar una trampa; armar lazo. **to fall into a t.,** *Fig.* caer en la trampa. **to pack one's traps,** liar el hato
trapeze /træˈpiz/ n trapecio (de gimnasia), m
trapper /ˈtræpər/ n cazador de animales de piel, m
trappings /ˈtræpiŋz/ n pl arneses, jaeces, m pl; arreos, aderezos, m pl, galas, f pl
trash /træʃ/ n paja, hojarasca, f; (of sugar, etc.) bagazo, m; trastos viejos, m pl; cachivaches, m pl; (literary) paja, f
trashy /ˈtræʃi/ a de ningún valor, inútil, despreciable
traumatic /trɔˈmætik/ a traumático
traumatism /ˈtrɔməˌtizəm/ n *Med.* traumatismo, m
travail /trəˈveil/ n dolores de parto, m pl. vi estar de parto; trabajar
travel /ˈtrævəl/ n el viajar, viajes, m pl. vi viajar; ver mundo; (of traffic) circular, pasar, ir. vt viajar por; recorrer; (with number of miles) hacer. **to t. over,** viajar por; recorrer. **t. worn,** fatigado por el viaje
travel agent n agente de viajes, mf
traveled /ˈtrævəld/ a que ha viajado, que ha visto muchas partes
traveler /ˈtrævələr/ n viajero (-ra); pasajero (-ra). **commercial t.,** viajante, mf **traveler's check,** cheque de viajeros, m. **traveler's joy,** *Bot.* clemátide, f
traveling /ˈtrævəliŋ/ n viajes, m pl. a viajero; para (or de) viajar; (itinerant) ambulante. **t. crane,** grúa móvil, f. **t. expenses,** gastos de viaje, m pl. **t. requisites,** objetos de viaje, m pl. **t. rug,** manta, f. **t. show,** circo ambulante, m
traversable /trəˈvɜrsəbəl/ a atravesable, transitable, practicable
traverse /n., a. ˈtrævərs; v. trəˈvɜrs/ n travesaño, m; *Law.* negación, f; (*Mil. Archit.*) través, m; (crossing) travesía, f, a transversal. vt atravesar, cruzar; *Law.* negar
travesty /ˈtrævəsti/ n parodia, f, vt parodiar

trawl /trɔl/ vt rastrear. vi pescar a la rastra. **t.-net,** red de arrastre, f
trawler /ˈtrɔlər/ n barco barredero, m; pescador a la rastra, m
trawling /ˈtrɔliŋ/ n pesca a la rastra, f
tray /trei/ n bandeja, f; (of a balance) platillo, m; (in a wardrobe, etc.) cajón, m; (trough) artesa, f
treacherous /ˈtretʃərəs/ a traidor, falso, pérfido, fementido; (of memory) infiel; engañoso; (of ice, etc.) peligroso
treacherously /ˈtretʃərəsli/ adv traidoramente, a traición
treachery /ˈtretʃəri/ n perfidia, traición, falsedad, f
treacle /ˈtrikəl/ n melado, m
tread /trɛd/ n pisada, f; paso, m; (of a stair) peldaño, m; (of tire) pastilla, f; (walk) andar, porte, m, vi pisar; (trample) pisotear; hollar; (oppress) oprimir. vt hollar; (a path) abrir; recorrer; caminar por; bailar. **to t. the grapes,** pisar las uvas. **to t. the stage,** pisar las tablas. **to t. under foot,** hollar; pisotear. **to t. on,** pisar. **to t. on one's heels,** pisarle los talones a uno; seguir de cerca. **to t. out,** (a measure) bailar
treading /ˈtrɛdiŋ/ n pisoteo, m
treadle /ˈtrɛdl/ n pedal, m; (of a loom) cárcola, f
treadmill /ˈtrɛdˌmil/ n molino de rueda de escalones, m; *Fig.* rueda, f
treason /ˈtrizən/ n traición, f. **high t.,** alta traición, lesa majestad, f
treasonable /ˈtrizənəbəl/ a desleal, traidor
treasonably /ˈtrizənəbli/ adv traidoramente
treasure /ˈtrɛʒər/ n tesoro, m; riqueza, f, caudal, m; *Fig.* perla, f. vt atesorar; acumular (or guardar) riquezas, (a memory) guardar. **t. trove,** tesoro hallado, m
treasurer /ˈtrɛʒərər/ n tesorero (-ra)
treasury /ˈtrɛʒəri/ n tesorería, f; (government department) Ministerio de Hacienda, m; (anthology) tesoro, m. **t. bench,** banco del Gobierno, m
treat /trit/ n (pleasure) gusto, placer, m; (present) obsequio, m; (entertainment) fiesta, f. vt tratar; *Med.* tratar, curar; (regale) obsequiar. vi (stand host) convidar; (of) tratar de, versar sobre; (with) negociar con
treatise /ˈtritis/ n tesis, monografía, disertación, f, tratado, m
treatment /ˈtritmənt/ n tratamiento, m; (of persons) conducta hacia, f, modo de obrar con, m; *Med.* tratamiento, m; (*Lit.*, *Art.*) procedimiento, m, técnica, f
treaty /ˈtriti/ n tratado, pacto, m; (bargain) contrato, m
treble /ˈtrɛbəl/ n *Mus.* tiple, m; voz de tiple, f. a triple; *Mus.* sobreagudo. vt triplicar; vi triplicarse. **t. clef,** clave de sol, f
trebling /ˈtrɛbliŋ/ n triplicación, f
tree /tri/ n árbol, m; (for shoes) horma, f; (of a saddle) arzón, m. **breadfruit t.,** árbol del pan, m. **Judas t.,** árbol de amor, m. **t. of knowledge,** árbol de la ciencia, m. **t.-covered,** arbolado. **t.-frog,** rana de San Antonio, f
treeless /ˈtrilis/ a sin árboles
trefoil /ˈtrifɔil/ n trébol, trifolio, m
trek /trɛk/ vi caminar, andar
trellis /ˈtrɛlis/ n enrejado, m; (for plants) espaldera, f. vt cercar con un enrejado; construir espalderas
tremble /ˈtrɛmbəl/ vi temblar; estremecerse; trepidar; vibrar; (sway) oscilar; (of flags) ondear; agitarse; ser tembloroso. **His fate trembled in the balance,** Su suerte estaba en la balanza. **to t. all over,** temblar de pies a cabeza
trembling /ˈtrɛmbliŋ/ n temblor, m; estremecimiento, m; trepidación, f; vibración, f; (fear) agitación, ansiedad, f; temor, m. a tembloroso; trémulo
tremendous /triˈmɛndəs/ a terrible, espantoso; formidable; grande; importante; *Inf.* tremendo; enorme
tremendously /triˈmɛndəsli/ adv terriblemente; *Inf.* enormemente
tremor /ˈtrɛmər/ n temblor, movimiento sísmico, m; (thrill) estremecimiento, m; vibración, f
tremulous /ˈtrɛmyələs/ a trémulo, tembloroso; vacilante; tímido
tremulously /ˈtrɛmyələsli/ adv trémulamente; tímidamente

tremulousness /'tremyələsnıs/ n lo tembloroso; vacilación, f; timidez, f

trench /trentf/ n zanja, f, foso, m; (for irrigation) acequia, f; Mil. trinchera, f. vt hacer zanjas (en); acequiar; Mil. atrincherar. **t.-fever,** tifus exantemático, m. **t.-foot,** pie de trinchera, m. **t.-mortar,** mortero de trinchera, m

trenchant /'trentfənt/ a mordaz

trencher /'trentfər/ n trinchero, m

trend /trend/ n curso, rumbo, m; Fig. tendencia, f; dirección, f. vi Fig. tender

trepan /trı'pæn/ vt Surg. trepanar

trepanning /trı'pænıŋ/ n Surg. trepanación, f

trepidation /,trepı'deifən/ n trepidación, f

trespass /'trespəs, -pæs/ n violación de propiedad, f; ofensa, f; pecado, m; (in the Lord's Prayer) deuda, f. vi (on land) entrar sin derecho, violar la propiedad; (upon) entrar sin permiso en; (with patience, etc.) abusar de; (against) pecar contra, infringir

trespasser /'trespəsər, -pæs-/ n violador (-ra) de la ley de propiedad. **"Trespassers will be prosecuted,"** «Entrada prohibida,» «Prohibido el paso»

tress /tres/ n (plait) trenza, f; rizo, bucle, m; pl **tresses,** cabellera, f

trestle /'tresəl/ n caballete, m; armazón, m. **trestle-table,** mesa de caballete, f

triad /'traiæd/ n terna, trinca, f; Mus. acorde, m

trial /'traiəl/ n prueba, f, ensayo, m; examen, m; (experiment) tentativa, f, experimento, m; (misfortune) desgracia, pena, f; (nuisance) molestia, f; Law. vista de una causa, f. **on t.,** a prueba; Law. en proceso. **to bring to t.,** procesar. **to stand one's t.,** ser procesado. **t. run,** marcha de ensayo, f. **t. trip,** Naut. viaje de ensayo, m

trial and error n tanteos, m. **by trial and error,** por tanteos.

triangle /'trai,æŋgəl/ n triángulo, m. **acute-angled t.,** triángulo acutángulo, m. **obtuse-angled t.,** triángulo obtusángulo, m. **right-angled t.,** triángulo rectángulo, m. **the eternal t.,** el eterno triángulo

triangular /trai'æŋgyələr/ a triangular, triángulo

triangulation /trai,æŋgyə'leifən/ n (in surveying) triangulación, f

tribal /'traibəl/ a tribal

tribe /traib/ n tribu, f

tribesman /'traibzmən/ n miembro de una tribu, m

tribulation /,trıbyə'leifən/ n tribulación, f; pena, aflicción, desgracia, f

tribunal /trai'byunl/ n (seat) tribunal, m; (court) juzgado, m; (confessional) confesionario, m

tribunate /'trıbyənıt/ n tribunado, m

tribune /'trıbyun/ n (person) tribuno, m; tribuna, f

tribunicial /,trıbyə'nıfəl/ a tribúnico

tributary /'trıbyə,teri/ a and n tributario m

tribute /'trıbyut/ n tributo, m; contribución, imposición, f

trice /trais/ n tris, soplo, m. **in a t.,** en un periquete, en un avemaría, en dos trancos

tricentennial /,traisen'tenıəl/ a de trescientos años; n tercer centenario, tricentenario, m

trick /trık/ n (swindle) estafa, f, engaño, m; (ruse) truco, m, estratagema, ardid, f; (mischief) travesura, f; burla, f; (illusion) ilusión, f; (habit) costumbre, f; (affectation) afectación, f; (jugglery) juego de manos, m; (knack) talento, m; (at cards) baza, f. vt engañar, estafar; (with out) adornar, ataviar; (with into) inducir fraudulentamente. vi trampear. **dirty t.,** Inf. mala pasada, perrada, f. **His memory plays him tricks,** La memoria le engaña. **to play a t. on,** gastar una broma (a). **to play tricks,** hacer travesuras. **t. riding,** acrobacia ecuestre, f

trickery /'trıkəri/ n maullería, superchería, f; fraude, engaño, m

trickle /'trıkəl/ n chorrito, hilo (de agua, etc.) m. vi gotear. **to t. down,** deslizar por, correr por, escurrir por

trickling /'trıklıŋ/ n goteo, m; (sound) murmullo, m

trickster /'trıkstər/ n embustero (-ra), trampeador (-ra). **to be a t.,** ser buena maula

tricky /'trıki/ a informal, maullero; (of things) difícil; complicado; (clever) ingenioso; (person) = **crafty**

tricolor /'trai,kʌlər/ a tricolor

tricycle /'traisıkəl/ n triciclo, m

tried /traid/ a probado

triennial /trai'enıəl/ a trienal

trifle /'traifəl/ n (object) baratija, fruslería, f; pequeñez, tontería, bagatela, f; cul, f; (small amount) pequeña cantidad, f, muy poco (de); (adverbially) algo. vi entretenerse, jugar. vt (away) malgastar. **to t. with,** jugar con

trifler /'traiflər/ n persona frívola, f; (with affections) seductor (-ra)

trifling /'traiflıŋ/ a insignificante, sin importancia, trivial

trigger /'trıgər/ n (of a fire-arm) gatillo, m; Mech. tirador, m

trigonometric /,trıgənə'metrık/ a trigonométrico

trigonometry /,trıgə'nomıtri/ n trigonometría, f

trilingual /trai'lıŋgwəl/ a trilingüe

trill /trıl/ n trino, m, vi trinar

trillion /'trılyən/ n trillón, m

trilogy /'trılədʒi/ n trilogía, f

trim /trım/ a aseado; bien arreglado; bien ajustado; elegante; bonito; (of sail) orientado. **She has a t. waist,** Inf. Tiene un talle juncal. n orden, m; buen estado, m; buena condición, f; (toilet) atavío, m. vt arreglar; (tidy) asear; pulir; (ornament) ornar, adornar; (adapt) ajustar, adaptar; Sew. guarnecer; (lamps) despabilar; (a fire) atizar; (hair, mustache) atusar, recortar; (trees) mondar, atusar; alisar; (sails) templar, orientar; (distribute weight in a boat) equilibrar; (of quill pens) tajar. vi (waver) nadar entre dos aguas. **to t. oneself up,** arreglarse

trimly /'trımli/ adv aseadamente; lindamente

trimmer /'trımər/ n guarnecedor (-ra); contemporizador (-ra)

trimming /'trımıŋ/ n arreglo, m; guarnición, f; (on a dress) pasamanería, f; adorno, m; Agr. poda, f; adaptación, f, ajuste, m; pl **trimmings,** accesorios, m pl

trimness /'trımnıs/ n aseo, buen orden, m; buen estado, m; elegancia, lindeza, f; (slimness) esbeltez, f

Trinidad and Tobago /'trınıdæd; tə'beigou/ Trinidad, f, y Tobago, m

Trinidadian /,trını'deidıən/ n and a trinitario

Trinity /'trınıti/ n Trinidad, f

trinket /'trıŋkıt/ n joya, alhaja, f; dije, m, chuchería, f; baratija, f

trinomial /trai'noumıəl/ a Math. de tres términos. n Math. trinomio, m

trio /'triou/ n trío, m

trip /trıp/ n excursión, f; viaje, m; (slip) traspié, tropiezo, m; (in wrestling) zancadilla, f; (mistake) desliz, m. vi (stumble) tropezar, caer; (move nimbly) andar airosamente, ir (or correr) ligeramente; (frolic) bailar, saltar; (wrestling, games) echar la zancadilla; (err) equivocarse; cometer un desliz. vt (up) hacer caer; echar la zancadilla (a); coger en una falta; hacer desdecirse; coger en un desliz; Naut. levantar (el ancla)

tripartite /trai'partait/ a tripartito

tripartition /,traipar'tıfən/ n tripartición, f

tripe /traip/ n callos, m pl; tripas, f pl; mondongo, m

triple /'trıpəl/ a triple. vt triplicar. vi triplicarse

triplet /'trıplıt/ n Poet. terceto, m; Mus. tresillo, m; cada uno (una) de tres hermanos (hermanas) gemelos (-as)

triplicate /a. 'trıplıkıt, v. -,keit/ a triplicado, m. vt triplicar

triplication /,trıplı'keifən/ n triplicación, f

tripod /'traipod/ n trípode, m

Tripoli /'trıpəli/ Trípoli, m

tripper /'trıpər/ n turista, excursionista, mf

tripping /'trıpıŋ/ a ligero, ágil

trippingly /'trıpıŋli/ adv ligeramente

triptych /'trıptık/ n tríptico, m

trite /trait/ a (overused) gastado, trivial

triteness /'traitnıs/ n trivialidad, vulgaridad, f

triumph /'traiəmf/ n triunfo, m. vi triunfar; (over) triunfar de, vencer

triumphal /trai'ʌmfəl/ a triunfal. **t. arch,** arco de triunfo, m

triumphant /trai'ʌmfənt/ *a* triunfante, victorioso
triumvirate /trai'ʌmvərɪt/ *n* triunvirato, *m*
trivet /'trɪvɪt/ *n* trébedes, *f pl*, trípode, *m*
trivial /'trɪvɪəl/ *a* trivial, frívolo; insignificante, sin importancia
triviality /ˌtrɪvi'ælɪti/ *n* trivialidad, frivolidad, *f*; insignificancia, *f*
trochlea /'trɒkliə/ *n* Anat. tróclea, *f*
trodden /'trɒdn/ *a* trillado, batido
troglodyte /'trɒgləˌdait/ *a* and *n* troglodita, *mf*
Trojan /'troudʒən/ *a* and *n* troyano (-na). **the T. War,** la guerra de Troya, *f*
trolley /'trɒli/ *n* Elec. trole, *m*; (for children) carretón, *m*. **t.-bus,** trolebús, *m*. *n* **t. car,** tranvía, *m*. **t.-pole,** trole, *m*
trollop /'trɒləp/ *n* tarasca, ramera, *f*
trombone /trɒm'boun/ *n* trombón, *m*. **t. player,** trombón, *m*
troop /trup/ *n* banda, muchedumbre, *f; Theat.* compañía, *f;* (of cavalry) escuadrón, *m; pl* **troops,** *Mil.* tropas, *f pl;* ejército, *m. vi* ir en tropel, congregarse; (with away) marcharse en tropel, retirarse; (with out) salir en masa. **fresh troops,** tropas frescas, *f pl.* **storm troops,** tropas de asalto, *f pl.* **t.-ship,** transporte de guerra, *m*
trooper /'trupər/ *n* soldado de caballería, *m*
trope /troup/ *n* tropo, *m*
trophy /'troufi/ *n* trofeo, *m*
tropic /'trɒpɪk/ *a* and *n* trópico, *m*
tropical /'trɒpɪkəl/ *a* tropical
tropism /'troupɪzəm/ *n* tropismo, *m*
trot /trɒt/ *n* trote, *m. vi* trotar. *vt* hacer trotar. **to t. out,** Inf. sacar a relucir
troth /trɒθ/ *n* fe, *f;* palabra, *f.* **to plight one's t.,** dar palabra de matrimonio, desposarse
trotting /'trɒtɪŋ/ *a* trotón. *n* trote, *m*
troubadour /'trubəˌdɔr/ *n* trovador, *m, a* trovadoresco
trouble /'trʌbəl/ *n* (grief) aflicción, angustia, *f;* (difficulty) dificultad, *f;* (effort) esfuerzo, *m;* pena, desgracia, *f;* (annoyance) disgusto, sinsabor, *m;* (unrest) confusión, *f,* disturbio, *m;* (illness) enfermedad, *f;* mal, *m;* (disagreement) desavenencia, *f.* **The t. is...,** Lo malo es; La dificultad está en que... **to be in t.,** estar afligido; estar en un apuro, estar entre la espada y la pared. **to be not worth the t.,** no valer la pena. **to stir up t.,** revolver el ajo; armar un lío. **to take the t. to,** tomarse la molestia de.
trouble /'trʌbəl/ *vt* turbar; agitar; afligir, inquietar; (badger) importunar; (annoy) molestar; (cost an effort) costar trabajo (e.g., Learning Spanish did not t. him much, No le costó mucho trabajo aprender el castellano). *vi* preocuparse; darse la molestia; inquietarse
troubled /'trʌbəld/ *a* agitado; inquieto; preocupado; (of life) accidentado, borrascoso. **to fish in t. waters,** pescar en agua turbia, pescar en río revuelto
troublemaker /'trʌbəlˌmeikər/ *n* Lat. Am. buscapleitos, *mf*
troublesome /'trʌbəlsəm/ *a* dificultoso; molesto; inconveniente; importuno; fastidioso
trough /trɒf/ *n* gamella, *f,* (for kneading bread) artesa, *f;* (of the waves) seno, *m;* (meteorological) mínimo, *m.* **drinking t.,** abrevadero, *m.* **stone t.,** pila, *f*
trounce /trauns/ *vt* zurrar, apalear; Fig. fustigar
troupe /trup/ *n* compañía, *f*
trousers /'trauzərz/ *n pl* pantalones, *m pl.* **plus four t.,** pantalones de golf, *m pl.* **striped t.,** pantalón de corte, *m.* **t. pocket,** bolsillo del pantalón, *m.* **t. press,** prensa para pantalones, *f*
trousseau /'trusou/ *n* ajuar de novia, *m*
trout /traut/ *n* trucha, *f*
trowel /'trauəl/ *n* Agr. almocafre, *m;* (mason's) paleta, *f,* palustre, *m*
troy weight /trɔi/ *n* peso de joyería, *m*
truant /'truənt/ *n* novillero, *m;* haragán (-ana). *a* haragán, perezoso. **to play t.,** (from school) hacer novillos; ausentarse
truce /trus/ *n* tregua, *f;* suspensión, cesación, *f*

truck /trʌk/ *n* camión, *m;* carretilla de mano, *f;* (railway) vagón de carga, *m;* (dealings) relaciones, *f pl;* (trash) cachivaches, *m pl,* cosas sin valor, *f pl*
truckage /'trʌkɪdʒ/ *n* camionaje, *m;* acarreo, *m*
truckle /'trʌkəl/ *vi* humillarse, no levantar los ojos. **t. bed,** carriola, *f*
truculence /'trʌkyələns/ *n* truculencia, agresividad, *f*
truculent /'trʌkyələnt/ *a* truculento, agresivo
trudge /trʌdʒ/ *vi* caminar a pie; andar con dificultad, caminar lentamente, andar trabajosamente, *n* caminata, *f*
true /tru/ *a* verdadero; real; leal, sincero; fiel; exacto; honesto; genuino; auténtico; alineado, a plomo. **That is t. of...** Es propio de... *adv* realmente; exactamente. **t.-bred,** de casta legítima. **t.-hearted,** leal, fiel, sincero
truffle /'trʌfəl/ *n* trufa, *f.* **to stuff with truffles,** trufar
truism /'truɪzəm/ *n* perogrullada, *f*
truly /'truli/ *adv* lealmente; realmente, verdaderamente; en efecto, por cierto; sinceramente, de buena fe. **Yours t.,** su seguro servidor (su s.s.)
trump /trʌmp/ *n* (cards) triunfo, *m;* son de la trompeta, *m; Inf.* gran persona, joya, *f. vt* ganar con el triunfo. **to t. up,** inventar. **t.-card,** naipe de triunfo, *m*
trumpery /'trʌmpəri/ *a* de pacotilla; ineficaz. *n* oropel, *m*
trumpet /'trʌmpɪt/ *n* trompeta, *f. vt* trompetear; Fig. pregonar. *vi* (of elephant) barritar. **ear.-t.,** trompetilla (acústica), *f.* **t. speaking t.,** portavoz, *m.* **t. blast,** trompetazo, *m.* **t. shaped,** en trompeta
trumpeter /'trʌmpɪtər/ *n* trompetero, trompeta, *m*
trumpeting /'trʌmpɪtɪŋ/ *n* trompeteo, *m;* (of elephant) barrito, *m*
truncate /'trʌŋkeit/ *a* truncado. *vt* truncar
truncheon /'trʌntʃən/ *n* porra (de goma), *f;* bastón de mando, *m.* **blow with a t.,** porrazo, *m*
trunk /trʌŋk/ *n* (Anat. Bot.) tronco, *m;* (elephant's) trompa, *f;* (railway) línea principal, *f;* baúl, *m;* cofre, *m;* (of a car) Lat. Am. baúl *m; pl* **trunks,** (Elizabethan, etc.) trusas, *f pl;* calzoncillos cortos, *m pl.* **wardrobe t.,** baúl mundo, *m.* **t.-call,** conferencia telefónica, *f.* **t.-line,** tronco, *m.* **t.-road,** carretera de primera clase, carretera mayor, *f*
truss /trʌs/ *n* Med. braguero, *m;* (of straw, etc.) haz, *m;* (of blossom) racimo, *m;* (framework) armazón, *f. vt* atar; Cul. espetar; (a building) apuntalar
trust /trʌst/ *n* fe, confianza, *f;* deber, *m; Law.* fideicomiso, *m;* (credit) crédito, *m;* esperanza, expectación, *f; Com.* trust, *m. vt* tener confianza en; confiar en; esperar; creer; Com. dar crédito (a). *vi* confiar, *Com.* dar crédito. **in t.,** en confianza, en administración, en depósito. **on t.,** al fiado
trustee /trʌs'sti/ *n* guardián, *m; Law.* fideicomisario, depositario, consignatario, *m*
trustful /'trʌstfəl/ *a* confiado
trusting /'trʌstɪŋ/ *a Lat. Am.* creído
trustingly /'trʌstɪŋli/ *adv* confiadamente
trust release *n* extinción de fideicomiso, *f*
trustworthiness /'trʌstˌwɜrðinɪs/ *n* honradez, probidad, integridad, *f;* (of statements) exactitud, *f*
trustworthy /'trʌstˌwɜrði/ *a* digno de confianza, honrado; fidedigno, seguro; exacto
trusty /'trʌsti/ *a* leal, fiel; firme, seguro
truth /truθ/ *n* verdad, *f;* realidad, *f;* exactitud, *f.* **the plain t.,** la pura verdad. **to tell the t.,** decir la verdad
truthful /'truθfəl/ *a* veraz; exacto, verdadero
truthfulness /'truθfəlnɪs/ *n* veracidad, *f;* exactitud, *f*
try /trai/ *vt* and *vi* procurar, tratar de; (test) probar, ensayar; (a case, Law.) ver (el pleito); (strain) poner a prueba; (tire) cansar, fatigar; (annoy) molestar, exasperar; (afflict) hacer sufrir, afligir; (attempt) intentar; (judge) juzgar; (the weight of) tomar a pulso; (assay) refinar. *n* tentativa, *f;* (football) tiro, *m.* **Try as he would...,** Por más que hizo... **to try hard to,** hacer un gran esfuerzo para. **to try one's luck,** probar fortuna. **to try on,** (clothes) probarse (un vestido, etc.). **to try out,** poner a prueba, probar. **to try to,** tratar de, procurar
trying /'traiɪŋ/ *a* molesto; fatigoso; irritante; (painful) angustioso, penoso

tryst /trɪst/ n cita, f; (affair) amorío, m; lugar de cita, m. vt citar. vi citarse

tsar /zɑr, tsɑr/ n zar, m

tsarina /zɑˈrinə, tsɑ-/ n zarina, f

tsetse fly /ˈtsetsi, ˈtitsi/ n mosca tsetsé, f

T-shirt /ˈtiˌʃɜrt/ n camiseta, f.; Dominican Republic poloché, m

tub /tʌb/ n cuba, f, artesón, m; cubeta, f. vi bañarse. **tub thumper,** Inf. gerundio, m

tuba /ˈtubə/ n Mus. tuba, f

tube /tub/ n tubo, m; Anat. trompa, f. **Eustachian t.,** Anat. trompa de Eustaquio, f. **Fallopian t.,** trompa de Falopio, f. **inner t.,** Auto. cámara de aire, f. **speaking t.,** tubo acústico, m. **test t.,** tubo de ensayo, m

tuber /ˈtubər/ n tubérculo, m. **kind of tuber resembling a sweet potato** Central America malanga, f

tubercular /tuˈbɜrkyələr/ a tuberculoso

tuberculosis /tuˌbɜrkyəˈlousɪs/ n tuberculosis, f

tuberose /ˈtubˌrouz/ n nardo, m, tuberosa, f

tubing /ˈtubɪŋ/ n tubería, f

tuck /tʌk/ n Sew. alforzar, f; pliegue, m. vt recoger; Sew. alforzar. vi hacer alforzas. **to t. in,** (in bed) arropar; Inf. tragar. **to t. under,** poner debajo; doblar. **to t. up,** (in bed) arropar; (skirt) sofaldar; (sleeves) arremangar

Tuesday /ˈtuzdei/ n martes, m. **Shrove T.,** martes de carnaval, m

tuft /tʌft/ n (bunch) manojo, m; (on the head) copete, moño, m, cresta, f; (tassel) borla, f; mechón, m

tufted /ˈtʌftɪd/ a Lat. Am. copetudo

tug /tʌg/ n tirón, m; sacudida, f; (boat) remolcador, m. vt tirar de; halar; sacudir. vi tirar con fuerza. **to give a tug,** dar una sacudida. **tug of war,** Lit. lucha de la cuerda, f; Fig. estira y afloja, msg

tuition /tuˈɪʃən/ n (teaching) instrucción, enseñanza, f; lecciones, f pl; (fee) cuota, f

tulip /ˈtulɪp/ n tulipán, m. **t. wood,** palo de rosa, m

tulle /tul/ n tul, m

tumble /ˈtʌmbəl/ n caída, f; (somersault) tumbo, m; voltereta, f. vi caer; (acrobats) voltear, dar saltos. vt hacer caer; desarreglar. **to t. down,** venirse abajo; caer por. **t. down,** ruinoso, destartalado. **to t. off,** caer de. **to t. out,** vt hacer salir; arrojar. vi salir apresuradamente. **to t. over,** vt tropezar con. vi volcarse. **to t. to,** Inf. caer en la cuenta

tumbler /ˈtʌmblər/ n (acrobat) volteador (-ra); vaso para beber, m

tumefaction /ˌtuməˈfækʃən/ n tumefacción, f

tumor /ˈtumər/ n tumor, m

tumult /ˈtumʌlt/ n alboroto, tumulto, m; conmoción, agitación, f; confusión, f

tumultuous /tuˈmʌltʃuəs/ a tumultuoso, alborotado; ruidoso; confuso; turbulento, violento

tumulus /ˈtumyələs/ n túmulo, m

tun /tʌn/ n tonel, m, cuba, f, vt entonelar, embarrilar

tuna /ˈtunə/ n atún, m

tune /tun/ n melodía, f; son, m; armonía, f; Fig. tono, m; Inf. suma, f. vt Mus. afinar, templar; Radio. sintonizar; (up, an engine) ajustar (un motor). vi (in) sintonizar el receptor; (up, Mus.) templar (afinar) los instrumentos. **in t.,** Mus. afinado, templado; Fig. armonioso; (agreement) de acuerdo, conforme. **out of t.,** Mus. desafinado, destemplado. **to be out of t.,** desentonar, discordar; Fig. no armonizar, no estar en armonía. **to go out of t.,** desafinar. **to put out of t.,** destemplar. **to change one's t.,** Inf. bajar el tono

tuneful /ˈtunfəl/ a melodioso

tunefully /ˈtunfəli/ adv melodiosamente, armoniosamente

tunefulness /ˈtunfəlnɪs/ n melodía, f

tuneless /ˈtunlɪs/ a disonante, discordante

tuner /ˈtunər/ n afinador, templador, m; Radio. sintonizador, m

tungsten /ˈtʌŋstən/ n tungsteno, m

tunic /ˈtunɪk/ n túnica, f, Lat. Am. also cusma, f

tuning /ˈtunɪŋ/ n afinación, f; Radio. sintonización, f. **t. fork,** diapasón normal, m. **t. key,** templador, m

Tunis /ˈtunɪs/ Túnez, m

Tunisian /tuˈniʒən/ a and n tunecino (-na)

tunnel /ˈtʌnl/ n túnel, m. vt hacer (or construir) un túnel por. vi hacer un túnel

tunneling /ˈtʌnlɪŋ/ n construcción de túneles, f; horadación, f

turban /ˈtɜrbən/ n turbante, m

turbid /ˈtɜrbɪd/ a turbio; Fig. confuso. **to make t.,** enturbiar

turbine /ˈtɜrbɪn, -bain/ n turbina, f

turbulence /ˈtɜrbyələns/ n turbulencia, f; desorden, m; agitación, f

turbulent /ˈtɜrbyələnt/ a turbulento; alborotado; (stormy) borrascoso; agitado

turf /tɜrf/ n césped, m; (fuel) turba, f; (racing) carreras de caballos, f pl

turgid /ˈtɜrdʒɪd/ a turgente, hinchado; (of style) pomposo

turgidity /tərˈdʒɪdɪti/ n turgencia, f; pomposidad, f

Turk /tɜrk/ n turco (-ca). **Turk's head,** (duster) deshollinador, m; Naut. cabeza de turco, f

Turkey /ˈtɜrki/ Turquía, f

turkey /ˈtɜrki/ n (cock) pavo, m; (hen) pava, f; **t. red,** rojo turco, m

Turkish /ˈtɜrkɪʃ/ a turco. n (language) turco, idioma turco, m. **T. bath,** baño turco, m. **T. slipper,** babucha, f. **T. towel,** toalla rusa, f

turmeric /ˈtɜrmərɪk/ n cúrcuma, f. **t. paper,** papel de cúrcuma, m

turmoil /ˈtɜrmɔil/ n alboroto, tumulto, desorden, m

turn /tɜrn/ n turno, m; (twist) torcimiento, m; (bend) recodo, m, vuelta, f; (in a river) meandro, m; (in a road) viraje, m; (revolution) vuelta, revolución, f; (direction) dirección, f; (in spiral stair) espira, f; Theat. número, m; (change) cambio, m; vicisitud, f; (appearance) aspecto, m; (service) servicio, m; (nature) índole, naturaleza, f; (of phrase) giro, m, expresión, f; (walk) vuelta, f, paseo, m; (talent) talento, m. **a sharp t.,** (in a road) un viraje rápido. **at every t.,** a cada instante; en todas partes. **bad t.,** flaco servicio, m. **by turns,** por turnos. **good t.,** servicio, favor, m. **in its t.,** a su vez. **in t.,** sucesivamente. **Now it's my t.,** Ahora me toca a mí. **The affair has taken a new t.,** El asunto ha cambiado de aspecto. **turn of the century,** vuelta del siglo, f; **turn of the millennium,** vuelta del milenio, f. **to a t.,** Cul. a la perfección. **to have a t. for,** tener talento para. **to take turns at,** alternar en. **t.-table,** (railway) plataforma, f; (of a record player) disco giratorio, m. **t. up,** barahúnda, conmoción, f; (of trousers) dobladillo (del pantalón), m

turn /tɜrn/ vt (on a lathe) tornear; (revolve) dar vueltas a, girar; (a key, door handle, etc.) torcer; (the leaves of a book) hojear; (the brain) trastornar; (a screw) enroscar; (the stomach) revolver (el estómago), marear; (go round) doblar, dar la vuelta a; (change) cambiar, mudar; (translate) traducir, verter; (dissuade) disuadir; (deflect) desviar; (apply) adaptar; (direct, move) volver; (concentrate) dirigir; concentrar; (turn over) volver del revés a lo derecho; (upside-down) volver de lo arriba abajo; (make) hacer, volver; (make sour) volver agrio; (transform) transformar convertir; Mil. envolver. **He has turned thirty,** Ha cumplido los treinta. **He said it without turning a hair,** Lo dijo sin pestañear. **He turned his head,** Volvió la cabeza. **They have turned the corner,** Han doblado la esquina; Fig. Han pasado la crisis. **"Please t. over,"** «A la vuelta de la página).» to **t. a deaf ear to,** no dar oídos a, no hacer caso de. **to t. one's hand to,** aplicarse a. **to t. to account,** sacar ventaja (de). **to t. adrift,** dejar a la merced de las olas; echar de casa, poner en la calle; abandonar. **to t. against,** causar aversión, hacer hostil. **to t. aside,** desviar. **to t. away,** despedir; rechazar; (the head, etc.) volver; desviar. **to t. back,** hacer volver; enviar de nuevo; (raise) alzar; (fold) doblar; (the clock) retrasar. **to t. down,** doblar; (gas) bajar; (a glass, etc.) poner boca abajo; (reject) rechazar; (a suitor) dar calabazas (a). **to t. from,** alejar de, desviar de. **to t. in,** doblar hacia dentro; entregar. **to t. in one's toes,** ser patizambo. **to t. inside out,** volver al revés. **to t. into,** (enter) entrar en; (change) cambiar en, transformar en; convertir en; (translate) traducir a. **to t. off,** (dismiss) despedir; (from) desviarse de, dejar; (light) apagar; (water) cortar; Mech. cerrar; (disconnect) desconectar; (avoid) evitar; (refuse) rechazar. **to t. off the tap,** (water, gas) cerrar la llave (del agua, del gas). **to t. on,** (light) encender; (water, gas, etc.) abrir la llave (del agua, del gas); (steam) dar (vapor); (electric current) establecer (la corriente eléctrica); (eyes) fijar. **to t. out,** (expel) expeler, echar; (dismiss) despedir; (animals) echar al campo; (produce) producir; (dress) vestir; (equip) equipar, guarnecer; (a light) apagar. **to t. over,** (the page) volver (la hoja); (transfer) ceder, traspasar; revolver; (upset) volcar; considerar, pensar. **to t. round,** dar vuelta (a); girar; (empty) descargar. **to t. up,** levantar; apuntar; hacia arriba; (the earth) labrar, cavar; (a glass) poner boca arriba; (one's sleeves, skirt) arremangar; (fold) doblar. **to t. up one's nose at,** mirar con desprecio. **to t. upon,** atacar, volverse contra, acometer; depender de, estribar en. **to t. upside down,** volver de lo arriba abajo; revolver; revolcar

turn /tɜrn/ vi (in a lathe) tornear; (revolve) girar, dar vueltas; (depend) depender (de); torcer; volverse; dar la vuelta; girar sobre los talones; dirigirse (a, hacia); (move) mudar de posición; (deviate) desviarse (de); (be changed) convertirse (en); (become) hacerse, venir a ser; (begin) meterse (a); (take to) dedicarse a; (seek help) acudir; (change behavior) enmendarse, corregirse; (the stomach) revolver (el estómago); (go sour) agriarse, avinagrarse; (rebel) sublevarse. **He turned to the left,** Dio la vuelta a la izquierda; Torció hacia la izquierda. **My head turns,** (with giddiness) Se me va la cabeza. **to t. about,** voltearse, dar la vuelta. **to t. against,** coger aversión (a), disgustarse con; volverse hostil (a). **to t. aside,** desviarse; dejar el camino. **to t. away,** volver la cabeza; apartarse; alejarse. **to t. back,** volver atrás; volver de nuevo; retroceder; volver sobre sus pasos. **to t. down,** doblarse; reducirse. **to t. from,** alejarse de; apartarse de, huir de. **to t. in,** doblarse hacia dentro; (retire) acostarse. **to t. into,** transformarse en; convertirse en. **to t. off,** (depart from) desviarse (de); (fork) torcer, bifurcarse. **to t. out,** estar vuelto hacia fuera; (leave home) salir de casa; (rise) levantarse (de la cama); (arrive) llegar, presentarse; (attend) asistir, acudir; (result) resultar. **to t. over,** mudar (or cambiar) de posición, revolverse; (upset) voltearse, volcarse. **to t. round,** girar; volverse; cambiar de frente; cambiar de dirección, dar la vuelta; (Auto., Aer.) virar; (change views) cambiar de opinión; (change sides) cambiar de partido. **to t. round and round,** dar vueltas, girar. **to t. to,** (apply to) acudir a; (begin) ponerse a; (become) convertirse en; (face) dirigirse hacia; (address) dirigirse a. **to t. up,** (crop up), surgir, aparecer; (arrive) llegar; (happen) acontecer; (be found again) volver a hallarse, reaparecer; (cards) venir; (of hats) levantar el ala; (of hair, etc.) doblarse. **His nose turns up,** Tiene la nariz respingona

turncoat /'tɜrn,kout/ n desertor (-ra), renegado (-da). **to become a t.,** volver la casaca

turned-up /'tɜrnd 'ʌp/ a (of hats) con el ala levantada; (of noses) respingona

turner /'tɜrnər/ n (craftsman) tornero, torneador, m

turning /'tɜrnɪŋ/ n (bend) vuelta, f; (turnery) tornería, f; (of milk, etc.) agrura, f; pl **turnings,** Sew. ensanche, m. **t.-point,** punto decisivo, m, crisis, f. **t. yellow,** Lat. Am. amarilloso

turnip /'tɜrnɪp/ n nabo, m. **t. field,** nabar, m

turnover /'tɜrn,ouvər/ n Com. ventas, f pl; Cul. pastelillo, m

turnpike /'tɜrn,paik/ n barrera de portazgo, f

turnstile /'tɜrn,stail/ n torniquete, m

turpentine /'tɜrpən,tain/ n aguarrás, m, trementina, f

turpitude /'tɜrpɪ,tud/ n infamia, maldad, f

turquoise /'tɜrkɔiz, -kwɔiz/ n turquesa, f

turret /'tɜrɪt/ n torrecilla, almenilla, f; Naut. torre blindada, f

turreted /'tɜrɪtɪd/ a con torres, guarnecido de torres; en forma de torre

turtle /'tɜrtl/ n (dove) tórtolo (-la); (sea) tortuga de mar, f. **to turn t.,** voltearse patas arriba, Naut. zozobrar. **t. soup,** sopa de tortuga, f

tusk /tʌsk/ n colmillo, m

tussle /'tʌsəl/ n lucha, f; agarrada, f. vi luchar, pelear; tener una agarrada

tutelage /'tutlɪdʒ/ n tutela, f

tutelar /'tutlər/ a tutelar

tutor /'tutər/ n (private) ayo, m; profesor (-ra); (Roman law) tutor, m; (supervisor of studies) preceptor. vt enseñar, instruir. vi dar lecciones particulares, ser profesor, dar clases

tutorial /tu'tɔriəl/ n (university) seminario, m; (private) clase particular, f

tutoring /'tutərɪŋ/ n enseñanza, instrucción, f

twaddle /'twɒdl/ n disparates, m pl, tonterías, patrañas, f pl

twain /twein/ a and n dos, m

twang /twæŋ/ n punteado de una cuerda, m; (of a guitar) zumbido, m; (in speech) gangueo, m. vt puntear; (las cuerdas de un instrumento) rasguear. vi zumbar. **to speak with a t.,** hablar con una voz gangosa

tweak /twik/ n pellizco, m; sacudida, f, tirón, m. vt pellizcar; sacudir, tirar

tweed /twid/ n mezcla, f, cheviot, m

tweezers /'twizərz/ n pl pinzas, tenacillas, f pl

twelfth /twelfθ/ a duodécimo; (of the month) (el) doce; (of monarchs) doce. n duodécimo, m; (part) dozavo, m, duodécima parte, f. **T.-night,** Día de Reyes, m, Epifanía, f

twelve /twelv/ a and n doce m; (of age) doce años, m pl. **t. o'clock,** las doce; (mid-day) mediodía, m; (midnight) media noche, f, las doce de la noche. **t.-syllabled,** dodecasílabo

twentieth /'twentiiθ/ a vigésimo; (of the month) (el) veinte; (of monarchs) veinte, n vigésimo, m; (part) vientavo, m, vigésima parte, f

twenty /'twenti/ a veinte; (of age) veinte años, m pl, n veinte, m; (score) veintena, f. **t.-first,** vigésimo primero; (of date) (el) veintiuno, m, (In modern Spanish the ordinals above décimo "tenth" are generally replaced by the cardinals, e.g. the twenty-ninth chapter, el capítulo veintinueve.)

twice /twais/ adv dos veces. **t. as many** or **as much,** el doble

twiddle /'twɪdl/ vt jugar con; hacer girar. vi girar; vibrar. n vuelta, f. **to t. one's thumbs,** dar vuelta a los pulgares, estar mano sobre mano

twig /twɪg/ n ramita, pequeña rama, f

twilight /'twai,lait/ n crepúsculo, m; media luz, f. a crepuscular. **in the t.,** en el crepúsculo; en la media luz. **t. sleep,** parto sin dolor, m

twin /twɪn/ a gemelo, mellizo; doble. n gemelo (-la), mellizo (-za); (of objects) pareja, f, par, m. **t.-engined,** bimotor. **t. screw,** (Naut. Aer.) de dos hélices

twine /twain/ n bramante, cordel, m; guita, f. vt enroscar; (weave) tejer; (encircle) ceñir; (round, about) abrazar. vi (of plants) trepar; entrelazarse; (wind) serpentear

twinge /twɪndʒ/ n punzada, f, dolor agudo, m; Fig. remordimiento, tormento, m. vi causar un dolor agudo

twining /'twainɪŋ/ a Bot. trepante, voluble. **t. plant,** planta enredadera (or trepante), f

twinkle /'twɪŋkəl/ vi centellear, chispear, titilar; (of eyes) brillar; (of feet) moverse rápidamente, bailar. n (in the eye) chispa, f

twinkling /'twɪŋklɪŋ/ n centelleo, m; titilación, f; (of the eye) brillo, m; (glimpse) vislumbre, m; Fig. instante, momento, m. a titilante, centelleador. **in a t.,** en un dos por tres. **in the t. of an eye,** en un abrir y cerrar de ojos

twin-tailed comet /'twɪn,teild/ n ceratias, m

twirl /twɜrl/ n rotación, vuelta, f, pirueta, f. vi hacer girar; voltear; torcer; (a stick, etc.) dar vueltas (a). vi girar, dar vueltas; dar piruetas

twirp /twɜrp/ n Inf. renacuajo, m

twist /twɪst/ n (skein) mecha, f; trenza, f; (yarn) torzal, m; (of tobacco) rollo, m; (of bread) rosca de pan, f; (act of twisting) torcimiento, m, torsión, f; (in a road, etc.) recodo, m, curva, vuelta, f; (pull) sacudida, f; (contortion) regate, esguince, m; (in a winding stair) espira, f; (in ball games) efecto, m; (in a person's nature) peculiaridad, *f*; falta de franqueza, *f*; (to words) interpretación, *f*. *vt* torcer; enroscar; (plait) trenzar; (wring) estrujar; (weave) tejer; (encircle) ceñir; (a stick, etc.) dar vueltas a; (of hands) crispar; (distort) interpretar mal, torcer. *vi* torcerse; enroscarse; (wind) serpentear; dar vueltas; (coil) ensortijarse; (writhe) undular, retorcerse; (of a stair) dar vueltas

twisted /'twɪstɪd/ *a* torcido, *Mexico* chueco; (of persons) contrahecho

twisting /'twɪstɪŋ/ *n* torcimiento, *m*; torcedura, *f*; serpenteo, *m*; (interlacing) entrelazamiento, *m*. *a* sinuoso, serpenteado

twitch /twɪtʃ/ *n* sacudida, *f*, tirón, *m*; (nervous) contracción nerviosa, *f*. *vt* tirar bruscamente, quitar rápidamente; agarrar; (ears, etc.) mover; (hands) crispar, retorcer. *vi* crisparse; (of ears, nose) moverse

twitching /'twɪtʃɪŋ/ *n* sacudida, *f*; (contraction) crispamiento, *m*, contracción nerviosa, *f*; (pain) punzada, *f*; (of conscience) remordimiento, *m*

twitter /'twɪtər/ *n* piada, *f*, gorjeo, *m*. *vi* piar, gorjear

two /tu/ *a* and *n* dos, *m*; (of the clock) (las) dos, *f pl*; (of age) dos años, *m pl*. *a* de dos. **in two,** en dos partes. **in two's,** de dos en dos. **one or two,** uno o dos; algunos, *m pl*; algunas, *f pl*. **two against two,** dos a dos. **two by two,** de dos en dos, a pares. **Two can live as cheaply as one,** Donde come uno comen dos. **to put two and two together,** atar cabos. **two-edged,** de dos filos. **two-faced,** de dos caras; *Fig.* de dos haces. **to be two-faced,** hacer a dos caras. **two-headed,** de dos cabezas; bicéfalo. **two hundred,** *a* and *n* doscientos, *m*. **two hundredth,** *a* ducentésimo. *n* ducentésima parte, *f*; doscientos, *m*. **two-legged,** bípedo. **two-ply,** de dos hilos. **two-seater,** *a* de dos asientos. **two-speed gear box,** cambio de marcha de dos velocidades, *m*. **two-step,** paso doble, *m*. **two of a kind,** (well-matched) tal para cual. **two-way switch,** *Elec.* interruptor de dos direcciones, *m*

twofold /a. 'tu,fould/ *adv.* -'fould/ *a* doble. *adv* doblemente, dos veces

twosome /'tusəm/ *n* partido de dos, *m*

two swords' theory *n* teoría de los dos gladios, *f*

tying /'taɪŋ/ *n* ligadura, *f*; atadura, *f*

tympanum /'tɪmpənəm/ *n* (*Anat., Archit.*) tímpano, *m*

type /taɪp/ *n* tipo, *m*; *Print.* carácter, *m*, letra de imprenta, *f*, tipo, *m*. *vt* and *vi* escribir a máquina. **t. case,** caja de imprenta, *f*. **t. founder,** fundidor de letras de imprenta, *m*. **t. foundry,** fundición de tipos, *f*. **t.-setter,** cajista, *mf* **t.-setting,** composición tipográfica, *f*

typewrite /'taip,rait/ *vt* and *vi* escribir a máquina

typewriter /'taip,raitər/ *n* máquina de escribir, *f*

typewriting /'taip,raitɪŋ/ *n* mecanografía, *f*, *a* mecanográfico

typewritten /'taip,ritn/ *a* escrito a máquina

typhoid /'taifɔid/ *n* tifoidea, fiebre tifoidea, *f*

typhoon /tai'fun/ *n* tifón, *m*

typhus /'taifəs/ *n* tifus, *m*, tabardillo pintado, *m*

typical /'tɪpəkəl/ *a* típico, característico; simbólico. **t. Mexican dish,** (of food) antojito, *m*

typify /'tɪpə,fai/ *vt* simbolizar, representar; ser ejemplo de

typist /'taipɪst/ *n* mecanografista, *mf*; mecanógrafo (-fa)

typographer /tai'pɒgrəfər/ *n* tipógrafo, *m*

typographic /,taipə'græfɪk/ *a* tipográfico

typography /tai'pɒgrəfi/ *n* tipografía, *f*

tyrannical /tɪ'rænɪkəl/ *a* tiránico, despótico

tyrannization /,tɪrənə'zeiʃən/ *n* tiranización, *f*

tyrannize /'tɪrə,naiz/ *vi* tiranizar

tyranny /'tɪrəni/ *n* tiranía, *f*, despotismo, *m*

tyrant /'taɪrənt/ *n* déspota, *m*, tirano (-na)

Tyre /taiᵊr/ Tiro, *m*

tyro /'tairou/ *n* novicio (-cia), tirón (-ona), advenedizo (-za), *mf*

Tyrol, the /tɪ'roul/ el Tirol

U

U /yu/ *n* (letter) u, *f*. **U-boat,** submarino, *m*. **u-shaped,** en forma de U

ubiquitous /yu'bɪkwɪtəs/ *a* ubicuo, omnipresente

ubiquity /yu'bɪkwɪti/ *n* ubicuidad, omnipresencia, *f*

udder /'ʌdər/ *n* ubre, teta, mama, *f*

ugh /ʊx, ʌg/ *interj* ¡uf!

ugliness /'ʌglinɪs/ *n* fealdad, *f*; (moral) perversidad, *f*; (of a situation) peligro, *m*, lo difícil

ugly /'ʌgli/ *a* feo, *Lat. Am. also* feroz; (morally) repugnante, asqueroso, perverso; (of a situation) peligroso, difícil; (of a wound) grave, profundo; (of a look) amenazador; *Inf.* desagradable; (of weather) borrascoso. **to make u.,** afear, hacer feo

Ukraine /yu'krein/ Ucrania, *f*

Ukrainian /yu'kreiniən/ *a* and *n* ucranio (-ia)

ukulele /,yukə'leili/ *n Mus.* ucelele, *m*

ulcer /'ʌlsər/ *n* úlcera, *f*, *Lat. Am. also* lacra

ulcerate /'ʌlsə,reit/ *vt* ulcerar. *vi* ulcerarse

ulceration /,ʌlsə'reiʃən/ *n* ulceración, *f*

ulcerous /'ʌlsərəs/ *a* ulceroso

ulterior /ʌl'tɪəriər/ *a* (of place) ulterior; (of time) posterior, ulterior; (of motives) interesado, oculto; **u. motive,** segunda intención, *f*

ultimate /'ʌltəmɪt/ *a* último; fundamental, esencial

ultimately /'ʌltəmɪtli/ *adv* por fin, al final; esencialmente

ultimatum /,ʌltə'meitəm/ *n* ultimátum, *m*

ultimo /'ʌltə,mou/ *adv* del mes anterior

ultra /'ʌltrə/ *a* exagerado, extremo. *prefix* ultra-. **u-red,** ultrarrojo. **u.-violet,** ultravioleta

ultramarine /,ʌltrəmə'rin/ *a* ultramarino. *n* azul de ultramar, *m*

ultramontane /,ʌltrəmɒn'tein/ *a* ultramontano

ululation /,ʌlyə'leiʃən/ *n* ululación, *f*, ululato, *m*

umbilical /ʌm'bɪlɪkəl/ *a* umbilical

umbilicus /ʌm'bɪlɪkəs/ *n* ombligo, *m*

umbra /'ʌmbrə/ *n Astron.* cono de sombra, *m*

umbrage /'ʌmbrɪdʒ/ *n Poet.* sombra, *f*; resentimiento, enfado, *m*. **to take u.,** ofenderse, resentirse

umbrella /ʌm'brelə/ *n* paraguas, *m*. **u. maker,** paragüero (-ra). **u. shop,** paragüería, *f*. **u. stand,** paragüero, *m*

umpire /'ʌmpaiᵊr/ *n Sports.* árbitro, *m*; *Law.* juez arbitrador, tercero en discordia, *m*. *vt* arbitrar

un- *prefix* Used before adjectives, adverbs, abstract nouns, verbs and translated in Spanish by **in-, des-, nada, no, poco, sin,** as well as in other ways

unabashed /,ʌnə'bæʃt/ *a* desvergonzado, descarado, insolente; (calm) sereno, sosegado

unabashedly /,ʌnə'bæʃɪdli/ *adv* sin rubor

unabated /,ʌnə'beitɪd/ *a* no disminuido; cabal, entero

unabbreviated /,ʌnə'brivi,eitɪd/ *a* íntegro, sin abreviar

unable /ʌn'eibəl/ *a* incapaz, impotente; (physical defect) imposibilitado. **to be u. to,** no poder, serle a uno imposible. **to be u. to control,** no poder controlar

unabridged /,ʌnə'brɪdʒd/ *a*. See **unabbreviated**

unaccented /,ʌn'æksentɪd/ *a* sin acento

unacceptability /,ʌnæk,septə'bɪlɪti/ *n* lo inaceptable

unacceptable /,ʌnæk,septəbəl/ *a* inaceptable

unaccepted /,ʌnæk,septɪd/ *a* rechazado, no aceptado

unaccommodating /,ʌnə'kɒmə,deitɪŋ/ *a* poco complaciente, nada servicial

unaccompanied /,ʌnə'kʌmpənid/ *a* solo, sin compañía; *Mus.* sin acompañamiento

unaccomplished /,ʌnə'kɒmplɪʃt/ *a* incompleto, sin terminar, inacabado; (not clever) sin talento

unaccountability /,ʌnə,kauntə'bɪlɪti/ *n* lo inexplicable; falta de responsabilidad, irresponsabilidad, *f*

unaccountable /,ʌnə'kauntəbəl/ *a* inexplicable; irresponsable

unaccountably /ˌʌnəˈkauntəbli/ *adv* inexplicablemente, extrañamente

unaccredited /ˌʌnæˈkrɛdɪtɪd/ *a* no acreditado, extraoficial

unaccustomed /ˌʌnəˈkʌstəmd/ *a* no habituado; (unusual) desacostumbrado, insólito, inusitado

unacknowledged /ˌʌnækˈnɒlɪdʒd/ *a* no reconocido; (of letter) sin contestación, por contestar; no correspondido, sin devolver; (of crimes, etc.) inconfeso, no declarado

unacquainted /ˌʌnəˈkweintɪd/ *a* que no conoce; que desconoce, que ignora; no habituado. **to be u. with,** no conocer; ignorar; no estar acostumbrado a

unadaptable /ˌʌnəˈdæptəbəl/ *a* inadaptable (also of persons)

unadorned /ˌʌnəˈdɔrnd/ *a* sin adorno sencillo, que no tiene adornos

unadulterated /ˌʌnəˈdʌltəˌreitɪd/ *a* sin mezcla, no adulterado, natural; genuino, verdadero; puro

unadventurous /ˈʌnædˈvɛntʃərəs/ *a* nada aventurero, que no busca aventuras, tímido; tranquilo, sin incidente

unadvisability /ˌʌnædˌvaizəˈbɪliti/ *n* imprudencia, *f*; inoportunidad, *f*

unadvisable /ˌʌnædˌvaizəˈbəl/ *a* imprudente, inoportuno, no conveniente

unadvisedly /ˌʌnædˌvaizɪdli/ *adv* imprudentemente

unaffected /ˌʌnəˈfɛktɪd/ *a* natural, llano, sin melindres; impasible; genuino, sincero. **u. by,** no afectado por

unaffectedly /ˌʌnəˈfɛktɪdli/ *adv* sin afectación

unaffectedness /ˌʌnəˈfɛktɪdnɪs/ *n* naturalidad, sencillez, *f*; sinceridad, franqueza, *f*

unaffiliated /ˌʌnəˈfɪliˌeitɪd/ *a* no afiliado

unafraid /ˌʌnəˈfreid/ *a* sin temor

unaided /ʌnˈeidɪd/ *a* sin ayuda, solo a solas

unalloyed /ˌʌnəˈlɔid/ *a* sin mezcla, puro

unalterability /ʌnˌɔltərəˈbɪliti/ *n* lo inalterable; constancia, *f*

unalterable /ʌnˈɔltərəbəl/ *a* inalterable; invariable, constante

unambiguous /ˌʌnæmˈbɪgyuəs/ *a* no ambiguo, nada dudoso, claro

unambitious /ˌʌnæmˈbɪʃəs/ *a* sin ambición; modesto

unamusing /ˌʌnəˈmyuzɪŋ/ *a* nada divertido

unanimity /ˌyunəˈnɪmɪti/ *n* unanimidad, *f*

unanimous /yuˈnænəməs/ *a* unánime

unanimously /yuˈnænəməsli/ *adv* unánimemente, por unanimidad. **carried u.,** adoptado por unanimidad

unanswerability /ʌnˌænsərəˈbɪliti/ *n* imposibilidad de negar, *f*; lo irrefutable

unanswerable /ʌnˈænsərəbəl/ *a* incontestable, incontrovertible, incontrastable, irrefutable

unanswered /ʌnˈænsərd/ *a* no contestado, sin contestar; (unrequited) no correspondido

unapparent /ˌʌnəˈpærənt/ *a* no aparente

unappealable /ˌʌnəˈpiləbəl/ *a* inapelable

unappeasable /ˌʌnəˈpizəbəl/ *a* implacable

unappeased /ˌʌnəˈpizd/ *a* no satisfecho; implacable

unappetizing /ʌnˈæpɪˌtaizɪŋ/ *a* no apetitoso; (unattractive) repugnante, feo

unappreciated /ˌʌnəˈpriʃiˌeitɪd/ *a* desestimado, no apreciado, tenido en poco; (misunderstood) mal comprendido

unapproachable /ˌʌnəˈproutʃəbəl/ *a* inaccesible

unapproachableness /ˌʌnəˈproutʃəbəlnɪs/ *n* inaccesibilidad, *f*

unappropriated /ˌʌnəˈproupriˌeitɪd/ *a* no concedido; libre

unapproved /ˌʌnəˈpruvd/ *a* sin aprobar, no aprobado

unarm /ʌnˈɑrm/ *vt* desarmar. *vi* desarmarse, quitarse las armas

unarmed /ʌnˈɑrmd/ *a* desarmado; indefenso; *Zool.,* *Bot.* inerme

unarranged /ˌʌnəˈreindʒd/ *a* no arreglado, sin clasificar; (accidental) fortuito, casual

unartistic /ˌʌnɑrˈtɪstɪk/ *a* no artístico

unascertainable /ˌʌnæsərˈteinəbəl/ *a* no verificable

unashamed /ˌʌnəˈʃeimd/ *a* sin vergüenza; tranquilo, sereno; insolente, descarado

unasked /ʌnˈæskt/ *a* sin pedir; no solicitado; espontáneo; (uninvited) no convidado

unassailable /ˌʌnəˈseiləbəl/ *a* inexpugnable; irrefutable; incontestable

unassisted /ˌʌnəˈsɪstɪd/ *a*. See **unaided**

unassuming /ˌʌnəˈsumɪŋ/ *a* modesto, sin pretensiones

unattached /ˌʌnəˈtætʃt/ *a* suelto; *Law.* no embargado; *Mil.* de reemplazo; independiente

unattainable /ˌʌnəˈteinəbəl/ *a* inasequible, irrealizable

unattainableness /ˌʌnəˈteinəbəlnɪs/ *n* imposibilidad de alcanzar (or realizar), *f*; inaccesibilidad

unattended /ˌʌnəˈtɛndɪd/ *a* solo, sin acompañamiento; (of ill person) sin tratamiento; (of entertainment, etc.) no concurrido

unattested /ˌʌnəˈtɛstɪd/ *a* sin atestación

unattractive /ˌʌnəˈtræktɪv/ *a* poco atrayente, desagradable, antipático, feo

unattractiveness /ˌʌnəˈtræktɪvnɪs/ *n* fealdad, falta de hermosura, *f*; lo desagradable

unauthentic /ˌʌnɔˈθɛntɪk/ *a* no auténtico, sin autenticidad; apócrifo

unauthorized /ʌnˈɔθəˌraizd/ *a* no autorizado

unavailable /ˌʌnəˈveiləbəl/ *a* inaprovechable

unavailing /ˌʌnəˈveilɪŋ/ *a* inútil, vano

unavenged /ˌʌnəˈvɛndʒd/ *a* no vengado, sin castigo

unavoidable /ˌʌnəˈvɔidəbəl/ *a* inevitable, preciso, necesario. **to be u.,** no poder evitarse, no tener remedio

unavoidableness /ˌʌnəˈvɔidəbəlnɪs/ *n* inevitabilidad, necesidad, *f*

unavoidably /ˌʌnəˈvɔidəbli/ *adv* irremediablemente

unaware /ˌʌnəˈwɛər/ *a* ignorante; inconsciente. **to be u. of,** ignorar, desconocer; no darse cuenta de

unawareness /ˌʌnəˈwɛərnɪs/ *n* ignorancia, *f*, desconocimiento, *m*; inconsciencia, *f*

unawares /ˌʌnəˈwɛərz/ *adv* (by mistake) sin querer, inadvertidamente; (unprepared) de sobresalto, de improviso, inopinadamente. **He caught me u.,** Me cogió desprevenido

unbalance /ʌnˈbæləns/ *vt* desequilibrar, hacer perder el equilibrio, *Fig.* trastornar

unbalanced /ʌnˈbælənst/ *a* desequilibrado; *Fig.* trastornado; *Com.* no balanceado

unbaptized /ʌnˈbæptaizd/ *a* no bautizado, sin bautizar

unbar /ʌnˈbɑr/ *vt* desatrancar; *Fig.* abrir

unbearable /ʌnˈbɛərəbəl/ *a* intolerable, insufrible, inaguantable, inllevable, insoportable

unbearably /ʌnˈbɛərəbli/ *adv* insoportablemente

unbeatable /ʌnˈbitəbəl/ *a* inmejorable

unbeaten /ʌnˈbitn/ *a* (of paths) no frecuentado, no pisado; (of armies) no derrotado, no batido; invicto

unbecoming /ˌʌnbɪˈkʌmɪŋ/ *a* impropio, inapropiado, inconveniente; indecoroso, indigno; indecente; (of clothes) que no va bien, que sienta mal

unbelief /ˌʌnbɪˈlif/ *n* incredulidad, *f*

unbelievable /ˌʌnbɪˈlivəbəl/ *a* increíble

unbelievably /ˌʌnbɪˈlivəbli/ *adv* increíblemente

unbeliever /ˌʌnbɪˈlivər/ *n* incrédulo (-la), descreído (-da)

unbeloved /ˌʌnbɪˈlʌvd/ *a* no amado

unbend /ʌnˈbɛnd/ *vt* desencorvar, enderezar; entretener, descansar; (*Naut.* of sails) desenvergar; (*Naut.* of cables) desamarrar. *vi* enderezarse; mostrarse afable

unbending /ʌnˈbɛndɪŋ/ *a* inflexible, rígido, tieso; *Fig.* inexorable, inflexible, duro, terco; (amiable) afable, jovial

unbiased /ʌnˈbaiəst/ *a* imparcial, ecuánime

unbidden /ʌnˈbɪdn/ *a* espontáneo; (uninvited) no convidado, no invitado

unbind /ʌnˈbaind/ *vt* desligar, desatar; (bandages) desvendar; (books) desencuadernar

unbleached /ʌnˈblitʃt/ *a* crudo, sin blanquear

unblemished /ʌnˈblɛmɪʃt/ *a* no manchado; (pure) sin mancha, inmaculado, puro

unblessed /ʌn'blɛst/ a no bendecido, no consagrado; (accursed) maldito; (unhappy) desdichado

unblushing /ʌn'blʌʃɪŋ/ a desvergonzado, insolente

unbolt /ʌn'boult/ vt descerrojar, desempernar

unborn /ʌn'bɔrn/ a sin nacer, no nacido todavía; venidero

unbosom /ʌn'buzəm/ vt confesar, declarar. **to u. oneself,** abrir su pecho (a) or (con)

unbought /ʌn'bɔt/ a no comprado; gratuito, libre; (not bribed) no sobornado

unbound /ʌn'baund/ a suelto, libre; (of books) en rama, no encuadernado

unbounded /ʌn'baundɪd/ a ilimitado, infinito; inmenso

unbowed /ʌn'baud/ a erguido; no encorvado; (undefeated) invicto

unbreakable /ʌn'breikəbəl/ a irrompible, inquebrantable

unbridled /ʌn'braidld/ a desenfrenado, violento; licencioso

unbroken /ʌn'broukən/ a no quebrantado, intacto, entero; continuo, incesante; no interrumpido; (of soil) virgen; (of a horse) indomado; inviolado; (of the spirit) indómito; (of a record) no batido

unbuckle /ʌn'bʌkəl/ vt deshebillar

unburden /ʌn'bɜrdn̩/ vt descargar; aliviar. **to u. oneself,** (express one's feelings) desahogarse

unburied /ʌn'bɛrid/ a insepulto

unburnt /ʌn'bɜrnt/ a no quemado; incombusto

unbusinesslike /ʌn'bɪznɪs,laik/ a informal; poco comercial, descuidado

unbutton /ʌn'bʌtn̩/ vt desabrochar, desabotonar

uncalled /ʌn'kɔld/ a no llamado, no invitado. **u.-for,** impertinente; innecesario

uncannily /ʌn'kænḷi/ adv misteriosamente

uncanniness /ʌn'kænɪnɪs/ n lo misterioso

uncanny /ʌn'kæni/ a misterioso, horroroso, pavoroso

uncared-for /ʌn'kɛard,fɔr/ a abandonado, desatendido, desamparado

uncarpeted /ʌn'karpɪtɪd/ a sin alfombra

uncaught /ʌn'kɔt/ a no prendido, libre

unceasing /ʌn'sisɪŋ/ a continuo, incesante, sin cesar, constante

unceasingly /ʌn'sisɪŋli/ adv incesantemente, sin cesar

uncensored /ʌn'sɛnsərd/ a no censurado

unceremonious /ˌʌnsɛrə'mouniəs/ a sin ceremonia, familiar; descortés, brusco

unceremoniousness /ˌʌnsɛrɛ'mouniəsnɪs/ n falta de ceremonia, familiaridad, f; incivilidad, descortesía, f

uncertain /ʌn'sɜrtn̩/ a incierto, dudoso; inseguro; precario; (hesitant) indeciso, vacilante, irresoluto

uncertainly /ʌn'sɜrtn̩li/ adv inciertamente

uncertainty /ʌn'sɜrtn̩ti/ n incertidumbre, duda, f; inseguridad, f; irresolución, f

uncertificated /ˌʌnsər'tɪfɪ,keitɪd/ a sin certificado (of teachers, etc.) sin título

uncertified /ʌn'sɜrtə,faid/ a sin garantía; no garantizado; (of lunatics) sin certificar

unchain /ʌn'tʃein/ vt desencadenar

unchallenged /ʌn'tʃæləndʒd/ a incontestable

unchangeable /ʌn'tʃeindʒəbəl/ a invariable, inalterable, inmutable

unchangeableness /ʌn'tʃeindʒəbəlnɪs/ n invariabilidad, inalterabilidad, f

unchanging /ʌn'tʃeindʒɪŋ/ a inmutable, invariable

uncharitable /ʌn'tʃærɪtəbəl/ a nada caritativo, duro; intolerante, intransigente

uncharitableness /ʌn'tʃærɪtəbəlnɪs/ n falta de caridad, f; intolerancia, intransigencia

uncharitably /ʌn'tʃærɪtəbli/ adv sin caridad; con intolerancia

unchaste /ʌn'tʃeist/ a incasto, incontinente; deshonesto, impuro, lascivo

unchecked /ʌn'tʃɛkt/ a desenfrenado; (unproved) no comprobado; Com. no confrontado

unchivalrous /ʌn'ʃɪvəlrəs/ a nada galante, nada caballeroso

uncircumcised /ʌn'sɜrkəm,saizd/ a incircunciso

uncircumscribed /ʌn'sɜrkəm,skraibd/ a incircunscripto

uncivil /ʌn'sɪvəl/ a descortés, incivil

uncivilizable /ʌn'sɪvə,laizəbəl/ a reacio a la civilización

uncivilized /ʌn'sɪvə,laizd/ a no civilizado, bárbaro, salvaje, inculto

uncivilly /ʌn'sɪvəli/ adv descortésmente

unclad /ʌn'klæd/ a sin vestir; desnudo

unclasp /ʌn'klæsp/ vt (jewelry) desengarzar; desabrochar; (of hands) soltar, separar

unclassifiable /ʌn'klæsə,faiəbəl/ a inclasificable

unclassified /ʌn'klæsə,faid/ a sin clasificar

uncle /'ʌŋkəl/ n tío, m; (pawnbroker) prestamista, m

unclean /ʌn'klin/ a sucio, puerco, inmundo; deseseado; impuro, obsceno; (ritually) poluto

uncleanliness /ʌn'klɛnlinɪs/ n suciedad, porquería, f; desaseo, m; falta de limpieza, f

uncleanly /ʌn'klɛnli/ a sucio, puerco; deseseado

uncleanness /ʌn'klɪnnɪs/ n suciedad, f; impureza, obscenidad, inmoralidad, f

unclench /ʌn'klɛntʃ/ vt (of hands) abrir

unclouded /ʌn'klaudɪd/ a sin nubes, despejado, claro

uncoil /ʌn'kɔil/ vt desarrollar. vi desovillarse; (of snakes) desanillarse

uncollected /ˌʌnkə'lɛktɪd/ a disperso; no cobrado; (in confusion) confuso, desordenado

uncolored /ʌn'kʌlərd/ a incoloro; Fig. imparcial, objetivo, sencillo

uncombed /ʌn'koumd/ a despeinado, sin peinar

uncomfortable /ʌn'kʌmftəbəl/ a incómodo; (anxious) intranquilo, inquieto, desasosegado, preocupado; (awkward) molesto, difícil, desagradable. **to be u.,** (people) estar incómodo; (anxious) estar preocupado; (of things) ser incómodo

uncomfortableness /ʌn'kʌmfərtəbəlnɪs/ n incomodidad, f; malestar, m; intranquilidad, preocupación, f; dificultad, f; lo desagradable

uncomfortably /ʌn'kʌmfərtəbli/ adv incómodamente; intranquilamente; desagradablemente

uncomforted /ʌn'kʌmfərtid/ a desconsolado, sin consuelo

uncommercial /ˌʌnkə'mɜrʃəl/ a no comercial

uncommon /ʌn'kɒmən/ a poco común, extraordinario, singular, raro, extraño; infrecuente; insólito

uncommonly /ʌn'kɒmənli/ adv extraordinariamente, muy; infrecuentemente, raramente

uncommonness /ʌn'kɒmənnɪs/ n infrecuencia, rareza, f; singularidad, f

uncommunicative /ˌʌnkə'myunɪkətɪv/ a reservado, poco expresivo

uncommunicativeness /ˌʌnkə'myunɪkətɪvnɪs/ n reserva, f

uncomplaining /ˌʌnkəm'pleinɪŋ/ a resignado, que no se queja

uncomplainingly /ˌʌnkəm'pleinɪŋli/ adv con resignación

uncompliant /ˌʌnkəm'plaiant/ a sordo, inflexible

uncomplicated /ʌn'kɒmplɪ,keitɪd/ a sencillo, sin complicaciones

uncomplimentary /ˌʌnkɒmplə'mɛntəri/ a descortés, poco halagüeño, ofensivo

uncompromising /ʌn'kɒmprə,maizɪŋ/ a inflexible, estricto, intolerante; irreconciliable

unconcealed /ˌʌnkən'sild/ a no oculto; abierto

unconcern /ˌʌnkən'sɜrn/ n indiferencia, frialdad, f; desapego, m; (lack of interest) apatía, despreocupación, f; (nonchalance) desenfado, m, frescura, f

unconcerned /ˌʌnkən'sɜrnd/ a indiferente, frío, despegado; apático; despreocupado; desenfadado, fresco

unconcernedly /ˌʌnkən'sɜrnɪdli/ adv con indiferencia; sin preocuparse; con desenfado

unconditional /ˌʌnkən'dɪʃən̩l/ a incondicional, absoluto. **u. surrender,** rendición incondicional, f

unconditionally /ˌʌnkən'dɪʃən̩li/ adv incondicionalmente; Mil. a discreción

unconfessed /ˌʌnkən'fɛst/ a inconfeso

unconfined /ˌʌnkən'faind/ a suelto, libre; ilimitado; sin estorbo

unconfirmed /ˌʌnkən'fɜrmd/ a no confirmado; (report) sin confirmar

uncongenial /ˌʌnkən'dʒinyəl/ a incompatible, antipático; desagradable, repugnante

uncongeniality /ˌʌnkənˌdʒini'æliti/ n incompatibilidad, antipatía, f; repugnancia, f; lo desagradable

unconnected /ˌʌnkə'nɛktid/ a inconexo; Mech. desconectado; (relationship) sin parentesco; (confused) incoherente

unconquerable /ʌn'kɒŋkərəbəl/ a invencible, indomable, inconquistable

unconquered /ʌn'kɒŋkərd/ a no vencido

unconscientious /ˌʌnkɒnʃi'ɛnʃəs/ a poco concienzudo

unconscionable /ʌn'kɒnʃənəbəl/ a excesivo, desmedido; sin conciencia

unconscious /ʌn'kɒnʃəs/ a inconsciente; (senseless) insensible, sin sentido; espontáneo; (unaware) ignorante. **to be u. of,** ignorar; perder la consciencia de. **to become u.,** perder el sentido

unconsciously /ʌn'kɒnʃəsli/ adv inconscientemente, involuntariamente

unconsciousness /ʌn'kɒnʃəsnɪs/ n inconsciencia, f; (hypnosis, swoon) insensibilidad, f; (unawareness) ignorancia, falta de conocimiento, f

unconsecrated /ʌn'kɒnsɪˌkreitid/ a no consagrado

unconsidered /ˌʌnkən'sɪdərd/ a indeliberado; sin importancia, trivial

unconstitutional /ˌʌnkɒnstɪ'tuʃənl/ a anticonstitucional, inconstitucional

unconstitutionally /ˌʌnkɒnstɪ'tuʃənli/ adv inconstitucionalmente

unconstrained /ˌʌnkən'streind/ a libre; voluntario; sin freno

uncontaminated /ˌʌnkəntæmɪ'neitid/ a incontaminado; puro, sin mancha, impoluto

uncontested /ˌʌnkən'tɛstid/ a sin oposición

uncontradicted /ˌʌnkɒntrə'dɪktid/ a sin contradicción; incontestable

uncontrollable /ˌʌnkən'trouləbəl/ a irrefrenable, incontrolable, inmanejable; (temper) ingobernable; indomable

uncontrolled /ˌʌnkən'trould/ a libre, no controlado; desenfrenado, desgobernado

unconventional /ˌʌnkən'vɛnʃənl/ n poco convencional; bohemio, excéntrico, extravagante; original

unconventionality /ˌʌnkənˌvɛnʃə'næliti/ a excentricidad, extravagancia, independencia de ideas, f; (of a design) originalidad, f

unconversant /ˌʌnkən'vɜrsənt/ a poco familiar, poco versado (en)

unconverted /ˌʌnkən'vɜrtid/ a no convertido; sin transformar

unconvinced /ˌʌnkən'vɪnst/ a no convencido

unconvincing /ˌʌnkən'vɪnsɪŋ/ a no convincente, poco convincente, que no me (nos, etc.) convence; frívolo

uncooked /ʌn'kʊkt/ a crudo, no cocido, sin cocer

uncork /ʌn'kɔrk/ vt destapar, descorchar, quitar el corcho

uncorrected /ˌʌnkə'rɛktid/ a sin corregir, no corregido

uncorroborated /ˌʌnkə'rɒbəˌreitid/ a no confirmado, sin confirmar

uncorrupted /ˌʌnkə'rʌptid/ a incorrupto; puro, no pervertido; (unbribed) no sobornado, honrado

uncorruptible /ˌʌnkə'rʌptəbəl/ a incorruptible

uncountable /ʌn'kauntəbəl/ a innumerable

uncounted /ʌn'kauntid/ a no contado, sin cuenta

uncouple /ʌn'kʌpəl/ vt soltar; desenganchar, desconectar

uncouth /ʌn'kuθ/ a grosero, chabacano, tosco, patán

uncouthness /ʌn'kuθnɪs/ n grosería, tosquedad, patanería, f

uncover /ʌn'kʌvər/ vt descubrir; (remove lid of) destapar; (remove coverings of) desabrigar, desarropar; (leave unprotected) desamparar; (disclose) revelar, dejar al descubierto. vi descubrirse, quitar el sombrero

uncovered /ʌn'kʌvərd/ a descubierto; desnudo; sin cubierta

uncreated /ˌʌnkri'eitid/ a increado

uncritical /ʌn'krɪtɪkəl/ a sin sentido crítico, poco juicioso

uncross /ʌn'krɔs/ vt (of legs) descruzar

uncrossed /ʌn'krɔst/ a (of check) sin cruzar

unction /'ʌŋkʃən/ n unción, f; untadura, f, untamiento, m; (unguent) ungüento, m; (zeal) fervor, m; (flattery) insinceridad, hipocresía, f; (relish) gusto, entusiasmo, m. **extreme u.,** extremaunción, f

unctuous /'ʌŋktʃuəs/ a untuoso, craso; insincero, zalamero

uncultivable /ʌn'kʌltəvəbəl/ a incultivable

uncultivated /ʌn'kʌltəˌveitid/ a inculto, yermo; (barbarous) salvaje, bárbaro; (uncultured) inculto, tosco; no cultivado

uncultured /ʌn'kʌltʃərd/ a inculto, iletrado

uncurbed /ʌn'kɜrbd/ a sin freno; Fig. desenfrenado

uncurl /ʌn'kɜrl/ vt desrizar vi desrizarse; desovillarse

uncurtained /ʌn'kɜrtn̩d/ a sin cortinas; con las cortinas recogidas

uncut /ʌn'kʌt/ a sin cortar, no cortado; (of gems) sin labrar

undamaged /ʌn'dæmɪdʒd/ a indemne, sin daño

undated /ʌn'deitid/ a sin fecha

undaunted /ʌn'dɔntid/ a intrépido, atrevido

undeceive /ˌʌndɪ'siv/ vt desengañar, desilusionar

undecided /ˌʌndɪ'saidɪd/ a (of question) pendiente, indeciso; dudoso; vacilante, irresoluto

undecipherable /ˌʌndɪ'saifərəbəl/ a indescifrable; ilegible

undeclared /ˌʌndɪ'klɛərd/ a no declarado

undefended /ˌʌndɪ'fɛndɪd/ a indefenso

undeferable /ˌʌndɪ'fɜrəbəl/ a inaplazable

undefiled /ˌʌndɪ'faild/ a impoluto, incontaminado; puro

undefinable /ˌʌndɪ'fainəbəl/ a indefinible; inefable, vago

undefined /ˌʌndɪ'faind/ a indefinido; indeterminado

undelivered /ˌʌndɪ'lɪvərd/ a no recibido; (speech) no pronunciado; (not sent) no enviado

undemonstrative /ˌʌndə'mɒnstrətɪv/ a poco expresivo, reservado

undeniable /ˌʌndɪ'naiəbəl/ a incontestable, innegable, indudable; excelente; inequívoco, evidente

undeniably /ˌʌndɪ'naiəbli/ adv indudablemente

undenominational /ˌʌndɪˌnɒmə'neiʃənl/ a sin denominación

undependable /ˌʌndɪ'pɛndəbəl/ a indigno de confianza

under /'ʌndər/ prep debajo de; bajo; (in) en; (less than) menos de, menos que; (at the orders of) a las órdenes de, al mando de; (in less time than) en menos de; (under the weight of) bajo el peso de; (at the foot of) al abrigo de; (for less than) por menos de; (at the time of) en la época de, en tiempos de; (according to) según, conforme a, en virtud de (e.g. under the law, en virtud de la ley); (of monarchs) bajo (or durante) el reinado de; (of rank) inferior a; (in virtue of) en virtud de; (of age) menor de; (with penalty, pretext, etc.) so; en; a (see below for examples); (Agr. of fields) plantado de, sembrado de. **u. arms,** bajo las armas. **u. contract,** bajo contrato. **u. cover,** al abrigo, bajo cubierto. **u. cover of,** bajo pretexto de, so color de. **u. fire,** bajo fuego. **u. oath,** bajo juramento. **u. pain of,** so pena de. **u. sail,** a la vela. **u. separate cover,** bajo cubierta separada, en sobre apartado, por separado. **u. steam,** al vapor. **u. way,** en camino; en marcha; en preparación. **to be u. an obligation,** deber favores; (to) tener obligacion de; estar obligado a

under /'ʌndər/ a inferior; (of rank) subalterno, subordinado; bajo, bajero. adv debajo; abajo; más abajo; menos; (for less) para menos; (ill) mal; (insufficient) insuficiente. **to bring u.,** someter. **to keep u.,** dominar, subyugar

underact /ˌʌndər'ækt/ vt hacer un papel sin fogosidad

underarm /'ʌndərˌɑrm/ n sobaco, m. a sobacal; (of bowling) de debajo del brazo. **to serve u.,** sacar por debajo

underbid /ˌʌndər'bɪd/ *vt* ofrecer menos que
underbred /ˌʌndər'brɛd/ *a* mal criado, mal educado
undercharge /ˌʌndər'tʃɑrdʒ/ *vt* cobrar menos de lo debido
underclothes /'ʌndər,klouz, -ˌklouðz/ *n* ropa interior, *f*, paños menores, *m pl*
undercurrent /'ʌndər,kərənt/ *n* corriente submarina, *f*; *Fig.* tendencia oculta, *f*
undercut /'ʌndər,kʌt/ *n* (of meat) filete, *m*
underdeveloped /ˌʌndərdɪ'vɛləpt/ *a* de desarrollo atrasado; *Photo.* no revelado lo suficiente
underdog /'ʌndər,dɔg/ *n* víctima, *f*; débil, paciente, *m*.
underdogs, los de abajo, *m pl*
underdone /'ʌndər'dʌn/ *a* (of meat) crudo, medio asado
underdress /ˌʌndər'drɛs/ *vt* and *vi* vestir(se) sin bastante elegancia
underestimate /ˌʌndər'ɛstəˌmeit/ *vt* tasar en menos; desestimar, menospreciar
underfeed /ˌʌndər'fid/ *vt* alimentar insuficientemente
underfoot /ˌʌndər'fʊt/ *adv* debajo de los pies, en el suelo
undergo /ˌʌndər'gou/ *vt* sufrir, padecer, pasar por.
undergo surgery, someterse a la cirugía
undergraduate /ˌʌndər'grædʒuɪt/ *n* estudiante no graduado, *m*
underground /a., n. 'ʌndər,graund; adv. -'graund/ *a* subterráneo; *Fig.* oculto, secreto. *adv* bajo tierra, debajo de la tierra; *Fig.* en secreto, ocultamente. *n* sótano, *m*
undergrown /'ʌndər,groun/ *a* enclenque
undergrowth /'ʌndər,grouθ/ *n* maleza, *f*
underhand /'ʌndər,hænd/ *adv Fig.* bajo mano, ocultamente, a escondidas. *a Fig.* secreto, oculto
underlie /ˌʌndər'lai/ *vt* estar debajo de; servir de base a, caracterizar
underline /'ʌndər,lain/ *vt* subrayar
underling /'ʌndərlɪŋ/ *n* subordinado (-da)
underlying /'ʌndər,laiŋ/ *a* fundamental, básico, esencial
undermentioned /ˌʌndər'mɛnʃən/d *a* abajo citado
undermine /ˌʌndər'main/ *vt* socavar, excavar; minar, destruir poco a poco
undermining /'ʌndər,mainɪŋ/ *n* socava, excavación, *f*; destrucción, *f*, *a* minador
underneath /ˌʌndər'niθ/ *adv* debajo. *prep* bajo, debajo de
undernourished /ˌʌndər'nərɪʃt/ *a* mal alimentado
undernourishment /ˌʌndər'nərɪʃmənt/ *n* desnutrición, *f*
underpaid /ˌʌndər'peid/ *a* insuficientemente retribuido, mal pagado
underpass /'ʌndər,pæs, -ˌpɑs/ *n* pasaje por debajo, *m*
underpay /ˌʌndər'pei/ *vt* pagar mal, remunerar (or retribuir) deficientemente
underpayment /'ʌndər,peimənt/ *n* retribución mezquina, *f*, pago insuficiente, *m*
underpin /ˌʌndər'pɪn/ *vt* apuntalar, socalzar
underpopulated /ˌʌndər'pɒpyə,leitɪd/ *a* con baja densidad de población
underprivileged /'ʌndər'prɪvəlɪdʒd/ *a* menesteroso, pobre, necesitado
underrate /ˌʌndər'reit/ *vt* tasar en menos; tener en poco, desestimar, menospreciar
underripe /'ʌndər,raip/ *a* verde
undersecretary /'ʌndər,sɛkrə,tɛri/ *n* subsecretario (-ia)
undersell /ˌʌndər'sɛl/ *vt* vender a un precio más bajo que
undershirt /'ʌndər,ʃrt/ *n Spain* camiseta, *Lat. Am.* franela, *f*
underside /'ʌndər,said/ *n* revés, envés, *m*
undersigned /'ʌndər,saind/ *a* infrascrito, suscrito.
the u., el abajo firmado, el infrascrito
undersized /'ʌndər'saizd/ *a* muy pequeño, enclenque, enano
underskirt /'ʌndər,skrt/ *n* enagua, *f*; refajo, *m*
understand /ˌʌndər'stænd/ *vt* comprender, entender; (know) saber; (be acquainted with) conocer; (hear) oír, tener entendido; (mean) sobrentender. *vi* com-

prender, entender; oír, tener entendido. **to u. each other,** comprenderse. **It being understood that...,** Bien entendido que...
understandable /ˌʌndər'stændəbəl/ *a* comprensible; inteligible. **It is very u. why he does not wish to come,** Se comprende muy bien por qué no quiere venir
understanding /ˌʌndər'stændɪŋ/ *n* (intelligence) entendimiento, *m*, inteligencia, *f*; (agreement) acuerdo, *m*; (knowledge) conocimiento, *m*; (wisdom) comprensión, sabiduría, *f*. *a* inteligente; sabio; (sympathetic) comprensivo, simpático. **to come to an u.,** ponerse de acuerdo
understandingly /ˌʌndərstændɪŋ/ *adv* con inteligencia; con conocimiento (de); con simpatía
understate /ˌʌndər'steit/ *vt* decir menos que, rebajar, describir sin énfasis
understatement /'ʌndərsteitmənt/ *n* moderación, *f*
understudy /'ʌndər,stʌdi/ *n* sobresaliente, *mf*. *vt* sustituir
undertake /ˌʌndər'teik/ *vt* comprometerse a, encargarse de; emprender, abarcar, acometer
undertaker /'ʌndər,teikər/ *n* empresario, director de pompas fúnebres, *m*
undertaking /ˌʌndər'teikɪŋ/ *n* empresa, tarea, *f*; garantía, promesa, *f*; (funerals) funeraria, *f*
undertone /'ʌndər,toun/ *n* voz baja, *f*; *Art.* color tenue (or apagado), *m*. **in an u.,** en voz baja
undervalue /ˌʌndər'vælyu/ *vt* tasar en menos; tener en poco, despreciar
underwater /'ʌndər'wɔtər/ *a* subacuático, submarino. **u. flipper,** aleta de bucear
underweight /'ʌndər'weit/ *a* de bajo peso, que pesa menos de lo debido, flaco
underworld /'ʌndər,wɜrld/ *n* (hell) infierno, averno, *m*; (slums) hampa, *f*, fondos bajos de la sociedad, *m pl*; heces de la sociedad, *f pl*. **u. slang,** *Peru* cantuja *f*
underwrite /ˌʌndər'rait/ *vt Com.* asegurar contra riesgos; reasegurar; obligarse a comprar todas las acciones de una compañía no subscritas por el público, mediante un pago convenido
underwriter /'ʌndər,raitər/ *n* asegurador, *m*; reasegurador, *m*
underwriting /'ʌndər,raitɪŋ/ *n* aseguro, *m*; reaseguro, *m*
undeserved /ˌʌndɪ'zɜrvd/ *a* inmerecido, no merecido
undeserving /ˌʌndɪ'zɜrvɪŋ/ *a* indigno, desmerecedor; que no merece
undesirable /ˌʌndɪ'zaiərəbəl/ *a* no deseable; nocivo, pernicioso; (unsuitable) inconveniente
undesired /ˌʌndɪ'zaiərd/ *a* no deseado; no solicitado, no buscado
undesirous /ˌʌndɪ'zaiərəs/ *a* no deseoso
undestroyed /ˌʌndɪ'strɔid/ *a* sin destruir, no destruido, intacto
undetected /ˌʌndɪ'tɛktɪd/ *a* no descubierto
undeveloped /ˌʌndɪ'vɛləpt/ *a* no desarrollado; rudimentario; inmaturo; (of a country) no explotado, virgen; *Photo.* no revelado; (of land) sin cultivar
undeviating /ʌn'divi,eitɪŋ/ *a* directo; constante, persistente
undigested /ˌʌndɪ'dʒɛstɪd/ *a* no digerido, indigesto
undignified /ʌn'dɪgnə,faid/ *a* sin dignidad; poco serio; indecoroso
undiluted /ˌʌndɪ'lutɪd/ *a* sin diluir, puro
undiminished /ˌʌndɪ'mɪnɪst/ *a* no disminuido, sin disminuir, cabal, íntegro
undiplomatic /ˌʌndɪplə'mætɪk/ *a* impolítico, indiscreto
undirected /ˌʌndɪ'rɛktɪd/ *a* sin dirección; (of letters) sin señas
undiscernible /ˌʌndɪ'sɜrnəbəl/ *a* imperceptible, invisible
undiscerning /ˌʌndɪ'sɜrnɪŋ/ *a* sin percepción, obtuso, sin discernimiento
undisciplined /ʌn'dɪsəplɪnd/ *a* indisciplinado
undisclosed /ˌʌndɪ'klouzd/ *a* no revelado, secreto
undiscouraged /ˌʌndɪ'skərɪdʒd/ *a* animoso, sin flaquear, sin desaliento

undiscovered /ˌʌndɪˈskʌvərd/ a no descubierto, ignoto

undiscriminating /ˌʌndɪˈskrɪməˌneitɪŋ/ a sin distinción; sin sentido crítico

undisguised /ˌʌndɪˈskaizd/ a sin disfraz; abierto, claro

undismayed /ˌʌndɪsˈmeid/ a intrépido, impávido; sin desaliento

undisposed /ˌʌndɪˈspouzd/ a desinclinado; (of property) no enajenado, no invertido

undisputed /ˌʌndɪˈspyutɪd/ a incontestable, indisputable

undistinguishable /ˌʌndɪˈstɪŋgwɪʃəbəl/ a indistinguible

undistinguished /ˌʌndɪˈstɪŋgwɪʃt/ a (of writers) poco conocido; indistinto; sin distinción

undisturbed /ˌʌndɪˈstɜrbd/ a sin tocar; tranquilo, sereno, impasible

undivided /ˌʌndɪˈvaidɪd/ a indiviso, íntegro; junto; completo, entero

undo /ʌnˈdu/ vt anular; reparar; desatar, deshacer; desasir; abrir

undoing /ʌnˈduɪŋ/ n anulación, f; (reparation) reparación, f; (opening) abrir, m; ruina, f

undomesticated /ˌʌndəˈmɛstɪˌkeitɪd/ a salvaje, no domesticado; poco casero

undone /ʌnˈdʌn/ a and part sin hacer; deshecho; arruinado, perdido. **I am undone!** ¡Estoy perdido! **to come u.,** desatarse. **to leave u.,** dejar sin hacer

undoubted /ʌnˈdautɪd/ a indudable, evidente, incontestable

undoubtedly /ʌnˈdautɪdli/ adv sin duda

undramatic /ˌʌndrəˈmætɪk/ a no dramático

undreamed /ʌnˈdrimd/ a no soñado. **u. of,** inopinado, no imaginado

undress /ʌnˈdrɛs/ vt desnudar, desvestir, Peru calatear. vi desnudarse. n traje de casa, m; paños menores, m pl; Mil. traje de cuartel, m

undressed /ʌnˈdrɛst/ a desnudo; en paños menores; (of wounds) sin curar; Com. en rama, en bruto

undrinkable /ʌnˈdrɪŋkəbəl/ a impotable

undue /ʌnˈdu/ a excesivo, indebido; injusto; impropio; (of a bill of exchange) por vencer

undulant /ˈʌndʒələnt/ a ondulante. **u. fever,** fiebre mediterránea, fiebre de Malta, f

undulate /ˈʌndʒəˌleit/ vi ondular, ondear

undulating /ˈʌndʒəˌleitɪŋ/ a ondulante

undulation /ˌʌndʒəˈleiʃən/ n ondulación, undulación, f, ondeo, m; fluctuación, f

undulatory /ˈʌndʒələˌtɔri/ a ondulatorio, undoso

unduly /ʌnˈduli/ adv excesivamente, demasiado, indebidamente; injustamente

undutiful /ʌnˈdutəfəl/ a desobediente, irrespetuoso

undutifulness /ʌnˈdutəfəlnɪs/ n desobediencia, falta de respeto, f

undying /ʌnˈdaiɪŋ/ a inmortal, imperecedero; eterno

unearned /ʌnˈɜrnd/ a no ganado; inmerecido

unearth /ʌnˈɜrθ/ vt desenterrar; Fig. descubrir, sacar a luz

unearthing /ʌnˈɜrθɪŋ/ n desenterramiento, m; Fig. descubrimiento, m, revelación, f

unearthly /ʌnˈɜrθli/ a sobrenatural; misterioso, aterrador, espantoso, Lat. Am. also extraterrenal

uneasily /ʌnˈizəli/ adv con dificultad; incómodamente; inquietamente

uneasiness /ʌnˈizinɪs/ n malestar, m; (discomfort) incomodidad, f; (anxiety) inquietud, intranquilidad, f, desasosiego, m

uneasy /ʌnˈizi/ a incómodo; inseguro; inquieto, intranquilo, desasosegado; aturdido, turbado. **to become u.,** inquietarse

uneaten /ʌnˈitn/ a no comido

uneconomical /ˌʌnɛkəˈnɒmɪkəl/ a poco económico, costoso, caro

unedifying /ʌnˈɛdəˌfaiɪŋ/ a poco edificante

unedited /ʌnˈɛdɪtɪd/ a inédito

uneducated /ʌnˈɛdʒəˌkeitɪd/ a ignorante; ineducado, inculto, indocto

unembarrassed /ˌʌnɛmˈbærəst/ a sereno, tranquilo, imperturbable; (financially) sin deudas, acomodado

unemotional /ˌʌniˈmouʃənl/ a frío, impasible

unemployable /ˌʌnɛmˈplɔiəbəl/ a sin uso, inservible; (of persons) inútil para el trabajo

unemployed /ˌʌnɛmˈplɔid/ a sin empleo; (out of work) sin trabajo, parado; desocupado, ocioso; inactivo. n paro obrero, m. **the u.,** los sin trabajo, los cesantes, los desocupados

unemployment /ˌʌnɛmˈplɔimənt/ n paro forzoso, m. **u. benefit,** subvención contra el paro obrero, f. **u. insurance,** seguro contra el paro obrero, m,

unencumbered /ˌʌnɛnˈkʌmbərd/ a libre, independiente; (of estates) libre de gravamen; (untaxable) saneado

unending /ʌnˈɛndɪŋ/ a perpetuo, eterno, sin fin; inacabable, constante, continuo, incesante

unendurable /ˌʌnɛnˈdʊrəbəl/ a insoportable, insufrible, intolerable

unenlightened /ˌʌnɛnˈlaitn̩d/ a ignorante

unenterprising /ʌnˈɛntərˌpraizɪŋ/ a poco emprendedor, tímido

unenthusiastic /ˌʌnɛnˌθuziˈæstɪk/ a sin entusiasmo, tibio

unenviable /ʌnˈɛnviəbəl/ a no envidiable

unequal /ʌnˈikwəl/ a desigual; inferior; (out of proportion) desproporcionado; injusto; insuficiente; incapaz; (of ground) escabroso. **to be u. to the task,** ser incapaz de la tarea; no tener fuerzas para la tarea

unequalled /ʌnˈikwəld/ a sin igual, incomparable, sin par, único

unequally /ʌnˈikwəli/ adv desigualmente

unequivocal /ˌʌniˈkwɪvəkəl/ a inequívoco; redondo, claro, franco

unerring /ʌnˈɜrɪŋ, -ˈɛr-/ a infalible; seguro

unerringly /ʌnˈɜrɪŋli, -ˈɛr-/ adv infaliblemente; sin equivocarse

unessential /ˌʌnəˈsɛnʃəl/ a no esencial

unesthetic /ˌʌnɛsˈθɛtɪk/ a antiestético

uneven /ʌnˈivən/ a desigual; (of roads) escabroso, quebrado; (of numbers) impar; irregular

unevenly /ʌnˈivənli/ adv desigualmente

unevenness /ʌnˈivənnɪs/ n desigualdad, f; desnivel, m, irregularidad, f. **the unevenness of the terrain,** lo desigual del terreno, lo accidentado del terreno, m

uneventful /ˌʌniˈvɛntfəl/ a sin incidentes, sin acontecimientos notables; tranquilo

unexaggerated /ˌʌnɪgˈzædʒəˌreitɪd/ a nada exagerado

unexamined /ˌʌnɪgˈzæmɪnd/ a no examinado, sin examinar

unexampled /ˌʌnɪgˈzæmpəld/ a sin igual, sin par

unexceptionable /ˌʌnɪkˈsɛpʃənəbəl/ a intachable, irreprensible; correcto; impecable, perfecto

unexhausted /ˌʌnɪgˈzɔstɪd/ a no agotado; inexhausto

unexpected /ˌʌnɪkˈspɛktɪd/ a inesperado, imprevisto, inopinado, impensado; repentino, súbito

unexpectedly /ˌʌnɪkˈspɛktɪdli/ adv inesperadamente; de repente

unexpectedness /ˌʌnɪkˈspɛktɪdnɪs/ n lo inesperado

unexpired /ˌʌnɪkˈspaiərd/ a (of bill of exchange) no vencido; (of lease) no caducado

unexplored /ˌʌnɪkˈsplɔrd/ a inexplorado

unexpressed /ˌʌnɪkˈsprɛst/ a no expresado; tácito, sobrentendido

unexpurgated /ʌnˈɛkspərˌgeitɪd/ a sin expurgar, completo

unfading /ʌnˈfeidɪŋ/ a inmarcesible, inmarchitable; eterno, inmortal

unfailing /ʌnˈfeilɪŋ/ a inagotable; inexhausto; seguro; indefectible

unfailingly /ʌnˈfeilɪŋli/ adv siempre, constantemente; sin faltar

unfair /ʌnˈfɛər/ a injusto; vil, bajo, soez; de mala fe, engañoso; (of play) sucio

unfairly /ʌnˈfɛərli/ adv injustamente; de mala fe

unfairness /ʌnˈfɛərnɪs/ n injusticia, f; mala fe, f

unfaithful /ʌnˈfeiθfəl/ a infiel; desleal; inexacto, incorrecto. **to be u. to,** ser infiel a; faltar a

unfaithfulness /ʌnˈfeiθfəlnɪs/ n infidelidad, f; deslealtad, f; inexactitud, f

unfaltering /ʌnˈfɔltərɪŋ/ a sin vacilar; resuelto, firme

unfamiliar /ˌʌnfə'mɪlyər/ a poco familiar; desconocido. **to be u. with,** ser ignorante de

unfashionable /ʌn'fæʃənəbəl/ a pasado de moda, fuera de moda; poco elegante

unfashionableness /ʌn'fæʃənəbəlnɪs/ n falta de elegancia, f

unfashionably /ʌn'fæʃənəbli/ adv contra la tendencia de la moda; sin elegancia

unfasten /ʌn'fæsən/ vt desatar; desabrochar, desenganchar; abrir; aflojar; soltar

unfathomable /ʌn'fæðəməbəl/ a insondable; impenetrable, inescrutable

unfavorable /ʌn'feivərəbəl/ a desfavorable, adverso, contrario

unfavorably /ʌn'feivərəbli/ adv desfavorablemente

unfeathered /ʌn'fɛðərd/ a implume, sin plumas

unfeeling /ʌn'filɪŋ/ a insensible, impasible, frío; duro, cruel

unfeigned /ʌn'feind/ a sincero, natural, verdadero

unfenced /ʌn'fɛnst/ a descercado, sin tapia; abierto

unfermented /ˌʌnfɜr'mɛntɪd/ a no fermentado;

unfetter /ʌn'fɛtər/ vt desencadenar, destrabar; poner en libertad, librar

unfilial /ʌn'fɪliəl/ a poco filial, desobediente

unfinished /ʌn'fɪnɪʃt/ a incompleto, inacabado; sin acabar; imperfecto

unfit /ʌn'fɪt/ a incapaz; incompetente, inepto; (unsuitable) impropio; (useless) inservible, inadecuado; (unworthy) indigno; (ill) enfermo, malo. vt inhabilitar, incapacitar. **u. for human consumption,** impropio para el consumo humano

unfitness /ʌn'fɪtnɪs/ n incapacidad, f; incompetencia, ineptitud, f; impropiedad, f; falta de mérito, f; falta de salud, f

unfix /ʌn'fɪks/ vt desprender, despegar, descomponer; soltar. **to come unfixed,** desprenderse

unflagging /ʌn'flægɪŋ/ a incansable, infatigable; persistente, constante

unflattering /ʌn'flætərɪŋ/ a poco halagüeño

unflinching /ʌn'flɪntʃɪŋ/ a inconmovible, resuelto, firme

unfold /ʌn'fould/ vt desplegar, desdoblar; tender; abrir; (plans) revelar, descubrir; contar, manifestar. vi abrirse

unfolding /ʌn'fouldɪŋ/ a que se abre. n despliegue, m; revelación, f; narración, f

unforced /ʌn'fɔrst/ a libre; espontáneo; fácil; natural

unforeseen /ˌʌnfɔr'sin/ a imprevisto, inesperado

unforgettable /ˌʌnfər'gɛtəbəl/ a involvidable

unforgivabѕe /ˌʌnfər'gɪvəbəl/ a inexcusable, imperdonable

unforgiving /ˌʌnfər'gɪvɪŋ/ a implacable, que no perdona, inexorable

unforgotten /ˌʌnfər'gɒtn̩/ a no olvidado

unformed /ʌn'fɔrmd/ a informe; rudimentario; inmaturo; (inexperienced) inexperto, sin experiencia

unfortunate /ʌn'fɔrtʃənɪt/ a desdichado, infortunado, desgraciado, desventurado. n desdichado (-da); pobre, mf; (prostitute) perdida, f

unfortunately /ʌn'fɔrtʃənɪtli/ adv por desdicha, desgraciadamente

unfounded /ʌn'faundɪd/ a infundado, inmotivado, sin fundamento, injustificado

unframed /ʌn'freimd/ a sin marco

unfrequented /ʌn'frikwəntɪd/ a poco frecuentado, solitario, retirado, aislado

unfriendliness /ʌn'frɛndlɪnɪs/ n hostilidad, falta de amistad, frialdad, f; huraña, insociabilidad, f

unfriendly /ʌn'frɛndli/ a hostil, enemigo; (of things, events) perjudicial; huraño, insociable

unfruitful /ʌn'frutfəl/ a estéril, infecundo; infructuoso, improductivo, vano

unfulfilled /ˌʌnfəl'fɪld/ a incumplido, sin cumplir; malogrado

unfurl /ʌn'fɜrl/ vt desplegar; Naut. izar (las velas)

unfurnished /ʌn'fɜrnɪʃt/ a desamueblado, sin muebles; desprovisto (de), sin

ungainliness /ʌn'geinlɪnɪs/ n falta de gracia, torpeza, f, desgarbo, m

ungainly /ʌn'geinli/ a desgarbado

ungallant /ʌn'gælənt/ a poco caballeroso, nada galante

ungenerous /ʌn'dʒɛnərəs/ a poco generoso; avaro, tacaño, mezquino; injusto

ungentlemanly /ʌn'dʒɛntḷmənli/ a poco caballeroso, indigno de un caballero

unglazed /ʌn'gleizd/ a sin vidriar; (paper) sin satinar; deslustrado

ungloved /ʌn'glʌvd/ a sin guante(s)

unglue /ʌn'glu/ vt desencolar, despegar

ungodliness /ʌn'gɒdlɪnɪs/ n impiedad, f

ungodly /ʌn'gɒdli/ a impío, irreligioso

ungovernable /ʌn'gʌvərnəbəl/ a ingobernable, indomable; irrefrenable

ungraceful /ʌn'greisfəl/ a desagraciado, desgarbado, sin gracia

ungracious /ʌn'greiʃəs/ a desagradable, poco cortés, desdeñoso

ungraciousness /ʌn'greiʃəsnɪs/ n descortesía, aspereza, inurbanidad, f

ungrammatical /ˌʌngrə'mætɪkəl/ a antigramatical, incorrecto

ungrateful /ʌn'greitfəl/ a ingrato, desagradecido; desagradable, odioso

ungratefulness /ʌn'greitfəlnɪs/ n ingratitud, f; lo desagradable

ungrounded /ʌn'graundɪd/ a infundado; sin motivo

ungrudging /ʌn'grʌdʒɪŋ/ a no avaro, liberal; generoso, magnánimo

ungrudgingly /ʌn'grʌdʒɪŋli/ adv de buena gana

unguarded /ʌn'gardɪd/ a indefenso, sin protección; descuidado; indiscreto, imprudente; sin reflexión

unguided /ʌn'gaidɪd/ a sin guía

unhallowed /ʌn'hæloud/ a impío, profano

unhampered /ʌn'hæmpərd/ a desembarazado, libre

unhappily /ʌn'hæpəli/ adv desafortunadamente, por desgracia

unhappiness /ʌn'hæpinɪs/ n infelicidad, desgracia, desdicha, tristeza, f

unhappy /ʌn'hæpi/ a infeliz, desgraciado, desdichado, triste; (ill-fated) aciago, funesto, malhadado; (remark) inoportuno, inapropiado

unharmed /ʌn'harmd/ a ileso, sano y salvo; (of things) indemne, sin daño

unharness /ʌn'harnɪs/ vt desaparejar; desenganchar; desarmar

unhealthiness /ʌn'hɛlθinɪs/ n falta de salud, f; (of place) insalubridad, f

unhealthy /ʌn'hɛlθi/ a enfermizo; malsano, insalubre

unheard /ʌn'hɜrd/ a no oído; sin ser escuchado; desconocido. **u.-of,** inaudito, no imaginado

unheeding /ʌn'hidɪŋ/ a distraído; desatento, sin prestar atención (a); descuidado

unhelpful /ʌn'hɛlpfəl/ a poco servicial; inútil

unhesitating /ʌn'hɛzɪˌteitɪŋ/ a resuelto, decidido; pronto, inmediato

unhesitatingly /ʌn'hɛzɪˌteitɪŋli/ adv sin vacilar

unhinge /ʌn'hɪndʒ/ vt desgoznar, desquiciar; (of the mind) trastornar

unhitch /ʌn'hɪtʃ/ vt desenganchar; descolgar

unholy /ʌn'houli/ a impío, sacrílego

unhonored /ʌn'ɒnərd/ a sin que se reconociese sus méritos; despreciado; (check) protestado

unhook /ʌn'hʊk/ vt desenganchar; desabrochar; descolgar

unhoped-for /ʌn'houpt fɔr/ a inesperado

unhurt /ʌn'hɜrt/ a ileso, incólume, sano y salvo; (of things) sin daño

unicellular /ˌyunə'sɛlyələr/ a unicelular

unicolored /'yunɪˌkʌlərd/ a unicolor

unicorn /'yunɪˌkɔrn/ n unicornio, m

unidentified /ˌʌnai'dɛntəˌfaid/ a no reconocido, no identificado

unification /ˌyunəfɪ'keiʃən/ n unificación, f

uniform /'yunəˌfɔrm/ a uniforme; igual, constante, invariable; homogéneo. n uniforme, m. **in full u.,** de gran uniforme. **to make u.,** uniformar, igualar, hacer uniforme

uniformity /ˌyunə'fɔrmɪti/ n uniformidad, igualdad, f

uniformly /'yunəˌfɔrmli/ adv uniformemente

unify /'yunə,fai/ vt unificar; unir
unilateral /,yunə'lætərəl/ a unilateral
unimaginable /,ʌnɪ'mædʒənəbəl/ a inimaginable, no imaginable
unimaginative /,ʌnɪ'mædʒənətɪv/ a sin imaginación
unimpaired /,ʌnɪm'pɛərd/ a no disminuido; sin alteración; intacto, entero; sin menoscabo
unimpeachable /,ʌnɪm'pitʃəbəl/ a irreprochable, intachable
unimportance /,ʌnɪm'pɔrtns̩/ n no importancia, insignificancia, trivialidad, f
unimportant /,ʌnɪm'pɔrtn̩t/ a sin importancia, nada importante, insignificante, trivial, Lat. Am. also intrascendente
unimpressive /,ʌnɪm'prɛsɪv/ a poco impresionante; nada conmovedor; (of persons) insignificante
uninflammable /,ʌnɪn'flæməbəl/ a no inflamable, incombustible
uninfluenced /,ʌnɪn'fluənsd/ a no afectado (por), libre (de)
uninformed /,ʌnɪn'fɔrmd/ a ignorante
uninhabitable /,ʌnɪn'hæbɪtəbəl/ a inhabitable
uninhabited /,ʌnɪn'hæbɪtɪd/ a deshabitado, inhabitado, vacío, desierto
uninjured /ʌn'ɪndʒərd/ a ileso; sin daño
uninspired /,ʌnɪn'spaɪərd/ a sin inspiración; pedestre, mediocre
uninstructive /,ʌnɪn'strʌktɪv/ a nada instructivo
uninsured /,ʌnɪn'ʃʊrd/ a no asegurado
unintelligent /,ʌnɪn'tɛlɪdʒənt/ a nada inteligente, corto de alcances, tonto
unintelligibility /,ʌnɪn'tɛlɪdʒə'bɪlɪti/ n incomprensibilidad, f, lo ininteligible
unintelligible /,ʌnɪn'tɛlɪdʒəbəl/ a ininteligible, incomprensible
unintentional /,ʌnɪn'tɛnʃənl/ a involuntario, inadvertido
unintentionally /,ʌnɪn'tɛnʃənli/ adv sin querer, involuntariamente
uninterested /ʌn'ɪntərəstɪd/ a no interesado, despreocupado
uninteresting /ʌn'ɪntərəstɪŋ/ a sin interés, poco interesante, soso
uninterrupted /,ʌnɪntə'rʌptɪd/ a ininterrumpido, sin interrupción; continuo, incesante
uninvited /,ʌnɪn'vaɪtɪd/ a no invitado, no convidado, sin invitación; (unlooked-for) no buscado
uninviting /,ʌnɪn'vaɪtɪŋ/ a poco atrayente; inhospitalario
union /'yunyən/ n unión, f; Mech. manguito de unión, m; conexión, f; (poverty) asociación, f; (trade) gremio de oficios, m; sindicato (obrero), m; (workhouse) asilo, m; (U.S.A.) Estados Unidos de América, m pl
unionism /'yunyə,nɪzəm/ n unionismo, m
unionist /'yunyənɪst/ n Polit. unionista, mf
unique /yu'nik/ a único, sin igual, sin par
uniqueness /yu'niknɪs/ n unicidad, f; lo singular
unisexual /,yunə'sɛkʃuəl/ a unisexual
unison /'yunəsən,/ n unisonancia, f. **in u.,** al unísono
unit /'yunɪt/ n unidad, f. **u.** bookcase, librería en secciones, f
Unitarian /,yunɪ'tɛərɪən/ a and n unitario (-ia)
Unitarianism /,yunɪ'tɛərɪə,nɪzəm/ n unitarismo, m
unite /yu'naɪt/ vt unir, juntar; combinar, incorporar; (of countries) unificar; (of energies, etc.) reunir. vi unirse, juntarse; reunirse, concertarse; convenirse
united /yu'naɪtɪd/ a unido; junto. **the U. Nations,** las Naciones Unidas, f pl
unitedly /yu'naɪtɪdli/ adv unidamente; armoniosamente, de acuerdo
United States of America los Estados Unidos de Norteamérica, m pl
unity /'yunɪti/ n unidad, f; Math. la unidad; unión, f; conformidad, armonía, f. **the three unities,** las tres unidades
universal /,yunə'vɜrsəl/ a universal; general; común. **to make u.,** universalizar, generalizar. **u. joint,** junta universal, f; Auto. cardán, m
universalize /,yunə'vɜrsə,laɪz/ vt universalizar

universe /'yunə,vɜrs/ n universo, m; creación, f; mundo, m
university /,yunə'vɜrsɪti/ n universidad, f. a universitario. **u. degree,** grado universitario, m
unjust /ʌn'dʒʌst/ a injusto
unjustifiable /ʌn,dʒʌstə'faɪəbəl/ a injustificable, indisculpable, inexcusable
unjustifiably /ʌn,dʒʌstə'faɪəbli/ adv injustificadamente, inexcusablemente
unjustly /ʌn'dʒʌstli/ adv injustamente, sin razón
unkempt /ʌn'kɛmpt/ a despeinado; desaseado, sucio
unkind /ʌn'kaɪnd/ a nada bondadoso, nada amable; poco complaciente; duro, cruel; desfavorable, nada propicio
unkindly /ʌn'kaɪndli/ adv sin bondad; con dureza, cruelmente
unkindness /ʌn'kaɪndnɪs/ n falta de bondad, f; severidad, crueldad, dureza, f, rigor, m; acto de crueldad, m
unknowable /ʌn'nouəbəl/ a impenetrable, incomprehensible, insondable
unknowingly /ʌn'nouɪŋli/ adv sin querer, involuntariamente; sin saberlo; insensiblemente
unknown /ʌn'noun/ a ignoto, desconocido; Math. incógnito. n lo desconocido, misterio, m; Math. incógnita, f; (person) desconocido (-da), forastero (-ra). Math. **u. quantity,** incógnita, f
unlabeled /ʌn'leibəld/ a sin etiqueta
unlace /ʌn'leis/ vt desenlazar; desatar
unladylike /ʌn'leidi,laik/ a indigno (or impropio) de una dama; vulgar, ordinario, cursi
unlamented /,ʌnlə'mɛntɪd/ a no llorado, no lamentado
unlatch /ʌn'lætʃ/ vt alzar el pestillo de, abrir
unlawful /ʌn'lɔfəl/ a ilegal, ilícito
unlawfulness /ʌn'lɔfəlnɪs/ n ilegalidad, f
unlearn /ʌn'lɜrn/ vt olvidar, desaprender
unleash /ʌn'liʃ/ vt soltar
unleavened /ʌn'lɛvənd/ a ázimo, sin levadura
unless /ʌn'lɛs/ conjunc a no ser que, a menos que, como no, si no (all followed by subjunc.); salvo, excepto, con excepción de
unlicensed /ʌn'laisənst/ a no autorizado, sin licencia
unlike /ʌn'laik/ a disímil, desemejante; distinto, diferente. prep a distinción de, a diferencia de, al contrario de. **They are quite u.,** No se parecen nada
unlikeliness /ʌn'laiklinɪs/ n improbabilidad, f
unlikely /ʌn'laikli/ a improbable, inverosímil; arriesgado
unlikeness /ʌn'laiknɪs/ n desemejanza, diferencia, f
unlimited /ʌn'lɪmɪtɪd/ a ilimitado, infinito, inmenso; sin restricción; excesivo, exagerado. **unlimited telephone,** teléfono no medido (Argentina)
unlined /ʌn'laind/ a no forrado, sin forro; sin rayas; (of face) sin arrugas
unlit /ʌn'lɪt/ a no iluminado, oscuro, sin luz
unload /ʌn'loud/ vt descargar; aligerar; Naut. hondear; (of shares) deshacerse de. vi descargar
unloading /ʌn'loudɪŋ/ n descarga, f, descargue, m
unlock /ʌn'lɒk/ vt desencerrar, abrir; Fig. revelar, descubrir
unlooked-for /ʌn'lʊktfɔr/ a inopinado, inesperado
unloose /ʌn'lus/ vt desatar; soltar; poner en libertad
unlovable /ʌn'lʌvəbəl/ a indigno del querer; antipático, poco amable; repugnante
unloveliness /ʌn'lʌvlinɪs/ n falta de hermosura, fealdad, f
unlovely /ʌn'lʌvli/ a nada hermoso, feo; desagradable
unluckily /ʌn'lʌkəli/ adv desafortunadamente, por desgracia
unluckiness /ʌn'lʌkɪnɪs/ n mala suerte, f; (unsuitability) inoportunidad, f; lo molesto, lo malo
unlucky /ʌn'lʌki/ a de mala suerte; desdichado, desgraciado, infeliz; (ill-omened) funesto, nefasto, fatal; inoportuno, inconveniente
unmanageable /ʌn'mænɪdʒəbəl/ a indomable, indócil; ingobernable, inmanejable; (unwieldy) difícil de manejar, pesado

unmannerliness /ʌn'mænərlinɪs/ n mala crianza, descortesía, f

unmannerly /ʌn'mænərli/ a mal educado, descortés

unmarketable /ʌn'mɑrkɪtəbəl/ a invendible

unmarriageable /ʌn'mærɪdʒəbəl/ a incasable

unmarried /ʌn'mærid/ a soltero, célibe

unmask /ʌn'mæsk/ vt desenmascarar; Fig. quitar la careta (a). vi quitarse la máscara; Fig. quitarse la careta, descubrirse

unmeaning /ʌn'minɪŋ/ a sin sentido, vacío, sin significación

unmelodious /ˌʌnmə'loudiəs/ a sin melodía, discorde

unmendable /ʌn'mɛndəbəl/ a incomponible

unmentionable /ʌn'mɛnʃənəbəl/ a que no se puede mencionar; indigno de mencionarse

unmerciful /ʌn'mɜrsɪfəl/ a sin piedad, sin compasión; cruel, despiadado, duro

unmerited /ʌn'mɛrɪtɪd/ a inmerecido, desmerecido

unmethodical /ˌʌnmə'θɒdɪkəl/ a poco metódico

unmindful /ʌn'maindfəl/ a olvidadizo; desatento; negligente. **u. of,** sin pensar en, olvidando

unmistakable /ˌʌnmɪ'steikəbəl/ a inequívoco; manifiesto, evidente, indudable

unmistakably /ˌʌnmɪ'steikəbli/ adv indudablemente

unmitigated /ʌn'mɪtɪˌgeitɪd/ a no mitigado; completo, absoluto; (of rogue) redomado

unmixed /ʌn'mɪkst/ a sin mezcla; puro, sencillo; (free) limpio

unmoor /ʌn'mʊr/ vt desamarrar

unmounted /ʌn'mauntɪd/ a desmontado

unmoved /ʌn'muvd/ a fijo; (unemotional) impasible, frío; (determined) firme, inflexible, inexorable

unmuffle /ʌn'mʌfəl/ vt desembozar, descubrir

unmusical /ʌn'myuzɪkəl/ a sin afición a la música; sin oído (para la música); inarmónico

unnamable /ʌn'neiməbəl/ a que no se puede nombrar, innominable

unnatural /ʌn'nætʃərəl/ a desnaturalizado; (of vices, etc.) contra natural; innatural; (of style) rebuscado; artificial; inhumano, cruel

unnaturalness /ʌn'nætʃərəlnɪs/ n lo monstruoso; lo innatural; artificialidad, f; inhumanidad, f

unnavigable /ʌn'nævɪgəbəl/ a innavegable, no navegable

unnecessarily /ˌʌnnɛsə'sɛrəli/ adv inútilmente, innecesariamente, sin necesidad

unnecessariness /ʌn'nɛsəˌsɛrinɪs/ n inutilidad, f; superfluidad, f; lo innecesario

unnecessary /ʌn'nɛsəˌsɛri/ a innecesario, superfluo, inútil

unneighborly /ʌn'neibərli/ a de mala vecindad, impropio de vecinos, poco servicial

unnerve /ʌn'nɜrv/ vt acobardar quitar el valor, desanimar

unnoticed /ʌn'noutɪst/ a inadvertido, no observado

unobjectionable /ˌʌnəb'dʒɛkʃənəbəl/ a Lat. Am. inobjetable

unobliging /ʌnə'blaidʒɪŋ/ a nada servicial

unobservable /ˌʌnəb'zɜrvəbəl/ a inobservable

unobservant /ˌʌnəb'zɜrvənt/ a inobservante

unobserved /ˌʌnəb'zɜrvd/ a sin ser notado, desapercibido

unobstructed /ˌʌnəb'strʌktɪd/ a no obstruido; sin obstáculos; libre

unobtainable /ˌʌnəb'teinəbəl/ a inalcanzable, inasequible

unobtrusive /ˌʌnəb'trusɪv/ a discreto, modesto

unobtrusiveness /ˌʌnəb'trusɪvnɪs/ n discreción, modestia, f

unoccupied /ʌn'ɒkyəˌpaid/ a (at leisure) desocupado, ocioso, sin ocupación; vacío, vacante, libre; (untenanted) deshabitado

unofficial /ˌʌnə'fɪʃəl/ a no oficial

unopened /ʌn'oupənd/ a sin abrir, cerrado; (of exhibitions, etc.) no inaugurado

unopposed /ˌʌnə'pouzd/ a sin oposición

unorganized /ʌn'ɔrgəˌnaizd/ a inorganizado; Biol. inorgánico

unoriginal /ˌʌnə'rɪdʒənl/ a poco original

unorthodox /ʌn'ɔrθəˌdɒks/ a heterodoxo

unostentatious /ˌʌnɒstən'teiʃəs/ a sencillo, modesto, sin ostentación

unostentatiousness /ˌʌnɒstən'teiʃəsnɪs/ n sencillez, modestia, falta de ostentación, f

unpack /ʌn'pæk/ vt desempaquetar; (trunks) vaciar; (bales) desembalar. vi desempaquetar; deshacer las maletas

unpacking /ʌn'pækɪŋ/ n desembalaje, m

unpaid /ʌn'peid/ a sin pagar, no pagado, Lat. Am. also impago

unpalatable /ʌn'pælətəbəl/ a de mal sabor; desagradable

unparalleled /ʌn'pærəˌlɛld/ a sin paralelo, sin par, sin igual

unpardonable /ʌn'pardnəbəl/ a imperdonable, inexcusable, irremisible

unpatriotic /ˌʌnˌpeitri'ɒtɪk/ a antipatriótico

unpaved /ʌn'peivd/ a sin empedrar

unperceived /ˌʌnpər'sivd/ a inadvertido, sin ser notado

unperturbed /ˌʌnpər'tɜrbd/ a impasible, sin alterarse, sereno

unpleasant /ʌn'plɛzənt/ a desagradable, desapacible; ofensivo; (troublesome) enfadoso, molesto

unpleasantly /ʌn'plɛzəntli/ adv desagradablemente

unpleasantness /ʌn'plɛzəntnɪs/ n lo desagradable; disgusto, sinsabor, m; (disagreement) disputa, riña, f

unpleasing /ʌn'plizɪŋ/ a nada placentero; desagradable, sin atractivos

unplug /ʌn'plʌg/ vt desenchufar

unpoetic /ˌʌnpou'ɛtɪk/ a poco poético

unpolished /ʌn'pɒlɪʃt/ a sin pulir, tosco, mate; Fig. inculto, cerril. **u. diamond,** diamante en bruto, m

unpolluted /ˌʌnpə'lutɪd/ a impoluto, incontaminado; puro, sin pervertir

unpopular /ʌn'pɒpyələr/ a impopular

unpopularity /ˌʌnpɒpyə'lærɪti/ n impopularidad, f

unpractical /ʌn'præktɪkəl/ a impracticable, imposible; (of persons) sin sentido práctico

unpracticed /ʌn'præktɪst/ a no practicado; inexperto, inhábil

unpraiseworthy /ʌn'preizˌwɜrði/ a inmeritorio

unprecedented /ʌn'prɛsɪˌdɛntɪd/ a sin precedente, inaudito

unprejudiced /ʌn'prɛdʒədɪst/ a sin prejuicios, imparcial

unpremeditated /ˌʌnpri'mɛdɪˌteitɪd/ a sin premeditación, indeliberado, impremeditado

unprepared /ˌʌnpri'pɛərd/ a sin preparación, no preparado; desprevenido; desapercibido (unready)

unpreparedness /ˌʌnpri'pɛəridnɪs/ n falta de preparación, imprevisión, f, desapercibimiento, m

unprepossessing /ˌʌnpripə'zɛsɪŋ/ a poco atrayente, antipático

unpresentable /ˌʌnprɪ'zɛntəbəl/ a impresentable

unpretentious /ˌʌnprɪ'tɛnʃəs/ a sin pretensiones, modesto

unpriced /ʌn'praist/ a sin precio

unprincipled /ʌn'prɪnsəˌpld/ a sin conciencia, sin escrúpulos

unprinted /ʌn'prɪntɪd/ a sin imprimir, no impreso

unprocurable /ˌʌnprou'kyʊrəbəl/ a inalcanzable, inasequible

unproductive /ˌʌnprə'dʌktɪv/ a improductivo; infructuoso, estéril

unproductiveness /ˌʌnprə'dʌktɪvnɪs/ n infructuosidad, f; esterilidad, f

unprofessional /ˌʌnprə'fɛʃənl/ a sin profesión; contrario a la ética profesional

unprofitable /ʌn'prɒfɪtəbəl/ a improductivo, infructuoso; sin provecho; inútil; nada lucrativo

unprogressive /ˌʌnprə'grɛsɪv/ a reaccionario

unpromising /ʌn'prɒməsɪŋ/ a poco halagüeño

unpronounceable /ˌʌnprə'naunsəbəl/ a impronunciable

unpropitious /ˌʌnprə'pɪʃəs/ a desfavorable, nada propicio, nada halagüeño

unprosperous /ʌn'prɒspərəs/ a impróspero

unprotected /ˌʌnprə'tɛktɪd/ a sin protección; (of persons) indefenso, desválido

unproved /ʌn'pruvd/ a no probado, sin demostrar

unprovided /ˌʌnprə'vaidid/ a desapercibido, desprovisto. u. **for,** sin provisión (para); sin medios de vida, desamparado

unprovoked /ˌʌnprə'voukt/ a no provocado, sin provocación; sin motivo

unpublished /ʌn'pʌblɪʃt/ a inédito, no publicado, sin publicar

unpunishable /ʌn'pʌnɪʃəbəl/ a no punible

unpunished /ʌn'pʌnɪʃt/ a impune, sin castigo

unpurchasable /ʌn'pɜrtʃɪsəbəl/ a que no puede comprarse

unqualified /ʌn'kwɒləˌfaid/ a incapaz, incompetente; (with professions) sin título; (downright) incondicional, absoluto

unquenchable /ʌn'kwɛntʃəbəl/ a inextinguible, inapagable; insaciable

unquestionable /ʌn'kwɛstʃənəbəl/ a indiscutible, indudable, indubitable

unquestionably /ʌn'kwɛstʃənəbli/ adv indudablemente

unravel /ʌn'rævəl/ vt deshilar; destejer; (a mystery, etc.) desentrañar, desembrollar, descifrar

unraveling /ʌn'rævəlɪŋ/ n deshiladura, f; aclaración, f

unreadable /ʌn'ridəbəl/ a ilegible

unreadiness /ʌn'rɛdinɪs/ n falta de preparación, f, desapercibimiento, m; lentitud, f

unready /ʌn'rɛdi/ a desapercibido, desprevenido; lento

unreal /ʌn'riəl/ a irreal; falso, imaginario, ilusorio; ficticio; artificial; insincero, hipócrita; ideal; incorpóreo

unreality /ˌʌnri'ælɪti/ n irrealidad, f; falsedad, f; artificialidad, f; lo quimérico

unreasonable /ʌn'rizənəbəl/ a irrazonable, irracional; disparatado, extravagante; (with price, etc.) exorbitante, excesivo

unreasonableness /ʌn'rizənəbəlnɪs/ n irracionalidad, f; exorbitancia, f

unreasonably /ʌn'rizənəbli/ adv irracionalmente

unreasoning /ʌn'rizənɪŋ/ a irracional; sin motivo, sin causa

unreceipted /ˌʌnri'sitid/ a sin recibo

unrecognizable /ʌn'rɛkəgˌnaizəbəl/ a que no puede reconocerse; imposible de reconocer

unrecognized /ʌn'rɛkəgˌnaizd/ a no reconocido

unreconciled /ʌn'rɛkənˌsaild/ a no resignado, no reconciliado

unrectified /ʌn'rɛktəˌfaid/ a no corregido, sin rectificar

unredeemed /ˌʌnri'dimd/ a no redimido; no mitigado; (of pledges) sin desempeñar

unrefined /ˌʌnri'faind/ a no refinado, impuro; inculto, grosero

unreformed /ˌʌnri'fɔrmd/ a no reformado

unrefuted /ˌʌnri'fyutid/ a no refutado

unregenerate /ˌʌnri'dʒɛnərɪt/ a no regenerado

unregretted /ˌʌnri'grɛtid/ a no llorado, sin lamentar

unrehearsed /ˌʌnri'hɜrst/ a sin preparación; Theat. sin ensayar; (extempore) improvisado

unrelated /ˌʌnrileitid/ a inconexo; (of persons) sin parentesco

unrelenting /ˌʌnri'lɛntɪŋ/ a implacable, inflexible, inexorable

unreliability /ˌʌnriˌlaiə'bɪliti/ n incertidumbre, f; el no poder confiar en, informalidad, inestabilidad, f

unreliable /ˌʌnriˌlaiəbəl/ a incierto, dudoso, indigno de confianza; (of persons) informal

unrelieved /ˌʌnri'livd/ a no aliviado, absoluto, complete, total

unremitting /ˌʌnri'mitɪŋ/ a incansable

unremunerative /ˌʌnri'myunərətɪv/ a sin remuneración, no remunerado

unrepealed /ˌʌnri'pild/ a vigente

unrepentant /ˌʌnri'pɛntn̩t/ a impenitente

unrepresentative /ˌʌnrɛpri'zɛntətɪv/ a poco representativo

unrepresented /ˌʌnrɛpri'zɛntid/ a sin representación

unrequited /ˌʌnri'kwaitid/ a no correspondido

unreserved /ˌʌnri'zɜrvd/ a no reservado; expresivo, comunicativo, expansivo, franco

unreservedly /ˌʌnri'zɜrvɪdli/ adv sin reserva; con toda franqueza

unresisting /ˌʌnri'zɪstɪŋ/ a sin oponer resistencia

unresolved /ˌʌnri'zɒlvd/ a sin resolverse, vacilante; incierto, dudoso, inseguro; sin solución

unresponsive /ˌʌnri'spɒnsɪv/ a flemático; insensible, sordo

unresponsiveness /ˌʌnri'spɒnsɪvnɪs/ n flema, f; insensibilidad, f

unrest /ʌn'rɛst/ n desasosiego, m, agitación, inquietud, f

unrestful /ʌn'rɛstfəl/ a agitado, inquieto, intranquilo

unrestrained /ˌʌnri'streind/ a desenfrenado; ilimitado, sin límites; sin reserva

unrestricted /ˌʌnri'strɪktɪd/ a sin restricción; ilimitado

unrevealed /ˌʌnri'vild/ a no revelado, por descubrir, no descubierto

unrewarded /ˌʌnri'wɔrdɪd/ a sin premio, no recompensado

unrighteous /ʌn'raitʃəs/ a injusto, malo, perverso

unrighteousness /ʌn'raitʃəsnɪs/ n injusticia, f; maldad, perversidad, f

unripe /ʌn'raip/ a verde, inmaturo

unripeness /ʌn'raipnɪs/ n falta de madurez, f

unrivaled /ʌn'raivəld/ a sin igual, sin par

unroll /ʌn'roul/ vt desarrollar. vi desarrollarse; (unfold) desplegarse (a la vista)

unromantic /ˌʌnrou'mæntɪk/ a poco (or nada) romántico

unruffled /ʌn'rʌfəld/ a sereno, plácido, ecuánime; no arrugado; (of hair) liso

unruliness /ʌn'rulinɪs/ n turbulencia, indisciplina, f; insubordinación, rebeldía, f

unruly /ʌn'ruli/ a ingobernable, revoltoso; refractario, rebelde; (of hair) indomable

unsaddle /ʌn'sædl/ vt desensillar; derribar (del caballo, etc.)

unsafe /ʌn'seif/ a inseguro; peligroso; arriesgado; (to eat) nocivo

unsafeness /ʌn'seifnɪs/ n inseguridad, f; peligro, riesgo, m

unsaid /ʌn'sɛd/ a sin decir, no dicho

unsalable /ʌn'seiləbəl/ a invendible

unsalaried /ʌn'sælərid/ a no asalariado

unsalted /ʌn'sɔltid/ a soso, sin sal

unsanitary /ʌn'sænɪˌteri/ a antihigiénico

unsatisfactoriness /ˌʌnsætɪs'fæktərinɪs/ n lo insatisfactorio

unsatisfactory /ˌʌnsætɪs'fæktəri/ a poco (or nada) satisfactorio; no aceptable

unsatisfied /ʌn'sætɪsˌfaid/ a no satisfecho; descontento; no convencido; (hungry) no harto; Com. no saldado

unsatisfying /ʌn'sætɪsˌfaiɪŋ/ a que no satisface

unsavoriness /ʌn'seivərinɪs/ n insipidez, f, mal sabor, m; lo desagradable; sordidez, suciedad, f

unsavory /ʌn'seivəri/ a insípido, de mal sabor; desagradable; sórdido, sucio

unscathed /ʌn'skeiðd/ a sin daño, ileso

unscented /ʌn'sɛntid/ a sin perfume, sin olor, no fragante

unscholarly /ʌn'skɒlərli/ a nada erudito; indigno de un erudito

unscientific /ˌʌnsaiən'tɪfɪk/ a no científico

unscrew /ʌn'skru/ vt destornillar, Lat. Am. desenroscar. vi destornillarse

unscrewing /ʌn'skruɪŋ/ n destornillamiento, m

unscrupulous /ʌn'skrupyələs/ a sin escrúpulos, poco escrupuloso, desaprensivo

unscrupulousness /ʌn'skrupyələsnɪs/ n falta de escrúpulos, desaprensión, f

unseal /ʌn'sil/ vt desellar, romper (or quitar) el sello (de)

unseasonable /ʌn'sizənəbəl/ a intempestivo, fuera de sazón; inoportuno, inconveniente. **at an u. hour,** a una hora inconveniente, a deshora

unseasonableness /ʌn'sizənəbəlnɪs/ n lo intempestivo, inoportunidad, f
unseasonably /ʌn'sizənəbli/ adv intempestivamente; a deshora; inoportunamente
unseasoned /ʌn'sizənd/ a Cul. sin sazonar, soso; (wood) verde; no maduro, sin madurar
unseat /ʌn'sit/ vt (from horse) tirar, echar al suelo; Polit. desituir
unseaworthy /'ʌn'si,wɜrði/ a innavegable
unseemliness /ʌn'simlinɪs/ n falta de decoro, f; indecencia, f
unseemly /ʌn'simli/ a indecoroso, indigno; indecente; impropio
unseen /ʌn'sin/ a no visto, invisible; inadvertido; secreto, oculto. n versión al libro abierto, f. **the u.**, lo invisible
unselfish /ʌn'sɛlfɪʃ/ a desinteresado, abnegado, nada egoísta; generoso
unselfishness /ʌn'sɛlfɪʃnɪs/ n abnegación, f; desinterés, m; generosidad, f
unsentimental /,ʌnsɛntə'mɛntl/ a no sentimental
unserviceable /ʌn'sɜrvɪsəbəl/ a inservible, inútil, que no sirve para nada, sin utilidad
unsettle /ʌn'sɛtl/ vt desarreglar; desorganizar; hacer inseguro; agitar, perturbar
unsettled /ʌn'sɛtld/ a inconstante, variable; Com. pendiente, sin pagar; incierto; sin resolver; (of estates) sin solucionar
unshackle /ʌn'ʃækəl/ vt desencadenar
unshakable /ʌn'ʃeikəbəl/ a inconmovible, firme
unshapely /ʌn'ʃeipli/ a desproporcionado
unshaven /ʌn'ʃeivən/ a sin afeitar
unsheathe /ʌn'ʃið/ vt desenvainar, sacar
unsheltered /ʌn'ʃɛltərd/ a desabrigado, desamparado; no protegido, sin protección; (of places) sin abrigo, expuesto; (from) sin defensa contra
unship /ʌn'ʃɪp/ vt desembarcar; (the oars) desarmar
unshod /ʌn'ʃod/ a descalzo; (of a horse) sin herraduras
unshrinkable /ʌn'ʃrɪŋkəbəl/ a que no se encoge
unshrinking /ʌn'ʃrɪŋkɪŋ/ a intrépido; resoluto, sin vacilar
unsightly /ʌn'saitli/ a feo, horrible, repugnante, antiestético
unsinkable /ʌn'sɪŋkəbəl/ a insumergible
unskilled /ʌn'skɪld/ a inexperto, inhábil, imperito, torpe
unsmokable /ʌn'smoukəbəl/ a (of tobacco) infumable
unsociability /,ʌnsouʃə'bɪlɪti/ n insociabilidad, huraña, esquivez, f
unsociable /ʌn'souʃəbəl/ a insociable, huraño, esquivo, arisco
unsocial /ʌn'souʃəl/ a insocial, antisocial
unsold /ʌn'sould/ a no vendido, sin vender
unsolder /ʌn'sodər/ vt desoldar, desestañar
unsoldierly /ʌn'souldʒɜrli/ a indigno de un soldado; poco marcial
unsophisticated /,ʌnsə'fɪstɪ,keitɪd/ a ingenuo, inocente, cándido
unsought /ʌn'sɔt/ a no solicitado; no buscado
unsound /ʌn'saund/ a enfermo; defectuoso; (rotten) podrido; (fallacious) erróneo, poco convincente; (of persons) informal, indigno de confianza; (of religious views) heterodoxo. **of u. mind,** insano
unsoundness /ʌn'saundnɪs/ n lo defectuoso; mal estado, m; falsedad, f; informalidad, f; heterodoxia, f
unsparing /ʌn'spɛərɪŋ/ a severo, implacable; generoso, pródigo
unspeakable /ʌn'spikəbəl/ a indecible, inefable; que no puede mencionarse, horrible
unspecified /ʌn'spɛsə,faid/ a no especificado
unspoiled /ʌn'spɔild/ a intacto; ileso, indemne; no corrompido; no estropeado; (of children) no mimado
unspoken /ʌn'spoukən/ a no pronunciado
unsportsmanlike /ʌn'spɔrtsmən,laik/ a indigno de un cazador; indigno de un deportista; nada caballeroso. **to play in an u. way,** jugar sucio
unstable /ʌn'steibəl/ a inestable; variable; inconstante; vacilante, irresoluto

unstained /ʌn'steind/ a no manchado; no teñido; inmaculado, sin mancha
unstamped /ʌn'stæmpt/ a sin sello; no sellado
unstatesmanlike /ʌn'steitsmən,laik/ a impropio (or indigno) de un hombre de estado
unsteadiness /ʌn'stɛdɪnɪs/ n inestabilidad, falta de firmeza, f; inconstancia, f
unsteady /ʌn'stɛdi/ a inestable, inseguro; inconstante
unstick /ʌn'stɪk/ vt desapegar
unstitch /ʌn'stɪtʃ/ vt desapuntar
unstressed /ʌn'strɛst/ a sin énfasis; (of syllables) sin acento
unstudied /ʌn'stʌdid/ a no estudiado; natural, espontáneo
unsubstantial /,ʌnsəb'stænʃəl/ a insubstancial; ligero; irreal, imaginario; incorpóreo; aparente
unsuccessful /,ʌnsək'sɛsfəl/ a sin éxito; infructuoso. **to be u.,** no tener éxito
unsuccessfully /,ʌnsək'sɛsfəli/ adv en vano, sin éxito
unsuitability /,ʌnsutə'bɪlɪti/ n impropiedad, f; inconveniencia, incongruencia, f; incapacidad, f; inoportunidad, f
unsuitable /ʌn'sutəbəl/ a inapropiado; inconveniente; impropio; inservible; incapaz; inoportuno
unsung /ʌn'sʌŋ/ a no cantado; no celebrado en verso
unsupported /,ʌnsə'pɔrtɪd/ a sin apoyo; sin defensa; no favorecido
unsurpassable /,ʌnsər'pæsəbəl/ a inmejorable, insuperable
unsurpassed /,ʌnsər'pæst/ a sin par
unsuspecting /,ʌnsə'spɛktɪŋ/ a no suspicaz, confiado, no receloso
unswerving /ʌn'swɜrvɪŋ/ a directo; sin vacilar, constante
unsymmetrical /,ʌnsɪ'mɛtrɪkəl/ a asimétrico
unsympathetic /,ʌnsɪmpə'θɛtɪk/ a indiferente, incompasivo; antipático
unsystematic /,ʌnsɪstə'mætɪk/ a sin sistema, asistemático, no metódico
untalented /ʌn'tæləntɪd/ a sin talento
untamed /ʌn'teimd/ a indomado, cerril, bravío, no domesticado; desenfrenado, violento. **u. horse,** Lat. Am. bellaco, m
unteach /ʌn'titʃ/ vt desenseñar
untenable /ʌn'tɛnəbəl/ a insostenible
untenanted /ʌn'tɛnəntɪd/ a desalquilado, deshabitado; vacío, desierto
unthankful /ʌn'θæŋkfəl/ a ingrato, desagradecido
unthinkable /ʌn'θɪŋkəbəl/ a inconcebible; imposible
unthinking /ʌn'θɪŋkɪŋ/ a sin reflexión; desatento; indiscreto
unthinkingly /ʌn'θɪŋkɪŋli/ adv sin pensar
unthread /ʌn'θrɛd/ vt deshebrar
untidily /ʌn'taidli/ adv en desorden, sin aseo
untidiness /ʌn'taidinɪs/ n desorden, m; desaseo, desaliño, m; falta de pulcritud, f
untidy /ʌn'taidi/ a desarreglado; desaseado; abandonado; en desorden, sin concierto
untie /ʌn'tai/ vt desatar, desanudar; (knots) deshacer
until /ʌn'tɪl/ prep hasta. conjunc hasta que. (The subjunc. is required in clauses referring to future time, e.g. No venga usted hasta que le avise yo, Don't come until I tell you. In clauses referring to past or present time the indicative is generally used, e.g. No la reconocí hasta que se volvió, I didn't recognize her until she turned around)
untilled /ʌn'tɪld/ a sin cultivar
untimeliness /ʌn'taimlinɪs/ n inoportunidad, f; lo prematuro
untimely /ʌn'taimli/ a inoportuno, intempestivo; prematuro
untiring /ʌn'taiᵊrɪŋ/ a incansable, infatigable
unto /'ʌntu; unstressed -tə/ prep hacia
untold /ʌn'tould/ a no revelado; no narrado; sin decir, no dicho; incalculable
untouchable /ʌn'tʌtʃəbəl/ a que no puede tocarse, intangible; (of castes) intocable
untouched /ʌn'tʌtʃt/ a sin tocar; intacto, incólume
untrained /ʌn'treind/ a indisciplinado; inexperto; no adiestrado

untranslatable /ˌʌntræns'leitəbəl/ a intraducible
untraveled /ʌn'trævəld/ a no frecuentado; (of persons) provinciano
untried /ʌn'traid/ a no experimentado. **u. knight,** caballero novel, m
untrodden /ʌn'trɒdn̩/ a no hollado, no frecuentado; inexplorado, virgen
untroubled /ʌn'trʌbəld/ a tranquilo, sosegado
untrue /ʌn'tru/ a mentiroso, falso, engañoso; ficticio, imaginario; traidor, desleal; infiel
untrustworthiness /ʌn'trʌst͵wɜrðinɪs/ n incertidumbre, inseguridad, f; (of persons) informalidad, f
untrustworthy /ʌn'trʌst͵wɜrði/ a indigno de confianza; incierto, dudoso; desleal
untruth /ʌn'truθ/ n mentira, falsedad, f; ficción, f
untruthful /ʌn'truθfəl/ a mentiroso; falso
untruthfulness /ʌn'truθfəlnɪs/ n falsedad, f
untwist /ʌn'twɪst/ vt destorcer
unused /ʌn'yuzd/ a no empleado; /ʌn'yust/ desacostumbrado; inusitado; (postage stamp) sin sellar
unusual /ʌn'yuʒuəl/ a fuera de lo común, desacostumbrado; extraño, raro, peregrino, extraordinario
unusually /ʌn'yuʒuəli/ adv excepcionalmente; infrecuentemente
unusualness /ʌn'yuʒuəlnɪs/ n lo insólito; rareza, f
unutterable /ʌn'ʌtərəbəl/ a indecible, inexpresable
unvarnished /ʌn'vɑrnɪʃt/ a sin barnizar; Fig. sencillo
unvarying /ʌn'vɛəriɪŋ/ a invariable, constante, uniforme
unveil /ʌn'veil/ vt quitar el velo; (memorial) descubrir; Fig. revelar. vi quitarse el velo; revelarse, quitarse la careta
unventilated /ʌn'vɛntʃleitɪd/ a sin ventilación; sin aire, ahogado; (of topics) no discutido
unverifiable /ʌn͵vɛrə'faiəbəl/ a que no puede verificarse
unverified /ʌn͵vɛrə'faid/ a sin verificar
unvisited /ʌn 'vɪsɪtɪd/ no visitado; no frecuentado
unvoiced /ʌn'vɔist/ a no expresado
unwanted /ʌn'wɒntɪd/ a no deseado; superfluo, de más
unwarlike /ʌn'wɔr͵laik/ a nada marcial, pacífico
unwarranted /ʌn'wɔrəntɪd/ a sin garantía; inexcusable, injustificable
unwashed /ʌn'wɒʃt/ a sin lavar; sucio
unwatched /ʌn'wɒtʃt/ a no vigilado
unwavering /ʌn'weivəriŋ/ a resuelto, firme; inexorable; (gaze) fijo
unwaveringly /ʌn'weivəriŋli/ adv sin vacilar; inexorablemente
unwearied /ʌn'wiərid/ a incansable; infatigable
unwelcome /ʌn'wɛlkəm/ a mal acogido; inoportuno; desagradable
unwell /ʌn'wɛl/ a indispuesto
unwholesome /ʌn'houlsəm/ a malsano, nocivo, insalubre
unwholesomeness /ʌn'houlsəmnɪs/ n insalubridad, f
unwieldiness /ʌn'wildinɪs/ n pesadez, dificultad de manejarse, f
unwieldy /ʌn'wildi/ a pesado, abultado, difícil de manejar
unwilling /ʌn'wɪlɪŋ/ a desinclinado, reluctante
unwillingly /ʌn'wɪlɪŋli/ adv de mala gana
unwillingness /ʌn'wɪlɪŋnɪs/ n falta de inclinación, repugnancia, f
unwind /ʌn'waind/ vt desenvolver; (thread) desdevanar, desovillar. vi desarrollarse; desdevanarse
unwise /ʌn'waiz/ a imprudente, indiscreto, incauto; (lacking wisdom) tonto
unwisely /ʌn'waizli/ adv imprudentemente, indiscretamente
unwitting /ʌn'wɪtɪŋ/ a inconsciente
unwittingly /ʌn'wɪtɪŋli/ adv sin darse cuenta
unwomanly /ʌn'wumənli/ a poco femenino
unwonted /ʌn'wɒntɪd/ a insólito, inusitado
unworkable /ʌn'wɜrkəbəl/ a impráctico
unworkmanlike /ʌn'wɜrkmən͵laik/ a chapucero, charanguero
unworldly /ʌn'wɜrldli/ a poco, mundano, espiritual
unworn /ʌn'wɔrn/ a sin llevar, nuevo

unworthiness /ʌn'wɜrðinɪs/ n indignidad, f
unworthy /ʌn'wɜrði/ a indigno
unwounded /ʌn'wundɪd/ a no herido, sin herida, ileso
unwrap /ʌn'ræp/ vt desenvolver, desempapelar
unwritten /ʌn'rɪtn̩/ a no escrito. **u. law,** ley consuetudinaria, f
unyielding /ʌn'yildɪŋ/ a duro, firme; (of persons) inflexible, terco, resuelto, obstinado
unyoke /ʌn'youk/ vt desuncir, quitar el yugo
up /ʌp/ adv (high) arriba, en alto; (higher) hacia arriba; (out of bed) levantado; (standing) de pie; (finished) concluido, terminado; (of time) llegado; (excited) agitado; (rebellious) sublevado; (of sun, etc.) salido; (come or gone up) subido; (of universities) en residencia; (for discussion) bajo consideración; (abreast of) al lado, al nivel; (incapable) incapaz, incompetente; (ill) enfermo, indispuesto. **"Up,"** (on elevators) «Para subir.» (For various idiomatic uses of **up** after verbs, see verbs themselves.) a (in a few expressions only) ascendente. prep en lo alto de; hacia arriba de; a lo largo de; (with country) en el interior de; (with current) contra. **to be up in arms,** sublevarse, rebelarse. **to be very hard up,** ser muy pobre, estar a la cuarta pregunta. **to drink up,** beberlo todo. **to go or come up,** subir. **to lay up,** acumular. **to speak up,** hablar en voz alta. **He has something up his sleeve,** Tiene algo en la manga. **It is all up,** Todo se acabó, Mi gozo en el pozo. **It is not up to much,** Vale muy poco; No es muy fuerte. **It is up to you,** Tú dirás, Tú harás lo que te parezca. **What is he up to?** ¿Qué está tramando? **What's up?** ¿Qué pasa? ¿Qué hay? **up and down,** adv bajando y subiendo, de arriba abajo; de un lado a otro; por todas partes. **up-and-down,** a fluctuante; (of roads) ondulante; (of life) accidentado, borrascoso. **ups and downs,** vicisitudes, f pl, altibajos, m pl. **up-grade,** subida, f. **up in,** versado en, perito en. **well up in,** fuerte en. **up North,** al norte; en el norte; hacia el norte. **up there,** allí arriba, allí en lo alto. **up to,** hasta; (aware) al corriente de, informado de. **up to date,** al día hasta la fecha. **up-to-date,** a de última moda; al día. **up to now,** hasta ahora. **up train,** tren ascendente. **Up with...!** ¡Arriba! **Up you go!** (to children) ¡Upa!
upbraid /ʌp'breid/ vt reprender, echar en cara
upbringing /'ʌp͵brɪŋɪŋ/ n crianza, educación, f
upcountry /n., a 'ʌp͵kʌntri; adv. ʌp'kʌntri/ n tierra adentro, f; lo interior (de un país). a de tierra adentro, del interior. adv tierra adentro, hacia el interior
update /'ʌp͵deit/ vt actualizar, poner al día
upheaval /ʌp'hivəl/ n solevantamiento, m; trastorno, m
uphill /a, adv. 'ʌp'hɪl; n. 'ʌp͵hɪl/ a ascendente; penoso, fatigoso, difícil. adv cuesta arriba, pecho arriba
uphold /ʌp'hould/ vt sostener, apoyar; (help) ayudar, consolar; (protect) defender; (countenance) aprobar; Law. confirmar
upholder /ʌp'houldər/ n sostenedor (-ra), defensor (-ra)
upholster /ʌp'houlstər, ə'poul-/ vt entapizar, tapizar
upholsterer /ʌp'houlstərər; ə'poulʇ/ n tapicero, m
upholstery /ʌp'houlstəri, ə'poulʇ/ n tapicería, f; (of car) almohadillado, m
upkeep /'ʌp͵kip/ n mantenimiento, m, conservación, f
upland /'ʌplənd/ n tierra alta, f, a alto, elevado
uplift /n. 'ʌp'lɪft; vt. 'ʌp͵lɪft/ vt elevar, n elevación, f; Inf. fervor, m
upon /ə'pɒn/ prep. See **on**
upper /'ʌpər/ a comp superior; alto; de arriba. n (of shoe) pala, f, Sports. **u.-cut,** golpe de abajo arriba, upper-cut, m. **U. Egypt,** Alto Egipto, m. **u. hand,** dominio, m; superioridad, ventaja, f. **u. house,** cámara alta, f; senado, m. **u. ten,** los diez primeros
upper classes /'klæsɪz/ a clases altas, capas altas, f pl
uppermost /'ʌpər͵moust/ a más alto, más elevado; predominante, principal; más fuerte. adv en primer lugar; en lo más alto. **to be u.,** predominar
upright /'ʌp͵rait/ a recto, derecho; vertical; (honorable) honrado, digno, recto. n (stanchion) mástil, so-

porte, palo derecho, montante, *m. adv* en pie; derecho

uprightly /'ʌp,raitli/ *adv* rectamente, honradamente

uprightness /'ʌp,raitnɪs/ *n* rectitud, honradez, probidad, *f*

uprising /'ʌp,raiziŋ/ *n* insurrección, sublevación, *f*

uproar /'ʌp,rɔr/ *n* alboroto, tumulto, estrépito, *m*, conmoción, *f*

uproarious /ʌp'rɔriəs/ *a* tumultuoso, estrepitoso

uproot /ʌp'rut/ *vt* desarraigar, *Lat. Am.* destroncar; *Fig.* arrancar; (destroy) extirpar

uprooting /ʌp'rutiŋ/ *n* desarraigo, *m*; arranque, *m*; extirpación, *f*

upset /*v.* ʌp'sɛt; *n.* 'ʌp,sɛt/ *vt* volcar; (overthrow) derribar, echar abajo; (frustrate) contrariar; desarreglar; (distress) trastornar, turbar; (of food) hacer mal. *vi* volcarse. *n* vuelco, *m*; trastorno, *m*. **u. price,** tipo de subasta, *m*

upsetting /ʌp'sɛtiŋ/ *a* turbante, inquietante

upshot /'ʌp,ʃɒt/ *n* resultado, *m*; consecuencia, *f*

upside /'ʌp,said/ *n* lado superior, *m*; parte superior, *f*; (of trains) andén ascendente, *m*. **u. down,** al revés, de arriba abajo; en desorden

upstairs /'ʌp'stɛarz/ *adv* arriba, en el piso de arriba; (with go or come) al piso de arriba

upstanding /ʌp'stændiŋ/ *a* gallardo, guapo. **an u. young man (woman),** un buen mozo (una buena moza)

upstart /'ʌp,stɑrt/ *n* arribista, *mf*; advenedizo (-za) insolente, *mf*; presuntuoso (-sa)

upstream /'ʌp'strim/ *a* and *adv* contra la corriente, agua arriba, río arriba

upturned /'ʌp,tɛrnd/ *a* (of noses) respingada

upward /'ʌpwərd/ *a* ascendente, hacia arriba

upwards /'ʌpwərdz/ *adv* hacia arriba; en adelante. **u. of,** más de

Urals, the /'yʊrəlz/ los Urales, *m pl*

uranium /yʊ'reiniəm/ *n Mineral.* uranio, *m*

Uranus /'yʊrənəs, yʊ'rei-/ *n Astron.* Urano, *m*

urban /'ɜrbən/ *a* urbano, ciudadano

urbane /ɜr'bein/ *a* cortés, urbano, fino

urbanity /ɜr'bænɪti/ *n* urbanidad, cortesía, finura, *f*

urbanization /,ɜrbənə'zeifən/ *n* urbanización, *f*

urbanize /'ɜrbə,naiz/ *vt* urbanizar

urban renewal *n* renovación urbana, renovación urbanística, *f*

urchin /'ɜrtʃin/ *n* galopín, granuja, pilluelo, *m*

ureter /yʊ'ritər/ *n Anat.* uréter, *m*

urethra /yʊ'riθrə/ *n Anat.* uretra, *f*

urge /ɜrdʒ/ *vt* empujar, impeler; incitar, estimular, azuzar, animar; pedir con urgencia, recomendar con ahínco, instar, insistir (en). *n* instinto, impulso, *m*; deseo, *m*; ambición, *f*

urgency /'ɜrdʒənsi/ *n* urgencia, *f*; importancia, perentoriedad, *f*

urgent /'ɜrdʒənt/ *a* urgente; importante, apremiante, perentorio. **to be u.,** urgir

urgently /'ɜrdʒəntli/ *adv* urgentemente

uric /'yʊrik/ *a* úrico

urinal /'yʊrənl/ *n* orinal, urinario, *m*

urinalysis /,yʊrə'næləsis/ *n* análisis de orina, urinálisis, *m*

urinary /'yʊrə,nɛri/ *a* urinario

urinary tract *n* conducto urinario, *m*, vías urinarias, *f pl*

urinate /'yʊrə,neit/ *vi* orinar

urine /'yʊrɪn/ *n* orín, *m*

urn /ɜrn/ *n* urna, *f*; (for coffee) cafetera, *f*; (for tea) tetera, *f*

Ursa /'ɜrsə/ *n Astron.* osa, *f.* **U. Major,** osa mayor, *f.* **U. Minor,** osa menor, *f*

urticaria /,ɜrti'kɛəriə/ *n Med.* urticaria, *f*

Uruguayan /,yʊrə'gweiən/ *a* and *n* uruguayo (-ya)

us /ʌs/ *pron* nos; (with prep.) nosotros, *m.* **He came toward us,** Vino hacia nosotros

usable /'yuzəbəl/ *a* aprovechable, servible

usage /'yusidʒ/ *n* (handling) tratamiento, *m*; uso, *m*, costumbre, *f*

use /yus/ *n* uso, *m*; manejo, empleo, *m*; (custom)

costumbre práctica, *f*; (need) necesidad, *f*; (usefulness) aprovechamiento, *m*; *Law.* usufructo, *m.* **directions for use,** direcciones para el uso, *f pl*, **for the use of...,** para uso de... **in use,** en uso. **out of use,** anticuado; fuera de moda. **to be of no use,** no servir; ser inútil. **to have no use for,** no tener necesidad de; *Inf.* tener en poco. **to make use of,** servirse de, aprovechar; *Law.* ejercer. **to put to use,** poner en uso, poner en servicio

use /yuz/ *vt* usar; (employ) emplear; (utilize) servirse de, utilizar; (handle) manejar; hacer uso de; (consume) gastar, consumir; (treat) tratar; practicar. **to use up,** agotar, acabar con; consumir. *vi impers* acostumbrar, soler (e.g. *It used to happen that...,* Solía ocurrir que...). (**Used to** and the verb which follows are often translated simply by the imperfect tense of the following verb, e.g. *I used to see her every day,* La veía todos los días. Use of the verbs *acostumbrar* or *soler* to translate *used to* adds emphasis to the statement)

used /yuzd/ *a* and *past part* /yust/ acostumbrado, habituado; empleado; (clothes) usado; (postage stamp) sellado. **to become u. to,** acostumbrarse a

useful /'yusfəl/ *a* útil; provechoso; servicial

usefully /'yusfəli/ *adv* útilmente; con provecho

usefulness /'yusfəlnɪs/ *n* utilidad, *f*; valor, *m*

useless /'yuslɪs/ *a* inútil; vano, infructuoso. **to render u.,** inutilizar

uselessness /'yuslɪsnɪs/ *n* inutilidad, *f*

user /'yuzər/ *n* el, *m*, (*f*, la) que usa, comprador (-ra)

usher /'ʌfər/ *n* ujier, *m*; (in a theater) acomodador (-ra). *vt* introducir, anunciar; acomodar

usual /'yuʒuəl/ *a* usual, acostumbrado, habitual; normal, común. **as u.,** como siempre. **in the u. form,** *Com.* al usado; como de costumbre. **with their u. courtesy,** con la cortesía que les es característica

usually /'yuʒuəli/ *adv* por lo general, ordinariamente. **We u. go out on Sundays,** Acostumbramos salir los domingos

usurer /'yuʒərər/ *n* usurero (-ra)

usurious /yu'ʒʊriəs/ *a* usurario

usurp /yu'sɜrp/ *vt* usurpar; asumir, arrogarse

usurpation /,yusər'peiʃən/ *n* usurpación, *f*; arrogación, *f*

usurper /yu'sɜrpər/ *n* usurpador (-ra)

usurping /yu'sɜrpiŋ/ *a* usurpador

usury /'yuʒəri/ *n* usura, *f.* **to practice u.,** usurear, dar (or tomar) a usura

utensil /yu'tɛnsəl/ *n* utensilio, instrumento, *m*; herramienta, *f.* **kitchen utensils,** batería de cocina, *f*

uterine /'yutərɪn/ *a Med.* uterino

uterus /'yutərəs/ *n* útero, *m*

utilitarian /yu,tɪlɪ'tɛəriən/ *a* utilitario

utilitarianism /yu,tɪlɪ'tɛəriə,nɪzəm/ *n* utilitarismo, *m*

utility /yu'tɪlɪti/ *n* utilidad, *f*; ventaja, *f*, beneficio, provecho, *m.* **u. goods,** artículos fabricados bajo la autorizacion del gobierno, *m pl*

utilizable /,yutʃ'aizəbəl/ *a* utilizable, aprovechable

utilization /,yutlə'zeifən/ *n* empleo, aprovechamiento, *m*

utilize /'yutl,aiz/ *vt* utilizar, servirse de; aprovechar

utmost /'ʌt,moust/ *a* (outermost) extremo; (farthest) más remoto, más distante; (greatest) mayor, más grande. *n* lo más; todo lo posible. **to do one's u.,** hacer todo lo posible, hacer todo lo que uno pueda

utopian /yu'toupiən/ *a* utópico

utter /'ʌtər/ *a* completo, total; terminate, absoluto; sumo, extremo. **He is an u. fool,** Es un tonto de capirote

utter /'ʌtər/ *vt* pronunciar, proferir, decir, hablar; (a sigh, cry, etc.) dar; (express) manifestar, expresar, explicar; (coin) poner en circulación, (a libel) publicar; (disclose) revelar, descubrir

utterance /'ʌtərəns/ *n* expresión, manifestación, *f*; pronunciación, *f*; (style) lenguaje, *m*

utterly /'ʌtərli/ *adv* enteramente, completamente

uttermost /'ʌtər,moust/ *a.* See **utmost**

uvula /'yuvyələ/ *n Anat.* úvula, *f*

uxorious /ʌk'sɔriəs/ *a* uxorio

V

v /vi/ n (letter) ve, f; pieza en forma de V, f
vacancy /'veikənsi/ n vacío, m; vacancia, f; (mental) vacuidad, f; (of offices, posts) vacante, f; (leisure) desocupación, ociosidad, f; (gap, blank) vacío, m, laguna, f
vacant /'veikənt/ a vacío; despoblado, deshabitado; (free) libre; (of offices, etc.) vacante; (leisured) ocioso; (absent-minded) distraído; (vague) vago; (foolish) estúpido, estólido
vacantly /'veikəntli/ adv distraídamente; estúpidamente
vacate /'veikeit/ vt dejar vacío; (a post) dejar; (a throne) renunciar a; dejar vacante; Mil. evacuar; Law. anular, rescindir
vacation /vei'keiʃən/ n (of offices) vacante, f; (holiday) vacaciones, f pl, f. **the long v.**, las vacaciones de verano. **to be on a v.**, estar de vacaciones
vaccinate /'væksə,neit/ vt vacunar
vaccination /,væksə'neiʃən/ n vacunación, f
vaccine /'væk'sin/ n vacuna, f
vacillate /'væsə,leit/ vi (sway) oscilar; (hesitate) vacilar, titubear, dudar
vacillating /'væsə,leitɪŋ/ a vacilante
vacillation /,væsə'leiʃən/ n vacilación, f
vacuity /væ'kyuti/ n vacuidad, f
vacuous /'vækyuəs/ a desocupado, ocioso; estúpido, vacío
vacuum /'vækyum/ n vacío, m. **v. brake,** freno al vacío, m. **v. cleaner,** aspirador de polvo, m. **v. flask,** termos, m. **v. pump,** bomba neumática, f. **vacuumshelf dryer,** secador al vacío, m
vade mecum /'vei'di mikəm, 'vɑ-/ n vademécum, m
vagabond /'vægə,bɒnd/ n vagabundo (-da); vago, m; (beggar) mendigo (-ga). a vagabundo, errante
vagabondage /'vægə,bɒndɪdʒ/ n vagabundeo, m, vagancia, f
vagary /və'gɛəri, 'veigəri/ n (whim) capricho, antojo, m, extravagancia, f; (of the mind) divagación, f
vagina /və'dʒainə/ n vagina, f
vaginal /'vædʒənl/ a vaginal
vagrancy /'veigrənsi/ n vagancia, f
vagrant /'veigrənt/ n vago, m, a vagabundo, errante
vague /veig/ a vago; indistinto; equívoco, ambiguo; (uncertain) incierto
vaguely /'veigli/ adv vagamente
vagueness /'veignɪs/ n vaguedad, f
vain /vein/ a vano; (fruitless) infructuoso; (useless) inútil; (unsubstantial) fútil, insubstancial; fantástico; (empty) vacío; (worthless) despreciable; (conceited) vanidoso, presumido. **in v.,** en vano, en balde, inútilmente. **v. about,** orgulloso de
vainglorious /vein'glɔriəs, -'glour-/ a vanaglorioso
vaingloriousness /vein'glɔriəsnɪs/ n vanagloria, f
vainly /'veinli/ adv vanamente; inútilmente; (conceitedly) vanidosamente, con vanidad
valance /'væləns/ n cenefa, f
vale /veil/ n (valley) valle, m. interj ¡adiós! n (goodbye) vale, m
valediction /,væli'dikʃən/ n despedida, f; vale, m
valedictory /,væli'diktəri/ a de despedida
Valencian /və'lɛnʃiən/ a and n valenciano (-na)
valency /'veilənsi/ n Chem. valencia, f
valet /væ'lei, 'vælɪt/ n criado, m. **v. de chambre,** ayuda de cámara, m
valetudinarian /,væli,tudɳ'ɛəriən/ a valetudinario
Valhalla /væl'hælə, vɑl'hɑlə/ n el Valhala, m
valiant /'vælyənt/ a valiente, esforzado, animoso, bravo
valiantly /'vælyəntli/ adv valientemente
valid /'vælɪd/ a válido, valedero; (of laws in force) vigente
validate /'væli,deit/ vt validar
validation /,væli'deiʃən/ n validación, f
validity /və'lɪdɪti/ n validez, f

validly /'vælɪdli/ adv válidamente
valise /və'lis/ n valija, f, saco de viaje, m
valley /'væli/ n valle, m
valor /'vælər/ n valor, m, valentía, f
valorous /'vælərəs/ a valoroso, esforzudo, intrépido
valuable /'vælyuəbəl/ a valioso; costoso; precioso; estimable; excelente. n pl **valuables,** objetos de valor, m pl
valuableness /'vælyuəbəlnɪs/ n valor, m
valuation /,vælyu'eiʃən/ n valuación, tasación, f; estimación, f
valuator /'vælyu,eitər/ n tasador, m
value /'vælyu/ n valor, m; precio, m; estimación, f; importancia, f; (Gram. Mus.) valor, m; pl **values,** valores morales, principios, m pl. vt tasar, valorar; estimar; apreciar; tener en mucho; hacer caso de; considerar. **to be of v.,** ser de valor
valued /'vælyud/ a apreciado, estimado; precioso
valueless /'vælyulɪs/ a sin valor; insignificante
valuer /'vælyuər/ n tasador, m
valve /vælv/ n (Elec., Mech., Anat.) válvula, f; (Bot., Zool.) valva, f
valved /vælvd/ a con válvulas; (in compounds) de... válvulas
valvular /'vælvyələr/ a valvular
vamp /væmp/ n (of a shoe) pala (de zapato), f; (patch) remiendo, m; Mus. acompañamiento improvisado, m; Inf. aventurera, f. vt (of shoes) poner palas (a); (patch) remendar; Mus. improvisar un acompañamiento; (of a woman) fascinar, engatusar
vampire /'væmpaiər/ n vampiro, m
van /væn/ n (Mil., Nav., Fig.) vanguardia, f; camión, m; (for delivery) camión de reparto, m; (for furniture) conductora de muebles, f; (removal) carro de mudanzas, m; (mail) camión postal, m; (for bathing) caseta de baño, f; (for guard on trains) furgón de equipajes, m; (railroad car) vagón, m
vandal /'vændl/ a and n vándalo (-la); bárbaro (-ra)
vandalism /'vændl,izəm/ n vandalismo, m
vane /vein/ n (weathercock) veleta, f; (of a windmill) aspa, f; (of a propeller) paleta, f; (of a feather) barba, f; (of a surveying instrument) pínula, f
vanguard /'væn,gɑrd/ n vanguardia, f. **in the v.,** a vanguardia; Fig. en la vanguardia
vanilla /və'nɪlə/ n vainilla, f
vanish /'vænɪʃ/ vi desaparecer; desvanecerse; disiparse
vanishing /'vænɪʃɪŋ/ n desaparición, f; disipación, f. **v. cream,** crema desvanecedora, f. **v. point,** punto de la vista, m
vanity /'vænɪti/ n vanidad, f. **v. case,** polvera de bolsillo, f
vanquish /'væŋkwɪʃ/ vt vencer, derrotar
vanquisher /'væŋkwɪʃər/ n vencedor (-ra)
vantage /'væntɪdʒ, 'vɑn-/ n ventaja (also in tennis), f. **v.-ground,** posición ventajosa, f, sitial de privilegio, m
vapid /'væpɪd/ a insípido, insulso; (of speeches, etc.) soso, aburrido, insípido
vapidity /væ'pɪdɪti/ n insipidez, sosería, f
vapor /'veipər/ n vapor, m; pl **vapors,** (hysteria) vapores, m pl. vi (boast) jactarse, baladronear; decir disparates. **v. bath,** baño de vapor, m
vaporizable /,veipə'raizəbəl/ a vaporizable
vaporization /,veipərə'zeiʃən/ n vaporización, f
vaporize /'veipə,raiz/ vt vaporizar. vi vaporizarse
vaporizer /'veipə,raizər/ n vaporizador, m
vaporous /'veipərəs/ a vaporoso
variability /,vɛəriə'bɪlɪti/ n variabilidad, f
variable /'vɛəriəbəl/ a variable. n Math. variable, f
variably /'vɛəriəbli/ adv variablemente
variance /'vɛəriəns/ n variación, f, cambio, m; desacuerdo, m, disensión, f; diferencia, contradicción, f. **at v.,** en desacuerdo, reñidos; hostil (a), opuesto (a); (of things) distinto (de), en contradicción (con)
variant /'vɛəriənt/ n variante, f

variation /ˌveəri'eiʃən/ n variación, f; cambio, m; variedad, f; diferencia, f; (Mus. magnetism) variación, f
varicose /'væri,kous/ a varicoso
varied success /'veərid/ éxito vario, m
variegate /'veərii,geit/ vt abigarrar, matizar, salpicar
variegated /'veərii,geitid/ a abigarrado; variado; mezclado
variegation /ˌveərii'geiʃən/ n abigarramiento, m; diversidad de colores, f
variety /və'raiiti/ n variedad, f; diversidad, f; (choice) surtido, m. **v. show,** función de variedades, f
various /'veəriəs/ a vario, diverso; diferente
variously /'veəriəsli/ adv diversamente
varix /'veəriks/ n várice, f
varnish /'varniʃ/ n barniz, m. vt barnizar; (pottery) vidriar; (conceal) disimular. **copal v.,** barniz copal, m. **japan v.,** charol japonés, m. **lacquer v.,** laca, f. **v. remover,** (for nails) quitaesmalte, m
varnishing /'varniʃiŋ/ n barnizado, m; (of pottery) vidriado, m
vary /'veəri/ vt variar; cambiar; diversificar; modificar. vi variar; cambiar; (be different) ser distinto (de); (deviate) desviarse (de); (disagree) estar en desacuerdo, distar, estar en contradicción. **to v. directly (indirectly),** Math. variar en razón directa (inversa)
varying /'veəriiŋ/ a variante, cambiante, diverso
vascular /'væskyələr/ a vascular
vase /veis, veiz, vaz/ n vaso, jarrón, m; urna, f
vaseline /'væsə,lin/ n vaselina, f
vassal /'væsəl/ n vasallo (-lla); esclavo (-va), siervo (-va). a tributario
vast /væst/ a vasto, extenso; enorme; grande. n vastedad, inmensidad, f
vastly /'væstli/ adv enormemente; muy; con mucho
vastness /'væstnis/ n vastedad, extensión, f; inmensidad, f; enormidad, f, gran tamaño, m; grandeza, f
vat /væt/ n cuba, tina, f; alberca, f, estanque, m. **dyeing vat,** cuba de tintorero, f. **tanning vat,** noque, m. **wine vat,** lagar, m
Vatican /'vætikən/ a and n Vaticano, m
vaticinate /və'tisə,neit/ vt and vi vaticinar, profetizar
vaticination /və,tisə'neiʃən/ n vaticinio, m, predicción, f
vaudeville /'vɔdvil/ n vodevil, m, zarzuela cómica, f
vault /vɔlt/ n Archit. bóveda, f; caverna, f; (for wine) bodega, cueva, f; (in a bank) cámara acorazada, f; (in a church) cripta, f; sepultura, f; (of the sky) bóveda celeste, f; (leap) salto, m; voltereta, f. vi (jump) saltar; (with a pole) saltar con pértiga; saltar por encima de; voltear. vt Archit. abovedar; saltar
vaulted /'vɔltid/ a abovedado
vaulter /'vɔltər/ n saltador (-ra)
vaulting /'vɔltiŋ/ n construcción de bóvedas, f; bóvedas, f pl; edificio abovedado, m; (jumping) salto, m. **v.-horse,** potro de madera, m
vaunt /vɔnt/ vi jactarse (de), hacer gala (de); triunfar (sobre). vt ostentar, sacar a relucir; (praise) alabar. n jactancia, f
veal /vil/ n ternera, f. **v.-cutlet,** chuleta de ternera, f
vector /'vektər/ n vector, m
Veda /'veidə/ n Veda, m
veer /viər/ vi (of the wind) girar; (of a ship) virar; Fig. cambiar (de opinión, etc.). vt virar
vegetable /'vedʒtəbəl/ n vegetal, m; legumbre, f; pl vegetables, (green and generally cooked) verduras, f pl; (raw green) hortalizas, f pl. **v. dish,** fuente de legumbres, f. **v. garden,** huerto de legumbres, m; **v. ivory,** marfil vegetal, m. **v. kingdom,** reino vegetal, m. **v. soup,** sopa de hortelano, f
vegetal /'vedʒitl/ a vegetal
vegetarian /ˌvedʒi'teəriən/ a and n vegetariano (-na)
vegetarianism /ˌvedʒi'teəriə,nizəm/ n vegetarianismo, m
vegetate /'vedʒi,teit/ vi vegetar
vegetation /ˌvedʒi'teiʃən/ n vegetación, f
vehemence /'viəməns/ n vehemencia, f; violencia, f; impetuosidad, f; pasión, f, ardor, m
vehement /'viəmənt/ a vehemente; violento; impetuoso; apasionado

vehemently /'viəməntli/ adv con vehemencia; violentamente; con impetuosidad; apasionadamente
vehicle /'viikəl/ n vehículo, m; (means) medio, m; instrumento, m
vehicular /vi'hikyələr/ a vehicular, de los vehículos; de los coches. **v. traffic,** circulación de los coches, f; los vehículos
veil /veil/ n velo, m; (curtain) cortina, f; (disguise) disfraz, m; (excuse) pretexto, m; (appearance) apariencia, f. vt velar; cubrir con un velo; (hide) tapar, encubrir; (dissemble) disimular; (disguise) disfrazar. **to take the v.,** tomar el velo, profesar
vein /vein/ n (Anat., Bot.) vena, f; (Geol., Mineral.) veta, f, filón, m; (in wood) fibra, hebra, f; (Fig. streak) rasgo, m; (inspiration) vena, f; (mood) humor, m
veined, veiny /veind/ 'veini/ a venoso; de venas; veteado
velar /'vilər/ a velar
vellum /'veləm/ n vitela, f
velocity /və'lɒsiti/ n velocidad, f; rapidez, f
velodrome /'vilə,droum/ n velódromo, f
velours /və'lʊr/ n terciopelo, m
velvet /'velvit/ n terciopelo, m, a hecho de terciopelo; aterciopelado
velveteen /ˌvelvi'tin/ n pana, f, velludillo, m
velvety /'velviti/ a aterciopelado
venal /'vinl/ a venal
venality /vi'næliti/ n venalidad, f
vend /vend/ vt vender
vendor /'vendər/ n vendedor (-ra)
veneer /və'niər/ vt chapear, taracear; (conceal) disimular, disfrazar. n taraceado, chapeado, m; (plate) chapa, hoja para chapear, f; (Fig. gloss) barniz, m, apariencia, f
venerability /ˌvenərə'biliti/ n venerabilidad, respetabilidad, f
venerable /'venərəbəl/ a venerable
venerate /'venə,reit/ vt venerar, reverenciar
veneration /ˌvenə'reiʃən/ n veneración, f
venerator /'venə,reitər/ n venerador (-ra)
venereal /və'niəriəl/ a venéreo. **v. disease,** enfermedad venérea, f
Venetian /və'niʃən/ a and n veneciano (-na). **v. blinds,** persianas, celosías, f pl
Venezuelan /ˌvenə'zweilən/ a and n venezolano (-na)
vengeance /'vendʒəns/ n venganza, f
vengeful /'vendʒfəl/ a vengativo
venial /'viniəl/ a venial
veniality /ˌvini'æliti/ n venialidad, f
Venice /'venis/ Venecia, f
venison /'venəsən/ n venado, m
venom /'venəm/ n veneno, m
venomous /'venəməs/ a venenoso; maligno, malicioso
venomously /'venəməsli/ adv con malignidad, maliciosamente
venomousness /'venəməsnis/ n venenosidad, f; malignidad, f
venous /'vinəs/ a venoso
vent /vent/ n abertura, f; salida, f; (air-hole) respiradero, m; (in pipes) ventosa, f; (in fire-arms) oído, m; Anat. ano, m; (Fig. outlet) desahogo, m; expresión, f. vt dejar escapar; (pierce) agujerear; (discharge) emitir, vomitar; (relieve) desahogar; expresar, dar expresión (a), dar rienda suelta (a)
venter /'ventər/ n Law. vientre, m
ventilate /'ventl,eit/ vt ventilar; discutir
ventilation /ˌventl'eiʃən/ n ventilación, f
ventilator /'ventl,eitər/ n ventilador, m
ventricle /'ventrikəl/ n ventrículo, m
ventriloquism /ven'trilə,kwizəm/ n ventriloquia, f
ventriloquist /ven'triləkwist/ n ventrílocuo (-ua)
venture /'ventʃər/ n ventura, f; riesgo, m; aventura, f; especulación, f. vt arriesgar, aventurar; (stake) jugar; (state) expresar. vi aventurarse; (dare) atreverse, osar; permitirse. **at a v.,** a la ventura. **to v. on,** arriesgarse a; probar ventura con; lanzarse a; (a remark) permitirse. **to v. out,** atreverse a salir

venturesome /'vɛntʃərsəm/ a atrevido, audaz; (dangerous) arriesgado, peligroso

venturesomeness /'vɛntʃərsəmnɪs/ n atrevimiento, m, temeridad, f; (risk) riesgo, peligro, m

Venus /'vinəs/ n (planet) Venus, m; (woman) venus, f

veracious /və'reiʃəs/ a veraz, verídico; verdadero

veracity /və'ræsiti/ n veracidad, f; verdad, f

veranda /və'rændə/ n veranda, f

verb /vɜrb/ n verbo, m. **auxiliary v.**, verbo auxiliar, m. **intransitive v.**, verbo intransitivo (neutro), m. **reflexive v.**, verbo reflexivo, m. **transitive v.**, verbo transitivo, m

verbal /'vɜrbəl/ a verbal

verbally /'vɜrbəli/ adv de palabra, verbalmente

verbatim /vɜr'beitim/ a textual. adv textualmente, palabra por palabra

verbiage /'vɜrbiidʒ/ n verbosidad, palabrería, f

verbose /vɜr'bous/ a verboso, prolijo

verbosity /vɜr'bɒsiti/ n verbosidad, f

verdancy /'vɜrdn̩si/ n verdura, f, verdor, m

verdant /'vɜrdnt/ a verde

verdict /'vɜrdɪkt/ n Law. veredicto, fallo, m, sentencia, f; opinión, f, juicio, m. **to bring in a v.**, fallar sentencia.

verdigris /'vɜrdɪˌgris/ n cardenillo, verdín, m

verdure /'vɜrdʒər/ n verdura, f, verdor, m; Fig. lozanía, f

verge /vɜrdʒ/ n (wand) vara, f; (edge) margen, borde, m; (of a lake, etc.) orilla, f; (horizon) horizonte, m; Fig. víspera, f, punto, m. **on the v. of**, al margen de, a la orilla de. **to be on the v. of**, Fig. estar a punto de; estar en vísperas de

verger /'vɜrdʒər/ n macero, m; (in a church) pertiguero, m

verifiable /ˌvɛrə'faiəbəl/ a verificable

verification /ˌvɛrəfɪ'keiʃən/ n verificación, f

verifier /'vɛrəˌfaiər/ n verificador (-ra)

verify /'vɛrəˌfai/ vt verificar, confirmar; probar

verily /'vɛrəli/ adv de veras, en verdad

verisimilitude /ˌvɛrəsɪ'mɪlɪˌtud/ n verosimilitud, f

veritable /'vɛritəbəl/ a verdadero

veritably /'vɛritəbli/ adv verdaderamente

verity /'vɛriti/ n verdad, f

vermicelli /ˌvɜrmɪ'tʃɛli/ n fideos, m pl

vermilion /vɜr'mɪlyən/ n bermellón, m

vermin /'vɜrmɪn/ n bichos dañinos, m pl; (insects) parásitos, m pl

vermouth /vɜr'muθ/ n vermut, m

vernacular /vɜr'nækyələr/ a vernáculo; nativo; vulgar. n lengua popular, f; lenguaje vulgar, m

versatile /'vɜrsətl/ a Zool. versátil; inconstante, voluble; (clever) de muchos talentos; de muchos intereses; adaptable; completo, cabal

versatility /ˌvɜrsə'tɪliti/ n (cleverness) muchos talentos, m pl; adaptabilidad, f

verse /vɜrs/ n verso, m; (stanza) estrofa, f; (in the Bible) versículo, m; (poetry) poesía, f, versos, m pl. **to make verses**, escribir versos

versed /vɜrst/ a versado, experimentado

versicle /'vɜrsɪkəl/ n versículo, m

versification /ˌvɜrsəfɪ'keiʃən/ n versificación, f

versifier /'vɜrsəˌfaiər/ n versificador (-ra)

versify /'vɜrsəˌfai/ vt and vi versificar

version /'vɜrʒən/ n versión, f; traducción, f; interpretación, f

versus /'vɜrsəs/ prep contra

vertebra /'vɜrtəbrə/ n vértebra, f

vertebral /'vɜrtəbrəl/ a vertebral

vertebrate /'vɜrtəbrɪt/ n vertebrado, m

vertex /'vɜrtɛks/ n (Geom., Anat.) vértice, m; Astron. cenit, m; cumbre, f

vertical /'vɜrtɪkəl/ a vertical

verticality /ˌvɜrtɪ'kæliti/ n verticalidad, f

vertiginous /vɜr'tɪdʒənəs/ a vertiginoso

vertigo /'vɜrtɪˌgou/ n vértigo, f

verve /vɜrv/ n brío, m, fogosidad, f

very /'vɛri/ a mismo; (mere) mero; (true) verdadero; (with adjective and comparative) más grande; Inf. mismísimo; (complete) perfecto, completo. **The v. thought of it made him laugh**, Sólo con pensarlo se

rió (or La mera idea le hizo reír). **this v. minute**, este mismísimo instante. **the v. day**, el mismo día

very /'vɛri/ adv muy; mucho; demasiado; (exactly) exactamente; completamente; absolutamente. **He is v. worried**, Está muy preocupado. **He is not v. well**, (i.e. rather ill) Está bastante bien. **This cloth is the v. best**, Esta tela es la mejor que hay. **I like it v. much**, Me gusta muchísimo. **He is v. much pleased**, Está muy contento. **so v. little**, tan poco; tan pequeño. **v. well**, muy bien

vesicle /'vɛsɪkəl/ n vesícula, f

vesper /'vɛspər/ n estrella vespertina, f, héspero, m; pl **vespers**, Eccl. vísperas, f pl

vessel /'vɛsəl/ n vasija, f, recipiente, m; (boat) barco, buque, m; (Anat., Bot.) vaso, m

vest /vɛst/ n camiseta, f; (waistcoat) chaleco, m. vt vestir; (with authority, etc.) revestir de; (property, etc.) hacer entrega de, ceder. vi tener validez; (dress) vestirse. **vested interests**, intereses creados, m pl. **v.-pocket**, bolsillo del chaleco, m. **v.-pocket camera**, cámara de bolsillo, f

vestal /'vɛstl/ a vestal; virgen, casto. n vestal, f; virgen, f

vestibule /'vɛstəˌbyul/ n vestíbulo, m; (anteroom) antecámara, f; (of a theatre box) antepalco, m; Anat. vestíbulo, m

vestige /'vɛstɪdʒ/ n vestigio, rastro, m; sombra, f; Biol. rudimento, m

vestment /'vɛstmənt/ n hábito, m; Eccl. vestidura, f

vestry /'vɛstri/ n vestuario, m, sacristía, f

vesture /'vɛstʃər/ n traje, hábito, m, vestidura, f

Vesuvius /və'suviəs/ Vesubio, m

veteran /'vɛtərən/ a veterano; de los veteranos; aguerrido; anciano; experimentado. n veterano (-na)

veterinary /'vɛtərəˌnɛri/ a veterinario. **v. science**, veterinaria, f. **v. surgeon**, veterinario, m

veto /'vitou/ n veto, m; prohibición, f. vt poner el veto; prohibir

vex /vɛks/ vt contrariar, irritar; enojar; (make impatient) impacientar; fastidiar; (afflict) afligir, acongojar; (worry) inquietar

vexation /vɛk'seiʃən/ n contrariedad, irritación, f; enojo, enfado, m; (impatience) impaciencia, f; fastidio, m; aflicción, f; inquietud, f; disgusto, m

vexatious /vɛk'seiʃəs/ a irritante; enojoso, enfadoso; fastidioso, molesto

vexatiousness /vɛk'seiʃəsnɪs/ n fastidio, m, molestia, f; incomodidad, f; contrariedad, f

vexed /vɛkst/ a discutido; contencioso; (thorny) espinoso, difícil

vexing /'vɛksɪŋ/ a irritante; molesto; enfadoso

via /'vaiə, 'viə/ n vía, f, prep por, por la vía de

viability /ˌvaiə'bɪliti/ n viabilidad, f

viable /'vaiəbəl/ a viable

viaduct /'vaiəˌdʌkt/ n viaducto, m

vial /'vaiəl/ n frasco, m, ampolleta, f

vibrant /'vaibrənt/ a vibrante

vibrate /'vaibreit/ vi vibrar; (of machines) trepidar; oscilar. vt hacer vibrar, vibrar

vibration /vai'breiʃən/ n vibración, f; trepidación, f; oscilación, f, Lat. Am. cimbrón, m

vibrator /'vaibreitər/ n Elec. vibrador, m; Radio. oscilador, m

vicar /'vɪkər/ n vicario, m; (of a parish) cura, m. **v.-general**, vicario general, m

vicarious /vai'kɛəriəs/ a vicario; sufrido por otro; experimentado por otro

vicariously /vai'kɛəriəsli/ adv por delegación; por substitución. **I know it only v.**, Lo conozco sólo por referencia

vice /vais/ n vicio, m; defecto, m; (in a horse) vicio, resabio, m; (tool) tornillo de banco, m, prefix vice. **v.-admiral**, vicealmirante, m. **v.-chairman**, vicepresidente (-ta). **v.-chancellor**, vicecanciller, m. **v.-consul**, vice-cónsul, m. **v.-consulate**, vice-consulado, m. **v.-president**, vicepresidente (-ta)

viceroy /'vaisrɔi/ n virrey, m

vice versa /'vaisə ˌvɜrsə, 'vais-/ adv viceversa

vicinity /vɪ'sɪnɪti/ n vecindad, f; (nearness) cercanía, proximidad, *f.* **to be in the v. of,** estar en la vecindad de

vicious /'vɪʃəs/ *a* vicioso. **v. circle,** círculo vicioso, *m*

viciousness /'vɪʃəsnɪs/ *n* viciosidad, *f*; (in a horse) resabios, *m pl*

vicissitude /vɪ'sɪsɪˌtud/ *n* vicisitud, *f*

vicissitudinous /vɪˌsɪsɪ'tudnəs/ *a* accidentado, vicisitudinario

victim /'vɪktəm/ *n* víctima, *f*

victimization /ˌvɪktəmə'zeɪʃən/ *n* sacrificio, *m*; tormento, *m*

victimize /'vɪktəˌmaiz/ *vt* hacer víctima (de); sacrificar; ser víctima (de), sufrir; (cheat) estafar, engañar

victor /'vɪktər/ *n* víctor (-ora), vencedor (-ora)

victoria /vɪk'tɔriə/ *n* victoria, *f*

Victorian /vɪk'tɔriən/ *a* victoriano

victorious /vɪk'tɔriəs/ *a* victorioso, triunfante. **to be v.,** triunfar, salir victorioso

victoriously /vɪk'tɔriəsli/ *adv* victoriosamente, triunfalmente

victory /'vɪktəri/ *n* victoria, *f*

victual /'vɪtl̩/ *n* vitualla, vianda, *f*; *pl* **victuals,** víveres, *m pl,* provisiones, *f pl. vt* avituallar; abastecer. *vi* tomar provisiones

victualler /'vɪtlər/ *n* abastecedor (-ra), proveedor (-ra)

victualling /'vɪtl̩ɪŋ/ *n* abastecimiento, *m*

vide /'wide, 'vaidi, 'videi/ *Latin imperative* véase, véanse

videlicet /wɪ'deilɪˌkɛt, vi'deləsɪt/ *adv* a saber

video /'vɪdiˌou/, *n* vídeo, *m*

videocassette /'vɪdioukəˌsɛt/ *n* videocasete, *f*

videotape /'vɪdiouˌteip/ *n* videograbación, videocinta, *f*

vie /vai/ *vi* (with) competir con; rivalizar con; (with a person for) disputar; luchar con

Vienna /vi'ɛnə/ Viena, *f*

Viennese /ˌviə'niz/ *a* and *n* vienés (-esa)

view /vyu/ *n* vista, *f*; perspectiva, *f*, panorama, *m*; (landscape) paisaje, *m*; escena, *f*; inspección, *f*; (judgment) opinión, *f*, parecer, *m*; consideración, *f*; (appearance) apariencia, *f*; aspecto, *m*; (purpose) propósito, *m*, intención, *f*; (sight) alcance de la vista, *m*; (show) exposición, *f. vt* examinar; inspeccionar; (look at) mirar; (see) ver, contemplar; considerar. **in v. of,** en vista de. **in my v.,** en mi opinión, según creo yo. **on v.,** a la vista. **to keep in v.,** no perder de vista; *Fig.* no olvidar, tener presente. **to take a different v.,** pensar de un modo distinto. **to v. a house,** inspeccionar una casa. **with a v. to,** con el propósito de. **v.-finder,** enfocador, *m.* **v.-point,** punto de vista, *m*

viewer /'vyuər/ *n* espectador (-ra); examinador (-ra)

viewing /'vyuɪŋ/ *n* inspección, *f*, examen, *m*

vigil /'vɪdʒəl/ *n* vela, vigilia, *f*; *Eccl.* vigilia, *f*

vigilance /'vɪdʒələns/ *n* vigilancia, *f*, desvelo, *m*

vigilant /'vɪdʒələnt/ *a* vigilante, desvelado

vigilantly /'vɪdʒələntli/ *adv* vigilantemente

vignette /vɪn'yɛt/ *n* viñeta, *f*

vigor /'vɪgər/ *n* vigor, *m*, fuerza, *f*

vigorous /'vɪgərəs/ *a* vigoroso, enérgico, fuerte; *Argentina* alentado

vigorously /'vɪgərəsli/ *adv* con vigor

Viking /'vaikɪŋ/ *n* vikingo, *m*

vile /vail/ *a* vil; bajo; despreciable; infame; *Inf.* horrible

vilely /'vaili/ *adv* vilmente; *Inf.* mal, horriblemente

vileness /'vailnɪs/ *n* vileza, *f*; bajeza, *f*; infamia, *f*

vilification /ˌvɪləfɪ'keiʃən/ *n* vilipendio, *m*, difamación, *f*

vilifier /'vɪləˌfaiər/ *n* difamador (-ra)

vilify /'vɪləˌfai/ *vt* vilipendiar, difamar

villa /'vɪlə/ *n* villa, torre, casa de campo, *f*; hotel, *m*

village /'vɪlɪdʒ/ *n* aldea, *f*, pueblo, *m*. **v. shop** *Lat. Am.* esquina, *f*

villager /'vɪlɪdʒər/ *n* aldeano (-na)

villain /'vɪlən/ *n* *Hist.* villano, *m*; malvado, *m*

villainous /'vɪlənəs/ *a* malvado; infame; vil

villainously /'vɪlənəsli/ *adv* vilmente

villainy /'vɪləni/ *n* vileza, infamia, maldad, *f*

vindicate /'vɪndɪˌkeit/ *vt* vindicar, justificar; defender

vindication /ˌvɪndɪ'keiʃən/ *n* vindicación, justificación, *f*; defensa, *f*

vindicative /vɪn'dɪkətɪv/ *a* vindicativo, vindicador, justificativo

vindicator /'vɪndɪˌkeitər/ *n* vindicador (-ra)

vindictive /vɪn'dɪktɪv/ *a* vengativo; rencoroso

vindictively /vɪn'dɪktɪvli/ *adv* vengativamente; rencorosamente

vindictiveness /vɪn'dɪktɪvnɪs/ *n* deseo de venganza, *m*; rencor, *m*

vine /vain/ *n* vid, parra, *f*; (twining plant) enredadera, *f.* **v.-arbor,** emparrado, *m.* **v.-branch,** sarmiento, *m.* **v.-clad,** cubierto de parras. **v.-grower,** vinicultor, *m.* **v.-growing,** vinicultura, *f.* **v.-leaf,** hoja de parra, *f.* **v.-pest,** filoxera, *f.* **v.-stock,** cepa, *f*

vinegar /'vɪnɪgər/ *n* vinagre, *m.* **v.-cruet,** vinagrera, *f.* **v.-sauce,** vinagreta, *f*

vinegary /'vɪnɪgəri/ *a* vinagroso

vineyard /'vɪnyərd/ *n* viña, *f*, viñedo, *m.* **v.-keeper,** viñador, *m*

vinification /ˌvɪnəfɪ'keiʃən/ *n* vinificación, *f*

vinosity /vai'nɒsɪti/ *n* vinosidad, *f*

vinous /'vainəs/ *a* vinoso

vintage /'vɪntɪdʒ/ *n* vendimia, *f*; (of wine) cosecha (de vino), *f*

vintner /'vɪntnər/ *n* vinatero, *f*

viola /vi'oulə/ *n* (*Mus., Bot.*) viola, *f.* **v. player,** viola, *mf*

violate /'vaiəˌleit/ *vt* (desecrate) profanar; (infringe) contravenir, infringir; (break) romper; (ravish) violar

violation /ˌvaiə'leiʃən/ *n* profanación, *f*; (infringement) contravención, *f*; (rape) violación, *f*

violator /'vaiəˌleitər/ *n* violador (-ra); (ravisher) violador, *m*

violence /'vaiələns/ *n* violencia, *f*

violent /'vaiələnt/ *a* violento

violently /'vaiələntli/ *adv* con violencia

violet /'vaiəlɪt/ *n* violeta, *f. a* violado, **v. color,** violeta, color violado, *m*

violin /ˌvaiə'lɪn/ *n* violín, *m*

violinist /ˌvaiə'lɪnɪst/ *n* violinista, *mf*

violoncellist /ˌvaiələn'tʃɛlɪst/ *n* violoncelista, *mf*

violoncello /ˌvaiələn'tʃɛlou/ *n* violoncelo, *m*

viper /'vaipər/ *n* víbora, *f*

viperish /'vaipərɪʃ/ *a* viperino

virago /vɪ'ragou/ *n* virago, *f*,

Virgilian /vər'dʒɪliən/ *a* virgiliano

virgin /'vɜrdʒɪn/ *n* virgen, *f*; (sign of the zodiac) Virgo, *m. a* virginal; (untouched) virgen. **the V.,** la Virgen. **v. soil,** tierra virgen, *f*

virginal /'vɜrdʒənl̩/ *a* virginal

virginity /vər'dʒɪnɪti/ *n* virginidad, *f*

Virgo /'vɜrgou/ *n* Virgo, *m*

virile /'vɪrəl/ *a* viril

virility /və'rɪlɪti/ *n* virilidad, *f*

virtual /'vɜrtʃuəl/ *a* virtual

virtue /'vɜrtʃu/ *n* virtud, *f*

virtuosity /ˌvɜrtʃu'ɒsɪti/ *n* virtuosidad, *f*

virtuoso /ˌvɜrtʃu'ousou/ *n* virtuoso (-sa)

virtuous /'vɜrtʃuəs/ *a* virtuoso

virulence /'vɪryələns/ *n* virulencia, *f*

virulent /'vɪryələnt/ *a* virulento

virulently /'vɪryələntli/ *adv* con virulencia

virus /'vairəs/ *n* virus, *m*

visa /'vizə/ *n* visado, *m*

visage /'vɪzɪdʒ/ *n* cara, *f*, rostro, *m*; semblante, aspecto, *m*

viscera /'vɪsərə/ *n* víscera, *f*

visceral /'vɪsərəl/ *a* visceral

viscid /'vɪsɪd/ *a* viscoso

viscosity /vɪ'skɒsɪti/ *n* viscosidad, *f*

viscount /'vai,kaunt/ *n* vizconde, *f*

viscountess /'vai,kauntɪs/ *n* vizcondesa, *f*

viscous /'vɪskəs/ *a* viscoso

visibility /ˌvɪzə'bɪlɪti/ *n* visibilidad, *f.* **poor v.,** mala visibilidad, *f*

visible /'vɪzəbəl/ *a* visible; aparente, evidente

visibly /'vɪzəbli/ *adv* visiblemente; a ojos vistas

Visigoth /'vɪzɪˌgɒθ/ *n* visigodo (-da)

Visigothic /ˌvɪzɪ'gɒθɪk/ *a* visigodo, visigótico
vision /'vɪʒən/ *n* visión, *f;* (eyesight) vista, *f.* **field of v.,** campo visual, *m*
visionary /'vɪʒə,nɛri/ *a* and *n* visionario (-ia)
visit /'vɪzɪt/ *n* visita, *f;* (inspection) inspección, *f;* (doctor's) visita de médico, *f. vt* visitar; hacer una visita (a); ir a ver; inspeccionar; (frequent) frecuentar; (Biblical) visitar. **to be visited by an epidemic,** sufrir una epidemia. **to go visiting,** ir de visita. **to pay a v.,** hacer una visita
visitation /ˌvɪzɪ'teɪʃən/ *n* visita, *f; Eccl.* visitación, *f;* (inspection) inspección, *f;* (punishment) castigo, *m*
visiting /'vɪzɪtɪŋ/ *a* de visita. **v. card,** tarjeta de visita, *f.* **v. card case,** tarjetero, *m.* **v. hours,** horas de visita, *f pl*
visitor /'vɪzɪtər/ *n* visita, *f;* (official) visitador, *m*
visor /'vaɪzər/ *n* visera, *f*
vista /'vɪstə/ *n* vista, perspectiva, *f*
visual /'vɪʒuəl/ *a* visual. **the v. arts,** las artes visuales
visualize /'vɪʒuə,laɪz/ *vt* and *vi* imaginarse, ver mentalmente
vital /'vaɪtl/ *a* vital; esencial; trascendental
vitalism /'vaɪtl,ɪzəm/ *n* vitalismo, *m*
vitality /vaɪ'tælɪti/ *n* vitalidad, *f*
vitalize /'vaɪtl,aɪz/ *vt* vitalizar, vivificar; reanimar
vitals /'vaɪtlz/ *n pl* partes vitales. *f pl; Fig.* entrañas, *f pl*
vitamin /'vaɪtəmɪn/ *n* vitamina, *f*
vitiate /'vɪʃi,eɪt/ *vt* viciar; corromper, contaminar
viticultural /ˌvɪtɪ'kʌltʃərl/ *a* vitícola
viticulture /'vɪtɪ,kʌltʃər/ *n* viticultura, *f*
vitreous /'vɪtriəs/ *a* vítreo, vidrioso
vitrification /ˌvɪtrəfɪ'keɪʃən/ *n* vitrificación, *f*
vitrify /'vɪtrə,faɪ/ *vt* vitrificar. *vi* vitrificarse
vitriol /'vɪtriəl/ *n* vitriolo, ácido sulfúrico, *m*
vitriolic /ˌvɪtri'ɒlɪk/ *a* vitriólico
Vitruvius /vɪ'truviəs/ Vitrubio, *m*
vituperable /vaɪ'tupərəbəl/ *a* vituperable
vituperate /vaɪ'tupə,reɪt/ *vt* vituperar
vituperation /vaɪ,tupə'reɪʃən/ *n* vituperio, *m*
vituperative /vaɪ'tupərətɪv/ *a* vituperador
vivacious /vɪ'veɪʃəs, vaɪ-/ *a* animado, vivaracho
vivaciously /vɪ'veɪʃəsli, vaɪ-/ *adv* animadamente
vivacity /vɪ'væsɪti, vaɪ-/ *n* vivacidad, animación, *f*
viva voce /'vaɪ'və vousi, 'vɪvə/ *a* oral. *n* examen oral, *m*
vivid /'vɪvɪd/ *a* vivo; brillante; intenso; (of descriptions, etc.) gráfico
vividly /'vɪvɪdli/ *adv* vivamente; brillantemente
vividness /'vɪvɪdnɪs/ *n* vivacidad, *f;* intensidad, *f;* (strength) fuerza, *f*
vivification /ˌvɪvəfɪ'keɪʃən/ *n* vivificación, *f*
vivify /'vɪvə,faɪ/ *vt* vivificar, avivar
vivifying /'vɪvə,faɪɪŋ/ *a* vivificante
vivisection /ˌvɪvə'sɛkʃən/ *n* vivisección, *f*
vixen /'vɪksən/ *n* raposa, zorra, *f;* (woman) arpía, *f*
viz. *adv* a saber
vizier /vɪ'zɪər, 'vɪzyər/ *n* visir, *m.* **grand v.,** gran visir, *m*
vocabulary /vou'kæbyə,lɛri/ *n* vocabulario, *m*
vocal /'voukəl/ *a* vocal. **v. cords,** cuerdas vocales, *f pl*
vocalist /'voukəlɪst/ *n* cantante, *mf.* voz, *f*
vocalization /ˌvoukələ'zeɪʃən/ *n* vocalización, *f*
vocalize /'voukə,laɪz/ *vt* vocalizar
vocation /vou'keɪʃən/ *n* vocación, *f;* oficio, *m;* empleo, *m;* profesión, *f*
vocational /vou'keɪʃənl/ *a* profesional; práctico. **v. guidance,** guía vocacional, orientación profesional, *f.* **v. training,** instrucción práctica, *f;* enseñanza de oficio, *f*
vociferate /vou'sɪfə,reɪt/ *vt* gritar. *vi* vociferar, vocear
vociferation /vou,sɪfə'reɪʃən/ *n* vociferación, *f*
vociferous /vou'sɪfərəs/ *a* (noisy) ruidoso; vocinglero, clamoroso
vociferously /vou'sɪfərəsli/ *adv* ruidosamente; a gritos
vodka /'vɒdkə/ *n* vodca, *m*
vogue /voug/ *n* moda, *f.* **in v.,** en boga, de moda
voice /vɔɪs/ *n* voz, *f. vt* expresar, interpretar, hacerse

eco de; hablar. **in a loud v.,** en voz alta. **in a low v.,** en voz baja
voiced /vɔɪst/ *a* (in compounds) de voz...; hablado
voice mail *n* correo de voz, *m*
void /vɔɪd/ *a* (empty) vacío; (vacant) vacante; deshabitado; (lacking in) privado (de), desprovisto (de); (without) sin; *Law.* inválido, nulo; sin valor. *n* vacío, *m. vt* evacuar; *Law.* anular; invalidar
voile /vɔɪl/ *n* espumilla, *f*
volatile /'vɒlətl/ *a* volátil; (light) ligero; (changeable) voluble, inconstante
volatility /ˌvɒlə'tɪlɪti/ *n* volatilidad, *f;* ligereza, *f;* volubilidad, *f*
volatilization /ˌvɒlətlə'zeɪʃən/ *n* volatilización, *f*
volatilize /'vɒlətl,aɪz/ *vt* volatilizar. *vi* volatilizarse
volcanic /vɒl'kænɪk/ *a* volcánico
volcano /vɒl'keɪnou/ *n* volcán, *m.* **extinct v.,** volcán extinto, *m*
volition /vou'lɪʃən/ *n* volición, *f;* voluntad, *f*
volley /'vɒli/ *n* (of stones, etc.) lluvia, *f;* (of firearms) descarga, *f;* (of cannon, naval guns) andanada, *f; Sports.* voleo, *m;* (of words, etc.) torrente, *m;* (of applause and as a salute) salva, *f. vt Sports.* volear; (abuse, etc.) dirigir. *vi* lanzar una descarga, hacer una descarga
volt /voult/ *n Elec.* voltio, *m;* (of a horse and in fencing) vuelta, *f.* **v.-ampere,** voltamperio, *m*
voltage /'voultɪdʒ/ *n* voltaje, *m.* **v. control,** mando del voltaje, *m*
voltaic /vɒl'teɪik/ *a* voltaico
Voltairian /voul'tɛəriən/ *a* volteriano
voltmeter /'voult,mitər/ *n* voltímetro, *m*
volubility /ˌvɒlyə'bɪlɪti/ *n* garrulidad, locuacidad, *f*
voluble /'vɒlyəbəl/ *a* gárrulo, locuaz
volume /'vɒlyum/ *n* (book) tomo, *m;* (amount, size, space) volumen, *m;* (of water) caudal (de río), *m;* (mass) masa, *f;* (of smoke) humareda, *f,* nubes de humo, *f pl*
volumed /'vɒlyumd/ *a* (in compounds) en... volúmenes, de... tomos
volumetric /ˌvɒlyə'mɛtrɪk/ *a* volumétrico
voluminous /və'lumənəs/ *a* voluminoso
voluminousness /və'lumənəsnɪs/ *n* lo voluminoso
voluntarily /ˌvɒlən'tɛrəli/ *adv* voluntariamente
voluntariness /ˌvɒlən'tɛrɪnɪs/ *n* carácter voluntario, *m*
voluntary /'vɒlən,tɛri/ *a* voluntario; espontáneo; libre; (charitable) benéfico; (intentional) intencional, deliberado. *n* solo de órgano, *m*
volunteer /ˌvɒlən'tɪər/ *n Mil.* voluntario (-ia). *a* de voluntarios. *vt* ofrecer; contribuir; expresar. *vi* ofrecerse para hacer algo; *Mil.* alistarse, ofrecerse a servir como voluntario
volunteering /ˌvɒlən'tɪərɪŋ/ *n* voluntariado, *m*
voluptuary /və'lʌptʃu,ɛri/ *n* voluptuoso (-sa); sibarita, *mf*
voluptuous /və'lʌptʃuəs/ *a* voluptuoso
voluptuously /və'lʌptʃuəsli/ *adv* voluptuosamente
voluptuousness /və'lʌptʃuəsnɪs/ *n* voluptuosidad, *f;* sensualidad, *f*
volute /və'lut/ *n Archit.* voluta, *f*
vomit /'vɒmɪt/ *n* vómito, *m. vt* vomitar; arrojar, devolver; *Central America, Mexico* deponer. *n* vómito, *m*
vomiting /'vɒmɪtɪŋ/ *n* vómito, *m*
voodoo /'vudu/ *n* vudú, *m*
voracious /vɔ'reɪʃəs/ *a* voraz
voracity /vɔ'ræsɪti/ *n* voracidad, *f*
vortex /'vɔrtɛks/ *n* torbellino, *m,* vorágine, *f; Fig.* vórtice, *m*
votary /'voutəri/ *n* devoto (-ta), adorante, *mf;* partidario (-ia)
vote /vout/ *n* voto, *m;* (voting) votación, *f;* (suffrage) sufragio, *m;* (election) elección, *f. vt* votar; asignar; nombrar; elegir; (consider) tener por. *vi* votar; dar el voto. **casting v.,** voto de calidad, *m.* **to put to the vote,** poner a votación. **to v. down,** desechar, rechazar. **v. of confidence,** voto de confianza, *m.* **v. of thanks,** voto de gracias, *m*
voter /'voutər/ *n* votante, *mf,* votador (-ra); elector (-ra)

voting /'voutɪŋ/ n votación, f; elección, f. a de votar; electoral. **v. paper,** papeleta de votación, f
votive /'voutɪv/ a votivo. **v. offering,** exvoto, m
vouch /vautʃ/ vi atestiguar, afirmar; garantizar; responder (de)
voucher /'vautʃər/ n (guarantor) fiador (-ra); (guarantee) garantía, f; (receipt) recibo, m; (proof) prueba, f; documento justificativo, m; vale, bono, m
vouchsafe /vautʃ'seif/ vt conceder, otorgar
vouchsafement /vautʃ'seifmənt/ n concesión, f, otorgamiento, m
vow /vau/ n voto, m; promesa solemne, f. vt hacer voto (de), hacer promesa solemne (de); jurar. **to take a vow,** hacer un voto
vowel /'vauəl/ n vocal, f
voyage /'vɔiidʒ/ n viaje (por mar), m; travesía, f. vi viajar por mar. **Good v.!** ¡Buen viaje!, Feliz viaje!
voyager /'vɔiidʒər/ n viajero (-ra)
vulcanite /'vʌlkə,nait/ n ebonita, f

vulcanization /,vʌlkənə'zeiʃən/ n vulcanización, f
vulcanize /'vʌlkə,naiz/ vt vulcanizar
vulgar /'vʌlgər/ a vulgar; (ill-bred) ordinario, cursi; (in bad taste) de mal gusto; trivial; adocenado; (coarse) grosero. n vulgo, populacho, m. **v. fraction,** fracción común, f
vulgarism /'vʌlgə,rɪzəm/ n vulgarismo, m; vulgaridad, f
vulgarity /vʌl'gærɪti/ n vulgaridad, f; grosería, f; mal tono, m, cursilería, f
vulgarize /'vʌlgə,raiz/ vt vulgarizar; popularizar
vulgarly /'vʌlgərli/ adv vulgarmente; comúnmente; groseramente
Vulgate /'vʌlgeit/ n Vulgata, f
vulnerability /,vʌlnərə'bɪti/ n vulnerabilidad, f
vulnerable /'vʌlnərəbəl/ a vulnerable
vulpine /'vʌlpain/ a vulpino; astuto
vulture /'vʌltʃər/ n buitre, Argentina carancho, m
vulva /'vʌlvə/ n vulva, f

W

w /'dʌbəl,yu/ n doble u, doble v, f
wabble /'wɒbəl/ vi. See **wobble**
wad /wɒd/ n (of straw, etc.) atado, m; (of notes, etc.) rollo, m; (in a gun) taco, m. vt Sew. acolchar; (furniture) emborrar; (guns) atacar; (stuff) rellenar
wadding /'wɒdɪŋ/ n borra, f; (lining) entretela, f; (for guns) taco, m; (stuffing) relleno, m
waddle /'wɒdl/ n anadeo, m, vi anadear
waddling /'wɒdlɪŋ/ a patojo, que anadea
wade /weid/ vi and vt andar (en el agua, etc.); vadear; (paddle) chapotear. **to w. in,** entrar en el agua, etc.); Fig. meterse en. **to w. through,** (a book) leer con dificultad; estudiar detenidamente; ir por
wader /'weidər/ n el, m, (f, la) que vadea; (bird) ave zancuda, f; pl **waders,** botas de vadear, f pl
wafer /'weifər/ n (host) hostia, f; (for sealing) oblea, f; (for ices) barquillo, m
waffle /'wɒfəl/ n Cul. fruta de sartén, f
waft /wɑft/ vt llevar por el aire o encima del agua; hacer flotar; (stir) mecer; (of the wind) traer. n (fragrance) ráfaga de olor, f
wag /wæg/ n (of the tail) coleada, f; movimiento, m; meneo, m; (jester) bromista, mf. vt mover ligeramente; agitar; (of the tail) menear (la cola), colear. vi menearse; moverse; oscilar; (of the world) ir. **And thus the world wags,** Y así va el mundo
wage, wages /weidʒ; 'weidʒɪz/ n salario, m; Fig. premio, galardón, m. **minimum wage,** salario mínimo, m. **wage-earner,** asalariado (-da);
wage /weidʒ/ vt emprender; sostener; hacer. **to w. war,** hacer guerra
wager /'weidʒər/ n (bet) apuesta, f; (test) prueba, f, vt (bet) apostar; (pledge) empeñar. **to lay a w.,** hacer una apuesta
wages /'weidʒɪz/ n pl. See **wage**
waggish /'wægɪʃ/ a zumbón, jocoso; cómico
waggishness /'wægɪʃnɪs/ n jocosidad, f
waggle /'wægəl/ vt menear; mover; agitar; oscilar. vi menearse; moverse; agitarse; oscilar. n meneo, movimiento, m; oscilación, f
wagon /'wægən/ n carro, m; carreta, f; (railway) vagón, m. **w.-lit,** coche cama, m. **w.-load,** carretada, f; vagón, m
wagoner /'wægənər/ n carretero, m
waif /weif/ n niño (-ña) sin hogar; animal perdido o abandonado, m; objeto extraviado, m; objeto sin dueño, m. **waifs and strays,** niños abandonados, m pl
wail /weil/ n lamento, gemido, m; (complaint) queja, f. vi lamentarse, gemir; quejarse (de). vt lamentar, deplorar
wailer /'weilər/ n lamentador (-ra)
wailing /'weilɪŋ/ n lamentaciones, f pl, gemidos, m pl, a lamentador, gimiente
wainscot /'weinskət, -skɒt/ n entablado de madera, m. vt enmaderar; poner friso de madera (a)

waist /weist/ n cintura, f; (blouse) blusa, f; (belt) cinturón, m; (bodice) corpiño, m; (narrowest portion) cuello, m, garganta, f; Naut. combés, m. **w.-band,** pretina, f. **w.-deep,** hasta la cintura. **w.-line,** cintura, f. **w. measurement,** medida de la cintura, f. **w.-coat,** chaleco, m. **w. strap,** trincha, f
wait /weit/ vi and vt esperar, aguardar; (serve) servir. **to keep waiting,** hacer esperar. **to w. at table,** servir a la mesa. **to w. on oneself,** servirse a sí mismo; cuidarse a sí mismo; hacer las cosas por sí solo. **to w. one's time,** aguardar la ocasión. **to w. for,** (until) esperar hasta que; (of persons) esperar (a), aguardar (a); (in ambush) acechar. **to w. on line,** hacer cola. **to w. upon,** (serve) servir (a); (visit) visitar; presentar sus respetos (a); (Fig. accompany) acompañar; (follow) seguir a
wait /weit/ n espera, f; (pause) pausa, f, intervalo, m; (ambush) asechanza, f; pl **waits,** coro de nochebuena, m. **to lie in w. for,** estar en acecho para
waiter /'weitər/ n camarero, mozo, m; (tray) bandeja, f
waiting /'weitɪŋ/ n espera, f. a que espera; de espera; de servicio. **lady-in-w.,** dama de servicio, f. **w.-room,** (of a bus station, etc.) sala de espera, f; (of an office) antesala, f
waitress /'weitrɪs/ n camarera, f
waive /weiv/ vt renunciar (a); desistir (de)
wake /weik/ vi estar despierto; despertarse; (watch) velar. vt despertar; (a corpse) velar (a). n vela, f; vigilia, f; (of a corpse) velatorio, m; (holiday) fiesta, f; (of a ship) estela, f. **in the w. of,** Naut. en la estela de; después de; seguido por
wakeful /'weikfəl/ a vigilante; (awake) despierto. **to be w.,** pasar la noche en vela
wakefulness /'weikfəlnɪs/ n vigilancia, f; (sleeplessness) insomnia, f
waken /'weikən/ vi despertarse. vt despertar; (call) llamar
waking /'weikɪŋ/ a despierto; de vela. n despertar, m; (watching) vela, f
wale /weil/ n (weal) verdugo, m, huella de azote, f, vt azotar
Wales /weilz/ (País de) Gales, m
walk /wɔk/ n (pace) paso, m; (modo de) andar, m; (journey on foot) paseo, m, vuelta, f; (long) caminata, f; (promenade) paseo, m, avenida, f; (path) senda, f; (rank) clase social, f; esfera, f; profesión, f; ocupación, f. **quick w.,** paseo rápido, m; (pace) andar rápido, m. **to go for a w.,** ir de paseo. **to take a w.,** dar un paseo (or una vuelta), pasear. **to take for a w.,** llevar a paseo, sacar a paseo. **w.-out,** (strike) huelga, f. **w.-over,** triunfo, m, (or victoria, f) fácil. **w. past,** desfile, m
walk /wɔk/ vi andar; caminar; ir a pie; (take a walk) pasear, dar un paseo; (of ghosts) aparecer; (behave) conducirse. vt hacer andar; (take for a walk) sacar a

paseo; andar de una parte a otra (de), recorrer; (a specified distance) hacer a pie, andar; (a horse) llevar al paso. **to w. abroad,** dar un paseo; salir. **to w. arm in arm,** ir de bracero. **to w. past,** pasar; (in procession) desfilar. **to w. quickly,** andar de prisa. **to w. slowly,** andar despacio, andar lentamente. **to w. the hospitals,** estudiar en los hospitales. **to w. the streets,** recorrer las calles; vagar por las calles. **to w. about,** pasearse; ir y venir. **to w. after,** seguir (a), ir detrás de. **to w. along,** andar por; recorrer. **to w. away,** marcharse, irse. **to w. away with,** (win) ganar, llevarse; (steal) quitar, tomar, alzarse con. **to w. back,** volver; volver a pie, regresar a pie. **to w. down,** bajar; bajar a pie; andar por. **to w. in,** entrar en; entrar a pie en; (walk about) pasearse en. **to w. on,** seguir andando; (step on) pisar. **to w. out,** salir. **to w. over,** andar por; llevar la victoria (a); triunfar fácilmente sobre. **to w. round,** dar la vuelta a. **to w. round and round,** dar vueltas. **to w. up,** subir andando; subir. **to w. up and down,** dar vueltas, ir y venir

walker /'wɔkər/ *n* (pedestrian) peatón, *m*; andador (-ra); (promenader) paseante, *mf*

walking /'wɔkɪŋ/ *n* el andar; (excursion on foot) paseo, *m*. *a* andante; de andar; a pie; ambulante. **at a w. pace,** a un paso de andadura. **w. encyclopedia,** enciclopedia ambulante, *f*. **w. match,** marcha atlética, *f*. **w.-stick,** bastón, *m*. **w. tour,** excursión a pie, *f*

Walkyrie /wal'kɪəri/ *n* valquiria, *f*

wall /wɔl/ *n* muro, *m*; (rampart) muralla, *f*; (*Fig.* and of an organ, cavity, etc.) pared, *f*. **partition w.,** tabique, *m*. **Walls have ears,** Las paredes oyen. **w. lizard,** lagartija, *f*. **w. map,** mapa mural, *m*. **w.-painting,** pintura mural, *f*. **w.-paper,** papel pintado, *m*. **w. socket,** *Elec.* enchufe, *m*

wall /wɔl/ *vt* cercar con un muro; amurallar. **to w. in,** murar. **to w. up,** tapiar, tabicar

wallet /'wɒlɪt/ *n* cartera, *f*; bolsa de cuero, *f*

wallflower /'wɔl,flauər/ *n* alhelí, *m*

Walloon /wɒ'lun/ *a* and *n* valón (-ona)

wallop /'wɒləp/ *n* golpe, *m*, *vt* tundir; zurrar

wallow /'wɒlou/ *vi* revolcarse; encenagarse; (in riches, etc.) nadar (en). *n* revuelco, *m*

walnut /'wɔl,nʌt/ *n* (tree and wood) nogal, *m*; (nut) nuez de nogal, *f*

walrus /'wɔlrəs/ *n* morsa, *f*

waltz /wɔlts/ *n* vals, *m*. *vi* valsar

wan /wɑn/ *a* ojeroso, descolorido; (of the sky, etc.) pálido, sin color

wand /wɒnd/ *n* vara, *f*; (conductor's) batuta, *f*. **magic w.,** varita mágica, *f*

wander /'wɒndər/ *vi* errar, vagar; (deviate) extraviarse; (from the subject) desviarse del asunto; divagar; (be delirious) delirar. *vt* vagar por, errar por, recorrer

wanderer /'wɒndərər/ *n* vagabundo (-da); hombre, *m*, (*f*, mujer) errante; (traveler) viajero (-ra)

wandering /'wɒndərɪŋ/ *a* errante; vagabundo; nómada; (traveling) viajero; (delirious) delirante; (of thoughts, the mind) distraído; (of cells, kidneys, etc.) flotante. *n* vagancia, *f*; viaje, *m*; (delirium) delirio, *m*; (digression) divagación, *f*; (of a river, etc.) meandro, *m*. **the w. Jew,** el judío errante

wane /wein/ *vi* (of the moon, etc.) menguar; (decrease) disminuir (*Fig.* decay) decaer. *n* (of the moon) menguante de la luna, *f*; mengua, *f*; disminución, *f*; decadencia, *f*

waning /'weiniŋ/ *a* menguante

wanly /'wɑnli/ *adv* pálidamente; *Fig.* tristemente

wanness /'wɑnnɪs/ *n* palidez, *f*; *Fig.* tristeza, *f*

want /wɒnt/ *vt* (lack) carecer de, faltar; (need) necesitar, haber menester de; (require or wish) querer, desear; (demand) exigir; (ought) deber; (do without) pasarse sin. *vi* hacer falta; carecer (de); (be poor) estar necesitado. **I don't w. to,** No quiero, No me da la gana. **to be wanted,** hacer falta; (called) ser llamado. **You are wanted on the telephone,** Te llaman por teléfono

want /wɒnt/ *n* (lack) falta, *f*; escasez, carestía, *f*; (need) necesidad, *f*; (poverty) pobreza, indigencia, *f*; (absence) ausencia, *f*; (wish) deseo, *m*; exigencia, *f*.

in w. of, por falta de; en la ausencia de. **to be in w.,** estar en la necesidad, ser indigente

wanted /'wɒntɪd/ se necesita; (advertisement) demanda, *f*. **Estelle wants me to write a letter,** Estrella quiere que escriba una carta. **What do you w. me to do?** ¿Qué quiere Vd. que haga?; ¿En qué puedo servirle? **What does Paul w.?** ¿Qué quiere Pablo?; (require) ¿Qué necesita Pablo? **He wants (needs) a vacation,** Le hacen falta unas vacaciones, Necesita unas vacaciones

wanting /'wɒntɪŋ/ *a* deficiente (en); falto (de); (scarce) escaso; ausente; (in intelligence) menguado. *prep* (less) menos; (without) sin. **to be w. in,** carecer de

wanton /'wɒntn/ *a* (playful) juguetón; (wilful) travieso; (loose) suelto, libre; (unrestrained) desenfrenado; extravagante; excesivo; caprichoso; (dishevelled) en desorden; (reckless) indiscreto; (of vegetation) lozano; (purposeless) inútil; imperdonable; frívolo; (unchaste) disoluto; lascivo. *n* mujer disoluta, *f*; ramera, *f*; (child) niño (-ña) juguetón (-ona)

wantonly /'wɒntnli/ *adv* innecesariamente; sin motivo; excesivamente; lascivamente

war /wɑr/ *n* guerra, *f*. *a* de guerra; guerrero. *vi* guerrear. **at war with,** en guerra con. **cold war,** guerra tonta, *f*. **on a war footing,** en pie de guerra. **We are at war,** Estamos en guerra. **to be on the war-path,** *Fig. Inf.* buscar pendencia, tratar de armarla. **to declare war on,** declarar la guerra (a). **to make war on,** hacer la guerra (a). **war to the death,** guerra a muerte, *f*. **war correspondent,** corresponsal en el teatro de guerra, *m*. **war-cry,** alarido de guerra, grito de combate, grito de guerra *m*. **war-dance,** danza guerrera, *f*. **war horse,** caballo de batalla, *m*. **war loan,** empréstito de guerra, *m*. **war-lord,** adalid, caudillo, jefe militar, *m*. **war material,** pertrechos de guerra, *m pl*; municiones, *f pl*. **war memorial,** monumento a los caídos, *m*. **war minister,** Ministro de la Guerra, *m*. **war neurosis,** neurosis de guerra, *f*. **War Office,** Ministerio de la Guerra, *m*. **war plane,** avión de guerra, *m*. **war-ship,** barco (o buque) de guerra, *m*. **war-wearied,** agotado por la guerra

warble /'wɔrbəl/ *vt* and *vi* trinar; gorjear; murmurar. *n* trino, *m*; gorjeo, *m*; murmurio, *m*

ward /wɔrd/ *n* guarda, *f*; (of a minor) pupilo (-la); (of locks, keys) guarda, *f*; (of a city) barrio, distrito, *m*; (of a hospital, etc.) sala, *f*; (of a prison) celda, *f*; (fencing) guardia, *f*. **w.-room,** cuarto de los oficiales, *m*. **w. sister,** hermana de una sala de hospital, *f*

ward /wɔrd/ *vt* proteger, defender. **to w. off,** desviar; evitar

warden /'wɔrdn/ *n* guardián, *m*; director (-ra); (of a prison) alcaide, *m*; (of a church) mayordomo de la iglesia, *m*; (of a port) capitán, *m*

warder /'wɔrdər/ *n* (jailer) guardián, *m*; alabardero, guardia, *m*

wardress /'wɔrdrɪs/ *n* guardiana, *f*

wardrobe /'wɔrdroub/ *n* guardarropa, ropero, *m*; (clothes) ropa, *f*; *Theat.* vestuario, *m*. **w. trunk,** baúl mundo, *m*

ware /wɛər/ *n* mercadería, *f*; (pottery) loza, *f*; *pl* **wares,** mercancías, *f pl*

war effort *n* esfuerzo bélico, esfuerzo de guerra, esfuerzo guerrero, *m*

warehouse /*n.* 'wɛər,haus; *v.* -,hauz/ *n* almacén, *m*, *vt* almacenar

warehouseman /'wɛər,hausmən/ *n* almacenero, *m*

warfare /'wɔr,fɛər/ *n* guerra, *f*; lucha, *f*; arte militar, *m*, or *f*. **chemical w.,** guerra química, *f*

warhead /'wɔr,hɛd/ *n* (of torpedo) cabeza de combate, punto de combate, *f*; (of missile) detonante, *m*

war hero *n* héroe de guerra, *m*

war heroine *n* heroína de guerra, *f*

warily /'wɛərəli/ *adv* con cautela, cautelosamente; prudentemente

wariness /'wɛərɪnɪs/ *n* cautela, *f*; prudencia, *f*

warlike /'wɔr,laik/ *a* belicoso, guerrero; militar, de guerra; marcial. **war-spirit,** espíritu belicoso, *m*, marcialidad, *f*

warm /wɔrm/ *a* caliente; (lukewarm) tibio; (hot) caluroso; (affectionate) cordial, cariñoso, afectuoso;

(angry) acalorado; (enthusiastic) entusiasta, ardiente; (art) cálido; (of coats, etc.) de abrigo; (fresh) fresco, reciente; *Inf.* adinerado. *vt* calentar; *Fig.* encender; entusiasmar. *vi* calentarse; *Fig.* entusiasmarse (con). **to have a w. at the fire,** calentarse al lado del fuego. **to be w.,** (of things) estar caliente; (of coats, etc.) ser de abrigo; (of the weather) hacer calor; (of people) tener calor. **to grow w.,** calentarse; (grow angry) excitarse, agitarse; (of a discussion) hacerse acalorado. **to keep w.,** conservar caliente; calentar. **to keep oneself w.,** estar caliente, no enfriarse. **to w. up,** calentar. **w.-blooded,** de sangre caliente; ardiente. **w.-hearted,** de buen corazón; generoso; afectuoso, cordial. **w.-heartedness,** buen corazón, *m*; generosidad, *f*; cordialidad, *f*

warming /'wɔrmɪŋ/ *n* calentamiento, *m*; calefacción, *f*. *a* calentador; para calentar. **w.-pan,** calentador, *m*

warmly /'wɔrmli/ *adv* (affectionately) cordialmente, afectuosamente; con entusiasmo; (angrily) acaloradamente. **to be w.** wrapped up, estar bien abrigado

warmonger /'wɔr,mʌŋgər/ *n* atizador de guerra, belicista, fautor de guerra, fomentador de guerra, propagador (-ra) de guerra

warmth /wɔrmθ/ *n* calor, *m*

warn /wɔrn/ *vt* advertir; prevenir; amonestar; (inform) avisar

warning /'wɔrnɪŋ/ *n* advertencia, *f*; aviso, *m*; amonestación, *f*; (lesson) lección, *f*, escarmiento, *m*; alarma, *f*. *a* amonestador; de alarma. **to give w.,** prevenir, advertir; (dismiss) despedir. **to take w.,** escarmentar

warningly /'wɔrnɪŋli/ *adv* indicando el peligro; con alarma; con amenaza

warp /wɔrp/ *vt* torcer; combar; *Naut.* espiar; (the mind) pervertir. *vi* torcerse; combarse, bornearse; *Naut.* espiarse. *n* (in a fabric) urdimbre, *f*; (in wood) comba, *f*, torcimiento, *m*; *Naut.* espía, *f*. **w. and woof,** trama y urdimbre, *f*

warping /'wɔrpɪŋ/ *n* (of wood) combadura, *f*; (weaving) urdidura, *f*; *Naut.* espía, *f*; (of the mind) perversión, *f*. **w. frame,** urdidera, *f*

warrant /'wɔrənt, 'wɒr-/ *n* autoridad, *f*; justificación, *f*; autorización, *f*; garantía, *f*; decreto de prisión, *m*; orden, *f*; *Com.* orden de pago, *f*; *Mil.* nombramiento, *m*; motivo, *m*, razón, *f*. *vt* justificar; autorizar; garantizar, responder por; asegurar. **pay w.,** boletín de pago, *m*

warrantable /'wɔrəntəbəl/ *a* justificable

warrantor /'wɔrən,tɔr/ *n* garante, *mf*

warranty /'wɔrənti/ *n* autorización, *f*; justificación, *f*; *Law.* garantía, *f*

warren /'wɔrən/ *n* (for hunting) vedado, *m*; (rabbit) conejera, *f*; vivar, *m*, madriguera, *f*

warrior /'wɔriər/ *n* guerrero, *m*; soldado, *m*

Warsaw /'wɔrsɔ/ Varsovia, *f*

wart /wɔrt/ *n* verruga, *f*

wary /'wɛəri/ *a* cauto, cauteloso; prudente

wash /wɒʃ/ *vt* lavar; (dishes) fregar; (lave) bañar; (clean) limpiar; (furrow) surcar; (wet) regar, humedecer; (with paint) dar una capa de color o de metal. *vi* lavarse; lavar ropa. **Two of the crew were washed overboard,** El mar arrastró a dos de los tripulantes. **Will this material w.?** ¿Se puede lavar esta tela? ¿Es lavable esta tela? **to w. ashore,** echar a la playa. **to w. away,** (remove by washing) quitar lavando; derrubiar; (water or waves) arrastrar, llevarse. **to w. one's hands,** lavarse las manos. **to look washed out,** estar ojeroso. **to w. down,** lavar; limpiar; (remove) llevarse; (accompany with drink) regar. **to w. off,** *vt* quitar lavando; hacer desaparecer; borrar; (of waves, etc.) llevarse; (of color) desteñir. *vi* borrarse; desteñirse. **to w. up,** lavar los platos, fregar la vajilla; (cast up) desechar. **w. one's dirty laundry in public,** sacar los más sucios trapillos a la colada

wash /wɒʃ/ *n* lavadura, *f*, lavado, *m*; baño, *m*; (clothes) ropa para lavar, ropa sucia, *f*; colada, *f*; (of the waves) chapoteo, *m*; (lotion) loción, *f*; (coating) capa, *f*; (silt) aluvión, *m*. **w.-basin,** palangana, *f*; lavabo, *m*. **w.-board,** tabla de lavar, *f*. **w.-house,** lavadero, *m*. **w.-leather,** gamuza, badana, *f*. **w.-out,** fracaso, *m*. **w.-stand,** aguamanil, lavabo, *m*. **w.-tub,** cuba de lavar, *f*

washable /'wɒʃəbəl/ *a* lavable

washer /'wɒʃər/ *n* lavador (-ra); (washerwoman) lavandera, *f*; (machine) lavadora, *f*; *Mech.* arandela, *f*

washerwoman /'wɒʃər,wʊmən/ *n* lavandera, *f*

washing /'wɒʃɪŋ/ *n* lavamiento, *m*; ropa sucia, ropa para lavar, *f*; ropa limpia, *f*; ropa, *f*; (bleaching) blanqueadura, *f*; (toilet) abluciones, *f pl*; *Eccl.* lavatorio, *m*; *pl* **washings,** lavazas, *f pl*. **There is a lot of w. to be done,** Hay mucha ropa que lavar. **w.-board,** tabla de lavar, *f*. **w.-day,** día de colada, *m*. **w.-machine,** lavadora, máquina de lavar, *f*. **w.-soda,** carbonato sódico, *m*. **w.-up,** lavado de los platos, *m*. **w.-up machine,** fregador mecánico de platos, *m*

wasp /wɒsp/ *n* avispa, *f*, *Lat. Am. also* jicote, *m*. **wasp's nest,** avispero, *m*. **w.-waisted,** (of clothes) ceñido, muy ajustado

waspish /'wɒspɪʃ/ *a* enojadizo, irascible; malicioso; mordaz

waste /weist/ *vt* desperdiciar, derrochar, malgastar; (time) perder; consumir; corroer; (devastate) asolar, devastar; echar a perder; malograr; disipar; agotar. *vi* gastarse; consumirse; perderse. **to w. time,** perder el tiempo. **to w. away,** (of persons) demacrarse, consumirse

waste /weist/ *n* (wilderness) yermo, desierto, *m*; (vastness) inmensidad, vastedad, *f*; (loss) pérdida, *f*; (squandering) despilfarro, derroche, *m*; disminución, *f*; (refuse) desechos, *m pl*; (of cotton, etc.) borra, *f*; disipación, *f*. *a* (of land) sin cultivar; yermo; inútil; desechado, de desecho; superfluo. **to lay w.,** devastar. **w. land,** yermo, *m*; tierras sin cultivar, *f pl*. **w. paper,** papel usado, papel de desecho, *m*. **w.-paper basket,** cesto para papeles, *m*. **w.-pipe,** desaguadero, tubo de desagüe, *m*

wasteful /'weistfəl/ *a* pródigo, derrochador, manirroto; antieconómico; ruinoso; inútil

wastefully /'weistfəli/ *adv* pródigamente; antieconómicamente; inútilmente

wastefulness /'weistfəlnɪs/ *n* prodigalidad, *f*, despilfarro, *m*; pérdida, *f*; gasto inútil, *m*; falta de economía, *f*

waster /'weistər/ *n* gastador (-ra); disipador (-ra); (loafer) golfo, *m*

watch /wɒtʃ/ *vi* velar; mirar. *vt* mirar; observar; guardar; (await) esperar; (spy upon) espiar, acechar. **to w. for,** buscar aguardar. **to w. over,** vigilar, guardar; (care for) cuidar; proteger. **watch out!** *Mexico* ¡abusado!

watch /wɒtʃ/ *n* (at night) vela, *f*; (wakefulness) desvelo, *m*; observación, vigilancia, *f*; (*Mil. Naut.*) guardia, *f*; (sentinel) centinela, *m*; (watchman) sereno, vigilante, *m*; (guard) ronda, *f*; (timepiece) reloj de bolsillo, *m*. **to be on the w.,** estar al acecho, estar al alerta, estar a la mira. **to keep w.,** vigilar. **dog w.,** media guardia, *f*. **pocket w.,** reloj de bolsillo, *m*. **wrist w.,** reloj de pulsera, *m*. **w.-case,** caja de reloj, relojera, *f*. **w.-chain,** cadena de reloj, leontina, *f*. **w.-dog,** perro guardián, *m*. **w.-glass,** cristal de reloj, *m*. **w.-making,** relojería, *f*. **w.-night,** noche vieja, *f*. **w.-spring,** muelle de reloj, *m*, espiral, *f*

watcher /'wɒtʃər/ *n* observador (-ra); espectador (-ra); (at a sick bed) el, *m*, (*f*, la) que vela a un enfermo

watchful /'wɒtʃfəl/ *a* vigilante, alerto; observador; atento, cuidadoso

watchfully /'wɒtʃfəli/ *adv* vigilantemente; atentamente

watchfulness /'wɒtʃfəlnɪs/ *n* vigilancia, *f*; cuidado, *m*; desvelo, *m*

watching /'wɒtʃɪŋ/ *n* observación, *f*; (vigil) vela, *f*

watchmaker /'wɒtʃ,meikər/ *n* relojero (-ra). **watchmaker's shop,** relojería, *f*

watchman /'wɒtʃmən/ *n* vigilante, sereno, *m*; guardián, *m*

watchword /'wɒtʃ,wɜrd/ *n* (password) consigna, contraseña, *f*; (motto) lema, *m*

water /'wɔtər/ *n* agua, *f*; (tide) marea, *f*; (of precious stones) aguas, *f pl*; (urine) orina, *f*; (quality) calidad, clase, *f*. *a* de agua; para agua; acuático; hidráulico. **fresh w.,** (not salt) agua dulce, *f*; agua fresca, *f*. **hard w.,** agua cruda, *f*. **high w.,** marea alta, *f*. **low w.,**

marea baja, *f.* **of the first w.,** de primera clase. **running w.,** agua corriente, *f.* **soft w.,** agua blanda, *f.* **to make w.,** *Naut.* hacer agua; orinar. **to take the waters,** tomar las aguas. **under w.,** *adv* debajo del agua. *a* acuático. **w.-bird,** ave acuática, *f.* **w. blister,** ampolla, *f.* **w.-boatman,** chinche de agua, *f.* **w.-borne,** flotante. **w.-bottle,** cantimplora, *f.* **w.-brash,** acedia, *f.* **w.-butt,** barril, *m,* pipa, *f.* **w.-carrier,** aguador (-ra). **w.-cart,** carro de regar, *m.* **w.-closet,** retrete, excusado, *m.* **w.-color,** acuarela, *f.* **w.-color painting,** pintura a la acuarela, *f.* **w.-colorist,** acuarelista, *mf* **w.-cooled,** enfriado por agua. **w.-cooler,** cantimplora, *f.* **w.-finder,** zahorí, *m.* **w.** front, (wharf) muelle, *m;* puerto, *m;* litoral, *m.* **w.-gauge,** indicador de nivel de agua, *m,* vara de aforar, *f.* **w.-glass,** vidrio soluble, silicato de sosa, *m.* **w. heater,** calentador de agua, *m.* **w.-ice,** helado, *m.* **w.-level,** nivel de las aguas, *m.* **w.-lily,** nenúfar, *m,* azucena de agua, *f.* **w.-line,** lengua de agua, *f;* (of a ship) línea de flotación, *f.* **w.-logged,** anegado en agua. **w.-main,** cañería maestra de agua, *f.* **w. man,** barquero, *m.* **w.-melon,** sandía, *f.* **w. mill,** aceña, *f.* **w.-nymph,** náyade, *f.* **w.-pipe,** cañería del agua, *f.* **w. pitcher,** jarro, *m.* **w. plant,** planta acuática, *f.* **w.-polo,** polo acuático, *m.* **w.-power,** fuerza hidráulica, *f.* **w.-rate,** cupo del consumo de agua, *m.* **w. snake,** culebra de agua, *f.* **w. softener,** generador de agua dulce, *m;* purificador de agua, *m.* **w. spaniel,** perro (-rra) de aguas. **w. sprite,** ondina, *f.* **w.-supply,** abastecimiento de agua, *m;* traída de aguas, *f.* **w. tank,** depósito para agua, *m.* **w. tower,** arca de agua, *f.* **w. wave,** ondulado al agua, *m.* **w.-way,** canal, río, *m,* o vía *f,* navegable. **w.-wheel,** rueda hidráulica, *f,* azud, *m;* (for irrigation) aceña, *f.* **w. wings,** nadaderas, *f pl*

water /ˈwɔtər/ *vt* (irrigate, sprinkle) regar; (moisten) mojar; (cattle, etc.) abrevar; (wine, etc.) aguar; diluir con agua; (bathe) bañar. *vi* (of animals) beber agua; (of engines, etc.) tomar agua; (of the eyes, mouth) hacerse agua. **My mouth waters,** Se me hace agua la boca

watercourse /ˈwɔtərˌkɔrs/ *n* corriente de agua, *f;* cauce, *m;* lecho de un río, *m*

watercress /ˈwɔtərˌkrɛs/ *n* berro, mastuerzo, *m*

watered /ˈwɔtərd/ *a* regado, abundante en agua; (of silk) tornasolado

watered-down /ˈwɔtərdˈdaun/ *Fig.* pasado por agua

waterfall /ˈwɔtərˌfɔl/ *n* salto de agua, *m,* cascada, catarata, *f*

wateriness /ˈwɔtərɪnɪs/ *n* humedad, *f;* acuosidad, *f*

watering /ˈwɔtərɪŋ/ *n* riego, *m;* irrigación, *f;* (of eyes) lagrimeo, *m;* (of cattle, etc.) el abrevar (a); *Naut.* aguada, *f.* **w.-can,** regadera, *f.* **w.-cart,** carro de regar, *m.* **w.-place,** (for animals) aguadero, *m;* (for cattle) abrevadero, *m;* (spa) balneario, *m;* (by the sea) playa de veraneo, *f*

watermark /ˈwɔtərˌmɑrk/ *n* (in paper) filigrana, *f;* nivel del agua, *m. vt* filigranar

waterproof /ˈwɔtərˌpruf/ *a* impermeable; a prueba de agua. *n* impermeable, *m. vt* hacer impermeable, impermeabilizar

water-repellent /ˈwɔtərrɪˌpɛlənt/ *a* repelente al agua

watershed /ˈwɔtərˌʃɛd/ *n* vertiente, *f;* línea divisoria de las aguas, *f;* (river-basin) cuenca, *f*

waterspout /ˈwɔtərˌspaut/ *n* bomba marina, manga, trompa, *f*

watertight /ˈwɔtərˌtait/ *a* impermeable, estanco; a prueba de agua; (of arguments, etc.) irrefutable

watertightness /ˈwɔtərˌtaitnɪs/ *n* impermeabilidad, *f*

waterworks /ˈwɔtərˌwɜrks/ *n* establecimiento para la distribución de agua, *m;* obras hidráulicas, *f pl*

watery /ˈwɔtəri/ *a* (wet) húmedo; acuoso; (of the sky) de lluvia; (of eyes) lagrimoso, lloroso; (sodden) mojado; (of soup, etc.) claro; insípido

watt /wɒt/ *n* vatio, *m.* **w. hour,** vatio hora, *m.* **w.-meter,** vatímetro, *m*

wattage /ˈwɒtɪdʒ/ *n* vatiaje, *m*

wattle /ˈwɒtl/ *n* zarzo, *m;* (of turkey) barba, *f;* (of fish) barbilla, *f*

wave /weiv/ *vi* ondear; ondular; flotar; hacer señales. *vt* (brandish) blandir; agitar; (the hair) ondular; ondear; hacer señales (de). **They waved goodby**

to him, Le hicieron adiós con la mano; Le hicieron señas de despedida; Se despidieron de él agitando el pañuelo

wave /weiv/ *n* (of the sea) ola, *f; Phys.* onda, *f;* (in hair or a surface) ondulación, *f;* (movement) movimiento, *m;* (of anger, etc.) ráfaga, *f.* **long w.,** onda larga, *f.* **medium w.,** onda media, *f.* **short w.,** onda corta, *f.* **sound w.,** onda sonora, *f.* **to have one's hair waved,** hacerse ondular el pelo. **w. band,** franja undosa, escala de longitudes de onda, *f.* **w. crest,** cresta de la ola, cabrilla, *f.* **w.-length,** longitud de onda, *f*

wavelet /ˈweivlɪt/ *n* pequeña ola, olita, *f;* (ripple) rizo (del agua), *m*

wave of immigration *n* una imigración, *f*

waver /ˈweivər/ *vi* ondear; oscilar; (hesitate) vacilar, titubear; (totter) tambalearse; (weaken) flaquear

waverer /ˈweivərər/ *n* irresoluto (-ta), vacilante, *m*

wavering /ˈweivərɪŋ/ *n* vacilación, irresolución, *f. a* oscilante; vacilante, irresoluto; flotante

waving /ˈweivɪŋ/ *n* ondulación, *f;* oscilación, *f;* agitación, *f;* movimiento, *m. a* ondulante; oscilante; que se balancea

wavy /ˈweivi/ *a* ondulado; flotante

wax /wæks/ *n* cera, *f;* (cobblers') cerote, *m;* (in the ear) cerilla, *f. a* de cera. *vt* encerar. *vi* crecer; hacerse; ponerse. **to wax enthusiastic,** entusiasmarse. **waxed paper,** papel encerado, *m.* **wax chandler,** cerero, *m.* **wax doll,** muñeca de cera, *f.* **wax modeling,** modelado en cera, ceroplástica, *f.* **wax taper,** blandón, *m*

waxen /ˈwæksən/ *a* de cera; como la cera; de color de cera

waxing /ˈwæksɪŋ/ *n* enceramiento, *m;* (of the moon) crecimiento, *m;* aumento, *m*

wax museum *n* museo de cera, *m*

waxwork /ˈwæksˌwɜrk/ *n* figura de cera, *f*

waxy /ˈwæksi/ *a.* See **waxen**

way /wei/ *n* camino, *m;* senda, *f;* paso, *m;* ruta, *f;* (railway, etc.) vía, *f;* dirección, *f;* rumbo, *m;* distancia, *f;* (journey) viaje, *m;* (sea crossing) travesía, *f;* avance, progreso, *m;* (*Naut.* etc.) marcha, *f;* método, *m;* modo, *m;* (means) medio, *m;* manera, *f;* (habit) costumbre, *f;* (behavior) conducta, *f,* modo de obrar, *m;* (line of business, etc.) ramo, *m;* (state) estado, *m,* condición, *f;* (course) curso, *m;* (respect) punto de vista, *m;* (particular kind) género, *m;* (scale) escala, *f.* **a long way off,** a gran distancia, a lo lejos. **a short way off,** a poca distancia, no muy lejos. **by way of,** pasando por; por vía de; como; por medio de; a modo de. **by the way,** de paso; durante el viaje; durante la travesía; a propósito, entre paréntesis. **in a small way,** en pequeña escala. **in a way,** hasta cierto punto; desde cierto punto de vista. **in many ways,** de muchos modos; por muchas cosas. **in no way,** de ningún modo; nada. **in the way,** en el medio. **in the way of,** en cuanto a, tocante a; en materia de. **I went out of my way to,** Dejé el camino para; Me di la molestia de. **Is this the way to...?** ¿Es este el camino a...? **Is that any way to speak to your mother?** ¿Hablas así con tu madre? **Make way!** ¡Calle! **Milky Way,** vía láctea, *f.* **on the way,** en camino; al paso; durante el viaje. **out of the way,** puesto a un lado; arrinconado; apartado, alejado; (imprisoned) en prisión; fuera del camino; remoto; (unusual) original. **over the way,** en frente; al otro lado (de la calle, etc.). **right of w.,** derecho de paso, *m.* **The ship left on its way to...,** El barco zarpó con rumbo a... **the Way of the Cross,** vía crucis, *f.* **This way!** ¡Por aquí!; De este modo, Así. **This way to...,** "Dirección a..." A... **under way,** en camino; en marcha; en preparación. **to bar the way,** cerrar el paso. **to be in the way,** estorbar. **to be out of the way of doing,** haber perdido la costumbre de hacer (algo). **to clear the way,** abrir paso, abrir calle; *Fig.* preparar el terreno. **to force one's way through,** abrirse paso por. **to find a way,** encontrar un camino; *Fig.* encontrar medios. **to find one's way,** hallar el camino; orientarse. **to get into the way of,** contraer la costumbre de. **to get under way,** *Naut.* zarpar, hacerse a la vela; ponerse en marcha. **to give way,** ceder; (break) romper. **to go a long way,** ir lejos; contribuir mucho (a). **to have one's own way,** salir con la suya. **to keep out of the way,** *vt* and *vi* esconder(se); mantener(se) alejado; mantener(se) apartado. **to lose one's way,** perder el camino; desorientarse; *Fig.* extraviarse. **to make one's way,** abrirse paso. **to make one's way down,** bajar. **to make one's way round,** dar la vuelta a. **to make one's way up,** subir. **to make way,** hacer lugar; hacer sitio; dar paso (a). **to pay one's way,** ganarse la vida; pagar lo que se debe. **to prepare the way for,** preparar el terreno para. **to put out of the way,** poner a un lado; apartar; (kill) matar; (imprison) poner en la cárcel; hacer cautivo (a). **to see one's way,** poder ver el camino; poder orientarse; ver el modo de hacer algo; ver cómo se puede hacer algo. **ways and means,** medios y arbitrios, *m pl.* **way back,** camino de regreso, *m;* vuelta, *f.* **way down,** bajada, *f.* **way in,** entrada, *f.* **way out,** salida, *f.* **way round,** camino alrededor, *m;* solución, *f;* modo de evitar..., *m.* **way through,** paso, *m.* **way up,** subida, *f*

wayfarer /'weɪ,feərər/ *n* transeúnte, *mf;* viajero (-ra)
wayfaring /'weɪ,feərɪŋ/ *a* que va de viaje; errante, ambulante
waylay /'weɪ,leɪ/ *vt* asechar, salir al paso (de)
wayside /'weɪ,saɪd/ *n* borde del camino, *m. a* (of flowers) silvestre; (by the side of the road) en la carretera. **gone by the w.,** despil farrándose la vida
wayward /'weɪwərd/ *a* caprichoso; desobediente; voluntarioso; travieso; rebelde
waywardness /'weɪwərdnɪs/ *n* desobediencia, indocilidad, *f;* voluntariedad, *f;* travesura, *f;* rebeldía, *f*
we /wi/ *pron* nosotros, *m pl;* nosotras, *f pl,* (Usually omitted except for emphasis or for clarity.) **We are in the garden,** Estamos en el jardín. **We have come, but they are not here,** Nosotros hemos venido pero ellos no están aquí
weak /wik/ *a* débil; flojo; frágil; delicado; (insecure) inseguro; (of arguments) poco convincente; (of prices, markets, etc.) flojo, en baja; (sickly) *Lat. Am.* farruto, *Central America, Mexico* fifiriche. **w.-eyed,** de vista floja. **w.-kneed,** débil de rodillas, *Fig.* sin voluntad. **w.-minded,** sin carácter; pusilánime; **w. spot,** debilidad, *f;* flaco, *m;* lado débil, *m;* desventaja, *f*
weaken /'wikən/ *vt* debilitar; (diminish) disminuir. *vi* debilitarse; flaquear, desfallecer; (give way) ceder
weakening /'wikənɪŋ/ *n* debilitación, *f. a* debilitante; enervante
weaker /'wikər/ *a comp* más débil. **the w. sex,** el sexo débil
weakling /'wiklɪŋ/ *n* ser delicado, *m,* persona débil, *f;* cobarde, *m; Inf.* alfeñique, *m*
weakly /'wikli/ *a* enfermizo, delicado, enclenque. *adv* débilmente
weakness /'wiknɪs/ *n* debilidad, *f;* imperfección, *f*
weal /wil/ *n* bienestar, *m;* prosperidad, *f;* (blow) verdugo, *m*
wealth /wɛlθ/ *n* riqueza, *f;* abundancia, *f;* bienes, *m pl*
wealthy /'wɛlθi/ *a* rico, adinerado, acaudalado; abundante (en)
wean /win/ *vt* destetar, ablactar; separar (de); privar (de); enajenar el afecto de; (of ideas) desaferrar (de)
weaning /'winɪŋ/ *n* ablactación, *f,* destete, *m*
weapon /'wɛpən/ *n* arma, *f; pl* **weapons,** (Zool., Bot.) medios de defensa, *m pl.* **steel w.,** arma blanca, *f*
wear /wɛr/ *n* uso, *m;* gasto, *m;* deterioro, *m;* (fashion) moda, boga, *f.* **for hard w.,** para todo uso. **for one's own w.,** para su propio uso. **for evening w.,** para llevar de noche. **for summer w.,** para llevar en verano. **w. and tear,** uso y desgaste, *m;* deterioro natural, *m*
wear /wɛr/ *vt* llevar; llevar puesto; traer; usar; (have) tener; (exhibit) mostrar; (be clad in) vestir; (waste) gastar; deteriorar; (make) hacer; (exhaust) agotar, cansar, consumir. *vi* (last) durar; (of persons) conservar(se); (of time) correr; avanzar. **She wears well,** Está bien conservada. **to w. one's heart on one's sleeve,** tener el corazón en la mano. **to w. the trousers,** *Fig. Inf.* llevar los pantalones. **to w. well,** durar mucho. **to w. away,** *vt* gastar, roer; (rub out) borrar; consumir. *vi* (of time) pasar lentamente, transcurrir despacio. **to w. down,** gastar; consumir; reducir; agotar las fuerzas de; destruir; (tire) fatigar.

to w. off, *vt* destruir; borrar. *vi* quitarse; borrarse; *Fig.* desaparecer, pasar. **to w. on,** (of time) transcurrir, correr, pasar. **to w. out,** *vt* usar; romper con el uso; consumir, acabar con; (exhaust) agotar; (tire) rendir. *vi* usarse; romperse con el uso; consumirse
wearable /'wɛərəbəl/ *a* que se puede llevar
wearer /'wɛərər/ *n* el, *m,* (*f,* la) que lleva alguna cosa
weariness /'wɪərɪnɪs/ *n* cansancio, *m,* fatiga, lasitud, *f;* aburrimiento, *m;* aversión, repugnancia, *f*
wearing /'wɛərɪŋ/ *n* uso, *m;* desgaste, *m. a* (tiring) agotador; cansado. **w. apparel,** ropa, *f*
wearisome /'wɪərɪsəm/ *a* cansado; laborioso; aburrido, tedioso, pesado
wearisomeness /'wɪərɪsəmnɪs/ *n* cansancio, *m;* aburrimiento, tedio, hastío, *m*
weary /'wɪəri/ *a* cansado, fatigado; aburrido; hastiado; impaciente; tedioso, enfadoso. *vt* cansar, fatigar; aburrir; hastiar; molestar. *vi* cansarse, fatigarse; aburrirse. **to w. for,** anhelar, suspirar por; (miss) echar de menos (a). **to w. of,** aburrirse de; (things) impacientarse de; (people) impacientarse con
weasel /'wizəl/ *n* comadreja, *f*
weather /'wɛðər/ *n* tiempo, *m;* intemperie, *f;* (storm) tempestad, *f. a Naut.* del lado del viento; de barlovento. *vt* (of rain, etc.) desgastar; curtir; secar al aire; *Naut.* pasar a barlovento; (bear) aguantar, capear; (survive) sobrevivir a; luchar con. *vi* curtirse a la intemperie. **Andrew is a little under the w.,** Andrés está algo destemplado; (with drink) Andrés tiene una mona; (depressed) Andrés está melancólico. **to be bad (good) w.,** hacer mal (buen) tiempo. **What is the w. like?** ¿Qué tiempo hace? ¿Cómo está el tiempo? **w.-beaten,** curtido por la intemperie. **w. chart,** carta meteorológica, *f.* **w. conditions,** condiciones meteorológicas, *f pl.* **w. forecast,** pronóstico del tiempo, *m.* **w. forecaster,** meteorologista, *mf.* **w.-hardened,** endurecido a la intemperie. **w. report,** boletín meteorológico, *m.* **w.-worn,** gastado por la intemperie; curtido por la intemperie
weathercock /'wɛðər,kɒk/ *n* veleta, *f*
weathering /'wɛðərɪŋ/ *n* desintegración por la acción atmosférica, *f*
weather-resistant /'wɛðərɪˌzɪstənt/ *a* resistente a la intemperie
weave /wiv/ *vt* tejer; trenzar; entrelazar; *Fig.* tejer. *vi* tejer. *n* tejido, *m;* textura, *f*
weaver /'wivər/ *n* tejedor (-ra)
weaving /'wivɪŋ/ *n* tejido, *m;* tejeduría, *f.* **w. machine,** telar, *m*
web /wɛb/ *n* tejido, *m;* tela, *f;* (network) red, *f;* (spider's) telaraña, *f;* (of a feather) barba, *f;* (of birds, etc.) membrana interdigital, *f;* (of intrigue) red, *f;* (snarl) lazo, *m,* trampa, *f.* **web-foot,** pie palmado, *m.* **web-footed,** palmípedo.
webbed /wɛbd/ *a* (of feet) unido por una membrana
Web site *n* Sitio en la Red, *m*
wed /wɛd/ *vt* casarse con; (join in marriage, cause to marry) casar; *Fig.* unir. *vi* estar casado; casarse
wedded /'wɛdɪd/ *a* casado; matrimonial, conyugal; *Fig.* unido (a); aficionado (a), entusiasta de; devoto (de); aferrado (a). **to be w. to one's own opinion,** estar aferrado a su propia opinión
wedding /'wɛdɪŋ/ *n* boda, *f,* casamiento, *m;* (with golden, etc.) bodas, *f pl;* (union) enlace, *m, a* de boda, nupcial, matrimonial, conyugal; de novios, de la novia. **golden w.,** bodas de oro, *f pl.* **silver w.,** bodas de plata, *f pl.* **w. bouquet,** ramo de la novia, *m.* **w.-breakfast,** banquete de bodas, *m.* **w.-cake,** torta de la boda, *f,* pan de la boda, *m.* **w.-day,** día de la boda, *m.* **w.-march,** marcha nupcial, *f.* **w.-present,** regalo de boda, regalo de la boda, *m, Lat. Am.* argolla, *f.* **w.-ring,** anillo de la boda, *m, Lat. Am.* argolla, *f.* **w. trip,** viaje de novios, *m*
wedge /wɛdʒ/ *n* cuña, *f;* (under a wheel) calza, alzaprima, *f; Mil.* cuña, mella, *f;* (of cheese) pedazo, *m. vt* acuñar, meter cuñas; (a wheel) calzar; (fix) sujetar. **to drive a w.,** *Mil.* hacer mella, practicar una cuña. **to w. oneself in,** introducirse con dificultad (en). **w.-shaped,** cuneiforme
wedlock /'wɛd,lɒk/ *n* matrimonio, *m*
Wednesday /'wɛnzdeɪ/ *n* miércoles, *m*

wee /wi/ *a* pequeñito, chiquito. **a wee bit,** un poquito

weed /wid/ *n* mala hierba, *f*; tabaco, *m*; (cigar) cigarro, *m*; (person) madeja, *f*; (*Fig.* evil) cizaña, *f*. *vt* carpir, desherbar, sachar, sallar, escardar. *Lat. Am.* desmalezar; *Fig.* extirpar, arrancar. **w.-grown,** cubierto de malas hierbas. **to w. out,** extirpar; quitar

weeder /'widər/ *n* (person) escardador (-ra); (implement) sacho, *m*

weedy /'widi/ *a* lleno de malas hierbas; *Fig.* raquítico

week /wik/ *n* semana, *f*. **in a w.,** de hoy en ocho (días); en una semana; después de una semana. **once a w.,** una vez por semana. **a w. ago,** hace una semana. **a w. later** *Lat. Am.* a la semana. **Michael will come a w. from today,** Miguel llegará hoy en ocho. **w. in, w. out,** semana tras semana. **w.-day,** día de trabajo, día laborable, día de la semana que no sea el domingo. **on weekdays,** entre semana, *m*. **w.-end,** fin de semana, *m*. **w.-end case,** saco de noche, *m*

weekly /'wikli/ *a* semanal, semanario; de cada semana. *adv* semanalmente, cada semana. *n* semanario, *m*, revista semanal, *f*

weep /wip/ *vt* and *vi* llorar. **to w. for,** (a person) llorar (a); (on account of) llorar por; (with happiness, etc.) llorar de. **They wept for joy,** Lloraron de alegría

weeping /'wipɪŋ/ *n* lloro, llanto, *m*, lágrimas, *f pl. a* lloroso, que llora; (of trees) llorón. **w.-willow,** sauce llorón, *m*

weevil /'wivəl/ *n* gorgojo, *m*

weigh /wei/ *vt* pesar; (consider) considerar, ponderar, tomar en cuenta; comparar; (the anchor) levar. *vi* pesar; ser de importancia. **to w. anchor,** zarpar, levar el ancla, hacerse a la vela. **to w. down,** pesar sobre; sobrecargar; hacer inclinarse bajo; *Fig.* agobiar. **to be weighed down,** hundirse por su propio peso; *Fig.* estar agobiado. **to w. out,** pesar. **to w. with,** influir (en). **w.-bridge,** báscula, *f*

weighing /'weiɪŋ/ *n* pesada, *f*; (weight) peso, *m*; (of the anchor) leva, *f*; (consideration) ponderación, consideración, *f*. **w.-machine,** báscula, *f*

weight /weit/ *n* peso, *m*; (heaviness) pesantez, *f*; cargo, *m*; (of a clock and as part of a system) pesa, *f*; *Fig.* peso, *m*, importancia, *f*. *vt* cargar; (a stick) emplomar; aumentar el peso (de); poner un peso (a). **gross w.,** peso bruto, *m*. **heavy w.,** peso pesado, *m*. **light w.,** peso ligero, *m*. **middle w.,** peso medio, *m*. **net w.,** peso neto, *m*. **to lose w.,** adelgazar. **loss of w.,** (of a person) adelgazamiento, *m*. **to put on w.,** cobrar carnes, hacerse más gordo. **to put the w.,** *Sports.* lanzar el peso. **to throw one's w. about,** *Inf.* darse importancia. **to try the w. of,** sopesar. **weights and measures,** pesas y medidas, *f pl.*

weightlifting, halterofilia, *f*

weighty /'weiti/ *a* (influential) influyente; importante, de peso; grave

weir /wɪər/ *n* presa, esclusa, *f*; (for fish) cañal, *m*

weird /wɪərd/ *a* misterioso, sobrenatural; fantástico; mágico; (queer) raro, extraño

weirdly /'wɪərdli/ *adv* misteriosamente; fantásticamente; (queerly) de un modo raro, extrañamente

weirdness /'wɪərdnɪs/ *n* misterio, *m*; cualidad fantástica, *f*; lo sobrenatural; (queerness) rareza, *f*

welcome /'wɛlkəm/ *a* bienvenido; (pleasant) grato, agradable. *n* bienvenida, *f*; buena acogida, *f*; (reception) acogida, *f*. *vt* dar la bienvenida (a); acoger con alegría, acoger con entusiasmo; agasajar, festejar; (receive) acoger, recibir; recibir con gusto. **W.!** ¡Bienvenido! **to bid w.,** dar la bienvenida (a). **You are w.,** Estás bienvenido. **You are w. to it,** Está a su disposición

welcoming /'wɛlkəmɪŋ/ *a* acogedor, cordial, amistoso

weld /wɛld/ *vt* soldar; combinar; unificar

welder /'wɛldər/ *n* soldador, *m*

welding /'wɛldɪŋ/ *n* soldadura, *f*; unión, fusión, *f*

welfare /'wɛl,fɛər/ *n* bienestar, bien, *m*; (health) salud, *f*; prosperidad, *f*; intereses, *m pl.* **w. state,** estado benefactor, estado de beneficencia, estado socializante, *m*. **w. work,** trabajo social, *m*

well /wɛl/ *a* bien; (in good health) bueno; (advantageous) provechoso; favorable; (happy) feliz; (healed) curado; (recovered) repuesto. **I am very w.,**

Estoy muy bien. **to get w.,** ponerse bien. **to make w.,** curar. **w. enough,** bastante bien

well /wɛl/ *adv* bien; (very) muy; favorablemente; convenientemente; (easily) sin dificultad. **as w.,** también. **as w. as,** tan bien como; además de. **That is all very w. but...,** Todo eso está muy bien pero... **to be w. up in,** estar versado en. **to get on w. with,** llevarse bien con. **Very w.!** ¡Está bien!; Muy bien. **w. and good,** bien está. **w. now,** ahora bien. **w. then,** conque; pues bien. **w.-advised,** bien aconsejado; prudente. **w.-aimed,** certero. **w.-appointed,** bien provisto; (furnished) bien amueblado. **w.-attended,** concurrido. **w.-balanced,** bien equilibrado. **w.-behaved,** bien educado; (of animals) manso. **w.-being,** bienestar, *m*; felicidad, *f*. **w.-born,** bien nacido, de buena familia. **w.-bred,** bien criado, bien educado; (of animals) de pura raza. **w.-chosen,** bien escogido. **w.-defined,** bien definido. **w.-deserved,** bien merecido. **w.-disposed,** bien dispuesto; favorable; bien intencionado. **w.-doing,** *n* el obrar bien; obras de caridad, *f pl.* a bondadoso, caritativo. **w.-done,** *a* bien hecho. *interj* ¡bravo! **w.-educated,** instruido, culto. **w.-favored,** guapo, de buen parecer. **w.-founded,** bien fundado. **w.-groomed,** elegante. **w.-grounded,** bien fundado; bien instruido. **w.-informed,** instruido; culto, ilustrado. **w.-intentioned,** bien intencionado. **w.-known,** bien conocido, notorio, *Lat. Am.* connotado. **w.-meaning,** bien intencionado. **w.-modulated,** armonioso. **w.-off,** acomodado, adinerado; feliz. **w.-read,** culto, instruido. **w.-shaped,** bien hecho; bien formado. **w.-shaped nose,** nariz perfilada, *f*. **w.-spent,** bien empleado. **w.-spoken,** bien hablado; bien dicho. **w.-stocked,** bien provisto. **w.-suited,** apropiado. **w.-timed,** oportuno. **w.-to-do,** acomodado, rico. **w.-wisher,** amigo (-ga). **w.-worn,** raído; (of paths) trillado

well /wɛl/ *n* pozo, *m*; (of a stair) caja, *f*; (of a ship) sentina, *f*. **w.-sinker,** pocero, *m*

well /wɛl/ *vi* chorrear, manar, brotar, fluir

Welsh /wɛlʃ/ *a* galés, de Gales. *n* (language) galés, *m*. **the W.,** los galeses

Welshman /'wɛlʃmən/ *n* galés, *m*

Welshwoman /'wɛlʃ,wumən/ *n* galesa, *f*

welt /wɛlt/ *n* (of shoe) vira, *f*, cerquillo, *m*; (in knitting) ribete, *m*; (weal) verdugo, *m*

Weltanschauung /'vɛltənˌʃauəŋ/ *n* cosmovisión, postura de vida, *f*

welter /'wɛltər/ *vi* revolcarse; bañarse (en), nadar (en). *n* confusión, *f*, tumulto, *m*; mezcla, *f*. **w.-weight,** peso welter, *m*

wench /wɛntʃ/ *n* mozuela, muchacha, *f*

wend /wɛnd/ *vt* dirigir, encaminar. *vi* ir. **to w. one's way,** dirigir sus pasos, seguir su camino

west /wɛst/ *n* oeste, *m*; poniente, *m*; occidente, *m*. *a* del oeste; occidental. *adv* hacia el oeste, a poniente; al occidente. **W. Indian,** de las Antillas, de las Indias Occidentales. **w.-north-w.,** oesnorueste, *m*. **w.-south-w.,** oessudueste, *m*. **w. wind,** viento del oeste, poniente, *m*

westerly /'wɛstərli/ *a* del oeste; hacia el oeste; occidental

western /'wɛstərn/ *a* occidental; del oeste. *n* (novel) novela caballista, *f*; (film) película del oeste, *f*

Western Hemispheric americano

westernized /'wɛstərˌnaizd/ *a* influido por el occidente

westernmost /'wɛstərnˌmoust/ *a* más al oeste

West Indies /'ɪndiz/ Indias Occidentales, *f pl*

westward /'wɛstwərd/ *a* que está al oeste. *adv* hacia el oeste; hacia el occidente

wet /wɛt/ *a* mojado; húmedo; (rainy) lluvioso. *vt* mojar; humedecer. *n* (rain) lluvia, *f*. **"Mind the wet paint!"** «¡Cuidado, recién pintado!» **to be wet,** estar mojado; (of the weather) llover. **to get wet,** mojarse.

wet blanket, *Fig.* aguafiestas, *mf* **wet through,** (of persons) calado, hecho una sopa. **wet-nurse,** nodriza, *Lat. Am.* criandera, *f*

wetting /'wɛtɪŋ/ *n* mojada, *f*; humectación, *f*; (soaking) remojo, *m*

whack /wæk/ n golpe, m; (try) tentativa, f; (portion) porción, parte, f. vt golpear, aporrear, pegar

whale /weil/ n ballena, f. **sperm w.,** cachalote, m.

w.-oil, aceite de ballena, m

whalebone /'weil,boun/ n barbas de ballena, f pl, ballena, f

whaler /'weilər/ n (man) ballenero, pescador de ballenas, m; (boat) buque ballenero, m

whaling /'weilɪŋ/ a ballenero. n pesca de ballenas, f. **w.-gun,** cañón arponero, m

wharf /wɔrf/ n muelle, embarcadero, descargadero, m, vt amarrar al muelle

what /wʌt/ unstressed wət/ a pron (interrogative and exclamatory) qué; cómo; (relative) que; el que, m; la que, f; lo que, neut; los que, m pl; las que, f pl; (which, interrogative) cuál, mf; cuáles, mf pl; (how many) cuantos, m pl; cuantas, f pl; (interrogative and exclamatory) cuántos, m pl; cuántas, f pl; (how much, interrogative and exclamatory) cuánto, m; cuánta, f. **And w. not,** Y qué sé yo qué más. **Make w. changes you will,** Haz los cambios que quieras. **W. confidence he had...,** La confianza que tenía... **W. is this called?** ¿Cómo se llama esto? **W. did they go there for?** ¿Por qué fueron? **W. do you take me for?** ¿Por quién me tomas? **That was not w. he said,** No fue eso lo que dijo. **to know what's w.,** saber cuántas son cinco. **You have heard the latest news, w.?** Has oído las últimas noticias, ¿verdad? **W. a pity!** ¡Qué lástima! **W., do you really believe it?** ¿Lo crees de veras? **W. else?** ¿Qué más? **W. for?** ¿Para qué? **what's-his-name,** fulano (-na) de tal, m. **W. ho!** ¡Hola! **W. if...?** ¿Qué será si...? **W. is the matter?** ¿Qué pasa? ¿Qué hay? **w. though...,** aun cuando...; ¿Qué importa qué? **w. with one thing, w. with another,** entre una cosa y otra. **What's more,...** Es más,...

whatever /wʌt'ɛvər/ a pron cuanto; todo lo que; cualquier cosa que; cualquier. **W. sacrifice is necessary,** Cualquier sacrificio que sea necesario. **W. I have is yours,** Todo lo que tenga es vuestro. **W. happens,** Venga lo que venga. **It is of no use w.,** No sirve absolutamente para nada

wheal /wil/ n. See **weal**

wheat /wit/ n trigo, m. a de trigo. **summer w.,** trigo tremesino, m. **whole w.,** a de trigo entero. **w.-ear,** espiga de trigo, f. **w.-field,** trigal, m. **w.-sheaf,** gavilla de trigo, f

wheedle /'widl/ vt lagotear, engatusar, Lat. Am. also engaratusar; (flatter) halagar; (with out) sacar con mimos

wheedling /'widlɪŋ/ a zalamero, mimoso; marrullero. n lagotería, f, mimos, m pl; (flattery) halagos, m pl; marrullería, f

wheel /wil/ n rueda, f; (bicycle) bicicleta, f; (for steering a ship) timón, m; rueda del timón, f; (for steering a car) volante, m; (for spinning) rueca, f; (potter's) rueda de alfarero, f; (of birds) vuelo, m; (turn) vuelta, f. Mil. conversión, f. **back w.,** rueda trasera, f. **front w.,** rueda delantera, f. **to break on the w.,** enrodar. **to go on wheels,** ir en ruedas; Fig. ir viento en popa. **to take the w.,** (in a ship) tomar el timón; tomar el volante. **w. of fortune,** rueda de la fortuna, f. **w.-chair,** silla de ruedas, f. **w.-house,** timonera, f. **w.-mark,** rodada, f

wheel /wil/ vt hacer rodar; (push) empujar; (drive) conducir; transportar; llevar; pasear; (turn) hacer girar. vi girar; dar vueltas; ir en bicicleta. **to w. about,** cambiar de frente; volverse; cambiar de rumbo

wheelbarrow /'wil,bærou/ n carretilla, f

wheeled /wild/ a de... ruedas; con ruedas. **w. chair,** silla de ruedas, f

wheeler-dealer /'wilər 'dilər/ n Lat. Am. ardilla, f

wheeling /'wilɪŋ/ n rodaje, m; Mil. conversión, f; (of birds) vuelos, m pl, vueltas, f pl. **free-w.,** rueda libre, f

wheelwright /'wil,rait/ n carpintero de carretas, ruedero, m

wheeze /wiz/ vi ser asmático, jadear, respirar fatigosamente, resollar

wheezing /'wizɪŋ/ n resuello, jadeo, m; respiración fatigada, f

whelp /wɛlp/ n cachorro (-rra). vi and vt parir

when /wɛn; unstressed wən/ adv cuando (interrogative, cuándo); (as soon as) tan pronto como, en cuanto; (meaning "and then") y luego, y entonces; (although) aunque. **I will see you w. I return,** Te veré cuando vuelva. **W. he came to see me he was already ill,** Cuando vino a verme estaba enfermo ya. **We returned a week ago, since w. I have not been out,** Volvimos hace ocho días y desde entonces no he salido. **Since w.?** ¿Desde cuándo?

whence /wɛns/ adv de donde (interrogative, de dónde); a donde (interrogative a dónde); por donde, de que; por lo que. **W. does he come?** ¿De dónde viene? **W. comes it that?** ¿Cómo es que...?

whenever /wɛn'ɛvər/ adv cuando quiera que, siempre que; cada vez que, todas las veces que; cuando

where /wɛər/ adv pron donde (interrogative, dónde); en donde; en que (interrogative, en qué); (to where with verbs of motion) a donde (interrogative, a dónde); (from where with verbs of motion) de donde (interrogative, de dónde). **W. are you going to?** ¿A dónde va Vd.? **This is w. we get out,** (of a bus, etc.) Nos apeamos aquí

whereabouts /'wɛərə,bauts/ adv (interrogative) dónde; (relative) donde. n paradero, m

whereas /wɛər'æz/ conjunc (inasmuch as) visto que, ya que; (although) mientras (que)

whereat /wɛər'æt/ adv por lo cual; a lo cual

whereby /wɛər'bai/ adv cómo; por qué; por el cual, con el cual

wherefore /'wɛər,fɔr/ adv (why) por qué; por lo cual. n porqué, m

wherein /wɛər'ɪn/ adv en donde (interrogative, en dónde); en que (interrogative, en qué)

whereinto /wɛər'ɪntu/ adv en donde; dentro del cual; en lo cual

whereof /wɛər'ʌv/ adv de que; (whose) cuyo

whereon /wɛər'ɒn/ adv sobre que; en qué

whereto /wɛər'tu/ adv adonde; a lo que

whereupon /,wɛərə'pɒn/ adv dónde; sobre lo cual, con lo cual; en consecuencia de lo cual

wherever /wɛər'ɛvər/ adv dondequiera (que), en cualquier sitio; adondequiera (que). **Sit w. you like,** Siéntate donde te parezca bien

wherewith /wɛər'wɪθ, -'wɪð/ adv con que (interrogative, con qué)

wherewithal /'wɛərwɪð,ɔl, -wɪθ-/ n lo necesario; dinero necesario, m

whet /wɛt/ vt (knives, etc.) afilar, amolar, aguzar; (curiosity, etc.) excitar, estimular

whether /'wɛðər/ conjunc si; que; sea que, ya que. **W. he will or no,** Que quiera, que no quiera. **w. or not,** si o no

whetstone /'wɛt,stoun/ n afiladera, amoladera, piedra de amolar, f

whetting /'wɛtɪŋ/ n aguzadura, amoladura, f; (of curiosity, etc.) estimulación, excitación, f

whey /wei/ n suero (de la leche), m

which /wɪtʃ/ a and pron cuál, mf; cuáles, mf pl; (interrogative, qué); el cual, m; la cual, f; lo cual, neut; los cuales, m pl; las cuales, f pl; el que, m; la que, f; lo que, neut; los que, m pl; las que, f pl; (who) quien. **all of w.,** todo lo cual, etc. **in w.,** en donde, en el que; donde. **W. of the cual, etc. W. would you like?** ¿Cuál quieres? **The documents w. I have seen,** Los documentos que he visto. **W. way have we to go?** ¿Por dónde hemos de ir?

whichever /wɪtʃ'ɛvər/ a and pron cualquiera (que), mf; cualesquiera, mf pl; el que, m; la que, f; (of persons only) quienquiera (que), mf; quienesquiera (que), mf pl Give me w. you like, Dame el que quieras. **I shall take w. of you would like to come,** Me llevaré a cualquiera de Vds. que guste de venir

whiff /wɪf/ n (of air) soplo, m; vaho, m; fragancia, f

while /wail/ n rato, m; momento, m; tiempo, m. **after a w.,** al cabo de algún tiempo, después de algún tiempo. **a little w. ago,** hace poco. **all this w.,** en todo este tiempo. **at whiles,** a ratos, de vez en cuando. **between whiles,** de cuando en cuando; entre tanto. **It is worth your w. to do it,** Vale la pena de hacerse. **Mary smiled the w.,** María mientras tanto se sonreía. **once in a w.**, de vez en cuando; en ocasiones

while /wail/ *conjunc* mientras (que); al (followed by an infinitive); al mismo tiempo que; a medida que; (although) aunque; si bien. **w. I was walking down the street,** mientras andaba por la calle, al andar yo por la calle. *vt* **to w.** (**away**), pasar, entretener. **to w. away the time,** pasar el rato

whim /wɪm/ *n* capricho, antojo, *m*; manía, *f*; extravagancia, *f*; fantasía, *f*

whimper /'wɪmpər/ *n* quejido, sollozo, gemido, *m*, *vi* lloriquear, quejarse, sollozar, gemir

whimpering /'wɪmpərɪŋ/ *n* lloriqueo, llanto, *m*, *a* que lloriquea

whimsical /'wɪmzɪkəl/ *a* antojadizo, caprichoso; fantástico

whimsicality /ˌwɪmzɪ'kælɪti/ *n* capricho, *m*, extravagancia, *f*; fantasía, *f*

whimsically /'wɪmzɪkli/ *adv* caprichosamente; fantásticamente

whine /wain/ *vi* gimotear, lloriquear; quejarse

whining /'wainɪŋ/ *n* gimoteo, lloriqueo, *m*; quejumbres, *f pl. a* que lloriquea; quejumbroso

whinny /'wɪni/ *n* relincho, hin, *m*, *vi* relinchar

whip /wɪp/ *vt* azotar; pegar; *Cul.* batir; *Sew.* sobrecoser; (ropes, etc.) ligar; (defeat) vencer. *vi* moverse rápidamente. **to w. down,** *vi* bajar volando, bajar corriendo. *vt* arrebatar (de). **to w. in,** entrar precipitadamente (en), penetrar apresuradamente (en). **to w. off,** cazar a latigazos, despachar a golpes; (remove) quitar rápidamente; (persons) llevar corriendo, llevar aprisa. **to w. open,** abrir rápidamente. **to w. out,** *vt* (draw) sacar rápidamente; (utter) saltar diciendo (que); proferir. *vi* escabullirse, escaparse, salir apresuradamente. **to w. round,** volverse de repente. **to w. up,** *vt* (horses, etc.) avivar con el látigo; (snatch) coger de repente agarrar; (gather) reunir. *vi* (mount) subir corriendo

whip /wɪp/ *n* azote, zurriago, *Lat. Am.* chicote, *m*; (riding) látigo, *m*. **blow with a w.**, latigazo, *m*. **to have the w.-hand,** mandar, tener la sartén por el mango; tener la ventaja. **w.-cord,** tralla del látigo, *f*

whippet /'wɪpɪt/ *n* especie de perro (-rra) lebrero (-ra)

whipping /'wɪpɪŋ/ *n* paliza, *f*, vapuleo, azotamiento, *m*. **w. post,** picota, *f*. **w. top,** trompo, *m*, peonza, *f*

whirl /wɜrl/ *n* vuelta, *f*, giro, *m*; rotación, *f*; *Fig.* torbellino, *m*. *vi* girar; dar vueltas; (dance) bailar, danzar. *vt* hacer girar; dar vueltas (a); (carry) llevar rápidamente. **to w. along,** volar (por), pasar aprisa (por); dejar atrás los vientos, correr velozmente. **to w. past,** pasar volando (por); pasar como una exhalación. **to w. through,** atravesar rápidamente, cruzar volando

whirligig /'wɜrlɪˌgɪg/ *n* perinola, *f*; (merry-go-round) tiovivo, *m*

whirlpool /'wɜrlˌpul/ *n* vórtice, remolino, *m*; *Fig.* vorágine, *f*

whirlwind /'wɜrlˌwɪnd/ *n* torbellino, *m*, manga de viento, *f*

whirr /wɜr/ *n* zumbido, *m*; (of wings) ruido (de las alas), *m*. *vi* girar; zumbar

whirring /'wɜrɪŋ/ *n* zumbido, *m*; ruido, *m. a* que gira; que zumba

whisk /wɪsk/ *n* cepillo, *m*; *Cul.* batidor, *m*; (movement) movimiento rápido, *m*. *vt Cul.* batir; (wag) menear, mover rápidamente; (with off, away) quitar rápidamente; sacudir; arrebatar; (take away a person) llevarse (a). *vi* moverse rápidamente; andar rápidamente

whiskered /'wɪskərd/ *a* bigotudo

whiskers /'wɪskərz/ *n pl* mostacho, *m*, patillas, barbas, *f pl*; (of a feline) bigotes, *m pl*

whisky /'wɪski/ *n* güisqui, *m*

whisper /'wɪspər/ *n* cuchicheo, *m*; (rumor) voz, *f*; (of leaves, etc.) susurro, murmullo, *m. vi* and *vt* cuchichear, hablar al oído; (of leaves, etc.) susurrar; (of rumors) murmurar. **in a w.**, al oído, en un susurro

whisperer /'wɪspərərsol/ *n* cuchicheador (-ra); (gossip) murmurador (-ra)

whispering /'wɪspərɪŋ/ *n* cuchicheo, *m*; susurro, *m*;

(gossip) murmurio, *m*. **w. gallery,** galería de los murmullos, *f. Inf.* sala de los secretos, *f*

whistle /'wɪsəl/ *n* (sound) silbido, silbo, *m*; (instrument) pito, silbato, *m*; *Inf.* gaznate, *m. vi* and *vt* silbar. **blast on the w.,** pitido, *m*. **to w. for,** llamar silbando; *Inf.* esperar sentado, buscar en vano

whistler /'wɪslər/ *n* silbador (-ra)

whistling /'wɪslɪŋ/ *n* silbido, *m*, *a* silbador

whit /wɪt/ *n* pizca, *f*, bledo, *m*. **not a w.,** ni pizca

white /wait/ *a* blanco; pálido; puro. *n* color blanco, blanco, *m*; (pigment) pintura blanca, *f*; (whiteness) blancura, *f*; (of egg) clara (del huevo), *f*; (person) blanco, *m*. **Elizabeth went w.,** Isabel se puso pálida. **the w.,** (billiards) la blanca. **the w. of the eye,** lo blanco del ojo. **w. ant,** hormiga blanca, termita, *f*. **w. cabbage,** repollo, *m*. **w. caps,** (of waves) cabrillas, *f pl*; (of mountains) picos blancos, *m pl*. **w. clover,** trébol blanco, *m*. **w. corpuscle,** glóbulo blanco, *m*. **w. currant,** grosella blanca, *f*. **w. elephant,** elefante (-ta) blanco (-ca). **w. ensign,** pabellón blanco, *m*. **w.-faced,** de cara pálida. **w. fish,** pescado blanco, *m*. **w. flag,** bandera blanca, *f*. **w.-haired,** de pelo blanco. **w. heat,** calor blanco, *m*, candencia, *f*; ardor, *m*. **w. horses,** cabrillas, palomas, *f pl*. **w.-hot,** incandescente. **W. House, the,** la Casa Blanca, *f*. **w. lead,** albayalde, *m*. **w. lie,** mentira inocente, mentira oficiosa, mentira piadosa, la mentirilla, *f*. **w. man,** blanco, hombre de raza blanca, *m*. **the white man's burden,** la misión sagrada de la civilización blanca, *f*. **w. meat,** carne blanca, pechuga, *f*. **w. paper,** libro blanco, *m*. **w. sauce,** salsa blanca, *f*. **w. slave,** víctima de la trata de blancas, *f*. **w. slavery,** trata de blancas, *f*. **w. sugar,** azúcar blanco, azúcar de flor, *m*. **w. woman,** mujer de raza blanca, *f*

whiten /'waitṇ/ *vt* blanquear. *vi* blanquearse

whiteness /'waitnɪs/ *n* blancura, *f*; palidez, *f*; pureza, *f*; *Poet.* nieve, *f*

whitening /'waitṇɪŋ/ *n* blanqueo, *m*; blanco de España, *m*; blanco para los zapatos, *m*

whitewash /'waitˌwɒʃ/ *vt* blanquear, jalbegar, encalar; (Fig. of faults) disculpar, justificar

whitewashing /'waitˌwɒʃɪŋ/ *n* blanqueo, *m*, encaladura, *f*

whither /'wɪðər/ *adv* (interrogative) adónde; (with a clause) adonde

whithersoever /ˌwɪðərsou'evər/ *adv* adondequiera

whiting /'waitɪŋ/ *n* blanco de España, *m*; blanco para los zapatos, *m*; (fish) pescadilla, *f*, merlango, *m*

whitish /'waitɪʃ/ *a* blanquecino

whitlow /'wɪtlou/ *n* panadizo, *m*

Whitsun /'wɪtsən/ *a* de Pentecostés

Whitsunday /'wɪt'sʌndei/ *n* domingo de Pentecostés, *m*

Whitsuntide /'wɪtsən,taid/ *n* pascua de Pentecostés, *f*

whittle /'wɪtḷ/ *n* navaja, *f. vt* cercenar, cortar; (sharpen) afilar, sacar punta (a); tallar; *Fig.* reducir. **to w. away, down,** *Fig.* reducir a nada

whizz /wɪz/ *n* silbido, zumbido, *m*, *vi* silbar, zumbar

whizzing /'wɪzɪŋ/ *n* silbido, *m*, *a* que zumba

who /hu/ *pron* (interrogative) quién, *mf*; quiénes, *mf pl*; (relative) quien, *mf*; quienes, *mf pl*; que; (in elliptical constructions the proper form, etc.) el que, *m*; la que, *f*; los que, *m pl*; las que, *f pl*

whoa /wou/ *interj* ¡so!

whoever /hu'evər/ *pron* quienquiera (que); cualquiera (que); quien. **Give it to w. you like,** Dáselo a quien te parezca bien

whole /houl/ *a* (healthy) sano; (uninjured) ileso, entero; todo. *n* todo, *m*; total, *m*; totalidad, *f*; conjunto, *m*. **on the w.,** por regla general, en general; en conjunto. **the w. week,** la semana entera, toda la semana. **w.-hearted,** sincero, genuino; entusiasta. **w.-heartedly,** de todo corazón. **w. length,** *a* de cuerpo entero. **w. number,** número entero, *m*

wholemeal /'houl'mil/ *n* harina de trigo entero, *f*, de trigo entero

wholeness /'houlnɪs/ *n* totalidad, *f*; integridad, *f*; todo, *m*

wholesale /'houl,seil/ *a Com.* al por mayor; en grueso; *Fig.* general; en masa. *n* venta al por mayor, *f.* **w. price,** precio al por mayor, *m.* **w. trade,** comercio al por mayor, *m*

wholesaler /'houl,seilər/ *n* comerciante al por mayor, *mf* mercader de grueso, *m*

wholesome /'houlsəm/ *a* sano; saludable; (edifying) edificante

wholesomeness /'houlsəmnıs/ *n* sanidad, *f;* lo sano; lo saludable

wholly /'houli/ *adv* completamente, enteramente, totalmente; integralmente; del todo

whom /hum/ *pron* quien; a quien, *mf;* a quienes, *mf pl;* (interrogative) a quién, *mf;* a quiénes, *mf pl;* al que, *m;* a la que, *f;* a los que, *m pl;* a las que, *f pl.* **from w.,** de quien; (interrogative) de quién. **the man w. you saw,** el hombre a quien viste

whoop /wup, wup/ *n* alarido, grito, *m;* estertor de la tos ferina, *m. vi* dar gritos, chillar; /hup/ (whooping-cough) toser

whooping cough /'hupıŋ/ *n* tos ferina, coqueluche, *f*

whore /hɔr/ *n* puta, ramera, *f, Lat. Am. also* araña, *f*

whorl /wɜrl, wɔrl/ *n* (of a shell) espira, *f; Bot.* verticilo, *m;* (of a spindle) tortera, *f*

whorled /wɜrld, wɔrld/ *a Bot.* verticilado; (of shells) en espira

whose /huz/ *pron* cuyo, *m;* cuya, *f;* cuyos, *m pl;* cuyas, *f pl;* de quien, *mf;* de quienes, *mf pl;* (interrogative) de quién, de quiénes; **W. daughter is she?** ¿De quién es ella la hija? **This is the writer w. name I always forget,** Este es el autor cuyo nombre siempre olvido

whosoever /,husou'evər/ *pron.* See **whoever**

why /wai/ *adv* (interrogative) por qué; (on account of which) por el cual, *m;* por la cual, *f;* por lo cual, *neut;* por los cuales, *m pl;* por las cuales, *f pl;* (how) cómo. *n.* ni porqué, *m., interj* ¡qué!; ¡cómo!; ¡toma!; si. **not to know the why or wherefore,** no saber ni el porqué ni el cómo, no saber ni el qué ni el por qué. **Why! I have just come,** ¡Si no hago más de llegar! **Why not?** ¿Por qué no? ¡Cómo no!

wick /wık/ *n* mecha, torcida, *f*

wicked /'wıkıd/ *a* malo; malvado, perverso; pecaminoso; malicioso; (mischievous) travieso

wickedly /'wıkıdli/ *adv* mal; perversamente; maliciosamente

wickedness /'wıkıdnıs/ *n* maldad, *f;* perversidad, *f;* pecado, *m;* (mischievousness) travesura, *f*

wicker /'wıkər/ *n* mimbre, *m, a* de mimbre

wicket /'wıkıt/ *n* postigo, portillo, *m;* (half-door) media puerta, *f;* (at cricket) meta, *f.* **w.-keeper,** guardameta, *m*

wide /waid/ *a* ancho; (in measurements) de ancho; vasto; extenso; grande; amplio; (loose) holgado; (distant) lejos; liberal; general, comprensivo. *adv* lejos; completamente. **far and w.,** por todas partes. **to be too w.,** ser muy ancho; estar muy ancho; (of garments) venir muy ancho. **two feet w.,** dos pies de ancho. **w.-awake,** muy despierto; despabilado; vigilante. **w.-eyed,** con los ojos muy abiertos; asombrado. **w.-open,** abierto de par en par

widely /'waidli/ *adv* extensamente; generalmente; (very) muy

widen /'waidn/ *vt* ensanchar; extender. *vi* ensancharse; extenderse

widening /'waidnıŋ/ *n* ensanche, *m;* extensión, *f*

widespread /'waid'sprɛd/ *a* universal, general; generalizado; extenso; esparcido. **to become w.,** generalizarse

widow /'wıdou/ *n* viuda, *f. vt* dejar viuda; dejar viudo; *Fig.* privar. **to be a grass w.,** estar viuda. **to become a w.,** enviudar, perder al esposo. **widow's pension,** viudedad, *f.* **widow's weeds,** luto de viuda, *m*

widowed /'wıdoud/ *a* viudo

widower /'wıdouər/ *n* viudo, *m.* **to become a w.,** perder a la esposa, enviudar

widowhood /'wıdou,hud/ *n* viudez, *f*

width /wıdθ/ *n* anchura, *f;* (of cloth) ancho, *m;* (of mind) liberalismo, *m.* **double w.,** (cloth) doble ancho, *m*

wield /wild/ *vt* (a scepter) empuñar; (power, etc.) ejercer; (a pen, sword) manejar

wife /waif/ *n* esposa, mujer, *f;* mujer, *f;* comadre, *f.* **husband and w.,** los cónyuges, los esposos. **old**

wives' tale, cuento de viejas, *m.* **The Merry Wives of Windsor,** Las alegres comadres de Windsor. **to take to w.,** contraer matrimonio con, tomar como esposa (a)

wifely /'waifli/ *a* de esposa, de mujer casada; de mujer de su casa; conyugal

wig /wıg/ *n* peluca, *f;* (hair) cabellera, *f.* **top wig,** peluquín, *m.* **wigmaker,** peluquero, *m*

wigged /wıgd/ *a* con peluca, de peluca

wigging /'wıgıŋ/ *n* (scolding) peluca, *f*

wigwam /'wıgwɒm/ *n* tienda de indios, *f*

wild /waild/ *a* (of animals, men, land) salvaje; (barren) desierto, yermo; (mountainous) riscoso, montañoso; (of plants, birds) silvestre; montés; (disarranged) en desorden, desarreglado; (complete) absoluto, completo; (dissipated) disipado; vicioso; (foolish) alocado; (of the sea) bravío; (of weather, etc.) borrascoso; (mad with delight, etc.) loco; (frantic, mad) frenético, loco; (with "talk," etc.) extravagante; insensato, desatinado; (shy) arisco; (incoherent) inconexo, incoherente; (frightened) alarmado, espantado; (willful) travieso, indomable. *n* tierra virgen, *f;* desierto, *m;* soledad, *f.* **It made me w.,** (angry) Me hizo rabiar. **to run w.,** volver al estado silvestre; (of persons) llevar una vida de salvajes; volverse loco. **to shoot w.,** errar el tiro. **to spread like w. fire,** propagarse como el fuego. **w. beast,** fiera, *f.* **w. boar,** jabalí, *m.* **w. cat,** gato montés, *Lat. Am.* lince, *m.* **w. duck,** pato silvestre, *m.* **w. goat,** cabra montesa, *f.* **w.-goose chase,** caza infructuosa, *f;* empresa quimérica, *f.* **w. oats,** avenas locas, *f pl; Fig.* indiscreciones de la juventud, *f pl.* **to sow one's w. oats,** andarse a la flor del berro

wilderness /'wıldərnıs/ *n* desierto, *m;* yermo, páramo, despoblado, *m;* soledad, *f;* (jungle) selva, *f;* (maze) laberinto, *m;* infinidad, *f*

wildly /'waildli/ *adv* en un estado salvaje; sin cultivo; (rashly) desatinadamente; sin reflexión, sin pensar; (incoherently) incoherentemente; (stupidly, of looking, etc.) tontamente; (in panic) con ojos espantados, con terror en los ojos; alarmado

wildness /'waildnıs/ *n* salvajez, *f;* estado silvestre, *m;* naturaleza silvestre, *f;* (ferocity) ferocidad, *f;* (of the wind, sea) braveza, *f;* (of the wind) violencia, *f;* (impetuosity) impetuosidad, *f;* (of statements, etc.) extravagancia, *f;* (incoherence) incoherencia, *f;* (disorder) desorden, *m;* (willfulness, of children) travesuras, *f pl;* (of the expression) gesto espantado, *m*

wile /wail/ *n* estratagema, *f,* engaño, *m,* ardid, *f*

wilily /'waulıli/ *adv* astutamente

wiliness /'wailınıs/ *n* astucia, *f*

will /wıl/ *n* voluntad, *f;* albedrío, *m;* (wish) deseo, *m;* (pleasure) discreción, *f,* placer, *m;* (legal document) testamento, *m.* **against my w.,** contra mi voluntad. **at w.,** a voluntad; a gusto, a discreción. **free w.,** libre albedrío, *m.* **of one's own free w.,** por su propia voluntad. **iron w.,** voluntad de hierro, *f.* **last w. and testament,** última disposición, última voluntad, *f.* **to do with a w.,** hacer con toda el alma, hacer con entusiasmo. **to make one's w.,** otorgar (hacer) su testamento. **w.-power,** fuerza de voluntad, *f*

will /wıl/ *vt* querer; disponer, ordenar; (bequeath) legar, dejar en testamento, mandar; (oblige) sugestionar (a una persona) para que haga algo; hipnotizar. *vi aux.* querer; (As a sign of the future it is not translated separately in Spanish) **I w. come tomorrow,** Vendré mañana. **John does not approve, but I w. go,** Juan no lo aprueba pero yo quiero ir. **Do what you w.,** Haga lo que a Vd. le parezca bien, Haga lo que Vd. quiera; Haga lo que haga. **Boys w. be boys,** Los niños son siempre niños. **He w. not (won't) do it,** No lo hará; No quiere hacerlo

willful /'wılfəl/ *a* rebelde, voluntarioso; (of children) travieso; (of crimes, etc.) premeditado

willfully /'wılfəli/ *adv* voluntariosamente; intencionadamente; (of committing crimes) con premeditación

willfulness /'wılfəlnıs/ *n* rebeldía, *f;* (obstinacy) terquedad, obstinación, *f*

willing /'wılıŋ/ *a* dispuesto, inclinado; (serviceable) servicial; deseoso; espontáneo; complaciente; gustoso; (willingly) de buena gana. **to be w.,** estar dispuesto (a), querer; consentir (en)

willingly /'wɪlɪŋli/ *adv* de buena gana, con gusto

willingness /'wɪlɪŋnɪs/ *n* buena voluntad, *f*; deseo de servir, *m*; complacencia, *f*; (consent) consentimiento, *m*

will-o'-the-wisp /'wɪləðə'wɪsp/ *n* fuego fatuo, *m*

willow /'wɪlou/ *n* sauce, *m*. **weeping w.**, sauce llorón, *m*. **w.-pattern china**, porcelana de estilo chino, *f*. **w. tree**, sauce, *m*

willowy /'wɪloui/ *a* lleno de sauces; (slim) cimbreño, esbelto, alto y delgado

willy nilly /'wɪli 'nɪli/ *adv* de buen o mal grado, mal que bien

wilt /wɪlt/ *vi* (of plants) marchitarse, secarse; *Fig.* languidecer; ajarse. *vt* marchitar; *Fig.* ajar; hacer languidecer

wily /'waili/ *a* astuto, chuzón

win /wɪn/ *vt* ganar; (reach) alcanzar, lograr; (a victory, etc.) llevarse; conquistar. *vi* ganar; triunfar. *n* triunfo, *m*. **to win back**, volver a ganar; recobrar

wince /wɪns/ *vi* retroceder, recular; (flinch) quejarse; (of a horse) respingar. *n* respingo, *m*. **without wincing**, sin quejarse; estoicamente

winch /wɪntʃ/ *n* cabria, *f*; (handle) manubrio, *m*

wind /wɪnd/ *n* viento, *m*; aire, *m*; (flatulence) flatulencia, *f*; (breath) respiración, *f*, aliento, *m*; (idle talk) paja, *f*. **breath of w.**, soplo de viento, *m*. **following w.**, viento en popa, *m*. **high w.**, viento alto, viento fuerte, *m*. **land w.**, viento terrenal, *m*. **It's an ill w. that blows nobody good**, No hay mal que por bien no venga. **There is something in the w.**, Hay algo en el aire, Se trama algo. **to get w. of**, husmear. **to sail before the w.**, navegar de viento en popa. **The w. stiffened**, Refrescó el viento. **You took the w. out of his sails**, Le deshinchaste las velas. **w.-instrument**, instrumento de viento, *m*. **w.-proof**, a prueba del viento. **w.-swept**, expuesto a todos los vientos. **w. storm**, ventarrón, *m*

wind /waind/ *vi* serpentear; desfilar lentamente; torcerse. *vt* (turn) dar vueltas (a); (a handle) manejar, mover; (a watch) dar cuerda (a); (wool, etc.) devanar, ovillar; (wrap) envolver; (of arms, embrace) rodear (con); (a horn) tocar. **to w. off**, devanar; desenrollar. **to w. round**, (wrap) envolver; (skirt) rodear; (embrace) ceñir con (los brazos); (pass by) pasar por; deslizarse por; (of snakes) enroscarse. **to w. up**, (a watch) dar cuerda (a); (thread) devanar; (conclude) concluir; *Com.* liquidar; (excite) agitar, emocionar

windbag /'wɪnd,bæg/ *n* pandero, *m*, sacamuelas, *mf*

winder /'waindər/ *n* (person) devanador (-ra); (machine) devanadera, *f*; (of a clock) llave, *f*

windfall /'wɪnd,fɔl/ *n* fruta caída del árbol, *f*; (good luck) breva, *f*; ganancia inesperada, lotería, *f*

windiness /'wɪndɪnɪs/ *n* tiempo ventoso, *m*; situación expuesta a todos los vientos, *f*; (of speech) pomposidad, verbosidad, *f*

winding /'waindɪŋ/ *a* tortuoso; (e.g., road) sinuoso; serpentino; en espiral. *n* tortuosidad, *f*; meandro, recoveco, *m*, vuelta, curva, *f*. **w. sheet**, mortaja, *f*, sudario, *m*. **w. stair**, escalera de caracol, *f*. **w.-up**, conclusión, *f*; *Com.* liquidación, *f*

windlass /'wɪndləs/ *n* torno, *m*

windless /'wɪndlɪs/ *a* sin viento

windmill /'wɪnd,mɪl/ *n* molino de viento, *m*

window /'wɪndou/ *n* ventana, *f*; (of a shop) escaparate, *Mexico* aparador, *m*; (in a train, car, bank, etc.) ventanilla, *f*; (booking office) taquilla, *f*; (of a church) vidriera, *f*. **casement w.**, ventana, *f*. **sash w.**, ventana de guillotina, *f*. **small w.**, ventanilla, *f*. **stained glass w.**, vidriera, *f*. **to lean out of the w.**, asomarse a la ventana. **to look out of the w.**, mirar por la ventana. **w. blind**, (Venetian) persiana, *f*; transparente, *m*; (against the sun) toldo, *m*. **w.-dresser**, decorador (-ra) de escaparates. **w. frame**, marco de ventana, *m*. **w.-pane**, cristal (de ventana), *m*. **w.-shutter**, contraventana, *f*. **w.-sill**, repisa de la ventana, *f*, alféizar, *m*

windpipe /'wɪnd,paip/ *n* tráquea, *f*

windshield /'wɪnd,ʃild/ *n* parabrisas, guardabrisa, *m*. **w.-wiper**, limpiaparabrisas, limpiavidrios, *m*

windward /'wɪndwərd/ *n* barlovento, *m*. *a* de barlovento. *adv* a barlovento

windy /'wɪndi/ *a* ventoso; expuesto al viento; (of style) hinchado, pomposo. **It is w.**, Hace viento

wine /wain/ *n* vino, *m*; zumo fermentado (de algunas frutas), *m*. *a* de vino; de vinos; para vino. **in w.**, *Cul.* en vino; (drunk) ebrio, borracho. **heavy w.**, vino fuerte, *m*. **light w.**, vino ligero, *m*. **local w.**, vino del país, *m*, **matured w.**, vino generoso, *m*. **red w.**, vino tinto, *m*. **thin w.**, vinillo, *m*. **white w.**, vino blanco, *m*. **w.-cellar**, bodega, cueva, *f*. **w.-colored**, de color de vino. **w.-cooler**, cubo para enfriar vinos, *m*. **w. country**, tierra de vino, *f*. **w. decanter**, garrafa para vino, *f*. **w.-grower**, vinicultor (-ra). **w.-growing**, *n* vinicultura, *f*. *a* vinícola. **w. lees**, zupia, *f*. **w. merchant**, comerciante en vinos, *mf*. vinatero, *m*. **w.-press**, lagar, *m*. **w.-taster**, catavinos, *m*. **w. waiter**, bodeguero, *m*

wineskin /'wain,skɪn/ *n* bota, *f*, odre, pellejo, *m*

wing /wɪŋ/ *n* (of a bird and *Zool.*, *Archit.*, *Aer.*, *Mil.*, *Bot.*) ala, *f*; (flight) vuelo, *m*; *Theat.* bastidor, *m*; *Fig.* protección, *f*. *vt* dar alas (a); llevar sobre las alas; (wound) herir en el ala; herir en el brazo; volar por. *vi* volar. **beating of wings**, batir de alas, aleteo, *m*. **in the wings**, *Theat.* entre bastidores. **on the w.**, al vuelo. **to clip a (person's) wings**, cortar (*or* quebrar) las alas (a). **under his w.**, bajo su protección. **w.-case**, élitro (de un insecto), *m*. **w. chair**, sillón con orejas, *m*. **w.-commander**, teniente coronel de aviación, *m*. **w.-span**, (*Zool.* and *Aer.*) envergadura, *f*. **w.-spread**, extensión del ala, *f*. **w.-tip**, punta del ala, *f*

winged /wɪŋd; *esp. Literary* 'wɪŋɪd/ *a* alado, con alas; (in compounds) de alas...; (swift) alado, (of style) elevado, alado

wink /wɪŋk/ *n* (blink) pestañear; (as a signal, etc.) guiñar; (of stars, etc.) titilar, parpadear, centellear. *vt* guiñar (el ojo). *n* pestañeo, *m*; guiño, *m*. **not to sleep a w.**, no pegar los ojos. **to take forty winks**, echar una siesta. **to w. at**, guiñar el ojo (a); (ignore) hacer la vista gorda

winking /'wɪŋkɪŋ/ *n* (blinking) parpadeo, *m*; (as a signal) guiños, *m pl*; (of stars, etc.) titilación, *f*, pestañeo, *m*. *a* (of stars, etc.) titilante. **like w.**, en un abrir y cerrar de ojos.

winner /'wɪnər/ *n* ganador (-ra); vencedor (-ra)

winning /'wɪnɪŋ/ *a* ganador; vencedor; (attractive) encantador. *n* ganancia, *f*. **w. number**, número galardonado, número premiado, número vencedor, *m*. **w.-post**, meta, *f*. **w. side**, *Sports.* equipo vencedor, *m*; (politics, etc.) partido vencedor, *m*

winnings /'wɪnɪŋz/ *n* ganancias, *f pl*

winnow /'wɪnou/ *vt* aventar, abalear; *Fig.* separar

winnower /'wɪnouər/ *n* aventador (-ra)

winnowing /'wɪnouɪŋ/ *n* ableo, aventamiento, *m*; *Fig.* separación, *f*. **w. fork**, bieldo, *m*. **w. machine**, aventador mecánico, *m*

winsome /'wɪnsəm/ *a* sandunguero; dulce, encantador

winsomeness /'wɪnsəmnɪs/ *n* sandunga, *f*; encanto, *m*, dulzura, *f*

winter /'wɪntər/ *n* invierno, *m*. *a* de invierno; hiemal. *vi* pasar el invierno, invernar. *vt* (of cattle, etc.) guardar en invierno. **in w.**, en invierno, durante el invierno. **w. clothes**, ropa de invierno, *f*. **w. palace**, palacio de invierno, *m*. **w. pasture**, *Lat. Am.* invernada, *f*. **w. quarters**, invernadero, *m*. **w. season**, invierno, *m*; temporada de invierno, *f*. **w. sleep**, invernada, *f*. **w. solstice**, solsticio hiemal, *m*. **w. sports**, deportes de nieve, *m pl*. **w. wheat**, trigo de invierno, *m*

wintry /'wɪntri/ *a* de invierno; invernal; (of a smile, etc.) glacial

wipe /waip/ *vt* limpiar; (rub) frotar; (dry) secar; (remove) quitar. *n* limpión, *m*; (blow) golpe de lado, *m*. **to w. one's eyes**, enjugarse las lagrimas. **to w. off, out**, limpiar; (remove) quitar; (erase) borrar; (kill) destruir completamente, exterminar; (a military force) destrozar; (a debt) cancelar

wire /waɪr/ *n* alambre, *m*; hilo metálico, *m*; telégrafo (eléctrico), *m*; *Inf.* telegrama, *m*. *vt* atar con alambre; (fence) alambrar; (snare) coger con lazo de alambre;

(of electrical equipment, etc.) instalar; (telegraph) telegrafiar. *vi* (telegraph) telegrafiar. **barbed w.,** alambre espinoso, *m.* **live w.,** alambre cargado (de electricidad), *m;* (person) fuerza viva, *f.* **w.-cutters,** cortaalambres, *m pl.* **w.-entanglement,** *Mil.* alambrada, *f.* **w. fence,** alambrera, *f,* cercado de alambre, *m.* **w. gauze,** tela metálica, *f.* **w. nail,** punta de París, *f.* **w.-netting,** malla de alambre, *f;* alambrado, *m.* **w.-pulling,** influencias secretas, *f pl;* intrigas políticas, *f pl*

wiredraw /'waiᵊr,drɔ/ *vt* estirar (alambre), tirar (el hilo de hierro, plata, etc.); (arguments, etc.) sutilizar

wiredrawer /'waiᵊr,drɔər/ *n* estirador, *m*

wireless /'waiᵊrlɪs/ *a* sin hilos; (of a message) radiotelegráfico; por radio. *n* telegrafía sin hilos, *f;* radiotelefonía, *f;* (telegram) radiocomunicación, *f;* (broadcasting) radio, *f. vt* radiotelegrafiar. **Let's listen to the w.,** Vamos a escuchar la radio. **portable w.,** radio portátil, *f.* **w. engineer,** ingeniero radiotelegrafista, *m.* **w. enthusiast,** radioaficionado (-da). **w. license,** permiso de radiorreceptor, *m.* **w. operator,** radiotelegrafista, *mf.* **w. room,** cuarto de telegrafía sin hilos, *m.* **w. set,** aparato de radio, *m.* **w. station,** estación de radiotelegrafía, *f;* (broadcasting) radioemisora, *f.* **w. telegraph,** telégrafo sin hilos, *m.* **w. telegraphy,** telegrafía sin hilos, radiotelegrafía, *f.* **w. telephony,** telefonía sin hilos, *f.* **w. transmission,** radioemisión, *f*

wiretap /'waiᵊr,tæp/ *vi* poner escucha. *vt* poner escucha a

wiring /'waiᵊrɪŋ/ *n* instalación de alambres eléctricos, *f*

wiry /'waiᵊri/ *a* semejante a un alambre; (of persons) nervudo

wisdom /'wɪzdəm/ *n* sabiduría, *f;* (learning) saber, *m;* (judgment) juicio, *m.* **Book of W.,** Libro de la Sabiduría, *m.* **w.-tooth,** muela del juicio, *f*

wise /waiz/ *a* sabio; juicioso, prudente; (informed) enterado, informado. **a w. man,** un sabio. **in no w.,** de ningún modo. **the W. Men of the East,** los magos. **w. guy,** *Inf.* toro corrido, *m*

wisely /'waizli/ *adv* sabiamente; prudentemente, con prudencia

wish /wɪʃ/ *n* deseo, *m.* **Best wishes for the New Year,** Los mejores deseos para el Año Nuevo. **w.-bone,** espoleta, *f*

wish /wɪʃ/ *vt* querer; desear; ansiar; (with "good morning", etc.) dar. **I w. he were here!** ¡Ojalá que estuviera aquí! **Theresa wishes us to go,** Teresa quiere que vayamos. **I w. it had happened otherwise,** Quisiera que las cosas hubiesen pasado de otra manera. **I w. you would make less noise,** Me gustaría que hicieses menos ruido. **I only w. one thing,** Solamente deseo una cosa. **I w. you good luck,** Te deseo mucha suerte. **I wished him a merry Christmas,** Le deseé unas Pascuas muy felices, Le felicité las Pascuas. **to w. a prosperous New Year,** desear un próspero Año Nuevo. **to w. good-by,** despedirse (de). **to w. good day,** dar los buenos días. **to w. for,** desear

wisher /'wɪʃər/ *n* el que, *m,* (f, la que) desea, deseador (-ra)

wishful /'wɪʃfəl/ *a* deseoso; ansioso; ávido. **w. thinking,** ilusiones, *f pl;* optimismo injustificado, optimismo exagerado, *m*

wisp /wɪsp/ *n* mechón, *m;* jirón, *m;* trozo, pedazo, *m*

wistaria /wɪ'stiəriə, -'steər-/ *n* vistaria, *f*

wistful /'wɪstfəl/ *a* ansioso; triste; patético; (envious) envidioso; (regretful) de pesar; (remorseful) de remordimiento; (thoughtful) pensativo

wistfully /'wɪstfəli/ *adv* con ansia; tristemente; patéticamente; con envidia; con pesar; con remordimiento; pensativo

wistfulness /'wɪstfəlnɪs/ *n* ansia, *f;* tristeza, *f;* (envy) envidia, *f;* (regret) pesar, *m;* (remorse) remordimiento, *m;* (thoughtfulness) lo pensativo, lo distraído

wit, to /wɪt/ *adv* a saber

wit /wɪt/ *n* (reason) juicio, *m;* agudeza, gracia, *f,* rasgo de ingenio, *m;* ingenio, *m;* inteligencia, *f,* talento, *m;* (person) hombre de ingenio, *m;* mujer de ingenio, *f.* **my five wits,** mis cinco sentidos. **to be at one's wits' end,** no saber qué hacer. **to live by one's**

wits, ser caballero de industria. **to lose one's wits,** perder el juicio

witch /wɪtʃ/ *n* bruja, *f.* **witches' sabbath,** aquelarre, *m.* **w.-doctor,** hechizador, mago, *m.* **witch-hazel,** carpe, *m;* loción de carpe, *f*

witchcraft /'wɪtʃ,kræft/ *n* brujería, *f;* sortilegio, encantamiento, *m*

witchery /'wɪtʃəri/ *n* brujería, *f;* *Fig.* encanto, *m,* magia, *f*

with /wɪθ, wɪð/ *prep* con; en compañia de; en casa de; (against) contra; (among) entre; en; (by) por; (towards) hacia; para con; (according to) según; (notwithstanding) a pesar de; a; (concerning) con respecto a; en el caso de. **Rose is w. Antony,** Rosa está con Antonio. **He was w. his dog,** Estaba acompañado por su perro. **He pulled at it w. both hands,** Lo tiró con las dos manos. **filled w. fear,** lleno de miedo. **to shiver w. cold,** temblarse de frío. **the girl w. golden hair,** la muchacha del pelo dorado. **They killed it w. one blow,** Lo mataron de un solo golpe. **It rests w. you to decide,** Tú tienes que decidirlo; Te toca a ti decidirlo. **to begin w.,** *adv* para empezar; *v* empezar por. **w. all speed,** a toda prisa. **to part w.,** desprenderse de; (of people) despedirse de; separarse de. **w. that...,** (at once) en esto... (disease and poverty, etc.) **are still with us,** están todavía en el mundo

withal /wɪð'ɔl, wɪθ-/ *adv* además; al mismo tiempo. *prep* con

withdraw /wɪð'drɔ, wɪθ-/ *vt* retirar; (words) retractar; (remove) quitar, privar (de); (a legal action) apartar. *vi* retirarse; retroceder; separarse; irse

withdrawai /wɪð'drɔəl, wɪθ-/ *n* retirada, *f;* (retirement) retiro, *m;* apartamiento, *m*

withdrawn /wɪð'drɔn, wɪθ-/ *a* (abstracted) ensimismado, meditabundo

wither /'wɪðər/ *vi* marchitarse, secarse, ajarse. *vt* marchitar, secar, ajar; *Fig.* hacer languidecer, matar; (snub) avergonzar

withered /'wɪðərd/ *a* marchito, mustio; muerto; (of persons) acartonado, seco

witheredness /'wɪðərdnɪs/ *n* marchitez, *f;* sequedad, *f*

withering /'wɪðərɪŋ/ *a* que marchita; (scorching) abrasador, ardiente; (scornful) despreciativo, desdeñoso; (biting) mordaz, cáustico

withers /'wɪðərz/ *n* cruz, *f*

withhold /wɪθ'hould, wɪð-/ *vt* retener; detener; (restrain) refrenar; apartar; (refuse) negar; abstenerse de; (refuse to reveal) ocultar

withholding /wɪθ'houldɪŋ/ *n* detención, *f;* (refusal) negación, *f*

within /wɪð'ɪn, wɪθ-/ *adv* dentro, adentro; en el interior; en casa; *Fig.* en su interior. **He stayed w.,** Se quedó dentro. **Is Mrs. González w.?** ¿Está en casa la Sra. González?

within /wɪð'ɪn, wɪθ-/ *prep* dentro de; el interior de; en; entre; (within range of) al alcance de; a la distancia de; (near) cerca de; a poco de; (of time) en el espacio de, en; dentro de; (almost) por poco, casi. **He was w. an inch of being killed,** Por poco le matan. **to be w. hearing,** estar al alcance de la voz. **seen from w.,** visto desde dentro. **twice w. a fortnight,** dos veces en quince días. **w. himself,** por sus adentros, entre sí. **w. an inch of,** *Fig.* a dos dedos de. **w. a few miles of Bogotá,** a unas millas de Bogotá. **w. a short distance,** en una corta distancia; a poca distancia

without /wɪð'aut, wɪθ-/ *prep* sin; falto de; (outside) fuera de; (beyond) más allá de. *adv* exteriormente; por fuera; hacia afuera; fuera. **It goes w. saying,** No hay que decir. **w. more ado,** sin más ni más. **w. my knowledge,** sin que yo lo supiese. **w. regard for,** sin miramientos por. **w. saying more,** sin decir más. **without batting an eyelash,** sin sobresaltos

withstand /wɪθ'stænd, wɪð-/ *vt* resistir, oponerse (a); soportar

withstanding /wɪθ'stændɪŋ, wɪð-/ *n* resistencia, oposición (a), *f*

witless /'wɪtlɪs/ *a* sin seso, tonto, necio

witness /'wɪtnɪs/ *n* (evidence) testimonio, *m;* (person) testigo, *mf;* espectador (-ra). **in w. whereof,** en

fe de lo cual. **to bear w.,** atestiguar, dar testimonio.
to bring forward witnesses, hacer testigos. **w. my hand,** en fe de lo cual, firmo. **w.-box,** puesto de los testigos, *m.* **w. for the defense,** testigo de descargo, *mf.* **w. for the prosecution,** testigo de cargo, *mf*

witness /'wɪtnɪs/ *vt* (show) mostrar, señalar; (see) ser testigo de, ver, presenciar; *Law.* atestiguar. *vi* dar testimonio; servir de testigo

witticism /'wɪtə,sɪzəm/ *n* rasgo de ingenio, donaire, *m*, agudeza, *f*

wittily /'wɪtļi/ *adv* ingeniosamente, donairosamente, agudamente

wittiness /'wɪtinɪs/ *n* viveza de ingenio, donosura, *f*

witty /'wɪti/ *a* salado, gracioso. **w. sally,** agudeza, *f*

wizard /'wɪzərd/ *n* mago, hechicero, *m*

wizardry /'wɪzərdri/ *n* magia, *f*

wizened /'wɪzənd/ *a* seco, arrugado; (of persons) acartonado

wobble /'wɒbəl/ *vi* tambalearse, balancearse; (quiver) temblar; oscilar; *Mech.* galopar; (stagger) titubear; *Fig.* vacilar

wobbly /'wɒbli/ *a* que se bambolea; inestable; *Fig.* vacilante

woe /wou/ *n* dolor, *m*; congoja, aflicción, *f*; mal, desastre, infortunio, *m.* **Woe is me!** ¡Ay de mí! ¡Desdichado de mí!

woebegone /'woubɪ,gɔn/ *a* angustiado

woeful /'woufəl/ *a* triste; doloroso; funesto

woefully /'woufəli/ *adv* tristemente; dolorosamente

wolf /wʊlf/ *n* lobo (-ba). **a w. in sheep's clothing,** un lobo en piel de cordero. **to cry w.,** gritar «el lobo!» **to keep the w. from the door,** ponerse a cubierto del hambre. **w.-cub,** lobezno, *m.* **w.-hound,** perro lobo, *m.* **w. pack,** manada de lobos, *f*

wolfish /'wʊlfɪʃ/ *a* lobuno, de lobo

woman /'wʊmən/ *n* mujer, *f*; hembra, *f*; (lady-inwaiting) dama de servicio, *f.* **a fine figure of a w.,** una real hembra. **w. doctor,** médica, *f.* **w.-hater,** misógino, *m.* **w. of the town,** mujer de la vida airada, *f.* **w. of the world,** mujer de mundo, *f*

womanhood /'wʊmən,hʊd/ *n* feminidad, *f*; sexo feminino, *m*

womanish /'wʊmənɪʃ/ *a* afeminado

womankind /'wʊmən,kaɪnd/ *n* el sexo femenino, las mujeres

womanliness /'wʊmənlinɪs/ *n* feminidad, *f*; carácter femenino, *m*

womanly /'wʊmənli/ *a* femenino, de mujer

womb /wum/ *n* útero, *m*, matriz, *f*; *Fig.* seno, *m*

women's dormitory /'wɪmɪnz/ *n* residencia para señoritas, *f*

wonder /'wʌndər/ *n* maravilla, *f*; prodigio, *m*; portento, milagro, *m*; (surprise) sorpresa, *f*; admiración, *f*; asombro, *m*; (problem) enigma, *m*; misterio, *m. vi* admirarse, asombrarse, maravillarse; sorprenderse. *vt* (ask oneself) preguntarse; desear saber. **I wondered what the answer would be,** Me preguntaba qué sería la respuesta. **It is no w. that...,** No es mucho que..., No es sorprendente que... **It is one of the wonders of the world,** Es una de las maravillas del mundo. **to work wonders,** hacer milagros. **to w. at,** asombrarse de, maravillarse de; sorprenderse de. **w.-working,** milagroso

wonderful /'wʌndərfəl/ *a* maravilloso; magnífico; asombroso; *Inf.* estupendo

wonderfully /'wʌndərfli/ *adv* maravillosamente; admirablemente

wondering /'wʌndərɪŋ/ *a* de asombro, sorprendido; perplejo

wonderingly /'wʌndərɪŋli/ *adv* con asombro

wonderland /'wʌndər,lænd/ *n* mundo fantástico, *m*; reino de las hadas, *m*; país de las maravillas, *m.* **"Alice in W.,"** Alicia en el país de las maravillas

wonderment /'wʌndərmənt/ *n.* See **wonder**

wondrous /'wʌndrəs/ *a* maravilloso. *adv* extraordinariamente

wont /wɒnt/ *n* costumbre, *f. vi* soler. **as he was w.,** Como solía

won't /wcount/ See **will not**

wonted /'wɒntɪd/ *a* sólito, acostumbrado

woo /wu/ *vt* galantear; hacer la corte (a), solicitar

amores a; cortejar, *Lat. Am.* afilar. *Fig.* solicitar; perseguir

wood /wʊd/ *n* bosque, *m*; madera, *f*; (for the fire, etc.) leña, *f*; (cask) barril, *m. a* de madera; (of the woods) selvático. **dead w.,** ramas muertas, *f pl; Fig.* paja, *f.* **w. alcohol,** alcohol metílico, *m.* **w.-anemone,** anémona de los bosques, *f.* **w.-block floor,** entarimado, *m.* **w.-borer,** xiló-fago, *m.* **w.-carver,** tallista, *mf* **w.-carving,** talla en madera, *f.* **w.-craft,** conocimiento del campo, *m.* **w.-cut,** grabado en madera, *m.* **w.-cutter,** leñador, *m.* **w.-engraver,** grabador (-ra) en madera. **w.-engraving,** grabado al boj, *m.* **w.-fibre,** fibra de madera, *f.* **w.-louse,** cochinilla, *f.* **w.-nymph,** ninfa de los bosques, *f.* **w.-pigeon,** paloma torcaz, *f.* **w.-pile,** pila de leña, leñera, *f.* **w.-pulp,** pulpa de madera, *f.* **w.-shaving,** acepilladura, *f.* **w.-splinter,** tasquil, *m*, astilla, *f.* **w.-wind,** *Mus.* madera, *f.* **w.-worm,** carcoma, *f*

wooded /'wʊdɪd/ *a* provisto de árboles, plantado de árboles, arbolado

wooden /'wʊdn/ *a* de madera; de palo; (of smiles) mecánico; (stiff) indiferente, sin emoción; (clumsy) torpe; (of character) inflexible. **He has a w. leg,** Tiene una pata de palo. **w. beam,** madero, *m*; viga de madera, *f.* **w. bridge,** pontón, *m.* **w. galley,** *Print.* galerín, *m*

woodland /n. 'wʊd,lænd/ *a* -lənd/ *n* bosques, *m pl. a* de bosque; silvestre

woodpecker /'wʊd,pekər/ *n* pájaro carpintero, picamaderos, *m*

woodshed /'wʊd,ʃed/ *n* leñera, *f*

woodwork /'wʊd,wɜrk/ *n* maderaje, *m*; molduras, *f pl*; carpintería, *f*

woody /'wʊdi/ *a* leñoso; arbolado, con árboles. **w. tissue,** tejido leñoso, *m*

wooer /'wuər/ *n* pretendiente, galanteador, *m*

woof /wʊf/ *n* trama, *f*

wooing /'wuɪŋ/ *n* galanteo, *m*

wool /wʊl/ *n* lana, *f. a* de lana; lanar. **to go w.-gathering,** estar distraído. **to pull the w. over a person's eyes,** engañar como a un chino. **w.-bearing,** lanar. **w.-carding,** cardadura de lana, *f.* **w.-growing,** cría de ganado lanar, *f.* **w. merchant,** comerciante en lanas, *mf*, lanero, *m.* **w.-pack,** fardo de lana, *m.* **w. trade,** comercio de lana, *m*

woollen /'wʊlən/ *a* de lana; lanar. *n* paño de lana, *m*; género de punta de lana, *m*

woolliness /'wʊlinɪs/ *n* lanosidad, *f*

woolly /'wʊli/ *a* lanudo, lanoso; de lana; *Bot.* velloso; (of hair) lanoso, crespo. *n* género de punta de lana, *m*; (sweater) jersey, *m*

word /wɜrd/ *n* palabra, *f; Gram.* vocablo, *m; Theol.* verbo, *m*; (maxim) sentencia, *f*, dicho, *m*; (message) recado, *m*; (news) aviso, *m*, noticias, *f pl; (Mil.* command) voz de mando, *f*; (order) orden, *f*; (password) contraseña, *f*; (term) término, *m. vt* expresar; formular; (draw up) redactar; escribir. **He was as good as his w.,** Fue hombre de palabra. **I do not know how to w. this letter,** No sé cómo redactar esta carta. **in a w.,** en una palabra; en resumidas cuentas. **by w. of mouth,** de palabra. **I give you my w. for it,** Le doy mi palabra de honor. **in effect,** en efecto. **the W.** (**of God**), el Verbo (de Dios). **to have a w. with,** hablar con; conversar con; entablar conversación con. **to leave w.,** dejar recado. **to have words with,** tener palabras con. **to keep one's w.,** cumplir su palabra

word index *n* índice de vocablos, *m*

wordiness /'wɜrdinɪs/ *n* palabrería, verbosidad, *f*

wording /'wɜrdɪŋ/ *n* fraseología, *f*; expresión, *f*; estilo, *m*; (terms) términos, *m pl*; (drawing up) redacción, *f*

word processor /'prɒsesər/ *n* procesador de palabra, *m*

wordy /'wɜrdi/ *a* verboso, prolijo

work /wɜrk/ *n* trabajo, *m*; (sewing) labor, *f*; (literary, artistic production and theological) obra, *f*; (behavior) acción, *f*, acto, *m*; (employment) empleo, *m*; (business affairs) negocios, *m pl; pl* **works,** obras, fortificaciones, *f, pl;* obras públicas, *f pl;* construcciones, *f pl*; (of a machine) mecanismo, *m*; motor, *m*; (factory) fábrica, *f*, taller, *m.* **w. of art,** obra de arte. **w.**

accident, accidente del trabajo, *m.* **w.-bag**, bolsa de costura, *f,* saco de labor, *m.* **w.-box**, (on legs) costurero, *m;* (small) neceser de costura, *m.* **w.-people,** obreros (-as). **w.-room,** taller, *m;* (study) estudio, *m;* (for sewing) cuarto de costura, *m.* **w.-table**, banco de taller, *m;* (for writing) mesa de escribir, *f*

work /wɜrk/ *vi* trabajar, *Central America also* laborar; *Sew.* hacer labor de aguja, coser; (embroider) bordar; *Mech.* funcionar, marchar; (succeed) tener éxito; ser eficaz; (be busy) estar ocupado; (be employed) tener empleo; (of the face) demudarse, torcerse; (ferment) fermentar; (operate) obrar *vt* trabajar; operar, hacer funcionar; mover; (control) manejar; (a mine) explotar; (embroider) bordar; (wood) tallar; (a problem) resolver; calcular; (iron, etc.) labrar; (the soil) cultivar; (a ship) maniobrar; (do) hacer; (bring about) efectuar; traer consigo; producir; (agitate oneself) agitarse, emocionarse, excitarse. **to w. in repoussé**, repujar. **to w. loose**, desprenderse. **to w. one's passage**, trabajar por el pasaje. **to w. overtime**, trabajar horas extraordinarias. **to w. two ways**, ser espada de dos filos. **to w. at**, trabajar en; ocuparse en; dedicarse a; elaborar. **to w. in**, *vt* introducir; insinuar. *vi* combinarse. **to w. into**, penetrar en. **to w. off**, usar, emplear; (get rid of) deshacerse de, librarse de. **to w. on, upon**, influir en; obrar sobre; estar ocupado en. **to w. out**, *vt* calcular; resolver; (a mine, topic, etc.) agotar; (develop) elaborar, desarrollar; trazar, planear; (find) encontrar. *vi* llegar (a); resultar; venir a ser. **to w. up**, crear; (promote) fomentar; producir; (excite) agitar, excitar; (fashion) dar forma (a), labrar; (finish) terminar

workable /'wɜrkəbəl/ *a* laborable; factible, practicable; (of a mine) explotable

workableness /'wɜrkəbəlnɪs/ *n* practicabilidad, *f*

workaday /'wɜrkə,dei/ *a* de todos los días; prosaico

workbench /'wɜrk,bɛntʃ/ banco de mecánico, *f,* banco de taller, banco de trabajo, *m,* mesa de trabajo, *f*

workday /'wɜrk,dei/ *n* día de trabajo, día laborable, *m,* jornada, *f*

worker /'wɜrkər/ *n* trabajador (-ra); (manual) obrero (-ra); (of a machine) operario (-ia). **w.-ant**, hormiga obrera, *f.* **w.-bee**, abeja obrera, *f*

workhouse /'wɜrk,haus/ *n* asilo, *m*

working /'wɜrkɪŋ/ *a* de trabajo; (of capital) de explotación; trabajador, que trabaja; obrero. *n* trabajo, *m;* (of a machine, organism, institution) funcionamiento, *m;* explotación, *f;* (of a mine) laboreo, *m;* (of a ship) maniobra, *f;* (of metal, stone, wood) labra, *f;* operación, *f;* (result) efecto, resultado, *m;* (calculation) cálculo, *m.* **"Not w.,"** «No funciona.» **to be in w. order**, funcionar bien. **w.-class**, clase obrera, *f;* pueblo, *m.* **w.-clothes**, ropa de trabajo, *f.* **w.-day**, día de trabajo, *m.* **w.-hours**, horas de trabajo, horas hábiles, *f pl.* **w. hypothesis**, postulado, *m.* **w.-man**, obrero, *m;* trabajador, *m.* **w.-out**, elaboración, *f;* ensayo, *m.* **w.-plan**, plan de trabajo, *m.* **w.-woman**, obrera, *f;* trabajadora, *f*

workless /'wɜrklɪs/ *a* sin trabajo

workman /'wɜrkmən/ *n* obrero, *m;* (agricultural) labrador, *m*

workmanlike /'wɜrkmən,laik/ *a* bien hecho, bien acabado; (clever) hábil

workmanship /'wɜrkmən,ʃɪp/ *n* trabajo, *m;* manufactura, *f;* hechura, *f;* (cleverness) habilidad, *f*

workshop /'wɜrk,ʃop/ *n* taller, *m*

world /wɜrld/ *n* mundo, *m.* **For all the w. as if...,** Exactamente como si... **to see the w.,** ver mundo. **to treat the w. as one's oyster**, ponerse el mundo por montera. **w. without end**, por los siglos de los siglos. **w.-power**, potencia mundial, gran potencia, *f.* **w.-wide**, mundial, universal

world almanac *n* compendio mundial, *m*

worldliness /'wɜrldlinɪs/ *n* mundanería, *f,* conocimiento del mundo, *m;* frivolidad, vanidad mundana, *f;* egoísmo, *m;* prudencia, *f*

worldly /'wɜrldli/ *a* de este mundo; mundano; humano; profano; frívolo. **to be w.-wise**, tener mucho mundo

World Wide Web *n* Red Mundial, Telaraña Global, *f*

worm /wɜrm/ *n* gusano, *m;* lombriz, *f; Chem.* serpentín, *m;* (of a screw) tornillo sinfín, *m;* (person)

gusano, *m; Fig.* gusano roedor, remordimiento, *m.* **intestinal w.,** lombriz intestinal, *f,* gusano de la conciencia. **w.-eaten,** carcomido. **w.-hole,** picadura de gusano, lombriguera, *f.* **w.-powder,** polvos antihelmínticos, *m pl.* **w.-shaped,** vermiforme. **having worms, suffering from worms,** *Lat. Am.* lombriciento

worm /wɜrm/ *vt* (a dog) dar un vermífugo (a). *vi* arrastrarse como un gusano. **to w. one's way into,** deslizarse en; *Fig.* insinuarse en, introducirse en. **to w. out,** (secrets, information) sonsacar

wormwood /'wɜrm,wʊd/ *n* ajenjo, *m*

wormy /'wɜrmi/ *a* gusanoso, lleno de gusanos

worn /wɔrn/ *a* (of garments) raído; estropeado; gastado; (of paths) trillado; (of the face) arrugado, cansado. **w. out,** acabado; muy usado; (tired) rendido; (exhausted) agotado

worrier /'wɜriər/ *n* inquietador (-ra); receloso (-sa); aprensivo (-va)

worry /'wɜri/ *n* preocupación, inquietud, ansiedad, *f;* problema, cuidado, *m. vt* (prey) zamarrear; preocupar, inquietar; molestar; importunar. *vi* estar preocupado, estar intranquilo, inquietarse. **Don't worry,** Pierda cuidado, No pase cuidado

worrying /'wɜriɪŋ/ *a* inquietante, perturbador; molesto

worse /wɜrs/ *a comp* peor; inferior. *adv* peor; menos. *n* lo peor. **so much the w.,** tanto peor. **to be w. off,** estar peor; estar en peores circunstancias; ser menos feliz. **to be the w. for wear,** ser muy usado; estar ajado; ser ya viejo. **to grow w.,** empeorarse; (of an ill person) ponerse peor. **w. and w.,** de mal en peor, peor que peor. **w. than ever,** peor que nunca

worsen /'wɜrsən/ *vt* agravar, hacer peor; exasperar. *vi* agravarse, empeorarse; exasperarse

worsening /'wɜrsənɪŋ/ *n* agravación, *f,* empeoramiento, *m;* exasperación, *f*

worship /'wɜrʃɪp/ *n* culto, *m;* adoración, *f;* veneración, *f. vt* adorar; reverenciar. *vi* adorar; rezar; dar culto (a). **place of w.,** edificio de culto, *m.* **Your W.,** vuestra merced

worshipful /'wɜrʃɪpfəl/ *a* venerable, respetable

worshipper /'wɜrʃɪpər/ *n* adorador (-ra); *pl* **worshippers,** (in a church, etc.) fieles, *m pl,* congregación, *f*

worshipping /'wɜrʃɪpɪŋ/ *n* adoración, *f,* culto, *m*

worst /wɜrst/ *a* el (la, etc.) peor; más malo. *adv* el (la, etc.) peor. *n* el (la, etc.) peor; lo peor. *vt* vencer; derrotar; triunfar sobre. **If w. comes to w.,** En el peor de los casos. **The w. of it is that...,** Lo peor es que... **to have the w. of it,** salir perdiendo, llevar la peor parte

worsted /'wʊstɪd, 'wɜrstɪd/ *n* estambre, *m, a* de estambre

worth /wɜrθ/ *n* valor, *m;* precio, *m;* mérito, *m, a* (que) vale; de precio de; cuyo valor es de; equivalente a; (que) merece; digno de. **He bought six hundred pesetas w. of sweets,** Compró seiscientas pesetas de dulces. **He sang for all he was w.,** Cantó con toda su alma. **It is w. seeing,** Es digno de verse, Vale la pena de verse. **to be w.,** valer. **to be w. while,** valer la pena, merecer la pena

worthily /'wɜrðɪli/ *adv* dignamente

worthiness /'wɜrðɪnɪs/ *n* mérito, valor, *m*

worthless /'wɜrθlɪs/ *a* sin valor; sin mérito; inútil; malo; (of persons) vil, despreciable, indigno

worthlessness /'wɜrθlɪsnɪs/ *n* falta de valor, *f;* falta de mérito, *f;* inutilidad, *f;* (of persons) bajeza, vileza, *f*

worthy /'wɜrði/ *a* digno de respeto, benemérito, respetable; digno, merecedor; meritorio. *n* varón ilustre, hombre célebre, *m;* héroe, *m;* (*Inf. Ironic.*) tío, *m.* **to be w. of,** ser digno de, merecer

would /wʊd/ *unstressed* wəd/ *preterite* and *subjunctive* of **will.** (indicating a conditional tense) **They w. come if...,** Vendrían si...; (indicating an imperfect tense) **Often he w. sing,** Muchas veces cantaba, **Now and then a blackbird w. whistle,** De vez en cuando silbó un mirlo; (expressing wish, desire) **What w. they?** ¿Qué quieren? **The place where I w. be,** El lugar donde quisiera estar. **When I were at home!** ¡Ojalá que estuviese en casa! **I thought that I w. tell you,** Se me ocurrió la idea de decírselo. **It w. seem that...,**

Parece ser que..., Según parece...; Se diría que... **He said that he w.** never have done it, Dijo que no lo hubiera hecho nunca. **They w.** have been killed if he had not rescued them, Habrían sido matados si él no los hubiese salvado. **He w.** go, Se empeñó en ir. **He w.** not do it, Rehusó hacerlo, Se resistió a hacerlo; No quiso hacerlo. **This w.** probably be the house, Sin duda esta sería la casa. **W.** you be good enough to..., Tenga Vd. la bondad de..., Haga el favor de...

would-be /'wʊdbi/ a supuesto; llamado; aspirante (a); en esperanza de (followed by infin.); (frustrated) frustrado, malogrado

wound /wund/ n herida, lesión, Lat. Am. also, lastimadura, f. vt herir; (the feelings) lastimar, lacerar. **deep w.**, herida penetrante, f. **the wounded,** los heridos.

wounding /'wundɪŋ/ n herida, f, a Fig. lastimador

wraith /reiθ/ n fantasma, espectro, m, sombra, f

wrangle /'ræŋgəl/ vi discutir; altercar, disputar acaloradamente; reñir; (bargain) regatear. n argumento, m; disputa, f, altercado, m; riña, f

wrangler /'ræŋglər/ n disputador (-ra)

wrangling /'ræŋglɪŋ/ n disputas, f pl, altercación, f; (bargaining) regateo, m

wrap /ræp/ vt envolver; arrollar; cubrir; abrigar; (conceal) ocultar. n envoltorio, m; abrigo, m; pl **wraps,** abrigos y mantas de viaje, m pl. **W.** yourself up well! ¡Abrígate bien! **to be wrapped up in,** estar envuelto en, Fig. estar entregado a, estar absorto en; (a person) estar embelesado con

wrapper /'ræpər/ n envoltura, f; embalaje, m; (of a newspaper) faja, f; (of a book) sobrecubierta, f; (dressing-gown) bata, f, salto de cama, m

wrapping /'ræpɪŋ/ n envoltura, cubierta, f. **w.-paper,** papel de envolver, m

wrath /ræθ/ n ira, f

wrathful /'ræθfəl/ a airado

wreak /rik/ vt ejecutar; (anger, etc.) descargar. **to w.** one's vengeance, vengarse

wreath /riθ/ n guirnalda, f; corona, f; trenza, f. **funeral w.,** corona funeraria, f

wreathe /rið/ vt trenzar; (entwine) entrelazar (de); (garland) coronar (de), enguirnaldar (con); (encircle) ceñir, rodear; (a face in smiles) iluminar

wreck /rɛk/ n naufragio, m; buque naufragado, m; destrucción, f; Fig. ruina, f; (remains) restos, m pl; (person) sombra, f. vt hacer naufragar; destruir; Fig. arruinar; hacer fracasar. **I am a complete w.,** Inf. Estoy hecho una ruina. **to be wrecked,** irse a pique, naufragar; Fig. arruinarse; frustrarse

wreckage /'rɛkɪdʒ/ n naufragio, m; restos de naufragio, m pl; ruinas, f pl; (of a car, plane, etc.) restos, m pl; accidente, m

wrecked /rɛkt/ a naufragado

wrecker /'rɛkər/ n destructor (-ra); (of ships) raquero, m

wrench /rɛntʃ/ n (jerk) arranque, m; (pull) tirón, m; (sprain) torcedura, f; (tool) llave, f; (pain) dolor, m. vt arrancar; forzar; torcer, dislocar. **He has wrenched his arm,** Se ha torcido el brazo

wrest /rɛst/ vt arrebatar, arrancar

wrestle /'rɛsəl/ vi luchar. n lucha grecorromana, f; Fig. lucha, f. **to w. with,** Fig. luchar con; luchar contra, Lat. Am. abrocharse (con...)

wrestler /'rɛslər/ n luchador, m

wrestling /'rɛslɪŋ/ n lucha grecorromana, f. **all-in-w.,** lucha libre, f. **w.-match,** lucha, f

wretch /rɛtʃ/ n infeliz, mf; (ruffian) infame, m; (playful) picaruelo (-la). **a poor w.,** un pobre diablo

wretched /'rɛtʃɪd/ a (unhappy) infeliz, desdichado; miserable; pobre; (ill) enfermo; horrible; malo; mezquino; despreciable; lamentable

wretchedly /'rɛtʃɪdli/ adv tristemente; pobremente; muy mal; ruinemente

wretchedness /'rɛtʃɪdnɪs/ n infelicidad, desdicha, f; miseria, pobreza, f; escualidez, f; ruindad, f

wriggle /'rɪgəl/ vi agitarse, moverse; menearse; serpear, culebrear; retorcerse. n See under **wriggling. to w. into,** insinuarse en, deslizarse dentro (de). **to w.**

out, escaparse. **to w. out of a difficulty,** extricarse de una dificultad

wriggling /'rɪglɪŋ/ n meneo, m; retorcimiento, m; serpenteo, culebreo, m

wring /rɪŋ/ vt torcer; estrujar; exprimir; arrancar; (force) forzar. **to w. one's hands,** restregarse las manos. **to w. the neck of,** torcer el pescuezo (a). **to w. out,** exprimir; estrujar

wringer /'rɪŋər/ n torcedor (-ra); (for clothes) exprimidor de ropa, m

wringing /'rɪŋɪŋ/ n torsión, f. **w.-machine,** exprimidor de ropa, m

wrinkle /'rɪŋkəl/ n arruga, f; pliegue, m; Inf. noción, f. vt arrugar. vi arrugarse. **to w. one's brow,** (frown) fruncir el ceño; (in perplexity) arrugar la frente

wrinkling /'rɪŋklɪŋ/ n arrugamiento, m

wrinkly /'rɪŋkli/ a arrugado

wrist /rɪst/ n muñeca, f. **w.-band,** tira del puño de la camisa, f. **w. bandage,** pulsera, f

wristlet /'rɪstlɪt/ n pulsera, f; manguito elástico, m. **w. watch,** reloj de pulsera, m

writ /rɪt/ n escritura, f; Law. decreto judicial, mandamiento, m; orden, f; título ejecutorio, m; hábeas corpus, m. **Holy W.,** la Sagrada Escritura. **to issue a w.,** dar orden. **to serve a w.,** notificar una orden. **w. of privilege,** auto de excarcelación, m

write /rait/ vt and vi escribir; Fig. mostrar. **He writes a good hand,** Tiene buena letra. **I shall w. to them for a list,** Les escribiré pidiendo una lista. **to w. back,** contestar por escrito; contestar a una carta. **to w. down,** poner por escrito; anotar, apuntar; describir. **to w. for,** escribir para; escribir para pedir algo; escribir algo en vez de otra persona. **to w. off,** escribir; escribir rápidamente; cancelar. **to w. on,** seguir escribiendo; escribir sobre. **to w. out,** copiar; redactar. **to w. over again,** escribir de nuevo, escribir otra vez, volver a escribir. **to w. up,** redactar; Com. poner al día; (praise) escribir alabando

writer /'raitər/ n escritor (-ra); autor (-ra). **the present w.,** el que, m, (f, la que) esto escribe. **writer's cramp,** calambre del escribiente, m

writhe /raið/ vi retorcerse

writhing /'raiðɪŋ/ n retorsión, f

writing /'raitɪŋ/ n escritura, f; (work) escrito, m; inscripción, f; documento, m; (style) estilo, m; (hand) letra, f; el arte de escribir; trabajo literario, m. **in one's own w.,** de su propia letra. **in w.,** por escrito. **w.-case,** escribanía, f. **w.-desk,** escritorio, m. **w.-pad,** taco de papel, m. **w.-paper,** papel de escribir, m. **w.-table,** mesa de escribir, f

written /'rɪtn/ a escrito

wrong /rɔŋ/ a injusto; mal; equivocado, erróneo; inexacto; falso; incorrecto; desacertado; inoportuno. **It is the w. one,** No es el que hacía falta; No es el que quería. **to be in the w. place,** estar mal situado; estar mal colocado. **to be w.,** estar mal; no tener razón; (mistaken) estar equivocado; (of deeds or things) estar mal hecho; (be unjust) ser injusto; (of clocks) andar mal. **to do w.,** hacer mal; obrar mal. **to get out of bed on the w. side,** levantarse del izquierdo. **to go w.,** (of persons) descarriarse; (of affairs) ir mal; salir mal; frustrarse; (of apparatus) estropearse, no funcionar. **We have taken the w. road,** Nos hemos equivocado de camino. **You were very w. to...,** Has hecho muy mal en... **w.-headed,** terco, obstinado; disparatado. **w.-headedness,** terquedad, obstinación, f. **w. number,** (telephone) número errado, m. **w. side,** revés, m. lado malo, m. **w. side out,** al envés; al revés

wrong /rɔŋ/ adv mal; injustamente; sin razón; incorrectamente; equivocadamente; (inside out) al revés. **to get it w.,** (a sum) calcular mal; (misunderstand) comprender mal

wrong /rɔŋ/ n mal, m; injusticia, f; perjuicio, m; ofensa, f, agravio, m; culpa, f; error, m. **to be in the w.,** no tener razon; haber hecho mal. **to put one in the w.,** echar la culpa (a), hacer responsable (de)

wrong /rɔŋ/ vt hacer mal (a); perjudicar; ser injusto con; ofender

wrongdoer /'rɔŋˌduər/ n malhechor (-ra); pecador (-ra); perverso (-sa)

wrongdoing /'rɔŋ,duɪŋ/ n maldad, maleficencia, f; pecado, m; injusticia, f
wrongful /'rɔŋfəl/ a injusto; perjudicial; falso
wrongfully /'rɔŋfəli/ adv injustamente; falsamente
wrongly /'rɔŋli/ adv injustamente; erróneamente, equivocadamente; perversamente; mal
wrongness /'rɔŋnɪs/ n mal, m; injusticia, f; falsedad, f; inexactitud, f, error, m
wrought /rɔt/ a forjado; labrado; (hammered) batido; trabajado. **w. iron,** hierro dulce, hierro forjado, m. **w. up,** muy excitado, muy agitado, muy nervioso
wry /rai/ a torcido; tuerto; triste; pesimista; desilusionado; irónico. **wry face,** mueca f, de desengaño, de ironía, de disgusto, etc. **make a wry face,** torcer el gesto, Mexico engestarse. **wry neck,** Ornith. torcecuello, m
wryly /'raili/ adv tristemente; irónicamente
wye /wai/ n (letter) ye, i griega, f; horquilla, cosa en forma de Y, f

X Y Z

x /ɛks/ n equis, f
x-ray /'ɛks,rei/ vt tomar una radiografía (de). **x-ray,** rayo x, m pl. **x-ray examination,** examen con rayos x, m. **x-ray photograph,** radiografía, f
xylophone /'zailə,foun/ n xilófono, m
y /wai/ n (letter) i griega, ye, f
yacht /yɒt/ n yate, m. **y. club,** club marítimo, m. **y. race,** regata de yates, f
yachting /'yɒtɪŋ/ n navegación en yate, f, paseo en yate, m
yachtsman /'yɒtsmən/ n deportista náutico, balandrista, balandrismo, m
yam /yæm/ n batata, f, Lat. Am. boniato, camote, m
yank /yæŋk/ n tirón, m, sacudida, f. vt dar un tirón (a); sacar de un tirón
Yankee /'yæŋki/ a and n yanqui, mf
yap /yæp/ vi ladrar. n ladrido, m
yapper /'yæpər/ n (yapping dog) gozque, gozquejo, m
yapping /'yæpɪŋ/ n ladridos, m pl, a que ladra
yard /yɑrd/ n (measure) yarda, f; Naut. verga, f; corral, m; (courtyard) patio, m. vt acorralar. **goods y.,** estación de mercancías, f. **y.-arm,** penol (de la verga), m. **y.-stick,** vara de medir de una yarda, f
yarn /yɑrn/ n hilaza, f; hilo, m; (story) historia, f, cuento, m. **to spin a y.,** contar una historia
yaw /yɔ/ vi Naut. guiñar; Aer. serpentear. n Naut. guiñada, f; Aer. serpenteo, m
yawn /yɔn/ vi bostezar; quedarse con la boca abierta; (of chasms, etc.) abrirse. n bostezo, m. **to stifle a y.,** ahogar un bostezo
yawning /'yɔnɪŋ/ a abierto. n bostezos, m pl
yea /yei/ adv en verdad, ciertamente; y aun... no sólo... sino. n si, m
year /yɪər/ n año, m; pl **years,** años, m pl, edad, f. **We are getting on in years,** Nos vamos haciendo viejos. **He is five years old,** Tiene cinco años. **all the y. round,** todo el año, el año entero. **by the y.,** al año. **every other y.,** cada dos años, un año sí y otro no. **in after years,** en años posteriores. **last y.,** el año pasado. **next y.,** el año próximo. el año que viene. **y. after y.,** año tras año. **New Y.,** Año Nuevo, m. **to see the New Y. in,** ver empezar el Año Nuevo. **New Year's Day,** día de Año Nuevo, m. **(A) Happy New Y.!** ¡Feliz Año Nuevo! **y.-book,** anuario, m. **a y. later,** Lat. Am. al año
yearling calf /'yɪərlɪŋ/ n becerra f
yearly /'yɪərli/ a anual. adv anualmente, cada año; una vez al año
yearn /yɜrn/ vi anhelar, suspirar (por); desear vivamente
yearning /'yɜrnɪŋ/ n sed, ansia, f; anhelo, deseo vehemente, m. a ansioso; anhelante; (tender) tierno
yeast /yist/ n levadura, f
yell /yɛl/ vi and vt chillar; gritar. n chillido, m; grito, m
yelling /'yɛlɪŋ/ n chillidos, m pl; gritos, m pl, gritería, f
yellow /'yɛlou/ a amarillo; (of hair) rubio; (cowardly) cobarde; (newspaper) amarillista, sensacionalista. **to turn y.,** vi ponerse amarillo; amarillear. vt volver amarillo. **y. fever,** fiebre amarilla, f. **y.-hammer,** Ornith. emberizo, m
yellowing /'yɛlouɪŋ/ n amarilleo, m
yellowish /'yɛlouɪʃ/ a amarillento, Lat. Am. amarilloso
yellowness /'yɛlouɪs/ n amarillez, f

yellow pages /'peidʒɪz/ n páginas amarillas, páginas doradas, f pl
yelp /yɛlp/ vi gañir. n gañido, m
yelping /'yɛlpɪŋ/ n gañidos, m pl
yen /yɛn/ n (currency) yen, m; (desire) deseo vivo, m
yeoman /'youmən/ n pequeño propietario rural, m; soldado de caballería, m. **Y. of the Guard,** alabardero de la Casa Real, m
yes /yɛs/ adv sí. **Yes?** ¿De verdad? ¿Y qué pasó después? ¿Y entonces? **to say yes,** decir que sí; dar el sí. **yes-man,** amenista, sacristán de amén, m
yesterday /'yɛstər,dei/ adv ayer. n ayer, m. **the day before y.,** anteayer
yet /yɛt/ adv aún, todavía. **as yet,** hasta ahora; todavía. **He has not come yet,** No ha venido todavía. **yet again,** otra vez
yet /yɛt/ conjunc sin embargo, no obstante, con todo; pero. **The book is well written and yet I do not like it,** El libro está bien escrito, y sin embargo no me gusta
yew /yu/ n tejo, m; madera de tejo, f
Yiddish /'yɪdɪʃ/ n yídis, yídish, yídico, m; a yídico
yield /yild/ vt producir; dar; (grant) otorgar; (afford) ofrecer; (surrender) ceder. vi producir; (submit) rendirse, someterse; (of disease) responder; (give way) flaquear, doblegarse; dar de sí; (consent) consentir (en); (to circumstances, etc.) ceder (a), sucumbir (a). n producción, f, producto, m; Com. rédito, m; (crop) cosecha, f. **to y. to temptation,** ceder a la tentación. **to y. up,** entregar; devolver
yielding /'yildɪŋ/ a flexible; (soft) blando; dócil, sumiso; fácil; condescendiente
yogurt /'yougərt/ n yogur, m
yoke /youk/ n yugo, m; (of oxen) yunta, f; (for pails) balancín, m; (of a garment) canesú, m; Fig. férula, f, yugo, m. vt uncir, acoplar. **to throw off the y.,** sacudir el yugo
yokel /'youkəl/ n patán, rústico, m
yolk /youk/ n (of an egg) yema, f
yonder /'yɒndər/ a aquel, m; aquella, f; aquellos, m pl; aquellas, f pl. adv allí; allí a lo lejos
yore /yɔr/ n **in days of y.,** antaño; en otro tiempo
you /yu/ unstressed yʊ, yə/ pers pron nominative (polite form) usted (Vd.), mf; ustedes (Vds.), mf pl; (familiar form) sing tu, mf; (plural) vosotros, m pl; vosotras, f pl; (one) uno, m; una, f; se (followed by 3rd pers. sing. of verb). pers pron accusative (polite form) le, m; la, f; les, m pl; las, f pl; a usted, a ustedes; (informal form) te, mf, os, mf pl; (after most prepositions) ti, mf; vosotros, m pl; vosotras, f pl. **Are you there?** (telephone) ¡Oiga! **I gave the parcel to you,** Te (os) di el paquete; Di el paquete a usted (a ustedes). **I shall wait for you in the garden,** Te (os) esperaré en el jardín; Esperaré a Vds. (a Vd.) en el jardín. **This present is for you,** Este regalo es para tí (para vosotros, para Vd. (Vds.)). **Away with you!** ¡Vete! ¡Marchaos! **Between you and me,** Entre tú y yo. **You can't have your cake and eat it too,** no hay rosa sin espinas. **You never can tell,** No se sabe nunca, Uno no sabe nunca
young /yʌŋ/ a joven; nuevo, reciente; inexperto; poco avanzado. n cría, f, hijuelos, m pl. **y. blood,** Inf. ojolo tres, a. **y. girl,** jovencita, f. **y. man** joven, m. **y. people,** jóvenes, m pl. **in his y. days,** en su juventud. **The night is y.,** La noche está poca avan-

zada. **to grow y. again,** rejuvenecer. **with y.,** (of animals) preñada f

younger /'yʌŋgər/ a más joven; menor. **Peter is his y. brother,** Pedro es su hermano menor. **to look y.,** parecer más joven

youngish /'yʌŋgɪʃ/ a bastante joven

youngster /'yʌŋstər/ n jovencito, chico, muchacho, m; niño, m

your /yʊr, yɔr; *unstressed* yər/ a *poss* (polite form) su (*pl* sus), de usted (Vd.), (*pl* de ustedes (Vds.)); (familiar form) tu (*pl* vuestro). **I have y. papers,** Tengo tus (vuestros) papeles; Tengo los papeles de Vd. (*or* de Vds.). **How is y. mother?** ¿Cómo está su (tu) madre? **It is y. turn,** Te toca a ti, Le toca a Vd.

yours /yʊrz, yɔrz/ *pron poss* (polite form) (el) suyo, m; (la) suya, f; (los) suyos, m pl; (las) suyas, f pl; el, m; la, f; lo, *neut*; los, m pl; las, f pl; de usted (Vd.), mf *sing* or de ustedes (Vds.), mf pl; (familiar form) (el) tuyo, m; (la) tuya, f; (los) tuyos, m pl; (las) tuyas, f pl; (el) vuestro, m; (la) vuestra, f; (los) vuestros, m pl; (las) vuestras, f pl. **This is a picture of y.,** (addressing one person), Este es uno de los cuadros de usted (Vd.), Este es uno de tus cuadros. **This hat is mine, it is not y.,** Este sombrero es el mío, no es el tuyo. **The horse is y.,** El caballo es tuyo (de Vd.). **Y. affectionately,** Un abrazo de tu amigo... **Y. faithfully,** Queda de Vd. su att. (atentísimo) s.s. (seguro servidor). **Y. sincerely,** Queda de Vd. su aff. (afectuoso)

yourself /yʊr'sɛlf, yɔr- yər-/ *pron pers* (familiar form *sing*) tú mismo, m; tú misma, f; (after a preposition) tí, mf; (polite form) usted (Vd.) mismo, m; usted misma, f; *pl* **yourselves,** (familiar form) vosotros mismos, m pl; vosotras mismas, f pl; (polite form) ustedes (Vds.) mismos, m pl; ustedes mismas, f pl. **This is for y.,** Esto es para ti; Esto es para Vd.

youth /yuθ/ n juventud, f; (man) joven, chico, mozalbete, m; (collectively) jóvenes, m pl, juventud, f

youthful /'yuθfəl/ a joven, juvenil; de la juventud

yowl /yaul/ n gañido, aullido, m. *vi* gañir, aullar

Yucatan /,yukə'tæn/ a yucateco

yucca /'yʌkə/ n *Bot.* yuca, f

Yugoslav /'yugou,slɑv/ n yugoeslavo (-va). a yugoeslavo

Yugoslavia /,yugou'slaviə/ Yugoeslavia, f

Yukon, the /'yukɒn/ el Yukón, m

Yule /yul/ n Navidad, f. **y.-log,** leño de Navidad, m. **y-tide,** Navidades, f pl

z /zi/ n (letter) zeda, zeta, f

zeal /zil/ n celo, entusiasmo, m; ardor, fervor, m

zealot /'zɛlət/ n fanático (-ca)

zealous /'zɛləs/ a celoso, entusiasta

zealously /'zɛləsli/ *adv* con entusiasmo

zebra /'zibrə/ n cebra, f

zenith /'zinɪθ/ n cenit, m; *Fig.* apogeo, punto culminante, m

zephyr /'zɛfər/ n céfiro, m, brisa, f

zero /'zɪərou/ n cero, m. **below z.,** bajo cero. **z. hour,** hora cero, f

zest /zɛst/ n sabor, gusto, m; entusiasmo, m. **to eat with z.,** comer con buen apetito. **to enter on with z.,** emprender con entusiasmo

zigzag /'zɪg,zæg/ n zigzag, m. a and adv en zigzag. *vi* zigzaguear, hacer zigzags, serpentear; (of persons) andar haciendo eses

Zimbabwe /zɪm'bɑbwei/ Zimbabue

zinc /zɪŋk/ n cinc, m. **z. oxide,** óxido de cinc, m

Zion /'zaiən/ n Sión, m

Zionism /'zaiə,nɪzəm/ n sionismo, m

Zionist /'zaiənɪst/ n and a sionista

zip /zɪp/ n (of a bullet) silbido, m; *Inf.* energía, f.

zip code n código postal, m

zipper /'zɪpər/ n cremallera, f, cierre relámpago, cierre, cerrador, m

zircon /'zɜrkɒn/ n circón, m

zither /'zɪθər/ n cítara, f

zodiac /'zoudi,æk/ n zodiaco, m

zone /zoun/ n zona, f; faja, f

zoo /zu/ n jardín zoológico, m

zoological /,zouə'lɒdʒɪkəl/ a zoológico. **z. garden,** jardín zoológico, m

zoologist /zou'ɒlədʒɪst/ n zoólogo, m

zoology /zou'ɒlədʒi/ n zoología, f

zoom /zum/ n zumbido, m; (photography) lente zoom. *vi* zumbar; *Aer.* empinarse

Zulu /'zulu/ a and n zulú mf

Spanish Irregular Verbs

Infinitive	Present	Future	Preterit	Past Part.
andar	ando	andaré	anduve	andado
caber	quepo	cabré	cupe	cabido
caer	caigo	caeré	caí	caído
conducir	conduzco	conduciré	conduje	conducido
dar	doy	daré	di	dado
decir	digo	diré	dije	dicho
estar	estoy	estaré	estuve	estado
haber	he	habré	hube	habido
hacer	hago	haré	hice	hecho
ir	voy	iré	fui	ido
jugar	juego	jugaré	jugué	jugado
morir	muero	moriré	morí	muerto
oir	oigo	oiré	oí	oído
poder	puedo	podré	pude	podido
poner	pongo	pondré	puse	puesto
querer	quiero	querré	quise	querido
saber	sé	sabré	supe	sabido
salir	salgo	saldré	salí	salido
ser	soy	seré	fui	sido
tener	tengo	tendré	tuve	tenido
traer	traigo	traeré	traje	traído
valer	valgo	valdré	valí	valido
venir	vengo	vendré	vine	venido
ver	veo	veré	vi	visto

Las formas del verbo inglés

1. Se forma la 3ª persona singular del tiempo presente exactamente al igual que el plural de los sustantivos, añadiendo -es o -s a la forma sencilla según las mismas reglas, así:

(1)	teach	pass	wish	fix	buzz
	teaches	passes	wishes	fixes	buzzes

(2)	place	change	judge	please	freeze
	places	changes	judges	pleases	freezes

(3a)	find	sell	clean	hear	love	buy	know
	finds	sells	cleans	hears	loves	buys	knows

(3b)	think	like	laugh	stop	hope	meet	want
	thinks	likes	laughs	stops	hopes	meets	wants

(4)	cry	try	dry	carry	deny
	cries	tries	dries	carries	denies

Cinco verbos muy comunes tienen 3ª persona singular irregular:

(5)	go	do	say	have	be
	goes	does	says	has	is

2. Se forman el tiempo pasado y el participio de modo igual, añadiendo a la forma sencilla la terminación -**ed** o -**d** según las reglas que siguen:

(1) Si la forma sencilla termina en -**d** o -**t**, se le pone -**ed** como sílaba aparte:

end	fold	need	load	want	feast	wait	light
ended	folded	needed	loaded	wanted	feasted	waited	lighted

(2) Si la forma sencilla termina en cualquier otra consonante, se añade también -**ed** pero sin hacer sílaba aparte:

(2a)
bang	sail	seem	harm	earn	weigh
banged	sailed	seemed	harmed	earned	weighed

(2b)
lunch	work	look	laugh	help	pass
lunched	worked	looked	laughed	helped	passed

(3) Si la forma sencilla termina en -**e**, se le pone sólo -**d**:

(3a)
hate	taste	waste	guide	fade	trade
hated	tasted	wasted	guided	faded	traded

(3b)
free	judge	rule	name	dine	scare
freed	judged	ruled	named	dined	scared

(3c)
place	force	knife	like	hope	base
placed	forced	knifed	liked	hoped	based

(4) Una -**y** final que sigue a cualquier consonante se cambia en -**ie** al añadir la -**d** del pasado/participio:

cry	try	dry	carry	deny
cried	tried	dried	carried	denied

3. Varios verbos muy comunes forman el tiempo pasado y el participio de manera irregular. Pertenecen a tres grupos.

(1) Los que tienen una sola forma irregular para tiempo pasado y participio, como los siguientes:

bend	bleed	bring	build	buy	catch	creep	deal
bent	bled	brought	built	bought	caught	crept	dealt

dig	feed	feel	fight	find	flee	get	hang
dug	fed	felt	fought	found	fled	got	hung

have	hear	hold	keep	lead	leave	lend	lose
had	heard	held	kept	led	left	lent	lost

make	mean	meet	say	seek	sell	send	shine
made	meant	met	said	sought	sold	sent	shone

shoot	sit	sleep	spend	stand	strike	sweep	teach
shot	sat	slept	spent	stood	struck	swept	taught

(2) Los que tienen una forma irregular para el tiempo pasado y otra forma irregular para el participio, como los siguientes:

be	beat	become	begin	bite
was	beat	became	began	bit
been	beaten	become	begun	bitten
blow	break	choose	come	do
blew	broke	chose	came	did
blown	broken	chosen	come	done
draw	drink	drive	eat	fall
drew	drank	drove	ate	fell
drawn	drunk	driven	eaten	fallen
fly	forget	freeze	give	go
flew	forgot	froze	gave	went
flown	forgotten	frozen	given	gone
grow	hide	know	ride	ring
grew	hid	knew	rode	rang
grown	hidden	known	ridden	rung
rise	run	see	shake	shrink
rose	ran	saw	shook	shrank
risen	run	seen	shaken	shrunk
sing	sink	speak	steal	swear
sang	sank	spoke	stole	swore
sung	sunk	spoken	stolen	sworn
swim	tear	throw	wear	write
swam	tore	threw	wore	wrote
swum	torn	thrown	worn	written

(3) Los que no varían del todo, la forma sencilla funcionando también como pasado/participio; entre éstos son de mayor frecuencia:

bet	burst	cast	cost	cut
hit	hurt	let	put	quit
read	set	shed	shut	slit
spit	split	spread	thrust	wet

Numbers/Números

Cardinal/Cardinales

one	1	uno, una
two	2	dos
three	3	tres
four	4	cuatro
five	5	cinco
six	6	seis
seven	7	siete
eight	8	ocho
nine	9	nueve
ten	10	diez
eleven	11	once
twelve	12	doce
thirteen	13	trece
fourteen	14	catorce
fifteen	15	quince
sixteen	16	dieciséis
seventeen	17	diecisiete
eighteen	18	dieciocho
nineteen	19	diecinueve
twenty	20	veinte
twenty-one	21	veinte y uno (or veintiuno)
twenty-two	22	veinte y dos (or veintidós)
thirty	30	treinta
thirty-one	31	treinta y uno
thirty-two	32	treinta y dos
forty	40	cuarenta
fifty	50	cincuenta
sixty	60	sesenta
seventy	70	setenta
eighty	80	ochenta
ninety	90	noventa

one hundred	100	cien
one hundred one	101	ciento uno
one hundred two	102	ciento dos
two hundred	200	doscientos, -as
three hundred	300	trescientos, -as
four hundred	400	cuatrocientos, -as
five hundred	500	quinientos, -as
six hundred	600	seiscientos, -as
seven hundred	700	setecientos, -as
eight hundred	800	ochocientos, -as
nine hundred	900	novecientos, -as
one thousand	1,000	mil
two thousand	2,000	dos mil
one hundred thousand	100,000	cien mil
one million	1,000,000	un millón
two million	2,000,000	dos millones

Ordinal/Ordinales

first	1st / 1°	primero
second	2nd / 2°	segundo
third	3rd / 3°	tercero
fourth	4th / 4°	cuarto
fifth	5th / 5°	quinto
sixth	6th / 6°	sexto
seventh	7th / 7°	séptimo
eighth	8th / 8°	octavo
ninth	9th / 9°	noveno
tenth	10th / 10°	décimo

Days of the Week/Días de la Semana

Sunday	domingo		Thursday	jueves
Monday	lunes		Friday	viernes
Tuesday	martes		Saturday	sábado
Wednesday	miércoles			

Months/Meses

January	enero		July	julio
February	febrero		August	agosto
March	marzo		September	septiembre
April	abril		October	octubre
May	mayo		November	noviembre
June	junio		December	diciembre

Useful Phrases/Locuciones Útiles

Good day, Good morning. Buenos días.
Good afternoon. Buenas tardes.
Good night, Good evening. Buenas
noches.
Hello. ¡Hola!
Welcome! ¡Bienvenido!
See you later. Hasta luego.
Goodbye. ¡Adiós!
How are you? ¿Cómo está usted?
I'm fine, thank you. Estoy bien, gracias.
I'm pleased to meet you. Mucho gusto
en conocerle.
May I introduce . . . Quisiera presentar . . .
Thank you very much. Muchas gracias.
You're welcome. De nada or No hay de
qué.
Please. Por favor.
Excuse me. Con permiso.
Good luck. ¡Buena suerte!
To your health. ¡Salud!

Please help me. Ayúdeme, por favor.
I don't know. No sé.
I don't understand. No entiendo.
Do you understand? ¿Entiende usted?
I don't speak Spanish. No hablo
español.
Do you speak English? ¿Habla usted in-
glés?
How do you say . . . in Spanish? ¿Cómo
se dice . . . en español?
What do you call this? ¿Cómo se llama
esto?
Speak slowly, please. Hable despacio,
por favor.
Please repeat. Repita, por favor.
I don't like it. No me gusta.
I am lost. Ando perdido; Me he
extraviado.

What is your name? ¿Cómo se llama
usted?
My name is . . . Me llamo . . .
I am an American. Soy norteamericano.
Where are you from? ¿De dónde es
usted?
I'm from . . . Soy de . . .
How is the weather? ¿Qué tiempo hace?
It's cold (hot) today. Hace frío (calor)
hoy.
What time is it? ¿Qué hora es?

How much is it? ¿Cuánto es?
It is too much. Es demasiado.

What do you wish? ¿Qué desea usted?
I want to buy . . . Quiero comprar . . .
May I see something better? ¿Podría ver
algo mejor?
May I see something cheaper?
¿Podría ver algo menos caro?
It is not exactly what I want. No es ex-
actamente lo que quiero.

I'm hungry. Tengo hambre.
I'm thirsty. Tengo sed.
Where is there a restaurant? ¿Dónde hay
un restaurante?
I have a reservation. Tengo una
reservación.
I would like . . . Quisiera . . .; Me
gustaría . . .
Please give me . . . Por favor, déme usted
. . .
Please bring me . . . Por favor, tráigame
usted . . .
May I see the menu? ¿Podría ver el
menú?
The bill, please. La cuenta, por favor.
Is service included in the bill?
¿El servicio está incluido en la cuenta?
Where is there a hotel? ¿Dónde hay un
hotel?
Where is the post office? ¿Dónde está el
correo?
Is there any mail for me? ¿Hay correo
para mí?
Where can I mail this letter? ¿Dónde
puedo echar esta carta al correo?

Take me to . . . Lléveme a . . .
I believe I am ill. Creo que estoy
enfermo.
Please call a doctor. Por favor, llame al
médico.
Please call the police. Por favor, llame a
la policía.
I want to send a telegram. Quiero poner
un telegrama.
As soon as possible. Cuanto antes.

Round trip. Ida y vuelta.
Please help me with my luggage. Por
favor, ayúdeme con mi equipaje.
Where can I get a taxi? ¿Dónde puedo
coger un taxi?
What is the fare to . . . ¿Cuánto es el
pasaje hasta . . . ?
Please take me to this address. Por

favor, lléveme a esta dirección.

Where can I change my money? ¿Dónde puedo cambiar mi dinero?

Where is the nearest bank? ¿Dónde está el banco más cercano?

Can you accept my check? ¿Puede aceptar usted mi cheque?

Do you accept traveler's checks? ¿Aceptan cheques de viaje?

What is the postage? ¿Cuánto es el franqueo?

Where is the nearest drugstore? ¿Dónde está la farmacia más cercana?

Where is the men's (women's) room? ¿Dónde está el servicio de caballeros (de señoras)?

Please let me off at. . . Por favor, déjeme bajar en . . .

Right away. ¡Pronto!

Help. ¡Socorro!

Who is it? ¿Quién es?

Just a minute! ¡Un momento no más!

Come in. ¡Pase usted!

Pardon me. Disculpe usted.

Stop. ¡Pare!

Look out. ¡Cuidado!

Hurry. ¡De prisa! *or* ¡Dése prisa!

Go on. ¡Siga!

To (on, at) the right. A la derecha.

To (on, at) the left. A la izquierda.

Straight ahead. Adelante.